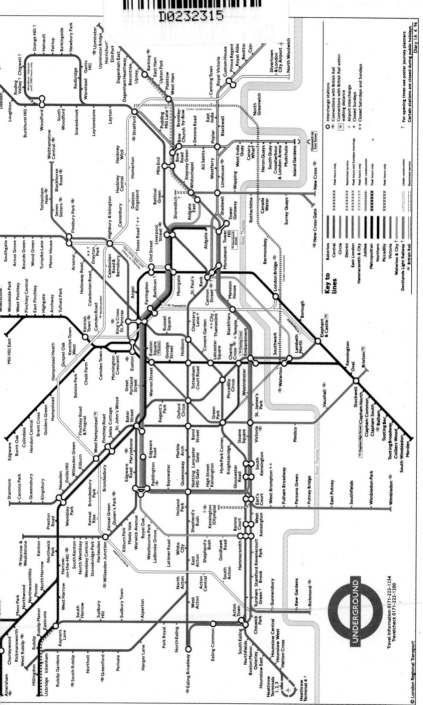

UNDERGROUND

Travel Information 0171-222-1234
Travelcheck 0171-222-1200

© London Regional Transport

LRT Registered User No. 97/2726

Key to lines

- Bakerloo
- Central
- Circle
- District
- East London
- Hammersmith & City
- Jubilee
- Metropolitan
- Northern
- Piccadilly
- Victoria
- Waterloo & City
- Docklands Light Railway
- British Rail

Peak hours only
Restricted service
Peak hours and Sundays mornings
Peak hours only
Under construction
Closed Sundays
Peak hours only
Under construction
Restricted service

◯ Interchange stations
● Central
⊖ Connections with British Rail
⊖ Connections with British Rail within walking distance
✈ Airport interchange
✱ Under construction
✱✱ Closed Saturdays and Sundays

† For opening times see poster journey planners
Certain stations are closed during public holidays

Diary J.4. 4. 96

London: Westminster and Whitehall

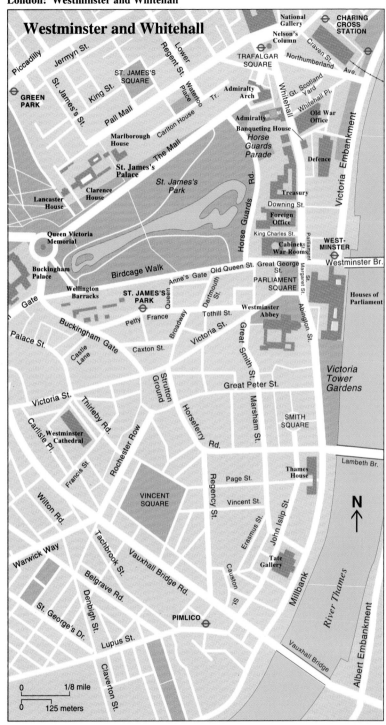

Westminster and Whitehall

Piccadilly

Jermyn St.

St. James's St.

King St.

ST. JAMES'S SQUARE

Pall Mall

Regent St.

Lower Regent St.

Waterloo Place

Carlton House Tce.

GREEN PARK

St. James's St.

Marlborough House

The Mall

St. James's Palace

Clarence House

Lancaster House

St. James's Park

Queen Victoria Memorial

Buckingham Palace

Wellington Barracks

ST. JAMES'S PARK

Birdcage Walk

Anne's Gate

Old Queen St.

Gate

Buckingham Gate

Palace St.

Castle Lane

Queen Anne's Gate

Dartmouth St.

Petty France

Broadway

Tothill St.

Victoria St.

Caxton St.

Victoria St.

Thirleby Rd.

Carlisle Pl.

Westminster Cathedral

Francis St.

Rochester Row

Strutton Ground

Horseferry Rd.

VINCENT SQUARE

Regency St.

Page St.

Vincent St.

Erasmus St.

Caston St.

John Islip St.

Wilton Rd.

Tachbrook St.

Belgrave Rd.

Denbigh St.

St. George's Dr.

Warwick Way

Vauxhall Bridge Rd.

PIMLICO

Lupus St.

Clayerton St.

National Gallery

Nelson's Column

CHARING CROSS STATION

Craven St.

Northumberland Ave.

TRAFALGAR SQUARE

Admiralty Arch

Whitehall

Gt. Scotland Yard

Whitehall Pl.

Admiralty

Banqueting House

Old War Office

Horse Guards Parade

Defence

Treasury

Downing St.

Foreign Office

King Charles St.

Cabinet War Rooms

Horse Guards Rd.

Parliament St.

WEST-MINSTER

Westminster Br.

Great George St.

PARLIAMENT SQUARE

Margaret St.

Abingdon St.

Houses of Parliament

Westminster Abbey

Great Smith St.

Great Peter St.

Marsham St.

SMITH SQUARE

Victoria Tower Gardens

Lambeth Br.

Thames House

N

Tate Gallery

Millbank

River Thames

Albert Embankment

Vauxhall Bridge

Victoria Embankment

0   1/8 mile

0   125 meters

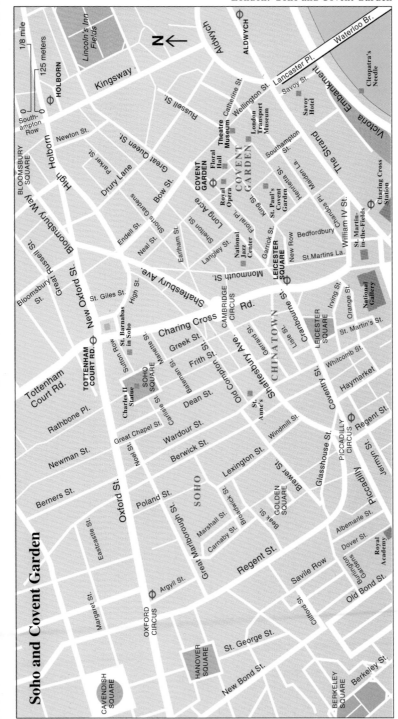

Soho and Covent Garden

London: Soho and Covent Garden

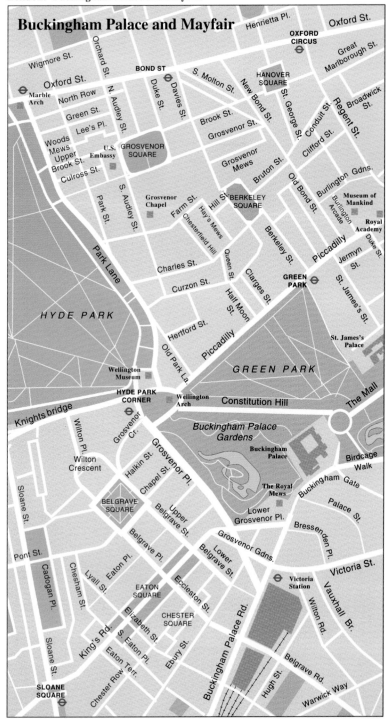

Buckingham Palace and Mayfair

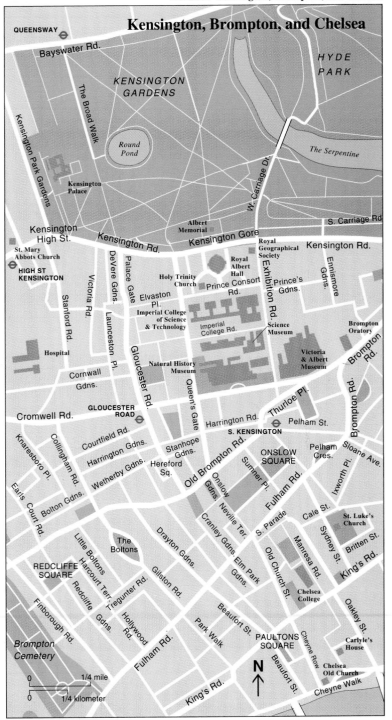

Kensington, Brompton, and Chelsea

QUEENSWAY

Bayswater Rd.

KENSINGTON GARDENS

HYDE PARK

The Broad Walk

Kensington Park Gardens

Round Pond

The Serpentine

Kensington Palace

W. Carriage Dr.

S. Carriage Rd.

Albert Memorial

Kensington High St.

Kensington Rd.

Kensington Gore

Kensington Rd.

St. Mary Abbots Church

HIGH ST KENSINGTON

DeVere Gdns.

Palace Gate

Holy Trinity Church

Prince Consort Rd.

Royal Albert Hall

Royal Geographical Society

Exhibition Rd.

Prince's Gdns.

Ennismore Gdns.

Victoria Rd.

Launceston Pl.

Elvaston Pl.

Imperial College of Science & Technology

Imperial College Rd.

Science Museum

Brompton Oratory

Stanford Rd.

Hospital

Cornwall Gdns.

Gloucester Rd.

Natural History Museum

Queen's Gate

Victoria & Albert Museum

Brompton Rd.

Cromwell Rd.

GLOUCESTER ROAD

Thurloe Pl.

Harrington Rd.

S. KENSINGTON

Pelham St.

Knaresboro Pl.

Collingham Rd.

Courtfield Rd.

Harrington Gdns.

Wetherby Gdns.

Stanhope Gdns.

Hereford Sq.

Old Brompton Rd.

ONSLOW SQUARE

Pelham Cres.

Sloane Ave.

Ixworth Pl.

Earls Court Rd.

Bolton Gdns.

Onslow Gdns.

Neville Ter.

Sumner Pl.

Fulham Rd.

S. Parade

Cale St.

St. Luke's Church

Little Boltons

Harcourt Terr.

The Boltons

Drayton Gdns

Cranley Gdns.

Elm Park Gdns.

Old Church St.

Manresa Rd.

Sydney St.

Britten St.

King's Rd.

REDCLIFFE SQUARE

Redcliffe Gdns.

Tregunter Rd.

Gilston Rd.

Hollywood Rd.

Beaufort St.

Chelsea College

Oakley St.

Finborough Rd.

Park Walk

PAULTONS SQUARE

Cheyne Row

Carlyle's House

Brompton Cemetery

Fulham Rd.

King's Rd.

Beaufort St.

Chelsea Old Church

Cheyne Walk

N

0   1/4 mile

0   1/4 kilometer

London: City of London

The City

N ←

Commercial St.
Leman St.
Mansell St.
Middlesex St.
Widegate St.
ALDGATE EAST
Houndsditch
Minories
Liverpool St. Station
St. Mary Axe
ALDGATE
Bishopsgate
Old Broad St.
Sun St.
London Stock Exchange
Leadenhall St.
Fenchurch St. Station
Royal Mint St.
E. Smithfield
St. Katharine's Way
Tower Br. Approach
Tower Br.
TOWER HILL
TRINITY SQUARE
Tower Hill
Pepys St.
Seething La.
St. Olave's
Mark La.
Mincing La.
St. Dunstan's
All Hallows
The Tower
Tower Pier
HMS Belfast
South Pl.
FINSBURY CIRCUS
London Wall
Throgmorton Ave.
Threadneedle St.
Lloyd's
Leadenhall Market
Lime St.
Fenchurch St.
Gracechurch St.
St. Mary at Hill
Gt. Tower St.
Lower Thames St.
Billingsgate Market
Ropemaker St.
Chiswell St.
Moorgate
MOORGATE
London Wall
St. Margaret's
Lothbury St.
Bank of England
BANK
Cornhill
Lombard St.
King William St.
St. Mary Abchurch
Eastcheap
MONUMENT
The Monument
Monument St.
St. Magnus Martyr
London Br.
Silk St.
Beech St.
Fore St.
Moorfields
Coleman St.
Bassinghall Ave.
Basinghall St.
Princes St.
Mansion House
Poultry
St. Stephen Walbrook
Walbrook
Temple of Mithras
Cloak La.
CANNON
Cannon St. Station
Southwark Br.
Barbican Centre
Aldersgate St.
Guildhall
Gresham St.
Bassishaw St.
King St.
St. Mary le Bow
Watling St.
Bread St.
St. Mary Aldermary
MANSION HOUSE
Cannon St.
Queen St.
Upper Thames St.
River Thames
BARBICAN
Long Lane
St. Giles without Cripplegate
Museum of London
London Wall
Wood St.
Milk St.
Cheapside
New Change
Queen Victoria St.
St. Bartholomew the Great
St. Martin's-Le-Grand
St. Paul's Cathedral
ST. PAUL'S
St. Andrew-by-the-Wardrobe
St. Benet's
Puddle Dock
Blackfriars Station
St. John St.
West Smithfield
Little Britain
Gilspur St.
Old Bailey
Newgate St.
Warwick La.
Ludgate Hill
FARRINGDON
Cowcross St.
Smithfield Market
Holborn Viaduct Station
Snow Hill
Holborn Viaduct
Fleet La.
Old Bailey
LUDGATE CIRCUS
New Bridge St.
Blackfriars Br.
BLACKFRIARS
Clerkenwell Rd.
Ely Pl.
Hatton Garden
Greville St.
Fetter La.
Farringdon Rd.
Shoe Lane
New Fetter La.
St. Bride St.
Fleet St.
GOUGH SQ.
Tudor St.
Temple Ave.
Temple Church
Middle Temple La.
BLACKFRIARS
Victoria Embankment
The Temple

0 ___ 1/4 mile
0 ___ 1/4 km

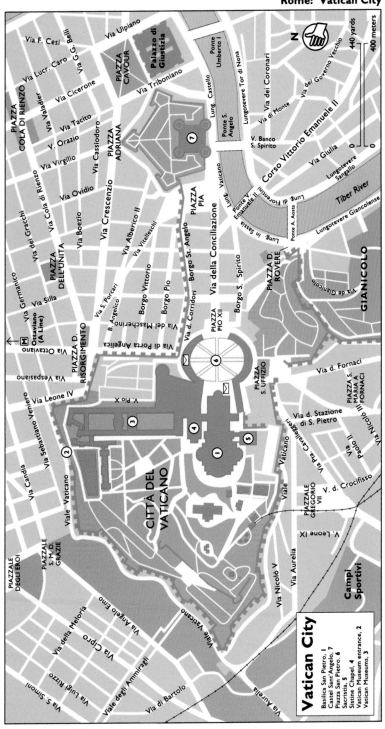

Rome: Vatican City

Vatican City

Basilica San Pietro, **1**
Castel Sant'Angelo, **7**
Piazza San Pietro, **6**
Sacristia, **5**
Sistine Chapel, **4**
Vatican Museum entrance, **2**
Vatican Museums, **3**

Rome Overview

Villa Borghese

Via Po

Via Salaria

V. Isonzo

Viale Regina Margherita

V. Dalmazia

Via Nizza

Via Nomentana

Corso d'Italia

Via Piave

Policlinico
Universita

Via V. Veneto

Via Boncompagni

XX Settembre

Viale Regina Elena

nish
ps

V. Ludovisi

Biblioteca
Nazionale

Via Palestro

Via del Policlinico

Via dell'Università

Sistina

SALARIO

Museo
Nazionale
Romano
PIAZZA DEL
CINQUECENTO

Via Castro Pretorio

ia del Tritone

Via Barberini

Via

PIAZZA
DELLA
REPUBBLICA

vi
ain

V. d. Quattro Fontane

Stazione
Termini

Via Marsala

Palazzo dei
Quirinale

Via Nazionale

Via Giovanni Giolitti

Via Tiburtina

Via Panisperna

Via Cavour

Via Merulana

V. dei Fori Imperiali

Via Cavour

Via Giovanni Lanza

PIAZZA
VITTORIO
EMANUELE

Forum

PIAZZA DEL
COLOSSEO

Via Labicana

Via Emanuele Filiberto

Viale Manzoni

V. S. Croce in Gerusalemme

Stazilia

PIAZZA
DI PTA.
MAGGIORE

**MONTE
PALATINO**

Colosseum

Via di S. Gregorio

Via Chiuda

*Parco del
Celio*

Via di S. Stefano Rotondo

P. DI SAN
GIOVANNI
IN LATERANO

San Giovanni in
Laterano

Via dei Cerchi

Circo Massimo

Circus Maximus

al Circo Massimo

CELIO

Via della
Navicella

Via dell'Amba Aradam

Via d. Laterani

Via Appia

INO

Via delle Terme

Via Druso

Viale Gallia

P. DEI RE
DI ROMA

Viale Aventino

Via Aventina

Viale Metronio

Via Cerveteri

Nuova

**Terme di
Caracalla**

Via di Porta Latina

Via Satrico

Via Etruria

esta

Viale di Terme di Caracalla

Via di Porta Sebastiano

Via Vetulonia

Via Concordia

Viale Giotto

Viale Guido Baccelli

Via Sina

Rome Transport

TO YOUTH
HOSTEL

FLAMINIO

A-LINE

Via G. Ferrari

Via Flaminia

•628•

•490•628•

•490•

•628•

Viale Angelico

•32•

•23•70•

Via Triomfale

Via Triomfale

Circ.

Via Lepanto

Via Mercanti
Colonna

PIAZZA
DEL
POPOLO

•70•490•

Viale delle Milizie

LEPANTO

Viale delle
Medaglie d'Oro

•490•

Via Andrea Doria

Viale Giulio Cesare

•70•

Via di Ripetta

Via di Ripetta

•628•

Via del Babuino

A-LINE

Via Cipro

Via Leone IV

V. Ottaviano

A-LINE

OTTAVIANO

Via Cola di Rienzo

•81•

•117•628•

Via del Corso

Via Cor

•32•81•

Via Cicerone

PIAZZA
CAVOUR

•70•32•

•32•

MOSCA

81 492

•23•492•

Via Crescenzio

•34•492•

•23•492•

Via d.
Conciliazione

PIAZZA
RISORGIMENTO

64

St. Peter's
Basilica

Castel
Sant'Angelo

34

•81•

•70•81•628•

PIA
SIL

•116•

PIAZZA
COLONNA

Viale
Vaticano

Tiber

Viale dei Coronari

870

•46•64•

•34•46•

Corso Vittorio Emanuele II

•70•81•116•
•492•628•

PIAZZA
NAVONA

•116•

Pantheon

Tiber

•23•870•

Via Giulia

•870•

CAMPO
DEI FIORI

•44•46•60•64•7
•81•170•492•62

V. d. Plebescito

•44•46•

Stazione
S. Pietro

34

Viale Gregorio VII

•870•

116

LARGO
ARGENTINA

Via Arenula

MONTE
DEL
GIANICOLO

Teatro
Marcello

Via Teatro Ma

Isola
Tiberina

Via Aurelia Antica

60

TRASTEVERE

PIAZZA
SONNINO

•44•170•

V. Nicola Fabrizi

Viale Glorioso

Via di S. Pancrazio

•44•870•

Via Giacinto Carini

•44•870•

Via
Dandolo

Viale di Trastevere

Porta
Portese

•23•

•23•715•

A

Via di Villa Pamphili

Via dei Quattro Venti

Via G. Barrilli

Via Alessandro Poerio

•13•170•

Via Marmorata

Via Vitelli

•870•

Via Fontejana

•13•313•715•

Via Giovanni Branca

Via Nicola Zabaglia

Via Galvani

•673•

Via

•44•

Via F. Ozanam

Parco
Testaccio

PIRAMID

13

Via di Donna Olimpia

•13•

Stazione
Trastevere

TESTACCIO

N

Circonvallazione

Gianicolense

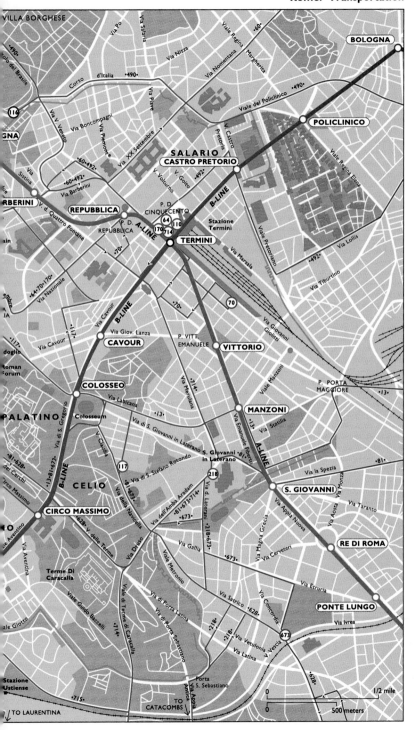

VILLA BORGHESE

BOLOGNA

POLICLINICO

Viale del Policlinico

Via Po

Via Salaria

Viale Regina Margherita

·60·

Via Nizza

Via Nomentana

·490·

Corso d'Italia ·490·

·490·

(116)

GNA

V. Castro Pretorio

Via V. Veneto

Via Boncompagni

Via Piemonte

XX Settembre

Via Piave

Viale Regina Elena

SALARIO

CASTRO PRETORIO

Via Pretoriano

Via Lollis

RBERINI

Via Sistina

·60·492·

Via XX Settembre

V. Volturno

V. Gaeta

·492·

Via Tiburtino

Via Barberini

·60·492·

B-LINE

·492·

REPUBBLICA

P. D. CINQUECENTO

Stazione Termini

V. d'Quattro Fontane

REPUBBLICA

A-LINE

(64) (110)

(170) (714)

ain

·70·

TERMINI

Via Marsala

·64·70·170·

Via Nazionale

B-LINE

Via Cavour

·70·

(70)

Via Giovanni Giolitti

·117·

Via Giov. Lanza

Via Cavour

CAVOUR

P. VITT. EMANUELE

VITTORIO

doglio

·117·

Roman Forum

ebbica IA

COLOSSEO

Via Labicana

·13·

Via Merulana

Viale Manzoni

P. PORTA MAGGIORE

·13·

PALATINO

Colosseum

V. Claudia

Via di S. Giovanni in Laterano

MANZONI

·13·

Via Statilia

A-LINE

Via di S. Gregorio

·81·628·

·13·81·673·

B-LINE

CELIO

(117)

Via di S. Stefano Rotondo

S. Giovanni in Laterano

·81·

·81·

Via la Spezia

del Cerchi

·81·673·

(218)

·81·673·71·

S. GIOVANNI

Via Aosta

Via Monza

Circo Massimo

CIRCO MASSIMO

·628·

Via delle Terme

Via della Navicella

Via dell'Amba Aradam

·673·

Via d. Laterani

·218·673·

Via Appia Nuova

Via Taranto

le Aventino

Via Aventina

·218·

RE DI ROMA

Terme Di Caracalla

Viale Guido Baccelli

·714·

Viale di Terme di Caracalla

Via Druso

Via di Porta Latina

Via Gallia

Via Metronio

·673·

Via Cerveteri

Via Magna Grecia

Via Etruria

PONTE LUNGO

le Giotto

Via Satrico

·628·

Via Concordia

Via Vescia

Via Ivrea

Stazione Ostiense

·218·

Via di Porta Sebastiano

·218·

Via Vetulonia

(673)

·628·

·715·

Via Latina

Porta S. Sebastiano

TO CATACOMBS

Via Appia Antica

TO LAURENTINA

0   1/2 mile

0   500 meters

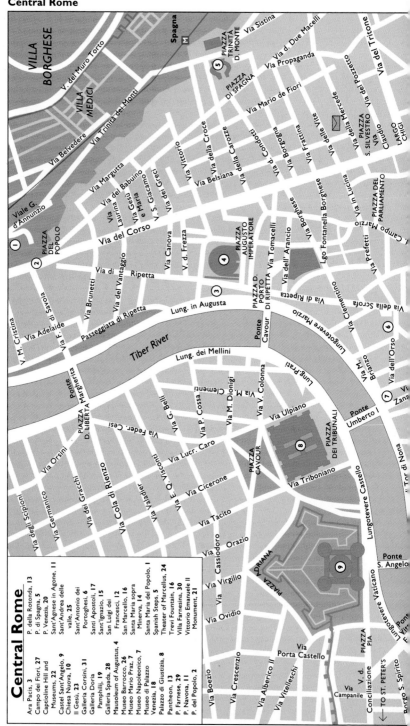

Central Rome

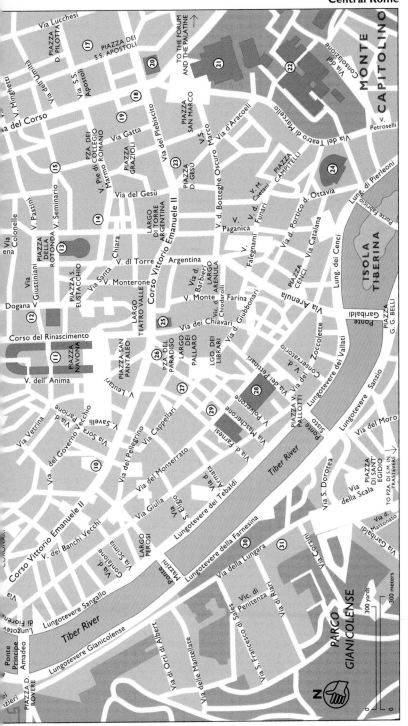

Central Rome

Rome: Villa Borghese

N

200 yards
200 meters

Corso d'Italia

V. Puglia
V. Romagna
Via Sardegna
Via Sicilia
Via Piemonte
Via Boncompagni
Via Quintina
Via Toscana
Via Marche
Via Vittorio Veneto
Via Emilia
Via Aurora
Via Ludovisi
Via Liguria

Giovanni Paisiello
Via S. Mercadante
V. Giovanelli
Via P. Raimondi
Via dei Daini
PIAZZALE DEI RAIMONDI
Galleria Borghese
Via dell'Uccelleria
V. Puzzi
Viale Museo Borghese
PIAZZA E. SIENKIEWICZ
Via di S. Teresa
Via Po
Via Pinciana

VILLA BORGHESE
GIARDINO ZOOLOGICO
Zoologico
Viale dei Cavalli Marini
Viale d. Canonica
PIAZZA DI SIENA
Pineta
Viale Goethe
PIAZZALE BRASILE
Porta Pinciana
Viale del Giardino
Viale Ulisse Aldrovandi
PIAZZALE D. CANESTRE
Viale Casina di Raffaello
Via di S. Paolo del Brasile
Via P. Raimondi

Galleria Naz. d'Arte Moderne
Via Omero
Via dell'Aranciera
V.-F. Laguardia
Via delle Belle Arti
Viale Valladier
Via di Muro Torto
GALOPPATOIO
Viale Galoppatoio
Via del Babuino
Spagna
A LINE

Museo Naz. di Villa Giulia
PIAZZALE PAOLA BORGHESE
Via Bernadotte
PIAZZALE DEL FIOCCO
Viale Madama
Via Washington
PIAZZALE DEI MARTIRI
VILLA MEDICI
Viale d. Belvedere
Viale Trinità dei Monti

VILLA STROHL FERN
VILLA RUFFO
Flaminio
PIAZZALE FLAMINIO
PIAZZA DEL POPOLO
Via del Babuino
Via del Corso
Via A. Canova
Via della Croce
Via Vittoria
PIAZZA AUGUSTO IMPERATORE
Via della Ripetta

V. di Villa Giulia
V. di S. Eugenio
Via Flaminia
Via Flaminia
Via Savoia
V. Disavoia
Via Brunetti
Via del Vantaggio
Lungo. in Augusta

PIAZZA DELLA MARINA
V. D. A. Azuni
V. G. Pisanelli
V. Romanosi
Ponte Margheria
Lungo. d. Mellini
Via Fed. Cesi
Via G. Belli

Lungotevere delle Navi
Lungo. Arnaldo da Brescia
Ponte Nenni
PIAZZA D. LIBERTA
Via Cola di Rienzo

Ponte d. Risorg
Fiume Tevere
Ponte G. Matteoti
Lungo. Michelangelo
PIAZZA COLA DI RIENZO
Via Boezio

PIAZZA MONTE GRAPPA
Lungotevere delle Armi
PIAZZA DELLE CINQUE GIORNATE
A LINE
Lepanto
Via Giulio Cesare
Via degli Scipioni
Via Pompeo Magno
Via dei Gracchi
PIAZZA D. LIBERTA
Viale Valladier
Via E. Q. Visconte
Via G. Belli

Viale Giuseppe Mazzini
Viale della Milizie
Via Settembrini
Via Marc. Colonna
Via Ezio

Villa **Borghese**

Paris Metro

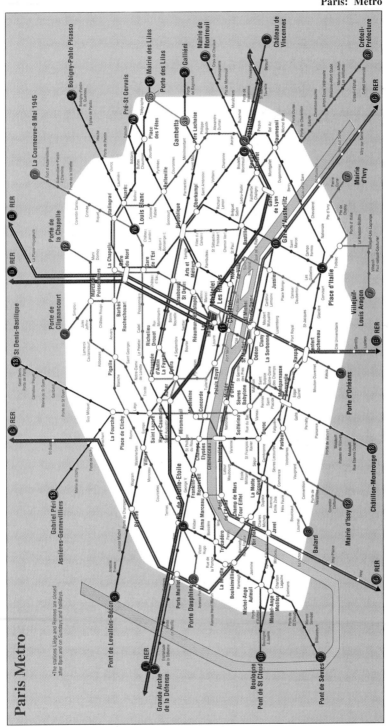

Paris: Metro

• The stations Liège and Rennes are closed after 8pm and on Sundays and holidays.

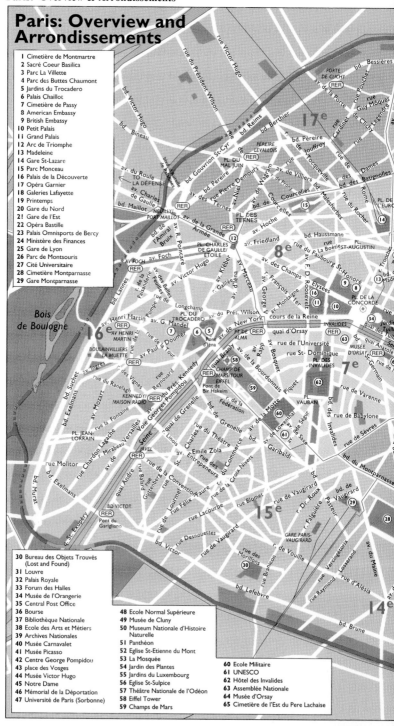

Paris: Overview and Arrondissements

1 Cimetière de Montmartre
2 Sacré Coeur Basilica
3 Parc La Villette
4 Parc des Buttes Chaumont
5 Jardins du Trocadero
6 Palais Chaillot
7 Cimetière de Passy
8 American Embassy
9 British Embassy
10 Petit Palais
11 Grand Palais
12 Arc de Triomphe
13 Madeleine
14 Gare St-Lazare
15 Parc Monceau
16 Palais de la Découverte
17 Opéra Garnier
18 Galeries Lafayette
19 Printemps
20 Gare du Nord
21 Gare de l'Est
22 Opéra Bastille
23 Palais Omnisports de Bercy
24 Ministère des Finances
25 Gare de Lyon
26 Parc de Montsouris
27 Cité Universitaire
28 Cimetière Montparnasse
29 Gare Montparnasse

30 Bureau des Objets Trouvés
(Lost and Found)
31 Louvre
32 Palais Royale
33 Forum des Halles
34 Musée de l'Orangerie
35 Central Post Office
36 Bourse
37 Bibliothèque Nationale
38 Ecole des Arts et Métiers
39 Archives Nationales
40 Musée Carnavalet
41 Musée Picasso
42 Centre George Pompidou
43 place des Vosges
44 Musée Victor Hugo
45 Notre Dame
46 Mémorial de la Déportation
47 Université de Paris (Sorbonne)

48 Ecole Normal Supérieure
49 Musée de Cluny
50 Museum Nationale d'Histoire
Naturelle
51 Panthéon
52 Eglise St-Etienne du Mont
53 La Mosquée
54 Jardin des Plantes
55 Jardins du Luxembourg
56 Eglise St-Sulpice
57 Théâtre Nationale de l'Odéon
58 Eiffel Tower
59 Champs de Mars

60 Ecole Militaire
61 UNESCO
62 Hôtel des Invalides
63 Assemblée Nationale
64 Musée d'Orsay
65 Cimetière de l'Est du Pere Lachaise

Paris: 1er and 2e

Gare St-Lazare

9e

R. d'Amsterdam

Rue de St-Lazare

Rue de la Chaussée d'Antin

Richelieu Drouot

M St Lazare

Rue du Havre

M

Havre-Caumartin

Chaussée d'Antin

M

La Fayette

M

Boulevard Haussmann

M

Bd. Haussmann

M

Rue Auber

Rue

Opéra

Boulevard des Italiens

Rue Favart

Rue Tronchet

RER **Auber**

Scribe

Bd. des Capucines

M **Opéra**

RER

Rue du Quatre

Septe

M

Quatre Septembre

Rue Daunou

R. Chabanais

Rue Pasquier

Rue des Capucines

Rue de la Paix

Rue D. Casanova

Rue des Petits C

Madeleine

Bd. de la Madeleine

M

Madeleine

Rue Boissy d'Anglas

Rue Royale

Bd. de la Madeleine

M

La Colonne

PLACE VENDÔME

Pyramides

Avenue de l'Opéra

Rue Thérèse

Rue St-Honoré

Rue de la Sourdière

Rue St-Roch

1er

8e

Rue Castiglione

Rue St-Honoré

Rue des Pyramides

M **Concorde**

R. de Mondovi

Rue du Mont Thabor

PLACE ANDRE MALRAU

M

Rue de Rivoli

Tuileries

M

Palais Musé Lou

Jeu de Paume

PLACE DE LA CONCORDE

JARDIN DES TUILERIES

PLAC CARR

L'Orangerie

Quai des Tuileries

Pt. de la Concorde

Seine

Pont Solférino

Pont Royal

Pont du Carrousel

Quai Anatole France

Quai Voltaire

Assemblée Nationale

Assemblée Nationale

M

Musée d'Orsay

RER

Musée d'Orsay

Rue de Lille

Bd. St-Germain

7e

Ecole Na Superie Bea

| 0 | | 1/8 mile |

| 0 | | 125 meters |

Solférino

M

Rue de l'Université

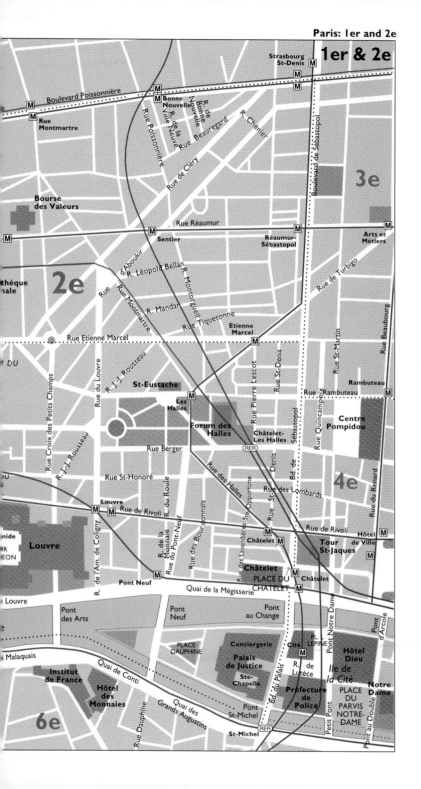

Strasbourg St-Denis Ⓜ

3e

Boulevard Poissonnière

Ⓜ Bonne Nouvelle

Rue Montmartre

Ⓜ Rue Montmartre

Rue Poissonnière

R. de la Ville Neuve

Rue Beauregard

R. Chénier

Boulevard de Sébastopol

Bourse des Valeurs

Rue Réaumur

Ⓜ Sentier

Réaumur-Sébastopol

Ⓜ

Arts et Métiers Ⓜ

thèque nale

2e

Rue de Cléry

d'Aboukir

R. Léopold Bellan

R. Montorgueil

Rue de Turbigo

Rue Beaubourg

Rue

Rue Montmartre

R. Mandar

Rue Tiquetonne

Rue Etienne Marcel

Etienne Marcel Ⓜ

DU

Rue du Louvre

R.-J.-J. Rousseau

St-Eustache

Les Halles Ⓜ

Rue Pierre Lescot

Rue St-Denis

Rue St-Martin

Rambuteau Ⓜ

Rue Rambuteau

Centre Pompidou

Rue Croix des Petits Champs

Forum des Halles

Châtelet-Les Halles

RER

Bd. de Sébastopol

Rue Quincampoix

Rue du Renard

R.-J.-J. Rousseau

Rue Berger

Rue St-Honoré

R. du Roule

Rue des Halles

Denis

Rue St-Denis

4e

Rue des Lombards

Louvre Ⓜ Ⓜ Rue de Rivoli

R. de la Monnaie

Rue du Pont-Neuf

Rue des Bourdonnais

Rue des Lavandières-Ste-Opportune

Rue de Rivoli

Hôtel de Ville Ⓜ

Louvre

Châtelet Ⓜ

Tour St-Jaques

Ⓜ

nide UR EON

Pont Neuf

Châtelet

PLACE DU CHATELET Ⓜ Châtelet Ⓜ

Louvre

Quai de la Mégisserie

Pont Neuf

Pont des Arts

Pont au Change

Pont Notre Dame

Pont d'Arcole

Malaquais

PLACE DAUPHINE

Conciergerie

Cité Ⓜ

PL. LEPINE

Hôtel Dieu

Institut de France

Quai de Conti

Palais de Justice

R. de Lutèce

Ile de la Cité

Notre Dame

Hôtel des Monnaies

Quai des Grands Augustins

Ste-Chapelle

Bd. du Palais

Préfecture de Police

PLACE DU PARVIS NOTRE-DAME

6e

Rue Dauphine

Pont St-Michel

St-Michel

RER

Petit Pont

Pont au Double

Paris: 5e and 6e

Pont Neuf

Châtelet — M

Palais du Louvre

Quai du Louvre

Pont des Arts

1er

Pont Neuf

Pont au Change

Pont du Carrousel

Conciergerie

Cité — M

Quai Malaquais

Quai de Conti

Ste-Chapelle

Ile de la Cité

Rue de la Cité

Ecole Nationale Supérieure des Beaux Arts

R. Bonaparte

Institut de France

Hôtel des Monnaies

Quai des Grands Augustins

Pont St-Michel

Pont St-Michel — RER

Rue des Sts-Pères

Rue Jacob

Rue de Seine

Rue Mazarine

Rue Dauphine

St-Michel

St-Michel

Pl. St-Michel

Rue St-Jacques

R. de l'Abbaye

Rue St-André des Arts

Rue Danton

PLACE ST-GERMAIN-DES-PRÉS — M

St-Germain Des Prés

Bd. St-Germain — M

Bd. St-Germain

Rue St-Michel

Bd. St-Germain

St-Germain des Prés — M

Mabillon

Odéon

Musée du Cluny

7e

R. du Four

Rue de l'Odéon

Boulevard

R. de Sèvres

R. du Vieux Colombier

Rue de Tournon

Rue de l'Odéon

Rue Racine

St-Michel

Sorbonne

R. du Saint Sulpice

PLACE ST-SULPICE

St-Sulpice

PLACE DE L'ODÉON

PLACE DE LA SORBONNE

R. du Cherche Midi

R. d'Assas

R. de Rennes

M — St-Sulpice

Rue Soufflot

Bd. Raspail

Palais du Luxembourg

Luxembourg — M

Rennes — M

R. de Vaugirard

6e

Rue Gay-Lu

St Placide — M

JARDIN DU LUXEMBOURG

Rue du Montparnasse

Notre-Dame des Champs — M

Rue d'Assas

Rue Vavin

Rue Notre-Dame des Champs

Boulevard St-Michel

Montparnasse Bienvenüe — M

Vavin — M

Boulevard du Montparnasse

Avenue de

Port Royal — M

14e

R. du Départ

Boulevard Raspail

la Observatoire

Edgar Quinet — M

Boulevard Edgar Quinet

Hôtel de Ville

4e

R. St-Paul

R. de l'Ave Maria

Bastille M

Boulevard Henri IV

Pont Marie
M
Quai des Célestins

Pont Louis Philippe

Pont Marie

e du re Dame

Rue St-Louis

Musée Mickiewicz

Rue des Deux Ponts

en l'Ile **Ile St-Louis**

M

Sully Morland

Notre Dame

Pont St-Louis

Pont de la Tournelle

Pont de Sully

Quai de la Rapeo

M

Montebello

Musée de l'Assistance Publique

R. de Bièvre

R. des Bernadins

R. de Pontoise

R. de Poissy

Boulevard St-Germain

Institut du Monde Arabe

Musée de la Sculpture en Plein Air

Seine

Quai

St-Bernard

RT

M

es Ecoles

R. Monge

R. du Cardinal Lemoine

Rue des Fossés St-Bernard

Musée de Minéralogie

Rue Cuvier

PLACE VALHUBERT

RER

M

Cardinal Lemoine
M

Rue

Jussieu M

Rue

Juissieu

Rue Lime

JARDIN DES PLANTES

Gare d'Austerlitz

St-Etienne du Mont

Arènes de Lutèce

○

Rue Cujas

Rue Rollin

5e

Rue Geoffroy

Saint Hilaire

Musée d'Histoire Naturelle

Gare d'Austerlitz

M

nthéon

Rue Lacepede

e l'Estrapade

Rue Mouffetard

Place Monge
M

PLACE MONGE

Rue Buffon

Rue Lhomond

Rue Monge

Institut Musulman et Mosque

Rue Poliveau

Rue Erasme Brossolette

St-Marcel M

Rue Claude Bernard

Censier Daubenton
M

Rue Bertholet

Boulevard St Marcel

Bd. de l'Hôpital

Campo Formio
M

Grâce

Gobelins
M

Boulevard de Port Royal

Avenue des Gobelins

13e

Paris: RER

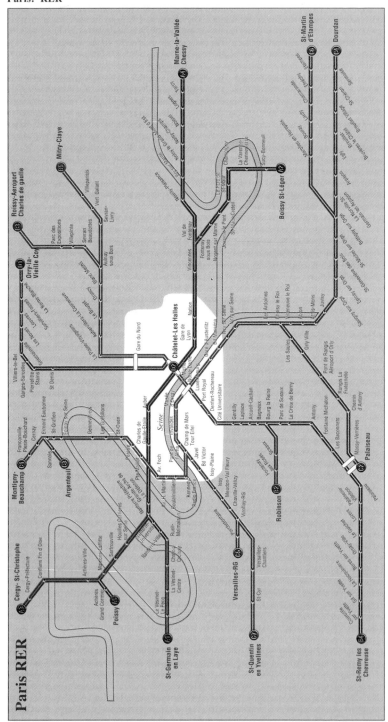

LET'S GO
Europe 1999

■ Let's Go writers travel on your budget.

"Guides that penetrate the veneer of the holiday brochures and mine the grit of real life."
—*The Economist*

"The writers seem to have experienced every rooster-packed bus and lunar-surfaced mattress about which they write."
—*The New York Times*

"All the dirt, dirt cheap."
—*People*

■ Great for independent travelers.

"The guides are aimed not only at young budget travelers but at the independent traveler, a sort of streetwise cookbook for traveling alone."
—*The New York Times*

"Flush with candor and irreverence, chock full of budget travel advice."
—*The Des Moines Register*

"An indispensable resource. *Let's Go*'s practical information can be used by every traveler."
—*The Chattanooga Free Press*

■ Let's Go is completely revised each year.

"Only *Let's Go* has the zeal to annually update every title on its list."
—*The Boston Globe*

"Unbeatable: good sight-seeing advice; up-to-date info on restaurants, hotels, and inns; a commitment to money-saving travel; and a wry style that brightens nearly every page."
—*The Washington Post*

■ All the important information you need.

"*Let's Go* authors provide a comedic element while still providing concise information and thorough coverage of the country. Anything you need to know about budget traveling is detailed in this book."
—*The Chicago Sun-Times*

"Value-packed, unbeatable, accurate, and comprehensive."
—*Los Angeles Times*

Let's Go Publications

Let's Go: Alaska & the Pacific Northwest 1999
Let's Go: Australia 1999
Let's Go: Austria & Switzerland 1999
Let's Go: Britain & Ireland 1999
Let's Go: California 1999
Let's Go: Central America 1999
Let's Go: Eastern Europe 1999
Let's Go: Ecuador & the Galápagos Islands 1999
Let's Go: Europe 1999
Let's Go: France 1999
Let's Go: Germany 1999
Let's Go: Greece 1999 **New title!**
Let's Go: India & Nepal 1999
Let's Go: Ireland 1999
Let's Go: Israel & Egypt 1999
Let's Go: Italy 1999
Let's Go: London 1999
Let's Go: Mexico 1999
Let's Go: New York City 1999
Let's Go: New Zealand 1999
Let's Go: Paris 1999
Let's Go: Rome 1999
Let's Go: South Africa 1999 **New title!**
Let's Go: Southeast Asia 1999
Let's Go: Spain & Portugal 1999
Let's Go: Turkey 1999 **New title!**
Let's Go: USA 1999
Let's Go: Washington, D.C. 1999

Let's Go Map Guides

Amsterdam	Madrid
Berlin	New Orleans
Boston	New York City
Chicago	Paris
Florence	Rome
London	San Francisco
Los Angeles	Washington, D.C.

Coming Soon: Prague, Seattle

Let's Go Publications

Let's Go Europe 1999

Alex Zakaras
Editor

Karen M. Paik & Elizabeth E. White
Associate Editors

Researcher-Writers:
Tom Davidson
Greg Halpern
Manjari Mahajan
Bede Sheppard

Macmillan

HELPING LET'S GO

If you want to share your discoveries, suggestions, or corrections, please drop us a line. We read every piece of correspondence, whether a postcard, a 10-page email, or a coconut. Please note that mail received after May 1999 may be too late for the 2000 book, but will be kept for future editions. **Address mail to:**

Let's Go: Europe
67 Mount Auburn Street
Cambridge, MA 02138
USA

Visit Let's Go at **http://www.letsgo.com,** or send email to:

feedback@letsgo.com
Subject: "Let's Go: Europe"

In addition to the invaluable travel advice our readers share with us, many are kind enough to offer their services as researchers or editors. Unfortunately, our charter enables us to employ only currently enrolled Harvard-Radcliffe students.

Published in Great Britain 1999 by Macmillan, an imprint of Macmillan General Books, 25 Eccleston Place, London, SW1W 9NF and Basingstoke.

Maps by David Lindroth copyright © 1999, 1998, 1997, 1996, 1995, 1994, 1993, 1992, 1991, 1990, 1989, 1988 by St. Martin's Press, Inc.

Published in the United States of America by St. Martin's Press, Inc.

ISBN: 0 333 74744 5

First edition
10 9 8 7 6 5 4 3 2 1

Let's Go: Europe is written by Let's Go Publications, 67 Mount Auburn Street, Cambridge, MA 02138, USA.

Let's Go® and the thumb logo are trademarks of Let's Go, Inc.
Printed in the USA on recycled paper with biodegradable soy ink.

ADVERTISING DISCLAIMER

All advertisements appearing in Let's Go publications are sold by an independent agency not affiliated with the production of the guides. Advertisers are never given preferential treatment, and the guides are researched, written, and published independent of advertising. Advertisements do not imply endorsement of products or services by Let's Go. If you are interested in purchasing advertising space in a Let's Go publication, contact: Let's Go Advertising Sales, 67 Mount Auburn St., Cambridge, MA 02138, USA.

About Let's Go

THIRTY-NINE YEARS OF WISDOM

Back in 1960, a few students at Harvard University banded together to produce a 20-page pamphlet offering a collection of tips on budget travel in Europe. This modest, mimeographed packet, offered as an extra to passengers on student charter flights to Europe, met with instant popularity. The following year, students traveling to Europe researched the first, full-fledged edition of *Let's Go: Europe,* a pocket-sized book featuring honest, irreverent writing and a decidedly youthful outlook on the world. Throughout the 60s, our guides reflected the times; the 1969 guide to America led off by inviting travelers to "dig the scene" at San Francisco's Haight-Ashbury. During the 70s and 80s, we gradually added regional guides and expanded coverage into the Middle East and Central America. With the addition of our in-depth city guides, handy map guides, and extensive coverage of Asia and Australia, the 90s are also proving to be a time of explosive growth for Let's Go, and there's certainly no end in sight. The maiden edition of *Let's Go: South Africa,* our pioneer guide to sub-Saharan Africa, hits the shelves this year, along with the first editions of *Let's Go: Greece* and *Let's Go: Turkey.*

We've seen a lot in 39 years. *Let's Go: Europe* is now the world's bestselling international guide, translated into seven languages. And our new guides bring Let's Go's total number of titles, with their spirit of adventure and their reputation for honesty, accuracy, and editorial integrity, to 44. But some things never change: our guides are still researched, written, and produced entirely by students who know first-hand how to see the world on the cheap.

HOW WE DO IT

Our series is completely revised and thoroughly updated every year by a well-traveled set of over 200 students. Every winter, we recruit over 160 researchers and 70 editors to write the books anew. After several months of training, researcher-writers hit the road for seven weeks of exploration, from Anchorage to Adelaide, Estonia to El Salvador, Iceland to Indonesia. Hired for their rare combination of budget travel sense, writing ability, stamina, and courage, these adventurous travelers know that train strikes, stolen luggage, food poisoning, and marriage proposals are all part of a day's work. Back at our offices, editors work from spring to fall, massaging copy written on Himalayan bus rides into witty yet informative prose. A student staff of typesetters, cartographers, publicists, and managers keeps our lively team together. In September, the collected efforts of the summer are delivered to our printer, who turns them into books in record time, so that you have the most up-to-date information available for your vacation. Even as you read this, work on next year's editions is well underway.

WHY WE DO IT

We don't think of budget travel as the last recourse of the destitute; we believe that it's the only way to travel. Living cheaply and simply brings you closer to the people and places you've been saving up to visit. Our books will ease your anxieties and answer your questions about the basics—so you can get off the beaten track and explore. Once you learn the ropes, we encourage you to put *Let's Go* down now and then to strike out on your own. You know as well as we that the best discoveries are often those you make yourself. When you find something worth sharing, please drop us a line. We're Let's Go Publications, 67 Mount Auburn St., Cambridge, MA 02138, USA (email: feedback@letsgo.com). For more info, visit our website, http://www.letsgo.com.

Contents

TRAVEL GUARD

INTERNATIONAL

America's leading travel insurance company.

How to get protection & make your family stop worrying.

1. Purchase our Special Student Program travel insurance (Ask for program #LG98) for your European trip.

2. Tell your parents you are covered for unforeseen circumstances such as: a medical emergency, theft or lost luggage.

3. Let them know there's a toll-free number you can call 24 hours a day, 7 days a week should you need Travel Guard Assistance.

4. Email them every day (ok, maybe every other day).

Protect yourself and your travel investment with America's #1 choice for travel insurance for as little as $24.

John M. Noel
President,
Travel Guard International

P.S. Traveling with a group? Call for our special group rates!

x

Maps

Color Maps

How to Use This Book

Once upon a time (well, actually, not all that long ago), the Grand Tour of Europe was the privilege of the aristocratic class. Often the finishing touch to an education, a trip around Europe was taken very seriously, with earnest intentions to broaden one's mind by meeting polite company in foreign lands, observing the countryside through the window of a coach, and recording curiosities in a journal to be passed around to friends at home. *Let's Go* believes that this kind of traveling only distances the traveler from the land—budget travel is not only a method for stretching your funds farther, but brings you closer to the actual people and culture of the country. Today you need not have a noble lineage (or even a Eurail pass) to experience the best of Europe—all that's required is an adventurous spirit and a trusty guide. Like this one.

Let's Go: Europe opens with a chapter of **Essentials** to guide you through the quagmire of preparations, with tips on passport and visa acquisition, packing, getting to Europe, and the budget travel opportunities once you're there. We've included a **Rail Planner** to help you map your path. The Essentials section also addresses specific concerns, such as those of women, bisexuals, gays, lesbians, travelers with disabilities, senior citizens, and travelers with children.

The rest of the book lists individual countries in alphabetical order. The 1999 guide covers roughly forty countries, including expanded coverage of Greece, Turkey, the Pyrenees, and Eastern Europe, and new coverage of the Former Yugoslavian Republic of Macedonia. England, Wales, and Scotland are grouped under Britain, while Northern Ireland is in the Ireland chapter (no political statement is intended by this arrangement). Map coverage has also been improved and expanded. Each chapter begins with a brief overview of that country's history and culture as well as country-specific Essentials, where you'll find such tidbits as visa requirements and the scoop on transportation, accommodations, regional cuisine, and a few helpful phrases in the national language.

For each major city, the **Orientation and Practical Information** section outlines the city's layout, shows you how to get there and to connecting cities, and explains how to communicate with folks back home. These sections also tell you where to go and whom to call in medical emergencies and crisis situations. Then we shower you with information on **Accommodations, Camping, Food, Sights,** and **Entertainment.** Smaller towns are usually divided in half: first we describe the sights, then we dig into the nitty-gritty: practical information, accommodations, and food. Gray boxes provide more detailed information on particular sights, history and art, as well as local customs and festivals.

Although our intrepid researcher-writers beat a trail across the continent annually, there are countless undiscovered travel gems in Europe. Keep an eye out for any amazing places we've missed, follow your own spirit and imagination, and feel free to write us about what you find.

A NOTE TO OUR READERS

The information for this book was gathered by *Let's Go*'s researchers from May through August of 1998. Each listing is derived from the assigned researcher's opinion based upon his or her visit at a particular time. The opinions are expressed in a candid and forthright manner. Other travelers might disagree. Those traveling at a different time may have different experiences since prices, dates, hours, and conditions are always subject to change. You are urged to check beforehand to avoid inconvenience and surprises. Travel always involves a certain degree of risk, especially in low-cost areas. When traveling, especially on a budget, always take particular care to ensure your safety.

Let's Go Picks

This book itself is a kind of "Greatest Hits" compilation—the best of Europe in under a thousand pages. But below we've chosen the true *crème de la crème:* the places and events that we'd most recommend. The list is subjective, of course; drop us a line and tell us what gets your thumb of approval.

Europe's Biggest Parties and Best Nightlife: The Love Parade (the second weekend of July), in Berlin, celebrates Germany's infatuation with techno (see p. 371), while beer flows (nay, gushes) at the annually inebriating **Oktoberfest** (Sept. 18-Oct. 3) in Munich (see p. 421). **Los San Fermines** (July 6-14) brings over a week of craziness in Pamplona, Spain (see p. 813). The Spanish island of **Ibiza's** world famous discos pump techno around the clock (see p. 831). Party naked at **Ios,** the most lively of the Greek islands (see p. 454). The antics of young people at the **Hungry Duck** in **Moscow** would make Vladimir Zhirinovsky blush (see p. 754).

Best Hiking: Iceland's **Interior** is the most forbidding and desolate wilderness in Europe (see p. 500). Stunning ocean views make **Pembrokeshire Coast National Park,** in England, and excellent place to don the hiking boots (see p. 165). Italy's **Dolomites** present stunning limestone spires and pine forests (see p. 559). In Switzerland, take your pick from the Alpine wonderlands of **Grindelwald** and **Zermatt** (see p. 886 and p. 887, respectively). The **Tirol** region in western Austria offers some of the world's most spectacular hiking (see p. 70).

Best Architecture: Spain's **Barcelona** (see p. 817) shocks with the bizarre splendor of Gaudí's creations, while to the north **Bilbao's** (see p. 809) miraculous new Guggenheim museum beckons from beyond winding streets. The skyline of **Istanbul,** Turkey (see p. 905), still dazzles with graceful minarets as it did five centuries ago. At **Mont-Saint-Michel** in Normandy, an abbey balances precariously on the jutting rock, surrounded by military fortifications (see p. 312). Amidst silver canals and rows of stone houses in **Bruges,** Belgium (see p. 109), reside some of the best examples of northern Renaissance architecture. The modest 16th-century monasteries with their painted frescoes await discovery in the green hills of **Bukovina,** Romania (see p. 737).

Best Food and Drink: Against the culinary dreamscape of Italy, **Naples** (see p. 588) earns its reputation for the world's best pizza. **Lyon** allows even budget travelers to partake in *haute cuisine* (see p. 343). Go tapas-bar hopping in **Seville,** the birthplace of this Spanish delicacy (see p. 837). Inside its coffeehouses, **Vienna** lovingly offers sumptuous pastries (see p. 76). To wash it all down, Europe is a continent of superlative spirits, with the exceptional ports of **Porto,** Portugal (see p. 724), and the best beers in Europe flowing from taps all around **Belgium.** Meanwhile, Hungary's **Valley of the Beautiful Women** overflows with wines and wineries open to the public for tastings.

Tomorrow's Hot Destinations: Having escaped mass Sovietization and retained its majestic, Baroque beauty, **Vilnius,** Lithuania, is experiencing a cultural and financial Renaissance (see p. 609). A fascinating and troubled past lends darkness and intrigue to trendy **Kraków,** Poland (see p. 695). The stunning **Dalmatian Coast** of Croatia, including Dubrovnik and the off-shore archipelago, are newly popular. Long protected from tourism, **Chios,** Greece, has gorgeous (and undiscovered) volcanic beaches and medieval villages (see p. 460). Discover **Berlin** all over again as restorations work their magic on this uniquely energetic and cutting-edge city (see p. 357).

Europe

- Honnigsvåg
- Rovaniemi
- neå

FINLAND

- L. Onega
- L. Ladoga
- *Gulf of Bothnia*

- Helsinki
- Tallinn
- St. Petersburg

- ockholm
- **ESTONIA**

Volga R.

- Nizhny Novgorod
- Rīga
- **LATVIA**
- Moscow

Baltic Sea

- **LITHUANIA**
- Vilnius
- **RUSSIA**
- **RUSSIA**
- Gdańsk
- Minsk
- **KAZAKHSTAN**

- arsaw
- **BELARUS**
- Volgograd

- **OLAND**
- Kraków
- Kiev
- Kharkiv

- **LOVAKIA**
- atislava
- Lviv
- **UKRAINE**
- *Dnieper River*

- Budapest
- **MOLDOVA**
- *Caspian Sea*

- **UNGARY**
- Chişinău
- Odessa
- *Sea of Azov*

- **ROMANIA**
- Rostov-na-Donu

- Belgrade
- Bucharest
- Yalta
- **GEORGIA**

- **YUGOSLAVIA**
- **ARMENIA**
- Sarajevo
- *Black Sea*

- **MONTENEGRO**
- **BULGARIA**
- **AZERBAIJAN**

- iranë
- Sofia
- Istanbul
- **IRAN**

- **FYR MACEDONIA**
- Ankara
- Thessaloniki

- **ALBANIA**
- **TURKEY**

- *Aegean Sea*

- onian Sea
- Izmir

- Athens
- **SYRIA**
- **IRAQ**

- **GREECE**
- Nicosia
- *Sea of Crete*
- Crete
- **LEBANON**
- **CYPRUS**

ESSENTIALS

Touring through the entirety of Europe, or even just a chunk of it, can be as daunting as it is exciting. Where to begin? Fortunately, there are countless resources devoted to helping travelers plan a journey through Europe. The organizations, publications, and tourist offices listed below can provide you with more than enough literature on your destination countries. All you need to do is dive in and plan a trip tailored to your specific interests and needs without losing sight of the fact that this is a vacation. Don't overplan your itinerary so that the trip becomes one big blur; just relax and wander through Europe at your own pace.

PLANNING YOUR TRIP

Give careful consideration to when and with whom you travel. Summer is the high season for traveling in Europe. *Everything* is crowded with tourists in July and August; June or September may be a better time to go. Traveling companions may insulate you from local culture, but they do share in food and lodging costs, as well as providing energy, comfort, and extra safety. If you choose to travel with others, discuss your trip in detail before you leave to make sure your interests are compatible. Going solo gives you freedom of movement but also the danger of loneliness and the need for extra safety precautions, particularly for women. A budget travel subculture fills Europe's hostels, ensuring that you will only be as lonely as you want to be.

■ Useful Information

GOVERNMENT INFORMATION OFFICES

> The following are **embassies** or **consulates** unless otherwise indicated.

Austria: Australia and New Zealand (National Tourist Office), 36 Carrington St. 1st fl., Sydney NSW 2000 (tel. (02) 92 99 36 21; fax 92 99 38 08). **Canada (National Tourist Office),** 1010 Ouest rue Sherbourne #1410, **Montreal,** Que. H3A 2R7 (tel. (514) 849-3709; fax 849-9577; email atcmtr@istar.ca); Granville Sq. #1380, 200 Granville St., **Vancouver,** BC V6C 1S4 (tel. (604) 683-8695; fax 662-8528; email atradebc.uniserve.com). **South Africa,** P.O. Box 95572 Waterkloof, Pretoria 0145 (tel. (012) 46 24 83; fax 46 11 51); **National Tourist Office,** Private Bag X18, Parklands, 2121 Johannesburg (tel. (011) 442 72 35; fax 442 83 04). **U.K. (Tourist Office),** 14 Cork St., London W1X 1PF (tel. (0171) 629 04 61; fax 499 60 38). **U.S. (National Tourist Office),** 500 Fifth Ave., Suite 800, **New York,** NY 10110 (tel. (212) 944-6880; fax 730-4568; email antonyc@ibm.net).
Belarus: U.K., 6 Kensington Court, London, W8 5DL (tel. (0171) 937 32 88; fax 361 00 05). **U.S.,** 1619 New Hampshire Ave. NW, Washington, D.C. 20009 (tel. (202) 986-1604; fax 986-1805).
Belgium: Belgium (Tourist Board), Grasmarkt 63, B-1000 Brussels (tel. (02) 504 03 90; fax 504 02 70). **Canada (Tourist Board),** P.O. Box 760, N.D.G., Montréal, QUE H4A 3S2 (tel. (514) 484-3594; fax 489-8965). **South Africa,** 625 Leyds St., Muckleneuk, Pretoria, 0002 (tel. (012) 44 32 01; fax 44 32 16). **U.K. (Tourist Office),** 31 Peper St., London E14 9RW. **U.S. (Tourist Board),** 780 Third Ave., #1501, New York, NY 10017 (tel. (212) 758-8130; fax 355-7675; http://www.visitbelgium.com).
Bosnia-Herzegovina: Australia (tel. (61 6) 257 5798); fax 257 7855) in Canberra. **U.K.,** 320 Regent St., London W1R 5AB (tel. (0171) 255 3758; fax 255 3760). **U.S.,** 2109 E St. NW, Washington, D.C. 20037 (tel. (202) 833-3612; fax 337-1502).
Britain: Australia (Tourist Authority), Level 16, Gateway Bldg., 1 Macquarie Pl., Sydney NSW 2000 (tel. (02) 9377 4400). **Canada (Tourist Authority),** 111 Ave-

nue Rd., Ste. 450, Toronto, Ont. M5R 3J8 (tel. (888) VISIT UK (847-4885) or (416) 925 6326). **New Zealand (Tourist Authority),** Dilworth Bldg., Ste. 305, Corner Customs and Queen St., Auckland 1 (tel. (09) 303 1446). **South Africa,** Southern Life Center, 8 Riebeeck St., Cape Town, 8000 (tel. (21) 25 36 70); **Tourist Authority,** Lancaster Gate, Hyde Ln. Manor, Hyde Park, Sandton 2196 (tel. (011) 325 0343; fax 325 0344). **U.S.,** 5551 Fifth Ave., Ste. 701, New York, NY 10176-0799 (tel. (800) GO2 BRIT (462 2748) or (212) 986 2200). On the **Internet,** http://www.vis-itbritain.com.

Bulgaria: Australia, 1/4 Carlotta Rd., Double Bay, Sydney, NSW 2028 (tel. (02) 9327 7581; fax 9327 8067; email lubo@tig.com.au). **Canada,** 325 Stewart St., Ottawa, ON K1N 6K5 (tel. (613) 789-3215; fax 789-3523). **U.K.,** 186-188 Queensgate, London SW7 5HL (tel. (0171) 584 9400; fax 584 4948); **Tourist Board,** Balkan Tourist, Osborne House, 111 Bartholomew Rd., London NW5 2BJ (tel. (0171) 485 5280; fax 485 5864). **U.S.,**1621 22nd St. NW, Washington, D.C. 20008 (tel. (202) 387-7969; fax 234-7973); **Tourist Board,** Balkan Holidays, 20 E. 46th St., #1003, New York, NY 10017 (tel. (212) 822-5900; fax 338-6830).

Croatia: Australia, 14 Jindalee Crescent, O'Malley, Canberra ACT 2606 (tel. (02) 6286 6988; fax 6286 3544). **Canada,**130 Albert St., #1700, Ottawa, ONT K1 P5 G4 (tel. (613) 230-7351; fax 230-7388). **New Zealand,** 131 Lincoln Rd., Henderson, P.O. Box 83200, Edmonton, Auckland (tel. (09) 836 55 81; fax 836 54 81). **South Africa,** 1160 Church Street, P.O. Box 11335, 0028 Hatfield, 083 Colbyn Pretoria (tel. (012) 342 12 06; fax 342 18 19). **U.K.,** 21 Conway St., London W1P 5HL (tel. (0171) 387 20 22; fax 387 05 74). **U.S.,** 2343 Massachusetts Ave. NW, Washington, D.C. 20008 (tel. (202) 588-5899; fax 588-8936).

Cyprus: South Africa, 1 Lakeside Pl., Ernest Oppenheimer Ave., Bruma 2198 (tel. (011) 622 45 17; fax 622 13 13). **U.K. (Tourist Office),** 213 Regent St., London W1R 8DA (tel. (171) 734 9822; fax 287 6534; email ctolon@ctolon.demon.co.uk). **U.S. (Tourist Office),** 13 E. 40th St., New York, NY 10016 (tel. (212) 683-5280).

Czech Republic: Australia, 38 Culgoa Circuit, O'Malley, Canberra, ACT 2606 (tel. (612) 290 13 86; fax 290 00 06; email canberra@embassy.mzv.cz). **Canada,** 541 Sussex Dr., Ottawa, ON K1N 6Z6 (tel. (613) 562-3875; fax 562-3878; email ottowa@embassy.mzv.cz). **Ireland,** 57 Northumberland Rd., Ballsbridge, Dublin 4 (tel. (3531) 668 1135; fax 668 1660; email dublin@embassy.mzv.cz). **New Zealand,** 48 Hair St., Wainuiomata, Wellington (tel./fax (644) 564 6001). **South Africa,** 936 Pretorius St., Arcadia, Pretoria 0083, or P.O. Box 3326, Pretoria 0001 (tel. (012) 342 34 77; fax 43 20 33). **U.K.,** 26 Kensington Palace Gardens, London W8 4QY (tel. (0171) 243 1115; fax 727 9654; email london@embassy.mzv.cz). **U.S. Embassy:** 3900 Spring of Freedom St. NW, Washington, D.C. 20008 (tel. (202) 274-9100; fax 966-8540; http://www.czech.cz/washington); **Tourist Board,** 1109-1111 Madison Ave., New York, NY 10028 (tel. (212) 288-0830; fax 288-0971).

Denmark: U.S. (Tourist Board), 655 Third Ave., New York, NY 10017 (tel. (212) 885-9700; fax 885-9710; http://www.visitdenmark.com). **South Africa,** P.O. Box 2942, Pretoria, 001 (tel. (012) 322 05 95; fax 322 05 96).

Estonia: On the Web: http://www.vm.ee. **Australia,** 86 Louisa Rd., Birchgrove 2041, NSW (tel. (612) 9810 7468; fax 9818 1779; email eestikon@ozemail.com.au). **Canada,** 958 Broadview Ave., Toronto, ON M4K 2R6 (tel. (416) 461-0764; fax 461-0353; email estconsu@inforamp.net). **Ireland,** Merlyn Park 24, Ballsbridge, Dublin 4 (tel. (3531) 269 1552; fax 260 5119; email asjur@indigo.ie). **South Africa,** 16 Hofmeyr St., Welgemoed 7530 (tel. (2721) 913 25 79; fax 933 50 48). **U.K.,** 16 Hyde Park Gate, London SW7 5DG (tel. (44171) 589 3428; fax 589 3430; email sekretar@estonia.gov.uk; http://www.estonia.gov.uk). **U.S.,** 2131 Massachusetts Ave. NW, Washington, D.C. 20008 (tel. (202) 588-0101; fax 588-0108; email info@estemb.org; http://www.estemb.org).

Finland: Australia (Tourist Board), Level 4, 81 York St., Sydney NSW 2000 (tel. (02) 9290 1950; fax (02) 9290 1981). **South Africa,** P.O. Box 443, Pretoria, 0001 (tel. (012) 343 02 75; fax 343 30 95). **U.K. (Tourist Board),** 30-35 Pall Mall, 3rd fl., London SW1Y 5LP (tel. (0171) 839 40 48; fax 321 06 96).**U.S. (Tourist Board),** 655 Third Ave., New York, NY 10017 (tel. (212) 885-9700; fax 885-9710; email mek.usa@mek.fi; http://www.travelfile.com/get/finninfo).

France: Australia, 31 Market St., 26th Fl., Sydney, NSW 2000 (tel. (02) 92 61 57 79); **Government Tourist Office,** 26 Perth Ave., Yarralumla, NSW 2000 (tel. (02) 6216-0100). **Canada (Tourist Office),** 1981 Ave., McGill College, #490, Montréal, PQ H3A 2W9 (tel. (514) 288-4264). **Ireland (Tourist Office),** 10 Suffolk St., Dublin 2 (tel. (01) 679 08 13). **New Zealanders** should contact the Consular Section of the French Embassy, 1 Willeston St., Wellington (tel. (64) 4 4720 200). **South Africa,** 807 George Ave., Arcadia, 0083 (tel. (012) 429 70 00; fax 429 70 29). **U.K. (Tourist Office),** 178 Piccadilly, London W1V OAL (tel. (0171) 629 1272). **U.S. (Tourist Office),** 444 Madison Ave., 16th fl., New York, NY 10022 (tel. (212) 838-7800).

Germany: Australia (National Tourist Office), German-Australia Chamber of Industry of Commerce, PO Box A 980, Sydney South, NSW 1235 (tel. (02) 9267 8148; fax 9267 9035). **Canada (National Tourist Office),** 175 Bloor St. E., North Tower, Ste. 604, Toronto, ONT M4W 3R8 (tel. (416) 968-1570; fax 968-1986; email germanto@idirect.com; http:www.germany-tourism.de). **South Africa (National Tourist Office),** 22 Girton Rd., Parktown, PO Box 10883, Johannesburg 2000 (tel. (11) 643 16 15; fax 484 27 50). **U.K. (National Tourist Office),** 34 Belgrave Sq.,London SW1X 8QB (tel. (0171) 824 13 00; fax 824 15 66; http://www.german-embassy.org.uk). **U.S. (National Tourist Office),** 122 E. 42nd St., 52nd Fl., New York, NY 10168 (tel. (212) 661-7200; fax 661-7174; email gntony@aol.com).

Greece: Australia (National Tourist Organization), 3rd Fl., 51 Pitt St., **Sydney,** NSW 2000 (tel. (02) 9241 1663; fax 9235 2174). **Canada (National Tourist Organization),** 300 Bay St., Toronto, ON M5R 3K8 (tel. (416) 968-2220; fax 968-6533; http://www.aei.ca/gntomtl); 1233 rue de la Montagne, Suite 101, Montréal, PQ, H3G 1Z2 (tel. (514) 871-1535; fax 871-1498; email gntomtl@aei.ca). **South Africa,** 995 Pretorius St., Arcadia, 0083 (tel. (012) 43 73 51; fax 43 43 13). **U.K. (National Tourist Organization),** 4 Conduit St., **London** W1R DOJ (tel. (171) 734 5997; fax 287 1369). **U.S. (National Tourist Organization),** Olympic Tower, 645 Fifth Ave., 5th Floor, **New York,** NY 10022 (tel. (212) 421-5777; fax 826-6940)

Hungary: Australia, Edgecliff Centre 203-233, #405, Head Rd., Edgecliff, Sydney, NSW 2027 (tel. (02) 9328 7859; fax 9327 1829). **Canada,** 299 Waverley St., Ottawa, ON K2P 0Z9 (tel. (613) 230-2717; fax 230-7560; email h2embott@docuweb.ca; http://www.docuweb.ca/hungary). **Ireland,** 2 Fitzwilliam Pl., Dublin 2 (tel. (01) 661 2903; fax 661 2880). **New Zealand,** Wellington, 151 Orangi Kaupapa Rd. 6005 Z (tel. (644) 475 85 74; fax 475 35 55). **South Africa,** 959 Arcadia St., Hatfield 0083, Postal address: P.O. Box 27077, Sunnyside 0132 (tel. (012) 43 30 30; fax 43 30 29). **U.K.,** 35 Eaton Pl., London SW1X 8BY (tel. (0171) 235 5218; fax 823 1348); **Tourist Board,** 46 Eaton Pl., London SW1 X8AL (tel. (0171) 823 1032; fax 823 1459). **U.S.,** 33910 Shoemaker St. NW, Washington, D.C. 20008 (tel. (202) 362-6730; fax 686-6412; http://www.hungaryemb.org); 11766 Wilshire Blvd., #410, Los Angeles, CA 90025 (tel. (310) 473-9344; fax 479-0456); **Tourist Board,** 150 E. 58th St., 33rd Fl., New York, NY 10155 (tel. (212) 355-0240; fax 207-4103; email huntour@gramercy.los.com).

Iceland: U.S. (Tourist Board), 655 THird Ave., New York, NY 10017 (tel. (212) 885-9700; fax 885-9710; http://www/arctic.is/ITB/)

Ireland: Australia (Tourist Board), Australia: Level 5, 36 Carrington St., Sydney NSW 2000 (tel. (02) 9299 6177; fax 9299 6323). **Canada,** 130 Albert St., Ste. 1105, Ottawa, Ontario K1P 5G4 (tel. (613) 233 6281; fax 233 5835). **South Africa,** Verite House, 20 DeKorte St., Braamfontein, Johannesburg (tel. (002711) 339 4865; fax 339 2474). **U.K. (Tourist Board),** 150 New Bond St., London W1Y 0AQ (tel. (0171) 518 0800; fax 493 9065). **U.S. (Tourist Board),** 345 Park Ave., New York, NY 10154 (tel. (800) 223 6470 or (212) 418 0800; fax 371 9052).

Italy: Canada (Tourist Board), 1 pl. Ville Marie, #1914, Montréal, Québec H3B 2C3 (tel. (514) 866 7667; fax 392 1429; email initaly@ican.net). **South Africa,** Embassy of Italy, 796 George Ave., Arcadia, Pretoria (tel. (12) 43 55 41; fax 43 55 47); Consulate General of Italy, 37 1st Ave., Houghton Estate 2196, Johannesburg (tel. (11) 728 13 92; fax 728 38 34). **U.K. (Tourist Board),** 1 Princess St., **London** WIR 9AY (tel. (0171) 408 12 54; fax 493 66 95). **U.S. (Tourist Board),** 630 Fifth Ave., Suite 1565, New York, NY 10111 (tel. (212) 245 5618; fax 586 9249; email enitny@bway.net; http://www.enit.it); 12400 Wilshire Blvd., #550, Los Angeles, CA 90025 (tel. (310) 820 1898 or 820 1959; fax 820 6357).

Latvia: Australia, P.O. Box 457, Strathfield NSW 2135 (tel. (02) 97 44 59 81; fax 97 47 60 55). **Canada,** 112 Kent St., Place de Ville, Tower B, #208, Ottawa, ON K1P 5P2 (tel. (613) 238-6014; fax 238-7044; email latvia-embassy@magmacom.com; http://www2.magmacom.com/latemb). **South Africa,** North Cliff Corner, DF Malan Ave. and Milner St., Roosevelt Park, Basement, Postal address: P.O. Box 48760, Roosevelt Park 2129 (tel. (011) 782 58 12; fax 888 55 00). **U.K.,** 45 Nottingham Pl., London W1M 3FE (tel. (0171) 312 0040; fax 312 0042). **U.S.,** 4325 17th St. NW, Washington, D.C. 20011 (tel. (202) 726-8213; fax 726-6785; http://www.virtual-globe.com/latvia).

Lithuania: Australia, 40B Fiddens Wharf Rd., Killara NSW 2071 (tel. (8) 8346 4775). **Canada,** 130 Albert St., #204, Ottawa, ON K1P 5G4 (tel. (613) 567-5458; fax 567-5315). **South Africa,** 1st Fl., Killarney Mall, Riviera Rd., Killarney 2193, Postal address: P.O. Box 1737, Houghton 2041 (tel. (011) 486 36 60; fax 486 36 50). **U.K.,** 84 Gloucester Pl., London W1H 3HN (tel. (0171) 486 6401; fax 486 6403). **U.S.,** 2622 16th St. NW, Washington, D.C. 20009 (tel. (202) 234-5860; fax 328-0466; email admin@ltembassyus.org; http://www.ltembassyus.org).

Luxembourg: Luxembourg, P.O. Box 1001, L-1010 Luxembourg (tel. (352) 40 08 08; fax 40 47 48; email tourism@ont.smtp.etat.lu). **South Africa,** P.O. Box 3431, Parklands 2121 (tel. (011) 447 64 34; fax 447 54 96). **U.K. (Tourist Office),** 122 Regent St., London W1R 5FE (tel. (0171) 434 28 00; fax 734 12 05; email tourism@luxembourg.co.uk; http://www.luxcentral.com). **U.S. (Tourist Office),** 17 Beekman Pl., New York, NY 10022 (tel. (212) 935-8888; fax 935-5896; email luxnto@aol.com).

Malta: Australia, 127 York St., Sydney NSW 2000 (tel. (02) 92 67 33 63; fax 92 64 28 74). **South Africa,** 1351 Morningside 2057, Parklands, 2121 (tel. (011) 706 05 12; fax 706 03 01). **U.K., Malta House,** 36-38 Piccadilly, London WIV OPP (tel. (0171) 292 49 00; fax 734 18 80; http://www.tourism.org.mt). **U.S.,** 2017 Connecticut Ave. NW, Washington DC 20008 (tel. (202) 462-3611; fax 387-5470); **Malta National Tourist Office,** Empire State Bldg., 350 Fifth Avenue, Ste. 4412, New York, NY 10118 (tel. (212) 695-9520).

Netherlands: Australia, 500 Oxford St., Plaza Tower #1, Level 19, Bombay Junc. 2022 (tel. (02) 93 87 66 44; fax 93 87 39 62), in Sydney. **Canada and U.S. (Board of Tourism),** 225 N. Michigan Ave., Ste. 1854, Chicago, IL 60601 (tel. (888) 464-6552, for a representative (312) 819-1500; fax 819-1740; http://www.goholland.com). **U.K.,** 38 Hyde Park Gate, London SW 7 5DP (tel. (0171) 590 32 00). **New Zealand** (tel. (09) 379 53 99), in Auckland. **South Africa,** P.O. Box 117, Pretoria, 0001 (tel. (012) 344 39 10; fax 343 99 50).

Northern Ireland Tourist Board: Head Office, 559 North St., Belfast, BT1 1NB, Northern Ireland (tel. (01232) 246609; fax 240960; http://www.ni-tourisim.com). **Canada,** 111 Avenue Rd., Ste. 450, Toronto, Ontario M5R 3J8 (tel. (416) 925 6368; fax 961 2175). **Ireland,** 16 Nassau St., Dublin 2 (tel. (01) 679 1977; CallSave (1850) 230230; fax (01) 677 1587). **U.K.,** British Travel Centre, 12 Lower Regent St., London SW1Y 4PQ (tel. (0171) 839 8417). **U.S.,** 551 Fifth Ave. #701, New York, NY 10176 (tel. (800) 326 0036 or (212) 922 0101; fax 922 0099).

Norway: South Africa, P.O. Box 9843, Pretoria, 0001 (tel. (012) 323 47 90; fax 323 47 89). **U.K. (Tourist Board),** Charles House, 5 Regent St., London SW1Y 4LR (tel. (0171) 839 62 55 or 839 26 50; fax 839 60 14). **U.S. (Tourist Board),** 655 Third Ave., New York, NY 10017 (tel. (212) 885-9700; fax 885-9710; email gonorway@interport.net; http://www.norway.org).

Poland: On the Web: http://www.polishworld.com/polemb. **Australia,** 7 Turrana St., Yarralumla ACT 2600 Canberra (tel. (06) 273 12 08 or 273 12 11; fax 273 31 84). **Canada,** 443 Daly St., Ottawa, ON, K1N 6H3 (tel. (613) 789-0468; fax 789-1218; email polamb@hookup.com). **Ireland,** 5 Ailesbury Rd., Dublin 4 (tel. (01) 283 08 55; fax 283 75 62). **New Zealand,** 17 Upland Rd., Kelburn, Wellington (tel. (04) 71 24 56; fax 71 24 55). **South Africa,** 14 Amos St., Colbyn, Pretoria 0083 (tel. (012) 43 26 31; fax 43 26 08). **U.K.,** 47 Portland Pl., London W1N 4JH (tel. (0171) 580 4324; fax 323 4018); 2 Kinnear Rd., Edinburgh EH3 5PE (tel. (0131) 552 0301; fax 552 1086). **U.S.,** 2640 16th St. NW, Washington, D.C. 20009 (tel. (202) 234-3800; fax 328-6271; email embpol@dgs.dgsys.com); 1240 Wilshire Blvd., #555, Los Angeles, CA 90025 (tel. (310) 442-8500; fax 442-8515).

Portugal: Canada (Trade and Tourist Office), 60 Bloor St. W., Suite 1005, **Toronto,** ON M4W 3B8 (tel. (416) 921 7376; fax 921 1353); **Ireland** (Trade and Tourist Office), 54 Dawson St., **Dublin** 2 (tel. (1) 670 91 33 or 670 91 34; fax 670 91 41; email info@icep.ie). **South Africa,** 4th fl., Sunnyside Ridge, Sunnyside Drive Parktown, 2193 Johannesburg (tel. (11) 484 34 87; fax 484 54 16). Send mail to: P.O. Box 2473, Houghton, 2041 Johannesburg. **U.K. (Trade and Tourist Office),** 2nd fl., 22-25A Sackville St., London W1X 2LY (tel. (171) 494 14 41; fax 494 18 68). **U.S.** (Trade and Tourist Office), 590 Fifth Ave., 4th fl., New York, NY 10036-4704 (tel. (212) 354 4403 or (800) 7678 8425; fax 764-6137; http://www.portugal.org).

Romania: Australia, 4 Dalmain, Canberra, Malloi ACT 2606 (tel. (02) 62 86 23 43; fax 62 86 24 33). **Canada,** 655 Rideau St., Ottawa, ON K1N 6A3 (tel. (613) 789-5345; fax 789-4365). **South Africa,** 117 Charles St., Brooklyn 0011, P.O. Box 11295, Pretoria (tel. (012) 466 941; fax 466 947). **U.K.,** 4 Palace Green, Kensington, London W8 4QD (tel. (0171) 937 9666; fax 937 8069); **Tourist Office,** 27 New Cavendish St., London W1M 7RL (tel. (0171) 224 3693; fax (0171) 487 2913). **U.S.,** 1607 23rd St. NW, Washington, D.C. 20008 (tel. (202) 332-4846; fax 232-4748); **Tourist Office,** Orbis 342 Madison Ave., #1512, New York, NY 10173 (tel. (212) 867-5011; fax (212) 682-4715).

Russia: Australia, 78 Canberra Ave., Griffith ACT 2603 Canberra (tel. (06) 295 90 33; fax 295 18 47). **Canada,** 285 Charlotte St., Ottawa, ON K1N 8L5 (tel. (613) 235-4341; fax 236-6342). For Visas call (613) 236-7220. **Travel Information Office,** 1801 McGill College Ave., #930, Montréal, PQ H3A 2N4 (tel. (514) 849-6394; fax 849-6743). **Ireland,** 186 Orwell Rd., Dublin 14 (tel. (01) 492 3525; fax 492-3525; email russiane.indigo.ie). **New Zealand,** 57 Messines Rd., Karori, Wellington (tel. (04) 476 61 13; fax 476 38 43). **U.K.,** 113 Kensington Palace Gardens, London W84 QX (tel. (0171) 229 3628; fax 727 8625); **Travel Information Office,** Kennedy House, 115 Hammersmith Rd., London W14 OQH (tel. (44) 17 16 03 10 00; fax 17 16 02 40 00). **U.S.,** 1706 18th St. NW, Washington, D.C. 20009 (info tel. (202) 298-5700 or 232-6020; fax (202) 483-7579; email russia@embassy.org; consular tel. 939-8907; fax 328-0137); **Travel Information Office,** 800 3rd Ave., #3101, New York, NY 10022 (tel. (212) 758-1162; fax 758-0933).

Slovakia: Australia, 47 Culgoa Circuit, O'Malley, Canberra ACT 2606 (tel. (6) 290 15 16; fax 290 17 55). **Canada,** 50 Rideau Terrace, Ottawa, ON K1M 2A1 (tel. (613) 749-4442; fax 749-4989). **South Africa,** 930 Arcadia St., Arcadia 0083, Postal Address: P.O. Box 12736, Hatfield 0028, Pretoria (tel. (012) 342 20 51; fax 342 36 88). **U.K.,** 25 Kensington Palace Gardens, London W8 4QY (tel. (0171) 243 0803; fax 727 5824). **U.S.,** 2201 Wisconsin Ave. NW, #250, Washington, D.C. 20007 (tel. (202) 965-5160; fax 965-5166; email svkemb@concentric.net; http://www.slovakemb.com); **Tourist Board,** 10 E. 40th St., #3604, New York, NY 10016 (tel. (212) 213-3865; fax 213-4461).

Slovenia: Australia, Level 6, Advance Bank Center, 60 Marcus Clarke St. 2608, Canberra ACT 2601 (tel. (6) 243 48 30; fax 243 48 27). **Canada,** 150 Metcalfe St., #2101, Ottawa, ON K2P 1P1 (tel. (613) 565-5781; fax 565-5783). **New Zealand,** Eastern Hutt Rd., Pomare, Lower Hutt, Wellington (tel. (644) 567 27; fax 567 24). **U.K.,** Cavendish Ct. 11-15, #1, Wigmore St., London W1H 9LA (tel. (0171) 495 7775; fax 495 7776). **U.S.,** 1525 New Hampshire Ave. NW, Washington, D.C. 20036 (tel. (202) 667-5363; fax 667-4563); **Tourist Board,** 345 E. 12th St., New York, NY 10003 (tel. (212) 358-9024; fax 358-9025; email info@sloveniatravel.com; http://www.sloveniatravel.com).

Spain: Canada (Tourist Board), 2 Bloor St. W., 34th fl., **Toronto,** ON M4W 3E2 (tel. (416) 961 3131; fax 961 1992). **South Africa,** 37 Shortmarket St., Cape Town 8001 (tel. (021) 22 24 15; fax 22 23 28). 169 Pine St., Arcadia, Pretoria 0083 (tel. (012) 344 3875; fax 343 48 91). **U.K. (Tourist Board),** Manchester Sq., 22-23, London W15 5AP (tel. (171) 486 80 77; fax 486 80 34). 24hr. brochure request line (tel. (891) 66 99 20). **U.S. (Tourist Board),** 6666 5th Ave., 35th fl., New York, NY 10103 (tel. (212) 265 8822; for info packet (888) 657 7246; fax 265 8864; http://www.OKSPAIN.org); San Vincente Plaza Building, 8383 Wilshire Blvd., Suite 960, **Beverly Hills,** CA 90211 (tel. (213) 658 7188; fax 658 1061).

Sweden: South Africa, P.O. Box 1664, Pretoria, 0001 (tel. (012) 321 10 50; fax 326 66 77). **U.K. (Tourist Board),** 11 Montagu Place, London W1H 2AL (tel. (0171)

724 58 68; fax 724 58 72). **U.S. (Tourist Board),** 655 Third Ave., New York, NY 10017-5617 (tel. (212) 885-9700; fax 885-9710).

Switzerland (including Liechtenstein): Canada (National Tourist Board), 9926 East Mall, Etobicoke, Ont. M9B 6K1 (tel. (416) 695-2090; fax 695-2774; sttoronto@switzerlandtourism.com; http://www.switzerlandtourism.com). **South Africa,** P.O. Box 724, Parkland, 2121 (tel. (11) 43 67 07; fax 442 78 91). **U.K. (National Tourist Board),** Swiss Centre, Swiss Court, London W1V 8EE (tel. (0171) 734 1921; fax 437 4577). **U.S. (National Tourist Board),** 608 Fifth Ave., **New York,** NY 10020 (tel. (212) 757-5944; fax 262-6116).

Turkey: Australia (Information Office), 428 George St., Rm. 17, Level 3, Sydney, NSW 2000 (tel. (2) 9223 3055; fax 9223 3204). **Canada (Information Office),** Constitution Square, 360 Albert St., #801, Ottawa, ON K1R 7X7 (tel. (613) 230-8654; fax 230-3683). **South Africa,** P.O. Box 56014, Arcadia, 0007 (tel. (012) 342 60 53; fax 342 60 52). **U.K. (Information Office),** 170-173 Piccadilly, 1st Fl., London W1V 9DD (tel. (0171) 355 4207; fax 491 0773; email tto@turkishtourism.demon.co.uk). **U.S. (Information Office),** Turkish Centre, 821 United Nations Plaza, New York, NY 10017 (tel. (212) 687-2194; fax 599-7568; email tourny@soho.ios.com); 1717 Massachusetts Ave. NW, #306, Washington, D.C. 20036 (tel. (202) 429-9844; fax 429-5649).

Ukraine: Australia, #3, Ground Floor, 902-912 Mt. Alexander Road, Essendon, Victoria 3040. **Canada,** 310 Somerset St. West, Ottawa, ON, K2P 0J9 (tel. (613) 230-2961; fax 230-2400; email ukremb@cyberus.ca). **South Africa,** 398 Marais St., Pretoria (tel. (12) 46 19 43; fax 46 19 44). **U.K.,** 60 Holand Park Rd., London W1 13SJ (tel. (0171) 727 6312; fax 792 1708). **U.S.,** 3350 M St. NW, Washington, D.C. 20007 (tel. (202) 333-0606; fax 333-0817); **Tourist Board,** Scope Travel, 1605 Springfield Ave., Maplewood, NJ 07040 (tel. (973) 378-8998; fax 378-7903; email info@scopetravel.com; http://www.scopetravel.com).

Yugoslavia: Australia, 11 Nuyts St., Red Hill, Canberra 2603 (tel. (06) 295 14 58 or 239 61 78). **Canada,** 17 Blackburn Ave., Ottawa, ON, KIN 8A2 (tel. (613) 233-6289; fax 233-7850). **U.K.,** 5-7 Lexham Gardens, London W8 5JU (tel. (0171) 370 6105; fax 370 3838). **U.S.,** 2410 California St. NW, Washington, D.C. 20008 (tel. (202) 462-6566; fax 462-2508).

USEFUL TRAVEL ORGANIZATIONS

Council on International Educational Exchange (CIEE), 205 E. 42nd St., New York, NY 10017-5706 (tel. (888) COUNCIL (268-6245); fax (212) 822-2699; http://www.ciee.org). A private, not-for-profit organization. Council administers worldwide work, volunteer, academic, internship, and professional programs. They also offer identification cards, (including the ISIC and the GO25) and publications such as the useful magazine *Student Travels* (free). Call or write for further information.

Federation of International Youth Travel Organizations (FIYTO), Bredgade 25H, DK-1260 Copenhagen K, Denmark (tel. (45) 33 33 96 00; fax 33 93 96 76; email mailbox@fiyto.org; http://www.fiyto.org), is an international organization promoting travel for young people. Member organizations include language schools, educational travel companies, national tourist boards, and accommodation centers. FIYTO sponsors the GO25 Card (http://www.go25.org).

International Student Travel Confederation, Herengracht 479, 1017 BS Amsterdam, The Netherlands (tel. (31) 20 421 2800; fax 20 421 2810; email istcinfo@istc.org; http://www.istc.org). A nonprofit confederation of student travel organizations that promote and facilitate travel among young people and students. Member organizations include International Student Surface Travel Association (ISSA), Student Air Travel Association (SATA), IASIS Travel Insurance, and the International Association for Educational and Work Exchange Programs (IAEWEP).

USEFUL PUBLICATIONS

Although *Let's Go* tries to cover all aspects of budget travel, we can't put *everything* in our guides. You might supplement your *Let's Go* library with more specific publications. Language tapes and **Handy Dictionaries** (US$9-15) can be obtained through Hippocrene Books, Inc., 171 Madison Ave., New York, NY 10016 (tel. (212) 685-

4371, orders (718) 454-2366; fax (718) 454-1391; email hippocre@ix.netcom.com; http://www.netcom.com/~hippocre). Books, cassettes, atlases, dictionaries, and maps are available from Travel Books & Language Center, Inc., 4931 Cordell Ave., Bethesda, MD 20814 (tel. (800) 220-2665; fax (301) 951-8546; email travel-bks@aol.com). Hard-to-find **maps** are stocked by Wide World Books and Maps, 1911 N. 45th St., Seattle, WA 98103 (tel. (206) 634-3453; fax 634-0558; email travel@speak-easy.org; http://www.wwbooks.com). **Michelin** publishes detailed road maps and atlases, as well as the **Green Guides** (US$18-20), with in-depth maps, suggested tours, and area background. Visit a bookstore or contact Michelin Tyre, the Edward Hyde Bldg., 38 Clarendon Rd., Watford WD1 1SX, U.K. (tel. (01923) 41 50 00; fax 41 52 50); in the U.S., Michelin North America, P.O. Box 19008, Greenville, SC 29602-9008 (tel. (800) 223-0987; fax 378-7471; http://www.michelin-travel.com). Travel gear, guidebooks, railpasses, and hostel memberships can be purchased from the **Forsyth Travel Library,** 1750 E. 131st St., P.O. Box 480800, Kansas City, MO 64148 (tel. (800) 367-7984; fax (816) 942-6969; email forsyth@avi.net; http://www.forsyth.com). Books on packing, global weather patterns, and safety concerns (US$9-10 each) are available from **Ten Speed Press,** P.O. Box 7123, Berkeley, CA 94707 (tel. (800) 841-2665; fax (510) 559-1629; email order@tenspeed.com). For *Background Notes* (US$2.50 each) on all countries, and *Health Information for International Travel* (US$20) contact the **Superintendent of Documents,** P.O. Box 371954, Pittsburgh, PA 15250 (tel. (202) 512-1800; fax 512-2250; email gpoaccess@gpo.gov; http://www.access.gpo.gov/su-docs).

   Festivals, a free booklet from the European Festivals Association, 120B, rue de Lausanne, CH-1202 Geneva, Switzerland (tel. (22) 732 28 03; fax 738 40 12; email aef@vtx.ch), lists the dates and programs of major European festivals. In the U.S., enclose 5 International Reply Coupons to order it from Dailey-Thorp Travel, Inc., 330 W. 58th St., New York, NY 10018-1817. Peruse **Mona Winks: Self-Guided Tours of Europe's Top Museums** (US$19) with "Professor" Rick Steves, a veteran traveler who offers great advice in **Europe Through the Back Door** (US$20). Both are available from John Muir Publications, P.O. Box 613, Santa Fe, NM 87504 (tel. (800) 888-7504; fax (505) 988-1680). For the inside story on **Charming Small Hotels** in England, France, Germany, Italy, Tuscany, or Switzerland (US$15 each), contact Hunter Publishing, P.O. Box 7816, Edison, NJ 08818 (tel. (908) 225-1900; fax 417-0482; email hunterpub@emi.net; http://www.hunterpublishing.com). The **Specialty Travel Index,** 305 San Anselmo Ave. #313, San Anselmo, CA 94960 (tel. (415) 459-4900; fax 459-4974; email spectrav@ix.netcom.com; http://www.spectrav.com) is an extensive listing of "off the beaten track" and specialty travel opportunities.

INTERNET RESOURCES

Budget travel is moving rapidly into the information age. On today's **Internet,** people can become their own budget travel agents by making airline, hostel, or car rental reservations, and by connecting personally with other travelers. **NetTravel: How Travelers Use the Internet,** by Michael Shapiro, is a very thorough and informative guide to all aspects of travel planning through the Internet (US$25). The forms of the Internet most useful to budget travelers are the World Wide Web and Usenet newsgroups.

The World Wide Web

The World Wide Web provides graphics, sound, and text, and is currently the most active and exciting use of the Internet. **Search engines,** which look for web pages under specific subjects, are the best way to navigate the expanse of available information. **Alta Vista** (http://www.altavista.digital.com), **Excite** (http://excite.com), and **Lycos** (http://a2z.lycos.com) are popular. **Yahoo!** is slightly more organized; check out its travel links at http://www.yahoo.com/recreation/travel. Visit the **Let's Go website** (http://www.letsgo.com) for our newsletter, a current list of links, a chatroom, a travel forum, information about our books, and more.

   If you know one good site, you can start "surfing" from there, through links from one web page to another. *Let's Go* recommends the following sites for budget travel info: **Shoestring Travel** (http://www.stratpub.com), **Microsoft Expedia** (http://expedia.msn.com), **City.Net** (http://www.city.net), **TravelHUB** (http://www.travelhub.com), **Cybercafe Guide** (http://www.cyberiacafe.net/cyberia/guide/ccafe.htm), **Foreign Language for Travelers** (http://www.travelang.com), **Rent-A-Wreck's Travel Links** (http://www.rent-a-wreck.com/raw/travlist.htm), **The CIA World Factbook** (http://www.odci.gov/cia/publications), and the **State Department travel page** (http://travel.state.gov).

We list other relevant web sites throughout the book, but as the turnover of good web sites is rapid, it is important that you head out on your own. But beware: the Web has become the newest path from corporate advertisers to the minds of the masses; be sure to distinguish between information and marketing.

Usenet Newsgroups

Newsgroups are forums for discussion of specific topics. One user "posts" a written question, to which other users read and respond. Information is available on almost any imaginable topic. But proliferation can become over-extension; the quality of discussion can be poor, and you often have to wade through piles of nonsense to find useful information. **Usenet,** the family of newsgroups, can be accessed easily from most Internet gateways. In UNIX systems, type "tin" at the prompt. Most commercial providers offer access to Usenet and often also have their own restricted versions of Usenet. There are a number of different hierarchies, including "soc" (society and culture), "rec" (recreation), and "alt" (alternative; varied topics). **Clarinet** posts AP news wires in the "clari" hierarchy. Since the quality of discussion changes so rapidly and new groups are always appearing, it's best to scan through to find appropriate topics.

▩ Documents & Formalities

All applications should be filed several weeks or months in advance of your planned departure date—remember that you are relying on government agencies to complete these transactions. Demand for passports is highest between January and August, so try to apply as early as possible. A backlog in processing can spoil your plans.

When you travel, always carry two or more forms of identification, including at least one photo ID. A passport combined with a driver's license or birth certificate usually serves as adequate proof of your identity and citizenship. Many establishments, especially banks, require several IDs before cashing traveler's checks. Never carry all your forms of ID together, however; you risk being left entirely without ID or funds in case of theft or loss. Also carry several extra passport-size photos that you can attach to the sundry IDs or railpasses you will eventually acquire. If you plan an extended stay, register your passport with the nearest embassy or consulate.

ENTRANCE REQUIREMENTS

Citizens of Australia, Canada, Ireland, New Zealand, South Africa, the U.K., and the U.S. all need valid **passports** to enter most countries and to re-enter their own country. Some countries do not allow entrance if the holder's passport expires in under six months; returning home with an expired passport is illegal, and may result in a fine. Some countries also require a **visa;** an **invitation** from a sponsoring individual or organization is required by several Eastern European countries. Some countries require children to carry their own passports.

Upon entering a country, you must declare certain items from abroad and must pay a duty on the value of those articles that exceed the allowance established by that country's **customs** service. Keeping receipts for purchases made abroad will help establish values when you return. It is wise to make a list, including serial numbers, of any valuables that you carry with you from home; if you register this list with customs before your departure and have an official stamp it, you will avoid import duty charges and ensure an easy passage upon your return. Be especially careful to document items manufactured abroad.

When you enter a country, dress neatly and carry **proof of your financial independence,** such as a visa to the next country on your itinerary, an airplane ticket to depart, enough money to cover the cost of your living expenses, etc. Admission as a visitor does not include the right to work, which is authorized only by a work permit. Entering certain countries to study requires a special visa, and immigration officers may also want to see proof of acceptance from a school and proof that the course of study will take up most of your time in the country, as well as proof that you can support yourself.

PASSPORTS

Before you leave, photocopy the page of your passport that contains your photograph, passport number, and other identifying information. Carry one photocopy in a safe place apart from your passport, and leave another copy at home. These measures will help prove your citizenship and facilitate the issuing of a new passport if you lose the original document. Consulates also recommend that you carry an expired passport or an official copy of your birth certificate in a part of your baggage separate from other documents.

If you do lose your passport, immediately notify the local police and the nearest embassy or consulate of your home government. To expedite its replacement, you will need to know all information previously recorded and show identification and proof of citizenship. A replacement may take weeks to process, and it may be valid only for a limited time. Some consulates can issue new passports within 24 hours if you give them proof of citizenship. Any visas stamped in your old passport will be irretrievably lost. In an emergency, ask for immediate temporary traveling papers that will permit you to reenter your home country.

Your passport is a public document belonging to your nation's government. You may have to surrender it to a foreign government official, but if you don't get it back in a reasonable amount of time, inform the nearest mission of your home country.

Australia Citizens must apply for a passport in person at a post office, a passport office, or an Australian diplomatic mission overseas. An appointment may be necessary. Passport offices are located in Adelaide, Brisbane, Canberra City, Darwin, Hobart, Melbourne, Newcastle, Perth, and Sydney. A parent may file an application for a child who is under 18 and unmarried. Adult passports cost AUS$120 (for a 32-page passport) or AUS$180 (64-page), and a child's is AUS$60 (32-page) or AUS$90 (64-page). For more info, call toll-free (in Australia) 13 12 32, or visit http://www.austemb.org.

Canada Application forms in English and French are available at all passport offices, Canadian missions, many travel agencies, and Northern Stores in northern communities. Citizens may apply in person at any 1 of 28 regional Passport Offices across Canada. Travel agents can direct applicants to the nearest location. Canadian citizens residing abroad should contact the nearest Canadian embassy or consulate. Children under 16 may be included on a parent's passport. Passports cost CDN$60, plus a CDN$25 consular fee, are valid for 5 years, and are not renewable. Processing takes approximately 5 business days for in-person applications; allow 3 weeks for mail delivery. For more info, contact the Canadian Passport Office, Department of Foreign Affairs and International Trade, Ottawa, ON, K1A 0G3 (tel. (613) 994-3500; http://www.dfait-maeci.gc.ca/passport). Travelers may also call (800) 567-6868 (24hr.); in Montréal (514) 283-2152; in Toronto (416) 973-3251; in Vancouver (604) 775-6250. Refer to the booklet *Bon Voyage, But...*, free at any passport office or by calling InfoCentre at (800) 267-8376 (within Canada), or (613) 944-4000 for further help and a list of Canadian embassies and consulates abroad. You may also find entry and background information for various countries by contacting the Consular Affairs Bureau in Ottawa (tel. (800) 267-6788 (24hr.) or (613) 944-6788). No charge for re-entering Canada with an expired passport.

Ireland Citizens can apply for a passport by mail to either the Department of Foreign Affairs, Passport Office, Setanta Centre, Molesworth St., Dublin 2 (tel. (01) 671 16 33; fax 671 10 92), or the Passport Office, Irish Life Building, 1A South Mall, Cork (tel. (021) 27 25 25; fax 27 57 70). Obtain an application at a local Garda station or request one from a passport office. The new Passport Express Service, available through post offices, allows citizens to get a passport in 2 weeks for an extra IR£3. Passports cost IR£45 and are valid for 5 years. Citizens under 18 or over 65 can request a 3-year passport that costs IR£10.

New Zealand Application forms for passports are available in New Zealand from travel agents and Department of Internal Affairs Link Centres in the main cities and towns. Overseas, forms and passport services are provided by New Zealand embassies, high commissions, and consulates. Applications may also be forwarded to the Passport Office, P.O. Box 10526, Wellington, New Zealand. Standard processing time in New Zealand is 10 working days for correct applications. The fees are adult NZ$80, and child under 16 NZ$40. An urgent passport service is also available for an extra NZ$80. Different fees apply at overseas post: 9 posts, including London, Los Angeles, and Sydney, offer both standard and urgent services (adult US$130, child US$65, plus US$130 if urgent). The fee at other posts is adult US$260, child US$195, and a passport will be issued within 3 working days. Children's names can no longer be endorsed on a parent's passport—they must apply for their own, which are valid for up to 5 years. An adult's passport is valid for up to 10 years. More information is available on the Internet at http://www.govt.nz/agency_info/forms.html.

South Africa Citizens can apply for a passport at any **Department of Home Affairs Office** or **South African Mission.** Tourist passports, valid for 10 years, cost SAR80. Children under 16 must be issued their own passports, valid for 5 years, which cost SAR60. If a passport is needed in a hurry, an **emergency passport** may be issued for SAR50. An application for a permanent passport must accompany the emergency passport application. Time for the completion of an application is normally 3 months or more from the time of submission. Current passports less than 10 years old (counting from date of issuance) may be **renewed** until December 31, 1999; every citizen whose passport's validity does not extend far beyond this date is urged to renew it as soon as possible, to avoid the expected glut of applications as 2000 approaches. Renewal is free, and turnaround is usually 2 weeks. For further info, contact the nearest Department of Home Affairs Office.

United Kingdom British citizens, British Dependent Territories citizens, British subjects, British Nationals (overseas), and British Overseas citizens may apply for a **full passport,** valid for 10 years (5 years if under 16). Application forms are available at passport offices, main post offices, many travel agents, and branches of Lloyds Bank and Artac World Choice. Apply by mail or in person (for an additional UK£10) to one of the passport offices, located in London, Liverpool, Newport, Peterborough, Glasgow, or Belfast. The fee is UK£31, children under 16 UK£11. The London office offers same-day, walk-in rush service; arrive early. The formerly available **British Visitor's Passport** has been abolished; every traveler over 16 now needs a 10-year standard passport. The U.K. Passport Agency can be reached by phone at (0990) 21 04 10.

United States Citizens may apply for a passport at any federal or state **courthouse** or **post office** authorized to accept passport applications, or at a **U.S. Passport Agency,** located in Boston, Chicago, Honolulu, Houston, Los Angeles, Miami, New Orleans, New York, Philadelphia, San Francisco, Seattle, Stamford, or Washington, D.C. Refer to the "U.S. Government, State Department" section of the telephone directory or the local post office for addresses. Parents must apply in person for children under age 13. You must apply in person if this is your first passport, if you're under age 18, or if your current passport is more than 12 years old or was issued before your 18th birthday. Passports are valid for 10 years (5 years if under 18) and cost US$65 (under 18 US$40). Passports may be **renewed** by mail or in person for US$55. Processing takes 3-4 weeks. **Rush service** is available for a surcharge of US$30 with proof of departure within 10 working days (e.g., an airplane ticket or itinerary), or for travelers leaving in 2-3 weeks who require visas. Given proof of citizenship, a U.S. embassy or consulate abroad can usually issue a new passport. Report a passport lost or stolen in the U.S. in writing to Passport Services, 1425 K St., N.W., U.S. Department of State, Washington D.C. 20524 or to the nearest passport agency. For more info, contact the U.S. Passport Information's **24-hour recorded message** (tel. (202) 647-0518). U.S. citizens may receive consular information sheets, travel warnings, and public announcements at any passport agency, U.S. embassy, or consulate, or by sending a self-addressed stamped envelope to: Overseas Citizens Services, Room 4811, Department of State, Washington,

D.C. 20520-4818 (tel. (202) 647-5225; fax 647-3000). Additional information (including publications) about documents, formalities, and travel abroad is available through the Bureau of Consular Affairs homepage at http://travel.state.gov, or through the State Department site at http://www.state.gov.

VISAS

A **visa** is an endorsement that a foreign government stamps into a passport which allows the bearer to stay in that country for a specified purpose and period of time. Most visas cost US$10-70 and allow you to spend about one month in a country, within six months to one year from the date of issue.

For more information, send for *Foreign Entry Requirements* (US$0.50) from the **Consumer Information Center,** Department 365E, Pueblo, CO 81009 (tel. (719) 948-3334; http://www.pueblo.gsa.gov), or contact the **Center for International Business and Travel (CIBT),** 25 W. 43rd St. #1420, New York, NY 10036 (tel. (800) 925-2428 or (212) 575-2811 from NYC), which secures visas for travel to and from all countries for a variable service charge.

CUSTOMS: GOING HOME

Upon returning home, you must declare all articles you acquired abroad and pay a **duty** on the value of those articles that exceed the allowance established by your country's customs service. Goods and gifts purchased at **duty-free** shops abroad are not exempt from duty or sales tax at your point of return; you must declare these items as well. "Duty-free" merely means that you need not pay a tax in the country of purchase.

Australia Citizens may import AUS$400 (under 18 AUS$200) of goods duty-free, in addition to 1.125L alcohol and 250 cigarettes or 250g tobacco. You must be over 18 to import alcohol or tobacco. There is no limit to the amount of Australian and/or foreign cash that may be brought into or taken out of the country, but amounts of AUS$10,000 or more, or the equivalent in foreign currency, must be reported. All foodstuffs and animal products must be declared on arrival. For information, contact the Regional Director, Australian Customs Service, GPO Box 8, Sydney NSW 2001 (tel. (02) 9213 2000; fax 9213 4000), or visit http://www.customs.gov.au.

Canada Citizens who remain abroad for at least 1 week may bring back up to CDN$500 worth of goods duty-free any time. Citizens or residents who travel for a period between 48 hours and 6 days can bring back up to CDN$200. Both of these exemptions may include tobacco and alcohol. You are permitted to ship goods except tobacco and alcohol home under the CDN$500 exemption as long as you declare them when you arrive. Goods under the CDN$200 exemption, as well as all alcohol and tobacco, must be in your hand or checked luggage. Citizens of legal age (which varies by province) may import in-person up to 200 cigarettes, 50 cigars or cigarillos, 200g loose tobacco, 1.14L wine or alcohol, and 24 355mL cans/bottles of beer; the value of these products is included in the CDN$200 or CDN$500. For more information, write to Canadian Customs, 2265 St. Laurent Blvd., Ottawa, Ontario K1G 4K3 (tel. (613) 993-0534), phone the 24hr. Automated Customs Information Service at (800) 461-9999, or visit Revenue Canada at http://www.revcan.ca.

Ireland Citizens must declare everything in excess of IR£142 (IR£73 per traveler under 15 years of age) obtained outside the EU or duty- and tax-free in the EU above the following allowances: 200 cigarettes, 100 cigarillos, 50 cigars, or 250g tobacco; 1L liquor or 2L wine; 2L still wine; 50g perfume; and 250mL toilet water. Goods obtained duty and tax paid in another EU country up to a value of IR£460 (IR£115 per traveler under 15) will not be subject to additional customs duties. Travelers under 17 may not import tobacco or alcohol. For more information, contact The Revenue Commissioners, Dublin Castle (tel. (01) 679 27 77; fax 671 20 21; email taxes@iol.ie; http://www.revenue.ie) or The Collector of Customs and Excise, The Custom House, Dublin 1.

New Zealand Citizens may import up to NZ$700 worth of goods duty-free if they are intended for personal use or are unsolicited gifts. The concession is 200 cigarettes (1 carton) or 250g tobacco or 50 cigars or a combination of all 3 not to exceed 250g.

You may also bring in 4.5L of beer or wine and 1.125L of liquor. Only travelers over 17 may import tobacco or alcohol. For more information, contact New Zealand Customs, 50 Anzac Ave., Box 29, Auckland (tel. (09) 377 35 20; fax 309 29 78).

South Africa Citizens may import duty-free: 400 cigarettes, 50 cigars, 250g tobacco, 2L wine, 1L of spirits, 250mL toilet water, and 50mL perfume, and other consumable items up to a value of SAR500. Goods up to a value of SAR10,000 over and above this duty-free allowance are dutiable at 20%; such goods are also exempted from payment of VAT. Items acquired abroad and sent to the Republic as unaccompanied baggage do not qualify for any allowances. You may not export or import South African bank notes in excess of SAR25,000. For more information, consult the free pamphlet *South African Customs Information,* available in airports or from the Commissioner for Customs and Excise, Private Bag X47, Pretoria 0001 (tel. (12) 314 99 11; fax 328 64 78).

United Kingdom Citizens or visitors arriving in the U.K. from outside the EU must declare goods in excess of the following allowances: 200 cigarettes or 100 cigarillos or 50 cigars or 250g tobacco; 2L still table wine; 1L strong liqueurs over 22% volume, or fortified or sparkling wine, 2L other liqueurs; 60 cc/mL perfume; 250 cc/mL toilet water; and UK£145 worth of all other goods including gifts and souvenirs. You must be over 17 to import alcohol or tobacco. These allowances also apply to duty-free purchases within the EU, except for the last category, other goods, which then has an allowance of UK£75. Goods obtained duty and tax paid for personal use (regulated according to set guide levels) within the EU do not require any further customs duty. More information is available from Her Majesty's Customs and Excise, Custom House, Nettleton Rd., Heathrow Airport, Hounslow, Middlesex TW6 2LA (tel. (0181) 910 36 02 or 910 35 66; fax 910 37 65) and on the Web at http://www.open.gov.uk.

United States Citizens may import US$400 worth of accompanying goods duty-free and must pay a 10% tax on the next US$1000. You must declare all purchases, so have sales slips ready. The US$400 personal exemption covers goods purchased for personal or household use (this includes gifts) and cannot include more than 100 cigars, 200 cigarettes (1 carton), and 1L of wine or liquor. You must be over 21 to bring liquor into the U.S. If you mail home personal goods of U.S. origin, you can avoid duty charges by marking the package "American goods returned." For more information, consult the brochure *Know Before You Go,* available from the U.S. Customs Service, Box 7407, Washington D.C. 20044 (tel. (202) 927-6724), or visit http://www.customs.ustreas.gov.

YOUTH, STUDENT, & TEACHER IDENTIFICATION

The **International Student Identity Card (ISIC)** is the most widely accepted form of student identification. Flashing this card can procure you discounts for sights, theaters, museums, accommodations, meals, train, ferry, bus, and airplane transportation, and other services. Present the card wherever you go, and ask about discounts even when none are advertised. It also provides insurance benefits, including US$100 per day of in-hospital sickness for a maximum of 60 days, and US$3000 accident-related medical reimbursement for each accident (see **Insurance,** p. 23). In addition, cardholders have access to a toll-free 24hr. ISIC helpline whose multilingual staff can provide assistance in medical, legal, and financial emergencies overseas (tel. (800) 626-2427 in the U.S. and Canada; elsewhere call collect (44) 181 666 9025 or 181 666 9025 from the U.K.).

Many student travel agencies around the world issue ISIC, including STA Travel in Australia and New Zealand; Travel CUTS and via the Web (http://www.isic-canada.org) in Canada; USIT in Ireland and Northern Ireland; SASTS in South Africa; Campus Travel and STA Travel in the U.K.; Council Travel, Let's Go Travel, STA Travel, and via the Web (http://www.ciee.org/idcards/index.htm) in the U.S.; and any of the other organizations under the auspices of the International Student Travel Confederation (ISTC). When you apply for the card, request a copy of the *International Student Identity Card Handbook,* which lists by country some of the available discounts. You can also write to Council Travel for a copy. The card is valid from September to December of the following year and costs US$20, CDN$15 or AUS$15. Applicants must be at least 12 years old and degree-seeking students of a secondary or post-secondary school. Because of the proliferation of phony ISICs, many airlines and some other services require other proof of student identity, such as a signed letter from the registrar attesting to your student status and stamped with the school seal or your school ID card. The **International Teacher Identity Card (ITIC)** offers the same insurance coverage, and similar but limited discounts. The fee is US$20, UK£5, or AUS$13. For more information on these cards, consult the organization's web site (http://www.istc.org; email isicinfo@istc.org).

Federation of International Youth Travel Organizations (FIYTO) issues a discount card to travelers who are under 26 but not students. Known as the **GO25 Card,** this one-year card offers many of the same benefits as the ISIC, and most organizations that sell the ISIC also sell the GO25 Card. A brochure that lists discounts is free when you purchase the card. To apply, you will need a passport, valid driver's license, or copy of a birth certificate; and a passport-sized photo with your name printed on the back. The fee is US$20. Information is available on the Web at http://www.ciee.org, or by contacting Travel CUTS in Canada, STA Travel in the U.K., Council Travel in the U.S., or FIYTO headquarters in Denmark (see **Useful Organizations,** p. 7).

DRIVING PERMITS AND CAR INSURANCE

If you plan to drive a car while abroad, you must have an **International Driving Permit (IDP),** though certain countries allow travelers to drive with a valid American or Canadian license for a limited number of months. Most car rental agencies don't require the permit. Call an automobile association to find out if your destination country requires the IDP. It may be a good idea to get one anyway, in case you're in a situation (an accident or stranded in a smaller town) where the police do not know English.

Your IDP, valid for one year, must be issued in your own country before you depart; AAA affiliates cannot issue IDPs valid in their own country. You must be 18 years old to receive the IDP. A valid driver's license from your home country must always accompany the IDP. An application for an IDP usually needs to include one or two photos, a current local license, an additional form of identification, and a fee. Australians can obtain an IDP by contacting their local **Royal Automobile Club (RAC),** or the **National Royal Motorist Association (NRMA)** if in NSW or the ACT, where a permit can be obtained for AUS$15. An application can be obtained by calling (08) 94 21 42 71 (fax 92 21 18 87; http://www.rac.com.au). Canadian license holders can obtain an IDP (CDN$10) through any **Canadian Automobile Association (CAA)** branch office in Canada, by writing to CAA, 1145 Hunt Club Rd., Suite 200, K1V 0Y3 Canada (tel. (613) 247-0117, ext. 2025; fax (613) 247-0118), or on the Web at http://www.caa.ca. Citizens of Ireland should drop into their nearest **Automobile Association (AA)** office where an IDP can be picked up for IR£4, or call (1) 283 35 55 (fax (1) 283 36 60) for a postal application form. In New Zealand, contact your local **Automobile Association (AA),** or their main office at P.O. Box 5, Auckland (tel. (9) 377 46 60; fax (9) 302 20 37); procedural information is also available at http://www.nzaa.co.nz. IDPs cost NZ$8, plus NZ$2 for return postage if mailed from abroad. In South Africa visit your local **Automobile Association of South Africa** office, where IDPs can be picked up for SAR28.50, or for more information call (11) 799 10 00, fax (11) 799 10 10, or write to P.O. Box 596, 2000 Johannesburg. In the U.K. IDPs are UK£4, and you can either visit your local **AA Shop,** call (1256) 49 39 32 (if abroad, fax (44-1256) 46 07 50), or write to AA, 5 Star Post Link, Freepost, Copenhagen Court, 8 New St., Basingstroke RG21 7BA, and order a postal application form (allow 2-3 weeks). For further information, call (44) 09 90 44 88 66 or visit http://www.theaa.co.uk/travel. U.S. license holders can obtain an IDP (US$10) at any **American Automobile Association (AAA)** office or by writing to AAA Florida, Travel Agency Services Department, 1000 AAA Dr. (mail stop 28), Heathrow, FL 32746 (tel. (407) 444-4245; fax 444-4247). You do not have to be a member of AAA to receive an IDP.

Most credit cards cover standard **insurance.** If you rent, lease, or borrow a car, you will need a **green card,** or **International Insurance Certificate,** to prove that you have liability insurance. Obtain it through the car rental agency; most include coverage in their prices. If you lease a car, you can obtain a green card from the dealer. Some travel agents offer the card; it may also be available at border crossings. Verify whether your auto insurance applies abroad; even if it does, you will still need a green card to certify this to foreign officials. If you have a collision abroad, the accident will show up on your domestic records if you report it to your insurance company. Rental agencies may require you to purchase theft insurance in countries that they consider to have a high risk of auto theft. Ask your rental agency about your destination countries. Italy is almost universally seen as a high-risk country; some agencies will add other countries such as Switzerland.

■ Money Matters

If you stay in hostels and prepare your own food, expect to spend US$10-60 per day plus transportation, depending on the local cost of living and your needs. Be careful—don't sacrifice safety and health for a cheaper tab.

CURRENCY AND EXCHANGE

On January 1, 1999, 11 members of the European Union—Austria, Belgium, Finland, France, Germany, Ireland, Italy, Luxembourg, the Netherlands, Portugal, and Spain—will accept the **euro** as their common currency. The national currency will continue to be accepted in each country until January 1, 2002, when the euro will become the only accepted currency. *Let's Go* lists all prices in the national currencies, as these will still be most relevant in 1999, but updated information on the euro can be found on the EU's website at http://www.europa.eu.int/.

Banks in Europe often use a three-letter code based on the name of the country and the name of the currency (for example, Norwegian kroner are NOK). We list this code at the beginning of each country's section with the abbreviation we use and the September 1998 exchange rates between local currency and U.S. dollars (US$), Canadian dollars (CDN$), British pounds (UK£), Irish pounds (IR£), Australian dollars (AUS$), New Zealand dollars (NZ$) and South African Rand (SAR). Check a large newspaper's financial pages for the latest exchange rates.

It is more expensive to buy foreign currency than domestic. In other words, Dutch guilders are cheaper in the Netherlands than in the U.S. However, converting some money before you arrive will allow you to zip through the airport rather than languish in exchange lines, and will prevent being stuck with no money after banking hours or on a holiday. You should bring enough foreign currency to last the first 24-72 hours, depending on the day of the week you arrive. Observe commission rates closely: banks generally have the best rates, but sometimes tourist offices or exchange kiosks are better. Airports and railroad stations generally have poor rates. A good rule of thumb is to go only to banks or bureaux de change which have no more than a 5% margin between buy and sell prices. Be sure that both prices are listed.

Since you lose money with every transaction, convert large sums (unless the currency is depreciating rapidly), but don't convert more of any currency than you'll need, since it may be difficult to change it back to your home currency, or to a new one. Some countries, such as the Czech Republic, Slovakia, and Russia, may require transaction receipts to reconvert local currency. A few (generally in Eastern Europe) will not allow you to convert local currency back at all.

If you are using traveler's checks or bills, be sure to carry some in small denominations (US$50 or less), especially for times when you are forced to exchange money at disadvantageous rates. However, you should generally carry a range of denominations since, in some countries, charges are levied per check cashed.

It may be difficult to exchange your home currency abroad—tellers may not recognize Australian and New Zealand dollars—so it's a good idea to have a few U.S. dollars or German marks on hand. In some places (e.g. Eastern European hotels), Western currency is preferred to local. Find out which establishments require hard currency, and don't use Western money when you don't have to. Throwing dollars around is offensive, attracts theft, and invites many locals to jack prices up.

TRAVELER'S CHECKS

Traveler's checks are one of the safest means of carrying money. Agencies and banks sell them for face value plus a 1% commission. (Members of the American Automobile Association can get American Express checks commission-free through AAA.) **American Express** and **Visa** are the most widely recognized. Order checks well in advance. If your checks get lost or stolen, you will be reimbursed by the check issuer; you may need a police report verifying the loss or theft. Inquire about toll-free refund hotlines and the location of refund centers when you purchase your checks. Keep check receipts and a record of which checks you've cashed in a separate place from the checks themselves. Leave a list of check numbers with someone at home in case of loss. Never countersign checks until you're ready to cash them. Be sure to keep cash for less touristy regions and emergencies. You may find it hard to change traveler's checks outside major cities in Eastern Europe. Finally, always bring your passport with you when you plan to use the checks.

American Express (AmEx): Call (800) 221-7282 in the U.S. and Canada; in the U.K. (0800) 52 13 13; in New Zealand (0800) 44 10 68; in Australia (800) 25 19 02. Elsewhere, call U.S. collect (801) 964-6665. AmEx Traveler's Cheques are widely recognized and easy to replace. Buy them for a small fee at AmEx Travel Service Offices, banks, and AAA offices (commission-free for AAA members). Cardmembers can also buy checks at AmEx Dispensers at Travel Service Offices, at airports, or by phone (tel. (800) 673-3782). AmEx offices cash their checks commission-free, with slightly worse rates than banks. "Cheques for Two" are available; request AmEx's *Traveler's Companion*. Checks available over America Online (tel. (800) 297-1234). Online travel offices at http://aexp.com.

Citicorp: Call (800) 645-6556 in the U.S. and Canada; in Europe, the Middle East, or Africa, (44) 17 15 08 70 07. Elsewhere, call U.S. collect (813) 623-1709. Citicorp and Citicorp Visa traveler's checks (1-2% commission). Worldwide delivery. Call 24hr.

Thomas Cook MasterCard: For 24hr. cashing or refund assistance: from the U.S., Canada, and the Caribbean, call (800) 223-7373; from U.K. (0800) 62 21 01 or collect (1733) 31 89 50. Elsewhere, call collect (44) 17 33 31 89 50. Checks (2% commission). Thomas Cook offices cash checks commission-free.

Visa: Call in U.S. (800) 227-6811; in U.K. (0800) 89 50 78. Elsewhere, call collect (44) 17 33 31 89 49. Any Visa traveler's check can be reported lost at the Visa number, and the addresses of local Visa offices can be located.

CREDIT CARDS

Credit cards can be invaluable or frustrating, as levels of acceptance vary. Major credit cards—**MasterCard** and **Visa** are the most welcomed—instantly extract cash advances from associated banks and teller machines throughout Western Europe (and sometimes elsewhere) in local currency. This can be a bargain because credit card companies get the wholesale exchange rate, which is generally better than the banks' retail rate, but you will be charged ruinous interest rates if you don't pay the bill quickly. **American Express** cards also work in some ATMs, as well as at AmEx offices and major airports.

All ATMs require a **Personal Identification Number (PIN).** Ask AmEx, MasterCard, or Visa to assign you one if they haven't upon issuing the card (see "Cash Cards" section below for more info). MasterCard and Visa have different names elsewhere ("EuroCard" or "Access" for MasterCard and "Carte Bleue" or "Barclaycard" for Visa). Credit cards are invaluable in a financial emergency and may offer other services, like insurance and emergency help.

American Express (tel. (800) 843-2273) has a hefty annual fee (US$55), but cardholders can cash personal checks at AmEx offices and use a 24-hour medical and legal assistance hotline (tel. (800) 554-2639 in U.S. and Canada; elsewhere call U.S. collect (202) 554-2639). Another benefit is the **AmEx Travel Service,** which sends mailgrams and cables, holds mail at AmEx offices, and helps change airline, hotel, and car rental reservations. **Visa** (tel. (800) 336-8472) and **MasterCard** are issued by individual banks and organizations, each with different services.

CASH CARDS

Cash cards—popularly called **ATM cards**—are widespread in Europe, especially the **Cirrus** (U.S. tel. (800) 424-7787) and **PLUS** (U.S. tel. (800) 843-7587) money networks. Cirrus has cash machines in 80 countries and territories and charges US$3-5 to withdraw abroad. PLUS covers 115 countries. Depending on your bank at home, you will probably be able to access your personal account. Happily, the ATM machines get the same wholesale exchange rate as credit cards. Unhappily, there is often a daily limit on withdrawal amounts, and computer network failures are common. Memorize your PIN code in numeral form, as machines abroad may not have letters on the keys, and talk to your bank if your PIN is longer than four digits. Many ATMs are outdoors; use discretion and don't get distracted while at the machine.

One innovation worth investigating is Visa's **TravelMoney,** an ATM card that doesn't require a bank or credit card account. Travelers buy it from one of over 20 banks worldwide by paying whatever they want to have on the card plus a commission of a few percent. The PIN and quick replacement policy (2 days) make TravelMoney a convenient and secure way to avoid changing money or having money sent from home. For more info, call from the U.S. and Canada (800) 847-2399; from the U.K. (0800) 96 38 33; elsewhere U.S. collect (410) 581-9091.

GETTING MONEY FROM HOME

One of the easiest ways to get money from home is to bring an **American Express** card. AmEx allows card holders to draw cash from their checking accounts at any of its major offices and many of its representatives' offices, up to US$1000 every 21 days (no service charge, no interest). AmEx cardmembers can also enroll in **Express Cash.** For a 2% transaction fee for each withdrawal, card holders may withdraw up to $1000 in a seven day-period from checking accounts or credit lines. Cardmembers in U.S. call (800) 227-4669; outside U.S. call (336) 668-5041. Unless using the AmEx service, avoid cashing checks in foreign currencies; they usually take weeks and a US$30 fee to clear.

Money can be wired abroad through **Western Union** (tel. (800) 325-6000). Credit card transfers do not work overseas; you must send cash. Some people also choose to send money abroad in cash via **Federal Express** to avoid transmission fees and taxes. FedEx is reasonably reliable; however, this method may be illegal, it involves an element of risk, and it requires that you remain at a legitimate address for a day or two to wait for the money's arrival—FedEx does not deliver to *Poste Restante* addresses. In general, it may be safer to swallow the cost of wire transmission and preserve your peace of mind.

In emergencies, U.S. citizens can have money sent via the State Department's **Overseas Citizens Service,** American Citizens Services, Consular Affairs, Room 4811, U.S. Department of State, Washington, D.C. 20520 (tel. (202) 647-5225; nights, Sundays, and holidays (202) 647-4000; fax (on demand only) (202) 647-3000; email ca@his.com; http://travel.state.gov). For US$15, the State Department forwards money within hours to the nearest consular office. Other travelers should contact their embassies for information on wiring cash.

■ Safety and Security

PERSONAL SAFETY

Blend in as much as possible. Walking inside to check your map is better than brandishing it on the street. Muggings are often impromptu; acting nervous implies that you have something valuable. Act confident and as if you know where you're going.

When exploring new **cities,** you need extra vigilance, but no city should turn precautions into panic. Find out about unsafe areas from *Let's Go,* tourist offices, lodging managers, or a local, but, above all, trust what your eyes tell you. If you feel uncomfortable, leave quickly, but don't let fear close off new worlds. Leave your itinerary with someone, especially if you are traveling alone, which you should never admit. A **whistle** can scare off attackers and attract attention. Know the police phone number. Police stations are shown as exclamation points on *Let's Go* maps. At night, stay near crowded, well-lit areas, and don't cross deserted neighborhoods.

If you take a **car,** park your vehicle only in a garage or well-traveled areas and learn local driving signals. The leading cause of travel deaths in many parts of the world is motor vehicle crashes. Wearing a seatbelt is the law in many areas. Children under 18kg should ride in specially designed carseats, obtainable from most car rental agencies. For long journeys, you may want to bring some spare parts. Learn your route before you depart; some roads have poor (or nonexistent) shoulders, few gas stations, or loose animals. In many regions, you will need to drive more slowly and cautiously than you would at home. Details and statistics on road safety are available from the **Association for Safe International Road Travel (ASIRT).** See **By Car,** p. 50.

Sleeping in a car is foolish, but if you must, do so close to a police station or 24-hour service station. Sleeping outside can be even more dangerous—camp only in campsites or wilderness backcountry. Exercise extreme caution when using **pools** or **beaches;** hidden rocks and shallow depths can cause injury or death. Heed warnings about undertows. If you rent scuba diving equipment, make sure that it works.

A good self-defense course might cost you more than the trip. **Impact, Prepare,** and **Model Mugging** (tel. (800) 345-KICK; US$50-400) can refer you to courses in the United States. Community colleges frequently offer inexpensive self-defense classes. Get more complete safety info from the **United States Department of State** (tel. (202) 647-5225 (24hr.); http://travel.state.gov). To order the free *A Safe Trip Abroad,* contact the Superintendent of Documents (see **Useful Publications,** p. 9). Find official warnings from the **United Kingdom Foreign and Commonwealth Office** at http://www.fco.gov.uk (tel. (0171) 238 45 03), from the **Canadian Department of Foreign Affairs and International Trade** (DFAIT) at http://www.dfait-maeci.gc.ca (tel. (800) 267-6788, in Ottawa (613) 944-6788), or from the **Australian Department of Foreign Affairs and Trade** (tel. 262 61 91 11; http://www.dfat.gov.au).

FINANCIAL SECURITY

Among the most colorful aspects of large cities are **con artists,** who often work in groups. Children are among the most effective. Don't respond or make eye contact, walk away quickly, and keep a grip on your belongings. Contact the police if a hustler is insistent or aggressive. *Don't put money in a wallet in your back pocket.* Carry as little money as possible and never count it in public. A **money belt,** sold at camping supply stores, is the best way to carry cash, especially the nylon, zippered pouch with belt that sits inside a waistband. A **neck pouch,** although less accessible, is equally safe. Avoid fanny-packs: even on your stomach, your valuables will be visible and easy to steal. Be alert in public telephone booths and discreet with your calling card number.

Be particularly watchful of your belongings on **buses** (carry your backpack in front of you), don't check baggage on trains, and don't trust anyone to watch your bag. **Trains** are notoriously easy for thieves, who strike when tourists fall asleep. When traveling in pairs, alternate sleeping; when alone, never stay in an empty compartment. Keep documents and valuables on you, and sleep on top bunks with your luggage stored above or with you. Try not to leave possessions in your **car** while away. If the tape deck or radio is not removable, conceal it under a lot of junk. Put baggage in the trunk if you must, but savvy thieves can tell a heavily loaded car by its tires.

Label every piece of luggage both inside and out. For packs, buy small combination **padlocks** to slip through the two zippers, securing the pack shut. Padlocks can also secure hostel lockers, which are useful but unwise for storing valuables. Never leave your belongings unattended anywhere, especially in hostels. If you feel unsafe, look for a place with a curfew or night attendant. Be extra-vigilant in low-budget hotels, where others may have keys, and in dorm-style lodgings. Making **photocopies** of important documents will let you recover them if they are lost or filched. Carry one copy separately and leave another copy at home. Keep some money separate as well.

Travel Assistance International by Worldwide Assistance Services, Inc., 1133 15th St. NW, #400, Washington, D.C. 20005-2710 (tel. (800) 821-2828 or (202) 828-5894; fax 828-5896; email wassist@aol.com; http://www.worldwide-assistance.com) provides its members with a 24-hour hotline for emergencies and referrals. Their Per-Trip (starting at US$65) and Frequent Traveler (starting at US$235) plans include medical, travel, and communication assistance services. The **American Society of Travel Agents,** 1101 King St., Alexandria, VA 22313 (http://www.astanet.com), publishes the free brochure, *Travel Safety*.

DRUGS AND ALCOHOL

Check alcohol, drunk driving, and drug laws for your destinations. The drinking age in Europe is lower than in the U.S. Avoid public drunkenness; it is often against the law and can jeopardize your safety. If you carry **prescription drugs**, keep a copy of the prescriptions—some drugs allowed in your home country may be illegal abroad. **Illegal drug laws** all over the world are different; such drugs are best avoided altogether. Remember that you are subject to the laws of the country you're traveling in and that it is your responsibility to familiarize yourself with those laws. Embassies will not help you if you are arrested on drug charges, which are punishable by anything from a prison sentence to the death penalty—a definite vacation-ruiner.

■ Health

BEFORE YOU GO

Take measures before leaving to prepare for emergencies. Write **emergency contact names,** allergies, and medical conditions in your passport. Always go prepared with any **medication** you take or may need, plus a copy of the prescription and/or a statement from your doctor, particularly for insulin, syringes, or any narcotics. Consult a doctor before leaving, especially for longer stays and rural or less industrialized regions. If you wear **glasses** or **contact lenses,** carry an extra prescription and arrange to have someone send a replacement pair in an emergency. If you wear contacts, take a pair of glasses in case of loss or simply to rest your eyes. Bring extra solutions, enzyme tablets, and eye drops, because prices can be sky-high. A **first-aid kit** should include bandages, pain killers, antiseptic soap or antibiotic cream, a thermometer, tweezers, motion sickness remedy, moleskin, sunscreen, insect repellent, burn ointment, and medicine for diarrhea, constipation, or stomach problems.

Look at your **immunization** records before you go; some countries require vaccination certificates. Travelers over two years old should be sure that the following vaccines are up to date: Measles, Mumps, and Rubella (MMR); Diphtheria, Tetanus, and Pertussis (DTP or DTap)—particularly advisable for those traveling to the former Soviet Union, where **diphtheria** is epidemic; Polio (OPV); Haemophilus Influenza B (HbCV); and Hepatitis B (HBV). A booster of Tetanus-diphtheria (Td) is recommended every 10 years, and adults traveling to the former Soviet Union should consider an additional dose of Polio vaccine if they have not had one during adulthood.

Hepatitis A vaccine and/or Immune Globulin (IG) is recommended for those going to Eastern or Southern Europe.

For information about region-specific vaccinations and health data, contact the **United States Centers for Disease Control and Prevention (CDC).** The CDC maintains an international fax info service for travelers; call 1-888-232-3299, select an international travel directory, and the requested information will be faxed to you. Similar information is available from the CDC website at http://www.cdc.gov. The CDC also publishes the booklet *Health Information for International Travelers* (US$20), a global rundown of disease, immunization, and health advice for particular countries. (Send a check or money order to the Superintendent of Documents. See **Useful Publications,** p. 9. Orders can also be made by phone with a credit card (D, MC, V).)

The **United States State Department** compiles Consular Information Sheets on health, entry requirements, and other issues for all countries; particularly helpful is the website at http://travel.state.gov. To receive these by fax dial (202) 647-3000 directly from a fax machine and follow the recorded instructions. For quick information on travel warnings, call the **Overseas Citizens' Services** (tel. (202) 647-5225). You can also get all of this info by contacting the State Department's regional passport agencies in the U.S., field offices of the U.S. Chamber of Commerce, and U.S. embassies and consulates abroad, or by sending a self-addressed, stamped envelope to the Overseas Citizens' Services, Bureau of Consular Affairs, #4811, U.S. Department of State, Washington, D.C. 20520. For general health info, contact the **American Red Cross,** 285 Columbus Ave., Boston, MA 02116-5114 (tel. (800) 564-1234), which publishes a *First-Aid and Safety Handbook* (US$5).

Travelers with specific medical conditions (diabetes, epilepsy, heart conditions, allergies, etc.) may want the **Medic Alert Identification Tag** (US$35 the first year, US$15 annually thereafter) from the Medic Alert Foundation, 2323 Colorado Ave., Turlock, CA 95382 (tel. (800) 825-3785). Membership in the foundation provides the disease-identifying tag and gives access to a 24-hour collect-call hotline. The **American Diabetes Association,** 1660 Duke St., Alexandria, VA 22314 (tel. (800) 232-3472), provides *Travel and Diabetes* and multilingual diabetic ID cards.

If you are concerned about access to medical support while traveling, contact one of these two services: **Global Emergency Medical Services (GEMS)** which provides 24-hour international medical assistance through registered nurses with on-line access to your medical information, primary physician, and a worldwide network of screened, credentialed English-speaking doctors. Subscribers also receive a personal medical record with vital information in case of emergencies. For more information call (800) 860-1111 (8:30am-5:30pm); fax (770) 475-0058; or write: 2001 Westside Drive, #120, Alpharetta, GA 30201. The **International Association for Medical Assistance to Travelers (IAMAT)** offers a free membership ID card, a directory of English-speaking doctors around the world who treat members for a set fee schedule, and detailed charts on immunization requirements, various tropical diseases, climate, and sanitation. Contact chapters in **Canada,** 40 Regal Road, Guelph, Ontario, N1K 1B5 (tel. (519) 836-0102) or 1287 St. Clair Avenue West, Toronto, M6E 1B8 (tel. (416) 652-0137; fax (519) 836-3412); **New Zealand,** P.O. Box 5049, Christchurch 5; and the **U.S.,** 417 Center St., Lewiston, NY 14092 (tel. (716) 754-4883, 8am–4pm EST; fax (519) 836-3412; email iamat@sentex.net; http://www.sentex.net/~iamat).

ON-THE-ROAD AILMENTS

Common sense is the simplest prescription for good health: eat well, drink lots of fluids, get enough sleep, and don't overexert yourself. Keep strong with high-protein, low-sugar snacks. You may experience fatigue, discomfort, or mild diarrhea as your body adapts to a new environment. Many people take over-the-counter remedies for **diarrhea,** although these can complicate infections. Avoid anti-diarrheals if you suspect exposure to contaminated food or water. The most dangerous side effect of diarrhea is **dehydration;** one anti-dehydration formula is 8oz. of water with ½ tsp. of sugar or honey and a pinch of salt. Also good are soft drinks without caffeine, and salted crackers. Down several of these remedies a day, rest, and wait for the malady to run its course. If you develop a fever or your symptoms last longer than five days, you may have a **food- or water-borne disease,** which can be quite serious—consult a doctor. **Cholera,** an intestinal bacterial disease carried in contaminated food, is a danger in Eastern Europe. First symptoms are watery diarrhea, dehydration, vomiting, and muscle cramps. Untreated cholera quickly becomes fatal. Antibiotics are available, but it is vital to rehydrate. **Hepatitis A** is an intermediate risk in Eastern Europe and the former Soviet Union. It is a viral infection of the liver acquired primarily through sexual contact or contaminated water, ice, shellfish, or unpeeled fruits or vegetables. Symptoms include fatigue, fever, loss of appetite, nausea, dark urine, jaundice, vomiting, aches and pains, and light stool. Ask your doctor about the vaccine "Havrix" or for an injection of immune globulin (IG). To avoid food- and water-borne diseases, watch what you eat and drink. Peel your own fruit and never eat raw foods, especially seafood. Be sure that the cooked food is hot (breads are safe cold). Bring to a rolling boil, treat with iodine, or pass through a water purifier all water, drink only bottled beverages, and don't trust ice. Be cautious with food from street vendors.

Watch out for **heatstroke** in which sweating stops, body temperature rises, and an intense headache develops. Left untreated, it is followed by confusion and ultimately death. Cool victims off with fruit juice or salted water, wet towels, and shade, then rush them to a hospital. For protection, wear a hat and light long-sleeved shirt. Extreme cold is also dangerous. Signs of **hypothermia** include rapidly dropping body temperature, shivering, poor coordination, irritability, and exhaustion, followed by slurred speech, sleepiness, hallucinations, and amnesia. *Do not let hypothermia victims fall asleep*—unconsciousness can lead to death. To avoid hypothermia, keep dry, wear wool or synthetics (most other fabrics, especially cotton, will make you colder), dress in layers, and wear a hat. **Frostbite** turns the skin white, cold, and waxy. Never rub or apply hot water to frostbite; frozen skin is easily damaged. Instead, slowly warm the frostbitten area in dry fabric or with steady body contact. Take serious cases to a doctor immediately. Take a few days to adjust to lower oxygen levels at **high altitudes** before exerting yourself on long hikes. Also be careful about alcohol, especially if you are used to U.S. standards for beer—many foreign brews and liquors pack more punch, and at high altitudes where the air has less oxygen, any alcohol will do you in quickly.

Wet or forested areas have **insects**—mosquitoes, fleas, ticks, and lice—which carry many diseases. **Ticks**—responsible for Lyme disease, among others—can be particularly dangerous. Brush ticks off when walking and inspect your scalp carefully. Wear repellent and clothing that covers as much skin as possible. To remove a tick, grasp it close to your skin and apply slow, steady traction. **Parasites** hide in unsafe water and food; some are also transmitted by insects. Symptoms of parasitic infections include swollen glands or lymph nodes, fever, rashes or itchiness, digestive problems, eye problems, and anemia. Wear shoes and follow the precautions for avoiding food- and water-borne diseases. Animal bites can mean **rabies;** clean wounds thoroughly and seek medical help right away.

Women traveling in unsanitary conditions are vulnerable to **urinary tract and bladder infections,** common bacterial diseases which cause a burning sensation and painful, difficult urination. Left untreated, they can pose serious kidney problems; see a doctor if these symptoms arise. To help avoid infection, drink lots of water and vitamin-C-rich juice, and urinate frequently. For more info, see **Women Travelers,** p. 27.

HIV, AIDS, AND STDS

HIV causes **AIDS,** crippling the immune system and making victims susceptible to even minor illnesses. While not everyone who is HIV-positive has AIDS, *any person who is HIV-positive can transmit this currently fatal virus*. The easiest mode of HIV transmission is through direct blood-to-blood contact: *never* share intravenous drug, tattooing, or other needles. The most common mode of transmission is sexual intercourse (contact of infected semen or vaginal secretions with blood or mucous membranes). The World Health Organization estimates that there are around 30 million people infected with the HIV virus, and women now represent 40% of all new HIV infections. Always assume your partner to be HIV-positive. Bring latex condoms with Nonoxynol-9 spermicide with you, and *use them*. Saliva, urine, and casual contact are not believed to be risky.

If you are HIV-positive, call (202) 647-1488 for country-specific entry requirements or write to the Bureau of Consular Affairs, #6831, Department of State, Washington, D.C. 20520. Many countries require an **HIV Antibody Test** for extended stays or work permits. For more information on AIDS, call the **U.S. Center for Disease Control's** 24-hour hotline at (800) 342-2437. In Europe, write to the **World Health Organization,** attn: Global Program on AIDS, Avenue Appia 20, 1211 Geneva 27, Switzerland (tel. (41 22) 791-2111; fax. (41 22) 791-0746), for statistical material on AIDS internationally. Or write to the **Bureau of Consular Affairs,** #6831, Department of State, Washington, D.C. 20520. Council's brochure, **Travel Safe: AIDS and International Travel,** is available at all Council Travel offices (see **Budget Travel Agencies,** p. 35).

Sexually transmitted diseases (STDs) such as gonorrhea, chlamydia, genital warts, syphilis, and herpes are a lot easier to catch than HIV, and some can be just as deadly. Safer sex involves following the guidelines recommended for avoiding HIV and using common sense, but remember that condoms can break or slip off. Try *looking* at your partner's genitals before sex, and if anything is amiss, just don't do it. The U.S. Center for Disease Control has an **STDs hotline** (tel. (800) 227-8922). If you may be sexually active, if you will be a health worker abroad, or if you are working or living in rural areas (particularly in Eastern Europe), you are advised to get the **Hepatitis B** vaccination, which begins six months before travel.

■ Insurance

Beware of buying unnecessary travel coverage—your regular policies may extend to travel-related accidents. **Medical insurance** (especially university policies) often covers costs incurred abroad. **Medicare's** "foreign travel" coverage is valid only in Canada and Mexico. The **Canadian** Department of Foreign Affairs and International Trade recommends its citizens to buy supplemental health insurance since the provincial health plans will only cover a portion of the total cost; check with your provincial Ministry of Health or Health Plan Headquarters for more details. **Australia** has Reciprocal Health Care Agreements (RHCAs) with several countries; when traveling in those nations, Australians are entitled to many services they receive at home. Contact the Commonwealth Department of Human Services and Health. An E111 form (available from local national health authorities) covers **EU citizens** for emergency treatment throughout the EU. **Homeowners' insurance** (or your family's coverage) often covers theft during travel and loss of travel documents (passport, plane ticket, etc.) up to US$500.

ISIC and **ITIC** provide US$3000 of accident-related medical reimbursement and US$100 per day up to 60 days of hospitalization. The cards give access to a toll-free 24-hour Traveler's Assistance hotline (tel. (800) 626-2427 in the U.S. and Canada; elsewhere U.S. collect (713) 267-2525) whose multilingual staff can help in emergencies. **Council** and **STA** offer a range of plans that can supplement your basic insurance coverage, including medical treatment and hospitalization, accidents, baggage loss, or even charter flights missed due to illness. **American Express** cardholders receive automatic car rental insurance and travel accident coverage on flight purchases made with the card. See **Budget Travel Agencies,** p. 35, or see **Money Matters,** p. 17.

Insurance companies usually require a copy of police reports for thefts, or evidence of having paid medical expenses before they will honor a claim. There may be time limits on filing for reimbursement. Check with each insurance carrier for specific policies. Always carry policy numbers and proof of insurance. Most carriers have 24-hour hotlines. Insurance companies include: **Access America,** 6600 West Broad St., P.O. Box 11188, Richmond, VA 23230 (tel. (800) 284-8300; fax (804) 673-1491), **The Berkely Group/Carefree Travel Insurance,** 100 Garden City Plaza, P.O. Box 9366, Garden City, NY 11530-9366 (tel. (800) 323-3149 or (516) 294-0220; fax (516)

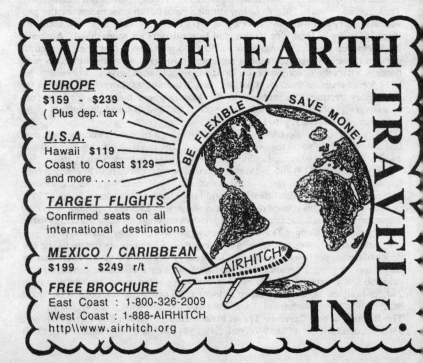

294-1095; email info@berkely.com; http://www.berkely.com), **Globalcare Travel Insurance,** 220 Broadway, Lynnfield, MA 01940 (tel. (800) 821-2488; fax (617) 592-7720; email global@nebc.mv.com; http://www.nebc.mv.com/globalcare), **Travel Assistance International,** by Worldwide Assistance Services, Inc., 1133 15th St. NW, Suite 400, Washington, D.C. 20005-2710 (tel. (800) 821-2828 or (202) 828-5894; fax (202) 828-5896; email wassist@aol.com; http://www.worldwide-assistance.com), **Travel Guard International,** 1145 Clark St., Stevens Point, WI 54481 (tel. (800) 826-1300; fax (715) 345-0525; http://www.travel-guard.com), and **Travel Insured International, Inc.,** 52-S Oakland Ave., P.O. Box 280568, East Hartford, CT 06128-0568 (tel. (800) 243-3174; fax (203) 528-8005; email travelins@aol.com).

■ Alternatives to Tourism

STUDY

Foreign study programs vary tremendously in expense, academic quality, living conditions, degree of contact with local students, and exposure to culture and language. There is a plethora of high school exchange programs. Most American undergraduates enroll in university-sponsored programs, and many colleges staff offices with study abroad information. Ask for the names of recent participants and get in touch.

American Field Service (AFS), 310 SW 4th Avenue, Suite 630, Portland, OR 97204-2608 (tel. (800) 237-4636; fax (503) 241-1653; email afsinfo@afs.org; http//www.afs.org/usa). AFS offers homestay exchange programs for high school students and graduating high school seniors. Financial aid available.

American Institute for Foreign Study, College Division, 102 Greenwich Ave., Greenwich, CT 06830 (tel. (800) 727-2437 ext. 6084; http://www.aifs.com). Programs for high school and college study in universities. Scholarships available.

College Semester Abroad, School for International Training, Admissions, Kipling Rd., P.O. Box 676, Brattleboro, VT 05302 (tel. (800) 336-1616 or 258-3267; fax 258-3500). Offers semester- and year-long programs, costing US$8200-10,300, all expenses included. Financial aid available and U.S. financial aid is transferable.

Council on International Educational Exchange sponsors over 40 study abroad programs throughout the world. Contact them for more information (see **Useful Travel Organizations,** p. 7).

Eurocentres, 101 N. Union St. #300, Alexandria, VA 22314 (tel. (800) 648-4809; fax (703) 684-1495; http://www.eurocentres.com), or Eurocentres, Head Office, Seestr. 247, CH-8038 Zurich, Switzerland (tel. +41 (1) 485 50 40; fax 481 61 24). Language programs and homestays. 2 weeks to a year for beginners to advanced.

Institute of International Education (IIE), 809 United Nations Plaza, New York, NY 10017-3580 (tel. (212) 984-5413; fax 984-5358). Book orders: IIE Books, Institute of International Educations, P.O. Box 371, Annapolis Junction, MD 20701 (tel. (800) 445-0443; fax (301) 953-2838; email iie-boks@iie.org). Publishes *Academic Year Abroad* (US$43; US$4 postage) and *Vacation Study Abroad* (US$37; US$5 postage). Write for a complete list of publications.

WORK AND VOLUNTEER

There's no better way to submerge yourself in a foreign culture than to become part of its economy. It's easy to find a **temporary job,** but it will rarely be glamorous or lucrative. Officially, you can hold a job in Europe only with a **work permit,** obtained by your employer, usually demonstrating that you have skills that locals lack. European friends can expedite permits or arrange work-for-accommodations swaps. Be an au pair; advertise to teach English. Many permit-less agricultural workers go untroubled. European Union citizens can work in any EU country, and if your parents were born in an EU country, you may be able to claim dual citizenship or the right to a permit, but beware of countries where citizenship entails military service. Check with universities' foreign language departments for job opening connections, and contact the Consulate or Embassy of your destination country for more information.

If you are a full-time student at a U.S. university, the simplest way to get a job abroad is through **Council on International Educational Exchange (CIEE)** and its member organizations (see **Useful Travel Organizations,** p. 7). Council can procure three- to six-month work permits (and a work and housing handbook) for France, Germany, and the U.K. (US$25 application fee). French and German positions require language skills; British and Irish programs are best for neophytes, since Council helps with finding accommodations, openings, and connections. **U.S. permanent residents** can get work permits for France and Ireland.

Vacation Work Publications, 9 Park End St., Oxford OX1 1HJ, UK (tel. (01865) 24 19 78; fax 79 08 85), publishes a wide variety of guides and directories with opportunities for summer or full-time work in numerous countries. Write for a catalogue of their publications. **Surrey Books,** 230 E. Ohio St., Chicago, IL 60611 (tel. (800) 326-4430; fax (312) 751-7330; email SurreyBk@aol.com; http://www.surreybooks.com), publishes *How to Get a Job in Europe: The Insider's Guide* (1995 edition US$18). **InterExchange,** 161 Sixth Ave., New York, NY 10013 (tel. (212) 924-0446; fax 924-0575; email interex@earthlink.net), provides information on international work and au pair programs. **Now Hiring! Jobs in Eastern Europe** (US$15), Independent Publishers Group, 814 N. Franklin St., Chicago, IL 60610 (tel. (800) 888-4741), covers finding work and accommodation in Eastern Europe. **Transitions Abroad Publishing, Inc.,** 18 Hulst Rd., P.O. Box 1300, Amherst, MA 01004-1300 (tel. (800) 293-0373; fax (413) 256-0373; email trabroad@aol.com; http://www.transabroad.com), publishes a bi-monthly magazine listing all kinds of opportunities and printed resources for those seeking to study, work, or travel abroad.

Volunteer jobs are readily available almost everywhere. You may receive room and board in exchange for your labor; the work can be fascinating (or stultifying). You can sometimes avoid the high application fees charged by the placement organizations by contacting the individual workcamps directly; check with the organizations. Listings in Vacation Work Publications's *International Directory of Voluntary Work* (UK£9; postage UK£2.50) can be helpful (see above). Also try:

Council on International Educational Exchange has a Voluntary Services Department offering 2- to 4-week environmental or community services projects in over 30 countries. Must be at least 18 years old. Minimum US$295 placement fee. See **Useful Travel Organizations,** p. 7.

Peace Corps, 1111 20th St. NW, Washington, D.C. 20526 (tel. (800) 424-8580; fax (202) 692-2231; http://www.peacecorps.gov). Write for their brochure, detailing applicant requirements. Opportunities in developing nations in Central and Eastern Europe and the former Soviet Union. Must be U.S. citizen, age 18 or over, and willing to make a 2yr. commitment. Bachelor's degree preferred.

Volunteers for Peace, 43 Tiffany Rd., Belmont, VT 05730 (tel. (802) 259-2759; fax 259-2922; email vfp@vfp.org; http://www.vfp.org), is a nonprofit organization that arranges speedy placement in 2-3 week workcamps comprising 10-15 people. Listings in annual *International Workcamp Directory* (US$15). Free newsletter.

World Trade Academy Press, 50 E. 42nd St., #509, New York, NY 10017-5480 (tel. (212) 697-4999). *Looking for Employment in Foreign Countries* (US$16.50) gives info on federal, commercial, and volunteer jobs abroad, and advice on resumes and interviews. Check your local library for their publications: *The Directory of American Firms Operating in Foreign Countries* (1996; US$200) and *The Directory of Foreign Firms Operating in the United States* (1995; US$150).

■ Specific Concerns

WOMEN TRAVELERS

Women exploring on their own inevitably face additional safety concerns. Trust your instincts: if you'd feel safer elsewhere, move on. Always carry money for a phone call, bus, or taxi. Consider staying in hostels with single rooms that lock from the inside or in religious organizations that provide rooms for women only; avoid "communal" showers. Stick to centrally located lodgings, and avoid late-night treks or metro rides. **Hitching** is never safe for lone women, even in pairs. Choose **train** compartments occupied by other women or couples; ask the conductor to put together a women-only compartment. In some parts of Europe, women are frequently beset by unwelcome followers. Exercise caution without avoiding all local men.

The less you resemble a tourist, the better off you'll be. Always look as if you know where you're going, and ask women or couples for directions if you're lost. Try to dress conservatively, especially in rural areas. Shorts and t-shirts may identify you as a foreigner and should be avoided. Trying to fit in can be effective, but may cause you to be ill at ease and a conspicuous target. Wearing a conspicuous **wedding band** may help prevent unwanted overtures, but in cities you may be harassed no matter how you're dressed. In crowds, you may be pinched or squeezed by over/under-sexed slimeballs. Your best answer to verbal harassment is no answer at all (a reaction is what the harasser wants). Feigning deafness or sitting motionless may do a world of good. The extremely persistent may be dissuaded by a firm, loud, and very public "Go away!" in the appropriate language. If need be, turn to an older woman for help; her rebukes will usually embarrass the most persistent jerks.

Women traveling alone should not attempt to challenge local custom or assert strong feminist beliefs. You won't change anything but may endanger yourself. You might even want to refer to your (fictional) "over-protective husband" who is waiting back at your hotel. Don't hesitate to seek out a police officer or a passerby. *Let's Go* lists emergency numbers (including rape crisis lines) in the **Practical Information** listings of most large cities; memorize the local numbers. Carry a whistle or an airhorn on your keychain for emergencies. A **model mugging** course will prepare you for a potential mugging and will raise your level of awareness and confidence (see **Safety and Security,** p. 19). Women also face additional health concerns when traveling (see **Health,** p. 20). These warnings and suggestions should not discourage you from traveling. Don't take unnecessary risks, but don't lose your spirit of adventure either.

For information in the U.S., contact the **National Organization for Women (NOW)** (email now@now.org; http://now.org), which has branches across the country. Main offices include 105 E. 22nd St., Suite 307, **New York,** NY 10010 (tel. (212) 260-4422); 1000 16th St. NW, Suite 700, **Washington, D.C.** 20036 (tel. (202) 331-0066); and 3543 18th St., Box 27, **San Francisco,** CA 94110 (tel. (415) 861-8960; fax 861-8969). The following publications offer tips for women travelers:

Directory of Women's Media is available from the National Council for Research on Women, 11 Hanover Sq., 20th Fl., New York, NY 10005 (tel. (212) 785-7335; fax 785-7350). The publication lists women's publishers, bookstores, theaters, and news organizations (mail orders, US$30).

A Journey of One's Own: Uncommon Advice for the Independent Woman Traveler, by Thalia Zepatos (US$17; US$2 shipping). Available from The Eighth Mountain Press, 624 Southeast 29th Ave., Portland, OR 97214 (tel. (503) 233-3936; fax 233-0774; email soapston@teleport.com). Interesting and full of good advice, with a bibliography of resources. In North American bookstores, or order direct.

Women's Travel in Your Pocket, Ferrari Guides, P.O. Box 37887, Phoenix, AZ 85069 (tel. (602) 863-2408; email ferrari@q-net.com; http://www.q-net.com), an annual guide for women (especially lesbians) traveling worldwide. Hotels, nightlife, dining, organizations, and outdoor adventure (US$14, plus shipping).

Active Women Vacation Guide, by Evelyn Kay (US$17.95; shipping is free for *Let's Go* readers). Blue Panda Publications, 3031 Fifth St., Boulder, CO 80304 (tel. (303) 449 8474; fax 449 7525). Has listings of 1,000 trips worldwide offered by travel companies for active women and true stories of women's traveling adventures.

MINORITY TRAVELERS

In general, minority travelers will find a high level of tolerance in large cities; the small towns and the countryside are more unpredictable. Western Europe tends to be more tolerant than Eastern Europe, though travelers should feel more comfortable in large, east/central cities like Budapest or Warsaw. Gypsies (*Romany*) encounter the most hostility throughout Eastern Europe, and travelers with darker skin of any nationality might be mistaken for Gypsies and face unpleasant consequences. Other minority travelers, especially those of African or Asian descent, will usually meet with more curiosity than hostility, and travelers of Arab ethnicity may also be treated more suspiciously. Skinheads are on the rise in Eastern Europe, and minority travelers, especially Jews and blacks, should regard them with caution. Anti-Semitism is still a problem in many countries, including Poland and the former Soviet Union; sad to say, it is generally best to be discreet about your religion. Still, attitudes will vary from country to country and town to town; travelers should use common sense—someone who flashes money around will become a target regardless of any racial or religious differences.

OLDER TRAVELERS

Senior Citizens are eligible for a wide array of discounts. If you don't see a senior citizen price listed, ask. Proof of senior citizen status is often required. Agencies for senior group travel such as **Eldertreks,** 597 Markham St., Toronto, ONT Canada, M6G 2L7 (tel. (800) 741-7956 or (416) 588-5000; fax 588-9839; email passages@inforamp.net; http://www.eldertreks.com) and **Walking the World** (P.O. Box 1186, Fort Collins, CO 80522, tel. (970) 498-0500; fax 498-9100; email walktworld@aol.com), are growing in popularity and enrollment.

AARP (American Association of Retired Persons), 601 E. St. NW, Washington, D.C. 20049 (tel. (202) 434-2277). Members 50 and over receive discounts, benefits, and services including the AARP Motoring Plan from AMOCO (tel. (800) 334-3300). Annual fee US$8 per couple; $20 for three years.

Elderhostel, 75 Federal St., 3rd Fl., Boston, MA 02110-1941 (tel. (617) 426-7788; email Cadyg@elderhostel.org; http://www.elderhostel.org). For those 55 or over (spouse of any age). Programs at colleges, universities, and other learning centers in over 70 countries on varied subjects lasting 1-4 weeks.

The Globe Piquot Press, P.O. Box 833, Old Saybrook, CT 06475-0833 (tel. (800) 243-0495; fax (800) 820-2329; email info@globe-piquot.com; http://www.globe-piquot.com). Publishes *Europe the European Way: A Traveler's Guide to Living Affordably in the World's Great Cities* (US $14), which offers general hints for the budget-conscious senior considering a long stay or retiring abroad.

National Council of Senior Citizens, 8403 Colesville Rd., Silver Spring, MD 20910-31200 (tel. (301) 578-8800; fax 578-8999). Memberships cost US$13 per year, US$33 for 3 years, or US$175 for a lifetime. Individuals or couples can receive hotel and auto rental discounts, a senior newspaper, and use of a discount travel agency.

Pilot Books, 127 Sterling Ave., P.O. Box 2102, Greenport, NY 11944 (tel. (516) 477-1094 or 1(800) 79PILOT (797-4568); fax (516) 477-0978; email feedback@pilotbooks.com; http://www.pilotbooks.com). Helpful guides including *Doctor's Guide to Protecting Your Health Before, During, and After International Travel* (US$10, postage US$2) and *Have Grandchildren, Will Travel* (US $10, postage US$2). Call or write for a complete list of titles.

No Problem! Worldwise Tips for Mature Adventurers, by Janice Kenyon. US$16 from Orca Book Publishers, P.O. Box 468, Custer, WA 98240-0468. Advice and info on insurance, finances, security, health, packing. Useful appendices.

Unbelievably Good Deals and Great Adventures That You Absolutely Can't Get Unless You're Over 50, by Joan Rattner Heilman. Great tips on senior discounts. US$10 from Contemporary Books or online at http://www.amazon.com.

BISEXUAL, GAY, AND LESBIAN TRAVELERS

Attitudes toward bisexual, gay, and lesbian travelers are, naturally, particular to each region. Listed below are organizations and publishers which address those concerns.

Damron Travel Guides, P.O. Box 422458, San Francisco, CA 94142-2458 (tel. (415) 255-0404 or (800) 462-6654; fax (415) 703-9049 or 703-8308; email damronco@damron.com; http://www.damron.com). The *Damron Address Book*

(US$15) lists bars, restaurants, guest houses, and services which cater to gay men. The *Damron Road Atlas* (US$16) contains color maps of major European cities and gay and lesbian resorts and listings of bars and accommodations. *The Women's Traveller* (US$13) lists over 7500 bars, restaurants, accommodations, bookstores, and services catering to lesbians. *Damron's Accommodations* lists gay and lesbian hotels around the world (US$19). Shipping US$5.

Ferrari Guides, P.O. Box 37887, Phoenix, AZ 85069 (tel. (602) 863-2408; fax 439-3952; email ferrari@q-net.com; http://www.q-net.com). *Ferrari Guides' Gay Travel A to Z* (US$16), *Ferrari Guides' Men's Travel in Your Pocket* (US$16), *Ferrari Guides' Women's Travel in Your Pocket* (US$14), *Ferrari Guides' Inn Places* (US$16), *Ferrari Guides' Gay Paris* (US$17.95). Available in bookstores or by mail (postage/handling US$5 for the first item, US$1 for each additional item mailed within the U.S; in Canada, first item $10; overseas, call or write for shipping cost).

Gayellow Pages, P.O. Box 533, Village Station, New York, NY 10014 (tel. (212) 674-0120; fax 420-1126; email gayellow@banet.net; http://gayellowpages.com). Annually updated listing of accommodations, resorts, hotlines, gay community centers, local switchboards, and other items of interest. U.S./Canada edition US$16.

Gay's the Word, 66 Marchmont St., London WC1N 1AB (tel. (0171) 278 7654). The largest gay and lesbian bookshop in the U.K. Mail order service available. No catalogue of listings, but they will provide a list of titles on a given subject. Open M-Sa 10am-6:30pm, Th 10am-7pm, Su 2-6pm. Nearest Underground: Russell Square.

Giovanni's Room, 345 S. 12th St., Philadelphia, PA 19107 (tel. (215) 923-2960; fax 923-0813; email giophilp@netaxs.com). International feminist, lesbian, and gay bookstore that carries publications listed here. Mail (and email) order service.

International Gay and Lesbian Travel Association, 4331 N. Federal Hwy., Suite 304, Fort Lauderdale, FL 33308 (tel. (954) 776-2626 or (800) 448-8550; fax (954) 776-3303; email IGLTA@aol.com; http://www.iglta.org). Organization of over 1350 companies serving gay and lesbian travelers worldwide. Call for lists of travel agents, accommodations, and events.

International Lesbian and Gay Association (ILGA), 81 rue Marché-au-Charbon, B-1000 Bruxelles, Belgium (tel./fax +32 (2) 502 24 71; email ilga@ilga.org; http://www.ilga.org). Not a travel service. Provides political information, such as homosexuality laws of individual countries.

Spartacus International Gay Guides, published by Bruno Gmunder, Verlag GMBH, Leuschnerdamm 31, 10999 Berlin, Germany (tel. +49 (30) 615 00 30; fax 615 90 07; email bgvtravel@aol.com). Lists bars, restaurants, hotels, bookstores, hotlines, and homosexuality laws in various countries. Available in bookstores and in the U.S. by mail from Lambda Rising, 1625 Connecticut Ave. NW, Washington D.C., 20009-1013 (tel. (202) 462-6969) for US$32.95.

The Gay Vacation Guide: The Best Trips and How to Plan Them, Mark Chesnut. Lists tour operators and travel companies along with advice on using gay-friendly businesses and avoiding problems while traveling. (US$14.95, shipping and handling US$4 for the first order, $1 for each additional title.) Carol Publishing, 120 Enterprise Ave., Secaucus, NJ 07094 (tel. (800) 447 2665; fax (201) 866 8159).

DISABLED TRAVELERS

Countries vary in accessibility to travelers with disabilities. Some national and regional tourist boards provide directories on the accessibility of various accommodations and transportation services. If these services are not available, contact institutions of interest directly. You should inform airlines and hotels of disabilities when making arrangements, so they can prepare special accommodations. Hotels and hostels are becoming more accessible to disabled persons, and many attractions are trying to make exploring the outdoors more feasible. Call ahead to restaurants, parks, and other facilities to find out about ramps, door widths, elevator dimensions, etc. **Diabetics** may wish to consult the short quarterly, **The Diabetic Traveler,** P.O. Box 8223 RW, Stamford, CT (tel. (203) 327-5832; subscription US$18.95).

Arrange transportation well in advance. If you give sufficient notice, some major car rental agencies (**Hertz, Avis,** and **National**) may offer hand-controlled vehicles. **Rail** is probably most convenient: large stations in Britain are equipped with wheel-

ESSENTIALS

chair facilities, and the French national railroad offers wheelchair compartments on all TGV (high speed) and Conrail trains. Guide dog owners will need to provide a certificate of immunization against rabies and should inquire as to the specific quarantine policies of destination countries. The following organizations provide info:

Access Project (PHSP), 39 Bradley Gardens, West Ealing, London W13 8HE, U.K. (Email Gordon Couch at gordon.couch@virgin.net). Distributes access guides to London and Paris for a donation of UK£7.50. Researched by persons with disabilities. They cover traveling, accommodations, and access to sights and entertainment. Includes a "Loo Guide" with a list of wheelchair-accessible toilets.

American Foundation for the Blind, 11 Penn Plaza, New York, NY 10001 (tel. (212) 502-7600). Provides information and services M-F 8:30am-4:30pm. For their *Consumer's Catalogue,* contact Lighthouse Enterprises, 36-20 Northern Boulevard, Long Island City, NY 11101 (tel. (800) 829-0500).

Directions Unlimited, 720 N. Bedford Rd., Bedford Hills, NY 10507 (tel. (800) 533-5343; in NY (914) 241-1700; fax (914) 241-0243). Individual and group vacations, tours, and cruises for the physically disabled. Group tours for blind travelers.

Flying Wheels Travel Service, 143 W. Bridge St., Owatonna, MN 55060 (tel. (800) 535-6790; fax 451-1685). Arranges trips for groups and individuals in wheelchairs or with other types of limited mobility.

Graphic Language Press, P.O. Box 270, Cardiff by the Sea, CA 92007 (tel. (760) 944-9594; email niteowl@cts.com). Publishes **Wheelchair Through Europe,** a guide covering accessible hotels, transportation, sightseeing and resources for disabled travelers in many European cities. $12.95 includes shipping and handling; make check payable to Graphic Language Press.

The Guided Tour Inc., Elkins Park House, 114B, 7900 Old York Rd., Elkins Park, PA 19027 (tel. (800) 783-5841 or (215) 782-1370; fax 635-2637; http://www.guided-tour.com). Travel programs for persons with developmental and physical challenges and those requiring renal dialysis. Call, fax, or write for a free brochure.

Mobility International USA (MIUSA), P.O. Box 10767, Eugene, OR 97440 (tel. (541) 343-1284 voice and TDD; fax 343-6812; email info@miusa.org; http://www.miusa.org). Sells the 3rd Edition of *A World of Options: A Guide to International Educational Exchange, Community Service, and Travel for Persons with Disabilities* (individuals US$35; organizations US$45).

Moss Rehab Hospital Travel Information Service, (tel. (215) 456-9600, TDD 456-9602). Telephone resource center on accessibility and other travel concerns.

Society for the Advancement of Travel for the Handicapped (SATH), 347 Fifth Ave., #610, New York, NY 10016 (tel. (212) 447-1928; fax 725-8253; email sath-travel@aol.com; http://www.sath.org). Publishes quarterly color travel magazine *OPEN WORLD* (free for members; subscription US$13) and info sheets on disability travel and accessible destinations. Annual membership US$45, students and seniors US$30.

Twin Peaks Press, P.O. Box 129, Vancouver, WA 98666-0129 (tel. (360) 694-2462; fax 696-3210; email 73743.2634@compuserve.com; http://netm.com/mall/info-prod/twinpeak/helen.htm). Publishes *Travel for the Disabled* (US$20), *Directory of Travel Agencies for the Disabled* (US$20), *Wheelchair Vagabond* (US$15), and *Directory of Accessible Van Rentals* (US$10). Postage US$4.00 for first book, US$2.00 for each additional book.

DIETARY CONCERNS

Vegetarians should have no problem finding suitable cuisine. In city listings, *Let's Go: Europe* notes many restaurants which cater to vegetarians or which offer good vegetarian selections. The **Vegetarian Society of the UK** (VSUK), Parkdale, Dunham Rd., Altringham, Cheshire WA14 4QG, U.K. (tel. (0161) 928 0793; fax 926 9182; http://www.vegsoc.org), publishes several titles; call or send a self-addressed, stamped envelope for a listing. **The Vegetarian Traveler,** P.O. Box 410205, Cambridge, MA 02141, U.S., sells a packet of 16 cards in 16 languages to be presented in restaurants, explaining your diet restrictions (US$9.95; US$1 shipping). Specify vegan (no meat, dairy, or eggs), lacto (no meat or eggs), or ovo-lacto (no meat).

Travelers who keep **kosher** should contact synagogues in larger cities about kosher restaurants; your own synagogue or college Hillel should have lists of Jewish institutions. **The Jewish Travel Guide** lists synagogues, kosher restaurants, and Jewish institutions in over 80 countries. It is available from Vallentine-Mitchell Publishers, Newbury House 890-900, Eastern Ave., Newbury Park, Ilford, Essex, U.K. IG2 7HH (tel. (0181) 599 88 66; fax 599 09 84), and in the U.S. ($15, shipping $3) from Sepher-Hermon Press, 1265 46th St., Brooklyn, NY 11219 (tel./fax (718) 972-9010).

TRAVELING WITH CHILDREN

Family vacations can be rewarding or frustrating. Plan ahead, slow the pace, and adapt plans to the interests and patience of all the travelers. Make sure your accommodations are child-friendly, or ask if a hostel has rooms for families. If you rent a car, ask if the rental company provides a car seat for younger children. Traveling by car is an easy way to keep an eye on young children, but teenagers may prefer the train. A papoose-style device for babies may be easier to maneuver than a stroller.

Restaurants often have children's menus and discounts, and virtually all museums and tourist attractions have a children's rate. Make your child carry some sort of ID in case of an emergency, and arrange a reunion spot in case of separation when sightseeing. Children under two generally fly for 10% of the adult airfare on international flights (not necessarily including a seat). International fares are usually discounted 25% for children ages two to 11. Finding a private place to **breastfeed** is often a problem; pack accordingly or search for mother-friendly spots wherever you end up. For information on traveling with breast-fed babies, check La Leche League's homepage (http://www.lalecheleague.org).

Backpacking with Babies and Small Children (US$9.95) is published by Wilderness Press, 2440 Bancroft Way, Berkeley, CA 94704 (tel. (800) 443-7227 or (510) 843-8080; fax 548-1355; email wpress@ix.netcom.com; http://wildernesspress.com). The **Kidding Around** series (US$8, postage under US$5), with illustrated children's books about Spain, Paris, and London, is available from John Muir Publications, P.O. Box 613, Santa Fe, NM 87504 (tel. (800) 285-4078; fax (505) 988-1680). **Take Your Kids to Europe,** by Cynthia W. Harriman (US$16.95, shipping US $3.95), published by Globe-Pequot Press, 6 Business Park Rd., Old Saybrook, CT 06475 (tel. (800) 285-4078; fax (860) 395-1418) is geared towards families. **Travel with Children** by Maureen Wheeler (US$12, postage US$2.50) is published by Lonely Planet Publications, 150 Linden St., Oakland, CA 94607 (tel. (800) 275-8555 or (510) 893-8555; fax 893-8563; email info@lonelyplanet.com; http://www.lonelyplanet.com), and P.O. Box 617, Hawthorn, Victoria 3122, Australia.

■ Packing

PACK LIGHT! Plan your packing according to the climate and the type of travel you'll be doing. Before you leave, strap your packed bag on and imagine yourself walking uphill on hot asphalt for three hours. A good rule is to pack what you need, then take half the clothes and twice the money. Leave room for souvenirs and gifts.

LUGGAGE

If you plan to cover most of your itinerary on foot, a sturdy **backpack** with padded hip belt and external compartments is unbeatable. In general, internal-frame packs are easier to carry and more efficient. For extensive camping or hiking, look into an **external-frame** pack, which offers added support, distributes weight better, and allows for a sleeping bag to be strapped on. Tie down loose straps to escape conveyor belt mangling. In any case, make sure your pack has a strong, padded hip belt, which transfers the weight from the shoulders to the legs. Sturdy backpacks cost anywhere from US$150-500. This is one area where it doesn't pay to economize—cheaper packs may be less comfortable, and the straps are more likely to fray or rip. A **suitcase** suffices for the less mobile, but weight and maneuverability should be con-

sidered. An empty, light-weight **shoulder bag** packed inside your luggage will be useful for purchases or laundry. A small **daypack** with secure closures allows you to dive into the city with just the essentials—lunch, camera, water bottle, and *Let's Go*. Guard money, passport, railpass, and other important articles in a **money belt** or **neck pouch,** and keep it with you always (see **Safety and Security,** p. 19).

CLOTHING AND FOOTWEAR

The **clothing** you bring will depend on when and where you plan to travel. If visiting places of worship, wear clothes that cover the shoulders and knees. Light natural fibers are the best in heat. For colder weather, you need a few heavier layers; have at least one layer that will insulate while wet. Make sure your clothing can survive wrinkles and repeated cleaning. Always bring a jacket or wool sweater. **Walking shoes** (well-cushioned sneakers and well-ventilated hiking boots) are not a place to skimp, and be sure to waterproof them. A double pair of socks—light silk or polypropylene inside and thick wool outside—will cushion feet, keep them dry, and help prevent blisters. Bring flip-flops for protection from fungi in showers. Talcum powder can prevent foot sores, and moleskin is bliss for blisters. *Break in your shoes before you leave home.* **Rain gear** is essential; a waterproof jacket and backpack cover will shield you and your stuff. A **poncho** is bulkier and may tear, but is lighter and can serve as a ground cloth or camper lean-to. Gore-Tex® is waterproof and breathable.

MISCELLANEOUS

The following list is not exhaustive: pocketknife, alarm clock, sewing kit, water bottle, flashlight, towel, compass, bungee cord, toilet paper (not always provided in toilets), plastic baggies, waterproof matches, moleskin, whistle, rubber bands, insect repellent, electrical tape (for patching tears), clothespins, maps and phrasebooks, tweezers, sunscreen, vitamins, cold medicine, tissues, an antiseptic, safety pins, and padlock. Condoms, tampons, and your favorite brand of deodorant and razor may be hard to find on the road. A **first-aid kit** is good but bulky. **Laundry** facilities are sometimes hard to find; washing clothes in hotel sinks is often a better option. Bring a bar of detergent soap, a sink-stopper (a squash ball works), and a travel clothesline or string. If staying in youth hostels, make the requisite **sleepsack** by folding a full-size sheet in half the long way, then sewing two sides closed. **Contact lens** supplies are rare and expensive, so bring saline and cleaner or wear glasses. **Film** is pricey, so buy it at home. Consider bringing a **disposable camera** or two rather than an expensive, permanent one. Despite disclaimers, airport security X-rays *can* fog film.

European **electricity** is usually 220V AC, which fries 110V North American appliances. Hardware stores have **adapters** (for the plug shape) and **converters** (which change the voltage). Use both, or you'll melt your appliance.

GETTING THERE

■ Budget Travel Agencies

Students and those under 26 qualify for reduced airfares from student travel agencies such as **Council Travel, STA, Let's Go Travel,** and **Travel CUTS.** These agencies resell bulk ticket purchases; in 1998, peak season student round-trips from the East Coast of North America to even the offbeat corners of Europe rarely topped US$800, with off-season fares considerably lower. Round-trip (regular) fares from Australia or New Zealand were about US$1600. Student travel agencies also serve people over 26, although many discounts are specifically for the young.

Council Travel (http://www.ciee.org/travel/index.htm), offers railpasses, discount airfares, hosteling cards, guidebooks, budget tours, travel gear, and student (ISIC), youth (GO25), and teacher (ITIC) identity cards. U.S. offices include: Emory Vil-

ESSENTIALS

lage, 1561 N. Decatur Rd., **Atlanta,** GA 30307 (tel. (404) 377-9997); 2000 Guadalupe, **Boston,** MA 02116 (tel. (617) 266-1926); 1138 13th St., 1153 N. Dearborn, **Chicago,** IL 60610 (tel. (312) 951-0585); 10904 Lindbrook Dr., **Los Angeles,** CA 90024 (tel. (310) 208-3551); 1501 University Ave. SE #300, **Minneapolis,** MN 55414 (tel. (612) 379-2323); 205 E. 42nd St., **New York,** NY 10017 (tel. (212) 822-2700); 953 Garnet Ave., **San Diego,** CA 92109 (tel. (619) 270-6401); 530 Bush St., **San Francisco,** CA 94108 (tel. (415) 421-3473); 1314 NE 43rd St. #210, **Seattle,** WA 98105 (tel. (206) 632-2448); 3300 M St. NW, **Washington, D.C.** 20007 (tel. (202) 337-6464). **For U.S. cities not listed,** call 800-2-COUNCIL (226-8624). Also 28A Poland St. (Oxford Circus), **London,** W1V 3DB (tel. (0171) 287 3337).

Rail Europe Inc., 226 Westchester Ave., White Plains, NY 10604 (tel. (800) 438-7245; fax 432-1329; http://www.raileurope.com). Sells all Eurail products and passes, national railpasses including Brit Rail and German Rail, and point-to-point tickets. Up-to-date info on rail travel, including Eurostar, the English Channel train.

STA Travel, 6560 Scottsdale Rd. #F100, Scottsdale, AZ 85253 (tel. (800) 777-0112 nationwide; fax (602) 922-0793; http://sta-travel.com). A student and youth travel organization with over 150 offices worldwide offering discount airfares, railpasses, accommodations, tours, insurance, and ISICs. Offices in the U.S. include: 297 Newbury Street, **Boston,** MA 02115 (tel. (617) 266-6014); 429 S. Dearborn St., **Chicago,** IL 60605 (tel. (312) 786-9050; 7202 Melrose Ave., **Los Angeles,** CA 90046 (tel. (213) 934-8722); 10 Downing St., Ste. G, **New York,** NY 10003 (tel. (212) 627-3111); 51 Grant Ave., **San Francisco,** CA 94108 (tel. (415) 391-8407); 4341 University Way NE, **Seattle,** WA 98105 (tel. (206) 633-5000); 2401 Pennsylvania Ave., **Washington, D.C.** 20037 (tel. (202) 887-0912); **Miami** (Coral Gables), FL (tel. (305) 284-1044). Overseas offices include: 10 High St., **Auckland** (tel. (09) 309 97 23); 6 Wrights Ln., **London** W8 6TA (tel. (0171) 938 47 11 for North American travel); 222 Faraday St., **Melbourne** VIC 3050 (tel. (03) 349 69 11).

Let's Go Travel, Harvard Student Agencies, 17 Holyoke St., Cambridge, MA 02138 (tel. (617) 495-9649; fax 495-7956; email travel@hsa.net; http://hsa.net/travel). Railpasses, HI-AYH memberships, ISICs, ITICs, FIYTO cards, guidebooks, maps, bargain flights, and travel gear. Call or write for a catalogue (or see insert).

Campus Travel, 52 Grosvenor Gardens, London SW1W 0AG (http://www.campus-travel.co.uk). Branches across U.K. Student and youth fares on transportation. Flexible airline tickets. Student/youth discount and ID cards and travel insurance. Also maps, guides, and travel suggestion booklets. Telephone bookings: in **Europe** call (0171) 730 34 02; in **N. America** call (0171) 730 21 01; **worldwide** call (0171) 730 81 11; in **Manchester** call (0161) 273 17 21; in **Scotland** (0131) 668 33 03.

Travel CUTS (Canadian Universities Travel Services Ltd.), 187 College St., Toronto, Ont. M5T 1P7 (tel. (416) 979-2406; fax 979-8167; email mail@travelcuts). Also 295-A Regent St., **London** W1R 7YA (tel. (0171) 637 31 61). Discounted airfares; student fares with ISIC. Issues ISIC, FIYTO, GO25, HI cards, and railpasses. Free *Student Traveller* and info on the Student Work Abroad Program (SWAP).

Travel Management International (TMI), 1129 East Wayzata, Wayzata MN 55391 (tel. (612) 404-7164 or (800) 245-3672). Student fares and discounts. Very helpful.

Unitravel, 117 North Warson Rd., St. Louis, MO 63132 (tel. (800) 325 2222; fax (314) 569 2503). Offers discounted airfares on major scheduled airlines.

Usit Youth and Student Travel, 19-21 Aston Quay, O'Connell Bridge, **Dublin** 2 (tel. (01) 677-8117; fax 679-8833). Also New York Student Center, 895 Amsterdam Ave., **New York,** NY, 10025 (tel. (212) 663-5435; email usitny@aol.com). Additional offices throughout Ireland and in Greece. Low-cost tickets and flexible travel arrangements all over the world. ISIC and FIYTO-GO 25 cards in Ireland only.

Wasteels, 7041 Grand National Drive #207, Orlando, FL 32819 (tel. (407) 351-2537). A huge chain in Europe, with 200,000 locations. Information in English can be requested from the **London** office (tel. (4471) 834 70 66; fax 630 76 28). Sells the Wasteels BIJ tickets, which are discounted (30-45% off regular fare) 2nd class international point-to-point train tickets with unlimited stopovers (must be under 26 on the first day of travel); sold *only* in Europe.

■ By Plane

The first budget challenge is getting there: after all, airlines are out to make money. Finding a cheap flight will be easier if you understand their byzantine pricing system. Call every toll-free number, and don't hesitate to ask about discounts, as it's unlikely they'll be volunteered. An hour or two of research can save you hundreds of dollars. Use several **travel agents,** preferably specialists in the region, but remember that they work on commission and may not want to spend a lot of time finding you the cheapest fares.

Students and those under 26 should never need to pay full price for a ticket. Seniors can also get great deals. Sunday newspapers may have travel sections with local bargains. Outsmart airline reps with the *Official Airline Guide* (US$359 per year; with fares US$479; check your local library; some info online at http://www.oag.com), a monthly guide listing nearly every scheduled flight in the world and toll-free phone numbers to call for reservations. More accessible is Michael McColl's *The Worldwide Guide to Cheap Airfare* (US$15).

There is a wealth of travel information available on the Internet. The **Air Traveler's Handbook** (http://www.cs.cmu.edu/afs/cs.cmu.edu/user/mkant/Public/Travel/airfare.html) is an excellent source of general information on air travel. **TravelHUB** (http://www.travelhub.com) has a directory of travel agents and a searchable database of fares from over 500 consolidators (see **Ticket Consolidators,** p. 41). Edward Hasbrouck maintains a **Consolidators FAQ** (http://www.travel-library.com/air-travel/consolidators.html) that provides great background on finding cheap international flights. Groups such as the **Air Courier Association** (http://www.aircourier.org) offer information about traveling as a courier and provide up-to-date listings of last minute opportunities. **Travelocity** (http://www.travelocity.com) operates a searchable online database of published airfares, which can be reserved online.

Most airfares peak between mid-June and early September. Midweek (M-Th morning) round-trip flights run about US$40-50 cheaper than on weekends, but weekend flights are generally less crowded. Traveling from hub to hub (for example, Los Angeles to London) will yield a more competitive fare than for smaller cities. Return-date flexibility is usually not an option for budget travelers; traveling with an "open return" ticket can be pricier than fixing a date and paying to change it. Whenever flying internationally, pick up your ticket well in advance of the departure date, have the flight confirmed within 3 days of departure, and arrive at the airport at least two hours before your flight.

COMMERCIAL AIRLINES

The commercial airlines' lowest regular offer is **APEX** (Advance Purchase Excursion Fare); advertised specials may be cheaper but have more restrictions and lower availability. APEXs provide confirmed reservations and allow "open-jaw" tickets (landing in and returning from different cities). Generally, reservations must be made seven to 21 days in advance, with seven- to 14-day minimum and up to 90-day maximum stay limits, and hefty cancellation and change penalties. Book APEX fares early for peak season; by May it may be difficult getting the summer departure date you want.

If you pay an airline's lowest published fare, you may waste hundreds of dollars; find out the average commercial price in order to assess your "bargain." Look into flights to less popular destinations or on smaller carriers. **Icelandair** (tel. (800) 223-5500; http://www.icelandair.com), which offers free 3-day Iceland stopovers on most flights to or from Europe, has last-minute offers and a low standby fare from New York to Luxembourg (June-Aug. $616; Sept.-May $369-$410; reserve within 3 days of departure; no Iceland stopover). **Finnair** (tel. (800) 950-5000; http://www.us.finnair.com) offers cheap round-trip fares to Helsinki and occasionally auctions tickets on its website. **Martinair** (tel. (800) 627-8462 or (800) MARTINAIR) offers one-way-only standby fares from New York to Amsterdam (you're responsible for the ticket home). **TowerAir** (tel. (800) 34-TOWER (86937); http://www.towerair.com) offers round-trip flights to Paris, Athens, and Rome.

TICKET CONSOLIDATORS

Ticket consolidators sell unsold tickets on commercial and charter airlines at unpublished fares—a 30-40% price reduction is not uncommon—and are the best deal for traveling on short notice, on a high-priced trip, to an off-beat destination, or in peak season. There are rarely age or stay constraints, but there is little to no flexibility in changing flights, and you must go back to the consolidator (not the airline) to get a refund. These tickets often are for connecting (not direct) flights on foreign airlines and do not credit frequent-flyer miles.

Consolidators come in three varieties: wholesale only; specialty agencies (both wholesale and retail); and "bucket shops," or discount retail agencies. As a private consumer, you can deal only with retail, but you can also have access to wholesale through a travel agent. Look for bucket shops' tiny ads in weekend papers (in the U.S., try the *Sunday New York Times;* in Australia, the *Sydney Times*). In London, the **Air Travel Advisory Bureau** (tel. (0171) 636 50 00) can provide names of reliable consolidators and discount flight specialists. Kelly Monaghan's *Consolidators: Air Travel's Bargain Basement* (US$8, shipping US$3.50), from the **Intrepid Traveler,** P.O. Box 438, New York, NY 10034 (tel. (212) 569-1081; email info@intrepidtraveler.com), lists consolidators by location and destination.

Be a smart and careful shopper. Phone around, and pay with a credit card (in spite of the 2-5% fee) so you can stop payment if you never receive your tickets. Research the agency and get a copy of their refund policy. Insist on a receipt that gives full details about the tickets, refunds, and restrictions, and record the name of the agent with whom you spoke and when. If they refuse to give you a receipt, or seem clueless or shady, use a different company. Beware the "bait and switch" gag: some firms will advertise a super-low fare and then tell a caller that it has been sold. Although this is a viable excuse, if they can't offer you a price near the advertised fare, it's a scam—report them to the Better Business Bureau. Since some consolidators have fingers in many pies, it's also worth asking about accommodation and car rental discounts.

Try **Airfare Busters** (tel. (800) 232-8783); **Cheap Tickets** (tel. (800) 377-1000); **Interworld** (tel. (305) 443-4929; fax 443-0351); **Pennsylvania Travel** (tel. (800) 331-0947); **Rebel** (tel. (800) 227-3235; email travel@rebeltours.com; http://www.rebeltours.com); or **Travac** (tel. (800) 872-8800; fax (212) 714-9063; email mail@travac.com; http://www.travac.com). **NOW Voyager,** 74 Varick St. #307, New York, NY 10013 (tel. (212) 431-1616; email info@nowvoyagertravel.com; http://www.nowvoyagertravel.com), acts as a consolidator and books discounted flights, mostly from New York, as well as courier flights, for an annual registration fee of US$50. For a processing fee, depending on the itinerary and number of travelers, **Travel Avenue** (tel. (800) 333-3335; http://www.travelavenue.com) will search for the lowest airfare available and give you a 5% rebate on fares over US$350.

STANDBY FLIGHTS

Very flexible budget travelers might try standby flights, for which you buy a promise that you will get to a destination near where you're going within a window of time (usually 5 days) from a location in a specified region. You call in before your date-range to hear all of your flight options for the next week or so, and your probability of boarding. You then decide which flights you want to try to make and present a voucher at the airport which grants you the right to board a flight on a space-available basis. This procedure repeats for the return trip. When flying standby, be sure to read all the fine print in agreements. It may be difficult to receive refunds, and vouchers will not be honored if the airline fails to receive payment in time. **Air.Tech.Com,** 588 Broadway #204, New York, NY 10012 (tel. (212) 219-7000; fax 219-0066; email fly@airtech.com; http://www.airtech.com), sells standby tickets for around US$169-229 one way, and also arranges courier flights and regular confirmed-reserved flights at discount rates. With **Airhitch,** 2641 Broadway, 3rd fl., New York, NY 10025 (tel. (800) 326-2009 or (212) 864-2000; fax 864-5489), and Los Angeles, CA (tel. (310) 726-5000), one-way flights to Europe run US$159-239. Several European offices can handle return registration; the main one is in Paris (tel. (1) 47 00 16 30).

CHARTER FLIGHTS

Charters are flights a tour operator contracts with an airline to fly extra loads of passengers to peak-season destinations. Charter flights fly less often and have more restrictions, notably on refunds. They are almost always fully booked, and schedules may change or be canceled last minute without a full refund. Pay with a credit card and consider insurance against trip interruption. Consolidators like **Interworld, Rebel, Travac,** and **Travel Avenue** (see above) often have charter options.

Eleventh-hour **discount clubs** and **fare brokers** offer members savings on European travel, including charters and tour packages. Study contracts closely and avoid overnight layovers. Some options are **Last Minute Travel Service,** 100 Sylvan Rd., Woburn, MA 01801, one of the few without a membership fee (tel. (800) 527-8646 or (617) 267-9800), and **Travelers Advantage,** Stamford, CT (tel. (800) 548-1116; http://www.travelersadvantage.com; US$49 annual fee).

COURIER COMPANIES

Those who travel light should consider being a **courier.** The company hiring the courier uses his or her checked luggage space for freight; the courier only brings carry-ons. You must be over 21 (sometimes 18), have a passport, and procure any necessary visas yourself. Most flights are round-trip with fixed-length stays (usually a week) and, if out of the U.S., depart from New York. Round-trip fares to Western Europe from the U.S. range from US$200-550. **NOW Voyager** (see **Ticket Consolidators,** p. 41), acts as an agent, with last-minute deals from US$200 round-trip plus US$50 registration fee. Another agent to try is **Halbart Express,** 147-05 176th St., Jamaica, NY 11434 (tel. (718) 656-5000; fax 917-0708; offices in Chicago, Los Angeles, and London). Check a bookstore or library for *Air Courier Bargains* (US$15, plus US$3.50 shipping from the Intrepid Traveler, see above). *The Courier Air Travel Handbook* (US$10, plus US$3.50 shipping) contains names and phone numbers of courier companies. Order it from Bookmasters, Inc., P.O. Box 2039, Mansfield, OH 44905 (tel. (800) 507-2665). Always read the fine print. There are cheap fares out there, but you won't get something for nothing.

ONCE THERE

■ Getting Around

BY TRAIN

European trains retain the charm and romance of an era that caught glimpses of the distances in between the destinations. But charm and romance don't satisfy those earthly needs. Bring food and a water bottle; the on-board cafe can be pricey, and train water undrinkable. Lock your compartment door and keep your valuables on your person.

Many train stations have different counters for domestic and international tickets, seat reservations, and info—check before lining up. Even with a railpass, you are not guaranteed a seat on a train unless you make a reservation (US $3-10); they are advisable during the busier holiday seasons, and often required on major lines. It will be necessary to purchase a supplement (US$10-50) or special fare for high speed or quality trains such as Spain's AVE, Cisalpino, Pendolino, and certain French TGV (Inter-Rail holders must also purchase supplements for trains like EuroCity, InterCity, InterCityExpress, and many of France's TGV, which are included in the Eurailpass and Europass). Check the brochure that came with your railpass for exact details on necessary supplements or special fares.

For overnight travel, a tight, open bunk called a **couchette** is an affordable luxury (about US$20). Both seat and couchette reservations can be made by your local travel

ESSENTIALS

agent, but they will probably cost a few dollars more than making them in person at the train station (reserve at least a few hours in advance for seats; at least a few days for couchettes). Not all countries give students or young people direct discounts on regular domestic rail tickets, but many will sell a student or youth card valid for 20-50% off all fares for an entire year.

RAILPASSES   Buying a railpass is a popular and sensible option under many circumstances. Ideally conceived, a railpass allows you to jump on any train in Europe, go wherever you want whenever you want, and change your plans at will. With your railpass you will receive a timetable for major routes and a map with details on possible ferry, steamer, bus, car rental, hotel, and **Eurostar** (the high speed train linking London and Paris or Brussels) discounts. In practice, it's not so simple. You still must stand in line to pay for supplements, seat reservations, and couchette reservations, as well as to have your pass validated when you first use it. More importantly, railpasses don't always pay off. For ballpark estimates, consult Rick Steves' **Europe Through the Back Door** newsletter or the **DERTravel** or **RailEurope** railpass brochure for prices of point-to-point tickets. Add them up and compare with railpass prices. If you're under age 26, the BIJ tickets are probably worth it (see **Rail tickets,** p. 47).

You may find it tough to make your railpass pay for itself in Belgium, Greece, Ireland, Italy, Luxembourg, the Netherlands, Portugal, Spain, Eastern Europe and the Balkans, where train fares are reasonable, distances short, and buses preferable. If, however, the total cost of your trips nears the price of the pass, the convenience of avoiding ticket lines may be worth the difference. Avoid an obsession with making the pass pay for itself; you may come home with only blurred memories of train stations.

A **Eurailpass** remains perhaps the best option for non-EU travelers. Eurailpasses are valid in most of Western Europe except for Britain: Austria, Belgium, Denmark, Finland, France, Germany, Greece, Hungary, Italy, Luxembourg, Netherlands, Norway, Portugal, Republic of Ireland, Spain, Sweden, and Switzerland. Eurailpasses and Europasses are designed by the EU itself, and are purchasable only by non-Europeans almost exclusively from non-European distributors. These passes must be sold at uniform prices determined by the EU, so no one travel agent is better than another as far as the pass itself is concerned. However, some agents tack on a $10 handling fee. Also, agents often offer different perks with purchase of a railpass, so shop around to see what you can get.

The first class **Eurailpass** rarely pays off; it is offered for 15 days (US$538), 21 days (US$698), one month (US$864), two months (US$1224), or three months (US$1512). Those traveling in a group of 2 to 5 might prefer the **Eurail Saverpass,** which allows unlimited first-class travel for 15 days (US$458 per person), 21 days (US$594), one month (US$734), two months (US$1040), or three months (US$1286). Travelers ages 12-25 can buy a **Eurail Youthpass,** good for 15 days (US$376), 21 days (US $489), one month (US$605), two months (US$857), or three months (US $1059) of second-class travel. The two-month pass is most economical. **Eurail Flexipasses** allow limited first-class travel within a two-month period: 10 days (US$634), 15 days (US$836). These prices drop to $540 and $710, respectively, when traveling in a group of 2 to 5. **Youth Flexipasses,** for those under 26 who wish to travel second-class, are available for US$444 or US$585, respectively. Children 4-11 pay half price, and children under 4 travel free.

The **Europass** combines France, Germany, Italy, Spain, and Switzerland in one plan. With a Europass you can travel in any of these five countries from five to 15 days within a window of two months. First-class adult prices begin at US$326 and increase incrementally by US$42 for each extra day of travel. With purchase of a first-class ticket you can buy an identical ticket for your traveling partner for 40% off. Second-class youth tickets begin at US$216 and increase incrementally by $29 for each extra day of travel. Children 4-11 travel for half the price of a first-class ticket. You can add associate countries (Austria/Hungary, Belgium/Luxembourg/Netherlands, Greece Plus (Greece and ADN/HML ferry between Italy and Greece), and Portugal) for a fee: $60 for 1 associated country, $90 for 2, $110 for 3, and $120 for all 4. The Europass

introduces planning complications; you must plan your routes so that they only make use of countries you've "purchased." They're serious about this: if you cut through a country you haven't purchased you will be fined.

You should plan your itinerary before buying a Europass. It will save you money if your travels are confined to between three and five adjacent Western European countries, or if you know that you want to go only to large cities. Europasses are not appropriate if you like to take lots of side trips—you'll waste rail days. If you're tempted to add lots of rail days and associate countries, consider the Eurailpass.

It is best to buy your Eurail or Europass before leaving. Otherwise, once in Europe, you'll probably have to use a credit card to buy over the phone from a railpass agent in a non-EU country (one on the North American east coast will be closest), who can send the pass to you by express mail. Contact Council Travel, Travel CUTS, Let's Go Travel (see **Budget Travel Agencies,** p. 35), or almost any travel agent handling European travel. Eurailpasses are not refundable once validated; if your pass is completely unused and unvalidated and you have the original purchase documents, you can get an 85% refund from the place of purchase. You can get a replacement for a lost pass only if you have purchased insurance on it under the Pass Protection Plan (US$10). All Eurailpasses can be purchased from a travel agent, or from **Rail Europe Group,** 500 Mamaroneck Ave., Harrison, NY 10528 (tel. (800) 438-7245; fax (800) 432-1329 in the U.S.; and tel. (800) 361-7245; fax (905) 602-4198 in Canada; http://www.raileurope.com), which also sells point-to-point tickets. They offer special rates for groups of ten or more traveling together. **DER Travel Services,** 9501 W. Devon Ave. Suite #301, Rosemont IL 60018 (tel. (800) 782-2424; fax (800) 282-7474; http://www.dertravel.com) also deals in rail passes and point to point tickets.

For EU citizens, there are **InterRail Passes,** for which six months' residence in Europe makes you eligible. There are 8 InterRail zones: A (Rep. of Ireland, Great Britain Passenger Railway, N. Ireland), B (Norway, Sweden, and Finland), C (Germany, Austria, Denmark, and Switzerland), D (Croatia, Czech Rep., Hungary, Poland, and Slovakia), E (France, Belgium, Netherlands, and Luxembourg), F (Spain, Portugal, and Morocco), G (Italy, Greece, Slovenia, Turkey, and the ADN/HML ferries between Italy and Greece), and H (Bulgaria, Romania, Yugoslavia, and Macedonia). You can buy a pass good for 22 days in one zone (under 26 UK£159, over 26 £229), or one month in two (£209, £279), three (£229, £309), or all 8 (£259, £349) zones. For information and ticket sales in Europe contact **Student Travel Center,** 1st Fl. 24 Rupert St., London, W1V7FN (tel. (0171) 437 01 21, 437 63 70, 437 81 01, or 434 13 06; fax 734 38 36; http://student-travel-centre.com). Tickets are also available from travel agents or main train stations throughout Europe.

If your travels will be limited to one country, consider a national railpass or regional pass such as the **ScanRail Pass,** which gives you unlimited rail travel in Denmark, Finland, Norway, and Sweden; the **Benelux Tourrail Pass** for Belgium, the Netherlands, and Luxembourg; the **Balkan Flexipass,** which is valid for travel in Bulgaria, Greece, the Former Yugoslavian Republic of Macedonia, Montenegro, Romania, Serbia, and Turkey; and the **European East Pass,** which covers Austria, the Czech Republic, Hungary, Poland, and the Slovak Republic. In addition to simple railpasses, many countries (and Europass and Eurail) offer rail-and-drive passes, which combine car rental with rail travel—a good option for travelers who wish both to visit cities accessible by rail and make side trips into the surrounding areas. Several national and regional passes offer companion fares, allowing two adults traveling together to save about 50% on the price of one pass. Some of these passes can be bought only in Europe, some only outside of Europe, and for some it doesn't matter; check with a railpass agent or with national tourist offices.

RAIL TICKETS For travelers under 26, **BIJ** tickets (Billets Internationals de Jeunesse) are a great alternative to railpasses. Available for international trips within Europe and for travel within France as well as most ferry services, they knock 20-40% off regular second-class fares. Tickets are good for 60 days after purchase and allow a number of stopovers along the normal direct route of the train journey. Issued for a specific international route between two points, they must be used in the direction and order of the designated route (side- or back-tracking must be done at your expense) and must be bought in Europe. Tickets are sold under the names **British Rail, Eurotrain,** and **Wasteels.** They are available from European travel agents, at Wasteels or Eurotrain offices (usually in or near train stations), or directly at the ticket counter in some nations. Contact Wasteels in Victoria Station, adjacent to Platform 2, London SW1V 1 JT (tel. (0171) 834 70 66; fax 630 76 28).

USEFUL RESOURCES   The ultimate reference for planning rail trips is the **Thomas Cook European Timetable** (US$28; with map of all European train and ferry routes US$39; postage US$5). This timetable, updated monthly, covers all major and most minor train routes in Europe. In North America, order it from **Forsyth Travel Library** (see **Useful Publications,** p. 7). In Europe find it at any **Thomas Cook Money Exchange Center;** in the rest of the world call (+44 1733 503 571) or write Thomas Cook Publishing, PO Box 227, Thorpe Wood, Peterborough, PE3 6PU, UK. Also available from Forsyth Travel library, or in bookstores, is **Traveling Europe's Trains** (US$15) by Jay Brunhouse, which includes maps and sightseeing suggestions. Available in most bookstores or from **Houghton Mifflin Co.,** 222 Berkeley St., Boston, MA 02116 (tel. (800) 225-3362; fax (800) 634-7568; http://www.hmco.com) is the annual **Eurail Guide to Train Travel in the New Europe** (US$15), giving timetables, instructions, and prices for international train trips, day trips, and excursions in Europe. The annual railpass special edition of the free Rick Steves' **Europe Through the Back Door** travel newsletter and catalogue, 120 Fourth Ave. N., P.O. Box 2009, Edmonds, WA 98020 (tel. (425) 771-8303; fax 771-0833; email rick@ricksteves.com; http://www.ricksteves.com) provides comparative analysis of European railpasses with national or regional passes and point-to-point tickets. Available by mail or on the Web. **Hunter Publishing,** P.O.Box 7816, Edison, NJ 08818 (tel. (800) 255-0343; fax (732) 417-1744; http://www.hunterpublishing.com), offers a number of rail atlases and travel guides. The huge online bookstore at **http://www.amazon.com** also sells and ships most of the above titles.

BY BUS

Though European trains and railpasses are extremely popular, the bus networks of Britain, Greece, Ireland, Portugal, and Turkey are more extensive, efficient, and often more comfortable; in Spain, Hungary, and the Baltics, the bus and train systems are on a par; and in Iceland and parts of northern Scandinavia, bus service is the only ground transportation available. In the rest of Europe, bus travel is more of a crapshoot; scattered offerings from private companies are often cheap, but sometimes unreliable. It may be difficult to negotiate the route you need, but short-haul buses can reach rural areas inaccessible by train. Amsterdam, Athens, Istanbul, London, Munich, and Oslo are centers for lines that offer long-distance rides across Europe.

Eurolines, 4 Cardiff Rd., Luton LU1 1PP (tel. (01582) 40 45 11; fax (01582) 40 06 94; in London, 52 Grosvenor Gardens, Victoria; (tel. (0171) 730 82 35); email welcome@eurolines.uk.com; http://www.eurolines.co.uk), is the largest operator of Europe-wide coach services, including Eastern Europe and Russia. A Eurolines Pass offers unlimited 30-day (under 26 and over 60 UK£159, 26-60 UK £199) or 60-day (under 26 and over 60, UK£199, 26-60 UK£249) travel between 30 major tourist destinations. Eurolines also offers **Euro Explorers,** seven complete travel loops throughout Europe with set fares and itineraries. **Eurobus UK Ltd.,** Coldborough House, Market Street, Bracknell, Berkshire RG121JA (tel.(01344) 300 301; fax (01344) 860 780; email info@eurobus.uk.com; http://www.eurobus.uk.com), offers cheap bus trips in 25 major cities in 10 major European countries for those between ages 18 and 38. The buses, with English speaking guides and drivers, stop door-to-door at one hostel or budget hotel per city, and let you hop on and off. Tickets are sold by zone; for any one zone US$195, for any two zones US$299, for all three zones US$319. Included with purchase of all three zones or added for a nominal fee with other tickets is **London Link,** a London/Paris return ticket. Travelers under 26 are eligible for discounts on all tickets. For purchase in the United States, contact Commonwealth Express (tel. (800) EUROBUS); in Canada contact Travel CUTS (see **Budget Travel Agencies,** p. 39). For discounted bus tickets between Athens and Rome check out **Magic Travel Services** in Athens (see **By Plane,** p. 53).

BY CAR

Yes, there really is no speed limit on the Autobahn. Cars offer speed, freedom, access to the countryside, and an escape from the town-to-town mentality of trains. Unfortunately, they also insulate you from the *esprit de corps* of rail traveling. Although a single traveler won't save by renting a car, four usually will. If you can't decide between train and car travel, you may benefit from a combination of the two; Rail Europe and other railpass vendors offer rail-and-drive packages for both individual countries and all of Europe. Travel agents may offer other options. Fly-and-drive packages are often available from travel agents or airline/rental agency partnerships.

You can **rent** a car from a U.S.-based firm (Alamo, Avis, Budget, or Hertz) with European offices, from a European-based company with local representatives (Europcar), or from a tour operator (Auto Europe, Europe By Car, Kemwel Holiday Autos, and Rob Liddiard Travel), which will arrange a rental for you from a European company at its own rates. Multinationals offer greater flexibility, but tour operators often strike better deals. Rentals vary by company, season, and pick-up point; picking up your car in Belgium, Germany or Holland is usually cheaper than renting from Paris. Expect to pay US$80-400 per week, plus tax (5-25%), for a teensy car. Reserve well before leaving for Europe and pay in advance if at all possible. It is always significantly less expensive to reserve a car from the U.S. than from Europe. Always check if prices quoted include tax and collision insurance; some credit card companies will cover this automatically. Ask about discounts and check the terms of insurance, particularly the size of the deductible. Rates are generally lowest in Belgium, Germany, Holland, and the U.K., and highest in Scandinavia and Eastern Europe. Ask your airline about special fly-and-drive packages; you may get up to a week of free or discounted rental. Minimum age varies by country, but is usually 21-25. At most agencies, all that's needed to rent a car is a U.S. license and proof that you've had it for a year. In Spain, Hungary, and parts of Eastern Europe you may need an international driver's license.

Try **Alamo,** available for Belgium, Czech Republic, Germany, Greece, Ireland, Malta, the Netherlands, Portugal, Slovak Republic, Switzerland, and the U.K., (tel. (800) 522-9696; http://www.goalamo.com); **Auto Europe,** 39 Commercial St., P.O. Box 7006, Portland, ME 04101 (tel. (800) 223-5555; fax (800) 235-6321; email webmaster@autoeurope.com; http://www.autoeurope.com); **Avis Rent a Car** (tel. (800) 331-1084; http://www.avis.com), with locations throughout Western and Eastern Europe; **Budget Rent a Car** (tel. (800) 472-3325; http://www.drivebudget.com); **Europe by Car,** One Rockefeller Plaza, New York, NY 10020 (tel. (800) 223-1516, (212) 581-3040, in California, (800) 252-9401; fax (212) 246-1458; http://www.europebycar.com); **Hertz Rent a Car** (tel. (800) 654-3001; http://www.hertz.com), throughout Europe; **Kemwel Holiday Autos** (tel. (800) 678-0678; email kha@kemwel.com; http://www.kemwel.com); **Maiellano Travel Auto** (specializing in rentals to/in Italy), 445 Forest Ave., Staten Island, NY 10301 (tel. (800) 223-1616; fax (718) 727-0399); **Payless Car Rental** (tel. (800) 729-5377) in the U.K.; **Rob Liddiard Travel** (tel. (800) 272-3299 or (818) 980-9133; email liddiard@jps.net).

For longer than 17 days, **leasing** can be cheaper than renting; it is often the only option for those ages 18-21. The cheapest leases are agreements to buy the car and then sell it back to the manufacturer at a prearranged price. As far as you're concerned, though, it's a lease and doesn't entail enormous financial transactions. Leases generally include insurance coverage and are not taxed, though they may include a VAT. The most affordable ones usually originate in Belgium, France, or Germany. Expect to pay at least US$1200 for 60 days. Contact **Auto Europe, Europe by Car, Kemwel Holiday Autos,** or **Rob Liddiard Travel.** You will need to make arrangements in advance.

If you're brave and know what you're doing, **buying** a used car or van in Europe and selling it just before you leave can provide the cheapest wheels for longer trips. Check with consulates for import-export laws concerning used vehicles, registration, and safety and emission standards. Camper-vans and motor homes give the advantages of a car without the hassle and expense of finding lodgings. Most of these vehicles are diesel-powered and deliver roughly 24 to 30 miles per gallon of diesel fuel, which is cheaper than gas. David Shore and Patty Campbell's **Europe by Van and Motorhome** (US$14, postage US$3, overseas US$6) guides you through the entire process of renting, leasing, buying, and selling vehicles in Britain and on the Continent, including buy-back options, registration, insurance, and dealer listings. To order: write, call, or email Shore/Campbell Publications, 1842 Santa Margarita Dr., Fallbrook, CA 92028 (tel./fax (800) 659-5222 or (760) 723-6184; email shore-cam@aol.com; http://members.aol.com/europevan).

Eric Bredesen's **Moto-Europa** (US$16, shipping US$5), available from Seren Publishing, 2935 Saint Anne Dr., Dubuque, IA 52001 (tel. (800) 387-6728; fax (319) 583-7853), is a thorough guide to all these options and includes itinerary suggestions, a motorists' phrasebook, and chapters on leasing and buying vehicles. More general info is available from the **American Automobile Association (AAA),** Travel Agency Services Dept., 1000 AAA Dr., Heathrow, FL 32746 (tel. (800) 222-4357, (407) 444-4300, or (407) 894-3333; http://www.aaa.com). For regional numbers of the **Canadian Automobile Association (CAA),** call (800) 222-4357 or go to their website at http://www.caa.ca.

Before setting off, know the laws of the countries in which you'll be driving (e.g., both seat belts and headlights must be on at all times in Scandinavia, and remember to keep left in Ireland and the U.K.). The **Association for Safe International Road Travel (ASIRT)** can provide more specific information about road conditions. They are located at 11769 Gainsborough Rd., Potomac, MD 20854 (tel. (301) 983-5252; fax 983-3663; email asirt@erols.com; http://www.asirt.org). ASIRT considers road travel (by car or bus) to be relatively safe in Denmark, Ireland, the Netherlands, Norway, Sweden, Switzerland, and the U.K.; and relatively unsafe in Turkey and Morocco. Scandinavians and Western Europeans use unleaded gas almost exclusively, but it's not available in many gas stations in Eastern Europe.

FLYING AROUND

Flying across Europe on regularly scheduled flights can devour your budget. **Alitalia** (tel. (800) 223-5730; http://www.alitalia.it) sells "Europlus": in conjunction with a transatlantic flight on Alitalia, for US$299 you may purchase a package of three flight coupons good for anywhere Alitalia flies within Europe; unlimited additional tickets cost $100. To non-Europe residents, **Lufthansa** (http://www.lufthansa.com) offers "Discover Europe," a package of three flight coupons which vary in cost, depending on country of origin. For U.S. residents, the tickets cost US$125-200 each depending on season and destination; up to six additional tickets are US$105-175 each (tel. (800) 399-LUFT (5838); fax (800) 522-2329). From London, **Go Fly Limited,** a subsidiary of **British Airways,** offers round-trip fares to Rome, Milan, and Copenhagen for UK£100 (tel. 84 56 05 43 21; http://www.go-fly.com).

U.S. citizens can also purchase **Eurair** passes (US$90 each, airport taxes not included, reservations recommended), to travel between 50 European cities (for information call (888) 387-2479; fax (512) 404 1291; http://www.eurair.com). Student travel agencies sell cheap tickets, and budget fares are frequently available in the spring and summer on high-volume routes between northern Europe and resort areas in Italy, Greece, and Spain. Consult budget travel agents and local newspapers. The **Air Travel Advisory Bureau** in London (tel. (0171) 636 50 00; http://www.atab.co.uk), can also point the way to discount flights. **Magic Travel Services** in Athens (tel. (01) 323 74 71; fax (01) 322 2021; email magic@magic.gr; http://www.magic.gr), which organizes bus and ferry excursions in Europe, also operates inexpensive flights. In addition, many European airlines offer visitor ticket packages, which give intercontinental passengers discounts on flights within Europe (as well as on accommodations and car rentals) after arrival. Check with a travel agent for details.

BY BOAT

Travel by boat is a bewitching alternative favored by Europeans but overlooked by most foreigners. Most European ferries are comfortable and well-equipped; the cheapest fare class sometimes includes a reclining chair or couchette where you can sleep. You should check in at least two hours early for a prime spot and allow plenty of time for late trains and getting to the port. Avoid the astronomically priced cafeteria cuisine by bringing your own food. Fares jump sharply in July and August. Ask for discounts; ISIC holders can often get student fares, and Eurail passholders get many reductions and free trips (check the brochure that comes with your railpass). You'll occasionally have to pay a small port tax (under US$10). Advance planning and reserved ticket purchases through a travel agency can spare you days of waiting in dreary ports for the next sailing.

Ferries in Europe divide into four major groups. **Mediterranean** ferries may be the most glamorous, but they can also be the most rocky. Reservations are recommended, especially in July and August. Bring toilet paper. Ferries run on erratic schedules, with similar routes and varying prices. Shop around, and beware of dinky, unreliable companies that don't take reservations. Ferries across the **English Channel** are frequent and dependable; see the Great Britain and Ireland **Getting There** sections. Ferries in the **North Sea** are reliable and go everywhere. Those content with deck passage rarely need to book ahead. **Riverboats** acquaint you with many towns that trains can only wink at. The Moselle, Rhine, and Danube steamers are overrun by tourists; other less commercial lines can be more attractive.

For complete listings of schedules and fares for ferries, steamers, and cruises throughout Europe find a copy of the quarterly **Official Steamship Guide International** at your travel agent. **Thomas Cook** also lists complete ferry schedules (see **By Train**, p. 48). Links to some major European ferry companies can be found at http://www.youra.com/intnlferries.html. For information on cruises throughout Europe and visa-free cruises to Russia contact **EuroCruises**, 303 W. 13th St., New York, NY 10014 (tel. (800) 688-3876 or (212) 691-2099; fax (212) 366-4747; email eurocruises@compuserve.com; http://www.eurocruises.com). They deal in both long river and sea cruises.

BY BICYCLE

Today, biking is one of the key elements of the classic budget Eurovoyage. With the proliferation of mountain bikes, you can do some serious natural sight-seeing. Remember that touring involves pedaling both yourself and whatever you store in the **panniers** (bags which strap to your bike). Take some reasonably challenging daylong rides at home to prepare yourself before you leave, and have your bike tuned up by a reputable shop. Wear visible clothing, drink plenty of water (even if you're not thirsty), and ride on the same side as the traffic. Learn the international signals for turns, and use them. Know how to fix a modern derailleur-equipped mount and change a tire, and practice on your own bike. A few simple tools and a good bike manual will be invaluable. For info about touring routes, consult national tourist offices or any of the numerous books available. **Michelin road maps,** available in bookstores, are clear and detailed (http://www.michelin-travel.com).

If you are nervous about striking out on your own, **Blue Marble Travel** (in Canada tel. (519) 624-2494; fax 624-4760; email blumarbl@mgl.ca; in Paris tel. (01) 42 36 02 34; fax (01) 42 21 14 77; email blumarbl@club-internet.fr; in U.S. tel. (800) 258-8689 or (973) 326-9533; fax 326-8939; email blumarbl@gti.net; http://www.blumarbl.com) offers bike tours designed for adults aged 20 to 50. Pedal with or without your 10 to 15 companions through the Alps, Austria, France, Germany, Italy, Portugal, Scandinavia, and Spain. Full-time graduate and professional students may get discounts, and standby fares may be obtained in Europe through the Paris office. **CBT Tours** offers one- to seven-week biking, mountain biking, and hiking tours, priced around US$95 per day, including all lodging and breakfasts, one-third of all dinners, complete van support, airport transfers, three staff, and extensive route notes and maps each day. Tours run May through August, with departures every seven to 10 days. In 1999, CBT will visit Belgium, the Czech Republic, England, France, Germany, Holland, Italy, Ireland, Luxembourg, Scotland, and Switzerland. Contact CBT Tours, 415 W. Fullerton, #1003, Chicago, IL 60614 (tel. (800) 736-BIKE (2453) or (773) 404-1710; fax (773) 404-1833; email adventure@cbt-tours.com; http://www.cbttours.com).

Many airlines will count your bike as your second free piece of luggage, a few charge. The additional or automatic fee runs about US$60-110 each way. Bikes must be packed in a cardboard box with the pedals and front wheel detached; airlines sell bike boxes at the airport (US$10). Most ferries let you take your bike for free or a nominal fee. You can always ship your bike on trains, though the cost varies from small to substantial.

Riding a bike with a frame pack strapped on it or your back is about as safe as pedaling blindfolded over a sheet of ice; panniers are essential. The first thing to buy, however, is a suitable **bike helmet.** At about US$25-50, they're a much better buy than head injury or death. U-shaped **Citadel** or **Kryptonite locks** are expensive (starting at US$30), but the companies insure their locks against theft of your bike for one to two years. **Bike Nashbar,** 4111 Simon Rd., Youngstown, OH 44512 (tel. (800) 627-4227; fax (800) 456-1223; http://www.nashbar.com), has excellent prices and cheerfully beats advertised competitors' offers by US$0.05. They ship anywhere in the U.S. or Canada.

Renting a bike beats bringing your own if your touring will be confined to one or two regions. *Let's Go* lists bike rental shops for most larger cities and towns. Some youth hostels rent bicycles for low prices. In Switzerland, train stations rent bikes and often allow you to drop them off elsewhere; check train stations throughout Europe for similar deals.

BY MOPED AND MOTORCYCLE

Motorized bikes have long spiced up southern European roads with their flashy colors and perpetual buzz. They offer an enjoyable, relatively inexpensive way to tour coastal areas and countryside, particularly where there are few cars. They don't use much gas, can be put on trains and ferries, and are a good compromise between the high cost of car travel and the limited range of bicycles. However, they're uncomfortable for long distances, dangerous in the rain, and unpredictable on rough roads and gravel. Always wear a helmet, and never ride with a backpack. If you've never been on a moped before, a twisting Alpine road is not the place to start. Expect to pay about US$20-35 per day; try auto repair shops, and remember to bargain. Motorcycles are more expensive and normally require a license, but are better for long distances. **Bosenberg Motorcycle Excursions,** Mainzer Str. 54, 55545 Bad Kreuznach, Germany (tel. 011 49 67 16 73 12; fax 011 49 67 16 71 53; email Bosenberg@compuserve.com; http://www.bosenberg.com) arranges tours in the Alps, Austria, France, Italy, and Switzerland; they also rent motorcycles April through October.

Before renting, ask if the quoted price includes tax and insurance, or you may be hit with an unexpected additional fee. Avoid handing your passport over as a deposit; if you have an accident or mechanical failure you may not get it back until you cover all repairs. Pay ahead of time instead.

BY THUMB

Let's Go strongly urges you to consider seriously the risks before you choose to hitch. **We do not recommend hitching** as a safe means of transportation, and none of the information presented here is intended to do so.

No one should hitch without careful consideration of the risks involved. Not everyone can be an airplane pilot, but any bozo can drive a car. Hitching means entrusting your life to a random person who happens to stop beside you on the road and risking theft, assault, sexual harassment, and unsafe driving. In spite of this, there are gains to hitching. Favorable hitching experiences allow you to meet local people and get where you're going, especially in northern Europe and Ireland, where public transportation is sketchy. The choice, however, remains yours.

Depending on the circumstances and the norms of the country, men and women traveling in groups and men traveling alone might consider hitching (called "autostop" in much of Europe) beyond the range of bus or train routes. If you're a woman traveling alone, don't hitch. It's just too dangerous. A man and a woman are a safer combination, two men will have a harder time, and three will go nowhere.

If you do decide to hitch, consider where you are. Britain and Ireland are probably the easiest places in Western Europe to get a lift. Hitching in Scandinavia is slow but steady. Long-distance hitching in the developed countries of northwestern Europe demands close attention to expressway junctions, rest stop locations, and often a destination sign. Hitching in southern Europe is generally mediocre; France is the worst. In some Central and Eastern European countries, the line between hitching and taking a taxi is quite thin.

Where one stands is vital. Experienced hitchers pick a spot outside of built-up areas, where drivers can stop, return to the road without causing an accident, and have time to look over potential passengers as they approach. Hitching (or even standing) on super-highways is usually illegal: one may only thumb at rest stops or at the entrance ramps to highways. In the **Practical Information** section of many cities, we list the tram or bus lines that take travelers to strategic points for hitching out.

Finally, success will depend on what one looks like. Successful hitchers travel light and stack their belongings in a compact but visible cluster. Most Europeans signal with an open hand, rather than a thumb; many write their destination on a sign in large, bold letters and draw a smiley-face under it. Drivers prefer hitchers who are neat and wholesome. No one stops for anyone wearing sunglasses.

Safety issues are always imperative, even for those who are not hitching alone. Safety-minded hitchers avoid getting in the back of a two-door car, and never let go of their backpacks. They will not get into a car that they can't get out of again in a hurry. If they ever feel threatened, they insist on being let off, regardless of where they are. Acting as if they are going to open the car door or vomit on the upholstery will usually get a driver to stop. Hitchhiking at night can be particularly dangerous; experienced hitchers stand in well-lit places, and expect drivers to be leery of nocturnal thumbers (or open-handers).

Most Western European countries offer a ride service (listed in the **Practical Information** for major cities), a cross between hitchhiking and the ride boards common at many universities, which pairs drivers with riders; the fee varies according to destination. **Eurostop International (Verband der Deutschen Mitfahrzentralen** in Germany and **Allostop** in France) is one of the largest in Europe. Riders and drivers can enter their names on the Internet through the **Taxistop** website (http://www.taxistop.be). Not all of these organizations screen drivers and riders; ask in advance.

BY FOOT

Europe's grandest scenery can often be seen only by foot. *Let's Go* describes many daytrips for those who want to hoof it, but native inhabitants (Europeans are fervent, almost obsessive hikers), hostel proprietors, and fellow travelers are the best source of tips. Many European countries have hiking and mountaineering organizations; alpine clubs in Germany, Austria, Switzerland, and Italy, as well as tourist organizations in Scandinavia, provide inexpensive, simple accommodations in splendid settings. **Walking Europe from Top to Bottom** by S. Margolis and G. Harmon details one of Europe's most popular trails (US$11); check your local bookstore for others.

ESSENTIALS

■ Accommodations

When arriving in a town without a reservation, stop first at the tourist office, which should distribute accommodations listings and reserve rooms for a small fee. Prices often rise each January. Hostel proprietors or locals with rooms may approach you in ports or train stations, an accepted custom with no guarantee of trustworthiness or quality. Carry your own baggage, ask for ID, and have them write down the price.

HOSTELS

Europe in the summer is overrun by young budget travelers. Hostels are the hub of this subculture, providing opportunities to meet youths from all over the world, find traveling partners, trade stories, and learn about places to visit. At US$10-25 per night, prices are low; only camping is cheaper. Guests tend to be in their teens and twenties, but most hostels welcome travelers of all ages. In northern Europe, where hotel prices are high, hostels have special family rooms. In the average hostel, though, you and 1-50 roommates will sleep in a gender-segregated room of bunk beds, with common bathrooms and a lounge down the hall. The hostel warden may be a laid-back student, a hippie dropout, or a crotchety disciplinarian. Most hostels have well-equipped kitchens; some serve hot meals. The **Internet Guide to Hostelling** (http://hostels.com) has more information, as does **Eurotrip** (http://www.eurotrip.com).

The basic disadvantage of hostels is their regimentation. Many have an early curfew—a distinct cramp in your style if you plan to rage in town. There is also often a lockout from morning to mid-afternoon. Conditions are generally spartan and crowded, and you may run into screaming pre-teen tour groups. Hostel quality varies dramatically. Some are set in gorgeous castles, others in run-down barracks far from the town center. Hostels usually prohibit sleeping bags: they provide blankets but make extra money by renting sheets to guests who don't have their own. To save money, make your own sleepsack from sheets (see **Packing,** p. 33) or order one (about US$15) from Let's Go Travel (see **Budget Travel Agencies,** p. 35) or a youth hostel federation. Large hostels are reluctant to take telephone reservations; citing an exact train arrival time or promising to call to confirm may help. In hostels in large Western European cities, make use of hostel-to-hostel booking services (US$2-5).

Privately owned hostels are found in major tourist centers and throughout some countries (particularly Ireland). No membership is required, and you won't always have to contend with early curfews or daytime lockouts, but their quality varies. **Young Men's Christian Association (YMCA)** rates are usually lower than a hotel's but higher than a hostel's and may include the use of TV, air conditioning, pools, gyms, access to public transportation, tourist information, safe deposit boxes, luggage storage, daily housekeeping, multilingual staff, and 24-hour security. Not all YMCA locations offer lodging; those that do are often located in urban downtowns, which can be convenient but a little gritty. Many YMCAs accept women and families (group rates often available), and some will not lodge people under 18 without parental permission. All reservations must be made and paid for in advance, with a traveler's check (signed top and bottom), U.S. money order, certified check, Visa, or MasterCard in US dollars. For more info, contact YMCA of the USA (tel. (800) 872-9622) or check out http://www.ymca.net or http://www.eay.org/Info/InfoTrav.htm.

You can also contact the **Young Women's Christian Association (YWCA) of the USA,** Empire State Building, Suite 301, 350 Fifth Avenue, New York, NY 10118 (tel. (212) 273-7800); their world-wide directory (US$10) features names, addresses, restrictions, and other info.

Hostel Membership

Hostelling International (HI) is a federation of national hosteling associations. All of the HI national affiliates listed below comply with HI standards and regulations. Official youth hostels will normally display a blue triangle with the symbol of the national hostel association. The International Youth Hostel Federation, 9 Guessens Road, Welwyn Garden City, Hertfordshire AL8 6QW, U.K., publishes **Hostelling International:**

Europe (UK£7/US$11, available from national hostel associations), which lists HI affiliated hostels throughout Europe and details the **International Booking Network (IBN)** which makes confirmed reservations at any of more than 300 hostels throughout the world (in the US, fee US$2-5; 1-week advance notice required, 1½ weeks when reserving from overseas). To make prepaid reservations, call or visit any hostel on the IBN or an HI branch. For a US$5 fee, reservations can be made for up to six nights and up to nine people, and changes can be made from three to eight days before the date of the reservation. Some hostels require a credit card (MC, Visa, Discover) guarantee, but credit card acceptance may vary across Europe.

A one-year HI membership permits you to stay at youth hostels all over Europe at unbeatable prices, and with few exceptions (such as Germany), you need not be a youth to take advantage of HI. Prospective hostel-goers should become members of the youth hostel association in their own country in order to become HI members. If you didn't get a membership at home, you can ask an HI hostel for a blank membership card with space for six validation stamps. Each night you'll pay a nonmember supplement (one-sixth the membership fee) and earn one Guest Stamp; get six stamps, and you're a member. This system works well in most of Western Europe, though in some countries you may need to remind the hostel reception. In Eastern Europe, many hostels are not HI members. (There is one HI hostel in Russia, but more in Poland, the Czech Republic, and Hungary.) Most student travel agencies (see **Budget Travel Agencies,** p. 35) sell HI cards; or contact one of the national hostel organizations listed below. The **Internet Guide to Hostelling** is at http://hostels.com.

Hostelling International-American Youth Hostels (HI-AYH), 733 15th St. NW, Suite 840, Washington, D.C. 20005 (tel. (202) 783-6161, ext. 136; fax 783-6171; email hiayhserv@hiayh.org; http://www.hiayh.org). Memberships also available at travel agencies: 1yr. US$25, under 18 US$10, over 54 US$15, family US$35.

Hostelling International-Canada (HI-C), 400-205 Catherine St., Ottawa, ONT K2P 1C3, Canada (tel. (613) 237-7884; fax 237-7868; email info@hostellingintl.ca; http://www.hostellingintl.ca). IBN booking centers in Edmonton, Montreal, Ottawa, and Vancouver. Membership: 1yr. CDN $25, under 18 CDN$12; 2yr. over 18 CDN$35; lifetime CDN$175.

Youth Hostels Association of England and Wales (YHA), Trevelyan House, 8 St. Stephen's Hill, St. Albans, Hertfordshire AL1 2DY, U.K. (tel. (01727) 85 52 15; fax 84 41 26). Enrollment fees: UK£10, under 18 UK£5, one parent with children under 18 enrolled free UK£10, UK£140 for lifetime membership. Overnight prices for under 18 UK£4-17.90, for adults UK£5.85-21.30.

An Óige (Irish Youth Hostel Association), 61 Mountjoy St., Dublin 7, Ireland (tel. (353) 1 830 4555; fax 1 830 5808; email anoige@iol.ie; http://www.irelandyha.org). 1yr. membership IR£7.50, under 18 IR£4, family IR£7.50 for each adult with children under 16 free. Rates from IR£4.50-9.50 per night. 37 locations.

Hostelling International Northern Ireland (HINI), 22-32 Donegall Rd., Belfast BT12 5JN, Northern Ireland (tel. (01232) 32 47 33 or 31 54 35; fax 43 96 99; email info@hini.org.uk; http://www.hini.org.uk). Annual memberships UK£7, under 18 UK£3, family UK£14 for up to 6 children.

Scottish Youth Hostels Association (SYHA), 7 Glebe Crescent, Stirling FK8 2JA (tel. (01786) 89 14 00; fax 89 13 33; email syha@syha.org.uk; http://www.syha.org.uk). Membership UK£6, under 18 UK£2.50.

Australian Youth Hostels Association (AYHA), Level 3, 10 Mallett St., Camperdown NSW 2050, Australia (tel. (02) 9565 1699; fax 9565 1325; email YHA@yha.org.au). Memberships AUS$44, renewal AUS$27, under 18 AUS$13.

Youth Hostels Association of New Zealand (YHANZ), P.O. Box 436, 173 Cashel St., Christchurch 1, New Zealand (tel. (643) 379 9970, fax 365 4476; email info@yha.org.nz; http://www.yha.org.nz). Annual membership fee NZ$24.

Hostelling International South Africa, P.O. Box 4402, Cape Town 8000, South Africa (tel. (021) 24 25 11; fax 24 41 19; email info@hisa.org.za; http://www.hisa.org.za). Membership SAR50, group SAR120, family SAR100, lifetime SAR250.

HOTELS, GUEST HOUSES, AND PRIVATE HOMES

Hotels are quite expensive in Britain, Switzerland, Austria, and northern Europe. Rock bottom for one or two people is US$25 each. Elsewhere, couples can usually get by fairly well (rooms with a double bed are generally cheaper than those with two twin beds), as can larger groups, but inexpensive European hotels may come as a shock to pampered North Americans. You'll share a hall bathroom; one of your own will cost extra. Hot showers may also cost extra. In Britain and Ireland, a large breakfast is often included; elsewhere a continental breakfast of a roll, jam, coffee or tea, and maybe an egg is served. Some hotels offer "full pension" (all meals) and "half pension" (no lunch). Unmarried couples will generally have no trouble getting a room together, although couples under 21 may encounter resistance.

Smaller **guest houses** and **pensions** are often cheaper than hotels. Even less expensive are rooms in **private homes**—the local tourist office usually has a list. If you're traveling alone, this is an economical way to get a single and meet real Europeans. The British and Irish **bed and breakfast** is a breed of private room that's extra heavy on the bacon and eggs. Private rooms are an excellent option in Eastern Europe, where youth hostels are non-existent outside of cities; tourist offices and travel agencies book most private rooms, and proprietors flag down tourists at the train station.

If you reserve in writing, indicate your night of arrival and the number of nights you plan to stay. The hotel will send you a confirmation and may request payment for the first night. Not all hotels take reservations, and few accept checks in foreign currency. Enclosing two International Reply Coupons will ensure a prompt reply (each US$1.05; available at any post office).

CAMPING

Organized campgrounds exist in most European cities, accessible by foot, car, or public transportation. Showers, bathrooms, and a small restaurant or store are common; some sites have more elaborate facilities. Prices are US$5-15 per person with an additional charge for a tent. Money and time spent in getting to the campsite may eat away at your budget and patience.

Europa Camping and Caravan Guide ($20), an annually updated German catalogue of European campsites, is available through **Recreational Equipment, Inc. (REI)** Mail Order, Sumner, WA 98352-0001 (tel. (800) 426-4840; http://www.rei.com). Automobile Association Publishing, c/o TBS Frating Distribution Centre, Colchester, Essex, CO7 7DW, U.K. (tel. (01206) 25 56 78; fax 25 59 16), publishes a wide range of maps, atlases, and travel guides, including **Camping and Caravanning: Europe** and **Camping and Caravanning: Britain & Ireland** (each UK£8). An **International Camping Carnet** (membership card) is required by some campgrounds (and provides discounts at others) but can usually be bought on the spot. It's available for US$35 through Family Campers and RVers, 4804 Transit Rd., Bldg. #2, Depew, NY 14043 (tel. (716) 668-6242; price includes their publication *Camping Today* and a membership fee).

Prospective campers will need to invest money in equipment and energy in carrying it. Use reputable mail-order firms to gauge prices; order from them if you can't do as well locally, and buy before you leave. In the fall, the previous year's merchandise may be discounted. **Campmor**, P.O. Box 700, Saddle River, NJ 07458-0700 (tel. (888) CAMPMOR (226-7667), outside the U.S. call (201) 825-8300; email customer-service@campmor.com; http://www.campmor.com), has brand name equipment at low prices. **REI** (see above) stocks a wide range of gear and has seasonal sales. **L.L. Bean,** Freeport, ME 04033 (tel. (800) 441-5713), supplies its own equipment and national-brand merchandise with a satisfaction guarantee.

Good **sleeping bags**—made of down (lightweight and warm) or synthetic (faster drying, heavier, more durable, and warmer when wet)—have ratings for minimum temperatures. The lower the mercury, the higher the price. Estimate the most severe conditions you may encounter, subtract a few degrees, and then choose your bag. Do not buy a down bag if you will be in a rainy climate. Expect to pay US$65-100 for a

summer synthetic bag and US$250-550 for a good down bag for sub-freezing temperatures. **Sleeping bag pads** cost US$15 and up, while **air mattresses** are about US$25-50. The best **tents** are free-standing, have their own frames and suspension systems, and require no staking. Low profile dome tents are good all-around, with little unnecessary bulk. Remember to seal the seams against water. Backpackers and cyclists will require small, lightweight models, costing US$130 and up. Try L.L. Bean or **Sierra Designs,** 1255 Powell St., Emeryville, CA 94608 (tel. (800) 635-0461 or (510) 450-9555; fax 654-0705), which carries all seasons and types of lightweight tent models.

For info on picking a pack, see **Packing,** p. 33. Weight should be centered on the hips for women and a little higher on the back for men. Tighten the hip strap on your pelvic bones. Be sure to wear **hiking boots** with good ankle support—see **Clothing and Footwear,** p. 35. Other camping basics include **rain gear,** which should be a jacket and pants, rather than a poncho which can catch and tear. **Synthetics,** like polypropylene tops, socks, and long underwear, along with a pile jacket, will keep you warm even when wet, unlike cotton. When camping in autumn, winter, or spring, bring along a **space blanket/bag,** which helps you to retain your body heat and doubles as a groundcloth (US$5-10). Plastic **water bottles** are virtually shatter- and leak-proof. Bring **water-purification tablets** for when you can't boil water. For those places that forbid fires or the gathering of firewood (this includes virtually every organized campground in Europe), you'll need a **camp stove.** The classic Coleman starts at about US$30. In Europe, consider the "GAZ" butane/propane stove (also about $30); its little blue cylinders can be purchased anywhere on the continent—just don't take them on a plane. A **first aid kit, Swiss army knife, insect repellent, calamine lotion,** and **waterproof matches** or a **lighter** are essential camping items. Other items include: a collapsible **water sack,** a battery-operated **flashlight,** a **plastic groundcloth,** a **nylon tarp,** a **waterproof backpack cover** (although you can also store your belongings in plastic bags inside your backpack), and a **"stuff sack"** and plastic bag to keep your sleeping bag dry. **Wilderness Press,** 2440 Bancroft Way, Berkeley, CA 94704 (tel. (800) 443-7227 or (510) 843-8080; fax 548-1355; email wpress@ix.netcom.com), publishes useful books like *Backpacking Basics* (US$11, postage included). **The Caravan Club,** East Grinstead House, East Grinstead, West Sussex, RH19 1UA, U.K. (tel. (01342) 32 69 44; fax 41 02 58), produces one of the most detailed English-language guides to campsites in Europe and the U.K.

The Great Outdoors

The first thing to preserve in the wilderness is yourself—health, safety, and food should be your primary concerns. See **Health** (p. 20) for info about basic concerns and first-aid. Many water bodies have bacteria like giardia, which causes gas, cramps, loss of appetite, and diarrhea and may last for months. To avoid this, always boil your water for at least five minutes or use an iodine solution. Filters do not remove all bacteria. *Never go camping or hiking by yourself for any significant time or distance.* If you're going into an area that is not well-traveled or marked, let someone know where you're hiking and for how long. **Stay warm, stay dry, and stay hydrated.**

The second thing to protect is the wilderness. Make small fires using only dead branches or brush; using a campstove is more prudent. Many parks and sites prohibit campfires. Pitch your tent on high, dry ground, don't cut vegetation, and don't clear sites. If there are no toilet facilities, bury human waste at least 4 in. deep and above the high-water line 150 ft. or more from any water supplies or campsites. Use only bio-safe soap or detergents. Always carry your trash to the next trash can; burning and burying pollute the environment.

ALTERNATIVE ACCOMMODATIONS

In university towns, **student dormitories** may be open to travelers when school is not in session. These dorms are often close to student areas—good sources for information on things to do, places to stay, and possible rides out of town—and are usually very clean. No one policy covers all these institutions. Getting a room may be

difficult, but rates tend to be low, and many offer free local calls. *Let's Go* lists colleges which rent dorm rooms among the accommodations for appropriate cities. The *Campus Lodging Guide* (18th Ed.) details 609 university and college accommodation options around the world, in addition to more general information. (Available in bookstores or via B&J Publications/Campus Travel Service, P.O. Box 5486, Fullerton, CA 96635; tel. (714) 525-6683.) College dorms are popular, especially with those looking for long-term lodging, so reserve ahead. Many **monasteries** and **convents** will open their doors, particularly in Italy. Though sleeping in train stations may be tolerated by authorities, it's neither comfortable nor safe, and don't spend the night in an urban park unless you place a similarly low value on your life. Several host networks can help you find lodging with families; see **Work and Volunteer**, p. 25.

■ Keeping in Touch

MAIL

Mail can be sent internationally through **Poste Restante** (the international phrase for General Delivery) to any city or town. Mark the envelope "HOLD" and address it, for example, "Daniel FERNHOLZ, Poste Restante, City, Country (with country code)." The last name should be capitalized and underlined. The mail will go to a special desk in the central post office, unless you specify a post office by street address or postal code. For towns in the Czech Republic and Slovakia, write a "1" after the city name to ensure that mail goes to the central post office. As a rule, it's best to use the largest post office in the area; sometimes, mail will be sent there regardless of what you write. When possible, it is safer and quicker to send mail express or registered.

It helps to use the appropriate translation of **Poste Restante** (*Lista de Correos* in Spanish, *Fermo Posta* in Italian, and *Postlagernde Briefe* in German). Bring photo ID, preferably your passport, to pick up your mail. If the clerk insists that there is nothing for you, check under your first name. Some places may charge a minimal fee. *Let's Go* lists post offices in the **Practical Information** section for larger cities.

Aerogrammes, printed sheets that fold into envelopes (no enclosures) and travel via airmail, are available at post offices. It helps to mark "airmail" in the appropriate language (*par avion* in French, *por avión* in Spanish, *mit luftpost* in German, *per via aerea* in Italian, *poczta lotnicza* in Polish, *leteky* in Czech), though *par avion* is universally understood. Airmail between Europe and the U.S. averages one to two weeks. Allow at least two weeks from Australia or N.Z., longer from most of Africa.

If regular airmail is too slow, there are a few faster, more expensive, options. Federal Express (U.S. tel. (800) 247-4747) can get a letter from New York to Paris in two days for US$28.50. By U.S. Express Mail, the same letter would arrive in two to three days and would cost US$21. FedEx rates from non-U.S. locations are prohibitively expensive (Paris to New York, for example, costs upwards of US$60). **Surface mail** is by far the cheapest and slowest way to send mail. It takes one to three months to cross the Atlantic, appropriate for sending large quantities of items you won't need for a while. Do not send items of great value (either monetary or sentimental) by surface mail. It is vital to distinguish airmail from surface mail by explicitly labeling "airmail" in the appropriate language. When ordering materials from abroad, always include one or two **International Reply Coupons (IRC)**—a way of providing the postage to cover delivery. IRCs should be available from your local post office as well as abroad (US$1.05).

American Express offices throughout Europe will act as a mail service for cardholders if you contact them in advance. Under this free **Client Letter Service,** they will hold mail for 30 days, forward upon request, and accept telegrams. The last name of the person to whom the mail is addressed should be capitalized and underlined. Some offices will offer these services to non-cardholders (especially those who have purchased AmEx Traveller's Cheques). Check the **Practical Information** section in *Let's Go* for cities you plan to visit. A complete list is available free from AmEx (tel. (800) 528-4800) in the booklet *Traveler's Companion* or online from links off of http://www.americanexpress.com.

TELEPHONES

> The **country code** is listed with exchange rates at the beginning of each chapter. **City codes** are listed at the beginning of the Practical Information section for large cities and in parentheses with the phone numbers for smaller cities and regions.

You can place **international calls** from most phones. To call from the U.S., dial the international access code (011), then the country code, the city code, and the local number. Country codes and city codes may sometimes be listed with a zero in front (e.g., 033), but when using 011 (or whatever your international access code happens to be), drop successive leading zeros (e.g., 011 33). You may have to go through the operator or wait for a tone after the international access code. Note: Wherever possible, save money by using a calling card (see below) for international phone calls.

You can usually make direct international calls from **pay phones,** but you may need to drop coins as quickly as words. Pay phones may be card-operated or accept major credit cards. Be wary of more expensive, private pay phones; look for pay phones in public areas, like train stations. In-room hotel phone calls often include a sky-high surcharge (up to US$10). It's a better idea to find a phone in the lobby.

English-speaking operators are often available for both local and international assistance. Operators in most European countries will place **collect calls** for you. It may be cheaper to find a pay phone and deposit just enough money to be able to say "Call me," but some pay phones in Europe can't receive calls. Some companies, seizing on this "call-me-back" concept, have created callback phone services. Under these plans, you call a specified number, ring once, and hang up. The company's computer calls back and gives you a U.S. dial tone. You can then make as many calls as you want, at rates reduced 20-60% (monthly US$10-25 minimum billing). For info, call **America Tele-Fone** (tel. (800) 321-5817), **Globaltel** (tel. (800) 370-4468), **International Telephone** (tel. (203) 634-4434), or **Telegroup** (tel. (800) 338-0225).

A **calling card** is a cheaper alternative; your local long-distance phone company will have a number for you to dial while in Europe (either toll-free or a local call) to connect to a company operator. The calls (plus a small surcharge) are then billed to your account. Call **AT&T** about its **US Direct** and **World Connect** service (tel. (888) 288-4685, from abroad (810) 262-6644 collect), **Sprint** (tel. (800) 877-4646, from abroad call (913) 624-5335 collect), or **MCI WorldPhone** and **World Reach** (tel. (800) 444-4141, from abroad dial the country's MCI access number). MCI's WorldPhone provides access to MCI's **Traveler's Assist** for legal and medical advice, exchange rate information, and translation services. For similar services for countries outside the U.S., contact your local phone company. In Canada, contact **Canada Direct** (tel. (800) 565-4708); in the U.K., British Telecom **BT Direct** (tel. (800) 34 51 44); in Ireland, Telecom Éireann **Ireland Direct** (tel. (800) 25 02 50); in Australia, Telsta **Australia Direct** (tel. 13 22 00); in New Zealand, **Telecom New Zealand** (tel. 123); and in South Africa, **Telkom South Africa** (tel. 09 03).

In many countries, you can also buy **pre-paid phone cards,** which carry a certain amount of phone time depending on the card's denomination. The time is measured in minutes or talk units (e.g. 1 unit/1 minute), and the card usually has a toll-free access telephone number and a personal identification number (PIN). To make a phone call, dial the access number, enter your PIN, and at the voice prompt, enter the phone number of the party you're trying to reach.

Phone rates are highest in the morning, lower in the evening, and lowest on Sundays and late at night. Remember **time differences** when you call. Britain, Ireland, Portugal, and Iceland are on Greenwich Mean Time (GMT)—five hours ahead of Eastern Standard Time. Bulgaria, Belarus, Estonia, Finland, Greece, Latvia, Lithuania, Moldova, Romania, western Russia, Turkey, and the Ukraine are two hours ahead of GMT. Moscow, St. Petersburg, and most of Russia are three hours ahead. Everywhere else in this book is one hour ahead of GMT. Some countries (like Iceland) ignore daylight savings time, and fall and spring switchover times vary.

OTHER COMMUNICATION

Domestic and international **telegrams** offer an option slower than phone but faster than post. Fill out a form at any post or telephone office from the U.S. only; cables arrive to international locations in one or two days. Telegrams can be quite expensive; **Western Union** (tel. (800) 325-6000), for example, adds a surcharge to the per-word rate depending on the country. You may wish to consider **faxes** for more immediate, personal, and cheaper communication. Major cities have bureaus where you can pay to send and receive faxes.

If you're spending a year abroad and want to keep in touch with friends, **electronic mail (email)** is an attractive option. Free **web-based accounts** are available from http://www.hotmail.com or http://www.yahoo.com. Check the Index of this book under "Internet Access" for places to get onto the electronic highway while you're on the road, or search through http://www.cyberiacafe.net/cyberia/guide/ccafe.htm to find a list of **cybercafes**. In some countries, **public libraries** offer free access to the Internet—call and investigate before parting with your money.

■ Parting Words

One of the quickest ways to learn about a different culture is to dissolve discreetly in it. As a foreigner, you will probably stand out, but a sincere effort to fit in will receive a warm reception. Hanging out exclusively with compatriots will insulate you from the local culture. You might as well stay home, an even cheaper alternative to budget travel. Get out and explore—culture shock may set in, but go for the *kringle* and goulash anyway and save McDonald's for home.

Language differences can be a bridge rather than a barrier between you and the people you meet, if you don't assume that other people speak English. Humbly asking "Do you speak English?"—or stumbling through the appropriate translation—expresses a genuine desire to communicate. Do your homework; play language tapes while you pack, and flip through a phrase book. You can learn the numbers from one to ten, how to order ice cream, and "please" and "thank you" in minutes.

But there is no substitute for practicing with native speakers and making friends in the process. While the history, architecture, and natural wonders of your destination country are fascinating, what makes your trip special is the people you'll meet. A photo of the Eiffel Tower, however elegantly silhouetted against the setting sun, won't evoke as many memories as a snapshot of Honza Vihan who put you up for the night in Prague. Part of meeting people is respecting their culture. Americans have acquired a reputation as arrogant boors, which may explain the little maple leaves that Canadian (and some American) tourists sew on their backpacks. However, the stereotype of the Ugly American need not haunt beer-swillling Yanks if they show that they're making an effort to understand your hosts. Europeans have a strong sense of their cultural history; if you belittle it, you'll only seem ignorant.

A word of warning: Many travelers succumb to a budget obsession on the road. Perhaps *Let's Go*'s greatest sin is that it perpetuates this mentality—to eat at the cheapest restaurant and stay at the cheapest hostel no matter how grimy or tacky. If you find yourself stuck in the doldrums, spend the extra 50 francs for a hearty meal or a night at a soothing pension. After all, your trip is supposed to be fun.

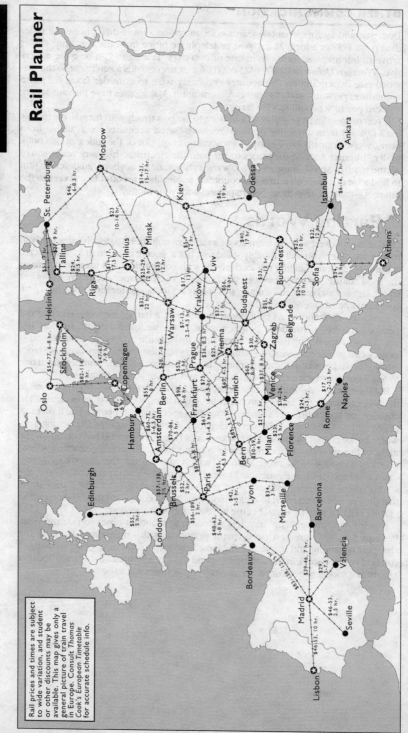

Rail Planner

Rail prices and times are subject to wide variation, and student or other discounts may be available. This map gives only a general picture of train travel in Europe. Consult *Thomas Cook's European Timetable* for accurate schedule info.

Andorra

Embracing fewer than 500 square km between France and Spain in the secluded confines of the Pyrenees, pint-sized Andorra (pop. 65,000) might sell its soul, duty-free, if it could get a good price. Tourists seeking souvenirs flock to the neon-lit streets for tax-free shopping, but outside the crowded boutiques await serene hamlets, mountain lakes, and some of the best ski slopes in Europe. Catalan is the official language, but French and Spanish are spoken widely. Every establishment is legally bound to accept both *pesetas* and *francs,* although *pesetas* are more prevalent. **Phones** require an STA *teletarjeta* (telecard; from 500ptas), available at post offices and kiosks. For **directory assistance,** dial 111. Andorra's **telephone code** is 376.

French and Spanish border police require presentation of a valid passport or an EU identity card to enter the country. All traffic from France must enter Andorra at the town **Pas de la Casa;** from Spain, traffic enters at **La Seu d'Urgell.** Andor-Inter/**Samar** buses (in Madrid tel. 914 68 41 90; in Toulouse 05 61 58 14 53; in Andorra 82 62 89) run to Madrid (9hr., 4700ptas). Andorra la Vella's main **bus station** is on C. Bonaventura Riberaygua. An efficient system of **inter-city buses** connects villages lying along Andorra's three major highways (90-590ptas). For a (tiny) **map** of Andorra, consult our map of Spain, p. 781.

Andorra la Vella
The capital, Andorra la Vella, is little more than a narrow, cluttered road flanked by shop after duty-free shop. To get to the **tourist office** (tel. 82 02 14), on Av. Doctor Villanova, from the bus stop on Av. Princep Benlloch, continue east just past the *plaça* on your left, then take C. Dr. Villanova. (Open July-Sept. M-Sa 9am-1pm and 3-7pm; Oct.-June M-Sa 10am-1pm and 3-7pm, Su 10am-1pm.) **Pensió La Rosa,** Antic Carrer Major 18 (tel. 82 18 10), just south of Av. Princep Benlloch, has immaculate rooms (singles 1700ptas; doubles 3000ptas; breakfast 350ptas). Try not to blow your budget here, but if you can't wait, hunt for restaurants along **Avinguda Meritxell** and the quieter streets near **Plaça Princep Benlloch.** The tourist office sells tickets to the annual **Festival Internacional de Música i Dansa** (mid-Nov. to May).

The Countryside
The *parròquia* (town) of **La Massana,** easily accessible by bus from Andorra la Vella (10min., 110ptas), provides an excellent base for exploring Andorra's spectacular mountains. The **tourist office** (tel. 83 56 93) is in a steep-roofed cabin just ahead of the bus stop (open M-Sa 9am-1pm and 3-7pm, Su 9am-1pm and 3-6pm). To reach the **Alberg Borda Jovell,** Av. Jovell (tel. 83 65 20; fax 83 57 76), in Sispony, walk 75m back toward Andorra la Vella from La Massana's bus stop and turn right at the main intersection, then follow the signs south for 1.3km (1600ptas; curfew midnight; call ahead July-Aug.). Convenient for hiking and the least populated of the parish towns, **Ordino,** 5km northeast of La Massana, has yet to be converted into a strip mall. Slink toward **Escaldes-Engordany,** just outside Andorra la Vella, for the pleasures of **Caldea Spa,** Parc de la Mola 10 (tel. 80 09 99), with massages and faux Roman baths (2500ptas for 3hr., plus fees per service; open daily 10am-9pm).

With its many trails, Andorra lends itself well to **hiking** and **mountain biking;** check at the tourist office for info on cycling routes and the *Grandes-Randonnées* hiking trails. The **Sports Activities** brochure, with suggested itineraries and helpful phone numbers, is essential. Several superb **ski** resorts lie within Andorra's boundaries, and all rent equipment. **Pal** (tel. 83 62 36), 10km from La Massana, is one of the largest; four buses leave daily from La Massana (last return 5pm; one-way 250ptas). Cross-country and downhill aficionados flock to **Soldeu-El Tarter** (tel. 85 11 51), 15km from the French border between Andorra la Vella and Pas de la Casa. Get the tourist office's winter edition of *Andorra: The Pyrenean Country,* or call **SKI Andorra** (tel. 86 43 89) for more info on the resorts.

Austria (Österreich)

US$1 = 12.15AS (Austrian Schillings)	**10AS = US$0.82**
CDN$1 = 8.00AS	**10AS = CDN$1.25**
UK£1 = 20.16AS	**10AS = UK£0.47**
IR£1 = 17.64AS	**10AS = IR£0.50**
AUS$1 = 7.20AS	**10AS = AUS$1.39**
NZ$1 = 6.23AS	**10AS = NZ$1.61**
SAR1 = 1.96AS	**10AS = SAR5.10**
Country Code: 43	**International Dialing Prefix: 00**
	from Vienna: 900

Surrounded by seven countries, the Federal Republic of Austria binds Eastern and Western Europe. Austria was once the heart of the mighty Austro-Hungarian Empire which dominated central Europe and Spain under the Habsburg dynasty. The mid-18th through early 20th centuries, however, were the real heyday of Viennese culture: Hadyn, Mozart, Beethoven, Schubert, the Strauss Family, and Mahler changed music forever. A mad, decadent, apocalyptic atmosphere of rampant artistic experimentalism and social flux descended on the capital at the turn of the century—and the center could not hold either culturally or politically. A weakened Austro-Hungary pulled the rest of Europe into the First World War, and at the war's end, the Empire ended. The glory of the 19th century gave way to Freud's analyses of middle class hysteria, and a troubled Austria did not resist the 1938 Nazi invasion. Yet the postwar years have nurtured an Austria that embraces EU membership, a strong environmentalism, and a thriving arts scene.

Despite Austria's political and economic importance and the rise of urban giants like Vienna and Salzburg, the country retains an overpowering physical beauty. With onion-domed churches set against snow-capped Alpine peaks, lush meadows blanketed with *Edelweiss*, pristine mountain lakes, dark forests, and mighty castles towering above the Danube, Austria generates tourism year-round. Alpine sports dominate the winter scene, while lakeside frolicking and hiking takes over during the summer.

For extensive and entertaining information on the country, pick up a copy of *Let's Go: Austria and Switzerland 1999.*

GETTING THERE AND GETTING AROUND

The **Österreichische Bundesbahn (ÖBB),** Austria's federal railroad, operates an amazingly efficient 5760km network of track accommodating frequent, fast, and comfortable trains. The ÖBB publishes the yearly *Fahrpläne Kursbuch Bahn-Inland,* a massive compilation of all rail, ferry, and cable-car transportation schedules in Austria (100AS). Over 130 stations accept major credit cards as well as AmEx Traveler's Checks and Eurocheques. **Eurail** passes are valid on the Austrian rail network. The **Austrian Railpass** allows four days of travel within any 10-day period on all rail lines, including Wolfgangsee ferries and private rail lines; it also entitles holders to a 50% discount on bicycle rental at train stations as well as the steamers of Erste Donau Dampfschiffahrtsgesellschaft operating between Passau, Linz, and Vienna (second class US$111; first class US$165).

The efficient Austrian bus system consists mainly of orange **BundesBuses,** which cover mountain areas inaccessible by train. They usually cost about as much as trains—railpasses are not valid. Buy tickets on-board or at a ticket office at the station. **Bikes** are also a great way to get around; countless private companies and over 160 train stations rent them (generally 150AS per day, 90AS with a railpass or valid train ticket from that day). If you get a bike at a train station, you can return it to any participating station. Look for the *Gepäckbeforderung* symbol (a little bicycle) on departure schedules to see if bikes are permitted in the baggage car. If your bike breaks down on the road, some auto clubs may rescue you; try the **Austrian Automobile, Motorcycle, and Touring Club (ÖAMTC)** (tel. 120) or **ARBÖ** (tel. 123).

Austria is a rough place to **hitchhike**—Austrians rarely stop, and many mountain roads are all but deserted. Generally, hitchhikers stand on highway *Knoten* (on-ramps) and wait. **Mitfahrzentrale** offices in larger cities match travelers with drivers heading in the same direction. **Drivers** must purchase a permit/sticker at Austria's border to place on the windshield (70AS per week) at the border or face a $130 fine.

ESSENTIALS

Virtually every town in Austria has a **tourist office,** most marked by a classy green "i" sign, and nearly all have a wealth of info on tourist attractions, activities, and accommodations. You may run into language difficulties in the small-town offices.

The unit of **currency** is the Schilling, abbreviated AS here and often simply S in Austria. **Exchange rates** are standardized among banks and exchange counters, while stores, hotels, and restaurants that accept U.S. dollars apply a slightly lower rate of exchange. Every establishment that exchanges currency charges at least 14AS. Many banks offer cash advances to Visa and MasterCard holders.

Most stores in Austria close Saturday afternoons and Sundays, and some museums close Mondays. Stores in many small towns close for lunch breaks from noon to 3pm. **Holidays** include January 1, Epiphany (Jan. 6), Easter (April 4 in 1999), Labor Day (May 1), Ascension Day (May 13), Whit Sunday and Monday (May 23-24), Corpus Christi Day (June 11), Feast of the Assumption (Aug. 15), National Day (Oct. 26), All Saints' Day (Nov. 1), and the Feast of the Immaculate Conception (Dec. 8).

COMMUNICATION Austria maintains an efficient **postal system.** Airmail letters take five to seven days to reach North America, although they make take up to two and a half weeks to reach Australia and New Zealand.

The Austrian **phone system** is equally reliable. You can usually make direct international calls from a pay phone, but remember to bring a handful of coins. A better option might be to buy **telephone cards** *(Wertkarten),* available in post offices, train stations, and *Tabak/Trafik* in 50AS and 100AS denominations (sold for 48AS and 95AS, respectively). The quickest and cheapest way to call abroad collect is to go to a post office and ask for a *Zurückrufen,* or return call. You will receive a card with a number on it. Call your party and tell them to call you back at that number, and at the end of the conversation pay for the original call. For **AT&T Direct,** dial 022 90 30 11; for **MCI WorldPhone,** 022 90 30 12; for **Sprint Access,** 022 90 30 14; for **Canada**

Direct, 022 90 30 13; for **BT Direct,** 022 90 30 44. Note that the use of these services is considered a local call, so you must have coins or a phone card. The number for the **police** is 133; for an **ambulance** 144; for **fire** 122.

English is the most common second language in Austria, but any effort to use the mother tongue will win fans. *Grüss Gott* is the typical Austrian greeting. For a language chart, see the Germany **Essentials,** p. 356.

ACCOMMODATIONS AND CAMPING

Rooms in Austria are usually spotless; even the most odious of Austria's **youth hostels** (*Jugendherbergen*) are quite tolerable. Most hostels charge US$8 to 25 a night for shared rooms. Nonmembers are normally charged an extra fee and sometimes turned away. Many hostels are somewhat cramped and offer little privacy; prepubescent hordes may also try your patience.

Hotels are usually quite expensive. If you're on a tight budget, look instead for *Zimmer Frei* or *Privatzimmer* signs; they advertise rooms in private houses for a more reasonable 150 to 350AS. Otherwise, smaller pensions and *Gästehäuser* are often within the budget traveler's range. With over 400 sites throughout the country, **camping** is another popular option. Pitching a tent, however, is often not wildly cheaper than staying in a hostel; prices range from 50 to 70AS per person and 25 to 60AS per tent, and a tax of 8 to 10AS is added for campers over 15 years old. Lists of all types of accommodations, including campgrounds, are available at tourist offices; many offices will also reserve rooms for a small fee.

SKIING AND HIKING

Western Austria is one of the world's best skiing and hiking regions, and the areas around Innsbruck and Kitzbühel in the Tirol are saturated with lifts and runs. High season runs from mid-December to mid-January and from February to March. Local tourist offices provide information on regional skiing and can point you to budget travel agencies that offer ski packages. Unless you're on top of a mountain, Austria doesn't usually get brutally cold. Nevertheless, warm sweaters are the rule from September to May, with a parka, hat, and gloves added in the winter months. Summertime brings frequent rains and high humidity—almost every three days in Salzburg, and nearly as often to the east—so suitable gear is a must.

Thanks to the extensive network of hiking trails and Alpine refuges, Austria's Alps are as accessible as they are gorgeous. A membership in the **Österreichischer Alpenverein** provides half-off the cost of staying at a series of **huts** across the Tirol and throughout Austria, all located a day's hike apart from each other. A place in any of the huts is always assured, along with use of the kitchen facilities and provisions. Third-party insurance, accident provision, travel discounts, and a wealth of maps and mountain information are also included with membership. For membership information call or write to: Österreichischer Alpenverein, Willhelm-Greil-Str. 15, A-6010 Innsbruck (tel. 58 78 28; fax 58 88 42). Membership (US$55, students under 25 US$40, one-time fee US$10) also includes use of some of the **Deutscher Alpenverein** (German Alpine Club) huts, all of which have beds.

Even if you're going for only a day hike, check terrain and weather conditions; weather in the Alps changes abruptly and often without warning. *Always* carry waterproof clothing and some high-energy food, wear durable footwear, and tell someone where you're going. Staying at Alpine refuges adds another safety precaution: you're expected to list your next destination in the refuge book, thus alerting search-and-rescue teams if you become lost or stranded.

FOOD AND DRINK

Although Austria has a solid and delicious national cuisine, somehow it is their heavenly desserts that travelers remember most nostalgically. Austrians flock to *Café-Konditoreien* to nurse the national sweet tooth with *Kaffee und Kuchen* (coffee and cake). Try *Sacher Torte,* a rich chocolate pastry layered with marmalade, *Linzer Torte,* a nutty pastry with raspberry filling, *Apfelstrudel,* and a multitude of other delights. Staple foods include *Schweinfleisch* (pork), *Kalbsfleisch* (veal), *Wurst* (sausage), *Eier* (eggs), *Käse* (cheese), *Brot* (bread), and *Kartoffeln* (potatoes). Austria's best-known dish is *Wiener Schnitzel,* a meat cutlet (usually veal or pork) fried expertly in butter with bread crumbs. The best discount supermarkets in Austria are **Billa** and **Hofer.** Most restaurants expect you to seat yourself. Although

AUSTRIA

Central Vienna

N

TO VOTIVKIRCHE ↑
Universität
Grillparzerstr.

Landesgerichtsstr.
Stadiongasse
Rathaus
RATHAUS. PL.
Parlament
Dr. K. Renner Ring
Dr. Karl Lueger Ring
Burg theater
Reichsratsstr.
Schmerlingpl.
Oppolzergasse
Löwelstr.
Bartensteing.
VOLKSGARTEN
Schottenstift
Schottengasse
Helferstorferstr.
Renngasse
Freyung
Herrengasse
Bankgasse
Tiefer Graben
Am Hof
Naglerg.
Wallnerstr.
Kohlmarkt
Fahnengasse
Schauflerg.
BALLHAUS-PL.
HELDENPLATZ
Burgtor
Burgring
Natürhistorisches Museum
MARIA THERESIENPL.
Messeplatz
Messepalast
Burggasse
Siebensterngasse
Mariahilfer Str.
Museumstr.
Auerspergstr.
Volkstheater
Hofburg
Neue Hofburg
Kunsthistorisches Museum
Opernring
Operngasse
Getreidemarkt
Eschenbachg.
Nibelungengasse
SCHILLERPL.
Akademie der Bildenden Künste
Secession Building
Linke Wienzeile
Friedrichstr.
Wiedner Hauptstr.
Bösendorferstr.
Elisabethstr.
ELISABETHPL.
Filmgoldpergasse
Maria im Gesiade
Wipplingerstr.
Farbergasse
Graben
JUDENPL.
Kirche am Hof
Marc-Aurel-Str.
Salvatorg.
Wiesinger
Maria am Gestade
MORZIN-PL.
Raben steig
Judengasse
Salzgries
Tuchlauben
Bräunerstr.
Dorotheerg.
Spiegelg.
Plankeng.
Seilerg.
St. Peter's
PETERSPL.
Goldschm.g.
Jasomirgstr.
Rotenturmstr.
Brandstätte
Landskrong.
Tuchlauben
Bauernmarkt
Fleischmarkt
Griecheng.
Köllnerhofg.
Laurenzerberg
Rabensteig
Stephansdom
Rotenturmstr.
Lugeck
Bäckerstr.
Sonnenfelsg.
Schönlaterng.
Postgasse
Wollzeile
Schulerstr.
Riemerg.
Grünangerg.
Singerstr.
Weihburggasse
Ballg.
Lilieng.
Burgg.
NEUER MARKT
Kärtner Str.
Plankeng.
Tegetthoffstr.
Spanish Riding School
Stallburg.
MICHAELER-PL.
Alte Hofburg
Reitschulg.
Augustinerstr.
Augustiner Kirche
Hanuschg.
Josefspl.
JOSEPH PL.
M. d. Franog.
Dorotheerg.
Führichgasse
ALBERTINA PL.
Albertina Museum
Staatsoper
Opern Passage
Kärntner Ring
Annagasse
Krugerstr.
Johannesgasse
Maysedergasse
Wallfischgasse
Mahlerstr.
Künstlerhaus
Musikverein PL.
Konzerthaus
SCHWARZENBERG-PL.
Schwarzenbergstr.
Fichtegasse
Schellinggasse
Seilerstätte
Himmelpfortgasse
Schubertring
Am Heumarkt
Lothringerstr.
STADTPARK
Parkring
Liebenberg.
Stubenbastei
Biberstr.
Dr. Karl Lueger Pl.
Weiskir-chnerstr.
Stubenring
Am Stadtpark
Beatrixgasse
Johannesgasse
Wien-Mitte Bahnhof
Landstraßer-Hauptstr.
Ireland
Invalidenstr.
Urbangasse
Rechte Bahngasse
Vord. Zollamtsstr.
Hint. Zollamtsstr.
Museum of Applied Art
Radetzkystr.
Weißgerbergasse
Untere Donaustr.
Donau Canal
Obere Donaustr.
Aspernbr.
Marienbr.
Schwedenbr.
SCHWEDENPL.
Ferry Docks
DDSG
Franz-Josefs-Kai
JULIUS-RAAB-PL.
Dominikanerbastei
Canada
Wiesingerstr.
Rosenburstr.
Biberstr.
Dominikanerbastei
Sterngasse
Wipplingerstr.
Jordang.

SCALE
0 ─ yards ─ 275
0 ─ meters ─ 250

a **tip** is not expected, it's customary to round up the bill. The server won't bring your check without first being asked; say *zahlen, bitte* (TSAH-len BIT-uh) to settle up.

Of course, you'll need something to wash all that down. The most famous Austrian wine is probably *Gumpoldskirchen* from Lower Austria, the largest wine-producing province. *Klosterneuburger,* produced near Vienna, is both reasonably priced and dry. The best wines are drunk outdoors in wine gardens *(Heurigen),* near the vine-yards where they were produced. Austrian beers are outstanding—try *Stiegl Bier,* a Salzburg brew, *Zipfer Bier* from upper Austria, and *Gösser Bier* from Graz. Austria imports lots of Budweiser beer (the famous Czech *Budvar,* not the American brew).

■ Vienna (Wien)

It was not without reason that home-grown satirist Karl Kraus once dubbed Vienna—birthplace of psychoanalysis, atonal music, functionalist architecture, Zionism, and Nazism—a "laboratory for world destruction." Vienna's heyday carried the seeds of its own decay, and did so in such a blatant way that cafe-goers analyzed the phenom-enon-in-process complacently over coffee. *Fin de siècle* Vienna had a cultural impor-tance that rivaled Paris, thanks to its enormous school of musicians (Mozart, Beethoven, Schubert, Strauss, Brahms) and imperial wealth and taste in imported Baroque art, architecture, and decor. At the height of its artistic ferment, during the smoky and caffeine-permeated days of the great cafe culture, the Viennese were already self-mockingly calling their city the "merry apocalypse." Now that the Cold War is over and the Iron Curtain has mostly crumbled, the city has been renewing business connections in the former Communist bloc and reestablishing itself as the political, cultural, and economic gateway to Eastern Europe.

ORIENTATION AND PRACTICAL INFORMATION

Vienna is in eastern Austria, 40km from the Hungarian, Czech, and Slovak borders. The city is divided into 23 **districts** *(Bezirke),* with the old *Innere Stadt* (inner city) occupying the first district. From this center, the city spreads out in a series of con-centric rings. The first ring, which surrounds the *Innere Stadt,* is the **Ringstraße,** known simply as the Ring. Along the southern section of the ring, the intersection of **Opernring, Kärntner Ring,** and **Kärntner Straße** forms the epicenter of the city; the Opera House, tourist office, and the **Karlsplatz** U-Bahn stop are nearby. Roman numerals have been added to most of the addresses listed below to indicate the dis-trict in which particular establishments are located.

Vienna is a metropolis with crime like any other; be extra careful in Karlspl., home to many pushers and junkies, and avoid sections of the Gürtel at night, when it becomes home to some of Vienna's skin trade.

Telephone Code: 0222 from within Austria, 1 from outside the country.

Flights: The **Wien-Schwechat Flughafen,** home of **Austrian Airlines** (tel. 17 89; open M-F 8am-7pm, Sa-Su 8am-5pm) is 18km from Vienna, accessible by public transport (S-7 to "Flughafen/Wolfsthal") or by the **Vienna Airport Lines Shuttle Bus** (70AS). Buses leave the airport for the City Air Terminal (at the Hilton across Land-str. and Hauptstr. from "Wien Mitte") every 20min. 6am to 11pm and every 30min. from 11pm to 6am. Travelers under 25 qualify for discounts for tickets bought 2 weeks in advance.

Trains: 3 main train stations in the city. For train information, call 17 17 (24hr.) or check times at http://www.bahn.at. The **Westbahnhof,** XV, Mariahilferstr. 132, runs trains west to destinations including Budapest (3-4hr., 9 per day, 374AS), Inns-bruck (6hr., every 2hr., 660AS), Munich (4½hr., 5 per day, 740AS), Salzburg (3hr., every hr., 410AS), and Zurich (9hr., 3 per day, 1160AS). The Westbahnhof train **information counter** is open daily 7:30am-8:40pm. The 2nd station, **Südbahnhof,** X, Wiedner Gürtel 1a, sends trains to Graz (2¾hr., every hr., 310AS), Prague (5hr., 3 per day, 524AS), and Venice (8hr., 5 per day, 760AS), along with trains to other cities in Poland, Germany, Russia, Greece, and Spain. The 3rd major station, **Franz-Josefs Bahnhof,** IX, Althamstr. 10, handles mostly domestic trains.

Ferries: Cruise with **DDSG Donaureisen** (tel. 523 80) to Austrian towns or as far away as Budapest (1 per day Apr. 8-Oct. 29, 750AS, round-trip 1100AS). Buy tickets at tourist offices. Boats dock at the *Reichsbrücke;* take U-1 to "Vorgartenstr."

Public Transportation: Excellent **U-Bahn** (subway), **bus, Strassenbahn** (tram), and **S-Bahn** (overground subway) systems cover the city. Single fare is 20AS (17AS if purchased in advance); a 24hr. pass costs 50AS, a 72hr. pass 130AS, a week pass 142AS. The 3-day **Vienna Card** (180AS) offers substantial discounts at many museums, sights, and events, and is useful for non-students. To validate a ticket, punch it immediately in the orange machine upon entering the bus, tram, etc. Unstamped ticket holders risk a 500AS fine. Tickets can be purchased from *Tabak* kiosks or *Automaten* in U-Bahn stations. Transport closes 12:30-5:30am, but **night buses** run on reduced routes (25AS, passes not valid). Night bus stops are designated by "N" signs. Information stands around the city will help you find your way, or check http://www.weinnet.at/efa.

Taxis: tel. 313 00, 401 00, 601 60, 814 00, or 910 11. Stands at Westbahnhof, Südbahnhof, and Karlspl. Rates generally 27AS plus 14AS per km. 27AS surcharge Su, holidays, and nights (11pm-6am); 13-26AS surcharge for heavy luggage.

Hitchhiking: For Salzburg, hitchers take U-4: Hütteldorf; the highway leading to the *Autobahn* is 10km farther. Hitchers traveling south ride tram 67 to the last stop and wait at the traffic circle near Laaerberg. **Mitfahrzentrale Wien,** VIII, Daung. 1a (tel. 408 22 10), off Laudong., organizes ride-sharing. Open M-F 8am-noon and 2-7pm, Sa-Su 1-3pm.

Bike Rental: At Wien Nord and the Westbahnhof. 150AS per day, 90AS with a train ticket from the day of arrival. **Pedal Power,** II, Ausstellungsstr. 3 (tel. 729 72 34; fax 729 72 35; http://www.pedalpower.co.at), rents bikes for 60AS per hr., 200AS per half day, 365AS for 24hr. with delivery. Open May-Oct. 8am-8pm.

Tourist Office: I, Kärntnerstr. 38, behind the Opera House, has an assortment of brochures, including a free city map. Books 300-400AS rooms for a 40AS fee plus deposit. Open daily 9am-7pm. **Branch offices** at the following locations offer similar services. **Westbahnhof,** open daily Apr.-Oct. 7am-10pm; Nov.-Mar. 7am-9pm **Airport,** open daily 8:30am-9pm. **Jugend-Info Wien** (Vienna Youth Information Service), Bellaria-Passage (tel. 17 99; email jugendinfo.vie@blackbox.ping.at), in the underground passage at U-Bahn: "Volkstheater." Hip staff has wide range of info and sells discount youth concert and theater tickets. Open M-Sa noon-7pm

Budget Travel: **Österreichisches Verkehrsbüro** (Austrian National Travel Office), I, Operng. 3-5 (tel. 588 62 38), opposite the Opera House. Though not intended exclusively for budget travelers, the office sells BIJ tickets. Open M-F 9am-6pm, Sa 9am-noon. **Ökista,** IX, Türkenstr. 8 (tel. 40 14 80), specializes in student travel. Open M-F 9am-7:30pm.

Embassies: Australia, IV, Mattiellistr. 2-4 (tel. 512 85 80), behind Karlskirche. Open M-Th 8:30am-1pm and 2-5:30pm, F 8:30am-1:15pm. **Canada,** I, Laurenzerburg 2, 3rd fl. (tel. 531 38, ext. 3000). Open M-F 8:30am-12:30pm and 1:30-3:30pm. Leave a message in an emergency. **Ireland,** III, Hilton Center, Landstraßer Hauptstr. 21, 6th fl. (tel. 715 42 47; fax 713 60 04). Open M-F 9:30-11:30am and 2-4pm. **New Zealand,** XIX, Springsiedleg. 28 (tel. 318 85 05; fax 318 67 17). No regular office hours; call in advance. If there is no answer, contact the consulate in Bonn at 0049 228 228 070. **South Africa,** XIX, Sandg. 33 (tel. 320 64 93). M-F 8:30am-noon. **U.K.,** III, Jauresg. 10 (tel. 716 13 53 38), near Schloß Belvedere. Open M-F 9:15am-noon. **U.S. Embassy,** IX, Boltzmanng. 16, off Währingerstr. and **Consulate** at I, Gartenbaupromenade 2 (tel. 313 39 for both), off Parkring. Phone hours M-F 8:30am-noon and 1-5pm. Open M-F 8:30am-noon. Call ahead.

Luggage Storage: Lockers (40AS per 24hr.) at all train stations. Adequate for sizable backpacks. **Luggage watch** 30AS. Open daily 4am-1:15am.

Currency Exchange: Banks and **airport exchanges** use the same official rates. Minimum commission: 65AS for traveler's checks, 10AS for cash. Most are open M-W and F 8am-12:30pm and 1:30-3pm, Th 8am-12:30pm and 1:30-5:30pm. **ATMs** are everywhere, offering excellent rates. **Train station** exchanges offer long hours and a 50AS charge for changing up to US$700 of traveler's checks. The 24hr. exchange at the **main post office** has excellent rates and a 80AS fee to change up to US$1100 in traveler's checks. **24-hour bill exchange** machines have horrid rates.

American Express: I, Kärntnerstr. 21-23, P.O. Box 28, A-1015 (tel. 515 40), down the street from Stephanspl. Cashes AmEx and Thomas Cook checks (3% commission), holds mail for 4 weeks for AmEx customers, and, for everyone, sells theater, concert, and other tickets. Open M-F 9am-5:30pm, Sa 9am-noon.

Bookstores: Shakespeare & Company, I, Sterng. 2 (tel. 535 50 53; fax 535 50 53 16; http://www.ping.at/members/shbook). Eclectic and intelligent. Great magazine selection. Occasional readings and signings. Open M-F 9am-7pm, Sa 9am-5pm.

Bisexual, Gay, and Lesbian Organizations: The bisexual, gay, and lesbian community in Vienna, though small, is more integrated than in other cities. The lovely **Rosa Lila Villa,** VI, Linke Wienzeile 102 (tel. 586 81 50), is a resource and social center for Viennese homosexuals and visitors to the city. Open M-F 5-8pm.

Laundromat: Schnell und Sauber, VII, Westbahnhofstr. 60 (tel. 524 64 60); U-6: Burgg. Stadthalle. Wash 60AS per 6kg. Soap included. Spin-dry 10AS. Open 24hr.

Public Showers and Toilets: At Westbahnhof, in Friseursalon Navratil downstairs from subway passage. Well-maintained. 30min. shower 48AS, with soap and towel 60AS (10AS extra for either on Sunday).

Emergencies: Ambulance, tel. 144. **Fire,** tel. 122. Alert your consulate of any emergencies or legal problems.

Police: tel. 133.

Medical Assistance: Allgemeines Krankenhaus, IX, Währinger Gürtel 18-20 (tel. 404 00). **Emergency care,** tel. 141.

24-hour Pharmacy: 15 50. Consulates can provide a list of English-speaking doctors.

Rape Crisis Hotline: tel. 523 22 22. Open M 10am-6pm, Tu 2-6pm, W 10am-2pm, Th 5-9pm. **24hr. immediate help,** tel. 717 19.

Post Offices: Hauptpostamt, I, Fleischmarkt 19. Exchange windows, phones, faxes, and mail services. Open 24hr. Address *Poste Restante* to "SVENDSEN, Christina; Postlagernde Briefe; Hauptpostamt; Fleischmarkt 19; A-1010 Wien." Branches throughout the city and at the train stations. **Postal Codes:** In the 1st district A-1010, in the 2nd A-1020, in the 3rd A-1030, and so on, to the 23rd A-1230.

Internet Access: National Library, I, Neue Burg 1 (tel. 53 41 00), in Heldenpl. at the Hofburg, provides free access at numerous terminals and long waits in long lines. Open M-Sa 10am-4pm, Su 10am-1pm. **Libro,** XXII, Donauzentrum (tel. 202 52 55). Free access at 6 terminals. Open Su-F 7am-7pm, Sa 9am-5pm.

ACCOMMODATIONS AND CAMPING

One of the few unpleasant aspects of Vienna is the hunt for cheap rooms during peak season (June-Sept.). Don't leave your shelter to the vagaries of chance; fax or call for reservations at least five days in advance. Otherwise, plan on calling from the train station between 6 and 9am during the summer to put your name down for a reservation. The summer crunch for budget rooms is slightly alleviated in July, when university dorms are converted into makeshift hostels.

Hostels

Myrthengasse (HI), VII, Myutheng. 7, and **Neustiftgasse (HI),** VII, Neustiftg. 85 (both tel. 523 63 16 or 523 94 29; fax 523 58 49). From the Westbahnhof take U-6 ("Heiligenstadt") to "Burggasse-Stadthalle," then bus 48A ("Ring") to "Neubaugasse." Walk back on Burgg. one block, and take the 1st right (15min.). From the Südbahnhof, take bus 13A ("Skodagasse/Alerstr.") to "Kellermanngasse," then walk 2 blocks to your left on Neustiftg. and turn left on Myrtheng. These Swedish-modern hostels are around the corner from each other and only a 20min. walk from the *Innenstadt.* 4- to 6-bed dorms with shower 165-180AS; 2-bed dorms 195-210AS. Non-members add 40AS. Breakfast and sheets included. Lunch or dinner 65AS. Laundry 50AS. Reception at Myrtheng. 7am-11:30pm. Curfew 1am. Lockout 9am-2pm. Reservations recommended (only by fax).

Believe It Or Not, VII, Myrtheng. 10, apt. 14 (tel. 526 46 58), across the street from the Myrtheng. hostel. Ring the bell. Funky and extremely social. 2 bedrooms, bunks rising to spacious ceilings, and a kitchen. Lockout 10:30am-noon. 160AS; Nov.-Easter 110AS. Reception 8am until early afternoon—call if in doubt. Reservations recommended.

Gästehaus Ruthensteiner (HI), XV, Robert-Hamerlingg. 24 (tel. 893 42 02; fax 893 27 96). Exit Westbahnhof at the main entrance (on Äußere Mariahilferstr., beyond the Gürtel), turn right and head to Mariahilferstr. Turn right again, continue until Haidmahnsg., and take a left on Robert-Hammerlingg. Sun-filled courtyard. Summer dorms 125AS; 10-bed dorms 145AS; 3- to 5-bed dorms 169AS; singles 245AS; doubles 470AS. Breakfast 25AS. Showers and sheets (except for 10-bed rooms) included. Lockers and kitchen available. Bike rental 89AS per day. **Internet access** from 20AS. Reception 24hr. Reservations recommended.

Hostel Zöhrer, VIII, Skodag. 26 (tel. 406 07 30; fax 408 04 09), about 10min. from the city center. From Westbahnhof, U-6 ("Heiligenstadt") to "Alserstr." then streetcar 43 ("Schottentor") to "Skodag." From Südbahnhof, bus 13A to "Alserstr./ Skodag." Kitchen. 5- to 8-bed dorms with showers 170AS; doubles 230AS. Breakfast, lockers, and sheets included. Laundry 60AS. Key deposit 100AS, with ID 50AS. Reception 7:30am-10pm. Check-out 9am. Lockout 11am-2pm.

Turmherberge Don Bosco, III, Lechnerstr. 12 (tel. 713 14 94), near U-Bahn: "Kardinal-Nagl-Pl." The cheapest beds in town in a hot and barren former bell tower. 75AS for hostel members. Curfew 11:45pm. Open Mar.-Nov.

Schloßherberge am Wilhelminenberg (HI), XVI, Savoyenstr. 2 (tel. 485 85 03, ext. 700; fax 485 85 03, ext. 702). U-6: "Thaliastr." then tram 46 ("Joachimsthalerpl.") to "Maroltingerg." Near the Vienna woods with a great view of the city. 4-bed dorms with bath 220AS. Keycard 25AS. Laundry 65AS. Group discounts. Reception 7am-11pm. Lockout 9am-2pm. Curfew 11pm. Reserve at least 2 days in advance.

University Dormitories

Porzellaneum der Wiener Universität, IX, Porzellang. 30 (tel. 31 77 28 20; fax 31 77 28 30). From Südbahnhof, tram D ("Nußdorf") to "Fürsteng." From Westbahnhof, tram 5 to "Franz-Josefs Bahnhof" then tram D ("Südbahnhof") to "Fürsteng." Flag display at entryway is worthy of the U.N. 10min. from the Ring. Singles 190AS; doubles 380AS. Sheets included. Reception 24hr. Reservations recommended.

Rudolfinum, IV, Mayerhofg. 3 (tel. 505 53 84; fax 505 53 85 450). U-1: Taubstummeng. Rock 'n' roll and MTV. More intense guests watch CNN. Great location. Singles 270AS; doubles 480AS; triples 600AS; quads 800AS. Breakfast included. Laundry facilities. Make arrangements to use the kitchen. Reception 24hr.

Studentenwohnheim der Hochschule für Musik, I, Johannesg. 8 (tel. 514 84 48; fax 514 84 49). 3 blocks down Kärnterstr. away from the Stephansdom and turn left onto Johannesg. Fabulous location. Cheap and yummy meals. Singles 420AS, with bath 490AS; doubles 760AS, with bath 980AS; triples 810AS; quads 1000AS; quints 1250AS. Breakfast and showers included. Reception 24hr.

Hotels and Pensions

Hotel Quisisana, VI, Windmühlg. 6 (tel. 587 71 55; fax 587 71 56 33). U-2 to "Babenbergerstr.," turn right on Mariahilferstr., go 3 blocks, then turn left on Windmühlg. An old-fashioned hotel run by a charming older couple. Singles 330-350AS, with shower 400AS; doubles 500-540AS, 660AS. Breakfast 40AS. 5% student discount.

Lauria Apartments, VII, Kaiserstr. 77, 3rd Fl. (tel. 522 25 55). From Westbahnhof, tram 5: "Burgg." From Sudbahnhof, tram 18: "Westbahnhof" then tram 5: "Burgg." Modern apartments offering rooms and dorm beds. Dorms 160AS; singles 480AS; doubles 530AS-700AS; triples 700AS-800AS; quads 850AS, with shower 940AS. The dorm beds might be the best deal: clean, cheap, modern, access to kitchen. Sheets and TV included. Phone reservations 24hr.; 2-night min. for reservations. Credit cards accepted except for dorm-beds.

Camping

Aktiv Camping Neue Donau, XXII, Am Kleehäufel 119 (tel./fax 202 40 10). U-Bahn 1 to "Kaisermühlen" then bus 91a to "Kleehäufel." 4km from the city center and adjacent to Neue Donau beaches. July-Aug. 73AS, tent 42AS, electricity 40AS. May, June, and Sept. 67AS, tent 37AS, electricity 40AS. Showers included. Laundry, supermarket, kitchen. Wheelchair accessible. Open May to mid-Sept.

FOOD AND COFFEE

In a world full of uncertainty, the Viennese believe that the least you can do is face things with a full stomach. Food in the city reflects the crazy patchwork empire of the Habsburgs. *Knödeln* (Czech-origin dumplings) and *Ungarische Gulaschsuppe* (Hungarian spicy beef stew) exemplify Eastern European influences; even the famed *Wiener Schnitzel* (fried and breaded veal cutlets) probably first appeared in Milan. Vienna is renowned for sublime desserts and chocolates—unbelievably rich, and priced for patrons who are likewise blessed. Most residents, however, maintain that the sumptuous treats are worth every *Groschen*. Gorge on *Sacher Torte, Imperial Torte, Palatschinken,* and *Apfel Strudel.*

Restaurants near **Kärntnerstraße** are generally expensive—a better bet is the neighborhood north of the university and near the Votivkirche (U-2: Schottentor). The area radiating from the **Rechte** and **Linke Wienzeile** near Naschmarkt (U-4: Kettenbrückeg.) houses a range of cheap eateries, and the **Naschmarkt** itself contains open-air stands vending aromatic delicacies (bread and a variety of ethnic food) to sample while shopping at Vienna's premier flea market (open M-F 7am-6pm, Sa 7am-1pm). For supermarket fare, try the ubiquitous **Billa, Hofer,** and **Sparmarkt.** Find kosher groceries at the **Kosher Supermarket,** Hollandstr. 10 (tel. 216 96 75). Be warned that most places close Saturday afternoons and all of Sunday.

Restaurants

Trzesniewski, I, Dorotheerg. 1, 3 blocks down the Graben from the Stephansdom. A famous stand-up restaurant, Trzes has been serving petite open-faced sandwiches for over 80 years. This was Franz Kafka's favorite place to eat. 10AS per *Brötchen.* Open M-F 9am-7pm, Sa 9am-1pm.

Levante, I, Wallnerstr. 2, near the Graben. This Greek-Turkish restaurant features street-side dining and heaps of affordable dishes, including vegetarian delights. Main courses 80-150AS. Open 11am-11pm.

Tunnel, VIII, Florianig. 39. U-2 to "Rathaus," then with your back to the *Rathaus* head right on Landesgerichtstr. and left on Florianig. Prized for its dilapidated hipness, live nightly music, and affordable food. Daily lunch *menüs* 45AS. Italian, Austrian, and Middle Eastern dishes, with many vegetarian options (45-125AS). Very cheap beer (0.50L *Gösser* 27AS). Open 10am-2am.

Bizi Pizza, I, Rotenturmstr. 4, on the corner of Stephanspl. Good food and a great deal in the heart of the city. Pizza (60-75AS, slices 28AS) and a salad bar. Open daily 11am-11:30pm.

Schnitzelwirt Schmidt, VII, Neubaug. 52 (tel. 523 37 71). U-2 or U-3 to "Volkstheater," then bus 49 to "Neubaug." Every kind of *Schnitzel* (60-110AS) imaginable. It's not gourmet *Schnitzel,* but the huge portions spill over the edges of the plate. Open M-Sa 11am-11pm.

Rosenberger Markt, I, Mayscderg. 2, behind Sacher Hotel. This large and chaotic subterranean buffet offers a gargantuan selection of decent food at reasonable prices. You pay by the size of your plate—pile high. Salads 29-64AS, waffles 55AS, vegetable dishes 24-64AS. Open 10:30am-11pm.

University Mensa, IX, Universitätsstr. 7, on the 7th floor of the university building, between U-2: "Rathaus" and "Schottentor." Take the elevator to the 6th floor and then the stairs up. 40-60AS. Open M-F 8am-6pm. Or try the **Music Academy,** I, Johannesg. 8 (tel. 512 94 70). Open M-F 7:30am-3pm. Food served 11am-2pm; in July and Aug. and Sa-Su 7:30-10am.

Coffeehouses and Konditoreien

The cafe was the centerpiece of Vienna's *fin de siècle* culture, and still is one of the main parts of the city's charm. The quintessential Viennese coffee is the *melange,* made with foamed cream or thick milk. Most cafes also serve hot food. When you're ready to leave, signal to the waiter by asking to pay: *"Zahlen bitte!"*

The *Konditoreien,* no less traditional, focus their attention on delectables instead. These pastries are something of a national institution—Switzerland may have its gold reserves, but Austria could back its currency with its renowned *Sacher Torte.*

mmm...coffee.

There is a steadfast rule for the Vienna coffeehouse—the drink matters, but the atmosphere *really* matters. 19th-century artists, writers, and thinkers fled badly heated apartments to surround themselves with the coffeehouse's dark wood and dusty velvet. There, they ordered a cup of coffee and stayed long into the night, composing operettas, writing books, and cutting into each other's work. The bourgeoisie followed suit, and the coffeehouse became the living room of the city. At its tables gathered the intellectual world of Vienna and, in many cases, Europe. A grand coffeehouse culture arose. Peter Altenberg, "the cafe writer," scribbled lines, Kokoschka grumbled alone, and exiles Vladimir Lenin and Leon Trotsky played chess. Here Theodor Herzl made plans for a Zionist Israel, and here Kafka came from Prague to visit the Herrenhof. Karl Kraus and a circle of minor writers baited Hugo von Hofmannsthal and Arthur Schnitzler. The original literary cafe was Cafe Griensteidl; after its 1897 zenith, the torch passed first to Cafe Central, then to Cafe Herrenhof. Of these, only Cafe Central looks like it used to. Coffeehouses now rest partway in the past. The best places resist massive overhauls, succumbing to a noble, comfortable decrepitude.

Café Central, I, at the corner of Herreng. and Strauchg. inside Palais Ferstel. Theodor Herzl, Sigmund Freud, satirist Karl Kraus, and Vladimir Ilych Ulianov (better known by his pen name, Lenin) all hung out here. Oh, and they serve coffee, too. Open M-Sa 9am-8pm. Live piano music 4-7pm.

Demel, I, Kohlmarkt 14, 5min. from the Stephansdom. The most luxurious Viennese *Konditorei,* Demel was confectioner to the imperial court until the empire dissolved. Chocolate is made fresh every morning. Waitresses in convent-black serve the divine confections (40-50AS). Open daily 10am-6pm.

Hotel Sacher, I, Philharmonikerstr. 4, around the corner from the main tourist office. Home of the world-famous Sachertorte (50AS), and a famous turn-of-the-century haunt. Open daily 7am-11:30pm.

Café Drechsler, VI, Linke Wienzeile 22, near Karlspl. Head down Operng. and continue on Linke Wienzeile. Early birds and night owls roost here over pungent cups of *mokka.* Great lunch menu. Open M-F 4am-8pm, Sa 4am-6pm.

Alte Backstube, VIII, Langeg. 34. Around the corner from Theater in der Josefstadt, this popular after-theater café/restaurant is also a museum of bakery art. Open Sept. to mid-July Tu-Sa 10am-midnight, Su 4pm-midnight.

Café Hawelka, I, Dorotheerg. 6, 3 blocks down Graben from the Stephansdom. Shabby and glorious. *Buchteln* (35AS) served fresh from the oven at 10pm. Coffee 30-50AS. Open M and W-Sa 8am-2am, Su 4pm-2am.

Café Savoy, VI, Linke Wienzeile 36. Scruffy *fin de siècle* cafe with dark wood and decrepit gold trim. A large gay and lesbian crowd moves in to make it a lively nightspot on weekends. Open Tu-F 5pm-2am, Sa 9am-6pm and 9pm-2am.

SIGHTS

Viennese streets are by turns scuzzy, startling, *gemütlich,* and grandiose. The best way to get to know the city streets is to get lost in them. The drivers of **Fiakers,** or horse-drawn carriages, are happy to taxi you wherever your heart desires, but be sure to agree on a price before you set out. **Cycling tours** occur every day; contact **Vienna-Bike,** IX, Wasag. (tel. 319 12 58), for bike rental (60AS) or a two- to three-hour tour (280AS). One of the best tours is simply a ride around the Ring on tram 1 or 2—buy a ticket and gawk to your heart's content.

The Innere Stadt

The **First District** (*Innere Stadt* or "inner city"), Vienna's social and geographical epicenter, is enclosed on three sides by the massive **Ringstraße** and on the northern end by the **Danube Canal.** If you begin your tour from the main tourist office, the first prominent building in view will be the world-renowned **State Opera House,** or

Pacts with the Devil: Not Good

Years ago, during the construction of the North Tower of the Stephansdom, a young builder named Hans Puchsbaum wished to marry his master's daughter. The master, rather jealous of Hans's skill, agreed on one condition: Hans had to finish the entire North Tower on his own within a year. Faced with this impossible task, Hans despaired until a stranger offered to help him. The good Samaritan required only that Hans abstain from saying the name of God or any other holy name. Hans agreed, and the tower grew by leaps and bounds. One day during construction the young mason spotted his love in the midst of his labor, and, wishing to call attention to his progress, he called out her name: "Maria." With this invocation of the Blessed Virgin, the scaffolding collapsed, and Hans plummeted 500ft. to his death. Rumors of a satanic pact spread, and work on the tower ceased, leaving it in its present condition.

Staatsoper. The cheapest way to see its glittering gold, crystal, and red-velvet interior may be to see an opera; standing-room tickets with excellent views are only 20AS. *(Open July-Aug. daily 11am-3pm on the hour; Sept.-June on request.)* If you can't find tickets, tours of the house cost 40AS, students 25AS. Alfred Hrdlicka's 1988 sculpture **Monument Gregen Krieg und Faschismus** (Memorial Against War and Fascism), on Albertinapl., memorializes the suffering of Austria's people—especially its Jews—during World War II. From Albertinapl., Tegetthoffstr. leads to the spectacular **Neuer Markt,** where a graceful fountain and 17th-century church greet visitors. Continue north from here to reach Vienna's most revered landmark, the Gothic **Stephansdom;** the cathedral's smoothly tapering South Tower has become Vienna's emblem. *(Tours of the cathedral in English M-Sa 10:30am and 3pm, Su 3pm. 30AS. July-Sept. also Sa 7pm. 100AS. North Tower open daily Apr.-Sept. 9am-6pm; Oct.-Mar. 8am-5pm. Elevator ride 50AS. Tours of the vault M-Sa 10am-noon and 2-4:30pm, Su 2-5pm. 50AS.)* Take a lap around the building before checking out the view from the **Nordturm** (North Tower). In the catacombs, the **vault** stores Habsburgs' innards. Their hearts and bodies are scattered in other crypts around town.

The **Hofburg** (Imperial Palace), rising from the southeast of the Michaelerpl., was inhabited by the Habsburg emperors until 1918, and now houses the President's office. The enormous complex also includes the **Burggarten,** the **Burgkapelle** (where the Vienna Boys' Choir sings Mass on Sunday and religious holidays), and the **Schauräume,** the former private rooms of Emperor Franz Josef and Empress Elizabeth. Also visit the **Nationalbibliothek** (National Library), which has outstanding papyrus scriptures and a zonkingly elaborate reading room. The Baroque **Josefsplatz** features an equestrian monument to Emperor Josef II and the stunning 14th-century **Augustinerkirche,** home to urns of the Habsburg's hearts. Augustinerstr. leads right past the **Albertina,** a palatial wing which now contains a film museum and the celebrated **Collection of Graphic Arts** (tel. 534 83), with drawings by the likes of Dürer, Michelangelo, da Vinci, Cezanne, and Schiele. *(Open Tu-F 10am-4pm, Sa 10am-6pm.)*

Between Josefspl. and Michaelerpl., the Palace Stables *(Stallburg)* are home to the famous Royal Lipizzaner stallions of the **Spanische Reitschule** (Spanish Riding School). Performances are always sold out; write for reservations six months in advance (do not send money) to Spanische Reitschule, Hofburg, A-1010 Wien. *(Tickets 250-900AS, standing-room 200AS. Performances Apr.-June and Sept. Su at 10:45am and W at 7pm; Mar. and Nov. to mid-Dec. Su at 10:45am.)* Watching the horses train is much cheaper. *(Mar.-June and Nov. to mid-Dec. Tu-Sa 10am-noon; Feb. M-Sa 10am-noon, except when the horses tour. Tickets sold at Josefspl., Gate 2, from about 8:30am. 100AS.)* Vienna's first modern building, the **Looshaus,** sits on **Michaelerplatz,** which is named for the **Michaelerkirche** on its eastern flank. Leopold "the Glorious" of Babenberg purportedly founded the church in gratitude for his safe return from the Crusades. In the middle of Michaelerpl. lie the **excavated foundations** of Roman Vienna—the Roman military camp called Vindobona where Marcus Aurelius penned *Meditations.*

The Hofburg's Heldenpl. gate presides over the Burgring segment of the **Ringstraße.** In 1857, Emperor Franz Josef commissioned this 187 feet wide and 2½ miles long boulevard to replace the medieval city walls that separated Vienna's center from the suburban districts. Follow Burgring west through the **Volksgarten's** hundreds of varieties of roses to reach the Neoclassical, sculpture-adorned **Parliament** building. Just up Dr.-Karl-Renner-Ring is the **Rathaus,** a lovely remnant of late 19th-century neo-Gothic with Flemish stylings and red geraniums in the windows. There are numerous art exhibits inside, and the city holds outdoor festivals in the square outside. Opposite the Rathaus, the **Burgtheater** contains frescoes by Klimt. Immediately to the north on Dr.-Karl-Lueger-Ring is the **Universität,** and the surrounding sidestreets overflow with cafes, bookstores, and bars.

Outside the Ring

Music lovers trek out to the **Zentralfriedhof** (Central Cemetery), XI, Simmeringer Hauptstr. 234; the second gate leads to the graves of Beethoven, Strauss, and Schönberg, and an honorary monument to Mozart. *(Open daily May-Aug. 7am-7pm; Mar.-Apr. and Sept.-Oct. 7am-6pm; Nov.-Feb. 8am-5pm.)* To reach the Zentralfriedhof, take streetcar 71 from Schwarzenbergpl. (35min.). Zentralfriedhof's Gate T or I leads to the **Jewish Cemetery** and the Austrian playwright Arthur Schnitzler's grave. If you need some cheering up after this experience, visit the **Hundertwasser Haus,** at the corner of Löwenstr. and Kegelg. in the third district. A wild fantasia of pastel colors, ceramic mosaics, and oblique tile columns contribute to the eccentricity of this blunt rejection of architectural orthodoxy.

Another must-see is the **Schloß Schönbrunn** and its surrounding gardens, which comprise one of the greatest palace complexes in Europe. Tours of some of the palaces' 1500 rooms reveal the elaborate taste of Maria Theresa's era. The six-year-old Mozart played in the **Hall of Mirrors** at the whim of the Empress, and to the profit of the boy's father. Outdoors, it's a pleasure to wander around the elaborate gardens and hilltop **Gloriette.** In summer, many concerts and festivals take place in the palace. *(U-4: Schönbrunn. Palace apartments open daily Apr.-Oct. 8:30am-5pm; Nov.-Mar. 8:30am-4:30pm. 100AS. Tours in English 40AS. Park free.)* The striking **Schloß Belvedere,** IV, whose sphinx-filled palace gardens begin just behind the Schwarzenbergpl. (tram D: Schwarzenberg), was once the summer residence of Prince Eugene of Savoy, Austria's greatest military hero. It now houses art by Klimt, Schiele, Kokoschka, and a wing of Baroque and medieval art.

Far to the north and west of Vienna sprawls the illustrious **Wienerwald,** made famous by Strauss's catchy waltz, "Tales of the Vienna Woods." The woods extend up to the slopes of the first foothills of the Alps. Take U-4 to "Heiligenstadt" then bus 38A to "Kahlenberg." **Kahlenberg** is the highest point of the rolling *Wienerwald,* and affords spectacular views of Vienna, the Danube, and even distant Alps. It was from here that the Turks besieged Vienna in 1683.

MUSEUMS

On the Burgring in what used to be the *Neue Hofburg* is the famous **Kunsthistorisches Museum.** (Open Tu-Su 10am-6pm. 100AS, students and seniors 70AS.) The building is home to one of the world's best art collections, including works by Brueghels, Vermeer, Holbein, Rembrandt, Titian, Dürer, and Velázquez. There's a superb collection of ancient art, a transplanted Egyptian burial chamber, and much more. Gustav Klimt decorated the lobby. Another **branch** of the museum resides in the Neue Burg (Hofburg) and contains the fabulous **Ephesus Museum,** which houses an ancient Greek temple and statues transported from the Ephesus. (Same hours as picture gallery. 30AS, students and seniors 15AS.) Across the way sits the **Naturhistorisches Museum,** featuring naturological fare and the beautifully over-proportioned Stone-Age statue the *Venus of Willendorf.* Fans of Klimt and fellow radicals Schiele and Kokoschka should visit the **Austrian Gallery,** in the **Belvedere Palace** (entrance at Prinz-Eugenstr. 27). The Lower Belvedere houses museums of Baroque and medieval art. (Both museums open Tu-Su 10am-5pm. 60AS, students 30AS.)

The greatest monument of *fin-de-siècle* Vienna is the **Secession Building,** I, Friedrichstr. 12, built by Wagner's pupil Josef Maria Olbrich to accommodate the artists, led by Gustav Klimt, who scorned the historical style and broke violently with the uptight Viennese art establishment. (Open Tu and Th-Su 10am-6pm, W 10am-8pm. 90AS, students 60AS.) Exhibits by contemporary artists adorn the walls, as does Klimt's 30m *Beethoven Frieze*. In the summer of 1998, guerrilla fans of the Secession painted the building a ragged red color overnight, in an attempt to celebrate the building's spirit of iconoclasm on its 100th anniversary. The **Künstlerhaus,** from which the Secession seceded, is to the east at Karlspl. 5. (Open M-W and F-Su 10am-6pm, Th 10am-9pm. 90AS, students 40AS.)

For some more Art Nouveau, visit the **Österreichisches Museum für Angewandte Kunst** (Museum of Applied Art), I, Stubenring 5, the oldest museum of applied arts in Europe. (Open Tu-W and F-Su 10am-6pm, Th 10am-9pm. 90AS, students 45AS.) Otto Wagner furniture and Klimt sketches sit amid crystal, furniture, and rugs from the Middle Ages to the present. Otto Wagner's **Kirche am Steinhof** resides at XIV, Baumgartner Höhe 1. (Take bus 48. Open M-F 8am-3pm, Sa 3-4pm. Free. Guided tours (in German) for 40AS.) The interior is stunning, combining Wagner's functionalism with a decidedly Byzantine influence. **Museum Moderner Kunst** (Museum of Modern Art; tel. 317 69 00; fax 317 69 01; http://www.MMKSLW.or.at) is split between two locations. The first is in the **Liechtenstein Palace,** IX, Fürsteng. 1, reached by tram D ("Nußdorf") to "Fürsteng." The *Schloß,* surrounded by a leafy garden, boasts a collection of 20th-century masters including Picasso, Miró, Kandinsky, Pollock, Warhol, and Klee. The second location is at the **20er Haus,** III, Arsenalstr. 1 (tel. 799 69 00), opposite the Südbahnhof. (Open Tu-Su 10am-6pm. 45AS, students 25AS for each exhibit; 60AS, children 30AS for both exhibits.) It sits in a large sculpture garden stocked with pieces by Giacometti, Moore, and others.

Kunst Haus Wien, III, Untere Weißgerberstr. 13, built for the works of Hundertwasser, is itself one of his greatest works. This crazily pastiched building also hosts international contemporary exhibits. (Open daily 10am-7pm. 90AS, students 50AS.) The **Historisches Museum der Stadt Wien** (Historical Museum of the City of Vienna), IV, Karlspl. 5, houses historical artifacts and paintings, including detritus from Roman Vienna and from the 1683 Turkish siege of the city. (Open Tu-Su 9am-6pm. 50AS, students 20AS, seniors 25AS. Free F 9am-noon.) The **Sigmund Freud Haus,** IX, Bergg. 19 (tel. 319 15 96), was Freud's home from 1891 until the *Anschluß.* (Open July-Sept. 9am-6pm; Oct.-June 9am-4pm. 60AS, students 40AS.) The house contains mostly photos and documents, including young Sigmund's report cards and circumcision certificate.

ENTERTAINMENT

Vienna is a city of music. Mozart, Beethoven, and Haydn created their greatest masterpieces in Vienna, as part of the First Viennese School. A century later, Schönberg, Webern, and Berg teamed up to form the Second Viennese School. All year, Vienna presents performances ranging from the above-average to the sublime, with much surprisingly accessible to the budget traveler. The **Staatsoper,** one of the world's top five companies, performs about 300 times from September through June. **Standing-room tickets** provide a glimpse of world-class opera for a pittance. (Balcony 20AS, orchestra 30AS. Formal dress not necessary, but no shorts. Line up 30min. before showtime (2-3hr. in tourist season) for tickets. Seats 100-850AS. Student discounts.)

The world-famous, top-notch **Wiener Philharmoniker** (Vienna Philharmonic Orchestra) included Gustav Mahler among its directors; a bust in his honor stands in the concert hall. Regular performances take place in the **Musikverein,** I, Dumbastr. 3 (tel. 505 81 90), off Karlspl. (Box office open Sept.-June M-F 9am-7:30pm, Sa 9am-5pm. Write Gesellschaft der Musikfreunde, Bösendorferstr. 12, A-1010 Wien for more information.) The Philharmoniker also play every Staatsoper production. Tickets to Philharmoniker concerts are mostly on a subscription basis, with a few tickets at the Musikverein box office. In summer, there is an **open-air cinema** in the Augarten park (all shows at 9:30pm; 70AS). The Austrian **Filmmuseum,** Augustinerstr. 1 (tel. 53 37 05 40), shows a rotating program of classic and avant-garde films.

Vienna hosts an array of important annual festivals, mostly musical. Look for the tourist office's monthly calendar for dozens of concerts and performances. The **Vienna Festival** (mid-May to mid-June) has a diverse program of exhibitions, plays, and concerts (for info call 58 92 20; fax 589 22 49; http://www.festwochen.or.at/wf). The Staatsoper and Volkstheater host the annual **Jazzfest Wien** during the first weeks of July. For information, contact Jazzfest Wien (tel. 503 56 47; http://jazz.at/). While other big guns take summer siesta, Vienna has held the **Klangbogen** every summer since 1952, featuring excellent concerts across Vienna. One final (free) treat is the **nightly film festival** of famous past concerts, operas, and ballet performances in July and August, shown in the Rathauspl. at dusk.

Nightlife

Pick up a copy of the indispensable **Falter** (28AS). Also, be sure to grab a schedule for the **night-bus** system, which runs all night after the regular public transportation shuts down at midnight. The traditional standby of loud, crowd-loving, and smoky types is the **Bermuda Dreieck** (Triangle), bounded by **Rotenturmstraße** and the area near U-Bahn: "Schwedenpl." Slightly outside of the Ring, the university area (8th and 9th districts) has tables in outdoor courtyards and loud, hip bars. DJs spin wax until 4 or even 6am, and some clubs will keep it going after hours until 11am the next morning. A fact of Viennese nightlife: it starts late.

Another late-night Viennese institution is the wine garden, or *Heuriger*. Marked by a hanging branch of evergreen at the door, *Heurigen* sell young wine (wine from the most recent harvest—typically grown and pressed by the *Heuriger* owner himself). It's ordered by the *Achtel* or (more commonly) the *Viertel* (eighth or quarter liter, respectively). *Heurigen* cluster together in the northern, western, and southern Viennese suburbs, such as **Grinzing, Sievering, Neustift am Walde, Stammersdorf,** and **Neuwaldegg.** One good place to taste the fruit of the vine is **Weingut Heuriger Reinprecht,** XIX, Cobenzlg. 22 (tel. 32 01 47 10). Take U-bahn 4 to "Heiligenstadt" then bus 38A to "Grinzing." It's a fairy-tale stereotype with picnic tables under an ivy-laden trellis, and *Schrammel* musicians strolling from table to table (*viertel* 30AS; open Mar.-Nov. daily 3:30pm-midnight).

> **Benjamin,** I, Salzgries 11-13. Just outside the Triangle area. Go down the steps from Ruprecht's church, left onto Josefs Kai, and left again on Salzgries. Persian rugs hang on the walls; candles shine from wine bottles. Student crowd and great beer—*Budvar* (37AS). Open Su-Th 7pm-2am, F-Sa 7pm-4am.
>
> **Jazzland,** I, Franz-Josefs-Kai 29 (tel. 533 25 75). U-1 or U-4: Schwedenpl. Serious live jazz of all styles and regions, extending to folk and blues—check the schedule first. Cover 50AS. Open Tu-Sa 7pm-2am. Music 9pm-1am.
>
> **Café MAK,** I, Stubenring 3-5, in the museum. Tram 1 or 2: Stubenring. The bar feels like another display case in the museum, but the people are stunning and the furniture is *Bauhaus* one step funkier. Hops with rowdy university students after 10pm. Open Tu-Su 10am-2am (hot food until midnight).
>
> **Zwölf Apostellenkeller,** I, Sonnenfelsg. 3, behind the Stephansdom. To reach this underground tavern, walk into the archway, take a right, go down the long staircase, and discover grottos that date back to 1561. Beer 37AS. *Viertel* of wine from 25AS. Open Aug.-June 4:30pm-midnight.
>
> **Alsergrunder Kulturpark,** IX, Alserstr. 4 (tel. 407 82 14). On the old grounds of a turn-of-the-18th-century hospital, Kulturpark is a favorite outdoor hangout for the Viennese, who flock to the beautifully landscaped grounds for the many bars and outdoor tables. Open Apr.-Oct. daily 4pm-2am. Call about the frequent concerts.
>
> **U-4,** XII, Schönbrunnerstr. 222. U-4: Meidling Hauptstr. A behemoth club with all the trappings, including cage dancers. Th is Gay Heaven Night. Cover 50-100AS. Open daily 11pm-5am.
>
> **Volksgarten,** I, Burgring/Heldenpl. Near the Volksgarten Park. Definite 70s vibe. In good weather, the place rolls back the roof so clubbers can pulse under the stars. Cover 70-100AS. Open Th-Su 10pm-5am.

■ Near Vienna: Eisenstadt

Joseph Haydn once called Eisenstadt "where I wish to live and die." He fulfilled both parts of this wish, thanks to the patronage of the powerful Esterházy family, Hungarian landholders descended from Attila the Hun who retained the composer as part of their provincial court. Their **Schloß Esterházy**, which dominates the old town center on Hauptstr., has magnificently preserved red silk salons and ducal bedchambers on view, but the star sight is the gorgeous wooden-floored **Hadynsaal**, whose perfectly calibrated acoustics make it a mecca for classical musicians. There are plenty of opportunities to hear the hall ring once more with music—*Hadynmatinees* are held biweekly (May-Oct. Tu and F at 11am; 80AS) and rather better *Hadynkonzerte* occur at night (July-Aug. Th at 8pm; May-June and Sept.-Oct. Sa at 7:30pm; 160-250AS). The Esterházy still own part of the castle, mainly to be in easy distance of the excellent local vineyards, which produce a wine often compared to France's Bordeaux.

Trains leave for Eisenstadt from **Wien Meidling** in Vienna (1hr., 2-3 per hr., 69AS) with a possible switch at Wulkaprodersdorf. You can also take a **bus** from Wien Mitte directly to Eisenstadt (1½hr., every hr. 6am-8:45pm, 70AS). The **tourist office** (tel. 673 90; fax 673 91; email tue.info@bnet.at) is sheltered in the right wing of the Schloß Esterházy, and has info about accommodations, vineyards, and music festivals.

■ Salzburg

Although it lies wedged between three wooded peaks and is dotted with church spires, medieval turrets, and resplendent palaces, Salzburg identifies itself not with its spectacular sights, but with the music of Wolfgang Amadeus Mozart. The city's adulation reaches a deafening roar every summer during the Salzburger Festspiele, a five-week festival featuring hundreds of operas, concerts, plays, and open-air performances. And no tour guide will let you forget that Salzburg is also the place to pay homage to *The Sound of Music*'s trilling von Trapp family.

ORIENTATION AND PRACTICAL INFORMATION

Salzburg hugs both sides of the **Salzach River** a few kilometers from the German border. On the west bank is the *Altstadt* (old city) and the heavily touristed pedestrian district; on the east side is the *Neustadt* (new city), with the **Mirabellplatz** at its heart. To reach the downtown area from the *Hauptbahnhof* (main train station), take bus 1, 5, 6, 51, or 55 to "Mirabellpl." or "Mozartsteg." On foot, exit the station, turn left, and follow Rainerstr. until it becomes Mirabellpl. (15min.).

Telephone Code: 0662.

Airport: The cheapest way to fly to Salzburg is to land in Munich and then take the train. Salzburg's own **Flughafen Salzburg** (tel. 858 00) is 4km west of the city center. Several airlines jet each day from such cities as Amsterdam, Paris, and Vienna. Bus 77 ("Bahnhof") runs to the train station every 15-30min. (5:32am-11:00pm).

Trains: Hauptbahnhof, Südtiroler Pl. (tel. 17 17), in the *Neustadt* north of town. To: Budapest (6¼hr., 10 per day, 525AS), Innsbruck (2hr., every 2hr., 350AS), Munich (2hr., every hr., 260AS), Prague via Linz (7hr., 4 per day, 415AS), Venice (6hr., 6 per day, 520AS), and Vienna (3½hr., 31 per day, 410AS).

Buses: The bus depot (tel. (0660) 51 88) is right outside the *Hauptbahnhof*. **BundesBuses** make outstanding connections to the Salzkammergut region.

Local Public Transportation: Extensive bus network. Info at the *Lokalbahnhof* (tel. 87 21 45), next to the station. Buy single-ride tickets from the driver or from vending machines (20AS). A day pass is 40AS from a *Tabak* (tobacco shop).

Bike Rental: At the train station, counter 3 (tel. 88 87 31 63). 70AS per half-day, 90AS per day, 670AS per week. Bike paths wind throughout the city.

Hitchhiking: Hitchers headed to Innsbruck, Munich, or Italy (except Venice) take bus 77 to the German border. Thumbers bound for Vienna or Venice take bus 29 ("Forellenwegsiedlung") to the *Autobahn* entrance at "Schmiedlingerstr." They also take bus 15 ("Bergheim") to the *Autobahn* entrance at "Grüner Wald."

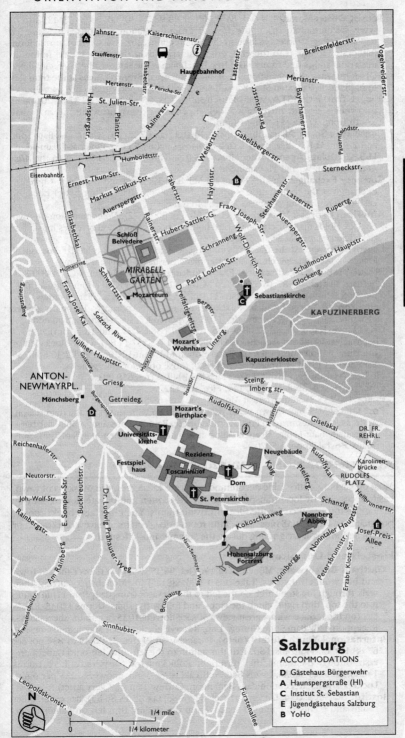

AUSTRIA

Salzburg

ACCOMMODATIONS

D Gästehaus Bürgerwehr
A Haunspergstraße (HI)
C Institut St. Sebastian
E Jügendgästehaus Salzburg
B YoHo

Tourist Office: Mozartpl. 5 (tel. 84 75 68 or 88 98 73 30; fax 88 98 73 42; http://www.salzburginfo.or.at), in the *Altstadt.* From the station, take bus 5, 6, 51, or 55 to "Mozartsteg," and curve around the building into Mozartpl. On foot, turn left on Rainerstr., follow it to the end, cross the river over the Salzach, and follow it upstream. Helps find rooms. The free hotel map is the same as the 10AS city map. Open July-Aug. daily 9am-8pm; Sept.-June 9am-6pm. **Branch offices** at the train station, platform 2a (open M-Sa 8:45am-8pm), and the airport (open daily 9am-9pm).

Budget Travel: ÖKISTA, Wolf-Dietrich-Str. 31 (tel. 88 32 52; fax 88 32 52 20; email info@oekista.co.at; http://www.oekista.co.at/oekista), near the International Youth Hotel. Open M-F 9am-5:30pm.

Consulates: South Africa, Buchenweg 14 (tel./fax 62 20 35). Open M-F 8am-1pm and 2-5pm. **U.K.,** Alter Markt 4 (tel. 84 81 33; fax 84 55 63). Open M-F 9am-noon. **U.S. Consulate Agency,** Alter Markt 1/3 (tel. 84 87 76; fax 84 97 77), in the *Altstadt.* Open M, W, and Th 9am-noon.

Currency Exchange: Banking hours are M-F 8am-12:30pm and 2-4:30pm. Currency exchange at the train station is open daily 7am-9pm. Banks offer better rates for cash than AmEx, but commissions are often higher.

American Express: Mozartpl. 5 (tel. 80 80; fax 80 81 72). No commission on own checks. Holds mail for check- or card-holders, books tours, and reserves music festival tickets. Open M-F 9am-5:30pm, Sa 9am-noon.

Luggage Storage: At the train station. Large lockers 30AS for 2 calendar days, small lockers 20AS. Luggage check 30AS per piece per day. Open 6am-10pm.

Bi-Gay-Lesbian Organizations: Frauenkulturzentrum (Women's Center), Elisabethstr. 11 (tel./fax 87 16 39). Open M 10am-12:30pm. **HOSI** (Homosexual Initiative of Salzburg), Müllner Hauptstr. 11 (tel. 43 59 27), holds regular meetings.

Laundromat: Norge Exquisit Textil Reinigung, Paris-Lodronstr. 16, on the corner of Wolf-Dietrich-Str. Wash and dry 110AS. Open M-F 7:30am-6pm, Sa 8am-noon.

Crisis Lines: Rape, tel. 88 11 00. **AIDS,** tel. 88 14 88 (M, W, and Th 5-7pm).

Pharmacies: Elisabeth-Apotheke, Elisabethstr. 1 (tel. 87 14 84), a few blocks left of the train station. Most pharmacies are open M-F 8am-12:30pm and 2:30-6pm, Sa 8am-noon. Closed pharmacies post lists of those open for emergencies.

Medical Assistance: Hospital, Dr. Franz-Rebirl-Pl. 5 (tel. 658 00).

Emergencies: Ambulance, tel. 144. **Fire,** tel. 122.

Police: tel. 133. Headquarters at Alpenstr. 90 (tel. 63 83).

Post Office: Mail your brown paper packages tied up with strings by the train station. Address *Poste Restante* to Postlagernde Briefe, Bahnhofspostamt, A-5020 Salzburg. Open daily 6am-11pm. **Branch office** at Residenzpl. 9. Open M-F 7am-7pm, Sa 8-10am. **Postal Code:** A-5020.

ACCOMMODATIONS AND CAMPING

Most of Salzburg's affordable accommodations are located on the outskirts of town, easily accessible by local transportation. For *Pensionen* and private homes, start by asking the tourist office for their list of private rooms. The office also books rooms, but charges a fee of 30AS plus 7.2% of the room price. You must have a reservation or plan of action if you are arriving during the summer music festival.

Hostels and Dormitories

Gasthaus Bürgerwehr, Mönchsberg 19c (tel. 84 17 29), towers over the old town and has wonderful views. Take bus 1 ("Maxglan") to "Mönchsbergaufzug" then walk through the stone arch on the left to the elevator (runs daily 9am-11pm). Ride it to the top, turn right, climb the steps, and follow the signs. Dorms 120AS. Breakfast (on the terrace with a great view) 30AS. Showers 10AS per 4min. Sheets 20AS. Reception daily 8am-9pm. Curfew 1am. Reserve ahead. Open May to mid-Oct.

International Youth Hotel (YoHo), Paracelsusstr. 9 (tel. 87 96 49 or 834 60; fax 87 88 10), off Franz-Josef-Str. Exit the station to the left, turn left onto Gabelsbergerstr. through the tunnel, then turn right. Rollicking frat party atmosphere. Dorms 140AS; doubles 360AS; quads 640AS. Breakfast 30-55AS. Showers 10AS per 6min. Lockers 1-10AS. Reception daily 8am-noon. Curfew 1am (not very strict).

Institut St. Sebastian, Linzerg. 41 (tel. 87 13 86; fax 87 13 86 85), has clean, quiet rooms and plenty of common space. From the station, turn left on Rainerstr., go past Mirabellpl., turn left onto Bergstr., and turn left at the end. The hostel is through the arch on the left. Dorms 180AS; singles 340-390AS; doubles 520-680AS; triples 900AS. Breakfast included. Call ahead for 60AS discount if you have your own sheets. Kitchen. Laundry 50AS. Reception 24hr. Call ahead.

Jugendgästehaus Salzburg (HI), Josef-Preis-Allee 18 (tel. 842 67 00; fax 84 11 01), southeast of the *Altstadt*. Take bus 5, 51, or 55 to "Justizgebäude." Outstanding wheelchair facilities. Dorms 164AS; doubles 528AS; quads 856AS; nonmembers add 40AS first night; breakfast and sheets included. Kitchen, laundry (40AS), and lockers. Strangely variable hours between 7am and midnight. Reserve ahead.

Eduard-Heinrich-Haus (HI), Eduard-Heinrich-Str. 2 (tel. 62 59 76; fax 62 79 80). Take bus 51 ("Salzburg Süd") to "Polizeidirektion." Walk down Billrothstr., turn left on the Robert-Stolz-Promenade, then right. Dorms 166AS with breakfast, nonmembers add 40AS. Reception daily 7-9am and 5pm-11pm. Lockout 9am-5pm.

Haunspergstraße (HI), Haunspergstr. 27 (tel. 87 50 30; fax 88 34 77), near the train station. Walk straight out Kaiserschützenstr., which becomes Jahnstr., and take the third left. Dorms 166AS, nonmembers add 40AS first night. Sheets, shower, and breakfast included. Laundry 80AS. Reception daily 7am-2pm and 5pm-midnight, but hostel fills by late afternoon. Curfew midnight. Open July-Aug.

Aigen (HI), Aignerstr. 34 (tel. 62 32 48; fax 232 48.13). From the station, take bus 5 to "Mozartsteg" then bus 49 ("Josef-Käut-Str.") to "Finanzamt," and walk 5min. along the road. It's the yellow building on your right. Large, sporty hostel with nearby bastketball hoop. Dorms 166AS; nonmembers add 40AS. Breakfast, showers, and sheets included. Reception daily 7-9am and 5-11pm. Curfew 11pm.

Hotels and Pensions

Distrust proprietors at the train station who offer rooms. *Pensionen* within the city are scarce and expensive; look on the outskirts for better prices and quality. The bargain rooms on **Kasern Berg** are officially outside the city; the tourist office doesn't list them. To reach this area, take any northbound regional train to "Salzburg-Maria Plain" (4min., every 30min. 6:17am-11:17pm, 17AS, Eurail valid), and walk up the road.

Haus Bankhammer, Moosstr. 77 (tel./fax 83 00 67). Take bus 1 to "Hanuschpl.," then bus 60 to "Marienbad" to reach this grand farmhouse on the moors. Doubles 440-500AS, with bath. Includes a scrumptious breakfast of homemade jam and fresh milk from the family dairy.

Haus Lindner/Christine, Panoramaweg 5/3 (tel. 45 67 73), in Kasern Berg. Gorgeous views from the mountaintop. Families welcome. Doubles 320-400AS; triples 480-600AS; quads 640-800AS. Reservations recommended.

Haus Seigmann, Kasern Berg 66 (tel. 45 00 01). Listen to birds singing from the stone terrace overlooking the Alps. Bright rooms with fluffy comforters. Doubles 340-400AS; triples 510-600AS. Breakfast included.

Germana Kapeller, Kasern Berg 64 (tel. 45 66 71), below Haus Lindner. Enchanting rooms and screenings of *The Sound of Music* upon group demand (guests only). Doubles 340-400AS; triples 510-600AS. Breakfast included. Call ahead.

Haus Ballwein, Moostr. 69 (tel./fax 82 40 29). Take bus 1 to "Hanuschpl.," then bus 60 to "Gsengerweg." Wonderful for hiking or as a relaxing rural reprieve from the bustle of city tourism. 200-240AS. Breakfast included.

Haus Elisabeth, Rauchenbichlerstr. 18 (tel./fax 45 07 03). Bus 51 to "Itzling-Pflanzmann" (last stop) then walk up Rauchenbichlerstr. over the footbridge and continue right along the gravel path. Plush rooms with TVs, balconies, and sweeping views of the city. Singles 300-330AS; doubles 500-550AS.

Haus Kernstock, Karolingerstr. 29 (tel. 82 74 69). Take bus 77 ("Flughafen") to "Karolingerstr.," and follow the signs. Spacious rooms far from the *Altstadt*. Doubles, triples, and quads 220-250AS per person. Breakfast included. Laundry 80AS.

Camping

Camping Stadtblick, Rauchenbichlerstr. 21 (tel. 45 06 52), next to Haus Elisabeth. The site offers a sweeping view of the city. 65AS per person; 15AS per tent; 80AS for a bed in a tent; 25AS per car. Ask about *Let's Go* discounts.

Camping Nord-Sam, Samstr. 22-A (tel. 66 04 94). Bus 33 ("Obergnigl") to "Lang-moosweg." Shady, flower-bedecked campground with a small swimming pool to boot. May to mid-June and Sept. 50AS; mid-June to Aug. 79AS. Laundry 75AS.

FOOD

Blessed with fantastic **beer gardens** and **Konditoreien** (pastry shops), Salzburg begs its guests to eat outdoors. The local specialty is the *Salzburger Nockerl*—a large souf-flé of eggs, sugar, and raspberry filling, baked into three mounds representing the three hills of Salzburg. **Mozartkugeln** (chocolate Mozart balls) are one of Salzburg's favorite confections. Supermarkets include the ubiquitous **SPAR**, e.g., at Mirabellpl. **EuroSPAR** is next to the train station (supermarkets generally open M-F 8am-6pm, Sa 8am-noon). Open-air **markets** fill the Universitätsplatz in the *Altstadt* (open M-F 6am-7pm, Sa 6am-1pm) and Mirabellpl. (open Th 5am-1pm).

Restaurant Zur Bürgerwehr-Einkehr, Mönchsberg 19c. The owners of the Bürger-wehr hostel (see above) run this appealing restaurant at the top of the Mönchs-berg. Take in some of the best views in town as you enjoy huge meals for 68-108AS. Kitchen open May-Oct. daily 10am-8:30pm.

Zum Fidelen Affen, Priesterhausg. 8, off Linzerg. Phenomenal food in a dark-wood, pleasantly crowded pub. Drinks 30AS. Spinach *Spätzle* (potato-based noodles) 88AS. Full meal of salad and main course 87-110AS. Open M-Sa 5pm-midnight.

Der Wilde Mann, Getreideg. 20, in the passage. Huge portions of *Wiener Schnitzel*, potatoes, and *Stiegl Bier* for the wild man (or woman) in all of us. Less touristed than nearby bistros. Main courses 75-145AS. Open M-Sa 11am-9pm.

Vegy, Schwarzstr. 21. Relaxing vegetarian restaurant with a plethora of filling options. Have a seat at a table or buy a quick meal to go. Daily *menu* with soup, coffee, and dessert 87AS. Open M-F 10:30am-6pm.

University Mensa (tel. 844 96 09), across from Sigmund Haffnerg. 16 and through the iron fence. A good deal for penny-pinchers. 2 hot entrees—one for carnivores (49AS) and one for herbivores (37AS). Desserts and drinks not included. Valid stu-dent ID required (ISICs accepted). Open M-Th 9am-4pm, F 9am-3pm. Get there early—ravenous students sometimes deplete the food supply.

Cafe im Kunstlerhaus, Hellbrunnerstr. 3. Low-key cafe popular with students, art-ists, and their fans. Wide variety of drinks—treat yourself. Local bands play Tuesday and Thursday nights. Saturday is lesbian night. Open M-F 11am-11pm.

SIGHTS

Salzburg sprang up under the protective watch of the hilltop fortress **Hohensalzburg,** built atop the Mönchsberg between 1077 and 1681 by the ruling archbishops. *(Open daily July-Sept. 8am-7pm; Nov.-Mar. 9am-5pm; Apr.-June 9am-6pm. 25AS. Castle tours in English and German July-Aug. daily 9:30am-5:30pm; Apr.-June and Sept.-Oct. 9:30am-5pm; Nov.-Mar. 10am-4:30pm. 35AS. Tour, museum, and fortress 70AS.)* Tours wind through staterooms, torture chambers, and the watchtower. The **Rainer Museum,** inside the fortress, dis-plays medieval weapons and instruments of torture. Walk up the hill to the fortress, or take the overpriced cable car from Festungsg. (every 10min., round-trip 69AS).

At the bottom of the Festungsbahn is **Kapitelplatz,** housing a giant chess grid and horse-bath fountain. If you're facing the mountain, the entrance to **St. Peter's Monas-tery** is at the back right corner, through the cemetery. The cemetery, **Petersfriedhof,** is one of the most peaceful places in Salzburg and is best known as the spot where Liesl's Nazi boyfriend Rolf blew the whistle on the von Trapp family in *The Sound of Music. (Open daily Apr.-Sept. 6:30am-7pm; Oct.-Mar. 6:30am-6pm.)* On the mountain side of the cemetery is the entrance to the **Katakomben** (catacombs), where Christians allegedly worshiped as early as 250. *(Open in summer Tu-Th 10:30am-4pm, F-Su until 5pm; off-season W-Su 10:30am-3:30pm.)* Past the arch near the catacombs stands **St. Peter's Church,** once a Romanesque basilica, which received a Rococo facelift in the 18th century. *(Open daily 9am-12:15pm and 2:30-6:30pm.)*

The distinctive dome of the **Universitätskirche** (University Church) stands watch over the Universitätspl., near the daily farmer's market. Generally considered Fischer von Erlach's masterpiece, this massive chapel is one of the largest Baroque chapels on the continent. From the Universitätsplatz, several passages lead through tiny courtyards filled with geraniums and ivy. They eventually give way to the stampede of **Getreidegasse**, a labyrinth of winding pathways and well-preserved facades dating from the 17th and 18th centuries.

Wolfgang Amadeus Mozart was unleashed upon the world from what is now called **Mozart's Geburtshaus** (birthplace), at Getreideg. 9. The house exhibits the boy wonder's first viola, first violin, some pictures, letters, and dioramas of stage sets for his operas. *(Open daily July-Aug. 9am-6:30pm; Sept.-June 9am-5:30pm; in summer show up before 11am to beat the crowds. 70AS, students and seniors 55AS.)* Turn right at the *Alter Markt* and venture down to Residenzpl. to find the 35-bell **Glockenspiel** which rings to one of Mozart's tunes at 7am, 11am, and 6pm, and Archbishop Wolf Dietrich's palace, the **Residenz,** featuring Baroque staterooms and a gallery emphasizing Baroque painting, especially the work of Poussin. *(Tours in English and German May-Oct. and Dec. daily every 30min. 10am-4:30pm; Jan.-Apr. and Nov. M-F every hr. 10am-4:30pm. 70AS, students 55AS. Gallery open Apr.-Sept. daily 10am-5pm; Oct.-Mar. Th-Tu 10am-5pm. 50AS, students 34AS.)* Mozart was christened in the adjacent Baroque **Dom** in 1756 and later worked there as *Konzertmeister* and court organist. The connecting **Dom Museum** holds the **Kunst- und Wunderkammer** (art and miracles chamber), which includes conch shells, mineral formations, and a two-foot whale's tooth. *(Open mid-May to mid-Oct. M-Sa 10am-5pm, Su 1-6pm. 70AS, students 25AS.)*

Cross the river on the Staatsbrücke into the *Neustadt;* it's the only bridge from the *Altstadt* over the Salzach open to motorized traffic. In the *Neustadt,* the bridge opens into **Linzergasse,** an enchanting medieval street. Ascend the stairs from under the stone arch on the right side of Linzerg. 14 to the **Kapuzinerkloster** (Capuchin Monastery). Legend has it that the resident monks clad in coffee-colored robes with white hoods inspired the world's first cup of *cappuccino.* Turning onto Dreifaltigkeitg. will bring you to Makartpl. and Mozart's **Wohnhaus** (residence). It suffered major damage in World War II air raids but was renovated and reopened on Mozart's 240th birthday, January 27, 1996. Continue down this street to Mirabellpl. to discover the marvelous 17th-century **Schloß Mirabell.** Next to the palace, the manicured **Mirabellgarten** includes extravagant rose beds, labyrinths of shrubs, and 15 grotesque marble likenesses of Wolf Dietrich's court jesters. Students from nearby Mozarteum often perform here, and Maria made this one of her stops in *The Sound of Music* as the children danced around and sang "do-re-mi." **Salzburg Sightseeing Tours** (tel. 88 16 16; fax 87 87 76) traces the movie through the city. Tours leave from Mirabellpl. daily at 9:30am and 2pm (350AS, 315AS with student ID or *Let's Go*). **Stiegl Brauwelt,** Bauhausstr. 1, is Salzburg's own beer museum, complete with a photo essay entitled "30 Ways to Open a Beer Bottle." Take bus 1 to "Brauhaus." *(Open W-Su 10am-5pm, last entrance 4pm. 75AS, students 50AS, children 40AS; includes 2 glasses of beer.)*

ENTERTAINMENT

The Music Festivals

The renowned **Salzburger Festspiele** run from late July to the beginning of September. During the festivities, almost every public space is overrun with operas, dramas, films, and concerts. The complete program of events, which lists all important concert locations and dates, is printed a year in advance (10AS) and is available from any tourist office. For the best seats, requests must be made in person or by mail months in advance. Write with orders to **Kartenbüro der Salzburger Festspiele,** Postfach 140, A-5010 Salzburg (tel. 84 45 01; fax 804 57 60; email info@salzb-fest.co.at; http://www.salzb-fest.co.at/salzb-fest), by early January. Cheap tickets (100-300AS) are gobbled up quickly; don't be surprised if you're offered tickets for 1000AS. Those under 26 can try writing eight months in advance to Direktion der Salzburger Festspiele, attn: Carl-Philip von Maldeghem, Hofstallg. 1, A-5020 Salzburg. American Express sells marked-up cheap tickets. If you have no luck, or can't afford what's offered, try to take advantage of the **Fest zur Eröffungsfest** (Opening Day Festival), when con-

AUSTRIA

certs, shows, and films are either very cheap or free. Tickets for these events are available on a first-come, first-serve basis the week of the opening.

Even when the *Festspiele* are not in full force, many other concerts and shows are staged throughout the city. The **Mozarteum** (Music School; tel. 87 31 54; fax 87 44 54) performs a number of concerts on a rotating schedule (available at the tourist office). For a bit more money, check out the **Mozart Serendaden** (Mozart's Serenades) in the Gothic Hall on Getreideg. These are evening concerts where Mozart favorites are performed with the musicians dressed in traditional Mozart-era garb; an intermission buffet is also included. For info and tickets, call or write Konzertdirektion Nerat, A-5020 Salzburg, Lieferinger Hauptstr. 136 (tel. 43 68 70; fax 43 69 70). For a particularly enchanting atmosphere, attend one of the nightly **Festungskonzerte** (Fortress Concerts; 590AS). For more info, contact Festungkonzerte Anton-Adlgasserweg 22, A-5020 Salzburg (tel. 82 58 58; fax 82 58 59; http:// alpin.or.at/festungskonzerte). The Mirabellgarten hosts various **outdoor performances** throughout the summer, including concerts, folk-singing, and dancing. The tourist office has info, but strolling through in the evening might be just as effective.

Beer Gardens and Bars

Salzburg prides itself on the charm of its beer gardens, many of which serve generous portions of food. They do, however, tend to close early. For those who want to tipple later, simply head to one of the more conventional bars.

Augustiner Bräu, Augustinerg. 4. From the *Altstadt,* pick up the footpath at Hanuschpl. and follow the river downstream. Go left up the flight of stairs past the Riverside Cafe, cross Müllner Hauptstr., continue up the hill, and take the first left. A Salzburg legend. Great beer is poured into massive steins from even more massive wooden kegs. Concession stands inside calm grumbling stomachs. Liters 56AS, half-liters 28AS. Open M-F 3-11pm, Sa-Su 2:30-11pm.

Sternbräu, Getreideg. 34. Located in the *Altstadt,* this place has two beer gardens, a restaurant, and a self-service snack bar. Get there by ducking into any number of passages at the end of Getreideg. Open daily 9am-midnight.

Pub Passage, Rudolfskai 22-26, under the Radisson Hotel by Mozartsteg bridge. A shopping promenade for youthful clubbing. All of these bars, located in the "mall" corridors, are open daily until 2-4am. Each has its own gimmick: **Tom's Bierklinik** brags beers from all over; **The Black Lemon** hosts Latino night on Wednesdays; **Bräu zum Frommen Hell** burns with 80s music; and **Hell** is a TV sports bar.

Vis à Vis, Rudolfskai 24. A swish lounge cut in the shape of an arched stone tunnel with plush, paisley armchairs, and smoking-room couches. Mixed gay and straight crowd. Open Su-Th 8pm-4am, F-Sa 8pm-5am.

2 Stein, Giselakai 9. A liquor bar with zebra print barstools catering primarily to a gay and lesbian scene. Open daily 5pm-4am.

Felsenkeller, in a cave in Toscaninihof next to the Festspielhaus. Card-playing locals and Austrian cabaret music complete the unusual mood. Open Su-F 3:30pm-midnight, Sa 10am-midnight.

■ Near Salzburg: Lustschloß Hellbrunn

Just south of Salzburg lies the unforgettable **Lustschloß Hellbrunn** (tel. 820 00 30; fax 82 03 72 31), a one-time pleasure dome for Wolf Dietrich's nephew, the Archbishop Markus Sittikus. The sprawling estate includes fish ponds, gardens, a gazebo, and tree-lined footpaths. The neighboring **Wasserspiele** (water fountains) are perennial favorites; Markus amused himself with elaborate water-powered figurines and a booby-trapped table which spouted water on drunken guests. (Open July-Aug. daily 9am-10pm; May-June and Sept. 9am-5:30pm; Apr. and Oct. 9am-4:30pm. Castle tour 30AS, students 20AS. Wasserspiele tour 70AS, 35AS. Tours of both 90AS, 45AS.) Bus 55 ("Untersberg") runs south to the **Untersberg peak,** where Charlemagne supposedly rests underground and prepares to return and reign over Europe. A **cable car** glides over Salzburg to the summit. (July-Sept. Th-Tu 8:30am-5:30pm, W until 8pm; Mar.-June and Oct. daily 9am-5pm; Dec.-Feb. daily 10am-4pm. Round-trip 215AS.)

■ Salzkammergut

East of Salzburg, the landscape swells into towering mountains interspersed with deep lakes. The region is remarkably accessible, with 2000km of footpaths, 12 cable-cars and chairlifts, and dozens of hostels.

The Vienna-Salzburg **rail** line skirts the northern edge of the Salzkammergut. Most **bus** routes run four to 12 times per day, and since the mountainous area is barren of rail tracks, buses are the most efficient method travel through the lake region. Dial 167 from Salzburg for complete schedule information. **Hitchers** from Salzburg reportedly take bus 29 to Gnigl and come into the Salzkammergut at Bad Ischl. The lake district is generally known as one of the rare Austrian regions in which hitchhikers make good time. Nevertheless, it's safer and more enjoyable to **bike** around the lake and through the mountain passes; most train stations in the region rent bikes. On the lakes themselves, reasonably priced **ferries** connect major towns. The **Wolfgangsee** line is operated by the Austrian railroad, so railpass holders enjoy free passage; other lines offer discounts to those with railpasses.

Hostels abound, though you can often find far superior rooms in private homes and *Pensionen* at just slightly higher prices. *"Zimmer Frei"* signs peek out from virtually every house. **Campgrounds** dot the region, but many are trailer-oriented; away from large towns, some travelers camp discreetly almost anywhere without trouble. Hikers can capitalize on dozens of **cable cars** in the area to gain altitude before setting out on their own, and almost every community has a local trail map posted in a public area or available at the tourist office.

Hallstatt In a valley surrounded on all sides by the sheer rocky cliffs of the Dachstein mountains, **Hallstatt** is quite simply, in the words of Alex V. Humboldt, "the most beautiful lakeside village in the world." In the 19th century, Hallstatt was the site of one of the largest Iron Age archeological finds in history, and the **Prähistorisches Museum** (Prehistoric Museum), across from the tourist office, displays artifacts unearthed in the region (open May-Sept. daily 10am-6pm; 50AS, students 25AS). The **Heimatmuseum** around the corner has exhibits on daily life in historic Hallstatt (same hours as Prähistorisches Museum). Depending on your particular brand of psychosis, a visit to St. Michael's Chapel at the **Pfarrkirche** can be poignant, intrusive, or fascinating; next to the chapel you can enter the parish "charnel house," a bizarre repository for skeletons. (Open May-Sept. daily 10am-5pm; off-season call (06134) 82 79 for an appointment. 10AS.) The 2500-year-old **Salzbergwerke** is the oldest saltworks in the world. (Open June to mid-Sept. 9:30am-4:30pm; Apr.-May and mid-Sept. to Oct. 9:30am-3pm. 135AS, students 60AS.) To reach the mines, climb the steep path near the Pfarrkirche to the top (1hr.), or follow the black signs with the yellow eyes to the train station and take the **Salzbergbahn.** (In service June to mid-Sept. 9am-6pm; Apr.-May and mid-Sept. to Oct. 9am-4:30pm. 60AS, round-trip 97AS.) Hallstatt is also the starting point for some of the most spectacular **hiking** trails in the region. The tourist office sells a 70AS guide which details over 35 additional trails, including the **Echental** hike and the **Glacier Gardens** hike, through valleys carved out by glaciers.

To reach Hallstatt from Salzburg, **buses** are the best option; you'll have to transfer in Bad Ischl and Gosamühle (130AS). The **train station** lies on the opposite bank of the lake from downtown; when you arrive, take the ferry into town (ferry 23AS; train from Salzburg via Attnang-Puchheim 210AS). The **tourist office,** Seestr. 169 (tel. (06134) 82 08; fax 83 52), in the Kultur und Kongresshaus, finds cheap rooms for no fee. (Open July-Aug. M-F 8:30am-6pm, Sa 10am-6pm, Su 10am-2pm; Sept.-June M-F 9am-noon and 2-5pm.) The **youth hostel,** Salzbergstr. 50, is limited to groups, but **Gasthaus zur Mühle,** Kirchenweg 36 (tel. (06134) 8318), is a quasi-hostel with lots of backpackers. (110AS. Showers and lockers included. Sheets 35AS. Reception 8am-2pm and 4-10pm.) **Frühstuckspension Sarstein,** Gosaumühlstr. 83 (tel. (06134) 82 17), offers the most charming accommodations in town. From the tourist office, head toward the ferry dock, and continue along the road nearest the lake past the Pfarrkircher steps (190-300AS; breakfast included).

AUSTRIA

Dachstein Ice Caves At the other end of the lake in Obertraun, the **Dachstein Ice Caves** give eloquent testimony to the geological hyperactivity that forged the region's natural beauty. (Open May to mid-Oct. 9am-5pm. Admission to either Giant Ice Cave or Mammoth Cave 90AS; combined "Gargantuan Experience" 130AS.) From Hallstatt, take the bus to Obertraun (22AS) and ride the Dachstein cable car up 1350m to Schönbergalm (runs 9am-5pm, round-trip 168AS). For more information on the caves, call (06131) 362.

■ Hohe Tauern National Park

The enormous **Hohe Tauern range** in the Austrian Central Alps encompasses 246 glaciers and 304 mountains over 3000m. The national park, the largest in all of Europe, encloses 29 towns with a total of 60,000 residents in Southern Austria. The **Glocknergruppe,** in the heart of the park, boasts the highest of the Hohe Tauern peaks (3797m) and dazzling glaciers. The **Krimmler Wasserfälle** is in the far west. For general information about the park, contact **Nationalparkverwaltung Hohe Tauern,** 5741 Neukirchen Nr. 306, Austria (tel. (06565) 655 80; fax 65 58 18). Heavy snowfall forces many roads to close from November to April.

More than a million visitors annually brave the hairpin-fraught **Großglockner Straße,** one of Austria's most popular attractions, which runs through the park from north to south. Skirting the country's loftiest mountains, Bundesstr. 107 (its less catchy moniker) winds for 50km amid silent Alpine valleys, meadows of (small and white, clean and bright) edelweiss, tumbling waterfalls, and a staggering glacier. The trip up to Kaiser-Franz-Josefs-Höhe (the midway point of the Großglockner Str.) and Edelweißspitze (the highest point) takes you from the flora and fauna of Austria into Arctic-like environments. Although tours generally run from **Zell am See** or **Lienz** to the park, the highway is officially only the 6.4km stretch from **Bruck an der Groß-glockner** to **Heiligenblut.** Coming from Zell am See, you'll pass the **Alpine Nature Exhibit** on the way up to Kaiser-Franz-Josefs-Höhe (open daily 9am-5pm; free). From Kaiser-Franz-Josefs-Höhe, you can gaze on Austria's highest peak, the **Großglockner** (3797m), and ride the **Gletscherbahn** funicular to Austria's longest glacier, the **Pasterze** (mid-May to Oct., every hr., round-trip 98AS). The **Gamsgrube Nature Trail** is a spectacular path (1½hr.) along the glacier, culminating in the roaring Wasserfall-winkel (2548m). Beware of quicksand, unique to this part of the Alps.

BundesBus offers daily return trips from Zell am See or Lienz to Kaiser-Franz-Josefs-Höhe. From the **north,** bus 3064 leaves from Zell am See's main bus station behind the post office, swinging by the stop directly across from the train station (145AS). For accommodations, see **Zell am See,** below, or contact the youth hostel in **Heiligenblut** (tel./fax (04824) 22 59). From the **south,** the odyssey begins in Lienz (120AS). For details, check *Der BundesBus ist WanderFreundlich,* available at the bus stations in Lienz and Zell am See and the tourist offices in Lienz and Heiligenblut.

■ Zell am See

Surrounded by a ring of snow-capped mountains that collapse into a broad, turquoise lake, Zell am See is a year-round resort for northern European tourists. **Boat tours** around the lake depart and return to the Zell Esplanade, off Salzmannstr. (40min., 8 per day, 10am-5:30pm, 80AS). You can conquer the local mountains on one of the town's five **cable cars.** The **Zeller Bergbahn** (780-1335m) is right in the center of town at the intersection of Schmittenstr. and Garternstr. (open June to late Sept. daily 9am-5pm; round-trip 140AS). Every winter, Zell am See is transformed into an Alpine ski resort. The **Zell/Kaprun Ski Pass** covers both Zell am See and nearby Kaprun (2 days 710-780AS, students 640-700AS). The Zell area also offers many opportunities to hike—pick up the *Three Panorama Round Trips of the Schmittenhöhe* or the *Wanderplan* at any cable-car station for suggestions.

Zell am See can be reached by **train** from Salzburg (1¾hr., 140AS) and Innsbruck (2hr., 240AS). The **tourist office,** Brucker Bundesstr. 1 (tel. (06542) 770) helps ferret out vacancies in local accommodations. (Open July to mid-Sept. and mid-Dec. to Mar. M-F 8am-6pm, Sa 8am-noon and 4-6pm, Su 10am-noon. Shorter hours off-season.) **Haus der Jugend (HI),** Seespitzstr. 13 (tel. (06542) 571 85; fax 571 854), has large rooms and lake-side terraces (140-165AS; sheets 25AS; reception 7-9am and 4-10pm). Lakefront **Camping Seecamp,** Thumerbacherstr. 34 (tel. (06542) 21 15) offers a restaurant, cafe, and even a small store (87AS per person, tents 45AS; guest tax 9AS; reception 7am-noon and 2-10pm). For food, try **Fischrestaurant "Moby Dick,"** Kreuzg. 16, the great white hope—with fries (open M-F 9am-6pm, Sa 8am-1pm).

■ Kitzbühel

Kitzbühel welcomes tourists with glitzy casinos and countless pubs, yet few visitors remain at ground level long enough to enjoy them. The mountains surrounding the city attract skiers and hikers of all stripes.

SIGHTS AND ENTERTAINMENT One of the best in the world, the Kitzbühel **ski area** challenges with its ethereal network of lifts, runs, and trails. In January, the city hosts the true *crème de la crème* during the **Hahnenkamm Ski Competition,** part of the annual World Cup (entry tickets available at the gate). For amateurs, a one-day ski pass (385-410AS) grants passage on 64 lifts and connecting shuttle buses. Passes may be purchased at any of the lifts or the Kurhaus Aquarena. The **Kitzbüheler Alpen Ski Pass** gives access to 260 lifts for six—not necessarily consecutive—days (1990AS, children 995AS). **Ski rental** is available from virtually any sports shop in the area; try **Kitzsport Schlechter,** Jochbergerstr. 7. Downhill equipment runs 170-500AS per day, and snowboards cost 180-350AS per day.

An extensive network of 70 **hiking trails** snakes up the mountains surrounding the city. The tourist office stocks English maps and organizes excellent hiking excursions for guest-card holders. Most of the trails are accessible by bus from the Hahnenkamm parking lot (1 per hr., 8am-5:10pm, 26AS, with guest card 20AS); after ski season, ride the **Hahnenkammbahn** to reach some of the loftier paths (daily 8am-5:30pm; 160AS, with guest card 140AS) or climb up to the trails yourself (about 2hr.). For budding botanists, the **Kitzbüheler Hornbahn** lift ascends to the **Alpenblumengarten,** where 120 different types of Alpine flowers blossom each spring (cable car 80AS per section; garden open late May to mid-Oct.). Before setting out for **mountain biking,** buy a booklet detailing the bike paths at the tourist office (54AS). If you need a bike, rent one at **Stanger Radsport,** Josef-Pirchlstr. 42 (tel. (05356) 25 49; 250AS per day).

PRACTICAL INFO, ACCOMMODATIONS, AND FOOD Most **phone numbers** in Kitzbühel have added a "6" to the beginning of the local number. Kitzbühel has two **train stations** (info tel. (05356) 64 05 53 85), one at each side of the "U" formed by the rail tracks. Direct connections are available to Innsbruck (1hr., 134AS), Salzburg (2½hr., 240AS), Vienna (6hr., 580AS), and other cities. The **tourist office,** Hinterstadt 18 (tel. (05356) 62 15 50 or 622 72; fax 623 07), offers tours and information; use the free telephone at the electronic accommodations board outside to secure a room. (Open July-Sept. and mid-Dec. to late Apr. M-F 8:30am-6:30pm, Sa 8:30am-noon and 4-6pm, Su 10am-noon and 4-6pm; Oct. to mid-Dec. and late Apr. to June M-F 8:30am-12:30pm and 2:30-6pm.) Kitzbühel has almost as many guest beds as inhabitants, but you'll pay for the convenience. Wherever you stay, be sure to ask for your **guest card** upon registration—it entitles you to discounts on many attractions. **Pension Hörl,** Josef-Pirchlstr. 60 (tel. (05356) 631 44), is quiet and unassuming. From the main train station, take a left after Hotel Kaiser (180-260AS per person; breakfast included; add 40AS in winter). To get to **Camping Schwarzsee,** Reitherstr. 24 (tel. (05356) 628 06; fax 644 79 30), take the train to "Schwarzsee" and walk toward the lake (88AS per person; 95AS per tent; 185-195AS per caravan; guest tax 6AS). Grocery shoppers can load up at the **SPAR Markt,** Bichlstr. 22, on the corner of Ehrenbachg. and Bichlstr. (open M-F 8am-6:30pm, Sa 7:30am-1pm).

■ Innsbruck

In 1964 and 1976 the Winter Olympics were held in Innsbruck, bringing international renown to the beautiful mountain city. The landscape is far more immediate here than in nearby Salzburg. Massive, snow-capped peaks seem to be advancing down cobblestoned streets at every turn. The tiny *Altstadt* is peppered with intricate facades and Baroque remnants of the Habsburg stronghold that emerged here under Emperor Maximilian I.

ORIENTATION AND PRACTICAL INFORMATION

Lying along the eastern bank of the **Inn River,** Innsbruck is very walkable. **Maria-Theresien-Straße,** the main thoroughfare, offers excellent mountain views. To reach the **Altstadt** from the main train station, turn right and walk until you reach Museumstr., then turn left and walk for about 10 minutes. You can also take tram 3 or 6, or city bus A, F, or K from the station to "Maria-Theresien-Str." Continue down Museumstr. and toward the river (curving to the left onto Burggraben, across Maria-Theresien-Str., and onto Marktgraben) to reach the **University district.**

> **Telephone Code:** 0512.
> **Trains: Hauptbahnhof,** on Südtirolerpl. (tel. 17 17; open 7:30am-7:30pm). Daily trains to Berlin (10hr.), Munich (2hr.), Paris (11hr.), Rome (8hr.), Salzburg (2hr.), Vienna (5¼hr.), and Zurich (4hr.).
> **Buses:** To get to the rest of Tirol, take a **Bundesbus** from the station on Sterzingerstr., next to the *Hauptbahnhof* and to the left of the main station.
> **Bike Rental:** At the main train station (tel. 503 53 95). 150-200AS per day, 96-160AS with Eurailpass or train ticket from that day. Open Apr. to early Nov. Su-F 7am-6:30pm, Sa 7am-6pm.
> **Ski Rental: Skischule Innsbruck,** Leopoldstr. 4 (tel. 58 17 42). 270AS including insurance.
> **Innsbruck Information Office,** Burggraben 3 (tel. 598 50; fax 598 07; email info@innsbruck.tub.co.at; http://tiscover.com/innsbruck), on the 3rd floor. Official and nonprofit, with tons of brochures and a helpful staff. Open M-F 8am-6pm, Sa 8am-noon. **Tirol Information Office** (tel. 56 18 82) gives Tirol info.
> **Currency Exchange: Innsbruck Information** tourist office, open M-Sa 8am-6:40pm, Su 9am-5:40pm. **Banks** generally open M-F 8am-noon and 2:30-4pm.
> **American Express:** Brixnerstr. 3 (tel. 58 24 91). Go right from train station, then first left. Mail held; all bank services. Open M-F 9am-5:30pm, Sa 9am-noon.
> **Emergencies: Ambulance,** tel. 142 or 144. **Fire,** tel. 122. **Mountain Rescue,** tel. 140.
> **Police:** tel. 133. Headquarters at Kaiserjägerstr. 8 (tel. 590 00).
> **Medical Assistance: University Hospital,** Anichstr. 35 (tel. 50 40).
> **Post Office:** Maximilianstr. 2 (tel. 500). Open 24hr. Branch next to train station. Open M-F 7am-8pm, Sa 8am-6pm. **Postal Code:** A-6010.
> **Telephones:** In post office or train station near info office.

ACCOMMODATIONS, CAMPING, AND FOOD

Beds are scarce in June—only two hostels are open. In July and August, university housing opens up to travelers, easing the crunch; try **Technikerhaus,** Fischnalerstr. 26 (tel. 28 21 10) or **Internationales Studentenhaus,** Recheng. 7 (tel. 50 15 92).

> **Hostel Torsten Arneus-Schwedenhaus (HI),** Rennweg 17b (tel. 585 814), along the river. Take bus C from the station to "Handelsakademie." Front-yard view of the river. 120AS, shower included. Breakfast 45AS. Reception 7-10am and 5-10:30pm. Lockout 9am-5pm. Curfew 10:30pm. Open July-Aug. Reserve ahead.

Jugendherberge Innsbruck (HI), Reichenauerstr. 147 (tel. 34 61 79 or 34 61 80). From the train station take bus R to "König-Laurin Str.," and then bus O to "Jugendherberge." Slick, corporate building. 146-176AS; nonmembers add 40AS. Price drops 30AS after one night. Breakfast and sheets included. Reception 7am-12:30pm and 5-10pm. Curfew 11pm. Phone reservations honored until 5pm.

Haus Wolf, Dorfstr. 48 (tel. 54 86 73), in the suburb of Mutters. Take the Stubaitalbahn tram to "Birchfeld" and walk down Dorfstr. in the direction the tram continues. Let proprietor Titti Wolf spoil you with comfy beds and great views. Singles, doubles, and triples 190AS per person. Breakfast and 7min. shower included.

Haus Kaltenberger, Schulg. 15 (tel. 54 85 76), just down the road from Haus Wolf in Mutters. Take the Stubaitalbahn to "Mutters," then walk towards the church, turn right on Dorfstr., and take the first left. Gorgeous mountain view. Doubles 360-400AS. Breakfast and shower included.

Jugenherberge St. Nikolaus (HI), Innstr. 95 (tel. 28 65 15; fax 28 65 15 14). From the train station take bus K to "Schmelzergasse" and walk across the street. Come for the happening scene, not the facilities. 145-160AS; doubles 390AS. **Internet access.** Reception 8-10am and 5-8pm. Get a key if you're out past 11pm.

Camping Innsbruck Kranebitten, Kranebitter Allee 214 (tel. 28 41 80). From train station, bus LK: "Klammstr." After hours, find a site and check in the next morning. 60AS per person, 40AS per tent, 40AS per car. Guest tax 6AS. Reception 8am-noon.

Rather than gawk at the overpriced delis and *Konditoreien* on Maria-Theresien-Str., cross the river to **Innstraße** to find a myriad of ethnic restaurants, cheap *Schnitzel Stuben,* and Turkish grocers. There's a farmer's **market** in the *Markthalle* next to the river on the corner of Innrain and Marktgraben (open M-F 7am-6:30pm, Sa 7am-1pm). Indulge in tasty veggie fare at **Philippine Vegetarische Küche,** Müllerstr. 9, at Lieberstr. one block from the post office (main dishes 82-168AS; specials 45-98AS; open M-Sa 10am-11pm). **Gasthof Weißes Lamm,** Mariahilfstr. 12, serves up Tirolian fare and is popular with the locals. (Soup, entree, and salad 80-115AS. Open M-W and F-Su 11:30am-2pm and 6-10pm.) **University Mensa,** Herzog-Siegmund-Ufer 15, on the 2nd floor of the university at Blasius-Hueber-Str., near the bridge, is a student cafeteria open to public (soup and main course 30-54AS). **Salute Pizza,** Innrain 35, is a popular student hangout (pizza 35-100AS; open daily 11am-midnight). Both **Churrasco la Mamma,** Innrain 2, and **Crocodiles,** Maria-Theresien-Str. 49, offer brick-oven pizza.

SIGHTS AND ENTERTAINMENT

Beneath 2657 gilded shingles, the **Goldenes Dachl** (Golden Roof) on Herzog-Friedrich-Str. is the center of the *Altstadt.* Inside the building, the new **Maximilianeum** museum commemorates Innsbruck's favorite ruler. (Open May-Sept. daily 10am-6pm; Oct.-Apr. Tu-Su 10am-12:30pm and 2-5pm. 50AS, students 20AS.) Many of the buildings surrounding the Goldenes Dachl are splendid 15th- and 16th-century structures. At Rennweg and Hofg. stand the **Hofburg** (Imperial Palace), **Hofkirche** (Imperial Church), and **Hofgarten** (take a guess). Built between the 16th and 18th centuries, the Hofburg brims with dynastic trappings (open daily 9am-5pm; last entrance 4:30pm; 55AS, students 35AS). The Hofkirche holds an intricate sarcophagus decorated with scenes from Maximilian I's life, as well as 28 mammoth bronze statues guarding the tomb. The punchline: the monument was never completed to Maxi's wishes, and he was buried near Vienna instead (open July-Aug. daily 9am-5:30pm; Sept.-June closes 5pm; 20AS, students 14AS). A special ticket (50AS) will also admit you to the collection of the **Tiroler Volkskunstmuseum,** which provides a thorough introduction to Tirolean culture (museum alone 40AS, students 25AS).

Backtrack a bit, cross the covered bridge over the Inn, and follow signs up to the **Alpenzoo,** with every vertebrate species indigenous to the Alps (zoo open daily in summer 9am-6pm; off-season 9am-5pm; 70AS, students 35AS). Descend on the network of trails that weave across the hillside, or catch tram 1 or 4 or bus C, D, or E to "Hungerbergbahn" and take the cable car up the mountain.

Outside the city proper, Archduke Ferdinand of Tirol left behind piles of 16th-century armor and artwork (including pieces by Velazquez and Titian) at **Schloß**

Ambras, one of the most beautiful Renaissance castles in Austria. Inside, a portrait gallery depicts European dynasties from the 14th to the 19th centuries. To reach the palace, take streetcar 6 ("Igls") to "Schloß Ambras," and follow the signs (open W-M 10am-5pm; 60AS, students 30AS). Also outside the city but well worth seeing is the **Swarovski Kristallwelten,** a multi-media crystal experience with a veneer of New-Age pretension. Take bus 4125 from the bus station to Waltens (open daily 9am-6pm; 75AS, students 65AS). On the hill overlooking the city perches the **Olympische Schischanze** (Olympic Ski Jump). Farther down the motorway, spanning the Sil River, is the tallest bridge on the continent, the **Europabrücke.**

A **Club Innsbruck** membership, available if you register at any central-Innsbruck accommodation, provides you with discounts on museums, free bike tours, **ski bus service,** and the option to join the club's fine **hiking** program (June-Sept.). Hikers meet in front of the Congress Center at 8:30am and return from the mountain range by 5pm. In winter, Club members hop on the complimentary ski shuttle (schedules at the tourist office) to any suburban cable car. The comprehensive **Innsbruck Glacier Ski Pass** to all 53 lifts in the region costs 1260AS for three days or 2270AS for six days (with Club membership 1040AS or 1880AS). Innsbruck-Information and its train station branch offer the most reliable daily **glacier ski packages:** 660AS in summer (including bus, lift, and ski rental) and 540AS in winter. The tourist offices also carry mountain guide booklets for hikers and plenty of info on skiing. In August, Innsbruck hosts the **Festival of Early Music,** with concerts by some of the world's leading soloists on period instruments at the Schloß Ambras, and organ recitals on the Hofkirche's 16th-century organ (for tickets call 53 56 21; fax 53 56 43).

Though most visitors collapse into bed after a full day of Alpine adventure, there is still enough action to keep a few party-goers from their pillows. Much of the lively nightlife revolves around the **university quarter. Hofgarten Cafe,** hidden inside the Hofgarten park, draws students and professionals alike. A series of tents shelter different bars and dance floors. Use the park's back entrance after 10pm to get to the cafe. (Snacks 50-100AS. Beer 28-48AS. Open in summer daily 10am-2am; off-season M-Sa 5pm-1am, Su 10am-6pm.) **Treibhaus,** Angerzellg. 8, is Innsbruck's favorite alternateen hangout and watering hole (food 50-95AS; open M-F 9am-1am, Sa-Su 10am-1am). Amber walls and sleek black railings line **Krah Vogel,** Anichstr. 12, a hip, modern bar (beer 29-41AS; open M-Sa 10am-2am, Su 5pm-2am). **Die Alte Piccolo Bar,** Seilerg. 2, is the only gay bar in Innsbruck (open Th-Tu 10pm-4am).

■ Bregenz

Bregenz is a kind of tourist nirvana, and thousands come—Speedo-clad—to bake on the banks of the Bodensee (Lake Constance) and hike in the nearby mountains. The **Martinturm,** begun in 1362, rules the Oberstadt and boasts Europe's largest onion dome. The walk up to **St. Gallus Pfarrkirche,** at the top of Kirchstr., provides a sweeping view of the *Oberstadt.* The 11th-century white stucco sanctuary now glows under lavish gold ornaments and a detailed painted ceiling that dates from 1738. The main attraction of the town is the **Bodensee,** where carefully groomed waterfront paths surround fantastic playgrounds and paddleboat rental shops. Hop aboard a ferry to the **Blumeninsel Mainau** (Mainau Flower Isle) and take a tour of the island's Baroque castle, tropical palm house, and butterfly house. (Ferries depart Bregenz May-Sept. daily at 9:20am, 10:20am, and 11:20am, and return at 2:40pm, 4pm, and 4:20pm. Round-trip 286AS.)

The **train station** (tel. (05574) 675 50) serves as the departure point for **BundesBus** connections to the rest of Austria. For maps and hotel reservations (30AS), head to the **tourist office** at Bahnhofstr. 14 (tel. (05574) 42 52 50; fax 42 52 55; email tourismus@bregenz.vol.at). A new youth hostel, **Jugendgästehaus Bregenz,** Mehreranerstr. 3-5 (tel. (05574) 428 67; fax 428 67 88), is scheduled to open in June 1999; call for details. A more expensive and nicer option is the **Pension Sonne,** Kaiserstr. 8 (tel. (05574) 425 72), off Bahnhofstr. (singles 350-440AS; doubles 640-800AS). **Seecamping** (tel. (05574) 718 95) is a long but pleasant walk from the train station, bearing left along Strandweg on the lake. (60AS per person and per tent, showers included. Guest tax 17AS. Open May 15-Sept. 15.) **Zum Goldenen Hirschen,** Kirchstr. 8, serves delicious Austrian specialties (open 10am-midnight).

■ Graz

Despite its impressive size and dignified medieval and baroque past, Graz remains surprisingly undertouristed, even during the festival season of late July and August. The ruins of the fortress perched on the **Schloßberg** (castle hill) withstood battering by the Ottoman Turks, Napoleon's armies (3 times), and the Soviet Union. The central *Altstadt* packs dozens of classical arches and domes into a twisting maze of cobblestone streets, while the stark modern buildings of Technical University a few blocks away demonstrate the influence of Graz's famous School of Architecture. A sight in itself, the **tourist office** is situated in the **Landhaus,** remodeled in 1557 in masterful Lombard style. Nearby, you'll find the **Landeszeughaus** (Provincial Arsenal), Herreng. 16, with enough scintillating spears, muskets, and armor to outfit 28,000 burly mercenaries. (Open Apr.-Oct. M-F 9am-5pm, Sa-Su 9am-1pm. 60AS includes admission to entire Landesmuseum Joanneum, students 40AS.) Dominating the inner city of Graz is the towering **Schloßberg,** the one-time site of a medieval fortress razed by Napoleon. Only the 16th-century **bell tower** and the 13th-century **clock tower** remain. The solemn 17th-century Habsburg **Mausoleum,** next to the cathedral, is one of the finest examples of Austrian Mannerism (open M-Sa 10am-12:30pm and 2-4pm; 10AS). Graz's remarkable **Opernhaus** (opera house; tel. (0316) 80 08), at Opernring and Burgg., sells standing-room tickets at the door an hour before curtain call (tickets 360-1490AS; standing-room from 100AS, student rush from 150AS).

The **Hauptbahnhof** (info tel. (0316) 17 17), Europapl., lies on the other side of the river, a short ride from Hauptpl. on tram 1, 3, or 6. **Trains** chug to Innsbruck (6hr., 560AS), Munich (6hr., 714AS), Salzburg (4¼hr., 410AS), and Vienna (2½hr., 310AS). The **Graz-Köflach Bus** (GKB; tel. (0316) 59 87) departs from Griespl. for West Styria. For the remainder of Austria, the **BundesBus** departs from Europapl. 6 (next to the train station) and from Andreas-Hofer-Pl. The **tourist office,** Herreng. 16 (tel. (0316) 807 50; fax 807 55 55), books rooms for a 30AS fee, gives away a map, and leads tours. (Open in summer M-F 9am-7pm, Sa 9am-6pm, Su 10am-3pm; off-season M-F 9am-6pm, Sa 9am-3pm, Su 10am-3pm.) There is a **branch office** (tel. (0316) 91 68 37) at the main train station (open M-Sa 9am-1pm and 2-6pm).

Sniffing out a cheap bed in Graz may require detective work. Ask the tourist office about *Privatzimmer* (most 150-300AS). **Hotel Strasser,** Eggenberger Gürtel 11 (tel. (0316) 71 39 77; fax 71 68 56), has large rooms. Exit the station, cross the street, and head right on Bahnhofgürtel. (5min. Singles 340-440AS; doubles 560-660AS; triples 840AS; quads 1000AS. Breakfast included.) For **Hotel Zur Stadt Feldbach,** Conrad-von-Hötzendorf-Str. 58, 2nd floor (tel. (0316) 82 94 68; fax 84 73 71), take tram 4 ("Liebnau") or 5 ("Puntigam") to "Jakominigürtel" (singles 350AS; doubles 500-650AS; triples 800AS; reception 24hr.). **University Mensa,** Sonnenfelspl. 1, just east of the Stadtpark at the intersection of Zinzendorfg. and Leechg., has the best deals (*menus* 47-53AS; open M-F 8:30am-2:30pm). **Kebap Haus,** Jakominstr. 16, is a superior Turkish restaurant with delicious pitas and Mediterranean pizza (open M-Sa 11am-midnight). After-hours activity is found in the **Bermuda Triangle,** an area of the old city behind Hauptpl. and bordered by Mehlpl., Färberg., and Prokopiag.

Belarus (Беларусь)

US$1 = 47,000BR (Belarusian rubles)	10,000BR = US$0.21
CDN$1 = 30,340BR	10,000BR = CDN$0.33
UK£1 = 77,100BR	10,000BR = UK£0.13
IR£1 = 44,800BR	10,000BR = IR£0.15
AUS$1 = 27,240BR	10,000BR = AUS$0.37
NZ$1 = 23,130BR	10,000BR = NZ$0.43
SAR1 = 7500BR	10,000BR = SAR1.32
DM1 = 26,170BR	10,000BR = DM0.38
Country Phone Code: 375	**International Dialing Prefix: 810**

> Inflation is rampant in Belarus, and the Belarusian ruble is likely to lose much of its value. We list many prices in U.S. dollars since they are likely to remain stable.

For as long as anyone can remember, Belarus has been the backwater of someone else's empire, and today it remains the black sheep of Eastern Europe. The fall of the USSR left Belarus directionless, grasping for a national identity; unable to find its own way, Belarus remains within Moscow's sphere. Soviet bureaucracy persists needlessly in much of the nation: businesses lack effective management and services, border and travel regulations discourage tourism and unnecessarily restrict natives, while taxes and an oppressive regime make living devastatingly difficult. If capitalism is seeping into Belarus, it's acting more like a nest of termites than the Big Bad Wolf. President Aleksandr Lukashenka, meanwhile, continues to harass, intimidate, and arrest his opposition, all the while proliferating an unrestrained cult of personality.

Lift the Belarusian curtain of your mind with *Let's Go: Eastern Europe 1999*.

ESSENTIALS

Belarus is very useful as a transportation link to Russia (see the Russia country map for a map of Belarus). If you're just passing through, **transit visas** (US$20-30; valid for 48hr.) are issued at consulates and at the border. For longer visits, you must secure an invitation and a visa—an expensive and head-spinning process. If an acquaintance in Belarus can procure you an invitation, you can get a single-entry (5-day service US$50, next-day US$100) or a multiple-entry (US$300) visa at an embassy or consulate (see **Government Information Offices,** p. 1). If you use **Host Families Association, HOFA,** 5-25 Tavricheskaya, 193015 St. Petersburg, Russia (tel./fax +7 (812) 275 19 92; email alexei@hofak.hop.stu. neva.ru), to find housing, they will provide invitations (homestays US$30-50). You may also obtain an invitation from a **Belintourist** office, which will give you documentation after you pre-pay all your hotel nights.

Be sure to carry a supply of hard **cash;** U.S. dollars, Deutschmarks, and Russian rubles are the preferred mediums of exchange; you will have a great deal of trouble with any other currency, even British pounds. There are one or two **ATM** machines in Minsk and some hotels do take **credit cards,** but traveler's checks are rarely accepted. Avoid the unreliable **mail** system at all costs. Local **phone calls** must be paid for with tokens, Belarusian rubles, or cards available at the post office. Long-distance phone calls

How Ivan Got His Hand Stuck in the Lighting Fixture

Because international trains are heavily taxed, the cheapest way to get to Warsaw from Moscow or Minsk is to reach Brest or Hrodna, catch an *elektrichka* across the border, and take Polish trains from there. If you choose this most budget of all routes, you will notice that as soon as the *elektrichka* embarks, quick-footed men with screwdrivers begin scaling walls and taking the train apart, hiding vodka of all shapes and sizes in the overhead compartments, the seats, and even, after unscrewing the lights, into the car ceiling. They then sit down quietly and wait. You may be asked to hold a bottle of liquor: you are allowed one duty-free liter, so it's all right to take a bottle provided you don't have your own (don't do this on international flights). At the border, guards board the train and take it apart again, impounding roughly a third of the smuggled vodka. If you don't snitch on these hard-working folk, you might get a little chocolate candy with some vodka in it.

usually must be made at a telephone office or from a hotel, and rates will be exorbitant. To reach the **BT Direct** operator, dial 8 800 44. For **AT&T Direct,** dial 8 800 101. For **MCI WorldPhone,** dial 8 800 103 from Minsk, Hrodna, Brest, and Vitebsk, or 8 10 80 01 03 from Gomel and Mogilev. Belarusians speak primarily Russian, but Polish is also fairly common in Hrodna and Brest. There are no hostels in Belarus, and many **hotels** charge a much higher rate for foreigners. If you do stay at a hotel, keep all the slips of paper you receive to avoid paying fines on your way out of the country. **Private rooms,** often US$10 or less, are worth a shot. The after-effects of **Chernobyl** are unlikely to harm short-term visitors, but it is wise to avoid cheap dairy products, mushrooms, and berries, and to drink bottled water.

■ Minsk (Мінск)

If you're looking for the supreme Soviet city, skip Moscow and head to Minsk, where the fall of Communism has meant only a reluctant shuffle toward the West. Most of the streets have been renamed, but Lenin's statue stands in pl. Nezalezhnastsi (Незалежнасці). Flattened in World War I, the city was redesigned as a showcase of Soviet style, with wide avenues and stereotypically Stalinist architecture.

SIGHTS AND ENTERTAINMENT Once named pl. Lenina and still bearing the mark of communist-era architecture, **Pl. Nezalezhnastsi** (Independence Square) is now the symbol of the independent Republic of Belarus. Standing out from the Soviet giants is the red Church of St. Simon, which provides a sanctuary amid the congestion outside. On pl. Svobody (Свободы) stands the dazzling and recently restored **Svetadukha Kafedralny Sobor** (Светадуха Кафедралный Собор; Cathedral of the Holy Spirit), vul. Mefodiya 3. Built in 1642 as a Bernardine monastery, the building later burned down, and was rebuilt by the Russian Orthodox Church.

Minsk's reconstructed **Old Town,** east of vul. Nyamiha on the north bank of the Svisloch, is a nice area for a mid-afternoon stroll through souvenir shops and beer gardens. A **Jewish memorial stone** stands on vul. Zaslavskaya (Заславская), behind Gastinitsa Yubileynaya, to commemorate the more than 5000 Jews who were shot and buried on this spot by the Nazis in 1941. The **Muzey Velikoy Otechestvennoy Voyny** (Музей Великой Отечественной Войны; Museum of the Great Patriotic War; tel. (0172) 26 15 44), pr. F. Skaryny 25a, explores World War II in Belarus, which lost 20% of its population (open Tu-Su 10am-6pm; 15,000BR; call for a tour in English, 200,000BR). The **National History and Culture Museum,** vul. K. Marxa 12 (К. Маркса), explores the history of everything Belarusian (open Th-Tu 11am-7pm; 7000BR). Soviet Minsk is completed by the city's parks; wander up pr. F. Skaryny to **Park Gorkoho** (Парк Горкого) and **Yanka Kupala Park** (Янка Купала Парк).

Minsk's world-renowned **Opera and Ballet Theater,** vul. E. Pashkevich 23 (Пашкевіч; tel. (0172) 233 17 90), showcases one of the best ballets in the former USSR. Tickets (15,000-20,000BR) can be purchased from the **Central Ticket Office,** pr. F. Skaryny 13 (open M-Sa 9am-8pm, Su 11am-5pm).

BELARUS

PRACTICAL INFO, ACCOMMODATIONS, AND FOOD The easiest way to buy advance **train** tickets to destinations outside Belarus is to go to the **Belintourist office** (Белінтурíст), pr. Masherava 19 (tel. (0172) 226 98 40), next to Gastsinitsa Yubileyni (metro: Nemiga; open M-Sa 8am-1pm and 2-8pm, Su 9am-5pm). The English, French, and German-speaking office also offers visa registration and extensions and sells plane tickets. Trains run to Moscow (10-14hr., 1,073,000BR), Vilnius (4½hr., 552,000BR), and Warsaw (12hr., US$35). There are two Minsk bus stations. **Avtovakzal Tsentralny** (Автовакзал Центральный; tel. (0172) 227 78 20), 200m to the right as you leave the train station at vul. Babruskaya 6 (Бабруйская), serves Vilnius (4hr., 119,000BR) and western cities. Take trolleybus 20 from vul. Kirava (Кірава), near Avtovakzal Tsentralny, to **Avtovakzal Vostochny** (Автовакзал восточный; tel. (0172) 248 08 81), at vul. Vaneyeva 34 (Ванэева), for buses within Belarus.

Hotels are universally expensive: pick up *Minsk in Your Pocket* for a fighting chance at a decent room. **Gastsinitsa Svisloch** (Гасцініца Свіслочь), vul. Kirava 13 (Кірава; tel. (0172) 20 97 83), has singles for 644,100BR (with shower 1,053,900BR) and doubles with shower for 1,394,400BR, but may not have hot water. **Gastsinitsa Minsk** (Гасцініца Мінск), pr. F. Skaryny 11 (tel. (0172) 20 07 03), in the center of town, offers renovated singles for 1,837,00BR and doubles for 2,410,000BR (breakfast included). Private rooms run about US$10. **Restaran Uzbekistan** (Рестаран Узбекістан), vul. Y. Kupaly 17, serves up Uzbek dishes in a tiny co-op restaurant (open daily 8am-11am, noon-4:30pm, and 6pm-midnight). *Plov po uzbeski* (плов по узбески) is a good rice dish with lamb for 158,600BR.

■ Brest (Брэст)

Traded to the Germans in the 1918 Treaty of Brest-Litovsk, Polish between the wars, and Russian again after 1939, Brest today is a hectic border town that sees legions of traders crossing back and forth across the Polish-Belarusian border. The massive brick walls, moats, and encasements of **Krepasts Brest-Litoisk** (Крэпасць Брест-Літоўск; Brest Fortress) withstood a six-week German siege during World War II. The monumental **Galoiny Ivakhod** (Галоўны Ўваход; Principal Entrance), at the end of vul. Maskaiskaya, welcomes each visitor in grand Soviet style. To the right lies **Uskhodni Fort** (Усходні Форт; Eastern Fort), a complex where isolated Russians held their ground for three weeks. Around the base of the soldier-in-the-boulder monolith to the right of the main gate are **memorials** to the defenders, including an impressive war obelisk and an eternal flame dedicated to all 13 of the Soviet Union's "Hero Cities." Past the museum, turn right and walk 50m to find **Painochnaya Brama** (Паўночная Брама; Northern Gate), the only gate still fully intact. To gain a sense of the fortress's former magnitude, remember that the whole place used to look like this.

The **train station**, north of vul. Ardzhanikidze (Арджанікідзе; tel. (0162) 005), connects to Minsk (4½-7hr., 110,000-150,000BR), Moscow (16hr., 800,000BR), Prague (18hr., US$96), and Warsaw (US$22). The **bus station** (tel. (0162) 225 51 36), at the corner of vul. Kuybyshava (Куйбышава) and vul. Mitskevicha (Міцкевіча), serves Hrodna (7½hr., 167,300BR) and Warsaw (6hr., 300,000BR). The best hotel for your money, **Gastsinitsa Vesta,** vul. Krupskay 16 (tel. (0162) 223 71 69), is located 200m behind the Lenin statue in pl. Lenin (singles 710,000BR; doubles 1,232,000BR). The hotel service bureau can arrange English speaking tours of the fortress. **Restaurant India** (Рестаран Індія), vul. Gogolya 29 (Гоголя), is said to be the best Indian restaurant between Warsaw and Moscow (open daily noon-11pm).

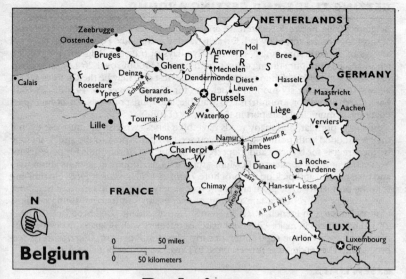

Belgium
(Belgique, België)

US$1	= 35.65BF (Belgian francs)	10BF =	US$0.28
CDN$1	= 23.45BF	10BF =	CDN$0.43
UK£1	= 59.13BF	10BF =	UK£0.16
IR£1	= 51.58BF	10BF =	IR£0.19
AUS$1	= 21.04BF	10BF =	AUS$0.48
NZ$1	= 18.26BF	10BF =	NZ$0.54
SAR1	= 5.74BF	10BF =	SAR 1.74
Country Code: 32		International Dialing Prefix: 00	

In many ways, Belgium is the heart of Western Europe. Situated between France, Germany, Holland, and with quick access to the British Isles, this small nation rubs shoulders with Europe's powerful cultural and intellectual traditions. But Belgium fights back: despite the fast urbanity of its capital and commercial centers, Belgium guards a charming provincialism. As you enter the country by train from the south or east, you may wonder if urban development will ever interrupt the countless miles of rolling countryside, rows of poplars, and occasional small farmhouses. Suddenly, the swift blur of gold and green gives way to compact urban centers—Antwerp bustles and thrives and the capital city Brussels, home to NATO and the European Union, buzzes with international decision-makers making the news you'll read about in tomorrow's paper. And near these cities, the cultural treasures of Bruges and Ghent await discovery. But if you don't get off the train, the urban hustle will vanish just as quickly into the wide, flat expanse of colorful Belgian countryside.

The first stop on the military tours of many would-be European conquerors, Belgium bears the scars of a troubled European history. Today division persists between Flemish-speaking nationalists of the northern province of Flanders and French-speaking Walloons. But some things transcend political tensions; from the Ardennes forests and the white sands of the North Sea coast to the cobblestoned medieval passageways, Belgium's beauty is even richer than its chocolate.

GETTING THERE AND GETTING AROUND

Belgium's **train network** is extensive and reliable. Prices are low, and the country is at most four hours across by rail. **Eurail** is valid; the **Benelux Tourrail Pass** does not always make economic sense, covering five days of travel in Belgium, the Netherlands, and Luxembourg during a one-month period (3100BF, over 26 4220BF). A five-day pass for travel in Belgium costs 2160BF. The best deal may be the **Go Pass,** which allows 10 trips over six months in Belgium for 1390BF (over 26, 1420BF). A **Half-Fare Card** (590BF for 1 month) is also available, and tourist offices sell a **24-hour pass** covering all municipal transport in the country (110BF).

Biking is popular, and many roads have bike lanes (which you must use even if they're studded with potholes). When you see two paths next to the street, the one by the street is for bicycles and mopeds, the one by the storefront is for pedestrians. You can rent bikes at many of Belgium's train stations. Inquire at stations about train and bike **passes,** and pick up the brochure *Train et Vélo/Trein en Fiets.* **Hitchhiking** is losing popularity in Belgium and is not recommended as a safe means of transport, but hitchers still report a fair amount of success in some areas. Bilingual signs ("please" is *s.v.p.* in French, *a.u.b.* in Flemish) are abundant. **Taxi Stop** (tel. (02) 223 23 10) has offices in major cities and matches travelers with Belgian drivers for destinations all over Europe (200-800BF per trip plus 1.3BF per km). **Ferries** from Zeebrugge and Oostende, near Bruges, cross to Dover and other British ports.

ESSENTIALS

Belgium's network of tourist offices is supplemented by **Infor-Jeunes/Info-Jeugd,** a service which helps young people secure accommodations. The weekly English-language *Bulletin* (85BF at newsstands) lists everything from movies to job openings.

Most pay **phones** require a 200BF phone card, available at **PTT** (post, telephone, and telegraph) offices and magazine stands; the rarer coin-operated phones are more expensive. Calls are cheapest from 8pm to 8am and on weekends. For operator assistance within Belgium-Netherlands-Luxembourg, dial 13 07; for international assistance, 13 04 (10BF). To reach an **AT&T Direct** operator, dial 0800 100 10; **MCI WorldPhone,** 0800 100 12; **Sprint Access,** 0800 100 14; **Canada Direct,** 0800 100 19; **BT Direct,** 0800 100 24; **New Zealand Direct,** 0800 104 23.

Public holidays in Belgium are New Year's Day (Jan. 1), Easter (Apr. 5), Labor Day (May 5), Feast of the Ascension (May 13), Whit Monday (May 24), Flemish Community Day (July 11), National Day (July 21), Feast of the Assumption (Aug. 15), French Community Day (Sept. 27), All Saints Day (Nov. 1), Armistice Day (Nov. 11), and Christmas (Dec. 25).

ACCOMMODATIONS, CAMPING, FOOD, AND DRINK
Hotels in Belgium are fairly expensive, with "trench-bottom" prices for singles starting at 800BF and doubles at 1000 to 1100BF. Avoid bankruptcy by staying in one of the 31 **HI hostels,** which charge about 385BF per night. They are generally modern and often boast extremely cheap bars. Pick up *Budget Holidays* or the free *Camping* at any tourist office for complete listings of hostels and campsites. **Campgrounds** charge about 130BF per night. Many visitors make the mistake of staying in Brussels and day-tripping to neighboring cities; try using the nearby Bruges, Ghent, or Antwerp as a base instead. Private hostels in Bruges are fun and lively, and the city is a welcoming refuge at night.

Belgian cuisine can be wonderful, but a native dish may cost as much as a night in a decent hotel. Steamed mussels *(moules)* are usually tasty and reasonably affordable (a whole pot for around 430BF). Other specialities include *lapin* (rabbit) and *canard* (duck). Belgian beer is both a national pride and a national pastime; more varieties (over 500, ranging from the ordinary Jupiler to the religiously brewed Chimay) are produced here than in any other country. Try Leffe, Kwak, and Duvel before you leave. Regular or quirky blonde goes for as little as 40BF, and dark beers cost about 60 to 90BF. Leave room in the wallet and belly for Belgian *gaufres* (waffles) and famous Godiva and Leonidas chocolates.

■ Brussels (Bruxelles, Brussel)

Instantly associated with NATO and the European Union, Brussels is more than just a political and economic capital. In the Grand-Place, center of the old city, you'll find the essence of Belgium, from waffles and beer to the *Mannekin Pis*. Where Antwerp claims Rubens, Brussels' cultural icon is no less than Hergé's androgynous comic strip creations Tintin and his dog Snowy, who peer at you from city shop windows. Architect Victor Horta was the innovator of and inspiration for many of Brussels' most fascinating interiors and exteriors, but Brussels' more recent architects have mingled garish glass and concrete behind gothic spires. Still, Brussels has carefully preserved its Old Town, to the delight of travelers who flock to its narrow streets.

ORIENTATION AND PRACTICAL INFORMATION

Brussels' trinity of train stations consists of **Brussels Midi** (the principal destination for international trains), **Brussels Central** (gateway to the Grand-Place), and **Brussels Nord** (near the Botanical Gardens). Most of Brussels' major attractions are clustered around these stations, near the **Bourse** (Stock Market) to the west and the **Parc de Bruxelles** to the east. Travel within the center of the city is easy, but trekking from the north end to the south is quite a hike. A 200BF **tourist passport** secures one day's public transportation, a map, a slew of reductions on museum admissions, and other bonuses (available at the TIB and almost every bookshop). If you're on an extended visit, you may want to attack the city area by area. Be aware that public transportation stops completely at midnight. Walking from a disco in the south back to Gare du Nord is not a good idea. Although Brussels is a bilingual city, some maps may only be in Flemish. *Let's Go* uses French as it is usually more familiar to travelers.

Telephone Code: 02.

Flights: tel. 722 31 11, info 723 60 10. Trains to **Brussels International Airport** (25min., every 20 min., 90BF) leave Gare Centrale 5:30am-11:20pm; all stop at Gare du Nord.

Trains: For info, call 555 25 55. All international trains stop at **Gare du Midi/Zuid;** many also stop at **Gare du Nord** or **Gare Centrale.** Traffic to other stations usually passes through one of the main stations. To: Amsterdam (3hr., 1040BF), Bruges (45-60min., 380BF), Antwerp (30min., 195BF), and Paris (2hr., 1900BF). **Eurostar** goes directly to London (3¼hr., from 5100BF one-way, under 26 1900BF).

Buses: STIB (Société des Transports Intercommunaux Bruxellois), has offices in Gare du Midi. Open M-F 7:30am-5pm, Sa 8:30am-4:30pm. Also at 20 Galeries de la Toison d'Or, 6th fl. (tel. 515 30 64). Call 515 20 00 for schedule info. **L'Épervier,** 50 pl. de Brouckère (tel. 217 00 25). M: Brouckère. Eurobus representative. Open M-F 9am-6pm, Sa 9am-noon and 1:30-4pm.

Public Transportation: 50BF buys 1hr. of travel on buses, the **Métro (M),** and trams. Day pass 130BF. 10-trip pass 330BF. Buy tickets at any Métro or train station, or on the bus. Public transportation runs daily 6am-midnight.

Hitchhiking: Hitchhiking is illegal on motorways and sliproads. To Antwerp or Amsterdam, hitchers reportedly take tram 52 or 92 from Gare du Midi or Gare du Nord to Heysel. To Ghent, Bruges, and Oostende, they take bus 85 from the Bourse to the stop before the terminus and follow E40 signs. To Paris, hitchers take tram 52, 55, or 91 to rue de Stalle and walk toward the E19.

Tourist Offices: National, 63 rue du Marché aux Herbes (tel. 504 03 90; fax 504 02 70), one block from the Grand-Place. Books rooms all over Belgium and has the free weekly *What's On* brochures. Open June-Sept. daily 9am-7pm; Apr., May, and Oct. 9am-6pm; Nov.-Mar. M-Sa 9am-6pm, Su 1-5pm. **TIB (Tourist Information Brussels)** (tel. 513 89 40), in the Town Hall, makes reservations at no charge, dispenses free maps, and sells tourist passports. Info on the 350BF guided walks. Theater, opera, and ballet tickets sold M-F 9am-1pm and 2-5pm. Open Easter-Oct. daily 9am-6pm; Nov.-Easter closed Su.

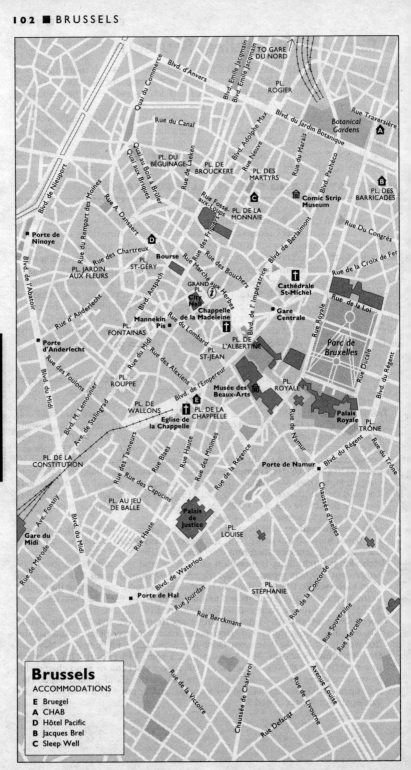

Brussels

ACCOMMODATIONS

- **E** Bruegel
- **A** CHAB
- **D** Hôtel Pacific
- **B** Jacques Brel
- **C** Sleep Well

Budget Travel: Acotra World, 51 rue de la Madeleine (tel. 512 55 40), finds cheap flights. Open M-F 8:30am-6pm. **Infor-Jeunes,** 27 rue du Marché-aux-Herbes (tel. 514 41 11). Budget bonanza. Open M-F 9:30am-5:30pm.

Embassies: Australia, 6 rue Guimard (tel. 286 05 00). **Canada,** 2 av. Tervueren (tel. 741 06 11). **New Zealand,** 47 bd. du Régent (tel. 512 10 40). **South Africa,** 26 rue de la Loi (tel. 285 44 00). Generally open weekdays between 9am and 5pm. **U.K.,** 85, rue Arlon (tel. 287 62 11). **U.S.,** 27 bd. du Régent (tel. 508 21 11); **consulate,** 25 bd. du Régent (tel. 508 25 32), for lost passport help. Open M-F 9am-noon.

Currency Exchange: Thomas Cook at the Grand-Place has good rates but a 5% commission. At **Gare du Nord** (150BF commission; open daily 8am-8pm) and **Gare du Midi** (30BF commission; open daily 6:45am-10:30pm). Most banks and change booths charge 100-150BF to cash checks, but banks have better rates.

American Express: 2 pl. Louise (tel. 676 27 27). M: Louise. Good exchange rates. Open M-F 9am-5pm.

Luggage Storage: Lockers and offices at the three major train stations. Bag check 60BF, lockers 60BF, 80BF, or 100BF.

Gay Services: tel. 733 10 24. Lists local events. Staffed daily 9am-9pm.

Laundromat: Salon Lavoir, 5 rue Haute, around the corner from Bruegel's youth hostel. M: Gare Centrale. Wash and dry 240BF. Open M-F 8am-6pm.

Emergencies: Ambulance or **First Aid,** tel. 112.

Police: tel. 101.

24-hour Medical Services: tel. 479 18 18.

Crisis Hotline: SOS-Jeunes, 27 rue Mercellis (tel. 512 90 20). For concerns about rape, drug use, and emotional trauma. Staffed 24hr. by English speaking operators.

Pharmacies: Pharma-Congrès, 56 rue du Congrès, at rue du Nord, near the Jacques Brel hostel. M: Gare Centrale. Open M-F 8:30am-1pm and 1:30-5:30pm. **Neos-Bourse Pharmacie** (tel. 218 06 40), bd. Anspach at rue du Marché-aux-Polets. M: Bourse. Open M-F 8:30am-6:30pm, Sa 9am-6:30pm.

Medical Assistance: Free Clinic, 154a chaussée de Wavre (tel. 512 13 14). Don't be misled by the name; you do have to pay for medical attention. Open M-F 9am-6pm.

Post Office: M: de Brouckère. **Main office** on the 2nd floor of the Centre Monnaie, the tall building on pl. de la Monnaie. Open M-F 9am-5pm, Sa 9am-noon. **Postal Code:** 1000 Bruxelles.

Internet Access: The hip **Cybertheater,** Av. de la Toison d'Or 4/5, boasts a bar, restaurant, and a DJ who spins urban techno. Open M-Sa 10am-1am, Su 3pm-1am. Also try **Cyber Bar de l'Amour Fou,** 185 ch. d'Ixelles (150BF per 30min.).

Telephones: 17 bd. de l'Impératrice, near Gare Centrale. Rates superior to those of privately owned competitors. Open daily 8am-10pm. Privately owned **Public Phone,** 30a rue de Lombard, has higher rates but a more pleasant atmosphere. Open daily 10am-10pm. For operator assistance, dial 1280.

ACCOMMODATIONS AND CAMPING

Accommodations in Brussels are fairly easy to come by. In general hotels and hostels are very well kept; any that you choose will provide a good springboard to the city.

Centre Vioncent Van Gogh-CHAB, 8 rue Traversière (tel. 217 01 58; fax 219 79 95). M: Botanique; walk toward the Jardin Botanique on rue Royale and turn right. 10min. walk from Gare du Nord; from Gare Centrale, take bus 65 or 66 to rue du Méridien. Colorful, artsy rooms. **Internet access.** Dorms 300-440BF; singles 650BF; doubles 1040BF. Sheets 100BF. Laundry 200BF. Reception 7am-2am.

Sleep Well, 23 rue du Daumier (tel. 218 50 50; fax 218 13 13). From Gare Centrale, walk right down bd. de l'Imperatrice, left on Stormstraat, right on Montagne aux Herbes, left onto Rue du Fosse Aux Loupes, then the 1st right. Clean, spacious rooms and private showers. **Internet access** and bar. Dorms (July-Aug.) 395BF; singles 690BF; doubles 1120BF; triples 1485BF. Reception 24hr. Lockout 10am-2pm.

Gîtes d'Etape: Auberge de Jeunesse "Jacques Brel" (HI), 30 rue de la Sablonnière (tel. 218 01 87), on the pl. des Barricades. 15min. from Gare Centrale. M: Botanique. Spacious, colorful rooms. Dorms 410BF; singles 695BF; doubles 1140BF; triples and quads 470BF per person. Dinner 275BF. Sheets 125BF. Reception 8am-7pm. Wheelchair accessible. Reserve ahead.

BELGIUM

Jeugdherberg Bruegel (HI), 2 Heilige Geeststr. (tel. 511 04 36; fax 512 07 11). From the back exit of Central Station, right on Cantersteen/bd. de l'Empereur, then the second left after Pl. de la Justice. Well-maintained, friendly, and quiet. Dorms 405BF; singles 695BF; doubles 1140BF; quads 1880BF. Sheets 125BF. Reception 7am-1am. Curfew 1am. Lockout 10am-2pm.

Hôtel Pacific, 57 rue Antoine Dansaert (tel. 511 84 59). M: Bourse; cross bd. Anspach. Excellent location, friendly, English-speaking staff. Singles 1000BF; doubles 1750BF. Showers 100BF. Breakfast included. Midnight curfew.

Camping: The best site is **Paul Rosmant,** 52 Warandeberg (tel. 782 10 09), in Wezembeck-Oppem. Take metro 1B to "Kraainem" or bus 30 to "Sint-Peterspl." Su take metro 1B to Stockel then tram 39 to Marcelisstr. Reception 9am-12:30pm and 2-10pm. 250BF per person. Open Apr.-Sept. North of Brussels in Grimbergen is **Veldkant,** 64 Veldkantstr. (tel. 269 25 97). Take bus G from Gare du Nord then follow signs. 125BF per person, 125BF per tent. Open Apr.-Oct.

FOOD

Although restaurants in Brussels can be expensive, much of the street food costs very little. For cheap cafeteria-style food and small cafes, check out the arcade across from the back entrance to the Central Station (open M-Sa 5pm). Many restaurants are near the Grand-Place. Visit the **rue des Bouchers,** just north of the Place, to admire the piles of exotic shellfish on ice. Just south of the Place, the **rue du Marché-aux-Fromages** is lined with inexpensive Greek eateries serving excellent pita sandwiches. The ubiquitous **Belgafraus** serves hot waffles (50-80BF). The open air **market** at pl. Ste–Catherine (open daily 7am-5pm) has fresh produce and other goodies. Load up on supplies at a **GB supermarket;** branches are at 248 rue Vierge Noire (M: Bourse), and in the "City 2" shopping center, 50m from Sleep Well (M: Rogier).

Dandon Biscuiterie, 31 rue au Beurre, serves delicious waffles, scrumptious crepes, and yummy pancakes, all for 75-210BF. Open daily 8:30am-7pm.

Ultième Hallutinatie, 316 rue Royale, serves simple Belgian meals starting at 150BF. Open daily noon-8pm.

Sole d'Italia, 67 rue Grétry. A huge serving of spaghetti with bread is only 195BF, and other specialties are only a bit more expensive. Open daily noon-late.

Maison des Crepes, 42 rue des Pierres. Popular among locals, this small restaurant serves specialty crepes starting at 80BF. Open daily 9am-6:30pm.

L'orfeo, 12 rue Haute. Comfortable restaurant serves up fresh salads and hot pita sandwiches (160-240BF). Lots of good vegetarian options.

L'Ecole Buissonnière, 13 rue de Traversière, opposite CHAB youth hostel. M: Botanique. Affordable traditional Belgian food (most meals 165-345BF). Ask to dine on the terrace or in the garden. Open M-F noon-2:30pm and 6-8pm.

SIGHTS

One look at Brussels' **Grand-Place** and you'll understand why Victor Hugo called it "the most beautiful square in the world." Framed by gold-trimmed architecture, the Place is a masterpiece, while the flower market and feverish tourist activity add color. The Gothic spires of the **Town Hall** pierce the sky. *(Tours Tu 11:30am and 3:15pm, W 3:15pm, Su 12:15pm; Oct.-Mar. closed Su. 75BF.)* Starting around 10 or 11pm in April through August and during December, 800 multi-colored floodlights give the Hall a psychedelic glow accompanied by the eerie pulsing of 15th-century chants.

Three blocks behind the Town Hall on rue de l'Etuve at rue du Chêne is Brussels' most giggled-at sight, the **Mannekin-Pis,** a statue of an impudent boy (with an apparently gargantuan bladder) steadily urinating. One story goes that a 17th-century mayor promised to build a statue in the position that his lost son was found; another says it commemorates a boy who (à la Gulliver) ingeniously defused a bomb. Locals have created hundreds of outfits for him, each with a little hole for you-know-what.

For more intellectual stimulation, visit the two **Royal Museums of Fine Arts.** The **Musée d'Art Ancien,** 3 rue de la Régence, houses a huge collection of the Flemish masters, including Brueghel the Elder's *Fall of Icarus* and *Census in Bethlehem* and

Rubens's *Martyrdom of St. Levinius* and *Calvary*. Next door at the **Musée d'Art Moderne,** you'll find everything from the brilliant to the banal—works by Miró, Picasso, Magritte, and Dalí, and Andy Warhol's portrait of hockey star Wayne Gretzky. *(M: Gare Centrale or Parc. Both museums open Tu-Su 10am-5pm. 150BF, students 100BF.)* The **Musées Royaux d'Art et d'Histoire,** 10 parc du Cinquantenaire (M: Mérode), cover a wide variety of periods and parts—Roman torsos without heads, Syrian heads without torsos, and Egyptian caskets with feet. *(Open Tu-Sa 9:30am-4:45pm, Su 9:30am-6pm. 120BF, students 90BF.)*

Victor Hugo described the **Saints Michel et Gudule Cathedral,** just north of Central Station at pl. St-Gudule, as the "purest flowering of the Gothic style." *(Open daily 8am-7pm. Free.)* Built over the course of six centuries, this magnificent cathedral represents Romanesque and modern architecture as well.

The **Musée Horta,** 25 rue Américaine, is early 20th century Art Nouveau master Baron Victor Horta's graceful home. *(Open Tu-Su 2-5:30pm. M-F 150BF, Sa-Su 200BF.)* For more Art Nouveau architecture, plus all the French and Belgian comic strips *(bande desinée)* you crave, visit the **Belgian Comic Strip Centre,** 20 rue des Sables, in a renovated Art Deco warehouse a few blocks from Sleep Well. Brussels, the "Comic Strip Capital of the World," even has a comic strip **library** complete with a reproduction of Tintin's rocket ship and works of over 700 artists. *(Open Tu-Su noon-6pm. 150BF.)* For Tintin souvenirs, check out the museum store or the **Tintin Boutique** near the Grand-Place. When you tire of ol' Tintin, escape to the **Botanical Gardens,** rue Royale. *(M: Botanique. Open daily 10am-10pm. Free.)*

The symbol of the 1958 World's Fair and Brussels' answer to the Eiffel tower, the shining aluminum and steel **Atomium** represents a cubic iron crystal structure 102m high, or magnified 165 billion times. *(M: Heysel, in the Bruparck entertainment complex. Open daily Apr.-Aug. 9am-8pm; Sept.-Mar. 10am-6pm. 200BF.)* It's now a **science museum** featuring fauna and minerals from around the world.

Consider spending some time exploring the rest of Brussels on foot: the chic **Sablon** is home to antique markets, art galleries, and lazy cafes. More frenetic activity can be found in **Marolles** where you can practice the fine art of bargaining at the morning flea market. The **Schuman** area houses the gleaming buildings of the European Parliament (called Caprice des Dieux—"Whim of the Gods"—perhaps because of their exorbitant cost).

ENTERTAINMENT

Theater and Cinema

The flagship of Brussels' theater network is the beautiful **Théâtre Royal de la Monnaie,** pl. de la Monnaie (M: de Brouckère; tel. 229 12 00). Renowned throughout the world for its opera and ballet, the theater actually has affordable performances (tourist office has schedules; tickets 250-3000BF; open Tu-Sa 11am-6pm). In the shadow of the Atomium, **Kinepolis** (M: Heysel), with 26 screens and a spectacular 600 square meter, Imax theater, is the largest movie theater in Europe (tickets from 300BF). In summer, concerts pop up on the **Grand-Place,** the **Place de la Monnaie,** and in the **Parc de Bruxelles.** The **Théâtre Royal des Galleries** offers popular theater in French (tel. 512 82 77; tickets 150-800BF). For info on events, snag *What's On* or call **BBB Agenda** (tel. 512 82 77).

Bars and Nightclubs

The scene in Brussels is intensely European—patrons dress stylishly but retain a casual air. At night the Grand-Place, the Bourse, and the streets surrounding them come to life with street performers and live concerts in the square. Leave your valuables at home if you join the nocturnal frenzy around **av. Louise.** The club scene changes very quickly—ask at bars and check *What's On* for the best spots.

BELGIUM

La Mort Subite, 7 rue Montagne-aux-Herbes-Potagères, and **La Bécasse,** rue de Tabora 11, are a couple of Brussels' oldest and best-known cafes. Beer 50-90BF. Coffee 60BF. Open daily 10:30am-midnight.

Le Fuse, 208 rue Blaes. One of Belgium's trendiest dance clubs. Pay homage to the gods of techno and rave. Open nightly 10pm-late.

L'Archiduc, 6 rue Dansaert. Trendy, expensive, art deco Jazz bar. No cover.

Le Cercueil (the coffin), 10 rue des Harengs, off the Grand-Place. Younger crowd illuminated by blacklights. Drinks are expensive as hell. Beer from 100BF, cocktails from 250BF. Open weekdays 11am-3am, weekends until 5am.

L'Incognito, 36 rue des Pierres. Gay men of all ages socialize in a mellow, friendly atmosphere that picks up as the morning draws near. Open nightly 4pm-dawn.

Chez Toone, hidden away at 21 Petite rue des Bouchers. Relaxed, smoky bar with great bartenders in an charming old puppet theater near the Grand-Place.

The Garage, 16 rue Dequesnoy. A swarm of sweaty bodies, and that's just to go through the cover charge line. Popular, fashionable crowd. Live bands often. Cover from 200BF includes a free drink. Open W-Su 11pm-late. Su is gay night.

■ Near Brussels: Waterloo

Napoleon was caught with both hands in his shirt at Waterloo, just south of Brussels. Modern residents are more likely to have their hands in your pockets, as history buffs and fans of the diminutive dictator pay for a glimpse at the town's little slice of history. For 385BF (students 315BF), you can buy a pass that grants admission to the six main sights: Wellington's Museum, Napoleon's Museum, the Waxwork Museum, the Lion's Mound, the Visitors Center, and the battlefield panorama. To get to Waterloo, take bus W or 365A (every 30min, one-way 76BF) from pl. Rouppe in Brussels (accessible via tram 90), or take the train from Brussels toward Nijvel and make sure it stops in Waterloo (round-trip 135-185BF), and then walk 1km to the center of town. You can purchase the discount pass at the **tourist office,** 149 chausée de Bruxelles, which will provide info on the apocalyptic reenactment of the battle planned for the year 2000 (tel. (02) 354 99 10; fax 354 22 23; open daily 9:30am-6:30pm).

FLANDERS (VLAANDEREN)

Nearly all the major Belgian cities are in Flanders, whose inhabitants speak Flemish, a language close to Dutch. Historically, the delta of the river Schelde at Antwerp provided the region with a major seaport, and the production and trade of linen, wool, and diamonds underwrote the cultural transformation of the Northern Renaissance. Flemish cities were among the largest in 16th-century Europe; today they are marvelously close together, rich in art, and vibrant with multilingual, friendly people.

▓ Mechelen

Mechelen, situated between Antwerp and Brussels, has enough sights to keep a visitor occupied for days. Lack of affordable accommodations and a mild nightlife, however, reduce it to an enjoyable daytrip. As the ecclesiatical capital of Belgium, Mechelen's main claim to fame is its *carillon* (set of 49 bells) performances (June-Sept. M 8:30pm). **St. Rumbold's Tower,** rising 97m over **Grote Markt,** down Consciencestr. from the station, contains two *carillons.* Climb to the top for a view of the town (100BF). The early Renaissance buildings in the Grote Markt include the 14th-century **Stadhuis** (city hall) and the stately **St. Rumbold's Cathedral.** The **De Wit Tapestry factory** on Schoutetstraat (off Wollemarkt) offers tours (Aug.-June Sa 10:30am; 50BF). Passing the factory and heading right on De Deckerstr., then left on Stassartstr., brings you to the **Museum of Nazi Deportation and Resistance;** during the Holocaust, Mechelen served as a temporary camp for Jews who were being sent to Auschwitz-Birkenau (open Su-Th 10am-5pm, F 10am-1pm). The **Gouden Carolus**

Brewery tours explain the brewing process used since 1471. The highlight, of course, is the tasting of one of its three beers (tours April-Aug. daily at 3pm; 100BF).

The **tourist office** (tel. (015) 29 76 55; fax 29 76 53), in the Stadhuis, is brochure-laden; request the free booklet with museum info and a map. (Open Easter-Sept. M-F 8am-6pm, Sa-Su 9:30am-12:30pm and 1:30-5pm; Oct.-Easter M-F 8am-5pm, Sa-Su 10am-noon and 2-4:30pm.) Ask about the frequent **music festivals;** the most raucous is **Op Signoorke** on the second Sunday of September. Frequent trains run to and from Brussels and Antwerp (each 15min., 120BF). **Carlton,** Grote Markt 3, serves simple dishes (75-200BF; daily 11am-8pm). You can also grab some grub at the **grocery store GB,** de Stassartstr. 30 (open M 8:30am-2pm, Tu-Sa 8am-6pm, and F until 7pm).

■ Antwerp (Antwerpen)

By the 16th century, Antwerp was a commercial city that claimed a place among the most powerful in Europe. It was the city of Rubens and Van Dyck, of wool and diamonds. Now Belgium's second largest city, Antwerp and its many museums offers some of Belgium's finest examples of art, architecture, and literature, and the city supports bars that stay open past sunrise.

SIGHTS AND ENTERTAINMENT Many of the best sights in Antwerp are free. A walk along the **Cogels Osylei** will take you past fanciful Art Nouveau mansions built with the wealth of the city's Golden Age. **Centraal Station** itself is beautiful, and the shops and buildings lining the **Meir** are excellent examples of Antwerp old and new. Not free but still impressive is the world-famous **Antwerp Zoo,** right next to the train station, a serene and exotic natural environment with fascinating wildlife (open daily 9am-6pm; 340BF, students 270BF). The **Stadhuis** (city hall), in Grote Markt in the **oude stad** (old city), is a dignified example of Renaissance architecture (open for tours M-W and F 9am-3pm, Sa noon-3:30pm; 30BF). The nearby **Kathedraal van Onze-Lieve-Vrouw,** Groenpl. 21, has a showy Gothic tower and an interior decorated with stained glass and Flemish masterpieces, notably Rubens's *Descent from the Cross* and *Exaltation of the Cross* (open M-F 10am-5pm, Sa 10am-3pm, Su 1-4pm; 70BF). The little-known **Mayer van den Bergh Museum** at Lange Gasthuisstr. 19 harbors Brueghel's *Mad Meg* (open Tu-Su 10am-5pm; 75BF, students 30BF). Antwerp's famed son built **Rubens Huis,** Wapper 9, off Meir, and filled it with art (open Tu-Su 10am-4:45pm; 100BF). The **Royal Museum of Fine Art,** Leopold De Waelpl. 1-9, has one of the best collections of Old Flemish Masters in the world (from the 14th-17th centuries). Natural lighting and the originality of its exhibit designs have made this gallery a model for many others (open Tu-Su 10am-5pm; 150BF, students 120BF, F free). The **Film Museum,** Meir 50 (tel. (03) 233 86 71), shows outdoor movies (100-150BF) in the summer. For an events guide, pick up *Antwerpen* at the tourist office.

Antwerp is famously well-endowed with 300 bars and nightclubs. International DJs spin house music in near-rave conditions at **Café d'Anvers,** Verversrui 16 (cover 200BF; open Sa-Su from midnight). Live rock and pop bands on Sunday and Monday nights feature at the **Swing Café,** on Suiker Rui (no cover; open daily noon-late). The streets behind the cathedral are always crowded. **Bierland,** Korte Nieuwstr. 28, is the most popular student hang-out, with special drink promotions. **Zottekot,** Vlaamse Kaai 23, indulges in theme nights, such as Monday's "DJ plays cupid" (cover 200BF; open Th-M 7pm-late). Alternatively, for a quiet evening of conversation, try the **Pelgrom,** Pelgrimstr. 15, a 16th-century cellar with vaulted ceilings (open daily noon-midnight). Most gay bars and discos cluster along Van Schoonhovenstr., just north of Centraal Station. Closer to Grote Markt is **Rotskam,** Vridagmarkt 12, where both men and women enjoy Belgian beer (open Sa-Th 3pm-late, F 9am-late).

PRACTICAL INFO, ACCOMMODATIONS, AND FOOD Trains run from Centraal Station to Amsterdam (2hr., 940BF), Brussels (45min., 195BF), and Rotterdam (1hr., 700BF). To reach the **municipal tourist office,** Grote Markt 15 (tel. (03) 232 01 03; fax 231 19 37), from Centraal Station, turn left onto De Keyserlei, which becomes

Meir, and follow it to Groenpl. (15min.; bear right at Meirbrug), then bear left down Bromstr. and past the cathedral to Maalderijstr. The office provides free hotel reservations and maps (open M-Sa 9am-6pm, Su 9am-5pm). **Globetrotter's Nest,** Vlagstr. 25 (tel. (03) 236 99 28), is a charming family-run hostel with clean, comfortable rooms. (Dorms 390BF. Sheets 90BF. Kitchen, bike rental, and a good video selection. Open May 10-Dec. 31.) To get to **Jeugdherberg Op-Sinjoorke (HI),** Eric Sasselaan 2 (tel. (03) 238 02 73), take tram 2 ("Hoboken") to "Bouwcentrum," walk right, take first left, and follow HI signs over the bridge, or take bus 27 to "Camille Huysmanslaan." The place is clean, modern, and somewhat strict (385BF, nonmembers 485BF. Breakfast included. Sheets 125BF. Lockout 10am-4pm). **Scoutel,** Stoomstr. 3 (tel. (03) 226 46 06; fax 232 63 92), has spacious singles (950BF) and doubles (1410-1610BF). **Beleejde Broodjes,** Melmarket 5, two minutes from Groenpl, has the best prices around for decent meals (spaghetti 195BF; open M-Sa 6:30am-8pm, Su 11am-7pm). **Gringo's Mexican Restaurant,** Ernest van Dijckaai 24, has colorful masks, colorful parrots, and colorful meals (from 200BF; open daily 6-11:30pm).

■ Ghent (Gent)

Ghent, once second only to Paris in size and prestige, is quite possibly the most underrated town in Belgium. The city has some of the best preserved Renaissance architecture in the country, and a large student population gives it a lively pulse.

SIGHTS AND ENTERTAINMENT Connoisseurs of fine architecture relish a trip to Ghent, which has the most protected monuments of any Belgian city. The tourist office offers guided city tours. **Gravensteen,** the Castle of the Counts, is a sprawling medieval fortress complete with ramparts, chambers, and a torture room. (Open Apr.-Sept. daily 9am-6pm; Oct.-Mar. 9am-5pm. Last admission 45min. before closing. 200BF, students 100BF.) Wind your way up the towering **Belfort** (belfry) and experience some classic Hitchcock vertigo (open daily 10am-12:30pm and 2-5:30pm; 100BF, students 60BF). The **Stadhuis** (town hall) is an arresting juxtaposition of Gothic and Renaissance architecture. A block away on Limburgstr. stands **Sint-Baafskathedraal,** built between the 14th and 16th centuries. Its claim to fame is Jan van Eyck's *Adoration of the Mystic Lamb,* an imposing polyptych on wood panels. (Open Easter-Oct. M-Sa 9:30-11:45am and 2-5:45pm, Su 1-5:45pm; Nov.-Easter M-Sa 10:30-11:50am and 2:30-4pm, Su 2-4:45pm. Cathedral free. *Adoration* 60BF, students 40BF.) Also worth a visit is the **Museum voor Schone Kunsten** (Museum of Fine Arts) in the Citadel Park, home to a strong Flemish collection and an exhibit of modern art (open Tu-Su 9:30am-5pm; 80BF).

Ghent is home to a large university, the **Rijksuniversiteit Ghent,** and the student population fuels a thriving nightlife. From October to July 15, young scholars cavort in the cafes and discos near the university restaurant on **Overpoortstraat. Vooruit,** a huge art-deco bar on St-Pietersnieuwstr., once the meeting place of the socialist party, was occupied by Nazis during World War II and is now popular with students (open Aug. 13-July 16 daily 10pm-3am). The bar's concert hall (tel. (09) 223 82 01) features everything from rock to jazz to avant-garde. **De Tap en de Tepal,** on Gewad by the youth hostel, serves wine and cheese (100-200BF). On the Vrijtagmarkt at the wood-paneled **Dulle Grief,** beer lovers lament that they can't sample every one of the over 250 Belgian beers (open M 4:30pm-1am, Tu-Sa noon-1am, Su 3-7pm). Ghent is a popular destination for gay men and women: the dance club **Parallax,** Vlannderenstr. 22, and **Dandy's,** Prinsesclementinalaar 195, are popular gay hangouts.

PRACTICAL INFO, ACCOMMODATIONS, AND FOOD Trains run from Sint-Pietersstation (accessible by tram 1 or 12) to Bruges (15min.) and Brussels (35min.) The **municipal tourist office** (tel. (09) 266 52 32), in the belfry, has guides to restaurants and sights and free maps (open Apr.-Oct. daily 9:30am-6:30pm; Nov.-Mar. 9:30am-12:30pm and 1:15-4:30pm). The elegant, modern, and clean **De Draeke (HI),** youth hostel, St-Widostr. 11 (tel. (09) 233 70 50; fax 233 80 01), is , and in the shadow of a castle, is the best place to stay in Ghent. From the station, take tram 1, 10, or 11 to "Gravensteen" (15min.). Walk left, then take the first right on Gewad, and then right on St-Widostr. The hotel offers **currency exchange** at good rates, and its dorms (385BF) and doubles (470BF) have bathrooms and showers (nonmembers 100BF extra; breakfast included; sheets 125BF; reception 7am-11pm). Rooms are also available at the **university** (singles 500BF; breakfast and shower included; open July 15-Sept. 15). Call the office at Stalhof 6 (tel. (09) 264 71 00; fax 264 72 96) for info. To get to **Camping Blaarmeersen,** Zuiderlaan 12 (tel. (09) 221 53 99), walk 15 blocks or ride bus 38 northwest of Sint-Pietersstation (120BF per person, 120BF per tent; open Mar. to mid-Oct.).

With luck, you'll be able to find a good meal for about 200BF. The best areas are around **Korenmarkt,** just in front of the post office, **Vrijtagmarkt,** a few blocks from the town hall, and **St.-Pietersnieuwstraat,** down by the university. The gay-friendly **Backstage,** on the corner of St.-Pietersnieuwstr. and J. Plateaustr., serves salads from 200BF and omelettes from 130BF, and doubles as a theater (open daily 11:30am-1am). Next door at **La Rustica,** the cooks dole out tasty pizza (200BF; open daily 6-11pm, also M-F 12:30-2:30pm).

■ Bruges (Brugge)

The capital of Flanders is one of the most beautiful cities in Europe, and tourists know it—Bruges has become the largest tourist attraction in the country. As you walk from the train station to the city center, silver canals carve their way through rows of stone houses; the entire city remains one of the best-preserved examples of northern Renaissance architecture. This beauty belies the destruction this region sustained in World War I; eight decades after the war, farmers still uncover 200 tons of artillery every year as they plough their fields.

ORIENTATION AND PRACTICAL INFORMATION

The dizzying **Belfort** (belfry) towers high at the center of town, presiding over the **Markt,** a handsome square. Outside the ring of canals, south of the center of the city, stands the train station.

Telephone Code: 050.

Trains: The station is on Stationsplein (tel. 38 23 82), 15min. south of the city center. To: Antwerp (1hr., 385BF), Brussels (1hr., 365BF), Ghent (15min., 175BF).

Bike Rental: At train station; 345BF per day. **Koffieboontje,** Hallestr. 4 (tel. 33 80 27), off the Markt by the belfry. 250BF a day, students 150BF; 850BF a week.

Hitchhiking: Those hitching to Brussels take bus 7 to St. Michiels or pick up the highway behind the station.

Tourist Office: Burg 11 (tel. 44 86 86; email toerisme@brugge.be), just east of the Markt. Turn left out of the station and walk to 't Zand Sq., then turn right on Zuidzandstr., then right through the Markt on Breidelstr. to Burg, another square (15min.). The office books rooms (400BF deposit) and sells a good map (25BF). Open Apr.-Sept. M-F 9:30am-6:30pm, Sa-Su 10am-noon and 2-6:30pm; Oct.-Mar. M-F 9:30am-1pm, 2-5:30pm, Sa 9:30am-12:45pm and 2-5pm. There's a smaller office at the **train station.** Open Mar.-Oct. M-Sa 2:45-9pm; Nov.-Feb. M-Sa 1:45-8pm.

Youth Information Center: JAC, Kleine Hertsbergestr. 1 (tel. 33 83 06), near the Burg, the 2nd right off Hoogstraat, lists cheap rooms and restaurants and has a youth crisis center. Open daily July-Aug. 10am-4pm; Sept.-June noon-6pm.

Currency Exchange: Master Change, at the corner of the Markt leading to Philipstockstr., has good rates (5% commission; open daily noon-5pm).

Luggage Storage: At the train station; 60BF. **Lockers** (15BF) at the tourist office.

Laundromat: Belfort, Ezelstr. 51, next to Snuffel's Sleep-In. Wash 'n' dry 150-250BF. Open daily 7:30am-10pm. **Mister Wash** is next door (160-280BF).

Emergencies: tel. 100.

Police: tel. 101.

Post Office: Markt 5. *Poste Restante.* Open M-F 9am-6pm, Sa 9am-noon. **Postal Code:** 8000.

Internet Access: Huysderkunsten, Kordevuldersstr. 30 (tel. 34 70 09). 150BF per 30min. Open M-F noon-8pm, Sa noon-5pm.

Telephones: Find a coin phone at the tourist office, post office, or your hostel; card phones dot the streets.

ACCOMMODATIONS AND CAMPING

Hostels fill up quickly in June, July, and August. Call ahead or show up early. The first two hostels listed here (plus Snuffel's Sleep-In) have standardized their prices: dorms 380BF; singles 550BF; doubles 950BF; triples 1290BF; and quads 1720BF.

The Passage, Dweersstr. 26 (tel. 34 02 32; fax 34 01 40). At 't Zand go right on Zuid-zandstr., then take the first left. Airy rooms, ideal location, good restaurant and bar (main courses 195BF-395BF; 1 free beer with full meal; open daily 6pm-midnight). Free city map. Dorms and doubles available. Sheets included, not breakfast. Reception 8:30am-midnight. Credit cards accepted. Free if it's your birthday. Or try **The Hotel Passage** next door. Singles 1200BF; doubles 1800BF. Reception 8am-10pm.

Bauhaus International Youth Hotel, Langestr. 135-137 (tel. 34 10 93 or 33 41 80); take bus 6 from the station to Kruispoort; ask bus driver to tell you when to get off (40BF). Clean rooms, always crowded and frenzied at night. Free beer with hearty dinners (200-400BF). Lockers 30BF. Reception (and bar) 8am-2am.

Europa International Youth Hostel (HI), Baron 143 (tel. 35 26 79; fax 35 37 72), 15min. walk from station, away from the Markt and the nightlife. Turn right from the station and follow Buiten Katelijnevest to Baron Ruzettelaan; or take bus 2 to the 3rd stop. Stay here for a quiet night's sleep. Dorms 385BF. Breakfast included.

Snuffel's Sleep-In, Ezelstr. 49 (tel. 33 31 33; fax 33 32 50), 10min. from the Markt; follow Sint-Jakobstr., which turns into Ezelstr. Or, take bus 3, 8, 9, or 13 from the station. Small rooms with few showers which you reach by trotting through the bar. All proceeds go to charity. Kitchen; laundromat and groceries next door. Reception 8am-midnight. Ask about doing chores for a free night's stay.

't Keizershof, Oostmeers 126 (tel. 33 87 28). 5min. walk from the station; walk left and take first right. Unexciting but clean and comfortable. Singles 925BF; doubles 1350BF; triples 1980BF; quads 2380BF. No credit cards.

Hotel Salvators, St-Salvatorsherhof 17 (tel. 33 19 21; fax 33 94 64). From 't Zand walk down Zuidzandstr. and take a right. Great for groups. Kitchen, TV, and common area. Bar open daily 5-10pm. Doubles 1500-2300BF; triples 2700BF; quads 3000BF, both with bath. Breakfast included. Free **Internet Access.**

Hotel Lybeer, Korte Vulderstr. 31 (tel. 33 43 55), just off 't Zand Sq.; take the first right off Zuidzandstr., then a quick left. Pleasant rooms and comfortable lounge area. Singles 900BF; with bath 1990BF; doubles 1500-1850BF; triples 2100-2700BF. Continental breakfast included, English breakfast 100BF. Half-hour free **Internet access** with 1 night's stay. Reception 8-10:30am and 3:30pm-midnight.

Camping: St. Michiel, Tillegemstr. (tel. 38 08 19; fax 80 68 24). Take bus 7 from the station. 25min. walk from the Markt. Camping with a restaurant, cafe, and style. 130BF per tent. Showers included.

FOOD

There are inexpensive eats around Bruges if you *search*. To avoid high prices, stay away from the Markt and 't Zand. Instead, look a block or two away from the town center. From the Burg, cross the river and turn left to find the **Vismarkt,** which sells fresh seafood. An even cheaper option is the **Nopri Supermarket,** Noordzandstr. 4, just off 't Zand or **Battard,** 55 Langestr., close to Bauhaus (both closed Su). **Markets** open on 't Zand every Saturday morning and the Burg every Wednesday morning.

Bistro de Kluiver, Hoogstr. 12. Tasty, diverse menu and cozy mood. Veggie pasta 220BF. Spare ribs and salad 350BF. Escargots 130BF. Open W-Su 11:30am-2:30pm and 6:30pm-midnight.

Ganzespel, Ganzestr. 37. From Burg, turn up Hoogstr.; 3rd right after the river. Hearty portions of traditional Flemish food for a local clientele. Open W-Sa noon-2pm and 6-10pm, Su noon-10pm.

Cafe Craenenburg, Markt 16. The exception to the rule that good location means high prices. Munch on simple meals and people-watch from the terrace. Sandwiches 150-200BF. Omelettes 200BF. Spaghetti 240BF. Open daily 7:30am-11pm.

The Lotus, Wappenmakerstr. 5, 3rd left off Philipstockstr. from the Markt. Serves vegetarian lunches in an attractive building. Meals from 280-300BF. Open mid-Aug. to July daily 11:45am-1:45pm.

Charlie Rockets, Hoogstr. 19. Large portions of Mexican and American food served in a lively rock cafe. Sandwiches 220BF. Open daily 11pm-late.

SIGHTS AND ENTERTAINMENT

Bruges is best seen on foot; the tourist office suggests excellent walking tours. Rising precipitously from the Markt, the **Belfort** towers above the center of the city. Climb its dizzying 366 steps during the day for a view of surrounding areas, then come back at night when it serves as the city's torch. (Open Apr.-Oct. daily 9:30am-5pm; Nov.-Mar. 9:30am-12:30pm and 1:30-5pm; tickets sold until 4:15pm. 100BF, students 80BF.) Up the street at the Burg, the 14th-century **Stadhuis** (town hall) has beautiful paintings and furniture behind its flamboyant Gothic front (open Apr.-Sept. daily 9:30am-5pm; Oct.-Mar. 9:30am-noon and 2-5pm; 100BF, students 80BF). More macabre personalities should check out the **Groeninge Museum** on Dijverstr., with works depicting decapitations, flaying, boiling in oil, and drawing and quartering by the Flemish Primitivists (Jan van Eyck and Hans Memling) and the master of medieval macabre, Hieronymus Bosch. (Open Apr.-Sept. daily 9:30am-5pm; Oct.-Mar. W-M 9:30am-noon and 2-5pm. 200BF, students 150BF.) Next door is the **Gruuthuse Museum,** 15th-century home of beer magnates, which shelters an amazing collection of weapons, tapestries, musical instruments, and coins dating back to the 6th century. (Open Apr.-Sept. daily 9:30am-5pm; Oct.-Mar. W-M 9:30am-noon and 2-5pm. 130BF, students 100BF.) Nearby, the **Memling Museum,** Mariastr. 38, showcases one of the oldest surviving medieval hospitals. (Open Apr.-Sept. daily 9:30am-5pm; Oct.-Mar. Th-Tu 9:30am-12:30pm and 2-5pm.)

Hidden away in the **Church of Our Lady** is the oft-photographed Michelangelo sculpture *Madonna and Child,* his only work to leave Italy during his lifetime. (Open Apr.-Sept. M-Sa 10-11:30am and 2:30-5pm, Su 2:30-5pm; Oct.-Mar. closes 30min. earlier in the evenings. Free.) A relic supposedly containing the blood of Christ is held in the **Basilica of the Holy Blood,** on the corner of the Burg. (Open Apr.-Sept. daily 9:30-noon and 2-6pm; Oct.-Mar. 10am-noon and 2-4pm; closed W afternoon. Free.) **Minnewater** (the Lake of Love) lies on the south side of the city. Don't get too excited—this romantic spot, once the home of an ammunition dump, is more for the contemplation, not the consummation, of love. For a view of an 18th-century windmill, head right on Rolweg to Kruisvest to the **Sint-Janshuismolen** (open May-Sept. daily 9:30am-12:30pm and 1:15-5pm).

If you're ready for cycling, the **Back Road Bike Co.** explores windmills, castles, and World War II bunkers. The excellent countryside tours leave from the main tourist office daily at 1pm (Mar.-Oct., 30km, shorter on weekends). Tours of the city leave at 5pm (Mar.-Oct.; 500-550BF for all tours). Call 34 30 45 for info (fax reservations to 34 57 18). **Boat tours** along Bruges's canals leave every 30 minutes (daily 10am-6pm; 150BF); call the tourist office for info.

The best nightlife in Bruges is just wandering through the romantic streets and over cobblestone bridges after sunset, but if that isn't intoxicating enough for you, sample some of the 300 varieties of beer at **Brugs Beertje,** Kemelstr. 5 (open M-Tu and Th 4pm-1am, F-Sa 4pm-2am; from 50BF). Next door, the *jenever,* Dutch gin, is tantalizingly fruity at **Dreiple Huis** (open daily 5pm-1am, F-Sa until 2am). The flavors slyly mask the very high alcohol content. **Rikka Rock,** on 't Zand, is where the twenty-something locals hang out (beers from 50BF; open daily noon-1am). After hours head next door to **L'ObCéDé** (The Pervert) for pulsating music and low purple lights (no cover; open daily 8pm-3am).

■ Near Bruges

Informative **Quasimodo** tours (tel. (050) 37 04 70) are a good way to explore Flanders while keeping Bruges as a base. The "Flanders Fields" tour somberly patrols the battlefields of World War I where thousands of soldiers died (open Su, Tu, and Th; 1400BF, under 26 1000BF), while the "Triple Treat" tour offers a little of everything, stopping for waffles, chocolate, and beer along the way (M, W, and F; same prices). Conducted in English, these tours leave various hostels and hotels as well as the central train station between 8:45 and 9:20am, returning around 5pm.

The towns along the North Sea coast of Belgium win fans largely for their beaches. **Zeebrugge** is little more than a port, but **Oostende** and the upscale **Knokke** boast beautiful beaches and stylish stores, just an hour's easy bike ride from Bruges. Ferries, ships, and jetfoils chug daily to the U.K. from Zeebrugge and Oostende, easily accessible by train from Bruges (30min., 1 per hr., 150BF). Get tickets from travel agents, at ports, or in the Oostende train station. **P&O European Ferries** (Brussels tel. (02) 231 19 37; Oostende tel. (059) 70 76 01; Zeebrugge tel. (050) 54 22 22) sail to Dover and Felixstowe. Another option is **Oostende Lines** and its mighty freighter, the *Prins Filip* (tel. (059) 55 99 55; fax 80 94 17), which goes to Ramsgate, England, two hours from London's Victoria Station (8 per day, 599BF in July-Aug., 499BF off-season). In Oostende, the **De Ploate Youth Hostel (HI)**, Langestr. 82 (tel. (059) 80 52 97), is close to the station (strict midnight curfew; 485BF). Campgrounds freckle the coast, including **De Vuurtoren,** Heistlaan 168 (tel. (050) 51 17 82), in Knokke (2 people 610BF; open mid-Mar. to mid-Oct.), and **Jamboree,** Polderlaan 55 (tel. (050) 41 45 45), in Blankenberge (tents 310-460BF; open mid-Mar.-Sept.).

WALLONIE

The dense forests of Belgium's middle marked the edge of Roman influence in the third century, and seventeen centuries later the division remains. While Germanic tribes settled the cities of modern day Flanders, Romanized Celts retained their French culture and language. Wallonie lacks the world-class cities of the north, but offers the peaceful beauty of the Ardennes instead.

Tournai The first city liberated by the Allied forces, Tournai's medieval old town escaped major damage in World War II. Once a Roman trading post, Tournai is a peaceful town less touristy than its Flemish counterparts. The city's most spectacular structure is the Romanesque and Gothic **cathedral,** whose **treasure room** houses a collection of medieval goldware and some of St. Thomas Becket's threads (open Apr.-Oct. 9am-noon and 2-6pm, off-season until 4pm; free.) Wander the **Grand-Place** area near the cathedral to take in most of the city's sights. The **Museum of Fine Arts,** Enclos Saint-Martin, is as remarkable for its Art Nouveau design as it is for its works by Breughel, Rubens, and Van Gogh.

To get to Tournai's **tourist office,** 14 Vieux Marché Aux Poteries (tel. (069) 22 20 45; fax 21 62 22), exit the station, walk straight for 15 minutes to the city center, and go around the left side of the cathedral. They have brochures and maps (open M-F 9am-7pm, Sa 10am-1pm and 3-6pm, Su 10am-noon and 2-6pm). The **Auberge de Tournai,** rue St-Martin (tel. (069) 21 61 36), housed in an 18th-century abbey, has tapestries worthy of museums and offers clean rooms (reception 8am-1pm and 5-10pm; 385BF, nonmembers 485BF; sheets 125BF). The **Pita Pyramid,** 7 rue de la Tête d'Or, stuffs its fare into pockets. (140-210BF. Open M-Th 11:30am-2:30pm and 5:30pm-1am, F-Su until 3am.) Nightlife centers around the Grand-Place and along the canals. **La Fabrique,** 13 Quai du Marché Aux Poissons, is a popular nightspot (open daily 11am-11pm, Su closes at 5pm).

Namur and the Ardennes The city of **Namur,** in the heart of Wallonie an hour's train ride from Brussels, is the last outpost before the vast wilderness of the

Ardennes. As such, the city serves as an excellent base for hiking, biking, caving, and climbing excursions. Its citadel, museums, and hospitable accommodations also make it a good place to escape the tourist hordes. The first noticeable sight is the foreboding **citadel,** rooted on the top of a rocky hill to the south. You can do the adventurous thing and climb to the top, or take a mini-train (Tu-Su 10am-4pm; 160BF, round-trip 190BF) or cable car (15min., 160BF). For another 195BF, you can check out the fortress (open daily 11am-5pm). For a little adrenaline, rent a mountain bike from the high station of the *télésiège* (150BF per hr., 600BF per day). For spiritual uplift, in both senses, check out the monastery and brewery of the imposing **Abbaye de Floreffe.** To get there, take bus 10 ("Chatelineau") to Floreffe (open Mar.-Oct. daily 10:30am-6pm; 80BF; beer 60BF). Consider biking to scenic **Dinant** for a daytrip. At the confluence of the rivers Lesse and Meuse, Dinant boasts an impressive citadel and an underground caves replete with cascades.

The **tourist office** (tel. (081) 22 28 59), just a few blocks to the left of the train station of Place Léopold, has discount packages for Namur's main attractions (open daily 9am-6pm). Get a free map here or at the train station. The **provincial tourist office,** 3 rue de Notre Dame (tel. (081) 22 29 98), helps plan trips deep into the Ardennes forest (open M-F 8am-noon and 1-5pm). Namur's youth hostel, the **Auberge Félicien Rops (HI),** 8 av. Félicien Rops (tel. (081) 22 36 88), named for one of Namur's best known artists, is among the friendliest and best equipped lodges around, with laundry facilities (240BF), a kitchen, bike rental (400BF per day), and tasty meals (260BF for dinner). To reach the hostel, take bus 3 directly to the door, or take bus 4 or 5 to "Les Marroniers" (385BF; doubles 970BF; breakfast included; reception 7:30am-1am). **Les Trieux,** 99 rue des Tris (tel. (081) 44 55 83), in Malonne, is the best camping option; to get there, ride bus 6 for 6km (75BF per person, 75BF per tent; cold showers free; open Apr.-Oct.). For a great view of the area, take bus 433 ("Lustin"; 50BF) to the **Belevdere** restaurant, 1 ave. Milieu du Monde, on a 300 ft. cliff overlooking the Meuse (meals from 320BF). Try the regional Ardennes ham at one of the sandwich stands throughout the city or stop at the enormous **Match** in the city center.

BELGIUM

Bosnia-Herzegovina

Bosnia-Herzegovina

US$1	= 1.80KM (convertible marks, or KM)	
CDN$1	= 1.16KM	
UK£1	= 2.95KM	
IR£	= 2.51KM	
AUS$1	= 1.04KM	
NZ$1	= 0.88KM	
SAR1	= 0.29KM	
DM1	= 1KM	
HRV KUNA1	= 0.28KM	

1KM =	US$0.56
1KM =	CDN$0.86
1KM =	UK£0.34
1KM =	IR£0.40
1KM =	AUS$0.96
1KM =	NZ$1.13
1KM =	SAR3.49
1KM =	DM1
1KM =	KUNA3.52

Country Phone Code: 387   **International Dialing Prefix: 00**

Defying the odds of centuries, Bosnia-Herzegovina, the mountainous centerpiece of the former Yugoslavia, persists. Bosnia's distinction—and its troubles—spring from its self-regard as a mixing ground for Muslims, Croats, and Serbs. In Sarajevo, Bosnia's cosmopolitan capital, that ideal is at least verbally maintained, but in the countryside and smaller towns, ethnic problems continue, and voting patterns continue to split along ethnic lines. Physically, Bosnia is a beautiful country of rolling green hills and valleys, but the past years have been deadly, with a bloody war played out on international television. The road to Sarajevo passes through endless fields guarded by roofless, abandoned houses, and many Bosnians have become refugees, displaced and scattered. The future of Bosnia is uncertain, particularly with the inevitable withdrawal of NATO troops within the next several years, but the process of rebuilding, at least for now, has begun.

Learn more about Bosnia's past and present in *Let's Go: Eastern Europe 1999*.

The U.S. Department of State issued a **Travel Warning** in June 1998 advising against unnecessary travel to Bosnia. The warning cites "risks from occasional localized political violence, landmines, unexploded ordnance, and carjacking," and notes that there may be as many as one million live landmines around Sarajevo and throughout the country. Check the U.S. State Department's web page at http://travel.state.gov/travel_warnings.html for updates.

ESSENTIALS

Citizens of Ireland and the U.S. do not need **visas** to enter Bosnia, but citizens of Australia, New Zealand, South Africa, and the U.K. do. Visa applications require you to submit your passport, a visa application, and a small fee (US$15). Register with your embassy upon arrival, and keep your papers with you at all times. **Croatia Airlines** (tel. in Zagreb (41) 42 77 52, in Split (21) 36 22 02) has service to Zagreb, Zurich, Ljubljana, and Istanbul. To buy a ticket in Sarajevo, you must pay in cash. **Trains** are barely functional, but **buses** run between Sarajevo and Dubrovnik, Split, and Zagreb.

Outside Sarajevo, **do not set foot off the pavement** under any circumstances. Even in Sarajevo, avoid venturing onto dirt or picking up anything from the ground you didn't drop yourself. Millions of **landmines** and **unexploded ordinances (UXOs)** lace the country. Many landmine injuries occur on **road shoulders.**

Tourist services are limited, although in Sarajevo, travelers are welcomed—a fledgling **tourist office** provides guidance. The **U.S. embassy,** equipped with full-time consul, is also useful. A new Bosnian currency, the **convertible mark (KM),** was introduced in summer 1998. It is fixed firmly to the **Deutschmark** at a 1:1 rate of exchange. Deutschmarks can be changed directly into convertible marks, without commission, at banks throughout Sarajevo. Beware of store clerks trying to pass unsuspecting foreigners old Bosnian dinars when making change: the dinar is no longer valid for payment. The Croatian **kuna** was also named an official currency in late summer 1997. **ATMs** are nonexistent. **Traveler's checks** can be exchanged in Sarajevo. **Cash** is almost exclusively the method of payment. *Poste Restante* is unavailable. Post offices are marked by yellow and white "PTT" signs. Dialing into and out of Bosnia is no longer a problem. To call **AT&T Direct,** dial 008 00 00 10. For **police,** dial 92 or 66 42 11; **fire,** dial 93; and **emergency,** dial 94.

■ Sarajevo

Tall, Communist-era buildings tower silently, abandoned, their windows jagged black holes. The city streets bear the marks of grenades and shrapnel. Sarajevans speak of their city's prewar beauty; now it possesses a sad and scarred nobility, and a determination to restore what was lost.

SIGHTS AND ENTERTAINMENT Many of Sarajevo's traditional tourist sites were damaged during the war; inquire at the U.S. Embassy or at the tourist agency for an update. **Maršala Tita** is the main street *(ulica)*, running east to west through town. The **eternal flame** burns for all the Sarajevans who died in World War II, but evidence of the recent four-year siege is not hard to find; the souvenir, cartoon-style map (10KM) sold at **Šahinpašić,** Mustafe Bašeskije 1, highlights points of interest. The **National Library,** at the east end of town on Obala Kulina Bana, was once regarded as the most beautiful building in Sarajevo. It is now an open-air structure housing piles of rubble. Up in the hills, a **treeline** is sharply evident, marking the front lines.

Central Sarajevo is packed with churches, mosques, and synagogues; their proximity to one another suggests the best and worst of what the city represents. The most active is the Catholic **Katedrala Srce Isusovo** (Cathedral of Jesus' Heart), on Ferhadija. The 16th-century **Gazi Husrev-Bey mosque,** perhaps Sarajevo's most famous building, dominates the Turkish Quarter skyline. The interior is closed to tourists for repair work, but it's still possible to visit the beautiful courtyard. The main Orthodox church, the **Saborna,** is closed for repairs as well, but the old Orthodox **Church of St. Michael the Archangel,** just north of the Turkish Quarter on Mula Mustafe Baseskije, remains open. The **old synagogue,** just to the west of St. Michael's on the same street, was turned into a museum, but it was still closed in summer 1998. The **Sephardic Synagogue,** however, remains open next to the JCC on Hamdije Kreševljakovića. On the corner of Obala Kulina Bana and Zelenih Beretki, a plaque on a building wall commemorates the birthplace of **World War I.** It was here that Gavrilo Princip shot Austrian Archduke Franz Ferdinand on June 28, 1914.

PRACTICAL INFO, ACCOMMODATIONS, AND FOOD Train service is limited: only a few lines run, the most helpful of which is to Skopje (10hr., M only, 60KM). The **bus station,** Kranjćevića 9 (tel. (071) 67 01 80 or 44 54 42, info tel. 21 31 00), is behind the Holiday Inn. **Centrotrans** (tel. (071) 21 12 82) runs to Dubrovnik (8hr., 40KM), Frankfurt (15hr., 180KM), Split (8hr., 35KM), and Zagreb (10hr., 60KM). Some kiosks and bookstores stock city **maps** (DM10). Incoming citizens should register immediately with their embassy: **Canada,** Logavina 7 (tel. (071) 44 79 00; fax 44 79 01); **U.K.,** Tina Ujevića 8 (tel. (071) 66 40 85; fax 44 44 29); and **U.S.,** Alipašina 43 (tel. (071) 44 57 00; fax 65 97 22). **Australians** should contact their embassy in Vienna (see p. 73), and **New Zealanders** should contact their embassy in Rome (see p. 536). A **tourist bureau,** Zelenih Beretki 22a (tel. (071) 53 26 06; fax 53 22 81), provides hotel info (open M-F 8am-3pm, Sa 9am-2pm). **Central Profit Banka,** Zelenih Beretki 24 (tel. (071) 53 36 88), exchanges money.

Housing is absurdly expensive, but prices are falling gradually as competition resumes. For now, private rooms are the best option. **UNIS Tours,** Ferhadija 16 (tel./fax (071) 20 90 89), finds private rooms (singles 40KM; doubles 35KM per bed; open M-F 9am-5pm). **Prenoćište "Konak,"** Mula Mustafe Baseskije 48 (tel. (071) 53 35 06), is somewhat rustic but has adequate rooms at great prices (singles 40KM, over 3 nights 30KM; doubles 60KM; reception 7am-midnight). For an authentic Bosnian meal, scour the Turkish quarter for **Čevabdžinića** shops. A convenient **market** lies on Mula Mustafe Baseskije (open M-Sa 8am-5pm, Su 8am-noon). **Aeroplan,** Sarci 6, east of Ferhadija in the Turkish Quarter, is a local favorite that now lures the international after-work crowd. (*Lonac*—vegetables and meat in a traditional small pot— 7KM. Main dishes 8-10KM. English menu. Open daily 8am-10pm.) The international crowd plugs in at the **Internet Cafe,** Maršala Titova 5, which boasts Czech *Budvar* (open Su-Th 10am-1am, F-Sa until 3am; live music most W and Th nights). One of Sarajevo's hippest nightspots is **Jazz Bar "Clou,"** Mula Mustafe Baseskije 5 (open daily 6pm-1am; live music Tu and Sa usually starts at 10pm). Every summer from July 1 to 25, the Turkish Quarter hosts an artistic festival, **Baščaršija Noći** (info tel. 44 51 49), featuring open-air music, theater, and film.

Britain

US$1 = £0.60 (British pounds)	£1 = US$1.66
CDN$1 = £0.39	£1 = CDN$2.53
IR£1 = £1.14	£1 = IR£0.87
AUS$1 = £0.36	£1 = AUS$2.81
NZ$1 = £0.31	£1 = NZ$3.24
SAR = £0.10	£1 = SAR10.31
Country Code: 44	International Dialing Prefix: 00

The 20th century has not been kind to the Empire. After Britain founded modern democracy, led the Industrial Revolution, conducted much of the world's trade, and, most recently, helped stave off a Nazi Europe in World War II, the United States, a former colony, replaced her as the world's economic leader. While overseas colonies claimed independence one by one, the Empire frayed at home as well: most of Ireland won independence in 1921, and Scotland and Wales were promised regional autonomy in 1975. Today, ongoing troubles in Northern Ireland underscore the problems of union and nationalism associated with empire.

And yet its lasting contributions to world culture are not, one hopes, well loved because they had rich, armored escorts. The minds of Shakespeare, Newton, and Locke, to name the ancestors, and of John Lennon, John Maynard Keynes, and, perhaps reluctantly, Virginia Woolf, have brought the language and its thought down in glory through the generations.

Travelers to Britain should remember that names hold political force. What you call this part of the world may incite local tempers and fuel debates. "Great Britain" refers to England, Scotland, and Wales; it's neither accurate nor polite to call a Scot or Welshman "English." The political terms "United Kingdom" and "Britain" refer to these regions, Northern Ireland, and the Isle of Man. Because of distinctions in laws and currency, *Let's Go* uses the term "Britain" to refer to England, Scotland, Wales, and the Isle of Man. Coverage of Northern Ireland is in the Ireland chapter for geographical convenience; no political statement is intended. Britain's topographical, cultural, and economic variety makes for an extremely rich journey. Look beyond London, allowing time for sparkling lakes, small towns, and the wild islands.

For more detailed, exhilarating coverage of Britain and London, pore over *Let's Go: Britain & Ireland 1999* or *Let's Go: London 1999*.

GETTING THERE

In 1994, the **Channel Tunnel** (Chunnel) was completed, physically connecting England and France (the horror!/*l'horreur!*). **Eurostar** operates rather like an airline, with similar discounts, reservations, and restrictions. Return tickets start at US$150, and 12 trains per day run from London and Paris. While France, Brit, BritFrance, Eurailpass, and Europasses are not tickets to ride, they are tickets to a discount, as is being a youth. From the U.S. call (800) EUROSTAR (387-6782) to purchase your ticket. In the U.K., call (01233) 61 75 75 for more information.

P&O Stena Line (tel. (0990) 98 01 11) offers **ferry** service across the channel between France (Calais and Dieppe) and England (Dover or Newhaven). Always ask about reduced fares—an HI card or ISIC with Travelsave stamps might mean a 25 to 50% discount. Book ahead June through August. Other routes between the Continent and England include Bergen, Norway to Lerwick or Newcastle; Esbjerg, Denmark to Harwich; Göteborg, Sweden to Harwich or Newcastle; Hamburg to Harwich or Newcastle; Oostende, Belgium to Ramsgate, near Dover; and Hook of Holland to Harwich.

Bus/ferry combinations are the best way to get from **Ireland** to Britain. **Supabus** (contact **Bus Éireann** in Dublin, tel. (01) 836 61 11) runs a bus/ferry deal from Dublin to London four times per day. Depart Dublin at 8:45, 10am (single IR£17, youth IR£15; tax IR£5), 7:30, or 8:45pm (single IR£26, youth IR£24; tax IR£5). Return

Britain

prices range from IR£30-43. Prices from London are the same, without the IR£5 tax. Supabus connects in London to the Eurolines network. **Bus Éireann** also offers daily service from Cork to London (IR£39-45, return IR£49-59; tax IR£5).

GETTING AROUND

Fares on all modes of public transportation in Britain are generally labeled either single (one-way) or return (round-trip). Period returns require you to return within a specific number of days; day returns are same-day round-trips.

Long-distance **coach** (bus) travel in Britain is more extensive than in most European countries and is the cheapest option. **National Express** (tel. (0990) 80 80 80) is the principal operator of long-distance coach services. For information contact **Eurolines**

(U.K.) Limited, 23 Crawley Rd., Luton LU1 1PP, England. Those 50 or over or 16 to 25 are eligible for Seniors' and Young Persons' **Discount Coach Cards** (£8), which reduce standard coach fares on National Express by about 30%.

Britain's **British Rail** service is extensive but expensive. If you plan to travel a great deal within Britain, the **BritRail Pass** can be a good buy. *You must buy BritRail Passes before arriving in Britain.* They allow unlimited travel in England, Wales, and Scotland; British Rail does not operate in Northern Ireland or the Republic of Ireland. In 1998, BritRail Passes cost US$259 for eight days (ages 16-25 US$205) and US$510 for 22 days (ages 16-25 US$410). BritRail Travel also offers **Flexipasses,** allowing travel on a limited number of days within a specific time period. The **Young Person's Railcard** (£16; valid for 1 year) offers 33% off most fares and discounts on Stena Sealink Line to Continental and Irish ports. You can buy this pass at major British Rail Travel Centres in the U.K. You must prove you're either between 16 and 25 (with a birth certificate or passport) or a full-time student over 23 at a British school, and submit two passport-sized photos. Families, seniors, and travelers in wheelchairs have their own Railcards. **The Eurail pass is not accepted in Britain.**

Much of Britain's countryside is well suited for **biking.** Many cities and villages have bike rental shops and maps of local cycle routes; ask at the tourist office. Large-scale Ordnance Survey maps detail the extensive system of long-distance **hiking** paths. Tourist offices and National Park Information Centres can provide extra information about routes. *Let's Go* does not recommend **hitchhiking,** but for those who decide to try, Vacation Work Publications publishes the *Hitch-Hikers' Manual: Britain,* which contains practical info on hitching laws, techniques, and the best places to hitch from 200 British towns (£4 plus £2.50 shipping).

ESSENTIALS

There are local **tourist offices** everywhere in Great Britain; most will book a place to stay for around £2. Most offices also offer a "book-a-bed-ahead" service; for about £2.50 (less in Wales), they will reserve a room in the next town you visit. Proprietors who have not paid a fee to be listed with a tourist office may be less visible.

The pound sterling (£) is the main unit of **currency** in the United Kingdom. One pound equals 100 pence (p). Northern Ireland, Scotland, and the Channel Islands have their own bank notes, which are identical in value to other British notes and can be used interchangeably with standard currency. You may have difficulty using Scottish £1 notes outside Scotland. Northern Ireland's currency is not accepted in the rest of Britain. Most banks are open Monday through Friday 9:30am to 5pm, although the hours in small villages may be reduced. Britain closes for **bank holidays** on January 1, Easter (Apr. 5 in 1999), May 3, May 31, August 25, and Christmas (Dec. 25-26). Discount rates for students, seniors, children, and the unemployed are often grouped under the catch-all term "concessions." The U.K. charges a **value-added tax (VAT),** a national sales tax on most goods and some services; the rate is 17.5% on many services and all goods except books, medicine, and food. This tax is generally included in the listed price. If you want a VAT refund, you must ask the shopkeeper from whom you buy your goods for the appropriate form, which customs officials will sign and stamp when you take your purchases through customs. Once home, send the form and a self-addressed, British-stamped envelope to the shopkeeper, who will mail your refund. You will, at some point, begin to wonder if that 17.5% is really worth it.

COMMUNICATION British **pay phones** charge 10p for local calls. A series of harsh beeps will warn you to insert more money when your time is up. For the rest of the call, a display ticks off your credit in suspenseful 1p increments. Unused coins (not change) are returned (maybe). You may use remaining credit on a second call by pressing the "follow on call" button (often marked "FC"). Phones don't accept 1p, 2p, or 5p coins. If you plan to make several calls, pick up a **Phonecard,** available in denominations of £2, £5, £10, and £20. Get them at post offices, newsagents, or John Menzies stationery shops. Phone booths that take cards are labeled in green and are common except in rural areas; coin booths are labeled in red.

BRITAIN

To make **international calls,** call direct or access an operator in the country you're dialing—rates for operator-assisted calls are often cheaper and the service a bit speedier. For **AT&T Direct,** dial 0800 89 00 11; **Australia Direct,** 0800 89 00 61; **Canada Direct,** 0800 89 00 16; **MCI WorldPhone,** 0800 89 02 22; **New Zealand Direct,** 0800 89 00 64. For the operator, dial 100; directory inquires, 192; international directory inquiries, 153; the international operator, 155. The general **emergency** number for Britain and Ireland is 999; no coins are needed.

ACCOMMODATIONS Britain has hundreds of **youth hostels,** both HI and independent. **YHA** (England and Wales) and **SYHA** (Scotland) are the national HI affiliates in Britain. Hostels here are sometimes closed from 10am to 5pm, and some impose an 11pm curfew. Some require sleep sacks; most prohibit sleeping bags. If these regulations cramp your style, stick to looser, independent establishments. Remember, quality can vary dramatically. Always book ahead in high season.

Native to Britain, the term **bed and breakfast** (B&B) generally means a small place that offers basic accommodations and breakfast at a reasonable price, often in private homes. B&Bs (usually £10-24, in London £16-60) are extremely widespread; when one is full, ask the owner for a referral. Some proprietors grant considerable rate reductions to guests who pay in advance or by the week and offer discounts between September and May. **Bed and Breakfast (G.B.),** P.O. Box 66, 94-96 Bell St., Henley-on-Thames, Oxon, England RG9 1XS (tel. (01491) 57 88 03; fax 41 08 06), covers London, England, Scotland, Wales, and Ireland from £30. Cheap hotels, often called guest houses, can sometimes offer even better bargains than B&Bs.

FOOD AND DRINK British cuisine's deservedly modest reputation redeems itself in a few areas. Britain is largely a nation of carnivores; the best native dishes are roasts—beef, lamb, and Wiltshire hams. And meat isn't just for dinner; the British like their famed breakfasts meaty and cholesterol-filled. Typical breakfast fare includes orange juice, cereal, eggs, bacon, sausage, toast, butter, grilled tomatoes, mushrooms, and, in winter, porridge. Veggies are the weakest, mushiest part of any meal. Salads often mean a mixture of mayo and something else. Before you leave the country, you must try any of the sweet, glorious British puddings.

Pub grub (food served in bars) is fast, filling, and generally cheap. The "ploughman's lunch" (a product of a 60s advertising campaign) consists of cheese, bread, pickle, chutney, and a tomato. Fish and chips are traditionally drowned in vinegar and salt. Caffs (full meals £5-6) are the British equivalent of U.S. diners. To escape English food, try Chinese, Greek, and especially Indian cuisines. Most restaurants figure a service charge into the bill, but if not, leave a 10 to 15% tip.

British "tea" refers both to a drink and a social ritual. Tea the drink is served strong and milky; if you want it any other way, say so in advance. Tea the social can be a meal unto itself. Afternoon high tea as served in rural Britain includes cooked meats,

---

Flakes and Smarties

British food has character (of one sort or another), and the traditional menu is a mad hodgepodge of candy, crisps, yeasts, and squashes. Britain has a greater variety of **candy** for sale than most countries. Brands to watch out for include Flake by Cadbury, Crunchies (which are made out of honeycombed magic), and the ever-popular Smarties. Watch out for the orange ones—they're made of orange chocolate. Potato chips, or **crisps** as they are known in England, are not just salted, but come in a range of flavors, including Prawn Cocktail, Beef, Chicken, Fruit 'n' Spice, and the more traditional Salt & Vinegar. All this sugar and salt can be washed down with pineapple and grapefruit flavored soda Lilt or a can of Ribena, a red currant syrup which has to be diluted with water. This latter beverage belongs to a family of drinks known as **squash,** all of which are diluted before consumption. But the food that expatriate Britons miss most is **Marmite,** a yeast extract which is spread on bread or toast. If you weren't fed Marmite as a baby, you'll never appreciate it; most babies don't either.

salad, sandwiches, and pastries. Cream tea, a specialty of Cornwall and Devon, includes toast, shortbread, crumpets, scones, jam, and clotted cream.

The British pub is a social institution where individuals and communities come together for conversation and relaxation. This attitude is reflected in the careful furnishing of pubs, which resemble the private living rooms they have come to replace. Drinks are generally served from 11am to 11pm, Sundays noon to 10:30pm. Beer is the standard drink. Bear in mind that British beer may have a higher alcohol content than you're accustomed to, and that British beer is usually served room temperature. Lager (the European equivalent of American beer) is served colder. Traditional cider, a fermented apple juice served sweet or dry, is a potent and tasty alternative to beer. Remember, tipping the barman is considered a come-on, but is usually appreciated.

ENGLAND

A land where there is the promise of a cup of tea just beyond even the darkest moor, England, for better or worse, has determined the meaning of "civilized" for many peoples and cultures. The driving force behind the brilliant expansion of the British empire, it is only since the end of World War II that England has been forced to play a more modest role and atone, culturally speaking, for its imperialist past. With its economy in trouble and Irish, Welsh, and Scottish nationalism on the rise, an uneasy sense of emptiness has settled over the land. Now that the sun has almost set on the British empire, the English, who have always termed themselves British, are searching for an identity of their own. Out of the decay has come a new culture—everyone from punk rockers to tabloid writers are defining "English" as the antithesis of everything that "British" used to mean. Tourists today can choose to linger in the glorious past, or to do as the English do and saucily throw off the burdens of civilization.

■ London

London is kind to those expecting bobbies and Beefeaters, "Masterpiece Theatre" and Sherlock Holmes. The Thamescape is still bounded by Big Ben in the west and the archetypal Tower Bridge in the east, and the whole world and all its double-decker red buses really *does* seem to whirl around Piccadilly Circus. But a glance between the bus fenders at the swirling crowd of peers and punks, or at a newsagent overflowing with music and style mags, reveals that London's "culture" stretches far beyond the Royal Opera. For all the "big sights" enclosed by the Circle Line, central London is just a speck on the Greater London map. In a city internalizing its imperial past, the Victorian doorway inscribed with an Anglican piety may belong to a Sikh or a Muslim. Part of what makes London fascinating is precisely this tension—between the cluttered, "familiar," sometimes fictional past of the heritage industry and a riotously modern present.

For an absolutely smashing little book packed with first-rate information on this city, grab a copy of *Let's Go: London 1999*.

ORIENTATION AND PRACTICAL INFORMATION

London is divided into boroughs, postal code areas, and informal districts. Both the borough name and postal code prefix appear at the bottom of most street signs. The city has grown by absorbing nearby towns, an expansion reflected in borough names such as "City of Westminster" and "City of London" (or "The City").

Central London, on the north side of the Thames and bounded roughly by the Underground's Circle Line, contains most of the major sights. Within central London, the vaguely defined **West End** incorporates the understated elegance of Mayfair, the shopping streets around Oxford Circus, the theaters and tourist traps of Piccadilly Circus and Leicester Squ., the exotic labyrinth of Soho, chic Covent Garden, and London's unofficial center, **Trafalgar Square.** East of the West End lies **Holborn,** center of legal activity, and **Fleet Street,** the journalists' traditional haunt.

BRITAIN

Around the southeastern corner of the Circle Line is **The City:** London's financial district, with the Tower of London at its eastern edge and St. Paul's Cathedral nearby. Farther east is the ethnically diverse and working-class **East End** and the epic construction site of **Docklands.** Moving back west, along the river and the southern part of the Circle Line is the district of **Westminster,** the royal, political, and ecclesiastical center of England, where you'll find Buckingham Palace, the Houses of Parliament, and Westminster Abbey. In the southwest corner of the Circle Line, below the expanse of **Hyde Park,** are gracious **Chelsea,** embassy-laden **Belgravia,** and **Kensington,** adorned with London's posher shops and restaurants.

Around the northwest corner of the Circle Line, tidy terraces border **Regent's Park;** nearby are the faded squares of **Paddington** and **Notting Hill Gate,** home to large Indian and West Indian communities. Moving east toward the Circle Line's northeast corner leads to **Bloomsbury,** which harbors the British Museum, London University colleges, art galleries, and specialty bookshops. Trendy residential districts stretch to the north, including **Hampstead** and **Highgate,** with the enormous Hampstead Heath and fabulous views of the city.

Trying to reach a **specific destination** in London can be frustrating. Numbers often go up one side of a street and down the other. One road may change names four times in fewer miles, and a single name may designate a street, lane, square, and row. **Postal code prefixes,** which often appear on London street signs and in street addresses, may help you find your way. The letters stand for compass directions, with reference to the central district (itself divided into WC and EC, for West Central and East Central). All districts that border this central district are numbered "1." There are no S or NE codes. A **good map** is key. For a day's walk, London Transport's free map will do, but visitors staying longer ought to buy a London street index. *London A to Z* (that's "ay to *zed*," by the way) and *Nicholson's Streetfinder* (from £2) are excellent. Refer also to this book's many **color maps** of London.

For the most part, London is a tourist-friendly city. It's hard to wander unwittingly into unnerving neighborhoods; these areas, in parts of Hackney, Tottenham, and South London, lie well away from central London. The areas around King's Cross/St. Pancras and Notting Hill Gate Tube stations are also a bit seedy at night.

Telephone Code: London has 2 **city codes:** 0171 (central London) and 0181 (outer London). Use the code only if you are calling from one area to the other. **All London numbers listed in** *Let's Go* **are 0171 unless otherwise indicated.**

Flights: Heathrow Airport (tel. (0181) 759 43 21) is the world's busiest airport. The **Heathrow Express** travels between Heathrow and Paddington Station every 15 minutes (15min., 5:10am-11:40pm, one-way £10); the express train departs from Heathrow terminal #1, 2, 3, and 4. London Transport's **Airbus** (tel. 222 12 34) zips from Heathrow to central points, including hotels (1hr., £6). From **Gatwick Airport** (tel. (01293) 53 53 53), take the BR Gatwick Express train to Victoria Station. (35min, daily 5am-midnight every 15min., midnight-5am every 30min; day return £8.50-11.) **National Express** (tel. (0990) 80 80 80) buses run from Victoria Station to Gatwick (1hr., every hr., 5:05am-8:20pm, £8.50, return £11). Taxis take twice as long and cost 5 times as much.

Trains: 8 major stations: Charing Cross, Euston, King's Cross, Liverpool St., Paddington, St. Pancras, Victoria, and Waterloo. All stations linked by Underground. For train info stop by ticket offices at the stations or any LTB or BTA tourist office, or call **British Rail** at (0345) 48 49 50 (24hr.). For info on traveling to Europe, try (0990) 84 88 48. For **Eurostar** info (through the Chunnel), call (0345) 88 18 81.

Buses: Victoria Coach Station (Tube: Victoria), located on Buckingham Palace Rd., is Britain's coach hub. **National Express** (tel. (0990) 80 80 80) services an expansive network. Greater London area served by **Green Line** (tel. (0181) 668 72 61), which leaves frequently from Eccleston Bridge behind Victoria Station. Purchase tickets from the driver. Deals include the one-day **Rover** ticket (£7, valid on almost every Green Line coach and London Country bus M-F after 9am, Sa-Su all day).

Public Transportation: London is divided into 6 concentric transport zones; fares depend on the distance of the journey and the number of zones crossed. Call the **24hr. help line** (tel. 222 12 34) for a live operator, who will help you plan subway and bus travel. The **Underground** (or **Tube**) is fast, efficient, and crowded (check out our **color map** of said Underground). It opens about 6am; the last train runs around midnight. Buy your ticket before you board and pass it through automatic gates at both ends of your journey. On-the-spot £10 fine if you're caught without a valid ticket. The **Travelcard** is a must for budget travelers. Travelcards can be used on the Underground, regular buses, British Rail (Network SouthEast), and the Docklands Light Railway. One-day Travelcards cannot be used before 9:30am M-F and are not valid on night buses (adult one-day Travelcard, zones 1 & 2, £3.50). The one-week and one-month Travelcards can be used at any time and are valid for Night Bus travel. (1-week Travelcard, zones 1&2, £16.60; 1-month Travelcard, zones 1&2, £65.80. Bring a passport-sized photo.) **Night buses** (the "N" routes) run frequently throughout London 11:30pm-6am. All pass through Trafalgar Sq. The free night bus brochure includes times of the last British Rail and Underground trains. The **bus** network is divided into 4 zones. In and around central London, one-way fares range from 50p to £1.20, depending on the number of zones you cross. Bus 11 (originating at Liverpool St. station) and Bus 14 (beginning in Riverside-Putney) offer excellent sightseeing opportunities. Pick up free maps and guides at **London Transport's Information Centres** (look for the lower-case "i" logo on signs) at the following Tube stations: Euston, Victoria, King's Cross, Liverpool St., Oxford Circus, Piccadilly, St. James's Park, and at Heathrow Terminals 1, 2, and 4.

Taxis: A light signifies that they're empty. Fares are steep, and 10% tip is standard.

Hitchhiking: Anyone who values safety will take a train or bus out of London. **Freewheelers** is a ride-share agency. Single-sex matching available. For more info, email freewheelers@freewheelers.co.uk or check out http://www.freewheelers.co.uk/freewheelers

Tourist Offices: London Tourist Board Information Centre, Victoria Station Forecourt, SW1 (tel. (0839) 123 432; recorded message only; 39-49p per min.). Tube: Victoria. Info on London and England and an accommodations service (£5 booking fee, plus 15% refundable deposit). Expect long waits. Open Apr.-Nov. daily 8am-7pm; Dec.-Mar. M-Sa 8am-7pm, Su 8am-5pm. Additional tourist offices located at Heathrow Airport (open daily Apr.-Nov. 9am-6pm; Dec.-Mar. 9am-5pm) and "Liverpool St." Underground Station (open M 8:15am-7pm, Tu-Sa 8:15am-6pm, Su 8:30am-4:45pm). **British Travel Centre** 12 Regent St. (tel. (081) 846 90 00). Tube: Piccadilly Circus. Down Regent St. from the "Lower Regent St." Tube exit. Ideal for travelers bound for destinations outside of London. Combines the services of the BTA, British Rail, and a Traveller's Exchange with an accommodations service (£5 plus 15% deposit). Open M-F 9am-6:30pm, Sa-Su 10am-4pm. **City of London Information Centre,** St. Paul's Churchyard, EC4 (tel. 606 30 30). Tube: St. Paul's. Info on the City of London. Open daily 9:30am-5pm.

Budget Travel: London is *the* place to shop for cheap bus, plane, and train tickets to anywhere. Browse ads in *Time Out* or the *Evening Standard.*

Embassies and High Commissions: Australia, Australia House, The Strand, WC2 (tel. 379 43 34). Tube: Aldwych or Temple. Open M-F 9:30am-3:30pm. **Canada,** MacDonald House, 1 Grosvenor Sq., W1 (tel. 258 66 00). Tube: Bond St. or Oxford Circus. **Ireland,** 17 Grosvenor Pl., SW1 (tel. 235 21 71). Tube: Hyde Park Corner. Open M-F 9:30am-1pm and 2:30-5pm. **New Zealand,** New Zealand House, 80 Haymarket, SW1 (tel. 930 84 22). Tube: Charing Cross. Open M-F 10am-noon and 2-4pm. **South Africa,** South Africa House, Trafalgar Sq., WC2 (tel. 451 72 99). Tube: Charing Cross. Open M-F 10am-noon and 2-4pm. **U.S.,** 24 Grosvenor Sq., W1 (tel. 499 90 00). Tube: Bond St. Phones answered 24hr.

Bisexual, Gay, and Lesbian Information: London Lesbian and Gay Switchboard, tel. 837 73 24. 24hr. advice and support service. **Bisexual Helpline,** tel. (0181) 569 75 00. Tu-W 7:30-9:30pm. **Lesbian Line,** tel. 251 69 11. M and F 2-10pm, Tu-Th 7-10pm.

Crisis Lines: Samaritans, 46 Marshall St., W1 (tel. 734 28 00). Tube: Oxford Circus. Highly respected 24hr. crisis hotline listens (rather than advises) to callers with suicidal depression and other problems. **Women's Aid,** 52-54 Featherstone St., EC1 (tel. 392 20 92). 24hr. hotline and emergency shelter for victims of domestic and sexual abuse. **Alcoholics Anonymous,** 352 30 01. **National AIDS Helpline,** tel. (0800) 567 123. 24hr.

BRITAIN

Information for Travelers with Disabilities: RADAR, 12 City Forum, 250 City Rd., EC1V 8AF (tel. 250 32 22). Open M-F 10am-4pm.

Pharmacies: Police stations keep lists of emergency doctors and pharmacists. Listings under "Chemists" in the Yellow Pages. **Bliss Chemists** 5 Marble Arch, (W1; tel. 723 61 16) at Marble Arch, is open daily 9am-midnight.

Medical Assistance: In an emergency, you can be treated at no charge in the A&E ward of a hospital. Socialized medicine has lowered fees here, so don't ignore any health problem merely because you are low on cash. The following have 24hr. walk-in A&E (a.k.a. casualty) departments: **Royal London Hospital,** Whitechapel, (tel. 377 70 00; Tube: Whitechapel); **Royal Free Hospital,** Pond St., NW3 (tel. 794 05 00; Tube: Belsize Park or British Rail: Hampstead Heath); **Charing Cross Hospital,** Fulham Palace Rd. (entrance St. Dunstan's Rd.), W6 (tel. (0181) 846 12 34; Tube: Baron's Ct. or Hammersmith); **St. Thomas' Hospital,** Lambeth Palace Rd., SE1 (tel. 928 92 92; Tube: Westminster); **University College Hospital,** Gower St. (entrance on Grafton Way), WC1 (tel. 387 93 00; Tube: Euston or Warren St.). Or, look under "Hospitals" in the gray Businesses and Services phone book.

Emergency: Dial 999; no coins required.

Post Office: Save hassle and have mail sent to **Post Restante,** Trafalgar Sq. Post Office, 24-28 William IV St., London WC2N 4DL (tel. 930 95 80). Tube: Charing Cross. Open M-Th and Sa 8am-8pm, F 8:30am-8pm.

Internet Access: Webshack, 15 Dean St., W1 (tel. 439 80 00). Tube: Leicester Sq. or Tottenham Ct. Rd. £3 per 30min. £5 per hr. Open M-Sa 10:30am-11pm.

Telephones: Most accept change and phonecards, but some take only phonecards.

ACCOMMODATIONS

Write well in advance to reserve rooms for summer—landing in London without reservations is like landing on a bicycle that has no seat. B&Bs are a bargain for groups of two or more, but hostels are the cheapest (and most social) option for small groups. Check for reduced weekly rates in hotels. Colleges and universities rent out rooms during the summer, offering the best deals to students with ID.

YHA/HI Hostels

Cheap and cheery, London's YHA hostels can be a welcome relief from dreary urban B&Bs. Reserve ahead for July and August; if not, it's still worth calling (central tel. 248 65 47; M-Sa 9:30am-5:30pm). Bring a padlock to secure your personal locker.

Oxford Street, 14-18 Noel St., W1 (tel. 734 16 18; fax 734 16 57). Tube: Oxford Circus. Walk east on Oxford St. and turn right on Poland St. As close as possible to the Soho action. Dorms £18.70, under 18 £15.25; doubles £40.60. Kitchen and laundry. Reception 7am-11pm. No curfew. Book 3-4 weeks in advance—very few walk-ins accepted. Full payment required to secure a reservation.

Hampstead Heath, 4 Wellgarth Rd., NW11 (tel. (0181) 458 90 54 or 458 70 96; fax 209 05 46). Tube: Golders Green, then bus 210 or 268 toward Hampstead, or on foot by turning left from the station onto North End Rd., then left again onto Wellgarth. More like a hotel than a hostel. Dorms, £15.60, under 18 £13.35; doubles £38.50; triples £55; quads £71. Breakfast included. Kitchen, laundry, fax, and **Internet** access. 24hr. security and reception. No curfew. Reserve ahead.

City of London, 36 Carter Ln., EC4 (tel. 236 49 65; fax 236 76 81). Tube: St. Paul's. Go left down Godliman St., then take the 1st right; look for the sign. Sleep in clean and quiet comfort a stone's throw from St. Paul's. Dorms £19-22, under 18 £17-18; singles £25, £21.50; doubles £49, £41; triples £67.50, £90; quads £57, £76. Luggage storage, currency exchange, and laundry. Reception 7am-11pm. Call ahead.

Earl's Court, Earl's Ct., 38 Bolton Gdns., SW5 (tel. 373 70 83; fax 835 20 34). Tube: Earl's Ct. Exit from the Tube station onto Earl's Ct. Rd. and turn right; it's the 5th street on your left. Very clean townhouse in a leafy residential neighborhood. £18.70, under 18 £16.45. Non-members £1.70 extra; student discount £1. Kitchen laundry, and currency exchange. All rooms single-sex. Reception 7am-11pm. 24hr. security. No curfew. Meals available in the large, colorful cafeteria 5-8pm.

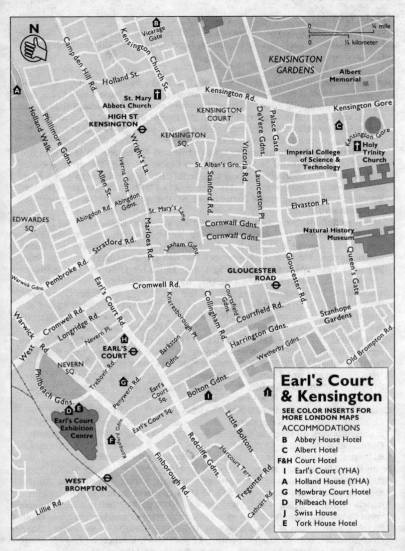

Earl's Court & Kensington

SEE COLOR INSERTS FOR MORE LONDON MAPS

ACCOMMODATIONS

B	Abbey House Hotel
C	Albert Hotel
F&H	Court Hotel
I	Earl's Court (YHA)
A	Holland House (YHA)
G	Mowbray Court Hotel
D	Philbeach Hotel
J	Swiss House
E	York House Hotel

BRITAIN

Holland House, Holland Walk, W8 (tel. 937 07 48; fax 376 06 67). Tube: High St. Kensington. Handsome 1607 Jacobean mansion in Holland Park offers lovely green views and a multi-lingual staff. HI membership required. Dorm £18.70, under 18 £16.45. Breakfast included. Laundry, kitchen, and luggage storage. 24hr. access.

King's Cross/St. Pancras, 79-81 Euston Rd., N1 (tel. 388 99 98; fax 388 67 66). Tube: King's Cross/St.Pancras or Euston. Spanking-new 8-story hostel boasts a convenient location and comfortable beds. Ask in advance about A/C. Dorms £18-21.30; doubles £19.40-22.50, with bath £21-24.30; quads £80; quints £97.50. Laundry, kitchen, and luggage storage. No curfew. Book in advance. Max. stay 1 week.

Private Hostels

Private hostels, which do not require an HI card, generally have a youthful clientele and often sport a vaguely bohemian atmosphere. Some have kitchen facilities and curfews are rare.

Ashlee House, 261-65 Gray's Inn Rd., WC1 (tel. 833 9400; fax 833 67 77; email ashleehouse@tsnxt.co.uk). Tube: King's Cross/St. Pancras. From King's Cross, turn right onto Pentonville Rd. and right again onto Gray's Inn Rd. Clean, bright rooms within easy walking distance of King's Cross. Dorms £13; 4- and 6-bed rooms £17; twins £22. Breakfast included (served M-F 7:30-9.30am, Sa-Su 8-10am). Kitchens and laundry available. Reception 24hr. No curfew or lockout. Check-out 10am.

Astor's Museum Inn, Montague St., WC1 (tel. 580 53 60; fax 636 79 48). Tube: Holborn, Tottenham Ct. Rd., or Russell Sq. Off Bloomsbury Sq. The prime location compensates for standard dorms. If they're full, they'll direct you to 1 of 3 other Astor's hostels. Coed dorms almost inevitable. £14-17; discounts available Oct.-Mar. Breakfast included. Adequate linens provided. Reception 24hr. No curfew. Book about a month ahead.

Tonbridge School Clubs, Ltd. (tel. 837 44 06), Judd and Cromer St., WC1. Tube: King's Cross/St. Pancras. Follow Euston Rd. to the site of the new British Library and turn left onto Judd St.; the hostel is 3 blocks down. Students with non-British passports only. No frills and no privacy, but dirt cheap. Blankets and foam pads provided. Floor space £5. Lockout 9am-9pm. Lights off 11:30pm. No admittance after midnight. Use caution when walking in the area at night.

Quest Hotel, 45 Queensborough Terrace, W2 (tel. 229 77 82). Tube: Queensway, then turn right onto Bayswater for 2 blocks, and left onto Queensborough. Communal, clean, and sociable. Dorms (co-ed and 1 women-only) £15-18. Breakfast (8-9:45am) and sheets included. Check-out 10am. No curfew or lockout.

Albert Hotel, 191 Queens Gate, SW7 (tel. 584 30 19; fax 823 85 20). Tube: Gloucester Rd., or Bus 2 or 70 from South Kensington. A substantial walk from the Tube, but deliciously close to Hyde Park; take a right on Cromwell and a left on Queen's Gate. Elegant and wood paneled, with sunny balconies. Dorms (single-sex or coed) £12-15; singles or doubles £40. Breakfast and sheets provided. Laundry. Reception 24hr. No lockout or curfew. Reserve ahead with 1 night's deposit.

Court Hotel, 194-196 Earl's Ct. Rd., SW5 (tel. 373 00 27; fax 912 95 00). Tube: Earl's Ct. Sister hostel at 17 Kempsford Gardens (tel. 373 2174). Very clean Australian-managed hostel. All single and double rooms have TV and tea/coffee set. Kitchen. Dorms (single-sex) £15; singles £26; doubles £35. Off-season discounts. Reception 8am-9pm. No curfew. Reservations not accepted; call for availability.

Hyde Park Hostel, 2-6 Inverness Terr., W2 (tel. 229 51 01; fax 229 31 70). Tube: Bayswater or Queensway. New and conveniently located. Pool room/lounge. Kitchen, laundry facilities. Dorms £12.50-15. Breakfast included. Reception 24hr.

Victoria Hotel, 71 Belgrave Rd. SW1 (tel. 834 3077; fax 932 0693). Tube: Pimlico. From the station, take the Bessborough St. (south side) exit and go left along Lupus St., then take a right at St. George's Sq. Belgrave Rd. starts on the other side. A clean, friendly, bohemian hostel with cool pool room. Kitchen. £12.50-15. Continental breakfast included. Luggage storage. Reception 24hr.

University Halls of Residence

London's university residences often accommodate visitors during the summer break (early June to mid-Sept.) and Easter vacations. Many of these halls have box-like rooms and institutional furniture. Most charge £18-25 and contain all singles. Call well in advance (by April for July reservations), as conference groups snatch up rooms early. The **King's Campus Vacation Bureau** (write to 127 Stanford Street, SE1 9NQ; tel. 928 37 77) controls bookings for a number of residential halls.

Stamford Street Apartments, 127 Stamford St., SE1 (tel. 873 29 60; fax 873 29 62). Tube: Waterloo. Take the exit marked "Waterloo Bridge," then the pedestrian subway marked "Subway to York Road," and follow it around the circle to reach Stamford St. 560 spacious singles with bathrooms. Each "apartment" shares a kitchen and TV lounge. Laundry facilities. Use of gym £5 per week. £32.50. 10% discount for stays over 7 days. Reception 24hr. Disabled access. Open July-Sept.

High Holborn Residence, 178 High Holborn, WC1 (tel. 379 55 89; fax 379 56 40). Tube: Holborn. An amazing combination of comfort and affordability. Singles are spacious and well furnished. You could eat off the bathroom floors, if so inclined. Lounge and bar. Usually booked far in advance. Singles £27; twins £45, with bath £52; discounts for longer stays. Breakfast included. Laundry facilities. Reception 7am-11pm. Open July to mid-Sept.

Wellington Hall, 71 Vincent Sq., Westminster, SW1 (tel. 834 47 40; fax 233 77 09). Tube: Victoria. Walk 1 block along Vauxhall Bridge Rd.; turn left on Rochester Row. Charming Edwardian hall on pleasant, quiet square. Reserve through King's Campus Vacation Bureau (see above). Singles £25; doubles £38.50. English breakfast included. Discounts for longer stays. Book in advance. Rooms generally available June-Sept. and Easter.

John Adams Hall, 15-23 Endsleigh St., WC1 (tel. 387 40 86; fax 383 01 64). Tube: Euston. Heading right on Euston Rd., take 1st right onto Gordon St. and 1st left onto Endsleigh Gdns.; Endsleigh St. is the 2nd right. Elegant Georgian building. Laundry facilities, TV lounge, and 5 pianos. Singles £22; doubles £37. 5 or more days: singles £19; doubles £33. English breakfast included. Reception daily 8am-1pm and 2-10pm. Open July-Aug. and Easter, but a few rooms free all year.

Bed & Breakfasts

The number of B&Bs boggles the mind. Some are dingy and indistinct, others feature unique furnishings and a warm, welcoming atmosphere.

Near Victoria Station

B&Bs around Victoria Station are close to London's attractions as well as transportation connections. In the summer, prudent visitors make reservations well in advance.

Melbourne House, 79 Belgrave Rd., SW1 (tel. 828 35 16; fax 828 71 20), past Warwick Sq. Tube: Pimlico. Take the Bessborough St. (south side) exit and go left along Lupus St. Turn right at St. George's Sq.; Belgrave Rd. starts on the other side of the square. All of the sparkling rooms come with TV, phone, and hot pot. Singles £30-50; doubles or twins with bath £70; triples £95; quads £110. Winter discounts. English breakfast with cereal option (7:30-8:45am). Book ahead. No credit cards.

Luna and Simone Hotel, 47-49 Belgrave Rd., SW1 (tel. 834 58 97; fax 828 24 78), past Warwick St. Tube: Victoria or Pimlico. Immaculate and well-maintained. Singles £25; doubles £50, with bath £60; triples with shower £75. 10% discount for long-term stays. Winter discount. English breakfast included. Luggage storage.

Georgian House Hotel, 35 St. George's Dr., SW1 (tel. 834 14 38; fax 976 60 85). Spacious rooms decorated with personality. Ask about the annex (about a block away) which is older but slightly cheaper and quieter. Singles £19-39; doubles £32-55; triples £45-68; quads £54-75. Breakfast included. Reception 8am-11pm.

Eaton House Hotel, 125 Ebury St., SW1 (tel./fax 730 87 81). Large, clean, pastel rooms with dark wood chairs, TV, and tea/coffee maker. Singles £35-55; doubles £55-70; triples £70-85. Ask about discounts. English breakfast included.

Earl's Court

The area feeds on the tourist trade: travel agencies, currency exchanges, and souvenir shops dominate. The area also has a vibrant gay and lesbian population. Rooms tend to be dirt cheap, but ask to see a room to make sure the "dirt" isn't literal. Beware of overeager guides willing to lead you from the station to a hostel.

York House Hotel, 27-28 Philbeach Gdns., SW5 (tel. 373 75 19; fax 370 46 41). Special features include a mod, 60s-style TV lounge and a lovely garden. Extraordinarily clean. Friendly staff, surroundings, and low prices. Singles £30; doubles £47, with bath £66; triples £58, with bath £79; quads £67. English breakfast included.

Mowbray Court Hotel, 28-32 Penywern Rd., SW5 (tel. 373 82 85 or 370 36 90; fax 370 5693; email mowbraycrthot@hotmail.com). This place is relatively expensive, but staff this helpful is a rarity in London; wake-up calls, tour arrangements, taxi-

BRITAIN

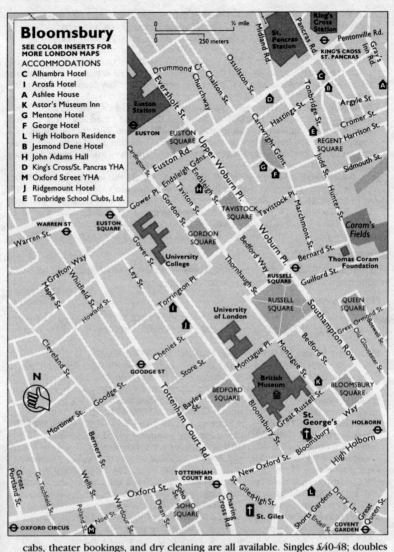

Bloomsbury

SEE COLOR INSERTS FOR
MORE LONDON MAPS

ACCOMMODATIONS

C Alhambra Hotel
I Arosfa Hotel
A Ashlee House
K Astor's Museum Inn
G Mentone Hotel
F George Hotel
L High Holborn Residence
B Jesmond Dene Hotel
H John Adams Hall
D King's Cross/St. Pancras YHA
M Oxford Street YHA
J Ridgemount Hotel
E Tonbridge School Clubs, Ltd.

cabs, theater bookings, and dry cleaning are all available. Singles £40-48; doubles £50-60; triples £63-72. Continental breakfast included. Reserve ahead if possible.

Philbeach Hotel, 30-31 Philbeach Gdns., SW5 (tel. 373 12 44; fax 244 01 49). The largest gay B&B in England, popular with both men and women. Gorgeous garden and an award-winning, upscale restaurant. Singles £45, with shower £55; doubles £58, with bath £75. Continental breakfast. 1-wk. advance booking recommended.

Kensington & Chelsea

These hotels prove convenient for those who wish to visit the stunning array of museums that line the southwest side of Hyde Park. Prices are a bit higher, but hotels here tend to be significantly more sober and comfortable than many at Earl's Ct.

Abbey House Hotel, 11 Vicarage Gate, W8 (tel. 727 25 94), off Kensington Church St. Tube: High St. Kensington. After a series of renovations, the hotel has achieved a level of comfort that can't be rivaled at these prices. Singles £40; doubles £65; triples £78; quads £90; quints £100. English breakfast. Book ahead. No credit cards.

Swiss House, 171 Old Brompton Rd., SW5 (tel. 373 27 69; fax 373 49 83; email recep@swiss-hh.demon.co.uk). Airy, spacious rooms, most with fireplaces. Singles £42, with bath £59; doubles with bath £75. Continental breakfast included.

Oakley Hotel, 73 Oakley St., SW3 (tel. 352 55 99 or 352 66 10; fax 727 11 90). Tube: Sloane Sq.; Victoria, then Bus 11, 19, or 22; or South Kensington. Turn left off King's Rd. at the Chelsea Fire Station. Just steps away from Albert Bridge, Battersea Park, and shopping on King's Rd. Amiable staff and lovely bedrooms. Dorms (women only) £14; singles £32; doubles £48, with bath £58; triples £63, £72; quads £72; quints £80. Breakfast included. Kitchen. Reserve ahead several weeks.

Bloomsbury

Despite its proximity to the West End, Bloomsbury maintains a fairly residential demeanor, with gracious, tree-filled squares and a prime location.

Arosfa Hotel, 83 Gower St., WC1 (tel./fax 636 21 15). All furnishings and fixtures are close to new, the rooms are spacious, and the facilities are immaculate. Singles £31; doubles £44, with bath £58; triples £59, £70. MC, V.

Ridgemount Hotel, 65-67 Gower St., WC1 (tel. 636 11 41 or 580 70 60; fax. 636 25 58). Bright rooms with firm beds. **Laundry** facilities, garden in back, free tea and coffee in the TV lounge. Singles £30, with bath £40; doubles £44, £55; triples £57, £72. English breakfast included. Call in advance. No credit cards.

Mentone Hotel, 54-55 Cartwright Gdns., WC1 (tel. 387 39 27; fax 388 46 71). Pleasantly decorated and newly renovated. Singles £42-60; doubles £60-75; quads with bath £90. Reduced rates Dec.-Apr. English breakfast included. AmEx, MC, Visa.

George Hotel 60 Cartwright Gdns., WC1 (tel. 387 87 77; fax 387 86 66). Pleasant proprietress manages newly-renovated hotel. Singles £43.50; doubles £59.50-75; triples £73-87; quads £80. English breakfast included. MC, Visa.

Alhambra Hotel, 17-19 Argyle St., WC1 (tel. 837 95 75; fax 916 24 76). Singles £30-40; doubles £40-55; quads £90. English breakfast included. AmEx, MC, Visa.

Jesmond Dene Hotel, 27 Argyle St., WC1 (tel. 837 46 54; fax 833 16 33; http://www.scoot.co.uk/jesmond-dene). Newly-renovated. Singles £28; doubles £38-55; triples £55-66; quads £75-85; quints £85. English breakfast. MC, Visa.

Paddington & Bayswater

B&Bs of variable quality cluster around Norfolk Square and Sussex Gardens.

Hyde Park Rooms Hotel, 137 Sussex Gdns., W2 (tel. 723 02 25 or 723 09 65). Tube: Paddington. Family run with airy rooms. An outstanding value. Singles £26, with bath £38; doubles £38, £48; triples £57, £72. English breakfast. Book in advance.

Dean Court Hotel, 57 Inverness Terr., W2 (tel. 229 29 61; fax 727 11 90). Tube: Bayswater or Queensway. Inverness is the 1st left off Bayswater Rd. Clean rooms with firm mattresses, and English breakfast (M-F 7:30-8:30am, weekends 8:30-9:30am). **New Kent** next door offers same rooms, prices, and management. No private facilities. Dorms £14 per night; doubles £38; twins £49; triples £54.

Garden Court Hotel, 30-31 Kensington Gdns. Sq., W2 (tel. 229 25 53; fax 727 27 49). Tube: Bayswater. From the Tube, make a left onto Queensway, a left onto Porchester Gdns., and then a right onto Kensington Gdns. Sq. A larger hotel in a pleasant, leafy neighborhood. Singles £34, with bath £48; doubles £48, £74; triples £68, £82. English breakfast. £25 deposit required. Check-out 11am.

FOOD

London presents a tantalizing range of foreign and English specialties. Indian, Lebanese, Greek, Chinese, Thai, Italian, West Indian, and African food is inexpensive and readily available. If you eat but one meal in London, let it be Indian—London's Indian food is rivaled only by India's. Meals are less expensive on Westbourne Grove (Tube: Bayswater) or near Euston Station than in the West End.

The West End

Mandeer, 8 Bloomsbury Way. W1. Tube: Tottenham Ct. Rd. North Indian food is exceedingly fresh, primarily organic, and all vegetarian. The best deal in the house is the lunch buffet (from £3.50). Open M-Sa noon-3pm and 5-10pm.

BRITAIN

West End Kitchen, 5 Panton St. Tube: Picadilly Circus. Perhaps the best deals going in London: a variety of ethnic and English dishes for under £3. 3-course set lunch £3.50. Open daily 7am-11:45pm.

The Stockpot, 18 Old Compton St., W1. Tube: Leicester Sq. or Piccadilly Circus. The cheapest place in Soho to soak up style. Open M-Tu 11:30am-11:30pm, W-Sa 11:30am-11:45pm, Su noon-11pm. Also at 40 Panton St.

The Wren Cafe at St. James's, 35 Jermyn St., SW1. Tube: Piccadilly Circus or Green Park. Wholefood/vegetarian delights served in the shadow of a Christopher Wren church. Open M-Sa 8:30am-6pm, Su 9am-5pm.

Cafe Emm, 17 Frith St., W1 (tel. 437 07 23). Tube: Leicester Sq. Large portions are served in an unpretentious and soothing atmosphere. A cheap and palatable way to sample Soho cafe-culture. Open M-Th noon-3pm and 5:30-11pm, F noon-3pm and 5:30pm-1am, Sa 5pm-1am, Su 5:30-11pm. Last orders 30min. before closing.

Lok Ho Fook, 4-5 Gerrard St., W1. Busy place with good prices and welcoming atmosphere. Extensive offerings with seafood, noodles, and vegetarian dishes. *Dim sum* (before 6pm) is made fresh when you order. Not to be confused with a nearby (and more expensive) place called Lee Ho Fook. Open daily noon-11:45pm.

Neal's Yard Salad Bar, 2 Neal's Yard, WC2. Take-away or sit outside at this simple vegetarian's nirvana. Tempting salads from £2. Open daily 11am-9pm.

Belgo Centraal, 50 Earlham St. WC2. Second branch, **Belgo Noord,** now open in Camden Town on 72 Chalk Farm Rd., NW1. Waiters in monk's cowls and bizarre 21st century beerhall interior make this one of Covent Garden's most popular restaurants. Daily noon-5pm, a fiver buys you wild boar sausage, Belgian mash, and a beer. Open M-Sa noon-11:30pm, Su noon-10:30pm. Wheelchair accessible.

City of London & East End

The Place Below (tel. 329 07 89), in St. Mary-le-Bow Church crypt, Cheapside, EC2. Tube: St. Paul's. Generous vegetarian dishes served to the hippest of City execs in a church basement. Menu changes daily. Quiche and salad £6. Food much cheaper to take-away and £2 is taken off when you sit in from 11:30am-noon. Serves as a cafe until lunch at 11:30am. Open M-F 7:30am-2:30pm.

Tinseltown 24 Hour Diner, 44/46 St. John St., EC1. Tube: Clerkenwell. All beer is about £1.50 and house wine £4.95. And best of all, it's open 24hr., 7 days a week.

Lahore Kebab House, 2 Umberston St., E1. Tube: Whitechapel or Shadwell DLR. Off Commercial Rd. Some of the best, cheapest Indian and Pakistani cuisine in the city. No dish over £4. Feel free to bring your own beer. Open daily noon-midnight.

Kensington, Knightsbridge, Chelsea, & Victoria

Ciaccio, 5 Warwick Way, SW1. An intimate Italian eatery whose prices and spices make it a giant for budget eaters. Pick a container of pasta and one of about 10 sauces (pesto, veggie, tomato and meat), and they'll heat it up in the microwave for £1.69-2.85. Open M-F 10am-7pm, Sa 9:30am-6pm.

Apadna, 351 Kensington High St., W8. A 10min. walk from the Tube and an escape from the street's commercial banality. Offers savory kebabs in fresh-baked *naan* (minced lamb kebab £2.80). Open daily 11am-11pm.

Chelsea Kitchen, 98 King's Rd., SW3. 7min. walk from the Tube. Eclectic, filling, and tasty. Breakfast 8-11:25am. Open M-Sa 8am-11:30pm, Su 9am-11:30pm.

Bloomsbury and North London

Wagamama, 4a Streatham St., WC1. Tube: Tottenham Ct. Rd. Fast food: waitstaff takes your orders on hand-held electronic radios that transmit directly to the kitchen. Noodles £4.50-5.70. Open M-Sa noon-11pm, Su 12:30-10pm.

Diwana Bhel Poori House, 121 Drummond St., NW1. Tube: Warren St. Tasty Indian vegetarian food in a clean and airy restaurant. Many vegetarian and liberal kosher options. Lunch buffet £4 (noon-2:30pm). Open daily noon-11:30pm.

Captain Nemo, 171 Kentish Town Rd., NW1. Tube: Kentish Town. Unassuming Chinese/chippie take-away rocks your world with tangy, delicious chips in curry sauce (£1.40). Open M-F noon-2:45pm and 5:30-11:30pm, Sa-Su 5:30-11:30pm.

Troubador Coffee House, 265 Old Brompton Rd., SW5, near Earl's Ct. and Old Brompton Rd. junction. Whirring espresso machines steam up the windows in this cafe. Live music. Assorted snacks, soups, and sandwiches under £4. Liquor available with food orders. Open M-Sa 9:30am-12:30am, Su 9:30am-11pm.

Notting Hill, Ladbroke Grove, and Earl's Court

The Grain Shop, 269a Portobello Rd., W11. Tube: Ladbroke Grove. Take-away shop with a large array of tasty foods and a long line of customers. Organic whole grain breads baked daily (80p-£1.40 per loaf). Groceries also available, many organic. Open M-Sa 9:30am-6pm.

Cockney's, 314 Portobello Rd., W10. Tube: Ladbroke Grove. "Traditional pie, mash, and eels," says the sign above the door, and they aren't joking (eels available F-Sa). Cups of liquor for only 30p. Open M-Th and Sa 11:30am-5:30pm, F 11:30am-6pm.

Bistro Benito, 166 Earl's Court Rd., SW5 (tel. 373 66 46). 20-yr. old family Italian bistro serves good cheer and hearty food in equal helpings. Most pastas £3.95. Open M-Sa noon-11:30pm, Su noon-11pm.

PUBS

The clientele of London's 700 pubs varies widely from one neighborhood to the next. Avoid touristy pubs near train stations. For the best prices head to the East End. Stylish, lively pubs cluster around the fringes of the West End. Many historic alehouses lend an ancient air to areas swallowed up by the urban sprawl, such as Highgate and Hampstead. Don't be afraid to leave a good pub—making a circuit, or **pub crawl,** lets you experience the diversity of a neighborhood's nightlife.

The Dog and Duck, 8 Bateman St., W1. Tube: Tottenham Ct. Rd. Frequent winner of the Best Pub in Soho award, its size keeps the crowd down. Inexpensive pints (£1.95-2.20). Evenings bring locals, theater-goers, and, yes, some tourists. Open M-F noon-11pm, Sa 6-11pm, Su 7-10:30pm.

The Three Greyhounds, 25 Greek St., W1. Tube: Leicester Sq. This medieval-style pub provides welcome respite from the posturing of Soho. Open M-Sa 11am-11pm, Su noon-10:30pm.

Riki Tik, 23-24 Bateman St., W1. Tube: Leicester Squ., Tottenham Ct. Rd., or Piccadilly Circus. A hyped, hip, and tremendously swinging bar specializing in orgasmic flavored vodka shots (£2.60). Come during happy hour (W-Sa noon-8pm) for near-bargains. Open M-Sa noon-1am. £3 cover after 11pm.

Lamb and Flag, 33 Rose St., WC2, off Garrick St. Tube: Covent Garden or Leicester Sq. A traditional pub, with 2 sections—the public bar for the working class, and the saloon bar for the businessmen, though today the classes mix. Live jazz upstairs Su from 7:30pm. Open M-Th 11am-11pm, F-Sa 11am-10:45pm, Su noon-10:30pm.

World's End Distillery, 459 King's Rd., near World's End Pass before Edith Grove. Tube: Sloane Sq. Enjoy pints in the comfy bookshelf-lined booths. Comedy every Su night at 8pm (£3.50). Open M-Sa 11am-11pm, Su noon-10:30pm.

The Old Crown, 33 New Oxford St., WC1. Tube: Tottenham Ct. Rd. A thoroughly untraditional pub with a lively crowd and cool jazz. Homemade food from £2.75. Open M-Sa 10am-11pm.

SIGHTS

London is best explored on foot. But if you have only one day here, a tour may be a good way to intensify your sight-seeing experience. The **Original London Sightseeing Tour** (tel. (0181) 877 17 22) provides a convenient, albeit cursory, overview of London's attractions from a double-decker bus. *(Tours daily in summer 9am-7pm; in winter 9:30am-5:30pm. £12, under 16 £6.)* Two-hour tours depart from Baker St., Haymarket (near Piccadilly Circus), Marble Arch, Embankment, and near Victoria Station. The route includes views of Buckingham Palace, the Houses of Parliament, Westminster Abbey, the Tower of London, St. Paul's, and Piccadilly Circus. A ticket allows you to ride the buses for a 24-hour period—permitting visitors to hop off at major sights and hop on a later bus to finish the tour. Walking tours can fill in the specifics of London that bus tours run right over. Among the best is **The Original London Walks** (tel. 624 39 78), two-hour tours led by well-regarded guides (£4.50, students £3.50).

Mayfair to Parliament

Piccadilly Circus and its towering neon bluffs (Tube: Piccadilly Circus) are an auspicious beginning to a day's wander. At the center of the Nash's swirling hub stands a fountain topped by a statue everyone calls Eros but is actually supposed to be the Angel of Christian Charity. North are the tiny shops of Regent St. and the renovated seediness of **Soho**, a region sporting a vibrant sidewalk cafe culture, where pornography once reigned supreme. Outdoor cafes, upscale shops, and slick crowds huddle in **Covent Garden** to the northeast. Paths across **Green Park** lead to **Buckingham Palace** (tel. 799 2331; http://www.royal.gov.uk), now partially open to tourists. *(Tube: Victoria, Green Park, and St. James's Park. Open daily Aug.-Sept. £9.50, seniors £7, under 17 £5. Tours may be available; call for details.)* The **Changing of the Guard** occurs daily (Apr. to late Aug.) or every other day (Sept.-Mar.) at 11:30am, unless it's raining. Arrive early or you won't see a thing.

The **Mall**, a wide processional, leads from the palace to **Admiralty Arch** and **Trafalgar Square.** South of the Mall, **St. James's Park** shelters a duck preserve and a flock of lawn chairs (70p per 4hr.). The center of a vicious traffic roundabout, Trafalgar Square (Tube: Charing Cross) centers on Nelson's Column, a 40 ft. high statue astride a 132 ft. column. Political Britain branches off **Whitehall**, just south of Trafalgar. Draped in black velvet, Charles I was led out of the **Banqueting House** (corner of Horse Guards Ave. and Whitehall) and beheaded. *(Open M-Sa 10am-5pm but closed for government functions. Last admission 4pm. £3.50, concessions £2.70.)* The building now hosts less lethal state dinners. The Prime Minister resides off Whitehall at **10 Downing Street,** now closed to tourists. In the middle of Whitehall is the **Cenotaph,** a monument to Britain's war dead. Whitehall ends by the sprawling **Houses of Parliament** (Tube: Westminster). Access to the House of Commons and the House of Lords is extremely restricted since a member was killed in a bomb blast in 1979. Queue up outside when either are in session in order to sit in the upper galleries of the Lords or Commons. You can hear **Big Ben** but not see him; Big Ben is neither the tower nor the clock, but the 14-ton bell, cast when a similarly proportioned Sir Benjamin Hall served as Commissioner of Works. Church and state tie the knot in **Westminster Abbey,** coronation chamber to English monarchs since 1066 and the site of **Poet's Corner,** the **Grave of the Unknown Warrior,** the **Stone of Scone,** and the elegantly perpendicular **Chapel of Henry VII.** *(Abbey open M-F 9am-4:45pm, last admission 3:45pm, some W until 7:45pm (call 222 7110), Sa 9am-2:45pm. £5, concessions £3, ages 11-18 £2, families £10. Tours (tel. 222 7110) £3. Photography permitted W evenings only.)* Britain bestows no greater honor than burial within these walls. The abbey plumber is buried here along with Elizabeth I, Darwin, Dickens, and Newton. Ask about the story surrounding the Stone of Scone.

Hyde Park & Kensington to Chelsea

Hyde Park shows its best face on Sundays from 11am to dusk, when soapbox orators take freedom of speech to the limit at **Speaker's Corner** (Tube: Marble Arch, *not* Hyde Park Corner). To the west, **Kensington Gardens,** an elegant relic of Edwardian England, celebrates the glories of model yacht racing in the squarish Round Pound. From the gardens, you can catch a glimpse of **Kensington Palace;** hourly tours visit uninhabited royal rooms and a collection of regal memorabilia, including Court dresses. *(Tours (1¼hr.) May-Sept. M-Sa 10am-5pm; call Ticketmaster at 344 44 44. £7.50, students £6.)* The **Royal Albert Hall,** on the south edge of Hyde Park, hosts the **Proms,** a gloriously British festival of music. Up Brompton Rd. near Knightsbridge, **Harrods** (Tube: Knightsbridge) vends under its humble motto, *Omnia Omnibus Ubique*— "All things for all people, everywhere." *(Open M-Tu and Sa 10am-6pm, W-F 10am-7pm.)* Still-fashionable **King's Road** (Tube: Sloane Sq.), south in **Chelsea**, attempts to do justice to its bohemian past—past residents include Oscar Wilde and the Sex Pistols.

Regent's Park to Fleet Street

Take a break from the city and picnic in the expanse of **Regent's Park,** northeast of Hyde Park across Marylebone (Tube: Regent's Park). The **London Zoo,** in the north end, harbors such exotic animals as mambos, Asian lions, and piranhas. *(Open daily*

Apr.-Sept. 10am-5:30pm; Oct.-Mar. 10am-4pm. Last admission 1hr. before close. £8.50, concessions £7.) **Camden Town** (Tube: Camden Town), bordering the park to the northeast, sports rollicking street markets. **Bloomsbury**—eccentric, erudite, and disorganized—is known for its literary and scholarly connections, including the **British Museum.** Although nearly all the papers have moved to cheaper real estate, **Fleet Street** is the traditional den of the British press. Close by are the **Inns of Court,** which have controlled access to the English Bar since the 13th century.

City of London & the East End

Once upon a time, "London" meant the square-mile enclave of the **City of London;** the rest of today's metropolis were far-flung towns and villages. The **Tower of London,** the grandest fortress in medieval Europe, was the palace and prison of English monarchs for over 500 years. Inside, the **Crown Jewels** include the Stars of Africa, cut from the enormous Cullinan Diamond, which was mailed third-class from the Transvaal in an unmarked brown paper package. The tower's best-known edifice, the **White Tower,** was begun by William the Conqueror. In 1483, the "Princes in the Tower" (Edward V and his brother) were murdered in the **Bloody Tower** in one of the great unsolved mysteries of British royal history. *(Tube: Tower Hill. Open M-Sa 9am-5pm, Su 10am-5pm; last ticket sold at 4pm. £9.50, concessions £7.15.)* Two of the wives of jolly King Henry VIII were beheaded in the courtyard, and in 1941 Rudolf Hess was sent to the Tower after his parachute dumped him in Scotland. Next to the tower is **Tower Bridge,** one of London's best-known landmarks. Other fragments of history are scattered throughout the City, among them 24 Christopher Wren churches interspersed among the soaring steel of modern skyscrapers. Peruse smaller churches, such as the Strand's **St. Clement Danes** of "Oranges and Lemons" fame or the superb **St. Stephen Walbrook** near the Bank of England (Tube: Bank). True-blue cockney Londoners are born within earshot of the famous bells of **St. Mary-le-Bow,** Cheapside. In the German Blitz in 1940, **St. Paul's Cathedral** stood firm in a sea of fire. *(Tube: St. Paul's. Open M-Sa 8:30am-4pm. Ambulatory and galleries open M-Sa 8:45am-4:15pm. Cathedral, ambulatory, crypt, and galleries £7.50, students £6.50.)* Climb above the graves of Wren, Nelson, and Wellington in the crypt to the dizzying top of the dome; the view is unparalleled. The **Barbican Centre** (Tube: Barbican or Moorgate) is one of the most impressive and controversial post-Blitz rebuilding projects.

The **East End** is a relatively poor section of London with a history of racial conflict. During the Industrial Revolution, a large working-class population moved into the district. A wave of Jewish immigrants fleeing persecution in Eastern Europe soon followed, settling around **Whitechapel.** Notable remnants of the community include the city's oldest standing synagogue, **Bevis Marks Synagogue.** *(Bevis Marks and Heneage Ln., EC3. Tel. 626 12 74. Tube: Aldgate; from Aldgate High St. turn right onto Houndsditch. Creechurch Lane on the left leads to Bevis Marks.)* In 1978, the latest immigration wave brought a large Muslim Bangladeshi community to the East End. **Brick Lane** (Tube: Aldgate East), the community's heart, is lined with Indian and Bangladeshi restaurants, colorful textile shops, and ethnic grocery stores. *(To reach Brick Lane, head left up Whitechapel as you exit the Tube station; turn left onto Osbourne St., which turns into Brick Lane.)* On Sundays, market stalls selling books, bric-a-brac, leather jackets, and sandwiches flank this street and Middlesex St., better known as **Petticoat Lane.**

The South & Outskirts

Lesser-known but equally rewarding treasures lie south of the river, the area currently experiencing a cultural and economic renewal. **Southwark Cathedral,** a smallish, quiet church, boasts London's second-best Gothic structure and a chapel dedicated to John Harvard (Tube: London Bridge). Not for the squeamish, **London Dungeon** lurks beneath the London Bridge with exhibits on execution, torture, and plague. *(Open daily Apr.-Sept. 10am-6:30pm, last entrance 5:30pm; Nov.-Feb. 10am-5:30pm, last entrance 4:30pm. £9.50, students £7.95.)* West along the riverbank, a reconstruction of **Shakespeare's Globe Theatre** (tel. 902 14 00) is used for performances. *(1hr. tours available May-Sept. M 9am-4pm, Tu-Sa 9am-12:30pm, Su 9am-2:30pm; Oct.-Apr. daily 10am-5pm. £5, concessions £4.)*

The genteel Victorian shopping and residential district of Brixton (Tube: Brixton) became the locus of a Caribbean and African community who followed large-scale Commonwealth immigration in the 1950s and 1960s. Most of the activity in Brixton centers around the **Brixton Market** at Electric Ave., Popes Rd., and Brixton Station Rd. Choose from among the stalls of fresh fish, vegetables, and West Indian cuisine, or browse through the stalls of African crafts and discount clothing. Nearby, on the corner of Coldharbor and Atlantic, the **Black Cultural Archives,** 378 Coldharbor Lane, SW9 (tel. 738 45 91), mounts small but informative exhibits on black history.

London **Docklands,** Europe's largest commercial development, is the only section of London built wholly anew—a break from the city's typically slow architectural evolution. Developers have poured tons of steel, reflective glass, and money onto the banks of the Thames east of London Bridge. The 800 ft. **Canary Wharf** building, Britain's tallest edifice and the jewel of the Docklands, is visible to the east from almost anywhere in London. The best way to see the area is via the **Docklands Light Railway (DLR)** (tel. 918 40 00), a driverless, totally automatic elevated rail system. All tickets, Travelcards, and passes issued by London Transport, London Underground, and British Rail are valid on the DLR, provided they cover the correct zones. The first stop for any Docklands tour should be the **Docklands Visitors Centre.** *(Tel. 512 11 11. DLR: Crossharbor, then left up the road. Open M-F 8:30am-6pm, Sa-Su 9:30am-5pm.)*

Head by train or boat to red-brick **Hampton Court Palace** (tel. (0181) 781 95 00) for a quirky change of pace. *(£8, return £12. Hampton Court open Mar. to late Oct. M 10:15am-6pm, Tu-Su 9:30am-6pm; late Oct. to Mar. M 10:15am-4:30pm, Tu-Su 9:30am-4:30pm; last admission 45min. before closing. Gardens open at the same time as the palace, but close at 9pm or dusk, whichever comes first. Free. All-encompassing admission £9.25, concessions £7; only to maze or Privy Garden £2.10.)* Its grounds contain the famous **hedgerow maze** (British Rail: Hampton Ct). From the Monday before Easter until the end of September, a boat runs from Westminster Pier to Hampton Court, leaving in the morning at 10:30, 11:15am, and noon, and returning from Hampton Court at 3, 4, and 5pm. The trip takes three to four hours one way.

Windsor Castle (tel. (01753) 86 82 86 or 83 11 18 for 24hr. info line) is the Queen's spectacular country retreat. *(Open daily Apr.-Oct. 10am-5:30pm, last entry 4pm; Nov.-Mar. 10am-4pm; last entry 3pm. £8.80, over 60 £6.20, under 17 £4.60.)* British Rail serves Windsor and Eton Central station and Windsor and Eton Riverside station, both of which are near Windsor Castle.

Just west of central London on the Thames lie the serene and exotic **Kew Gardens** (tel. (0181) 940 1171). Lose yourself in the controlled wilderness of the grounds, or explore the Victorian and modern glasshouses containing thousands of plant species. *(Tube or British Rail: Kew Gardens. Gardens open M-F 9:30am-6:30pm, Sa-Su and bank holidays 9:30am-7:30pm; last admission 30min. before closing. Conservatories close at 5:30pm. Closing times may vary by season; call ahead. £5, students and seniors £3.50. Daily tours £1. Kew also hosts summer jazz concerts—tickets £18-25. Call Ticketmaster at 344 44 44 for details.)*

The transport system that encouraged London's urban sprawl blurs the distinction between city and surroundings. If Hyde Park seemed small, **Highgate** and **Hampstead Heath** will prove that there is an English countryside. In the Eastern Cemetery, Karl Marx and George Eliot repose in the Gothic tangle of **Highgate Cemetery,** Swains Lane. *(Tube: Archway.* **Eastern Cemetery** *open M-F 11am-4:30pm, Sa-Su 10am-4:30pm. £1.* **Western Cemetery** *access by guided tour only M-F at noon, 2, and 4pm, Sa-Su every hr. 11am-4pm. £3. Camera permit £1.)*

MUSEUMS

British Museum, Great Russell St., WC1 (info tel. 323 82 99). Tube: Tottenham Ct. Rd. or Holborn. The closest thing to a complete record of the rise and ruin of world cultures. Among the plunder on display are the **Rosetta Stone** (whose inscriptions allowed French scholar Champollion to decipher hieroglyphics) and Elgin Marbles. Open M-Sa 10am-5pm, Su 2:30-6pm. Free, suggested donation £2.

National Gallery, Trafalgar Sq., WC2 (tel. 839 33 21 or 747 28 85 for recorded info). Tube: Charing Cross, Leicester Sq., Embankment, or Piccadilly Circus. One of the world's best collections of Western paintings. The Micro Gallery can print out a free personalized tour. Open M-Sa 10am-6pm, W until 8pm, Su noon-6pm. Free.

National Portrait Gallery, St. Martin's Pl., WC2, opposite St.-Martin's-in-the-Fields. Tube: Charing Cross or Leicester Sq. Mugs from Queen Elizabeth II to John Lennon. Doubles as *Who's Who in Britain.* Open M-Sa 10am-6pm, Su noon-6pm. Free.

Tate Gallery, Millbank, up the Thames from Parliament Sq. (tel. 887 80 00 for recorded info). Tube: Pimlico. The best of British artists, along with Monet, Dalí, Picasso, and Matisse. The best place for contemporary art fans in London. The vast J.M.W. Turner collection rests in the Clore Gallery. Open daily 10am-5:50pm. Free.

Victoria and Albert Museum, Cromwell Rd. (tel. 938 84 41 for recorded info). Tube: South Kensington. An array of fine and applied arts. Open M noon-5:50pm, Tu-Su 10am-5:50pm. £5, concessions £3, students free.

Madame Tussaud's, Marylebone Rd., NW1. Tube: Baker St. The classic waxwork museum. Might not be worth the wait and the cost. Open M-F 10am-5:30pm, Sa-Su 9:30am-5:30pm. Winter M-F opens 1hr. later. £9.75, seniors £7.45.

Museum of London, 150 London Wall, EC2 (tel. 600 08 07 for 24hr. info). Tube: St. Paul's or Barbican. From Londinium to the 1996 European Soccer Championships. Free lectures W-F; check for times. Open Tu-Sa 10am-5:50pm, Su noon-5:50pm, last entry 5:30pm. £4, concessions £2. Free after 4:30pm. Wheelchair accessible.

Museum of the Moving Image (MOMI), South Bank Centre, SE1 (tel. 401 26 36 for 24hr. info). Tube: Waterloo. The entertaining museum charts the development of image-making with light, from shadow puppets to film and telly. Open daily 10am-6pm. Last admission 5pm. £6.25, students £5.25, seniors £4.50.

Science Museum, Exhibition Rd., SW7. Tube: South Kensington. Closet science geeks will be outed by their orgasmic cries as they enter this wonderland of motors, springs, and spaceships. This 5-story collection rivals the best science museums around. Open daily 10am-6pm. £6.50, concessions £3.50. Free 4:30-6pm.

London Transport Museum, Covent Garden, WC2 (tel. 565 72 99 for recorded info). Tube: Covent Garden. Although ground floor traffic flows through a maze of historic trains, trams, and buses, the museum offers much more than a history of public transport vehicles. Open M-Th and Sa-Su 10am-6pm, F 11am-6pm, last admission 5:15pm. £4.95, concessions £2.95. Wheelchair accessible.

Imperial War Museum, Lambeth Rd., SE1 (tel. 416 50 00). Tube: Lambeth North or Elephant & Castle. The atrium is filled with tanks and planes; gripping exhibits illuminate every aspect of two world wars in every possible medium. Open daily 10am-6pm. £5, students £4. Free daily 4:30-6pm. Wheelchair accessible.

The Wallace Collection, Hertford House, Manchester Sq., W1 (tel. 935 06 87). Tube: Bond St. Outstanding works include Hals's *The Laughing Cavalier,* Delacroix's *Execution of Marino Faliero,* Fragonard's *The Swing,* and Rubens's *Christ on the Cross.* Home to the largest armor and weaponry collection outside of the Tower of London. Open M-Sa 10am-5pm, Su 11am-5pm. Guided tours M-Tu 1pm, W 11:30am and 1pm, Th-F 1pm, Sa 11:30am, Su 3pm. Free.

ENTERTAINMENT

On any given day or night, Londoners and visitors can choose from the widest range of entertainment. For guidance consult *Time Out* (£1.80) or *What's On* (£1.30).

Theater, Music, & Film

London **theater** is unrivalled. Seats cost £8-30 and up, and student/senior standby (with an "S," "concessions," or "concs" in newspaper listings) puts even the best seats within reach—£7-10 just before curtain (come two hours early with ID). **Day seats** are sold cheaply (9-10am the day of performance) to all; queue up earlier. The **Leicester Square Ticket Booth** sells half-price tickets on the day of major plays (open M-Sa 11am-6:30pm; long wait; £2 fee; credit cards accepted). Standby tickets for the **Royal National Theatre** (tel. 452 34 00; Tube: Waterloo), on the South Bank Centre, sell two hours beforehand (£10-14; students £7.50, 45min. before). The **Barbican Theatre** (24hr. info tel. 382 72 72, reservations 638 88 91; Tube: Barbican or Moorgate), London home of the Royal Shakespeare Company, has student and senior standbys for £6 from 9am on the performance day. For a mere £5, you can stand as a groundling and watch Shakespearean productions in the meticulously reconstructed **Shakespeare's Globe Theatre** (call 401 99 19 for tickets), New Globe Walk, Bankside SE1 (Tube: London Bridge. Box office open M-Sa 10am-8pm.) Exciting cheaper performances are found on the **Fringe,** in less commercial theaters.

Most major **classical music** is staged at the acoustically superb **Royal Festival Hall** (tel. 960 42 42; Tube: Waterloo) and the **Barbican Hall. Marble Hill House** has low-priced outdoor concerts on summer Sundays at 2pm (tel. 413 14 43). Londoners have been lining up for standing room in the **Royal Albert Hall's "Proms"** (BBC Henry Wood Promenade Concerts; tel. 589 82 12) for nearly a century. **Pop music** performers from the world over cannot keep away from London. **Brixton Academy** (tel. 924 99 99; Tube: Brixton) is a larger, rowdy venue for a variety of music including rock and reggae (advance tickets £8-25). **Ronnie Scott's,** 47 Frith St., W1 (tel. 439 07 47; Tube: Leicester Sq. or Piccadilly Circus), has London's greatest jazz (cover from £15).

The Prince Charles, Leicester Pl., WC2 (tel. 437 81 81; Tube: Leicester Sq.), is a Soho institution. The four shows a day (cheerily deconstructed on the recorded phone message) are generally second runs but also include a sprinkling of classics for only £2-2.50. The **Institute of Contemporary Arts (ICA) Cinema,** Nash House, The Mall, W1 (tel. 930 36 47; Tube: Piccadilly Circus or Charing Cross) plays cutting-edge contemporary cinema and an extensive list of classics (£6.50), and the **National Film Theatre (NFT),** South Bank Centre, SE1 (tel. 928 32 32; Tube: Waterloo) boggles the mind with its array of film, TV, and video (most screenings £5).

Nightclubbing

London pounds to 100% groovy Liverpool tunes, ecstatic Manchester rave, hometown soul and house, U.S. hip-hop, and Jamaican reggae. Many clubs host a variety of provocative one-night stands (like "Get Up and Use Me") throughout the week. Check listings in *Time Out* for the latest.

Iceni, 11 White Horse St., W1 (tel. 495 53 33). Tube: Green Park. Off Curzon Street. 3 floors of funk in this Mayfair hotspot. £10-12. Open F 11pm-3am, Sa 10pm-3am.

Ministry of Sound, 103 Gaunt St., SE1. Tube: Elephant and Castle. Night Buses N12, N62, N65, N72, N77, or N78. Mega-club with beefy covers and beautiful people, but beware—bouncers concoct the "most appropriate" crowd. One of the first major rave spots. Cover F £10, Sa £15. Open F 10:30pm-6:30am, Sa midnight-9am.

The Roadhouse, Jubilee Hull, 35 The Piazza, WC2. Tube: Covent Garden. Excellent live cover bands every night (2 bands on Saturday) spice up the place and let you know that everyone is getting what they want, what they really really want—a good time. Cover £3-10. Open M-Th 5:30pm-3am, F 4:30pm-3am, Sa 6:30pm-3am.

The Hanover Grand, 6 Hanover St., W1 (tel. 499 7977). Tube: Oxford Circus. Loud funk atmosphere. £5-15, W before 11pm £3. W-F 10:30pm-4am, Sa 10:30pm-5am.

The Fridge, Town Hall Parade, Brixton Hill, SW2. Tube: Brixton. Night bus N2. A serious dance dive with a stylish multi-ethnic crowd. Saturday's "Love Muscle," the ultimate London one-nighter, packs in a beautiful and shocking mixed-gay clientele. £10, with flyer £8. Open F-Sa 10pm-6am.

BISEXUAL, GAY, AND LESBIAN LONDON

London has a very visible gay scene, covering everything from the flamboyant to the mainstream. *Time Out* has a section devoted to gay listings, and gay newspapers include *Capital Gay* (free, caters to men), *Pink Paper,* and *Shebang* (for women). *Gay Times* (£3) is the British counterpart to the *Advocate; Diva* (£2) is a monthly lesbian mag. Islington, Earl's Ct., and Soho (especially **Old Compton Street**) are all gay-friendly areas. For further info contact the **gay, lesbian, bisexual helplines,** p. 123.

Balans, 60 Old Compton St., W1. Tube: Leicester Sq. Another branch at 239 Old Brompton Rd. (tel. 244 88 38; open daily 8am-2am). Ruthlessly glamorous ambience for a mostly gay male clientele. Lots of veggie options. Open daily 8am-5am.

The Candy Bar, 4 Carlisle St., W1. Tube: Tottenham Ct. Rd. 3 floors of women (men welcome as guests) at London's first all-lesbian bar. Bar downstairs becomes dance floor W-Sa. Cover £5 F-Sa after 10pm.

Old Compton Cafe, 35 Old Compton St., W1 (tel. 439 33 09). Tube: Leicester Sq. In the geographic epicenter of Soho, this is *the* gay cafe. Tables and people (predominantly 20- and 30-something males) overflow onto the street. Open daily 7am-5am.

Heaven, Villiers St., WC2, underneath The Arches. Tube: Embankment or Charing Cross. The oldest and biggest gay disco in Europe. Bumping garage music F-Sa 10pm-3am. Cover F £6, after 11:30pm £7.50. Sa £7; after 11:30pm £8.

"G.A.Y.," at London Astoria 1 (Sa), and 2 (Th and M), 157 Charing Cross Rd., WC2. Tube: Tottenham Ct. Rd. Pop extravaganza amidst chrome and disco balls. Unpretentious mixed clientele. Open, Th and Sa from 10:30pm, Sa from 11pm. Cover £3-6. Discounts with flyers.

SOUTH ENGLAND

■ Kent

Canterbury Six hundred years ago, Geoffrey Chaucer saw enough irony in flocks of tourists to capture them in verse. His sometimes lewd, sometimes reverent tales speak of the pilgrims of Middle Ages, en route from London to **Canterbury Cathedral** on England's busiest road. Here, Archbishop Thomas à Becket met his demise after an irate Henry II asked, "Will no one rid me of this troublesome priest?" and a few of his henchmen took the hint. (Open Easter-Oct. M-Sa 8:45am-7pm, Su 11am-2:30pm and 4:30-5:30pm; Nov.-Easter daily 8:45am-5pm. Choral evensong M-F 5:30pm, Sa-Su 3:15pm. Donation £2.50. Check nave pulpit for times of guided tours. £3, students £2. Headphone tour £2.50.) The **Canterbury Tales** visitor attraction, St. Margaret's St., recreates the tales with a gap-toothed Wife of Bath, her waxen companions, and authentic olfactory stimulation. (Open July-Aug. daily 9am-6pm; Mar.-June and Sept.-Oct. daily 9:30am-5:30pm; Nov.-Feb. Su-F 10am-4:30pm, Sa 9:30am-5:30pm. £4.95, students £4.25.) On Stour St., the **Canterbury Heritage Museum** features medieval pilgrim badges and reconstructions of the historical Canterbury. (Open Nov.-May M-Sa 10:30am-5pm; June-Oct. also Su 1:30-5pm. £2.20, students £1.25.) The **Roman Museum,** Butchery Ln., houses artifacts from Canterbury's Roman inhabitants (open M-Sa 10am-5pm, last admission 4pm; £2.20, students £1.25). Little remains of **St. Augustine's Abbey,** but older Roman ruins and the site of St. Augustine's first tomb can be viewed near the cathedral (open daily Apr.-Nov. 10am-6pm; Nov.-Mar. 10am-4pm; £2.50, students £1.90). Around the corner, **St. Martin's** is the oldest parish church in England.

Trains from London's Victoria Station arrive at Canterbury's East Station; trains from Charing Cross and Waterloo Station arrive at West Station (1½hr., £13.10). **Buses** (tel. (01227) 47 20 82) to Canterbury leave London's Victoria Coach Station (1¾hr., £8). The **tourist office,** 34 St. Margaret's St. (tel. (01227) 76 65 67; fax 45 98 40), books lodgings for a £2.50 fee and 10% deposit, and carries maps and guides to Kent (open daily Apr.-June 9:30am-5:30pm; July-Aug. 9am-6pm; Sept.-Mar. 9:30am-5pm). **B&Bs** cluster near both train stations and on London and Whitstable Rd. The **YHA Youth Hostel** at 54 New Dover Rd. (tel. (01227) 46 29 11), may be packed and chaotic. (£9.75. Reception 7:30-10am and 1-11pm. Open Feb.-Dec.; call for off-season openings.) **The Tudor House,** 6 Best Ln. (tel. (01227) 76 56 50), offers rooms in an attractive 16th-century home (£18) and **Let's Stay,** 26 New Dover Rd. (tel. (01227) 46 36 28), has beds for £10. The streets around the cathedral teem with bakeries and sweet shops. **Cafe Venezia,** 60-61 Palace St., serves pizza (£1 per slice; open daily 9am-6pm; July-Aug. 9am-11pm), while **The Famous Sandwich Shop,** 16 St. Dunstan's St., makes fresh sandwiches (open M-Sa 8:15am-4pm). The pub **Simple Simon's,** 3-9 Church Ln., draws students to sample its wares (open daily 11am-11pm).

BRITAIN

Dover The roar of the English Channel at Dover has been drowned out by the put-tering of ferries, the hum of hovercraft, and the chatter of French families *en vacan-ces.* Yet despite the clamor of tourist traffic, the city has retained its dignified maritime identity. The view from Castle Hill Rd. reveals why **Dover Castle** is famed both for its setting and for its impregnability.

Trains for Dover's Priory Station leave from London's Victoria, Waterloo East, Lon-don Bridge, and Charing Cross stations approximately every 45 minutes (2hr., £17). Beware when you board as many trains branch off en route; check schedules and dis-plays to see which trains split. National Express **buses** run regularly from London's Victoria Coach Station to the Eastern Docks after stopping at the bus station (tel. (01304) 24 00 24, info (01813) 58 13 33) on Pencester Rd. (2¾hr., £13). Buses also make trips to Canterbury (£4). Major **ferry** companies operate ships from Dover to Calais, and the Dover tourist office offers a ferry booking service. The **P&O Stena Line** (tel. (0990) 98 01 11) sends ferries to Calais. **Hovercraft** leave for Calais from Dover's Hoverport at the Prince of Wales Pier; book a few days in advance. The **Channel Tunnel (Chunnel)** provides passenger service on **Eurostar** (tel. (01233) 61 75 75) and car transport on **Le Shuttle** to and from the Continent.

The **tourist office** (tel. (01304) 20 51 08), on Townwall St., has lodgings info and ferry and hovercraft tickets (open daily July-Aug. 8:30am-7:30pm; Sept.-June 9am-6pm). The **YHA Charlton House Youth Hostel,** 306 London Rd. (tel. (01304) 20 13 14), is a half-mile from the train station (£9.75; lockout 10am-1pm; curfew 11pm). **Amanda Guest House,** 4 Harold St. (tel. (01304) 20 17 11), and **Victoria Guest House,** 1 Laureston Pl. (tel./fax (01304) 20 51 40), offer gracious Victorian lodgings (£24-54). Cheap **food** fries from dawn to dusk in the fish-and-chip shops on London Rd. and Biggin St. Enjoy a decent pub lunch almost anywhere in the city center.

■ Sussex

Brighton According to legend, future King George IV scuttled into Brighton for some hanky-panky around 1784. Today, Brighton is still the unrivaled home of the "dirty weekend"—it sparkles with a risqué, tawdry luster all its own. Before indulg-ing, check out England's long-time fascination with the Far East incarnate at the **Royal Pavilion** on Pavilion Parade, next to Old Steine (open daily June-Sept. 10am-6pm; Oct.-May 10am-5pm; £4.50, students £3.25). Around the corner on Church St. stands the **Brighton Museum and Art Gallery,** with paintings, English pottery, and a wild Art Deco and Art Nouveau collection. Leer at Salvador Dalí's sexy red sofa, *Mae West's Lips* (open M-Tu and Th-Sa 10am-5pm, Su 2-5pm; free). Before heading out to the rocky **beach,** stroll the **Lanes**—a jumble of 17th-century streets that form the heart of Old Brighton.

Brighton brims with nightlife options. It is *the* gay nightlife spot in Britain outside London. Check out *The Punter, What's On, Gay Times* (£2.20), or *Capital Gay* for info on the rapidly changing club and bar scenes. In the early evening, folks gather to drink at **Fortune of War** and **Cuba,** both on the beach between West Pier and Palace Pier. The most massively populated clubs are **Paradox** and **Event II,** both on West St. Paradox gets dressy toward the end of the week, and the monthly "Wild Fruit" gay night is popular with a mixed crowd. **Casablanca,** Middle St., plays live jazz to a mostly student crowd. The converted World War II tunnels of **Zap Club,** King's Rd, provide space for dark rendezvous and hard-core dirty dancing.

Trains roll regularly from London to Brighton (50min., £13.70) on their way to Arundel via Ford (50min., £6) and Portsmouth (1½hr., £11.10). National Express **buses** also head to London (2hr., £9). The **tourist office,** 10 Bartholomew Sq. (tel. (01273) 29 25 99), offers a free map and books rooms for a £1 fee per adult plus a 10% deposit (open M-F 9am-5pm, Sa 10am-5pm, Su 10am-4pm). Brighton's best bets for budget lodging are its hostels. Cheaper, shabbier **B&Bs** collect west of West Pier and east of Palace Pier. **Brighton Backpackers Hostel,** 75-76 Middle St. (tel. (01273) 77 77 17; email backpackers@fastnet.co.uk), is an independent hostel just 50m from the waterfront (£9; free **Internet access**). **Baggies Back-packers,** 33 Oriental Pl. (tel. (01273) 73 37 40), has mellow vibes and exquisite murals (dorms £9-10; doubles £23; no lockout; no curfew). The **YHA Youth Hostel,** Patcham Pl. (tel. (01273) 55 61 96), has rooms that look new even though they're 400 years old (£9.75, students £8.75; curfew 11pm). Take Patcham Bus 5 or 5A from Old Steine in front of the Royal Pavilion to the Black Lion Hotel. The area around the Lanes is filled with trendy and expensive places waiting to gobble up tourist dollars; for cheaper fare, try the fish and chip shops along the beach or north of the Lanes. **Food for Friends,** 17a Prince Albert St., has well-seasoned vegetarian meals (£3-6; open daily 8am-10pm).

Arundel and Chichester The tea rooms and antique shops of **Arundel** surround its castle-like stone minions, always in the shadow of towers, ramparts, and cathedral spires. **Arundel Castle** is the third oldest in Britain and the seat of the Duke of Norfolk, Earl Marshal of England (open Apr.-Oct. Su-F noon-5pm; last admission 4pm; £5.70). In late August, the castle hosts the **Arundel Festival,** 10 days of concerts, jousting, and outdoor theater; a fringe schedule offers less expensive events (info tel. (01903) 88 36 90). **Trains** leave London's Victoria Station for Arundel (1¼hr., day return £15.50). Most other train and bus routes require connections at Littlehampton to the south or Barnham to the east. The **tourist office,** 61 High St. (tel. (01903) 88 22 68), offers the free *Town Guide* (open in summer M-F 9am-5pm, Sa-Su 10am-5pm; off-season closes at 3pm). If you're up for the 1½-mile walk from town, the **YHA Warningcamp Youth Hostel** (tel. (01903) 88 22 04) is a cheerful place to prop up your feet. (£8.80, camping £3.85. Curfew 11pm. Open July-Aug. daily; Apr.-June M-Sa; Sept.-Oct. Tu-Sa; Nov.-Dec. F-Sa. Closed Jan.-Mar.) Otherwise, prepare to pay at least £20-25 for **B&Bs** along the River Arun. Locals frequent **Belinda's,** 13 Tarrant St., a 16th-century tea room with a bird-filled garden and large wine selection (open Tu-Sa 6am-5:30pm, Su 11am-5:30pm).

The remains of Roman walls and an imposing Norman cathedral provide the backdrop for **Chichester's** superb theater, arts festival, and gallery exhibits. The **Cathedral,** started in 1091, features a glorious stained-glass window by Marc Chagall (open daily 7:30am-6pm; off-season until 5pm; £2 donation encouraged). During the first half of July, the cathedral hosts the **Chichester Festivities,** one of the finest spells of concentrated musical and artistic creativity in all of England (info tel. (01243) 78 57 18). The **Roman Palace** in nearby Fishbourne is the largest Roman residence excavated in Britain. Go west along Westgate, which becomes Fishbourne Rd. (the A259) for 1½ miles, or take bus 700 or 701 from Chichester center. (Open Mar.-July and Sept.-Oct. daily 10am-5pm; Aug. 10am-6pm; Nov.-Dec. and Feb. 10am-4pm; Jan. Su only 10am-4pm. £3.80, students and seniors £3.20.)

Trains run to Brighton (1hr., £8.70), London's Victoria Station (1½hr., £17.20), and Portsmouth (1hr., £6). National Express **buses** run less frequently to London (period return £10); Coastline buses 700 and 701 serve Brighton (2hr., £4.40) and Portsmouth (1hr., £3.90). The bus station (tel. (01903) 23 76 61) lies diagonally across from the train station on Southgate. The **tourist office** (tel. (01243) 77 58 88; fax 53 94 49), South St., has a 24-hour information computer (open M-Sa 9:15am-5:15pm; July-Aug. also Su 10am-4pm). Rooms for under £15 are virtually nonexistent here. **Hedgehogs,** 45 Whyke Ln. (tel. (01243) 78 00 22), offers cozy rooms near the town center (£18-26). Camp at **Southern Leisure Centre** (tel. (01243) 78 77 15), Vinnetrow Rd., a 15-minute walk southeast of town (£8-10 per tent, plus £2 per person; open Apr.-Oct.). **Maison Blanc Boulangerie and Patisserie,** 56 South St., will make any Francophile's mouth water.

■ Hampshire

Portsmouth Over 900 years old and site of the D-Day launching in 1944, Portsmouth boasts an incomparable naval heritage and magnificent seafaring relics. Henry VIII's beloved **Mary Rose** set sail in 1545 only to keel over and sink before the monarch's eyes. The vessel, raised from its watery grave in 1982, and Tudor artifacts salvaged from the wreck are now on display at the **Naval Heritage Center** in the naval Base (entrance next to The Hard tourist office). Nearby, Admiral Nelson's flagship **HMS Victory** won the Battle of Trafalgar against the French and Spanish in 1805; a careful look reveals the dismal, cramped conditions endured by recruits. Entrance to just the **Historic Dockyard** is free. (Open daily July-Aug. 10am-7pm; Mar.-June and Sept.-Oct. 10am-6pm; Nov.-Feb. 10am-5:30pm.) Each ship within charges admission (£5.25-5.75, students £4.25-5.25).

Trains (tel. (01705) 22 93 93) arrive from London Waterloo (1½hr., return £19.40); National Express **buses** run from London (2½hr., return £12.50) and Salisbury (2hr., £7). Portsmouth has **tourist offices** (tel. (01705) 82 67 22) on The Hard, by the entrance to the ships (open daily 9:30am-5:45pm), and at 102 Commercial Rd. (tel. (01705) 83 83 82), near the Portsmouth and Southsea station (open M-Sa 9:30am-5:30pm). **B&Bs** clutter Southsea, a resort town 1½ miles east; cheaper lodgings lie two or three blocks inland. The **Southsea Backpackers Lodge,** 4 Florence Rd. (tel. (01705) 83 24 95), offers ample facilities (dorms £9; singles £15; doubles £25). The **YHA Youth Hostel** (tel. (01705) 37 56 61) is in Wymering Manor, Old Wymering Lane, Medina Rd., in Cosham. Take any bus to Cosham and follow the signs. (£8.80. Lockout 10am-5pm. Curfew 11pm. Open Feb.-Aug. daily; Sept.-Nov. F-Sa; closed Dec.-Jan.). Mrs. Parkes watches over her spotless **Testudo House,** 19 Whitwell Rd., Southsea (tel. (01705) 82 43 24; £17.50-34). **Restaurants** line Osborne, Palmerston, and Clarendon Rd. in the Southsea shopping district. Near The Hard, **pubs** greet weary sailors and tourists.

Winchester

Winchester's glory days echo from Roman times, when it was a walled city known as "Venta Belgrum." William the Conqueror and Alfred the Great (whose statued image still looms) based their kingdoms here, and monks painstakingly prepared the *Domesday Book* for William here. Today, the city makes a great daytrip from Salisbury or Portsmouth. The 556 ft. long **Winchester Cathedral** is the longest medieval building in Europe; the interior holds magnificent medieval tiles and Jane Austen's tomb. (Open daily 7:15am-6:30pm; East End closes 5pm. £2.50 voluntary donation, students £2.) Founded in 1382, most of **Winchester College's** 14th-century buildings remain intact (tour booking tel. (01962) 62 12 17).

Trains (tel. (0345) 48 49 50) run to Chichester via Fareham (1hr., £9.30-9.80), London (1hr., £15.90-16), and Portsmouth (1hr., £6.50-7). National Express **buses** run to London via Heathrow (1½hr., £9.25-12.50) and Oxford (2½hr., £7.50-9); Hampshire buses head to Portsmouth and Salisbury (each 1½hr., round-trip £3.90). The **tourist office,** The Guildhall, Broadway (tel. (01962) 84 05 00 or 84 81 80; fax 85 03 48), books rooms for a £2.50 fee and a 10% deposit, gives out maps, and arranges guided tours (open June-Sept. M-Sa 10am-6pm, Su 11am-2pm; Oct.-May M-Sa 10am-5pm).

Great Traditions of British Sport I

Though cricket often seems incomprehensible to those not raised on Marmite, crumpets, and full English breakfasts, its rules are actually quite simple. Teams are composed of 11 players. The game is played on a 22-yard green, marked by two **wickets** at each end. (Wickets consist of 3 vertical stumps and 2 bails.) One team acts as **batsmen** and the other as **fielders.** The batting team sends up its first two batsmen. Their goal is to make as many runs as they can while protecting their wicket; as the fielders run for the ball, the two batsmen switch places. If they switch once, they score a single; twice a double; and so on. The goal of the fielders is to try to get the batsmen out by hitting or **taking** the wickets with the ball or by catching the ball while it is in the air. A good pitcher or **bowler** will force the batsmen to protect his wicket. Once the batsmen is knocked out, the next one in the batting order replaces him until the whole team has been up to bat. Then the teams switch places. Innings can take a long time: teams have been known to score 500 runs during one inning. In a normal match, both teams bat only twice.

Expect a chore or two at the well-located **YHA youth hostel,** 1 Water Ln. (tel. (01962) 85 37 23; £8.80; lockout 10am-5pm; curfew 11pm; call ahead). **B&Bs** cluster on Christchurch and St. Cross Rd. near Ranelagh Rd. **Mrs. Tisdall's,** 32 Hyde St. (tel. (01962) 85 16 21), is comfortable and convenient (£20-32; 10% *Let's Go* discount; breakfast included). Restaurants line Jewry St., and most pubs serve good fare. **Royal Oak,** off High St., claims fame as the country's oldest pub.

Salisbury and Stonehenge

Salisbury is centered around the **Salisbury Cathedral,** whose spire rises 404 ft. from its grassy close. (Open daily May-Aug. 8am-8:15pm; Sept.-Apr. 8am-6:30pm. Suggested donation £3, students and seniors £2. Tours M-Sa 11:15am and 2:15pm. Tower tours M-Sa 11am, 2, 3, and 6:30pm, Su 4:30pm. £2.) One of four surviving copies of the *Magna Carta* rests in the **Chapter House,** which is surrounded by detailed medieval friezes. (Open Mar.-Oct. M-Sa 9:30am-4:45pm, Su 1-4:45pm; Nov.-Feb. M-Sa 11am-3pm, Su 1-3:15pm. Free.)

Trains depart Salisbury Station, South Western Rd. (tel. in Southampton (0345) 48 49 50), for London (1½hr., £22.10-30), Portsmouth and Southsea (1½hr., £10.80-12.60), and Winchester (change at Southampton; 1½hr., £9.30-9.80). National Express **buses** run from London's Victoria Station (2¾hr., £9.25). Wilts and Dorset buses serve Bath and Stonehenge. The helpful and busy **tourist office,** Fish Row (tel. (01722) 33 49 56; fax 42 20 59), Guildhall in Market Sq., books rooms (with a deposit) and offers tours. (1½hr., £2. Open July-Aug. M-Sa 9:30am-7pm, Su 10:30am-5pm; June and Sept. M-Sa 9:30am-6pm, Su 10:30am-4:30pm; Oct.-May M-Sa 9:30am-5pm; May also Su 10:30am-4:30pm.) The **YHA youth hostel,** Milford Hill House (tel. (01722) 32 75 72), Milford Hill, is surrounded by two acres of gardens (£9.75; camping £4.70 per person; curfew 11:30pm; call ahead). **Matt and Tiggy's,** 51 Salt Ln. (tel. (01722) 32 74 43), is just up from the bus station (£9.50; breakfast £2). **The Old Bakery,** 35 Bedwin St. (tel. (01722) 32 01 00), is a comfy resting spot (singles £15; doubles £14-18; breakfast £3). Sip your brew at the **Old Mill** or the not-so-**New Inn,** two of the 60-odd watering holes.

The 22 ft. high boulders of **Stonehenge** (tel. (01980) 62 53 68) were carried and placed from 2800 to 1500 BC, some from as far away as Ireland. Capture a good view from Amesbury Hill, 1½ miles up the A303, or pay admission for a closer look. (Open daily June-Aug. 9am-7pm; Sept. to mid-Oct. and mid-Mar. to May 9:30am-6pm; mid-Oct. to mid-Mar. 9:30am-4pm. £3.90, students £2.90.)

SOUTHWEST ENGLAND

The mist of legends shroud the counties of Dorset, Somerset, Devon, and Cornwall in England's West Country, home to Bronze Age barrows and King Arthur. Although you will undoubtedly encounter industrial cities and annoying "Mayflour" bake shops, the region's timeless terrain is unfailingly beautiful.

British Rail **trains** from London frequently pass through Exeter and Plymouth on their way to Penzance. From Glasgow and Edinburgh, a line passes though Bristol and Exeter before ending at Plymouth. National Express **buses** run to major points along the north coast via Bristol and to points along the south coast via Exeter and Plymouth. Local bus service is less expensive and more extensive than the local trains. For hikers and bikers, the longest coastal path in England, the **South West Peninsula Coast Path,** originates in Dorset and runs through South Devon, Cornwall, and North Devon, ending in Somerset. The path is divided into four, more manageable parts based on the national parks and counties through which it passes.

Exeter

Exeter withstood an 18-day siege by William the Conqueror in 1068 but was flattened during a few perilous days of German bombing in 1942. Frantic rebuilding has resulted in an odd mixture of the venerable and the banal: Roman and Norman ruins poke up from delicatessen parking lots, and department store cash registers ring atop medieval catacombs. This jigsaw cityscape and a large university community may have fostered Exeter's diverse population, noteworthy in the homogenous hills of Devon. **Exeter Cathedral,** low-slung and lovely, overlooks the commercial clutter of High St. Although the cathedral was heavily damaged in World War II, intricate details abound: a gilded ceiling boss depicts the murder of St. Thomas à Becket, the west front holds hundreds of stone figures, and misericordia (small seats against a wall) retain carvings of elephants and basilisks. On display in the cathedral library, the **Exeter Book** is the richest treasury of early Anglo-Saxon poetry in the world. (Cathedral open daily 7am-6:30pm. Library open M-F 2-5pm. £2 donation. Free guided tours Apr.-Oct. M-F 11:30am and 2:30pm, Sa 11am.)

Trains arrive at Exeter St. David's Station, St. David's Hill, from London's Paddington and Waterloo Stations (3hr., £36 and £39.10 respectively). National Express **buses** (tel. (0990) 80 80 80) provide the cheapest transportation to Exeter; a student coach card grants passage from London's Victoria Coach Station for £21-25 (4hr.). Buses also drive from Bristol (£9.10-11) and Bath (£11.35-13.75). The bus station (tel. (01392) 562 31) is on Paris St., off High St. just outside the city walls. The **tourist office,** Civic Centre, Paris St. (tel. (01392) 26 57 00), books rooms (10% deposit; open M-F 9am-5pm, Sa 9am-1pm and 2-5pm). The **YHA youth hostel,** 47 Countess Wear Rd. (tel. (01392) 87 33 29; fax 87 69 39), is spacious and cheery (£9.80; breakfast £2.95). Cheap eateries cluster along Queen St., near the Central Station. If you're heading north or west to one of the national parks, pick up supplies at **Marks and Spencer** on High St. The best watering hole is the airy **Imperial,** New North Rd., just up from St. David's Station (two dinners for £5). Travel cyberspace, coffee in hand, at **Internet Express,** in the Central Station building (£2.50 per 30min.).

■ Dartmoor National Park

> The Ministry of Defense uses much of the northern moor for target practice; consult the *Dartmoor Visitor* or an Ordnance Survey map for the boundaries of the danger area, or call (01392) 27 01 64 for recorded info, cowboy.

The lush, green forests and windy moors of Dartmoor National Park challenge visitors with treacherous terrain and capricious weather, but reward hearty explorers with unparalleled serenity and beauty. Prehistoric remains lurk about the moor near **Princetown,** at the southern edge of the park's north-central plateau. The moor was the setting for the famous Sherlock Holmes tale, "The Hound of the Baskervilles." The rugged eastern part of the park centers on **Hay Tor.** Two miles north of this village lies **Hound Tor,** where excavations have unearthed the remains of 13th-century huts and longhouses. Don't be surprised if a weary traveler approaches you and asks for a rubber stamp (or "traveler"). Yes, a rubber stamp. Throughout the park are hidden **Dartmoor Letterboxes,** containing stamps to prove you were here; finding them is hardly elementary (stamp and clue books are available in area stores), and the quest captivates some avid Dartmoorians.

Contact the Exeter **bus station** (tel. (01392) 42 77 11), the Plymouth bus station (tel. (01752) 22 26 66), or the Devon County Council's **Public Transportation Helpline** (tel. (01392) 38 28 00; M-F 8:30am-5pm) for info on transportation to Dartmoor. **Hiking** and **cycling** are the way to go once inside the park. Whatever method you choose, make sure you have an Ordnance Survey Map (about £5), waterproof gear, and a compass. Ask questions and pick up the essential *Dartmoor Visitor* from one of the National Park Information Centres: **Tavistock** (tel. (01822) 61 29 38), **Ivybridge** (tel. (01752) 89 70 35), **Newbridge** (tel. (01364) 63 13 03), **Okehampton** (tel. (01837) 530 20), **Postbridge** (tel. (01822) 88 02 72), and **Princetown** (High Moorland Visitor Centre; tel. (01822) 89 04 14).

B&B signs are frequently displayed in pubs and farmhouses along the roads, and the information centers hand out free accommodation lists. **YHA Steps Bridge** (tel. (01647) 25 24 35) is in Dunsford, near the eastern edge of the park (£7.20; open Apr.-Sept.). The popular **YHA Bellever** (tel. (01822) 88 02 27), in Yelverton, is one mile southeast of Postbridge village; take bus 82 or 359 from Exeter or bus 82 from Plymouth and ask to be let off as close to the hostel as possible (£8.80; open Apr.-June M-Sa; Sept.-Oct. Tu-Sa). Although official campsites exist, many travelers camp on the open moor. Ask permission before crossing or camping on private land.

Plymouth Plymouth has long been a city of departures: Sir Francis Drake, Captain Cook, the Pilgrims, Lord Nelson, and millions of emigrants to the United States and New Zealand have immortalized Plymouth in their haste to get away from it. The city offers only a few attractions for stranded travelers. Climb the spiral steps and leaning ladders to the balcony of **Smeaton's Tower** for ferocious blasts of wind from the Channel and a magnificent view (open Easter-Sept. 10:30am-5pm; 75p). The blackened shell of **Charles Church,** largely destroyed by a bomb in 1941, stands in the middle of the Charles Cross traffic circle as a memorial to the Plymouth citizens killed during World War II.

Trains run hourly to Bristol (3½hr., £25), London (3½hr., £53), and Penzance (1¾hr., £10). National Express **buses** (tel. (0990) 80 80 80) also serve Bristol (2½hr., £18) and London (4½hr., £27). Stagecoach Devon buses connect to Exeter (1¼hr., £4.15). **Ferries** leave Millbay Docks (tel. (0990) 36 03 60) for Roscoff, France (6hr., £20-58), and Santander, Spain (24hr., £80-145). Check in an hour before departure; disabled travelers should arrive two hours early. The **tourist office,** Island House, 9 The Barbican (tel. (01752) 26 48 49; fax 25 79 55), answers questions and dispenses a free city map (open M-Sa 9am-5pm, Su 10am-4pm). Low-priced **B&Bs** grace Citadel Rd. and Athenaeum St. between the west end of Royal Parade and the Hoe; prices run £12-15. Check on availability at the tourist office. Call ahead for the excellent YHA Youth Hostel, **Belmont House,** Belmont Place, Stoke (tel. (01752) 56 21 89), which has spacious rooms and an elegant dining hall. Take bus 15 or 81 to Stoke, and the hostel will appear on your left (£9.75; breakfast £2.95; lock-out 10am-5pm; curfew 11pm). The closer **Plymouth Backpackers Hotel,** 172 Citadel Rd., The Hoe (tel. (01752) 22 51 58), has basic hostel dorm rooms from £8. Reel in the catch of the day at **Cap'n Jaspers,** a stand by the Barbican side of the Harbor (open M-Sa 6:30am-11:45pm, Su 10am-11:45pm).

■ The Cornish Coast

Penzance On Cornwall's Penwith Peninsula, sunny Penzance is the very model of an ancient English pirate town. A stone sailor greets visitors to the life of 18th-century seamen at the **Maritime Museum,** halfway down Chapel St. (open May-Oct. M-Sa 10:30am-4:30pm; £2). Across the bay from Penzance at Marazion, **St. Michael's Mount** monastery was built on the site of a supposed sighting of Archangel Michael by 5th-century fishermen. (Open Apr.-Oct. M-F 10:30am-5:45pm; in summer also most weekends; off-season as weather permits. Admission to island £3.90.) Penzance's **train station** (tel. (0345) 48 49 50) and **bus station** (tel. (01209) 71 99 88) stand conveniently together in the same square on Wharf Rd., at the head of Albert Pier. The **tourist office** (tel. (01736) 36 22 07), also in the square, books rooms for a 10% deposit (open M-F 9am-5pm, Sa 10am-1pm; in summer also Sa 9am-4pm and Su 10am-1pm). The super-friendly YHA Youth Hostel, **Castle Horneck** (tel. (01736) 36 26 66), provides newly refurbished rooms in a restored 18th-century mansion (£9.75; campsites £4.95; reception 5-11pm). **The Turk's Head,** 46 Chapel St., serves yummy food in a 13th-century pub. (Meals from £4-5. Open M-Sa 11am-2:30pm and 6-10pm, Su noon-2:30pm and 6-10pm.)

St. Ives Ten miles north of Penzance, St. Ives perches on a rounded spit of land lined with pastel beaches and azure waters. A white **lighthouse,** thought to be an inspiration for Virginia Woolf's masterpiece *To The Lighthouse,* watches over the town. **Trains** on the Plymouth-Penzance line stop at St. Erth, a 10-minute shuttle from St. Ives. **Buses** run to St. Ives from Penzance (£1.80). The **tourist office** (tel.

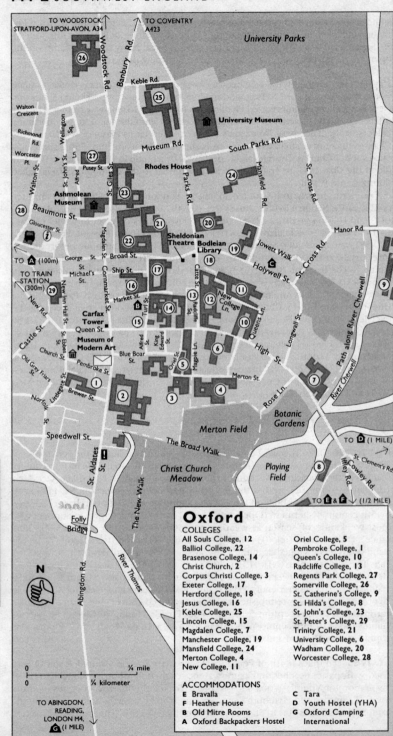

TO WOODSTOCK,
STRATFORD-UPON-AVON, A34

TO COVENTRY
A423

University Parks

Woodstock Rd.

Banbury Rd.

Keble Rd.

26

25

Walton
Crescent

Richmond
Rd.

Worcester
Pl.

University Museum

Museum Rd.

South Parks Rd.

St. Cross Rd.

Wellington Sq.

St. John's Ln.

Alfred St.

27

Pusey St.

Rhodes House

Parks Rd.

Mansfield Rd.

Walton St.

Ashmolean
Museum

St. Giles St.

23

24

28

Beaumont St.

Gloucester St.

21

Manor Rd.

TO (A) (100m)

George St.

St. Michael's
St.

22

Sheldonian
Theatre Bodleian
Library

20

19

Jowett Walk

St. Cross Rd.

TO TRAIN
STATION
(300m)

New Inn Hall St.

Magdalen St.

Cornmarket St.

Broad St.

Ship St.

18

Holywell St.

9

29

Market St.

16

17

Catte St.

Turl St.

13

12

11

New College
Ln.

Queen's Ln.

Longwall St.

Path along River Cherwell

River Cherwell

Carfax
Tower

B

14

Radcliffe
Sq.

10

Castle St.

Queen St.

15

Alfred St.

King Edward St.

Oriel St.

Magpie Ln.

6

High St.

Museum of
Modern Art

Church St.

Pembroke St.

Blue Boar
St.

5

Rose Ln.

7

Old Grey Friars
St.

1

Brewer St.

2

3

4

Merton St.

Botanic
Gardens

Norfolk St.

Littlegate St.

St. Ebbe's
St.

Merton Field

Speedwell St.

The Broad Walk

8

TO (D) (1 MILE)

St. Clement's Rd.

Cowley Rd.

St. Aldates St.

Christ Church
Meadow

Playing
Field

TO (E) & (F) (1/2 MILE)

N

The New Walk

Folly
Bridge

River Thames

Abingdon Rd.

0   ¼ mile

0   ¼ kilometer

TO ABINGDON,
READING,
LONDON M4,
(G) (1 MILE)

Oxford

COLLEGES

All Souls College, 12
Balliol College, 22
Brasenose College, 14
Christ Church, 2
Corpus Christi College, 3
Exeter College, 17
Hertford College, 18
Jesus College, 16
Keble College, 25
Lincoln College, 15
Magdalen College, 7
Manchester College, 19
Mansfield College, 24
Merton College, 4
New College, 11

Oriel College, 5
Pembroke College, 1
Queen's College, 10
Radcliffe College, 13
Regents Park College, 27
Somerville College, 26
St. Catherine's College, 9
St. Hilda's College, 8
St. John's College, 23
St. Peter's College, 29
Trinity College, 21
University College, 6
Wadham College, 20
Worcester College, 28

ACCOMMODATIONS

E Bravalla
F Heather House
B Old Mitre Rooms
A Oxford Backpackers Hostel

C Tara
D Youth Hostel (YHA)
G Oxford Camping
   International

BRITAIN

(01736) 79 62 97) is in the Guildhall on Street-an-Pol (open M-Sa 9:30am-5:30pm, Su 10am-1pm; off-season closed Sa-Su). Although the closest youth hostel beckons from Penzance, **B&Bs** line every alley and cluster on Park Ave. and Tregenna Terr. (from £14). Prices dip farther from the water and higher up the gusty hillside. Campsites are abundant in nearby Hayle; try **Trevalgan Camping Park** (tel. (01736) 79 64 33), with cooking facilities and access to the coastal path. Storefront blackboards will tempt you with **Cornish cream tea** (a pot of tea with scones, jam, and Cornish clotted cream). Try it at **Bumble's Tea Room** at Digey Sq. near the Tate (£2.50; open M-Sa 10am-4:30pm, Su 11am-4:30pm; off-season closed Su).

Falmouth Two spectacular castles eye each other across the world's third largest natural harbor in Falmouth, situated along the Penryn River. **Pendennis Castle,** built by Henry VIII to keep out French frigates, now features a walk-through diorama and superb views (open daily Apr.-Oct. 10am-6pm; Nov.-Mar. 10am-4pm; £3, students £2.30). **St. Mawes Castle,** a 20-minute ferry ride from Falmouth to St. Mawes village (for ferry info, call (01326) 31 32 01 or 31 38 13; return £4), was expected to gun down any Frenchmen Pendennis spared. (Open Apr.-Oct. daily 10am-6pm; Nov.-Mar. F-Tu 10am-4pm. £2.50, students and seniors £1.90.) Falmouth is accessible by **rail** from any stop on the London-Penzance line, including Exeter and Plymouth; change at Truro and go three stops (30min., £9.50). Western National **buses** (tel. (0990) 80 80 80) serve Falmouth from Truro (£2.20) and Penzance (£3.50). The **tourist office,** 28 Killigrew St. (tel. (01326) 31 23 00), will help you find a room. (Open Apr.-Sept. M-Th 9am-5pm, F 9am-4:45pm; July-Aug. also Su 10am-4pm; shorter hours off-season.) The **YHA Youth Hostel,** Pendennis Castle (tel. (01326) 31 14 35; fax 31 54 73), is 30 minutes from town ending with an uphill seaside hike. Book far ahead. (£8.80. Reception 8:30am-10am and 5-10:30pm. Curfew 11pm. Open Feb.-Sept. daily; Oct.-Nov. Tu-Sa; closed Dec.-Jan.)

Newquay An outpost of surfer subculture, **Newquay** (NEW-key) draws both neon youth and tourists to its world-class shores. All **trains** to Newquay run through the small town of Par on the main London-Penzance line. National Express **buses** (tel. (0990) 80 80 80) run directly to Newquay from London; Western National buses connect Newquay and St. Ives. The town's **tourist office** (tel. (01637) 87 13 45) sits atop Marcus Hill (open M-Sa 9am-6pm, Su 10am-5pm; shorter hours off-season). Get a crash course in surfer life at **Fistral Backpackers,** 18 Headland Rd. (tel. (01637) 87 31 46) or **Newquay Backpackers International,** 69-73 Tower Rd. (tel. (01637) 87 93 66; £6-9). The restaurants in Newquay are expensive; keep an eye out for three-course "early bird" specials. **Food for Thought,** 33A Bank St., at the corner of Beachfield Ave., offers takeout "Californian" salads and sandwiches (£2-3; open daily 8:30am-10pm). Newquay's nightlife rises at 9pm and reigns until dawn; clubs are open until 1am. Those on the trail of surfer bars begin at **The Red Lion,** wash over to pubs on Fore St., and crash at **The Newquay Arms.**

HEART OF ENGLAND

■ Oxford

Named for the place where oxen could ford the Thames, Oxford, the city of dreaming spires, is a furiously rushing commercial town which shelters England's oldest university. Despite an appalling number of buses and bikes, the hordes of commercial and professional people are largely concentrated in a small district in the city center. To escape, leave the busy streets and alleys and enter into the quiet world of the medieval college quadrangle, enhanced by meticulously cared-for lawns and vibrantly colorful gardens, or walk along Christ Church meadow down to the Thames, obscurely called the Isis for these few miles only.

ORIENTATION AND PRACTICAL INFORMATION

Queen, High, St. Aldates, and Cornmarket St. meet at right angles in **Carfax,** the town center. The colleges surround Carfax to the east along High St. and Broad St.; the train and bus stations lie to the west.

Telephone Code: 01865.

Trains: Station on Park End St., west of Carfax (tel. (0345) 48 49 50, recording 79 44 22). Local trains run from London's Paddington Station (1hr., every 30min, £11.80 day return). Ticket office open M-F 6am-8pm, Sa 6:45am-8pm, Su 7:45am-8pm.

Buses: Station on Gloucester Green (follow arrows up Cornmarket St. from Carfax). **Oxford Tube** (tel. 77 22 50) and **Oxford CityLink** (tel. 78 54 00 or 77 22 50 for timetable; desk open daily 6:30am-6:30pm) send buses to and from London. **Stagecoach Oxford** (tel. 77 22 50) and **National Express** (tel. (0990) 80 80 80) offer national routes. Most **local services** board on the streets around Carfax. Fares are low (most 60p), but day and week passes are well worth the purchase; buy them from the bus driver or at the bus station.

Tourist Office: The Old School, Gloucester Green (tel. 72 68 71; fax 24 02 61). Located beside the bus station. A pamphleteer's paradise. Accommodations list 50p. Street map 70p. Books rooms for a £2.50 fee and a 10% deposit. Open M-Sa 9:30am-5pm, Su 10am-3:30pm.

Currency Exchange: Banks and **ATMs** abound on Carfax. **Barclays,** 54 Cornmarket St. Open M-F 9:30am-4:30pm, W until 5pm, Sa 10am-noon.

American Express: 4 Queen St. (tel. 79 20 66). Open M-Tu and Th-F 9am-5:30pm, W 9:30am-5:30pm, Sa 9am-5pm; also open Su 11am-3pm in summer.

Luggage storage: Pensioners' Club in Gloucester Green (tel. 24 22 37), by the bus station. £1-2 donation requested. Open M-Sa 9am-4:45pm.

Emergency: Dial 999; no coins required.

Police: tel. 26 60 00. St. Aldates and Speedwell St.

Hotlines: Samaritans (crisis), 123 Iffley Rd. (tel. 24hr. 72 21 22); drop-in daily 8am-10pm. **Gay Switchboard,** Oxford Friend (tel. 79 39 99). Open daily 7am-9pm.

Pharmacy: Boots, 6-8 Cornmarket St. (tel. 24 74 61). Open M-F 8:45am-6pm, Th until 7pm, Su 11am-5pm.

Hospital: John Radcliffe Hospital, Headley Wy. (tel. 74 11 66). Bus 13B or 14A.

Post Office: 124 St. Aldates St. (tel. 20 28 63). Open M-F 9am-5:30pm, Sa 9am-6pm. Bureau de change. **Postal Code:** OX1 1ZZ.

Internet Access: Daily Information, 31 Warnborough Rd. (tel. 31 00 11). £6 per hr., £1 minimum. Open M-W 9am-9pm, Th-Sa 9am-6pm. If possible, call beforehand.

ACCOMMODATIONS AND CAMPING

B&Bs line the main roads out of town, all of them a vigorous walk (15-20min.) from Carfax. You'll find cheaper B&Bs on Iffley Rd. (Cityline bus 3 or 4), Cowley Road (Cityline buses in the 50s). Expect to pay £18-22 per person.

YHA Youth Hostel, 32 Jack Straw's Ln., Headington (tel. 76 29 97; fax 76 94 02). Catch Citylink bus 13 or 14 heading away from Carfax on High St. and ask the driver to stop. The hostel is an 8min. walk up the hill. One of England's largest hostels (114 beds), with kitchen, laundry, lockers, and food shop. £10.25, under 18 £7.05, student ID £1 off. Call ahead.

Bravalla, 242 Iffley Rd. (tel. 24 13 26; fax 24 97 57). 6 sunny rooms. Breakfast in a conservatory; sign the breakfast board the night before (vegetarian options). Singles £25; doubles with bath £38-44. Reserve ahead.

Old Mitre Rooms, 4b Turl St. (tel. 27 98 00), next to Past Times. Recently refurbished. Singles £23; doubles £42-46; triples £55-60. Open July to early Sept.

Heather House, 192 Iffley Rd. (tel./fax 24 97 57). Take the bus marked "Rose Hill" from the bus station, train station, or Carfax Tower (65p). Friendly Australian proprietor; clean, modern rooms. Dorms £18-20; singles £22; doubles £46.

Tara, 10 Holywell St. (call *Typetalk* (free) at (04451) 494 20 22; within the U.K. (0800) 51 51 52; give the operator Tara's phone number (01865) 20 29 53; fax 20 02 97). Basin in each room. Singles £28; doubles £46; triples £55. Reserve ahead.

Oxford Backpacker's Hotel, 9a Hythe Bridge St. (tel. 72 17 61). Between the bus and train stations. Social atmosphere. £9-11 per night. Laundry facilities. Kitchen.

Camping: Oxford Camping International, 426 Abingdon Rd. (tel. 24 65 51, after 5:30pm call 72 56 46), behind the Touchwoods camping store. 129 nondescript sites. £2.80 per tent, £1.65 per person. Toilets and laundry. Showers 20p. The **YHA Youth Hostel** may also offer limited camping; call to find out.

FOOD

Oxford offers a mix of typical college-town eateries and more upscale ethnic restaurants. **Harvey's of Oxford,** 58 High St., is one of the better take-aways. (Mighty sandwiches £1.50-2.75. Open M-F 8:30am-5:30pm, Sa until 6pm, Su 9am-6pm.) **Fasta Pasta,** in the covered market, hawks cheap, gourmet sandwiches and bagels and an impressive selection of olives. When students tire of burgers and pizza, they stock up at the **Co-op** supermarket on Cornmarket St. (open M-F 8am-7pm, Sa 8am-6pm) or at the all day Wednesday **market** at Gloucester Green, by the bus station.

The **Nosebag,** 6-8 St. Michael's, overcomes a silly name with gourmet meals served cafeteria-style. The **Saddlebag Cafe** downstairs sells sandwiches, salads, and cakes during the day. (Open M 9:30am-5:30pm, Tu-Th 9:30am-10pm, F-Sa 9:30am-10:30pm, Su 9:30am-9pm.) Across Magdalen Bridge, **Hi-Lo Jamaican Eating House, Dhaka,** and **The Pak Fook,** all on Cowley Rd., are good bets. **Heroes,** 8 Ship St., serves up sandwiches on a variety of fresh breads with a super selection of stuffings (£1.70-3.30; open M-F 8am-5pm, Sa 8:30am-6pm, Su 10am-5pm).

SIGHTS AND ENTERTAINMENT

Start your walking tour at Carfax ("four-forked"), the center of activity; hike up the 99 spiral stairs of **Carfax Tower** for an overview of the city (open daily Apr.-Oct. 10am-5:30pm; Nov.-Mar. 10am-3:30pm; £1.20).

King Henry II founded Britain's first university in 1167; today, Oxford's alumni register reads like a who's who of British history, literature, and philosophy. Just down St. Aldates St., **Christ Church** names 13 prime ministers among its former students. (Open M-Sa 9am-5pm, Su 1-5pm. Services Su 8, 10, 11:15am, 6pm; weekdays 7:30am, 6pm. £3, students £2.) The 13th-century **University College,** on High St., welcomed Bill Clinton during his Rhodes Scholar days, but expelled Percy Bysshe Shelley for writing about atheism; a monument recalls his watery death. Nearby, the idyllic **Botanic Garden** is perfect for a late-afternoon stroll (open daily 9am to 4:30 or 5pm; glasshouses open daily 2-4pm; £1.50). Flamboyant Oscar Wilde attended **Magdalen College,** considered by many Oxford's most handsome college. (Open daily July-Sept. noon-6pm; Oct.-June 2-5pm; Apr.-Sept. £2, students £1; Oct.-Mar. free.)

Follow Catte St. to the **Bodleian Library;** with over five million books, it is Oxford's principal reading and research library (open M-F 9am-6pm, Sa 9am-1pm). No one has ever been permitted to check one out, not even Cromwell. Well, especially not Cromwell. Across Broad St. you could browse for days at **Blackwell's,** the world-famous bookstore (open M-Sa 9am-6pm, Su 11am-5pm). The **Sheldonian Theatre,** set beside the Bodleian, is a Roman-style jewel of an auditorium. Graduation ceremonies, conducted in Latin, take place here. The cupola of the theater affords an inspiring view of the spires of Oxford (open M-Sa 10am-12:30pm and 2-4:30pm, subject to change; £1.50). The **Cast Gallery,** behind the **Ashmolean Museum** on Beaumont St., stores over 250 casts of Greek sculptures. While the museum undergoes renovation, the entire collection is exhibited—the finest classical collection outside London (open Tu-Sa 10am-4pm, Su 2-4pm; free). The five blocks of **Cowley Road** closest to Magdalen Bridge feature a fascinating clutter of ethnic restaurants, small bookstores, and alternative shops.

Music and drama at Oxford are cherished arts. Try to attend a concert at one of the colleges or a performance at the **Holywell Music Rooms,** the oldest in the country. **City of Oxford Orchestra,** the city's professional symphony orchestra (tel. 74 44 57, tickets 26 13 84), plays in the Sheldonian Theatre and various college chapels (shows

BRITAIN

at 8pm; tickets £12-15, 25% student discount). The **Apollo Theatre,** George St. (tel. 24 45 44), presents performances ranging from lounge-lizard jazz to the Welsh National Opera (tickets from £6, discounts for seniors and students). During summer, college **theater groups** stage productions in local gardens and cloisters.

Pubs far outnumber colleges in Oxford; *Good Pubs of Oxford* (£3 at the tourist office) is an indispensable guide to the town's offerings. Sprawling underneath the city, the 13th-century **Turf Tavern** hides on Bath Pl., off Holywell St, and **The King's Arms,** Holywell St, is Oxford's unofficial student union. **The Eagle and Child,** 49 St. Giles St., known to all as the Bird and Baby, served C.S. Lewis and J.R.R. Tolkien for a quarter-century. For more sober entertainment, head to the River Thames, where **punting** is a favorite pastime among Oxford students and visitors.

■ Near Oxford: Woodstock

The largest private home in England and one of the loveliest, **Blenheim Palace** (tel. (01993) 81 13 25) features rambling grounds, a nearby lake, and a fantastic garden. While attending a party here, Churchill's mother gave birth to the future Prime Minister in a closet. (Open daily mid-Mar. to Oct. 10:30am-5:30pm; grounds open year-round 9am-5pm. £7.80, students £5.80, includes a boat trip on the lake.) Blenheim sprawls in **Woodstock,** eight miles north of Oxford on the A44. **Stagecoach Express** (tel. 77 22 50) runs to Blenheim Palace from Gloucester Green bus station (20min., return £3). The same bus also goes to Stratford and Birmingham. Another service, **Blenheim Palace Shuttle** (tel. (01993) 81 38 88), offers hourly buses from George St. The £10 ticket includes transport, palace admission, and a guided tour. Winston Churchill rests in the nearby village churchyard of **Bladon.**

■ Cotswolds

Stretching across western England, the whimsical hills of the **Cotswolds** enfold old Roman settlements and tiny Saxon villages hewn from the famed Cotswold stone. Although not readily accessible by public transportation, the glorious Cotswolds demand entry into any itinerary. The hills lie mostly in **Gloucestershire,** bounded by **Banbury** in the northeast, **Bradford-upon-Avon** in the southwest, **Cheltenham** in the north, and **Malmesbury** in the south. **Trains** and **buses** frequent the area's major gateways—Cheltenham, Bath, and Gloucester—but buses between the villages are rare. Snag the comprehensive *Connection* timetable free from all area bus stations and tourist offices. *Getting There from Cheltenham* is also invaluable. Local roads are perfect for **cycling,** and the closely spaced villages make ideal watering holes. **Cotswold Way,** spanning 100 miles from Bath to Chipping Camden, should appeal to those interested in **hiking** the hills. When you're ready to call it a day, the *Cotswold Way Handbook* (£1.50) lists **B&Bs** along the Cotswold Way. Most **campsites** are close to Cheltenham, but Bourton-on-the-Water, Stow-on-the-Wold, and Moreton-on-the-Marsh also have places to put your Tent-on-the-Ground. The annually updated *Gloucestershire Caravan and Camping Guide* is free at local tourist centers.

Stow-on-the-Wold, Winchcombe, and Cirencester Experience

the Cotswolds as the English have for centuries by treading well-worn footpaths from village to village. **Stow-on-the-Wold** is a sleepy town with fine views, cold winds, and authentic stocks. The **YHA youth hostel** (tel. (01451) 83 04 97) stands just a few yards from the stocks. (£8.80, students £7.80. Call ahead. Open Apr.-Aug. daily; Sept.-Oct. M-Sa; Nov.-Dec weekends; closed Jan.-Mar.) West of Stow-on-the-Wold and six miles north of Cheltenham on the A46, **Sudeley Castle,** once the manor of King Ethelred the Unready, enserfs the town of **Winchcombe** and holds regular falconry shows (open Apr.-Oct. daily 10:30am-5pm; £5.50). Archaeologists have discovered prehistoric paths and habitation sites across the Cotswolds. **Belas Knap,** a 4000-year-old burial mound, lies less than two miles southwest of Sudeley Castle.

The Cotswolds boast some of the best examples of Roman settlements in Britain, most notably in **Cirencester.** Its **Corinium Museum,** Park St., houses a formidable collection of Roman artifacts. (Open Apr.-Oct. M-Sa 10am-5pm, Su 2-5pm; Nov.-Mar.

Tu-Sa 10am-5pm, Su 2-5pm. £2.50, students £1.) The **tourist office** is in Corn Hall, Market Pl. (tel. (01285) 65 41 80). Stay in Cheltenham (see below) and make the ruins a daytrip. On Fridays, the town becomes a mad **antique marketplace.** Quaff a pint at the **Golden Cross,** on Black Jack St., or the **Crown,** at West Market Pl. near the abbey.

Cheltenham

A spa town second only to Bath, Cheltenham epitomizes elegance and proudly possesses the only naturally alkaline water in Great Britain. Enjoy the diuretic and laxative effects of the waters at the **Town Hall** (open M-F 9am-1pm and 2:15-5pm; free) or at the **Pittville Pump Room** (tel. (01242) 52 38 52) in Pittville Park. Sip it, don't gulp. Manicured gardens adorn shops and houses around town, but for a real floral fix, sunbathe at the exquisite **Imperial Gardens,** just past The Promenade away from the center of town. **Trains** run regularly to Bath (1½hr., £11.40), Exeter (2hr., £25.70), and London (2hr., £26). National Express **buses** run to Exeter (3½hr., £17) and London (3hr., £9.50) as well. The **tourist office,** Municipal Offices, 77 The Promenade (tel. (01242) 52 28 78), one block east of the bus station, posts vacancies after-hours. (Open July-Aug. M-Sa 9:30am-6pm, Su 9:30am-1:30pm; Sept.-June M-Sa 9:30am-5:15pm.) The well-situated **YMCA,** Vittoria Walk (tel. (01242) 52 40 24), is clean and accepts both men and women. From Town Hall, turn left off the Promenade and go three blocks (singles £14; reception 24hr.). **Bentons Guest House,** 71 Bath Rd. (tel. (01242) 51 74 17), and **Cross Ways,** 57 Bath Rd. (tel. (01242) 52 76 83), offer well-kept rooms (£18-30). Fruit stands and **bakeries** dot High St. For a relaxing pint, try **Dobell's,** 24 The Promenade (open M-Sa 11am-11pm, Su noon-2:30pm and 7-10:30pm).

■ Stratford-upon-Avon

Former resident William Shakespeare is now the area's industry. Knick-knack huts hawk "Will Power" t-shirts, and all the perfumes of Arabia will not sweeten the tour-bus-exhausted air in Stratford's center. Diehard fans should purchase the **combination ticket** (£10, students £9), which offers admission to five Shakespeare sights, but the least crowded way to pay homage is to visit Shakespeare's grave in **Holy Trinity Church,** Trinity St. (60p, students 40p). Bring your *Complete Works* to the riverbank outside. In town, begin your walking tour at **Shakespeare's Birthplace** (tel. (01789) 20 40 16) on Henley St., half period recreation and half life-and-work exhibition. **New Place,** High St., was Stratford's hippest home when Shakespeare bought it in 1597 after writing some hits in London. Only the foundation remains—it can be viewed from the street above. Down Chapel Lane, the **Great Garden** and the more attractive exterior of New Place can be viewed for free from the bowers around back.

Recent sons of the world-famous **Royal Shakespeare Company** include Kenneth Branagh and Ralph Fiennes; get thee to a performance. To reserve seats (£5-49), call the box office (tel. (01789) 29 56 23, phones open at 9am; 24hr. recording 26 91 91; fax 26 19 74). The box office opens at 9:30am; a group gathers outside at about 9:10am for same-day sales. Student and senior standbys for £11 exist in principle. The **Stratford Festival** (2 weeks in July) manages to celebrate artistic achievement other than Shakespeare's. The festival typically features world-class art from all arenas of performance (ticket info (01789) 41 45 13).

Stratford lies about two hours from London by **Thames trains** (tel. 57 94 53). National Express **buses** run to and from London's Victoria Station (3hr., 3 per day, return £17). The **tourist office** (tel. (01789) 29 31 27), Bridgefoot, across Warwick Rd. at Bridge St. toward the waterside park, books rooms for a £3 fee and a 10% deposit. (Open Apr.-Oct. M-Sa 9am-6pm, Su 11am-5pm; Nov.-Mar. M-Sa 9am-5pm.)

To B&B or not to B&B? If you can find one with a vacancy it's probably a good investment; the nearest youth hostel is more than two miles out of town and, with a return bus fare, costs as much as an inexpensive B&B. Guest houses (£15-22) line **Grove Road, Evesham Place,** and **Evesham Road. Field View Guest House,** 35 Banbury Rd. (tel. (01789) 29 26 94), offers clean singles (£16) and doubles (£32). Warm and attentive proprietors run **The Hollies,** 16 Evesham Pl. (tel. (01789) 26 68 57; doubles £35-45). The **YHA youth hostel,** Hemmingford House, Wellesbourne Rd.,

Alveston (tel. (01789) 29 70 93), has large, attractive grounds; take bus 18 or X18 (£1.50) from Bridge St., across from the McDonald's (£13.45, under 18 £10; breakfast included; reception 7am-midnight). Closer to town, **Nando's,** 18 Evesham Pl. (tel./fax (01789) 20 49 07), has delightful owners and comfortable rooms (£22-44). **Riverside Caravan Park,** Tiddington Rd. (tel. (01789) 29 23 12), one mile east of Stratford on the B4086, has **camping** grounds (£6 per tent, £1 extra per person; open Apr.-Oct.).

Hussain's Indian Cuisine, 6a Chapel St., is Stratford's best Indian cuisine, with a slew of tandoori (lunch £6; entrees from £6; open daily 12:30-2pm and 5pm-midnight). **Dirty Duck Pub,** Waterside, serves a traditional pub lunch for £2-4.50; double that for dinners (open M-Sa 11am-11pm, Su noon-10pm). A Safeway **supermarket** awaits on Alcester Rd.

Near Stratford lurks one of England's finest medieval castles, **Warwick Castle** (open daily Mar.-Oct. 10am-6pm; Nov.-Feb. 10am-5pm; £9). Trains (20min., £2.20) journey frequently from Stratford to Warwick, and Stagecoach Midland Red buses run every hour (20-40min., return £2.50).

■ Bath

A visit to the elegant Georgian city of Bath remains *de rigueur,* even though it's now more of a museum (or perhaps a museum's gift shop) than a resort. But expensive trinkets can't hide Bath's sophistication. Immortalized by Fielding, Smollet, Austen, and Dickens, Bath once stood second only to London as the social capital of England.

SIGHTS AND ENTERTAINMENT The excellent **Roman Baths Museum** (tel. (01225) 47 77 59; http://www.romanbaths.co.uk) explores the architectural remains, engineering achievements, and bits and pieces from the daily life of the Roman spa city Aquae Sulis. The ruins of the city were discovered by sewer-diggers in 1880. (Open daily Apr.-July and Sept. 9am-6pm; Aug. 9am-6pm and 7-9pm; Oct.-Mar. 9am-5pm. £6.30. Partially wheelchair accessible.) Penny-pinching travelers can view one of the baths in the complex for free by entering through The Pump Room (see below); look for explanatory posters. The museum, however, is decidedly worth the admission price. Next door to the baths, the towering and tombstone 15th-century **Bath Abbey** has a whimsical west facade showing several angels climbing ladders up to heaven and, curiously enough, two climbing down (open daily 9am-4:30pm; £1.50). The dazzling **Museum of Costume** on Bennett St. will satisfy any fashion fetish. (Open daily 10am-5pm. £3.80, joint ticket to Museum and Roman Baths £8.40.) Walk up Gay St. to **The Circus,** which has attracted illustrious residents for two centuries; blue plaques mark the houses of Thomas Gainsborough, William Pitt, and David Livingstone. **Royal Crescent,** a half-moon of Gregorian townhouses, lies up Brock St. **Royal Victoria Park,** nearby, contains one of the finest collections of trees in the country, and its **botanical gardens** nurture 5000 species of plants (open M-Sa 9am-dusk, Su 10am-dusk; free). The renowned **Bath International Festival of the Arts,** over two weeks of concerts and exhibits, induces merriment all over town from late May to early June. A night on the town could begin and end at the cafe/bar **P. J. Peppers** on George St. (open daily 8am-11pm). The **Hat and Feather,** on Walcot St. at London St., rocks with two levels of funk and rave (open daily 11am-11pm).

PRACTICAL INFO, ACCOMMODATIONS, AND FOOD From Bath, **trains** travel to Bristol (15min., £4.40), Exeter (1¾hr., £19), and London Paddington (1½hr., £27). National Express **buses** (tel. (0990) 80 80 80) run to and from London Victoria (3hr., return £11-18.50) and Oxford (2hr., £12). The train and bus stations are near the south end of Manvers St. From either terminal, walk up Manvers St. to the Terrace Walk roundabout, and turn left onto York St. to reach the efficient **tourist office** (tel. (01225) 47 71 01) in the Abbey Churchyard. (Open June-Sept. M-Tu and F-Sa 9:30am-6pm, W-Th 9:45am-6pm, Su 10am-4pm; Oct.-May M-Sa 9am-5pm, Su 10am-4pm.)

B&Bs (from £18) cluster on Pulteney Rd. and Pulteney and Crescent Gardens. For a more relaxed setting, take the footpath behind the rail station to **Widcombe Hill,** where rooms start at £17. The **YHA youth hostel,** Bathwick Hill (tel. (01225) 46 56

74), is in a secluded and clean mansion overlooking the city (£9.75). Badgerline "University" Bus 18 runs to the hostel from the bus station and the Orange Grove roundabout (until midnight, return £1). Take bus 14 to **Lynn Shearn,** Prior House, 3 Marlborough Lane (tel. (01225) 31 35 87), and look for the *Let's Go* sign in the window; warm proprietors will welcome you as friends (doubles £30; breakfast included). The **International Backpackers Hostel,** 13 Pierrepont St. (tel. (01225) 44 67 87), has a great location (£8-10; breakfast £1). **The White Guest House,** 23 Pulteney Gardens (tel. (01225) 42 60 75), will knock £2 off if you tell them *Let's Go* sent you (singles £20-22; doubles £36-40).

Fruits and vegetables are ripe for the picking at the **Guildhall Market,** between High St. and Grand Parade (open M-Sa 8am-5:30pm). Indulge in a cream tea (£5.25) at the palatial Victorian **Pump Room,** Abbey Churchyard (open daily Apr.-Sept. 9am-6pm; Oct.-Mar. 9:30am-5pm), or an excellent vegetarian dish at **Demuths Restaurant,** 2 North Parade Passage, off Abbey Green (open daily 10-11:30am, noon-4pm, and 6:30-10pm).

EAST ANGLIA

The plush green farmlands and watery fens of East Anglia stretch northeast from London, cloaking the counties of Cambridgeshire, Norfolk, and Suffolk. Although industry is modernizing the economies of Cambridge and Peterborough, the college town and cathedral city are still linked by flat fields sliced into irregular tiles by windbreaks, hedges, and stone walls. East Anglia's flat terrain and relatively low annual rainfall are a boon to bikers and hikers. The area's two longest walking trails, **Peddar's Way** and **Weaver's Way,** together cover over 200 miles.

■ Cambridge

Cambridge's university began a mere 786 years ago when rebels defected from nearby Oxford to this settlement on the River Cam. Today these rebels can be seen maneuvering around the prohibited lush campus lawns and scurrying nightly to meet the closing college gates. Since third-year finals shape many students' futures, most colleges close to visitors during official quiet periods in May and early June. But when exams end, cobblestoned Cambridge explodes with gin-soaked glee. May Week (in mid-June, naturally) launches a dizzying schedule of cocktail parties and festivities, including The Bumps (rowing races where the winners celebrate by burning a boat) and the aptly named Suicide Sunday.

ORIENTATION AND PRACTICAL INFORMATION

Cambridge (pop. 105,000), 60 miles north of London, has two main avenues. The main shopping street starts at **Magdalene Bridge** and becomes **Bridge Street, Sidney Street, St. Andrew's Street, Regent Street,** and finally **Hills Road.** The other main street also suffers from an identity crisis, changing names four times from **St. John's Street** to **Trumpington Road.** This is the academic thoroughfare, with several colleges lying between the road and the River Cam. From the bus station, a quick walk down **Emmanuel Street** leads to a shopping district near the tourist office. To reach the center of town from the train station, go west along Station Rd. and turn right onto Hills Rd.

Telephone Code: 01223.
Train Station: Station Rd. (British Rail tel. (0345) 48 49 50). Open daily 5am-11pm for ticket purchases. Trains to Cambridge run from both London's King's Cross and Liverpool Street stations (1hr., £15.10).
Bus Station: Drummer St. **National Express** (info tel. (0990) 80 80 80) arrives from London's Victoria Station (2hr., from £8). National Express and **Stagecoach Express** buses run between Oxford and Cambridge (2¾hr., £6.40). **Cambus** (tel. 42 35 54) handles local service (60p-£1).

Bike Rental: Geoff's Bike Rental, 65 Devonshire Rd. (tel. 36 56 29) and in the bus and train stations. £6 per day, £12-15 per week. Open daily 9am-6pm.

Tourist Office: Wheeler St. (tel. 32 26 40; fax 45 75 88), a block south of the marketplace. Books rooms for a £3 fee and a 10% deposit. *Cambridge: The Complete Guide* has a street-indexed map (£1.30). Open Apr.-Sept. M-F 10am-6pm, Sa 10am-5pm, Su 11am-4pm; Nov.-Mar. M-F 10am-5:30pm, Sa 10am-5pm. Info on city events is available at **Corn Exchange box office,** Corn Exchange St. (tel. 35 78 51), adjacent to the tourist office.

Currency Exchange: Lloyds Bank and the American Express office cluster on Sidney St. **Thomas Cook** is at 18 Market St.

American Express: 25 Sidney St. (tel. 35 16 36). Open M-W and F 9am-5:30pm, Th 9:30am-5:30pm, Sa 9am-5pm.

Emergency: Dial 999; no coins required.

Police: Parkside (tel. 35 89 66).

Crisis Lines: Crime Victims, tel. 36 30 24. **Rape Crisis,** tel. 35 83 14.

Medical Assistance: Addenbrookes Hospital, Hill Rd. (tel. 24 51 51). Catch Cambus 95 from Emmanuel St. (95p).

Post Office: 9-11 St. Andrew's St. (tel. 32 33 25). Open M-Tu and Th-F 9am-5:30pm, W 9:30am-5pm, Sa 9am-12:30pm. *Poste Restante* and currency exchange. **Postal Code:** CB2 3AA.

Internet Access: CBI, 32 Mill Rd. (tel. 57 63 06). 10p per min., £6 per hr. Open daily 10am-8pm.

ACCOMMODATIONS, CAMPING, AND FOOD

The lesson this university town teaches is to book ahead. Many of the **B&Bs** around Portugal St. and Tenison Rd. are open only in July and August. Check the comprehensive list at the tourist office, or pick up the guide to accommodations there (50p).

YHA Youth Hostel, 97 Tenison Rd. (tel. 35 46 01; fax 31 27 80). Relaxed, welcoming atmosphere. Well-equipped kitchen, laundry room, and TV lounge. Spiffy cafeteria. 3- to 4-bed rooms £10.70, students £9.70, under 18 £7.30. Crowded Mar.-Oct.; in summer call ahead with a credit card.

Mrs. McCann, 40 Warkworth St. (tel. 31 40 98). A jolly hostess with comfortable twin rooms in a quiet neighborhood near the bus station. Rates go down after 3 nights. £15 per person. Breakfast included.

Warkworth Guest House, Warkworth Terr. (tel. 36 36 82). Sunny rooms with TV near the bus station. Singles £22.50; twins £35. Breakfast included.

Tenison Towers Guest House, 148 Tenison Rd. (tel. 56 65 11). Fresh flowers grace impeccable rooms near the train station. Singles £15-22; doubles £28-32; triples £42; quads £48-56.

Home from Home B&B, Liz Fasano, 39 Milton Rd. (tel. 32 35 55). Sparkling rooms and an accommodating hostess. Singles £30; doubles £40. Breakfast included.

Highfield Farm Camping Park, Long Rd., Comberton (tel. 26 23 08); take Cambus 118 from the Drummer St. station. Flush toilets, showers, and laundry facilities. £4-5 per tent. Open Apr.-Oct.

Tatties, 26-28 Regent St., serves delectable baked potatoes to please any palate (platters with vegetable skewers £4-5; open daily 10am-10:30pm). **Rainbow's Vegetarian Bistro,** 9A King's Parade, is a tiny burrow serving vegetarian fare (open daily 9am-9pm). **Nadia's,** 11 St. John's St., is an uncommonly good bakery at commoner's prices (take-out only; open M-Sa 7:30am-5:30pm, Su 7:30am-5pm). Foreigners and beautiful people meet for cappuccino and quiche at **Clowns Coffee Bar,** 54 King St. (open daily 9am-midnight). **Hobbs' Pavillion,** Parker's Piece, off Park Terr., is renowned for delicious pancakes (open Tu-Sa noon-2:15pm and 7-9:45pm). **Market Square** has bright pyramids of fruit and vegetables (open M-Sa 8am-5pm). Students buy their gin and corn flakes at **Sainsbury's,** 44 Sidney St., the only grocery store in the middle of town (open M-F 8am-8pm, Sa 8am-7pm, Su 10am-4pm). The alcohol-serving **curry houses** on Castle Hill are also popular.

SIGHTS AND ENTERTAINMENT

Cambridge is an architect's dream, packing some of the most breathtaking examples of English architecture into less than 1 sq. mile. If you are pressed for time, visit at least one chapel (preferably King's), one garden (try Christ's), one library (Trinity's is the most interesting), and one dining hall. Cambridge is most exciting during the university's three terms: Michaelmas (Oct.-Dec.), Lent (Jan.-March), and Easter (April-June). Most of the colleges are open daily from 9am to 5:30pm, although a few are closed to sightseers during the Easter term and virtually all are closed during exam period (mid-May to mid-June). The colleges' hours may vary and are often mysteriously obscure; call to find out.

Cambridge's colleges stretch along the River Cam. **King's College** (tel. 33 11 00), on King's Parade, possesses a spectacular Gothic chapel. Rubens's magnificent *Adoration of the Magi* hangs behind the altar. (College open M-F 9:30am-4:30pm, Su 10am-5pm. £3, students £2. Chapel open term-time M-Sa 9:30am-3:30pm, Su 1:15-2:15pm and 5-5:30pm; chapel and exhibitions open during college vacations 9:30am-4:30pm. Free.) **Trinity College** (tel. 33 84 00), on Trinity St., of *Chariots of Fire* fame, is the University's purse and houses the stunning **Wren Library,** which keeps such notable treasures as A.A. Milne's handwritten manuscript of *Winnie-the-Pooh* and less momentous achievements by Milton, Byron, Tennyson, and Thackeray (library open M-F noon-2pm; £1.75, students £1). **Queens' College** (tel. 33 55 11) possesses the only unaltered Tudor courtyard in Cambridge (college open daily 1:45-4:30pm; in summer also 10:30am-12:45pm; £1), while **Christ's College** (tel. 33 49 00), founded as "God's house" in 1448, boasts gorgeous gardens (open M-F in summer 10:30am-noon; in session 10:30am-12:30pm and 2-4pm). The **Fitzwilliam Museum,** Trumpington Rd., houses paintings by da Vinci, Michelangelo, Picasso, Monet, and Seurat and an eclectic collection of antiques only the Brits could have assembled (open Tu-Sa 10am-5pm, Su 2:15-5pm; free).

Just 15 miles north of Cambridge, the massive **Ely cathedral** and its **stained glass museum** merit a morning or afternoon excursion. (Cathedral open Easter-Sept. daily 7am-7pm; Oct.-Easter M-F 7:30am-6pm, Su 7:30am-5pm. £3, students £2.20. Museum open daily 10:30am-4:30pm. £2.50, students £1.50.) Trains run from Cambridge to Ely daily (20min., round-trip £3.80).

The best source of information on student activities is the *Varsity;* the tourist office's free *Cambridge Nightlife Guide* is helpful as well. Cambridge hangouts offer good pub-crawling year-round, though they lose some of their character and their best customers in the summer. Students drink at the **Anchor,** Silver St., and **The Mill,** Mill Ln., pouring out with their pints onto Silver St. Bridge and a riverside park when weather permits. **Pickerel,** on Bridge St., is Cambridge's oldest pub. **The Eagle,** Benet St., is where Nobel laureates Watson and Crick rushed in breathless to announce their discovery of the DNA double helix—unimpressed, the barmaid insisted they settle their four-shilling back-tab before she'd serve them a toast. **Burleigh Arms,** 9-11 Newmarket Rd., serves up beer and lager to its primarily gay clientele. Dancing rears its rocking rump at **The Junction,** Clifton Rd., off Cherry Rd. (F-Sa), and at **5th Avenue,** upstairs at Lion Yard, every night except Sunday (cover £3-6; open 9pm-2am).

■ Norwich

One of England's largest and most populous cities before the Norman invasion, Norwich (NOR-ridge, like porridge) now conceals its medieval heritage behind modern facades. The 11th-century **Norwich Cathedral** and the 12th-century **Norwich Castle,** where King John signed the *Magna Carta* in 1215, reign over puzzling, winding streets unaffected by modern gridding. (Cathedral open daily mid-May to mid-Sept. 7:30am-7pm; mid-Sept. to mid-May 7:30am-6pm. Free.) **Regional railways** (tel. (0345) 48 49 50) run trains to the station at the corner of Riverside and Thorpe Rd. from Cambridge (1½hr., £10.20) and London (2hr., £32). National express **buses** (tel. (0990) 80 80 80) travel from the station on Surrey St. to and from Cambridge (2½hr., round-trip £8.75) and London (3hr., £14.50) as well. The **tourist office** is at Guildhall, Gaol Hill (tel. (01603) 66 60 71), in front of city hall. (Open June-Sept. M-F 9:30am-5pm, Sa 10am-5pm; Oct.-May M-F 9:30am-4:30pm, Sa 9:30am-1pm and 1:30-4pm.) The **YMCA,** 46-52 Giles St. (tel. (01603) 62 02 69), has gender-segregated wings (dorms £8.50; singles £12.50). In the heart of the city is one of England's largest and oldest open-air **markets** (open M-Sa 8am-4:30pm).

CENTRAL ENGLAND

The 19th century swept into central England in an industrial sandstorm, revolutionizing quiet village life. By the beginning of the 20th century, the "dark satanic mills" foreseen by William Blake had indeed overrun the Midlands. Yet several cities preserved their architectural and artistic treasures, and others embraced artists and musicians to counterbalance the harms of industrialization. Today, Manchester and Liverpool are home to innovative music and arts scenes as well as some of the U.K.'s most vibrant nightlife, while Lincoln and Chester tell many of their tales in Latin.

Lincoln Medieval streets, half-timbered Tudor houses, and a 12th-century cathedral are all relative newcomers to **Lincoln,** a town originally built for retired Roman legionnaires. The king of the hill is undoubtedly the magnificent **Lincoln Cathedral.** (Open May-Aug. M-Sa 7:15am-8pm, Su until 6pm; Sept.-Apr. M-Sa 7:15am-6pm, Su until 5pm. Free tours May-Aug. daily 11am and 2pm; Sept.-Apr. Sa only. £2.) **Lincoln Castle** still retains its Norman walls and houses one of the four surviving copies of the *Magna Carta.* (Open Apr.-Oct. M-Sa 9:30am-5:30pm, Su 11am-5:30pm; Nov.-Mar. M-Sa 9:30am-4pm. £2.50.)

The station (tel. (01522) 34 02 22) on St. Mary's St. welcomes **trains** from London's King's Cross Station (2hr., £36.50). National Express **buses** (tel. (0990) 80 80 80) roll to London from the Melville St. station, across from the train station (5hr., £18). The main **tourist office,** 9 Castle Hill (tel. (01522) 52 98 28), atop the hill near the cathedral, distributes *Where to Stay* and *What's On In Lincoln* (open M-Th 9am-5:30pm, F 9am-5pm, Sa-Su 10am-5pm). Carline and Yarborough Rd., west of the cathedral, are lined with **B&Bs** (£16-18). **Bradford Guest House,** 67 Monks Rd. (tel. (01522) 52 39 47), across from North Lincolnshire College, is only five minutes from the town center (singles £16; doubles £30; breakfast included). A **YHA youth hostel,** 77 S. Park (tel. (01522) 52 20 76), is opposite South Common at the end of Canwick Rd. (£8.80, students £7.80. Reception closed daily 10am-5pm. Open Feb.-Oct. daily; Nov.-Dec. F-Sa.) **The Spinning Wheel,** 39 Steep Hill Rd., just south of the tourist office, serves vegetarian dishes (£3.95-5; open daily 11:30am-10pm).

■ Peak District National Park

Covering 555 square miles, Peak District National Park lies at the southern end of the Pennines, with the industrial giants Manchester, Sheffield, and Nottingham at its corners. In the northern Dark Peak area, deep gullies gouge the hard peat moorland against a backdrop of gloomy cliffs. Well-marked public footpaths (sometimes turning into small steams) lead over mildly rocky hillsides to village clusters in the Northern Peak area. Abandoned milestones, derelict lead mines, and country homes are scattered throughout the southern White Peak.

Public transport and bus tours bring mobs of visitors on sunny summer weekends; for a more tranquil visit, try to catch the infrequent buses to the more remote northern moors. Two **rail lines** originate in Manchester and enter the park from the northwest: one line stops at Buxton near the park's western edge, while the Hope Valley line continues across the park to Sheffield, via Edale, Hope, and Hathersage. **Bus TP** winds through the park (3½ hours, every 2hr.) from Manchester to Nottingham, stopping at Buxton, Bakewell, Matlock, Derby, and other towns. Those who plan to ride frequently should buy a **Derbyshire Wayfarer** (£7.25), which covers virtually all transport services. The invaluable *Peak District Timetable* (60p, available in Peak tourist offices) has bus and train routes and a map.

Write to Peak District National Park, National Park Office, Aldern House, Barlow Rd., Bakewell DE4 5AE for info and publications. The **National Park Information Centres** at **Bakewell** (tel. (01629) 81 32 27), **Castleton** (tel. (01433) 62 06 79), and **Edale** (tel. (01433) 67 02 07) have walking guides and some have accommodations services. You can also ask questions at **tourist offices** in **Ashbourne** (tel. (01335) 34 36 66), **Buxton** (tel. (01298) 251 06), and **Matlock Bath** (tel. (01629) 550 82). Many farmers allow camping on their land; **YHA youth hostels** in the park cost from £8 to £10. **Bakewell** (tel. (01629) 81 23 13), **Buxton** (tel. (01298) 222 87), **Castleton** (tel. (01433) 62 02 35), **Edale** (tel. (01433) 67 03 02), and **Matlock** (tel. (01629) 58 29 83) are all good options. The park authority operates six **Cycle Hire Centres**, where you can rent bikes (about £8). Call **Ashbourne** (tel. (01335) 34 31 56) or **Hayfield** (tel. (01663) 74 62 22) for info.

Bakewell, Edale, and Castleton
The Southern Peak is better served than the Northern Peak by buses and trains, and is consequently more trampled than its counterpart. Thirty miles southeast of Manchester, **Bakewell** is the best base for exploring the southern portion of the park. Located near several scenic walks through the White Peaks, the town is known for its delicious Bakewell pudding, created when a flustered cook, trying to make a tart, poured an egg mixture over strawberry jam instead of mixing it into the dough. **The Old Original Bakewell Pudding Shop,** on Rutland Sq., sells lunches and delicious desserts in addition to the pudding. (Supremely sinful cream tea £3.60. Open July-Aug. daily 8:30am-9pm; Sept.-June M-Th 9am-6pm, F-Su 8:30am-6pm.) Bakewell's **National Park Information Center** is at the intersection of Bridge and Market St. The intimate and cozy **YHA Youth Hostel,** Fly Hill, is a five-minute walk from the tourist office (open mid-June to Aug. daily; Apr. to mid-June and Sept.-Oct. M-Sa; Nov.-Mar. F-Sa).

The northern Dark Peak area contains some of the wildest and most rugged hill country in England. Cradled in the deep dale of the River Noe, with gentle, gray-green hills sweeping up on two sides, **Edale** offers little in the way of civilization other than a church, cafe, pub, school, and nearby youth hostel. Its environs, however, are arguably the most spectacular in Northern England. If there's no room at the youth hostel, try camping at **Fieldhead** (tel. (01433) 67 03 86), behind the tourist office (£3.20 per person). From Edale, the 3½-mile path to **Castleton** affords a breathtaking view of both the dark gritstone Edale Valley (Dark Peak) and the lighter limestone Hope Valley (White Peak) to the south. If picturesque Castleton persuades you to stay for awhile, check out the amazing caverns in the area. The **Blue John Cavern** (tel. (01433) 62 06 42) and **Treak Cliff Cavern** (tel. (01433) 62 05 71) are about 1½ miles west of town on the A625. (Blue John open daily 10am-5pm; 50min. tours every 20min. £5. Treak Cliff open daily Easter-Oct. 9:30am-5pm; Nov.-Easter 10am-4pm. £4.95.) Right in town, the gigantic **Peak Cavern** (tel. (01433) 62 02 85) was known in the 18th century as the "Devil's Arse" and features the second-largest aperture in the world (open Easter-Nov. daily 10am-4pm; Dec.-Easter. Sa-Su 10am-4pm; £4.50). In town, stay at the excellent **YHA Youth Hostel** (£9.75; open Feb. to late Dec.) or **Cryer House** (tel. (01433) 62 02 44), across from the tourist office (doubles £36).

BRITAIN

■ Manchester

The Industrial Revolution quickly transformed this once unremarkable village into a bustling northern hub. Derided by Ruskin as a "devil's darkness," the partially gentrified city is still considered slightly dangerous but draws thousands with its pulsing nightlife and vibrant arts scene.

SIGHTS AND ENTERTAINMENT The towering neo-Gothic **Manchester Town Hall** in St. Peter's Sq., behind the tourist office, is a gem in a city not known for its architecture, but is surpassed by the **Central Library** behind it. One of the largest municipal libraries in Europe, the domed building houses a music and theater library, an exceptional language and literature library, and an extensive Judaica collection (open M-Th 10am-8pm, F-Sa 10am-5pm). In the **Museum of Science and Industry**, Castlefield, on Liverpool Rd., working steam engines and looms provide a dramatic vision of Britain's industrialization (open daily 10am-5pm; £5, students £3).

Manchester has notably energetic and exciting theater and music scenes. For a list of everything that's going on, get *City Life* (£1.60) at newsstands, or hang around Oldham St. during the day to get a whiff of what's on for the evening. The **Royal Exchange Theatre** (tel. (0161) 833 98 33), back at St. Ann's Sq., performs a diverse program though it was destroyed by an IRA bomb only two years ago. (Box office open M-Sa 10am-7:30pm. £7-23, concessions £5 with 3-day advance booking.) Manchester's clubbing and live music scene remains a national trendsetter. Most clubs lie within a few blocks of Whitworth St. Indie/alternative spins at **The Venue**, 17 Whitworth St., an appropriately small, dark club. **Generation X,** 11-13 New Wakefield St., plays house and breakbeat; Sunday is "Regeneration," an *aprés*-clubbing chill-down. East of Princess St., the **Gay Village** rings merrily all night. Evening crowds drink at the bars lining **Canal Street;** the purple **Manto's** fills up with all ages, genders, and orientations, with its Saturday "Breakfast Club" lasting until 6am.

PRACTICAL INFO, ACCOMMODATIONS, AND FOOD **Trains** leave Piccadilly Station on London Rd. and Victoria Station on Victoria St. for Chester (1hr., £7.20), Liverpool (50min., £6), and London (2½hr., £61). **Buses** serve about 50 stops around Piccadilly Gardens; pick up an immense, free, fold-out route map at the station (open M-Sa 7am-6:30pm, Su 10am-6pm). National Express buses use the Chorlton St. Coach Station (to London 4½hr., £22). The **tourist office** (tel. (0161) 234 31 57), Town Hall Extension on Lloyd St., provides guides to accommodations, food, and sights (open M-Sa 10am-5:30pm, Su 11am-4pm). **Cyberia,** 12 Oxford St., offers web access and a popular bar (open M-Sa 11am-11pm, Su 2-9pm). The highest concentration of budget accommodations is located two to three miles south of the city center in the suburbs of **Fallowfield, Withington,** and **Didsbury** (consult *Where to Stay* from the tourist office). Closer to the city, the **YHA Manchester Youth Hostel** (tel. (0161) 839 99 60), near the Museum of Science, offers modern, efficient facilities including a huge kitchen, laundry, and cafeteria (from £13; reception 7am-11pm). Manage a meal at the pricey Chinatown restaurants by eating their multi-course "Businessman's Lunch." **Cornerhouse Cafe,** 70 Oxford St., sports a bar (open until 11pm), art galleries, cinemas, and trendy crowds (main courses from £3.50; hot meals served noon-2:30pm and 5-7:30pm). **Spice,** on Whitworth St. West, offers fast food, a 10% student discount, and long hours for late-night revelers. (Pizza and burgers £1.60-3.70. Open M-Tu 5pm-2:30am, W-Th 5pm-3am, F-Sa 5pm-4am, Su 5pm-midnight.)

■ Chester

With fashionable shops tucked in medieval houses, tour guides in full Roman armor, a town crier in Georgian uniform, and a Barclays bank occupying a wing of the cathedral, Chester at times resembles an American theme-park pastiche of Ye Olde English Towne. Originally built by frontier-foraging Romans and later a Plantagenet base for campaigns against the Welsh, the crowded but lovely city now allows foreigners within its fortified walls while maintaining a watchful eye on Wales.

The famous **city walls** completely encircle the town, and you can walk on them for free. Just outside Newgate lies the unimpressive base of the largest **Roman amphitheater** in Britain (open daily Apr.-Sept. 10am-6pm; Oct.-Mar. 10am-1pm and 2-4pm; free). Fight your way through the throngs for a visit to the awe-inspiring **cathedral** (open daily 7am-6:30pm). Every aspect of the cathedral is outstanding, from the intersecting stone arches to the brilliant stained-glass windows. The cloisters, with their garden, should not be missed. During the last week in June and first week of July, a river carnival and raft race highlight the **Sports and Leisure Fortnight;** contact the tourist office for more details. The **Chester Summer Music Festival** draws musical groups from across Britain into the cathedral during the third and fourth weeks of July. Contact the Chester Summer Music Festival Office, 8 Abbey Sq., Chester CH1 2HH (tel. (01244) 32 07 00 or 34 12 00). Chester has 30-odd **pubs** to assuage thirst (and hunger). Watering holes group on **Lower Bridge** and **Watergate St.**

British Rail **trains** run from the station on City Rd. to Holyhead (1 per hr., £13.70), London Euston (3hr., £38.50), and Manchester (1hr., £7.20). National Express **buses** leave from Delamere St. for London (5½hr., £12) and Manchester (1hr., £4.05). The **tourist office,** Town Hall, Northgate St. (tel. (01244) 40 23 85; fax 40 04 20), offers a useful city map for 50p. (Open May-Oct. M-Sa 9am-7:30pm, Su 10am-4pm; Nov.-Apr. M-Sa 9am-5:30pm, Su 10am-4pm.) A smaller branch is located at the train station (open daily 10am-8pm). Decent **B&Bs** (from £13.50) line Hoole Rd., a five-minute walk from the train station (or take bus 21, C30, or 53 from the city center). The **YHA youth hostel,** Hough Green House, 40 Hough Green (tel. (01244) 68 00 56; fax 68 12 04), one mile from the city center, is a beautiful Victorian house; take bus 7 or 16 and ask for the youth hostel (£9.75; closed late Dec.). **Laburnum Guest House,** 2 St. Anne St. (tel. (01244) 38 03 13), has four sparkling rooms with TV and bath (£19). **Tesco supermarket** is hidden at the end of an alley off Frodsham St. (open M-Sa 8am-10pm, Su 11am-5pm). **Hattie's Tea Shop,** 5 Rufus Ct., off Northgate St., offers homemade cakes and snacks (open M-F 9am-5pm, Sa 9am-7pm, Su 11am-4pm).

■ Liverpool

On the banks of the Mersey, Liverpool boasts an enormous cathedral, docklands transformed to attract tourists instead of ships, a modern, thriving cultural scene, and—oh yeah—the Beatles. Begun in 1904, the Anglican **Liverpool Cathedral,** Upper Duke St., boasts the highest Gothic arches ever built, the largest vault and organ, and the highest and heaviest bells in the world. Climb to the top of the 300 ft. tower for a view to North Wales. (Cathedral open daily 9am-6pm. Tower open daily 11am-4pm, weather permitting. £2.) In contrast, the **Metropolitan Cathedral of Christ the King,** Mt. Pleasant, looks more like a rocket launcher than a house of worship (open daily 8am-6pm; in winter Su until 5pm). **Albert Dock,** at the western end of Hanover St., is a series of 19th-century warehouses transformed into a complex of shops, restaurants, and museums. A cornerstone of this development is the **Tate Gallery** (a branch of the London institution), with scads of modern art (open Tu-Su 10am-6pm; free). Also at Albert Dock, **The Beatles Story** pays tribute to the group's work with John Lennon's white piano, a recreation of the Cavern Club, and, of course, a yellow submarine (open daily Apr.-Oct. 10am-6pm; Nov.-Mar. 10am-5pm; £6.45). Pick up the **Beatles Map** (£2) at the tourist office, which leads you to Strawberry Fields and Penny Lane. Nearby, the **Beatles Shop,** 31 Matthew St., is loaded with souvenirs and memorabilia (open M-Sa 9:30am-5:30pm, Su 11am-4pm).

Trains run to Birmingham (2hr., £14.80), London (2hr., £38.50), and Manchester (1½hr., £6). National Express **buses** (tel. (0990) 80 80 80) also serve Birmingham (2½hr., £10 return), London (4-5hr., £12.50), and Manchester (1hr., £6). The **tourist office** (tel. (0151) 709 36 31), in the Clayton Sq. Shopping Centre, stocks a guide to the city (£1), books rooms for a 10% deposit, and they do appreciate you comin' 'round (open M-Sa 9:30am-5:30pm). A smaller branch is located at **Atlantic Pavilion,** Albert Dock (tel. (0151) 708 88 54; open daily 10am-5:30pm). For a hard day's night, head to Lord Nelson St., adjacent to the train station, or Mt. Pleasant, for modest hotels. The **Embassie Youth Hostel,** 1 Faulkner Sq. (tel. (0151) 707 10 89), is a beautiful old house in the southeast part of town (£10.50). Single women will find clean rooms at the **YWCA,** 1 Rodney St. (tel. (0151) 709 77 91; singles £12; doubles £22). A **YHA Hostel** is scheduled to open by the end of 1998 on Chalenor St. near Albert Dock (call (0171) 248 65 47 for details). Cheap take-out eateries cluster on Hardman St. and Berry St. **Cafe Tabac,** 126 Bold St., serves an inexpensive menu (£3 and under) and eclectic international wines (open M-Sa 9:30am-11pm, Su 10am-5pm).

Liverpool has a thriving arts scene and an energetic nightlife. *In Touch* (£1), available at the tourist office and newsstands, and *Liverpool Echo* (28p), sold on street corners, detail the city's offerings. **Cream,** Wolstenholme Sq., off Parr St., is Liverpool's super-club—people travel for miles to come here. The **Cavern Club,** Matthew St., where the Fab Four first gained prominence, pumps out club most of the time, but showcases live music Saturdays 2-6pm (free before 10pm). The bookstore **News From Nowhere,** 96 Bold St., has info on special events at gay and lesbian clubs. The **Baa Bar,** 43-45 Fleet St., off Bold St., attracts a lesbian, gay, trendy, and far from sheepish crowd for cappuccino and cheap beers (open M-Sa 10am-2am, Su 11am-6pm).

NORTH ENGLAND

Between Central England's industrial belt and Scotland's rugged wilderness is a quiet area of natural beauty. Sliced by the Pennine Mountains, North England's main attractions lie enshrined in four national parks and several calm coastal areas. Walkers and ramblers flock here, and no trail tests their stamina more than the Pennine Way, the country's first official long-distance path and still its longest. Isolated villages along the trails continue a pastoral tradition that contrasts with the polluted enormity and din of many English cities to the south.

■ Pennine Way

The Pennine Peaks form the spine of England, arching south to north up the center of Britain from the Peak National Park to the Scottish border. The 268-mile **Pennine Way** crowns the central ridge. Hard-core hikers have completed the hike in 10 days, but most walkers spend three weeks on the long, green trail. The classic Wainwright's *Pennine Way Companion* (£10), available from bookstores, is a good supplement to the Ordnance Survey maps, which run about £6 at National Park Information Centers and tourist offices. **YHA youth hostels** are spaced within a day's hike (7-29 miles) of one another. Send a self-addressed envelope to YHA Northern Region, P.O. Box 11, Matlock, Derbyshire DE4 2XA (tel. (01629) 82 58 50), for info on the **Pennine Way Package** that allows you to book a route of 18 or more hostels along the walk (50p booking fee per hostel). Any National Park Information Centre or tourist office can also supply details on trails and alternative accommodations, or you can consult the invaluable *Pennine Way Accommodations Guide* (90p). In the High Pennines, YHA operates three **camping barns.** To book, call (01200) 42 83 66 and send a check to YHA Camping Barns, 16 Shawbridge St., Clitheroe, BB7 1LZ.

South Pennines In the midst of the gorse-strewn moorland of the **South Pennines,** the tiny villages of **Haworth** and **Hebden Bridge** provide hospitable civilization breaks for an overnight or daytrip from Manchester. From Hebden Bridge, you can make day-hikes to the nearby villages of Blackshaw Head, Cragg Vale, or **Hepstonstall,** where you'll find the restless remains of Sylvia Plath, the ruins of a 13th-century church, and a 1764 octagonal church, the oldest Methodist house of worship in the world. Two **rail** lines go through the region—get the free *West Yorkshire Train Times.* Hebden Bridge's **tourist office,** 1 Bridge Gate (tel. (01422) 84 38 31), is equipped with many free town maps, walking guides, and leaflets on local attractions (open Apr.-Oct. M-Sa 10am-5pm, Su 11am-5pm; Oct.-Mar. daily 10am-4pm). Brontësaurs should head for the Brontë **parsonage,** behind the church in Haworth, where

Emily, Charlotte, Anne, and Branwell lived with their father (open Apr.-Oct. daily 10am-5:30pm). Haworth's **tourist office,** 2/4 West Ln. (tel. (01535) 64 23 29), at the summit of Main St., stocks maps and guides (open daily Easter-Nov. 9:30am-5:30pm; Nov.-Easter 9:30am-5pm). The town's **YHA Youth Hostel,** Longlands Dr. (tel. (01535) 64 22 34), is located a mile from the tourist office. (£8.80. Open mid-Feb. to Oct. daily; Nov. to mid-Dec. M-Sa.) **B&Bs** are on Main St., down the hill from the tourist office (about £15-17).

High Pennines This largely untouristed area stretches about 20 miles west of Durham City, from below Barnard Castle in the south to Hadrian's Wall in the north. The High Pennines are best suited to **hiking** or **biking;** cars can successfully navigate the roads, but buses tackle the region with distressing hesitancy. Twenty miles southwest of Durham by the River Tees, the peaceful market town of **Barnard Castle** makes an excellent base for exploring the castles of Teesdale and the North Pennine peaks and waterfalls. Along the river sprawl the ruins of the 13th-century Norman **castle.** (Open Apr.-Sept. daily 10am-1pm and 2-6pm; Oct. daily 10am-1pm and 2-4pm; Nov.-Mar. W-Su 10am-1pm and 2-4pm. £2.20, students £1.70.) A remarkable collection of European art merits a visit to the **Bowes Museum,** a 17th-century-style French château. (Open Apr.-Oct. M-Sa 10am-5pm, Su 2-5pm; Nov.-Mar. call (01833) 69 06 06 for hours. £3.90.) Barnard Castle has no youth hostel but boasts many excellent **B&Bs,** including **Mrs. Williamson,** 85 Galgate (tel. (01833) 63 87 57; singles £18-24; doubles with bath £42). Guided walks leave from the **tourist office,** Woodleigh, Flatts Rd. (tel. (01833) 69 09 09; open daily Apr.-Oct. 10am-6pm; Nov.-Mar. 10am-4pm).

■ Durham City

Twisting medieval streets, footbridges, and restricted vehicle access make cliff-top Durham a foot-friendly area, although its only claim to being a "city" is the presence of **Durham Cathedral,** England's greatest Norman cathedral. At one end lies the **tomb of the Venerable Bede,** author of *The Ecclesiastical History of the English People.* The view from the **tower** compensates for the 325-step climb. (Cathedral open daily 7:15am-8pm; Sept.-Apr. 7:15am-6pm. Suggested donation £2.50. Tower open daily 10am-4pm. £2.) **Durham Castle,** once a key defensive fortress, has become a residence for university students and summer travelers. (B&B £20.50. Tours daily July-Sept. 10am-12:30pm and 2-4:30pm; Oct.-June 2-4:30pm. £3.) If your legs are Wear-y, rent a rowboat from **Brown's Boathouse Centres,** Elvet Bridge, and explore the winding River Wear while dodging scullers and ducks (£2.50).

    Trains leave from the station (tel. (0191) 232 62 62) west of town to London (3hr., £63), Newcastle (20min., £2.40), and York (1hr., £15.90). **Buses** also regularly serve London and Newcastle from the station on North Rd. The **tourist office** (tel. (0191) 384 37 20) is at Market Place; if you're arriving at the train station, call ahead for directions. (Open July-Aug. M-Sa 10am-6pm, Su 2-5pm; June and Sept. M-F 10am-5:30pm, Sa 9:30am-5:30pm; Oct.-May M-F 10am-5pm.) A large supply of cheap and often beautiful dormitory rooms, available from July to September and during school vacations, rings the cathedral. **University College,** Durham Castle (tel. (0191) 374 38 63), and **St. John's College,** 3 South Bailey (tel. (0191) 374 35 66), provide rooms (£18-20.50). **Mrs. Koltai** runs an attractive B&B at 10 Gilesgate (tel./fax (0191) 386 20 26; singles £16; doubles £32). Bakeries with £1 pastries crowd the center of town, while vegetables and fruits fill the stands of **Market Hall** (open daily 9am-5pm). Grab a sandwich from **Marks and Spencer,** on Silver St. (open M-Th 9am-5:30pm, F-Sa 8:30am-5:30pm). Students gather to dance and drink at **Hogshead,** 58 Saddler St.

Newcastle-upon-Tyne Hardworking Newcastle is not known for dreamy spires or evening hush, but for the legendary local pub and club scene. While you can still see straight, explore the masterful **Tyne Bridge** and the elegant tower of the **Cathedral Church of St. Nicholas.** (Cathedral open M-F 7am-6pm, Sa 8am-4pm, Su 9am-noon and 4-7pm. Free.) At night, the rowdy area of **Bigg Market** frowns on underdressed student types. Some of the milder pubs are **Blackie Boy** and **Macy's.** The **Quayside** is a slightly more relaxed, student-friendly area of town; **The Red House,** 32 Sandhill, and **The Cooperage,** opposite the Guildhall, offer good drinks. Revelers sway even before they've imbibed at **The Tuxedo Royale,** a boat/dance club under the Tyne Bridge. Gays and lesbians flock to the corner of Waterloo and Sunderland St. to drink at **The Village** and dance at **Powerhouse.**

Trains (tel. (0191) 232 62 62) leave Central Station for Edinburgh (1½hr., £26.40) and London (3hr., £40.50). National Express **buses** leave Gallowgate Coach Station for Edinburgh (3hr., £18.50 return) and London (6hr., £27 return) as well. The **tourist office** (tel. (0191) 261 06 10), at the Central Library off New Bridge St., offers an essential street map (open M and Th 9:30am-8pm, Tu-W and F 9:30am-5pm, Sa 9am-5pm). A branch office sits in Central Station. **B&Bs** typically begin at £15, but the crowded **YHA youth hostel,** 107 Jesmond Rd. (tel. (0191) 281 25 70), offers cheap rooms. (£9.15, under 18 £6.20. Lockout 10am-5pm. Curfew 11pm; ask for the late entry code. Closed Dec.-Jan.) **Don Vito's,** 82 Pilgrim St., stands out among the many Italian eateries. Expect cheap food and paranormal activity at the **Supernatural Vegetarian Restaurant,** 2 Princess Sq. (open M and Sa 10:30am-7pm, Tu-F until 7:30pm).

■ York

York looks and feels as different from nearby Manchester and Liverpool as it does from its American namesake. Yet the well-preserved city walls that once foiled marauding invaders cannot protect York from hordes of equally determined tourists, who come to conquer York's medieval thoroughfares, Georgian townhouses, and Britain's largest Gothic cathedral.

SIGHTS AND ENTERTAINMENT The best introduction to the city is a 2½-mile walk along its medieval walls; you can sign up for one of countless **walking tours** at a tourist center. The **Association of Voluntary Guides** runs a particularly good architectural tour. (2hr.; daily Nov.-Mar. 10:15am, Apr.-Oct. also 2:15pm. Meet in front of the York City Art Gallery directly across from the tourist office.) The tourist stampede abates in the early morning and toward dusk, but everyone and everything converges at the enormous **York Minster,** built between 1220 and 1470. Half of all the medieval stained glass in England glitters here. The **Great East Window,** depicting the beginning and end of the world, holds over a hundred scenes and is the largest medieval glass window on Earth. It's a mere 275 steps to the top of the **Central Tower,** from which you can stare down on York's red roofs. (Cathedral open daily in summer 7am-8:30pm; off-season 7am-5pm. Donation £2. Tower open daily 9:30am-6:30pm or until dark in winter. £2.) The **Yorkshire Museum,** in the gardens off Museum St., presents an elaborate display of Roman, Anglo-Saxon, and Viking art galleries, as well as the gorgeous £2.5 million **Middleham Jewel.** (Open daily 10am-5pm; last admission 4:30pm. £3.60. Wheelchair accessible.) In the museum gardens, peacocks strut among the haunting ruins of **St. Mary's Abbey,** once the most influential Benedictine monastery in northern England. The fascinating **Jorvik Viking Center,** on Coppergate, travels even further back in time (open daily Apr.-Oct. 9am-5:30pm; Nov.-Mar. until 3:30pm; £4.99, students £4.59).

Not many pubs can boast an original Roman bath in their basement, but the **Roman Bath** (tel. 62 04 55) on St. Sampsons can. For other entertainment options, pick up the weekly *What's On* guide and the seasonal *Evening Entertainment* brochure from the tourist office.

Near York, the English Baroque **Castle Howard** (tel. (01653) 64 83 33) presides over 999 acres of even more stunning grounds, including gardens, fountains, and lakes. **York Pullman** (tel. (01904) 62 29 92) in Bootham Tower, Exhibition Square, offers half-day excursions to the castle for £3.75. (Castle open Mar.-Oct. daily 11am-4:30pm. Grounds open from 10am. Call for off-season hours. £7, students £6.)

BRITAIN

PRACTICAL INFO, ACCOMMODATIONS, AND FOOD Trains arrive at Station Rd. from Edinburgh (2-3hr., £45), London's King's Cross Station (2hr., £54), and Manchester's Piccadilly Station (1½hr., £13.30). National Express **buses** (tel. (0990) 80 80 80) run less often to Edinburgh (5hr., £20.25), London (4hr., £17.50), and Manchester (3hr., £7.50) from the station on Rougier St. The main **tourist office** (tel. (01904) 62 17 56), in De Grey Rooms, Exhibition Sq., finds rooms for a £3 fee plus 10% deposit (open July-Aug. M-Sa 9am-7pm, Su 9am-6pm; Sept.-June daily 9am-6pm).

Competition for inexpensive **B&Bs** (from £16) can be fierce in the summer. Try side streets along Bootham/Clifton or The Mount area (past the train station and down Blossom St.). **Avenue Guest House,** 6 The Avenue (tel. (01904) 62 05 75), and **Queen Anne's Guesthouse,** 24 Queen Anne's Rd., ¾ mile from town, both provide comfortable rooms (£13-18 per person). **YHA Youth Hostel,** Water End, Clifton (tel. (01904) 65 31 47), 1 mile from the town center, is a super-grade hostel with excellent facilities. From the tourist office, walk about ¾ mile out Bootham/Clifton and take a left at Water End, or take a bus to Clifton Green and walk ¼ mile down Water End. (£14.40; singles £17.50; doubles £37; family rooms £52 or £78. Breakfast included. Reception 7am-11:30pm. Closed Dec. 5-Jan 15.) **The Old Dairy,** 10 Compton St. (tel. (01904) 62 38 16), and **York Youth Hostel,** 11-15 Bishophill Senior (tel. (01904) 62 59 04 or 63 06 13), provide cheap, dorm-style accommodations.

Expensive tea rooms, medium-priced bistros, fudge shops, and cheap eateries bump elbows even in the remote alleyways of York. Fruit and vegetable grocers peddle their wares at the **market** between Parliament St. and the Shambles (open M-Sa 9am-5pm; Apr.-Dec. also Su 9am-4:30pm). **Oscar's Wine Bar and Bistro,** 8 Little Stonegate, serves massive portions of delicious food (£5-7; open daily 11am-11pm). Eat upstairs overlooking the market at **Little Shambles Cafe,** Little Shambles off Shambles, open for English breakfast (£2), lunch, and tea (open M-Sa 7am-5:30pm, Su 9am-5pm). **La Romantica,** 14 Goodramgate, is open later and serves delicious pastas and pizzas (£5-7) in a candlelit setting (open daily noon-2:30pm and 5:30-11:30pm).

■ Lake District National Park

Although rugged hills make up much of England's landscape, only in the Lake District of the northwest corner do sparkling waterholes fill the spaces in between. Windermere, Ambleside, Grasmere, and Keswick make good bases for exploring. In summer, tourists in exhaust-spewing tour buses can be as numerous as sheep and cattle, so ascend into the hills and wander through the smaller towns, especially those in the more remote northern and western areas. The farther west you go from the busy bus route serving the towns along the A591, the more countryside you'll have to yourself.

The best way to reach the Lake District is to take public transportation to Windermere or Oxenholme, and then hike or take a local bus from more remote regions. **Trains** service Oxenholme; National Express **buses** run to Windermere from Birmingham, Manchester, and London (call the Windermere tourist office for info, tel. (015394) 464 99). Two rail lines flank the park: the **Preston-Lancaster-Carlisle line** runs south to north along the east edge, while the **Barrow-Carlisle line** serves the west coast. **Stagecoach Cumberland buses** (tel. (01946) 632 22) serve over 25 towns and villages; tourist offices provide the essential and free *Lakeland Explorer*, which has timetables. **YHA** (tel. (015394) 323 04) also offers a door-to-door **minibus** service between its hostels (£2).

Psych yourself up for a hilly challenge if you decide to **bike.** Two-wheelers can be rented in most towns. **Hikers** will find an abundance of trails and often an overabundance of fellow walkers. If you plan to take a long or difficult hike, check first with the Park Service, get a good map (e.g. Ordnance Survey), call for **weather** information (tel. (017687) 757 57), and leave your route with your B&B or hostel proprietor.

For an introduction to the Lake District, visit the beautiful grounds and house of the **National Park Visitor Centre** (tel. (015394) 466 01) in **Brockhole,** halfway between Windermere and Ambleside (open Apr.-Nov. daily 10am-5pm). The following **National Park Information Centres** provide expert info, sell a camping guide (£1), and book accommodations: **Ambleside (Waterhead)** (tel. (015394) 327 29), **Bowness Bay** (tel. (015394) 428 95), **Coniston** (tel. (015394) 415 33), **Grasmere** (tel. (015394) 350 57), **Hawkshead** (tel. (015394) 365 25), **Keswick** (tel. (017687) 726 45), **Pooley Bridge** (tel. (017684) 865 30), **Seatoller Barn** (tel. (017687) 772 94), and **Ullswater** (tel. (017684) 824 14). **B&Bs** line nearly every street in every town (£13-18), and the Lakes have the highest concentration of **YHA youth hostels** in the world, but lodgings fill in July and August. Campers should pick up the National Park's *Caravan and Tent Guide* (£1) and the free *Camping Barns in England*, which list campground locations.

Windermere and Bowness
A first stop for many travelers, **Windermere** and **Bowness** fill to the gills in summer as myriad boaters and water-skiers swarm over Lake Windermere. **Windermere Lake Cruises** (tel. (015394) 433 60) runs a Lake Information Centre at the north end of the pier, rents boats, and books passage on popular cruises to Ambleside (return £5.50) and south to Lakeside (return £5.70). The Windermere **tourist office** (tel. (015394) 464 99), next to the rail station, books National Express buses, exchanges foreign currency (£2.50 commission), and dispenses guides to lake walks and local restaurants (open daily Easter-Oct. 9am-6pm; Nov.-Easter 9am-5pm). Bowness and Windermere are chock-full of convenient **B&Bs**, but you'll still have to book ahead. In Bowness, try **Brendan Chase**, 1-3 College Rd. (tel. (015394) 456 38; £10-15), **The Haven**, 10 Birch St. (tel. (015394) 440 17; £16-17.50), or **Dalecott**, 13 Upper Oak St. (tel. (015394) 451 21; £13.50-16.50). In Windermere, the social **Lake District Backpackers Hostel** (tel. (015394) 463 74), on High St., is a two-minute walk from the train station (£9.50). The nearest campground, **Limefitt Park** (tel. (015394) 323 00), 4½ miles north of Bowness on the A592, offers every amenity except public transport (2-person tent £15). In Windermere, stop in the espresso-sized **Coffee Pot,** 15 Main Rd., for sandwiches (open M-W and F-Sa 10am-5:30pm, Su 1-5pm). In Bowness, try the **Hedgerow Teashop** on Lake Rd. for a ploughman's lunch (£4; open W-M 10:30am-5pm).

Ambleside and Grasmere
The villages of **Ambleside** and **Grasmere** offer Lake District beauty at a less frenetic pace than Windermere. *Ambleside Walks in the Countryside* (20p) lists three gentle walks from the town's center. The Ambleside **tourist office** (tel. (015394) 325 82) sits on Church St. (Open Easter-Oct. daily 9am-5pm; Nov.-Easter Tu-Th 10am-1pm and 2-5pm, F-Sa 9am-1pm and 2-5pm.) **B&Bs** cluster on Church St. and Compston Rd. but fill up quickly (£14.50-16). Ambleside's **YHA youth hostel** (tel. (015394) 323 04), one mile south on Windermere Rd. (the A591), is the mother of all hostels; you can even swim off the pier (£10.70). On Compton Rd., **Scoffs** serves up a huge selection of sandwiches on baguettes (from £1.40; open daily 9am-3pm).

During quiet mornings in **Grasmere,** you can savor the peace that Wordsworth so enjoyed here. Visit **Dove Cottage** where the poet lived with his wife, his sister, Samuel Taylor Coleridge, De Quincey, and assorted children, opium-eaters, and literati. (Open mid-Feb. to mid-Jan. daily 9:30am-5pm. £4.40, students £3.75; includes admission to museum next door.) The 6-mile **Wordsworth Walk** circumnavigates the two lakes of the Rothay River, passing by the poet's grave, Dove cottage, and Rydal Mount along the way. Star-seeking fell-climbers can tackle the path from Rydal to Legburthwaite (near Keswick) in an athletic day, passing the towering Great Rigg and Helvellyn on the way. Bus 555 will bring you back to Ambleside. There are two **YHA youth hostels** within an eight-minute walk of Grasmere. **Butterlip How** (tel. (015394) 353 16) is a Victorian house with flowering gardens (£8.80; open Apr.-Oct. daily; Jan.-Mar. Tu-Sa). **Thorney How** (tel. (015394) 355 91) is a converted farmhouse; follow the road to Easedale and turn right at the fork (£8.80; open daily Apr.-Sept.; mid-Feb. to Mar. and Oct.-Dec. Th-M). For a tasty snack, try Sarah Nelson's famous Grasmere Gingerbread at **Church Cottage,** just by St. Oswald's Church.

Keswick Sandwiched between towering Skiddaw peak and the northern edge of Lake Derwentwater, **Keswick** (KEZ-ick) rivals Windermere as the region's tourist capital. The **tourist office,** Moot Hall, Market Sq. (tel. (017687) 726 45), finds B&Bs for a 10% deposit and sells both a £1 lodgings booklet and a 20p map (open daily July-Aug. 9:30am-6pm; Sept.-June 9:30am-5pm). **B&Bs** nestle between Station St., St. John St., and Penrith Rd. (£14-19.50).

Nine miles south of Keswick lies the harrowing **Honister Pass,** gateway to the wildest parts of the Lake District, including craggy Great Gable and Green Gable (take bus 79 1½ miles south of "Seatoller"). **Honister Hause youth hostel** (tel. (017687) 772 67) sits at the Pass' summit (£6.50; open June-Aug. daily; Apr.-May and Sept.-Oct. F-Tu). No serious mountain climber's Lakeland experience would be complete without a hike up nearby **Scafell Pike** in the magnificent Langdale Fells. At 3162 ft., it's the highest peak in England.

WALES

As churning coal and steel mines fall victim to Britain's faltering economy, Wales has turned its economic base from heavy industry to tourism. Travelers from near and far crowd Welsh towns on their way to miles of sandy beaches, grassy cliffs, and dramatic mountains. Nevertheless, Wales clings steadfastly to its Celtic heritage, continuing a struggle for independence that has been active for over a millennium. The Welsh language endures in conversation, commerce, and literature, especially in the North, which is even more fiercely nationalistic and linguistically independent than southern Wales. Enjoy the landscapes and cultures that make this area unique, and avoid calling the Welsh "English" at all costs.

■ Cardiff (Caerdydd)

One of the few urban centers in a land of small villages, Cardiff mined its wealth out of the coal industry. Today, it mixes youthful flair and traditional culture: Cardiff has a cutting-edge music scene and a rich national museum. Begin with tradition by visiting the opulent interior, beautiful gardens, and Norman keep of **Cardiff Castle** (open daily Mar.-Oct. 9:30am-6pm; Nov.-Feb. until 4pm; £5, students £3.60). The domed **National Museum and Gallery of Wales** includes a hoard of western European art and startling audio-visual exhibits outlining "The Evolution of Wales" (open Tu-Su 10am-5pm; £3.25, students and seniors £2).

National Express **Rapide coaches** (tel. (0990) 80 80 80) roll to Cardiff from London's Victoria Station (3hr., 8 per day, £22.75), Heathrow Airport (3hr., 11 per day, £27), and Gatwick Airport (4hr., 11 per day, £29); buses also arrive from Glasgow (8½hr., 3 per day, £44). British Rail **trains** chug into the station in Central Square (tel. (0345) 48 49 50) from London's Paddington Station (2hr., 1-2 per hour, £35). The **tourist office** (tel. (01222) 22 72 81) at the train station provides a free accommodations list, and books rooms in reasonably priced **B&Bs** (£16-18) on the outskirts of town for a £1 fee and 10% deposit. (Open Apr.-Sept. M and W-Sa 9am-6:30pm, Tu 10am-6:30pm, Su 10am-4pm; Oct.-Mar. M and W-Sa 9am-5:30pm, Tu 10am-5:30pm, Su 10am-4pm.) Hook into the Internet at **Cardiff Cybercafé,** 9 Duke St. for £4.50 per hour (open M-F 11am-7pm, Sa 10am-6pm).

The best deals are found in the smaller neighborhoods around Cathedral Rd. (take bus 32 or walk 15min. from the castle). With its purple and yellow exterior, the colorful and modern **International Cardiff Backpacker** hostel, 98 Neville St., is hard to miss, and its 24-hour liquor license means you won't want to. (Tel. (01222) 34 55 77. Fax 23 04 04. Single sex dorm rooms £12.50 per night; doubles £29; triples £35. Breakfast included. Kitchen. No curfew.) If arriving late, don't walk; call for pickup service from the hostel.

Cardiff's specialty is **Brains S.A.** (Special Ale), known by locals as "Brains Skull Attack." Tours of **Brains Brewery** on Caroline St. can be arranged by calling (01222) 39 90 22 in advance and asking for the marketing department. **Celtic Cauldron Wholefoods,** 47-49 Castle Arcade, offers traditional Welsh food, including faggots, and a good selection of vegetarian fare. (£3.50-4.50. "Mighty Vegetarian" meal £8.10. Open Jun.-Aug. M-Sa 8:30am-9pm, Sun. 11am-4pm; Sept.-May M-Sa 8:30am-6pm, Su 11am-4pm.) Head to the Welsh-speaking **Clwb Ifor Bach** (the Welsh Club) 11 Womanby St. (tel. (01222) 23 21 99), for the local music scene. (Cover £2-3, plus a £1 "associate membership." Sa night fluent Welsh only. Open M-Th until 2am, F varies, Sa until 4am, Sun. until 10:30pm.) Cardiff's gay and lesbian crowd dances and drinks at the **Exit Bar,** 48 Charles St. (open M-Tu 6pm-2am, no entry after midnight, W-Sa 6pm-midnight, Su 7pm-midnight).

■ Wye Valley

Wordsworth once came to the Wye Valley to escape the "fever of the world"; the region's tranquility has since been disturbed by a feverish tourist trade. Even so, much of this region, where the Wye River (Afon Gwy) winds down the hills of central Wales, remains unsullied. Below Monmouth, the Wye forms the border between England and Wales and flows between Wordsworth's "steep cliffs," "tufted orchards," and "pastoral farms."

Stagecoach Red and White **buses** (tel. (01633) 26 63 36) are the primary means of transport in the area (there is virtually no Sunday service), but hikers enjoy walks of all difficulties and lengths. The **Wye Valley Walk** starts from Chepstow and goes to Tintern Abbey and other sites. The **Offa's Dyke Path** encompasses 177 miles of trails and runs along the entire English/Welsh border.

Chepstow Chepstow's strategic position at the mouth of the river and the base of the English border made it an important fortification and commercial center in Norman times. **Chepstow Castle,** built by a companion of William the Conqueror, is Britain's oldest stone castle, and offers awesome views of the Wye River. (Open daily Apr. to late Oct. 9:30am-6:30pm, late Oct. to Mar. M-Sa 9:30-4pm, Su 11am-4pm; last admission 30min. before closing. £3, students £2.) Nearby, the **tourist office** (tel. (01291) 62 37 72) provides info on the castle and the valley's treasures (open daily May-Sept. 10am-5:45pm; Oct.-Apr. 10am-4pm). **Trains** arrive at Station Rd.; **National Express** buses stop above the town gate in front of the Somerfield supermarket. Ask about bus tickets at **Fowlers Travel,** 9 Moor St. The **YHA Youth Hostel** (tel. (01594) 53 02 72; fax 53 08 49), 4 miles northeast of Tintern, occupies a 12th-century castle with a dungeon. To get there from the A466 (bus 69 from Chepstow) or the Offa's Dyke Path, follow signs for 2 miles from Bigsweir Bridge to St. Briavel's (£9.75, under 18 £6.55; curfew 11pm; closed Jan.). In Chepstow, stay at **Lower Hardwick House** (tel. (01291) 62 21 62), on Mt. Pleasant, 300 yd. up the hill from the bus station (singles £15-18; doubles £30-35; camping £5 per tent).

Tintern, Hereford, and Hay-on-Wye Five miles north of Chepstow on the A466, the delicate arches of **Tintern Abbey** (tel. (01291) 68 92 51) shade crowds of tourists in the summer. (Open mid-Mar. to mid-Oct. daily 9:30am-6:30pm; mid-Oct. to mid-Mar. M-Sa 9:30am-4pm, Su 11am-4pm. £2.20, students and seniors £1.70.) Wordsworth's praise is fitting; the windswept abbey is beautiful against the open sky and surrounding hills. Near the iron footbridge, a path leads to the **Devil's Pulpit** (1hr.), a huge stone from which Satan is said to have tempted the monks working in the fields. Ideally situated for excursions into Wales, **Hereford** attracts visitors for its own sake with an 11th-century **cathedral** and the 13th-century **Mappa Mundi. Trains** arrive from Cardiff (1hr., £11.40) and London's Paddington Station (3hr, £31). Stagecoach Red and White **bus** 39 connects to Hay-on-Wye (1¾hr.) from 20 Broad St. The helpful staff at the **tourist office,** 1 King St. (tel. (01432) 26 84 30), in front of the cathedral, books beds for a 10% deposit (open M-Sa 9am-5pm). The **Somerville,** Bodenham Rd. (tel. (01432) 27 39 91), offers singles (£18-25) and doubles (£30-40).

Hay-on-Wye boasts 35 second-hand and antiquarian book shops, and hosts a 10-day **literary festival** in late May at which luminaries like Toni Morrison give readings while Salman Rushdie darts about nervously. The **tourist office,** Oxford Rd. (tel. (01497) 82 01 44), books beds for a £2-3 fee (open daily Apr.-Oct. 10am-1pm and 2-5pm; Nov.-Mar. 11am-1pm and 2-4pm). The 16th-century **Brookfield,** Brook St. (tel. (01497) 82 05 18), offers singles for £18 and doubles for £30.

■ Brecon Beacons National Park (Bannau Brycheiniog)

Brecon Beacons National Park (Bannau Brycheiniog) encompasses 519 square miles of barren peaks, thick forests, and spectacular waterfalls. The park is crisscrossed by four mountain ranges. At the center is the impressive **Brecon Beacons;** the most pleasant hiking route starts in nearby **Llanfaes** and follows leafy roads up to trails past streams and waterfalls. The **Black Mountains,** in the easternmost section of the park, offer long and lofty ridges and 80 square miles of solitude; **Crickhowell,** on the A40, is the easiest starting point for forays into this area. About seven miles southwest of the Beacons, the **waterfall district** features forest rivers tumbling through rapids, gorges, and amazing falls. Near **Abercrave,** off the A4067, the stunning **Dan-yr-Ogof Showcaves** (tel. (01639) 73 02 84) showcase enormous stalagmites.

The market towns on the fringe of the park, especially **Brecon** and **Abergavenny,** make pleasant touring bases. The Paddington Station (London)-South Wales **train** line runs via Cardiff to Abergavenny at the park's southeast corner; call National Rail Inquiries at (0345) 48 49 50. Red and White **buses** (tel. (01633) 26 63 36) cross the park regularly en route from Brecon, on the northern side of the park, to Abergavenny or Hay-on-Wye. Once in town, stop at a **National Park Information Centre.** Ordnance Survey maps 12 and 13 (£6 each) are indispensable, both for exploring and for reaching safety in bad weather. The centers also provide weather reports and brochures on hiking. In **Abergavenny,** the info center is on Monmouth Rd., in the tourist office opposite the bus station (tel. (01873) 85 32 54; open Easter-Oct. daily 9:30am-5:30pm). In **Brecon,** go to Cattle Market Car Park, next to the tourist info office off Lion St. (tel. (01874) 62 31 56; open Apr.-Oct. daily 9:30am-5:30pm). The main park office is around the corner on Glamorgan St.

The Brecon tourist office's free *Where to Stay in Brecon's National Park* maps 14 campsites in the park (about £2-5.50 per tent). Several HI youth hostels are scattered throughout the park. **Capel-y-ffin HI Youth Hostel** (tel. (01873) 89 06 50), at the eastern edge of the Black Mountains near Hay-on-Wye, is an excellent base for ridge-walking (£6.50; **camping** allowed). **Llwyn-y-Celyn HI Youth Hostel** (tel. (01874) 62 42 61), seven miles south of Brecon (take bus 43), is convenient to the Beacons range. (£7.20. Lockout 10am-5pm. Open July-Aug. daily; Sept.-Oct. Tu-Sa; Nov F-Sa; mid-Feb. to Mar. F-Tu; Apr.-June M-Sa.) **Ystradfellte HI Youth Hostel** (tel. (01639) 72 03 01) is near the waterfall district. (£6.50. Open Apr. to mid-July and Sept.-Oct. F-W; mid-July to Aug. daily; Nov. and Feb.-Mar. F-Sa.)

■ Pembrokeshire Coast National Park

The Pembrokeshire Coast National Park features harbors, hills, and quaint villages amid 225 square miles of beautiful coastal scenery. The best way to enter the region is from **Haverfordwest,** on the main **rail** line from Cardiff (£13.60) and London (£42-54). **Buses** have more frequent and extensive service; schedules are compiled in the helpful *Public Transport Timetables from Pembrokeshire,* available at regional tourist offices. In town, the **Tourist Information Centre,** 19 Old Bridge (tel. (01437) 76 31 10), has park info (open May-Aug. daily 10am-5:30pm; Sept.-Apr. M-Sa 10am-5pm).

Pembroke is another point of entry into the park. **Pembroke Castle,** birthplace of Henry VII, is among the most impressive fortresses in South Wales. (Open daily Apr.-Sept. 9:30am-6pm; Mar. and Oct. 10am-5pm; Nov.-Feb. 10am-4pm. £3.) The **tourist office** (tel. (01646) 62 23 88), Commons Rd., books ferries and lodgings. (Open May-Oct. daily 10am-5:30pm; Mar.-Apr. Tu, Th, and Sa 10am-4pm; Nov.-Feb. often closed.) Stay at the **Merton Place House,** 3 East Back (tel. (01646) 68 47 96; £15).

Once in the park, check out one of the **Outdoor Activity Centres,** which rent canoes, kayaks, and bicycles (£10-20 per day). For short hikes, stick to the more accessible St. David's Peninsula in the northwest; otherwise, set out on the coastal path, which is marked with acorn symbols. Near the western extremity of the coastal path is **St. David's,** medieval Wales's largest and richest diocese. A chest in the **cathedral** holds the bones of St. David, patron saint of Wales (donation £2). The **Bishop's Palace** resembles a castle. (Open Apr.-Oct. daily 9:30am-6:30pm; Nov.-Mar. M-Sa 9:30am-4pm, Su 2-4pm. £1.70, students £1.20.) **YHA youth hostels** are spaced along the coastal path. **Marloes Sands** (tel. (01646) 63 66 67) is near the Dale Peninsula (£6.50; open Apr.-Oct.). **Broad Haven** (tel. (01437) 78 16 88), on St. Bride's Bay, has 75 beds (£9.75; open mid-Feb. to Oct.). **Hamilton Backpacker's Lodge,** 21/33 Hamilton St. (tel. (01348) 87 47 97), has dorms (£9), singles (£12), and doubles (£22).

■ Aberystwyth

Along the sweeping Cardigan Bay coastline, the university town of Aberystwyth offers easy access to all of Wales and plenty of pubs to entertain you as you wait for your connection. If it's a long wait, check out the **National Library of Wales,** off Penglais Rd., which houses the earliest surviving manuscript of the *Canterbury Tales* and almost every book written in Welsh or pertaining to Wales (open M-Sa 10am-5pm; free). Aberystwyth's charming beachfront and promenade remain much as they were in the Victorian era. The city rests at the western end of the Heart of Wales rail line; the **train station,** Alexandra Rd. (tel. (0345) 48 49 50), provides service to major cities. For destinations on the northern coast, change at Machynlleth (30min., £3.80). The **tourist office,** Lisburne House, Terrace Rd. (tel. (01970) 61 21 25), has B&B info (open July-Aug. daily 10am-6pm; Sept.-June M-Sa 10am-5pm). The nearest **HI youth hostel** is nine miles north in Borth (tel. (01970) 87 14 98; £8.80). Take the train to Borth Station (10min.) or Crosville bus 511 or 512. In town, **Mrs. E. V. Williams,** 28 Bridge St. (tel. (01970) 61 25 50), has staggeringly comfortable beds (£12.50). Aberystwyth abounds with good pubs… go wild!

■ Snowdonia National Park

The 840 sheep-dotted square miles of Snowdonia National Park, stretching north from Machynlleth to Bangor and Conwy, embrace narrow-cut valleys, elevated moorland, and the sun-pierced coves of Harlech and the Llŷn Peninsula, but are dominated by the rough countenance of the ancient mountains. At 3560 ft., **Mount Snowdon** is one of the highest peaks in Britain and the most popular mountain for hiking.

Tourist offices and National Park Information Centres stock leaflets on walks (40p), drives, and accommodations, as well as Ordnance Survey maps (£5-6). Contact the **Snowdonia National Park Headquarters,** Penrhyndeudraeth, Gwynedd, Wales LL48 6LF (tel. (01766) 77 02 74), for full details. Among the other information centers, **Betws-y-coed,** the Old Stables (tel. (01690) 71 06 65 or 71 04 26), is the busiest and best stocked (open daily Apr.-Oct. 10am-6pm; Nov.-Mar. 9:30am-4:30pm). Call **Mountaincall Snowdonia** (tel. (01839) 50 53 30) for the local forecast, ground conditions, and a three- to five-day weather report. If hiking isn't your thing, the coal-fired steam locomotives of the **Snowdon Mountain Railway** (tel. (01286) 87 02 23) chug from Llanberis to Snowdonia's summit. (2hr. round-trip; 30min. stop at the peak. Return £14.80. Weary hikers can try for a £10.70 standby back down.) The **Ffestiniog Railway** (tel. (01766) 51 23 40) romps through the mountains from Porthmadog (round-trip £8.20-12.40). A **Red Rover ticket** (£4.40) buys unlimited travel on the Snowdon Sherpa **buses** that run between the park's towns and trailheads.

The eight **YHA youth hostels** in the mountain area are some of the best in Wales. Plenty of sheep, cows, and bulls keep hostelers company at **Llanberis** (tel. (01286) 87 02 80; fax 87 09 36) as they take in the splendid views of Llyn Peris and Llyn Padarn below and Mt. Snowdon above (£8; open Apr.-Aug. daily; Sept.-Oct. and Jan.-Mar. Tu-Sa). **Snowdon Ranger,** Llyn Cwellyn (tel. (01286) 65 03 91; fax 65 00 93), is at the base of great hiking trails; take bus 95 (£8.80; open Apr.-Aug. daily; mid-Feb. to Mar. and Nov.-Dec. F-Su; Sept.-Oct. W-Su). In the mountains, **camping** is permitted as long as you leave no mess, but the Park Service discourages it because of recent erosion. In the valleys, owner's consent is needed.

Llanberis and Harlech Distinguished mainly by the mountain looming over it, **Llanberis** is the largest town in the park and has flocks of B&Bs. To reach **Ceunant Mawr,** one of Wales's most impressive waterfalls, walk along the footpath on Victoria Terr. by Victoria Hotel, take the first right, then the first left (about 1 mile). Llanberis is a short ride from Caernarfon (KMP **bus 88**; tel. (01286) 87 08 80) or Bangor (Williams Peinioien **bus 77**; tel. (01286) 87 04 84). The **tourist office,** 41B High St. (tel. (01286) 87 07 65), books rooms and doles out maps and hiking tips (open Apr.-Oct. daily 10am-6pm; Nov.-Mar. W and F-Su 10:30am-4:30pm).

Just shy of the Llŷn Peninsula, the tiny town of **Harlech** affords a haunting view of the misty, craggy mountains of Snowdonia to the north. Edward I chose the strategic spot for his in-your-face fortress—**Harlech Castle.** (Open Apr.-Oct. daily 9:30am-6:30pm; Nov.-Mar. M-Sa 9:30am-4pm, Su 11am-4pm. £3, students £2.) The **tourist office** (tel./fax (01766) 78 06 58) at Gwyddfor House, Stryd Fawr, will book you a room; otherwise, try the **YHA Llanbedr Hostel** (tel. (01341) 24 12 87), four miles south; take the train to Llanbedr or bus 38. (£14-28. Open May-Aug. daily; Sept.-Oct. and mid-Feb. to Apr. Th-M; Jan. to mid-Feb. F-Su.)

■ Llŷn Peninsula and Northern Coast

The Llŷn has been a hotspot for tourism since the Middle Ages, when crowds of religious pilgrims tramped through on their way to Bardsey Island off the peninsula's western tip. Now sun worshippers make the trek to the endless, sandy beaches along the coast. **Porthmadog** is the southeast gateway to the peninsula. The town's principal attraction is the steam **Ffestiniog Railway** (tel. (01766) 51 23 40), which runs through the hills of Snowdonia (1hr., £12.80). The **tourist office** (tel. (01766) 51 29 81) is on Stryd Fawr, next to the rail station. An eccentric landmark of Italy-fixation, the private village of **Portmeirion** stands two miles east of Porthmadog. The various buildings, all of which were transported from faraway places, are washed with cool Mediterranean colors. Statues in classical, Indian, and mythical styles await discovery.

The Menai Strait Perched on the edge of the bay of the same name, **Caernarfon** (can-AR-von) lures visitors with Wales's grandest medieval castle. Built by Edward I in 1283, the overwhelming **Caernarfon Castle** features decorative bands of colored stone and the world's only surviving rapid-arrow slits. (Open Apr.-Oct. daily 9:30am-6:30pm; Nov.-Mar. M-Sa 9:30am-4pm, Su 11am-4pm. £4, students £3.) The **tourist office** (tel. (01286) 67 22 32), on Castle St., Oriel Pendeitsh, offers a helpful street map and accommodations listings (open Apr.-Oct. daily 10am-6pm; Nov.-Mar. Th-Tu 9:30am-4:30pm). Stay in wood bunks at **Totters Hostel,** 2 High St. (tel. (01286) 67 29 63; £9.50; no curfew or lockout). The delightful B&B **Bryn Hyfryd** (tel (01286) 67 38 40), on St. David's Rd., offers spacious rooms (£14-16). Cafes and pubs crowd inside the town walls. Watch the sunset, pint in hand, at **Anglesey Arms** on the Promenade.

Buses 5 and 5B run every 15 minutes between Caernarfon and **Bangor,** a convenient base for exploring the nearby Isle of Anglesey. The **YHA Bangor Youth hostel,** Tan-y-Bryn (tel. (01248) 35 35 16), near the town center, has bunks for £8.80. **Beaumaris,** across the Menai Strait, features the magnificent **Beaumaris Castle,** the largest of Edward I's chain of Welsh fortresses. (Open Apr.-Oct. daily 9:30am-6:30pm; Nov.-Mar. M-Sa 9:30am-4pm, Su 11am-4pm. £2.70, students £1.40.)

BRITAIN

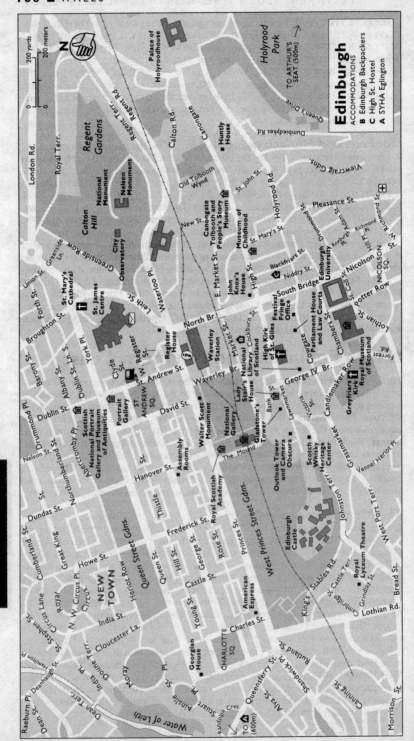

Holyhead and Conwy On the Isle of Anglesey, **Holyhead** has one sure lure for the traveler: ferries to Ireland. **Irish Ferries** leave Holyhead daily for Dublin (4hr., one-way £25), and accepts bookings at its Holyhead offices. For more info, call (0990) 17 17 17 or check http://www.irish-ferries.ie. **Stena Line** (tel. (01233) 64 70 47) sails to Dun Laoghaire, with bus/rail connections to Dublin (4hr., £26-35). **National Express** hits Holyhead from most major cities. The town is also the terminus of the North Wales Coast **rail** line with hourly trains to Bangor (30min., £5.40), Chester (1½hr., £13.70), and London (6hr., £48.50). If you miss your boat, check room vacancies at the **tourist office** (tel./fax (01407) 76 26 22), in a booth in the rail station (open daily Apr.-Oct. 10am-6pm; Nov.-Mar. 10am-5pm).

Edward I's 13th-century **castle** solemnly guards the walled town of **Conwy,** a town with an agelessness that countless tourist buses cannot kill. On tilted floors, the 14th-century **Aberconwy House,** on High St. and Castle St., displays armor and period furnishings (open Apr.-Oct. W-M 10am-5pm; £2). Arriva Cymru (tel. (01492) 59 69 69) **buses** 5 and 5B follow a coastal route from Caernarfon to Llandudno, stopping in Bangor and Conwy along the way. Conwy's **tourist office** (tel. (01492) 59 22 48) is at the entrance to the castle. (Open Easter-Oct. daily 9:30am-6:30pm; Nov.-Easter M-Sa 9:30am-4pm, Su 11am-4pm.) **B&Bs** cluster in the Cadnant Park area, a 10-minute walk from the castle. To get to the fabulous **YHA Conwy** (tel. (01492) 59 35 71) from Lancaster Sq., head down Bangor Rd., turn left up Mt. Pleasant, and go right at the top of the hill (£9.75).

SCOTLAND

At its best, Scotland is a world apart, a defiantly distinct nation within the United Kingdom with a culture and worldview all its own. Exuberant Glasgow has mind-bending nightlife, Aberdeen's grand architecture sprawls regally, and Edinburgh is the epicenter of Scottish culture during its famed International Festival in August. A little over half the size of England but with one-tenth its population, Scotland revels in stark, open spaces. The heather-covered mountains and glassy lochs of the west coast and luminescent mists of the Hebrides demand worship, while the farmlands to the south and the rolling river valleys of the east coast display a gentler beauty. The frayed northwest coast, cut by sea lochs and girded by islands, remains the most beautiful region in Scotland and one of the last stretches of true wilderness in Europe. Even in tourist season, you can easily hike for a full day without seeing another human being.

▓ Edinburgh

In the early 18th century, the dark alleys of Edinburgh (ED-in-bur-ra) yielded an outpouring of talent that turned this Calvinist Kingdom of God into a capital of the Enlightenment. The philosopher David Hume presided over a republic of letters that included Adam Smith, Robert Louis Stevenson, and Sir Walter Scott, and the New Town city planning project rejected the Old Town's tenements, closes, and wynds in favor of the graceful Gregorian symmetry and orderly gridwork. Today, Edinburgh is a meeting place of opposing forces—natural rock and hewn stone, wild landscapes and terraced gardens, distant bagpipes and roaring traffic.

ORIENTATION AND PRACTICAL INFORMATION

Edinburgh lies 45 miles east of Glasgow and 405 miles northwest of London on Scotland's east coast. **Princes Street** is the main road in the **New Town,** in the northern section of the city; the **Royal Mile** (Lawnmarket, High St., and Canongate) is the main street in the Old Town. **North Bridge, Waverly Bridge,** and **The Mound** connect the Old and New Towns. The train station lies between North Bridge and Waverley Bridge near the center of town; the bus station is three blocks from the east end of Princes St. Edinburgh is easily explored on foot, but **Lothian Regional Transport** (tel. 554 44 94) and **SMT** (tel. 557 50 61) sell bus passes for extensive travel.

Telephone Code: 0131.

Trains: Waverley Station (tel. (0345) 484 49 50), in the center of town. To: Aberdeen (£32), Glasgow (£7.10), Inverness (£29), Oban (£24), and other cities. For schedules, call **Scotrail** at (0345) 48 49 50.

Buses: St. Andrew Square Bus Station, St. Andrew Sq. (tel. 663 92 33). **Scottish Citylink** (tel. (0990) 50 50 50) serves Glasgow (£4.50), Inverness (£12.30), and Aberdeen (£13), and London (£18). **National Express** (tel. 452 87 77) also goes to London. To avoid long lines, simply buy your ticket on the bus.

Taxis: City Cabs (tel. 228 12 11); **Central Radio Taxis** (tel. 229 24 68). Taxi stands are located at both stations and on almost every corner on Princes St.

Bike Rental: Edinburgh Rent-a-Bike, 29 Blackfriars St. (tel. 556 55 60), off High St. Bikes £5-15 per day.

Tourist Office: Edinburgh and Scotland Information Centre, Waverley Market, 3 Princes St. (tel. 557 17 00), next to Waverley train station. Busy but efficient accommodations service (£4); outside, a 24hr. computer gives availability updates. Pick up *The Essential Guide to Edinburgh and the Lothians* (50p). Bus and theater tickets. **Currency exchange.** Open July-Aug. M-Sa 9am-8pm, Su 10am-8pm; Sept.-June closes at 6pm.

Budget Travel Services: Edinburgh Travel Centre, Potterow Union, Bristo Sq. (tel. 668 22 21). Branch at 92 St. Clerk St. (tel. 667 94 88). Both open M-W and F 9am-5:30pm, Th 10am-5:30pm, Sa 10am-1pm. **Campus Travel,** 5 Nicolson Sq. (tel. 668 33 03). Open M-Tu and Th-F 9am-5:30pm, W and Sa 10am-5:30pm.

Currency Exchange: Try **Barclays,** 18 S. St. Andrews St., and the **Royal Bank of Scotland** on North Bridge. Both have **ATM** machines.

American Express: 139 Princes St. (tel. 225 78 81), 5 blocks from Waverley Station. Mail held. Open M-W and F 9am-5:30pm, Th 9:30am-5:30pm, Sa 9am-4pm.

Bisexual, Gay, and Lesbian Services: Gay Switchboard, (tel. 556 40 49). Staffed daily 7:30-10pm. **Lesbian Line,** (tel. 557 07 51). Staffed M and Th 7:30-10pm. Pick up *Gay Scotland* or drop by the **Nexus Café-Bar,** 60 Broughton St. (tel. 478 70 69). Open daily 11am-11pm.

Emergency: Dial 999; no coins required.

Police: 5 Fettes Ave. (tel. 311 31 31).

Crisis Lines: Nightline, tel. 557 44 44. Staffed daily 6pm-8am. **Rape Crisis Center,** tel. 556 94 37. Staffed M-W and F 7-9pm, Th 1-3pm, Sa 9:30-11am. **Women's Aid,** tel. 229 14 19. Staffed M, W, and F 10am-3pm, Tu 1:30-3:30pm.

Hospital: Royal Infirmary of Edinburgh, 1 Lauriston Pl. (tel. 536 10 00). From The Mound, take bus 23 or 27.

Post Office: 8-10 St. James Centre (tel. 556 95 46), near the bus station. Open M 9am-5:30pm, Tu-F 8:30am-5:30pm, Sa 8:30am-6pm. **Postal Code:** EH1 3SR.

Internet Access: Cafe Cyberia, 88 Hanover St. (tel. 220 44 03). £2.50 per 30min., students and seniors £2. Open M-Sa 10am-10pm, Su noon-7pm.

ACCOMMODATIONS

The tourist office will find you a room for a £4 fee. During festival season (Aug. 15-Sept. 4 in 1999) there are few available rooms. Most of Edinburgh's countless **B&Bs** are open between May and September, cost £15 to 30, and are clustered in three areas: **Bruntsfield, Newington,** and **Leith.** Edinburgh's hostels are cheap and convenient but fill up fast. Call ahead when possible.

Castle Rock Hostel, 15 Johnston Terr. (tel. 225 96 66). Walking toward the Castle on Royal Mile, turn left onto Johnston Terr. Gigantic gold-mine of a hostel with regal views of the castle. 380 beds in rooms of 6-10, co-ed bathrooms, private showers. Free tea, coffee, and hot chocolate. **Internet access** available. £10-12.50. Breakfast £1.40. Laundry £2.30. Reception 24hr.

High St. Hostel, 105 High St. (tel. 557 61 20). Spiffy new fittings in this 35-bed facility. Free tours of the Royal Mile, pub crawls, and wonderful staff. Access to sister hostel, Castle Rock. £10.50-12.50.

Edinburgh Backpackers, 65 Cockburn St. (tel. 220 17 17). Excellent location; from North Bridge, turn right on High St. and take the first right. £10.50-12.50. Reception 24hr. Doubles and twins with kitchen and laundry at 34a Cockburn (£35).

Argyle Backpackers, 14 Argyle Pl. (tel. 667 99 91), south of the Meadows and the Royal Mile. Expect a welcoming cup of tea and excellent advice on sights. TVs. Dorms £10; twins £24; doubles £30.

SYHA Eglinton, 18 Eglinton Crescent (tel. 337 11 20), about 1 mile west of town center, near Haymarket train station. Take bus 3, 4, 12, 13, 22, 26, 28, 31, 33, or 44 from Princes St. to Palmerston Pl. £11.50-12.50. Continental breakfast included. Evening meal £4.20. Reception 7am-midnight. Curfew 2am. Open Jan.-Nov.

Avondale Guest House, 10 S. Gray St. (tel. 667 67 79). From Waverley Station, turn right onto Princes St. and right again onto N. Bridge St. Catch bus 69 or any Newington bus to the corner of Minto St. and W. Mayfield. Turn right onto W. Mayfield and right again onto S. Gray St. Friendly proprietors keep a small, comfortable house. Singles £20; doubles £30-50. Full Scottish breakfast included.

FOOD

As the capital of Scottish tourism, Edinburgh offers traditional fare with much ceremony and expense. You can get haggis cheap in many pubs; many offer student and hosteler discounts in the early evening. Sandwich shops sell baguettes and filled rolls (30p-£2). Take-away shops on S. Clerk St. offer reasonably priced Chinese or Indian fare. For groceries, try **Presto's,** St. James Shopping Centre (tel. 556 11 90; open M-W and F-Sa 8am-6pm, Th 8am-8pm).

Ndebele, 57 Home St. Delicious meals for under £5. Try an avocado, mushroom, and cucumber sandwich (£2.60), or sample the daily African specialty. Huge array of African and South American coffees and juices. Open daily 10am-10pm.

Lost Sock Diner, 1 E. London St. My Beautiful Launderette goes a step further at this new restaurant-launderette, where you can order a delicious meal for under £3.50 while your pants finish drying. Open daily 8am-9pm.

The Basement, 10a-12a Broughton St. "Restaurant quality food at pub-grub prices." Salmon fillet £4. A lively mix of students, musicians, and members of the gay and lesbian community. Food served daily noon-10pm.

The Last Drop, 72-74 Grassmarket, serves good "haggis, tatties, and neeps" (haggis, potatoes, and turnips) in omnivorous and vegetarian versions. Everything on the menu (save the steak) is £2.50 for students and hostelers until 6:30pm. A packed and comfortable pub in the evening. Open daily 10am-2am.

The Baked Potato, 56 Cockburn St., a small take-away wholefoods shop, sells slightly pricey potatoes with endless topping choices (£2.15-2.80). Veggie kebab pitas, pastries, and stuffed rolls. Student discounts. Open M-Sa 9am-9pm.

Haggis: What's in There?

Although restaurants throughout Scotland produce steamin' plates o' haggis for eager tourists, we at *Let's Go* believe all should know what's inside that strange-looking bundle before taking the plunge. An age-old recipe calls for the following ingredients: the large stomach bag of a sheep, the small (knight's hood) bag, the pluck (including lights (lungs), liver, and heart), beef, suet, oatmeal, onions, pepper, and salt. Today's haggis is available conveniently canned (!) and includes: lamb, lamb offal, oatmeal, wheat flour (healthy, no?), beef, suet, onions, salt, spices, stock, and liquor (1%).

SIGHTS

The **Royal Mile** (Lawnmarket, High St., and Canongate) defines the length of Old Town, the medieval center of Edinburgh. At the top of the Royal Mile, **Edinburgh Castle** glowers over the city from the peak of an extinct volcano. *(Open daily Apr.-Sept. 9:30am-6pm; Oct.-Mar. 9:30am-5pm; last admission 45min. before closing. £6, seniors £4.50, children 1.50.)* The Scottish Crown Jewels lie within, as well as **St. Margaret's Chapel,** a 12th-century Norman church. The walk along Royal Mile from the castle passes some of Edinburgh's oldest attractions. The 1617 tenement **Gladstone's Land** is well worth a visit; everything inside remains as it was almost 400 years ago. *(Open Apr.-Oct.*

BRITAIN

M-Sa 10am-5pm, Su 2-5pm; last admission 4:30pm. £3, students £1.90.) Through the passage at 477 Lawnmarket awaits **Lady Stair's House,** a 17th-century townhouse home to **The Writer's Museum,** with memorabilia of Robert Burns, Sir Walter Scott, and Robert Louis Stevenson. *(Open M-Sa 10am-5pm; during Festival also Su 2-5pm. Free.)*

Where Lawnmarket becomes High St., the Mile is dominated by **St. Giles Cathedral.** *(Open Easter to mid-Sept. M-F 9am-7pm, Sa 9am-5pm, Su 1-5pm; mid-Sept. to Easter M-Sa 9am-5pm, Su 1-5pm. £1 donation requested.)* From the pulpit of St. Giles, John Knox delivered fiery Presbyterian sermons to rally the populace against Mary, Queen of Scots. **Canongate,** the steep hill at the of the Mile, has three free museums; but if you've had your fill of museum etiquette, check out the toys and games at the **Museum of Childhood,** 42 High St. The spectacular **Palace of Holyroodhouse** at the eastern end of the Mile, once the home of Mary, Queen of Scots, is now Queen Elizabeth II's official residence in Scotland. *(Open Apr.-Oct. daily 9:30am-5:15pm; Nov.-Mar. M-Sa 9:30am-3:45pm; closed during official residences in late May and late June. £5.30, seniors £3.70, under 17 £2.60.)* While in town, royalty attend services at **Canongate Kirk,** a 17th-century chapel and the resting place of Adam Smith.

On the way to the New Town, on The Mound, the **National Gallery of Scotland** has a small but superb collection of Renaissance, Romantic, and Impressionist works. *(Open M-Sa 10am-5pm, Su 2-5pm; during Festival M-Sa 10am-6pm, Su 11am-6pm. Free.)* Edinburgh's New Town is a masterpiece of Georgian planning. James Craig won the city-planning contest in 1767 with his rectangular gridiron of three main parallel streets (Queen, George, and Princes) linking two large squares (Charlotte and St. Andrew). The **New Town Conservation Centre,** 13a Dundas St., can answer questions about the area. *(Open M-F 9am-1pm and 2-5pm.)* A must-see is the elegant **Georgian House,** 7 Charlotte Sq. *(Open Apr.-Oct. M-Sa 10am-5pm, Su 2-5pm; last admission 4:30pm. £4.20, students, seniors, and children £2.80.)* The chandeliered **Assembly Rooms,** east of Charlotte Sq. on George St., shine as one of the glories of classical Edinburgh and host varied performances during the summer. On Princes St., between The Mound and Waverley Bridge, sits the **Walter Scott Monument**—a grotesque Gothic "steeple without a church" with statues of Scott and his dog inside. Climb the winding 287-step staircase and get an eagle's-eye view of Princes St. Gardens, the castle, and Old Town's Market St. *(Open Apr.-Sept. M-Sa 9am-6pm; Oct.-Mar. M-Sa 9am-3pm. £2.)* The **Scottish National Portrait Gallery,** 1 Queen St., north of St. Andrew Sq., mounts the mugs of famous Scots. *(Open M-Sa 10am-5pm, Su 2-5pm. Free.)*

ENTERTAINMENT AND FESTIVALS

The summer season overflows with music in the gardens and many theater and film events around town. In winter, shorter days and the crush of students sustain a flourishing nightlife. For details, find a copy of *The List* (£1.90).

Theater, Music, and Nightlife

In Bruntsfield, **King's Theatre,** 2 Leven St. (tel. 529 60 00), sponsors touring productions of musicals and plays, while the **Royal Lyceum Theatre,** 30 Grindlay St. (tel. 229 96 97), presents well-known comedies. The **Playhouse Theatre,** 18-22 Greenside Pl. (tel. 557 25 90), often hosts musicals. Jazz enthusiasts crowd **L'attache,** Rutland St., **Navaar House Hotel,** Mayfield Gardens, and **The Cellar Bar,** Chambers St. For rock and progressive shows, try **The Venue** (tel. 557 30 73) and **Calton Studios** (tel. 556 70 66), both on Calton Rd. **Whistle Binkies,** 4 Niddry St. (tel. 557 51 14), has nightly live music from country to punk rock (open daily 5pm-3am). You'll find Scottish bands and country dancing at the **Ross Open-Air Theatre** (tel. 529 41 47), under the tent in Princes St. Gardens (from about 7pm), and at a number of smaller pubs.

There's a pub in sight from everywhere in Edinburgh. Royal Mile pubs draw an older crowd, but **Scruffy Murphy's,** 50 George IV Bridge, near St. Giles, and **The Tron Ceilidh Bar,** off High St. at South Bridge, attract many students. Some of the best pubs in the Old Town are clustered around the university. Students booze it up at the **Pear Tree,** 38 W. Nicolson St., with a large outdoor courtyard, and **Greyfriars Bobby's Bar,** 34 Candlemaker Row. Nearby, at 9B Victoria St., are **Finnigan's Wake** and its neighbor **Buddy Mulligan's.** The New Town has several gay pubs, concentrated in the Broughton St. area.

Festivals

In August, the spectacular **Edinburgh International Festival** (Aug. 15-Sept. 4 in 1999) features a kaleidoscopic program of music, drama, dance, and art. For tickets and a schedule of events, contact the **Festival Box Office,** 21 Market St. EH1 1BW (inquiries tel. 473 20 01, bookings 473 20 00; fax 473 20 03). Tickets (£4-44) are sold by phone and over the counter starting the third week in April, and by post or fax from the second week in April. You can also get tickets at the door for most events. Look for half-price tickets after 1pm on the day of the performance.

   Around the festival has grown a more spontaneous **Festival Fringe** (Aug. 8-30 in 1999), which now includes over 500 amateur and professional companies presenting theater, comedy, children's shows, folk and classical music, poetry, dance, opera, and various exhibits (tickets £3-16). The *Fringe Programme* (available from mid-June) and the *Daily Diary* list performances; get brochures and tickets by mail from the **Fringe Festival Office,** 180 High St., Edinburgh EH1 1QS. (tel. 226 52 57, bookings 226 51 38). Bookings can be made by post starting mid-June, by phone (with credit card) beginning late June, and in person from July 28. Include 75p postage from Britain, £1.50 from EU countries, £3.50 from everywhere else. Cash, stamps, and foreign currency are accepted (box office open M-Sa 10am-6pm; Aug. and during the Festival daily 9am-9pm). The concurrent **Military Tattoo** is performed every Monday to Saturday night in the Esplanade—a spectacle of military bands, bagpipes, and drums. For tickets (£7.50-16), contact the **Tattoo Ticket Sale Office,** 33-34 Market St. (tel. 225 11 88; fax 225 86 27), which accepts bookings from early January (open M-F 10am-4:30pm or until the show).

Great Traditions of British Sport II (Last in Series)

What golf is to St. Andrews, curling is to Edinburgh. Conceived by Flemish immigrants in the 15th century, curling quickly became a Scottish favorite, appearing in native prose and verse and surfacing in the paintings of Bruegel. Modern curling involves a heavy granite stone, several small brooms, and a long sheet of ice. Curlers compete in teams of four; one member of each team, "the Skip," tells a second curler to hurl the stone down the ice; the other two curlers hop in front of the stone, using their brooms to smooth the surface of the ice, guiding the stone to a spot chosen by the Skip. The winner is the team that gets more of its stones close to the designated spots. Sadly, Scotland has all but abandoned its brooms to Canada. Well over one million of today's curlers hail from the Commonwealth nation; the rest of the world boasts fewer than a quarter million mad sweepers.

■ Glasgow

Glasgow is a city of cultural opportunity. A gaggle of museums and galleries, all free, compete for the attention of locals as well as tourists. The city center's vital grid of Victorian buildings thrives with reawakened energy and urban commerce; Glasgow, which has suffered a reputation of industrial lackluster, is back on track. A center of shipbuilding and steel production in the 19th century, Glasgow fell into a long depression which only began to lift in the 1980s. Today, the city pours millions of pounds into the arts; the West End seethes with trendy creativity and energy. Though not as heavily touristed as Edinburgh, Glasgow, Scotland's largest city and the 1999 European City of Architecture, is unique and unforgettable.

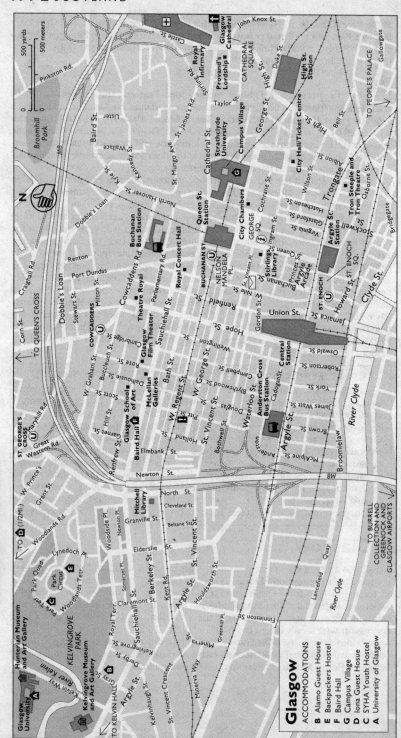

Glasgow

ACCOMMODATIONS

- B Alamo Guest House
- E Backpackers Hostel
- F Baird Hall
- G Campus Village
- D Iona Guest Hosue
- C SYHA Youth Hostel
- A University of Glasgow

ORIENTATION AND PRACTICAL INFORMATION

George Square is the center of town; the tourist office, train and bus stations, and cathedral are all within a few blocks. To reach the tourist office from Central Station, exit on **Union Street,** turn left and walk two blocks, then take a right on **St. Vincent Street.** From Buchanan Station, exit onto **North Hanover** and take a right.

Telephone Code: 0141.

Flights: Glasgow Airport (tel. 887 11 11), 10 miles west in Abbotsinch. Citylink runs to Glasgow's Buchanan station (20min., £2) and to Edinburgh (1¾hr., £6.50).

Trains: Central Station, Gordon St., serves southern Scotland, England, and Wales. U: St. Enoch. To: Stranraer (2½hr., £19.50), Dumfries (1¾hr., £16.40), and London via York and Newcastle (5-6hr., about £65). **Queen St. Station,** beside Coppthorne Hotel, George Sq., covers routes to the north and east. U: Buchanan St. To: Edinburgh (50min., £7.10), Aberdeen (2½hr., £34), Inverness (3¼hr., £29), and Fort William (3¾hr., £22.70). Credit card purchases (tel. (0800) 45 04 50).

Buses: Buchanan Station, N. Hanover St. (tel. 332 71 33), 2 blocks north of George Sq. Buses are much cheaper than trains. National Express (tel. (0990) 80 80 80) and/or Scottish Citylink (tel. (0990) 50 50 50) serve Edinburgh (50min., £4.50), Inverness (4hr., £11.50), London (8hr., £16), and Oban (3hr., £10).

Public Transportation: Glasgow's transportation system includes suburban rail, a dazzling variety of private bus services, and the **Underground (U),** a circular subway line, a.k.a. the "Clockwork Orange" (runs M-Sa 6:30am-11pm, Su 11am-6pm; 65p). Wave wildly to stop buses and carry exact change (usually 55-80p).

Tourist Office: 11 George Sq. (tel. 204 44 00). U: Buchanan St. Free local accommodations and bus bookings. Pick up the *Essential Guide to Glasgow* and *Where To Stay* (both free). Open July-Aug. M-Sa 9am-8pm, Su 10am-6pm; June and Sept. M-Sa 9am-7pm, Su 10am-6pm; Oct.-May 9am-6pm.

Currency Exchange: At tourist office. **Thomas Cook,** 15-17 Gordon St. (tel. 204 44 84), is in Central Station. Open daily 9:30am-9:30pm. Most banks are open M-F 9:30am-4:30pm; some are also open Sa.

American Express: 115 Hope St. (tel. 221 43 66; fax 204 26 85). Client mail held. Open M-F 8:30am-5:30pm, Sa 9am-noon.

Gay and Lesbian Switchboard: tel. 332 83 72. Staffed daily 7-10pm.

Laundry: Coin-Op Laundromat, 39-41 Bank St. U: Kelvinbridge. Soap and change available. Open M-F 9am-7:30pm, Sa-Su 9am-5pm.

Emergencies: Dial 999; no coins required.

Police: Stewart St. (tel. 532 30 00).

Pharmacy: Boots, 200 Sauchiehall St. (tel. 332 07 74 or 332 19 25). Open M-W and F-Sa 8:30am-6pm, Th 8:30am-7pm, Su 11am-5pm.

Post Office: Post offices are sprinkled about. Near George Sq., try 47 St. Vincent St., open M-F 8:30am-5:45pm, Sa 9am-5:30pm. **Postal Code:** G2 5QX.

Internet Access: The Internet Cafe, 569 Sauchiehall St. (tel. 564 10 52). £2.50 per 30min., students, seniors, and children £2. Open M-Th 9am-11pm, F 9am-9pm, Sa 10am-9pm, Su 10am-11pm.

ACCOMMODATIONS

In the summer, try to reserve rooms a month in advance, or call the **SYHA hostel** in Loch Lomond, less than an hour north (see p. 179). In addition to the places listed below, the universities in town provide dorm accommodations during the summer. The **University of Glasgow,** 52 Hillhead St. (tel. 330 53 85; open M-F 9am-5pm), offers housing in six dorms, including **Queen Margaret Hall,** 55 Bellshaugh Rd. (tel. 334 21 92), near Byres Rd. (£20.50, students £14.75). The **University of Strathclyde** has rooms at **Baird Hall,** 460 Sauchiehall St. (tel. 332 64 15; singles £18; twins £31); and at the **Campus Village** dorms (tel. 552 06 26; £9-22.50), off Cathedral St. Glasgow's **B&Bs** cluster on both sides of Great Western Rd. in the University area, or east of the necropolis near Westercraigs Rd.

SYHA Youth Hostel, 7-8 Park Terr. (tel. 332 30 04), in a beautiful residential area. U: St. George's Cross. From Central Station, take bus 44 or 59 to the first stop on Woodlands Rd. (at Lynedoch St.); from Queen St. Station or Buchanan bus station, take bus 11. Once the home of an English nobleman, the hostel retains an air of luxury. £11.50-12.50, under 18 £10-11. All rooms with bath. Breakfast included.

Alamo Guest House, 46 Gray St. (tel. 339 23 95). Quiet, spacious rooms and plenty of bathrooms. Singles £19; doubles £36.

Glasgow Backpackers Hostel, Kelvin Lodge, 8 Park Circus (tel. 332 90 00). U: St. George's Cross. Beautiful Georgian terrace house with an experienced, friendly staff. Dorms £9.50; twins £22. Open July-Sept.

Iona Guest House, 39 Hillhead St. (tel. 334 23 46), near Glasgow University, on a street lined with B&Bs. U: Hillhead. Convenient to reach Byres Rd. Stunning front hall, subterranean breakfast nook, and floral rooms. Haggis available for breakfast. Singles £22; doubles £36.

FOOD

Like many university towns, Glasgow has many cheap restaurants with great food. Cafes cluster behind Byres Rd. on **Ashton Lane,** a cobblestone alley lined with 19th-century brick facades. For groceries, try **Safeway,** 373 Byres Rd. (open M-Sa 8am-8pm, Su 9am-7pm), or **Grassroots,** 20 Woodlands Rd. (open M-W and F 8:45am-6pm, Th 8:45am-7pm, Sa 9am-6pm, Su 11am-3pm).

Insomnia Cafe, 38-40 Woodlands Rd., near the hostels. Sleepless students. Samosas with riata and onion £2.45. Breakfast quesadilla £2.75. Open 24hr.

Cafe Antipasti, 337 Byres Rd. and 305 Sauchiehall St. Excellent Italian food and bustling atmosphere. Pizzas, pastas, and fancy caesar salads £4.45-6.25. Open daily 8am-midnight, if it's busy enough.

Grosvenor Cafe, 31-35 Ashton Ln., behind U: Hillhead. Stuff yourself silly from the endless menu—most dishes under £1. More elaborate dinner menu Tu-Sa 7-11pm. Open M 9am-7pm, Tu-Sa 9am-11pm, Su 11am-5:30pm and 7-11pm.

Pierre Victoire, 167 Hope St. and 91 Miller St. French, reasonably priced, and delicious. 2-course meal and coffee £7. Open M-Sa noon-3pm and 5-11pm, Su 5-9pm.

The Willow Tea Room, 217 Sauchiehall St., upstairs from Henderson the Jewellers. Over 28 kinds of tea (£1.30 a pot) and marvelous sweets. Meringues with strawberries and cream £2. Open M-Sa 9:30am-4:30pm, Su noon-4:15pm.

SIGHTS

The Gothic **Glasgow Cathedral,** at the eastern end of Cathedral St., which runs behind Queen St. Station, was the only full-scale cathedral spared the fury of the 16th-century Scottish Reformation. *(Open Apr.-Sept. M-Sa 9:30am-6pm, Su 2-5pm; Oct.-Mar. M-Sa 9:30am-4pm, Su 2-4pm. Free.)* Next door is the entrance to the giant **necropolis,** a terrifying hilltop cemetery. Nearby, the **St. Mungo Museum of Religious Life and Art** surveys world religions from Hindu to Yoruba and boasts an impressive array of sacred objects. *(Open M-Sa 10am-5pm, Su 11am-5pm. Free.)* Charles Rennie Mackintosh, Scotland's most famous architect, designed the **Glasgow School of Art,** 167 Renfrew St. *(Tours M-F 11am-2pm, Sa 10:30am. £3.50, students £2.)*

The West End's residential **Park Circus** area features elegant parks and intact examples of early Victorian terracing. A block west, students come to tan on the grassy slopes of **Kelvingrove Park,** a large wooded expanse on the banks of the River Kelvin. In the southwest corner of the park, just off the intersection of Argyle and Sauchiehall St., the spired **Art Gallery and Museum** displays works by Rembrandt and Van Gogh as well as exhibits on armor, bee-keeping, and natural history. *(Open M-Sa 10am-5pm, Su 11am-5pm. Free.)* The **Museum of Transport,** on Dumbarton Rd., displays a collection of full-scale original trains, trams, and automobiles in a huge warehouse. *(Open M-Sa 10am-5pm, Su 11am-5pm. Free.)* To the west, on the bridge over the river, you can see the soaring tower of the **University of Glasgow's** central building. Founded in 1451, the university is Britain's fourth oldest. The central university building is off Byres Rd. on University Ave. These newly refurbished arches support the **Hunterian Museum,** the oldest museum in town, which includes an interesting ancient coin collection. *(Open M-Sa 9:30am-5pm. Free.)*

ENTERTAINMENT

Glaswegians play more and party harder than Edinburgh's inhabitants. The **Ticket Centre,** City Hall, Candleriggs (tel. 287 55 11; phones staffed M-Sa 9am-9pm, Su noon-5pm), will tell you what's playing at the city's dozen-odd theaters. Pick up a free copy of the *City Live!* events calendar here as well (open M-Sa 9:30am-6:30pm, Su noon-5pm). The arts scene intensifies during several spring and summer festivals. The **Mayfest** arts festival offers a good program of Scottish and international theater and music; for information, write to 18 Albion St., Glasgow, G1 1LH (tel. 552 84 44). The annual **Glasgow International Jazz Festival** (late June to early July) brings such greats as B. B. King and Betty Carter to town (same address as Mayfest; tel. 552 35 52). In early August, the city hosts the largest **International Early Music Festival** in the U.K. During the **World Pipe Band Championships** in mid-August, the skirling of bagpipes is heard for miles.

No matter where you end your day of sight-seeing, you won't be more than a block or so from a welcoming pub. The infamous Byres Road pub crawl usually starts with a trip to **Tennant's Bar** and then proceeds toward the River Clyde. **Cul de Sac Bar,** 46 Ashton Ln., is *the* artsy hangout, serving chic, young clientele on two floors (open Su-Th noon-11pm, F-Sa noon-midnight). **Halt Bar,** 160 Woodlands Rd., 2 blocks from the youth hostel, attracts all sorts. One side is dark and deafening, the other hot and humid (open M-Th 11am-11pm, F-Sa 11am-midnight). **The Horseshoe Bar,** 17-21 Drury St., in the city center, is a magnificent Victorian bar with etched mirrors and carved wooden walls. As many as 25 bartenders are needed to preside over the longest continuous bar in the U.K. (open M-Sa 11am-midnight, Su 12:30pm-midnight).

The city's sizable student population guarantees a lively club scene as well. *The List* (£1.90 from news agents) is the best source of info. Unless specified otherwise, club hours are generally 11pm to 3am; cover charges run £2 to 8 with occasional student discounts. Head to **Nice 'n' Sleazy,** 421 Sauchiehall St., where patrons enjoy music and choose from 15 flavors of Absolut vodka (open daily 11:30am-midnight). Look for two skeletons just outside the windows of **Archaos,** 25 Queen St. With frequent student discounts, musical variety, and several floors, it's no wonder that it's packed. Across the street, **Garage,** 490 Sauchiehall St., swallows hordes of students into its vortex of Mad Hatter decor. Grunge and indie resound in the **Cathouse,** 15 Union St., with mostly student patrons.

■ Near Glasgow: Stranraer

Located on the westernmost peninsula of Dumfries and Galloway, Stranraer is the port for ferries serving Northern Ireland. **Stena Line** (tel. (0990) 70 70 70) leaves for Belfast (2hr.; return £46, students £34, children £24). Arrive an hour before departures; ferries sometimes leave early depending on weather conditions. The **Seacat** (tel. (0990) 52 35 23) skims across the Irish Sea (1½hr., £25, students £16, children £14). **Trains** connect Glasgow to Stranraer (2½hr., £18.50); **buses** run to Glasgow (3hr.) and to London (9hr.) via Manchester (6½hr.). The **tourist office,** 1 Bridge St. (tel. (01776) 70 25 95), posts a list of **B&Bs** and books rooms for a deposit. (Open June-Sept. M-Sa 9:30am-6pm, Su 10am-6pm; Apr.-May and Oct. M-Sa 9:30am-5pm, Su 10am-4pm; Nov.-Mar. M-Sa 10am-4pm.) Should you fancy some munchies for the ride, visit the **Tesco supermarket** near the ferry terminal.

■ Arran

Called "Scotland in Miniature" for its gentle hills and dramatic peaks, the **Isle of Arran** is easily accessible from Glasgow's Central Station. Take the **train** west to Ardrossan on the Firth of Clyde (45min., £4), and from there take the **Calmac ferry** (tel. (01770)

30 21 66) which makes the crossing to **Brodick,** Arran's largest town. Brodick's **tourist office** (tel. (01770) 30 21 40), in the round building at the base of the pier, distributes free maps and info on the island's numerous **hiking options** (open May-Sept. M-Sa 9am-7:30pm, Su 10am-5pm). **Brodick Cycles** (tel./fax (01770) 30 24 60), down Shore Rd., rents bikes. (£2-5 per hr.; £4.50-9 per day. Open mid-Mar. to early Oct. M-Sa 9am-1pm and 2-6pm, Su 10am-1pm and 2-6pm.) The popular ascent of **Goatfell** (2866 ft.; 4-5hr.) happens between the **Brodick castle** and the heritage museum; the views from the top are stellar. As the ancient seat of the Dukes of Hamilton, the castle has a fine porcelain collection and scores of dead beasties. (Open Apr.-Oct. daily 11:30am-5pm. Last admission 4:30pm. Castle and gardens £4.50, students £1.50.) Rest at **Mrs. Wilkie** (tel. (01770) 30 28 28) at Cala Sona at the top of Alma Pk. (£14), and stock up on necessities at the **Co-op,** across from the ferry terminal (open M-Sa 8am-8pm, Su 10am-6pm). The small northern town of **Lochranza,** 14 miles from Broddick, offers a 13th-century castle and access to Loch Tanna, while **Blackwaterfoot,** is a good base for jaunts to the prehistoric sites in the west. **Bus** transport throughout the island is easy and cheap; just flag down a driver and hop on.

■ Stirling

Sitting atop a triangle formed by Glasgow to the southwest and Edinburgh to the southeast, Stirling has historically controlled north-south movement in central Scotland. Crowning a defunct volcano, **Stirling Castle** is now being restored to its original splendor. (Open daily Apr.-Oct. 9:30am-6pm; Nov.-Mar. 9:30am-5pm; last admission 45min. before closing. £4.50, seniors £3.50, under 16 £1.20.) The castle also contains the **Regimental Museum of the Argyll and Sutherland Highlanders.** (Open Easter-Sept. M-Sa 10am-5:45pm, Su 11am-4:45pm; Oct.-Easter daily 10am-4:45pm. Free.) Down Castle Hill Wynd, the **Church of the Holy Rude** witnessed the fire and brimstone of John Knox. (Open daily May-Sept. 10am-5pm. Su service July-Dec. 10am; Jan.-June 11:30am. Frequent organ recitals. Donations requested.) Cross the Abbey Rd. footbridge over the River Forth to find the ruins of the 12th-century **Cambuskenneth Abbey.** (Open Apr.-Sept. M-Sa 9:30am-6pm, Su 2-6pm, grounds open all year. Free.) Nearby, the 200 ft. **Wallace Monument** has the 66 inch sword William Wallace wielded against King Edward I of England at the 1297 Battle of Stirling Bridge. (Open daily July-Aug. 9:30am-6:30pm; June and Sept. 10am-6pm; Mar., May, and Oct. 10am-5pm; Nov.-Feb. Sa-Su only 10am-4pm. £2.50, seniors and children £1.50.) Back at sea-level (or closer to it, anyway), buses leave from the parking lot at the base of Abbey Craig for Stirling's train and bus stations (£1). Two miles south of Stirling at **Bannockburn,** a statue of Robert the Bruce overlooks the field where his men charged the fields and won their freedom in 1314.

The train station is on Goosecroft Rd. with **trains** to Edinburgh (50min., £4.50), Glasgow (30min., £5.60), and Inverness (3hr., £27). The bus station is down the road; buses run to the same cities for about half the price. The **tourist office** (tel. (01786) 47 50 19) greets visitors warmly at 41 Dumbarton Rd. (Open July-Aug. M-Sa 9am-7:30pm, Su 9:30am-6:30pm; June and Sept. M-Sa 9am-6pm, Su 10am-4pm; call for off-season hours.) **SYHA Stirling** (tel. 473442; fax 445715), is on St. John St. (£11-12.50. Reception 7:30am-11pm. Bedroom lockout 10am-2pm. Curfew 2am.)

■ St. Andrews

In St. Andrews, golf is the game. St. Andrews's **Old Course,** the golf pilgrim's Canterbury and frequent venue for the British Open, stretches out regally to a gorgeous beach at the northwest edge of town. (Call (01334) 46 66 66 or fax 47 70 36 to enter the lottery for starting times or make a reservation for a nearby course. £70 per round on the Old Course, £15-30 on other courses.) The **British Golf Museum,** next to the Old Course, details the origins of the game. (Open Easter-Oct. daily 9:30am-5:30pm; Nov.-Easter Th-M 11am-3pm. £4, students and seniors £2.75.)

Despite the onslaught of pastel and polyester, one need not worship the wedge to love St. Andrews. With its restored medieval streets, ruins of an enormous cathedral, ancient university, and magnificent beaches, St. Andrews possesses a rare and compelling beauty. In the Middle Ages, pilgrims journeyed to **St. Andrews Cathedral** to pray at the Saint's Shrine; today, only a facade and the outline of the walls remain. Nearby, **St. Andrews Castle** maintains secret tunnels, bottle-shaped dungeons, and high stone walls to keep out (or in) rebellious heretics. (Cathedral and castle open daily Apr.-Sept. 9:30am-6:30pm; Oct.-Mar. 9:30am-4:30pm. Joint ticket £3.50, seniors £2.70.) **St. Andrews University,** founded in the 15th century, lies just west of the castle between North St. and The Scores.

Fife Scottish buses (tel. (01334) 47 42 38) follow the scenic coastal route every day from Edinburgh to St. Andrews (2hr., £5.50). ScotRail **trains** (tel. (0345) 55 00 33) stop five miles away at **Leuchars** (from Edinburgh 1hr., £7); from there, buses travel to St. Andrews. The marvelous **tourist office** (tel. (01334) 47 20 21) is at 70 Market St.; from the bus station, turn right on City Rd. and take the first left. (Open July-Aug. M-Sa 9:30am-8pm, Su 11am-6pm; Sept.-June M-Sa 9:30am-6pm, Su 11am-4pm.) The office gives out lists of local **B&Bs,** but the thrifty traveler should make St. Andrews a daytrip from Edinburgh or Glasgow. Though less than attractive, **Gannochy House** (tel. (01334) 46 48 70), next to Younger Hall on North Street, is centrally located (£10; reception 2-6pm; open June- Aug.). **Cadzow Guest House,** 58 North St. (tel. (01334) 47 69 33) is comfy but expensive (singles with bath £23; doubles £32-42; phone and mail reservations accepted).

■ Loch Lomond and the Trossachs

Loch Lomond The hills of the Scottish uplands begin to swell 30 miles from Glasgow and grow into majestic peaks as they undulate northward. Just 45 minutes northwest of Glasgow, **Loch Lomond** is the closest that most foreigners get to the Highlands. Visitors who undertake hikes in such roadless areas as the northeastern edge of Loch Lomond are rewarded with quiet splendor. Small, rough beaches make fine spots for lazy picnics and paddles. **West Highland Way** snakes along the entire eastern side of the Loch, 95 miles from Milngavie north to Fort William.

Balloch, at the Loch's south tip, is the "major" town in the area. Across the River Leven, the Balloch Castle Country Park provides 200 acres of beach, lawn, woods, gardens, ancient ruins, and a Visitor's Centre/Ranger Station (open Easter-Oct. daily 10am-6pm). **Trains** run from the station across the street from the tourist office to Glasgow's Queen Station (45min., £3). The **bus station** is a few paces down Balloch Rd., but buses bypassing the town pick up passengers on the A82 near the roundabout. To reach the eastern side of the loch, take bus 309 from to **Balmaha** (40min.). Buses 305 and 307 also make the trek (£2.80) and continue to **Luss** on the Loch's western side (from Glasgow £3.70). **Sweeney's Cruises** run boat tours of Loch Lomond starting on the tourist office's side of the River Leven (1hr., £4.50). The town's **tourist office,** Old Station Building, Balloch Rd. (tel. (01389) 75 35 33), books rooms and sells walking guides and maps. (Open daily July-Aug. 9:30am-7:30pm; June 9:30am-6pm; Sept. 9:30am-7pm; Apr.-May and Oct. 10am-5pm.)

The **SYHA Loch Lomond Youth Hostel** (tel. (01389) 85 02 26) is a stunning 19th-century castle-like building two miles north of Balloch. Call ahead to book a room (£9.60). In Balloch, **B&Bs** congregate on Balloch Rd. The **Tullichewan Caravan and Camping Site** (tel. (01389) 75 94 75) is located on Old Luss Rd. up Balloch Rd. from the tourist office and rents mountain bikes (£10 per 8hr.; tent and 2 people £9; closed Nov.). The **SYHA Rowardennan Youth Hostel** (tel. (01360) 87 02 59) is the first hostel along the West Highland Way (£7.75; open Mar.-Oct.). To get there, take the Inverberg ferry (tel. (01301) 70 23 56) across the Loch to Rowardennan (Apr.-Sept. 3 per day; £4).

Trossachs The gentle mountains and lochs of the **Trossachs** form the southern boundary of the Highlands, northeast of Loch Lomond. A few buses link Glasgow to **Aberfoyle** and **Callander,** the area's two main towns. The A821 winds through the

---

Know Your Whisky

An old Highland saying proclaims that "there are two things a Highlander likes naked, and one is malt whisky." Whisky producers fawn over their ancient distilleries (sometimes refusing to clean them, for fear of losing mysterious but tasty bacteria) and speak dreamily of the Scotch water which feeds them. One malt whisky, Laphroaig's, is said to taste like iodine and is so powerful that some natives violate all propriety and mix it in with oatmeal. The founder of Laphroaig loved the whisky so much that he fell into a vat of it and died.

With only three ingredients, the whisky-making process seems simple, but the barley, water, and yeast actually undergo an elaborate transformation. **Malting:** The barley is soaked in water until it begins to grow, and then is smoked dry. **Mashing:** Just what you think. The barley is ground into grist and then turned into liquid wort. **Fermentation:** The fun part; here's where the mixture becomes alcoholic. **Distillation:** The low-alcohol liquid passes through large stills to be refined into the strong stuff. Whiskies develop individual qualities at this stage. **Maturation:** The whisky is poured into large oak casks and left alone for a number of years. **Bottling:** From oak to glass, from warehouse to bar.

---

heart of the Trossachs between Aberfoyle and Callander, passing near beautiful **Loch Katrine,** the Trossachs' original lure and the setting of Scott's *The Lady of the Lake*. A road for walkers and cyclists traces the Loch's shoreline. Cyclists can rent bikes on the pier (tel. (01877) 38 26 14; £12 per day; open Apr.-Sept. daily 10am-5:30pm). Nearby, 1207 ft. **Ben A'an'** hulks over the Trossachs; the rocky one-hour hike up begins a mile from the pier, along the A821. The **S.S. Sir Walter Scott** (tel. (0141) 955 01 28) steams between Loch Katrine's Trossachs Pier and Stronachlachar (Apr.-Oct.; £3.50-5). Getting to this area is tough: your best bet is to ask in Aberfoyle or Callander about **post buses.** Or try **The Trossachs Trundler,** a 1950s-style bus that creaks to Callander, Aberfoyle, and Trossachs Pier in time for the sailing of the *Sir Walter Scott* (buses run July-Sept.; Day Rover £5.40). Service bus 59 leaving from Stirling bus station connects with the Trundler in Callander (Stirling-Trossachs Trundler Rover £8.10). Call the **Stirling Council Public Transport Helpline** at (01786) 44 27 07 for information.

■ Fort William and the Road to the Isles

Fort William, built in the 17th century to keep out "savage clans and roving barbarians," today suffers under a constant seige of tourists and outdoorsmen. Mountaineers come for the challenge of 4406 ft. **Ben Nevis,** one of the highest peaks in Britain. The main trail starts just past the town park; allow eight to nine hours for the hike to the top and back. Visitors to the **Nevis Range** ski area (tel. (01397) 70 58 25) enjoy Scotland's longest ski run and a state-of-the-art **gondola** (round-trip £6.25). The **tourist office** (tel. (01397) 70 37 81) provides information on the area's attractions. (Open May-Sept. M-Sa 9am-8pm; Su 9am-6pm; Oct.-Dec. M-Th 10am-4pm, F 10am-5pm; Jan.-Apr. Sa-Su 10am-1pm.) Just five minutes from town, the **Fort William Backpackers Guesthouse** (tel. (01397) 70 07 11), on Alma Rd., welcomes visitors with a hot cup of tea and a cozy bed (£10). The **SYHA Glen Nevis Youth Hostel** (tel. (01397) 70 23 36) stands 3 miles east of town on the Glen Nevis Rd., right across from the trail up Ben Nevis (£8.10-9.60). On the opposite side of the River Nevis, the **Ben Nevis Bunkhouse** (tel. (01397) 70 22 40) lies 2 miles from town along Achintee Rd. (£8). B&Bs cluster on Fassifern Rd., behind the Alexandra Hotel. The **Glen Nevis Caravan & Camping Park** (tel. (01397) 70 21 91) is on Glen Nevis Rd. east of the SYHA hostel (£1.30, tents £4.60-5.70, reduced prices off-season; open mid-Mar. to Oct.).

Trains wind coastward through the mountains from Fort William to **Mallaig** along the famous "Road to the Isles." On the way, disembark at Arisaig or Morar to reach the **Silver Sands** (white beaches). Walk 3 miles along the A830 from the station at Arisaig or Morar to reach a **campsite** near secluded beaches. The **tourist office** (tel. (01687) 46 21 70) in Mallaig is around the block from the rail station. (Open July-Aug.

M-Sa 9am-8pm; Su 10am-5pm; Easter-June and Sept. M-Sa 9am-6:30pm, Su 10am-5pm; mid-Mar. to Easter and late Sept. to mid-Oct. M-Sa 10am-6:30pm.) In town, catch up on sleep at **Sheena's Backpackers Lodge** (tel. (01687) 46 27 64; £8.50-11).

■ Oban and the Lower Hebrides

Three hours by bus or train from Glasgow, **Oban** (OH-ben), the busiest ferry port on the west coast, endears itself with sporadic outbursts of small-town warmth. If you tire of the busy pier, gaze at the bay from **McCaig's Tower,** built between 1902 and 1906 to employ local masons, or walk 15 minutes north of town to the crumbling tower of **Dunollie Castle. Trains** from Glasgow (3hr., £17) stop at the station (tel. (01631) 56 30 83) at Railway Quay. Citylink **buses** (tel. (01631) 56 28 56) from Glasgow (3hr., £10) and Inverness via Fort William (4hr., £10) stop at 1 Queens Park Pl. The **tourist office,** Argyll Sq. (tel. (01631) 56 31 22), is friendly but very busy (open July-Aug. M-Sa 9am-9pm, Su 9am-5pm; off-season reduced hours). Sleep in peach bunkbeds at **Oban Backpackers Lodge,** 21 Breadalbande St. (tel. (01631) 56 21 07; £8.90). The **SYHA Youth Hostel,** Corran Esplanade (tel. (01631) 56 20 25), hugs the waterfront (£8.10-9.60; open Mar.-Dec.).

    Caledonian MacBrayne Ferries (tel. (01475) 65 01 00; fax 65 02 62), known locally as "Cal-Mac" sail from Oban to most southern Hebrides islands. Ferries go to Craignure on Mull (40min., £3.75); Coll and Tiree, two islands west of Mull (to Coll 3hr. or Tiree 4hr., 0-1 per day, £10.50); and Barra (5hr., M and W-Sa, £16).

■ Skye

Often described as the shining jewel in the Hebridean crown, the island of Skye radiates unparalleled natural splendor. The **Cuillin Hills,** volcanic peaks surging boldly into a halo of clouds, offer perhaps the most dramatic mountain vistas in Britain. Lush peninsulas and bays mark the extremes of the island near Staffin and Armadale. The new **Skye Bridge** includes a footpath for pedestrians and sends shuttle buses (55p) to Skye. Four Scottish Citylink and Skye-Ways **coaches** run daily from Glasgow and Inverness to **Kyle of Lochalsh,** on the western edge of mainland Scotland. **Trains** arrive from Inverness (2½hr.). Transportation on the island is tough; bus service is infrequent and pricy. Biking or hiking may be better options; many hitch. Minibus tours are also an option: **Nick's Tour** (tel. (01599) 53 40 87) leaves Kyleakin daily at 10:30am and covers the scattered sites of Skye (7hr., £12). The **tourist office** in Kyle of Lochalsh (tel. (01599) 53 42 76) books B&Bs on either side of the channel.

    Once you've seen the harbor in Kyleakin, move on to the ruins of the **Castle Moil;** legend relates that the original castle on this site was built by "Saucy Mary," a Norwegian princess who stretched a stout chain across the Kyle and charged ships a fee to come through the narrows. Eight miles east along the A87, on an islet in Loch Duich, perches **Eilean Donan Castle,** the restored 13th-century seat of the MacKenzies (and the castle in *Highlander!*). Visit the ruins of **Duntulm Castle,** which guard the tip of the northeast peninsula. The castle was the MacDonald's formidable stronghold until a nurse dropped the chief's baby from the window, cursing the house.

    Skye's attractive **SYHA hostels** are distressingly oversubscribed in the summer; call in advance. **Glenbrittle** (tel. (01478) 64 02 78) is in the heart of the Cuillins, accessible only to hikers and those with their own transportation (£6.10; open mid-Mar. to Oct.). **Uig** (tel. (01470) 54 22 11), overlooking the bay on the northern peninsula, is a tough 45-minute walk from the ferry on the A586 (£6.10; open mid-Mar. to Oct.). **Broadford** (tel. (01471) 82 24 42) is the most central, close to both mountains and beaches (£7.75; open Apr.-Dec.). **Armadale** (tel. (01471) 84 42 60; £6.10; open mid-Mar. to Sept.), on the southern tip of Skye, is near the Mallaig ferry and serves as a base for touring the verdant **Sleat Peninsula.** The top-notch **Kyleakin** (tel. (01599) 53 45 85) fills very quickly (£9.60). Several independent hostels also await. The **Skye Backpackers** (tel. (01599) 53 45 10) in Kyleakin offers relaxed comfort for £10. Near Broadford, **Fossil Bothy** (tel. (01471) 82 26 44 or 82 22 97) sleeps eight cozily (£7; bring a sleeping bag). In Portree, Skye's capital, stay at the **Portree Backpackers Hostel,** 6 Woodpark, Dunvegan Rd. (tel. (01478) 61 36 41; £8.50).

■ Outer Hebrides

The landscape of the Outer Hebrides is astoundingly ancient; much of the exposed rock here is about three billion years old. The culture and customs of the Hebridean people have also resisted change. Most old and some young islanders still speak Gaelic among themselves. The vehemently Calvinist islands of Lewis and Harris observe the Sabbath strictly: all shops and restaurants close, and public transportation stops on Sundays. Television and tourism are diluting some local customs, but the islands are large and remote enough to retain much of their beauty and charm.

Caledonian MacBrayne ships travelers out. Ferries and infrequent buses connect the islands, and hitchers and cyclists enjoy success except during frequent rain storms. Since ferries arrive at odd hours, try to arrange a bed ahead. The Outer Hebrides are home to the Gatliff Hebridean Trust Hostels (Urras Osdailean Nan Innse Gall Gatliff), four 19th-century thatched croft houses converted into simple hostels, open year-round, with enough authenticity and atmosphere to compensate for crude facilities (each £4.65). Camping is allowed on public land, but freezing winds and sodden ground often make it miserable. For more information, snag a copy of *The Outer Hebrides Handbook and Guide* (£8 at tourist offices).

Lewis and Harris

The island of Lewis is famous for its atmosphere: pure light and drifting mists off the Atlantic Ocean shroud the untouched miles of moorland and small lochs in quiet luminescence. The unearthly setting is ideal for exploring the Callanish Stones, an extraordinary (and isolated) Bronze Age circle. Caledonian MacBrayne ferries from Ullapool on the mainland serve Stornoway, the biggest town in the Outer Hebrides (M-Sa, £12). The tourist office (tel. (01851) 70 30 88) is at 26 Cromwell St.; turn right from the ferry terminal, then left on Cromwell St. (open Mar.-Sept. 9am-6pm and 8-9pm; Oct.-Feb. 9am-5pm). The Stornoway Backpackers Hostel, 47 Keith St. (tel. (01851) 70 36 28), has free tea, coffee, and cereal, and is always open (£8).

Although Harris is part of the same island as Lewis, it preserves its separate identity behind the curiously treeless Forest of Harris (actually a mountain range). Open hills, softened by a carpet of *machair* and wildflowers, make for wonderful off-trail rambling. Ferries (tel. (01859) 50 24 44) serve unlovely Tarbert from Uig on Skye (£7.85). The chipper tourist office awaits on Pier Rd. (Tel. (01859) 50 20 11. Open early Apr. to mid-Oct. M-Sa 9am-5pm and for late ferry arrivals.) Rent a bike from Mr. Mackenzie (tel. (01859) 50 22 71), across from the tourist office (£6 per day). The nearest SYHA Youth Hostel is 7 miles away in Stockinish (tel. (01859) 53 03 73; £4.65; open mid-Mar. to Sept.), but there are many B&Bs near the tourist office.

Barra

Little Barra, the southern outpost of the outer isles, is indescribably beautiful—but we'll try. On a sunny day, the island's colors are unforgettable: grassy sand dunes and flawless beaches complement dazzling blue waters wreathed below by dimly visible red, brown, and green kelp. Kisimul Castle, bastion of the old Clan Mac-Neil, inhabits an islet in Castlebay Harbor (boat trips out M, W, and Sa 2-5pm; £2.20). West of Castlebay, near Borve, is one squat standing stone which was allegedly erected in memory of a Viking galley captain who lost a bet with a Barra man; Archaeologists who excavated the site did indeed find a skeleton and Nordic armor. To see the whole island, rent a bike from Castlebay Cycle Hire (tel. (01871) 81 02 84; £8-15) and follow A888, which makes a 14-mile circle around the rather steep slopes of Ben Havel. A Caledonian MacBrayne ferry makes the trip between Castlebay on Barra and Oban or Mallaig on the mainland (5-6hr.; Tu, Th-F, and Su; £17). The Castlebay tourist office (tel. (01871) 81 03 36) is around the bend to the right from the pier. (Open roughly mid-Mar. to mid-Oct. M-Sa 9am-5pm, Su 11:30am-12:30pm, and for late ferry arrivals.)

■ Aberdeen

The center of Britain's North Sea oil industry, Aberdeen offsets its dirt and smog with attractive parks, a vibrant university, and proximity to some of the finest castles and least crowded Scottish countrysides. **Old Aberdeen** and **Aberdeen University** are a short bus ride (1, 2, 3, 4, or 15) from the city center. The intricately carved "misery seats" in the 16th-century **King's College Chapel** make visitors squirm (open daily 9am-4:30pm). The twin-spired, 14th-century **St. Machar's Cathedral** has less torturous features, including a heraldic ceiling and stained glass (open daily 9am-5pm). The impressive **Aberdeen Art Gallery,** Schoolhill (tel. (01224) 64 63 33), houses many English, French, and Scottish paintings, and hosts summertime drama and music performances (open M-Sa 10am-5pm, Su 2-5pm; free). Aberdeen's largest park, **Hazlehead,** off Queen's Rd., has an aviary and extensive woodlands. Take bus 14 or 15 to Queen's Rd. and walk one mile on Hazlehead Ave. A sandy **beach** stretches north for about two miles from Aberdeen's old fishing community at Footdee.

Trains zip from the station on Guild St. to Edinburgh (£31), Glasgow (£34), Inverness (£18.50), and London (£78). National Express and Scottish Citylink **buses** travel from the station on Guild St. (tel. (01224) 21 22 66) to the same cities for about half the price. The **Aberdeen Ferry Terminal,** Jamieson's Quay (tel. (01224) 57 26 15), is the only place on mainland Britain where ferries go to Lerwick on the Shetland Islands and Stromness on the Orkney Islands. The **tourist office,** St. Nicholas House, Broad St. (tel. (01224) 63 27 27), books rooms. (Open July-Aug. M-F 9am-7pm, Sa 9am-5pm, Su 10am-4pm; Sept.-June M-Sa 9am-5pm, Su 10am-2pm.) Great Western Rd. bursts with **B&Bs** (£15-23). Take bus 17, 18, or 19 or walk 20 minutes from the train and bus stations. The **SYHA George VI Memorial Hostel,** 8 Queen's Rd. (tel. (01224) 64 69 88), accessible by bus 14, 15 or 27, has spacious dorms (£7.10-9.60; lights out 11:30pm; curfew 2am; lockout 9:30am-1:30pm). Campers try **Hazlehead Park** (tel. (01224) 32 12 68) on Groats Rd. (£3.50-7 per tent). Take bus 14 or 15. The **Safeway supermarket** is at 215 King St. (open M-F 8am-8pm, Sa 8am-7pm).

■ Inverness

The charms of Inverness, like the Loch Ness monster herself, are somewhat elusive, but persistent visitors won't be disappointed. In town, don't expect many reminders of Shakespeare's *Macbeth;* nothing of the "auld Castlehill" remains, and Banquo's ghost has no ruins to haunt. Instead, visit the **Balnain House,** 40 Huntley St., try your hand at the bagpipe or *clarsach* (harp), and hear live Highland music daily. (July-Aug. M-F 10am-8pm, Sa-Su 10am-6pm; June Tu-Su 10am-5pm; Sept.-May Tu-Sa 10am-5pm. £2, students and seniors £1.50.) Just five miles south of Inverness lies the unfathomably deep and mysterious **Loch Ness.** An easy way to see the loch is on the tour run by **Inverness Traction,** leaving from the tourist office at 10:30am, 11:15am, and 2:30pm (£7.50, students, seniors, and children £6). A mile south of **Culloden,** to the east of Inverness, the chambered cairns (mounds of rough stones) of the **Cairns of Clava** recall Bronze Age civilizations. Nearby, **Moniack Castle,** built in 1580 as the home of the Frasers, houses the family and their winery (open Mar.-Oct. M-Sa 10am-5pm; Nov.-Feb. M-Sa 11am-4pm; £2). The **Cawdor Castle** and its stunning garden maze have entertained the Thane's descendants since the 15th century (open May to mid-Oct. daily 10am-5:30pm; £5.20, students and seniors £4.20).

Trains run from Station Sq. to Aberdeen (£18), Edinburgh and Glasgow (£28), and London (£78). Scottish Citylink has frequent **bus** service to most destinations, including Edinburgh (£12.30), Glasgow (£11.50), and London (£41). The **tourist office,** Castle Wynd (tel. (01463) 23 43 53), can put you on Nessie's trail. (Open July to mid-Sept. M-Sa 9am-8:30pm, Su 9:30am-6pm; mid-May to June M-Sa 9am-6pm, Su 9:30am-5:30pm; call for off-season hours.) Buy a **Tourist Trail Day Rover** (£6, students £4) to travel by bus from Inverness to Cawdor Castle, Castle Stuart, other sites near Culloden, and back. The extroverted staff of the **Inverness Student Hotel,** 8 Culduthel Rd. (tel. (01463) 23 65 56), also runs a resource center (£8.50-8.90; reception

BRITAIN

6:30am-2:30am). From the stations, walk left along Academy St., turn right onto Union and left on the pedestrian Drummond St., then look for signs for the **Ho-Ho Hostel,** 23a High St., (tel. (01463) 22 12 25; dorms £8.50; twins or doubles £9.50).

■ Orkney Islands

Orkney rarely fails to enchant visitors with its natural wonders, ancient and medieval artifacts and monuments, and hospitality. Several ferries connect mainland Scotland to the islands. The **Orkney Bus,** which departs daily (May to early Sept.) from the Inverness bus station's platform at 10am and 2:20pm, rides to **John O'Groats,** where ferries sail for **Burwick** on the southern tip of Orkney. From Burwick, a local bus travels up the Churchill Barriers to Kirkwall (round-trip £37, buy tickets on the bus). A **P&O Scottish** ferry originating in Aberdeen stops in Stromness most weeks on its way to Lerwick, Shetland. (June-Aug. Su and Tu noon; May and Sept. Sa noon; Oct.-Dec. Sa 6pm; Jan.-Apr. times vary. Call (01224) 57 26 15 for exact schedule.) On the main island, the largest and busiest city, Kirkwall, lies north of Burwick and east of Stromness; frequent buses link the three. From the Kirkwall pier, the **Orkney Islands Shipping Co.** (tel. (01856) 87 20 44) ferries passengers to **Sanday** and the smaller islands.

Kirkwall and Stromness Kirkwall is the administrative and social center of

the Orkney Islands. The sandstone **St. Magnus Cathedral,** begun in 1137, and a few age-old structures at the town center attest to the city's long history. The **tourist office,** 6 Broad St. (tel. (01856) 87 28 56), down the main road from the cathedral, books B&Bs and dispenses advice. (Open mid-Apr. to Sept. daily 8:30am-noon and 4-8pm; Oct. to mid-Apr. M-Sa 9:30am-5pm.) The friendly **Kirkwall Youth Hostel (SYHA),** Old Skapa Rd. (tel. (01856) 87 22 43), has affordable prices (£7.75; open mid-Mar. to Oct.). For quiet rooms, try **Vanglee** (tel. (01856) 87 30 13), on Weyland Park off Cromwell Rd. (£13-15). Camping is available off the A965 at the **Pickaquoy Caravan & Camping Site** (tel. (01856) 87 35 35; £3.50-4.65). Stock up on supplies at the **Safeway Supermarket** on Broad St.

Stromness was founded in the 16th century as a fishing and whaling port. The helpful **tourist office** (tel. (01856) 85 07 16) resides in an old warehouse on the pier (usually open for ferry arrivals and departures; call for hours). Nearby, **Brown's Hostel,** 45-7 Victoria St. (tel. (01856) 85 06 61), offers warm, comfortable rooms (£7.50-8). The **SYHA hostel** (tel. (01856) 85 05 89) on Hellihole Rd. doesn't deserve its infernal address (£5-6.10; open mid-Mar. to Oct.). **The Cafe** at 22 Victoria St. serves cheap meals (£3-6; open M-Sa 9am-9pm, Su 10am-9pm). The bars at **The Ferry Inn** and **The Stromness Hotel** are popular nightspots for both locals and tourists.

Many important archaeological sites are around Stromness and Kirkwall. **Skara Brae** was once a busy Stone Age village. Nearby on A965, **Standing Stones of Stenness** may have been the site of a priests' settlement. On the southern tip of Ronaldsay, 35 miles from Stromness, perches the **Tomb of Eagles** where you can handle Stone Age tools and skulls and walk through a Bronze Age house (call ahead (01856) 83 13 39; £2.50).

Bulgaria (България)

US$1	= 1790 lv (leva, or BGL)		100 lv=	US$0.06
CDN$1	= 1150 lv		100 lv=	CDN$0.09
UK£1	= 2930 lv		100 lv=	UK£0.03
IR£1	= 2500 lv		100 lv=	IR£0.04
AUS$1	= 1095 lv		100 lv=	AUS$0.10
NZ$1	= 879 lv		100 lv=	NZ$0.11
SAR1	= 285 lv		100 lv=	SAR0.35
DM1	= 995 lv		100 lv=	DM0.10

Country Phone Code: 359   **International Dialing Prefix: 00**

From the pine-clad slopes of the Rila, Pirin, and Rodop mountains in the southwest, to the lush Valley of Roses traversing the middle of the country, to the rocky and sandy beaches of the beautiful Black Sea, Bulgaria pleases the eye. Once the most powerful state in the Balkans and the progenitor of the Cyrillic alphabet and Slavic Orthodoxy, to which its many storied monasteries attest, it spent 500 years under Ottoman Turk rule. These years yielded minarets above crosses and underground monasteries, but also, finally, the National Revival of the 19th century, when Bulgarians reestablished an independent church and championed the use of the Bulgarian language. This was the time when much of the most majestic, very European architecture now gracing its cities was built. The 20th century has not been kind to Bulgaria, however, as the post-communist era has brought little except rampant inflation and massive unemployment. It is today among the poorest countries in Europe, but in many ways the most hospitable to the budget traveler: profoundly rich in religious history, cheap even by Eastern European standards, filled in summer with fresh apricots and cherries, Bulgaria is at the same time only barely affected, despite its own efforts, by the pace of Western consumerism.

For more detailed coverage of Bulgaria, peruse *Let's Go: Eastern Europe 1999*.

GETTING THERE

U.S. and EU citizens can visit Bulgaria **visa-free** for up to 30 days. Citizens of other countries, or anyone planning to stay longer than 30 days, must obtain a 90-day visa (single-entry US$53, multiple-entry US$123, transit US$43) from their local consulate (see **Government Information Offices,** p. 2). Visas take about 10 days to process, unless you opt for rush service (US$68-88). The application requires a passport, a photograph, and payment by cash or money order. Visas can be extended at a Bureau for Foreigners, located in every major Bulgarian city. The visa price includes a US$20 border tax which the visa-less are required to pay upon entering the country.

Bulgarian **trains** run to Budapest, Romania (enter through Ruse), Yugoslavia, Greece, and Turkey. **Balkan Air** flies directly to Sofia from New York and other cities. **Rila** is the main international train ticket company. **Group Travel** buses run to Prague, Budapest, and Istanbul. There are ferries from coastal cities to Istanbul and other cities on the Black Sea, including Odessa.

GETTING AROUND

The **train** system is comprehensive but slow, crowded, and aged. Direct trains run from Sofia to major towns throughout the country. There are three train types: express (експрес), fast (бърз; *burz*), and slow (пътнически; *putnicheski*). Avoid the slow trains, which stop at any sign of civilization. Arrive early for a seat. Stations are poorly marked, often only in Cyrillic. Some useful words are: влак (*vlak,* train); автобус (*avtobus,* bus); гара (*gara,* station); перон (*peron,* platform); колвоз (*kolovoz,* track); билет (*bilet,* ticket); заминаващи (*zaminavashti,* departure); пристигащи (*pristigashti,* arrival); спални вагон (*spalen vagon,* sleeping car); първа класа (*purva klasa,* first class); and втора класа (*vtora klasa,* second class).

Slow trains and rising ticket prices make **bus** travel an attractive option. For long distances, the private companies **Group Travel** and **Etap** offer modern buses with bathrooms, A/C, and even VCRs at around 1.5 times the price of train tickets. Buy a seat in advance from the agency office or pay when boarding. Some buses have set departure times; others leave when full. Private companies have great package deals on international travel. **Balkan Air** fares have swollen enormously (Sofia to Varna or Burgas US$138), and there are no youth discounts on domestic flights.

Taxis are everywhere in cities and larger towns. Avoid private taxis, refuse to pay in dollars, and insist on a metered ride *(sus apparata).* Ask the distance and price per km to do your own calculations. **Hitchhiking** is risky, but the patient may succeed.

ESSENTIALS

Balkantourist, the former national tourist bureau, still has some offices, though many have been privatized. The agency often changes money and books hotel rooms and private accommodations. In a few cities, it may be difficult to get information unless you're booking an expensive excursion or room, but at least they speak English. If you have no luck at the tourist offices, keep in mind that many hotels also provide valuable tourist info.

The **lev** (lv, plural *leva*) is the standard monetary unit, but *Let's Go* lists some prices in U.S. dollars due to recent chaos in the lev's value. On July 1, 1997, the lev was pegged to the Deutschmark; 1000lv=DM1. Inflation is still high, however—the prices listed here will likely have changed. Private **exchange bureaus** may be open 24 hours, but often buy only U.S. dollars and major European currencies. Exchange bureaus have a lower rate for AmEx Traveler's Checks than for cash. You can also change currency or cash AmEx Traveler's Checks in *leva* (sometimes US$) at major **banks** such as **BulBank** or **Biohim Bank,** and **Obedinena Bulgarska Banka.** Some banks also accept major credit cards for cash advances (especially MC); otherwise you can use credit cards in larger hotels and more expensive resorts. **ATMs** are becoming an alternative to carrying Deutschmarks or US$; most are linked to Cirrus, EC, and MC. Bills from before 1974 are worthless—check carefully.

Public **bathrooms** are often nothing more than a hole in the ground; pack a small bar of soap and toilet paper, and expect to pay 50-200lv for the toilet paper. **Safety concerns** are of special importance in a country where hard currency is desirable; avoid walking alone after dark, even if you know where you're going. *Pedestrians do not have the right of way* in Bulgaria, and some drivers choose to park on sidewalks. Despite its legality, acceptance of **homosexuality** is very slow in coming.

COMMUNICATION Making international **telephone** calls from Bulgaria can be challenging, and is definitely expensive. To call collect, dial 0123 for an international operator or have the telephone office or hotel receptionist order the call for you. The operator invariably won't speak English. You can also make international calls at most post offices, but connections are poor outside large cities. Calls to the U.S. average US$2 per minute, but expect to pay up to US$4 per minute at major hotels and resorts. **AT&T Direct** (tel. 008 00 00 10), **British Telecom** (tel. 00 800 99 44), **Sprint Access** (tel. 008 00 10 10), and **MCI** (tel. 008 00 00 01) provide direct calling card connections via English-speaking operators. **Betkom** or **Bulfon** direct-dial phones with digital displays (for English usually press "i") are all over, and probably the easiest way to make international calls, either using the AT&T direct number or just calling directly. These phones require special cards, sold in kiosks, restaurants, shops, and in all post offices and telephone offices (places selling them will have stickers saying so; the 400 unit, 20,000lv cards can make international calls anywhere—just pop the card in, dial the country's international code and then the number). In an **emergency,** dial 160 for **fire,** 166 for **police,** and 150 if you need an **ambulance.**

Some English is often spoken by young people and in tourist areas, but in the countryside you're on your own. The Bulgarian transliteration is much the same as the Russian except that x is *h*, щ is *sht*, and ь is sometimes transliterated as *â* (pronounced as in English b*u*g). For Cyrillic characters, see p. 743. Keep in mind that Bulgarians shake their heads to indicate "yes" and nod to indicate "no." Also, be aware that many street names will be changed as the country moves further from its communist past; try to find the most recent map.

Yes/no	Да/Не	dah/neh
Hello	Добър ден	DOH-bur den
Please	Моля	MOE-lya
Thank you	Благодаря	blahg-oh-dahr-YA
Where is...?	Къде е...?Ё	kuh-DEH EH
How much does this cost?	Колко струва	KOHL-ko STROO-va
Do you speak English?	Говорите ли английски?	goh-VOH-rih-tih lih ahn-GLIH-skih
I don't understand	Не разбирам	neh rahz-BIH-rahm
Help!	Помощ	POH-mosht

ACCOMMODATIONS AND CAMPING When you cross the border you will probably be given a yellow **statistical card** to document where you stay each night. If you get one and lose it, you may have difficulty getting a hotel room. If you don't get a card at all (which could be the case if you don't need a visa to enter), don't worry. Ask hotels or private room bureaus to stamp your passport, or to stamp a receipt-like paper that you can keep with you and show upon border re-crossing.

Private rooms are arranged through Balkantourist or other tourist offices for US$5 to 15 per night. Be sure to ask for a central location and try to find out if any family members speak English. Or, look for signs reading частни квартири (private rooms). Bulgarian **hotels** are classed by stars; rooms in one-star hotels are almost identical to those in two- and three-star hotels but have no private bathrooms; they average about US$20 for singles and US$30 for doubles. Foreigners are always charged much higher prices than Bulgarians. The majority of Bulgarian **youth hostels** are located in the countryside and are popular with student groups; try to make reservations through **ORBITA,** Hristo Botev 48 (Христо Ботев; tel. (02) 80 01 02; fax 88 58 14), which can also find rooms in university dorms. Outside major towns, **campgrounds** give you a chance to meet backpackers. Freelance camping is popular, but you risk a fine (and your safety).

BULGARIA

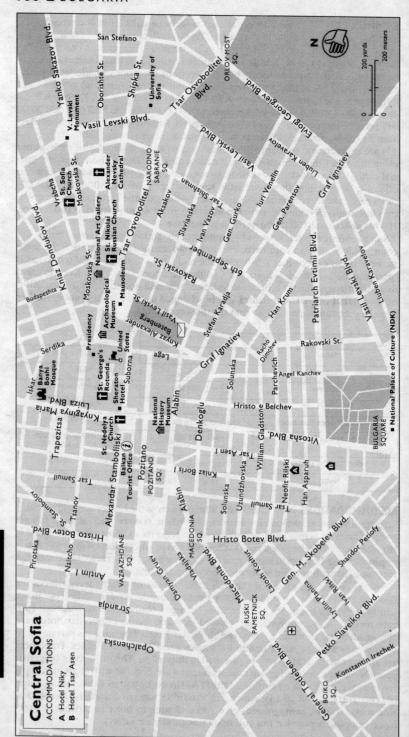

Central Sofia

ACCOMMODATIONS

A Hotel Niky
B Hotel Tsar Asen

BULGARIA

San Stefano

Yanko Sakazov Blvd.

Oborishte St.

Shipka St.

University of Sofia

Tsar Osvoboditel Blvd.

 ORLOV MOST SQ.

Evlogi Georgiev Blvd.

N

200 yards
200 meters

V. Levski Monument

Vasil Levski Blvd.

Vasil Levski Blvd.

Liuben Karavelov

Graf Ignatiev

Vrabcha

St. Sofia Church

Moskovska St.

Alexander Nevsky Cathedral

NARODNO SABRANIE SQ.

Aksakov

Tsar Shishman

Slavianska

Ivan Vazov

Gen. Gurko

Iuri Venelin

Gen. Parensov

Kniaz Dondukov Blvd.

National Art Gallery

St. Nikolai Russian Church

Tsar Osvoboditel

6th September

Rakovski St.

Patriarch Evtimii Blvd.

Vasil Levski Blvd.

Liuben Karavelov

Budapeshta

Moskovska St.

Archaeological Museum

Mausoleum

Vasil Levski St.

Stefan Karadja

Han Krum

Presidency

United States

Kniaz Alexander Batenberg

Graf Ignatiev

Racho Dimchev

Rakovski St.

Serdika

St. George's Rotunda

Lège

Angel Kanchev

Iskar

Banya Boshi Mosque

Sheraton Hotel

Suborna

National History Museum

Alabin

Solunska

Parchevich

Hristo Belchev

Kniaginya Maria Luiza Blvd.

Trapezitsa

St. Nedelya Church

Alexander Stamboliiski

Balkan Tourist Office

Pozitano

POZITANO SQ.

Denkoglu

Kniaz Boris I

Tsar Asen I

Uzundzhovska

William Gladstone

Neofit Rilski

Solunska

Victosha Blvd.

BULGARIA SQUARE

National Palace of Culture (NDK)

Tsar Samuil

Tsanov

Tsar Samuil

Alabin

Solunska

Tsar Asen I

Han Asparuh

Pirotska

Naitcho

Hristo Botev Blvd.

VAZRAZHDANE SQ.

Strandja

Antim I

Damyan Gruev

Macedonia Blvd.

Vladaiska

Laiosh Koshut

Hristo Botev Blvd.

Gen. M. Skobelev Blvd.

Shandor Petofy

Opalchenska

RUSKI PAMETNICK SQ.

Lyulin planina

Ivan Riiski

Petko Slaveikov Blvd.

General Totleben Blvd.

BOIKO SQ.

Konstantin Irechek

FOOD AND DRINK Food from kiosks is cheap (600-2000lv), and restaurants average 6000lv per meal. Kiosks sell *kebabcheta* (кебабчета; small sausage-shaped hamburgers), salami sandwiches, pizzas, *banitsa sus sirene* (баница със сирене; cheese-filled pastries), and filled rolls. Fruits and vegetables are sold in a *plod-zelenchuk* (плод-зеленчук), *pazar* (пазар), and on the street. In summer, Bulgaria is blessed with delicious fruits and vegetables, especially tomatoes and peaches. Try *shopska salata* (шопска салата), an addictive salad of tomatoes, peppers, cucumbers, onions, and feta cheese. *Gyuvech* (гювеч) is mixed stew with meat, onion, peppers, potatoes, and other veggies. Also try *tarator* (таратор)—a cold soup made with yogurt, cucumber, and garlic. Notwithstanding these vegetarian delights, Bulgarians put a heavy emphasis on meat. Try *kavarma* (каварма)—a meat dish with lots of onions and sometimes an egg on top. There are also many organ-based dishes such as *mozik* (мозик; brain) or *ezik* (език; tongue). Local cheeses and yogurts are often delicious.

Well-stirred *airan* (айран; yogurt with water and ice cubes) and *boza* (боза; same ingredients as beer, but sweet and thicker) are popular national drinks, excellent with breakfast. Bulgaria exports mineral water; locals swear by its healing qualities (good brands are Gorna Banya and Hissaria). Melnik is famous for its red wine. A 10% **tip** is appreciated but not obligatory.

▓ Sofia (София)

On the main thoroughfares and squares of Sofia, at nearly any time of day, there is a wild stir of bustling activity. Pedestrians dodge slamming tram doors and cars weaving indiscriminately across streets and sidewalks lined with vendors. Centuries-old churches stand alongside Soviet-era concrete blocks, and the steel trolley lines link 19th-century elegance with pre-fab fast food chains. In the midst of it all, Sofia's 1.2 million inhabitants manage to keep their cool—they move through their 1500-year-old capital with a reassuring ease and composure that invites visitors from around the world to sample the city's eclectic culture and history.

ORIENTATION AND PRACTICAL INFORMATION

Current **maps** are sold in hotels, tourist agencies, kiosks, and exchange bureaus. **Bulevard Patriarh Evtimii** (бул. Патриарх Евтемий), **bulevard Hristo Botev** (Христо Ботев), **bulevard Aleksandr Stamboliiski** (Александър Стамболийски), **bulevard Knyaz Aleksandr Dondukov** (Княз Александър Дондуков), and **bulevard Vasil Levski** (Васил Левски) surround most administrative and tourist sights. **Ploshtad Sveta Nedelya** (пл. Света Неделя), the center of Sofia, is recognizable by St. Nedelya Church, the Sheraton Hotel, and Tsentralen Universalen Magazin (TSUM). South from pl. Sveta Nedelya runs the pedestrian **bulevard Vitosha** (Витоша). To the north, **bulevard Knyaginya Maria Luiza** (Княгиня Мария Луиза) connects to the central **train station,** (Централна Гара; *tsentralna gara*). **Bulevard Vitosha** (Витоша) is one of the main shopping and nightlife thoroughfares, linking pl. Sveta Nedelya to the huge concrete landmark **Natsionalen Dvorets Kultura** (**NDK;** Национален Дворец Култура; National Palace of Culture). Young people meet at **Popa,** the irreverent nickname of **Patriarch Evtimii's monument,** where Patriarh Evtimii meets Vasil Levski and **Graf Ignatiev** (Граф Игнатиев). Pick up the *Sofia City Guide* (free at the airport, hotels, and travel agencies) and the *Sofia Guide* (1000lv at Balkan Tour) for sight guides and phone numbers.

Telephone Code: 02.

Flights: Airport Sofia (tel. 72 06 72, domestic flights info tel. 72 24 14, international flights tel. 79 32 22 11). To get to the city center, take bus 84 (250lv). The bus stop is on the left from international arrivals; ask for *tsentur* (център). Some airlines offer youth fares. **Balkan Airlines,** pl. Narodno Subranie 12 (reservations and information tel. 981 51 70), flies to Athens, Istanbul, London, Moscow, Prague, and Warsaw. Open M-F 8am-7pm, Sa 8am-2pm. **Lufthansa,** Suborna 9 (tel. 980 41 41; fax 981 29 11). Open M-F 9am-5:30pm.

Trains: Sofia's central **train station** is north of the center on Knyaginya Maria Luiza. Trams 1 and 7 travel to pl. Sv. Nedelya; trams 9 and 12 head down Hristo Botev. Buses 85, 213, 305, and 313 get you there from different points in town. Tickets for northern Bulgaria are sold on the ground floor, while tickets for southern Bulgaria and international destinations are in the basement. Or pick up domestic and international tickets at the all-purpose **ticket office** (domestic tickets tel. 843 42 80, international tel. 843 53 80), down the stairs in front of the main entry of NDK. Trains run to Athens (56,000lv), Budapest (74,000lv), Istanbul (36,200lv), and Thessaloniki (24,000lv). Open M-F 7am-3pm, Sa 7am-2pm.

Buses: The bus station at **Ovcha Kupel** (Овча Купел), along Tsar Boris III bul. (Цар Борис III), serves domestic and international travelers. The station can be reached by tram 5 from the Natsionalen Prirodonauchen Muzey near Sv. Nedelya or tram 4 from the train station. For info and tickets, try the office under the NDK (tel. 65 01 42 or 65 02 42). Private **international and domestic** buses leave from the parking lot across from the central train station. Get tickets at the Billetni Tsentur (Биллетни Център) kiosks, or check on the buses themselves. Pay in leva, US$, or DM. **Matpu** (Матпу), ul. Damyan Gruev 23 (Дамян Груев; tel. 52 50 04 or 51 92 01), services Balkan connections and Athens (US$37, students US$30), Belgrade (32,000lv), Istanbul (US$25), Skopje (50,000lv), and Tirana (US$26). Pay in leva.

Public Transportation: The system of trams and buses is extremely cheap (250lv per ride, day-pass 1000lv). Buy tickets at kiosks marked with yellow and brown signs saying "билети" (*bileti;* tickets) or from the driver. Operating hours are officially 5am-1am, but most lines don't run later than 11pm or earlier than 6am.

Hitchhiking: It is said that hitching in the Sofia area is becoming increasingly dangerous, and drivers rarely stop.

Tourist Office: BalkanTour Ltd., Stamboliiski 27/37 (tel. 88 06 55; fax 88 07 95 or 83 20 88), 3 blocks from pl. Sveta Nedelya. Books rooms (US$16-30), exchanges currency and traveler's checks, and sells current maps. Arranges bus travel to Budapest, Istanbul, Prague, and other cities. Open daily 8am-7pm.

Budget Travel: ORBITA Travel, Hristo Botev 48 (tel. 80 15 06 or 80 01 02; fax 988 58 14). From pl. Sveta Nedelya, walk up Stamboliiski, and take a left. Finds rooms. Issues and renews ISICs. Open M-F 8am-7pm.

Embassies: Citizens of **Australia, Canada,** and **New Zealand** should contact the British embassy. South African citizens should contact the embassy in Greece. **U.K.,** Vasil Levski 38 (tel. 980 12 20 or 980 12 21), 3 blocks northwest of the Palace of Culture (NDK). Open M-Th 8:30am-12:30pm and 1:30-5pm, F 8:30am-1pm. Consular and visa services open M-F 9am-noon and M-Th 2-4pm. **U.S.,** ul. Suborna 1a (Съборна; tel. 980 52 41), 3 blocks from pl. Sveta Nedelya behind the Sheraton. Americans are advised to register with the **Consular section,** Kapitan Andreev 1 (Капитан Андреев; tel. 963 00 89), behind Economic Tehnikum. Open M-F 8:30am-5pm.

Currency Exchange: A large concentration of exchange bureaus lies along bul. Vitosha, Stamboliiski, and Graf Ignatiev. **Bulbank** (Булбанк), pl. Sv. Nedelya 7 (tel. 84 91), across from the Sheraton, cashes traveler's checks (US$1 per transaction). Open M-F 8:30am-12:30pm and 1-4:30pm. **ATMs** accepting Cirrus, EC, and MC are located at Bulbank and at **Purva Investitsionna Banka** (Първа Инвестиционна Банка), Stefan Karadzha 51 (Стефан Караджа), next to the telephone office.

Luggage Storage: Downstairs at the central train station. Look for "гардероб" (*garderob)* signs. 500lv per piece. Open 5:30am-midnight.

Laundromats: None really. Hosts of private rooms may do it for a minimal charge, but sinks work too. A good dry cleaner is **Svezhest** (Свежест), Solunska 19 (Солунска). Open M-Sa 7:30am-6:30pm.

Pharmacies: Purva Chastna Apteka (Първа Частна Аптека), Tsar Asen 43 (Цар Асен). Open *dyenonoshte* (деноноще; 24hr.). **Megapharma,** Vitosha 69 (tel. 980 53 99), across from the NDK. Open daily 8am-11pm.

Medical Assistance: State-owned hospitals offer foreigners emergency aid free of charge. **Pirogov emergency hospital,** Gen. Totleben bul. 21 (Ген. Тотлебен; tel. 515 31), across from Hotel Rodina. Open 24hr. Dr. Anton Filchev is an English-speaking **dentist** (tel. 66 29 84). Embassies have more info about medical care.

Emergencies: Ambulance, tel. 150. **Police,** tel. 166.

Post Office: General Gurko 2 (Гурко). Walk down Suborna behind pl. Sv. Nedelya, turn right on Knyaz Batenberg, then left on Gurko. Open for *Poste Restante* (60lv) M-F 8am-8pm. Many hotels also provide postal services. **Postal Code:** 1000.

Internet Access: ICN (tel. 916 62 213), on the lower floor of NDK. 5000lv per hr. Open daily 9am-7pm. Also in the **Business Center** in the basement of the Sheraton. US$6 per hr. Open M-Th 7:30am-8pm, Sa 8am-2pm.

Telephones: ul. Stefan Karadzhna 6, near the post office. Use 10lv coins. Open 24hr.

ACCOMMODATIONS AND CAMPING

Hotels are rarely worth their price, but private rooms are better. Check with ORBITA (see above). If you do choose a hotel, avoid the expensive, sometimes unpleasant hotels in central Sofia. Many choose the suburb **Dragalevtsi** (Драгалевци), which offers many private, clean, and cheap hotels. Take tram 9 or 12 to the last stop, then bus 64; get off after 5 stops in the main square. **Hotel Orhideya** (Орхидея), Angel Bukoreshtliev 9 (Ангел Букорещлиев; tel. 67 27 39), and **Hotel Darling** (Дарлинг), Yabulkova Gradina 14 (tel. 67 19 86), next door, are good bets.

Hotel Baldjieva (Балдиева), Tsar Asen 23 (Цар Асен; tel. 87 29 14 or 87 37 84). Walking from pl. Sv. Nedelya to the NDK, Tsar Asen is on the right, parallel to Vitosha (Витоша). Light and airy rooms with direct-dial phones. US$40 for one person, US$50 for two; apartment US$70. Breakfast included. Pay in dollars or leva.

Hotel Niky, Neofit Rilski 16 (Неофит Рилски; tel. 51 19 15 or 951 51 04), off Vitosha (Витоша). Wood-paneled rooms have private showers and satellite TV. Shared toilets. Singles US$22; doubles US$40. Pay in DM, dollars, or leva.

Hotel Tsar Asen (Цар Асен), Tsar Asen 68 (tel. 54 78 01 or 70 59 20). Walking toward the NDK on Tsar Asen, cross Patr. Evtimii and continue 40m. Ring doorbell at the gate. Cable TV and private shower. Singles US$28; doubles US$34.

Orbita Hotel, James Baucher bul. 76 (Джеймс Баучер; tel. 639 39), on the hill. Take tram 9 south past NDK to Anton Ivanov. A 2-star behemoth. Clean, plain rooms have private baths and fridges. Singles US$35; doubles US$46. Orbita Travel arranges rooms here for students at discounted rates (see **Budget Travel,** p. 190).

FOOD

From fast food to Bulgarian specialties, inexpensive meals are easy to find. Supermarket **Zornitsa** (Зорница), Denkogli 34 (Денкогли), off Vitosha, is well-stocked (open M-Sa 8am-8pm). All-night markets lie along Vitosha. An **open market,** known as the women's market (женски пазар, *zhenski pazar*), extends for several blocks. Take Knyaginya Maria Luiza from pl. Sveta Nedelya and make a left on Ekzarh Yosif (Екзарх Иосиф); bring a bag for fresh fruit and vegetables (open daily).

Kushtata (Къщата; House), Verila 4 (Верила), off Vitosha near the NDK. The menu offers a wide range of "dishes with character," including *spaghetti mafiosa* (спагети мафиоса; meat, tomato sauce, zucchini; 5490lv). Main dishes 5000-9000lv, salads 1700-3000lv, soups 950-1500lv. English menu. Open daily noon-midnight.

Eddy's Tex-Mex Diner, Vitosha 4. Break through the saloon doors into one of Sofia's hippest eateries. Buffalo wings (3500lv) and fajitas (7000lv). English menu. Open 12:30pm until the last customer leaves. Live music nightly from 9:30pm.

Chinese Restaurant Chen, Rakovski 86, across from the Opera house. Main dishes 2500-6000lv, vegetarian 1500-8000lv, seafood 5000-20,000lv, spring rolls 2500lv. All in a cheery atmosphere. Chinese/English/Bulgarian menu. English spoken. Open daily noon-11pm.

Korona (Корона; the Crown), Rakovski 163A. Go up Rakovski from pl. Slaveikov. Vegetarians may like *grutski sumichki* (stuffed vine leaves, 1500lv) or "cheeses on grill Bella" (4000lv). Main dishes 5000-8000lv. A/C. English menu and English spoken. Open daily 11:30am-10:30pm.

SIGHTS AND ENTERTAINMENT

Sofia's two most venerable churches, the late Roman **Sveta Georgi** (Св. Георги; St. George's Rotunda) and the early Byzantine **Sveta Sofia**, date from the 4th and 6th centuries, respectively. St. George's hides in the courtyard of the Sheraton Hotel, accompanied by a complex of ruins that used to be an ancient canal system. St. Sofia, the city's namesake since the 14th century, has Byzantine floor mosaics. Across the square from St. Sofia looms the gold-domed **Sveta Aleksandr Nevsky** (Св. Александър Невски), erected between 1904-1912 in memory of the 200,000 Russians who died in the 1877-78 Russo-Turkish War. The **crypt** houses a spectacular array of painted icons and religious artifacts. (Cathedral open daily 9:30am-7pm. 1500lv. English tour 4500lv. Crypt open W-M 10:30am-12:30pm and 2-6:30pm.) In an underpass between pl. Sveta Nedelya and Tsentralen Universalen Magazin, the tiny 14th-century **Tsurkva Hram Sveta Petya Samardzhiiska** (Църква Храм Св. Петя Самарджийска; Church of St. Petya Samardzhiiska) has fascinating, layered frescoes (open M-Sa 8am-6pm, Su 8am-3pm; 5000lv).

Along the way to the central train station from pl. Sveta Nedelya sits the 16th-century **Banya Bashi Mosque** (Баня Баши; open daily 8am-10pm; no shorts, remove shoes at door, women need head covering). Across the street, the **Tsentralen Sinagog** (Централен Синагог), Ekzarh Yosif 16, is one of Europe's largest synagogues. Down Tsar Osvoboditel from pl. Sv. Nedelya, the beautiful 1913 **Sv. Nikolai** (Св. Николай) has five onion domes and was built in accordance with Russian architectural and decorative styles (open Th-Su 9am-10pm). A few interesting museums complement the city's architectural monuments. The **Natsionalen Istoricheski Muzey** (Национален Исторически Музей; National History Museum), Vitosha 2, has everything from Thracian treasures to medieval war exhibits. (Open May-Sept. M-F 9:30am-7:15pm; Oct.-Apr. M-F 9:30am-4:30pm. 5000lv, students 2500lv.) Traditional Bulgaria is preserved at the **Natsionalen Etnograficheski Muzey** (Национален Етнографически; Ethnographic Museum) in the Royal Palace building (open W-Su 10:30am-6pm; 2500lv, students 1200lv). The **Natsionalna Hudozhestvena Galeriya** (Национална Художествена Галериа; Museum of Fine Arts), with a permanent exhibit of Bulgarian masterpieces, is also located in the Royal Palace (open Tu-Su 10am-5pm; 3000lv, students free). The **Suyuz na Bulgarskite Hudozhnitsi** (Съюз на Българските Художници; Bulgarian Artists' Union) has a four-floor gallery on Shipka, behind the University (open M-Sa 10am-6pm; free).

Rakovski is Bulgaria's Broadway, with half a dozen theaters along a half-mile stretch. The **National Opera House**, Rakovski 59 (main entrance at Vrabcha 1; Врабча; tel. 87 13 66), has tickets at the box office to the right of the main entrance (1000-15,000lv; open M and Sa 9am-6pm, Tu-F 8:30am-7:30pm). The **Natsionalen Dvorets Kultura** (Национален Дворец Култура; National Palace of Culture, NDK), at the end of Vitosha, contains restaurants, theaters, and the country's best cinema; subtitled American movies run 2000lv. The nightlife in Sofia gets wilder every year. Before you pick any fights, remember that the mafia runs the show in these parts. Smartly dressed Sofians fill the cafes and outdoor bars around **bulevard Vitosha** and the **park** outside the NDK. **Frankie's Jazz Club/Piano Bar**, Kurnigradska 15 (Кърниградска), off Vitosha across from the American Center, hosts some of Bulgaria's best jazz musicians (cover from 500lv; no music in summer; open 10am-2am). Another popular option for live music, food, and liquor is **Mr. Punch**, 20 Stefan Karadzha, a club made up of several bars, a restaurant, and a theater (open daily noon-3pm and 6pm-late). Regulars head to **Yalta** (Ялта), one of Sofia's most venerable discos on the corner of Tsar Osvoboditel and Vasil Levski (cover 1000lv). The exceedingly exclusive **Spartakus** (Спартакус), under the Grand Hotel Sofia by pl. Narodno Subranie (Народно Събрание), serves gay and straight clientele.

■ Near Sofia: Rila Monastery

Rilski Manastir (Рилски Манастир), 120km south of Sofia, is the largest and most famous monastery in Bulgaria. (Open daily 6am to around 4:30pm; services 6:30am and 4:30pm. 4000lv, students 2000lv; English tours 10,000lv.) Built by Holy Ivan of Rila in the 10th century, the monastery maintained the arts of icon painting and manuscript copying through Byzantine and Ottoman occupations. The 1200 frescoes on the central **chapel** and surrounding walls form an outdoor gallery. The monastery also houses **museums** with religious objects, coins, weapons, and jewelry. Maps and suggested routes for excellent **hiking** in the nearby hills are posted outside the monastery. Trails are marked by colored lines on a white background.

The quickest way to get to Rila town is to take a **bus** from Sofia's Novotel Europa to Blagoevgrad (2hr., 8-10 per day, 1200lv), then from Blagoevgrad to Rila town (50min., 6 per day, 600lv), and then catch the bus up to the monastery (45min., 2 per day, 500lv). To stay the night, inquire in room 170 (tel. (099 7054) 22 08) or ask any monk for a heated **monastery cell** (27,000lv per person; reception 9am-noon and 2-4pm, after 6pm try Room 74). The three-star **Hotel Rilets** (Рилец; tel. (099 7054) 21 06), a 20-minute walk out the back entrance from the monastery (follow the signs), has fairly clean singles with bath for US$16 and doubles for US$32. **Restaurant Rila**, by the monastery, serves *kavarma*, monk-style (каварма по манастирски; 4500lv; open daily 7:30am-11:30pm). The **monastery bakery** sells delicious fried dough (open daily 7am-6:30pm).

■ Melnik (Мелник)

Tiny Melnik sits in a deep sandstone gorge, locked in time, with exquisitely preserved National Revival houses and an emphasis on traditional culture and ways of life. **Kordopulova Kushta** (Кордопулова Къща; Kordopulova's House), the biggest National Revival house in Bulgaria, with a comparably sized wine cellar, was built in 1754. To get there, take the right fork of the town's road and look for the biggest house on the hillside to your left (open daily dawn-dusk; 1000lv). Mitko Manolev's **Izba za Degustatsiya na Vino** (Изба за Дегустация на Вино; wine tasting cellar; tel. (0997437) 399) is a 200-year-old establishment offering the freshness of its naturally air-conditioned caverns and some of the best Melnik wine (glass 600lv, bottle 3000lv; open daily 8am-9pm). To visit, turn left at the fork and climb the hillside on the right through the ruins of the 10th-century **Bolyarska Kushta** (Болярска Къща; Bolyar's House). More ruins dot the hills overlooking the town.

Buses arrive here via Sandanski from Sofia-Sandanski (2½hr., 1 per day, 3000lv), Sandanski-Melnik (40 min., 4 per day, 800lv), and Blagoevgrad (1hr., 1 per day, 800lv). Although there is no tourist office, **maps** are sold at hotels and restaurants (1000lv). **Private rooms** cost US$5 to 7: there are signs advertising "rooms to sleep" or "rooms" on houses and restaurants all over town. **Hotel-Vinarna MNO** (МНО; tel. 249), with a sign reading "Ресторан/Винарна" in front, is on the left, 50m past the post office (15,000lv or US$10 per person). The **Mencheva Kushta** (Менчева Къща) serves up a host of traditional Bulgarian dishes (2500-8500lv), salads and vegetarian dishes (800-2500lv), and local beers and wines (600-7000lv). The owner also rents doubles (shared bath; 10,000lv per person).

■ Plovdiv (Пловдив)

While Plovdiv is second in size to Sofia, it is widely hailed as the cultural capital of Bulgaria. Pass quickly by Soviet-style apartment blocks and stroll into the convoluted **Stari Grad** (Стари Град; Old Town), where National Revival houses protrude over the cobblestones below, windows stare into alleys at impossible angles, and churches and mosques hide in secluded corners.

SIGHTS AND ENTERTAINMENT Most of Plovdiv's historical and cultural treasures are concentrated among Stari Grad's three hills (the **Trimontium**). The area's most ancient treasure is the 2nd-century Roman marble **Antichen Teatr** (Античен Театр; amphitheater). Take a right off Knyaz Aleksander (Княз Алецандър) to Stanislav Dospevski (Станислав Доспевски) and walk ahead. In the middle of pl. Dzhumaya

BULGARIA

(Джумая) lies the **Philipoplis Stadium;** see if you can spot the ancient stones beneath the more recent trash. The mosque that gave its name to pl. Dzhumaya is the **Dzhumaya Dzhamiya** (Джамия), whose colorful minaret peeks between other buildings. Head past the Dzhumaya Dzhamiya up Suborna to the **Durzhavna Hudozhestvena Galeria** (Държавна Художествена Галерия; State Art Gallery) to gain insight into 20th-century Bulgaria through the eyes of master artists, many of them Plovdiv natives (open Tu-Su 9-11am and 1-5pm; 1000lv, students 100lv). At the end of Suborna (Съборна), the **Etnografski Muzei** (Етнографски Музей; Museum of Ethnography) displays ancient Bulgarian crafts including an interesting exhibit on the production of precious rose oil (open Tu-Su 9am-noon and 1-5pm; 3000lv). On a cool evening, head to the fountainside cafe in the **Tsentralni Park** (Централни Парк), near pl. Tsentralen (пл. Централен), illuminated by multicolored strobes. One of the many **movie theaters** on Knyaz Aleksander is bound to be showing a film in English.

PRACTICAL INFO, ACCOMMODATIONS, AND FOOD **Trains** arrive from Sofia (2½hr., every hr., 2900lv) on their way to Burgas; **buses** arrive from and leave for Sofia at Yug (Юг) station on the north side of Hristo Botev (Христо Ботев; 1hr., every hour, 4000lv). English-speaking **Puldin Tours** (Пълдин), bul. Bulgaria 106 (България; tel. (032) 55 38 48), offers maps in English (but usually with Communist-era street names), finds rooms (US$13-20), and changes money. From the train station, ride trolley 2 or 102 (150lv) nine stops to bul. Bulgaria and backtrack a block (open M-F 9am-5:30pm; until 9pm during fairs). **Prima Vista Agency** (Прима Виста), Ivan Vazov 74 (Иван Вазов; tel. (032) 27 27 78; fax 27 20 54), finds private lodgings for visitors (open daily 10am-6pm). Located in a National Revival building listed among Plovdiv's monuments, **Hostel Touristicheski Dom** (Туристически Дом; tel. (032) 63 32 11), P.R. Slaveykov 5 (П.Р. Славейков) in the Old Town, has spacious, attractive dorms with sinks. From Knyaz Aleksander, take Patriarch Evtimii (Патриарх Евтимий), passing under Tsar Boris, into town and hang a left on Slaveykov (18,000lv per person; lockout midnight). From pl. Tsentralen, walk across Tsar Boris to reach **Hotel Feniks** (Феникс), Kapitan Raicho 79, 3rd fl. (Капитан Райчо; tel. (032) 22 47 29), which has laundry, shared bathrooms, and unintentionally antique furniture (singles US$15; doubles US$20). **Kambanata** (Камбаната), Suborna 2B (tel. (032) 26 06 65), has a large number of traditional vegetarian dishes, but the chef's specialty is *Kambanata,* a concoction of filet of pork or veal, cream, mushrooms, smoked cheese and spaghetti (US$2-5; open daily 10:30am-midnight). **Alafrangite** (Алафрангите), Kiril Nektariev 17 (Кирил Нектариев; tel. 26 95 95), cooks up classic Bulgarian dishes (3000-9000lv; English menu; open daily 11:30am-midnight).

■ Near Plovdiv: Bachkovo Monastery

About 28km south of Plovdiv lies the 11th-century Bachkovski Manastir (Бачковски Манастир), the second largest in the country. The monastery's treasure is the miracle-working icon of the Virgin Mary and Child, kept in the **Holy Trinity Church** (open daily 7am-dark). To get to Bachkovo, take a **train** from Plovdiv to Asenovgrad (25min., every 30min., 500lv), then catch a **bus** to the monastery (10min., 300lv). Inquire about the spartan **accommodations** at the administrative office on the monastery's second floor (tel. (03327) 277; dorms 2000lv). The monks allow visitors to pitch tents on the lawn for free.

■ Valley of Roses

Stretching across central Bulgaria along the rail line east from Sofia, the famed Valley of Roses preserves much of the architecture and heritage of the 19th-century National Revival. Unsurprisingly, the smell of roses wafts through the area.

Koprivshtitsa The seemingly sleepy little wood and stone houses of **Koprivshtitsa** (Копривщица) conceal its revolutionary roots. Todor Kableshkov's 1876 "letter of blood" announcing the uprising against Ottoman rule was drafted here; the Turks' brutal oppression led to the Russo-Turkish War of 1877-78 and, eventually, Bulgarian independence. Many homes of the uprising leaders are now museums (Къщата-музей): the 1845 house of **Todor Kableshkov** (Тодор Каблешков) has ingeniously carved ceilings and an impressive facade (open Tu-Su 8am-noon and 1:30-5:30pm). The house of **Georgi Benkovski** (Георги Бенковски) pays tribute to the leader of the "Flying Troop" of horsemen (closed Tu). The birthplace of **Dimcho Debelyanov** (Димчо Дебелянов) showcases one of Bulgaria's best lyric poets (closed M). A 1500lv ticket grants entry to all museum houses. The 1817 **Uspenie Bogorodichno** (Успение Богородично; Assumption Church) is said to have been built in 11 days.

Trains from Sofia (2½hr., 1500lv) stop 10km from Koprivshtitsa. Get off at the stop after Anton, or, on a *burz* (бърз; fast) train, the one after Pirdop. An idling bus awaits to take you into town (10min., 500lv), but it drives off quickly, so hurry. Get off at the Koprivshtitsa **bus station** (a dark wooden building), which posts the bus and train schedules. To reach the main square, backtrack along the river. **Hotel Byalo Konche** (Бялото Конче; tel. (07184) 22 50), up the steep street from the main square, has five doubles, with shared shower and toilet, in a classic Koprivshtitsa house (US$8 per person, breakfast included). **Hotel Dalmatinets** (Далматинец), Georgi Benkovski 62 (Георги Бенковски; tel. (07184) 29 04), is near the end of town, upstream from the Biohim Bank. Five sparkling doubles with private showers and 24-hour hot water go for US$10 (with breakfast US$12). Arrange **private rooms** through the English-speaking owner of the Mlechkov (Млечков) souvenir shop (tel. (07184) 21 64) in the main square (US$10 per person; open daily 10am-6pm). **Byaloto Konche** has a separate tavern offering splendid full meals for around 4200lv (open daily 8am-late). The **food market** by the stream, past the buses and post office, stocks essentials.

Kazanluk

The town of **Kazanluk** (Казанлък)—despite the typical concrete-block skyline—has long been the center of Bulgaria's rose-growing world. During the Rose Festival in the first week of June, the town drowns in a sweet scent which lovingly envelops the song-and-dance troupes, comedians, and soccer stars. Half an hour away from pl. Sevtopolis (Севтополис) awaits the **Muzey na Rozata** (Музей на Розата; Rose Museum), which illustrates the history of rose oil production. Next door are **gardens** with over 250 rose varieties (museum open Mar. 15-Oct. 15 daily 9am-5pm; US$1, students US$0.50). To reach the museum from the square, take Gen. Skobelev (Скобелев), go right at the fork, and continue on bul. Osvobozhdenie (Освобождение) towards Gabrovo; buses 5 and 6 run irregularly across from Hotel Kazanluk (150lv). Kazanluk's **Trakiiska Grobnitsa** (Тракийска Гробница; Thracian Tomb) is a 10-minute walk from pl. Sevtopolis. The resting place of the original tomb dates from the turn of the 3rd century BC. The inside has been recreated 20m away (open Mar.-Oct. daily 8am-noon and 1:30-6pm; 2000lv, students 1000lv). As you walk back down the stairs out of the park, take the first left onto General Radetski (Генерал Подецки) and the first right onto the cobblestone Knyaz Mirski (Княз Мирски), which leads into the heart of **Koulata** (Кулата), the oldest part of Kazanluk, which preserves the architecture and traditions of the National Revival.

More Precious than Gold

More expensive by weight than gold and used in luxurious perfumes, over 70% of the world's rose oil is produced in Bulgaria. Workers in the famed Valley of Roses fields pick rose petals, one by one, in late May and early June. A single gram of "attar of roses" (rose oil) requires 2000 petals picked before sunrise. The first roses were grown here by Thracians, and modern rose cultivation began in the 17th century under the Ottomans. Apart from perfume and rose water, Bulgarian rose petals have been used in medicine, jam, tea, vodka, sweet liquor, and syrup. Rose-picking season ends with the annual **rose festival** (Прозник на Розата), held during the first June weekend in Karlovo and Kazanluk.

BULGARIA

Trains arrive often from Burgas (3hr., 1960lv), Karlovo (1½hr., 4100lv), and Sofia (3hr., 1960lv); **buses** make the trip from Plovdiv's Sever station (2500lv). From the train station, bul. Rozova Dolina (Розова Долина) leads to pl. Sevtopolis. Off the square at 23 Pehoten Shipchenski Polk 16 (23ти Пехотен Шипченски Полк), the **Bookstore Tezi** (Тези) sells English maps of town. The best deal in Kazanluk is **Hotel Arsenal** (Арсенал; tel. (0431) 205 83). Head away from pl. Sevtapolis on the small road behind Hotel Kazanluk, take a left onto Iskra (Искра), continue past the museum on the right, and take Oreshaka (Орешака) around to the right. Hotel Arsenal is 10 minutes past Hotel Vesta, inside the yellow and white sports complex on the left. Take a taxi if it's dark. Large rooms include bath and fridge (15,000lv per person; doubles 20,000lv; triples 24,000lv). For a peaceful, if pricey, setting, try **Hotel Vesta** (Веста; tel. 477 40), Chavdar Voivoda 3 (Чавдар Войвода), before Hotel Arsenal on Iskra, the hotel is in a parking lot behind the cultural center (singles US$50; doubles US$60; breakfast included). Part of a new tourist complex, **Campground Krunsko Hanche** (Крънско Ханче; tel. (0431) 242 39 or 270 91), 3km from the city (take a bus to Gabrovo or city bus 6; ask the driver to stop), charges US$3 per person and US$15 per tent. For budget dining, search out **Starata Kushta** (Старата Къща), Dr. Baev 2. From pl. Sevtapolis, take a left on Gen. M. Skobelev, then right on Gen. Gurko (Гурко); Dr. Baev (Др. Баев) is the first right (open 24hr.).

Etura Etura (Етъра) is a worthwhile two-hour stopover en route from Kazanluk (40min., 7 buses each way per day) to Veliko Turnovo. Buses stop in **Gabrovo**. Once there, take trolley 32 or bus 1 to the end-stop at "Bolshevik" (15min., 150lv), then ride bus 7 or 8 and ask to be dropped off at Etura (5min., 150lv). The town's attraction is a little **outdoor museum** (complex open daily May-Sept. 8:30am-5:30pm; off-season 8am-4pm; 4500lv, students 2300lv) with National Revival style buildings, workshops, and mills. Climb through tiny doors and narrow staircases into artisan shops that look as they did a hundred years ago. Visit the candy store for sticky sesame and honey bars (300lv), or the bakery for sweet breads and pastries.

■ Veliko Turnovo (Велико Търново)

Perched high above the Yantra River, Veliko Turnovo has been watching over Bulgaria for 5000 years. The city's residents led the national uprising against Byzantine rule in 1185, and the fortress walls and battle towers have stood since Veliko Turnovo was the capital of Bulgaria's Second Kingdom. Bulgaria's biggest treasure trove of ruins also has a relaxed atmosphere beyond the narrow streets of the Old Town.

The remains of the **Tsarevets** (Царевец), a fortress which once housed a cathedral and the royal palace, stretch across an overgrown hilltop overlooking the city (open daily in summer 8am-7pm; off-season 8am-5pm; 3500lv, students 2000lv). At the top of the hill stands **Tsurkva Vuzneseniegospodne** (Църква Възнесениегосподне; Church of the Ascension), restored in 1981 on the 1300th anniversary of the Bulgarian state. Near the fortress off ul. Ivan Vazov (Иван Вазов), the **Muzey Vtoroto Bulgarsko Tsarstvo** (Музей Второто Българско Царство; Museum of the Second Bulgarian Kingdom) traces the region's history with Thracian pottery, a collection of medieval crafts, and copies of religious frescoes (open Tu-Su 8am-noon and 1-6pm; 3500lv, students 2000lv). Next door, the **Muzey na Vuzrazhdaneto** (Музей на Възраждането; National Revival) documents Bulgaria's 19th-century cultural and religious resurgence (open W-M 8am-noon and 1-6pm; 3500lv, students 2000lv).

Veliko Turnovo sends frequent **trains** to Burgas (5100lv), Pleven (1½hr., 2200lv), Ruse (2200lv), Sofia (5800lv), and Varna (3½hr., 5100lv). Almost any city bus from the station goes to the town center (200lv), but ask *"za tsentur?"* to be sure. There is no official tourist office, but **Kingi** (Кинги), a bookstore at Rakovski 15, has good maps (2000lv; open daily 10am-6:30pm). Fortunately, you shouldn't need a lot of help finding a room. **Hotel Trapezitsa (HI)** (Хотел Трапезица), Stefan Stambolov 79 (tel. (062) 220 61), is an excellent youth hostel with clean rooms, some with views of the river. From the post office, walk straight, and turn right with the street (doubles

13,300lv; nonmembers 19,000lv). **Hotel Comfort** (Панайот Типографов), Panayot Tipografov 5 (tel. (062) 287 28), has tidy rooms and beautiful bathrooms. From Stambolov, walk left of Rakovski (Раковски), turn left on the small square, and search for the street sign (25,000lv per person). A large outdoor **market** sells fresh produce daily from dawn to dusk at the corner of Bulgaria (България) and Nikola Gabrovski (Никола Габровски). Several taverns occupy the balconies of old houses overlooking the river.

■ Ruse (Русе)

For centuries, foreigners drifted down the Danube to Ruse, bringing art, music, and architecture. Recently, the war in the former Yugoslavia has weakened Ruse's links to the west, and today most of the city's museums are closed, but the city center remains one of the liveliest and most beautiful in all of Bulgaria. **Pl. Svoboda** (Свобода), in the city center, is marked by elegant and colorful Baroque, Renaissance, and Art Deco architecture. On the right side lies another square, **pl. Sv. Troitsa** (Св. Троица), on which stand the **Opera House** and **Sveta Troitsa** (Holy Trinity Church), erected in 1632 during the Ottoman occupation (church open daily 6:30am-7pm). **Sveti Pavel** (Свети Павел; St. Paul's), one of the few Catholic churches in Bulgaria, is on a small street off Knyazheska (Княжеска). In the evening, come for a stroll in the popular **Mladezhki Park** (Младежки Парк) on the east side of the city, complete with a swimming pool. At night, try one of the **movie theaters** on Aleksandrovska (Александровска) or the **discos** in the Riga and Dunav Hotels.

Trains run to Bucharest (6hr., 9700lv), Sofia (7hr., 6500lv), and Varna (4hr., 4400lv). Ruse is accessible by **bus** from Pleven (2hr., 2600lv) and Varna (3½hr., 4000lv); **Group Travel,** pl. Svoboda (tel. (082) 82 29 49), at the Dunav Hotel, sends buses to Sofia (5hr., 8300lv). **Dunav Tours** (Дунав Турс), pl. Han Kubrat (Хан Кубрат; tel. (082) 22 30 88 or 22 52 50), arranges private rooms (singles US$10.50; doubles US$16) and provides maps and brochures; from pl. Svoboda, take Aleksandrovska in the direction indicated by the statue's left hand. Securing a private room through Dunav Tours is the best bet for accommodations. **Hostel Prista** (Хижа Приста; tel. (082) 23 41 67), is in Prista Park, 8km west of the city center by the Danube. Buses 6 and 16 run here from the center at extremely unpredictable intervals (10min., 200lv). Get off at the stop after the campground, backtrack about 30m, follow the side road to the restaurant, and take a right. Then take the first left (10,000lv per person includes cold shower and private bath; lockout 11:30pm). Food in Ruse centers around Aleksandrovska, with the **Hali** (Хали) supermarket at the intersection with Tsar Osvoboditel (Цар Освободител; open M-Sa 7am-8pm, Su 8am-2pm). **Leventa** (Левента; tel. (082) 282 90), underneath the tallest TV tower in the Balkans (take bus 17), serves main courses (2500-5000lv) and vegetarian dishes (1200-2800lv; open daily 11:30am-midnight).

BLACK SEA COAST

The Black Sea, the most popular destination in Bulgaria for foreign and native vacationers alike, bundles centuries-old, thumbnail-sized fishing villages with clear, secluded bays, energetic seaside towns, and some ugly Soviet resorts. In between, you find warm, sandy beaches in the south and rockier shores with white cliffs to the north. You're bound to run into more English-speakers than in any other region of Bulgaria, along with higher, though still reasonable prices.

■ Varna (Варна)

Bulgaria's sea capital is still a commercial and transport hub that attracts a growing summer population with extensive beaches hidden behind sprawling seaside gardens on its fringes. Long experience as a tourist hub has taught the city countless ways to squeeze out a traveler's last cent. The beautiful, sandy, family-dominated **beaches** can be reached through the seaside gardens. The well-preserved **Rimski Termi** (Римски Терми; Roman Baths) stand on San Stefano in the city's old quarter—**Grutska Mahala** (Гръцка Махала; open Tu-Su 10am-5pm; 1000lv). **Nightlife** centers around bul. Slivnitsa and bul. Knyaz Boris I. The **Festivalen Complex,** with a cinema (3500lv), is a popular hangout for younger crowds.

Trains roll to Burgas (3hr., 4200lv), Plovdiv (5½-7hr., 7300lv), and Sofia (7hr., 10,000lv, *couchette* 4000lv extra). The helpful **Rila** international train bureau, Preslav 13 (tel. (052) 22 62 73 or 22 62 88), sells tickets to Athens, Budapest, and Istanbul (open M-F 8am-5:30pm, Sa 8am-3pm). **Buses** are the best means of getting to and from Burgas (3hr., 3500lv). The Varnenski Bryag (Владислав Варенчик) **tourist office,** Musala 3 (Мусала, tel. (052) 22 55 24; fax 25 30 83), between Preslav and Knyaz Boris I off pl. Nezavisimost, has transportation info and arranges private rooms for US$10 to 14 (open daily June 8am-7pm; July-Aug. 7am-8pm; Sept.-May 8am-5pm). **Solvex** (tel. 60 58 61), near track 4 at the train station, finds rooms for US$5 to 10 per person (open daily 5:30am-9:30pm). **Hotel Musala** (Мусала), Musala 3 (tel. (052) 22 39 25), next to Varnenski Bryag, has small, simple but affordable rooms, in a cool old building with a beautiful (and long) staircase inside. (Singles with sink US$14; doubles US$20; triples US$24.) Tiled bathrooms are shared.

■ Near Varna: Balchik

An overlooked jewel among the northern seaside resorts, **Balchik** (Балчик) captivates with a simple and unspoiled beauty, dotted with white houses and orange roofs carved into rocky cliffs. The **public beach** is small but clean, with showers, changing rooms, bar, volleyball, umbrellas, and paddleboat rental (3000lv per 30min.). A smaller, less-crowded beach lies 0.5km in the other direction. Above the slightly rocky shoreline lies Romanian Queen Marie's **summer palace,** where you can sit in her marble throne and explore the **garden** and the largest **cactus collection** in the Balkans (open daily 8am-8pm; entry to both 4000lv). To reach Balchik, take a **bus** or a quicker **minivan** from Varna (45min.-1hr., 1560lv), then walk down Cherno More (Черно Море) to the main square; Primorska (Приморска) runs to the shore. **Hotel Esperanza** (Хотел Есперансаа), Cherno More 16 (tel. (0579) 51 48), is a small establishment with spacious rooms (US$8-10 per person). Dozens of summer restaurants serve 3000lv meals along the beach. At night, relax at a beachside cafe or dance at **Cariba disco,** right on the beach (open 10pm-sunrise; no cover).

■ Burgas (Бургас)

Used mainly as a transport link to the south coast, Burgas is still packed with people strolling, especially through the lively, colorful center (Aleksandrovska and Bogoridi) and its seaside gardens. The **Archeological Museum,** Bogorodi 21, displays artifacts dating back to the 5th century BC. (Open daily in summer 9am-10pm; off-season M-F 9am-5pm. 2000lv, students 1600lv. Free English guidebook.)

Daily **trains** travel to Ruse (6hr., 6500lv), Sofia (7hr., 8300lv) via Plovdiv or Karlovo, and to Varna (4½hr., 4100lv). **Primorets Tourist,** pl. Garov (Гаров; tel. (056) 84 27 27), a block east of Aleksandrovska under the sign "Частни Квартири," offers private rooms (US$6; open M-F 6:30am-8pm, Sa-Su noon-5pm). **Camping Kraimorie** (Къмпинг Краймори; tel. (056) 240 25), 10km from Burgas by hourly bus 17, rents out motel rooms by wide, clean beaches (doubles US$14; bungalows US$10). **Ul. Bogoridi** and **Aleksandrovska** are full of restaurants and cafes. **Art Restaurant,** on Bogoridi, serves healthy portions of fish in the shade of a huge fig tree.

Nesebur A museum town atop the peninsula at the south end of Sunny Beach, **Nesebur** (Несебър) is a nice alternative to generic coastal resorts, but it too gets crowded during the summer. A walk through the **Stari Grad** (Old Town) is a walk through time. Stone fortress walls from the 3rd century AD stand on the north shore,

as well as a Byzantine gate from the 5th century. The 6th-century church **Starata Mitropoliya** (Старата Митрополия; Old Metropolitan) survives roofless in the center of town, and the 11th-century **Tsurkvata Sveti Stefan** (Църквата Свети Стефан; Church of St. Stephen) is covered with 16th-century frescoes. The **Archaeological Museum,** to the right of the town gate, exhibits a collection of ceramics, coins, and naval implements (open May-Oct. daily 9am-7:30pm; Nov.-Apr. M-F 9am-7pm; 2100lv, students 850lv).

Buses from Burgas (40min., every 40min., 1600lv) stop at the Old Nesebur port and gate leading to town. **Tourist Bureau Mesembria** (Менабрия; tel. (0554) 70 91), on Mesembria, has a free map (open daily 9am-8pm). The bureau arranges rooms at US$14 per person. In high season, it may be difficult to find accommodations for fewer than three nights, but families can be approached on the street to ask about rooms (US$3-5). **Mesembria Hotel,** Ribarska 2 (Рибарска; tel. (0554) 32 55), near the post office, has rooms for 60,000lv per person. **Kapitanska Sreshta** (Капитанска Среща; Captain's Meeting), on Chayka (Чайка), serves up superb seafood (open daily 9am-midnight; live music 6-11pm). Other edibles are sold at kiosks along the harbor.

Sozopol
Once the resort of choice for Bulgaria's artistic community, **Sozopol** (Созопол) still caters to a more creative set than its Black Sea neighbors—the town is quieter and less expensive than Nesebur. To reach Sozopol from Burgas, take the hourly **bus** (45min., 6am-8pm, 1200lv). From the bus station, walk to the end of the park, turn left on Republikanska (Републиканска), and walk toward the New Town. The tourist bureau **Lotos** has offices at the bus station (tel./fax (5514) 282) and at Ropotamo 1 (tel. (5514) 429), in the **Novi Grad** (New Town) main square. The clerks dole out info on campsites, organize trips, and arrange private rooms for US$7-12 per person (open daily 8am-5pm). The cheapest hotel is the **Voennensko Club** (Военненско Клуб; tel. (5514) 283), at the intersection of Republikanska and Ropotamo (singles 20,000lv; doubles 40,000lv). **Apolonia** is the site of a crafts fair and home to many **kiosks** offering fresh fish and calamari. For a delicious meal, walk to **Vyaturna Melnitsa** (Вятърна Мелница), Morski Skali 27a (Морски Скали), the street running along the peninsula tip (meals 1400-16,300lv; open daily 10am-midnight).

Ahtopol
Twenty-five kilometers from the Turkish border, **Ahtopol** (Ахтопол) is a humble town of 1400 inhabitants. Hidden rocky bays with crystal-clear water and the highest seawater temperature of all Bulgarian resorts make for a truly relaxing beach experience. The public **beach** competes with several small bays (try the one at the lighthouse). **Buses** run from Burgas (2½hr., 2 per day, 3100lv). The bus station is on the main drag, **Trakia** (Тракия). All points of interest are within 15 minutes on foot. To get to the beach from the bus station, take Levski (Левски) to the end, then follow the paved path past the "жп район пловдив" sign. **Tourist bureau CREDO-OK** (tel. (05563) 340) is at the bus station. Helpful staff gives out maps, finds **private rooms** (US$4-6 per person), and sells **bus tickets** to Sofia (7½hr., 2 per day, 15,000lv). An **exchange bureau** is on the way to the post office (open daily 9am-1pm and 4-7pm).

Private rooms are the accommodations of choice (US$3.50-6), but a few private hotels also exist. Try **Berlin,** Cherno More 22a (Черно Море; tel. (05563) 320). From Trakia, go left on Veleka (Велека) then right on Cherno More (clean doubles with shower and breakfast 50,000lv). The small town leads a surprisingly active culinary life. It is busiest along **Kraymorska** (Крайморска)—left and right off Trakia at the quay. To the right, **Restaurant Sirius** (Сириус), Kraymorska, offers cheap grills (700-1000lv) and fish (750-3000lv) amid live music and mythic Greek scenes painted on the fence (open daily 11am-midnight). Left and up the street is **Chetirimata Kapitana** (Четирмата Капитана), Kraymorska 29. Draped in fishing nets, it offers imaginatively named and prepared dishes (2200-4800lv; open daily 11am-3pm and 6pm-midnight). A couple of **discos** by the beach operate until sunrise.

BULGARIA

Croatia

Croatia (Hrvatska)

US$1	= 6.50kn (kuna)	1kn =	US$0.15
CDN$1	= 4.21kn	1kn =	CDN$0.24
UK£1	= 10.65kn	1kn =	UK£0.09
IR£1	= 9.08kn	1kn =	IR£0.11
AUS$1	= 3.77kn	1kn =	AUS$0.26
NZ$1	= 3.20kn	1kn =	NZ$0.31
SAR1	= 1.02kn	1kn =	SAR0.98
DM1	= 3.62kn	1kn =	DM0.28

Country Phone Code: 385   **International Dialing Prefix: 00**

Croatia, where the Mediterranean, the Alps, and the Pannonian plain converge, is a country of unearthly beauty. Traced with thick forests, karst, wispy plains, underground streams, and the translucent sea, it has for centuries attracted such self-proclaimed luminaries as George Bernard Shaw, who wrote of the largest archipelago in the Mediterranean that "the gods wanted to crown their creation and on the last day they turned tears, stars, and the sea breeze into the isles of Korrati." An independent state from the 9th to the 12th centuries, Croatia has been situated historically on divides—between the Frankish and Byzantine empires in the 9th century, between the Catholic and Orthodox churches beginning in the 11th century, and between Christian Europe and Islamic Turkey from the 15th to the 19th centuries. Most recently, its split from Yugoslavia led to war with Serbia and the shelling of lovely Dubrovnik. The damage now is hardly visible—although the hills are still fraught with mines—and the coast and islands are again pearls in the Adriatic, even if the prices are only slightly, shall we say, Eastern European.

For more detailed coverage of Croatia, refer to *Let's Go: Eastern Europe 1999.*

GETTING THERE AND GETTING AROUND

Citizens of Australia, Ireland, New Zealand, the U.K, and the U.S. do not need visas to enter Croatia. South African citizens require visas; send a visa application, two passport-sized photos, and a $29 check or money order to the nearest embassy and consulate (see **Government Information Offices,** p. 2). Citizens of any country staying more than 90 days should fill out an extension of stay form at a local police station.

By land or air, Zagreb is the main entry point. **Croatia Airlines** (tel. (01) 455 13 40) flies here from many cities, including Chicago, Frankfurt, London, New York, Paris, and Toronto. **Trains** travel to Zagreb from Budapest, Ljubljana, and Vienna, and continue to cities throughout Croatia. **Buses** are sometimes more convenient than trains, but are usually slow and crowded. **Ferry** service is run by **Jadrolinija.** Boats sail the Rijeka-Split-Dubrovnik route, stopping at some islands along the way. Ferries also chug from Split to Ancona, Italy, and from Dubrovnik to Bari, Italy.

ESSENTIALS

Most major cities have a tourist office *(turist biro),* which generally does not arrange accommodations. Private agencies include the two conglomerates **Kompas** and **Atlas** (associated with American Express). Croatia's monetary unit, the **kuna,** is theoretically convertible, but impossible to exchange abroad (except in Hungary and Slovenia). Most tourist offices, banks, hotels, and transportation stations offer **currency exchange** and accept traveler's checks. **ATMs** have become common on the mainland. Most banks also give Visa or MC **cash advances,** but only pricey stores, restaurants, and hotels accept plastic.

Post offices usually have **telephones** available to the public. Phones requiring **telekarta** (phone card), available at most newspaper stands and the post office, are gradually phasing out token phones. For **AT&T Direct,** dial 0 800 22 01 11; **BT Direct,** 0 800 22 00 44; **MCI World Phone,** 0 800 22 01 12. The Croats speak a southern Slavic language very similar to Serbian, but write in Latin rather than Cyrillic characters. In Zagreb and tourist offices, many know English, but the most popular coastal languages are Italian and German.

> Although Croatia is currently at peace, travel to Slavonia and Krajina is extremely dangerous due to **unexploded land mines.** Travel to the coast and islands is considered relatively safe, but check on the situation in nearby Bosnia.

The police require foreigners to register with them within 24 hours of arriving in a new city; hotels, campsites, and accommodation agencies should do this for you. Women travelers usually feel safe. Tolerance for homosexuality, while growing, is low; discretion is advisable.

Most **hotels** are expensive, and a 20 to 50% tourist surcharge will be added to your bill, but you can often avoid the surcharge by asking to pay in kuna. *Sobe* (rooms to let) can be great, but prices are increasing. Organized **campgrounds** speckle the country but are usually packed. Keep in mind that all rooms are subject to a tourist tax of 5 to 10kn, and that arriving during the weekend may cause lodging problems.

■ Zagreb

After bearing much of the weight of the war, Zagreb is embracing its new role as a modern central European capital. This mid-sized city still has a magic to it, from the towering arches of St. Stephen's cathedral to the Austro-Hungarian architecture of many of the downtown buildings. Organized **tours** of Zagreb leave from the TIC office at Trg bana J. Jelačića 11, every Wednesday at 10am. Solo strolls through old Zagreb should start around the huge statue and beautiful facades of **Trg bana Josipa Jelačića.** The **Cathedral of the Assumption of the Virgin Mary,** visible from many parts of the city, lies just around the corner (tours M-Sa 10am-5pm, Su and holy days 1-5pm). The **Mimara Museum,** Rooseveltiv trg 4, has a vast and varied collection, from ancient Egyptian artifacts to Rembrandt (call (01) 482 81 00 for hours). Today, the former clerical city of **Kapitol** and the craftsmen's province of **Gradec**—the twin seeds that grew into modern-day Zagreb—comprise the area called **Gornji Grad** (Upper Town). The medieval core remains the same, including such structures as the **Kamenita Vrata** (Stone Gate) on Radićeva, and **Crkva sv. Marka** (Church of St. Mark), with its Gothic entrance and the multi-colored tile roof. It contains works by Ivan Meštrovič, Croatia's most famous modern sculptor. Visitors tend to head straight for the **Lotrščak tower,** Strossmayerovo šetalište 9, with its splendid city panorama (open M-F 10am-6pm, Sa 10am-3pm; 10kn).

The Glavni Kolodvor **train station,** Trg kralja Tomislava 12 (tel. (01) 98 30), provides efficient service to coastal Croatia as well as Budapest (7hr., 182kn), Ljubljana (2½hr., 60kn), Venice (8hr., 227kn), and Vienna (6½hr., 304kn). The **bus station** (tel. (060) 31 33 33), on Držićeva Cesta, east of the train station, serves Frankfurt (8 per week, 529kn), Ljubljana (3hr., 63kn), Sarajevo (9hr., 218kn), and Vienna (8hr., 175kn). The main **tourist office,** Trg J. Jelačića 11 (tel. (01) 481 40 54; fax 481 40 56), in the main square's southeast corner, has free maps and will call around to find vacant rooms (open M-F 8:30am-8pm, Sa 10am-6pm, Su 10am-2pm). Rooms in Zagreb are expensive, but **Student Hotel Cvjetno,** Odranska 8 (tel. (01) 619 12 45), has converted dorm rooms available from July 15 through October (singles 214kn; doubles 280kn). **Omladinski Turistički Centar (HI),** Petrinjska 77 (tel. (01) 484 12 61 or 484 12 47), has clean but worn rooms and a great location (dorms 70kn, non-members 75kn; singles 152-205kn; doubles 200-270kn). **Melong,** Petrijnska 9, has great vegetarian budget eating in glass and oak refinement (open M-Sa 7am-11pm). The **Bulldog Pub,** Bogoviceva 6, is hip, young, and central (open daily 9am-11pm).

DALMATIAN COAST

The Dalmatian coast is the apogee of the Mediterranean. The waters of the north and central Adriatic combine and deepen to a vibrant cobalt along this south central stretch of coastline, and the cities seem untouched by war.

■ Rab

An extraordinarily beautiful town (on an island of the same name) whose white-washed stone houses and scintillating narrow streets seem to rise out of the sea, Rab will likely become one of your favorite places on earth. A stroll along the city's **Gornja ul** (Upper St.) takes you from the remains of **Crkva sv. Jvana** (St. John's Church), an outstanding Roman *bazilika,* to **Crkva sv. Justine** (St. Justine's Church), which houses a museum dedicated to Christian art (open M-Sa 9am-noon and 7:30-10pm, Su 7:30-10pm; 7kn). Sunset from the zenith of **St. Mary's Bell Tower,** built in the beginning of the 13th century, is truly stupendous (open daily 10am-1pm and 7:30-10pm; 5kn). The 12th-century **Katedrala Djevice Marije** (Virgin Mary Cathedral) and nearby 14th-century **Samostan sv. Antuna** (St. Anthony Monastery), farther down Gornja ul, complete the tour of this history-laden quarter. However, Rab's real assets are its tiny, craggy beaches, perfectly isolated from the madding crowd. These are best reached by **taxi-boats** waiting in the harbor.

Buses run to Zagreb (6hr, 108kn). The friendly, English-speaking staff at **Turistička Zejednica-Informationi Centar** (tel. 77 11 11) can help you with **ferry** schedules (ferry F 9:25pm for Split/Dubrovnik; office open 7am-10pm). **Tourist Agency Katurbo,** Palit 491 (tel./fax 724 45), one block from the bus station toward the har-

Love on the Dalmatian Coast

One of the most famous love stories of the 20th century moved to its denouement in Dalmatia more than 60 years ago. The Dalmatian holiday of the British sovereign Edward VIII and the American divorcee Wallis Simpson scandalized the worlds of politics and fashion. When Edward chose love (and the lovely Adriatic) over the crown, the attention of the British and American press-vultures turned to Dalmatia. Subsequently, stylized aspects of Dalmatian folk costume appeared on the catwalks and streets of New York. As for Edward, though forced to abdicate, he learned the popular Dalmatian game "balote," which is similar to bowling.

bor, arranges accommodation (54kn per person plus 7.60kn tourist tax). **Camping III Padova** (tel. 72 43 55; fax 72 45 39), 1km east of the bus station, is close to town (18kn per person, 14kn per tent). For eats, try the hunter's cutlet (50kn) on table-clothed picnic tables at **Gostiona Labirint,** Srednja ul 9, in an alcove off Stjepara Radića (open daily 11am-2pm and 6-11pm).

■ Poreč

More than two thousand years ago, Roman soldiers built their fortified colony Parentium in Poreč (PO-retch); today Roman churches huddle alongside Gothic and Baroque houses on the polished stone streets. On the coast near Poreč, beautiful villas built for the repose of Roman patricians (the *villae rusticae*) glint in the sun. The Old Town's main street is the historic **Dekumana,** lined with shops and restaurants. From Trg Slobode, walk past the **Peterokutna kula** (Pentagon Tower), a relic of Poreč's Venetian days; the emblematic lion remains visible today on the 15th-century Gothic tower. The **Euphrasius Basilica,** one block north of Dekumana, is the city's most important monument. The basilica has late Gothic choir stalls, a Renaissance belltower, and stunning Byzantine mosaics. The best beaches are south of the Marina, around the **Plava Laguna** (Blue Lagoon) and **Zelena Laguna** (Green Lagoon). Shed your fig leaf at nudist camp **Solaris** (tel. (052) 44 34 00) in nearby Laterna.

The **bus station,** five minutes south of the town center at Rade Končara 1 (tel. (052) 321 53), serves Laterna (10 per day), Ljubljana (4½hr., 83kn), and Zagreb (5hr., 74-105kn). The **information center,** Zagrebačka 11 (tel. (052) 45 14 58; fax 45 16 65), provides free maps and pamphlets (open daily in summer 8am-9pm; off-season 9am-4pm). Ask at the info center about Poreč's several hotels, most with a 7.60kn per day tourist tax. For **private rooms,** try **Turizam Vits,** Zagrebačka 17 (tel./fax (052) 43 17 38), near the tourist office (singles 55-77kn; doubles 77-120kn; apartments 120-180kn; open daily 8am-10pm). If these rooms are full, there are other agencies on every streetcorner. **Laternacamp** (tel. (052) 43 49 00; fax 44 30 93), far to the east, has good facilities (50kn per night plus 24kn per person; open Apr.-Oct.).

■ Split

With an Old Town wedged between a high mountain range and a palm-lined waterfront, Split lures visitors with Roman ruins, multiple museums, and, above all, stirring natural beauty. Split also allows easy access to the nearby islands of Hvar and Korčula. The eastern half of the **Old Town** was once the summer residence of the Roman Emperor Diocletian. A **portal,** just past the line of taxis on the south side of the city, leads into the cellars of the city; at the entrance, turn either direction to wander around the labyrinth and explore the archaeological finds (portal open daily 10am-9pm). Straight through the cellars and up the stairs, you will find yourself in the open-air **peristyle,** a colonnaded square. The phenomenal **cathedral** on the west end of the peristyle is one of architecture's great ironies—it was originally the mausoleum of Diocletian, an emperor known largely for his violent persecution of Christians (open daily 7am-noon and 4-7pm). Split has **beaches** on both its north and south ends. The best ones require a ride on bus 60 outside the city.

Trains (tel. (021) 485 88) don't serve many cities, but do run to Zagreb (9hr., 90kn); **buses** run to Dubrovnik (4½hr., 65-77kn) and Zagreb (6½-9hr., 80-100kn). **Ferries** also run to Hvar and Korčula (see below) From the train or bus station, follow Obala kneza Domagoja to Obala hrvatskog narodnog preporoda, where the **tourist office** (tel. (021) 33 22), at #12, answers questions (in English), provides maps, and arranges accommodations (singles 160kn; doubles 240kn; open M-Sa 7:30am-9pm, Su 7:30am-2pm). **Prenoćište Slavija,** Buvinova 1 (tel. (021) 470 53), in the Old Town, is clean but has seen better days (singles 160-200kn; doubles 200-240kn; tourist tax 8kn). Inquire at the tourist office about **camping** in and around Split. **Dionis,** Marmontaova 3, on the west side of the Old Town, pleases with a large, hearty *menü* for 30kn (open daily 8am-midnight).

Hvar The vineyards, olive groves, and lavendar on Hvar, the longest Adriatic island, are nourished by numerous springs and more sunny hours per year than anywhere else in Croatia. Its old town, founded in 385 BC as the Greek colony Pharos, is situated at the deepest end of 6km bay. The only easy way to get here is on the **Jadrolinija Ferry,** which connects to Split (2hr., 23kn). Another ferry stops by Hvar on its way from Split to Dubrovnik (2hr., Tu, W, F, and Su, 50kn) or back. Walking left along the harbor from the ferry landing, the **tourist office** (tel. (021) 74 22 50) rents singles for 90kn and doubles for 140kn (open M-Sa 9am-noon and 6-9pm, Su 6-8pm). The nearby **Mengola** (tel. (021) 74 20 99) also has private rooms (singles 120kn; doubles 160kn). The well-stocked **Razvitka market** is on the north side of the main square (open M-Sa 6am-9:30pm, Su 7am-noon).

Korčula The central Dalmatian island of Korčula (KOR-chula), stretching parallel to the nearby mainland, is an island of exceptional grace, history, and culture. Its sacral monuments and churches date from the time of the Apostles, and its exquisite natural beauty is aromatically tousled by indigenous sage, rosemary, lavendar, mint, and marjoram. The town of Korčula is situated beside the sea on the northeast end of the island. **Buses** run to Sarajevo (8hr., 140kn) and Zagreb (11-13hr., 2 per day, 130-145kn). **Ferries** run to Split (5½hr., 7 per week, 26kn) and other coastal cities. **Atlas,** Trg 19 travnja (tel. 711 060, 711 061), arranges accommodation for 87kn per person (30% more for 1-2 nights, although you pay directly and this *may* be negotiable).

▓ Dubrovnik

Picturesquely wedged between the Dinaric Alps and the calm Adriatic, Dubrovnik has a chic character that's more Mediterranean than Eastern European—the local dialect blends Croatian with Italian and Latin, the streets and buildings of the Stari Grad (old town) are all made from the same pale stone, and cafe-goers on the central plaza still stand and fall silent when a religious procession passes. The most impressive legacy of this former naval city-state are the awesome **city walls.** Stretching up to 25m high, they were mostly completed in the 14th century. Climbing to the top affords a glorious view of the old city and the sparkling blue Adriatic; budget an hour if you want to walk the full 2km circumference (open daily 9am-7pm). Entering the Stari Grad at the Pile gate, the **Franjevački samostan** (Franciscan monastery) is on the left and the **Dominikanski samostan** (Dominican monastery) awaits at the other end. The latter has a rich collection of Renaissance paintings, art, and books (open daily 9am-6pm; 10kn). Nearby, the street opens onto a large square, with **Crkva sv. Vlaha** (St. Blaise's Church) sitting on the same side as the **katedrala.** Between the two is the town's best museum, the 1441 **Knežev dvor** (Rector's Palace), which holds furniture, paintings, coins, and weaponry, all dating from the 16th and 17th centuries (open M-Sa 9am-1pm and 4-7pm, Su 9am-1pm; 10kn).

As tempting as it may be to stroll in the hills above the city, there may still be **land mines** in the area: hiking there is *not* safe.

The **bus station** (*Autobusni Kolodvor;* tel. (020) 42 30 88), about 2km north of the Stari Grad along Dr. Ante Starčević, serves Split (5hr., 65-77kn) and Zagreb (11hr., 135kn). A few hundred meters north of the station, the **ferry** landing (ticket info tel. (020) 41 80 00) sends boats to Split (8hr., 61kn). From this area, you can take a bus to the Old Town gates (any except bus 7; 6kn on board, 5kn from kiosks). The **Dubrovnik tourist board** (tel. (020) 42 63 03 or 42 63 04) is at Cvijete Zuzorić ½ (open M-F 8am-4pm, Sa 9am-1pm). Walk to the end of the Placa, Stari Grad's main street, go right between St. Blaise's Church *(Crkva Svetog Vlaha)* and the coffee shop Gradska Kavana, and take the first right. The **HI youth hostel,** Bana J. Jelačića 15/17 (tel. (020) 43 22 41; fax 41 25 92), is ultra-clean and friendly. From the bus station, go up Ante Starčevića about 10min. and turn right at the traffic light. After 40m, turn right again onto Bana J. Jelačića. Look for a hidden sign on the left. (63-73kn; breakfast included. Hostel and reception open July-Aug. daily 24hr. Call ahead in off-season.) At the bus station, owners hawk **private rooms** (singles 80-100kn; doubles 130kn; negotiate a lower price for longer stays). **Raguse 2,** Zamanjina 2, cooks up seafood spaghetti (45kn) and doles out a free glass of *prošek* (open daily 8am-midnight). Dubrovnik has a vibrant music scene; a billboard just outside the west end of the old town is plastered with upcoming events. The **Dubrovnik Summer Festival's** 50th anniversary will be held in 1999, with more drama, ballet, jazz, and opera than usual (call (020) 41 22 88 for info; http://www.dubrovnik-festival.hr). Dubrovnik youth flock to bars like **Ferrari** and **Burbon Street,** near the hostel on Bana J. Jelačića.

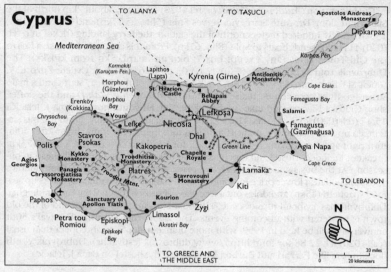

Cyprus (Κυπρος)

US$1 = C£0.51 (Cypriot Pounds)	C£1 = US$1.96
CDN$1 = C£0.34	C£1 = CDN$2.94
UK£1 = C£0.84	C£1 = UK£1.19
IR£1 = C£0.74	C£1 = IR£1.35
AUS$1 = C£0.30	C£1 = AUS$3.33
NZ$1 = C£0.26	C£1 = NZ$3.85
SAR1 = C£0.08	C£1 = SAR12.50
Country Code: 357	International Dialing Prefix: 080

> Journeys to northern Cyprus require careful planning and must usually begin in Turkey. For info on northern Cyprus, see *Let's Go: Turkey 1999*.

Aphrodite blessed the island of Cyprus with an abundance of natural beauty, from the sandy beaches of Agia Napa to the serene Troodos Mountains. Unfortunately, the beautiful is also desirable, and the ancient temples, Roman mosaics, crusader castles, Arab and Ottoman mosques, and English street signs all attest to the succession of settlements by those who would have control over the spectacular isle. The events of 1974 have left the island partitioned with Greeks in the south and Turks in the north divided by the UN manned Green Line. The island's future is still in question.

For more extensive coverage of this lovely isle, dig *Let's Go: Greece 1999*.

ESSENTIALS

The third largest island in the Mediterranean after Sicily and Sardinia, Cyprus lies 64km from Turkey and 480km from the nearest Greek island. The Greek southern side constitutes 63% of the island, and restrictions prohibit travel from north to south except for tourists making short daytrips across the **Green Line** in Nicosia (p. 209).

Olympic Airlines (tel. (800) 223-1226), **Egypt Air** (tel. (800) 334-6787), and **Cyprus Airways** (tel. (212) 714-2310) offer **flights** to the Republic of Cyprus; student fare from Athens is about US$190 round-trip. Weekly **ferries** run from Peiraias in Greece, through Rhodes, to Limassol, proceeding to Haifa Israel. Inquire at ferry docks and tourist offices for more information. Once in Cyprus, cars drive on the *left* side of the road and driving conditions can be intimidating. **Buses** and **service** (shared) **taxis** connect towns, and tourist offices stock an island-wide bus schedule. Transportation is largely nonexistent after 7pm—not even taxis run.

Cyprus' extremely helpful **tourist offices** provide free maps and plenty of info on buses, museums, and cultural activities. Cyprus has a fairly good **telephone** system; direct overseas calls can be made from nearly all public phones with convenient tele-cards sold at banks and kiosks. To call **AT&T Direct,** dial 080 900 10; **MCI World-Phone,** 080 900 00; **Sprint Access,** 080 900 01. Nicosia, Paphos, Troodos, and Larnaka all have **HI youth hostels.** Cyprus has only a few **campgrounds,** but you may sleep on beaches and in forests; exercise caution.

■ Larnaka (Λαρνακα)

One of the oldest continuously inhabited cities in the world, **Larnaka** draws tourists not with history but with **beaches.** The city does, however, house the uncovered treasures of several archaeological digs. Larnaka was built over ancient Kition, whose ruins reveal the foundations of the (rather residual) **Temple of Astarte** (open M-F 9am-12:30pm, Th until 5pm; £0.75). The **Larnaka District Archaeological Museum** boasts local Neolithic finds (open M-F 9am-2:30pm, Th until 6pm; £0.75). The private **Pierides Foundation Museum** on Zinonos St. showcases artifacts from 3000 years of Cypriot history, including prehistoric idols and antique maps. (Open in summer M-F 9am-1pm and 3-6pm, Sa 9am-1pm, Su 10am-1pm; reduced hours in winter. £1.) The remains of Lazarus lie (permanently, this time) in the **Church of St. Lazarus,** at the first left north of the fortress. Find lively company at night in the beachfront pubs on Athinon Ave. and in the cafes in town.

Most **flights** into Cyprus land at the Larnaka airport; take bus 19 (M-F in summer 6:20am-7pm, in winter until 5:45pm, reduced Sa service; £0.50) or a taxi (about £3) from the airport into town. From Athinon Ave., **buses** leave for Limassol (3-4 per day, £1.70) and Nicosia (4-7 per day, £1.50). A **tourist office** is located at the airport (open 24hr.), and another resides at Vasileos Pavlou Sq. (tel. (04) 65 43 22; hours vary). The **HI youth hostel** (tel. (04) 62 11 88), Nikolaou Rossou St. in St. Lazarus Sq., has three 10-bed dorms (£3.50, sheets £1; bring bug repellent; guests can sign in 24hr.). Exchange ideas over carafes of local wine (£2.50) at the vegetarian-friendly **1900 Art Cafe,** 6 Stasinou St., or have a virtual experience at the **Web Internet Cafe,** 54 Lordou Vyronou St. (access to the web and email £2 per hr.).

Two kilometers west of Larnaka Airport (bus #19 to Kiti; tell the driver your stop), the **Hala Sultan Tekke Mosque** is set on the shore of a gorgeous salt lake. From Lar-naka, many visitors bus north (£1) to **Agia Napa** (Αγια Ναπα), a tourist center with white sandy beaches and a raucous nightlife dominated by foreigners. Flats above the **Cinderella Leather Shop** (tel. (04) 72 21 48), on Makariou Ave., are simple and close to the nightlife (singles £13; doubles £15; inquire within the shop).

■ Limassol (Lemesos; Λεμεσος)

The island's second largest city and port of entry for most passenger ferries, industrial yet cosmopolitan **Limassol** is a cordial introduction to a striking island. **Limassol Cas-tle** has changed hands many times since its construction in the 12th century, but its latest incarnation is as the **Cyprus Medieval Museum.** (Open in summer M-F 7:30am-5pm, Sa 9am-5pm, Su 10am-1pm; off-season M-Sa 7:30am-5pm. £1.) For sunbathing, the gorgeous **Dassoudi Beach,** 3km east of town (bus 3 from the market on Kanaris St.), and the ebullient **Ladies Mile Beach,** just west of the new port (bus 1), are pop-ular. The extensive Roman and Hellenistic ruins of **Kourion,** 12km out of town, boast a **sanctuary of Apollo** from the 8th century BC and a **stadium** built in the 2nd century AD. Buses to Kourion leave from Limassol Castle (every hr. on the hr. 9am-2pm, return at 11:50am, 2:50 and 4:50pm; £0.60). Most shops, services and sights can be found within a few blocks of the waterfront, especially **Agiou Andrew Street** (also called St. Andrew Street).

The **bus terminal,** at the corner of Irinis and Enosis St. (400m north of castle), serves and Larnaka (4 per day, £1.70), Nicosia (3-5 per day, £1.50), and Paphos (1 per day, £1.50). **Service taxis** run to Larnaka (£3), Nicosia (£3.45), and Paphos (£2.50); contact Kyriakos (tel. (05) 36 41 14) or Makris (tel. (05) 36 55 50). Limassol's **tourist office,** 15 Spiro Araouzos St. (tel. (05) 36 27 56), on the waterfront one block east of the castle, provides maps and schedules. (Open July-Aug. M and Th 8:15am-2:15pm and 4-6:30pm, Tu-W and F 8:15am-2:15pm, Sa 8:15am-1:15pm; call for off-season hours.) Rooms at the well-located **Luxor Guest House,** 101 Agiou Andreou St. (tel. (05) 36 22 65), have a simple elegance. The **Guest House Ikaros,** 61 Eleftherias St. (tel. (05) 35 43 48), has large, pleasant rooms (singles £5; doubles £10). The **municipal market** is the best option for the health- and wealth-conscious traveler (open M-F 6am-1pm and 4-6pm, closed W 4-6pm). Limassol residents host a spirited **wine festival** from late August to early September (Dionysian revelries 6-11pm; £1.50).

■ Paphos (Παφος)

Paphos' glory days as the capital of the (Egyptian) Ptolemaic empire ended with an earthquake in the 4th century, and the city remained a small village until recently. But Paphos, combining the best of beaches and historic sites, has risen again as the tourist capital of Cyprus. Just inland from the conspicuous **Paphos Fort** (open daily 10am-5:45pm; £0.75), the **House of Dionysus,** the **House of Theseus,** and the **House of Aion** are the city's most dazzling ancient remains. To reach the houses, take Sophias Vembo St., off A. Pavlou Ave. (admission to all 3 £1). The musty **Catacombs of Agia Solomoni,** along the road between Ktima (upper) and Kato (lower) Paphos, include a chapel with deteriorating Byzantine frescoes. A tree with handkerchiefs draped from its branches marks the entrance to the catacombs on A. Pavlos Ave. St. Paul was allegedly whipped for preaching Christianity at **St. Paul's Pillar** (both free and open 24hr.). In Ktima Paphos, don't miss the **Ethnographic Museum,** 1 Exo Vrysi St., just outside of Kennedy Sq. (open M-Sa 9am-6pm, Su 10am-1pm; £1; English guidebooks £3). Across the way, the **Byzantine Museum,** 26 25th Martiou St., has icons and religious relics (open M-F 9am-5pm, Sa 10am-1pm; reduced hours in winter; £1).

Service taxis go to Limassol (£2.50); contact Makris (tel. (06) 23 25 38) or Kyriakos (tel. (06) 23 25 38). From Limassol, both make connections with Nicosia service taxis, and Makris connects to Larnaka. The **tourist office,** 3 Gladstone St. (tel. (06) 23 28 41), is across from Iris Travel (hours vary). The **HI youth hostel,** 37 Eleftheriou Venizelou Ave. (tel. (06) 23 25 88), is on a residential street northeast of the town center; from the square, follow Pallikaridi and make a right (£4; sheets £1). Close to nightlife, **Violetta Fields,** 7 Dionissiou St. in Kato Paphos (tel. (06) 23 41 09), offers home-like studios with kitchen facilities (singles £15; doubles £18). **Hondros** is one of the older restaurants in the area, founded long before the town's tourist boom (open daily 11am-4pm and 7pm-midnight). Kato Paphos is home to virtually all of the area's nightlife, centering around Aglas Napas St. The club **Summer Cinema** is on the waterfront, just past Geroskipou beach.

■ Polis (Πολις)

Blessed with hiking trails in the nearby Akamas peninsula and some of the country's most beautiful beaches, **Polis** is also smaller, cheaper and more relaxed than other coastal towns. The road from Polis to the **Baths of Aphrodite,** 10km west, leads past pristine **beaches** and some cheap lodgings, but the beaches to the east are just as beautiful. Next to the Baths of Aphrodite, signs mark the beginning of **hiking** trails called Aphrodite and Adonis. In town, the church of **Agios Andronikos** was turned into a mosque during Ottoman rule but is currently being converted back. To see its frescoes being recovered from under the plaster, ask for a key in the *platia* from the helpful and enthusiastic **tourist office,** at the end of the winding main street (open M-Sa 9am-1pm and 2:30-5:45pm). The **Lemon Garden** (tel. (06) 32 14 43), past the *platia* to the right, has quality rooms and a restaurant/bar (doubles £14-16). Also look for

CYPRUS

inexpensive rooms in private households on the road to Latchi or inquire at a cafe (£5-6 per person). Beyond the parking lot to Baths of Aphrodite, a large field provides practically beachside **camping** for free. In town, the family-owned **Arsinoe,** across from the church, sells its daily catch (open daily 8am-1pm and 7pm-1am).

■ Nicosia (Lefkosia; Λευκωσια)

CYPRUS

Landlocked Nicosia, the capital of the Republic of Cyprus, is a city of walls. The ramparts and barbed wire of the **Green Line** run east-west at the north end of the city to separate it from the Turkish-occupied area, and the imposing circular walls left by the Venetians distinguish the New City from the Old. Geared more towards bureaucrats than backpackers, Nicosia may be preferable as a daytrip. The **Makarios Cultural Center** occupies the Old City buildings of Archbishopric Kyprianos Sq., where several interesting museums are clustered, including the **Byzantine Art Gallery,** with the island's largest collection of icons (open M-F 9am-4:30pm; £1), the **Folk Art Museum** (open M-F 9am-5pm, Sa 10am-1pm; £1), and the Greek **Independence War Gallery,** with relics from the struggle for *enosis,* the union of Cyprus with Greece (open M-F 9am-4:30pm, Sa 9am-1pm; £0.50). Nearby is the **Ömeriye Mosque,** easily recognizable by its large minaret, and the **Turkish Baths,** 8 Tillirias St. (Open for women W and F 8am-3pm. Open for men W and F 3-7pm, Tu, Th, and Sa-Su 8am-7pm. £4.) In the *Laiki Yitonia,* the pedestrian shopping district, the **Leventis Municipal Museum** on Hippocratis St. chronicles the history of Nicosia (open Tu-Su 10am-4:30pm; free). In the New City, the **Cyprus Museum** has the most extensive collection of ancient artifacts on the island (open M-Sa 9am-5pm, Su 10am-1pm; £1.50).

Crossing the Green Line into northern Nicosia for the day is possible at the **Ledra Palace Checkpoint,** northwest of the city walls off Markou Drakou St. You must leave between 8am and 1pm and return before 5pm. Do not let authorites on the otherside stamp your passport or else you will never be able to return to the south side; have them stamp a piece of paper instead. When you are on the Turkish side, notice a different approach to urban planning in the development of parts of the old city.

There are three bus stations in town. **Kallenos,** in Solonos Sq. (tel. (02) 65 48 50), runs to Larnaka (£1.50); **Kemek,** 34 Leonider, south of Solonos Sq. (tel. (02) 46 39 89), and **ALEPA,** in Tipolis Bastion, near Solonos Sq. (tel. (02) 62 50 27), run to Limassol (£1.50) and Paphos (£3). **Zingas** (tel. (02) 46 39 89), at the Kemek office, and **Clarios** (tel. (02) 45 32 34), at Costanza Bastion, serve various towns in the Troodos Mountains. **Service taxis** provide service to and Larnaka (£2.40), Limassol (£3.45), and Paphos (£5.95); contact Makris (tel. (02) 46 62 01) or Kyriakos (tel. (02) 44 41 41). The **tourist office,** 11 Aristokypros St. (tel. (02) 44 42 64), in the *Laiki Yitonia,* has maps, bus info, and free copies of *Nicosia: This Month* (open M-F 8:30am-4pm, Sa 8:30am-2pm). Most of Nicosia's accommodations are within the city walls, but the New City is the center of the nightlife. The **youth hostel (HI),** I Hadjidaki St. (tel. (02) 44 48 08), 1km into the New City, has a communal kitchen (£4; sheets £1). **Sans Rival,** 7 Solon St. (tel. (02) 47 43 83), has modern rooms in the *Laiki Yitonia* (singles £10; doubles £13). The **municipal market** on the corner of Digenis Akritas and Kallipolis Ave. has a variety of food stands. The cafe **Ta Kala Kathoumena,** 21 Nikokleous St., in an alley near Phaneromeni Church, is a late-night gathering spot.

In the serene **Troodos Mountains,** isolated villages nestled amid cool, pine-covered hills provide refuge from the sun-baked coastal cities. Spectacular **hikes** originate near **Troodos Village;** detailed maps are available at tourist offices. The town itself, accessible only by bus from **Clarios** in Nicosia (see above), is essentially a cluster of tourist and camping facilities. **Troodos Youth Hostel** (tel. (05) 42 24 00) is the roomiest, most relaxing of the island's hostels (£4 per person; sheets £1). The nearby **Jubilee Hotel Bar** rents bicycles.

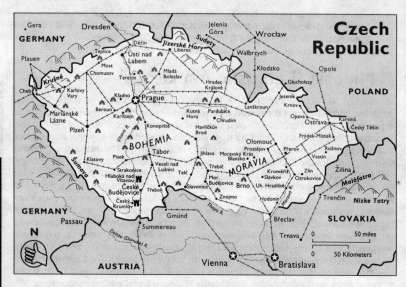

The Czech Republic (Česká Republika)

US$1 = 33Kč (koruny)	10Kč = US$0.30
CDN$1 = 21.30Kč	10Kč = CDN$0.47
UK£1 = 54.10Kč	10Kč = UK£0.19
IR£1 = 46.14Kč	10Kč = IR£0.22
AUS$1 = 19.10Kč	10Kč = AUS$0.52
NZ$1 = 16.20Kč	10Kč = NZ$0.62
SAR1 = 5.26Kč	10Kč = SAR0.19
DM1 = 18.40Kč	10Kč = DM0.55
Country Phone Code: 420	**International Dialing Prefix: 00**

Culturally and politically, it has been a decade of rapid change for the Czech people. In November of 1989, following the demise of Communist governments in Hungary and Poland and the fall of the Berlin Wall, Czechs peacefully threw off the communists and chose dissident playwright Václav Havel to lead them westward. Havel attempted to preserve the Czech-Slovak union, but the two nations split bloodlessly in 1993. Czechs continue to admire their playwright-president and for the most part are embracing the dizzying pace the westernization, though the notion of self-determination is relatively new to them: from the Holy Roman Empire up to the Nazis and the Soviets, foreigners have driven the Czechs' internal affairs; even the 1968 Prague Spring was frozen by the iron rumble of Soviet tanks. Today, the Czech Republic is facing a more benevolent but by no means figurative invasion, led by enamored tourists sweeping in to savor the magnificent capital and the world's best beer. Even if the locals become increasingly less pleased with the foreign presence and Prague's August streets become ever less penetrable, the sheer gingerbread magic of the Czech Republic's prize towns will continue to draw us here, will we or no.

Check out the Czech Republic in majestic detail in *Let's Go: Eastern Europe 1999.*

GETTING THERE AND GETTING AROUND

U.S. citizens may visit the Czech Republic **visa-free** for up to 30 days; citizens of the U.K., Canada, or New Zealand for up to 180 days, and Ireland for up to 90 days. Australians and South Africans need visas, valid for 30 days and available at a Czech embassy or consulate (see **Government Information Offices,** p. 2), or at one of three border crossings: **Rozvadov, Dolní Dvořiště,** or **Hatí.** Single-entry or transit visas cost US$22 (US$60 at the border), double-entry visas US$36, and 90-day multiple-entry visas US$50. They require two photos, a passport, and three days to process (1 day in person). South Africans can get a 30-day, single-entry visa free of charge. Apply for visa extensions of up to six months at the Local Passport and Visa Authorities.

Eastrail is accepted in the Czech Republic, but **Eurail** is valid only with a special supplement. The fastest trains are the *expresný.* The *rychlík* trains cost as much as the express, while the few *spěšný* (semi-fast) trains cost less. Avoid *osobný* (slow) trains. **ČSD,** the national transportation company, publishes the monster *Jízdní řád* (train schedule; 74kč), with a two-page English explanation in front. *Odjezd* (departures) are printed in train stations on yellow posters, *přijezd* (arrivals) on white. If you're heading to Austria or Hungary, it's often less expensive to buy a Czech ticket to the border, then, at the border, buy a separate ticket to your destination. **Seat reservations** (*místenka;* 10kč) are recommended on most express and international trains and for all first-class seating; snag them at the counter with the boxed "R." IC and EC trains require an additional supplement which can double the ticket price.

Buses can be significantly faster for trips between smaller cities and are only slightly more expensive than trains. **ČSAD** runs national and international bus lines. From Prague, buses run a few times per week to Munich, Milan, and other transport hubs; buses leave Brno for many destinations in Austria. Consult timetables at stations or buy one (25kč) from a kiosk. **Hitchhiking** remains popular, especially during the morning commute (6-8am).

ESSENTIALS

Čedok, the official state tourist company and relic of the centralized Communist bureaucracy, has been transformed into a travel agency. **CKM,** its junior affiliate, is very helpful for the student and budget traveler, serving as a clearinghouse for youth hostel beds and issuing ISICs and HI cards. The quality of private tourist agencies varies. **Tourist offices** in major cities provide printed materials on sights, cultural events, hotels, and hostels. City maps *(plán města)* are available for 30 to 60kč. Bookstores sell *Soubor Turistických Map,* a great hiking map with an English key.

ATMs abound wherever there are banks. Traveler's checks can be exchanged in every town, thanks to the ubiquitous **Komerční banka,** which accept all sorts of checks. **Banks** are generally open weekdays from 9am to 5pm. The Czech unit of currency is the **korun,** plural *koruny* (kč). Czech money is not valid in Slovakia. If you're carrying money with you, beware purse-snatchers and pickpockets in Prague's Old Town Square, on the way to the Castle, and on trams. Lost wallets and purses sometimes appear at embassies with only the cash missing.

Internet access is popping up everywhere in the Czech Republic. The **postal system** is usually reliable and efficient; letters reach the U.S. in under 10 days. For calls within the country, a **phone card** (150kč for 50 units) is invaluable. It's used in any of the blue phones—the old phones demand coins but rarely give them back. Local calls cost 2kč regardless of length. Use an international long-distance system to avoid the expensive Czech telephone bureaucracy—calls run 31kč per minute to the U.K., 63kč per minute to the U.S., Canada, or Australia, and 94kč per minute to New Zealand. To reach the **AT&T Direct** operator, dial tel. 00 42 00 01 01; **MCI WorldPhone,** 00 42 00 01 12; **Canada Direct,** 00 42 00 01 51; and **BT Direct,** 00 42 00 44 01.; **Sprint International,** tel. 00 42 08 71 87. In **emergencies,** try contacting your consulate, since police may not be well-versed in English. The number for **police** is 158; for **fire** 150; for **ambulance** 155.

Many Czechs, especially students, speak at least a little English; German phrases go even further, especially in Prague, but might earn you some resentment.

Yes/no	*Ano/Ne*	AH-noh/neh
Please/You're welcome	*Prosím*	PROH-seem
Thank you	*Děkuji*	DYEH-koo-yih
Hello	*Dobrý den*	DOH-bree den
Where is...?	*Kde je...?*	k-DEH YEH
Do you speak English?	*Mluvíte anglicky?*	MLOO-vit-eh AHNG-lits-kih
I don't understand.	*Nerozumím*	NEH-roh-zoo-meem
Check, please.	*Prosím, účet*	PRO-seem, OO-chet

Czechs celebrate: New Year's Day (Jan. 1); Easter (Apr. 12-13); Labor Day (May 1); Liberation Day (May 8); Cyril and Methodius Day (July 5); Jan Hus Day (July 6); Republic Day (Oct. 28); and Christmas.

ACCOMMODATIONS AND CAMPING

Converted **university dorms** run through CKM are the cheapest option in July and August. Comfy two- to four-bed rooms go for 200 to 400kč per person. CKM's **Junior Hotels** (year-round hostels which give discounts to both HI and ISIC holders) are comfortable but often full. Private youth lodgings have broken CKM's monopoly, but may not surpass its reliability. Showers and bedding are usually included, breakfast sometimes too, especially outside Prague.

Across the country, **private homes** have become a legal and feasible lodging option. In Prague, hawkers offer expensive rooms (US$16-30, but don't agree to more than US$20), often including breakfast. Scan train stations for "hostel," *"zimmer frei,"* or "accommodations" ads. Quality varies widely; *do not* pay in advance. Be prepared for a healthy commute to the center of town. Outside of Prague, **local tourist offices** and **CKM/GTS** handle private room booking, although private agencies are popping up around train and bus stations. If you're sticking to **hotels,** and **hostels** reserve a week ahead from June to September in Prague and Český Krumlov, even if pre-payment is required. In less touristed towns, it's easier to find a bed on the spot. **Camping** is available everywhere for 60 to 100kč per person plus 50 to 90kč per tent (most sites open only mid-May to Sept.). The book *Ubytování ČSR,* in decodable Czech, lists accommodations in Bohemia and Moravia.

FOOD AND DRINK

Anyone in the mood for true Czech cuisine should start learning to pronounce *knedlíky* (k-NED-lee-kee). The thick pasty loaves of dough serve as staples of Czech meals, soaking up *zelí* (sauerkraut) juice and the unbelievably thick sauces that smother almost any local dish. The Czech national meal is *vepřové* (roast pork), *knedlíky,* and *zelí;* but *guláš* (stew) runs a close second. The main food groups have become *hovězí* (beef), *sekaná pečeně* (meatloaf), and *klobása* (sausage). Meat can be *pečené* (roasted), *vařené* (boiled), or *mleté* (ground). *Ryby* (fish) include *kapr* (carp) and *pstruh* (trout). If you are in a hurry, you can grab a pair of *párky* (frankfurters) or some *sýr* (cheese) at either a *bufet, samoobsluha,* or *občerstvení,* all variations on a fast-food stand. Vegetarian restaurants do exist, serving *šopský salat* (mixed salad) and other *bez masa* (no meat) specialties. *Káva* (coffee) is almost always served Turkish-style. A beloved dessert is *koláč,* a tart filled with either poppy-seed jam or sweet cheese.

How to Tip in Czech

The Western convention of tipping waiters a percentage (often 15%) of the meal cost makes little sense to Czechs, and it can be downright offensive. Nevertheless, waiters make little, and tipping is expected for adequate service. When it's time to pay, your waiter will tell you the cost of the meal. You should respond by rounding up; your figure will be the total cost, including the tip—learn to say your numbers. For example, if the bill comes to 322Kč, say "330Kč." Tipping is a way of saying "thank you," and you should tip more for better service, or not at all if the service is lousy. And do not just leave a few *koruny* on the table.

CZECH REPUBLIC

■ Prague (Praha)

According to legend, Princess Libuše stood on Vyšehrad above the Vltava and declared, "I see a city whose glory will touch the stars; it shall be called Praha (threshold)." Medieval kings, benefactors, and architects fulfilled the prophecy, building soaring cathedrals and lavish palaces which gave notice of Prague's status as the capital of the Holy Roman Empire. But the city's character differed sharply from the holy splendor of Rome and Constantinople: legends of demons, occult forces, and mazes of shady alleys lent this "city of dreams" a dark side that inspired Franz Kafka's tales of paranoia. Only this century has the spell been broken, as the fall of the Iron Curtain brought hordes of Euro-trotting foreigners to the once-isolated capital. Tourists and entrepreneurs have long since explored and exploited every nook and cranny of the city, yet these visitors give Prague a festive air matched by few places in the world.

ORIENTATION AND PRACTICAL INFORMATION

Straddling a bend in the Vltava, Prague is a gigantic mess of suburbs and curvy streets. **Staré Město** (Old Town) sits on the southernmost bend of the river as it curves east. Across the Vltava sits **Hradčany** castle, with **Malá Strana** (Lesser Side) at its southern base. South of Staré Město spreads **Nové Město** (New Town), and farther east across **Wilsonova** and **Legerova** lie the **Žižkov** and **Vinohrady** districts. **Holešovice** in the north has an international train terminal; **Smíchov**, the southwest end, is the student-dorm neighborhood. All train and bus terminals are on or near the metro system. Don't just refer to your map: study it—and take a look at this book's **color map** of the city. *Tabak* stands and bookstores vend the indexed *plán města* (map). The English-language weekly *The Prague Post* provides news and tips for visitors.

> Prague continues to reform its phone system. Businesses often receive no more than three weeks' notice before their numbers change. The 8-digit numbers provided in these listings are least likely to be obsolete by the time you read this—but then again, nothing is sacred.

Telephone Code: 02.

Flights: Ruzyně Airport (tel. 20 11 11 11), 20km northwest of the city. Take bus 119 from Dejvická or the **airport bus** (tel. 20 11 42 96) from nám. Republiky (90kč) or Dejvická (60kč). From midnight-5am, night tram 51 to "Divoká Šárka" then night bus 510 will bring you to the airport. Taxis to the airport are exorbitant. Many carriers fly into Prague, including **ČSA** (Czech National Airlines; tel. 20 10 43 10).

Trains: info tel. 24 22 42 00, international fares tel. 24 61 52 49. 4 terminals. **Praha Hlavní Nádraží** (tel. 24 61 72 50; Metro C: Hlavní Nádraží) is the biggest, but most international trains run out of **Holešovice** (tel. 24 61 72 65; Metro C: Nádraží Holešovice). To: Berlin (5hr., 5 per day, 1574kč, Wasteels 1346kč); Budapest (8hr., 6 per day, 1279kč, Wasteels 1040kč); Bratislava (5hr., 9 per day, 426kč); Vienna (5hr., 4 per day, 735kč, Wasteels 521kč); and Warsaw (10hr., 3 per day, 937kč, Wasteels 651kč). Domestic trains go from **Masarykovo** (tel. 24 61 72 60; Metro B: nám. Republiky) on the corner of Hybernská and Havlíčkova, or from **Smíchov** (tel. 24 61 72 55; Metro B: Smíchovské Nádraží), opposite Vyšehrad. **B.I.J. Wasteels** (tel. 24 61 74 54; fax 24 22 18 72), at Hlavní Nádraží, on the 2nd floor, to the right of the stairs, sells cheap international tickets to those under 26 and books couchettes. Open in summer M-F 7:30am-8pm, Sa 8-11:30am and 12:30-3pm; winter M-F 8:30am-6pm. Wasteels tickets also available at **Czech Railways Travel Agency** (tel. 80 08 05; fax 80 69 48) at Holešovice. Open daily 7-11:25am, noon-5:40pm, 6:20-9:45pm, 10:35pm-2am, and 3:15-6:35am.

Buses: ČSAD has several *autobusové nádraží* (bus stations). The biggest is **Florenc**, Křižíkova 4 (tel. 24 21 49 90; info 24 21 10 60; Metro B or C: Florenc). The staff speaks little English, and the tricky timetables require study (no symbol key in English). Look for the bus stop number of your destination and get tickets in advance. To Berlin (6hr., 1 per day, 820kč) and Vienna (8½hr., 6 per week, 400kč). Students may get a 10% discount. The **Tourbus** office upstairs (tel. 24 21 02 21) has Eurolines and airport bus tickets. Open M-F 8am-8pm, Sa-Su 9am-8pm.

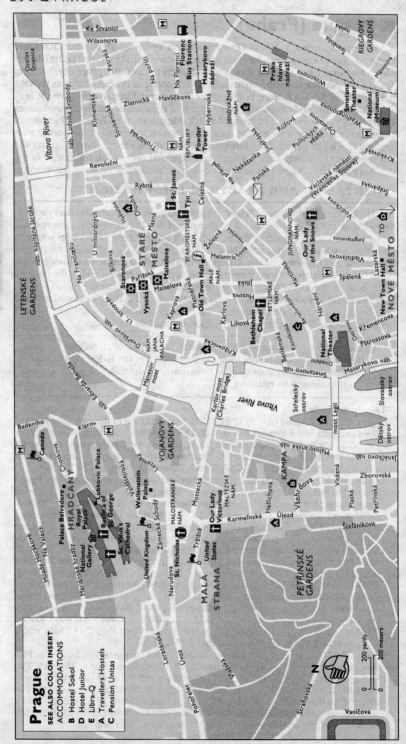

CZECH REPUBLIC

Prague
SEE ALSO COLOR INSERT
ACCOMMODATIONS
B Hostel Sokol
D Hotel Junior
E Libra-Q
A Travellers' Hostels
C Pension Unitas

Ferries: PPS, Rašínovo Nábřeží (tel. 29 38 03; fax 24 91 38 62), between the Jiráskův and Palackého bridges. Various river trips daily; 2hr. Vltava cruise 200kč.

Public Transportation: The **metro, tram,** and **bus** services are pretty good, and share a ticket system. Buy tickets from newsstands, *tabák,* machines in stations, or **DP** (*Dopravní Podnik;* transport authority) kiosks. A 12kč ticket is valid for 1hr. anywhere in the city with unlimited bus, tram, and metro connections, as long as you keep heading in the same direction. An 8kč ticket is good for 30min. or 4 stops on the metro. Large bags 6kč each, as are bikes and prams without babies in them (*with* babies free, so don't forget the baby). If a plainclothes DP inspector issues you a 200kč spot fine, make sure you see their official badge and get a receipt. **Night trams** 51-58 and **buses** run all night after the metro quits at midnight; look for dark blue signs at bus stops. **DP offices** by the Jungmannovo nám. exit of Můstek station (tel. 24 22 51 35; open daily 7am-9pm) or by the Palackého nám. exit of Karlovo nám. station (tel. 29 46 82; open M-F 7am-6pm) sell **tourist passes** (24hr. 50kč, 3 days 130kč, 1 week 190kč).

Taxis: Cab drivers are notorious; before getting in, check that the meter is set to zero, and ask the driver to start it by saying *"Zapněte taximetr."* For longer trips, agree on a price before starting. Always ask for a receipt (*"Prosím, dejte mi paragon"*) with distance traveled, price paid, and the driver's signature. If the driver doesn't write the receipt or reset the meter, you aren't obligated to pay. Prague has instituted set rates: 17kč per km with a 25kč flat rate for getting into the taxi. You're likelier to get ripped off if you hail a taxi on the street, so stick to public transport or call. **Taxi Praha** (tel. 24 91 66 66) and **AAA** (tel: 24 32 24 32) run 24hr.

Hitchhiking: Hitching in the area has become increasingly dangerous and is not recommended. Those going east take tram 1, 9, or 16 to the last stop. To points south, they walk left from Metro C: Pražskeho povstání to 5. května (highway D1). To the north, they take a tram or bus to "Kobyliské nám.," then bus 175 up Horňátecká. To Munich, hitchers take tram 4 or 9 to Plzeňská at Kukulova/Bucharova.

Tourist Offices: Signs with "i"s indicate tourist agencies that book rooms, arrange tours, and sell maps, bus tickets, and guidebooks. Be wary: these private firms didn't appear out of sheer benevolence. **Pražská Informační Služba** (Prague Info Service; tel. 24 48 25 62, English tel. 54 44 44), Staroměstské radnice, in the old town hall, sells **maps** (39-49kč) and **tickets** to shows. Open M-F 9am-7pm, Sa-Su 9am-6pm; closes 1hr. earlier in winter. Other offices at Na příkopě 20, Hlavní nádraží, and in the tower on the Malá Strana side of the Karlův most (same hours).

Budget Travel: CKM, Jindřišská 28 (tel. 24 23 02 18; fax 26 86 23; email ckm-prg@mbox.vol.cz). Metro A or B: Můstek. Sells budget air tickets for students and those under 26 and the discount cards to qualify for them (ISIC, GO25, and Euro26 180kč). Also books rooms in Prague (from 350kč). Open M-Sa 9:30am-1pm, M-Th also 1:30-6pm, F also 1:30-4pm. For HI cards and bookings, go to **KMC,** Karoliny Světlé 30 (tel. 24 23 06 33). Metro B: Národní Třída. Open M-Th 9am-noon and 2:30-5pm, F 9am-noon and 2:30-3:30pm.

Passport Office: Foreigner police, Olšanská 2 (tel. 683 17 39). Metro A: Flora. Turn right onto Jičinská so that the cemetery is on your right, and turn right onto Olšanská, or take tram 9 ("Spojavací") to "Olšanská." Visa extensions involve a 90kč stamp and up to a 2hr. wait. Little English spoken. Open M-Tu and Th 7:30-11:45am and 12:30-2:30pm, W 7:30-11:30am and 12:30-5pm, F 7:30am-noon.

Embassies: Travelers from **Australia** and **New Zealand** have honorary consuls (tel. 24 31 00 71 and 25 41 98, respectively) but should contact the British embassy in an emergency. **Canada,** Mickiewiczova 6 (tel. 24 31 11 08). Metro A: Hradčanská. Open M-F 8am-noon and 2-4pm. **Hungary,** Badeního 1 (tel. 36 50 41). Metro A: Hradčanská. Open M-W and F 9am-noon. **Ireland,** Tržiště 13 (tel. 53 09 02). Metro A: Malostranská. Open M-F 9:30am-12:30pm and 2:30-4:30pm. **Poland,** Valdštejn-ská 8 (tel. 57 32 06 78). Metro A: Malostranská. Open M-F 7am-noon. **Russia,** Pod Kaštany 1 (tel. 38 19 45). Metro A: Hradčanská. Open M, W, and F 9am-1pm. **Slovakia,** Pod Hradbani 1 (tel. 32 05 21). Metro A: Dejvická. Open M-F 8:30am-noon. **South Africa,** Ruská 65 (tel. 67 31 11 14). Metro A: Flora. Open M-F 9am-noon. **U.K.,** Thunovská 14 (tel. 57 32 03 55). Metro A: Malostranská. Open M-F 9am-noon. **U.S.,** Tržiště 15 (tel. 57 32 06 63, emergency after hours tel. 53 12 00). Metro A: Malostranská. From Malostranské nám., head down Karmelitská and take a right onto Tržiště. Open M-F 8am-1pm and 2-4:30pm.

Currency Exchange: The best rates are for AmEx and Thomas Cook traveler's checks, cashed commission-free at the appropriate office. Exchange counters are everywhere, and rates vary wildly. **Chequepoints** mushroom around the city center, and may be the only places open when you need to change cash, but they can take off a 10% commission. **Komerční Banka,** Na přlkopě 33, buys notes and checks for 2% commission. Open M-F 8am-5pm. **ATMs** are all over the place.

American Express: Václavské nám. 56 (tel. 22 80 02 51; fax 22 21 11 31). Metro A or C: Muzeum. Mail held. MC and Visa cash advances (3% commission). **ATM.** Open July-Sept. M-F 9am-6pm, Sa 9am-2pm; Oct.-Apr. M-F 9am-5pm, Sa 9am-noon. Another office near the Karlův most at Mostecká 12. Open daily 9:30am-7:30pm.

Thomas Cook: Národní tř. 28 (tel. 21 10 52 76; fax 24 23 60 77). Cashes Cook's checks commission-free. MC and Visa cash advances. Open M-Sa 9am-7pm, Su 10am-6pm. Also Staroměské nám. 5 (tel. 24 81 71 73). Open daily 9am-7pm.

Luggage Storage: Lockers in all train and bus stations take two 5kč coins. If these are full, or if you need to store your pack for longer than 24hr., use the left luggage offices in the basement of **Hlavní nádraží** (15kč per day for first 15kg) and halfway up the stairs at **Florenc** (10kč per day for first 15kg). Open daily 5am-11pm.

English Bookstore: The Globe Bookstore, Janovského 14 (tel. 66 71 26 10). Metro C: Vltavská. New and used books, a big noticeboard, and a coffeehouse. A legendary (pick-up) center of anglophone Prague. Open daily 10am-midnight.

Gay Information: SOHO (tel. 24 22 03 27), the Association of Organizations of Homosexual Citizens in the Czech Republic.

Laundromat: Laundry Kings, Dejvická 16 (tel. 312 37 43), Metro A: Hradčanská. Cross the tram *and* railroad tracks, then left on Dejvická. Wash 60kč. Dry 15kč per 8min. Soap 10-20kč. Beer 11kč (ah, Prague). A hang-out/pick-up spot for dirty backpackers. Bulletin board for apartment seeking, English teaching, and friend locating. Open M-F 6am-10pm, Sa-Su 8am-10pm.

Emergencies: Na Homolce (hospital for foreigners), Roentgenova 2 (tel. 52 92 21 46, after hours 57 21 11 11). Open M-F 8am-4pm. **American Medical Center** (tel. 80 77 56). **Canadian Medical Centre** (tel. 316 55 19).

24-Hour Pharmacies: At Koněvova 210 (tel. 644 18 95) and Štefánikova 6 (tel. 24 51 11 12). If you don't see something, ask. Common items: *kontrcepční prostředky* (contraceptives), *náplast* (bandages), or *dámské vložky* (tampons).

Post Office: Main office, Jindřišská 14, 110 00 Praha 1. Metro A or B: Můstek. *Poste Restante* at window 17. For stamps, window 16; letters and parcels under 2kg., windows 12-14. Open daily 7am-8pm. Parcels over 2kg can be mailed only at **Celní stanice** (customs office), Plzeňská 139. Tram 4, 7, or 9 from Metro B: "Anděl" to "Klamovka." Open M-F 7am-3pm, W till 6pm. **Postal Code:** 110 00.

Internet Access: Terminal Bar, Soukenická 6 (tel. 21 87 11 15; http://www.terminal.cz). Metro B: nám. Republiký. A multimedia cafe with style. 100kč per hr., half-price for members. Only 8 computers; be prepared to wait. Open daily noon-1am. **Internet Cafe,** Národní třída 25 (tel. 21 08 52 84; email internetcafe@highland.cz; http://www.internetcafe.cz). Metro B: Národní třída. 11 PCs (2kč per min.) and virtually no wait. Open M-F 9am-10pm, Sa-Su 2-10pm.

Telephones: Everywhere, especially at the post office. Phone cards are 150kč for 50 units at kiosks, the post office, and some exchange places: don't get ripped off.

ACCOMMODATIONS AND CAMPING

While hotel prices rise, the hostel market is glutted; prices have stabilized around 250-350kč per night. The smaller hostels are homey but often full. The Strahov complex and other student dorms bear the brunt of the summer's backpacking crowds. A few bare-bones hotels are still cheap, and a growing numbers of residents are renting rooms. Sleeping on Prague's streets is too dangerous to consider. Don't do it.

Accommodations Agencies

Hawkers and agents besiege visitors at the train station with offers of rooms for around US$15-30 (500-1000kč), depending on location. Haggling is possible. Arrangements made in this way are generally safe, but if you're wary of bargaining on the street, call around or try a private agency. Make sure any room you accept is close to public transport; ask where the stop is. Don't pay until you know what you're getting—if in doubt, ask for details in writing. You can often pay in US$ or DM, though prices are generally lower in kč.

Konvex 91, Ve Smečkách 29 (tel. 96 22 44 44 or 22 21 04 73; fax 22 21 15 02). Metro A or C: Muzeum. Specializes in apartment rental, around 450-600kč per person per night near the TV tower or 590-720kč in Staré Město. Hostels from 340kč per night. English and French spoken. Open M-F 9am-12:30pm and 1:30-6pm.

Ave., Hlavní Nádraží (tel. 24 22 32 26; fax 24 23 07 83), on the 2nd fl. of the train station next to the leftmost stairs. Offers hundreds of shared or private rooms from 440kč per person; books hostels from 360kč. Open daily 6am-10pm. AmEx, MC, V.

Hello Travel Ltd., Senovážné nám. 3 (tel. 24 21 26 47), between Na příkopě and Hlavní Nádraží. Arranges every sort of housing imaginable. Singles in pensions from US$23 (low season) or US$35 (high); doubles US$38-56; hostels US$10-13. Pay in kč, DM, or by credit card (AmEx, DC, MC, V). Open daily 10am-9pm.

Hostels

In the Strahov neighborhood, west of the river next to the Olympic stadium, an enormous block of dorms frees up for travelers from June to August. These rooms may be the best bet for those arriving in the middle of the night without a reservation, but many prefer the smaller, more personable hostels. Unfortunately, too many no-shows have forced many places to refuse reservations. To snag a bed, call the night before you arrive or around check-out at 10am. Staffs generally speak good English.

Penzion v podzámčí, V podzámčí 27 (tel. 472 27 59). From Metro C: Budějovická, take bus 192 to the 3rd stop—ask for "Nad Rybníky." Eva & co. run the homiest hostel in Prague. Kitchen, satellite TV, and killer cat. About 40 beds; 2 to 4-person dorms 240kč per person. Laundry service 100kč per 5kg.

Hostel Boathouse, V náklích 1a (tel. 402 10 76). From the train station, Karlovo nám., Staro Město, or the Charles Bridge, take tram 3 or 17 south ("Sídliště Modřany") to "Černý Kůň," then follow the yellow signs to the Vltava. Amazingly clean. 70 beds; 3- to 5-bed dorms 250kč (300kč for just one night). Big breakfast 50kč, dinner 70kč. Laundry service 100kč per load. 50kč key deposit. Call ahead.

Domov Mládeže, Dykova 20 (tel. 25 06 88; fax 25 14 29). From Metro A: nám. Jiřího z Poděbrad, follow Nitranská and go left on Dykova. 80 beds in the peaceful, tree-lined Vinohrady district. Clean but not sterile 2- to 7-person dorms 350kč per person (lone double 400kč). Breakfast included. If they're full, try one of their sister hostels: **Amadeus,** Slavojova 108/8. From Metro C: Vyšehrad, descend the bridge to Čiklova, then turn left onto Slavojova. **Máchova,** Máchova 11. From Metro A: Náměstí Míru, walk down Ruská, then turn right onto Máchova. **Košická,** Košická 12. Same as to Máchova, but continue on Ruská; turn right on Moskevská and then right again on Košická. All use the same reservation number as Domov Mládeže.

Libra-Q, Senovážné nám. 21 (tel. 24 23 17 54; fax 24 22 15 79). Metro B: nám. Republiky. From nám. Republiky, walk down Hybernská to Senovážná, which brings you to Senovážné nám. Tidy, spartan rooms; great location near Staré Město. Triples and quads 330kč per person; 8-bed dorms 310kč per person.

Hotel Junior, Žitná 12 (tel. 29 29 84; fax 24 22 39 11). From Metro B: Karlovo nám, head towards the *radnice* and go right onto Žitná just before the park ends. Neat rooms and central location. Dorm beds 500kč, with ISIC or HI 400kč (400/300kč off-season). Breakfast included. Check-in 2pm.

Hostel Sokol, Všehrdova 10 (tel. 57 00 73 97), in the sports complex. From Metro A: Malostranská, take tram 12 or 22 ("Hlubočepy" or "Nádraží Hostivar," respectively) to "Hellichova" and walk a block down Újezd to Všehrdova; follow the signs. On top of a Malá Strana sports club. 220kč per person. Reservations accepted.

Traveller's Hostels (email hostel@terminal.cz; http://www.terminal.cz/~hostel). These summertime big-dorm specialists round up travelers at bus and train stations and herd them to one of 8 central hostels. **Dlouhá 33** (tel. 231 13 18), in Staré Město, is in the same building as the Roxy club. Dorms 300kč; doubles 900kč; triples 1170kč. **Neklanova 32** (tel. 24 91 55 32), Metro C: Vyšehrad; head down Slavojova. Dorms 270kč. Stop at Metro B: Národní třída for **Mikulandská 5** (tel. 24

91 07 39;270kč), **Střelecký ostrov** (tel. 24 91 01 88), on the island off most Legii (300kč), and **Husova 3** (tel. 24 21 53 26), smack dab in Staré Město and the classiest of the lot. Dorms 400kč; breakfast included. From the metro, turn right onto Spálená (which turns into Na Perštýně after Národní). **Křížovnická 7** (tel. 232 09 87). Metro A: Staroměstská. 230kč. **Růžova 5** (tel. 26 01 11). Metro C: Hlavní nádraží. 220kč. **U lanové drahy 3** (tel. 53 31 60). Tram 6, 9, 12 to "Újezd" and up the stairs. 200kč.

Hotels and Pensions

With so many tourists in Prague, hotels are upgrading service and appearance, and budget hotels are now scarce. Beware: hotels may try to bill you for a more expensive room than the one you stayed in. The good, cheap ones require reservations up to a month ahead, but as with hostels, many places no longer accept reservations. Call, then confirm by fax.

B&B U Oty, Radlická 188 (tel./fax 57 21 53 23). From Metro B: Radlická, up the slope, 400m. Kitchen facilities and free laundry service after 3 nights. Singles 500kč; doubles 770kč; triples 950kč; quads 1250kč. Additional 100kč per person if staying only 1 night.

Hotel Standart (HI), Přístavní 2 (tel. 87 52 58 or 87 56 74; fax 80 67 52). From Metro C: Vltavská, take tram 1 ("Spojavací"), 3 ("Lehovec"), 14 ("Vacovna Kobylisy") or 25 ("Střelničná") to "Dělnická." Continue along the street, then left onto Přístavní. Spotless hall showers. Singles 595kč; doubles 750kč; triples 995kč; quads 1090kč. All rooms 350kč per person for HI members. Breakfast included.

Pension Unitas/Cloister Inn, Bartolomějská 9 (tel. 232 77 00; fax 232 77 09; email cloister@cloister-inn.cz; http://www.cloister-inn.cz), in Staré Město. Metro B: Národní. Cross Narodní and head down Na Perštýně away from Tesco's, then turn left on Bartolomějská. An old monastery where Beethoven once performed, then a Communist jail. Singles US$65-90; doubles US$85-105; triples US$100-125.

Hotel Kafka, Cimburkova 24 (tel. 27 31 01 or 22 78 04 31; fax 27 29 84 or 22 78 13 33), in Žižkov near the TV tower. From Metro C: Hlavní Nádraží, take tram 5 ("Harfa"), 9 ("Spejovací"), or 26 ("Nádraží Hostivar") to "Husinecká." Go uphill on Seifertova and left onto Cimburkova. Mar. 15-Aug. 1: singles 1250kč; doubles 1700kč; triples 2000kč; quads 2400kč. August and New Year's: singles 1500kč; doubles 2050kč; triples 2400kč; quads 2850kč. Off-season roughly half Aug. rates.

Camping

Tourist offices sell a guide to campsites near the city (15kč). For a tranquil setting, try **Císařská Louka,** on a peninsula on the Vltava. Metro B: Smíchovské nádraží, then tram 12 ("Hlubočepy") to "Lihovar." Walk toward the river and onto the shaded path. **Caravan Park** (tel. 54 09 25; fax 54 33 05), near the ferry, has two- (480kč) and four-bed (720kč) bungalows. **Caravan Camping** (tel. 54 56 82), near the tram, has singles (365kč), doubles (630kč), and triples (945kč). Both Caravans are 100kč per person, 100-150kč per tent. **Sokol Troja,** Trojská 171 (tel./fax 688 11 77), is Prague's largest campground. From Metro C: Nádraží Holešovice, take bus 112 to "Kazanka," the fourth stop. 100kč per person, 80-160kč per tent. Dorm, bungalow, and flat accommodations at 165kč, 175kč, and 150kč per person respectively. If it's full, at least four nearly identical places are on the same road. If you've ever felt like crawling into a barrel of *Budvar*, **Na Vlachovce,** Zenklova 217 (tel./fax 688 02 14), has two-person barrels at 250kč per person. Take bus 102 or 175 from Nádraží Holešovice to "Okrouhlická" and continue in the same direction. Reserve a week ahead.

FOOD

The general rule is that the nearer you are to the tourist throngs on Staroměstské nám., Karlův most, and Václavské nám., the more you'll pay. Check your bill carefully—you'll pay for anything the waiter brings, including ketchup and bread. In Czech lunch spots, *hotová jídla* (prepared meals) are cheapest. Traditional Czech meals are increasingly difficult to find near the center. Vegetarian eateries are opening up, but in many restaurants veggie options are still limited to fried cheese dishes and cabbage. For groceries, try the basement level of the **Krone department store,** at Václavské nám. and Jindřišská (Metro A or B: Můstek; open M-F 8am-9pm, Sa 9am-8pm), or **Kotva department store** on the corner of Revoluční and nám Republiky (Metro B: nám. Republiky; open M-F 7am-8pm, Sa 8am-6pm, Su 10am-6pm). Also look for the daily **vegetable market** at Havelská and Melantrichova in Staré Město.

Restaurants

Universal, V jirchářích 6. From Metro B: Národní Třída, turn left onto Spálená, right on Myslíkova, then right on Křemencova; it's on the left-hand corner. The biggest and freshest salads (87-125kč) in Prague; stoplights and acid jazz make the fondue (140kč) taste that much better. Open daily noon-11pm.

Lotos, Platnéřská 13. Metro A: Staroměstská. Turn left down Valentinská, then right onto Platnéřská. Vegetarian restaurant that deserves applause for its innovative and organic food (bean goulash 49kč). Wheat-yeast *Pilsner* 22kč for 0.5L. Open M-Sa 11am-10pm.

Velryba (The Whale), Opatovická 24 (tel. 241 23 91). Metro B: Národní tř, then go left on Spálená, take an immediate right onto Ostrovní, then walk left down Opatovická. Locals, American expats, business types, and tourists enjoy inexpensive Czech dishes (33-89kč) and adventurous vegetarian platters. Open daily 11am-2am.

Massada, Michalská 16 (tel. 24 21 34 18). Metro A or B: Můstek. Walk down Na můstek, turn left onto v. Kotcích, then right onto Michalska. The first kosher restaurant in Prague, Massada is the only place in town to get falafel (105kč) and hummus (95kč). Separate dining areas and kitchens for meat and dairy. Open daily 10am-midnight. Reservations required for F night and Sa afternoon.

Góvinda Vegetarian Club, Soukenická 27, upstairs at the back of the building. Metro B: nám. Republiky. Delicious vegetarian stews; a plate with the works is 75kč. Menu changes daily. Open M-Sa 11am-5pm.

Restaurace U Pravdů, Žitná 15. Metro B: Karlovo nám. A deservedly popular Czech lunch spot, with a shady beer garden. Fish dishes 59-83kč, soya "meat" 41kč, pork 80-99kč, potato *knedlíky* 15kč. Big glass of *Staropramen* beer 13kč, *Radegast* 17kč. Open M-F 10am-11pm, Sa-Su 11am-11pm.

Malostranská Hospoda, Karmelitská 25, just by Malostranské nám. Metro A: Malostranská. Chairs spill out onto the street from the pub's vaulted interior. Good *guláš* (68kč) and even better sauerkraut (7kč). Draft *Staropramen* 15kč per 0.5L. English menu. Open daily 10am-midnight.

Bar bar, Všehrdova 17. Metro A: Malostranská. Follow the tram tracks from the metro station down Letenská, through Malostranské nám., and down Karmelitská. Turn left on Všehrdova after passing the museum. Salads (54-89kč) and pancakes (18-92kč). Good vibe, good music, and 40 varieties of good whiskey (from 41kč). Open M-F 11am-midnight, Sa-Su noon-midnight.

Bohemia Bagel, Újezd 16. Metro A: Malostranská, and take tram 12 or 22 to "Újezd." Fast on the heels of Budapest's New York Bagels, this is a 2nd place in Eastern Europe for bagelophiles to get their fixes. All the usual flavors and more. Bagel with exceptional cream cheese 35kč. Open M-F 7am-2am, Sa-Su 9am-2am.

Cafes

When Prague journalists are bored, they churn out another "Whatever happened to cafe life?" feature. Ignore their complaints and try some of the places listed below.

U malého Glena, Karmelitská 23. Metro A: Malostranská. Their motto: "Eat, Drink, Drink Some More." Light menu has 70kč veggie plates and delicious stuffed pita breads 70-95kč. Great margaritas (50kč). Basement bar has nightly jazz or blues at 9pm. Cover 50-70kč. Open daily 7:30am-2am.

Cafe Gulu Gulu, Betlémské nám. 8 (tel. 90 01 25 81). From Metro A: Staroměstská, turn left on Křižovnická toward the Charles Bridge. Turn left again onto windy Karlova, then right onto Husova. A chill hangout for Prague's hippest twenty-somethings. Fun-loving, from the Miro-esque wall characters to the frequent impromptu musical jams and blaring ska. By 11pm, people are hanging out of windowsills to get a place to sit. *Eggenberg* 25kč. Great food 20-45kč. Open daily 10am-1am.

Unamuno Lounge, Mánesova 79, in the U Knihomola bookstore basement. From Metro A: Jiřího z Poděbrad, walk 1 block down Slavíkova to Mánesova. The only place in town for a real latte. Jazz lulls patrons to nirvana. Coffee 20-40kč; carrot cake 75kč. Open M-Th 10am-11pm, F-Sa 10am-midnight, Su 11am-8pm.

Andy's Cafe, V Kolkovně 3. Metro A: Staroměstská. Walk down Dlouhá; when it becomes Kozí, turn left on V Kolkovně. Stay late enough drinking beer (25kč) and soup (20kč) to skip the night buses and catch the morning metro. Open M-F 10am-6am, Sa-Su noon-6am.

SIGHTS

Central Prague is structured by three streets that form a leaning "T." The long stem of the T is the boulevard **Václavské nám.** (Wenceslas Sq.). The **Národní Muzeum** sits at the bottom of the T. The busy, pedestrian **Na příkopě** forms the right arm, leading to **nám. Republiky.** On the left, **28. října** becomes **Národní** after a block, leading to the **Národní Divadlo** on the river. From the tip of the T-end of Václavské nám. opposite the museum, **Na Můstku** turns into **Melantrichova** after one block and leads to **Staroměstské nám.,** northwest of Václavské nám. There are two prominent **St. Nicholas churches**—in Malá Strana near the castle and in Staroměstské nám.—and two **Powder Towers**—one in the castle and another in nám. Republiky. Strollers will find that Prague has plenty of green space along Malá Strana's **Petřínské Sady.** Miles of pathways traverse the Kinsky, Strahov, Lobkowic, Schönborn, and Seminář **gardens,** but most are badly eroded. Many try the promenade on the banks of the Vltava south of **most Legií** along Nové Město's **Masarykoro nábřeží.** On hot or humid days, the river is known to give off quite a stench. Gorgeous greenery lies southeast of Staré Město in **Vinohrady.** This quarter's hills also offer great views of the town.

Václavské náměstí (Wenceslas Square)

Not so much a square as a broad boulevard, **Václavské nám.** owes its name to the equestrian statue of the Czech ruler and saint **Václav** (Wenceslas), in front of the National Museum. Václav has presided over a century of turmoil and triumph, witnessing no fewer than five revolutions from his pedestal since 1912. The new Czechoslovak state was proclaimed here in 1918, and in 1969, Jan Palach set himself on fire in protest against the 1968 Soviet invasion. Václavské nam. sweeps down from the National Museum past department stores, overpriced discos, posh hotels, sausage stands, and trashy casinos. The **Radio Prague Building,** behind the National Museum, was the scene of a tense battle during Prague Spring between Soviet tanks and Prague citizens trying to protect the radio studios by human barricade. North of the Václav statue, the Art Nouveau style, expressed in everything from lampposts to windowsills, dominates the square. The premier example is the 1903 **Hotel Europa.**

From the north end of Václavské nám., turn left onto 28. rijna and take a quick detour to Jungmannovo nám. and **Panna Marie Sněžná** (Church of Our Lady of the Snows). The Gothic walls are highest of any church in Prague, but the rest of the structure is still unfinished. Enter **Františkánská zahrada** through the arch at the intersection of Jungmannova and Národní. *(Open daily Apr. 15-Sept. 14 7am-10pm; Sept. 15-Oct. 14 7am-8pm; Oct. 15-Apr. 14 8am-7pm. Free.)* No one knows how the Franciscans who tend the rose gardens have managed to maintain such a bastion of serenity in Prague's commercial district, perhaps because most friars are too busy talking to the birds to answer questions. Under the arcades halfway down Národní stands a **memorial** honoring the hundreds of Prague's citizens beaten by the police on November 17, 1989.

Staroměstské náměstí (Old Town Square)

A labyrinth of narrow roads and Old World alleys lead to **Staroměstské nám.,** Staré Město's thriving heart since 965. **Jan Hus,** the Czech Republic's most famous martyred theologian, sweeps across the scene in bronze. No less than eight magnificent towers surround the square. The building with a bit blown off is the **Staroměstská radnice** (Old Town Hall), partially demolished by the Nazis in the final week of World

War II. *(Open for tours in summer daily 9am-5:30pm; 30kč, students 15kč.)* **Crosses** on the ground mark the spot where 27 Protestant leaders were executed on June 21, 1621 for staging a rebellion against the Catholic Hapsburgs. Crowds gather on the hour to watch the wonderful **astronomical clock** *(orloj)* chime with its procession of apostles, a skeleton, and a thwarted Turk. Across from the *radnice,* the spires of **Matka Boží před Týnem** (Týn Church) rise above a huddled mass of medieval homes. The famous astronomer **Tycho Brahe** is buried inside. To the left of the church, the austere **Dům U kamenného zvonu** (House at Stone Bell) shows the Gothic core that lurks beneath many of Prague's Baroque facades (see **Museums,** p. 223). The flowery **Goltz-Kinský palác** on the left is the finest of Prague's Rococo buildings and the official birthplace of Soviet Communism in the Czech Republic: on February 21, 1948, Klement Gottwald declared communism victorious from its balcony. **Sv. Mikuláš** (Church of St. Nicholas) sits just across Staroměstské nám. *(Open Tu-F 10am-5pm, closes early in summer for daily concerts.)* Between Sv. Mikuláš and Maiselova, a plaque marks **Franz Kafka's** former home.

Josefov

Prague's historic Jewish neighborhood, Josefov, is located north of Staromětstské nám. along Maiselova and several side streets. In 1180, Prague's citizens complied with a pope's decree to avoid Jews by surrounding the area with a 12-foot wall, which stood until 1848. The closed city bred disease but also stories, many focusing on **Rabbi Loew ben Bezalel** (1512-1609) and his legendary *golem,* a creature made from mud that came to life to protect Prague's Jews. Hitler's decision to create a "museum of an extinct race" resulted in the preservation of the old cemetery and five synagogues despite the destruction of Prague's Jewish community in the holocaust. *(Open Su-F 9am-5:30pm; closed on Jewish holidays; museums and synagogues 450kč, students 330kč.)* At the 90-degree bend in U Starého hřbitova, **Starý židovský hřbitov** (Old Jewish Cemetery) remains the quarter's most popular attraction. Between the 14th and 18th centuries, 12 layers of 20,000 graves were laid. The 700-year-old **Staronová synagóga** (Old-New Synagogue) is Europe's oldest operating synagogue. The Hebrew clock in exterior of the neighboring **Židovská radnice** (Jewish Town Hall) runs counterclockwise. Walking down Maiselova and turning right on Široka leads you to the **Pinkasova synagóga,** whose walls list the names of victims of Nazi persecution.

Karlův most (Charles Bridge)

Head out of Staroměstské nám. on Jilská, and go right onto Karlova. Wandering left down Liliová leads to **Betlémské nám.,** where the **Betlémské kaple** (Bethlehem Chapel) stands. The present building is a reconstruction of the medieval chapel made famous by Jan Hus, the great Czech religious reformer. Turning back onto Karlova and left toward the river will lead to **Karlův most,** mobbed with tourists and people trying to sell them things. At the center of the bridge is the statue of legendary hero **Jan Nepomucký** (John of Nepomuk), confessor to Queen Žofie. Brave Jan was tossed over the side of the Charles for faithfully guarding his queen's extra-marital confidences from a suspicious King Václav IV. The right-hand rail, where Jan was supposedly ejected, is now marked with a cross and five stars between the fifth and sixth statues. It is said that if you make a wish with a finger on each star you will return to Prague. Climb the Gothic **defense tower** on the Malá Strana side of the bridge or the tower on the Old Town side for a superb view of the city. *(Both towers open daily 10am-6:30pm. 35kč, students 20kč.)* The stairs on the left side of the bridge (as you face the castle district) lead to **Hroznová,** where a crumbling mural honors John Lennon and the 60s peace movement.

Malá Strana (Lesser Side)

The seedy hangout of criminals and counter-revolutionaries for nearly a century, the cobblestone streets of Malá Strana have, in the strange sway of Prague fashion, become the most prized real estate on either side of the Vltava. From Karlův most, continue straight up Mostecká and turn right into **Malostranské nám.** Dominating the square is the magnificent Baroque **Chrám sv. Mikuláše** (Church of St. Nicholas) with its remarkable high dome. Classical concerts (many of which are frankly not worth the price of admission) take place nightly. *(Church open daily 9am-4:30pm; 30kč, students 15kč. Concert tickets an absurd 390kč, students 290kč.)* Nearby on Karmelitská rises the more modest **Panna Maria Vítězna** (Church of Our Lady Victorious). The famous polished-wax statue of the **Infant Jesus of Prague** resides within. *(Open in summer daily 7am-9pm; off-season 8am-8pm; English mass Su noon.)* A simple wooden gate just down the street at Letenská 10 opens onto **Valdštejnská zahrada** (Wallenstein Garden), one of Prague's best-kept secrets. This tranquil 17th-century Baroque garden is enclosed by old buildings that glow golden on sunny afternoons.

Pražský Hrad (Prague Castle)

Founded 1000 years ago, Pražský Hrad has always been the seat of the Bohemian government. Give the castle a full day—just don't make it Monday. From Metro A: Hradčanská, cross the tram tracks and turn left onto Tychonova, which delivers you to the glorious and newly renovated **Královský Letohrádek** (Royal Summer Palace) and the serene and shady 1534 **Královská zahrada** (Royal Garden). The **castle entrance** lies at the other end of the garden and across the **Prašný most** (Powder Bridge). Before entering the palace, you'll pass the **Šternberský palác,** home of the National Gallery's European art collection, featuring Goya, Rubens, and Rembrandt. *(Gallery open Tu-Su 10am-6pm. 45kč, students 25kč.)*

Inside the castle walls stands Pražský Hrad's centerpiece, the colossal **Katedrála sv. Víta** (St. Vitus's Cathedral), which may look Gothic but was actually finished in 1929—600 years after it was begun. The cathedral's stained glass windows were created by some of the most gifted Czech artists, including Alphonse Mucha. To the right of the high altar stands the **tomb of sv. Jan Nepomucký,** 3m of solid, glistening silver, weighing two tons. Look for an angel holding a silvered tongue. Emperor Karel IV's tomb is in the **Royal Crypt** below the church along with a handful of other Czech kings and all four of Karel's wives, who are tactfully buried in the same grave to his left. Back up the stairs in the main church, the walls of **Svatováclavská kaple** (St. Wenceslas's Chapel) are lined with precious stones and a painting cycle depicting this saint's legend. The 287 steps of the Cathedral Tower lead to the best view of the entire city. *(All sights open daily summer 9am-5pm; Sept.-Mar. 9am-4pm. Ticket office across from St. Vitus's Cathedral, inside the castle walls. Ticket valid for 3 days; 100kč, students 50kč.)*

The **Starý královský palác** (Old Royal Palace), to the right of the cathedral behind the Old Provost's House and the statue of St. George, houses the lengthy expanse of the **Vladislav Hall,** where jousting competitions once took place; upstairs is the **Chancellery of Bohemia,** the site of the second Defenestration of Prague. On May 23, 1618, angry Protestants flung two Habsburg officials (and their secretary) through the windows and into a steaming dungheap which broke their fall, signalling the start of the extraordinarily bloody Thirty Years' War in Europe.

Directly behind the cathedral stand the **convent** and **basilika sv. Jiří** (St. George). The convent is home to the **National Gallery of Bohemian Art,** from the Gothic to the Baroque. *(Open Tu-Su 10am-6pm. 50kč, students and seniors 15kč. First Friday of each month free.)* The palace street Jiřská begins to the right of the basilica. Halfway down, the tiny **Zlatá ulička** (Golden Lane) heads off to the left. Alchemists once worked here, later Kafka lived at #22, and today there is a small forest of cramped souvenir shops for tourists to squeeze in and out of. Back on Jiřská, the **Lobkovický Palác** contains a replica of Bohemia's coronation jewels and a history of the Czech lands. *(Open Tu-Su 10am-6pm. 40kč, students 20kč.)* After passing between the two armed sentries on your way out of the castle, peer over the battlements on the right for a fine cityscape, then descend the Staré Zámecké Schody (Old Castle Steps) into the Malá Strana.

Outer Prague

The **Petřínské sady,** the largest gardens in central Prague, are topped by a model of the Eiffel Tower and the wacky castle **Bludiště.** *(Castle open Tu-Su 10am-7pm.)* Take a cable car from just above the intersection of Vítězná and Újezd for spectacular views (8kč; look for *lanová dráha* signs).

The former haunt of Prague's 19th-century romantics, **Vyšehrad** is clothed in nationalistic myths and the legends of a once-powerful Czech empire. It is here that Princess Libuše foresaw Prague and embarked on her search for the first king of Bohemia. The 20th century has passed the castle by, and Vyšehrad's elevated pathways now escape the flood of tourists in the city center. Quiet walkways lead between crumbling stone walls to a magnificent **church,** a black Romanesque rotunda, and one of the Czech Republic's most celebrated sites, **Vyšehrad Cemetery,** where Dvořák and other national heroes are laid to rest. To reach the complex, take Metro C: Vyšehrad (complex open 24hr.).

Museums

Prague is not known for its museums—the city's magic emanates from the streets themselves. But if you can't stay outdoors, try one of the nine locations of **Národní galérie.** The **Šternberský palác** and **Klášter sv. Jiří** are described above in the "Pražký Hrad" section. The other major gallery is the **Klášter sv. Anežky** (St. Agnes's Cloister), where the 19th-century Czech art collection is displayed. *(Metro A: "Staromwstská." All 3 museums open Tu-Su 10am-6pm. 50kč, students 15kč.)* The **Mucha Museum,** Panská 7, is devoted entirely to the work of Alphone Mucha, the Czech Republic's most celebrated artist. *(Open daily 10am-6pm. 120kč, students and children 60kč. English guidesheet 30kč.)* Take Metro A or B to "Můstek," then walk down Václavské nám. toward the museum. Turn left onto Jindřišska, then left onto Panská. The **Uměleckoprůmyslové muzeum** (Decorative Arts), 17. listopadu 2 (tel. 24 81 12 41), across the street from Rudolfinum, exhibits fun furniture with detailed English handouts so you know what's what. *(Metro A: Staroměstská. Open M noon-6pm, Tu-Su 10am-6pm. 40kč, students 10kč.)* The **Muzeum hlavního města Prahy** (Municipal), Na poříčí 52, holds the original calendar board from the town hall's astronomical clock and a scale model of old Prague, precise to the last window pane of more than 2000 houses. *(Open Tu-Su 9am-6pm. 20kč, students 5kč. 100kč deposit for an English guidebook.)* From Metro B or C: "Florenc," exit to the left onto Sokolovská, which turns into Na poříčí. Other exhibits from the collection reside in the **Dům U kamenného zvonu** (House at Stone Bell), Staroměstské nám., left of Matka Boží před Týnem. *(Open Tu-Su 10am-6pm. 75kč, students 35kč.)*

ENTERTAINMENT

For a list of current concerts and performances, consult *The Prague Post, Threshold,* or *Do města-Downtown* (the latter two are free and distributed at most cafes and restaurants). Most shows begin at 7pm; unsold tickets are sometimes available 30 minutes before showtime. **Národní Divadlo** (National Theater), Národní třída 2/4 (tel. 24 91 34 37), is perhaps Prague's most famous theater. (Box office open M-F 10am-6pm, Sa-Su 10am-12:30pm and 3-6pm, and 30min. before performances.) Equally impressive is **Stavovské Divadlo** (Estates Theater), Ovocný trh 1 (tel. 24 21 50 01), where Mozart's *Don Giovanni* premiered (same box office as National Theater, or show up 30min. before a performance). Most of Prague's theaters shut down in July and return in August with attractions for tourists. Around mid-May to early June, the **Prague Spring Festival** draws musicians from around the world. Tickets (300-2000kč) may sell out a year in advance; try **Bohemia Ticket International,** Salvátorská 6 (tel. 24 22 78 32), next to Čedok. *(Open M-F 9am-6pm, Sa 9am-4pm, Su 10am-3pm.)*

The most authentic way to enjoy Prague at night is through an alcoholic fog; the venues below should satisfy the need for a *pivo* and a sweaty dance floor. Gay bars distribute the linguistically confused *Amigo* (15kč), a guide to gay life in the Czech Republic and Slovakia.

Kozička (The Little Goat), Kozí 1 (tel./fax 231 08 52). Metro A: Staroměstské nám. This giant cellar bar is always packed, and you'll know why after your first super-cheap 0.5L Krušovice (20kč). Twenty-something crowd comes early and stays all night. Open M-F noon-4am, Sa-Su 4pm-4am.

Cafe Marquis de Sade, a.k.a. **Cafe Babylon,** Templová 8. Metro B: nám. Republiky. Relax on the red velvet couches with a beer (25kč), while the band strikes up old pops or mellow jazz for a packed house. Open M-F noon-2am, Sa-Su 3pm-2am.

Jáma (The Hollow), V Jámě 7. Metro A or C: Muzeum. Walk down Václavské nam. away from the museum, turn left on Vodičkova, then left again on V Jámě. While the crowd is mainly American, Jáma is the closest thing to a sports bar in Prague. Enjoy *Staropramen* (25kč) with satellite TV. Open daily 11am-1am.

Újezd, Újezd 18. Metro B: Národní třída. A mid-20s crowd smokes the night away at this mecca of mellowness—a giant mushroom chandelier hangs above the bar. DJ or live acid jazz 3 times a week. Open nightly 6pm-3am.

Molly Malone's, U obecního dvora 4. Metro A: Staroměstská. Very green, but very cozy. A draft of *Staropramen* is 30kč, and Guinness is cheaper than in Ireland at 65kč per pint. Open Su-Th noon-midnight, F-Sa noon-1:45am.

Roxy, Dlouhá 33. Metro B: nám. Republiky. Walk up Revoluční toward the river and turn left on Dlouhá. Experimental DJs, theme nights, and endless dancing. Open Tu-Su from 8pm. Cover starts at 50kč.

U Staré Paní, Michalská 9. Metro A or B: Můstek, then walk down na Můstku at the end of Václavské nám through its name change to Melantrichova. Turn left on Havelská and right on Michalská. "At the Old Lady's" showcases some of the finest jazz vocalists in Prague in a classy upstairs venue. Shows nightly 9pm-midnight. Cover 90kč; with ISIC or GO25 45kč, plus 10% off drinks. Open daily 7pm-4am.

Radost FX, Bělehradská 120. Metro C: I.P. Pavlova, then walk towards the church and turn right on Bělehradská. Heavily touristed, but still plays bad-ass music and remains packed. *Staropramen* 35kč. Cover from 50kč. Open nightly 8pm-dawn.

U Střelce, Karoliny Světlé 12. Metro B: Národní Třída, then walk down Národní towards the river, and turn right on Karoliny Světlé; the club is under the archway on the right. Gay club pulls a diverse crowd with F and Sa night cabarets, when fabulous female impersonators take the stage. Cover 100kč. Open nightly 6pm-4am.

L-Club, Lublaňská 48. Metro C: I. P. Pavlova. Great fun for both guys and dolls, with a blacklit disco, bar, and cafe. Mostly gay men. Cover 75kč. Open nightly 8pm-4am.

■ Near Prague: Karlštejn, Kutná Hora, and Terezín

The Bohemian hills around Prague contain 14 castles, some built as early as the 13th century. A train ride southwest from Hlavní nádraží or Praha-Smíchov (45min., 20Kč) brings you to **Karlštejn** (tel. (0311) 68 46 17), a walled and turreted fortress built by Karel IV to house his crown jewels and holy relics. The **Chapel of the Holy Cross** is decorated with more than 2000 inlaid precious stones and 128 apocalyptic paintings by medieval artist Master Theodorik (open Tu-Su 9am-5pm; mandatory tour; English guide 90Kč, Czech 20Kč). Ask at tourist information in Prague whether they've finished restoring the chapel before setting out.

An hour and a half east of Prague is the former mining town of **Kutná Hora** (Mining Hill). A 13th-century abbot sprinkled soil from Golgotha on the cemetery, which made the rich and superstitious keen to be buried there. In a fit of whimsy, the monk in charge began designing flowers out of pelvi and crania. He never finished, but the artist František Rint completed the project in 1870 with flying butt-bones, femur crosses, and a grotesque chandelier made from every bone in the human body. (Open daily Apr.-Sept. 8am-noon and 1-6pm; Oct. 9am-noon and 1-5pm; Nov.-Mar. 9am-noon and 1-4pm. 30kč, students 15kč.) The *kostnice* (ossuary) is 2km from the bus station: take a local bus to "Sedlec Tabák" and follow the signs. **Buses** arrive regularly from Prague's Florenc station (1½hr.) and from station 2 at Metro A: "Želivského" (1¾hr.).

In 1940 Hitler's Gestapo set up a prison in the Small Fortress in Theresienstadt, and in 1941 the town itself became the **Terezín** concentration camp—by 1942, the civilian population had been evacuated. Some 35,000 Jews died here and 85,000 others were transported to death camps in the east, primarily Auschwitz. Twice, Terezín was beautified in order to deceive delegations from the Red Cross. The **Ghetto Museum,** Komenského, displays contemporary documents and harrowing children's art from the ghetto. (Open daily 9am-6pm; closes at 5:30 in off-season. 90kč, including Small Fortress 100kč, students 60kč. Guided tour in English 220kč.) East of the town, the **Small Fortress** is the other major sight (open daily May-Sept. 8am-6pm; Oct.-Apr. 8am-4:30pm). The Prague-Florenc **bus** (1hr., every 1-2hr., 20kč) stops by the central square, where the **tourist office** sells a map (25kč; open until 6pm).

WEST BOHEMIA

West Bohemia overflows with curative springs: over the centuries, emperors and intellectuals have soaked in the waters of Karlovy Vary and Mariánské Lázně. The Czech Republic's two most popular drinks also have their home here—the spicy green *Becherovka* and Plzeň's world-famous *Pilsner*.

■ Karlovy Vary

Once a vacation spot for such diverse personalities as Sigmund Freud, Peter the Great, and Karl Marx, Karlovy Vary now attracts aging German tourists seeking out the therapeutic powers of the spas and springs. Younger visitors are known to indulge in its other "therapeutic" waters.

SIGHTS AND ENTERTAINMENT In the heart of the pedestrian spa area, you're free to drink from the **Pramen svobody** (Freedom Spring) or the five more spas that cluster along the **Mlýnská kolonáda** (Mill Colonnade). Bring your own cup or buy one for 40-180kč. Across the river, the Baroque dome of the **Kostel sv. Maří Magdalená** (Church of Mary Magdalene) and the Art Nouveau **Zawojski House** deserve a look. The most potent of the springs, the **Vřídlo Spring** spurts 30L of 72°C water several meters into the air every second. Follow Stará Louka (Old Meadow) until you reach Mariánská; at the dead end, a **funicular** rises to the **Diana Watchtower** (runs daily 9am-6pm, every 15min.; round-trip 30kč). The tower opens its spiraling staircase daily until 6:30pm (10kč). Pop into **Lázně** (Bath) **3** (tel. 322 56 41) to get an underwater massage (110kč). Karlovy Vary's **International Film Festival** runs July 2-10.

E&T, Zeyerova 3 (tel. (017) 322 60 22), serves meat dishes and salads on an outdoor terrace (main dishes 80-130kč; open M-Sa 10am-midnight, Su 11am-midnight). **Propaganda,** Jaltská 5 (tel. (017) 322 22 92), attracts Karlovy Vary's hippest young crowd (drinks from 20kč; open M-Th 5pm-3am, F-Sa 5pm-6am, Su 5pm-2am).

PRACTICAL INFO, ACCOMMODATIONS, AND FOOD The town is referred to in German as *Karlsbad,* and prices are often listed in DM. **Trains** arrive from Prague (4½hr., 5 per day, 126kč). **Buses,** quicker than trains, serve Prague (2½hr., 25 per day, 95kč) and Plzeň (1½hr., 16 per day, 70kč). The white **City-Info booth** (tel. (017) 322 33 51; fax 322 57 61) on Masaryka across from the post office, books rooms starting at 450kč per person. Exchange traveler's checks at banks (2% commission) or at **American Express,** Vřídelní 51, for free (AmEx open M-Su 9am-7pm). **Karlovarsky Autorent,** nám. Dr. Horákové 18 (tel. (017) 332 28 33), can book a double for 900kč (open M-F 9am-5pm, Sa 9am-noon; off-season closed noon-1pm). **Pension Kosmos,** Zahradní 39 (tel. (017) 322 31 68), in the center of the spa district offers singles 440kč (with bath 750kč) and doubles 720kč (with bath 1340kč). **Pension Romania,** Zahradní 49 (tel. (017) 322 28 22), is a great deal, offering singles, doubles, and triples for 895kč per person, 616kč for students and children, breakfast included. Most of Karlovy Vary's eateries are over-priced and over-bland; try the supermarket **Městská Tržnice,** Horova 1 (open M-F 6am-7pm, Sa 7am-5pm, Su 10am-6pm). The (mostly) **Vegetarian Restaurant,** I.P. Pavlova 25, has fruit kebab (45kč) and spicy veggie goulash and dumplings (35kč; open daily 11am-9pm).

SOUTH BOHEMIA

■ České Budějovice

No amount of beer can help you correctly pronounce České Budějovice (CHESS-kay BOOD-yay-yov-ee-tzeh). Luckily for pint-guzzlers, the town was known as Budweis in the 19th century when it inspired the name of the popular but pale North American *Budweiser,* which bares little relation to the malty local *Budvar.* Nestled in lush Bohemian countryside with endless bus and train connections, České Budějovice makes a terrific launchpad for day trips to the region's many wonders.

Surrounded by Renaissance and Baroque buildings, cobbled **nám. Otakara II** is the largest square in the Czech Republic. Near the square's northeast corner, **Černá věž** (Black Tower) looms over the town. Beware: the treacherous stairs, rising 72m, are difficult even for the sober. (10kč. Open Tu-Su July-Aug. 10am-7pm; Sept.-Nov. 9am-5pm; Mar.-June 10am-6pm.) The tower once served as a belfry for the neighboring 13th-century **Chrám sv. Mikuláše** (Church of St. Nicholas; open daily 7am-6pm). The city's most famous attraction, the **Budweiser Brewery,** Karoliny Světlé 4, offers tours of the factory for groups of six or more; arrange them at the tourist office. To reach the brewery, take bus 2 or 4 from the center of town. České Budějovice also sports a super-hip **second-hand shopping** scene. Shops with large "Second Hand" signs pop up everywhere, but are particularly abundant along Riegrova, off nám. Otakara II.

The **train** station welcomes travelers from Brno (4½hr., 126kč), Plzeň (2hr., 72kč), and Prague (2½hr., 92kč). To reach the gigantic nám. Otakara II from the station, take a right out of the main entrance onto Nádražní and turn left at the pedestrian Lannova tř., which becomes Kanovnická. The **tourist office,** nám. Otakara II 2 (tel./fax (038) 594 80), books private rooms. (Around 350kč. Open May-Sept. M-F 8am-6pm, Sa 8am-3pm, Su 8am-1pm; Oct.-Apr. closes 1hr. earlier.) **Pension U Výstaviště,** U Výstaviště 17 (tel. (038) 724 01 48), is a clean, friendly establishment; take tram 1 from the station to "U parku" and continue 150m along the street that branches right (250kč first night, 200kč thereafter; they may offer you a free lift from the station). The University of South Bohemia **dorms** (tel. (038) 777 44 00) on Studenstská open to travelers in July and August. Take tram 1 from the bus station five stops to "U parku," then head back down Husova, and turn right (doubles 300kč).

This Bud's for EU

Many Yankees, having tasted the malty goodness of a Budvar brew, return home to find it conspicuously unavailable. That Budvar was the Czech Republic's largest exporter of beer in 1995 makes its absence from American store shelves even stranger. Where's the Budvar? The answer lies in a tale of trademarks and town names. České Budějovice (Budweis in German) had been brewing its own style of lager for centuries when the Anheuser-Busch brewery in St. Louis came out with its Budweiser-style beer in 1876. Not until the 1890s, however, did the Budějovice Pivovar (Brewery) begin producing a beer labeled "Budweiser." International trademark conflicts ensued, and in 1911 the companies signed a non-competition agreement: Budvar got markets in Europe and Anheuser-Busch took North America. But the story continues...

A few years ago, Anheuser-Busch tried to end the confusion by buying a controlling interest in the makers of Budvar. The Czech government replied "nyeh." In response, the following year Anheuser-Busch didn't order its normal one-third of the Czech hop crop. Anheuser-Busch is now suing for trademark infringement in Finland, while Budvar is petitioning the EU to make the moniker "Budweiser" a designation as exclusive as that of "Champagne," meaning that any brand sold in the EU under that name would have to come from the Budweiser region. As long as the battle continues on European fronts, there is little chance that a Budvar in America will be anything but an illegal alien.

Restaurants abound along the Old Town's back streets, but it's hard to find anything but meat, dumplings, and *Budvar*. There's a grocery store, **Večerka,** at Plachého 10 (entrance on Hroznova; open M-F 7am-8pm, Sa 7am-1pm, Su 8am-8pm). Aid your digestion of Tábor steak (95kč) or veggie dishes (50-70kč) with a tall *Budvar* (19kč per 0.5L) at **Vinárna U paní Emy,** Široká 25, near the main square. In summer, lakes around the town host open-air **disco concerts** (ask at the tourist office).

■ Český Krumlov

Winding medieval streets, scenic promenades, and the looming presence of Bohemia's second-largest castle make Český Krumlov one of the most popular spots in the Czech Republic. The town's wonderful location on the banks of the Vltava also makes it ideal for hiking, bicycling, canoeing, and kayaking.

SIGHTS AND ENTERTAINMENT Perched high above the town, the **castle's** stone courtyard is free to the public, and two tours cover the lavish interior, which includes frescoes, a Baroque theater, and crypt galleries. (Open Apr. and Oct. Tu-Su 9am-noon and 1-3pm; May, June, and Sept. Tu-Su 9am-noon and 1-4pm; July-Aug. Tu-Su 9am-noon and 1-5pm. Tours in English 50kč.) You can also ascend the 147 steps of the castle **tower** (25kč, students 15kč) for a magnificent view of the town. Housed in an immense Renaissance building, the **Egon Schiele International Cultural Center,** Široká 70-72, contains hours of browsing material, including works by Picasso and other 20th-century artists (open daily 10am-6pm; 120kč, students 80kč). The **Five-Petal Rose Festival,** Krumlov's medieval fair, happens the third weekend in June and provides a great excuse to dress up in tights and joust with the locals. **U Baby,** Rooseveltova 66, pours hefty steins of *Eggenberg* (18kč; open Tu-Su 6pm-midnight).

PRACTICAL INFO, ACCOMMODATIONS, AND FOOD Sixteen kilometers southwest of České Budějovice, the town is best reached by frequent **buses** (35min.; M-F 22 per day, Sa 8 per day, Su 12 per day; 20kč). The **tourist office,** nám. Svornosti 1 (tel. (0337) 71 11 83), in the town hall, books rooms in pensions from 550kč and cheaper private rooms (open daily 9am-6pm). From the bus station, head to the upper street (where stops #20-25 are located) and turn right. As the road curves right, follow the dirt path uphill to the left. At the path's intersection with Kaplická, turn right. At the light, cross the highway and go straight onto Horní, which brings you into the square. **U vodnika,** Po vodě 55 (tel. (0337) 71 19 35; email vodnik@ck.bohem-net.cz), located in a lush 13th-century home, has a quad (200kč per person) and two doubles (250kč per person) near the river (**Internet access** 100kč per hr.). For a livelier stay, try **Krumlov House,** just up the road at Rooseveltova 68 (same tel., same rates as U vodnika). From the station, follow directions to the tourist office but go left on Rooseveltova after the street light. The 17-bed **Ryba Hostel,** Rybářska 5 (tel. (0337) 71 18 01), on the banks of the Vltava, offers dorm-style rooms for 200kč per bed. Overlooking the castle tower, **Vegetarian Restaurant,** Parkán 105 (tel. (0337) 71 25 08) serves up heaping portions of tasty veggie dishes (50-60kč; open daily 11am-8:30pm). The **Cikanská jízba** (Gypsy bar), Dlouhá 31 (tel. (0337) 55 85), serves traditional gypsy fare to a faithful crowd of American ex-pats and locals. The spicy goulash (57kč) should not be missed (main dishes around 60kč; open M-Th 2-11pm, F-Sa 3pm-1am).

MORAVIA

Wine-making Moravia makes up the easternmost third of the Czech Republic. Home to the country's finest folk-singing tradition and two of its leading universities, Moravia is also the birthplace of a number of Czech notables: Tomáš Masaryk, first president of Czechoslovakia; composer Leoš Janáček; and psychologist Sigmund Freud.

■ Brno

Second city of the Czech Republic, Brno (bruh-NO) industrialized early and still attracts keen business interest in its frequent trade fairs—as well as the attention of motorcycling fans fixated on the annual **Grand Prix**. The city also offers a fine collection of Gothic and Baroque churches, splendidly cheap opera, techno raves all summer long, and amazing ice cream. While there are more exciting and beautiful places to visit in the Czech Republic, Brno offers travelers the opportunity to escape the hordes of tourists and experience a living Czech city.

SIGHTS AND ENTERTAINMENT Monks at the **Hrobka Kapucínského Kláštera** (Capuchin Monastery Crypt), just to the left of Masarykova as you come up from the station, developed a revolutionary embalming technique, preserving 100-plus 18th-century monks and assorted worthies. The results are now on display. (Open M-Sa 9am-noon and 2-4:30pm, Su 11-11:45am and 2-4:30pm. 40kč, students 20kč.) At Radnická 8, the tower of the **Stará radnice** (Old Town Hall) looms large over a vegetable market. The dragon hanging on one wall was said to have ravaged the town in medieval times. A knight tricked it into eating quick-lime, and when the dragon tried to quench its thirst, its belly exploded—thus the seam that marks his stomach today (*radnice* open daily Apr.-Oct. 12 9am-5pm; tower 10kč). Towering above Zelný trh on Petrov Hill is the **Biskupská Katedrála sv. Petra a Pavel** (Cathedral of St. Peter and St. Paul), whose bells ring twelve times at 11am to commemorate a ruse which once held off Swedish invaders (open daily 10am-6pm). Head down Husova and up the hill on the right to reach **Hrad Špilberk**, the mighty Hapsburg fortress-turned-prison where Hungarian, Italian, Polish and Czech patriots and revolutionaries were incarcerated in grim conditions. (Open daily June-Sept. 9am-6pm; Oct.-Mar. 9am-5pm. 20kč, students 10kč. English leaflet available. English-speaking guide 200kč.)

Head downhill from the castle on Pellicova, take the stairs on the right leading to Sladová, then left on Úvez to reach the heart of Old Brno, **Mendlovo nám.** The high Gothic **Basilika Nanebevzetí Panny Marie** (Basilica of the Assumption of the Virgin Mary) houses the 13th-century *Black Madonna*, the Czech Republic's oldest wood icon, which purportedly held off the Swedes in 1645 (church open daily 5pm-7:15pm, Su also 7am-12:15pm). The Augustinian monastery next door was the home of **Johann Gregor Mendel**, who laid out the fundamental laws of modern genetics. The **Mendelianum**, Mendlovo nám. 1a, documents Mendel's life and works, explaining his remarkable experiments with peas and bees. (Open daily July-Aug. 9am-6pm; Sept.-June 8am-5pm. 8kč, students 4kč. English pamphlet 5kč.) Check out the posters plastered around town for info on films, shows, and techno raves, Brno students' favorite summer entertainment. Or stop by the **Divadelní Hospoda Vesdá Husa** (Merry Goose Theatrical Pub), Zelný trh 9, for impromptu performances and improv games (open M-F 11am-midnight, Sa-Su 3pm-midnight). Inside **H46**, Hybešova 46, a mostly gay, partly lesbian, others-welcome bar pours beer (20kč; ring bell if door is locked; open nightly 4pm-4am).

PRACTICAL INFO, ACCOMMODATIONS, AND FOOD **Trains** (tel. (05) 42 21 48 03) run to Bratislava (2hr., 97kč), České Budějovice (4½hr., 104kč), and Prague (3hr., 132kč). **Buses** also make frequent trips to Prague (120kč) from Zvonařka station (tel. (05) 43 21 77 33). The **tourist office**, Radnická 8 (tel. (05) 42 21 10 90; fax 42 21 07 58), in the old town hall, books rooms and sells guidebooks and maps (39-60kč; open M-F 8am-6pm, Sa-Su 9am-5pm). **GTS International,** Skrytá 2 (tel. (05) 42 21 31 47), sells ISICs (180kč) and books dorm rooms in July and August (from 400kč). To reach the lackluster **Interservis (HI)**, Lomená 48 (tel. (05) 45 23 31 65; fax 33 11 65), take tram 9 or 12 from the train station to the end at "Komárov," continue along Hněvkovského, and turn left onto the unmarked Pompova, the last turn before the railroad overpass (230-270kč per person, without HI or ISIC 275kč. Watch for bugs.) **Pension Bulharský Klub,** Skrytá 1 (tel. (05) 42 21 10 63), has one hall of doubles with a shared shower and toilet (doubles and triples 300kč per person; reception varies, call ahead). A young Czech crowd angsts at **Livingstone,** Starobrněnská 1. (*Kuřeci prsa* (chicken) 45kč; *Krušovice* beer 17.50kč. Open M-F noon-1am, Sa-Su 6pm-1am.) Follow the rainbow-colored hot-air balloon murals to **Aviatik Klub and Restaurace,** Jakubská 7, for traditional Czech favorites (30-75kč) and tea (open M-Sa 11am-11pm). Brno's lone cybercafe, **@InternetCafe,** Lidická 17, serves great coffee (25kč; Internet access 2kč per min.; open M-F 10am-10pm, Sa-Su 2-10pm).

■ Olomouc

Olomouc (OH-lo-mots), the historic capital of North Moravia, is a town more chic than Brno, but more quaint than Prague. Tourists will likely find themselves outnumbered by local students. The imposing spires of **Metropolitní Kostel sv. Václava** (Metropolitan Church of St. Wenceslas), tucked away in the northeast corner of the Old Town, features a high-vaulted interior in impeccable condition. Downstairs, the crypt museum exhibits the gold-encased skull of St. Pauline (open M-Th and Sa 9am-5pm, F 1-5pm, Su 11am-5pm; donations accepted). The massive 1378 **radnice** (town hall) dominates Horní nám.; the saints in its wonderful astronomical clock on the north side were replaced with steel workers in 1954.

Trains connect to Brno (1½hr., 53-68kč) and Prague (3½hr., 127kč). The **tourist office** (tel. (068) 551 33 85), Horní nám. in the town hall, has tons of info, offers 4 tours a day, and books rooms from 230kč per person (open daily 9am-7pm). The dorm **Hostel Envelopa,** 17. listopadu 54 (tel. (068) 522 38 41), was recently refurbished. From the train station, take any inbound tram two stops to "Žižkovo nám." and go down the road to the left of Masaryk's statue (singles 215kč; doubles 500-612kč, with ISIC 310-406kč; open July-Aug.). For **Hostel Palavecký Stadión,** Legionářská 11 (tel. (068) 41 31 81; fax 541 32 56), at the swimming stadium, take any tram from the train station to "nám. Národních hrdínů," backtrack through the bus park, head left under the airplane, and go around the pool buildings (doubles 400kč; triples 440kč; swimming 30kč). **U červeného volka,** Dolní nám. 39, serves delicious soy dishes (48kč) and porky plates (48-71kč; open M-Sa 10am-11pm). **Depo No. 8,** nám. Republiky 1, offers Czech food (with some tofu) and turns into a popular dance club at night (open M-Th 10am-4am, F-Sa 10am-6am, Su 4am-1am). A 24-hour **grocery** store sits at Komenského 3.

The World's Most Difficult Sound

Not quite a Spanish "r" and simply not the Polish "rz" (pronounced like the second "g" in "garage"), Czech's own linguistic blue note, the letter "ř," lies excruciatingly in between. Although many of Prague's ex-pats would sacrifice a month of Saturdays at Jo's Bar to utter the elusive sound just once, few manage more than a strangely trilled whistle. Most foreigners resign themselves to using the "ž" (akin to the Polish "rz") in its place, but what we consider a subtle difference often confuses Czechs. For all those linguistic daredevils in the audience, here's a sure-fire method of tackling the randy Mr. Ř: roll your tongue and quickly follow with a "ž", then repeat. Oh, yeah—and start when you're two.

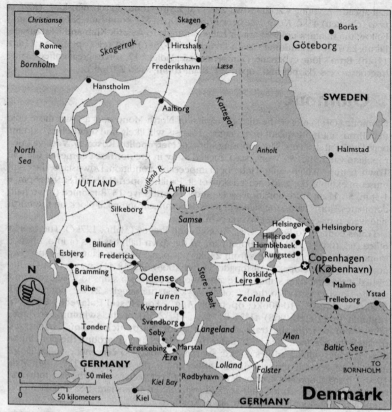

Denmark (Danmark)

US$1	= 6.57kr (Denmark kroner)		10kr =	US$1.52
CDN$1	= 4.33kr		10kr =	CDN$2.31
UK£1	= 10.92kr		10kr =	UK£0.92
IR£1	= 9.54kr		10kr =	IR£1.05
AUS$1	= 3.89kr		10kr =	AUS$2.57
NZ$1	= 3.37kr		10kr =	NZ$2.97
SAR1	= 1.06kr		10kr =	SAR9.43
Country Code: 45			**International Dialing Prefix: 00**	

Denmark is clean, safe, and has one of the most supportive social security structures in the world. The Danes levy high taxes to provide everyone with quality education, health care, and retirement benefits. They were also the first to legalize gay and lesbian marriages and have accepted immigrants from around the world. As a result, Denmark is no longer a homogeneous blonde, blue-eyed landscape; even the new Princess Alexandra boasts Austrian and Hong Kong lineage. Though Danes are proud of their green farmland, beech forests, chalk cliffs, and sand dunes, they are also endowed with a sense of self-criticism, which is reflected in the Danish literary canon: the more famous voices are Søren Kirkegaard, Hans Christian Andersen, Isak Dinesen, and, more recently, Peter Høeg. Contrary to the suggestion of a certain English playwright, very little seems to be rotten in the state of Denmark.

Wedged between Sweden and Germany, Denmark is the cultural and geographic bridge between Scandinavia and continental Europe. Well into the 16th century, the Danish crown ruled an empire uniting Norway, Sweden, Iceland, and parts of Germany; Christianity, the Protestant Reformation, and the socialist movements of the late 19th century also entered into Scandinavia via Denmark. During World War I, Denmark remained neutral, but in 1940 the Danes capitulated to Hitler rather than risk a full invasion; however, they did not compromise their humanitarianism, smuggling 7000 Danish Jews into neutral Sweden. Today, Denmark beckons with the pristine beaches of Funen and the hip, progressive scene in Copenhagen.

Finally—high-brow generalities aside—Denmark has a pub-culture that is unrivaled among its Scandinavian neighbors. Home to the famous beers Carlsberg and Tuborg, this just, gentle country knows how to have a good time.

GETTING THERE AND GETTING AROUND

Eurail passes are valid on all state-run **DSB** routes. The *buy-in-Scandinavia* **Scanrail Pass** allows five days within 15 (1350kr, under 26 1000kr, 60 and over 1200kr) or 21 consecutive days (2100kr, under 26 1550kr, 60 and over 1850kr) of unlimited rail travel through Denmark, Norway, Sweden, and Finland, as well as many free or 20-50% discounted ferry rides. This differs from the *buy-outside-Scandinavia* **Scanrail Pass,** which offers five out of 15 days (US$182, under 26 US$137), 10 days out of one month (US$292, under 26 US$219), or 30 consecutive days (US$426, under 26 US$320) of unlimited travel. Seat reservations, compulsory on many international trains (20-68kr), can be made at central stations or by phone. For domestic schedules, reservations, and info, call 70 13 14 15; for international call 70 13 14 16. Remote towns may be served by **buses** from the nearest train station.

With the completion of the **Great Belt Fixed Link,** Zealand is for the first time connected to Funen by an 18km underwater tunnel for trains and parallel bridge for cars. Later phases of this project will link southern Zealand to Germany and make Malmö, Sweden the newest suburb of Copenhagen. These projects are significantly reducing travel time to, within, and through Denmark. Eurail and Scanrail Passes secure discounts and some free rides on many Scandinavian **ferries,** and the free *Ni Rejser* newspaper, available at tourist offices, can help you sort out the dozens of smaller ferries that serve Denmark's outlying islands. See **Ferries,** p. 235.

Flat terrain, well-marked national and local bike routes, bike paths in the countryside, and bike lanes in towns and cities make Denmark a cyclist's dream. Cyclists are required to obey traffic signals; failure to do so will result in fines. You can rent **bicycles** (35-50kr per day) from some tourist offices (not Copenhagen's), ubiquitous bicycle rental shops, and a few railway stations in north Zealand. A 200kr deposit is usually required. The **Dansk Cyklist Førbund** (Danish Cycle Federation), Rømersg. 7, 1362 Copenhagen K (tel. 33 32 31 21; fax 33 32 76 83; http://www.dcf.dk; email dcf@inet.uni-c.dk), sells repair and touring products, cycling maps (free-80kr), and helpful literature, and can hook you up with longer-term rental companies. You can take your bike on specially marked cars of most trains. (Look for the white bicycle sign painted on the doors, or consult *Bikes and Trains,* available at most train stations. Free-50kr; check with conductor.)

ESSENTIALS

Stacks of free brochures in English, available from **tourist offices** and Danish Tourist Boards abroad (see **Government Information Offices,** p. 2), will help you find your way around. The easiest way to get cash is from **ATMs: Cirrus** and **PLUS** cash cards are widely accepted, and many machines give advances on credit cards. PIN numbers are four digits long. Most banks charge a commission of 10-35kr per traveler's check, but the **American Express** office in Copenhagen (the only one in Denmark) can exchange checks of smaller denominations for larger ones. Danish **phone** numbers have no city codes. From pay phones, local calls require 2kr. Phone cards are sold at post offices and kiosks in denominations of 30, 50, and 100kr. Denmark's **emergency** number is 112; no coins are required. For domestic directory info, dial 118 (10kr per min.); for international info, 113 (8kr per min.). For **collect calls**, dial 141; for direct international calls, 00 then the country code. For **AT&T Direct** dial 80 01 00 10; **MCI WorldPhone** 80 01 00 22; **SprintExpress** 80 01 08 77; **Canada Direct** 80 01 00 11; **BT Direct** 80 01 02 90; **New Zealand Binary Systems** 80 88 02 45. The country celebrates national **holidays** on Easter (Apr. 5), Common Prayer Day (Apr. 30), Ascension Day (May 13), Whit Sunday and Monday (May 23-24), Constitution Day (June 5), Midsummer (June 23-24), Christmas (Dec. 24-26), and New Year's Eve (Dec. 31).

The Danish alphabet adds *æ* (like the "e" in "egg,"), *ø* (like the "i" in "first,"), and *å* (still sometimes written as *aa*; like the "o" in "lord") at the end; thus Århus would follow Viborg in an alphabetical listing of cities. Knowing *ikke* ("not") will help you figure out such signs as "No smoking" *(ikker ryger)*, and *åben/lukket* (O-ben/loock-eh, "open/closed") is also useful. Nearly all Danes speak flawless English, but a few Danish words might help break the ice: try *skål* (skoal, "cheers"). Danish has a distinctive glottal stop known as a *stød*, indicated in the chart below as an apostrophe.

Yes/no	*Ja/Nej*	Ya/Ny
Hello/good-bye	*Dav/Farvel*	Dow'/fah-VEL
Hi/bye (informal)	*Hej/Hejhej*	HIGH/HIGH-high
Please	*Vær venlig*	VER VEN-li
Thank you	*Tak*	tak
Excuse me	*Undskyld*	UND-scoold
Do you speak English?	*Taler De engelsk?*	TA' lor dee ENG' elsg
I don't speak Danish.	*Jeg taler ikke dansk.*	Yai TA' lor IG-ge dan'sg
Where is...?	*Hvor er...?*	Vaw' ayr
How much does it cost?	*Hvad koster det?*	Va KOS' tor dey
I would like...a room.	*Jeg vil gerne have... et værelse.*	Yai vil GAYR-ne HAY-ve it VAYR-el-se
Help!	*Hjælp!*	Yel'b

Emergency health care in Denmark is free, but those in less dire straits must pay an initial fee of 200-400kr. **Wheelchairs** and **strollers** are allowed on trains and buses at no additional cost. All Copenhagen buses are equipped for wheelchair access and many street lights nationwide click slow for "don't walk" and fast for "walk" to help **vision-impaired** pedestrians. For more info, contact the **Danish Association for the Handicapped** *(Dansk Handicap Ferbund)*, Hans Knudsens Plads 1A, 1st floor, 2100 Copenhagen Ø (tel. 39 29 35 55; fax 39 29 39 48; email dhf@dhf-net.dk), and ask for a free copy of *Access in Denmark.* **DSB** publishes *Handicappede*, available at all ticket offices, which details wheelchair access to every train station in the country. **Women** travelers who take normal precautions should find Denmark safe. **Lesbian, bisexual, and gay** travelers will be amazed at the level of tolerance in Denmark, although more rural areas may still harbor hostility. Contact the **Danish Association for Gays and Lesbians** (see p. 236).

ACCOMMODATIONS AND CAMPING

While Denmark's hotels are generally expensive (250-850kr), the country's 101 **HI youth hostels** *(vandrerhjem)* are well run, have no age limit, and generally include rooms for families at the same per person rate. The 1-5 star rating system doesn't take lovely settings, friendly owners, or serendipitous encounters into account, but higher rated hostels may have in-room bathrooms and longer opening hours. All charge less than 100kr per bed; nonmembers pay 25kr extra. Sheets cost about 35kr more. You can generally feast on an unlimited breakfast for 38kr. Kitchen facilities are often available. Reception desks normally take a break between noon and 4pm and close for the day at 9 or 11pm. Because hostels cater primarily to families and school groups, they may be booked far ahead, and may be far from cities. Reservations are required in winter and highly recommended in summer, especially near beaches. They can be made by phone without a deposit, but you will be asked to show up by 5pm or call that day to confirm. Official hostel guides are available at hostels and tourist offices. For more info, contact the **Danish Youth Hostel Association** (tel. 31 31 36 12; fax 31 31 36 26; email ldv@danhostel.dk; http://www.danhostel.dk). Many tourist offices book rooms in **private homes** (125-175kr), which are often in suburbs.

Denmark's 525 official **campgrounds** (about 60kr per person) rank from one star (toilets and drinking water) to three (showers and laundry) to five (swimming, restaurants, and stoves). You'll need a **camping pass,** available at all campgrounds and valid for a year (30kr, families 60kr, groups 120kr). One-time guest passes are 7.50kr (families 15kr); international passes are also accepted. The **Danish Camping Council** (*Campingrådet*), Hesseløg. 16, DK-2100 Copenhagen Ø (tel. 39 27 88 44), sells a campground handbook (*Camping Denmark;* 100-130kr by mail-order, 95kr in bookstores and tourist offices) and passes. The free *Camping/Youth and Family Hostels* from the Danish Youth Hostel Association is also adequate. Sleeping in train stations and parks is illegal, as is camping on private property, beaches, and protected lands.

FOOD AND DRINK A "Danish" in Denmark is a *wienerbrød* ("Viennese bread") and can be found in bakeries alongside other flaky treats. Danish ice cream cones are freshly made from thin waffles. For more substantial fare, Danes favor small, open-faced sandwiches called *smørrebrød*. Look for lunch specials called *dagens ret* and all-you-can-eat buffets (*spis alt du kan* or *tag selv buffet*). Beer (*Øl*) is usually served as a *lille* or *stor fadøl* (0.25L or 0.5L draft), but bottled beer tends to be cheaper. National brews are Carlsberg and Tuborg. Shots of hard liquor like *akvavit* are usually reserved for special occasions. The drinking age in bars in Denmark is 18, but many clubs have higher age limits; you must be 15 to buy beer and wine in stores. Restaurant checks and bar tabs include tax and service. Many **vegetarian** (*vegetarret*) options are the result of Indian and Mediterranean influences, but salads and vegetables (*grøntsaker*) can be found on most menus. For more info, contact **Dansk Vegetarforening,** Borups Allé 131, 2000 Frederiksberg (tel. 38 34 24 48).

■ Copenhagen (København)

"Wonderful, wonderful Copenhagen!" sings Danny Kaye in the 1952 film *Hans Christian Andersen,* but despite the swan ponds and cobblestone clichés that Andersen's fairy-tale imagery brings to mind, Denmark's capital is a fast-paced modern city which offers cafes to rival Paris, nightlife to rival London, and style to rival New York—all at half the cost of Oslo or Stockholm. Some of the most beautiful (and best dressed) people on the planet can be seen walking down Strøget. Copenhagen today is a cosmopolitan city where mythic blonde children walk to school with their Inuit, Turkish, Greek, Vietnamese, and Ethiopian classmates. But if you are still craving Andersen's Copenhagen, the *Lille Havfrue* (Little Mermaid), *Tivoli,* and *Nyhavn*'s Hanseatic gingerbread houses are also yours to discover. And despite Danny Kaye's penchant for calling the city "CopenhAHgen," most Danes will agree that in English, København is most definitely (and no less wonderfully) "CopenhAYgen."

ORIENTATION AND PRACTICAL INFORMATION

Copenhagen lies on the east coast of the island of **Zealand** (Sjælland); Malmö, Sweden, is just across the sound (Øresund). Copenhagen's **Hovedbanegården** (Central Station) lies close to the city's heart. One block north of the station, **Vesterbrogade** passes **Tivoli** and **Rådhuspladsen** (the city's central square, where most bus lines begin) and then cuts through the city center as **Strøget** (STROY-yet), the world's longest pedestrian thoroughfare. Outlying districts fan out from the center: **Østerbro** is known as affluent, while working-class **Nørrebro** draws students. **Vesterbro** is considered Copenhagen's rougher side because of its red-light district (near the train station on Istegade). **Christianshavn** is known as "little Amsterdam" for its waterways and its hippie-hash artists' colony, **Christiania,** in the district's south-central half.

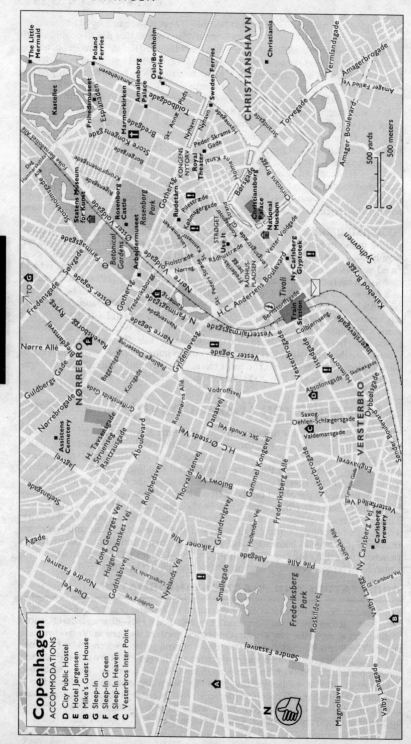

Copenhagen
ACCOMMODATIONS

D City Public Hostel
E Hotel Jørgensen
B Mike's Guest House
G Sleep-In
F Sleep-In Green
A Sleep-In Heaven
C Vesterbros Inter Point

At the end of 1999, Copenhagen will change all phone numbers that begin with "31." Call toll-free 80 80 80 80 for the new numbers, but snag someone who speaks Danish.

Flights: For schedule info, call 32 47 47 47 or 32 54 17 01. Bus 250S (40min., 17kr) from Rådhusplådsen and the Central Station, and the SAS bus (20min., 35kr) from Central Station both run to and from **Kastrup Airport,** 11km away. SAS buses run daily to the airport 5:40am-9:45pm every 15min., and back 6:30am-11:10pm every 10-15min. By 1999, a new subway (S-bana) at the airport should also be open.

Trains: All trains stop at **Hovedbanegården.** 4-5 per day to Stockholm (9hr., 760kr, under 26 540kr), Oslo (9hr., 2 per day, 735kr, under 26 530kr), Berlin (8hr., 4 per day, 550kr, under 26 450kr). Seat reservations required (20kr). Call **DSB** at 70 13 14 15 for domestic schedules and reservations; 70 13 14 16 for international travel. For holders of BIJ, Scanrail, and Eurail passes, the **InterRail Center** in the station is a friendly haven, with a relaxing lounge, telephones, showers (10kr), a stove (no utensils), maps, and free condoms. Open June to mid-Sept. daily 6:30-10:30am and 4-10pm; late June to mid-Aug. also open afternoons.

Public Transportation: For bus info, dial 36 45 45 45 (daily 7am-9:30pm); for **train** info, call 70 13 14 15 (daily 7am-9pm). Buses and S-trains (subways and suburban trains) operate on a zone system. 3 zones cover central Copenhagen; 11 zones get you to Helsingør. Buy tickets (2 zones 11kr, each additional zone 6kr, children half-price) or, better, a *rabatkort* (rebate card), which gets you 10 "clips," each good for one journey within a specified number of zones. The blue 2-zone *rabatkort* (70kr) will get you around the city and can be clipped more than once for longer trips. Cards must be clipped in the machines upon beginning a journey. A ticket or clip (available from kiosks or bus drivers) gives 1hr. of transfers. The 24hr. bus and train pass buys use of public transport in greater Copenhagen (70kr from the Tivoli tourist office or any railway station). Railpasses are good on S-trains but not buses. Buses and trains run M-Sa 5am-12:30am, Su 6am-12:30am; **night buses** run on different routes during the remaining hours and charge double fare. A comprehensive map of public transport over North Zealand (5kr) is available at the bus info-center on Rådhauspladsen. The **Copenhagen Card,** sold in hotels, tourist offices, and train stations, buys unlimited travel in North Zealand, discounts on ferries to Sweden, and free admission to most sights, including Tivoli (140kr for 24hr., 255kr for 48hr., 320kr for 72hr.).

Ferries: The tourist office has details on the mind-boggling variety of ferry services from Copenhagen. To **Norway: Scandinavian Seaways** (tel. 33 42 30 00; fax 33 42 30 01) departs daily at 5pm for Oslo (16hr., 480-735kr, under 26 315-570kr, Eurail and Scanrail 50% off). To **Sweden:** trains cross over on the Helsingør-Helsingborg ferry at no extra charge. Hourly **Hydrofoils** (tel. 33 12 80 88) go between Havnegade (at the end of Nyhavn) and Malmö (40min., 19-49kr). Both **Flyve-bådene** and **Pilen** run hourly hydrofoils to Malmö from 9am-11pm (45min., 50kr). Bus 999 (60kr) from the Central Station goes to Lund via ferry at Dragør. To **Poland: Polferries** (tel. 33 11 46 45; fax 33 11 95 78) set out M and W-F at 10pm, Su at 10:30am from Nordre Toldbod, 12A (off Esplanaden) to Świnoujście, where there are rail connections to the rest of Poland (10hr., 315kr, with ISIC 260kr). To **Bornholm** (7hr., 1-2 per day, 189kr), call **Bornholmstrafikken** (tel. 33 13 18 66; fax 33 93 18 66).

Taxis: tel. 35 35 35 35, 38 77 77 77, or 38 10 10 10. 22kr base, 8.50kr per km during the day; 10kr per km at night. Central Station to airport 150kr.

Bike Rental: The **City Bike** program lets you borrow bikes for free. Deposit 20kr in any of the 150 bike racks around the city, release the bike, and retrieve the coin upon return at any rack. **Dan Wheel,** Colbjørnsensgade 3 (tel. 31 21 22 27). 35kr per day, 165kr per week; 200kr deposit. Open M-F 9am-5:30pm, Sa-Su 9am-2pm. Also in Central Station near track 13.

Hitchhiking: Try Use It's ride boards (see **Tourist Offices,** below) instead.

Tourist Offices: The invaluable **Use It,** Rådhusstræde 13 (tel. 33 73 06 20; fax 33 73 06 49; email useit@ui.dk; http://www.useit.dk) is a super-friendly tourist office specifically for budget travelers. From the station, follow Vesterbrogade, cross

DENMARK

Rådhuspladsen onto Strøget then take a right on Rådhusstræde. Free maps, bed-finding, ride board (also on website), and luggage storage (not overnight). Mail held. Has *Playtime,* a budget guide to the city, and the biweekly *Use It News,* listing cultural events. Building also houses a cafe, restaurant, cinema, and housing/job placement office. Open mid-June to mid-Sept. daily 9am-7pm; mid-Sept. to mid-June M-W 11am-4pm, Th 11am-6pm, F 11am-2pm. Less helpful is the **Wonderful Copenhagen Tourist Office,** Bernstorffsgade 1 (tel. 33 11 13 25; fax 33 93 49 69), opposite the train station, in a corner of Tivoli. Open July-Aug. 9am-8pm; May-June and early Sept. 9am-6pm; mid-Sept. to Apr. M-F 9am-4:30pm, Sa 9am-1:30pm.

Budget Travel: Wasteels Rejser, Skoubogade 6 (tel. 33 14 46 33). Youth fares for trains and planes. Open M-F 9am-7pm, Sa 10am-3pm. **Kilroy Travels,** Skindergade 28 (tel. 33 11 00 44). Low ferry and plane fares. Changes dates for CIEE plane tickets. Open M 9am-7pm, Tu-F 9am-5:30pm, Sa 10am-1pm.

Embassies: Australian Consulate, Strand Boulevarden 122, 5th floor (tel. 39 29 20 77; fax 39 29 60 77). **Canada,** Kristen Bernikowsgade 1 (tel. 33 48 32 00; fax 33 48 32 21). **Estonia,** Aurehøjvej 19 (tel. 39 40 26 66; fax 39 40 26 30). **Ireland,** Øster-banegade 21 (tel. 35 42 32 33; fax 35 43 18 58). **Latvia,** Rusbæksvej 17 (tel. 39 27 60 00; fax 39 27 61 73). **Lithuania,** Bernstorffsvej 214 (tel. 39 63 62 07; fax 39 63 65 32). **New Zealanders** contact the embassy in Brussels at Boulevard du région 47-48, 1000 Brussels (tel. (+00 322) 512 1040; fax 513 4856). **Poland,** Richelieus-allé 12 (tel. 39 62 72 45; fax 39 62 72 96). **South Africa,** Gammel Vartovvej 8 (tel. 39 18 01 55; fax 39 18 40 06). **U.K.,** Kastelsvej 36-40 (tel. 35 44 52 00; fax 35 44 52 93). **U.S.,** Dag Hammarskjölds Allé 24 (tel. 35 55 31 44; fax 35 43 02 23).

Currency Exchange: Forex, in the central station. 20kr commission on cash, 10kr per travelers check. Open daily 8am-9pm. Also at the **airport** (open daily 6:30am-8:30pm). Change counters on Strøget charge up to 10% commission. **Banks** cluster in the pedestrian district and on Vesterbrogade near the train station. Most charge a 25kr commission. Regular banking hours M-W and F 9:30am-4pm, Th 9:30am-6pm. High commissions on traveler's checks (30-35kr min.), except at American Express (see below).

American Express: Nørreg. 7A, 3rd floor (tel. 33 12 23 01; fax 33 12 29 80), near Strøget. Best exchange rates. No commission on AmEx cheques. 15kr commission on cash. Mail held for those with AmEx cards or Traveler's Cheques. Open June-Aug. M-F 9am-5pm, Sa 9am-2pm; Sept.-May M-F 9am-5pm, Sa 9am-noon.

Luggage Storage: Free at Use It and most hostels. At **Central Station,** 20-35kr per 24hr. Open M-Sa 5:30am-1am and Su 6am-1am. At **DSB Garderobe,** suitcases 25kr, packs 35kr per 24hr. Open daily 6:30am-12:15am.

Lost Property: Police (tel. 38 74 52 61); **bus** (tel. 36 45 45 45); **train** (tel. 33 16 21 10); **planes** (tel. 32 32 32 60). For credit cards: **AmEx** (tel. 80 01 00 21); **Master-Card and Visa** (tel. 44 89 25 00).

Bookstores: Atheneum, Nørregade 6, has a good-sized English collection. Open M-F 9am-5pm, Sa 10am-2pm. **Use It** also operates a book swap.

Laundromats: Lots; look for *Vascomat* and *Møntvask* chains. At Borgergade 2, Nansensgade 39, and Istedgade 45. Most open 8am-10pm (wash and dry 40-50kr).

Women's Centers: Kvindehuset, Gothersgade 37 (tel. 33 14 28 04), runs an info center and 2nd-hand shop. Open M-F noon-5:30pm. **Kvindecentret Danner-huset,** Nansensgade 1 (tel. 33 14 16 76). Shelter for battered women. Call 24hr.

Gay and Lesbian Services: National Association for Gay Men and Women, Teglgaardsstr. 13 (tel. 33 13 19 48). Small bookstore/library. Open M-F 5-7pm. The monthly *PAN Homoguide,* published in English every summer, lists clubs, cafes, and organizations, and is available at **PAN** (see **Entertainment**).

Crisis Hotlines: The 24hr. **Den Sociale Døgnvagt** hotline (tel. 33 66 33 33) will help you find help. **Lifeline** (suicide hotline tel. 70 20 12 01; daily 4-8pm). **AIDS hotline** (tel. 33 91 11 19; daily 9am-11pm). **Alcoholics Hotline** (tel. 33 33 06 10; daily 9am-midnight).

Emergencies: Ambulance and fire, tel. 112. No coins needed at public phones.

Police: tel. 112. **Headquarters** at Polititorvet (tel. 33 14 14 48).

Pharmacy: Steno Apotek, Vesterbrogade 6c (tel. 33 14 82 66), and **Sønderbro Apoteket,** Amagerbrogade 158 (tel. 32 58 01 40). Open 24hr.; ring for entrance.

Medical Assistance: Doctors on Call (tel. 33 93 63 00), open M-F 8am-4pm; after hours, call 38 88 60 41. Visits 120-350kr. **Emergency rooms** at **Rigshospitalet,** Blegsdamsvej 9 (tel. 35 45 31 93); **Sundby Hospital,** Italyvej 1 (tel. 32 34 32 34); and **Bispebjerg Hospital,** Bispebjerg Bakke 23 (tel. 35 31 35 31).

Post Office: Tietgensgade 37-39, 1500 København V, behind Central Station. *Poste Restante.* Open M-F 11am-6pm, Sa 10am-1pm. Branch office in Central Station open M-F 8am-10pm, Sa 9am-4pm, Su 10am-4pm. *Poste Restante* also at **Use It:** last name first, 13 Rådhusstræde, 1466 København K.

Internet Access: Free at **Use It** (see **Tourist Offices,** above) and the **Copenhagen Central Library** *(Hovedbibliotek),* Krystalgade 15 (tel. 33 93 60 60); open M-F 10am-7pm, Sa 10am-2pm. Also at the cafe **Babel,** Frederiksborggade 33 (tel. 33 33 93 38). Open M-Sa 2-11pm; 30kr per hr., 30min. minimum.

Telephones: Phone cards (30, 50, or 100kr for 30, 53 and 110 units, respectively) for sale in post offices and shops near card phones.

ACCOMMODATIONS AND CAMPING

Like all of Scandinavia, Copenhagen is rich in hostels and campgrounds but poor in budget hotels. Because Danish youth hostels are used by families and school groups, the HI hostels fill early, despite their sometimes remote locations (allow 20-30kr for bus fare). Reservations are especially advisable during Karneval (mid-May), the Roskilde Festival (late June), the Copenhagen Jazz Festival (early July), and national vacations in early August. If the hostels are booked, consult the **Use It** tourist office. Sleep-Ins are temporary summertime hostels set up by the city to provide cheap and central places to sleep. All are open 24-hour and are the accommodation of choice for young travelers. Slumbering in a park or the station is neither legal nor wise.

Hotel Jørgensen, Rømersgade 11 (tel. 33 13 81 86; fax 33 15 51 05), in a quiet area, 20min. walk from Central Station. S-train to "Nørreport," then walk along Frederiksborggade and turn left on Rømersgade. Somewhat cramped rooms of 6-14, all with TV. Centrally located and friendly. 115kr includes huge breakfast. Oct.-June 100kr; singles 380kr; doubles from 480kr; quads 520kr. Lockers free with own lock. Sheets 30kr. Reception 24hr. No credit cards.

City Public Hostel, Absalonsgade 8 (tel. 31 31 20 70; fax 31 23 51 75), in the Vesterbro Youth Center. From the station, walk away from the Rådhuspladsen on Vesterbrogade, then take a left on Absalonsg. Younger clientele in dorms of 6-70. 110kr, with breakfast buffet 130kr. Kitchen, BBQ and supplies, happening lounge. Lockers free with own padlock. Sleeping bags allowed, sheets 30kr. Reception 24hr. Open early May-late Aug. No credit cards.

Vesterbros Inter Point, Vesterbros KFUM (YMCA), Valdemarsgade 15 (tel. 31 31 15 74). From Central Station, walk away from Rådhuspladsen on Vesterbrogade. Take a left on Valdemarsgade. 65kr. Sheets 20kr. Breakfast 29kr. Locked luggage storage; small kitchen; 2 pianos. Reception daily 8:30-11:30am, 3:30-5:30pm, 8pm-12:30am. Beware 12:30am curfew. Open late June-early Aug. No credit cards.

Sleep-In, Blegdamsvej 132 (tel. 35 26 50 59; fax 35 43 50 58). Take the S-train to "Østerport," then bus 1, 6, or 14 (night bus 906 or 914) to "Trianglen" or walk 10min. up Hammerskjölds (hostel is across the square from the 7-11). Close to the centre and the nightlife in Østerbro. Badminton and tennis courts. No pillows or private showers. Free lockers. Wheelchair accessible. Kitchen. 75kr. Breakfast 30kr. Sheets 30kr. Reception 24hr. Open July-Aug. No credit cards.

Sleep-In Green, Ravnsborggade 18, Baghuset (tel. 35 37 77 77). Take bus 16 from the station. Cozy, eco-friendly walk-up with dorms of 10-38. Central location, just outside city center. 68 beds. 70kr. Organic breakfast 25kr. Sheets 20kr. Free locked storage. Reception 24hr. Check-out noon. Open June-Sept. No credit cards.

Sleep-In Heaven, H.V. Nyholmsvej 6 (tel. 38 10 44 45), just off Peter Bangsvej, in Frederiksberg. Take bus 1 from Central Station or night bus 85N (10min. from the city center). Friendly and fun, with pool and foosball tables, and a funky cafe. 80kr includes breakfast and sheets. Free locked luggage storage. Reception 24hr. Open May-Oct. No credit cards.

København Vandrerhjem Bellahøj (HI), Herbergvejen 8 (tel. 38 28 97 15; fax 38 89
02 10; email bellahoj@danhostel.dk), in Bellahøj. Call for directions. Rooms of 6-12
in a big, modern hostel, far from the city center. Lockers; optional lock rental 5kr.
Sheets 30kr. Laundry 20kr. Breakfast 40kr. No kitchen. Reception 24hr. No credit
cards. Wheelchair accessible. Open Mar. to mid-Jan.

København Vandrerhjem Amager (HI), Vejlandsallé 200 (tel. 32 52 29 08; fax 32
52 27 08). Take bus 46 (M-F 6am-5pm) from Central Station or the S-train to "Valby"
and then bus 37. Night bus 96N. Huge and far from the city center in enormous
nature reserve. 2- to 5-bed rooms. 80kr, nonmembers 105kr. Kitchen. Free use of
safe; no lockers. No sleeping bags. Sheets 30kr. Laundry 25kr. Reception 24hr.
Check-in 1-5pm. No credit cards. Wheelchair accessible. Closed Dec. to mid-Jan.

Lyngby Vandrehjem (HI), Råduad 1 (tel. 45 80 30 74). Take S-train line A or L from
Central Station to "Lyngby" (40min.), then bus 187 to "Råduad" or 182/183 to
"Hjortakær" (1hr.). Inconveniently far, but in the beautiful Jægersberg Deer Park.
Dorms 88kr; doubles 210kr; triples 310kr; quads 372kr. Sheets 30kr. Reception
8am-noon and 4-9pm. Open Easter-Oct. 15.

Mike's Guest House, Kirkevænget 13 (tel. 36 45 65 40). 10min. by bus or train from
the station; get directions when you call ahead. Singles 200kr; doubles 290kr; triples 400. Rooms in Mike's big house, some with terraces. No credit cards.

Bellahøj Camping, Hvidkildevej 66 (tel. 38 10 11 50; fax 38 10 13 32), 5km from
the city center. Bus 11: Bellahøj. Bike rental 40kr. 50kr per person. Cabins for two
280kr, for four 410kr. Kitchen. Free showers. Reception 24hr. Cafe and market
open daily 7am-noon and 4-10pm. Open June-Aug.

Charlottenlund Strandpark, Strandvejen 144B, Charlottenlund (tel. 39 62 36 88;
fax 39 61 08 16), in a park with beach, 8km from center. Take bus 6 from Rådhuspladsen (30min.). 60kr per person. Shower 5kr. Laundry: wash 20kr, dry 5kr per
10min. Reception 7am-10pm. Open May 15-Sept. 15.

Absalon Camping, Korsdalsvej 132, Rødovre (tel. 36 41 06 00; fax 36 41 02 93),
9km from the city center. Take bus 5508 from Central Station; tell the driver where
you're going. Store, laundry, and kitchen. 50kr per person; 7.50kr per site; cabins
195kr plus 50kr per person.

FOOD

Copenhagen's fare has much improved since the Vikings slobbered down mutton
and salted fish. Stroll down the **Strøget** with peach juice dripping down your chin,
munch pickled herring by the waterfront, and sample the goodies in every bakery
window. Around **Kongens Nytorv,** elegant cafes serve sandwiches (smørrebrod) at
lunchtime for around 35kr. All-you-can-eat buffets (40-70kr) are popular, especially at
Turkish, Indian, and Italian restaurants. The **Fakta** and **Netto** supermarket chains are
a budget fantasy; one is located at Fiolstræde 7, a few blocks north of Strøget (open
M-F 9am-7pm, Sa 8am-5pm). Open-air **markets** like the one at Israels Plads near Nørreport Station (open M-F 7am-6pm, Sa 7am-2pm) provide fresh fruits and veggies;
fruit stalls also line Strøget and the side-streets to the North.

La Bella Notte, Rådhustræde 13. Tasty pasta dishes (70-80kr) served in a courtyard
around the corner from Huset on Magstræde. Open mid-May to Aug. M-Sa noon-
2pm and 5-11pm. Round out the evening at the disco upstairs F-Sa 11pm-2am.

Restaurant Stedet, Lavendelstræde 13, near Strøget and Rådhuspladsen. Affordable
Danish fare. Gay and straight clientele. Lunch specials Tu-Th 68kr (12:30-7pm). Su
brunch 58kr (12:30-4pm). Open Tu-Su noon-10:30pm.

Det Lille Apotek, St. Kannike Stræde 15, has been serving traditional Danish delicacies to local luminaries and tourists alike since 1720. Lunchtime special 59kr
(11:30am-5pm), 2 course dinner 138kr. Wash down your pickled herring with
homemade schnapps (20kr). Open M-Sa 11am-midnight, Su noon-midnight.

Nyhavns Færgekro, Nyhavn 5. Sit along the canal as you lunch on all-you-can-eat
herring (11 varieties; 78kr). Dinners 145kr. Open daily 11:30am-midnight.

Den Grønne Kælder, Pilestræder 48. Popular, classy vegetarian and vegan dining.
Hummus 18-35kr, veggie burgers 28kr. Open M-Sa 11am-10pm.

Southern California, Vester Voldgade 87, just south of Rådhuspladsen. The healthiest and tastiest fast food option in town. Excellent burritos (33-79kr), quesadillas (27-43kr), and salads (15-45kr). Open Tu-F noon-9pm; Sa-Su 4-9pm.

Cafes

Cafe Norden, Østergade 61, on Strøget and Nicolaj Plads, in sight of the fountain. A French style cafe with dark wood interior. The best vantage point on Strøget. Crepes 59-62kr, sandwiches 16-58kr, Danish and French pastries 15-40kr. Pricey coffee and beer. Open daily 9am-midnight.

Cafe Europa, Amagertorv, on Nicolaj Plads opposite Cafe Norden. As Norden is the place to see, trendy Europa is where to be seen. Sandwiches 23-44kr, beer 45kr per pint. Open M-W 9am-midnight, Th-Sa 9am-1am.

Kafe Kys, Læderstræde 7, on a quiet street running to the south of and parallel to Strøget. Minimalist Mediterranean look. Sandwiches 38-58k, beer 35kr per pint. Open M-Th 11am-1am, F-Sa 11am-2am, Su noon-10pm.

Bankeråt, Ahlefeldtsg. 29, is a busy, artsy cafe popular with busy, artsy locals, near the Hotel Jørgensen. Beer 28kr per pint. Open daily until midnight.

SIGHTS

A fairly compact city, Copenhagen is best seen on foot or by bike; the free **city bikes** (20kr deposit) provide access to the city's stunning architecture. Guided and self-guided tours of all sorts are described in Use It's *Playtime* and in brochures available at the tourist office. Ascend the ramp of the **Rundetårn** (Round Tower, built in 1642 by King Christian IV) on Købmagergade for a fantastic panorama of Copenhagen's copper spires and cobbled streets. *(Open June-Aug. daily 10am-8pm; Sept.-May M-Sa 10-5pm, Su noon-5pm.)* **Strøget,** the pedestrian street that transects the entire city center, is lively, especially at its major squares: **Nytorv, Nicolaj Plads,** and **Kungens Nytorv.** Opposite Kungens Nytorv is **Nyhavn,** the "new port" where Hans Christian Andersen wrote his first fairy tale, lined with Hanseatic houses, sailing boats in dock, and **ferries** leaving for tours of Copenhagen's waterways. **Nette** tour boats offer the best deal. *(Tours late Apr. to mid-Sept. 10am-5pm, every 20min., 20kr.)* From their departure at Holmen's Church opposite Nyhavn at Heibergsgade, they make their way past Amalienberg Palace, Christiansborg Palace, and the Lille Havfrue.

The varied attractions of the famed 19th-century **Tivoli** amusement park, Vesterbrogade 3, include botanical gardens and marching toy soldiers, as well as the expected rides. *(Open late Apr. to mid-Sept. Su-W 11am-midnight, Th-Sa 11am-1am. Children's rides open at 11:30am, others at 12:30pm. 45kr, 10kr discount before 1pm. Children under 12 20kr. Single-ride tickets 10-20kr. Ride-pass 168kr.)* On Wednesdays and weekends the night culminates with music and fireworks. Next to Tivoli, the **Ny Carlsberg Glyptotek,** Dantes Plads 7, displays ancient and Impressionist art and sculpture. *(Open Tu-Su 10am-4pm. 15kr, free with ISIC, W and Su free.)* Nearby, the **National Museum,** Ny Vestergade 10, contains Danish and European archaeological discoveries, including treasures from the Viking Age. *(Open Tu-Su 10am-5pm. 30kr, students 20kr, W free.)* Across the canals on Slotsholmen Island, the *Folketing* (Parliament) meets at **Christiansborg Castle.** *(Castle tours May-Sept. W-F at 11am and 3pm; June-Aug. also at 1pm; Oct.-Apr. Tu-Th and Sa-Su at 9:30am and 3:30pm. 37kr. Also ask about the free Parliament tours.)*

The **Royal Theater** is home to the world-famous Royal Danish Ballet. Half-price theater tickets are available the afternoon of the performance at the Tivoli ticket office, Vesterbrog. 3. *(Tel. 33 15 10 12. Open mid-Apr. to mid-Sept. daily 9am-9pm, off-season 10am-7pm. Royal theater tickets available at 4 or 5pm, others at noon.)* Call **Arte,** Hvidkildevej 64, at 38 88 22 22; ask about student discounts. Post offices also sell tickets for theater and concerts throughout Denmark. The changing of the palace guard takes place at noon on the brick plaza of the queen's **Amalienborg Palace.** Although most of the interior is closed to the public, you can view the royal apartments of Christian VII. *(Open daily June-Aug. 10am-4pm; May 11am-4pm; Jan.-Apr. Tu-Su 11am-4pm. 35kr.)* The western approach to the plaza frames a view of the impressive dome of the 19th-century Romanesque Baroque **Marmorkirken** (marble

DENMARK

church). The inside of the dome is almost as elaborate. *(Open M-Tu and Th-F 11am-2pm, W 11am-6pm, Sa 11am-4pm, Su noon-4pm. Free.)*

A few blocks north of Amalienborg is the **Frihedsmuseet** (Resistance Museum), Churchillparken, which chronicles the 1940-45 Nazi occupation. While documenting Denmark's rescue of almost all its Jews, the museum also examines the period of acceptance of German "protection," when the Danish government arrested anti-Nazi saboteurs. *(Open May to early Sept. Tu-Sa 10am-4pm, Su 10am-5pm; mid-Sept. to Apr. Tu-Sa 11am-3pm, Su 11am-4pm. Free.)* Across a bridge is **Kastellet,** a 17th-century fortress-turned-park. *(Open daily 6am-dusk.)* Edvard Eriksen's statue **Den Lille Havfrue** (The Little Mermaid) honors H. C. Andersen at the harbor's opening.

The area around Øster Voldgade and Sølvgade houses Copenhagen's finest parks and gardens. The **Botanisk Have** (Botanical Gardens), Gothersgade 128, at the corner of Øster Voldgade and Gothersgade, are open daily from 8:30am to 6pm. *(Sept. to late Mar. 8:30am-4pm. Free.)* Across the street the **Rosenborg Palace and Gardens** *(Rosenborg Slot)*, Øster Volgade 4A, houses much of the collection of royal treasures, including the crown jewels. *(Open June-Aug. daily 10am-4pm; Sept. to mid-Oct. and May 11am-3pm; late Oct. to Apr. Tu, F, and Su 11am-2pm. 45kr.)* Nearby, at Rømersgade 22, the gripping **Arbejdermuseet** (Workers' Museum) portrays the lives of the non-royal. *(Open July-Oct. daily 10am-4pm; Nov.-June Tu-Su 10am-4pm. 30kr.)* Three blocks north at Østervoldgade and Sølvgade is the **Statens Museum for Kunst** (State Museum of Fine Arts), Sølvgade 48-50, which displays works by Matisse and Dutch masters.

In the southern Christianshavn district lies **Christiania** (entrances on Prinsessegade). This "free city," founded in 1971 by youthful squatters in abandoned military barracks, still keeps the hippie spirit alive with its young population of artists and "free-thinkers." With dogs roaming free and hash and marijuana sold from booths on Pusher Street (joints 10-30kr), it's not everyone's cup (or pot…) of tea; always ask before taking pictures, never take pictures on Pusher Street, and exercise caution at night. Infrequent police raids rarely result in serious charges (the dogs usually raise the alarm in time), but remember that all forms of cannabis are illegal in Denmark and possession of even small amounts is enough to get you arrested. For legalized substance abuse, try the **Carlsberg Brewery,** Ny Carlsbergvej 140, accessible by taking bus 6 west from Rådhuspladsen to Valby Langgade (tours M-F at 11am and 2pm; meet at Elephant Gate). The tour is free and offers beer (about 2 bottles per person) and soda at the end of the tour. If the breweries haven't confused your senses enough, try the **Experimentarium,** Tuborg Havnevej 7 (bus 6 north from Rådhuspladsen), where you can dance in the "reverse disco" or miraculously lose 20kg in seconds. *(Open late June to mid-Aug. daily 10am-5pm; late Aug.-early June M and W-F 9am-5pm, Tu 9am-9pm, Sa-Su 11am-5pm. 69kr, students 55kr.)*

The collection of contemporary art in the new **Arken Museum of Modern Art** (in Ishøj Strandpark just south of the city) is as striking as the white marble frigate-shaped building in which it is housed. *(Take S-train to "Ishøj" and then walk or take bus 138. Open Tu and Th-Su 10am-5pm, W 10am-9pm. 40kr.)* To watch exquisite hand-painted porcelain being crafted, tour the **Royal Copenhagen Porcelain Factory** in nearby Frederiksberg. Take bus 1 or 14 from Rådhuspladsen. *(15min. Tours at 9, 10, 11am, 1, and 2pm; 25kr.)* The **Assistens Kirkegård** is the final resting place of Hans Christian Andersen, Søren Kirkegaard, and many other famous Danes.

ENTERTAINMENT

Copenhagen's weekends often begin on Wednesday, and nights rock until 5am. Come Thursday, though, as most bars and night clubs have reduced cover and *cheap* drinks. The central pedestrian district reverberates with crowded bars and discos, **Kongens Nytorv** boasts fancier joints, and Nyhavn exudes salty charisma. A popular option is to buy beer at the supermarket and head to the boats and cafes of Nyhavn. For current events, consult *Copenhagen This Week* (free at hostels and tourist offices) or contact Use It for *Use It News* with (English) listings of concerts and entertainment. The **Scala** complex across the street from Tivoli features a multitude of bars and restaurants. University students liven up the cheaper bars in the Nørrebro area.

The relaxed **Kul-Kaféen,** Teglgårdsstræde 5 (open M-Sa 11am-midnight), is a great place to meet other young people, see live performers, and get info on music, dance, and theater. During the world-class **Copenhagen Jazz Festival** (July 2-11 in 1999; http://www.cjf.dk), the city fairly drowns in excellent jazz, with many free concerts on sidewalks and squares complementing the more refined venues. Copenhagen's lesbian and gay scene is one of the best in Europe, and gay Danish men and women report equal comfort in straight establishments.

Rust, Guldbergsgade 8, in the Nørreboro. Long lines by midnight at this disco. 20-something crowd dances the night away. Open Tu-Su 10pm-5am. Cover 50kr.

Cafe Pavillionen, Fælleaparken, Borgmester Jensens Allé. Refreshingly unsmoky summer-only outdoor cafe features live local bands from 8-10pm, then a disco from 10pm-5am. Open May-Aug. Tu-Sa. No disco on Tu. Su concert 2:30-5pm, then tango lessons and dancing until midnight. No cover.

Le Kitsch, 13 Gothersgade. Underground in the literal sense. Chart music until late keeps the place packed. 50kr cover after midnight F-Sa. Open Th-Su 10pm-3am.

Woodstock, 12 Vestergade, just north of Strøget and Nytorv. Fifties and sixties vintage music attracts a mixed crowd of younger and older couples. A good starter club. Open Th-Sa 9pm-6am.

IN Bar, Nørreg 1. Dance on the speakers! No, wait, drink *cheap* and then dance on the speakers! Th 10pm-5am, 30kr cover, beer and wine 10kr; F-Sa 10pm-10am, 150kr cover includes open bar.

Australian Bar, Vesterg 10. Pool tables, live music, and your favorite Aussie beers. Open Su-W 6pm-2am; Th-Sa 6pm-5am. Cover 30-40kr. Th 10kr drinks.

Park, Østerbrog. 79, in Østerbro. Lose your inhibitions and your friends in this enormous club with 2 packed dance floors, live music hall, and rooftop patio. Pint 40kr. Su-W 10am-2am, Th 10am-4am, F-Sa 10am-5am. Cover F-Sa 50kr.

PAN Club and Cafe, Knabrostræde 3. Combination gay cafe, bar, and disco which publishes the comprehensive *Homoguide.* Cafe opens daily at 8pm, disco at 11pm. Both stay open late. Cover Th 20kr; F-Sa 40kr.

Sebastian Bar and Cafe, 10 Hyskenstræde, off Strøget. The city's best-known gay and lesbian hangout. Copies of *Homoguide* available. Beer 17-31kr. Happy hour 5-9pm. Open daily noon-2am.

■ Near Copenhagen

Stunning castles, white sand beaches, and a world-class museum are all within easy reach of Copenhagen by train. Two rail lines go north from the city: a coastal line up to Helsingør (paralleled by the more scenic bus 388) and an S-train line to Hillerød. **Klampenborg** and **Charlottenlund,** close by on the coastal line (and at the end of S-train line C), feature topless beaches. **Bakken,** Dyrehaven, Klampenborg (tel. 39 63 73 00), the world's oldest amusement park, though less ornate than Tivoli, delivers more thrills (including untranslated warnings). Just north from the Klampenborg train station, turn left, cross the overpass, and head through the park (open Mar. 25-Aug. daily 11am-midnight; rides begin at 2pm and cost 10-25kr; free entry). Bakken borders the **Jægersborg Deer Park,** the royal family's former hunting grounds, and still home to their **Eremitage** summer château, miles of wooded paths, and over 2000 red deer.

Rungsted and Humlebæk The quiet harbor town, **Rungsted,** where Isak Dinesen wrote *Out of Africa,* houses the author's abode at the **Karen Blixen Museum,** Rungsted Strandvej 111 (open May-Sept. daily 10am-5pm; Oct.-Apr. W-F 1-4pm, Sa-Su 11am-4pm; 30kr). A path from the gardens leads to Blixen's tree-shaded grave. Trains leave from the courtyard (every 20min.); buy tickets inside. **Humlebæk,** farther up the coast, distinguishes itself with the spectacular **Louisiana Museum of Modern Art.** Named for the three wives (each named Louisa) of the estate's original owner, the museum contains works by Picasso, Warhol, Lichtenstein, Calder, and other 20th-century masters. Overlooking the Swedish coast, the building and its sculpture-studded grounds are themselves well worth the trip. Follow signs 1.5km

north from the Humlebæk station or snag bus 388 (10kr). Classical music concerts ring out on Wednesday evenings in summer (90kr includes museum); call 49 19 07 19 for info (museum open daily 10am-5pm, W until 10pm; 55kr, students 47kr).

Helsingør, Hornbæk, and Hillerød Farther north, (45min. from Copenhagen) castles evince the Danish monarchy's fondness for lavish architecture. The most famous of these is undoubtedly **Kronborg Slot** in **Helsingør,** also known as Elsinore, the setting for Shakespeare's *Hamlet*. This castle was built in the 15th century to collect tolls from passing merchant ships. Viking chief Holger Danske is buried in the castle's dungeon; legend has it that he still rises to face any threat to Denmark's safety. The self-guided tour includes a church and impressively furnished royal apartments. The castle also houses the Danish maritime museum with many model ships and the world's oldest sea biscuit from 1853. (Open May-Sept. daily 10:30am-5pm; Apr. and Oct. Tu-Su 11am-4pm; Nov.-Mar. Tu-Su 11am-3pm. Combined ticket 45kr.) The **tourist office** (tel. 49 21 13 33; fax 49 21 15 77) in Helsingør is inside **Kulturhuset,** to the left of the train station as you exit. The office books rooms for a 25kr fee and has ferry info. (Open mid-June to late Aug. M-F 9:30am-6pm, Sa 10am-4pm; Sept. to mid-June M-F 9am-4pm, Sa 10am-1pm.) The waterfront **HI youth hostel Villa Moltke,** is at Ndr. Strandvej 24 (tel. 49 21 16 40; fax 49 21 13 99); take bus 340 from the station. (74kr, nonmembers 84kr. Sheets 40kr. Breakfast 40kr. Free showers and kitchen. Reception 8am-noon and 4-9pm. Open Feb.-Nov.) **Cafeteria San Reno,** Stengade 53, offers a huge menu, or try Kulturhuset's **Kammer Cafeen** (sandwiches 25-30kr) near the train station.

Very near Helsingør, **Hornbæk** is a relaxed beach town about an hour north of Copenhagen. The town comes alive during the summer when city-weary urbanites flock to the beach—see Danes at their most beautiful on display. Wild antics surround the **harbor party** on the fourth weekend in July. Accommodations are generally out of budget reach. Bus 340 runs from Hillerød to Hornbæk (20min., 20kr).

Moated **Frederiksborg Slot** in **Hillerød** is the most impressive of the castles north of Copenhagen, featuring exquisite gardens, brick ramparts, and the **National Historical Museum,** which displays portraits of prominent Danes. Free concerts are given on the famous 1610 **Esaias Compenius organ** in the chapel on Thursdays 1:30-2pm. Call 48 26 04 39 for information. (Castle open May-Sept. daily 10am-5pm; Oct. and Apr. 10am-4pm; Nov.-Mar. 11am-3pm. 40kr, students 10kr.) Along the train line halfway between Hillerød and Helsingør is **Fredensborg Castle,** built in 1722 and still used as the spring and autumn royal residence. The park is free and open year-round (castle open only July daily 1-5pm; 10kr). Peek into the palace gardens from the **Fredensborg Youth Hostel (HI),** Østrupvej 3 (tel. 48 48 03 15; fax 48 48 16 56), 1km from the train station. (93kr, nonmembers 118kr. Sheets 45kr. Reception 7am-9pm. No credit cards.) Hillerød is at the end of S-train lines A and E (40min. via Lyngby, 38kr), and accessible directly from Helsingør by train (30min.).

Roskilde West of Copenhagen (25-30min., 35kr or 3 clips on the yellow *rabatkort;* free with railpasses), **Roskilde** served as Denmark's first capital when King Harald Bluetooth built the first Christian church in Denmark here in 980. Thirty-eight other Danish monarchs repose in the ornate sarcophagi of **Roskilde Domkirke** (cathedral). (Open Apr.-June 16 Tu-F 9am-4:45pm, Sa 9am-noon, Su 12:30-3:45 pm; Oct.-Mar. Tu-F 10am-3:45pm, Sa 11:30am-3:45pm. Concerts June-Aug. Th at 8pm, Su 12:30pm-3:45pm. 6kr.) The **Viking Ship Museum,** Strandengen on the harbor, houses the recovered remains of five trade- and warships sunk around 1060 and their less skeletal reconstructions moored in the outside harbor, as well as a working Viking-era shipyard. From June 15 through August you can book a ride on one of these Viking long boats, but be prepared to take an oar—Viking conquest is no spectator sport (open daily Apr.-Oct. 9am-5pm; Nov.-Mar. 10am-4pm; 40kr). A fruit, flea, and flower **market** transforms Roskilde on Wednesdays and Saturdays (open 8am-2pm). From July 1-4 (1999), Roskilde hosts one of northern Europe's largest **music festivals** (tel. 70 10 17 17; http://www.Roskilde-Festival.dk), drawing over 90,000 fans to see bands such as Beck, U2, Radiohead, Smashing Pumpkins, and David Bowie. The **tourist office**, Gullandsstræde 15 (tel. 46 35 27 00), sells festival tickets, books rooms for a 25kr fee, and offers the 7-day **Roskilde Card** (100kr, children 50kr) which provides admission to 10 sites. (Open Sept.-Mar. M-Th 9am-5pm, F 9am-4pm, Sa 10am-1pm; Apr.-June M-F 9am-5pm, Sa 10am-1pm; July-Aug. M-F 9am-6pm, Sa 9am-3pm, Su 10am-2pm.) Roskilde's **HI youth hostel**, Hørhusene 61 (tel. 46 35 21 84; fax 46 32 66 90), has beach access but is booked during the festival. (Bus 601 from train station to Låddenhøj, then walk 0.8km. 90kr, nonmembers 115kr. Reception 9am-noon and 4-8pm. Closed Jan.). Camp by the beach at **Roskilde Camping**, Baunehøjvej 7-9 (tel. 46 75 79 96; fax 46 75 44 26), 4km north; take bus 603 towards Veddelev (reception 8am-10pm; 50kr per person; open Apr. to mid-Sept.). Near Roskilde, the **Lejre Research Centre**, Slangealleen 2, reconstructs Viking agrarian life in an open-air museum. Take the S-train from Copenhagen to **Lejre**, then bus 233 to Lejre Experimental Centre (open daily 10am-5pm; closed M in off-season; 50kr).

Møn To see what Andersen called one of the most beautiful spots in Denmark, travel south from Copenhagen two hours to the white cliffs of the isle of **Møn**. Take the train to Vordingborg, bus 62 or 64 to Stege, and then bus 54 to Møn Klint. Plan carefully: only three buses go out and back a day; the last often leaves Møn before 4pm. For more info contact the **Møns Turistbureau**, Storegade 2 (tel. 55 81 44 11; fax 55 81 48 46), in Stege. (Open June 15-Aug. M-F 10am-6pm, Sa 9am-6pm, Su 10am-noon; Sept.-June 14 M-F 10am-5pm, Sa 9am-noon.)

■ Bornholm

Southwest of Sweden, the gorgeous island of Bornholm lures vacationers to its sand beaches and cozy fishing villages. A dreamland for avid bikers and nature lovers, the red-roofed cliffside villas may remind you of southern Europe, but the flowers and half-timbered houses are undeniably Danish. Walking through Bornholm's tidy capital town, **Rønne**, it's hard to imagine the devastation wrought by relentless bombing during World War II. Bornholm's unique **round churches**, built as both places of worship and fortresses for waiting out pirate attacks, are worth checking out. The sandiest and longest **beaches** are at Dueodde, on the island's southern tip. Of the four towns, Østerlars is the largest, and Nylors the best-preserved.

Bornholmstrafikken (tel. in Bornholm 56 95 18 66; in Copenhagen 33 13 18 66; in Ystad, Sweden +46 (411) 180 65, in Sassnitz; Germany +49 383 92 352 26; fax 56 91 07 66; email info@bornholmferries.dk; http://www.bornholmferries.dk) offers transport to Bornholm from Denmark, Sweden, and Germany. The combo bus and ferry route via Sweden is the fastest way to reach the island (5hr., 190kr). If you're in Sweden, a ferry departs daily from Ystad, just one hour southeast of Malmö (2½hr., 98-122kr, 50% Scanrail discount); from Germany, ferries depart from Sassnitz-Mukran to Rønne (3½hr., 50-100kr).

On Saturdays in July and August, **Polferries** (tel. 56 95 10 69; fax 56 95 89 10) sails to and from Swinoujscie, Poland (6hr., 180kr). All ferries run to the harbor in Rønne, where you can rent a **bike** at **Bornholms Cykeludlejning**, Ndr. Kystvej 5, in the center of Rønne (55kr per day, 215kr per week; open May-Sept. daily 7am-4pm). Bornholm has an efficient local BAT **bus** service. (30kr to Gudhjem or Sandvig-Allinge, 37.50kr to Svaneke. Unlimited travel for 24hr. 90kr, 7 days or 5 periods of 24hr. 330kr. More than one person can share the same multi-ride ticket.) There are numerous cycling paths; pick up a guide at the tourist office (see below). Rooms in Bornholm should be reserved in advance.

Rønne and Sandvig-Allinge Amid cafes and cobblestoned streets, Rønne, on Bornholm's southwest coast, is the island's principal port of entry. The Rønne **tourist office**, Nordre Kystvej 3 (tel. 56 95 95 00; fax 56 95 95 68; email turist@bornholminfo.dk), a mirrored-glass building behind the Q8 gas station by the Bornholm-strafikken terminal, books rooms in private homes (150-200kr) and provides free copies of the helpful *Turist Bornholm Guide* and *Bornholm This Week*. (Open May M-F 9am-5pm, Sa 11am-3pm, Su noon-4pm; June-Aug. M and Sa 7am-8pm, Tu-F 7am-6pm, Su 1-6pm; Sept.-Dec. M-F 9am-4pm, Sa 11:30am-2:30pm.) The **youth hostel (HI),** Arsenalvej 12 (tel./fax 56 95 13 40), is in a quiet, woodland area; from the ferry terminal, walk along Munch Petersens Vej, turn left up Zahrtmannsvej, and go up the steps to the junction with Skansevej, then follow the signs. (95kr, nonmembers 120kr. Reception 9am-noon, 4-6pm, and 10-10:30pm. Reserve ahead.) **Galløkken Camping,** Strandvejen 4 (tel. 56 95 23 20; fax 56 95 37 66), charges 49kr per person and 40kr per tent (open mid-May-Aug.). Shop for groceries at **Kvickly,** in the Snellemark Centret shopping center across from the tourist office, which also has a second-floor cafeteria with affordable sandwiches. (25-35kr. Supermarket open M-F 9am-7pm, Sa 9am-4pm, Su 10am-4pm. Cafeteria open M-F 9am-7pm, Su 9am-4pm.) Lively **Cafe Gustav,** on the busy Store Torv Square, hosts a disco Th-Sa (open Su-W 11am-2am, Th-Sa 11am-5am).

The smaller town of **Sandvig-Allinge** is perched at the tip of Bornholm's spectacular north coast, whose white-sand beaches attract bikers and bathers. Down Hammershusvej and perched above the sea, **Hammershus** is northern Europe's largest castle ruin. The **Nordbornholms Turistbureau,** Kirkeg. 4 (tel. 56 48 00 01; fax 56 48 02 26), in Allige, provides free maps, brochures, and accommodation info. **Internet access** is free at the library, Pingels Allé 1 (book ahead at 56 95 07 04; open M-Th 10am-7pm, F 10am-5pm, Sa 10am-2pm). Just outside of Sandvig is the **Sandvig Vandrerhjem (HI),** Hammershusvej 94. (Tel. 56 48 03 62; fax 56 48 18 62. 100kr, nonmembers 125kr. Reception 9:30-11am and 4-5:30pm. Open Apr.-Oct.) **Sandvig Familie Camping,** Sandlinien 5 (tel. 56 48 04 47; fax 56 48 04 57), has camping sites on the sea (45kr per person, 10kr per tent; reception 8am-10pm; open Apr.-Oct).

FUNEN (FYN)

Situated between the island of Zealand to the east and the Jutland peninsula to the west, Funen is Denmark's garden. And yet this remote bread basket is no longer isolated from the rest of Denmark—a bridge and tunnel now connect it to Zealand. Pick up maps of the bike paths covering the island at all Funen tourist offices (75kr).

■ Odense

Hans Christian Andersen, the famous fairy tale writer, was born in this manufacturing metropolis in 1805 but left at the earliest opportunity; you might find yourself doing the same. Though home to a few interesting museums, Odense (OH-n-sa) Denmark's third largest city, doesn't have much to recommend an extended visit.

SIGHTS AND ENTERTAINMENT At **H.C. Andersens Hus,** Hans Jensens Stræde 37-45, learn about the author's eccentricities and see free performances of his work (June 22-Aug. 2 11am, 1, and 3pm) in the garden behind the museum (open daily June-Aug. 9:30am-7pm; Sept.-May 10am-4pm). A few scraps from his ugly duckling childhood are on view in **H.C. Andersens Barndomshjem** (Childhood Home), Munkemøllestræde 3-5 (open daily June-Aug. 10am-4pm; Sept.-Mar. 11am-3pm; 5kr). Don headphones and listen to the classical compositions of another Great Dane at the **Carl Nielsen Museum,** Claus Bergs Gade 11 (open Tu-Su 10am-4pm; 15kr). At the other end of the pedestrian district, **Brandts Klædefabrik,** Brandts Passage 37-43 (tel. 66 13 78 97), hosts an outstanding modern art gallery, the worthwhile **Museum of Photographic Art,** and the **Danish Press/Graphic Arts Museum** (all open daily 10am-5pm; Sept.-May closed M; joint ticket 40kr). Also worth a visit is the collection of Danish art in the **Fyns Kunstmuseum,** Jernbaneg. 13 (open July-Aug. daily 10am-5pm; Sept.-June Tu-Su 10am-5pm; 25kr). In southern Odense the **Den Fynske Landsby** (Funen Village), Sejerskovvej 20, is a collection of 18th- and 19th-century buildings brought from around the island. (Take bus 42. Open June-Aug. daily

9:30am-7pm; Sept.-Oct. and Apr.-May Tu-Su 10am-4pm; Nov.-Mar. Su 11am-3pm. 30kr.) In late June, **Ringe**, 30km away, hosts the **Midtfyn Festival** (tel. 65 96 25 12 or 65 96 25 01 for info, or the Ringe tourist office at 62 62 52 23; http://www.mf.dk), one of the largest rock/folk festivals in Denmark. The Black Crowes, Sting, and Jamiroquai have played here (350kr per day, 625kr for F-Su; free camping).

PRACTICAL INFO, ACCOMMODATIONS, AND FOOD Buses depart from behind the train station (11kr). The **tourist office**, Rådhuspladsen (tel. 66 12 75 20; fax 66 12 75 86; email otb@odenseturist.dk), provides free maps, exchanges currency, and books rooms for a 25kr fee (125kr per person). From the train station, walk on Nør- reg. to Vesterg., turn left, and continue to Rådhurpladsen. (Open June 15-Aug. M-S 9am-7pm, Su 11am-7pm; Sept. to mid-June M-F 9:30am-4:30pm, Sa 10am-1pm.) The **Odense Eventyrpas**, available at the tourist office, station, youth hostel, and camp- ground, is good for travel on municipal buses and trains and a 75% discount on most museum admissions (24hr. pass 50kr; 48hr. pass 90kr). **Vandrerhjem Kragsbjerg- gården (HI)**, Kragsbjergvej 121 (tel. 66 13 04 25; fax 65 91 28 63), is 2km from the town center; take bus 61, 62, 63, or 64 from the train station. (85kr, nonmembers 110kr. Reception 8am-noon and 4-8pm. Open mid-Jan. to Nov. Reserve ahead. 1999 will see a new hostel built next to the train station; call the same number.) You can camp next to the enticing Fruens Boge park at **DCU Camping**, Odensevej 102 (tel. 66 11 47 02; fax 65 91 73 43); hop on bus 41 or 81 (50kr per person; reception 7am- 10pm; open late Mar. to Sept.)

   Den Grimme Ælling (The Ugly Duckling), across the street from H.C. Andersens Hus, at Hans Jensen Stræde 1, serves a huge buffet of "proper Danish food" and bot- tomless beer and wine at lunch (30kr, lunch 70kr, dinner 100kr; open daily noon- 2:30pm and 5:30-10:30pm). **Cafe Biografen**, Brandt's Passage 39-41, has a daily large brunch (45kr; M-Sa 11am-1pm, Su noon-2pm), and is the front office for a 3-screen art house cinema with films in English (45-50kr; cafe closes M-Th at 1am, F-Sa at 2am, Su at midnight). For a full veggie dinner, arrive by 6pm at the communal kitchen **Kærne- huset**, Nederg. 6 (40kr; open M-F; closed July). Groceries are available at **Aktiv Super,** corner of Nørreg. and Skulkenborg (open M-F 9am-7pm, Sa 8:30am-4pm). The central library in the train station has free **Internet access.** (Open Oct.-Apr. M-Th 10am-7pm, F-Su 10am-4pm; May-Sept. M-Th 10am-7pm, F 10am-4pm, Sa 10am-2pm.)

■ Egeskov Slot and Svendborg

About 45 minutes south of Odense on the Svendborg rail line is the town of **Kværndup** and its most famous edifice, **Egeskov Slot,** a stunning 16th-century castle that appears to float on the lake that surrounds it—it's actually supported by an entire forest of 12,000 oak piles. The castle's interior features opulent furnishings from the 18th through the 20th centuries and the grounds are a wonderland of formal gardens and a large bamboo labyrinth. On summer Sundays at 5pm, classical concerts resound in the castle's **Knight Hall.** (Castle open daily May 25-June and Aug.-Sept. 10am-5pm; July 10am-7pm. 100kr. Grounds open daily May and Sept. 10am-5pm; June and Aug. 10am-6pm; July 10am-8pm. 55kr, combined castle and grounds ticket 100kr.) To get to Egeskov, exit the Svendborg-bound train at Kværndup; leave the station, and turn right until you reach Bøjdenvej, the main road. You can then wait for the hourly bus 920 (11kr), or turn right and walk the 2km through wheat fields to the castle. A picnic lunch might be the most pleasant budget move you ever made.

   On Funen's south coast, an hour from Odense by rail, **Svendborg** is a beautiful har- bor town and a major departure point for ferries to the south Funen islands. Retrace Svendborg's nautical history at the **Maritime Museum,** Strang. 1. (Open May-Sept. daily 10am-5pm; Jan.-Apr. and Oct.-Dec. M-F 2-5pm, Sa 9am-noon. 20kr.) Or visit the regal 17th-century estate of **Valdemars Slot,** built by Christian IV for his son and whose grounds hold a new Yachting Museum and a beach open to visitors. (Open May-Sept. daily 10am-5pm; Apr. and early Oct. Sa-Su 10am-5pm. 45kr.) Bus 200 (every hr. 35min. after the hr.) goes to both, as do the cruises of the **M/S Helge** (tel. 62 21 09 80; 2hr., 50kr) that leave from Jensens Mole.

Ferries to Ærø leave from the docks behind the train station (see **Aero**, below, for times and prices). The **tourist office** (tel. 62 21 09 80; fax 62 22 05 53) is on the cafe-filled Centrum Pladsen; the office books ferries, hotel rooms and hostels for free, and finds rooms in private homes for 25kr. (Open late June-Aug. M-F 9am-7pm, Sa 9am-3pm; Sept. to mid-June M-F 9am-5pm, Sa 9:30am-12:30pm.) The five-star **HI youth hostel**, Vesterg. 45 (tel. 62 21 66 99; fax 62 20 29 39), is centrally located. (88kr. Breakfast, sheets, and laundry 40kr each. Free lockers. Kitchen. Bike rental 50kr per day. Reception 8am-9pm. Check-out 9:30am.) To get there from the station, take a left onto Jernbaneg., then turn left at Valdemarsg., which becomes Vesterg. (20min.). **Carlsberg Camping,** Sundbrovej 19 (tel. 62 22 53 84; fax 62 22 58 11), is across the sound on Tåsinge (51kr; reception 8am-10pm; open May-Oct). **Den Grimme Ælling,** Korsg. 17, serves all-you-can-eat lunch (70kr) and dinner (100kr).

ÆRØ

Ærø's (EH-ruh) wheat fields, busy harbors, and cobblestoned hamlets quietly preserve an earlier era in Danish history. A small island off the south coast of Funen, Ærø is a place where cows, rather than real estate developers, lay claim to the most beautiful waterfront land. Several **trains** from Odense to Svendborg are timed to meet the ferry from Svendborg to Ærøskøbing. (70min. Departs Svendborg daily 7:30, 10:25am, 1:25, 4:25, 7:25 and 10:30pm. Ferry 64kr one-way, 109kr round-trip; buy ticket on board. Call 62 52 40 00 or fax 62 52 20 88.) The **M/S Fair Lady** sails from Marstal, on Ærø's west tip, to Kiel, Germany (3hr., 2 per day, 50kr). From Mommark, on Jutland, **Ærø-Als** (tel. 62 58 17 17) sails to Søby (1hr., Apr.-Sept. 2-5 per day, Mar.-Oct. Sa-Su only, 60kr). Bus 990 rides between the main towns of Ærøskøbing, Marstal, and Søby (15kr, day pass 44kr), but Ærø is best explored on bike.

Thanks to economic stagnation followed by conservation efforts, the town of **Ærøskøbing** appears today almost as it did 200 years ago. The ubiquitous rosebushes and half-timbered houses attract tourist yachts from Sweden and Germany, as well as vacationing Danes, but you don't have to get too far out of town to find your own serene spot. The **tourist office** (tel. 62 52 13 00; fax 62 52 14 36; email Turistar@post1.tele.dk), just across from the ferry landing, arranges rooms in private homes. (170kr per person. Open June 15-Aug. M-F 9am-5pm, Sa 10am-3pm, Su 11am-1pm; Sept.-June 14 M-F 9am-4pm, Sa 10am-1pm.) The gracious **HI youth hostel,** Smedevejen 15 (tel. 62 52 10 44; fax 62 52 16 44), is a 10-minute walk from the ferry; walk left on Smedeg., which becomes Nørreg., then Østerg., and then Smedevejen. (85kr, nonmembers 110kr. Breakfast 40kr. Sheets 35kr. Reception 8am-noon and 4-8pm. Check-in by 5pm or call ahead. Reservations recommended. No credit cards. Open Apr. to mid-Oct.) **Ærøskøbing Camping,** Sygehusvejen 40b (tel. 62 52 18 54; fax 62 52 14 36), is 10 minutes to the right as you leave the ferry (44kr per person; reception 7am-10pm; open May-Sept.).

Musicians come to **Cafe Andelen** at Sønderg. 28 to play for appreciative crowds and to enjoy the delectable 22kr rhubarb pie. (Music daily 9pm-midnight. Food 50-120kr. Cafe open daily noon-6pm.) Generally pricy restaurants line Vesterg., the street leading into town from the ferry port. Affordable Danish seafood is available at **Ærøskøbing Røgeri,** Havnen 15. (Open daily May to mid-June and Aug. 10am-6pm; late June to July 10am-7pm.) Thrifty shoppers head to the supermarket **Emerko,** Statene 3 (open M-F 8am-7pm). You can rent a **bike** at the hostel or at the campground (40-50kr per day) to explore the towns of **Marstal** and **Søby,** on the more remote shores of the island.

JUTLAND (JYLLAND)

Homeland of the Jutes who joined the Angles and Saxons in the conquest of England, the Jutland peninsula is Denmark's largest land mass. Beaches and campgrounds mark the peninsula as prime summer vacation territory, while low rolling hills, marshland, and sparse forests add color and variety. Jutland may not be suitable for a whirlwind tour, but the plentiful supply of hostels will allow you to take a weekend beach fling without denting your budget. Frequent **trains** connect major Danish cities with **Esbjerg,** on Jutland's west coast. **Ferries** travel to Norway and Sweden; **DFDF** sails to Harwich, England (18hr., 3-4 per week, 429-870kr depending on time of year, Eurail 50% off). Those stuck waiting for connections may try the **HI youth hostel,** Gammel Vade Vej 80. (Tel. 75 12 42 58; fax 75 13 68 33. 85kr, nonmembers 110kr. Reception 8am-noon and 4-8pm. Open Feb.-Dec.)

■ Århus

Århus (ORE-hoos), Denmark's second largest and many Danes' favorite city, bills itself as "the world's smallest big city," but this slogan, along with the town's "Little Tivoli" and other Copenhagen-inspired touches, reveals a thriving rivalry with its big sibling to the east. Still, travelers to this manageably-sized and laid-back student and cultural center may find themselves believing that size doesn't matter.

SIGHTS AND ENTERTAINMENT Queen Margarethe II's summer home here at **Marselisborg Castle** opens its exquisite rose garden to the public. From the train station, take bus 1, 18, or 19. (Closed July and whenever else the Queen is in residence and needs to frolic unaccompanied.) At the town center, the 13th-century **Århus Domkirke** (cathedral) dominates Bispetorv and the cafe- and shop-lined pedestrian streets that fan out around its Gothic walls. (Open May-Sept. M-Sa 9:30am-4pm; Oct.-Apr. 10am-3pm. Free.) Nearby Åboulevarden is Århus' answer to Copenhagen's Nyhavn, with trendy cafes lining the street along the newly reopened canal.

The **Århus Kunstmuseum,** Vennelystparken, has a fine collection of Danish Golden Age painting as well as American and German Realist and Impressionist art (open Tu-Su 10am-5pm; 30kr). Next door, reclaim "herstory" at the **Women's Museum,** Domkirkeplads 5 (open June-Aug. daily 10am-5pm; Sept.-May Tu-Su 10am-4pm; 20kr). Near the cathedral, just off Domkirkeplads, in former Gestapo headquarters, the Århus **Museet for Besættelsen** (Occupation Museum) has collections of military equipment, propaganda, and items used for sabotage (open daily June-Aug. 10am-4pm; Jan.-May and Sept.-Dec. Sa-Su 10am-4pm; 20kr). Two millennia ago, people living near Århus killed some of their own and threw them into nearby bogs, where antiseptic acidity mummified the bodies. Take bus 6 from the train station to the end of the line to reach the **Moesgård Museum of Prehistory,** where Graballe Man, a completely preserved bog body, makes his home. (Open Feb.-Sept. daily 10am-5pm; Oct.-Jan. Tu-Su 10am-4pm; Jan.-May 9 also W until 9pm. 35kr.) From behind the museum, the **Prehistoric Trail** leads through mock settings to a **sand beach** (3km). In summer, bus 19 (last bus 7:40pm) returns from the beach to the Århus station. Buses 3, 14, or 15 go to **Den Gamle By** (Old Town), Viborgvej 2, a reconstructed 16th-century Jutland village. (Open daily June-Aug. 9am-6pm; May and Sept. 9am-5pm; Apr., Oct., and Dec. 10am-4pm; Jan.-Mar. and Nov. 11am-3pm. 50kr.)

The **Århus Festuge,** a rollicking week of theater, dance, and music, will run from Aug. 27-Sept. 5 in 1999 (tel. 89 31 82 70; fax 86 19 13 36; http://www.aarhusfestuge.dk). In mid-July Århus holds a week-long **Jazz Festival** (tel. 86 12 24 69; fax 86 12 28 89; http://www.musikhuset-aarhus.dk; tickets free-120kr). You can visit a smaller replica of Tivoli, the **Tivoli Friheden,** at Skovbrynet. (Bus 1, 4, 6, 8, 18, or 19. Open daily Apr. 25-June 20 and Aug. 4-17 2-10pm; June 21-Aug. 3 1-11pm. 35kr.) The **Bent J** jazz club, Nørre Allé 66, jams Monday evenings and occasionally other weekdays (call 86 12 04 92 M-F 2-6pm for tickets and info). **Valdemar,** Store Torv 3, is a popular disco in the middle of town with no cover and a somewhat flexible minimum age of 23 (Th-Sa 10pm-5am). The **Pan Club**, Jægergårdsg. 42, has a cafe, bar, and largely gay and lesbian dance club. (Cafe open Su-Th 6pm-midnight, F-Sa 6pm-5am. Dance club open W-Sa 11pm-4am; F-Sa 45kr cover.)

PRACTICAL INFO, ACCOMMODATIONS, AND FOOD The **tourist office** (tel. 89 40 67 00; fax 86 12 95 90; email aarhconv@inet.uni-c.dk) in the town hall, a block down the street at the left-hand end of the train station, dispenses free maps and city guides and books accommodations in private homes for a 25kr fee. (Rooms 125-150kr. Open late June to early Sept. M-F 9:30am-6pm, Sa 9:30am-5pm, Su 9:30am-1pm; reduced hours off-season.) Århus is eminently walkable, but the tourist office sells one-day bus passes (45kr). Also available at the tourist office is the **Århus Pass**, good for travel on public transit in the city and free admission to all sights (48hr. 110kr, 1 week 155kr). The main library, at Mølleparken, has English-language periodicals and free **Internet access.** (Open May-Aug. M-Th 10am-7pm, F 10am-6pm, Sa 10am-2pm; Sept.-Apr. M 10am-10pm, Tu-Th 10am-8pm, F 10am-6pm, Sa 10am-2pm.)

Ten minutes from the train station, the hip **Århus City Sleep-In,** Havneg. 20 (tel. 86 19 20 55; fax 86 19 18 11; email sleep-in@mail1.stofanet.dk), doubles as an unofficial cultural and info center. (Dorms 85kr; doubles 200kr, with shower 250kr. Breakfast 25kr. Sheets 30kr. Laundry 25kr. Free lockers. Wheelchair accessible. Bike rental 50kr per day. Reception 24hr. Check-out noon.) The Sleep-In runs in conjunction with the helpful **Kutturgyngen student center,** around the corner at Mejlg. 53, which has a cafe/club. Århus's **HI youth hostel "Pavillonen,"** Marienlundsvej 10 (tel. 86 16 72 98; fax 86 10 55 60), rests in the Risskov forest 3km from the city center and five minutes from the beach. Take bus 1, 6, 9, or 16 to Marienlund then walk 300m into the park. (78kr, nonmembers 103kr. Breakfast 40kr. Sheets 30kr. Wheelchair accessible. Reception 7:30-10am and 4-11pm.) Camp at the beautiful **Blomme-havenn Camping Århus,** Ørneredevej 35 (tel. 86 27 02 07; fax 86 27 45 22), located near a beach in the Marselisborg forest and near the Royal Family's summer residence. Take bus 19 (summer only) from the rail station directly to the grounds, or bus 6 to Hørhavevej. (50kr plus 15kr per site in high season. Reception Apr. to early Sept. 7am-10pm; mid-Sept. to Mar. 8am-8pm.)

Cheap groceries are at **Fakta,** Østerg. 8-12 (open M-F 9am-7pm, Sa 9am-4pm). The all-you-can-eat buffet at the comfortable yet classy **Den Grønne Hjørne,** Frederiksg. 60, includes fruit and always has veggie options (buffet 59kr before 4pm, 79kr after; open M-Sa 11:30am-10pm).

■ Near Århus: Legoland and Silkeborg

Billund is renowned as the home of **Legoland**—an amusement park built of 40 million Lego pieces, best seen as a daytrip. More than just baby-babble, "Lego" is an abbreviation of *leg godt* (have fun playing). Don't skip the impressive indoor exhibitions. Unfortunately, private buses make Legoland a bit expensive. To get there, take the train from Århus to **Vejle** (45min., 1 per hr.), then bus 912 or 44, marked "Legoland." A combined ticket for the bus and park admission (including rides) costs 165kr. (Tel. 75 33 13 33; http://www.legoland.dk. Open daily late June to Aug. 10am-9pm; Apr. to mid-June and Sept.-Oct. 10am-8pm; rides close 2hr. earlier.)

An hour west of Århus by train (62kr), **Silkeborg** floats in perhaps the most scenic part of Denmark. The Tollund Man, a remarkably preserved 2200-year-old bog man, rests in the **Silkeborg Museum,** Hovedgården (open May-Oct. 18 daily 10am-5pm; Oct.19-Apr. W and Sa-Su noon-4pm; 20kr). The **tourist office,** Åhavevej 2A (tel. 86 82 19 11; fax 86 81 09 83), offers free maps and town guides. From the train station, turn right on Drewsensvej, make a left on Chr. 8 Vej, a right on Rosenørns Allé, and a left on Åhavevej. (Open June 15-Aug. M-F 9am-5pm, Sa 9am-3pm, Su 9:30am-12:30pm; Sept.-June 14 M-F 9am-4pm, Sa 9am-noon.)

■ Aalborg

The site of the earliest known Viking settlement, Aalborg (OLE-borg) is now Denmark's fourth-largest city. Its spotless streets and white church garnered it the title of Europe's Tidiest City in 1990. By contrast, **Lindholm Høje**, Vendilavej 11, in nearby Nørresundby, was filled with unkempt, rowdy Vikings around 700. Today, it's covered with 700 of their gravestones and a museum of Viking life. To reach the site, take bus 6 (11kr) from near the tourist office. (Site open daily dawn-dusk. Museum open from Apr. to mid-Oct. daily 10am-5pm; late Oct. to mid-Mar. Tu-Su 10am-4pm. 20kr.) The frescoed **Monastery of the Holy Ghost,** C.W. Obelsplads, is Denmark's oldest welfare institution (1431; English tours late June to mid-Aug. Tu and Th at 1:30pm; 25kr). The **Budolfi Church,** on Algade, has a brilliantly colored interior with ringing *carillon.* (Open May-Sept. M-F 9am-4pm, Sa 9am-2pm; Oct.-Apr. M-F 9am-3pm, Sa 9am-noon.) The **Nordjyllands Kunstmuseum,** Kong Chr. Allé 50, houses 20th-century painting (open July-Aug. daily 10am-5pm; Sept.-June closed M; 30kr). For serious rollercoasters visit **Tivoliland,** Karolinelundsvej (open daily Apr.-Sept. noon-10pm; 40kr, full-day "Funcard" 160kr).

The **tourist office, Østerå.** 8 (tel. 98 12 60 22; fax 98 16 69 22), gives out maps and brochures. From the station, cross the street and J.F.K. Plads, then turn left on Boulevarden, which becomes Østerå. (Open June 15-Aug. 14 M-F 9am-6pm, Sa 9am-5pm; rest of year M-F 9am-4:30pm, Sa 10am-1pm.) **Aalborg Vandrerhjem and Camping (HI),** Skydebanevej 50 (tel. 98 11 60 44; fax 98 12 47 11), sits next to a beautiful fjord. Take bus 8 ("Fjordparken") to the end. (75kr, nonmembers 100kr; camping 49kr. Laundry 35kr. Reception late Jan. to mid-June and early Aug. to mid-Dec. 8am-noon and 4-9pm; late June to mid-Aug. 7:30am-11pm.) Bars, restaurants, and nightclubs line **Jomfru Ane Gade.** Lunch can be had for about 40kr; a 3-course dinner for 100kr.

■ Frederikshavn

Despite noble efforts to showcase its admittedly charming streets and hospitality, Frederikshavn is best known for its ferry links. **Stena Line** ferries (tel. 96 20 02 00) leave here for Göteborg, Sweden (2-3¼hr., 100-115kr, round-trip 150-165kr, Scanrail 50% off), as well as for Oslo (10hr., 350kr, round-trip 400kr, Scanrail 50% off) and other points in Norway. **SeaCat** (tel. 98 42 83 00) offers cheaper service to Göteborg (2hr., 3 per day, 90-100kr). **Color Line** (tel. 99 20 40 60) also sails to Norway, but offers no railpass discounts. Ferries are cheaper but less frequent off-season. The **tourist office,** Brotorvet 1 (tel. 98 42 32 66; fax 98 42 12 99), near the Stena Line terminal south of the rail station, has a currency exchange, free maps and guides, and reserves rooms for a 25kr fee. (Open mid-June to mid-Aug. M-Sa 8:30am-8:30pm, Su 11am-8:30pm; mid-Aug. to mid-June M-F 9am-4pm, Sa 11am-2pm.) The **HI youth hostel,** Buhlsvej 6 (tel. 98 42 14 75; fax 98 42 65 22), is group-oriented and packed. From the bus or train station, walk right, then follow the signs (15min.). (Dorms 53kr, nonmembers 78kr. Wheelchair accessible. Reception in summer 7am-noon and 4-9pm; off-season closes at 6pm. Open Feb.-Dec.) Camp at **Nordstrand Camping,** Apholmenvej 40 (tel. 98 42 93 50; fax 98 43 47 85; 49kr; open Apr.-Sept.15).

■ Skagen

Perched on Denmark's northernmost tip, sunny Skagen (SKAY-en) is a beautiful summer retreat amidst long stretches of white-sand dunes and sea. The powerful currents of the North Atlantic and Baltic Seas collide at **Grenen.** Do not try to swim in these dangerous waters; every year some hapless soul is carried out to sea. To get to Grenen, take bus 99 from the Skagen station to Gammel (11kr) or walk 3km down Fyrvej. The spectacular **Råberg Mile** sand dunes were formed by a storm in the 16th century and migrate eastward 15m each year. From here, you can swim along 60km of beaches whose endless summer light attracted Denmark's most famous late 19th-century painters. Their works can be seen in the wonderful **Skagen Museum,** Brøndumsvej 4 (open June-Aug. daily 10am-6pm; shorter hours off-season; 40kr). You can also tour the artists' homes at **Michael og Anna Archers Hus,** Markvej 2-4, and **Holger Drachmanns Hus,** Hans Baghsvej 21. Skagen hosts a large annual folk, brass, and **Dixieland music festival** in late June (free-150kr); contact the tourist office.

The **tourist office** (tel. 98 44 13 77; fax 98 45 02 94) is in the train station. (Open June 1-20 and Aug. 11-31 M-Sa 9am-5:30pm, Su 10am-2pm; June 21-Aug.10 9am-7pm; May and Sept. M-F 9am-4pm, Sa-Su 10am-2pm; Jan.-Apr. and Oct.-Dec. M-F 9am-4pm, Sa 10am-1pm.) Nordjyllands Trafikselskab (tel. 98 44 21 33) runs both **buses** and **private trains** from Frederikshavn to Skagen (1hr., 33kr, 50% off with Scanrail). The **Skagen Ny Vandrerhjem,** Rolighedsvej 2 (tel. 98 44 22 00; fax 98 44 22 55), not to be confused with the somewhat inconvenient **Gammel Skagen Vandrerhjem** (tel. 98 44 13 56; fax 98 45 08 17; open Mar.-Nov.), 4km west, serves as a springboard for nocturnal forays in town (75-85kr, nonmembers 100-110kr; reception 10am-noon and 4-9pm; open Feb.-Dec.). Most **campgrounds** around Skagen are open late April to mid-September (55kr); try **Grenen** (tel. 98 44 25 46; fax 98 44 65 46) or **Østerklit** (tel./fax 98 44 31 23), not far from the city center. To sample Skagen's famous seafood, try the kiosks lining **Nordkaj** on the harbor, **Skagen Fiske Restaurant,** Fiskehuskaj 13, or **Pakhuset Fiskerestaurant og Harnecafe,** Rødspættevej 6. Come summer, dance the night away at **Hyttefadet,** Jens Bergsvej 2 (disco open daily until 5am).

■ Southwestern Jutland

Popular with tourists from the rest of the continent as well as vacationing Danes, the region's lovely beaches, marshland, and ancient towns are well-trafficked. The area south of the river Konge Åen (including Tønder and Ribe) was German territory from 1864 until a plebiscite in 1920, when residents decided to rejoin Denmark; the result is something of a gradual border. A new rail connection from Nieböll, Germany to Tønder should be operational by 1999, making travel in the region simpler.

■ Ribe

After centuries of wrestling with the North Sea, Ribe, Denmark's oldest town, is now separated from the water by flat salt meadows and boasts migratory seasonal birds, half-timbered medieval houses, and red-tiled roofs. For a great view, climb the 248 steps through the clockwork and huge bells of the 12th-century **cathedral** tower. (Open Apr. and Oct. M-Sa 11am-4pm, Su noon-4pm; May and Sept. M-Sa 10am-5pm, Su noon-5pm; June-Aug. M-Sa 10am-6pm, Su noon-6pm; Nov.-Mar. M-Sa 11am-3pm, Su noon-3pm. 10kr.) Next to the **Rådhus,** Van Støckens Plads (tel. 75 42 00 55), a former debtor's prison houses a small museum on medieval torture (open June-Aug. daily 1-3pm; May and Sept. M-F 1-3pm; 15kr). Follow the **night watchman** on his rounds for an English or Danish tour of town beginning in Torvet, the main square (35min.; June-Aug. 8pm and 10pm; May and Sept. 10pm; free). **Ribe's Vikinger,** Udin Plads 1, houses an impressive collection of artifacts recovered from archaeological excavation of the town, once an important Viking trading post. (Open Apr.-May and late Sept. to Oct. daily 10am-4pm; June to mid-Sept. daily 10am-5pm; Nov.-Mar. Tu-Su 10am-4pm. 40kr.) Two kilometers south of town, the open-air **Ribe Vikingcenter,** Lustrupvej 4, has authentic recreations of a Viking market, farm and town (open mid-May to Sept. Tu-Su 11am-4pm; 40kr). The **Vadehavscentret** (Wadden Sea Center), Okholmvej 5, Vestervedsted (tel. 75 44 61 61), has exhibits on and tours of the local marshes, dikes, and sea (bus 711; open daily June-Oct. 10am-6pm; Apr.-May and Oct.-Nov. 10am-4pm; 30kr). You can also rent a bike and explore on your own.

The **tourist office,** Torvet 3 (tel. 75 42 15 00; fax 75 42 40 78), has free maps and arranges accommodations for a 20kr fee. (Open mid-June to Aug. M-F 9:30am-5:30pm, Sa 9:30am-5pm, Su 10am-2pm; Sept.-Oct and Apr. to early June M-F 9am-5pm, Sa 10am-1pm; Nov.-Mar. M-F 9:30am-4:30pm, Sa 10am-1pm.) From the train station, walk down the street to the left of the Viking museum. At the Torvet (main square), the office is on your right. The centrally located **Ribe Vandrerhjen (HI),** Sct.

Pedersg. 16 (tel. 75 42 06 20; fax 75 42 42 88), has **bike rental** (50kr per day) and a view of the flatlands. It will *make* room for you in busy season, even if it's only a mattress on the floor at a reduced rate. (90kr, nonmembers 115kr. Breakfast 40kr. Sheets 36kr. Wheelchair accessible. Reception 8am-noon and 4-8pm; longer hours May-Sept. Open Feb.-Nov.) **Ribe Camping,** Farupvej 2 (tel. 75 41 07 77), 1.5km from the town center, has showers, laundry, a grocery store, cafeteria, and campfires (50kr per person; 2-person cabins 175kr). Somehow, Ribe's tiny population supports 5 large supermarkets, which cluster around Seminarievej, near the hostel. Netto and Rema 1000 are cheapest; Kvickly has an affordable cafeteria upstairs. **Valdemar,** Sct. Nicolajg 6, is a cozy pub with live music in summer (open M-Th 1pm-1am, F-Sa 11am-3am).

How the Vikings Became Christian

While the Viking name still brings to mind vicious horned helmets, iron mesh, and uncouth table manners, this ancient people was not alone in its ruthless tactics. Ansgar, the German missionary who is largely credited with the 9th-century Christianization of Viking Scandinavia, was himself a brutal converteer. Upon arriving in a Viking village, Ansgar set immediately to accusing all the old women of witchcraft and having them burned at the stake. Old Viking women were the keepers of clan and village lore, and their deaths eliminated generations of Viking history and tradition, and with these the religious heritage. Though opposed, like all good liberals, to capital punishment, Danes to this day burn witches in effigy in great seaside bonfires during Midsummer celebrations. As for "the Apostle of the North," he became Saint Ansgar after his death in 865.

DENMARK

Estonia (Eesti)

US$1	= 14.37EEK (Estonian Kroons)	
CDN$1	= 9.30EEK	
UK£1	= 23.56EEK	
IR£1	= 20.09EEK	
AUS$1	= 8.35EEK	
NZ$1	= 7.08EEK	
SAR1	= 2.26EEK	
DM1	= 8.00EEK	

10EEK =	US$0.70	
10EEK =	CDN$1.07	
10EEK =	UK£0.42	
10EEK =	IR£0.50	
10EEK =	AUS$1.20	
10EEK =	NZ$1.41	
10EEK =	SAR4.42	
10EEK =	DM1.25	

Country Phone Code: 372   **International Dialing Prefix: 800**

German cars, cellular phones, designer shops, and ever more stylish youngsters seem to attest that Estonia is benefiting from its transition to democracy and capitalism. Material trappings, however, mask declining living standards in the face of growing inflation. Historically and culturally identifying with its Nordic and Lutheran German neighbors, Estonia is redefining and European-izing its identity and forgetting its Soviet past, to the chagrin of the 35% ethnically Russian population. Tallinn's tiny old town is immensely charming and uncannily resembles Kraków's, while Tartu is a rollicking college town that produced the great literary critic Yuri Lotman, and the bikeable islands off the coast offer some of the former Soviet Union's least trammeled wilderness. Having overcome successive centuries of domination by the Danes, Swedes, and Russians, the Estonians' serene, patient pragmatism has matured into a dynamic and, some would say, Scandinavian attitude.

Estonians can't resist a man with a copy of *Let's Go: Eastern Europe 1999*.

GETTING THERE AND GETTING AROUND

Citizens of Australia, Ireland, New Zealand, the United Kingdom, and the United States do not need a visa to visit Estonia for 90 days. South Africans can obtain a visa at the border for 400EEK. When arranged before departure, 30-day, single-entry visas are US$10, and multiple-entry visas US$50. To obtain a visa extension, contact the visa department of the Immigration Department, Endla 4, in Tallinn (tel. 612 69 79).

Several **ferry lines** connect to Tallinn's harbor (info tel. 631 85 50). For specific information, see Tallinn's **Practical Information: Ferries,** p. 255. By air, **Finnair** (tel. 611 09 50) connects Tallinn to Helsinki (round-trip 1700EEK), and **SAS** (tel. 631 22 40) flies to Stockholm (2180EEK).

Three **train** lines cross the Estonian border; one heads from Tallinn through Tartu to Moscow, another goes to Rīga and on to Warsaw, and the third goes through Narva to St. Petersburg. The **Baltic Express** is the only train from Poland that skips Belarus, linking Tallinn to Warsaw via Kaunas, Rīga, and Tartu (one per day, 21hr., 477-680EEK). Major towns such as Pärnu and Haapsalu are all connected to Tallinn, but trains can be scarce. **Buses** thoroughly link all towns, often more cheaply and efficiently than the trains. During the school year (Sept.-June 25), students receive half-price bus tickets. On the islands, where buses have up to 12-hour gaps between trips, **bike** and **car rentals** can be a relatively inexpensive way of exploring the remote areas. Those who **hitchhike** stretch out an open hand.

ESSENTIALS

Larger towns and cities in Estonia have well-equipped **tourist offices** which often arrange tours and make reservations. Smaller information booths, marked with a green "i," sell maps and give away free brochures. The unit of currency is the **kroon** (EEK), divided into 100 **senti.** Most banks *(pank)* cash **traveler's checks,** and credit card acceptance is increasing, mostly with **Visa** and **MasterCard.** Hotel Viru in Tallinn and many banks across the country provide Visa cash advances. **ATMs** are common in all of the towns listed below.

To use a pay **phone,** you must insert a digital card, obtainable at any bank or newspaper kiosk. **AT&T Direct** is available in Estonia by dialing 80 08 00 10 01. **International long-distance** calls can be made at post offices. Calls to the Baltic states and Russia cost 8.50EEK per minute (10.50EEK with a digital card); calls to the U.S. run 30-36EEK per minute (40.80EEK with a digital card). The system of adding prefixes and codes to Estonian phone numbers proves that the universe tends towards disorder. There are three phone systems (old, new, and cellular), each with its own area codes. In Tallinn, for the **old** system, phone numbers have six digits, and the area code is 22. For the **new** system, in which phone numbers have seven digits (the first of which is a 6 and is often mistakenly placed in parentheses), the area code is 2. For **cellular** phones, the area code is 25. The new (digital) system and the old system can call each other within a given city without the area code. To call Tallinn from outside Estonia on the old system, dial 37 22 before the number; on the digital system, dial 372. To call a cell phone anywhere in Estonia, dial 37 25. To call out of Estonia on the old system, dial 8, wait for two tones, then dial 00, the country code, and the number. From digital phones, dial 800 without waiting for a tone. From a cell phone, just dial 00 and the number. If you can't figure it out call the English-language **Ekspress Hotline** at 631 32 22 in Tallinn; elsewhere dial 8, then 11 88 after the two tones. In a true **emergency,** dial 01 for fire (001 in Tallinn), 02 for police (002 in Tallinn), and 03 for an ambulance (003 in Tallinn).

Estonians speak the best English in the Baltics; most young people know at least a few phrases. German and Russian are more common among the older set.

Yes/no	*Jaa/Ei*	yah/ay
Hello	*Tere*	TEH-re
Please	*Palun*	PA-lun
Thank you	*Tänan*	TEH-nan
Excuse me	*Vabandage*	vah-pan-TAGE-euh
Do you speak English?	*Kas te räägite inglise keelt?*	Kas te RA-A-gite ING-lise keelt
I don't speak Estonian.	*Ma ei oska eesti keelt.*	Ma ei OS-ka Ees-ti keelt
Where is...?	*Kus on...?*	kuhs on

ESTONIA

ESTONIA

Tallinn

Gulf of Finland

Song Festival Grounds

Pirita tee

Kadriorg Park

Kadriorg Palace

Peter the Great Museum

A. Weizenbergi

Mäekalda

Lasnamäe

Kuristiku

Oktobri tee

Pae

Pallasti

Lasnamäe

500 yards

500 meters

Vesi värava

J. Vilmsi

J. Poska

Gonsiori

K. Türnpu

Tartu mnt.

Lastekodu

Juhkentali

Filtri tee

Karu

F. R. Kreutzwaldi

Pronksi

Tartu mnt.

Lembitu

Liivalaia

Herne

Veerenni

Suur-Patarei

City Concert Hall

Sadama

Ahtri

Mere pst.

Pōhja pst.

Narva mnt.

"Estonia" Theater and Concert Hall

Pärnu mnt.

Estonia pst.

Skela

Soo

Pōhja pst.

Maritime Museum

Vana-Kalamaja

Rannamäe cee

Nunne Puppet Theater

City Museum

L. Pikk

Town Hall and Museum

RAEKOJA PLATS

Harju

Vabaduse väljak

Kaarli pst.

Luise

Endla

Suur Ameerika

Pärnu mnt.

Koidu

Luha

Lilleküla

Kopli

Telliskivi

Train Station

Toompuiestee

Rohu

Tehnika

Paldiski mnt.

Toompea Castle

Falgi tee

Toompuiestee

TOOMPEA

Dome

"Kiek in de Kök"

Alexander Nevski Cathedral

Rüütli

How much?	*Kui palju?*	Kwee PAL-you
I would like…a single/double.	*Ma sooviksin…übelist/ kahelist.*	Ma SOO-vik-sin…EW-hel-ist/ KA-hel-ist
Help!	*Appi!*	APP-pi

Tourist offices have listings of all accommodations and prices in their respective towns and can often arrange a place for visitors. For info on HI hostels around Estonia, contact the **Estonian Youth Hostel Association,** Tatari (tel. 646 14 57; fax 646 15 95; email puhkemajad@online.ee). Many hotels provide laundry services for an extra charge. Go into any **restaurant** and you'll see the same assortment of drab sausages, lifeless *schnitzel,* greasy bouillon, and cold fried potatoes that plague the former USSR. But there is more fish on the menus in Estonia, and beer is the national drink for good reason—not only is it inexpensive, it's also delicious and nutritious. The national brand *Saku* is downright excellent, as is the darker *Saku Tume.*

■ Tallinn

Tallinn's hip, cosmopolitan shops and fashionably dressed, young crowd complement the ancient beauty and charming serenity of Estonia's capital; German spires grace the skyline while vendors below pour glasses of *Saku* and visitors wind their way through the cobblestone streets. The most renowned town of the German Hanseatic league in the 14th and 15th centuries, Tallinn is beginning to boom again. Nonetheless, the prosperity of the Old Town cannot hide Tallinn's drab outskirts, which remain squalid as if frozen in Soviet rule.

ORIENTATION AND PRACTICAL INFORMATION

Tallinn's **Vanalinn** (Old Town) is ringed by four streets—**Põhja puiestee, Mere puiestee, Pärnu maantee,** and **Toom puiestee.** From the junction of Mere pst. and Pärnu mnt., **Narva maantee** runs east to **Hotel Viru,** the central landmark. The Old Town peaks at the fortress-rock **Toompea,** whose 13th-century streets are level with church steeples in **All-linn** (Lower Town). To reach the Old Town from the **ferry terminal,** walk along Sadama to Põhja pst., then south on Pikk between the stone towers. From the train station, cross Toom pst. and go straight through the park along **Nunne**—the stairway up **Patkuli trepp** on the right leads to Toompea. In Vanalinn, **Pikk tee** (Long street), the main artery, runs from the seaward gates of All-linn to Toompea via **Pikk Jalg** tower. **Raekoja plats** (Town Hall Sq.) is the scenic center of All-linn. The second-floor shop in Hotel Viru stocks *Tallinn This Week.*

Telephone Codes: see Estonia's **"Essentials"** section above.

Flights: Bus 2 runs every 20min. from the **airport,** Lennujaama 2 (tel. 21 10 92), to near Hotel Viru.

Trains: Toompuiestee 35 (tel. 615 68 51); trams 1 and 2 travel to Hotel Viru. Service to St. Petersburg (10hr., 1 per day, 155EEK) and Warsaw via Rīga (1 per day; Rīga 7hr., 162 EEK; Warsaw 21hr., 477 EEK).

Buses: Lastekodu 46 (tel. 642 25 49), just south of Tartu mnt. Tram 2 or 4 and bus 22 connect to the city center. Buy tickets at the station or from the driver. To Rīga (7hr., 4 per day, 132EEK), St. Petersburg (9hr., 155EEK), and the entire country.

Ferries: At the end of Sadama, 15min. from the center. A variety of vessels cross to Helsinki. **Eckerö Line,** Terminal B (tel. 631 86 06; fax 631 86 61): 3½hr., 3 per day, June 27-Aug. 16 325EEK, students 200EEK; Aug. 17-June 26 250EEK, students 150EEK. **Silja Line,** Terminal D (tel. 631 83 31; fax 631 82 64): daytime crossing 3½hr., nighttime 8½hr., 2 per day, June 12-Aug. 9 410EEK; Aug. 10-June 11 Su night-F day 270EEK, F night-Su day 430EEK. Cabin supplement from 540EEK.

Public Transportation: Buses, trams, and trolleybuses run daily 6am-midnight. Tickets *(talong)* can be bought from the driver (7EEK in exact change), but to save money and avoid the wrath of the driver pick some up first from any kiosk (5 EEK). Punch your ticket aboard. Tram 2 connects the bus and train stations.

Taxis: Find a *Takso* stand, or call 612 00 00, 630 01 34, 655 60 00, or 55 79 05. Check that the cab has a meter and expect to pay 4-6EEK per km.

Tourist Office: The **Tourist Information Center,** Raekoja plats 10 (tel. 631 3940; fax 631 3943; email info@tallin.turism.ee; http://www.tallinn.ee), across the square from the town hall. Get a *Tallinn in your Pocket* (14EEK), an info-packed guide to local sights, restaurants, and pubs with a useful map (open M-F 9am-5pm, Sa-Su 10am-4pm). A **branch office,** Sadama 25 (tel. 631 83 21), at Tallinn Harbor (terminal A), has info on smaller hotels. The **Tallinn Card,** available form either office, entitles holders to a sightseeing tour, unlimited public transport, and entry to most museums (1 day 195EEK, 2 days 270EEK).

Embassies: Canada, Toomkooli 13 (tel. 631 79 78; fax 631 35 73). Open M-F 9am-4:30pm. **Latvia,** Tõnismägi 10 (tel. 646 13 13; fax 631 13 66). Open M-F 10am-noon. **Russia,** Pikk 19 (tel. 646 41 69; fax 646 41 78). Open M-F 9am-noon. **U.K.,** Kentmanni 20 (tel. 631 34 61; fax 631 33 54). Open Tu-Th 10am-noon. **U.S.,** Kentmanni 20 (tel. 631 20 21; fax 631 20 25). Open M-F 8:30am-5:30pm.

Currency Exchange: Windows 11 and 47 at the central post office exchange currency, offering some of the best rates in Tallinn. **ATM** machines can be found on nearly every street in the old town.

American Express: Suur-Karja 15, EE-090 (tel. 626 62 62; fax 631 36 56; email sales@estravel.ee). Sells and cashes traveler's checks, exchanges currency, books hotels and tours, sells airline, ferry, and rail tickets, and arranges visas. Members can receive mail and get cash advances. Open M-F 9am-6pm, Sa 10am-5pm.

Luggage Storage: Lockers in the train station cost 15EEK. Open daily 5am-12:30pm. At the bus station 3-12EEK per day. Open daily 5am-noon and 12:30-11:40pm.

Emergencies: Fire, tel. 001. **Ambulance,** 003.

Police: tel. 002.

Pharmacy: RAE Apteek, Pikk 47 (tel. 44 44 08). A broad selection of Scandinavian medical supplies. Open M-F 9am-6pm, Sa 10am-4pm.

Post Office: Narva mnt. 1, 2nd fl., across from Hotel Viru. Open M-F 8am-7pm, Sa 9am-5pm. **Postal Code:** EE-0001.

Internet Access: Küber-kohuik, Gonsiori 4. 40EEK per hr., students 20EEK per hr. Open Su-F 11am-8pm, Sa 3-8pm.

Telephones: Narva 1 (tel. 640 26 66), ground fl. of central post office building. For all phone services, telegrams, and faxing (2-page fax to US 45 EEK). Open M-F 8am-7pm, Sa 9am-4pm.

ACCOMMODATIONS

At the height of summer, hostels fill fast, so book as far in advance as possible. **Bed & Breakfast,** Sadama 11 (tel./fax 641 22 91), finds rooms in private homes in Tallinn, throughout the Baltics, and in St. Petersburg (from 180EEK per person).

Hotell Küün (HI), Väike-Karja 1, 2nd fl. (tel. 44 34 65), in Vanalinn. From behind the town hall walk downhill, turn right up Vana turg, left on Suur-karja, and then veer left. The hostel is through an arch on your left. A find for budget travelers, with unbeatable cleanliness and location (even though it's in the same building as a strip club). Dorms 160EEK; sheets 20EEK. Doubles with shared baths 535EEK. Nonmembers add 15EEK. Call ahead.

Hotell Gasthaus Eeslitall, Dunkri 4, 2nd fl. (tel. 631 37 55; fax 631 32 10). Colorful and clean rooms just off Raekoja plats. Singles 350EEK; doubles 485EEK. Couples can stay in the singles with double beds for the same price. Communal bathrooms. Breakfast in the restaurant 36EEK (see **Food** below).

Pääsu, Sõpruse pst. 182 (tel. 52 00 34; fax 654 20 13), in Mustamäe. Catch trolley bus 4 from the railway station to the "Linn tee" stop. Backtrack a little, and turn left on Linnu tee, then left again on Nigri and follow the signs. Comfortable rooms with cable TV and fridge. Sauna. Singles 360EEK; doubles 460EEK. Breakfast included.

Merevaik (HI), Sõpruse pst. 182, 5th fl. (tel. 52 96 04; fax 52 96 47). Enter from the messy stairwell behind the Pääsu Hotell (see directions above). This hostel's only attractions are its price and friendly atmosphere. 90-100EEK per person.

FOOD

Although cheaper than in Western Europe, restaurants in Tallinn are becoming increasingly expensive. The most central supermarket is **Spar**, Aia 7, near the Viru Gates (open daily 9am-9pm).

Eeslitall, Dunkri 4. The "Donkey Stable" is the best place in Tallinn for Balto-Russian cuisine; there's been a restaurant here since 1362. Meat and veggie dishes 25-132EEK. Open Su-Th 11am-11pm, F-Sa 11am-1am.

Rüütli Baar, Kohtu 2, in the portico across from the Toomkirik. A budget traveler's dream. The Germanic menu includes *schnitzel* (26EEK). Open M-F noon-6pm

Linnaisa Juunes, Aia 2 (tel. 44 09 10). Proud of Estonia's future EU membership, this restaurant presents a dish from each member state (45-115EEK), as well as a few Estonian options (*schnitzel* 49EEK). Open daily 10am-10pm.

SIGHTS

Get acquainted with **Vanalinn** (Old Town) by starting at Hotel Viru, walking down Narva mnt., then continuing along Viru through the 15th-century **Viru City Gate.** Continue up Viru to **Raekoja plats** (Town Hall Square), where folk songs and dances are performed on summer evenings, and the beer flows freely in the outdoor cafes. The **raekoda** (town hall) was built between 1371 and 1404 and is topped by **Vana Toomas** (Old Thomas), a cast-iron weather vane figurine of Tallinn's legendary defender. Thomas has done a good job so far; this is the oldest surviving town hall in Europe. On the north side of the square, Saia Kang (Bread Alley) twists onto Pühavaimu, where the 14th-century **Pühavaimu kirik** (Church of the Holy Ghost) holds an intricate 17th-century wooden clock. *(Open M-Sa 10am-4:30pm.)*

From Viru, head up Vene, take a left on Olevimägi, then a right down Pikk for a view of the medieval city's north towers and bastion. Along the way, the history of Tallinn from its founding in 1219 until the 1940's first republic is all condensed into the **Linnamuuseum** (City Museum), Bene 17. *(Open W-M 10:30am-5:30pm. 7EEK, students 3EEK.)* Founded by Dominicans in 1246, **Dominiiklaste Klooster,** Vene 16, across the street and through a courtyard, contains a Gothic limestone courtyard, two Catholic churches, a windmill, stone carvings, and a granary. At the northern end of Pikk, in the large squat tower known as **Paks Margareeta** (Fat Margaret), the **Meremuuseum** (Maritime Museum) houses changing exhibits on Tallinn's history as a port. *(Open W-Su 10am-5:30pm. 7EEK, students 3EEK.)*

Go to the end of Pikk and hang a left on Rataskaevu to see the mighty spire of **Niguliste kirik** (St. Nicholas's Church). Inside, check out the decidedly ghoulish 150 gravestone of Johannes Ballivi. *(Open Th-Su 11:30am-6pm, Tu 5-8pm, W 3-9pm. 12-15EEK, students 5EEK.)* Travel farther south along Rüütli, then loop to the right around the outside of the city walls. The 1475 **Kiek in de Kök** (Peek in the Kitchen) tower, Komandandi 2, is aptly named—in the 16th century, it offered voyeuristic views into virtually every home in the area. The museum in the tower maintains six floors of less titillating art and historical exhibits. *(Open Tu-F 10:30am-5:30pm, Sa-Su 11am-4pm; 7EEK, students 3.50EEK.)*

Following Lühike jalg uphill onto Toompea from St. Nicholas's Church leads to Lossi plats (Castle Sq.), a square dominated by **Aleksander Nevski katedraal,** begun under Tsar Alexander III and finished a few years before the Bolshevik Revolution. A marble marker from 1910 recalls Peter the Great's 1710 victory over Sweden. *(Open daily 8am-7pm.)* **Eesti Kunstimuuseum** (Estonian Art Museum), Kiriku plats 1, across from **Toomkirik** higher up on Toompea, displays Estonian art from the 19th century to the 1940s. *(Open W-Su 11am-5:30pm. 10EEK, students 5EEK.)*

In **Rocca-al-mare,** a peninsula 12km west of Tallinn, the **Vabaõhumuuseumi** (Estonian Open-Air Museum), Vabaõhumuuseumi 12 (tel. 656 02 30; fax 656 02 27), recreates 18th- to 20th-century wooden mills and farmsteads with all the trimmings. *(Open May-Oct. daily 10am-8pm, some buildings close at 6pm. 21EEK, students 7EEK.)* From Tallinn's train station, take bus 21 (regular ticket; 30min.).

ESTONIA

ENTERTAINMENT

Check *Tallinn This Week* to begin planning your night. **Eesti Kontsert,** Estonia pst. 4 (ticket office tel. 44 31 98; fax 44 53 17; staffed M-F noon-7pm, Sa-Su noon-5pm), features symphonies almost every night (tickets from 30EEK). **Estonia teater,** Estonia pst. 4 (tel. 626 02 15), offers opera, ballet, musicals, and chamber music (ticket office open daily noon-7pm). **Old Town Days** are June 6 to 10, when open-air concerts take place throughout Vanalinn, and a stage on Raekoja plats is erected for fashion shows, singing, and skit performances. The first week of July brings **Beersummer,** a celebration of the good stuff.

Bars have sprouted on almost every street of Vanalinn, and nightclubs are multiplying. By 11pm, the local scene moves from the bars to the clubs. **Von Krahli Teater/ Baar,** Rataskaevu 10, is a bar, club, and avant-garde theater showcasing talent from Lithuanian jazz to experimental dance (tickets 35-40EEK; open Su-Th noon-1am, F-Sa noon-3am). **Nimeta Baar,** Suur-Karja 4, draws a large, boisterous crowd (open Su-Th 11am-2am, F-Sa until 4am). **Hell Hunt** (The Gentle Wolf), Pikk 39, a rocking Irish pub, has Guinness and Kilkenny on tap and occasional live music (open Su-M 11am-1am, Tu-Th until 2am, F-Sa until 3am). **Hollywood,** Vanna-Posti 8, spins house and techno (cover up to 100EEK; open Tu and Su 10am-3am, W-Th until 4am, F-Sa until 6am).

■ Pärnu

The beach pavilions and grand old summer houses of Pärnu were built in the late 19th century when the city was famed throughout Russia for its therapeutic waters and mud baths. Today, a sassy young crowd parties in beachside bars trying to revive the resort. The tree-lined street leading south from the **Tallinn Gate,** the only surviving Baltic town wall gate from the 17th century, takes you to a pedestrian zone just behind the **beach.** The famous **mud baths** still function in the Neoclassical bath house at the southern end of Supeluse pst. (Open daily 8am-3pm; baths stay open until 1am. Mud bath 120EEK, massage 200EEK.) The **Lydia Koidula Museum,** Jannseni 37 (tel. 416 63), across Pärnu river, honors the 19th-century poet who led a revival in Estonian verse and drama (open W-Su 11am-5pm; 3EEK, students 1EEK).

The **train station,** east of the city center by the corner of Riia mnt. and Raja, serves Tallinn (3½hr., 30EEK). Closer to the center of town, **buses** leave the station (at Ringi 3) for Kuressaare (3hr., 87EEK), Rīga (4hr., 76EEK), Tallinn (2-3hr., 55EEK), and Tartu (5hr., 70-76EEK). The **tourist office,** Mungu 2 (tel. (244) 406 39; fax 456 33), has maps of the city and other information (open June-Aug. M-F 9am-6pm, Sa 9am-4pm, Su 10am-3pm; Sept.-May M-F 9am-5pm). **Hotell Kajakas,** Seedri 2 (tel. (244) 430 98), provides a sauna and old but spacious rooms (singles 180EEK; doubles 290EEK). **Hotell Seedri,** Seedri 4 (tel. (244) 433 50), near the beach, has rather worn common bathrooms but a fridge and sink in every room (doubles 220-240EEK; reservations

ESTONIA

The Dirtiest Bath This Side of the Baltics

Mud has never looked or felt better than at Pärnu's Neo-Classical Mudaravila, Ranna pst. 1 (tel. 424 61). Since 1838, when the mud baths and health resort were founded, the privilege of rolling around in gooey mud has not been limited to pigs and small children. Workers at the mud bath and many health professionals insist that Pärnu's sea mud has a curative effect on disorders of the bones, joints, and peripheral nervous system. There's even a special ward for patients with myocardial infarction and cardiovascular diseases. After a brief consultation, patients can choose between General Mud, Local Mud, and Electric Mud (95-120EEK). And, for those tough-to-reach areas, there's the ever-so-popular mud tampon (70EEK). No day at the mud bath is complete without a massage (200EEK), a "curative" bath or shower (60-75EEK), and a cup of restorative herb tea—no mud added (open daily 8am-3pm).

recommended). A popular spot for a cheap meal is **Georg,** on the corner of Rüütli and Hommiku, a cafeteria-style restaurant offering various Estonian staples (open M-F 7:30am-7:30pm, Sa-Su 9am-7:30pm). On summer evenings, drinking, partying, and sunset-watching center around the temporary bars that set up along the beach. **La Pera Vida,** Mere 22, is a disco housed in a sprawling wooden 1930s dancehall (cover 25EEK; open daily 10pm-5am), while **Diskoklubi "Hamilton,"** Rüütli 1, boasts DJs from all over Estonia every night (cover 50EEK; open daily 9pm-5am).

▒ Tartu

Tartu—Estonia's second largest city—is the oldest city in the Baltics. Yet despite its age, Tartu has an inescapable youthful exuberance and energy, due largely to some 10,000 university students. **Raekoja plats** (Town Hall Square) is the center of the city. Ülikooli runs north-south behind the town hall; to the north, it passes **Tartu Ülikool** (Tartu University), founded in 1632 and key to the development of Estonian nationalism. Farther up Ülikooli, the 14th-century **Jaani-kirik** (St. John's Church) is barely standing, but a few hundred terra-cotta figurines still adorn the outside walls. The **Toomemägi** (Cathedral Hill) dominates Tartu from behind the town hall; on the western hump are majestic remains of the 15th-century **Toomkirik** (Cathedral of St. Peter and Paul). Today, it houses the **Museum Historicum Universitatis Tartuensis** (Tartu University Museum), an in-depth series of displays, including scientific instruments and a social history of the university (open W-Su 11am-5pm; 10EEK, students 5EEK). The **Eesti Rahva Muuseum** (Estonian National Museum), J. Kuperjanov 9, holds hordes of ethnographic exhibits from across Estonia (open W-Su 11am-6pm; 5EEK, students 3EEK).

    Trains roll out of the station at Vaksali 6, 1.5km from the city center, for Moscow (18hr., 284-416EEK), Rīga (5hr., 111EEK), and Tallinn (3hr., 70EEK). Local buses 5 and 6 shuttle from the train station to Raekoja plats and the bus station. **Buses** run from Turu 2, 300m south of Raekoja plats, to Pärnu (4hr., 70-74EEK) and Tallinn (2-5hr., 75EEK). Everything the traveler needs is located within a square kilometer bordered by the bus and train stations. The **tourist office,** Raekoja plats 14 (tel./fax (7) 43 21 41), provides info and organizes travel and transportation (open M-F 10am-6pm, Sa 10am-3pm). **Tartu Hotell,** Soola 3 (tel. (7) 43 20 91), in the center of town, behind the bus station, has large rooms with newly tiled communal showers and a sauna (singles 370EEK, with HI membership 180EEK). **Külalistemaja Tähtvere,** Laulupeo pst. 19 (tel. (7) 42 17 08), northwest of the historic center, in front of the looming beer factory, has singles (150EEK) and doubles (250EEK). A newly redone **market** is on the corner of Vabaduse and Vanenmuise, opposite the bus station (open M-F 7:30am-4pm, Sa until 2pm, Su until 1pm). **Rüütli Birstoo,** Rüütli 2, has cheap eats, cafeteria style (open M-Sa 7:30am-10pm, Su 8:30am-9pm).

▒ Haapsalu

In the early 13th century Haapsalu became the seat of the Saare-Lääne bishopric encompassing most of West Estonia. Today, it's a sleepy town known for its sailing and rapid westernization. From Lossiplats, the square just northeast of Kavja, you can enter **Lossi Park** (open 7am-11pm), where the limestone **Piiskopilinnus** (Bishop's Castle) adjoins the historical museum (open daily 10am-6pm; 10EEK, students 5EEK). The **Aafrikarand** (Africa Beach) promenade, northeast of the castle at the end of Rüütli, runs 2km to the yacht club. **Kaluri,** farther east, makes for beautiful walks amid weathered Baltic wooden houses, marsh grasses, and ducks. **Buses** run from the defunct train station at Rantee 2 to Kärdla (3hr., pay 40EEK on the bus), Pärnu (2-3hr., 48EEK), and Tallinn (2hr., 42EEK). From **Rohuküla,** 9km west of Haapsalu (take bus 1), **ferries** (tel. (247) 336 66) head to Heltermaa on Hiiumaa. The elaborate train platform houses the **tourist information office** (tel. (247) 332 48; fax 334 64; email ht@webs.ee). The helpful English-speaking staff sells **maps** (25EEK) and hands out brochures (open May-Sept. 15 M-F 9am-6pm, Sa 10am-2pm; Sept. 16-Apr. M-F 10am-

5pm). The **Jahtklubi** (Yacht Club), Holmi 5a (tel. (247) 455 82; fax 455 36), sports ship-shape rooms and a well-polished bar (singles 170EEK; doubles 350 EEK; hall bathrooms). The **Laine Sanatorium**, Sadama 9/11 (tel. (247) 441 91; fax 456 39), has nice views (singles with bath, balcony, and breakfast 300EEK). The new **Restoran Central,** Karja 21, has a beer cellar downstairs and a dining room that serves fried trout with cream and spinach (89EEK; open M-Th noon-midnight, F-Sa noon-2am; bar opens 1hr. earlier).

■ Estonian Islands

Saaremaa Off-limits to outsiders during the Soviet occupation, the island of Saaremaa is reckoned to be more Estonian than Estonia itself. **Kuressaare,** its largest city, was a thriving resort—complete with a medieval castle—before Soviet occupation and is now making a comeback. **Piiskopilinnus** (Bishopric Castle), the town's main attraction, lies south of the Raekoja plats (town hall square) through a sleepy park. Inside the castle, the excellent **Saaremaa Regional Museum** displays an eclectic collection of chariots, ceramic masks, and trinkets from the island's history. (Museum and castle open May-Aug. daily 11am-7pm, last entry 6pm; Sept.-Apr. W-Su 11am-7pm, last entry 6pm. 30EEK, students 15EEK.) Rent a bike at the bus station or behind the city hall, and pedal south to the quiet, clean beaches of **Mändjala** and **Järve,** which cover an 8 to 12km stretch west of Kuressaare.

    Buses, Pihtla tee 2 (info tel. 573 80), at the corner of Tallinna, go to Pärnu (3hr., 2 per day, 87EEK) and Tallinn (9 per day, 4hr., 110EEK). To get to the mainland, it's easier and cheaper to take a direct bus (which gets first priority on the ferries). A new **ferry** route allows you to island-hop between north Saaremaa's Triigi port and south Hiiumaa's Orjaku port (65min., Th-Tu 2 per day, 50EEK). The **tourist office,** Tallinna 2 (tel. (245) 337 66), inside the town hall, sells maps (10EEK; open daily 9am-7pm, reduced hours off-season). Clean, institutional **Mardi Öömaja,** Vallimaa 5a (tel. (245) 332 85), has the cheapest rooms in town (singles 125EEK; doubles 170EEK; cash only). **"Kämping,"** Mändjala (tel. (245) 751 93), 11km outside of Kuressaare on the bus to Järve, offers camping near a clean beach and secluded pine woods (tent sites 15EEK per person; dorms 145EEK per person; open May-Sept.).

Hiiumaa Because the Soviets closed off Hiiumaa for 50 years, the area's rare plant and animal species, as well as its unhurried local lifestyle, have been preserved. The island's flat terrain and beautiful, peaceful forests make it ideal for biking. **Kärdla,** the only real city, has a good **tourist office,** Keskväljak 1 (tel. (246) 330 33; http://www.hiiumaa.ee), which has info on hiking and ferry schedules (open May-Sept. M-F 9am-6pm, Sa-Su 10am-2pm; off-season M-F 9am-4pm). The pyramid-shaped **Kõpu Lighthouse,** over Hiiumaa's west peninsula, offers gorgeous views of the entire island. **Buses** (tel. (246) 965 02) go from Hiiumaa to Tallinn (4hr., 80EEK), and **ferries** cross to the island from Rohuküla; call (246) 316 30 for schedule info. **Hotell Sõnajala,** Leigri väljak 3 (tel. (246) 312 20), has clean and comfortable rooms. From Keskväljak, head south on Rookopli, turn right on Kõrgessaare mnt. (the major intersection with a big stone head on the corner), and left on Sõnajala; the hotel is in the complex on the right (singles 150EEK; breakfast 45EEK; shared modern bathrooms). Stock up on groceries at **Tiigi Pood,** Tiigi 5 (open daily 9am-10pm).

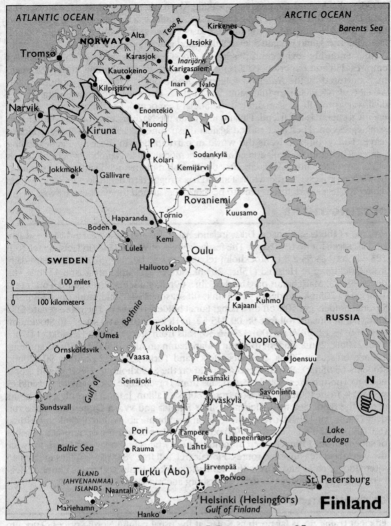

Finland (Suomi)

US$1 = 5.27mk (Finnish markka)	1mk = US$0.19
CDN$1= 3.47mk	1mk = CDN$0.29
UK£1 = 8.73mk	1mk = UK£0.11
IR£1 = 7.62mk	1mk = IR£0.13
AUS$1 = 3.11mk	1mk = AUS$0.32
NZ$1 = 2.70mk	1mk = NZ$0.37
SAR1 = 0.85mk	1mk = SAR1.17
Country Code: 358	**International Dialing Prefix: 00**

Between the Scandinavian peninsula and the Russian wilderness, Finland is a land of coniferous trees, astounding summer clouds, and five million taciturn souls. Outside the Helsinki metropolitan area, nature reigns. The west coast is dotted with old wooden shacks, and the Swedish-speaking Åland Islands are a biker's paradise. The Lake District in southeast Finland also offers outdoor activities—sailing, skiing, and music festivals. Lapland, in the north, boasts rugged terrain and rolling fells, boundless wilderness, and Finland's several thousand indigenous Sami people.

After enduring seven centuries in the crossfire of warring Swedish and Russian empires, Finland experienced a romantic nationalistic awakening in the 19th century, nurtured by the *Kalevala* folk epic, Jean Sibelius's rousing symphonies, and Akseli Gallen-Kallela's mythic paintings. In 1917, however, the Finns fought a bitter civil war as the Right slaughtered the Social Democrats. On the principle that my enemy's enemy is my friend, Finland invited in the Nazis in an effort to counter Russian aggression. They later turned against these same "allies" who were reluctant to leave. Today, Finland leads the world in participation in the U.N. Peacekeeping Forces. The nation's mediation efforts are memorialized in Namibia, where hundreds of children are named Ahtisaari after the Finnish diplomat who supervised the independence process. All the while, Finland has struggled to maintain a delicate Nordic neutrality. Its eastern towns tend to be more Russian and the west more Swedish.

GETTING THERE

Citizens of the U.S., Canada, U.K., Ireland, Australia, and New Zealand can visit Finland **visa-free** for up to 90 days. The festive vessels of **Viking Line** (in Helsinki tel. (09) 123 51, fax 123 53 27; in Stockholm tel. (08) 452 40 00, fax 452 42 40) steam daily from Stockholm to Helsinki (15hr., 205mk, students 155mk; off-season 119mk, students 89mk), Mariehamn on Åland (6½hr., 69mk, students 52mk), and Turku (11-12hr., 149-205mk, students 99-155mk, off-season 85-105mk, students 65-85mk). Scanrail holders get 50% off on Viking; Eurail holders ride free. The more sedate **Silja Line** (tel. in Finland toll free 98 00 745 52, in Helsinki (09) 180 44 22, in Stockholm (08) 666 35 12, in Vaasa (06) 323 36 30) sails from Stockholm to Helsinki (14½hr., from 210mk, 25mk student discount), Mariehamn on Åland (5½hr., 130mk, students 120mk, off-season 70mk, students 60mk), and Turku (11hr., 2 per day, 90-120mk, students 65-95mk). Eurail tickets are valid on the Stockholm to Helsinki and Stockholm to Turku routes. Silja Line also sails from Travemünde, Germany to Helsinki (3 per week, from 460mk, off-season from 280mk). Tallinn, Estonia sits only a few hours across the Baltic Sea from Helsinki. Silja's **Finnjet** and **Wasa Queen** make the run daily (3½hr., or 12½hr. overnight, 75-100mk without cabin), and **Tallink** in Helsinki (tel. (09) 22 82 12 11; fax 64 98 08) offers a number of cruising options at a number of speeds (from 110mk). Keep in mind that ferry rates on Friday can be up to twice the weekday rates on some routes. **Finnair** (tel. toll free 98 00 34 66) flies in from 45 international cities and covers the domestic market. Buses and trains connect Helsinki and other Finnish cities to St. Petersburg and Moscow.

GETTING AROUND

Efficient **trains** zip as far north as Kolari at the usual painful Nordic prices (Turku to Helsinki 94mk, Helsinki to Rovaniemi 320mk); railpasses are valid and seat reservations (15-30mk) are not required except on the luxurious InterCity trains. Couchettes cost 60mk from Monday to Thursday, 90mk from Friday to Sunday. The *buy-outside-of-Scandinavia* **Scanrail Pass** offers five out of 15 days (US$182, under 26 US$137), 10 days out of one month (US$292, under 26 US$219), or one month (US$426, under 26 US$320) of unlimited travel in Denmark, Finland, Norway, and Sweden, as well as free or discounted ferry rides. This differs from the *buy-in-Scandinavia* **Scanrail Pass,** which allows 21 consecutive days (1700mk, under 26 1280mk) or five days within 15 of unlimited rail travel (1120mk, under 26 840mk). A **Finnrail Pass** offers unlimited rail travel throughout Finland during a one month period (3 days 570mk, 5 days 770mk, 10 days 1040mk).

Buses cost about the same as or more than trains, and often take longer. They are, however, the only way to reach some smaller towns and to travel in northern Finland. For bus information anywhere in Finland, call 02 00 40 00 (6.34mk per min.).

ISIC holders can purchase a student card (34mk and photo required) from bus stations that ensures a 50% discount on tickets. Railpasses are valid on some buses that follow discontinued train routes.

Finnair gives a discount for those under 25 and has special summer rates that reduce fares by up to 70%. **Steamers** link many cities in the lake district. **Hitchhikers** report finding more rides in Finland than elsewhere in Scandinavia, but **cyclists** hanker for Denmark's shorter distances. Some campgrounds, youth hostels, and tourist offices rent bikes. Rates average 40-55mk per day or 190mk per week, plus a deposit.

ESSENTIALS

Most **shops** close at 5pm on weekdays (10pm in Helsinki; Sa around 1pm), but urban supermarkets may stay open until 9pm (Sa 4-6pm). **Kiosks** sell basic food, snacks, and toiletries until 9 or 10pm. **Banks** are typically open weekdays 9:15am to 4:15pm. Finnish **holidays** include Epiphany (Jan. 6), Good Friday (Apr. 2), May Day (May 1), Ascension Day (May 21), Midsummer (June 20), All Saints Day (Nov. 1), Independence Day (Dec. 6), Christmas Day (Dec. 25), and Boxing Day (Dec. 26). Many stores and museums, as well as all banks and post offices, are also closed for Easter (April 10-13), Second Easter (Apr. 11), Christmas (Dec. 24-26), and New Year's Day. During Midsummer, when Finns party all night to the light of *kokko* (bonfires) and the midnight sun, virtually the entire country shuts down.

With more computers connected to the **Internet** per capita than anywhere else in the world, Finland is a webhead's dream. But don't automatically run to the Internet cafes—your best bet is to hit the public library, where a connection is usually free, although you may have to register or pay a small fee (around 40mk per 30min.).

Local and short long-distance calls within Finland usually cost 2mk; most pay **phones** take 1, 5, and 10mk coins. Phone cards are available from R-kiosks and post offices in 30, 50, 70, and 100mk denominations. "Tele" or "Nonstop" cards work nationwide; other cards only work in the city in which you purchase them. Some card telephones accept credit cards. Call 118 for domestic information, 112 in an **emergency**, and 100 22 for the **police**. For international calls, dial 00, 990, or 999 first (all identical). For **AT&T Direct**, call 9800 100 10; **MCI WorldPhone**, 0800 11 02 80; **Sprint Access**, 9800 1 0284; **Canada Direct**, 0800 11 00 11; **BT Direct**, 0800 11 04 40; and **New Zealand Direct**, 0800 1 2141. The mail service is fast and efficient.

The Finnish language, which is not Indo-European, is virtually impenetrable to foreigners. Watch out for town names that modify their form on train and bus schedules due to the lack of prepositions in Finnish. Swedish, often seen on signs, is the official second language; many Finns speak English, but fluency decreases in the north. The stress is always on the first syllable.

Please/ Thank you	*Olkaa hyvä/Kiitos*	AWL-kah HU-va/KEE-tohss
Do you speak English?	*Puhutteko englantia?*	POO-hoot-teh-kaw ENG-lan-ti-ah
I don't understand.	*En ymmärrä*	ehn ÜM-mar-ra
Where is...?	*Missä on...?*	MEESS-ah OWN
I would like...	*Haluaisin...*	HAH-loo-eye-seen
train station	*rautatieasema*	RAO-tah-tee-AH-sehma

ACCOMMODATIONS AND CAMPING Finland has 140 **youth hostels** (*retkeily-maja*; RET-kay-loo-MAH-yah), 80 of which are open year-round. Prices generally range from 55 to 110mk; non-HI-members add 15-35mk. Most have laundry and kitchen facilities and prohibit sleeping bags; many have saunas. **Hotels** are often exorbitant (over 250mk); *kesähotelli* (summer hotels) offer doubles for around 300mk. **Private room** rental is less common than in Sweden, but local tourist offices will help you find the cheapest accommodations. The **Finnish Youth Hostel Association** (Suomen Retkeilymajajärjestö; SRM) is located at Yrjönkatu 3B 15, Helsinki (tel.

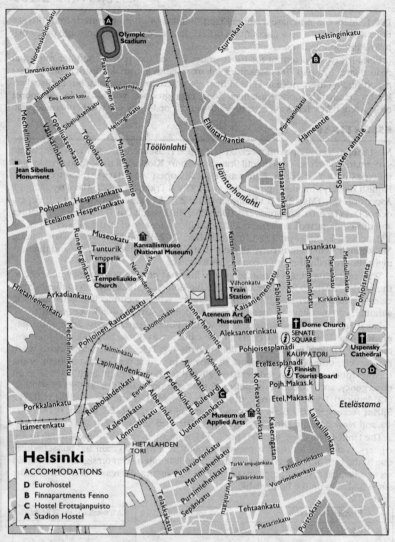

Helsinki
ACCOMMODATIONS

D Eurohostel
B Finnapartments Fenno
C Hostel Erottajanpuisto
A Stadion Hostel

(09) 694 03 77; fax 693 13 49; email info@srm.inet.fi; http://www.srmnet.org). As in much of Scandinavia, you may camp anywhere (except in Åland) as long as you respect flora and fauna, stay a polite distance away from homes, and do not light a fire without the landowner's permission. Well-equipped official **campgrounds** dapple the country, some with saunas (tent sites 25-75mk per night, *mökit* (small cottages) 100mk and up).

FOOD AND DRINK   A *kahuila* is a cafe that serves food, coffee, and perhaps beer, while a *grilli* is a fast-food stand. A *ravintola* is a restaurant; some evolve into dance-spots or bars later in the evening (cover 15mk and up). You must be at least 18 years old to purchase beer, and 20 for hard liquor; the age limit in bars and pubs is usually 18, but it can be as high as 25. Despite the stereotype of the drunken Finn, alcohol is no bargain. Beer (*olut*) is divided into several groups. Olut IV is the strongest and most expensive (at least 25mk per *iso tuoppi*; half-liter). Olut III (the best value) is slightly weaker and cheaper (18-20mk). Outside bars and restaurants, all alcohol stronger than Olut III must be purchased at the state-run **Alko** liquor stores. You need not tip servers.

Among the less expensive supermarkets are **Alepa** and **Antilla.** The best budget dining options are the common all-you-can-eat lunch buffets (35-45mk), often found at more pricey restaurants. The Finns are proud of their fish; popular options include *kirjolohi* (rainbow trout), *silakka* (Baltic herring), and *lohi* (salmon)—cured, pickled, smoked, poached, or baked. Finnish dietary staples include robust rye bread, potatoes, sour milk, Karelian pastries, and squirming yogurt-like *viili.* In July and August, the land blossoms with blueberries, cranberries, lingonberries, and—in the far north—Arctic cloudberries.

■ Helsinki (Helsingfors)

With its broad avenues, grand architecture, and well-tended parks, Helsinki is a model of 19th-century city planning. The city distinguishes itself, however, with a decidedly multicultural flair. Lutheran and Russian Orthodox cathedrals stand almost face to face, Baltic Sea produce fills the marketplaces and restaurants, and St. Petersburg and Tallinn are but a short cruise across the Gulf of Finland.

ORIENTATION AND PRACTICAL INFORMATION

Helsinki's main street, **Mannerheimintie,** passes between the bus and train stations as it runs toward the city's center, eventually meeting **Esplanadi.** This wide promenade leads east to **Kauppatori** (Market Square) and the harbor. All street signs and maps are in both Finnish and Swedish. The free English language papers *Helsinki This Week, Helsinki Happens,* and *City* provide lists of lodgings, restaurants, and events.

Telephone Code: 09.

Flights: For info, call 96 00 81 00 (3.40mk per min.). Buses 615 and 616 run regularly between the **Helsinki-Vantaa** airport and station square (15mk); bus 615 is more direct. The Finnair bus shuttles between the airport and the Finnair building at Asemaaukio 3, next to the train station (35min., every 20min. 5am-midnight, 25mk).

Trains: Dial 707 57 00 for info. Trains chug to Moscow (15hr., daily at 5:32pm, 2nd class 523mk), Rovaniemi (10hr., 8 per day, 320mk), St. Petersburg (7hr., 2 per day, 2nd class 261mk), Tampere (2hr., every hr. 6am-10pm, 94mk), and Turku (2hr., 12 per day, 94mk). The train station, which has **lockers** (10mk per day), is open M-F 5:15am-1:30am, Sa-Su 5:15am-midnight.

Buses: Call 02 00 40 00 (6.34mk per min.) for info. The bus station sits between Salomonkatu and Simonkatu; from the railway station, turn right and head up Kaivokatu for two blocks. Services run to Lahti (1½hr. on express line, every 30min., 87mk), Tampere (2½hr., every hr., 94mk), and Turku (2½hr., every 30min., 105mk). Buy tickets at the station or on the bus. Station open M-F 7am-7pm, Sa 7am-5pm, Su 9am-6pm.

Ferries: For details, see **Getting There,** p. 262. **Silja Line,** Mannerheimintie 2 (tel. 180 44 22). **Viking Line,** Mannerheimintie 14 (tel. 123 51). **Tallink,** Erottajankatu 19 (tel. 22 82 12 11). Viking Line and **Finnjet** (contact Silja Line) ferries leave from Katajanokka island east of Kauppatori (take tram 2 or 4). The departure point for Silja Line and Tallink ferries is South Harbor, south of Kauppatori (take tram 3T). For more info about touring the Baltic, call 63 05 22.

Local Transportation: The metro and most trams and buses run approximately 5:30am-11pm (certain bus and tram lines, including the indispensable tram 3T, continue to 1:30am). Single fare tickets can be bought on buses and trams (10mk) or from machines at the metro station (8mk); 10-trip tickets (75mk) are available at R-kiosks and at the City Transport office in the Rautatientori metro station (open M-Th 7:30am-6pm, F 7:30am-4pm). All tickets are valid for one hour (transfers free); punch your ticket on board. Ask on trams or at the City Transport office for maps; some routes are more direct than others. The **Tourist Ticket,** available at City

FINLAND

Transport and tourist offices, provides boundless bus, tram, metro, and local train transit in Helsinki (1-day 25mk, 3-day 50mk, 5-day 75mk). For transit information, call 010 01 11 (2mk per min.).

Tourist Offices: City Tourist Office, Pohjoisesplanadi 19 (tel. 169 37 57; fax 169 38 39; http://www.hel.fi). From the train station, walk 2 blocks south on Keskuskatu and turn left on Pohjoisesplanadi. Open May-Sept. M-F 9am-7pm, Sa-Su 9am-3pm; Oct.-Apr. M-F 9am-5pm, Sa 9am-3pm. The **Finnish Tourist Board,** Eteläesplanadi 4 (tel. 41 76 93 00; fax 41 76 93 01; http://www.mek.fi), has info on transportation routes and accommodations. Open June-Aug. M-F 8:30am-5pm, Sa 10am-2pm; Sept.-May M-F 8:30am-4pm, W until 5pm. **Hotellikeskus** (Hotel Booking Center; tel. 17 11 33; fax 17 55 24), in the train station, has maps and books rooms for a fee. Open June-Aug. M-Sa 9am-7pm, Su 10am-6pm; Sept.-May M-F 9am-5pm. The **Helsinki Card,** sold by the tourist office, Hotellikeskus, central R-kiosks, and most hotels, provides museum discounts and unlimited local transportation (1-day 110mk, 3-day 170mk).

Budget Travel: Kilroy Travels, Kaivokatu 10 (tel. 680 78 11), sells domestic and international tickets and ISICs. Open M-F 10am-6pm, Sa 10am-4pm.

Embassies: For emergencies, **Australians** and **New Zealanders** should contact the British Embassy. **Canada,** Pohjoisesplanadi 25B (tel. 17 11 41). Open M-F 8:30am-4:30pm. **Estonia,** Itäinen Puistotie 10 (tel. 622 02 60). **Ireland,** Erottajankatu 7A (tel. 64 60 06). **Latvia,** Armfeltintie 10 (tel. 47 64 72 22). **Lithuania,** Rauhankatu 13A (tel. 60 82 10). **Poland,** Armas Lindgrenintie 21 (tel. 684 80 77). **Russia,** Tehtaankatu 1B (tel. 66 18 76). **South Africa,** Rahapajankatu 1A (tel. 65 82 88). **U.K.,** Itäinen Puistotie 17 (tel. 22 86 51 00). Open M-F 8:30am-5pm. **U.S.,** Itäinen Puistotie 14A (tel. 17 19 31). Open M-F 8:30am-5pm.

Currency Exchange: Forex, in the train station, charges a 10mk fee for cash, 10mk per traveler's check, but no fee to exchange markka into foreign currency. Open daily 8am-9pm. Visa credit card advances and Plus/Cirrus withdrawals available from the bright orange Otto **ATM** machines.

American Express: Area Travel, Mikonkatu 2D, 2nd floor (tel. 62 87 88). No commission on their traveler's checks. Arranges for wiring of money for members. Open M-F 9am-1pm and 2:15-4:30pm.

Bookstore: Akateeminen Kirjakauppa (Academic Bookshop), Pohjoisesplanadi 39 (tel. 121 41). Dazzling selection of books in English (including travel guides) and classic novels from 15mk. Open M-F 9am-9pm, Sa 9am-6pm.

Laundromat: Your best bet is to check for facilities at youth hostels (5-40mk). Otherwise, look for the words *Itsepalvelu Pesula.*

Travelers With Disabilities: Rullaten Ry, Pajutie 7 (tel. 805 73 93).

Pharmacy: Yliopiston Apteekki, has branches at Mannerheimintie 5 (tel. 17 90 92; open daily 7am-midnight), and Mannerheimintie 96 (tel. 41 57 78; open 24hr.).

Medical Assistance: Aleksin lääkäriasema, Mannerheimintie 8 (tel. 77 50 84 00). Receives and refers foreigners. Open M-F 7:30am-7pm.

Emergencies: tel. 112.

Police: tel. 100 22. Stations at Pasilanraitio 13, 2 Pikku Roobertinkatu 1-3, and the train station near platform 11.

Post Office: Mannerheiminaukio 1A (tel. 195 51 17). Open M-F 9am-6pm. *Poste Restante* office in the same building also sells stamps and accepts packages; open M-F 7am-9pm, Sa 9am-6pm, Su 11am-9pm. **Postal Code:** 00100.

Internet Access: The multimediaphiles at **dose,** on the corner of Aleksanterinkatu and Mikonkatu, let you surf the Internet for free on the computers in their store. Five min. limit when others are waiting. Open M-F 10am-8pm, Sa 10am-6pm.

Telephones: In the same building as the post office; open M-F 9am-5pm. Public phones also circle the outside of the building. See also (**Essentials,** p. 263).

ACCOMMODATIONS AND CAMPING

During the summer, it's wise to make reservations, but just showing up is not extraordinarily risky. Most hostels offer laundry facilities and provide breakfast for a fee. Extra summer hostels are open from June to August; try **Hotel Satakuntatalo (HI),** Lapinrinne 1 (tel. 69 58 52 31; fax 685 42 45), **Academica (HI),** Hietaniemenkatu 14 (tel. 13 11 43 34; fax 44 12 01), and **Kallio Youth Hostel,** Porthaninkatu 2 (tel. 70 99 25 90; fax 70 99 25 98).

Hotel Erottanjanpuisto (HI), Uudenmaankatu 9 (tel.64 21 69; fax 680 27 57). Exiting the train station, turn right, then turn left on Mannerheimintie until the road veers right, becoming Erottajankatu; Uudenmaankatu is on the right. Centrally located and welcoming hostel in a century-old building. Fifty beds and only 1 shower (basins in rooms). Kitchen. Dorms 120mk per person; singles 195mk; doubles 280mk; nonmembers add 15mk per person. Breakfast 25-35mk. Reservations essential during the summer.

Eurohostel (HI), Linnankatu 9, Katajanokka (tel. 622 04 70; fax 65 50 44; email euroh@icon.fi; http://www.eurohostel.fi). With Uspensky Cathedral to your left, head down Kanauakatu; take the third road on the left (it veers directly into Linnankatu). Largest hostel in Finland. Kitchen and cafe. Sauna. Singles 170mk; doubles 206mk; nonmembers add 15-17mk per person. Student discounts in winter. Reception 24hr.

Finnapartments Fenno, Franzeninkatu 26 (tel. 773 16 61; fax 701 68 89). From the train station, walk north on Unioninkatu (which becomes Siltasaarenkatu) or catch the metro to Hakaniemi. Then head right on Porthaninkatu, left onto Fleminginkatu, then left again. Simple rooms, with or without private facilities. Kitchen and sauna. Singles 165-230mk; doubles 320mk. Wheelchair accessible.

Stadion Hostel (HI), Pohj. Stadiontie 3B (tel. 49 60 71; fax 49 64 66), in the Olympic Stadium complex. Take tram 3T or 7A from the train station. 150-bed hostel has high ceilings, huge windows, a kitchen, and TV. Pool and sauna nearby. Dorms 60mk; doubles 160mk; nonmembers add 15mk. Breakfast 25mk. Locked room for luggage. Paper sheets 15mk. Reception June to early Sept. daily 7am-2am; mid-Sept. to May 8-10am and 4pm-2am.

Camping: Rastila Camping (tel. 31 65 51), 14km east of the city center. Take the metro to Itäkeskus and then catch bus 90, 90A, or 96 (first stop after a long bridge). Vast, cheap, municipal campground with washing and cooking facilities, showers, and toilets. One person 60mk; cabins 80mk per person. Reception 24hr.

FOOD

In Finland, even groceries are expensive; find relief at the **Alepa** chain (the branch under the train station is open M-Sa 8am-10pm, Su 10am-10pm). **Kauppatori** (Market Square; open June-Aug. M-Sa 7am-2pm and 4-8pm; Sept.-May M-F 7am-2pm), by the port, and the nearby **Vanha Kauppahalli** (Old Market Hall; open M-Th 8am-5:30pm, F 8am-6pm, Sa 8am-3pm), offer a variety of fresh foods, including fruit, veggies, and fish. The food court in the basement of **Forum,** at the corner of Mannerheimintie and Simonkatu, quells all fast food cravings (open M-F 9am-9pm, Sa 9am-6pm). If you're not traveling farther east, be sure to try one of Helsinki's many excellent Russian restaurants.

Zetor, Kaivokatu 10, up the steps. The very essence of Finland: food, drinks, music, dancing, and of course, a tractor. Main dishes 40-65mk; beer 18mk. Open Su-M 3pm-1am, Tu-F 3pm-3am, Sa 1pm-3am.

Ravintola Tempura, through the arch at Mikonkatu 2. Restaurant in the heart of the city, specializing in fish and vegetarian dishes. Lunch special 39mk; namesake vegetarian tempura 39mk. Open M-F 11am-8pm; in summer also Sa noon-4pm.

Suola Ja Pippuri, Snellmaninkatu 17. On a quiet side street. Lunch from 40mk. Mainly seafood. Open M-F 11am-midnight, Sa 1pm-midnight; bar open 4pm-1am.

Kappeli, Eteläesplanadi 1, in the park strip. Parisian fantasy cafe that's catered to trendies since 1837 (Sibelius had a favorite table). Though expensive, it's where to see and be seen. Pie from 20mk; beer 27mk. Open Su-Th 9am-1am, F-Sa 9am-3pm.

Kasvis, Korkeavuorenkatu 3. Serves organically grown vegetable dishes (39-45mk) and amazing homemade bread that they've been perfecting for 20 years. Open M-F 11am-8pm, Sa-Su noon-8pm; kitchen closes at 7:30pm.

Cafe Engel, Aleksanterinkatu 26. Sip coffee (11mk) or try the delicious lingonberry pie (17mk) while gazing at the cathedral. Open M-F 7:45am-midnight, Sa 9:30am-midnight, Su 11am-midnight.

Unicafe, Fabianinkatu 33. The cheapest place in town; main dishes 20mk. This is the university cafeteria, so students only. Open M-F 10am-4:30pm.

FINLAND

SIGHTS

Tram 3T offers the city's cheapest tour (pick up a free itinerary on board). Better yet, just walk—most sights are packed within 2km of the train station, and the city has few hills. Pick up a copy of the booklet *See Helsinki on Foot* before you go. The famed architect Alvar Aalto once said of Finland, "Architecture is our form of expression because our language is so impossible," and the bold 20th-century creations amid slick Neoclassical works that suffuse the region prove him right. Much of the layout and architecture of the old center, however, is the brainchild of a German: Carl Engel. After Helsinki became the capital of the Grand Duchy of Finland in 1812, Engel was chosen to design an appropriately grand city. In **Senaatin Tori** (Senate Square), on the corner of Unioninkatu and Aleksanterinkatu, his work is well represented by the **Tuomiokirkko** (Dome Church), completed in 1852. After marveling at the Neoclassical exterior, the austere interior of the Lutheran cathedral comes as quite a contrast. *(Open June-Aug. M-Sa 9am-6pm, Su noon-4pm; Sept.-May Su-F 10am-4pm, Sa 10am-6pm.)* A few blocks to the east, on Katajanokka island, the spectacular Byzantine-Slavonic **Uspenskinkatedraadi** (Uspensky Orthodox Cathedral) guards the island with its red and gold cupolas. *(Ornate interior open MWF 9:30am-4pm, Tu 9:30am-6pm, Sa 9am-4pm, Su noon-3pm.)*

Across from the train station stands Finland's largest art museum, the **Ateneum Taidemuseo**, Kaivokatu 2, with predominantly Finnish art from the 1700s to the 1960s. *(Open Tu and F 9am-6pm, W-Th 9am-8pm, Sa-Su 11am-5pm. 15mk, students and seniors 10mk; special exhibits 30-35mk.)* The controversial new museum of contemporary art, **Kiasma**, Mannerheiminaukio 2, next to the statue of Mannerheim, is the latest addition to Helsinki's culture beat. *(Open Tu and F 9am-6pm, W-Th 9am-8pm, Sa-Su 11am-5pm. 25mk.)* The **Suomen Kansallismuseo** (National Museum of Finland), 500m northwest of the train station at Mannerheimintie 34, displays intriguing bits of Finnish culture, from Gypsy and Sami costumes to *ryijyt* (rugs), along with a magnificent roof mural by Akseli Gallen-Kallela. *(The museum will be closed until late 1999 for repairs. Until then, parts of the exhibition are displayed at temporary locations. Consult the board outside the museum, or call 94 05 01 for info on current locations.)*

Across the street, **Finlandia Talo,** Mannerheimintie 13e (tel. 402 41), stands as a testament to the skill of **Alvar Aalto**, who designed not only the building, but also the interior and furnishings. The gently undulating white marble exterior of the concert hall is currently being repaired (guided tours 20mk). The intriguing **Temppeliaukio Kirkko**, Lutherinkatu 3, designed in the late 60s by Tuomo and Timo Suomalainen, is built into a hill of rock with only the roof visible from the outside. *(Open M-F 10am-8pm, Sa 10am-6pm, Su midday-1:45pm and 3:20-5:45pm. Services conducted in English Su 2pm.)* From the Natural History Museum, continue down Pohj. Rautatiekatu, then turn on Fredrikinatu, which leads to the square where the church is buried. The striking **Jean Sibelius Monument**, 750m north of the church in Sibelius Park, on Mechelininkatu, was dedicated to one of the 20th century's greatest composers by sculptor Eila Hiltunen in 1967. The monument looks like a cloud of organ pipes ascending to heaven. If you don't want to walk there, catch bus 24 ('Seurasaari") from Mannerheimintie; look for the monument on your left. Follow the sea gulls to **Market Square** and **Old Market Hall** at the harbor end of Esplanadi, where fresh fish, flowers, berries, and souvenirs are sold daily, or check out the cacti and palms at the **City Wintergarten**, Hammarskjöldintie 1. *(Open M-Sa noon-3pm, Su noon-4pm; free.)*

Surrounding islands provide welcome relief from the fast pace of Helsinki's center. Ferries leave hourly from Market Square for the now-demilitarized fortress island of **Suomenlinna,** built by the Swedes in the 18th century on five interconnected islands to repel attacks on Helsinki. Explore the dark passageways of the old fortress or visit one of the island's museums. Best bets include the model ship collection of the **Ehrensvärd**, the submarine **Vesikko**, and the **Rannikkotykistömuseo** (Coastal Artillery Museum). *(Most museums open in summer daily 10am-5pm; Mar.-May Sa-Su 11am-4pm. 10mk, students 5mk; some have additional admission. Ferries to museum area 25mk round-trip.)* If museumed-out, relax on the rocky **beach** or head to **Seurasaari,** linked to the mainland by a walkway, for a picnic, swim, or saunter. Seurasaari's **open-air museum** contains redwood churches and farmsteads transplanted from the country-side. *(Open M-F 9am-3pm, Sa-Su 11am-5pm. 20mk; W free.)* Visit during Midsummer to witness the *kokko* (bonfire) and Finnish revelry in its full splendor. To reach Seurasaari, take bus 24 from Erottaja, outside the Swedish Theater, to the last stop. There's also summer boat service from Market Square. A 15-minute train ride (take H, K, P, or R from the railway station to Tikkurila, Vantua; 15mk) takes you to the **Heureka Science Center** (tel. 857 99), with hands-on exhibits, a planetarium, and a fascinating presentation on the Finno-Ugric languages. *(Open F-Tu 10am-6pm, W 10am-8pm; 75mk, students 45mk; planetarium extra.)*

ENTERTAINMENT

Much of Helsinki nods off early, but only because the days are packed. Sway to afternoon street music in the leafy **Esplanadi** or party on warm nights at **Kaivopuisto park** or **Hietaniemi beach.** Kaivopuisto also hosts open-air concerts on summer Sundays. Consult the free English language papers *Helsinki This Week, Helsinki Happens,* and, in summer, *City* for popular cafes, bars, nightclubs, and the latest happenings. Finland is one of a few European countries in which the drinking age—18 for beer and wine, 20 for hard alcohol—is usually enforced. Both bouncers and cover charges usually relax on weeknights; speaking English may help you get in. With the exception of licensed restaurants and bars, the state-run liquor store **Alko** holds a monopoly on sales of any alcohol more potent than lighter beers. (Branches at Mannerheimintie 1 and Salomonkatu 1. Open M-Th 10am-6pm, F 10am-8pm, Sa 9am-4pm.) Starting in the last week of August, the two-week **Helsinki Festival** (tel. 135 45 22; email info@helsinkifestival.fi; http://www.helsinkifestival.fi) brings together a melange of arts events, from ballet to theater to rock concerts.

Vanha (Old Students' House), Mannerheimintie 3. A 19th-century establishment with pubs, dancing, restaurant, and sociable students. Beer 15-20mk. Cover 20-50mk for live bands. Open M-Th 7:45am-2am, F-Sa 7:45am-3am, Su 9am-2am.

Manala (Hell), Dagmarinkatu 2, just behind the National Museum. Live bands, celebrity acts, and a multi-roomed interior. Rock, disco, and tango. Because Manala's main drawing power is its late closing time, "Hell" gets more crowded as the night goes on. Cover varies. Open M-F 11am-4am, Sa-Su 4pm-4am.

Storyville, Museokatu 8, near the National Museum. Promises "hot jazz to cool blues," with live music after 10pm. Cover varies. Jazz club open daily 8pm-4am; Tin Roof Bar open M-Sa 5pm-4am, Su 8pm-4am; piano bar open M-Th 7-10pm.

Happy Days, P. Esplanadi 2, right between the two Esplanadi. As American in style as the sitcom. Age 24 and up. Open daily 11am-4am. F-Sa cover 25mk after 10pm.

DTM (Don't Tell Mama), Annankatu 32. Dance club with disco, techno, and rock that attracts a gay and mixed crowd. Open daily 2pm-4am, club from 11pm.

Con Hombres, Eerikinkatu 14. A predominantly male gay bar. Open daily 4pm-2am.

■ Near Helsinki

The cobblestone streets of **Porvoo,** Finland's second oldest town, lie 50km east of Helsinki along Old King Road, which continues to Russia. In 1809, Tsar Alexander I granted Finland its autonomy at the Porvoo **cathedral,** in the old town. (Open May-Sept. M-F 10am-6pm, Sa 10am-2pm, Sun 2-5pm; Oct.-Apr. Tu-Sa 10am-2pm, Su 2-4pm.) At **Runeberg's Home,** Aleksanterinkatu 3, poet Johan Ludvig Runeberg ate his wife's delicious apple pastry, now known as "Runeberg's delight" and served by cafes on Aleksanterinkatu. (Open May-Aug. M-Sa 10am-4pm, Su 11am-5pm; Sept.-Apr. W-Sa 10am-4pm, Su 11am-5pm. 15mk.) The main **tourist office,** Rihkamakatu 4 (tel. (019) 58 01 45; http://www.porvoo.fi), gives out free maps (open June-Aug. M-F 8am-4pm, Sa 10am-2pm; Sept.-May M-F 9am-6pm). **Buses** leave for Porvoo every 30 minutes from Helsinki's bus station (1hr., 41mk). **Porvoo Camping Kokonniemi** (tel. (019) 58 19 67), 1.5km from the center, has cabins, tent sites, sauna, showers, laundry, and cooking facilities (tents 75mk per person, cabins from 290mk; open June 5- Aug. 16).

FINLAND

Jean Sibelius tormented himself in **Järvenpää**, 40km north of Helsinki. At his home, **Ainola** (tel. 28 73 22), the composer drank and brooded, his perfectionism so exacting that he destroyed much of his late work (open May-Sept. W-Sa 11am-5pm; 20mk). **Buses** to Tuusula pass by the home from platforms 9, 11, or 12 in the Helsinki bus station (20mk).

At Finland's southernmost point, the seaside resort of **Hanko,** founded as a spa in 1874, juts out into a beautiful archipelago. The spectacular residences that line the miles of sandy beaches reflect the splendor and decadence of the now-vanished Russian nobility. At the end of Mannerheimintie, **Neljän Tuulen Tupa** (The House of the Four Winds) sits on Little Pine Island. Previously owned by Finland's great war hero, Marshal Mannerheim, it is now a cafe and a great place to grab a beer (14mk). Though there are over 30km of **beaches** to choose from, the best are southwest of the town. Bicycles can be rented almost anywhere. Buses run to Hanko from Helsinki bus station (2¼hr., 7per day, round-trip 148mk). The helpful **tourist office,** Bulevardi 10 (tel. (019) 220 34 11; fax 248 58 21), has free maps. Hanko has numerous guest-houses, many situated along Appelgrenintie; **Villa Doris,** Appelgrenintie 23 (tel. (019) 248 12 28), is open year-round (in summer 170-200mk per person; off-season from 120mk). **Hanko Camping Silversand** (tel. (019) 248 55 00), Hopeahietikko, 2.5km northeast of the town center, has its own beach. From town, follow Santalantie, then turn left on Lähteentie (75mk per person; open June-Aug.).

ÅLAND ISLANDS (AHVENANMAA)

The 6500 islands that make up the Åland (OHR-land) archipelago have long been a cultural and geographic bridge between Sweden and Finland. Although Åland became part of Finland in 1807, it has achieved a unique autonomy from the mainland, sporting its own flag, parliament, and postal system. Many islanders work to minimize Finnish influence, and the island remains fiercely monolingual: all signs are in Swedish. Political controversy seems out of place here, though. The gentle landscape more befits leisurely hikes, bike rides, and sun-soaking.

For information on traveling to Mariehamn on the **Viking Line** or **Silja Line,** see **Getting There,** p. 262. **Birka Lines** (tel. in Mariehamn (018) 170 27, in Stockholm (08) 714 55 20) launches its *Princess* daily for 24hr. cruises from Stockholm to Mariehamn (125mk in a 4-person cabin). **Eckerö Line** (tel. in Mariehamn (018) 283 00, in Grisslehamn (0175) 309 20) travels from Eckerö in Åland to Grisslehamn, Sweden (June 18-Aug. 9 56mk, students 28mk; Aug. 10-June 17 35mk, students 18mk).

Inter-island ferries are free for walk-on and biking passengers; cars cost 30-40mk (100mk if landing on Åland, Uårdö, or mainland Finland). You can pick up the *Skärgårdstrafiken* **ferry** schedule or the *Ålandstrafiken* **bus** schedule for free at the Mariehamn tourist office. The main island, with its extensive paths and wide roads, is best explored by bike. **RoNo Rent,** (tel. (018) 128 26) facing the ferry terminal in Mariehamn and also in the Eastern habor, rents bikes (30mk), mopeds (200mk) and various kinds of boats (open June-Aug. daily 9am-noon and 1-6pm; May and Sept. by appointment).

Most places accept both Swedish and Finnish currencies. Due to Åland's popularity during the summer, **accommodations** should be booked in advance. **Ålandsresor,** Torggatan 2 (tel. (018) 280 40; fax 283 80; http://www.alandsresor.fi), books rooms and cottages for all the islands, and publishes a helpful brochure available at tourist offices nationwide. (Open M-F 8:30am-5pm. Rooms start at 120mk and go way up from there. 35mk booking fee.)

■ Mariehamn

On the south coast of the main island, Mariehamn is the center of activity on Åland and the only town with a significant number of shops and restaurants. Travelers would do well to stock up on groceries here, as most of the island consists of small campgrounds, beaches, and a few cafes. Just 500m north of the ferry terminal, the moored ship **Pommern**, the only surviving four-masted cargo vessel, gives visitors a feel for life on the high seas. The adjacent **Sjöfartsmuseum** displays a collection of mastheads and recovered booty. (Both open May-June and Aug. 9am-5pm, July 9am-7pm. Pommern also Sept.-Oct. 10am-4pm. 20mk each or 30mk for both.) Local artwork and history springs to life at the **Åland Museum**, at Stadshusparken off Storagatan (open W-M 10am-4pm, Tu 10am-8pm; 15mk, students 10mk).

For maps of Åland and info on Åland activities, head to the **tourist office** at Storagatan 8 (tel. (018) 240 00; fax 242 65; http://www.turist.aland.fi). From the ferry terminal, head left up Hamngatan then right onto Storagatan. (Open June-Aug. daily 9am-6pm; July until 7pm; Sept.-May M-F 9am-4pm, Sa 10am-4pm.) **Alida** (tel. (018) 137 55), a boat docked on the Eastern harbor, has a popular pub/cafe, and offers sardine-sized doubles for 70mk (sheets 20mk; reception open 8am-10pm; closed Oct.-April). Otherwise, visit **Ålandsresor** (see above). **Gröna Uddens Camping** (tel. (018) 190 41) relaxes by the water, 10 minutes down Skillnadagatan from the town center (20mk per person; showers, laundry, cafe; open mid-May to Aug.). Mariehamn's restaurant prices make **supermarket** food suddenly alluring; try **Fokus** at Torggatan 14 (open M-F 9am-7pm, Sa 9am-4pm). **Cafe Nero**, Strandgatan 12, handles any size appetite with local Finnish recipes (29-80mk; open M-Th 10am-11pm, F 10am-midnight, Sa 11am-midnight, Su noon-10pm). For lunch, the best deal in town is the 40mk buffet at the otherwise pricey **Arkipelag** hotel, Strandgatan 31 (buffet M-F 11am-3pm). Bite into *Ålandspannkakor*, covered with berry sauce and whipped cream, for 10mk at **Cafe Julius**, Torggatan 10 (open daily 8am-10pm). The pub upstairs from Cafe Nero has an outside terrace and dancing (open daily 8pm-4am).

■ Near Mariehamn

The rest of the Åland Islands are very accessible from Mariehamn by a combination of ferries, buses and bikes. To the northeast of Mariehamn, and easily accessible by bike (follow the cycling route to Godby), lies the province of **Sund**. Bike, or take bus 4 (30min., 7 per day, 18mk) to the Kastelholm stop and follow the sign to the 13th-century **Kastelholms Slott** (Castle). (Open May-June and mid Aug.-Sept. daily 10am-4pm; July-mid Aug. 10am-5pm. 20mk, students 14mk, including guided tour.) Nearby lurks the **Vita Björn** museum, which features prison cells from various centuries (open May-Sept. daily 10am-5pm; 6mk, students 4mk), as well as an open-air museum, **Jan Karlsgården** (open May-Sept. daily 10am-5pm; free). Ten kilometers farther down the road, **Bomarsund** (bus 4, 23mk from Mariehamn, 10mk from Kastelholm) displays the ruins of an Tsarist Russian fortress blown up by the British and French during the Crimean War. **Puttes Camping** (tel. (018) 440 16; fax 440 47), at Bomarsund, rents bikes and boats and has laundry, showers, and a kitchen. Beyond Bomarsund, **Prästö** also has a campground, **Prästö Stugor & Camping** (tel./fax (018) 440 45; 10mk per tent; cabins, bathrooms, laundry, showers, and sauna).

From Prästö, a bike-friendly ferry runs to **Lumpo** in northern **Lumparland,** leaving at 12:30pm from June through mid-August, and also 5pm in July (July ferries cost 30mk, free June-Aug.). Lumparland offers many cycling and walking trails through forest and along the coast. Trails begin from Svinö and Lågnäsbyn. From **Langnäs** and Svinö, on Lumparland's east coast, ferries leave to many of the surrounding islands (40mk; free if on foot). **Föglo** has a campground with kitchen, showers, sauna, and laundry called **C.C. Camping** (tel. (018) 514 40; 10mk per tent; open June-Aug.). **Kökar's Sandvik Camping,** near Hamno in the southeast (tel. (018) 559 11), charges 40mk for a tent and access to a kitchen, showers, laundry, bathrooms, and saunas. Northwest of Sund is **Geta,** the northernmost district of Åland. A 2.5km "culture trail" begins at Geta kyrka (church), and the 4km **Trail of Djupvik** links Soltuna and Getabergen. **Tourist information** (tel. (018) 496 01) may be found in Östergeta (open June 1-Aug. 7 M-F 10am-5pm). **Kasvikens Camping** (tel. (018) 414 10), in Geta, has campgrounds for 65mk (laundry, bathrooms, sauna, and showers).

Åland's second real town, **Eckerö,** in the west, is also a port for departures to Stockholm. Take bus 1 from Mariehamn (24mk) to get there. Eckerö's stone church has its foundations in the 12th century, while the 1826 **Post and Customs House** was designed by Finland's favorite Tsarist Russian—C.L. Engel—who is also responsible for the Helsinki Senate Square. The Eckerö **tourist office,** Storby Centrum (tel. (018) 380 95; fax 381 95), has info on island ferries, buses, and campgrounds (open June 9-Aug. 31 daily 10am-7pm). About 4km off the main bus route to Eckerö is **Notvikens Camping,** Överby 57 (tel. (018) 380 20), with tent sites (60mk), cafe, showers, laundry, bathrooms, and sauna.

SOUTHWEST FINLAND

■ Turku (Åbo)

Turku, Finland's oldest city, was once the country's capital. The ascendancy was short-lived, though; in 1812 Tsar Alexander I snatched Finland away from Sweden and declared Helsinki the capital. Shortly thereafter, Scandinavia's worst fire devoured Turku's wooden buildings. Despite these losses, Turku remains a flourishing cultural and academic center and serves as a welcome excursion from Helsinki.

SIGHTS AND ENTERTAINMENT Still under Swedish influence, the oldest of Turku's two universities, **Åbo Akademi,** operates in Swedish. Nearby, the massive **cathedral** in Tuomiokirkkotori (Cathedral Square), completed in 1300, speaks of the era when Turku was a center for the spiritual and commercial colonization of the Finnish hinterland. (Open daily mid-Apr. to mid-Sept. 9am-8pm; mid-Sept. to mid-Apr. 9am-7pm. Regular organ concerts in summer.) Sheltered from the ferry ports by a screen of trees, the 700-year-old **Turunlinna** (Turku Castle), along the Aura River about 3km from the city center, impresses with its thick walls, sleek lines, medieval artifacts, and **historical museum.** (Open mid-Apr. to mid-Sept. daily 10am-6pm; mid-Sept. to mid-Apr. M 2-7pm, Tu-Su 10am-3pm. 30mk, students 20mk.) **Luostarinmäki,** the only part of Turku to survive the 1827 fire, now stands as an open-air **handicrafts museum** with over 30 workshops. (Open mid-Apr. to mid-Sept. daily 10am-6pm; mid-Sept. to mid-Apr. Tu-Su 10am-3pm. 20mk, students 15mk.) On Puolalanmäki hill, under the spires of the imperial **Turun Taidesmuseo** (Art Museum), Aurakatu 26, hang some of Akseli Gallen-Kallela's vibrant *Kalevala* paintings. (Open Apr.-Sept. Tu and F-Sa 10am-4pm, W-Th 10am-7pm, Su 11am-6pm; Oct.-Mar. Tu-W and F-Sa 10am-4pm, Th 10am-7pm, Su 11am-6pm. 30mk, students 20mk.) **Ruissalo Island,** with Finland's biggest oak forest, turn of the century villas, sunbathing, boat rentals at Saaronniemi Beach, and access to over 20km of nature trails, makes a refreshing daytrip. Catch bus 8 from Market Square (9mk). The weekend after Midsummer finds crowds swarming Turku's Ruissalo Island for **Ruisrock** (tel. (02) 251 15 96; http://ruisrock.weppi.fi), Finland's oldest and largest rock festival, which attracts names like Björk, the Beastie Boys, David Bowie, and Sting (admission 190mk, 2-day pass 300mk). The **islands** surrounding Turku are best seen on a short cruise through the archipelago. The *S/S Ukkopekka,* Linnankatu 38 (tel. (02) 233 01 23; fax 233 09 23), offers daily **cruises** (3 hr., cruises leave at 9am, 12:30, and 8pm; 60-95mk).

The groovy **Downtown,** 17 Linnankatu, is a nightclub with live music (beer 15mk; cover F-Sa from 20mk; open Su-Tu 4pm-4am, F-Sa 4pm-5am). **Dynamo,** Linnankatu 7, gets down to live funk, soul, and ska (cover 20-25mk; open W-Sa 9pm-3am). The cafe **Opera,** Aurakatu 10, turns into a nightclub after 10pm (the fat lady sings at 4am).

PRACTICAL INFO, ACCOMMODATIONS, AND FOOD The **tourist office,** Aurakatu 4 (tel. (02) 233 63 66; fax 233 64 88; http://www.turku.fi), arranges local accommodations and gives away maps (open M-F 8:30am-6pm, Sa-Su 9am-4pm). Free **Internet access** is available on the second floor of the city **library,** Linnankatu 2 (open M-F 10am-7pm). Turku is a two-hour **train** ride from Helsinki (12 per day, 94mk); if you're

(**take in a rock show**)

and use **AT&T Direct**^{SM} Service
to tell everyone about it.

 It's all within **AT&T** your reach.

Exploring lost cultures? You better have an

AT&T Direct^{SM} Service wallet guide.

It's a list of access numbers you need to call home fast and clear from

around the world, using an AT&T Calling Card or credit card.

What an amazing planet we live on.

For a list of **AT&T Access Numbers,**
take the attached wallet guide.

It's all within **AT&T** your reach.

w w w . a t t . c o m / t r a v e l e r

For your calling convenience tear off and take with you!

AT&T Direct℠ Service

WALLET GUIDE

Inside you'll find simple instructions on how to use AT&T Direct Service to place calling card or collect calls from outside the U.S.

All you need are the AT&T Access Numbers when you travel outside the U.S., because you can access us quickly and easily from virtually anywhere in the world. And if you need any further help, there's always an AT&T English-speaking Operator available to assist you.

Calling From Specially Marked Telephones

Throughout the world, there are specially marked phones that connect you to AT&T Direct℠ Service. Simply look for the AT&T logo. In the following countries, access to AT&T Direct Service is *only* available from these phones: Ethiopia, Mongolia, Nigeria, Seychelles Islands.

Public phones in Europe displaying the red 3C symbol also give you quick and easy access to AT&T Direct Service. Just lift the handset and dial ✳60 (in France dial M60) and you'll be connected to AT&T.

Pay phones in the United Kingdom displaying the New World symbol provide easy access to AT&T. Simply lift the handset and press the pre-programmed button marked AT&T.

Customer Care

If you have any questions, call 800 331-1140, Ext. 707.

When outside the U.S., dial the AT&T Access Number for the country *you are in* and ask the AT&T Operator for Customer Care.

108-25   © AT&T 6/98

Printed in the U.S.A. on recycled paper.

Special Features

Just dial the AT&T Access Number for the country *you are in* and follow the instructions listed below.

● To call U.S. 800 numbers: Enter the 800 number you are calling. (Note: Based upon the 800 number dialed, calls may be toll-free or AT&T Direct℠ Service charges may apply for the duration of the call; some numbers may be restricted.)

● To set up conference calls: Dial AT&T TeleConference Services at 800 232-1234. (Note: One conferee must be in the U.S.)

● To access language interpreters: Dial AT&T Language Line® Services at 408 648-5871.

● To record and deliver messages: Dial #123 if you get a busy signal or no answer, or dial AT&T True Messages® Service at 800 562-6275.

Here's a time-saving tip for placing additional calls: When you finish your conversation, or if there is a busy signal or no answer, <u>don't hang up</u> – press # and wait for the voice prompt or an AT&T Operator.

To Call the U.S. and Other Countries Using Your AT&T Calling Card* or credit card,°° Follow These Steps:

1. Make sure you have an outside line. (From a hotel room, follow the hotel's instructions to get an outside line, as if you were placing a local call.)

2. If you want to call a country other than the U.S., make sure the country *you are in* is highlighted in blue on the chart like this:

3. Enter the AT&T Access Number listed in the chart for the country *you are in*.

4. When prompted, enter the telephone number you are calling as follows:

● For calls to the U.S., dial the Area Code (no need to dial 1 before the Area Code) + 7-digit number.

● For calls to other countries,† enter 01 + the Country Code, City Code, and Local Number.

5. After the tone, enter your AT&T Calling Card* or credit card number (not the international number). If you need help or wish to call collect, hold on for an AT&T Operator.

 * You may also use your AT&T Corporate Card, AT&T Universal Card, or most U.S. local phone company cards.
 † The cost of calls to countries other than the U.S. consists of basic connection rates plus an additional charge based on the country you are calling.
 °° Credit card billing subject to availability.

AT&T Access Numbers

AT&T Access Numbers (Refer to footnotes before dialing.) From the countries highlighted in blue below, like this ☐, you can make calls to virtually any location in the world; and from *all* the countries listed, you can make calls to the U.S.

It's all within your reach.

AT&T

Country	Number
Albania ●	00-800-0010
American Samoa	633 2-USA
Angola	0199
Anguilla ✦	1-800-872-2881
Antigua ✦	1-800-872-2881
(Public Card Phones)	#1
Argentina ●	0-800-54-288
Armenia ● ▲	8◆10111
Aruba ●	800-8000
Australia ○	1-800-881-011
Austria ●	022-903-011
Bahamas	1-800-872-2881
Bahrain	800-001
Bahrain †	800-000
Barbados ✦	1-800-872-2881
Belarus ✖ ● ▬	8◆800101
Belgium ●	0-800-100-10
Belize ▲	811
(From Hotels Only)	555
Benin ●	102
Bermuda ✦	1-800-872-2881
Bolivia ●	0-800-1112

Country	Number
Bosnia ▲	00-800-0010
Brazil	000-8010
British V.I. ✦	1-800-872-2881
Brunei ●	800-1111
Bulgaria ● ▲	00-800-0010
Cambodia ✱	1-800-881-001
Canada	1 800 CALL ATT
Cape Verde Islands ●	112
Cayman Islands ✦	1-800-872-2881
Chile	800-800-311
	or 800-800-288
China, PRC ▲	10811
Colombia	980-11-0010
Cook Island	09-111
Costa Rica	0-800-0-114-114
Croatia ▲	99-385-0111
Cyprus ●	080-90010
Czech Rep. ●	00-42-000-101
Denmark	8001-0010
Dominica ✦	1-800-872-2881

Country	Number
Dom. Rep. ✱, ☐	1-800-872-2881
Ecuador ▲	999-119
Egypt● (Cairo)	510-0200
(Outside Cairo)	02-510-0200
El Salvador ○	800-1785
Estonia	800-0001-0011
Fiji	004-890-1001
Finland ●	9800-100-10
France	0800 99 0011
French Antilles	0800 99 0011
French Guiana	0800 99 0011
Gabon ●	00◆001
Gambia ●	00111
Georgia ▲	8◆0288
Germany ●	0130-0010
Ghana	0191
Gibraltar	8800
Greece ●	00-800-1311
Grenada ✦	1-800-872-2881
Guadeloupe ✦, ✱ (Marie Galante)	0800 99 00 11

Country	Number
Guam	1 800 CALL ATT
Guantanamo Bay † (Cuba)	935
Guatemala ○, ✱	99-99-190
Guyana ★	165
Haiti	183
Honduras	800-0-123
Hong Kong	800-96-1111
Hungary ●	00◆800-01111
Iceland ●	800 9001
India ✖ ▲	000-117
Indonesia→	001-801-10
Ireland ✓	1-800-550-000
Israel	1-800-94-94-949
Italy ●	172-1011
Ivory Coast●	00-111-11
Jamaica □	872
Jamaica ○	1-800-872-2881
Japan IDC● ▲	0066-55-111
Japan KDD●	005-39-111
Kazakhstan	8◆800-121-4321
Korea † 550-HOME or 550-2USA	
Korea →	0030-911

Country	Number
Kuwait	800-288
Latvia (Riga)	7007007
(Outside Riga)	8◆27007007
Lebanon ○ (Beirut)	426-801
(Outside Beirut)	01-426-801
Liechtenstein ●	0-800-89-0011
Lithuania ✖, ▬	8◆196
Luxembourg†	0-800-0111
Macao ▲	0800-111
Macedonia, F.Y.R. of ● ▲, ○	99-800-4288
Malaysia ○	1800-80-0011
Malta	0800-890-110
Marshall Isl.	1 800 CALL ATT
Mauritius	73120
Mexico ▽† 01-800-288-2872	
Micronesia	288
Monaco ●	800-90-288
Montserrat ✦	1-800-872-2881
Morocco	002-11-0011
Netherlands Antilles ● ◆	001-800-872-2881

Country	Number
Netherlands ●	0800-022-9111
New Zealand	000-911
Nicaragua	174
Norway	800-190-11
Pakistan ▲	00-800-01001
Palau	02288
Panama	109
(Canal Zone)	281-0109
Papua New Guinea 0507-12880	
Paraguay ■, ▲ (Asunción City)	008-11-800
Peru ▲	0-800-50000
Philippines●	105-11
Poland ●	0◆0-800-111-1111
Portugal ▲	05017-1-288
Qatar	0800-011-77
Reunion Isl.	0800 99 0011
Romania ●	01-800-4288
Romania †	01-801-0151
Russia ● ▲, ○ (Moscow)	755-5042
(Outside Moscow)	8-095-755-5042

Country	Number
Russia ● ▲, ○ (St. Petersburg)	325-5042
(Outside St. Petersburg)	8-812-325-5042
St. Kitts/Nevis & St. Lucia ✦	1-800-872-2881
St. Pierre & Miquelon	0800 99 0011
St. Vincent △	1-800-872-2881
Saipan ▲	1 800 CALL ATT
San Marino ●	172-1011
Saudi Arabia ◇	1-800-10
Senegal	3072
Sierra Leone	1100
Singapore ●	800-0111-111
Slovakia ▲	00-42-100-101
Solomon Isl.	0811
So. Africa	0-800-99-0123
Spain	900-99-00-11
Sri Lanka ▬	430-430
Sudan	800-001
Suriname △	156

Country	Number
Sweden	020-795-611
Switzerland ●	0-800-890011
Syria	0-801
Taiwan	0080-10288-0
Thailand ●	001-999-111-11
Trinidad/Tob. ▲	1-800-872-2881
Turkey ●	00-800-12277
Turks & Caicos ✦, ▬	01-800-872-2881
Uganda	800-001
Ukraine ▲	8◆100-11
U.A.E. ▲, ✦	0800-121
	or 0500-89-0011
U.K. ▲	0500-89-0011
Uruguay ▬	000-410
U.S. ▽	1 800 CALL ATT
Uzbekistan 8◆641-7440010	
Venezuela	800-11-120
Vietnam ●	1-201-0288
Yemen	00 800 101
Zambia	00-899
Zimbabwe ▲	110-98990

● Public phones require coin or card deposit. ❷ Press red button ❸ Additional charges apply when calling outside of Moscow. ■ **AT&T Direct℠** calls cannot be placed to this country from outside the U.S. ✱ Available from pay phones. Phnom Penh and Siem Reap only. ✖ Not available from public phones. ⊕ From St. Maarten or phones at Bobby's Marina, use 1-800-872-2881.

◇ From this country, **AT&T Direct℠** calls terminate to designated countries only. ➤ From U.S. Military Bases only. ▬ Not yet available for all areas. ○ Select hotels. ▲ May not be available from every phone/public phone. † Collect calling from public phones. ✓ Available from phones with international calling capabilities or from most Public Calling Centers. ✓ From Northern Ireland use U.K. access code.

◇ Collect calling only. ○ Public phones require local coin payment through the call duration. ▽ Await second dial tone. ▽ When calling from public phones, use phones marked "Lastdel." If call does not complete, use 00-800-462-4240. △ Available from public phones. ◆ Public phones use phones marked ▬. ◀ When calling from public phones use phones marked Lenso.

☐ Calling Card calls available from select hotels. ↪ Use phones allowing international access. ✦ Including Puerto Rico and the U.S. Virgin Islands. ▼ **AT&T Direct℠** Service only from telephone calling centers in Hanoi and post offices in Da Nang, Ho Chi Minh City and Quang Ninh. ✤ If call does not complete, use 0800-013-0011.

WE GIVE YOU THE WORLD...AT A DISCOUNT

LET'S GO®

TRAVEL

MERCHANDISE
CATALOG FOR 1999

LET'S GO

Travel Gear

World Journey

Equipped with Eagle Creek Comfort Zone Carry System which includes Hydrofil nylon knit on backpanel and lumbar pads. Parallel internal frame. Easy packing panel load design with internal cinch straps. Lockable zippers. Detachable daypack. Converts into suitcase. 26x15x9", 5100 cu. in., 6 lbs. 12 oz. Black, Evergreen, or Blue. $30 discount with railpass. **$225.00**

Security Items

Undercover Neckpouch Ripstop nylon with a soft Cambrelle back. Three pockets. 5 1/2" x 8 1/2". Lifetime guarantee. Black or Tan. **$10.50**

Undercover Waistpouch Ripstop nylon with a soft Cambrelle back. Two pockets. 12" x 5" with adjustable waistband. Lifetime guarantee. Black or Tan. **$10.50**

Continental Journey

Carry-on size pack with internal frame suspension. Comfort Zone padded shoulder straps and hip belt. Leather hand grip. Easy packing panel load design with internal cinch straps. Lockable zippers. Detachable daypack. Converts into suitcase. 21x15x9", 3900 cu. in., 4 lbs. 5 oz. Black, Evergreen, or Blue. $20 discount with railpass. **$175.00**

Travel Lock Great for locking up your World or Continental Journey. Two-dial combination lock. **$5.25**

Hostelling Essentials

Hostelling International Membership
Cardholders receive priority, discounts, and reservation privileges at most domestic and international hostels.

Youth (under 18)..................... free
Adult (ages 18-55)................**$25.00**
Senior (over 55)....................**$15.00**

European Hostelling Guide
Offers essential information concerning over 2500 European hostels. **$10.95**

Sleepsack
Required at many hostels. Washable polyester/cotton. Durable and compact. **$14.95**

International ID Cards
1999

Provide discounts on airfares, tourist attractions and more. Includes basic accident and medical insurance. **$20.00**

International Student ID Card (ISIC)
International Teacher ID Card (ITIC)
International Youth ID Card (GO25)

1-800-5LETSGO
http://www.hsa.net/travel

---- Prices are in US dollars and subject to change.----

Euralpass

Euralpass Unlimited travel in and among all 17 countries: **Austria, Belgium, Denmark, Finland, France, Germany, Greece, Holland, Hungary, Italy, Luxembourg, Norway, Portugal, Republic of Ireland, Spain, Sweden, and Switzerland.**

First Class	15 days	21 days	1 month	2 months	3 months	10 days	15 days
	consecutive days					*in two months*	
1 Passenger	$554	$718	$890	$1260	$1558	$654	$862
2 or More Passengers	$470	$610	$756	$1072	$1324	$556	$732
Youthpass (Second Class)							
Passengers under 26	$388	$499	$623	$882	$1089	$458	$599

Europass Travel in the five Europass countries: **France, Germany, Italy, Spain, and Switzerland.** Up to two of the four associate regions (Austria and Hungary; Benelux (Belgium, Netherlands, and Luxembourg); Greece; Portugal) may be added.

First Class	5 days	6 days	8 days	10 days	15 days	first	second
	in two months					*associate country*	
1 Passenger	$348	$368	$448	$528	$728	+$60	+$40
2 to 5 Passengers traveling together	$296	$314	$382	$450	$620	+$52	+$34
Youthpass (Second Class)							
Passengers under 26	$233	$253	$313	$363	$513	+$45	+$33

Pass Protection For an additional $10, insure any railpass against theft or loss.

Discounts with the purchase of a railpass
- $30 off a World Journey backpack
- $20 off a Continental Journey backpack
- Any *Let's Go* Guide for 1/2 Price
- Free 2-3 Week Domestic Shipping

Call about Eurostar–the Channel Tunnel Train–and other country-specific passes.

Airfares & Special Promotions

Call for information on and availability of standard airline tickets, student, teacher, and youth discounted airfares, as well as other special promotions.

Publications & More

Let's Go Travel Guides—
The Bible of the Budget Traveler

USA • India and Nepal • Southeast Asia............22.99
Australia • Eastern Europe • Europe.................21.99
Britain & Ireland • Central America • France •
Germany • Israel & Egypt • Italy • Mexico •
Spain & Portugal...19.99
Alaska & The Pacific Northwest • Austria &
Switzerland • California & Hawaii • Ecuador
& The Galapagos Islands • Greece • Ireland.....18.99
South Africa • Turkey..17.99
New York City • New Zealand • London •
Paris • Rome • Washington D.C. 15.99

Let's Go Map Guides
Know your destination inside and out!
Great to accompany your Eurailpass.

Amsterdam, Berlin, Boston, Chicago, Florence, London, Los Angeles, Madrid, New Orleans, New York, Paris, Rome, San Francisco, Washington D.C.   8.95

Michelin Maps

Czech/Slovak Republics • Europe • France • Germany • Germany/Austria /Benelux • Great Britain & Ireland • Greece • Italy • Poland • Scandinavia & Finland • Spain & Portugal 10.95

LET'S GO Order Form

Last Name*   First Name*   Home and Day Phone Number*
(very important)

Street*   (Sorry, we cannot ship to Post Office Boxes)

City*   State*   Zip Code*

Citizenship‡§□   School/College§   Date of Birth‡§   Date of Travel*
(Country)

Qty	Description	Color	Unit Price	Total Price

Shipping and Handling

2-3 Week Domestic Shipping		
Merchandise value under $30	$4	
Merchandise value $30-$100	$6	
Merchandise value over $100	$8	
2-3 Day Domestic Shipping		
Merchandise value under $30	$14	
Merchandise value $30-$100	$16	
Merchandise value over $100	$18	
Overnight Domestic Shipping		
Merchandise value under $30	$24	
Merchandise value $30-$100	$26	
Merchandise value over $100	$28	
All International Shipping	$30	

Total Purchase Price	
Shipping and Handling	+
MA Residents add 5% sales tax on gear and books	+
TOTAL	

☐ Mastercard   ☐ Visa

Cardholder name:

Card number:

Expiration date:

When ordering an International ID Card, please include:
1. Proof of birthdate (copy of passport, birth certificate, or driver's license).
2. One picture (1.5" x 2") signed on the reverse side.
3. (ISIC/ITIC only) Proof of current student/teacher status (letter from registrar or administrator, proof of tuition, or copy of student/faculty ID card. FULL-TIME only).

* Required for all orders
‡ Required in addition for each Hostelling Membership
§ Required in addition for each International ID Card
□ Required in addition for each railpass

Prices are in US dollars and subject to change.

Make check or money order payable to:
Let's Go Travel
17 Holyoke Street
Cambridge, MA 02138
(617) 495-9649

1-800-5LETSGO

Hours: Mon.-Fri., 10am-6pm ET

going to the **ferry** terminal at the southwestern end of Linnankatu, take the train (3 per day) to Turku *satama* (harbor) or bus 1 from Turku's Market Square (8mk). From there, the Viking and Silja Line ferries ply to Mariehamn in the Åland Islands and beyond to Stockholm (see **Getting There,** p. 262).

Boisterous and amicable, the **Hostel Turku (HI),** Linnankatu 39 (tel. (02) 231 65 78; fax 231 17 08), is midway between the ferry terminals and the train station. From the station, walk west three to four blocks on Ratapihankatu, take a left on Puistokatu to the river, and make a right on Linnankatu; or from the ferry, walk 20 minutes up Linnankatu. (Dorms 45mk, singles 105mk, doubles 140mk. Nonmembers add 15mk per person. Sheets 30mk. Laundry 5mk per hour. Bikes 50mk per day.) For immaculate singles (190mk) and doubles (290mk), as well as impeccable hospitality, stay at **Bridgettine Sisters' Guesthouse,** Ursininkatu 15A (tel. (02) 250 19 10). Nearby, **Majatalo Kultainen Turrsti,** Käsityöläiskatu 11 (tel./fax (02) 250 02 65), offers 200mk singles and 250mk doubles (breakfast included; reception open 24hr.). **Ruissalo Camping** (tel. (02) 533 46 53; summer only) is located on Ruissalo island.

Find groceries at **Kauppatori** (Market Square) or walk southwest on Eerikinkatu to the red-brick **Kauppahalli** (Market Hall) for pricey pastries (both closed Su). The bakery of **Valintalo Supermarket,** Eerikinkatu 19, may be more affordable (open M-F 9am-9pm, Sa 9am-6pm). **Verso,** upstairs at Linnankatu 3, is a veggie bistro extraordinaire. (Lunches until 2pm, 35mk; large set menu 36mk; 10% student discount; open M-Sa 11am-5pm.) **Tolmuset,** Hämeenkatu 8, practically gives away hearty meals (23mk lunch special; open M-F 7:30am-5pm.) Festive Turku swims in cafes and riverside beer gardens.

■ Near Turku: Naantali (Nådendal)

Naantali, a peaceful enclave of old wooden houses 15km west of Turku, bills itself as the "sunshine town." The town and harbor are scenic, but the hordes of vacationing Finnish families put a strain on Naantali's serenity and make accommodations scarce. The buildings of the **Old Town,** some dating back to the late 18th century, are centered around Mannerheiminkatu, south of the **Convent Church,** built in 1462 (open daily May to mid-Aug. noon-6pm; mid-Aug. to Apr. noon-3pm). Try to catch a glimpse of Finland's president lounging in his fortress-like summer home, **Kultaranta,** visible from Naantali's harbor. The tourist office offers daily guided tours of the home. (By boat from the small west harbor 10am and 2pm; 45mk. From the main gate 3pm, 30mk. For more info, call (02) 435 08 50.) Even if you've never read *Finn Family Moomintroll,* you can recapture your youth at **Moomin Valley,** a harborside fantasy land (open early June to mid-Aug. daily 10am-8pm; admission 80mk, kids 60mk). Mini-trains chug around Naantali daily from Moomin Valley (10mk or free with a Moomin Valley admit ticket). For more info check out the **Moomin shop,** Mannerheiminkatu 3, in the center of town, or call (02) 511 11 11. The **Naantali Music Festival** (tel. (02) 432 53 63; fax 434 54 25; http://www.festivals.fi/naantali) brings chamber music to the holiday resort for the first two full weeks of June. Be warned that on **Sleepyhead Day** (July 27), the residents of Naantali get up at 6am and wake anyone

FINLAND

Naked Northerners

True to the stories, the sauna is an integral part of almost every Finn's life. More than simply a place to cleanse oneself thoroughly after a shower, saunas have evolved an entire mystique and are immortalized in *Kalevala,* the Finnish national epic. They are associated with cleanliness, strength, and endurance. The country now boasts over 1.5 million saunas, or one for every 3 people. Modern saunas are found in every hotel, most hostels, and many campgrounds. These wooden rooms reach temperatures around 100°C, so hot that no metal parts may be exposed, or the bathers will be burned. Water thrown on heated stones brings humidity to 100%. Finland's electricity use skyrockets on Friday and Saturday evenings, when hundreds of thousands of saunas are heated.

still sleeping. Dressed in carnival costumes, they proceed to crown the year's Sleepyhead and throw him or her into the harbor.

Buses 11 and 110 run to Naantali from the marketplace in Turku every five to 15 minutes, less frequently on weekends (25min., 16mk). Some buses also pick up at the train station, and the S/S *Ukkopekka* steams from Turku, Linnankatu 38 (tel. (02) 233 01 23), three times per day (tickets 75-95mk). The helpful **tourist office,** Kaivotori 2 (tel. 024 35 08 50; fax 435 08 52; http://www.travel.fi/naantali), can book accommodations and arrange tours. From the bus station, walk southwest on Tullikatu to Kaivokatu, then go right 300m; the tourist office is on your left (open June to mid-Aug. daily 9am-6pm; mid-Aug. to May M-F 9am-4pm). For tourist info, call the 24-hour hotline (tel. 060 09 21 10; 2.20mk per min.). There are no youth hostels, but **Naantali camping** (tel. (02) 435 08 55), 500m south of town, maintains year-round cabins (from 140mk) and summer tent sites (40mk per person). Another option is the **Summerhotel,** Opintie 3 (tel. (02) 445 56 60), which has dormitory style rooms. (Open June M-F 180mk per person, Sa-Su 200mk; July 200mk. Breakfast, sauna, and pool use at the nearby Spa Hotel included.) The best local bargain resides at **Seurahuone,** Tullikatu 6b, with its lovely terrace and filling lunch menu for 38mk (beer 16mk; open M-Th from 3pm, F from noon, Sa-Su from 9am, closes late).

■ Lahti

Located at the southern tip of the Lake District, Lahti will give you a taste of what lies north: scenic lakeside vistas, an active marketplace, and pleasant bars and pubs, all combined in a modern if uninspired city center. Lahti is at its prime in the winter, but is still active over the summer. The **Ski Museum** at the Sports Center has nifty ski-jump and biathalon simulators (open M-F 10am-5pm, Sa-Su 11am-5pm; 15mk, students 10mk). From the complex, 150km of trails radiate through hills cut during the ice age. If you can't get enough of Aalto architecture, visit the towering, macabre **Church of the Cross,** Kirkkokatu 4 (open daily 10am-3pm). Cruise boats go to Jyväskylä at 10am from the passenger dock (207mk).

Lahti serves as a transportation center. **Buses** depart for Jyväskylä (3hr., 118mk) and Savonlinna (4hr., 149mk). **Trains** chug to Helsinki (1½hr., 62mk), Jyväskylä (156mk), Savonlinna (152mk), Tampere (2hr., 88mk), and St. Petersburg, Russia (6hr., 226mk). The **tourist office,** Torikatu 3B, 2nd floor (tel. (03) 814 45 66; fax 814 45 64; email matkailu@lahti.fi; http://www.lahti.fi), has transportation and city info. (Open June-Aug. M 8am-6pm, Tu-F 8am-5pm, Sa 9am-2pm; Sept.-May M 8am-5pm, Tu-F 8am-4pm.) The **Lahden Kansanopisto hostel (HI),** Harjukatu 46 (tel. (03) 752 33 44; fax 752 33 22), is a high school during the year. From the train station, walk north on Vesijärvenkatu one block and then right on Harjukatu. (Dorms 75mk, nonmembers 90mk; singles 150mk. Reception open M-F 8am-9pm, Sa-Su 8am-noon and 4-9pm. Open June-Aug. 16.) There is a **campground** at the **Mukkula Tourist Center** (tel. (03) 882 35 00, or May-Aug. 882 36 00; fax 882 35 22; tents 40-70mk, year-round 4-person cabins 220-450mk), accessible by bus 30 (3 per hr., 11mk). **Bellmanni,** Kauppakatu 9, has cheap eats (main dishes 30-55mk). For nightlife, check out **Open House** in Hotelli Cumulus, Vapaudenkatu 24 (cover around 40mk for live bands; open 10pm-4am).

■ Lappeenranta

Lappeenranta was built in the 1600s around a harbor which still thrives today. First ruled by the Swedes, then the Russians, the town's rich culture is reflected in the architecture and the many museums of the old town. A 10-minute walk from the train station up Kauppakatu brings you to **Linnoitus** (the old town) which sits on a small hill. The area has been restored, and the only reminders of modern times are the cafes, museums, and shops occupying the old forest and buildings which once made up the Russian **fortress.** The **South Karelian Museum,** in the fortress at Kristiinankatu 15, has a scale model of the fortress and collections from Viipuri (Vyborg in

Russia). The **Calvary Museum,** Kristiinankatu 2, housed in the oldest building in the fortress, illustrates garrison life in the 1880s with its collection of uniforms and weapons. Just down the street, the **South Karelian Art Museum,** Kristiinankatu 8-10, in the yellow barracks, displays Finnish art along with a small postmodern collection. (All museums open June-Aug. M-F 10am-6pm, Sa-Su 11am-5pm; Sept.-May Tu-Th, Sa-Su 11am-5pm. 30mk ticket good for all museums in the fortress, students 20mk.) The fortress's **Russian Orthodox Church,** built in 1785, is the oldest in Finland (open Tu-Su 10am-4pm). In 1870, A Russian serf-turned-merchant family built the **Wolkoff house,** Kauppakatu 26, now beautifully decorated with Russian relics. (Open June-Aug. M-F 10am-5pm, Sa-Su 11am-5pm; Sept.-May F-Sa 11am-5pm. 20mk, students 15mk, includes tour.)

Karelia Lines (tel. (05) 453 03 80; fax 411 90 96), at the harbor, cruises the eight locks of the 43km Saimaa canal (60mk), and offers visa-free trips to Vyborg, Russia (110mk; passport and reservation required). Daily **trains** run to Helsinki (3hr., 6 per day, 138mk), Savonlinna (2hr., 5 per day, 80mk), and St. Petersburg (4hr., 155mk). The **tourist offices** (tel. (05) 66 77 88) are on Kauppakatu in the bus station (open June-Aug. M-F 9am-6pm; off-season M-F 9:30am-5:30pm) and by the harbor (open daily June 9am-8pm, July-Aug. until 9pm). **Huhtiniemi (HI),** Kuusimäenkatu 18 (tel. (05) 451 55 55), is situated near the lake, close to town. Take bus 5 or 6 from Valtakatu (11mk). (Dorms 40mk, nonmembers 55mk; doubles 250mk. Camping 85mk. Call ahead in winter.) Simple but cheap food is served at **Lounaskahvila Kuutti,** Kauppakatu 52 (open M-F 8:30am-8pm, Sa 9am-8pm, Su 10am-6pm).

LAKE DISTRICT

■ Savonlinna

The tsarist aristocracy turned Savonlinna's sandy beaches and numerous harbors into a fashionable resort 150 years ago, and travelers today come here for the laid-back waterside atmosphere and for the many vestiges of Finland's turbulent history scattered across this scenic part of the Lake District. Go east from the bus and train stations on Olavinkatu and cross the bridge, then hug Linnankatu along the south shore until you reach the elegant **Olavinlinna Castle,** a weather-worn medieval fortress, where you can tour the steep defense passages and winding stairways. (Open daily June to mid-Aug. 10am-5pm; mid-Aug. to May 10am-3pm. 25mk, students 15mk.) During the magnificent **Opera Festival** in July, divas come from all over the world to perform in the castle's courtyard. Tickets (180-550mk) should be ordered as early as October. Write to Savonlinna Opera Festival, Olavinkatu 27, FIN-57130 Savonlinna (tel. (015) 47 67 50; fax 476 75 40; http://www.operafestival.fi), or contact the tourist office (see below). For peaceful bathing, cross the footbridges north to the pine-covered isle of **Sulosaari.**

Savonlinna is yours by **train** from Helsinki (5hr., 5 per day, 170mk) or **bus** from Kuopio (2½ hr., 7 per day, 105mk) or Pieksämäki (2hr., 3 per day, 98mk). Most trains to Savonlinna stop at Retretti if you ask; during July, **express trains** shuttle between the city and caves (30min., 20mk, students 10mk). Once in Savonlinna, the train stops first at Savonlinna-Kauppatori in the center of town and near the tourist office and all lodging, then continues to the Savonlinna stop by the out-of-the-way main train station. **Water travel** provides the best access to the pristine lake regions; vessels cruise between Savonlinna and Kuopio (11½hr, Tu-Su 9:30am, 250mk). Daily cruises leave from the harbor on the **M/S Timppa** and **M/S Timppa 2** (9 per day, 30mk). The busy **tourist office,** across the bridge from the market at Puistokatu 1 (tel. (015) 51 75 10; fax 517 51 23; email savonlinna@touristservice-sul.fi; http:// www.travel.fi/fin/savonlinna), will help you find accommodations (reservations 50mk; open June 9-Aug. 9 daily 8am-6pm, July until 10pm, Aug. 10-June 8 M-F 9am-4pm). The bookstore **Knut Posse,** Olavinkatu 44, lets you browse the **Internet** (open M-F 9am-6pm, Sa 9am-2pm).

Despite its location behind the casino, **Vuorilinna Hostel (HI)**, Kylpylaitoksentie, Kasinosaari (tel. (015) 739 50; fax 27 25 24), snoozes peacefully on the island 200m across the footbridge from the market (95mk, nonmembers 110mk; kitchen; reception daily June-Aug. 7am-11pm). **Malakias (HI)**, Pihlajavedenkuja 6 (tel./fax (015) 53 32 83), is 1.5km from town. Going up Tulliportinkatu, veer right on Savonkatu (95mk, nonmembers 110mk; kitchen). **Vuohimäki Camping** (tel. (015) 53 73 53) is 7km out of town, but bus 3 runs there twice every hour (75mk per person; open early June to late Aug.). Eating and imbibing center on **Olavinkatu**. The **Steakhouse San Martin**, Olavinkatu 46, has salads (30mk) and pasta as well (main dishes 58-70mk; open M-F 10:30am-8pm, Sa-Su 11am-5pm). Across Olavinkatu from the market, visitors throw back a few beers at **Happy Time Pub**, Kauppatori 1 (open Su-M noon-1am, Tu-Th until 2am, F-Sa until 3am).

■ Near Savonlinna

The stretch of land and water between Savonlinna and Kuopio includes many worthwhile stops. At the handsome **Valamo Monastery** (tel. (017) 57 01 11), 35km from Heinävesi along the Savonlinna-Kuopio boat route, guests often outnumber monks 20 to one (guided tours 15mk). Take the bus to Heinävesi (80mk) and then the bus to the monastery (30mk). You can stay in their guest house (dorms 95mk; doubles 350mk), and chow down at the restaurant (55mk). The largest wooden church in the world is in **Kerimäki**, 24km east of Savonlinna, and seats over 3000 people (open M-F and Su 9am-8pm, Sa 9am-6pm). A more worldly retreat is **Rauhalinna**, a wooden palace built in the 19th century by a Russian commander for his wife. Cruises to this elegant island leave the market square in Savonlinna daily (35min., 5 per day, 40mk round-trip; open June-Aug. M-Sa noon-7pm and Su noon-4pm, July M-Sa 11am-8pm and Su 11am-6pm). The 130 islands of the **Linnansaari National Park**, about 50km from Savonlinna, are best seen by canoe; rent them at **Holiday Village Järvisydän** (tel. (015) 44 09 99). The **Forest and Park Service** (tel. (015) 57 68 10) and the Savonlinna tourist office have information on hiking trails, camping sites, and huts (4 people 100mk) throughout the park. To get to the park, take the boat going to Kuopio.

■ Tampere

Though it was once Finland's most industrialized city, machines and factories are no longer the centerpieces of "the Manchester of Finland," and the city's energetic nightlife, frequent cultural festivals, and pleasant beaches make it well worth a short stay.

SIGHTS AND ENTERTAINMENT The proletarian spirit burns brightly at the **Lenin Museum**, Hämeenpuisto 28, 3rd floor, established and still managed by the **Finnish-Soviet Friendship Society** also at Hämeenpuisto 28, site of the first conference of Lenin's revolutionary party. It was here that Lenin and Stalin first met (open M-F 9am-6pm, Sa-Su 11am-4pm; 15mk; bourgeois intellectuals 10mk). **Amuri Museum**, Makasiininkatu 12, has an evocative showcase of 25 workers' living quarters between 1873 and 1973 (open early May to mid-Sept. Tu-Su 10am-6pm; 20mk). Take bus 27 (9mk) to climb up the world's highest *esker* (a glacier-formed ridge) at **Pyynikki** park for a view of both Näsijärvi and Pyhäjärvi lakes from the observation tower (open daily 9am-8pm; 3mk). The simple, powerful paintings that line the interior of the 1907 **cathedral**, Tuomiokirkonkatu 3, are worth a look (open daily May-Aug. 8am-8pm, Sept.-Apr. 11am-3pm).

Tampere's **Short Film Festival** (early March; tel. (03) 219 61 49), featuring contestants from 30 countries, is rivaled in urbanity only by the **International Theater Festival** (early August; tickets 40-140mk; tel. (03) 31 46 69 58; http://tampere.fi/festival/theatre). Unpretentious **Papaan Kapakka**, Koskikatu 9, across from the tourist office, has live jazz nightly starting around 9pm (no cover; open M-Sa May-Aug. noon-2am, Sept.-Apr. 3pm-2am). **Doris**, Aleksanterinkatu 20, is a popular rock club (cover 10mk; open Tu-Su 11pm-3am), and **Mixei**, Otavalankatu 3, becomes a gay disco Friday and Saturday nights (open Tu-Su 10pm-3am).

The nearby coastal town of **Pori** comes alive during the famous **Pori Jazz Festival** in mid-July (tentatively July 10-18 in 1999; tickets 30-250mk; tel. (02) 550 55 50; http://www.porijazz.fi).

PRACTICAL INFO, ACCOMMODATIONS, AND FOOD Trains head south to Helsinki (2hr., 9 per day, 94mk) and Turku (2hr., 7 per day, 84mk), and north to Oulu (5hr., 6 per day, 224mk). **Boats** cruise to Ruovesi (4½hr., Tu, Th, and Sa, 167mk) and beyond to Virrat (7½hr., 226mk) or to Hämeenlinna (8hr., 1 per day, 202mk). For info, call (03) 212 48 04. The **tourist office,** Verkatehtaankatu 2 (tel. (03) 31 46 68 00; fax 31 46 64 63; email touristbureau@tampere.fi; http://www.tampere.fi.), is exceptionally helpful. From the train station, walk up Hämeenkatu, turn left just before the bridge, and look for the sign. (Open June-Aug. M-F 8:30am-8pm, Sa 8:30am-6pm, Su 11am-6pm; Sept.-May M-F 8:30am-5pm.) At the R-kioski in the train station, ask about the **Tampere Tourist Card,** which allows unlimited access to public transit.

When you become alienated by the tourism industry, achieve solidarity with the masses at the **Tampereen NNKY (HI),** Tuomiokirkonkatu 12 (tel. (03) 254 40 20; fax 254 40 22), a block from the train station. (Dorms 55mk; singles 125mk; doubles 170mk. Nonmembers add 15mk. Sheets 25mk. Reception daily 8-10am and 4-11pm.) Five kilometers southwest, **Camping Härmälä** (tel. (03) 265 13 55) overlooks Lake Pyhäjärvi (tents 75mk; cabins 160mk-240mk; open late May to late Aug.).

Sample *mustamakkara,* a Tampere sausage made with flour and cow's blood, at **Kauppahalli** (Market Hall), Hämeenkatu 19 (open M-Th 8am-5pm, F 8am-5:30pm, Sa 8am-3pm). **Pleuna,** Itäinen katu 8, dishes up hearty food and lots of sausage in a brewery (30-65mk; open M-Th 11am-1am, F-Sa 11am-2am, Su noon-10pm). The buffet and salad bar at **Bon Appétit,** Hämeenkatu 1, 2nd floor, are a budget traveler's dream (from 29mk; buffet M-F 5-7pm).

■ Jyväskylä

Tightly encircled by dense forest and an enchanting lake, Jyväskylä (OO-vas-kill-ah), the capital of Finland's lake district, is famous as the home of architect Alvar Aalto. If you like his work, this town's for you. The compact and modern city is sprinkled liberally with buildings designed by Aalto; if you can't pick them out yourself, pick up a guide (10mk) or free map at the **tourist office,** Asemakatu 6 (tel. (014) 62 49 03; fax 21 43 93; email matkailu@jkl.fi; http://www.jkl.fi), one block up from the train station. (Open June-Aug. M-F 9am-6pm, Sa-Su 9am-3pm; Sept.-May M-F 9am-5pm, Sa 9am-2pm.) The **Alvar Aalto Museum,** Alvar Aallon Katu 7, follows the development of his style through furniture, photographs, plans, and models (open Tu-Su 11am-6pm, Aug. until 8pm; 10mk, students free, F free). The **University of Jyväskylä,** largely designed by you-know-who, occupies an isolated campus in piney woods and lilacs near the Aalto Museum. Jyväskylä keeps a late schedule; many buildings don't open until 11am. Stay out late and sleep in.

In the third week of July, Jyväskylä hosts the **Jyväskylän Kesä arts festival,** with concerts, film screenings, and exhibitions. (Tel. (014) 62 43 78; fax 21 48 08; http://www.jkl.fi/festivals/kesa. Tickets 30-120mk, student discounts 25-50%.) Two-hour **cruises** on Lake Päijänne run 55mk (departing daily June-mid Aug. 11:30am and 3:30pm); the **Blue and White Line** offers more elaborate cruises (June-Aug. 20 W-Sa 8pm from the dock; 70mk). Cruises also sail to Lahti (10hr., 207mk).

Trains arrive from Tampere (2hr., 8 per day, 80mk) and Helsinki (3½hr., 8 per day, 140mk), while **buses** arrive from several Lake District towns. Sporty **Laajari (HI),** Laajavuorentie 15 (tel. (014) 62 48 85; fax 62 48 88), has a ski slope with a great view and a free sauna in the basement; take bus 25 (2 per hour, 11mk) from stop 6. (Dorms 85mk, no breakfast; singles 165mk and doubles 240mk, breakfast included; 15mk discount for HI members June-Aug.) Lakeside **Tuomiojärvi Camping** (tel. (014) 62 48 95), 2km north of town, is accessible by bus 8, 22, or 27 (38mk per person, 4-person cabins 200mk; open June-Aug.). Right across from the campus, **Sohwi,** Vaasankatu 21, attracts students with a 30mk lunch special, huge pasta dishes, salads, and happy hours (happy hours M-F 4-7pm; restaurant open M-F 11am-3am, Sa noon-3am, Su noon-midnight). On Kauppakatu, drop by **Hemingway's**, a lively bar, (ages 22 and up; open Su-Tu 3pm-1am, W-Th until 2am, F-Sa until 3am). **Club 73**, Vapaudenkatu, has a hip disco (ages 23 and up; open M-Tu 7pm-midnight, W-Su 7pm-4am).

■ Kuopio

With nine flea markets and 22 outdoor dining spots, bustling Kuopio lures merchants from the west, chefs from the east, and tourists from all over. Located at the edge of Finland's northern tundra in the Lake District, Kuopio suffers seemingly endless winter darkness but rejoices under the midnight sun when it arrives. The festivities begin in late June when flamenco, bolero, ballet, modern, and Arabian dancers parade into the city for Kuopio's **Dance and Music Festival** (tel. (017) 282 15 41; fax 261 19 90; email Kuopio.dance.festival@travel.fi; http://www.travel.fi/kuopiodancefestival; tickets 40-220mk). Seat of the Orthodox archbishop of Finland, Kuopio houses spectacular Russian icons and textiles; don't miss the **Orthodox Church Museum** on Karjalankatu 1 (open May-Aug. Tu-Su 10am-4pm; Sept.-Apr. M-F noon-3pm, Sa-Su noon-5pm). Take in the beauty of the northern Lake District from atop the 75m tall **Puijo** tower (15mk). Follow Puistokatu north, or catch bus 6 (tower open daily 9am-9pm). On Vajasalo Island, 5km from Passenger Harbor, the **Alahovi Berry Farm** (tel. (017) 362 11 29) produces sweet currant and strawberry wines and offers tours of its winery and samples of its wares (open May 29-Aug.9 Tu-Sa noon-9pm, Su noon-5pm). The ferry leaves regularly from the Passenger Harbor for the island (round-trip 50mk).

Kuopio is easily accessible by **train** from Oulu (5hr., 4 per day, 168mk) and Rovaniemi (7hr., 3 per day, 248mk) to the north, and Helsinki (5hr., 8 per day, 208mk), Lahti (4hr., 5 per day, 160mk), and Tampere (4hr., 6 per day, 156mk) to the south. Consult the **tourist office,** Haapaniemenkatu 17 (tel. (017) 18 25 84; fax 261 35 38), on the corner of Market Square, for info on weekly events (open June-Aug. 15 M-F 9am-6pm, Sa 9am-4pm; Aug. 16-May M-F 9am-5pm). For enthusiastic help, maps, and brochures, look for tourist advisors dressed in green uniforms at the train station, harbor, market place, and **Puijo**. The hostel **Hermannin Salit** (tel. (017) 364 49 61; fax 364 49 11), is the cheapest stay in Kuopio. From the train station, go right on Asemakatu and then left on Haapaniemenkatu. Continue about 1km, veer left onto Haapaniementie, and turn left on Hermaninaukio. (Dorms 80mk; singles 135mk; doubles 190mk. Breakfast 25mk. Sheets 15mk. Free laundry). Bus 6 in front of the Sokos on Haapaniemenkatu leads to **Hostelli Rauhalahti (HI)**, Katiskaniementie 8 (tel. (017) 47 34 73; fax 47 34 70; 105mk, nonmembers 120mk). **Kuopio Camping Rauhalahti,** Kiviniementie (tel. (017) 361 22 44; fax 262 40 04), has a kitchen, showers, and minigolf (tents 40mk, cottages 130-260mk; open May-Aug.).

Pick up warm loaves of *kalakukko*, a local specialty of small pike baked in rye bread, from the market square. The lunch special is only 37mk at **Ravintola Rose,** Haapaniemenkatu 15 (daily 11am-3pm). Next door, **Melly's** pub lures customers with happy hour (3pm-6pm, beer 15mk; open M-F 3pm-2am, Sa noon-2am, Su 3pm-1am).

■ Kuhmo

The quiet town of Kuhmo near the Russian border draws travelers with its hiking opportunities and *rönttöset* (lingonberry pie). The beautiful paths along Lake Lammasjärvi are approachable from town near the **Arts Center,** Koulakatu 1, which hosts the **Kuhmo Chamber Music Festival** in late July (tickets 25-200mk; tel. (08) 655 67 50; fax 655 67 54; http://www.kuhmofestival.fi). The Arts Center's modern facade contrasts with the bucolic charm of Kuhmo's **Kalevalakylä** (tel. (08) 655 45 00), a re-created traditional Finnish village. Within the complex are various galleries and workshops. (Open daily June-Aug. 9:30am-6pm. 60mk.) Even the most inexperienced hikers can enjoy the excellent trails around Kuhmo. The easy-going 2.5km **Kämärä nature trail** winds its way through the Pönkävaara hill and is 10km from Kuhmo's center. Follow the road to Hukkajärvi and look for signs. The must-do 12km

Elimyssalo path meanders through swamps, spruce woods, and wildflowers and is part of the longer **UKK Reitti.** The entire UKK trail is dotted with free overnight shelters and a few rental cabins. For hiking info, call the **Finnish Forest and Park Service** (tel. (08) 877 63 80) or the **Kuhmo Recreational Service** (tel. (08) 655 04 95).

Kuhmo is accessible by **bus** only, via Joensuu, Kajaani, and Oulu. The **tourist office** (tel. (08) 655 63 82; fax 655 63 84), 1km away from town on Kainuuntie after the Shell station, also has a few basic hiking maps and info on lodgings (open June-Aug. M-F 8am-6pm, Sa 9am-4pm; Sept.-May M-F 8am-5pm). Lodging is available in July in the dormitory of the Piilola School at the **Kuhmo Youth Hostel (HI)** (tel. (08) 655 63 82, in July 655 62 45) on Kainuuntie. From the bus station walk right on Koulukatu, then left on to Kainuuntie; it is on the block between Vienantie and Peuranpolku (dorms 70mk; singles 150mk; doubles 90mk; sheets 30mk). The **Kuhmo Matkak-ievari KY Motel,** Vienantie 3 (tel. (08) 655 02 71) is open all year (singles 110-170mk; doubles 190-230mk). To get to the **Kalevala Camping Site** (tel. (08) 655 63 88, in winter 655 63 82; fax 655 63 84), go 4km from the center of town in the direction of Suomussalmi (2-person cabin 150mk; camping 65mk; sauna 60mk; boat rental 100mk per day). Stock up for the trails at **S-market,** on the corner of Koulukatu and Kainuuntie (open M-F 9am-9pm, Sa 9am-6pm). Before leaving town, stop by **Neljä Kaessa,** Koulukatu 3, for some *rönttöset* (8mk; open M-F 8am-5pm, Sa 8am-1pm).

OSTROBOTHNIA

■ Oulu (Uleåborg)

A lively university city by Finnish standards, Oulu's flower-bordered streets and well-tended bike paths lend it elegance in the summer months. See exotic flora in the twin glass pyramids of the **Botanical Gardens,** 7km north of the center, 15 minutes along bus route 19. (Pyramids open June-Aug. Tu-F 8am-4pm, Sa-Su 10am-4pm; Sept.-May Tu-F 8am-3pm, Sa-Su noon-3pm. Open-air gardens open in summer daily 8am-9pm; off-season 7am-5pm. Free.) **Nallikari,** Finland's Côte d'Azur, rims an island 5km northwest of town. Despite its tacky amusement park, the splendid beach is the best place in Northern Finland to enjoy the Bothnian waters. Take the hourly bus 5 (11mk) from Rotuaari in the center of town (11am-6pm). Despite its current renovation project, you can stay at nearby **Nallikari Camping** (tel. (08) 554 15 41; 40mk per person; 4-person cabins 350-550mk). With multi-colored cottages, the island of **Pikisaari,** connected by bridges to the harbor, offers idyllic strolling and picnicking.

All **trains** between north and south Finland pass through Oulu; four or five per day leave for Helsinki (276mk) and north to Rovaniemi (108mk). The station also rents **bikes** (30mk per day). The **tourist office,** Torikatu 10 (tel. (08) 314 12 94; fax 314 12 69; http://www.ouka.fi), greets visitors with info on the entire Ostrobothnia region. Take Hallituskatu, the broad avenue perpendicular to the train station, for six blocks, then take a left. (Open late June-early Aug. M-F 9am-6pm, Sa 10am-3pm; early Aug.-late June M-F 9am-4pm.) The well-equipped **Uni Hostel (HI),** Kajaanintie 36 (tel. (08) 313 63 11; fax 313 67 54), has bargain rooms with cooking facilities (dorms 55mk, add 15mk for nonmembers, singles 200mk, doubles 270mk; 13mk for use of sauna, gym, and pool; open June-Aug.). For a quick bite, go south on Isokatu to the corner of Saaristonkatu, where you'll find **Fantasia,** with all-you-can-eat pizza and salad buffets (lunch buffet 39mk; open M-Tu 10:30am-9pm, W-Th until 10pm, F-Sa until 8pm, Su noon-9pm). The dungeon-like club **45 Special,** Saaristonkatu 12, complete with iron bars and shackles, hosts Finnish bands (open daily 8pm-4am; cover F-Sa 15-20mk).

LAPLAND (LAPPI)

The sun never sets on Lapland during the pleasant two- to three-month summer. In winter, the sun rises for only a few hours a day: clear sky, moonlight, and white snow produce an eerie blue glow, and the green, red, and yellow streaks of the Northern Lights illuminate a surreal snowscape. In the south you'll find river rapids and white-fish. To the north lies 80km-long **Inarijärvi** (Lake Inari) and its countless islands; even farther north, the land rises with the steep tundra slopes of the **Teno River Valley**. **Skiing** is ideal from February to mid-May, with facilities and rental outlets at almost every tourist center (including **Ounasvaara,** near Rovaniemi). In summer, guides lead **hiking expeditions** from the same places; only experienced groups should undertake independent excursions. Hikers should plan their routes around the mountain huts run by the Finnish Youth Hostel Association. **Etiäinen** (tel. 02 05 64 78 20), in Santa Claus's Village (see **Rovaniemi,** below), provides maps, hiking routes, info about locations of huts and cabins, and sells fishing and hunting permits (open June-Aug. M-Sa 9am-7pm, Sept.-May M-F 10am-5pm).

■ Rovaniemi

Tucked 8km south of the Arctic Circle, Rovaniemi is the capital of Finnish Lapland. As a farewell gesture, retreating Germans razed Rovaniemi to the ground in 1944. The city was rebuilt using blueprints conceived in the mind of our friend Aalto, who shaped the layout to resemble reindeer antlers. You can meet the jolly man and his reindeer at **Santa Claus's Village,** if you can fight your way through the hordes of eager tourists. A visit to the **Arktikum** center, Pohjoisranta 4, is a must; it houses the **Arctic Science Center,** with exhibits on life and culture in the north, as well as the **Provincial Museum of Lapland.** (Open May-June daily 10am-6pm; July-Aug. daily 10am-8pm; Sept.-Apr. Tu-Su 10am-6pm. 50mk, students 40mk.) The **Ranua Wildlife Park** (tel. (016) 355 19 21), one hour from Rovaniemi (catch a direct bus from the bus station), has 3km of paths through areas of fenced-in Arctic elk, bears, and wolves. (Open daily May 10am-6pm, June-mid Aug. 9am-8pm, mid Aug.-Sept. 10am-6pm, Oct.-Apr. 10am-4pm. 45mk.)

 Buses head to Kuusamo (2½hr., 2 per day, 116mk), Kilpisjärvi (6½hr., 1 per day, 233mk), Muonio (3½hr., 4 per day, 136mk), and north to Ivalo (5hr., 168mk), with connections to Norway. Rovaniemi is also easily accessible by trains from Oulu (Helsinki-Rovaniemi 4 per day, 280mk), and by southbound buses from Inari, Muonio, Enontekiö, and Karasjok, Norway. Travel to Sweden by **train** to Kemi, then by bus (railpasses valid) 25km west to the border town of **Tornio.** Some buses continue across the border into Haparanda, Sweden. If you choose that route, the Tornio **HI hostel** (tel. (016) 48 16 82; fax 48 00 48), at Kirkkokatu, 1.6km north of the Finnish customs post, is scheduled to reopen in summer 1999 after renovations.

 The **tourist office** at Koskikatu 1 (tel. (016) 34 62 70; fax 342 46 50; http://www.rovaniemi.fi/rovaseu/rovaseu.htm) dishes up a weekly events listing happily titled *Let's Go* (open June-Aug. M-F 8am-6pm, Sa-Su 11:30am-4pm; Sept.-May M-F 8am-4pm). For info on short hiking trails, ask for the free brochure, *Walk the Wonders of the Arctic Circle*. From the train station, head right on Ratakatu and turn right on Hallituskatu just after the bus station. Follow Hallituskatu to Korkalonkatu, where you go left, then go right on Koskikatu and follow it to the river (about 15min. total). **Lapland Safaris,** Koskikatu 1 (tel. (016) 331 12 00), leads groups up the River Ounasjoki to a reindeer farm (6hr., 720mk) and offers cruises (165mk), mountain bike trips (3hr., 260mk), and huskie and snowmobile safaris (2-6hr., 290-780mk). Rovaniemi's **HI youth hostel,** Hallituskatu 16 (tel. (016) 34 46 44), is friendly if somewhat spartan. Follow directions to the tourist office until Hallituskatu (70mk, nonmembers 85mk). Across the river from the town center sits **Ounaskoski Camping** (tel. (016) 34 53 04; 60mk; open June-Aug.). Fill up at **Max Buffet,** Koskikatu 9, (open M-Tu 11am-9pm, W-F until 10pm, Sa–Su noon-10pm), or sample reindeer meat in lingonberry sauce

(79mk) at **Martina**, Korkalonkatu 27 (open M-Th 11am-11pm, F-Sa until 1am, Su noon-11pm). The **Panimo and Pub**, Koskikatu 13, has a noisy crowd that starts drinking early (beer 20mk; open M-Th 11am-2am, F-Sa until 3am, Su noon-2am).

■ Northern Hiking Regions

Finland has preserved large sections of its northern wilderness by turning them into **national parks** which serve as ideal locations for summer and fall hiking. The **Urho Kekkonen National Park** is one of the nicest areas. Located in northeastern Finland, it is accessible by bus from Ivalo, Rovaniemi, or Sodankylä. A popular week-long hike begins its circular trail from Kiilopää, and shorter nature trails leave from Kiilopää and Tankauaara. Main points of entry include **Vuotso** on the west side and **Tulppio** on the east. Contact the main visitor center in Tankauaara (tel (016) 62 62 51) for more info (open daily June-Sept. 10am-7pm, Oct.-May 10am-4pm). Just west of Inari, **Lemmenjoki National Park,** Finland's largest, is also a popular spot for hikers, offering a large wilderness section for experienced hikers. Contact the park service of Ivalo (tel. (9697) 68 77 00) for news about transportation and services in the park. For accommodations in Ivalo try **Montelli Petsamo Hostel (HI),** Petsamontie 16 (tel. (016) 66 11 06; fax 66 16 28; 80-200mk), or for north of Inari in Kaamanen try the **Jokitörmä Hostel (HI),** Lomakylä (tel. (016) 67 27 25; fax 67 27 45; 50-155mk).

The more commercial **Kuusamo,** northeast of Oulu, is accessible from there or Rovaniemi. Kuusamo includes the scenic **Oulanka National Park,** suitable for day hikes, and offers such attractions as superb fishing, whitewater rafting, a water park, and rock climbing at **Ruoppivaara Fell**. The Rukatunturi Fell in **Ruka,** one of the leading winter sports centers in Finland, is also the finish of the internationally famous 80km **Bear's Ring** hiking route (begins at Hautajärvi visitor center; tel. (016) 83 96 51). From the top of the fell (reached by chair lift or on foot), speed demons can shoot down Finland's longest summer toboggan slope (1001m). To get to Rukatunturi Fell, take the daily bus from Rovaniemi to Kuusamo. Call the Kuusamo **tourist office,** Torangintaival 2 (tel. (08) 850 29 10; fax 850 29 01), for info.

FINLAND

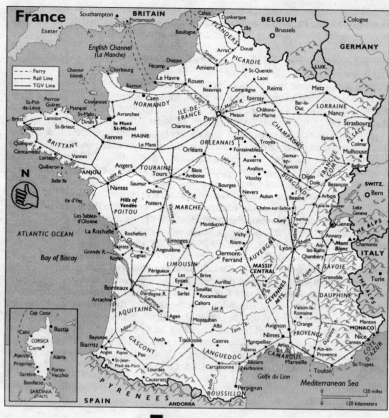

France

US$1	= 5.79F (francs)	1F =	US$0.17
CDN$1	= 3.81F	1F =	CDN$0.26
UK£1	= 9.61F	1F =	UK£0.10
IR£1	= 8.38F	1F =	IR£0.12
AUS$1	= 3.42F	1F =	AUS$0.29
NZ$1	= 2.96F	1F =	NZ$0.34
SAR1	= 0.93F	1F =	SAR 1.08

Country Code: 33   **International Dialing Prefix: 00**

The French celebrate the senses like no one else. Most conventional images of France are steeped in such pleasures: the vineyards of Bordeaux and Burgundy, the elaborate dishes of Dijon, the lavender slopes and sandy expanses of the Riviera, the crisp Alpen air, and the priceless treasures of the country's trillion art museums. Against such notions runs the Rationalism that has dominated French intellectual life for over 400 years. Philosopher Descartes, chemist Lavoisier, and mathematician Poincaré arose from a flourishing culture of methodical inquiry. These competing qualities—sensuality and reason—meet, quite literally, in neighborhood brasseries and cafes, where lively conversation is enjoyed no less than wine and the *plat du jour*.

The regions of France are culturally and historically diverse. The cliffs and fertile countryside of Normandy posed for the Impressionists and embraced Anglo-American liberators, while Brittany and Corsica still cling to distinct cultural identities. The Loire Valley chateaux blossom with the architecture of the French Renaissance, while the Alps illustrate the architecture of raw geological force. The Dordogne River Valley shelters 20,000-year-old cave paintings, while the Riviera is just too glorious for its own good.

Long ago, France was inhabited by the Gauls, a Celtic people who fell prey to decentralized turmoil after the fall of the Roman Empire. The coming of Charlemagne in the 8th century, and the feudal lords' consolidation of regions into nation over the next several centuries gave meaning to Napoleon's later quip "Impossible? The word is not French." The Renaissance witnessed mushrooming chateaux in the Loire Valley under the care of François I, and the opulence crescendoed during the reign of Louis XIV, the Sun King. By 1789, the French citizens could no longer support such extravagance; the ensuing years of furious rabble-rousing and violence inspired later revolutions in France and across Europe. In the afterglow of the Revolution, Napoleon's armies gained mastery over Europe, but eventually fell, and a Republic was established. Impressionists Monet and Renoir redefined painting, and after World War I Paris became the stomping ground of the Lost Generation. Today, as France grapples with its own post-colonial identity, the doors are still wide open to Europe's largest tourist industry.

For more detailed fact- and flavor-filled coverage, pick up a copy of *Let's Go: France 1999* or *Let's Go: Paris 1999*.

GETTING THERE AND GETTING AROUND

France does not require **visas** of U.S., Canadian, New Zealand, or EU citizens, but it does of South Africans and Australians (see **Government Information Offices,** p. 3).

The **Société Nationale de Chemins de Fer (SNCF)** manages one of Europe's most extensive rail networks. Timetables are complicated but well-organized, with color-designated periods. Blue periods have lower train traffic, usually Monday afternoon through Friday morning and Saturday afternoon to Sunday afternoon; white periods coincide with heavier train use (most other times) and cost more. Train tickets are not valid for use until punched in the orange machine at the entrance to the platforms at the *gare* (train station). Seat **reservations,** recommended for international trips, are mandatory on EuroCity (EC), InterCity (IC), and TGV *(train à grande vitesse)* trains. All three require a ticket supplement (US$3-18; railpass holders exempt) and a reservation fee (US$2-3). The SNCF's premier pass offering, the **France Railpass,** allows 3 days of travel within one month (first-class US$185, second-class US$145), with up to 6 additional days available (US$30 each), and must be bought outside France.

French **buses,** usually affordable, are useful for filling the gaps in the rail network. The bus station, usually near the train station, is called the *gare routière.* **Hitching** in France reportedly requires patience. **Allostop-Provoya** is a service that pairs drivers and riders. It charges 250F for eight trips within a two-year period, or 30-70F for individual trips depending on the distance traveled. Gas and tolls are extra. Their main office at 84 passage Brady, 75010 Paris (tel. within Paris 01 42 46 00 66, outside Paris 01 47 70 02 01), can give you the addresses of offices throughout the country. With a wealth of well-paved minor routes, French roads are terrific for **cycling.** Prime regions include the Loire Valley, Normandy, Provence, the Dordogne River Valley, Alsace-Lorraine, and Burgundy. SNCF's pamphlet *Guide du train et du vélo* offers details on bike-and-rail trips in France. Bike rentals require a 100-2000F deposit; some train stations rent bikes and allow you to drop off at another station.

FRANCE

ESSENTIALS

The extensive French tourism support network revolves around **syndicats d'initiative** and **offices de tourisme** (in the smallest towns, the **Mairie,** the mayor's office, deals with tourist concerns), both of which *Let's Go* labels as "tourist office." Both will help you find accommodations, distribute maps, and suggest excursions to the countryside. The basic unit of currency in France is the franc, subdivided into 100 centimes and issued in both coins and paper notes.

Just about everything snoozes from noon to 2pm and closes on Sundays, and many provincial areas also shut down on Mondays. Museums close at least one day a week, usually Tuesday. The major national **holidays** are: January 1, Easter Monday (April 5 in 1999), Labor Day (May 1), Victory in Europe Day (May 8), Ascension Day (May 13), Whit Monday (May 24), Bastille Day (July 14), Assumption Day (Aug. 15), All Saints' Day (Nov. 1), Armistice Day (Nov. 11), and Christmas (Dec. 25).

Summer brings daytime highs of around 24°C to most of France, although it is cooler in the North and the Alps, and southern France basks in 32°C scorchers every summer. Winters are generally mild, with temperatures rarely dipping below freezing, although frequent rains will dampen more than just spirits.

COMMUNICATION To operate payphones, buy a *télécarte* (telephone card), available in denominations of 41 and 98F at train stations, post offices and *tabacs.* Phone numbers starting with 0 800 are toll-free; those starting with 08 charge high rates. To call collect, tell the operator *"en PCV"* (ahn-PAY-say-VAY). For **AT&T Direct,** dial 0800 99 00 11; **MCI WorldPhone,** 0800 99 00 19; **SprintExpress,** 0800 99 00 87; **Australia Direct,** 00 33 11; **Canada Direct,** 0800 99 00 16; **BT Direct,** 0800 99 02 44; **New Zealand Direct,** 0800 906 296. Anywhere in France, dial 10 for an operator, 12 for directory assistance, and 00 33 11 for an international operator. In an **emergency,** dial 15 for **medical** assistance, 17 for **police,** and 18 for the **fire** department.

Contrary to popular opinion, even flailing efforts to speak French will be appreciated, especially in the countryside. Be lavish with your *Monsieurs, Madames,* and *Mademoiselles,* and greet people with a friendly *bonjour* (*bonsoir* after 6pm).

Yes/no	*Oui/Non*	wee/nohn
Hello	*Bonjour*	bohn-ZHOOR
Please/Thank you	*S'il vous plaît/Merci*	seel voo PLAY/mehr-SEE
Excuse me	*Excusez-moi*	ehks-KOO-ZAY MWAH
Do you speak English (sir, madam)?	*Parlez-vous anglais, (Monsieur, Madame)?*	PAHR-lay VOO zahn-GLAY (muh-SYUR, mah-DAHM)
I don't understand.	*Je ne comprend pas.*	ZHUH NUH kohm-PRAHN pah
I don't speak French.	*Je ne parle pas français.*	zhuh nuh PAHRL pah frahn-SAY
Where is/are...?	*Où est/sont...?*	oo ay/sohn
How much?	*Combien?*	kohm-BYEHN
I would like...	*Je voudrais...*	ZHUH voo-DRAY
I would like a room for one/two.	*Je voudrais une chambre simple/pour deux.*	ZHUH voo-DRAY oon SHAHM-bruh SAM-pluh/poor DEUH
Help!	*Au secour!*	OH suh-COOR

ACCOMMODATIONS AND CAMPING Youth hostels (*auberges de jeunesse*) cover France, ranging from well-kept, centrally located castles to run-down barracks. Most are affiliated with HI and charge nonmembers slightly more. Hostels run 45-80F per person, with breakfast about 15F (usually not obligatory). The quality of **hotels** in France generally matches their standardized rating on the government scale of one to four stars. Expect to pay at least 105F for singles and 130F for doubles. Showers are usually not included and can run 10-25F. Inquire whether the breakfast or meals at the hotel are *obligatoire*. Breakfast (15-25F) usually means bread, jam, and coffee or hot chocolate. Make reservations (confirm with one night's deposit) in summer.

Campgrounds, plentiful in France, are also rated on a four-star system. The *Guide Officiel Camping/Caravaning* is available from the **Fédération Française de Camping et de Caravaning,** 78 rue de Rivoli, 75004 Paris (tel. 01 42 72 84 08). The **Club Alpin Français** maintains mountain huts in upland regions. Contact the office at 24 av. de Lumière, 75019 Paris (tel. 01 53 72 88 00; fax 01 42 02 24 18), for more information. Tourist offices list local *gîtes d'étape* (shelters inaccessible to motorists) and, in many rural areas, *campings à la ferme* (campsites on private farms).

FOOD AND DRINK French chefs cook for one of the most finicky clienteles in the world. Traditionally, the complete French dinner includes an *apéritif* (pre-dinner drink), an *entrée* (appetizer), a *plat* (main course), salad, cheese, dessert, fruits, coffee, and a *digestif* (after-dinner drink). The French generally take wine with their meals; *boisson comprise* entitles you to a free drink (usually wine) with your meal. For an occasional 90F spree you can have a marvelous meal.

In restaurants, fixed-price three-course meals (called *menus*) generally begin at 60F. Service is usually included (*service compris*). Be careful when ordering *à la carte*; *l'addition* (the check) may exceed your weekly budget. Do as the French do: go from one specialty shop to another to assemble a picnic, or find an outdoor market (*marché*). Cafés are a forum for long chats, but you pay for the right to sit and watch the world go by: drinks and food are often 10-30% more if served in the dining room (*salle*) or outside (*sur la terrasse*) rather than at the bar (*comptoir*).

Boulangeries, pâtisseries, and *confiseries* tempt with bread, pastries, and candy, respectively. *Fromageries* and *crémeries* present an astonishing array of cheeses. *Charcuteries* sell meats. For supermarket shopping, look for **Carrefour, Casino, Monoprix, Prisunic, Stoc,** and **Rallye.** The many local markets (*marchés*) are picturesque, animated, and often offer better quality than supermarkets.

■ Paris

France is often described as *Paris et la Province*—Paris and the provinces, Paris and everything else. Like New York or London, the city is a bit self-absorbed, but for good reason; few cities are so beautiful and alive, and none do it like Paris does. From tiny alleys hiding the world's best bakeries to broad avenues flaunting the highest of *haute couture,* from the old stone of Notre-Dame Cathedral to the metal and plastic of the Centre Pompidou, from street performers to the *Comédie Francaise*, Paris presents itself as a city that has always tried hard and succeeded. But as Parisians know and visitors soon learn, Paris is much more than its aesthetic delights. Seductive, arch, and sassy, the real Paris lies in the *joie de vivre* and—yes—romance that seem to gush from the Seine and soak all who cross its bridges. While it is possible to go to Paris and neither fall in love nor write a novel, let yourself be carried away. With the right attitude, you can get away with almost anything.

For dazzling, detailed, definitive coverage of Paris and its environs, pick up a copy of *Let's Go: Paris 1999.*

ORIENTATION AND PRACTICAL INFORMATION

Flowing languidly from east to west, the Seine River bisects the heart of Paris. Two islands in the Seine, the **Ile de la Cité** and **Ile St-Louis,** form the geographical center of the city. The rest of Paris spreads onto two banks—the renowned **Rive Gauche** (Left Bank) to the south, and the **Rive Droite** (Right Bank) to the north. By the time of Louis XIV, the city had grown to 20 *quartiers.* Haussmann's 19th-century reconstructions shifted their boundaries but kept the number, dividing Paris into 20 *arrondissements* (districts) which spiral clockwise like a snail's shell around the **Louvre.** In the majority of *Let's Go* listings, the *arrondissement* is included; thus 8ème signifies the *huitième,* or eighth, *arrondissement. Arrondissements* correspond only roughly to the original neighborhoods. The Right Bank starts with the **Louvre-Palais Royal** area in the 1er; the northwest 2ème and southwest 9ème comprise the **Opéra** district. The **Marais** overlaps the 3ème and the 4ème, while **Bastille** encompasses the southern 11ème and the eastern 4ème. **République** refers to the northern 11ème and the western 3ème and 10ème; **Montmartre** is in the 18ème. **Montparnasse** rides the border of the 14ème and 15ème. On the Left Bank, the **Latin Quarter** takes up the 5ème and 6ème; **St-Germain-des-Prés** is in the 6ème; and the **Tour Eiffel** area is the 7ème. For further detail, see the **Sights** section. If you get lost while roaming around, remember that Paris metro stops usually have a detailed neighborhood map posted near the exits or ticket counters. Refer also to this book's **color maps** of the city.

Flights: Most transatlantic flights land at **Aéroport Roissy-Charles de Gaulle,** 23km northeast of Paris. As a rule, terminal 2 serves Air France and its affiliates (for 24hr. English language passenger info, call 01 48 62 22 80). The cheapest, fastest way to get to town is by public transportation. Roissy Rail runs to central Paris; take the free shuttle bus from Aérogare 1, gate 28; Aérogare 2A, gate 5; Aérogare 2B, gate 6; or Aérogare 2D, gate 6 to the Roissy train station, and ride the RER B3 to the city (45min., 47F includes transfer to metro). **Aéroport d'Orly** (tel. 01 49 75 15 15), 12km south of Paris, handles charters and many European flights. From Orly Sud, gate H or gate I, platform 1; or Orly Ouest, arrival level gate F, take the free shuttle bus to Orly train station and the RER C2 to central Paris (30min., 30F).

Trains: Buy **SNCF** tickets at one of Paris's main stations. Guard your valuables and don't buy tickets from anyone except the uniformed personnel in the booths. **Gare du Nord** covers northern France, Belgium, Britain, the Netherlands, Scandinavia, much of the former USSR, and northern Germany. To: Amsterdam (5hr., 366F), Brussels (2hr., 220F), Cologne (5-6hr., 332F), Copenhagen (16hr., 1343F), and London (by the Eurostar chunnel, 2hr., 360-740F). **Gare de l'Est** for eastern France, Austria, Luxembourg, southern Germany, Hungary, and northern Switzerland. To Zurich (6hr., 412F). **Gare de Lyon** for southern France, parts of Switzerland, Italy, and Greece. To Geneva (3½hr., 498F) and Rome (12hr., 630F). **Gare d'Austerlitz** for the Loire Valley, southwestern France, Spain, and Portugal. To Barcelona (9hr., 600F) and Madrid (12-13hr., 600F). **Gare St-Lazare** for Normandy. To Rouen (1½hr., 102F). **Gare de Montparnasse** for Brittany and the TGV to southwestern France. All train stations are stops on metro lines.

Buses: Most international buses arrive at **Gare Routière Internationale,** 28 av. du Général de Gaulle, Bagnolet (tel. 01 49 72 51 51). M: Gallieni. **Hoverspeed Voyages** runs buses to England (reservations tel. 0800 90 17 77). Its Paris terminal is at 165 av. de Clichy, 17ème (tel. 01 40 25 22 00). M: Porte du Clichy.

FRANCE

Public Transportation: The Paris subway, **Métropolitain** or **Métro (M)**, is speedy and efficient. Lines are numbered but referred to by their final destinations; connections are called *correspondences.* Tickets to anywhere within the city cost 8F; a *carnet* of 10 is 46F. Ticket windows close as early as 10pm, so keep extras. *Hold onto your ticket* until you exit the metro. If caught without one, you must pay a hefty fine. Special passes include the *Paris Visite* tourist ticket, which is valid for unlimited travel on bus, metro, and RER, and discounts on sightseeing trips, bicycle rentals, etc. (2 days 70F, 3 days 105F, 5 days 165F). *Formule 1* lasts one day and covers the metro, RER, and bus lines (30F). The weekly *(hebdomadaire)* **Coupon Vert** allows unlimited travel (starting on the first day of the week) but must be accompanied by the ID-style **Carte Orange**. To get your *carte orange,* bring an ID photo to the ticket counter and then buy your swanky *coupon vert* (75F). Changing to and getting *off* the **RER** (Réseau Express Régional—commuter train to the suburbs, express subway within central Paris) require sticking your validated (and uncrumpled) ticket into a turnstile. Watch the signboards next to the RER tracks and check that your stop is lit up before riding. Metro service runs roughly 5:30am-12:30am. The *Principes de Tarification* poster in the center of each station gives each line's last train. **Buses** use the same 8F tickets (which the driver sells), but tickets are only good for one ride and a transfer requires a new ticket. Validate tickets in the machine by the driver. Buses run 7am-8:30pm, *Autobus du Soir* until 12:30am, and *Noctambus* (3-4 tickets) run 1:30-5:30am to the *portes* (city exits) from the Châtelet stop. Refer to this book's **color maps** of Paris' transit network.

Taxis: Cab stands are located near train stations and major bus stops. 3-person max. Taxis are pricey (13F plus 4-8F per km), and even pricier if you don't speak French and/or are an out-of-towner. The meter starts running when you phone (tel. 01 47 39 47 39, 01 45 85 85 85, or 01 41 27 27 27).

Hitchhiking: Traffic at *portes* (city exits) is too heavy for cars to safely stop. **Allostop-Provoya**, 8 rue Rochambeau, 9*ème* (tel. 01 53 20 42 42). M: Cadet. Matches folks with drivers heading in the same direction. Geneva 177F. Frankfurt about 186F. Open M-F 9am-7:30pm, Sa 9am-1pm and 2-6pm.

Tourist Offices: Bureau d'Accueil Central, 127 av. des Champs-Elysées, 8*ème* (tel. 01 49 52 53 54). M: Charles-de-Gaulle-Etoile. English-speaking and mobbed in summer. Open Apr.-Oct. daily 9am-8pm; Nov.-Mar. M-Sa 9am-8pm, Su 11am-6pm. **Branches** at Gare du Nord (open May-Oct.), Gare de Lyon (open all year), the Eiffel Tower (open May-Sept.), Orly and Roissy-Charles de Gaule Airports. **Tourist Information,** tel. 01 49 52 53 56 (English). Recorded list of the week's big events.

Budget Travel: Accueil des Jeunes en France (AJF), 119 rue St-Martin, 4*ème* (tel. 01 42 77 87 80), across from the Centre Pompidou. M: Rambuteau. Discount student plane, train, and bus tickets; also ISICs. Staff will book rooms in Paris hotels and hostels for a 10F fee. Open M-Sa 10am-6:45pm. Also at 139 bd. St-Michel, 5*ème* (tel. 01 43 54 95 86). M: Port-Royal. Open M-Th 10am-12:30pm and 1:45-6pm, F 10:30am-12:30pm and 1:45-6pm. **Council Travel,** 1 pl. Odéon, 6*ème* (tel. 01 44 41 89 89). M: Odéon. English-speaking budget travel service for those under 26. Books international flights and student train tickets, as well as selling guidebooks and ISICs. BIJ/Eurotrain tickets. Open M-F 9am-7pm, Sa 9:30am-2:30pm.

Embassies: Australia, 4 rue Jean-Rey, 15*ème* (tel. 01 40 59 33 00; fax 01 40 59 33 10). M: Bir-Hakeim. Open M-F 9am-6pm. **Canada,** 35 av. Montaigne, 8*ème* (tel. 01 44 43 29 00). M: Franklin-Roosevelt or Alma-Marceau. Open M-F 9am-5pm. **Ireland,** 12 av. Foch, 16*ème* (tel. 01 44 17 67 48). M: Argentine. Open 9:30am-noon. **New Zealand,** 7ter rue Léonard de Vinci, 16*ème* (tel. 01 45 00 24 11). M: Victor-Hugo. Open M-F 9am-1pm and 2-5:30pm. **South Africa,** 59 quai d'Orsay, 7*ème* (tel. 01 53 59 23 23). M: Invalides. Open M-F 9am-noon. **U.K.,** 35 rue du Faubourg-St-Honoré, 8*ème* (tel. 01 44 51 31 00). M: Concorde. Open M-F 9:30am-12:30pm and 2:30-5pm. **U.S.,** 2 av. Gabriel, 8*ème* (tel. 01 43 12 22 22). M: Concorde. Open M-F 9am-6pm.

Currency Exchange: Hotels, train stations, and airports offer poor rates but have long hours; Gare de Lyon, Gare du Nord, and both airports are open from 6:30am until 10:30-11:30pm. MC and Visa work in most **ATMs;** check for stickers saying **CB/VISA** (Carte Bleue; for Visa) or **EC** (Eurocard; for MC). **AmEx** works in ATMs at **Crédit Lyonnais** banks. **Cirrus** cards work in **Crédit Mutuel** and **Crédit Agricole** ATMs. The **PLUS** system works in most Visa ATMs. Institutions supporting

FRANCE

Paris: Accommodations

SEE COLOR INSERTS FOR MORE PARIS MAPS

MM Aloha Hostel
R Auberge Internationale des Jeunes
O Auberge de Jeunesse "Jules Ferry" (HI)
U Castex Hôtel
GG CISP "Kellerman"
S CISP "Ravel"
HH FIAP Jean-Monnet
V Grand Hôtel Jeanne d'Arc
RR Grand Hôtel Lévêque
X Henri IV
FF Hôtel des Alliés
Z Hôtel des Argonauts
E Hôtel Beauharnais
K Hôtel Bellevue et du Chariot d'Or

P Hôtel de Belfort
KK Hôtel de Blois
II Hôtel de Chevreuse
AA Hôtel d'Esmeralda
DD Hôtel Gay Lussac
BB Hôtel Gerson
W Hôtel des Jeunes (MIJE)
G Hôtel Lion d'Or
SS Hôtel Malar
H Hôtel Montpensier
Y Hôtel Nesle
N Hôtel de Nevers
JJ Hôtel du Parc
M Hôtel Picard
PP Hôtel Printemps
J Hôtel de Roubaix
L Hôtel du Séjour

F Hôtel Vivienne
T Mistral Hôtel
LL Ouest Hôtel
I Paris Louvre
CC Paris Quartier Latin
OO Practic Hôtel
Q Résidence Bastille
C Résidence Hôtel des Trois Poussins
QQ Royal Phare Hôtel
NN Three Ducks Hostel
A UCJF (Union Chrétienne de Jeunes Filles, YWCA)
B Village Hostel
D Woodstock Hostel
EE Young and Happy (Y&H) Hostel

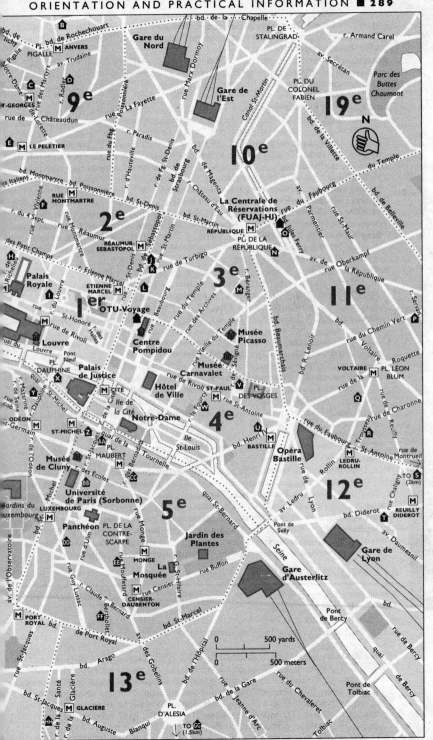

PLUS are: **Crédit Commercial de France, Banque Populaire, Union de Banque à Paris, Point Argent, Banque Nationale de Paris, Crédit du Nord, Gie Osiris,** and ATMs in many **post offices.**

American Express: 11 rue Scribe, 9ème (tel. 01 47 77 77 07), across from the back of the Opéra. M: Opéra. Middling rates, long lines. Receives moneygrams and holds mail for cardholders or those with AmEx Traveler's Checks; otherwise 5F per inquiry. English spoken. Open M-F 9am-6pm, Sa 9am-6:30pm.

Lost Property: Bureau des Objets Trouvés, 36 rue des Morillons, 15ème (tel. 01 55 76 20 20). M: Convention. No info given by phone. Open July-Aug. M-Th 8:30am-5pm; Sept.-June M and W 8:30am-5pm, Tu and Th 8:30am-8pm.

Bookstores: Shakespeare and Co., 37 rue de la Bûcherie, 5ème, across the Seine from Nôtre-Dame. M: St-Michel. No relation to Sylvia Beach's 1920s bookstore, but a quirky, wide-ranging selection of new and used books. Open daily noon-midnight. **Gibert Jeune,** 5 pl. St-Michel, 5ème. M: St-Michel. Best bookstore in town; books in all languages for all tastes. Open M-Sa 9:30am-7:30pm.

Gay and Lesbian Services: Centre Gai et Lesbien, 3 rue Keller, 11ème (tel. 01 43 57 21 47 or 01 43 57 75 95). M: Ledru Rollin. Info hub of all gay services and associations in Paris. English spoken. Open M-Sa noon-8pm, Su 2-7pm. **Les Mots à la Bouche,** 6 rue Ste-Croix-de-la-Bretonnerie, 4ème (tel. 01 42 78 88 30). M: St-Paul or Hôtel-de-Ville. A gay/lesbian bookstore with info on current activities and events. Open M-Sa 11am-11pm, Su 2-8pm.

Public Baths: Beat the high cost of hotel showers at 8 rue des Deux Ponts, 4ème. M: Pont-Marie. Showers 8F, with soap and towel around 16F. Clean and popular. Open Th noon-7pm, F-Sa 7am-5pm, Su 8am-noon.

Emergencies: Ambulance, tel. 15. **Fire,** tel. 18. **Poison,** tel. 01 40 37 04 04.

Police: tel. 17. Call the operator (tel. 12) to find the closest *arrondissement* police station. Note: French cops have not been called *gendarmes* since 1947.

Crises: SOS Friendship (tel. 01 47 23 80 80). For depressed, lonely English-speakers. Open daily 3-11pm. **Rape, SOS Viol** (tel. 0 800 05 95 95). Call free anywhere in France for counseling (medical and legal, too). Open M-F 10am-6pm.

24-hour Pharmacies: Pharmacie Dhéry, 84 av. des Champs-Elysées, 8ème (tel. 01 45 62 02 41). M: George V. **Grande Pharmacie Daumesnil,** 6 pl. Félix-Eboué, 12ème (tel. 01 43 43 19 03). M: Daumesnil. Visible as you exit the metro.

Medical Assistance: Hôpital Franco-Britannique de Paris, 3 rue Barbès, in the suburb of Levallois-Perret (tel. 01 46 39 22 22). M: Anatole-France. English-speaking doctors of good repute. **Hôpital Americain,** 63 bd. Victor Hugo, Neuilly (tel. 01 46 41 25 25), also in the 'burbs. M: Porte Maillot, then bus 82 to the end of the line. More expensive. Blue Cross accepted; fill out the forms first. Dental service.

Post Office: 52 rue du Louvre, 1er. M: Châtelet-les-Halles. *Poste Restante.* Open daily 7:30am-6:30pm. For postal info, call 01 40 28 20 40. For urgent telegrams and calls, dial 01 40 28 20 00. **Postal Code:** Formed by adding the *arrondissement* to the number 750 (e.g., the code for 3ème is 75003).

Internet Access: See **Café Orbital** and **Hammam Café** in **Cafés,** p. 297.

Telephones: Paris has as many phones as lovers. Buy a *télécarte* at post offices, metro stations, and *tabacs;* coin-operated phones are scarce. To call to or from anywhere in France, dial the ten digit number. All Paris numbers begin with 01.

ACCOMMODATIONS

If at all possible, make a reservation *before* coming to Paris, but if you haven't yet done so, don't panic. Tourist offices (see **Tourist Offices,** p. 287) can book rooms, although the lines are usually long and the selections are not the cheapest. Try calling around or visit one of these booking services:

La Centrale de Réservations (FUAJ-HI), 4 bd. Jules Ferry, 11ème (tel. 01 43 57 02 60; fax 01 40 21 79 92). M: République. Follow the rue du Faubourg du Temple away from pl. de la République until you reach the park-like entity which divides bd. Jules Ferry in 2. Cross to the far side and turn right. One of the best ways to secure a cheap bed (113-125F) in Paris. Same-day reservations. The earlier you show up the better. Open M-Sa 9am-6pm. If closed, the 24hr. reception at the Jules Ferry Hostel, 2 doors down, may be able to help you.

OTU-Voyage (Office du Tourisme Universitaire), 119 rue St. Martin, 4ème (tel. 01 40 12 12 29). Across the pedestrian mall from the Pompidou. Even in the busiest months, OTU-Voyage guarantees "decent and low-cost lodging" in Résidence Bastille and hotels for same-day reservation and immediate use. You must pay the full price of the *foyer* room when making your reservation, even before seeing the room. Employees speak English. 10F service charge. Open M-F 9:30am-7pm and Sa 10am-noon and 1:15-5:30pm.

Hostels and Foyers

Paris's hostels skip many standard restrictions—sleep sheets, curfews, and the like—but they do tend to have (flexible) maximum stays. The hostels below are open daily and include showers unless otherwise noted. The six HI hostels in the city proper are for members only. The rest of Paris's dorm-type lodgings are either private hostels or *foyers* (student dorms; usually quieter and more private than regular hostels).

CISP "Kellerman," 17 bd. Kellerman, 13ème (tel. 01 44 16 37 38; fax 01 44 16 37 39). M: Porte d'Italie. Cross the street and turn right. Ultra-modern and impeccably clean. Laundry. Dorms 113-138F; singles 156-186F; doubles 310F. Breakfast included (served 7-9:30am). Lockout 1:30-6:30am. Reserve ahead.

Village Hostel, 20 rue d'Orsel, 18ème (tel. 01 42 64 22 02; fax 01 42 64 22 04). M: Anvers. Go up the hill on Steinkerque and turn right. Newly renovated with beautiful interiors, furniture, and views of Sacré Coeur. Toilet and shower in every room. Dorms 117-127F; doubles 147F. Curfew 2am. Call ahead, even if same day.

Woodstock Hostel, 48 rue Rodier, 9ème (tel. 01 48 78 87 76). M: Anvers. Walk against traffic on pl. Anvers, go right on av. Trudaine and then left on rue de Rodier. Conveniently located. Spotless rooms and relatively peaceful atmosphere. Clean hall showers. Summer: dorms 87F; doubles 194F. Off-season: 75F; 174F. In summer, call or stop by in the morning; call ahead in winter.

Hôtel des Jeunes (MIJE), 6 rue de Le Fourcy, 4ème (tel. 01 42 74 23 45; fax 01 40 27 81 64), books "Le Fourcy," "Le Fauconnier," and "Maubuisson," 3 small, charming hostels in old Marais aristocratic residences. Ages 18-30. Dorms 125F; singles 198F; doubles 304F; triples 401F. Breakfast included. 7-day max. stay. Reception 7am-1am. Lockout noon-4pm. Curfew 1am. Quiet after 10pm.

Auberge de Jeunesse "Jules Ferry" (HI), 8 bd. Jules Ferry, 11ème (tel. 01 43 57 55 60; fax 01 43 14 82 09). M: République. Walk east on rue du Faubourg du Temple and turn right on the far side of bd. Jules Ferry. Wonderfully located. Clean, large rooms with bunk beds. Friendly party atmosphere. Single-sex lodging but can accommodate couples. Dorms 120F; doubles 250F. Lockers 5F. Sheets 5F. Wash 20F, dry 10F. Flexible 4-night max. stay. Reception open 24hr. Lockout 10am-2pm. No curfew. No reservations, so arrive by 7am, especially in summer.

Auberge Internationale des Jeunes, 10 rue Trousseau, 11ème (tel. 01 47 00 62 00; fax 01 47 00 33 16). M: Ledru-Rollin. Walk east on rue du Faubourg St-Antoine then turn left. Lively atmosphere, lots of backpackers in the sunny breakfast room. Very clean, cramped rooms. Friendly staff. Common rooms downstairs. Safebox for valuables. Luggage storage. Mar.-Oct. 91F per person; Nov.-Feb. 81F per person. Breakfast (served 7-9:30am) included. Sheets 5F. Lockout 10am-3pm. Show up by 8am.

UCJF (Union Chrétienne de Jeunes Filles, YWCA), 22 rue Naples, 8ème (tel. 01 53 04 37 47; fax 01 53 04 37 54). M: Europe. Take rue de Constantinople and turn left. Organized, homey environment for women 18-26 only. June-Aug. 2-day min. stay. 30F YWCA membership fee and a 50F processing fee for stays over a week. Singles 155F; doubles 270F; triples 405F. Weekly: singles 950F; doubles 1500F. Breakfast and dinner included. Kitchen and laundry. 200F key deposit. Reception M-F 8am-12:30am, Sa-Su 9am-12:30pm and 1:30pm-12:30am. Flexible curfew 12:30am. Reserve with deposit. Another location at 168 rue Blomet, 15ème (tel. 01 53 53 63 00; fax 01 53 53 63 12). M: Convention. Men should contact the YMCA *foyer* **Union Chrétienne de Jeunes Gens,** 14 rue de Trévise, 9ème (tel. 01 47 70 90 94).

Centre International de Paris (BVJ) runs a chain of friendly hostels. Reserve well in advance and confirm, especially in summer, or check for available rooms around 9am. **Paris Louvre,** 20 rue J.-J. Rousseau, 1er (tel. 01 53 00 90 90; fax 01 53 00 90 91). M: Louvre. Take rue du Louvre away from river, turn left on rue St-Honoré and then right. 120F, no singles. Breakfast included. *Call if you'll be late.* **Paris Quart-**

ier Latin, 44 rue des Bernardins, 5ème (tel. 01 43 29 34 80; fax 01 53 00 90 91). M: Maubert-Mutualité. Walk with traffic on bd. St-Germain then turn right. Immense and ultra-modern. Dorms 120F; singles 130F. Showers in rooms. Lockers 10F. Reception 24hr. Check-in by 2:30pm. Reserve in advance or arrive by 9am.

FIAP Jean-Monnet, 30 rue Cabanis, 14ème (tel. 01 45 89 89 15; fax 01 45 81 63 91). M: Glacière. From metro, turn left off bd. Auguste-Blanqui onto rue de la Santé, then right. A large, fast-moving tourist machine. Well-furnished, impeccable rooms. Laundry room, piano bar, and restaurant. Dorms 131F; singles 281F; doubles 368F; triples 483F; quads 644F. Curfew 2am. Reserve 2-4 weeks ahead.

Centre International du Séjour de Paris: CISP "Ravel," 6 av. Maurice Ravel, 12ème (tel. 01 44 75 60 00; fax 01 43 44 45 30). M: Porte de Vincennes. Walk east on cours de Vincennes, take the 1st right on bd. Soult, left on rue Jules Lemaître, then right. Large rooms, art exhibits, and access to outdoor pool (25F). Self-serve restaurant. Dorms 138F; singles 186F; doubles 312F. Breakfast included. Flexible 3-day max. stay. Reception 7:30am-1:30am. Reserve a few days ahead.

Résidence Bastille, 151 av. Ledru-Rollin, 11ème (tel. 01 43 79 53 86; fax 01 43 79 35 63). M: Voltaire. Walk across the pl. Léon Blum and head south onto av. Ledru-Rollin. More subdued than most. Ages 18-35 (flexible). Flexible curfew 1am. Dorms Mar.-Oct. 120F; Nov.-Feb. 110F; 10% ISIC and GO25 discount. Reception 7am-10pm. Lockout noon-3pm. No phone reservations; write or fax.

Three Ducks Hostel, 6 pl. Etienne Pernet, 15ème (tel. 01 48 42 04 05; fax 01 48 42 99 99). M: Félix Faure. Walk against traffic on the left side of the church. One of Paris's rowdiest summer hangouts for young backpackers, a 15min. walk from the Eiffel Tower. Brand new kitchen, lockers, and renovated dorm-style rooms for 2-8 people. Mar.-Oct. 107F; Nov.-Feb. 87F. Sheets 15F. Towels 5F. Breakfast included. Curfew 2am. Reservations with 1 night's credit card deposit.

Young and Happy (Y&H) Hostel, 80 rue Mouffetard, 5ème (tel. 01 45 35 09 53; fax 01 47 07 22 24). M: Monge. From the metro, cross rue Gracieuse and take rue Ortolan to rue Mouffetard. Clean, cheerful rooms in the heart of a raucous student quarter. Doubles 254F; quads 428F. Breakfast included. Sheets 15F. Lockout 11am-5pm. Curfew 2am. Reserve with 1 night's deposit by mail (by phone only on the day you arrive); otherwise show up at 8am.

Aloha Hostel, 1 rue Borromée, 15ème (tel. 01 42 73 03 03; fax 01 42 73 14 14). M: Volontaires. Walk against traffic on rue de Vaugirard, then turn right on rue Borromée. Centrally located and colonized by English-speaking backpackers. Apr.-Oct. dorms 97-107F; Nov.-Mar. 107-127F. Reserve by credit card or arrive by 8am.

Hotels

Among Parisian budget accommodations, hotels may be the most practical for the majority of travelers. There are no curfews, no school groups, total privacy, and often concerned managers—features hostels and *foyers* can't offer. Groups of two, three, and four may find it more economical to stay in a hotel. Note that there are usually rules against bringing food into your room. Expect to pay at least 150F for a single, and 200 to 400F for a double. In inexpensive hotels, few rooms come with private bath and hall showers can cost between 15 and 25F per use. Rooms fill quickly after morning check-out (generally 10am-noon), so arrive early or reserve ahead. Most hotels accept reservations and generally require one night's deposit payable by credit card. Instead of parading yourself and your bags around town all morning, call first.

Louvre-Palais Royal: 1er and 2ème Arrondissements

Central to the **Louvre,** the **Seine,** the **Faubourg St-Honoré,** and the ritzy **Place Vendôme,** this area still has a few less expensive hotels. Avoid rue St-Denis.

Henri IV, 25 pl. Dauphine, 1er (tel. 01 43 54 44 53). M: Cité. Walk toward the Conciergerie, turn right on bd. du Palais, left on quai de l'Horloge, then left at the front of the Conciergerie onto pl. Dauphine. Last outpost of cheap accommodations on Ile de la Cité. Inconvenient 1st-floor toilets. Singles 120-125F; doubles 150-265F; triples 240-260F; quads 280F. Reserve 2 months ahead.

Hôtel Lion d'Or, 5 rue de la Sourdière (tel. 01 42 60 79 04; fax 01 42 60 09 14). M: Tuileries. Walk down rue du 29 Juillet away from the park, right on rue St-Honoré, then left. Quiet, simple, carpeted rooms, with phones and TVs. English-speaking staff. Singles 230-300F; doubles 380-420F; extra bed 60F. Breakfast 35F. 5% off for stays of more than 3 nights.

Hôtel Montpensier, 12 rue de Richelieu (tel. 01 42 96 28 50; fax 01 42 86 02 70). M: Palais-Royal. Walk around the left side of the Palais-Royal to rue de Richelieu (directly ahead). Spacious, with clean rooms, most with showers. Singles and doubles 285-400F; extra bed 70F. Breakfast 37F. Shower 25F.

Hôtel Vivienne, 40 rue Vivienne (tel. 01 42 33 13 26; fax 01 40 41 98 19). M: Rue Montmartre. Follow the traffic on bd. Montmartre past the Théâtre des Variétés and turn left on rue Vivienne. Gracious living at budget rates. Singles and doubles, all with shower or bath, 360-440F; 3rd person 30% extra. Breakfast 40F.

The Marais: 3ème and 4ème Arrondissements

Lined with 17th-century mansions, narrow streets, and hidden courtyards, the Marais is home to the **Jewish quarter,** the **Gay Community,** and all that is chic and fabulous.

Hôtel de Roubaix, 6 rue Greneta, 3ème (tel. 01 42 72 89 91; fax 01 42 72 58 79). M: Réaumur-Sébastopol. Walk against traffic on bd. de Sébastopol then turn left. Very clean rooms with shower and toilet, some noisy. Singles 305-330F; doubles 390-410F; triples 415-480F; quads 500F; quints 525F. Breakfast included.

Grand Hôtel Jeanne d'Arc, 3 rue de Jarente, 4ème (tel. 01 48 87 62 11; fax 01 48 87 37 31; http//www.hoteljeannedarc.com). M: St-Paul. Walk against traffic on rue de Rivoli, turn left on rue de Sévigné, then right. Stylish rooms with TV, toilet, and shower. Singles 300-395; doubles 305-490F; triples 530F; quads 590F; extra bed 75F. Breakfast 35F. Reserve 2 months ahead. 2 rooms are wheelchair accessible.

Castex Hôtel, 5 rue Castex, 4ème (tel. 01 42 72 31 52; fax 01 42 72 57 91). M: Bastille. Exit on bd. Henri IV and take the 3rd right. Spotless, quiet rooms. Singles 240-290F; doubles 320-360F; triples 460F; extra bed 70F. Breakfast 25F. Reception 7am-noon. Check-in 1pm. Reserve 2 months ahead with deposit.

Hôtel du Séjour, 36 rue du Grenier St-Lazare, 3ème (tel. 01 48 87 40 36). M: Etienne Marcel. Follow traffic on rue Etienne Marcel which becomes rue Grenier St-Lazare. Under renovation; ask for a new room. Singles 160F; doubles, some with showers, 240-300F; extra bed 150F. Showers 20F. Reception 7am-10:30pm, or call ahead.

Hôtel Bellevue et du Chariot d'Or, 39 rue de Turbigo, 3ème (tel. 01 48 87 45 60; fax 01 48 87 95 04). M: Etienne Marcel. Walk against traffic on rue Turbigo. Belle Epoque elegant. Lovely rooms with toilet, bath, and TV. Singles 310F; doubles 340F; triples 410F; quads 440F. Breakfast 35F. Reserve 2 weeks ahead by fax.

Hôtel Picard, 26 rue de Picardie, 3ème (tel. 01 48 87 53 82; fax 01 48 87 02 56). M: République. Walk down rue du Temple, turn left on rue Béranger, right on rue de Franche-Comté, then left. Tasteful rooms, central location. Singles 200-250F; doubles 240-320F; triples 510F. 10% *Let's Go* discount. Breakfast 30F. Showers 20F. Apr.-Sept. reserve 1 week ahead.

The Latin Quarter: 5ème and 6ème Arrondissements

Revolving around the **Sorbonne** and the **Ecole des Beaux-Arts,** the *Quartier Latin* shelters bookstores, student cafes, cinemas, markets, and nightlife.

Hôtel d'Esmeralda, 4 rue St-Julien-le-Pauvre, 5ème (tel. 01 43 54 19 20; fax 01 40 51 00 68). M: St-Michel. Walk along the Seine on quai St-Michel toward Nôtre-Dame and turn right at parc Viviani. Friendly staff, homey rooms. Singles 160F; doubles 420-490F; triples 550F; quads 600F. Breakfast 40F. No credit cards.

Hôtel des Argonauts, 12 rue de la Huchette, 5ème (tel. 01 43 54 09 82; fax 01 44 07 18 84). M: St-Michel. Walking away from the Seine take the first left off bd. St-Michel. Above a Greek restaurant, but surprisingly quiet, with clean, newly decorated rooms. Singles 255F; doubles 285-360F. Breakfast 25F.

Hôtel Nesle, 7 rue du Nesle, 6ème (tel. 01 43 54 62 41). M: Odéon. Walk up rue de l'Ancienne Comédie, onto rue Dauphine and take a left. Whimsical, warm management. Beautiful Moroccan tiled rooms with showers. Singles 275F; doubles 350-450F. Breakfast included. Laundry. Reservations recommended.

Hôtel des Alliés, 20 rue Berthollet, 5ème (tel. 01 43 31 47 52; fax 01 45 35 13 92). M: Censier-Daubenton. Walk south on rue Monge, turn right onto rue Claude Bernard, then left. Clean and comfy rooms, away from the bustle. Singles and doubles 220-300F. Hall showers 15F. Breakfast 28F.

Hôtel de Chevreuse, 3 rue de Chevreuse, 6ème (tel. 01 43 20 93 16; fax 01 43 21 43 72). M: Vavin. Walk up bd. Montparnasse away from the Eiffel Tower and take a left. Great neighborhood, clean rooms. Singles 220F; doubles 270-330F; triples 510F. Breakfast 32F. Reserve 1 week in advance with credit card.

Hôtel Gerson, 14 rue de la Sorbonne, 5ème (tel. 01 43 54 28 40; fax 01 44 07 13 90). M: Cluny-Sorbonne. Left on bd. St-Michel, left on rue des Ecoles, then right. Fairly spacious rooms are bright and clean. Singles 225-306F; doubles and triples 250-400F. Breakfast 25F. Reserve 3 weeks ahead.

Hôtel Gay Lussac, 29 rue Gay-Lussac, 5ème (tel. 01 43 54 23 96). M: Luxembourg. Creaky floors and spacious, sunny rooms. Singles and doubles 185F; triples 450-480F; quads 580F. Breakfast included. Reserve 2-4 weeks ahead. No credit cards.

Eiffel Tower, Invalides, Musée d'Orsay, Musée Rodin: 7ème Arrondissement

Quieter and more expensive, hotels in this area are indeed close to the **Eiffel Tower,** though the best views of the tower are from further away.

Royal Phare Hôtel, 40 av. de la Motte-Picquet (tel. 01 47 05 57 30; fax 01 45 51 64 41). M: Ecole Militaire. Next to the metro. Blink and you'll miss the small entryway. Small, tidy, colorful rooms with TVs, phones, and hair dryers. Friendly reception. Singles 310-400F; doubles 355-420F; extra bed 100F. Breakfast 32F. Reserve 1 week ahead with 1 night's deposit.

Grand Hôtel Lévêque, 29 rue Cler, 7ème (tel. 01 47 05 49 15; fax 01 45 50 49 36; http://www.interresa.ca/hotel/leveque). M: Ecole Militaire. Walk on av. de la Motte-Picquet then turn left. Completely renovated and aiming for luxury. Singles 250F; doubles 350-420F; triples 515F. Breakfast 30F.

Hôtel Malar, 29 rue Malar, 7ème (tel. 01 45 51 38 46; fax 01 45 55 20 19). M: Latour Maubourg. Follow traffic on bd. de la Tour Maubourg, turn left on rue St. Dominique, then right. Provincial family hotel with inner courtyard. Singles 290-395F; doubles 330-480F; extra bed 100F. Breakfast 32F.

The Opéra: 9ème Arrondissement

The northern part of this district, around **Pigalle** and bd. de Clichy is a red-light district, but the elegant southern half boasts the **Opéra Garnier** and affordable hotels.

Hôtel Beauharnais, 51 rue de la Victoire, 9ème (tel. 01 48 74 71 13). M: le Peletier. Follow traffic on rue de la Victoire and look for flower boxes; there is no hotel sign. Each elegant room is decorated by Mme Bey with antiques and has a shower. Singles and doubles 320F; triples 490F. Breakfast free with *Let's Go.* No credit cards.

Résidence Hôtel des Trois Poussins, 15 rue Clauzel, 9ème (tel. 01 53 32 81 81; fax 01 53 32 81 82). M: St-Georges. Uphill on rue Nôtre-Dame-de-Lorette, right on rue H. Monnier, then right. Clean, well-furnished rooms and studios, all with bath. Singles 360F; doubles 480F; triples 740F. Weekly and monthly rates available. Reserve 2 weeks ahead.

Place de la Bastille and République: 11ème and 12ème Arrondissements

These *arrondissements* offer inexpensive hotels near the Gare de Lyon and the Bastille nightlife. Be careful at night, especially north of the av. de la République.

Hôtel de Nevers, 53 rue de Malte, 11ème (tel. 01 47 00 56 18; fax 01 43 57 77 39). M: République. Down av. de la République and right. Spotless rooms. Singles and doubles 170-260F; triples 310F; quads 380F. Breakfast 25F. Hall showers 20F. Reception 24hr. Reserve 2 weeks ahead by credit card deposit.

Hôtel de Belfort, 37 rue Servan, 11ème (tel. 01 47 00 67 33; fax 01 43 57 97 98). M: Père-Lachaise. Left off rue du Chemin Vert. Functional rooms with showers and toilets. *Let's Go* special: 100F per person (rooms for 2, 3, or 4) and 15F breakfast.

Mistral Hôtel, 3 rue Chaligny, 12ème. (tel. 01 46 28 10 20; fax 01 46 28 69 66). M: Reuilly-Diderot. West on bd. Diderot, then left. One of the best deals in Paris. Spectacularly clean. Singles 205-250F; doubles 210-290F; triples 320F; quads 500F. Breakfast 35F. Hall showers 15F. Reserve 1 week ahead.

Montparnasse: 14ème and 15ème Arrondissements

Areas closest to flashy **bd. du Montparnasse** maintain the vitality that drew Picasso, Sartre, and Hemingway, while adjoining neighborhoods are residential and sedate.

Hôtel de Blois, 5 rue des Plantes, 14ème (tel. 01 45 40 99 48; fax 01 45 40 45 62). M: Mouton-Duvernet. Left onto rue Mouton Duvernet; left at the end. Unquestionably one of the best deals in Paris. Quality decor. Singles and doubles 230-360F; triples 360F. Breakfast 27F. Reserve at least 10 days in advance.

Ouest Hôtel, 27 rue de Gergovie, 14ème (tel. 01 45 42 64 99; fax 01 45 42 46 65). M: Pernety. Against traffic on rue Raymond Losserand, then right. Clean and friendly. Singles and doubles 120-230F. Breakfast 20F. Hall showers 20F.

Hôtel du Parc, 6 rue Jolivet, 14ème (tel. 01 43 20 95 54; fax 01 42 79 82 62). M: Edgar-Quinet. Facing the Tour Montparnasse, turn left on rue de la Gaîté, right on rue du Maine, then right on rue Jolivet. TVs and views of the courtyard or park. Singles and doubles 265; triples 450F. Breakfast 30F. Shower 20F.

Hôtel Printemps, 31 rue du Commerce, 15ème (tel. 01 45 79 83 36; fax 01 45 79 84 88). M: La Motte-Picquet. In a busy neighborhood with shops and restaurants. Clean rooms at hostel prices. Singles and doubles 140-220F. Breakfast 20F. Hall showers 15F. Reserve 3-4 weeks ahead.

Practic Hôtel, 20 rue de l'Ingénieur Keller, 15ème (tel. 01 45 77 70 58; fax 01 40 59 43 75). M: Charles Michels. From pl. Charles Michels, walk up rue Linois, turn left on rue des 4-Frères Peignot, then right. Bright, clean, elegant rooms worthy of Sheraton. Singles and doubles 260-390F; triples 460F. Breakfast 39F.

FOOD

With *pâtisseries* on every corner, daily open-air markets, and a history of *haute cuisine*, strong cheeses, and fine wine, dining is a high-profile, high-quality affair. In addition to traditional French bistros, Paris is filled with wonderful and inexpensive Vietnamese, North African, and Middle Eastern restaurants. **CROUS (Centre Regional des Oeuvres Universitaires et Scolaires),** 30 av. Georges Bernanos, 5ème, has info on university restaurants (tel. 01 40 51 37 10; M: Port-Royal; open Tu-Sa 11:30am-1:30pm and 6-8pm). Every *arrondissement* has a morning outdoor market; ask at your hotel for the nearest one. When assembling a picnic, visit the specialty shops of the **Marché Montorgueil,** 2ème, **rue Mouffetard,** 5ème, and the **Marché Bastille** on bd. Richard-Lenoir (M: Bastille; open Th and Su 7am-1:30pm).

Restaurants

Louvre-Palais Royal: 1er and 2ème Arrondissements

Near the Louvre, the small streets of the 2ème teem with traditional bistros. Cheaper options surround Les Halles, which, though lively by day, can be sketchy at night.

Le Vieil Ecu, 166 rue St-Honoré, 1er. M: Palais-Royal. Walk toward the Palais-Royal and turn right. Everything you'd expect from a Parisian restaurant: checkered tablecloths and exposed beams. Bistro *menu.* Live music upstairs M-Sa nights. Open M-Sa 11:30am-3pm and 6:30-11pm.

Le Loup Blanc, 42 rue Tiquetonne, 2ème. M: Etienne Marcel. Walk against traffic on rue de Turbigo and turn left on rue Tiquetonne. The charming owner-couple offers huge portions of grilled and marinated entrées. Sunday brunch 75-95F. Open M-Sa noon-3pm and 8-11:30pm, Su brunch 11am-5pm.

Aux Lyonnais, 32 rue St-Marc, 2ème. M: Bourse. Walk with traffic on rue Vivienne and turn left. Copious, traditional French food like *caille rôtie* (roast quail; 75F) or *lapin aux échalotes* (rabbit with shallots; 75F) amid antique mirrors. Ideal for a romantic dinner. Open M-F 11:30am-3pm and 6:30-11:45pm, Sa 7pm-midnight.

FRANCE

Ile St-Louis and The Marais: 3ème and 4ème Arrondissements

The **Ile St-Louis** is charming but not cheap. The Marais offers chic bistros, kosher delis, and gay cafes. **Rue de Rosier** transects the Marais's traditional Jewish quarter.

Les Fous de l'Isle, 33 rue des Deux-Ponts, on Ile St-Louis. M: Pont Marie. A mellow cafe-bistro for the young local crowd. Main courses 60-98F. Open Tu-F noon-midnight, Sa 6pm-midnight, Su noon-4pm for brunch.

Le Temps des Cerises, 31 rue de la Cerisaie. M: Bastille or Sully-Morland. From bd. Henri IV, turn right. A neighborhood bistro, cafe, and wine bar run situated in the former banquet hall of a Celestine convent. Hearty 3-course lunch *menu* (68F), *pot au feu* (a rich beef stew; 65F), sandwiches (12F), and coffee (10F). Open for lunch M-F 11:30am-2:30pm; bar open M-F 7:45am-8pm.

Chez Jo Goldenberg, 7 rue des Rosiers. M: St-Paul. In the heart of the Marais's Jewish quarter, the famous Goldenberg's (est. 1920) serves **kosher** soups (20-32F), *blini* (18F), beef goulash (80F), borscht (25F per L), gefilte fish (45F), and bagels (6F). Open daily noon-midnight.

The Latin Quarter: 5ème and 6ème Arrondissements

Affordable French, Greek, and Lebanese restaurants line **rue Mouffetard, rue de la Huchette,** and **rue du Pot-de-Fer.** In the 6ème, tiny restaurants with rock-bottom *menus* crowd the area bounded by bd. St-Germain, bd. St-Michel, and the Seine.

Le Jardin des Pâtes, 4 rue Lacépède, 5ème. M: Jussieu. From the metro, walk up rue Linné and turn right. This bright Mediterranean restaurant dishes organic gourmet pastas, like *pâtes de seigle* (ham, white wine, and sharp *comté* cheese; 56F). Open daily noon-2:30pm and 7-11pm.

Restaurant Perraudin, 157 rue St-Jacques, 5ème. M: Luxembourg. Take rue Collard to rue St-Jacques. Burgundy and wood interior and classic French dishes like *sautée d'agneau aux flageolets* (sauteed lamb with white beans; 59F). Open Tu-F noon-2:15pm and 7:30-10:15pm, M and Sa 7:30-10:15pm.

L' Estrapade, 15 rue de l'Estrapade, 5ème. M: Luxembourg. From pl. du Panthéon turn right on rue Clotaire, then left. Near the Panthéon, this tiny *fin de siècle* bistro specializes in French cuisine like *fricassée de volaille* and *soupe à l'oignon.* Open Su-F noon-2:30pm and 7-11pm, Sa 7-11pm.

Crêperie Saint Germain, 33 rue St-André-des-Arts, 6ème. M: St-Michel. This *crêperie* offers live jazz and wheat-flour *crêpes noirs,* and sweet dessert *crêpes* (26-56F). A 49F *menu* (served until 6pm) includes 2 *crêpes* and a glass of bubbly apple spiked *cidre.* Open daily noon-1am.

Crémerie Restaurant Polidor, 41 rue Monsieur-le-Prince, 6ème. M: Cluny-Sorbonne. Walk away from the river, turn right on rue Racine, then left. Rimbaud, Verlaine, Hemingway, and Joyce came here for bistro cuisine like *escargots* (74F). Open M-Su noon-2:30pm and 7pm-12:30am.

Eiffel Tower and Champ de Mars: 7ème Arrondissement

The 7ème's restaurants are a bit pricey, but make for a great splurge.

La Varangue, 27 rue Angereau. M: Ecole Militaire. From av. de la Bourdonnais, turn right on rue de Grenelle, then left. Close to the Eiffel Tower, with an intimate bistro menu. Open M-F noon-10pm, Sa 6:30-10pm.

Le Club des Poètes, 30 rue de Bourgogne. M: Varenne. Walk north on av. Bosquet ad turn left. Dine on simple bistro fare while the owners read Rimbaud and other French poets. Dinner 100-150F. Open M-Sa noon-3pm and 8pm-1am.

Fontaine de Mars, 129 rue St-Dominique. M: Ecole Militaire. A splurge, but worth every *centime* for goat cheese, roast a duck, and marinated plums in Armagnac (67-95F). Open daily noon-3pm and 7:30-11pm.

Opéra, Bastille, and République: 9ème, 10ème, and 11ème Arrondissements

The 10ème has a high concentration of ethnic restaurants: **Passage Brady** overflows with Indian eateries. Restaurants in the 11ème fill to capacity with young, chic regulars who stay through the night; try to reserve ahead.

Haynes Bar, 3 rue Clauzel, 9ème (tel. 01 48 78 40 63). M: St-Georges. Uphill on rue Nôtre-Dame-de-Lorette, turn right on rue Monnier, then right. Since 1947, a center for African-American expats like Armstrong, Baldwin, and Wright. Generous portions of fried chicken, BBQ, and cornbread (70-100F). Jazz on F nights. Open Sept.-Aug. Tu-Sa 7:30pm-12:30am.

Paris-Dakar, 95 rue du Faubourg St-Martin, 10ème (tel. 01 42 08 16 64). M: Gare de l'Est. Senegalese cuisine served with West African charm. Lunch and dinner *menus* (59-179F) feature *tiébou dieune* (fish with rice and veggies). Open Tu-Th and Sa-Su noon-3pm and 7pm-2am, F 7pm-2am.

Au Petit Keller, 13 rue Keller, 11ème. M: Charonne. From rue Charonne, turn left on rue Keller. Hip bistro in the heart of the Bastille. Lunch *menus* 50-70F. Open M-Sa noon-2pm and 7pm-midnight.

A la Banane Ivoirienne, 10 rue de la Forge-Royale, 11ème (tel. 01 43 70 49 90). M: Faidherbe-Chaligny. Walk west on rue du Fbg. St-Antoine and turn right. African prints from the Ivory Coast complement West African specialties like *attieke* and *aloko*. Dinner *menus* (95-140F). Open Tu-Sa 7pm-midnight.

Pause Café, 41 rue de Charonne, 11ème. M: Ledru-Rollin. This ultra-hip bar had a starring role in the recent film *Chacun cherche son chat*. Excellent salads (40-80F) and cheap beer (20F). Open Tu-Sa 8:30am-2am, Su 8:30am-8:30pm.

Montparnasse: 14ème Arrondissement

At the turn of the century, Bretons flocked to Montparnasse bringing their speciality *crêpes*. French bistros, Corsican, African, and Asian restaux also line the 14ème.

La Route du Château, 123 rue du Château. M: Pernety. Walk with traffic on rue Raymond Losserand. The romantic Parisian bistro *par excellence:* soft lighting, lace curtains, and bistro classics like *lapin* (rabbit) sautéed in cider and mustard (80F). Open Tu-Sa noon-2pm and 7pm-midnight.

Crêperie de Josselin, 67 rue du Montparnasse. M: Edgar Quinet. On a street full of *crêperies,* locals come here for *crêpes salées* and *crêpes sucrées* (22-70F). Open Tu-F noon-3pm and 6-11:30pm, Sa-Su noon-midnight.

Sampieru Corsu, 12 rue de l'Amiral Roussin. M: Cambronne. Walk into the pl. Cambronne, turn left on rue de la Croix Nivert, then left. Cheap, copious 3-course *menu* (41F, wine included). Open M-F 11:45am-1:30pm and 6:30-9:30pm.

Montmartre: 18ème Arrondissement

Monmartre's charming bistros line the streets between M: Abbesses and pl. St-Pierre. The touristed cafes on pl. du Tertre are perfect for coffee breaks but pricey for meals.

Chez les Fondues, 17 rue des Trois Frères. M: Abbesses. Walk down rue Yvonne le Tac and turn left. A cross between a cabaret and a mead hall, this restaurant serves only 2 main dishes: *fondue bourguignonne* (meat fondue) and *fondue savoyarde* (cheese fondue) and wine (87F). Open W-M 7pm-2am.

Au Grain de Folie, 24 rue la Vieuville. M: Abbesses. Eating here is like dining in the kitchen of an unpretentious French family. Serves huge portions of vegetarian couscous, hummus, salads and cheese. Main courses 50-70F. Open M-F 12:30-2:30pm and 7-10:30pm, Sa-Su 12:30-2:30pm and 7-11pm.

Chez Claude et Claudine, 94 rue des Martyrs. M: Abbesses. Walk down rue Yvonne le Tac and turn right. This plant-filled restaurant serves large portions of solid, standard French fare like onion soup and *boeuf bourgignon* (79F). Open daily noon-2pm and 6-11:30pm.

Classic, Hip, and Cyber Cafes

French cafes have long been suffused with the glamor of languid leisure time, conjuring images of writers and long afternoons. Popular cafe drinks include coffee, wine, *citron pressé* (freshly squeezed lemon juice), tea, and vast selections of spring, mineral, and soda waters. Cafes also serve affordable light lunches and snacks: a *croque monsieur* (grilled ham-and-cheese sandwich) runs about 15 to 20F. Salads usually cost a bit more. Cafe prices are two-tiered; it's cheaper at the counter (*comptoir* or *zinc*) than in the seating area.

FRANCE

La Closerie des Lilas, 171 bd. du Montparnasse, 6ème. M: Port-Royal. This lovely flower-filled cafe was home to Hemingway (a scene in *The Sun Also Rises* takes place here), Picasso, the Dadaists, and the Surrealists. *Crêpes* (90F). Open daily noon-2:30pm and 7pm-1:30am.

La Coupole, 102 bd. du Montparnasse, 6ème. M: Vavin. La Coupole's Art Deco interior has hosted Lenin, Stravinsky, Hemingway, and Einstein. You can probably still afford coffee (11F) and a *croque monsieur* (28F). Open M-Th 7:30am-2am, F 9:30pm-4am, Sa 3-7pm and 9:30pm-4am.

Les Deux Magots, 6 pl. St-Germain-des-Prés, 6ème. M: St-Germain-des-Prés. Sartre's 2nd-choice cafe and Beauvoir's 1st, it was here that they met. Coffee and pastries (12-24F). Open daily 7am-1:30am.

Café Beaubourg, 100 rue St-Martin, 4ème. M: Hôtel de Ville. This would be your neighborhood cafe if the boy next door was a Calvin Klein model. Coffee 16F. Open daily 8am-1am.

Café de la Mosquée, 39 rue Geoffroy St-Hilaire, 5ème. M: Censier Daubenton. In the Mosquée de Paris, this café offers mint tea (22F) and *Mahgrebin* pastries (10F). Indulge at the *hammam*. Open daily 10am-midnight.

Amnésia Café, 42 rue Vieille du Temple, 4ème. M: Hôtel de Ville. In the heart of the Marais, the Amnésia attracts a gay crowd on Sa nights and a mixed scene for Su brunch (70-130F). Open daily 10am-2am.

Café Orbital, 13 rue du Médicis, 6ème. M: Odéon. France's first cyber cafe offers **Internet access** 1F per min., 55F per hr. Open M-Sa 10am-10pm, Su noon-8pm.

WebBar, 23 rue de Picardie, 3ème. M: République. One of coolest spots to surf the web. **Internet access** 40F per hr., 250F for 10hr.—nerd. Open M-F 8:30am-2am, Sa-Su 11am-2am.

Salons de Thé, Wine Bars, and Pubs

Salons de thé provide tea and low-key refinement, while wine bars are the way to sample good French wine by the glass. Pubs offer nightlife without the cover at clubs.

Angelina's, 226 rue de Rivoli, 1er M: Concorde. Audrey Hepburn's favorite. Afternoon tea (33F) and pastries (6-35F), including the meringue *Mont Blanc*. Open M-F 9am-7pm, Sa-Su 9:30am-7:30pm.

Marriage Frères, 30 rue du Bourg-Tibourg, 4ème. M: Hôtel de Ville. Founded by 2 brothers who loathed British tea. Sandwiches, cakes, and 400 varieties of tea (35-55F). Open daily 10:30am-7:30pm.

Le Bar du Caveau, 17 pl. Dauphine, 1er, facing the front steps of the Palais de Justice. M: Cité. Luscious cheeses and wines attract fashionable Parisians. Wines by the glass 12-23F. Plate of cheese 47F. Open M-F 8:30am-8pm.

Le Franc Pinot, 1 quai de Bourbon, 4ème. M: Pont Marie. A fixture on Ile St-Louis since the 17th century. Burgundy wines are a specialty; by the glass 15-36F. Live jazz W-Sa. Open Tu-Sa 10am-2am, Su 2pm-2am.

Jacques Mélac, 42 rue Léon Frot, 11ème. M: Charonne. A family-owned wine bar and bistro, with an annual wine-harvest fête in Sept. Wine 18F per glass. Open Sept.-July M 9am-5pm, Tu-F 9am-10:30pm.

Finnegan's Wake, 9 rue des Boulangers, 5ème. M: Cardinal Lemoine. Walk up rue des Boulangers to this Irish pub set in a 14th-century wine cellar. Best Guinness in the city (25-35F). Open M-F 11am-2am, Sa-Su 4pm-2am.

Chez Richard, 37 rue Vieille-du-Temple, 4ème. M: Hôtel-de-Ville. Inside a courtyard off rue Vieille-du-Temple, this Marais bar features a swank, plush red-leather. Beer and cocktails 22-55F. Open M-Sa 5pm-2am.

SIGHTS

In a few hours, you can walk from the heart of the Marais in the east to the Eiffel Tower in the west, past almost every monument there is. Try to reserve one day for wandering: you don't have a true sense of Paris until you know how close medieval Nôtre Dame is to the modern Centre Pompidou, and the *Quartier Latin* of students to the Louvre of kings. After dark, the glamour increases: spotlights go up over everything from the Panthéon to the Eiffel Tower, Nôtre Dame to the Obélisque. Until midnight, the city glows like a galaxy of multicolored, glittering chandeliers.

Ile de la Cité and Ile St-Louis

If any one location is the heart of Paris, the **Ile de la Cité** is it. Since the 3rd century BC, when it was inhabited by the *Parisii*, a Gallic tribe of hunters, sailors, and fishermen, the Ile de la Cité has been the administrative center of Paris and the home of kings. In the 12th century work commenced on the **Cathédrale de Nôtre-Dame de Paris** (M: Cité) and the **Ste-Chapelle** under the direction of Bishop Maurice Sully. *(Tours in English W and Th noon; in French M-F noon, Sa 2:30pm. Free. Towers open daily Apr.-Sept. 10am-6pm; Oct.-Mar. 10am-5pm. Last admission 30min. before closing. 32F, students 12-25F. Cathedral open daily 8am-6:45pm. High mass with Gregorian chant Su 10am. Confession heard in English.)* Completed in the 14th century, the cathedral is one of the most famous and beautiful examples of medieval architecture. After the Revolution, the building fell into disrepair and was even used to shelter livestock, but Victor Hugo's 1831 novel *Nôtre-Dame-de-Paris (The Hunchback of Notre Dame)* inspired thousands of citizens to push for restoration. Modifications, including the addition of the spire and the gargoyles, were made by the architect Eugène Viollet-le-Duc. The first thing you see is the intricately carved apocalyptic **facade.** Inside, the soaring light and apparent weightlessness of the walls—Gothic effects produced by brilliant engineering and optical illusions—are inspiring even for the most church-weary. The cathedral's biggest draw is the enormous stained-glass **rose windows** dominating the north and south ends of the transept. A perilous and claustrophobic staircase inside the **towers** emerges onto a spectacular perch from which weather-worn gargoyles survey the city. Once outside again, take a moment to walk around back to see the spectacular, spidery **flying buttresses,** which support the weight of the structure.

The **Palais de Justice** has harbored Paris district courts since the 13th century. Inside its courtyard, the flamboyant Gothic **Ste-Chapelle** was built by Saint Louis (Louis IX) to house his most precious possession, Christ's crown of thorns (now in Nôtre Dame). *(Open daily Apr.-Sept. 9:30am-6:30pm; Oct.-Mar. 10am-5pm. 32F, students and seniors 21F, with the Conciergerie 50F.)* The chapel contains some of the most beautiful stained-glass in the world. The **Conciergerie,** once one of Paris's most infamous prisons, lurks around the corner of the Palais from Ste-Chapelle's entrance. *(Open daily Apr.-Sept. 9:30am-6:30pm; Oct.-Mar. 10am-5pm. 28F, students 21F.)* Marie-Antoinette and Robespierre were imprisoned here during the Revolution.

Across the Pont St-Louis is the **Ile St-Louis,** which some of the most privileged of Paris's privileged elite, like the Rothschilds and Pompidou's widow, call home. Check the plaques on the sides of buildings for famous former residents (e.g., Voltaire, Baudelaire, Marie Curie). At night, the Ile St-Louis glows in the light of its cast-iron lamps and candlelit bistros. Paris's best ice cream can be found at Ile St-Louis's **Berthillon,** 31 rue St-Louis-en-Ile. *(M: Cité. Open Sept.-July W-Su 10am-8pm.)*

The Latin Quarter and St-Germain-des-Prés

Home since the 13th century to the **Sorbonne,** the *Quartier Latin* is filled with bookish bohemians scribbling works-in-progress in attic apartments and corner cafes. However, after the violent student riots in protest of the outmoded university system in May of 1968, the University of Paris split into 13 campuses. With decentralization the *quartier* lost many of its youthful, scholarly inhabitants, but many bookstores, cafes, and students remain.

The **Panthéon** towers at the highest point on the Left Bank (M: Cardinal Lemoine). In the **crypt** you'll find the tombs of Voltaire, Rousseau, Victor Hugo, Emile Zola, Jean Jaurès, and Louis Braille, which can be seen from behind locked iron gates at each of their niches. The **dome** features neoclassical frescoes. *(Open daily 10am-6:30pm; last admission 5:45pm. 32F, students 21F.)*

Even if an average walk in the park bores you, stroll through the **Jardin des Plantes,** pl. Valhubert (M: Jussieu). Opened in 1640 for the purpose of growing medicinal plants for King Louis XIII, it now features natural science museums and a **zoo** which Parisians raided for food during the siege of 1871. The **boulevard St-Michel,** flooded with cafes, restaurants, bookstores, and cinemas, is the center of the Latin Quarter and the divider between the 5ème and 6ème. **Place St-Michel,** at the northern tip of this *grand-avenue,* is filled with bookstores, students, cinemas, and tourists.

West of the Panthéon, the formal French gardens of the **Jardin du Luxembourg** are fabulous for strolling, reading, and the famous **guignol** puppet theater. Scarred by centuries of attack, weather, revolution, and war, the **Eglise St-Germain-des-Prés,** pl. St-Germain-des-Prés is the oldest standing church in Paris, dating from 1163. *(M: St-Germain-des-Prés. Open daily 8am-7:30pm.)*

The Faubourg St-Germain

The green, tree–lined **Esplanade des Invalides** runs from the grand **Pont Alexandre III** to the gold-leaf dome crowning the **Hôtel des Invalides** (M: Invalides). The Hôtel, built under Louis XIV for retired and wounded veterans, now houses the **Musée de l'Armée** and **Napoleon's Tomb.** Nearby on rue Varenne is the excellent **Musée Rodin** (see **Museums,** p. 302).

Of the **Tour Eiffel** (Eiffel Tower; M: Bir-Hakeim), Gustave Eiffel wrote in 1889, "France is the only country in the world with a 300m flagpole." *(Open daily June-Aug. 9am-midnight; Sept.-June 9:30am-11pm. Elevator to: 1st floor 20F, 2nd floor 42F, 3rd floor 59F.)* Maupassant liked to eat lunch there because it was the one place in Paris where he didn't have to look at it. Built in 1889 as the centerpiece of the World's Fair (held in Paris for the centennial jubilee of the French Revolution), the structure has come to symbolize the city. Despite criticism, the only thing tacky about the elegant tower are the souvenirs that bear its image. Climb to the top for a view of the city. At night, even the most jaded tourists will be impressed.

The Louvre, the Opéra, the Marais, and the Bastille

World-famous art museum and former residence of kings, the **Louvre** occupies about one-seventh of the surface area of the 1er *arrondissement* (see **Museums,** p. 302). **Le Jardin des Tuileries** (M: Palais-Royal/Musée du Louvre), at the western foot of the Louvre, was commissioned by Catherine de Médicis in 1564, improved by André Le Nôtre (designer of the gardens at Versailles) in 1649, and is popular for walks and outdoor leisure. Three blocks north along rue de Castiglione, **Place Vendôme** hides 20th-century offices and luxury shops behind 17th-century facades. In the center of the *place* is a column cast from 1250 Austrian and Russian bronze cannon captured in battle by Napoleon (that's him on the top, in the toga). Commissioned in 1632 by Cardinal Richelieu, the **Palais-Royal** became royal when the Cardinal gave it to Louis XIII. In 1784 the elegant buildings enclosing the palace's formal garden became *galleries,* the prototype of a shopping mall. The revolutions of 1789, 1830, and 1848 all began with angry crowds in that same garden.

North of the Louvre, Charles Garnier's grandiose **Opéra** was built under Napoleon III in the eclectic style of the Second Empire. *(M: Opéra. Open for visits daily 10am-5pm; last admission 4:30pm. 30F, students 20F.)* The magnificent interior is adorned by Gobelin tapestries, gilded mosaics, a 1964 Marc Chagall ceiling, and the six-ton chandelier which fell on the audience in 1896. East of the Opéra lie the 3ème and 4ème *arrondissements,* known together as the **Marais.** With Henri IV's construction of the elegant **place des Vosges** (M: St-Paul) at the beginning of the 17th century, the area became *the* place to live. Several of the many mansions left in the area now house museums. Today, the Marais's small streets house the city's Jewish and Gay communities, as well as chic restaurants and shops. At the meeting point of the 1er, 2ème, 3ème, and 4ème, the **Centre Pompidou** looms like an oversized factory abandoned next to the Seine. *(Closed until Dec. 31, 1999; see **Museums** p. 302.)* In afternoon and early evening, the vast cobblestone *place* in front of this museum and cultural center gathers a mixture of artists, musicians, and pick-pockets. Be careful at night.

Farther east, Charles V built the **Bastille** prison to guard the eastern entrance to his capital; it became a state prison under Louis XIII, housing religious heretics and political undesirables. On July 14, 1789, revolutionaries stormed the Bastille for its supply of gunpowder. By 1792, nothing was left of the prison but its outline on the *place.* On July 14, 1989, François Mitterrand inaugurated the glittering **Opéra Bastille,** 120 rue de Lyon (M: Bastille) to celebrate the destruction of Charles's fortress. Alas, the ugly Opéra Bastille is almost as hated as its predecessor.

Champs-Elysées, Bois de Boulogne, and La Défense

The **place de la Concorde** (M: Concorde), Paris's largest and most infamous public square, is at the western edge of the Tuileries. Constructed between 1757 and 1777 to hold a monument to Louis XV, the vast area soon became the place de la Révolution, site of a guillotine that severed 1343 necks. After the Reign of Terror, the square was optimistically renamed—*concorde* means peace. The huge, rose granite **Obélisque de Luxor** dates from the 13th century BC and depicts the deeds of Ramses II. Given to Charles X by the Viceroy of Egypt in 1829, it is Paris's oldest monument.

Stretching west, the **avenue des Champs-Elysées** is lined with luxury shops, *haute couture* boutiques, cafes, and cinemas. The avenue is the work of Baron Haussmann, who was commissioned by Napoleon III to convert Paris into a grand capital with broad avenues, wide sidewalks, new parks, elegant housing, and sanitary sewers. At its western terminus, the **Arc de Triomphe**, pl. Charles de Gaulle was commissioned in 1806 by Napoleon in honor of his Grande Armée. *(M: Charles de Gaulle-Etoile. Open daily Apr.-Sept. 9:30am-11pm; Oct.-Mar. 10am-6pm; last admission 30min. before closing. 35F, students and seniors 23F. Use the safe underpass and buy your ticket before going upstairs.)* In 1940, Parisians were brought to tears as Nazis goose-stepped through the Arc. After four years of Nazi occupation, the city was liberated by British, American, and French troops, who marched through on August 26, 1944, to the roaring cheers of thousands. The terrace at the top has a fabulous view.

Avenue Foch, one of Haussmann's finest creations, runs from the Arc de Triomphe to the **Bois de Boulogne,** 16ème (M: Porte Maillot, Sablons, Pont de Neuilly), a popular place for daytime picnics. Joggers and walkers can find maps at regular intervals on the periphery of the park. Although the police recently cleaned out many of the drug dealers and prostitutes, it's still a risky choice for a moonlit stroll.

Outside the city limits, the skyscrapers and modern architecture of **La Défense** (M: "La Défense," zone 2; RER, zone 3) make up Paris's newest (unofficial) *arrondissement.* Home to many of the city's corporate offices, La Défense boasts the headquarters of 14 of France's top 20 corporations. The stunning **Grande Arche**, inaugurated in 1989, completes the *axe historique* running through the Louvre, the pl. de la Concorde, and the Arc de Triomphe. *(Open daily 10am-7pm; roof closes 6pm. 40F, under 18, students, and seniors 30F.)* There's a yet another wonderful view from the top. Shops, galleries, trees, and sculptures by Miró and Calder line the pedestrian esplanade.

Montmartre and Père-Lachaise

The **Basilique du Sacré-Coeur,** 35 rue du Cheval de la Barre, 18ème (M: Anvers, Abbesses, or Château-Rouge), crowns the **butte Montmartre** like an enormous white meringue. *(Open daily 7am-11pm. Free. Dome and crypt open 9am-7pm. Admission 8F, students 6F.)* Its onion dome is visible from almost any corner of the city down below, and its 112m bell tower is the highest point in Paris, with a view that stretches as far as 50km. Nearby, **place du Tertre** features touristed outdoor cafes and sketch artists.

The **Cimetière Père-Lachaise,** on bd. de Ménilmontant, 20ème (M: Père-Lachaise), holds the remains of Balzac, Colette, Seurat, Danton, David, Delacroix, La Fontaine, Haussmann, Molière, Sarah Bernhardt, and Proust within its peaceful, winding paths and elaborate sarcophagi. Foreigners buried here include Chopin, Gertrude Stein, Modigliani, and Oscar Wilde, though the most visited grave is **Jim Morrison's,** covered with his fans' graffiti, flowers, joints, and poetry. French Leftists make ceremonious pilgrimage to the **Mur des Fédérés** (Wall of the Federals), where 147 revolutionary *Communards* were executed and buried. *(Open daily Mar.-Oct. 9am-6pm; Nov.-Feb. 9am-5:30pm; last admission 15min. before closing.)*

MUSEUMS

In addition to the **Louvre,** Paris is home to hundreds of wonderful museums, most notably the **Musée d'Orsay,** the **Musée Rodin,** the **Centre Pompidou,** the **Institut du Monde Arabe, La Villette,** and the **Musées Cluny, Picasso, Dalí,** and **Marmottan.** For updated info, check the bimonthly *Paris Museums and Monuments,* available at the Champs-Elysées tourist office. The weekly magazines *Pariscope* and *L'Officiel des*

Spectacles list museum hours and temporary exhibits. Frequent museum-goers may want a **Carte Musées et Monuments,** which grants entry to 65 Parisian museums without waiting in line. The card is sold at major museums and metro stops (1 day 80F, 3 consecutive days 160F; 5 consecutive days 240F).

Musée du Louvre, 1*er*. M: Palais-Royal/Musée du Louvre. The short list of master-pieces includes the Code of Hammurabi, the *Venus de Milo,* the *Winged Victory of Samothrace,* Vermeer's *Lacemaker,* David's enormous and brilliant Revolutionary paintings, Ingres's *Odalisque,* Géricault's *Raft of the Medusa,* Delacroix's *Liberty Leading the People,* and that lady with the mysterious smile, the *Mona Lisa.* (Impressionist works and most late 19th-century art are at the Musée d'Orsay.) Enter through I.M. Pei's **Pyramid** in the Cour Napoléon, or skip lines by entering directly from the metro. Open Th-Su 9am-6pm, M and W 9am-9:45pm. Last admission 45min. before closing. M and W evenings are quiet. 45F before 3pm, 26F after 3pm and on Su, first Su of each month free. A 100F **Carte Louvre Jeune** is good for a year for those under 26. English tours M and W-Sa 17F. Wheelchair accessible.

Musée d'Orsay, 62 rue de Lille, 7*ème*. M: Solférino; RER Musée d'Orsay. While the Musée d'Orsay is considered *the* Impressionist museum, this former railway station is dedicated to presenting all of the major artistic movements between 1848 and WWI. Incorporating painting, sculpture, decorative arts, architecture, and photography, the museum's collection includes Manet's *Olympia* and *Déjeuner sur l'Herbe,* Monet's *Gare St-Lazare* and *Rouen Cathedral,* Degas's *Absinthe Drinker,* and Whistler's *Mother,* as well as works by Rodin, Renoir, Cézanne, Van Gogh, Toulouse-Lautrec, Gaugin, and Seurat. Open June 20-Sept. 20 Tu-W and F-Su 9am-6pm, Th 9am-9:45pm; Sept. 21-June 19 opens at 10am. Last admission 45min. before closing. 40F, Su 30F. Wheelchair accessible.

Centre National d'Art et de Culture Georges-Pompidou (Palais Beaubourg), 4*ème*. M: Rambuteau. This inside-out building has inspired debate since its inauguration in 1977. The Centre Pompidou's interior exhibition halls, library, and museum spaces (including the **Musée National d'Art Moderne**) will be closed for renovations until December 31, 1999. Still, it's a sight from the outside: colored piping and ventilation ducts run up, down, and sideways along the outside (blue for air, green for water, yellow for electricity, red for heating).

Musée Rodin, 77 rue de Varenne, 7*ème*. M: Varenne. The elegant 18th-century Hôtel Biron holds hundred of sculptures by Auguste Rodin (and his lover, Camille Claudel), including the *Gates of Hell, The Thinker,* the *Burghers of Calais,* and *The Kiss.* Open Apr.-Sept. Tu-Su 9:30am-5:45pm; Oct.-Mar. Tu-Su 9:30am-4:45pm. Last admission 30min. before closing. 28F, students, seniors, and Su 18F.

Musée de l'Orangerie, 1*er*. M: Concorde. In the southwest corner of the Tuileries. Smaller and less crowded than the Musée d'Orsay, the Impressionist collection includes works by Renoir, Cézanne, and Mattisse, and features Monet's water lilies murals, *Les Nymphéas.* Open W-M 10am-5pm. 30F, under 25 18F.

Hôtel de Cluny, 6 pl. Paul-Painlevé, 5*ème*. M: Cluny-Sorbonne. One of the world's finest collections of medieval art, housed in a medieval monastery, built on top of Roman baths. *La Dame et La Licorne* (The Lady and the Unicorn) is one of the most beautiful extant medieval tapestry series. Open W-M 9:15am-5:45pm. 30F, under 25, over 60, and Su 20F, under 18 free.

Musée Salvador Dalí (Espace Montmartre), 11 rue Poulbot, 18*ème*. M: Anvers or Abbesses. Just off pl. du Tertre, the museum features work by the Spanish surrealist, laid out in "Surrealist surroundings"—wonderful spacing, funky lighting, and eerie background music. Open daily 10am-6pm. 35F, students 25F.

Musée Picasso, 5 rue de Thorigny, 3*ème*. M: Chemin Vert. Catalogues the life and career of one of the century's most prolific, inventive artists, from his early work in Barcelona to his Cubist and Surrealist years in Paris and his Neoclassical work on the Riviera. Open W-M 9:30am-5:30pm. 30F, ages 18-25 and Su 20F, under 18 free.

Musée des Égouts de Paris (The Sewers of Paris), 7*ème* (tel. 01 47 05 10 29). M: Pont de l'Alma. Inside the sewers, at the corner of the quai d'Orsay and pl. de la Résistance. Like Jean Valjean in Victor Hugo's *Les Misérables,* you can visit, but don't breathe deep—the smell can be overwhelming. Tours May-Sept. Sa-W 11am-5pm; Oct.-Apr. Sa-W 11am-4pm. 25F, students and under 10 20F.

Les Catacombs, 1 pl. Denfert-Rochereau, 14ème. M: Denfert-Rochereau. Contains the bones of 5-6 million Parisians in former limestone mines—including those of a guy who got lost here in 1793 and wasn't found for 9 years. Bring a sweater and don't get lost. Open Tu-F 2-4:45pm, Sa-Su 9-11am and 2-4pm. 27F, ages 7-25 19F.

La Villette, 19ème. M: Porte de la Villette or Porte de Pantin. An urban renewal project in the northeastern corner of Paris, la Villette's 55 hectares enclose a landscaped park, a huge science museum (open daily 10am-6pm, 55F), an Omnimax cinema (57F, M-F students 44F), a conservatory, an exhibition hall, a jazz club, a concert, theater space, and a brand-new high-tech music museum (open Tu-Th noon-6pm, F-Sa noon-7:30pm, Su 10am-6pm. 35F, students 25F).

Musée d'Art Moderne de la Ville de Paris, 11 av. du Président Wilson, in the Palais de Tokyo, 16ème. M: Iéna. While the Pompidou is closed, this is Paris's best collection of 20th-century art, with works by Matisse *(The Dance)* and Picasso *(The Jester);* temporary exhibits vary dramatically. Open Tu-F 10am-5:30pm, Sa-Su 10am-6:45pm. 27-35F, students and seniors 17-25F.

Musée Marmottan, 2 rue Louis-Boilly, 16ème. M: La Muette. Follow Chaussée de la Muette (av. Ranelagh) through the Jardin (park) du Ranelagh. A hunting lodge turned stately mansion, furnished with Empire furniture and an eclectic collection of Impressionist Monet and Renoir canvases, and medieval illuminations. Open Tu-Su 10am-5pm. 40F, students and seniors 25F.

Institut du Monde Arabe, 23 quai St-Bernard, 5ème (tel. 01 40 51 38 38). M: Jussieu. Paris's most architecturally innovative museum. The riverside facade is shaped like a boat, representing the migration of Arabs to France. The opposite side has camera-lens windows with Arabic motifs that open and close with the sunlight. Houses art from the Maghreb, the Near and Middle East and hosts Arab movies (25F, students 20F) and theater (80-100F). The rooftop terrace has a fabulous and free view of Montmartre and the Seine. Open Tu-Su 10am-6pm. 25F, ages 12-18 20F.

ENTERTAINMENT

Paris's cabarets, discos, jazz clubs, cinemas, theaters, and concert halls offer the best of French and world culture. Consult the weekly magazines **Pariscope** (3F) and the **Officiel des Spectacles** (2F), both on sale at any newsstand, for updated listings. Or contact **Info-Loisirs,** a recording that keeps tabs on what's on in Paris (English tel. 01 49 52 53 56, French 01 49 52 53 55).

Theater tickets can run high, but reduced student rates are nearly always available, and some theaters sell rush tickets an hour before curtain. Most theaters close for August. *Pariscope* and *l'Officiel des Spectacles* print complete listings of current shows. The best place for cut-rate theater tickets is the **Kiosque-Théâtre,** 15 pl. de la Madeleine, 8ème (M: Madeleine; also in 1er, M: Châtelet-Les Halles), which sells half-price, same-day tickets (16F fee; open Tu-Sa 12:30-8pm, Su 12:30-4pm). **Alpha FNAC: Spectacles** at 136 rue de Rennes, 6ème (tel. 01 49 45 30 00; M: Montparnasse-

FRANCE

Paris 2000

To signal the beginning of the next Millennium, Paris will take center stage with a year-long program of celebrations, events, exhibitions, and festivals all centered around the theme *Paris, City of Lights.* The Eiffel Tower's **Countdown Clock** has already begun the digital countdown to January 1, 2000. On New Year's Eve, the twelve *avenues* that span out from the Arc de Triomphe will be lit up to create a huge **Millennium Clock** that will count down the last hours of the Millennium. Paris will build a huge 200m **Tour de la Terre** (Earth Tower) near the Seine that will feature exhibitions on technology, history, culture, and the environment. Paris's museums are planning special exhibitions, including the Grand Palais's **Future Visions, The Year 1000 in Europe,** and **Europe 1900,** the Centre Pompidou's **Time throughout the Ages,** and the Louvre's **Invention of Time.** For more information, contact the **Mission pour la Célébration de l'An 2000,** 32, Quai des Célestins, 4^{éme} (tel. 01 42 76 73 90; email dircom@celebration.2000.gouv.fr) or surf the official website, **http://www.tour-eiffel.fr/teiffel/an2000_fr/.**

Bienvenue); Forum des Halles, 1-7 rue Pierre Lescot, 1er (tel. 01 40 41 40 00; M: Châtelet-Les Halles); and 71 bd. St-Germain, 5ème (tel. 01 44 41 31 50), sells tickets for theater, concerts, and festivals (open M-Sa 10am-7:30pm). The **Comédie Française**, 2 rue de Richelieu, 1er (tel. 01 44 58 15 15), features classic comedies by Molière (tickets 45-120F, student tickets 60-70F, rush tickets 30F). The **Odéon Théâtre de l'Europe**, 1 pl. Odéon, 6ème (tel. 01 44 41 36 36), offers productions from the classics to the avant-garde (tickets 50-165F, student rush 60F). The **Théâtre de la Huchette**, 23 rue de la Huchette, 5ème (tel. 01 43 26 38 99), still performs Ionesco's *La Cantatrice Chauve (Bald Soprano)* and *La Leçon*. (M-Sa at 7pm and 8pm, respectively. Tickets 100F, students M-F 80F. Both shows 160F, 120F.) *Café-théâtres* like **Au Bec Fin**, 6 rue Thérèse, 1er (tel. 01 42 96 29 35; tickets 80F), perform low-budget, high-energy skits but require good French language skills to enjoy.

Cinema

Cinema was invented in Paris (by the Lumière brothers, Auguste and Louis), and the first movie premiered at the Grand Café (14 bd. des Capucines) in 1895. Paris, of all the cities in the world, probably plays the greatest number of films each week. Cinemas offer a range of ticket discounts, especially on Mondays and Wednesdays. Check *Pariscope* for listings. Film festivals are listed separately. The notation **v.o.** *(version originale)* after a non-French movie listing means that the film is being shown in its original language with French subtitles; **v.f.** *(version française)* means that it has been dubbed—an increasingly rare phenomenon.

La Pagode, 57bis rue de Babylone, 7ème (tel. 01 36 68 75 07). M: St-François-Xavier. From bd. des Invalides, turn right. A monument to 19th-century Orientalism, the *Salle Japonaise* is Paris's most charming cinema. 45F, students and seniors M-F before 6pm 38F.

L'Entrepôt, 7-9 rue Francis de Pressensé, 14ème (tel. 01 45 40 78 38). M: Pernety. Turn right off rue Raymond Losserand. A venue for independent films with festivals and director forums. 3 screens show films in *v.o.* 40F, students and seniors 30F. The delightful bar (open daily 3pm-1am) makes this great for a date.

Cinémathèque Française, pl. du Trocadéro, 16ème (tel. 01 45 53 21 86). M: Trocadéro. At the Musée du Cinéma in the Palais de Chaillot; enter through the Jardins du Trocadéro. Recording (tel. 01 47 04 24 24) lists all shows. A must for film buffs. 2-3 classics, near-classics, or soon-to-be classics per day. Foreign films usually in *v.o.* Buy tickets 15-20min. early. Open W-Su 5-9:45pm. 28F, students 17F.

Jazz

Ever since the arrival of American Expatriate jazz musicians in the 30s and 40s, Paris has become one of the jazz capitals of the world. Frequent summer festivals sponsor free or nearly free jazz concerts. French mags *Jazz Hot* (45F), *Jazz Magazine* (35F), and *LYLO (Les Yeux, Les Oreilles;* free) have the most complete listings.

Au Duc des Lombards, 42 rue des Lombards, 1er. M: Châtelet. Murals of Ellington and Coltrane swathe the exterior of this premier jazz joint. The best in French jazz in a dark and smoky atmosphere. Cover 80-100F, music students 50-80F. Drinks 28-55F. Music starts at 10pm. Open daily 7:30pm-4am.

Caveau de la Huchette, 5 rue de la Huchette, 5ème. M: St-Michel. For those who have always felt jazz was meant to be danced to. Come prepared to listen, watch, and dance. Dance lessons M-F evenings. The caves served as a prison during the Revolution. Cover Su-Th 60F, F-Sa 70F. Students 55F. Drinks 22-30F. Open M-Th 9:30pm-3am, F 9:30pm-2:30am, Sa 9:30pm-4am.

New Morning, 7-9 rue des Petites-Ecuries, 10ème. M: Château d'Eau. Dark, smoky, and crowded, it's everything a jazz club should be. All the greats have played here—from Chet Baker and Miles Davis to Wynton Marsalis. Open Sept.-July from 8pm. Cover 110-140F. Drinks 30-55F.

Dance and Rock Clubs

Some clubs here are small, private, and nearly impossible to sniff out unless you're a native. Many Parisian clubs are officially private, which means they have the right to choose and refuse their clientele. Parisians dress up to go out, so wear black. Haggard backpackers might want to try the friendlier and cheaper bar scene instead.

L'Arapaho, 30 av. d'Italie, Centre Commercial Italie 2, 13ème. M: pl. d'Italie. It's the gray door on the right, just past Au Printemps. Since 1983, the best hard-core, rap, pop, and metal in Paris. A pitstop for indie rock bands' tour itineraries. Tickets 60-130F. Beer 20F. Cocktails 50F. F Asian, Sa Cuban. Cover 80F.

Les Bains, 7 rue du Bourg l'Abbé, 3ème. M: Réaumur-Sébastopol. Ultraselective, super-crowded, and very expensive, it used to be a public bath, visited at least once by Proust. Madonna's been here. House and garage grunge. Cover and 1st drink 100F. Open daily midnight-6am.

Le Cithéa, 114 rue Oberkampf 11ème. M: Parmentier. More of a bar with live music and an intimate floor than a pulsing, flash-dancing club. In the very hip Oberkampf *quartier* and full of young, artsy folk. Jazz, hip hop, and free jack fusion bands. No cover. Drinks 25F-60F. Open daily 9:30pm-5:30pm.

Folies Pigalle, 11 pl. Pigalle, 9ème. M: Pigalle. This club is the largest and most popular in the once-sleazy Pigalle *quartier*. A former strip joint, popular among gay and straight clubbers. Mostly house and techno. Open Th-Sa 11pm-7am, Su 3-8pm. Cover 100F. Drinks 50F.

Le Queen, 102 av. des Champs-Elysées, 8ème. Come taste the fiercest funk in town where drag queens, superstars, models, moguls, and buff go-go boys get down. Her majesty is open 7 days a week, midnight to dawn. M Disco (50F cover plus 50F drink); Tu Gay (50F cover, 50F drink); W Latin House (no cover); Th House (no cover); F-Sa House (80F, 50F drink); Su 80s Retro (no cover).

Gay and Lesbian Paris

Paris's fabulous gay and lesbian scene is centered in the **Marais** (3ème and 4ème), with cafes, bars, and shops on rue Vieille du Temple, rue Ste-Croix de la Bretonnerie, and rue des Archives. For the most comprehensive listing of bi, gay, and lesbian establishments, organizations, and services, consult Gai Pied's *Guide Gai 1999* (in English and French, 79F at any kiosk), *Lesbia*'s ads (25F), and *Pariscope*. Anyone seeking the hippest club scene in Paris will want to drop in at **Le Queen** on the Champs-Elysées. **Pulp!,** 25 bd Poissonnière (2ème), is the glamorous gal alternative.

Open Café, 17 rue des Archives, 4ème. M: Hôtel-de-Ville. Recently redone, the Open Café is the most popular of the Marais gay bars. Grit your teeth, grip your handbag, and bitch your way onto the terrace. Beer 18F, cocktails 35F. Su brunch 70-105F. Open daily 10am-2am.

Amnésia Café, 42 rue Vieille-du-Temple, 4ème. M: Hôtel-de- Ville. A classy, relaxed bar where friends gather and gossip. Crowded, but less cruisy, the Amnésia will help you forget your troubles. Beer 18-45F. Open daily 10am-2am. Su brunch noon-4pm (50-70F).

Le Champmeslé, 4 rue Chabanais, 2ème. M: Pyramides or Quatre Septembre. This intimate lesbian bar is Paris's oldest. No cover. Drinks 25-45F. Open M-W 5pm-2am, Th-Sa 5pm-5am.

L'Unity, 176/178 rue St Martin, 4ème. M: Rambuteau. Bright punk graffiti fronts this large and loud lesbian bar. Next to the Pompidou Center with reggae, rock, and techno. Drinks 17-40F. Open daily 4pm-2am.

■ Near Paris: Versailles, Chartres, and Disneyland

Louis XIV, the Sun King, built and held court at **Versailles** (tel. 01 30 84 74 00) his extraordinary palace and gardens, 12km west of Paris. The incredibly lavish château embodies the Old Regime's extravagance. Louis XVI and Marie Antoinette held fabulous fêtes in the château's **Hall of Mirrors, Grand and Petit Trianons,** and faux **Hameau.** (Château open May-Sept. Tu-Su 9am-6:30pm; Oct.-Apr. Tu-Su 9am-5:30pm.

FRANCE

Last admission 30min. before closing. 45F; after 3:30pm, ages 18-25, and over 60 35F.) Le Nôtre's geometric **gardens** are studded with fountains, which spurt to music every Sunday, May through September. Tours (1hr., 25F, leaves from entrance D) are worth it (gardens open sunrise-sundown; free, except May-Sept. Su 20F). Take **RER** C5 from M: Invalides to the Versailles Rive Gauche station (30-40 min., every 15min., round-trip 28F). Take any train whose label begins in "V" (Vick, Vora, etc.). Buy your RER ticket *before* getting to the platform; though your metro ticket will get you onto the train, it will not get you through the RER turnstiles at Versailles.

The stunning **Cathédrale de Chartres** survives today as one of the most beautiful creations of the Middle Ages (open M-Sa 7:30am-7:15pm, Su 8:30am-7:15pm). Arguably the finest example of early Gothic architecture in Europe, the cathedral retains several of its original 12th-century stained-glass windows. The rest of the windows and the magnificent sculptures on the main portals date from the 13th century. Malcolm Miller, an authority on Gothic architecture, leads fantastic tours of the cathedral in English (1¼min.; Apr.-Jan. M-Sa noon and 2:45pm; 30F, students 20F). The town of **Chartres** celebrates the medieval crafts showcased in its cathedral. Frequent **trains** run to Chartres from Gare Montparnasse. (1hr., roughly one per hour, but call 08 36 35 35 35 for schedule info, round-trip 142F.) To reach the cathedral from the station, walk straight to pl. de Châtelet, turn left into the *place,* right onto rue Ste-Même, and then left onto rue Jean Moulin. The **tourist office** across from the cathedral can give you all the info you need.

It's a small, small world and Disney seems bent on making it even smaller. When EuroDisney opened, it was met by the jeers of French intellectuals and the popular press. Resistance to the park has subsided since Walt & Co. renamed it **Disneyland Paris;** a touch of class goes a long way (Apr.-Sept. and Jan.-Feb. 200F, under 12 155F; off-season 155F. Open in summer daily 9am-11pm; in winter hours vary.) Buy *"passeports"* (tickets) at the 50 windows on Disneyland Hotel's ground floor, at the Paris tourist office, or at any major station on RER line A; buy ahead to avoid lines if you'll be visiting on a weekend. To reach Disneyland Paris from Paris, take **RER** A4 "Marne-la-Vallée" to the last stop, "Marne-la-Vallée/Chessy" (45min., every 30min., round-trip 76F). The last train to Paris leaves Disney at 12:22am but doesn't reach Paris before the metro closes. **Eurail** holders take notice: the TGV runs from Roissy/Charles de Gaulle Airport to the park in 15 minutes.

THE NORTH (LE NORD)

■ The Channel Ports

Calais Ever since Richard the Lionheart and his crusaders passed through, **Calais** has been the continent's primary portal to Britain. Hovercrafts to Dover are faster than ferries and similarly priced; contact **Hoverspeed,** Hoverport (tel. 0 800 90 17 77 within France; to Dover 35min., one-way or 5-day return 150F, with InterRail 75F), or **P&O Stena Line** (tel. 03 21 46 04 40; ferries to Dover 75min., every 45min.-1hr., one way or 5-day return 145F). During the day, free buses connect the hoverport, ferry terminal, and **train station** (tel. 08 36 35 35 35), bd. Jacquard, where trains leave for Paris (3½hr., 198F), Boulogne (30min., 39F), and Dunkerque (45min., 44F). The **tourist office,** 12 bd. Clemenceau (tel. 03 21 96 62 40; fax 03 21 96 01 92), a block from the train station, books rooms and exchanges currency (open M-Sa 9am-7pm, Su 10am-1pm). Rodin's famous sculpture, **The Burghers of Calais,** stands in front of the Hôtel de Ville at bd. Jacquard and rue Royale. **Centre Européen de Séjour (HI)** (tel. 03 21 34 70 20), av. Maréchal Delattre de Tassigny, a block from the beach, has 84 doubles. From the train station, take bus 3, or turn left, following the main road. Cross the bridge and go left at the monument onto bd. de Gaulle, then right onto rue Alice Marie. (78F; nonmembers 88F and 1-night max. stay; breakfast included. Sheets 16F. Reception 24hr.). **Hotel Victoria,** 8 rue du Commandant Bonningue (tel. 03 21 34 38

32), has cheerful rooms (singles 152F; doubles 204-254F). To fill your stomach, find a **boulangerie** on bd. Gambetta, bd. Jacquard, or rue des Thermes, or go to the **Match supermarket**, pl. d'Armes (open M-Sa 8:30am-7:30pm, Su 10am-7pm).

Boulogne-sur-Mer

Legend has it that a boat carrying a statue of the Virgin Mary washed onto the beach in 636, making **Boulogne-sur-Mer** a pilgrimage site. Today, France's most important fishing port serves as a major point of entry for Brits fleeing their soggy isle. The hilltop *vieille ville* offers great views of the city. The massive **Château-Musée**, rue de Bernet, houses an eclectic and impressive art collection. (Open May 15-Sept. 15 M-Sa 9:30am-12:30pm and 1:30-6:15pm, Su 9:30am-noon and 2:30-6:15pm; Sept. 16-May 14 M-Sa 10am-12:30pm and 2-5pm, Su 10am-12:30pm and 2:30-5:30pm. 20F.) The towering **Basilique de Notre-Dame** contains precious religious objects and the remains of a Roman temple (open M-Sa 9am-noon and 2-6pm; crypt and basilica 10F). When the locals aren't catching fish, they're admiring them at **Le Grand Nausicaä** (tel. 03 21 30 98 98; http://www.nausicaa-sea-centres.com), on bd. Ste-Beuve, a fantastic aquarium featuring a clear underwater tunnel. It can be crowded; arrive late in the day. (Open July-Aug. 9:30am-8pm; Sept.-May 9:30am-6:30pm; closed for 2 weeks in Jan. 65F, ages 3-12 45F.)

Trains leave the station on bd. Voltaire for Paris (3hr., 159F) and Calais (30min., 39F). **Hoverspeed** (tel. 0 800 90 17 77 within France) runs car ferries to Folkestone, England (every 3hr., one-way or 5-day return 150F). To reach the **tourist office** (tel. 03 21 31 68 38; fax 03 21 33 81 09; email boulogne@tourisme.norsys.fr), on pl. Frédéric Sauvage, exit the train station and go left on bd. Voltaire until you reach the canal, then turn right and follow bd. Diderot past the shopping center and post office; helpful staff books rooms (open M-Sa 8:45am-6pm, Su 9:30am-1pm and 2:30-5:30pm). The **auberge de jeunesse (HI)**, 1 pl. de Lisle (tel. 03 21 99 15 30; fax 03 21 80 45 62), opposite the train station, has a kitchen and **Internet access,** and all rooms have private bath. (HI members only. 68F in triple, breakfast included. Reception 7:30am-1am. Curfew 1am. Reserve ahead in July-Aug.) Charming **restaurants** cluster on rue de Lille in the *vieille ville*, while cheap food abounds on the waterfront around bd. Gambetta. Escape the fish and ferries in the bars and brasseries of **pl. Dalton**, which also has a great market (W and Sa 7:30am-12:30pm).

■ Lille

With a rich Flemish ancestry and exuberant nightlife, the unsullied and largely untouristed Lille flaunts its big city charms without the usual accompanying big city hassle. One of France's finest museums, Lille's **Musée des Beaux-Arts,** on pl. de la République, has an encyclopedic display of early- and mid-19th century French paintings (open M 2-6pm, W-Su noon-6pm, F until 8pm; 30F, under 25 20F). To get to the companion **Musée d'Art Moderne,** 1 allée du Musée, which houses an impressive Cubist and Postmodern collection, take bus 10 or 41 to "Parc Urbain-Musée" (open W-M 10am-6pm; 25F, students 15F). The Flemish Renaissance **Vieille Bourse** (Old Stock Exchange), at pl. Général de Gaulle, now houses flower and book markets. Nearby stand two other masterpieces: the **Chamber of Commerce and Industry** and its tower on pl. du Théâtre, and the 14th-century **Eglise St-Maurice** (M: "Rihour;" church open M-Sa 9am–6pm, Su 2-6pm, except during mass).

The **tourist office**, pl. Rihour (tel. 03 20 21 94 21), occupies a 15th-century castle and offers currency exchange, a free map, and an accommodations service (open M 1-6pm, Tu-Sa 10am-6pm, Su 10am-noon and 2-5pm). **Trains** leave from **Gare Lille Flandres** on pl. de Gare (tel. 08 36 35 35 35; M: Gare Lille Flandres) for Arras (40min., 51F), Brussels (1½hr., 100F), and Paris (1hr., 199F). Lille's other station, **Gare Lille Europe,** rue Corbusier (tel. 03 20 87 30 00; M: Gare Lille Europe), services Eurostar (to London or Brussels) and all TGV trains headed for the south of France. The **Auberge de Jeunesse (HI),** 12 rue Malpart, (tel. 03 20 57 08 94; fax 03 20 63 98 93), is in an old hospital. From Gare Lille Flandres, circle around the station to the left and take rue du Molinel, then the second left onto rue de Paris, and the third right onto rue

Malpart. (69F; singles 76-111F. Breakfast included. Sheets 18F. Reception 7-11am and 4pm-1am. Lockout 10:30am-4pm. Curfew 1am. Closed Dec. 20-Jan. 25.) Spacious **Hôtel de France**, 10 rue de Béthune (tel. 03 20 57 14 78; fax 03 20 57 14 78), is in the heart of the pedestrian district (singles 135-200F; doubles 150-285F; triples 285-300F; extra bed 30F; breakfast 27F). **Les 3 Brasseurs**, 22 pl. de la Gare (tel. 03 20 06 46 25), makes its own beer every morning (open daily 11am-midnight). **Aux Moules**, 34, rue de Béthune, is a local favorite with mussels from 51F (open daily noon-midnight). Pubs line **rue Solférino** and **rue Masséna**, and the *vieille ville* boasts popular dance clubs and wine bars. Stumble down Jean-Jacques Rousseau to **La Piroge**, or try your luck with the bouncer at nearby **Les Visiteurs du Soir** for experimental bands.

■ Near Lille: Arras and Vimy

Built over the fascinating **Les Boves tunnels** that have sheltered both medieval chalk miners and British World War I soldiers, **Arras** lies 40 minutes by train (51F) from Lille. The friendly folks at the **tourist office** (tel. 03 21 51 26 95), in the 15th-century Hôtel de Ville, find rooms (no charge) and organize tours of the tunnels. (Open May-Sept. M-Sa 9am-6:30pm, Su 10am-1pm and 2:30-6:30pm; Oct.-Apr. M-Sa 9am-noon and 2-6pm.) Spend the night at the central **auberge de jeunesse (HI)**, 59 Grande Place (tel. 03 21 22 70 02; 46F; sheets 22F; reception daily 7:30-noon and 5-11pm). Elegant **restaurants** are located near the hostel. Ten kilometers northeast of Arras lies the monument of **Vimy**, a memorial to the 66,000 plus Canadians killed in World War I. The peaceful 11,285 trees planted in the park represent the number of the soldiers whose final resting place is unknown. **Stay on marked trails; undetonated mines lie beyond.** (Sunrise to sunset. Free tours of the tunnels Apr.-Nov. 10am-6pm in English or French. Interpretive center open daily 10am-6pm.) Frequent **buses** (one-way 8F) and **trains** (16F) arrive from Arras.

NORMANDY (NORMANDIE)

Fertile Normandy is a land of gently undulating fields, tiny fishing villages along a jagged coastline, and soaring cathedrals. Vikings seized the region in the 9th century, and invasions have twice secured Normandy's place in military history: in 1066, when William of Normandy conquered England, and on D-Day, June 6, 1944, when Allied armies began the liberation of France here.

   Normandy supplies much of the country's butter; try the creamy, pungent *camembert* cheese, but be sure it's ripe (soft in the middle). The province's traditional drink (*cidre*) comes both dry (*brut*) and sweet (*doux*). A harder cousin is *calvados*, aged apple brandy, which ranks with the finest cognacs.

■ Rouen

Best known as the city where Joan of Arc was burned and Emma Bovary was bored, Rouen is no provincial hayseed town. The city enjoyed prosperity and status from the 10th through 12th centuries as the capital of the Norman empire, and Victor Hugo later dubbed it "the city of a hundred spires."

SIGHTS AND ENTERTAINMENT The most famous of these spires are those of the **Cathédrale de Notre-Dame**, which has the tallest tower in France (151m). The now-grimy Gothic facade so fascinated Monet that he painted it over and over again in varying lights and seasons (open M-Sa 8am-7pm, Su 7:30am-6pm). Behind the cathedral, the flamboyant **Eglise St-Maclou** features an elaborately carved pipe organ. (Open Mar.-Oct. M-Sa 10am-noon and 2-6pm, Su 3-5:30pm; Nov.-Feb. M-Sa 10am-noon and 2-5:30pm, Su 3-5:30pm.) Nearby, at 186 rue de Martainville, **Aitre St-Maclou** served as the church's charnel house and cemetery through the later Middle Ages; visitors gape at the perfectly preserved cadaver of a cat buried alive to exorcise spirits (open daily 8am-8pm; free). From the cathedral, turn onto rue du Gros Horloge to see the charmingly inaccurate 14th-century **Gros Horloge** (Big Clock).

Joan of Arc died on **place du Vieux Marché,** east of the city center. A cross marks the spot near the unsightly **Eglise Ste-Jeanne d'Arc,** designed to resemble an overturned boat. A block up rue Jeanne d'Arc, the **Musée des Beaux-Arts,** square Verdrel, houses an excellent collection of European masters from the 16th through 20th centuries (open W-Su 10am-6pm; 20F, ages 18-25 13F). If you're ill from Monet overdose, be happy that you won't be treated at the **Musée Flaubert et d'Histoire de la Médecine,** 51 rue de Lecat, whose exhibits showcase a gruesome array of pre-anesthesia medical instruments, including gallstone crushers and a battlefield amputation kit (open Tu-Sa 10am-noon and 2-6pm; 12F, ages 18-25 8F). Possessions of the former occupant, writer Gustave Flaubert, are also on display.

On the way to or from Paris, stop by **Giverny,** where the **Musée Claude Monet** preserves the artist's gardens and Japanese prints (open Apr.-Oct. Tu-Su 10am-6pm; 35F, students 25F). Buses run to the museum from **Vernon** (10min., M-Sa 6 per day, Su 3 per day, 12F), 40 minutes from Rouen by train (every 2hr., 52F).

PRACTICAL INFO, ACCOMMODATIONS, AND FOOD Trains run from Rouen to Caen (via Serquigny; 2hr., every 2hr., 113F), Le Havre (1hr., every hr., 72F), Lille (3hr., 3 per day, 160F), and Paris (1½hr., every hr., 102F). From the station, walk down rue Jeanne d'Arc and turn left onto rue du Gros Horloge to reach pl. de la Cathédrale and the **tourist office** (tel. 02 32 08 32 40; fax 02 32 08 32 44), which changes currency and traveler's checks with no commission. (Open Apr.-Sept. M-Sa 9am-7pm, Su 9:30am-12:30pm and 2:30-6pm; Oct.-Mar. M-Sa 9am-6:30pm, Su 10am-1pm.) For 24-hour accommodation service, call **Club Hôtel Rouennais** (tel. 02 35 71 76 77). **Hôtel Normandya,** 32 rue du Cordier (tel. 02 35 71 46 15), offers hospitality near the train station off rue Donjon (singles and doubles 100-110F, with shower 140-150F). **Hôtel des Arcades,** 52 rue de Carmes (tel. 02 35 70 10 30; fax 02 35 70 08 91), is pricier but sparkling (doubles 145-230F). **Camping Municipal de Déville** (tel. 02 35 74 07 59) is on rue Jules Ferry in Déville-les-Rouen, 4km from Rouen; take bus 2 from the station to "Mairie" (22.50F per person; 7F per tent; open May-Sept. for tents). If you crave *moules* (mussels), **Le Queen Mary,** 1 rue du Cercle, off pl. du Vieux-Marché, is for you (44-75F; open July-Aug. daily 11:30am-2pm and 7:30-11pm; Sept.-June closed M). **La P'tite Flambée,** 24 rue Cauchoise, off pl. du Vieux-Marché, makes crepes right before your eyes (12-49F; open Tu-Sa 11:30am-2:30pm and 6:30-11:30pm). Find tasty organic food at **Natural Gourmand'grain,** 3 rue du Petit Salut, off pl. de la Cathédrale (*menu* 41F or 64F; open Tu-Sa noon-6pm). A **market** enlivens pl. du Vieux Marché (open Tu-Su 7am-12:30pm). Packaged foods crinkle at the **Monoprix supermarket,** 73-83 rue du Gros Horloge (open M-Sa 8:30am-9pm).

■ Normandy Coast

Dieppe Hordes of sun-starved Britons flock to Dieppe's long pebbly **beach,** bordered by protective cliffs to the west and the port to the east, which Canadian forces struggled to retake in 1942. **Trains** leave from bd. G. Clémenceau (tel. 02 35 06 69 33) for Rouen (45min., 54F) and continue to Paris St-Lazare (129F) and Caen (145F). (Ticket office open M-F 5:45am-6:30pm, Sa 6:15am-7:35pm, Su 7:15am-8:50pm. Info office open M-Sa 9am-12:30pm and 1:30-6:30pm.) Free buses run to the ferry terminal for ferry ticket holders. The **tourist office,** pont Jehan Ango (tel. 02 35 84 11 77; fax 02 35 06 27 66), is on the waterfront in the *centre ville.* (Open July-Aug. daily 9am-1pm and 2-8pm; May-June and Sept. M-Sa 9am-1pm and 2-7pm, Su 10am-1pm and 3-6pm; Oct.-Apr. M-Sa 9am-noon and 2-6pm.) The **auberge de jeunesse (HI),** 48 rue Louis Fromager (tel. 02 35 84 85 73), has spacious, clean rooms; take bus 2 ("Val Druel") to "Château Michel," backtrack a bit, and take the first left, or call ahead for directions for the 30-minute walk (65F; sheets 16F; reception 8-10am and 5-10pm). Stena **ferries** (tel. 08 02 01 00 20), in the *gare maritime* across the canal at the outer port, cross the English Channel to Newhaven (2¼-4¼hr., June-Sept. 4 per day; Oct.-May 1 per day, 100-240F, bikes free).

Fécamp The port town of Fécamp has its own scenic beach as well as two architectural marvels. The magnificent, Renaissance-inspired **Palais Bénédictine,** 110 rue Alexandre Le Grand, houses impressive collections of medieval and Renaissance religious artifacts. The palace is famous for its after-dinner liqueur, originally distilled from 27 plants and spices by the town's monks. (Open daily May-Sept. 20 9:30am-6pm; Sept. 21-Nov. 11 10am-noon and 2-5:30pm; Nov. 12-Mar. 15 at 10:30am and 2-5pm; Mar. 16-Apr. 10am-noon and 2-5:30pm. 27F, sample included.) The enormous 11th-century **Abbatiale de la Trinité** houses an even rarer liquid: the relic of the *précieux-sang,* a fig trunk that allegedly carried a few drops of Christ's blood to the shores of Fécamp in the 6th century, rests within the massive nave (open daily 9am-7pm; free). The **train station,** bd. de la République (tel. 02 35 28 24 82), serves Paris (2½hr., 144F) and Rouen (1¼hr., 68F) daily. The **tourist office,** 113 rue Alexandre Le Grand (tel. 02 35 28 51 01; fax 02 35 27 07 77), books rooms for a 10F fee and dispenses maps. (Open July-Sept. daily 10am-6pm; Oct.-June M-Sa 9am-12:15pm and 1:45-6pm, Su opens 10am.) The most affordable rooms are located around the Eglise St-Etienne. **Hôtel Martin,** 18 pl. St-Etienne (tel. 02 35 28 23 82), has six clean, bright rooms (singles and doubles 140-210F; breakfast 30F).

■ Caen

Although Allied bombing leveled three quarters of its buildings, Caen restored its architectural treasures and revitalized its tourist industry. The energy from international voyagers and a large student population has made the city a major rail, ferry, and party hub. Caen's biggest draw is the powerful **Mémorial: Un Musée pour la Paix,** in the northwest corner of the city, which includes footage from World War II, displays on pre-war Normandy, a tribute to Nobel Peace Prize laureates, and high-tech exhibits. (Open daily July-Aug. 9am-9pm; Feb. 15-June and Sept.-Oct. 9am-7pm; Nov.-Jan. 4 and Jan. 20-Feb. 14 M-Sa 9am-6pm, Su 9am-7pm. 67F, students 59F, veterans free.) The city's twin abbeys, **Abbaye-aux-Hommes** and the adjacent **Abbatiale-St-Etienne,** both off rue Guillaume le Conquérant, were financed by William the Conqueror as penance for marrying his distant cousin. (Tours of Abbaye-aux-Hommes in French daily 9:30, 11am, 2:30, and 4:30pm. 10F, students 5F. Abbatiale-St-Etienne open daily 8:15am-noon and 2-7:30pm.) Opposite the tourist office sprawl the ruins of William's **château** (open May-Sept. daily 6am-9:30pm; Oct.-Apr. 6am-7:30pm).

Trains leave pl. de la Gare (tel. 08 36 35 35 35) for Paris (2½hr., 152F), Rouen (2hr., 113F), and Tours (3½hr., 168F). Local **buses** run from the station (6.10F) to near the Eglise St-Pierre, where the **tourist office** (tel. 02 31 27 14 14) distributes maps and finds rooms for a 10F fee. (Open July-Aug. M-Sa 9:30am-7pm, Su 9:30am-1pm and 2-5pm; Sept.-June M-Sa 10am-1pm and 2-6pm, Su 10am-1pm.) The clean, popular **auberge de jeunesse (HI),** 68bis rue Eustache-Restout (tel. 02 31 52 19 96), is at Foyer Robert Reme. Take a right from the train station, then take the second right onto rue de Vaucelles and walk up a block. From the bus stop on your left, take bus 5 or 17 ("Fleury" or "Grâce de Dieu") to "Lycée Fresnel" (60F; sheets 15F; reception 5-10pm). For renovated rooms in the *centre ville,* try **Hôtel de la Paix,** 14 rue Neuve-St-Jean (tel. 02 31 86 18 99; singles 155-200F; doubles 165-210F). **Terrain Municipal,** route de Louvigny (tel. 02 31 73 60 92), has riverside campsites (18F per person; 13F per tent; open May-Sept.).

Ethnic restaurants, *crêperies,* and *brasseries* line the streets of the **quartier Vaugueux** near the château. There are morning markets in pl. St-Sauveur (F) and in front of the Eglise St-Pierre (Su). **Le Filao,** 2 av. de la Liberation, serves African specialties in huge quantities (dishes 60F; *menus* 85F and 120F; open Tu-Su noon-2pm and M-Sa 6-11pm). Caen's old streets pulsate in moonlight, especially around **rue de Bras, rue des Croisiers,** and **rue St.-Pierre.** Locals head to **Joy's Club,** 10 rue Strasbourg (tel. 02 31 85 40 40), to flail to techno (open daily 10am-5am; 60F cover includes 1st drink).

■ Cotentin Peninsula

Bayeux An ideal base for exploring the D-Day beaches, **Bayeux** is renowned for its **Tapisserie de Bayeux** (Bayeux Tapestry), 70m of embroidery depicting the Norman conquest of Britain in 1066. The **Centre Guillaume le Conquérant** on rue de Nesmond displays the tapestry. (Open daily May-Aug. 9am-7pm; Sept.-Oct. 15 and Mar.15-Apr. 9am-6:30pm; Oct. 16-Mar. 14 9:30am-12:30pm and 2-6pm. 38F, students 15F.) The **Musée de la Bataille de Normandie** (tel. 02 31 92 93 41), bd. Fabian Ware, recounts the summer of 1944 with old newspaper clippings, photographs, films, and uniforms. (Open May-Sept. 15 daily 9:30am-6:30pm; Sept. 16-Apr. 10am-12:30pm and 2-6pm. 30F, students 15F.)

Trains (tel. 02 31 92 80 50) roll into pl. de la Gare from Caen (20min., 33F), Cherbourg (50min., 78F), and Paris (2½hr., 164F). To walk the 10 minutes to the town center, turn left onto the highway (bd. Sadi-Carnot) and then bear right, following the signs to the *centre ville*. Once there, continue up rue Larcher to rue St-Martin. On your right, the **tourist office** (tel. 02 31 51 28 28; fax 02 31 51 28 29), pont St-Jean, books rooms (open M-Sa 9am-noon and 2-6pm; July-Sept. 15 also Su 9:30am-noon and 2:30-6pm). **Centre d'Accueil Municipal,** 21 rue des Marettes (tel. 02 31 92 08 19), has small singles for 75F (reception 8:30am-noon and 2-7pm). From the station, follow bd. Sadi-Carnot and bear left at the rotary onto bd. Maréchal Leclerc, which metamorphoses into bd. Fabien Ware. **Hôtel Notre-Dame,** 44 rue des Cuisiniers (tel. 02 31 92 87 24; fax 02 31 92 67 11), across from the cathedral, has comfy rooms with cathedral views (singles and doubles 160-270F; breakfast 30F; shower 50F). **Le Table du Terroir,** 42 rue St-Jean, is one of the heartiest restaurants in the region (*menus* 55-95F; open daily noon-2:30pm and 7-10pm).

D-Day Beaches

The record of the 1944 Allied invasion of Normandy can be read in the sobering gravestones and the pockmarked landscape of the D-Day beaches. Ten kilometers north of Bayeux on D514 is **Arromanches,** easternmost of the beaches, where the British sank old ships to create a harbor. The **Musée du Débarquement** on the beach houses relics and photographs of the Allied landings and explains the logistics of the attack. (Open daily May 6-Sept. 5 9am-6:30pm; Sept. 6-Mar. 9 11:30am and 2-5:30pm; Apr.-May 5 9-11:30am and 2-6pm; Sept.-May opens 10am on Su. 32F, students 27F.) At **Omaha Beach,** just east of the Pointe du Hoc, almost 10,000 American graves stretch over a 172.5-acre coastal reserve. A memorial and chapel are dedicated to the fallen Allied troops (open daily Apr.-Nov. 8am-6pm; Dec.-Mar. 9am-5pm). The Canadian Cemetery is located at **Bény-sur-Mer-Reviers;** British cemeteries are at **Ranville** and **Hermanville-sur-Mer. Normandy Tours,** 26 pl. de la Gare (tel. 02 31 92 10 70), runs flexible three- to four-hour tours (60F). **Bus Fly** (tel. 02 31 22 00 08) runs half- and full-day tours, and will pick you up at your hotel (call in advance for availability and reservations).

Cherbourg

Northwest of Bayeux at the northern tip of the Cotentin peninsula, **Cherbourg,** World War II's "Port de la Libération," shuttles passengers to and from Ireland and England. Contact **P&O European Ferries** (tel. 02 33 88 65 70) for connections to Portsmouth and **Brittany Ferries** (tel. 02 33 88 44 88) for Poole. **Irish Ferries** (tel. 02 33 23 44 44) runs to Rosslare three times per week (rotating days; call well in advance for info; office open M-F 9am-noon and 2-6pm). The **train station,** a 20-minute walk from the ferry terminal, serves Bayeux (1hr., 79F), Caen (1½hr., 97F), Paris (3½hr., 212F), and Rouen (3hr., 177F). The helpful **tourist office** (tel. 02 33 93 52 02), at the northern end of the Bassin du Commerce near the bridge Pont Tournant, has a map, plenty of brochures, and a free reservation service (open M-Sa 9am-6:30pm; off-season M-F 9am-noon and 2-6pm, Sa 9am-noon). The new **auberge de jeunesse (HI),** 57 rue de l'Abbaye (tel. 02 33 78 15 15; fax 02 33 78 15 16), is your cheapest option (57F includes required sheets; reception 8am-2pm and 5-10pm). Popular restaurants line quai de Caligny. **Les Baladins,** in an inconspicuous courtyard off rue au Blé, offers Norman *menus* for 50-98F (open daily noon-2pm and 7-10pm). Or stock up at **Continent supermarket,** quai de l'Entrepôt, next to the station (open M-Sa 8:30am-9:30pm).

■ Mont-Saint-Michel

Rising abruptly from the sea directly west of Paris, the island of Mont-St-Michel is visible for kilometers. An **abbey** balances precariously on the jutting rock, surrounded by military fortifications and a *ville basse* built to serve medieval pilgrims. Just as overwhelming as the Mont's beauty, though, are its crowds; try to make the trip during the off-season or late in the day. Start your visit on the **Porte de l'Avancée,** then walk along the **Porte du Roy** to **Grande Rue,** a winding pedestrian street full of souvenir stands and restaurants. A climb up several flights of stairs places you at the abbey entrance, the departure point for tours. (Open daily May-Sept. 9am-5:30pm; Oct.-Apr. 9:30am-4:30pm. 40F, under 26 25F. Tour times vary.) After the tour, escape down the ramparts to the abbey **garden** or the **Porte du Bavole.** Beware the water, though; the tides can rush in at 2m per second. The Mont is stunning at night; view the illumination from the causeway entrance or from across the bay at **Avranches.** Mont-St-Michel is best explored from **St-Malo** (see p. 313), from which run Courriers Bretons **buses** (tel. 02 99 56 79 09; 1½hr.; 106F).

BRITTANY (BRETAGNE)

Brittany is lined with spectacular beaches and misty, almost apocalyptic headlands. This peninsula, its cliffs gnawed by the sea into long crags and inlets, has always tugged away from mainland France, intent on its own direction. Locals speak lilting *Brezhoneg* (Breton) and sustain a rich traditionalism that dates back to Brittany's centuries as an independent duchy. The region's 1800-odd *crêperies* set their tables with the regional specialty, accompanied by the local *cidre.* **Cycling** is the best way to travel. **Hikers** can wander along the long-distance footpaths (*Grandes Randonnées*) GR341, GR37, GR38, GR380, and the spectacular GR34 along the northern coast.

■ Rennes

The administrative center of Brittany and home to two major universities, Rennes mixes Parisian sophistication with traditional Breton charm. The lovely *vieille ville* (old town), the only section to survive the fire that devastated the wood-heavy city in 1720, now teems with hip cafes, bars, and clubs.

SIGHTS AND ENTERTAINMENT The **Musée des Beaux-Arts,** 20 quai Emile Zola, houses an impressive collection of paintings and artifacts dating from the 14th century to the day before yesterday (open W-M 10am-noon and 2-6pm; tours Jul.-Aug. W and F at 2:30pm; 30F). Concerts are often held in the lush and gorgeous **Jardin du Thabor** (open June-Sept. daily 7am-9:30pm), behind the Renaissance **Eglise Notre-Dame** and **Cloître Ste-Melaine.** The **Cathédrale St-Pierre,** in the *vieille ville,* boasts a magnificent ceiling and chandeliers (open daily 9am-noon and 2-5pm). Across the street from the cathedral, down rue Porte Mordelaise, stands the **Porte Mordelaise** itself, the last remaining piece of the town's medieval wall. In early July, Rennes holds the **Tombées de la Nuit** festival (tel. 02 99 79 01 98 or 02 99 30 38 01), nine days of non-stop music, dance, partying, and theater; for info, write the Office de Tourisme, Festival de TN, 8, pl. du Maréchal Juin, 35000 Rennes. Rennais nightlife, known to attract even Parisian students, centers around **pl. Ste-Anne** and **pl. St. Michel.** Check out **La Marina,** 16 pl. St. Anne (until 1am), **L'Espace,** 45 bd. La Tour d'Auvergne (until 5am), or **Le Dejazey,** 54 rue St. Malo (until 3am), for hip late-night activity.

PRACTICAL INFO, ACCOMMODATIONS, AND FOOD The **train station** (tel. 02 99 65 50 50, reservations 08 36 35 35 35), pl. de la Gare, serves Caen (4hr., 11 per day, 163F), St. Malo (1hr., 14 per day, 68F), and Paris (2hr., 15 per day, 277F, all TGV). **Les Courriers Bretons** (tel. 02 99 56 79 09) run to Mont-St-Michel (2½hr., M-Sa 2 per day, Su 1 per day, 62F), while **Anjou Bus** (tel. 02 41 69 10 00 in Angers) goes to Angers (3hr., 1-2 per day, 96F). The **tourist office**, 11, rue Saint-Yves (tel. 02 99 67 11 11. Fax 02 99 67 11 10, has free maps and info on local events (open M-F 9am-6pm, Sa 2-6pm, Su 10am-6pm). Pick up a copy of *La Griffe* for events info.

The **auberge de jeunesse (HI)**, 10-12 Canal St-Martin (tel. 02 99 33 22 33; fax 02 99 59 06 21) is a 30-minute walk from the train station, so take bus 20 ("Centre Commercial Nord"; on weekends, 1 or 18) to "Hôtel Dieu." From there, continue down the road, turn right on rue St-Malo and follow it to the intersection; the hostel is on the right. (49F; singles 85F; doubles 130F, with shower 160F. Reception open daily 7am-11:30pm. Dorm sheets 17F. Breakfast 19F for dorm, included with single or double.) **Hôtel Venezia,** 27 rue Dupont des Loges (tel. 02 99 30 36 56; fax 02 99 30 78 78), off quai Richemont, has well-decorated rooms in a great location. Singles and doubles 110-190F if you show your copy of *Let's Go: Europe.* Take av. Jean Janvier from the station and turn right on rue Dupont des Loges. Rennes is a *gourmand*'s dream—seek out your fancy on **rue St-Malo, pl. St-Michel, rue St-Georges,** or **rue Ste-Melaine. Crêperie au Boulingrain,** 25 rue St. Melaine, a former prison, now serves galettes worth jail time (open M-F 11:30am-2pm and 6:30-11pm, Sa-Su 6:30-11pm).

■ St-Malo

St-Malo is the ultimate oceanside getaway—and everybody knows it. Tourists converge on the miles of warm, brown, sandy beaches that frame crystalline blue waters, and on the town's hoppin' nightlife. The best view of St-Malo is from its ramparts—the old town on one side and a long stretch of sea on the other. **Trains** run from pl. de l'Hermine to Dinan via Dol (1hr., 46F), Paris-Montparnasse (5hr., 294F), and Rennes (1hr., 68F). Courriers Bretons **buses** run to Mont-Saint Michel (tel. 02 99 56 79 09; 1½hr., 106F). The **tourist office** (tel. 02 99 56 64 48), on esplanade St-Vincent near the entrance to the old city, offers a free map and list of accommodations and restaurants (open July-Aug. M-Sa 8:30am-8pm, Su 10am-7pm; shorter hours off-season). **Auberge de Jeunesse/Centre de Rencontres Internationales (HI),** 37 av. du Révérend Père Umbricht (tel. 02 99 40 29 80), is three blocks from the beach (68F; singles and doubles 74F per person; sheets 16F). **Hôtel Gambetta,** 40 bd. Gambetta (tel. 02 99 56 54 70), is pretty and calm (singles 110-150F; doubles 140-220F). **Le Capri,** 10 rue de Boyer, serves traditional *crêpes* at nontraditional prices (open daily 11:30am-3pm and 6:30pm-midnight). For karaoke and 20F sangria, head to the **Cutty Sark,** 20 rue de la Herse (tel. 02 99 40 85 70), where there's jazz on Friday and Saturday (open July-Sept. daily 5pm-3am; Oct.-June M-Sa only). **L'Aviso,** 12 rue Point du Jour boasts 300 different beers (open daily until 2am).

■ Dinan

Tranquil Dinan may be the best-preserved medieval town in Brittany. In the *vieille ville* (old city), 15th-century houses line cobblestone streets, and artisans ply their trades as generations before them have done. The **Promenade des Petits-Fossés** begins near the post office and follows the ramparts to the 13th-century **Porte du Guichet,** the entrance to the **Château de la Duchesse Anne.** Inside the oval tower, the **Musée de Dinan** displays old furniture, paintings, and religious statuettes. (Château and museum open June-Oct. 15 daily 10am-6:30pm; closed Tu and shorter hours off-season. 25F, under 18 10F.) As you enter the *vieille ville* from the port, you'll pass through the **Porte du Jerzual,** formerly the main gate to the city. Recent restorations of the **parapet** have allowed visitors to climb up and stroll along the ramparts with a view of the **Rance River** to one side and of the *vieille ville* to the other.

Trains run to Paris (5hr., 312F), Rennes (1¼hr., 70F), and St-Brieuc (1hr., 54F). **Buses** service Mont-St-Michel (summer only, round-trip 105F). The **tourist office,** 6 rue de l'Horloge (tel. 02 96 39 75 40; fax 02 96 39 01 64), in the *vieille ville*, offers tours (July-Aug. daily 10am and 3pm; 25F) and a guide with a map. (15F. Open June-Sept. M-Sa 9am-7:00pm, Su 10am-noon and 3-5pm; Oct.-May M-Sa 8:30am-12:30pm and 2-6pm.) The wonderful **Auberge de Jeunesse (HI),** Moulin du Méen in Vallée de la Fontaine-des-Eaux (tel. 02 96 39 10 83; fax 02 96 39 10 62), has 70 beds in small, clean rooms. Call from the station and the owner may pick you up; if you're walking (30min.), turn left from the station's main exit, then left across the tracks, turn right, and follow the tracks and signs (49F; sheets 16F; camping 26F; reception 9-11am and 3-11pm). **Hôtel du Théâtre,** 2 rue Ste-Claire (tel. 02 96 39 06 91), across from the tourist office, offers pleasant rooms (singles and doubles 80-150F; breakfast 22F). At 6 rue Ste-Claire, **Le Cantorbery** pleases with a delicious 70F *menu* (open June-Aug. daily noon-2pm and 7-10pm; Sept.-May closed M). Feast on *galettes* and crepes at the **Crêperie des Artisans,** 6 rue du Petit Fort (open June-Aug. daily noon-2:30pm and 7-10:30pm; Sept.-June closed M).

■ Northern Coast (Côtes d'Armor)

Brittany's northern coast features some of the most spectacular scenery in France. Transportation poses problems, but many tourist offices offer lists of regional bus, train, and boat connections, as well as information on tours and hiking trails.

Côte d'Emeraude and Côte de Granite Rose
Between the Côte d'Emeraude and the Côte de Granite Rose, **St-Brieuc** provides a base for trips to the scenic countryside. **Trains** arrive from Dinan (1hr., 56F), Morlaix (1hr., 85F), and Rennes (1hr., 92F); CAT **buses** serve Cap Fréhel (July-Sept., 1½hr., 46F) and Paimpol (1½hr., 38F). To get to **Manoir de la Ville Guyomard (HI)** (tel. 02 96 78 70 70; fax 02 96 78 27 47), take bus 3 ("Les Villages") to "Van Meno" or "Jean Moulin" (6F, last bus 8:15pm; dorms 68F; sheets 20F; camping 26F).

Northeast of St-Brieuc, gorgeous **Cap Fréhel** marks the northern point of the Côte d'Emeraude. The tip of this windswept peninsula drops 70m into the ocean below, while the coastline features the scenic GR34 **hiking trail.** If your spirit is as rugged as the cape's cliffs, you'll love the **Auberge de Jeunesse Cap Fréhel (HI),** la Ville Hadrieux, Kerivet (tel. 02 96 41 48 98; Sept. 16-Apr. 02 98 78 70 70), near Plévenon, where many guests choose to camp out. Take a bus to the Cap and walk toward Plévenon on D16, then follow the inconspicuous signs bearing the fir-tree hostel symbol (30-40min; 44F; sheets 20F; camping 25F; open May-Sept.). The hostel also rents **bikes** (25F per half-day); if you ask at St-Brieuc's hostel, you can leave a rented bike at Cap Fréhel and vice-versa.

Paimpol, at the eastern end of the Côte de Granite Rose, offers access to nearby hiking trails, islands, and beaches. CAT **buses** run to St-Brieuc (1¼hr., 42F). The **tourist office** (tel. 02 96 20 83 16) is at pl. de la République (open July-Aug. M-Sa 9am-7:30pm, Su 10am-1pm; shorter hours off-season). The **auberge de jeunesse/gîte d'étape (HI)** (tel. 02 96 20 83 60) is at Château de Kéraoul (46F; camping 25F; sheets 17F), and organizes sea kayaking trips. Just six kilometers north of Paimpol, the dramatic pink granite **Pointe de l'Arcouest** and the tranquil **Île de Bréhat** merit a visit.

Finistère Nord
Although it is often used simply as a base for exploring Northern Brittany, **Brest** is a lively home to boisterous sailors and students who attend Brittany's second largest university. Brest's **château** was the only building to survive World War II and is now the world's oldest active military institution. **Trains** arrive from Morlaix (45min., 54F), Nantes (4hr., 210F), Paris (4½hr., 313F plus 10F TGV reservation), and Rennes (1½hr., 161F). The **tourist office,** pl. de la Liberté (tel. 02 98 44 24 96; fax 02 98 44 53 73), offers free maps. (Open June 15-Sept. 15 M-Sa 9:30am-12:30pm and 2-6:30pm, Su 10am-noon and 2-4pm. Shorter hours off-season.) To get to the **auberge de jeunesse (HI),** rue de Kerbriant (tel. 02 98 41 90 41; fax 02 98 41

82 66), take bus 7 (6F; last bus 7:30pm, 6pm on Su) to "Port de Plaisance"; facing the port, take your first right, then another right, and the hostel is on the right. (69F. Reception M-F 7-9am and 5-8pm, Sa-Su 7-10am and 5-8pm. Curfew midnight; off-season 11pm.) **Camping du Goulet** (tel. 02 98 45 86 84), is 6km out of Brest and 1km from the sea; take bus 14 to "Le Cosquer" or bus 7, 11, 12, or 26 to "Route de Conquet" (17F per person, 20F per tent; free hot showers). Brest-feed at the **Restaurant l'Hermine,** 9 rue Bois d'Amour (open Tu-Su noon-2:30pm and 7-9:30pm).

For an idyllic retreat, look into excursions to **Ile de Batz,** just north of Roscoff. Ferries run every 30 minutes between 7:45 am and 8pm from Roscoff. Call **CFTM** (tel. 02 98 61 79 66) for info. The island's charming **auberge de jeunesse (HI)** (tel. 02 98 61 77 69) is just two minutes from the beach.

Crozon Peninsula

To the north and south, Finistère's two larger peninsulas overshadow **Crozon,** a tiny point of land between the profiles of Léon and La Cornouaille. From its jagged cliffs, you can gaze across azure pools and feel a million miles from Brittany's tourist hubs. Bikers may find the terrain challengingly hilly, but hitchers report easy success all over the peninsula. **Boats** sail from Brest's *gare maritime* to Le Fret on the peninsula (49F, 56F with shuttles to the peninsula's main towns: Crozon, Morgat, and Camaret). **Buses** connect Brest to Crozon or Camaret (1½hr., 68F). From Quimper, the peninsula is best reached by bus (58F). The bus between Camaret and Crozon or Morgat costs 11F. **ULAMIR** (tel. 02 98 27 01 68), in Crozon, has info on the peninsula's four **gîtes d'étape,** which offer beds for 45F.

Just beyond the edge of **Camaret** on the D8 sit the **Alignements de Lagatjar,** rocky monoliths from 2500 BC. Nearby, the ruins of **Château de St-Pol Roux** afford a magnificent view of the bay. A memorial to the Bretons of the Free French forces stands on the 76m cliff on the **Pointe de Penhir,** just 3.5km away on the D8. Climb out onto the rocks for a blood-curdling view of the isolated rock masses of the **Tas de Pois.** Each Monday in July and August, Camaret hosts **Les Lundis Musicaux** (tel. 02 98 27 90 49), with concerts from classical music recitals to gospel jams. Camaret's **tourist office** (tel. 02 98 27 93 60), is in the Gendarmerie next to pl. de Gaulle (open July-Aug. M-Sa 9am-7pm, Su 9am-noon and 2-6pm; shorter hours off-season). **Hôtel le Styvel** (tel. 02 98 27 93 06) and **Hôtel Vauban** (tel. 02 98 27 91 36), next to each other on quai du Styvel, offer the most affordable rooms (singles and doubles 160F).

Crozon is a good base from which to explore the peninsula. The **tourist office** (tel. 02 98 27 07 92) faces the beach on bd. de la Plage (open July-Aug. M-Sa 9:15am-7:30pm, shorter hours off-season). Presqu'île Loisirs, opposite the tourist office, rents **bikes. Hôtel Moderne,** 61 Rue Alsace Lorraine (tel. 02 98 27 00 10), has reasonable rooms, if somewhat inconsistent decor (doubles 184F). **Morgat** has splendid beaches that attract throngs of summer vacationers. **Camping du Bouis** (tel. 02 98 26 12 53), is 1.5km outside town on the way to the Cap. (35F, 2 people 62F, each extra person 15F. Showers 5F. Gates closed 11pm-8am. Open Easter-Sept.)

■ Southern Brittany

Southern Brittany is most easily accessible through its hub, **Quimper,** but travelers in the know move on quickly to the smaller, more remote communities along the coast.

Quiberon

All roads in **Quiberon** lead to the smooth, sandy, wonderfully clean **Grande Plage** at the heart of town. Connected to the mainland by only a narrow strip of land, this *presqu'île* (literally, "almost island") is a great place to relax with an ice cream, check out your neighbor's tan, and make plans for a trip to Belle-Ile. To escape the masses of tourists, there's always the smaller, rockier **Plage du Goviro** near the campgrounds—from the port, follow bd. Chanard east along the water as it becomes bd. de la Mer and then bd. du Goviro. For a walk on the wild side, head to the **Côte Sauvage,** a craggy, windy 10km along the western edge of the peninsula—but mind the *Baignades Interdites* (no swimming) signs; these waters can be very treacherous.

Trains (tel. 02 97 50 07 07) run only in July and August, to Auray; TIM **buses** (tel. 02 97 47 29 64) also run to Auray (1hr., 35F) via Carnac (30min., 22F). To get to the **tourist office,** 14 rue de Verdun (tel. 02 97 50 07 84; fax 02 97 30 58 22), from the train station, turn left and go down rue de la Gare. When you see the church on your left, bear right down rue de Verdun; the tourist office is on the left and has a guide to area accommodations and restaurants. (Open M-Sa 9am-12:30pm and 2-6:30pm; June-Sept. also Su 9:30am-12:30pm and 3-7pm.) To reach the small, centrally located **auberge de jeunesse (HI),** 45 rue du Roch-Priol (tel. 02 97 50 15 54), from the station, turn left, then take rue de la Gare through pl. du Repos, take rue de Lille, turn left onto rue Roch-Priol where the road splits at the "Itinéraire Conseillée" sign and go uphill to the hostel. (49F. Breakfast 19F. Sheets 17F. Reception open daily May-Sept. 8:30-10am and 6-8:30pm.) **Hôtel de l'Océan,** 7 quai de l'Océan (tel. 02 97 50 07 58; fax 02 97 50 27 81), offers clean, plain rooms (singles and doubles 170-300F). Follow directions to the tourist office, but take rue de Verdun to its end and turn right on rue de Port Maria, which meets quai de l'Océan. Spacious **Camping Bois d'Amour** (tel. 02 97 50 13 52, off-season 02 97 30 24 00) has a heated swimming pool (23-37F per person, camping location 37-69F; electricity 19F; open Apr.-Sept.).

Belle-Ile

At least five boats depart daily from Quiberon's Port-Maria (45min., round-trip 105F, 47F per bike) for **Belle-Ile,** an island with high cliffs, narrow creeks, and crashing seas. The massive 16th- to 17th-century **Citadelle Vauban,** now a museum, will catch your eye from the boat (open daily May-Oct. 9:30am-6pm; Nov.-Apr. 9:30am-noon and 2-6pm; 35F). The **Plage de Donnant** is the island's widest and most popular beach, but don't miss gems like the tiny **Plage Port Maria** on the eastern shore or the powdery white expanse of **Plage Grands Sables,** southeast of **Le Palais,** the island's port and largest town. The **tourist office** (tel. 02 97 31 81 93; fax 02 97 31 56 17) is on the left end of the *quai* as you disembark. (Open July-Aug. M-Sa 8:30am-8pm, Su 9am-12:30pm; Sept.-June M-Sa 9am-noon and 2-6pm, Su 10am-noon.) **Cyclotour** (tel. 02 97 31 80 68), quai de Bonnelle, near the tourist office, rents bikes for 60-80F per day. (Passport deposit. Open July-Aug. daily 8:15am-7pm; Sept.-June M-Sa 9am-noon and 2-7pm.) Head 6km northwest to **Sauzon,** a picturesque fishing village, and then on to **Pointe des Poulains** on the northernmost tip of the island. Massive rock formations rise over crystalline waters at the **Grotte de l'Apothecairerie,** just southwest of the Pointe.

A hostel and campsite are located near the citadel, a 10-minute hike from Le Palais' port. Turn right from the port and follow the quay to the footbridge leading to the citadel; cross the bridge, walk diagonally left through the parking lot, follow the street to the left and enter **Camping Les Glacis.** (Tel. 02 97 31 41 76. Fax 02 97 31 57 16. 19F per person, 12F per tent, 4F per bike. No credit cards.) To reach the **HI youth hostel** (tel. 02 97 31 81 33), continue on, climb another hill, and follow the road through a residential neighborhood (49F, sheets 17F, tents 25F per person; reception open daily 8-10am and 6-8pm). **La Frégate** (tel. 02 97 31 54 16), quai de l'Acadie, in front of the dock, has rooms above a lively restaurant and bar (singles and doubles 120-170F, with shower and toilet 230F; breakfast 30F; open Apr.-Oct.).

■ Nantes

While Nantes is part of the Pays de la Loire, most *Nantais* feel a cultural allegiance to Brittany. The city is defined by its high-tech industries, bountiful greenery, and 27,000 college students, and while there aren't many must-see sights, its ideal location, year-round festivals, and vibrant nightlife make Nantes a smart stop between Brittany and points south. Built in the 15th century by François II, Nantes' heavily fortified **Château des Ducs de Bretagne** once held Gilles de Retz (the original Bluebeard). In 1598, Henri IV composed the Edict of Nantes here to soothe national religious tensions. The château has two museums: the **Musée des Arts Populaires Régionaux,** with traditional Breton clothing, and the **Musée des Salorges,** which explores Nantes' colonial and commercial history. (Open July-Aug. daily 10am-7pm;

Sept.-June W-M 10am-noon and 2-7pm. Courtyard and ramparts open July-Aug. daily 10am-7pm; Sept.-June 10am-noon and 2-7pm. Château and museums 20F, students 10F, under 12 free.)

The **train** station (tel. 08 36 35 35 35) has two entrances: north (27 bd. de Stalingrad and cours John Kennedy) and south (bus connections at rue de Loumel) across the tracks. Trains run to Bordeaux (4hr., 224F), La Rochelle (2hr., 122F), Paris (3-4hr., 220-265F; by TGV 2hr., add 36-90F), and Rennes (2hr., 115F). **Cariane Atlantique**, 5 allée Duquesne (tel. 02 40 20 46 99), sends **buses** to Rennes (2hr., 95F) and Vannes (1½hr., 93.50F). The **tourist office**, pl. du Commerce (tel. 02 40 20 60 00; fax 02 40 89 11 99), has good maps and info (open M-Sa 10am-7pm).

Nantes has lots of good hotels and, in the summer, student dorm space. Try the 200-bed **Foyer des Jeunes Travailleurs, Beaulieu (HI)**, 9 bd. Vincent Gâche (tel. 02 40 12 24 00; fax 02 51 82 00 05; 57F, higher for nonmembers, sheets 16F; reception 8am-midnight). The **Cité Internationale/Auberge de Jeunesse (HI)**, 2 pl. de la Manufacture (June-Aug. tel. 02 40 29 29 20; Sept.-May tel. 02 40 20 57 25; fax 02 40 20 08 94), has 70F rooms. **Hôtel du Tourisme**, 5 allée Duquesne (tel. 02 40 47 90 26; fax 02 40 35 57 25; singles and doubles 140-220F), has a great location. Restaurants on **rue Kervégan** and **rue de la Juiverie,** in the St-Croix quarter, will sautée, boil, skewer, and grill almost anything. There are **open-air markets** on **pl. du Bouffay** and at the **Marché de Talensac,** along rue de Bel-Air near pl. St-Similien behind the post office (Tu, F, and Su 9am-1pm). A **Monoprix** is at 2 rue de Calvaire (open M-Sa 9am-9pm). For nightlife listings, check the weekly *Nantes Poche* (6F at any *tabac*). The **rue Scribe** is full of late-night bars and cafes—try Le Duo, Le Scribe, or Le Corneille.

LOIRE VALLEY (PAYS DE LA LOIRE)

Between Paris and Brittany, the fertile valley of the Loire, France's longest river, practically overflows with châteaux, which run the gamut from dilapidated medieval fortresses to elegant Renaissance homes reflected in pools and surrounded by spectacular gardens. Most châteaux were built in the 16th and 17th centuries, when French monarchs left Paris for the countryside around Tours in order to enjoy hunting excursions while attending to their state duties. The history of many of these dignified mansions presents a mixed bag of genius, promiscuity, and dirty dealings.

The hostels in Blois, Saumur, and Orléans are comfortable bases, but pose daunting challenges to the car-less; public transportation routes fan out of the larger cities, but infrequent service can strand you. Tours is the region's best rail hub. Distributed at train stations, the invaluable *Les Châteaux de la Loire en Train Eté '99* and *Châteaux pour Train et Vélo* have train schedules and info on bike and car rental.

■ Orléans

Orléans, with its fairy-tale castles, expansive vineyards, and rich forests, has been besieged by jealous foreigners for millennia—today, its prominence is gradually waning as nearby Tours steals the show. Come to Orléans to get better acquainted with St. Joan of Arc or to explore the châteaux a daytrip away. The stained-glass windows of the stunning **Cathédrale Ste-Croix** depict Joan's dramatic story, from her liberation of the city to the flames that consumed her (open daily June-Sept. 9:15am-7pm; Oct.-May 10am-noon and 2:15-6:45pm). The **Maison de Jeanne d'Arc,** 3 pl. de Gaulle, off pl. du Martroi, explores Orléans's obsession with the formidable female fighting machine. (Open daily May-Oct. Tu-Su 10am-noon and 2-6pm; Nov.-Apr. Tu-Su 2-6pm. 13F, students 6F50.) A pleasant daytrip down the Loire lies the region's second-oldest castle, the imposing 14th-century fortress **Sully-sur-Loire,** accessible by bus from the *gare routière* (1hr., 44F).

Trains stop at Gare d'Orléans on their way to Blois (40min., 104F), Paris (1¼hr., 180F), and Tours (1¼hr., 178F). A second train station, Gare Les-Aubrais (tel. 02 38 79 91 00), is 30 minutes north of the *centre ville* on rue Pierre Semar; a free and frequent train shuttles between the two stations. The **tourist office,** pl. Albert 1er (tel. 02 38 24 05 05; fax 02 38 54 49 84), off the mall above the Gare d'Orléans, offers city tours and local info. (Open July-Aug. M-Sa 9am-7pm, Su 9:30am-12:30pm and 3-6:30pm; off-season closed Su afternoon and M-Sa at 6:30.) The budget accommodation of choice is the **Auberge de jeunesse (HI),** 14 rue du Faubourg Madeleine (tel. 02 38 62 45 75); take bus B ("Paul-Bert") from the Gare d'Orléans. (Members only. 42F. Reception 7-9:30am and 5:30-10pm. Oct.-May closed Sa.) Wander **rue de Bourgogne** for inexpensive *brasseries,* restaurants, and bars. **Ste-Catherine,** 64 rue Ste-Catherine, and **Le Brin de Zinc,** next door, are both good, cheap places to eat. **Monoprix,** 46 rue de Faubourg Bannier, stocks groceries (open M-Th 8:30am-12:45pm and 2:30-7:30pm, F 8:30am-8pm, Sa 8:30am-7pm).

■ Blois

Blois relishes its position as gateway to the Loire Valley and welcomes visitors with bucolic charm and proximity to the important châteaux. Home to French monarchs Louis XII and François I, Blois's **château** was the Versailles of the late 15th and early 16th centuries. (Château open daily Mar.15-June and Sept. 9am-6:30pm; July and Aug. 9am-8pm; Oct.-Mar. 14 9am-12:30pm and 2-5:30pm. 35F, students 20F.)

Trains run to Orléans (30min., 51F) and Paris (1¾hr., 121F), but not to most châteaux. Rent a **bike** instead at **Atelier Cycles,** 44 levée des Tuileries (tel. 02 54 74 30 13; 25-100F per day), near the "Verdun" bus stop on line 4, and explore. The **tourist office,** 3 av. Jean Laigret (tel. 02 54 90 41 41), can direct you to local sights and has complete info on nearby châteaux. (Open May-Sept. M-Sa 9am-7pm, Su and holidays 10am-7pm; Oct.-Apr. M-Sa 9am-12:30pm and 2-6pm, Su 9:30am-12:30pm.) **Point Bus,** 2 pl. Victor Hugo (tel. 02 54 78 15 66), sends buses to Chambord and Cheverny (65F, students 50F; bus passes include reduced admission) and other châteaux. For hot showers and a jovial, countryside atmosphere, make the 5km trip to the **auberge de jeunesse (HI),** 18 rue de l'Hôtel Pasquier (tel. 02 54 78 27 21). Follow Porte Côté then rue Denis Papin to the river, then take bus 4 ("Les Grouets") and get off at the bottom of the hill, after the large stone church. (61F, discounts after first night. Reception 6:45-10am and 6-10:30pm. Curfew 10:30pm. Open Mar.-Nov. 15. Reserve ahead.) **Auberge de Jeunesse Verte** (tel. 02 38 44 61 31) is 10km away in Montivault. **Le Pavillon,** 2 av. Wilson (tel. 02 54 74 23 27), has clean, bright rooms (singles 100-130F; doubles 220F). **Hôtel du Bellay,** 12 rue des Minimes (tel. 02 54 78 23 62), at the top of porte Chartraine, has clean rooms and spotless bathrooms (singles and doubles 130-185F; breakfast 25F; call ahead).

Blois drowns its citizens in chocolate. Sumptuous *pavé du roi* (chocolate-almond cookies) and *malices du loup* (orange peels in chocolate) peer invitingly from *pâtisseries* along rue Denis Papin. For those who cling foolishly to the dinner-before-dessert convention, restaurants cluster on **rue St- Lubin** and **pl. Poids du Roi,** near the cathedral, while *boulangeries* and fruit stands line **rue des Jacobins,** below the château. **Les Arcades,** pl. Louis XII, has good, cheap *menus* from 57F.

■ Near Blois: Chambord, Cheverny, and Amboise

Built by François I to satisfy his egomania, **Chambord** is the largest and most extravagant of the Loire châteaux. Seven hundred of François I's trademark stone salamanders lurk on Chambord's walls, ceilings, and staircases, and 365 fireplaces are scattered through the 440 rooms. The central staircase is a double helix. (Open daily July-Aug. 9:30am-6:45pm; Apr.-June and Sept. 9:30am-5:45pm; Oct.-Mar. 9:30am-4:45pm. 40F, students 25F. Grounds and wildlife preserve free.) By **bike** from Blois, take route D956 south 2-3km, then go left on D33.

Cheverny, accessible by bus or bike from Blois (take D956 south), soothes with manicured grounds and a magnificent interior: Spanish leather walls, delicate Delft vases, and an elaborate royal bedchamber still await the visit of their first French king.

(Open daily June-Sept. 15 9:15am-6:45pm; late Sept. 9:30am-noon and 2:15-6pm; Oct. and Mar. 9:30am-noon and 2:15-5:30pm; Apr.-May 9:15am-noon and 2:15-6:30pm; Nov.-Feb. 9:30am-noon and 2:15-5pm. 33F, students 21F.)

The battlements of the 15th-century château at **Amboise** (tel. 02 47 57 00 98) stretch out across the hill above the town like protective arms—an unsettling sight to those who considered attacking the place that four French kings called home. Two of those kings did meet their end here: the four-foot tall Charles VIII bumped his head on a *really* low door and died a few hours later, and the equally clumsy Charles V tripped over a torchbearer and burned himself alive. Today, the jewel of the grounds is the late 15th-century **Chapelle St-Hubert.** A plaque inside marks Leonardo da Vinci's supposed resting place. (Open daily July-Aug. 9am-7:30pm; Apr.-June 9am-6:30pm; late Mar. and Sept.-Oct. 9am-6pm; Nov.-Jan. 9am-noon and 2-5pm; Feb.-Mar. 13 9am-noon and 2-5:30pm. 37F, students 30F.) **Trains** pass through on their way to Blois (15min. 32F), Paris (2¼hr., 140F), and Tours (20min., 28F). The **auberge de jeunesse (HI),** Ile d'Or (tel. 02 47 57 06 36), sits on an island in the middle of the Loire (members only; 50F; reception Tu-Su 3-8pm; call ahead).

■ Tours

Tours is the urban centerpiece of the Loire region, and its fabulous nightlife, diverse population, and great food will free scenery-imprisoned souls. **Cathédrale St-Gatien,** rue Jules Simon, may have the most dazzling collection of stained glass in the Loire. (Open daily Easter-Sept. 8:30am-noon and 2-8pm; Oct.-Easter 8:30am-noon and 2-5:30pm.) Other than the cathedral, though, Tours' sights are low-key. Check out the wax reenactments at the **Historial de Touraine,** 25 av. André Malraux, if you so desire. Otherwise, kick back and enjoy the cafe scene and nightlife.

Trains run to Amboise (20min., 28F), Bordeaux (2½hr., 224F), Paris-Austerlitz (2¼hr., 153F). The **tourist office,** 78/82, rue Bernard Palissy (tel. 02 47 70 37 37; fax 02 47 61 14 22), distributes maps, books accommodations, and leads a detailed historical tour on foot. (Open June-Aug. M-Sa 8:30am-7pm, Su 2:30-5pm; Sept.-May M-Sa 8:30am-6pm, Su 2:30-5pm.) **Hotel Foch,** 20 rue du Maréchal Foch (tel. 02 47 05 70 59; fax 02 47 20 95 10), has large rooms, a marvelous location, and a friendly proprietor (singles 120-220F; doubles 150-260F; triples 290F). The small **Hôtel St-Eloi,** 79 bd. Béranger (tel. 02 47 37 67 34), offers a pleasant atmosphere (singles and doubles 140-180F). Local favorite **Chez Jean Michel,** 123 rue Colbert, features new culinary creations every day (*menu* 70F; open M-Sa 7:30-10:30pm, Tu-Sa also noon-2pm). **Pl. Plum'** is a peach of a place to find cheerful students sipping drinks and chattering at countless cafés and bars. **Dépanneur** features 13F half-pint beers amid industrial decor. A lively, youthful crowd frequents the alternative, techno-pop, and jazz nights at **Rhythm and Blues,** 19 rue Petit Soleil open daily 11pm-4am; 30-50F cove).

■ Near Tours: Villandry, Loches, and Chenonceau

Villandry (tel. 02 47 50 02 09) maintains fantastic gardens with waterfalls, vine-covered walkways, and over 120,000 plants, but the château itself pales before its regal cousins. (Gardens open June-Aug. daily 8:30am-8pm; Sept.-May 9am-dusk. Château open daily July-Aug. 9am-6:30pm; off-season 9:30am-5:30pm. Château and garden 45F.) Villandry is difficult to get to: from Tours, take the **train** to Savonnières (10min., 15F) and walk 4km along the Loire. **Cyclists** follow D16.

The walled medieval town of **Loches** surrounds its grand château, which consists of two distinct wings at opposite ends of a hill. To the south, the 11th-century **donjon** (keep) and watchtowers went from keeping enemies out to keeping them in when Charles VII turned it into a state prison, complete with suspended cages. (Open daily July-Sept. 15 9am-7pm; Mar. 15-June and Sept. 16-30 9:30am-1pm and 2:30-7pm; Feb.-Mar. 14 and Oct. 9:30am-1pm and 2:30-6pm. 30F, students 20F.) Four **buses** per day make the 50-minute trek from in front of the Tours train station to Loches (45F; pay on board). Nine trains also make the journey (1hr., 45F).

A series of women created the graceful beauty of château **Chenonceau** (tel. 02 47 23 90 07): first the wife of a tax collector distracted by war, then, in succession, the lover (Diane de Poitier) and wife (Catherine de Medici) of Henri II. Its internal bridge over the river Cher marked the border between annexed and Vichy France during World War II (open Mar. 16-Sept. 15 daily 9am-7pm; call for off-season hours; 45F, students 35F). **Trains** roll from the station 2km away to Tours (45min., 34F).

■ Saumur

Saumur's 14th-century **château** stands aloof above the city's skyline. Charles V's brother, Louis I of Anjou, built this pre-Renaissance edifice as a country residence. Inside, the **Musée des Arts Décoratifs** features medieval and Renaissance paintings and tapestries, and the **Musée du Cheval** will appeal to even the lukewarm equestrian. (Château and museums open daily June-Sept. 9:30am-6pm; July-Aug. also W and Sa 8:30-10:30pm; Oct.-May 9:30am-noon and 2-5:30pm; Oct.-Mar. closed Tu. 37F, students 26F.) Don't leave Saumur without tasting the region's specialties: *les vins* and *les champignons* (mushrooms). An impressive *cave* is **Gratien et Meyer**, route de Chinon (tel. 02 41 83 13 30). Take bus D from pl. Bilange to "Beaulieu." Check out the bottles of wine in the *cave*, then try some. (Open Apr.-Sept. daily 9am-6:30pm; Oct.-Mar. M-F 9am-noon and 2-6pm, Sa-Su 10am-12:30pm and 3-6pm. 15F; 1hr. *dégustation* 50F.) The **Champignonnière du Saut-aux-Loups** (tel. 02 41 51 70 30), a local mushroom *cave*, offers tastings (open Mar. to mid-Nov. daily 10am-6:30pm; 25F). Near Saumur, the awesome Abbaye de Fontevraud (tel. 02 41 51 71 41), known as a refuge for women (e.g. Eleanor of Aquitaine), is the largest extant monastic city in Europe. (Open daily June to the 3rd Su in Sept. 9am-6:30pm; off-season reduced hours and closed noon-2pm.)

Trains roll out of the station on av. David d'Angers for Angers (30min., 42F) and Tours (45min., 56F). The **tourist office,** pl. Bilange (tel. 02 41 40 20 60; local bus A), next to pont Cessart, books beds for a 5F fee. (Open mid-May to mid-Oct. M-Sa 9:15am-7pm, Su 10:30am-12:30pm and 3:30-6:30pm; mid-Oct. to mid-May M-Sa 9:15am-12:30pm and 2-6pm.) The modern **Centre International de Séjour (HI),** rue de Verden (tel. 02 41 40 30 00), on Ile d'Offard, has a superb view of the château (8-berth rooms 82.50F; 2-berth rooms 106F; reception 8am-8pm). At **Le 30 Février,** 9 pl. de la Républic, add a day to your life with healthy salads, pizzas, and vegetarian plates (35-65F; open M-Sa noon-2pm and 7-10:30pm, Su 7-10:30pm).

■ Angers

From behind the massive stone walls of Angers's 15th-century **château,** the Dukes of Anjou ruled the surrounding countryside and an island across the Channel; Henry II held court here as often as in London. (Open daily June-Sept. 15 9:30am-7pm; Sept. 16-Oct. and Lent-May 10am-6pm; Nov.-Lent 10am-5pm. 35F, students 23F.) Inside, the 14th-century **Tapisserie de l'Apocalypse,** thought to be the world's largest woven masterpiece, depicts the Book of Revelations. The **Musée de la Tapisserie Contemporaine** has an amazing textile and tapestry collection. (Open mid-June to mid-Sept. daily 9am-6:30pm; off-season Tu-Su 10am-noon and 2-6pm. 20F.)

Trains leave the station on rue de la Gare for Orléans (3-4hr., 164F), Paris-Austerlitz (4hr., 239F), Saumur (30min., 42F), and Tours (1hr., 86F). **Buses** run to Saumur (1½hr., 46F) and Rennes (3hr., 96F). The **tourist office,** pl. Kennedy (tel. 02 41 23 51 11; fax 02 41 23 51 66), opposite the château, organizes tours and reserves rooms. (Open June-Sept. M-Sa 9am-7pm, Su 10am-1pm and 2-6pm; Oct.-May M-Sa 9am-12:30pm and 2-6:30pm.) The **Auberge de Jeunesse Darwin (HI),** 3 rue Darwin (tel. 02 41 72 00 20; fax 02 41 48 51 91), has 320 beds. Take bus 1 ("Belle Baille") to its end (members 61F; kitchen). The family-run **Royal Hôtel,** rue d'Iéna (tel. 02 41 88 30 25; fax 02 41 81 05 75), off pl. de la Visitation, has immaculate rooms (singles 100-210F; doubles 150-240F). For cafes and *pâtisseries*, stroll along rue St-Laud. The **mar-**

ket in the basement of Les Halles, rue Plantagenêt, sells inexpensive produce and baked goods (open Tu-Sa 7am-8pm, Su 7am-1:30pm). **La Soufflerie,** 8 pl. du Pilori, has great dinner and dessert soufflés (34-53F; open Tu-Sa noon-2:30pm and 7-10pm).

■ La Rochelle

With white sand beaches, refined 14th-century architecture, and annual festivals, La Rochelle is the perfect vacation spot. Climb around the fortifications of the 14th-century **Tour St-Nicolas,** on the left as you face the harbor. (Open Apr.-Sept. daily 10am-7pm; Oct.-Mar. 10am-12:30pm and 2-5:30pm. 25F, students 15F.) During the last week of June and the first week of July, the city hosts the **Festival International du Film de la Rochelle** (admission to all 100 films 490F; tel. 01 48 06 16 66; fax 01 48 06 15 40). Then, in the third week of July, La Rochelle turns around and holds its **FrancoFolies,** a massive six-day music festival with francophone performers from all around the world (call 05 46 50 55 77 or the tourist office). **Île de Ré,** an island known for its 70km of white sand beaches, lies only 10km from downtown La Rochelle. Look into excursions (by bike, bus, or ferry) to the island. **Trains** leave daily for Bordeaux (2hr., 131F) and Paris (5hr., 256F). The **tourist office,** pl. de la Petite Sirène (tel. 05 46 41 14 68; fax 05 46 41 99 85), is in the quartier du Gabut. (Open July-Aug. M-Sa 9am-8pm, Su 11am-7pm; June and Sept. M-Sa 9am-7pm, Su 11am-5pm; Oct.-May M-Sa 9am-12:30pm and 2-6pm, Su 10:30am-12:30pm.) Take bus 10 ("Port des Minimes") to "Auberge de Jeunesse" to reach **Centre International de Séjour, Auberge de Jeunesse (HI)** (tel. 05 46 44 43 11; 72F), av. des Minimes.

AQUITAINE

Forested hills, tranquil river valleys, and dramatic cliffs have drawn people to Aquitaine for some 150,000 years. Today, the Dordogne, Vézère, Isle, and Lot rivers wind past limestone caves painted with scenes of Paleolithic life, 12th-century Romanesque churches and chapels clinging to the rocks of pilgrimage towns, and through *bastides* (fortified mountaintop towns) built during the Hundred Years War. Bus and train connections to smaller towns can be inconvenient, but a bike makes for pleasant touring if a car is not an option.

■ Bordeaux

Once as darkened with age as its vintages, Bordeaux has found that one of its greatest treasures is the city itself; the local government has scrubbed Bordeaux's splendid mansions, Gothic cathedrals, and *places* clean, and the city's restaurants, art galleries, and concerts reflect the diversity of the local population.

SIGHTS AND ENTERTAINMENT It takes time to undo the effects of time, however, and restoration work obscures monuments such as the city's Gothic masterpiece, the **Cathédrale St-André.** Two blocks from cours de Maréchal Foch in the Entrepôt Laine gallery at 7 rue Ferrère, the far-out **Musée d'Art Contemporain** and the **Arc en Rêve Centre d'Architecture** exhibit modern painting, sculpture, design and photography (open Tu-Su 11am-6pm, W until 8pm; 30F, students and seniors free). Bordeaux is, of course, famous for **wine.** The most efficient and comprehensive way to get a glimpse of Bordeaux's wine country is with the tourist office's afternoon guided tours that rotate between Les Côtes de Bourg et de Blaye, L'Entre-Deux-Mers, Médoc, and St. Emilion (May-Oct. daily 1:30pm; Nov.-Apr. W and Sa 1:30pm; 160F, 140F for students). The **Maison du Vin/CIVB,** 1 cours du 30 Juillet (tel. 05 56 00 22 66 or 05 50 00 22 88), gives a two-hour "Initiation to Wine Tasting" course in French and English for those wanting to learn more. (Twice weekly June-Aug.; 100F. *Maison* open May-Oct. M-F 8:30am-6:30pm; Nov.-Apr. M-Th 8:30am-6pm, F 8:30am-5:30pm.) In grapespeak, "château" means "vineyard," and many of the area's châteaux are also private homes. It is always best to call ahead and politely ask if they are open to visitors. Approach your meeting as a customer, not a tourist. The free *Clubs and Concerts* (at the tourist office) or *Bordeaux Plus* (2F at any *tabac*) gives an overview of nightlife. Sweaty students dance off angst at clubs on **quai Ste-Croix** and **quai de Paludade**.

PRACTICAL INFO, ACCOMMODATIONS, AND FOOD Trains leave from the Gare St-Jean, rue Charles Domercq, for Nice (9½hr., 4 per day, 440F), Paris (5-8hr.,10-20 per day, 290F, TGV 330-380F), and Toulouse (2½hr., 10 per day, 159F). From the train station, take bus 7 or 8 to "Grand Théâtre" and walk toward the Monument des Girondins to reach the **tourist office,** 12 cours du 30 Juillet (tel. 05 56 00 66 00; fax 05 56 00 66 01; http://www.mairie-bordeaux.fr), which has info on lodgings and winery tours. (Open May-Sept. M-Sa 9am-8pm, Su 9am-7pm; Oct.-Apr. M-Sa 9am-7pm, Su 9:15am-4:30pm. Branch office at train station.) An **American Express** office is at 14 cours de l'Intendance (tel. 05 56 00 63 33; open M-F 8:45am-noon and 1:30-6pm).

Relatively inexpensive hotels and an elegant student *maison* highlight the city's abundant budget options. Sidestreets around **place Gambetta** and **cours d'Albret** are good places to look for rooms. Reserve a couple of days in advance in June through August. To get to the clean, classy, and central **Maison des Etudiantes,** 50 rue Ligier (tel. 05 56 96 48 30), take bus 7 or 8 from the train station to "Bourse du Travail," and continue in the same direction on cours de la Libération to rue Ligier. Alternatively, walk along cours de la Marne through pl. de la Victoire to cours Aristide Briand, and the hostel will be on the right after the street turns into a mini parking lot (71F, with ISIC 51F; shower and sheets included; reception 24hr.). The **auberge de jeunesse (HI),** 22 cours Barbey (tel. 05 56 91 59 51; fax 05 56 94 02 98), has single-sex dorms and immaculate bathrooms in a worn building. To get there, take cours de la Marne from the right end of the station for about five blocks and turn left onto cours Barbey; women may feel uncomfortable walking alone. (56F; breakfast included. Reception M-Th 8-10am and 3-11pm, F 9-10am and 3-11pm, Sa-Su and holidays 8-9am and 3-11pm. Lockout 10am-2pm. Flexible curfew 11pm.) For airy rooms with shower and TV, consider **Hôtel la Boétie,** 4 rue de la Boétie (tel. 05 56 81 76 68; fax 05 56 81 24 72), off rue Bouffard between pl. Gambetta and the Musée des Beaux-Arts (singles 120F; doubles 135-60F; triples 180F; reception 24hr.). The same family that runs Boétie also runs 11 other nearby hotels with good rates.

Bordeaux, known as *la Région de Bien Manger et de Bien Vivre* (The Region of Fine Eating and Living), has affordable restaurants in which to do so, especially along the pedestrian streets between **place St. Pierre** and **place Gambetta.** Bring a plate and knife and descend into the cool cellar of **Baud et Millet,** 19 rue Huguerie, off pl. Tourny, to consume as much as you can from 200 kinds of *fromage* (105F; open M-Sa 9am-midnight). Crowd into **La Casuccia,** 49 rue St-Rémi, for pizza (from 30F) or the filling *menus* (from 65F; opens daily at 11:30am for lunch, 6:30pm-midnight for dinner). Head to **Le Jardin Gourmand,** 15 rue de Faussets, for the three-course lunch. (50F, wine and coffee included; dinner from 70F; open M-Sa noon-2:30pm and 7pm-midnight, Su 7pm-midnight.)

■ Périgueux

Encircled by the river Isle, Périgueux preserves significant architecture in both the medieval and Roman halves of the town. The city is also a good base for visiting local prehistoric caves. The town's *vieille ville* sports Renaissance architecture and the multi-domed **Cathédrale St-Front** combines the styles of several eras (open daily 8am-7:30pm; free tours in French upon request). The **Tour de Vésone** is a remarkable Roman ruin; it was a *cella*, the holiest place and center of worship of a Roman temple (open daily Apr.-Sept. 7:30am-9pm; Oct.-Mar. 7:30am-6:30pm).

The town sends several **trains** per day to Bordeaux (1½hr., 97F), Paris via Limoges (5-7hr., 271-368F), and Toulouse (4hr., 179F). The **tourist office,** 26 pl. Francheville (tel. 05 53 53 10 63; fax 05 53 09 02 50), organizes tours and distributes useful info (open July-Aug. M-Sa 9am-7pm, Su 9:30am-5:30pm; Sept.-June M-Sa 9am-6pm). The

Foyer des Jeunes Travailleurs Résidence Lakanal (tel. 05 53 53 52 05), off bd. Lakanal, offers comfortable beds. From the tourist office, turn left down cours Fénélon and take a right on bd. Lakanal; after the intersection with bd. Bertran de Born, the Municipal Bridge and Billiard Club will appear on your right. Walk through the parking lot on the left side of the club. (73F. Sheets, showers, and breakfast included; no breakfast on Su. Reception M-F 4-8pm, Sa-Su 7-8pm.) **Au Bon Coin/Chez Pierrot,** 8 rue Chanzy (tel. 05 53 53 43 22), manages 10 slightly musty but clean rooms (singles and doubles 100F; reception M-Sa 24hr.). Camp 1.5km away in Boulazac at **Barnabé-Plage,** 80 rue des Bains (tel. 05 53 53 41 45). Take city bus D ("Cité Belaire"; 6F, last one about 7:30pm) from cours Montaigne to "rue de Bains" (16F per person, 15F per tent, 10F per car; reception 9am-midnight).

■ Near Périgueux: Les Eyzies-de-Tayac

A perfect daytrip, **Les Eyzies-de-Tayac** is served by five trains a day from Périgueux (30min., 40F). **Prehistoric caves**—bursting with tourists from June to mid-September—house fascinating paintings and carvings, as well as spectacular stalagmites and stalactites. Call at least two weeks in advance to get tickets in summer. The best paintings near town are at the **Grotte de Font-de-Gaume** (tel. 05 53 06 90 80), 1km outside Les Eyzies on D47, where 15,000-year-old horses, bison, reindeer and woolly mammoth cavort along the cave walls. (Open Tu-Th Apr.-Sept. 9am-noon and 2-6pm; Mar. and Oct. 9:30am-noon and 2-5:30pm; Nov.-Feb. 10am-noon and 2-5pm. 35F, ages 12-25 21F, artists and art students free.) Commanding a panoramic view of the valley, **Grotte du Grand Roc,** 1.5km northwest of town, contains millions of stalactites, stalagmites, and *eccentriques*—small, crooked calcite accretions. (Open July-Aug. daily 9:30am-7pm; Apr.-June and Sept.-Nov. 10 daily 9:30am-6pm; Feb. 9-Mar. and Nov. 11-Jan. 10 Su-F 10am-5pm. 35F.) About 9km northwest of Les Eyzies on route D66, the **Roque St-Christophe** (tel. 05 53 50 70 45) is the most extensive cave dwelling yet discovered. A 45-minute visit (brochures in English) allows you to examine tools, ovens, monastic remains, and weapons (open daily Mar.-Nov. 10 10am-6:30pm; Nov. 11-Feb. 11am-5pm; 31F). The **tourist office,** pl. de la Mairie (tel. 05 53 06 97 05; fax 05 53 06 90 79), rents bikes, changes currency, and has info on hiking. (Open July-Aug. M-Sa 9am-7pm, Su 9am-noon and 2-6pm; call for hours off-season.)

■ Sarlat

Even with the dense mobs swarming **Sarlat** each summer, the town's remarkable *vieille ville* of golden sandstone merits a mosey. Sarlat's movie-set medieval perfection has attracted the gaze of more than a few cameras—*Cyrano de Bergerac* and *Manon of the Spring* were both shot here. **Trains** run to Bordeaux (2½hr., 116F) and Périgueux (3hr., 73F) via le Buisson. SCETA and STUB **buses** truck to Souillac (35min., 29F), and from there trains chug to Toulouse or Paris. Stop by the **tourist office,** pl. de la Liberté (tel. 05 53 59 27 67), for a self-serve smorgasbord of info (open M-Sa 9am-noon and 2-7pm, Su 10am-noon and 2-6pm). Sarlat's **Auberge de Jeunesse (HI),** 77 av. de Selves (tel. 05 53 59 47 59 or 05 53 30 21 27), is 30 minutes from the train station but only five to 10 minutes from the *vieille ville*. Go straight along rue de la République until it becomes av. Gambetta; follow it for another 100m, then bear left at the fork onto av. de Selves. It's on your right, behind a gray gate. (45F. Sheets 16F. Camping 30F. Reception 6-8pm or so. Open Mar. 15-Nov. Reserve ahead.)

BASQUE COUNTRY (PAYS BASQUE)

Bayonne A grand port with small town appeal, Bayonne enjoys a prominent position on the Gulf of Gascony, near the Spanish border. The 13th-century **Cathédrale Ste-Marie,** twin steeples needling the sky, intimidates from afar and impresses from within. (Cloister open daily 9:30am-12:30pm and 2-5pm. Free. Church open M-Sa

FRANCE

10am-noon and 3-6pm, Su 3:30-6pm.) Highlights of the unbeatable **Musée Bonnat,** 5 rue Jacques Laffitte, in Petit-Bayonne, include the Rubens' lecherous mythical men, a ghoulish El Greco, and Goya's grim *La Dernière Communion de San José de Calasanz* (open W-M 10am-noon and 2:30-6:30pm, F until 8:30pm; 20F, students 10F).

Bayonne is linked by **train** to Biarritz (10min.,12F), Bordeaux (1½-2½hr., 130-138F), and Paris (5½hr., 406-456F). **STAB** buses also connect Bayonne, Biarritz, and Anglet (every 30-40min, 7.50F). The **tourist office** (tel. 05 59 46 01 46; fax 05 59 59 37 55), pl. des Basques, provides a free city map and can help find rooms. (Open July-Aug. M-Sa 9am-7pm, Su 10am-1pm; Sept.-June M-F 9am–6:30pm, Sa 10am-6pm.) Decent lodgings dot the area around the train station and pl. de la République. The **Hôtel Paris-Madrid,** pl. de la Gare (tel. 05 59 55 13 98; fax 05 59 55 07 22), has cheerful rooms. (Singles and doubles 95-170F. Reception July-Sept. 24hr.; Oct.-June 6am-12:30am.) Huge portions of delicious regional cuisine are served in an elegant atmosphere at **Le Bistrot Ste-Cluque,** 9 rue Hugues, across from the station (*menu* 55F; *paella* 65F; open daily noon-2pm and 7-11pm).

Anglet Anglet's *raisons d'être* are its nine beaches of fine-grained white sand, from the perfect waves of the **plage Les Cavaliers** to the rocky jetty of the **Chambre d'Amour.** All swimmers should beware the strong undertow. The **Rainbow Surfshop,** 18-21 av. Chambre d'Amour, gives lessons and rents the colorful tools of the trade: bodyboards (100F per day, 1000F deposit), surfboards (100F per day, 2000F deposit), and wetsuits (50F per day, 1000F deposit). The carefree **Auberge de Jeunesse (HI),** 19 rte. de Vignes (tel. 05 59 58 70 00; fax 05 59 58 70 07), lies directly uphill from the beach (80F; camping 58F; breakfast included; reception 8:30am-10pm). From the Hôtel de Ville in Biarritz, take bus 4 ("Bayonne Sainsontain;" every 50min.) to Auberge. From pl. de la République or pl. de Réduit in Bayonne, take bus 4 to "La Barre," then change to bus 4N ("Mairie Biarritz"); in summer, bus 4 runs to "Auberge" without the transfer.

Biarritz Biarritz is not a budgeteer's dream, but its free beaches make a daytrip *de luxe.* At the **Grande Plage,** you'll find a wealth of surfers and bathers, and just north are the less-crowded **plage Miramar** and **Pointe St-Martin,** where bathers repose *au naturel.* Trains cruise through **Biarritz-la-Négresse,** 3km out of town (tel. 05 59 24 00 94). To get to the *centre ville,* take blue bus 2 ("Bayonne via Biarritz") or green bus 9 ("Biarritz HDV"). Another option is to get off the train in Bayonne and hop a bus to downtown Biarritz (30min.). All buses cost 7.50F. The **tourist office,** 1 sq. d'Ixelles (tel. 05 59 24 20 24), will track down accommodations and dispense the *Biarritz-cope* with events listings (open daily June-Sept. 8am-8pm; Oct.-May 9am-6:45pm). The friendly staff of the **Auberge de Jeunesse (HI),** 8 rue de Chiquito de Cambo (tel. 05 59 41 76 00; fax 05 59 41 76 07), makes the 40-minute walk to Biarritz worth it (singles 90F; doubles 180F; breakfast included). **Hôtel Barnetche,** 5bis rue Charles-Floquet (tel. 05 59 24 22 25; fax 05 59 24 98 71), has dorm accommodations for just 100F (doubles 250-280F; triples and quads 130F per person; open May-Sept.).

THE PYRENEES

Ice-capped mountains and plunging slopes of forested greenery make the French Pyrénées a paradise for lovers of the outdoors. Hiking, mountain climbing, skiing, and mountain biking opportunities await at every turn, and the national park remains the last refuge of *isards* (mountain antelopes), royal eagles, vultures, and the endangered *ours des Pyrénées* (pint-sized brown bears).

Cauterets Tiny Cauterets nestles in a narrow, breathtaking valley on the edge of the **Parc National des Pyrénées Occidentales.** Romans first discovered the therapeutic effects of Cauterets's hot sulfuric *thermes,* but most visitors now come to take advantage of the skiing and hiking (for all levels of hikers) in the surrounding mountains. **SNCF buses** run from pl. de la Gare to Lourdes (1hr., 6 per day, 37F; tickets at the station), where you can catch **trains** to Bordeaux (3hr., 7 per day, 170F) or Paris (7-9hr., 5 per day, 439F). Buses also run to Luz-St-Sauveur (6 per day, 38F). The **tourist office**, pl. Foch (tel. 05 62 92 50 27; http://www.cauterets.com), has lists of available hotels, but is not the best source of info on outdoor activities (open daily July-Aug. 9am-7pm; Sept.-June 9am-12:30pm and 2-6:30pm). For **hiking info** (tel. 05 62 92 52 56), head to Maison du Parc on pl. de la Gare, where regional maps and day-hike maps are for sale. **Equipment rental** shops are all over town.

   Centre UCJG (Unions Chrétiennes des Jeunes Gens de France), av. Docteur Domer (tel. 05 62 92 52 95), has dorms and bungalows. From the bus station, walk across the square and take the path running uphill past the cable car. Turn left as it hits the unmarked av. de Det. Domer, and walk past the tennis courts. (55F per person. Sheets, kitchen, and laundry included. **Camp** in your own tent for 20F or in one of their 4 12-bed tents for 40F. Open June 15-Sept. 15. Reserve well ahead.) The **Gîte d'Etape: Le Pas de l'Ours**, 21 rue de la Raillère (tel. 05 62 92 58 07), a few blocks up the street opposite the tourist office, welcomes hikers, climbers, and skiers. (65F. 3-person hotel rooms 90F per person. Breakfast 40F. Sauna 45F for 1 person, 70F for 2. Clothes laundered 50F. Reception 8am-noon and 2-11pm. Open Dec.-Apr. 14 and May 16-Oct.) The covered **Halles market**, in the center of town on av. Général Leclerc, has fresh produce (daily 8:30am-12:30pm and 2:30-7:30pm).

Luz and the Parc National des Pyrénées

One of France's seven national parks, the **Parc National des Pyrénées** soothes with sulfur springs, frustrates with unattainable peaks, changes dramatically with the seasons, and never fails to awe a constant stream of visitors. Before heading off on any trail, it is important to procure an intelligible map of the area. Experienced hikers can pick up maps at sporting goods stores, but the friendly and helpful **Parc National Office**, Maison du Parc (tel. 05 62 92 52 56; fax 05 62 92 62 23), sells *Promenades en Montagne* maps (35F) of 15 different trails beginning and ending in Cauterets, all labeled with estimated duration (1hr.-2 days) and difficulty. These trails have been designed for a range of hiking aptitudes, from rugged outdoor enthusiasts to geeky publishing types. Morning hikes are a good way to beat the crowds, and the *Parc National* knows about less frequented paths.

   From Cauterets, the GR 10 connects to **Luz-St-Saveur** just over the mountain and then on to **Gavarnie**, another day's hike up the valley. These towns are also accessible by SNCF bus. Circling counter-clockwise from Cauterets to Luz-St-Sauveur, the **Refuges Des Oulettes** is the first shelter past the **Lac de Gaube** (on the IGN map; tel. 05 62 92 62 97; 78F per night; open June-Sept.). Dipping into the **Vallée Lutour**, the **Refuge Estom** rests peacefully near **Lac d'Estom** (in winter tel. 05 62 92 75 07; in summer tel. 05 62 92 72 93; 60-70F per night, open all year). The **Refuge Jan Da Lo** (tel. 05 62 92 40 66) in **Gavarnie**, near the loop's halfway mark, costs 48F per night.

   Luz-St-Sauveur is actually two villages combined: Luz caters mostly to skiers and St-Saveur deals in close encounters of the thermal kind. Set in the wide, grassy **Vallée du Toy**, Luz itself offers few challenging hikes in the immediate vicinity, but its proximity to Gavarnie and Bagnées and its accessibility on the **SNCF bus line** make it an excellent launching pad into the Pyrénées. The **tourist office**, pl. du 8 Mai 45 (tel. 05 62 92 30 30; fax 05 62 92 87 19), will provide you with a rough map and a list of hotels and send you to the **Maison de la Vallée** for everything else (open M-Sa 9-noon and 2-6:30pm). In winter, the **Bureau des Guides, l'Ecole de Ski Français**, pl. Clemenceau (in winter tel. 05 62 92 55 06), provides guides and assistance. The tourist office has free *plans des pistes*, maps of downhill and cross-country ski paths with varying levels of difficulty. Many nearby skiing towns are accessible by SNCF buses from Cauterets or Lourdes.

LANGUEDOC-ROUSSILLON

Languedoc and Roussillon, rugged southern lands where culture and personal origins are as much Spanish as French, have never been comfortable with Parisian authority. Once, an immense region called Occitania (today Languedoc) stretched from the Rhône all the way to the foothills of the Pyrénées, and from the Catalan coastal region of Roussillon in the southeast to Toulouse in the west. Its people spoke the *langue d'oc*, not the *langue d'oïl* spoken in northern France (which evolved into modern French). The region was eventually overwhelmed and integrated into the French kingdom, and the Cathar religion persecuted. The *langue d'oc* faded, and in 1539, the Edict of Villiers-Cotterets made the northern *langue d'oïl* official.

■ Toulouse

Just when all the French towns on your itinerary start to look alike, Toulouse's eclectic architecture, streets, alleys, squares, and diverse population greet you like a breath of fresh air. The highbrow elegance of the shopping district flows into the old-school grandeur of pl. du Capitole; from there, the pizzeria intimacy of rue du Tour spills into the cafe and moped chit-chat of the student quarter.

SIGHTS AND ENTERTAINMENT The **Basilique St-Sernin,** the longest Romanesque structure in the world, was the seat of St. Dominique's Cathar-hunting inquisition. (Open July-Sept. M-Sa 9am-6:30pm, Su 9am-7:30pm; Oct.-June M-Sa 8:30-11:45am and 2-5:45pm, Su 9am-12:30pm and 2-7:30pm. Tours July-Aug. twice daily; 35F.) The 13th-century **Les Jacobins,** rue Lakanal, is an excellent example of the southern Gothic style. Flamboyant decorations are tempered by the elegance of the stained glass and serenity of the cloister. A modest crypt inside contains the ashes of St. Thomas Aquinas (open daily June-Sept. 10am-6:30pm; Oct.-Mar. 10am-noon and 2-6pm; cloister 10F). Housed in the **Hôtel d'Assézat,** rue de Metz, near the river, the **Foundation Bemberg** displays an impressive collection of Bonnards, Dufys, Pisarros, and Gauguins, supplemented by European pieces spanning five centuries (open Tu-Su 10am-6pm, W until 9pm; 25F, groups 15F). Away from the river, the **Musée des Augustins,** 21 rue de Metz, has an unsurpassed collection of Romanesque and Gothic sculptures (open Th-M 10am-6pm, W 10am-9pm; 12F, students free). For greener pastures, head to **Jardin Royal** and less formal **Jardin des Plantes,** on the outskirts of town, which offer benches and lots of shade. For bicyclists, the **Grand Rond** unfurls into allée Paul Sabatier, which keeps rolling to the Canal du Midi.

Toulouse has something to please almost any nocturnal whim, though things are liveliest when the students are in town. Numerous **cafes** flank pl. St. Georges and pl. du Capitole, and late-night **bars** line rue St-Rome and rue des Filatiers. **La Ciguä,** 6 rue de Colombette, just off bd. Lazare Carnot, is a friendly gay bar (open Tu-Su 9pm-2am, Sa 9pm-4am). From July to September, **Musique d'Eté** brings classical concerts, jazz, and ballet to a variety of venues (tickets 80-140F at the tourist office and on location).

PRACTICAL INFO, ACCOMMODATIONS, AND FOOD Trains, bd. Pierre Sémard (tel. 08 36 35 35 35), go to Bordeaux (2¼hr., 160F), Lyon (6hr., 295F), Marseille (4½hr., 234F), and Paris (7hr., 425F). To reach the **tourist office** (tel. 05 61 11 02 22; fax 05 61 22 03 63) from the station, turn left along the canal and then right onto the broad allée Jean Jaurès. Walk a third of the way around pl. Wilson (bearing right), then take a right onto rue Lafayette. The office, in a park near the intersection with rue d'Alsace-Lorraine, finds rooms and gives out free maps. (Open May-Sept. M-Sa 9am-7pm, Su 10am-1pm and 2-6:30pm; Oct.-Apr. M-F 9am-6pm, Sa 9am-12:30pm and 2-6pm, Su 10am-12:30pm and 2-5pm.)

To reach the **Hôtel des Arts,** 1bis rue Cantegril (tel. 05 61 23 36 21; fax 05 61 12 22 37), at rue des Arts near pl. St-Georges, take the metro ("Basso Cambo") to "pl. Esquirol." Spacious, spotless rooms and a friendly staff (singles and doubles 80-135F, with shower 125-160F; reserve ahead). **Hôtel du Grand Balcon,** 8 rue Romiguières (tel. 05 61 21 48 08), on the corner of pl. du Capitole, has a wonderful location and bright rooms (singles 110-150F; doubles 130-190F; closed first 3 weeks of Aug.). New beds and sparkling bathrooms highlight the offerings at **Hôtel Beauséjour,** 4 rue Caffarelli (tel. 05 61 62 77 59), just off allée Jean Jaurès halfway between the train station and pl. Wilson (singles 75-135F; doubles 95-115F; call ahead).

Markets line pl. des Carmes, pl. Victor Hugo, and bd. de Strasbourg (open Tu-Su 6am-1pm), and inexpensive eateries lie along rue du Taur on the way to the university. The *brasseries* that crowd pl. Wilson offer 50-80F *menus* and ambience. **Le Bar à Pâtes,** 8-10 rue Tripière, off rue St-Rome, lets you choose your own delicious pasta and sauce for 39F (open M-Sa noon-2pm and 7:15-11:30pm, Su 7:15-11:30pm). **Mille et Une Pâtes,** at 3 pl. du Peyrou, two blocks from St-Sernin, has unique and varied salads and pasta (33-58F; open M-Sa 11:30am-2pm and 7:30pm-10pm, closed M nights).

■ Carcassonne

The Cité de Carcassonne has had a rough go of it. Attacked at various times by Romans, Visigoths, and Moors, Europe's largest fortress has come to exemplify stalwart opposition in the face of the enemy. Today, the Cité de Carcassonne rises from a precipitous plateau in the Garonne Valley and stands as one of the most spectacular and most popular sights in France.

SIGHTS AND ENTERTAINMENT The *cité* perches imperiously above the modern *basse ville*, where shops, hotels, and the train station are located. To reach the fortress, take bus 4 to "pl. Gambetta" and switch to bus 2 or 8 to get to the *cité* (5F40), or hike 30 minutes up the hill. Originally constructed as a palace in the 12th century, the **Château Comtal** was transformed into a citadel following Carcassonne's submission to royal control in 1226. (Open July-Aug. 9am-7:30pm; Sept. and June 9am-7pm; Oct.-May 9:30am-12:30pm and 2-6pm. 32F, ages 18-25 21F. Obligatory guided tour.) The privately-run **Musée de l'Inquisition,** 5 rue du Grand Puits, displays the objects of gentle persuasion used by the Catholics to show the Cathars the light (open July-Aug. 9am-11pm; Sept.-June 10am-7pm; 40F, students 30F). At the other end of the *cité,* the beautiful **Basilique St-Nazaire** is the coolest place in the fortress on a sultry summer afternoon (open July-Aug. daily 9am-7pm; Sept.-June 9:30am-noon and 2-5:30pm). On Bastille Day (July 14), a lighting effect makes the fortress look as if it's going up in flames when viewed from the *basse ville*, commemorating the villages burned under Carcassonne's stern mandate when the city's *Tour de l'Inquisition* was the seat of the Inquisition's jury. In early August, the entire *cité* returns to the Middle Ages for the **Spectacles Médiévaux,** complete with daily jousts. Though nightlife is limited, several bars and cafes along rue Omer Sarraut and pl. Verdun offer some excitement. Locals dance the night away at **La Bulle,** 115 rue Barbacane.

PRACTICAL INFO, ACCOMMODATIONS, AND FOOD Trains arrive from Toulouse (50min., 72F) on their way to Lyon (5½hr., 258F), Marseille (3hr., 195F), and Nice (6hr., 288F). For bus info, check at the tourist office or the station at bd. de Varsovie. To reach the **tourist office,** 15 bd. Camille Pelletan, sq. Gambetta (tel. 04 68 10 24 30; fax 04 68 10 24 38), from the train station, walk over the canal on rue G. Clemenceau, turn left onto rue de la Liberté, then turn right onto bd. Jean Jaurès (open July-Aug. 9am-7pm; Sept.-June 9am-12:15pm and 1:45-6:30pm). In the old, walled *cité,* the **auberge de jeunesse (HI),** rue de Vicomte Trencavel (tel. 04 68 25 23 16; fax 04 68 71 14 84), has friendly dorms. (70F; sheets 15F. Members only. Reception M-F 7am-1am, Sa-Su 7am-noon and 5pm-1am. Curfew 1am; off-season 11pm.) The **Hôtel Astoria** (tel. 04 68 25 31 38), at the intersection of rue Montpellier and rue Tourtel, has pleasant rooms in a quiet location (singles and doubles 100-190F; reception 7:30am-10pm; reserve ahead). **Le Cathare,** 53 rue Jean Bringer (tel. 04 68 25 65 92), near the post office, has cozy, bright rooms (singles and doubles 117-168F).

Most restaurants in Carcassonne serve the regional specialty *cassoulet*, a stew of white beans, herbs, and meat. On rue du Plo, 60 to 70F *menus* abound, but save room for dessert at one of the many outdoor *crêperies* on pl. Marcou. **Les Fontaines du Soleil**, 32 rue du Plo, offers indescribably good food in a little garden courtyard (open daily July-Aug. 11:30am-2am; Sept.-June 11:30am-3pm and 6pm-2am).

PROVENCE: RHÔNE VALLEY

■ Avignon

The walled city of Avignon sparkles with artistic brilliance among the lush vineyards of the Rhône Valley. Film festivals, street musicians, and Europe's most prestigious theatrical gathering, the famed Festival d'Avignon, keep this university town shining. The **Palais des Papes,** built in the 14th century when the popes moved here from Rome, stands in white granite majesty at the highest point in Avignon. (Open daily Apr.-Oct. 9am-7pm, until 9pm during festival; Nov.-Mar. 9am-12:45pm and 2-6pm. 35F, students 27F. Guided tour 43F, students 35F.) From early July to early August, the **Festival d'Avignon** (also known as the **IN**) puts on drama, dance, mime, and everything from Gregorian chants to all-night readings of the *Odyssey* (50-190F per event; reservations accepted from mid-June). The cheaper, more experimental **Festival OFF** presents over 400 plays, some in English, from mid-July to early August. For info, call the tourist office or the Bureau de Festival (tel. 04 90 82 67 08). The beautiful town of **Fontaine de Vaucluse** is just 50 minutes from Avignon by bus (36F).

The **tourist office,** 41 cours Jean Jaurès (tel. 04 90 82 65 11; fax 04 90 82 95 03), has a free brochure listing rooms, restaurants, and museums (open M-F 9am-1pm and 2-7pm, Sa closes 5pm; during festival daily 10am-7pm). The **Foyer YMCA/UCJG** is at 7bis chemin de la Justice (tel. 04 90 25 46 20; fax 04 90 25 30 64), in Villeneuve, across Pont Daladier. Ask for one of the new rooms. Take bus 10 ("Les Angles-Grand Angles") to "Général Leclerc" or bus 11 ("Villeneuve-Grand Terme;" 6F50) to "Pont d'Avignon" (singles 120-150F; doubles 144-180F; triples 192-240F; reception 8:30am-8pm). **Foyer Bagatelle** (tel. 04 90 86 30 39; fax 04 90 85 78 45), Ile de la Barthélasse, has 250 beds (59F; **camping** 19-24F; 8-11F per tent). **Camping Municipal: St-Bénezet** (tel. 04 90 82 63 50; fax 04 90 85 22 12), 10 minutes past Foyer Bagatelle, has hot showers, laundry, a restaurant, a supermarket, and tennis courts. (18-26F; 16-19F per tent. Reception June-Sept. 8am-10pm; Apr.-May 8am-8pm; Oct. and Mar. 8am-6pm. Open Mar.-Oct.)

Buy provisions at the **open-air market** outside the city walls near porte St-Michel (open Sa-Su 7am-noon), or at **Codec supermarket,** 23 rue de la République (open M-Sa 8:30am-8pm). **Woolloomooloo,** 16bis rue des Teinturiers, has huge portions and a funky, mellow ambience (meals 63-79F; open Tu-Sa noon-2pm and 8pm-2am). **Gambrinus,** 62 rue Carreterie, 200m down the street from porte St-Lazare, specializes in *moules.* (Mussels and fries 45F. Draft beer 14F. *Menu* 75F. Open daily 7am-1:30am. Closed Aug. 10-25 and Jan. 1-15.) **Took Took,** 74 rue de Lices, at rue des Teinturiers, has nothing but good karma (salads 25-50F; Indian *plats* 60F; open Tu-Su 10am-2am; daily during the festival).

■ Arles

Roman grandeur haunts the sun-baked remnants of Arles's **arènes** (now used for bull-fights) and endures in the **Cloître St-Trophime.** The city celebrates the **Fête d'Arles** (the last weekend in June and the first in July) in local costume with bonfires blazing. Arles's beautiful vistas lured both Picasso and Van Gogh, who dropped two years—and his ear—here. Be sure to get an English copy of *Arles et Vincent,* which explains the markers that stand where Van Gogh once planted his easel. The amazing **Fondation Van Gogh,** 26 Rond-Point des Arènes (tel. 04 90 49 94 04), houses tributes to the master by over 700 artists, poets, and composers (open daily in summer 10am-7pm; call for winter hours; 30F, students 20F). During the second week in July, the **Rencontres Internationales de la Photographie** (tel. 04 90 96 76 06) courts photographers and agents (20-30F per exhibit, students 10-20F; global ticket 140F and 70F).

Frequent **buses** run from the *gare routière* (next to the train station) to the 30km of beaches at **Les Stes-Maries-de-la-Mer.** Trains roll from the **train station,** av. P. Talabot, to Aix-en-Provence (1¾hr., 93F), Avignon (20min., 35F), Marseille (1hr., 71F), and Nîmes (25min., 41F). The **tourist office** (tel. 04 90 18 41 20; fax 04 90 18 41 29), in esplanade Charles de Gaulle at bd. des Lices, finds rooms for a 5F fee. (Open Apr.-Sept. M-Sa 9am-7pm, Su 9am-1pm; Oct.-Mar. M-Sa 9am-6pm, Su 10am-noon.) There's also a **branch** at the train station (tel. 04 90 49 36 90; open M-Sa 9am-1pm and 2-6pm, reduced hours Oct.-Mar.). Inexpensive **hotels** cluster around rue de l'Hôtel de Ville and pl. Voltaire, and fill in a flash during the photography festival. The **Auberge de Jeunesse (HI),** av. Maréchal Foch (tel. 04 90 96 18 25; fax 04 90 96 31 26), is a 20-minute walk from the station. (1st night 77F, thereafter 65F. Reception 7-10am and 5pm-midnight. Curfew midnight, 1-2am during festival. Call ahead Apr.-June.) Sweet-smelling **Hotel Gauguin** sits at 5 pl. Voltaire (tel. 04 90 96 14 35; fax 04 90 18 98 87; singles and doubles 160-220F; triples 260F). **Hôtel Mirador,** 3 rue Voltaire (tel. 04 90 96 28 05; fax 04 90 96 59 89), has impeccable rooms (singles and doubles 200F-265F; extra bed 60F). Regional produce fills the **open markets** on bd. Emile Courbes (open W 7am-1pm) and bd. des Lices (open Sa 7am-1pm). A **Monoprix supermarket** is on pl. Lamartine. **Vitamine,** 16 rue du Docteur Fanton, has good pasta, great salads, and fabulous desserts (*nougat glacé* 30F; open daily noon-3pm and 7-10pm, in summer midnight). At the cafes on **pl. du Forum,** everyone knows everyone else by midnight; in summer, the cafes on **pl. Voltaire** have music on Wednesdays.

■ Near Arles: The Camargue

Between Arles and the Mediterranean coast stretches the Camargue. Pink flamingos, black bulls, and the famous white Camargue horses roam freely across this flat expanse of wild marshland, protected by the confines of the natural park. Aspiring botanists and zoologists should stop at the **Centre d'Information de Ginès** (tel. 04 90 97 86 32) along D570, which distributes information on the region's unusual flora and fauna (open Apr.-Sept. daily 9am-6pm; Oct.-Mar. Sa-Th 9:30am-5pm). Next door, on the bus line from Arles to Les Saintes-Maries-de-la-Mer, the region's capital, the **Parc Ornithologique de Pont de Gau** (tel. 04 90 97 82 62; to "Pont de Gau," 7F from Les Stes-Maries-de-la-Mer) provides paths through marshland and offers views of marsh birds and grazing bulls. Rarer bird species are housed in aviaries (park open daily Apr.-Sept. 9am-sunset; Oct.-Mar. opens 10am; 33F). The best way to see the Camargue is on **horseback** (70F per hr., 180-200F for 3hr., 320-350F per day; meal usually included). **Jeep safaris** (100F for 1½hr., 150F for 2½hr.) and **boat trips** (Bateau de Promenade tel. 04 90 97 84 72; 1½hr., 60F) are also great ways to see this area, and while many trails are only for horseback riders, **bicycle touring** is also an option. Trail maps indicating length, level of difficulty, and danger spots are available from the Les Saintes-Maries-de-la-Mer **tourist office,** 5 av. Van Gogh (tel. 04 90 97 82 55). Frequent **buses** run to the Camargue from Arles' *gare routière* (1hr., 35F50).

■ Aix-en-Provence

Blessed with plentiful restaurants, elegant cafes, and exuberant festivals, Aix (pronounced "Ex") truly marks the spot as the cultural core of Provence. The international student population of the nearly 600-year-old Université d'Aix spawns a frenzied intellectual energy that makes the city feel smart, safe, and friendly.

SIGHTS AND ENTERTAINMENT Pass the afternoon in a cafe on **cours Mirabeau,** or walk the **Chemin de Cézanne,** which transforms the city into an open-air museum of the native artist and his work, including his studio at 9 av. Paul Cézanne. Pick up *In*

FRANCE

the Footsteps of Cézanne at the tourist office and follow the bronze markers in the sidewalk. The **Musée Granet,** pl. St-Jean-Marie-de-Malte, displays Dutch and French works and several Cézannes (open July-Aug. daily 10am-noon and 2-6pm; Sept.-June closed Tu; 18F, students 10F). **Cathédrale St-Sauveur,** rue Gaston de Saporta, on the *place,* is a dramatic melange of carvings (open W-M 8am-noon and 2-6pm). The lovely gardens at the **Pavillon de Vendôme,** 32 rue Célony, are worth a visit. At the **Videothèque d'Art Lyrique** in the **Cité des Livres,** 8-10 rue des Allumettes, you can watch operas and concerts of past Festivals d'Aix for free (open Tu-Sa noon-6pm).

Aix en Musique (tel. 04 42 21 69 69), a casual, five-week jamboree of big-band jazz and chamber music, begins the second week of June. But those gen-Aix-ers can't get enough: they also host an **International Music Festival** (July to early Aug.), a **Jazz Festival** (early July), and a **Dance Festival** (first 2 weeks of July). The **Comité Officiel des Fêtes** (tel. 04 42 63 06 75), on cours Gambetta at the corner of bd. du Roi René, can fill you in on festival info. When the sun sets, **Le Scat,** 11 rue Verrerie, is a terrific club with live music (open M-Sa 11pm-whenever). A little outside town, **La Chimère,** montée d'Avignon, quartier des Plâtrières, attracts a sizeable gay crowd to its bar and disco (open Tu-Su 10pm-6am). **Bistro Aixois,** 37 Cours Sextius, off La Rotonde, packs students and bands in cramped quarters (open daily 6:30am-4am).

PRACTICAL INFO, ACCOMMODATIONS, AND FOOD To get virtually anywhere by **train** from Aix, you must pass through Marseille (40min., 1 per hr. until 9:23pm, 36F) or on the cheaper **bus** (30min., 22F). Four buses a day run to Avignon (1½hr., 70-80F). From the train station, follow av. Victor Hugo (bear left at the fork) to La Rotonde and the central bus terminus and **tourist office,** 2 pl. du Général de Gaulle (tel. 04 42 16 11 61; fax 04 42 16 11 62), which books rooms for a 5F fee and has the guides *Le Mois à Aix* and *Aix la Vivante.* (Open daily July-Aug. 8:30am-10pm; May-June and Sept. 8:30am-8pm; Oct.-Apr. 8:30am-7pm.)

To get to the crowded **auberge de jeunesse (HI),** 3 av. Marcel Pagnol (tel. 04 42 20 15 99; fax 04 42 59 36 12), quartier du Jas de Bouffan, follow av. de Belges from La Rotonde and turn right on av. de l'Europe. At the first rotary after the highway overpass, bear left and climb the hill. The hostel is on your left (35min.). Alternately, take bus 6 (bus A on weekends; every 15-30min. until 8pm, 7F) from La Rotonde to "Vasarely." (1st night 79F, thereafter 68F. Sheets 11F. Lockout 10am-4pm. Curfew midnight. Arrive before noon or after 4pm.) All of the rooms of **Hôtel des Arts,** 69 bd. Carnot (tel. 04 42 38 11 77; fax 04 42 26 77 51), have shower and phone (singles and doubles 180-205F). French decor prevails at the **Hôtel Vigouroux,** 27 rue Cardinale (tel. 04 42 38 26 42), between pl. des Dauphins and Musée Granet.

The streets north of cours Mirabeau are packed with restaurants for all palates and wallets. **Hacienda,** 7 rue Mérindol, in the pl. des Fontêtes, offers a delicious three-course *menu* (75F; open M-Sa noon-2pm and 7-10pm). **Autour d'une Tarte,** 13 rue Gaston de Saporta, off pl. de l'Hôtel de Ville, has quiches galore (12-40F; open M-Sa 8:30am-7:30pm). Find 56 flavors of ice cream at hip **La Rose D'Aix,** 44 rue Espariat. Buy a picnic lunch at the **markets** on pl. de Verdun, pl. de la Madeleine, and pl. Richelme (open Tu, Th, and Sa 7am-1pm), or stock up at the **Casino supermarkets** at 1 av. de Lattre de Tassigny (open M-Sa 8:30am-8:30pm) and 3 cours d'Orbitelle (open M-Sa 8am-1pm and 4-8pm). Be sure to sample Aix's famed almonds, used in cakes and cookies, at one of the *pâtisseries* along rue d'Italie or rue Espariat.

FRENCH RIVIERA (CÔTE D'AZUR)

Paradises are made to be lost. Sparkling between Marseille and the Italian border, the sun-drenched beaches and waters of the Mediterranean form the backdrop for this fabled playground of the rich and famous. But its seductive loveliness has almost been its undoing, as shrewd developers have turned the coast's beauty to profit and its pleasures into big business. Today, the area is as crammed with low-budget tourists as with high-handed millionaires, and many French condemn it as a shameless Fort Lauderdale, a mere shadow of its former self.

The coast is well served by frequent, inexpensive **trains** and **buses.** Trains for the Côte leave Paris's Gare de Lyon every hour in summer; the trip takes five hours on the TGV to Marseille and eight hours to Nice. Trains and roads are packed in summer; you might want to base yourself in the less expensive coastal towns and take daytrips to the purse-emptying cities. Like western Provence, the Riviera is best visited during early June and in September when the crowds diminish somewhat.

■ Marseille

France's third largest city is like its famous *bouillabaisse:* steaming hot and spicy. Colorful, chaotic Marseille enjoys a reputation for roguishness and danger. Its large immigrant population creates a stew of cultures, but also fuels ethnic tensions. A mix of wild nightclubs, beaches, gardens, and big-city adventure, Marseille bites its thumb at manicured Monaco and winks across the Atlantic to New York City. Use cosmopolitan caution, and after dark avoid the *vieux port,* the North African quarter, and the areas around the train station, in front of the opera, and around rue Curiol.

To get a sense of *le vrai* Marseille, amble down **rue Paradis, rue St Ferréol, cours Julien,** and the North African **rue des Feuillants.** The majestic 19th-century **Basilique de Notre Dame de la Garde** perches on a hill above the city. To reach the site, take bus 60, or follow rue Breteuil from the *vieux port,* turn right on bd. Vauban, and then right again on rue Fort du Sanctuaire (open daily in summer 7am-8pm; off-season 7am-7pm; free; no shorts or tank tops). Marseille's public **beaches** are accessible on bus 83 ("Rond point du Prado") from the *vieux port.* Both **plage du Prado** and **plage de la Corniche** offer wide beaches, clear waters, and scenic views.

Trains leave pl. Victor Hugo for Lyon (3½hr., 202F) and Paris (4¾hr., 400F), while **buses** serve Aix-en-Provence (25F), Avignon (2hr., 89F, round-trip 134F), Cannes (2¼-3hr., 120F, students 85F), and Nice (2¾hr., 133F, students 90F). **SNCM,** 61 bd. des Dames (tel. 08 36 67 95 00), runs **ferries** to Corsica (254-286F, students 156-172F), Sardinia, and North Africa. The **tourist office,** 4 La Canebière (tel. 04 91 13 89 00; fax 04 91 13 89 20), has a free accommodation service and maps (open July-Aug. daily 9am-8pm; Oct.-June M-Sa 9am-7pm, Su 10am-5pm). The **Auberge de Jeunesse de Bois-Luzy (HI)** (tel./fax 04 91 49 06 18), allée des Primevères, has clean rooms. Take bus 6 from cours J. Thierry at the top of La Canebière to "Marius Richard" and follow the signs, or bus 8 from "La Canebière" to "Bois-Luzy." At night, take bus T from "La Canebière" to "Marius Richard." (68F. Breakfast included. Sheets 7F. Reception 7:30-10am and 5-10:30pm. Curfew 10:30-11pm. Call ahead.) The **Auberge de Jeunesse Bonneveine (HI)** (tel. 04 91 73 21 81; fax 04 91 73 97 23), impasse Bonfils, a left turn after 47 av. J. Vidal, has a bar, restaurant, and travel agency (dorms 60-70F; doubles 160-180F; members only; reception 6am-1am; closed Jan.). **Hôtel du Palais,** 26 rue Breteuil (tel. 04 91 37 78 86; fax 04 91 37 91 19), has air conditioning and firm beds (singles and doubles 185F; triples 280-300). **Hôtel Béarn** is at 63 rue Sylvabelle (tel. 04 91 37 75 83; singles 134-200F).

The restaurant population soars around the *vieux port;* for a more artsy crowd and cheaper fare, head up to **cours Julien** and the pedestrian mall. **L'Écailler,** 10 rue Fortia, has true *marseillaise* cuisine and a three-course *menu* for 65F (open daily 11:45am-2:30pm and 7-11:30pm). Nightlife centers on cours Julien, northeast of the harbor, and pl. Thiers near the *vieux port.* **Trolleybus,** 24 quai de Rive Neuve, is a mega-club (cover 64F on Sa only; open Th-Sa 11pm-7am).

■ St-Tropez

Once a fishing hamlet, *St. Trop d'Aise* (St. Too-Much-Luxury) now exhibits a religious devotion to the holy trinity of sun, sand, and big white boats. To reach the **beaches,** take a Sodetrav bus from the *gare routière* on av. Général Leclerc ("St-Tropez-Ramatuelle;" M-Sa 3 per day, 9F). Or rent wheels from **Louis Mas,** 3-5 rue Quarenta. (Bikes 50-80F per day, deposit 1000-2000F. Mopeds 110F, deposit 2500-5000F. Open Easter-Oct. 15 M-Sa 9am-7pm, Su 9am-5pm.)

FRANCE

To reach St-Tropez take the **bus** (tel. 04 94 97 88 51) from St-Raphaël (1½-2¼hr., 48F). The faster, more scenic boat ride from St-Raphaël is much more suave, but not much more expensive (50min., 100F round-trip, only 80F if you stay at the Fréjus hostel). Call **Gare Maritime de St-Raphaël** at 04 94 95 17 46 for details. **Hitching** is poor—"they'd soil the Porsche's upholstery, dahling." The **tourist office** (tel. 04 94 97 45 21; fax 04 94 97 82 66), overlooking the frenzied port from quai Jean Jaurès, has transportation and sights info (open daily 9:30am-1:30pm and 3:30-11pm). Budget hotels do not exist in St-Tropez; the closest **HI youth hostel** is in Fréjus. **Camping** is the cheapest option, but make reservations. The tourist office can help you find sites with vacancies. Try the four-star **La Croix du Sud** (tel. 04 94 79 80 84; fax 04 94 79 89 21), route des Plages, in Ramatuelle (85F for 1-2 people, 120F for 3; open Easter-Sept.), or **Kon Tiki** (tel. 04 94 79 80 17; 113F for 2 people, car, and tent). Both lie just behind the Pampelonne beach.

The **Vieux Port** and the narrow cobblestone streets of the hillside *vieille ville* behind the waterfront form the hub of St-Tropez's culinary activity. **Lou Regalé,** 12 rue du Colonel Guichard, next to the Eglise Paroissiale, serves pasta, roast chicken and *ratatouille* on its 50F *menu* (open daily noon-2:30pm and 7-11pm). To create your own ambience, head to the **grand marché** on pl. des Lices (open daily 5am-2pm) or the **Prisunic supermarket,** 7 av. du Général Leclerc (open M-Sa 8am-8pm; in summer also Su 8:30am-1pm and 3-8pm). Dance all night at **Le Pigeonnier,** 13 rue de la Ponche (80F cover includes 1st drink; drinks 70F; open daily 11:30pm-dawn).

■ St-Raphaël and Fréjus

Sandwiched between St-Tropez and Cannes, the twin cities of St-Raphaël and Fréjus boast all the wide beaches, seafood restaurants, and coastal charm of their swanky Côte d'Azur cousins at half the cost. Bake in the sun along the long and sandy **Plage Fréjus,** just 10 minutes along the waterfront from the St-Raphaël train station. Ask at the tourist office for info on bullfights and rock concerts at the **Roman amphitheater** on rue Henri Vadon. (Open daily Apr.-Sept. 9:30-11:45am and 2-6:15pm; Oct.-Mar. 9-11:45am and 2-4:15pm. Free.) The first weekend in July is the **Competition Internationale de Jazz New Orleans** in St-Raphaël. Hundreds of musicians face off in the streets and around the port—and it's free (call the tourist office for more info).

St-Raphaël sends **trains** to Cannes (25min., 32F) and Nice (1hr., 54F). **Sodetrav buses** connect St-Raphaël to St-Tropez (1½hr., 15 per day, 48F), and **Forum Cars** (tel. 04 94 95 16 71) makes the trip from Cannes to St-Raphaël (70min., 33F). **Les Bateaux de Saint Raphaël** (tel. 04 94 95 17 46), at the *vieux port,* cruise to St-Tropez four to five times per day in summer (50min., round-trip 70-100F). If you are staying at the youth hostel in Fréjus, ask about ticket discounts. The **tourist office** (tel. 04 94 19 52 52; fax 04 94 83 85 40) in St-Raphaël, across the street from the train station, has the scoop on transportation and room availability (open July-Aug. daily 8:30am-7pm; Sept.-June closed Sa-Su).

Kind managers run the **Auberge de Jeunesse de St-Raphaël-Fréjus (HI),** chemin du Counillier (tel. 04 94 53 18 75; fax 04 94 53 25 86), 4km from the St-Raphaël train station. A direct shuttle bus runs from quai 7 of the *gare routière* to the hostel at 6pm (6F50); a return shuttle leaves at 8:30am and 6 and 7pm (66F; camping 32; curfew 11pm; ask about bike rental and boat discounts). **Le Mistral,** 80 rue de la Garonne (tel. 04 94 95 38 82), is next to the beach and offers discounts for longer stays and *Let's Go*ers. Their restaurant has 65 and 75F *menus* (singles 140-190F; doubles 150-260F; triples 210-330F; quads 240-360F). **Le Bishop,** 84 rue Jean Aicard, serves paella and delicious pasta (40-55F; open daily noon-2pm and 7-11pm).

■ Cannes

All stereotypes of the French Riviera materialize in Cannes, a favorite stop of the international jet-set. Less reclusive than St-Tropez, Cannes allows even unshaven budget travelers to tan like the stars.

SIGHTS AND ENTERTAINMENT In May, Cannes's **Festival International du Film** brings Hollywood's *crème de la crème* from across the sea. None of the festival's 350 screenings are open to the public, but the sidewalk show is free. Most of Cannes's daytime activity (and spending) pulses between rue Félix-Faure and the waterfront. **Rue d'Antibes,** running parallel to the sea, and **boulevard de la Croisette,** passing right along the shore, front high-price displays with the familiar names of Dior, Hermès, and Versace. Farther west, the **Castre Cathédrale** and its courtyard stand on the hill on which *vieux* Cannes was built.

Of Cannes's three casinos, the most accessible is **Le Casino Croisette,** 1 jetée Albert Eduoard (tel. 04 93 38 12 11), next to the Palais des Festivals, with slots, blackjack, and roulette (gambling daily 5pm-4am; open for slots at 10am; no shorts; ages 18 and up). If your luck sours, take to the clubs, but be sure to dress to impress or you may be turned down at the door. From 11pm to dawn, dance at **Jane's,** 38 rue des Serbes, in the Hôtel Gray d'Albion (cover and drink 120F; subsequent drinks 70F). Or for a more mellow feel, try **Kylian's Pub,** 8 rue des Frères Pradignac, for drinkin' and dancin' (15F *demi-pressions,* cover 20F; open daily 9:30pm-2:30am).

PRACTICAL INFO, ACCOMMODATIONS, AND FOOD On the major coastal **train** line, Cannes's station, 1 rue Jean-Jaurès, sends trains to Monaco (50min., 44F), Nice (35min., 31F), and TGV to Paris via Marseille (about 440F, ask for student fares; call regarding prices). Buz Azur **buses** (tel. 04 93 39 18 71) leave from the *gare routière* to Antibes (30min., 12F50), Nice (1½hr., 30F), and St-Raphaël (70min., 32F). The **tourist office,** 1 bd. de la Croisette (tel. 04 93 39 24 53; fax 04 92 99 84 23), has a free lodging service (open July-Aug. daily 9am-7pm; Sept.-June M-Sa 9am-6:30pm). The **branch office** is at the train station. (Open July-Sept. M-Sa 8:30am-12:30pm and 3-7pm; Oct.-June M-F 9am-12:30pm and 2-6:15pm.)

A few bargain accommodations lurk near the train station, but the area is less than safe at night. Try to book ahead—an absolute must in July and August. From the train station, take a right on bld. Carnot, another right on av. 11 November, and then a left onto av. Galliéni. Follow signs to the **Auberge pour la Jeunesse-Le Chalit,** 27 av. Maréchal Galliéni (tel. 04 93 99 22 11; fax 04 93 39 00 28; 90F; sheets 15F). The new **Auberge de la Jeunesse de Cannes,** 35 av. de Vallauris (tel./fax 04 93 99 26 79; follow the signs from under the train station), offers big, comfy beds (70-80F; curfew midnight; reception 8am-noon and 3-10pm). The best **camping** is the three-star site at **Le Grand Saule,** 24 bd. Jean Moulin (tel. 04 93 90 55 10; fax 04 93 47 24 55), in nearby **Ranguin.** Take bus 9 (7F) from pl. de l'Hôtel de Ville toward Grasse (70F per person, 124F for 2 people and tent; open Apr.-Oct.).

Morning markets tempt you with fresh foodstuffs on the *place* between rue Mimont and av. de la République (open daily 7am-noon). You can also buy your supplies at **Monoprix supermarket,** 9 rue Maréchal Foch, across from the station (open M-Sa 8:30am-8:30pm), and then picnic in the breezy Jardin de la Croisette. **Le Lion d'Or,** 45 bd. de la République, serves an unbeatable three-course 67F *menu* (open Su-F noon-2pm and 7-9:30pm). **Restaurant des Artistes,** 5 rue Rouguière, and **Papa Nino's,** 15 bd. de la République, can also tame the hungry beast.

■ Near Cannes

Antibes is like Nice but quieter and more serene: the beaches are sandy, the museums close by, and the city itself is clean and pleasant. Once you've gotten your share of the sun, retreat to the charming *vieille ville* (old town). Old Antibes, which stretches between bd. Maréchal Foch and the port d'Antibes, is a haven for museums and pricey boutiques. The **Musée Picasso,** in the Château Grimaldi on pl. Mariejol, displays works by the master and his contemporaries. (Open Tu-Su June-Sept. 10am-6pm; Oct.-May 10am-noon and 2-6pm. 30F, students 18F.) Drawings by local artist Raymond Peynet can be found in the **Museé Peynet,** pl. Nationale (open Tu-Su 10am-noon and 2-6pm; 20F, students 10F). **Trains** connect Antibes with Cannes (10min., 13F), Juan-les-Pins (5min., every 30min. until 12:25am, 7F), Marseille (2½hr., 135F), and Nice (18min., 21F). **Buses** go to Cannes (30min., 12F50) and Nice (1¼hr.,

FRANCE

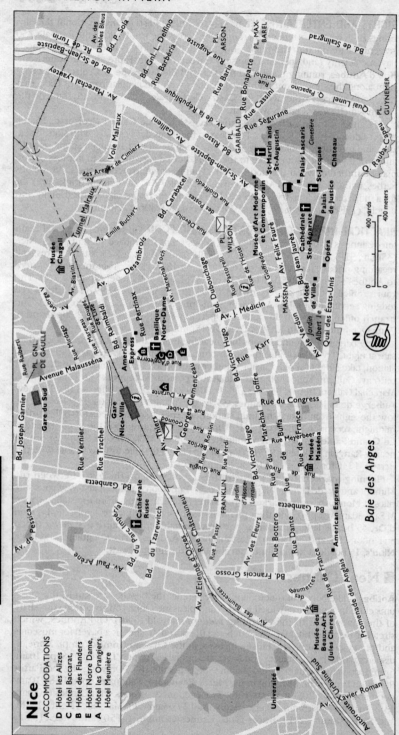

Nice

ACCOMMODATIONS

D Hôtel les Alizés
C Hôtel Baccarat
B Hôtel des Flanders
A Hôtel Notre Dame,
  Hôtel les Orangiers,
  Hôtel Meunière

24F50). To get to the **tourist office**, 11 pl. de Gaulle (tel. 04 92 90 53 00), exit the train station, turn right onto av. Robert Soleau, and follow signs for the *Maison du Tourisme.* (Open July-Sept. daily 8:45am-7:30pm; Sept.-June M-F 9am-12:30pm and 2-6pm, Sa 9am-noon and 2-6pm.) The **Hôtel Brasserie Nouvelle,** 1 av. Niguet (tel. 04 93 34 10 07), is within sight of the *gare routière* (bus station; singles and doubles 150-230F; breakfast 25F; reception 7am-8pm). *Vieille* Antibes packs in *boulangeries,* fruit stands, and restaurants ranging from reasonable to ridiculous.

Though joined as one—the city is known as Antibes-Juan-les-Pins (pop. 70,000)—Antibes and **Juan-les-Pins** are 3km apart and use separate train stations, post offices, and tourist offices. Juan-les-Pins is the younger, hipper, and more hedonistic of the two. Boutiques remain open until midnight, cafes until 2am, and nightclubs until past sunrise. The streets are packed with seekers of sea, sun, and sex (the order varies), and nightclubs pulse with promises of decadence. The cafes are much cheaper and almost as lively, so even the most miserly traveler can be included in the nightly bash. In winter, Juan-les-Pins becomes a ghost town.

Discothèques open around 11pm, and their cover charges average 100F (1st drink included). Look for advertisements for special events, including the *mega-mousse* party where clubbers dance in a sea of foamy bubbles. Check out the psychedelic **Whiskey à Gogo,** la Pinède, and fluorescent **Voom Voom,** 1 bd. de la Pinède. **Joy's Discothèque,** av. Dautheville, has dance revues as well as a disco. Mingle with chic young locals at **Le Ten's Bar,** 25 av. du Dr. Hochet, off Av. Guy de Maupassant away from the beach (beer 15F), or pay homage to that famous Cuban at **Ché's Café,** 1 bd. de la Pinède, where a beer will liberate your mind for 16F. The dress code at all the clubs is simple: look good.

The **train station** is on av. l'Esterel at av. du Maréchal Joffre. Trains leave every 20 minutes for Nice and Cannes (11F). To get from Antibes's pl. du Général de Gaulle to Juan-les-Pins by foot, follow bd. Wilson (about 1.5km) and turn left on av. Dautheville. Rather than make the post-party trek back to Antibes, take a right out of the train station and sack out at **Hôtel Trianon,** 14 av. de L'Estérel (tel. 04 93 61 18 11; singles 150-200F; doubles 180-200F; triples 250-280F).

■ Nice

Cosmopolitan and chic, sun-drenched and spicy, Nice sparkles as the unofficial capital of the Riviera. The city's pumping nightlife, top-notch museums, and bustling beaches enhance the native *provençal* charms: flowery, palm-lined boulevards, casual affluence, and soothing sea breezes. During its **Carnaval** (Feb. 13-28 in 1999), the city celebrates spring with wild floral revelry, grotesque costumes, and raucous song and dance. Prepare to have more fun than you'll remember.

ORIENTATION AND PRACTICAL INFORMATION

The **train station,** Gare Nice-Ville, is in the center of town, next to the tourist office on **avenue Thiers.** To the left, **avenue Jean-Médecin** runs toward the water to **place Masséna.** Heading right from the train station, you'll find **boulevard Gambetta,** the other main street running directly to the water. Sweeping along the coast, the **promenade des Anglais** is a noisy people-watching paradise. Cafes, boutiques, and expensive restaurants line the **pedestrian zone** west of pl. Masséna. Women should avoid walking alone after sundown, and everyone should exercise caution around the train station and *Vieux Nice* (Old Nice). Never leave your belongings unattended.

Flights: Aéroport Nice-Côte d'Azur (tel. 04 93 21 30 30). Take Sunbus 23 ("St-Laurent") from the train station (every 20min., 6am-9pm, 9F). The airport bus (tel. 04 93 56 35 40) runs from the bus station by pl. Masséna every 20min. (21F).

Trains: Gare SNCF Nice-Ville, av. Thiers (tel. 08 36 35 35 35). Trains run frequently to Antibes (25min., 26F), Cannes (40min., 37F), Monaco (25min., 22F), and elsewhere in France, Italy, and Spain. In summer, 10 trains per day connect with the TGV to Paris (7hr., 420-522F plus 20F required reservation fee). **Lockers** 15-30F. **Luggage storage** 30F per day per piece (open daily 7am-10pm).

Buses: Gare Routière, 5 bd. Jean Jaurès (tel. 04 93 85 61 81). To Antibes (1hr., 25F), Cannes (1¼hr., 30F), Juan-les-Pins (1hr., 27F), and Monaco (45min., 17-19F).

Public Transportation: Sunbus, 10 av. Félix Faure (tel. 04 93 16 52 10), near pl. Leclerc and pl. Masséna. Tickets 8F. Day pass 22F; *carnet* of 10 tickets 68F; 5-day pass 85F. Buy passes at the agency or kiosk at pl. Leclerc. Bus 12 goes from the train station to pl. Masséna and the beach every 12min. The tourist office's *Le Plan Sunbus* and *Guide Infobus* list other routes.

Ferries: SNCM, quai du Commerce (tel. 04 93 13 66 66; fax 04 93 13 66 81). Take bus 1 or 2 ("Port") from pl. Masséna. To: Bastia (3hr., 300F, students 191-209F) and Ajaccio (6-7hr., same prices). Open M-F 8am-7pm, Sa 8am-noon.

Bike Rental: JML Location, 34 av. Auber, across from the train station. Bikes 60-80F per day. Scooters 130-310F per day. Open daily 8am-noon and 2-6:30pm. **Cycles Arnaud,** 4 pl. Grimaldi, near the pedestrian zone. Bikes 100F, deposit 2000F or credit card. Open M-Sa 9am-noon and 2-7pm.

Tourist Office: av. Thiers (tel. 04 93 87 07 07; fax 04 93 16 85 16; email otc@nice-coteazur.org; http://www.nice-coteazur.org), beside the station. Books a limited number of rooms. Ask for the English-language *Nice: A Practical Guide* and the city map. Open daily June 15-Sept. 15 8am-8pm; Sept. 16-June 14 8am-7pm.

Currency Exchange: Cambio, 17 av. Thiers (tel. 04 93 88 56 80), across from the station. No commission. Open daily 7am-midnight.

American Express: 11 promenade des Anglais (tel. 04 93 16 53 53), at the corner of rue des Congrès. The office has an **ATM** machine. Open daily 9am-9pm.

Laundromat: Laverie Automatique, rue de Suisse, between rue Paganini and rue d'Angleterre. Wash 20F, dry 2F per 5min. Open daily 7am-9pm.

Emergency: tel. 17. **Medical emergency,** tel. 18.

Police: (tel. 04 93 17 22 22), at opposite end of bd. M. Foch from bd. Jean Médecin.

Hospital: St-Roch, 5 rue Pierre Devoluy (tel. 04 92 03 33 75). From av. Jean Médecin, turn left on rue Pastorelli, which turns into rue P. Devoluy.

Post Office: 23 av. Thiers (tel. 04 93 82 65 22). Open M-F 8am-7pm, Sa 8am-noon. **Telephones** and *Poste Restante*. **Postal Code:** 06000.

Internet Access: see Cyber Café La Douche, **Entertainment,** p. 338.

ACCOMMODATIONS

Don't make your first *niçois* experience regrettable—come with **reservations.** Affordable places cluster around the train station, but without reservations (made 3-5 days in advance), you'll be forced to join the legions outside the train station, which moonlights as one of the largest and most dangerous bedrooms in France.

Hôtel Les Alizès, 10 rue de Suisse (tel. 04 93 88 85 08), off rue d'Angleterre. From the train station, turn left, walk to av. Jean Médecin and turn right. Friendly owners keep comfortable, spotless rooms, all with showers. Singles 70-80F; doubles 150-200F; triples 220-260F. Free breakfast and discounts with *Let's Go.*

Relais International de la Jeunesse "Clairvallon," 26 av. Scudéri (tel. 04 93 81 27 63; fax 04 93 53 35 88), in Cimiez, 4km away. Take bus 15 ("Remiez") to "Scudéri" from the train station or pl. Masséna, walk uphill, and take your first left. You and 160 new friends in the luxurious villa of a deceased Marquis. Dorms 70F. Breakfast included. Check-in 5pm. Lockout 9:30am-5pm. Curfew 11pm. No credit cards.

Hôtel Baccarat, 39 rue d'Angleterre (tel. 04 93 88 35 73; fax 04 93 16 14 25). Turn left from the train station, walk 50m, and turn right. Large, clean, beautifully renovated rooms and a friendly staff. All rooms and dorms come with bath. Dorms 83F; singles 153F; doubles 206F. Breakfast 15F. Prices 10-20F cheaper off-season.

Hôtel Les Orangiers, 10bis av. Durante (tel. 04 93 87 51 41; fax 04 93 82 57 82). Walk down the steps by the Thomas Cook agency, cross the street and go down the ramp. The hotel is up on the left. Large, bright dorms and rooms, some with balconies, most with showers. English-speaking owner offers free luggage storage. Dorms 85F; singles 85-100F; doubles 200-210F; quads 360F. Breakfast 20F.

Hôtel des Flanders, 6 rue de Belgique (tel. 04 93 88 78 94; fax 04 93 88 74 90). Large, clean rooms with bathrooms and well-worn carpets. Student dorms 90F; singles 200F; doubles 220-250F; triples 340F; quads 360-400F. Breakfast 25F.

Hôtel Notre Dame, 22 rue de Russie (tel. 04 93 88 70 44; fax 04 93 82 20 38), corner of rue d'Italie one block west of av. Jean Médecin. Good-sized, quiet rooms. Owners also rent studios. Singles 130-180F; doubles 150-240F; triples 240-320F; quads 350F. Apartments (4 people) 350F. Breakfast 20F. Showers 10F.

Hôtel Lyonnais, 20 rue de Russie (tel. 04 93 88 70 74; fax 04 93 16 25 56). Singles 145-220F; doubles 120-220F; triples 180-290F; quads 240-390F. Breakfast 22F. Showers 15F. No lockout. *Let's Go*ers get a 10% off-season discount.

Auberge de Jeunesse (HI), route Forestière du Mont-Alban (tel. 04 93 89 23 64; fax 04 92 04 03 10), 4km from the city center. Take bus 14 ("Mont Baron") to "l'Auberge" from the *gare routière* off bd. Jean Jaurès (last bus 7:30pm). Otherwise, from the train station, take bus 17 and tell the driver you need to switch to bus 14. 66F, including shower and breakfast. Kitchen. Reception opens at 5pm. Lockout 10am-5pm. Curfew midnight.

Hôtel Belle Meunière, 21 av. Durante (tel. 04 93 88 66 15), near the *gare*. Hostelers hang out in the gardens and jest with the owner. Singles 76-101F; doubles 243-266F; triples 326F. Breakfast included. Luggage storage 10F. Free parking.

FOOD

Nice offers a smorgasbord of seafood and North African, Asian, and Italian gastronomic delights. Avoid the touristy places near the train station in favor of the restaurants that cluster around the *vieux port*, or stock up at the **Prisunic supermarket**, 42 av. Jean Médecin (open M-Sa 8:30am-8:30pm).

La Braisière, 11 rue de l'Abbaye. Mouth-watering delicacies at reasonable prices. 10% discount for *Let's Go*ers. Open daily 10am-3pm and 6-11:30pm.

Lou Pilha Leva, 10 rue du Collet, in *Vieux Nice*. Hustling and bustling order counter will provide a lot for 30F. 15F quiche. 10F *socca*. Open daily 8am-11pm.

Nissa Socca, 5 rue Ste-Réparate, has filling *niçois* dishes (35F) and a homey aura. Open M-Sa noon-2pm and 7-11pm.

Le Faubourg Montmartre, 39 rue Pertinax, off av. Jean Médecin. *Cuisine niçoise* at low prices. Open daily 11:30am-3pm and 5:30pm-late.

SIGHTS

Nice's **promenade des Anglais,** which stretches the length of the waterfront, is a sight in itself. Private beaches crowd the water between bd. Gambetta and the Opéra, but plenty of public space remains. Whatever dreams you've had of Nice's beach, the hard reality is an endless stretch of smooth rocks; bring a beach mat. Between av. Verdun and bd. Jaurès off the Promenade des Anglais and quai des Etats-Unis, **Jardin Albert 1er** and **Espace Masséna** offer a break from the heat with benches, plenty of shade, and an ornate 18th-century Triton fountain. Promenade des Anglais leads east to **La Colline du Château,** a flowery hillside park crowned with the remains of an 11th-century cathedral. *(Park open daily 8am-7:30pm.)*

Even burn-hard sunbathers will have a hard time passing by Nice's excellent museums. The **Musée des Beaux-Arts,** 33 av. Baumettes, exhibits the work of Fragonard, Monet, Sisley, Bonnard, and Degas, and also features sculptures by Rodin and Carpeaux. Take bus 38 from the train station to "Chéret," or bus 12 to "Grosseo." *(Open Tu-Su 10am-noon and 2-6pm. 25F, students 15F.)* The elegant **Musée National Marc Chagall,** av. du Dr. Ménard, a 15-minute walk north of the station or a ride on bus 15 ("Rimiez" and "Les Sources"; 8F), showcases the artist's work. *(Open W-M July-Sept. 10am-6pm; Oct.-June 10am-5pm. 30-38F, students 18-28F.)* The **Musée Matisse,** 164 av. des Arènes de Cimiez, perhaps Nice's most exciting museum, displays the colorful designs of Henri Matisse, who lived and worked in Nice from 1917 until his death in 1954. *(Open W-M Apr.-Sept. 10am-6pm; Oct.-Mar. 10am-5pm. 25F, students 15F.)* Finally, the **Musée d'Art Moderne et d'Art Contemporain,** promenade des Arts, at the intersection of av. St-Jean Baptiste and Traverse Garibaldi (bus 5 "St-Charles" from the station), features over 400 French and American avant-garde pieces from 1960 to the present. *(Open W-Th and Sa-M 11am-6pm, F 11am-10pm. 25F, students 15F.)*

The gorgeous **Cathédrale Orthodoxe Russe St-Nicolas,** 17 bd. du Tsarévitch, off bd. Gambetta, is a reminder of the days when the Côte d'Azur was a favorite retreat for Russian nobility. *(Open daily June-Aug. 9am-noon and 2:30-6pm; Sept.-May 9:30am-noon and 2:30-5pm. 12F.)* The **Monastère Cimiez,** pl. du Monastère, housed Nice's Franciscan brethren from the 13th to the 18th centuries. The monastery's cloister, peaceful gardens, cemetery (in which Matisse is buried), and museum are free. *(Open M-Sa 10am-noon and 3-6pm.)* Take bus 15 or 17 from the station, or follow the signs from the Musée Matisse.

ENTERTAINMENT

Nice's **Jazz Festival** (tel. 04 93 21 68 12; fax 04 93 18 07 92), in mid-July at the Parc et Arènes de Cimiez near the Musée Matisse, is one of the best in the world (tickets 40-170F). The **Théâtre du Cours,** 2 rue Poissonnerie, stages traditional drama (75F), while the **Théâtre de Nice** on Promenade des Arts hosts concerts and theater (50-200F). The **FNAC** in the Nice Etoile shopping center, 24 av. Jean Médecin, sells tickets for virtually every performance in town.

Nice guys do finish last—the city's party crowd swings long after the folks in St-Tropez and Antibes have called it a night. The bars and nightclubs around rue Masséna and *Vieux Nice* rollick with rock, jazz, and pizzazz, but the area around *Vieux Nice* can be dangerous at night, so don't visit clubs in this area alone.

Chez Wayne, 15 rue de la Préfecture. Attracts an English-speaking crowd with live music every summer night and the double whammy of karaoke and undubbed *The Simpsons* on Su nights. Beers 28-36F. Open daily 2:30pm-midnight.

Master Home, next to Chez Wayne. Too-sexy club where a pint is 28F day or night. Open daily 11am-2:30am.

The Hole in the Wall, 3 rue de l'Abbaye. Tiny but loads of fun. Mellow live music every night. Open daily 8pm-1am.

Cyber Café La Douche, 34 cours Saleya. A dark, black-lit bar/club where you can check your email for 25F (30min.). Open daily 4pm-2:30am.

■ Near Nice

The narrow streets and pastel houses of **Villefranche-sur-Mer,** only two stops from Nice on the local train, have enchanted Aldous Huxley, Katherine Mansfield, and a bevy of other writers. Strolling from the train station along the quai Ponchardier, a sign to the *vieille ville* points the way to **rue Obscure,** the oldest street in Villefranche. Two excellent museums are located in the 16th-century **Citadelle,** near the waterfront: the **Musée Volti** displays the contemporary art and sculpture of resident Antoniucci Volti, while the **Musée Goetz-Boumeester** traces the work of Villefranche painter Henri Goetz and his wife, Christine Boumeester. (Both open W-M July-Aug. 10am-noon and 3-7pm, Su 3-7pm; June and Sept. 9am-noon and 3-6pm; Oct.-May 10am-noon and 2-5pm. Free.) **Trains** run from Nice every 30 minutes (9F). The **tourist office** (tel. 04 93 01 73 68; fax 04 93 76 63 65), on Jardin François Binon, gives out free maps and info on sights. (Open July to mid-Sept. daily 8am-8pm; mid-Sept. to June M-Sa 8:30am-noon and 2-7pm.)

St-Jean-Cap-Ferret, is a lovely town with lovelier beaches. The **Fondation Ephrussi di Rothschild,** however—a stunning Italianate villa with an impressive, eclectic collection of artwork—is the town's main draw. (Open July-Aug. daily 10am-7pm; Sept.-Oct. and Feb. 14-June daily 10am-6pm; Nov.-Feb.14 M-F 2-6pm, Sa-Su 10am-6pm. 46F, students 35F.)

On the way to Monaco, **Cap d'Ail** has 3km of cliff-framed foamy seashore. **Les Pissarelles** draws hundreds of nudists, while the more modest frequent **plage Mala.** The beachside **Relais International de la Jeunesse** on bd. de la Mer (tel. 04 93 78 18 58), has an amazing location for 70F per night.

■ Monaco/Monte-Carlo

Wealth and casual luxury drip from every ornate street lamp and newly-scrubbed sidewalk of sumptuous Monaco. The money and mystery of the Monte-Carlo *quartier* revolve around the Casino, where Mata Hari shot a Russian spy and Richard Burton wooed Liz Taylor.

SIGHTS AND ENTERTAINMENT The **Casino's** interior, ablaze with red velvet curtains, gilded ceilings, and gold and crystal chandeliers, is worth visiting. If you feel lucky, the slot machines open at 10am, while blackjack, craps, and roulette (25F min.) open at 5pm. These games are also played next door at the **Café de Paris,** where admission to the main room is free (you must be over 21; no shorts, sneakers, sandals, or jeans), but a peek at the high-stakes *salons privés* costs 50-100F.

After losing your shirt, admire the royal robes at the **Palais Princier,** the sometime home of Prince Rainier and his family. When the flag is down, the prince is away and visitors can tour the lavish palace (open daily June-Sept. 9:30am-6pm; Oct. 10am-5pm; 30F, students 20F). Next door is the stately **Cathédrale de Monaco,** 4 rue Colonel Bellando de Castro, where former Princes of Monaco are buried. Grace Kelly's simple grave is behind the altar (open daily 9am-12:30pm and 1:30-4:30pm; free). Once run by Jacques Cousteau, the **Musée Océanographique,** av. St-Martin, houses thousands of species of marine animals. (Open daily July-Aug. 9am-8pm; Apr.-June and Sept. 9am-7pm; Oct. and Mar. 9:30am-7pm; Nov.-Feb. 10am-6pm. 60F, students 30F.) The **Exhibition of H.S.H. the Prince of Monaco's Private Collection of Classic Cars,** les Terraces de Fontvieille, features 105 of the most sexy and stately cars ever made (open daily Dec.-Oct. 10am-6pm; 30F, students 15F).

PRACTICAL INFO, ACCOMMODATIONS, AND FOOD Monaco is 18km east of Nice and 12km west of the Italian border. The **train station,** on av. Prince Pierre (tel. 08 36 35 35 35), connects to Antibes (45min., 36F), Cannes (70min., 44F), and Nice (25min., 18F). When you exit the station, turn right onto av. du Port, then left onto bd. Albert 1er overlooking the harbor. On the right sits the *quartier* of **Monaco-Ville** with its *vieille ville* and the palace; to the left rises the fabled *quartier* of **Monte-Carlo.** *To call Monaco from outside, dial the international prefix (00 in France) then 377.* The **tourist office,** 2a bd. des Moulins (tel. (377) 92 16 61 16; fax 92 16 60 00), near the casino, provides a map and makes room reservations (open M-Sa 9am-7pm, Su 10am-noon). Summertime annexes are set up at the train station and port.

To afford a room in Monaco, you'll need to seduce royalty or win big. Try the **Centre de Jeunesse Princesse Stéphanie,** 24 av. Prince Pierre (tel. (377) 93 50 83 20; fax 93 25 29 82), 100m up the hill from the train station. (80F, breakfast and sheets included. Age limit is 32. 5-night max stay. Reception 7am-1am; off-season 7am-midnight.) Picnickers should stop by the fruit and flower **market** on pl. d'Armes, at the end of av. Prince Pierre (open daily 6am-1pm). The **Carrefour supermarket** is in Fontvieille's *centre commercial* (shopping plaza). From the train station, turn right onto rue de la Colle; at pl. du Canton cross the street and go down one level (open M-Sa 8:30am-10pm).

CORSICA (CORSE)

Appropriately called *Kallysté,* "the most beautiful," by the Greeks, Corsica combines the mountainous splendor of the Alps with the beaches and crystal-blue Mediterranean waters of the Riviera. Although ferries and other tourist services multiply between June 15 and the end of September, prices soar by 50%. Half the island's one million annual tourists visit then, packing the beaches and hotels along the coast.

The **Société National Maritime Corse Méditerranée (SNCM)** sends ferries from Marseille and Nice to Ajaccio, Bastia, Calvi, and Propriano on Corsica. About two boats per day travel between Corsica and the mainland in the off season, a few more during summer; the trip usually takes six to 12 hours. Schedules and prices vary, so call ahead. SNCM has offices in Ajaccio, quai L'herminier (tel. 04 95 29 66 88; fax 04 95 29 66 77); Bastia, Nouveau Port (tel. 04 95 54 66 88; fax 04 95 54 66 69); Nice, quai du Commerce (tel. 04 93 13 66 99); Marseille, 61 bd. des Dames (tel. 04 91 56 30 10); and Paris, 12 rue Godot-de-Mauroy (tel. 01 49 24 24 24). **Corsica Ferries** cross from the Italian ports of Livorno and Savona to Bastia (140-200F). The central reservation office is at 5 bd. Chanoine-Leschi (tel. 04 95 32 95 95), in Bastia.

Air France and **Air Inter** fly to Ajaccio, Bastia, and Calvi from Paris (round-trip 1390F, discounts up to 300F), Nice (653-952F), Marseille (705-1051F), and Lyon (1325-2337F). Call Air France's offices in Marseille (tel. 04 91 39 36 36) or Paris (tel. 01 45 46 90 00) for more information about flights. Air Inter's offices are at the airports in Ajaccio (tel. 04 95 29 45 45) and Bastia (tel. 04 95 65 88).

Trains in Corsica are slow and limited; they don't serve all the major towns (no rail south of Ajaccio) and don't accept any railpasses. **Buses** connect major towns but are neither cheaper nor more frequent. Call **Eurocorse Voyages** (tel. 04 95 21 06 30) for more info. **Car rental** may be convenient for groups of three or four; the least expensive models cost 350-530F per day, plus 2-4F per kilometer. Weekly rentals (1450-1806F) usually include unlimited free mileage. **Hiking** is the best way to explore the island's mountainous interior. The longest marked route, the **GR20**, is a difficult 160km, 13- to 15-day trail going from Calenzana (southeast of Calvi) to Conca (northeast of Porto-Vecchio). Two other popular routes are the **Mare e Monti**, a seven-day trail from Calenzana to Cargèse, and the easier **Da Mare a Mare**, which crosses the southern part of the island between Porto-Vecchio and Propriano (4-6 days). The **Parc Naturel Regional de la Corse**, 2 rue Major Lambrashini, Ajaccio (tel. 04 95 51 79 10), publishes maps and has info on staying at *gîtes d'étapes* near the trails.

Ajaccio and Calvi

The urban bustle of **Ajaccio** balances the Mediterranean calm of the city's beachside resort—this place swings like no other Corsican city. The **tourist office**, pl. Maréchal Foch (tel. 04 95 51 53 03; fax 04 95 51 53 01), in the Hôtel de Ville, hands out free maps (open in summer daily 8:30am-8:30pm; off-season M-F 8:30am-6pm, Sa 8:30am-1pm). **Hôtel le Dauphin**, 11 bd. Sampiero (tel. 04 95 21 12 94; fax 04 95 21 88 69), has clean rooms with TV, shower, and toilet (singles from 202F; doubles from 238F), but women may feel uncomfortable at the bars along the street. **Hôtel Napoleon,** 4 rue Lorenzo Vero (tel. 04 95 51 54 00), is a three-star hotel, and you'll pay for it (rooms from 310F). Bag a baguette at the **Monoprix supermarket,** 31 cours Napoléon (open M-Sa 8:30am-7:15pm).

With its well-preserved Genoan citadel, stretches of white-sand beaches, and 2400 hours of sunshine a year, **Calvi** could well be paradise—but no benevolent god would charge these prices. If you tire of the 6km stretch of expensive **public beach**, head to the citadel's rocks to bask in seclusion. Check out the view of the pink and cream Eglise Sainte-Marie-Majeure from the **Chapelle de Notre Dame de la Serra** (open daily 9am-noon and 2-7pm; 45F). The **tourist office** (tel. 04 95 65 16 67), is at Port de Plaisance (open July-Aug. daily 7am-7pm; Sept.-June M-F 7am-noon and 2-6pm). July and August bring the tourists, and rooms may become prohibitively expensive. The friendly, refreshingly quiet **Relais International de la Jeunesse U Carabellu** (tel. 04 95 65 14 16), rte. de Pietra-Maggiore (75F; breakfast included; open May-Sept.), is in the middle of nowhere—call for directions. The clean and airy **BVJ Corsotel,** av. de la République (tel. 04 95 65 14 15; 120F; breakfast included; open late Mar.-Oct.), is also a good bet. **Hôtel Belvédère,** av. de l'Uruguay (tel. 04 95 65 01 25) features bright Art Deco halls and small, fresh, recently renovated rooms (doubles 200-350F; open Apr.-Oct.). **Les Tamaris,** rte. d'Ajaccio (tel. 04 95 65 00 26), has peaceful, shady camping by a beach (25F per person; 10F per tent). For grub, try **La Galère,** at the end of rue Clemenceau.

Bastia and Cap Corse

Littered with square, graceless buildings, **Bastia** has little in the way of Mediterranean charm, but offers supplies and a base for excursions to more scenic Cap Corse. Before setting out, meander through pl. de l'Hôtel de Ville and gaze at the immense proportions and gilded domes of the 18th-century **Eglise St-Jean-Baptiste**. The **tourist office**, pl. St-Nicolas (tel. 04 95 55 96 96), has info on hotels, camping, and transportation (open M-Sa 8am-6pm, Su 8am-noon and 2-6pm). The **Hôtel Central**, 3 rue Miot (tel. 04 95 31 71 12), has many beautifully renovated rooms (singles 200-250F; doubles 200-300F). Camp at **Les Orangiers**, Quartier Licciola-Miomo (tel. 04 95 33 24 09; 22F per person; 12F per tent).

Cap Corse is a 48km peninsula north of Bastia, strung with fishing villages and quiet inlets. From Calvi, **Autocars Mariani** (tel. 04 95 65 05 32) runs tours of the Cap, leaving at 7am and returning at 7:30pm on Fridays (145F; June-Sept.). On Cap Corse, **Macinaggio** is one of the few port towns where you can find services and supplies. Nearby, serene **Rogliano** features the ruins of a Genoese castle and a large 16th-century church. The town of **Erbalunga** really *is* paradise.

THE ALPS

After countless museum corridors, the Alps come as a refreshing relief. Snow-capped crests and tumbling waterfalls exhilarate the weary soul, and crystal-clear air makes Paris smog seem a distant memory. **Skiing** in the Alps has always been expensive; make arrangements months in advance. The least crowded and cheapest months to go are January, March, and April. Most resorts close in October and November. **FUAJ**, the French Youth Hostel Federation, offers week-long winter skiing and summer sports packages. For more info, contact local FUAJ offices, youth hostels, or the central office at 27 rue Pajol, 75018 Paris (tel. 01 46 07 00 01).

The beauty of the Alps does little good to the traveler who wants to go anywhere quickly or directly. While TGV **train** service will whisk you from Paris to Aix-les-Bains or Annecy at the gateway to the serious mountains, from there it's either slow trains, special mountain trains, or torturously slow **buses**. **Hiking** ranges from simple strolls through mountain meadows to some of the most difficult climbing in the world. Many towns maintain chalet dorms, as well as hostels and campgrounds; in less accessible spots, the **Club Alpin Français** runs refuges. Get a list from one of their offices: 136 av. Michel-Croz, Chamonix (tel. 04 50 53 16 03); or 32 av. Félix Viallet, Grenoble (tel. 04 76 87 03 73). *Always* check with local hiking bureaus before setting out on *any* hike; even in summer, you can encounter snowstorms and avalanches.

▨ Grenoble

Stendhal, Grenoble's most famous bookworm, grumbled about his hometown that "at the end of every street, there is a mountain." Few are so rancorous about this lively university city and its majestic surroundings. The bubble-shaped cable car (*Téléphérique Grenoble Bastille;* tel. 04 76 44 33 65; round-trip 34F, students 27F) to the **Bastille** has a great view of the landscape that inspired Shelley to ethereal free verse; you can hike down through the maze-like **Jardin Léon Monet**. Several mountain **hikes** begin here. Grenoble's museums include the regional **Musée Dauphinois**, 30 rue Maurice Gignoux (open W-M May-Oct. 10am-7pm; Nov.-Apr. 10am-6pm; 20F, students 10F), and the half-pipe-shaped **Musée de Grenoble**, 5 pl. de Lavalette (open Th-M 11am-7pm, W 11am-10pm; 25F, students 15F).

The **tourist office**, 14 rue de la République (tel. 04 76 42 41 41), has good maps, accommodations info, and *Grenoble Magazine*, a guide to local events (open M-Sa 9am-12:30pm and 1:30-6pm, Su 10am-1pm). The *Guide DAHU*, written by hip Grenoble students, is useful for longer stays (20F). To reach the **Auberge de Jeunesse (HI)**, 18 av. du Grésivaudan (tel. 04 76 09 33 52; fax 04 76 09 38 99), 4km out of town, take bus 8 ("Pont Rouge") to "La Quinzaine;" the hostel is one block behind the Casino supermarket (68F; reception M-Sa 7:30am-11pm, Su 7:30-10am and 5:30-11pm). **Le Foyer de l'Etudiante**, 4 rue Ste-Ursule (tel. 04 76 42 00 84; fax 04 76 44 36 85), is a great place to meet friendly students. (Dorms 50F; singles 90F; doubles 140F. Reception 24hr. Accepts men and women mid-June to mid-Sept.; off-season women only for month-long stays.) **Hôtel de l'Europe,** 22 pl. Grenette (tel./fax 04 76 46 16 94), has a perfect location. (Singles from 140-190F; doubles from 150-210F; triples 340F; quads 360F. Reception 24hr.) Cafes and restaurants cluster around **pl. Notre-Dame** and **pl. St-André,** both in the heart of the *vieille ville.* **Le Valgo,** 2 rue St-Hughes, at pl. Notre-Dame, has excellent food (open Tu-W lunch, Th-Sa lunch and dinner). The **Prisunic supermarket** sits across from the tourist office.

■ Chamonix

In other alpine villages, people dip in cold, still waters that reflect the distant peaks; in Chamonix, the Arne river looks like fluid ice, and daggers of mammoth glaciers menace the town. Lying within skiing distance of two countries, Chamonix buzzes with climbers and skiers swapping tall tales of the town's slopes, among the world's toughest. **Mont Blanc,** Western Europe's highest peak (4807m), reigns just to the east, and the first modern Winter Olympics were held here in 1924.

SKIING AND HIKING Skiers should reserve a spot on the *téléphérique* in high season (tel. 04 50 53 30 80, 24hr. reservations 04 50 53 40 00) or arrive *early.* **Balme** (tel. 04 50 54 00 58), on the southern tip of the valley, is the best intermediate slope (1-day lift pass 120F). Insane experts ski **Vallée Blanche,** a 20km, unmarked, unpatrolled run (*téléphérique* 144F). Check conditions before you go, don't ski alone, and bring means to call for aid. Bring warm clothes, lunch, and your camera, and remember that mountain weather can change rapidly.

In summer, special trains run from a small station next to the main train station to the huge **Mer de Glace** glacier (56F, round-trip 73F; May-Sept. daily 8:30am-5:30pm), but you might prefer the two-hour hike. Serious hikers should buy the IGN topographic map, available at the Office de Haute Montagne (see below) and bookstores. Mont Blanc is a two- to three-day expedition for the experienced. Don't do it alone, and get info about storm fronts and avalanches before hiking at high altitudes. If you're just in it for the views, take the spectacular cable car to **l'Aiguille du Midi** (180F; additional 13F to go to the summit), and then to **Helbronnes** (90F extra), in Italy, from which you can see three countries, Mont Blanc, and the Matterhorn.

PRACTICAL INFO, ACCOMMODATIONS, AND FOOD The **tourist office,** pl. du Triangle de l'Amitié (tel. 04 50 53 00 24; fax 04 50 53 58 90), lists hotels, dorms, and campgrounds. (Open daily July-Aug. and winter vacation 8:30am-7:30pm; off-season 8:30am-12:30pm and 2-7pm.) Next to the church on pl. de l'Eglise, the **Maison de la Montagne** houses the **Office de Haute Montagne** (tel. 04 50 53 22 08), a good place to start planning your hike. Downstairs, the **Compagnie des Guides** (tel. 04 50 53 00 88) organizes lessons and guided hikes and trips.

When you can get a spot, the *gîtes* and dorms are a budget traveler's dream. During summer weekends, call the tourist office for availability. Hotels and many dorms require reservations (preferably 6 weeks ahead) for school vacations (Dec. and Feb.). The **auberge de jeunesse (HI)** (tel. 04 50 53 14 52; fax 04 50 55 92 34), in Les Pélerins, has breathtaking views and a vibrant crowd. Take the bus ("Les Houches") from pl. de l'Eglise to "Pélerins Ecole" (7F), and follow signs uphill. By train, get off at "Les Pélerins" and follow the signs. (76F; singles 98F; doubles 170F. Sheets 19F. Reception 8am-noon, 4-7:30, and 8:30-10pm. Offers winter ski packages.) The new **Gîte le Vagabond,** 365 av. Ravanel-le-Rouge (tel. 04 50 53 15 43; fax 04 50 53 68 21), is near the downtown (dorms 65F; 100F key deposit; reception noon-2pm and 4pm-1am). **Red Mountain Lodge,** 435 rue Joseph-Vallot (tel. 04 50 53 94 97), is a great cozy chalet in the middle of town (singles 100F; doubles 200F). **Hôtel le Touring,** 95 rue Joseph-Vallot (tel. 04 50 53 59 18), has big rooms with showers (singles 165-210F; doubles 215-275F; higher mid-summer and mid-winter). The same management runs **Hotel du Midi** (tel. 04 50 53 05 62; fax 04 50 53 67 25) around the corner (singles 165-215F; doubles 200-280F; receptions for both hotels 8am-10pm).

Straight out of Dublin, **The Jekyll**, 71 rte des Pélerins, provides Guinness (33F), huge burgers, and awesome salads (30-64F; open daily 4pm-2am). Bring your bathing suit to **Wild Wallabies**, rue de la Tour; the pool is free to patrons. They have excellent calamari (35F) and barbecue (65F; open daily 11am-2am). Frugal folks retreat to **Super U**, 117 rue Joseph Vallot (open M-Sa 8:15am-7:30pm, Su 8:15am-12:15pm).

■ Annecy

With narrow cobblestone streets, overstuffed flower boxes, and the purest mountain lake in Europe, Annecy feels more like a fairy-tale fabrication than a real city. Hordes of vacationers enjoy the lakeside beaches and stroll along the flower-dotted canals around the **Palais d'Isle**, a 12th-century fortress rising out of a tiny island. The **château** houses a museum, but is far more impressive from the outside. A stroll through the *vieille ville* may cost you several rolls of film; all of Annecy is one big, beautiful sight. Cross the street from the tourist office to walk through the **Champ de Mars**, a long, grassy field dotted with *boules* players, sunbathers, and picnickers stretching out to the lake. For a dip in the cold, crystalline lake, you can choose between the free but crowded **plage des Marquisats** or the 18F waterslide wonderland of **Parc Public de l'Impérial** (open May-Sept. 10am-7:30pm). Take the bus to Lovagny (10min., 3-4 per day, 12F) and then walk 800m to the **Gorges du Fier**, a canyon carved by glaciers. (Open daily June 15-Sept. 15 9am-6:15pm; Mar. 15-June 14 and Sept. 16-Oct. 15 9am-noon and 2-5:15pm. 24F. For info, call 04 50 46 23 07.)

The **tourist office**, 1 rue Jean Jaurès (tel. 04 50 45 00 33 or 04 50 45 56 66), at pl. de la Libération, gives out brochures on Annecy and nearby towns. (Open July-Aug. daily 9am-6:30pm; Sept.-June M-Sa 9am-noon and 1:45-6:30pm, Su 3-6pm.) Room reservations are recommended. The **Auberge de Jeunesse "La Grande Jeanne" (HI)** (tel. 04 50 45 33 19; fax 04 50 52 77 52), rte de Semnoz, is a super-chalet tucked away in the woods. In summer, take bus 91 ("Semnoz;" last bus 6pm, 7F). From the tourist office, walk down quai Chappuis, turn right on av. de Trésun, and follow D41; after an uphill hike (15min.) the hostel will be on your right (70F; sheets 17F; reception 7am-11pm). **Hôtel Savoyard**, 41 av. de Cran (tel. 04 50 57 08 08), behind the train station, is rustic and hospitable (singles and doubles 100-180F; breakfast 20F). **Hôtel Rive du Lac**, 6 rue des Marquisats (tel. 04 50 51 32 85), is ideally located (singles and doubles from 138F; triples 186F). Close to the HI youth hostel is the *busy* **camping area**, 8 rte de Semnoz (tel. 04 50 45 48 30; fax 04 50 45 55 56; 60F for tent and 1-2 people; closed Oct. 16-Dec. 14). Dozens of campgrounds border the lake in **Albigny**, reachable by Voyages Crolard buses or by following av. d'Albigny from the tourist office (1.5km).

A **Prisunic supermarket** fills the pl. de Notre-Dame (open M-Sa 8:30am-7:30pm), and **open-air markets** are held on pl. Ste-Claire (Tu, F, and Su mornings) and bd. Taine (Sa mornings). **Quoi de n'Oeuf**, 19 fbg. Ste-Claire, has a 50F all-you-can-eat tartiflette, salad, and dessert offer (open noon-2pm and 7-10pm). **Taverne le Freti**, 12 rue Ste-Claire, is *the* place for fondue (56-98F; open Tu-Su 7-11:30pm).

CENTRAL FRANCE

■ Lyon

France's second-largest city is second in little else. With industrial and culinary *savoir faire*, Lyon (pop. 1.5 million) has established itself as a cultural and economic alternative to the capital. Despite its historical reputation as aloof and bourgeois, Lyon is friendlier and more relaxed than Paris, with a few centuries more history. And unlike so many other European cities, Lyon's focus is the present: its best art collections are contemporary, and the whole metropolis overflows with a dynamic creativity.

quai St-Vincent

Pont St-Vincent

rue de Constantine

rue Lanterne

rue Longue

rue Neuve

rue Gentil

r. Claudia

r. A. Sallès
r. de la
Bourse d'Argent

CORDELIERS Ⓜ

PL. DES CORDELIERS

quai de Bondy

Pont de la Feuillée

quai de la Pêcherie

rue de Brest

rue du Président Edouard Herriot

r. du Président Carnot

rue Grolée

rue St-Paul

Gare St-Paul

Saône

quai St-Antoine

Grenette

r. Tupin

r. Palais Grillet

rue de la

r. Fr. Vernay

M. des Carmes

rue Juiverie

M. St-Barthélémy

PL. DU CHANGE

quai Romain Rolland

rue Mercière

rue Ferrandière

rue Thomassin

M. Nicolas Lange

Musée de la Marionette

Pont Alphonse Juin

r. de la Monnaie

r. J. de Tournes

r. Childebert

PL. DES JACOBINS

American Express

République

rue du Bœuf

rue St-Jean

Palais de Justice

P. du Palais de Justice

quai des Célestins

r. de Savoie

r. Ch. Dullin

r. des Archers

Emile Zola

Gasparin

Théâtre des Célestins

Tour Métallique

M. des Chazeaux

rue de la Bombarde

Cathédrale St-Jean

r. G. André

r. d'Amboise

BELLECOUR Ⓜ

Chemin du Rosaire

Ⓘ Ⓜ FOURVIÈRE

Basilique Notre-Dame de Fourvière Ⓘ

PL. ST-JEAN Ⓘ

rue de la Barre

PLACE BELLECOUR Ⓘ

Montée du Chemin Neuf

Ⓜ ave A. Max
VIEUX LYON

Pont Bonaparte

quai du Plat

rue R. Radisson

rue Cléberg

Musée de la Civilization Gallo-Romaine

Ⓜ MINIMES

Tramassac

quai Tilsitt

rue A. Fochier

rue Roissac

r. Fr. Dauphin

rue Victor Hugo

r. A. Comte

Théâtres Romains

rue de l'Antiquaille

rue des Farges

P. St. Georges

quai Fulchiron

rue Sala

PL. ANTOINE VOLLAN

rue Ste-Hélène

rue d'Auvergne

ST-JUST Ⓜ

Saône

quai Tilsitt

rue Guynemer

rue Vaubecour

rue Jarente

rue des Remparts

AMPÈRE VICTOR HUGO Ⓜ

d'Ainay

PL. AMPÈRE

r. Henri IV

r. de Castries

r. d'Enghien

PLACE CARNOT

Chemin de Choulans

Chemin de Choulans

quai du M. Joffre

rue G. Plessier

PERRACHE Ⓜ

Montée des Genovefains

P. Kitchener

Marchand

autoroute A7

Gare de Perrache Ⓘ

cours de Verdun

N

rue Dugas Montbel

Lyon

ORIENTATION AND PRACTICAL INFORMATION

The Saône and the Rhône rivers cradle the city in a huge "Y." East of the Rhône resides the **Part-Dieu** train station, its commercial complex, and most of the city's population. Between the two rivers, the *centre ville* is home to the **Perrache** train station, **pl. Bellecour,** the main tourist office, and the old Terraux neighborhood. To the river's west, the **Fourvière hill** and its basilica overlook the city as **Vieux Lyon** (Old Lyon) unfolds below to the banks of the Saône. Lyon is divided into nine *arrondissements;* the first, second, and fourth lie between the rivers, the third includes Part-Dieu, the fifth encompasses *Vieux Lyon* and Fourvière, and the sixth is to the north.

Flights: Aéroport Lyon-Satolas (tel. 04 72 22 72 21), 25km east of Lyon. **Satobuses** leave from Perrache via Part-Dieu until 9pm (every 20min., 46F).

Trains: TGV trains to Paris pass through both the Part-Dieu and Perrache stations. Check schedule posters about other destinations. **Perrache,** between the Saône and Rhône rivers, is more central. SNCF info and reservation desk open M-Sa 8am-7:30pm. **Part-Dieu** is in the business district on the east bank of the Rhône. SNCF info desk open M-F 9am-7pm, Sa 9am-6:30pm. To Dijon (2hr., 131F), Geneva (2hr., 159F), Grenoble (1¼hr., 95F), Marseille (3hr., 203F), Nice (6hr., 295F), Paris (all TGV, 2hr., 250-300F), and Strasbourg (6hr., 287F).

Buses: in the Perrache train station. Open July-Aug. M-Sa 7:30am-6:30pm; Sept.-June M-Sa 6:30am-5pm. To Annecy and Grenoble. **Philbert** (tel. 04 78 98 56 00) handles many domestic routes. **Eurolines** (tel. 04 72 41 09 09) and **Iberbus** (tel. 04 72 41 09 09) travel throughout Europe.

Public Transportation: TCL (tel. 04 78 71 80 80) has info offices at both train stations and major Metro stops. The **Metro (M)** operates 5am-midnight. Tickets, good for 1hr. in 1 direction, bus and trolley connections included, are 8F each (*carnet* of 10 tickets 68F, students 55F). *Ticket Liberté* (20F) offers 1 day of unlimited travel—buy at tourist and TCL offices, not in stations. **Trolleys** *(funiculaires)* operate until 10pm and run from pl. St-Jean to St-Just and the top of Fourvière. **Buses** run 5am-9pm (a few until midnight), later on theater performance nights.

Taxis: Taxi Radio de Lyon (tel. 04 72 10 86 86). 24hr. service. 200F to the airport.

Hitchhiking: Travelers find that *autoroute* ramps to Paris are hard places to find a ride but offer longer hauls. Taking buses #2, 5, 19, 21, 22, or 31 and standing past Port Mouton at the intersection with N6 may be easier but with shorter rides. To Grenoble take bus #39 to Moselle Trinité and the entrance to A43.

Tourist Office: pl. Bellecour, 2*ème* (tel. 04 72 77 69 69; fax 04 78 42 04 32). M: Bellecour. Smorgasbord of info. Ask about the "key to the city" (90F) which allows admission to 7 museums. Open mid-June to mid-Sept. M-F 9am-7pm, Sa 9am-6pm; mid-Sept. to mid-June M-F 9am-6pm, Sa 9am-5pm, Su 10am-6pm. If you're arriving at the **Perrache station,** pick up a map at the annex in the Centre d'Echanges. Open M-F 9am-1pm and 2-6pm, Sa 9am-5pm.

Budget Travel: Wasteels (tel. 04 78 37 80 17), in the Perrache's Galerie Marchande. BIJ tickets. Long lines. Open M-F 9am-6:30pm, Sa 9am-5pm.

Currency Exchange: AOC, in the tourist offices on pl. Bellecour and Perrache. **Thomas Cook** (tel. 04 72 33 48 55), in the Part-Dieu train station. Open 24hr.

American Express: 6 rue Childebert, 2*ème* (tel. 04 72 77 74 50). Open May-Sept. M-F 9am-noon and 2-6:15pm, Sa 9am-noon; Oct.-Apr. closed Sa. Currency exchange closes at 5:30pm.

English Bookstore: Eton, 1 rue du Plat, 2*ème* (tel. 04 78 92 92 36), 1 street west of pl. Bellecour. Open M 2-7pm, Tu-Sa 10am-12:30pm and 1:30-7pm.

Laundromat: Lavadou, 19 rue Ste-Hélène. Open 7:30am-8:30pm.

Emergencies: tel. 17. **Medical emergency:** tel. 15.

Police: 47 rue de la Charité (tel. 04 78 42 26 56).

Crisis Lines: CISL (tel. 04 78 01 23 45), an international center for visitors to Lyon. **SOS Racisme** (tel. 04 78 39 24 44). Open M-F 6:30-8:30pm. **AIDS Lyon Rhône-Alps,** 21 pl. Tolozan, 3*ème* (tel. 04 78 28 61 32).

Medical Assistance: Hôpital Edouard Herriot, 5 pl. Arsonval (tel. 04 72 11 73 00). M: Grange Blanche. Well-equipped for serious emergencies, but far from the city center. For non-emergencies, go to **Hôpital Hôtel-Dieu,** 1 pl. de l'Hôpital, 2*ème* (tel. 04 72 41 30 00), near quai du Rhône.

Post Office: pl. Antonin Poncet (tel. 04 72 40 65 22), next to pl. Bellecour. Open M-F 8am-7pm, Sa 8am-noon. **Postal Codes:** 69000-69009; main post office and *centre ville* is 69002. The last digit indicates *arrondissement*.

Internet Access: Connectix Café, 19 quai St-Antoine, *2ème* (tel. 04 72 77 98 85). 75F per hr.; includes popular bar. Open 10am-8pm, until 1am weekends.

ACCOMMODATIONS AND CAMPING

As a financial center, Lyon has few empty beds during the work week but openings on the weekends. "Low season" is actually considered to be July and August. If the hotels near Perrache are full, rooms should be available near pl. des Terreaux.

Auberge de Jeunesse (HI), 41-45 Montée du Chemin Neuf (04 78 15 05 50; fax 04 78 15 05 51; http://www.iyhf.orh). From place Bellecour, walk west toward the old city and cross the Saône at Pont Bonaparte. Turn right though Place St. Jean and then left onto Rue de la Bombarde. Follow the hairpin turn left onto Montée du Chemin Neuf and prepare for a good climb. The hostel is 8min. up on the right (15min. from Bellecour, 25min. from Perrache). Features a beautiful courtyard and a fun-loving staff who lead nightlife tours of Lyon. Bar, **Internet access,** kitchen. 69F. Breakfast included. Sheets 17F. Reception 24hr. Reservations recommended.

Résidence Benjamin Delessert, 145 av. Jean Jaurès, *7ème* (tel. 04 78 61 41 41; fax 04 78 61 40 24). Metro: Macé. From Perrache, take any bus going to "J. Macé," walk under the train tracks, and look left after 2½ blocks. Bright, clean dorms, all with phones. TV room and laundry. Singles 90F-95F. Reception 24hr. Reserve ahead.

Hôtel d'Ainay, 14 rue des Remparts d'Ainay, *2ème* (tel. 04 78 42 43 42). M: Ampère-Victor Hugo. Near the station, on top of Place Ampère. Cheap, sunny, comfortable rooms with very firm beds. Happy anglophone staff. Singles from 137-208F; doubles 175-218F. Breakfast 25F. Shower 15F. Reception 7am-11pm.

Le Celtic, 10 rue Francois Vernay, *5ème* (tel. 04 78 28 01 12; fax 04 78 28 01 34). M: Terreaux. The affordable option in Vieux Lyon, and a good one. Singles 135-165F; doubles 160-200F; triples 300F. Breakfast 35F. Shower 30F. Reception 24hr.

Camping: Dardilly (tel. 04 78 35 64 55). From the Hôtel de Ville, take bus 19 ("Ecully-Dardilly") to "Parc d'Affaires." Hot showers, swimming pool, grocery store, bar, and restaurant. 55F per tent and car. Reception mid-June to mid-Sept. 8am-noon and 4-9pm; mid-Sept. to mid-June 8am-11pm. Open year-round.

FOOD

The galaxy of *Michelin* stars adorning Lyon's restaurants confirm the city's reputation as the culinary capital of Western civilization. There are plenty of options for budget travelers. Cozy *bouchons*, descendants of inns, serve *andouillettes* (sausages made of cow intestines) and other local treats in the Terreaux district and along rue Mercière in the second *arrondissement*. Finish off your dinner with *torte tatin*, an upside-down apple pie *à la mode*, or *cocons*, chocolates wrapped in marzipan. Chocolate lovers swoon at **Bernachon,** 42 cours Franklin Roosevelt, *6ème*. Ethnic restaurants cluster around the streets off **rue de la République** (*2ème*).

The market at **Les Halles,** 102 cours Lafayette, *3ème*, counts Paul Bocuse—the culinary messiah—as well as mere mortals among its patrons (open Tu-Sa 7:30am-noon and 3-7pm, Su 7:30am-noon). **Open markets** are held at quai St-Antoine and on bd. de la Croix Rousse (open Tu-Su 7:30am-12:30pm). The **Prisunic supermarket** is on rue de la République, at pl. des Cordeliers, 2ème (open M-Sa 8:30am-7:30pm).

Le Sud, 11 pl. Antonin Porcet, *2ème* (tel. 04 72 77 80 00), off pl. Bellecour. Highly praised. Provençal and Italian cuisine with Mediterranean ambiance. 90F *plat du jour* and 115F *menu*. Open noon-2pm and 7-midnight. Reserve 2 days in advance.

Chez Mounier, 3 rue des Marrioniers, *2ème*. Generous portions of traditional specialties on a four-course *menu* starting at 59F. Open noon-2pm and 7-10:30pm; closed Sunday night and all day Monday.

Comptoir du Boeuf, 3 pl. Neuve St. Jean, 5ème (tel. 04 78 92 82 35). Specialties include lentil and herring patés, lamb sautéed in ginger chutney, and *andouillette* (of course...). *Menus* 89F-119F. Open daily noon-2pm and 7pm-midnight.

L'Acteur, 5 Charles Dullin, 2ème (tel. 04 78 92 88 53). The gourmet *menu* has included rabbit paté, smoked salmon salad, and other delicacies. Lunchtime menu 65F, dinner starts at 82F. Open M-Sa noon-2pm, 7-11pm.

Chez Carlo, 22 rue du Palais Grillet, 2ème. Locals call it the best pasta and pizza (46F) in Lyon. Open Tu-Sa noon-2pm and 7-11pm, Su noon-2pm.

SIGHTS AND ENTERTAINMENT

Nestled up against the Saône at the bottom of the Fourvière hill, the cobblestone streets of *Vieux Lyon* are lined with lively cafes and magnificent medieval and Renaissance townhouses. The 12th-century **Cathédrale St-Jean,** at the south end of *Vieux Lyon,* towers over pl. St-Jean. Henri IV met and married Marie de Médici here in 1600 (open M-F 8am-noon and 2-7:30pm, Sa-Su 2-5pm; free).

From the corner of rue du Boeuf and rue de la Bombarde, ascend the stairs leading to the **Fourvière Hill,** the nucleus of Roman Lyon. It's quite a walk up from **Vieux Lyon;** most prefer to take the *funiculaire* (dir: "Fourvière") from the head of av. Max, off pl. St-Jean, in the old town. When you've reached the top of the hill, admire the view on the **Esplanade Fourvière,** where a model of the cityscape points out local landmarks. Behind the Esplanade is the **Basilique Notre-Dame de la Fourvière.** Multicolored mosaics, gilded pillars, and elaborate carvings adorn every square inch of the interior. If you walk down the hill making a left as you exit the church, you'll see signs for the **Musée Gallo-Romain,** 17 rue Cléberg, 5ème, which displays mosaics, helmets, swords, jewelry, and tablet inscribed with a speech by Emperor Claudius (open W-Su 9:30am-noon and 2-6pm; 20F, students 10F). Just next door is the **Théâtre Romain,** a 2000-year-old amphitheater that is still in use.

Monumental squares, statues, and fountains are the trademarks of the **presqu'île,** the lively area between the Rhône and the Saône. The heart of the area is **place Bellecour,** a barren expanse of red gravel fringed by shops and flower stalls and dominated by an equestrian statue of Louis XIV. Across the square, the spectacular Renaissance **Hôtel de Ville** stands guard opposite the **Musée des Beaux-Arts,** which includes a small but distinguished collection of French painting, works by Spanish and Dutch masters, an Italian Renaissance wing, and a sculpture garden (open W-Su 10:30am-6pm; 25F, students 12F). A few blocks north of the museum on rue Burdeau, 1er, lie the ruins of the Roman **Amphithéâtre des Trois Gaulles,** where an unfortunate band of Christians met their demise in 177.

Historically, Lyon dominated the European silk industry, and by the 18th century, 28,000 looms operated in the city. Although the silk industry is now based elsewhere, an extraordinary collection of silk and embroidery remains at the **Musée Historique des Tissus,** 34 rue de la Charité (open Tu-Su 10am-5:30pm; 26F, students 13F, W free). **La Maison des Canuts,** 10-12 rue d'Ivry, 4ème, demonstrates the actual weaving techniques of the *canuts lyonnais* (open M-F 8:30am-noon and 2-6:30pm, Sa 9am-noon and 2-6pm; 15F).

The **Centre d'Histoire de la Résistance et de la Déportation,** 14 av. Bertholet, 7ème, has assembled documents and photos of the Lyon-based resistance to the Nazis (open W-Su 9am-5:30pm; 25F, students 15F). The **Musée d'Art Contemporain,** in the futuristic *Cité Internationale de Lyon* on quai Charles de Gaulle, 6ème (M: Masséna), has an extensive collection of modern art. The *Cité* is a sight itself—the super-modern complex houses offices, shops, theaters, and—don't jaywalk—Interpol's world headquarters. Nearby is the massive **Parc de la Tête d'Or,** a 259-acre park with a zoo, botanical garden, and beautiful rose garden (park open daily Apr.-Sept. 6am-11pm; Oct.-Mar. 6am-9pm).

Lyon's major theater is the **Théâtre des Célestins,** 4 rue Charles Pullin, 2ème (tel. 04 78 42 17 67; 70-200F). The **Opéra,** pl. de la Comédie, 1er (tel. 04 72 00 45 45), has 70F standing-room-only tickets the evening of the show. In the summer, Lyon bursts with festivals and special events nearly every week. Highlights include the **Fête de la**

Musique in early June, when performers take over the city streets, and the **Bastille Day** celebration on July 14. The **Festival de Musique du Vieux Lyon,** slated for 1999, brings artists from around the world to perform in the churches of Lyon's old town (Tel. 04 78 42 39 04. Fax 04 78 42 39 28. Mid-Nov. to mid-Dec. Tickets 90-230F. For info, contact the Festival at 5 pl. du Petit Collège, 5ème.) Lyon, considered by some to be the birthplace of cinema, shows silver screen classics. The **Cinéma Opéra,** 6 rue J. Serlin (tel. 04 78 28 80 08), and **Le Cinéma,** 18 impasse St-Polycarpe (tel. 04 78 39 09 72), show black-and-white oldies, all in *v.o.* (original language; 30-40F).

Nightlife in Lyon is fast and furious. Local students spend their nights at Lyon's bars—pound 10F tequilas like everyone else at **L'Abrevoir,** 18 rue Ste-Catherine (open Su-Th until 1am, F-Sa until 2am). The terrace at **Le Voxx,** 1 rue d'Algerie, is the latest in a series of rotating hotspots just off of pl. des Terreaux. The city's best and most accessible late-night meatmarkets are a strip of riverboat dance clubs on the east side of the Rhône. **Le Fish,** across from 21 quai Augagneur, has theme nights with salsa, jungle, house, garage, and disco. (Open Th 7pm-4:30am, F-Sa 10pm-6am. Free until 10pm, after which point 60-80F includes a drink.) **La Ruche,** 22 rue Gentil, 2ème (tel. 04 78 39 03 82), does a gay bar British pub-style.

BURGUNDY (BOURGOGNE)

Burgundy is best known for its annual 40 million bottles of wine, which graciously represent a landscape green and gold, traversed by lazy streams and dense forests, splashed with vineyards and peppered with monasteries, cathedrals, and châteaux.

▓ Dijon

Dijon's prospects looked bleak in 1513, as a Swiss siege gripped the city. Negotiations faltered until the *Dijonnais* sent wine casks across enemy lines—the foes, with inebriated generosity, retreated. Today, Dijon is famous for its wine-based mustards, and the city, with myriad museums and a lively international student population, is almost as spicy as its Grey Poupon. Should you visit Dijon? But of course.

SIGHTS AND ENTERTAINMENT A 30F card admits you to all of Dijon's museums, including the **Musée des Beaux-Arts,** occupying a wing of the colossal **Palais des Ducs de Bourgogne.** The palace's **Salle des Gardes** gallery is dominated by the huge sarcophagi of Philippe le Hardi and Jean sans Peur (open W-M 10am-6pm; 22F, students and Su free). With a façade of gargoyles, the **Eglise Notre-Dame** exemplifies the Burgundian Gothic style, while the **Eglise St-Michel** on pl. St-Michel is a melange of Gothic and Renaissance artistry. On pl. St-Bénigne, the elegant **Cathédrale St-Bénigne** memorializes the 2nd-century missionary priest whose martyred remains were exhumed near Dijon. Nearby, the **Musée Archéologique,** 5 rue Docteur Maret, unearths Gallo-Roman sculpture, jewelry, and weapons. (Open June-Sept. W-M 10am-6pm; Oct.-May W-M 9am-noon and 2-6pm. 14F, students and Su free.) A trip to the **Grey Poupon store,** 32 rue de la Liberté, where *moutarde au vin* has been made since 1777, should not be considered a mere condiment to your Dijon excursion.

In June, Dijon's **Eté Musical** (tel. 03 80 30 61 00) hosts many of the world's best symphony orchestras and chamber groups. From mid-June to mid-August, **Estivade** (tel. 03 80 30 31 00) brings dance, music, and theater to the streets. Operas and classical music are performed mid-October through late April at the 18th-century **Théâtre de Dijon,** pl. du Théâtre (tel. 03 80 67 20 21; 110-240F, student rush 50F). Evenings, try **Atmosphère,** 7 rue Audra, a combination bar, pool hall, nightclub, and disco (open daily 2pm-3am; no cover), or **L'Univers,** 47 rue Berbisey, where crowds often spill out onto the sidewalk (open M-Sa 11am-2am, Su 5pm-2am). The *cavo* downstairs rocks to a different (gay) beat 9pm-2am.

PRACTICAL INFO, ACCOMMODATIONS, AND FOOD Trains chug steadily to the station at cours de la Gare, at the end of av. Maréchal Foch, from Lyon (1½hr., 10 per day, 131F), Paris by TGV (2hr., 12 per day, 217-257F), and Strasbourg (4hr., 4 per day, 199F). The **tourist office,** pl. Darcy (tel. 03 80 49 11 44), a 5-minute walk from the train station along av. Maréchal Foch, finds accommodations (10F and 10% deposit), exchanges currency, and gives out info on sights and events (open daily 9am-9pm).

Reservations for accommodations are advised in summer. Students can call CROUS (tel. 03 80 40 40 40) for info on university housing. The enormous **Auberge de Jeunesse (HI),** 1 av. Champollion (tel. 03 80 72 95 20; fax 03 80 70 00 61), offers a laundry facility, bar, and disco. Take bus 5 ("Epirey") from pl. Grangier to the end of the line (dorms 68F, nonmembers add 6F; singles 138F; doubles 288F; 24hr. reception). Find spotless, air-conditioned rooms at **Hôtel Montchapet,** 26-28 rue Jacques Cellerier (tel. 03 80 53 95 00; fax 03 80 58 26 87), north of av. Première Armée Française (singles 140-205F; doubles 215-265F; quads 360F; reception 6am-midnight). **Hôtel Monge,** 20 rue Monge (tel. 03 80 30 30 15; fax 03 80 30 63 87), has cozy rooms and friendly owners (singles 125F; doubles 180F). Take bus 12 ("Fontaine d'Ouche") to "Hôpital des Chartreux" for the lakeside **Camping Municipal du Lac,** 3 bd. Kir (tel. 03 80 43 54 72; 16F per person, 12F per tent; open Apr.-Oct. 15).

The pedestrian area from pl F. Rude north to rue Bannelier explodes into a colorful **market** on Tuesday and Friday mornings (6am-1pm), and all day Saturday. University cafeterias stay open all summer; **R.U. Maret,** 3 rue Docteur Maret, has an all-you-can-eat dinner for 14F with student ID. (Open M-F 11:30am-1:30pm and 6:30-8pm, Sa-Su 11:40am-1:15pm and 6:40-7:45pm.) **Le Rapido,** 102 rue Berbisey, has generous entrees and salads (around 30F), as well as *plats* (49-59F). Vegetarians and vegans will enjoy **L'Entresol,** 27-29 rue Musette, off pl. Grangier (salad and dessert bar 55F; open M-Sa 11:45am-2:30am).

■ Near Dijon: Beaune and the Côte d'Or

The well-touristed town of **Beaune,** a half-hour south of Dijon on the Lyon rail line (36F), has disgorged wine for centuries. Surrounded by the famous **Côte de Beaune** vineyards, the town itself is packed with wineries offering free *dégustations* (tastings). Try the **Marché aux Vins,** near the Hôtel-Dieu, where you can descend into a candle-lit cave and follow a trail of 20 wine kegs, each with a different vintage for your sampling delight (50F; open M-Th 9:30am-noon and 2-6:30pm, F-Su 9:30am-7pm). The town's biggest non-potable attraction is the **Hôtel-Dieu,** a regional architectural icon built in the 15th century as a hospital for the poor. (Open daily Mar. 22-Nov. 16 9am-6:30pm; Nov. 17-Mar. 21 9-11:30am and 2-5:30pm. 32F, students 25F.) The **tourist office** (tel. 03 80 26 21 30), rue de l'Hôtel-Dieu, lists *caves* in the region offering tours (open M-Sa 9am-8pm, Su 9am-6pm; June 15-Sept. 15 Su until 7pm).

The 60km **Côte d'Or,** with its rolling vineyards, has produced some of the world's best wines. Tour the 10th-century **Château de Gevrey-Chambertin** (tel. 03 80 34 36 13), 10km south of Dijon, before visiting its *cave,* favored by both Napoleon I and Louis XIV. (Open Apr.-Oct. daily 10am-noon and 2-6pm; Nov.-Mar. M-Sa 10am-noon and 2-5pm, Su 11am-noon and 2-5pm. 30min. Tour 20F.)

ALSACE-LORRAINE

■ Strasbourg

A few kilometers from the Franco-German border, Strasbourg has spent much of its history being annexed by one side or the other. Today the city is seen as a symbol of French-German détente; German is heard on the streets almost as often as French, and as many *Weinstuben* line the squares as *pâtisseries*. Several European Union offices, including the European Parliament, add to its cosmopolitan credentials.

FRANCE

SIGHTS AND ENTERTAINMENT Built between the 11th and 15th centuries, the ornate, deep-red, Gothic **Cathédrale de Strasbourg** thrusts its heaven-tickling tower 142m into the sky (open M-Sa 7-11:45am and 12:45-7pm, Su 12:45-6pm). Inside, the **Horloge Astronomique** demonstrates the wizardry of 16th-century Swiss clockmakers; each day at 12:30pm, the apostles troop out of the face while a cock crows to greet St. Peter (tickets on sale at 11:50am at the cathedral entrance; 5F). While you wait, check out the **Pilier des Anges** (Angels' Pillar), a masterpiece of Gothic sculpture. Across the way, the **Maison de l'Oeuvre Notre-Dame** houses some of the cathedral's statues and reconstructed stained glass (closed M). Also across from the cathedral, the **Musée d'Art Moderne,** scheduled to reopen in the fall of 1998, has an excellent collection. The **Château des Rohan,** 2 pl. du Château, houses the small but noteworthy **Musée des Beaux-Arts, Musée des Arts Décoratifs,** and **Musée Archéologique** (all 3 museums 40F, students 20F). Le Nôtre designed the inviting grounds of **l'Orangerie,** Strasbourg's largest park, after cutting his teeth on Versailles.

PRACTICAL INFO, ACCOMMODATIONS, AND FOOD Strasbourg is a major European rail junction. **Trains** (tel. 03 88 22 50 50) run to Frankfurt (3hr., 307F), Luxembourg (2½hr., 154F), Milan (7hr., 491F), Paris (4hr., 210F), and Zurich (3hr., 226F). **Tourist offices** next to the cathedral (tel. 03 88 52 28 28) and across from the station (tel. 03 88 32 51 49) dispense maps (3F) and have accommodation listings as well as the free *Shows and Events* and *Strasbourg Actualités* (open June-Sept. M-Sa 9am-7pm, Su 9am-6pm; Oct.-May daily 9am-6pm). Crédit Commerciale de France on pl. Gutenberg at rue des Serruriers has a 24-hour automatic **currency exchange.**

Everyone stays the night in Strasbourg, so make reservations or arrive early. **CIARUS (Centre International d'Accueil de Strasbourg),** 7 rue Finkmatt (tel. 03 88 15 27 88; fax 03 88 15 27 89), boasts sparkling rooms, a central location, and **Internet access.** From the train station, take rue du Maire-Kuss to the canal, turn left, follow quais St-Jean, Kléber, and Finkmatt, and take a left onto rue Finkmatt. (Dorms 86-98F; singles 185F; doubles 236F. Breakfast included. Reception 6:30am-10pm. Check-in 3:30pm. Check-out 9am.) At the **Auberge de Jeunesse René Cassin (HI),** 9 rue de l'Auberge de Jeunesse (tel. 03 88 30 26 46; fax 03 88 30 35 16), 2km from the station, you can find clean, slightly worn rooms. Take bus 3 ("Holtzheim-Entzheim Ouest") or 23 ("Illkirch") from rue du Marché-aux-Vins. (Dorms 69F, sheets 17F; doubles 198F, sheets included. Camping 42F. Breakfast included. Reception 7am-12:30pm, 1:30-7:30, and 8:30-11pm. Curfew 1am. Closed Jan.) **Hôtel Michelet,** 48 rue du Vieux Marché aux Poissons (tel. 03 88 32 47 38), has dim, tidy rooms and a great location (singles 140-205F; doubles 165-250F; reception 7am-8pm).

Strasbourgeois restaurants are known for *choucroute garnie,* spiced sauerkraut with meat. *Weinstuben* are informal places traditionally affiliated with wineries. **Poêles de Carottes,** 18 rue de la Krute, has tempting vegetarian food (lunch *menu* 59F; dinner *menu* 98F; open M-Sa noon-2:30pm and 7-10:30pm). **Trudie,** 9 rue des Dentelles-Cour Rathsamhausen, is adorable but not cutesy; the food is *stub*-pendous (*menu* 89F; open Tu-Sa noon-2pm and 6:30-10pm, Su noon-2pm).

■ Nancy

Bustling Nancy reigns as the cultural heart of Lorraine, with a resident symphony, ballet and opera companies, and lots of museums. The city's 30,000 students fuel a passion for jazz, manifest both in the live bands at bars and restaurants and in Nancy's many festivals. The 18th-century **pl. Stanislas** wraps Baroque gilded-iron arms around a statue of the "Good Duke" Stanislas Lesczynski, a dethroned Polish king relocated to Lorraine by his son-in-law Louis XV. Nancy's **Musée des Beaux-Arts,** 3 pl. Stanislas (tel. 03 83 85 30 72), spent 1998 doubling its gallery to show works by Matisse, Modigliani, and Dufy. **Trains** roll to Metz (40min., 50F), Paris (3hr., 203F), and Strasbourg (1hr., 108F). The **tourist office,** pl. Stanislas (tel. 03 83 35 22 41), runs tours and exchanges currency. Request a copy of *Le Fil d'Ariane,* a 160-page yearly guide written and researched by a squad of university students (open M-Sa 9am-7pm, Su

10am-5pm; Oct.-May closed Su afternoon). **Centre d'Accueil de Remicourt (HI),** 149 rue de Vandoeuvre (tel. 03 83 27 73 67; fax 03 83 41 41 35), is in Villers-lès-Nancy, 4km southwest of town in the Château de Remicourt. Call for directions (75F; reception M-Sa 9am-10pm; members only). **Hôtel de l'Académie,** 7 rue des Michottes (tel. 03 83 35 52 31; fax 03 83 32 55 78), is centrally located (doubles 150-170F). Restaurants cluster around **rue des Maréchaux.** The tunnels of **Le Blue Note III,** 3 rue des Michottes, echo with live jazz and rock (open M-Th 6pm-4am, F until 5am, Sa-Su from 8pm; 30F cover).

■ Metz

Originally a Roman settlement, attractive Metz maintains classic fountains, sculptured gardens, verdant canals, and golden cobblestone streets. In pl. d'Armes, marvel at the stained-glass windows of the **Cathédrale St-Etienne,** built between the 13th and 16th centuries. The 6500 square meters of glass, including windows by Chagall, have earned the cathedral the moniker "Lantern to God" (open daily 7:30am-noon and 2-6:30pm; 12F). Metz's patchwork of gardens and promenades offers a refreshingly green alternative to the yellow urban core—pick up the tourist office's trail map. Down the steps from the Esplanade, shady paths wind their way through the wooded park along the **Lac aux Cygnes.**

Trains run to Lyon (5hr., 255F), Nancy (40min., 51F), Paris (3hr., 204F), and Strasbourg (1½hr., 112F). The **tourist office,** pl. d'Armes (tel. 03 87 55 53 76), has maps and books rooms. (Open July-Aug. M-Sa 9am-9pm, Su 10am-1pm and 2-5pm; Sept.-June M-Sa 9am-7pm.) Take bus 3 ("Metz-Nord") or 11 ("St-Eloy") to "Pontiffroy," where the excellent **auberge de jeunesse (HI),** 1 allée de Metz Plage (tel. 03 87 30 44 02; fax 03 87 33 19 80), offers free bike and boat loan, ping-pong, fishing, and more (members only; dorms 49F; reception 7am-10pm; Sept.-June 7-10am and 5-10pm). The **Association Carrefour/Auberge de Jeunesse (HI),** 6 rue Marchant (tel. 03 87 75 07 26; fax 03 87 36 71 44), also offers superb facilities; from the station take the minibus to "Ste-Ségolène" and take a left up the hill (members only; dorms 69F; singles and doubles 81F per person). **Crêperie St-Malo,** 14 rue des Clercs, serves hundreds of *crêpes* and *galettes* (open M-Sa 11:45am-11pm).

CHAMPAGNE

Champagne, the region between Lorraine and Paris, is under French law the only source of real champagne, which must be aged according to the rigorous *méthode champenoise.* The best way to see and taste the results is to visit the underground *caves* of Reims and Epernay, both a little over an hour from Paris's Gare de l'Est.

■ Reims

Though most travelers put Reims on their maps for its fabulous *caves,* the city's other sights—most notably the Cathédrale de Notre-Dame and the Basilique St-Remi—should not be overlooked. The **cathedral,** ornamented with dreamlike Chagall windows, was built with blocks of golden limestone quarried in the Champagne *caves* beginning in 1211 (open daily 7:30am-7:30pm). The **Palais du Tau** next door contains wonderful treasures, including Charlemagne's 9th-century talisman and the extravagant gold and velvet coronation vestments of Charles X. (Open July-Aug. daily 9:30am-6:30pm; reduced hours off-season; 32F, students 21F). South of the cathedral area stands the **Basilique St-Remi,** a Gothic renovation of a Carolinginan Romanesque church believed to contain the tombs of many of France's earliest kings (open M-W, F, and Su 8am-7pm or dusk, Th and Sa opens at 9am). Four hundred kilometers of *crayères* (Roman chalk quarries) wind underground through the countryside around Reims. Today, they shelter bottles emblazoned with the great names of Champagne—Pommery, Piper-Heidsieck, Mumm, and Taittinger. The tourist office has a map with a list of the **caves** open to the public. Many houses give tours by appointment only, so call ahead. The most engaging *caves* and greatest wines belong to **Pommery,** pl. du Général Gouraud (tel. 03 26 61 62 55), set in a magnificent group of 19th-century English-style buildings. (Tours by appointment Apr.-Oct. daily 10am-5:30pm; Nov.-Mar. M-F 10am-4:30pm. 40F, students 20F.) For an affordable taste of the bubbly, order a *coupe de champagne* at any bar in town (25-30F) or look for sales at wineshops (from 70F per bottle of the good stuff).

The **train station,** bd. Joffre (tel. 08 36 35 35 35), serves Paris (1½hr., 118F). The **tourist office,** 2 rue Guillaume de Machault (tel. 03 26 77 45 25), is near the cathedral. For local events pick up *Les Rendez-vous Remois.* (Open July-Aug. M-Sa 9am-8pm, Su 9:30am-7pm; Easter-June and Sept. M-Sa 9am-7:30pm, Su 9:30am-6:30pm; Oct.-Easter M-Sa 9am-6:30pm, Su 9:30am-5:30pm.) The **auberge de jeunesse (HI),** chaussée Bocquaine (tel. 03 26 40 52 60; fax 03 26 47 35 70), is a 15-minute walk from the station. Cross the park in front of the train station, then turn right onto bd. Général Leclerc. Follow it to the canal and cross the first bridge (pont de Vesle); chaussée Bocquaine is your first left. The hostel has attractive rooms and great facilities (singles 85F; doubles and triples 65F per person; reception 24hr.). **Au Bon Accueil,** 31 rue Thillois (tel. 03 26 88 55 74, fax 03 26 05 12 38), off of pl. d'Erlon, has clean rooms with comfy beds (singles 80-110F; doubles 120-170F; reception 24hr.). The place to be for food is the **Place Drouet d'Erlon**—try **Boeuf ou Salade?,** which serves huge salads for 45F (open daily 11am-midnight). **Monoprix supermarket** is housed in a graceful 19th-century building on the corner of rue de Vesle and rue de Talleyrand (open M-Sa 8:30am-9pm). Beer drinkers crowd the popular **Jour et Nuit,** 81 pl. d'Erlon.

■ Near Reims: Epernay

Unlike the more metropolitan Reims, Epernay strips away all the distractions of the city and devotes itself heart and soul to the production of the bubbly. One of the richest streets in the world, **avenue de Champagne,** is distinguished by its mansions, lush gardens, and monumental champagne firms. The best known, **Moët & Chandon,** 20 av. de Champagne (tel. 03 26 51 20 20), produces the king of wines, Dom Pérignon (open Apr.-Nov. 15 daily 9:30-11:45am and 2-4:45pm; tours 35F). **Mercier,** 70 av. de Champagne (tel. 03 26 51 22 22), just down the street, has a slick, silly "film," but a clinical, rather dull tour (25-30F). Epernay is also a good base from which to explore the countryside; the "Champagne route" is a set of **hikes** through nearby vineyards, châteaux, and mountains. Frequent **trains** connect Epernay to Reims (20min., 33F).

No Preservatifs Added

Having invented the French kiss and the French tickler, the speakers of the language of love have long had *savoir faire* in all things sexual—safety included. In the age of responsibility, French pharmacies (those flashing green crosses) provide 24-hour condom (*preservatif*) dispensers. They aren't hidden in dark, smoky bar bathrooms; instead, in typical French style, they unabashedly adorn the public streets. But don't ask for foods *sans preservatifs.*

Germany (Deutschland)

US$1 = DM1.73 (Deutschmarks)	DM1 = US$0.58
CDN$1 = DM1.14	DM1 = CDN$0.88
UK£1 = DM2.86	DM1 = UK£0.35
IR£1 = DM2.51	DM1 = IR£ 0.40
AUS$1 = DM1.02	DM1 = AUS$0.98
NZ$1 = DM0.89	DM1 = NZ$1.12
SAR1 = DM0.28	DM1 = SAR3.57
Country Code: 49	International Dialing Prefix: 00

Ten years after the fall of the Berlin Wall, Germany's story is still a parable for life in the modern era—the nation's history encapsulates all of the promises and betrayals of the 20th century and exposes the fissures beneath Western civilization's veneer. Despite its history of reactionary politics, Germany has always been a wellspring of revolutionaries and innovators: to name Charlemagne, Martin Luther, Beethoven, Marx, and Nietzsche is just to begin breaking the surface. And then there's Adolf Hitler, one of the most loathsome figures in Western history, who organized in this country the capacity to perform deeds—the brutal conquest of Europe, the Holocaust—that will always elude explanation. This last image, of course, colors all subsequent German history indelibly; Germans must grapple with the fact that the cradle of Bach and Goethe also spawned Dachau and Buchenwald. Although burdened by this troubling history, Germany is also blessed with an incomparable cultural tradition. Every major European movement of the past 500 years was, to some extent, influenced by the Germans—the wealth of artistic, historical, and cultural treasures that Germany has accumulated throughout centuries of war and division defines a healthy chunk of Western history.

For the most part, stereotypes of the German people are ridiculous; having finally emerged from World War II and the bipolarism of the Cold War, Germany is decidedly non-stereotypical. There are, to be sure, certain "German" characteristics—industriousness, efficiency, and a mystifying refusal to cross the street against the light. But with rapid globalization, the nation has become more and more multicultural and now defies easy categorization.

Meanwhile, Germany's global influence continues to grow. In the wake of Europe's most recent wave of revolution, Germany's pivotal position between East and West is even more important than it was during the Cold War. Germany brings a unique perspective and motivation to the project of an integrated Europe, as it faced many of the same issues within its own borders just ten years ago. Despite the troubles of reunification, Germany has maintained its role as the dominant economic power on the Continent. The nation will be especially festive this year, with parties celebrating Goethe's 250th birthday, Weimar's designation as Europe's Cultural Capital, the 10th anniversary of German reunification, and the 50th anniversary of the ally-created Federal Republic.

For more comprehensive and stimulating coverage of the country, treat yourself to *Let's Go: Germany 1999*.

GETTING THERE AND GETTING AROUND

The **Deutsche Bahn (DB)** integrated the Deutsche Bundesbahn and old eastern Reichsbahn. Integration is still taking place; many connections are as of yet incomplete. Traveling from a western city to a nearby eastern one often requires unusually tricky connections. The DB network is one of Europe's finest (and most expensive) systems, averaging over 120km per hour with stops. "S-Bahn" trains are commuter rail lines that run through the city center and may be integrated with the local subway or streetcar system. "RE" or "RB" trains run between neighboring cities. "Interregio" (IR) trains cover larger networks between cities quickly and comfortably, while

Germany

N

North Sea

Baltic Sea

DENMARK

Sylt
North Frisian Islands
Flensburg
Schleswig
Fehmarn
Saßnitz
Rügen
Stralsund
Greifswald
Kiel
SCHLESWIG-HOLSTEIN
Travemünde
Rostock
Cuxhaven
Lübeck
Wismar
MECKLENBURG-VORPOMMERN
East Frisian Islands
Bremerhaven
Schwerin
Neubrandenburg
Norden
Oldenburg
Bremen
Hamburg
Lüneburg
Plauersee
Müritzsee
NETHER-LANDS
Lüneburger Heide
Elbe
BRANDENBURG
POLAND
LOWER SAXONY
Celle
Osnabrück
Hannover
Wolfenbüttel
Berlin
Bernau
Frankfurt a.d. Oder
TEUTOBURG FOREST
Hameln
Braunschweig
Magdeburg
Brandenburg
Potsdam
SPREEWALD
Münster
Bielefeld
Detmold
Hildesheim
Goslar
Quedlinburg
SAXONY-ANHALT
Dessau
Wittenberg
Lübben
Cottbus
NORTH RHINE-WESTPHALIA
Göttingen
Harz Mountains
Essen
Dortmund
Halle
Leipzig
Bautzen
Düsseldorf
Wuppertal
Kassel
Naumburg
SAXONY
Meissen
Dresden
Cologne (Köln)
Solingen
Frankenberg
THURINGIA
Chemnitz
Aachen
Marburg
HESSE
Eisenach
Erfurt
Weimar
Jena
Gera
Erz Mountains
Bonn
Limburg
Fulda
THURINGIAN FOREST
Gotha
Zwickau
Plauen
BEL.
Koblenz
Eifel Massif
Wiesbaden
Frankfurt-am-Main
Bayreuth
CZECH REPUBLIC
Prague
LUX.
Mainz
Main
Darmstadt
Würzburg
Bamberg
Trier
Mosel
RHINELAND-PALATINATE
Worms
SAARLAND
Mannheim
Heidelberg
Fürth
Nuremberg (Nürnberg)
BAVARIAN FOREST
Saarbrücken
Speyer
Heilbronn
Rothenburg
Regensburg
Straubing
Passau
Karlsruhe
Pforzheim
Stuttgart
Dinkelsbühl
BAVARIA
Landshut
Strasbourg
Baden-Baden
Schwäbisch Gmünd
Danube
FRANCE
Rhine
Tübingen
Freudenstadt
Ulm
Augsburg
Inn
Danube
Breisach
BLACK FOREST
BADEN-WÜRTTEMBERG
Munich (München)
Berchtesgaden
Freiburg
Swabian Jura
Ammersee
Starnbergersee
Chiemsee
AUSTRIA
Konstanz
Lake Constance (Bodensee)
Wangen
Lindau
Garmisch-Partenkirchen
Füssen
Bavarian Alps
SWITZERLAND

0   50 miles
0   50 kilometers

"IC" (intercity) trains zoom along between major cities every hour. You must buy a supplementary "IC Zuschlag" to ride an IC or EC train (DM7 when bought in the station, DM9 on the train). The pricey, futuristic **InterCity Express (ICE)** zips as fast as 260km per hour. For these, railpass users don't usually pay a *Zuschlag* unless the seat requires a reservation. "D" trains are usually non-German trains on international trips.

Non-Germans can purchase the **German Railpass** in their home countries. The pass allows a selected number of days of rail travel within a one-month period on all DB trains. The second-class version costs US$188 for five days, US$304 for 10 days, and US$410 for 15 days in a month; the first-class version costs US$276, US$434, and US$562, respectively. Children 4 to 11 pay half of adult rates; those under 4 travel free. The **German Rail Youth Pass,** available to non-Germans aged 12 to 25, offers second-class passage at US$146 for five days, US$200 for 10, and US$252 for 15. For anyone under age 27, the **Tramper-Ticket** allows 10 days of unlimited second-class rail travel in a month on all DB trains, the railroad-run buses *(Bahnbusse),* and the local S-Bahns in cities—all for DM369. This pass, available between June 15 and October 15, may be purchased *only* in Germany. Also available only in Germany, the **BahnCard** is valid for one year and secures a 50% discount on all rail tickets, including the ICE. Students under 27 and anyone under 23 or over 60 can get a second-class pass for DM120; first-class cards are DM240. Normal rates are DM240 second-class, DM480 first-class. These cards require a passport-sized photo.

BUSES, FLIGHTS, BIKES, AND EURAIL
Buses between cities and to small, outlying towns usually run from the **Zentral Omnibus Bahnhof (ZOB),** often located near the train station. Buses are usually slightly more expensive than the train for comparable distances. Check university bulletin boards or the classified pages of local magazines for occasional deals. Railpasses are not valid on any buses other than those (relatively few) run by the DB. Although more than 100 international **airlines** serve Germany, flying across the country is generally expensive and unnecessary.

Bikes are sight-seeing power tools; Germany makes it easy with its wealth of trails and bike tours. Cities and towns usually have designated bike lanes. The **Fahrrad am Bahnhof** ("bikes at the train station") program offers cycle rentals throughout the country for DM10 to 15 per day. Usually bikes can be rented from one station and returned at another for a small deposit. For information about bike routes, regulations, and maps, contact **Allgemeiner Deutscher Fahrrad-Club,** Postfach 10 77 47, 28077 Bremen. A bike tour guidebook, including extensive maps, is available from **Deutsches Jugendherbergswerk (DJH)** (tel. (05231) 740 10).

Although *Let's Go* does not recommend **hitchhiking** as a safe means of transportation, it is permitted and quite common on the German *Autobahnen* (expressways). Hitchers may stand only at *Raststätten* (rest stops), *Tankstellen* (gas stations), and in front of the *Autobahn* signs at on-ramps. **Mitfahrzentralen** offices in many cities pair drivers and riders for a fee to the agency (about US$20) and to the driver (per km).

Eurail is valid in Germany and provides free passage on S-Bahns in cities and DB bus lines but not on the U-Bahn. Urban **public transit** is excellent in the western and decent in the eastern regions. You'll see four types: the **Straßenbahn** (streetcar), **S-Bahn** (commuter rail), **U-Bahn** (subway), and regular **buses.** Consider purchasing a day card *(Tageskarte)* or multiple-ride ticket *(Mehrfahrkarte);* they usually pay for themselves by the third ride. Public transportation tickets must be validated by placing the correct end of the ticket into a small validator machine (usually blue) on subway platforms before boarding or on buses immediately upon boarding. Failure to do this can result in a DM60 fine due on the spot to plain-clothes officers who patrol public transit at random.

ESSENTIALS

Every city in western Germany has a **tourist office,** usually located near the main train station *(Hauptbahnhof)* or central market square *(Marktplatz)*. They go by a bewildering variety of names (often *Verkehrsamt* or *Verkehrsverein*), but they are all marked by a thick lowercase "i" sign. The offices provide city maps and info on cycling routes and local sights, and often book rooms (usually for a small fee).

The **Deutschmark** (abbreviated DM, or occasionally M) and **Pfennig** (Pf) are the primary units of currency in Germany. One DM equals 100Pf. Coins come in 1, 2, 5, 10, and 50Pf, and DM1, 2, and 5 amounts. Bills come in DM5, 10, 20, 50, 100, 200, 500, and 1000 denominations. **Currency exchange** *(Geldwechsel)* is available in all large train stations, though banks generally offer the best rates. **Credit card** acceptance is markedly less common in Germany than in the U.S. or U.K., but **ATMs,** especially linked to Cirrus and Plus, are widespread. Most locals carry large wads of hard cash, but for tourists, **traveler's checks** are probably a better option. **Bank hours** are often quite bizarre; a typical work week might be Monday through Wednesday and Friday 9am to 12:30pm and 2:30 to 4pm, Thursday 9am to 12:30pm and 2:30 to 5pm.

Store hours are usually Monday through Friday 9am to 6:30pm, Saturday 9am to 2pm. Some stores remain open until 8:30pm on Thursday and until 4pm on the first Saturday of each month. In larger cities, shops inside train stations are open longer.

Many smaller shops take a mid-day break from noon to 2pm. Germany celebrates the following public **holidays:** January 1, Easter (Apr. 2-5 in 1999), May 1, Ascension Day (May 13), Whit Monday (May 24), October 3, and December 25-26.

> Although violent crime is relatively uncommon in Germany, homosexuals and for-eigners, particularly non-whites and members of certain religious groups, may feel threatened by local residents in certain regions. Neo-Nazi skinheads are most active in larger northern cities of the former East Germany. Be aware that some who subscribe to skinhead aesthetics are actually vehemently anti-Nazi punks.

COMMUNICATION The main **post office** in a town generally has the longest hours; all accept *Poste Restante,* known as *Postlagernde Briefe.* Local calls should be made with a *Telefonkarte;* cards are sold in all post offices in DM12, DM20, and DM50 denominations. In the booth, pick up the receiver, deposit coins or stick in your card (even if your call is toll-free) and dial. **Local calls** cost 30Pf. Phones accept 10Pf, DM1, and DM5 coins, but not 50Pf or DM2. Sometimes you can also pay by credit card. The **national information** number is 11 833. For information in EU nations, call 00 11 88. Pay phones marked with a bell allow you to receive calls. From anywhere in Ger-many, the number for the **AT&T Direct** operator is 0130 00 10; for **SprintExpress,** 0130 00 13; **Canada Direct,** 0130 00 14; **BT Direct,** 0130 80 00 44; and **New Zealand Direct,** 0130 80 00 64. You must pay for the local connection time to the operator; if you don't have a phone card, be sure to have 30Pf in change. In case of an **emergency,** call the police at 110; fire or ambulance at 112.

English **language** ability is common in western Germany, but far less so in the east. Keep in mind that the letter **ß** is equivalent to double *s.* To make more friends, try:

Yes/No	*Ja/Nein*	ya/nine
Good day/evening	*Guten Tag/Abend*	GOO-ten tahg/AH-bend
Please	*Bitte*	BIT-teh
Thank you	*Danke*	DAHN-keh
Excuse me	*Entschuldigung*	ent-SHUL-di-gung
Do you speak English?	*Sprechen Sie englisch?*	SHPREK-en zee AYN-glish
I don't understand.	*Ich verstehe nicht.*	ikh fair-SHTAY-uh nikht
Where is...?	*Wo ist...?*	Vo ist
How much does that cost?	*Wieviel kostet das?*	vee-feel KOHS-tet das
I would like...	*Ich möchte...*	ikh MURKH-teh
I would like a room for one/two	*Ich möchte ein Zimmer für ein/zwei*	ikh MURKH-teh ine TZIM-mehr fyur INE/TSVIH
Bill, please.	*Zahlen, bitte*	TZAHL-en, BIT-tuh
Help!	*Hilfe!*	HIL-feh

ACCOMMODATIONS AND CAMPING A German schoolteacher founded the world's first youth hostel in 1908, and there are now more than 600 *Jugendherber-gen* throughout the country. **Deutsches Jugendherbergswerk (DJH)** (tel. (05231) 740 10; fax 74 01 49) oversees hosteling in Germany. Rates hover around US$8 to 20. The DJH has, in recent years, initiated a growing number of **Jugendgästehäuser** (youth guest houses); with higher prices (around DM32 for a bed in a 4-person dorm) and additional facilities, these cater more to young adults than to schoolchildren. Keep in mind that hostels in Bavaria do not accept guests over the age of 26. DJH publishes *Deutsches Jugendherbergsverzeichnis* (DM14.80), which details all feder-ated German hostels; it is available at all German bookstores and many newsstands, or by writing DJH-Hauptverband, Postfach 1455, 32704 Detmold, Germany.

There are about 2600 **campgrounds** in Germany, about 400 of which are open in the winter. Prices run about DM4 to 5 per person with additional charges for tents and vehicles. Most tourist offices have lists of nearby sites.

FOOD AND DRINK Though German cuisine is neither as sophisticated as French cooking nor as sultry as Italian food, it is far from taste bud torture. *Deutsche* delights often include *Schnitzel* (a lightly fried veal cutlet), *Spätzle* (a southern noodle), and tasty seafood. However, pork and potatoes are the more steady staples of the family table. Most notable is Germany's broad palette of breads and cheeses that puts baguettes to shame. The fresh rolls (*Brötchen* or *Semmeln*) sold in any bakery will satisfy even the most discriminating of dough connoisseurs. Though Germany is quite carnivorous, vegetarians can easily find food in medium- to large-sized cities.

German breakfasts (*Frühstück*) consist of coffee or tea, rolls, butter, marmalade, slices of bread, cheese, and *Wurst* (cold sausage). The main meal, *Mittagsessen,* is served at noon. Around 4pm, many Germans head to the *Konditorei* for *Kaffee und Kuchen* (coffee and cake). The evening meal, *Abendbrot* or *Abendessen,* is traditionally a reprise of breakfast, but with beer instead of coffee. Restaurant prices include tax and service (*Mehrwertsteuer und Bedienung),* but it is customary to round up the bill to the next *Mark.* For inexpensive food, try a department-store cafeteria or, with a student ID, a *Mensa* (university dining hall). Stop at an *Imbiß* for anything fast.

The average German beer is, very generally, relatively malty and "bread-like." From the south comes *Weißbier,* a smooth, refreshing, richly brown brew. Sampling local brews numbers among the finest of Germany's pleasures. On hot summer days, lightweight drinkers prefer *Radler,* a Bavarian mix containing half beer and half lemon-lime soda. Also try the largely overlooked German wines, particularly the sweet (*lieblich* or *süß*) whites of the Rhine and Mosel Valleys.

■ Berlin

Contemporary Berlin is an inchoate tangle of experiences in search of an identity. Long recognized as the cultural capital of Germany, Berlin has not yet resumed its status as political capital. Split into eastern and western sectors, the city acted as the focal point of the Cold War in Europe, then symbolized its end when the Wall came down in 1989. Even as money is finally allocated to rebuild the eastern sectors, the disparity between east and west is troubling to residents of both. Raised in the shadow of global conflict, Berliners respond with a glorious storm of cultural activity and the nightlife you might expect from a population that has its back against the wall. A kaleidoscope of GDR apartment blocks and designer boutiques, decaying buildings and gleaming modern office complexes, Berlin's gritty melancholy is balanced by the exhilaration of being on the cutting edge.

ORIENTATION AND PRACTICAL INFORMATION

Berlin is an *immense* conglomeration of two once-separate cities: the former East, containing most of Berlin's landmarks, historic sites, and pre-fab concrete socialist architectural monsters, and the former West, which functioned for decades as an isolated Allied protectorate. Western Berlin is still the commercial heart of united Berlin, but this is changing rapidly as many businesses and embassies move their headquarters to **Potsdamer Platz** and Mitte in the east.

Western Berlin's commercial district lies at one end of the huge **Tiergarten** park, centering on **Bahnhof Zoo** and **Kufürstendamm** (Ku'damm for short), and marked by the bombed-out **Kaiser-Wilhelm-Gedächtniskirche,** next to the boxy tower of the **Europa Center.** The grand, tree-lined **Straße des 17. Juni** runs west-east through the Tiergarten and ends at the triumphant **Brandenburg Gate,** opening onto **Pariser Platz,** a site of landmark public addresses. Heading south from the Brandenburg Gate and nearby **Reichstag,** Ebertstr. runs haphazardly through the construction sites to **Potsdamer Platz.** Toward the east, the gate opens onto **Unter den Linden,** Berlin's most famous boulevard, which in turn empties into socialist-realist **Alexanderplatz,** center of the East's growing commercial district and the home of Berlin's most visible landmark, the **Fernsehturm.** Southeast of Mitte lies the eclectic **Kreuzberg** district, a newly central (and thus slowly gentrifying) former fringe neighborhood. The **Spree**

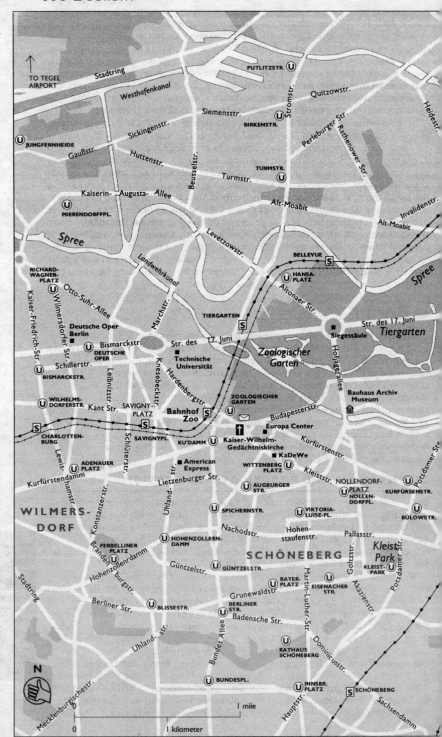

Berlin

River snakes its way from west to east through the center of Berlin, forming the northern border of the Tiergarten and splitting just east of Unter den Linden to close off the **Museumsinsel** (Museum Island), East Berlin's cultural epicenter.

For visits of more than a few days, the blue-and-yellow **Falk Plan** (DM11) can be useful. Dozens of streets and subway stations in Eastern Berlin were named after Communist heroes and heroines. Many, but not all, have been renamed in a process only recently completed; be sure your map is up-to-date. Refer also to this book's **color map** of Berlin's transit network.

> Although Berlin is by far the most tolerant city in Germany, economic chaos has unleashed a new wave of right-wing extremism, particularly in the outer boroughs of eastern Berlin. While it's unlikely that you'll encounter neo-Nazi skinheads, it is important for people of color as well as gays and lesbians to take precautions when traveling in suburban east Berlin or on the S-Bahn late at night.

Telephone Code: 030.

Flights: Flughafen Tegel (tel. 41 01 23 06) is Western Berlin's main airport. Express bus X9 from Bahnhof Zoo, bus 109 from U-Bahn 7: "Jakob-Kaiser-Pl.," or bus 128 from U-Bahn 6: "Kurt-Schumacher-Pl." **Flughafen Tempelhof** (tel. 69 51 22 88) is mostly used for domestic travel and flights within Europe. U-Bahn 6: Pl. der Luftbrücke. **Flughafen Schönefeld** (tel. 60 91 51 66) is southeast of Berlin. S-Bahn 9 or 45, or bus 171 from U-Bahn 7: "Rudow."

Trains: Trains to and from Berlin are serviced by **Zoologischer Garten** (best known as **Bahnhof Zoo**) in the West and **Ostbahnhof** (formerly *Hauptbahnhof*) in the East. Most trains go to both, although some connections to cities in the former GDR only stop at the latter. For late night arrivals, Bahnhof Zoo is preferable; the Ostbahnhof environs can be unsavory. Be prepared for a long wait when calling **Deutsche Bahn Information** (tel. 194 19), or at the stations' *Reisezentren.*

Buses: ZOB, the central bus station (tel. 301 80 28), is by the *Funkturm* near Kaiserdamm. U-Bahn 2: "Kaiserdamm" or S-Bahn 4, 45, or 46: "Witzleben." *Zitty* and *Tip* list deals for long-distance buses, uncomfortable but often much cheaper than rail.

Public Transportation: The **bus, Straßenbahn** (streetcar), **U-Bahn** (subway), and **S-Bahn** (surface rail) networks of the **BVG** *(Berliner Verkehrsbetriebe)* form one of the world's most efficient public transport systems. Berlin has 3 transit zones. Since almost everything is in Zone A (downtown) or B, an AB ticket is the best deal; you can buy regional tickets for outlying areas (Zone C contains the suburbs of Potsdam, Oranienburg, and Bernau). A single ticket for the combined network (*Langstrecke* AB or BC, DM3.90, or *Ganzstrecke* ABC, DM4.20) lasts 2hr. after validation. A transit pass is almost always a better deal. A **Tageskarte** (AB DM7.80, ABC DM8.50) is valid from cancellation until 3am the next day. Up to 5 can travel together on a **Gruppentageskarte** (AB DM20, ABC DM22.50). The **WelcomeCard** (DM29) is valid on all lines for 72hr. The **7-Tage-Karte** (AB DM40, ABC DM48) is good for 7 days of travel. You can buy tickets from machines, bus drivers, or U- and S-Bahn station windows. Fines are a stiff DM60, and inspections have increased sharply in the last 2 years. *Validate tickets in the red or yellow validation box marked "hier entwerten" before boarding.* The U- and S-Bahn generally don't run 1-4am, though most S-Bahn lines run once an hour on weekend nights, and the **U9** and **U12** run all night F and Sa. Last runs on most regular lines start by 12:15am. The extensive **night bus** system, detailed in the free *Nachtliniennetz* map, centers on Bahnhof Zoo and runs every 20-30min. or so. All-night bus numbers are preceded by the letter **N.**

Taxis: Tel. 21 02 02, 26 10 26, or 690 22. Call at least 15min. in advance. Women may request a female driver.

Car Rental: For Avis, Hertz, Europcar, and Sixt, the *Mietwagenservice* (counter 21 at Bahnhof Zoo *Reisezentrum*). Most companies also have offices at Tegel airport.

Bike Rental: Bahnhof Zoo, next to the lost and found. DM13-23 per day; DM60 for 3 days; DM120 per week. Open daily 6am-11pm.

Hitchhiking: Those who hitch west and south take S-Bahn 1 or 7 to "Wannsee," then bus 211 to the *Autobahn* entrance ramp. Those headed north, ride U-Bahn 6 to

"Alt-Tegel" or S-Bahn 25 to "Tegel," then bus 224; ask the driver to be let out at the "Trampenpl." Both have crowds, but someone generally gets picked up every few minutes. **City Netz,** Joachimstalerstr. 17 (tel. 194 44; fax 882 44 20) has a computerized **ride-share** database. U-Bahn 2 or 9: Kurfürstendamm. To Vienna DM79, Paris and Budapest DM109. Open 9am-7pm, M-F till 8pm. **Mitzfahrzentrale Alex,** in the Alexanderpl. U-Bahn station (tel. 241 58 20 or 241 58 21), specializes in the East. Open M, W, and F 10am-6pm, Th 10am-8pm, Sa-Su 11am-4pm.

Tourist Offices: For info, call 25 00 25. The two most convenient offices are **Europa Center** (from Bahnhof Zoo, 5min. along Budapester Str. past the Kaiser-Wilhelm-Gedächtniskirche, on your right), open M-Sa 8am-10pm, Su 9am-9pm, and **Brandenburger Tor** (S-Bahn 1 or 2: Unter den Linden), open daily 9:30am-6pm. Useful city map DM1; sights and transit stations more clearly marked than on the *Falk Plan.* Free copies of *030* and (for gays and lesbians) *Siegessäule* and *Sergej,* which have entertainment listings. *Tip* and *Zitty* are better, but in German (DM4 each).

Tours: The Walk is one of the best. Tours leave from the taxi stand at Bahnhof Zoo, May 25-Oct. 10 at 9:45am and 2pm (DM10). The **Insider Tour** also enjoys a very good reputation. 3hr. tours leave from the McDonald's by Bahnhof Zoo at 10am and 2:30pm daily late Mar. to Nov. (DM15, students DM10). A 4hr. bike version leaves May-Sept. at 10am and 3pm (DM 29 and 25).

Budget Travel: Kilroy Travels, Hardenbergstr. 9 (tel. 313 04 66; fax 312 69 75), across from the Technical University; many others. **STA,** Goethestr. 73 (tel. 311 09 50; U-Bahn 2: Ernst-Reuter-Pl.). Open M-W and F 10am-8pm, Th 10am-6pm.

Embassies and Consulates: Embassy and consulate locations will be in flux for the next 5 years. The **Auswärtiges Amt Dienststelle Berlin** (tel. 20 18 60; fax 20 18 62 52), a general office for foreign service, has the most recent info. U- or S-Bahn stop names match street names except where noted. **Australia,** Uhlandstr. 181-183 (tel. 880 08 80; fax 88 00 88 99). Open M-F 9am-noon. **Canada,** Friedrichstr. 95 (tel. 261 11 61; fax 262 92 06). Open M-F 8:30am-12:30pm and 1:30-5pm. **Ireland,** Ernst-Reuter-Pl. 10 (tel. 34 80 08 22; fax 34 80 08 63). Open M-F 10am-1pm. **New Zealand** citizens should contact the embassy in Bonn at Bundeskanzlerpl. 2-10 (tel. 22 80 70; fax 22 16 87). **South Africa,** Douglasstr. 9 (tel. 82 50 11; fax 826 65 43). Open M-F 9am-noon. **U.K.,** Unter den Linden 32-34 (tel. 20 18 40; fax 20 18 41 58). Open M-F 9am-noon and 2-4pm. **U.S. Citizens Service,** Clayallee 170 (tel. 832 92 33; fax 831 49 26). U-Bahn 1: Oskar-Helene-Heim. Open M-F 8:30am-noon. Phone advice available M-F 9am-5pm; recorded emergency instructions after hours. **U.S. Consulate,** Neustädtische Kirchstr. 4-5 (tel. 238 51 74; fax 238 62 90).

Currency Exchange: Wechselstube, Breitscheidpl. near the Gedächtniskirche; also at Alexanderpl. train station. Good rates, no commission. Open M-F 9am-6pm, Sa 9am-4pm. **Geldwechsel,** Joachimtal Str. 7-9 (tel. 882 63 71), has decent rates and no commission. Also **ReiseBank** at Bahnhof Zoo (tel. 881 71 17; open daily 7:30am-10pm) and Ostbahnhof (tel. 296 43 93; open M-F 7am-10pm, Sa 7am-6pm, Su 8am-4pm).

American Express: Main Office, Uhlandstr. 173 (tel. 88 45 88 21). U-Bahn 15: Uhlandstr. Mail held; banking services. Long lines F-Sa. Open M-F 9am-5:30pm, Sa 9am-noon. **Branches** at Bayreuthstr. 23 (tel. 21 49 83 63; no mail held), and Friedrichstr. 172 (tel. 20 17 40 12; full services). Both open M-F 9am-5:30pm (Bayreuthstr. until 6pm), Sa 10am-1pm.

Luggage Storage: In the **Bahnhof Zoo** train station (lockers DM2 per day, larger lockers DM4; 72hr. max.). Also at the **Ostbahnhof** (same terms).

Bookstores: Marga Schoeler Bücherstube, Knesebeckstr. 33 (tel. 881 11 12), at Mommsenstr., between Savignypl. and the Ku'damm. Many books in English. Open M-W 9:30am-7pm, Th-F until 8pm, Sa until 4pm. The **British Bookshop,** Mauerstr. 83-84 (tel. 238 46 80), by Checkpoint Charlie. Open M-F 10am-6pm, Sa 10am-4pm.

Laundromat: Wasch Centers at Leibnizstr. 72 (Charlottenburg); Wexstr. 34 (Schöneberg); Bergmannstr. 109 (Kreuzberg); Behmstr. 12 (Mitte); and Jablonskistr. 21 (Prenzlauer Berg). Wash DM6 per 6kg, soap included; dry DM2 per 30min. All open daily 6am-11pm.

Emergency: Ambulance and **Fire,** tel. 112.

Police: Tel. 110. Station at Pl. der Luftbrücke 6 (tel. 69 90).

Pharmacy: Europa-Apotheke, Tauentzienstr. 9-12 (tel. 261 41 42), by Europa Center near Bahnhof Zoo; open M-F 9am-8pm, Sa 9am-4pm. Signs on closed *Apotheken* direct you to the nearest open one. Call 011 41 for late-night pharmacy info.

Medical Assistance: Lists of English-speaking doctors at U.K. and U.S. embassies. **Emergency Doctor,** tel. 31 00 31. **Emergency Dentist,** tel. 89 00 43 33. English-speaking dentists available.

Crisis Lines: English speakers at most lines. **Sexual Assault Hotline,** tel. 251 28 28. Open Tu and Th 6-9pm, Su noon-2pm. **Schwules Überfall** (gay bashing) hotline and legal help, tel. 216 33 36. Open daily 6-9pm. Gay and lesbian counseling at **Schwulenberatung,** tel. 194 46, and **Lesbenberatung,** tel. 215 20 00, respectively. **Drug Crisis,** tel. 192 37. Open M-F 8:30am-10pm, Sa-Su 2-9:30pm. **Frauenkrisen-telefon** (women's crisis line), tel. 615 42 43. Open M and Th 10am-noon, Tu-W and F 7-9pm, Sa-Su 5-7pm. **Deutsche AIDS-Hilfe,** Dieffenbachstr. 33 (tel. 690 08 70).

Post Offices: In the **Bahnhof Zoo** (tel. 311 00 20). Interminable lines, but the best hours. Open M-F 6am-midnight, Sa-Su 8am-midnight. Address **Poste Restante** (held at window 7) thus: Hauptpostlagernd, Postamt Bahnhof Zoo, 10612 Berlin. Also at **Tegel Airport** and near the **Ostbahnhof.**

Internet Access: Website, Joachimstaler Str. 41 (tel. 88 67 96 30; http://www.vrcafe.de). U-Bahn 9 or 15: Kufürstendamm. Berlin's trendiest cybercafe (DM7 per 30min.; open daily 10am-2am). **Cyberb@r,** in the Karstadt Sport store at Joachimstaler Str. 5 (DM5 per 30min.; open M-F 10am-8pm, Sa 9am-4pm).

ACCOMMODATIONS

Tourists mob Berlin in the summer, but same-day accommodations are still possible to find. As always, it's best to call ahead; during the **Love Parade** (see p. 371), booking ahead is a must. For DM5, a **tourist office** will find you a room, but prepared to pay at least DM70 for a single or DM100 for a double. Tourist offices also control most of the city's 4000-plus private rooms *(Privatzimmer);* expect to pay DM80 for singles and DM100 for doubles, plus a single-night DM5 surcharge.

For visits over 4 days, a **Mitwohnzentrale** can arrange for you to housesit or sublet someone's apartment. Prices start at DM40 per night, plus a percentage fee. The **Home Company Mitwohnzentrale,** Joachimstalerstr. 17 (tel. 194 45; U-Bahn 9 or 15: Kufürstendamm) is the biggest (open M-F 9am-6pm, Sa 11am-2pm; Amex, Visa, MC).

Hostels and Dormitory-Style Accommodations

Hostels fill quickly with German school groups (especially in summer and on weekends)—always call ahead. Most HI hostels are members-only; some will accept non-members for an extra DM6. You can buy an **HI card** (DM30 for non-Germans) either at the hostels or at Tempelhofer Ufer 32 (tel. 264 95 20; fax 262 04 37; open M, W, and F 10am-4pm, Tu and Th 1-6pm). HI hostels have strict curfews. Many accept written or faxed reservations; you can also contact the above office.

The Backpacker, Chausseestr. 102 (tel. 262 51 40 or 28 39 09 65; fax 28 39 09 35). U-Bahn 6: Zinnowitzer Str. This place has *style.* Kitchen, laundry, **Internet access,** bike rentals. Hip staff has nightlife, travel, and sight-seeing tips. Great walking tour in English leaves hostel daily at 9am and 2pm (4hr., DM10). 5-7-bed room DM25; 4-bed DM28; 3-bed DM30; 2-bed DM38 (all prices per person). Sheets DM5. Reception 7am-noon and 1:30-11pm. No curfew.

Circus, Am Zirkus 2-3 (tel. 28 39 14 33; fax 28 39 14 84; email circus@mind.de). U-Bahn 6 or S-Bahn 1-3, 5, 7, 9, or 75: Friedrichstr. **Internet access,** laundry, bike rental; the lobby has a disco ball. Same tour that leaves the Backpacker at 9am and 2pm leaves Circus 30min. later. 4-5-bed room DM25; 3-bed DM28; single DM38; double DM30 (all prices per person). One-time DM3 for sheets. No curfew.

Die Fabrik, Schlesische Str. 18 (tel. 611 71 16; fax 617 51 04). U-Bahn 1 or 15: "Schlesisches Tor" or night bus N65: "Taborstr." Beautifully converted factory; walking distance from Kreuzberg's mad nightlife. Surprisingly comfortable dorms DM30; singles DM66; doubles DM94 (honeymoon suite DM110); triples DM120; quads 144. Breakfast DM10. Reception 24hr. No curfew. Reserve or call ahead.

Jugendgästehaus (HI), Kluckstr. 3 (tel. 261 10 97 or 261 10 98; fax 265 03 83), in the Schöneberg/Tiergarten area. From Ku'damm, bus 129 ("Hermannpl.") to "Gedenkstätte," or U-Bahn 1: "Kurfürstenstr.," then up Potsdamerstr., left on Pohlstr., right on Kluckstr. Clean and modern with lockers and laundry. DM32, over 26 DM41; breakfast and sheets included. Key deposit DM10. Reception 1pm-midnight except 1:45-2:35 and 9:45-10:15pm; ring bell. Lockout 9am-1pm. Curfew midnight; door opens at 12:30 and 1am. Call at least 2 weeks ahead.

CVJM-Haus, Einemstr. 10 (tel. 264 91 00; fax 261 43 08). U-Bahn 1, 2, or 4: Nollendorfpl. YMCA one block from Nollendorfpl.'s gay nightlife. Dorms, singles, and doubles DM40 per person. Quiet hours 10pm-7am and 1-3pm. Breakfast included. Reception 8-11am and 4-9pm. Get a key for curfew-free revelry. Book ahead.

Jugendgästehaus am Zoo, Hardenbergstr. 9a, 5th floor (tel. 312 94 10; fax 401 52 83), opposite Technical Univ. *Mensa.* Bus 145 to "Steinpl.," or down Hardenbergstr. from Bahnhof Zoo's back exit. Well-located, but spartan and poorly lit. Dorms DM35; singles DM47; doubles DM85. Over 26 add DM5. Reception 24hr. Check-in 10am. Check-out 9am. No curfew. No reservations, but try calling in the morning.

Jugendgästehaus Tegel, Ziekowstr. 161 (tel. 433 30 46; fax 434 50 63), by the Tegel parks in the north end of town. U-Bahn 6: "Tegel," then bus 222 (night bus N22) to "Titusweg." New, bright inside. DM37.50. Breakfast, sheets included. Laundry DM5. Reception 7:30am-11pm. No curfew. Same-day rooms sometimes available.

Jugendgästehaus Nordufer, Nordufer 28 (tel. 45 19 91 12; fax 452 41 00). U-Bahn 9: "Westhafen," left over bridge, then left on Nordufer about 15min. Away from the center, but on the pretty, swimmable Plötzensee. Some singles; mostly 4-bed rooms. DM37.50 includes breakfast, sheets. Reception 7am-midnight. No curfew.

Hotels and Pensionen

Many small *Pensionen* and hotels are within budget range, especially when they are amenable to *Mehrbettzimmer,* where extra beds are moved into a large double or triple. Most affordable hotels are in Western Berlin; the hotels in Mitte are ridiculously expensive. The best places to find cheap rooms are around Savignypl. and along Wilmersdorfer Str.

Hotel-Pension Cortina, Kantstr. 140 (tel. 313 90 59; fax 31 73 96). S-Bahn 3, 5, 7, 75, or 9 or bus 149 or X34: Savignypl. High-ceilinged, bright, convenient, and hospitable. Small singles DM70; doubles DM120, with shower DM130. Extra beds in rooms upon agreement. Breakfast included. Reception 24hr.

Pension Knesebeck, Knesebeckstr. 86 (tel. 312 72 55; fax 313 34 86). S-Bahn 3, 5, 7, or 9: Savignypl. Just north of the park. Large *Alt-Berliner* rooms, many with couches and sinks. Singles with showers DM80; doubles DM120, with showers DM140; big *Mehrbettzimmer* DM50-60 per person. Breakfast included. Laundry DM2.50. Reception 24hr. Must confirm phone reservations by fax or letter.

Charlottenburger Hof, Stuttgarterpl. 14 (tel. 32 90 70; fax 323 37 23). S-Bahn 3, 5, 7, or 9: "Charlottenburg" (across the street) or U-Bahn 7: "Wilmersdorferstr." Slick but expensive. Spotless rooms with bathroom, TV. Singles DM80-120; doubles DM110-160; quads DM160-220. Nov.-Dec. 20-30% off. Laundry DM5.

Hotel Sachsenhof, Motzstr. 7 (tel. 216 20 74; fax 215 82 20). U-Bahn 1, 15, 2, or 4: Nollendorfpl. Small, plain rooms, but clean and well-furnished. Singles DM57-65; doubles DM99-156; DM30 per extra bed. Breakfast DM10. Reception 24hr.

Pension Kreuzberg, Grossbeerenstr. 64 (tel. 251 13 62; fax 251 06 38). U-Bahn 6 or 7 to "Mehringdamm" or bus 119. Small but well-decorated rooms in an old but grand building close to the Kreuzberg scene. Singles DM65; doubles DM85; *Mehrbettzimmer* DM37 per person. Breakfast DM5. Reception 8am-10pm.

Hotel Transit, Hagelberger Str. 53-54 (tel. 785 50 51; fax 785 96 19). U-Bahn 6 or 7: "Mehringdamm," or bus 119 (night bus N19). Party hard and crash gently in this stylin' *Pension.* Singles DM90; doubles DM105; triples DM140; quads DM180; all with showers. "Sleep-In" deal lets you share a *Mehrbettzimmer* with any other traveler for DM33. Breakfast included. Reception 24hr.

GERMANY

Camping

Deutscher Camping-Club runs two of the major city campgrounds (both adjacent to former Berlin Wall site). Reserve by writing the Deutscher Camping-Club Berlin, Geisbergstr. 11, 10777 Berlin. Otherwise, call in advance. Both sites DM9.50 per person, DM7 per tent. **Dreilinden** (tel. 805 12 01). S-Bahn 7: "Griebnitzsee;" then walk back between the station and lake. City campsite surrounded on 3 sides by Wall vestiges. Open Mar.-Oct. **Kladow,** Krampnitzer Weg 111-117 (tel. 365 27 97). U-Bahn 7: "Rathaus Spandau," then bus 135 to "Alt-Kladow" (the last stop). Switch to bus 234 to "Krampnitzer Weg/Selbitzerstr.," then follow Krampnitzer Weg 200m. Relaxed atmosphere; swimmable lake. Open year-round.

Internationales Jugendcamp Fließtal, Ziekowstr. 161 (tel. 433 86 40). U-Bahn 6: "Tegel;" then bus 222 or night bus N22: "Titusweg." Next to Jugendgästehaus Tegel. Blanket and thermal pad under tent DM10. Officially under 27 only, but they aren't into that conformist stuff here. No reservations. Open July-Aug.

FOOD

Berlin's cuisine has joined the melting pot, with many delectable international options saving you from the ubiquitous *Würste* and *Schnitzel*s of other German cities. Almost every street has its own Turkish **Imbiß** or restaurant. A second wave of immigration has brought quality Indian restaurants to Berlin; Italian is always a safe choice. A gloriously civilized tradition in Berlin cafes is **Frühstück,** breakfast served well into the afternoon, sometimes 24 hours. Leisurely natives read the paper and linger over their fruity, fatty breakfasts; join them and relax with *Milchkaffee.*

Aldi, Plus, Edeka, and **Penny Markt** are the cheapest supermarket chains, followed by the more up-market **Bolle, Kaiser's,** and **Reichelt.** The best **open-air market** fires up Saturday mornings on Winterfeldtpl., though almost every neighborhood has one; there's a kaleidoscopic **Turkish market** in Kreuzberg, along Maybachufer on the banks of the Landwehrkanal every Friday. Take U-Bahn 8: Schönleinstr.

Western Berlin

Cafe Hardenberg, Hardenbergstr. 10. Big *belle époque* spot. Funky music, artsy interior, lots of students. Breakfast 9am-5pm (DM4-8). Most meals under DM13. Also good for a drink (grog DM4). Open daily 9am-1am, F-Sa till 2am.

Amrit, Oranienstr. 202-203. U-Bahn 1 or 15: Görlitzer Bahnhof. Fabulous Indian food, possibly the city's best, near Kreuzberg's bar and club scene. Veggie-friendly. English menu available. Open Su-Th noon-1am, F-Sa noon-2am.

Baharat Falafel, Winterfeldtstr. 37. U-Bahn 1, 2, or 4: Nollendorfpl. Superlative falafel (DM5-7). Open M-Sa 10am-2am, Su 11am-2am; closed last week in July.

Sushi am Winterfeldtplatz, Goltzstr. 24. U-Bahn 1, 2, or 4: Nollendorfpl. Standing-room only Japanese cuisine in Schöneberg's heart. A la carte sushi DM3-5; filling nigiri lunch platters DM15. Open M-Sa noon-1am, Su 3pm-midnight.

Kurdistan, Uhlandstr. 161. U-Bahn 15: Uhlandstr. One of Berlin's most exotic and appetizing offerings. Fabulously spiced *Yekawe* (meat with rice, raisins, and cinnamon) DM15. Most main courses DM15-20. Open M-Sa after 5pm.

Schwarzes Cafe, Kantstr. 148, near Savignypl. Dark walls, big-band music, and dapper waiters. It's not cool to pay DM4.20 for 0.2L of apple juice, but they have breakfast at all hours (DM7-15). Open daily 11am-3am.

Die Rote Harfe, Oranienstr. 13, on Heinrichpl. U-Bahn 1 or 15: Görlitzer Bahnhof. Leftists and grizzled types eating solid German food bound to spark the radical in you. 3-course lunch DM15. Open Su-Th 10am-2am, F-Sa 10am-3am.

Café Voltaire, Stuttgarterpl. S-Bahn 3, 5, 7, or 9: "Charlottenburg," or U-Bahn 7: "Wilmersdorfer Str." Cafe-bistro-gallery with a talkative crowd. Extensive menu with great breakfasts (DM6-8; served 5am-3pm). Open daily 24hr.

Ashoka, Alt-Moabit 49. U-Bahn 9: Turmstr. Friendly, entirely vegetarian, neighborhood Indian place. Huge portions DM6-10. Open noon-midnight.

Mensa TU, Hardenbergstr. 34. Bus 145: "Steinpl." or a 10min. walk from Bahnhof Zoo. Berlin's mightiest *Mensa.* Pretty good vegetarian *(Bio Essen)* fare. Meals DM4-5, non-students DM6-7. Cafeteria downstairs has longer hours, slightly higher prices. *Mensa* open M-F 11:15am-2:30pm. Cafeteria open M-F 8am-7:45pm.

Eastern Berlin

Trattoria Ossena, Oranienburger Str. 65. Ossena serves more substantial fare than surrounding cafes. Delicious Italian pastas and enormous pizzas. Try the *pizza treccose* or *lasagne con verdura,* each DM14. Open daily from 5pm.

Beth Cafe, Tucholskystr. 40, just off Auguststr. S-Bahn 1, 2, or 25: Oranienburger Str. Genuine kosher restaurant in the Scheunenviertel. DM5-15. Open Su-Th 11am-10pm, F 9am until 2hr. before shabbat, closed Sa.

Taba, Chausseestr. 106. U-Bahn 6: Zinnowitzer Str. Big portions of delicious, spicy Mexican and Brazilian food, spiced up further by live salsa music on W. Most entrees DM15-20. On W all entrees DM10. Open Su-Th from 4pm, Tu-Sa from 6pm.

Die Krähe, Kollwitzstr. 84, off Kollwitzpl. U-Bahn 2: Senefelderpl. Menu changes weekly. Filling breakfasts under DM10, giant salads DM12. Popular all-you-can-eat Su buffet DM13.50. Open M-Th 5:30pm-2am, F-Sa till 3am, Su 10:30am-2am.

Ostwind, Husemannstr. 13. U-Bahn 2: Senefelderpl. Prenzlauer hipsters down *dim sum* or *Shao-Lin Min* (DM13). Open M-Sa 6pm-1am, Su 10am-1am.

Village Voice, Ackerstr. 1a. U-Bahn 8: Rosenthaler Pl. Cafe/bar/bookstore trying hard for NYC hip. Inexpensive fare beats the campy books. Cafe open M-F 11am-2am, Sa-Su noon-2am; bookstore open M-F till 8pm, Sa noon-4pm.

Humboldt University Mensa, Unter den Linden 6, in back of the main building. Full meals from DM1.50. Student ID required. Open M-F 11:30am-2:30pm.

SIGHTS

Many of central Berlin's major sights lie along the route of **bus 100,** which goes from Bahnhof Zoo to Prenzlauer Berg, passing the Siegessäule, Brandenburg Gate, Unter den Linden, the Berliner Dom, and Alexanderpl. along the way. To add an element of thrill, climb up to the second floor of this double-decker bus and sit in the very first row: the view is unbeatable, and you'll feel like you're on an amusement park ride.

Between Eastern and Western Berlin

For decades a barricaded gateway to nowhere, the opened **Brandenburg Gate** (Brandenburger Tor) symbolizes reunited Berlin, connecting Unter den Linden on the east with the Tiergarten park and Str. des 17. Juni on the west. Built during the reign of Friedrich Wilhelm II as an emblem of peace, the locked gate embedded in the Berlin Wall was a symbol of Cold War division. The **Berlin Wall** itself is a dinosaur, with only fossil remains. Fenced overnight on August 13, 1961, the 165km wall separated families and friends, sometimes even running through homes. Portions are preserved near the *Ostbahnhof* and by Potsdamer Pl.; the longest remaining bit is the brightly painted **East Side Gallery** (S-Bahn 3, 7, or 9: Ostbahnhof).

The demolished wall has left an incompletely healed scar across the city center. **Potsdamer Platz,** cut off by the wall, was once a major Berlin transportation hub, designed under Friedrich Wilhelm I to approximate Parisian boulevards; the surrounding area is now a mess of construction. Just south of Potsdamer Pl. stands the **Martin-Gropius-Bau,** at Stresemannstr. 110. The decorous edifice was designed by Martin Gropius, a pupil of Schinkel and uncle of *Bauhausmeister* Walter Gropius. The popular **Haus am Checkpoint Charlie,** Friedrichstr. 44 (U-Bahn 6: Kochstr. or bus 129), a museum on the site of the famous border crossing point, is a fascinating, uneasy mixture of blatant Western tourist kitsch and didactic Eastern earnestness. *(Open daily 9am-10pm. DM8, students DM5.)*

Western Berlin

The Reichstag and Tiergarten

Just north of the Brandenburg Gate sits the imposing, stone-gray **Reichstag** building, former seat of the parliaments of the German Empire and the Weimar Republic, and future home of Germany's governing body, the *Bundestag.* Shortly after Hitler became Chancellor in 1933, a mysterious fire in the Reichstag provided a pretext to declare a state of emergency, giving the Nazis broad powers to arrest and intimidate opponents. The eventual result, the infamous Enabling Act, established Hitler as legal dictator and abolished democracy. A monument outside recalls the Reichstag members executed by the Nazis.

The lush **Tiergarten** in the center of old Berlin is a relief from the neon lights of the Ku'damm to the west and the din and dust of construction work to the east. In the heart of this vast landscaped park, the slender 70m **Siegessäule** (victory column), topped by a gilded statue of winged victory, commemorates Prussia's triumph over France in 1870. Climb 285 steps to the top for a panorama of the city. *(Open Apr.-Nov. M 1-6pm, Tu-Su 9am-6pm. DM2, students DM1.)* Radiating from the column, the **Straße des 17. Juni** bisects the park from west to east. At the eastern end stands the **Soviet Army Memorial** (yes, it's still Western Berlin), flanked by a pair of giant toy tanks.

Ku'damm, Schöneberg, and Charlottenburg

A sobering reminder of the devastation caused by World War II and one of Berlin's most striking sights, the shattered **Kaiser-Wilhelm-Gedächtniskirche** now houses an exhibit dedicated to peace. *(Exhibit open M-Sa 10am-4pm.)* However, the exhibit loses some didactic force amid the giddy neon of the **Ku'damm,** Berlin's biggest and fanciest shopping strip. The renowned **Zoo,** with entrances across from the train station and at Budapesterstr. 34 (the famous Elephant Gate), houses an exotic collection of fauna. The excellent **Aquarium** is next door at Budapesterstr. 32. *(Zoo open daily May-Sept. 9am-6:30pm; Oct.-Feb. 9am-5pm; Mar.-Apr. 9am-5:30pm. Aquarium open daily 9am-6pm. Each DM12, students DM10; combination ticket DM19, students DM16.)*

South of Nollendorferpl. is the **Rathaus Schöneberg,** where West Berlin's city government met in the 1960s. On June 26, 1963, 1.5 million Berliners swarmed beneath the sleek tower to hear John F. Kennedy reassure them of the Allies' commitment to the city. Kennedy's speech concluded with the now famous "All free men, wherever they may live, are citizens of Berlin. And therefore, as a free man, I take pride in the words *"Ich bin ein Berliner"* (colloquially, "I am a jelly doughnut").

Schloß Charlottenburg (U-Bahn 2: Sophie-Charlotte-Pl. or bus 145 from Bahnhof Zoo), the vast, bright Baroque palace built by Friedrich I for his second wife, Sophie-Charlotte, presides over a carefully landscaped park. *(Castle open Tu-F 9am-5pm, Sa-Su 10am-5pm. Mausoleum open Apr.-Oct. Tu-Su 10am-noon and 1-5pm. Entire palace complex Tageskarte DM15, students DM10, under 14 free.)* Seek out the **Palace Gardens,** with their small lakes, footbridges, fountains, and carefully planted rows of trees surrounding the **Royal Mausoleum.** *(Gardens open Tu-Su 6am-9pm. Free.)*

Kreuzberg

Indispensable for a sense of Berlin's famous *alternative Szene,* or counter-culture, is a visit to **Kreuzberg,** an area long proud of its diverse population and liberal leanings. Much of the area was occupied by *Hausbesetzer* (squatters) during the 60s and 70s; their forcible eviction in the early 80s provoked riots and upheaval in the city. For a look at the district's more respectable face, take U-Bahn 6 or 7 to "Mehringdamm" and wander. At night, many bohemian cafes and punk clubs spill onto **Gneisenaustraße,** which heads west from the intersection with Mehringdamm. The cafes and bars on Oranienstr. boast a more radical element; the May Day parades always start on Oranienpl. The **Landwehrkanal** bisects Kreuzberg; the tree-dotted strip of the canal near Hallesches Tor, **Paul-Linke Ufer,** may be the most beautiful street in Berlin, with its shady terraces and old facades. The east end of Kreuzberg near the old Wall is home to Turkish and Balkan neighborhoods, with a wealth of ethnic restaurants popular with radicals, students, and shabby genteel gourmets. From the "Schlesisches Tor" U-Bahn stop, a three-minute walk leads across the **Oberbaumbrücke,** through a fragment of the wall and into the Friedrichshain district of the former East.

Eastern Berlin

Unter den Linden and Gendarmenmarkt

The Brandenburg Gate opens east onto **Unter den Linden,** once one of Europe's best-known boulevards and the spine of pre-war Berlin. Beyond Friedrichstr., many neighboring 18th-century structures have been restored to their original splendor, though GDR excesses continue to mar the landscape. As the main thoroughfares of downtown East Berlin, the intersection of Friedrichstr. and Unter den Linden became a proletarian showcase of glitzy hotels and restaurants. Amidst the architectural terror rises the stately **Deutsche Staatsbibliothek** (library); the shady, ivy-covered courtyard houses a pleasant cafe. Beyond the library is the **Humboldt Universität,** whose hallowed halls have been trodden by the likes of Einstein, Hegel, Marx, and the Brothers Grimm. Next door, the **Neue Wache** (new guard house) was designed by Schinkel in unrepentant Neoclassical style. Buried inside are urns filled with earth from the Buchenwald and Mauthausen concentration camps, as well as the battlefields of Stalingrad, El Alamein, and Normandy. Under renovation in 1998, it is scheduled to reopen in 1999.

Across the way is **Bebelplatz,** where on May 10, 1933, Nazi students burned nearly 20,000 books by "subversive" authors. The building with the curved facade is the **Alte Bibliothek.** On the other side of the square is the handsome **Deutsche Staatsoper,** fully rebuilt after the war from original sketches. The distinctive blue dome at the end of the square belongs to the **St.-Hedwigs-Kathedrale.**

Back on Unter den Linden, the heavily ornamented **Zeughaus,** once the Prussian Army Hall of Fame and military museum, has become the **Museum of German History.** Berlin's most impressive ensemble of 19th-century buildings is a few blocks south of Unter den Linden at **Gendarmenmarkt.** The twin cathedrals **Deutscher Dom** and **Französischer Dom** grace opposite ends of the square; in between lies the Neoclassical **Schauspielhaus,** Berlin's most elegant concert space.

Museumsinsel and the Lustgarten

After crossing the Schloßbrücke over the Spree, Unter den Linden passes by the **Museumsinsel** (Museum Island), home of four major museums and the **Berliner Dom.** The beautifully bulky cathedral was severely damaged by an air raid in 1944; it emerged from its 1973-1993 restoration with a gaudily stunning interior. *(Open daily 9am-7:30pm. Dom DM5; Dom, tower, and galleries DM8. Students DM3 and DM5. Free organ recitals M, Th, and F at 3pm. Frequent concerts in summer.)*

Immediately to the left stands the pillared **Altes Museum.** The **Lustgarten** in front, normally a pleasant collection of trees and benches, will be completely overhauled in the next few years to look as it did in the 19th century. Behind the Altes Museum lie three other enormous museums: the **Pergamon,** the **Bodemuseum,** and the **Alte Nationalgalerie.** Across the street, the Lustgarten turns into Marx-Engels-Pl. under the glaring amber **Palast der Republik,** where the GDR parliament met. Crossing the Liebknecht-Brücke leads you to a small park on the right-hand side of the street; in the middle of the park stands a memorial consisting of steel tablets dedicated to the world-wide workers' struggle against fascism and imperialism. The exhibit is dwarfed by a huge statue of a seated Santa Claus-like Marx and a standing Engels. The park and the street behind it used to be collectively known as the **Marx-Engels Forum;** the park has not been renamed, but the street is now called Rathausstr.

Alexanderplatz, Nikolaiviertel, and Scheunenviertel-Oranienburger Str.

On the other side of the Museumsinsel, Unter den Linden becomes Karl-Liebknecht Str., and leads into the monolithic **Alexanderplatz.** Formerly the frantic heart of Weimar Berlin, the plaza was transformed in GDR times into an urban wasteland of fountains and pre-fab office buildings. The undisputed landmark of the district is the **Fernsehturm** (television tower), the city's tallest structure. An elevator whisks tourists to the top. *(Open daily Mar.-Oct. 9am-1am; Nov.-Feb. 10am-midnight. DM8.)*

The graceful 15th-century **Marienkirche** stands on the open plaza in front of the Fernsehturm. *(Open M-Th 10am-4pm, Sa-Su noon-4pm, closed F.)* Nearby is the gabled **Rotes Rathaus,** Berlin's famous red-brick town hall. Have your own Poseidon Adventure in the aquamarine **Neptunbrunnen** in front. A few blocks down Spandauer Str. is the **Nikolaikirche,** whose twin spires mark Berlin's oldest building. The church gives the surrounding **Nikolaiviertel,** a carefully reconstructed *Altstadt,* its name.

Northwest of Alexanderpl. lies the **Scheunenviertel,** once the center of Berlin's Orthodox Jewish community (S-Bahn 1,2, or 25: "Oranienburger Str." or U-Bahn 6: "Oranienburger Tor"). Today, the area is better known for its outdoor cafes and punk clubs than its historical significance as. The shell of the **Neues Synagoge,** a huge "oriental-style" building designed by the famous Berlin architect Knoblauch, stands at Oranienburger Str. 30. The synagogue was destroyed by bombing, but its restoration, largely financed by international Jewish organizations, began in 1988. The temple's beautiful gold-laced domes have been reconstructed, and two first-class exhibits are housed here. *(Open Su-Th 10am-6pm, F 10am-2pm. DM5, students DM3.)* **The New Synagogue 1866-1995** display chronicles the synagogue's history; the **Jewish History in Berlin** exhibit documents the history of Jews in Berlin since the 1660s.

Prenzlauer Berg

Northeast of Oranienburger Str. and Alexanderpl. lies **Prenzlauer Berg,** a former working-class district largely neglected by Eastern Germany's reconstruction efforts. Many of its old buildings are falling apart; others still have shell holes and embedded bullets from World War II. The result is aged charm and graceful decay, slightly less charming for phoneless local residents with bad plumbing. Unlike the loud, raucous scene in Kreuzberg and Mitte, Prenzlauer Berg is more sedate and cerebral—not to say that it isn't lively. The streets here are studded with hip but casual cafes, bars, and squats, frequented by an ever-burgeoning crowd. Especially worthy of a stroll is the restored **Husemannstraße.** The scene around **Kollwitzplatz** is especially vibrant.

The powerful **Sowjetisches Ehrenmal** (Soviet War Memorial) is a mammoth promenade built with marble taken from Hitler's Chancellery (S-Bahn 4, 6, or 8-10: Treptower Park). The Soviets dedicated the site in 1948, honoring the Red Army soldiers who fell in the "Great Patriotic War." The memorial sits in the middle of **Treptower Park,** a spacious wood ideal for morbid picnics. The neighborhood adjoining the park is known for its pleasant waterside cafes and handsome suburban mansions.

MUSEUMS

Berlin is one of the world's great museum cities, with collections encompassing all subjects and eras. The **National Prussian Cultural Foundation** (*Staatliche Museen Preußischer Kulturbesitz* or **SMPK**) runs the four major complexes—**Museumsinsel** (S-Bahn 3, 5, 7, or 9: Hackescher Markt), **Tiergarten** (U-Bahn 2 or S-Bahn 1, 2, or 25: Potsdamer Pl. On your right up Potsdamer Str.), **Charlottenburg** (U-Bahn 2: "Sophie-Charlotte-Pl." or bus 145), and **Dahlem** (U-Bahn 2: Dahlemdorf)—that form the hub of the city's museum culture. These government-run museums have standardized prices: DM4, students DM2. The first Sunday of every month offers free admission. A *Tageskarte* (DM8, students DM4) is valid for all the SMPK museums on the day of purchase; the *Wochenkarte* (DM25, students DM12.50) is valid for the whole week.

Pergamonmuseum, Kupfergraben, on Museumsinsel. One of the world's great ancient history museums. Exhibits on a mind-boggling scale: the entire Babylonian Ishtar Gate, the Roman Market Gate of Miletus, and the majestic Pergamon Altar of Zeus. Extensive collections of Greek, Assyrian, Islamic, and Far Eastern art. Entry requires *Tageskarte*. Open Tu-Su 9am-5pm; last entry 4:30pm.

Alte Nationalgalerie, Bodestr. 1-3, on Museumsinsel. 19th-century art, mostly German, but also a sizable French Impressionism collection. Open Tu-Su 9am-5pm.

Bodemuseum, Monbijoubrücke, on Museumsinsel. World-class exhibit of Egyptian art, as well as early Christian art, Byzantine masterpieces, 15th- to 18th-century paintings, and an ancient history exhibit. *Kindergalerie.* Open Tu-Su 9am-5pm.

Altes Museum, Lustgarten, on Museumsinsel. Converted into a special-exhibit museum; recent powerhouse showings of 20th-century avant-garde, political art. *Tageskarte* not valid; exhibits up to DM10, students DM5. Open Tu-Su 10am-5pm.

Gemäldegalerie (Painting Gallery), Tiergarten. Rightly one of Germany's most famous museums. Stunning and enormous collection of works by Dutch, Flemish, German, and Italian masters, including 26 Rembrandts. Open Tu-F 10am-6pm, Th till 8pm, Sa-Su 11am-6pm. SMPK ticket.

Neue Nationalgalerie, Potsdamer Str. 50, Tiergarten. Sleek van der Rohe building gives quantity its own quality in a collection devoted to large art. Special exhibits often supersede permanent collection. SMPK ticket will get you in, but exhibitions are DM12, students DM6. Open Tu-F 10am-6pm, Th till 8pm, Sa-Su 11am-6pm.

Schloß Charlottenburg, Spandauer Damm, holds several museums set against the romantic *Schloßgarten.* Special exhibits in the **Kleiner Orangerie.** *Schloß* DM8, students DM4; *Tageskarte* for gardens but non-SMPK areas DM15, students DM10. **Galerie der Romantik,** in the *Neuer Flügel* (new wing), holds a dynamic collection of 19th-century art. Open Tu-F 10am-6pm, Sa-Su 11am-8pm. SMPK prices.

Ägyptisches Museum, Schloßstr. 70, across Spandauer Damm from the castle. Fascinating, dramatically lit collection of ancient Egyptian art, including the 3300-year-old bust of Queen Nefertiti. Open Tu-F 10am-6pm, Sa-Su 11am-6pm. SMPK prices.

Sammlung Berggruen, Schloßstr. 1, in an identical building across the street from the Egyptian museum. Incredible collection of modernists; equally impressive special exhibits. Open Tu-F 10am-6pm, Sa-Su 11am-6pm. SMPK ticket valid.

Bröhan Museum, Schloßstr. 1a. Two floors of *Jugendstil* and Art Deco pieces dating from 1889 to 1939. Open Tu-Su 10am-6pm. DM8, students DM4.

Brücke Museum, Bussardsteig 9 (tel. 831 20 29). From Bahnhof Zoo, bus 249 to "Güntzelstr.," then bus 115 to "Clayallee/Pücklerstr." (30min., 13 stops). Along with the *Neue Nationalgalerie,* this is *the* Expressionist museum in Berlin, with works by the *Brücke* school. Open M and W-Su 11am-5pm. DM7, students DM3.

Martin-Gropius Bau, Stresemannstr. 110 (tel. 25 48 60). S-Bahn 1, 2, or 25: Anhalter Bahnhof. Museum for the industrial arts. Includes **Berlinische Galerie,** devoted to contemporary German art, and **Jüdisches Museum,** exhibiting art on the German Jewish experience. Open Tu-Su 10am-6pm. DM12, students DM6.

Topographie des Terrors, in back of the Martin-Gropius-Bau, on the ruins of a Gestapo kitchen. Comprehensive exhibit in German details the development of Nazism. English guides DM2. Open Tu-Su 10am-6pm. Free.

Bauhaus Archiv-Museum für Gestaltung, Klingenhöferstr. 13-14. U-Bahn 1, 15, 2, or 4: Nollendorfpl. Exhibits on the development of *Bauhaus* and questions of art theory. Open M and W-Su 10am-5pm. DM5, students DM2. Free on Monday.

Deutsches Historisches Museum (Museum of German History), Unter den Linden 2, opposite Museumsinsel. Permanent displays on German history; rotating exhibits on the last 50 years. Lots of "happy worker" GDR art. Th-Tu 10am-6pm. Free.

Museum für Verkehr und Technik (Transportation and Technology), Trebbiner Str. 9. U-Bahn: Gleisdreieck or Möckernbrücke. Tu-F 9am-6pm, Sa-Su 10am-6pm. DM5.

ENTERTAINMENT

Berlin has one of the most vibrant cultural scenes in the world. Exhibitions, concerts, plays, and dance abound. Varied festivals spice up the regular offerings. Tickets are usually reasonable, especially with student discounts (always ask); you can reserve by calling the box office directly. Major theaters and operas close from mid-July to late August. **Hekticket,** on Hardenbergstr. next to the Zoo-Palast cineplex (tel. 230 99 30), has last-minute half-price tickets (open M-F 9am-8pm, Sa 10am-8pm, Su 4-8pm). **Berliner Festspiele,** next door, also sells tickets (open M-F 10am-6pm, Su 10am-2pm). Find theatre, cinema, nightlife, and music listings in *Tip* or *Zitty* (both DM4 and in German), and *030* (free in cafes, bars). Berlin has **de-criminalized marijuana possession** of up to 8g. Smoking in public, however, has not been officially accepted; puffing clouds of hash smoke into the face of police officers is not wise.

Concerts, Opera, and Dance

Berlin reaches its musical zenith during the fabulous **Berliner Festwochen,** lasting almost all of September and drawing the world's best orchestras and soloists, and the **Berliner Jazztage** in November. For more information on these events (and tickets, which sell out months ahead), contact *Berliner Festspiele,* Budapester Str. 50, D-10787 Berlin (tel. 25 48 92 50; http://www.berlinerfestspiele.de). In mid-July, **Bachtage** (Bach Days) offer an intense week of classical music; every Saturday night in August, **Sommer Festspiele** turns the Ku'damm into a multi-faceted concert hall with punk, steel-drum, and folk groups competing for attention.

In the monthly pamphlets *Konzerte und Theater in Berlin und Brandenburg* (free) and *Berliner Programm* (DM2.80), you'll find notices of concerts in the courtyard of the old Arsenal on the **Schloßinsel Köpenick** (castle island) or in the parks.

GERMANY

Tickets for the *Philharmonie* and the *Oper* are often impossible to acquire through conventional channels. Try standing out in front before performances with a small sign saying, *"Suche Karte"* (I seek a ticket). **Berliner Philharmonisches Orchester,** Matthäikirchstr. 1 (tel. 25 48 81 32; fax 25 48 81 35), is one of the world's finest. Check for seats an hour before curtain. Closed from late June until early Sept. (U-Bahn 2 or S-Bahn 1, 2 or 25: "Potsdamer Pl." and up Potsdamer Str. Cheapest tickets DM14-30. Ticket office open M-F 3:30-6pm, Sa-Su 11am-2pm.) **Deutsche Oper Berlin,** Bismarckstr. 35 (info tel. 341 02 49, tickets 343 84 01; fax 343 84 55) is Berlin's best opera. (U-Bahn 2: Deutsche Oper. Tickets DM15-140. Students up to 50% off within a week of performance. Evening tickets 1hr. before show. Main box office open M-Sa 11am-1hr. before show, Su 10am-2pm. Closed July-Aug.) Eastern Berlin's leading opera company, **Deutsche Staatsoper,** Unter den Linden 7 (tel. 20 35 45 55; fax 20 35 44 83), also does ballet and classical music. (Tickets DM18-35, students 50% off. Box office M-F 10am-6pm, Sa-Su 2-6pm. *Abendkasse* open 1hr. before show. Closed mid-July to early Sept.)

Theater and Film

Theater listings are available in the monthly pamphlets *Kultur!news* and *Berlin Programm,* as well as in *Zitty* and *Tip.* Look for listings marked *in englischer Sprache* (in English); Berlin has a lively English-language theater scene. On any night, you can also choose from 100 different films, many in the original languages. (*"O.F."* next to a movie listing means original version. *"O.m.U."* means original with German subtitles. Everything else is dubbed.) Check the ubiquitous *Kinoprogramm* posters plastered throughout the city. **Odeon,** Hauptstr. 116 (tel. 781 26 82; U-Bahn 4: Rathaus Schöneberg), shows a mixture of mainstream American and British films, all in English. Berlin hosts the international **Berlinale** film festival in February (Feb. 10-21 in 1999) and a **Theater Festival** in May. **Deutsches Theater,** Schumannstr. 13a (tel. 28 44 12 25), is the best theater in the country, with innovative productions of both classics and newer works. (U-Bahn 6 or S-Bahn 1-3, 5, 7, 25, 75, or 9: Friedrichstr. Tickets DM15-40; ask about 50% student discounts. Box office open M-Sa noon-6pm, Su 3-6pm.) **Friends of Italian Opera,** Fidicinstr. 40 (tel. 691 12 11), is Berlin's leading English-language theater and has a penchant for the grotesque. (U-Bahn 6: "Pl. der Luftbrücke;" tickets DM15-20; most shows at 8pm.)

NIGHTLIFE

Berlin's nightlife is sheer madness. Bars, clubs, and cafes typically jam until at least 3am and often stay open until daylight. In Western Berlin, the best places to look are **Savignyplatz, Nollendorfplatz,** and particularly **Kreuzberg.** The Ku'damm is best avoided at night, unless you enjoy the company of drunken businessmen and dirty old men. Savignypl. is rife with cafes and bars. Schöneberg nightlife focuses on Nollendorfpl., encompassing cafe-Kneipen on Winterfeldtpl., Akazienstr., and Goltzstr., and more bars on Kleiststr. East Kreuzberg is wild; radically alternative clubs from laid-back to breathtakingly salacious lie along Oranienstr. between U-Bahn 1, 12, or 15 "Kottbusser Tor" and "Görlitzer Bahnhof." Farther east, Schlesisches Tor is home to a more punkish heap of bars. On the opposite bank of the Spree in Friedrichshain, check out the venues along Mühlenstr. (U-Bahn 1, 12, or 15: Warschauer Str.)

As funky as Kreuzberg is, its alterna-charm has become a tad passé as clubs flee east and north. Low rents and a fascinating new "alternative" population have make the East hot. The **Scheunenviertel** has some of the more interesting bars, especially along **Oranienburger Straße** (not to be confused with Kreuzberg's Oranienstr.) near the synagogue. The **Prenzlauer Berg** area has places worth checking out along Schönhauser Allée, Kastanienallée, and Kollwitzpl. Streetlights are sparse on many eastern residential streets; avoid empty alleys and parks and travel in groups when possible.

Sage Club, Brückenstr. 1. U-Bahn 8: "Heinrich-Heine-Str." or night bus N8. Sage Club has dealt a one-two punch to its Kreuzberg competitors in cornering the techno and house market. Th-Su from 11pm. Cover DM10-25.

GERMANY

The Love Parade

Every year during the second weekend in July, the Love Parade brings Berlin to its knees—its trains run late, its streets fill with litter, and its otherwise patriotic populace scrambles to the countryside in the wake of a wave of West German teenagers dying their hair, dropping ecstasy, and getting down *en masse*. What started in 1988 as a DJ's birthday party, with only 150 people, has mutated into an annual techno Woodstock, the world's only million-man rave, and a massive corporate event. A huge "parade" takes place on Saturday afternoon, involving a snail-paced procession of tractor-trailers loaded with blasting speakers and topped by gyrating bodies that slowly works it from Ernst-Reuter-Pl. to the Brandenburg Gate. The city-wide party turns the Str. des 17 Juni into a riotous dance floor, and the Tiergarten into a garden of original—and sometimes quite creative—sin. To celebrate the licentious atmosphere, the BVG offers a "No-Limit-Ticket," useful for getting around from venue to venue during the weekend's 54 hours of nonstop partying (DM10, condom included). Unless you have a fetish for tall people's hairy and sweaty armpits, the best way to see and enjoy the parade is to be up high (literally, of course)—the porta-potties are supreme watch towers. Club prices skyrocket for the event as the best DJs from Europe and Detroit are imported for a frantic weekend of beat-thumping madness. It's an experience that you'll never forget, unless you consume something that leaves you in a hazy cloud of oblivion. Keep an ear out for updates on the 1999 event; although past Love Parades have been held in the Tiergarten, the authorities might move it after environmentalists raised concerns about the 750,000 liters of urine which the park must absorb every year. Regardless of the locale, the techno world trembles in eager anticipation of next year's incarnation.

Tresor/Globus, Leipziger Str. 126a (tel. 229 06 11 or 612 33 64). U-Bahn 2 or S-Bahn 1, 2, or 25: "Potsdamer Pl." or night bus N5, N29 or N52. One of the most rocking techno venues in Berlin. **Globus** chills with house; **Tresor** rocks to techno. Open W and F-Sa 11pm-6am. Cover DM5 on W, DM10 on F, DM15-20 on Sa.

E-Werk, Wilhelmstr. 43 (tel. 617 93 70). U-Bahn 2, S-Bahn 1, 2, or 25, or night bus N52: Potsdamer Pl. After several years' absence, it remains to be seen whether or not the world's most famous techno club (scheduled to reopen in late 1998) can still pack them in (cover DM15-20); call for up-to-date information.

Hackesche Höfe, Rosenthaler Str. 40-41. S-Bahn 3, 5, 7, 75, or 9: Hackescher Markt. One of the few truly successful attempts to revitalize northern Mitte. 6 connected courtyards of restaurants, cafes, clubs, galleries, and more. *Klezmer* bands vie with street performers for attention. The low-key **Oxymoron** club (tel. 28 39 18 85) has daily jazz concerts (open M and W-Sa after 11pm, Tu after 8:30pm, Su after 10pm).

Tacheles, Oranienburger Str. 53-56 (tel. 282 61 85). U-Bahn 6: "Oranienburger Tor" or S-Bahn 1, 2, or 25: "Oranienburger Str." or night bus N6 or N84. Galleries, bars, and vicious raves; a playground for artists, punks, and curious tourists from nearby hostels. Always a threat it'll be evicted in favor of office buildings. Open daily 24hr.

Kulturbrauerei, Knaackstr. 97 (tel. 441 92 69 or 441 92 70). U-Bahn 2: Eberswalder Str. Variety of concerts and parties in enormous former brewery; call ahead for info. Open Th-Su and Tu after 10pm. Cover DM3-5, more for special events.

Metropol, Nollendorfpl. 5 (tel. 217 36 80). U-Bahn 1, 15, 2, or 4: "Nollendorfpl.," or night buses N5, N19, N26, N48, N52, or N75. Berlin's largest disco. Funk, house, and soul F-Sa nights from 9pm. Cover DM20. Sometimes concerts between dances (ticket prices vary; call 215 54 63 for info). Open M-F 11am-3pm and 3:30-6pm.

Quasimodo, Kantstr. 12a (tel. 312 80 86; http://www.quasimodo.de). S-Bahn: Savignypl. Unassuming basement pub with attached *Biergarten* is one of Berlin's most crucial jazz venues; big names, lively crowds. Cover free-DM30; concert tickets available from 5pm or at Kant Kasse tickets (tel. 313 45 54). Open daily from 8pm.

SO 36, Oranienstr. 190 (tel. 61 40 13 06; http://www.SO36.de). U-Bahn 1, 12, or 15: "Görlitzer Bahnhof" or night bus N29: "Heinrichpl." or N8: "Adalbertstr." Berlin's only *truly* open club. A mixed gay/straight clientele grooves to a mish-mash of genres; weekends range from techno to live concerts. Open after 11pm.

GERMANY

Junction Bar, Gneisenaustr. 18 (tel. 694 66 02). U-Bahn 7: "Gneisenaustr." or night bus N4 or N19: "Zossener Str." Live jazz and blues accompany American-style breakfast served until 2:30am. "Eat Real Late!" Showtimes at 7:30, 8:30, and 9:30pm, and DJ parties after 1am. Open Su-Th 6pm-3am, F-Sa 5pm-5am.

Insel der Jugend, Alt Treptow 6 (tel. 53 60 80 20), on an island in the middle of the park. S-Bahn 4, 6, 8-10: "Treptower Park," then bus 166, 167, or 265 or night bus N65: "Alt-Treptow." Reggae, hip-hop, ska, and house; basement techno. Open W after 7pm, Th after 9pm, F-Sa after 10 pm. Cover Th- Sa DM5-15.

GAY AND LESBIAN BERLIN

Berlin is by far the most open city on the continent. **Nollendorfplatz,** the so-called "Pink Village," has traditionally been the social nexus of gay and lesbian life; Schöneberg and Kreuzberg are also heavily gay districts. **Spinnboden-Lesbenarchiv,** Anklamerstr. 38 (tel. 448 58 48), has culturally hip offerings and info on lesbian life (open W and F 2-7pm). With the fall of the Wall, Berlin's *Szene* was revitalized by the emergence of East Berlin's previously heavily oppressed homosexual community; many of the new clubs of the past few years are situated in the eastern half of the city. The free *Siegessäule,* and for men, *Sergej,* have current listings.

Bierhimmel, Oranienstr. 183. U-Bahn 1, 15, or 8: Kottbusser Tor. Very popular hang-out for Berlin's gays and lesbians. Heavenly beer in abundance. Open 6pm-late.

SO 36, see above.

Die Busche, Mühlenstr. 12. U-Bahn 1, 12, or 15 or S-Bahn 3, 5, 6, 7, 75 or 9: Warschauer Str. East Berlin's largest queer disco serves up techno, top 40, and *Schlager.* Open W and F-Su from 9:30pm. Gets going around midnight; *really* heats up around 3am. Cover DM8-10.

SchwuZ, Mehringdamm 61 (tel. 694 10 77). U-Bahn 6 or 7: Mehringdamm. Cafe/club in southern Kreuzberg with a gay, mostly male, clientele. Ballroom and tango Th from 8pm; house, techno, and top 40 F-Sa from 11pm. Cover DM5-10.

BRANDENBURG

Surrounding Berlin on all sides, the province of Brandenburg is overshadowed by the sprawling metropolis within it. Many believe that Brandenburg, now an agrarian hinterland, will unite with Berlin in the future to form a single federal state, Berlin-Brandenburg. Brandenburg's lakes and forests are all easily accessible from Berlin, and provide a soul-saving break from the overloaded circuits of the capital.

■ Potsdam

Visitors discomfited by Berlin's sprawling urban demeanor could do no better than to catch the S-Bahn to nearby Potsdam, the glittering city of Frederick the Great. Between the early 1920s and World War II, Potsdam was Germany's "Little Hollywood," and in 1945 it was where the Allies divided up Germany. The 600-acre **Sanssouci Park,** with its countless marble fountains, exotic pavilions, and Baroque castles, stands as a monument to Frederick the Great's (sometimes dubious) aesthetic taste. A **day ticket** gives you access to all of the park's four royal castles (DM20, students DM15). The largest of the castles, the **Neues Palais,** contains a glittering 19th-century reception room, the *Grottensaal.* (Open Su-Th Apr.-Oct. 9am-5pm; Nov.-Mar. 9am-4pm. DM6, students DM4. Tour DM2.) Frederick escaped his wife and other troubles at **Schloß Sanssouci,** at the opposite end of the park. (Open Apr.-Oct. daily 9am-5pm; Feb.-Mar. 9am-4pm; Nov.-Jan. 9am-3pm. DM10, students DM5.) The most exotic of the park's pavilions is the **Chinesisches Teehaus,** a gold-plated opium dream, complete with a parasol-toting rooftop Buddha (DM2). Try to arrive at the park early.

Potsdam's second park, the **Neuer Garten,** contains several former royal residences. Built in the image of an English country manor, **Schloß Cecilienhof** hosted the signatories of the 1945 Potsdam Treaty. To get there, take tram 96 to "Pl. der Einheit" then take tram 95 to "Alleestr." (open Tu-Su 9am-noon and 12:30-5pm; DM6, with tour DM8, students DM4). Take tram 93-95 to "Burgstr." for the **Glienicker Brücke** ("The James Bond Bridge"), used until 1989 to exchange spies between the GDR and West Berlin.

The **tourist office,** Friedrich-Ebert-Str. 5 (tel. (0331) 27 55 80, accommodations info 275 58 16; fax 275 58 99), is between the "Alter Markt" and "Pl. der Einheit" streetcar stops. The office books rooms (DM20-40) for a DM5 fee. (Open Apr.-Oct. M-F 9am-8pm, Sa 9am-6pm, Su 9am-4pm; Nov.-Mar. M-F 10am-6pm, Sa-Su 10am-2pm.) The S-Bahn 7 runs directly from Berlin's Bahnhof Zoo to Potsdam-Stadt, the town center (30min.). Potsdam lies in zone C of Berlin's transport system (a ticket for zone C costs DM2.80, zones B and C DM7.80).

SAXONY (SACHSEN)

Saxony is known to foreigners primarily for Leipzig and Dresden, but the entire region reveals a great deal about life in the former East. The castles around Dresden attest to the lavish history of Saxony's prince-electors, while the socialist monuments of Chemnitz reflect the colorless world of the GDR. On the eastern edge, Sächsiche Schweiz and the Zittauer Gebirge provide a respite from the aesthetic violence of GDR city planners with hiking trails that march through a land of escapism to the borders of the Czech Republic and Poland.

■ Dresden

Dresden pulses with an intensity that is both sublime and vicious, and remains an emblem of everything that was and is East Germany. Allied bombings shattered the "Baroque Jewel" in 1945, and the city still houses spectacular ruins. Today, as palaces and churches burst forth from the rubble left uncleared throughout the GDR years, Dresden acts as a focal point for Germany's reunification; a skyline of over 200 cranes steadily assists the reconstruction, scheduled for completion by 2006, the city's 800-year anniversary. But while you'll hear tourists everywhere waxing pretentious about "the hope of tomorrow," the raw Dresden of today offers a vitality that transcends the process of reconstruction.

ORIENTATION AND PRACTICAL INFORMATION

The capital of Saxony, Dresden stands magnificently on the Elbe River 80km northwest of the Czech border and 180km south of Berlin. The **Altstadt** lies on the same side of the river as the **Hauptbahnhof** (main train station); the **Neustadt** to the north, having escaped most of the bombing, is now ironically one of the oldest parts of the city. Many of Dresden's tourist attractions are located between the *Altmarkt* and the Elbe, a mere five-minute walk from the *Neustadt.* For longer outings, public transportation offers rides for DM1.30 and day passes for DM8.

Telephone Code: 0351.

Trains: For info, call 194 19, or use the computerized schedule center in the main hall of the *Hauptbahnhof.* To: Berlin-Lichtenberg (1½-2½hr.), Budapest (11hr.), Frankfurt am Main (5hr.), Leipzig (1½hr.), Munich (7½-9hr.), Paris (10-13hr.), Prague (3hr.), and Warsaw (10hr.). **Bahnhof Dresden Neustadt** sits on the other bank of the Elbe; trains leave from here to Gorlitz and other eastern cities.

Bike Rental: (tel. 461 32 85) in the *Hauptbahnhof* near the luggage storage. DM10 per day. Open M-F 6am-10pm, Sa 6am-9pm.

Hitchhiking: Hitchers stand in front of the *"Autobahn"* signs at on-ramps. To Berlin: streetcar 3 or 6 to "Liststr.," then bus 81 to "Olter." To Prague or Frankfurt am Main: bus 72 or 76 to their last stops ("Lockwitz" or "Luga," respectively). **Mitfahr-**

zentrale, Antonstr. 41 (tel. 194 40), 400m from *Bahnhof-Neustadt.* DM0.10 per km plus finder's fee. Berlin DM21. Open M-F 9am-7pm, Sa 9am-1pm, Su 11am-4pm.

Tourist Office: Dresden Information, Pragerstr. (tel. 49 19 21 16; http://www.dres-den-online.de). A new tourist office on Pragerstr., opposite the *Hauptbahnhof,* is scheduled to open in 1999. It will find private rooms (DM30-50) or hotel rooms for a DM5 fee, and offer guided tours. Open M-F 9am-8pm, Sa 9am-4pm, Su 10am-2pm.

Currency Exchange: ReiseBank, in the main hall of the train station. DM3 for cash exchange, DM7.50 for traveler's checks. Open M-F 7:30am-7:30pm, Sa 8am-noon, 12:30-4pm, Su 9am-1pm. There are also a number of banks on Pragerstr.

American Express: Hoyerzwalderstr. 20 (tel. 80 70 30), in front of the Frauen-kirche. Standard AmEx offerings. Open M-F 7:30am-6pm.

Gay and Lesbian Organizations: Gerede-Dresdner Lesben, Schwule und alle Anderen, Wienerstr. 41 (tel. 464 02 20), in Haus der Jugend, near the station.

Laundromat: Groove Station, Katharinenstr. 11/13. DM5-6. Open Su-F 11am-2am, Sa 10am-late. **Jugendherberge Rudi Arndt,** in the cellar. DM3-4.

Women's Center: Frauenzentrum "sowieso," Dornblüthstr. 18 (tel. 33 77 09). Phone line (tel. 281 77 88) for confidential crisis counseling. Office open M 10am-noon, Tu 10am-6pm, F 9am-noon.

Emergencies: Ambulance, tel. 115. **Fire,** tel. 112.

Police: tel. 110.

Post Office: Hauptpostamt Königbrückerstr. 21/29, 01099 Dresden (tel. 444 10), in Dresden-Neustadt. Open M-F 8am-6pm and Sa 8am-noon.

Internet Access: ComPet, Obergraben 7, right off the *Neustadt's* Hauptstr. DM7 per 30min. Open daily 11am-midnight.

ACCOMMODATIONS, CAMPING, AND FOOD

Dresden is prepared for a convergence of all the citizens of the world, if need be—new hotels and hostels are constantly being planned, built, and opened. The excess of rooms means that you can often find same-day deals at the hotels on Pragerstr.

Jugendgästehaus Dresden (HI), Maternistr. 22 (tel. 49 26 20; fax 492 62 99). Turn left out of the Pragerstr. exit of the *Hauptbahnhof,* following the streetcar tracks along Annonstr. to Freibergerstr. Turn right then take another quick right. Over 400 beds; singles and family rooms available. DM33, over 26 DM38. Nonmembers DM5 extra. Breakfast and sheets included. Reception 4-10pm.

Mondpalast Backpacker, Katharinenstr. 11-13 (tel./fax 804 60 61), a 5min. walk from *Bahnhof-Neustadt,* above Down Town and Groove Station. A brand-new backpacker's paradise. Dorms DM29; doubles DM70. Sheets included. Huge Kitchen. Reception 24hr.

Hostel Die Boote, Louisenstr. 20 (tel. 801 33 61; fax 801 33 62). A renovated apartment building set back in a small courtyard, this new hostel offers 54 beds in immaculate rooms in the middle of the *Neustadt.* Rent bikes here. DM27. Breakfast DM8. One-time fee of DM5 for sheets. Reception 24hr. Call ahead.

Jugendherberge Dresden Rudi Arndt (HI), Hübnerstr. 11 (tel. 471 06 67; fax 472 89 59). From the *Hauptbahnhof,* walk down Fritz-Löffler-Str., bear right onto Münchenerstr., turn right onto Nürnbergerstr. Walk 1 block and turn left. Members only. Central and laid-back. Crowded rooms for 3-5 don't detract from the convenience. DM24, over 26 DM29. Mandatory one-time linen fee DM5. Check-in 3-10pm. Curfew 1am. Lockout 10am-3pm. Reserve ahead Mar.-Aug.

Camping: Campingplatz Altfranken (tel. 410 24 00), in Altfranken, 7km outside of Dresden. Take streetcar 7 to "Julius-Valdrecht," then bus 70 to the end. DM10 per tent. Reception 24hr.

The surge in Dresden tourism has also meant a surge in food prices. The cheapest eats are at **supermarkets** or *Imbiß* stands on Pragerstr. **Raskolnikow,** Böhmischestr. 34, beneath a sign for Galerie Erhard, is a Dostoevskian haunt serving Russian and Afghan fare for DM8-15 (open daily 10am-2am). The chain **Nordsee,** Hauptstr. 14, cooks up every variety of seafood (meals DM8-14; open M-F 9am-7pm, Sa 11am-4pm, Su 8am-3pm). **Tio Pepe,** Louisenstr. 28, serves good Spanish fare (dinners DM15-25; open daily 11am-2am).

SIGHTS AND ENTERTAINMENT

From the banks of the Elbe, the Electors of Saxony once ruled almost all of central Europe. The extravagant art collection of Emperor Augustus the Strong and the incredible palace he built to house it, the **Zwinger,** once rivaled the Louvre. The Semper Wing contains the **Gemäldegalerie Alte Meister,** still one of the world's premier collections of paintings from 1500 to 1800 (open Tu-Su 10am-6pm; DM7, students DM4). Gottfried Semper also designed the **Semper-Oper** (Opera House). The interior is open for fascinating tours (DM8, students DM5; ask at the tourist office for times). Across from the Zwinger lies the nearly restored **Dresdnerschloß** (Dresden Palace), featuring a display on the Renaissance and Baroque eras of the palace and the history of its reconstruction (open Tu-Su 10am-6pm; DM5, students DM3). The nearby **Katholische Hofkirche** (Catholic Royal Chapel), was built to hide the ruling family's Catholic pageantry from Protestant subjects, but is undergoing renovations until early 1999. From the Cathedral, the 16th-century **Brühlsche Terrasse** offers a prime photo opportunity of the Elbe. Turn right at the end to reach the **Albertinum,** another fabulous museum complex. In **Gemäldegalerie der Neuen Meister,** a solid ensemble of German and French Impressionists, including many Renoirs and Gauguins, leads into a collection of Expressionists and *Neue Sachlichkeit* Modernist works that is hard to match. **Grünes Gewölbe,** on the second floor of the Albertinum, has a dazzling collection of completely gratuitous refinements owned by the House of Sachsen (both open F-W 10am-6pm; DM7, students DM4). From the Albertinum, a walk to the *Neumarkt* leads to the shell of the **Frauenkirche,** once Germany's most splendid Protestant church.

A cobblestone, tree-lined pedestrian avenue of shops and restaurants, **Hauptstraße** (Main Street) stretches from the magnificent **Augustus Brücke** (bridge) over the Elbe past the **Goldener Reiter,** a gold-plated vision of Frederick August II (a.k.a. Augustus the Strong). At the other end of Hauptstr., **Albertplatz** (formerly Pl. der Einheit) is surrounded by handsome 19th-century mansions.

Much of the nighttime hustle and bustle takes place around Albertpl. in the *Neustadt,* with the big time bar and hard-core music scene on Alaunstr. At last count, there were over 50 bars packed into this area, bounded by Königsbrückestr., Bischofsweg, Kamenzerstr., and Albertpl. Pick up *Kneipen Surfer* or check out the back of *SAX* magazine (DM2.50) for info. At **Scheune,** Alaunstr. 36-40 (tel. 802 66 19), you can eat Indian food in the garden or candlelit pool hall, then disco to Baltic or Yiddish music (club opens at 8pm; call for a schedule of events). **DownTown and Groove Station,** Katharinenstr. 11-13, is *the* place to shake your booty and indulge in Dresden's neon techno scene with straight, gay, and lesbian co-revelers (cover DM5-7; open Th-M 9pm-5am). The club **AZ Conni,** Rudolf-Leonhard-Str. 39, occupies an old Kindergarten, but that doesn't stop things from getting pretty naughty (open 9pm until late).

■ Near Dresden: Pillnitz

August the Strong must have led a happy life. Among his many castles (almost as numerous as his mistresses), the magnificent gardens of **Schloß Pillnitz** produce a singularly fantastic effect. The turrets of the **Bergpalais** and **Wasserpalais** (modeled on Chinese architectural forms) swim in an amazing setting, surrounded on one side by the Elbe, and the other by gardens in English, Chinese, and just plain decadent styles. The residences now house Dresden's **Kunstgewerbmuseum** (arts and crafts museum), some modern art displays, and lots of porcelain amidst the sumptuously sensual and suggestively salacious summer-like colors of the courtly rooms. (Museum open May-Oct. 9:30am-5:30pm. Bergpalais and Kunstgewerbmuseum closed M, Wasserpalais closed Tu. DM3, students and seniors DM2. Permission to take photos DM3. Grounds open 5am-sunset year round.) To reach Pillnitz from Dresden, take *Straßenbahn* 14 from Pirnaischerpl. ("Kleinzschachwitz") to the last stop (30min.). Get off the *Straßenbahn* and walk towards the banks of the Elbe, where you'll see a ferry shuttling passengers every 15 minutes (DM1.30, children DM1; surcharge DM1 for bicycles, DM5.50 for cars).

■ Sächsische Schweiz (Saxon Switzerland)

One of Eastern Germany's most beloved holiday destinations, Sächsische Schweiz is Germany's newest national park. The region is "Swiss" because of the stunning landscape—sandstone cliffs emerge from dense vegetation, while sumptuous summits and excellent hiking beckon adventurous tourists.

Rathen and Hohnstein Just around the first bend in the Elbe, the magnificent sandstone begins. The first cliffs are called *"Die Bastei"* and were once the roaming grounds of—you guessed it—August the Strong. Closest to Pirna lies Wehlen, and on the other end of the Bastei you'll find **Rathen.** Because of its location on the edge of **Sächsische Schweiz National Park,** hiking trails of all lengths and difficulties (well, they're all pretty steep) abound. Rathen also boasts the **Felsenbühne,** one of Europe's most beautiful open-air theaters, with stone pillars looming over the stage and 2000 seats carved into a cliff. Tickets and schedules are available from the **Theaterkasse** (DM6-39; tel. (035024) 77 70; fax 77 735). A **tourist office** (tel./fax (035024) 704 22), upstairs in the *Gästeamt,* sells maps, finds private rooms, and will help you sort out hiking options (open M-F 9am-noon and 2-6pm, Sa 9am-2pm, closed Sa in winter).

The small village of **Hohnstein** ("high stone" in old Sachsen), with its grand forest vistas on all sides, is linked to Rathen by a beautiful hike through one of the national park's most stunning valleys. To get there from Rathen, follow the path of the red stripe (the trail, not a Maoist paramilitary club). Or take the S-Bahn to "Pirna," and then bus 236 or 237 from the *Bahnhof* to "Hohnstein Eiche" (DM4.10). The town encircles the **Hohnstein Jugendburg,** Am Markt 1 (tel. (035975) 202; fax 203), a fortress which holds a history and nature museum, *Aussichtsturm* (lookout tower), cafe-restaurant, outdoor garden, and **youth hostel** (tel. (035975) 812 02; DM26-37). The **tourist office,** Rathausstr. 10 (tel. (035975) 194 33; fax 868 10), in the *Rathaus,* finds rooms and doles out information on trails and the *Burg* (open M-F 9am-noon and 12:30-5pm, Th until 4pm).

Königstein The next stop on the Dresden S-Bahn journey into the hills and dales of the Sächsische Schweiz is **Königstein.** The *Weiße Flotte* boats also alight on these shores. Above the town looms the **fortress,** whose huge walls are built right into the same stone spires that made Sächsiche Schweiz famous. (Open daily Apr.-Sept. 9am-8pm; Oct. 9am-6pm; Nov.-Mar. 9am-5pm. DM7, students and seniors DM5. Pamphlets in English available at the information office in the castle.) Paths also lead from the town up to the challenging 415m **Lilienstein,** hiked by August the Strong in 1708. The steep 2km hike takes 30 minutes.

The **tourist office,** Schreiberberg 2 (tel. (035021) 682 61; fax 688 87), two blocks uphill from the "Festungs Express" stop, books rooms (DM25-45), but in summer it's wise to call ahead. They have a list of available rooms, vacation houses, and *Pensionen;* prices are in the window when they're closed (open M-Tu and Th-F 9am-noon and 2-6pm, W 2-6pm, Sa 9am-noon; Nov.-Mar. may be open shorter hours). Königstein's **Naturfreunde Jugendherberge,** Halbestadt 13 (tel. (035022) 424 32), is nicer than most hostels but also more expensive. (DM38.40-46.20. Breakfast included. Reception 6am-10pm.) The **campground** (tel. (035021) 682 24), in the shadow of the fortress, is on the banks of the Elbe about 10 minutes upstream from the station. It has washing facilities, a small supply shop, and a playground (DM6.80 per person, DM4 per tent).

■ Leipzig

Leipzig gained fame for its role as the crucible of *die Wende,* the sudden toppling of the GDR in 1989. The city currently jumps out from the calm Eastern German landscape in a fiery blaze of nowNowNOW. The glitzy nightlife and glassy skyscrapers set amidst concrete blights cast a decidedly Western flavor, while the *Uni*-culture spawned by over 20,000 students harkens back to the days when Goethe, Nietzsche, and Leibniz stalked these ivory (well...gray) towers.

ORIENTATION AND PRACTICAL INFORMATION

Most of the sights dwell in the ringed *Innenstadt*. It's a 10-minute walk from the main train station on the north edge of the *Innenstadt* to the **Augustus Platz,** the center surrounded by the *Gewandhaus,* the university, and the main post office. The cavernous **Leipziger Hauptbahnhof** is a sight in itself—its curved-beam roofs enclose one of Europe's largest train stations and recall the grander days of rail travel.

Telephone Code: 0341.
Trains: tel. 194 19. Leipzig lies on the Berlin-Munich line with regular IC service to Frankfurt am Main. Info counter on the platform near track 15.
Public Transportation: Streetcars and **buses** cover the city; the hub is on Pl. der Republik, in front of the train station. 4 1hr. tickets DM8, day card DM7.
Tourist Office: Leipzig Information, Richard-Wagner-Str. 1 (tel. 710 42 60; fax 710 42 76), across Willy-Brandt-Pl. from the station. Brochures, a free map, and accommodations service (M-Sa only). *Kreuzer* (DM2.50) is the best guide to nightlife. Open M-F 9am-8pm, Sa 9am-4pm, Su 9am-2pm.
Currency Exchange: Dresdner Bank, Goethestr. 3-5, just off Augustuspl. Open M-Th 8:30am-7:30pm, F 8:30am-4pm. Several **ATMs.**
Laundromat: Maga Pon, Gottschedstr. 11 (tel. 960 79 22), takes the cake as the jazziest laundromat in Saxony—it doubles as a hep-cat bar and restaurant, so come in your coolest dirty clothes. Wash DM6, dry DM1. Open daily 9am-3am.
Emergencies: Fire, tel. 112. **Ambulance,** tel. 115.
Police: tel. 110.
Pharmacy: Löwen Apotheke, Grimmaischestr. 19 (tel. 960 50 27). Open M-F 8am-8pm, Sa 9am-4pm. After hours, push the button for emergency service.
Post Office: Hauptpostamt 1, across from Augustuspl. on Grimmaischestr. Open M-F 8am-8pm, Sa 9am-4pm. **Postal Code:** 04109.
Internet Access: Cafe le bit, Kohlgartenstr. 2 (tel. 998 20 20; email le-bit@wilder.osten.de).

ACCOMMODATIONS AND FOOD

Budget accommodations in Leipzig are a mess; be sure to book ahead, especially during the summer. Private rooms are reasonable at around DM35 a person, but the tourist office charges a DM10 booking fee per night. The **Jugendherberge Leipzig Centrum (HI),** Volksgartenstr. 24 (tel. 245 70 11; fax 245 70 12) is a 15-minute streetcar ride from the city. Take car 17, 27, or 57 to "Löbanerstr.," then take a right just in front of the supermarket (DM 24, over 26 DM29; breakfast included; reception until 1am; curfew 1am).

To reach **Campingplatz Am Auensee,** Gustav-Esche-Str. 5 (tel. 465 16 00), from the train station, take streetcar 10, 28, or 30 ("Wahren") to "Rathaus Wahren." Turn left at the city hall and then turn right at the end of the street. (Camping DM40 per tent. Small 2-bed bungalows DM50-55. Two-person huts with bath DM80.)

The **Innenstadt** is well supplied with *Imbiß* (snack joints), bistros, and restaurants, although an ever-increasing number are not exactly of the budget variety. The Brühl, running in front of Sachsenpl., offers a lifesaver in the form of **Kaiser's Supermarket.** Sachsenpl. also offers a **market** (Tu and F). **Maga Pon,** Gottschedstr. 11 (tel. 960 79 22), has delicious spaghetti dishes (DM7-9.50; open daily 9am-3am). **Dreiundzwanzigstunden,** on the corner of Emilienstr. and Petersteinweg, heaps up German food at great prices (schnitzel DM5.50-6.90) 23 hours a day (open daily 6am-5am).

SIGHTS AND ENTERTAINMENT

The heart of the city beats in the **Marktplatz,** a colorful square guarded by the 16th-century **Altes Rathaus.** Inside the *Rathaus,* the **Stadtgeschichtliches Museum Leipzig** offers entrancing temporary exhibits and a straightforward look at Leipzig's history (open Tu 2-8pm, W-Su 10am-4pm; DM5, students DM2.50). Just behind the *Altes Rathaus,* on Grimmaische Str., is the temporary home of the **Museum der Bildenden Künste Leipzig** (Museum of Fine Arts; tel. 21 69 90), which chronicles German art from the 18th century to the present. Since World War II, the museum was housed in the supreme court building; however, recently, when the court decided to move back, the museum was left on the street. Close by, on Nikolaistr., the 800-year-old **Nikolaikirche** witnessed the birth of Bach's *Johannes Passion* as well as the GDR's peaceful revolution (open M-Sa 10am-6pm, Su after services; free). Continuing away from the *Marktplatz,* take Universitätsstr. to the former Karl Marx University, now rechristened **Universität Leipzig.**

Just north of the *Neues Rathaus* and close to the *Marktplatz* is the **Thomaskirche,** where Bach served as cantor. Mozart and Mendelssohn also performed in this church, and Wagner was baptized here in 1813. The church is currently undergoing massive restorations for the Bach festival of year 2000. (Open daily in summer 8am-6pm; off-season 9am-5pm; services Su 9:30am and 6pm.) Across the street, the **Johann-Sebastian-Bach-Museum,** Thomaskirchhof 16, chronicles Bach's activities in Leipzig from 1723-1750 (open daily 10am-5pm; last admission 4:30pm; DM4, students DM2.50). North of the Thomaskirche lies Leipzig's most fascinating museum, the **Museum der "Runden Ecke,"** Dittrichring 24. Once the headquarters of the feared East German Ministry for State Security or *Stasi,* the building is now home to an exhibit on the history, doctrine, and tools of the *Stasi* (open W-Su 2-6pm; free).

The tourist office has info on **Bach festivals** in July and August and performances by the famous **Gewandhaus Orchestra** and Leipzig's **Opera** (tel. 126 10; tickets DM8-50; student discounts available). **Moritzbastei,** Universitätsstr. 9 (tel. 702 59 13, tickets tel. 70 25 90), next to the university tower, is one of the more fascinating sights in Leipzig. University students spent two years excavating this series of medieval tunnels so that they could get their groove on, and their hard work definitely didn't go to waste. A totally groovin', yet chill atmosphere presides over the multiple bars and dance-floors. **Karl-Liebknecht-Straße** is just as *Szene*-ic without being claustrophobic. Take streetcar 10 or 11 to "Arndtstr." At night, bars along the street pour drinks for Irish lovers (**Killiwilly** at #44), Francophiles (**Maître** at #62), tough art-house film types (**nato** at #46), caffeine addicts (**KAHWE** at the corner of Arndtstr. and Karl-Liebknecht-Str.), and everyone else (**Weisses Rössel,** next door).

THURINGIA (THÜRINGEN)

Affectionately dubbed the "Green Heart of Germany," Thuringia is certainly the most beautiful of the new Federal States. Echoes of Thuringia are heard throughout Europe's cultural canon: Bach, Goethe, Schiller, Luther, and Wagner all left their mark on this landscape. The Thuringian Forest is the deep green, hilly nucleus of the *Land,* and a necklace of historical cities—among them Jena, Weimar, Erfurt, and Eisenach—are joined by a direct east-west rail line. Relatively unexplored by foreign tourists, Thuringia is the perfect destination for an authentic German experience.

■ Weimar

1999 is a big year for Weimar. It's Goethe's 250th birthday; the Bauhaus movement's 80th birthday; the FRG's 50th birthday; the 10th anniversary of reunification; and Weimar is the designated Cultural Capital of Europe for 1999. In short, the city is going to be one big party. The activity bespeaks a new dynamism which will breath new life into a city whose intellectual ghosts used to dominate: Weimar once was the home to Goethe, Schiller, and Herder; it also expanded the boundaries of the avantgarde in the 20th century, spawning both the Bauhaus architectural movement, as well as the Weimar Republic's remarkably liberal constitution of 1919. On a darker note, Weimar also became the site of Buchenwald. To cap off this century of contradictions, Weimar will exceed all expectations.

SIGHTS AND ENTERTAINMENT One hundred and fifty years after their deaths, Goethe and Schiller still loom large. The **Goethehaus,** on Frauenplan 1, has flawless original manuscripts and letters (open Tu-Su 9am-5pm; DM8, students DM5). Between the Frauenplan and the **Marktplatz** is the beginning of **Schillerstraße,** a vivacious shop-lined pedestrian zone. Nearby, the **Schillerhaus,** at Schillerstr. 12, displays original drafts and early editions of plays (open daily in summer 9am-6pm; in winter 10am-4pm; DM5, students DM3). One block away on Hummelstr., Schiller and Goethe are memorialized in bronze before the **Deutsches Nationaltheater,** which first breathed life into their stage works and where the Weimar Constitution emerged in 1919 (tickets DM9-44; 50% student discounts). Directly across from the theater is the slick new **Bauhaus-Museum** featuring works produced by the Bauhaus School of Design and Architecture (open Tu-Su 10am-6pm; DM5, students DM3).

Steps away from the **Bauhaus Universität** on Marienstr. (connected to the Bauhaus of the 1920s in name only) is the **Franz Liszt Haus,** where the composer spent his last years (open Tu-Su 9am-1pm and 2-6pm; DM4, students DM3). The **Nietzsche-Archiv,** Humboldtstr. 36, was founded by Nietzsche's sister Elisabeth, who helped the Nazis distort her brother's philosophy (open Tu-Su in summer 1-6pm; in winter 1-4pm; DM4, students DM3). **Park an der Ilm** on the river, landscaped by Goethe, sports 18th-century pavilions. Of particular note are the fake ruins built by the Weimar shooting club and the eerie Soviet war memorial. South of the town center, Goethe and Schiller lie in rest together at the **Historischer Friedhof** cemetery (open Mar.-Sept. 8am-9pm; Oct.-Feb. 8am-6pm). The cultural offerings during the **Cultural Capital celebrations** range from the opening of a new museum of modernity to the "universal couch"—a daily five-minute reading of Goethe on a red couch at random and unannounced sites in the city. For a full bill of the action, write **Ticket Service Weimar, 1999 GmbH,** Markt 10, D 99 423 Weimar (tel. (03643) 24 00 24; http://www.weimar1999.de).

PRACTICAL INFO, ACCOMMODATIONS, AND FOOD Weimar is on the Dresden-Frankfurt and Berlin-Frankfurt rail lines; call (03643) 33 30 for schedules and prices. **Weimar Information,** Marktstr. 10 (tel. (03643) 240 00; fax 24 00 40), within view of the *Rathaus,* offers maps and books rooms for a DM5 fee (open M-F 10am-7pm, Sa-Su 10am-4pm). **Walking tours** leave the office daily at 11am and 2pm (DM12, students DM8). Finding a cheap place to stay in town is not difficult. **Jugendhotel Hababusch,** Geleitstr. 4 (tel. 85 07 37; email yh@larry.scc.uniweimar.de), smack in the middle of the sights and run by a bunch of architecture students, is the best-located and coolest place to stay. From Goethepl., turn left on Geleitstr. and follow its rightward twist to the clearing with the statue on the left (DM15; doubles DM20 per person; reception 24hr.). **Jugendherberge Germania (HI),** Carl-August-Allee 13 (tel. 85 04 90; fax 85 04 91), offers newly renovated facilities, and is within spitting distance of the train station (DM23, over 26 DM27, breakfast included; sheets DM7; reception 24hr.).

Weimar is best at cooking for the wealthy; the light of pocket should try the daily **produce market** in the *Marktplatz* or the **Rewe grocery store** at the corner of Frauenplan and Wielandpl. (open M-F 7am-8pm, Sa 7am-4pm). **Da Toni Ristorante Pizzeria,** Windsichenstr. 12 (tel. 50 27 19), serves delicious, no-foolin' Italian food close to Schiller's house—so Italian they hardly understand German (pizzas from DM5.50; open daily 10am-1am). **Bistro Donecker,** Theaterpl. 1, is a cafeteria-style restaurant that serves German and international foods (DM5-12; open M-Sa 7am-6pm, Su 7am-4pm).

■ Near Weimar: Buchenwald

It is especially tragic that a city which reached such heights in humanistic and artistic expression also witnessed one of the greatest failures of human reason and conscience. From 1937 to 1945, the concentration camp at Buchenwald, overlooking Weimar, held over 250,000 Jews, political prisoners, gypsies, and gays. Most did not survive the Holocaust. That the horrors took place behind this barbed wire, on the gravel path on which you stand, is enough to shake the most devout faith. What remains is the **Nationale Mahn-und Gedenkstätte Buchenwald** (National Buchenwald Memorial). At the memorial, signs point to two destinations: the **KZ Lager** and the **Gedenkstätte.** The former refers to the camp, while the latter is a monument overlooking a valley, 20 minutes away. The camp is now a vast, flat, gravel plain. In the large storehouse building, a **museum** documents the history of Buchenwald and Nazism. **Memorial stones** near the former children's barracks read in English, German, and Hebrew: "So that the generation to come might know; that the children, yet to be born, may rise and declare to their children" (camp open May-Sept. Tu-Su 9:45am-5:15pm; Oct.-Apr. Tu-Su 8:45am-4:15pm). To reach the camp, take bus 6 from the station or downtown Weimar (only buses with "B" or "EB" on the schedule and whose front reads "Buchenwald" take you there; M-F 1 per hr.; Sa-Su 1 per 2hr.).

■ Erfurt

The capital of Thuringia, Erfurt surprises its guests with an exquisitely renovated and quirky *Altstadt,* many cosmopolitan cafes, and an abundance of verdant parks. A lot of money has been funneled into Erfurt recently, allowing the cultural offerings to flourish and creating a strikingly picturesque look all too rare in the cities of the east. Dominating the view from the *Marktplatz* atop its perch on Domhügel Hill, the mammoth Erfurt **Dom** is one of Germany's most impressive cathedrals. Martin Luther was invested as a priest here and interrupted his first mass by hurling his Bible across the altar. He claimed the target was the devil himself, impressing his audience if not the Bishop. The *Dom* is further enriched by the adjacent **Church of St. Severi.** (Both open May-Oct. M-F 9am-5pm, Sa 9am-4:30pm, Su 2-4pm; Nov.-Apr. M-Sa 10-11:30am, Su 2-4pm. Mass Su 11am and 6pm.) From the *Domplatz,* Marktstr. leads down to the breezy, open **Fischmarkt,** bordered by restored guild houses sporting wildly decorated facades. Farther down Markstr., the Gera River is spanned by the **Krämerbrücke,** a medieval bridge covered by small shops, some of which date from the 12th century. From the far side of the bridge, follow Gotthardtstr. and cut left through Kircheng. to reach the **Augustinerkloster,** where Martin Luther spent 10 years as a Catholic priest and Augustine monk. He ultimately had the last laugh—the cloister now functions as a Protestant college (ask for times of tours; DM4.50, students DM3).

From Erfurt's Hauptbahnhof, **trains** shoot off to Dresden, Frankfurt (2½hr.), Leipzig (3hr.), and Würzburg (2½hr.). The **tourist office,** Fischmarkt 27 (tel. (0361) 664 00; fax 664 02 90), down the street from the *Rathaus,* has the monthly *Erfurter Magazine,* a useful guide to the city. The office also books rooms (singles DM30-50) for a DM5 fee (open M-F 10am-7pm, Sa-Su 10am-4pm). The best bet for budget beds is the **Jugendherberge Karl Reiman (HI),** Hochheimerstr. 12 (tel. (0361) 562 67 05), an old mansion a fair distance from the city center. From the station, take streetcar 5 ("Steigerstr.") to the last stop, then backtrack a little, and turn left onto Hochheimerstr. (DM24, over 26 DM28; reception 6-9am and 3-10pm; curfew midnight). In a pinch, Weimar's hostels are a 15-minute train ride away. Sample the succulent regional specialty *Thüringer Bratwurst* at markets, street corners, and train stations throughout the city (DM2-3). **Internet-Cafe,** across from the *Hauptbahnhof* at Willi-Brandt-Pl. 1, has pricey but super-fast access (DM12 per hr.; open M-F 7am-8:30pm, Sa-Su 10am-6pm).

■ Eisenach

Birthplace of Johann Sebastian Bach and home-in-exile to Martin Luther, Eisenach boasts impressive humanist credentials. High above Eisenach's half-timbered houses, the **Wartburg Fortress** sheltered the excommunicated Luther in 1521 while he worked on his German translation of the Bible. Check out the amazing view of the Thuringian Forest from the walls of the courtyard. A plethora of city-sponsored **tourist buses** runs from the city center up the enormous hill to the castle (round-trip

DM2.50); for the more adventurous, there are several well-cleared **footpaths** leading up the steep incline. From the train station, a stroll down **Wartburger Allee** leads to the foot of the hill. (Castle open Mar.-Oct. daily 8:30am-5pm; Nov.-Feb. 9am-3:30pm. DM11, students DM6, seniors and disabled DM8.) Town life centers on the pastel **Markt,** bounded by the **Rathaus** and the latticed **Lutherhaus,** Lutherpl. 8, where young Martin lived from 1498 to 1501 (open daily 9am-5pm; DM5, students DM2).

Frequent **train** connections link Eisenach to Erfurt (1hr.) and Weimar (1¼hr.). If you arrive by train, Eisenach's *Bahnhof* provides services for travelers, including **luggage storage, an ATM,** and a **grocery store** open until 8pm. Eisenach's **tourist office,** Bahnhofstr. 3-5 (tel. (03691) 67 02 60), a short walk from the train station, has plenty of info on the castle and books rooms (DM30-40) in private homes (open M 10am-6pm, Tu-F 9am-6pm, Sa 10am-2pm). **Jugendherberge Artur Becker (HI),** Mariental 24 (tel. (03691) 74 32 59), fills a comfortable villa near the castle. From the station, take Bahnhofstr. to Wartburger Allee, which runs into Mariental, or grab bus 3 ("Mariental") to "Lilienstr." (DM22, over 26 DM26; breakfast included; reception 4-9pm). The nearest **camping, Am Altenberger See** (tel./fax (03691) 21 56 37), is about 10km away; from the station, take a bus toward Bad Liebenstein and tell the driver your destination (DM7 per person, DM5 per tent; reception until 10pm).

SAXONY-ANHALT (SACHSEN-ANHALT)

Saxony-Anhalt's endless, mesmerizing grass plains offer one of the more tranquil landscapes in Eastern Germany. Once serving as the stronghold of the Holy Roman Empire, the region today suffers from high unemployment rates and pollution. Yet the area is cleaning up its act. The grand cathedrals filling the skyline attest to the region's former importance, and, with the help of Western tourist dollars, the many construction sites mushrooming across the *Land* point toward the future.

Wittenberg The Protestant Reformation, which initiated centuries of religious conflict, began quietly in Wittenberg on October 13, 1517, when local professor and priest Martin Luther nailed his 95 theses to the wooden door of the Schloßkirche (castle church). All the major attractions are accessible from **Collegienstraße.** At #54 lies Luther's home, **Lutherhalle,** where he lived from 1508. The museum inside chronicles the history of the Reformation (open Tu-Su Apr.-Sept. 9am-6pm; Oct.-Mar. 10am-5pm; DM7, students DM4). Turning right on leaving Lutherhaus brings you to the sickly **elm tree** by Lutherstr. under which Luther defiantly burned a papal decree of excommunication. Farther down Collegienstr., the **Schloßkirche,** crowned by a sumptuous Baroque cupola, holds a copy of the complaints that Luther nailed to its doors. (Open May-Oct. M 2-5pm, Tu-Sa 10am–5pm; Su 11:30am-5pm; Nov.-Apr. M 2-4pm, Tu-Sa 10am-4pm, Su 11:30am-4pm.)

Wittenberg, a mere hour and a half by **train** from Berlin, Halle, and Leipzig, is an excellent daytrip. Instead of disembarking at the *Hauptbahnhof,* get off at the more central *"Haltepunkt Lutherstadt Wittenberg-Elbtor."* Walk straight down Elbstr. to the second intersection. To the right lies Collegienstr. Turn left here instead onto Schloßstr., and walk five minutes to the *Schloß.* Directly across the street, the new **Wittenberg Information,** Schloßpl. 2 (tel. (03491) 49 86 10; fax 49 86 11), caters to all your info, map, and room (for a DM3 fee) needs (open M-F 9am-6pm, Sa 10am-2pm, Su 11am-3pm). The **Jugendherberge (HI)** (tel./fax (03491) 40 32 55) is located in the castle. Newly renovated but often filled with schoolkids, the hostel features some two- to four-bed rooms and many spacious 10- to 18-bed rooms. (DM20, over 26 DM25. Breakfast included. Sheets DM6. Reception 5-10pm.) Cheap yet delectable food is found along the Collegienstr.-Schloßstr. strip.

Dessau Some 30km west of Wittenberg, **Dessau** is worth a daytrip for those interested in the *Bauhaus* school or native son and musician Kurt Weill. A number of buildings in Dessau reflect the *Bauhaus* aesthetic. The school began in Weimar in

GERMANY

Hamburg

ACCOMMODATIONS

- **B** Hotel Alt-Nürnberg
- **C** Hotel Terminus Garni
- **A** Jugendherberge

ST. GEORG

Museum für Kunst und Gewerbe

Außenalster

Binnenalster

Kunsthalle

St. Jacobikirche

St. Petrikirche

Chilehaus

Klosterwall

Johannis Wall

BURCHARDPL.

DEICHTOR PL.

Deichtor-hallen

RATHAUS-MARKT

Rathaus

American Express

St. Nikolaikirche Spire

Katharinen-kirche

ALTSTADT

Speicherstadt

Staatsoper

GÄNSE-MARKT

Hanse Viertel

RÖDINGS MARKT

Stadthausbr.

NEUSTADT

Musikhalle

KARL-MUCK-PLATZ

GROSS NEUMARKT

St. Michaelis-kirche

SCHAAR-MARKT

Stein Hof

Neust Neuerweg

Kleine Wallanlagen

TO PLANTEN UN BLOMEN

Alter Botanischer Garten

TO UNIVERSITY

Wallring Park

Große Wallanlagen

Karolinenstrasse

Heiligengeistfeld

ST. PAULI

PAULINEN-PL.

TO FERNSEHTURM

Budapester Str.

TO ALTONA

FISCHMARKT

St. Pauli Landungsbrücken

Ferry Dock

Elbe

TO FISCHMARKT

400 yards

400 meters

1919 but moved to Dessau from 1925 to 1932, before its exile by the Nazis. American skyscrapers were the highpoint of *Bauhaus,* whose teachers were intrigued by the possibilities of glass and steel. The **tourist office,** Zerbster str. 2c (tel. (0340) 204 14 42), has more info (open M-F 9am-7pm, Sa 9am-noon). After a day of Bauhausing at the **Bauhaus,** Gropiusallee 38, the school for international architecture which houses works of legendary *Bauhausmeisters* Gropius, Klee, and Co., take a rest at the **Jugendherberge (HI),** Waldkaterweg 11 (tel. (0340) 61 94 52). The hostel has a woodsy entrance and is a 25-minute walk from the train station. (DM21, over 26 DM26. Sheets DM6. Check-in M-F 8am-4pm and 7:30-9:30pm, Sa-Su 6-9pm. Check-out 9am.) Every year, the **Kurt Weill Festival** (tel. (0810) 251 13 33) alienates a new generation of fans (Feb. 27-Mar. 8 in 1999; DM10-60).

SCHLESWIG-HOLSTEIN

The only *Land* to border on two seas, Schleswig-Holstein's past and present liveli-hood is based on the trade generated by its port towns. In between the coasts, peace-ful, verdant plains contrast with the often stormy seascapes. Schleswig-Holstein became a Prussian province in 1867 as step one of Bismarck's unification plan, and chose, after World War I, to remain part of Germany, but the *Land* retains close cul-tural and commercial ties with Scandinavia.

Those traveling to Scandinavia by ferry can go through **Kiel.** From the wharf on the west bank, **Baltic Line** (tel. (0431) 98 20 00) ferries go to Sweden (60hr., weekly, DM430), **Color Line** (tel. (0431) 97 40 90) sails to Oslo (18hr., daily, DM150, students 50% off selected sailings), and **Langeland-Kiel** (tel. (0431) 97 41 50; fax 945 15) cruises to Bagenkop, Denmark (2½hr., DM7-9).

■ Hamburg

With a fiercely activist population and a licentious, reckless sex industry, modern Hamburg is a crazy coupling of the progressive and the perverse. A proud tradition of autonomy dates back to 1618, when Hamburg gained the status of Free Imperial City, and even today the city is a politically autonomous *Land.* Restoration and riots deter-mined the post-World War II landscape, but recently Hamburg, the largest port town in Germany, has become a harbor for lonesome sailors, contemporary artists, and rev-elling party-goers who absorb Germany's self-declared "capital of lust."

ORIENTATION AND PRACTICAL INFORMATION

Hamburg's harbor is 100km inland on the north bank of the **Elbe River,** but most major sights lie between the **St. Pauli Landungsbrücken** ferry terminal in the west and the *Hauptbahnhof* (central train station) in the east.

Telephone Code: 040.

Flights: For info, call 507 50. **Lufthansa** (tel. (01803) 80 38 03) and **Air France** (tel. 50 75 24 59) are the two heavy-hitters that fly to Hamburg. **Jasper** (tel. 227 10 60) makes the 25min trip from the Kirchenalle exit of the Hauptbahnof to **Fuhlsbüttel Airport** (every 20min. from 5am-9:20pm, DM8). Or, take U-Bahn 1 or S-Bahn 1 to "Ohlsdorf" and catch the express bus to the airport.

Trains: For train info, call 194 19. The **Hauptbahnhof** handles most traffic, with connections to: Berlin (2¾hr., DM93), Copenhagen (6hr.), Frankfurt (3¾hr., DM182), and Munich (5½hr., DM256). **Dammtor** station is across the Kennedy/ Lombards bridge; **Altona,** the end station for most InterCity trains, is in the west.

Buses: The **bus station (ZOB),** is located across Steintorpl. from the *Hauptbah-nhof;* buses go to Berlin (6 per day, DM40), Copenhagen (5 per week, DM55), and Paris (3 per week, DM90).

Public Transportation: Efficient buses, the U-Bahn, and the S-Bahn cost DM1.80 for single tickets within downtown. 1- and 3-day tickets cost DM 9.50 and 23.30, respectively; consider the **Hamburg Card** instead (see **Tourist Offices,** below). Tickets available at orange *Automaten*. Public transit is closed midnight to 4:30am. For a diagram of Hamburg's public transit network, see this book's **color map.**

Ferries: Scandinavian Seaways, Van-der-Schmissenstr. 4 (tel. 38 90 30; fax 38 90 31 20), about 1km west of the *Fischmarkt* (U-Bahn: Königstr.), runs ferries every other day to England and elsewhere. Tickets from DM183, students DM147. Open M-F 10am-4:30pm; phone reservations M-F 10am-6pm, Sa 10am-2pm. Ferries to Scandinavia leave from Kiel (see p. 383).

Taxis: Taxiruf, tel. 44 10 11.

Tourist Offices: Hamburg's 2 tourist offices supply free maps and pamphlets. The **Hauptbahnhof office,** near the Kirchenallee exit (tel. 30 05 12 01; fax 30 05 13 33; http://www.hamburg-tourism.de), books rooms for a DM6 fee. Open daily 7am-11pm. The less crowded **St. Pauli Landungsbrücken office** (tel. 30 05 12 00), between piers 4 and 5, is open daily 10am-7pm. Both offices sell the **Hamburg Card** (single day DM12.50, 3-day DM24.50, DM10 without public transit), which provides free public transportation and up to 50% off of museums and tours. For advance reservations and info call the **Hamburg Hotline** (tel. 30 05 13 00).

Consulates: Ireland, Feldbrunnenstr. 43 (tel. 44 18 62 13). U-Bahn: Hallerstr. Open 9am-noon. **New Zealand,** Heimhuder Str. 56 (tel. 442 55 50). **U.K.,** Harvestehuder 8a (tel./fax 448 03 20), near U-Bahn: "Hallerstr." Open 9am-noon and 2-4pm. **U.S.,** Alsterufer 27 (tel. 41 17 10), Außenalster's west side. Open M-F 9am-noon.

Currency Exchange: ReiseBank, on the second floor of the central train station, near the Kirchenallee exit, arranges Western Union money transfers, cashes traveler's checks, and exchanges money for a DM3 fee. Open daily 7:30am-10pm. Otherwise, try one of the dozens of banks downtown. Most banks are open M-W and F 9am-1pm and 2:30-4pm, Th 9am-1pm and 2:30-6pm.

American Express: Ballindamm 39, 20095 Hamburg (tel. 30 90 80, refund service (0130) 85 31 00; fax 30 90 81 30). Mail held for cardmembers (no charge). All banking services. Open M-F 9am-5:30pm, Sa 10am-1pm.

Lesbian and Gay Services: Hein und Fiete Gay & Lesbian Information Center, Pulverteich 17-21 (tel. 24 03 33). Open M-F 4-9pm, Sa 4-7pm. **Magnus Hirschfeld Centrum,** Borgweg 8 (tel. 279 00 69). U-Bahn 3 or bus 108: "Borgweg." Open M and F 2-6pm, Tu-W 7-10pm; cafe open daily 5pm-midnight.

Laundromat: Schnell und Sauber, Grindelallee 158, in the university district. Wash DM6 per 6kg, soap included. Dry DM1 per 15min. Open daily 6am-11pm.

Rape Crisis Line: tel. 25 55 66. Phones staffed M and Th 9:30am-1pm and 3-7pm, Tu-W 9:30am-1pm and 3-4pm, F 9:30am-1pm.

Emergencies: Ambulance, tel. 112.

Police: Tel. 110. Station at Kirchenallee 46, opposite the train station.

Pharmacy: Exit the Hauptbahnhof on Kirchenallee and turn right. The staff of the **Senator-Apotheke** speaks English. Open M-F 7am-8pm, Sa 8am-4pm.

Post Office: At the Kirchenallee exit of the train station. Open M-F. 8am-8pm, Sa 8am-6pm, Su 10am-4pm. *Poste Restante,* Gr. Burstah 3, 20097 Hamburg, at main branch. Open M-F 8am-6pm, Sa 8am-noon.

Internet Access: On the 2nd floor of the **Staats- und Universitäts-bibliotek,** Von Melle Park 3. Open M-F 9am-9pm; Aug. M-F 9am-7:30pm, Sa 10am-1pm.

Telephones: Make international calls (with German phone card) at the post office in the train station. Phone cards are available in denominations of DM12 or DM50.

ACCOMMODATIONS AND CAMPING

Hamburg is expensive: single rooms start at around DM60, doubles at DM75. A slew of small, relatively cheap *Pensionen* line **Steindamm, Steintorweg, Bremer Weg,** and **Bremer Reihe** around the *Hauptbahnhof*. While the area is filled with drug-addicts and wannabe mafiosi, the hotels are relatively safe. Women traveling alone, however, should investigate other alternatives. Check out your hotel before you accept a room, or let the tourist office's *Hotelführer* (DM1) help steer you clear. For longer stays, try the **Mitwohnzentrale** at Lobuschstr. 22 (tel. 194 45).

Schanzenstern Übernachtungs-und-Gasthaus, Bartelsstr. 12 (tel. 439 84 41; fax 439 34 13; http://www.schanzenstern.de). U- and S-Bahn 3 or S-Bahn 21: Sternschanze. Walk left onto Schanzenstr., right on Susannenstr., left to Bartelsstr. Run by a progressive co-op in the student district. Clean, quiet, bright, and tastefully decorated. Dorms DM33; singles DM60; doubles DM90; triples DM110. Breakfast buffet DM11. Reserve ahead in summer and at New Year's. Wheelchair accessible.

Jugendherberge auf dem Stintfang (HI), Alfred-Wegener-Weg 5. (tel. 31 34 88; fax 31 54 07; email jh-stintfang@t-online.de). Reservations via Internet at http://www.schoelzel.com/jh-hamburg/index.shtml. S-Bahn 1, 2, or 3, or U-Bahn 3: Landungsbrücke. Great location near the Reeperbahn and the U-Bahn; harbor view. DM29.50, over 26 DM35. Sheets and breakfast included. Doubles and family rooms available. Reception 7-9:30am and 12:30pm-1am. Curfew 1am. Stragglers admitted at 2am. Reservations essential.

Hotel Alt Nurnberg, Steintorweg 15 (tel. 24 60 23; fax 280 46 34). From station, go straight ahead from Kirchenalle, veering off toward Steintorpol on the right. In the heart of Hamburg's somewhat sketchy *Hauptbahnhof* neighborhood. Clean, fairly safe, and smallish rooms with telephones. Singles DM60-90; doubles DM90-130.

Hotel Terminus Garni, Steindamm 5 (tel. 280 31 44; fax 24 15 18). From the *Hauptbahnhof*'s Kirchenalle exit, turn right. Doubles DM45, with shower DM60; triples with bath DM165. Breakfast included. Reception 24hr.

Camping: Campingplatz Rosemarie Buchholz, Kielerstr. 374 (tel. 540 45 32). From Altona train station, bus 182 or 183: "Basselweg," then walk 100m in the same direction as the traffic. Leafy setting near a very busy access road. DM7 per person. Showers DM1.50. Reception 7am-10pm. Call ahead.

FOOD

The most interesting part of town from a culinary standpoint is **Sternschanze,** where Turkish fruit stands, Asian *Imbiße*, and avant-garde cafes entice the hungry passersby with good food and atmosphere. Slightly cheaper establishments abound in the **university** area, especially along Rentzelstr., Grindelhof, and Grindelallee. In **Altona,** the *Fußgängerzone* (pedestrian zone) leading up to the train station is packed with ethnic food stands and produce shops. Check out the **Mercado** mall, whose 30 eateries include everything from sushi bars to Portuguese fast-food. There's even a **Safeway** (open M-F 10am-8pm, Sa 9am-4pm). In a pinch, the shopping arcade at the **Hauptbahnhof** has about a dozen fast food joints (open daily 6am-11pm).

Mensa, Schlüterstr. 7. S-Bahn: "Dammtor," then head north on Rothenbaumchaussee, left on Moorweidenstr., then right onto Schlüterstr. University cafeteria. Hang with students and check bulletin boards for special events. Meals DM1.70-6 with student ID; more for non-students. Open M-F 11am-2pm and 4-7pm.

Asia Imbiß Bok, Bartelstr. 29. U-Bahn 3: Sternschanze. *Imbiß* is a misnomer here—this joint serves restaurant food. Try the spicy Thai noodles, or other savory Korean and Chinese options (DM6-12). Full Korean dinner DM25. Open daily 10am-8pm.

Noodles, Schanzenstr. 2-4. Serves up veggie dishes and innovative pasta creations alongside a full bar. Open Su-Th 10am-1am, F-Sa 10am-3am.

Falafel-König, Schanzenstr. 113. Serves all varieties of falafel and other Lebanese fare (from DM5). Open daily 10am-11pm.

Machwitz, Schanzenstr. 121. Hip student crowd. *Tagesmenu* (daily special) DM 9.80. Occasional concerts by local bands. Open daily 10am until everyone leaves.

Geo Pizza aus dem Holzbackofen, Beim Schlump 27. Delectable pizzas (DM8-15), baked in an oven hot enough to make steel glow. Try the Inferno Pizza if you're feeling brave. Open Su-Th 11am-1am, F-Sa 11am-2am.

SIGHTS

The **Hamburg Hafen** lights up nightly with ships from around the world. After sailing the East Indies, the 19th-century **Windjammer Rickmer Rickmers** was docked at Pier 1 and restored as a museum. *(Open daily 10am-6pm; DM6, students DM5.)* Inside the

GERMANY

building behind Pier 6 resides the elevator to the **Old Elbe Tunnel.** With all its machinery exposed, the building looks like a nautilus machine for the gods.

The copper spires of the **Rathaus,** a richly ornamented 19th-century monstrosity, rises above the city center. For English tours, call 36 81 24 70. *(Every hr.; M-Th 10:15am-3:15pm, F-Su 10:15am-1:15pm.)* Built in 1932, the **column** to the left of the *Rathaus* stands in memorial to the 40,000 Hamburg men who died in World War I. To the north of the *Rathaus* are the two **Alster lakes** bordered by arbored paths, elegant promenades, commercial facades, and water sport fiends. To the west, the **Planten un Blomen** park provides a bucolic sanctuary on the edge of the downtown. From May to September daily performances from Irish step-dancing to the police orchestra resound from the outdoor **Musikpavillon.**

Just south of the *Rathaus,* off Ost-Weststr., stand the somber ruins of the **St. Nikolaikirche.** An early example of neo-Gothic architecture, the church was flattened by Allied bombing in 1943. The area behind the church is a zig-zagging maze of canals and bridges centered on the **Alte Börse** (old stock market). The buildings along the nearby **Trostbrücke** sport huge copper models of clipper ships on their spires—a reminder of the importance of sea-trade in the making of Hamburg's wealth. The gargantuan 18th-century **Große Michaelskirche** is the grandaddy of all Hamburg churches. *(Tower and church open Apr.-Sept. M-Sa 9am-6pm, Su 11:30am-5:30pm; Oct.-Mar. M-Sa 10am-4:30pm, Su 11:30am-4:30pm. Church DM1.)*

The pedestrian shopping zone which stretches from the *Rathaus* to the *Hauptbahnhof* along **Mönckebergstraße,** is punctuated by two spires. The first belongs to the **St. Petrikirche,** site of the oldest church in Hamburg. *(Open M-F 9am-6pm, Sa 9am-5pm, Su 9am-noon and 1-5pm. English services 1st Su of every month at 5pm.)* The second church in the area is the **St. Jakobikirche,** known for its 14th-century **Arp-Schnittger organ.** *(Open daily 10am-5pm.)*

The dozens of museums in Hamburg range from the erotic to the Victorian. **Hamburger Kunsthalle,** Glockengiesserwall 1, one block north of the *Hauptbahnhof,* holds an extensive and dazzling collection of art from the medieval to the modern. *(Open Tu-Su 10am-6pm, Th 10am-9pm. DM15, students DM10.)* Hamburg's contemporary art scene resides at **Deichtorhallen Hamburg,** Deichtorstr. 1-2, with mind-boggling architecture. *(U-Bahn: Steinstr. Open Tu-Su 11am-6pm. DM10, students DM8.)* The **Erotic Art Museum,** Nobistor 12, has a stimulating collection of art and porn. *(S-Bahn: "Reeperbahn" or U-Bahn: "St. Pauli." Open Tu-Su 10am-midnight. DM15, students DM10.)* The **Museum für Kunst und Gewerbe,** Steintorpl. 1, one block south of the *Hauptbahnhof,* has exhibits of Egyptian, Roman, and Asian handicrafts, china, and furnishings, as well as a Lego reconstruction of the life and times of the ancient Egyptians. *(Open Tu-W and F-Su 10am-6pm, Th 10am-9pm. DM10, students and seniors DM6, Hamburg Card holders DM5.)*

ENTERTAINMENT AND NIGHTLIFE

The cultural capital of the North, Hamburg patronizes the arts generously with both money and attention, keeping ticket prices down. For DM20, the **Kulturkarte** offers steep discounts at theatres, concert halls, museums, and even churches. Call 300 51 300 for details. The **Staatsoper,** Dammtorstr. 28 (tel. 35 17 21; tickets from DM7), houses one of the best opera companies in Germany, and the associated **ballet** company is the acknowledged dance powerhouse of the nation. **Orchestras** abound—the **Philharmonie,** the **Hamburg Symphony,** and the **Nord-Deutscher-Rundfunk** are the big three. Lighter music, popular musicals, and transvestite cabarets play at the **Operettenhaus Hamburg,** the **Neue Flora Theater,** and other smaller venues. Call the tourist office for info. Traditional jazz can be found at the Fish Auction Hall of the **Fischmarkt.** International rock groups play at **Docks,** Spielbudenpl. 19 (tel. 319 43 78). The renowned **Fabrik,** Barnerstr. 36 (tel. 39 10 70; cover around DM12), in Altona, features everything from funk to punk. Pick up a copy of *Szene, Oxmox,* or *Prinz* (free at hostels) for the latest info on the music scene.

The heart of Hamburg's nightlife lies in St. Pauli on the **Reeperbahn,** featuring the best clubs and bars, as well as porn theaters and sex shops to satisfy the naval libido.

Mojo Club, Reeperbahn 1, has more attitude than it knows what to do with and was labeled "Germany's Best Club" by MTV. The attached **Jazz Cafe** also attracts the trendy (club open W-Th 10pm-4am, F-Su 11pm-4am; DM10 cover on weekends). **Große Freiheit 36/Kaiser Keller,** Große Freiheit 36 (tel. 31 42 63), featured the Beatles back in the day downstairs and today showcases the Wu-Tang Clan upstairs (open daily; call for info). **Molotow,** Spielbudenpl. 5, parallel to the Reeperbahn, spins an eclectic mix of hip-hop, garage, salsa, and industrial (open Th-Sa 10pm-late; cover DM10). **Herbertstraße,** south of the Reeperbahn off Davidstr., is a legalized prostitution strip, open only to men over 18. If you're female and out late in the area, take a cab.

Students avoiding the debauchery of the Reeperbahn head north to the spiffy streets of **Sternschanze** and **Altona.** Unlike St. Pauli, these areas are centered around cafes and weekend extravaganzas of the alternative flavor. **Rote Flora,** Schulterblatt 71, a cafe during the week and a night club during the weekend is the nucleus of the Sternschanze scene (cafe open M-F 5pm-10pm; weekend cover from DM8). Much of the Hamburg gay scene is located in the **St. Georg** area of the city, near the *Hauptbahnhof.* **Front,** Heidencampsweg 32 (U-Bahn 3: Berliner Tor), is a jungle and house haven for both the gay and lesbian scene and straight people just trying to stay hip (open W and F-Sa at 11pm; cover DM10-12), while **Frauenkneipe,** Stresemannstr. 60 (S-Bahn: Altona), is a bar for gay and straight women (open M-F 8pm-1am, Sa 9pm-3am, Su 8pm-1am).

■ Lübeck

With a skyline of neo-classical townhouses punctuated by 13th-century copper spires, Lübeck is easily Schleswig-Holstein's most beautiful city. The *Altstadt,* though leveled in 1942 and rebuilt with Marshall Plan funds, has successfully staved off inroads by modern architecture, giving it a slightly anachronistic feeling. Between the inner city and the train station is the massive **Holstentor,** one of the four gates built in the 15th century and the symbol of Lübeck. The centerpiece of the *Altstadt* is the **Rathaus,** a 13th-century structure of glazed brick (tours M-F at 11am and noon; DM4, students DM2). Lübeck is world famous for its organ concerts, and behind the *Marktplatz,* the Romanesque/Gothic **Marienkirche** boasts the largest mechanical organ in the world. (Church open daily 10am-4pm; in summer until 6pm. Free. Several concerts per week Apr.-Dec., including Sa 6:30pm. DM9, students DM6.) Also of note is the church's reproduction of its famous **Totentanzbild,** a mural depicting the era of the plague. Opposite the Marienkirche is the **Buddenbrookhaus,** Mengstr. 4, a museum dedicated to the life and work of local heroes and literary giants Heinrich and Thomas Mann (open daily 10am-5pm; DM7, students DM4). At the **Behnhaus** and **Drägerhaus** museums, modern art clashes with the neoclassical architecture of an 18th-century townhouse. (Open Tu-Su 10am-4pm; Apr.-Sept. until 5pm. DM5, students DM3, free first F of month.) On Schmiederstr., the steeple of the 750-year-old **Petrikirche** gives a sweeping view. (Church open daily noon-7pm. Tower open Apr.-Oct. 9am-7pm. DM3.50, students DM2.)

Frequent **trains** serve Lübeck from Hamburg (40min.) and Berlin (4hr.). Skip the **tourist office** in the train station; their maps are DM4 and their room booking fee is a stiff DM5 plus 10% of your hotel bill. Instead, try the office in the *Altstadt* at Breiterstr. 62 (tel. (0451) 122 54 13 or 122 54 14). They don't book rooms, but the helpful staff will point you in the right direction and give you a free map (open M-F 9:30am-6pm, Sa-Su 10am-2pm). **Rucksack Hotel,** Kanalstr. 70 (tel./fax (0451) 70 68 92), in the *Altstadt* by the canal, has bright, cheery rooms (dorms DM24-28; double DM80; quad DM136; reception 9am-1pm and 3-10pm). **Jugendgästehaus Lübeck (HI),** Mengstr. 33 (tel. (0451) 702 03 99; fax 770 12), is a superb hostel (DM26.50-40; call ahead). **Sleep-In (CVJM),** Große Petersgrube 11 (tel. (0451) 789 82), near the Petrikirche, is a clean, laid-back YMCA. (Dorms DM15; doubles DM40. Sheets DM5. Reception M-F 8am-5pm, Sa-Su 8am-noon.) **Tipasa,** Schlumacher. 12-14, serves pizza and pasta for a hungry student crowd. (Tipasa-topf stew DM11. Open noon-1am, F-Sa till 2am;

Insults for Sale

The concept of free speech in Germany does not imply *cost-free* speech. While doling out compliments requires no budget, dropping insults will unload your wallet in no time. Public humiliation in Germany carries such destructive force that officials have created an insult price list. Angry, offended, or drunk budget travelers should beware. The heaviest fines are incurred by mouth-flappers who put down a female police officer's respectability: belting out *Trottel in Uniform* (fool in uniform) costs DM3000, while the lesser insult *Dumme Kuh* (dumb cow) requires a mere DM1200 payoff. Call any uniformed official *Idiot* (idiot), and you'll be out a whopping DM3000. The budget traveler's insult, *Holzkopf* (wood-headed), goes for DM1500. Equivalent insults in English are not exempt; stories abound of policemen who've doled out thousands of *Marks* in fines to tourists who think that Germans don't understand what "asshole" means. We tell you this merely as a warning—and prices, of course, are subject to change, you idiot.

---

kitchen closes 30min. before close.) **Cafe Affenbrot,** Kanalstr. 70, serves veggie dishes (open daily 9am-midnight; kitchen closes 11:30pm). **I. G. Niederegger,** Breitestr. 89, opposite the *Rathaus,* is famous for its marzipan. For entertainment listings, pick up *Piste, Szene, Zentrum,* or *Zimtzicke* (for women) from the tourist office.

■ Schleswig

Schleswig, at the southern end of the **Schlei inlet,** has picture-perfect fishing settlements, a 16th-century castle, and extensive museum collections. Towering over the meandering cobblestoned streets of the *Altstadt* is the 12th-century **St. Petri-Dom,** famous for its intricately carved wooden altarpiece (open M-Sa 9am-5pm, F closes 3pm; Su 1-5pm; tower DM2). The 16th-century **Schloß Gottorf** houses the **Landesmuseen,** a treasure trove of Dutch, Danish, and Art Deco pieces. On the other side of the castle, the **Kreuzstall** houses the **Museum des 20. Jahrhunderts,** devoted to *Brücke* school artists. The surrounding park is an **outdoor sculpture museum** (all daily 9am-5pm; Nov.-Feb. 9:30am-4pm; DM7, students DM3). Get answers to those burning questions on Viking life at the **Wikinger Museum Haithabu** (Apr.-Oct. daily 9am-5pm; Nov.-Mar. Tu-Su 9am-4pm; DM2, students DM1; round-trip ferry DM6).

Schleswig's **train station** is far from the city center; take bus 1, 2, 4, or 5 from the stop outside the *ZOB,* close to the *Altstadt* (15 min., DM1.80). Trains go hourly to Kiel, Flensburg, Husum, and Hamburg (via Neumünster). The **tourist office,** Plessenstr. 7 (tel. (04621) 248 78 or 207 03), up the street from the harbor, books private and hotel rooms on the spot for DM2. (Open M-F 9:30am-12:30pm and 1:30-5pm, Sa 9am-noon; Oct.-Apr.closed F afternoons and Sa.) The **Jugendherberge (HI),** Spielkoppel 1 (tel. (04621) 238 93), is close to the town center. Take bus 2 ("Hühnhauser-Schwimmhalle") to "Schwimmhalle." Great location and an inlet view (DM20-25; sheets DM7; reception 7am-1pm and 5-11pm). Try the fresh, cheap seafood at the *Imbiße* down by the *Stadthafen.*

LOWER-SAXONY (NIEDERSACHSEN)

Extending from the Ems River to the Harz Mountains and from the North Sea to the hills of central Germany, Lower-Saxony has two distinct flavors. Along the northern coast, descendants of the Frisians run their fishing boats from ports built on foggy marshland, while the vast remainder of the *Land* is a broad plain which supports agricultural communities.

■ Hanover (Hannover)

Defying its relatively small size, Hanover puts on a magical display of cultural and cosmopolitan charm. With great economic vigor, a wealth of museums, an unmatched concert hall, and a tradition of outdoor festivals, the city reigns as the political and cultural capital of Lower Saxony. To fully experience Hannover, follow the **Red Thread,** a 4km walking tour guided by a red line connecting all the major sites. Painstakingly recreated after World War II, the modern **Neues Rathaus** offers an amazing tower view. (Tower open Apr.-Oct. M-F 9:30am-5:30pm, Sa-Su 10am-5pm. DM3, students DM2.) While wandering through the wild and ambitious landscaping of the **Herrenhausen Gardens** you'll pass exotic vegetation, Europe's highest garden fountain (80m), and the 18th-century **Herrenhausen Palace.** Take U-Bahn 4 to "Herrenhäuser Gärten." (Gardens open Apr.-Oct. M-Tu 8am-8pm, W-Su 8am-11pm; Nov.-Mar. daily 8am-dusk. DM3. Fountains open M-F 11am-noon and 3-5pm, Sa-Su 11am-noon and 2-5pm. DM3. Light show W 5-7:30pm. DM5.) The **Sprengel Museum,** Kurt-Schwitters-Pl., is a modern art lover's dream—Turrell, Dalí, Picasso, Magritte, and Antes highlight the impressive collection (open Tu 10am-8pm, W-Su 10am-6pm; DM7, students DM3.50).

The **tourist office,** Ernst-August Pl. 2 (tel. (0511) 30 14 20 or 21; fax 30 14 14), near the train station, dispenses maps, and organizes 16 different tours (open M-F 9am-7pm, Sa 9:30am-3pm). To avoid the exorbitant DM10 room-finding fee, ask for the free hotel list. **Naturfreundehaus Misburg,** Am Fahrhorstfelde 50 (tel. (0511) 58 05 37; fax 958 58 36), offers rooms close to a beautiful lake brimming with ducks. Take U-Bahn 4 ("Roderbruch") to "Misburger Str.," then take bus 631 to "Misburg Waltfriedhof," and follow Am Fahrhorstfelde to the end (DM30; sheets DM7.50; reception Tu-F 2-8pm; reservations needed). **Naturfreundehaus Stadtheim,** Hermann-Bahlsen-Allee 8 (tel. 69 14 93; fax 69 06 52), has relatively tiny rooms, but their breakfast is superior. Take U-Bahn 3 or 7 to "Spannhagengarten," backtrack 15m to the intersection, and follow Hermann-Bahlsen-Allee (15min.) until you see the sign pointing towards the hostel on the right hand side of the road (DM35; breakfast included; reception 8am-10:30pm; no curfew). The **Kröpcke,** a world-renowned cafe/food court in the center of the pedestrian zone, can provide ample eats. The **Peach Pit,** Lister Meile 5 (tel. 34 34 32), is a late night/early morning haven for the drunk, tired, and hungry. (Open W 8pm-2am, Th 6am-2am, and 6pm on F to 2pm on Su; yes, that's 56hr. straight of service!) Check *Prinz* (DM4.50) or the free *MagaScene* for a guide to nightlife, or head to **The Capitol,** Schwarzer Bär 2 (tel. (0511) 44 40 66; call for a schedule). A hip student joint, **The Loft,** Georgstr. 50b, is close to Kröpcke.

■ Bremen

Bremen's cultural flair, liberal politics, and strong desire to remain an independent *Land* have caused Germans to coin the adjective *bremisch,* which simply means something unusual. Bremen has given up its Hanseatic ambience for a rebellious cosmopolitan flair—people here flaunt high-flying don't-thread-on-me attitudes. The *Altstadt* revolves around the ornate **Rathaus,** which was spared during World War II by a pilot who could not bear to bomb it. (Tours usually M-F 10, 11am, and noon, Sa-Su 11am and noon. Ask at the tourist office.) The **St. Petri Dom,** Sandstr. 10-12, next to the *Rathaus,* has a mosaic interior of orange, gold, and gray stone arches (open M-F 10am-5pm, Sa 10am-1:45pm, Su 2-5pm; free). If you can't resist the yeasty smell of brewing beer, head across the Weser to **Beck's Brewery** for tours (DM5).

Bremen lies below the mouth of the Weser River at the North Sea, just over an hour from Hamburg and Hanover by train. The **tourist office** (tel. (0421) 308 00 51; fax 308 00 30), across from the train station, offers info and books rooms for a DM3 fee plus a DM10-20 deposit (open M-W 9:30am-6:30pm, Th-F 9:30am-8pm, Sa 9:30am-4pm). Inexpensive hotels fill fast in Bremen, so call ahead. To reach the sleek **Jugendgästehaus Bremen (HI),** Kalkstr. 6 (tel. (0421) 17 13 69; fax 17 11 02), take bus 26 or streetcar 1 or 6 to "Am Brill," then walk along Bürgermeister-Smidt-Str. to

GERMANY

the river, turn right, and walk two blocks (DM27, over 26 DM32; reception 24hr.). **Hotel-Pension Garni Weidmann,** Am Schwarzen Meer 35 (tel. (0421) 498 44 55), has plush comforters and cavernous rooms fit for royalty. Take streetcar 10 to "St.-Jürgen-Str." and continue down the tracks for 300m. (Singles from DM40; doubles from DM80. 2-week advance reservations recommended.) In the *Rathaus,* Bremen's renowned **Ratskeller** is one of the oldest wine bars in Germany. (From DM4.40 per glass; meals DM40. Open 24hr.; kitchen open noon-2:30pm and 6-11pm.) For a cheap meal, try the open-air **market** nearby (open daily 8am-2pm).

■ Göttingen

Göttingen, home of Europe's first free university, remains a college town to the bone. Its scenic **Altstadt** lies within the confines of the horseshoe-shaped **Ernst-Hönig Wall.** At its center, you can find the **Altes Rathaus** (town hall), which serves as a meeting spot for the whole town. Make sure you kiss the little **Gänsliesel** (goose-girl) on the fountain—she's known as the "most-kissed girl in the world" after centuries of graduates have lined up to embrace her on receiving their diplomas. **Bismarckturm** (Bismarck tower), im Hainberg, in the *Stadtforest,* commemorates the troublemaking of political giant Otto von Bismarck and offers a splendid view of the town (open Sa-Su 11am-6pm; free). The **Städtisches Museum,** Ritterplan 7 (tel. (0551) 400 28 43), gives a detailed examination of the city over the past few millennia. Theater buffs have excellent options with the world-class **Deutsches Theater,** Theaterpl. 11 (tel. (0551) 49 69 11), and the innovative **Junges Theater** (tel. (0551) 551 23).

Situated in the southern part of Niedersachsen, Göttingen is easily reached by train from Frankfurt (2½hr.), Hamburg (2hr.), and Hannover (1hr.). The **tourist office,** Markt 9 (tel. (0551) 540 00; fax 400 29 98; email tourismus@goettingen.de), in the Altes Rathaus, books rooms (from DM45) and dispenses information. (Open Apr.-Oct. M-F 9:30am-6pm, Sa-Su 10am-4pm; Nov.-Mar. M-F 9am-6pm, Sa 10am-1pm.) **Jugendherberge (HI),** Habichtsweg 2 (tel. (0551) 576 22; fax 438 87), puts most hostels to shame with immaculate rooms and many singles. Take bus 8, 10, 11, 15, or 18 to "Kornmarkt" and then bus 6 ("Theaterpl./Klausberg") to "Jugendherberge" (DM22, over 26 DM27; reception 6:30am-11:30pm). **Nudelhaus,** Rotestr. 13 (tel. (0551) 442 63), has a fully-stocked international menu and a backyard beer garden (DM8-13; open daily noon-11:30pm). Göttingen's student population gives the town a hyperactive nightlife: try **Outpost,** Königsallee 243 (tel. (0551) 662 51), the best dance club in the city (open Tu, F-Sa 9pm-1am). Or hit **Blue Note,** Wilhelmspl. 3 (tel. (0551) 469 07), for live music and big name DJs (open M-F 6pm-2am, Sa-Su 8pm-3am). **Irish Pub,** Mühlenstr. 4, is a popular student hangout (open daily 6pm-2am).

■ Harz Mountains

Heinrich Heine wrote that even Mephistopheles trembled when he approached the Harz, the devil's dearest mountains. It's easy to see why Heine—as well as Goethe, Bismarck, and a host of others—fell in love with the mist-shrouded woodlands, which stretch from the western **Oberharz** to the eastern **Ostharz.** Germany's 45-year political division allowed the Harz to flourish in an artificial time warp. Since the region straddled the Iron Curtain, both East and West declared much of it off-limits, sparing its natural gifts and mist-shrouded health resorts in the south from development. Spring thaws turn ski slopes into webs of hidden hiking trails. The **Harzerquerbahn** and **Brockenbahn,** antique narrow-gauge railways, steam through gorgeous Harz scenery from Nordhausen to Wernigerode. The Harzer Verkehrsverband **regional tourist office,** Marktstr. 45 (tel. (05321) 340 40; fax 34 04 66), inside the Industrie und Handels Kammer building, sells the indispensable *Grüner Faden fur den Harz-Gast* pamphlet (DM5), which lists nearby attractions. Also pick up *Reiseführer "Harz"* (DM9.80), a guide to the mountains' main attractions, and the *Taschen-Fahrplan "Harz"* (DM3), which tells you how to get to all of them via public transportation (open M-F 8am-4pm).

Goslar Forty minutes by train from Hanover, **Goslar's** *Altstadt* is congested with immaculate half-timbered houses and winding narrow streets, which have changed little since the town lost its mining rights in the 16th century. Goslar's postcard perfection, with its divine location at the edge of the lush, green Harz Mountains, has turned it into something of a tourist trap. The hub of an extensive bus network, Goslar allows easy access to any part of the region. **Kaiserpfalz** (Imperial Palace), Kaiserbleek 6, is a massive Romanesque palace that served as the ruling seat for 11th- and 12th-century emperors (open daily Apr.-Oct. 10am-5pm; Nov.-Mar. 10am-4pm; DM3.50, children DM2). The interior of the great hall is plastered with 19th-century murals; the huge paintings display carefully selected historical incidents in a mythic, pompous manner. The **Mönchehaus,** Mönchestr. 3, exhibits a grand modern art collection including the works of Miró and Calder (open Tu-Sa 10am-1pm and 3-5pm, Su 10am-1pm; donations requested).

The **tourist office,** Markt 7 (tel. (05321) 780 60; fax 230 05), across from the *Rathaus,* finds rooms (from DM30) for free. To get there from the station, turn left and walk to the end of Rosentorstr., which becomes Hokenstr. (Open May-Oct. M-F 9:15am-6pm, Sa 9:30-4pm, Su 9:30-2pm; Nov.-Apr. M-F 9:15am-5pm, Sa 9:30am-2pm.) The **Jugendherberge (HI),** Rammelsbergerstr. 25 (tel. (05321) 222 40), wins the prize for most confusing location, but there's a shortcut: from the Marktpl., take Bergstr. southwest until it ends at Clausthalerstr. Directly across the street, follow the stairway between the trees, head right at the fork halfway up (20min.). (DM20, over 26 DM25. Breakfast included. Members only. Reception 9:30am-10pm. Check-in after 3pm. Curfew midnight.) **Campingplatz Sennhütte,** Clausthalerstr. 28 (tel. (05321) 224 98), 3km from town along the B241, has a restaurant and sauna (DM5.50 per person, DM4 per tent; showers DM1).

Bad Harzburg and Torfhaus Offering few other attractions, **Bad Harzburg** is the gateway to the **Harz National Park,** a stunning nature and wildlife preserve. The **Haus der Natur** (tel. (05322) 17 74; fax 17 94), in the Kurpark, has a plethora of pamphlets and an exhibition detailing the park's history and wildlife (open W-M 10am-5pm; DM5 donation requested, children DM3). By the station, the **tourist office** (tel. (05322) 29 27) finds rooms (from DM30) for a DM5 fee (open M-F 9am-1pm and 3-6pm, Sa 10am-1pm). **Torfhaus** offers an airy mountain hostel, near-perfect hiking trails, and the Harz's highest mountain, the 1142m **Brocken.** The town marks the midpoint of the Bad Harzburg-Braunlage bus route 63 (20min., daily 7:45am-8:25pm, DM3.80). An alternative to the 16km hike along the **Goethe Weg** is the expensive **Schmalspurchbahn,** a train that carries the fatigued from Weingerode to Brocken's peak (see below; 1½hr., DM42, round-trip DM42). The **Nationalpark Torfhaus,** Torfhaus 21 (tel./fax (05320) 263), sells maps of the trails around Brocken (open daily 9am-5pm). Walking away from Bad Harzburg, turn right at the "Altenau-8km" sign for the **Jugendherberge (HI),** Torfhaus 3. (Tel. (05320) 242. DM22, over 26 DM27. Members only. Reception noon-1:30pm and 5-7pm. Curfew 10pm.)

Wernigerode One of Goethe's secret spots in the hills, and now a stop on the Harzquerbahn route, **Wernigerode** still charms with half-timbered houses and a magnificent hilltop **castle.** The Kaiser came to the *Schloß* for hunting; his room is wildly brocaded green and gold. From the flower-trimmed terrace, you can see straight to the peak of Brocken. (Open May-Oct. daily 10am-6pm; Nov. Sa-Su only; Dec.-Apr. Tu-Su 10am-6pm. Last entry 5pm. DM8, students DM7. Tour DM1 extra.) Wernigerode's busy **tourist office,** Nicolaipl. 1 (tel. (03943) 63 30 35), around the corner from the *Rathaus,* books rooms (from DM35) for a 10% commission. (Open May-Oct. M-F 9am-7pm, Sa 10am-4pm, Su 10am-3pm; Oct.-Apr. M-F 9am-6pm, Sa-Su 9am-3pm.) To reach the **Jugendgästehaus,** Friedrichstr. 53 (tel. (03943) 63 20 61), walk from Westerntor station right on Unter den Zindeln, then turn right on Friedrichstr. (25min.); or, take bus 1, 4, or 5 to "Kirchstr." (DM24, over 26 DM29. Breakfast included. Sheets DM6. Reception M-F 6:30am-3pm and 5-7pm, Sa-Su 6:30-10am and 4:30-7pm.)

Thale Behind the dramatic front of **Thale's** jagged cliffs lurks a region of myths and witches. Legend dates Thale's cultic past back to prehistoric times, when a sorceress named **Watelinde** led pagan rituals to indoctrinate young witches-to-be. A few thousand years later a whirlwind threw a startled Watelinde into some rocks which now comprise the **Hexentanzplatz** (the place where witches dance). Down the hill from Hexentanzpl. is the **Walpurgishalle,** a museum commemorating the Harz history of witchcraft (open daily May-Sept. 9am-5pm; Oct.-Apr. 9am-1pm; DM2, students DM1). Next to the museum is **Harzer Bergtheater Thale** (tel. (03947) 23 24), a huge outdoor amphitheater with performances ranging from Broadway musicals and operas to Goethe's *Faust* and the *Hexenkonzerts* (witches' concerts; shows run sporadically May-Sept.; tickets DM15-32, 30% student discount). One can ascend to the Hexentanzpl. either by following the **trail** that begins by the hostel (30min.) or by **cable car;** the cable car, departing from a station at the foot of the valley, offers spectacular views of the Bodental. (Cable car runs in summer daily 9:30am-6pm; in winter Sa-Su 10am-4:30pm. Round-trip DM8, children DM6.)

Trains leave every hour for Thale from Halberstadt (30min.) and Quedlinburg (10min.). Across from the train station, the **tourist office,** Rathausstr. 1 (tel. (03947) 25 97 or 22 77; fax 22 77), books rooms (DM25-40) for free. (Open May-Oct. M-F 9am-6pm, Sa 9:30am-4:30pm, Su 9:30am-3:30pm; Nov.-Dec. M-F 9am-4pm; Jan.-Apr. M-F 9am-5pm.) The cavernous rooms of the **Jugendherberge,** Bodetal-Waldkater 1 (tel./fax (03947) 28 81), look out into the mountains and the running river below. From the train station, cut diagonally through the park, go past the *Opfer des Fascismus* statue on the right and the cathedral on the left; then turn right and continue walking along the river. (DM16, over 26 DM21, plus either breakfast (DM6) or dinner (DM7). Sheets DM6. Reception 3-6 and 8-10pm.) Check out the many food stands by Hexentanzpl. Thale explodes in nuptial bliss and revelry every year on April 30 (the wedding anniversary of the Nordic gods of the seasons) for the **Walpurgisnacht.**

NORTH RHINE-WESTPHALIA

In 1946, the victorious Allies attempted to speed Germany's recovery by merging the traditionally distinct regions of Westphalia, Lippe, and the Rhineland to unify the economic nucleus of post-war Germany. The resulting *Land,* North Rhine-Westphalia, meets no typical German stereotype. With its 17 million inhabitants and the mighty Ruhr Valley, North Rhine-Westphalia is the most heavily populated and economically powerful area in Germany. Despite downturns in heavy industry and high unemployment, the great industrial wealth of the region continues to support a multitude of cultural offerings. While the region's squalor may have inspired the philosophy of Karl Marx and Friedrich Engels, the area's natural beauty and intellectual energy of Cologne and Düsseldorf spurred the muses of Goethe, Heine, and Böll.

■ Cologne (Köln)

Founded by Romans in 48 AD, Cologne gained fame and fortune in the Middle Ages as an elite university town and the center of important trade routes. While most of the inner city was destroyed during World War II, the magnificent Gothic cathedral survived no fewer than 14 bombings and remains Cologne's main attraction. Today, tourists come to see this symbol of Cologne's rebirth, participate in libatious celebrations, and indulge in the burgeoning fine arts scene.

PRACTICAL INFORMATION

Telephone Code: 0221.
Flights: Info tel. (02203) 40 25 38. Bus 170 runs from stop 4 of the *Hauptbahnhof* to the **Köln-Bonn Airport** (15min., DM8.20, children DM4.50).
Trains: Direct train lines connect Cologne with Berlin (5½-7½hr.), Düsseldorf (30min.), Frankfurt (2½hr.), Hamburg (4hr.), and Munich (6-8hr.).

Public Transportation: VRS (Verkehrsverbund Rhein-Seig) offices carry plans of the S- and U-Bahn lines, as well as maps of city bus and streetcar lines. One office is located downstairs in the train station. Tickets priced by distance: 1-ride tickets DM1.55-13.50; day cards DM11-33. The DM11 card gets you anywhere in Cologne.

Hitchhiking: Hitchers take bus 132 to the last stop for all destinations. **Citynetz Mitfahrzentrale,** Maximistr. 2 (tel. 194 40), to the left of the train station, lists rides. Open M-F 9am-6pm, Sa 9am-2pm.

Tourist Office: Verkehrsamt, Unter Fettenhennen 19 (tel. 221 33 45; fax for hotel reservations 221 33 20; http://www.koeln.org/koelntourismus), across from the cathedral. Free maps. Books rooms for a DM5-6 fee. *Monatsvorschau* (DM2) has info and events schedules. Open May-Oct. M-Sa 8am-10:30pm, Su 9am-10:30pm; Nov.-Apr. M-Sa 8am-9pm, Su 9:30am-7pm.

Currency Exchange: You can exchange money at the train station (open daily 7am-9pm), but the service charges are lower at the post office (see below).

American Express: Burgmauerstr. 14 (tel. 925 90 10), near the cathedral. **ATM.** Cardholders' mail held for free. Open M-F 9am-5:30pm, Sa 9am-noon.

Laundry: Öko-Express, Neue Weyerstr. 1. Wash DM6; dry DM1 per 10min. Soap included. Open M-Sa 6am-11pm. Also at Zülpicher Wall 2.

Pharmacy: Dom Apotheke, Komodienstr. 5 (tel. 257 67 54), near the station. Their *Pharmacie-Internationale* advises in English. Open M-F 8am-6:30pm, Sa 8:30am-4pm. List of after-hours pharmacies posted outside.

Emergency: Police, tel. 110. **Hospital,** 112.

Post Office: Main office, WDR Arkaden. From the *Dom* exits of the train station, head down Breitestr., then An den Ruhr. Open M-Sa 8am-6pm, Su 8am-1pm. **Postal Code:** 50667.

ACCOMMODATIONS AND FOOD

Most hotels fill up in the spring and fall when conventions come to town, and the two hostels are filled to the beams from June to September. Call ahead.

Jugendherberge Köln-Deutz (HI), Siegesstr. 5a (tel. 81 47 11; fax 88 44 25), just over the Hohenzollern Bridge. From the station, S-Bahn 6, 11, or 12: "Köln-Deutz." Small but clean rooms, prime location and free laundry. DM32, over 26 DM37. Sheets included. Reception 6-9am and 12:30pm-12:30am.

Jugendgästehaus Köln-Riehl (HI), An der Schanz 14 (tel. 76 70 81; fax 76 15 55), on the Rhine north of the zoo. From the station, U-Bahn 16 or 18 ("Ebertpl./Mül-heim"): "Boltensternstr." More posh but less central than Köln-Deutz. DM38.50; singles DM63.50. Sheets and breakfast included. Reception 24hr.

Jansen Pension, Richard-Wagner-Str. 18 (tel. 25 18 75). U-Bahn 1, 2, 6, 15, or 19: "Rudolfpl." and head west out of the U-bahn (2-3 blocks). Infinitely charming rooms in this Victorian row-house make this a Grand Hotel style *pension* in an equally grand neighborhood. Singles DM45-60; doubles DM95. Breakfast included.

Camping: Campingplatz Poll (tel. 83 19 66), southeast of the *Altstadt* on the Rhine. U-Bahn 16: "Marienburg," then cross Roddenkirchener Bridge. DM6 per person; DM5 per tent. Reception 8am-noon and 3-10pm.

Students pack cafes and diners from Zülpicherstr. into the university complex; the mid-priced restaurants and ethnic eateries center on the *Altstadt*. The city's best inexpensive eats are found in the Turkish district on Weideng. Don't leave Cologne without trying the city's smooth **Kölsch beer.** An open-air **Markt** on Wilhelmspl. takes over the northern Nippes neighborhood to offer farm-fresh joys (open M-Sa 7-11:30am). **Cafe Waschsalon,** Friesenstr. 80, serves breakfast (from DM6.50) until 4pm (open M-Th 8am-1am, F 8am-3am, Sa 10am-3am, Su 10am-1am). At **Brauhaus Früh am Dom,** Am Hof 12-14, patrons enjoy a number of Kölner and German specialties: *Schnitzel, Brats, Kartoffeln*—it's all here (most dishes DM9-22; open daily 8am-midnight). **Cafe Rendezvous,** Heinsberg 11a, capitalizes on silver-screen glitz with classic Hollywood decor and starving actor prices (all under DM10; open Su-Th 8am-1am, F-Sa 8am-3am).

SIGHTS AND ENTERTAINMENT

Cologne celebrated **Gothic Year in Köln** in 1998 to honor the 750th anniversary of the **Dom** (cathedral). Visitors exiting Cologne's *Bahnhof* are immediately confronted by the building, overwhelming in both intricacy and scale. Inside, the stained-glass windows cast an intense play of colored light over a gilded altarpiece, magnificent woodcuts, and other treasures. The enormous sculpture shining brilliantly in the dim light is the **Shrine of the Magi,** a reliquary of the Three Kings in blinding gold, brought to the city in 1164. Look for the 976 **Gero Crucifix,** the oldest intact sculpture of Christus patiens. A mere 509 steps lead to the top of the **Südturm** (south tower); catch your breath 400 steps up at the *Glockenstübe,* where the 24-ton **Der große Peter,** the world's heaviest swinging bell, roosts. (Cathedral open daily 6am-7pm. English tours Su-F 2pm, Sa 10:30am. DM6. Free organ concerts mid-June to Sept. Tu 8pm. Tower open daily May-Sept. 9am-6pm; Mar.-Apr. and Oct. 9am-5pm; Nov.-Feb. 9am-4pm. DM3, students DM1.50.)

The 12th-century **Groß St. Martin** rises like a medieval castle beside the *Dom* despite extensive wartime damage. (Open M-F 10:15am-6pm, Sa 10am-12:30pm and 1:30-6pm, Su 2-4pm. Crypt DM1, students DM0.50.) Farther on, the squares and crooked streets of the old **Fischmarkt** district open onto paths along the Rhine, and crowded cafes give way to riverside stretches of grass. If you've skimped on hostel showers, stop by the famous **house #4711,** Glockeng., where a small fountain dispenses the fragrant liquid that made Cologne a household word.

A three-day pass for entry into all of the city's museums, the DM15 **Köln Bonbon,** is available at most upscale hotels in the city center, including the **Dom Hotel,** across from the cathedral. The **Römische-Germanisches Museum,** Roncallipl. 4, was built over Roman ruins (open Tu-Su 10am-5pm; DM7, students DM4). The **Heinrich-Böll-Platz,** Bischofsgartenstr. 1, behind the Römische-Germanisches Museum, houses three museums: the **Wallraf-Richartz Museum** has pieces from the 13th to 19th centuries; the **Museum Ludwig** travels from Impressionism through Picasso, Dalí, and Klee, and ends with art fresh off the easel; and the **Agfa Foto-Historama** chronicles chemical art of the last 150 years. (All open Tu 10am-8pm, W-F 10am-6pm, Sa-Su 11am-6pm. DM10 for all three, students DM5.) Take U-bahn 12, 16, or 18 to "Barbarossapl." to find **The Beatles Museum,** Heinsbergstr. 13, which is crammed with Fab Four memorabilia (open Sept.-July W-Sa 10am-7pm; DM5). Even better than Willy Wonka's chocolate factory, **Das Museum (Imhoff-Stollwerk Museum),** Rheinauhafen 1a, makes its visitors writhe in ecstasy at the sight of the gold fountain spurting streams of chocolaty goo.

Cologne becomes a living spectacle during **Karneval,** a week-long pre-Lenten festival. The weekend builds up to a bacchanalian parade on **Rosenmontag,** the last Monday before Lent (Feb. 11 in 1999). Everyone's in costume and gets and gives a couple dozen *Bützchen* (kisses on a stranger's cheek). For info and tickets to events, ask at the **Festkomitee des Kölner Karnevals,** Antwerpenerstr. 55 (tel. 57 40 00). The *Köln, Karneval* booklet at the tourist office also has helpful tips.

Students congregate in the **Quartier Lateng,** the area bounded by Zülpicherstr., Zülpicherpl., Roonstr., and Luxemburgstr. Gay nightlife runs up Matthiasstr. to Möhlenbach, Hohe Pforte, Marienpl., and up to Heumarkt by the Deutzer Brücke. The only science going on at **Museum,** Zülpicherpl. 9, are blood alcohol level experiments, under the watchful eye of the local dinosaur (open Su-Th 7pm-1am, F-Sa 7pm-3am). **MTC,** Zülpicherstr. 10, has varied musical offerings (cover DM6; open Su-Th 9pm-2am, F-Sa 9pm-3am). At **Päffgen Brauhaus,** Friesenstr. 64-66, *Kölsch* is brewed on the premises and consumed in cave-like halls and the *Biergarten* (0.2L shot DM2.20; open daily 10am-midnight). **Broadway,** Ehrenstr. 11, is a funky cafe haunted by Köln's hippest artists and intellectuals (open daily 10am-1am). At **Gloria,** Apostelnstr. 11, a gay and lesbian cafe fronts a popular disco (call 25 44 33 for info).

■ Bonn

Derisively called the *"Hauptdorf"* (capital village), Bonn has been Germany's whipping boy for 50 years simply because it's not Berlin. Unimportant for most of its 2000 years, Bonn made it big by chance: since Konrad Adenauer, the postwar chancellor, had a house in the suburbs, the ever-considerate occupying powers promoted humble Bonn to capital status. Since reunification, the city lost the seat of government to Berlin but remains a worthy destination with a spread of museums, bustling *Altstadt*, and respected university.

SIGHTS AND ENTERTAINMENT Bonn's old town center winds into a lively pedestrian zone littered with historic niches. The **Beethoven Geburtshaus** (birthplace), Bonng. 20, attracts music aficionados of all sorts. (Open M-Sa 10am-5pm, Su 11am-4pm. DM8, students DM4. Call ahead for English tours.) The museum is Bonn's biggest draw after the *Bundestag*. The castles, palaces, and most museums lie just outside the inner city. The **Kurfürstliches Schloß**, an 18th-century palace, was later converted into the central building of Bonn's university. Down the Poppelsdorfer Allee promenade, the 18th-century **Poppelsdorfer Schloß** sports a French facade, an Italian courtyard, and manicured **Botanical Gardens.** (Gardens open May-Sept. M-F 9am-6pm, Su 9am-1pm; Oct.-Apr. M-F 9am-4pm. Free.) A **Bonncard** (DM12), available at the tourist office, provides public transport and admission to the museums of the **Museum Mile** (U-Bahn 16, 63, or 66: Heussallee). The **Kunstmuseum Bonn,** Friedrich-Ebert Allee 2, has superb Expressionist and contemporary German art (open Tu-Su 10am-6pm; DM5, students DM3), while the art in the **Kunst- und Ausstellungshalle der BRD** is so new that you can smell the paint (open Tu-W 10am-9pm, Th-Su 10am-7pm; DM8, students DM4). The futuristic **Haus der Geschichte** offers an interactive look at German history (open Tu-Su 9am-7pm; free). For cultural and entertainment listings, check out the *Schnüss* guide, or hang at the *über*-hip **Cafe Göttlich**, Franziskanerstr. (beer DM3.50-6; desserts DM5-8; open daily 9am-1am).

PRACTICAL INFO, ACCOMMODATIONS, AND FOOD Trains run regularly from Bonn to Cologne (30min.) and Frankfurt (2hr.). Bonn's **tourist office,** Münsterstr. 20 (tel. (0228) 77 34 66 or 19 44 33; fax 77 31 00), books hotels for a DM3-5 fee. Take the "Stadtmitte" exit from the station, walk up Poststr., and turn left (open M-F 9am-6:30pm, Sa 9am-5pm, Su 10am-2pm). For the first-rate **Jugendgästehaus Bonn-Venusberg (HI),** Haager Weg 42 (tel. (0228) 28 99 70; fax 289 97 14), take bus 626 ("Ippendorf Altenheim") to "Jugendgästehaus." (DM37. Sheets and breakfast included. Laundry DM10. Reception 9am-1am. Curfew 1am.) **Hotel Virneburg,** Sandkaule 3a (tel. 63 63 66; U-Bahn 62, 64, or 66: Bertha-von-Suttner-Pl.) has functional rooms, unbeatable prices, and a terrific location (singles DM35–65; doubles DM65-90; breakfast included).

Münsterpl. features several fast-food counters, small cafes, and an open-air market (M-Sa 9am-6pm). The **University Mensa,** Nassestr. 11, a 15-minute walk from the train station along Kaiserstr., also offers cheap meals. (DM2-5. Open for lunch M-Th 11:30am-2:15pm, F 11:30am-2pm, Sa noon-1:45pm. Dinner M-F 5:30-8pm. Closed mid-July to late Aug.) Fulfill your wildest vegetarian fantasies at **Cassius Garten,** Maximilianstr. 28d, at the edge of the *Altstadt* (DM2.58 per 100g; open M-W and F 9am-8pm, Th 8am-9pm, Sa 9am-4pm).

■ Aachen

Charlemagne sang the mantra of multiculturalism when he made Aachen the capital of his Frankish empire in the 8th century, and the tunes are still heard today—Aachen jives day and night in four different languages, and a flux of students and international travelers continually renew the city's vibrant atmosphere. The world-famous neo-Byzantine **cathedral** sits in the center of the city circle. Stained glass rings the 15th-century Gothic choir; beneath the chancel lie the bones of Charlemagne himself (open daily 7am-7pm). The 14th-century stone **Rathaus** looms over the wide *Marktplatz* beside the cathedral. On the northern facade stand 50 statues of former German sovereigns, 31 of whom were crowned in Aachen (open daily 10am-1pm and 2-5pm; DM3, students DM1.50). The **Ludwig Forum für Internationales Kunst,** Jülicherstr. 97-109, in a converted *Bauhaus* umbrella factory, showcases modern masters, American pop art, and an ironic Eastern European collection. (Open Tu and Th 10am-5pm, W and F 10am-8pm, Sa-Su 11am-5pm. Last entrance 30min. before closing. DM6, students DM3.)

Aachen sits at the crossroads between Germany, Belgium, and the Netherlands, and is one hour from Cologne by **train.** The **tourist office** (tel. (0241) 180 29 60; fax 180 29 31), in the Atrium Eliserbrunnen on Friedrich-Wilhelm-Pl., finds rooms from DM35. From the train station, head up Bahnhofstr., turn left on Theaterstr., and then right onto Kapuzinergraben, which becomes Friedrich-Wilhelm-Pl. (open M-F 9am-6pm, Sa 9am-2pm). The **Jugendherberge (HI),** Maria-Theresia-Allee 260 (tel. (0241) 711 01; fax 70 82 19), has old rooms but a friendly atmosphere. From the station, walk left on Lagerhausstr. until it intersects Kareliterstr. and Mozartstr. From there, take bus 2 ("Preusswald") to "Ronheide" or bus 12 ("Diepenbendem") to "Colynshof" (DM25, over 26 DM30; reception until 10pm; curfew 11:30pm). To get to **Hotel Marx,** Hubertusstr. 33-35 (tel. (0241) 375 41; fax 267 05), walk down Lagerhausstr. (which becomes Boxgarden), take a right on Stephanstr., and be won over to the left on Hubertusstr. (singles DM60-85; doubles DM100-130; breakfast included).

Pontstraße is lined with restaurants and pubs. Treat yourself to some fine baked goods at **Van Den Daele,** Büchel 18, off the Markt (open M-W 9am-6:30pm, Th-Sa 9am-9pm, Su noon-6pm). Eat and drink in Charlemagne's shadow at **Egmont,** Pontstr.1 (open daily 9am-3am). **Tam-phat,** Pontstr. 100, offers Chinese and Thai dishes (DM7-14; open M-F 11am-3pm and 5pm-11pm, Sa-Su noon-11pm).

■ Düsseldorf

The capital of North Rhine-Westphalia and the headquarters of Germany's largest corporations and fashion industry, Düsseldorf is a stately, modern metropolis, pulsating with an energy unlike anything found in most other German cities. The city has rebounded from war-time destruction with resilience and fierce pride. By day, crowds line "the Kö," a 1km-long fashion runway that sweeps down either side of the old town moat. At night, propriety (and sobriety) are cast aside as thousands of Düsseldorfers flock to the 500 pubs of the *Altstadt,* trading their monocles and Rolexes for beer goggles and a damn good time.

PRACTICAL INFORMATION

Telephone Code: 0211.

Flights: Call 421 22 23 for flight info. 24hr. emergency service tel. 421 66 37. Frequent S-Bahns and a Lufthansa shuttle travel from the station to the international **Flughafen Düsseldorf.** Open 5am-12:30am.

Trains: All trains go through **Düsseldorf Hauptbahnhof** (tel. 194 19). To: Frankfurt am Main (2½hr.), Hamburg (3½hr.), and Köln (29min.).

Public Transportation: Call 582 28 for schedule info. The **Rheinbahn** includes subways, streetcars, buses, and the S-Bahn. Single tickets DM1.90-1-1.70. Closes by 1am. The *Tagesticket* (from DM10) is the best value around—up to 5 people can travel 24hr. on any line. Tickets sold at vending machines; pick up the *Fahrausweis* brochure in system, which connects surrounding areas.

Tourist Office: Main office, Konrad-Adenauer-Pl. (tel. 17 20 20; fax 35 04 04). Up and to the right from the station. Pick up the free *Düsseldorfer Monatsprogram.* Open M-F 8:30am-6pm, Sa 9am-noon; open for hotel reservations (DM5) M-Sa 8am-8pm, Su 4-10pm. The **branch office,** Heinrich-Heine-Allee 24 (tel. 899 23 46), specializes in cultural listings. Open M-F 9am-5pm.

Currency Exchange: Deutsche Verkehrs Credit Bank, in the *Hauptbahnhof* and airport. Open M-Sa 7am-9pm, Su 8am-9pm.

American Express: Neusserstr. 111 (tel. 90 13 50). Mail held for members. All financial services. Open M-F 9am-5:30pm, Sa 8:30am-noon.

Gay and Lesbian Organizations: Gay male hotline tel. 77 52 42; lesbian hotline tel. 54 42. Call hotlines for daytime hours; evenings usually Tu-Sa 8pm-1am.

Laundromat: Wasch Center, Friedrichstr. 92, near the Kirchpl. S-Bahn. Wash DM6, dry DM1 per 15min. Soap included. Open daily 6am-11pm.

Pharmacy: In the *Hauptbahnhof.* Closed pharmacies post lists of nearby open ones. **Emergency pharmacy,** tel. 115 00.

Emergency: Ambulance and **Fire,** tel. 112. **Emergency Doctor,** tel. 192 92.

Police: tel. 110.

Post Office: Hauptpostamt, Konrad-Adenauer-Pl., to right of the tourist office. Open for most services M-F 8am-6pm, Sa 9am-2pm, Su noon-1pm. A **branch office** is located in the *Hauptbahnhof.* **Postal Code:** 40210.

Internet Access: g@rden, Rathansurfer 8 (tel. 86 61 60; email gsg@garden.de; http://www.garden.de). Open daily 11am-1am.

ACCOMMODATIONS, CAMPING, AND FOOD

Düsseldorf is a convention city where corporate crowds make rooms scarce and costly; it's imperative that you call as far in advance as possible. Most rooms go for at least DM50 per person even in the off-season. Check around the train station.

Jugendgästehaus Düsseldorf (HI), Düsseldorferstr. 1 (tel. 55 73 10; fax 57 25 13), just over the Rheinkniebrücke bridge from the *Altstadt.* Take U-Bahn 70, 74, 75, 76, or 77 to "Luegpl.," then walk 500m down Kaiser-Wilhelm-Ring. Unbeatable location. DM33.50, over 26 DM37. Laundry DM9. Private lockers. Reception 7am-1am. Curfew 1am, but doors open every hour on the hour 2-6am.

Jugendherberge Duisburg-Wedau, Kalkweg 148E (tel. (0203) 72 41 64; fax 72 08 34). Take S-Bahn 1 or 21 to "Duisburg Hauptbahnhof," then bus 934 to "Jugendherberge." Old but clean rooms. DM22.50, over 26 DM27.50. Reception 8:30-9am, 12:30-1, and 6:30-7pm. Open mid-Jan. to mid-Dec.

Hotel Manhattan, Graf-Adolf-Str. 39 (tel. 37 71 38; fax 37 02 47), 2 blocks from the station. The spacious, comfortable rooms offer convenient respite from a hard day's shopping. Singles DM68-120; doubles DM100-180. Breakfast buffet included. Reception 24hr.

CVJM-Hotel, Graf-Adolf-Str. 102 (tel. 17 28 50; fax 361 31 60), down the street, left of the train station. Clean, modern rooms in a location convenient to both the station and the Kö. Singles DM70; doubles DM117. Reception 24hr. No credit cards.

Camping: Kleiner Torfbruch (tel. 899 20 38). S-Bahn to "Düsseldorf Geresheim," then bus 735 ("Stamesberg") to "Seeweg." DM6 per person, DM9 per tent.

The streets of the *Altstadt* are lined with restaurants and fast-food joints. **Linanon Express,** Bergerstr. 21, in Düsseldorf's *echt Deutsch Altstadt,* is probably the last place you'd expect to find Lebanese food, but this hip cafe serves up great falafels (DM4.50), among other dishes, in the heart of *Kneipe*-land. Dine with the glitzy in the *Biergarten* at **Galerie Burghof,** Burgallee 1-3 (open daily 11am-1am). **La Copa,** Bergerstr. 4, serves 50 tasty dishes (DM8-15) and *sangria* (open daily noon-1am). The cool, swanky cafeteria, **Marché,** Königsalle 60, is cheap (main courses from DM6.80) and generous with its portions (open daily 7:30am-11pm).

SIGHTS AND ENTERTAINMENT

The **Königsallee** ("the Kö"), the fashionable shopping district outside the *Altstadt,* embodies the vitality and glamour of Düsseldorf. If you can resist the chi-chi shops, the **Hofgarten** park adds an oasis of green and culture at the upper end of the promenade. West of the Hofgarten is the mirror-glass **Kunstsammlung Nordrhein-Westfalen,** Grabbepl. 5, an exceptional modern art museum with the definitive Paul Klee collection. Take U-Bahn 70 or 75-79 to Heinrich-Heine-Allee and walk north two blocks (open Tu-Th and Sa-Su 10am-6pm, F 10am-8pm; DM5, students DM3). Düsseldorf has had mixed luck with its cultural heroes. Beloved poet Heinrich Heine's manuscripts are on display at **The Heinrich Heine Institut,** Bilkerstr. 12-14 (open Tu-F and Su 11am-5pm, Sa 1-5pm; DM4, students DM2). **Robert Shumann** was so miserable that he tried to drown his sorrows by jumping off a town-bridge. Farther from the city center, in **Kaiserwerth,** are the ruins of Emperor Friedrich's **palace.** Take U-Bahn 79 to "Klemenspl.," follow Kaiserwerther Markt to the Rhine, and walk left (open daily 8am-12:30pm; free). The **Art Ticket** (DM20) gives free entrance to all museums, and can be purchased at the tourist office or at a museum.

Prinz magazine (DM4.50, often free at the youth hostel) is Düsseldorf's fashion cop and scene detective; the free cultural guides *Coolibri* and *Biograph* are less complete but still helpful. The gay and lesbian nightlife magazine, *Facolte,* is available at most newsstands. **Das Kommödchen** (tel. 32 94 43) is a tiny, extraordinarily popular theater behind the Kunsthalle at Grabbepl. (Box office open M-Sa 1-8pm, Su 3-8pm. Tickets DM33, students DM23. Call at least two days ahead.) Purchase ballet and opera tickets at the **Opernhaus** (tel. 890 82 11), on Heinrich-Heine-Allee (open M-F 11am-6:30pm, Sa 11am-1pm, and 1hr. before performances).

Folklore holds that Düsseldorf's 500 pubs make up *die längste Theke der Welt,* the longest bar in the world. **Stahlwerk,** Ronsdorfer 134 (U-Bahn 75: Ronsdorferstr.), a classic factory-turned-disco in one of the city's grittiest neighborhoods, packs in 1500 every night (cover DM10; open F-Sa and last Su of every month at 10pm). **g@rden** (see **Practical Information,** above) is one of Düsseldorf's best jazz venues; gigs here tend much more toward progressive jazz than most German jazz clubs. Plan transport home from **Tor 3,** the techno club at Ronsdorferstr. 143, across from Stahlwerk—public transportation will stop long before you leave (cover DM15; open F-Sa 10pm-5am). **Engelchen,** Kurzestr. 11, a mellow oasis papered with posters, emanates Seattle grunge (open M-F 9am-1am, Sa 10am-3am, Su 10am-3am). **Cafe Rosa,** Oberbilker Allee 310, is the mecca of Düsseldorf's gay community, offering a cafe, bar, and disco. (Tu, Th, and most Sa mixed, F lesbians only, last Sa of each month gay men only.)

HESSE

Prior to the 20th century, Hesse was known for exporting mercenary soldiers to rulers such as King George III, who sent them off to put down an unruly gang of colonial hicks in 1776. Today, Hesse is the busiest commercial center in the country, led by the banking metropolis of Frankfurt. Fortunately, the medieval delights and Baroque elegance of areas outside the city attract little attention from tourists.

■ Frankfurt am Main

Known to some Germans as "Bankfurt" or "Mainhattan," Frankfurt is a thriving financial and commercial center, one of the most Americanized cities in Europe, and, perhaps not coincidentally, the crime capital of Germany. Anne Frank, Goethe, and the social theorists of the Frankfurt School enriched the city's cultural treasury, and the *Kulturszene* is diverse and cosmopolitan.

SIGHTS AND ENTERTAINMENT Almost all of Frankfurt was destroyed by Allied bombings during World War II—what's left of the old city is in the **Römerberg** area. The towering **Dom** (cathedral) served as the coronation site for German emperors between 1562 and 1792, and the view from its tower is well worth the punishing climb. (Cathedral open Sa-Th 9am-noon and 2:30-6pm, F 2:30-6pm. Tower closed in winter. DM3.) Frankfurt's city hall since 1405, the red sandstone **Römer** stands at the west end of the *Römerberg.* The upper floors contain the **Kaisersaal,** adorned with portraits of the 52 German emperors from Charlemagne to Franz II (open daily 10am-1pm and 2-5pm; mandatory hourly tour DM3, students DM1). From *Römerberg,* walk across the Eiserner Steg footbridge to the **Museumsufer,** home to seven museums. Elsewhere, the **Museum für Moderne Kunst** (Museum of Modern Art), Domstr.

10 (tel. (069) 21 23 04 47; fax 21 23 78 82), is a must-see; the building itself is an architectural wonder, and appropriate to the stunning collection.

In the northwest part of town, the lush **Palmengarten** houses an extensive variety of native and exotic birds, and offers refuge from the city's commercial bustle. Take U-Bahn 6 or 7 to "Bockenheimer Warte" (admission DM7, students DM3). Enjoy animal antics at the world-famous **zoo**. (U-Bahn 6 or 7. Open mid-Mar. to Sept. M-F 9am-7pm, Sa-Su 8am-7pm; Oct. to mid-Mar. daily 9am-5pm. DM11, students DM5. Show your U-Bahn ticket for a discount.) The *Journal Frankfurt* (DM2.80), *Fritz*, or *Strandgut* (both free) have info on Frankfurt's **theatrical performances.**

For pubs and taverns, try the **Alt Sachsenhausen** district, between Brückenstr. and Dreieichstr. Frankfurt's thriving disco scene (and its gay nightlife) centers around Zeil and Bleichstr.; check out **Sinkkasten** on Brönnerstr., or **Nachtleben** on Kurt-Schumacher-str. The renowned jazz scene happens on Kleine Bockenheimer Str., also known as **Jazzgasse** (Jazz Alley). The most famous venue is **Der Jazzkeller,** Kleine Bockenheimer Str. 18a (tel. (069) 28 85 37; cover varies; live music on Th and Sa).

PRACTICAL INFO, ACCOMMODATIONS, AND FOOD

From the **airport,** S-Bahn 8 and 5 travel to the train station (4 per hour; DM5.80; Eurail valid). Frequent **trains** service major cities including Berlin (5-6hr., every hr.), Munich (3½-4½hr., every hr.), and Paris (6-8hr., every 2hr.); call (069) 194 19 for more info. For a diagram of Frankfurt's transit network, check this book's **color map.** The **tourist office,** in the station (tel. (069) 21 23 88 49), books rooms for a DM5 fee (tel. (069) 21 23 08 08) and sells the **Frankfurt Card,** which gives unlimited public transportation as well as a 50% discount to museums and the zoo (DM10-15; tourist office open M-F 8am-9pm, Sa-Su and holidays 9am-6pm). **Currency exchange** is available in the station and in Airport Hall B, but rates are better at the **main post office,** Zeil 90 (open M-F 9:30am-8pm, Sa 9am-4pm), or at any bank. Log on at the **CyberRyder Internet Cafe,** Töngesg. 31 (6DM per 30min.; M-F 10am-9pm, Sa 10am-10pm).

Hotel prices in Frankfurt rise as high as the skyscrapers. For affordable, convenient rooms, try the **Jugendherberge (HI),** Deutschherrnufer 12 (tel. (069) 61 90 58; fax 61 82 57). To reach the hostel, take bus 46 to "Frankensteinerpl." and turn left along the river; after 7:30pm, take S-Bahn 2-6 or tram 16 to "Lokalbahnhof," turn right on Darmstädter Landstr. (which becomes Dreieichstr.), and turn left. (DM 25, over 20 DM32, doubles DM84. Required sheet deposit DM10. Reception 24hr. Curfew is officially midnight.) **Pension Brüns,** Mendelssohnstr. 42 (tel. (069) 74 88 96; fax 74 88 46), has sunny rooms with TVs and phones. From the train station, take a left onto Düsseldorferstr., and after two blocks, veer right on Beethovenstr. At the circle, go right (doubles DM79, triples DM105; breakfast included; showers DM2). Farther along, **Pension Backer,** Mendelssohnstr. 92 (tel. (069) 74 79 92), is bright and clean (singles DM50, doubles DM60, triples DM68; breakfast included; showers DM3).

Frankfurt is famous for its *Ebbelwei* (large mugs of apple wine, also called *Äpfelwein*). **Zum Gemalten Haus,** Schweizerstr. 67, is known for its classic, greasy German fare (*Ebbelwei* DM2.50 for 0.3L; open W-Su 10am-midnight).

■ Marburg

Almost two centuries ago, the Brothers Grimm spun their fairy tales in Marburg's rolling hills, and from a distance, the city seems more like their world than ours. Tough terrain and dense forests surround the town, and the *Oberstadt* is still a maze of tiring staircases and narrow alleys. Founded in the heart of Marburg in 1527, the world's first Protestant **university** boasts alumni Martin Heidegger, Boris Pasternak, and T.S. Eliot. Climb 250 steps or take bus 16 from Rudolphspl. to the exalted **Landgrafenschloß,** former haunt of the Teutonic knights. The castle now houses the university's **Museum für Kulturgeschichte** (Cultural Museum), with exhibits on Hessian history and religious art (open Apr.-Oct. Tu-Su 10am-6pm; Nov.-Mar. Tu-Su 11am-5pm; DM3, students DM2). To reach the 13th-century **Elisabethkirche,** Elisabethstr. 3, the oldest Gothic church in Germany, exit the train station, walk down Bahnhofstr. (5min.), and take a left at Elisabethstr. (Open daily Apr.-Sept. 9am-6pm; Oct. 9am-5pm; Nov.-Mar. M-Sa 10am-4pm, Su after 11am. Church free; reliquary DM3, students DM2.)

The **tourist office,** Pilgrimsteinstr. 26 (tel. (06421) 991 20; fax 99 12 12), sells maps and hotel lists (DM0.50-1.50) and books rooms for free. Take buses 1-6 to "Rudolphspl." and exit to the north along Pilgrimsteinstr.; the office is on the left (open M-F 9am-6pm, Sa 10am-2pm). If the tourist office is closed, call **hotel info** at (06421) 194 14. Marburg is served by frequent **trains** from Frankfurt (1hr., every hr.) and Kassel (1hr., every 30min.). The riverside **Jugendherberge (HI),** Jahnstr. 1 (tel. (06421) 234 61; fax 121 91), features beautiful rooms, some with bath. From Rudolphspl., cross the bridge and turn right onto the riverside path until you reach the small wooden bridge (DM25, over 27 DM30; reception 9am-noon and 1:30-11:30pm). **Camping Lahnaue,** Trojedamm 47 (tel. (06421) 213 31), is on the Lahn River; to reach the campsite, follow directions to the hostel and continue downriver (DM7 per person, DM5 per tent; open Apr.-Oct; call ahead). **Cafe Barfuß,** Barfüßerstr. 33, serves big breakfasts until 3pm (DM6-13) and beer aplenty (open daily 10am-1am). **Cafe News/Hemingways/Down Under Dance Club,** Reitg. 5 (tel. (06421) 212 05), is a trendy meeting spot, bar, and dance club all in one (open daily 6pm-1am, dance floor F-Sa 9pm-1am).

■ Kassel

When Napoleon III was captured by Prussian troops and brought to the Schloß Wilhelmshöhe prison in 1870, Aacheners jeered *"Ab nach Kassel"* ("off to Kassel"). Today, hordes answer the call to see this ultra-sophisticated city. **Wilhelmshöhe park** is a hillside park with one giant Greek hero, two castles, three museums, and waterfalls galore. From the Wilhelmshöhe station, take bus 43 ("Herkules") to the endstation. **Schloß Wilhelmshöhe,** in the park, was the mammoth home of the local rulers. (Open Mar.-Oct. Tu-Su 10am-5pm; Nov.-Feb. Tu-Su 10am-4pm. DM6, students DM4.) All of the park's paths lead up to the large **Riesenschloß,** an amphitheater topped by the figure of **Herkules,** Kassel's emblem. Hordes of art-lovers and curiosity seekers descend on Kassel every five years to take part in **documenta,** the world's preeminent contemporary art exhibition, next scheduled for 2002. The remains of previous exhibitions sprawl across the city—even the *Hauptbahnhof* (train station) gets a piece of the action—check out the **caricatura,** its self-proclaimed "museum of bizarre art." **Museum Fridericianum,** Friedrichspl. 18, contains most of the *documenta*-related exhibitions, along with other exhibits (open W-Su 10am-6pm, Th until 8pm; DM8, students DM5, free Th 6-8pm).

The **Wilhelmshöhe station,** an ICE hub, is the point of entry to Kassel's ancient castles on the west side; the older **Hauptbahnhof** is the gateway to the *Altstadt* (old town). Kassel is accessible by **trains** from Frankfurt (2hr.) and Hamburg (2hr. with ICE). The **tourist office,** Königspl. 53, 2nd fl. (tel. (0561) 707 71 07; fax 707 71 69), sells maps, a hotel list (rooms from DM45), and brochures in English (open M-Th 9:15am-6pm, F 9:15am-4:30pm). The **Jugendherberge am Tannenwäldchen (HI),** Schenkendorfstr. 18 (tel. (0561) 77 64 55; fax 77 68 32), offers huge common areas and eight-bed rooms. Take streetcar 4 or 6 from Wilhelmshöhe station or the town hall, walk up Friedrich-Ebert-Str., and go right on Schenkendorf. (DM25, over 26 DM30. Breakfast included. Sheets DM6. Reception until 11pm. Sunday and winter curfew 12:30am. No phone reservations.) **Hotel-Restaurant Palmenbad,** Kurhausstr. 27 (tel./fax (0561) 326 91), is comfortable and clean. Take streetcar 3 to "Wiganstr." and walk five minutes uphill on An den Eichen. (Singles DM49; doubles DM90. Reception M 5:30-11pm, Tu-Sa 10am-11pm, Su 10am-3pm.) One of Kassel's oldest beer gardens, **Lohmann Biergarten,** Königstor 8, is the only outdoor beer garden that stays open until 2am (cheap but limited menu; opens at noon). The free magazine *Infotip,* available at tourist offices, is a useful guide to Kassel's nightlife.

RHINELAND-PALATINATE

A trip to the Rhineland-Palatinate to see the castles and wine towns along the Rhine is an obligatory tourist tromp. The region is a visual feast—the Mosel River curls downstream to the Rhine Gorge, a soft shore of castle-backed hills. But it also provides a literal feast; a rich agricultural tradition keeps fresh fruits and vegetables in abundance, and the vineyards of the Rhine and Mosel Valleys produce sweet, delicious wines.

■ The Rhine: Mainz to Koblenz

The Rhine River may run from Switzerland to the North Sea, but in the popular imagination it exists only in the 80km of the **Rhine Gorge** that stretch from Mainz to Bonn. This is the Rhine of legend: a sailor's nightmare, a poet's dream, and often the center of rhetorical storms of nationalism. From the Lorelei Cliffs, poet Heinrich Heine's legendary siren lured passing sailors to their deaths on the sharp rocks below, while the vineyards along the hillsides have inspired many a lesser illusion.

The best way to see the sights is probably by **boat,** if you're willing to put up with lots of tourists. The **Köln-Düsseldorfer line** (tel. (0211) 258 30 11) sails to 40 Rhine landings between Cologne and Mainz, including the cliffs and waterfalls at **Königswinter,** and offers connections to Mosel ferries. (Round-trip DM40, students half-price. Eurail and German Railpasses are valid on trips between Cologne and Mainz.)

Mainz The capital of the Rhineland-Palatinate region, **Mainz** is an elegant mix of modern and ancient—concrete and cobblestone mesh seamlessly to carry a wide variety of visitors through its vibrant streets. Across Liebfrauenpl. stands the colossal **Martinsdom,** the final resting place of several Archbishops of Mainz, whose extravagant tombs line the walls. (Open Apr.-Sept. M-F 9am-6:30pm, Sa 9am-4pm, Su 12:45-3pm and 4-6:30pm; Oct.-Mar. M-F 9am-5pm, Sa 9am-4pm, Su 12:45-3pm. Free.) Mainz's favorite son and the father of movable type, Johannes Gutenberg, is immortalized along with his creations in the marvelous **Gutenberg Museum** on Liebfrauenpl. (open Tu-Sa 10am-6pm, Su 10am-1pm; DM5, students DM2.50, Su free). On a hill several blocks to the south, in the opposite direction from the river, the **Stephanskirche** is noted for its stunning stained-glass windows by Marc Chagall (open daily 10am-noon and 2-5pm).

To make the maze of Mainz more maneuverable, streets running parallel to the Rhine have blue nameplates; those running towards it have red ones. The **tourist office,** Bahnhofstr. 15 (tel. (06131) 28 62 10; fax 286 21 55), on the *Brückenturm* of the *Rathaus,* reserves rooms for a DM5 fee (open M-F 9am-6pm, Sa 9am-1pm). Mainz's well-run **Jugendgästehaus (HI),** Otto-Brunsfels-Schneise 4 (tel. (06131) 853 32; fax 824 22), in the *Volkspark* in Weisenau, is clean and relatively safe; take bus 22 to "Jugendherberge/Viktorstift." (Doubles DM36; quads DM27. Reception 7am-midnight. Lockout midnight-6:30am. Closed until Apr. 1999 for renovations.) Near the *Dom,* **Central Cafe,** on the corner of Rheinstr. and Heug. (tel. (06131) 22 56 66), cooks up everything from burgers to traditional German fare, all for under DM 10 (open Su-Th 10am-midnight, F-Sa 10am-1am).

Bacharach On the west bank of the Rhine between Mainz and Koblenz, the gorgeous town of **Bacharach** brims with *Weinkeller* (wine cellars) and *Weinstuben* (wine pubs) that do justice to its name—"altar to Bacchus." Locals and tourists alike seem to favor **Die Weinstube,** located right behind the stunning **Altes Haus** (an original half-timbered house) in the center of town at Oberstr. From the late-Romanesque **Peterskirche** in the center of town, stairs lead up to the **Wernerkapelle,** the red sandstone frame of a chapel that took 140 years to build (1294-1434) but only a few hours to destroy during the War of Palatine Succession in 1689. The **tourist office,** Overstr. 1 (tel. (06743) 12 97; fax 31 55), has maps of hiking trails and a list of wine cellars and pubs (open M-F 9am-12:30pm and 1:30-5pm, Sa 10am-1pm). Hostels get no better than the unbelievable **Jugendherberge Stahleck (HI)** (tel. (06743) 12 66; fax 26 84), a gorgeous 12th-century castle with a panoramic view of the Rhine gorge. From the station, turn left at Peterskirche and take any of the marked paths leading up the hill. The painful 20-minute hike is worth every step (DM23.50; breakfast included; laundry DM9; curfew 10pm; call ahead).

Koblenz The beauty of Koblenz—not to mention its strategic value at the confluence of the Rhine and the Mosel—has attracted Roman, French, Prussian, and German conquerors over the past 2000 years. Before reunification, the city served as a large munitions dump, but now the only pyrotechnics are during the **Rhein in Flammen** (Rhine in Flames) fireworks festival, held each August.

The city's focal point is the **Deutsches Eck** (German Corner), the peninsula that purportedly saw the birth of the German nation when the Teutonic Order of Knights settled here in 1216. The tremendous **Mahnmal der Deutschen Einheit** (Monument to German Unity), erected in 1897 in honor of Kaiser Wilhelm I's forced reconciliation of the German Empire, dominates the peninsula. Most of the nearby *Altstadt* was flattened during World War II, but several attractive churches have been carefully restored. The **Florinskirche** towers shine with bursts of vibrant color, while the **Liebfrauenkirche** features oval Baroque towers, emerald and sapphire stained glass, and intricate ceiling latticework. If ground-level viewing has you down, head for **Festung Ehrenbreitstein**, a Brobdingnagian fortress at the highest point in the city. The Prussians used it to accommodate French troops in past centuries; today, the German state uses it to accommodate *you* (see **Jugendherberge Koblenz,** below).

Trains run regularly from Koblenz to Bonn (30min.) and Frankfurt (1½hr.). The **tourist office** (tel. (0261) 313 04 or 331 34; fax 129 38 00), opposite the train station, has boat schedules and city maps complete with hotel, restaurant, and pub listings (open May-Sept. M-F 9am-8pm, Sa-Su 10am-8pm). The **Jugendherberge Koblenz (HI)** (tel. (0261) 97 28 70; fax 972 87 30), inside the fortress, has standard four- to six-bed rooms, but is arguably the best-located hostel in Germany (DM23.50; breakfast included; reception 7am-11pm; curfew 11:30pm). **Campingplatz Rhein-Mosel** (tel. (0261) 827 19) is across the Mosel from the *Deutsches Eck;* a ferry crosses the river during the day. (DM5.50 per person, DM4.50-6 per tent. Reception 8am-noon and 2-8pm. Open Apr.-Oct. 15.) **Marktstübchen,** Am Markt 220, serves up *real* German food for *real* budget prices (most dishes under DM11; open daily 9am-midnight). **Salat Garten,** where Casinostr. becomes Gymnasiumstr. in the *Altstadt* just off Zentralpl., has a good salad bar (daily specials DM8; open M-F 11am-7pm, Th until 9pm, Sa 11am-3pm).

■ The Mosel Valley (Moseltal)

As if trying to avoid its inevitable surrender to the Rhine at Koblenz, the Mosel meanders slowly past the sun-drenched hills, pretty towns, and ancient castles of the softly cut Mosel Valley. The valley's slopes aren't as steep as the Rhine's narrow gorge, but the arresting landscape, ancient castles, and vineyards easily compensate.

See the splendid scenery by boat, bus, or bicycle; the **train** line between Koblenz and Trier often strays from the river into unremarkable countryside. Some train stations will rent you a sturdy three-speed **bike** for DM11 if you have a ticket or railpass. Although passenger **boats** no longer make the Koblenz-Trier run, several companies still run summer trips along shorter stretches; inquire at local tourist offices.

Cochem and Beilstein Like so many precious German wine-making villages, the hamlet of **Cochem** has become a repository of German nostalgia, its quintessential quaintness eaten up voraciously by busloads of city-dwellers. Yet the impressive vineyard-covered hills and majestic **Reichsburg** castle, perched high on a hill above town, simply can't be cheapened. The 11th-century castle was destroyed in 1689 by French troops led by Louis XIV, but was rebuilt in 1868 and is now open to the public for frequent 40-minute tours. (Written English translations available. Open Mar. 15-Oct. daily 9am-5pm. DM6, students DM5.)

The **tourist office**, Endertpl. 1 (tel. (02671) 39 71 or 39 72; fax 84 10), is right next to the bridge; from the train station, head to the river and turn right. The office makes free same-day room reservations (open May-Nov. 15 M-F 10am-5pm, Sa 10am-3pm). Cochem's friendly, basic **Jugendherberge (HI)**, Klottenerstr. 9 (tel. (02671) 86 33; fax 85 68), is 10 to 15 minutes from the station on the opposite shore. (DM21; breakfast included. Reception noon-1pm and 5-10pm; late arrivals ring the bell. Curfew 10pm.) **Campingplatz am Freizeitzentrum** (tel. (02671) 44 09) is on Stadionstr. below the youth hostel (DM6.50 per person, DM6-12 per tent; reception 8am-9pm).

Ten kilometers upstream from Cochem lies tiny **Beilstein**, with its half-timbered houses and crooked cobblestone streets. The ruins of **Burg Metternich,** another casualty of French troops in 1689, offer a sweeping view of the valley (open Apr.-Oct. daily 9am-5pm; DM2, students DM1.50). The Baroque **Karmelitenkirche** has an intricate wooden altar and famous 16th-century sculpture. **Buses** to Beilstein depart about once an hour from both the Endertpl. and train station in Cochem (DM3.50). The **passenger boats** of Personnenschiffahrt Kolb (tel. (02673) 15 15) also travel between the two towns (1hr., May-Oct. 4 per day, round-trip DM19).

Trier The oldest town in Germany, **Trier** was founded by the Romans during the reign of Augustus, and reached its heyday in the 4th century as the capital of the western Roman Empire and the residence of Emperor Constantine. Today, the city preserves several Roman ruins and a beautiful and dignified *Altstadt.* The natural point of departure for any tour of the city is the 2nd-century **Porta Nigra** (Black Gate), named for the centuries of grime that have turned its sandstone face varying shades of gray (DM4, students DM2). From here, stroll down Simeonstr. to the **Hauptmarkt,** a shopping district packed with fruit stalls and lined with architecturally diverse buildings. The masses may want to make a pilgrimage to **Karl-Marx-Haus,** Brückenstr. 10, where young Karl first walked, talked, and dreamed of labor alienation. (Open Apr.-Oct. M 1-6pm, Tu-Su 10am-6pm; Nov.-Mar. M 3-6pm, Tu-Su 10am-1pm and 3-6pm. DM3, students DM2.) Make a left onto Sternstr. and explore the impressive interior of the 11th-century **Dom** (open 6:30am-6pm; Nov.-Mar. closes 5:30pm; daily tours at 2pm; free). A walk down Liebfrauenstr. and uphill along Olewigerstr. brings you to the remains of the 2nd-century **amphitheater,** an enormous 20,000-seat venue.

Frequent **trains** go to Koblenz (1½hr.) and nearby Luxembourg (45min., DM12.80). **Personnenschiffahrt ferries** (tel. (0651) 15 15) mosey along the Mosel from beside Kaiser-Wilhelm Brücke (May-Oct. 9:15am, round-trip DM44). Trier's **tourist office** (tel. (0651) 97 80 80; fax 447 59), in the shadow of the Porta Nigra, hands out free maps, books rooms, and offers **tours** in English daily at 1:30pm. (DM9. Open Apr.-Nov. M-Sa 9am-6:30pm, Su 9am-3:30pm; Nov.-Dec. M-Sa 9am-6pm, Su 9am-3:30pm; Jan.-Feb. M-Sa 9am-5pm; Mar. M-Sa 9am-6pm, Su 9am-1pm.)

Trier's **Jugendgästehaus (HI),** An der Jugendherberge 4 (tel. (0651) 14 66 20; fax 146 62 30), has an extensive array of vending machines and ping-pong tables. Take bus 2 or 8 ("Trierweilerweg" or "Pfalzel/Quint") to "Moselbrücke," and walk 10 minutes downstream on the path along the river. (Singles DM50-60; doubles DM72; quads DM107.20; all with toilet and shower. Breakfast, sheets included. Reception generally open 7am-midnight.) The well-located **Jugendhotel Kolpinghaus,** Dietrichstr. 42 (tel. (0651) 97 52 50; fax 975 25 40), is one block off the Hauptmarkt. (Dorms DM27; singles DM37; doubles DM74. Breakfast included. Reception 8am-11pm. Call ahead.) To reach **Trier City Campingplatz,** Luxemburgerstr. 81 (tel. (0651) 869 21), from the Hauptmarkt, follow Fleischstr. to Bruckenstr. to Karl-Marx-Str. to the Römerbrücke; from here, cross the bridge and head left. If you end up in Luxembourg, you've gone too far. (DM7 per person. Reception 8-11am and 6-10pm in Gortätle Kranich, up from the river.) **Astarix,** Karl-Marx-Str. 11, is a relaxed student hangout with wonderfully inexpensive meals (open M-Th 11am-1am, F-Sa 11am-2am, Su 6pm-1am; kitchen closes at 11:30pm). The **wine information office,** Konstantinpl. 11 (tel. (0651) 736 90), will help you make decisions about wine tasting in the Mosel region (open M-F 10:15am-6:30pm, Sa 10am-4pm, Su 1-5pm).

■ Saarbrücken

For centuries, Saarbrücken's proximity to the French border has made it a center of one violent conflict after another, leaving virtually none of the *Altstadt* intact. One of the last undiscovered centers of the modern European cultural scene, Saarbrücken's focus is on the future, and today's shambles are products only of the creation of a slick DM500-million rail transit system, scheduled for completion by 2000. The figures on the bronze doors of the **Basilika St. Johann** are writhing either in hell-fire or heavenly bliss (opens M, W, and F at 8:30am, Tu, Th, and Su 9:30am, Sa 9am). A walk along Am Stadtgarten with the river on the right leads you to the **Saarland Museum,** Bismarckstr. 11-19, which displays Picasso, Matisse, and Beckmann. Medieval Madonnas repose across the street at **Alte Sammlung,** Karlstr. 1. (Both open Tu and Th-Su 10am-6pm, W noon-8pm. Joint admission DM3, students DM1.50.) The 9th-century **Saarbrücker Schloß,** on the other side of the Saar river, has tall sparkling glass columns (tours in German Sa-Su 4pm; free). Around the Schloßpl., the **Historisches Museum** includes a disturbing collection of war propaganda. (Open Tu-W, F, and Su 10am-6pm, Th 10am-8pm, Sa noon-6pm. DM4, students DM2, free Th after 5pm.)

From Saarbrücken, trains chug to Trier (1hr.), Frankfurt (2hr.), and Koblenz. The **tourist office,** Am Hauptbahnhof 4 (tel. (0681) 365 15; fax 905 33 00), to the left of the train station, finds rooms for a DM3 fee and gives out free maps (open M-F 9am-6pm, Sa 9am-3pm). The **Jugendgästehaus "Europa" (HI),** Meerwiesertalweg 31 (tel. (0681) 330 40; fax 37 49 11), is a 25-minute walk from the station; you can also take bus 19 to "Prinzenweiher" and backtrack. (DM26.80-36. Breakfast and sheets included. Reception 7:30am-1am. Curfew 1am.) **Gästehaus Weller,** Neugrabenweg 8 (tel. (0681) 37 19 03; fax 37 55 65), offers huge rooms with bath, phone, and TV. Go down Ursulinenstr., right on Mozartstr., on to Schumannstr., left on Fichtestr., and cross the bridge. (Singles DM59-79; doubles DM89-105. Reception M-Sa 8am-11pm, Su 6-11pm. Call ahead.) For **Campingplatz Saarbrücken,** Am Spicherer Berg (tel. (0681) 517 80), take bus 42 to "Spicherer Weg," cross Untertürkheimstr., and head uphill (DM6 per person; DM8 per tent; open Apr.-Sept.). The streets around **St. Johannis Markt** brim with bistros and beer gardens. **Hela,** at the end of Ursulinenstr., is a supermarket-drugstore-hair salon (open M-F 8am-8pm, Sa 8am-4pm).

BADEN-WÜRTTEMBERG

Two of the most prominent of German icons—the Brothers Grimm and the Mercedes-Benz—duke it out in Baden-Württemberg. Rural custom and tradition are still widely evident in the scenic, foreboding hinterlands of the Black Forest and the Swabian Jura, while the modern capital city of Stuttgart is rooted in the ascendancy of the German industrial machine. The land *(province)* is also the home of the snooty millionaires' resort of Baden-Baden, the vacation getaways of Lake Constance, and the ancient university towns of Freiburg, Tübingen, and Heidelberg.

■ Stuttgart

Visiting Stuttgart is like stepping into a little piece of Utopia. Blown to bits in World War II, the city had nowhere to aim but the future; it continues on its path with vibrant optimism. Despite its rampant modernization, the home of Porsche and Daimler-Benz and the capital of Baden-Württemberg is a blissfully livable metropolis, boasting one of the most verdant settings of any major German city.

SIGHTS AND ENTERTAINMENT At Stuttgart's core lies an enormous pedestrian zone, with shops and restaurants stretching as far as the eye can see. **Königstraße** and **Calwerstraße** are the main pedestrian thoroughfares; from the train station, both are accessible through the underground **Arnulf-Klett-Passage.** The main municipal park, the tranquil **Schloßgarten,** runs south from the station to the elegant Baroque **Neues**

GERMANY

Schloß. The north end of the park contains the **Rosensteinpark** and **Wilhelma,** Stuttgart's famous zoo and botanical garden. (Wilhelma open daily 8:15am-5:30pm; Nov.-Feb. closes at 4pm. DM14, students DM7; lower off-season.) Across from the *Schloß-garten* at Konrad-Adenauer-Str. 30-32 is the superb **Staatsgalerie Stuttgart,** containing works by Picasso, Kandinsky, Beckmann, and Dalí (open Tu-Su 10am-5pm, Tu and Th till 8pm; DM5, students DM3). For artistry of a different sort, the **Mercedes-Benz Museum** covers the history of the luxury automobile from its creation to modern experimental models. (S-Bahn 1: "Neckarstadion;" go left under the bridge and left at the next intersection. Open Tu-Su 9am-5pm. Free.) The **Porsche Museum** tells a similar story with curvier cars. (S-Bahn 6 ("Weil-der-Stadt"): Neuwirtshaus. Open M-F 9am-4pm, Sa-Su till 5pm. Free.) The recently-reopened 58m **clock tower** in the *Hauptbahnhof* has a great view of the city (open daily until 7pm; free). The **Staatstheater** (tel. (0711) 197 03 or 01 15 17), across from the plaza from the *Neues Schloß,* is Stuttgart's most famous. (Box office open M-F 10am-6pm, Sa 9am-1pm. Tickets DM16-90, student discounts available.) Other local theaters are usually much cheaper (DM10-25, students DM5-15); the tourist office has info and tickets.

PRACTICAL INFO, ACCOMMODATIONS, AND FOOD

As the transportation hub of southwest Germany, Stuttgart has direct **trains** to most major cities, including Berlin (6hr.), Frankfurt (1½hr.), Munich (2½hr.), and Paris (6hr.); dial (0711) 194 19 for 24-hour schedule info. Single-ride tickets for Stuttgart's **public transportation** system (buses, streetcars, U-Bahns, and S-Bahns) range from DM3.20 to 9.60. A *Tageskarte* (day pass—not valid for night buses), costs DM12-20. Those staying in city accommodations can get a great deal—3 days of travel on the U-Bahn for DM12; on the entire transport system for DM19. For more info, contact the **tourist office, I-Punkt,** Königstr. 1 (tel. (0711) 222 80; fax 222 82 53), in front of the escalator down to the Klett-Passage, which also books rooms for free and sells the *Monatsspiegel* (in German; DM3.50) guide to museums, events, food, and nightlife. (Open M-F 9:30am-8:30pm, Sa 9:30am-6pm, Su and holidays May-Oct. 11am-6pm; Nov.-Apr. 1-6pm). **Tips 'n' Trips,** Rotebühlpl. 26/27 (tel. (0711) 222 27 30; fax 222 27 33), in the underground U-Bahn passage at Theodor-Heuss-Str. and Fritz-Elsas-Str., is also a great resource (open M-F noon-7pm, Sa 10am-4pm). An **American Express** office is at Schillerpl. 4 (tel. (0711) 162 49 20), by the Schloßpl. (open M-F 10am-6:30pm, Sa 9:30am-12:30pm). For **Internet access,** try Tips 'n' Trips (DM5 per hr.) or the top floor of the **Kaufhof** near the train station (DM3 per 30min; open M-F 9:30am-9pm, Sa 9am-4pm).

Most of Stuttgart's budget beds are on the two ridges surrounding the downtown area and are easily accessible by streetcar. The busy **Jugendherberge Stuttgart (HI),** Haußmannstr. 27 (tel. (0711) 24 15 83; fax 236 10 41), is out the "ZOB" exit of the Klett-Passage, through the Schloßgarten, and past the signs going uphill via the paved path. Or take U-Bahn 15 ("Heumaden") to "Eugenspl.," go down the hill, bear left and enter on Kernerstr. (DM22, over 26 DM27. Sheets DM5.50. Reception 7-9am and noon-11pm. Lockout 9am-noon. Strict curfew 11:30pm, but doors reopen briefly at 1am and 5am for hard-core partiers. *Always* call ahead.) The **Jugendgästehaus Stuttgart,** Richard-Wagner-Str. 2 (tel. (0711) 24 11 32), in a quiet residential neighborhood, is less central. Streetcar 15 ("Heumaden"): Bubenbad. (Singles DM30-50; extra person DM35-45; add DM5 each for one-night stays. Breakfast included. Reception M-F 9am-8pm, Sa-Su 11am-8pm. No curfew.)

Iden, Eberhardstr. 1 (U-Bahn: Rathaus), serves good vegetarian fare cafeteria-style (salads DM2.68 per 100g; open M-F 11am-9pm, Sa 10am-5pm). **UDO-Snack,** Calwerstr. 23, has cheap, greasy favorites for DM2.80-5.80 (open M-Tu 11am-11pm, W-Th till midnight, F-Sa till 1am, Su 3-11pm). At the **University Mensa,** Holzgartenstr. 11, quantity compensates for quality. (Meals DM4-5. Open during school M-F 11:15am-2:30pm; the rest of the year M-F 11:15am-1:30pm.)

The soothing waters of Stuttgart's **mineral baths** are an ideal remedy for budget travel exhaustion. The **Mineralbad Leuze,** Am Leuzebad 2-6 (tel. (0711) 216 42 10), has spectacular facilities (open daily 6am-9pm; day card DM15.50, students DM10.50). Once refreshed, join the crowd for drinks at **Palast der Republik,**

GERMANY

Heidelberg
ACCOMMODATIONS

B Hotel-Pension Elite
C Jeske Hotel
A Jugendherberge

Wehrsteg
Karlstor
Ziegelhäuser Landstr.
Karl-Theodor (Alte) Brücke
Am Hackteufel
Hauptstr.
Schlossberg-Höhenweg
Schloß
Schlossberg-Höhenweg
Schloss-Hof-Weg
Neckar-Höhenkurweg
BERGBAHN
Molkenkur
TO KÖNIGSTUHL
BERGBAHN
Brückentor
MARKT-PLATZ
Rathaus
KARLS-PLATZ
KORN-MARKT
Heiliggeistkirche
Haus zum Ritter
Unterestr.
Alte Universität
Augustinerg.
Zwingerstr.
Seminarstr.
Schlossberg
UNIVERSITÄTS-PLATZ
Grabeng.
Kupfälzisches
Theaterstr.
Hauptstr.
Friedrichstr.
Karl-Ludwig-Str.
Plöck
Neckarstaden
Neckar
Philosophenweg
Neuenheimer Landstr.
Ziegelgasse
Marzgasse
Friedrich-Ebert-Anlage
Gaisbergtunnel
Hauptstr.
Akademiestr.
Plöck
Theodor-Heuss-Brücke
Sofien-Str.
American Express
BISMARCK-PLATZ
Gaisbergstr.
Rohrbacherstr.
Bunsenstr.
Häusserstr.
B
Bruckenstr.
Lutherstr.
Ladenburger Str.
Uferstr.
Schurmannstr.
Bergheimerstr.
Poststr.
Kurfürstenanlage
Bahnhofstr.
Blumenstr.
Kaiserstr.
Monchhofstr.
Keplerstr.
Schröderstr.
Neckar
Romerstr.
RÖMER-KREIS
Römerstr.
Jahnstr.
Uferstr.
Ernst-Walz-Brücke
Iqbal-Ufer
Vangerowstr.
Bergheimerstr.
Alte Eppelheimer Str.
Kurfürsten-Anlage
Hauptbahnhof
Berlinerstr.
TO
A
Mittermeierstr.

N

Friedrichstr. 27 (beer DM4-6; open M-W 11am-2am, Th-Sa till 3am, Su 3pm-2am; in winter Su-W till 1am, Th-Sa till 2am), or dancing at **Zap,** Hauptstätlerstr. 40, in the *Schwabenzentrum* (cover DM8-15; open Tu and Th 11pm-3am, W and Su 9pm-4am, F-Sa 10pm-6am). **Laura,** Kronprinzstr. (Th-Su 10pm-6am; Sa men only), and **Kings,** Calwerstr. 21 (tel. (0711) 226 45 58), are the premier gay and lesbian locales.

▨ Heidelberg

Believe the tourist propaganda—Heidelberg is surrounded by magnificence that truly shines. In 1386, the sages of Heidelberg turned from illuminating manuscripts to illuminating young German minds, and founded Germany's first and greatest university. Set against a backdrop of wooded hills along an ancient river, the crumbling edifices of the once-majestic *Schloß* and the *Altstadt*'s lively nightlife exert a magnetism that draws thousands of shutter-clicking tourists daily.

ORIENTATION AND PRACTICAL INFORMATION

Heidelberg occupies both sides of the Neckar River about 20km east of the river's convergence with the Rhine, but most of its attractions are clustered on the southern shore. To reach the *Altstadt* from the train station, take any bus or streetcar going to "Bismarckpl.," where the **Hauptstraße,** known as the longest shopping street in Germany, runs straight through the heart of the city.

Telephone Code: 06221.

Trains: Frequent trains run from Stuttgart (45min.) and Frankfurt (1hr.); Mannheim is less than 10min. away. Trains also serve towns in the Neckar Valley.

Public Transportation: To get to, from, and around Heidelberg, buy a 24hr. pass good on all streetcars and buses (DM10). The pass is available at the tourist office or from any bus or streetcar conductor. Single-ride tickets cost DM3.30.

Bike Rental: Per Bike, Bergheimerstr. 125 (tel. 16 11 48). Half-day DM15, full day DM25. Open M-F 9am-6pm, Sa 9am-1pm; Nov.-Mar. closed Sa.

Hitchhiking: Hitchers walk to the western end of Bergheimerstr. for all directions. The **Mitfahrzentrale,** Bergheimerstr. 125 (tel. 246 46; fax 14 59 59), matches drivers and riders. Hamburg DM54. Köln DM28. Paris about DM51. Open M-F 9am-5pm, Sa 9am-noon; Nov.-Mar. closed Sa.

Tourist Office: (tel. 142 20; fax 14 22 22), in front of the train station. Sells maps (DM1) and reserves rooms (7% deposit), but the staff steers guests towards pricier places. *Meier* (DM2) and *Fritz* (free) list local events and attractions. Open M-Sa 9am-7pm, Su 10am-6pm; Jan-Feb. closed Su.

Currency Exchange: If banks and the post office are closed, try the *Hauptbahnhof.* Open M-Sa 8am-8pm, Su 9am-1pm.

American Express: Brückenkopfstr. 1 (tel. 450 50; fax 41 03 33), at the end of Theodor-Heuss Bridge. Mail held for members and those with AmEx traveler's checks. All banking services. Open M-F 10am-6pm, Sa 10am-1pm.

Laundromat: Wasch Salon SB, Poststr. 49, next to Kurfürst Hotel. Wash DM7; dry DM1 per 20min. Open daily 6am-3am.

Emergencies: tel. 110. **Women's Emergency Hotline,** tel. 18 36 43.

Police: tel. 990. Station at Römerstr. 2-4.

Post Office: The main office is on Belfortstr., diagonally to the right across from the train station. Held mail can be picked up at counters 15-17. Open M-F 8am-6pm, Sa 8am-noon. **Postal Code:** 69115.

ACCOMMODATIONS, CAMPING, AND FOOD

Finding accommodations in Heidelberg (even expensive ones) can be a nightmare. In the summer, call ahead or arrive early in the day. Those with a railpass might try the little towns and villages scattered short distances from Heidelberg. Many Neckar Valley towns with youth hostels lie along the reliable Heidelberg-Heilbronn railroad.

Jugendherberge (HI), Tiergartenstr. 5 (tel. 41 20 66). From the station or Bismarckpl., take bus 33 ("Zoo-Sportzentrum") to "Jugendherberge." Crowded and noisy, but still popular. Members only. Small disco open nightly. DM22, over 26 DM27. Sheets DM5.50. Lockout 9am-1pm. Flexible curfew 11:30pm. Partially wheelchair accessible. Reserve a week ahead or forget it.

Jeske Hotel, Mittelbadg. 2 (tel. 237 33). From the train station, take bus 33 ("Köpfel") or 11 ("Karlstor") to "Bergbahn," then follow Zwingerstr. west back toward the *Hauptbahnhof;* Mittelbachg. is the first right after Oberbadg. An unbeatable location at a great price draws students to this quiet overnighter. DM24. Open Feb. to mid-Nov.; at other times call ahead.

Hotel-Pension Elite, Bunsenstr. 15 (tel. 257 33). From Bismarckpl., follow Rohrbacherstr. away from the river and turn right onto Bunsenstr. Victorian decor and pastoral views. Bath and TV in each room. Singles DM75-85; doubles DM95-100; DM15 per extra person. Breakfast included. Reserve by mail or phone.

Camping: Haide (tel. (06223) 21 11), between Ziegelhausen and Kleingemünd. Take bus 35 to "Orthopedisches Klinik," then cross the river. DM15-20 per person; DM6-12 per tent; cabins DM15-20. Open Apr.-Oct. Camp on the other side of the river at **Camping Heidelberg-Schlierbach** (tel. 80 25 06); take bus 35 ("Neckargmünd") to "Im Grund." DM10 per person; DM4-12 per tent; DM2 per car.

Eating out is costly in Heidelberg, especially around Hauptstr. Student pubs and restaurants beyond the pedestrian zone offer better value. Buy groceries at **Handelshof,** Kurfürsten-Anlage 60, 200m in front of the train station on the right (open M-F 7:30am-8pm, Sa 7:30am-4pm).

The **Mensa** on Marstallstr. serves cheap food and beer in a state-subsidized cafeteria and cafe. Take bus 35 to "Marstallstr.," or from the Alte Brücke take a left along the river; it's the huge stone installation on the left. (Open M-F 11:30am-2pm, Sa 11:30am-1:30pm. During vacations, alternates hours with the *Mensa* on Universitätspl.) **Gastätte Essighaus,** Plöck 97 (tel. 224 96), serves tasty specials in a traditional German setting (open daily 11:30am-12:30am, food available until 11:30pm). **Zum Schwarzen Wal,** Bahnhofstr. 27 (tel. 201 85), is *the* place in Heidelberg for big, delicious breakfasts (DM6-15), but also serves lunch and dinner (DM10-20; open M-F 7:30am-1am, Sa 8:30am-1am, Su 9am-1am).

SIGHTS AND ENTERTAINMENT

The remarkable Gothic and High Renaissance **Heidelberger Schloß,** at the southeast corner of town, was built over a period of 400 years, beginning in the early 13th century. The obligatory tour includes a visit to the **Faß,** reputedly the world's largest wine barrel. Also in the castle, the **Apothekenmuseum** features a 17th-century alchemist's lab. (Grounds open daily 8am-dusk; before 5:30pm DM3, students DM1.50. Tours in English daily at 11:30am, 2pm, and 3:45pm. DM4, students DM2. Apothekenmuseum open daily 10am-5:30pm. Free with entrance to castle.) The castle is accessible by foot or by *Bergbahn* (cable car), which runs from the "Bergbahn/Rathaus" stop (bus 11 or 33; round-trip DM4.70).

In town, several sights cluster near the **Marktplatz,** a cobbled square that holds an open-air market every Wednesday and Saturday. In the center stands **Hercules' Fountain,** where accused witches and heretics were burned during the Middle Ages. Two of the oldest structures in the city border the Marktpl.: the 14th-century **Heiliggeistkirche,** a Gothic church with an ancient library, and the 16th-century **Hotel zum Ritter.** The stately **Rathaus** presides over the far end of the square. From the square, take Hauptstr. west for more Heidelbergian beauty; five blocks down, a stone-lion fountain oversees activities on **Universitätsplatz,** where the **Alte Universität** (Old University) was once headquartered. At Hauptstr. 97, the **Kurpfälzisches Museum** features the jawbone of *Homo heidelbergensis* ("Heidelberg Man," one of the oldest humans unearthed), other fascinating archaeological exhibits, and works of art by Van der Weyden and Dürer (open Tu-Su 10am-5pm, W until 9pm. DM5, students DM3, Su discounts).

No trip to Heidelberg would be complete without a visit to the northern bank of the Neckar, opposite the *Altstadt*. A stroll across the elegant **Karl-Theodor-Brücke** finds a statue of the Prince-Elector himself; Theodor commissioned it as a symbol of his modesty. From the far end of the bridge, clamber up the **Schlangenweg**, a winding stone stairway, to the **Philosophenweg**, a famous pedestrian walkway where Hegel and Max Weber indulged in afternoon promenades. Atop the **Heiligenberg**, the mountain traversed by the *Philosophenweg*, lie the ruins of the 9th-century **St. Michael Basilika**, the 13th-century **St. Stephen Kloster**, and an **amphitheater**, built under Hitler's order, on the site of an ancient Celtic gathering place.

Heidelberg is home to a number of merry festivals. The **Faschings Parade (Carnival)** struts through the city on Shrove Tuesday. The Spring Festival spices up the last few days of May. The **Handschuhsheim Fest** lures revelers across the river on the third weekend in June, while the **Schloßfestspiele Heidelberg** features a series of concerts and plays at the castle for five weeks, beginning in late July (call 583 52 for info and tickets). On September 30th, the **Heidelberger Herbst** brings a medieval market to the *Altstadt*. For drinks and entertainment year-round, visit the popular, historical **student taverns;** the two best-known are **Roter Ochsen,** Haupstr. 217, and **Zum Sepp'l** next door. (Meals DM12-31; beer DM4.50-5. Roter Ochsen open Apr.-Oct. M-Sa 11:30am-2pm and 5pm-midnight; Nov.-Mar. M-Sa 5pm-midnight. Zum Sepp'l open daily 11am-midnight.) Much of Heidelberg's nightlife centers on Hauptstr. and the Marktpl. **Little Heaven,** Fahrtg. 18, is the local outpost of Euro-dance music culture (open daily 10pm-3am), while **O'Reilly's,** on the corner of Brückenkopfstr. and Uferstr., is a hoppin' Irish pub (open M-F 4pm-1am, Sa-Su noon-1am).

■ Near Heidelberg: Speyer and Neckar Valley

The **Neckar Valley,** a scenic stretch of narrow, thickly wooded ridges along the Neckar River, encompasses several medieval castles and untouristed small towns. At the north end of the valley, 14km upstream from Heidelberg, **Neckarsteinach** is notable for its four medieval castles, all within 3km of one another along the north bank of the river. Set against the ruins of a Roman imperial castle on a ridge high above the Neckar, **Bad Wimpfen** is one of the best-kept secrets in southwest Germany. It lies along one of two train lines between Heidelberg and Heilbronn. One of the best ways to explore the valley is along the 85km **bike** route. Alternatively, the **Rhein-Neckar Fahrgastschiffahrt** (tel. (06221) 201 81 or (06229) 526) runs boat tours from Easter through late October beginning in front of the *Stadthalle* in Heidelberg (DM4-19.50).

Just into Rhineland-Palatinate, **Speyer** is most easily accessed from Heidelberg by **rail** (1-1½hr.) or by **bus** 7007 (1½hr.). Spared during the two world wars and, until recently, well off the beaten path of mass tourism, the city boasts a gracefully ramshackle *Altstadt* and several glorious churches. Since its construction in the 12th century, the enormous **Kaiserdom** (Imperial Cathedral) has been the symbol of Speyer. The crypt under the east end coddles the remains of eight Holy Roman Emperors and their wives (open daily Apr.-Oct. 9am-7pm; Nov.-Mar. 9am-5pm). Just south of the *Dom*, the **Historisches Museum der Pfalz** displays ancient artifacts, cathedral treasures, and the oldest bottle of wine in the world (open Tu-Su 10am-6pm, W 10am-8pm; DM8, students DM5). Speyer's **tourist office,** Maximilianstr. 11 (tel. (06232) 14 23 92; fax 14 23 32), is two blocks from the cathedral's main entrance (open M-F 9am-5pm, Sa 10am-4pm; May-Oct. also Su 11am-3pm).

■ Tübingen

Situated on the willow-lined Neckar River near the Black Forest, Tübingen has gracefully retained the aloofness of its intellectual origins. Nearly half the city's residents are affiliated with the 500-year-old university, and students energize the city center.

SIGHTS AND ENTERTAINMENT The 15th-century **Stiftskirche,** the focal point of the *Altstadt*, houses the tombs of 14 members of the former House of Württemberg in the chancel. The church's tower affords an amazing view of the city. (Church open

GERMANY

daily 9am-5pm. Chancel and tower open Aug.-Sept. daily 10:30am-5pm; Apr.-July and Oct. F-Su 10:30am-5pm. Chancel and tower DM2, students DM1.) Just down the road from the Stiftskirche is the **Tübingen Evangelischer Stift.** Built as an Augustinian monastery, it later became a seminary which housed such academic luminaries as Kepler, Hölderlin, Hegel, Schelling, and Mörike. Alas, the historical interest of this building outweighs its aesthetic appeal. The ornate, painted facade of the **Rathaus** faces the old market square in the middle of the *Altstadt.* On top of the hill that separates the university from most of the city stands the **Schloß Hohentübingen,** a castle with a rough stone balcony overlooking the old town. On the north riverbank is the **Hölderlinturm,** a tower where 18th-century poet Friedrich Hölderlin lived out the final 36 years of his life. (Open Tu-F 10am-noon and 3-5pm, Sa-Su 2-5pm. Tours Sa-Su 5pm. DM3, students DM2.) The tower now houses a memorial museum.

The *Altstadt*'s zig-zagging streets are lined with excellent pubs and cafes. **Tangente-Night,** Pfleghofstr. 10, is a premier Tübingen student hangout; during the school year, DJs spin house, acid jazz, hip-hop, and techno Thursday through Sunday nights (open daily 10am-3am). **Marktschenke,** Am Markt 11, and **Neckarmüller,** Gartenstr. 4, are popular with the young folks.

PRACTICAL INFO, ACCOMMODATIONS, AND FOOD Tübingen's **tourist office,** Neckarbrücke (tel. (07071) 913 60; fax 350 70), books hotel or private rooms for a DM5 fee (DM30-100). From the front of the train station, turn right and walk to Karlstr., turn left, and walk to the river (open M-F 9am-7pm, Sa 9am-5pm, Su 2-5pm). The recently renovated **Jugendherberge (HI),** Gartenstr. 22/2 (tel. (07071) 230 02; fax 250 61), overlooks the Neckar and has a great breakfast. Take bus 11 (DM2.50) from the station to "Jugendherberge." (DM23, over 26 DM28. Breakfast included. Reception 5-8pm and 10-10:15pm. Curfew 10pm. Members only.) Camp at **Rappernberghalde** (tel. (07071) 431 45) on the river. Go upstream from the old town or left from the station, cross the river on the Alleenbrücke, and turn left again (20-25min.). Follow the blue camping signs. (DM9.50 per person; DM5.50-7 per tent. Reception 8am-12:30pm and 2:30-10pm. Open Mar. to mid-Oct.)

Tübingen's students keep a number of superb yet inexpensive restaurants busy. **Marquardtei,** Herrenbergstr. 34, serves whole-wheat pizza and a vast selection of vegetarian and meat dishes (main courses DM10-14; open M-Sa 11:30am-1am, Su 10am-1am). **Die Wurstküche,** Am Lustnauer Tor 8, dishes up regional (DM13-27) and vegetarian specialties (DM13-15; open daily 11am-midnight).

■ Freiburg im Breisgau

Freiburg may be the "metropolis" of the Schwarzwald, but it has not succumbed to the hectic rhythms of city life. Its palpably relaxed air may result from the surrounding hills, which brim with greenery and fantastic hiking trails.

SIGHTS AND ENTERTAINMENT The pride of Freiburg is the **Münster,** a tremendous stone cathedral with a 116m spire built at intervals between the 13th and 16th centuries. (Cathedral open M-Sa 10am-7pm, Su 1-6pm. Tower open May-Oct. M-F 9:30am-5pm, Su 1-5pm; Nov.-Apr. Tu-Sa 9:30am-5pm, Su 1-5pm. DM2, students DM1.) A stroll through the surrounding *Altstadt* will reveal several **Bächle,** narrow streams of swiftly flowing water that run through the city. In medieval times, these open gutters were used to water cattle and protect against fires; today, they exist only to soak the shoes of unwary tourists. Two medieval gates—the **Schwabentor** and the **Martinstor**—still stand within a few blocks of one another in the southeast corner of the *Altstadt.* From the Schwabentor, take the pedestrian overpass across the heavily trafficked Schloßbergring and climb the **Schloßberg** for an excellent view of the city.

Freiburg's museums cater to a variety of interests. The **Augustiner Museum,** housed in a former monastery on Augustinerpl., has a large collection of mostly medieval artifacts (open Tu-Su 10am-5pm; DM4, students DM2). Farther south, the **Museum für Neuekunst** (Museum of Modern Art), Marienstr. 10a, displays the work of 20th-century German artists such as Otto Dix (open Tu-Su 10am-5pm; free).

The brewery **Brauerei Ganter,** Schwarzwaldstr 43 (tel. (0761) 218 51 81), conducts one-hour tours tracking the production process of the malt beverage; the grand finale consists of food and lots of beer atop one of the factory buildings (free). For less structured entertainment, Freiburg's nightlife revolves around the Martinstor. **Jazzhaus,** Schnewlingstr. 1, features live performances almost every night, while **Greiffenegg-Schlößle,** Schloßbergring 3, offers beer (DM5-7) on a hillside terrace.

PRACTICAL INFO, ACCOMMODATIONS, AND FOOD The **tourist office,** Rotteckring 14 (tel. (0761) 388 18 82; fax 388 18 87), two blocks down Eisenbahnstr. from the train station, distributes the comprehensive *Freiburg Official Guide* (DM6) and maps of hiking trails. (Open June-Sept. M-F 9:30am-8pm, Sa 9:30am-5pm, Su 10amnoon; Oct.-May M-F 9:30am-6pm, Sa 9:30am-2pm, Su 10am-noon.) The **Jugendherberge (HI),** Kartäuserstr. 151 (tel. (0761) 676 56; fax 603 67), provides rooms in an arboreal setting. Take S-Bahn 1 ("Littenweiler") to "Römerhof," then cross the tracks, walk down Fritz-Geiges-Str., cross the stream, and follow the footpath to the right. (DM23, over 26 DM28. Reception 7am-11:30pm. Curfew 11:30pm. Members only.) **Hotel Zum Löwen,** Breisgauerstr. 62 (tel. (0761) 809 72 20; fax 840 23), doesn't feel like a budget hotel. Take S-Bahn 1 to "Padua-Allee" and walk down Breigauerstr. for 5 minutes; enter from the parking lot (singles DM45-60; doubles DM80-130; breakfast included). To find the attractive **Haus Lydia Kalchtaler,** Peterhof 11 (tel. (0761) 671 19), take S-Bahn 1 ("Littenweiler") to "Lassbergstr.," then hop on bus 17 ("Kappel") to "Kleintalstr.," and follow Peterhof up to the wooden farmhouse (DM15-21). **Freiburger Salatstuben,** Löwenstr. 1, offers imaginative salads and health foods, while **Milano,** Schusterstr. 7, serves tasty pizza (DM7-8) and pasta (DM7.50-15.50).

■ Black Forest (Schwarzwald)

Throughout its rocky development, the German cultural consciousness dreamed of the dark, from the earliest fairy tales to Franz Kafka's disturbing fiction. Nowhere are such nightmarish thoughts more at home than in the southwest corner of Baden-Württemberg—the Black Forest, so named because of the eerie gloom that prevails under its canopy of evergreens. Inspiration for *Hänsel and Gretel,* the Black Forest draws travelers and skiers to its trails, now marked by more than bread crumbs.

The main entry points to the Black Forest are Freiburg at its center; Baden-Baden to the northwest; Stuttgart to the east; and Basel, Switzerland to the southwest. The **Freiburg tourist office** is the best place to gather info about the Black Forest. The longest slope is at Feldberg (near Titisee), and the most scenic route is the stretch from northern Waldkirch to southeastern Hinterzarten. **Rail lines** run along the perimeter from Baden-Baden to Freiburg and east from Freiburg to Donaueschingen and Stuttgart, but many of the innermost regions are accessible only by infrequent **buses.** Check return connections in advance before setting off on daytrips. Many bus lines are privately owned, rendering railpasses invalid.

Titisee and Schluchsee The touristed town of **Titisee** (TEE-tee-zay), 30km east of Freiburg, is set against dark pine-forested ridges and a lake of the same name. Hourly **trains** connect Freiburg to Titisee. The **tourist office,** Strandbadstr. 4 (tel. (07651) 980 40; fax 98 04 40; http://www.titisee.de), is in the *Kurhaus.* To reach the building, turn right in front of the train station, walk to the first intersection, and turn right before the entrances to the pedestrian zone. The office books rooms (DM3) and sells maps of the 130km of hiking trails around the lake. (DM1-15. Open May-Oct. M-F 8am-5:30pm, Sa 10am-noon and 3-5pm, Su 10am-noon; Nov.-Apr. M-F 8am-noon and 1:30-5:30pm.) **Paddleboats** can be rented from several vendors along Seestr. (DM7 per 30min.). Guided **boat tours** of the lake (25min., DM6) leave from the same area. **Jugendherberge Veltishof (HI),** Bruderhalde 27 (tel. (07652) 238; fax 756), is beautifully if inconveniently located at the far end of the lake. From the train station, take Südbaden bus 7300 to "Feuerwehrheim" (every 1-3hr., DM3.30). By foot, it's a 30-minute walk along the main road from the *Kurhaus* (DM25.10, over 26 DM30.10;

members only; reception 5-8pm; curfew 10pm). Several campgrounds lie along the same road; **Naturcamping Weiherhof,** Bruderholde 26 (tel. (07652) 14 68; fax 14 78), has laundry facilities and great, tree-shaded places to pitch a tent. (DM8 per person, DM6.50 per tent, *Kurtaxe* DM2.10. Free showers. Open mid-May to Sept.)

South of Titisee is the comparably picturesque, less-touristed **Schluchsee.** Hourly **trains** make the 30-minute jaunt from Titisee. The **tourist office** (tel. (07656) 77 32; fax 77 59; http://www.schluchsee.de), a block into the pedestrian zone in the *Kurhaus,* sells hiking maps and finds rooms. (Open July-Aug. M-F 8am-6pm, Sa 10am-noon and 4-6pm, Su 10am-noon; Sept.-Oct. and May-June M-F 8am-noon and 2-6pm, Sa 10am-noon.; Nov.-Apr. closed Sa.) The **Jugendherberge Schluchsee-Wolfsgrund (HI),** Seeweg 28 (tel. (07656) 329; fax 92 37), is situated on the shore; from the station, cross the tracks, hop the fence, then follow the path right, over the bridge parallel to the tracks. (DM23, over 26 DM28. Reception closed daily 2-5pm. Curfew 11pm. *Kurtaxe* DM2.50 May-Oct.)

St. Peter, St. Märgen, and Triberg

North of Titisee and about 15km east of Freiburg, the twin villages of **St. Peter** and **St. Märgen** lie within the High Black Forest. **Bus** 7216 runs occasionally from Freiburg to St. Märgen via St. Peter; the more timely route requires a train ride on the Freiburg-Neustadt line to "Kirchzarten," where bus 7216 whisks you up to St. Peter. **St. Peter,** closer to Freiburg and surrounded by a cherry orchard, appears where a halo of green farmland breaks through the dark crust of pine forests. The abbey's **Klosterkirche** is aflutter with Baroque angels inside (tours given Su 11:30am, Tu 11am, and Th 2:30pm; July-Sept. also W 11am). From the "Zähringer Eck" bus stop, the **tourist office** (tel. (07660) 91 02 24; fax 91 02 44) is right in front of the church (open M-F 8am-noon and 2-5pm; June-Oct. also Sa 11am-1pm). Well-marked **trails** cover the surrounding area; an 8km trail from the abbey leads to St. Märgen.

Nestled in a valley 800m above sea level and 1½ hours by train from Konstanz, the touristy whistle stop of **Triberg** has Germany's highest **waterfalls,** a series of white cascades tumbling over mossy rocks for 163 vertical meters (park admission DM2.50, students DM2). **Hiking trails** abound throughout the outskirts of town, including a portion of the Pforzheim-Basel *Westweg.* Triberg's **tourist office** (tel. (07722) 95 32 30; fax 95 32 36), on the ground floor of the local *Kurhaus,* sells town maps (DM1) and hiking maps (DM5.50; open M-F 9am-5pm; May-Sept. also Sa 10am-noon). The town's sparkling, modern **Jugendherberge (HI),** Rohrbacherstr. 35 (tel. (07722) 41 10; fax 66 62), requires a masochistic 30-minute climb up Friedrichstr. (which turns into Rohrbacherstr.) from the tourist office. (DM22, over 26 DM27. Sheets DM5.50. Reception 5-7pm and at 9:45pm. Call ahead.) For those avoiding the climb, the **Hotel Zum Bären,** Hauptstr. 10 (tel. (07722) 44 93), offers worn-in rooms, most with showers, closer to the town center. The jolly staff has been dealing with American students for decades (singles DM45; doubles DM84).

■ Baden-Baden

If you're fabulously wealthy, Baden-Baden can be a lot of fun. Minor royalty and the like convene here to bathe in the curative mineral spas and drop fat sums of money in the casino. Backpackers will feel a bit out of place, but the haughtiness may be worth tolerating long enough to enjoy the affordable baths and pretty downtown area.

SIGHTS AND SPAS Baden-Baden's history as a resort goes back nearly two millennia, when the Romans built the first **thermal baths** here. The **Friedrichsbad,** Römerpl. 1, is a palatial 19th-century bathing palace where you can enjoy a three-hour Roman-Irish Bath. No clothing is permitted. (Open M-Sa 9am-10pm, Su noon-8pm; last entry 3hr. before closing. Baths are co-ed all day W, Sa, and Su; Tu and F 4-10pm. Bath DM36, with soap and brush massage DM48.) More modest and budget-minded cure-seekers should try next door at the beautiful **Caracalla-Thermen,** Römerpl. 11, which offers placid soaking—in bathing suits (open daily 8am-10pm;

DM19 for 2-3hr.). When not getting wrinkled at the baths, Baden-Baden's affluent guests head to the **Casino,** whose lavish decor, modeled on Versailles, can be viewed during guided tours. (Open daily Apr.-Sept. 9:30am-noon; Oct.-Mar. 10am-noon. Last tour at 11:45am. DM6.) To enter during gaming hours (Su-Th 2pm-2am, F-Sa 2pm-3am), you must be 21, pay DM5, and wear semi-formal attire.

For a sumptuous view of the Black Forest, mount the 668m **Merkur** peak east of town. Take bus 4 or 5 from Leopoldspl. to "Merkurwald," then take the railway to the top (round-trip DM7). On the hill, the **Neues Schloß** houses a museum of the town's history (open Tu-Su 10am-12:30pm and 2-5pm; DM2, students DM1; tours M-F 3pm). From the neighboring garden, Baden-Baden lies at your feet. The 12th-century ruins of the **Altes Schloß** in the upper hills, a few kilometers from the Neues Schloß, afford a view extending all the way to France. Take bus 15 from Augustapl. (open Tu-Su 10am-10pm; free).

PRACTICAL INFO, ACCOMMODATIONS, AND FOOD The **tourist office** is at Augustapl. 8 (tel. (07221) 27 52 00; fax 27 52 02), in the building next to the Kongreßhaus (open daily 9:30am-6pm). Baden-Baden's **train station** is 7km northwest of town. To avoid the 1½hr. walk, take bus 201 ("Lichtental/Oberbeuren") to "Augustapl." (DM3, 24hr. pass DM8). The **post office,** in the Wagener department store in the pedestrian zone, has phones and changes money, as does the casino. The cheapest bed in town is at the modern **Jugendherberge (HI),** Hardbergstr. 34 (tel. (07221) 522 23; fax 600 12), halfway between the station and the town center; take bus 201, 205, or 206 to "Große-Dollen-Str." and follow the signs uphill. (DM23, over 26 DM28. Reception 5-11pm. Curfew 11:30pm. Members only. Wheelchair accessible.) Most rooms in the center of town are ritzy and overpriced, but the **Hotel am Markt,** Marktpl. 18 (tel. (07221) 270 40; fax 27 04 44), offers reasonable prices and a great location uphill from the main pedestrian area. (Singles DM52-90; doubles DM95-140. Breakfast included. Reception 7am-10pm.) Most restaurant prices aren't compatible with budget travel, but daily specials often run for under DM12. Another option is to fill up a picnic basket at **Pennymarkt** at the Große-Dollenstr. bus stop.

■ Lake Constance (Bodensee)

The third-largest lake in Europe, Lake Constance forms a graceful three-cornered border at the conjunction of Austria, Switzerland, and Germany. Ancient castles, manicured islands, and great sunbathing provide an excellent escape during the summer.

Spanning the Rhine's exit from the lake, the elegant university city of **Konstanz** is among the few German cities to have escaped Allied bombing. Narrow streets wind around painted Baroque and Renaissance facades in the town's center. Particularly inspiring is the Konstanz **Münster;** sadly, its soaring spire is under renovation until 2003 (open daily 10am-5pm; free). For lovely views of the water, wander down Seestr. or Rheinstag, or find the Stadtgarten, next to the main harbor. Konstanz's free **beaches** are packed in good weather. **Strandbad Horn** is the largest and most popular (bus 5). Twenty-somethings frolic on the beach at the university; take bus 4 to "Egg" and walk past the playing fields. The sublime garden island of **Mainau,** 15 minutes from Konstanz (bus 4), has an unparalleled view of the Bodensee. Students can get in free on summer evenings, when the island is at its tranquil best. (Open 7am-8pm. DM17, students DM9; after 6pm and off season hours DM9, students free.)

The **tourist office,** Bahnhofspl. 13 (tel. (07531) 13 30 30; fax 13 30 60), in the arcade to right of the train station, has an excellent walking map. (Open May-Sept. M-F 9am-6:30pm, Sa 9am-1pm; Oct.-Apr. M-F 9am-12:30pm and 2-6pm; Apr. and Oct. also Sa 9am-1pm.) Ask about the one-day **Gästekarte,** which provides bus fares within Konstanz and reduced admission to some sights. The marvelous **Jugendherberge Kreuzlingen (HI),** Promenadenstr. 7 (tel. (0041) 71 688 26 63; in Switzerland (071) 688 26 63), is south of the border in Kreuzlingen, Switzerland. (Call for directions. Reception 8-9am and 5-9pm. First night 21.20SFr/DM26.50, then 18.70SFr/DM23.40. Open Mar.-Nov.) It's both more luxurious and more conveniently located than **Jugendherberge "Otto-Moericke-Turm" (HI),** zur Allmannshöhe 18 (tel. (07531) 322 60), which has cramped rooms in a former water tower (terrific view, though). Bus 4 from the station: "Jugendherberge." (Reception Apr.-Oct. 3-10pm; Nov.-Mar. 5-10pm. DM21.50, over 26 DM26.50. Members only. Call ahead.) **Sedir,** Hofhaldestr. 11, serves delectable vegetarian noodles for DM9.50 (open M-F 11:30am-2pm, Sa noon-3pm, daily 6pm-1am; kitchen closes 1:45pm and 11:30pm). The **University Mensa** dishes out the city's cheapest food; take bus 9 from the station: "Universität" (open M-Th 7:45am-6:30pm, F closes 5pm; Aug. M-F 11am-2pm).

Lindau im Bodensee

Connected to the lake shore by a narrow causeway, the romantic medieval city of **Lindau** looks out across the Bodensee, where the aquamarine waters and the small detachment from the mainland contribute to the resort-like ambience. The **Städtische Kunstsammlung** (town art museum) is in **Cavazzen-Haus,** an ornate Baroque mansion in the *Marktplatz* (Market Square; open Apr.-Oct. Tu-Su 10am-noon and 2-5pm; DM4, students DM1). The harbor is framed by a 19th-century **Bavarian Lion** and the **New Lighthouse,** the latter offering an illuminating overview of the neighborhood (open daily 10am-7pm; DM2, students DM1). For those over 21 and well-dressed, the **casino** by the Seebrücke bridge can be fun (open daily 3pm-4am; DM5 and a passport). Lindau has three **beaches.** (All open June to mid-Aug. daily and weekends year-round 10am-8pm; other times 10:30am-7:30pm. Last admission 1hr. before closing.) **Römerbad,** left of the harbor, is the smallest and most familial (DM4, students DM3).

Ferries chug to Konstanz (3hr., 3-6 per day, DM18.40, under 24 11.20), as does the **train** (2hr., DM13). Rent **boats** (tel. (08382) 55 14) 50m to the left of the casino, right next to the bridge. (Open mid-Mar. to mid-Sept. daily 9am-9pm. Paddleboats DM14-18 per hr.; motor boat DM45 per hr.) One-hour excursions on a boat leave from the dock behind the casino at 11:30am, 1, 2:30, and 6pm (DM12). The **tourist office,** across from the train station at Ludwigstr. 68 (tel. (08382) 26 00 30; fax 26 00 26), finds rooms for a DM5 fee and leads English tours Monday at 10am (DM3-5; open mid-June to early Sept. M-Sa 9am-1pm and 2-7pm; shorter hours off-season).

The spectacular **Jugendherberge** (youth hostel), Herbergsweg 11 (tel. (08382) 967 10), lies across the Seebrücke off of Bregenzerstr. (DM29; breakfast, sheets, and *Kurtaxe* (guest tax) included. Reception 7am-midnight. Curfew midnight. Under 27 and families with small children only.) **Campingplatz Lindau-Zech,** Frauenhoferstr. 20 (tel. (08382) 722 36), is 3km south of the island on the mainland. Take bus 1 or 2 from the station to "Anheggerstr.," then bus 3 ("Zech"). (DM9.50 per person, DM4 per tent. *Kurtaxe* DM1.50. Showers included. Open May-Oct.) Sit down for Greek at **Taverna Pita Gyros,** Paradiespl. 16, which offers big platters (DM6-19; open daily 10am-9pm).

BAVARIA (BAYERN)

Bavaria is the Germany of Teutonic myth, Wagnerian opera, and fairy tales. From the Baroque cities along the Danube to the turreted castles perched high in the Alps, the region draws more tourists than any other part of the country. Indeed, when most foreigners conjure up images of Germany, they imagine Bavaria, land of beer halls, oom-pah-pah bands, and *Lederhosen.* Though mostly rural, Catholic, and conservative, this largest of Germany's federal states nurtures flourishing commerce and industry, including Bayerische Motor Werke (BMW). The region's independent residents have always been Bavarians first and Germans second.

Reminder: HI-affiliated hostels in Bavaria do not admit guests over age 26.

■ Munich (München)

As Germany's second city, Munich's sensual air of merriment—most obvious during the wild *Fasching* and the legendary *Oktoberfest*—contrasts with Berlin's starker, more cutting-edge energy. The modern city emerges from a powerful and troubled history: the Bavarian Golden Age of the 18th and 19th centuries, characterized by the wildly extravagant castles of Ludwig II, ended abruptly with Germany's defeat in World War I, and World War II shattered the city, leaving less than 3% of its center intact. But Munich has proved resilient—today, it shines unabashedly with Western German postwar economic glory. World-class museums, handsome parks and architecture, a rambunctious arts scene, and an urbane population combine to create a city of astonishing vitality.

ORIENTATION AND PRACTICAL INFORMATION

A map of Munich's center looks like a skewed circle quartered by one horizontal and one vertical line. The circle is the main traffic **Ring**, within which lies the lion's share of Munich's sights. The east-west and north-south thoroughfares cross at Munich's epicenter, the **Marienplatz** (home to the **Neues Rathaus**), and meet the traffic ring at **Karlsplatz** in the west, **Isartorplatz** in the east, **Odeonsplatz** in the north, and **Sendlinger Tor** (Sendlinger Gate) in the south. The **Hauptbahnhof** (main train station) is just beyond Karlspl. outside the Ring in the west. To get to Marienpl. from the train station, go straight on Schützenstr. to Karlspl., then continue through Karlstor to Neuhauserstr., which becomes Kaufingerstr. before it reaches Marienpl. (15-20min.). Or take S-Bahn 1-8 two stops from the main train station to "Marienpl."

The **Residenz** palace sprawls at Odeonspl.; **Ludwigstraße** stretches north to the university district. **Leopoldstraße**, Ludwigstr.'s continuation, goes farther into the student area, **Schwabing** ("Schwabylon"). West is the **Olympiazentrum;** farther still, the posh **Nymphenburg** is built around the **Schloß Nymphenburg** (Nymphenburg palace). Southwest of Marienpl., **Sendlingerstraße** leads past shops to the Sendlinger Tor. From there, Lindwurmstr. proceeds to Goethepl., from which Mozartstr. leads to **Theresienwiese,** site of the annual beer extravaganza—*Oktoberfest.*

Telephone Code: 089.

Flights: For flight info, call 97 52 13 13. **Flughafen München** is accessible from the train station by S-Bahn 8, which runs daily every 20min. 3:35am-12:35am (DM14 or 8 strips; Eurail, InterRail and German railpasses valid).

Trains: Munich is the transportation hub of southern Germany. The **Hauptbahnhof** (tel. 22 33 12 56) has connections throughout Europe several times per day: Amsterdam (9hr.), Berlin (7½hr.), Frankfurt (3½hr.), Hamburg (6hr.), Paris (10hr.), Prague (6-8½hr.), and Vienna (4-5hr.). Call 194 19 for schedules, fare information, and reservations (6am-10:30pm); you can also get a **destination booklet** *(Städteverbindungen)* from the Reisezentrum info counters.

Public Transportation: The **MVV** system runs 5am-12:30am, Sa-Su until 2:30am. Eurail, InterRail, and German railpasses are valid on any S-Bahn (commuter rail) but *not* on the U-Bahn (subway), *Straßenbahn,* or buses. Single ride tickets (with transfers) are DM3.50 within the *Innenraum* (city center). A *Streifenkarte* (11-strip ticket) costs DM15. Use 2 strips per person. Single-day tickets give one person unlimited travel (city center DM8.50). The **Innenraum 3-day pass** (DM21) is available at the Hauptbahnhof MVV office behind tracks 31 and 32. Stamp your ticket in the boxes marked with an "E" *before you go to the platform* (or on board a bus). If you cheat, the fine is DM60. For a diagram of Munich's transit network, see this book's **color map.**

Bike Rental: Radius Bikes (tel. 59 61 13), in the rear of the *Hauptbahnhof* near tracks 30-31. 2hr. DM10; full day DM30. DM100 deposit. 10% student or Eurail discount. Offers **biking tours** (DM12-19). Open daily Apr. to early Oct. 10am-6pm.

Hitchhiking: Those offering rides post info in the **Mensa** (cafeteria), on Leopoldstr. 13. Otherwise, hitchers try *Autobahn* on-ramps. Hitchers heading to E11 "Salzburg-Vienna-Italy" take U-Bahn 1 or 2 to "Karl-Preis-Pl." For E11 in the other

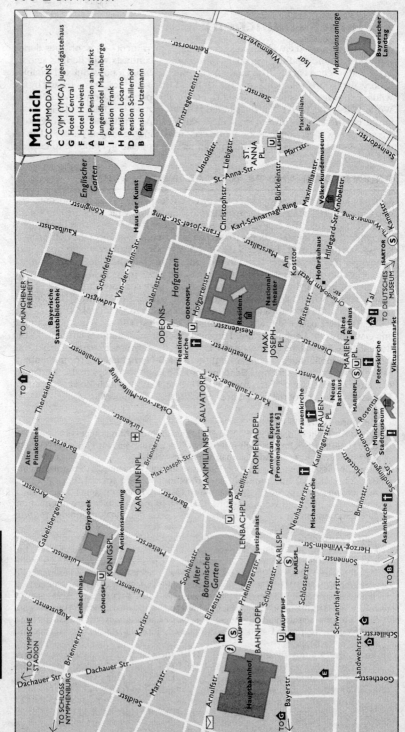

Munich

ACCOMMODATIONS

C CVJM (YMCA) Jugendgästehaus
G Hotel Central
F Hotel Helvetia
A Hotel-Pension am Markt
E Jungendhotel Marienberge
I Pension Frank
H Pension Locarno
D Pension Schillerhof
B Pension Utzelmann

GERMANY

direction ("Stuttgart/France"), they take streetcar 17 "Amalienburgstr." Those aiming for the E6 interchange north to Berlin take U-Bahn 6 to "Studentenstadt" and walk 500m to the Frankfurter Ring. A safer bet is **McShare Treffpunkt Zentrale,** Klenzestr. 57b and Lämmerstr. 4 (tel. 59 45 61) which matches drivers with passengers (Berlin DM54; open daily 8am-8pm). **Frauenmitfahrzentrale,** Klenzestr. 57b, is for **women only.** Take U-Bahn 1 or 2 to "Fraunhoferstr.," up Fraunhoferstr. away from the river and turn right. Open M-F 8am-8pm.

Tourist Offices: Fremdenverkehrsamt (tel. 23 33 02 56 or 23 33 02 57; fax 23 33 02 33; http://www.munich-tourist.de), on the main train station's east side. Books rooms (free with a 10-15% deposit) and sells accommodations lists (DM1) and excellent city maps (DM0.50). *München Infopool* (DM1) is aimed at young tourists. Open M-Sa 9am-10pm, Su 10am-6pm. A **branch office** (tel. 233 03 00), at the airport in the *Zentralgebäude*, provides general info, but no room bookings. Open M-Sa 8:30am-10pm, Su 1-9pm. **EurAide in English** (tel. 59 38 89; fax 550 39 65; http://www.cube.net/kmu/euraide.html), along Track 11 (room 3) of the *Hauptbahnhof*, is good for transportation needs. Room reservations DM7. Open from June-*Oktoberfest* daily 7:45am-noon and 1-6pm; Oct.-Apr. M-F 7:45am-noon and 1-4pm, Sa 7:45am-noon; May daily 7:45am-noon and 1-4:30pm.

Tours: Mike's Bike Tours (tel. 651 42 75). 4hr. tours 1-2 times daily Mar.-Oct. from the *Altes Rathaus* (6hr. tours daily June-Aug.); DM31-45. **Munich Walks** (tel. (0177) 227 59 01). 2½hr. guided tours in English provide a historical overview (1-2 times daily), or emphasize Nazi history (1-3 times weekly Apr.-Oct.). DM10-15.

Budget Travel: Council Travel, Adalbertstr. 32 (tel. 39 50 22; fax 39 70 04), near the university, sells ISICs. Open M-F 10am-1pm and 2-6:30pm.

Consulates: Australia, contact the Bonn consulate: Godesberger Allee 105-107 (tel. (0228) 810 30; fax 810 31 30). **Canada,** Tal 29 (tel. 219 95 70). Open M-Th 9am-noon and 2-5pm, F 9am-noon and 2-3:30pm. **Ireland,** Mauerkircherstr. 1a (tel. 98 57 23). Open M-F 9am-noon and 1-4pm. **New Zealand,** contact the Bonn consulate: Bundeskanzlerpl. 2-10 (tel. (0228) 22 80 70; fax 22 16 87). **South Africa,** Sendlinger-Tor-Pl. 5 (tel. 231 16 30). Open M-F 9am-noon. **U.K.,** Bürkleinstr. 10 (tel. 21 10 90), 4th fl. Consular section open M-F 8:45-11:30am and 1-3:15pm. **U.S.,** Königinstr. 5 (tel. 288 80). No longer handles visas; call (0190) 27 07 89 for recorded info, (0190) 91 50 00 M-F 7am-8pm for an official. Open M-F 8-11am.

Currency Exchange: American Express is cheapest; otherwise pick up a copy of EurAide's free publication *Inside Track* and take it to the **Reise Bank** (tel. 55 10 80), at the main station, in front of the main entrance on Bahnhofpl., for a 50% discount on commission (regularly DM3-10) if cashing US$50 or more in U.S. traveler's checks (open daily 6am-11pm). Also at track 11 (open M-Sa 7:30am-7:15pm, Su 9:30am-12:30pm and 1-4:45pm).

American Express: Promenadepl. 6 (tel. 29 09 00; 24hr. hotline (0130) 85 31 00; fax 29 09 01 18), in the Hotel Bayerischer Hof. Holds mail, cashes traveler's checks, no fee. Open M-F 9am-5:30pm, Sa 9:30am-12:30pm.

Luggage Storage: At the **train station;** staffed storage room *(Gepäckaufbewahrung)* open daily 6am-11pm. DM4 per piece per day. Lockers DM2-4 per 24hr.

Bookstore: Anglia English Bookshop, Schellingstr. 3 (tel. 28 36 42). Reams of books in a gloriously chaotic atmosphere. Open M-F 9am-6:30pm, Sa 10am-2pm.

Gay and Lesbian Organizations: Gay services info tel. 260 30 56. Lesbian info tel. 725 42 72 (F 6-10pm), or **Lesbentraum LeTra,** (tel. 725 42 72, Th 7-10pm).

Laundromat: The **City SB-Waschcenter,** Paul-Heyse-Str. 21, near the station; wash and soap DM6. Open daily 7am-11pm. **Münz Waschsalon,** Amalienstr. 61, near the university. Wash DM6.20. Open M-F 8am-6:30pm, Sa 8am-1pm.

Emergency: Police, tel. 110. **Ambulance,** tel. 192 22. **Emergency medical service,** tel. 55 17 71. **Fire,** tel. 112. **Poison Control,** tel. 192 40.

Crisis Lines: Rape Crisis, Frauennotruf München, Güllstr. 3 (tel. 76 37 37). **AIDS Hotline,** tel. 520 73 87 or 520 74 12 (M-Th 8am-3pm, F 8am-noon) or 194 11 (M-Sa 7-10pm).

Pharmacy: Bahnhof Apotheke, Bahnhofpl. 2 (tel. 59 41 19 or 59 81 19), outside the station. Open M-F 8am-6:30pm, Sa 8am-2pm. 24hr. service rotates—call 59 44 75 for info in German, or get a schedule at the tourist office or EurAide.

Medical Assistance: Klinikum Rechts d.Isar, Ismaningerstr., across the river. U-Bahn 4 or 5: Max-Weber-Pl. List of English-speaking doctors at U.K. or U.S. consulates.

Internet Access: Internet-Café (see **Food,** p. 420). **Hotel Kurpfalz** (guests only; see **Accommodations and Camping,** p. 419).

Post Office: Post/Telegrafenamt, Arnulfstr. 32., 80074 München (tel. 54 54 23 36). *Poste Restante* and money exchange. Go out of the train station and turn left onto Arnulfstr.; the post office will be on your right. Open M-F 8am-8pm, Sa 8am-noon. EurAide (see **Tourist Offices,** p. 417) offers a "message-forwarding service."

ACCOMMODATIONS AND CAMPING

Munich's accommodations fall into one of three categories: seedy, expensive, or booked. Reserve in advance in summer and during *Oktoberfest,* when all three often apply. Sleeping in the *Englischer Garten* or train station is unsafe and illegal. Augsburg's hostel (40min. by train; see page 425) is an option, but mind the 1am curfew. The Ebersberg hostel (tel. (8092) 225 23; 30min. by train) closes at 10pm. HI hostels are not supposed to accept solo travelers over 26, although families may book rooms. For railpass holders, a final option is to catch the 11:17pm train to Heidelberg, and, upon arriving at 3:12am, catch the 3:19am train back to Munich. Arrive in Munich at 7:16am, and start looking for a real room immediately. Be sure to *double check* an up-to-date train schedule before attempting this stunt.

Hostels and Camping

Jugendlager Kapuzinerhölzl ("The Tent"), In den Kirschen 30 (tel. 141 43 00). Streetcar 17 ("Amalienburgstr.") from the *Hauptbahnhof* to "Botanischer Garten," go straight on Franz-Schrank-Str., then turn left. Sleep with 400 others on a foam pad under a circus tent with ping pong and its own beer garden. DM13 with breakfast. Actual "beds" DM17. Lockers provided; bring a lock or rent one for DM2. Reception 24hr. Reservations for groups over 15. Open mid-June to early-Sept.

4 you münchen (ökologisches Jugendgästehaus), Hirtenstr. 18 (tel. 55 21 660; fax 55 21 66 66), 200m from the *Hauptbahnhof.* Beautiful and ecological, with facilities for the handicapped. Dorms DM24-29; singles DM54; doubles DM76; over 27 15% surcharge. Breakfast DM7.50. Sheets DM5. Key deposit DM20. In adjoining hotel, singles DM79; doubles DM110; breakfast included. Reception 7am-1:30pm, 3-7pm, and 7:30-10pm.

Jugendherberge Pullach Burg Schwaneck (HI), Burgweg 4-6 (tel. 793 06 43; fax 793 79 22). S-Bahn 7 ("Wolfratshausen") to "Pullach." Romantic, but swarming with schoolchildren. Dorms DM19.50-22.50; breakfast included. Sheets DM5. Reception 4-11pm. Curfew 11:30pm. Try to make reservations 7:30-10am.

Jugendherberge München (HI), Wendl-Dietrich-Str. 20. (tel. 13 11 56). U-Bahn 1 to "Rotkreuzpl." then cross Rotkreuzpl. towards the Kaufhof store. Best located hostel. Dorms DM23-25.50. Breakfast and sheets included. Mandatory key deposit DM20. Safes with DM50 deposit. Check-in at 11am, but lines start before 9am. Reception 24hr. Reservations only accepted a week in advance; if you get one, arrive by 6pm or call first.

Jugendgästehaus Thalkirchen, Miesingstr. 4 (tel. 723 65 50). U-Bahn 1 or 2 to "Sendlinger Tor," then 3 ("Fürstenrieder West") to "Thalkirchen" (Zoo). Take the Thalkirchnerpl. exit, follow Schäftlarnstr. toward Innsbruck and bear right, follow Frauenbergstr., then left on Münchnerstr. Dorms DM27; singles DM35.50; doubles DM63; quads DM118. Breakfast included. Reception 7am-1am. Curfew 1am.

Jump In, Hochstr. 51 (tel. 48 95 34 37), S-Bahn 1-8 "Rosenheimerpl."; take the Gasteig exit. Small and delightfully informal. Accessible location; spartan rooms. DM29-35; doubles DM78. Kitchen. Reception 10am-1pm and 5-10pm. No curfew.

Jugendhotel Marienberge, Goethestr. 9 (tel. 55 58 05), less than a block from the train station, staffed by merry nuns. **Women under 26** only. Kitchen and laundry facilities (wash/dry DM2 each). Dorms DM30; singles DM40; doubles DM70. Breakfast included. Reception 8am-midnight. Curfew midnight.

CVJM (YMCA) Jugendgästehaus, Landwehrstr. 13 (tel. 552 14 10; fax 550 42 82; email muenchen@cvjm.org). Take the Bayerstr. exit from the station, and go straight down Goethestr. Spic'n'span rooms. Coed rooms for married couples only.

Singles DM50; doubles DM86; over 27 add 15%. Breakfast included. Reception 8am-12:30am. Curfew 12:30am. Closed Easter and Dec.20-Jan. 7.

Haus International, Elisabethstr. 87 (tel. 12 00 60). U-Bahn 2 ("Feldmoching") to "Hohenzollernpl.," then streetcar 12 ("Romanpl.") or bus 33 ("Aidenbachstr.") to "Barbarastr." It's the 5-story beige building behind the BP gas station. Singles DM55-85; doubles DM104-144; larger rooms DM138-200. Reception 24hr.

Camping: Campingplatz Thalkirchen, Zentralländstr. 49 (tel. 723 17 07; fax 724 31 77). U-Bahn 1 or 2 to "Sendlinger Tor," then 3 to "Thalkirchen," and change to bus 57. Laundry facilities and a restaurant (meals DM3-8); showers DM2. DM7.90 per person; tent DM5.50-7. Curfew 11pm.

Hotels and Pensions

When the city is full, finding clean singles under DM55-65 and doubles under DM80-100 in a safe area is nearly impossible. Reserving *months* ahead is particularly important during *Oktoberfest.* The tourist office and EurAide find rooms for a deposit/fee. Calling ahead for a price quote is an absolute *must.*

Hotel Helvetia, Schillerstr. 6 (tel. 590 68 50; fax 59 06 85 70), to the right as you exit the station. Recently renovated. Dorms DM19-24; singles DM53-62; doubles DM68-115; triples DM99-120. Sheets DM4. Laundry DM8.50. *Oktoberfest* 10-15% higher. Reception 24hr.

Pension Frank, Schellingstr. 24 (tel. 28 14 51; fax 280 09 10). U-Bahn 3 or 6: "Universität." Dorms DM35; singles DM55-65; doubles DM78-85; during *Oktoberfest* add DM5. Breakfast included. Reception 7:30am-10pm.

Pension Utzelman, Pettenkoferstr. 6 (tel. 59 48 89; fax 59 62 28). From the train station, walk 4 blocks down Schillerstr. and go left on Pettenkofer. Nostalgically elegant rooms. Hall showers DM5. Singles DM50-125; doubles DM90-145; triples DM125-175; quads DM160-180. Breakfast included. Reception 7am-10pm.

Pension am Kaiserplatz, Kaiserpl. 12 (tel. 34 91 90), close to the nightlife. U-Bahn 3 or 6 to "Münchener Freiheit." Exit onto Herzogstr., turn left onto Viktoriastr. and walk to the end. Elegantly decorated rooms. Singles DM49-59; doubles DM82-89; larger rooms DM120-170. Breakfast included. Reception 7am-9pm.

Hotel Kurpfalz, Schwanthalerstr. 121 (tel. 540 98 60; fax 54 09 88 11; email hotel-kurpfalz@munich-online.de). Exit the station onto Bayerstr., turn right down Bayerstr., and veer left onto Holzapfelstr. Free **Internet access.** Singles DM89; doubles DM129, with extra cot DM165; breakfast included. Reception 24hr.

Pension Locarno, Bahnhofpl. 5 (tel. 55 51 64; fax 59 50 45), right outside the train station, under the AGFA sign. Plain rooms with TVs and phones. Hall showers. Singles DM55-75; doubles DM85; triples DM125; quads DM140. Breakfast included. DM5 less if you arrange to skip breakfast. Reception 7:30am-midnight.

Hotel-Pension am Markt, Heiliggeiststr. 6 (tel. 22 50 14; fax 22 40 17), right in the city center. S-Bahn 1-8 to "Marienpl.," walk through the *Altes Rathaus,* and turn right. Singles DM62-110; doubles DM110-160; triples DM165-205. Breakfast included. Reserve rooms at least 3-4 weeks in advance.

Pension Schillerhof, Schillerstr. 21 (tel. 59 42 70; fax 550 18 35). Two blocks right from the Bahnhofspl. train station exit. Tidy rooms in a sea of neighborhood sex shops and *kinos.* Singles DM50-75; doubles DM80-110; extra bed DM20. Breakfast included. *Oktoberfest* surcharge DM25-40 per person. Reception 6am-10pm.

Hotel Central, Bayerstr. 55 (tel. 543 98 46; fax 543 98 47), 5min. to the right from the Bayerstr. exit of the train station. Spacious, plain rooms. Singles DM50-85; doubles DM85-130; ask for low group rates of DM35-45 per person. Reception 24hr.

FOOD

Munich's gastronomic center is the vibrant **Viktualienmarkt,** two minutes south of Marienpl., with a rainbow of bread, fruit, meat, pastry, cheese, wine, vegetable, and sandwich shops (open M-F 9am-6:30pm, Sa 9am-2pm). Otherwise, look for cheap meals in the **university district** off Ludwigstr. You can find groceries at **Tengelmann,** Bayerstr. 5, near the train station (open M-F 8:30am-8pm, Sa 8am-4pm).

GERMANY

Türkenhof, Türkenstr. 78. Smoky and buzzing from noon till night. Creative dishes (*Schnitzel,* omelettes, soups) DM7-14. Vegetarian-friendly. Open Su-Th 11am-1am, F-Sa 11am-3am.

Schelling Salon, Schellingstr. 54. Bavarian *Knödel* and billiard balls since 1872; Lenin, Rilke, and Strauss used to drop in. Breakfast DM5-9; *Wurst* DM6-7. Restaurant and billiards museum open Th-M 6:30am-1pm.

News Bar, Amalienstr. 55, at the corner of Schellingstr. Bustling, trendy, and youthful new cafe. Crepes DM7-11. Open daily 7:30am-2am.

Shoya, Orlandostr. 5, across from the Hofbräuhaus. Japanese restaurant/take-out. *Teriyaki* DM8-16, sushi DM5-30. Open daily 10:30am-midnight.

"La Fiorentina" Trattoria Pizzeria Cafe, Goethestr. 41. Calzones DM11.50, pizza DM7-12.50, Maß 8.60.

buxs, Frauenstr. 9, on the Viktualienmarkt. Vegetarian cafe/restaurant with salads (DM3 per 100g) and tasty pastas. Open M-F 11am-8:30pm, Sa 11am-3:30pm.

Beim Sendlmayr, Westenriederstr. 6, off the Viktualienmarkt. A slice of Little Bayern. Specials DM7-25. Beer DM5.60 for 0.5L. Open daily 11am-11pm.

Internet-Cafe, Nymphenburgerstr. 145 (http://www.icafe.spacenet.de). U-Bahn 1 to "Rotkreuzpl." Unlimited free **Internet access** with an order of pasta (DM9.50), pizza (DM7.50-10), or beer (DM4.90 for 0.5L). Open daily 11am-4am.

SIGHTS

The **Marienplatz** is an interchange for major S-Bahn and U-Bahn lines as well as the social nexus of the city. On the square, the onion-domed towers of the 15th-century **Frauenkirche** (church) have long been one of Munich's most notable landmarks. *(Towers open Apr.-Oct. M-Sa 10am-5pm. DM4, students DM2.)* At the neo-Gothic **Neues Rathaus** (new city hall), the **Glockenspiel** marks the hour at 11am, noon, 5, and 9pm with jousting knights and dancing barrel-makers. At 9pm, a mechanical watchman marches out and a Guardian Angel escorts the *Münchner Kindl* ("Munich Child," the city's symbol) to bed. *(Tower open M-F 9am-7pm, Sa 9am-7pm, Su 10am-7pm. DM2.50.)*

The 11th-century **Peterskirche** is at Rindermarkt and Peterspl.; 302 steps scale the saintly tower, christened *Alter Peter* (Old Peter) by locals. *(Tower open M-Sa 9am-7pm, Su 10am-7pm. DM2.50, students DM1.50.)* Nearby, Ludwig II of Bavaria rests in a crypt of the 16th-century Jesuit **Michaelskirche,** on Neuhauserstr. *(Crypt DM2, students DM1.)* A Bavarian Rococo masterpiece, the **Asamkirche,** Sendlingerstr. 32, is named after brothers Cosmas and Egid, who vowed to build it if they survived a shipwreck. The magnificent **Residenz,** Max-Joseph-Pl. 3, boasts richly decorated rooms built with the wealth of the Wittelsbach dynasty, Bavaria's ruling family from the 12th to the early 20th century. The grounds now house several museums, and the **Schatzkammer** (treasury) contains jeweled baubles, crowns, swords, and ivory from as early as the 10th century. *(Open Tu-Su 10am-4:30pm; last admission 4pm. DM6, students (with ID) and seniors DM4.)* To reach the *Residenz,* take U-Bahn 3, 4, 5, or 6 to "Odeonspl."

Ludwig I's summer residence, **Schloß Nymphenburg,** is worth the trip northwest of town; take streetcar 17 ("Amalienburgstr.") to the "Schloß Nymphenburg" stop. *(Open Tu-Su Apr.-Sept. 9am-noon and 1-5pm; Oct.-Mar. 10am-12:30pm and 1:30-4pm. Main palace DM6, students and seniors DM4; entire complex DM8, students DM5. Grounds free.)* A Baroque wonder set in a winsome park, the palace hides treasures like a two-story granite marble hall seasoned with stucco, frescoes, and a Chinese lacquer cabinet. Check out Ludwig's "Gallery of Beauties"—whenever a woman caught his fancy, he would have her portrait painted. Next door is the immense **Botanischer Garten,** where greenhouses shelter rare and exotic flora. *(Open daily 9am-8pm; greenhouses 9-11:45am and 1-7:30pm. DM4, students DM2.)* Abutting the city center is the **Englischer Garten,** one of Europe's oldest landscaped parks.

Museums

Munich is a supreme museum city. The **Deutsches Museum,** on the Museumsinsel (Museum Island) in the Isar River (S-Bahn 1-8 to "Isartor"), is one of the world's largest, most exciting museums of science and technology. *(Open daily 9am-5pm. DM10, students DM4.)* Particularly interesting are the mining exhibit, which winds through a labyrinth of recreated subterranean tunnels, the planetarium (DM3), and the daily electrical show. The **Neue Pinakothek,** Barerstr. 29, exhibits the work of 18th- to 20th-century masters such as Van Gogh and Klimt, while the **Alte Pinakothek,** next door, shows Giotto, da Vinci, Raphael, Rembrandt, Dürer, Rubens, and others. *(Both open Tu and Th 10am-8pm, W and F-Su 10am-5pm. DM7, students DM4.)* **Lenbachhaus,** Luisenstr. 33, houses Munich cityscapes, along with works by Kandinsky, Klee, and other members of the *Blaue Reiter* school, which forged the modernist abstract aesthetic. *(Open Tu-Su 10am-6pm. DM8, students DM4.)* Between them, **Glyptohek,** Königspl. 3, and **Antikensammlung,** Königspl. 1, hold Munich's finest collection of ancient art. *(Glyptohek open Tu-Su 10am-5pm, Th until 8pm. Antikensammlung open Tu-Su 10am-5pm, W till 8pm. Joint admission DM10, students DM5.)* **Staatsgalerie moderner Kunst,** Prinzregentenstr. 1, in the **Haus der Kunst,** has a excellent 20th-century collection including Klee, Picasso, and Dalí. *(Open Tu-Su 10am-5pm, Th until 8pm. DM6, students DM3.50.)* The **Haus der Kunst** was built by Nazis and opened with the famous exhibit on "degenerate art." The **ZAM: Zentrum für Außergewöhnliche Museen** (Center for Unusual Museums), Westenriederstr. 41, includes favorites like the Corkscrew Museum, Museum of Easter Bunnies, and the Chamberpot Museum. *(Open daily 10am-6pm. DM8, students DM5.)* If you're looking for the kinky rather than the quirky, try the **Museum für erotische Kunst** (Museum of Erotic Art), Odeonspl. 8. *(U-Bahn 3-6: "Odeonspl." or bus 53. Open Tu-Su 11am-7pm. DM8, students DM6.)*

ENTERTAINMENT

Munich's streets erupt with bawdy beer halls, rowdy discos, and cliquish cafes every night. Pick up *Munich Found* (DM4), *In München* (free), or the hip and hefty *Prinz* (DM5) at any newsstand to find out what's up.

Beer

To most visitors, Munich means beer. The six great city labels are *Augustiner, Hacker-Pschorr, Hofbräu, Löwenbräu, Paulaner-Thomasbräu,* and *Spaten-Franzinskaner;* each brand supplies its own beer halls. Beer is served by the *Maß* (about a liter; DM8-11). The world's biggest keg party, Munich's **Oktoberfest** (Sept. 18-Oct. 3 in 1999) features speeches, a parade of horse-drawn beer wagons, and the mayor tapping the first ceremonial barrel. The Hofbräu tent is the rowdiest (for more Oktoberfest info: http://www.munich-tourist.de). Most *Müncheners* claim that **Augustiner Keller,** Arnulfstr. 52 (S-Bahn 1-8: "Hackerbrücke"), is the finest beer garden in town, with lush grounds and 100-year-old chestnut trees. *(Maß DM11. Open daily 10am-1am; beer garden open 10:30am-midnight. Food (DM10-28) served until 10pm.)* The world-famous **Hofbräuhaus,** Am Platzl 9, two blocks from Marienpl., has been tapping barrels for commoners since 1897 and now seems reserved for drunken tourists; 15,000-30,000L of beer are sold each day *(Maß DM10.40; sausages and sauerkraut DM10; open daily 9:30am-midnight).* The newer **Augustiner Bräustuben,** Landsbergerstr. 19 (S-Bahn 1-8: "Hackerbrücke"), in the Augustiner Brewery's former horse stalls, offers delicious Bavarian food at excellent prices (DM6-20; open daily until 11pm). The largest beer garden in Europe, **Hirschgarten,** Hirschgartenallee 1 (U-Bahn 1: "Rotkreuzpl.," then streetcar 12: "Romanpl."), is boisterous and verdant *(Maß DM8.60; open daily 11am-11pm; restaurant open Nov.-Feb. Tu-Su).* **Chinesischer Turm,** in the **Englischer Garten** next to the pagoda (U-Bahn 3 or 6: "Giselastr.") is a fair-weather tourist favorite swarming with kids *(Maß DM9.50; salads DM7-13.50; open daily in good weather 10:30am-11pm).*

Theater, Music, and Nightlife

Stages sprinkled throughout the city span styles and tastes from dramatic classics at the **Residenztheater** and **Volkstheater** to comic opera at the **Staatstheater am Gärtnerplatz** to experimental works at the **Theater im Marstall** in Nymphenburg. The tourist office's *Monatsprogramm* (DM2.50) lists schedules for all of Munich's stages. Standing tickets sell for about DM10. Munich's **Opera Festival** (in July) is held in the **Bayerische Staatsoper** (tel. 21 85 19 20), accompanied by a concert series in the

Nymphenburg and Schleissheim palaces. (Regular season standing-room and student tickets DM6-20. Box office open M-F 10am-6pm, Sa 10am-1pm.) **Gasteig Kulturzentrum,** Rosenheimerstr. 5 (tel. 48 09 80, box office 54 89 89), hosts diverse musical performances on the former site of the *Bürgerbräukeller,* where Adolf Hitler launched his abortive Beer Hall Putsch. (Box office in the Glashalle open M-F 10:30am-2pm and 3-6pm, Sa 10:30am-2pm, and 1hr. before curtain.) The **Muffathalle,** Zellerstr. 4 (tel. 45 87 50 00), in Haidhausen, a former power plant, still generates energy with techno, hip-hop, jazz, and dance performances (DM30; M-Sa until 4am, Su until 1am).

Munich's nightlife is a curious mix of Bavarian *Gemütlichkeit* (snugness) and trendy cliquishness, so dress well. **Münchener Freiheit** is the most famous and touristy bar/cafe district. More low-key is the southwestern section of **Schwabing,** directly behind the university on Amalienstr. The center of Munich's homosexual scene lies within the "Golden Triangle" of Sendlinger Tor, the Viktualienmarkt/Gärtnerpl. area, and Isartor. Mingle with an English-speaking crowd at **Günther Murphy's,** Nikolaistr. 9a, (Guinness DM6; open M-F 5pm-1am, Sa 2pm-3am, Su noon-1am). **Ball Haus,** Klenzestr. 71, is more relaxed. Things get rolling late at **Nachtcafe,** Maximilianspl. 5, with live jazz, funk, soul, and blues until the wee hours (beer DM8 for 0.3L). Dance clubs include the huge complex **Kunstpark Ost,** Grafingerstr. 6 (Hours, cover, and themes vary—call 49 00 29 28 for info and tickets) and **Nachtwerk and Club,** Landesbergerstr. 185, twin clubs spinning mainstream dance tunes for sweaty crowds (beer DM6; cover DM10; open daily 10pm-4am). **Oly Disco,** Helene-Mayer-Ring 9, is the place to rock out cheap after midnight (student ID required). **Backstage,** Helmholzstr. 18, has a wide range of music and funky theme nights (open W-Th until 3am, F-Sa until 5am). **Club Morizz,** Klenzestr. 43, reminiscent of *Casablanca* scenes, is frequented by gay men and a few lesbians (open Su-Th 7pm-2am, F-Sa 7pm-3am).

■ Near Munich: Dachau

"Once they burn books, they'll end up burning people," wrote the 19th-century German poet Heinrich Heine. This eerily prophetic statement is posted at **Konzentrationslager-Gedenkstätte,** the concentration camp at **Dachau,** next to a photograph of one of Hitler's book burnings. The walls, gates, and crematorium have been restored since 1962 in a chillingly sparse memorial to the victims of the first Nazi concentration camp. The horrors of the camps are mourned in the several memorials and chapels on the grounds, and in photographs and letters housed in the Dachau **museum.** Take S-Bahn 2 ("Petershausen") to "Dachau" (20min., round-trip DM14) then catch bus 724 ("Kräutgarten") or 726 ("Kopernikusstr.") in front of the station to the *KZ Gedenkstätte* (20min., DM 1.80). The grounds are open Tu-Su 9am-5pm. Free 2hr. tours in English leave the museum at 12:30pm (June-Sept. daily; Oct.-May Sa-Su). Call (08131) 17 41 for more info.

■ The Chiemsee

For almost 2000 years, artists and musicians have marveled at the picturesque islands, mountains, and forests of the Chiemsee region. The main attractions are the two inhabited islands on Lake Chiem, the largest lake in Bavaria. Ferries ply the waters from the port in Prien to the **Herreninsel** (Gentlemen's Island), the **Fraueninsel** (Ladies' Island), and towns on the other side of the lake (DM10-12). On Herreninsel, the architecture of **Königsschloß Herrenchiemsee,** King Ludwig II's third and last "fairy-tale castle," is fabulously overwrought. Candlelit concerts are given in the **Hall of Mirrors** throughout the summer. (Open Apr.-Sept. daily 9am-5pm; Oct.-Mar. 10am-4pm. Admission and obligatory tour DM8, students and seniors DM5.) Fraueninsel offers subtler pleasures. Its miniature world has no room for cars; only footpaths wander through this village of fishermen and nuns (a walk around the island is well worth the 45min.). The **abbey** dates back to at least 866. Various artifacts, including the impressive 8th-century Merovingian **Cross of Bischofhofen,** are on display in the room above the Torhalle, the oldest surviving part of the cloister (open daily 11am-6pm; Oct. to mid-June closed Su; DM4, students DM1.50).

The town of **Prien** works as a base for excursions on the lake. The **tourist office,** Alte Rathausstr. 11 (tel. (08051) 690 50 or 69 05 55), offers free maps and brochures and finds rooms in private houses (DM20-40) for no fee (open M-F 8:30am-6pm, Sa 9am-noon). The cheapest beds in town are at the raucous **Jugendherberge (HI),** Carl-Braun-Str. 66 (tel. (08051) 687 70; fax 68 77 15), a 10-minute walk from the lake. (DM25; sheets DM5.50. Reception 8-9am, 5-7pm, and 9:30-10pm. Curfew 10pm. Open early Feb. to Nov.) **Campingplatz Hofbauer** is at Bernauerstr. 110 (tel. (08051) 41 36; fax 626 57). Walk right from the station, turn left at Seestr., left again at the next intersection and follow Bernauerstr. out of town past the gas station and McDonald's (DM10.50 per person, DM10 per tent; open Apr.-Oct.). **La Piazzo,** Seestr. 7, serves up yummy pasta (DM11-13) and pizza (DM9.80). Grab groceries at **HL Markt,** Seestr. 11 (open M-F 8am-8pm, Sa 8am-4pm).

■ Nuremberg (Nürnberg)

Although few visible scars remain and historical landmarks shine in splendor, Nuremberg is a city inextricably bound to its troubled past. The very mention of Nuremberg, backdrop of the massive annual Nazi party rallies from 1933-1938 and namesake of the 1935 racial purity laws that paved the way for the Holocaust, still conjures up totalitarian imagery of the sort immortalized in Leni Riefenstahl's film *Triumph des Willens* (Triumph of the Will). For these reasons, the 1949 war criminal trials were held here to reestablish justice in a world of horror. Thanks largely to the Marshall Plan, the city today is a model of postwar prosperity, known for its connection to Albrecht Dürer, its toy-fair and Christmas-Markt, and its sausages and gingerbread.

SIGHTS AND ENTERTAINMENT Allied bombing reduced 90% of Nuremberg to rubble in 1945, but restoration projects have recaptured some of the city's charm and majesty. The **Lorenzkirche** on St. Lorenzpl., destroyed during the war, has now been completely restored and once again displays its priceless works of art. Of particular interest is the 20m high tabernacle, with delicate stone tendrils curling up into the roof vaulting (open M-Sa 9am-5pm, Su 1-4pm). Across the river on Hauptmarktpl. is the **Frauenkirche** (Church of Our Lady), Catholic since 1916, and the **Schöner Brunnen** (Beautiful Fountain), with 40 imaginatively carved figures. Walk uphill from the fountain to find the **Rathaus,** built between 1616 and 1622 in early Baroque style with a little Renaissance Classicism thrown in. Beneath the building, the **Lochgefängnisse** (dungeons) contain an exhibit of medieval torture instruments. (Obligatory 30min. tour every 30min. Open M-F 10am-4:30pm, Sa-Su 10am-1pm. DM4, students DM2.) Across from the *Rathaus* is the **Sebalduskirche,** a Protestant Church. (Open June-Aug. daily 9:30am-8pm; Nov. and Jan-Feb. 9:30am-4pm; Mar.-May 9:30am-6pm.) The Catholic congregation morbidly celebrates the feast day of St. Sebaldus by parading through town with his relics. During the other 364 days, his bits rest in his gilded cast bronze tomb in front of the altar. Up the hill is a three-part castle: the **Kaiserburg** (Emperor's fortress), the **Burggrafenburg** (fortress count's fortress), and the **Stadtburg** (city fortress). (Open Apr.-Sept. daily 9am-noon and 12:45-5pm; Oct.-Mar. 9:30am-noon and 12:45-4pm. Last tour 30min. before closing. DM5.) The **Albrecht Dürer Haus,** Albrecht-Dürer-Str. 29, was the last residence of Nuremberg's favorite son. The *Fachwerk* house has period furniture, Dürer etchings, and copies of his paintings (open Tu-W and F-Su 10am-5pm, Th 10am-8pm; DM5, students DM3).

The ruins of **Dutzendteich Park,** site of the Nazi *Parteitage* (Party Convention) rallies in the 1930s, remind visitors of a darker time in German history. To reach the park, take S-Bahn 2 to "Dutzendteich." **Zeppelin Field** sits on the far side of the lake near the massive marble platform from which Hitler addressed throngs. The exhibit *Faszination und Gewalt* (Fascination and Terror), located inside the **Zeppelin Tribune** in the Golden Hall, attests to the emotional power of these events (open mid-May to Oct. Tu-Su 10am-6pm; DM2, students DM1).

The weekly *Plärrer* (DM4) lists musical events, bars, and discos. **Cince Citta,** Gewerbemuseumpl. 3 (tel. (0911) 20 66 60), packs 7 cafes, 12 movie theaters, and a disco into an eight-story, multimedia mega-complex (open daily until 3am or later).

PRACTICAL INFO, ACCOMMODATIONS, AND FOOD Trains (tel. (0911) 194 19) leave the station frequently for Berlin (6hr., every 2-3hr.), Munich (2hr., 2-3 per hr., DM53), and Würzburg (1hr., 2-3 per hr., DM28). Nuremberg's **tourist office** (tel. (0911) 233 60; fax 233 61 66), in the *Hauptbahnhof*, finds rooms for a DM5 fee (open M-Sa 9am-7pm). The comfortable and well-run **Jugendgästehaus (HI),** Burg 2 (tel. (0911) 230 93 60; fax 23 09 36 11), was once a grain storage house of the imperial castle. From the train station, take the escalator down into the tunnel passage and walk straight, then left up to the sloping exit. Follow Königstr. to the marketplace, then head toward the golden fountain on the left and bear right on Burgstr., up the hill (reception 7am-1am; curfew 1am; DM29; reserve ahead). **Jugend-Hotel Nürnberg,** Rathsbergstr. 300 (tel. (0911) 521 60 92), is rustic and cheerful but far from the city center; take bus 212 to "Hernhütte," then bus 21 to "Ziegelstein." (Singles DM37; doubles DM58. Breakfast DM7.50. Reception 8am-10pm. Call ahead). **Campingplatz im Volkspark Dutzenteich,** Hans-Kalb-Str. 56 (tel. (0911) 81 11 22), is behind the soccer stadium; take S-Bahn 2 to "Frankenstadion" (DM8 per person, DM5 per tent; open May-Sept.; call ahead).

Nuremberg is famous for its *Rostbratwurst* (grilled sausage). The place to try some is beneath the crowded, popular **Bratwurst Häusle,** Rathauspl. 1, next to St. Sebaldus Church. (6 *Rostbratwürste* with sauerkraut or spiced potato salad DM9.50. Open M-Sa 10am-9:30pm.) The crowded **Internetcafe Falkens Maze,** Färberstr. 11 (email max@maximum.de; http://www.maximum.de), on the 3rd floor of the *Maximum* complex, invites you to grab a cup of coffee (DM3), then email or chat the night away (open M-Sa 11am-10pm; DM5 per 30min., DM9 per hr.). **Cafe Mohr,** Färberstr. 3, is a fun place to meet people and enjoy crepes (DM5-8.50) and salads (DM6.50-11.50; open M-Th 9am-midnight, F-Sa 9am-1am, Su 2pm-midnight).

■ Romantic Road (Romantische Straße)

Between Würzburg and Füssen, in the foothills of the Alps, lies a beautiful country-side of castles, walled cities, elaborate churches, and dense forest. Sensing opportunity, the German tourist industry christened these bucolic backwaters the Romantic Road in 1950. The world has responded—this is the most visited region in Germany, so be prepared for a group experience. Deutsche Bahn's **Europabus** runs from April to October daily between Frankfurt and Munich (12hr.; change at Dinkelsbühl for Füssen), stopping at most towns in the area along the way. Eurail and German Rail-pass holders ride free after a DM10 registration fee, but otherwise the service is fairly slow and costly (Frankfurt to Rothenburg DM58; to Dinkelsbühl DM69; to Munich DM113). A more economical way to see the region for those without railpasses is to use the faster and more frequent **trains,** which run to every town except Dinkelsbühl. Tourist offices can provide maps and info to the many travelers who **bike** the route. For general information, contact the **Romantische Straße Arbeitgemeinschaft,** Marktpl., 91550 Dinkelsbühl (tel. (09851) 902 71).

Würzburg Surrounded by vineyard slopes and bisected by the Main River, **Würzburg** is the bustling center of the Franconian wine region. A testament to the immense secular powers of Würzburg's prince-bishops, the imposing 13th-century **Marienburg Fortress** overshadows the town from across the river. Inside, German paintings and furniture grace the **Fürstenbau Museum.** (Open Apr.-Sept. Tu-Su 9-12:30am and 1-5pm; Oct.-Mar. Tu-Su 10-12:30am and 1-4pm. DM4, students DM3.) The fortress also houses the **Mainfränkisches Museum,** with statues by Würzburg's native son, Tilman Riemenschneider. (Open Apr.-Oct. Tu-Su 10am-5pm; Nov.-Mar. Tu-Su 10am-4pm. DM3.50, students DM2.) Climb to the fortress or take bus 9 from "Spitäle" (DM2). The **Residenz** palace, a Baroque masterpiece containing the largest ceiling fresco in the world, stands over the sweeping Residenzpl. (Open Apr.-Oct. Tu-Su 9am-5pm; Nov.-Mar. Tu-Su 10am-4pm. Last admission 30min. before closing. DM5, students and seniors DM3.50.) The **Residenzhofkirche** is simply astounding: the gilded moldings, pink marble, and frescoes place this little church at the apex of

Baroque fantasy. (Open Apr.-Oct. Tu-Su 9am-noon and 1-5pm; Nov.-Mar. Tu-Su 10am-noon and 1-4pm. Free.)

Trains (tel. (0931) 344 25) roll to Frankfurt (1½-2hr., 1 per hr., DM37), Munich (2½hr., 2 per hr., DM75), Hamburg (3½hr.), and Rothenburg (1hr.); **buses** head to Rothenburg (DM26) and Munich (DM84). In front of the train station, the **tourist office** (tel. (0931) 374 36) provides a hotel list (DM0.50) and a free map, and finds rooms for a DM5 fee (open M-Sa 10am-6pm). Call the 24-hour **accommodations hotline** at (0931) 194 14. Würzburg's **Jugendgästehaus (HI),** Burkarderstr. 44 (tel. (0931) 425 90; fax 41 68 62), is across the river; take tram 3 ("Heidingsfeld") or 5 ("Heuchelhof") from the station to "Löwenbrücke." (Check-in 2-5:15pm and 6:30-10pm. Under 27 only. DM29. Breakfast included. Reception 8am-10pm.) **Uni Café,** Neubaustr. 2, has a relaxed student atmosphere and outdoor seating (baguettes and salads DM3.50-9.50; open M-Sa 8am-1am, Su 9am-1pm). Adventurous souls should snoop around the bohemian back alleys of the city's south side, especially on Sandestr., the heart of the university subculture, where idiosyncratic people and curious food abound in smoky dens and grottoes. To sample the region's distinctive wines try **Haus des Frankenweins Fränkischer Weinverband,** Krankenkai 1 (tel. (0931) 120 93), or stop by during the **Wine Festival** (early June and late Sept.-early Oct.).

Rothenburg to Augsburg

Although **Rothenburg ob der Tauber** has got to be the most touristed spot in Germany, it may be your only chance to see a walled medieval city without a single modern building. **Trains** run every hour from major cities to Steinach, where you can transfer for a quick trip to Rothenburg (15min.). Call (09861) 46 11 for train information. *"Zimmer frei"* signs mark private rooms for rent (DM20-45). The **tourist office,** Marktpl. 2 (tel. (09861) 404 92), supplies handy maps and books rooms (DM35-60); from the station, bear right on Ansbacherstr. and follow it to the *Marktplatz* (open M-F 9am-12:30pm and 1-6pm, Sa-Su 10am-3pm; Nov.-Apr. M-F 9am-12:30pm and 1-5pm, Sa 10am-1pm). To reach the exemplary **Jugendherberge Rossmühle (HI),** Mühlacker 1 (tel. (09861) 941 60; fax 94 16 20), from the *Marktplatz,* make a left onto Obere Schmiedg. and go straight until you see the sign to the right (under 27 only; DM22; reception 7am-midnight). Not as prepackaged as Rothenburg, the old town of **Dinkelsbühl,** 40km south, maintains a full complement of medieval half-timbered houses. The walled city of **Nördlingen im Ries,** 35km south of Dinkelsbühl, sits on the plain where a kilometer-wide meteorite smashed into the earth with the power of 250,000 atomic bombs 15 million years ago. You can view the crater from **Der Daniel,** the tower of the 15th-century **St. Georgskirche** (tower open M-F 9am-noon and 2-5pm, Sa-Su 2-5pm).

Rising from the slumber of the dark medieval days, **Augsburg** radiates an air of youthfulness without forgetting about its past. Founded by Caesar Augustus in 15 BC, it was the financial center of the Holy Roman Empire and a major commercial city by the end of the 15th century. Jakob Fugger the Rich, personal financier of the Hapsburg Emperors, founded the **Fuggerei** quarter in 1519 as the first welfare housing project in the world. The **Fuggerei Museum** documents this classic piece of urban planning, as well as the financial adventures of its patrons (open Mar.-Oct. daily 9am-6pm; DM1, students DM0.70). Augsburg's medieval past unfolds at the brightly frescoed **Guildhaus,** down Bürgermeister-Fischer-Str.; from here, a left down Maximilianstr. leads to the huge Renaissance **Rathaus** (open daily 10am-6pm; free). The **Bertolt Brecht Haus** on Auf dem Raim was renovated in 1998, the 100th anniversary of Brecht's birth. (Open Tu-Su May-Sept. 10am-5pm; Oct.-Apr. 10am-4pm. DM2.50, students DM1.50.)

Augsburg's **tourist office,** Bahnhofstr. 7 (tel. (0821) 50 20 70 or 502 07 24; fax 502 07 45), about 300m in front of the station, books rooms for a DM3 fee (open M-F 9am-6pm). There's another office at Rathauspl. (tel. (0821) 502 07 24; also open Sa 10am-4pm, Su 10am-1pm). The **Jugendherberge (HI),** Beim Pfaffenkeller 3 (tel. (0821) 339 03; fax 151 11 49), is cramped but well-located (DM20; reception 7-9am and 5-10pm; open late Jan. to early Dec; call ahead).

■ Bavarian Alps (Bayerische Alpen)

South of Munich, the land buckles into dramatic peaks and valleys which stretch through Austria into Italy. Mountain villages, glacial lakes, icy waterfalls, and ski resorts dot the landscape. Rail lines are scarce, but buses fill in the gaps. For regional information, contact the **Fremdenverkehrsverband Oberbayern,** Bodenseestr. 113 (tel. (089) 829 21 80), in Munich (open M-F 9am-4:30pm, Sa 9am-noon).

Füssen and the Royal Castles Curled up at the base of the Alpine foothills at the southern end of the Romantic Road, **Füssen** provides easy access to Mad King Ludwig's famed **Königsschlösser** (royal castles). The town also boasts impressive architectural monuments of its own. The inner walls of the **Hohes Schloß** (High Castle) courtyard are decorated with arresting *trompe l'oeil* windows and towers; the **Staatsgalerie** inside displays regional late Gothic and Renaissance art (open Apr.-Oct. Tu-Su 11am-4pm; Nov.-Mar. Tu-Su 2-4pm; DM3, students DM2). Just below the castle rests the 8th-century Baroque basilica **St. Mangkirche** and its abbey. An ancient fresco discovered during 1950 renovations lights up the church's 10th-century subterranean crypt (call (08362) 48 44 for info on tours). Füssen is also a haven for cyclists: one of the most scenic daytrips is the 32km **Forgensee Cycle Route** which follows the grassy shoreline of the alpine lake. Any daytrip from Füssen should include the **Wieskirche** (Church of the Meadows), a splendid rococo pilgrimage church surrounded by fields and forest. Buses run regularly from Füssen station.

The **tourist office,** Kaiser-Maximilian-Pl. 1 (tel. (08362) 938 50; fax 93 85 20), dispenses maps (under DM8), advises on hikes, and finds rooms (open M-F 8am-6pm, Sa 9am-noon). Budget singles in *Gästhäuser* run DM35-40. The **Jugendherberge (HI),** Mariahilferstr. 5 (tel. (08362) 77 54; fax 27 70), is often packed; turn right from the station and follow the train tracks. (DM21.90. Under 27 only. Reception 7-9am, 5-7, and 8-10pm. Closed Nov. Reserve ahead.) Stock up on groceries at **Plus,** on the corner of Bahnhofstr. and Luitpoldstr. (open M-F 8:30am-7pm, Sa 8am-2pm).

The *Königsschlösser* lie 5km across the Lech River in the village of **Hohenschwangau.** Ludwig II's building spree culminated with the construction of the **Schloß Neuschwanstein;** the castle was the inspiration for Disney World's "Fantasyland" castle and now draws lines just as long as its American counterpart. Consider taking the tour early in the morning and then spending the afternoon hiking around the spectacular **Pöllat Gorge** behind the castle. (Castle open daily Apr.-Sept. 9am-5:30pm; Oct.-Mar. 10am-4pm. DM11, students, seniors, and disabled DM8.) From Füssen, take the "Königsschlösser" **bus,** which departs from the train station hourly (DM2.40). Buses also run from the Garmisch-Partenkirchen train station (daily at 8:05am, 1:05, 4:15, and 5:05pm; M-F also at 9:35 and 11:15am); the two-hour journey costs DM13 round-trip with a *Tagesticket.* From Munich, take a **train** to Buchloe and transfer to the regional train to Füssen (2hr., DM30).

Berchtesgaden At the easternmost point of the Bavarian Alps, Berchtesgaden profits from a sinister and overtouristed attraction—Hitler's **Kehlsteinhaus,** also called "Eagle's Nest." The only real reason to stop by this retreat-turned-restaurant is because it's en route to the spectacular view from the mountain's 1834m peak. On your way back down, inspect the remains of the **Berghof.** It was at Berghof that Hitler browbeat Austrian Chancellor Kurt von Schuschnigg into giving up control of the Austrian police, paving the way for the *Anschluss.* The Berchtesgaden **Schloß,** a monastic priory until Bavarian rulers appropriated the property, now houses a mixture of art and weaponry. (Open Su-F 10am-12pm and 2-4pm; Oct.-Easter M-F 10am-1pm and 2-5pm. Last entry 4pm. DM7, students DM3.50.) Berchtesgaden is also a good base town for some amazing hikes. Buses run to Obersalzburg, a popular winter ski resort, and Ramsau, a tiny, beautiful town with terrific hiking opportunities. A DM6.40 (round-trip) bus ride will take you to the **Königssee,** wedged into extraordinary Alpine cliffs and calmly mirroring the landscape on its blue-green surface.

The **tourist office,** Königsseestr. 2 (tel. (08652) 96 71 50), opposite the train station, sells hiking passes (DM5) with tips on trails (open M-F 8am-5pm, Sa 9am-noon). Hourly **trains** (tel. (08652) 50 74) run to Munich (2½hr.) and Salzburg (1hr.); change at Freilassing for both. The **Jugendherberge (HI)** (tel. (08652) 943 70; fax 94 37 37) is at Gebirgsjägerstr. 52; from the station, take bus 9539 ("Strub Kaserne," DM2.40) to "Jugendherberge." (DM23 with tax. Breakfast included. Sheets DM5.50. Reception 8am-noon and 5-7pm; check-in until 10pm. Closed Nov.-Dec. 26.) Pick up a *Wurst* from vendors or groceries at **Edeka Markt,** Dr.-Imhof-Str. near Griesstätterstr. (open M-F 8am-6pm, Sa 8am-12pm).

■ The Danube

The Danube Valley, with Baroque Passau and Gothic Regensburg, is every bit as inviting as the Romantic Road. Northeast of Munich, the valley's rolling hills and lovely riverscapes attract Germans and international tourists year-round.

Regensburg and the Bavarian Forest Once the capital of Bavaria,
Regensburg later became the administrative seat of the Holy Roman Empire and then the site of the first German parliament. The (Holy Roman) Imperial Parliament met in the **Reichstags Museum,** housed in the Gothic **Altes Rathaus.** The different heights of the chairs reflect the political hierarchy of the legislators. (English tours May-Sept. M-Sa 3:15pm. German tours daily year-round. DM5, students DM2.50.) The splendid high-Gothic **St. Peter's Cathedral** towers over the city (open Apr.-Oct. Tu-Su 6:30am-6pm; DM3, students DM1.50).

Trains chug to Munich via Landshut (1½hr., every hr.), Nuremburg (1-1½hr., every 30min.-1hr.), and Passau (1-1½hr., every 1-2hr.). The **tourist office** Altes Rathaus (tel. (0941) 507 44 10; fax 507 44 19), on Rathauspl., finds rooms for free and provides a free map. From the train station, walk down Maximilianstr. to Grasg. and take a left. Follow it as it turns into Obermünsterstr., then turn right at the end to Obere Bachg., and walk straight to Rathauspl. The **Jugendherberge (HI),** Wöhrdstr. 60 (tel. (0941) 574 02), offers pleasant but sterile rooms. (Under 27 only. DM27. Reception 6am-11:30pm. Partially wheelchair accessible. Closed mid-Nov. to mid-Jan.) Campers should head for the **Azur-Camping,** Am Weinweg 40 (tel. (0941) 27 00 25); take bus 11 ("West Bad") to "West-heim" from Albertstr. (DM10 per person, DM7 per tent). **Hinterhaus,** Roe-Hahnen-Gasse 2, off Haidpl., is a politically grooving grove of left-leaning tables that offers excellent vegetarian dishes and salads (DM5-15); jazz bands occasionally perform in the garden (open M-F 11am-1am, Sa-Su 6pm-1am). A grocery store, **Tengelmann,** is on Untere Brückg. 2, on the way to the tourist office from the train station (open M-F 8am-8pm, Sa 7:30am-4pm).

Northeast of Regensburg and Passau along the Austrian and Czech borders, the **Bavarian Forest** *(Bayerischer Wald)* is Central Europe's largest range of wooded mountains. The **Bavarian Forest National Park** is strictly protected from any activities that may alter its ecosystem; this includes camping or building fires outside designated areas. Clearly marked trails lace 20,000 sylvan acres. You can hoof it alone, or take a free guided walking, botanical, or natural history tour; sign up at least a day in advance by contacting **Hans-Eisenmann-Haus,** Bömstr. 35, 94556 Neuschönau (tel. (08558) 961 50; open daily Jan.-Oct. 9am-5pm). For general info, contact either the **Nationalparkverwaltung Bayerischer Wald,** Freyunstr., 94481 Grafenau (tel. (08552) 960 00; fax 46 90) or the **Tourismusverband Ostbayern,** Luitpoldstr. (tel. (0941) 58 53 90; fax 585 39 39), in Regensburg. The park's thick woods hide palaces and 17 **HI** youth hostels. Regensburg's tourist office has a helpful brochure.

An abundance of train connections and great **hiking** trails makes **Zweisel** an excellent hub for scouting the heart of the forest. The **youth hostel** at Hindenburgstr. 26 (tel. (09922) 10 61; fax 601 91) is the choicest accommodation in the Bavarian Forest.

Passau Poised on two peninsulas forged by the confluence of the Danube, Inn,
and Ilz Rivers, **Passau** embodies the ideal Old World European city. Its Baroque architecture reaches its apex in the sublime **Stephansdom** (St. Stephen's Cathedral),

where hundreds of cherubs sprawl across the ceiling, and the world's largest **church organ** looms above the choir. (Open M-Sa 8-11am and 12:30-6pm. Free. Organ concerts May-Oct. M-Sa noon. DM4, students and seniors DM2. Also Th 7:30pm. DM10 and DM5.) The **Domschatz** (cathedral treasury), inside the **Residenz** behind the cathedral, houses an extravagant collection of gold and tapestries (open May-Oct. M-Sa 10am-4pm; DM2, students DM1). The 13th-century Gothic **Rathaus** contains a stunning Great Hall. (Open May 16-Sept. daily 10am-5pm; Easter-May 15 10am-4pm; Oct. M-F 10am-4pm. DM2, students DM1.) A former palace of the bishopric, the **Veste Oberhaus** (open early Apr.-Oct. Tu-Su 11:30am-5pm) now houses the **Cultural History Museum** (open Mar.-Jan. 9am-5pm, Sa-Su 10am-6pm; DM6, students DM3), spanning 2000 years. The **Museum Moderner Kunst,** Bräug. 17, has excellent rotating art exhibits (open Tu-Su 10am-6pm; DM 10, students DM6).

The **train station** (tel. (0851) 194 19), west of downtown on Bahnhofstr., serves Regensburg (1-2hr.), Nuremburg (2hr.), Munich (2hr.), and Vienna (3½hr.). The **tourist office,** Rathauspl. 3 (tel. (0851) 95 59 80), has maps and books rooms for a DM5 fee. (Open Apr.-Oct. M-F 8:30am-6pm, Sa-Su 10am-2pm; Nov.-Mar. M-Th 8:30am-5pm, F 8:30am-4pm.) The **Jugendherberge (HI),** Veste Oberhaus 125 (tel. (0851) 413 51; fax 437 09), is a long, steep walk for adequate facilities, but has the cheapest beds in town. (DM16.50. Breakfast included. Sheets DM5.50. Reception 7am-11:30am and 4-11:30pm; new arrivals after 6pm only. Curfew 11:30.) **Rotel Inn** (tel. (0851) 951 60; fax 951 61 00) has wide beds in tiny rooms overlooking the Danube. To get there, go through the tunnel in front of the station, toward the blue head of this hotel built in the shape of a sleeping man (singles DM30; doubles DM50; reception 24hr.). **Pension Rößner,** Bräug. 19 (tel. (0851) 93 13 50; fax 931 35 55), has homey rooms on the Danube, all with bath (singles DM60-85; doubles DM80-100; breakfast included).

The popular **Innsteg: Cafe Kniepe,** Innstr. 13, is a block from Nikolastr. (menu DM5-21; open daily 10am-1am). **Wirtshaus Bayersche Löwe,** Dr.-Hans-Kapfinger-Str. 3, has big German food for big appetites (open daily 9am-1am). The **Mensa,** Innstr. 29, offers cafeteria meals for DM2.40-4.50; any student ID will do. From Ludwigspl., follow Nikolastr. and turn right (open M-Th 8am-4pm, F 8:15am-2:30pm).

▓ **Bamberg and Bayreuth**

Bamberg Packed with sights but largely overlooked by travelers, this little city on the Regnitz River boasts a history spanning a thousand years. The residents of Bamberg are proud of their picturesque home, and they celebrate by drinking an astounding amount of beer—330 liters per capita every year, the highest consumption rate in the world. The 15th-century **Altes Rathaus** guards the middle of the river like an anchored ship (open Tu-Su 9:30am-4:30pm). Stand on one of the two bridges to gaze at the half-timbered, half-Baroque facade with a Rococo tower in between. Across the river and up the hill is the **Dom,** dating from the early 11th century. The most famous object inside is the 13th-century equestrian statue, the **Bamberger Reiter** (Bamberg Knight), embodying the chivalric ideal of the medieval warrior-king. (Open Apr.-Oct. daily 8am-6pm; Nov.-Mar. 8am-5pm; closed during services. 30min. organ concerts May-Oct. Sa noon. Free.) Across the square, the **Neue Residenz,** Dompl. 8, boasts lavish furnishings and a prim rose garden outside. (Open Apr.-Sept. daily 9am-noon and 1:30-5pm; Oct.-Mar. 9am-noon and 1:30-4pm. Last entry 30min. before closing. DM4, students DM3.)

The **train station** (tel. (0951) 194 19), on Ludwigstr., serves Munich (2½-4hr., 1-2 per hr.), Nuremberg (30min.-1hr., 2-4 per hr.), and Würzburg (1hr., 1 per hr.). The **tourist office,** Geyerwörthstr. 3 (tel. (0951) 87 11 61; fax 87 19 60), on an island in the Regnitz River, offers a free hotel list and booklet with a map (open M-F 9am-6pm, Sa 9am-3pm; Apr.-Oct. also Su 10am-2pm). Though far away, **Jugendherberge Wolfsschlucht (HI),** Oberer Leintritt 70 (tel. (0951) 560 02; fax 552 11), is clean and pleasant; take bus 18 from the Zentral Omnibus Bahnhof to "Am Regnitzufer." (Under 27 only. DM20. Sheets DM5.50. Breakfast included. Reception 4-10pm. Curfew 10pm. Open Feb. to mid-Dec. Reserve well in advance.) Rooms in the **Maisel-Bräu-Stübl,** Obere Königstr. 38 (tel./fax (0951) 255 03), overlook a serene courtyard 10 minutes from the station (singles DM39; doubles DM70-80; breakfast included; reception 9am-midnight). Also convenient is **Hospiz,** Promenadestr. 3 (tel. (0951) 98 12 60), off Schönleinspl. (Singles DM50, with bath DM70; doubles with shower DM80, with bath DM90-100. Reception 7am-10pm. Call ahead.) The **University Mensa,** Austr. 37, off Obstmarkt, serves cheap meals (DM5 with any student ID; open daily 11:30am-2pm). **Polarbär,** Judenstr. 7, a beer graden with aromatic atmosphere, has baguettes (DM7.30; open daily 11am-midnight). The **Tengelmann supermarket,** Langestr. 14, sells groceries (open M-F 8:30am-7pm, Sa 7:30am-4pm). The **Jazzclub,** Obere Sandstr. 18, plays a funky mix (cover DM11-14; live jazz F-Sa 9pm-1am).

Bayreuth

Bayreuth Once you've turned off Tristanstr. onto Isoldenstr. and passed Walküreg., there will be little doubt that you're in Bayreuth, the adopted home of **Richard Wagner.** Every summer from July 25 to August 28, thousands of visitors pour in for the **Bayreuth Festspiele,** a vast, bombastic celebration of Wagner's works. Tickets go on sale three years in advance and sell out almost immediately (DM40-300; write to Bayreuther Festspiele, 95402 Bayreuth). The avid fan can tour Wagner's house (Haus Wahnfried), now the **Richard Wagner Museum,** Richard-Wagner-Str. 48 (open M, W, and F 9am-5pm, Tu and Th 9am-8:30pm; DM4-5, students DM2). Bayreuth is an easy daytrip by hourly **trains** from Nuremberg (1hr.). The **tourist office,** Luitpoldpl. 9 (tel. (0921) 885 88), about four blocks to the left from the station, provides maps and hotel listings (open M-F 9am-6pm, Sa 9:30am-12:30pm). You'll need the map to reach the friendly but regimented **Jugendherberge (HI),** Universitätsstr. 28 (tel. (0921) 25 12 62), near the university. (DM20. Under 27 only. Reception 7am-noon and 5-9:30pm. Strict curfew 10pm. Open Mar. to mid-Dec.)

Greece (Ελλας)

US$1 = 295dr (Greek Drachmes)
CDN$1 = 194.08dr
UK£1 = 490dr
IR£1 = 428.47dr
AUS$1 = 174.74dr
NZ$1 = 151.25dr
SAR1 = 47.56dr
Country Code: 30

100dr = US$0.34
100dr = CDN$0.52
100dr = UK£0.20
100dr = IR£0.23
100dr = AUS$0.57
100dr = NZ$0.66
100dr = SAR2.10
International Dialing Prefix: 00

Greece is known to its celebrants less as a place than a state of soul. Sometime between Homer and Plato, Greek poets and philosophers came upon the notion of the human soul, and the Western imagination has not been the same since. The intensely rational beauty that inspired the ancients still calls countless backpackers to commune with the column as they wander through the unearthed temples, theaters, palaces, and stadia of lost civilizations.

The same culture that taught us the Doctrine of the Mean has sent its ecstatics—monks and hedonists—to the extremes of human experience. The memory of Dionysus, god of the vine, still fuels the island circuit—a blur of sun, sand, and sex, framed in the blues of the clear sky and the golds of the endless beach. Back from the shore, in Greece's austere hills, monks and hermits lurk in structures that have aged a millennium, offering hospitality to the wanderers who seek them out.

Over the centuries, Greece has occupied a unique position at the crossroads of Europe and Asia. The relics of Crete's Minoan civilization betray the influence of flowering contemporary cultures in Egypt and Babylon. The Byzantine era saw the preservation—in the bushy beards and long black robes of Orthodox priests—of the mores of an Eastern empire. Four hundred years under the Ottoman Turks left a certain spice in Greek food, an Oriental flair in the strains of its *bouzouki* music, and minaret tips in its skylines. Greece emerged independent in 1821 under the dual veneer of Classical Athens and Imperial Byzantium, but Ottoman folkways still persist.

Greece's beauty and traditions have drawn one of the heaviest tourist industries in Europe, surrounding its monuments with camera-flashing hordes and cheap junk-shops. Today, as the country moves toward the European Monetary Union and overhauls its infrastructure for the 2004 Summer Olympics in Athens, development has accelerated at a blistering pace. Still, when you climb above the concrete resorts and whirring tour buses—when you hear the wind's lonely, persistent whistle—you'll know that Greece remains oracles' ground.

For coverage of Greece rivaling that of Pausanias, why not *Let's Go: Greece 1999?*

GETTING THERE

Certainly the most popular way of getting to Greece is by **ferry** from Italy. Boats travel primarily from Italy (Ancona and Brindisi) to Corfu (10hr.), Igoumenitsa (12hr.), and Patras (20hr.). Seats run L50,000 to 105,000 (US$31-66; in low season L22,000-45,000 or US$13-29). Rhodes is connected by ferry to Marmaris, Turkey; Limassol, Cyprus (18,500-22,000dr); and Haifa, Israel (28,500-33,000dr in low season). If you plan to travel from Brindisi in the summer, make reservations and arrive at the port well before your departure time. ISIC holders can often get student fares, and Eurail pass holders get many reductions and free trips. Everyone pays the port tax (L10,000, or US$6.25, in Brindisi) and, in high season, a supplementary fee of L19,000 (US$12).

Flying from northern European cities is also a popular way of getting to Greece. From North America, an indirect flight through Brussels or Luxembourg may cost less than a flight going directly to Athens. **Olympic Airways,** 96-100 Singrou St., 11741 Athens (tel. (01) 926 72 51), serves many large cities and islands within Greece.

Greece is served by a number of relatively cheap international **train** routes that connect Athens, Thessaloniki, and Larissa to most European cities, but count on at least a three-day journey from Trieste or Vienna to Athens. Buses are even cheaper, but a real marathon. **Eurolines,** 4 Cardiff Rd., Luton LU1 1PP, U.K. (tel. (01582) 40 45 11), is Europe's largest operator of Europe-wide coach services.

GETTING AROUND

Train service in Greece is limited and sometimes uncomfortable, and no lines go to the western coast. The new, express, air-conditioned intercity trains, though slightly more expensive and rare, are well worth the price. **Eurail passes** are valid on Greek trains. **Hellenic Railways Organization (OSE)** connects Athens to other major Greek cities. In Greece, call 145 or 147 for schedules and prices.

Faster, more extensive, and reasonably priced, **buses** are a good alternative to train travel; most are run through **KTEL.** Smaller towns may use cafes as bus stops; ask for a schedule. Confirm your destination with the driver; signs may be wrong. Along the road, little blue signs marked with white buses or the word "ΣΤΑΣΗ" indicate stops, but drivers usually stop anywhere if you flag them down. Let the driver know ahead of time where you want to get off; if your stop is passed, yell "Stasi!"

Greeks are not eager to pick up foreigners. Sparsely populated areas have little or no traffic. Visitors who choose to **hitchhike** write their destination on a sign in both Greek and English, and hitch from turn-offs rather than along long stretches of straight road. Women should *never* hitch alone. The mountainous terrain and unpaved roads make **cycling** in Greece difficult. **Mopeds** can be great for exploring, but they also make you extremely vulnerable to the carelessness of other drivers. The majority of tourist-related accidents each year occur on mopeds.

There is frequent **ferry** service to the Greek islands, but schedules are irregular and exasperating; misinformation is common. In some places, fierce competition will keep one ferry agent silent about another ferry line's schedule; the government tourist office should provide complete, or at least unbiased, ferry info. To avoid hassles, go to **limenarheio** (port police)—every port has one, and they all carry ferry schedules. **Flying dolphins** (hydrofoils) are a speedier but more expensive alternative to ferry transport. Finally, if you're planning a trip to Turkey, keep in mind that information about Turkey is sketchy in Greece; gather info outside of the country.

The national airline, **Olympic Airways** (tel. (01) 926 72 51), operates efficient and reasonably priced flights between many islands. Note that these flights are often booked weeks in advance in summer. Coverage to remote areas is spotty.

ESSENTIALS

Tourism in Greece is overseen by two national organizations: the **Greek National Tourist Organization (GNTO)** and the **tourist police** *(touristiki astinomia)*. The GNTO can supply general information about sights and accommodations throughout the country. The main office is at 2 Amerikis St., Athens (tel. (01) 322 41 28). Remember that the GNTO is known as **EOT** in Greek. The **tourist police** (tel. in Athens 171, elsewhere in Greece 922 77 77) deal with more local and immediate problems: where to find a room, what the bus schedule is, or what to do when you've lost your passport. They are open long hours and are willing to help, although their English is often limited. The **emergency** number for **police** is 100 in most of Greece; for **first aid,** 166; for **U.S. citizens emergency aid,** (01) 722 36 52.

Women traveling in Greece, as in other Mediterranean countries, are likely to experience verbal harassment. Ignore it, or turn to an older woman for help. In an emergency, call out "vo-EE-thee-a" ("help"). Modest dress (no shorts, short skirts, or revealing tops) is likely to reduce unwanted attention, and is required of both sexes at monasteries and churches. Normal **business hours** in Greece include a break from about 2pm until 6pm or so. Hours vary from place to place. Banks are normally open Monday through Friday 8am to 1:30pm, and also 3:30-6pm in some larger cities. The major **national holidays**—during which all banks and shops are closed—are New Year's Day, Epiphany (Jan. 6), independence day (Mar. 25), a day celebrating resistance to Italy in WWII (Oct. 28), Good Friday (Apr. 10), Easter (Apr. 12), Labor Day (May 1), The Assumption of the Virgin Mary (Aug. 15), and Christmas (Dec. 25).

COMMUNICATION Greece's **telephone** company is **OTE.** Their offices are usually open 7:30am to 3pm in villages, 7:30am to 10pm in towns, and 24 hours in larger cities. For **AT&T Direct,** dial 00 800 13 11; **MCI WorldPhone,** 00 800 12 11; **Sprint Access,** 00 800 14 11; **Canada Direct,** 00 800 16 11; **BT Direct,** 00 800 44 11; and **Ireland Direct,** 155 11 74. **Post offices** are generally open Monday through Friday 7:30am to 2pm. A letter to the U.S. costs 120dr and usually takes four to 14 days.

Although many Greeks in Athens and other heavily touristed areas speak English— particularly young people—those living off the beaten path are unlikely to. The following transliteration table should help you decipher things, although prepare for some exceptions (for instance, Φ and φ are often spelled *ph*).

Greek	Roman	Greek	Roman	Greek	Roman
A, α	A, a	I, ι	I, i	P, ρ	R, r
B, β	V, v	K, κ	K, k	Σ, σ, ς	S, s
Γ, γ	G, g; Y, y	Λ, λ	L, l	T, τ	T, t
Δ, δ	D, d	M, μ	M, m	Y, υ	Y, y; I, i
E, ε	E, e	N, ν	N, n	Φ, φ	F, f
Z, ζ	Z, z	Ξ, ξ	X, x	X, χ	Ch, ch; H, h
H, η	I, i; Ē, ē	O, o	O, o	Ψ, ψ	Ps, ps
Θ, θ	Th, th	Π, π	P, p	Ω, ω	O, o; Ō, ō

To avoid misunderstandings, it is also important to know Greek body language. To say no, Greeks lift their heads back abruptly while raising their eyebrows. To indicate a yes, they emphatically nod once. A hand waving up and down that seems to say "stay there" actually means "come."

Yes/No	Ναι/Οχι	NEH /OH-hee
Hello	Γεια σας	YAH-sas
Excuse me.	Συγνωμη	seeg-NO-mee
Do you speak English?	Μιλας Αγγλικα;	mee-LAHS ahn-glee-KAH
I don't speak Greek.	Δεν μιλαω Ελληνικα;	dhen mee-LAHO el-leen-ee-KAH
Where is...?	Που ειναι;	pou EE-neh
How much?	Ποσο κανει;	PO-so KAH-nee
I would like...	Θα ηθελα	thah EE-the-lah
Can I see a room?	Μπορω να δω ενα δωματιο;	bo-RO nah DHO E-nah dho-MAH-tee-o
Help!	Βοηθεια!	vo-EE-thee-ah

ACCOMMODATIONS AND CAMPING Lodging in Greece is a bargain. At the time of publication, Hostelling International (HI) had yet to reach an agreement with Greek hostels, and they endorse only one hostel in the entire country (in Athens). Nevertheless, hostels that are not currently endorsed by HI are in most cases still safe and reputable. Curfews in hostels are strict, and they may leave you on the street. Hotel prices are regulated, but proprietors may try to push you to take the most expensive room. Check your bill carefully, and threaten to contact the tourist police if you think you are being cheated. GNTO offices usually have a list of inexpensive accommodations, with prices. In many areas, *domatia* (rooms to let) are an attractive and perfectly dependable option. Although you may sacrifice some amenities, the possibility of sharing coffee or some intriguing conversation with your proprietor is worth it. Often you'll be approached by locals as you enter town or disembark from your boat; Greek tourist officials consider this illegal. Greece hosts plenty of official **campgrounds,** and discreet freelance camping—though illegal—is common in July and August, but may not be the safest way to spend the night.

FOOD AND DRINK Greek food is simple and healthy. Most restaurants in Greece work from the same culinary palette, but create original masterpieces with subtle shadings. A restaurant is known as either a *taverna* or *estiatorio,* while a grill is a *psistaria.* Breakfast can be bread, *tiropita* (cheese pie), or a pastry with *marmelada* (jam) or *meli* (honey), and a cup of coffee (*elliniko* is Turkish style and *frappe* is a frothy iced drink). Lunch, the largest meal of the day, is eaten in the mid- to late afternoon. The evening meal is a leisurely affair, usually served after 8 or 9pm, and as late as 11pm to 1am during the summer in the larger cities. It is customary to round up the bill in restaurants. Greek restaurants divide food into two categories: *magiremeno,* meaning cooked, and *tis oras,* to indicate grilled meat. The former is generally cheaper. *Tis oras* includes grilled *moskari* (veal), *arni* (lamb), or *kotopoulo* (chicken), served with *tiganites patates* (french fries), *rizi* (rice), or *fasolia* (beans). Popular *magiremeno* dishes include *mousaka* (chopped meat and eggplant mixed with a cheese and tomato paste), *pastitsio* (a lasagna-like dish of thick noodles covered with a rich cream sauce), *yemista* (stuffed tomatoes and peppers), *dolmadhes* (stuffed grape leaves), and *youvrelakia* (meatballs in egg and lemon sauce). You can hardly avoid *souvlaki,* a large skewer of steak, generally pork or lamb. A *souvlaki pita,* known as "the budget food of the masses," is a pita crammed full of skewered meat and fillings (about 300dr). *Gyros* also abound in street vendor fast-food stands (approximately 350dr). A favorite Greek snack combination is *ouzo* with *mezes,* tidbits of cheese, sausage, cakes, and octopus. *Ouzo* is a distilled spirit to which anise is added, giving it a licorice taste. Mixed with water, it's sweet but not overwhelming.

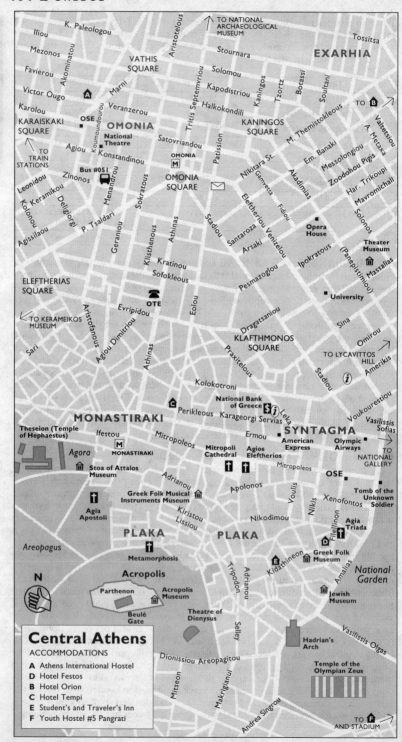

TO NATIONAL ARCHAEOLOGICAL MUSEUM

K. Paleologou
Iliou
Mezonos
Favierou
Victor Ougo
Karolou
KARAISKAKI SQUARE
Leonidou
Kolonou
Agissilaou

Akominatou
Marni
Veranzerou
Koumoundourou
Agiou K. Konstandinou
Zinonos
Menandrou
Keramikou
Deligiorgi
P. Tsaldari
Geraniou

VATHIS SQUARE
Aristotelous
Stournara
Solomou
Kapodistriou
Halkokondili
Tritis Septemvriou
Satovriandou
Patission
Klisthenous
Athinas
Stadiou
Sokratous

EXARHIA
Tossitsa
Solonos

KANINGOS SQUARE
Kaningos
Tzortz
Borassi
Soultani

M. Themistokleous
Valtetsiou
A. Metaxa

OMONIA
National Theatre
Bus #051
OSE

OMONIA SQUARE

Em. Banaki
Messolongiou
Zoodohou Pigis
Akadimias
Nikitara St.
Gamveta
Fidiou
Eleftheriou Venizelou
Santaroza
Arsaki
Pesmazoglou
Eolou

Har. Trikoupi
Mavromichali
Solonos
Opera House
Ipokratos
(Panepistimiou)
Massalias
Theater Museum

ELEFTHERIAS SQUARE
TO KERAMEIKOS MUSEUM
Sari
Aristofanous
Evripidou
Agiou Dimitriou
Athinas
Kratinou
Sofokleous
OTE

University
Sina

KLAFTHMONOS SQUARE
Dragatsaniou
Praxitelous
Stadiou

TO LYCAVITTOS HILL
Omirou
Ameriklis

Kolokotroni
National Bank of Greece
Karageorgi Servias
Leka
Perikleous
MONASTIRAKI
Theseion (Temple of Hephaestus)
Ifestou
Mitropoleos
Ermou
Agora
Stoa of Attalos Museum
MONASTIRAKI

SYNTAGMA
American Express
Olympic Airways
Voukourestiou
Vasilissis Sofias
TO NATIONAL GALLERY

Adrianou
Greek Folk Musical Instruments Museum
Mitropoli Cathedral
Agios Eleftherios
Apolonos
Mitropoleos
Voulis
Xenofontos
OSE
Tomb of the Unknown Soldier

Agia Apostoli
Kiristou
Lissiou
Nikodimou
Nikis
Filellinon
Agia Triada

PLAKA
Areopagus
Metamorphosis
PLAKA
Tripodon
Adrianou
Kidathineon
Greek Folk Museum
Amalias
National Garden

N
Acropolis
Parthenon
Acropolis Museum
Beulé Gate
Theatre of Dionysus
Selley
Jewish Museum

Dionissiou Areopagitou
Mitseon
Makriglanni
Hadrian's Arch
Vasilissis Olgas

Temple of the Olympian Zeus

Andrea Singrou
TO AND STADIUM

Central Athens

ACCOMMODATIONS

A Athens International Hostel
D Hotel Festos
B Hotel Orion
C Hotel Tempi
E Student's and Traveler's Inn
F Youth Hostel #5 Pangrati

One of the great arts in Greece is wine-making, and every region has its own specialty. Long ago, the Greeks discovered that when wine was stored in pine pitch-sealed goatskins, it developed a fresh, sappy flavor. After much deduction, and perhaps after a nagging disgust at drinking out of a carcass, they discovered that adding pine resin in varying amounts during fermentation achieved the same result. The resulting wine became known as *retsina*. Resinated wines now come in three varieties: white, rosé, and red *(kokkineli)*.

■ Athens (Αθηνα)

In contemporary Athens, the Fates have patched together a mosaic of Byzantine churches, ancient ruins, chic cafes, traditional outdoor *tavernas,* and modern shopping centers. Visitors harboring mental images of togas and philosophers may be disappointed to find that Athens is a 20th-century city in every sense of the word—crowded, noisy, and polluted. Plaka, the neighborhood which borders the Acropolis, is one of the few remnants of the ancient grandeur: column-bound temples stand as proud reminders of the faith of the ancient Athenians. The incessant roar and exhaust from buses, cars, and motorcycles in certain areas can be deafening and suffocating, but the urban charm of this cosmopolitan capital's lively neighborhoods makes Athens truly endearing.

ORIENTATION AND PRACTICAL INFORMATION

The center of modern Athens, **Syntagma Square** is a bustling plaza packed with overpriced outdoor cafes, luxury hotels, and flashy banks. The **Greek National Tourist Office (EOT), post office, American Express office, transportation terminals,** and a number of **travel agencies** and **banks** surround the square. **Filellinon Street** and **Nikis Street,** which run parallel from Syntagma toward Plaka, contain the city's budget travel offices, cheap hotels, and dance clubs. Plaka, bounded by the **Temple of Olympian Zeus** and the **Acropolis,** is the oldest section of the city and now houses the junkshops and *tavernas* that define Greek tourism. Northwest of Syntagma, **Omonia Square** is the site of the city's central subway station. Cheap shops and lodgings abound, but in recent years, this cosmopolitan area has become increasingly unsafe. *Do not travel alone at night in Omonia Square.*

Athens is impossible to negotiate without a **map.** Make use of the free maps from the tourist office: the city map is clear and includes bus and trolley routes, while the magazine *Greece-Athens-Attica* has a more detailed street plan. Cultural listings appear in the English-language newspaper *Athens News* (250dr). Be alert when crossing streets, and remember that Athenian streets often have multiple spellings.

Telephone Code: 01.

Flights: East Terminal, foreign airlines and some charters; **West Terminal,** Olympic Airways domestic and international service; **New Charter Terminal,** most charters. From Athens, take the express bus 090 or 091 from either Syntagma Sq. or Stadiou St. near Omonia Sq. Buses run every 20min. 7:30am-9:50pm, plus 12 per night 10:15pm-6:45am. A taxi costs 2500-3000dr, with an extra 50dr charge for each piece of luggage over 10kg, and a 300dr surcharge from the airport. Express buses and taxis are the most reliable travel option.

Trains: Call 145 or 147 for timetables. **Larissis Train Station** (tel. 524 06 01) serves northern Greece (Thessaloniki 4100dr) and Europe. Take trolley bus 1 from Panepistimiou St. in Syntagma (every 10min. 5am-midnight, 100dr). **Peloponnese Train Station** (tel. 513 16 01) serves Patras (1580dr) and major towns in the Peloponnese. Also has OSE **buses** (tel. 323 62 73) to Bulgaria, Albania, Turkey. From Larissis, exit to your right and go over the footbridge, or take blue bus 057 from Panepistimiou St. (every 15min. 5:30am-11:30pm, 100dr).

Buses: Terminal A, 100 Kifissou St. (tel. 512 49 10), serves most of Greece, including the Peloponnese, and can be reached by blue bus 051 at the corner of Zinonos and Menandrou near Omonia Sq. **Terminal B,** 260 Liossion St. (tel. 831 71 81), sends buses to central Greece. Take blue bus 024 at El. Venizelou (Panepistimiou St.). Buy a blue bus ticket at a kiosk and stamp it at the orange machine on board.

Ferries: Most dock at **Peiraias.** Boats to Andros, Tinos, and Mykonos leave from **Rafina,** east of Athens. Always check schedules, available at the tourist office, in the *Athens News,* or with the **Port Authority of Peiraias** (tel. 422 60 00).

Hydrofoils: Ceres' Flying Dolphins (tel. 428 00 01) serves the mainland and the Argosaronic, Sporades, and Cyclades islands. Open M-Sa 8am-6:30pm, Su 8am-1pm. Hydrofoils, roughly twice as fast and twice as expensive as ferries, leave from **Zea Port** near Peiraias, Agios Konstantinos, and Volos.

Public Transportation: Tickets for all public transportation—blue **buses,** designated by 3-digit numbers, yellow **trolley** rides (1-2 digits), and the **subway** system *(elektriko)*—cost 100dr. Buy tickets ahead of time at a kiosk or from automated machines in the station, and hold on to your ticket.

Taxis: Hail your taxi by shouting your destination—not the street address, but the area (i.e., "Kolonaki"). Base fare of 250dr, plus 62dr per km within the city limits.

Tourist Office: The **central office** and **information booth,** 2 Amerikis St. (tel. 331 04 37, 331 05 61, or 331 05 62; fax 325 28 15), off Stadiou St. near Syntagma Sq. Bus, train, and ferry schedules and prices. Ask for the detailed Athens map. Open M-F 9am-7pm, Sa 10am-2pm. There is also an office in the **East Terminal** of the airport (tel. 961 27 22; fax 964 16 27). After exiting baggage claim, the office is on the left before the exit. Open M-F 9am-7pm, Sa 11am-5pm.

Budget Travel: Magic Travel Agency (formerly **Magic Bus**), 20 Filellinon St. (tel. 323 74 71, 323 74 72, 323 74 73, or 323 74 74; fax 322 02 19), stands out. Extremely competent, English-speaking staff. Open M-F 9am-6pm, Sa 10am-2pm. You might also visit **Consolas Travel,** 100 Aiolou St. (tel. 325 49 31; fax 321 09 07), next to the post office. They have a 2nd office at 18 Filellinon St. (tel. 323 28 12). Generally, it's best to shop around and look for specials at the agencies.

Embassies: Australia, 37 D. Soutsou St. (tel. 721 30 39). Open M-F 8:30am-12:30pm. **Canada,** 4 Ioannou Genadiou St. (tel. 727 34 00; fax 727 34 60). Open M-F 8:30am-12:30pm. **Ireland,** 7 Vas. Konstandinou St. (tel. 723 27 71). Open M-F 9am-3pm. **South Africa,** 60 Kifissias St. (tel. 680 66 45). Open M-F 8am-1pm. **U.K.,** 1 Ploutarchou St. (tel. 723 62 11), at the intersection of Ypsilantou St. Open for visas M-F 8:30am-1pm. **U.S.,** 91 Vas. Sofias St. (tel. 721 29 51; fax 645 62 82). Open M-F 8:30am-5pm, for visas 8-11am.

Currency Exchange: National Bank of Greece, 2 Karageorgi Servias St. (tel. 344 00 18), on Syntagma Sq. Open for full service M-Th 8am-2pm, F 8am-1:30pm. Open for currency exchange only M-Th 3:30-5:30pm, F 3-5:30pm, Sa 9am-3pm, Su 9am-1pm. Also try AmEx, the post office, hotels, and other banks.

American Express: 2 Ermou St., P.O. Box 3325 (tel. 324 49 75 or 324 49 79), above McDonald's in Syntagma Sq. Cashes traveler's checks at no commission, holds mail for 1 month, and provides other special services for cardholders. Open M-F 8:30am-4pm, Sa 8:30am-1:30pm (Sa, travel and mail services only).

Luggage Storage: At the airport for 1000dr per piece per day; keep your ticket stub. Several offices on Nikis and Filellinon St. charge 500dr per piece per day.

English Bookstore: Eleftheroudakis Book Store, 17 Panepistimiou St. (tel. 331 41 80). Open M and W 9am-4pm, Tu and Th-F 9am-8:30pm, Sa 9am-3pm.

Laundromats: The Greek word for laundry is *plinitirio.* At 10 Angelou Geronta St. in Plaka and 41 Kolokinthous and Leonidou St. (tel. 522 62 33), near the train stations. One load (wash, dry, and detergent) costs about 2500dr.

Emergencies: Ambulance, tel. 166.

Police, tel. 100. Broken English spoken. **Tourist Police,** tel. 171. Station on 77 Dimitrakopoulou St., great for info and in emergencies. Open daily 7am-11pm.

Pharmacies: Indicated by a green cross extending out over the street. The daily *Athens News* (300dr) lists each day's emergency pharmacies and their hours in its "Useful Information" section. For pharmacy info, dial 107.

Medical Assistance: Near Kolonaki is a **public hospital** at 45-47 Evangelismou (tel. 722 01 01; fax 729 18 08). In Greek, "hospital" is *nosokomio.*

Post Offices: 100 Aiolou St., **Omonia Square** (tel. 321 60 23). **Postal Code:** 10200. **Syntagma Square** (tel. 322 62 53), on the corner of Mitropolis. **Postal Code:**

10300. Both open M-F 7:30am-8pm, Sa 7:30am-2pm, Su 9am-1:30pm. An **Acropolis** branch is open M-F 8am-5:30pm, Sa 7:30am-2pm, Su 9am-2pm.

Telephones: OTE, 85 Patission St. (tel. 821 44 49 or 823 70 40). Offers overseas collect calls and currency exchange (until 3pm). Open M-F 7am-9pm, Sa 8am-3pm, Su 9am-2pm. **Telephone cards** for local phone booths are sold for 1700, 7000, or 11,500dr. Push the "i" button on the phones for English-language instructions. For telephone info, call 134; for info on overseas calls, dial 161; for directory assistance, 132; for a domestic operator speaking English, 151.

ACCOMMODATIONS

Many hotel hawkers meet trains at the station. Some distribute pamphlets for decent places near the station, others lure tourists to expensive dumps far from town. Have the hawker point out the place on a large map of the city and set a firm price, ideally in writing, *before* leaving the station. When you arrive at a hotel, ask for a room that faces away from noisy streets. Men arriving by bus should beware of "friendly barkeepers" who may deceitfully lead you to brothels. Most budget hotels cluster in Plaka-Syntagma; stay here if nightlife matters to you. If you stay fewer than three nights, an Athenian hotel owner can legally add a 10% surcharge to your bill. Athens proper has **no camping** facilities. Do not sleep in the parks, even as a last resort; it's illegal and extremely unsafe. *Note that the prices quoted below are from mid-1998 and are expected to increase in the next year. In 1999, expect a 10 to 20% price increase. Prices are 20 to 40% less in the off season (Sept.-May).*

Student's and Traveler's Inn, 16 Kidathineon St. (tel. 324 48 08; fax 321 00 65), in the heart of Plaka. Convenient locale, friendly owner and staff, and outdoor courtyard. **Internet access.** 24hr. hot showers. Singles 7000dr; doubles 9000dr; triples 12,000dr; quads 14,000dr. 10% discount with student ID or youth card.

Hotel Festos, 18 Filellinon St. (tel. 323 24 55). Come as a guest and stay as an employee! Hotel Festos hires travelers to work in the lounge and behind the desk. The restaurant has a rotating menu at reasonable prices. 24hr. hot water. Dorms 3000dr; doubles 8000dr; triples 12,000dr; quads 14,000dr. Check-out 10am.

Athens International Hostel (HI), 16 Victor Hugo St. (tel. 523 41 70; fax 523 40 15). From Omonia Sq., walk down Tritis Septembriou St. and take a left on Veranzerou St.; it will become Victor Hugo after crossing Marni St. Hot water 6-10am and 6-10pm. Dorms 1500dr; non-members add 600dr. Reserve ahead in summer.

Hotel Tempi, 29 Aiolou St. (tel. 321 31 75; fax 325 41 79). From Syntagma Sq., follow Ermou St. and take a right on Aiolou St. (also spelled Eolu and Eolou). 24hr. hot water. Singles 5000-6500dr; doubles 8500dr-9500dr; triples 10,500dr.

Hotel Orion, 105 Em. Benaki St. (tel. 382 73 62 or 382 01 91; fax 380 51 93). From Omonia Sq., walk up Em Benaki St. or take bus 230 from Syntagma Sq. Abutting Strefi Hill, Orion has small rooms and shared baths. 24hr. hot water. Singles 6000dr; doubles 8000dr; triples 9000dr.

Youth Hostel #5 Pangrati, 75 Damareos St. (tel. 751 95 30; fax 751 06 16). Take trolley 2 or 11 from Syntagma Sq. to Filolaou St., or walk through the National Garden, down Eratosthenous St. to Plastira Sq., 3 blocks on Efthidiou St. to Frinis St., and down Frinis St. until Damareos St. (40min.). Look for the number "75" on a green door. Dorms 1800dr; roof beds 1500dr. Check-out 10am.

FOOD

Athens offers a melange of stands, open-air cafes, outdoor sidestreet *tavernas,* and intriguing dim restaurants frequented by grizzled Greek men. *Souvlaki* (250-400dr), either on a *kalamaki* (skewer) or wrapped in *pita,* is the Greek alternative to fast-food. A *tost,* a grilled sandwich of variable ingredients (normally ham and cheese) for 300 to 600dr is another portable option. Beer, usually Amstel or Heineken, runs about 350dr per bottle. *Tiropita* (hot cheese pie) and *spanakopita* (hot spinach pie) go for around 300dr. Ice cream is sold at almost every kiosk. A *koulouri,* a doughnut-shaped, sesame-coated roll, makes a quick breakfast (50-100dr).

Tourists eat in Plaka. Crowded in peak season, the outdoor *tavernas* and roof gardens make for terrific people-watching, and there are numerous good places up Adrianou and Kidatheneon St. Women should know that Plaka is frequented by *kamakia* (literally, "octopus spears") who enjoy making catcalls at women as they walk by. Ignore them, and they should pose no physical danger. Restaurants tend to be deserted at 6pm, near-empty before 10pm, and crowded from 11pm to 1am.

Savas, 86 Mitropoleos St. Tucked into a corner off Ermou St. with vegetarian *gyros* (150dr). Near the Acropolis and the flea market. Open daily 7am-3am.

O Barba Giannis, 94 Em. Benaki St. Menu includes a wide variety of fish (from 950dr) and vegetarian dishes (950dr). Open M-Sa noon-1am, Su noon-7pm.

Kouklis Ouzeri a.k.a. **To Gerani,** 14 Tripodon St. From Kidatheneon, one of Plaka's busiest strips, Tripodon is a side street. The rotating menu limits your choices, but any 2 dishes make a good meal (900-1100dr each).

Eden Vegetarian Restaurant, 12 Lissiou St. On the corner of Minissikleous on the western side of Plaka. Airy, secluded, and popular. Spinach special 1700dr.

Kentrikon, 3 Colocotroni St., near Stadiou St. Traditional Greek meal for 1800dr. Open M-F 11am-6pm, Sa 11am-4pm.

Healthy Food Vegetarian Restaurant, 57 Panepistimiou St. Everything is made without any preservatives. Potato carrot pie (400dr). After your meal, browse through the adjoining shop. Open M-F 8am-10pm, Sa 8am-9pm, Su 10am-4pm.

SIGHTS

The **Acropolis,** or "high city," with its strategic position overlooking the Aegean Sea and Attic Plains, has served throughout history as both a military fortress and a religious center. *(Open in summer M-F 8am-7:30pm, Sa-Su and holidays 8:30am-7:30pm; off-season daily 8:30am-4:30pm. 2000dr, students 1000dr.)* Today, the hilltop's remarkable (if scaffolded) ruins grace otherwise rubble-strewn grounds. The ramp that led to the Acropolis in classical times no longer exists: today's visitors make the five-minute climb to the ticket-window, enter through the crumbling **Beulé Gate** (added by the Romans), and continue through the **Propylaea,** the ancient entrance. The site is not wheelchair accessible. The marble can be slippery, so wear appropriate shoes. At the cliff's edge, the tiny **Temple of Athena Nike** was built during a respite from the Peloponnesian War, the so-called Peace of Nikias (421-415 BC). Looming over the hillside, the **Parthenon,** or "Virgin's Apartment," keeps vigil over Athens. The temple features many almost imperceptible intentional irregularities; the Doric columns bulge in the middle, and the stylobate (pedestal) of the building bows slightly upward in order to compensate for the optical illusion in which straight lines, viewed from a distance, appear to bend. The **Erechtheion,** to the left of the Parthenon as you face it, was completed in 406 BC, just prior to Athens's defeat by Sparta. This unique two-level structure housed a number of cults. On the south side of the Erechtheion, facing the Parthenon, are the **caryatids,** six columns sculpted in the shape of women. The **Acropolis Museum** (tel. 323 66 65), footsteps away from the Parthenon, contains a superb sculpture collection, including five of the original Erechtheion caryatids. *(Open M-F 8am-7:30pm, Sa-Su and holidays 8:30am-7:30pm; in winter daily 8:30am-4:30pm.)*

The **Athenian Agora,** at the foot of the Acropolis, was the administrative center and marketplace of Athens from the 6th century BC through the late Roman Period (5th and 6th centuries AD). The **Temple of Hephaestos,** on a hill in the northwest corner, is the best-preserved Classical temple in Greece. Built around 440 BC, it is notable for its friezes depicting the labors of Hercules and the adventures of Theseus. To the south, the elongated **Stoa of Attalos,** a multi-purpose building for shops, shelter, and informal gatherings, was rebuilt between 1953 and 1956 and now houses the **Agora Museum.** *(Agora and museum open Tu-Su 8:30am-2:30pm. 1200dr, students 600dr.)* The museum contains a number of relics from the site and offers sanctuary from the sweltering summer sun. There are several entrances to the Agora, including one at the edge of Monastiraki, one on Thission Sq., and one on Adrianou St. Fifteen majestic columns are all that remain of the **Temple of Olympian Zeus,** Vas. Olgas and Amalias

Ave., the largest temple ever built in Greece. *(Open Tu-Su Nov.-Apr. 8:30am-3pm; May-Oct. 8am-2:30pm. 500dr, students 300dr.)* Next to the Temple, **Hadrian's Arch** marked the 2nd-century boundary between the ancient city of Theseus and the new city built by Hadrian. One of the world's finest selections of classical sculpture, ceramics, and bronzework is found in the **National Archeological Museum,** 44 Patission St. Pieces that would shine elsewhere seem almost unremarkable amid the general magnificence. The "Mask of Agamemnon," from Heinrich Schliemann's Mycenae digs and the larger-than-life bronze statue of Poseidon are must-sees. *(Open Apr.-Oct. M 12:30-7pm, Tu-F 8am-7pm, Sa-Su and holidays 8:30am-3pm; Nov.-Mar. M 11am-5pm, Tu-F 8am-5pm, Sa-Su and holidays 8:30am-3pm. 2000dr, students 1000dr, seniors 1500dr, free Su and holidays. No flash photography.)* The **Chapel of St. George,** on top of **Lycavittos Hill,** offers a beautiful view of the city. The **National Gallery** (Alexander Soutzos Museum), 50 Vasileos Konstandinou (tel. 723 58 57), exhibits works by Greek artists, including El Greco, supplemented by periodic international displays. *(Open M and W-Sa 9am-3pm, Su 10am-2pm. 1000-1500dr, students and seniors 500dr. Consult This Week in Athens or call for info on exhibits.)* Walk along the tranquil paths and visit the duck pond and zoo of the pleasant **National Garden,** adjacent to Syntagma Sq. Women should avoid strolling alone. *(Open daily sunrise to sunset.)* Don't miss the changing of the guard every hour on the hour in front of the **Parliament** building. Unlike the British equivalents, *evzones* occasionally wink or even smile. Every Sunday at 10:45am, the pomp-filled ceremony occurs with the full troop of guards and a band. Byzantine churches in Athens include the **Agia Apostoli,** at the east edge of the Agora; **Metamorphosis,** in Plaka near Pritaniou St.; **Agia Triada,** on Filellinon St., a few blocks from Syntagma; and **Agios Eleftherios,** next to the **Mitropoli Cathedral,** on Mitropoleos St. Viewing hours are at the discretion of each church's priest; mornings are the best bet. Dress appropriately: skirts for women, pants for men, and sleeved shirts for everyone.

ENTERTAINMENT

During the summer, hip Athenians head to the numerous seaside clubs on Poseidonos Ave. in **Glyfada** (past the airport). Many do not admit anyone in shorts. Covers range from 2000 to 3000dr, and beers run as high as 1000 to 2000dr (cocktails 1500-3000dr). Nearby, off the water, on Vouliagmenis St. in Glyfada, the best bars are all lined up. Some good hotspots include **King Size** for dance beat, **Camel Club** for rock, and **Bo** for people watching. You will wait in line on Friday and Saturday for the current hot spot **Privilege.** Cover charges are roughly 3000kr, and taxi fare to and from the city center is 1500 to 2500dr each way. Other parts of the city have good clubs as well. Try venturing to the posh **Kolonaki** district, where a coffee or beer at any of the outdoor *tavernas* is manageable. **Jazz in Jazz,** on Deinokratous St., up from the British Embassy, is nearby. **Kifissia,** a hip residential area north of Athens, has many slick *tavernas* and discos. For gay (primarily male) clubs, try **Lembessi Street** off Singrou.

The **Athens Festival** runs annually from June until September, featuring classical theater groups performing in the Odeon of Herodes Atticus, the Lycavittos Theater at the top of Lycavittos Hill, and in Epidavros. The Greek Orchestra plays during this festival regularly; visiting artists have ranged from the Bolshoy to B.B. King. The **Festival Office** (tel. 322 14 59 or 322 31 11, ext. 240) is in the arcade at 4 Stadiou St. Student tickets are generally affordable. (Open M-F 8:30am-2pm and 5-7pm, Sa 8:30am-1pm, Su 10am-1pm. Tickets 3000-5000dr.)

The bazaar-like **Athens Flea Market,** adjacent to Monastiraki Sq., offers a potpourri of the second-hand, the costly, and everything in between (market open M, W, and Sa-Su 8am-3pm, Tu and Th-F 8am-8pm). Sunday is the grand bazaar: the flea market overflows the square and Fillis Athinas St. A huge indoor-outdoor **food market** lines the sides of Athinas St. between Evripidou and Sofokleous St. The **meat market** is huge, but not for the faint of heart.

■ Near Athens

The view of the Aegean from the **Temple of Poseidon** makes a visit here a sublime experience (open daily 9am-sunset; 800dr, students 400dr, EU students free). The remaining Doric columns of the sanctuary, built by Pericles in 440 BC, sit on a promontory above the coast at **Cape Sounion,** 70km from Athens. Two **buses** go to Cape Sounion. One travels the Apollo Coast, leaving every hour on the half-hour from 14 Mavromateon St. (2hr., 6:30am-6:30pm, 1200dr). The other bus, on a less scenic route, leaves from Areos Park (2¼hr., every hr. on the hr. 6am-6pm, 1200dr). Bring water and a lunch. Check return schedules at the bus station upon arrival.

In 490 BC, when the Athenians defeated the Persians at the bloody battle of **Marathon,** the messenger Pheidippides ran 42km to announce the victory and then collapsed, dead from exhaustion. Even though modern marathoners regularly repeat this feat (without the fatal collapse), the sane among us reach Marathon by **bus** from 29 Mavromateon St. by Areos Park in Athens (1hr., roughly every hr. 5:30am-10:30pm, 700dr). To get to the fascinating **Archaeological Museum of Marathonas,** ask the driver to let you off at the sign for the museum ("Mouseion and Marathonas." Open Tu-Su 8am-2:30pm. 500dr, students 250dr, EU students and students of classics or archaeology free, Oct.-Mar. Su free.)

Troubled denizens of the ancient world journeyed to the Oracle of Apollo at **Delphi,** where the *Pythia* (priestess of Apollo) gave them profound, if cryptic, advice. If modern Delphi is the center of anything, it's the tour-bus circuit—visit early in the morning. **Buses** leave Athens for Delphi from the 260 Liossion St. station (3½hr., 5 per day, 2800dr). If you have a railpass, take the **train** to Levadia and catch the Delphi bus from there (750dr).

The Irony of Oracles

The Delphic Oracle was renowned for giving obscure, deceptively metaphorical answers. Many a suppliant went home more confused than he came, having failed to draw meaning from the answer, or—worse still—having drawn the wrong meaning from it. In the 6th century BC, King Croesus of Sardis, ruler of most of Asia Minor and known in antiquity as the richest man in the world, came to the oracle to ask about the threat the Persians posed to his kingdom. The oracle's answer: "A great Empire will be destroyed." Croesus returned to Sardis thinking that he would conquer the Persian Empire, which even at that time was as large as his own. Of course, as he realized while watching his kingdom and capital fall to the Persians, the empire the oracle had meant was his own. Later, Themistocles, leader of Athens during the first Persian War, asked the oracle how to prepare for approaching war. He was told to "build wooden walls." Most took this to mean that wooden walls should be built around the city. Themistocles, however, set to work building a fleet of ships. Only after Athens' decisive victory over the Persians at the great naval battle of Salamis did the Athenians realize Themistocles' great wisdom. Such stories show that the nature of the oracle was not simply to answer questions. This was part of the meaning of the exhortation once inscribed on the Temple of Apollo: "Know thyself."

NORTHERN GREECE

The northern provinces of Macedonia, Thessaly, Thrace, and Epirus seldom find their way onto postcards, but not for lack of beauty. Greece's forgotten half is graced with pine-filled mountains and winding trails that lead to some of the country's most precious Byzantine treasures, graceful springs, and breathtaking scenery. Robust and unpretentious, the region waits to be discovered by adventurous travelers.

■ Thessaloniki (Θεσσαλονικη)

Thessaloniki has a more Western European feel than any other Greek city. Its broad tree-lined avenues, spacious squares, and cosmopolitan atmosphere make it seem, in fact, more Parisian than Athenian. And yet there is an older, more traditional world as well—particularly in the quiet, winding streets of the old town, in the seemingly infinite stone Byzantine churches, and in the thick-walled ruins of the ancient Romans. Adventurous visitors may discover a deeply gratifying anomaly: a Greek urban center that succeeds in showing off its history without being overshadowed by it.

ORIENTATION AND PRACTICAL INFORMATION

Running parallel to the water, the main streets are **Nikis, Mitropoleos, Tsimiski, Ermou, Egnatia,** and **Agiou Dimitriou.** Cheaper hotels dwell on Egnatia, and waterfront bars and cafes are on Nikis. Facing inland, head left on Mitropoleos to reach the **Ladadika** district. Roughly 15 blocks inland, north of Athinas St. and flanked by ancient castle walls, wind the streets of the **old town.**

Telephone Code: 031.

Flights: The airport (tel. 47 39 77) is 16km east of town. Take bus 78 (120dr) or a taxi (2200dr). **Olympic Airways Office,** 3 Koundouriotou St. (tel. 26 01 22; fax 22 97 25). Open M-Sa 8am-3:30pm. Call 28 18 80 for reservations M-Sa 7am-9pm. To: Athens (22,100dr), Crete (30,000dr), Lesvos (21,000dr), Rhodes (32,000dr), and elsewhere in Europe.

Trains: The **main terminal** (tel. 51 75 17) is on Monastiriou St., in the western part of the city. Take any bus down Egnatia St. (80dr). To: Athens (8hr., 10 per day, 4100dr), Istanbul (12hr., 1 per day, 12,730dr), Larissa (4½hr., 11 per day, 1370dr), and Sofia (7hr., 1 per day, 6310dr). A **ticketing office** (tel. 27 63 82) is at the corner of Aristotelous and Ermou. Open Tu-F 8am-8pm, Sa and M 8am-3pm.

Buses: **KTEL** has dozens of stations. Departure times posted above ticket counters. To Athens (7hr., 17 per day, 8000dr). Call 142 for Greek language info.

Ferries: Ticketing at **Karacharisis Travel and Shipping Agency,** 8 Kountourioti St. (tel. 52 45 44; fax 53 22 89). Open M-F 9am-9pm, Sa 9am-3pm. To: Crete (24hr., 11,900dr), Mykonos (13hr., 9200dr), and Santorini (17hr., 9900dr). Ferries travel twice a week to Chios (12hr., 8300dr), Kos (18hr., 12,300dr), Lesvos (9hr., 8000dr), and Rhodes (20hr., 14,500dr). In July and August, reserve 2-3 days in advance. Ferry service reduces significantly in the winter.

Hydrofoils: Flying Dolphins travel daily (June-Sept. only) to Alonissos (5hr.), Skiathos (3hr.), and Skopelos (4hr.). Buy tickets (average 10,000dr) at **Crete Air Travel,** 1 Dragoumi St. (tel. 54 74 07 or 53 43 76), across from the main port. Open M-F 9am-9pm, Sa 9am-3pm.

Public Transportation: Office across from the EOT gives info. Buses 8, 10, 11, and 31 run along Egnatia St. Buy ticket on board (price varies with distance; 80-220dr).

Tourist Offices: EOT, Aristotelous Sq. #8 (tel. 27 18 88 or 26 55 07; fax 26 55 04), one block from the water. Take any bus on Egnatia St. to Aristotelous Sq. Free city maps, hotel listings, and transportation schedules. Inquire about Thessaloniki's **festivals** (Sept.-Nov.). Open M-F 8am-8pm, Sa 8:30am-2pm. **United Travel System,** 28 Mitropoleos St. (tel. 28 67 56; fax 28 31 56), near Aristotelous Sq. Ask for English-speaking Liza and carry *Let's Go.* Open M-F 9:30am-5pm. Other offices at the port (tel. 59 35 78) and the airport (tel. 42 50 11, ext. 215).

Currency Exchange: National Bank, 11 Tsimiski St. (tel. 53 86 21). Open for exchange M-F 8am-2pm and 6-8pm, Sa 9am-1pm, Su 9:30am-12:15pm. Smaller banks charge slightly higher commissions. Many line Tsimiski.

American Express: 19 Tsimiski St. (tel. 26 15 21). Open M-F 10am-4pm, Sa 9am-2pm. Another AmEx is at **Memphis Travel,** 23 Nikis St. (tel. 22 27 96), on the waterfront.

Laundromat: Bianca, 3 L. Antoniadou St. (tel. 20 96 02). 1400dr per load includes wash, dry, and soap. Open M-F 8am-8:30pm, Sa 8am-3pm.

Hospital: Ippokration Public Hospital, 50 A. Papanastasiou (tel. 83 79 20), some doctors speak English. **Red Cross First Aid Hospital,** 6 Kountourioti St. (tel. 53 05 30), at the entrance to the main port, gives free minor medical care.

Post Office: The main branch is on Aristotelous St., right before Egnatia. Open M-F 7:30am-8pm, Sa 7:30am-2pm, Su 9am-1:30pm. **Postal Code:** 54101.

Internet Access: Globus Internet Cafe, 12 Amynta (tel. 23 29 01) offers web access and email. 1300dr per hr.

Telephones: OTE, 27 Karolou Diehl St., at the corner of Ermou, 1 block east of Aristotelous Sq. Open 24hr.

ACCOMMODATIONS AND FOOD

Most of Thessaloniki's less expensive hotels are clustered together along the western end of Egnatia St., between Vardari Sq. (500m east of the train station) and Dikastirion Sq. Be aware that Egnatia, a major thoroughfare, is loud at all hours. Prices rise about 25% between September and November. Single women should avoid offers for cheap rooms from English-speaking "tourist officials" at the train station.

Hotel Argo, 11 Egnatia St. (tel. 51 97 70). Clean rooms, good bargains, and classical music. Singles 5000dr, with bath 6000dr; doubles 6000dr, with bath 8000dr.

Youth Hostel, 44 Alex. Svolou St. (tel. 22 59 46; fax 26 22 08). Tram 8, 10, 11, or 31 from Egnatia St. to the Arch of Galerius. Walk toward the water; 2 blocks later turn left onto Svolou St. 2000dr, hot shower included. Lockout 11am-6:30pm. 3-night max. stay, 1-night without membership.

Hotel Atlantis, 14 Egnatia St. (tel. 54 01 31). Old-fashioned pink pastel exterior and patriotically decorated blue and white rooms with shared baths. Singles 6000dr; doubles 8000dr; triples 11,000dr.

Hotel Emporikan, 14 Singrou (tel. 52 55 60 or 51 44 31), at intersection with Egnatia. Clean rooms with shared bath. Singles 6000dr; doubles 9000dr.

Hotel Averof (tel. 53 88 40; fax 54 31 94), at the intersection of Egnatia St. and 24 L. Sofia St. Friendly staff and new furniture. Communal living room with TV. Singles 6000-8000dr; doubles 8000-10,000dr.

Thessaloniki is known throughout Greece for its excellent *mezedes.* **Open-air markets** line Vati Kioutou St. just off Aristotelous Sq. The Aretsou Area, along the bay about 4km toward the airport, boasts excellent **seafood.** Explore the old town and Ladadika district for inexpensive, family-oriented *tavernas.* **The Brothers,** in Navarino Sq. (open daily noon-midnight), and **To Chriso Pagoni,** 42 Alex. Svolou St., next to the hostel, offer traditional Greek meals for 1500dr. **Dell Arco,** on Egnatia St. right next to Arch of Galerius, specializes in pizza, pasta and calzone (main courses 1350-2250dr).

SIGHTS AND ENTERTAINMENT

Thessaloniki's array of museums, churches and ruins is surpassed only by Athens. The superlative **Archaeological Museum** displays a collection of Macedonian treasures, including gold myrtle wreaths found in Derveni and the cemetery at Pydna. Also notable is the Derveni papyrus—an Orphic poem about the underworld and the only surviving papyrus in Greece. Take bus 3 from the railway station to HAN Sq. (Open in summer M 12:30-8pm, Tu-Sa 8am-8pm, Su 8am-7pm; off-season M 10:30am-5pm, Tu-F 8am-5pm, Sa-Su 8:30am-3pm. 1500dr, non-EU students 800dr, EU students free.) Next door, the **Museum of Byzantine Culture** has fascinating exhibits on the evolution of Byzantine churches, the nature of everyday Byzantine life, and the attitudes of the Byzantines towards death and burial. (Open M noon-8pm, Tu-Su 8am-8pm. 1500dr, non-EU students 800dr, EU students free.) The **International Fairgrounds,** across from the Archaeological and Byzantine museums, hold a variety of **festivals** in the fall, including the International Trade Fair in September (for info call 23 92 21). On the other side of the park looms Thessaloniki's best-known landmark, **White Tower** (Lefkos Pirgos), all that remains of a 16th-century Venetian seawall

Street Smart in Northern Greece

Travel through Northern Greece for long enough, and you'll notice something odd about the street and square names—they're all the same. Here's a guide for all those who have wondered what it *really* means to stand at the corner of **25 Martiou** and **Pavlou Melas.**

25 Martiou: March 25, 1821—Greece's national holiday, celebrating Greece's declaration of independence from the Ottoman Empire.

3 Septemvriou: September 3, 1863—Greeks riot against monarchical rule and demand a constitution.

11 Noemvriou: November 11, 1912—Thessaloniki liberated from the Ottomans.

28 Octovriou: October 28, 1940—"Ohi Day!" President Metaxas refused to surrender to Mussolini's Italians.

Athanassiou Diakou: A hero of the Greek Revolution roasted on a spit after being captured by the Turks.

Pavlou Melas: Guerrilla leader who freed Macedonian villages from Bulgarians.

Iroon Polytehniou: The heroes of the Polytechnio—students who rioted against the military *junta* in 1974 and contributed to its downfall.

Riga Ferreou: The great Greek poet before the Revolution who wrote "Better one day of freedom than 40 years of slavery and oppression."

Averof: The name of one of Greece's oldest, richest, and most munificent families. The primary recipient of their generosity is the mountain village of Metsovo.

whose blood-stained walls were painted white to obliterate wartime memories. The tower houses a museum of early Christian art (open Tu-Su 8am-2:30pm; free). The **Eptapirgion Walls,** erected during the reign of Theodosius the Great, stretch along the north edge of the old city. Take bus 22 from Eleftherias Sq. on the waterfront.

The celebrated but scaffolded **Arch of Galerius** stands at the end of Egnatia St. at the corner of Gounari St. For further historical pursuits, head north of Dikastirion Sq. to the **Roman Market** between Filippou and Olibou St. The centerpiece of the remains of the **Palace of Galerius,** near Navarino Sq., is the octagonal hall. Thessaloniki boasts a large number of churches; a walk down Egnatia makes it seem as if small stone Byzantine churches reside in every corner. The city's oldest and most famous is **Agios Dimitrius,** built in the 5th century AD and named for Dimitrius, the patron saint of Thessaloniki. Explore the **catacombs** beneath the church (open Su 10:30am-8pm, M 12:30-7pm, Tu-Sa 8am-8pm). The 7th-century **Agia Sophia,** located just below the intersection of Prassanaki St. and Egnatia St., has a splendid 9th-century mosaic of the Ascension. Nearby, **Panagia Ahiropoeitos** is one of the first known basilica-style churches, and **Agios Yiannis Prodromos** hides an underground church in its crypts. You can also visit the beautiful **Old Synagogue** at 35 Singrou St.; the caretaker at the **Jewish Community Center,** 24 Tsimiski St., will let you in.

Thessaloniki's varied and dynamic nightlife rivals that of Athens. There are three main hubs for late-night *glendi* in Thessaloniki: the Ladadika district, the bustling waterfront, and the area around the exit for the airport. **Mylos,** 56 Andreou Georgiou (tel. 52 59 68), is a massive entertainment center, containing art exhibits, a restaurant, bars, and an area for live shows. Disco lives on at **Tataboo Disco,** right on the exit for the airport (cover 2000dr). **Theatron** (tel. 47 11 60) is arguably the most sophisticated club in Thessaloniki (cover 4000dr), and **Iguana,** 45 L-Nikis, is one of the largest bars on the waterfront (beer 1000dr). **Taboo,** on Kastritsiou St., one block from Egnatia, caters to gay and lesbian partiers.

■ Mount Olympus and Meteora

Greece's loftiest peak, **Mt. Olympus** (Ολυμπος; 2917m) rises from the coastal plain 90km southwest of Thessaloniki. This summit of the gods requires two days of challenging hiking (May-Oct. only) but no special equipment. To reach the small town of **Litohoro,** the gateway to Olympus, take the train from Thessaloniki to Katerini, then

GREECE

walk 1km to catch the bus that will take you the remaining 5km into town. From the main square, follow signs to the **EOS Greek Mountaineering Club** (tel. (0352) 845 44) and **SEO Mountaineering Club** (tel. (031) 224 710), which provide maps and have **refuges** on the mountain (EOS open June-Aug. M-F 9am-12:30pm and 6:30-8:30pm, Sa-Su 9am-noon). The **tourist office** (tel. (0352) 831 00) has free maps of the area (open daily mid-June to Sept. 9am-8pm). The **Hotel Park** (tel. (0352) 812 52), is on the main road to the right just after the entrance to town (singles 6000dr; doubles 7000dr). **Do not freelance camp** on the north side of the road connecting the town and the highway: this is training ground for the armored units of the Greek army.

Southwest of Olympus lies **Meteora** (Μετεωρα), where several exquisite Byzantine monasteries grip the tops of enigmatic black spires. The monasteries have staggered their closing days, but all are open Saturday, Sunday, and Wednesday from April until the end of September (9am-6pm; each 500dr). No photography or revealing dress allowed. The **Grand Meteoron Monastery** is the oldest, largest and most important of the monasteries and has brilliant frescoes of the Roman persecution of Christians. **Varlaam Monastery** has 16th-century frescoes in its chapel, including a particularly disturbing rendition of the Apocalypse. The most popular base for exploring Meteora is the town of **Kalambaka** (Καλαμπακα). There will be **no train service** to Kalambaka through 1999 due to construction; call the station (tel. (0432) 224 51) for info on replacement routes by bus. **Buses** run daily to Kalambaka from Athens (5200dr), Thessaloniki (3500dr), and Volos (2900dr); others depart for Meteora (20min., 2 per day, 220dr). Most people walk back to town (6km downhill), visiting the monasteries along the way. The awe-inspiring view of the Meteora from **Koka Roka** (tel. (0432) 245 54) is worth the 15-minute walk up from the bus station in Kalambaka (singles 3000-4000dr; doubles 6000-7000dr; triples 7500dr).

■ Ioannina (Ιωαννινα)

Now Epirus' largest city and capital, Ioannina displays the most marked Turkish influence of all of the cities in Greece—an Eastern flavor reflected in the city's distinctive museums, architecture, and way of life. The city's **castle** makes a logical starting point for your excursions. Rising ominously from the surrounding waters, the castle's massive stone walls contain the old city, complete with museums, shops, a **mosque,** and a **synagogue,** mutely attesting to the former prominence of the city's Jewish population. Within the **Its Kale,** the inner sanctum of the castle, lie the **tomb of Ali Pasha** and the **Inner Acropolis** with eerie stone tunnels just waiting to be explored (open Tu-Su 7am-10pm). At the northern corner of the castle is the splendid **Aslan Pasha Mosque,** built in 1618 to celebrate the failed 1611 Greek insurrection led by the fanatical Bishop of Trikala, Dionysos Skilosofos. Outside of the castle, behind the clock tower in a park south of Averof St., you'll find the **Archaeological Museum,** whose collection is a must-see for those visiting Dodoni. (Open M noon-6pm, Tu-F 8am-6pm, Sa-Su 8:30am-3pm. Admission 500dr, students 300dr.) The museum features lead tablets etched with political, romantic, and cosmological questions asked of the oracle at Dodoni between the 6th and the 3rd century BC. Catch a boat (10min; In summer, every 30min. 8am-11pm; 200dr) across the lake to **Nisi** (island) to explore its three Byzantine monasteries.

The main bus station is between Sina St. and Zossimadon St. From there, **buses** run regularly to Athens (7hr., 7000dr) and Thessaloniki (6½hr., 5850dr). To find the **EOT tourist office** (tel. 25 086; fax 72 148), turn right onto Dodonis St. (an extension of Averof St.) from 28 Octovriou St., with the central park on your left (open daily in summer 7:30am-2:30pm and 5:30-8:30pm; in winter 7:30am-2:30pm). Staying in Ioannina unfortunately carries a pretty hefty price, as hotels here generally cater to deep-pocketed business travelers. **Hotel Paris,** 6 Tsirigoti St. (tel. (0651) 205 41), on a side street by the main bus terminal, offers large traditional Greek rooms (singles 5000-7000dr; doubles 8000-9000dr). **Hotel Tourist,** 18 Koletti St. (tel. (0651) 264 43 or 250 70), has spotless rooms with TVs (singles 10,000dr; doubles 14,000dr). Little *souvlaki* stands can be found throughout Ioannina. The dining scene centers on the waterfront and old town areas of the city.

■ Near Ioannina: Dodoni (Δωδωνη)

Ancient Dodoni, the site of Greece's oldest oracle, is located at the base of a mountain 22km southeast of Ioannina (site open daily 8am-7pm; admission 500dr, students 400dr). According to myth, Zeus resided in Dodoni as the roots of a giant oak while courting a nearby cypress tree (Zeus was an omnivore). With the oracle long-gone, however, the chief attraction at Dodoni today is the well-preserved **amphitheater,** which in its heyday was grander than that of Epidauros. In the summer, two **buses** a day come from Ioannina–but at very inconvenient times (25min., F-W 6:30am and 4pm, 4pm on Su.; 360dr).

THE PELOPONNESE (Πελοποννεσος)

Connected to the mainland only by the narrow isthmus of Corinth, the Peloponnese contains the majority of Greece's best archaeological sites, including Olympia, Mycenae, Messene, Mystra, and Epidavros. It also offers some of Greece's most stunning landscapes, from the barren crags of the Mani to the forested peaks and flower-blanketed pastures of Arcadia. By heavenly happenstance, this rich, beautiful land is also sparsely populated and relatively untouristed.

■ Argolis and Corinthia (Αργολιδα Και Κονινθια)

Chronicled in the pages of ancient writers, the 100-eyed Argos once roamed the northern Peloponnese, subduing unruly satyrs and rampaging bulls. Today, the greatest threat comes from heat and crowds: try to visit early in the day.

Corinth Most visitors to the Peloponnese stop first at Corinth (Κορινθος), where a green bus drives 7km to the ruins of **Ancient Corinth** (every hr. 6am-9pm, 220dr), where the **Ministry of Culture Archaeological Museum** houses artifacts from the archaeological site. To the left as you exit the museum is the 6th-century BC **Temple of Apollo.** (Both open daily in summer 8am-8pm; in winter 8am-5pm. 1200dr, students 600dr, Su free.) The lower peak of the **Acrocorinth** is the site of an ancient fortress; the upper summit once held a **Temple to Aphrodite.** The walk up is 1½ hours, or a taxi (tel. (0741) 314 64) can take you (round-trip 2500dr).

Back in New Corinth, **trains** arrive on Demokratias St. from Athens (2hr., 15 per day, 800dr) and connect to all major Peloponnesian towns. The spotless rooms at **Hotel Acti,** 3 Ethnikis Antistasis St. (tel. (0741) 233 37; singles 3000dr; doubles 6000dr), and the private baths at **Hotel Apollon,** 18 Pirinis St. (tel. (0741) 225 87; singles 4000dr; doubles 8000dr; triples 9000dr) comfort the weary. **Kanita,** on Damaskinov, is the best harbor eatery (open 24hr.), and at night motorcycling teenagers and vacationing families alike head down to the cafes and bars of **Kalami beach.** In the ancient city, walk away from the ruins, turn right onto Sisyphos St., and right again at the sign for Argos to reach **Rooms Marinos** (tel. (0741) 312 09; singles 7500dr; doubles 11,000), or try **Taverna Tassos,** on the road to Corinth (tel. (0741) 312 25), with crisp white rooms (singles 4000dr; doubles 5000dr).

Nafplion A favorable location and beautiful old town make **Nafplion** an ideal base for exploring nearby ruins. The town itself boasts impressive monuments, most notably the **Palamidi Fortress.** Visitors can travel a 3km road or walk up 999 steps to the fortress, with its well-preserved walls and stunning views. (Open in summer M-F 7:45am-7pm, Sa-Su 8:30am-3pm; off-season daily 8:30am-3pm. 800dr, students 400dr, EU students free.) The **bus station,** at the base of the hill on Singrou St., serves Athens (3hr., 2450dr), Corinth (2hr., 1100dr), Epidavros (1hr., 550dr), and Mycenae (45min., 550dr). **Pension Acronafplia,** 23 Vasileos Konstandinou St. (tel (0752) 244 81), has clean, charming rooms and an excellent old city location (singles 5000dr; doubles 7500dr; triples 13,500dr). **Hotel Argolis,** 32 Argos St. (tel. (0752) 277 21), is a 15-minute walk from the bus station on the road coming into town—save yourself the trouble of walking by asking to be let off at the Thanasenas stop, just up the street from the hotel (singles 4000dr; doubles 6000dr; sometimes less for students). Dining options cluster around Syntagma Sq. **Taverna O Vasiles,** on Staikopoulou St., serves wonderful fresh fish and a rabbit in onions (1500dr) that will delight even the most avid Beatrix Potter fan.

Mycenae and Epidavros
Greece's supreme city from 1600 to 1100 BC, **Mycenae** (Μυκηναι) was once ruled by Agamemnon, leader of the Greek forces during the Trojan War. Find the gory details in Homer's *Iliad* and Aeschylus' *Oresteia*. Most of the treasures from the excavation are in Athens, but the **Lion's Gate** and the **Treasury of Atreus** are among the most celebrated modern archaeological finds. (Site open daily Apr.-Sept. 8am-10pm; Oct.-Mar. 8am-5pm. 1500dr, students 800dr, EU students free. Keep your ticket or pay again at Agamemnon's tomb.) **Buses** arrive daily from Argos (30min., 260dr) and Nafplion (40min., 550dr). The **Belle Helene Hotel** (tel. (0751) 762 25) serves as a bus stop on the main road (singles 6000dr; doubles 7000dr; triples 10,000dr).

Try to visit **Epidavros** (Επιδαυρος) on Friday or Saturday night from late June to mid-August, when the **National Theater of Greece** and visiting companies perform plays from the classical Greek canon (in Greek). Performances start at 9pm, and you can buy tickets (4000-6000dr, students 2000dr) at the site (open M-Sa 9am-5pm, F-Sa until 9pm). Contact the **Athens Festival Box Office** (tel. (01) 322 14 59) for advance ticket sales. The **theater** itself, built in the 2nd century BC, is remarkable. Henry Miller wrote that he heard "the great heart of the world" beat here; at the very least, you can still stand on the top row of seats and hear a *drachma* dropped on stage. Near the theater and other classical ruins, Epidavros's **museum** houses painted decorations from the ruins and huge stones with inscriptions of hymns to Apollo. (Theater, site, and museum open in summer Tu-Su 8am-7pm and M noon-7pm; off-season closes 5pm. 1500dr, students 800dr, EU students free.) **Buses** connect to Nafplion (1hr., 6 per day, 550dr).

▓ Patras (Πατρας)

Sprawling Patras, Greece's third largest city, is known mainly as a transportation hub, but during **Carnival** (mid-Jan. to Ash Wednesday), the port becomes one vast dance floor. At other times, visitors spend time exploring the 13th-century Venetian **castle** and park (follow Ag. Nikolaou St. inland from town) or the **Ancient Odeum,** a Roman theatre west of the castle (open Tu-Su 8:30-2:30; free). The largest Orthodox cathedral in Greece, the **Agios Andreas,** holds magnificently colored frescoes and an unusual relic—St. Andrew's head. To get there, follow the water to the west end of town (open daily 9am-dusk). Sweet black grapes produce *Mavrodaphne* wine at the **Achaïa Clauss winery.** (Bus 7 from the intersection of Kolokotroni and Kanakari St. Tours in summer daily 9am-7:30pm; off-season 9am-5pm. Free.)

The **tourist office** (tel. (061) 62 22 49), on the waterfront at the entrance to the customs complex, helps with accommodations and has free maps and timetables (open M-Sa 7am-10pm). **Trains** (tel. (061) 27 36 94) depart from Othonos Amalias St. for Athens (8 per day, 1600dr) via Corinth (1000dr). The **bus terminal** (tel. (061) 62 38 86), on Othonos Amalias between Aratou and Zaïmi, serves Athens (3hr., 3350dr), Thessaloniki (8000dr), Tripoli (3000dr), and other cities. Several **ferry** lines go to Cephalonia, Corfu, and Ithaka, as well as Italy's Ancona, Bari, Brindisi, and Venice (prices vary; ask about student discounts); check in the travel offices along Iroon Politechniou/Othonos Amalias St. for particulars. If you have a railpass, go to **HML** (tel. (061) 45 25 21) on Iroon Politechinou. **Strintzis Tours,** 14 Othonas Amalias St. (tel. (061) 62 26 02; open daily 9am-10pm), has info on Ionian island ferries.

Cheap accommodations are scattered around Ag. Andreas St., a block up and parallel to the waterfront. **Pension Nikos,** 3 Patreos St., 3rd floor (tel. (061) 22 16 43), has clean rooms (singles 4000dr; doubles 6500dr). There is also a cramped **youth hostel** at 68 Iroon Polytechniou St. (tel. (061) 42 72 78). A good pick for vegetarians and omnivores alike is the traditional **Taverna Nicolaras,** three blocks inland on Ag. Nikolaou (meals 800-1300dr).

▓ Olympia (Ολυμπια)

Beginning in 776 BC, leaders of rival city-states in ancient Greece shed their armor every four years and congregated to enjoy the Olympic games and make offerings to the gods. Today, the remains of a gymnasium, palaestra, stadium, and several temples and treasures are scattered around **Ancient Olympia,** although they are not labeled or particularly well-preserved. Dominating the site, the gigantic **Temple of Zeus,** once held a statue of the god so beautiful it was one of the seven wonders of the ancient world. On the north edge of the Altis lie the remains of the 7th-century BC **Temple of Hera,** the site's best-preserved structure and the location of the quadrennial lighting of the **Olympic flame.** The **New Museum,** across the street from the site, houses a vast array of sculpture, including the Nike of Paionios, the **Hermes of Praxiteles,** and the pedimental sculptures from the Temple of Zeus. (Site open daily 8am-8pm. Museum open Tu-F 8am-8pm, Sa-M noon-8pm. Each 1200dr, students 600dr, EU students free. No flash cameras in museum.)

Buses run to Pirgos (40min., 380dr) and Tripoli (3½hr., 2300dr). In new Olympia, the **tourist office** (tel. (0624) 231 00), Kondili Ave., on the east side of town, provides maps (open daily noon-8pm; July-Aug. 9am-9pm). The **youth hostel,** 18 Kondili Ave. (tel. (0624) 225 80), charges 1600dr per person. **Camping Diana** (tel. (0624) 223 14), uphill from the Sports Museum, has a clean pool and hot water (1400dr per person, 900-1300dr per tent). A walk toward the railroad station or up the hill, away from the busloads of tourists, reveals some charming and inexpensive *tavernas.*

▓ Arcadia and Messenia (Αρκαδια και Μεσσηνια)

Poets since Theocritus have fancied Arcadia as the archetypal pastoral setting. Tripoli and a few other towns now rumble with buses and other traffic, but rural serenity persists among the hidden bays, dramatic mountains, and vast fir forests in this area. In adjacent Messenia, olives, figs, and grapes spring from the rich soil along the rocky coastline, and towns like Pylos and Methoni offer easy access to the region's sparkling beaches and turquoise waters.

Arcadia Urban **Tripoli** (Τριπολιη) intimidates with crowded sidewalks and perilous streets, but the town provides pleasant squares and cafes for those awaiting transportation to other points in Arcadia. For overnight stays, your best bet is **Hotel Anactoricon** (tel. (071) 22 25 45), along Ethnikis Antistasis two blocks before the park (singles 4000dr; doubles 8000dr). The new **Archaeological Museum,** Evangelistrias St., has pottery from Mycenaean tombs (open Tu-Su 8:30am-2pm; 500dr, students free). Westward, the little villages of **Dimitsana** (Δημητσανα) and **Stemnitsa** (Στεμνιτσα) are good bases for **hiking** and walking excursions, and will entice you to stay awhile with their chalet-like houses and natural beauty. Dimitsana has been a center of Greek learning and revolutionary activity since the 16th century. A better option than a hotel is to let a room in town. The rooms above the grocery store in the main square are newly remodeled with bathrooms, balconies, and TVs (singles 5000dr; doubles 8000dr). In Stemnitsa, enjoy a comfy night at the gorgeous **Hotel Triokolonion** (tel. (0795) 812 97), on the main road (singles 7500dr; doubles 9000dr; triples 11,500dr).

Messenia The Peloponnese's second largest city, **Kalamata** (Καλαματα) is a fine base for exploring the southwestern coast. **Trains** (tel. (0721) 950 56) leave the end of Sideromikou Stathmou St. for Athens (7hr., 2400dr) via Tripoli (2½hr., 840dr), Corinth (5¼hr., 1700dr), Patras (5½hr., 1500dr), and other cities. **Buses** (tel. (0721) 285 81 and 228 51) run to Athens (4hr., 4100dr), Sparta (2hr., 1040dr), and Tripoli (2hr., 1500dr). **Hotel Nevada** is at 9 Santa Rosa (tel. (0721) 824 29); get off bus 1 when it turns left along the water (singles 4000dr; doubles 5000dr; triples 7000dr). The well-preserved remains of Ancient Messene at Mavromati (transport is tricky) are one of Greece's most impressive archaeological sites. West of Kalamata (1½hr. by bus, 900dr), beautiful **Pylos** (Πυλος) offers beaches and considerable charm. Buses continue to **Methoni** (Μεθωνη; 15min., 220dr), where hibiscus-lined streets wind around the impressive 13th-century **Venetian fortress. Hotel Galini** (tel. (0723) 314 67) is in the beachside square (singles 5000dr; doubles 7000dr; triples 8000dr; higher in July, roughly double in Aug.). Crowded **Camping Methoni** (tel. (0723) 312 28) has attractive beach-side sites (1100dr per person, 750-950dr per tent).

■ Laconia (Λακωνια)

Although Laconia boasts three of the Peloponnese's most popular sights—Mani's Pirgos Dirou caves, the Byzantine ruins at Mystra, and Monemvassia's "rock"—the region remains low-key; even the tourist industry here is far less businesslike than on the islands or in Athens. As a result, Laconia's friendly villages are a welcome break from the urban atmosphere of other, more touristed areas in Greece.

Sparta and Mystra While **Sparta** (Σπαρτη) has been immortalized in the annals of military history, the modern city is noted mostly for its olive oil and orange trees and serves best as a base for visits to more impressive **Mystra** (Μυστρας), just 6km away. The center of Constantinople's rule over the Peloponnese during the 14th and 15th centuries, Mystra overflows with Byzantine churches and well-labeled castle ruins. Don't miss the **Metropolis of St. Demetrios** in the lower tier, with its courtyard and museum of architectural fragments. The **Church of Peribleptos** is perhaps Mystra's most stunning relic—every inch of the church is covered in exquisitely detailed paintings of religious scenes and figures. (Site open daily in summer 8am-8pm; off-season 8:30am-3pm. 1200dr, students 600dr.) **Buses** (tel. (0731) 264 41) head to Athens (3hr., 3600dr), Pirgos Dirou and the caves (1½hr., 1350dr), and many other towns. For buses to Mystra (220dr), head to the station at the corner of Lykourgou and Kythonigou, two blocks past the town hall; call the tourist office to verify departures. In Sparta, the **tourist office** (tel. (0731) 248 52), to the left of the town hall in the square, helps with bus schedules and hotels (maps 400dr; open daily 8am-

---

A Hard-Knock Life

A young Spartan's training for a life of war began early, even before conception. Lycurgus believed two fit parents produced stronger offspring, so he ordered all Spartan women to undergo the same rigorous training endured by men. Furthermore, newlyweds were permitted only an occasional tryst on the theory that the heightened desire of the parents would produce more robust children. If they weren't winnowed out as weak or deformed, boys began a severe regimen of training under an adult Spartan. The young were forced to walk barefoot to toughen their feet and wore only a simple piece of clothing in both summer and winter to expose them to drastic weather changes. The Spartan creed dictated that young men be guarded against temptations of any kind—strict laws forbidding everything from drinking to sodomy governed Spartans' actions. Moreover, young Spartans were given the plainest and simplest foods for fear that rich delicacies would stunt their growth. One visitor to Sparta, upon sampling the fare, allegedly quipped, "Now I know why they do not fear death."

2pm). Attractive rooms are available at the lemon-yellow **Hotel Cecil** (tel. (0731) 249 80), on the corner of Paleologou and Thermopilion St. (singles 6000dr; doubles 8000dr), or at the air-conditioned **Hotel Laconia** (tel. (0731) 289 52), also on Paleologou St. (singles 5000-6000dr; doubles 8000-10,000dr).

Mani Once known for violent family feuds and savage piracy, sparsely settled **Mani** (Μανη) remains a stark and rugged place, where bald mountains provide the backdrop for a jagged coast and austere settlements, and forbidding towers add muted greys and greens to the landscape. The port town of **Gythion** (Γυθειο), the self-proclaimed "Gateway to Mani," offers easy access to Areopolis and the rest of the coast. The **bus station,** on the north end of the waterfront, serves Areopolis (1hr., 460dr), Athens (4350dr) via Sparta (1hr., 750dr), Kalamata (1300dr) via Itilo (1hr., 650dr), and the caves near Pirgos Dirou (1¼hr., 600dr). **Ferries** depart from the quay to the right of Mavromichali Sq. for Crete (2 per week, 4560dr) and Kythera (1 per day, 1535dr). In Gythion, you can rent **mopeds** to explore the hard-to-reach Mani. In town, try the spacious and clean rooms of **Xenia Karlafti's** (tel. (0733) 227 19), near the causeway (doubles 6000dr; triples 7000dr). The most luxurious campgrounds are **Meltemi** (tel. (0733) 228 33; 1200dr per person, 1000dr per tent) and **Mani Beach** (tel. (0733) 234 50; 1100dr per person, 750-950dr per tent). The campgrounds are south of town and accessible by bus. **Mavromichali Square** is the perfect place for lunch or a cheap dinner, and **Masouleri Kokkalis,** at the center of the square behind the plastic chairs, serves delicious gyros for 300dr.

From **Areopolis** (Αρεοπολη), along the western coast, you can make daytrips to the spectacular **Glyfatha Lake Cave** (also known as Spilia Dirou or Pirgos Dirou). The boat ride down the subterranean river passes a forest of stalactites and stalagmites (30min.). After the boat docks, a five-minute walk through the caves takes you to the exit. (The exit is different from the entrance. Caves open daily June-Sept. 8am-5pm; Oct.-May 8am-2:45pm. 3500dr.) From Areopolis, **buses** drive to the caves (3 per day, 220dr), Sparta (1½hr., 1200dr) via Gythion (30min., 460dr), and other towns. For a bed in Areopolis, find **Tsimova** (tel. (0733) 513 01), off Kapetan Matapan St. (singles 5000dr; doubles 6000dr).

Monemvassia The ancient Byzantine city of **Monemvassia** (Μονεμβασια) is dominated by a huge rock with vertical cliffs. The narrow streets of this wonderfully preserved city, replete with child-sized doorways, stairways, and flowered courtyards, should be explored. **Buses** connect to Corinth (5hr., 3950dr), Sparta (2½hr., 1750dr), and Tripoli (4hr., 2750dr) via Molai; the express bus to Athens costs 5350dr. In summer, **Flying Dolphins** leave for Kythera (1¼hr., 4910dr). Rooms in the medieval village tend to be expensive; there are many *domatia* along the waterfront. **Hotel Sophos** (tel. (0732) 613 60), across the street from the post office, has recently renovated rooms (singles 5000dr; doubles 7000dr). Pitch a tent at **Camping Paradise** (tel. (0732) 611 23), 3½km along the water on the mainland (1100dr per person, 800-1100dr per tent; prices lower off-season).

IONIAN ISLANDS
(Νησια Του Ιονιου)

Situated on Greece's western edge, the Ionian islands escaped Turkish occupation during the Middle Ages only to be overrun by the Venetians, Napoleon, the Russians, and the British. These uninvited visitors left a lasting cultural, commercial, and architectural imprint, and today their legacy complements an equally impressive array of beaches, flowers and trees, and hiking trails around the islands.

■ Corfu (Kerkyra; Κερκυρα)

Since Odysseus washed ashore and praised the lush beauty of **Corfu,** the seas have brought Crusaders, conquerors, and colonists to this verdant Ionian Island. Today, international visitors ramble through the shuttered alleys of an *ersatz* Venice, stroll along a Parisian esplanade, and sip tea on the grounds of a British imperial palace. Fortunately, the hedonistic mayhem has declined a bit in recent years, making Corfu's fine sandy beaches, sparkling blue waters, and verdant flower-strewn hillsides more accessible than ever.

All ferries and most buses originate in **Corfu Town,** the logical base for touring the island. **Ferries** travel to and from Ancona (23hr., 15,800dr), Bari (10hr., 12,000dr), Brindisi (8hr., 5600-11,500dr), and Venice (26hr., 15,800-19,600dr) in Italy, as well as Patras (9hr., 5800dr) and several other Greek towns and islands. The **National Tourist Office** (tel. (0661) 375 20), on the second floor of the building at Rizospaston Voulefton and Iak. Polila, dishes out info in several languages. Keep in mind that the office has moved since the publication of the map dispensed around town (open May-Sept. M-F 7:30am-2:30pm). **Tourist agencies** along Arseniou and Stratigou St. find single rooms from 4000dr, doubles from 5000dr, and triples from 6000dr. Walk west along the coast towards the Igoumenitsa port, bear left on Xenofonto Stratigou right after Hotel Atlantis, and then take your fourth left to find **Hotel Europa,** 10 Giantsilio (tel. (0661) 393 04; singles 4000-7000dr; doubles 7000dr; triples 9000dr). At the new port, **Hotel Ionina,** 46 Xen. Stratigou (tel. (0661) 399 15 or 306 28), offers singles (7000dr), doubles (10,000dr), and triples (12,000dr).

The premier restaurant areas are at the two ends of **N. Theotoki Street,** near the Spianada and by the old port. For a visual treat and inexpensive fresh produce, head to the open-air **market** on Dessila St. near the base of the New Fortress (open daily 6am-2pm). Try the delicious feta and tomato sandwiches (500dr) at the **Art Cafe** in a garden behind the palace of St. Michael and St. George. Below the palace on a small pier reside the **En Plo Cafe** and the **Faliraki Restaurant.**

KTEL **buses** leave frequently from Corfu Town's New Fortress for most of the island's major spots; other buses leave from Sanrocco Sq. A trip west takes you to **Paleokastritsa beach** and its white mountaintop monastery, **Panagia Theotokos.** The monastery houses a collection of Byzantine icons and a skeleton of a sea monster. Buses run to Paleokastritsa from behind the new fortress (45min., 420dr). South of Paleokastritsa is **Pelekas,** a base town with access to beaches. **Pelekas beach** is a 30-minute downhill walk from town. The **Glyfada Beach,** 5km up the coast from Pelekas Town, is served directly by bus from behind the New Fortress. The isolated beach of **Moni Myrtidon** and the unofficial nude beach **Myrtiotissa** are also nearby.

Agios Gordios, accessible by bus 7 (45min., 280dr), with its steep cliffs and impressive rock formations, is the setting for the **Pink Palace** (tel. (0661) 530 24; fax 530 25). The resort has legendary status among English-speaking hedonists for weekend toga parties, which groove all night as pink *ouzo* flows. Rooms vary significantly in quality (6000dr per person; breakfast, dinner, and nightclub included).

■ Cephalonia (Κεφαλλωνια)

Dubbed "The Island of Peculiarities" for its disparate but beautiful sandy beaches, subterranean caves, rugged mountains, and shady forests, Cephalonia is ideal for a week-long stay. **Argostoli,** the capital of Cephalonia and Ithaka, is a busy, noisy town whose palm tree-lined streets are regularly jammed with traffic. The surprisingly interesting **Historical and Folk Museum** shows pictures and relics of the city before it was destroyed by an earthquake in 1953 (open M-Sa 9am-2pm; 500dr). **Buses** (tel. (0671) 222 81) leave from the station at the south end of the waterfront. Argostoli has the most frequent bus service and thus is a convenient base from which to explore the rest of the island, but check schedules carefully or risk being stranded—service is reduced on Saturday and non-existent on Sunday. The **tourist office** (tel. (0671) 222 48 or 224 66), at the port, has maps and advice on lodgings, restaurants, and beaches.

(Open July to late Aug. M-F 7:30am-2:30pm and 4-10pm, Sa 9am-1pm and 5pm-9pm; late Aug. to June M-F 7:30am-2pm.) **Hotel Allegro** (tel. (0671) 286 84), up from the water on Andrea Choïda, has private baths (singles 5000dr; doubles 7000dr).

A small town on a harbor surrounded by steep, lush hills, **Sami** offers a white-pebble beach, proximity to **Melissani Lake** and **Drograti Cave,** and a break from the bustle of Argostoli. **Buses** run from Argostoli (500dr). From the port, **ferries** travel to Astakos (daily at 8:45am, 1948dr), Ithaka (1350dr), Patras (daily at 8:30am, 3095dr), as well as Bari and Brindisi in Italy. The friendly **Hotel Kastro** (tel. (0674) 230 01; fax 230 04), is on the waterfront near the ferry docks (singles 4000-8000dr; doubles 8000-1600dr).

■ Ithaka (Ithaki; Ιθακη)

The least touristed and quite possibly the most beautiful of the Ionian Islands, Ithaka is all too often passed over for the tourist havens of Lefkada and Cephalonia. Those who do not make this sad mistake have Ithaka's pebbled coves, rocky hillsides, and terraced olive groves quietly at their disposal. Ithaka's largest town and capital, **Vathi,** wraps around a circular bay skirted by precipitous, green hillsides. Those of a poetic bent and sturdy footwear may want to climb to the **Cave of the Nymphs,** where Odysseus hid the treasure the Phaeacians gave him; bring a flashlight (200dr). Back in Vathi, **ferries** go to Sami on Cephalonia (1hr., 950dr), and Astakos on the mainland (2½hr., 1850dr). **Delas Tours** (tel. (0674) 321 04; fax 330 31), in the main square, can help you find a room and decipher mercurial fares and schedules. The proprietors of private *domatias* may meet the ferry (6000-8000dr in summer), and **camping** is generally tolerated on the nearby beach.

The island's only **bus** runs north from Vathi, passing through the scenic villages of Lefki, Stavros, Platrithiai, Frikes, and Kioni. Schedules are erratic, but in high season the bus usually runs three times daily; check return times before you go (1hr., 350dr to Frikes). The road skirts both sides of the isthmus, and offers stunning views of the strait. On the way to Frikes and Kioni, in **Stavros,** high in the mountains, classicists will enjoy the alleged site of **Odysseus's Palace,** which overlooks three bays, just as Homer related. Close to Vathi is **Daxa beach,** Odysseus's mythical landing point and still a sunning spot.

CYCLADES (Κυκλαδες)

When people wax rhapsodic about the Greek islands, chances are they're talking about the Cyclades. Whatever your idea of Greece—whitewashed houses, *ouzo* sipped outside through warm sunsets, inebriated revelry—you can find it here. Most of the islands are practically international colonies during the summer, when countless hippies, backpackers, and businesspeople convene for the post-Eurailpass party.

■ Mykonos (Μυκονος)

Coveted by pirates in the 18th century for its blonde beaches, chic Mykonos is still lusted after by those seeking revelry and Bacchanalian excess amidst the charm of a rich history. Social life, both gay and straight, may abound, but it's not cheap on this choicest of Cyclades—you'll need a wallet thicker than your *Let's Go* to afford all the festivities. Mingle with the *kosmopolitikos,* and then savor the beaches and labyrinthine streets of Mykonos Town and the surrounding coastline.

During the day, the beaches are the island's main attraction. **Megali Ammos,** 1km past the windmills on the southwest corner of the harbor, the crowded **Psarou Beach,** and the fab (topless) **Ornos Beach** are all close to Mykonos Town. All beaches on Mykonos are technically nudist, but the degree of bareness is as varied as the specimens you'll inevitably see. Take a bus to **Plati Yialos** (220dr), not a bad beach in its own right, and a *caïque* from there to join the crowds at **Paradise** (300dr) and **Super**

Paradise (380dr), the most popular of the gay beaches. Excursion boats leave Mykonos Town for 4 round-trips per day to Apollo's birthplace, the island of **Delos** (25min., Tu-Su departing every 30-45 minutes 8:30am-11:30am, returning 11am-3pm, 1700dr round-trip). At night, *everyone* passes through the **Skandinavian Bar,** near the waterfront, where mellowness winds into madness around midnight (beer 800dr, cocktails 1600dr; open nightly 10:30pm-3am, Sa until 4am). At **Pierro's,** on Mato-gianni St., the mainly gay crowd spills out into the square with dancing and music (beers 1000dr, cocktails 2000dr). Step into a Toulouse-Lautrec and sip a glass of wine (800dr) at **Montparnasse,** 24 Agion Anargyron St., in the Little Venice district (open nightly 7pm-3am).

Ferries travel to Ios (4hr., 3200dr), Naxos (3hr., 1850dr), Paros (2hr., 1800dr), San-torini (6½hr., 3500dr), and many other islands. North Station, uphill from the ferry dock, sends **buses** to the northern and eastern beaches; at the opposite end of town, South Station serves the south (tel. for both (0289) 233 60). Everything you'll need is near the waterfront—banks, travel agencies, shops, cafes, and bars. If you still have questions, the **tourist police** (tel. (0289) 224 82), in an office at the ferry landing, have English speakers (open daily 8am-9pm).

Accommodations-hawking is a full-blown industry on Mykonos; if you're aggressive and undaunted, you may find a good deal. Otherwise, push past the solicitors at the ferry port and bear right 10m along the water; you can't miss the offices for **hotels** (tel. (0289) 245 40), **rooms-to-let** (tel. (0289) 248 60), and **camping** (tel. (0289) 235 67), which have plenty of info and will telephone proprietors on your behalf. **Chez Maria Pension,** 27 N. Kalogera St. (tel. (0289) 224 80), off Matogianni St., is above Chez Maria Restaurant (doubles 10,000-15,000dr; triples 12,000-18,000dr). The **campground** (tel. (0289) 221 29 or 228 52; fax 243 50) on Paradise Beach often feels crowded and has the occasional nude bather traipsing through (1700dr per person, 1000-1300dr per tent). On Mykonos, self-consciously trendy food is the rule, but sev-eral affordable options remain. **Klimataria,** on Florou Zouganeli St., has tasty *mous-saka* (1100dr) and rabbit stew (1700dr; open daily 9am-1am), while **Alexi** will put on a show as he cooks up your *gyro-pita* (350dr) at his eponymous restaurant at the back of Taxi Sq. (open daily 21hr.—closed 7am-10am for cleanup). **Niko's Taverna,** inland from the excursion boat docks, hops with traditional Greek cuisine (baked *kalamari* 2500dr; open daily noon-2am).

■ Paros (Πάρος)

The geographical center of the Cyclades and a convenient base for excursions to the other islands, Paros is a favorite for its golden beaches and tangled whitewashed vil-lages. The island has struck a careful balance between new world nightlife and old world serenity, and gracefully absorbs hordes of summer tourists. Behind the com-mercial facade of **Paroikia,** the island's main port, flower-filled streets wind past an *agora,* a basilica, and windmills. Byzantine architecture buffs will be enraptured by the **Panagia Ekatontapiliani** (Church of Our Lady of 100 Gates), an imposing 6th-century edifice that houses three adjacent churches, cloisters, and a large peaceful courtyard (open daily 8am-9pm; dress appropriately, no shorts). Ten kilometers south of town is the cool, spring-fed **Valley of the Butterflies,** home to an enormous swarm of the winged creatures (they mate in June). Take the bus from Paroikia to Aliki (10min., 200dr), ask to be let off at the butterflies *(petaloudes),* and follow the signs (open M-Sa 9am-8pm, Su 9am-1pm and 4-8pm; 230dr). You can also take a tour from one of the various travel agents (2500dr).

Ferries sail to many islands in the area, including Crete (8hr., 4800dr), Ios (2½hr., 2480dr), Mykonos (2hr., 1710dr), Naxos (1hr., 1370dr), Rhodes (16hr., 6820dr), and Santorini (3½hr., 3080dr). Since the Paros tourist office has closed, your best bet for info is probably one of the travel agencies littering the port area. Many hotels and pri-vate rooms are located near the waterfront and in the old town, but a slew of cheaper accommodations have opened up behind the town beach. Rooms may still be scarce in summer. To reach **Festos Pension** (tel. (0284) 216 35; fax 241 93) from the dock, walk left and diagonally back toward the church. Head for the far right corner of the main square (the church will be to your left) and look for the side street marked "the Festos" (2500-4500dr per person; call ahead). **Parasporos Camping** (tel. (0284) 222 68 or 211 00), 1.5km south of the port with shuttle service, has showers, laundry, and kitchen (1000dr per person, 500dr per tent). **Koula Camping** (tel. (0284) 220 81 or 220 82), 400m north of town on the beach, also has a market (1400dr per person, 1000dr per tent). **Apollo Garden Restaurant,** by Hotel Dina on Market St., has exquisite traditional Greek food. The psychedelic **Happy Green Cow,** behind the National Bank, has delicious vegetarian food (open daily 6pm-midnight).

■ Naxos (Ναξος)

After Ariadne, daughter of King Minos of Crete, saved Theseus from her father's labyrinth, the young prince expressed his gratitude by abandoning her on Naxos. Today, rocky promontories, squat windmills, and demure villages tucked between rolling hills dot this largest and most fertile island of the Cyclades. The streets of Old **Naxos Town** offer glimpses of the brilliant blue sea as they wind around stone archways and gardens. Be sure to stroll around the old **Venetian Castle,** a series of mansions still inhabited by the descendants of Frankish and Venetian nobility. Writer Nikos Kazantzakis once studied at the **Archaeological Museum,** which displays Cycladic artifacts, Mycenaean jewels, and Geometric chamber tombs (open Tu-Su 8am-2:30pm; 500dr, students 300dr, Su free). The **Portara,** a marble archway on the hilltop peninsula near the port, is one of the best star-watching and picnic spots in town.

Ferries travel to Ios (1½hr., 2100dr), Mykonos (2hr., 1880dr), Paros (1hr., 1400dr), Santorini (3hr., 2900dr), and many other islands; **buses** run to Chalki (30min., 320dr) and other towns on the island. Offices, stores, and agencies meet travelers' needs along the waterfront in Naxos Town. There is a privately run tourist office on the dock, but the *real* **tourist office** (tel. (0285) 243 58 or 252 01; fax 252 00) is 300m up by the bus depot. It offers bus and ferry schedules, currency exchange, luggage storage, and advice on accommodations (open daily 8am-midnight). People who meet ferries offer singles for 3000-4500dr and doubles for 4000-8000dr; it's virtually assured you can get a better deal if you haggle. For clean rooms with cooking facilities and bath, try **Irene Studios** (tel. (0285) 231 69; fax 252 00), 300m from Agio Georgios beach in newer Naxos (doubles 10,000dr, 5000dr in June). If you have a few extra *drachmes,* try the sparkling **Hotel Anixis** (tel. (0285) 221 12; fax 229 32; 12,000-13,000dr; breakfast 900dr), or the lovely **Hotel Chateau Zevgoli** (tel. (0285) 229 93); follow the light blue signs from the old town (doubles 15,000dr; triples 18,000dr). **Naxos Camping** (tel. (0285) 235 00), 1.5km along St. George's beach, has a swimming pool (1000dr per person, 500dr per tent; *Let's Go* discount).

Restaurants in the old town are more scenic and have traditional, tasty food; those near the waterfront are a bit more pricey. **Galini,** 500m down the inland road past Hotel Hermes, is an exceptional fish taverna; to try it all order the *peekeelia,* an assortment of bite-size morsels (open daily noon-2am). High up in the old city, **Koutouki** serves huge entrees with veggies, fries, and rice (*souvlaki* and stuffed peppers 1300dr each). Naxos's nightlife isn't as frenetic as some of the other islands; try **The Jam** or **The Rocks** behind the OTE.

Naxos's bewitching **interior** features rolling hills, staggering rock formations, tranquil villages, and herds of sheep and goats. The ideal way to appreciate the landscape is on foot; you can also traverse the terrain by bus or, with some difficulty, by moped. The main road across the island passes through the resplendent **Tragea,** a vast Arcadian olive grove. Stop in **Chalki's** parish church, **Panagia Protothonis,** where restoration work has uncovered wall paintings from the 11th through 13th centuries. If the church is closed, find a local priest to admit you. Drive from Naxos Town via Melanes to **Flerio,** where one of the *kouroi* (colossal statues of nude males dating from as early as the 7th century BC) sleeps in a woman's garden.

■ Ios (Ιος)

If you're not drunk by the time you get here, you will be by the time you leave. There is little to do in Ios but sleep late, sunbathe in the afternoon, and join the cavorting at night. It's your mother's worst nightmare—people swilling from wine bottles at 3pm; condoms scattered on dirt roads, people dancing naked in bars, and oh-so-much more. Ios's wild and famous bar scene centers on the old village area. **Sweet Irish Dream** is in a large building near the "donkey steps." Come here to dance on the tables after 2am (no cover before 2am; beers 500-600dr, cocktails 1000dr). Across the street, **The Slammer Bar,** just uphill from the main square in the village, serves tequila slammers to a full house (900dr), while **Kalimera,** lower down off the main strip, features jazz and reggae (beers 500-800dr; cocktails 1000-1200dr). **Dubliner** has a pub-like wooden section and a large outdoor terrace (beers 500dr, cocktails 1000dr). If you can still stand up straight, **Scorpion Disco,** outside of town on the way to the beach, is a dance emporium, and one of the craziest spots on the island (1000dr cover after 2am includes first drink).

Ferries travel to Mykonos (4-5hr., 3040dr), Naxos (80min., 2100dr), Paros (2½hr., 2400dr), Santorini (1¼hr., 1500dr), and many other islands. **Buses** shuttle every 10 to 20 minutes. between the port (Yialos), village (Hora), and Mylopotas beach (8am-2am, 220dr). The **Tourist Information Center** (tel. (0286) 911 35), right next to the bus stop, sells ferry and hydrofoil tickets, provides currency exchange, helps with accommodations, and offers free maps, luggage storage, and safety deposit boxes (open daily 7:30am-midnight). Also next to the bus stop is the **Medical Center** (tel. (0286) 912 27; open daily 10am-1pm and 6-7pm). Along the road heading to Kolitsani Beach are the English-speaking **police** (tel. (0286) 922 22; open 24hr.).

It helps to arrive on Ios sober, so you can bargain intelligently with the swarm of room hawkers that will meet you at the port. Depending on how the season is going, prices fluctuate between 2000 and 7000dr for singles and 2500 and 10,000dr for doubles. The owner of **Francesco's** (tel./fax (0286) 912 23), uphill from the National Bank, will do his best to see that you enjoy Ios (doubles 5000dr, with bath 8000dr; triples 6000-9000dr; reservations encouraged). To get to the friendly **Pension Markos** (tel. (0286) 910 59; fax 910 60) from the bus stop, take the right (uphill) just before the supermarket, and watch for a sign which directs you to a side street (doubles 8000dr; triples 10,000dr; reserve a few days in advance). You won't be roughing it at **Far Out Camping** (tel. (0286) 923 01 or 923 02; fax 923 03), at the far end of Mylopotas beach: the site has a restaurant, bar, swimming pool, and water slides (1400dr per person; tent rental 500dr; open Apr.-Sept.). If you arrive late, go to **Camping Ios** at the port (1700dr per person; open June-Sept.). For divine Greek cuisine look for **Lordos Byron,** uphill from the National Bank on the street below the main drag (Greek omelette 1200dr, *fava* dip 1000dr; open daily 7pm-midnight).

■ Santorini (Σαντορινη)

Santorini's landscape is as dramatic as the cataclysm that shaped it—a massive volcanic eruption that gave rise to the Atlantis legend and is believed by many to have destroyed the Minoan civilization on Crete. In Fira (Φηρα), the island's capital, the **Archaeological Museum** holds an impressive collection of vases, most from the site of ancient Thira (open Tu-Su 8am-2:30pm; 800dr, students 400dr). More fascinating are the excavations at **Akrotiri,** a late Minoan city preserved virtually intact under layers of volcanic rock (open daily 8:30am-2:30pm; 1200dr, students 600dr). Breeze through on your own or join a guided tour. Bus tours (4000-4500dr) are often coupled with a visit to the **Profitias Ilias Monastery** and a local wine-tasting. From Profitias Ilias, it's an hour's hike to **ancient Thira,** where the ancient theater, church, and forum of the island's old capital are visible (open Tu-Su 8am-3:30pm; free). The most frequented black sand beaches are **Perissa** and **Kamari,** both accessible by bus.

Ferries leave Santorini for Ios (1½hr., 1687dr), Mykonos (7hr., 3543dr), Paros (4hr., 3187dr), Peirais (9hr., 6081dr), Thessaloniki (10,090dr), and many other ports. Most ferries land at **Athinios** harbor—be clear with the hawkers at the port who sometimes misrepresent the rooms they peddle. Try for one of the small towns near Fira. **Thira Youth Hostel** (tel. (0286) 223 87 or 238 64), about 300m north of the square, offers clean mixed-gender and single-sex dorm rooms. Hot showers are available 24 hours, but bring toilet paper. (Dorms 1500dr; doubles 5000-8000dr. 24hr. reception. Quiet after 11pm enforced. Open Apr.-Oct.) Share bottles of wine with Petros at the **Pension Petros** (tel. (0286) 225 73; fax 226 15), one block east of the main square. (Follow the blue signs for Santorini Camping. Doubles and triples with bath 14,000-15,000dr, off-season 7000-8000dr. Free transportation from port.) In quieter Perissa, **Stelio's Place** (tel. (0286) 818 60; fax 817 07) offers 15 immaculate rooms 50m from the beach. Take the road out of town, turn left before the travel agencies, and follow the signs (2000-4000dr; reservations recommended; open May-Sept.). From Fira, follow blue "camping" signs to **Santorini Camping** (tel. (0286) 229 44; 1500dr per person, 800dr per tent; 24hr. reception; open Apr.-Oct.).

THE SPORADES (Σποραδες)

Lush islands of fragrant pines, luxurious beaches, and abundant fruit orchards, the Sporades offer travelers a smorgasbord of earthly delights. Tourism is on the rise, but there are spots on this archipelago that remain relatively quiet and inexpensive.

■ Skiathos (Σκιαθος)

Although less idyllic than the other Sporades, cosmopolitan Skiathos compensates by hosting the archipelago's largest social scene. Tourists pack the streets of **Skiathos Town,** but in the residential neighborhoods, balconies still burst with white gardenias over undisturbed terraces. A bus leaves the harbor in Skiathos Town (every 15-30min. 7:15am-1am, 280dr) and stops at beaches along its southern route, including **Megali Ammos, Nostros, Platanias,** and **Vromolimnos.** The bus route and the road end where more secluded beaches begin, such as Koukounaries, Banana Beach and the nude Little Banana Beach (not for everyone).

Ferries arrive from Agios Konstantinos, Alonissos, and Skopelos; if you're coming from Athens, take the bus from the station at 260 Liossion St. to Agios Konstantinos (2½hr., 2650dr), and then the ferry (3½hr., 3300dr). In town, the **tourist police** (tel. (0427) 231 72), on the right side of Papadiamantis St., have brochures with a map (open daily 8am-9pm). The police, across the street, can also help you arrange *domatia* rooms. Most tourists book accommodations ahead; if you are having trouble locating a room, contact **Rooms to Let** (tel. (0427) 229 90 or 242 60; fax 238 52) in the wooden kiosk by the port (open daily 8:30am-midnight). **Pension Anglea** (tel. (0427) 229 62), to the left at the end of Papadiamantis St., offers clean doubles with bath (7000-10,000dr). **Camping Koukounaries** (tel. (0427) 492 50) lies close to the beach on the bus route between stops 19 and 20, and has a restaurant and minimarket (1700dr per person, 1000dr per tent). The cheapest dining option is to hit the *gyros/souvlaki* stands (350dr) lining Papadiamantis and the waterfront, or forage in the numerous **supermarkets.** Bars cluster on Polytechniou St., Evangelistra St., and Papadiamantis Sq., and dance clubs line the far right side of the coast. The rowdy **Banana Bar,** on a small street parallel to Papadiamantis, sloshes out beer for only 600dr.

■ Skopelos (Σκοπελος)

Looming cliffs rise from the coastline of Skopelos, but inland acres of pine, olive, and plum trees blanket the hills and temper the mountains' starkness. Roads and **hiking** paths wind through the terrain and lead to monasteries and beaches. **Ferries** connect to Skiathos (1½hr., 1400dr) and other islands. Except for the inevitable front line of tourist offices and *tavernas*, **Skopelos Town** is a complex and delightful cobblestone maze stacked up against the hillside. The Thalpos **tourist agency** (tel. (0424) 229 47; fax 230 57), behind Restaurant Akteon, is on the second floor (open daily 9am-2pm and 6-8pm; extended hours July-Aug.). Wander around the narrow streets behind the waterfront to find lodging, or try asking friendly faces for *domatia*. **Pension Sotos,** (tel. (0424) 225 19; fax 236 68), 10m left of Thalpos travel, has a common kitchen and a book exchange. (Doubles 6500-10,000dr; triples 9000-15,000dr; quads 11,000-16,500dr; singles also available.) Platanos Sq. is home to the 350dr gyro, but **Greca's Crêperie** may well be the highlight of Skopelos (*crêpes* 600-1400dr).

■ Alonissos and Skyros (Αλοννησος και Σκυρος)

Alonissos Though it lacks polished beauty, **Alonissos** is one of the friendliest and least touristed islands in the Sporades. A **National Marine Park** protects its unruffled atmosphere. Boats dock at **Patitiri,** but a trip to the island is not complete without a visit to the rebuilt **Hora** (old town), set high on the hillside to ward off pirate attacks. The parching walk from Patitiri (1hr.) requires a liter of water per person, but affords glorious views. A 30-minute downhill walk from Patitiri leads to four sandy **beaches.** **Ferries** arrive from Athens via Agios Konstantinos (5½hr., 4300dr), Skiathos (2hr., 1800dr), and Skopelos (30min., 1100dr). In Patitiri, **Alonissas Travel** (tel./fax (0424) 655 11) helps you find rooms, change money, book excursions, and buy ferry tickets (open daily 9am-midnight). A **Rooms to Let** office helps with accommodations (tel./fax (0424) 655 77; open daily 9:30am-3pm and 6-10pm), though it may be cheaper to negotiate with locals and look for EOT signs on inland streets. Inquire at Boutique Mary, on the right side of Pelsagon, for rooms at **Dimakis Pension** (tel. (0424) 652 94; singles 5000-7000dr; doubles 6000-7500dr). Ten meters down the road towards the waterfront, **La Bricola** serves cheap sandwiches and salads (100-1200dr).

Skyros Rolling purple hills, sandy beaches, fragrant pine groves, and gnarled cliffs form the spectacular backdrop for daily life on **Skyros.** Tourism is beginning to encroach, but the island remains the quietest and most isolated of the Sporades. Perched above **Skyros Town,** the **Monastery of St. George** and the ruins of the Byzantine **Castle of Licomidus** afford spectacular views of the eastern coast. Down the steps and to the left of the statue of English poet Rupert Brooke, the fascinating **Faltaits Museum** has a superior folk art collection (open daily 10am-1pm and 6-9pm; free). There are no ferries to the rest of the Sporades, but expensive **Flying Dolphins** travel to Alonissos (1¼hr., 7250dr), Skiathos (2¼hr., 7150dr), and Skopelos (1¾hr., 6850dr). **Skyros Travel** (tel. (0222) 911 23 or 916 00), Agoras St., organizes boat and bus excursions, rents mopeds (3500dr), helps find rooms, and sells maps (500dr; open daily 9:15am-2:15pm and 6:30-10pm). Marble-floored **doubles** (tel. (0222) 914 59), below the National Bank of Greece, go for 6000 to 8000dr.

CRETE (Κρητη)

Greece's largest island embraces an infinite store of mosques and monasteries, mountain villages, gorges, grottoes, and beaches. Since 3000 BC, Crete has tended to maintain a distinct identity from the rest of Greece, first expressed in the language, script, and architecture of the ancient Minoans.

Most travelers arrive in Crete by **ferry.** From Iraklion, boats connect to Athens (12hr., 7000dr), Naxos (7hr., 5185dr), Paros (8½hr., 5185dr), Rhodes (12hr., 6442dr), Santorini (4hr., 5185dr), and other islands. Ferries also dock at Agios Nikolaos, Hania, and Rethymnon. If you prefer to fly, **Olympic Airways** sends planes from the island to Athens (45min., 22,000dr), Rhodes (30min., 18,500), and other destinations; **Air Greece** has less frequent but less expensive service to Crete.

■ Iraklion (Ηρακλιο)

As Crete's capital, **Iraklion** sports a chic native population, a nightlife more diverse than those of nearby beach resorts, and an ideal location as the base for a cultural tour of Crete. The phenomenal **Archaeological Museum,** off Eleftherias Sq., has appro-

Half-breeds, High Taxes, and Wax Wings

One of the most complex and resonant myths in all Greek mythology, that of **King Minos**, begins with a simple crime of ingratitude. When Minos withheld the sacrifice of a fine white bull which Poseidon had granted him for that exclusive purpose, Aphrodite was dispatched to exact a twisted retribution: an unconquerable lust in Minos' queen **Pasiphaë** for the bull itself. To woo the bull she hired master engineer **Daedalus** to build a sexy cow costume that might rouse the bull's affections. After a lusty roll in the hay, Pasiphaë bore—to King Minos' disgust and dismay—the **Minotaur**, a fearsome beast which had the head of a bull and a human body, and a taste for human flesh. The Minotaur was kept in the inescapable **labyrinth** designed by Daedalus, and to feed his queen's child Minos imposed an annual tax of seven maidens and seven youths upon mainland Greece. **Theseus**, an Athenian prince, volunteered for the sacrifice and, once within its labyrinth, slew the minotaur. With a ball of string given him by **Ariadne**, Minos' daughter (who had conspired with Daedalus to save her Athenian squeeze), Theseus retraced his path out of the labyrinth and escaped with Ariadne by ship. Although he had promised her marriage, he later left Ariadne on the beach of Naxos to be swept off by Dionysus. Meanwhile, Minos imprisoned Daedalus and his son **Icarus** as conspirators. Always resourceful, Daedalus constructed wings of wax for the two of them, with which they took flight into the ultimate jailbreak. With freedom in sight, Icarus, in a fit of hubris, flew straight at the sun, melting his wings and sending him plummeting to his death.

priated the major finds from all over the island and presents a comprehensive island history from the Neolithic period to Roman times. The highlight is the **Hall of the Minoan Frescoes**, which depicts ancient Minoan life. (Open M 12:30-8pm, Tu-Su 8am-8pm; off-season closes Tu-Su 5pm. 1500dr, students 800dr, EU students free.)

Inquire at **Travel Hall Travel Agency**, 13 Hatzimihali Yiannari St. (tel. (081) 28 21 12 or 34 18 62; fax 28 33 09), for **Olympic Airways** and **Air Greece** tickets (open daily 9am-9pm). There are several **bus terminals** in town. Terminal A, between the old city walls and the harbor near the waterfront, serves Ag. Nikolaos (1½hr., 1350dr) and Malia (1hr., 750dr); Terminal B serves Matala (2hr., 1500dr) and other towns. A third terminal sends buses to Hania (2800dr) and Rethymnon (1500dr); walk down 25th Augustou Ave. to the waterfront, turn right, and walk about 500m. Across from the Archaeological Museum, the **tourist office**, 1 Xanthoudidou St. (tel. (081) 22 82 03 or 24 44 62), has maps, hotel lists, and transportation schedules (open M-F 8am-2:30pm). The **tourist police**, 10 Dikeosinis St. (tel. (081) 28 31 90), provide info for those who arrive late (open daily 7am-11pm). With **Internet access,** cheap coffee, and late hours, **Polykentro,** on Androgeou St., is the best virtual time in town (open Su-Th 9am-1am, F-Sa 10am-2am). **Rent a Room Hellas** is at 24 Handakos St. (tel. (081) 28 88 51; dorms 1700dr; singles 4000dr; doubles 5500dr). The **youth hostel,** 5 Vyronos St. (tel. (081) 28 62 81; fax 22 29 47), has standard, quiet hostel rooms (1500dr per person; doubles 3000-4000dr). Techno, house, and Greek pop pulses at **Yacht, Limenico,** and **Bahalo.**

■ Near Iraklion: Knossos

Knossos is undoubtedly the most famous archaeological site in Crete—few visitors escape the island without at least a quick visit. Excavations here revealed remains of a Minoan city that thrived 3500 years ago. Sir Arthur Evans, who financed and supervised the excavations, eventually restored large parts of the **palace** in Knossos; his work often crossed the line from preservation to artistic interpretation, but the site is impressive nonetheless. (Open daily in summer 8am-8pm; off-season 8am-5pm. 1500dr, students 800dr; off-season Su free.) To reach Knossos from Iraklion, take bus 2 at 25th Augustou Ave. (every 20min., 230dr); look for the signposts on the street.

■ Western Crete

While the resort towns of Crete's eastern half seem to have sprung from the brains of British booking agents, the vacation spots of Western Crete have grown naturally around towns with rich histories and distinctive characters.

Rethymnon and Hania The Ottoman and Venetian influences that pervade northern Crete's towns are best appreciated at the scenic harbor of **Rethymnon** (Ρεθυμνο). Arabic inscriptions lace the walls of the town's narrow, arched streets, and minarets highlight the old city's skyline. Keeping watch over the harbor's west end, the walls of the 16th-century **Venetian Fortezza** are in excellent condition (open Tu-Su 8am-7pm; 700dr), and now protect a lively **Renaissance Festival** (July and Aug.). The **Wine Festival** (in July or Aug.) is a crowded all-you-can-drink fest. (first night admission 1000dr; required souvenir glass 150dr). The **tourist office** (tel. (0831) 291 48), on the waterfront, supplies maps and bus and ferry schedules (open M-F 8am-4:30pm, Sa 9:30am-3pm). The cheerful **youth hostel,** 41-45 Tombazi St. (tel. (0831) 228 48), at the center of the old town, teems with international youngsters in the summer (1500dr; reception in summer 8am-noon and 5-9pm; off-season until 9:30pm). **Olga's Pension** (tel. (0831) 298 51) is at 57 Souliou St., off Antistaseos (singles 4500-5000dr; doubles 6000-7000dr; triples 10,000dr). Pitch tents at **Elizabeth Camping** (tel. (0831) 286 94), 3km east of town. The staff lends kitchen and camping supplies (1300dr per person, 1000dr per tent; open mid-Apr. to Oct.).

Narrow, four-story Venetian buildings and Ottoman domes mingle in the lively harbor town of **Hania** (Χανια). The **tourist office,** on the first floor of the Megaro Pantheon, 1866 Sq. (tel./fax (0821) 926 24), behind the Greek Agricultural Bank, has info on ferries, buses, and hotels in town (open M-F 7:30am-2:30pm). To get to **Hotel Fidias,** 6 Sarpaki St. (tel. (0821) 524 94), from Halidon St., turn right at the cathedral on Athinagora St., which becomes Sarapaki St. (Dorms 1500-2000dr; singles 2000-4000dr; doubles 3000-4500dr; triples 4500-6000dr.) For a truly Cretan experience, replete with mustachioed old men dancing to traditional music, head east to **Cafe Kriti,** 22 Kalergon St. (beer 500dr; open daily 6pm-3am; not recommended for women traveling alone).

Samaria Gorge The most popular excursion from Hania, Rethymnon, or Iraklion is the five- to six-hour hike down the 16km **Samaria Gorge,** a spectacular ravine that cuts through heavy forests and sheer granite cliffs. Be sure to bring lots of water and good hiking boots (open May-Oct. 15 daily 6am-4pm; 1200dr). For gorge info call **Hania Forest Service** (tel. (0821) 922 87). Buses run from Hania to **Xyloskalo** (1½hr.) at the start of the trail. The trail ends in **Agia Roumeli** on the south coast; from here, take a boat to Hora Sfakion and then a bus back to Hania.

▓ Eastern Crete

The endlessly winding main highway joining Malia and Hersonissos to Agios Nikolaos, Ierapetra, and Sitia is spectacular—it grips the side of the mountains, ascending and descending deep valleys. Destinations along this highway are equally impressive. The white villages along the coast are colored by small green gardens, olive plains, and an astonishingly blue sea.

Malia and Hersonissos Malia (Μαλια) has been increasingly encroached upon by self-aggrandizing hotels, neon signs, and billboard advertisements. Nonetheless, the palatial Minoan site at Malia merits a visit. The **Minoan Palace** lacks the labyrinthine architecture and magnificent interior decoration of Knossos, but it's still imposing. To reach this area, follow the road to Agios Nikolaos 3km to the east and turn left toward the sea, or walk along the beach and then 1km through the fields (open daily 8am-2:30pm; 800dr, students free). **Pension Aspasia** (tel. (0897) 312 90), and **Pension Menios** (tel. (0897) 313 61), both on 25th Martiou St., have clean doubles (6000-7000dr). Nightlife is the only draw of **Hersonissos** (Χερσονησος); the town is free of ancient ruins, monasteries, and decent beaches. As night progresses, visitors head to Main St., the Paraliakos, and the waterfront. The hottest club in town is the **Camelot Dancing Club,** featuring international rave and house (open daily 10pm-5:30am).

Agios Nikolaos An intense nightlife, diverse selection of glamorous shops, and remnants of an indigenous Cretan culture make Agios Nikolaos (Αγιος Νικολαος) an appealing mix of humility and pretension. The **tourist office** (tel. (0841) 223 57 or 241 65; fax 825 34), at the bridge between the lake and the port, changes money, finds rooms, has a free brochure with a map, and provides boat and bus schedules (open Apr.-Oct. daily 8:30am-9:45pm). From the tourist office, walk up 25th Martiou St. and go left onto Manousogianaki. After four uphill blocks, go right onto Solonos to find **Argiro Pension,** 1 Solonos St. (tel. (0841) 287 07), with its jasmine-scented garden (doubles 4800-5500dr; triples 7000dr). Off the main square, **Itanos** serves large portions of fresh Greek salads (700dr) and homemade barreled wine (1500dr per L). For **nocturnal pursuits,** stroll around the harbor on I. Koundourou St. or go up 25th Martiou St. From the left side of the harbor, near the tourist office, Nostos Travel cruisers (3000dr) and smaller fishing boats (1000dr) make daytrips to the small but striking **Spinalonga,** formerly a leper colony.

NORTHEAST AEGEAN ISLANDS

The intricate, rocky coastlines of the Northeast Aegean Islands enclose thickly wooded mountains and isolated valleys. Proximity to Turkey explains the presence of guns, camouflage, and large numbers of young soldiers.

■ Samos (Σαμος)

With its sultry landscape and engrossing archaeological remains, quiet Samos is perhaps the most beautiful and certainly the most touristed island in the Northeast Aegean. The waterfront of **Samos Town** (Vathi) is a snarl of tourist shops and cafes, but the town itself has wide sidewalks, garden-laced residential lanes, and picturesque red-roofed houses nestled against the mountainside. **Olympic Airways** (tel. (0273) 272 37) flies to Athens (1hr., 14,000dr) from Samos's airport (2500dr by taxi from Samos Town). **Ferries** travel to Chios (5½hr., 2940dr), Lesvos (8hr., 4090dr), Naxos and Paros (6hr., 4370dr), and other islands. Ferries also go daily to **Kuşadası,** Turkey. (2hr., 8am and 5pm, 8000dr. Greek port tax 5000dr. Turkish port tax 3000dr. Turkish entrance visas must be purchased at the Turkish port by Irish (IR£15), U.K. (UK£10), and U.S. (US$45) citizens.) The **tourist office** (tel. (0273) 285 30 or 285 82), is on a side street one block before Pythagoras Sq. (open July-Aug. M-Sa 8:30am-2pm). To get to **Pension Ionia,** 5 Manoli Kalomiri St. (tel. (0273) 287 82), turn right at the end of the ferry dock, take a left onto E. Stamatiadou St. before the Hotel Aiolis on the waterfront, and then take the second left (singles 4000-5000dr; doubles 5000 to 7000dr). Just up the road, **Pension Trova,** 26 Kalomiris St. (tel. (0237) 277 59), has singles (4000dr) and doubles with baths (5500-7000dr).

Buses from Samos Town and boats from Patmos and points south arrive at **Pythagorion,** the former capital of Samos. Near the town, you can see the magnificent remains of Polykrates's 6th-century BC engineering projects: the **Tunnel of Eupalinos,** which diverted water from a natural spring to the city, a 40m deep **harbor mole,** and the **Temple of Hera** (temple open Tu-Su 8:30am-3pm; 800dr, students 400dr).

■ Lesvos and Chios (Λεσβος και Χιος)

Lesvos Once home of the sensual poet Sappho, Lesvos is still something of a mecca for lesbians. The island mixes horse breeding, serious *ouzo* drinking, and leftist politics. Most travelers pass through crumbling but picturesque **Mytilini,** the capital and central port city. Ubiquitous signs point tourists to various sights. The enormous **Church of St. Therapon** presides benignly over the fish market, while the **Archaeological Museum,** 7 Argiri Eftalioti St., houses an impressive collection of the island's archaeological finds (open Tu-Su 8:30am-3pm; 500dr, students 300dr, EU students free, Su free). **NEL Lines,** 67 Pavlou Koudoutrioti St. (tel. (0251) 222 20), runs ferries to Chios (3hr., 3250dr), Peiraias (12hr., 7030dr), Thessaloniki (12hr., 8300dr), Çesme, Turkey, and elsewhere. The **tourist office,** 6 James Aristarchou (tel. (0251) 425 11; fax 425 12), has info, free brochures, and maps (open M-F 8:30am-3pm). The **Rooms to Let** office, one block inland from the center of the waterfront, can secure singles for 5000-6000dr and doubles for 7000-8000dr (open M-Su 9am-10pm). The towns of **Petras** and **Molyvos** are also frequently touristed. The red-tiled stone houses of Molyvos cluster at the base of the castle-peaked hill, conveying picture-perfect charm, while Petra stretches along a fine sand beach and presses into the fertile plain behind. Just up from the Moylvos bus stop, the **tourist office** (tel. (0253) 713 47) will help you find a room. In Petra, contact the **Women's Cooperative,** on the same street as the National Bank, to find rooms.

Chios When the mythical hunter Orion drove the wild beasts off **Chios** (Χιος), grand pine and cypress trees sprouted on the vast mountainsides. Chios has only recently been opened to tourism, but as its striking volcanic beaches and medieval villages become more accessible, the island is slowly becoming a vacation hotspot. **Ferries** travel to Samos (4½hr., 2800dr), other islands, and the Turkish coast. In **Chios Town,** the tourist office, 11 Kanari St. (tel. (0271) 443 44), will answer questions and provide brochures and an accommodations list.

THE DODECANESE ISLANDS

An endless succession of conquerors and explorers, from the Turks and Knights of St. John in the Middle Ages to the Italians and Germans of this century, has left an indelible imprint on the Dodecanese Islands. The landscape is dotted with classical ruins, Italian buildings, and restored medieval homes. Rhodes in particular endures frenzied tourism from both the Greek and Turkish coasts.

■ Rhodes (Ροδος)

While the resort towns of Rhodes suffer from the maladies brought on by crowds and commercialism, the interior regions and the smaller coastal towns retain a sense of serenity and dignity. Beaches stretch along the east coast, jagged cliffs skirt the west, and green mountains dotted with villages fill the interior. At the northern tip of the island, the **City of Rhodes** welcomes visitors with tourist amenities as well as medieval turrets and archways, decaying mosques and minarets, and soothing palm trees. Encapsulated within the fortress walls, the **Old Town** features an incredible array of medieval castles and fortresses left by the Knights of St. John. The best place to begin exploring this quarter is at **Symi Square,** inside **Eleftherias Gate** at the base of the Mandraki. Nearby, in **Argykastrou Square,** the beautiful halls and courtyards of the former **Hospital of the Knights** now house the **Archaeological Museum,** where most of the island's archaeological treasures are located (open Tu-Su 8:30am-3pm; 800dr, students 400dr, EU students free). At the top of the hill, an archway leads to Kleovoulou Sq.; to the right sits the pride of the city, the **Palace of the Grand Masters,** a complex of 300 rooms, moats, drawbridges, watch towers, and colossal battlements (open Tu-F 8am-7pm, Sa-Su 8:30am-3pm; 1200dr, students 600dr).

Rhodes is the most accessible island in the Dodecanese. **Planes** soar to Athens (21,500dr), Karpathos (9400dr), Kos (11,000dr), and other cities. The airport (tel. (0241) 917 71) is on the west coast, 17km from town near the city of Paradisi; public buses run hourly (daily 7am-midnight, 300dr). Regular **ferries** connect to Crete (6221dr), Kos (3900dr), Patmos (5366dr), and virtually every other major island and coastal city in the area. A weekly **international ferry** passes through Rhodes on the way to Limassol, Cyprus (17hr., 20,500dr), and Haifa, Israel (36hr., 33,500dr). **Hydrofoils** travel to other Dodecanese islands, the Northeast Aegean islands, and Turkey; schedules vary from day to day and should be checked at travel agencies. The **City of Rhodes tourist office** (tel. (0241) 359 45), in Rimini Sq., helps with accommodations and changes money (open M-Sa 8am-9pm, Su 8am-3pm). The **Greek tourist office (EOT)** (tel. (0241) 232 55 or 236 55) is a few blocks up Papagou St. (open M-F 7:30am-3pm). In the Old Town, stay at **Hotel Andreas,** 28D Omirou St. (tel. (0241) 341 56; fax 742 85; doubles 6000-8000dr; triples 10,000dr; quads 12,000dr), or the spotless **Pension Olympos,** 56 Ag. Fanouriou St. (tel./fax (0241) 335 67; doubles 8000dr; triples 10,000dr). In a quiet area of the New Town, **Hotel Capitol,** 65-67 Dilberaki St. (tel. (0241) 620 16), has private showers in all rooms (singles 7000dr; doubles 8000dr; triples 12,000dr; breakfast included).

Excursion boats follow the coast south from Rhodes to Lindos, making several stops along the way. Schedules and prices are posted at the dock along the lower end of the Mandraki; most cost roughly 3500dr round-trip. **Buses** also connect to smaller towns on the island. Ten kilometers south of Rhodes at **Kalithea,** an exceptional beach lies next to a deserted spa for European aristocrats. Another 5km south, **Faliraki** is a popular resort with a sandy beach and rocking nightlife. About halfway down the eastern coast, **Lindos** is perhaps the most picturesque town on Rhodes. Beautiful whitewashed houses cluster beneath a soaring castle-capped acropolis, but the town's charms are no secret; in summer the population and prices skyrocket. If you make it to the island's southwestern tip, you can see the impressive ruins of the **Castle of Monolithos,** which crumble at the summit of a 160m rock pillar.

■ Kos (Κως)

In summer, visitors to Kos throng to the classical and Hellenic ruins, fill the beaches, and frisk about booming bars and nightclubs. In **Kos Town,** minarets from Turkish mosques stand alongside grand Italian mansions and the massive walls of a Crusader's fortress. **Ferries** travel to Patmos (4hr., 2768dr), Rhodes (4hr., 3460dr), and the usual set of islands in the area. The **tourist office** (tel. (0242) 287 24), at the meeting point of Akri Miaouli, Hippokratous St., and Vas. Georgiou, has info on accommodations and ferry schedules (open M-F 7:30am-9pm, Sa 7:30am-3pm). The room hawkers in Kos are notorious; it's best to seek out your own room unless you arrive very late. **Pension Alexis,** 9 Herodotou St. (tel. (0242) 287 98), the first right off Meg. Alexandrou, has incomparable hospitality and a jasmine-vined patio (doubles 5500-7000dr; triples 7500dr; breakfast 800dr). **Hotel Afendoulis,** 1 Evripolou St. (tel./fax (0242) 253 21), has well-kept rooms in a quiet part of town near the beach; go down Vas. Georgiou and look for Evripolou (doubles with private bath 7500-9000dr). **Rooms to Let Nitsa,** 47 Averof St. (tel. (0242) 258 10), near the beach north of town, has super-clean rooms with baths and kitchenettes (doubles 7000dr; triples 9000dr). The nightlife in Kos can be heard pounding all over the Dodecanese. The **Exarhia** area is packed with bars. The other party zone is on **Porfiriou Street** in the north, near the beach. The most popular island discos, **Kahlua** and **Heaven,** both on the beach, reside here. Beers (500dr) at **Pub Cuckoo's Nest** are accompanied by free shots.

The **Asclepion,** an ancient sanctuary dedicated to the god of healing, lies 4km west of Kos Town (open June-Sept. Tu-Su 8:30am-7pm; 800dr, students 400dr). In the 5th century BC, Hippocrates opened the world's first medical school here. The most interesting remains are in the three central terraced planes, called *andirons.* These contain the **School of Medicine,** statues of deities, and a figure of Pan. Climb the 30 steps to the second *andiron* to see the best preserved remains of the Asclepion—the elegant white columns of the **Temple of Apollo** and the **Minor Temple of Asclepios.** The climb to the third *andiron* leads to the **Main Temple of Asclepios** and affords a view of the whole site, Kos Town, and the Turkish coast. Sixteen **buses** a day make the short jaunt to the Asclepion during the summer.

Patmos The holy island of **Patmos** (Πατμος) balances its weighty religious past (St. John supposedly wrote the Book of Revelation here) with excellent beaches and traces of an artistic community. The sprawling Monastery of St. John the Theologian, just above the charming and labyrinthine hilltop village of **Hora,** presides over the island. **Ferries** depart from the port town of **Skala** for Kos (4hr., 2720dr), Rhodes (10hr., 5600dr), and nearby islands. If you prefer not to haggle for a room at the dock, contact **Captain's House Hotel** (tel. (0247) 317 93) or **Maria Paschalidis** (tel. (0247) 321 52). Both have clean doubles for 6000 to 7000dr. To get to **Flower Stefanos Camping at Melloi** (tel. (0247) 318 21), follow the waterfront road all the way to the right, facing inland, and look for the signs (1500dr per person, 750dr per tent).

Karpathos The friendly island of **Karpathos** (Καρπαθος) boasts a charming port town and some of the most beautiful, non-touristed beaches in Greece. **Pigadia** (Karpathos Town) is the island's administrative and transportation center; from here, **Olympic Airways** (tel. (0245) 221 50) flies to Athens (22,600dr) and elsewhere, and **ferries** run to Paros (17hr., 5025dr), Rhodes (5hr., 4175dr), and Santorini (12hr., 4860dr). **Mertonas Studios** (tel. (0245) 226 22 or 230 79), two blocks uphill and left from the bus station, rents gorgeous, furnished studios (doubles 5000-7000dr).

Hungary (Magyarország)

US$1	= 225 forints (Ft, or HUF)	100Ft =	US$0.45
CDN$1	= 145Ft	100Ft =	CDN$0.69
UK£1	= 369Ft	100Ft =	UK£0.27
IR£1	= 314Ft	100Ft =	IR£0.32
AUS$1	= 130Ft	100Ft =	AUS$0.77
NZ$1	= 111Ft	100Ft =	NZ$0.90
SAR1	= 35.80Ft	100Ft =	SAR2.79
DM1	= 125Ft	100Ft =	DM0.80
Country Phone Code: 36		**International Dialing Prefix: 00**	

Forty-five years of isolation and relative powerlessness under Soviet rule are a mere blip in Hungary's 1100-year history, and traces of socialism are evaporating with each passing iron-free day. Three hundred years as a somewhat reluctant partner in the Habsburg domination of Europe has left Hungary, especially Budapest, with a large-scale, almost monumental architecture. Budapest still dominates the country, though by no means has a monopoly on cultural attractions; the countryside around it offers fine wines and well-preserved Baroque. Through it all course the incomprehensible strains of the Magyar tongue, a distant relation of Finnish and Estonian, whose strangeness in a strange linguistic land has largely determined the course of Hungarian literature and culture; one non-linguistic medium has produced world-renowned contributors heavily influenced by folk and particularly Gypsy music, including Franz Liszt and Béla Bartók. One of this century's towering Marxist theoreticians, Georg Lukács, also hails from Hungary. Well-kept though not without its traces of socialist gray, Hungary is probably the most modernized, though still highly affordable, of the Central European countries—for whatever that's worth.

For everything Hungarian, ask to dance with *Let's Go: Eastern Europe 1999*.

GETTING THERE AND GETTING AROUND

With a valid passport, citizens of the U.S., Canada, and Ireland can travel to Hungary **visa-free** for 90 days; citizens of the U.K. for six months; and citizens of South Africa for 30 days. Australians and New Zealanders must obtain 90-day tourist visas from their Hungarian embassy or consulate (see **Government Information Offices,** p. 3); no border-control posts issue visas. For U.S. residents with a green card, visas cost US$40 (single-entry), US$75 (double-entry), US$180 (multiple-entry), or US$38 (48hr. transit visa). Nonresidents pay US$65, US$100, US$200, and US$50, respectively. Obtaining a visa takes one day and requires proof of means of transportation (such as a plane ticket), a valid passport, three photographs (5 for double-entry), payment by cash or money order, and a self-addressed, stamped (certified mail) envelope. Visa extensions are rare, but can be applied for at police stations in Hungary.

Budapest's **Ferihegy airport** handles all international traffic, including **Malév,** the national airline. Hungarian **trains** *(vonat),* many of which pass through the capital, are reliable and inexpensive; Eurail and EastRail are valid. *Személyvonat* are excruciatingly slow; *gyorsvonat* trains (listed on schedules in red) cost the same and move at least twice as fast. Air-conditioned InterCity trains are the fastest. Large provincial towns are accessible by the blue *expressz* rail lines. Seat reservations are required on trains marked with an "R" on schedules. Travelers under 26 are eligible for a 33% discount on some domestic train fares, and an ISIC earns 30% discounts on international tickets from IBUSZ, Express, and station ticket counters. Flash your card and state "DEE-ahk" *(diák,* student)—sometimes you need to be persistent. Other important words to know include *érkezés* (arrival), *indulás* (departure), *vágány* (track), and *állomás* or *pályaudvar* (station, abbreviated *pu*).

The extensive **bus** system is cheap but crowded; it links many towns whose only rail connection is to Budapest. Buy inter-city bus tickets on board (get there early if you want a seat); purchase **public transportation** tickets in advance from a newsstand and punch them on board. There is a fine if you're caught ticketless. The Danube **hydrofoil** goes to Vienna via Bratislava (12,700Ft); Eurailpass holders get 50% off. Either IBUSZ or Tourinform can provide a brochure about **cycling** in Hungary that includes all the details you'll need to plan an excursion. Write the **Hungarian Tourist Board,** 1065 Budapest, Bajcsy-Zsilinszky út 31, or the **Hungarian Cycling Federation,** 1146 Budapest, Szabó J. u. 3, for more info.

ESSENTIALS

IBUSZ offices throughout the country will find rooms, change money, sell train tickets, and charter tours. Snare the pamphlet *Tourist Information: Hungary* and the monthly entertainment guides *Programme in Hungary* and *Budapest Panorama* (all free and in English). **Express,** the former national student travel bureau, handles youth hostels and changes money. Regional travel agencies are helpful in outlying areas; knowledgeable **Tourinform** has branches in every county.

Change money only as you need it, and keep some dollars in cash on hand. **American Express** offices in Budapest and IBUSZ, OTP banks, and Postabank offices cash traveler's checks. Cash advances on credit cards are available at most major OTP branches, but as the number of ATMs increases, this service is becoming less common. Major credit cards are accepted at more expensive hotels and at many shops and restaurants. New Zealand dollars cannot be exchanged here, so pack another currency. At the few exchange offices with extended hours, the rates are generally poor. Hungary swarms with **ATMs,** which have great rates.

Business hours in Hungary are expanding gradually; right now, shops are typically open Monday through Friday 9am to 5pm (7am-7pm for food stores). Banks close around 3pm on Friday. Tourist bureaus are usually open Monday through Saturday 8am to 8pm in summer (some are open until noon on Su); off-season these hours shrink to Monday through Friday 10am to 4pm. Museums are usually open Tuesday through Sunday 10am to 6pm, with occasional free days on Tuesday. With an ISIC you can often get in free or pay 50%. Nothing is open on Christian and national **holidays,** including May 1, August 20, and October 23.

Over 600 street names in Budapest alone have changed since the 1989 revolution, but maps in tourist offices are generally up to date. Hungarian addresses usually involve one of the following: *utca,* abbreviated *u.* (street); *út,* or *útja* (avenue); *tér,* or *tere* (square, but may be a park, plaza, or boulevard); *híd* (bridge); and *körút,* abbreviated *krt.* (ring-boulevard). Some streets are odd-numbered on one side and even on the other, while others are numbered up one side and down the other.

COMMUNICATION

Hungarian belongs to the Finno-Ugric family of languages. English is the country's very distant third language after Hungarian and German—much of Hungary is accustomed to German-speaking tourists. A few starters for pronunciation: *c* is pronounced "ts" as in ca*ts*; *cs* is "ch" as in *ch*urch; *gy* is "dy" as in fri*dg*e; *ly* is "y" as in *y*am, *s* is "sh" as in *sh*ovel; *sz* is "s" as in "*S*amantha"; *zs* is "jh" as in plea*s*ure, and *a* is "a" as in *a*lways. The first syllable always gets the emphasis.

Yes/No	*Igen/Nem*	EE-gen/nem
Hello/Goodbye	*Jó napot/Szia*	YOH naw-pot/SEE-ya
Please	*Kérem*	KAY-rem
Thank you	*Köszönöm*	KUR-sur-num
Excuse me	*Sajnálom*	shoy-na-lawm
Do you speak English/German?	*Beszél angolul/németül?*	BES–el AWN-gohlul/NAY-met-yuhl
I don't understand.	*Nem értem*	NEM AYR-tem
Where is…?	*Hol van…?*	hawl von
How much does this cost?	*Mennyibe kerül?*	menyeebeh keh rewl
Do you have a vacancy?	*Van szabad szobájuk?*	von sub-od soh-bah-yook
Bill, please.	*Kérem a számlát*	KAY-rem o SAAM-laat
Men/Women	*Férfi/Nói*	FAIR-fee/NOY-ee
Help!	*Segítség!*	SHEH-gheet-shayg

Almost all phone numbers in the countryside have six digits. For inter-city calls, wait for the tone and dial slowly; a "06" goes before the city code. **International calls** require red phones or new, digital-display blue ones, found at large post offices, on the street, and in metro stations. Though the blue phones are more handsome than their red brethren, they tend to cut you off after three to nine minutes. Pay phones devour coins so fast you may need a companion to feed them. The public phones throughout the country increasingly require **phone cards,** available at kiosks, train stations, and post offices in units of 800 or 1600Ft. Direct calls can also be made from Budapest's phone office. To call collect, dial 190 for the international operator. To make a direct call, put in a 10 and a 20Ft coin (which you'll get back), dial 00, wait for the second dial tone, then for **AT&T Direct** dial 80 00 11 11; **MCI WorldPhone,** 80 00 14 11; **Sprint Access,** 80 00 18 77; **Canada Direct,** 80 00 12 11; **BT Direct,** 80 00 44 11; **Mercury Call UK,** 80 00 44 12; **Ireland Direct,** 80 00 35 31; **Australia Direct,** 80 00 61 11; **New Zealand Direct,** 80 00 64 11. For **ambulance,** call 104; **police,** call 107; and **fire,** call 105.

The **mail** service is perfectly reliable; airmail *(légiposta)* to the U.S. takes five to 10 days. Hungarians put the family name first; hence *Poste Restante* or a phone directory would list "Gabor Zsa Zsa." When using hand signals for numbers, remember to start with the thumb for "1"—holding up your index finger means "wait."

ACCOMMODATIONS AND CAMPING

Most travelers stay in **private homes** (look for *"Zimmer Frei"* or *"Kiadó Szoba"* signs) booked in person or through a tourist agency. Singles are scarce; it's worth finding a roommate, because solo travelers often must pay for a double room. Agencies may initially try to foist off their more costly quarters. Outside Budapest, the best and cheapest office is usually the regional one (such as Eger-Tourist in Eger). These agencies will often call ahead to make reservations at your next stop. Making arrangements with the owner yourself avoids the tourist agencies' 20 to 30% commission.

Some towns have cheap **hotels,** but most are disappearing. As the hotel system develops and room prices rise, **hostels** become more attractive, although year-round hostels are rare outside of Budapest. Many can be booked at Express or sometimes the regional tourist office after you arrive. From late June through August, **university dorms** change into hostels. Locations change annually; book with an Express office. The staff at Express can generally speak German, sometimes English. Over 300 **campgrounds** are sprinkled throughout Hungary. If you rent bungalows, you must pay for unfilled spaces. Most sites are open May to September. Tourist offices offer the annual *Camping Hungary.* For more info, contact **Tourinform** in Budapest.

FOOD AND DRINK

Paprika, Hungary's chief agricultural export, colors most dishes red. In Hungarian restaurants, called *étterem,* you may begin with *gulyásleves,* a delicious and hearty beef soup seasoned with paprika. *Borjúpaprikás* is a veal dish with paprika, often accompanied by small potato-dumpling pasta. Vegetarians can find the tasty *rántott sajt* (fried cheese) and *gombapörkölt* (mushroom stew) on most menus. *Túrós rétes* is a chewy pastry pocket filled with sweetened cottage cheese.

Finding a genuine, "local" eatery is hard. Gypsy music often spells tourist trap. Rounding the bill up as a tip is standard for a job well done. Tip as you pay—leaving it on the table is rude. A *csárda* is a traditional inn, a *bisztró* an inexpensive restaurant, and an *önkiszolgáló étterem* a cheap cafeteria. Since few menus outside Budapest are written in English, a dictionary can spare you from point-and-pray meals. *Salátabárs* vend deli concoctions. Fresh fruit and vegetables abound on stands and in produce markets. For pastry and coffee, look for a *cukrászda,* where you can fulfill relentless sweet-tooth desires for dangerously few forints. Hungarians are justly proud of their wines; most famous are the red *Egri Bikavér* ("Bull's Blood of Eger") and the sweet white *Tokaji.* Fruit schnapps *(pálinka)* are a national specialty. Local beers are good; the most common is *Dreher. Kávé* means espresso.

▓ Budapest

At once a cosmopolitan European capital and the stronghold of Magyar nationalism, Budapest awakened from its Communist cocoon with the same pride that rebuilt the city from the rubble of World War II and endured the Soviet invasion of 1956. Endowed with an architectural majesty befitting the Hapsburg Empire's number one city, Budapest is graceful and multifaceted. Today, the city maintains its charm and vibrant spirit alongside a thoroughly liveable, and lived-in, atmosphere: no toy-land Prague, this, but a city with an ancient culture that yields only partially to superficial inspection—though neon lights and hordes of tourists have added a new twist to the Budapest rhapsody, it remains one of Eastern Europe's most sophisticated tunes.

ORIENTATION AND PRACTICAL INFORMATION

Previously two cities, Buda and Pest (PESHT), separated by the **Duna** (Danube), modern Budapest straddles the river in north-central Hungary 250km downstream from Vienna. On the west bank, **Buda** inspires countless artists with its hilltop citadel, trees, and cobblestone **Castle District,** while on the east side **Pest** pulses as the heart of the modern city. Three bridges bind the two halves together: **Széchenyi lánchíd,** slender, white **Erzsébet híd,** and green **Szabadság híd.**

Moszkva tér (Moscow Square), just down the north slope of the Castle District, is where virtually all trams and buses start or end their routes. One metro stop away in the direction of Örs vezér tere, **Batthyány tér** lies opposite the Parliament building on the west bank; this is the starting node of the **HÉV commuter railway.** Budapest's three metro lines converge at **Deák tér,** at the core of Pest's loosely concentric ring boulevards, next to the main international bus terminal at **Erzsébet tér.**

Many street names occur more than once in town; always check the district as well as the type of street. Moreover, streets arbitrarily change names from one block to the

HUNGARY

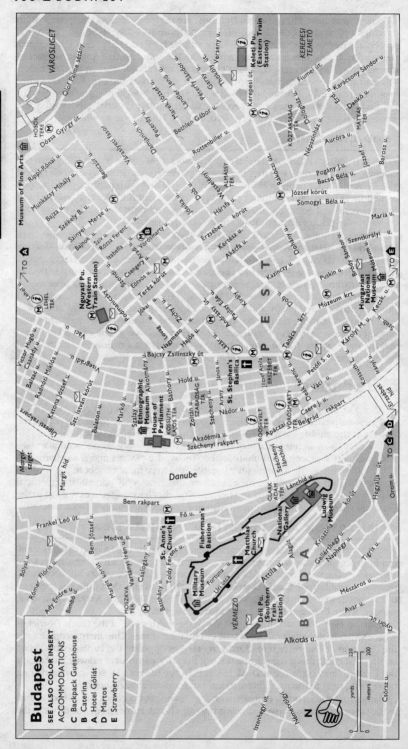

Budapest
SEE ALSO COLOR INSERT
ACCOMMODATIONS
C Backpack Guesthouse
B Caterina
A Hotel Góliát
D Marós
E Strawberry

next. Because many have shed their Communist labels, an up-to-date **map** is essential. To check if your map of Budapest is useful, look at the avenue leading from Pest toward the City Park (Városliget) in the east: the name should be Andrássy út. Refer also to this book's **color map** of central Budapest. The **American Express** and **Tourinform** offices have reliable and free tourist maps, while *Belváros Idegenforgalmi Térképe* is available at any metro stop (199Ft).

Telephone Code: 1.

Flights: Ferihegy Airport (tel. 267 43 33, info tel. 357 71 55, reservations tel. 357 91 23). Volánbusz (every 30min. between 5:30am and 9pm) takes 30min. to terminal 1 and 40min. to terminal 2 (500Ft) from Erzsébet tér. The **airport minibus** (tel. 296 85 55) will pick you up anywhere in the city, or take you anywhere from the airport (1200Ft). Call for pick-up 24hr. in advance. Youth and stand-by discounts available at the **Malév office** (see **Budget Travel,** below).

Trains: For domestic info, call 461 54 00, international 461 55 00. The word for train station is *pályaudvar,* often abbreviated "pu." Those under 26 get a 33% discount on international tickets. Show your ISIC and tell the clerk *"diák"* (*DEE-ak,* student). The three main stations—**Keleti pu., Nyugati pu.,** and **Déli pu.**—are also metro stops. Each station has schedules for the others. To: Belgrade (8hr., 7500Ft), Berlin (13hr., 20,400Ft, reservation 2500Ft), Prague (6hr., 11,000Ft, reservation 1600Ft), Vienna (3hr., 6800Ft, reservation 620Ft), and Warsaw (11hr., 12,000Ft, reservation 2300Ft). The **Orient Express** arrives daily from Paris and continues on to Istanbul. **Luggage storage** at Keleti pu. (80Ft).

Buses: Info tel. 117 29 66. **Volánbusz main station,** V, Erzsébet tér (tel. 317 25 62). M1, 2, or 3: Deák tér. Buses to the Czech Republic, Slovakia, Poland, Romania, Turkey, and Ukraine depart from the **Népstadion** terminal on Hungária körút 48/52, as do most domestic buses to eastern Hungary. M2: Népstadion. Buses to the Danube Bend leave from the **Árpád híd** station. To: Berlin (14½hr., 15,400Ft), Bratislava (4hr., 1970Ft), Prague (8½hr., 5100Ft), and Vienna (3½hr., 4390Ft).

Public Transportation: The **Metro (M)** is rapid and punctual. There are 3 lines—M1 is yellow, M2 is red, and M3 is blue. "M" indicates a stop, but you won't always find the sign on the street; look for stairs leading down. Most public transportation stops about 11:30pm. The subway, buses, and trams all use the same blue **tickets** which are sold in Metro stations, *Trafik* shops, and by some sidewalk vendors. A single-trip ticket costs 70Ft; punch it in the orange boxes at the gate of the Metro or on board buses and trams (10-trip *tíz jegy* 630Ft; 1-day pass 560Ft; 3-day pass 1120Ft). The **HÉV commuter rail** runs between Batthyány tér in Buda and Szentendre, 40min. north on the Danube Bend, every 15min.

Hydrofoils: MAHART International Boat Station, VI, Belgrád rakpart (tel. 318 19 53; fax 318 77 40), on the Duna near Erzsébet híd, has info and tickets. Open M-F 8am-4pm. **IBUSZ,** VII, Dob u. (tel. 322 16 56; fax 322 72 64), is open M-F 8am-4pm. M2: Astoria. Be at the docks 1hr. before departure for customs and passport control. 50% Eurailpass discount. To Vienna (6½hr., 12,700Ft, students 10,000Ft).

Taxis: Budataxi, tel. 233 33 33. 100Ft base fare plus 80Ft per km. **Főtaxi,** tel. 222 22 22. These companies are generally much cheaper than taxis hailed in the street. Always make sure the driver starts his meter, and ask about rates before getting in.

Tourist Offices: All tourist offices have *Budapest Kártya,* which buys 3 days of public transportation use, entrance to all museums, and other discounts (2900Ft). **Tourinform,** V, Sütő u. 2 (tel. 317 98 00; fax 317 95 78), off Deák tér just behind McDonald's. M1, 2, or 3: Deák tér. Busy and multilingual. Open M-F 9am-7pm, Sa-Su 9am-4pm. Accommodation bookings available at **IBUSZ** and **Budapest Tourist** (offices in train stations and tourist centers). The 24hr. IBUSZ central office is at V, Fererciek tér 10 (tel. 337 09 39; fax 318 49 83).

Budget Travel: Express, V, Szabadság tér 16 (tel. 131 77 77). Some reduced international air and rail fares for the under-26 crowd (reductions also available at train stations). ISIC for 700Ft. Open M-F 8am-6pm, Sa 8am-noon. Amazing discounts for those under 26 available at the **Malév office,** V, Dorottya u. 2 (tel. 235 38 04; fax 266 27 84), on Vörösmarty tér. Open M-F 7:30am-5pm.

Embassies: Australia, XII, Királyhágó tér 8/9 (tel. 201 88 99). M2: Déli pu., then bus 21 to "Királyhágó tér." Open M-F 9am-noon. **Canada,** XII, Budakeszi út 32 (tel. 275 12 00). Take bus 158 from Moszkva tér to the last stop. **New Zealanders** should contact the British embassy. **U.K.,** V, Harmincad u. 6 (tel. 266 28 88), off the corner of Vörösmarty tér. M1: Vörösmarty tér. Open M-F 9:30am-noon and 2:30-4pm. **U.S.,** V, Szabadság tér 12 (tel. 267 44 00). M2: Kossuth Lajos; walk down Akademia and turn left on Zoltán. Open M and W 8:30am-11am; Tu, Th, and F 8:30-10:30am.

Currency Exchange: The bureaus with longer hours generally have less favorable rates. **GWK Tours** (tel. 322 90 11), in the Keleti Station. Good rates and convenient for rail travelers. Open daily 6am-9pm. **Magyar Külkereskedelmi Bank,** V, Váci u. 38 (tel. 269 09 22). Two blocks north of the Metro, at the basilica's entrance. Perhaps the most comprehensive exchange place in town, with very good rates and outdoor **ATMs.** Open M-Th 8am-2pm and F 8am-1pm. **Budapest Bank,** V, Váci utca 1-3. Cash advances on credit cards, Western Union services, cash traveler's checks in US$ (3.5% commission) and has possibly the best exchange rates in town. Open M-F 8:30am-5pm, Sa 9am-2pm.

American Express: V, Deák Ferenc u. 10 (tel. 235 43 30; fax 267 20 28). M1: Vörösmarty tér, next to Hotel Kempinski. Sells traveler's checks and cashes checks in US$ for variable commission. Cash advances only in forints. Mail held free for cardholders. AmEx **ATM.** Office open June-Sept. M-F 9am-6:30pm, Sa 9am-2pm; Oct.-May M-F 9am-5:30pm, Sa 9am-1pm. Currency Exchange open daily 9am-6:30pm.

English Bookstore: Bestsellers KFT, V, Október 6 u. 11, near Arany János u. M: Deák tér or M1: Vörösmarty tér. Open M-F 9am-8pm, Sa 10am-6pm.

Gay and Lesbian Organizations: Cruise Victory Co., II Váci u., 9 (tel./fax 267 38 05). Eponymous free brochure with gay listings. Open M-F 9am-5pm.

Laundromats: Irisz Szalon, V, Városház u. 3-5 (tel. 317 20 92). M3: Ferenciek tere. Wash: 5kg 700Ft. Dry: 270Ft per 15min. Pay the cashier before you start. Open M-F 7am-7pm, Sa 7am-1pm. Many hostels let you use their machines for a fee.

Emergencies: Ambulance, tel. 104. **Fire,** tel. 105.

Police: tel. 107. For tourist police, call 343 00 34 and ask for "K.E.O."

24-Hour Pharmacies: II, Frankel L. út 22 (tel. 212 44 06); III, Szerterdrei út 2/A (tel. 388 65 28); IV, Pozsonyi u. 19 (389 40 79); VII, Rékóczi út 39 (314 36 95); IX, Boráras tér 3 (217 07 43); X, Liget tér 3 (260 16 87); XII, Alkotás u. 1/B (355 46 91). At night, call the number on the door, or ring the bell to summon the manager.

Medical Assistance: Falck Személyi Olvosi Szolgálat KFT, II, Kapy út 40/B (tel. 200 01 00 or 275 15 35). English spoken. Open 24hr. First aid is free for foreigners.

Post Office: *Poste Restante* at V, Városház u. 18 (tel. 318 48 11). Open M-F 8am-8pm, Sa 8am-2pm. Open 24hr. **Branches** at Nyugati station, VI, Teréz krt. 105-107, and Keleti station, VIII, Baross tér 11c. English generally spoken. Sending mail via American Express may be better. **Postal Code:** 1052.

Telephones: V, Petőfi Sándor u. 17. English-speaking staff. Fax service. **Internet access** (500Ft per hr.). Open M-F 8am-8pm, Sa-Su 8am-2pm. Also try the post office. Many public phones use **phone cards,** available at newsstands, post offices, and Metro stations. 50-unit card 800Ft, 120-unit card 1600Ft. **Card phones** are better than coin phones for **international calls,** but both will probably cut you off.

ACCOMMODATIONS AND CAMPING

Travelers arriving in Keleti station enter a feeding frenzy of hostel solicitors. Don't be drawn in by promises of free drinks or special discounts, and keep in mind that the best options are not always represented at Keleti. The newly formed **Hungarian Youth Hostel Association** has consolidated a number of Budapest hostels and has a booth at Keleti. Make sure that the room is easily accessible by public transportation, preferably by Metro. Ask to be shown on a map where the lodging is located and see the room before you hand over any cash.

Accommodations Agencies

Accommodation services are overrunning Budapest. Rates (1200-5000Ft per person) depend on location and quality. Haggle stubbornly. Arrive around 8am, and you may get a single for 1400Ft or a double for 2200Ft. Travelers who stay for more than four nights can obtain a somewhat better rate.

Pension Centrum, XII, Szarvas Gábor út 24 (tel. 200 88 70). Rents private apartments starting at 3600Ft. Open daily 10am-10pm.

Welcome Hotel Service, V, Apáczai Csere J. u. 1 (tel. 318 39 25; fax 317 90 99). A 24hr. tourist office and accommodation service. Rents private doubles from 5000Ft; off-season 3500Ft. Triples and quads from 6000Ft; off-season 4000Ft. Also rents apartments.

Budapest Tourist, V, Roosevelt tér 5 (tel. 317 35 55; fax 318 60 62), near Hotel Forum, 10min. from Deák tér on the Pest end of Széchenyi lánchíd. A well-established enterprise. Singles 3000Ft; doubles 4000-5000Ft; triples 6000Ft; 1-bedroom apartment with 2 beds, kitchen, and bathroom 5000Ft; 2-bedroom apartment with 4 beds, kitchen and bath 8000Ft. Open M-F 9am-5pm.

Cooptourist, XI, Bartók Béla út 4 (tel. 209 66 67; fax 386 82 40) rents doubles (2500-4000Ft) and apartments, 1-bedroom (2 beds, from 4000Ft), and 2-bedroom (3-4 beds, from 4500Ft). Open M-F 9am-5pm, Sa 9am-1pm.

IBUSZ, V, Ferenciek tere 10, 3rd fl. #318, entrance from Parizsi Court (tel. 317 35 00; fax 337 12 05). Rents private rooms (2-bed 3000-4000Ft; 3-bed 4000-5500Ft; 4-bed 5000-7000Ft), and apartments (1-bedroom doubles from 5000Ft, 2-bedroom triples and quads from 6000Ft). Open M-Th 8am-4pm, F 8am-3pm.

Hostels

If you're eager to meet young people, hostels are the place to be. Be especially paranoid about theft, though, and always make sure that you lock up your belongings.

Open year-round

Backpack Guesthouse, XI, Takács Menyhért u. 33 (tel. 209 84 06; tel./fax 385 89 46). From Keleti pu. or the city center, take bus 1, 7, or 7A (black numbers) heading toward Buda and disembark at "Tétényi u.," after the rail bridge. Go back under the bridge, turn left, and follow the street parallel to the train tracks for 3 blocks. Look for the most colorful house on the block. Carpeted rooms, clean bathrooms, and humor in every niche. 1100-1400Ft; doubles 1700Ft. Showers, private locker, and use of kitchen, TV, and VCR. **Internet access.**

Station Guest House, XIV, Mexikói út 36/B (tel. 221 88 64; email station@free-mail.c3.hu). From Keleti, take 7 bus one stop to "Hungária Körút," go under an overpass, then right on Mexikói út for 2 blocks. Close to the train station with clean rooms, eclectic decor, and a friendly Doberman. Live music W and Su nights. Dorms 1400-2000Ft. Laundry 300Ft per 4kg.

Nicholas's Budget Hostel, XI, Takács Menyhért u. 12 (tel. 385 48 70). Follow the directions to the Backpack Guesthouse, then continue a half block down the road. Not as corporate as the competition, but more spacious and clean, and just as friendly. TV, garden, kitchen, lockers and laundry (700Ft per 5kg). Doubles 4000Ft; 12-bed dorms 1200Ft per person. Bedding 600Ft. Reservations accepted.

Summer Hostels

Technical University (Műegyetem) dorms become youth hostels in July and August; these are conveniently located in district XI, around Móricz Zsigmond Körtér. From M3: "Kálvin tér," ride tram 47 or 49 across the river to "M. Zsigmond."

Strawberry Youth Hostels, IX, Ráday u. 43-45 (tel. 218 47 66), and Kinizsi u. 2/6 (tel. 217 30 33). M3: Kálvin tér. Two converted university dorms within a block of one another in Pest, off Kálvin tér. Spacious rooms with refrigerators and sinks. Disco on the premises. Doubles 2600Ft; triples and quads 2300Ft per person. 10% off with HI card. Laundry 300Ft. Check-out 10am.

Martos, XI, Stoczek u. 5/7 (tel. 463 37 76; tel./fax 463 36 50; email reception@hotel.martos.bme.hu), near the Technical University. From Keleti pu. take red bus 7 to Moric Zsigmond Körtér and trek back 300m toward the river on Kainthy F. u. Take a left on Egri Tózset and another left onto Stoczek u. Free use of washers and kitchens. **Internet access** available. Singles 2000Ft; doubles 3000Ft. Comfy 6-person apartment 10,000Ft. Reception 24hr. No curfew. Check-out 9am.

Universitas, XI, Irinyi József u. 9-11 (tel. 463 38 25 or 463 38 26). First stop after crossing the river on tram 4 or 6. In-room fridges and communal bathrooms. Satellite TV, active nightlife in the disco and bar on weekends. Doubles 5200Ft. Laundry 200Ft. HI members 10% off. Fine cafeteria with 540Ft *menü*. Check-out 9am.

Guest Houses

Guest houses and rooms for rent in private homes include a personal touch for about the same as an anonymous hostel bed. Proprietors carry cellular telephones so they can always be reached for reservations. In stations, bypass the pushier hostel representatives and look for the quieter ones hanging around in the background.

Caterina, V, Andrássy út 47, III. 48 (tel. 291 95 38, cellular tel. 06 20 34 63 98). Take M1 or tram 4 or 6 to "Oktogon." A century-old building only a few min. from downtown Pest. Two guest bathrooms. Dorms 1200Ft; doubles 4400Ft. TV in all rooms. Owners speak only some English.

Weisses Haus, III, Erdőalja u. 11 (cellular tel. 06 20 34 36 31; tel./fax 387 82 36). Take bus 137 from Flórián tér to "Iskola." On a hillside in residential Óbuda. Panoramic view across the Danube. Doubles 4400Ft. Breakfast included.

Mrs. Ena Bottka, V, Garibaldi u. 5, 5th fl. (tel. 302 34 56, cellular tel. 06 30 518 763; email viktor.bottka@stud.bke.hu), a block south of M2: Kossuth tér. Live the Bohemian life in tiny rooms overlooking gabled rooftops and the Parliament building. Small kitchen. 2 common bathrooms. Singles 2600Ft; doubles 4400Ft. Also rents rooms in a few attractive, spacious apartments in central Pest (3300Ft per person); these have kitchen facilities, cable TVs, and private bathrooms. Call in the morning or evening to reserve.

"Townhouser's" International Guesthouse, XVI, Attila u. 123 (cellular tel. 06 30 44 23 31; tel./fax 405 25 96). M2: Örs Vezér tere, then 5 stops on bus 31 to Diófa u. Quiet residential area in east Pest, 30min. from downtown. Doubles 4400-5200Ft; triples 5400Ft. Also available: 3 apartments at Vaci utca 44, in the middle of downtown (6800-11,000Ft per night). Béla takes guests to and from the train station.

Hotels

Budapest's few affordable hotels are frequently clogged with groups, so call ahead. Proprietors often speak English. All hotels should be registered with Tourinform (see **Practical Information,** above).

Hotel Góliát, XIII, Kerekes út 12-20 (tel. 270 14 55; fax 349 49 85). M1: Árpád híd, then take the tram away from the river and get off before the overpass. Walk down Reitler Ferere ut. until you see the 10-story yellow building on the right. Clean, spacious rooms with sinks. Singles 3000Ft; doubles 4000Ft; quads 4800Ft.

Hotel Citadella, Citadella Sétány (tel. 466 57 94; fax 386 05 05), atop Gellért Hill. Take tram 47 or 49 three stops into Buda to "Móricz Zsigmond Körtér," then catch bus 27 to "Citadella." Perfect location and spacious rooms. Doubles 7400Ft; quads 10,680Ft. Usually packed, so write or fax well in advance to reserve.

Camping

Camping Hungary, available at tourist offices, describes Budapest's campgrounds.

Római Camping, III, Szentendrei út 189 (tel. 368 62 60; fax 250 04 26). M2: Batthyány tér, then take the HÉV commuter rail to "Római fürdő," and walk 100m toward the river. Tip-top security with grocery, swimming pool, and huge park on the site. Communal showers. 1700Ft per tent, 10% off with HI card. Bungalows 1050-1600Ft per person. Open Apr. to mid-Oct.

Zugligeti "Niche" Camping, XII, Zugligeti út 101 (tel./fax 200 83 46). Bus 158 from "Moszkva tér" to last stop. Closest camping to central Budapest. Beautiful camping site, partially forested. Restaurant and buffet. Communal showers. 700Ft per person; 450Ft per tent; 650Ft per car; 400Ft for electricity. English-speaking reception.

FOOD

Most restaurants in Budapest will fit your budget, though the food at family eateries may be cheaper and tastier than more elegant repasts. An average meal runs 700-900Ft, a 10% tip is usual, plus another 10% for live music. Seek out a *kifőzde* or *vendéglő* for a taste of Hungarian life. Cafeterias lurk under **Önkiszolgáló Étterem** signs (vegetarian meals 180Ft; meat meals 300-400Ft). Travelers may also rely on mar-

kets and tiny 24-hour stores labeled *Non-Stop* for staples. The king of them all is the
Central Market, V, Kőzraktár tér u. 1 (M3: Kálvin tér). Two great markets can be
found near central Pest. **Hold utcai piac,** V, Hold u. 13, is just off of Szabadság tér
(open M 6:30am-5pm, Tu-F 6:30am-6pm, Sa 6:30am-2pm). **Vámház vásárcsarnok,**
IX, Vámház krt. 1/3 is at Fövám tér (open M 6am-5pm, Tu-F 6am-6pm, Sa 6am-2pm).
Take a gander at the **ABC Food Hall,** I, Batthyány tér 5/7 (open Su 7am-1pm).

Gandhi, V, Vigyázó Ferenc u. 4. Take a right at the northern end of Roosevelt tér.
Outstanding vegetarian restaurant. New menu every day, herb teas, organic wines,
and wheat beers. Main dishes 560-780Ft. Open daily noon-10:30pm.

Korona Passage, V, Kecskeméti u. 14. M3: Kálvin tér, in the Mercure Korona Hotel.
Giant Hungarian crepes served with a large variety of toppings (350-510Ft) make
filling meals in and of themselves. Open daily 10am-10pm.

Söröző a Szent Jupáthoz, II, Dékán u. 3. 50m from M2: Moszkva tér; entrance on
Retek u. Down the modest stairway, then right back up into an open-air hall. Huge
portions; friendly staff. Main courses 545-1419Ft. *Holstein* 0.5L 229Ft. Open 24hr.

Fatâl Restaurant, V, Váci u. 67. One of the most popular restaurants in Budapest.
Large, hearty, and delicious Hungarian meals in pleasant, rustic surroundings. Main
dishes from 900Ft. Open daily 11am-11pm.

Marxim, II, Kis Rókus u. 23. M2: Moszkva tér. With your back to the Lego-like castle,
walk along Margit krt. Food prepared by the staff according to their abilities, consumed by the patrons according to their needs. Salads 170-190Ft. Pizza 260-610Ft.
Open M-Th noon-1am, F-Sa noon-2am, Su 6pm-1am.

Remiz, II, Budakeszi út 8 (tel. 275 13 96). Take bus 22 from "Moszkva tér" to "Szépi-
lona" (about 10min.), and walk three stores past the stop. Traditional and tasty
Hungarian cuisine in a yuppie setting. Main dishes 800-1600Ft. Outdoor seating in
warm weather. Live music. Open daily 9am-1am. Call for reservations.

New York Bagels (The Sequel), VI, Bajcsy-Zsilinszky út 21. M3: Arany János u.
Assorted bagels baked hourly, freshly made spreads, sandwiches, salads, and cookies. Bagel sandwich specials 300-500Ft. Open M-F 7am-10pm, Sa-Su 9am-10pm.

Fészek Müvész Klub Étterem, VII, Kertész u. 36, corner of Dob u. 2 blocks southwest of Erzsébet krt. M1: Oktogon, or tram 4 or 6 to "Király u." Excellent Hungarian food and decent prices. Main courses 490-1370Ft, but 300Ft cover. In summer,
walk through to the leafy courtyard. Open daily noon-1am.

Kisharaig Étkezde, VI, Október 6 u. 17. Just off Szabadság tér, this little eatery is central, cheap, and quick. Main dishes 350-500Ft. English and German menus available. Open M-F 11am-8pm, Sa-Su 11:30am-4:30pm.

Cafes

These amazing establishments were once the pretentious haunts of Budapest's literary, intellectual, and cultural elite. A cafe repose is a must for every visitor; the
absurdly ornate pastries are inexpensive, even in the most genteel establishments.

Cafe New York, VII, Erzsébet krt. 9-11. M2: Blaha Lujza tér. Resplendent with velvet, gold, and marble, this is one of the most beautiful cafes in Budapest. Cappuccino 250Ft. Ice cream and coffee delights 400-900Ft. Open daily 9am-midnight.

Müvész Kávéház, VI, Andrássy út 29, diagonally across the street from the State
Opera House. M1: Opera. Golden Age wood panelling and gilded ceilings. One of
Budapest's most elegant. Cappuccino 170Ft. Open daily 9am-midnight.

Ruszwurm, I, Szentháromság u. 7, just off the square on Várhegy in the Castle District. Confecting since 1826 and strewn with period furniture. Stop by to relax
after the majesty of Mátyás Cathedral down the street. You won't be hurried. Ice
cream 50Ft per scoop. Cakes 80-280Ft. Open daily 10am-7pm.

Café Pierrot, I, Fortuna u. 14. Antique clown dolls hang from the curvaceous walls.
Espresso 120Ft. Fabulous crepes *(palacsinta)* 350Ft. Live piano music daily from
8pm. Open daily 11am-1am.

HUNGARY

SIGHTS

Buda

Budapest's designated tourist zone, the **Castle District** rests 100m above the Duna, atop the 2km mound called **Várhegy** (Castle Hill). Find a path up the hill, or cross the **Széchenyi lánchíd** (Széchenyi Chain Bridge) from Pest and ride the *sikló* (cable car) to the top. *(Operates daily 7:30am-10pm. Closed 2nd and 4th M of each month. 250Ft.)* Built in the 13th century, the hilltop castle was leveled in sieges by Mongols then by Ottoman Turks. Christian Hapsburg forces razed the rebuilt castle while ousting the Turks after a 145-year occupation. A reconstruction was completed just in time to be destroyed by the Germans in 1945. Determined Hungarians pasted the castle together once more, only to face the new Soviet menace—bullet holes in the palace facade recall the tanks of 1956. The current **Budavári palota** (Royal Palace) houses several notable museums. During recent reconstruction, excavations revealed artifacts from the earliest castle here; they are now displayed in Wing E in the **Budapesti Történeti.** *(Budapest History Museum. Open Mar.-May 15 M and W-Su 10am-6pm; May 16-Sept. 15 daily 10am-6pm; Sept. 16-Oct. M and W-Su 10am-8pm; Nov.-Feb. M and W-Su 10am-4pm. 100Ft, students 50Ft, W free.)* Wing A contains the **Kortárs Művészeti Múzeum** (Museum of Contemporary Art) and the **Ludwig Museum,** a collection of international modern art. *(Open Tu-Su 10am-6pm. 100Ft, students 50Ft.)* Wings B-D hold the **Magyar Nemzeti Galéria** (Hungarian National Gallery), a vast hoard of the best Hungarian painting and sculpture. *(Open Tu-Su 10am-6pm. 150Ft, students 50Ft, for all wings. W free. English tour 200Ft.)*

From the castle, stroll down Színház u. and Tárnok u. to **Szentháromság tér** (Trinity Square), site of the Disney-esque **Fisherman's Bastion.** This arcaded stone wall supports a squat, fairy-tale tower, but you'll have to pay for the magnificent view across the Danube (100Ft, free on M). Behind the tower stands the delicate, neo-Gothic **Mátyás templom** (Matthias Church); it served as a mosque for 145 years after the Turks seized Buda. These days, high mass is celebrated Sundays at 7am, 8:30am, 10am, noon, and 8:30pm with orchestra and choir. On occasional summer Fridays at 8pm, organ concerts reverberate in the resplendent interior. Intricate door-knockers and balconies adorn the Castle District's other historic buildings; wander along **Úri u.** (Gentlemen's Street) among Baroque townhouses, or **Táncsics Mihály u.** in the old Jewish quarter. Enjoy a terrific view of Buda from the Castle District's west walls.

The **Szabadság Szobor** (Liberation Monument) crowns neighboring **Gellérthegy,** just south of the castle. This 30m bronze woman honors Soviet soldiers who died while liberating Hungary from the Nazis. The **Citadella,** adjacent to the Liberation Monument, was built as a symbol of Hapsburg power after the 1848 revolution; climb the hill to it from Hotel Gellért (bus 27 also drives up). The hill itself is named for the 11th-century bishop sent by the Pope to help King Stephen convert the Magyars. Unconvinced Magyars hurled poor St. Gellért to his death from atop the hill. His statue overlooks the **Erzsébet híd** (Elizabeth Bridge).

Like a Troubled Bridge over Water...

The citizens of Budapest are justly proud of the bridges that bind Buda to Pest. The four great lions that have guarded the **Széchenyi lánchíd** (Széchenyi Chain Bridge) since 1849 make the bridge one of the most recognizable. These beasts were created by János Marschalkó in a naturalistic style, with the tongues resting far back in their gaping mouths. The anatomical correctness of their new mascots did not impress Budapestians—distraught by public laughter over the seemingly missing tongues, Marschalkó jumped from the bridge to his death. Another version of the story has the king reprimanding Marschalkó, with the same result. *Let's Go* does not recommend sculpting lions without visible tongues.

North of the castle, the **Margit híd** spans the Danube and connects to the **Margitsziget** (Margaret Island). Off-limits to private cars, the island offers capacious thermal baths, luxurious garden pathways, and numerous shaded terraces. According to legend, the *sziget* is named after King Béla IV's daughter; he vowed to rear young Margit as a nun if the nation survived the Mongol invasion of 1241. The Mongols decimated Hungary but did not destroy it, and Margaret was confined to the island convent. Take bus 26 from "Szt. István krt." to the island.

The **Szoborpark Múzeum** (Statue Park Museum), XXII, on the corner of Balatoni út and Szabadkai út, is a unique collection of the statues removed from Budapest's parks and squares after the collapse of Communist rule. Take the yellow long-distance bus from Kosztelányi tér toward Érd. *(Open daily 10am-dusk. 100Ft, students 50Ft.)*

Pest

Across the Danube lies Pest, the capital's throbbing commercial and administrative center. The old **Belváros** (Inner City), rooted in the pedestrian zone of Váci u. and Vörösmarty tér, is a tourist haven. On the riverbank, a string of modern luxury hotels leads up to the magnificent neo-Gothic **Ovszágház** (Parliament) in Kossuth tér. *(Tours available in English W-Su 10am. 750Ft, students 350Ft. Purchase tickets at gate #10 at the Parliament. Reservations recommended; call 268 49 04.)* Nearby, at Kossuth tér 12 in the former Hungarian Supreme Court, the **Néprajzi múzeum** (Museum of Ethnography) hosts an outstanding exhibit of pre-World War I Hungarian folk culture. *(Open Tu-Su Mar.-Nov. 10am-5:45pm; Dec.-Feb. 10am-4pm. 200Ft, students 100Ft. Tu free.)*

Sz. István Bazilika (St. Stephen's Basilica), two blocks north of Deák tér, is by far the city's largest church, with room for 8500 worshippers. Climb 302 spiraling steps to the Panorama tower for a 360-degree view of the city. *(Open Apr.-Oct. daily 10am-6:30pm. 200Ft, students 100Ft.)* St. Stephen's holy **right hand,** one of Hungary's most revered religious relics, is displayed in the **Basilica museum.** *(Basilica open M-Sa 9am-5pm, Su 1-5pm. 120Ft, students 60Ft. Museum open Apr.-Sept. M-Sa 9am-4:30pm, Su 1-4:30pm; Oct.-Mar. M-Sa 10am-4pm, Su 1-4pm.)* At the corner of Dohány u. and Wesselényi u., the **Zsinagóga** (Synagogue) is the largest active temple in Europe and the second-largest in the world. *(Open M-Sa 10am-2:30pm, Su 10am-1:30pm. 400Ft, students 200Ft.)* Next door, the **Jewish Museum** juxtaposes magnificent exhibits dating back to the Middle Ages with haunting documentation of the Holocaust. *(Open Apr.-Oct. M-F 10am-3pm, Su 10am-1pm.)*

To the east of the basilica, **Andrássy út,** Hungary's grandest boulevard, extends from the edge of Belváros in downtown Pest to **Hősök tere** (Heroes' Square), some 2km away. The **Magyar Állami Operaház** (Hungarian State Opera House), VI, Andrássy út 22 (M1: Opera), is laden with sculptures and paintings in the ornate Empire style of the 1880s. If you can't actually see an opera, at least take a tour. *(Daily at 3 and 4pm. 700Ft, students 300Ft.)* The **Millenniumi emlékmű** (Millennium Monument), commemorating the nation's most prominent leaders and national heroes from 896 to 1896, dominates Hősök tere. The **Szépművészeti Múzeum** (Museum of Fine Arts) on the square maintains a splendid collection; highlights include an entire room devoted to El Greco and an exhaustive display of Renaissance works. *(Open Tu-Su 10am-6pm; Jan.-Mar. 15 until 4pm. 200Ft, students 100Ft. Tours for up to 5 people 1500Ft.)*

Behind the monument, the **Városliget** (City Park) is home to a circus, an amusement park, a zoo, a castle, and the impressive **Széchenyi Baths.** The **Vajdahunyad Vára** (Castle), created for the Millenary Exhibition of 1896, incorporates Romanesque, Gothic, Renaissance, and Baroque styles. Outside the castle broods the hooded statue of **Anonymous,** the secretive scribe to whom we owe much of our knowledge of medieval Hungary. Rent a **rowboat** (June to mid-Sept. daily 9am-8pm) or **ice skates** (Nov.-Mar. daily 9am-1pm and 4-8pm; 150Ft) on the lake by the castle.

The ruins of the north Budapest garrison town of **Aquincum** crumble in the outer regions of the third district. To reach the area, take M2: Batthyány tér, then the HÉV to "Aquincum"; the site is about 100m south of the HÉV stop. Here are the most impressive vestiges of the Roman occupation which spanned the first four centuries

HUNGARY ·

AD. The **museum** on the grounds contains a model of the ancient city, musical instruments, and other household items. *(Open Apr.-Oct. daily 10am-6pm. 300Ft, students 60Ft.)* The remains of the **Roman Military Baths** are visible to the south of the Roman encampment, beside the overpass at Flórián tér near the "Árpád híd" HÉV station. From the stop, follow the main road away from the river.

ENTERTAINMENT

Budapest hosts cultural events year-round. Pick up a copy of the English-language *Programme in Hungary, Budapest Panorama,* or *Pestiest,* all available free at tourist offices; they contain daily listings of all concerts, operas, and theater performances in the city. The "Style" section of the weekly English-language *Budapest Sun* is another excellent source for schedules of entertainment happenings.

Theater, Music, & Dance

The **Central Theater Booking Office,** VI, Andrassy út 18 (tel. 312 00 00), next to the Opera House, and the branch at Moszkva tér 3 (tel. 212 56 78; both open M-Th 9am-6pm, F until 5pm), sell commission-free tickets to almost every performance in the city. An extravaganza at the gilded, neo-Renaissance **State Opera House,** VI, Andrássy út 22 (tel. 332 81 97; M1: Opera), costs only US$8-10; the box office (tel. 353 01 70), on the left side of the building, sells unclaimed tickets at even better prices 30min. before showtime (open Tu-Sa 11am-1:45pm and 2:30-7pm, Su 10am-1pm and 4-7pm). The **Philharmonic Orchestra** is also world-renowned; concerts thunder through town almost every evening September to June. The ticket office (tel. 317 62 22) is located at Vörösmarty tér 1. (Open M-F 10am-6pm, Sa-Su 10am-2pm. Tickets 1000-1500Ft; less on the day of performance.)

In late summer, the Philharmonic and Opera take sabbaticals, but summer theaters and concert halls are ready to pick up the slack. In July, classical music and opera are performed at 8:30pm in the **Hilton Hotel Courtyard,** I, Hess András tér 1/3 (tel. 214 30 00), next to Mátyás templom in the Castle District. The **Margitsziget Theater,** XIII, Margitsziget (tel. 340 41 96), features opera and Hungarian-music concerts on its open-air stage. Take tram 4 or 6 to "Margitsziget." Try **Zichy Mansion Courtyard,** III, Fő tér 1, for orchestral concerts, or the **Pest Concert Hall** (Vigadó), V, Vigadó tér 2 (tel. 318 99 03; fax 375 62 22), on the Danube bank near Vörösmarty tér, for operettas (cashier open M-Sa 10am-6pm; tickets 3200Ft). Folk-dancers stomp across the stage at the **Buda Park Theater,** XI, Kosztolányi Dezső tér (tel. 366 99 16); brochures and concert tickets flood from the ticket office at Vörösmarty tér 1 (open M-F 11am-6pm; tickets 200-300Ft). For a psychedelic evening, try the laser shows at the **Planetarium.** (Tel. 334 11 61. M3: Népliget. W-Th and Sa 6:30, 8, and 9:30pm; M and F 8 and 9:30pm; Tu 6:30 and 9:30pm.) The **Budapest Spring Festival** in late March and the **Budapest Arts Weeks** each fall showcase Hungarian art and music. Check with **Music Mix 33 Ticket Service,** V, Vaci u. 33 (tel. 266 70 70), for pop concerts.

Thermal Baths

To soak away weeks of city grime, crowded trains, and yammering camera-clickers, sink into a thermal bath, an essential Budapest experience. The post-bath massages vary from a quick three-minute slap to a royal half-hour indulgence. Some baths are meeting spots, though not exclusively, for Budapest's gay community.

Gellért, XI, Kelenhegyi út 4-6 (tel. 466 61 66). Take bus 7 or tram 47 or 49 to Hotel Gellért, at the base of Gellért-hegy. Venerable indoor thermal baths, segregated by sex, where you may soak nude if you like, plus a co-ed (and clothed) indoor pool surrounded by statues. Outside awaits a rooftop sundeck and a wave pool. Also a huge range of inexpensive *à la carte* options, from mudpacks to pedicures. Thermal bath 600Ft, with pool privileges 1200Ft. 15min. massage 550Ft. Open May-Sept. M-F 6am-6pm, Sa-Su 6am-4pm; Oct.-Apr. M-F 6am-6pm, Sa-Su 6am-2pm. Pools open daily until 7pm except weekends Oct.-Apr., when they close at 5pm.

Király, I, Fő u. 84 (tel. 202 36 88). M2: Batthány tér. Bathe in the splendor of Turkish cupolas and domes. Thermal bath 400Ft. Massage 550Ft per 15min. Men only M,W, and F 6:30am-6pm. Women only Tu and Th 6:30am-6pm and Sa 6:30am-noon.

Széchenyi Fűrdő, XIV, Állatkerti u. 11-14 (tel. 321 03 10), in Városliget, 7min. north of M1: Hősök tere. These public thermal baths (400Ft) have a devoted following among the city's gentry; the **outdoor swimming pool** delights their grandchildren. Bring a swimsuit. Massage 550Ft per 15min. In July-Aug. the baths are men-only M, W, and F; women-only Tu, Th, and Sa. Open M-F 6am-7pm, Sa 6am-1pm.

Rudas, Döbrentei tér 9 (tel. 375 83 73), on the river under a dome built by Turks 400 years ago. Take bus 7 to the first stop in Buda. The centuries haven't altered the dome, the bathing chamber, or the "men only" rule. Swimming pool open to women, too (400Ft); bath (1½hr. 450Ft). Open M-F 6am-6pm, Sa-Su 6am-1pm.

NIGHTLIFE

An unenforced drinking age and cheap drinks draw old and young alike to Budapest's clubs and bars. As clubs become more and more sophisticated, the cover prices are rising—a night of techno may soon cost the same as an opera ticket. To find out what's going on and when, pick up a copy of *Budapest Week* (96Ft).

Old Man's Pub, VII, Akácfa u. 13. M2: Blaha Lujza tér. Live blues and jazz in a classy and upscale environment. Kitchen serves pizza, spaghetti, and salads. Occasional free samples of beer. Open M-Sa 3pm-dawn.

Fat Mo's Speakeasy, V, Nyári Pal Utca 11. M3: Kálvin tér. Pricey food, but hip bands and a large selection of tap beer (12 varieties, 250-540Ft for 0.5L). Su-Tu live music, Th-Sa DJ after 11:30pm. Open M-F noon-3am, Sa-Su 6pm-3am.

Morrison's Music Pub, VI, Révay u. 25, left of the State Opera House. M1: Opera. Pub and dance club with a young, international crowd. Beer 240Ft. June-Aug. cover 400Ft. Open daily 8:30am-4pm.

The Long Jazz Club, VII, Dohány u. 22-24. A club with orange painted walls, David Lynchean atmosphere, and a young jazz-loving crowd. Live music every night starting at 9:30pm. *Gösser* 0.5L 260Ft. Cover 100-300Ft. Open daily 6pm-2am.

Bahnhof, north side of Nyugati train station. M3: Nyugati pu. No technical wizardry, but two superb dance floors (rock and disco). Well ventilated. Guaranteed NO TECHNO. Cover 300Ft. Open M-Sa 6pm-4am.

Made-Inn Music Club, VI, Andrássy út 112. M1: Bajza u. Crowds come for the frequent live bands in this cavernous disco/funk club. Different nightly themes, including Wednesday half-priced drinks, "happy music" Friday, and funk/soul Saturday nights. Disco open W-Sa 10pm-5am. Cover 300Ft. Greek/Italian/Hungarian restaurant upstairs open daily 11am-3am.

Piaf, VI, Nagymező u. 25. Popular after-hours place and the final destination of any decent pub crawl in Budapest. Guests are admitted after knocking on a rather inconspicuous, though large, door and meeting the approval of the person behind the peephole. Open 4pm-4am. Cover 500Ft—good for a drink.

Angel Bar, VII, Szövetség u. 33. A giant 3-level, mostly gay disco, cafe and bar. Lowest floor plays loud eardrum-shattering music; bring your earmuffs. Only Sa is exclusively gay. Back room. Cover 400Ft. Open daily 1pm-sunrise.

■ Danube Bend (Dunakanyar)

On its way from Vienna along the Slovak border, the Danube sweeps south in a dramatic arc known as the Danube Bend (*Dunakanyar*) before reaching Budapest. This lush and relaxed region is deservedly one of the great tourist attractions in Hungary.

Szentendre By far the most touristy of the Danube Bend cities, Szentendre's proximity to Budapest, narrow cobblestone streets, and wealth of art galleries keep the visitors coming. On **Templomdomb** (Church Hill), above Fő tér, sits the 13th-century Roman Catholic **parish church.** Facing it, the **Czóbel Museum** exhibits works of Hungary's foremost Impressionist, Béla Czóbel. (Open Mar. 15-Oct. Tu-Su 10am-4pm; off-season F-Su 10am-4pm. 90Ft, students 50Ft.) To the north across Alkotmány u., the Baroque **Szerb Ortodox Templom** (Serbian Orthodox Church) displays Serbian religious art (open W-Su 10am-4pm; 60Ft). The **Kovács Margit Múzeum,** Vastagh György u. 1, exhibits brilliant ceramic sculptures and tiles by 20th-century Hungarian artist Margit Kovács. (Open Mar. 17-Oct. Tu-Su 10am-6pm; Nov.-Mar. 14 Tu-Su 10am-4pm. 250Ft, students 150Ft.) **Szabó Marcipán Múzeum,** Dumtsa Jenő u. 7, details marzipan's history and production with clever, tasty displays (open daily 10am-6pm; 100Ft, students and seniors 50Ft).

The HÉV, train, and bus station is south of the Old Town; to get to **Fő tér,** use the underpass, and head up Kossuth u. The HÉV **commuter rail** leaves for Budapest's Batthyány tér (45min., every 20min., 190Ft). Hourly **buses** run from Budapest's Árpád bridge station to Szentendre (30min., 146Ft), many continuing on to Visegrád (45min. farther) and Esztergom (1½hr. from Szentendre). The **MAHART boat pier** is a 10-minute walk north of Fő tér (to Budapest: 3 per day, 520Ft; May 17-Aug. only). The helpful staff of **Tourinform,** Dumsta Jenő u. 22 (tel. (26) 31 79 65 or 31 79 66), has brochures and 50Ft maps (open M-F 10am-5pm, Sa-Su 10am-2pm). **IBUSZ,** Bogdányi u. 4 (tel. (26) 31 03 33), changes money and finds private doubles (2000-3000F; open M-F 9am-4pm; June 15-Sept. also Sa-Su 10am-2pm). **Ilona Panzió,** Rákóczi Ferenc u. 11 (tel. (26) 31 35 99), near the center of town, has clean doubles with private baths (4000Ft, one person 3000Ft; breakfast included). **Pap-szigeti Camping** (tel. (26) 31 06 97), north of the town center on Pap-sziget Island, has bungalows (2500-4500Ft) and tent sites (2200Ft for 2 people, 900Ft per extra person).

Esztergom If you can't find the Esztergom **cathedral,** you're either too close or in the wrong town; step back and look up. Hungary's largest church, consecrated in 1856, is responsible for the town's nickname "The Hungarian Rome." On a smaller scale, the red marble **Bakócz Chapel** on the south side of the cathedral is a masterwork of Renaissance Tuscan stone-carving. Climb to the 71.5m high **cupola** for a view of Slovakia (80Ft), or descend into the **crypt** to honor the remains of Hungary's archbishops (open daily 9am-5pm; 50Ft). The **cathedral treasury** (Kincstár), on the north side of the main altar, protects Hungary's most extensive ecclesiastical collection. The jewel-studded cross labeled #78 is the **Coronation Cross,** on which Hungary's rulers pledged their oaths until 1916 (open daily 9am-4:30pm; 150Ft, students 75Ft). Nearby stands the restored 12th-century **Esztergom Palace.** (Open in summer Tu-Su 9am-4:30pm; off-season 10am-3:30pm. 60Ft, students 10Ft, free with ISIC.) For an extra 25Ft, you can ascend to the roof to survey the kingdom. At the foot of the hill, **Keresztény Múzeum** (Christian Museum), Berenyi Zsigmond u. 2, houses exceptional Renaissance religious artwork (open Tu-Su 10am-6pm; 100Ft, students 50Ft).

Trains connect to Budapest (1½hr., 312Ft). Catch **buses** a few blocks south of Rákóczi tér on Simor János u. to Budapest (1½hr., 326Ft) and Szentendre (1hr., 237Ft). **MAHART boats** depart from the pier (tel. (33) 31 35 31) at the end of Gőzhajó u., on Primas Sziget island in the south, for Visegrád (1½hr., 450Ft) and Szentendre (3½hr., 915Ft) on the way to Budapest (5hr., 1270Ft). Twice a day on weekends a **hydrofoil** leaves from the same pier and scoots directly to Budapest (1hr.) and Visegrád (40min.). To reach the central Rákóczi tér from the train station, walk up Baross Gábor út (go left out of the station), make a right onto Kiss János Altábornagy út, and keep going straight as it becomes Kossuth Lajos u. **Gran Tours,** Széchenyi tér 25 (tel./ fax (33) 31 37 56), at the edge of Rákóczi tér, provides maps and arranges rooms for 1400Ft (open M-F 8am-6pm, in summer also Sa 9am-noon). One of several centrally located pensions, **Platán Panzió,** Kis-Duna Sétány 11 (tel. (33) 31 13 55), between Rákóczi tér and Primas Sziget, rents singles (1300Ft) and doubles (2644Ft) with shared bath. **Gran Camping,** Nagy-Duna Sétány (tel. (33) 31 13 27), is in the middle of Primas Sziget (250Ft per person, 380Ft per tent). **Szalma Csárda,** in the middle of Primas Sziget near the pier at the end of Cőzhajó 4, cooks up fish straight from the Danube for 400Ft (open daily noon-midnight). **Julius Meinl,** on Rákóczi, sells the usual supermarket fare (open M-F 6:30am-6:30pm, Sa until 1:30pm).

■ Eger

Eger is blessed with a splendid combination of endless sunshine and overflowing jugs of wine. Indeed, the city's lively wine cellars, cobblestone streets, and magnificent Baroque monuments seduce visitors with a warm giddiness.

SIGHTS AND ENTERTAINMENT With good company or sheer determination, you can spend an entire afternoon and evening in the wine cellars of **Szépasszonyvölgy,** the Valley of the Beautiful Women. The valley is lined with the doors of cellars dug into the hills; 25 are open for wine tasting. Most open after 10am and begin to close around 6 to 7pm; some stay open as late as 10pm. The best time to go is late afternoon. Little glasses for tasting are free; 100mL glasses run 30-50Ft. One liter of wine costs 300Ft. To reach the wine cellars, walk west from Deák u. down Telekessy u., which with a quick jog to the left takes you to Király u. and then Szépasszonyvölgy u. When the road forks (about 10min. from Deák), go left.

Wander back to Eszterházy tér to explore the wealth of Baroque architecture around town. The yellow **basilica** here, the second-largest church in Hungary, was built in 1837 by Joseph Hild, who also built Hungary's largest—the Esztergom cathedral. Organ concerts are held here May to mid-October (M-Sa 11:30am, Su 12:45pm; 200Ft, students 60Ft). Opposite the cathedral is the Rococó **Lyceum.** The fresco in the magnificent library on the first floor depicts an ant's-eye view of the Council of Trent (open Tu-Su 9:30am-2:30pm; 200Ft, students 100Ft). On the south side of Dobó tér stands the luxuriously Baroque **Minorite Church,** which overlooks a statue of Captain Dobó and two co-defenders, one of them a woman poised to hurl a rock at an unfortunate Turk. Hungarians revere medieval **Eger Castle;** it was here that Dobó István and his 2000 men held off the unified Ottoman army, halting their advance for another 44 years (grounds open daily 8am-8pm; 80Ft, students 40Ft). A 200Ft ticket (students 100Ft) buys admission to the **picture gallery,** the **Dobó István Castle museum,** which displays excavated artifacts and an impressive array of weapons, and the **Dungeon Exhibition,** a collection of torture equipment to inspire sadists and masochists alike (museums open Tu-Su 9am-5pm). Climb the nearby **Turkish minaret** for a great view, but be careful on the steep, narrow staircase (open daily in summer 10am-6pm; 40Ft). In summer, the city's **open-air baths** (a.k.a. swimming pools) offer a desperately needed respite from the sweltering city. (Open daily 8:30am-7pm. Full day swimming ticket 200Ft, students 130Ft. 6-8am or 4:30-8:30pm 100Ft.) Eger revels in its heritage during the **Baroque Festival** held throughout August. Nightly performances of operas and operettas and medieval and Renaissance court music are held in the courtyard of the Franciscan church, the cathedral, and Dobó tér.

PRACTICAL INFO, ACCOMMODATIONS, AND FOOD **Trains** bound for Budapest's Keleti station (2hr., 820Ft) split in Hatvan; make sure you're in the right car. The **bus station** (tel. (36) 41 05 52), five minutes west of Dobó tér, provides transport to Aggtelek (3hr., 790Ft) and Budapest (2hr., 940Ft). The **Tourinform** office at Dobó tér 2 (tel./fax (36) 32 18 07), has brochures, English newspapers, and maps (60Ft), as well as accommodations info (open M-F 9am-6pm, Sa-Su 9am-2pm).

The best and friendliest accommodations are private rooms; look for *"Zimmer Frei"* signs outside the city center. Several are on Almagyar u. and Mekcsey u., near the castle. **Eger Tourist,** Bajcsy-Zsilinszky u. 9 (tel. (36) 41 17 24), can arrange private rooms for about 1400Ft per person (open June-Sept. M-F 9am-6pm, Sa 9am-noon; Oct.-May M-F 8:30am-5pm). Eger Tourist also operates the very basic **Tourist Motel,** Mekcsey u. 2 (doubles 2800-3600Ft; triples 3400-4300Ft; quads 3600-4800Ft) and **Autós Caravan Camping,** Rákóczi u. 79, 20 minutes north of the city center on bus 5, 10, 11, or 12 (320Ft per person, 250Ft per tent; open Apr. 15-Oct. 15).

For quick gourmet food, go to the **HBH Bajor Söház,** Bajcsy-Zsilinszky u. 19, off Dobó tér, a Bavarian beer house that serves Hungarian specialties (meals 450-1000Ft; English menu; open daily 10am-10pm). In the Valley of the Beautiful Women, the vine-draped courtyard of **Kulacs Csárda Borozó** keeps the crowds coming for the roasted fish with fries (370Ft) and Parisian pork (540Ft; open Tu-Su noon-10pm).

■ Near Eger

Just 70 minutes away from Eger by **train** (140Ft) or 45 minutes away by **bus** (218Ft), **Szilvásvárad** is beloved for its 400-year-old race of Lipizzaner horses and surrounding national parks. **Horse shows** kick into action on weekends usually at 2 and 4pm in the arena on Szalajka u. (300Ft). If you prefer more active participation, **Péter Kovács**, Egri út 62 (tel. (36) 35 53 43), lends horses for 1500Ft per hour and horse-drawn carriages for 2000 to 3500Ft per hour. The nearby **Bükk mountains** (45min. walking, 20min. by train) entices hikers with the **Fátyol waterfalls** and the **Istálósk cave**, which housed a bear cult in the Stone Age.

The **Baradla caves** (tel./fax (48) 35 00 06) are a 25km long system of limestone tunnels that wind between Hungary and Slovakia. Each chamber is a forest of dripping stalactites and stalagmites and fantastically shaped stone formations. Cave **tours** begin from the town of **Aggtelek**. A large chamber with perfect acoustics has been converted into an auditorium, and the tours pause here for a dazzling light-and-sound show. (Bring a jacket. Hour-long tours leave daily 10am, 1, 3, and 5pm. 350Fr, students 200Ft.) The daily **bus** from Eger (450Ft) leaves at 8:40am, whizzes through Szilvásvárad at 9:20am, arriving in Aggtelek at 11:20am in front of Hotel Cseppkő, 200m uphill from the cave entrance. The bus back to Eger leaves at 3pm.

■ Tokaj

Locals say that King Louis XIV called Tokaj (toke-EYE) wine "the wine of kings and the king of wines." While Tokaj is just one of the 28 villages that take advantage of the local volcanic yellow soil and sunny climate to produce unique whites, it lends its name to the entire class of wine. Signs reading *"Bor Pince"* herald **private wine cellars.** Owners are generally pleased to let visitors sample their wares (50mL 90-300Ft, depending on the cellar)—walk on in, or ring the bell if the cellar looks shut. Explore the less touristy side streets for higher-quality wines. Serious **tasting** takes place at the best-respected and largest of the lot: **Rákóczi Pince**, Kossuth tér 15 (tel. (47) 35 27 09), a 1.5km long system of 24 tunnels dug from volcanic rock in 1502. A jacket is a good idea down here, even in summer. **Wine-tastings** and **group tours** of the cellar are usually held on the hour. (English-speaking guides available July-Aug. 300Ft for a 30min. tour; 950Ft for the tour and 6-glass wine tasting. Open daily 10am-8pm.) The young **Tokaji Hímesudvar cellars**, Bem u. 2 (tel. 35 24 16), makes phenomenal Aszú wines and offers immense tastings (400-600Ft; open daily 9am-9pm).

Trains, Baross G. u. 18 (tel. (47) 35 20 20), puff to Miskolc (1hr., 302Ft), which connects Tokaj to the rest of the country. The train station sits 15 minutes southwest of town; with your back to the station, walk left along the railroad embankment until you reach an underpass, then turn left on Bajcsy-Zsilinszky u. At the Hotel Tokaj fork, stay on the left road. The only **bus** service is to local towns. **Tokaj Tours, Tourinform**, Serház u. 1 (tel./fax (47) 35 23 23), at Rákóczi u., arranges private and hotel rooms (for free) and organizes tours of the region and wine-tastings (open M-Sa 9am-5pm). *"Zimmer Frei"* and *"Szoba Kiadó"* signs abound—your best bet is to walk along Rákóczi u. and its side streets (singles about 1200Ft-1400Ft; doubles 2750Ft). **Graf Széchenyi István Students Hostel**, Bajcsy-Zsilinszky u. 15-17 (tel. (47) 35 23 55), between the train station and the center, is the best hotel deal around, with fresh, recently renovated doubles (3800Ft with bath) and sparse but clean quads (reception is usually gone for lunch; open July-Aug. only). **Makk-Marci Panzió-Pizzéria**, Liget Köz 1 (tel. (47) 35 23 36; fax 35 30 88), facing Rákóczi u., has relaxing, bright rooms with bath. (Singles 2688Ft; doubles 3808Ft; triples 5600Ft; quads 6496Ft. Breakfast included. Reserve ahead.) The mega-center **Camping Tisza**, on the right as you cross the river, rents out river-side campsites (a.k.a. mosquito breeding grounds; tents 470Ft per person). **Gödör**, in the Tisza Vízisport complex, cooks up heavy meat dishes and some veggie ones (meals 200-400Ft; open M-F 9am-11pm, Sa-Su 7am-11pm).

■ Kecskemét

Nestled amid vineyards, fruit trees, and sandy *puszta* (plains), Kecskemét (CATCH-keh-MATE) lures tourists with its salmon-colored center and famous *barack pálinka* (apricot brandy). The **town hall,** Kossuth tér 1, built in 1897 during the height of the Hungarian Art Nouveau movement, is Kossuth tér's most impressive building. (Tours by appointment daily 7:30am-6pm; call (76) 48 36 83 and ask for Földi Margit. 50Ft, in English 300Ft.) You can brave the rickety wooden floors and wobbly stairs of the Neoclassical **Roman Catholic Big Church** on Széchenyi tér for a superb view at the top of the tower (tower open June-Aug. daily 10am-8pm; 200Ft). The Art Nouveau **Kecskeméti Képtár** (Gallery), Rákóczi út 1, displays the works of local artists (open Tu-Su 10am-5pm; 100Ft, students 60Ft, Th free). The **Katona József Színház** (Theater), Katona tér 5 (tel. (76) 48 32 83), not only puts on excellent drama, but is located in a magnificent 1896 building (off-season operettas 400-500Ft).

Trains run from the station at the end of Rákóczi út (tel. (76) 32 24 60) to Budapest (1¼hr., 770Ft). The station around the corner (tel. (76) 32 17 77) sends **buses** to Budapest (1½hr., 710Ft), Eger (2½hr., 1290Ft), and Pécs (5hr., 1507Ft). **Local buses** head into town from the train station (63Ft). **Tourinform,** Kossuth tér 1 (tel./fax (76) 48 10 65), in the town hall, has maps and lots of info on the *puszta*. (Open in summer M-F 8am-6pm, Sa-Su 9am-1pm; off-season M-F 8am-5pm, Sa 9am-1pm.) **Cooptourist,** Kettemplom kőz 9 (tel. (76) 48 14 72), rents singles and doubles (around 2000Ft for two people). **Hotel Pálma,** Arany János u. 3 (tel./fax (76) 32 10 45), is as close to the heart of the city as possible, with newly redone and super-clean rooms (dorm-style triples; one person 2400Ft, two 4200Ft, three 4900Ft). **Caissa Panzió,** Gyenes tér 18 (tel. (76) 48 16 85), has small but clean and modern rooms (singles 2200-3400Ft; doubles 2700-4200Ft; triples 4800Ft; curfew 10pm; call ahead). Enjoy Greek and Hungarian food at **Göröd Udvar Étterem,** Hornyik J. 1 (veggie dishes 550Ft; open daily 11am-11pm). **Kilele Music Cafe,** Jokai 34, offers a mellow good time (beer 160Ft; cover 100-150Ft; open M-F noon-2am, Sa 6pm-4am, Su 6pm-1am).

■ Szeged

Szeged straddles the Tisza River about 10km north of the Yugoslav border. The town's easygoing charm belies its status as Hungary's only planned city; after an 1879 flood wiped out the town, streets were laid out and lined with row after row of colorful neo-Renaissance and Art Nouveau buildings.

SIGHTS AND ENTERTAINMENT Street names recall the many cities which helped Szeged rebuild. Walk east to the river to find the **Móra Ferenc Múzeum,** Roosevelt tér 1/3, which boasts an exhibit of folk art from the 18th century to the present (open Tu-Su 10am-5pm; 100Ft, students 25Ft). On Dóm tér, the red brick **Fogadalmi Templom** (Votive Church) pierces the city's skyline with its twin 91m towers (open M-Sa 9am-6pm, Su 12:30-6pm; sometimes closes early). Beside the church is the 12th-century **Dömötör Torony** (Demetrius Tower). Smaller and brighter than the Votive Church is the 1778 **Palánki Szerb Templom** (Serbian Orthodox Church), across the street, home to 60 gilt-framed paintings (open whenever there's someone around to collect the 100Ft admission fee). At the corner of Hajnóczi u. and Jósika u. stands the beautiful and eclectic **Great Synagogue,** built in 1903. The building is used now mainly for concerts and memorials (open May-Sept. Su-F 9am-noon and 1-6pm; 100Ft, students 50Ft). The Szeged **Open-Air Theater Festival** (mid-July to mid-Aug.) is the country's largest outdoor theatrical festival. Traveling troupes perform folk dances, operas, and musicals in the amphitheater in Dóm tér. Tickets (400-1500Ft) are sold at Déak u. 28/30 (tel. (62) 47 14 66; fax 47 13 22).

PRACTICAL INFO, ACCOMMODATIONS, AND FOOD Trains chug to Belgrade (6hr., 4427Ft) and Budapest (2½hr., 1215Ft). **Buses** leave the terminal on Mars tér just west of Londoni krt., a 10-minute walk west of the center, for Budapest (3½hr.,

1450Ft) and Pécs (4½hr., 1510Ft). **Tourinform,** Victor Hugo út. 1 (tel./fax (62) 31 17 11), has free maps and heaps of info on the town and region (open M-F 9am-8pm, Sa 9am-2pm). Ask about private rooms and other budget accommodations. **Fortuna Panzió,** Pécskai u. 8 (tel./fax (62) 43 15 85), across Belvárosihíd bridge to the northeast, is a bit tricky to find but boasts spacious rooms and sparkling bathrooms (doubles with bath and TV 4500Ft). **Apáthy Kollégium,** Apáthy u. 4 (tel. (62) 45 40 00; fax 45 57 29), is a centrally located dorm (singles 2300Ft; doubles 3000Ft; triples 3800Ft; open July-Aug.). **Napfény,** Dorozsmai u. 4 (tel./fax (62) 42 18 00), is a hotel and campground. Take tram 1 to the last stop, climb the overpass behind you, and walk 10 minutes (300Ft per person, 200Ft per tent; bungalow doubles 1900F).

Aranykorona Étterem, Déak Ferenc u. 29, at the corner of Victor Hugo u., offers mouth-watering Hungarian dishes that are the cheapest of their kind. (Red wine and fish with tomato sauce 370Ft. Open M-Th 11am-11pm, F-Sa 11am-2am, Su 11am-10pm.) **Roosevelt téri Halászcsárda (Sótartá Étterem),** Roosevelt tér 14, on the square's southeast side next to the river, is the place to sample Szeged's famous spicy fish soup (open daily 11am-11pm).

■ Pécs

At the southern foot of the Mecsek mountain range, Pécs (PAY-ts) offers an incomparably scenic view of hilly Transdanubia. One of the largest towns of southwest Hungary, Pécs' downtown walkways teem with local college students and tourists. With a 2000-year history, there is much to see indeed, and the monuments of the city reveal a rich legacy of Roman, Ottoman, and Hapsburg influence.

SIGHTS AND ENTERTAINMENT Ornate buildings surround Széchenyi tér, centered on the **Gazi Khasim Pase Belvarosi templom** (Gazi Khasim Pasha Inner City Parish Church), a converted Turkish mosque. On the southwest corner of the square, the **Patika Múzeum** (Pharmacy Museum), Apáca u. 1, tries to convince visitors that leeches and blood-letting were sound techniques to cure anything from stubbornness to political incorrectness (open M-F 8am-4:30pm; free). Stroll along Ferencesek u. until you reach the quasi-Baroque **Franciscan Church;** nearby, Szent István tér is surrounded by trees and offers a welcome rest during a hot summer afternoon. On the square's east side, 4th-century **Roman ruins** slowly crumble in the shadow of the Romanesque **cathedral,** Pécs's centerpiece. Below the ruins lie the largest known burial site in Hungary (open Tu-Su 10am-6pm). East of the Old Town, **Várostörténeti Múzeum** (History Museum), Felsőmalom u. 9, chronicles Pécs's subordination under foreign rule from the Middle Ages through the 20th century. The exhibit on the local industrial revolution showcases Pécs determination to turn out elegance—porcelain, musical instruments, and champagne—in an age of conveyor belts and smokestacks (open Tu-Su 10am-4pm; 120Ft, students 50Ft).

Nightlife centers around Széchenyi tér, especially on the first two blocks of Király u. **Rózsakert Sörkert/Rosengarten Biergarten,** Janus Pannonius u., east of the cathedral, features outdoor live music in an outdoor setting (open daily 11am-11pm). **Kioszk Eszpresszo,** opposite Janus Pannonius u. 1 next to Dóm tér, is a popular cafe/beer garden with a mixed gay and straight crowd (open daily 11am-11:45pm).

PRACTICAL INFO, ACCOMMODATIONS, AND FOOD Pécs sits on the knees of the Mecsek mountain range; north and south correspond to up and down the hillside. The Pécs **train station** is located just beyond the bottom of the city's historic district, a 10-minute bus ride (30, 32, or 33) from the center of town. **Trains** (tel. (72) 31 24 43) run to Budapest (3½hr., 1330Ft, plus 250Ft for IC trains). The middle of the inner city is **Széchenyi tér,** where most of the tourist offices are located. **Tourinform,** Széchenyi tér 9 (tel. (72) 21 33 15), sells tourist maps (250Ft) and an informative historical guide (60Ft; open daily June-Aug. 9am-2pm; Sept.-May 8am-4pm).

Private rooms can be arranged at the Old Town's tourist offices. For stays of less than three nights, a 30% fee is added to the first night's price. **Mecsek Tours,** Széchenyi tér 1 (tel. (72) 21 33 00; fax 21 20 44), seeks out singles (1200Ft) and doubles

(1800Ft). **Szent Mór Kollégium,** 48-es tér 4 (tel. (72) 31 11 99), offers doubles in a gorgeous old building for 800Ft; take bus 21 to "48-es tér." From the train station, take bus 34 to **Hotel-Camping Mandulás,** Angyán János u. 2 (tel. (72) 31 59 81), in the hills above the city. The one-star hotel has tent sites (500Ft per person, 450Ft per tent), three-bed bungalows (3600Ft.), and doubles with shower (4000Ft) at the entrance to **hiking trails** into the Mecsek Hills (open mid-Apr. to mid-Oct.).

Low prices, choice beers, and local students lurk in a cellar at **Liceum Söröző,** off Király u. 35 opposite the Liceum church (meals from 400Ft; open M-Th 11am-10pm, F-Sa until 11pm). **Caflisch Cukrászda Cafe,** Király u. 32, is possibly the best and trendiest cafe in town (pastries from 60Ft; open Su-Th 8am-10pm, F-Sa 8am-11pm).

■ Lake Balaton

Shallow Lake Balaton is the largest lake in Central Europe and one of the region's most coveted vacation spots. Villas first sprouted along its shores during the Roman Empire, and in the 1860s, rail connections transformed the lake into a favored summer playground. Be aware, though, that storms roll in over Lake Balaton quickly. Amber lights on tall buildings give storm warnings: 60 revolutions per minute means swimmers must be within 100m of shore.

Siófok The largest town on Lake Balaton, Siófok attracts countless surf-starved Germans and Austrians each summer. All attractions pale in comparison with the **Strand,** which is not a beach but a series of park-like lawns running to the concrete shoreline. There are public and private sections, with some private spots charging at least 100Ft per person. Nightclubs of varying seediness line the lakefront, while amphibious boppers revel on the **Disco Boat** from July 9 to August 21 (leaves harbor at 9:30pm; 750Ft). If you're out of Dramamine, dance at **Flört Disco,** Sió u. 4 (open nightly 9pm-5am), or the **Kajman Pub Disco,** Fő u. 212 (cover 400Ft; open nightly 10pm-4am).

The **bus** and **train stations** are next to each other off the town's main drag, **Fő u.** A *gyorsjárat* (fast bus) leaves for Budapest six times a day (2½hr., 927Ft), while trains go every hour (2½hr., 684Ft). **Tourinform** (tel. (84) 31 53 55), inside the base of the water tower at Fő u. 41, will find rooms for free (open July-Aug. M-Sa 8am-8pm, Su 8am-1pm; Sept.-June M-F 9am-4pm). **IBUSZ,** Fő u. 174 (tel. (84) 31 10 66), has doubles for 3000Ft in July and August. (30% surcharge for stays of less than 4 nights. Open June-Aug. M-Sa 8am-6pm, Su 9am-1pm; Sept.-May M-F 8am-4pm.) **Tuja Panzió,** Szent László u. 74 (tel. (84) 31 49 96), has well-equipped rooms with shower and TV (3000Ft per person; less off-season). **Hunguest Hotel Azúr,** Vitorlás u. 11 (tel. (84) 31 20 33 or 31 22 59; fax 31 21 05), off Erkel Ferenc u., offers bright doubles with bathrooms (2400Ft). The **Csárdás Restaurant,** Fő u. 105, offers Hungarian dishes in a friendly atmosphere (600-900Ft; open daily 11am-11pm).

Keszthely The pride of **Keszthely** (KESS-tay), on the southern tip of Balaton, is the Helikon Kastélymúzeum, inside the **Festetics Kastély** (palace; open Tu-Su 9am-6pm; 700Ft, students 500Ft). Built by a powerful Austro-Hungarian family, the palace contains 360 rooms (only the central wing is open to tourists) full of artwork and period furniture, including the 90,000-volume **Helikon Library.** Concerts are held in the mirrored ballroom hall during summer. The surrounding **English park** is a vast and well-kept strolling ground. Keszthely's **strand** is rocky and swampy, but still manages to attract a crowd. The **train station** and **bus terminal** are adjacent to each other, near the water. **Trains** head to Budapest (3hr., 920Ft), while **buses** zip to Pécs (3hr., 650Ft). To reach the main square, Fő tér, walk up Mátirok u. and turn right on Kossuth Lajos u. **IBUSZ,** Kossuth Lajos 27 (tel. (83) 31 29 51), finds doubles. (2500Ft. Open June-Aug. M-F 8am-8pm, Sa 9am-6pm, Su 9am-1pm; Sept.-May M-Th 8am-4pm, F 8am-3pm.) **Mr. Atila Lukic's** cozy *panzió*, Jókai Mór u. 16 (tel. 31 12 32), has attractive rooms (2500Ft per person). **Castrum Camping,** Móra Ferenc u. 48 (tel. 31 21 20), has tent sites with all the amenities (920Ft per person, students 720Ft; 480Ft per tent; open May-Sept.). **Oázis-Reform Restaurant,** Rákóczi tér 3, serves tasty, fresh vegetarian dishes including several Hungarian specialties (open daily 11am-8pm).

Tihany With its lush vegetation, luxurious homes, and great views, **Tihany** (TEE-hawn) is the pearl of Lake Balaton. Lording over the peninsula, the 1754 **Benedictine Abbey** features Baroque altars, pulpit, and organ (open daily 9am-6pm; 140Ft; students 70Ft). Next door, an 18th-century monastery now houses the **Tihany Museum,** with psychedelic dreamscapes, colorized etchings, and Roman inscriptions (open Mar.-Oct. Tu-Su 10am-6pm; 80Ft). The promenade behind the church leads to the **beach** (follow the "strand" signs; open daily 7am-7pm; 100Ft). Frequent **buses** pass by the beaches at both Tihany and the more popular Tihanyi-rév. If you're enchanted by the town, **Balatontourist,** Kossuth u. 12 (tel. (86) 44 85 19), arranges private rooms (2800-3800Ft; open M-Sa 8:30am-6:30pm, Su 8:30am-1pm).

■ Győr

Some of Hungary's finest 17th- and 18th-century buildings crowd Győr's inner city, and the occasional horse-drawn cart still plods through rush-hour traffic. The **city hall,** a few steps from the train station, is the most magnificent building in Győr. Most sights, however, lie within a rough triangle between Bécsi Kapu tér, Káptalandomb, and Széchenyi tér. Bécsi Kapu tér is the site of the yellow **Carmelite church** and the remains of a medieval **castle** built to defend Győr against the Turks. At the top of Káptalandomb is the **Székesegyház** (Episcopal Cathedral), originally built in 1030. Generations of embellishments have resulted in a hybrid of architectural styles. The miraculous **Weeping Madonna of Győr** in the altar in the north nave, brought from Ireland in the 1650s, is said to have spontaneously wept blood and tears for three hours on St. Patrick's Day, 1697. The **Kovács Margit Gyűjtemény** (Margit Kovács Museum), Rózsa Ferenc u. 1, just past Gutenberg tér on the left, is one of Győr's hidden treasures, displaying the artist's distinctive ceramic sculptures and tiles (open Tu-Su Mar.-Oct. 10am-6pm; Nov.-Feb. 10am-5pm; 80Ft, students 40Ft). The marketplace on the river erupts into a **bazaar** on Wednesday, Friday, and Saturday mornings.

From the station south of the inner city, **trains** roll to Budapest (2½hr., 800Ft) and Vienna (2hr., 4116Ft). **Buses** depart from the terminal beside the train station for Budapest (2½hr., 800Ft). Packed with free **maps** and brochures, the **Tourinform kiosk** at Árpád u. 32 (tel. (96) 31 17 71), one block north of the train station, also helps find accommodations (open M-Sa 8am-8pm, Su 9am-1pm). The English-speaking staff of **Hotel Szárnyaskerék,** Révai Miklós u. 5 (tel. 31 46 29), right outside the train station, rents clean doubles (3350Ft, with bath 5100Ft). The enthusiastic teenage waitstaff at **Sárkányluk** (Dragon's Hole), Arany János u. 27, runs a popular bistro that fills quickly (main courses 250-950Ft; open M-Sa 11am-9pm, Su 11am-3pm).

■ Sopron

With its soaring spires and winding cobblestone streets, the medieval quarter of Sopron (SHO-pron) feels decidedly German. In 1920, however, the Swabians of Ödenburg (as Sopron was then called) voted to remain part of Hungary instead of joining their linguistic brethren in Austria.

SIGHTS AND ENTERTAINMENT The **Tűz Torony** (Fire Tower), on the north side of Fő tér (the main square), consists of a 17th-century spire atop a 16th-century tower, sitting on a 12th-century base that straddles a Roman gate (open Tu-Sa 10am-6pm; 120Ft, students 60Ft). Across the square is the **Bencés Templom** (a.k.a. Goat Church), built in the 13th century with funds from a happy herder whose goats found gold. The **Chapter's Hall** in the small **monastery** next door is a room of textbook Gothic architecture enriched by 10 sculptures of human sins and recorded Gregorian chants (church and hall open daily 10am-noon and 2-5pm).

At Fő tér 8, the **Storno-ház** (Storno House) is the best museum in town. The Stornos were 19th-century Swiss-Italian restorers of monuments and cathedrals; their taste in churches is often less than impressive, but their home and personal collections of furniture and artwork are exquisite. (Open Tu-Su 10am-6pm. Compulsory pre-recorded tour; English fact sheet. 80Ft, students 40Ft.) For a brief but enchanting tour of Old Sopron, walk down Templom u. to the **Evangélikus Templom** (Evangelical Church) and admire the late Baroque interior, especially the organ. Return to Fő tér via Szent György u. and peek inside **Szent György Templom** (St. George's Cathedral); its interior is a lovely blend of Gothic and Baroque ornamentation.

PRACTICAL INFO, ACCOMMODATIONS, AND FOOD Frequent **trains** run to Budapest (3-4hr., 1300Ft), Győr (1hr., 500Ft), and Vienna (1hr., 2340Ft). The **bus station** is two blocks left of the center on Lackner Kristóf, and the train station is a 10-minute walk away from the city center on either Erszébet u. or Mátyás Király út, both off of Széchenyi tér. **Ciklámen Tourist,** Ógabona tér 8 (tel. (99) 31 20 40), offers maps and advice (in German or Hungarian) and finds private rooms (singles 1600Ft; doubles 2000Ft; open M-F 8am-4:30pm, Sa 8am-1pm). **Locomotiv Turist,** Új u. 1 (tel. (99) 31 11 11), near Fő tér, arranges singles (1800Ft) and doubles (3500Ft; open M-Sa 9am-5pm). **Talizmán Panzió,** Táncsics u. 15 (tel. (99) 31 16 20), offers small, tidy doubles with showers (but shared toilet) for 3000Ft. **Középiskolai Fiú Kollégium,** Erzsébet u. 9 (tel. (99) 31 12 60), off of Széchenyi tér in the city center, and its sister dorm, **Középiskolai Leány Kollégium,** Ferency János u. 60 (tel. (99) 31 43 66), to the right off Lackner Kristóf near the bus station, offer four-bed dorms (1204Ft per person, students 972Ft; open June 20-Aug. 20 and off-season weekends). **Lővér Campground** is at the south end of town on Kőszegi u. (tel. (99) 31 17 15; open Apr. 15-Oct. 15). **Várkerület Restaurant,** Várkerület 38 near Széchenyi tér, serves tasty *sertés pörkölt* (stews), home-made dumplings, and vegetarian entrees (450-630Ft; open daily 10am-midnight). **Julius Meinl grocery,** Várkerület 100-102, is one of the town's best-stocked shops (open M-F 6:30am-8pm, Sa 6:30am-3pm).

■ Near Sopron: Fertőd

Twenty-seven kilometers east of Sopron in tiny **Fertőd** stands the magnificent Baroque **Eszterházy Palace,** Bartók Béla u. 2 (tel. (99) 37 09 71). Miklós Eszterházy, known as Miklós the Sumptuous before he squandered his family's vast fortune, ordered the palace built in 1766 to hold his multi-day orgiastic feasts. (Open Tu-Su mid-Apr. to mid-Dec. 9am-5pm; mid-Dec. to mid-Apr. 9am-4pm. 600Ft, students 240Ft.) Josef Haydn composed and conducted here, and stellar concerts still resound within. **Buses** leave hourly for Fertőd from platform 11 of Sopron's Lackner Kristóf station (45min., 218Ft). They continue on to Győr every two hours (2hr., 498Ft). Book **rooms** in Fertőd with Ciklámen Tourist in Sopron.

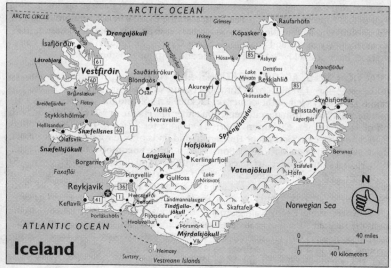

Iceland (Island)

US$1   = 70.35Ikr (Icelandic krónur)
CDN$1 = 46.33Ikr
UK£1 = 116.52Ikr
IR£1   = 101.84Ikr
AUS$1 = 41.57Ikr
NZ$1 = 35.97Ikr
SAR1 = 11.30Ikr
Country Code: 354

100Ikr =   US$1.42
100Ikr = CDN$2.16
100Ikr = UK£0.86
100Ikr =   IR£0.98
100Ikr = AUS$2.41
100Ikr = NZ$2.78
100Ikr = SAR8.85
International Dialing Prefix: 00

Perpetually rent asunder and forged anew by volcanoes, gorged and scarred by the glaciers that continue to advance tiny tendrils, and whipped by seemingly never-ending wind, rain, and snow, Iceland's landscape is uniquely warped and contorted. Nature, in its primeval fury, is the greatest attraction: desolate moonscapes, thundering waterfalls, spouting geysers, and smothering icecaps dominate the territory. Vegetation stands little chance, and the twisted shadows of the few existing trees provide mute evidence of the environment's brutality.

Surprisingly, humans have survived here and bent nature to their will. Geothermal power provides hot water and electricity to Iceland's settlements, roads are carved through the inhospitable terrain, and planes battle the whipping winds or wait for better weather. Yet much of Iceland remains in a rugged, unspoiled state; Reykjavík is Europe's least polluted capital city. Several major roads are not paved, and the combination of strict immigration laws and the interior's inaccessibility has kept Iceland's entire population to 272,000.

Much of the strong Viking heritage that inspired the world's first democracy still exists today, though Icelanders may not disembowel enemies over slander anymore. A language committee systematically banishes foreign words, and, instead of surnames, people follow the patronymic custom of identifying themselves as the sons or daughters of their fathers (the phone book is ordered by first name). The determination and work ethic that led Leif Ericsson to discover North America persists as well—all Icelandic children are expected to work summer jobs from the age of 13. The deep sense of community, strong economy, booming tourist industry, and pollution-free environment ensures one of the highest standards of living in the world.

GETTING THERE

Icelandair (tel. (800) 223-5500) flies to Reykjavík from Baltimore, Boston, Halifax, Ft. Lauderdale (not in summer), New York, and Orlando. The planes often continue to other European cities: Amsterdam, Copenhagen, Glasgow, Hamburg, London, Luxembourg, Oslo, Stockholm, and, in summer only, Frankfurt and Paris. Icelandair charges no extra airfare for travelers who stop over up to three days in the country—ask about their "Take-A-Break" special offers. **SAS** from Copenhagen and **Lufthansa** from Frankfurt also fly to Iceland.

The best way to feel the sea wind off Iceland's rugged shores is on the ferry *Norröna*, which circles the North Atlantic via Seyðisfjörður, East Iceland; Tórshavn in the Faroe Islands; Bergen, Norway; and Esbjerg, Denmark; for more information, see **East Iceland,** p. 498. **Eimskip** (tel. 525 7000) offers more expensive ferry rides on cargo ships from Reykjavík to Immingham, Rotterdam, and Hamburg.

GETTING AROUND

BUSES Iceland has no trains, and although flying is more comfortable, **buses** are often cheaper and offer a close-up look at the terrain. Within Iceland, one tour company, **BSÍ** (tel. 552 2300; fax 552 9973), in the Reykjavík bus terminal, coordinates all schedules and prices. Free schedules are available at hostels and tourist offices. The *Iceland 99* brochure lists selected bus schedules as well as tours and ferry routes; the *Leiðabók* lists all bus schedules and is an absolute must for anyone traveling the **Ring Road.** Land travel focuses on the 1411km **Highway I,** completed in 1974, which circles the island (only 30% paved—the going is slow). Plan on at least 10 days if you want to circle the country on the Ring Road; buses do it in several five- to nine-hour stages, with daily service on each leg from mid-June through August. Frequency drops dramatically off season. You can buy tickets in the stations (*umferðarmiðstöð*) in Reykjavík and Akureyri, or from the driver.

BSÍ sells passes that simplify bus travel greatly. The **Full Circle Passport** (14,600Ikr) allows you to circle the island at your own pace on the Ring Road (available mid-May to Sept.). You cannot change directions with the Full Circle Passport (you must continue clockwise or counter-clockwise around the country), though few travelers actually do backtrack along the long and arduous roads. For an additional 7000Ikr, the pass allows you to visit the Westfjords. If you don't complete the circle you can finish it on your next trip to Iceland. The **Omnibus Passport** (available all year) entitles you to a period of unlimited travel on all scheduled bus routes including non-Ring roads (1-week 16,400Ikr, 2-weeks 23,800Ikr, 3-weeks 31,200Ikr, 4-weeks 34,800Ikr). All passes entitle you to 10% discounts on many ferries, campgrounds, farms, *Hótel Edda* sleeping-bag accommodations, and guided bus tours. Unless you plan to go off the Ring Road two or three times or do some backtracking, the Full Circle passes are still best. During the off season, Omnibus passes prices drop because fewer routes are available. Keep in mind that neither pass covers the interior bus routes. BSÍ does offer a **Highland Pass** for hardy inland explorers (see **The Interior,** p. 500). Although they are often quite expensive, Iceland's guided bus tours are considered exceptional.

FLIGHTS The only quick way to travel in Iceland is by air; flights are on propeller planes and can have terrific views of glaciers, mountains, and lava fields—though brooding storm clouds often ruin the view. Planes can be cheaper than buses, but if you want to see the land, take the bus. **Flugleiðir** (the domestic service) flies between Reykjavík and major towns, **Flugfélag Norðurlands** out of Akureyri, and **Flugfélag Austurlands** among towns in the east. The **Air Rover,** sold at Icelandair offices, offers four stops from Reykjavík, Ísafjörður, Akureyri, Egilsstaðir, and the Vestmann Islands for 21,890Ikr, and the **Four Sector Icelandair Pass,** allows three destinations from Reykjavík (US$190). Both are also valid on the regional airlines. Another option is the **Air/Bus Rover** (fly one way, bus the other), offered by Icelandair and BSÍ Travel (June-Sept.; Reykjavík to Akureyri US$212). Icelandair offers some student discounts, including half-price on standby flights. The dicey weather can ground flights, so *do not* plan to fly back to Reykjavík the day before your plane leaves Iceland.

ICELAND

DRIVING, BIKING, AND HIKING Seeing the country by **car** (preferably 4-wheel-drive) allows you the most freedom. Car rental *(bílaleiga)* starts at about 5000Ikr per day and 30Ikr per km after the first 100km (ask about special package deals). Determined **hitchers** try the roads in summer, but sparse traffic and harsh weather exacerbate the inherent risks of hitching. Nevertheless, for those who last, the ride does come (easily between Reykjavík and Akureyri; harder in the east and the south). **Cycling** is becoming increasingly popular, but ferocious winds, driving rain, and non-existent road shoulders make the going difficult. You can put the bike on the bus for 500Ikr. **Trekking** is even more arduous; well-marked trails are rare, but several suitable areas await the truly ambitious (see **The Interior,** p. 500).

ESSENTIALS

Iceland's tourist season doesn't start until mid-June, and it isn't really high season until July, when the interior opens up, snow almost disappears, and all the bus lines are running. Things begin to wind down in mid-August and more or less come to a halt by the end of the month. Except for truly hard-core travelers, winter is not a time to visit; virtually all tourist services are closed, and the sky is dark all the time. In the summer, the sun dips below the horizon for a few hours each night, but it never gets really dark, and it's warm enough to camp and hike. An eye-shade may make sleeping easier. The Gulf Stream keeps temperatures moderate: it rarely gets hotter than 60°F (16°C) in summer, or dips below 20°F (-6°C) in winter. Bring watertight, windproof, lightweight clothing that can be layered. Capricious weather means a rain jacket, woolen sweaters, ski gloves, a wool hat, and sturdy shoes are *musts* at any time of year. Stormclouds are a common evil; it *will* rain, and the wind will howl unmercifully. Think of any trip outside of Reykjavík as a camping trip in cold weather. Iceland's geothermal springs make for an outdoor bathing culture, so pack a swimsuit. Film is expensive; bring plenty with you.

Tourist offices in large towns have schedules, maps, and brochures; check at hotel reception desks in smaller towns for local info. Must-haves are the free brochures *Around Iceland* (accommodation, restaurant, and museum listings for every town), *The Complete Iceland Map,* and the *Leiðabók* (with bus schedule). The Icelandic language has changed little from Old Norse. Icelandic has two extra letters: Þ (lowercase þ) as in *th*orn; Ð (lowercase ð) as in *th*em. All young people and most adults speak English proficiently, but knowing a few phrases may endear you to them.

Hello / Good morning	Góðan dag	GO-than die-in
Thank you	Takk fyrir	tahk FIH-rihr
Yes / No	Já / Nei	yow / nei
Excuse me	Afsakið	ahf-sahk-ith
Where is…?	Hvar er…?	hvahr air
How much does it cost?	Hvað kostar það?	hvath koh-star thath
Do you speak English?	Talar þú ensku?	tah-lar thoo EN-skoo
Can you help me please?	Getur þú hjálpað mér?	geh-tur thoo HYOWL-pohth myehr
Goodbye	Bless	bless
Help!	Hjálp!	Hyoulth

June 17 sees Independence Day festivals all over Iceland; the best are in Reykjavík. Other legal **holidays** in 1999, when most everything closes, include January 1, Easter (Apr. 1-5), Labor Day (May 1), Ascension Day (May 13), Whit Sunday and Monday (May 23-24), Bank Holiday Monday (Aug. 2), and Christmas (Dec. 24-26). Regular business hours are weekdays 9am to 5pm, 6pm in summer. **Banks** are usually open weekdays 9:15am to 4pm. Currency exchange commissions vary only slightly between banks (except at the airport); the government sets the rates. **Post offices** *(póstur)* are generally open weekdays 8:30am to 4:30pm, as are **telephone** *(sími)* offices, often in the same building. Post offices and hostels normally hold mail. Pay phones take 10 or 50Ikr pieces; local calls are 20Ikr. For the best prices and connections, make calls from the telephone offices; next best is a prepaid phone card. Before making any international call, you must deposit at least 10Ikr or insert a phonecard (available at the tourist office; 100 units for 500Ikr). To reach the **operator,** call 115, and for **information,** call 118. For **AT&T Direct** dial 800 9001; **MCI World-Phone** 800 9002; **Canada Direct** 800 9011; **New Zealand Direct** 800 9064; **Sprint Access** 800 9003; and **BT Direct** 800 9044. In case of **emergency,** dial 112. Iceland does not observe daylight savings time—the time is even with London in winter but an hour behind in summer.

ACCOMMODATIONS AND CAMPING Iceland has 28 **HI youth hostels,** invariably clean, with kitchens and common rooms. **HI hostels are uniformly priced** at 1050Ikr for members, 1350Ikr for non-members (sheet rental not included). Pick up the free *Hostelling in Iceland* brochure at tourist offices for a complete listing. **Sleeping-bag accommodations** *(svefnpokapláss),* widely available on farms, at summer hotels, and in guesthouses *(gistiheimili),* are viable and competitively priced (most often you get at least a mattress); the free *Around Iceland* and *Icelandic Farm Holidays* brochures list about 100 farms nationwide, though many of the farms are only accessible by car. Starting in early June, many schoolhouses become *Hótel Eddas,* which offer sleeping-bag accommodations from 900 to 1450Ikr (no kitchens, 10% discount for bus pass holders). Most of these places also offer breakfast and made-up beds (both *quite* expensive). Be warned: while staying in a tiny farm or hostel may be the highlight of your Iceland trip, the nearest bus may be 20km away and run once a week. Check the bus schedules carefully and try not to hurry through your trip. Many remote lodgings offer to pick up tourists at the nearest town for a small fee.

In cities and nature reserves, **camping** is permitted only at designated campsites. Outside of official sites, camping is free but discouraged; watch out for *Tjaldstæði bönnuð* (No Camping) signs, and *always* ask at the nearest farm before you pitch tent. Use gas burners; Iceland has no firewood, and it is illegal to burn the sparse vegetation. Always bring your waste with you to the nearest disposal. **Official campsites** (summer only) range from rocky fields with cold water taps to the sumptuous facilities in Reykjavík. Upper-crust sites may cost 500Ikr per person; more basic ones start at about 250Ikr. Many offer discounts for students and bus pass holders.

FOOD AND DRINK Icelandic cuisine celebrates animals you might normally envision in a zoo or at your local aquarium. Traditional foods include *lundar* (puffin), *rjúpa* (ptarmigan), and *selshreifar* (seal flippers). You can stick to fish and lamb, or bust out and try *svið* (singed and boiled sheep's head), *hrútspungur* (ram's testicles), or *hákarl* (rotten, years-old shark). Icelanders usually limit their consumption of these delicacies to a four-week period beginning in mid-January, preferring Italian, American, and Chinese food for much of the year. If you just can't get that last bite of puffin down, rejoice: Iceland has some of the purest water in Europe. Beer, legalized in 1989, costs 350-600Ikr at most pubs and is consumed mostly on weekends. The national drink is *Brennivín,* a type of schnapps known as "the Black Death." Alcohol is sold only in a few state-run outlets and in pubs and restaurants. The rarely-enforced drinking age is 20. Drunk driving is severely punished.

Grocery stores are the basic hunting grounds for travelers in Iceland; virtually every town has a **Kaupfélag** (cooperative store) and often also a fast-food kiosk. Gas stations (usually open from 9am until 10 or 11pm) sell snacks too. Grocery stores sometimes close for an hour at noon, especially outside Reykjavík. Larger towns commonly have supermarkets: **Bonus** and **Netto** are cheaper alternatives to the ubiquitous **Hagkaup.** Some supermarkets stay open until 11pm. Food is very expensive in Iceland; a *cheap* restaurant meal will cost at least 600Ikr. Tipping is not customary.

ICELAND

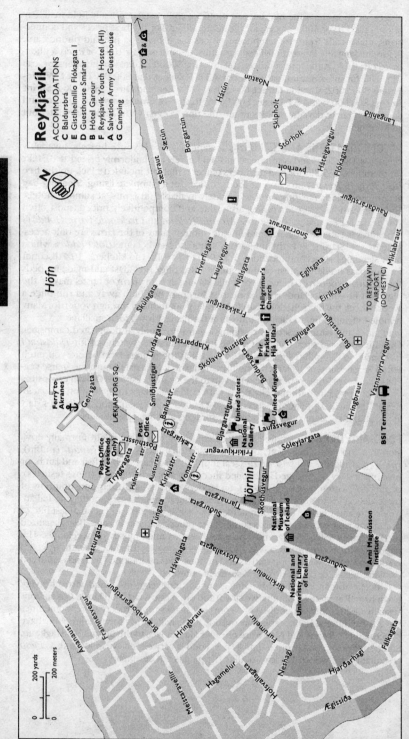

Reykjavik

ACCOMMODATIONS
C Baldursbrá
E Gistiheimilið Flókagata I
D Guesthouse Smárar
B Hotel Garður
F Reykjavik Youth Hostel (HI)
A Salvation Army Guesthouse
G Camping

TO F & G

N

Höfn

Hátún
Nóatún
Skipholt
Borgartún
Stórholt
Sætún
Háteigsvegur
Flókagata
Þverholt
Langahlíð
Raudarárstígur

Snorrabraut

Hverfisgata
Laugavegur
Njálsgata
Egilsgata
Eiriksgata
Hallgrímur's Church
Skúlagata
Lindargata
Frakkastígur
Freylugata
Skólavördustígur
Klapparstígur
Þrir
Frakkar
Hjá Úlfari
Baldursgata
Barónsstígur
Miklabraut

TO REYKJAVIK
AIRPORT
(DOMESTIC)

Geirsgata
Ferry to
Akranes
LÆKJARTORG SQ
Smidjustigur
Bankastr.
Bjargarstígur
United States
United Kingdom
Laufásvegur
Hringbraut
Vatnsmyrarvegur
BSI Terminal
Post Office
Post
Office
(Weekends Only)
Pósthússtr.
Lækjargata
National Gallery
Soleyjargata
Tryggvagata
Hafnar-
str.
Austurstr.
Kirkjustr.
Fríkirkjuvegur
Vesturgata
Tüngata
Vonarstr.
Skothúsvegur
Tjarnargata
Suðurgata
Tjörnin
Hávallagata
Ljósvallagata
National Museum
of Iceland
Árni Magnússon
Institute
Suðurgata
Bræðborgarstígur
Hringbraut
Birkimelur
National and
Univeristy Library
of Iceland
Framnesvegur
Ánanaust
Meistaravellir
Furumelur
Neshagi
Hagamelur
Hofsvallagata
Hjardarhagi
Fálkagata
Ægissíða

200 yards
200 meters
0
0

■ Reykjavík

"To ill purpose we crossed good land to settle this spit," lamented Reykjavík's founder, the Norwegian Ingólfur Arnarson, upon arriving in the desolate "Smoky Bay" in 874. Today, the "smoke" (geothermal steam) heats the houses of Iceland's capital, home to almost 40% of the country's population of 272,000. Reykjavík's charm more than makes up for its modest size. Bold modern architecture complements the backdrop of snow-dusted purple mountains, and the air is refreshingly sweet, thanks to the legions of youngsters sweeping the streets by 7am. Reykjavík's inhabitants pride themselves on their up-to-dateness: black-clad bohemians brood in cafes while weekend Vikings skateboard outside. On Friday nights, the *runtur,* the city's walking streets, fill with a bar-hopping, partying, and bottle-smashing crowd; breaking glass echoes at 3am, when the bars close and the night *really* begins. Inviting and virtually crime-free, Reykjavík's only weakness is the often blustery weather.

ORIENTATION AND PRACTICAL INFORMATION

Lækjartorg, the main square of old Reykjavík, sits on the northern side of a peninsula on Iceland's southwest coast. To the north, across the harbor, looms Mount Esja. South of Lækjartorg are the lake, the long-distance bus station, and the Reykjavík Airport on the shore. Extending east and west from Lækjartorg is the pedestrian thoroughfare which forms the axis of the city; the street name changes from **Austurstræti** in the west to **Bankastræti** to the east and finally to **Laugavegur.**

All international flights arrive at **Keflavík Airport,** 55km from Reykjavík. Forty-five minutes after each arrival, a "Flybus" (tel. 562 10 11; 650Ikr) shuttles passengers to the domestic, downtown **Reykjavík Airport** and the adjacent Hótel Loftleiðir, from which bus 1 (100Ikr) leaves every 30 minutes for Lækjartorg downtown. Outgoing Flybuses leave the Grand Hotel Reykjavík two and a half hours and Hótel Loftleiðir two hours before each departure from Keflavík; buses also leave the youth hostel at 4:45am and 1:15pm from June to August. Many flights depart before city buses run, so allow time for walking to the Flybus stops or book a cab in advance. It is reportedly quite easy to hitch from the airport. If purchasing an Omnibus Pass from **BSÍ Travel** (a 10-15min. walk south of the city, halfway to the airport), be aware that the Flybus fare is covered by the pass and can be refunded at either BSÍ Travel or the Reykjavík Excursions desk in the Hotel Loftleiðir (open 24hr.). This is not true of the Full Circle Passport. Pick up free copies of *What's On in Reykjavík* and *Around Reykjavík* almost anywhere.

Flights: International **Keflavík Airport** (see above). Icelandair is at Laugavegur 7 (info tel. 505 01 00; staffed M-F 9am-5pm). From **Domestic Reykjavík Airport,** just south of town, **Flugleiðir** (Icelandair; tel. 505 02 00) flies all over Iceland, Greenland, and the Faroe Islands, while **Íslandsflug** (tel. 570 80 90) flies to several small towns in Iceland, including the Vestmann Islands. Bus 1 or walk 15min. from town.

Buses: Umferðarmiðstöð (local), Vatnsmýrarvegur 10 (tel. 552 23 00), off Hringbraut near Reykjavík Airport. Terminal open 7:30am-11:30pm; tickets sold 7:30am-11pm. Upstairs, **BSÍ Travel** (in main BSÍ bus station) has passes and schedules, as well as bike rentals. Open June-Aug. Su-F 7:30am-7pm, Sa 7:30am-2pm.

Public Transportation: Strætisvagnar Reykjavíkur (SVR) (tel. 551 27 00) runs yellow city buses (120Ikr). Ask the driver for a free transfer ticket *(skiptimiði),* good for 30-45min. Kiosks at 4 terminals sell tickets; the 2 main ones are at Lækjartorg (in the building on the north side of the square) and at Hlemmur (in the building between Hverfisg. and Laugavegur at Rauðarárstígur). A map and schedule are printed in *Around Reykjavík;* the tourist office has maps of routes. Buses run every 20-30min. Buses run M-F 7am-7pm, Sa 7am-midnight, Su and holidays 10am-midnight. Some night buses (rare and tricky to find) with limited routes run until 4am on weekends.

Taxis: BSR, Skolatröð 18 (tel. 561 00 00). 24hr. service. The ride costs about 650Ikr from Lækjartorg to Hótel Loftleiðir, but rates are slightly higher at night.

Bike Rental: BSÍ Travel. Mountain bikes 1200Ikr per day, 7500Ikr per week. 50% off for Omnibus Passport holders; 20% for Full Circle Passport holders. Reservations required. The youth hostel also rents bikes (1000Ikr per day).

Hitchhiking: Those hitching take buses 15, 10, or 110 to the east edge of town, then stand on Vesturlandsvegur for the north, Suðurlandsvegur to go southeast.

Tourist Office: Upplýsingamiðstöð Ferðamála í Íslandi, Bankastr. 2 (tel. 562 30 45), at the end of a courtyard on the corner of Lækjartorg and Bankastr. Free maps and info galore. Open May 15-Sept. 15 daily 8:30am-7pm; Sept. 15-May 15 M-F 8:20am-6pm, Sa-Su noon-6pm. A small **tourist office** (tel. 563 20 05; http://www.arctic.is) is in the new city hall on Vonarstr. Open in summer M-F 8:30am-4:30pm, Sa-Su noon-6pm. Also a tiny branch at Keflavík Airport (tel. 421 55 51).

Budget Travel: Ferðaskrifstofa Stúdenta (tel. 561 56 56; fax 551 91 13), Hringbraut, next to National Museum. ISICs, rail, and bus passes. Open M-F 9am-5pm.

Embassies and Consulates: Canada, Suðurlandsbraut 10, 3rd fl. (tel. 568 08 20; fax 568 08 99; email kristbj@mmedia.is). Open M-F 8am-4pm. **Ireland,** Kringlan 7 (tel. 588 66 66; fax 588 65 64; email mottaka@chamber.is). Open M-F 8am-4pm. **South Africa,** Kringlan 7 (tel. 520 33 00; fax 520 33 99). Open M-F 9am-5pm. **U.K.,** Laufásvegur 31 (tel. 550 5100; fax 550 51 05). Open M-F 9am-noon; phones staffed until 4pm. **U.S.,** Laufásvegur 21 (tel. 562 91 00; fax 562 91 10; email amemb@iin.is). Open M-F 8am-12:30pm and 1:30-5pm; for visas, passports M, W, and F 9am-noon.

Currency Exchange: Banks open M-F 9:15am-4pm; many are located on Austurstr. and Laugavegur. Best rates at **Landsbanki Íslands** branches; no commission. Other banks: 90-100Ikr commission for cash, 165Ikr for traveler's checks. After hours, try the tourist office until 8pm or the **McDonald's** on Austurstr. until 11pm.

American Express: Úrval-Útsýn Travel, Lágmúli 4, P.O. Box 8650, 128 Reykjavík (tel. 569 93 00; fax 588 02 02). Open M-F 9am-5pm. Mail held for members. No wired money accepted.

Camping Equipment: Sport Leigan (tel. 551 30 72), next to the BSÍ station. Open M-Th 9am-6pm, F 9am-7pm, Sa 10am-3pm. **Skátabúðin,** Snorrabraut 60 (tel. 511 20 30). Try **Hagkaup** groceries for gas ovens, sleeping pads, and basic supplies.

Luggage Storage: At the HI hostel: 50Ikr per day, 300Ikr per week, even for nonguests. Also at the BSÍ terminal: 150Ikr per day, 400Ikr per week.

English Language Bookstore: Mál og Menning, Laugavegur 18 (tel. 552 42 40). Books on Iceland and a great selection of fiction, non-fiction, and poetry. Open daily 9am-11pm.

Gay/Lesbian Organizations: SAMTÖKIN 78, in a yellow house at Lindarg. 49 (tel. 552 85 39; fax 552 75 25). Small cafe, large library. Info office open M-F 11am-noon; library M and Th 8-11pm; coffeeshop open library hours and Sa 9:30pm-1am.

Disabled Services: Icelandic Association of the Disabled (tel. 581 4999).

Laundromat: Many hostels have arrangements with nearby cleaners. Otherwise, visit **Þvoið Sjálf,** Barónsstígur 3 (tel. 552 74 99), below Hverfisg. Wash 400Ikr, dry 400Ikr; 10% student discount. Open M-F 8am-7pm, Sa 10am-6pm.

Weather Conditions: 94.3FM 8am-10am (in summer Tu-Sa) for a report in English. Also try the tourist office at 562 30 45. For a recording, call 902 06 00, ext. 44.

Emergencies: tel. 112.

Police: tel. 569 90 00, after hours 369 90 11.

Crisis Lines: Women's Hotline (tel. 800 62 05) has English-speaking operators.

Pharmacies: Look for *apótek* signs. Call 551 88 88 for the current 24hr. pharmacy. **Reykjavík Apótek** Austurstraeti 16 (tel. 551 17 60), across from the central post office. **Lyfia Apótek,** Lágmúli 5 (tel. 533 23 00). Open daily 9am-midnight.

Medical Assistance: Borgarspítalinn (City Hospital), on Sléttuvegur (tel. 525 17 00; staffed 24hr.). Take bus 6, 7, 8, or 9. **The Medical Center,** Barónsstígur 47 (tel. 552 12 30). Open M-F 4pm-8am and on Sa-Su. Call 525 1000 from 8am-4pm.

Post Office: ÍSLANDSPÓSTUR, Pósthússtr. 5, at Austurstr. (tel. 550 70 10). *Poste Restante.* Open M-F 8am-4:30pm; June-Aug. also Sa 10am-2pm. **Postal Code:** 101.

Internet: National and University Library, across from the National Museum. Free for 1hr. intervals. Open June-Aug. M-F 9am-5pm, Sa 1-5pm; Sept.-May M-F 8:15am-7pm, Sa 10am-5pm.

Telephones: Landssiminn, opposite Kirkjustr. 8. Open M-F 9am-6pm.

ACCOMMODATIONS AND CAMPING

The city has dozens of guesthouses offering sleeping-bag accommodations. In most cases, this means you get a nice room with a nice bed, no sheets or blanket. A cheap hotel will cost no less than 5000Ikr; breakfast usually costs an extra 550-600Ikr, but most people take advantage of Iceland's cheap cereal and yogurt instead. Virtually all of Reykjavík's lodgings are packed from mid-June through August, so reserve in advance and ask about student discounts. Prices drop in the off season. The tourist office has loads of info on all accommodations.

Hjálpræðisherinn Gisti-og Sjómannaheimili (Salvation Army Guest and Seamen's Home), Kirkjustr. 2 (tel. 561 32 03), a pale yellow house in the center of town near Tjörnin (the pond). Filled with backpackers enjoying the spacious rooms and free soap and towels. Sleeping-bag accommodations 1300Ikr; singles 2600Ikr; doubles 3600Ikr. Sheets 300Ikr. Laundry wash and dry 750Ikr. Reception 7am-1am; use the doorbell after hours. It's always a struggle to get a bed; reserve in advance.

Reykjavík Youth Hostel (HI), Sundlaugavegur 34 (tel. 553 81 10; fax 588 92 01). Bus 5 from Lækjarg. to Sundlaugavegur. Strict no-shoe policy spares spiffy hardwood floors. Sells tourist card, Circle Passes. Rents bikes. Kitchen. Luggage storage 50Ikr per day, 300Ikr per week. Sleeping bags allowed; sheets 300Ikr. Reception 8am-midnight, Sa-Su closed 11am-4pm; ring bell after hours.

Baldursbrá, Laufásvegur 41 (tel. 552 66 46; fax 562 66 47; email heijfis@centrum.is), in a nice residential area 5-7min. from BSÍ. Well-stocked kitchen. Jacuzzi, sauna (100Ikr). Sleeping-bag accommodations 1600Ikr; singles 5000Ikr; doubles 7000Ikr.

Guesthouse Smárar, Snorrabraut 52 (tel. 562 33 30; fax 562 33 31). Spacious singles; doubles have refrigerators. TV, kitchen. Laundry 400Ikr. Sleeping-bag accommodations 1500Ikr; singles 3600Ikr; doubles 4900Ikr; triples 6400Ikr.

Gistihemlð Flókagata I, Flókag. 1 (tel. 552 11 55; fax 562 03 55; email guesthouse@skyrr.is), with an entrance on Snorrabraut. Bus 1 from BSÍ terminal. Spotless rooms with coffeemakers, tea bags, fridges. Sleeping-bag accommodations on attic mattresses 1300Ikr, with breakfast 1900Ikr; singles 4200Ikr; doubles 6400Ikr. Breakfast included. Reception 24hr.

Camping: Behind Sundlaugavegur Hostel (tel. 568 69 44). Bus 1 from the central BSÍ station to Hlemmur bus station; from there, bus 5 to the campsite. You can also take the Flybus, but it runs irregularly. Exceptional campsite. Kitchen and barbeque; grocery store nearby. Great geothermal swimming pool next door (200Ikr). 500Ikr per tent, 250Ikr per extra person; 2-bed cabins 2800Ikr. Showers 100Ikr. Laundry (wash 200Ikr; dry 100Ikr). Call ahead. Open May 15-Sept. 15.

FOOD

Hunting down affordable cuisine in Reykjavík can be quite a challenge, especially for those seeking typical Icelandic fare. A real experience of traditional foods (centered on seafood and lamb) will cost at least 1000Ikr. Supermarket giant **Hagkaup** has a branch at Laugavegur 59 (open M-F 9am-9pm, Sa 10am-6pm, Su noon-6pm). Other major chains: **Bonus,** at Faxafen 14 (open M-Th noon-6:30pm, F until 7:30pm, Sa 10am-4pm), and **10/11** (open daily 10am-11pm), which has the most central branch in town (on Austurstr. next to the post office). Smaller convenience stores throughout the city stay open until 10pm.

Restaurants

Jómfrúin, Laekjarg. 4. Danish restaurant serving filling open-faced sandwiches and Icelandic specialties for 750Ikr. Open daily 11am-10pm.

One Woman Restaurant, Laugavegur 20B, at the intersection with Klapparstígur. One flight up, this colorful, peaceful veggie restaurant is as soothing as its food. Different cuisine daily (F and Sa usually Pakistani and Indian). Su night hot buffet 900Ikr. Open M-F 11:30am-2pm and 6-10pm, Sa 11:30am-9pm, Su 6-10pm.

Grænn Kostur, Skólavörðustígur 8B, through the parking lot off Bergstaðstr. Vegetarian fare without sugar, yeast, or white flour. Dishes 395-550Ikr. Cake 280Ikr. Open M-Sa 11:30am-9pm, Su 1-11pm.

Gott Í Gogginn, Laugavegur 4, just after Bankastr. turns into Laugavegur. A cute and popular little take-out delicatessen with only 4 stools. Baguettes 330-450Ikr.

Devito's Pizza, in a parking lot off Rauðarastigur, opposite Hlemmur bus station. Take-out stand with great lunch special—9" pizza with 3 toppings and soda 450Ikr. Slices 230Ikr. Open M-Th 11:30am-midnight, F-Sa noon-5am, Su 1pm-midnight.

Cafes

The cafes of Reykjavík transform from quiet places for an early breakfast by day to boisterous coffeehouses and bars at night. Here you can try the light, creamy Icelandic ice cream, grab a quick lunch, enjoy a beer, or even have a cup of coffee. It's fun to arrive at a cafe early on a weekend night (9-10pm) and watch the place fill up around you. Pick up a copy of *Efst á Baugi* for its listings of live shows.

Kaffi Barinn, on Bergstatastr. near Laugavegur. Fantastic small cafe; largely local crowd. Always busy; *packed* on weekend nights, especially after the DJ shows up. Coffee 160-250Ikr, beer 500-600Ikr, cake 300Ikr, lunch sandwiches 300-650Ikr.

Cafe Frank, 1 Lækjarg. A nice mellow place with huge windows for people-watching. Coffee 170Ikr, beer 450Ikr, soup 300Ikr, sandwiches 350Ikr.

Sólon Íslandus, Bankastr. 7a. Students and literati congregate in this hip cafe/gallery. Occasional live jazz upstairs (1000Ikr cover). Coffee 200Ikr, beer 450-550Ikr, soup 450Ikr, children cake (made from chocolate) 300-420Ikr.

Cafe Paris, opposite Parliament. Yuppie-ish crowd. One of the few places where you can eat outside on a sunny day.

Kaffi Thomsen, Hafnarstr. 17. Young, informal crowd. DJ most weekend nights. Coffee 180Ikr, beer 350Ikr, huge slices of cake 390Ikr. Open 11am-1am, F-Sa till 3am.

SIGHTS AND ENTERTAINMENT

Hyperactive travelers might want to investigate the **Reykjavík Card,** which allows free public transportation and admission to many of the city's sights. You can buy the card at the tourist office (1-day 600Ikr, 2-day 800Ikr, 3-day 1000Ikr). Most travelers, however, simply use Reykjavik as a base for exploring Iceland's stunning landscape, and have no need for the card.

For a good view of Reykjavík, hike up Skólavörðustígur to **Hallgrímskirkja** (Hallgrímur's Church) which rises high above the city. The church's design was inspired by Iceland's ubiquitous basalt columns, but its steeple more closely resembles a rocket ship preparing to lift off. (Open in summer M-F 9am-6pm, Sa-Su 10am-6pm; in winter daily 10am-6pm. 200Ikr.) The **Þjóðminjasafn Íslands** (National Museum of Iceland), at Hringbraut and Suðurg. beside the university, should re-open by August 2000. The outdoor **Laugardalslaug,** on Sundlaugavegur next to the campground, is the largest of Reykjavík's geothermally heated pools (open M-F 6:45am-10pm, Sa-Su 8am-10pm; 200Ikr). The **Ásmundur Sveinsson Sculpture Museum,** Sigtún, celebrates Sveinsson's huge concrete monuments to the working man (open daily June-Sept. 10am-4pm; Oct.-Apr. 1-4pm; 200Ikr). For a relaxing break, lounge on one of the benches next to **Tjörnin** (the pond) in the center of the old city.

On the east shore of the pond, the bright **Listasafn Íslands** (National Gallery of Iceland), at Fríkirkjuvegur 7 (entrance on Skálholtsstígur), shows Icelandic paintings and hosts international exhibits. The building itself, a stunning construction of glass, marble and stainless steel, outdoes the paintings inside (open Tu-Su 11am-5pm; 300Ikr). The **Árbaer Open-Air Folk Museum** depicts life in Iceland through the ages. Take bus 10 or 110 (open Tu-F 9am-5pm, Sa-Su 10am-6pm; 300Ikr, students 150Ikr). Well-marked trails lead to the salmon-filled Elliðaár river.

If you follow the river to **Lake Elliðavatn,** you will find **Heiðmörk reserve,** a popular picnic spot and photo stop. On a sunny, warm, and non-windy day (it could happen), **Viðey Island** provides an excellent opportunity for hiking and picnicking. The island has been inhabited since the 10th century and boasts Iceland's second-oldest church. Ferries run to the island regularly.

If you have the idea that Icelanders are austere and staid people, visit as the work week winds down. Reykjavík nightlife breaks out during the Friday night *runtur,* as alcohol and music flow in bars and clubs around the city. Unfortunately, a fat wad of *krónur* is needed; cover charges run 500 to 1000Ikr, and beers can cost 550Ikr. The city's cafes are the hottest nightspots, though Reykjavík has its fair share of pubs and discos as well. **22,** Laugavegur 22, is an artsy hangout that attracts a large gay crowd on weekends with its upstairs disco (open daily noon-1am, F-Sa until 3am). **Gaukur á Stöng,** Tryggvag. 22, is Iceland's first pub and has live music every night at 11pm; at midnight serves sandwiches on weekends (food served until 10pm; open Su-Th 6pm-1am, F-Sa until 3am). A younger punk crowd jams at **Bióbarinn,** Klapparstig 26, on the corner of Hverfisg. (open daily 4pm-1am, F-Sa until 3am).

■ Near Reykjavík

Some of Iceland's stellar attractions lie within an hour or two from downtown Reykjavík. BSÍ runs many tours of the area; the "Golden Circle" guided bus tour departs from Hotel Lofteiðir in Reykjavík daily at 9am (May-Sept.) for an eight hour tour of Hveragerði, Kerið, Skálholt, Geysir, Gullfoss, and Þingvellir National Park (4800Ikr); book ahead with Reykjavík Excursions (tel. 562 1011). Scheduled buses can also get you around.

Þingvellir National Park, 50km east of Reykjavík, commemorates the world's first democracy and Iceland's ancient parliament, the Alþing. For almost nine centuries, Icelanders gathered once a year in the shadow of **Lögberg** (Law Rock) to discuss matters of blood, money, and justice. The geology of the area is equally interesting. Straddling the junction of the European and North American tectonic plates, the park spreads 2cm apart every year, and massive rifts abound. The river Öxará slices through the lumpy lava fields and jagged fissures on its way to the **Drekkingarhylur** (Drowning Pool), where convicted witches were drowned, and to **Lake Þingvallavatn,** the largest lake in Iceland. The river, according to legend, portends doom by changing into blood, and changes mysteriously into wine for one hour every year. Buses run daily from Reykjavík to Þingvellir (May 15-Sept. 15 at 1:30pm, returning at 5pm; one-way 570Ikr). The **tourist office** (tel. 482 26 60), a 20-minute walk north, sells a brochure and hiking map for 100Ikr (open in summer daily 8:30am-8pm). **Campgrounds** are located by the info center and the lake (450Ikr per person; no showers); the grounds farther north are cheaper but have no bathrooms (300Ikr).

The bus from Reykjavík traverses lush green valleys and bright red clay paths to **Geysir,** a favorite attraction. The Geysir area is a rocky, rugged tundra, with steaming pools of hot water every few meters. Most merely bubble, and the Geysir itself, etymological parent of geysers and one of the world's largest (the spray used to reach 80m high), now has to be induced to erupt with large quantities of soap, which breaks the surface tension. Eruptions are announced in the papers and at tourist offices. Just a few steps away, the smaller **Strokkur** makes up for its size with the energetic frequency of its eruptions (every 5-10min.). Look for the water beginning to swell, and then take cover. You can also find azure and rust-colored boiling mud baths near the geysers—but at over 120°C they're too hot for a dip. Across the road, **Hotel Geysir** (tel. 486 89 15; fax 486 87 15) has sleeping-bag accommodations and a pool with a panoramic view of the valley (650Ikr; sleeping-bag doubles 2800Ikr; singles 3100Ikr; doubles 4300Ikr). The hotel also runs the nearby **campsite,** where falling water serenades you on a soft, grassy field (350Ikr per person; bus pass discounts). A **tourist shop,** which runs a snack bar, grocery store, gas station, and bus stop, sells all the supplies you'll need (open daily 10am-7pm).

Nine kilometers further along on the same road roars the torrential **Gullfoss** (Golden Falls), named for the hue the fall acquires as it carries mud downstream. The glacial river drops 30m in two stages through a gorge, sending billowing mist high into the air—get as near as you dare, but bring raingear. Nearby, a small museum/info shack details the geology and history of the falls. **Buses** leave Reykjavík for Geysir (1210Ikr) and Gullfoss. (1290Ikr. May-June 15 daily at 9am; June 16-Aug. daily at 11:30am; Oct.-Apr. F-Sa at 9am. They return from Gullfoss May-June 15 at 12:45pm, June 16-Aug. at 12:45pm, from Geysir at 2:30pm year-round.)

VESTMANN ISLANDS
(VESTMANNAEYJAR)

Vaulting boldly and majestically from the icy blue depths of the North Atlantic, the precipitous black cliffs off the Vestmann Islands (named after the Irish slaves of the first Viking settlers) are the newest product of the volcanic fury that created Iceland. Forged in fire and baptized in the salty sea water, these 16 jagged monoliths fascinate visitors and welcome thousands of seabirds from all over the north. The newest island, Surtsey, was created during an underwater volcanic explosion in 1963. An annual eruption of another sort, the three-day *Þjódhátíð* (people's feast), held the first weekend in August, brings a hefty percentage of Reykjavík's livelier, drinkinger, dancinger population to the island's spanking new shores.

Heimaey The town of **Vestmannaeyjar**, on island of **Heimaey**, is one of the most important fishing ports in the country. In 1973, a fiery volcanic fault tore through the northern sector of the island, spewing forth glowing lava and hot ash in a five-month eruption. Though the encroaching lava threatened to close off the natural harbor, a bit of ingenuity saved the island's commercial viability, as a massive effort was undertaken to spray sea water on the advancing lava front, slowing and redirecting its flow. The harbor was preserved and actually improved. When the eruption of the volcano **Eldfell** finally ceased, the town was 20% smaller, and the island was 20% larger. Today, the town is rebuilt and modernized, framed by still-cooling lava and the black and green mountains that shelter its harbor, but the chilling remnants of buildings half-crushed by the lava still stand.

Hiking in the area is encouraged; the tourist office distributes a free map outlining hiking trails. The most spectacular spot is on the cliff's edge at **Há.** The view of the town below, the twin volcanic peaks across, and the snow-covered mainland afar is stunning. Both volcanic peaks await the intrepid hiker, but beware the biting winds that howl over their summits. If you head over to one of the country's two **aquariums** on Heidarvegur (near the gas station on the second floor), you can ogle at strange and wonderful creatures without getting your feet wet (open in summer daily 11am-5pm; 200Ikr).

Despite its insular reputation, getting to and from Vestmannaeyjar is relatively easy. Flugleiðir has daily flights from Reykjavík (round-trip from 6300Ikr). A slower but much cheaper option is the **ferry** (tel. 481 28 00), a potentially stomach-churning two- or three-hour ride that leaves from Þorlákshöfn. (Ferries leave daily at noon; Th, F, and Su also 7pm. 1500Ikr. Ferries return daily at 8:15am, Th, F, and Su also at 3:30pm.) Buses from Reykjavík connect to the dock and leave from the BSÍ terminal one hour before the ferry sails (550Ikr). Vestmannaeyjar's **tourist office** is at Vestmannabraut 38 (tel. 481 1271), in the Samvinnuferðir-Landsýn travel agency (open June-Sept. M-F 9am-5pm, Sa-Su 1-5pm). Ask there about island bus tours (2 per day, 1500Ikr) and boat tours (1500Ikr). The **HI hostel,** Faxastígur 38 (tel. 481 2915), is a typical Icelandic hostel: meticulously clean, warm and friendly, with a TV that gets one channel (sheets 300Ikr; open June to mid-Sept.). The **campground** (tel. 481 20 75), 10 minutes west of town on Dalvegur, near the golf course, has showers and cooking facilities (200Ikr per tent and per person). There are **K.A. supermarkets** on Strandvegur and on Vestvegur (open M-Sa 9am-7pm, Su 10am-6pm).

SNÆFELLSNES AND THE WEST FJORDS

Nowhere in Iceland is the awesome power of the Ice Age glaciers more vividly expressed than in the deeply striated northwest. Raking through the Greenland Sea like the curved talons of a hawk, the Snæfellsnes Peninsula and the Vestfirðir (West Fjords) are Iceland's most isolated coastal landscapes. With mossy, snow-covered cliffs rising high above the sea, the West Fjords allow little permanent settlement. Towns are few and far between, yet amid this desolation beats the heart of Iceland's vital fishing industry. At the tip of Snæfellsnes, the extinct glacier-capped volcano **Snæfellsjökull** provides the dramatic entrance to the mysterious, subterranean world of Verne's *Journey to the Center of the Earth.* To the north, **Breiðafjörður,** a bay of some thousand islands, separates Snæfellsnes from the **West Fjords,** whose ever-changing terrain lends a dramatic backdrop to glacier-carved valleys and waterfalls.

Snæfellsnes is served by **bus** (from Reykjavík daily 9am and 7pm), but the West Fjords are not as easily accessible. To reach Stykkishólmur (3hr., 2000Ikr, round-trip 3600Ikr), transfer buses near the end of the trip. To see Snæfellsjökull, disembark at Hellisandur (3½hr., 2250Ikr, round-trip 4000Ikr) or Ólafsvík (3¼hr., 2150Ikr, round-trip 3750Ikr). Ask at the Reykjavík tourist office about glacier **snowmobile** tours (about 4000Ikr). On the rare clear day, you can hike out for a view of the mountains of ice. Buses return daily to Reykjavík from Ólafsvík (daily at 5pm, M and Sa also 8am) and Stykkishólmur (Su-F 5:20pm, M and Sa also 8:20am). Be sure to check schedules in advance, and expect many hours on unpaved roads.

■ Stykkishólmur

Stykkishólmur, the peninsula's largest town and principal port, is a tiny but attractive fishing community with a bustling harbor. It is rich in folk history and home to the mysterious **Helgafell,** the Holy Mountain. According to legend, anyone who climbs this hill for the first time will be granted three wishes, as long as the wisher hikes silently, doesn't look back on the way up the hill, faces east while silently making the wishes (bring a compass), and never reveals them to anyone. The turn-off to Helgafell is 5km south of town off the main highway; a round-trip hike to the mountain takes at least four hours. Stykkishólmur's modern **church,** which resembles a giant praying mantis, sits on a hill above the town (open M-F 1-5pm; free). Summer concerts, held every second Monday (usually at 9pm; 500Ikr), take advantage of the church's great acoustics. The **Norwegian House,** Hafnarg. 5, hosts exhibits from local artists as well as historical displays (open June-Sept. daily 11am-5pm; 200Ikr). For a beautiful view of the sun's descent over the Breiðafjörður islands, take the short climb up to the top of **Súgandisey,** a former island now connected to the harbor by a narrow road.

The **tourist office,** Borgarbraut 4 (tel. 438 11 50), books private rooms in local houses and also runs a **campground** next door (230Ikr; bathrooms and showers on site; office open June-Aug. 20 10am-9pm). To get there, follow Aðalg. (the main street and continuation of the intercity road) 150m past the bus/gas station. Continue on Aðalg. around to the left, and then take another left up the hill on the dirt road to reach the **HI hostel,** Höfðag. 1. (Tel. 438 10 95. Sleeping bags allowed. 1050Ikr, non-members 1350Ikr. Sheets 250Ikr. Open June-Sept. Reserve ahead.) The hostel also runs a **fishing tour** (2000Ikr, 2½hr.)—hungry backpackers can fry their catch on the grill or use the kitchen. Feed yourself at the gas station grill, the **Stykkiskaup** super-market, or the bakery across from the gas station.

Your link to the West Fjords is the car-ferry *Baldur* (tel. 438 11 20), which chugs across the bay to the tiny settlement of **Brjánslækur,** to the south of the fjords. The ride is cheap, scenic, and generally calm. (June-Aug. leaves Stykkishólmur daily at 9am and 4pm, returns from Brjánslækur at 12:30pm and 7:30pm. 1400Ikr one way. Cars 1400-2100Ikr. Book in advance.) Buses run between Ísafjörður and Brjánslækur (3hr. each way, mid-June to Aug. M, W, Th, and Sa). The *Baldur* stops briefly (too short to disembark unless you want to wait for the later ferry) at the small, rocky island of **Flatey,** once home to a monastery where many of Iceland's great works of literature were composed. Today, a few beautifully preserved houses are clustered near a bird sanctuary of puffins, ducks, and Eider geese. The island's remote, magical aura draws summer residents from Reykjavík, but the winter population hovers around ten. For a truly relaxing 24 hours, spend a night on the island in the big blue farmhouse in "town," which offers sleeping bag accommodations 9100Ikr) and one double. The first floor of the farmhouse is **Cafe Vogur** (tel. 438 14 13) which runs the hostel, stocks food, and serves hearty meals.

ICELAND

■ Ísafjörður

In Ísafjörður, a sense of the frontier is particularly keen—the ocean stretches uninterrupted all the way to Greenland and the North Pole. In the highlands above the walls of the fjord that enclose the city, awesome vistas of snow-covered mountains and vast, glacial valleys extend on either side of the narrow road. Ísafjörður offers an array of outdoor activities and excursions; just pray for good weather. For organized ferry, fishing, hiking or birdwatching tours (or any combination thereof), contact **West Tours** (tel. 456 51 11 or 456 51 85) or the tourist office, or just pick up one of their brochures at the summer hotel. Boat tours last from 2-4 hours and cost about 3000Ikr. Ask about the excursion to the island Vigur.

Flugfélag Islands flies 2-3 times daily from Reykjavík (call the tourist office for details). All **buses** to Hólmavík (Tu, F, and in summer Su 11:45am; W and Sa 1:30pm; 2800Ikr) connect easily with buses to Reykjavík (5800Ikr) and Akureyri. The **tourist office**, Aðalstr. 7 (tel. 456 51 21), is in a big green house (open M-F 8am-6pm, Sa-Su 10am-2pm). The **Islandsbanki** at Hafnarstr. 1-3 has an **ATM**. The excellent **summer hotel** (tel. 456 44 85), the *Framhalosskói á Ísafirði*, on Skutulsfjarðarbraut (the main highway), has a helpful management and sleeping-bag accommodations ranging from a well-equipped double to a mattress on the floor (900-1500Ikr; reception 24hr.; open mid-June to Aug.). Next door, the hotel runs a small, quiet **campsite** (tel. 456 41 11 or 456 44 85; 450Ikr for 1 tent and 1 person; 10% bus pass discount). **Áslanger guesthouse** (tel. 456 38 68), which has no sign, is right in the town square on Hafnarstr., above a little flower shop (sleeping-bag accommodations 1500Ikr; singles 1900Ikr). **Gallery Pizza** is about 100Ikr more expensive—but has a touch more charm—than **Pizza 67**, which offers 9" pizzas from 830Ikr and burgers from 400Ikr. Both are on Hafnarstr. The **Hotel Ísafjörður** has a relatively cheap tourist menu (lunch 800-1000Ikr, dinner 1100-1700Ikr), and is located in the town square on Hafnarstr. **Samkaup camping** lies just north on Hafnerstr.

NORTH ICELAND (NORÐURLAND)

Dipping its toes into the Arctic Circle and basking in the glow of the midnight sun, North Iceland can have a surprisingly mild climate, thanks to well-placed mountains and warm southern currents. Wispy birch trees thrive amidst the volcanic melee of steam and stone.

■ Akureyri

Set against the snowy banks of Eyjafjörður, Akureyri's forested hills make for a soothing oasis amid otherwise rocky environs. Despite a size that would hardly make it a midsized town elsewhere in the world, Akureyri is the nerve center of northern Iceland. Galleries, museums, and coffee shops provide a dose of bohemian culture that contrasts with the region's hearty fishing tradition.

SIGHTS AND ENTERTAINMENT A stroll down **Aðalstræti** gives visitors a good introduction to the city's layout and character. The 3.6-hectare **Lystigarður Akureyrar botanical garden** flaunts Iceland's finest flora (open in summer M-F 8am-10pm; Sa-Su 9am-10pm; free). Traditional Icelandic music is performed in the **church** next to the museum (July-Aug. 28 Tu and Th 9pm; 600Ikr includes museum admission). Four **galleries** at Kaupvangsstr. 12 display contemporary Icelandic work (open Tu-F 2-6pm). If you're after a more strenuous afternoon, **Mt. Súlur** offers a spectacular view of the Eyjafjörður region; to access the 5km (one-way) trail, take any bus except 3a to Súluvegur and walk up the road 1.5km. **Kjarnaskógur,** 5km out of town on bus 3a, is ideal for jogging and picnicking. If your muscles need relaxing, take a dip in the **swimming pool**, Þingvallastr. 7, adjacent to a small amusement park replete with waterslides, electric cars, and mini-golf (open M-F 7am-9pm, Sa-Su 8am-6pm; 200Ikr).

In summer, free **jazz** concerts are held every Thursday night on Kaupvangsstr. After the show, musicians and fans move to **Cafe Karólína** to continue the merriment. Akureyi has an annual summer **festival of the arts** in July and August. Pick up a copy of the *Listasummar* brochure for dates and times. **Sjallinn**, Geislag. 14, with bars on three floors, is popular with beautiful people of all ages. At night, Akureyri's cafes turn into bars as well, most notably Cafe Karólína (see above), Góði Dátinn, 14 Geislag., and Ráðhlískaffi, in the town square.

PRACTICAL INFO, ACCOMMODATIONS, AND FOOD Flugfélag Íslands (tel. 461 22 00), flies to and from Reykjavík (one-way 4755Ikr), and a few times a week to Isafjöður (one-way 4855Ikr) and Grimsey (one-way 3655Ikr). The **bus station** is at Hafnarstr. 82 (tel. 462 44 42), in the same building as the tourist office. **FMN Saefari** (tel. 461 15 22) sends ferries to Grímsey from the neighboring village of Dalvik (M and Th at 11pm). A connecting bus leaves from the BSÍ station on Hafnarstr. at 10am, and the bus from Dalvik returns to Akureyri at 9:30pm (round-trip 3200Ikr). **Saevar** (tel. 852 22 11) runs boats to the island Hrísey from Árskógssandur (round-trip 500Ikr). The bus from Akureyri to Árskógssandur is 450Ikr each way. The **tourist office,** Hafnarstr. 82, (tel. 462 77 33; fax 461 18 17; email tourinfo@est.is), also serves as the BSÍ station. The English-speaking staff will book accommodations and sightseeing excursions (open daily 7:30am-8:30pm). If planning a trip to Akureyri, try to reserve a room in advance—believe it or not, the town is always busy. **Salka,** Skipg. 1 (tel. 461 23 40; fax 462 26 97), has spacious rooms filled with books, magazines, and games (singles 1900Ikr; doubles 3000Ikr; quads 5200Ikr). The **Farfuglah Youth Hostel (HI),** Storholt 1 (tel. 462 36 57 or 854 42 99; fax 461 45 29), is a bit far. From the tourist center, go through the heart of town and down Glerag.; Storholt is the right after the river. If you're tired, take a bus or call to see if the owner can pick you up. (Sleeping-bag accommodations 1050Ikr, non-members 1500Ikr; family-sized room 1000Ikr per person; doubles 4400Ikr. Breakfast 600Ikr. Sheets 250Ikr. Reception 8am-midnight.) The nearest **campsite** (tel. 462 33 79; fax 461 20 30) lies between the swimming pool and grocery store, across the street from the Hótel Edda (500Ikr per person; showers at the pool 160Ikr; laundry). Akureyri's food prices are steep— supermarkets are the best bet. **KEA Nettó,** at the intersection of Óseyri and Krossanesbraut, is the cheapest. The pedestrian street in the heart of town has snack kiosks and a **bakery.**

■ Near Akureyri: Hrísey, Grímsey, and Ósar

An island nestled inside a fjord, **Hrísey** is famous for its bird preserve, lush, green walking trails, and quarantined cattle (many come for the great steaks). In Hrísey, the restaurant **Brekka** (tel. 466 17 51; fax 466 30 51) also offers accommodations (sleeping-bag accommodations 1200Ikr; singles 2500Ikr; doubles 4400Ikr). Call **Saevar** (tel. 852 22 11) for ferry information. Besides its Arctic circle location, **Grímsey** is well-known for its bird population and, surprisingly enough, chess players. The American philanthropist Willard Fiske donated chess sets, money, and a library in the late 19th century, thereby establishing himself as something of the island's patron saint. **Básar Guesthouse** (tel. 467 31 03) offers meals and accommodations. **Ferries** run from Dalvik, near Akureyri; call **FMN Saefsari** (tel. 461 15 22) for info. Ask at the tourist office in Akureyri about hikes, river rafting, and other activities. A word of caution: the local fowl, having taken a cue from Hitchcock's *The Birds,* are in the habit of divebombing pedestrians. While these "attacks" present no real danger, a sturdy cap is advised. The **Sunset Youth Hostel (HI),** 531 Hvammstangi, Ósar Vatsnses (tel. 451 26 78; email osar@isholf.is), is an absolute gem. Located in a beautiful old house on a working farm in the middle of nowhere, it's well-situated for hikes into the hills or along the coast. If you give the owner, Knutur Óskarsson, advance notice, he'll be there to pick you up at the Viðilið gas station (tell the bus driver you need to get off there). The 20min. ride is an extra 1000Ikr, but well worth it.

■ Mývatn

The beauty and fury of Iceland's fiery past, present, and future explode into view in the area surrounding Mývatn, a shallow volcanic lake 100km east of Akureyri. Like þingvellir in the south, Mývatn straddles the juncture of European and American tectonic plates. Although the continental bump and grind has produced jagged fissures, bizarre lava formations, and boiling springs, the lake itself sits placidly amid the tumult. Its marshy shores are home to dozens of bird species, some rare, making the protected nesting area on the north-west side a bird-watcher's paradise. Directly east, the gnarled lava towers of **Dimmuborgir** disappear over the hills. Nearby, inside the lip of a deep fissure, the underground pool **Grjótagja** simmers with geothermal heat. To the north, plumes of steam rise from dark red lava fields, still warm from the most recent eruption, and an extremely odiferous, luminous **Blue Lagoon** surrounds the geothermal power plant. The surface at Vindbelgur on the south end of the lake is pockmarked by **pseudo-craters** created 2300 years ago when a lava flow was cooled by the lake water. The **Krafla** volcanic region, 13km from Reykjahlið, smolders from subterranean activity and holds the explosion crater **Víti** (Hell).

Two towns lie on the edge of lake Mývatn, **Reykjahlið** to the north and the smaller, southern **Skútustaðir**. On foot you'll need several days to appreciate the area's sights, but renting a bike will speed your progress. In Reykjahlið, **mountain bike rental** is located at the gas station in front of the Hótel Reynihlíð (700Ikr per ½day, 1100Ikr per day) or for the same prices at **Eldá** on route 1. In Reykjahlið the **tourist office** (tel. 464 4390) is about a kilometer from town down Hliðarvegur, next to the swimming pool (open June 6-Aug. 25 daily 9am-9pm). Sleeping-bag accommodations are available at the **Gistiheimilið Bjarg** (also called Eldá; tel. 464 42 20; 1400Ikr) with camping available on premises (450Ikr; free showers). **Hlið** (tel. 464 41 03), north past Hotel Reynihlíð at the edge of a lichen-stained lava flow, also offers camping (400Ikr) and sleeping-bag accommodations (1300Ikr; free showers; laundry 800Ikr). In Skútustaðir, **Sel Mývatn** (tel. 464 41 64; fax 464 4365) has sleeping-bag accommodations (1500Ikr) and **campsites** (400Ikr) with free showers (tel. 464 42 12).

EAST ICELAND (AUSTURLAND)

Crossing the inland road to East Iceland from Akureyri, you may think vegetation has made a dash for friendlier fjords. Flat planes of barren earth stretch their way to the horizon, and only jagged lava flows and hills of unbroken beige color the landscape. Suddenly, though, across gravel fields and blasted heaths, glacial rivers carve their way to the coast, where small ports and fishing villages dot the mighty fjords.

Egilsstaðir The main town in this area is landlocked Egilsstaðir, at the northern tip of the narrow lake **Lögurinn** (actually just a widening of the river Lagarfljót). The town is principally a transportation hub, and everything of use to the tourist is in the center. Buses depart from the **campground/tourist office** (tel. 471 23 20; open June-Aug. 9am-9pm). Shell out 450Ikr to camp. The campground also offers sleeping-bag accommodation in a small thatch-roofed **guesthouse** with warm, tidy rooms and a small kitchen (1000Ikr, 3500Ikr for the whole house). Across the parking lot from the campground, a **supermarket** stocks the basics (open M-Th 9am-6pm, F 9am-7pm, Sa 10am-4pm). Facing the supermarket, the gas station offers late-night **groceries** and a grill (open daily 8am-11:30pm).

Seyðisfjörður Cradled between the massive cliffs of a winding fjord lies Seyðisfjörður, 26km over a snowy mountain pass from Egilsstaðir. This tiny town gets very big on Thursdays when the **Norröna** (tel. 472 11 11; in Reykjavík 562 63 62), Iceland's only international car and passenger ferry, calls at the port. The ship departs on the same day (June-Aug.) for Tórshavn in the Faroe Islands (18hr., 14,640Ikr), and continues to Hanstholm, Denmark (32hr. from Tórshavn, 24,480Ikr). Those continuing on to Bergen, Norway (36hr., 20,280Ikr), have a three-day layover in the Faroe Islands. Students get a 25% discount on all trips. Find the **tourist office** at Vesturvegur 8 (tel. 472 15 51; open daily 2-6pm and Th 9am-noon). The excellent **HI Hostel** (tel. 472 1410; fax 472 1610; email thora@eldhorn.is) is in the mauve house on the north shore of the fjord and fills quickly on Wednesdays. **Snaefell** (tel. 472 1460; fax 472 1570), in the blue house on Austurvegur, has live music on Wednesday nights and is good for family stays. (Sleeping-bag accommodations 1250Ikr. Breakfast 500Ikr.) The **campground** next to the tourist office is 400Ikr per person.

SOUTHERN ICELAND (SUÐURLAND)

Throughout southern Iceland, a flat strip of land of varying width, formed from the silt of snow and glacial outwash, skirts the jagged cliffs and glaciers of the Icelandic interior. The occasional farm appears, lost in the sea of green and humbled by the towering cliffs. Blessed with good weather, the journey from Höfn to Selfoss is argu-ably the most stunning in Iceland.

■ Höfn

The small fishing town of **Höfn** (*HUH*-pin) spreads out on a flat spit of land a few kilo-meters in front of the icy tendrils of **Vatnajökull,** Europe's largest glacier. A good base for exploring Vatnajökull and the surrounding mountains, Höfn is the link between the south coast and the eastern fjords and the terminus for buses to and from Egilsstaðir (4-5hr., to Egilsstaðir mornings and returning afternoons, one-way 3700Ikr) and Reykjavík (8½hr., 1 per day, 4700Ikr). The **campsite** (tel. 478 1000; fax 478 19 01), on your left as you come into town (450Ikr per person; 10% bus pass dis-count), doubles as a **tourist info center** (open daily 7:30-11am and 3-10pm). Showers (150Ikr), washers (250Ikr), and dryers (300Ikr) are available. Most establishments are located on Víkurbraut and Hafnarbraut, which form a ring that passes by the harbor. The **HI youth hostel,** Hafnarbraut 8 (tel. 478 17 36), has a nice dining room but can be a bit claustrophobic (reception 7:30-11:30am and 5-11pm; open May-Sept.). There is a **pool** with hot tubs across the street (200Ikr). The **Gistihus Asgaður,** Ránarslóð 3 (tel. 478 13 65), has dorm-style sleeping-bag accommodations (1450Ikr) and sleeping-bag doubles (2900Ikr, both with breakfast), big lounges, a TV room, and laundry (400Ikr). If arriving the first weekend of July, get stuffed at the **Lobster Festival;** if not, head for the **grocery store** on the corner of Álaugareyjarvegur and Víkurbraut (open M-F 8am-10pm, Sa-Su 10am-10pm). **Osinn,** on Hafnarbraut past the intersec-tion with Víkurbraut, serves as a gas station, convenience store, and restaurant (9 in. pizza 550Ikr).

■ Skaftafell National Park

Perched between two icy tongues of the Vatnajökull ice cap are the numerous hiking paths and birch forests of **Skaftafell National Park.** The park is ideal for day-hikes, offering well-marked trails and spectacular views of the nearby glacier-capped moun-tains, the flat, fan-like alluvial plain which reaches toward the sea, and many cascad-ing waterfalls. The most impressive of these is **Svartifoss** (Black Falls), where gray glacial water pours out over vaulting basalt columns (1-2hr. round-trip by foot from the campground). To the east, **Sjónarnípa** (1hr. one-way) and **Gláma** (3hr. one-way) offer fantastic views of the glacier, and **Sjonarsker** is also worthy of a roll of film or two. A **map** with all the hiking routes is available at the info center (100Ikr, free for those staying at the campsite).

The park is just off Highway 1, three hours west of Höfn. Skaftafell becomes a swarming hive of frenzied activity as foreigners and Icelanders alike descend during July and the first half of August. Plan carefully, especially for the weekends. The often crowded **campsite** (tel. 478 16 27; 500Ikr per person; showers 200Ikr) serves as base for exploration and houses a well-stocked **info center** (open 8am-7pm and 9-10pm) and **restaurant/grocery store** (open 9am-10pm). Following the main road out of the campsite and then turning right for a 30-minute uphill hike brings you to the cozy farmhouse **Bolti** (tel. 478 16 26), which offers all the comforts of home and fantastic views over the vast sandy plains (sleeping-bag accommodations 1500Ikr; cabins 1500Ikr per person; dinner 1200Ikr).

Between Skaftafell and Höfn, buses stop for 20 minutes at the glacial lake **Jökulsár-lón,** where large chunks of calved glacial ice ground themselves in the shallow bay on their inexorable journey to the sea. Surreal, natural sculptures appear as the sun does its thing, and the blue "bergs" slowly melt away. **Fjölnir Torfason** (tel./fax 478 1065) offers boat tours from the lagoon (35-40min., 1200Ikr), but the timing only works if you take a bus from Höfn in the morning and continue on to **Kirkjubæjarklaustur** ("Klaustur" for short) to spend the night, as there is nowhere to sleep in Jökulsárlón. More convenient (and more expensive) is one of the full-day **glacier tours** of the area which leave from the info center in Höfn (6800-9200Ikr).

■ Vík in Mýrdalur

Vík, at the bottom of a green valley beneath the Mýrdalsjökull glacier, is Iceland's southernmost village. Its long black volcanic beach was hailed by *Island Magazine* as one of the world's top ten island beaches; sadly, the cold water precludes anything beyond toe-dipping. **Hiking** trails lead from Vík to the 120m cliffs above the ocean, as well as to inland waterfalls and views of the hulking glacier. Just offshore, the jagged rock columns of **Reynisdranger** tower above the churning water, where hundreds of birds (allegedly a band of magical "little people") make their homes. Further west, the natural rock arch of **Dyrhólaey** forms the southern tip of Iceland. **Mýrdaelingur Ltd** (tel. 487 13 34) leads tours to both in amphibious boats-on-wheels (1500Ikr for 1hr., 2500Ikr for 2hr.), as well as jeep tours into the mountains (2500Ikr).

The **tourist office** (tel. 487 13 95), inside the main service center/bus station, has info on the area and on private lodgings, as well as hiking maps. The **youth hostel (HI)** (tel. 487 1106; fax 487 13 03) is in the one-house locale of Reynisbrekka, 10km from the bus station, high up in a breathtaking valley. The owner is also the local police chief; his wife picks up guests at the bus station in the squad car. Breakfast is 600Ikr; guests are advised to bring their own food due to the hostel's inaccessibility. The newly opened **Hotel Lundi,** Víkurbrant 26 (tel. 487 12 12; fax 487 14 04), offers sleeping-bag accommodations in the kitchen-equipped annex next door (1200-1400Ikr). The **campground** (tel. 487 13 45), 200m from the bus station, has an airy indoor pagoda with a kitchen, big windows, and plenty of seats (400Ikr per person; showers 50Ikr; **hot tub** and shower 250Ikr; washing machine 300Ikr). Outside of hotels, the only place to eat in Vík is the restaurant/snack bar inside the bus station (open daily 9am-10pm). In summer, two **buses** shuttle daily between Reykjavík and Vík (3-4 hr., in winter 4 per week, 1800Ikr) and between Vík and Höfn (5-6 hr., in winter 3 per week, 2700Ikr).

THE INTERIOR

The abode of elves and outlaws, Iceland's interior is the most forbidding and desolate wilderness in Europe. It remains uninhabited to this day; the truly adventurous, or lost, can tramp for leagues without glimpsing another soul. No paved roads, bridges, or gas stations—just limitless stretches of sand rising into mountains, peaked with glaciers, which unleash tumbling waterfalls evolving into rivers. Four-wheel-drive buses trundle through the emptiness, plow through rivers, and are overtaken by jeeps sporting balloon-like tires and 9m antennas. At times obscured by swirling clouds of red dust, the landscape is so otherworldly that Apollo astronauts trained here for their moon rendezvous.

Iceland's most magnificent and popular hike is the four-day trek between the technicolor rhyolite mountains of **Landmannalaugar** and the green valley of **Þórsmörk** (Thor's Forest), both within easy striking distance of Reykjavík. Þórsmörk is packed with beer-guzzling crowds on weekends; it's advisable to decline any friendly offers to fight. **Kerlingarfjöll**, in the center of the island, is accessible by bus from the north. It offers summer skiing, good hikes, a great ice cave tour (1700Ikr), and a restaurant. If you can deal with the terrain's intensity, spending the night and returning on the next day's bus can be a good way to sample the eeriness of the moon-like interior. Reserve through BSÍ travel. Other attractions include the **Hekla** volcano, the mudfilled volcanic crater **Askja,** approachable from Mývatn, and, past Laudmannalaugar, the **Eldgjá** volcanic fissure.

You *must* pack all food and gas needed for your trip since there are *no* places to buy anything (Kerlingarfjöll excepted). Anyone driving in the interior should get a free copy of *Mountain Roads* (available at most tourist offices), which details all the "cans" and "cannots" of interior driving. Never venture out without a detailed map, an all-season sleeping bag, a sturdy windproof tent, and a compass.

The **Ferðafélag Íslands** (Icelandic Touring Club), Mörkinni 6, 108 Reykjavík (tel. 568 25 33; fax 568 25 35), organizes a range of interior tours or can help you plan your own (open M-F 9am-6pm). BSÍ runs a **guided tour** across the interior from Reykjavík to Lake Mývatn. (12hr., 2 per week, returning next morning, US$108, round-trip US$185. Reservations recommended.) BSÍ also organizes **self-guided trekking tours** of the interior for those with their own gear who want only to be dropped off and picked up several days later. If undertaking a truly hard-core interior journey, leave an itinerary with the **Association of Icelandic Rescue Teams,** Stangarhylur 1 (tel. 587 40 40; fax 587 40 10), in Reykjavík. Topographic maps of the entire interior are available from **Landmælingar Íslands** (the Iceland National Land Survey) at their Reykjavík store at Laugavegur 178 (tel. 533 40 00; fax 533 40 11; open M-F 9am-5pm).

Buses traverse interior routes daily in July and August (weather permitting); some are guided tours. Find listings in the ubiquitous *Iceland 99* brochure (Reykjavík to Akureyri or vice versa is about 5000Ikr). BSÍ Travel's (tel. 552 23 00) **Highland Pass** (19,700Ikr), consists of units used to "pay" for individually priced interior bus routes The pass, valid all summer, is a bad deal for a one-time visit, although there is a discount for Omnibus Pass holders.

From June to September 15, **buses** run from Reykjavík to Landmannalaugar (4½hr., 1 per day at 8:30am, returning at 2:30pm, round-trip 5800Ikr), Þórsmörk (3½hr., 1 per day at 8:30am, returning at 2:30pm, round-trip 4500Ikr), and Eldgjá passing through Landmannalaugar and continuing to Skaftafell (11hr., at 8:30am, returning from Skaftafell at 8am, 5100Ikr, discounts of around 30% for Full Circle pass holders).

Accommodations in the interior consist of campgrounds (600Ikr per person) and huts (sleeping bag accommodation 1200Ikr per person) run by **Ferðafélag Íslands** (see above). It can be a wonderfully twisted experience to get off the bus in the middle of nowhere) spend the night at one of the huts, then get on the next day's bus for no extra charge (Kerlingarfjöll is a worthwhile destination). Those hiking between Landmannalaugar and Þórsmörk will find tent sites and heated huts every 15km or so. Reservations are essential; contact the Ferðafélag Íslands office in Reykjavík. BSÍ Travel and the Reykjavík tourist office can also help with info on interior huts.

Ireland (Éire and Northern Ireland)

US$1 = IR£0.69 (Irish Pounds)
CDN$1 = IR£0.46
UK£1 = IR£0.89
AUS$1 = IR£0.41
NZ$1 = IR£0.35
SAR = IR£0.11

IR£1 = US$1.45
IR£1 = CDN$2.17
IR£1 = UK£1.12
IR£1 = AUS$2.44
IR£1 = NZ$2.85
IR£1 = SAR9.09

Country Code: Republic of Ireland: 353   International Dialing Prefix: 00
Northern Ireland (UK): 44, 08 from the Republic of Ireland

It can be hard to see Ireland through the mist of stereotypes that surrounds it even on the clearest of days. Much of the island is rural and deeply religious, although a developing urban culture has formed links to England and the Continent. Long hiking trails, roads, and cliff walks link a chain of windy, watery, spectacular scenery around the coast, while Dublin and Belfast diffuse their uniquely Irish modernity and sophistication to all in their orbits. Travelers visit the Republic of Ireland for its "trad" (traditional Irish) music and unique pub culture, as well as to study the language and literature. The Irish language lives in small, secluded areas known as *gaeltacht* as well as on road signs and in national publications.

Current tensions and conflicts in Ireland continue centuries-old disputes. Following the Reformation in England, the defiant Catholic population was ruthlessly suppressed by the English. The Potato Famine of the late 1840s resulted in the death or emigration of one third of the population, and the malicious negligence of the English government during those years exacerbated tensions. Turn of the century Fenians agitated passionately for home rule and fighting degenerated into civil war. The island was provisionally partitioned into the Irish Free State and Northern Ireland, which remained part of the United Kingdom. In 1949, the Free State officially proclaimed itself the Republic of Ireland (*Éire* in Irish), an independent country that still stakes a (nominal) territorial claim over the six counties that remain under British rule.

By the end of the 1960s, the tension in Northern Ireland between Catholic Nationalists, who considered themselves Irish, and Protestant Unionists, who considered themselves British, again erupted into violence. For years, the British and Irish governments' attempts to defuse the situation only led to sectarian attacks by paramilitaries on both sides of the debate. In the spring of 1998, the British and Irish governments formulated a peace accord, which was then adopted by popular vote. The agreement mandates full disarmament of paramilitary groups and recognizes Northern Ireland as remaining under British jurisdiction but links its long-term status to the will of the majority. While some problems remain, many in Ireland and around the world are optimistic about the prospects of a lasting peace under the new accord.

For more detailed coverage of Ireland, snag a copy of *Let's Go: Ireland 1999* or *Let's Go: Britain & Ireland 1999*.

GETTING THERE

Ferries journey between Britain and Ireland several times per day; fares vary depending on time of year, time of day, and type of boat. Adult single tickets usually range from IR£20 to IR£35, and a world of discount rates is waiting to be plundered. Bikes can usually be brought on board for no extra charge. Be aware that the **ferry** prices listed below exclude an IR£5 government travel tax. **Irish Ferries** (tel. (01) 661 05 11, holidays tel. (01) 661 05 33) sail between Rosslare Harbour and Pembroke, Wales (4hr.), and between Dublin and Holyhead, North Wales (3½hr.). Inquire about HI member discounts. **Stena Sealink ferries** (tel. (01) 204 77 77, 24hr. recorded info tel.

Ireland:
Republic of Ireland
and Northern Ireland

IRELAND

(01) 204 77 99) sail from Holyhead to Dún Laoghaire, a Dublin suburb, and serve Fishguard Harbor, South Wales, from Rosslare Harbour. **Cork-Swansea Ferries** (tel. (021) 27 11 66) run between Swansea, Wales, and Cork (10hr.). The **Hoverspeed SeaCat** (tel. (0345) 52 35 23, in the U.K. (0800) 55 17 43) leaves from Stranraer, Scotland for Belfast (1½hr.), and the **SuperSeaCat Ferry** sails from Liverpool, England to Dublin (4hr.). **Supabus** connects Dublin with London (where Supabus connects with Eurolines) in a combination bus/ferry deal (UK£10-25). Book tickets at any Bus Éireann office, Irish Ferries, Stena Line, or any Eurolines or National Express office in Britain (tel. (0990) 80 80 80).

En route to France? Sail between Cork and Roscoff, France with **Brittany Ferries,** Tourist House, 42 Grand Parade, Cork (tel. (021) 27 78 01; 14hr., IR£51-66). **Irish Ferries** also sail from Cork (tel. (021) 55 19 95) and Rosslare Harbour (tel. (053) 331 58) to Le Havre and Roscoff, France (20-22hr., IR£40-65). Eurailpasses grant passage (no seats) on ferry service between Rosslare and Cherbourg/Le Havre.

You can combine a ferry across the Irish Sea with a stopover on the Isle of Man, which also allows you to ferry into Dublin and ferry out of Belfast at no extra charge. The **Isle of Man Steam Packet Co.** (Douglas info tel. (01624) 64 56 45, reservations 66 16 61; fax 66 10 65; http://www.steam-packet.com) uses Heysham and Liverpool as its principal ports (one-way UK£23-33).

British Airways, British Midlands, and **Manx Air** offer flights from Britain (including Gatwick, Stansted, Heathrow, Luton, Manchester, Birmingham, Liverpool, and Glasgow) to Dublin, Shannon, Cork, Kerry, Galway, Knock, Sligo, Waterford, Belfast, and Derry. The **Air Travel Advisory Bureau,** 28 Charles Sq., London N16ST, England (tel. (0171) 636 50 00), can point out the cheapest carriers out of London.

GETTING AROUND

Trains run by **Iarnród Éireann** (Irish Rail) branch out from Dublin to larger cities, but service is limited. For schedule information, pick up an *InterCity Rail Traveler's Guide* (50p), available at most train stations. By far the most useful student travel pass in Ireland is the **TravelSave stamp,** available from USIT (see **Dublin,** p. 507) with an ISIC and IR£8. Affixed to your ISIC, this stamp decreases fares by about 50% on rail lines and 15% on bus services in Ireland (except fares less than IR£1). The **Eurailpass** is valid on trains (but not buses) in the Republic but not in Northern Ireland.

Buses in the Republic of Ireland reach more destinations than trains, but are less frequent, less comfortable, and slower. **Bus Éireann,** the national bus company, operates **Expressway** buses, which link larger cities, and **Local** buses, which serve the countryside and smaller towns. The bus timetable book (IR£1) is available at Busáras Station in Dublin and many tourist offices. Ireland has **Rambler** tickets, offering unlimited bus travel in Ireland for three out of eight days (IR£28), eight out of 15 days (IR£68), or 15 out of 30 days (IR£98)—you have to move fast to make them pay off.

Northern Ireland Railways (tel. (01232) 89 94 11) service isn't extensive, but covers the northeast coastal region well. The major line connects Dublin to Belfast (UK£17, round-trip UK£26), where lines run to Bangor and Larne. There is a **TravelSave stamp** (UK£6) in Northern Ireland similar to the one offered in the Republic of Ireland. The **Freedom of Northern Ireland** ticket allows unlimited travel by train and Ulsterbus for seven days (UK£35), three days (UK£25), or one day (£10).

Much of Ireland and Northern Ireland's countrysides are well suited for **cycling. Irish Cycle Hire,** Mayoralty St., Drogheda, Co. Louth (tel. (041) 410 67, 439 82, or 423 38; fax 353 69), with offices in Dublin, Cork, Killarney, Dingle, Galway, and Donegal, rents bikes for IR£6 per day, IR£30 per week (deposit IR£30; 10% off with ISIC). Ireland offers rugged hills and small mountains to its **hikers.** The best hiking maps are the **Ordnance Survey** series (IR£4.20 each), available at tourist offices.

ESSENTIALS

Bord Fáilte (Irish Tourist Board) operates a nationwide network of offices, selling maps and local guidebooks. Most tourist offices will book a room for a small fee (IR£1-3) and a 10% deposit, but many fine hostels and B&Bs are not "approved," so the tourist office can't tell you about them. **Weather** in Ireland is temperate (summer averages 15-18°C; 60-65°F) yet temperamental. Keep a poncho or umbrella handy, and carry a sweater as sunshine often yields suddenly to chilly rain.

Banks are open Monday through Friday from 9am to 4pm, sometimes later on Thursdays. Dial 114 in the Republic or 153 in the North for an **international operator.** For **Australia Direct,** call (1800) 55 00 61 in the Republic and (0800) 89 00 61 in the North; **British Telecom** (1800) 55 01 44 in Ireland; **Ireland Direct** (0800) 89 03 53 in the North; **Telecom New Zealand** (1800) 55 00 64 in the Republic and (0800) 89 00 64 in the North; **Telekom South Africa** (1800) 55 00 27 in the Republic and (0800) 89 00 27 up North; **AT&T Direct** (1800) 55 00 00 in the Republic and (0800) 89 00 11 in the U.K.; **MCI World Phone** (1800) 55 10 01 in Ireland and (0800) 89 02 22 in the North. Dial 190 for the operator; for directory inquiries 1190 in the South and 192 in the North. In an **emergency,** dial 999.

Much of Southern Ireland closes for **holidays** on January 1, St. Patrick's Day (Mar. 17), Easter (Apr. 2-5 in 1999), June 1, August 3, October 26, and Christmas (Dec. 25-26). Northern Ireland celebrates January 1, St. Patrick's Day, Easter, May Day (May 1 and 3 in 1999), Spring or Whitsun Holiday (May 25), Orange Day (June 12), August 31, and Christmas.

ACCOMMODATIONS, CAMPING, AND FOOD Hosteling is the way to go in Ireland. **An Óige,** the Irish Hostelling International affiliate, runs 37 hostels that are often relatively bare and somewhat out of the way. The North's HI affiliate is **YHANI** (Youth Hostel Association of Northern Ireland). It operates nine nicer hostels. The *An Óige Handbook* (IR£1.50) lists and details all An Óige and YHANI hostels; its standard pricing system isn't always followed by every hostel listed. A number of hostels in Ireland belong to the **Independent Holiday Hostels (IHH).** These hostels have no lockout or curfew (with a few exceptions), accept all ages, require no membership card, and have a comfortable atmosphere; all are Bord Fáilte-approved. **B&Bs** provide a luxurious break from hosteling. Expect to pay IR£15 to 25 for singles and IR£20 to 36 for doubles. "Full Irish breakfasts" are often filling enough to get you through to dinner.

Camping in Irish State Forests and National Parks is not allowed; camping on public land is permissible only if there is no official campsite in the area. Most caravan and camping parks are open April through October, though some stay open year-round. The *Caravan and Camping Ireland,* available from any Bord Fáilte office (IR£4), lists all approved campgrounds in the Republic.

Food in Ireland is expensive. The basics are simple and filling. "Take-away" (take-out) fish and chips shops are quick, greasy, and very popular. Many pubs serve food as well as drink; typical pub grub includes Irish stew, burgers, soup, and sandwiches. Soda bread is delicious and keeps well, and Irish dairy products are addictive. Pubs in Ireland are the forum for banter, singing, and *craic* (a good time). In the evening, many pubs play impromptu or organized traditional music (trad); there's quite a bit of variety to these watering holes. Guinness, a rich, dark stout, is the most revered brew in Ireland. Irish whiskey (with an 'e') is sweeter and more stinging than its Scotch counterpart. Pubs are usually open Monday to Saturday 10:30am to 11 or 11:30pm, Sunday 12:30 to 2pm and 4 to 11pm (in the North Su 12:30-2:30pm and 7-10pm).

■ Dublin

In a country known for its quiet and lackadaisical pace, Dublin is fast, urban, and energized. The city and its suburbs, home to one-third of Ireland's population, are at the vanguard of the country's rapid social change: countercultures flourish here in a way the rest of the Emerald Isle would summarily reject, and cutting-edge, world-renowned music bursts from within the city's pub doors. Yet despite Dublin's progressive pace and rocking nightlife, the old Ireland still courses through its citified veins. Statues of writers like Joyce, Swift, Burke, and Beckett pepper the streets with literary landmarks, and beneath the urban bustle, majestic cathedrals and quaint pubs welcome visitors with Ireland's trademark friendliness and zeal.

ORIENTATION AND PRACTICAL INFORMATION

The **River Liffey** cuts central Dublin in half from west to east. Better food and the more famous sights reside on the **South Side,** though hostels and the bus station inhabit the grittier **North Side.** When streets split into "Upper" and "Lower" sections, "Lower" is closer to the Liffey's mouth (east). Most attractions are in the area circumscribed by North and South Circular Rd. **Trinity College Dublin (TCD)** functions as the nerve center of Dublin's activity. Heading west on Dame St., **Temple Bar** is a lively nightspot area. The **North Side** has the reputation of being a rougher part of town; avoid walking in unfamiliar areas at night. Streets change names often; get a good map with an index. Dundrum's *Handy Map of Dublin* (IR£4) is superb.

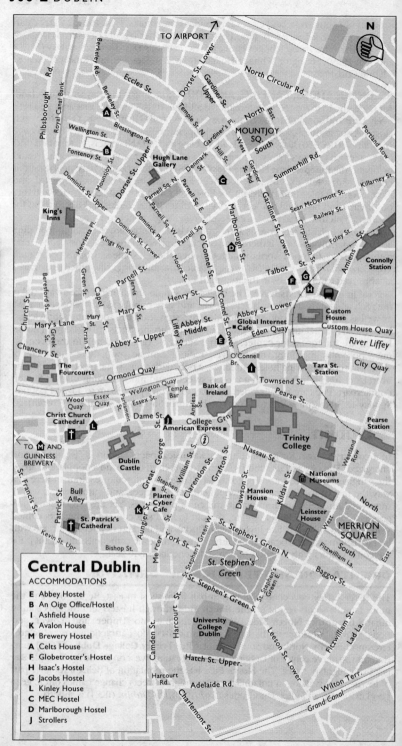

TO AIRPORT

N

MOUNTJOY SQ.

Hugh Lane Gallery

King's Inns

Connolly Station

Custom House

Custom House Quay

River Liffey

City Quay

The Fourcourts

Christ Church Cathedral

TO M AND GUINNESS BREWERY

Bull Alley

St. Patrick's Cathedral

Dublin Castle

Planet Cyber Cafe

Bank of Ireland

American Express

Trinity College

Pearse Station

National Museums

Mansion House

Leinster House

MERRION SQUARE

St. Stephen's Green

University College Dublin

Global Internet Cafe

O'Connell Br.

Tara St. Station

Central Dublin

ACCOMMODATIONS

- E Abbey Hostel
- B An Oige Office/Hostel
- I Ashfield House
- K Avalon House
- M Brewery Hostel
- A Celts House
- F Globetrotter's Hostel
- H Isaac's Hostel
- G Jacobs Hostel
- L Kinley House
- C MEC Hostel
- D Marlborough Hostel
- J Strollers

IRELAND

Telephone Code: 01.

Flights: Dublin Airport (tel. 844 49 00). Catch Dublin bus 41, 41A, or 41C (every 20min., IR£1.30) to Eden Quay in the city center, or try **Airport Express** buses (tel. 704 42 22; IR£2.50), which go to Busáras and sometimes Heuston stations.

Trains: Most intercity trains arrive at **Heuston Station** (tel. 703 21 32), just south of Victoria Quay. Buses 26, 51, and 79 go to the city center. The other main terminus is **Connolly Station** (tel. 836 33 33), centrally located on Amiens St. **Pearse Station,** on Pearse St. and Westland Row, is served by fewer trains. **Irish Rail Information,** 35 Lower Abbey St. (tel. 836 62 22). Open M-F 9am-5pm, Sa 9am-1pm; phones staffed M-Sa 9am-6pm, Su 10am-6pm.

Buses: Busáras, Store St. (tel. 836 61 11), next door to Connolly Station, is the central station for inter-city buses. **Luggage storage** IR£1.50-2 per day.

Ferries: Stena Sealink ferries arrive in Dún Laoghaire, where the DART shuttles to the city center (IR£1.30). **B&I** ferries dock at the mouth of the Liffey; from there, buses 53 and 53A run along Alexandra Rd. (80p). **Irish Rail,** 35 Lower Abbey St. (tel. 836 62 22), handles bookings. Open M-F 9am-5pm, Sa 9am-1pm; phones staffed M-Sa 9am-6pm, Su 10am-6pm.

Public Transportation: Dublin Bus (Bus Átha Cliath). Distressingly lime green. Fares 55p-IR£1.50. Buses run daily 6am-11:30pm. **NiteLink** service runs express routes to the suburbs (Th-Sa midnight, 1, 2, and 3am; IR£2.50, no passes valid). **Dublin Area Rapid Transportation (DART)** serves coastal suburbs from Howth to Bray; fares 75p-IR£2. DART runs daily 6:30am-midnight. Among passes, the **One Day Travel Wide** (IR£3.50; Dublin buses only), the **One Day Bus/Rail** (IR£4.50; valid on buses, DART, and rail service between Kilcoole, Balbriggan, and Maynooth), and the **Four Day Explorer** (IR£10; like a One Day Bus/Rail plus 3 days) are good bets. Insert your pass into the scanner near the bus entrance as you get on.

Car Rental: Thrifty, 14 Duke St. (tel. 679 94 20). Another office at the airport. Summer from IR£35 per day, IR£210 per week; in winter IR£30-175. Ages 23 and over.

Bike Rental: C. Harding for Bikes, 30 Bachelor's Walk (tel. 873 24 55; fax 873 36 22). Bikes IR£7 per day, IR£30 per week. Deposit IR£40. For IR£12, return your bike to other depots. Bike repair. Open M-Sa 8:30am-6pm.

Tourist Offices: Main office on Suffolk St. (international tel. 666 12 58; domestic tel. 18 50 23 03 30; fax 605 77 87). From Connolly Station, walk left down Amiens St. to the Quay, turn right past Busáras, and make a left over O'Connell Bridge. Go past TCD; Suffolk St. is on the right. Accommodations service (IR£1 and 10% booking deposit). *Map of Greater Dublin* (IR£3.90). Open mid-June to mid-Sept. M-Sa 8:30am-7:30pm, Su 9am-3:30pm; mid-Sept. to mid-June M-Sa 9am-5:30pm, Tu opens at 9:30am.

Budget Travel: USIT (Irish Student Travel Agency), 19-21 Aston Quay (tel. 679 88 33), near O'Connell Bridge. ISICs, HI cards. TravelSave stamps IR£8. Many discounts, especially for those under 26. Open M-F 9am-6pm, Sa 10am-5:30pm.

Embassies: Australia, 2nd fl., Fitzwilton House, Wilton Terr. (tel. 676 15 17). Open M-Th 8:30am-12:30pm and 1:30-3:30pm, F 9am-noon. **Canada,** 65 St. Stephen's Green South (tel. 478 19 88). Open M-F 9am-noon and 1-4:30pm. **New Zealand's** embassy is in London: New Zealand House, Haymarket, London SW1Y 4QT. From Ireland, dial +44 (171) 930 84 22. **South Africa,** 2nd fl., Alexander House, Earlsford Centre (tel. 661 55 53; fax 661 55 90). Open 9am-12:30pm and 2-4pm. **U.K.,** 29 Merrion Rd. (tel. 269 52 11). Open M-F 9am-12:45pm and 2-5pm. **United States,** 42 Elgin Rd., Ballsbridge (tel. 668 87 77). Open M-F 8:30am-5pm.

Currency Exchange: Best rates at banks; try the **Bank of Ireland** or **AIB** on Lower O'Connell St. Also in the General Post Office and at the main tourist office.

American Express: 116 Grafton St. (tel. 677 28 74). Currency exchange. Client mail held. Open M-Sa 9am-5pm; June-Sept. also Su 11am-4pm.

Gay and Lesbian Information: Gay Switchboard Dublin (tel. 872 10 55); open Su-F 8-10pm, Sa 3:30-6pm. **Lesbian Line** (tel. 661 37 77); open Th 7-9pm. Get *Gay Community News,* covering Ireland, from the **National Gay and Lesbian Federation,** Hirschfeld Centre, 10 Fownes St.

Laundromat: The Laundry Shop, 191 Parnell St. (tel. 872 35 41). Wash IR£2.40, dry IR£1.30. Soap 60p. Open M-Sa 8am-7pm.

Emergency: Dial 999 for police, fire, or ambulance; no coins required.

Crisis Lines: Alcoholics Anonymous, 109 South Circular Rd. (tel. 453 89 98 or 453 76 77). **Samaritans,** 112 Marlborough St. (tel. (1850) 60 90 90 or 872 77 00), for the depressed or suicidal. Staffed 24hr. **Rape Crisis Centre,** 70 Lower Leeson St. (tel. 661 49 11; freephone 1 800 77 88 88). **Women's Aid** (tel. (1800) 34 19 00 or 860 00 33). Lines staffed M-F 10am-10pm, Sa 10am-6pm.

Pharmacy: O'Connell's, 55 Lower O'Connell St. (tel. 873 04 27). Convenient to city bus routes. Open M-Sa 8:30am-10pm, Su 10am-10pm.

Medical Assistance: Meath Hospital, Heytesbury St. (tel. 453 65 55, 453 60 00, or 453 66 94). Open 24hr. **AIDS Resource Centre,** 14 Haddington Rd. (tel. 660 21 49), off Baggot St. Advice, counseling, and anonymous HIV testing.

Post Office: General Post Office (G.P.O.) (tel. 705 70 00), O'Connell St., on the left from the Liffey. *Poste Restante* at bureau de change window. Open M-Sa 8am-8pm, Su 10am-6:30pm. **Postal Code:** Dublin 1.

Internet Access: Cyberia Cafe, Temple Ln. South, provides sustenance for the email starved. Open M-Sa 10am-11pm, Su noon-8pm. IR£1.50 per 15min., students IR£1.25. **Global Internet Cafe,** 8 Lower O'Connell St., a block north of the Liffey. Techno-happy in every sense of the word. IR£1.25 per 15min., students IR£1. Open M-Sa 10am-11pm, Su noon-10pm. **Planet Cyber Cafe,** 23 South Great Georges St. IR£1.50 per 15min. Open Su-W 10am-10pm, Th-Sa 10am-midnight.

Telephones: On every corner and in the General Post Office. Post office public pay phones open M-Sa 8am-8pm, Su and holidays 10:30am-6:30pm.

ACCOMMODATIONS

Dublin's accommodations overflow, especially during Easter, holidays, and July and August—reserve well ahead. Summertime singles in B&Bs are especially hard to come by. Dorms range from IR£7 to 12 per night. Quality **B&Bs** blanket Dublin and the surrounding suburbs; most charge IR£15 to 25, and many cluster along Upper and Lower Gardiner St., on Sherriff St., and near the Parnell Sq. area. Phoenix Park may tempt the desperate, but camping there is a bad idea. If the *garda* or park rangers don't get you to leave, the threat of thieves and drug dealers should. Dublin Tourism's annual *Dublin Accommodation Guide* (IR£3) lists all approved B&Bs.

Avalon House (IHH), 55 Aungier St. (tel. 475 00 01; fax 475 03 03; http://www.avalon-house.ie). From Dame St., take Great Georges St. until it becomes Aungier St. Groovy comforters and clean bathrooms. Co-ed showers, toilets, and dorms. **Internet access.** Dorms IR£11-13.50; doubles IR£16; cheaper off-season. Breakfast included. All meals under IR£5 (open daily noon-10pm).

Kinlay House (IHH), 2-12 Lord Edward St. (tel. 679 66 44; fax 679 74 37), on the continuation of Dame St. Comfy beds and excellent security. Dorms IR£9.50-13; singles IR£17-18; doubles IR£27-32. Breakfast and luggage storage included.

Isaac's Hostel, 2-5 Frenchman's Ln. (tel. 855 62 15; fax 855 65 74), off the lower end of Gardiner St. behind the Customs House. Simple, clean rooms; part of a biblical chain that includes the nearby Jacob's (see below). Cafe and laundry. Dorms IR£8-9.25; doubles IR£32; triples IR£43.50; cheaper off-season.

Ashfield House, 19/20 D'Olier St. (tel. 679 77 34). You can't beat the location or the condition of the bright, airy rooms, all with bath. Kitchen open 24hr. Dorms IR£10; doubles IR£32; triples IR£48. Winter discounts. Wheelchair accessible.

Jacob's Inn, 21-28 Talbot Place (tel. 855 56 60; fax 855 56 64), on a narrow north-south street 2 blocks north of the Customs House. Bright and airy reception area with a cafe. Dorms IR£10.95-15.50; doubles IR£19.50; triples IR£50; cheaper off-season. Sheets included. Bed lockout 11am-3pm.

Abraham House, 82 Lower Gardiner St. (tel. 855 06 00; fax 855 05 98). Dorms IR£8.50-11; singles IR£18; doubles IR£32; quads IR£50; cheaper off-season. Laundry IR£5. Light breakfast and towels included.

Globetrotter's Tourist Hostel (IHH), 46 Gardiner St. Lower (tel. 873 58 93). Comfortable beds in high bunks. Smoking room, TV room, civilized kitchen. Free luggage storage. Dorms IR£11-15. Great breakfast included. Towels 50p.

Abbey Hostel, O'Connell Bridge, 29 Bachelors Walk (tel. 878 07 00 or 878 07 19; http://indigo.ie/~abbeyhos), in an emphatically yellow building. Well-kept hostel in a great location. Dorms IR£13-17; doubles IR£40-60; lower rates off-season.

Strollers, 58 Dame St. (tel. 677 56 14 or 677 54 22; fax 839 04 74). Super location and bright rooms, though cars whiz by at all hours. Live music 4 nights a week. Dorms IR£12-14.50; doubles IR£34. Breakfast included. Wheelchair accessible.

Marlborough Hostel (IHH), 81-82 Marlborough St. (tel. 874 76 29; fax 874 51 72), up the street from the Protestant cathedral. Large rooms, mediocre showers, and a barbecue. Dorms IR£7.50; doubles IR£26. Breakfast included. Check-out 10:30am.

Mrs. M. Ryan, 10 Distillery Rd. (tel. 837 41 47), off Clonliffe Rd. The oft-dyed proprietor welcomes all with warm comforters. Singles IR£15; doubles IR£28.

Mrs. R. Casey, Villa Jude, 2 Church Ave. (tel. 668 49 82), off Beach Rd. Bus 3 or DART to "Lansdowne Rd." Every room is immaculate and has a TV. Singles IR£14.

Mrs. Bermingham, 8 Dromard Terr. (tel. 668 38 61). Take bus 3 from O'Connell St. or the DART to "Sandymount." Old-fashioned rooms and a TV in the sitting room. Soft beds and great comforters. Singles IR£15; doubles IR£28.

Glen Court, 67 Gardiner St. Lower (tel. 836 4022), 1 block west of Busáras, 2 blocks east of O'Connell. A clean, cheap, and well located old Georgian house. Singles IR£18; doubles IR£30; triples IR£42; quads IR£49.

Backpackers EuroHostel, 80/81 Lower Gardiner St. (tel. 836 49 00). This "campsite" is really a big room behind the hostel of the same name. IR£4 gets you a mattress on the floor and use of all the hostel facilities.

FOOD

Dublin's open-air **Moore Street Market,** which runs between Henry St. and Parnell St., provides fresh, cheap fixings (open M-Sa 9am-5pm). **Dunnes Stores** offer cheap wares at three locations: St. Stephen's Green Shopping Center, the ILAC Center off Henry St., and on North Earl St. off O'Connell St. (all open M-Sa 9am-6pm, Th until 8pm). Cheap, creative eateries fill the Temple Bar area.

La Mezza Luna, 1 Temple Ln., corner of Dame St. The food *is* celestial. *Paglia* IR£5.50. Lunch special IR£5. Open M-Sa 12:30-11pm, Su 4-10:30pm.

Bad Ass Cafe, Crown Alley, off Temple Bar. Colorful, exuberant atmosphere. Sinéad O'Connor once worked here; the food fits right in. Lunch IR£3-5. Pizza IR£5.75-7.75. Student menu (with ISIC) IR£5.75. Open daily 9am to past midnight.

Marks Bros., 7 South Great Georges St., off Dame St. Thick sandwiches (IR£1.30-1.70) and salads for starving artists and punks. Popular gay hang-out. Legendary cinnamon buns 40p. Open daily 11am until late.

Cornucopia, 19 Wicklow St. This vegetarian horn of plenty overflows with huge portions (meals for IR£5). Open M-W and F 9am-8pm, Th 9am-9pm, Sa 9am-6pm.

Chez Jules, 16a D'Olier St. Fun atmosphere amidst pasta and seafood consumption. 3-course lunch IR£7. 3-course dinner IR£12. Garlic mussels IR£5. Open M-F noon-3pm and 6-11pm, Sa 1-4pm and 6-11pm, Su 5-10pm.

Leo Burdock's, 2 Werburgh St., uphill from Christ Church Cathedral. Take-out only. Eating Burdock's fish and chips is a religious experience from which walking shouldn't distract. Open M-F 11am-11pm, Sa 2-11pm.

Bewley's Cafes, A Dublin institution: delightful crowd, dark wood paneling, marble table tops, and mirrored walls. Wildly complex pastries (IR£1), superb coffee, and plain but cheap meals. Largest branch at 78 Grafton St. (open Su-Th 7:30am-1am, F-Sa 7:30am-2am). James Joyce frequented 12 Westmoreland St. (open M-Sa 7:30am-9pm, Su 9:30am-8pm). Also at 13 South Great Georges St. (open M-Sa 7:45am-6pm) and Mary St., past Henry St. (open M-W 7am-9pm, Th-Sa 7am-2am, Su 10am-10pm).

SIGHTS

Dublin is a walkable city; most of the sights lie less than a mile from O'Connell Bridge. The tourist office sells *Visitor Attractions in Dublin* (IR£2.25) outlining the main sights. The **Historical Walking Tour** (tel. 845 02 41) inundates you with Dublin's history from the Celts to the present. *(June-Sept. M-Sa 11am, noon, and 3pm; Su also at 2pm; Oct.-May Sa-Su noon. 2hr. IR£5, students IR£4.)* The irreverent **Trinity College Walking Tour** covers Dublin's history but concentrates on university lore. *(June-Sept. daily every 15min. from 10am-4pm. 30min. IR£5, students IR£4.)*

Trinity College

Through the late 16th century, the English toyed with the idea of an Irish university. In 1592, a small group of Dubliners obtained a charter from Queen Elizabeth to found Trinity College. The city granted the new foundation the lands and run-down buildings of a monastery just southeast of the city walls. The late-17th century brought turmoil to its hallowed halls: the Provost fled in 1641, the college had to pawn its plate in 1643, and all fellows and students were expelled in order to turn the college into a barrack for James II's soldiers in 1689.

Trinity was up and running again by the beginning of the 18th century with the construction of the library underway. As the university of the Protestant Ascendancy, Trinity met few disturbances save the small number of boisterous Jacobites who unsuccessfully tried to introduce radical politics into this burgeoning intellectual aristocracy. In 1793, Trinity went avant-garde and admitted Roman Catholic students. By the late 19th century, the tumultuous political climate had finally seeped into the college grounds. The government made numerous attempts to incorporate Trinity into a federated university with several other Irish academic institutions; the college vehemently opposed and ultimately terminated such threats to its independence. In 1904, the university first admitted women, who comprised 16% of the student population only ten years later. World War I and the creation of the Republic left Trinity without resources or strength in a divided Ireland, while newer universities in the U.K. quickly gained prestige. With the help of a long-needed annual state grant finally secured in 1947, however, Trinity has continued to prosper through its fourth century.

Sprawling at the center of Dublin, **Trinity College,** *alma mater* of Swift, Moore, Beckett, and Wilde, houses the *Book of Kells* (c. 800 AD) in its **Old Library,** built in 1712. *(Open M-Sa 9:30am-5pm, Su noon-4:30pm. IR£3.50, students IR£3.)* South of the college, on the block between Kildare St. and Upper Merrion St., Irish history and culture reign. The **National Museum** protects the Ardagh Chalice and the Tara brooch. Down the street on Merrion Sq., portraits of Lady Gregory, Eliza O'Neill, Joyce, Shaw, and Yeats line the **National Gallery's** staircase. *(Open M-Sa 10am-5:30pm, Th 10am-8:30pm, Su 2-5pm. Free.)*

Kildare, Dawson, and Grafton St. all lead from Trinity south to **St. Stephen's Green.** *(Open M-Sa 8am-dusk, Su 10am-dusk.)* Bequeathed to the city by the Guinness clan, this 22-acre park boasts arched bridges, a lake, fountains, gazebos, swans, and waterfalls. On summer days, half of Dublin fills the lawns, in various stages of undress, and outdoor theatrical productions are held near the old bandstand.

West of Trinity College, between Dame St. and the Liffey, the **Temple Bar** neighborhood bustles with cheap cafes, hole-in-the-wall theaters, rock venues, and used clothing and record stores. Next to this hipster scene is the **Dublin Viking Adventure,** Essex St. West, where you can walk through the recreated Dublin of the 9th and 10th centuries. *(Open Th-M 9:30am-4pm. IR£4.75, students IR£3.95.)*

At the west end of Dame St., where it meets Parliament and Castle St., hovers **Dublin Castle.** *(State Apartments open M-F 10am-12:15pm and 2-5pm, Sa-Su and holidays 2-5pm. IR£2, students IR£1; rest of castle free.)* Built in 1204 by King John, the castle was the seat of English rule in Ireland for more than 700 years. Strangely, Dublin's two official cathedrals, **Christ Church Cathedral** on Dame St. and **St. Patrick's Cathedral** down Nicholas St., are owned by the Church of Ireland, not the Catholic Church. *(Christ Church open daily 10am-5pm except during services; choral evensong Sept.-May Th 6pm. IR£1. St. Patrick's open M-F 9am-6pm, Sa 9am-5pm, Su 10-11am and 12:45-4:30pm. IR£1.20).* Christ Church hosts **Dublinia,** a life-size recreation of parts of medieval Dublin. *(Open daily Apr.-Oct. 10am-5pm; Nov.-Mar. 11am-4pm. IR£4, students and children IR£3).*

Those craving alcoholic ambrosia are drawn to the giant **Guinness Brewery,** St. James Gate. To get there from Christ Church, follow High St. west as it becomes Cornmarket, Thomas and then James St. The **Hop Store,** on Crane St. off James St., perpetuates the Guinness mystique and gives complimentary beer with tours. *(Take* *bus 68A or 78A from Ashton Quay or bus 123 from O'Connell St. Open Apr.-Sept. M-Sa 9:30am-5pm (last admission), Su 10:30am-4:30pm; Oct.-Mar. M-Sa 9:30am-4pm, Su noon-4pm. IR£3, students IR£2.)* On the North Side, the **Dublin Writer's Museum,** 18 Parnell Sq. North, introduces visitors to the city's rich literary legacy with manuscripts, memorabilia, and caricatures of pen-wielding Dubliners. *(Open June-Aug. M-F 10am-6pm, Sa 10am-5pm, Su 11am-5pm; Sept.-May M-Sa 10am-5pm, Su 11am-5pm. IR£2.95, students IR£2.50.)*

ENTERTAINMENT

The *Dublin Event Guide* (free at Temple Bar restaurants) and *In Dublin* (IR£1.50) detail a smorgasbord of events. Hostel workers are also a good, if sometimes biased, source of information on entertainment options.

Music, Theater, and Festivals

Hot Press (IR£1.50) has the most up-to-date listings for Dublin's music scene. Traditional music (trad) is a vibrant component of the musical offerings. Pubs in the city center resound with clapping, the drone of a pipe, and roll of a *bodhrán* drum. **Whelan's,** 25 Wexford St. (tel. 478 07 66), is one of the hottest spots in Dublin. Excellent bands frequent the **Baggot Inn,** 143 Baggot St. (tel. 676 14 30)—U2 played here in the early 80s. The **National Concert Hall,** Earl's Fort Terrace (tel. 671 15 33), is the venue for classical music (concerts July-Aug. at 8pm; IR£8-15, students half-price).

Part of the National Theater, the **Abbey Theatre,** 26 Lower Abbey St. (tel. 878 72 22), was founded in 1904 by Yeats and Lady Gregory to promote Irish culture and modernist theater. (Box office M-Sa 10:30am-7pm. Tickets IR£10-25; student standby IR£8 1hr. before M and Th shows.) The **Gate Theatre,** 1 Cavendish Row (tel. 874 40 45), produces everything from Restoration comedies to Irish classics. (Box office M-Sa 10am-7pm. Tickets IR£10-12; student standby IR£6 M-Th at curtain.)

The city returns to 1904 on **Bloomsday,** June 16, the day on which the action of Joyce's *Ulysses* takes place. Festivities are held all week long. The **James Joyce Center,** 35 North Great Geroges St. (tel. 873 19 84), sponsors a mock funeral and wake, a lunch at Davy Byrne's, and a breakfast with Guinness as part of its Bloomstime program. On the day itself, a Messenger Bike Rally culminates in St. Stephen's Green with drink and food and readings from *Ulysses.* To find Joyce's works head to Dublin's premier bookdealer, **Fred Hanna's,** 27-29 Nassau St. (open M-Sa 9am-5:30pm).

Pubs

The **Dublin Literary Pub Crawl** (tel. 454 02 28) traces Dublin's liquid history in reference to its literary one. Meet at **The Duke,** 2 Duke St. (June-Aug. M-Sa 3pm and 7:30pm, Su noon and 7:30pm; May and Sept. daily 7:30pm; Oct.-Apr. F-Sa 7:30pm, Su noon. IR£6, students IR£5.) *Let's Go* recommends beginning your personal journey at Trinity College Gates, moving onto Grafton Street, stumbling onto Camden, teetering down South Great Georges St., and crawling (triumphantly) into the Temple Bar area.

The Stag's Head, 1 Dame Ct. The entrance is marked by "Stag's Head" written in tile on the sidewalk. Beautiful Victorian pub with stained glass, mirrors, and brass. Shiny. Huge mounted whiskey kegs. Truly excellent grub.

The Mean Fiddler, Wexford St., next door to Whelan's. Live music regularly with a hip crowd. At 11pm the gates of the attached nightclub open (cover IR£5). Bar open daily noon-2am.

Whelan's, 25 Wexford St., continue down South Great Georges St. Nightly music makes it one of the hot spots for live rock in Dublin, despite its dark interior and uncomfortable church pews. Nightly Irish indie rock or blues. Cover IR£2-4.

The Porter House, 16-18 Parliament St. Dublin's only microbrewery brews 6 different kinds of porter, stout, and ale, including Wrasslers 4X Stout.

Mulligan's, 8 Poolbeg St., behind Burgh Quay off Tara St. *Let's Go* pick for the best pint of Dublin Guinness. This low-key favorite is your typical Irish pub: smoke and chat with mellow middle-aged men.

The White Horse, 1 Georges Quay. For the early morning urge, the White Horse opens at 7:30am. Small, simple, frequented by regulars who come for the trad and rock (starts around 9:30pm; no cover). Low-key—yet to be invaded by tourists.

Know Your Whiskey

Anyone who drinks his whiskey as it's meant to be drunk—"neat," or straight—can tell you that there's a huge difference between Irish whiskeys (Bushmills, Jameson, Power and Son, and the like), Scotch whiskys (spelled without an e), and American whiskeys. But what makes an Irish whiskey *Irish?* The basic ingredients in whiskey—water, barley (which becomes malt once processed), and heat from a fuel source—are always the same. It's the quality of these ingredients, the way in which they're combined, and the manner in which the combination is stored that gives each product its distinct flavor. The different types of whiskey derive from slight differences in this production process. American whiskey is distilled once and is often stored in oak, bourbon is made only in Kentucky, scotch uses peat-smoked barley, and Irish whiskey is triple distilled. After this basic breakdown, individual distilleries will claim that their further variations on the theme make their product the best of its class. We could get more technical, but at *Let's Go* we realize that the best way to understand the distinctions between brands is to taste the various labels in close succession to one another. Line up those shot glasses, sniff and then taste each one (roll the whiskey in your mouth like a real pro), and have a sip of water between each brand. **"But I don't have the money to buy a shot of each brand,"** our budget-traveling readers murmur. Well, then, get thee to a distillery tour and when the tour guide asks for volunteers, stick your hand in the air and squeal, "Me! Me!" If you're lucky, you'll be selected to be an "Irish Whiskey Taster," trying no less than five kinds of Irish, two scotch, and one bourbon whiskey under the supervision of your highly trained tour guide. Sure, the certificate is nice, but the haze is even better (up to a point, of course).

McDaid's, 3 Harry St., off Grafton St., across from Anne St. Books adorn the walls, inspiring conversations of love and honor among young Dubliners. Crowded downstairs, spacious upstairs areas. Ballads, blues, jazz, and occasional rock gigs.

The George, 89 South Great Georges St. Dublin's first gay bar. A mixed crowd of old and young. Mostly gay men. Lesbians welcome any time but most come W nights to dance at the attached nightclub. Cover IR£4-7.

Clubs

Clubs open at 10:30 or 11pm, but the action gets moving after 11:30pm; pubs close around 2 or 3am. Covers run IR£4-8; pints IR£3.

The Kitchen, The Clarence Hotel, Wellington Quay, Temple Bar. With 2 bars and a dance floor, this U2-owned club is the coolest spot in town. Hard to get in on F-Sa because it's filled with "VIPs." Dress to fit in with the rocker/model crowd. Cover IR£8, students IR£3 on Tu.

Rí-Rá, 1 Exchequer St., in the Central Hotel, pumps out pop favorites. 2 floors, several bars, and more nooks and crannies than an English muffin. Open daily 11pm-2:30am. Cover IR£6.

Club M, Blooms Hotel, Anglesea St., Temple Bar. One of Dublin's largest clubs, attracting a crowd of diverse ages and styles. Cover around IR£6.

Stonewall, Griffth College, South Circular Rd., is a large and lively gay club. Dancing, a video screen, and pool tables make it worth the trip. Some nights are male or female only—check *In Dublin* for details. Bus 19, 19A, or 22. Cover £5.

■ Near Dublin: Howth and Boyne Valley

Nine miles north of Dublin and easily accessible by DART trains (30min., IR£1.10) and buses, Howth provides a bit of countryside—scenic paths, a castle, and great pubs—near the capital city. Orient yourself with the *Guide to Howth Peninsula*, posted at the harbor entrance across from the St. Lawrence Hotel. Howth's primary attraction is the **Howth Castle** on the outskirts of town; take a right on Harbour Rd. as you leave the DART station. A patchwork of architectural styles give it an awkward charm. Farther up the hill, follow the path to the right around the Deer Park Hotel to reach the fabulous **Rhododendron Gardens**. A one-hour **cliff walk** rings the peninsula; the slope's views and springtime blooms are amazing. To get to the trail head, turn left at the station and follow Harbour Rd. around the corner and up the hill. Howth's **B&Bs** make a fine base for hopping to Dublin. **Glenn Na Smol** (tel. (01) 832 29 36), at the end of Nashville Rd., off Thormanby Rd., and **Highfield** (tel. (01) 832 39 36), a 20-minute walk up Thormanby Rd., offer convenient bases (IR£20). **Ye Olde Abbey Tavern**, Abbey St., pumps out trad (M-Su at 9pm; cover IR£4).

The thinly populated **Boyne Valley** safeguards some of Ireland's greatest historical treasures. The massive Neolithic tomb-mounds of **Newgrange, Knowth**, and **Dowth** puzzle experts and amaze more casual visitors. Newgrange, the most spectacular, is the prime example of a passage-tomb. Built over 5000 years ago, using stones believed to have been carted from Wicklow 40 miles away, Newgrange is covered with elaborate patterns and symbols mystifying to archaeologists. Possession of the **Celtic Hill of Tara** used to convey the Kingship of Ireland upon its owner. **Slane** and **Trim** boast well-preserved medieval castles. **Buses** from Dublin hit the major Boyne towns, but service between towns is spotty (return IR£3-6). **Cyclists** will find the terrain between the sights welcomingly gentle. Several tours herd visitors through the circuit of sites. **Celtic Twilight** (tel. (088) 547 87) offers a full sight-seeing "Tour of the Royal Meath" (June-Aug. Su; IR£14). The coach leaves the Nassau St. entrance to Trinity College Dublin at 10am and returns to Dublin at 5:30pm. **Sightseeing Tours** (tel. (01) 283 99 73) visits Newgrange and Knowth on its Boyne Valley tour. The bus leaves the Dublin Tourist Office (June-Sept. daily at 1:20pm, return at 6pm; IR£14).

SOUTHEAST IRELAND

The Wicklow Mountains Over 2000 feet high and laced with scenic trails, the Wicklow Mountains provide a perfect opportunity to earn that tall drink back in Dublin. The 70 miles **Wicklow Way** hiking trail starts near Dublin and jogs south all the way to Clonegal in Co. Carlow. Although the path is well-posted with yellow arrows, you should get the *Wicklow Way Map Guide* (IR£5), available at tourist offices, bookstores, and mountaineering stores. **Glendalough** (GLEN-da-lock), a spectacularly uninhabited valley in the midst of the mountains, cradles two lakes, a pine forest, and the remains of a medieval monastic settlement. Stay at **Glendalough Hostel (HI)** (tel. (0404) 453 42), or in nearby **Laragh** at **Gleannailbhe B&B** (tel. (0404) 452 36; IR£14-16), Main St., or the **Wicklow Way Hostel** (tel. (0404) 453 98; co-ed dorms IR£8). **St. Kevin's Bus Service** (tel. (01) 281 81 19) runs to Laragh from Dublin (IR£6, return IR£10) and from the Bray town hall (return IR£6).

Rosslare Harbour Jutting out along St. George's Channel in southeast Ireland, **Rosslare Harbour** offers little in the way of Irish charm, but serves as an important transportation link to Wales, France, and the Irish coast. **Irish Ferries** (tel. (053) 331 58; http://www.irish-ferries.ie) chug to Le Havre in France (22hr.). **Buses** run to Cork (IR£13), Dublin (3hr., IR£9), Limerick (IR£12), and Wexford (20min., IR£2.50). The quicker **trains** have similar prices. The **tourist office** in the ferry terminal (tel. (053) 336 23) is overworked but provides free maps (open daily 10am-8pm). If you stay overnight, try the **Rosslare Harbour Youth Hostel (An Óige/HI)** (tel. (053) 333 99; fax 336 24; IR£6.50-7.50), Goulding St.

Kilkenny Touted as the best-preserved medieval town in Ireland, **Kilkenny** offers rocking nightlife too—nine churches line the same street as 78 pubs. Thirteenth-century **Kilkenny Castle** evokes images of flowing robes and clashing swords. (Open daily June-Sept. 10am-7pm; Oct.-Mar. Tu-Sa 10:30am-5pm, Su 11am-5pm; Apr.-May daily 10:30am-5pm. IR£3, students IR£1.50.) **St. Canice's Cathedral** has medieval tombstones embedded in the floor and walls (open daily 10am-6pm, except during services). **Trains** (tel. (056) 220 24) and **buses** (tel. (056) 649 33) stop at **McDonagh**

Station, Dublin Rd. The **tourist office,** Rose Inn St. (tel. (056) 515 00; fax 639 55), offers a free map and city guide and has info on B&Bs. (Open June-Sept. M-Sa 9am-6pm, Su 11am-5pm; shorter hours and closed Su off season.) **Kilkenny Town Hostel (IHH),** 35 Parliament St. (tel. (056) 635 41), is always brimming with activity (IR£8). **Foulksrath Castle (An Óige/HI),** Jenkinstown (tel. (056) 676 74), may be far, but it's one of the nicest hostels in Ireland (IR£6; curfew 10:30pm). Half a block from the train station, the friendly **Matt the Miller's,** John St., is always packed.

Waterford First impressions of **Waterford** are, as a rule, unimpressive. Fortunately, behind its industrial facade lie winding, narrow streets filled with shops and amiable pubs. The best way to get a feel for the city is to take one of the **Walking Tours of Historic Waterford** that depart from the front of the Granville Hotel on the Quay (45min., Mar.-Oct. daily at noon and 2pm, IR£3). The **Waterford Crystal Factory** (tel. (051) 37 33 11) is one mile out of town on the N25 (Cork Rd.). Forty-minute tours allow you to witness the transformation of molten glass into polished crystal. Admire the finished products—and their outrageous prices—in the gallery. (Tours daily Apr.-Oct. 8:30am-4pm, every 10min., showroom open 8:30am-6pm; Nov.-Mar. 9am-3:15pm, showroom 9am-5pm. IR£3.50, students IR£1.75.)

Trains (tel. (051) 87 62 43) and buses (tel. (051) 87 90 00) connect to **Plunkett Station,** across the bridge from The Quay, from Dublin, Kilkenny, and Rosslare Harbor. Between Hanover St. and Gladstone St., the **tourist office,** 41 Merchant's Quay (tel. (051) 87 57 88), dispenses a free map and the *Waterford Touring Guide.* (IR£2. Open July-Aug. M-Sa 9am-6pm, Su 11am-1pm and 2-5pm; June and Sept. M-Sa 9am-6pm; Oct.-Feb. M-F 2-5pm; Mar.-Apr. M-Sa 9am-1pm and 2-6pm.) A spacious lounge and friendly staff await at the **Viking House Hostel (IHH),** Coffee House Ln. (Tel. (051) 85 38 27; fax 87 17 30. Dorms IR£8-12; doubles IR£27; cheaper off-season.) Though smaller, **Waterford Hostel,** 70 The Manor (tel. (051) 85 01 63), is clean and comfortable (IR£8). **Cafe Luna,** 53 John St., offers cheap food with a trendy touch (open M-F until 2:30am, Sa-Su until 4am), while **Haricot's Wholefood Restaurant,** 11 O'Connell St., keeps the peace between vegetarians and carnivores with innovative dishes (open M-F 9:30am-8pm, Sa 9:30am-5:45pm). **Pubs** cluster on the Quays, John St., and Barron Strand.

Cashel Magical when seen from a distance or when lit at night, the commanding **Rock of Cashel** rises above the town. The dark limestone hill bristles with an elaborate complex of medieval buildings 300 feet above the plain. **Cormac's Chapel,** a majestic, dual-towered structure, was consecrated in 1134. The interior displays gorgeous Romanesque carvings and a richly decorated sarcophagus. The 13th-century **Cashel Cathedral** overshadows all the other ruins in grandeur. The museum at the entrance to the complex preserves the 12th-century **St. Patrick's Cross.** Kings of Munster were crowned on the site marked by the *croix faux.* (Complex open daily mid-June to mid-Sept. 9:30am-7:30pm; mid-Mar. to mid-June 9:30am-5:30pm; mid-Sept. to mid-Mar. 9:30am-4:30pm. Last admission 45min. before closing. IR£3, students IR£1.25.) The plush **Cashel Holiday Hostel (IHH),** 6 John St. (tel. (062) 623 30), off Main St., features comfortable rooms and friendly management (IR£7-8; private rooms IR£10). The stunning **O'Brien's Farmhouse Hostel** (tel. (062) 610 03), off Dundrum Rd., is on the way to **Hore Abbey** (IR£8; private rooms IR£10; **camping** IR£4 per person). Bushels of *craic* entice locals to **Feehan's,** on Main St.

SOUTHWEST IRELAND

Life in the southwest is leisurely and localized. The newly settled foreign expatriates, the remote pubs that stay open until 3am, the crumbling, ancient spiritual monuments, and the stretches of wild, open, undeveloped land all contribute to the region's informal and decidedly anti-urban atmosphere.

■ Cork City

As Ireland's second-largest city, Cork is the center of the southwest's sports, music, and arts scenes. Unfortunately for the visitor, culture barely conceals its ugly but dependable twin: commerce. Wise visitors will exploit the city's resources, and use Cork as a place to eat, drink, shop, and sleep while filling their lungs with country air.

SIGHTS AND ENTERTAINMENT Downtown Cork is the tip of an arrow-shaped island in the River Lee; bridges link the island to Cork's residential south side and less affluent north side. The dynamic **Triskel Arts Centre,** Tobin St. (tel. (021) 27 20 22), maintains two small galleries, runs an excellent cafe, and organizes many cultural events (open M-W and F-Sa 10am-5:30pm; free). On the other side of the river, **St. Anne's Church** is Cork's most famous landmark. The church earned the nickname of "the four-faced liar" because the four tower clocks are notoriously out of sync with each other (open in summer M-Sa 10am-5pm; off-season M-Sa 10am-4pm). The **Crawford Municipal Art Gallery,** Emmet Pl., boasts an exceptional collection of Irish art and features traveling exhibits (open M-Sa 10am-5pm; free). Go directy to the **Cork City Gaol** for a tour of jail as it appeared in the 1800s; cross the footbridge at the western end of Fitzgerald Park, turn right on Sunday's Well Rd., and follow the signs. (Open daily 9:30am-6pm; in winter M-F 10:30am-2:30pm, Sa-Su 10am-4pm. Admission IR£3.50, students IR£2.50.)

Cork is the proud producer of both **Murphy's** and **Beamish,** which you can enjoy in the pubs along Oliver Plunkett St., Union Quay, and South Main St. **An Spailpín Fánach,** 28 South Main St., is one of Cork's most popular bars (live music Su-F; meals served M-F noon-3pm). **The Lobby,** 1 Union Quay (tel. (021) 31 11 13), arguably the most famous venue in Cork, has given some of Ireland's biggest folk acts their starts (live music nightly; occasional cover IR£4-5). The hardwood floors and stained glass cathedral ceilings strain to contain the crowd in **The Old Oak,** Oliver Plunkett St. **Loafer's,** 26 Douglas St., is Cork's sole gay and lesbian pub. Steps away from campus, **The Thirsty Scholar,** Western Rd., is always full of local students. Nightclubs fill up when the pubs close. **Sir Henry's,** South Main St., is crowded and intense (open W-Sa; cover IR£2-11). Head to **City Limits,** Coburg St., for a mixed-age crowd (open Th and Su 11pm-2am, F-Sa are comedy nights, 9pm-2am).

PRACTICAL INFO, ACCOMMODATIONS, AND FOOD Trains leave from Kent Station, Lower Glanmire Rd. (tel. (021) 50 67 66), for Dublin (3hr., IR£32, students IR£13.50), Limerick (1½hr., IR£15.50, students IR£5.50), and Killarney (2hr., IR£13.50, students IR£6). **Buses** drive from Parnell Pl. (tel. (021) 50 81 88), two blocks east of Patrick's Bridge on Merchants' Quay, to Belfast (7½hr., IR£17, students IR£13), Dublin (4½hr., IR£12, students IR£8.50), and other cities. **Ferries** to England dock at Ringaskiddy Terminal, 9 miles south of the city. Pick up a city map and sights guide (IR£1.50) at the **tourist office** (tel. (021) 27 32 51), Tourist House, Grand Parade (open in summer M-Sa 9am-6pm; off-season M-Sa 9:30am-5pm).

The **Cork City Independent Hostel,** 100 Lower Glanmire Rd. (tel. (021) 50 90 89), is super-relaxed and entertaining (dorms IR£6; doubles IR£14). Positively packed with perks, **Sheila's Budget Accommodation Centre (IHH),** 3 Belgrave Pl. (tel. (021) 50 55 62), lures visitors with a huge kitchen, **Internet stations,** and a sauna (dorms IR£6.50-8; singles IR£18; doubles IR£20; reception 24hr.). Immaculate and modern bunkrooms await in **Cork International Hostel, An Oige (HI),** 1-2 Redclyffe, Western Rd. (tel. (021) 54 32 89; dorms IR£7.50-8.50; reception 8am-midnight), or prepare to be pampered at **Garnish House,** Western Rd. (tel. (021) 27 51 11; singles from IR£20; doubles from IR£40). **Bienvenue Ferry Camping** (tel. (021) 31 27 11), very near the airport, is located 5 miles south of town on Kinslade Rd. (Take the airport bus from the bus station. Tents IR£5 plus IR£1 per person. Open year-round.)

Restaurants and cafes cluster near the city center. **Kafka's,** 7 Maylor St., has cheap but delicious Euro-American hybrid cuisine (open M-Sa 8am-6pm). Sink into cool jazz and heavenly breads at the **Gingerbread House,** Paul St. (Open in summer M-Th 8am-

10:30pm, F-Sa 8am-11pm, Su 8am-6pm; off-season M-Th 8am-9:30pm, F-Sa 8am-10:30pm, Su 8am-6pm.) Find scrumptious vegetarian delights in the **Quay Co-op,** 24 Sullivan's Quay (open M-Sa 9am-9pm; table service 7-10:30pm). The health food store downstairs caters to all your organic needs, and the **Tesco Supermarket** on Paul St. is the biggest grocery store in town.

■ Near Cork City: Blarney

Busloads of tourists travel 5 miles northwest of Cork to see **Blarney Castle** and its overrated **Blarney Stone.** But the view from the top of the castle, if you get one, makes up for all the tour groups. (Open M-Sa May 9am-6:30pm; June-Aug. 9am-7pm; Sept. 9am-6:30pm; Oct.-Apr. 9am-sundown. Su: summer 9:30am-5:30pm; off-season 9:30am-sundown. IR£3, students IR£2.) Adjacent to the castle lies the **Rock Close,** a beautiful and relatively quiet rock-and-plant garden. **Bus Éireann** runs buses from Cork to Blarney (10-16 per day, round-trip IR£2.60).

■ Southwest Coast

Kinsale A 30-minute drive southwest of Cork lies the ritzy seaside town of **Kinsale. Charles Fort** (tel. (021) 77 22 63), 2 miles east of town, offers spectacular views of the town and its watery surroundings. (Open mid-June to mid-Sept. daily 9am-6pm; mid-Apr. to mid-June and mid-Sept. to mid-Oct. M-Sa 9am-5pm, Su 9:30am-5:30pm. IR£2, students IR£1.) Reach the fort by following the sylvan, coastal **Scilly Walk.** Across the harbor, the ruins of **James Fort** delight with secret passageways and panoramic views of Kinsale (open 24hr.; free). Near James Fort, the **Castlepark Marina Centre** (tel. (021) 77 49 59) has rooms with beautiful marina views (IR£8; open Mar.-Nov.). Closer to town, stay at **Dempsey's Hostel (IHH)** (tel. (021) 77 21 24), Cork Road (IR£5). With its renowned eateries of the **Good Food Circle,** Kinsale is Ireland's gourmet food capital. From the hills on Scilly Peninsula, **Spaniard** (tel. (021) 77 24 36), on the road to Charles Fort, rules over the Kinsale pub scene.

Mizen Head Peninsula The seaside hamlet of **Schull** is an ideal base for exploring the craggy, windswept, beach-laden, and gloriously unspoiled southwest tip of Ireland. **Hiking** and **biking** trails snake along the water and up the nearby hills; inquire at the Backpackers' Lodge (see below) for maps and info. **Freewheelin',** Cotter's Yard, Main St., rents bikes for IR£8 per day (open M-Sa 10am-noon). A calm harbor and numerous shipwrecks are a diver's paradise; the **Watersports Centre** rents dinghies, wind-surfboards, wetsuits, and air tanks (open M-Sa 9:30am-8:30pm). **Buses** travel to Cork and from Griffin's Bar on Main St. **Ferries** chug to Cape Clear and Sherkin; contact Captain O'Driscoll for more info (tel. (028) 391 35). If the **tourist office,** occasionally found on Main St., poses too much of an existential dilemma for you, pick up the lengthy **Schull Guide** from any store in town (IR£1.50). **The Schull Backpackers' Lodge (IHH),** Colla Rd. (tel. (028) 286 81), is bright and immaculate (dorms IR£7-8; doubles IR£20-24; bike rental IR£7 per day). The **Courtyard,** on Main St., sells a variety of gourmet foods, whole foods, soups and sandwiches (open M-Sa 10am-4pm and 6:30-9:30pm), and the adjacent **pub** features trad, jazz, and blues. The grocery store **Spar Market** is on Main St. (open daily 7am-9pm).

Ring of Kerry The Ring of Kerry once embodied the tough, romantic spirit of Ireland, but today seems the epitome of package tourism. Lively **Killarney** is a good base for exploring the impressive national park nearby. B&Bs are easy to come by, and good hostels reside in town. Try **Neptune's (IHH),** Bishop's Lane (tel. (064) 352 55), the first walkway off New St. on the right (dorms IR£8.50; doubles IR£20; 10% discount with ISIC), or the **Bunrower House Hostel (IHH)** (tel. (064) 339 14), right next to the park (dorms IR£7-8.50; doubles IR£20; camping IR£3.50). **The Súgán (IHH),** Lewis Rd. (tel. (064) 331 04), is a two-minute walk from the bus or train station (dorms IR£8). **Yer Mans,** Plunkett St., is the unequivocal best pub in town and the only bar in Ireland licensed to sell Guinness in jam jars. From June through September, buses leave Killarney for the **Ring of Kerry Circuit,** which stops in Killorglin, Cahirsiveen, Caherdaniel, and other towns (IR£8 if booked in a hostel).

The spectacular **National Park** offers some respite from the crowds. Get a decent map from the Killarney **tourist office,** Beach St. (tel. (064) 316 33), off New St. **Muckross House** (tel. (064) 314 40), a 19th-century manor, is three miles south of Killarney on Kenmare Rd. (open daily July-Aug. 9am-7pm; Sept.-June 9am-6pm). You can bike to the hallowed **Gap of Dunloe,** which divides the epic **Macgillycuddy's Reeks** (Ireland's tallest mountain range) from the **Purple Mountains.** Take a **motorboat** to the head of the Gap (£7.50; £7 if booked at the tourist office or a hostel), which will leave you and your bike at **Lord Brandon's Cottage.** The 1½-mile stretch before arriving at the head of the Gap is a steep climb well-rewarded by the 7-mile downhill coast through the park's most breathtaking scenery. At the foot of the Gap, you'll pass **Kate Kearney's Cottage** and droves of tourists (open daily 9am-midnight; food until 9pm; frequent live trad). The 8-mile ride back to Killarney (bear right after Kate's, turn left on the road to Fossa, then right on Killorglin Rd.) passes the ruined **Dunloe Castle,** an Anglo-Norman stronghold demolished by Cromwell's armies.

What tiny **Caherdaniel** lacks in excitement it makes up for with two miles of white sand in **Derrynane Strand** and the 19th-century patriot Daniel O'Connell's **Derrynane House** (IR£2, students IR£1). The new **Traveller's Rest Hostel** (tel. (066) 751 75) sits near the crossroads (IR£7; call ahead). The town of **Cahersiveen** is worth a stop for the extraordinarily friendly **Sive Hostel (IHH),** 15 East End, Main St. (tel. (066) 727 17; IR£7-18), the very Irish **Anchor Bar** and **Mike Murt's,** and the nightlife provided by another 28 pubs. In **Killorglin,** the **Laune Valley Farm Hostel** (tel. (066) 614 88; 1½ miles from town off the Tralee road) shares its land with a barnyard full of cats, dogs, and chickens (IR£6; doubles from IR£16; camping IR£3).

Dingle Peninsula

Dingle Peninsula Touristy Dingle Peninsula, County Kerry's northernmost, combines striking scenery with some of the few surviving *gaeltacht* communities. Base yourself in **Dingle Town,** rich in traditional culture and famous for **Fungi the dolphin,** permanent resident of Dingle Bay. While the town is well-connected to Killarney and Tralee, public transport on the peninsula is scarce. **Buses** run daily in July and August, but only two or three times per week the rest of the year. For info, call the Tralee **bus station** (tel. (066) 235 66) or stop in the Dingle town **tourist office** (tel. (066) 511 88), at the corner of Main and Dykegate St. (Open July-Aug. M-Sa 9am-7pm, Su 9am-1pm and 2:15-7pm; Apr.-June and Sept.-Oct. 9:30am-6pm.) **Ballintaggart Hostel (IHH)** (tel. (066) 514 54), 25min. east of town on Tralee Rd., is set in the grand stone mansion where the Earl of Cork poisoned his wife in an upstairs room that her ghost now supposedly haunts. Gloriously renovated with an enclosed cobblestone courtyard, a crystal chandelier, and a high-quality restaurant. (Dinners IR£7-9. 10- to 12-bed dorms IR£7; 4-bed dorms IR£8; private rooms from IR£13 per person. **Camping** IR£3.50 per person.) Try **An Droichead Beag** on Lower Main St. for drinks and the best trad in town. For tasty food and Irish patriotism, go to the bookstore/cafe **An Café Liteartha,** on Dykegate St. (open M-F 10am-5:30pm, Sa-Su 11am-5:30pm).

No matter how tight your schedule is, you will inevitably be waylaid by glorious **Slea Head.** *Ryan's Daughter* and parts of *Far and Away* were filmed amid the green hills, sheep, and jagged cliffs of this area. Stone houses and plenty of spoken Irish fill the scattered settlement of **Dunquin. Kruger's** (tel. (066) 561 27) features pub grub, music sessions, and fantastic views. The adjacent **B&B** has pretty and comfortable rooms (IR£15 per person). Just outside of "town" on the road to Ballyferriter, the **Blasket Centre** recreates life on the isolated Blasket Islands with writings and photographs of the Great Blasket authors. (Open daily July-Aug. 10am-7pm; Easter-June and Sept. 10am-6pm. IR£2.50, students IR£1.) A winding cliffside road runs northward from Dingle via the **Connor Pass** and affords tremendous views of bays and valleys.

Tralee

Tralee While tourists see Killarney as the core of Kerry, residents are proud to identify Tralee as the county's economic center. **Kerry the Kingdom,** Ashe Memorial Hall, Denny St., uses modern technology to chronicle the history of Co. Kerry

IRELAND

from 8000 BC to the present. (Open Mar.-June and Sept.-Oct. daily 9am-6pm; July-Aug. M-Sa 9am-7pm, Su 10am-6pm; Nov.-Mar. daily 9am-5:30pm. IR£5.50, students IR£4.75.) Near the museum, the radiant **Roses of Tralee** in the town park and the famous **Siamsa Tíre Theatre** (tel. (066) 230 55), Ireland's national folk theater, draw many visitors. (Productions July-Aug. M-Sa at 8:30pm; May-June and Sept. M-Th and Sa at 8:30pm. IR£9, students IR£8.) During the last week of August, the **Rose of Tralee International Festival** (info tel. (066) 213 22) brings a maelstrom of entertainment to town, as young Irish women compete for the title "Rose of Tralee."

Trains go to Cork (2½hr., IR£17, students IR£7), Dublin (4hr., IR£33.50, students IR£12.50), and Killarney (40min., IR£5.50, students IR£3.50). **Buses** run to Cork (2½hr., IR£10, students IR£6), Dingle (1¼hr., IR£6, students IR£4), Killarney (40min., IR£4.40, students IR£3), and Limerick (2¼hr., IR£9, students IR£5). The **tourist office** (tel. (066) 212 88) is in Ashe Memorial Hall on Denny St. (open in summer M-Sa 9am-7pm, Su 9am-6pm; off-season Tu-Sa 9am-5pm). **Finnegan's Hostel (IHH),** 17 Denny St. (tel. (066) 276 10), is in a majestic 19th-century townhouse that contains part of the old town castle (IR£7.50; doubles IR£18).

WESTERN IRELAND

Even Dubliners will tell you that the West is the "most Irish" part of Ireland. It was hardest hit by the potato famine in the 19th century, and the population is still less than half of what it was in 1841. But from Connemara north to Ballina, hikers, and cyclists enjoy boggy, rocky, or brilliantly mountainous landscapes. Booming Galway City remains an enclave of carousing in this otherwise quiet, traditional region.

■ Limerick

Although high unemployment and grimy industry have long kept it sagging, **Limerick City** is completing a multi-year facelift. Attractive Georgian architecture and **King John's Castle** on Nicholas St. are worth exploring (castle open daily 9:30am-6pm; IR£3.80, students IR£2.10). **Buses** (tel. (061) 31 33 33) leave from Colbert Station, just off Parnell St., for Cork (2hr., IR£9, students IR£5.30), Dublin (3hr., IR£10, students IR£7.50), Galway (2hr., IR£9, students IR£3.50), Killarney (2½hr., IR£9.30, students IR£5.30) Sligo (6hr., IR£14, students IR£8.50). **Trains** (tel. (061) 31 55 55) also leave from Colbert Station. The **tourist office,** Arthurs Quay (tel. (061) 31 75 22), has IR£1 city maps. (Open July-Aug. M-F 9am-7pm, Sa-Su 9am-6pm; Mar.-June and Sept.-Oct. M-Sa 9:30am-5:30pm; Nov.-Feb. M-F 9:30am-5:30pm, Sa 9:30am-1pm.) From the station, walk down Davis St. and turn left onto Pery Sq. to reach the hostel **Finnegan's (IHH),** 6 Pery Sq. (tel. (061) 31 03 08; dorms IR£7.50; private rooms IR£10 per person). Or try the pleasant rooms at **St. Anthony's,** 8 Coolraine Terrace, Ennis Rd. (tel. (061) 45 26 07; IR£16-17). **The Green Onion Cafe,** Evlen St., serves excellent bistro food (open daily noon-10pm). Trad music is played nightly around town.

Eight miles northwest of Limerick along Ennis Rd. (N18), **Bunratty Castle** claims to be Ireland's most complete medieval castle, with superbly restored furniture, tapestry, and stained-glass windows.

■ Clare Coast

Europe's best traditional Irish music, highest cliffs, and strangest landscapes are to be found on the superlative coast of Co. Clare. **Bus Éireann** (tel. (065) 241 77) runs a coastal bus from Ennis to Galway, through most of the small towns and past the Cliffs of Moher and Doolin. The spectacular **Westend Cliff Walk** and a famously fun pub crawl make **Kilkee** worth a visit. **Kilkee Hostel (IHH)** (tel. (065) 562 09), among the pubs on O'Curry St., makes friends of strangers (dorms IR£7; sheets 50p). Just 20 miles up the coast from Kilkee and two miles inland from the Spanish Point beach is **Milltown Malbay,** probably the best place for Irish music. During **Willie Clancy**

Week, July 3-10, 1999, Milltown turns into a traditional music festival; thousands of musicians and *craic* addicts converge for a week of recitals, lectures, and nonstop sessions. Central **Ward's B&B** (tel. (065) 846 84) has beautiful rooms (IR£12-13).

The tiny seaside resort of **Lahinch** sits on smooth sand in a crook of the bay. Near the water on Church St. is the comfortable **Lahinch Hostel** (tel (065) 810 40; dorms IR£7.50; doubles IR£22). A 20-minute bus ride goes around the coast to the extraordinary **Cliffs of Moher,** justifiably one of Ireland's most famous sights. Standing 700 feet above the Atlantic spray, you'll peer below onto gulls circling limestone spires. **Doolin** (pop. 600) is a rural backpackers' mecca eight miles up the coast from the Cliffs of Moher. It's lower village is a handful of buildings near the sea; the tiny upper village is a mile up the road. Fifteen years ago, Doolin was the trad capital, and its three legendary pubs—**McGann's** and **McDermott's** in Upper Village and **O'Connor's** in the Lower—still have fantastic sessions and tasty food nightly. By the river between the two villages is the **Aille River Hostel (IHH)** (tel. (065) 742 60), a small cottage with a groovy ambience. (Dorms IR£6.50; private rooms IR£8 per person; **camping** IR£3.50. Open mid-Mar. to mid-Nov.) Doolin is within easy biking distance of the Burren and the Cliffs; the **Doolin Bike Store** (tel. (065) 742 60) rents bikes (IR£6 per day).

North and east of Doolin, bare limestone pops up amid the grasses and sheep. This region, encompassing 100 square miles, is the **Burren,** where an elaborate moonscape includes jagged hills, ruined churches and castles, thousands of miles of stone walls, rare wildflowers, disappearing lakes, and ancient megaliths. It's notoriously difficult to get around the Burren. Yellow arrows mark a 26 mile hiking trail from Liscannor to Ballyvaughan; Doolin and Kinvara are the best bases for biking tours. **Kinvara,** a gem of a fishing village just north of the Burren, has an excellent music scene, a vibrant artistic community, pubs with character, and a well-preserved medieval castle. **Johnston's Hostel (IHH)** (tel. (091) 371 64), on Main St., is a relaxing retreat where dozens have met their spouses (dorms IR£7.50; sheets IR£1; **camping** IR£4.50; lockout 12:30-7am; open June-Sept). **Tully's** and **The Pierhead** have the best trad.

■ Galway City

Galway (pop. 60,000) is a college town on *craic*. In the past few years, a huge influx of young Irish, over 13,000 students, a transient population of 20-something Europeans, and droves of backpackers have turned this small town into a vibrant cultural mecca overflowing with youth. Casinos and amusement parks overlook the mile-long beachfront promenade in neighboring Salthill, while musicians work the cobblestoned medieval streets straddling the Corrib River in the city center.

SIGHTS AND ENTERTAINMENT Sightseers find Galway a convenient base for trips to the Clare coast or the Connemara, backpackers appreciate its large number of fine hostels, and pubcrawlers find inspiration in its wondrous variety of drinking establishments. The town's main attractions are its nightlife and setting; *Galway Magazine* (IR£1) describes its few notable sights, and *The List* has music and restaurant listings. The **Film Fleagh, Salthill Air Show, Galway Arts Festival,** and **Galway Races** follow one another in rapid succession in July, making it impossible to find accommodation without advance booking.

Choosing from among the Galway's endless variety of fantastic pubs is a difficult challenge even for residents (nightclubs lag far behind in quality and value). Experienced drinkers solve their dilemma by visiting as many as possible until the perfect pint meets the perfect atmosphere. Generally speaking, Quay St. pubs cater to vacationers and students. Don't miss the spectacular interiors of the third floor of **The Slate House,** a converted convent on Kirwin's Lane off Cross St., and **The Quays,** a converted church on Quay St. (open 10pm-1am). The **Front Door** across the street seems small, but opens more rooms as it gets busy, eventually rising three stories and sprouting appendages all over the block, while the bunch at **Seaghan Ua Neachtain** (Knockton's) next door trade personal space for warmth and energy. The Dominick St. pubs across the river are much better for music. The second floor of **The Crane,** 2

Sea Rd., just off Dominick St., is the place to hear trad. The best Irish bands play down the street at **Roisín Dubh. The Blue Note** between them pulsates every night with acid jazz from funky guest DJs. **Le Graal,** on Lower Dominick St., is a candle-lit wine bar that draws a crowd of beautiful continentals and other sophisticates (open until 1am). The gigantic **Skeffington Arms,** on Eyre Sq., is a pup crawl unto itself, while **Padraig's** on the docks opens at 7:30am for the die-hards (you know who you are).

PRACTICAL INFO, ACCOMMODATIONS, AND FOOD From the Eyre Sq. Station (tel. (091) 56 14 44; open M-Sa 7:40am-6pm), **trains** run to Dublin (3hr., IR£15-21). **Citylink** (tel. (091) 56 41 63) sends **buses** to Dublin (IR£5); **Bus Éireann** (tel. (091) 56 20 00) leaves for Belfast (IR£16.30), and Cork (IR£12). The main **tourist office** (tel. (091) 56 30 81) is at Victoria Pl. southeast of Eyre Sq. (open daily 9am-5:45pm; later in summer). Access the **Internet** at **Cyberzone,** southwest of Eyre Sq. (IR£3 per hr.).

Galway boasts excellent hostels. **Kinlay House** (tel. (091) 56 52 44), on the south-east corner of Eyre Sq., is modern, spotless, fun, secure, and big (dorms IR£8-10; doubles IR£26-32; breakfast included; 10% ISIC discount). The **Quay Street Hostel** (tel. (091) 56 86 44) has a darkwood common room, impressive kitchen, and "kick-ass" location in pub central (dorms IR£7-9.50; doubles IR£24-29). The **Salmon Weir Hostel** (tel. (091) 56 11 33), a five-minute walk west of Eyre Sq. on St. Vincent's Ave., sucks newcomers into a fun-loving, comfortable atmosphere (dorms IR£7.50; doubles IR£20; no smoking; curfew 3am). Across from the station, the **Galway Hostel** (tel. (091) 56 69 59) has attractive rooms and a cozy kitchen (dorms IR£7-8.50; doubles with bath IR£26-28). The **Eyre Square Hostel** (tel. (091) 56 84 32), west of the square on Eyre St., is cozy with giant windows (dorms IR£7-8; doubles IR£22-24). For affordable eats, stay east of the river near Quay St. or the west part of Abbeygate St. **Scotty's Casual Gourmet,** Middle St., casually beams you down to foot-long subs (IR£2.50). **Java's,** Upper Abbeygate, serves IR£4 baps and cappuccino until 4am.

■ Aran Islands (Oileáin Árann)

The harsh limestone landscapes of the Aran Islands guard the entrance to Galway Bay. Awesome Iron Age forts sit top the stark cliffs while mazes of stone walls divide deserted fields. Although islanders still fish, speak Irish, and produce traditional sweaters and *curraghs* (tar-bottomed boats), tourism and modernization are gradually changing their ways. **Island Ferries** (tel. (091) 56 17 67) leaves from **Rossaveal** (return IR£15; return bus from Galway IR£4) and **O'Brien Shipping** (tel. (091) 56 72 83) leaves from the Galway pier (return IR£12, students IR£10); both have booths in the Galway tourist office. **Doolin Ferries** (tel. (065) 744 55) leaves from Doolin (return £20 to all islands).

Of the dozens of ruins, forts, churches, and holy wells which rise from the stony terrain of Inishmore, the most amazing is the **Dún Aengus** ring fort, where a small semicircular wall surrounds a thought-provoking 300-foot drop. Inishmore is still a fairly isolated place despite an increase in tourists. Ferries land at **Kilronan,** where the tourist office (tel. (099) 612 63) sells maps, holds bags (75p), and changes money (open May to mid-Sept. daily 10am-7pm). Beds at **Mainistir House (IHH)** (tel. (099) 611 69) come with superb fresh breakfasts and a cool atmosphere (IR£8; doubles IR£24). A free hostel minibus meets the ferries. The **Spar Market,** past the hostel, is the island's social center (open M-Sa 9am-8pm, Su 10am-6pm). **Inishmaan** is a wind-swept, barren place where tourists are considered a necessary evil. **Inisheer,** the smallest island, is less rugged and budget-friendly. The **Brú Hostel (IHH)** (tel. (099) 750 24) is clean, spacious, and a limestone slab's throw from the pier (dorms IR£7; private rooms IR£9-10 per person; breakfast IR£2-3.50).

■ The Connemara

Spanning from Galway City to the Atlantic, the rugged Connemara comprises lacy coastline and rough mountains, with squishy bogs in between. Ireland's largest Irish-speaking region *(gaeltacht)* stretches along the southern coast, where a developed strip from Galway to Rossavel gives way to long beaches and pretty fishing villages. One nice village is **Roundstone,** which curves along a colorful harbor. Buses regularly service the main road from Galway to Clifden; the coastal road through Roundstone; and, during summer, the more scenic route north of Lough Corrib. Biking is a rewarding way to see the Connemara.

The rugged **Twelve Bens** (Na Benna Beola; Twelve Pins) range, in the Connemara National Park (tel. (095) 410 54), reaches 2400-foot heights and is not recommended for single or beginning hikers. Hikers should obtain Jos Lynam's book of 18 hikes through the Bens and the adjoining Maamturks. The park's entrance is just outside the three-pub crossroads of Letterfrack, home to one of the finest hostels in Ireland. Sturdy pine bunks, desks, and couches fit the spacious high-ceilinged rooms of the **Old Monastery Hostel** (tel. (095) 411 32; dorms IR£7-9; **bikes** IR£6 per day).

Alone in the Atlantic seven miles from the western tip of the Connemara, the island of **Inishbofin** keeps time according to the ferry and the tides. There's little to do on the island but watch birds fish among the coves, scramble up the craggy hills, commune with the seals, sunbathe on a secluded white strand, and sleep under a blanket of bright stars. **Michael Nee's bus** (tel. (095) 510 82; return IR£10) connects Clifden to the ferry port; the **Island Discovery** (tel. (095) 446 42; return IR£12) and the **M.V. Dun Aengus** (tel. (095) 458 06) both serve the island 2-3 times a day. The **Inishbofin Island Hostel (IHH)** (tel. (095) 458 55), a 10-minute walk right from the harbor, blesses hostelers with pine bunks, entertaining views, and kind management (dorms IR£6.40; private rooms IR£9-10 per person; sheets IR£1; **camping** IR£4).

Clifden (An Clochán) Picturesque Clifden, embedded in spectacular scenery,

dozes during the winter and explodes with tourists in peak season. Despite its recent commericalization, it remains a bastion of traditional Irish culture, music, and language. **Buses** run to Clifden from Galway through Oughterard (1½hr., June-Aug. 2-6 per day, fewer off-season, IR£6.50). The **tourist office**, Market St. (tel. (095) 211 63), has plenty of info (open M-Sa 9am-6pm; July-Aug. also Su noon-4pm). **Connemara Walking Center,** Market St. (tel. (095) 213 79), plans forays into the bogs, islands, and mountains (IR£8-24; **bike rental** IR£6 per day; open Mar.-Oct. M-Sa 10am-6pm).

The central **Clifden Town Hostel,** Market St. (tel. (095) 210 76), has spotless rooms, great facilities, and a friendly atmosphere (dorms IR£7; private room IR£8-10 per person). **Leo's Hostel (IHH)** (tel. (095) 214 29), Sea View, is beginning to show its age, but a turf fire and astounding "loo with a view" more than compensate (July-Aug. dorms IR£7; private rooms IR£8; **camping** IR£3; bikes IR£5 per day). The **Brookside Hostel,** Hulk St. (tel. (095) 218 12), has spacious common rooms and friendly sheep (dorms IR£6-7). **Mannion's,** Market St., hosts seemingly spontaneous trad sessions nightly, while **King's,** the Square, pulls the best pint. **E.J. King's** next door is a touristy pub that rocks the casbah. **Humpy's,** rumored to have its own dance, gets busy on the weekends in the panoramic back room.

Westport A pleasant town with a more-than-satisfactory pub life and plenty of

good cafes, Westport is nestled in the elbow-crook of **Clew Bay,** with Connemara to its south and Co. Mayo's islands a short jaunt northwest. The **Westport Quay** tourist trap, with its Heritage Centre, stately Westport House, and ferry service to Clare Island, is a mile west of town on Quay Rd. **Croagh Patrick's** perfect cone of a mountain, holy for millennia, rises 2510 feet over Clew Bay. Most climbers start from the village of **Murrisk,** west of Westport on R395 and accessible by bus or cab, and continue on to Louisburgh. **Trains** (tel. (098) 252 53 or 253 29) arrive in Westport from Dublin (IR£15, F and Su IR£20); the town is a 10-minute walk away on the left. **Buses** leave from the Octagon for Galway (IR£8.80). The **tourist office** (tel. (098) 257 11) sits on the North Mall by the river (open M-F 9am-6pm, Sa 10am-6pm). Rent **bikes** from **Breheny & Sons,** Castlebar St. (tel. (098) 250 20). Drinking while driving on the information superhighway is encouraged at **Dunning's Cyberpub,** the Octagon.

The **Old Mill Holiday Hostel (IHH),** James St. (tel. (098) 270 45), between the Octagon and the tourist office, keeps firm beds in a renovated mill and brewery (IR£6.50; laundry IR£3). **Club Atlantic (IHH),** Altamont St. (tel. (098) 266 44 or 267

17), across from the station and a five-minute walk from the Mall, is a 140-bed complex with a huge kitchen, snooker, and video games (dorms IR£5.50-6.50; singles IR£9; doubles IR£11.80-13.80; rates vary). Bop down Bridge St. for a night of drinking and carousing. **McCormack's,** Bridge St., is praised as the exemplary teahouse. Join the crowds at **Matt Molloy's,** owned by the Chieftains' flautist.

NORTHWEST IRELAND

Sligo is a bay town close to the heart of poet William Butler Yeats, Donegal is the most remote county of the Republic, with windy mountains and winding coasts, and the inspiring Inishowen Peninsula can be a gateway to Northern Ireland.

Sligo Town Childhood haunt of W.B. Yeats, Sligo Town is a busy commerical center with a happening pub life. In **Drumcliff churchyard,** four miles northwest of Sligo on N15 Bundoran Rd., Yeats is buried under his epitaph: "Cast a cold eye/On life, on death./Horseman, pass by!" To the southeast, **Lough Gill** has enough sights to fill a daytrip. The Sligo **tourist office,** Temple St. (tel. (071) 612 01), on the corner of Charles St., covers the region. (Open June M-Sa 9am-6pm; July-Aug. M-Sa 9am-8pm, Su 9am-2pm; Sept. M-F 9am-8pm, Su 9am-1pm; Oct.-May M-F 9am-5pm.) The **bus** and **train station,** Lord Edward St., sends trains to Dublin (IR£13.50) and buses to Belfast (4hr., IR£13.50), Derry (3hr., IR£10), and Galway (2½hr., IR£10.50). Reserve ahead for room. The awesome **Harbour House,** Finisklin Rd. (tel. (071) 715 47), and the convenient **White House Hostel (IHH),** Markievicz Rd. (tel. (071) 451 60 or 423 98), offer accommodations (IR£6.50-10). **Hargadon Bros.,** O'Connell St. is the most traditional of traditional pubs; **Shoot the Crows,** Castle St., and **McGarrigle's,** O'Connell St., have younger crowds and great music.

Sink or Sin

Stand by the shore of Lough Gill and listen carefully. What do you hear? The lapping of the waves? The wind rustling in trees? The soft peal of a pure silver bell, sounding distantly from the bottom of the lake? No? That's because you're a sinner. When Sligo's Dominican Friary was wrecked during the Ulster rebellion of 1641, worshippers saved its bell and hid it on the bottom of Lough Gill. Legend insists that only those free from sin can still hear it. Don't worry, neither can we.

Donegal Town and the Donegal Coast Gateway to the splendor of the north and west, **Donegal Town** features an energetic nightlife. **Buses** travel to Dublin (4hr., IR£10) and Galway (4hr., IR£13) via Sligo (1hr., IR£7.30). Be sure to stop at the superb **tourist office,** Quay St. (tel. (073) 211 48), for brochures and advice before heading north. (Open July-Aug. M-F 9am-8pm, Sa 9am-6pm, Su 9am-5pm; Sept.-Oct. and Easter-June M-F 9am-5pm, Sa 10am-2pm.) The **Donegal Town Hostel (IHH),** Killybegs Rd. (tel. (073) 228 05), presents a great community for the road-weary backpacker (IR£7; doubles IR£16; camping IR£4; the owners will pick you up in town). **The Blueberry Tea Room,** Castle St., and **Errigal Restaurant,** Main St., serve popular, affordable meals.

During the day, your hours are best spent visiting nearby **Lough Eske Castle** (ask at the tourist office for info), but Donegal puts on a good show by night. **Schooner's,** upper Main St., has the best trad sessions in town in the summer, while **The Cellar Bar,** down the street, offers nightly trad and ballads. **The Voyager Bar,** the Diamond, draws crowds with live bands on the odd weekend and no cover. During the last weekend of June and first week of July, the **International Arts Festival** features drama, storytelling, traditional music, and parachuting.

The road west along Donegal's southern edge, the N56, snakes along the Atlantic coast, then inland around weather-beaten cliffs and tiny villages. Although not very appealing, the fishing harbor of **Killybegs** has some of the only services in the area. A breathtaking eight miles past Killybegs is tiny **Kilcar,** in which you can rest and enjoy impromptu music at **Piper's Rest Pub & Restaurant** on Main St. a mile and a half out of town, the charming **Derrylahan Hostel (IHH)** (tel. (073) 380 79) welcomes guests with hot showers and an amiable staff (IR£6; private rooms IR£8 per person; camping IR£3). Still farther north, the small town of **Carrick** offers great fishing and access to **Slieve League**, a 2000-foot mountain which drops precipitously into Donegal Bay, set on a coastline of 1000-foot sea cliffs. For info, talk to the locals at the **Tweed Factory Craft Shop and Tea Room** in Kilcar (open June-Sept. M-F 9am-6pm, Sa 10am-4pm). Just south of Carrick, **Teelin Bay House** (tel. (073) 390 43) is deservedly famous for its hospitality (IR£13; book ahead).

Dungloe and Crohy Head

Many miles north of Carrick on N56, **Dungloe** (dun-LO; An Clochan Liath) is a busy market town near Crohy Head where travelers stock up before hurrying on to the mountains. North and west of Dungloe stretch the Rosses, a haunting, largely untouched area and bog ecologist's paradise jutting into the sea. Stony soil dotted with tiny ponds covers the glacially crumpled ground of this headland. The Dungloe **tourist office** (tel. (073) 212 97), on a well-marked side street off Main St. toward the shore, has free town maps. It's a good idea to stop in here before heading into the Rosses and Gweedore—the office is the last Bord Fáilte you'll find in the area (open June-Sept. M-Sa 10am-1pm and 2-6pm). **Greene's Independent Holiday Hostel (IHH),** Carnmore Rd. (tel. (073) 219 43), is right off Main St. away from the waterfront. (Dorms £7; singles £8; doubles £16; family room £25-30. **Bike rental** £5 per day. Laundry £3. Curfew Tu-Th 1am, F-M 2am.) **Crohy Head,** the peninsula six miles southwest of Dungloe, collects strangely shaped rock formations around a jagged coast. To reach the peninsula and the hostel from Dungloe, turn onto Quay Rd. halfway down Main St. and follow the bumpy road along the sea.

Derryveagh Mountains and Letterkenny

The imposing **Derryveagh Mountains** isolate the northwest corner of Donegal, the country's largest Irish-speaking area. **Letterkenny** is Donegal's commercial center and one of the fastest growing towns in Europe. Stop here between peninsular jaunts, or on your way to Glenveagh National Park or Donegal. The **Chamber of Commerce Visitors Information Centre,** 40 Port Rd. (tel. (074) 248 66 or 255 05), doles out pamphlets (open M-F 9am-5pm). **The Manse Hostel (IHH),** High Rd. (tel. (074) 252 38), is comfortable, with dated decor in a central location (dorms IR£6). Fourteen miles northwest of Letterkenny stretches the **Glenveagh National Park** (tel. (074) 370 90 or 372 62)—37 square miles of glens, mountains, and nature walks, plus a castle. (Both open Easter to early Nov. daily 10am-6:30pm, opens late on Su in July and Aug. IR£2, students IR£1.)

Donegal Peninsulas

Between Lough Swilly and Mulroy Bay, the **Fanad Peninsula** juts into the Atlantic, favoring drivers with beautiful views from remote roads. North of Rathmullan, the road narrows and winds through dense wildlife as it rises over the Knockalla Mountains and Glenvar. Beyond this stretch of road, the coast arcs dramatically between mountain and shore. Follow the signs to the peaceful **Bunnaton Hostel,** Glenvar (tel. (074) 501 22; IR£6.50; private rooms IR£8.50 per person).

A mosaic of rugged mountains, lush forests, and sumptuous beaches, the **Inishowen Peninsula** is a microcosm of Ireland. An excellent place to begin is the 4000-year-old cultural center of the peninsula, the hilltop ringfort of **Grianán Ailigh,** which was originally a Druidic temple of sun worship. **Buncrana,** on the west side of the peninsula along the shores of Lough Swilly, is an energetic resort where sweeping beaches repose in the long shadow of **Slieve Snacht,** a 2019 ft. peak. About six miles north of Buncrana and 800 feet above sea level, the **Mamore Gap** offers a view over the mountains to the Atlantic. From **Malin Head,** the northernmost point in Ireland, you can see across to the Paps of Jura, Scotland, on a clear day. A path to the left of the car park leads to **Hell's Hole,** a 250 ft. chasm which roars with the incoming tide.

Situated on a lovely estuary, the village of **Culdaff** exudes a warmth from its beaches. **McGrory's Pub** (tel. (077) 791 04) offers renowned trad as well as B&B lodgings (IR£15). Glorious **Culdaff Strand,** best seen at sunrise or sunset, is a short walk from McGrory's. Nearby **Kinnagoe Bay,** site of the 1588 wreck of the Spanish

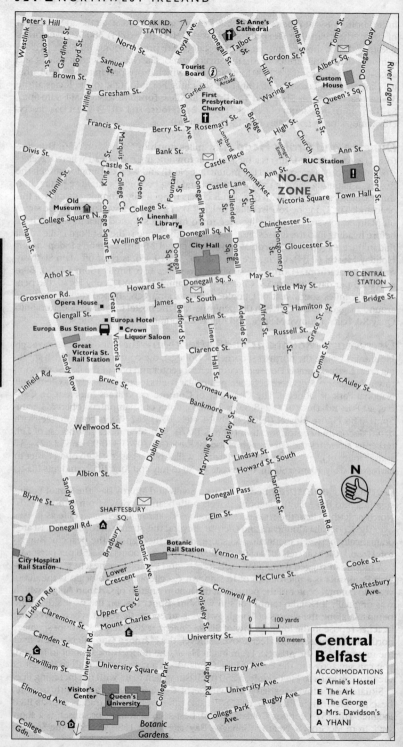

Central Belfast

ACCOMMODATIONS

C Arnie's Hostel
E The Ark
B The George
D Mrs. Davidson's
A YHANI

Armada, offers breathtaking views. On the southeast coast of the Inishowen Peninsula sits the **Moville Holiday Hostel (IHH)** (tel. 823 78), lovingly converted from old stone-walled farm buildings. The hostel's forested grounds, ideal for camping, contain the oldest bridge in Ireland (dorms IR£6; private rooms IR£11; **camping** IR£4).

NORTHERN IRELAND

The strife that makes Northern Ireland infamous hides the land's beauty and appeal. Underneath the sometimes violent history rest a string of seaside villages on the Ards Peninsula; the pockets of green collectively called the Glens of Antrim; the Giant's Causeway, one of the world's strangest geological sights; and the beautiful Fermanagh Lake District. Always a major industrial center, Belfast has recently become a fun, hip destination for a range of travelers and students. Pub culture and urban neighborhoods show everyday life in a divided but generally peaceful society. Despite setbacks, the widespread support of the 1998 Peace Agreement raises hopes of a resolution to the struggles that have divided the island for centuries.

The **currency** in Northern Ireland is British pounds ("pounds sterling"). Notes printed in Northern Ireland have the same value as those printed in England and Scotland, but are *not* accepted in the rest of the U.K. English, Scottish, and Manx notes, however, *are* accepted in Northern Ireland and on the border. Most towns have shops that take "punt for pound" or vice versa. **Hitching** in the North is less common and less safe than in the Republic. Border check-points have recently been removed, and there are fewer and fewer armed soldiers in the cities. A fear of bombs still lingers, however; don't leave your luggage unattended—it will be viewed suspiciously.

■ Belfast

The second-largest city on the island, Belfast is the center of the North's cultural, commercial, and political activity. Victorian architecture, acclaimed theater, and the annual arts festival in November maintain Belfast's reputation as a thriving artistic center, and West Belfast's political graffiti art and famous murals are both informative and truly moving. The burgeoning bar scene—a mix of British and Irish pub culture—entertains locals, foreigners, and the lively student population. The past few years have brought a chic cosmopolitan edge to this growing city, which, despite a significant visitor presence, seems unlikely to succumb to tourist culture.

ORIENTATION AND PRACTICAL INFORMATION

Belfast is loosely centered on **City Hall** in **Donegall Square,** six blocks west of the River Lagan and the harbor. To the north lies the city's snazzy shopping district, while two blocks west of the center, the **Golden Mile** follows Great Victoria St. from Shaftesbury Sq. to the Opera House. South of Donegall Square, **University Road** and **Botanic Ave.** lead to Queen's University and a neighborhood of B&Bs, pubs, and cafes. Divided from the rest of the city by the Westlink Motorway, **West Belfast** is both poorer and more politically volatile than the city center. If you plan on visiting the docks for the nightlife, it is best to travel to and from there in a taxi.

> Tourists should avoid Belfast around **July 12,** when the Protestant Orangemen hold their parades. These days have seen riots and violence, and tourists hold no special amnesty when passions are high. It is also prohibited to take **photographs** of soldiers or any sort of military item year-round; this rule *is* enforced.

Telephone Code: 01232.
Flights: Belfast International Airport, Aldergrove (tel. 42 28 88). **Airbus** (tel. 33 30 00) runs to Europa/Glengall Station (M-Sa every 30min., Su every hr., UK£4.50).
Trains: Belfast Central Station, East Bridge St. (tel. 89 94 00). To: Derry (2¼hr., UK£5.50, return UK£9.50) and Dublin (2½hr., UK£15, return UK£24). Some also stop at **Botanic Station** or the **Great Victoria Station.**

Buses: Europa/Glengall St. Station (tel. 33 30 00). To: Derry (UK£6.50, return UK£11.50) and Dublin (UK£10.50, return UK£14). Buses from Northern Ireland's east coast arrive at the **Laganside Station** (tel. 33 30 00). **Leaping Leprechaun** (tel. (015047) 42 65 55) goes to hostels on the Antrim coast (UK£18).

Public Transportation: Provided by the red **Citybus Network** (24hr. tel. 24 68 85), supplemented by the **Ulsterbus** "blue buses" to the suburbs. The green **Centrelink** buses connect all of the major areas of Belfast. Tickets for the late **Nightline** buses must be bought in advance in Shaftesbury Sq. (UK£2).

Taxis: Huge **black cabs** run set routes to West and North Belfast (standard 60p charge). Cabs heading to Catholic neighborhoods are marked with a Falls Rd., Andersontown, or Irish-language sign; those going to Protestant neighborhood are marked with a Shankil sign or a red poppy. Or try **City Cab** (tel. 24 20 00).

Tourist Office: St. Anne's Court, 59 North St. (tel. 24 66 09). Free map with bus schedules. Books rooms. 24hr. info computer outside. Open July-Aug. M-F 9am-7pm, Sa 9am-5:15pm, Su noon-4pm; Sept.-June M-Sa 9am-5:15pm.

Budget Travel Office: USIT, 13b The Fountain Centre, College St. (tel. 32 40 73), near Royal Ave. Open M and W-F 9:30am-5:30pm, Tu 10am-5:30pm, Sa 10am-1pm. Also at Queen's University Student Union (tel. 24 18 30).

Consulates: None for **Australia, Canada,** or **Republic of Ireland. U.S.,** Consulate General, Queens House, Queen St. (tel. 22 82 39). Open M-F 1-4pm.

Currency Exchange: Thomas Cook, 22/24 Lombard St. (tel. 23 60 44). No fee to cash own traveler's checks; others at 2% commission. Open M-F 9am-5:30pm. Most banks and post offices change currency and cash traveler's checks for a small fee.

Bisexual, Gay, and Lesbian Information: Rainbow Project N.I. (tel. 31 90 30).

Emergency: Dial 999; no coins required.

Police: 65 Knock Rd. (tel. 65 02 22).

Crisis Lines: Samaritans, tel. 66 44 22. Open 24hr. **Rape Crisis Center,** 29 Donegall St. (tel. 32 18 30). Open M-F 10am-6pm, Sa 11am-5pm.

Medical Assistance: Belfast City Hospital, 9 Lisburn Rd. (tel. 32 92 41).

Post Office: 25 Castle Pl. (tel. 32 37 40). Open M-Sa 9am-5:30pm. *Poste Restante* mail arrives here. **Postal Code:** BT1 1NB.

Internet Access: Revelations Internet Cafe, 27 Shaftesbury Sq. UK£5 per hr, students UK£4 per hr. Open M-F 10am-10pm, Sa 10am-8pm, Su noon-10pm.

ACCOMMODATIONS AND FOOD

Look for generally safe and convenient lodgings near Queen's University, south of the city center. Buses 59, 69-71, 84, and 85 run from Donegall Sq. East to areas farther south. From the bus station, it's a 15-minute walk to accommodations.

Arnie's Backpackers (IHH), 63 Fitzwilliam St. (tel. 24 28 67). Relaxed, friendly atmosphere. 24hr. kitchen. Luggage storage. UK£7.50.

The Ark, 18 University St. (tel. 32 96 26). New, with that college co-op feel. 24hr. Kitchen. Dorms UK£7.50-9.50; doubles UK£28. Luggage storage.

YHANI Belfast Hostel (HI), 22 Donegall Rd. (tel. 32 47 33). Clean, spacious, modern dorms, some with bath. UK£8-10. Wheelchair accessible. Reception 24hr.

Mrs. Davidson's East-Sheen Guest House, 81 Eglantine Ave. (tel. 66 71 49). The best deal in Belfast, if you can get a room. Enormous breakfast included. UK£19.50.

The George, 9 Eglantine Ave. (tel. 68 32 12). Immaculate rooms, each with shower and TV. Singles UK£20; doubles UK£36, with bath UK£38.

Dublin Rd., Botanic Rd., and the **Golden Mile** (of Great Victoria St.) have the highest concentrations of places to eat. The **Mace Supermarket** on the corner of Castle and Queen St. has cheap groceries (open M-Sa 9am-6pm, Th until 9pm). **Bookfinders,** 47 University Rd., a smoky bookstore/cafe, offers soup and bread (UK£2) amid stacks of old books (open M-Sa 10am-5:30pm). At **Maggie May's Belfast Cafe,** 50 Botanic Ave., you can relax with tea and free newspapers. Great food available to order any time (open M-Sa 8am-10:30pm, Su 10am-10:30pm). Chill with travelers and expats at **Spuds,** 23 Bradbury Pl. (open M-Th and Sa 11am-3am, F 11am-4am, Su 11am-1am).

SIGHTS AND ENTERTAINMENT

Belfast's **City Hall,** Donegall Sq., is the administrative and geographical center of the city, regally set apart from the crowded streets by a grassy square. Its 173-foot-high green copper dome can be seen from anywhere in the city. (Tours of City Hall June-Sept. M-F at 10:30, 11:30am, and 2:30pm, Sa 2:30pm; Oct.-May M-Tu and Th-F at 2:30pm, W 10:30am. Free.) At the northwest corner of Donegall Square, the **Linen Hall Library** is famous for its comprehensive collection of political materials relating to the Troubles (open M-W and F 9:30am-5:30pm, Sa 9:30am-4pm). West of City Hall, the **Golden Mile** (Great Victoria St.) passes Belfast's pride and joy, the oft-bombed and restored **Grand Opera House.** Down the street, the huge, plush (and also oft-bombed) **Europa Hotel** faces the beautifully restored Victorian **Crown Liquor Saloon.** Follow Great Victoria St. south from City Hall to **Queen's University,** whose attractive Tudor buildings overlook the meticulously groomed **Botanic Gardens.**

The neighborhoods of **West Belfast** are the historic heart of the political tension in the North. Visitors are often amazed by the intense political **murals** found on the ends of row houses; the best way to see these is through a **black cab tour** (see **Taxis,** p. 526). Particularly well done is the **Backpacker's Tour** (tel. (0421) 06 77 52; UK£5 per person for a 6-person tour); your hostel can recommend a favorite driver.

The best sources of info on Belfast's many arts and entertainment offerings are the *Arts Council Artslink,* the Thursday issue of *Irish News,* and the daily *Belfast Telegraph.* The **Grand Opera House** (tel. 24 04 11) boasts a mix of opera, ballet, and drama. Stop by the box office at 2-4 Great Victoria St. (Tel. 24 19 19 for reservations; 24 91 29 for info. Open M-W 8:30am-8pm, Th 8:30am-9pm, F 8:30am-6:30pm, Sa 8:30am-5:30pm. Tickets UK£8-160, 50% student discount M-Th after noon on performance days.) In November, Queen's University hosts the **Belfast Festival at Queen's,** a three-week extravaganza of drama, music, and art. (Contact the Festival House, 25 College Gardens, Belfast BT9 6BS, by Aug. Ticket sales by mail begin Sept. 15; after Oct. 14 call 66 76 87.) Pubs cluster around Great Victoria St., the city center, and the university. The rather unattractive **Lavery's Gin Palace,** 12 Bradbury Pl., is one of the hottest spots in town, and **The Botanic Inn,** 23 Malone Rd, packs in the students. Despite frequent bomb damage, the **Crown Liquor Saloon,** 46 Great Victoria St., has gas lamps and "snugs" (booths) perfect for that special drink. The friendly **Queens Bar,** 4 Queen's Arcade, draws a gay and straight crowd, and **The Parliament Bar,** 2-6 Dunbar St., transplants its gay patrons to the Greek islands with disco (Tu and F-Sa), live music (Th), and bingo (M).

In Cultra, seven miles east of the city on A2 Bangor Rd., the fascinating **Ulster Folk and Transport Museum** stretches over 176 acres. The Folk Museum is the best part: over 32 buildngs from the past three centuries have been moved from their original locations all over Ulster and reconstructed here. (Open July-Aug. M-Sa 10:30am-6pm; Apr.-June and Sept. M-F 9:30am-5pm, Sa 10:30am-6pm, Su noon-6pm; Oct.-Mar. M-F 9:30am-4pm, Sa-Su 12:30-4:30pm. UK£4, students and seniors UK£2.50. Transport Museum is wheelchair accessible; Folk Museum is partially wheelchair accessible.)

A Primer of Symbols in the Murals of West Belfast

The Red Hand: the symbol of Ulster, symbolizing the hand of the first Norse King, which he supposedly cut off and threw on a Northern Ireland beach to establish his primacy. **Blue, White, & Red:** the colors of the British flag; painted to demarcate Unionist murals and neighborhoods. **King Billy/William of Orange:** sometimes depicted on a white horse; the Orange Order was founded in his honor; a major Protestant icon. **Orange & Green:** colors of the Irish Republic's flag; painted to demarcate Republican murals and neighborhoods. **Tiocfaidh ár lá:** (CHOCK-ee-ar-LA) "Our day will come." Words in Irish are a good sign of a Nationalist mural.

■ Derry (Londonderry)

Despite a history of internal conflict and the shadow of "Bloody Sunday," Derry is now engaged in a determined effort to cast off the legacy of the Troubles. New growth and a thriving rock scene attract young tourists. Derry's **city walls**, 18 feet high and 20 feet thick, were erected between 1614 and 1619. They've never been breached, hence the nickname "the Maiden City." The stellar **Tower Museum**, just inside Magazine Gate, offers a detailed city history. (Open July-Aug. M-Sa 10am-5pm, Su 2-5pm; Sept.-June Tu-Sa 10am-5pm. Last entrance 4:30pm. UK£3.50, students UK£1.20.) Brilliant **Murals** throughout town bring the turbulent past to life.

Unfortunately, Derry's present is still turbulent: avoid the city on and around **Marching Day** (July 12). **Ulsterbus** (tel. (01504) 26 22 61) serves all destinations in Northern Ireland and some in the Republic, including Belfast (1½-3hr., UK£6.50), Dublin (UK£10.50), Galway (5½hr.). The **tourist office,** 44 Foyle St. (tel. (01504) 26 72 84), distributes a city guide and free maps. (Open July-Sept. M-F 9am-7pm, Sa 10am-6pm, Su 10am-5pm; Oct.-Easter M-Th 9am-5:15pm, F 9am-5pm; Easter-June M-Th 9am-5:15pm, F 9am-5pm, Sa 10am-5pm.) **Oakgrove Manor (YHANI/HI),** Magazine St. (tel. (01504) 37 22 73), is within the city walls (dorms UK£7.50-8; singles UK£15). **Aberfoyle Hostel (HI),** 29 Aberfoyle Terrace, Strand Rd. (tel. (01504) 37 00 11) is an intimate hostel in the university quarter (dorms UK£7.50; open June-Sept.) **The Sandwich Co.,** on the corner of Ferryquay and Bishop St., offers tasty sandwiches (UK£1.50-2.50; open M-Sa 8:30am-5pm). **Peadar O'Donnell's,** 53 Waterloo St., is a popular pub with live trad, and **The Strand Bar,** 35-38 Strand Rd., has multiple levels, including a hip nightclub.

■ Causeway Coast

As the Northern Irish coast rounds Torr Head, between Ballycastle in the east and Portstewart in the west, 600-foot cliffs plummet into the restless surf. The scenic **A2**, suitable for cycling, connects the main towns along the Causeway. **Ulsterbus** 172 also runs along the coast from Ballycastle to Portrush with connections to Portstewart (1hr.). In good summer weather, take the open-topped **Bushmills Bus** (tel. (01265) 433 34), which follows the coast between Coleraine, 5 miles south of Portrush, and the Giant's Causeway (July-Aug. 5 per day).

The Glens of Antrim and the Causeway Coast meet at T-shaped **Ballycastle,** a bubbly seaside town with a popular beach. The **tourist office,** 7 Mary St. (tel. (012657) 620 24), is in Sheskburn House. (Open July-Aug. M-F 9:30am-7pm, Sa 10am-6pm, Su 2-6pm; Sept.-June M-F 9:30am-5pm.) The **Castle Hostel (IHH),** 62 Quay Rd. (tel. (012657) 623 37), has a central location and cozy bunk room (UK£6-7.50; laundry UK£1). The new **Ballycastle Backpackers Hostel,** 4 North St. (tel. (012657) 636 12 or 694 58), is spacious and extra-friendly (UK£6-7.50). From Ballycastle, a ferry runs to **Rathlin Island,** the ultimate in escapism for 20,000 puffins, one golden eagle, and about 100 people. Five miles west of Ballycastle, the modest village of **Ballintoy** features a picturesque church and a tiny harbor. Crossing the flimsy bridge that connects the mainland to **Carrick-a-rede Island** (over a dizzying 30m drop to rocks and sea) is a popular tourist activity. Take the sign-posted turnoff from the coast road ½ miles east of Ballintoy. Three miles south of Ballycastle, **Fair Head** draws international hikers to its heather- and rock-covered headland.

Advertised as the eighth natural wonder of the world, the **Giant's Causeway** is Northern Ireland's most famous sight. Two miles west of Ballintoy, the 40,000 hexagonal columns of basalt form a honeycomb path from the foot of the cliffs into the sea. The **Causeway Visitors Centre** (tel. (012657) 318 55) has tourist info, a *bureau de change,* and a post office. (Open July-Aug. daily 10am-7pm; June 10am-6pm, Sept. and Mar.-May 10am-5pm; Nov.-Feb. 10am-4:30pm.) Two miles farther west, **Bushmills** is the home of the oldest functioning whiskey distillery in the world. (Open M-Sa 9:30am-5:30pm. Tours, with free sample, every 15-20min. Apr.-Oct. 9:30am-4pm; Nov.-Mar. M-F 5 per day. UK£3, students UK£2.50).

IRELAND

■ Glens of Antrim

Between Belfast and the Causeway Coast, the rolling green hills and moors of County Antrim drop through nine lush valleys—the Glens of Antrim—down to the rocky coast. Scant **bus** lines serve the area: Ulsterbus 162 starts at Belfast and sometimes continues to Waterfoot, Cushendall, and Cushendun, while the Antrim Coaster runs in summer from Belfast to Coleraine (June-Sept. M-Sa 2 per day; July-Sept. Su 2 per day). Most rides within the Glens average UK£2-5. Call **Ulsterbus** in Belfast (tel. (01232) 32 00 11) for details. Many also bike or hitch a ride along these lovely roads.

The small village of **Glenarm,** once the chief dwelling place of the MacDonnell clan, offers a string of centuries-old houses and pubs. **Glenarm Castle** is the current residence of the 13th Earl of Antrim. Its 17th-century gate is visible from Castle St. but is open to the public only on July 14 and 15; the gardens can be explored year-round. A rock formation called **madman's window** appears on the right just before you enter town. **Nine Glens B&B,** 18 Toberwine St. (tel. (841590) 84 15 90), makes for a comfortable stay overnight (IR£15).

Five miles down the coast, the village of **Waterfoot** guards Antrim's broadest glen, part of the **Glenariff Forest Park,** 4 miles south of the village along Glenariff Rd. There waterfalls feed the River Glenariff among steep, tree-shaded hills. Camp at **Glenariff Forest Park Camping,** 98 Glenariff Rd. (tel. (012667) 582 32; tents UK£6-9), or find a farmer who welcomes campers (ask in town). The Ballymena-Cushendun **bus** (M-F 5 per day, Sa 3 per day) stops at the park entrance.

One mile north of Waterfoot, **Cushendall** offers plenty of rooms and practical convenience for the glen explorer. The **HI youth hostel** (tel. (012667) 713 44) is a 10-minute walk from town on Layde Rd. (UK£7-11.50; open Mar.-Dec.). You'll receive a warm welcome from Mrs. O'Neill at the **Glendale B&B,** 46 Coast Rd. (tel. (012667) 714 95; UK£17 per person). **Bikes** can be rented from **Ardclinis Activity Center,** 11 High St. (tel. (012667) 713 40; UK£10 per day).

Farther north via an inland road that rises through the moors, the National Trust preserves the tiny seaside village of **Cushendun.** Vast sandy beaches and amazing stone sea caves make the village a terrific afternoon stopover. The town's most popular attraction is **Mary McBride's,** 2 Main St., with slightly unusual pub grub (mac and cheese UK£3.50) and Thursday trad sessions. One mile toward Cushendall is **Sleepy Hollow B&B,** 107 Knocknacarry Rd. (tel. (01266) 76 15 13; UK£18-20).

Italy (Italia)

US$1 = L1710 (lire)	L1000 = US$0.58
CDN$1 = L1126.30	L1000 = CDN$0.89
UK£1 = L2832.62	L1000 = UK£0.35
IR£1 = L2472.75	L1000 = IR£0.40
AUS$1 = L1009.50	L1000 = AUS$0.99
NZ$1 = L873.47	L1000 = NZ$1.14
SAR1 = L274.69	L1000 = SAR3.64
Country Code: 39	**International Dialing Prefix: 00**

Italy is more than your average boot. Throughout the centuries, natural barriers and hand-made medieval stone walls have insulated communities, nurturing local dialects and customs. Unified in 1870, Italy's regional and city bonds often prove stronger than nationalist sentiment—the split between the wealthy, industrial north and the poorer, agrarian south is particularly pronounced. The political scene is equally varied: since the fall of Mussolini and the fascists, Italy has seen no fewer than 50 governments, the result of an electoral system that gives power to even the smallest of parties and necessitates unwieldy, tenuous coalitions. In the midst of this volatile political system, and even in the face of the still powerful mafia, Italy perseveres with all of its pleasures and laid-back elegance intact.

A trip through the history of Italy begins beneath the grassy hills of Tarquinia, in the brightly painted tombs of the Etruscans—this highly developed civilization ruled central Italy centuries before the birth of Christ. Meanwhile, in Sicily, the Greeks honored their gods with soaring temples of white marble. Traces of the vast Roman Empire define the landscape, from the monumental amphitheaters of Rome and Verona to the volcanically embalmed towns of Pompeii and Herculaneum. Early Christian churches sparkling with Byzantine frescoes distinguish Ravenna as a treasure house of early medieval culture, while San Gimignano bristles with the forbidding towers of the later Middle Ages. In Florence, the Italian Renaissance continues to make its intoxicating presence known.

Glean fistfuls of informative tips by reading *Let's Go: Italy 1999*.

GETTING THERE AND GETTING AROUND

Alitalia (tel. (800) 223 57 30) is Italy's national airline and may offer off-season youth fares. **Ferry** services in the port towns of Bari, Brindisi, and Ancona connect Italy to Greece. Unless you have a Eurailpass (honored only at Brindisi), Bari and Ancona services are cheaper and don't involve Brindisi's chaotic hordes of tourists.

The **Ferrovie dello Stato (FS),** the Italian State Railway, runs more or less on time and its network is comprehensive. A *locale* train stops at nearly every station; the *diretto* goes faster but serves fewer stations, while the *espresso* stops only at major stations. The *rapido,* an InterCity (IC) train, zips along but costs a bit more. If you plan to travel extensively in Italy and are under 26, the **Cartaverde** should be your first purchase (L40,000, valid for 1 year). Showing this card entitles you to a 20% discount on any state rail fare. When traveling in groups, sleep in shifts, and always keep documents and valuables concealed on your person.

Intercity **buses** are often more convenient for shorter hauls off the main rail lines, and they serve countryside points inaccessible by train. For **city buses,** buy tickets in *tabacchi,* newsstands, or kiosks, and validate them on board. An *Autostrada* (superhighway) is a worthy successor to the Appian Way, but gas and tolls are prohibitive, and Italian driving frightens some foreigners. **Mopeds** (L40,000-60,000 per day) can be a great way to see the islands and the more scenic areas of Italy, but are potentially disastrous in the rain and on rough roads or gravel. **Bicycling** is a popular national

Italy

sport, but bike trails are rare, drivers often reckless, and, except in the Po Valley, the terrain challenges even the fittest. Although hitchhiking is relatively common, *Let's Go* urges travelers to consider the safety risks. Women should never hitchhike alone.

ESSENTIALS

In provincial capitals, look for a branch of the **Ente Provinciale per il Turismo (EPT)** for info on the entire province. The city tourist board, **Azienda Autonoma di Sog-giorno e Turismo (AST)** is generally the most useful. Keep an eye out for the **Centro Turistico Studentesco e Giovanile (CTS)** and **Compagnia Italiana Turismo (CIT).**

Italy closes on the following **holidays:** New Year's Day (Jan. 1); Epiphany (Jan. 6); Easter Monday (Apr. 5 in 1999); Liberation Day (Apr. 25); May Day (May 2-4); Assumption of the Virgin (Aug. 15); All Saints' Day (Nov. 1); Immaculate Conception (Dec. 8); Christmas Day (Dec. 25); and Santo Stefano (Dec. 26). August, especially the weeks around the 15th, is vacation month for Italians; the cities shut down and empty out. At other times of the year, nearly everything closes from around 1 to 3 or 4pm for *siesta*. Most museums are open from 9am to 1pm and some again from 4 to 7pm; Monday is often their *giorno di chiusura* (day of closure). Banks are usually open from 8:30am to 1:30pm and 3 to 4pm. Food shops have a different *giorno di chiusura* from province to province.

Summers are humid and hot in the north, drier and hotter in the south. Winters are ferocious in the Alps and cold and damp in Venice and Florence, but Sicilian waters are swimmable year-round. Italy's cathedrals and churches are religious institutions and not museums. Don't visit during mass, and *cover your knees and shoulders;* the more conservative your appearance, the more likely you are to see what you came for. Italian men, generally speaking, have earned their tarnished reputation. For tips on handling unwanted attention and harassment, see **Women Travelers,** p. 27.

COMMUNICATION Fermo Posta is Italian for *Poste Restante*. There are three types of phone in Italy. Some take only coins—put more in than you think you'll need, or risk getting cut off. *Scatti* calls (often available only from telephone offices) are made from a phone run by an operator. A meter records the cost of the call, and you pay when you finish. Check first for a service fee. The most common type of phone accepts **phone cards** (L5000, L10,000, or L15,000 from *tabacchi*, newsstands, bars, post offices, and the occasional machine). A collect call is a *contassa a carico del destinatario* or *chiamata collect.* The English-speaking **operator** in Italy (dial 170) can put through collect calls. For **AT&T Direct,** dial 172 10 11; **MCI WorldPhone,** 172 10 22; **Sprint Access,** 172 18 77; **Canadian International,** 172 10 01; **BT Direct,** 172 00 44; **Telestra (Australia),** 172 10 61; and **NZ Direct,** 1 67 87 57 64. In an **emergency,** call the state **police** at 112, **fire** department at 115, and **medical** help at 113.

Any knowledge of Spanish, French, Portuguese, or Latin will help you understand Italian. Pig Latin will *not* help. The tourist office staff usually speaks some English.

Yes/No	*Sì/No*	see/no
Hi/Bye	*Ciao*	chow
Please	*Per favore*	pehr fah-VOH-ray
Thank you	*Grazie*	GRAHT-syeh
Excuse me	*Scusi?*	SKOO-zee
You're welcome.	*Prego.*	PRAY-go
Do you speak English?	*Parla (Parli) inglese?*	par-LA (par-LEE) in-GLAYZ-ay
I don't speak Italian.	*Non parlo italiano*	nohn PAR-loh ee-tahl-YAHN-o
Where is...?	*Dov'è...?*	doh-VAYY
I would like...	*Vorrei...*	vohr-RAY
I would like a room (with single bed) (with double bed) (with two beds).	*Vorrei una camera (singola) (matrimoniale) (doppia).*	vohr-RAY oo-NA ka-MEHR-ah (seen-GO-la) (mah-tri-moh-nee-o-NAHL-ay) (doh-PEE-uh)
Help!	*Aiuto!*	ah-YOO-toh

ACCOMMODATIONS AND CAMPING Associazione Italiana Alberghi per la Gioventù (AIG), the Italian **hostel** federation, operates dozens of youth hostels *(ostelli Italiani)* across the country, especially in the north. A complete list is available from most **EPT** and **CTS** offices and from many hostels. Prices average about L25,000 per night, including breakfast. Hostels are the best option for solo travelers (single rooms are relatively scarce in hotels), but curfews, lockouts, out-of-the-way locations, and less than perfect security detract from their appeal.

Italian hotel rates are set not by private owners but by the state. Under Italian law all guests must be registered by passport on a special form; check the room *first,* and then don't be afraid to hand the passport over for a while (usually overnight), but ask for it as soon as you think you will need it. One-star *pensioni* are the best budget option. Prices fluctuate by region, but singles usually start around L30,000, doubles L50,000. By law, the price must be posted behind the door of each room; if it isn't, get it in writing. Always check to see if breakfast and shower privileges are additional and/or mandatory. A room with a private bath *(con bagno)* usually costs 30 to 50% more. A new breed of tourist office, the **Azienda di Promozione Turismo (APT),** presents you with a list of hotels that have paid to be listed; some of the hotels we recommend may not be on the list. **Affitta camere** (rooms to let in private residences) can be significantly less.

An even better value in most large cities are the **Protezione della Giovane,** dorms for women travelers run by religious orders. Quality is high, but the curfew is generally early. Try to reach your destination and begin looking for accommodations before noon, especially in summer. If you must arrive late, call and reserve a day ahead. **Monasteries** are an alternative to hostels; for more info contact the province's archdiocese or tourist board. **Camping** sites tend to be loud and modern and cost around L8000 per person (or tent) plus L7000 per car, much more near big cities.

FOOD AND DRINK

"Mangia, mangia!" The production, preparation, and loving consumption of food are all close to the core of Italian culture. For simple, hearty, and inexpensive eating, try *alimentari* stores; they often prepare *panini* (sandwiches) with fresh local cold cuts and slices of excellent Italian cheese: *Bel Paese, provolone, La Fontina,* or *mozzarella. Rosticcerie* sell hot food to take out and are often the cheapest option for a filling dinner. A *tavola calda* is a cheap, sit-down option. The student *mensa* in every university town is a great deal but not always accessible by foreigners. *Osterie, trattorie,* and *ristoranti* are, in ascending order, fancier and more expensive. They are usually open 12:30 to 2pm and 7 to 11pm (later in the south). Pizza can be sold by the *etto* (100g) or the *fetta* (slice) in a *pizza a taglio* place, although you can order a whole round pizza at a sit-down pizzeria. Menus in smaller restaurants are often incomplete or nonexistent; ask for the *piatti del giorno* (daily specials). A *menù turistico,* when offered, might run only L15,000 to 20,000 for a full meal, but variety is limited. Sit-down establishments often charge *pane e coperto* (a bread and cover charge), usually not much more than L2000. Check whether service is included *(servizio compreso).*

A full meal consists of an *antipasto* (appetizer), a *primo piatto* (pasta or soup), a *secondo piatto* (meat or fish) occasionally with a *contorno* (vegetable), and usually salad, fruit, and/or cheese. In the north, butter and cream sauces dominate. Rome and central Italy are notoriously spicy regions. As one travels south, tomatoes play an increasingly significant role. Pastries also become progressively sweeter toward the south, reaching an all-time glucose high in the sinfully sugary *marzipan* of Sicily.

Coffee is another rich and varied focus of Italian life. Espresso is meant to be quaffed quickly. *Cappuccino,* a mixture of espresso and hot, frothy milk, is the normal breakfast beverage. Order it after 11:30am and expect sneers of *"turista." Caffè macchiato* ("spotted") is espresso with a touch of milk, while *latte macchiato* is milk with a splash of coffee. Perhaps the best finish to a meal is a *caffè corretto* ("corrected"), espresso spiked with your favorite liqueur. When you order at a *caffè* or *bar* (both "cafes" in Italy), you'll get a receipt, which you should then give to the bartender who makes your coffee.

Wines from the north of Italy, such as the Piedmont's *Asti Spumante* or Verona's *Soave,* tend to be heavy and full-bodied; stronger, fruitier wines come from the hotter climate of south Italy and the islands. *Moretti* and *Peroni* are popular beers, although many Italians prefer Guinness or German imports. Those who do drink Italian beer reportedly order *Peroni*. Bars are good places to sample wines, eat breakfast, stop for snacks, or watch locals socializing. They also serve a wide collection of Italian liqueurs. Try *grappa,* a gut-wrenching liqueur often flavored with various fruits, and Roman *sambuca,* a sweet anise concoction served flaming, with coffee beans floating on top. Sitting down at a table generally doubles the price of anything you order.

ITALY

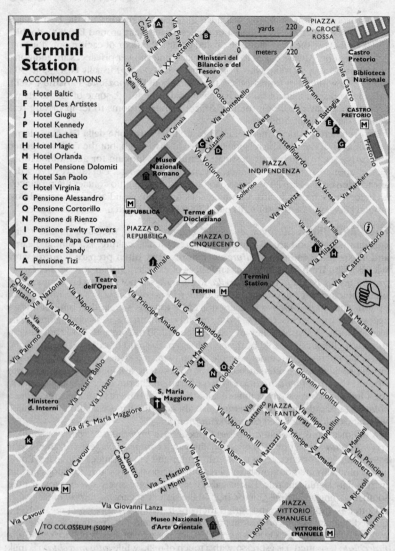

Around Termini Station

ACCOMMODATIONS

B Hotel Baltic
F Hotel Des Artistes
J Hotel Giugiu
P Hotel Kennedy
E Hotel Lachea
H Hotel Magic
M Hotel Orlanda
E Hotel Pensione Dolomiti
K Hotel San Paolo
C Hotel Virginia
G Pensione Alessandro
O Pensione Cortorillo
N Pensione di Rienzo
I Pensione Fawlty Towers
D Pensione Papa Germano
L Pensione Sandy
A Pensione Tizi

In almost every Italian town you can find numerous shops selling Italy's greatest contribution to civilization: *gelato* (ice cream). Look for the *produzione propria* (homemade) sign. Also delicious on hot summer days are *granite* ("Italian ices") and *frullati* (cool fruit shakes), both guaranteed to please.

■ Rome (Roma)

Rome is like a sensory overload, rushing down the hills of Lazio to knock you flat on your back, gasping for air, and dying for more. Even amidst today's flip historical and artistic scepticism, Rome's glory is not dimmed, its head not bowed, its ruins not—well, ruined. Augustus boasted that he found Rome a city of brick and left it one of marble, but his work was only the start. For two thousand years, Caesars and popes built forums, churches, temples, palaces, and *piazze*, all testifying to monumental ambitions and egos. Although today the Colosseum crumbles from pollution and the screech of maniacal scooters precludes any semblance of tranquility, Romans revel in their city rather than letting it stagnate as a museum. Concerts animate monuments, kids play soccer around the Pantheon, and august *piazze* serve as movie theaters. Decline and fall seems ridiculous here; all of Rome's empires live on and leave the city undefined by any single epoch. The millions of pilgrims who try to conquer Rome every year may find themselves wearied by its twisting, hot alleyways, and multi-layered design. But why worry about what has been missed? Everything in sight is sweet, everything tastes good, and the eternal city isn't going anywhere.

For more detailed information about Rome (or for steamy gossip about its former inhabitants), curl up with a copy of *Let's Go: Rome 1999*.

ORIENTATION AND PRACTICAL INFORMATION

Rome is a sea of one-way streets, dead ends, clandestine *piazze*, incongruous monuments, and incurable traffic. Getting lost is inevitable, but not necessarily undesirable.

Rome is loosely divided into nine neighborhoods, used as headings throughout. Most visitors arrive by train in **Termini** and the area of **San Lorenzo.** The central artery, **Via Nazionale,** connects Termini to **Piazza Venezia.** To the east lie the ruins of the **Ancient City.** The west claims the **Centro Storico,** home to P. Navona, the Pantheon, and countless museums. Just north of P. Venezia, the trendy **Piazza di Spagna** and the Spanish Steps border on the urban museum-park, **Villa Borghese.** South of P. Venezia, find the blue-collar **Testaccio** and **Aventino** as well as Mussolini's project, **EUR.** The far south is home to the outlying **Monti** and the **Appian Way.** West of the Centro Storico, across the Tiber, expats create art in **Trastevere.** To its north, **Vatican City** is a country unto itself.

Rome's circuitous streets make **maps** indispensable. Use the detailed **Tax Free For Tourists** map (available at tourist offices), or try the one published by **AmEx.** The **Metro/Bus/Tram** map is free from tourist offices or the info office at Stazione Termini. If you are willing to pay for a map, **Roma: Nuova Pianta della Città** is for you.

For a major city, Rome is quite safe. Exercise common sense and be especially aware around the Forum and the Colosseum, and on the crowded buses such as 64 and 492. At night women and men will generally feel safe walking through the historic center of town, but use caution beyond these well-lit, crowded areas. The area around Termini and to its south (especially near P. Vittorio Emanuele and the Oppian Hill) and Testaccio deserve special care, as do the streets around the Olympic Village in the north. For more detail, refer to this book's many **color maps** of the city.

Flights: Most flights arrive at **Leonardo da Vinci Airport (Fiumicino)** (tel. 06 659 51). After leaving customs, follow the signs to your left for **Stazione FS/Railway Station.** The Termini line goes directly to the city's main transportation station (30min., 1 per hr. at 8min. past the hr. 8:08am-10:08pm, L15,000). Trains run from Termini Station to the airport from track 22 (every hr., L15,000). Most charter and some domestic flights arrive at **Ciampino** (tel. 06 79 49 41). From here take the blue COTRAL bus to the Anagnina stop on Metro A (every hr. 6am-11pm, L1500).

Trains: Termini, is the focal point of train and Metro lines. Be wary of pickpockets and con-artists. **Railway Info,** right at the front entrance, facing P. dei Cinquecento where all the buses are, and facing tracks 1 and 9. Home to Eurail Office (windows 9 and 10). Open daily 7am-10pm. The **EPT tourist office** (tel. 06 487 12 70), in the middle of the main concourse has many brochures and lists of events. Open daily 8:15am-7:15pm. To Bologna (3¼-4hr., L50,000), Florence (2-3hr., L38,500), Genova (5-5½hr., L59,500), Milan (5-6hr., L68,000), Naples (2-2½hr., L28,500), Palermo (11-12hr., L71,000), Venice (5hr., L74,500).

Public Transportation: Efficient and extensive. The network of bus routes may seem daunting at first, but the **ATAC** (*Aziende Tramvie Autobus Comunali*) intra-city bus company (tel. 167 55 56 66; daily 8am-8pm) has a myriad of booths. Each stop (*fermata*) is marked by yellow signs listing all routes that stop there and key stops on these routes. Tickets, good for 1¼hr. of travel on a bus or one ride on the Metro, cost L1500; buy them at newsstands, *tabacchi*, and machines in stations. Daily (L6000) and weekly bus/metro passes (L24,000) are valid everywhere in the *Comune di Roma*, including Ostia but not Fiumicino. You must board buses from the back door and immediately stamp your ticket in the yellow machine. Night routes are indicated by black shields or by the letter "N" following the number. The two lines of the **Metropolitana (M)** subway intersect at Termini. **Linea A** runs from Mosca, near the Vatican, to Anagnina. **Linea B** runs from the suburbs through the university to Termini, Magliana (change for trains to Ostia and the beach), ending at Laurentina. The subway runs daily 5:30am-11:30pm.

Taxis: Ride only in yellow or white taxis with meters. Meter starts at L4500. Night surcharge L5000; Su L2000; airport L11,500-14,000; luggage L2000. **Cosmos Radio Taxi,** tel. 06 88 177 or **Societa Cooperativa Autoradio Taxi,** tel. 06 35 70.

Bike and Moped Rental: Rent-a-Scooter, Via Filippo Turati 50 (tel. 064 46 92 22; fax 064 81 59 37), near Termini. Mopeds from L35,000 per day. Open Su-F 9am-7pm. **Scooters for Rent,** Via della Purificazione 84 (tel. 064 88 54 85), off P. Barberini. Bicycles L20,000 per day, mopeds L50,000 per day. Open M-Sa 9am-7pm, Su 9am-6pm. AmEx, MC, V.

Tourist Offices: EPT, (tel. 06 482 40 70) in the Termini Station in the middle of the main concourse. Lines can be horrendous. **Central Office,** Via Parigi 5 (tel. 06 48 89 92 55 or 06 48 89 92 53; fax 06 48 89 92 50). Walk from the station diagonally to the left across bus-filled P. Cinquecento and go straight across P. della Repubblica. Via Parigi starts on the other side of the church. Offices open M-Sa 8:15am-7pm. **Enjoy Rome,** Via Varese 39 (tel. 064 45 18 43; fax 064 45 07 34; email info@enjoyrome.com; http://www.enjoyrome.com). From Termini station with trains behind you, head right and cross Via Marsala. Head 3 blocks on Via Milazzo to Via Varese and turn right. Hotel accommodations and short-term lodging. Books 3hr. walking and cycling tours and shuttle service to Pompeii. Open M-F 8:30am-2pm and 3:30-6:30pm, Sa 8:30am-2pm.

Budget Travel: Centro Turistico Studentesco (CTS), Via Genova 16 (tel. 064 62 04 31), off Via Nazionale, and other branch offices throughout the city. Free map, currency exchange (at great rates), and free accommodations service. Open M-F 9:30am-1pm and 2:30-6:30pm, Sa 9:30am-1pm.

Embassies and Consulates: Australia, Via Alessandria 215 (tel. 068 5 27 21; fax 85 27 23 00). Consular and passport services around the corner at Corso Trieste, 25. Open M-Th 8:30-12:30 and 1:30-5:30, F 8:30-1:15. **Canada,** Consulate at Via Zara 30, 5th fl. (tel. 06 44 59 84 21; fax 06 44 59 89 12). Open M-F 10am-noon and 2-4pm. Embassy at Via G.B. De Rossi 27 (tel. 06 44 59 81). **Ireland,** Consulate at P. Campitelli 3 (tel. 066 97 91 21). Open in summer M-Sa 8-2; in winter daily 10am-12:30pm. **New Zealand,** Via Zara 28 (tel. 06 441 71 71; fax 064 40 29 84). Open M-F 8:30am-12:45pm and 1:45-5pm. **South Africa,** Via Tenaro 14 (tel. 068 41 97 94; fax 06 85 25 43 00). **U.K.,** Via XX Settembre 80a (tel. 064 82 54 41; fax 06 48 90 30 73), near Porta Pia and the corner of Via Palestro. Open mid-July to Aug. M-F 8am-1pm; Sept. to mid-July M-F 9:15am-1:30pm and 2-4pm. **U.S.,** Via Veneto 119a (tel. 064 67 41; fax 06 46 74 22 17). Open M-F 8:30-noon and 1:30-3:30pm.

Currency Exchange: CTS and the banks often have the best rates. Banking hours are often M-F 8:30am-1:30pm with an extra hour in the afternoon. Decent deals are found at the **Banca di Roma** or the **Banca Nazionale del Lavoro.** Or, **Numismatica Internazionale, Numismatica Internazionale,** P. d. Cinquecento 57/58 (tel. 064 88 50 05), in the arcade on the left side of the *piazza* as you face away from the station. No commissions. Open M-Sa 8am-7pm. **Thomas Cook,** P. Barberini 21A (tel. 064 82 80 82/3). Also at Via della Conciliazione, 23/25 (tel. 06 68 30 04 35), in front of St. Peter's; open M-Sa 8:30am-6pm, Su 9am-5pm. Via del Corso 23 (tel. 063 23 00 67); open in summer M-Sa 9am-8pm, Su 9am-1:30pm; off-season open M-F 9am-5pm with 1hr. lunch break, Sa 9am-1pm.

American Express: P. di Spagna 38 (tel. 066 76 41, lost or stolen cards and/or checks issued in the U.S. toll-free 24hr. tel. 167 87 43 33, others call 06 72 281; fax 06 67 64 24 99). Perfect English is spoken. The office holds mail and offers excellent free maps, but it's wiser to change checks at the small *cambio* booths. Open Sept.-July M-F 9am-7:30pm, Sa 9am-3pm; Aug. M-F 9am-6pm, Sa 9am-12:30pm.

Laundromat: OndaBlu, Via G. de Mattheis 7 (tel. 06 44 25 14 91, main number 167 86 13 46), at P. Bologna. Wash L6000 per 6.5kg load; dry L6000 per 6.5kg load. Open daily 8am-10pm. Also at 50/52 Via Vespasiano (Prati/S. Pietro, near the Ottaviano Metro stop) and 10/12 Via La Marmora (P. Vittorio).

Bookstore: Economy Book and Video Center, Via Torino 136 (tel. 064 74 68 77), off Via Nazionale. Enormous selection of English language books. Open June-Aug. M-F 9am-8pm, Sa 9am-2pm; Sept.-May same hours except M 3-8pm only.

Crisis Line: Samaritans, Via San Giovanni in Laterano 250 (tel. 06 70 45 44 44). Native English speakers. Open for calls and visits daily 1-10pm. Call before visiting.

24-Hour Pharmacies: Farmacia Internazionale, P. Barberini 49 (tel. 06 48 54 56). **Farmacia Piram,** Via Nazionale 228 (tel. 064 88 07 54).

Medical Assistance: Ospedale San Camillo in Monteverde, Circonvallazione Gianicolense 87 (tel. 06 587 01), in Gianicolo. Does pregnancy tests, STD tests, gynecological exams, and pap smears. Open M-Sa 8-11am, open for info daily 8am-7pm. **Unione Sanitaria Internazionale,** Via V. Orsini 18 (tel. 06 321 50 53), north of the Vatican, off P. della Libertà; or Via Machiavelli 22 (tel. 06 70 45 35 44). Metro Linea A: Vittorio Emanuele. English spoken. Open for tests daily 7-11am; open for info daily 7am-7pm.

Emergency: First Aid, tel. 118. **Fire,** tel. 115. **Ambulance (Red Cross),** tel. 55 10.

Police: tel. 113 (English interpreter). **Carabinieri,** tel. 112. **Ufficio Stranieri** (Foreigners' Office), Via Genova 2 (tel. 06 46 86 27 11), around the corner from Questura. English spoken. Report thefts here in person. Open 24hr.

Bisexual, Gay, and Lesbian resources: The Roman branch of **ARCI-GAY** (tel. 06 855 55 22) is located at Via Primo Acciaresi 7, off of Via Tiburtina. Open M-F 3-7pm, Sa 4:30-7:30pm.

Post Office: Main office at P. San Silvestro 19, south of P. di Spagna. Stamps at booths 23-25. *Fermo Posta* at booth 72. Open M-F 9am-6pm, Sa 9am-2pm. **Postal Code:** 00187 for *Fermo Posta* at the post office and AmEx office.

Internet Access: Internet Cafe, Via dei Marrucini 12 (tel./fax 06 445 49 53; http://www.internetcafe.it), in San Lorenzo (bus 492). Lunch deal 11am-3pm: sandwich, drink, and 1hr. of computer for L10,000. Otherwise L8,000 per hr., L10,000 after 9 pm. Open M-F 9am-2am, Sa-Su 5pm-2am.

Telephones: Telecom, in the main gallery of Termini. 2 metered phones; tell the manager you're calling, dial direct, and pay afterwards. Open daily 8am-9:45pm. Booths are located throughout Rome. **Phone cards** are available in L5000, L10,000, and L15,000 denominations at *tabacchi*, newsstands, bars, and post offices.

ACCOMMODATIONS AND CAMPING

Rome swells with tourists from May through August; Easter is also tremendously busy. The **tourist offices** in Rome will scrounge (sometimes reluctantly) to find you a room, as will **Enjoy Rome** (see above) and the **Centro Turistico Studentesco (CTS).** Termini is full of "officials" swarming around to find you a place. Those who are genuine have photo IDs issued by the tourist office—others are hucksters. Ask for maps and directions (real officials will have maps), and always insist on seeing a room first. It is illegal and stupid to "rough it" in public areas of Rome; be careful even at designated campgrounds.

North of Termini

There are clusters of clean *pensioni* and hotels within five to 15 minutes of Termini. The area has recently become a trendy haven for budget travelers.

Pensione Fawlty Towers, Via Magenta 39 (tel./fax 064 45 03 74). Exit Termini to the right and cross Via Marsala to Via Marghera. Walk 1 block up Via Marghera, turn right on Via Magenta, and look for the yellow sign. Fabulous! Co-ed dorm-style quads L30,000; singles L55,000, with shower L70,000; doubles L80,000, with shower L95,000, with bath L110,000; triples with shower L110,000. Check-out 9am for dorm rooms and 10am for private rooms. No curfew; night keys available. Frequently full, but the reception will do their utmost to find you a place.

Pensione Papa Germano, Via Calatafimi 14A (tel. 06 48 69 19). With the trains behind you, exit the station to your right and turn left on Via Marsala, which shortly becomes Via Volturno; Via Calatafimi will be on your right. Clean, affordable rooms and outstanding service. Singles L45,000; doubles L65,000, with bath L85,000; triples L75,000, with bath L100,000. Nov.-Mar. 10% reduction. Check-out 11am. No curfew. Reservations encouraged.

Hotel Des Artistes, Via Villafranca 20 (tel. 064 45 43 65; fax 064 46 23 68; email artistes@tin.it). From Termini Station, make a left onto Via Marsala and a right onto Via Vicenza; the hotel is on the 5th cross-street, to the left. Luxury for a budget price. Singles L60,000; doubles L90,000, with bath L170,000; triples L120,000, with bath L210,000; quads L140,000, with bath L260,000. Breakfast L5000. Reception open until midnight. Check-out 10am. No curfew.

Hotel Virginia, Via Montebello 94 (tel. 064 88 17 86 or 064 45 76 89; fax 064 88 17 86). Exit Termini to the right onto Via Marsala, turn left and follow the street until it turns into Via Volturno. Via Montebello will be on your right. Each *camera* is truly unique. Singles L45,000, with shower L50,000; doubles with shower L50,000-65,000, with full bath L75,000-80,000; triples L75,000-90,000. Washing machine available, L5000 per load. Check-out 12pm.

Pensione Alessandro, Via Vicenza 42 (tel. 064 46 19 58). Across the street from *a pizzeria rustica,* near the corner with Via Palestro. 60 beds, 4-6 beds per room. Apr.-Sept. L25,000 per person; Oct.-Mar. L20,000 per person. L5,000 for breakfast and use of the full kitchen. Reception 7am-midnight. Check-out 10am. No curfew.

Hotel Magic, Via Milazzo 20 (tel./fax 064 95 98 80). Upstairs from Galli and Fenicia. Clean, well-furnished, and affordable. Alacazam! Prices include private baths and TVs. Singles L90,000; doubles L120,000; triples L150,000; quads L200,000.

Pensione Tizi, Via Collina 48 (tel. 064 82 01 28; fax 064 74 32 66). A 15min. walk from the station. Take Via Goito from P. dell'Indipendenza, cross Via XX Settembre onto Via Piave, then take the first left onto Via Flavia, which leads to Via Collina on the right. Recently renovated, spacious, well-kept rooms. Singles L55,000; doubles L75,000, with bath L95,000; triples L100,000, with bath L120,000; quads L120,000, with bath L140,000. Breakfast L9000. Check-out 11am.

Hotel Lachea and **Hotel Pensione Dolomiti,** Via San Martino della Battaglia 11 (tel. 064 95 72 56 or 06 49 10 58; fax 064 45 46 65), off P. dell'Indipendenza. 3 rooms with a balcony over Via S.M. della Battaglia. TVs in most rooms, phones in all. **Lachea:** Singles L60,000-70,000, with bath L85,000; doubles with bath L105,000-110,000; triples with bath L130,000-150,000; quads available upon request; bargaining possible. **Dolomiti:** prices for doubles and triples are L40,000-50,000 more. Breakfast for L8000-10,000 extra, but with the bigger rooms, it's included. Check-out 11am.

Hotel Baltic (ex Sant'Andrea), Via XX Settembre 89 (tel. 064 81 47 75; fax 064 8 55 09). Up Via XX Settembre just past the intersection with Via Palestro. Great views. Singles L50,000-70,000; doubles with shower L80,000, with bath L100,000; triples with shower L100,000, with bath L120,000; quads with bath L160,000. Check-out 11am. Traveler's checks accepted.

South of Termini

The area south of Termini is often portrayed as noisier and seedier than other parts of central Rome, but lately the neighborhood has started to clean up its act. Nevertheless, exercise caution, especially at night. Prices tend to be very flexible in this area; they depend on the season, length of stay, and how many people are in your group.

Pensione di Rienzo, Via Principe Amedeo 79A (tel. 064 46 71 31 and 064 46 69 80). Tranquil, spacious, newly renovated rooms with large windows. Singles L28,000-70,000, with bath up to L80,000; doubles L29,000-79,000, with bath L35,000-96,000. Check-out 10am. No curfew.

Hotel Kennedy, Via Filippo Turati 64 (tel. 064 46 53 73; fax 064 46 54 17; email hotelkennedy@micanet.it; http://www.panservice.it/alfasoft/kenn.htm). Private bath, color TV with satellite, phone, and even A/C. Singles L65,000-120,000; doubles L85,000-199,000; triples L120,000-249,000. Breakfast included. 10% discount to *Let's Go* travelers. Check-out 11am. No curfew.

Pensione Cortorillo, Via Principe Amedeo 47 (tel. 064 88 09 54; fax 064 81 76 13). Family room with double bed, twin bed, and crib available. Singles L70,000, with bath L100,000; doubles with bath L100,000, with bath L135,000; triples L135,000, with bath L150,000. 10% off in the winter. Check-out 11am. No curfew.

Hotel Orlanda, Via Principe Amedeo 76 (tel. 064 88 01 24, 064 88 01 83, or 064 88 06 37; fax 064 88 01 83; email orlandohotelrom@cdc.it), at Via Gioberti. English spoken. Singles L50,000, with bath L80,000; doubles L100,000, with bath L150,000; triples L130,000, with bath L190,000. Reception 24 hr. Check-out 10am. No curfew.

West of Termini

Pensione Sandy, Via Cavour 136 (tel. 064 88 45 85), near S. Maria Maggiore. No sign; look for the Hotel Valle next door. Plain, hostel-style shared rooms, usually for 3-5 people, in a central location. L25,000 in summer, less in the winter. Individual lockers in each room.

Hotel San Paolo, Via Panisperna 95 (tel. 064 74 52 13; fax 064 74 52 18). Follow Via S. Maria Maggiore, just off Via Cavour to your right after S. Maria Maggiore. Recently renovated. Hall baths are clean and private. House special: 6-person, L300,000. Frat-style suite of rooms. Free luggage storage after check-out. English spoken. Singles L65,000; doubles L90,000, with bath L120,000; triples L120,000. Check-out 9am. Reservations accepted.

Hotel Giugiu, Via del Viminale 8 (tel./fax 064 82 77 34). Steps away from Termini. 18 large, quiet rooms with high ceilings. Singles without bath L55,000; doubles L85,000, with bath L95,000; triples L128,000; quads L160,000. *Let's Go* discount. Breakfast L8000. Check-out 10am.

Centro Storico: Near Piazza Navona and Campo dei Fiori

Il Centro Storico (the Historic Center) is the ideal, if expensive, base for living as the Romans do. From Stazione Termini, take bus 64, 170, or 75 to Largo Argentina, the transportation hub of the historic center.

Hotel Navona, Via dei Sediari 8 (tel. 066 86 42 03; fax 06 68 80 38 02; call before faxing). Take Via dei Canestrari off of the southern end of P. Navona, cross over C. del Rinascimento, and continue straight. Large rooms that are quiet and clean, and most have bathrooms. Singles L95,000, with bath L125,000; doubles L130,000, with bath L150,000, with air conditioning L210,000; triples L195,000, with bath L210,000. Free breakfast and parking. Checkout 10am.

Albergo della Lunetta, P. del Paradiso 68 (tel. 066 86 10 80 or 066 87 76 30; fax 066 89 20 28), near the Church of Sant'Andrea della Valle. Take Via Chiavari off C. Vittorio Emanuele II, then the first right off Via Chiavari. Clean, well-lit rooms. Great value in a great location (between Campo dei Fiori and P. Navona). Singles L70,000, with bath L90,000; doubles L100,000, with bath L150,000; triples L145,000, with bath L195,000. Reservations accepted with a credit card.

Albergo Pomezia, Via dei Chiavari 12 (tel./fax 066 86 13 71). Clean rooms with telephones. Singles L90,000, with bath L130,000; doubles L130,000, with bath L180,000; triples L145,000, with bath L210,000. Prices drop Nov.-Feb., except at Christmas. Breakfast included (served 8-11am).

Hotel Mimosa, Via Santa Chiara 61 (tel. 06 68 80 17 53; fax 066 83 35 57), off P. della Minerva behind the Pantheon. Spacious rooms and central location offset cramped bathrooms. English spoken. Singles L80,000; doubles L110,000, with bath L130,000; triples L160,000. 10% price reduction in winter. Curfew 1am.

Piazza di Spagna

Sure, the accommodations in this area might run you a few thousand more *lire* per day, but can you really put a price tag on living a scant few steps away from Prada?

Pensione Panda, Via della Croce 35 (tel. 066 78 01 79; fax 06 69 94 21 51), between P. di Spagna and Via del Corso. Huge rooms, arched ceilings, and real beds. Singles L60,000, with bath L80,000; doubles L95,000, with bath L130,000; triples L120,000, with bath L160,000; quads L160,000, with bath L200,000. No curfew; night keys available. Check-out 11am. Reservations recommended. Small discount for *Let's Go* readers.

Pensione Jonella, Via della Croce 41 (tel. 066 79 79 66), between P. di Spagna and Via del Corso. Beautiful rooms with a bird's eye view of the pedestrian traffic on Via della Croce. There is no reception, so arrange ahead of time for someone to meet you. Singles L60,000; doubles L90,000. Reservations recommended.

Hotel Boccaccio, Via del Boccaccio 25 (tel. 064 88 59 62; http://www.webeco.it/hotelboccaccio). Off Via del Tritone down from P. Barberini. Spacious rooms, each with unique furnishings. Singles L80,000; doubles L100,000, with bath L130,000; triples L120,000, with bath L165,000.

Across the Tiber: Borgo and Prati

The *pensioni* on the other side of the Tiber are fairly expensive but also tend to be comfortable, clean, and friendly. Those in **Prati,** near the Vatican, are attractive for their proximity to popular sights. Bus 64 from Termini ends right near St. Peter's and Metro A runs to Ottaviano and Mosca, the Metro stops in the area.

Pensione Ottaviano, Via Ottaviano 6 (tel. 06 39 73 72 53 or 06 39 73 81 38; http://www.enjoyrome.it/ottavhtl.htm), off P. del Risorgimento north of P. San Pietro. Free email access for guests. Friendly staff. Dorm-style rooms L25,000 in the summer, L20,000 in the winter. 2 doubles are available for L70,000 in summer and L45,000 in winter. No curfew.

Hotel Pensione Joli, Via Cola di Rienzo 243, 6th floor (tel. 063 24 18 54; tel./fax 06 324 18 93), at Via Tibullo, *scala* A. Nice beds and gorgeous views of the Vatican. All rooms come with a bath and telephone. Singles L80,000; doubles L120,000; triples L160,000; quads L200,000. Breakfast included. Curfew 1am.

Hotel Florida, Via Cola di Rienzo 243 (tel. 063 24 18 72 or 063 24 16 08; fax 06 324 18 57), on the 2nd and 3rd fl. Bathrooms are delightfully clean. Singles L70,000, with bath L120,000; doubles L100,000, with bath L150,000; triples with bath L190,000. Rooms without bath still have sinks. 10% discount in low season; a 6-day stay in the low season will get you a 15% discount.

Ostello del Foro Italico (HI), Ostello del Foro Italico, Via delle Olimpiadi 61 (tel. 06 323 62 67 or 063 23 62 79; fax 063 24 26 13). Take Metro Linea A to Ottaviano (last stop) and then exit onto Via Barletta and take bus 32 (in the middle of the street) to Cadorna. It's the 7th stop; get off as soon as you see the pink Foro Italico buildings. The entrance is across the street. Inconvenient location with 350 beds. Bring earplugs. L23,000 with HI card (buy one at the desk for L30,000, or pay L5000 extra per night); in groups up to 14, only one person, the designated leader, has to buy a card. Continental breakfast and showers included. Reception noon-11pm. Check-out 7-9am, but they have storage space for luggage. Lockout 9am-2pm. Curfew midnight. Wheelchair accessible.

Camping

Several campgrounds around Rome are downright luxurious, with everything from swimming pools to campground bars. In August, arrive well before 11am.

Seven Hills, Via Cassia 1216 (tel. 06 30 36 27 51 or 063 03 31 08 26; fax 063 03 31 00 39), 8km north of Rome. Take bus 907 from P. Risorgimento to Via Cassia, or 201 from Flaminio. Ask where to get off—it's 3-4km past the big highway known as the GRA. From here, follow the country road about 1km until you see the sign. Houses a bar, market, BBQ, restaurant, and pizzeria. You can't use money, though; you buy a Seven Hills card which you can use all over the campground. Daily Vatican shuttles leave at 8 and 9:30am, round-trip L6000. L12,500 per person, L8000 per tent, L6000 per car. Camper L14,000. Bungalow L70,000-110,000. Check-in 7am-11pm. Open late Mar. to late Oct.

Flaminio, Via Flaminia Nuova 821 (tel. 063 33 26 04), about 8km outside of Rome. Take bus 910 from Termini to P. Mancini, then transfer to 200. Get off on Via Flaminia Nuova when you see the "Philips" or EUCLID building on your right; there are several stops on Via Flaminia Nuova, so keep your eyes peeled. Outfitted with a pool, market, restaurant, bar, and a disco. L13,000 per person, L8000 per tent. Bungalows L38,000; doubles L64,000; triples L102,000; quads L128,000. Coin-operated washing machines L500. Open Mar.-Oct.

FOOD

Meals in Rome are prolonged affairs, each course often continuing for hours on end. When you're ready to indulge, stay away from the area near the train station; "bargain" restaurants are often tourist snares. Instead, hop on the bus to reach the nearby university district of **San Lorenzo** or **Testaccio,** the last truly untouristed neighborhoods in Rome. Closer to the city center, **Piazza Navona** and **Campo dei Fiori** boast some romantic *trattorie,* and **Trastevere** harbors the best *pizzerie* in the city.

Get a taste of local produce and local haggling techniques at Rome's many outdoor **markets,** the largest of which are at P. Campo dei Fiori, P. Vittorio Emanuele II, and P. San Cosimato in Trastevere. The **STANDA supermarkets** at Via Cola di Rienzo 173 (near the Vatican) and Via di Trastevere 62, (information tel. 167 358 758), has all you could desire, including clothing, food, and housewares. If you can't eat another plate of pasta, head to **Castroni,** Via Cola di Rienzo, 196/198 (tel. 066 87 43 83). Not only a great coffee bar, but also a phenomenal foreign foods market.

Restaurants

Pizzeria Baffetto, Via del Governo Vecchio 114, at Via Sora. Once a meeting place for 1960s radicals, now just radically crowded. Pizzas L5000-9000. Vino L6000. Cover L1000. Open M-F 10am-noon and 7:30pm-1am, Sa-Su 10am-noon and 7:30pm-2am.

Hostaria Grappolo d'Oro, P. della Cancelleria 80-81, on Via Cancelleria off C. Vittorio Emanuele II. Words are too cheap for the *antipasti* (L10,000-12,000) and *penne all'arrabbiata* (L10,000). House white wine L9000. Cover L2000. Open M-Sa noon-3pm and 7-11:30pm.

L'Insalata Ricca, Largo di Chiavari 85, off C. Vittorio Emanuele near P. Sant'Andrea della Valle. Over 20 meal-sized salads, including the *cacio e pere* (cheese and pear). 6 other locations (P. Pasquino 72; Via del Gazometro 62; P. Albania 3; Via Polesine 16; P. Risorgimento 5; and Via Freancesca Grinaldi 52). Cover L1500. Open daily 12:30-3:30 and 6:45-11:30pm.

Margherita, P. delle Cinque Scole 30, right next to the Santa Maria del Pianto church. Delicious, affordable cuisine that is worth the wait. *Primi* L8000-13,000; *secondi* L12,000-14,000. Cover L1000. Open M-F noon-3pm.

Margutta Vegetariano RistorArte, Via Margutta 119, off Via del Babuino, near P. del Popolo. Innovative veggie dishes like *risotto giallo ai fiori di zucca e piscilli* (rice with saffron, zucchini blossoms, and peas; L14,000). All-you-can-eat brunch Su 11am-3pm for L30,000. Open Sept.-July M-Sa 1-3:30pm and 7:40-11:40pm.

Al Piccolo Arancio, Vicolo Scanderbeg 112. Facing Trevi Fountain, make a right on Via del Lavatore; Vicolo Scanderbeg is on the right. The sign says "Hostaria." *Gnocchi al salmone* (L10,000). Cover L2000. Open Tu-Su noon-3pm and 7-11:30pm. Closed in Aug.

Taverna dei Quaranta, Via Claudia 24. Shaded by the trees of the Caelian Park, outdoor dining at this corner *taverna* is a must. The ever-changing menu features an outstanding *bruschetta al pomodoro* (L3000) and creations like *ravioli al amalfitana* (L9000). Open daily noon-3pm and 8pm-midnight.

Gran Caffè Rossi Martini, P. del Colosseo 3a & 3b. Go up Via dei Fori Imperiali one block from the Metro stop, cross the train tracks to P. del Colosseo. More wine, liquors, liqueurs, and elixirs than you would believe. *Gnocchi* in meat sauce (L18,000) and sandwiches (L5000) are especially good. Open daily 8:30am-1am.

Pizzeria Panattoni, Via Trastevere 53-59. Crispy pizzas (L9000-11,000), fantastic appetizers, including ascolane olives (stuffed with meat and breaded; L6800) and the "fabulous fancy salad" with just about everything you can imagine (L8900). No cover. Open daily 6pm-2:30am.

Ristorante Max, P. dell'Unita 26/27, just east of P. del Risorgimento at Via dei Gracchi and Via C. Mario. The big ol' pizzas are L8000-12,000, but the pasta musn't be overlooked at L6000-8000 for large portions. Delicious *bruschetta* with olive spread L2000. *Secondi* L7000-16,000. House wine L5000-10,000 per liter. Open Tu-Su noon-3pm and 7-11pm.

Armando, Via Plauto 38-39, off Borgo Angelico. Sing the praises of the delicious lasagna, the house specialty (L15,000); *primi* L10,000-15,000. *Saltimbocca alla Romana* L16,000. Cover L2500. Open Th-Tu 12:30-3pm and 7-11pm.

Pulcino Ballerino, Via degli Equi 66/68, off Via Tiburtina. *Tagliolini al limone* (pasta in a lemon cream sauce, L9000) or *risotto* (various types, L10,000-12,000). You can also skip the chef altogether and prepare your own meal on a warm stone. Cover L1000. Open M-Sa 1pm-3:30pm and 8pm-midnight. Closed first week of Aug.

Pizzeria Ficini, Via Luca della Robbia 23. Take Via Vanvitelli off Via Marmorata, then take your first left. A no-frills pizzeria befitting this working-class community. Cheap, delicious pizzas L6000-8000, *calzone* L8000. Wine L6000 per liter. Open Sept.-July Tu-Su 6-11:30pm.

Il Giardinetto, Via del Governo Vecchio 125. Verdant courtyard houses a French-Tunisian influenced establishment. The *risotto all pescatora* is unbeatable (L12,000). *Secondi* L12,000-15,000. Open Tu-Su 10:30am-3pm and 6pm-midnight.

La Capricciosa, Largo dei Lombardi 8. Right off Via del Corso, across from its intersection with Via della Croce. Unique pizzas (L8000-14,000). *Primi* L8000-11,000. Desserts L6000. Cover L2000. Open W-M 12:30-3pm and 7:30pm-1am. Reservations necessary for large groups.

Taverna della Scala, P. della Scala 19. Facing Santa Maria in Trastevere, take the road on the right until you come to P. di Egidio. Go through the *piazza* to Via della Scala. Take Via della Scala to P. della Scala. Specials like *gnocchi con crema di carciofi* (potato dumplings in artichoke cream sauce). Cover L2000. Open W-M 12:30-3pm and 7pm-midnight.

Il Capellaio Matto, Via dei Marsi 25. From Via Tiburtina take Via degli Equi and take the 4th right onto Via dei Marsi. Vegetarians, rejoice! Salads (L7000), numerous pasta and rice dishes (L8000-11,000), crepes (around L7500), and spinach and ricotta ravioli (L9000) will all give you good reason. Menu available in English. Cover L2000. Open W-M 8pm-midnight.

Armando, P. Tiburtino 5. Near Porta di San Lorenzo at the beginning of Via Tiburtina. A one-trip-only buffet of cold *antipasti* and desserts, L14,000. Pizza L7000-15,000. Try the *Cernia con porcini* (L20,000). Menus in English. Open Th-Tu 12:30-3pm and 7:30pm-1am. Reservations accepted.

Desserts and Caffè

Creamy and flaky pastries and *gelato* rainbows taunt passersby from countless bakery windows; if you can't resist any longer, try one of the revered places listed below. *Caffè* and Campari make up the fifth food group in Rome, the others being pasta, *caffè*, campari, and pasta. In most *caffè* and bars, you pay one price to stand at the bar, and a higher price (as much as double) if you sit down at a table. To get the most for your *caffè* buck, see the following.

Da Quinto, Via di Tor Millina 15, west of P. Navona. Every combination of ice, milk, fruit, and ice cream imaginable. Prices range from L2500-10,000. Open daily noon-2am. Closed W in winter. Hours may vary.

Sant'Eustachio, Il Caffè, P. Sant'Eustachio 82. Take a right on Via Palombella behind the Pantheon on the right as you face it. Rome's "coffee empire." *Granita di caffè* with all the works (L8000, at the bar L6000), or their very own *gran caffè speciale* (L5000, at the bar L3000). Open Tu-F and Su 8:30am-1am, Sa 8:30am-1:30am.

Giolitti, Via degli Uffici del Vicario 40. From the Pantheon, follow Via del Pantheon (at the northern end of the *piazza*) to its end and then take Via della Maddelena to its end; Via degli Uffici del Vicario is on the right. An old-fashioned ice cream shoppe, Giolitti is the St. Peter's Basilica for ice cream worshippers. Small cone L2500, medium L3000, large L4000. Open 7am-1am. Nov.-Apr. closed M.

Palazzo del Freddo Giovanni Fassi, Via Principe Eugenio 65/67, off P. Vittorio Emanuele, southeast of Termini. Another location at Via Vespasiano 57, near the Vatican. A confectionery altar, duly worshiped by both kids and adults. Cones L2500-5000. *Frulatti* L3000-5000. Open Tu-Su noon-12:30am; in summer also M noon-12:30am.

Caffè della Pace, Via della Pace 3/7, off P. Navona. *Cappuccino*: daytime L3000 at bar, L5000 at table; nighttime L4000 at bar, L8000 at table. Red wine L7000 at bar, L10,000 at table. Open daily 9am-8pm.

Cul de Sac, P. Pasquino 73, off P. Navona. Everything a wine bar should be and more—snacks, outdoor tables, and a huge selection of wines. Ask about their lunch special. Open M 6:30pm-12:30am, Tu-Su 12:30-3pm and 6:30pm-12:30am.

Dolce Trastevere, P. Sonino 29, in Trastevere. The best *gelati* in Trastevere. Get a waffle cone full (L6000) and go home happy.

SIGHTS

Rome wasn't built in a day, and it's not likely that you'll see any substantial portion of it in 24 hours either. Ancient temples and forums, medieval churches, Renaissance basilicas, Baroque fountains, 19th- and 20th-century museums, and futuristic space monkeys all cluster together in a city bursting with masterpieces from every era of western civilization. No other city in the Western world can lay claim to so many masterworks of architecture from so many different epochs, not to mention the countless paintings and sculptures found inside each of them. Nor can any other city claim enough nooks and crannies to cram in the 981 churches and 280 fountains that Rome possesses. From Etruscan busts to cities of tomorrow, there is more than enough in the Rome to captivate even the least curious for months, even years, on end.

The Ancient City

Across the Tiber, the ancient city of Rome centered on the Capitoline and Palatine Hills in the southern part of the modern city center. To reach the Capitoline Hill, head down Via dei Fori Imperiali from the "Colosseo" Metro stop, and walk around the Vittorio Emanuele II monument. The ancient city is also accessible on any of the buses that stop at P. Venezia. The original capitol and one of the most sacred parts of the city, the **Campidoglio** (Capitoline Hill) still serves as the seat of the city's government, perched in a spectacular *piazza* designed by Michelangelo. Here you can also enjoy unforgettable views of the Forum and Palatine, as well as several superb museums. The **Musei Capitolini,** in the twin *palazzi* on either side of the *piazza,* display one of the largest collections of ancient sculpture in the world, including the Capitoline Wolf, the centuries-old symbol of Rome. *(Open Tu-Su 9am-7pm; holidays 9am-1:30pm. L10,000, students L5000.)*

The **Roman Forum** and **Palatine** mark the geographical and commercial center of the ancient city. *(Complex open in summer M-Sa 9am-7pm, Su 9am-1pm; in winter M-F 9am-1hr. before sunset, Su and holidays 9am-noon. Forum free. Palatine L12,000; last admittance 1hr. before closing.)* From the entrance gate on Via dei Fori Imperiali (across from the end of Via Cavour), a ramp descends past the Temple of Antoninus and Faustina on the left and the remains of the **Basilica Aemilia** on the right. The **Curia,** or Senate House, to the right of the Basilica Aemilia as you exit, was one of the oldest buildings in the Forum, although the present structure dates from the time of Diocletian (303 AD). The broad space in front of the Curia was the **Comitium,** or assembly place, where male citizens came to vote and representatives of the people gathered for public discussions. The brick platform to the left of the arch was the **Rostra,** or speaker's platform, erected by Caesar in 44 BC, which any citizen could mount to voice his opinion. Cicero's head and hands were displayed here after his assassination, and Augustus' rebellious daughter Julia allegedly engaged in amorous activities with some of her father's greatest enemies on this platform. Proceed along Via Sacra, the main thoroughfare of the Forum and oldest street in Rome. At the end, the **Arch of Septimius Severus** (203 AD) commemorates the emperor's victories in the Middle East.

This part of the Forum also has several shrines and sacred precincts. The three great temples of the lower Forum have been closed for restorations, but the eight columns of the **Temple of Saturn** have at last shed their scaffolding. This was the site of the public treasury and an underground stash of sacred treasures. Around the corner to the left, justice was administered at Caesar's **Basilica Julia** (54 BC). Look for inscribed grids and circles in the steps where Romans awaiting judgement distracted themselves with a form of tic-tac-toe. At the east end of the Basilica Julia, the **Temple of Castor and Pollux** celebrates the Roman rebellion against the Etruscan king.

The **House of the Vestal Virgins** occupied the sprawling complex of rooms and courtyards behind the temple of Vesta. As long as they kept their vows of chastity, the Vestal Virgins remained among the most respected people in Ancient Rome. But if a virgin strayed from celibacy, she was buried alive. The best way to reach the **Palatine Hill,** whose flowering sculpture gardens provide a welcome respite from the dusty Forum, is by the stairs to the right after the street turns at the Arch of Titus. When you're ready to tackle the ruins again, check out the **Domus Augustana,** the imperial palace built by Domitian (81-96 AD) and used subsequently as the empire headquarters.

Across the street from the old Forum Romanum sprawl the **Fori Imperiali,** a vast conglomeration of temples, basilicas, and public squares. Caesar, Augustus, Vespasian, Nerva, and Trajan all built capacious monuments in this area to glorify the city and, more often, themselves. The **Forum of Trajan** (107-113 AD), the largest and most impressive of the lot, spreads across Via dei Fori Imperiali below two Baroque churches at the eastern end of P. Venezia. Down the street, with an entrance on Via IV Novembre 94, the three-floors of the fascinating **Markets of Trajan** once sheltered dozens of single-room stores along cobblestone streets. *(Open in summer Tu-Sa 9am-6:30pm, Su 9am-1:30pm; winter hours vary depending on when the sun sets, and closing may be as early as 1pm. L3750, students L2500, EU citizens under 18 and over 60 free.)* Farther up Via dei Fori Imperiali, stairs over the Colosseo Metro station lead up to an ill-kept park that contains the remains of Nero's **Domus Aurea.**

The **Colosseum** stands as the city's grandest symbol. *(Metro: Colosseo. Ground level open in summer M-Tu and Th-Sa 9am-7pm, W and Su 9am-2pm; in winter, closes 1hr. before sunset—as early as 3pm. Free. Upper level closes 1hr. before ground level. L8000, EU citizens under 18 and over 60 free.)* At its opening in 80 AD, the Colosseum could hold as many as 50,000 spectators; its first 100 days saw some 5000 wild beasts perish in the bloody arena, and the slaughter of animals and people continued for three centuries. The outside of the arena is well-preserved around three-quarters of its circumference. Inside, the missing floor reveals a labyrinth of underground cells, corridors, ramps, and elevators used for transporting animals up to the arena level. Built to commemorate Constantine's victory over his rival Maxentius in 312, the amazingly preserved **Arch of Constantine** lies between the Colosseum and the Palatine Hill.

At the bend of Via del Portico d'Ottavia, a shattered pediment and a few disembodied ivy-covered columns in the shadow of the Teatro di Marcello are all that remain of the once magnificent **Portico d'Ottavia.** Farther down Via di Teatro di Marcello toward the Tiber, the **Church of Santa Maria in Cosmedin** harbors some of Rome's most beautiful medieval decoration and the famed **Bocca della Verità** in the portico. *(Open Sept.-July M-Sa 7:30am-noon and 4-7pm, Su 10am-1pm.)* Originally a drain cover, the relief was credited with supernatural powers in the Middle Ages. It's said that the hoary face will chomp on the hand of a liar, severing his fingers.

Cradled in the valley between the Palatine and Aventine Hills, today's **Circus Maximus** offers only a grassy shadow of its former glory. From the P. di Porta Capena, at the eastern end of the Circus, Via delle Terme di Caracalla passes the remains of the **Baths of Caracalla,** the largest and best-preserved baths in the city. *(Baths open in summer Su-M 9am-2pm, Tu-Sa 9am-7pm; in winter closes 1hr. before sunset. Last admittance 1hr. before closing. Admission L8000.)*

Pantheon and Piazza Navona

Between Via del Corso and P. Navona, in the *centro storico,* the **Pantheon** has stood for nearly 2000 years: the marble columns (brought whole from Egypt in the 2nd century AD), bronze doors, and soaring domed interior remain largely unchanged from the day the building was erected by Hadrian. *(Open June M-Sa 9am-6pm, Su 9am-1pm; July-Aug. M-Sa 9am-6:30pm, Su 9am-1pm; Oct.-May M-Sa 9am-4pm, Su 9am-1pm. Free.)* Around the left side of the Pantheon, an obelisk supported by Bernini's winsome elephant statue marks the center of **Piazza Minerva.** In back, the unassuming facade of the **Church of Santa Maria Sopra Minerva** hides Renaissance masterpieces, including a brilliant fresco cycle by Filippino Lippi. Michelangelo's great *Christ Bearing the Cross* stands guard near the altar. *(Open M-Sa 7am-7pm, Su 7am-1pm and 3:30-7pm.)* North of the P. della Rotonda, stands the **Church of San Luigi dei Francesi,** the French national church in Rome and home to three of Caravaggio's most famous ecclesiastical paintings. *(Open F-W 7:30am-12:30pm and 3:30-7pm, Th 7:30am-12:30pm.)*

Once the site of an ancient racetrack, the **Piazza Navona,** a few blocks west across Corso del Rinascimento, evolved into a glorious Baroque *piazza* as the result of a century of one-upmanship. Innocent X, who came to the papal throne in 1644, was only too eager to distract the Roman people from the achievements of his predecessor, the ubiquitous Urban VIII Barberini. He therefore cleared out the stadium on the site and constructed a new *piazza* and palace to rival those of the Barberini across town. The towering, rippling bodies in Bernini's **Fountain of the Four Rivers** command the center of the *piazza* with the grandeur that Innocent intended. Of course, Bernini himself was competing with a rival as well; one story holds that he designed the Nile and Plata statues on the fountain to block the view of the nearby **Church of Sant'Agnese in Agony,** designed by Bernini's great rival Borromini.

Off Via del Corso, Via Lata leads into P. del Collegio Romano and to another stunning *palazzo* and museum. The **Palazzo Doria Pamphilj** hides the Rococo frivolity of the stunning **Galleria Doria Pamphilj,** P. del Collegio Romano 2. *(Open F-W 10am-5pm. L12,000, students and seniors L9000.)* On nearby C. del Rinascimento, the **Chiesa di Sant'Ivo's** corkscrew cupola hovers over the **Palazzo della Sapienza,** the original home of the University of Rome.

Campo dei Fiori, Via Giulia, and Piazza Mattei

Across Corso Vittorio Emanuele II from P. Navona, down Via della Cancelleria, the **Campo dei Fiori** saw countless executions during papal rule; now the only carcasses that litter the *piazza* are those of the fish in the colorful **market** that springs up (M-Sa 6am-2pm). Continuing southwest, away from P. Navona, you'll reach **Piazza Farnese,** where two amazing palaces merit a visit. Towering over the *piazza* is the huge, stately **Palazzo Farnese,** begun in 1514 with an elaborate cornice by Michelangelo (interior not open to the public). To the east, the **Palazzo Spada** represents a masterpiece of Baroque stucco. Room 2 of the **Galleria Spada** inside has works by Tintoretto and Titian. *(Open Tu-Sa 9am-6:30pm, Su 9am-12:30pm. L8000.)*

South of P. Farnese and these palaces begins **Via Giulia,** commissioned by Pope Julius II in the early 16th century as a straight road leading directly to the Vatican. Throughout the 16th century, this luxurious expanse remained a refined neighborhood, and today it is one of the most peaceful and exclusive roads in Rome, with well-maintained *palazzi,* antique stores, and art galleries.

Just east of Campo dei Fiori and accessible by bus 64, **Piazza Mattei,** with the 16th-century **Fontana delle Tartarughe** (Tortoise Fountain) by Taddeo Landini, marks the center of the **Jewish Ghetto,** the lowland quarter where Jews were confined from the 16th to the 19th centuries. The **Sinagoga Ashkenazita** stands at Via Catalana and Lungotevere Cenci. Built between 1874 and 1904, the building incorporates Persian and Babylonian architectural devices. *(Open for services only.)* Following a 1982 attack on the synagogue, *carabinieri* armed with machine guns search and question all visitors before they enter.

Piazza del Popolo, Piazza di Spagna, and Villa Borghese

The traditional northern entrance to the city, **Piazza del Popolo** (the people's square) is a favorite arena for communal antics. Tucked away on the north side of the *piazza* near the Porta del Popolo, the small **Church of Santa Maria del Popolo** contains two exquisite canvases by Caravaggio, the *Conversion of St. Paul* and the *Crucifixion of St. Peter,* among other notable works. *(Open daily 7am-noon and 4-7pm.)*

Designed by an Italian, paid for by the French, occupied by the British, and now under the sway of American ambassador-at-large Ronald McDonald, the **Spanish Steps** (Scalinata di Spagna) exude a truly international atmosphere as a tourist attraction and hangout for foreigners and Italians alike. Today, you're more likely to see con artists, but in its day the area attracted Stendhal, Balzac, Wagner, and Liszt; Henry James and the Brownings lived on Via Bocca di Leone, a small sidestreet in the area. A small plaque on the side of P. di Spagna, 26, marks the place where Keats died in 1821. The second floor of the house now features the charming **Keats-Shelley Memorial Museum,** full of curious relics from the poets' lives. *(Open May-Sept. M-F 9am-1pm and 3-6pm, Sa 11am-2pm and 3-6pm; Oct.-Apr. M-F 9am-1pm and 2:30-5:30pm. Closed 2nd and 3rd weeks of Aug. L5000.)* From P. del Popolo, Via di Ripetta leads south toward the Tiber, ending in the **Piazza Augusto Imperatore.** The circular brick mound of the **Masoleo d'Agosto** once housed the funerary urns of the Imperial Roman family. *(Open sporadically for tours.)*

Immediately north of the Spanish Steps and northeast of the P. del Popolo, the park of the **Villa Borghese** features cool, shady paths, countless fountains and statues, three major museums, and a zoo. To get to Villa Borghese, take Metro A to "Flaminia." In the park, the **Galleria Borghese** has reopened its marvellous doors and brims with gold, crystal, and marble. Inside are Bernini's greatest early sculptures, including *Apollo and Daphne,* the *Rape of Proserpina,* and *David. (Open Tu-Sa 9am-7pm, Su and holidays 9am-1pm. Last admission 30min. before closing. L10,000.)* The **Galleria Nazionale d'Arte Moderna** is filled with the best Italian and European art of the 19th and 20th centuries. *(Open Tu-Su 9am-7pm, holidays 9am-1pm.)*

Trevi Fountain to Piazza Barberini

Nicola Salvi's famed and now sparkling-clean **Fontana di Trevi** (Trevi Fountain) emerges from the back wall of Palazzo Poli, dwarfing the already narrow *piazza.* In the foreground of the fountain, two enormous Tritons struggle out of the rough-hewn stone and guide the winged chariot of Neptune. **Piazza del Quirinale,** southeast of Trevi Fountain at the end of Via del Quirinale, occupies the summit of the tallest of Rome's seven hills. In the *piazza,* the heroic statues of **Castor and Pollux** flank yet another of Rome's many obelisks.

Just north of Trevi Fountain and a few blocks north of P. del Quirinale, Via del Tritone runs east to **Piazza Barberini.** Bernini's **Fontana del Tritone** (Triton Fountain) spouts a stream of water high into the air over the bustling traffic circle of this *piazza.* The *piazza* is also home to Bernini's **Fontana delle Api** (Bee Fountain), which buzzes with the same motif that graces the aristocratic Barberini family's coat of arms. Follow Via Veneto from the *piazza* to reach the **Church of Santa Maria della Concezione,** a mausoleum built in 1626 as part of the Counter-Reformation. In the **Capuchin Crypt** downstairs, the arranged bones of 4000 Capuchin friars make this one of the most bizarre and elaborately macabre settings in Rome. *(Open F-W 9am-noon and 3-6pm. L1000 minimum donation requested.)* On the side of P. Barberini opposite the church, up Via delle Quattro Fontane, Palazzo Barberini's **Galleria Nazionale d'Arte Antica** houses a superb collection of paintings from the 12th to 17th century. *(Open Tu-Sa 9am-2pm, Su 9am-1pm. L8000, under 18 and over 60 free.)*

From the Chiesa di S. Susanna, Via Orlando lead towards **Piazza della Repubblica,** home to the turn-of-the-century **Fontana delle Naiadi** (Fountain of Nymphs) and the ruins of the **Baths of Diocletian.** From AD 298 to 306, 40,000 Christian slaves were kept busy building the latter, the grandest community center of ancient Rome

Monti and the Appian Way

The grandiose **Church of San Giovanni in Laterano,** the cathedral of the diocese of Rome, lies east of the Colosseum at the end of Via San Giovanni in Laterano, in the *piazza* of the same name. *(Metro A: San Giovanni. Open in summer daily 7am-6:45pm; off-season 7am-6pm. Dress appropriately.)* The traditional pilgrimage route from St. Peter's ends here, at the city's oldest Christian basilica. Four blocks down Via Cavour from Termini, the Basilica of **Santa Maria Maggiore** occupies the summit of the Esquiline Hill. Both the front and rear facades are Rococo works, but the interior is the best example of a paleo-Christian basilica in the city.

The Via Appia Antica was built in 312 BC and has rightly been called the "queen of roads" ever since. Bus 218 proceeds down Via Appia Antica from S. Giovanni to the Chiesa di Santa Maria in Palmis, also known as **Domine Quo Vadis,** where a fleeing St. Peter had a vision of Christ. *(Open daily 9am-noon and 4-7pm.)*

Outside the city proper lie the **catacombs,** mysterious multi-story condos for the dead. Of the 60 such tunnels around Rome, the most notable are **San Sebastiano, San Callisto,** and **Santa Domitilla,** next door to one another on Via Appia Antica south of the city. *(Catacombs open 8:30am-noon and 2:30-5:30pm; off-season until 5pm. San Sebastiano closed Th and Nov., Santa Domitilla closed Tu and Jan., San Callisto closed W and Feb. Each L8000.)* Buses 218 and 660 serve this part of the city. San Sebastiano is perhaps the most impressive of the three: the tunnels here run for 7 mi. on three levels and accommodate 174,000 bodies, and the passageways are eerily decorated with animal mosaics, disintegrating skulls, and early Christian iconography.

Trastevere

Across the river, Trastevere boasts a proud, independent vitality, giving the neighborhood a character and atmosphere unlike that of the rest of central Rome. To reach Trastevere, take bus 75 or 170 from Termini, or bus 56 or 60 from Via Claudio in front of P. San Silvestro, near the Spanish Steps. Buses to Trastevere stop at **Piazza Sonnino,** which is close to most attractions in the historic center. The *piazza* itself draws crowds of tourists for its restaurants, *pizzerie,* and bars, although the buses and bus terminals here diminish some of the charm. Near the *piazza,* Via dei Genovesi runs toward the river to the intersection with Via di Santa Cecilia; turn right here to find the **Basilica of Santa Cecilia in Trastevere,** up ahead on the right. *(Open Tu and Th 10am-noon and 4-5:30pm.)* Stefano Maderno's famous statue of Santa Cecilia reclines under the high altar. From Viale di Trastevere take Via della Lungaretta to P. di Santa Maria in Trastevere, home to the grandiose 4th-century **Church of Santa Maria in Trastevere.** Although the church is being restored, the 12th-century mosaics in the apse and the chancel arch still glimmer in their full splendor. *(Open daily 7:30am-7pm.)*

Isola Tiberina, the island situated between Trastevere and Centro Storico, has been continuously inhabited for nearly 3000 years. The bridge leading from the east bank of the river, the **Ponte Fabricio,** commonly known as the **Ponte dei Quattro Capi** (Bridge of Four Heads), is the oldest in the city, built by Lucius Fabricius in 62 BC. In the island's one *piazza,* the 10th-century **Chiesa di San Bartolomeo** has been flooded and rebuilt many times, resulting in the eclectic mix of a Baroque facade, a Romanesque bell tower, and 14 antique columns. *(Open daily 9am-1pm and 4-6:30pm. Undergoing restoration in 1999.)*

To ascend the **Janiculan Hill (Gianicolo),** where the beautiful **Botanical Gardens** lie, take Via della Scala in Trastevere up to Via Garibaldi (about 10min.). Atop the hill sits the **Church of San Pietro in Montorio,** built on the spot once believed to be the site of St. Peter's upside-down crucifixion. *(Open daily 9am-noon and 4-6:30pm.)*

Vatican City

Occupying 108.5 acres entirely within the boundaries of Rome, Vatican City is the last toehold of a church that once wheeled and dealed as a mighty European power. Under the Lateran Treaty of 1929, the pope exercises all legislative, judicial, and executive powers over this tiny theocracy, but must remain neutral in Italian national politics and Roman municipal administration. On the western bank of the Tiber, the Vatican can be reached from Rome's center by Metro A to "Ottaviano" or "Mosca"; after leaving the station, walk south on Via Ottaviano toward the distant colonnade. You can also take buses 64 and 492 from Termini and Largo Argentina, bus 62 from P. Barberini, bus 23 from Testaccio, or bus 19 from San Lorenzo.

The **Basilica di San Pietro** (St. Peter's Basilica) rests on the reputed site of St. Peter's tomb. *(Open daily Apr.-Sept. 7am-6pm; Oct.-Mar. 7am-5pm. Free. Dome closes 1hr. earlier and may be closed on W morning. Admission to dome on foot L5000, by elevator—part of the way—L6000.)* In 1506, Pope Julius II called on Donato Bramante to improve on the aging brick basilica on the site, and through the years Bramante, Sangallo, Michelangelo, and Raphael had a hand in designing the church. Today, Michelangelo's sorrowful **Pietà** greets visitors to the basilica, though unfortunately from behind bullet-proof glass. Further down the nave on the right, toward the intersection of the two arms of the church, a medieval bronze **statue of St. Peter** presides over the crossing. In the center of the crossing of the two arms, Bernini's **baldacchino** rises on spiraling solomonic columns over the plain marble altar, which only the Pope may use. Steps at the crossing, below Bernini's spear-wielding statue of St. Longinus, lead down to the **Vatican Grottoes,** the final resting place of countless popes and saints. The grottoes lead to the stairs that climb to the **cupola;** at the top, you will find perhaps the most expansive and breathtaking view of Rome.

When in town, the Pope grants **public audiences** in P. San Pietro on Wednesdays, usually at 10:30am. To attend an audience, apply in writing to the **Prefettura della Casa Pontificia,** 00120 Città del Vaticano, specifying the number of tickets desired and the preferred date. Otherwise, stop by the office on the Monday or Tuesday before the audience you wish to attend and see if tickets are available. The office is beyond the bronze doors to the right of the basilica at the beginning of the colonnade, past the Swiss guards. *(Open M-W 9am-1pm; tickets free.)*

A 10-minute walk around the Vatican City walls or bus ride from the *piazza* brings you to the extraordinary **Vatican Museums.** *(Major galleries open M to Sa 8:45am-1pm. Extended hours Mar. 16-Oct. 30 M-F 8:45am-3:45pm, Sa 8:45am-1:45pm. Last admittance 1hr. before closing. Museums are closed on major religious holidays. L15,000, with ISIC L10,000, children under 1m tall free. Free last Su of each month 8:45am-1:45pm.)* Of the four color-coded paths through the museums, Tour A hits only the barest essentials, while Tour D covers absolutely everything. Several of the greatest extant works of classical sculpture adorn the **Pio-Clementine Museum,** including the sublime Apollo Belvedere, the evocative Laocoön, and the sarcophagus of St. Helen. A floor above, the remarkable **Etruscan Museum** displays artifacts from Tuscany and northern Lazio. Several routes lead through the breathtakingly frescoed **Raphael Rooms,** the sumptuous papal apartments built by Pope Julius II in the 16th century. The **Stanza della Segnatura** contains Raphael's splendid School of Athens, in which Plato and Aristotle stroll through an airy architectural fantasy as other famous scholars and artists converse around them. The climax of any tour of the Vatican Museums is the **Sistine Chapel.** The barrel vault of the ceiling, some 70 feet above the floor, gleams with the undaunted genius, brave simplicity, and brilliant coloring of Michelangelo's masterpiece. The altar wall is covered by Michelangelo's restored The Last Judgment. **Refrain from taking flash photos;** it's detrimental to the frescoes and you can buy much better shots on postcards. Once out of the Sistine Chapel, explore several more masterpieces at the **Pinacoteca.**

A short walk down Via della Conciliazione from St. Peter's stands the massive **Castel Sant'Angelo.** Built by the Emperor Hadrian (117-138 AD), the edifice has served the popes as a fortress, prison, and palace. The enormous complex now contains a museum of arms and artillery, but the papal apartments and the incomparable views of Rome are the real reasons to visit. *(Open in summer Tu-F 9am-10pm, Sa-Su 9am-8pm; in winter Tu-Su 9am-2pm. Admission L8000, EU citizens under 18 or over 60 free.)* The marble **Ponte Sant'Angelo,** lined with Bernini's angels, leads back across the river.

ENTERTAINMENT

Whatever happened to the days when you could swing by the Colosseum to watch a man viciously clawed to death by a bear? Today, Romans seeking diversion are more likely to go to a nightclub in Testaccio than fight a man to the death. Is this progress?

You will have to content yourself by checking **Trovaroma,** in Thursday's edition of *La Repubblica,* and **Roma C'è** for a comprehensive lists of concerts, plays, clubs, and movies. The latter has a special English-language section.

Music, Theater, and Cinema

The classical scene in Rome goes wild in summer. The smaller festivals that run from mid-May to August are just parts of the larger Roma Estate (for full information about the summer's events, consult the website http://www.romaestate.com). It all starts with the **Festa Europea della Musica,** a weekend of non-stop music at the end of June—most concerts are free. In July, the **Accademia Nazionale di Santa Cecilia** (tel. 063 61 10 64 or 066 79 36 17) holds concerts in the **Villa Giulia,** P. della Villa Giulia 9 in Villa Borghese. For concert information and schedules, call or visit the Villa Giulia/ Santa Cecilia **ticket office** in Villa Borghese (tel. 063 61 10 64 or 063 61 18 33, credit card reservations 06 68 80 10 44; open Tu-Sa 10am-2pm, Su 10am-1pm, and on the day of the performance). Buy tickets at Villa Giulia or from the **Agenzia Tartaglia** in P. di Spagna 12 (tel. 066 78 45 65). For information on **plays** and musicals in English, check the tourist office or the English section of *Roma C'è.* Useful websites include http:// www.musical.it and http://www.comune.rome.it. **Teatro Argentina,** Via di Torre Argentina 52 (tel. 06 68 80 46 01 or 06 687 54 45), accessible by bus 64 from Termini, hosts plays (Italian or translated into Italian) concerts, and ballets (box office open M-F 10am-2pm and 3-6pm, Sa 10am-2pm). In summer, especially July, huge screens come up in various *piazza* for **outdoor film festivals.** The single best resource for cinema in Rome is the **I Love Rome home page,** which has a searchable database of movie theaters and showtimes (http://www.alfanet.it/welcomeItaly/roma/default.html).

Music Clubs, Discos, and Jazz

Although Italian discos can be a thrilling, flashy, sweaty good time, travelers must overcome several obstacles before putting on their dancing shoes. Italians still pay over L20,000 to get into laughable discotheques suspended in 1984. The really cool club scene changes as often as Roman phone numbers, and bigger clubs flee in terror during Rome's steaming summer by closing up shop and bounding beachward to **Fregene, Ostia,** or **San Felice Circeo.** Make sure that a club exists and is open before heading out. **Akab,** Via Monte Testaccio 69 (tel. 06 574 44 85), in Testaccio, is an extremely popular hip-hop and R&B club. Be prepared to wait in line (open F-Sa 10pm-4am; cover L10,000 includes first drink). Many clubs are in the Testaccio area, so if this is a miss for you, others nearby may satiate your need to get down. **Alexanderplatz Jazz Club,** Via Ostia 9 (tel. 06 39 74 21 71), is a Jazz club that has hosted some of the greats. Guests must buy a *tessera,* L10,000, good for two months (open Sept.-June daily 10pm-1:15am; shows start at 10:30pm). Take Metro Linea A to Ottaviano, and from there head west on Via Giulio Cesare, take the second right onto Via Leone IV and the first left onto Via Ostia. Night buses to P. Venezia and Termini leave from P. Clodio. If you wondered where many of the clubs go during the summer, **Villagio Globale,** Lungotevere Testaccio, is one of the primary possibilities. Take bus 27 from Termini, get off right before it crosses the river, and head left down the river; after midnight take night bus 20N/21N from Piramide back to Termini. In Testaccio, **RadioLondra,** Via di Monte Testaccio 67, is one of the best gay clubs in town (mixed drinks L15,000). Take Metro Linea B to the Pyramide Metro stop.

Pubs

There are many pubs in Rome, quite a few with some sort of Irish theme. Drinks often go up in price after 9pm, so imbibe accordingly. The pubs and *birrerie* in Trastevere offer the best mix of foreigners and Romans.

Pub Hallo'Ween, P. Tiburtino 31 at the corner of Via Tiburtina and Via Marsala. Abandon all hope of not having fun, ye who enter here. Draft beer L6000-8000, bottles L7000-10,000. Cocktails L8000-9000. Open daily 8:30pm-12:30am. Closed in Aug. Happy Hour, featuring free appetizers, 8:30-10:30pm. Boo.

Jonathan's Angels, Via della Fossa 16. West of P. Navona. Take Vicolo Savelli Parione Pace off Via Governo Vecchio. Lively, loud clientele. You won't believe the bathroom. Beer on tap L10,000. Cocktails/long drinks L15,000. Open daily 1pm-2am.

Julius Caesar, Via Castelfidardo 49, just north of Termini near P. dell'Indipendenza, near the train station. Live music, cheap drinks, and good times. Beer on tap L6000-8000. During Happy Hour (9-10pm), a beer and sandwich are only L10,000. Pitchers L15,000. Cocktails L10,000. Wine L20,000 per bottle. Inquire about the *Let's Go* discount. Open daily 9pm-3am.

Druid's Den, Via San Martino ai Monti 28 (tel. 06 48 90 47 81). Traveling south on Via Merulana from Via Santa Maria Maggiore, take your second right. Pints of Guinness and Strong Bow cider on tap, L7500. Open daily 5pm-12:30am.

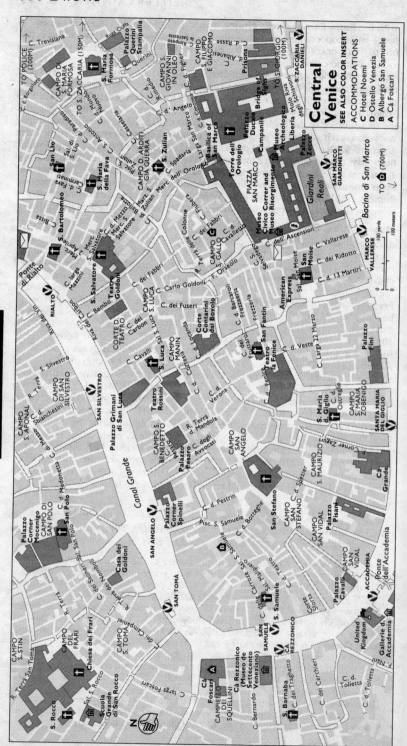

ITALY

Central Venice

SEE ALSO COLOR INSERT

ACCOMMODATIONS

C Hotel Noemi
D Ostello Venezia
B Albergo San Samuele
A Cà Foscari

■ Near Rome

In **Tivoli,** water is the inspiration and principal attraction. Ancient Roman literati such as Catullus and Horace enjoyed the delicious cold of the cascades. From Largo Garibaldi, the gardens of the 16th-century **Villa d'Este** spill over watery terraces from the entrance in P. Trento. (Open May-Aug. 9am-6:45pm; Sept.-Apr. 9am-1hr. before sunset. Admission L8000, EU citizens under 18 and over 60 free). Just outside of Tivoli is the **Villa Adriana,** where Emperor Hadrian reconstructed the architectural wonders of his far-flung empire (open daily 9am-1½hr. before sunset; admission L8000). **COTRAL buses** depart from the "Rebibbia" metro stop for Tivoli (every 30min., L4100). To get to Villa Adriana, get off the COTRAL bus headed for Giudonia from Largo S. Angelo (L2000) or take bus 4 (L1500) from Largo Garibaldi in Tivoli.

The remains of **Ostia Antica** offer a cooler, closer, and cheaper alternative to the more famous ruins at Pompeii and Herculaneum. Take Metro B to "Magliana," change to the Lido train, and get off at Ostia Antica (25min., same metro ticket for both legs of trip). Cross the overpass, go left when the road ends, and follow the signs (open daily in summer 9am-7pm; in winter 9am-5pm; L8000).

THE VENETO

The Veneto encompasses a wide range of geographical terrains, from the rocky foothills of the Dolomites and the Alps to the fertile valleys of the Po River. These territories were linked only loosely under the Venetian Empire, and regional dialects testify to the relative isolation in which the towns developed. The sense of local culture and custom that remains quite strong in each town may surprise visitors lured to Italy's most-touristed region primarily by Venice, the *bella* of the north.

■ Venice (Venezia)

It is with good reason that Venetians call their city *La Serenissima*—the most serene. Venice awakens each morning with a refreshing absence of the cars and mopeds that infest other Italian cities; her citizens make their way on foot or by boat through an ancient maze of narrow streets and winding canals. The serenity is broken only by tourists, who swarm in the city's *campi* (squares) and thoroughfares, searching out its wealth of museums and landmarks. As you follow the crowds to Venice's many architectural and artistic attractions, be sure to save some time to explore the quiet backstreets and lively residential quarters of the city as well.

ORIENTATION AND PRACTICAL INFORMATION

At the northern tip of the Adriatic, Venice is linked by ferry to Greece and the Middle East, and by rail to major European cities. The **Santa Lucia train station** lies on the northwest edge of the city; the bus terminals are across the Grand Canal in nearby **Piazzale Roma.** If you're in a rush to get to **Piazza San Marco** and the central tourist office, take *vaporetto* (canal boat) 82 from the station or Piazzale Roma. If you prefer to walk to San Marco (about 40min.), head left from the station onto Lista di Spagna, and follow the signs and crowds.

The main part of Venice is divided into *sestieri* (districts): **San Marco, Castello, San Polo, Santa Croce, Santa Elena, Cannaregio,** and **Dorsoduro.** Within each section, there are no individual street numbers, but one long sequence of numbers (roughly 6000 per *sestiere*) that winds its way haphazardly through the district. Every building is located on a "street"—*fondamenta, salizzada, calle, campo, canale, rio, ponte,* and *rio terrà. Let's Go: Europe* lists these wherever possible. Always be sure you're in the proper *sestiere;* some street names are duplicated and no *sestiere* boundaries are marked. Yellow signs posted all over town will direct you to and from P. San Marco (at the border of San Marco and Castello), the **Rialto Bridge** (linking San Marco to San Polo), the **train station** (*Ferrovia;* in Cannaregio), the **bus station** (*Piazzale Roma;* in Santa Croce), and the **Accademia** (in Dorsoduro). If you haven't figured it out already, you're going to need a detailed map to navigate Venice successfully. The color-coded *Storti Edizioni* map (L4000-5000) shows all the major streets, has an invaluable street index, and is more useful than anything you'd get for free. Refer also to this book's **color map** of the city.

The **Grand Canal,** the central artery of Venice, can be crossed on foot only at the **ponti** (bridges) **Scalzi, Rialto,** and **Accademia.** *Traghetti* (gondola-like ferry boats) cross the canal fairly frequently where there is no bridge (L1400). High tides (particularly Nov.-Apr.) cause *acque alte,* periodic floods that swamp parts of the city. San Marco is sometimes under three feet of water for two or three hours.

Telephone Code: 041.

Flights: Aeroporto Marco Polo, tel. 541 54 91. ACTV (tel. 528 78 86) local bus 5 runs to the airport (30min., L1400), or take the ATVO coach (tel. 541 51 80), with luggage space, for L5000. Times vary with flight schedule, so call ahead.

Trains: Stazione di Santa Lucia. Info office across from the station's tourist office. Open daily 7:15am-9:15pm. To: Bologna (2hr., 1 per hr., L14,000); Florence (3hr., 5 direct per day, L22,00-43,500); Milan (3hr., 1 per hr., L22,000-34,000); Padua (30min., 1-3 per hr., L3900); and Rome (4-5hr., 6 per day, L45,500). **Luggage Storage** L5000 for 12hr. Open 3:45am-12:30am. **Lost and Found,** tel. 78 52 38.

Buses: ACTV (tel. 528 78 86), the local line for buses and boats in P. Roma. Open daily 7:30am-8pm. **ACTV long distance carrier,** to Padua (1hr. 20min., 2 per hr., L5000) and Treviso (1hr., 2 per hr., L3800, round-trip 7000). Ticket office open daily in summer 8am-8pm; off-season 7:40am-7pm. Info office open M-Sa 7am-8pm.

Public Transportation: The alternative to walking is taking the *vaporetti* (motorboat buses), which cruise waterways. Most principal boats run 24hr. but frequency is reduced after 11pm. The 24hr. or 3-day *biglietto turistico* is good for unlimited travel on all boats (L15,000-30,000). The ACTV office offers a special 3-day ticket for holders of the Rolling Venice Card (L20,000). Not all stations sell tickets all the time—buy extras and get the type that can be machine-validated at any station. Buy tickets at booths in front of *vaporetti* stops and at self-serve dispensers (located at the ACTV office in P. Roma and at the Rialto stop). Buy tickets on board for an L800 surcharge. The fine for riding the *vaporetti* without a ticket is L24,000.

Tourist Offices: APT, Palazzina del Santi (Gardinetti Reali; tel. 522 63 56; fax 52 99 87 30), just past the park. Exit P. San Marco between the columns and turn right along the waterfront. Open daily 10am-noon and 2-4pm. There is a second office in P. San Marco, **Ascensione** (tel. 520 89 64), in the building directly opposite the Basilica. Open daily 9:30am-5:30pm. The office at the **train station** (tel./fax 041 71 90 78) is usually mobbed. Get in line at the left side of the booth. Open daily 8:10am-6:50pm. The office at the **Lido,** Gran Viale 6/A (tel. 526 57 21), is open during the high season only (open M-Sa 10am-1pm). If you're in Venice for more than a couple of days, check out **Youth Discount Card: Rolling Venice,** Comune di Venezia, Assessorato alla Gioventù, San Marco 1529 (tel. 270 76 51; fax 270 76 42), on Corte Contarina. The card (L5000) offers discounts at many hotels, restaurants, shops, and museums, and comes with a map that lists participating establishments.

Walking Tours: Enjoy Venice (toll-free 167 27 48 19) gives walking tours in English. Under 26 L25,000, 26 and up L30,000.

Budget Travel: CTS, Dorsoduro 3252 (tel. 520 56 60; fax 523 69 46), on Fondamenta Tagliapietra. Off the Dorsoduro-to-San Marco route, near Campo S. Margherita. Open M-F 9:30am-1:30pm and 3-6:30pm. **Transalpino** (tel./fax 71 66 00), for international train tickets, is to the right as you exit the station. Open M-F 8:30am-12:30pm and 3-7pm, Sa 8:30am-12:30pm.

Currency Exchange: Banco di Sicilia, San Marco 5051 (tel. 66 37 11). Changes cash and traveler's checks. Open daily 8:30am-1:30pm, F-W also 3-4pm. Many automatic change machines located next to **ATMs** outside banks offer 24hr. service, low commission, and decent rates.

American Express: San Marco, Sal. S. Moise 1471 (tel. 167 87 20 00). Exit P. San Marco opposite the basilica and head toward the Accademia (look for the AmEx directional mosaic underfoot). Free mail service for members or those with AmEx Traveler's Checks. Mediocre exchange rates; no commission. Office open M-F 9am-5:30pm, Sa 9am-12:30pm. Exchange service open in summer M-Sa 8am-8pm.

English Bookstores: Libreria Editrice Cafoscarina, Dorsoduro 3259 (tel. 523 89 69; fax 522 81 86), on Cà Foscari near the university. The largest selection in Venice. 10% Rolling Venice discount. Open M-F 9am-7pm, Sa 9am-12:30pm.

Emergency: tel. 113. **First Aid,** tel. 118.

Police: Carabinieri, tel. 112 in an emergency, station in Castello 4693/a (tel. 520 47 77).

24-Hour Pharmacy: Look at the display on the door of any pharmacy, or check *A Guest in Venice,* available at the tourist office.

Hospital: Ospedale Civili, Campo SS. Giovanni e Paolo (tel. 529 45 17).

Post Office: S. Marco 5554 (tel. 271 7111), on Salizzada Fontego dei Tedeschi to the east of the Rialto bridge, off Campo San Bartolomeo. *Fermo Posta* at #4, stamps at #9 and 10 or *tabacchi* all over town. Open M-Sa 8:15am-7pm. Housed in an old palace, the building merits a visit on its own. **Branch office** (tel. 528 59 49) through the arcades at the end of P. San Marco, opposite the basilica. Open M-F 8:10am-1:30pm, Sa 8:10am-12:30pm. **Postal Codes:** San Marco, 30124; Castello, 30122; Canareggio, 30121; Dorsoduro, 30123.

Telephones: San Marco, Fontego dei Tedeschi, 5550, next to the main post office. Open M-F 8am-12:30pm and 4-7pm.

ACCOMMODATIONS AND CAMPING

Plan to spend slightly more for rooms here than elsewhere in Italy. Reservations, ideally made as much as a month in advance, will preserve your sanity in the summer. If your plans are more uncertain, dormitory-type accommodations are sometimes available in Venice without reservations, even during August and September. Such accommodations often have irregular operating seasons, so check with the tourist offices to see which are open. In *pensioni*, be wary of L12,000 breakfasts and other forms of bill-padding, and always agree on what you'll pay before surrendering your passport. In a pinch, you might want to visit Venice while based in one of the nearby towns; Padua is just 30 minutes away and a good place to secure a room.

Hostels and Dormitories

Ostello Venezia (HI), Fondamenta di Zitelle 86 (tel. 523 82 11; fax 523 56 89), on Giudecca. Take *vaporetto* 82 from the station (40min.) or take 82 or 52 from S. Zaccaria near San Marco (5min.). Get off at Zitelle and walk right along the waterfront. Institutional, but bright and cheerful. L25,000 per person. Breakfast and sheets included. Reception 7-9:30am and 1-10:30pm. Lockout 9am-2pm. Curfew 11:30pm. Members only. Reservations through IBN from another HI hostel.

Foresteria Valdese, Castello 5170 (tel./fax 528 67 97). Take *vaporetto* 82 to San Zaccharia or 1 to Rialto, then go to Campo Santa Maria Formosa. From the *campo,* take Calle Lunga S. M. Formosa over the first bridge. 18th-century building with frescoed ceilings. Dorms L28,000-29,000; doubles L80,000-120,000. Breakfast included. Reception M-Sa 9am-1pm and 6-8pm, Su 9am-1pm. Lockout 10am-1pm. Phone reservations strongly suggested. Closed 15 days in Nov.

Domus Civica, ACISJF, San Polo 3082 (tel. 72 11 03), on the corner of Calle Chiovere, Calle Campazzo, and S. Rocco, between the Basilica dei Frari and P. Roma. Follow the yellow arrows between P. Roma and the Rialto. Ping-pong tables, TV room, and piano. Singles L42,000; doubles L70,000. 20% discount with Rolling Venice or ISIC. Curfew 11:30pm. Open mid-June to Sept.

Suore Cannosiano, Fondamenta del Ponte Piccolo 428 (tel. 522 21 57). Take *vaporetto* 82 to the Guidecca/Palanca, and walk left over the bridge. Run by nuns. Women only. Dorms L20,000. Check-out 7:30-8:30am. Strict curfew 10:30pm.

Hotels

Casa Gerotto, Campo S. Germia 283 (tel./fax 71 53 61), in Cannaregio. Make a left after leaving the station and walk along Main St. to Campo S. Germia (2min.) for the city's best bargain. Wonderful owner is justly proud of her huge, bright rooms. Clean bathrooms/showers. Owner matches solo travelers and puts them into larger rooms for L25,000-30,000 each. Singles L50,000-60,000; doubles L80,000-130,000; triples L90,000-160,000. Lower prices off-season. Curfew 12:30am.

Hotel Calderan, (tel. 71 55 62) is in the same building as Casa Gerotto, with the same prices and virtually the same rooms.

Hotel Noemi, Calle dei Fabbri 909 (tel. 523 81 44). Leave P. San Marco through the bell towers, turn left at the dead end and cross the bridge, then turn left on Calle dei Fabbri. One of the best located budget hotels in Venice—just one minute from the *piazza*. Singles L75,000; doubles L90,000; triples L112,000.

Hotel Rossi, Cannaregio 262 (tel. 71 51 64; fax 71 77 84), right off Lista di Spagna. Continue from the train station and make a left under the arch onto Calle della Procuratie. Tiled floors and phones in the rooms. Singles L70,000-90,000; doubles L110,000-140,000; triples with bath L175,000; quads with bath L210,000. Breakfast included. Curfew 1am.

Cà Foscari, Dorsoduro 3887b (tel. 71 04 01; fax 71 08 17), on Calle della Frescada. Take *vaporetto* 1 or 82 to San Tomà. Turn left at the dead end, cross the bridge and turn right, then take a left into the little alleyway. In a quiet neighborhood near the ferry. Singles 80,000; doubles L100,000-135,000; quads L164,000-200,000. Breakfast included. Curfew 1am. Rooms held until 2pm. Open Feb.-Nov.

Locanda Antica Casa Carettoni, Cannaregio 130 (tel. 71 62 31; fax 041 71 69 94), along Lista di Spagna. From the station, head left on the main street. Good, firm mattresses perfect for weary backpackers. Singles L85,000, off-season 40,000; doubles L125,000, off-season L70,000. Midnight curfew M-F. No curfew Sa-Su.

Albergo San Samuele, San Marco 3358 (tel./fax 522 80 45). Follow Calle delle Botteghe from Campo S. Stefano (near the Accademia) and turn left on Salizzada S. Samuele. Lovely polychromatic stone floors, and some rooms with flowered balconies. Singles L60,000; doubles L100,000-125,000; extra bed 40% more. Breakfast L7000. Reserve 1-2 months ahead with 1 night's deposit.

Albergo Adua, Cannaregio 233a (tel. 71 61 84; fax 244 01 62), on Lista di Spagna. Young patrons tread on old floors in Adua, whose sometimes tiny rooms are well-priced for Venice. Singles L40,000-65,000; doubles L75,000,-154,000. Breakfast L7500. Curfew 1am. MC, V costs 5% more.

Camping

Camping Miramare, Punta Sabbioni (tel. 96 61 50; fax 530 11 50), about 700m along the beach to your right as you descend from the Punta Sabbioni *vaporetto* stop. L8500 per person; L18,500 per tent. 4-person bungalows L55,000; 5-person bungalows L88,000. Open Mar. to mid-Oct.

Campeggio Fusina (tel. 547 00 55), Via Moranzani 79, in Malcontenta. From P. Roma, take bus 2 to the Fusino stop of S. Marta (1hr., last bus 9pm, L1100), or boat 16 from the Zatteri stop. Call ahead. L10,000 per person, L7000 per tent.

FOOD

While tourists flock to the mediocre restaurants that line the main streets, the best and cheapest food can be found a few feet away in the less traveled alleyways. For an alternative to restaurants, visit any bar or *osteria* in town and make a meal from the vast display of meat- and cheese-filled pastries, tidbits of seafood, rice, and meat, and *tramezzini,* triangular slices of soft white bread with every imaginable filling. Good deals on tourist *menù* abound in the university area, **Dorsoduro.**

Located in the area surrounding the Rialto (San Polo side), the city's most famous **market** was once the center of trade and merchandise for the old Venetian Republic. Fruit stands line the Ruga degli Orefici, and on the right are the vegetable and fish markets. Locals shop around **Campo Beccarie** in San Polo near the Rialto. In Cannaregio, **STANDA,** on Strada Nuova 3660, near Campo S. Felice, has groceries in the back (open daily 8:30am-7:20pm). In Castello near San Marco, stock up on the basics at **Su. Ve.,** Calle del Mondo Novo 5816, off Campo Santa Maria Formosa (open M-Tu and Th-Sa 8:30am-1pm and 4-7:30pm, W 8:30am-1pm). **Kosher food** is served in Europe's oldest Jewish quarter, the **Ghetto Vecchio.**

Vino, Vino, San Marco 2007a, on Calle del Sartor da Veste, off Calle Larga XXII Marzo along the S. Marco to Accademia route. Perhaps the tastiest budget restaurant in Venice. *Primi* L8000. *Secondi* L15,000. 10% Rolling Venice discount on food. Cover L1000. Open for food W-M noon-2:30pm and 7-11pm.

Bora Bora, San Marco 5251. From the Rialto, walk along Salizzada Alla Fava, turn right on Merceria 2 Aprile, then left on Calle Stagneri. Huge pizzas and *primi* L8000-13,000. *Secondi* from L9000. 10% Rolling Venice discount. Open daily noon-3pm and 7:15pm-2:20am.

Trattoria/Pizzeria All'Anfora, Santa Croce 1223, on Lista dei Bari. From the station, cross the Grand Canal, go straight, and then cross the first bridge on the left. Walk around Chiesa di S. Simeon, take the first right, and then the first left. A hearty eatery with a vine-covered patio. *Primi* L8000-16,000. *Secondi* L13,500-25,000. Pizzas L7000-14,500. Cover L3000, service 12%. Open W-M noon-11pm.

Crepizza, Dorsoduro 3760, on Calle San Pantalon. From Campo S. Margherita, walk across Rio di Cà Foscari and around the right side of Chiesa di S. Pantalon. *Primi* L6000-12,000. *Secondi* L9000-17,000. *Menù* L14,500. Pizzas L4000-10,000. Cover L1500. Service 10%. Open W-M noon-2:30pm and 7-10:30pm.

Cip Ciap, Ponte del Mondo Nuovo 5799a, off Fondamenta S. Maria Formosa southwest of the *campo,* in Castello. Grab an incredibly inexpensive pizza (from L4000) or slice (L1600 per *etto*) from this take-out joint and enjoy it on the steps in S. Marco. Open W-M 9am-9pm.

Ai Pugni, Dorsoduro 2839, along Rio di S. Barnaba and Fondamenta Gherardini, off Campo S. Barnaba. Take *vaporetto* 1 to Cà Rezzonico. Sandwiches, salads, and huge, tasty pizzas. *Primi* L7000-8000. *Secondi* L13,000. Pizzas L5500-8000. *Menù* L20,000. No cover. Open for drinks Tu-Su 11am-1am.

Caffè Poggi, Campo della Maddalena 2103, in Cannaregio. Take a left from the station and cross two bridges. Student-friendly and loud, this popular university hangout charges no service or cover for students from Venice or elsewhere. *Panini* L4000-5000, pizza/beer special L13,000. Open Tu-Su 6:30am-1am.

Gelati Nico, Dorsoduro, 922 near the Zattere *vaporetto* stop. Venice's pride. *Gianduiotto,* chocolate-hazelnut ice cream dunked in whipped cream L4000. Cones from L2000. Open in summer daily 7am-11pm; mid-Jan. to mid-Dec.W-M 7am-9pm.

SIGHTS

In Venetian churches a strict dress code applies. No shorts, sleeveless shirts, or miniskirts are allowed. Also, be aware that many of the sights have student, youth, senior, and group discounts; don't be afraid to ask if policies aren't posted.

San Marco and Environs

Piazza San Marco is the city's pigeon-infested, *campanile*-punctuated nucleus. In contrast to the narrow, maze-like streets that cover most of Venice, the *piazza* is an expanse of light and space, framed all around by museums and medieval buildings. Construction of the **Basilica di San Marco** began in the 9th century, when two Venetian merchants stole St. Mark's remains from Alexandria by hiding them in a barrel of pork to hoodwink Arab officials. The basilica's main treasure is the **Pala d'Oro,** a Veneto-Byzantine gold bas-relief encrusted with precious gems. To the right of the altar is the small **treasury,** with a hoard of gold and relics from the Fourth Crusade. *(Basilica open daily 9:45am-7:30pm. Free. Pala d'Oro open M-Sa 10am-4:30pm, Su 2-5pm. L3000. Treasury open M-Sa 10am-4:30pm, Su 2-5pm. L4000, reduced L2000.)* The 15th-century **Torre dell'Orologio** (clock tower), left of San Marco, a florid arrangement of sculpture and sundials, is closed for renovations.

Next to San Marco stands the **Palazzo Ducale** (Doge's Palace). *(Open 9am-7pm, last entry at 5:30pm. L17,000, reduced 10,000.)* Rebuilt in the 14th century after a fire, the palace epitomizes the Venetian Gothic with elegant arcades and light-colored stone cladding. Facing the palace are Sansovino's masterpieces, the elegant **Libreria** and the **Zecca** (coin mint). The main reading room of the **Biblioteca Marciana,** on the second floor, is adorned with frescoes by Veronese and Tintoretto. *(Entrance at #12. Open M-F 9am-7pm, Sa 9am-1pm. Prior permission required.)* Farther north, Calle Lunga and Calle Cicogna lead to Campo **SS. Giovanni e Paolo** and to the church of the same name. This grandiose Gothic structure, built by the Dominican order from the mid-13th to mid-15th centuries, has a wonderful polyptych by Bellini and several marvelous paintings. If you cross the Ponte Rosso and go straight, you'll come to the Lombardos' masterpiece, the **Chuch of Santa Maria dei Miracoli.**

For a real treat, make your way through the *calli* to the **Scuola Dalmata S. Giorgio degli Schiavoni,** Ponte dei Greci 3259. *(Open Tu-Sa 10am-12:30pm and 3-6pm, Su 10am-12:30pm. L7000, reduced L5000.)* Here, between 1502 and 1511, Carpaccio decorated the ground floor with some of his finest paintings, depicting episodes from the lives of St. George, St. Jerome, and St. Trifone.

Art Galleries and Museums

The **Accademia** in Dorsoduro, southwest of San Marco across the Ponte dell'Accademia, displays the best of Venetian painting. *(Open M 9am-2pm, Tu-Sa 9am-10pm, Su 9am-8pm. L12,000.)* The world-class collection includes the superb Bellini *Pala di San Giobbe,* Giorgione's enigmatic *La Tempesta,* and Titian's last work, a brooding *Pietà.* Go early to get your money's worth. For art of a different flavor, visit the **Collezione Peggy Guggenheim,** Dorsoduro 701, housed in the late Ms. Guggenheim's Palazzo Venier dei Leoni. *(Open W-M 11am-6pm. L12,000, students with ISIC or Rolling Venice L8000.)* All the major names in modern art are here, in glorious surroundings. Another art-filled area surrounds the Gothic **Basilica dei Frari** in San Polo across the Rialto. *(Open M-Sa 9am-noon and 2:30-6pm, Su 3-6pm. L2000; holidays free.)* The basilica houses a moving wooden sculpture of St. John by Donatello, Bellini's *Madonna and Saints,* and Titian's famous *Assumption.* The *scuole* of Venice, a cross between guilds and religious fraternities, erected ornate "clubhouses" throughout the city. The richest, the **Scuola Grande di San Rocco,** across the *campo* at the end of the Frari, boasts 56 Tintorettos. *(Open in summer daily 9am-5:30pm; off-season M-F 10am-1pm, Sa-Su 10am-4pm. L8000, with Rolling Venice L6000.)* To see the paintings in chronological order, start on the second floor in the Sala dell'Albergo and follow the cycle downstairs.

The Lagoon and Outlying Sights

Many of Venice's most beautiful churches are a short boat ride away from San Marco. Two of Palladio's most famous churches are visible in the distance from the *piazza.* The **Church of San Giorgio Maggiore,** across the lagoon (boat 52 or 82, L4500), graces the island of the same name. *(Open M-Sa 10am-12:30pm and 2:30-6:30pm, Su 9:30-10:30am and 2:30-6:30pm. L3000.)* The church houses Tintoretto's famous *Last Supper.* A bit farther out on the next island, Giudecca, is Palladio's famous **Church of Il Redentore.** *(Open daily 8am-noon and 3-7pm.)* During the pestilence of 1576, the Venetian Senate swore that they would build this devotional church and make a yearly pilgrimage here if the plague would leave the city. To make your own pilgrimage, take *vaporetto* 82 from S. Zaccharia.

North of Venice stretches the **lagoon.** With a *vaporetto* ticket you can visit the island of **Murano** (*vaporetto* 12 or 52), famous for its glass since 1292, the fishing village of **Burano,** and **Torcello** (both *vaporetto* 12), an island with an enchanting Byzantine cathedral and some of the finest mosaics in Italy. The **Lido,** the setting for Thomas Mann's *Death in Venice,* is accessible by *vaporetto* 1, 6, 14, or 52.

ENTERTAINMENT

Mark Twain may have called the **gondola** "an inky, rusty canoe," but it's a canoe that only the gentry can afford to ride. The authorized rate, which increases after sunset, starts at L80,000 for 50 minutes. Most romantic around sundown, the ride is only affordable if you and your significant other squeeze on with two or three strangers. If you can't afford a long trip, there are several points along the canal where *gondole* operate a one- or two-minute cross-canal service for locals (L2000).

The weekly booklet *A Guest in Venice* (free at hotels and at the tourist office) lists current festivals, concerts, and gallery shows. For theatrical entertainment, **Commedia in Campo** performs outdoors in various *campi* throughout the city; contact Teatro Goldoni for more info (tel. 520 54 22; tickets 520 75 83; fax 520 52 41; tickets L30,000). The famed **Venice Beinnale** (tel. 521 87 11; fax 521 00 38), centered in the Giardini di Castello, takes place every odd-numbered year, with a gala exhibit of international modern art (admission to all exhibits L16,000). Contact the tourist office for info on Venice's several **movie theaters** and the **Mostra Internazionale del Cinema** (Venice International Film Festival) in late August and early September. Venice's selection of **nightclubs** is rather paltry, but several cluster around San Marco. The principal after-midnight stop is **Fondamenta della Misericordia,** in Cannaregio, just past the "Ghetto," where you'll find **Paradiso Perduto,** a young, hip bar, jazz club, and restaurant (open Th-Tu 7:30am-late), and **Iguana,** a favorite hangout for Venetian students (open Th-Tu 12:30pm-3pm and 7pm-1am).

■ Padua (Padova)

Brimming with student life and bursting with art, Padua is a treasury of strident frescoes, sculpture-lined *piazze,* and ethereal nighttime festivals. Here, art eludes the canvas, covering churches from floor to ceiling, and high culture blends with a bustling university scene.

SIGHTS AND ENTERTAINMENT You can buy a **Biglietto Unico,** good at most of the museums in Padua and valid for one year (L15,000, students L10,000). The **Cappella degli Scrovegni** (Arena Chapel) contains Giotto's breathtaking floor-to-ceiling fresco cycle, illustrating the lives of Mary and Jesus. The adjoining **Museo Civico,** where you buy tickets for both sights, features Giorgione's *Leda and the Swan* and a restored Giotto crucifix. (Open daily Feb.-Oct. 9am-7pm; Nov.-Jan. 9am-6pm. L10,000, students L7000. The museum is closed on M, but the chapel remains open.) Next door, the 13th-century **Church of the Eremitani** boasts an imposing exterior and a beautifully carved wooden ceiling. Pictures near the alter show the aftermath of a 1944 bombing which literally tore the church in half. (Open Apr.-Sept. M-Sa 8:15am-noon, Su 9am-noon and 3:30-6:30pm; Oct.-Mar. M-Sa 8:15am-noon, Su 9am-noon and 3:30-5:30pm. Free.) Thousands of pilgrims are drawn to see St. Anthony's jawbone and well-preserved tongue at the **Basilica di Sant'Antonio,** where he is entombed (open daily 7:30am-7pm). The Basilica itself is a medieval conglomeration of eight domes and filled with devastatingly beautiful frescoes. The fascinating yet somewhat bizarre **Palazzo della Ragione** (Hall of Justice), built in 1218, marks the city's center (open Tu-Su 9am-7pm; off-season 9am-1pm and 3-6pm; L9000, students L7000). The interior is lined with astrological mythologies, and such oddities as a golden sun-face and a giant wooden horse. Next door to the **Duomo** in P. Duomo lies the **Battistero,** built in the 12th centrury and perhaps the most beautiful of Padua's structures (open daily in summer 9:30am-1:30pm and 3-7pm; off-season 9:30am-1pm and 3-6pm). Seek out the buildings of the ancient **university,** which are scattered throughout the city but centered in Palazzo Bó.

At night, locals flood the central *piazze* for late dinners and walks. Check out **Lucifer Young,** Via Altinate 89, a hip bar whose decorator took lessons in the Divine Comedy's lowest circle (open Su-Tu and Th-F from 7pm, Sa from 6pm).

PRACTICAL INFO, ACCOMMODATIONS, AND FOOD Trains depart from P. Stazione for Bologna (2hr., L9,100), Milan (2½hr., L20,000-31,500), Venice (30min., L3900), and Verona (1hr., L7400). The **bus station,** Via Trieste 42 (tel. 04 98 20 68 44 or 04 98 76 30 35), offers rides to Venice (45min., every 30min., L5100). The **tourist office** is in the train station (tel. 04 98 75 20 77; open M-Sa 9am-7pm, Su 9am-12:30pm). Pick up a map and a copy of the free *Padua Today.* Be sure to ask about festivals during your stay.

Cheap lodgings abound in Padua, but they tend to fill up quickly. If you can't get into the places listed below, try any of the hotels near **Piazza del Santo.** Better yet, reserve ahead. **Antonianum** offers summer university housing for men (tel. 04 98 76 87 11 from 9:30am-2pm or 5-7pm). The **Ostello Città di Padova (HI),** Via Aleardi 30 (tel. 04 98 75 22 19; fax 049 65 42 10), near Prato della Valle, has an English-speaking staff. Take bus 3 or 8 from the station. (L22,000. Hot showers and breakfast included. Reception 7-9:30am and 2:30-11pm. Lockout 9:30am-4pm. Curfew 11pm.)

ITALY

Albergo Verdi, Via Dondi dall'Orologio 7 (tel. 04 98 75 57 44), has large, comfortable rooms in the center of town (singles L40,000; doubles L60,000; reserve ahead), while **Albergo Pavia,** Via dei Papafava 11 (tel. 049 66 15 58), features newly renovated rooms and a kitchen (singles L42,000; doubles L57,000; quads L100,000).

Prepare for culinary bliss at **Trattoria da Paccagnella,** Via del Santo 113. (*Primi* L10,000-12,000. *Secondi* L15,000-25000. Open daily 7:30am-11pm. Cover L3000. Service 10%.) Otherwise, try **Pizzeria al Borgo,** Via Luca Belludi 56, for creative pizza on an outdoor terrace (open W-M noon-3pm and 6:45pm-12:15am). Supermarket wares are available at **PAM,** on Via Cavour in P. della Garzeria (open M–Sa 8:30am-8pm).

■ Verona

Traversing the old Roman Ponte Pietra on a summer's evening, with the gentle rush of the Adige River below and the illuminated towers of churches and castles glowing in the distance, you'll hardly wonder why Shakespeare set his *Romeo and Juliet* in Verona. Its monumental city gates and ancient amphitheater memorialize its Roman past, while the Scaligeri bridge and tombs hark back to Verona's Gothic glory.

SIGHTS AND ENTERTAINMENT In July and August, the city resounds with music, as tourists and singers from around the world descend for the annual **Opera Festival.** The performances, staged in the majestic first-century **Arena** in P. Brà, are unforgettable. (Arena open Tu-Su 8am-7pm; during opera season 8:15am-3:30pm. L6000, students L4000, 1st Su of the month free. For opera info, call (045) 800 32 04; for tickets call (045) 800 51 51 or check the website at http://www.arena.it.) The heart of the city lies on the southern side of the Adige River, between P. delle Erbe and the Arena. From P. Brà, Via Mazzini leads to **Piazza delle Erbe,** the former Roman Forum. Today the *piazza* offers views of a fountain, several medieval buildings, and countless fruit vendors. The 83m **Torre dei Lambertini,** down Via Capello from P. Erbe, offers perhaps the most stunning view of Verona (open Tu-Su 9:30am-6:30pm; L3000). At **Casa di Giulietta** (Juliet's House), Via Cappello 23, you too can stand on a diminutive balcony and have your photo snapped by camera-happy tourists only to find out that the dal Capello (Capulet) family never lived here (open Tu-Su 9am-7pm; L6000, students L4000). The **Giardino Giusti,** Via Giardino Giusti 2, is a magnificent 16th-century garden with a labyrinth, mysteriously diverging passages, and statues of mythological creatures (open daily Apr.-Sept. 9am-8pm; Oct.-Mar. 9am-7pm). The della Scala fortress, the **Castelvecchio,** at the end of Via Roma from P. Brà, is decked out with walkways, parapets, and an extensive collection of art including Pisanello's *Madonna and Child* and Luca di Leyda's *Crucifixion* (open Tu-Su 9am-7pm. L6000, students L2000, 1st Su of each month free).

PRACTICAL INFO, ACCOMMODATIONS, AND FOOD The **train station** at P. XXV Aprile (tel. (045) 59 06 88 or (1478) 880 88), linked with P. Brà by Corso Porta Nuova, serves Bologna (2hr., L10,100), Milan (2hr., L12,100), Venice (2hr., L10,100), and other cities. **Buses** leave from P. XXV Aprile (tel. (045) 800 41 29) for Brescia (L10,000), Riva del Garda (L9300), and Sirmione (L4800). The **tourist office,** Via Leoncino 61 (tel. (045) 806 86 80; fax 800 36 38), is in a large yellow building opposite the Arena. (Open M-Sa in summer 9am-8pm; in winter 9am-6pm. During the opera season—June 26 to Aug. 30—the office is also open Su 9am-noon and 3-6pm.)

To reach the unbeatable **Ostello della Gioventù (HI), "Villa Francescatti,"** Salita Fontana del Ferro 15 (tel. (045) 59 03 60; fax 800 91 27), from the station, hop on bus 73 or night bus 90 to "P. Isolo," then turn right and follow the yellow signs up the hill. The hostel is located in a renovated 16th-century villa with gorgeous gardens, where you may **camp** for L8000. (Beds L20,000. Hot showers, breakfast, and sheets included. 5-night max. stay. Check-in begins at 5pm. Checkout and rebooking 7-9am. Lockout 9am-5pm. Curfew 11:30pm, flexible for opera-goers. No reservations.) Women should also try the beautiful **Casa della Giovane (ACISJF),** Via Pigna 7 (tel. (045) 59 68 80), in the historic center of town. (Dorms L22,000; singles L32,000; doubles L50,000. Curfew 11pm, extended for opera-goers for an extra L3000. Checkout 9:30am. Call ahead.) To get to **Locanda Catullo,** Vicolo Catullo 1 (tel. (045) 800 27 86), walk along Via Mazzini until you reach #40, turn onto Via Catullo, and then left onto Vicolo Catullo. (Singles L55,000; doubles L80,000-100,000. 3-day min. stay for reservations in high season. No credit cards.)

Vendors in P. Isolo sell Verona's famous wines: *soave* (dry white), *valpolicella,* and *bardolino* (both red). For a large sampling, try **Oreste dal Zovo,** Via S. Marco in Foro, 7/5, off Corso Porta Borsari (open Tu-Su 8:30am-1:30pm and 2:30-10pm). **Ristorante Brek,** P. Brà 20, is the site of a cafeteria-style feeding frenzy (no cover; open M-Sa 11:30am-3:30pm and 6:30-10pm). **Cantore,** Via A. Mario 2, a block from the Arena, has some of Verona's best pizza (open M-Tu and Th-Su 11:45am-3pm and 6-11pm).

FRIULI-VENEZIA GIULIA

■ Trieste (Triest)

Evidence of Trieste's multinational history lingers in the numerous buildings and monuments of Hapsburg origin and the Slavic influence on local cuisine. The 15th-century Venetian **Castle of San Giusto** presides over **Capitolin Hill,** the city's historic center. Take bus 24 (L1200) from the station to the last stop at the fortress, or ascend the hill by way of the daunting **Scala dei Giganti** (Steps of the Giants—all 265 of them). Take a right on Via Capitalina, which will take you to **Piazza della Cattedrale,** with a great view of the sea and downtown. Directly below are the remains of the old Roman city center, and across the street is the restored **Cathedral of San Giusto.** Down the other side of the hill lies the **Museo di Storia de Arte** and the **Orto Lapidario,** Via Cattedrale 15, in P. Cattedrale. The museum provides exhibits on Trieste's ancient history and boasts a growing collection of Egyptian art as well as artifacts from southern Italy (open Tu-Su 9am-1pm; L3000).

Trieste is a departure point for many travelers to Eastern Europe. Pick up travel info at the **tourist office** in the train station (tel. (040) 42 01 82; open M-Sa 9am-7pm, Su 10am-1pm and 4-7pm). **Trains** (tel. (147) 880 88) depart from P. della Libertà for Budapest (13hr., L97,000), Milan (5hr., L50,000), Venice (2hr., L14,000), and other cities. **Agemar Viaggi,** P. Duca degli Abruzzi 1/A (tel. (040) 36 37 37), arranges ferries to the former Yugoslavia and other locales. The **Valeria,** Via Nazionale 156 (tel. (040) 21 12 04) offers clean rooms in a peaceful suburb. Catch the tram to Opicina from P. Oberdan (singles L35,000; doubles L50,000). **Blaue Krone,** Via XXX Ottobre 12 (tel. (040) 63 18 82), is in the center of town (singles L40,000; doubles L60,000). For amazing pizza, head to **Pizzeria Barattolo,** P. Sant'Antonio 2 (open Tu-Su 8am-1am).

THE LAKES AND THE DOLOMITES

When Italy's monuments and museums all start to blur together, explore the natural beauty of the country's lakes and mountains. The Dolomites dominate the landscape in the province of Trentino-Alto Adige, rising from Austrian-influenced valley communities to lofty peaks perfect for skiing and hiking. The Lake Country lends itself to relaxation by the lakeside or in nightclubs; windsurfing and water sports are also popular throughout the region.

■ The Lakes

With its romantic shores and inexpensive hostels, **Lake Como** (Lago di Como) is one hour north of Milan by train (L9200) near the Swiss border. Situated at the southwest tip of the lake, **Como** is the largest urban outpost. Swimmers should head up the lake for cleaner waters, but Como's harbor permits boats to reach the shore. For excellent hiking and stunning views, take the *funicolare* up to **Brunate;** the cars leave from the far end of Lungo Lario Trieste, in front of P. Cavour (round-trip L7200, at the hostel L5000). Como's **tourist office,** P. Cavour 16 (tel. 031 26 20 91), near the waterfront, has maps and currency exchange and reserves rooms (open M-Sa 9am-12:30pm and 2:30-6pm, Su 9am-12:30pm). **Ostello Villa Olmo (HI),** Via Bellinzona 2 (tel. 031 57 38 00), offers clean rooms and discounts on various attractions in Como; from the station, it's a 20-minute walk left down Via Borgovico, which becomes Bellinzona. (L16,000. Breakfast included. Reception Mar.-Nov. 7:30-10am and 4-11pm; Dec.-Feb. open to groups by reservation only. Call ahead.) In nearby Menaggio, **Ostello La Prinula (HI),** Via IV Novembre 86 (tel./fax 034 43 23 56), is one of the jollier and better-kept hostels around (L17,000; lockout 10am-5pm; curfew 11:30pm; open mid-Mar. to early Nov.). The laid back **hostel (HI)** in Domaso, 50km (2hr.) from Como by bus and also accessible by boat, comforts backpackers and windsurfers at Via Case Sparse 12 (tel. 034 49 60 94; L14,000; open Mar.-Oct.). The tourist office in Como has info on the many **campsites** that dot the region.

Lake Garda (Lago di Garda) is one of the grandest and most popular of Italy's lakes. To explore the region, travel to **Desenzano** along the Milan-Venice train line; from there, the lake towns are easily accessible by buses, hydrofoils, and ferries. You can also reach the lake by bus from Brescia (1hr., L5400) and Verona (1hr., L4600). Along the southern edge of the lake, near most bus and rail lines, **Sirmione** boasts extensive Roman ruins and a beautifully situated medieval **castle,** although it is more commercial than its neighbors. Sleep right next to the castle at **Albergo Grifone,** Vicolo Bisse 5 (tel. (030) 91 60 14; singles L50,000; doubles L78,000), or pick up info on other accommodations at the **tourist office** (tel. (030) 91 61 14). In **Gardonne Riviera,** the **Il Vittoriale,** the villa of poet, novelist, and latter-day Cassanova, Gabriele D'Annunzio, is Lake Garda's famous sight. At the north end of the lake, secluded **Riva** offers splendid hiking, swimming, and windsurfing.

■ The Dolomites

An hour north of Verona on the Bologna-Brenner train line, beautiful **Trent** (Trento, Trient) balances Germanic and Mediterranean flavors. Trent's sights are few and far between, but for a sampling of northern Italian life, superb restaurants, and strolls between luxuriously decorated buildings, Trent merits a visit. For an introduction to Trent's history, take a right at the end of Via Belenzani onto Via Roma and head to the **Castello del Buonconsiglio.** The castle features beautiful gardens and an impressive art museum, while the towers offer a panoramic view of the city. (Open Apr.-Sept. Tu-Su 9am-noon and 2-5:30pm; Oct.-Mar. closes at 5pm. L9000, students and seniors L5000.) Trent's Gothic-Romanesque *duomo* (cathedral), atop the **Cathedral of Saint Vigilio,** completes the looming structure that wraps partly around the P. Duomo. The *piazza* and its **Fontana del Nettuno** mark the vital center of Trent. The **tourist office,** Via Alfieri 4 (tel. (0461) 98 38 80; fax 98 45 08), is across the park from the train station. **Ostello Giovane Europa (HI),** Via Manzoni 17 (tel./fax (0461) 23 45 67), has sparkling rooms and a friendly staff (dorms L20,000). **Hotel Venezia,** P. Duomo 45 (tel. (0461) 23 41 14), has pleasant, large rooms (singles L45,000-59,000; doubles L65,000-86,000). **Monte Bondone** rises majestically over Trent and begs for pleasant excursions. In summer and winter, check at the **tourist office** (tel. (0461) 94 71 28; fax 94 71 88; open Dec.-Easter and June 20-Sept. 20) in **Vaneze,** halfway up the mountain, about accommodations and skiing. The cable car from Ponte di San Lorenzo (L1500-4000 one-way), between the train tracks and the river, will take you to **Sardagna,** a great picnic spot.

Only an hour by train from Trent (every 30-40min., L9000) and en route to the Brenner Pass, **Bolzano's** (Bozen) bilingual street signs and mandatory instruction in both Italian and German betray the city's true Austrian bent. The historic center is a combination of spacious *piazze/plätze* and arcaded alleys, and is an ideal place to stock up on essentials for excursions to the Dolomites. With its prickly, spined tower and diamond-patterned roof, the foreboding Gothic **duomo** is an awesome sight. The

tourist office, P. Walther 8 (tel. (0471) 30 70 00; fax 98 01 28), offers hiking and accommodations advice (open M-F 9am-6:30pm, Sa 9am-12:30pm). To prep for serious mountaineering, go to the **Provincial Tourist Office for South Tyrol,** P. Parrocchia 11 (tel. (0471) 99 38 08), just down from P. Walther across from the *duomo.* The spacious **Croce Bianca,** P. del Grano (Kornpl.) 3 (tel. (0471) 97 75 52), has old-style charm (rooms L40,000-90,000). In Bolzano, pizza and gelato take a back seat to Knödel, strudel, and other Austrian fare. **Hopfen & Co.,** Via Argentieri 36, serves a filling goulash for L8000.

For a taste of small town Italy (and the potent local *grappa*), consider a day trip to **Bassano del Grappa,** an hour by train from Padua (L10,100). The **tourist office,** Largo Corona d'Italia 35 (tel. 52 43 51), has info and a map. The lovely **Ponte degli Alpini,** a covered wooden bridge dating from 1209, leads to a charming downtown.

LOMBARDY (LOMBARDIA)

Although urbane Milan looms largest in foreigners' image of Lombardy, Mantua and smaller regional towns also offer artistic and culinary treasures. The foothills of the Alps are close by, mixing an Italian climate with Swiss and Austrian culture, and the region has become a magnet for North African and Middle Eastern immigrants.

■ Milan (Milano)

Once the capital of the western half of the Roman Empire, modern Milan retains few reminders of its distinguished pedigree. The city has forged toward modernity with more force than any other major Italian city, creating a fast-paced life—even the requisite *siesta* is shortened. Although success has also brought petty crime and drugs, Milan remains a vibrant city on the cutting edge of high finance and fashion.

ORIENTATION AND PRACTICAL INFORMATION

The layout of Milan resembles a giant target, encircled by remnants of concentric ancient city walls. The **duomo** and **Galleria Vittorio Emanuele II** comprise the bull's-eye, roughly at the center of the downtown circle. From the train station, a scenic ride on bus 60 or quick commute on metro line 3 takes you to the downtown hub. Refer to this book's **color map** of the city.

Flights: For flight information, call 02 74 85 22 00. **Malpensa Airport,** 45km from town, handles intercontinental flights. Buses connect to the airport from P. Luigi di Savoia, on the east side of Stazione Centrale (1-2 per hr., L13,000). **Linate Airport,** 7km from town, covers domestic and European routes. The cheapest trip to this airport is on bus 73 from MM1: P. San Babila (L1500).

Trains: Stazione Centrale, P. Duca d'Aosta (tel. 147 88 80 88). To: Florence (2½hr., L37,000), Genoa and Turin (each 1½-2hr., L22,500), Rome (4½hr., L68,000, IC L79,500), and Venice (3hr., L34,000). Info office open daily 7am-9:30pm. Eurail-passes and *Cartaverde* available outside the building. **Luggage storage** L500 per 12hr. Open 24hr.

Buses: Many buses leave from Stazione Centrale. Intercity buses are often less convenient and more expensive than trains. **SAL, SIA, Autostradale,** and other carriers leave from P. Castello and nearby (MM: Cairoli).

Public Transportation: ATM (tel. 167 016 857 toll-free or 02 48 03 24 03), in P. del Duomo MM station. Municipal buses require pre-purchased tickets (L1500). Day passes L5000. Info office open M-Sa 7:30am-7:30pm; ticket office open daily 7:30am-7:30pm.

Tourist Office: APT, Via Marconi 1 (tel. 02 72 52 43 00; fax 02 72 52 43 50), in the Palazzo di Turismo in P. del Duomo, to the right as you face the *duomo.* Comprehensive local and regional info, a useful map, and a museum guide (in Italian). Doesn't reserve rooms, but will check for vacancies. Be sure to pick up *Milano: Where, When, How* as well as *Milano Mese* for info on activities and clubs. Open

ITALY

Milan

SEE ALSO COLOR INSERT

PIAZZA ASCOLI

Viale dei Mille
Viale Piceno
Viale Umbria

Via Bronzetti

Stazione Porta Vittoria

TO LINATE AIRPORT (6KM)

Corso XXII Marzo

300 yards
300 meters

Via Belotti
Via Carlo Goldoni

Viale Piave
Viale Premuda
Viale B. Maria

Luigi Maino

Via Anfossi
Via Campionesi

Via Spartaco
PIAZZALE LIBIA

Vle. Lazio

Nero
Viale Reg. Margherita
Via Monte Nero
Via Caldara
Vle. Caldara
PORTA ROMANA

Museo di Storia Naturale
Via Cappucini
Via Mozart
Damiano Corso Monforte
Conservatorio
Via Conservatorio
Corso di Vittoria
Via della Pace

Via Palestro
Galleria d'Arte Moderna
PALESTRO
Palazzo del Senato
Via Senato
Corso Venezia

Via della Spiga
Museo di Milano
S. BABILA
Via Borgogna
Corso Monforte
Via Cavallotti
Via San Barnaba
Via d. Commenda
Corso di Porta Romana
ROCETTA

Via Fatebenefratelli
Via Manzoni
MONTE NAPOLEONE
Via Monte Napoleone
Via Bigli
Corso Matteotti
Duomo
Palazzo Arcivescovado
Via F. Sforza
Policlinico
Corso Porta Vignetina

Pinacoteca di Brera
Via Monte di Pietà
Museo Poldi-Pezzoli
PIAZZA DELLA SCALA
Galleria
V. Emanuele II
United Kingdom
Corso Vitt. Emanuele II
Via Larga
Teatro Lirico
Via Festa del Perdono
Ospedale Maggiore (University)
Via San Nazaro
Corso di Porta Romana

Via Brera
La Scala
Via Verdi
Via Mercanti
CORDUSIO
Palazzo Reale
PIAZZA DEL DUOMO
DUOMO
Via Paola
Via Mazzini

Via Pontaccio
American Express
LANZA
CAIROLI
PIAZZA CORDUSIO
Oreficio
PIAZZA CORDUSIO
Via Spadari
Via S. Sofia
Via Savoia

Via Mercado
Via Dante
Via Meravigli
Pinacoteca Ambrosiana
Via Torino
Via Amedei
Corso Italia
Viale Beatrice d'Este

PARCO SEMPIONE
Castello Sforzesco
Buses to Malpensa Airport
Foro Buonaparte
CAIROLI
Via Giani
Via Orsola
Via Stampa
San Lorenzo
Via San Vito
PIAZZA VETRA
Via del Fante
Via Mercalli
Viale Col di Lana

Via Gadio
CADORNA
Via G. Carducci
Via Agnese
Via Valeria
Basilica di Sant'Ambrogio
Via Correnti
San Lorenzo
San Eustorgio
PORTA TICINESE

Palazzo dell'Arte
Via Palestro
Stazione Monti Nord
Santa Maria delle Grazie
Via Boccaccio
AMBROGIO
Via Lanzone
Via Edmondo De Amicis
Corso Porta Ticinese
Via Arena
Via G. d'Annunzio
Viale Gorizia
PIAZZALE XXIV MAGGIO

Via Vincenzo Monti Nord
CONCILIAZIONE
Corso Magenta
Via San Vittore
Via Olivetani
Museo Nazionale della Scienza e della Tecnica "da Vinci"
Via Olona
Via Ariberto
PIAZZA CANTORE
Colombo
Via Vigevano
PORTA GENOVA

Via L. Mascheroni
Via Ariosto
Via Vercellina
Viale Vercellina
CARCERI
Via S. Agostino
Via Papiniano
Viale Conti Zugna
Stazione Porta Genova
PORTA GENOVA

Via Pagano
Via Togni
PARCO SOLARI
Viale Solari
Via Solari
Via Savona
Via Tortona

M-F 8:30am-8pm, Sa 9am-1pm and 2-7pm, Su 9am-1pm and 2-5pm. **Branch office** at Stazione Centrale (tel. 02 72 52 43 70 or 02 72 52 43 60). Open M-Sa 9am-6pm, Su 9am-12:30pm, 1:30-6pm.

Currency Exchange: Banca di San Paolo, at Stazione Centrale, has standard rates and charges a L6000 fee. Open M-Sa 8:30am-12:30pm and 2-7:30pm.

American Express: Via Brera 3 (tel. 02 72 00 36 93), on the corner of Via dell'Orso. Mail held free for AmEx members for 1 month. Accepts wired money (a L2500 fee if over US$100). Open M-Th 9am-5:30pm, F 9am-5pm.

Laundromat: Vicolo Lavandai, Via Monte Grappa 2. MM2: Garibaldi. Self-service wash or dry L5000 for 7kg. Open daily 8am-10pm.

Pharmacy: In Stazione Centrale (tel. 02 669 07 35 or 02 669 09 35). Open 24hr.

Hospital: Ospedale Maggiore di Milano, Via Francesco Sforza 35 (tel. 02 550 31), 5min. from the *duomo* on the inner ring road.

Emergencies: tel. 113. **First Aid,** tel. 02 38 83. **Ambulance,** tel. 118.

Police: tel. 112 or 02 772 71.

Post Office: Via Cordusio 4 (tel. 02 869 20 69), near P. del Duomo toward the castle. Stamps, *fermo posta,* and money exchange. Open M-F 8:30am-7:30pm, Sa 8:30am-1pm. **Postal Code:** 20100.

Internet Access: Hard Disk Cafe, Corso Sempione 44 (tel. 02 33 10 10 38). L10,000-15,000 per hr. Open M-Sa 9am-2am.

Telephones: In Galleria Vittorio Emanuele. Open daily 8am-7:30pm. Phones are also available in Stazione Centrale. Open daily 8am-9:30pm.

ACCOMMODATIONS AND CAMPING

Every season is high season in Milan, except August when locals vacation and much of the city shuts down. For the best deals, check out the area east of the train station or go to the city's southern periphery. When possible, make reservations.

Ostello Pietra Rotta (HI), Via Salmoiraghi 1 (tel. 02 39 26 70 95). Take MM1 to QT8, and go right (so the round church is to the left, across the street) for 10min. Modern facilities and 350 beds. L24,000. Breakfast, sheets, and lockers included. Members only; HI cards L30,000. Reception 7-9am and 3:30pm-midnight, but no morning check-in. Curfew 11:30pm. Open Jan. 13-Dec. 20.

Hotel Ca' Grande, Via Porpora 87 (tel./fax 02 26 14 40 01 or 02 26 14 52 95), about 7 blocks in from P. Loreto in a yellow house. MM1 or 2: Loreto. Clean rooms with phones, plain beds, and a wonderful proprietor. Street below can be noisy. Singles L60,000-80,000; doubles L90,000-100,000. Breakfast included. Reception 24hr.

Viale Tunisia, 6. MM1: Porta Venezia. This building houses 2 separate hotels equidistant from the station and the city center. Ask for keys if going out at night. **Hotel San Tommaso** (tel./fax 02 29 51 47 47), 3rd fl. Large, clean, renovated, tile-floored rooms, some overlooking a courtyard. English spoken. Singles L60,000; doubles L90,000. Prices may fluctuate. **Hotel Kennedy** (tel. 02 29 40 09 34), 6th fl. Pristine rooms with light blue dreamscape decor. Renovations planned for 1999. Some English spoken. Check-out 10am. Singles L50,000-70,000; doubles L70,000-130,000; triples L40,000 per person; quads L40,000 per person. Reserve ahead.

Hotel San Marco, Via Piccinni 25 (tel. 02 204 95 36; fax 02 29 51 32 43). From MM1 or 2: Loreto, head left on P. Luigi di Savoia. Take a right at the post office on Via Pergolesi, which crosses P. Caiazzo, C. Buenos Aires, and finally becomes Via Piccinni (20min.). Comfy retro rooms with TV and telephone compensate for street noise. Singles L68,000-90,000; doubles L88,000-120,000; triples L150,000.

Hotel Aurora, C. Buenos Aires 18 (tel. 204 79 60; fax 204 92 85). MM1: Lima. Spotless rooms with phone and TV. English-speaking owner. Singles L70,000, with bath L80,000-85,000; doubles with bath L120,000-125,000. Reception 24hr.

Camping di Monza (tel. 039 38 77 71), in the park of the Villa Reale in Monza. Take a train or bus from Stazione Centrale to Monza, then a city bus. Restaurant/bar nearby. L5000 (L8000 in Sept.) per person and per tent. Hot showers L500. Open Apr.-Sept. Call ahead.

FOOD

Like its fine *couture,* Milanese cuisine is sophisticated and overpriced. The largest **markets** are around Via Fauché and Viale Papiniano on Saturdays and Tuesdays, and along P. Mirabello on Mondays and Thursdays. The **Fiera di Sinigallia,** a 400-year-old market extravaganza, occurs on Saturdays on the banks of the Darsena, a canal in the Navigli district (Viale d'Annunzio). Splurge on a local pastry at **Sant'Ambroeus,** a Milanese culinary shrine, under the arcades at C. Matteotti 7 (open 8am-8pm). Pick up groceries at **Pam,** off C. Buenos Aires at Via Piccinni 2 (open daily 8:30am-9pm). In the center, there's a **STANDA** supermarket near the *duomo,* in the basement of the department store at Via Torino 45 (open M 1-7:30pm, Tu-Sa 9am-7:30pm). For a balanced meal, try one of the self-service restaurants that cater to city professionals.

Ciao, on the 2nd floor of the Duomo Center in P. del Duomo. Convenient, with *secondi* for L8000. Open daily 11:30am-3pm and 6:30-11pm.

Brek, Via Lepetit 20 (with another location in P. Cavour). A more elegant self-service restaurant. Fresh ingredients are cooked before your eyes into tasty dishes. *Secondi* around L7500. Open M-Sa 11:30am-3pm and 6:30-10:30pm.

Pizzeria Grand'Italia, Via Palermo 5. Fabulous pizza (L7000-10,000) and big salads (L12,000). Open W-M 12:15-2:45pm and 7pm-1:15am.

Ristorante "La Colubrina," Via Felice Casati 5. MM1: Porta Venezia. A neighborhood restaurant with pizza for L6000-10,000, daily specials for L9000-20,000, and a liter of wine for L8000. Cover L2000. Open Sept.-July Tu-Su noon-2:30pm and 7-11:30pm. Closed lunch Tu and Su.

Le Briciole, Via Camperio 17, off Largo Cairoli, near the *duomo.* Pizza L9000-16,000. Spectacular *antipasto* buffet L13,000. Cover L3000. Open Tu-Su 12:15-2:30pm and 7:15-11:30pm. Closed Sa lunch.

Ristorante Asmara, Via Lazzaro Palazzi 5. Serves Eritrean food, eaten with thin spongy falt-bread (injera). Delicious vegetarian meals L14,000-16,000. A/C. Open Th-Tu noon-3pm and 6pm-midnight.

Viel, Via Marconi 3E, next to the tourist office. Fresh fruit *gelati* (L3000-6000) and *frullati* (whipped fruit drinks; L3000-8000).

SIGHTS AND ENTERTAINMENT

The **Piazza del Duomo** marks the geographical center of Milan, and makes a good starting point for a walking tour of the city. The **duomo,** a looming Gothic creation, presides over the *piazza.* More than 3400 statues, 135 spires, and 96 gargoyles grace this third-largest church in the world. (Open daily June-Sept. 7am-5pm; Oct.-May 9am-4pm. Free. Tower L6000, with elevator L8000. Proper dress required.) Beside the *duomo* is the entrance to the **Galleria Vittorio Emanuele II,** a four-story arcade of *caffè* and shops. Meander through this beautiful gallery to the **Teatro alla Scala (La Scala),** the world's premier opera house where Maria Callas, among other opera titans, became a legend. Enter the lavish hall through the **Museo Teatrale alla Scala,** which includes such opera memorabilia as Verdi's famous top hat (open daily 9am-noon and 2-5:30pm; L6000).

From La Scala, Via Verdi leads to Via Brera, another charming street lined with small, brightly colored palaces and art galeries. The 17th-century **Pinacoteca di Brera,** which features works by Caravaggio, Bellini, and Raphael (open Tu-Sa 9am-9:45pm, Su 9am-12:45pm and 2-7:45 pm; L8000). The **Museo Poldi-Pezzoli,** Via Manzoni 12, contains an outstanding private art collection; the museum's signature piece is Antonio Pollaiolo's *Portrait of a Young Woman.* (Open Tu-F 9:30am-12:30pm and 2:30-6pm, Sa 9:30am-12:30pm and 2:30-7:30pm, Su 9:30am-12:30pm; Oct.-Mar. also open Su 2:30-6pm. L10,000.) For a taste of Italian sculpture, visit the enormous **Castello Sforzesco** (MM1: Cairoli), one of Milan's best known monuments, which houses Michelangelo's unfinished *Pietà Rondanini* and other excellent works (open Tu-Su 9:30am-5:30pm; free). Finally, marvel at Leonardo Da Vinci's immensely famous *Last Supper* on the refectory wall of the **Church of Santa Maria delle Grazie.** (MM1: Cairoli. Open Tu-Su 8am-2pm; June-Aug. also Tu-Sa 7-10pm and Su 5-8pm.

L12,000.) For more da Vinci genius, explore the **Museo Nazionale della Scienza e della Tecnica "Leonardo da Vinci,"** Via San Vittore 21, off Via Carducci (MM1: San Ambrogio, or bus 50 or 54). Wooden models of Leonardo's most ingenious and visionary inventions fill a huge room (open Tu-F 9:30am-4:50pm, Sa-Su 9:30am-6:20pm; L10,000). Following Via Spadari off Via Tornio and making a left onto Via Cantú will deposit you at the tiny but lovely **Pinacoteca Ambrosiana,** P. Pio XI 2, with art from the 15th through 17th centuries, including works by Botticelli, Leonardo, Raphael, and Caravaggio (open Tu-Su 10am-5:30pm; L12,000).

While seats at the famed **La Scala** are expensive, 200 standing room tickets go on sale 45 minutes before the show starts. (L10,000. Opera season is Dec.7-June; fewer shows July-Sept. Box office tel. 86 07 87; open daily 12-6pm.) If you've come to Milan to (window) **shop,** as many do, the city's most elegant boutiques are between the *duomo* and P.S. Babila, especially on the glamorous **Via Monte Napoleone** and off P.S. Babila on Via Spiga and Via Sant'Andrea.

At night, excellent people-watching can be had in the **Navigli district** (the Venice of Lombardy), through the Neoclassical Arco di Porta Ticinese, a lively area with many *caffè, gelaterie,* and bars. Another fun place to wander at night is the safe and chic area along **Via Brera.** Younger *Milanese* migrate to the areas around **Porta Ticinese** and **Piazza Vetra** (north of Navigli) to sip beer at one of the many *birrerie* (pubs). Most clubs charge a cover of around L20,000. For rock music, hit the trendy **Hollywood,** Corso Como 15 (open Tu-Su 11pm-4am), or **Plastic,** Viale Umbria 120, Milan's premier disco-pub (open Tu-Su 10:30pm-4am). The city's best jazz spot is **Le Scimmie,** Cia Ascanio Sforza 49 (open W-M 8pm-2am). For disco, head to **City Square,** Via Castelbarco 11, with some of the biggest dance floors in Milan and occasional live music (open nightly until 4am). **Grand Cafe Fashion,** Corso di Porta Ticinese, on the corner of Via Vatere, has the requisite beautiful people and good music (mandatory first drink L15,000; open Tu-Sa 6:30pm-3am). For gay and lesbian nightlife, women head to **Cicip e Ciciap,** Via Gorani 9 (open Tu-Su 7pm-2am), and men head to **Nuovo Idea,** Via de Castilla 30 (MM2: Gioia; women welcome Sa), and a mixed crowd fills **Uitibar,** Via Monvisa 14 (open Tu-Su 8:30pm-2am).

■ Mantua (Mantova)

Although Mantua's first claim to fame was as the hometown of the great poet Virgil, the city enjoyed its heyday as the court of the extravagant, 400-year Gonzaga dynasty. Beginning in 1328, the Gonzagas loaded Mantua with palaces, churches, and towers and lured some of the most important Renaissance artists to their court. While industry and commercial agriculture now rule the city, the historic center preserves much of the rustic flavor and artistic flair of this earlier age.

The cobblestone **Piazza Sordello** forms the center of a vast complex built by the Gonzagas. Towering over the *piazza*, **Palazzo Ducale** is one of the largest and most sumptuously decorated palaces in Europe, with no less than 500 rooms and 15 courtyards. Marvel at Antonio Pisanelli's frescoes in the palace's **Hall of Dukes,** discovered in 1969 under thick layers of plaster. (Open Tu-Sa 9am-2pm and 2:30-6pm, Su 9am-1pm and 4-10pm. L12,000 for the entire palace.) A trek through P. Veneto and down Largo Parri leads to the opulent **Palazzo del Tè,** widely regarded as the finest building of the Mannerist period. Once the Gonzaga family's suburban villa, the palace now exhibits works by modern Italian artists and a collection of Egyptian art (open Tu-Su 9am-6pm; L12,000, students L5000). Near P. delle Erbe, south of P. Sordello, the **Church of Sant'Andrea** is acclaimed as the crowning achievement of Florentine architect Leon Battista Alberti.

Trains pass through the station at P. Don Leoni, southwest of town, bound for Milan (2hr., L15,000) and Verona (40min., L3900). The **bus station** at P. Mondadori serves Brescia (1½hr., L9500). The **tourist office,** P. Mantegna 6 (tel. (0376) 32 82 53; fax 36 32 92), adjacent to the church of Sant'Andrea, offers maps and brochures (open M-Sa 8:30am-12:30pm and 3-6pm). Accommodations in Mantua will break your budget; those willing to stay in smaller nearby towns will be able to find less

ITALY

expensive lodgings. Ask at the tourist office about **agriturismo** lodgings (around L20,000) if rooms are scarce. Or take bus 2M, which runs from P. Cavallotti into Virgiliana (6:45am-7:45pm, 10min.) to **Albergo Marago,** Via Villanova De Bellis 2 (tel. (0376) 37 03 13), on the left just past P. San Isidro (singles L30,000; doubles L45,000, with bath L65,000). Feast on pizza, salami, and seafood all in one sitting at **Piedigrotta 2,** Via Verdi 5, off P. Mantegna (*primi* from L6000 and *secondi* from L11,000). **Antica Osteria ai Ranari,** Via Trieste 11, near Porto Catena, specializes in regional dishes. (*Primi* L8000, *secondi* L9000-14,000. Closed for 3 weeks in late July and early Aug. Call for reservations.)

■ Bergamo

Glimmering in the distance, an entire medieval city is nestled in the hills over Bergamo, complete with palaces, churches, and a huge stone fortification. **Via Pignolo,** in the *città bassa* (lower city), winds past a succession of handsome 16th- to 18th-century palaces. Turning right on Via San Tommaso brings you to the astounding **Galleria dell'Accademia Carrara,** with works by virtually every Italian notable, as well as Breughel, van Dyck, and El Greco (open W-M 9:30am-12:30pm and 2:30-5:30pm; L5000, Su free). From the Galleria, the terraced **Via Noca** ascends to the *città alta* through Porta Sant'Agostino. Perched above the modern city and also accessible by **funicular** from **Viale Vittorio Emanuele II** (every 7min., L1500), the *città alta* is a wonderfully preserved medieval town. Via Gambito ends in **Piazza Vecchia,** a majestic mix of medieval and Renaissance buildings. Climb the **Torre Civica** (L2000) for a marvelous view of Bergamo and the surrounding hills. Under the arcade is **Piazza del Duomo,** with the multicolored marble facade of the 1476 **Colleoni Chapel,** designed for the Venetian mercenary Bartolomeo Colleoni (open daily Apr.-Oct. 9am-noon and 2-6:30pm; Nov.-Mar. 9am-noon and 2:30-4:30pm).

The train station, bus station, and numerous budget hotels are in the *città bassa.* **Trains** run from P. Marconi to Brescia (1hr., L5200) and Milan (1hr., L6000). **Buses** leave from across the train station for Milan (L7300) and local cities. Take bus 1 or 1a to the funicular, then follow Via Gambito to the P. Vecchia to find the **tourist office,** Vicolo Aquila Nera 2 (tel. (035) 23 27 30), in the *città alta* (open daily 9am-12:30pm and 2:30-5:30pm). Take bus 14 from Largo Porto Nuova to "Leonardo da Vinci" to reach **Ostello Città di Bergamo (HI),** Via G. Ferraris 1 (tel. (035) 34 30 38; fax 36 17 24), with spotless rooms. (L25,000 per person, breakfast included. Singles L35,000; doubles L60,000. Members only.) **Albergo S. Giorgio,** Via S. Giorgio 10 (tel. (035) 21 20 43; fax 31 00 72), nearer the train station, has small, neat rooms. Go left on Via Pietro Paleocopa, which becomes Via S. Giorgio after a few blocks (15min.), or take bus 7 (singles L35,000-55,000; doubles L65,000-90,000). In the *città bassa,* **Trattoria Casa Mia,** Via S. Bernardino 20, off Via Zambonate, offers a full "home-style" meal for L15,000 (open Sept.-July M-Sa 8am-3pm and 5:30-10:30pm). In the *città alta,* the former prison **Circolino Cooperativa Città Alta,** Via S. Agata 19, is now a lush garden cafe with bocce and a view (open Th-Tu 11am-2:30pm and 7:30pm-2:20am).

ITALIAN RIVIERA (LIGURIA)

Liguria is the Italian Riviera, with lemon trees, almond blossoms, and turquoise water. Genoa divides the area neatly in half—**Riviera di Ponente** (setting sun) and the more splendid **Riviera di Levante** (rising sun) lie to the west and east respectively. This crescent-shaped coastal stretch differs greatly from its hyped French counterpart; here you'll find elegance, not arrogance. Especially lovely are the **Portofino peninsula** (about 30min. by train from Genoa) and the **Cinque Terre** area (immediately west of La Spezia). In July and August, only reservations will get you a place for the night.

■ Genoa (Genova)

Genoa's leading families began prospering in the 13th century, when the port town's international trade flourished. The sudden riches went to furnish the city with parks, palaces, and countless works of art. Genoa's financial glory was matched by its citizens' accomplishments: native sons include Chistopher Columbus, Giuseppe Mazzini, and Nicolò Paganini. After falling into decline in the 18th century, modern Genoa has turned its attentions to restoring the city to its former grandeur.

SIGHTS AND ENTERTAINMENT Via Garibaldi, the most impressive street in Genoa, is lined with elegant *palazzi*. Approaching from the west from Via Cairoli, you'll first see the **Palazzo Bianco** (#11), which houses Ligurian, Dutch, and Flemish art. Across the street, the **Palazzo Rosso** (#18) has magnificent furnishings and frescoes. (Both open Tu and Th-F 9am-1pm, W and Sa-Su 9am-7pm. L6000 for one, L10,000 for both, free on Su.) Farther along Via Garibaldi, the **Palazzo Tursi** (#9) now serves as the city hall and houses Paganini's violin (ask one of the guards to see it). **Palazzo Podestà** and **Palazzo Parodi** boast beautiful courtyards and doorways. Don't miss the incredibly rococo **Palazzo Reale,** on Via Balbi (open Su-Tu 9am-1:45pm, W-F 9am-7pm, L8000). From P. Marose, take the public elevator *(ascensore)* to **Piazza Castelletto** for a panoramic view (open 6:40am-midnight, L600 or a validated bus ticket).

From P. Corvetto, Via Roma leads to the **Palazzo Ducale,** P. Matteotti, where the city's rulers once lived; on the opposite corner stands the ornate **Church of the Gesù,** which holds two Rubens. The historical center of town *(centro storico),* a twisting maze of alleys south and west of Via Garibaldi, is generally safe for tourists only during the day. There, the **Duomo San Lorenzo** features a Gothic facade and a carved central portal (open M-Sa 8:30am-noon and 3:30-6pm, Su noon-6:30pm; free). On the eastern side of town, Via San Luca leads past the **Church of San Siro,** Genoa's first cathedral (open M-F 4-6pm; free). With twin towers and arched entryway, the medieval **Porta Soprana** is the supposed boyhood home of Christopher Columbus (his father was the gatekeeper). Through the archway to the left rest the ruins of the 12th-century **Cloister of San'Andrea.**

PRACTICAL INFO, ACCOMMODATIONS, AND FOOD Genoa is easily accessible by rail from Rome (6hr., L40,000) and Turin (2hr., L14,000). There are two train stations: **Stazione Principe,** P. Acquaverde, and **Stazione Brignole,** P. Verdi. Call 147 88 80 88 for train info. Buses 33 and 37 connect the stations. Bus 40 from Brignole and bus 41 from Principe run to the center of town (P. de Ferrari). **Via Balbi** extends from Stazione Principe to the central **Piazza de Ferrari,** while **Via XX Settembre** runs east towards Stazione Brignole. Procure a decent map (L6000) in the train station or at any newsstand to make sense of the tangled streets. The **tourist office** is at Porto Antico, P. Santa Maria (tel. 01 02 48 71; fax 01 02 46 76 58; open daily 9am-6:30pm); there is also a **branch** at the Principe train station (open M-F 8am-8pm, Sa 9am-noon).

For accommodations, head for the hostel or stick to the safer areas around Stazione Brignole. **Ostello per la Gioventù (HI),** Via Costanzi 120 (tel./fax 01 02 42 24 57), offers panoramic views and incredible facilities. From Stazione Principe, walk to P. della Nunziata, catch bus 40 (which goes directly from Brignole), and ride to the end. (L22,000. Members only. Reception 7-11:30am and 3:30pm-midnight. Wheelchair accessible.) A beautiful and secure *palazzo* on Via Gropallo houses both **Pensione Mirella,** 4/4 (tel. 01 08 39 37 22; singles L37,000; doubles L65,000), and **Albergo Carola,** 4/12 (tel. 01 08 39 13 40; singles L45,000; doubles L65,000-75,000). Genoa is famous for its *pesto* and *focaccia.* **La Locanda,** Via Borgo Incrociati 45r, behind Satzione Brignole, serves a delicious Genovese *menu* for L15,000 (open daily 8am-4pm and 7pm-12:30am).

■ Riviera di Ponente and Riviera di Levante

Finale Ligure Eschewing the glamor and arrogance of other Riviera towns, Finale Ligure welcomes weary backpackers with soft sands and luxurious flora. The city is divided into the three sections. **Finalborgo** (the old village), to the west, is enclosed within solid ancient walls. **Finalpia** is to the east, while **Finalmarina,** in the center, includes the train station and most other sights. Follow your nose to the Genovese Baroque **Basilica di San Giovanni Battista,** in the beautiful, gardenia-filled *piazza* of the same name. The best free **beach** is on Via Aurelia.

From P. Vittorio Veneto, **trains** (tel. 147 88 80 88) offer frequent service to Genoa (1hr.). **SAR buses** (tel. 019 69 22 75), near the train station, travel to neighboring beachside towns. The **IAT tourist office,** Via San Pietro 14 (tel. 019 68 10 19; fax 019 68 18 04), offers a great map and can arrange rooms in private homes (open M-Sa 9am-12:30pm and 3:30-7pm; in summer also Su 9am-noon). **Castello Wuillerman (HI)** (tel. 019 69 05 15), on Via Generale Caviglia, is worth the tough uphill hike from the station. From the station, take a left onto Via Mazzini, which turns into Via Torino, turn left onto Via degli Ulivi, and on the left is a seemingly endless set of stairs: the Gradinata delle Rose. Follow the sign at the top. (L19,000 for members. Reception 7-10am and 5-10pm. Curfew 11:30pm. No phone reservations. Open Mar. 15-Oct. 15.) **Albergo San Marco,** Via della Concezione 22 (tel. 019 69 25 33), offers singles for L45,000. Camp at **Del Mulino** (tel. 019 60 16 69), on Via Piemonte. From the station take the bus for Calviso from "P. Vittorio Veneto" and get off at the Boncardo Hotel, Corso Europa 4. Turn left at P. Guglielmo Oberdan, right onto Via Porra, and left onto Via Castelli. Take the stairs up to the left and follow signs (L10,000 per person, L8000-14,000 per tent; open Apr.-Sept.). *Trattorie* and *pizzerie* line the streets closest to the beach, but you'll pay less farther inland along Via Rossi and Via Roma.

Camogli A small, peaceful resort town, **Camogli** takes great pride in its ancient maritime traditions. The name is a contraction of "Casa Mogli," meaning "Wives' House," from the women who ran the town while their husbands manned its once-huge fishing fleet. **Trains** arrive from Genoa (20min., L2200) and Santa Margherita (10min., L1700); **Tigullio buses** (tel. 167 01 48 08) depart from P. Schiaffino to nearby towns. The **tourist office,** Via XX Settembre 33 (tel. 01 85 77 10 66), is to the right as you leave the station. (Open June-Sept. daily 8:30am-12:30pm and 3-7pm; Oct.-May M-Sa 9am-noon and 4-7pm, Su 9am-1pm.) Your best bet for accommodations is unquestionably **Albergo La Camogliese,** Via Garibaldi 55. (Tel. 01 85 77 14 02. Singles with bath L50,000-70,000; doubles L80,000-100,000; 10% discount for cash-paying *Let's Go* readers.) The pleasant **Albergo Augusta,** Via Schiaffino 100 (tel./fax 01 85 77 05 92), and **Albergo Selene,** Via Cuneo 16 (tel. 01 85 77 01 49), offer singles (L50,000-75,000) and doubles (L75,000-119,000). For an affordable meal, the restaurants on Via Repubblica should suffice, or try the **Picasso Supermercato,** Via XX Settembre 35 (open M-Sa 8am-12:30pm and 4-7pm; closed W 4-7pm).

Santa Margherita Ligure Once accessible only to wealthy vacationers, **Santa Margherita Ligure** now welcomes budget travelers and provides an ideal, serene base for exploring the rest of the Italian Riviera. There are two main squares that cover the waterfront: **Piazza Martiri della Libertà** and the smaller **Piazza Vittorio Veneto.** Both are lovely parks lined with palm trees. **Trains** arrive at P. Federico Raoul Nobili, at the summit of Via Roma, from Genoa (L3100). **Buses** depart from P. Vittorio Veneto for Camogli (L2000) and Portofino (L1700). The **tourist office,** Via XXV Aprile 2b (tel. 01 85 28 74 85), gives a town map and has an accommodations service. Turn right from the train station onto Via Roma, then right on Via XXV Aprile (open M-Sa 9am-12:30pm and 3:30-6:30pm, Su 9:30am-12:30pm).

When looking for a room, sacrifice a waterfront view for peace, quiet, and an extra L30,000-40,000 in your pocket. The proprietor of **Hotel Terminus**, P. Nobili 4 (tel. 01 85 28 61 21; fax 01 85 28 25 46), is dedicated to the comfort of his guests (singles L70,000; doubles L140,000). **Hotel Conte Verde,** Via Zara 1 (tel. 01 85 28 71 39), on your right as you come down Via Roma, has clean, functional rooms (singles L45,000-70,000; doubles L80,000-120,000). Supermarkets, bakeries, fruit vendors, and butcher shops line Corso Matteotti. **Trattoria Baicin,** Via Algeria 9, offers hearty delicious meals, while **Cutty Sark Pub,** Via Roma 35, has filling *panini* and beer.

Portofino and San Fruttuoso

Scenic yacht- and boutique-filled **Portofino** merits a daytrip from Santa Margherita. Trek up to the **Chiesa di San Giorgio** or the **castle** for enchanting vistas of the bay, or follow the "Al faro" signs to reach the **lighthouse.** There's no train to Portofino, but Tigullio **buses** run along the coastline to and from Santa Margherita (L1700; take the bus to Portofino Mare, not Portofino Vetta). The gorgeous but expensive **San Fruttuoso** is set in a natural amphitheater of pines, olive trees, and green oaks. Boats make the trip every hour from Camogli (round-trip L13,000), or you can walk from Portofino (1½hr.). Be sure to visit the 10th-century **Abbazia di San Fruttuoso di Capo di Monte,** for which the town is named.

Cinque Terre and La Spezia

A group of five connected villages clinging to the cliffs above the sea, **Cinque Terre** is justly famed for impressive vistas, clear waters, and the sweet *sciacchetrà* wine. The towns, in order of increasing distance from Genoa, are **Monterosso, Vernazza, Corniglia, Manarola,** and **Riomaggiore,** of which Monterosso is the biggest, easiest to reach, and least charming. Enjoy the best views from the narrow goat paths that link the towns; the best and most challenging **hike** lies between Monterosso and Vernazza (1½hr.), while the trail between Vernazza and Corniglia passes through some of the area's most gorgeous scenery (2hr.). Cinque Terre's two public **beaches** reside on the south side of Monterosso and on the long strip of pebbles between Corniglia and Manarola. You can reserve parts of Monterosso's beach (L5000), or head to Guvano Beach to chill with nudist hippies. To get to Guvano for free, hike down off the road between Corniglia and Vernazza. Tiny trails off the road to Vernazza lead to hidden coves popular among the locals.

The **tourist office** (tel. 01 87 81 75 06), in Monterosso below the train station, provides an accommodations service and info on boats and hikes (open Apr.-Oct. M-Sa 10am-noon and 4-6pm, Su 10am-noon). For accommodations, check out the *affitta camere* (private rooms) throughout the Cinque Terre. In Manarola, the new **Albergo Della Gioventu-Ostello "Cinque Terre,"** V.B. Riccobaldi 21 (tel. 01 87 92 02 15; fax 01 87 92 02 18), is to the right and up the hill from the train station. (L25,000. Reception June-Sept. 15 7am-10am and 5pm-1am; Sept. 16-May 7am-10am and 4pm-midnight. Closed Nov. 5-Dec. 5.) The **Albergo Barbara,** P. Marconi 21 (tel. 01 87 81 22 01), at the port in Vernazza, offers bright, airy rooms (singles L60,000; doubles L80,000-90,000; triples L115,000; quads L130,000). **Hotel Souvenie,** Via Gioberti 24 (tel. 01 87 81 75 95), in Monterosso, is a quiet family-run hotel (L40,000). Cinque Terre's seafood is swimmingly fresh, and *sciacchetrà,* the sweet local white wine, complements it deliciously. To get to **Ristorante Cecio** (tel. 01 87 81 20 43), in Corniglia on the small road that leads to Vernazza, follow the signs at the top of the stairs that lead to town from the train station (*primi* from L8000; cover L3000). Spend the night there, too (doubles L90,000).

La Spezia, more commercial and less pleasant than the smaller towns of the surrounding coast, serves as a departure point to Corsica. **Corsica Ferries** (tel. 01 87 77 80 97), at the Molo Italia dock, serve Bastia, Corsica (5hr., L36,000-48,000). **Tirrenia** sends ferries to Olbia, Sardinia (5½hr., L110,000). The **tourist office** (tel. 01 87 77 09 00) sits beside the port at Via Mazzini 45; a branch office is in the train station (tel. 01 87 71 89 97). If you must stay here, **Albergo Terminus,** Via Paleocapa 21 (tel. 01 87 70 34 36; fax 01 87 71 49 35), has singles and doubles for L32,000 to 65,000.

EMILIA-ROMAGNA

Come to Emilia-Romagna to eat. Italy's wealthiest wheat- and dairy-producing region covers the fertile plains of the Po river valley and fosters the finest in culinary traditions. Here, enjoy Parmesan cheese and *prosciutto*, Bolognese fresh pasta and *mortadella*, and the region's sparkling red wines, such as *lambrusco*.

■ Bologna

With one forkful of Bologna's *tortellini*, it becomes clear that this city appreciates the better things in life. The city founded the first university in Europe 900 years ago, and the **Università di Bologna** has since graduated the likes of Dante, Petrarch, Copernicus, and Tasso. Today, social tolerance and student energy fan both local nightlife and strong political activism.

SIGHTS AND ENTERTAINMENT Bologna's most remarkable sights are its endless series of porticoed buildings, a 14th-century solution to the housing crisis of a growing city. The tranquil expanse of **Piazza Maggiore** is the heart of the city. The Bolognese originally plotted to make the **Basilica di San Petronio** larger than St. Peter's in Rome, but jealous Church officials diverted the funds to a different project (open daily 7:15am-1pm and 2:30-6:30pm). Nearby, the **Piazza del Nettuno** features the Romanesque **Palazzo del Podestà** and the famous 16th-century *Neptune and Attendants* statue and fountain. Behind the fountain of Neptune are displayed the photos of those who lost their lives fighting for Italian freedom from Germany; also remembered are those who lost their lives in the right-extremist attacks of 1974, 1980, and 1984. Via Rizzoli leads from P. Nettuno to **Piazza Porta Ravegnana**, where seven streets converge in Bologna's medieval quarter. The two towers here are the emblem of the city; climb the **Torre degli Asinelli** for an amazing view of the city (open daily in summer 9am-6pm; off-season 9am-5pm; L3000). From the two towers, the Strada Maggiore leads east past the **Basilica of San Bartolomeo.** Stop here and see the exquisite *Madonna* by Guido Reni before proceeding to the **Church of Santa Maria dei Servi** (open daily 7-11:45am and 3:30-7:45pm). Down Via Santo Stefano, the triangular **Piazza Santo Stefano** opens onto a complex of beautiful Romanesque churches. Under the pulpit of the **Chiesa del San Sepolcro**, in the center of the group, is buried San Petronio, patron saint of Bologna. The **Museo Civico Archeologico**, Via Archiginnasio 2, has a fascinating collection of antiquities (open Tu-F 9am-2pm, Sa-Su 9am-1pm and 3:30-7pm; L8000, students L4000).

Bologna's huge student population makes for lively nighttime diversion during the academic year. To reach **Made in Bo**, a complex of open-air discos raving from mid-March through July in Parco Nord, take bus 25 (free; starts 10pm). Look for posters about **Bepop**, a free festival in July and August with events ranging from poetry reading to raves (bus 38 or 91A to "Fiera"). **Kinky Discoteca,** Via Zamboni 1, near the Two Towers, offers alternative music and gay and lesbian night on Saturday (cover L25,000-40,000). To get drunk with the locals head to **Irish Times Pub,** Via Paradiso 1d (open daily 7:30pm until no one is left standing). On Sunday afternoons September through June, the Bolognese **soccer team** plays in the **Stadio Comunale,** Via Adrea Costa 174 (tel. 051 22 50 90 or 051 39 88 54). Take bus 21 from the station or 14 from Porta Isaia.

PRACTICAL INFO, ACCOMMODATIONS, AND FOOD Treat Bologna as you would a big city—be plenty cautious at night and watch your wallet, especially in the university area, where shady characters abound. **Trains** run to Florence (1½hr., L8200), Milan (3hr., L18,000), Rome (4hr., L35,000), Venice (2hr., L14,000), and other cities. Buses 25 and 30 shuttle between the train station and **Piazza Maggiore** (L1500). The **tourist office,** P. Maggiore 6 (tel. 051 23 96 60; fax 051 23 14 54; http://www.comune.bologna.it), in Palazzo Comunale, is modern, genial, and efficient (open M-Sa 9am-7pm, Su until 2pm). Prices are high and rooms scarce in Bologna.

A Pasta Primer

For Italians, the desecration of pasta is a mortal sin. Pasta must be chosen correctly and cooked *al dente* (firm, literally "to the tooth"). To avoid embarrassment, get to know the basics. The *spaghetti* family includes all variations that require twirling, from hollow cousins *bucatini* and *maccheroni* to the more delicate *capellini*. Flat *spaghetti* include *fettuccini, taglierini* and *tagliatelle*. Short pasta tubes can be *penne* (cut diagonally and occasionally *rigate* or ribbed), *sedani* (curved), *rigatoni* (wider), or *cannelloni* (usually stuffed). *Fusilli* (corkscrews), *farfalle* (butterflies or bow-ties), and *ruote* (wheels) are fun as well as functional. Don't be alarmed if you see pastry displays labeled "pasta"; the Italian word refers to anything made of dough and vaguely edible.

The clean, new **Ostello di San Sisto (HI),** Via Viadagola 5 (tel./fax 051 50 18 10), is in the Località di San Sisto, 6km northeast of the center of town, off Via San Donato; ask at the tourist office for a map with directions. (L20,000, nonmembers L25,000. Reception 7am-midnight. Lockout 10am-3:30pm.) **Pensione Marconi,** Via Marconi 22 (tel. 051 26 28 32), has clean rooms and a desk monitored all night (singles L50,000-62,000; doubles L78,000-95,000). **Albergo Panorama,** Via Livraghi 1 (tel. 051 22 18 02), has views of the hills behind Bologna (singles L70,000; doubles L95,000-120,000). **Albergo Apollo,** Via Drapperie 5 (tel./fax 051 22 39 55), couldn't be closer to the center of town (singles L55,000; doubles L92,000-120,000; closed in Aug.). **Protezione della Giovane,** Via S. Stefano 45 (tel. 051 22 55 73), is a women-only dorm often filled with students (L20,000 per person; L600,000 per month).

Don't miss Bologna's namesake dish, *spaghetti alla bolognese*—pasta with a hefty meat and tomato sauce. The areas around Via Augusto Righi and Via Piella, as well as the neighborhood of Via Saragozza, are good for *trattorie*. **Nuovo Pizzeria Gianna,** Via San Stephano 76a, serves excellent pizza (from L5000; open M-Sa for lunch and dinner). **Trattoria De Marro,** Via Broccaindosso 71/D, has a *menù* for L20,000 (cover L2500; open M-Sa noon-2:30pm and 8-10:15pm). At **Ristorante Clorofilla,** Strada Maggiore 64, the food is innovative and almost exclusively vegetarian (open Sept.-July M-Sa 12:15-3pm and 7:30pm-midnight; in winter tea served 4-7pm). **Mensa Universitaria Irnerio,** Via Zamboni 47, is amazingly cheap for students (L6000; open M-F noon-2:30pm and 7-9pm, Sa-Su 12:30-2pm).

■ Parma

Parma enjoys a rich history and robust cultural activity, but the city is best known for its incomparable delicacies: luscious *prosciutto* ham, sharp *parmigiano* cheese, and the sparkling white wine *Malvasia*. Try to arrive in Parma famished. In **Piazza Duomo,** the cathedral contains such masterpieces as *Descent from the Cross,* sculpted by Benedetto Antelami in 1178, and the spectacular dome with *Ascent of the Virgin* frescoed by Correggio (open daily 7:30am-12:30pm and 3-7pm). Next door, the **baptistery** features carved wooden portals by Antelami and stunning 13th-century frescoes (open daily 9am-12:30pm and 3-6pm; L3000, students L1000). Behind the *duomo*, in P. San Giovanni, the **Church of San Giovanni Evangelista** features frescoes by Correggio and Parmigianino (open daily 6:30am-noon and 3:30-8pm; free). A few blocks from the *duomo*, the **Palazzo della Pilotta** houses the **Galleria Nazionale,** with works by da Vinci, Parmigianino and Correggio (open daily 9am-1:45pm; L8000). Make sure to see Parma's premier opera house, the **Teatro Regio,** Via Garibaldi 16 (tel. 05 21 21 89 10), next to P. della Pace; a visit is free if you call ahead. Or just sit and people-watch at the nearby **Piazza Garibaldi.**

Trains connect Parma to Bologna (1hr., L7400), Florence (3hr., L25,500), and Milan (1½hr., L12,100). The train station is located on P. Carlo Alberto della Chiesa. The **tourist office,** Via Melloni 1b (tel. 05 21 21 88 89; fax. 05 21 23 47 35), off Strada Pisacane, has info on nearby towns (open M-Sa 9am-7pm, Su 9am-1pm). The **Ostello Cittadella (HI)** (tel. 05 21 96 14 34), Via Passo Buole, occupies a 15th-century fortress. To get there, bus 9 in front of the station or snag bus 6 or 9 from P. Garibaldi,

Central Florence

SEE ALSO COLOR INSERT

ACCOMMODATIONS
B Albergo Montreal
E Hotel il Perseo
C Hotel Visconti
G Locanda Orchidea
A Locanda La Romagnola and
   Soggiorno Gigliola
D Soggiorno Abaco
H Soggiorno Bavaria
F Soggiorno Panerai

ITALY

and get off when the bus turns left on Via Martiri della Libertà. (L16,000. Members only, but may accept student ID. 3-night max. stay. Lockout 9:30am-5pm. Strict curfew 11pm.) For women under 25 only, **Casa Della Giovane,** Via del Conservatorio 11 (tel. 05 21 28 32 29), offers rooms for L25,000. **Locanda Lazzaro,** Borgo XX Marzo 14 (tel. 05 21 20 89 44), off Via della Repubblica, has a restaurant downstairs and comfortable rooms upstairs (singles L49,000; doubles L82,000; reserve ahead).

The cuisine of Parma is wonderfully affordable, and local specialties fill the windows of many *salumerie* along Via Garibaldi. For lunch, try **Le Sorelle Picchi,** Strada Farini 27, a traditional *salumeria* with a hidden *trattoria* in back. (*Salumeria* open 8:30am-1pm and 4-7pm. *Trattoria* open M-Sa noon-3pm.) For dinner, head to **Trattoria Corrieri,** Via Conservatorio 1 (cover L3000; open M-Sa noon-2:30pm and 7:30-10:30pm). **K2,** at the corner of Borgo Cairoli and Borgo Coreggio, has Parma's creamiest gelato (open Th-Tu 11am-midnight).

TOSCANA (TUSCANY)

Tuscany is the stuff Italian dreams (and more than one romantic Brits-in-Italy movie) are made of. Gazing out over rolling hills, fields of sunflowers, and inviting cobblestone streets, it's hard not to wax poetic. Tuscany's Renaissance culture became Italy's heritage, and its regional dialect, the language of Dante, Petrarch, and Machiavelli, became today's textbook Italian. After a tumultuous medieval period, Tuscany came under the astute (though despotic) rule of the Medici family, who presided over the nascent Humanist philosophy and the flowering of the Renaissance. The newly rich Tuscans commissioned huge *palazzi* and incredible works of art and left a trail of resplendent artistic excess. Protected by centuries of serenity, the cities and towns of Tuscany remain virtually unchanged as they watch the area once again grow in importance—this time because of its thriving tourism industry.

▓ Florence (Firenze)

In Florence, the sun glows yellow on the orange sea of roofs; even in the rainy season, alleyways sparkle. Although Dante Alighieri bemoaned his hometown's greed and viciousness in the 13th century, nearly every visitor to walk the city's cobblestone streets since has fallen under its singular spell. Stimulated by an innovative banking system, the city evolved from a busy 13th-century wool- and silk-trading town into a center of political experimentation and artistic rebirth. Under Lorenzo the Magnificent in the 15th century, Florentine Renaissance culture peaked in a flurry of splendid productivity. No other place offers such a concentration of beauty; each serendipitous turn hides some scintillating jewel.

ORIENTATION AND PRACTICAL INFORMATION

From Stazione Santa Maria Novella, it's a short walk on Via de' Panzani and then left on Via de' Cerrentari to the center of Florence. This area, the heart of the city, is bounded by the *duomo* on the north, the Arno River on the south, and the Bargello and Palazzo Strozzi on the east and west. Major arteries radiate from the *duomo* and its two *piazze*: **Piazza San Giovanni** encircles the baptistery and **Piazza del Duomo** the cathedral. **Via dei Calzaiuoli,** a lively pedestrian walkway, runs from the *duomo* to **Piazza Signoria** and the Arno. Parallel to Via dei Calzaiuoli on the west, **Via Roma** leads from P. San Giovanni through **Piazza della Repubblica** (the city's largest open space) to the **Ponte Vecchio,** which spans the Arno to the **Oltrarno** district.

Florence's streets are numbered in red and black sequences. Black addresses appear here as a numeral only, while red addresses are indicated by a number followed by an "r." If you reach an address and it's not what you're looking for, you've probably got the wrong color; just take a step back and look around for the other sequence. For guidance through Florence's tangled center, grab a **free map** (preferably with a street index) from a tourist office. Refer also to this book's **color map.**

Trains: Santa Maria Novella Station (tel. 055 27 87 85), across from the Church of Santa Maria Novella. Info office open daily 7am-9pm; after hours go to ticket window #20. Trains depart every hr. to Bologna (1hr., L13,500), Milan (3½hr., L36,500), Rome (2½hr., L36,600), and Venice (3hr., L32,000).

Buses: LAZZI, P. Adua 1-4r (tel. 055 21 51 55), goes to Pisa (L10,600) and Rome (L24,000). **SITA,** Via S. Caterina da Siena, 15r (tel. 055 48 36 51), sends frequent buses to Siena (L11,000).

Public Transportation: Orange ATAF city buses traverse all of Florence, generally 6am-1am. Tickets: L1500 for 1hr. of unlimited use; L5800 for 4 such tickets; L2500 for 3hr.; L6000 for 24hr.; and L11,000 for 3 days. You must buy tickets before boarding and validate them using the orange machine on board. If you're caught without one, or with a ticket that has not been stamped, you'll be fined L70,000. Many bus stops are equipped with ticket-vending machines; you can also buy tickets at *tabacchi*.

Taxis: tel. 055 43 90, 055 47 98, or 055 42 42. Taxis wait outside the train station.

Bike and Moped Rental: MotoRent, Via San Zanobi 9r (tel. 055 49 01 13). Mountain bikes run about L5000 per hr., L30,000 per day. Mopeds begin at L10,000 per hr., L50,000-75,000 per day, L220,000 per week. Ages 18 and up.

Hitchhiking: For the A-1 south to Rome and the extension to Siena, hitchers take bus 31 or 32 from the station to Exit #23, Firenze Sud. As always, *Let's Go* does not recommend hitchhiking, as it is *extremely* risky. **The International Lift Center,** Borgo dei Greci 40r (tel. 055 28 06 21), pairs passengers with drivers for a fee. Open daily 10am-7pm. You must call 1 week in advance.

Tourist Offices: Consorzio ITA (tel. 055 28 28 93 and 055 21 95 37), in the train station by track 16, next to the pharmacy. Accommodations service for L3000-10,000 commission. A bulletin board lists travelers trying to find each other. Open daily 8:30am-8:30pm. **Currency exchange** 7:30am-1:30pm and 2:30-8pm.

Tours: Enjoy Florence (toll-free tel. 167 27 48 19). Walking tours in English meet daily in summer at 10am in front of the Thomas Cook office at the Ponte Vecchio. Reduced winter hours. L30,000, under 26 L25,000.

Consulates: U.K., Lungarno Corsini 2 (tel. 055 28 41 33). Open M-F 9:30am-12:30pm and 2:30-4:30pm. Answering machines give after-hours instructions. **U.S.,** Lungarno Vespucci 38 (tel. 055 239 82 76), at Via Palestro near the station. Open M-F 8:30am-noon and 2-4pm. Canadians, Australians, and New Zealanders should contact their consulates in Rome (see p. 536) or Milan.

Currency Exchange: Local banks have the best exchange rates. Most open M-F 8:20am-1:20pm and 2:45-3:45pm, some open Sa morning. **Cassa di Risparmio di Firenze** now has 24hr. **ATMs** at: Via de' Bardi 73r, Via Nazionale 93, Via de' Tornabuoni 23r, Via degli Speziali 16r, and Via dei Servi 40r.

American Express: Via Dante Alighieri 20-22r (tel. 055 509 81). From the *duomo,* walk down Via dei Calzaiuoli and turn left onto Via dei Tavolini. The office is in the little *piazza* at its end. Cashes personal checks for cardholders. Holds mail for free for card- and checkholders; otherwise L3000 per inquiry, whether you have mail or not. Open M-F 9am-5:30pm, Sa 9am-12:30pm.

Luggage Storage: at the train station, track #16. L500. Open daily 4:15am-1:30am.

Emergencies: tel. 113. **Medical Emergency,** tel. 118. **Fire,** tel. 115.

Police: tel. 112. **Questura,** Via Zara 2 (tel. 055 497 71), or P. del Duomo 5. Open M-F 8am-8pm, Sa 8am-2pm.

24-Hour Pharmacies: Farmacia Comunale (tel. 055 28 94 35), at the train station by track 16. **Molteni,** Via dei Calzaiuoli 7r (tel. 055 28 94 90). **Farmacia all'Insegna del Moro,** P. San Giovanni 20r (tel. 055 21 13 43).

Post Office: (tel. 055 21 61 22) on Via Pellicceria off P. della Repubblica. *Fermo Posta* at window #24. To send packages, go to Via dei Sassetti 4. Open M-F 8:15am-7pm, Sa 8:15am-12:30pm. 24hr. telegram service. **Postal Code:** 50100.

Internet Access: Internet Train, Via dell'Orvio 25r (tel. 055 234 53 22; email info@fionline.it; http://www/fionline.it). L6000 per 30min., L10,000 per hr., students L8000. Open M-F 10am-11pm, Sa 12:30am-7:30pm, Su 3-7pm. Second, larger location at Via Guelfa 24/a (tel. 055 21 47 94).

ACCOMMODATIONS

Florence abounds with one-star *pensioni* and private *affitta camere*. If you arrive late in the day, check with the train station's accommodations service for available rooms and going rates. Sleeping in train stations, streets, or parks is a bad idea, and police actively discourage it. Make reservations *(prenotazioni)* at least 10 days in advance if you plan to visit at Easter or in summer. Expect higher prices than those listed here; rates uniformly increase by 5% or so every year and take effect in March or April.

Via Nazionale and Environs

Via Faenza 56, houses 6 separate *pensioni,* among the best budget lodgings in the city. From the station, turn right toward P. della Stazione. Turn left onto Via Nazionale, and Via Faenza will be the 1st intersecting street. **Pensione Azzi** (tel. 055 21 38 06) has friendly management, large, immaculate rooms, and an elegant dining room. Singles with shower L48,000; doubles L80,000, with bath L88,000; triples L98,000. Breakfast L6000. No curfew. Wheelchair accessible. **Albergo Anna** (tel. 055 239 83 22). Lovely rooms: frescoes for the aesthetes, and fans for the physicalists. Management and prices the same as the Pensione Azzi. **Albergo Merlini** (tel. 055 21 28 48; fax 055 28 39 39). Murals and red geraniums adorn the lounge/solarium. Singles L50,000; doubles L75,000, with bath L95,000; triples L105,000; quads L120,000. Breakfast L7,000. Curfew 1:30am. **Albergo Marini** (tel. 055 28 48 24). Polished wood hallway leads to inviting, spotless rooms. Singles L60,000-70,000; doubles L80,000-100,000; triples L110,000-130,000; quads L120,000-140,000. Breakfast L7000. Curfew 1am. **Albergo Armonia** (tel. 055 21 11 46). Posters of American films bedeck these clean rooms. Singles L60,000; doubles L100,000; triples L130,000; quads L150,000. Breakfast L7,000. **Locanda Paola** (tel. 055 21 36 82). Minimalist rooms, some with views of Fiesole and the surrounding hills. Curfew 2am. Management same as Pensione Azzi.

Hotel Nazionale, Via Nazionale 22 (tel. 055 238 22 03), near P. Indipendenza. Sunny rooms with blue carpets and comfy beds. Singles L65,000, with bath L75,000; doubles L95,000, with bath L115,000; triples L128,000 and L155,000. Breakfast included. Door locks at midnight, but a key is available on request.

Via Faenza 69: Hotel Soggiorno d'Erico, 4th fl. (tel./fax 055 21 55 31). Small rooms with views of the hills around Florence. Singles L55,000; doubles L75,000; triples L95,000; quads L110,000. Free kitchen use. Laundry L6000 per wash (no dryer). **Locanda Giovanna** (tel. 055 238 13 53). 7 basic, well-kept rooms, some with garden views. Singles L50,000; doubles L75,000. **Locanda Pina and Albergo Nella** (tel. 055 21 22 31), the 1st and 2nd floors. Twin establishments offering basic rooms at a good price. Singles L45,000; doubles L75,000; quads L110,000. Free kitchen use. Laundry L5000 per load (no dryer).

Old City (Near the Duomo)

Locanda Orchidea, Borgo degli Albizi 11 (tel. 055 248 03 46). Take Via de' Panzani from the tip of P. della Stazione and follow it straight to the *duomo,* then take a left off Via Proconsolo, which begins behind the *duomo.* 7 cozy, nicely decorated rooms, 4 of which open onto a garden. Singles L48,000; doubles L70,000; triples L110,000. Closed 2 weeks in mid-Aug. Reserve ahead.

Soggiorno Bavaria, Borgo Albizi 26 (tel./fax 055 234 03 13). Walk down Via del Proconsolo. Borgo Albizi is the first intersecting street. Newly renovated rooms, some with balconies, in a cool, quiet 15th-century *palazzo.* Singles L85,000; doubles L115,000-135,000; triples L148,000-160,000. Breakfast L5000.

Soggiorno Panerai, Via dei Servi 36 (tel./fax 055 26 41 03). Facing the *duomo,* Via dei Servi radiates out from back-left side of the cathedral. Serene rooms with shared baths. Doubles L75,000; triples L100,000; quads 115,000.

Hotel Il Perseo, Via Cerretani 1 (tel. 055 21 25 04; fax 055 28 83 77). From the station, walk down Via de'Panzani, which becomes Via de'Cerretani. The hotel is opposite Feltrinelli. Bright, immaculate rooms, all with fans. Cozy bar and TV lounge. Singles L75,000-85,000; doubles L100,000-110,000; triples L150,000-170,000; quads L170,000-200,000. Ample breakfast included. Parking L30,000 per day. If they're full, they'll call around to find you a room.

ITALY

Piazza Santa Maria Novella and Environs

Locanda La Romagnola and Soggiorno Gigliola, Via della Scala 40 (tel. 055 21 15 97 or 055 28 79 81). Leave the station by track 5, cross the street to Via Santa Caterina da Siena, and turn right one block later onto Via della Scala. Simple, spacious rooms. Singles L40,000, with bath L50,000; doubles L68,000, with bath L85,000; triples L90,000, with bath L100,000. Curfew midnight.

Albergo Montreal, Via della Scala 43 (tel./fax 055 238 23 31). Cozy hotel with ebullient staff. 14 bright, noisy rooms. TV lounge with perfect couch-potato seats. Singles L70,000; doubles with shower L84,000, with bath L96,000; triples with bath L130,000; quads with bath L150,000. Curfew 1:30am.

Hotel Visconti, P. Ottaviani 1 (tel./fax 055 21 38 77), on the corner diagonally across the *piazza* from the church. Bar, TV lounge, and rooms with carefully planned color schemes. Singles L62,000; doubles L94,000, with bath L124,000. Friendly management serves breakfast (L12,000) on the roof garden. Open 24hr.

Soggiorno Abaco, Via dei Banchi, 1 (tel./fax 055 238 19 19). From the station, walk straight into P. Santa Maria Novella. With the church on your right, Via dei Banchi will be on the left. 7 well-kept rooms with a medieval feel, polished wood-beamed ceilings, fans, and TVs. Singles L75,000; doubles L100,000, with bath L120,000; triples L130,000, with bath L140,000; quads available. Laundry service L5000 per load. Kitchen facilities L10,000. No curfew.

Near Piazza San Marco and the University Quarter

Hotel Tina, Via San Gallo 31 (tel. 055 48 35 19 or 055 48 35 93). Small *pensione* with high ceilings and new furniture. Amicable owners will find you another place if they're full. Singles L80,000, with bath L90,000; doubles L100,000, with bath L120,000; triples with bath L130,000; quads with bath L140,000.

La Colomba, Via Cavour 21 (tel. 055 28 43 23). Italo-Austrian proprietor leads you to spic und span rooms overlooking the city. A/C. Singles L80,000; doubles L125,000, with bath L150,000. Breakfast included. Negotiable curfew 1:30am.

Albergo Sampaoli, Via San Gallo 14 (tel. 055 28 48 34). Peaceful *pensione* is an American backpacker's "home away from home." Fridge on each floor. Singles L90,000-100,000; doubles L110,000-160,000; triples L170,000; quads L180,000. No written reservations; call the night before you arrive.

Hostels

Ostello Santa Monaca, Via Santa Monaca 6 (tel. 055 26 83 38; fax 055 28 01 85), off Via dei Serragli in the Oltrarno. Crowds up to 10 beds into high-ceilinged rooms. Kitchen facilities but no utensils. Dorms L23,000. Laundry L12,000 per 5kg. 7-night max. stay. Reception 6-9:30am and 2pm-12:30am. Check-in 9:30am-1pm and after 2pm. Curfew 12:30am. Written reservations must arrive at least 3 days in advance.

Istituto Gould, Via dei Serragli 49 (tel. 055 21 25 76), in the Oltrarno. Leave the station by track 16, turn right, and walk to P. della Stazione. Go straight down Via degli Avelli, with the Church of Santa Maria Novella on your right. Cross P. Santa Maria Novella and continue straight on Via dei Fossi, over the Ponte alla Carraia, and down Via dei Serragli (15min.). Or take bus 36 or 37 from the station to the 1st stop across the river. One of the best lodgings in Florence, with 2 minor drawbacks: you can't check in or out on Sa afternoons or on Su, and the rooms overlooking the street are often noisy. Singles L45,000-50,000; doubles L66,000-70,000; triples L90,000-96,000; quads with bath L120,000; quints with bath L125,000. Reception M-F 9am-1pm and 3-7pm, Sa 9am-1pm. No curfew.

Pensionato Pio X, Via dei Serragli 106 (tel./fax 055 22 50 44). Follow the directions to the Istituto Gould (above) then walk a few blocks farther. Clean rooms and bathrooms. 4 comfortable lounges. Dorms with shower L25,000, with bath L5000. 2-night min. stay, 5-night max. stay. Check-in before 9am. Check-out 9am. Curfew midnight. No reservations. Busy in summer, but turnover is high.

Ostello Archi Rossi, Via Faenza 94r (tel. 055 29 08 04; fax 055 230 26 01), 2 blocks from the train station. Exit left from the station onto Via Nazionale and turn left at Via Faenza. Look for the blue neon *Ostello* sign. A funky hostel with floor-to-ceiling graffiti, ceramic tiles, and brick archways. Very popular, and justifiably so. TV room and courtyard patio. Dorms L20,000-27,000. Continental breakfast L2500. Dinner L12,000. Laundry L10,000. Room lockout 9:30am, hostel lockout 11am. Curfew 12:30am. No reservations; arrive by 11am in summer. Wheelchair accessible.

Ostello della Gioventù Europa Villa Camerata (HI), Via Augusto Righi, 2-4 (tel. 055 60 14 51; fax 055 61 03 00), northeast of town. Take bus 17 from outside the train station (near track 6), from P. dell'Unità across from the train station, or from P. del Duomo (20-30min.). Ask bus driver to alert you to the stop. Tidy and popular, though far away. In a gorgeous villa with *loggia* and gardens. Dorms L23,000. Nonmembers add L5000. Sheets and breakfast included. Dinner L14,000. Self-service laundry L10,000. Reception 1-11pm. Check-out 7-9:30am. Strict midnight curfew. Reserve in writing.

Camping

Michelangelo, Via Michelangelo 80 (tel. 055 681 19 77), near P. Michelangelo. Take bus 13 from the station (15min., last bus 11:25pm). Extremely crowded, but offers a spectacular panorama of Florence. Fantastic facilities, including a well-stocked food store and bar. L10,000 per person; L8000 per tent, L6000 per car, L4000 per motorcycle. Open Apr.-Nov. 6am-midnight.

Villa Camerata, Via A. Righi 2-4 (tel. 055 60 03 15), outside the HI youth hostel on the 17 bus route (HI directions above). L8000 per person, L6800 with a camping card; L8000 per small tent, L16,000 per large tent. Open 1pm-midnight. If the office is closed, stake your site and return later (before midnight) to register and pay. Breakfast at hostel L2500. 7-night max. stay. Check-out 7-10am.

FOOD

White beans and olive oil are the two main staples, and most regional dishes come loaded with one or the other, if not both. Florentine specialties include the Tuscan classics *minestra di fagioli* (a delicious white bean and garlic soup), *ribollita* (a hearty bean, bread, and black cabbage stew), and *bistecca alla Fiorentina* (thick sirloin steak). Genuine Florentine *chianti classico* commands a premium price.

For lunch, visit a *rosticceria gastronomia*, peruse the city's pushcarts, or stop by the **students' mensa** at Via dei Servi 52, where a filling meal costs only L14,000 (open M-Sa noon-12:15pm and 6:45-9pm; closed mid-July to Aug.). Buy your own fresh produce and meat at the **Mercato Centrale,** between Via Nazionale and the back of San Lorenzo (open June-Sept. M-Sa 7:30am-2pm; Oct.-May Sa 7am-2pm and 4-8pm). For staples, head over to the **STANDA supermarket,** Via Pietrapiana 1r (open Tu-Sa 8:30am-8pm, Su 8:30am-1:30pm).

I Latini, Via Palchetti 6r. From the Ponte alla Carraia, walk up Via del Moro; Via Palchetti is on the right. Be prepared to wait. Delicious Tuscan classics (*ribollita* L8000) served beneath dangling cured hams. *Primi* L8000-12,000; *secondi* L15,000-20,000. Cover L2500. Open Tu-Su 12:30-2:30pm and 7:30-10:30pm.

Amon, Via Palazzuolo 26-28r. Scrumptious Middle Eastern food. Try the mousaka or the *foul,* which, despite its name, is delicious. English menu. Falafel L4000, shish kebab L5000. Stand-up or take-out only. Open M-Sa noon-3pm and 6:30-11pm.

Trattoria da Zà-Zà, P. del Mercato Centrale 26r. Soups are a specialty in this hopping *trattoria.* Cover L2000. Open M-Sa noon-3pm and 7-11pm. Reservations recommended

Trattoria da Garibaldi, P. del Mercato Centrale 38r. Locals crowd this huge place, and with good reason. Vegetarian options. Open in summer M-Sa noon-3:30pm and 7pm-midnight; in winter M-Sa noon-3pm and 7-10pm.

Ristorante Il Vegetariano, Via delle Ruote 30, off Via San Gallo. Self-service place with fresh, inventive meat-free dishes (not all cheese-dependent). *Primi* from L6000; *secondi* from L9000. Amazing desserts L5000. Cover L2000. Open Tu-F 12:30am-3pm and 7:30pm-midnight, Sa-Su 8pm-midnight.

Acqua al Due, Via Vigna Vecchia 40r, behind the Bargello. Florentine specialties in a cozy place popular with young Italians. Getting a table always demands a reservation. A/C. *Primi* L8000-10,000; *secondi* L10,000-20,000. Cover L2000. Open June-Sept. daily 8pm-1am; Oct.-May Tu-Su 8pm-1am.

Oltrarno Trattoria Casalinga, Via Michelozzi 9r, near P. Santo Spirito. Tuscan specialties in a pleasant, family atmosphere. Excellent *pasta al pastore* (L9000). *Primi* L4500-9000; *secondi* L7500-16,000. Menu changes daily. Cover L1500. Open M-Sa noon-3pm and 7pm-midnight.

SIGHTS

Florence's museums have recently doubled their prices, offer no student discounts, and stop selling tickets 30 minutes to an hour before closing—but none of this should prevent you from indulging in the finest Renaissance art in the world.

Piazza del Duomo

The red brick of Florence's **Duomo** is visible from virtually every part of the city. *(Open M-F 10am-5pm, Sa 10am-4:45pm, Su 1-5pm; 1st Sa of every month 10am-3:30pm. Mass 7-10am and 5-7pm.)* Filippo Brunelleschi designed the cathedral's sublime dome, the world's largest when it was built. To accomplish this feat, the architect developed a revolutionary double-shelled construction, using interlocking bricks that supported themselves as the dome was being built. The *duomo* claims the world's third-longest nave, after Rome's St. Peter's and London's St. Paul's. Climb the 463 steps inside the dome to the **lantern,** which offers an unparalleled view of the city. *(Open M-Sa 8:30am-7pm. L8000.)*

Most of the *duomo*'s art resides behind the *duomo* in the **Museo dell'Opera di Santa Maria del Fiore,** P. del Duomo. *(Open in summer M-Sa 9am-6:50pm; in winter M-Sa 9am-6:20pm. L10,000. Look for the English tours in summer W-Th 4pm.)* Up the first flight of stairs is a late *Pietà* by Michelangelo. According to legend, he severed Christ's left arm with a hammer in a fit of frustration. Soon after, a diligent pupil touched up the work, leaving visible scars on parts of Mary Magdalene's head.

Although it was built in the 5th through 9th centuries, by Dante's time the Florentines believed their **battistero** (baptistry) had originated as a Roman temple. *(Open M-Sa 1:30-6pm, Su 9am-12:30pm. Mass at 10:30 and 11:30am. L3000.)* The interior Byzantine-style mosaics inspired details of Dante's *Inferno.* Incidentally, the author was christened in this very baptistery. Florentine artists competed fiercely for the commission to execute the baptistery's famous **bronze doors.** In 1401, Brunelleschi (then 23) and Ghiberti (then 20) were asked to work in partnership on the doors, but Brunelleschi, unwilling to compromise, left in a huff shortly thereafter. When Ghiberti completed his project in 1425, his work was so admired that he immediately received the commission to forge the last set of doors, which he finished in 1452 after 28 years of labor. The **"Gates of Paradise,"** as Michelangelo reportedly called them, are nothing like the two earlier portals; they abandon the 28-panel design for 10 large, gilded squares, each incorporating mathematical perspective to create the illusion of deep space. They have been under restoration since the 1966 flood and will eventually reside in the Museo dell'Opera del Duomo. Next to the *duomo* rises the 82m-high **campanile.** *(Open daily Apr.-Oct. 9am-6:50pm; Nov.-Mar. 9am-5:30pm. L8000.)* The 414-step climb to the top earns ineffably beautiful views.

Palazzo Vecchio and Piazza della Signoria

From P. del Duomo, **Via dei Calzaiuoli,** one of the city's oldest streets, leads to P. della Signoria. At the far end, the area around the **Palazzo Vecchio** forms Florence's civic center. *(Open M-W and F-Sa 9am-7pm, Su 8am-1pm. L10,000.)* Arnolfo del Cambio designed this fortress-like *palazzo* in the late 13th century as the seat of the *comune*'s government.

A vast space by medieval standards, **Piazza della Signoria** came into being in the 13th century and soon became Florence's civic center. In 1497, religious leader and social critic Savonarola convinced Florentines to light the **Bonfire of the Vanities** in the square, a grand roast that consumed some of Florence's best art. A year later, disillusioned citizens sent Savonarola up in smoke on the same spot, marked today by a granite disc. Monumental sculptures cluster in front of the *palazzo,* including Michelangelo's *David* (a copy now stands in place of the original). The awkward *Neptune* to the left of the Palazzo Vecchio so revolted Michelangelo that he insulted the artist: "Oh Ammannato, Ammannato, what lovely marble you have ruined!" The graceful 14th-century **Loggia dei Lanzi,** built as a stage for civic orators, became a misogynistic sculpture gallery under the Medici dukes. It holds Benvenuto Cellini's *Perseus*

Slaying Medusa, Giambologna's *Rape of the Sabines,* whose spiral composition invites viewing from any angle, and the violent *Rape of Polyxena* by Pio Fedi.

The heart of medieval Florence lies between the *duomo* and P. della Signoria at the 13th-century **Bargello** in P. San Firenze. This fortress was once the residence of the chief magistrate and later became a brutal prison. Restored in the 19th century, it now houses the **Museo Nazionale,** a treasury of Florentine sculpture, including Donatello's bronze *David* and several of Michelangelo's early works. *(Open daily 9am-1:30pm; closed on the 1st, 3rd, and 5th Su and the 2nd and 4th M of every month. L8000.)* The **Badia,** across Via del Proconsolo from the Bargello, was the site of medieval Florence's richest monastery. *(Open M-Sa 5-7pm, Su 7:30-11:30am.)* Filippino Lippi's *Apparition of the Virgin to St. Bernard,* one of the most famous paintings of the late 15th century, greets you on the left as you enter.

In nearby **Piazza Santa Croce,** the Franciscans built the **Chiesa di Santa Croce** which, despite their stark asceticism, is quite possibly the most splendid church in the city. *(Open daily 8am-6:30pm.)* Among the famous Florentines buried here are Michelangelo, Macchiavelli, and Galileo.

The Uffizi and the Ponte Vecchio

In May of 1993, terrorists set off a bomb in the **Uffizi,** killing five people in nearby buildings and destroying priceless works of art. *(Open Tu-Sa 8:30am-6:50pm, Su 8:30am-1:50pm. L12,000. For an extra L1600, save hours of queueing by purchasing advance tickets; call 055 47 19 60 to reserve by phone with a credit card, or visit the Informazione Turistica in the train station M-F 8am-6:30pm.)* A few rooms in the Uffizi are closed to the public and will remain that way for the next few years while reconstruction progresses, but the museum still displays an unparalleled collection of Renaissance art. Botticelli, da Vinci, Michelangelo, Raphael, Titan, Giotto, Caravaggio, Cimabue, even Rubens and Rembrandt—you name it, they have it. Vasari designed the palace in 1554 for the new Tuscan administration of Duke Cosimo. Upstairs, a long corridor wraps around the building and holds an impressive collection of Hellenistic and Roman marbles, the inspiration for many Renaissance works. From the Uffizi, Via Georgofili leads left to the river; a right will take you to the nearby **Ponte Vecchio** (Old Bridge); an apt name for the oldest bridge in Florence. The Medici kicked out the butchers and tanners, whose shops lined the bridge in the 1500s and who had been dumping pig's blood and intestines in the river for decades. In their place, the ruling family installed goldsmiths and diamond-carvers.

Piazza della Repubblica and Santa Maria Novella

The 1547 **Mercato Nuovo** (New Market) arcades housed the gold and silk trades. Pietro Tacca's pleasantly plump statue, *Il Porcellino* (The Little Pig), actually a wild boar, appeared some 50 years later. Said to bring good luck, its snout remains brightly polished by tourist rubbing. **Piazza della Repubblica** replaced the Mercato Vecchio (Old Market) as the site of the town market in 1890. A single column remains from the Mercato Vecchio, topped off by a statue representing *Abundance.* In this area, you'll find several of the city's most popular cafes: the pricey, decadent **Gilli,** Florence's most famous coffeehouse (established in 1733), and the nearby **Giubbe Rosse,** once the haunt of Italian Futurist writers and artists.

The wealthiest merchants built their chapels in the 13th- and 14th-century **Church di Santa Maria Novella,** near the train station. *(Open M-Sa 7am-12:15pm and 3-6:30pm, Su 3-5pm.)* Frescoes covered the interior until the Medici commissioned Vasari to paint new ones in their honor, ordering the other walls white-washed so their rivals would not be remembered. Vasari removed all but Masaccio's powerful *Trinity,* the first painting to use geometric perspective.

The Medici used an entire portion of the city north of the *duomo* for their own church, the spacious **Basilica di San Lorenzo,** and the **Palazzo Medici.** *(Open daily 8am-noon and 5:30-6pm.)* The family cunningly placed Cosimo's grave in front of the high altar, making the entire church his personal mausoleum. Michelangelo designed the church's exterior, but, disgusted by the murkiness of Florentine politics, he ran off to Rome to study architecture in the middle of the project. The **Laurentian Library** next door contains one of the largest and most valuable manuscript collections in the world. *(Open M-Sa 9am-1pm. Free.)*

To reach the **Cappella dei Medici,** walk around to the back entrance on P. Madonna degli Aldobrandini. *(Open daily 9am-2pm; closed the 2nd and 4th Su and the 1st, 3rd, and 5th M of every month. L10,000.)* The architectural simplicity of Michelangelo's **Sacrestia Nuova** (New Sacristy, 1524) reveals his study of Brunelleschi. The **Accademia** lies near the church at Via Ricasoli 60. *(Open Tu-Sa 8:30am-6:15pm, Su 8:30am-2pm. L12,000. Wheelchair accessible.)* Michelangelo's triumphant *David* stands under the rotunda designed just for him. In the hallway leading up to the *David* are Michelangelo's four *Prisoners.* The master left these intentionally unfinished; he chipped away only enough to liberate them.

In the Oltrarno

Historically disdained by downtown Florentines, the far side of the Arno remains a lively, unpretentious quarter, even in high season. Start your tour a few blocks west of P. San Spirito at the **Chiesa di Santa Maria del Carmine.** *(Open M and W-Sa 10am-4:30pm, Su 1-4:30pm. L5000.)* Inside, the **Brancacci Chapel** holds, in glorious restored form, Masaccio's stunning and influential 15th-century frescoes, declared masterpieces even in their own time. With such works as the *Tribute Money,* this chapel became a school for many artists, including Michelangelo.

Luca Pitti, a nouveau riche banker of the 15th century, built his *palazzo* east of Santo Spirito against the Boboli hill. The Medici acquired the *palazzo* and the hill in 1550 and enlarged everything possible. Today, the **Pitti Palace** houses seven museums. *(All museums, except as noted, open daily 9am-2pm; closed on the 1st, 3rd, and 5th M and the 2nd and 4th Su of each month. Admission to both the Museo degli Argenti and the Museum of Costumes L8000; admission to the Porcelain Museum L4000.)* The **Museo degli Argenti** on the ground floor exhibits the Medici family treasures, including gems, ivories, silver pieces, and Lorenzo the Magnificent's famous collection of vases. The **Museum of Costumes** and the **Porcelain Museum** host other items of Medici fortune. The **Royal Apartments** and the **Carriage Museum** boast lavish reminders of the time when the *palazzo* was the House of Savoy's living quarters. *(Open Tu-Sa 8:30am-7pm, Su 8:30am-2pm. L12,000.)* The **Galleria Palatina** includes a number of works by Raphael, Titian, Andrea del Sarto, Caravaggio, and Rubens. In the **Galleria d'Arte Moderna** lies one of Italian art history's big surprises: the early 19th-century proto-Impressionist works of the Macchiaioli school. *(Admission L4000.)*

Spanning several vistas of the Florentine skyline and surrounding hills, the elaborately landscaped **Boboli Gardens** are an exquisite example of stylized Renaissance gardening. *(Open daily June-July 9am-7:30pm; Sept.-Oct. and Apr.-May 9am-6:30pm; Nov.-Feb. 9am-4:30pm; Mar. 9am-5:30pm. Closed first and last M of the month. L4000. Fort open daily in summer 9am-10pm; in winter 9am-5pm.)* You'll want to get lost in this seraglio of green that eventually stretches up the hilltop to **Forte Belvedere,** once the Medici fortress and treasury. Ascend Via di Costa San Giorgio from P. Santa Felicità, to the left after crossing Ponte Vecchio, to reach the villa, an unusual construction with a central *loggia* designed by Ammannati. Built by Buontalenti for Grand Duke Ferdinand I, the fortress now hosts summer exhibitions and tanning exhibitionism.

The splendid view of Florence from the fort is equal only to the picture-perfect panorama from **Piazzale Michelangelo.** *(Ask the sacristan to let you into the chapel. Church open daily 7:30am-7pm.)* Go at sunset for the most spectacular lighting of the city. Cross the Ponte Vecchio and take a left, walk through the *piazza* and fork right up Via de' Bardi, and follow uphill as it becomes Via del Monte alle Croci. There's a staircase to your left that heads directly to the *piazzale.*

ENTERTAINMENT

For reliable information on what's hot and what's not, consult the city's entertainment monthly, *Firenze Spettacolo* (L2700). Street performers draw crowds to the steps of the *duomo,* the arcades of the Mercato Nuovo, and P. Michelangelo. **Caffè La**

Dolce Vita in P. del Carmine draws a respectable evening crowd and is convenient to the budget lodgings in the Oltrarno. Just two blocks away, P. Santo Spirito hops with a good selection of bars and restaurants.

The Red Garter, Via dei Benci 33r. A raucous mix of American students and the Italian youth who pursue them. Flying peanut shells and classic American rock. If you have what it takes, they might let you on stage. Happy hour 8:30pm. Open nightly.

Auditorium Flog, Via Mercati 24. The hottest place in Florence for live rock and jazz. Come in your skin-tight, metallic blue cat-suit.

Eskimo, Via dei Canaccii 12r, near Santa Maria Novella. Live music and occasional alternative theater. Sip sangria and cocktails. Open Tu-Su 9:30pm-3:30am.

Fuori Porta, Monte alle Croce 10r. For those who prefer a quieter evening. An impressive selection of *vino* by the glass from L4000. Open M-Sa 10am-midnight.

Meccanò, Via degli Olmi 1 (tel. 055 33 13 71), near Parco delle Cascinè. The most popular of Florence's discos among locals and tourists alike. Take bus 17c from the *duomo* or train station. L30,000 cover includes 1 drink; each subsequent drink L10,000. Call for the weekly music schedule. Open Tu-Sa 11pm-4am.

Tenax, Via Pratese 46a, Perètola. Florence's biggest club has the flex to attract a lot of big bands, which play in its multiple dance floors. Open W-Su nights.

Every June the various *quartieri* of Florence turn out in costume to play their own medieval version of soccer, known as **Calcio Storico.** Two teams of 27 players face off over a wooden ball in one of the city's *piazze.* Tickets (from L20,000) are sold at the **Chiosco degli Sportivi** (tel. 055 29 23 63) on Via dei Anselmi. Real games occur at the **stadio,** north of the city center. You can buy tickets (from L20,000) from the bar across the street from the stadium.

May brings the classical **Maggio Musicale.** The **Festival of San Giovanni Battista** on June 24 features a tremendous fireworks display in P. Michelangelo (easily visible from the Arno) that starts at about 10pm. From June to August, the **Estate Fiesolana** fills the Roman theater in nearby Fiesole with concerts, opera, theater, ballet, and film. In September, Florence hosts the **Festa dell'Unità,** an organized music and concert series at Campi Bisenzia (take bus 30). The **Florence Film Festival** is generally held in December; call 055 24 07 20 for details. *Funghi*-lovers should check out the annual **Festa dei Porcini,** a three-day long mushroom festival in August. The **Festa del Grillo** (Festival of the Cricket) is held the first Sunday after Ascension Day.

■ Siena

After centuries of often violent rivalry with its neighbors, especially the Florentines, Siena today shines peacefully amidst its more touristed sibling cities. The city lingers complacently as a living masterpiece—even in Italy, few places are as aesthetically harmonious.

SIGHTS AND ENTERTAINMENT The salmon-colored, shell-shaped **Piazza del Campo** is the focus of Sienese life. At the bottom of the shell is the **Palazzo Pubblico,** a graceful Gothic palace over which soars the **Torre del Mangia** clock tower, named for the gluttonous bellringer Mangiaguadagni. (Literally, "eat the profits." Palazzo open Mar.-Oct M-Sa 9:30am-6:15pm, Su 9am-1:30pm; Nov.-Feb. daily 10am-5pm. L8000, students L6000. Torre del Mangia open M-Sa in summer 9:30am-6:30pm, Su 9:30am-1:30pm; in winter M-Sa 10am-5pm. L7000.) Inside, the **Museo Civico** contains excellent Gothic painting; the **Sala del Mappamondo** and the **Sala della Pace** have particularly stellar works. (Open Mar.-Oct. M-Sa 9am-6:15pm, Su 9am-12:45pm; Nov.-Feb. daily 9am-12:45pm. L8000, students L6000.)

The construction of Siena's **duomo** spanned two architectural eras, incorporating Romanesque arches and Gothic pinnacles. (Open daily Jan.-Mar. 14 7:30am-1:30pm and 2:30-5pm; Mar. 15-Oct. 9am-7:30pm; Nov.-Dec. 7:30am-1:30pm and 2:30-5pm. Free. Modest dress required.) The **pulpit** is one of Andrea Pisano's best, with allegorical and biblical reliefs, and the **baptistery** has carvings by some of the greatest Italian sculptors. The lavish **Libreria Piccolomini,** off the left aisle, holds frescoes by Pinturicchio and 15th-century illuminated musical scores. (Open mid-Mar. to Oct. 9am-7:30pm; Nov. to mid-Mar. 10am-1pm and 2:30-5pm. L2000. Proper dress required.) The **Museo dell'Opera della Metropolitana,** next to the cathedral, displays art formerly held in the cathedral, including Duccio di Buoninsegna's splendid *Maestà* (open mid-Mar. to early Nov. 9am-7:30pm; Nov. to mid-Mar. 9am-1:30pm).

All day during the **Palio di Siena,** July 2 and August 16, Sienese parade around in 15th-century costume. The central event is a traditional bare-back horse race around the packed P. del Campo. Get there three days early to watch the rambunctious horse selection in the *campo* (10am) and to pick a *contrada* (neighborhood) to root for. The night before the race everyone revels until 3am or so, strutting and chanting their way around the city, pausing only to eat and drink. You can stand in the "infield" of the *piazza* for free, but access closes early, so stake out a spot early in the day. For tickets and a list of rooms-to-let, write to the tourist office by March; arrive without a reservation and you'll be sleeping on the streets.

PRACTICAL INFO, ACCOMMODATIONS, AND FOOD Siena lies off the main Florence-Rome **rail line.** Direct trains run from Florence (L10,000); from Rome (L22,000) you must change at Chiusi. Take any bus passing across the street from the station to the center of town (L1500), or prepare for a 45-minute uphill trek. Express TRA-IN/SITA **buses,** faster than the train, link Siena with Florence (L11,000) and other Tuscan destinations. The **tourist office,** Il Campo 56 (tel. 05 77 28 05 51), provides info on local sights, hotels, and other Tuscan towns. (Open in summer M-Sa 8:30am-7:30pm, Su 8:30am-2pm; off-season M-Sa 8:30am-1pm and 3-7:30pm.) Finding a room in Siena is usually simple, but call a few days ahead during July and August and months ahead for either Palio. The pricey but beautiful **Albergo Bernini,** Via della Sapienza 15 (tel./fax 05 77 28 90 47), has incredible views of the *duomo.* (Singles L80,000; doubles L110,000-130,000; triples L148,000; quads available; cheaper off-season. Curfew midnight.) The inconveniently located **Ostello della Gioventù "Guidoriccio" (HI),** Via Fiorentina 89 (tel. 057 75 22 12; fax 057 75 61 72), in Località Lo Stellino, is a 20-minute ride on bus 15, 35, or 36 across from the station at P. Gramsci; if coming from Florence by bus, get off at the stop just after the large black-and-white sign announcing entry into Siena (L20,000; breakfast included; curfew 11:30pm). **Locanda Garibaldi,** Via Giovanni Dupré 18 (tel. 05 77 28 42 04), behind the Palazzo Publico and P. del Campo, has homey rooms and a restaurant downstairs (singles L45,000; doubles L80,000, triples L110,000; curfew midnight).

Siena specializes in rich pastries, most notably *panforte,* a concoction of honey, almonds, and citron. Sample it at **Bar/Pasticceria Nannini,** Via Banchi di Sopra 22-24. Pick up supplies at the **Consortio Agrario supermarket,** Via Pianigiani 5, off P. Salimberi (open M-F 7:45am-1pm and 4:30-8pm, Sa 7:45am-1pm). **Grotta del Gallo Nero,** Via del Porrione 67, serves medieval Tuscan dishes in a *menú assaggio,* which allows varied sampling (from L25,000; open Tu-Su noon-2:30pm and 7pm-1am). **Mensa Universitaria,** Via Sant' Agata 1, has full meals for L10,000 and pasta for L4000-7000 (open daily noon-2pm and 6:45-9pm; closed Aug.).

San Gimignano

Only an hour from Siena by bus (L8600), the medieval towers of **San Gimignano** reach skyward. The towers and the walled *centro* testify to a 13th-century building competition between San Gimignano's wealthiest families. Of the original 72 edifices, 14 remain. Scale the **Torre Grossa,** the tallest of the remaining towers, attached to **Palazzo del Popolo,** for a panorama of Tuscany. (Torre open Mar.-Oct. daily 9:30am-7pm; Nov.-Feb. Tu-Su 9:30am-12:30pm and 1:30-4:30pm. L6000-8000. Palazzo open Tu-Su 9am-7:30pm.) In Torre Grossa's shadow, the **Museo Civico** houses an amazing collection of Sienese and Florentine works, most notably Lippi's *Annunciation* (open same hours as the tower; L5000-7000). *Affitte camere* (singles around L60,000) are an alternative to overpriced hotels. Get a list from either the **tourist office,** P. del Duomo 1 (tel. 05 88 94 00 08), or the **Associazione Strutture Extralberghiere,** P. della Cisterna 6 (tel. 05 77 94 31 90; open daily Mar.-Nov.

9:30am-7:30pm). The hostel, **Ostello di San Gimignano,** Via delle Fonti 1 (tel. 05 77 94 19 91), is refreshingly peaceful. (L20,000-24,000. Breakfast and sheets included. Reception Mar.-Oct. 7-9am and 5-11:30pm.) **Albergo/Ristorante Il Pino,** Via S. Matteo 102 (tel. 05 77 94 04 15), offers simple rooms in a quiet quarter near the convent (doubles L70,000). Pitch a tent at **Il Boschetto,** (tel. 05 77 94 03 52) at Santa Lucia, 2½km downhill from Porta San Giovanni. Buses run from town to the site (L1500), but it's not a bad hike. (L8000 per person, L7500 per small tent. Reception 8am-1pm, 3-8pm, and 9-11pm. Open Apr.-Oct. 15.) Find take-out fare at the **market,** Via S. Matteo 19 (open M-Sa Mar.-Oct. 8am-8pm; Nov.-Feb. 8am-1pm and 4-7pm).

Elba If you've had it with city-hopping, soak in a few days of sun and swimming just off the coast of Tuscany on the island of **Elba,** where Napoleon spent his exile, but avoid the overcrowded island in July and August. Take the train to **Piombino Marittima** (also called Piombino Porto) where you can hop on one of the frequent Toremar or Navarma **ferries** (1hr., about 16 per day, L10,000-15,000). Talk directly to Toremar (tel. 05 65 91 80 80) or Navarma (tel. 05 65 22 12 12) at Piazzale Premuda, 13, in Piombino. The **APT tourist office,** Calata Italia 26 (tel. 05 65 91 46 71), is across from the Toremar boat landing (open daily in summer 9am-1pm and 2:30-7:30pm; off-season 9am-1pm and 3-7pm)

■ Pisa

Tourism wasn't always Pisa's prime industry: throughout the Middle Ages this city was a major port with an empire extending to Corsica, Sardinia, and the Balearics. But when the Arno River silted up, the city's power and wealth declined accordingly. Today, the city resigns itself to welcoming tourists and countless t-shirt and ice cream vendors to the **Piazza del Duomo,** also known as the **Campo dei Miracoli** (Field of Miracles), a grassy expanse on the northern side of the Arno where most of the major attractions are located. A L17,000 ticket admits you to the Campo's sights.

The famous **Leaning Tower** continues to slip one to two millimeters every year. Although many tourists come to Pisa simply to marvel at the tower's odd appearance, more perceptive visitors also note that it is a prime example of the innovative architecture of the Pisan Romanesque period. Unfortunately, visitors are no longer allowed to enter the tower. Also on the Campo, the dazzling **duomo** is a treasury of fine art, including Giovanni Pisano's greatest pulpit (open M-Sa 10am-7:45pm; L2000). Next door is the **baptistery,** where precision acoustics allow an unamplified choir to be heard 20km away (open daily in summer 8am-7:30pm; off-season 9am-4:40pm). The adjoining **Camposanto,** a long, white-walled cemetery, has many classical sarcophagi and a series of haunting frescoes by an unidentified 14th-century artist known only as the "Master of the Triumph of Death" (open daily in summer 9am-5:40pm; off-season 9am-4:40pm). The **Museo delle Sinopie,** across the square from the Camposanto, displays *sinopie* (preliminary fresco sketches) discovered during restoration after World War II, while the **Museo dell'Opera del Duomo,** behind the Tower, displays artworks from three buildings of the P. del Duomo. (Both open daily in summer 8am-7:45pm; off-season 9am-12:30pm and 3-4:30pm. Combined ticket L10,000, EU citizens free.) One hidden treasure in town is the Gothic church of **Santa Maria della Spina,** which faces Lungarno Gambacorti against the river. Its bell tower allegedly holds a thorn from Christ's crown.

Trains run to Florence every hour (1hr., L7200) from P. della Stazione (tel. 05 04 13 85), in the southern part of town; the main coastal line links Pisa to Genoa and Rome. The **tourist office,** P. della Stazione (tel. 05 04 22 91), to your left as you exit the station, doles out maps (open M-Sa 8am-8pm, Su 9am-1pm). There's a **branch office** (tel. 050 56 04 64) at P. del Duomo in the Museo dell'Opera (open daily Apr.-Oct. 8am-8pm; Nov.-Mar. 9am-5:30pm). The **Centro Turistico Madonna dell'Acqua** hostel, Via Pietrasantina 15 (tel. 050 89 06 22), awaits beneath an old sanctuary. Take bus 3 from the station and ask to be let off at the *ostello* (dorms L20,000; doubles L62,000; reception 6-11pm; check-out 9am). The **Albergo Gronchi,** P. Archivescovado 1 (tel. 050 56 18 23), just off P. del Duomo, has frescoed ceilings and a pretty garden (singles L32,000; doubles L52,000; triples L70,000). The **Casa della Giovane (ACISG),** Via F. Corridoni 29 (tel. 05 04 30 61), a 10-minute walk from the station (turn right immediately), offers beds to women only (L25,000; curfew 10pm). **Campeggio Torre Pendente,** Viale delle Cascine 86, is 1km away. Follow the signs from P. Manin (L10,000 per person, L3500-6000 per tent; open Easter-Oct. 15).

For more authentic restaurants than those by the touristy *duomo,* head to the river or university area. Pisans prefer the **open-air market** in P. Vettovaglie. At **Trattoria da Matteo,** Via l'Aroncio 46, off Via S. Maria, *gnocchi al pesto* goes for L7000 and pizza starts at L6500 (open Su-F noon-3pm and 7-11pm). Walk through the Palazzo d'Orlogio and turn right to reach the **Mensa Universitaria,** Via Martiri; one ticket (L6000) buys two filling meals (open daily noon-2pm and 7-9pm).

UMBRIA

Christened the "Green Heart of Italy," Umbria has enjoyed renown since ancient times for its wooded hills, valleys, and riverbanks. Often shrouded in an ethereal silvery haze, the landscape has enticed mystics from St. Benedict to Umbria's most famous visionary, the nature-adoring ascetic St. Francis. Generations of visual artists also clambered about these hills, among them Giotto, Signorelli, and Perugino.

■ Perugia

The extremely polite residents of Perugia may be trying to make up for two millennia of excessive nastiness, during which Perugians regularly stoned each other and even threw tree-hugging St. Francis of Assisi into a dungeon. The city earns more dubious fame as the birthplace of the Flagellants, who wandered Europe whipping themselves, and as the site of two popes' death by poisoning. But Perugia now attracts visitors with steep medieval streets and mellow university atmosphere.

SIGHTS AND ENTERTAINMENT The city's most noteworthy sights frame **Piazza IV Novembre.** The **Fontant Maggiore** in the center is adorned with sculptures and bas-reliefs by Nicolà and Giovanni Pisano. The 13th-century **Palazzo dei Priori** presides over the *piazza* and shelters the **Galleria Nazionale dell'Umbria,** Corso Vannucci 19. Inside, the immense collection includes fine works by Fra Angelico, Piero della Francesca, and a definitive collection of Umbrian art. Perugino's *Adoration of the Magi* is the gallery's premier piece (open M-Sa 9am-7pm, Su 9am-1pm; L8000, students free). Perugia's austere Gothic **duomo** looms at the end of the *piazza;* its facade was never completed because the *Perugini* were forced to return the marble they had stolen to build it. At the far end of Corso Vannucci, the well-tended **Giardini Carducci** offer a broad view of the Umbrian countryside. Around the gardens and down Via Marzia, stands the 16th-century fortress, the **Rocca Paolina.** Every July, the fantastic **Umbria Jazz Festival** draws performers and crowds to Perugia (L15,000-50,000, some events free; contact the tourist office for more info).

PRACTICAL INFO, ACCOMMODATIONS, AND FOOD The **train station,** P. Veneto, serves Assisi (25min., L3500), Florence (2½hr., L20,700), and Rome via Terontola (3hr., L26,000). From the station, city buses 28, 29, 36, 42, and CD make the trip to town (L1200). The **tourist office,** P. IV Novembre (tel. 07 55 72 53 41 or 07 55 72 33 27), offers info on accommodations and the jazz festival (open M-Sa 8:30am-1:30pm and 3:30-6:30pm, Su 9am-1pm). To get to the **Ostello della Gioventù/Centro Internazionale di Accoglienza per la Gioventù,** Via Bontempi 13 (tel. 07 55 72 28 80), from P. Italia, walk to P. IV Novembre, continue through P. Dante, taking the farthest street to the right through P. Piccinio, and right again onto Via Bontempi. (L16,000. Showers included. Sheets L2000. Curfew midnight. Open mid-Jan. to mid-Dec.) The clean, cool rooms in **Albergo Anna,** Via dei Priori 48, 4th fl. (tel. 07 55 73

63 04), off Corso Vannucci, offer great views of the city (singles L36,000-56,000; doubles L56,000-75,000). **Paradis d'Ete** (tel. 07 55 17 21 17), 5km away in Colle della Trinità, has hot showers and a pool at no extra charge. Take bus 36 from the station (L7000 per person, L6000 per tent).

Trattoria Dal Mi Cocco, Corso Garibaldi 12, writes its menu in a Perugian dialect, but enjoys well-deserved popularity (*menù* L25,000; open Tu-Su 1-2:30pm and 8:15-10:30pm). **L'Oca Nera,** Via dei Priori 78/82, serves everything from *gnocchi* to burgers (around L6500; open Th-Tu 7:30pm-1am). Though renowned for chocolate, Perugia also serves up a variety of delectable breads and pastries; try **Ceccarani,** P. Matteotti 16 (open M-Sa 7:30am-2pm and 4:30-8pm), or the **Co.Fa.Pa.** bakery two doors down (open M-Sa 7:30am-1pm and 5-7:30pm). **Pasticceria Sandri,** Corso Vannucci 32, serves local confections amid old-world elegance (open M-Sa 7:30am-8pm).

■ Assisi

Assisi's serenity originates with the legacy of St. Francis, the eco-friendly monk who preached poverty, obedience, and love eight centuries ago. After his death in 1226, Florentine and Sienese painters decorated the **Basilica di San Francesco** with a spectacular ensemble of frescoes illustrating his life. The upper level is elaborate and sumptuously decorated, while the lower level, built around the crypt housing the saint's tomb, is more modest. The walls of the church are almost completely covered with Giotto's *Life of St. Francis* fresco cycle. Call 075 81 22 38 to arrange a free, English language tour. (The upper church is open daily sunrise to sunset, and closed on Holy Days; the lower church will be closed for the next 1-2 years for restoration. English language Mass Sa-Su 6:30pm. Modest dress. No photography.) Towering above town, the restored fortress **Rocca Maggiore** overwhelms visitors with its tremendous views (open daily 10am-dusk; closed in bad weather; L5000, students L3500). On the other side of Assisi stands the pink-and-white **Basilica of Santa Chiara,** where St. Francis attended school and St. Clare now rests (open M-F 10am-noon and 3:30-5:30pm, Sa-Su 9:30-11:30am and 3:30-5:30pm).

Assisi is on the Foligno-Terontola **rail** line; trains go to Ancona (L12,100), Florence, and Rome (L25,500). **Buses** run to Perugia (L4900) and other Umbrian towns. The **tourist office,** P. del Comune 12 (tel. 075 81 25 34), offers an accommodations service and posts train and bus schedules outside. (Open M-F 8am-2pm and 3:30-6:30pm, Sa 9am-1pm and 3:30-6:30pm, Su 9am-1pm.) The **Ostello della Pace (HI),** Via di Valecchi 177 (tel./fax 075 81 67 67), has large rooms and spotless bathrooms. (L22,000-27,000 per person; breakfast included. Reception 7-9:15am and 3:30-11:30pm.) From the top of P. Matteotti, Via Eremo leads to the Porta Cappuccini and the superb **Ostello Fontemaggio** (tel. 075 81 36 36), Via per l'Eremo delle Carceri (L17,000; camping L7000 per person, L6000 per tent). **Carmere Annalisa Martini**, Via San Gregorio 6 (tel. 075 81 35 36), is a peaceful refuge in the medieval core of Assisi (singles L40,000; doubles L60,000). **Pizzeria Otello,** Via San Antonio 1, off P. del Comune, is a no-nonsense family-run pizzeria with a garden (open 7:30am-11pm).

THE MARCHES (LE MARCHE)

■ Urbino

With humble stone dwellings huddled around an immense turreted palace, Urbino's fairy tale skyline has changed little over the past 500 years. The city's most remarkable monument is the Renaissance **Palazzo Ducale** (Ducal Palace), a looming structure more thrilling on the outside than on the inside. The interior **courtyard** is the essence of Renaissance balance and proportion; to the left, a large staircase leads to the private apartments of the Duke, which now house the **National Gallery of the Marches.** Among the works here are Piero della Francesca's *Flagellation of Christ,* Berruguete's famous portrait of Duke Federico, Raphael's *Portrait of a Lady,* and

Paolo Uccello's tiny, strange *Profanation of the Host.* The most intriguing room of the palace is the Duke's study on the second floor, where inlaid wooden panels give the illusion of real books and shelves covered with astronomical and musical instruments. Don't leave the palace without heading underground to see the well-documented "works" of the *palazzo.* This meandering maze includes the Duke's baths, kitchen, washroom, and freezer (entire palace open M 9am-2pm, Tu-Sa 9am-7pm, Su 9am-10pm). At the end of Via Barocci lies the 14th-century **Oratorio di San Giovanni Battista,** decorated with brightly colored Gothic frescoes representing events from the life of St. John. (Open M-Sa 10am-12:30pm and 3-5:30pm, Su 10am-12:30pm. L3000, but you will be obliged to see S. Giuseppe next door for another L2000.) **Raphael's house,** Via Raffaello 57, is now a vast and delightful museum with period furnishings. His earliest work, a fresco entitled *Madonna e Bambino,* hangs in the *sala* (open Mar.-Oct. M-Sa 9am-1pm and 3-7pm, Su 10am-1pm; L5000).

The SAPUM **bus** from Pesaro (on the main Bologna-Lecce line along the Adriatic coast) to Urbino is cheap and direct (1hr., L3700). After winding up steep hills, the bus will deposit you at Borgo Mercatale; a short uphill walk leads to **Piazza della Repubblica,** the city center. The **tourist office,** P. Rinascimento 1 (tel. 07 22 26 13; fax 07 22 24 41), across from the palace, dispenses a list of hotels and a map. (Open in summer M-Sa 9am-1pm and 3-6pm, Su 9am-1pm; off-season M-Sa 8:30am-2pm.)

Cheap lodging is rare in Urbino; reservations are key. **Pensione Fosca,** Via Raffaello 67 (tel. 07 22 32 96 22 or 07 22 25 42), has charming, high-ceilinged rooms (doubles L59,000). The **Hotel San Giovanni,** Via Barocci, 13 (tel. 07 22 28 27) has a restaurant downstairs (doubles L50,000-80,000; closed July). **Camping Pineta,** Via San Donato (tel./fax 07 22 47 10), is 2km from the city in Cesane; take bus 7 from Borgo Mercatale and tell the driver your destination (L9500 per person; L19,500 per tent; open Apr. to mid-Sept.). Many *paninoteche, gelaterie,* and burger joints cluster around P. della Repubblica. **Morgana,** Via Nuova 3 (open daily noon-3pm and 7pm-12:30am), and **Pizzeria Le Tre Piante,** Via Voltaccia della Vecchia 1, off Via Budassi (open daily noon-3pm and 7pm-2am), serve pizzas (L5000-10,000) and other dishes. A **Margherita** supermarket is at Via Raffaello 37 (open M-Sa 7:30am-2pm and 4:30-8pm). At night, drinkers and dancers pack **The Bosom Pub** on Via Budassi (no cover).

ADRIATIC PORTS

Ancona, Bari, and Brindisi—all on the Bologna-Lecce train line—are Italy's principal departure points for Greece, Cyprus, and Israel.

Ancona Ancona is the center point of Italy's Adriatic Coast—a major port in a small, whimsical, and largely unexplored city. **Piazza Roma** is dotted with yellow and pink buildings, and **Piazza Cavour** is the heart of the town. **Trains** arrive at P. Rosselli from Rome and all points along the Bologna-Lecce rail line. From the station, take bus 1 to P. Cavour (10min., L1200); from here, Corso Garibaldi and Corso Mazzini lead to the port. Detailed **ferry** schedules are available at the **Stazione Marittima,** on the waterfront just off P. Kennedy. All the ferry lines operate ticket and information booths. Make reservations for travel in July or August, and always arrive at the station at least two hours before departure. The main lines are: **Adriatica** (tel. 071 20 49 15; fax 071 20 22 96), **ANEK** (tel. 07 12 07 32 22; fax 07 15 46 08), **Jadrolinija** (tel. 071 20 45 16; fax 07 15 62 56), **Minoan/Strintzis** (tel. 071 20 17 08; fax 071 56 00 09), **SEM Maritime Co.** (tel. 07 15 52 18; fax 071 20 26 18), and **Superfast** (tel. 071 20 20 33; fax 071 20 22 19).

The ferry station closes with the last departure, so no sacking out on a bench, but you'll find many reasonably priced hotels around the train station and in the town center. Make reservations or arrive early in the summer. **Pensione Centrale,** Via Marsala 10 (tel. 07 15 43 88), one block from P. Roma, is a quick 10-minute stroll from the Stazione Marittima (singles L37,000; doubles L55,000, with bath L85,000). For hearty Italian fare, head to **Da Nando,** Via Calatafimi 2b, on the corner of P. Cavour and C. Mazzini (open M-Sa noon-3:30pm and 8-10:30pm). The supermarket **SIDIS,** Via Matteotti 115, offers the best grocery deals around (open M-W and F-Sa 8:15am-12:45pm and 5-7:30pm, Th 8:15am-12:45pm).

Bari While most tourists only stay in Bari long enough to buy a ferry ticket to Greece, Apulia's capital is a vibrant, modern city, home to a university, historic sights, and the world's most organized backpacker welcoming committee. **Stop-Over in Bari** (summer hotline tel. (080) 577 23 49) lures backpackers by doling out irresistible amounts of **free stuff,** including city bus passes, bicycle rentals, luggage storage, hotel bookings, campsites with tents and showers, excursions, concerts, and **Internet access.** At their **information bus** outside the train station, hip, multilingual gen-Xers will tell you everything known about city sights and attractions. Be careful of pickpockets and petty thieves; do not venture into the old city alone, especially at night. Bari is connected by **train** to Brindisi (2hr., L10,100), Milan (10hr., L80,000-90,000), and Rome (4½-6hr., L38,500-65,500). There are no discounts for Eurailpass holders, but **Ventouris Ferries** (tel. (080) 521 76 99) and **Marlines** (tel. 080 523 18 24; fax 523 02 87) have student rates.

To party in Bari, chat with the expat owners of **Bohémian,** Via de Napoli 17, a popular British pub, or enjoy Guinness stout on tap at **Joy's Shop,** C. Sonnino 118. Local students cram into **Largo Adua** and the other *piazze* along the Lungomare, where **Deco** serves American food and has live music. Most bars are open from around 8pm until 1 or 2am, 3am on Saturdays, and close down during the August holidays. Near Bari, **Alberobello's** famous *trulli* (mortarless conical roofs) and the spectacular **Castellana Grotte** are worth a daytrip (train to "Grotte di Castellana Grotte" 1hr.).

Brindisi Every year, about a million Eurailers get off the train at Brindisi, walk to the port, and catch a boat to Greece. If you're one of them, arrive in the afternoon, as the ferries leave in the evening. **Trains** arrive from Milan via Ancona and Bologna (12hr., L80,000), Naples (7hr., L31,000), and Rome via Barletta (7hr., L49,000). **Corso Umberto,** a frenetic jumble of ferry offices and tourist restaurants, runs 1km from the station to the port, becoming **Corso Garibaldi** midway. The *stazione marittima* is on the right at the end, the **tourist office** a block to the left, at Via Regina Margherita 5 (open M-F 8am-2pm, Tu also 3-6:30pm). Eurailers and InterRailers should go straight to **Adriatica,** Via Regina Margherita 13 (tel. (0831) 52 38 25) or **Hellenic Mediterranean Lines,** C. Garibaldi 8 (tel. (0831) 52 85 31). Both offer free deck passage on a space-available basis to Corfu (8hr.), Igoumenitsa (9hr.), and Patras (17hr.). At their offices on the main drag, pay the L29,000 **port tax** (Oct.-June 9 or with InterRail L10,000), pick up your ticket, and be sure to clear your passport with the police at the port before you leave. Don't be fooled by the signs; there are no official Eurail or InterRail offices in town. Non-Eurailers can buy tickets from one of the many competing lines—expect to pay L40,000-80,000. A **Sidis** supermarket sits on C. Garibaldi near the port. Deck passage is less appealing in the rain, so bring warm clothes or a sleeping bag and check the weather. During August, consider arriving early or buying a reservation in another city. Board the ferry two hours in advance.

Brindisi quiets down two blocks from the frenzied C. Garibaldi. A pleasant walk along the water to the left of C. Garibaldi leads to a staircase with a column marking the end of the **Appian way;** ascending the stairs and continuing straight takes you to P. del Duomo and Brindisi's **archaeological museum** (open daily 9:30am-1:30pm, M-F also 3:30-6:30pm; free). Or, call **Ostello della Gioventù** (tel. (0831) 41 31 23), 1km away in Casale, where you can get a room for the day (L9000). After they've picked you up, you can leave luggage, do laundry, nap, check email, and take the shuttle to the beach before getting a ride back to the port. Stay the night for L18,000 with breakfast and sheets. In town, try **Albergo Venezia,** Via Pisanelli (tel. (0831) 52 75 11; singles L25,000). **Pizzeria da Michele,** Via B. Giorgio 8, has traditional Apulian fare in casual atmosphere (open M-Sa noon-2:30pm and 5pm-midnight). If stuck in Brindisi, make a daytrip by train to **Lecce,** with its distinctive Baroque architecture made from soft local stone (30min., L3900).

SOUTHERN ITALY

South of Rome, the sun gets brighter, the meals longer, and the passions more intense. Though long subject to the negative stereotypes and prejudices of the more industrialized North, the so-called "Mezzogiorno" (midday) region remains justly proud of its open-hearted and generous populace, strong traditions, classical ruins, and enchanting, relatively untouristed beaches.

■ Naples (Napoli)

Naples has gotten a bad rap. True, mopeds race down sidewalks like they were streets, stoplights are taken as mere suggestions, and markets are mile-long hordes of shoppers and shouting merchants. Yet somehow the Neapolitans thrive on this chaos. The city has a palpable vitality; you can see it at the street markets off P. Dante, and taste it in the world's best pizza. If you're patient with Naples's rough edges, and there are many, you will be rewarded with great food, superb museums, and wonderful Renaissance and Baroque churches.

ORIENTATION AND PRACTICAL INFORMATION

Naples is on the west coast of Italy, two hours south of Rome. The main train and bus terminals cram immense **Piazza Garibaldi,** on the east side of Naples. Broad **Corso Umberto I** leads southwest ending at **Piazza Bovio.** From here Via De Pretis leads left to **Piazza Municipio,** the city center, and the **Molo Beverello** ferry port. **Via Toledo** (also called **Via Roma**) leads up from regal **Piazza Plebiscito** through the picturesque Spanish quarter to **Piazza Dante.** The narrow streets in the historical area between P. Garibaldi and Via Toledo—densely packed with *piazze,* churches, and monuments—are the best place to start a tour. Along the coast past P. Plebiscito, you'll find the **Santa Lucia** and **Mergellina** districts and the public gardens, **Villa Comunale.**

While violence is rare in Naples, petty theft is relatively common (unless you're in the mafia, in which case the opposite is true). Always be careful. Young women walking alone or in groups are harassed; travel in mixed company whenever possible.

Trains: FS (tel. 08 11 47 88 80 88). To: Brindisi (5hr., L34,500), Milan (8hr., L95,000), and Rome (2hr., L18,000). **Circumvesuviana** (tel. 08 17 72 24 44) runs to Herculaneum (L2200), Pompeii (L3100), and Sorrento (L4700).

Ferries: Caremar, Molo Beverello (tel. 08 15 51 38 82). To: Capri (1½hr., 5 per day, L9500) and Ischia (1½hr., 8 per day, L9500). **Tirrenia,** Molo Angioino (tel. 08 17 20 11 11). To: Cagliari (15 hr., 1-4 per week, L98,000, port tax L10,000) and Palermo (11hr., L80,500, port tax L10,000).

Public Transportation: L1500 ticket works for buses, Metropolitana (subway), trams, and funiculars; one-day pass L4500. R1, R2, R3, and R4 buses connect the center to Vomero, P. Garibaldi, Mergellina, and Capodimonte, respectively.

Tourist Office: EPT (tel. 081 26 87 79; fax 081 20 66 66), at the central train station. English spoken. Helps with hotels and ferries. Pick up *Qui Napoli* and a free city map. Open M-Sa 8am-8pm. **Main office,** P. Martiri 58 (tel. 081 40 53 11). Open M-Sa 8:30am-8pm, Su 8am-2pm. **AAST information office,** P. Gesù Nuovo (tel. 08 15 52 33 28), on the R1 bus line. Open M-Sa 9am-7pm, Su 9am-2pm.

Consulates: South Africa, Corse Umberto I (tel. 08 15 51 75 19). **U.K.,** Via Crispi 122 (tel. 081 66 35 11). Metro: P. Amedeo. Open M-F July-Aug. 8am-1:30pm; Sept.-June 9am-12:30pm and 2:30-4pm. **U.S.,** P. della Repubblica (tel. 08 15 83 81 11 or 08 17 61 43 03, 24hr. emergency 03 37 94 50 83). Open M-F 8am-5pm.

Currency Exchange: Thomas Cook, P. Municipo 70 (tel. 08 15 51 83 99), and at the airport, has decent rates. Open M-F 9:30am-1pm and 3-6:30pm.

Emergencies: tel. 113. **Ambulance,** tel. 08 17 52 06 96. **Hospital, Cardarelli** (tel. 08 17 47 11 11), north of town on the R4 bus line.

Police: tel. 113 or 08 17 94 11 11. English speakers always available.

Post Office: P. Matteotti (tel. 08 15 51 14 56), on Via Diaz (R2 line). Also in Galleria Umberto and Stazione Centrale. Notoriously unreliable *Fermo Posta* L1500. P. Matteotti office open M-F 8:15am-6pm, Sa 8:15am-noon. **Postal Code:** 80100.

Internet Access: Internet Cafe, Via Giancardo Tramontano 12. M-F L5000 per hr. until 8pm; L7000 after 8pm; Sa-Su L10,000. Open M-Sa 10:30am-1am, Su 8pm-3am.

ACCOMMODATIONS AND FOOD

The shoddy area around P. Garibaldi is packed with hotels; many solicit customers at the station. Following a hawker is usually safe as long as you don't give up your passport before seeing the room and you always agree on a price before unpacking. Try bargaining. The **ACISJF/Centro D'Ascolto** (tel. 081 28 19 93), at the Stazione Centrale, helps women find safe, inexpensive rooms (open M, Tu, and Th 3:30-6:30pm).

Ostello Mergellina (HI), Salita della Grotta 23 (tel. 08 17 61 23 46; fax 08 17 61 63 91). Make two sharp rights onto Via Piedigrotta from M: Mergellina. Turn left on via Salita della Grotta, then right into the long driveway just after the overpass. The 2-, 4-, and 6-bed rooms are well maintained but vary in quality. Dorms L22,000; doubles L52,000. Lockout 9am-3pm. Curfew 12:30am.

Casanova Hotel, Via Venezia 2 (tel./fax 081 26 82 87). Take Via Milano from P. Garibaldi and turn left at its end. Clean, airy rooms and a rooftop terrace. Singles L30,000; doubles L55,000, with bath L69,000-80,000. 10% *Let's Go* discount.

Hotel Eden, Corso Novara 9 (tel. 081 28 53 44), down the street to the right of the station. Well-maintained rooms on a noisy thoroughfare. Singles L42,000; doubles L66,000; triples L90,000; quads L104,000. All with bath. 20% *Let's Go* discount.

Soggiorno Imperia, P. Miraglia 386 (tel. 081 45 93 47). Take the R2 from the station, walk up Via Mezzocannone through P. San Domenico Maggiore, and look for the first set of large green doors to the left. Bright rooms in a 16th-century *palazzo*. Singles L30,000; doubles L50,000. Call 1-2 days in advance July-Aug. and Easter.

Hotel Ideal, P. Garibaldi 99 (tel. 081 26 92 37 or 081 20 22 23), to the left of the station. Well-furnished rooms are modern and secure. Singles L40,000-50,000; doubles L60,000, with bath L90,000. Breakfast included.

Pizza-making is an art born in Naples. **Antica Pizzeria da Michele,** nine blocks to the right off C. Umberto from P. Garibaldi, is one of the city's most traditional pizzerias (open M-Sa 8am-11pm). *Pizza margherita* (L5000), the most common pizza in Italy, was invented in 1889 at **Pizzeria Brandi,** Salita S. Anna di Palazzo 1 (open daily noon-3pm and 7pm-midnight). **Pizzeria Di Matteo,** Via Tribunali 94, has bred a cult of aficionados (open M-Sa 9am-midnight). Try the large and innovative selections at **Pizzeria Trianon da Ciro,** Via Pietro Colletta 42/46 (open daily 10am-4:30pm and 6:30pm-midnight), or let the 21 Sorbillo children cook you the cheapest pizza in town at **Pizzeria Sorbillo,** Via dei Tribunali 35. If you tire of pizza, head to the **Piazza Amadeo** and explore the side streets for alternatives.

SIGHTS AND ENTERTAINMENT

Although the unpleasant region around the train station is often disheartening for visitors, much of Naples is beautiful, interesting, and friendly. The renowned **Museo Archeologico Nazionale,** near M: "Cavour," houses a stunning collection of mosaics, frescoes, and jewelry excavated from Pompeii and Herculaneum. Look for the tender *Portrait of a Woman,* and the famous wall-sized Alexander Mosaic, which portrays a young and fearless Alexander routing the Persians (open M and W-Sa 10am-10pm, Su 8am-8pm; L12,000, EU citizens free). Take buses R4, 24, or 110 to the **Museo e Gallerie di Capodimonte,** a newly restored museum in an 18th-century royal palace in the northern hills (open Tu-Sa 10am-10pm, Su 8am-8pm; L9500). You can also tour the Royal Apartments and the San Carlo Theater in the **Palazzo Reale,** commissioned by the Bourbon King Charles III to imitate Versailles (open M-Tu and Th-Sa 9:30am-10pm, Su 9:30am-8pm; L8000). Next door, the massive **Castel Nuevo** contains the impressive **Museo Civico,** which displays paintings of Neapolitan history of the nativity and crucifixion (open M-Sa 9am-6pm; L10,000). Up the funicular to Voremo's villas, the **Museo Nazionale di San Martino** documents the art, history, and life of 16th-century Naples (open Tu-Su 9am-2pm; L9500, EU citizens free), while the parks of **Villa Floridiana** are on a hill overlooking the bay.

Walk along the bay in the late afternoon or early evening to see the **Villa Comunale,** a waterfront park with the oldest aquarium in Europe, fill with locals taking their *passeggiata.* To the west, the hills of Posillipoto offer nicer walks. A fascinating alternative is to see Naples from beneath; **LAES** (tel. 081 40 02 56) offers subterranean tours on weekend mornings (L10,000, foreign language tours L100,000 extra).

The hippest downtown area is **Piazza Bellini,** near P. Dante. The small streets off **Piazza Amedeo** also beckon with nightlife and a night bus returning to P. Garibaldi after the Metro stops running. The city's hotspots include **Camelot,** Via Petrarca 101; **Chez Moi,** Parco Margherita 13 (Metro: P. Amedeo); and the larger **Madison Street,** Via Sgambati 47, in Voremo. They feature dancing Friday through Sunday starting at 10pm and charge a L25,000-30,000 cover (Camelot closed Su). **ARCI-Gay/Lesbica** (tel. 08 15 51 82 93) has free info on gay and lesbian goings-on about town.

■ Near Naples: Pompeii and Herculaneum

Immense **Mount Vesuvius,** the only active volcano on the European continent, looms over the area east of Naples. Its infamous eruption in 79 AD buried the nearby Roman city of Herculaneum (Ercolano) in mud, and its neighbor Pompeii (Pompei) in ashes. Excavations, beginning in 1784, have unearthed a stunningly well-preserved picture of Roman daily life. The frescoed houses, colonnaded forum, wide roads, and small brothels haven't changed much since then. Neither have the victims, some of whose ghastly remains were preserved by plaster casts in the hardened ash.

Take the Circumvesuviana **train** from Naples, Salerno, or Sorrento to the **"Pompeii Scavi"** station (about L3000; Eurail not valid). To reach the archaeological site, head downhill and take your first left to the west (Porta Marina) entrance. Guided tours are expensive, but some sneaky folks have been known to successfully freeload. Otherwise, pick up one of the **guidebooks** (L8000-20,000) at the entrance and a free **map** of the site at the **tourist office** at the bottom of the hill outside the western entrance. Pack a lunch and a water bottle, as the cafeteria is expensive.

At the Porta Marina entrance to your right, the **basilica** (law court) walls are decorated with stucco to imitate marble. Walk farther to reach the **Forum,** which is surrounded by a colonnade. Once dotted with statues of emperors and gods, this site was the commercial, civic, and religious center of the city. Showcases along the near-side display some of the gruesome body casts of the volcano's victims. At the **Forum Baths** on Via di Terme, parts of the body casts here have chipped away to reveal the teeth and bones underneath. The **House of the Vettii** is home to some of the most vivid frescoes in Pompeii. The vestibule contains a depiction of Priapus (the god of fertility) displaying his colossal member. Phalli were believed to scare off evil spirits in ancient times, but now they seem only to invite hordes of tittering tourists. On Vico di Vetti, there is a small **brothel** with several bed-stalls. Above each of the stalls a pornographic painting depicts with unabashed precision the specialty of the stall's occupant (or so archaeologists fantasize). The **amphitheater,** the oldest in the world still standing (80 BC), held 12,000 spectators. (Entrances to Pompeii open daily 9am until 1hr. before sunset; June-July until 7pm; Nov.-Dec. until 3pm. L12,000.)

Herculaneum is 500m downhill of the Ercolano stop on the Circumvesuviana Line (20min. from Naples). Stop at the **tourist office** on the way for a free **map.** Less of the city has been excavated, but the 15 or so houses open to the public were so neatly dug up that the tour feels like an invasion of privacy (L12,000).

■ Amalfi Coast

The bold, arresting bluffs and picturesque towns scattered into the ravines of the **Amalfi coast** merit every tourist brochure superlative. A calm sea, delicious seafood, and sumptuous fruits temper the rugged shore, while the tiny towns exude rustic character. The mountains above the peninsula are wonderful for **hiking** expeditions inland and between towns; pick up the *Club Alpino Italiano* map. **Trains** connect Naples to Sorrento on the northwestern side of the peninsula (1hr., L4700) and Salerno at its southeastern base (1hr., L5000), but the coastal towns can only be reached by ferry or a more tortuous (and torturous) bus ride. The **SITA bus** (tel. 089 22 66 04) runs from Corso Garibaldi 117 in Salerno to the Circumvesuviana station in Sorrento and back, stopping in Vietri, Maiori, Minori, Atrani, Amalfi, Praiano, and Positano. A bus to inland Ravello runs from Amalfi. Buy tickets at the *tabac*, and don't go after lunch. Frequent, inexpensive **ferries** connect Salerno, Amalfi, Positano, and Sorrento.

Paestum

Paestum Forty-five minutes south of Salerno by train (L4700), **Paestum** boasts three spectacularly preserved Doric temples and rare examples of Greek wall painting. Once a flourishing mercantile center, epidemics and attacks forced out its population by the 10th century, and the ruins have been lying in the grass ever since (ruins L8000, museum L8000).

Salerno, Vietri sul Mare, Maiori, and Minori

Salerno, Vietri sul Mare, Maiori, and Minori Industrial **Salerno** has few worthwhile sights, but it's a good base for daytime excursions to nearby towns. Pick up a map and the *MEMO* entertainment guide at the **tourist office** in the *piazza* outside the station (tel. (089) 23 14 32). The **Ostello della Gioventù "Irno" (HI),** Via Luigi Guercio 112 (tel. (089) 79 02 51), is the cheapest sleep in town (L17,500 with breakfast and sheets). Closer to the station, **Albergo Santa Rosa,** C. Vittorio Emanuele 14 (tel. (089) 25 53 46), is a safe *pensione* with a grandmotherly proprietor (singles L42,000; doubles L65,000). Head to the restaurant row on the western end of Via Roma for **food,** or check your email at **Mailboxes, Etc.,** Via Diaz 19 (tel. (089) 23 12 95). West of Salerno, **Vietri sul Mare** is a charming seaside resort. **Maiori's** half-mile beach partly makes up for its ugly postwar concrete, while nearby **Minori** has a smaller beach and generic family atmosphere.

Amalfi and Atrani

Amalfi and Atrani Snuggled into a small coastal ravine, **Amalfi** exudes noise and chaos worthy of a city many times its size. Visitors indulge in swims off its pebbly beach, strolls on bayside promenades, forays into the hills of the surrounding coast, and visits to the elegant, Moorish-influenced 9th-century **duomo,** rebuilt in the 19th century. **A'Scalinatella,** P. Umberto 12 (tel. 089 87 19 30 or 089 87 14 92), lets hostel beds and regular rooms in both Atrani and Amalfi (dorms L20,000-40,000; doubles L80,000-100,000; camping L15,000 per person). The cheapest double runs L55,000 at **Pensione Proto** (tel. (089) 87 10 03). **Trattoria La Perla,** Salita Truglio 5, is the place to eat. A 10-minute walk around the bend from Amalfi is **Atrani,** a tiny ravine town which tourism hasn't changed a bit. Look into the many spectacular **hikes** that lead up from Amalfi and Atrani through lemon groves and across mountain streams.

Ravello

Ravello Capping a promontory 1000 feet above Amalfi, **Ravello** is an ideal spot for quiet contemplation or an afternoon stroll. Its tranquil setting and exquisite gardens have attracted a long list of great writers and celebrities. The Moorish cloister and meandering gardens of **Villa Rudolfo** (off P. Duomo), inspired Boccaccio's *Decameron* and Wagner's *Parsifal* (open 9am-sunset; L5000). On the small road passing to the right, signposts lead to the more impressive **Villa Cimbrone.** Its floral walkways and gardens hide temples and statued grottos. Ravello hosts numerous acclaimed classical **music festivals,** shattering the tranquility with pompous Wagnerian operatics. The two-hour **hike** up to Ravello from Amalfi is spectacular, but a **bus** carries the weary and lazy (20min., L1700). With bath, balcony, and breakfast, the best rooms are at **Villa Amore** (tel. (089) 85 71 35; doubles L115,000).

Praiano

Praiano Halfway between Amalfi and Positano, **Praiano** is a small residential community with hearty food and an active nightlife. Enjoy the panorama from the campground **Villaggio La Tranquillità** and the **Hotel Continental,** Via Roma 10 (tel. 089 87 40 84; fax 089 87 47 79), on the road to Amalfi. (Ask the bus driver to stop at the Ristorante Continenta. Camping L35,000 for one; L50,000 for two. With *Let's Go,* renovated singles and new bungalows are L75,000; doubles L100,000-120,000.) Around the bend towards Amalfi is **Marina di Praia,** a 400-year-old fishing village turned local hot spot. At **Africana,** fish swim under the glass dance floor as the nightly live music echoes off the dimly lit cave above (cover L25,000; women free on W). Farther on, the SITA **bus** services the spectacular **Grotto dello Smeraldo** (Emerald Grotto), which rivals Capri's azure equivalent (open daily 10am-4pm; L5000).

Positano The idyllic setting, cliffside homes, and idiosyncratic locals of **Positano** began to lure writers, artists, painters, and actors in the beginning of the century. Soon afterwards, its artsy cachet made it a popular destination for high rollers. It's best enjoyed by those who have money to throw around, but budget travelers can also rub elbows with the jet set here. Positano's nearby majestic mountains are good for **hiking,** its sandy beaches are always crowded, and its window shopping is almost as satisfying as the real thing. The **tourist office** (tel. (089) 87 50 67), in the reddish building below the *duomo,* has maps and accommodations info. **Pensione Maria Luisa,** Via Fornillio 40 (tel. (089) 87 50 23), has seaside terraces and the jolliest owner in Italy (singles L50,000; doubles L80,000-90,000). **Casa Guadagno** (tel. (089) 87 50 42), next door, earns praise for spotless rooms and sublime views (with *Let's Go,* doubles L100,000-110,000). Take the local bus and ask to be let off at either hotel. The **Music on the Rocks** disco off Spiaggia Grande is expensive but classy … dude.

Sorrento The largest, most touristy town on the peninsula, **Sorrento** is charming despite its reputation as a retirement home for Neapolitan grandparents. The old town is lively and a convenient base for daytrips around the Bay of Naples. Caremar **ferries** (tel. 08 18 07 30 77) go to Capri (L6200), and a local bus shuttles between P. Tasso and the port. **Ostello Le Sirene,** Via degli Aranci 160 (tel. 08 18 07 29 25), has clean, six-bed rooms right behind the train station (L25,000; breakfast and sheets included). Halfway to the free beach at Punta del Capo on the "A" bus, **Hotel Elios,** Via Capo 33 (tel. (081) 878 18 12), has clean rooms in a tranquil area (singles L35,000; doubles L70,000). **Terlizzi,** C. Italia 30, is the only **laundromat** in the area (L15,000 per load). Good, affordable food is easy to find in Sorrento. At **Ristorante Giardiniello,** Via Accademia 7, off Via Giuliani, Mamma Luisa's *gnocchi* are served in a peaceful garden (cover L1500; open June-Sept. daily 11am-2am, off-season closed Th). **Taverna Azzura,** Via Marina Grande 166, along the fisherman's wharf, has fresh seafood and pasta cooked to perfection (cover L2500; open daily noon-3pm and 7pm-midnight). Off C. Italia two blocks from P. Tasso, **Davide,** Via Giuliani 39, makes divine gelato and masterful mousse (55-80 flavors daily). At night, a crowd gathers upstairs in the rooftop lemon grove above **The English Inn,** C. Italia 56.

■ Bay of Naples Islands

Capri The sheer bluffs, divine landscapes, and azure waters of **Capri** have beckoned wayfarers from the Italian mainland since Imperial times. **Capri town** is above the ports, while **Anacapri** sits higher up the mountain. From P. Umberto in Capri Town, Via Roma leads up to Anacapri; buses also make the trip. The **Grotta Azzurra** (Blue Grotto) is a must-see—light enters the cavern though a hole in the rock under the water, causing the whole grotto to glow a fantastic neon blue. The blue light is best seen from 11am-3pm on sunny days (closed Nov.-Mar. and in bad weather). Take the bus from Capri to Anacapri and a second bus to the Grotto (L1500). An unfortunate ban on swimming into the grotto ensures fat profits for Caprisian boat tours (L16,000 plus tip). Up the stairs from P. Vittoria in Anacapri, **Villa San Michele** has lush gardens and a remarkable view of the island (open daily in summer 9am-6pm; in winter 10:30am-3:30pm; L6000). To appreciate Capri's Mediterranean beauty from higher ground, take the **chairlift** up Monte Solaro from P. Vittoria (round-trip L7500; may be closed for repairs until spring 1999). Alternately, take Via Longano from P. Umberto in Capri Town and make the trek up to the left on Via Tiberio to **Villa Jovis** (1hr.), the most magnificent of the 12 villas that the emperor Tiberius scattered throughout Italy (open daily 9am to 1hr. before sunset; L4000).

Caremar **ferries** run from Naples' Beverello port (5 per day, L9500); **Alilauro** services Ischia (2 per day, L20,000) and the Amalfi coast; both run from Sorrento (9 per day, L6000). **Hydrofoils** are faster, costlier, and run longer hours. **Tourist offices** are located on the dock (tel. 08 18 37 06 34) and in P. Umberto (tel. 08 18 37 06 86) in Capri; also at Via Orlandi 19a (tel. (081) 837 15 24) in Anacapri, to the right from the P. Vittoria bus stop (all open M-Sa 9am-1:30pm and 3:30-6:45pm; June-Sept. 8:30am-8:30pm). With its luxurious gardens, elegant pool, and beautiful rooms, **Villa Eva,** Via della Fabbrica 8 (tel. 08 18 37 15 49 or 08 18 37 20 40), in Anacapri, is the island paradise you came for. Call from the dock, then take the bus to P. Vittoria and wait for Eva's car (L30,000-35,000; reserve early and confirm often; open Mar.-Nov. 15). **Il Girasole** (tel. 08 18 37 23 51; L40,000 per person), in Anacapri, has a comfortable terrace, a pool, and **Internet access.** Also in Anacapri, the deluxe **Hotel Caesar Augustus,** Via Orlandi 4 (tel. 08 18 37 14 21), has a spectacular view (singles L60,000, with view L80,000; doubles L80,000 and L120,000). **Pensione Stella Maris,** Via Roma 27 (tel. 08 18 37 04 52), is Capri's cheapest (singles with bath L50,000-70,000; doubles from L80,000). Elegant yet affordable **Buca di Bacco,** Via Longano 35, has incredible *pennette alla bacco* (L10,000). **Il Grottino Ristorante,** Via G. Orlandi 95, a few blocks from P. Vittoria, has delicious *ravioli alla caprese,* a local specialty (L13,000; cover L2000). Dine in style in Anacapri at **Ristorante Il Cucciolo,** Via Fabbrica 52, on the way to the Grotta Azzurra (cover L3000; *Let's Go* discounts). At night, droves of beautiful, dressed-to-kill Italians come out for Capri's *passegiatta,* and the pricey bars and discos lining the streets around P. Umberto keep the music pumping late. **Buses** return to Anacapri until 1:40am, and **taxis** are reasonable.

Ischia Across the bay from overrun Capri, larger, less glamorous Ischia (EES-kee-yah) offers a variety of landscapes, including beautiful beaches, natural hot springs, ruins, forests, and vineyards. Buses 1, CD, and CS follow the coast in a counterclockwise direction from **Ischia Porto,** a port formed by the crater of an extinct volcano. Along the way, you can stop at **Casamicciola Terme,** with its overcrowded beach and legendary thermal waters, or **Lacco Ameno,** the oldest Greek settlement in the Mediterranean, now known for the island's cleanest boardwalk. The bus continues to **Forio,** the hippest area on Ischia, thanks to its tree-lined streets and popular bars.

Caremar **ferries** (tel. 081 98 48 18) arrive from Naples (L18,000). **Linee Lauro** (tel. 081 99 18 88) runs from Sorrento to Ischia (L18,000) and connects the island to Capri with a **hydrofoil** (1 per day, L20,000). SEPSA **buses** run from P. Trieste (one-way tickets L1700, full-day L5000). Stay in Ischia Porto only if you want to be close to the ferries—most *pensioni* are in Forio. The floral **Pensione Di Lustro,** Via Filippo di Lustro 9 (tel. 081 99 71 63), for instance, is just a short walk from the beach (doubles with bath June L90,000; July-Aug. L110,000; Oct.-Mar. L80,000). In Ischia Porto, the **Albergo A. Macri,** Via Iasolino 96 (tel. 081 99 26 03), is on a quiet side street (singles L30,000-38,000; doubles L55,000-65,000; higher prices July-Sept.). **Eurocamping dei Pini** is at Via delle Ginestre 28 (tel. 081 98 20 69), 20 minutes from the port. Take Via del Porto to Via Alfredo de Luca, walk uphill, turn right on Via delle Terme, and follow the arrow (L12,000 per person, L7000 per tent).

SICILY (SICILIA)

Every great Mediterranean civilization of the past 2500 years has left its mark on Sicily: the ancient Greeks scattered temples and theaters; the Romans, bridges and aqueducts; the Saracens, mosques and towers; and the Normans, churches and castles. Sicilians, however, don't revel in their island's traditions. Today, they speed unchecked toward the future, installing condom-vending machines in front of medieval cathedrals and demonstrating against their most well known institution, the Mafia. The tempestuousness of Sicilian history and political life is matched only by the island's dramatic landscapes and climate. The countryside is dominated by sheer, rock-strewn crags, and Europe's highest volcano, Mt. Etna, serves as an uneasy reminder that Sicily rests on the edge of the European geologic plate.

La Famiglia

Pin-striped suits, machine guns, horse heads, and the Godfather are a far cry from the reality of the Sicilian Mafia. The system has its roots in the *latifondi* (agricultural estates) of rural Sicily, where land managers and salaried militiamen (a.k.a. landlords and bouncers) protected their turf and people. Powerful because people owed them favors, strong because they supported one another, and feared because they did not hesitate to kill offenders, they founded a tradition that has dominated Sicilian life since the late 19th century. Since the mid-80s, the Italian government has worked to curtail Mafia influence, with visible results. Today Sicilians shy away from any Mafia discussion, referring to the system as *Cosa Nostra* (our thing). Unfortunately, "their thing" expanded to include a rigid structure of national politics, drug-smuggling, and assassination. But hey, *Ch' t' le dich'à fa'*.

· **Tirrenia,** in Palermo (tel. 091 33 33 00), the largest private ferry service in Italy, is the most extensive and reliable, though you should still beware the summer tourist rush and strikes. Tickets can often be purchased at travel agencies, either in foreign countries or within Italy. Prices and schedules vary according to specific dates; approximations are given below. From Rome, first take a train to Reggio di Calabria on the southern tip of Italy, and then the ferry to Messina on Sicily's northeast coast (ferry L5000). Ferries also offer direct service to Palermo from Caligari (14hr., L29,000-69,500) and Naples (11hr., L51,700-80,500). Call Tirrenia for departure times and other routes. Once on the island, **Cuffaro, SAIS,** and **Segesta** serve many destinations inaccessible by train. Expect delays and confusion. **Hitchhiking** is difficult and very risky, especially for long trips.

■ Palermo

As Sicily's capital, Palermo is notorious as the cradle of Italian organized crime. Since the election of Palermo's first avowedly anti-mafia mayor in 1993, however, the city has begun cleaning up its politics and revitalizing its historic district, much of which was destroyed in World War II. Although Palermo has its share of sketchy neighborhoods, it is also sports the attractions of a modern metropolis.

Venturing from the Quattro Canti onto Corso Vittorio Emanuele, heading away from the harbor, you will confront the striking exuberance of Palermo's **Church of San Cataldo.** Begun by the Normans in 1185, it absorbed elements of every architectural style from the 13th through 18th centuries (open M-F 9:30am-1pm, Su 8:30am-1pm). Nearby, the **Palazzo dei Normanni** contains the **Cappella Palatina,** which features a carved wooden stalactite ceiling and an outstanding cycle of golden Byzantine mosaics. Perhaps the most romantic spot in Palermo is the garden of the **Church of San Giovanni degli Eremiti,** Via dei Benedettini 3, with fountains, vines, and stone archways. To get there from the station, take bus 122 and get off before P. Indipendenza (open M-F 9am-1pm and 3-7pm, Su 9am-12:30pm; L4000).

The **tourist office,** P. Castelnuovo 34 (tel. 09 16 05 83 51 or 09 16 05 81 11), is 2km up Via Maqueda; turn right on Via Maqueda from the station or take bus 101 or 107 going toward Teatro Politeama (open M-F 8:30am-2pm and 3-6pm, Sa 8am-2pm). **Hotel Luigi,** Salita Santa Caterina 1 (tel. 091 58 50 85), is well located and has simple rooms (singles L30,000-40,000; doubles L50,000-60,000). **Hotel Lampedusa,** Via Roma 111 (tel./fax 09 16 17 14 09), has great prices on the main drag (singles L40,000-50,000; doubles L60,000-70,000). The quiet and clean **Petit Hotel,** Via Principe di Belmonte 84 (tel. 091 32 36 16), is to the left off Via Roma, three blocks after Via Cavour from the station (singles L35,000; doubles L60,000). Camp at **Trinacria,** Via Barcarello 25 (tel. (091) 53 05 90); take bus 101 to "Gasperifour Teatro Politeama," then 628 to "Sferracavallo" (L7000-8000 per person and per tent).

Palermo is famous for its *pasta con le sarde* (with sardines and fennel) and *rigatoni alla palermitana* (with a sauce of meat and peas). At **Lo Sparviero,** Via Sperlinga 23, trust the amicable staff for their suggestions on the *pasta del giorno* (open daily 11am-2pm and 7:30-midnight). The 92-year-old **Osterio Lo Bianco,** Via E. Amari 104, off Via Roma heading toward the port, has delectable fare (*calamari* L9000; pasta from L5000; open M-Sa noon-3pm and 7-10pm).

■ Near Palermo

About 10km southwest of Palermo, **Monreale's** magnificent Norman-Saracen cathedral, **Santa Maria la Nuova** (c. 1174), was the largest cathedral in Europe at the time of its construction. The church features incredible mosaics and intricate arches, and the **cloister** next door houses a renowned collection of Sicilian sculpture. (Cathedral open daily 8am-noon and 3:30-6pm. Cloister open July-Sept. M, W, and F 9am-1pm and 3-6pm, Tu, Th, Sa 9am-1pm, Su 9am-12:30pm; Oct.-June ask at cathedral. Cloister L4000.) **Buses** 389 and 309 drive here from Palermo's P. Indipendenza.

An hour from Palermo by train (L5700), **Cefalù** guards a cache of Arab, Norman, and medieval architecture. In P. Duomo off Corso Ruggero you'll find the town's 11th-century Norman **cathedral.** Inside, 16 Byzantine and Roman columns support superb capitals, and the elegant horseshoe arches exemplify the Saracen influence on Norman architecture in Sicily (open 8:30am-noon and 3:30-6:30pm; proper dress required). For a bird's-eye view of the city, make the 30-minute haul up the **Rocca** by way of the Salita Saraceni, which begins near P. Garibaldi off Corso Ruggero. Follow the brown signs for *"pedonale Rocca."* On the mountain, ancient walls and crumbling cisterns lead to the **Tempio di Diana,** dating from the 4th century BC. The **tourist office,** C. Ruggero 77 (tel. 092 12 10 50; fax 092 12 23 86), in the old city, has maps and finds rooms. (Open June-Sept. M-Sa 8am-8:30pm, Su 8am-2pm; Oct.-May M-F 8am-2pm and 4-7pm, Sa 8am-2pm.)

■ Agrigento

Among Sicily's classical remains, the **Valle di Templi** at Agrigento shares top honors with those at Syracuse. Take bus 1, 2, or 2/ from the train station (L1000) and ask to be dropped off. The **Tempio della Concordia,** one of the world's best-preserved Greek temples, owes its survival to consecration by St. Gregory of the Turnips. Uphill from the ruins, the **Museo Nazionale Archeologico di San Nicola** contains a notable collection of artifacts, especially vases from central Sicily (open M-Sa 8am-12:30pm; L8000). Revisit modern fashion and convenience at the **centro storico,** a cobblestone web of welcoming streets and shops.

Trains arrive from Palermo (1½hr., L11,500). The swanky staff at the **tourist office,** Via Battista 13, left off Via Atenea, will outfit you with maps and brochures (open in summer daily 8:30am-1:30pm and 5:30-7:30pm). **Hotel Bella Napoli,** P. Lena 6 (tel./fax 092 22 04 35 or 092 22 05 92), off Via Bac Bac, has a terrace overlooking the valley (singles L25,000-40,000; doubles L55,000-75,000). Take your first left off Via Imera and follow signs up the hill to **Hotel Concordia,** Via San Francesco 11 (tel. 09 22 59 62 66; singles L30,000-35,000; doubles L60,000-70,000). **Trattoria Atenea,** Via Ficani 32, the fourth right off Via Atenea from P. Moro, has a quiet courtyard and seafood offerings (*calamari* L9000; open M-Sa noon-3pm and 7pm-midnight).

▒ Syracuse (Siracusa)

Founded in 734 BC by Greeks who fancied the splendid harbor, ancient Syracuse cultivated such luminaries as Pindar, Archimedes, and Theocritus. The city just hasn't been the same since the Romans sacked it in 211 BC, but several ancient monuments still remain. Cross the bridge on Corso Umberto to the island of **Ortigia** to pay homage to the Temples of **Apollo** and **Athena.** The latter, now part of the city's cathedral, has a richly embellished facade added in the 18th century. From P. del Duomo, a trip down Via Picherale leads to the ancient **Fonte Aretusa,** a freshwater spring by the sea. Syracuse's larger monuments are in or near the **Archaeological Park** on the north side of town; follow Corso Gelone until it meets Viale Teocrito, then walk down Via Augusto to the left (open daily 9am-2hr. before sunset; L4000). The park contains an enormous ancient **Greek theater** where Aeschylus premiered his *Persians*. Check out the **Orecchio di Dionigi** (Ear of Dionysius), a giant artificial grotto with exceptional acoustics and an earlobe-shaped entrance. The tyrant Dionysius reputedly put all his prisoners here so he could eavesdrop on their conversations. Nearby, the **Altar of Hieron II** (241-215 BC) is the largest known altar, while the **Roman amphitheater,** constructed in the 2nd century AD, is stunningly well-preserved. If you prefer tans to temples, bus the 18km to **Fontane Bianche** (bus 21, 22, or 24; L600), a silken beach frequented by the jet-set.

Trains arrive from Messina (4hr., L15,500) and Taormina (2¼hr., L12,700), while **buses** pull into town from Palermo (4hr., L20,000, round-trip L30,000). Near the **Catacombe di San Giovanni** (open daily Mar. 15-Nov. 14 9am-12:30pm and 2-5pm; Nov. 15-Mar. 14 9am-1pm; L4000), the **tourist office,** Via San Sebastiano 43 (tel. 09 31 46 14 77), distributes maps and brochures (open M-Sa 8:30am-1:30pm and 3:30-6:30pm). Solo travelers should be wary of the train station area at night. **Pensione Bel Sit,** Via Oglio 5 (tel. 093 16 02 45), is close to the train station and has modern, basic rooms (singles L35,000-40,000; doubles L45,000-55,000). **Hotel Milano,** C. Umberto I 10 (tel. 09 36 69 81), has well-kept rooms (singles L30,000-50,000; doubles L55,000-80,000). Budget eateries center on Ortigia, or try the **market** on Via Trento, near the Temple of Apollo (open M-Sa 8am-early afternoon). For grub, try the **Linguanti** supermarket, C. Umberto I 174 (open M-Tu and Th-Sa 5:30am-8:30pm, W 5:30am-1:30pm). **Spaghetteria do Scugghiu,** Via D. Sciná 11, off P. Archimede, serves up 18 delicious kinds of spaghetti (most L7000; open Tu-Su noon-3pm and 5pm-midnight).

■ Taormina

A cliff-top of mansions, pine trees, and flowers, leaning over a hazy blue coastline, Taormina is a city of unsurpassed beauty. The 3rd-century **Greek theater,** at the very edge of the cliff, is one of the most dramatic spots in Italy. To get there, walk up Via Teatro Greco, off C. Umberto I at P. Vittorio Emanuele (open daily 9am-sunset; L4000). On the other side of P. Vittorio Emanuele, the Church of Santa Caterina hides the small **Roman Odeon** theater. Walk down Via di Giovanni and follow the signs for a momentary escape among the sculpted hedges of the **Villa Comunale's** English garden. A short trip away lies **Gole Alcantara,** a haven of gorgeous gorges, freezing waterfalls, and crystal rapids (your camera will need a waterproof bag). SAIS runs 6 **buses** there, but only one back, at 2pm (round-trip L8500).

Reach Taormina by **bus** from Catania or Messina (L5000-6000). **Trains** are more frequent and only L4700, but the train station is far below town with access controlled by buses (L2000) that make the climb every 15 minutes until 10:20pm. A helpful and well-organized **tourist office** waits on P. Santa Caterina (tel. (0942) 232 43; fax 249 41), in Palazzo Corvaia off C. Umberto (open M-Sa 8am-2pm and 4-7pm; July-Aug. also on Su). Accommodations can be hard to come by in August, so call ahead in July. **Villa Pompei,** Via Bagnoli Croci 88 (tel. (0942) 238 12), overlooks the public gardens (singles L35,000; doubles L52,000-60,000). **Pensione Svizzera,** Via Pirandello 26 (tel. (0942) 237 90), has gorgeous views of the coastline and impressively clean rooms (singles L65,000; doubles 110,000-120,000; open Feb.-Nov.). Dining can be expensive; consider stocking up at the **STANDA supermarket,** Via Apollo Arcageta 49, at the end of C. Umberto (open M-Sa 8:30am-1pm and 5-9pm). The sign in front of **Trattoria da Nino,** Via Pirandello 37, reads "Stop, you have found the best homemade cooking and pasta in Taormina." It may well be correct (open daily 11:30am-3pm and 6:30-11:30pm; in winter closed F).

■ Aeolian Islands (Isole Eolie)

Home of the wind god Aeolus and the Sirens, the Aeolian (or Lipari) Islands, with their fiery volcanos and long, rocky beaches, comprise one of the last areas of unspoiled seashore in Italy. To reach the archipelago from Sicily, first travel to the town of **Milazzo** on the Messina-Palermo train line (from Messina 40min., L5400;

from Palermo 3hr., L15,500). From the Milazzo train station, take the orange AST bus to the port (L600). From there, **Siremar** (tel. 09 09 28 32 42) and **Navigazione Generale Italiana (NGI)** (tel./fax 09 09 28 34 15) run reliable ferries to the islands. The increasingly popular **hydrofoils** make the trip in half the time but cost twice as much.

Lipari On **Lipari,** the largest and most developed of the islands, pastel-colored houses dot a small promontory crowned by the walls of a medieval *castello,* the site of an ancient Greek acropolis. Many of the artifacts found here decorate the exterior of the superb **Museo Archeologico Eoliano,** in the two buildings flanking the cathedral. (Open M-Sa 9am-2pm and 4-7pm, Su 9am-1pm and 4-7pm; last entrance 30min. before closing. Free.) Farther from town, the island features everything from nude beaches to churches to pumice mines; rent a bike or moped and explore at your own pace. The **tourist office,** C. Vittorio Emanuele 202 (tel. 09 09 88 00 95), is up the street from the ferry dock. (Open July-Aug. M-Sa 8am-2pm and 4:30-10pm, Su 8am-2pm; Sept.-June M-Sa 8am-2pm and 5:30-7:30pm. Closed Sa evenings.) Next to the cathedral, the **Ostello Lipari (HI),** Via Castello 17 (tel. 09 09 81 15 40; off-season 09 09 81 25 27), is one of the best deals on the islands. (L14,000. Reception 7-10am and 6pm-midnight. Check-out 10am. Strict midnight curfew. Open Mar.-Oct.) A few steps up from the hydrofoil port, **Locanda Salina,** Via Garibaldi 18 (tel. 09 09 80 55; fax 09 09 81 23 32), has beautiful rooms overlooking the water (singles L35,000; doubles L70,000). **Hotel Europeo,** C. Vittorio Emanuele 98 (tel. 09 09 81 15 89), has airy rooms of spartan simplicity (singles L30,000-45,000; doubles L85,000-100,000).

Vulcano and Stromboli The island of **Vulcano** offers an intriguing daytrip of thermal springs and bubbling mud baths. A good way to start your visit is to tackle the challenging one-hour **hike** to the **Gran Cratere** (Great Crater) along the snaking footpath beside the crater's fumaroles. On a clear day, you'll be able to see all the other islands from the top. Just up Via Provinciale from the port sits the **Laghetto di Fanghi** (mud pool); you can't miss the smell. If you would prefer not to bathe in mud, wade in the nearby waters of the **acquacalda** just behind the *laghetto,* where underwater volcanic outlets make the sea percolate like a jacuzzi. For cooler pleasures, visit the crowded beach and crystal-clear waters of **Sabbie Nere,** just down the road from the *acquacalda* (follow the signs off Via Ponente through the black sand). Stop by the **tourist office,** Via Provinciale 41 (tel. 09 09 85 20 28; July-Aug. only), for more info on these sights. **Ferries** make the trip to Vulcano from Lipari (L2400) and Milazzo (L9900); **hydrofoils** cost L4500 and L20,000, respectively.

Viewed from Lipari or Vulcano, **Stromboli** looks like a giant iceberg jutting out of the water. In reality, the island is a volcano—an active one at that. **Società Navigazione Pippo** (tel. 090 98 61 35) operates daily tours of the island (10am-1pm and 3-6pm; L25,000). Hiking the volcano is illegal and dangerous (someone was burnt to death after getting too close to the opening), but that doesn't seem to have stopped people. **Guide Alpine Autorizzate** (tel. 090 98 62 11) leads guided (and legal) hikes. Hikers should bring sturdy shoes, a flashlight, warm clothes, and water. Reaching the summit (about 3hr.) around dusk allows adventurers to camp out and see the brilliant lava bursts by night. The **ferry** from Lipari to Stromboli costs L25,500.

SARDINIA (SARDEGNA)

Sardinia is the perfect antidote to Italy-overdose. Inspired by the island's mountainous terrain and rustic villages, D. H. Lawrence declared that Sardinia, like Russia, had "escaped the net of European civilization." Much of the area south of over-touristed **Costa Smeralda** persists in its untamed state, and Sardinia's beaches rival Europe's finest. Ancient civilizations that settled in Sardinia some 3500 years ago built **nuraghe,** cone-shaped fortified tower-houses. Constructed of huge blocks of stone and assembled without the aid of mortar, over 7000 *nuraghe* survive today.

Tirrenia runs the most extensive ferry network, including service to Cagliari from Genoa (L82,500-95,500) and Palermo (L48,500-66,500). For info, call the Cagliari *Stazione Marittima* (tel. 070 66 60 65). **Flights** are quicker but much more expensive; check local tourist offices for details. On the island, **ARST** buses link villages while **PANI** buses connect only major cities. Bus and train service has improved the last few years, but **car rental** is still the only way to reach many locations (L50,000-195,000 per day). Ask at tourist offices for the comprehensive and dependable *Alberghi e Campeggi,* which lists prices for all hotels, pensions, and campsites. Decent singles go for L35,000, but rooms are scarce in August.

Cagliari, Alghero, and Oristano
At the island's southern tip, **Cagliari** gracefully combines the vigor of a bustling city, the rich history of a medieval town, and natural panoramic splendor. The cramped medieval quarter and impressive **duomo,** with dazzling gold mosaics atop each entryway, rest on a hill above the modern port. If you prefer to worship the sun, take city bus P, PQ, or PF to **Il Poetto,** Cagliari's most popular beach (20min., L1300). The **tourist office,** P. Matteotti (tel. 070 66 92 55), helps find rooms and offers info on local sites (open M-Sa in summer 8am-8pm; off-season 8am-1:30pm). Elegant **Pensione Vittoria,** Via Roma 75 (tel. 070 65 79 70), has mosaic floors (singles L55,000-60,000; doubles L85,000-100,000). **Allogio Firenze,** Viale Trieste 56, on the 5th floor (tel. 070 65 36 78 or 070 65 52 22), has large singles (L38,000-40,000) and doubles (L50,000-54,000).

The sea breezes and twisting streets of **Alghero** grant a respite from the sun's glare. The F.S. bus brings visitors to the nearby **Grotte di Nettuno,** an eerie cavern complex. (Round-trip bus ticket L6300. Grottoes open daily Apr.-Sept. 9am-7pm; Oct. 10am-5pm; Nov.-Mar. 9am-2pm. L10,000.) The **tourist office** in Alghero, P. Porta Terra 9 (tel. 079 97 90 54), is the most organized in Sardinia (open May-Sept. M-Sa 8am-8pm, Su 9am-1pm; reduced hours off-season). **Ostello dei Giuliani (HI),** Via Zara 3 (tel./fax 079 93 03 53), is 7km from the city center but near the beach (take the orange AF city bus from Via La Marmora; L14,000; reserve ahead).

Situated on the western coast, **Oristano** is a quiet base for excursions to stunning beaches and archaeological sites. The **tourist office** is at Via Cagliari 278, 6th floor (tel. 078 37 31 91 or 078 37 41 91; open M-F 8am-2pm, Tu-W also 4-8pm). **Marco Moto,** Via Cagliari 99/101, rents mopeds (L25,000 per half day) and motorcycles. (L75,000 per day. Open M-F 8:30am-1pm and 3:30-8pm, Sa 8:30am-1pm. Ages 18 and up.) The nearby **Sinis Peninsula** and **Costa Verde** offer everything that the better-known resorts do—except the crowds and concrete. At the tip of the peninsula, 17km west of Oristano, lie the ruins of the ancient city of **Tharros.**

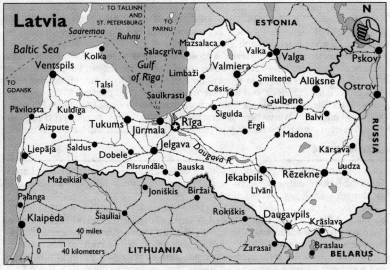

Latvia (Latvija)

US$1 = 0.60Ls (lats)		1Ls = US$1.66
CDN$1 = 0.39Ls		1Ls = CDN$2.58
UK£1 = 0.99Ls		1Ls = UK£1.01
IR£1 = 0.84Ls		1Ls = IR£1.19
AUS$1 = 0.35Ls		1Ls = AUS$2.89
NZ$1 = 0.30Ls		1Ls = NZ$3.86
SAR1 = 0.09Ls		1Ls = SAR10.55
DM1 = 0.33Ls		1Ls = DM2.99
Country Phone Code: 371		**International Dialing Prefix: 00**

Except for 20 years of independence that ended with the 1939 Molotov-Ribbentrop Pact, Latvia has been ruled by Germans, Swedes, and Russians from the 13th century until 1991. The country (pop. 2.6 million) is now rebuilding after almost 50 years of Soviet occupation that caused a massive exodus of Latvians and a huge influx of Russians. With the smallest majority of natives of the three Baltic States, Latvia remains the least affluent and developed. Attitudes toward the many Russians who still live in the country are softening, but evidence of national pride abounds, from patriotically renamed streets bleeding with crimson-and-white flags, to a reemergence of native holidays predating even the Christian invasions. Rīga, Latvia's only large city, is a westernizing capital where many corporations have established their Baltic headquarters. The rest of the country is mostly a provincial expanse of deep green hills dominated by tall birches and pines, dairy pastures, and quiet settlements.

Latvia is covered in delightful detail in *Let's Go: Eastern Europe 1999*.

GETTING THERE AND GETTING AROUND

Irish, U.K., and U.S. citizens can visit Latvia visa-free for up to 90 days. Citizens of Australia, Canada, New Zealand, and South Africa require 90-day visas, obtainable at a Latvian consular office (see **Government Information Offices,** p. 4) or at Rīga's airport. Single-entry visas cost US$15; multiple-entry cost US$30; 24-hour rush processing costs US$60 (single-entry) or US$90 (multiple-entry). Multiple-entry visas are issued only if an official invitation from a Latvian government agency or an officially registered organization is submitted with the visa application. Allow 10 days for standard processing. With the application, send your passport, one photograph, and payment by check or money order. For extensions, apply to the Department of Immigration and Citizenship and Immigration, Raina iela 5 (tel. 721 91 81) in Rīga.

Latvia is well-connected by **train** to Moscow, St. Petersburg, Tallinn, Vilnius, and even Berlin; efficient long-distance **buses** travel to Prague, Tallinn, Vilnius, and Warsaw. **Ferries** run to Rīga from Stockholm and Kiel, but from Stockholm the train through Tallinn is cheaper, and from Germany a bus passes through Klaipėda on its way to Rīga. **Flights** to Latvia use Rīga Airport, 8km southwest of Rīga. Once in Latvia, buses and trains run everywhere; getting from town to town is rarely a problem. The suburban train system based in Rīga stretches to the Lithuanian and Estonian borders.

ESSENTIALS

Look for the big green "i" marking some tourist offices. The **Tourist Club of Latvia** offers the best information. Stores often close between noon and 3pm. **Homosexuality,** though legal, is not always tolerated.

The Latvian currency unit is the **Lat** (100 santīmu = 1 Lat, abbreviated Ls). There are many **ATM** machines in Rīga linked to Cirrus and MasterCard, and in most towns there are a few establishments that accept **Visa** and **MasterCard.** It's difficult to cash **traveler's checks,** but AmEx and Thomas Cook checks can be converted in Rīga.

Buy slick **phone cards** for the newly digitalized telephones at the local post office and anywhere sporting a phone-card sticker (lowest denomination 2Ls). The **AT&T Direct** number in Latvia is 700 70 07; it's not a free call, but it's your best option for an English speaking operator. The gradual switch to digital phones has left some travelers feeling like safe-crackers—sometimes you must dial a 2 before a number to make a connection, sometimes a 1, and sometimes 8. Check a phone office or *Rīga in Your Pocket* for the latest in digit disaster. In an **emergency,** dial 01 for **fire,** 02 for **police,** and 03 for an **ambulance.**

Many young Latvians study English, while the older set knows some German. Latvians speak Russian, although the language may inspire some hostility.

Yes/No	*Jā/Nē*	yah/ney
Hello	*Labdien*	LAHB-dyen
Please	*Lūdzu*	LOOD-zuh
Thank you	*Paldies*	PAHL-dee-yes
Where is...?	*Kur ir...?*	kuhr ihr
How much does this cost?	*Cik maksā?*	sikh MAHK-sah
I don't understand	*Es nesaprotu*	ehs NEH-sah-proh-too
Help!	*Palīdzājiet!*	PAH-leedz-ah-yee-eht

Heavy and filling, Latvian **food** tries to fatten you for winter. National specialties, simple and tasty on the whole, include smoked *sprats* (similar to sardines), the holiday dish *zirņi* (gray peas with onions and smoked fat), *maizes zupa* (bread soup usually made from cornbread and full of currants, cream, and other goodies), and the warming *Rīgas balzams* (a sweet black liquor great on ice cream or in coffee). Dark rye bread is an essential staple of the Latvian table, and homemade bread and pastries are deliciously worth asking for. Try the *speķa rauoi,* a warm pastry, or *biezpien-maize,* bread with sweet curds. Beer is quite good, plentiful, and inexpensive; standouts include the Aldaris brewery's *Porteris* labels.

June 23 brings the amorous Midsummer's Eve Festival (Līgo) to Rīga, while November 18 sees feasts on Latvian National Day.

■ Rīga

Founded in 1201 by the Teutonic Order of the Knights of the Sword, Rīga was later ruled by Poles, Swedes, and then Russians, and grew to be the most prosperous city in the Baltics. The famed Art Nouveau architecture reveals German influences, while the population and atmosphere reflect the inescapable legacy of the Soviet era. Tensions between disenfranchised Russians, *nouveau-riche* businesspeople with cellular phones, and returning Latvians who fled in the 40s after Stalin's takeover make Rīga a hotbed of post-Soviet politics. The growing tourist population attests to the city's changing face—toward a celebration of its pre-war past and bright future.

ORIENTATION AND PRACTICAL INFORMATION

Rīga's center consists of a series of concentric half-circles along the banks of the **Daugava** River, surrounding **Vecrīga** (Old Riga). The train and bus stations sit on the southeast edge of the city. With the train station behind you, walk left on the busy Marijas iela; once you pass the canal's terminus, you are in the Old Town. A city map (1Ls) and *Rīga in Your Pocket* (0.50Ls) will help you out the rest of the way.

Telephone Code: 2 (8 for digital lines).
Flights: For flight info, call 20 70 09. **Lidosta Rīga** (Rīga Airport) is 8km southwest of the Old Town. Take bus 22 from Gogol iela.
Trains: The **station** (info tel. 23 21 34) is east of the Old Town and north of the canal. To: Moscow (17hr., 2 per day, *coupé* 28Ls), St. Petersburg (13hr., 1 per day, *coupé* 23Ls), Tallinn (8½hr., 1-2 per day, *coupé* 14Ls), and Berlin via Vilnius.
Buses: The **station** (tel. 721 36 11) lies 200m south of the train station along Prāgas iela, across the canal from the Central Market. To Tallinn (5-6hr., 5-6Ls) and Vilnius (6hr., 6Ls). **Eurolines,** to the right of the ticket window, serves Prague (30hr., 38Ls) and Warsaw (14hr., 15Ls).
Public Transportation: Buses, trams, and trolleys cost 0.14Ls; buy tickets on board.
Ferries: Transline Balt Tour, Eksporta iela 1a (tel. 732 23 11), 1km north of the castle at the passenger port. To Stockholm (17hr., M, W, and F 6pm, 20-40Ls).
Tourist Office: The English-speaking **Tourist Club of Latvia,** Skārņu iela 22 (tel. 722 17 31; fax 722 76 80), behind St. Peter's Church, arranges Russian visas and walking tours. Open 24hr. (knock on the window if the door is locked). **Balta Tourist Agency,** Basteja 10 (tel. 721 64 44; fax 724 31 00), gives out maps and pamphlets. Open M-F 9am-6pm, Sa 10am-2pm.
Embassies: Belarus, Jēzusbaznīcas 12 (tel. 732 25 50; fax 73 22 89). Open M-F 9am-1pm. **Canada,** Doma laukums 4, 4th fl. (tel. 722 63 15, emergency tel. 755 11 81). Open M-F 9am-5:30pm. **Russia,** Antonijas iela 2 (tel. 721 25 79). Open M-F 10am-1pm. **Ukraine,** Kalpaka bulv. 3 (tel. 33 29 56). Open M-F 10am-1pm. **U.K.,** Alunāna iela 5 (tel. 733 81 26). Visa section open M-F 9:30am-noon; embassy open 9am-5pm. **U.S.,** Raiņa bulv. 7 (tel. 721 00 05). Open M-F 9am-noon and 2-4pm.
Currency Exchange: At any of the *Valutos Maiņa* kiosks or shops in the city. **Unibanka,** Kaļķu iela 13, gives MC and Visa cash advances, and cashes traveler's checks. Open M-F 9am-9pm, Sa 9am-6pm. Cirrus/MC/Visa **ATMs** are common.
American Express: Latvia Tours, Kaļķu iela 8 (tel. 721 36 52; fax 782 00 20). Cashes traveler's checks and holds mail. Open M-F 9am-6pm, Sa 10am-2pm.
Gay and Lesbian hotline: 951 95 51 (24hr.), or email GayLatvia@hotmail.com.
Laundromat: Miele, Elizabetes iela 85a (tel. 721 76 96), in the courtyard opposite the bookstore. The wash takes about 2hr. Wash 1.84Ls. Dry 0.63Ls. Open 24hr.
Emergencies: Ambulance, tel. 03. **Fire,** tel. 01.
Police: tel. 02.
Post Office: Stacijas laukums 1 (tel. 721 32 57), near the train station. *Poste Restante* window 1. Open M-F 8am-8pm, Sa 8am-4pm, Su 8am-4pm. **Postal Code:** LV-1050.
Internet Access: Latnet, Raiņa 29 (tel. 721 12 41; http://www.latnet.lv). 0.22Ls per hr. Open M-Th 9am-6pm, F 9am-5pm. **Bilteks,** Jēkaba 20 (tel. 732 22 08). 2Ls per hr. Open daily 10am-9pm. **Internet Cafe Audalūzijas Suns,** Elizabetes iela 83/85 (tel. 724 28 26). 1.80Ls per hr. Open daily noon-10pm.
Telephones: Office at Brīvības bulv. 21 and at main post office. Open 24hr.

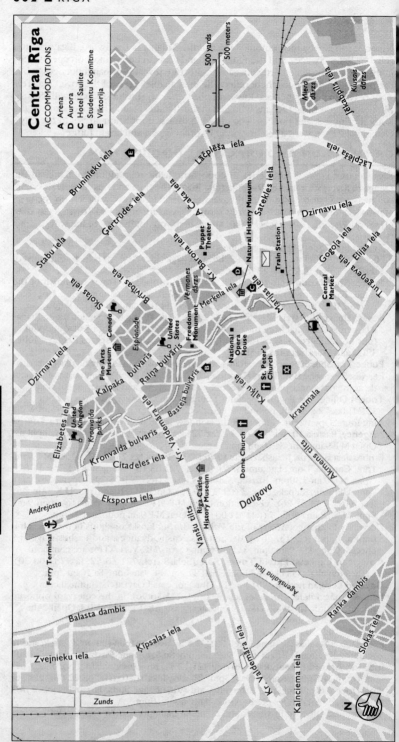

Central Rīga

ACCOMMODATIONS
A Arena
D Aurora
C Hotel Saulite
B Studentu Kopmītne
E Viktorija

500 yards
500 meters

LATVIA

Miera dārzs
Jēkabpils iela
Klusais dārzs
Lāčplēša iela
Bruņinieku iela
Gertrūdes iela
Sarekles iela
Dzirnavu iela
A. Čaka iela
Stabu iela
Puppet Theater
Natural History Museum
Kr. Barona iela
Train Station
Gogoļa iela
Elijas iela
Skolas iela
Vērmanes dārzs
Merķeļa iela
Tērbatas iela
Central Market
Turgeņeva iela
Brīvības iela
Māriņas iela
Canada
Esplanade
Fine Arts Museum
United States
Freedom Monument
National Opera House
St. Peter's Church
Kalpaka bulvāris
Raiņa bulvāris
Kaļķu iela
Elizabetes iela
United Kingdom
Kronvalda parks
Basteja bulvāris
Kr. Valdemāra iela
Krastmala
Citadeles iela
Kronvalda bulvāris
Dome Church
Akmens tilts
Eksporta iela
Rīga Castle History Museum
Daugava
Andrejosta
Vanšu tilts
Ferry Terminal
Agenskalna līcis
Ranka dambis
Slokas iela
Balasta dambis
Ķīpsalas iela
Zvejnieku iela
Kr. Valdemāra iela
Kalnciema iela
Zunds

N

ACCOMMODATIONS

Rīga's prices for decent rooms are generally the highest in the Baltics. However, there are a number of very cheap, if grim, places to stay in town.

Arena, Palasta iela 5 (tel. 722 85 83), an unmarked building in the heart of Vecrīga. Hall shower and communal kitchen. 3Ls per person. Open Apr.-Oct. Cash only.

Saulite, Merķela iela 12 (tel. 22 45 46), across from train station. Clean halls, rooms, and communal showers and toilets. Singles 4-6Ls; doubles 10Ls.

Studentu Kopmītne (Student Dormitories), Basteja bulvarīs 10 (tel. 721 62 21), above the Europcar Interrent office, on the edge of Vecrīga. Clean and well-maintained. Mostly new communal bathrooms. 3-4Ls, with private bath and refrigerator 6-8Ls. Call ahead—this place is popular.

Viktorija, Čaka iela 55 (tel. 701 41 11; fax 731 06 29), 8 blocks from the train station on Marijas iela (which becomes Čaka iela), or 2 stops on trolleybus 11 or 18. Plain rooms with common toilets. Low-end singles from 8-9Ls; doubles 10-12Ls.

Aurora, Marijas iela 5 (tel. 722 44 79), across from the train station. Rooms are old but livable. Common toilets tend to smell. Hall bathrooms. All rooms have sinks with hot water. Singles 3.80Ls; doubles 6Ls; triples 8.10Ls. Cash only.

FOOD

Bleary-eyed women tend an insomniac's daydream: 24-hour food and liquor stores. **Interpegro,** Raiņa bulv. 33 (tel. 722 90 44), for one, stocks liquor, water, fruits and vegetables, and more (open 24hr.). In five immense zeppelin hangars behind the bus station, **Centrālais Tirgus** (Central Market), one of the largest in Europe, has by far the best selection at the cheapest prices. Shop around and haggle, as vendors' prices vary quite a bit (open M-Sa 8am-5pm, Su 8am-3pm).

Alus Arsenāls, at Pils Laukums 4. Descend from the entrance on Arsenāla. Romantic dates and business dinners take place in this low-ceilinged restaurant with heavy, oak furniture. Beef filet 2.30Ls. Salad 0.95Ls. Scrumptious crab sticks in beer dough 1.30Ls. 0.3L of *Aldaris* 0.40Ls. Open 11am-midnight.

Lido Bistro-Piceria, Elizabetes 65. Very popular fast-food. Greasy but good meals 1.30-1.85Ls; salads 0.45Ls. Open daily 8am-11pm.

Rozamunde, Mazā Smilšu 8, 1 block off Filharmonija laukums. An upscale pub with an older crowd. Good beef tenderloin stuffed with mushrooms and cheese 3.80Ls. Open daily 11am-11pm.

Fredis Cafe, Ģertrūdes iela 62. Sophisticated patrons enjoy the smoky, faded atmosphere. Tiny subs 1Ls. *Aldaris* 0.65Ls. Open daily 9am-midnight.

LuLu Pizza, Ģertrūdes iela 27. Large pizzas enough for 3 moderately hungry people 2.99-3.99Ls. Slices 0.69-0.95Ls. *Aldaris* 0.65Ls. Open daily 8am-midnight.

Hotel Latvija Express Bar, Elizabetes iela 55, at the corner of Brīvības bulv. past the Freedom Monument. Renowned breakfast joint. Small portions of pancakes with jam 0.96Ls. 32 varieties of omelettes 0.81-4.21Ls. Big windows overlook the Orthodox Cathedral's park. Open daily 7am-11pm. Cash only.

SIGHTS AND ENTERTAINMENT

Most of Rīga's monuments are located in Vecrīga (Old Rīga). At the end of Audēju iela, **Sv. Pētera baznīca** (St. Peter's Church) towers with a dark spire visible throughout the city. First built in 1209, the church now standing dates from 1408. From the top of the 103m tower, you can see the Baltic Sea (open Tu-Su 10am-7pm; church free; tower 1.20Ls, students 0.80Ls). Just behind at Skārņu iela 10/20 stands the 1208 **Juras Kirik** (St. George's Church), the oldest stone edifice in Rīga. Constructed for the German Knights of the Sword, the church was secularized in the 1500s and divided into warehouses by German merchants. It now houses the magnificent **Museum of Applied Arts,** showcasing Latvian ceramics, bookmaking, and tapestries. (Open Tu-Su 11am-5pm. Museum 0.40Ls, students 0.20Ls. Exhibition 0.50Ls, students 0.20Ls.)

LATVIA

Farther right on Skārņu iela at the corner with Jāņa iela stands **Sv. Jāņa baznīca** (St. John's Church), a small 13th-century chapel embellished as late as the 1830s in a medley of architectural styles, from Gothic to Baroque to Neoclassical (open Tu-Su 10am-1pm). Through a tiny alleyway to the left, **Jāņa Sēta** (St. John's Courtyard) is the oldest site in Rīga, where the first city castle stood. Nearby rise the ominous black walls of the **Okupācijas muzejs-fonds** (Occupation Museum Fund) Strēlnieku laukums 1, one of Rīga's finest museums. The initial Soviet occupation is depicted so vividly you can almost hear the Red Army marching, and a model gulag helps explain why the Germans were welcomed as liberators.

The cobblestone expanse of **Doma laukums,** Vecrīga's central square, remains timelessly serene despite several vast new outdoor bars serving tourists and Rīga's *nouveau riche.* Rīga's centerpiece, **Doma Baznīca** (Dome Cathedral), begun in 1226, stands on one side of the square. Inside lies one of Europe's largest, finest pipe organs. (Open Tu-F 1-5pm, Sa 10am-2pm. 0.50Ls, students 0.20Ls. Concerts W and F 7pm. Call 721 34 98 for ticket info.) Next door, the **History and Maritime Museum,** Palasta iela 4, thoroughly explores Rīga's complex history (open W-Su 11am-5pm; 1Ls, students 0.40Ls). **Rīga Pils** (Rīga Castle), Pils laukums 2, at the street's end, houses three modest museums (art, history, and literature) labeled in Latvian only.

At Jēkaba iela 11, Latvia's **Saeima** (Parliament) was barricaded with trucks, barbed wire, sandbags, and nationalism during the 1991 struggle for independence. A couple blocks away and though the **Zviedru vārti** (Swedish Gate), Torņa iela leads to **Pulvertornis** (Powder Tower), one of Rīga's oldest landmarks and the only city tower left. Nine cannonballs are still lodged in its 14th-century walls; it's not clear why they're on the side facing *into* the city. Inside, the **Latvijas Kara Muzejs** (Latvian Museum of War), Smilšu iela 20, explores the Latvian resistance to Soviet rule (open Tu-Su 10am-6pm; 0.50Ls, students 0.25Ls; English tours 3Ls).

At the north end of the park, on Kr. Valdemāra iela, lies the **National Theater,** where Latvia first declared its independence on November 18, 1918 (open M-F 10am-7pm, Sa-Su 11am-6pm). In the park, Kaļķu iela widens to become Brīvības bulv., where the beloved **Brīvības Piemineklis** (Freedom Monument), nicknamed "Milda," was dedicated in 1935 while Latvia was an independent republic.

Proud birthplace of Mikhail Baryshnikov, Rīga is home to the excellent **Rīga Ballet** and the **Latvian National Opera.** The theaters are closed during the summer, but during the rest of the year, get tickets at Teātra 10/12 (tel. 722 57 47; open daily 10am-7pm). A prime evening plan is to hop from dinner to the beer gardens in Doma laukums and then to a dance club. At **Paddy Whelan's,** Grēcineku iela 4, fast-flowing beer satisfies a noisy, friendly crowd of local students, backpackers, and expats (beers 1.20Ls; open nightly 5pm-midnight; food served until 8pm). **Pulkuedim Neviens Neraksta,** Peldu 26/28, is a restaurant by day and a trendy bar at night (F-Sa cover 1-2Ls; open Su-Th noon-3am, F-Sa noon-5pm). **Groks Stacija** (tel. 721 63 81), Kaļķu iela 22, has a "metro stop" disco, complete with fluorescent graffiti (open daily noon-5am, F and Sa until 6am). **Purrs,** Matisa 60/62, and **808,** Kalmiņa 8, are gay nightspots.

■ Sigulda

Sigulda, 50km east of Rīga, boasts the ruins of medieval castles, legendary caves, and other goodies connected by nature trails in the picturesque Gauja Valley. Perched on a ridge to the right of Gauja iela on the near side of the gorge is **Siguldas dome,** the new "castle." Behind it, the **Siguldas pilsdrupas** (Siguldas Castle), now in ruins, was constructed by the German Knights of the Sword between 1207 and 1226 and destroyed in the Great Northern War. Down the slope and to the left along Turaidas iela about 500m, the chiseled maw of **Gūtmaņa ala** (Gūtman's Cave), is inscribed with coats of arms and phrases by generations of Latvians and other visitors since the 16th century. The wooden building up the hill to the right is the 1750 **Turaida Church,** now home to a small archaeological museum (open daily 10am-6pm). Farther out rise the towers and walls of **Turaidas pils** (Turaidas Castle), begun in 1214. Restored earlier in this century, the red tower is home to the **Sigulda History Museum,** Turaidas iela 10 (0.80Ls).

Hiking options here are numerous. One excellent 2km walk follows the Gauja River to the steep **Piķenes Slopes,** where two more caves merit a look. Another good hike goes from the Sigulda castle down to the Gauja, then upstream to cross **Vējupite creek.** Another 100m upstream on Vējupite, stairs rise to **Paradīzes Kalns** (Paradise Hill), where 19th-century Latvian painter Jānis Rozentāls made the valley view famous. Visible from the commuter rail, the Olympic-size **bobsled and luge run** plummets from Sveices iela 13 (tel. (29) 739 44). You can take the plunge year-round for 1Ls (open Sa-Su 10am-8pm). Try **Dukšte Gunars** (tel. (29) 761 16 14, mobile phone 934 03 20) for **hot-air balloon** rides (60Ls per person per hr.).

Trains roll to Sigulda from Rīga (1hr., 0.58Ls). The town center is up **Raiņa iela** from the main train station. For affordable lodging, take bus 12 to **Hotel Senleja,** Turaidas iela 4 (tel. (29) 721 62; fax 790 16 11; singles 15Ls; doubles 22Ls). **Kafejuīca/ Bistro,** Raiņa iela 1, next to the bank, a cafeteria-style eatery, has salads, chicken shish kebabs, and rice, all sold by weight. (Meals about 1.5Ls. *Aldaris* beer 0.35Ls. Open daily 7am-10pm, F-Sa later.)

■ Cēsis

In the 1930s, Cēsis (TSEH-siss) became a popular resort, and today it is making a comeback among vacationers charmed by its medieval streets, majestic castle ruins, and the lovely countryside nearby. Built by the Germans in 1209 to rule the region, the **castle** (tel. (0241) 226 15) was a mighty fortress with walls 4m thick by its completion in the 1280s (open Tu-Su 10am-5pm; 0.50Ls, students 0.40Ls; mandatory tour 2Ls). The Gauja river flows on the east side of town, and a number of good **hiking** trails lead along the many cliffs lining the river. Bus 9 from the hotel on Vienības laukums takes you the 3km along Gaujas iela to the base of the trails. The best cliffs are to the south. From Rīga, Cēsis is easily reached via suburban **trains** (1½-2hr., 10 per day, 0.93Ls) and **buses** (2hr., 17 per day, 1.10Ls). **Raunas iela** runs to the town center from the stations, then empties into the main square, **Vienības laukums.** The **tourist office,** Uzvaras Bulvaris 8 (tel. (0241) 222 46), in a small white building, functions best as a travel agency (open M-Sa 10am-6pm, Su 10am-3pm; closed daily 1-2pm). The best and most central hotel in town is the Danish-French-run **Cēsis Hotel,** Vienības Lakums 1 (tel. (0241) 223 92). The beautiful, spacious rooms have hardwood floors (singles 14Ls, with bath 19Ls; doubles 19Ls, 24Ls; breakfast 2Ls; English spoken).

LATVIA

Liechtenstein

Famous chiefly for its wines, royal family, and yes, postage stamps, Liechtenstein's minute size (160 sq. km) and population (30,629) make the principality itself more of an attraction than any sight it contains. With the only German-speaking monarchy in the world, Liechtenstein remains the last vestige of the Holy Roman Empire. Although the official language is German, many residents also speak English and French; the **currency** is the Swiss franc (SFr). **Biking** is a dream in flatter areas, and an efficient and cheap **postal bus** system links all 11 villages (most trips 2.40SFr, 1-week pass 10SFr; Swisspass valid). To enter the principality, catch a postal bus from Sargans or Buchs in Switzerland, or Feldkirch just across the Austrian border (each 3.60SFr). The **postal code** is FL-9490. The **telephone code** for all of Liechtenstein is 075. For international calls, use the Swiss **country code** (41) and **international dialing prefix** (00). For the **police,** call 117, and for **medical emergencies,** call 144. For a **map** of Liechtenstein, see our map of Switzerland p. 875.

Vaduz

More a hamlet than a national capital, Vaduz is not a budget-friendly place. Above the town sits the 12th-century **Schloß Vaduz,** regal home to Hans-Adam II, Prince of Liechtenstein. The **Staatliche Kunstsammlung** (State Art Museum), Städtle 37, is next to the tourist office (5SFr, students 3SFr). Nearby, philatelists salivate over (not on) the collection in the **Briefmarkenmuseum.** (Stamp Museum. Free. Both museums open daily Apr.-Oct. 10am-noon and 1:30-5:30pm; Nov.-Mar. until 5pm.)

Liechtenstein's **national tourist office,** Städtle 37 (tel. 392 11 11), up the hill and to the right from the Vaduz-Post bus stop, stamps passports (2SFr), finds rooms, and advises on hiking, cycling, and skiing. (Open June-Oct. M-F 8am-noon and 1:30-5:30pm, Sa 9am-noon and 1-4pm, Su 10am-noon and 1-4pm; Nov.-May closed weekends). Liechtenstein's lone **jugendherberge (HI),** Untere Rütig. 6 (tel. 232 50 22; fax 232 58 56), is in nearby **Schaan.** Take the bus to "Mühleholz" and turn down Marianumstr. (Members only. 26.30SFr; doubles 64.60SFr. Reception M-Sa 5-10pm, Su 6-10pm. Curfew 10pm. Open Mar.-Nov. 15.) If the hostel is full, walk 10 minutes back toward Vaduz to **Hotel Falknis** (tel. 232 63 77; singles 50SFr). Buy groceries at **Denner Superdiscount,** Äulestr. 20 (closed Su).

Upper Liechtenstein

With gorgeous views and great hiking, the villages in the upper country are far more rewarding to visitors than Vaduz. **Triesenberg,** the principal town, was founded in the 13th century by the Walsers, a group of Swiss immigrants fleeing poverty and oppression. The **Walser Heimatmuseum** chronicles their customs and crafts. (Open June-Aug. Tu-F 1:30-5:30pm, Sa 1:30-5pm, Su 2-5pm; Sept.-May closed Su; 2SFr.) The **tourist office** (tel. 262 19 26) is in the same building and has the same hours. **Pension Alpenblick,** Neudorf 383 (tel. 262 35 77), offers spacious rooms 10 minutes (downhill) from the tourist office (singles 40SFr; doubles 70SFr). **Camping Mittagspitze** (tel. 392 26 86) is between Triesen and Balzers on the road to Aargans (reception 8am-noon and 2-10pm; 8.50SFr per person, 5SFr per tent).

Malbun, on the other side of the mountain from Triesenberg, offers great skiing (day pass 33SFr; week pass 136SFr) and hiking: contact the **tourist office** (tel. 263 65 77) for more info (open M-F 9am-noon and 1:30-5pm, Sa 9am-noon and 1-4pm). The superb duo of chalet-*cum*-hotels **Hotel Alpen** (tel. 263 11 81; fax 263 96 46) and **Hotel Galina** offer the best accommodations. (Singles and doubles 40-65SFr per person. Reception at Hotel Alpen for both. Open mid-May to Oct. and Dec. 15-Apr. 15.)

Lithuania

Lithuania (Lietuva)

US$1	= 4.00Lt (Litai)		1Lt =	US$0.25
CDN$1	= 2.56Lt		1Lt =	CDN$0.39
UK£1	= 6.55Lt		1Lt =	UK£0.15
IR£1	= 5.56Lt		1Lt =	IR£0.18
AUS$1	= 2.28Lt		1Lt =	AUS$0.44
NZ$1	= 1.96Lt		1Lt =	NZ$0.51
SAR1	= 0.63Lt		1Lt =	SAR1.60
DM1	= 2.21Lt		1Lt =	DM0.45

Country Phone Code: 370   **International Dialing Prefix: 810**

Long ago, Lithuania was the largest country in Europe, stretching into modern-day Ukraine, Belarus, and Poland. It chose Roman Catholicism and allied itself with Poland, and this, coupled with its ability to withstand foreign incursions, insulated it from both the good and ill effects of German influence. Avoiding the Protestant Reformation, the Lithuanian Church remained strong, but the country missed out on the technological and political advances of Northwestern Europe. Since then, Lithuania has faced oppression from tsarist Russia, Nazi Germany, and Soviet Russia. After becoming the first Baltic nation to declare its independence from the USSR in 1990, though, Lithuania has moved to apply its vast experience in statecraft. It is now less Sovietized than Latvia and less Lutheran-Scandinavian than Estonia. The spectacular capital city, Vilnius, known among those in the know as the "New Prague," welcomes hordes of tourists into the largest old town in Europe, recently covered in a bright new coat of paint from city-wide renovations. Sun, fun, and the Baltic's best beaches can be found where the mighty Baltic Sea washes up at Palanga and Kuršių Nerija (Curonian Spit).

Tune in to *Let's Go: Eastern Europe 1999* for more madcap Lithuanian know-how.

GETTING THERE AND GETTING AROUND

Citizens of the U.S., Canada, the U.K., and Australia can visit Lithuania **visa-free** for up to 90 days. New Zealand and South African citizens without visas for Estonia or Latvia need a 90-day visa. Border posts do not issue visas. Send a photo, passport, and check or money order (single-entry US$20, multiple-entry US$40, transit visa US$10) to the nearest embassy or consulate (see **Government Information Offices**, p. 4). Regular service takes two weeks (rush costs US$15-20 extra). For visa extensions, contact the Immigration Dept. at Virkių g. 3 #6, Vilnius (tel. 75 64 53).

Trains are slow, noisy, and often crowded. Two major rail lines cross Lithuania: one runs north-south from Latvia through Šiauliai and Kaunas to Poland; the other runs east-west from Belarus through Vilnius and Kaunas to Kaliningrad, or on a branch line from Vilnius through Šiauliai to Klaipėda. Slightly more expensive and faster **buses,** however, radiate from all the cities of Lithuania.

Klaipėda, Kaunas, and Vilnius are accessible by **train** or **bus** from Belarus, Estonia, Latvia, Poland, and Russia. Most trains from Poland to Vilnius go through Belarus, requiring a transit visa (US$30). The *Baltic Express* chugs from Warsaw to Tallinn, departing Warsaw at 2:30pm every other day, passing through Kaunas at 11:55pm, and arriving in Tallinn the next day at 1:10pm. There is also one overnight train running between Warsaw and Šeštokai, Lithuania; it arrives at 6:30pm, two hours before a Šeštokai-Kaunas-Vilnius train departs. These two trains, as well as buses from Poland, do not go through Belarus. **Planes** fly to Vilnius from Berlin, Moscow, Stockholm, and Warsaw. **Ferries** connect Klaipėda with Kiel and Muhkran in Germany.

ESSENTIALS

Litinterp offices arrange private accommodations, rent cars, and stock city information. The three big Lithuanian cities have helpful guidebooks. *Vilnius in Your Pocket* (4Lt), thoroughly updated every two months and available at newsstands, is a bestseller, as are sister guides *Kaunas in Your Pocket* and *Klaipėda in Your Pocket.*

The unit of **currency** is the Litas (Lt); 1 Lt equals 100 centų. Since March 1994, Litai have been tied to the U.S. dollar (4Lt=US$1). Traveler's checks can be cashed at most banks (usually for a 2-3% fee). Cash advances on a **Visa** card can usually be obtained with a minimum of hassle in banks; **Vilniaus Bankas,** with outlets in major Lithuanian cities, accepts major credit cards and traveler's checks and charges no higher than a 0.5% commission. Most cities have 24-hour **ATMs.**

Lithuania's Independence Day falls on February 16. Other **holidays** include March 4, St. Kazimieras's Day; April 12-13, Easter Sunday and Monday; first Sunday in May, Mother's Day; June 23, Rasos Šventi (Midsummer Night); June 24, Joninės (St. John's Day); July 6, Mindaugas Day; November 1, All Saints' Day; November 2, All Souls' Day; December 25-26, Kalėdos (Christmas).

ACCOMMODATIONS AND FOOD
Be sure to take advantage of the eight **Lithuanian Youth Hostels (LJNN/HI).** HI membership is nominally required, but an LJNN guest card (US$3 at any of the hostels) will suffice. The LJNN main office is in Vilnius at Filaretų g. 17 (tel./fax 25 46 27). Grab a copy of their *Hostel Guide,* a handy booklet with info on bike and car rentals, advance booking, and maps.

Lithuanian **cuisine** is generally heavy, filling, and sometimes very greasy. Many restaurants serve various types of *blynai* (pancakes) with *misa* (meat) or *varške* (cheese). *Cepelinai* are heavy, potato-dough missiles stuffed with meat, cheese, and mushrooms, most prominent in West Lithuania. *Šaltibarščiai* is a beet and cucumber soup prevalent in the eastern half of the country. *Karbonadas* is fried breaded pork fillet, and the blissful *koldunai* are spiced meat dumplings. Most restaurants and shops stock the Lithuanian **beer** *Kalnapilis,* which is very good. *Baltijos* reigns supreme around Klaipėda, and the award-winning *Utenos* is often available.

COMMUNICATION Public phones come in two varieties: the long, rectangular ones that accept magnetic strip cards and the newer, rounded ones that accept chip cards. Both types of card are sold at phone offices and many kiosks in denominations of 3.54Lt, 7.08Lt, and 28.32Lt. Calls to Europe are 5.80Lt per minute; to the U.S. 7.32Lt per minute. You can book international calls through the operator at the central phone office (pay when finished), but you may have to wait 20 to 45 minutes for the call to go through. Most countries can be dialed directly. Dial 8, wait for the second tone, dial 10, then dial the country code and number. For countries to which direct dialing is not available, dial 8, wait for the second tone, and dial 194 or 195 (English-speaking operators available). For the **AT&T Direct operator,** dial (8), wait for a dial tone, then 196; for **Sprint Express,** dial (8), wait for a dial tone, then 197.

 English-language books can be cheap but not plentiful. The English-language *Lithuanian Weekly* (2Lt) covers Lithuanian events in some depth, but is increasingly hard to find and not available at all outside Vilnius. The Tallinn-based *Baltic Independent* and Rīga's *Baltic Observer* are both available in Vilnius, Kaunas, and Klaipėda, and the ever-informative *City Paper—The Baltic States* can be picked up at hotels, kiosks, and tourist info points (US$1.50). In Vilnius, pick up **Voice of America Radio** 24 hours at 105.6 FM.

Yes/No	Taip/Ne	TAYE-p/neh
Hello	Labadien	Lah-bah-DEE-yen
Please/You're welcome	Prašau	prah-SHAU
Thank you	Ačiu	AH-chyoo
Excuse me	Atsiprašau	ahtsy-i-prah-SHAoo
Do you speak English?	Ar Jūs kalbate angliškai?	ahr yoos KAHL-bah-te AHNGL-ish-kī
I don't understand.	Aš nesuprantu.	AHSH neh-soo-PRAHN-too
Where is...?	Kur yra....?	Koor EE-rah
How much does this cost?	Kiek kainuoja?	KEE-yek KYE-new-oh-yah
I'd like a room.	Aš norėčiau kambario.	ahsh no-RYEH-chi-aoo KAHM-bah-ri-o
I'd like to pay.	Aš norėčiau užmokėti	ahsh no-RYEH-chi-aoo ush-moh-KYEH-TI
Help!	Gelbfkite	GYEL-beh-kyi-te

■ Vilnius

Once a minor city within the vast Soviet Empire, Vilnius was able to escape mass Sovietization and retain its majestic, Baroque beauty. In the 19th century, Wilno, as it was called, was the world center of Jewish scholarship. Today, foreign investment is pouring into this "new Prague," and new stores and restaurants are opening daily. See it for yourself, before everyone else gets in on the secret.

ORIENTATION AND PRACTICAL INFORMATION

From the **train** or **bus stations** (the two face each other), walk east on **Geležinkelio g.** (to your right as you exit the train station) and turn left at its end. **Aušros Vartų g.** leads north from here through the south gates of **Senamiestis** (Old Town). **Gedimino pr.**, the commercial artery, leads west from the square in front of the cathedral. Kiosks and hotels sell the excellent *Vilnius in Your Pocket* (4Lt).

LITHUANIA

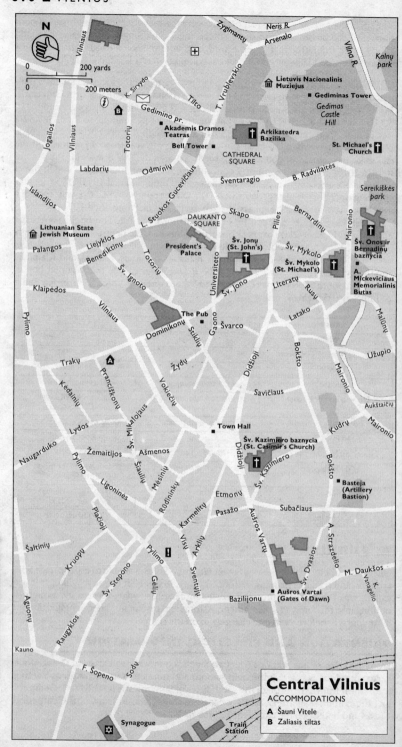

N

0 ____ 200 yards
0 ____ 200 meters

Vilniaus

Neris R.

Žygimantų

Arsenalo

Vilna R.

Kalnų park

Lietuvis Nacionalinis Muziejus

■ Gediminas Tower

Gedimas Castle Hill

Jogailos

Vilniaus

K. Sirvydo

Tilto

T. Vrublevskio

Gedimino pr.

Akademis Dramos Teatras ■

Bell Tower ■

Arkikatedra Bazilika

CATHEDRAL SQUARE

St. Michael's Church

Labdarių

Odminių

Šventaragio

B. Radvilaitės

Sereikiškės park

Islandijos

L. Stuokos-Gucevičiaus

DAUKANTO SQUARE

Skapo

Pilies

Bernardinų

Maironio

Lithuanian State Jewish Museum

Liejyklos

Benediktinų

Totorių

Palangos

Šv. Ignoto

President's Palace

Universiteto

Šv. Jonų (St. John's)

Šv. Jono

Šv. Mykolo

Šv. Mykolo (St. Michael's)

Literatų

Rusų

Latako

Šv. Onos ir Bernadinų baznycia

A. Mickevičiaus Memorialinis Butas

Klaipėdos

Pylimo

Vilniaus

Dominikonų

The Pub

Stiklių

Gaono

Švarco

Didžioji

Bokšto

Maironio

Užupio

Aukštaičių

Maironio

Trakų

Pranciškonų

Žydų

Vokiečių

Savičiaus

Kudrų

Kedainių

Šv. Mikalojaus

Lydos

Ašmenos

Town Hall ■

Šv. Kazimiero baznycia (St. Casimir's Church)

Bokšto

Žemaitijos

Mėsinių

Didžioji

Šv. Kazimiero

Basteja (Artillery Bastion)

A. Strazdelio

Naugarduko

Pylimo

Ligonines

Rūdininkų

Etmonų

Pasažo

Subačiaus

Plačioji

Karmelitų

Visų

Arklių

Aušros Vartų

Šaltinių

Kruopų

Šv. Stepono

Pylimo

Šventųjų

Gelių

Šv. Dvasios

Bazilijonu

Aušros Vartai (Gates of Dawn)

M. Daukšos

K. Vanagelio

Aguonų

Raugyklos

Kauno

F. Šopeno

Sodų

Train Station

Synagogue

LITHUANIA

Central Vilnius

ACCOMMODATIONS

A Šauni Vitele
B Zaliasis tiltas

Telephone Code: 02.

Flights: Aerouostas (airport; flight info tel. 63 02 01), Rodūnės Kelias 2, 5km south of town. Take bus 1 from the train station, or bus 2 from the "Sparta" stop of trolley bus 16 on Kauno g. **LOT** (tel. 73 90 20) flies to Warsaw; **SAS** (tel. 23 60 00) to Copenhagen. **Estonian Air** (tel. 73 90 22) to Tallinn (1½hr., daily). **Lithuanian Airlines** (tel. 75 25 88) to Berlin, Kiev, London, and Moscow.

Trains: Geležinkelio g. 16 (tel. 63 00 86 or 63 00 88). Tickets sold in the yellow addition to the left of the main station. **Reservation Bureau** (tel. 62 69 47), in the station hall (open M-F 9am-4pm). To: Berlin via Belarus (transit visa required; 19½hr., 309Lt), Kaliningrad, Russia (7hr., 40Lt, *coupé* 65Lt), Minsk (5hr., 32Lt, *coupé* 52Lt), Moscow via Belarus (transit visa required; 17hr., 80Lt, *coupé* 128Lt), Rīga (7½hr., 41Lt, *coupé* 67Lt), St. Petersburg (18hr., 64Lt, *coupé* 108Lt), Warsaw via Belarus (transit visa required; 12hr., 60Lt, *coupé* 115Lt).

Buses: Autobusų Stotis, Sodų g. 22 (info tel. 26 24 82, reservations 26 29 77 or 63 52 77), opposite the train station. **Tarpmiestinė Salė** covers long-distance and has an info booth open daily 7am-8pm. To: Kaliningrad (8hr., 34-40Lt), Minsk (4hr., 19Lt), Rīga (5-6hr., 25-40Lt), Tallinn (10hr., 81Lt), and Warsaw (10hr., 60-65Lt).

Public Transportation: Buses and **trolleys** don't run in Senamiestis but link Vilnius's train and bus stations, its suburbs, and Senamiestis's edges (daily 6am-midnight). Buy tickets at any kiosk (0.60Lt; 0.75Lt from the driver; punch on board).

Taxis: Former State Taxis (tel. 22 88 88; 1.30Lt per km). **Private taxis** show a green light in the windshield; debate the fare before you go.

Tourist Offices: The **Tourist Information Centre,** Gedimino pr. 14 (tel. 61 68 67; fax 22 61 18), organizes tours and sells *Vilnius in Your Pocket.* Open M-F 9am-6pm, Sa 10am-3pm. **Lithuanian Youth Hostels Head Office,** Filaretų g. 17 (tel. 25 46 27; email filaretai@post.omnitel.net), at the Filaretai Hostel (see below). Arranges trips, hostel reservations, and ISICs (20Lt). Open daily 8am-5pm.

Embassies: Australia (consulate), Radvilaites 4 (tel./fax 22 33 69). **Belarus,** P. Klimo g. 8 (tel./fax 26 34 43). Visa services at Muitinės g. 41 (tel. 63 06 26). Open M-Tu and Th-F 10am-4:30pm. **Canada,** Gedimino pr. 64 (tel. 22 08 98). Open M-F 10am-1pm. **Russia,** Latvių g. 53/54 (tel. 72 17 63, visa info 72 38 93). Open M-Tu and Th-F 10am-1pm. **Ukraine,** Turniškių g. 22 (tel./fax 76 36 26). Visa services on Kalvarijų 159, 2nd fl. (tel. 77 84 13). Open M-Tu and Th-F 10am-1pm. **U.K.,** Antakalnio g. 2 (tel. 22 20 70). Open M-F 9:30am-12:30pm. **U.S.,** Akmenų g. 6 (tel. 22 30 31; fax 31 28 19). Open M-Th 8:30am-5:30pm.

Passport Office: Imigracijos Taryba, Verkių 3, #3, (tel. 75 64 53), 2km north of Senamiestis. Extends visas for 61Lt for travelers with proof of their need to stay in the country. Open M-F 9am-4:30pm.

Currency Exchange: Vilniaus Bankas, Gedimino pr. 12 (tel. 61 07 23). Cash advances with no commission from Diners Club, MC, or Visa. Cashes AmEx and Thomas Cook traveler's checks. Visa-linked **ATM.** Open M-Th 8am-3:30pm, F 8am-3pm. **The Lithuanian Savings Banks** at Vilniaus 16 and Pilies 9 have **ATMs** that accept MC and Cirrus.

Gay Information Line: tel. 63 30 31. Info about organizations, events, and accommodations for gay men. **Lithuanian Gay and Lesbian Homepage** (http://cs.ektaco.ee/~forter) lists gay and lesbian establishments in Lithuania.

Laundromat: Slayana, Latvių g. 31 (tel. 75 31 12), in Žvėrynas. Do-it-yourself wash and dry 12Lt. Detergent 3Lt. Open M-F 8am-8pm, Sa 8am-3pm.

Emergencies: Police: 02. **Ambulance:** 03. **Information:** 09.

24hr. Pharmacy: Gedimino Vaistinė, Gedimino pr. 27 (tel. 61 01 35 or 62 49 30).

Medical Services: Baltic-American Medical & Surgical Clinic, Antakalnio g. 124 (tel. 34 20 20), at Vilnius University Hospital. Open 24hr.

Post Office: Centrinis Paštas, Gedimino pr. 7 (tel. 61 67 59), west of Arkikatedros aikštė. *Poste Restante* at the window that says *"iki pareikalavimo."* 0.50Lt to pick up mail. Open M-F 7am-7pm, Sa 9am-4pm. **Postal Code:** LT-2000.

Internet Access: Send free email from the offices of the **Soros Foundation,** Šv. Jono g. 3/5 (tel. 22 38 06; call 22 37 01 to reserve a terminal). Gets very busy and may require an appointment scheduled a week in advance. Open M-F noon-8pm.

Telephones: In the main post office (info. tel. 62 55 11). Phones take phone cards (3.54Lt and up) and allow direct dialing abroad. Open M-F 7am-7pm, Sa 9am-4pm.

ACCOMMODATIONS

Few of the accommodations in Vilnius cater to budget travelers. **Litinterp,** Bernardinų 7, #2 (tel. 22 38 50; fax 22 35 59; email litinterp@post.omnitel.net), arranges homestays. (Reserve ahead. Singles 60-100Lt. Doubles 100-140Lt. Open M-F 9am-6pm, Sa 9am-4pm.) In a pinch, head to the overnight office in the main train station (tel. 69 24 72), to the left of the ticket info office, for a **couchette in a non-working stationary train** (check-in after 7pm; check-out 7am; 15Lt).

Filaretai Youth Hostel (HI), Filaretų g. 17 (tel. 25 46 27; fax 22 01 49; email filareta@post.omnitel.net). Take bus 34, leaving from the right of the station to the 7th stop. Clean kitchen, satellite TV, and oodles of Vilnius info. Dorms 20-24Lt; doubles 56-64Lt. Reception open 7am-midnight. Curfew 1am.

Old Town Hostel, Aušros vartų 20-15a (tel. 62 53 57; fax 22 03 05; email filaretai@post.omnitel.net). Small hostel near the train station. 32Lt per person.

Žaliasis tiltas (The Green Bridge), in the center of downtown at 2 different locations around the corner from each other. **Gedimino pr. 12** (tel. 61 54 50; fax 22 17 16) has sumptuous rooms. Singles 200-250Lt; doubles 160-320Lt. **Vilniaus g. 2, #15** (tel. 61 54 60, info and reservations tel./fax 22 17 16). Small but clean singles from 80Lt; doubles from 120Lt. Breakfast included. AmEx, Diners Club, MC, and V.

Šauni Vietelė, Pranciškonų g. 316 (tel./fax 22 41 10), in a former monastery. Excellent location and very comfortable. Singles 130Lt; doubles 250Lt. Reserve ahead.

FOOD

The four French **Iki** supermarkets stock foreign foods. The most convenient one is at Žirmūnų g. 68, 1.5km north across the Neris (open M-Sa 9am-9pm, Su 9am-8pm). Trendy yet inexpensive restaurants are popping up everywhere, and a full meal can be as cheap as US$4-6. The more English words on the menu, the more you'll pay.

Ritos Sléptuvė (Rita's Hideaway), A. Goštauto g. 8, west of Senamiestis along the Neris. *The* place to go. Pasta 5-10Lt. Transforms into a **bar** by night with live music and disco on F and Sa. Open Su-Th 7:30am-2am, F-Sa 7:30am-4am.

Ritos Smuklė (Rita's Tavern), Žirmūnų g. 68. Rita's newest creation is this traditional Lithuanian restaurant. Take trolley bus 12, 13, or 17. Try the meat or mushroom koldūnai (6.90Lt). Live folk music F and Sa 8-10pm. Open daily 11am-2am.

Prie Parlamento, Gedimino pr. 46. An extremely popular, if slightly pricey, eatery. Hefty servings of your favorite Eastern European dishes for 10Lt and up. Open M-F 8am-midnight, Sa-Su 10am-2pm.

Cafe Filharmonija, Aušros vartų g. 5. The best of the sidewalk cafes near Aušros Vartai. Offers great people watching with a relaxed crowd and tasty ice cream desserts. Main dishes 7-12Lt. Open daily 9am-11pm.

SIGHTS

With the largest Old Town in Eastern Europe, Vilnius has no shortage of architectural or historic sights. Through **Aušros Vartai** (Gates of Dawn), the first door on the right leads to the 17th-century **Aušros Vartų Koplyčia** (Chapel). The miraculous reputation of the icon inside fuels Catholic pilgrimages. Farther along, the crown-topped **Šv. Kazimiero bažnyčia** (St. Casimir's Church) has an utterly Lithuanian history: in 1832, the church gained a Russian Orthodox dome; in World War I, the Germans made it Lutheran; after World War II, the Soviets turned it into a museum of atheism; and in 1989, it was restored as a Catholic church. *(Open M-Sa 4-6:30pm, Su 8am-1:30pm.)*

Didžioji g. broadens into **Rotušės aikštė,** an ancient marketplace dominated by the 18th-century **town hall,** now home to the **Lietuvos Menininkų Rūmai** (Lithuanian Artists Center). Just down the street at Didžioji g. 4 lies the beautiful **Vilniaus Paveikslu Gallerija.** *(Open Tu-Su noon-6pm. 4Lt, students 2Lt, Sept.-May W free.)* As Didžioji g. continues north, it passes **Šv. Mikalojaus bažnyčia** (St. Nicholas's Church), Lithuania's oldest. A bit farther, Didžioji g. widens into a triangular square and merges with the pedestrian **Pilies g.,** lined with souvenir shops and cafes. At the corner of Pilies and Šv. Jono g. stands the **University of Vilnius.** Founded in 1579, the Jesuit university was a major player in the Counter-Reformation. Through the arches opposite St. John's Church waits the remarkable 17th-century **Astronomical Observatory.**

North on Pilies g. (or Universiteto g.), the picturesque **Arkikatedros aikštė** (Cathedral Square) has had a church here since 1387; the present 18th-century **Arkikatedra** resembles a Greek temple. Gedimino pr. leads west from here; at its far end sits the **parliament.** In January 1991, the world watched as Lithuanians raised barricades to protect their parliament from the Soviet army. Behind the Cathedral, up on Castle Hill, **Gedimino pilis** (tower) affords a great view of Vilnius's spires. Descending the hill, meander to the south through the park until Maironio g., which leads south to the Gothic **Šv. Onos ir Bernardinų bažnyčia** (St. Anne's Church and Bernardine Monastery), so beautiful that Napoleon wanted to carry it back to France. On Maironio g., follow the stairs up to Bokšto g. for a view of **Užupio,** the oldest part of the city outside the medieval walls. The **Bastėja** (Artillery Bastion), Bokšto g. 20/18, is a restored section of the 17th-century fortifications that once surrounded the city. The high Baroque **St. Peter and Paul Church,** on Antakalnio g., northeast of Cathedral Square, is a must-see; the ceiling is covered with two thousand intricately carved figures.

ENTERTAINMENT

Vilnius's breakneck economic development has opened the gates for a fast and furious arts scene. For a list of performances, check *Vilnius in Your Pocket* (available at the tourist office) or the paper *Lietuvos Rytas.* The tourist office at Gedimino pr. 14 (tel. 61 68 67; fax 22 61 18) has ticket info. The posters in Senamiestis and Prie Parlamento's bulletin board are often the best source of information. Lithuanian hipsters Eduardas and Vladimiras organize a **gay disco** every Saturday night at a different venue. Call them (tel. 63 30 31) for more info (cover 15Lt).

Mingle with the locals at the lively pub, **Amatininkų Užeiga,** Didžioji g., 19 #2, or descend into the cozy, medieval basement for a more intimate atmosphere (open M-F 8am-5am, Sa-Su 11am-5am). **The Pub (Prie Universiteto),** Dominikonų g. 9, is an immensely popular traditional English pub (pint of *Pilsner Urquell* 10Lt; open daily 11am-2am). **Ultra,** Goštauto g. 12, is a hip spot for a younger crowd of technodancing fools (open Th-Sa 8pm-5am; cover 5Lt). **Ministerija,** Gedimino pr. 46, is a perenially popular club with a small, cozy floor and a "no techno" rule (open M-Th 5pm-2am, F-Sa 5pm-4am; ages 20 and up; cover 5Lt).

■ Near Vilnius: Trakai

The capital of the Grand Duchy of Lithuania in the 14th and 15th centuries, Trakai, 28km west from Vilnius, is a lakeside village full of intricate wooden cottages, castles, and ruins. Eight **trains** to run to Trakai from Vilnius every day (1hr., 2Lt), as well as over 25 **buses** (45min., 2.30-2.60Lt). Trakai's train station is on Vilniaus g., 500m south of the bus station; follow the crowd into town. The exquisite **Trakai Castle** sits on an island in Lake Galvė, accessible by a footbridge on Karaimų g. The 30m high watchtower is stocked with historical displays (open daily 10am-7pm; 2.50-5Lt).

▓ Kaunas

Burnt to the ground 13 times, Kaunas, Lithuania's second-largest city, has been repeatedly reincarnated and still seems to embody Lithuania's true heart and soul. The capital city from 1918 until 1940, it is now a serene place whose unhurried pace has been little changed by the growing number of bars, restaurants, and shops.

SIGHTS AND ENTERTAINMENT Where Laisvės al. ends, Kaunas's Old Town begins; follow Vilniaus g. through an underpass and you'll be inside the medieval city walls. The **Kauno Arkikatedra Bažnyčia** is a shockingly large 15th-century cathedral with a Gothic and Renaissance interior. Wander up Karaliaus dvaro off the north end of the square and you'll arrive at **Santakos Parkas,** a tree-dotted chunk of land where the Neris and Nemunas rivers meet and site of Kaunas's 13th-century **castle.**

The massive **St. Michael the Archangel Church** commands the east end of Laisvės al., a 2km pedestrian avenue. Two blocks down Laisvės al. and right on Daukanto g. lies **Vienybės aikštė** (Unity Sq.), depicted in etched glory on the back of the 20Lt note. Surrounding the square are several museums. The **M. K. Čiurlionis Museum,** Putvinskio g. 55, honors the avant-garde artist who sought to combine image and music to express an idea without words (open Tu-Su noon-6pm, closed last Tu of every month; 3Lt, students 1.50Lt). Across the street, the hellish (yet wonderful) **Velnių muziejus** (Devil Museum), Putvinskio g. 64, houses a collection of nearly 2000 devils, most of them folk carvings. Don't miss Devil Hitler and Devil Stalin chasing each other across bone-covered Lithuania (open Tu-Su noon-6pm, closed last Tu of every month; 4Lt, students 2Lt).

The **Pažaislis Monastery and Church,** a vibrant Baroque complex with rich frescoes, sits on the Nemunas's right bank, 10km east of central Kaunas. Used as a KGB-run "psychiatric hospital," the monastery was returned to the Catholic Church in 1990 (open Su 11am-6pm; call (027) 75 64 85 for info on tours during the week). Take trolleybus 5 or 9 to the end of the line; then walk 1km down the road.

PRACTICAL INFO, ACCOMMODATIONS, AND FOOD Trains arrive at Čiurlionio g. 16 (tel. (027) 29 22 60) on their way to Rīga (6hr., 36-58Lt) and Vilnius (1½-2hr., 7.30-8.70Lt). The **bus station,** Vytauto pr. 24/26 (tel. (027) 22 19 42), services cities including Vilnius (2hr., 10.40Lt). In summer, a daily **hydrofoil** leaves Raudondvario pl. 107 for Nida (4hr., 49Lt). **Delta/Tourist Information,** Laisvės al. 88 (tel. (027) 20 49 11), sells maps (8Lt) and gives info on accommodations and sights (open M-F 9am-6pm, Sa 10am-2pm). **Litinterp,** Kumelių 15, apt. 4 (tel./fax (027) 22 87 18), in the Old Town, finds private rooms (singles 60Lt; doubles 100Lt; open M-F 9am-6pm, Sa 9am-4pm). The **Svečių Namai (HI),** Prancūzų g. 59 (tel. (027) 74 89 72; fax 22 41 85), offers excellent facilities a bit far from town. From the train station, cross the tracks, and head left at the end of the bridge to Prancūzų g. (dorms 28Lt; singles 44Lt, nonmembers 80Lt). **Hotel Baltijos,** Vytauto pr. 71 (tel. (027) 28 32 02), offers aging rooms at the end of Laisvės al. (singles 70Lt; doubles 104-58Lt). At **Liepaitė,** Donelaičio 66, the food is decent and service impeccable (chicken filet with apricots 19Lt; open Su-Th noon-midnight, F-Sa noon-3am). **Pieno Baras,** Laisvės al. at S. Daukanto, serves up *blyneliai* (3.40Lt) and whipped milk (2Lt; open daily 8am-8pm).

■ Near Kaunas: Šiauliai and Druskininkai

On a sunny morning in 1236, German Knights of the Sword, returning after a campaign to Christianize Lithuania, were ambushed and massacred. To commemorate the bloodshed, people began placing crosses on eerie **Kryžių Kalnas** (Hill of Crosses), 10km northwest of the city. After uprisings in 1831 and 1863, Lithuanians brought crosses to remember the dead and the deported. Under the Soviets, more crosses appeared and the hill became a mound of anti-Russian sentiment, whose crosses were replaced despite the best effort of Soviet bulldozers. Since independence, crosses have been placed by or in honor of emigrated Lithuanians. **Trains** arrive from Kaunas (2hr., 6Lt). From the train station, walk left on Dubijos g., right on Višinskio and left on Stoties to the bus station, Tilžės 109. From there, **buses** running north to Joniškis, Meškuičiai, Rīga, or Tallinn pass by at Kryžių Kalnas; ask the driver to stop. From where the bus drops you, a marked road leads down for about 2km. Be aware that the buses stop running to Kaunas in late afternoon—plan ahead.

"You hear the murmur of the pines, so solemn, as if they were trying to tell you something," avant-garde artist, composer, mystic, and native son Mikolojus Konstantinas Čiurlionis wrote of **Druskininkaiin** in 1905. The artist's unique works are kept alive at **M. K. Čiurlionio Memorialinis Muziejus,** Čiurlionio g. 35 (open Tu-Su noon-6pm, closed last Tu of the month; 1Lt, students 0.50Lt). **Piano concerts** on Sunday evenings in summer feature Čiurlionis's own compositions, as well as those of Bach, Debussy, and Beethoven (5pm, 1hr., 5Lt). **Buses** head from the station at Gardino g. 1 (tel. (233) 513 33) to Kaunas (3hr., 13.20Lt) and Vilnius (2½hr., 13.20Lt). To get to town, make a left after exiting the station and walk down Gardino g. For maps and info, go to the **Tourist Information Center**, Vilnaius 18 (tel./fax (233) 517 77; open M-F 9am-12:30pm and 1:15-5:30pm). **Druskininkai Hotel**, Kudirkos g. 43 (tel. (233) 525 66; fax 522 66), on the corner of Taikos g., offers spartan, clean rooms and balconies (singles 40Lt; doubles 30-46Lt; triples 66Lt).

■ Palanga

Every summer, Lithuanians flock to Palanga, one of the former Soviet Union's prime beach resorts, to crowd its streets and brave the icy Baltic. Visitors enjoy sandy beaches, extensive botanical gardens, mineral springs, and a relaxing small-town feel. The best way to spend a day here is at the **beach**, which runs from Girkeliai, 5km south of town, all the way to the border, 18km north. **Nude bathing** is allowed—women control the section starting 200m north of the pier, men head south. At the end of Basanazičiaus g., a plaza opens onto the boardwalk which stretches behind the dunes for the length of the town. Its cafes and bars let you sip away the evening and dance away the weekends. Alternatively, wander through the **Botanical Park** at Palanga's south end. Well-marked paths and flowering trails make for romantic walks around sunset. In the park, Count Tiškevičius's **palace** contains the glittering **Amber Museum**, a gargantuan collection of more than 35,000 pieces of amber (open Tu-Su 10am-8pm, ticket office until 7pm; 5Lt, students 2.5Lt). For recreation along Palanga's many paths, street vendors offer **bikes** (10Lt per hr.), **in-line skates** (7Lt per hr.), and a host of other wheeled vehicles to rent.

Buses run from the station at Jasinsko 1 to Kaunas (3hr., 29Lt), Klaipėda (20min., 2.50Lt), and Vilnius (4-5hr., 39Lt). Get **tourist information** on the second floor of Kretingos 54 (tel./fax (236) 570 40 or 483 79) from a very helpful, mulitlingual staff (open M-F 9am-5pm). **"Palangos Žuvėdra" Viešbutis,** Birutės alėja 52 (info tel. (236) 538 52, registration tel. 532 53), is close to the shore, and offers clean, comfortable but bare doubles with shared bath (50Lt per person). **Vyturio Korpusas,** Dariaus ir Girėno g. 20 (tel. (236) 538 07), offers clean, livable rooms as well as a sauna and pool (singles 60Lt; doubles 90Lt). From the bus station, go left on Vytauto g. to Danaus ir Gireno g. and left again; the hotel is by the soccer fields. Vytauto g. and J. Basanavičiaus g., among others, are lined with **cafes** blaring their music out into the street.

■ Klaipėda

This busy port was always the apple of Lithuania's eye, and centuries of foreign control could not shake the country's hopes of one day reclaiming Klaipėda. That dream has now come true, and proud Lithuanians are softening the lingering effects of Soviet occupation with comfortable cafes, elegant restaurants, and bars throughout the city. Before settling in for the evening, check out the **Klaipėda Theater** in the Old Town center, Teatro aikštė. Built in 1857, the theater is famous as one of Wagner's favorite haunts and infamous for the *Anschluss* (annexation) speech Hitler gave from its balcony in 1939. For tickets, call (026) 21 25 89 (open Tu-Su 10am-2pm and 4-6pm). In front stands the **Simon Dach Fountain**, at the center of which is the symbol of Klaipėda, a statue of Ännchen von Tharau. The **Paveikslų** (Picture Gallery), Liepų 33, has excellent 20th-century Lithuanian art (open Tu-Su noon-6pm; 3Lt, students 1.50Lt; tours 20Lt). Forest paths lead west about 500m to the **beaches.** Signs mark gender-restricted areas for **nude bathing**—*moterų* is women, *vyrų* men. Bars in the Old Town are a staple of Klaipėda nightlife, and a growing number of discos provide evening fun. **Nova,** Janonino 27, a neon palace of a disco, is the most popular place in town (cover 10-20Lt; open W-Su 10pm-late).

The **Danė River** divides the city into the southern **Senamiestis** (Old Town) and northern **Naujamiestis** (New Town), while a lagoon cuts off **Smiltynė,** Klaipėda's Curonian Spit quarter. **Trains** roll from Priestočio g. 7 (tel. (026) 21 46 14, reservations 29 62 91) to Kaunas (7½hr., 23Lt) and Vilnius (5hr., 38Lt). **Buses** also serve Kaunas (2-4hr., 20-25Lt), Nida (2hr., 8Lt), and Vilnius (4-7hr., 30-37Lt) from Butkų Juzės 9 (tel. (026) 21 48 63, reservations 21 14 34). Frequent **ferries** go to Smiltynė (round-trip 1.40Lt). The Litinterp **tourist office,** S. Šimkaus g. 21/8 (tel. (026) 31 14 90; fax 21 98 62), arranges private rooms in and around Klaipėda (doubles 100Lt), rents bikes (20Lt per day with a US$100 deposit), and sells maps and guidebooks (open M-F 9am-6pm, Sa 10am-4pm). **Hotel Viktorija,** S. Šimkaus g. 2 (tel. (026) 21 36 70), offers the best location at the best price (singles 45Lt; doubles 60-65Lt; private bath 120Lt). The central **market** on Turgaus aikštė, at the south end of *Senamiestis,* is open daily 8am to 6pm. **Skandalas,** Kanto 44, is a change from most Lithuanian food; tasty grilled steaks are 20Lt before 6pm, 28Lt after (live jazz at night; open daily noon-3am). **Restoranas Luiza,** Puodžių 4, opposite the Hotel Klaipėda, has a pleasant outside bar (stuffed squid 22Lt; open daily noon-midnight).

■ Nida

If you're watching the sunrise from a high white dune as the crisp smell of smoked fish rises into the air, you must be in Nida. The town lies on the **Curonian Spit** (Kuršiçe Nerija), a 3km wide strip of dunes, unspoiled beaches, and thick pine and birch forests. The **Drifting Dunes of Parnidis** rise south of town. You can hike out and climb the 60m high dune for a spectacular, desert-like view. All of the **wooden houses** clustered along Naglių g. and Lotmiškio g. are classified historic monuments. From the center of town, walk north on Pamario or along the waterfront promenade to reach the **Thomas Mann House** at #17 (open Tu-Su 10am-6pm; 1Lt), where Mann wrote *Joseph and his Brother.* **Buses** from Kaunas and Vilnius run to Naglių 18, just north of Taikos g., but the easiest way to travel may be to take one of the regular **minibuses** to Klaipėda and move from there. The **tourist office,** Taikos g. 4 (tel. (0259) 523 45), opposite the bus and ferry stations, sells maps (3Lt) and arranges accommodations (20-40Lt per person). **Urbo Kalnas,** Taikos g. 32 (tel. (0259) 524 28), will accommodate you in big, high-ceilinged rooms with hot showers (singles 150Lt; doubles 210Lt; breakfast included). **Litinterp** (tel. (26) 21 69 62) in Klaipėda hikes its prices for Nida **private rooms** (singles 100-120Lt; doubles 140-150Lt). The local specialty is *rūkyta žuvis* (smoked fish); selection varies from nondescript "fish" to eel and perch. **Seklyčia,** Lotmiškio 1, is considered to be the best restaurant in town (tomato salad 4Lt; open daily 9am-3pm). **Ešerinė,** Naglių 2, is a wacky thatched-roofed collection of glass-wall huts (pork chops 16.50Lt; *Baltijos* 4Lt).

Luxembourg

US$1= 35.63LF (francs, or LUF)
CDN$1= 23.47LF
UK£1= 59.02LF
IR£1= 51.58LF
AUS$1= 21.05LF
NZ$1= 18.24LF
SAR1= 5.72F
Country Code: 352

10LF =US$0.28
10LF =CDN$0.43
10LF =UK£0.17
10LF =IR£0.19
10LF =AUS$0.48
10LF =NZ$0.55
10LF =SAR1.74
International Dialing Prefix: 00

Founded in 963, the Grand Duchy of Luxembourg was first named *Luclinburhuc*, or "little castle." By the time successive waves of Burgundians, Spaniards, French, Austrians, and Germans had receded, the little castle had become a bristling armored mountain, and the countryside was saturated with fortresses. Only after the last French soldier returned home in 1867 and the Treaty of London restored its neutrality did Luxembourg begin to cultivate its current image of peacefulness. Today Luxembourg is an independent constitutional monarchy, a member of the European Union, and a tax haven for investors world-wide. The Grand Duke and his Cabinet of 12 ministers still wield supreme executive power over the country's 400,000 residents and 2600 sq. km. From the wooded and hilly Ardennes in the north to the fertile vineyards of the Moselle Valley in the south, the country's unspoiled rural landscapes provide a sharp contrast to the high-powered banking of the capital city.

ESSENTIALS

The tiny territory is split into five travel zones: the capital (Luxembourg City), the Moselle, the Mullerthal (Little Switzerland), the Ardennes, and the Land of Red Rocks. The **Luxembourg Card,** if it is still available, allows free use of public transport throughout the Duchy, and free admission to 32 tourist sites (1 day 300LF, family 600LF; 2 days 500LF; 3 days within 1 week 700 LF). The **Billet Réseau** (160LF) allows a day's unlimited second-class travel on any train or national bus. A **billet courte distance** (short distance ticket) is useful for travel within Luxembourg City (40LF, 10 tickets 320 LF). A **Benelux Tourrail Pass,** good for unlimited travel any five days in a month-long period in Belgium, the Netherlands, and Luxembourg, costs 4400LF (under 26 3300LF). **Bicycles** are permitted on many trains for a 40LF fee. **Hitchhiking** has mixed results, as traffic is light and safety is never guaranteed.

The many **tourist offices** are skilled at finding cheap rooms. Hostels frequently give discounts on tours. Luxembourg francs are worth the same as Belgian francs; you can use Belgian money in

Luxembourg

↑ TO LIÈGE

BELGIUM

Troisvierges

Clervaux

Our R.

Clerf R.

GERMANY

Esch-sur-Sûre

Vianden

Sûre R.

Sûre R.

Ettelbrück

Diekirche

Beaufort

Echternach

Berdorf

TO TRIER

Sûre R.

Alzette R.

Hollenfels

Bourglinster

Arlon

Grevenmacher

Mosel R.

Luxembourg City

Remich

Longwy

FRANCE

0   10 miles

0   10 kilometers

TO METZ ↓

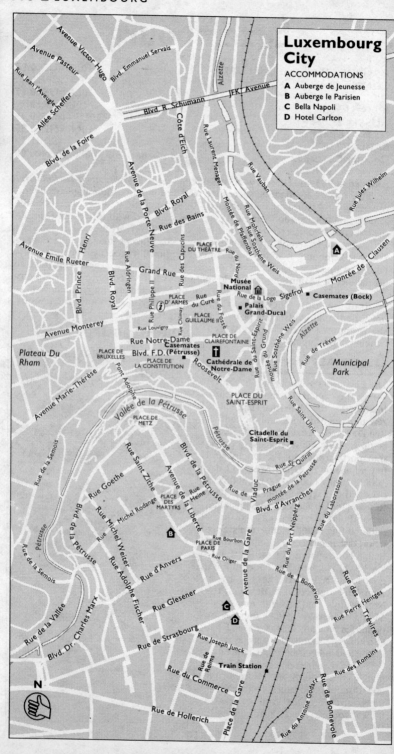

Luxembourg City

ACCOMMODATIONS

A Auberge de Jeunesse
B Auberge le Parisien
C Bella Napoli
D Hotel Carlton

Luxembourg, and vice versa. Most **banks** are open Monday through Friday 8:30am to 4:30pm; most shops are open Monday 2 to 6pm and Tuesday through Saturday 9:30am to 6pm. Many shops close at noon for two hours, especially in the countryside, where only taverns may be open after 6pm.

Luxembourg's official **languages** are French and German, but the most common is Letzebuergesch, a German dialect with French loanwords. French is often preferred to German; English is heard nearly everywhere. For **AT&T Direct,** call 08 00 01 11; **MCI WorldPhone** 08 00 01 12; **Sprint Access** 08 00 01 15; **Canada Direct** 08 00 01 19; **BT Direct** 08 00 00 44; and **NZ Direct** 08 00 57 84.

Citizens of most Asian, African, Eastern European, and South American countries need a visa to enter the country. Australians, Canadians, and U.S. citizens need only a valid passport.

ACCOMMODATIONS, CAMPING, AND FOOD The 11 **HI youth hostels** in Luxembourg charge 355-650LF, over 26 435-650LF; nonmembers 100LF extra. Breakfast is included, a packed lunch costs 125LF, and dinner 260LF—eating a meal in the hostel earns a 15LF discount. All but one of the hostels have kitchen facilities. Sheets are 125LF. Hostels will usually hold your bag for the day free of charge. Many hostels close during December and January. Call ahead to verify hours, since check-in at the smaller hostels is often limited to 5-11pm. You can, however, drop off your bags in the common rooms, which are open all day. **Hotels** advertise 800-1500LF per night but often try to persuade tourists to take more expensive rooms. **Campgrounds** abound; nearly all have hot showers. Two people with a tent will pay 250-300LF. Restaurant prices will devour your budget. Luxembourg cuisine is closely linked to that of the neighboring Lorraine region of France, and sliced Ardennes ham is the national specialty. The sparkling wines of the Moselle Valley will please most gourmets.

■ Luxembourg City (Ville de Luxembourg)

Overlooking the lush valleys of the Pétrusse and Alzette Rivers, Luxembourg City is one of the most attractive and dramatic capitals in Europe. Its diversity of languages, varied cuisines, and chic clubs reflect its status as an international banking capital and European Community center. But there is a quieter, more intimate Luxembourg City worth seeking out in the small cafes and bars, in the valleys, and in the patrician houses that line the narrow streets.

PRACTICAL INFORMATION

Flights: Bus 9 to the airport (40LF plus a rarely enforced 40LF charge for baggage) is cheaper than the Luxair bus (120LF) and runs the same airport-hostel-train station route more frequently (every 20min.).

Trains: Gare CFL, av. de la Gare (tel. 49 24 24), near the foot of av. de la Liberté in the southern part of the city (10min. from the city center). Bus 9 runs between the railway station, the HI hostel, and the airport. Pick it up on your right as you leave the station, in front of the Luxair office. To: Amsterdam (5¾hr., 16,342LF), Brussels (2¾hr., 890LF, under 26 520LF), and Frankfurt (5hr.). Call 49 90 49 90 (free) or consult http://www.cfl.lu for national and international train schedules.

Buses: Buy tickets from the driver (40LF; valid 1hr. or 160LF for full day), or get a package of 10 (320LF) at banks.

Taxis: (tel. 48 22 33). 64LF per km. 10% more 10pm-6am. 25% more on Su. 700-800LF from city center to airport.

Bikes: Rent bikes from 8 rue Bisserwé (tel. 22 27 52). Open M-F 1-8pm, Sa-Su 9am-noon and 1-8pm. 100LF per hr., 400LF per day. 20% discount for those under 26, and groups of 4 or more.

Tourist Offices: Grand Duchy National Tourist Office, in the train station (tel. 48 11 99; fax 40 47 48; email touristinfo@luxembourg-city.lu; http://www.luxembourg-city.lu/touristinfo/). Free map and reservations service. Open 9am-noon and

2-6:30pm. The **Municipal Tourist Office,** pl. d'Armes (tel. 22 28 09; fax 47 48 18), in the center of town, offers more specific city info. Open M-Sa 9am-7pm, Su 10am-6pm. At either location grab *La Semaine à Luxembourg* (free).

Budget Travel: SOTOUR, 15 pl. du Théâtre (tel. 46 15 14). BIJ and other discount tickets; plane, train, and hotel reservations. Open M-F 9am-6pm, Sa 9am-noon.

Embassies: Travelers from **Australia, Canada, New Zealand,** and **South Africa** should contact their embassies in France or Belgium. **Ireland,** 28 rue d'Arlon (tel. 45 06 10; fax 45 88 20). Open M-F 9am-12:30pm and 2-5pm. **U.K.,** 14 bd. Roosevelt (tel. 22 98 64; fax 22 98 67). Same hours as Ireland. **U.S.,** 22 bd. E. Servais (tel. 46 01 23). Open M-F 8am-5pm.

Currency Exchange: Mediocre rates at the train station *bureau de change.* Open M-Sa 8:30am-9pm, Su 9am-9pm. Banks have similar rates. The HI youth hostel will exchange many currencies for comparable or better rates. An automatic **currency exchange machine** is across from the station at Banque UCL.

ATM: Most of the automatic tellers accept PLUS, Cirrus, Visa, and MC.

American Express: 34 av. de la Porte-Neuve (tel. 22 85 55). Mail held. Traveler's checks cashed, sold, and replaced; wired money accepted. Exchange rates slightly better than banks. Open M-F 9am-1pm and 2-5:30pm, Sa 9:30am-noon.

Luggage Storage: At the station. Check and insure your bags for up to 1 month. 100LF per day. Open daily 4am-1am. Lockers, good for 2 days, are 60-100LF. Hotels and hostels will often hold bags for the day free of charge.

Laundromat: Quick Wash, 31 rue de Strasbourg, near the station. Wash 290LF, dry 90LF. Open M-F 8:30am-7pm, Sa 8am-6pm. Cheaper at the HI hostel (250F).

Police: tel. 113. The station is at 60 rue Glesner (tel. 40 94 01).

Crisis Lines: tel. 54 16 16; M-Tu and Th-F 9am-5pm, W noon-5pm; English-speaking. **SOS Distress,** tel. 45 45 45; daily 3-11pm; English-speaking. **SOS Drogue,** tel. 49 60 99, for drug problems; 24hr.; usually no English assistance.

Pharmacy: Pharmacie du Globe, 12 rue Jean Origier (tel. 48 70 09), off av. de la Gare. Open M-F 8am-6pm. Dial 112 on weekends to find a pharmacy, or look in any pharmacy window for the address of the current *pharmacie de garde.*

Medical Emergencies: tel. 112. English spoken. Open 24hr.

Post Office: Main office, 38 pl. de la Gare, across the street and to the left of the train station. Open M-F 6am-7pm, Sa 6am-noon. **Branch office** at 25 rue Aldringern, 2 blocks from pl. d'Armes. Open M-F 7am-8pm, Sa 7am-6pm. *Poste Restante* available at both offices. **Postal Code:** For *Poste Restante,* address mail L-1009 for main office and L-1118 for the branch office in the center.

Telephones: Outside both post offices and in two locations at the train station. Buy a phone card at the train station or post office for 50 units (50 short calls in the city), 250LF. Coin phones are only in hostels and hotels.

ACCOMMODATIONS AND CAMPING

Inexpensive hotels jam the streets near the train station, but they become increasingly pricey and posh as you move north of the ravine. Both the main and branch tourist offices will help you find cheap rooms.

Auberge de Jeunesse (HI), 2 rue du Fort Olisy (tel. 22 68 89). Take bus 9 from the airport or train station; ask the driver to let you off at the hostel. From the stop, walk under the bridge and turn right down the steep path. Can be noisy, with lots of students. Bar, pool table, and laundry. Clean dorms and rooms for groups. Dorms 415-465LF, over 26 500-560F; singles 630LF, over 26 730LF; doubles 1100LF, over 26 1120LF. Nonmembers add 110LF. Breakfast included. Sheets 125LF. Reception 7am-10pm. Lockout 10am-1:30pm. Curfew 2am.

Hotel Carlton, 9 rue de Strasbourg (tel. 48 48 02; fax 29 96 64). From the station, walk up av. de la Liberté and turn left on rue de Strasbourg. Beautiful hotel; friendly staff. Singles 750LF; doubles 1400LF, with bath 1700LF. Breakfast included. (Prices may rise after current renovations.) Wheelchair accessible. 24hr. reception.

Bella Napoli, 4 rue de Strasbourg (tel. 48 46 29; fax 48 64 80), opposite Hotel Carlton. Plain rooms, all with showers and toilets. Singles 1500LF; doubles 1800LF; triples 2400LF. Breakfast included.

Auberge Le Parisien, 46 rue Ste-Zithe (tel. 49 23 97; fax 40 20 92). From the station walk down av. de la Liberté to pl. de Paris. Small, clean rooms, all with a TV. Singles 1350LF; doubles 1850LF; triples 2300LF; quads 2800LF. Breakfast included. Call ahead for reservations. Open Jan. 9-Dec. 22.

Camping: Kockelscheuer (tel. 47 18 15). Bus 2 from the station. 140LF, children 50LF. Tents 120LF. Showers included. Wheelchair accessible. Open Easter-Oct.

FOOD

Most restaurants are crowded by Luxembourgeois with cash to spare, but with a little searching, you can actually afford to eat. The area around **Place d'Armes,** blanketed with outdoor terraces and frequent live music, is great for dining. **La Fournée Dorée** on Rue du Cuse sells excellent sandwiches for 80F. For a touch of class without high prices, try **Restaurant Bacchus,** 32 Marché-aux-Herbes, down the street from the Grand-Ducal palace (excellent pizza 300LF; open Tu-Su noon-10pm). **Bella Napoli,** 4 rue de Strasbourg, has an extensive Italian menu: 250LF for a pizza, and dinner-size pastas start at 320LF. **Girogio,** 11 rue du Nord, has veggie options (330LF), while **Maybe Not Bob's,** 107 rue de la Tour Jacob, complements its veggie fare (340-425LF) with burgers (305LF) and spare ribs (355LF). Gather up the fixings for a picnic in the parks by the ravine at the subterranean supermarket **Nobilis,** 47 av. de la Gare (open M-F 9am-7:30pm, Sa 8:30am-1pm).

SIGHTS AND ENTERTAINMENT

The tourist office provides free leaflets for a 2½-hour self-guided tour through the historic city center. Guided tours of the **city promenade** are available (2hr. tour Easter-Oct. daily at 2:30pm; meet at the Municipal tourist office; 240LF). The **Wenzel walk** takes you through 1000 years of history in 100 minutes as it winds around the walls of the old city and down into the casemates. Tours are held every Saturday at 3pm (280LF, children 140LF) and begin at the **Bock-Casemates.** Looming imposingly over the Alzette River valley, this fortress (part of Luxembourg's original castle, dating back to the 10th century) sheltered 35,000 people while the rest of the city was pounded during World War II. (Entrance on rue Sigefroi near the bridge leading to the hostel. Open Mar.-Oct. daily 10am-5pm. 70LF.) If that isn't enough, descend into the **Pétrusse Casemates,** on the place de la Constitution. Dating back to the 1600s, these fortifications were built by the Spanish and later improved by the Austrians (open July-Sept.; daily guided tours 11am-4pm; 70LF). Back above ground, check out the imposing medieval **Citadel of the Holy Ghost,** midway up the side of a cliff. The 17th-century **Notre Dame Cathedral,** incorporating features of the Dutch Renaissance and early Baroque styles, reflects the town's varied history in its architecture. (Open Easter-Oct. M-F 10am-5pm, Sa 8am-6pm, Su 10am-6pm; Nov.-Easter M-F 10-11:30am and 2-5pm, Sa 8-11:30am and 2-5pm, Su 10am-5pm. Free.) The **Musée National d'Histoire et d'Art** houses an eclectic mix of Roman relics, modern art of local painters, and collections of weapons, coins, ceramics, and decorative crafts of Luxembourg (open Tu-Su 10am-5pm; 100LF, children 50LF). The city's most beautiful sights may well be in the many parks lining the valleys. Take the lift down from Constitution Square, turn right on rue St-Ulric and then right on rue St-Quirin to reach the tranquil valley of the Pétrusse river. *La Semaine à Luxembourg,* free at the tourist office, lists the week's events, including free summer concerts in the city center.

Luxembourg's nocturnal debauchery centers around the numerous bars that line the valley in Grund and Rue de Hollerich near the train station. Wednesday, Friday, and Saturday nights are the most popular. Check the monthly **Nightlife.lu,** available at most newsstands, for the happening sites. Warm up for the night with a jolly older crowd at **Cafe des Artistes,** 22 Montée du Grund, a candle-lit piano bar. Then climb up the valley for a drink in the cavernous **Yesterday's Pub,** 6 Rue de la Loge. **Chiggeri,** 11 rue de Nord, parties until dawn, and **Cafe-Club David,** 30 av. Emile Reuter, is popular with gay men. Chic **Marx,** 42-44 Rue de Hollerich, is where to be seen. If clubs are more your style, groove at **Down Under,** 10 Rue de la Loge.

THE COUNTRYSIDE

In 1944 the Battle of the Bulge raged through Luxembourg, mashing the Ardennes into slime and mud. Now, 50 years later, the forest is verdant again, its thick greenery broken only by the many small, shallow rivers. The valleys and castles draw thousands of Deutsch and Dutch tourists as well as travelers from around the world.

Miles of hiking trails cut through dark wooded areas up mountainsides and past waterfalls. A web of **bus** and **train** routes blanket the countryside, especially in July and August when extra routes are added. The one-day *Billet Réseau* pass (160LF) makes it possible to visit many towns in a day. Take a bus from the city to **Grevenmacher** (35min.), continue on to **Echternach** (40min.) and then to **Diekirch** (25min.) All buses going to **Vianden** stop in Diekirch (15min.). The bus to **Ettelbrück** (10min.), where you can catch a train back to the city, completes the loop (1hr., 50LF). You can also head north from Ettelbrück to **Clervaux** (30min.), and stay in the **HI hostel** (tel. 980 18) across from the train station in **Troisvierges** (10min. by train from Clervaux; 435LF, under 26 355LF).

■ Echternach

Best known for its impressive 7th-century Benedictine monastery, Echternach is a beautiful town next to the German border in an area known as **Petite Suisse Luxembourgeoise** (Little Switzerland in Luxembourg). As you exit the bus station, turn left at the marketplace on av. de la Gare, take the last left, and walk past the church to see the **Abbaye**, whose museum provides a short but interesting history of the monastery. Echternach also serves as a base for hiking, mountain biking, windsurfing, and spelunking. The **tourist office**, 9-10 Parvis de la Basilique (tel. 72 02 30), offers information on outdoor activities. From the bus station, walk down av. de la Gare and follow the signs to your left (open M-F 9:30am-noon and 2-5pm, Sa 10am-noon and 2-4pm). The **HI youth hostel**, 9 rue André Drechscher (tel. 72 01 58), has clean rooms and a genial management. Turn left on av. de la Gare as you leave the bus station, and make the last right (10min.; 435LF, under 26 355LF; sheets 125LF; reception 5-9pm). Cheap **eateries** line the central av. de la Gare, including a little *friture* that serves German *bratwurst* with Belgian *frites*. Stop at the **Cafe de Philo'soff**, 31 av. de la Gare, to check signs for local jazz and classical concerts.

■ The Moselle and Sûre Valleys

The **Moselle Valley,** with its sunny weather and abundance of water, was discovered by French winemakers as a suitable substitute for the Champagne region of France. Now, the valley is renowned not only for its sparkling wines (often marked *méthode champenoise*), but also for its still wines such as *Riesling* and *Pinot Gris*. The village of **Grevenmacher,** once home to a training ground for the *greven* (a second-class form of nobility), is right in the center of this wine culture and makes a convenient base from which to explore the famous vineyards. Begin with a tour of the **Bernard-Massard winery,** rue du Vin, right next to the bridge. You'll learn all about the Champagne method, but more importantly, you'll indulge in a glass of excellent sparkling wine at the end of the tour (open Apr.-Oct. daily 9:30am-6pm; 90LF). A **Jardin des Papillons** (butterfly garden) lies nearby (open Apr. to mid-Oct. daily 9:30am-5pm; 180LF, with winery 240LF). Grevenmacher is the site of an **international wine festival** that takes place the second weekend of September.

To reach Grevenmacher's **HI youth hostel,** 15 Gruewereck (tel. 75 02 22; fax 75 91 46), from the bus stop, turn left on Route de Trèves, then make a right on R. P d'Osbourg, which becomes R. des Remparts, and follow that road to the end. At the "T" turn right, and 10m away a staircase will take you up to the hostel (15-20min.). Call ahead for reservations (435LF, under 26 355LF; reception 5-9pm). Few buses or trains run through this secluded valley, but **riverboats** glide along regularly on the placid Moselle (Grevenmacher-Remich 240LF, round-trip 370LF). **Buses** run to Grevenmacher from Echternach throughout the day (40min.).

If you tire of the Moselle, tackle the **Sûre River**, where kayaking is readily available. The **Outdoor Center**, 10 rue de la Sûre, L-6350 Dillingen (tel. 86 91 39; fax 86 91 43), has everything you'll need. The shop will pick up kayaks but not people at the final destination. In summer, call ahead to reserve. (1-person kayak 700LF; 2-person kayak 1000LF; Dillingen-Echternach about 2-5hr. paddling). In **Diekirch** (15min. from Dillingen by bus), the **Historical Museum,** 10 Bamental, around the corner from the tourist office, presents a powerful exhibition of relics from World War II's Battle of the Bulge. The 6th-century **Vieille Église Saint-Laurent** (Old Church of St. Laurence) is built like a compact Roman vestibule and has beautiful 15th-century frescoes. Around the corner from the 15th-century **Église Saint-Laurent,** the **Municipal Museum,** Place Guillaume, houses three wonderful Roman mosaics. (Museum open Easter-Oct. F-W 10am-noon and 2-6pm.) The **tourist office**, 1, Esplanade (tel. 80 30 23), across from the church, has museum info and makes hotel reservations (open M-Sa 9am-6pm). There is no hostel here, so stay in Echternach or Luxembourg City.

■ Vianden

Just across the river from Germany, Vianden was the ancestral home of the Orange-Nassau dynasty, rulers of Holland and (in the person of William III) England as well. Nestled within rocky cliffs and the dense Ardennes woods, this quiet and beautiful town makes for an idyllic retreat from the frenzy of city life. It's a good base from which to visit neighboring Diekirch and Clervaux, or launch bike, hiking, or kayak excursions. The village spills down a steep hill beneath a renovated 9th-century **château.** (Open daily Apr.-Sept. 10am-6pm.; Mar. and Oct. 10am-5pm; Nov.-Feb. 10am-4pm. 180LF, students 130LF.) For a great view of the château, ride the **télésiège** (chairlift) from rue de Sanatorium, 500m upstream from the tourist office, down rue de Victor Hugo. (Open spring and summer daily 10am-5pm. Round-trip 160LF; one-way with easy hike down 90LF.) With a small hike, the ascent also affords a view of Europe's largest hydroelectric plant, the **Barrage.**

Buses arrive from Echternach and Ettelbrück via Diekirch about once an hour. Rent bikes from Beltendorf René (tel. 84 92 22; 550LF per day). The **tourist office** (tel. 842 57; fax 84 90 81) is in the **Victor Hugo House,** on rue de la Gare beside the bridge over the River Our (open Easter-Sept. daily 9:30am-noon and 2-6pm; Oct.-Easter M-Sa same hours). To reach the **HI youth hostel,** 3 Montée du Château (tel. 83 41 77; 5min. downhill from the château), cross the bridge from the tourist office and follow the Grande Rue until it curves to the left and ends. Clean, intimate rooms; friendly staff. (435LF, under 26 355LF. Sheets 125LF. Reception 5-9pm, later if you call ahead. Accepts many groups in early summer; closed Dec.-Feb. to all but groups.) Numerous hotels litter Grande Rue, and the tourist office lists rooms in private homes (singles from 800LF, doubles 1000LF). **Camp op dem Deich** (tel. 84 92 91), a five-minute walk downstream from the tourist office, offers campsites in the shadow of the château (130LF per person and per tent; open Easter-Aug.).

Food in Vianden is good, cheap, and plentiful, with a strong Germanic influence. Try one of the local **grasseries** for a full meal of soup, salad, meat (like *entrecôte* or *wiener schnitzel*), and dessert for 400LF, or head to one of the many smoked meat shops on Grande Rue. Get groceries at **Economart,** 1 rue de la Gare (open M-Sa 8am-6pm and Su 10am-noon).

Near Vianden, nestled in the northern town of **Clervaux,** the **château** houses the striking **Family of Man exhibition.** This collection of over 500 pictures from 68 countries depicts all aspects of human life and emotions. It was compiled in 1955 by Edward Steichen, a photographer born in Luxembourg, and has been displayed around the world (open Mar.-Dec. Tu-Su 10am-12pm and 1-6pm; 150LF).

Former Yugoslav Republic of Macedonia (Македонија)

US$1	= 39dn (denars)		10dn =	US$0.26
CDN$1	= 25dn		10dn =	CDN$0.40
UK£1	= 64dn		10dn =	UK£0.16
IR£1	= 54dn		10dn =	IR£0.18
AUS$1	= 22dn		10dn =	AUS$0.45
NZ$1	= 19dn		10dn =	NZ$0.52
SAR1	= 6.12dn		10dn =	SAR1.63
DM1	= 22dn		10dn =	DM0.46

Country Phone Code: 389   **International Dialing Prefix: 99**

Although years of U.N.- and Greek-enforced trade embargoes damaged its economy, Macedonia is slowly regaining its place among Southern European resorts. Its greater problem now may be the escalating unrest between the country's different ethnic groups—especially its large, underprivileged Albanian minority. Current problems notwithstanding, Macedonia's historical and geographical treasures remain intact, accessible, and welcoming. The lively capital and the spectacular mountain basin that is home to Lake Ohrid make Macedonia a necessary and memorable addition to any Balkan itinerary.

> For brevity's sake, *Let's Go* uses the name "Macedonia" to refer to the Former Yugoslav Republic of Macedonia. *Let's Go* does not endorse any perceived claims of the former Yugoslav Republic to the Greek territory of the same name.

ESSENTIALS

Irish and U.K. citizens need only a valid passport to enter Macedonia. Citizens of Australia, Canada, and the U.S. can procure visas at any border crossing at no cost. New Zealanders and South Africans must submit their passports to a Macedonian embassy or consulate (US$14 for 90-day single-entry). Allow 10 days for processing.

You can reach Macedonia by air, bus, or train. The airlines **Adria** (Slovenian), **CRO** (Croatian), **Balkan** (Bulgarian), and **MAT** (Macedonian) fly to Skopje, the capital. Many people prefer to travel by land from Sofia, Bulgaria, or Thessaloniki, Greece, though the **train** system is not extensive. Luckily, **buses** run frequently and reliably to most destinations. Be warned: border crossings can take a long time, as there are often traffic backups for miles. **Hitchhiking** in Macedonia, which *Let's Go* does not recommend, is uncommon.

Changing money on the street is illegal. Most hard currency prices in Macedonia are given in **Deutschmarks (DM)**, although most banks will readily accept U.S. dollars or British pounds and cash **AmEx** traveler's checks. Few places accept **credit cards**, and some major hotels accept only cash. **ATMs** take MC and Cirrus.

Place international collect calls via Macedonia's **AT&T Direct** operator (tel. (99) 800 42 88). International calls may be a challenge at card-operated phones; try an assigned phone at the post office instead. To get an international line, dial 99. To make local calls from public phones, you must buy a microchip **phone card** (100 or 200dn) at a post office. Some kiosks also sell them or lend their own phones for a fee.

Macedonian and **Bulgarian** are mutually intelligible. **Russian** is widely understood, as are **Serbian** and **Croatian. English** is quickly becoming the second language of choice in Macedonia, and many young people in urban areas are fluent. Older Macedonians may reverse the Western style of **head movements** for "yes" and "no;" confirm everything with words.

> Recent political events have made it inadvisable to enter Albania or the Kosovo Region of Serbia; even traveling near the border may be dangerous, due as much to bandits as to soldiers and police.

A hotel or hostel will take your passport at check-in: all businesses offering accommodations are required by law to **register** passports with the police. You'll get the passport back at the end of your stay; try to get it back earlier if you are expecting *Poste Restante* or if you plan to cash traveler's checks. Free-lance **camping** is popular, but you risk a fine and it's not safe. Camping in reserve areas is prohibited.

Tipping in small amounts is customary—5% is a good guideline for decent service. When restaurants are crowded, share a table with the locals and practice your Macedonian. **Homosexuality** is illegal in Macedonia, and there is a general lack of tolerance toward lesbians and gay men. Life here will be easier if you do not express views or preferences openly.

■ Skopje (Скопје)

The rolling hills, tilled fields, and orange-roofed suburbs that surround Skopje lend the city a sense of rural serenity—an impression quickly corrected upon the first choking attempt to breathe the smog-filled air in the nation's bustling capital. Miraculously, the earthquake that destroyed most of Skopje in 1963 preserved the Old Bazaar and some of the city's ancient churches and mosques.

SIGHTS AND ENTERTAINMENT Most of Skopje's historical sights are an easy walk from the bus station. The domes of the 15th-century **Daut-Pashin Amam** (Даут-Пашин Амам; Turkish baths), now an art gallery, are visible from the bus station. The baths serve as a gateway to the enchanting streets of the **Stara Charshiya** (Old Bazaar). Largely Albanian and Muslim, the Old Bazaar stands in stark contrast to the modern side of town. Climb the stairs on the left side of the shopping center "Most," climb the stairs, and turn right onto Samoilova (Самоилова) until you reach a small square with a fountain. Across the square is **Sveti Spas** (Свети Спас; tel. 23 38 12), an orthodox church where frescoes of God and a few angels hover over marble floors and a masterful walnut iconostasis (open Tu-F 7am-7pm, Sa-Su 9am-5pm; 60dn, students 30dn). Farther up Samoilova, **Mustafa Pashina Jamiya** (Мустафа Пашина џамија; Mustafa Pasha Mosque), marks its 504th year. The mosque's key-holder will let you in any time he's around, usually between 5am and 10pm. Every Friday at 1pm, hundreds gather to listen to the preaching of the *Hodzha*, or *Imam*. Skopje has a long-standing fascination with jazz, but blues is the craze of the moment. **Lady Blue I,** just off pl. Makedonija at Louis Pasteur 3, is the most popular blues venue (music Tu-Su 9pm-3am; arrive early to avoid huge crowds). A more bohemian clientele congregates at **Van Gogh,** an artsy bar at Mihali Chokov 4 (Михали Чоков); turn left off Ilinden immediately past Hertz.

PRACTICAL INFO, ACCOMMODATIONS, AND FOOD Despite being a city of half a million, Skopje has managed to consolidate many points of interest along a small stretch of the **Vardar River.** Flights arrive at **Skopje Airport/Aerodrome Petrovec** (tel. (91) 77 10 23 and 23 51 56) near the hamlet Petrovec. Trains run from the new **train station** (Нова Железница Станица; *nova zheleznitsa stanitsa*), Bulevar Kuzman Yosifovski bb (Кузман Јосифовски) to Budapest (2650dn) and Thessaloniki, Greece (700dn). The easiest way to purchase tickets is through **Feroturist**

(Феротурист; tel. (91) 11 62 48), in the station (open M-F 7am-8pm, Sa 7am-3:30pm). Catch **buses** at the entrance to the Old Town (info tel. (91) 23 62 54). The cheery English speakers at the **tourist office** (Скопје Туристичка Информација; tel. (91) 11 68 64; fax 23 08 03), around the corner from the bus station (in the shopping center), provide maps and book private rooms (open M-Sa 8am-7:30pm). Skopje has three Cirrus/MC **ATMs,** the most convenient of which is in the shopping center.

Accommodations are scarce and overpriced. Most hotels are still state-run and charge 3000-5000dn per person. Private pensions and rooms are better options (700-1200dn, but frequently negotiable), and can be booked through the tourist office and tourist agencies. Friendly students, **Internet access,** and a hopping social scene await at the **Student Dorm Gotse Delchev** (Гоце Делчев; tel. 36 33 06), Ivo Ribar Lola bb (Иво Рибар Лола), 4km from the city center. Take a taxi for 100dn or less on your first trip (300-450dn; dorms open only to foreign travelers June-Aug.). Or try the private **Hotel Laki** (Хотел Лаки), Leninova 79 (Ленинова; tel. 23 55 97). Go west on Ivo Ribar Lola, cross St. Klement Ohridski, and take the first right on Leninova. Insist on a room in the reception building, or they may stick you in a poorly lit apartment 2 blocks away (from 1100dn per person; reception 7am-11pm).

You'll find some of Skopje's best dishes toasting over coals in the streets of **Stara Charshiya.** Finding vegetarian food in Skopje's eateries is somewhat like searching for intelligent life in the universe—it may be out there, but don't hold your breath while you look. Request *"neshto bez meso"* (something without meat). **Idadiya III** (Идадија III), Rade Konchar bb (Раде Кончар; tel. 11 05 22), has classic Macedonian cuisine (open daily 8am-midnight).

■ Ohrid (Охрид)

Ohrid is Macedonia's premier summer resort, and arguably its most beautiful town. A profusion of cafes fan out from the main square by the shore, giving way to small shops on narrow streets up the sloping Old Town.   To get to the center from the bus station, make a right onto Partizanska (Партизанска). The collection of white, orange-roofed houses on the hill is the Old Town. Ohrid's many churches and monasteries are worth exploring. **Sveta Sofia** (Света Софија), Ohrid's oldest church, has 11th-century frescoes of scenes from both the Old and New Testaments. To get there, walk toward the lake on Kliment Ohridski, turn right on Tsar Samoil, and continue for about 300m (open Tu-Su 9am-1pm and 5-10pm; 50dn, students 30dn). Performances of the **Festival Ohridsko Leto** (July 12-Aug. 20) are held with the church as a backdrop. **Sveti Kliment** (Свети Климент) is high on the hill above town and has revisionist frescoes of a vegetarian last supper (open daily 9am-7pm in summer, shorter hours off-season). The 13th-century **Sveti Yovan** (Свети Јован) perches on the lip of a cliff overlooking the lake. Take the steps behind Sveta Sofia (to the left as you exit) to Kocho Ratsin (Кочо Рацин), then follow the cliff path to the church.

Buses go to Istanbul (1600dn), Skopje (3½-5hr., 10 per day, 260-300dn), and Sofia (900dn). The **tourist office AD Galeb-Bilyana** (АД Галеб-Билјана), Partizanska 3 (tel. 224 94; fax 241 14), in the bus station building and one of many tourist bureaus in the center, finds private rooms (300-700dn per person; apartments from 1350dn) and sells new maps. **Exchange money** and cash AmEx **traveler's checks** at **Ohridska Banka** (Охридска Банка), on the corner of Makedonski Prosvetiteli and Turistichka bul. (Туристичка; tel. (096) 314 00; open daily 8am-5pm); there are **no ATMs** in Ohrid. The rates for **private rooms** are good (300-400dn), but lower-end prices usually don't include the 20dn daily tax. **Pop Markov Dimitar,** Kosta Abrash 48 (Коста Абраш; tel. (096) 09 62 00 or 26 12 00), offers two triples with common bath and kitchen near the lake and the town center (US$10 per person). The exceptionally helpful family will refer you to neighbors if they are booked. **Hotel Park** (tel. 26 15 21 or 26 36 71; fax 26 00 61), 2km south of Ohrid, has camping for only 9dn (reception 24hr.). **Restoran Antico,** Tsar Samoil 30, sits at the base of the old town and serves excellent local food (open daily 10:30am-2am). The **gradsko pazarishte** (градско пазариште; town market), between Gotse Delchev and Turistichka, sells fruit and vegetables (open daily 8am-8pm), and the mellow **Jazz Inn,** Kosta Abrash 74, has good music and a great location (open daily 9pm-2am).

Malta

Malta is a fairy-tale island, in whose crowded past lurk knights in shining armor, pirates, and the salvation of Christian Europe. The archipelago, consisting of the islands of Malta, Gozo, and Comino, as well as the uninhabited islets of Cominotto in the north and Fifla to the south, has become a major tourist destination. Maltese is the official language, but everyone knows English. The Maltese **lira** (Lm) is divided into 100 **cents** (¢). One U.S. dollar is worth about Lm0.40; one U.K. pound is worth about Lm0.65. Visitors must declare foreign currency upon arrival, and may take no more than Lm25 in unspent Maltese currency out of the country. Dial 190 for **telephone assistance.** The **emergency** number is 196. Malta's **country code** is 356.

Citizens of Australia, Canada, EU countries, New Zealand, and the U.S. can stay in Malta without a visa for up to three months. South African citizens need to obtain a visa (see **Government Information Offices**, p. 4). **Island Seaway** runs from Catania in Sicily and Reggio Calabria in Italy to Valletta. **Virtu Ferries** sends speedy catamarans to Catania and Syracuse (each round-trip Lm36). Reach Reggio Calabria by **train** from Naples (5hr., L38,500), Catania from Syracuse (1½hr., L8000). **Flights** leave from Rome (round-trip about Lm130) on **Air Malta** (tel. 69 08 90) and **Alitalia** (tel. 24 67 82). In Valletta, **NSTS** travel service, 220 St. Paul's St. (tel. 24 49 83), has cheap plane fares (open M-Sa 9am-1pm; irregular afternoon hours). Buses 8 and 39 run between the airport and Valletta (6am-8pm, 11¢). If taking a **taxi,** agree on a price in advance.

Valletta Capital of the nation, Valletta is located on a narrow finger of land on Malta's southeast side. **Republic Street,** the city's backbone, has shops and restaurants, and most of the important sights are not far away. **St. John's Co-Cathedral** (1573-1577) vaunts an absurdly ornate Baroque interior and contains Caravaggio's two final masterpieces. The historical residence of Malta's rulers since 1574, the opulent **Grand Master's Palace** is just beyond the cathedral. **The Malta Experience,** at the Mediterranean Conference Center along the Grand Harbor, gives an introduction to the islands (shows every hr. M-F 11am-4pm, Sa-Su 11am-1pm; Lm2.50).

The **tourist office** (tel. 23 77 47) is just inside the City Gate. (Open Apr.-Oct. M-Sa 8:30am-6:30pm, Su 8:30am-1pm; Nov.-Mar. M-Sa 8:30am-5:30pm, Su 8:30am-1pm.) There is another office at the airport, and the **NSTS** office (see above) is also extremely helpful. The **Asti Guest House,** 18 St. Ursula St. (tel. 23 95 06; Lm5.50), and **Coronation Guest House,** 10 E.M.A. Vassalli St. (tel. 23 76 52; Lm4-5), are in Valletta. The suburbs of **Sliema, St. Julian's,** and **Paceville** offer better nightlife (take bus 62, 64, 67, 68, 667, 662, or 671 from the fountain outside Valletta's main gate; 5:30am-11pm). Reserve ahead through NSTS for Sliema's **Hibernia House** (tel. 33 38 59), Depiro St. (Lm2.70-3.70). **Agius Pastizzeria,** 273 St. Paul's St. in Valletta, has cheap take-out. **Axis,** on Saint George's Road, is Paceville's best disco.

Near Valletta Once the island's capital, **Mdina** (em-DEE-nah) hasn't changed much since its glory days. Inside Mdina's 9th-century Saracen fortifications lies a preserved 17th-century Baroque world. **St. Paul's Catacombs** and **St. Agatha's Catacombs** offer Christian and Jewish relics. Take bus 80 or 81 to Mdina from Valletta, or bus 65 from Sliema. The popular **Blue Grotto** hides near the end of bus route 38. Boats leave the harbor for the phosphorescent wonder (call 82 99 25 in advance; Lm2.50). The astonishing megalithic temples of **Hagar Qim** and **Mnajdra** are a 20-minute walk away. The best bet for **beaches** is the west coast, where crowded **Golden Bay** (bus 47 from Valletta, 652 from Sliema) leads to quieter **Gnejna Bay.** Try the **Marfa** peninsula in the northwest, or take bus 11 to **Pretty Bay** in the east.

The Netherlands (Nederland)

US$1	= fl.95 (guilders)		fl =	**US$0.51**
CDN$1	= fl.28		fl =	**CDN$0.78**
UK£1	= f3.23		fl =	**UK£0.31**
IR£1	= f2.83		fl =	**IR£0.35**
AUS$1	= fl.15		fl =	**AUS$0.87**
NZ$1	= fl.00		fl =	**NZ$1.00**
SAR1	= f0.31		fl =	**SAR3.23**
Country Code: 31			**International Dialing Prefix: 00**	

The Dutch say that although God created the rest of the world, they created the Netherlands. The country is truly a masterful feat of engineering: since most of the country is below sea level, vigorous pumping and a series of dikes were used to create thousands of square kilometers of land (including Amsterdam). What was once the domain of seaweed and cod is now sprinkled with windmills, cheese, tulips, and the occasional wooden shoe.

During the Age of Exploration, Dutch conquerors fanned out over the globe, as the Dutch East and West India Companies traded as far afield as Java, the Caribbean, and Africa, and set up a small colony they called "New Amsterdam" which eventually burgeoned into New York. The wealth flowing into the country from these commercial ventures contributed to the Dutch Golden Age in the 17th century. During this time, Holland also served as a sanctuary for Europe's religious and political dissidents, and this atmosphere of freedom and tolerance spawned the masterpieces of Rembrandt and Vermeer, as well as the philosophies of Descartes and Spinoza.

The Dutch have continued to race ahead and push the boundaries of social frontiers. Recovering from the devastating effects of two world wars, residents rebuilt their cities with the stark, modernistic influence of Mondrian's De Stijl school and the architecture of Mies van der Rohe. Now, where rubble once lay, modern buildings gleam and tower. Yet the country has by no means abandoned its medieval and Renaissance heritage; ancient canals wind through the countryside and centuries-old buildings and cathedrals still grace small towns.

GETTING THERE AND GETTING AROUND

TRAINS, BUSES, AND TRAMS The efficient rail authority, **NS,** runs up to four trains an hour between major cities. Intercity trains are generally nonstop, *sneltreins* take the fastest route, and *stoptreins* pause in most of the villages along the way. Call 09 00 92 92 (f0.75 per min.) for info on domestic trains and 09 00 92 96 (f0.50 per min.) for international trains. **Eurail** is valid throughout the country. A round-trip ticket is valid only on the day of issue. **Day Trip (Rail Idee)** programs, available at train stations in spring and summer, allow you to pay an all-inclusive reduced price for a round-trip train ticket, attraction entrance fees, and often also connecting transport.

The **Euro Domino Holland** card allows three (f130, under 26 f100), five (f200 and f150), or 10 days (f350 and f275) of unlimited rail travel in a one-month period; it's economical only if you will make *long* one-way or round-trips in a day. For group travel, consider the **Meerman's Kaart,** which grants one day of unlimited travel for two to six people (f108-186). One-day passes cost f71.50. A "plus" option on many passes offers use of trams and other services for an extra f18-47.

A nationalized fare system covers city buses, trams, and long-distance buses. The country is divided into zones; the number of *strippenkaart* (strip tickets) required depends on the number of zones through which you travel. The base charge is two strips, and travel to some smaller towns can exceed 20 strips. Bus and tram drivers sell two-strip (f3), three-strip (f4.50), and eight-strip tickets (f12). Tickets are *much* cheaper from public transportation counters, post offices, and some tobacco shops and newsstands (15-strip ticket f11.50, 45-strip ticket f34). Alternatively, *daskaartan* (day tickets) are available for one to nine days. The one-day ticket (f16), is worth it, especially if you are traveling between towns. Riding without a ticket can result in a f60 fine plus the original cost of the ticket.

CYCLING AND HITCHHIKING Cycling is the way to go in the Netherlands. Distances between cities are short, the countryside is flat, and most streets have separate bike lanes. You can rent one-speed bikes for about f8 per day or f30 per week (deposit f50-100, discount with railpass); the flatness of the terrain (except near the coast) renders three-speeds unnecessary. Many train stations rent bikes upon presentation of your ticket or railpass. Call the station a day ahead to reserve; phone numbers are listed in the free booklet *Fiets en Trein.* Purchasing a used bike (about f140) at a station and then reselling it may prove more thrifty. However, you must take care to secure your bike, especially in cities. **HEMA,** a large, fairly ubiquitous department store, sells locks from f25. **Hitchhiking** is risky but somewhat effective in many areas, although competition on roads out of Amsterdam is cutthroat. The **International Lift Center,** Nieuwezijds Voorburgwal 256, 1st fl., Amsterdam (tel. (020) 622 43 42), matches riders and drivers for destinations all over Europe (f10 membership, plus gas money; open M-F 10am-6pm, Sa 10am-2pm).

ESSENTIALS

VVV tourist information offices are marked by triangular blue signs. These offices, along with museums themselves, sell passes which cover admission to most of the hundreds of museums in the Netherlands.

Dutch **currency** includes the *stuiver* (5¢), *dubbeltje* (10¢), *kwartje* (25¢), and *rijksdaalder* (f2.50). Post offices, generally open weekdays 9am to 5pm, exchange currency at reasonable rates for a commission. **Banks** are usually open weekdays 10am to 4pm and occasionally Thursdays 6 to 8pm or 7 to 9pm. **GWK** often has the best rates and does not charge a commission to ISIC holders. Otherwise, expect a flat fee of about f2-5 and a 1-2% commission. **Quick Change** exchange centers are open later than banks, but commissions are often 8-10%. You can make international **calls** from pay phones, which take 25¢ and f1 coins. A **phone card** (in denominations of f10) is more economical than change (overseas calling around 25¢ for 15 seconds). For directory assistance, dial 06 80 08 within the Netherlands or 06 04 18 from outside the country; for collect calls, dial 06 04 10. To reach an **AT&T Direct** operator, call 0800 022 91 11; **MCI WorldPhone**, 0800 022 91 22; **Sprint Access**, 0800 022 91 19; **Canada Direct**, 0800 022 91 16; **BT Direct**, 0800 02 20 44; and **New Zealand Direct**, 0800 022 23 13.

Although most Dutch speak English extremely well, do try out their native tongue. The language of food is essential: *dagschotel* means "dinner special," *broodje* means "bread" or "sandwich," *bier* is "beer," and *kaas* is "cheese." Eventually you'll need directions to the *wissel kantor* meaning "money exchange" or *toiletten*, "bathroom."

Yes/No	Ja/Nee	Ya/nay
Hello	Hallo or das	hallo
Please	Als't u blieft	ALST oo bleeft
Thank you	Dank u wel	Dank oo vel
How much does it cost?	Wat kost dit?	Vat kost dit
Where is...?	Waar is....?	Vahr ees
What can you recommend?	Wat kunt u aanbevelen?	Vat kunt oo ahn-bev-ay-len
Are there rooms available?	Zijn er nog kamers vrij?	Zij-n er nock kamers vrij
Do you speak English?	Sprecht u engels?	Sprect oo engels

ACCOMMODATIONS AND CAMPING The VVV offices which supply accommodations lists can nearly always find a room, and will make reservations in other cities (f4 fee). Rooms in private homes cost about two-thirds as much as hotels but are hard to find; check with the VVV. During July and August many cities add a f2.50 "tourist tax" to the price of all rooms. The country's best values are the 34 **HI youth hostels** run by the **NJHC (Dutch Youth Hostel Federation),** divided into three price categories based on quality. Most cost f25-30 for bed and breakfast, plus high-season and prime-location supplements. The VVV has a hostel list, and the useful *Jeugdherbergen* brochure describes each one (both free). For more info, contact the NJHC at Prof. Tupelstr. 2, Amsterdam (tel. (020) 551 31 55; fax (020) 623 4986; open M-F 9am-5pm). Youth hostel cards are available at hostels (f28). **Camping** is available country-wide, but many sites are crowded and trailer-ridden in summer.

FOOD AND DRINK Dutch food is hearty and simple. Pancakes, salted herring, and pea soup are national specialties. Dutch cheeses transcend *gouda* and *edam;* nibble *leiden*, the mild *belegen*, and the creamy *kernhem*, too. Thin slices of cold meat and cheese on bread with a soft-boiled egg are a typical breakfast. For a hearty brunch, order an *uitsmijter* (literally "bouncer"), which packs in salad, ham, cheese, and fried eggs. Sweet bread toppings like *hagelslag* (chocolate sprinkles) and chocolate spread are also extremely popular. At dinner, reap the benefits of Dutch imperialism: *rijsttafel* is an Indonesian specialty comprising up to 25 different dishes, including curried chicken or lamb with pineapple, served on a mountain of rice. Or try *pannekoeken*, the traditional Dutch lunch of buttery, sugary, golden brown pancakes. Wash it all down with a foamy mug of hometown beers Heineken and Amstel (f2-2.50 per glass, f5-6 per pint), or try *jenever* (usually f3), a strong gin made from juniper berries and traditionally accompanied by smoked eel. During the school year in the many university towns, you can eat cheaply and plentifully at student *mensas*.

Despite what you may see, hear, and smell, drugs are illegal in this country. Although police largely ignore the soft drug scene, possession of up to 30g of hashish can incur hefty fines, and possession of more than this amount is a serious offense. Police consider hard drugs (acid, cocaine, heroin, ecstasy, etc.) a different category altogether and punish offenders accordingly. Avoid pot milkshakes and space cakes; the government cannot control their contents and they have been known to cause serious damage, including paralysis. Never buy anything from street pushers; ignore them and keep walking.

■ Amsterdam

After enduring both Spanish and French rule, Amsterdam now has the last laugh as it lures nationals of every country to its never-never land of bacchanalian excess. The aroma of cannabis wafts from coffeeshops, and the city's infamous sex scene swathes itself in red light. However, one need not be naughty to enjoy Amsterdam. Art enthusiasts will delight in the troves of Rembrandts, Vermeers, and van Goghs, and romantics can stroll along endless cobbled streets and canals which sparkle with the reflected city lights.

ORIENTATION AND PRACTICAL INFORMATION

Amsterdam is a major hub for budget flights from around the world (especially southeast Asia) and train service throughout Europe. **Schiphol Airport,** 5m below sea-level, is connected to the city by trains to **Centraal Station** (every 20min., f6.25) and by Interliner buses to Leidsepl. (every 30min. past the hr., f5). Emerging from the central train station, you'll hit **Damrak,** a key thoroughfare that leads to the **Dam,** the main square. Concentric canals ripple out around the Dam and Centraal Station, so that the city resembles a horseshoe with the station at the open north end. Radiating from the station, the canals lined by streets of the same name are **Singel, Herengracht, Keizergracht,** and **Prinsengracht.** Street names change capriciously; buy a good **map** of the city (f2.75-4) at the VVV tourist office or from most magazine stands. *Use It* (f2.50) includes a map, info on cheap lodgings, an index of youth agencies, and city news.

   The areas around the train station and up Damrak are the easiest places to "lose" valuables: pickpockets abound here. Do not head into the **red-light district,** immediately left of the train station, until you've locked up your bags either at the train station or where you'll be staying. Lone travelers should be wary of the train station at night. The police are extremely helpful, so report all thefts. While illegal, marijuana and hashish are generally tolerated and readily available at cafes and coffeeshops. For info on the legal ins and outs of the drug scene, call the **Jellinek clinic** at 570 23 55.

Telephone Code: 020.
Flights: Schiphol Airport (tel. (06) 350 33 08 for charters, 350 34 05 for other flights). Trains connect to Centraal Station (20min., every 10min., f6.25).
Trains: Centraal Station, Stationspl. 1, at the Damrak's end. For international info and reservations, get a number at the booth, then wait until you're called. In summer, expect waits as long as 1hr. Open for info M-F 8am-10pm, Sa-Su 9am-8pm; reservations M-F 8am-8pm, Sa-Su 9am-5pm. For international info, call 09 00 92 96 (f0.50 per min), for domestic info 09 00 92 92. Timetables are available online at http://www.ns.nl/reisplan2a.asp. **Lockers** f4-6.
Buses: Trains are quicker. The **GVB** (see **Public Transportation,** below) will direct you to a bus departure point if your destination isn't on a rail line. **Muiderpoort** (2 blocks east of Oosterpark) goes east; **Marnixstation** (at the corner of Marnixstr. and Kinkerstr.), west; and the **Stationsplein depot,** north and south.

Amsterdam

ACCOMMODATIONS

- **Y** The Arena
- **D** BA Hostel
- **H** Bob's Youth Hostel
- **W** Casa Cara
- **O** Christian Youth Hostel Eben Haëzer
- **J** Christian Youth Hostel "The Shelter"
- **R** Euphemia Budget Hotel
- **E** The Flying Pig: Downtown
- **U** The Flying Pig: Vondelpark
- **I** The Globe
- **A** Hotel Arrivé
- **Q** Hans Brinker
- **V** Hotel Bema
- **C** Hotel Brian
- **G** Hotel Crown
- **M** Hotel Monopole
- **S** Hotel Museumzicht
- **N** Hotel van Onna
- **P** International Budget Hotel
- **B** International Student Center
- **X** Liliane's Home
- **K** Nelly's B&B
- **T** NJHC City Hostel Vondelpark
- **L** NJHC-Herberg-Stadsdoelen
- **F** Old Nickel

Public Transportation: Trams, buses, *nachtbussen* (night buses), and 2 subway lines. Most tram and bus lines radiate from Centraal Station and stop running at midnight; get a separate *nachtbussen* schedule. Don't buy your *strippenkaart* and *dagkaart* (Amsterdam day passes f12) on the bus; you'll pay dearly. The 15-strip card (f11.50) is the best deal for light travel over several days. The **GVB** (public transportation company; tel. (06) 92 92), on Stationspl., sells tickets and distributes the *Public Transport* flyer. Open daily 8am-10:30pm.

Taxis: Tel. 677 77 77. Fares from f6 plus f2.80 per km or min.; prices higher at night.

Bike Rental: All train stations rent plain ol' bikes for f10 per day, f30-40 per week with a train ticket. **Damstraat Rent-a-Bike,** Pieter Jacobstr. 11 (tel. 625 50 29), just off Damstr. near the Dam, charges f12 per day, f50 per week (deposit f50 and passport); used bikes are sold for f140-200. **Yellow Bike Tours,** Nieuwezijds Voorburgwal 66 (tel. 620 69 40), offers 3hr. city (9:30am and 1pm, f29) and 6½hr. countryside (11am, f42.50) tours.

Hitchhiking: Those hitching to Utrecht, central and southern Germany, and Belgium take tram 25 to the end and start at the bridge. Those heading to Groningen and northern Germany take bus 56 to Prins Bernhardpl. or the metro to Amstel and start along Gooiseweg. Those going to the airport, Leiden, and The Hague take tram 16 or 24 to Stadionpl. and start on the other side of the canal on Amstelveenseweg. Those going to Haarlem, Alkmaar, and Noord Holland take bus 22 to Haarlemmerweg and start from Westerpark.

Tourist Office: VVV, Stationspl. 10 (tel. 551 25 12; fax 625 28 69), to the left and in front of Centraal Station. Charges a hefty f5 fee plus a f5 deposit for room booking. Sells maps, tickets, changes money (poor rates), and plans excursions. Get *What's On* (f4), a fabulous listing of events. Go early to avoid long lines. Open daily 8am-8pm; Sept.-June 10am-5pm. **Branch offices:** at Centraal Station (open daily 8am-8pm), Leidsepl. 1, Stadionpl. (both open daily 9am-5pm), and Schiphol Plaza (airport; open daily 7am-10pm). Buy phone cards and *strippenkaart* here.

Budget Travel: NBBS, Rokin 38 (tel. 624 09 89 or 620 50 71). Budget student flights. Open mid-May to mid-Aug. M-F 9:30am-5:30pm, Sa 10am-4pm; mid-Aug. to mid-May closes Sa at 3pm. No credit cards. **Budget Bus/Eurolines,** Rokin 10 (tel. 627 51 51), has Eurolines bus deals. Open M-F 9:30am-5:30pm, Sa 10am-4pm. **Wasteels,** on Rokin as well, has cheap plane tickets.

Consulates: The **Australian, Canadian, New Zealand,** and **South African** embassies are in The Hague. **U.K.,** Koningslaan 44 (tel. 676 43 43). Open M-F 9am-noon and 2-3:30pm. **U.S.,** Museumpl. 19 (tel. 664 56 61). Open M-F 8:30am-noon and 1:30-4:30pm.

Currency Exchange: Best rates at the American Express office (see below). The **GWK** offices at Centraal Station and Schiphol have good rates, and no commission for traveler's checks with ISIC or student ID (open 24hr.). **Change Express,** Kalverstr. 150 (open daily 8am-8pm) or Leidestr. 106 (open daily 8am-midnight) has good rates and a 3% commission. Avoid **Chequepoint's** outrageous commissions.

American Express: Damrak 66 (tel. 520 77 77; fax 504 87 07). Excellent rates and no commission on any traveler's checks. Open M-F 9am-5pm, Sa 9am-noon. Cash machine for cardholders. Be careful; the area's thieves are notorious. **Branch office:** Van Baerlestr. 28 (tel. 671 41 41). Safer area and much less crowded. Both cash checks, but only Damrak holds mail. Open M-F 9am-5pm, Sa 9am-noon.

Bookstores: The Spui, near the Amsterdam University, is lined with bookstores and holds an open-air *Boekemarkt* every F 10am-6pm. Mountains of paperbacks at the **American Discount Book Center,** 185 Kalverstr. 10% student discount. Open M-Sa 10am-8pm, Th until 10pm, Su 11am-6pm. **Ako,** Regulierbreestr. 19. Extensive collection and international newspapers. Open M-Sa 9am-10pm, Su 9:30am-8pm.

Gay and Lesbian Services: COC, Rozenstr. 14 (tel. 626 30 87), is the main info source. Open M-F 9am-5pm. Coffee shop open Tu and Sa 1-5pm. *Best Guide to Amsterdam & The Benelux* is reliable. **Intermale,** Spuistr. 251 (tel. 625 00 09), is a gay bookstore. Open M noon-6pm, Tu-Sa 10am-6pm. **Gay and Lesbian Switchboard** (tel. 623 65 65) is answered daily 10am-10pm.

Laundry: Look for a *Wasserette* sign. **Enzo Clean,** Jorge Roelensteeg Ya., between Nieuwezijds Voolburgwal and Spuistr. Wash and dry f12. Open daily 9am-7pm.

NETHERLANDS

Condoms: Find the widest variety of colors, flavors, and styles at the **Condomerie,** Warmoesstr. 141, next to the red-light district. Open M-Sa 11am-6pm.

Emergencies: tel. 112 (police, ambulance, and fire brigade).

Police: Headquarters, Elandsgracht 117 (tel. 559 91 11).

Crises: Rape crisis hotline for women, tel. 613 02 45; staffed M-F 9:30am-11pm, Sa-Su 4-11pm. **Drug counseling,** Jellinek clinic (tel. 570 23 55).

Pharmacies: Most are open M-F 8:30am-5pm. When closed, each *apotheek* (pharmacy) posts a sign directing you to the nearest open one.

Medical Assistance: Tourist Medical Service, tel. 695 56 38. Open 24hr. For hospital care, call **Academisch Medisch Centrum,** Meibergdreef 9 (tel. 566 91 11), near the Holendrecht Metro stop. For free emergency medical care, visit the **Kruispost,** Oudezijds Voorburgwal 129 (tel. 624 90 31). Open M-F 6:45am-11pm. **Sexually Transmitted Disease Clinic** at Groenburgwal 44 (tel. 622 37 77); free and confidential. Open daily 8-10:30am. **STD Line,** tel. 623 22 52.

Post Office: Singel 250-256 (tel. 556 33 11), at Raadhuisstr. behind the Dam. *Poste Restante.* Open M-F 9am-6pm, Sa 10am-1:30pm. **Postal Code:** 1016 AB.

Internet Access: Cybercafé, Nieuwendijk 19 (tel. 020 623 51 46; email cyber@cybercafe.euronet.nl). f3 per 20min. Open Su-Th 10am-1am, F-Sa 10am-3am. **Internet Center,** Weteringschans 165 (tel. 08 00 04 03). f2.50 per 15min. Open M 1-6pm, Tu, W, F 9am-6pm, Th 9am-9pm, Sa 9am-5pm.

Telephones: Outside Centraal Station, at Leidsepl., or at the post office. Call first and pay afterward at **Telehouse,** Raadhuisstr. 48-50, near the Dam (open 24hr.), or the safer **TeleTalk Center,** Leidsestr. 101, near the Leidsepl. (open daily 10am-midnight). Both handle faxes. Most public phones require prepaid phone cards, available at the tourist office, the post office, cigarette shops, and currency change offices. Coin phones can be found in hostels, hotels, and the post office.

ACCOMMODATIONS AND CAMPING

Amsterdam is packed from mid-June to mid-September, but several enormous hostels help accommodate most visitors. Reserve in advance. For HI hostels, book (and pay for) rooms in advance from any other HI hostel (free within the Netherlands, f4 outside). Many hostels do not accept reservations for dorms; arrive between 9 and 10am in the summer. The Christian hostels' single-sex dorms are safer, less wild, and easily the best bargain in town; they do, however, have a troublesome midnight or 1am curfew. Private hostels generally charge more, set later curfews (or none at all), and have more laid-back atmospheres. Almost all places are about f2.50 cheaper in the off-season. At the station and tourist office you'll be accosted by accommodations pushers; many are from reputable hostels, but be cautious. The legitimate ones often carry printed cards with their hostel's address and prices; ask to see the card. Carry your own luggage, and never pay before you look. If you arrive at night and can't find a room, consider staying in a neighboring city (such as Haarlem; 15 min. by train).

Staying in a hotel or hostel (by Amsterdam's standards) part of town, such as near the Leidsepl. or in the Jordaan, may be enjoyable. These areas have their share of bars and coffeeshops and are close to the large museums. Accommodations here are found on safer, peaceful side streets. The red-light district and city center are about a 15-minute walk from these areas. Accommodations closer to the station often take good security measures. If you need to buy your own padlock (f7-25), stop by **HEMA,** a department store behind the Damrak American Express.

Leidseplein/Museumplein
Hostels

International Budget Hotel, Leidsegracht 76 (tel. 624 27 84; fax 626 18 39). Tram 1, 2, or 5 to Prinsengracht. Turn right down the next street, cross the bridge, and turn left on Leidsegracht. Beautiful location, friendly staff, and an addictive cartoon network in TV lounge. 4-bed dorms f40; doubles f120.00. Breakfast f2.50-6. Min. 2-night stay in summer. Reception 9am-11pm. No curfew. Reservations advised.

The Flying Pig: Vondelpark, Vossiusstr. 46-47 (tel. 400 41 87; fax 400 41 05; email palace@flyingpig.nl; http://www.flyingpig.nl). Tram 1-2 or 5 to Leidsepl. Cross the street and canal; turn left at the Marriott. Vossiusstr. is the first street on the right after passing the Vondelpark's entrance. Relaxed atmosphere. Kitchen. Bar. Dorms from f25. Breakfast included. Free Internet access and lockers. No curfew.

NJHC City Hostel Vondelpark (HI), Zandpad 5 (tel. 589 89 99 or 589 89 55; email vondelpark@njhc.org), bordering Vondelpark. Tram 1, 2, or 5 to Leidespl. Head toward the Marriott and turn left on Stafhouderskade. Turn right at the 2nd street before the park entrance. Clean, spacious rooms with full baths. Dorms f34.50; singles f72; doubles f90; quads f158; nonmembers add f5. Breakfast included. Laundry and kitchen. Reception 7am-12:30am. No curfew. Avoid the park after dark.

The Arena, 's-Gravesandestr. 51-53 (tel. 694 74 44; fax 663 26 49). Tram 3, 6, 7 or 10 from Leidespl., 9 from Centraal Station, or 14 from the Dam to Mauritskade; take the right after the "Weesperpl." Metro stop. Palatial hostel has marble columns, Art Deco staircases, concert hall, and art gallery. Crowded and crazy. **Bike rental** (f10 per day) open daily 10am-noon and 7-8pm. DJs Th-Sa. Dorms f27; doubles f115; triples f150; quads f200. Breakfast and sheets not included. Lockers free with f20 deposit. Reception 9am-1pm and 4-9pm. No dorm reservations.

Euphemia Budget Hotel, Fokke Simonszstr. 1-9 (tel. 622 90 45; fax 622 90 45; email euphemia-hotel@wxs.nl; http://www.channels.nl/amsterdam/euphemia.html), 10min. walk from Leidespl. Tram 16, 24, or 25 to 6th stop, near the Heineken Brewery. Relatively safe and comfy. Dorms f25-45; doubles f80-150; triples f110-180. Seasonal prices. Reception 8am-11pm.

Hans Brinker, Kerkstr. 136 (tel. 622 06 87; fax 638 20 60). Tram 1, 2, 5, or 11 to Prinsengracht; walk one block back toward the city center. Clean, sparse, and comparatively safe. Dorms a bit pricey at f40.50-43; singles f75-90; doubles f122-148.

Hotels

Hotel Museumzicht, Jan Luijkenstr. 22 (tel. 671 29 54; fax 671 35 97). A lovely little hotel in a quiet neighborhood across the street from the Rijksmuseum. Singles f60-110; doubles f115-150; triples f135-180. Breakfast included.

Hotel Bema, Concertgebouwpl. 19 (tel. 679 13 96; fax 662 36 88), across from the Concertgebouw. Take tram 5 or 16 to Museumpl. Showing its age a bit, but still spacious and spotless rooms in a posh area. Singles f65-75; doubles f100-125. Breakfast included. Reception 8:30am-11pm. No credit cards.

Liliane's Home, Sarphatistr. 119 (tel./fax 627 40 06). Tram 3, 6, 9, or 14 (about 10min. from Leidespl.). Classy guesthouse for women. TV in all rooms. Singles f75; doubles f130; triples f185-215. Breakfast included. Free tea and coffee. 2 night min. stay on weekends. Always call ahead for reservations and arrival. No credit cards.

Casa Cara, Emmastr. 24 (tel. 662 31 35; http://www.com-all.nl/hotels/casa-cara), 10min. behind Rijksmuseum; from Concertegebouwpl. walk down Verhulststr. and take the 4th right. Simple rooms in a quiet area. Singles f65-100; doubles f100; triples f155; quads f175. Breakfast included. Call ahead.

Red-light District and Rembrandtsplein

Hostels

Flying Pig: Downtown, Nieuwendijk 100 (tel. 420 68 22; fax 421 08 02; email downtown@flyingpig.nl). All rooms with bath. Crowded, laid-back, but clean. Lively bar. 20-bed dorm f25; 6-bed dorm f35.50; doubles f55; quads f36.50. Blanket f4.50. Breakfast included. Free lockers. No curfew, but f15 key deposit.

NJHC-herberg Stadsdoelen (HI), Kloveniersburgwal 97 (tel. 624 68 32; fax 639 01 35; email vondelpark@njhc.org), between Nieuwmarkt and Rembrandtspl. Tram 4, 9, 16, 24, or 25 to Muntpl. Walk down Amstel and cross the bridge on your left. Large, clean dorms. Lounge area with cable TV. f25.25, nonmembers add f5. July-Aug. f2.50 surcharge. Breakfast included. Free lockers. Kitchen and laundry (f8.50). Reception 7am-12:30am. Flexible curfew 2am. No groups over 10.

BA Hostel, Martelaarsgracht 18 (tel. 638 71 19; fax 638 88 03). Friendly staff; sunny, clean rooms. Meals f8.50-22; happy hour 6-7pm. Bright and airy 8-12 bed dorms f25-45, prices vary by season. Includes showers, sheets, towels, breakfast, luggage storage, and a locker/safe-deposit box. Reception 7:30am-1am. No curfew.

The Globe, Oudezijds Voorburgnal 3 (tel. 421 74 24; fax 421 74 23). From Centraal Station, cross the bridge, turn left on Prins Hendrikkade, right on Warmoestr., and then take the first left. Clean, comfortable hostel connected to a large, lively sports cafe. Dorms f35 (f30 in winter); doubles f120; triples f150. English breakfast f7.50-15. Reception 24hr.

Nelly's Inn B&B, Warmoesstr. 115/117 (tel. 638 01 25; fax. 633 44 01; email nellys@xs4all.nl). From Centraal Station, it's an easy walk 2 blocks to the left of the Damrak. Small, cozy hostel in the heart of the red-light district. Dorms f25-35.

Arrive as close to 9am as possible—no reservations taken. Breakfast and sheets included. Reception 24hr. Connected to **Dirty Nelly's,** a Irish pub with live bands and lots of, guess what…Guinness.

Bob's Youth Hostel, Nieuwezijds Voorburgwal 92 (tel. 623 00 63; fax 675 64 46), near Centraal Station and the police station. Tram 1, 2, 5, 13, or 17. No smoking in the rooms; you'll inhale enough on the stairs. This place keeps the Amsterdam myths going. Mattress on floor f20. Dorms f24. Key and locker deposit f25. Breakfast and sheets included. Vegetarian dinner available. Reception 8am-3am. No reservations, no credit cards.

Hotel Crown, Oudezijds Voorburgwal 21 (tel. 626 96 64). Simple, clean accommodations in the red light district. Attached bar stays open until 5am nightly. Dorms f40; singles f80; doubles f120; quads f55. Reception 24hr. No curfew.

Christian Youth Hostel "The Shelter," Barndesteeg 21-25 (tel. 625 32 30), off the Nieuwmarkt. Virtue amid the red lights. Snack bar, cozy courtyard, and religious slogans. Ages 16-35 f25. Showers, sheets, and breakfast included. Lockers f10; deposit f1. Reception 7:30am-midnight. Enforced midnight curfew, F-Sa 1am.

Hotels

International Student Center, Keizersgracht 15-17 (tel. 625 13 64; fax 624 70 12), 10min. from Centraal Station. Peaceful hotel overlooking a canal. Nice rooms; beds have thick mattresses. Singles f80; doubles f120; triples f135-158. Breakfast f10. 50% advance payment for reservations. Reception 7am-3am. Flexible 3am curfew.

Hotel Brian, Singel 69 (tel. 624 46 61). Nothing fancy, but clean, friendly, and comfortable. TV lounge. 2-4 bed rooms Apr.-Aug. f40 per person; Sept. f35; Oct.-Mar. f25. Sheets, towels, luggage storage, and all-you-can-eat breakfast included—with eggs cooked to order. Reception 24hr. No curfew. No credit cards. Management also owns **Hotel Hortus** (tel 625 99 96) near the zoo.

Hotel Monopole, Amstel 60 (tel. 624 62 71; fax 624 58 97). Gay-friendly hotel overlooking the canal near Rembrandtspl. Well-furnished, spacious rooms with bath. Singles f75; doubles f125 (f110 off-season); triples f180. Reception 8:30am-11pm.

Old Nickel, Nieuwebrugsteeg 11 (tel. 624 19 12; fax 620 76 83). Quiet hotel assures a friendly welcome. Singles f55-65; doubles f80-110. Luggage storage, sheets, and towels included. Reception 8am-4am. No curfew. No credit cards.

The Jordaan

Christian Youth Hostel Eben Haëzer, Bloemstr. 179 (tel. 624 47 17; fax 627 61 37; email eben@globalxs.nl), 1 street from Rozengracht in the Jordaan (tram 13 or 17: Marnixstr.). Good bargain with clean-cut, cheery staff. Huge single-sex dorms with few showers. f20; showers, sheets, and breakfast included. Lockers f1; deposit f10. Free luggage storage. Midnight curfew; F-Sa 1am.

Hotel van Onna, Bloemgracht 104 (tel. 626 58 01). Tram 13 or 17 from Centraal Station. Charming hotel, recommended by *The New York Times* as the best budget hotel in Amsterdam. f70 per person. Breakfast included. Reception 8am-10pm.

Hotel Arrivé, Haarlemmerstr. 65 (tel. 622 14 39; fax 622 19 83). Convenient location between the Jordaan and Centraal Station. Family-run with clean rooms. 4-bed dorms f40 per person; singles f75-80; doubles f100-120; triples 150-180. Reception 24hr. No curfew.

Pensions and Private Accommodations

Roommate's snoring keeping you up all night? Hate being part of the masses (or Bible-reading sessions) at the local hostels? Head out to the cheap and wonderful pensions surrounding the city; it's usually worth the travel time.

Gerda Rikker-Kouwenhoren, Iepenlaan 16 (tel. (02993) 639 33). About 35min. by bus in beautiful downtown Volendam. Knowledgeable, friendly owner. Central to Edam, Hoorn, and Zaanse Schaus for all you windmill lovers. f29.50 per person.

Pension Kil, Volendammerpad 19 (tel. (0299) 37 18 27). Take the NZH bus to Edam. Violently verdant, eclectically eccentric; living room was transformed into a replica of the jungle, complete with aviary of songbirds. Doubles f70, breakfast included. Reserve 1-2 weeks ahead June-Sept.

NETHERLANDS

Camping

Camping Zeeburg, Zuider-Ijdijk 20 (tel. 694 44 30), next to the Amsterdam Rijncanal. Direct ferry from Centraal Station, or bus 22 or 37, or night bus 170. Backpacker-oriented. Live music regularly. Campsites f6.75 per person, f3.50 per tent; f12.25 for 2 people and tent. Showers f1.50. Reception July 8am-11pm; Apr.-June and Sept.-Aug. 9am-1pm and 5-9pm.

Gaaspercamping, Loosdrechtdreef 7, (tel. 696 73 26; fax 696 93 69) in Gaasper Park. 20min. from Centraal Station by metro ("Gaasperplas") to the end; or night bus 75. Vast and fully rigged. f6.50 per person, f15 per tent. Showers f1.50. Laundry f13. Reception 9am-12:30pm and 1:30-9pm. Open mid-Mar. to Dec.

FOOD

Dutch food ranges from the hopelessly bland to the oddly tasty. **FEBO,** a reasonably priced self-service fast food chain, won't remind you of home cooking, but will give local flavor to your junk food frenzy. *Frikandel* (fried sausage) usually costs as little as f1.50. If you're feeling adventurous, stop at a fish stall to try the summer specialty of herring—raw, salted, with a squeeze of lemon, and best when swallowed whole in one mouthful. Sample Surinamese, Indonesian, Chinese, and Indian food in the red-light district around the Nieuwmarkt and off the Dam, on streets such as Hartenstr. Indonesian *rijsttafel* (a collection of rice, meats, and spices) is blissful here and can be a good bargain if you go with a group. Many cheap restaurants cluster around the Leidsepl., the Rembrandtspl., and the Spui. *Eetcafés,* especially in the Jordaan, purvey good meat-and-potatoes fare for f12-20. Bakeries selling inexpensive cheese croissants and magnificent breads congregate along Utrechtsestr., south of Prinsengracht. Some restaurants close during school vacations.

Fruit, cheese, flowers, and sometimes even live chickens populate the **markets** on Albert Cuypstr., behind the Heineken brewery (open M-Sa 10am-4:30pm). The cheapest groceries are found at **Aldi Supermarket,** Nieuwe Weteringstr., off of Vijizelgracht, near the Heineken brewery (closed Su). The ubiquitous **Albert Heijns** are centrally located at Koningspl., and 226 Nieuwezijds Voorburwal, besides the Magna Plaza. **De Eenhoorn,** Warmoesstr. 16, adds a touch of class with its fresh meats and cheeses and broad selection of wines. Health food addicts rejoice at **De Natuurwinkel,** Weteringschans 135.

Leidseplein and the Museum District

Bojo, 51 Lange Leidsedwar. Generous servings of delicious Indonesian food at reasonable prices. Meals f13-20. Open M-F until 2am, Sa-Su until 4am.

Dionysos, Overtoom 176 (tel. 689 44 41). From Leidsepl., walk right on the Stadhouderskade (past the Marriott); Overtoom is on the left. Tasty Greek dishes served daily from 5am-1am. Call ahead if you arrive after 12:30am on a weekday.

Paviljoen de Carrousel, Weteringschans. Feast on scrumptious pancakes (f6) after your Heineken tour. Open daily 10am-10pm.

Cafe 't Hoekje, Frans Hals Str., corner of Eerst Jacob Can Campen Str. Chill with the locals on your way from the Rijksmuseum to the Heineken brewery. Sandwiches f3.50-6. Open daily 10am-10pm.

Brasserie van Gogh, Hoofstr. 28. Pleasant spot down from the Rijksmuseum towards Leidsepl. Salads f17.50-22.50, lasagna f19.50. Open daily 10am-7pm.

Petite Bordeaux, Keizersgracht 594, corner of Nieuwe Spiegel. Classy restaurant with reasonable prices. Lasagna f18, pancakes f10-12, sandwiches and burgers f6.50. Open daily 11am-9pm.

Cafe Meden, 422 Prinsengracht. Enjoy a languid lunch along the canal. Sandwiches f7.50-8.50, salads f14-16.

Pannekoekhuis Upstairs, Grimburgwal 2. Indulge in a true Dutch tradition. Pancakes f6-12. Open Su-F until 7pm, Sa until 6pm.

Esoterica, Overtoom 409. Serves home-made vegetarian food. Most meals f12.50-19. Open W-Su noon-9pm.

Red Light/Rembrandtsplein

Atrium, Oudezijds Achterburgwal 237, at Binnengasthuisstr. A huge, spotless university trough on the fringe of the red-light district. Dinners f8.50. Meals served M-F noon-2pm and 5-7pm. Snack bar open 9am-7pm. Closed July.

Say Saté, Amstelstr. 26. Specializes in *rijsttafel* and its signature *saté* (skewered meat). Delicious meals f18-25. Open Su-Th 5-11pm, F-Sa 5pm-2:30am.

Keuhen Van 1870, Spuistr. 4. A soup kitchen in the 19th century, Keuhan now serves traditional Dutch food at the cheapest prices around. Open M-F noon-8pm, Sa-Su 4pm-9pm.

Bolhoed, 60-62 Prinsengracht, across the canal from the Anne Frank Huis. Specializes in organic vegetarian food (f10-20). Open daily noon-10pm.

Sukabumi, Geelvincksteeg 2, on Singel canal. Get an outdoor table at this tiny Indonesian restaurant market. Simple meals f12.50-25. Open daily noon-11pm.

Thai Pohchana, 83 Harlemmerstr. Each dish is prepared with exquisite care. Most meals f13-20. Open daily 1-11pm.

Kam Yin, 6 Warmoesstr. This Chinese/Surinamese landmark serves cheap, heaping portions. Meals f8-16. Open daily noon-midnight.

Vishandel de Kreeft, Vijzelstr. 3, near Muntpl. Stand-up seafood counter that satisfies your salty, wet desires cheaply. Open M-Sa 10am-6pm.

La Place, on Rokin near Muntpl., and at Vroom Dreesman, Kalverstr. 201. Make up for your vegetable and fresh meat deficiency at this buffet-style restaurant. Meals around f10. Open daily 10am-9pm.

Café de Jaren, Nieuwe Dodenstr. 20-22. A great place to chill with a magazine/newspaper—which you can borrow from their collection. Meals f12-32, served until 10pm. Open Su-Th 10am-midnight, F 10am-1am, Sa 10am-2am.

Café Restaurant Turquoise, Wolvenstr. 30. Turkish cuisine at unbeatable prices. Sandwiches and crepes f4. Most meals f5-15. Open daily noon-11pm.

C.O.C. Koffieshop, Rozenstr. 14. (open Tu-Sa 1pm-5pm) and **Downtown,** Reguleersdwarsstr. 21 (open daily 10am-8pm) are popular with the gay community. Sandwiches and simple meals f2-5.

Cybercafé, Nieuwendijk 19. Munch on sandwiches (f4-10) and sip coffee as you log on. **Internet access** f3 per 20min. Open M-Sa 10am-10pm.

SIGHTS

Amsterdam is fairly compact—most of its sights are within walking distance form Centraal Station. Although bike theft is very common in Amsterdam, many people prefer to get around the city with a **bike** rented from the train station. **Circle Tram 20** stops at 30 attractions throughout the city (buy tickets on the tram or at VVV offices; runs daily every 10min, 9am-6pm, f10). A more peaceful way to explore is on the **canal bus** which allows you to hop on or off (every 45min., f19.75 per day). You can also rent a **canal bike** and power your own way through the canals. *(2 people f19.50 per hr.; 4 people f29.50. f50 deposit.)* Pick up and drop off points for both the bus and bikes are at Rijksmuseum, Anne Frank Huis, Leidsepl., Centraal Station, and City Hall/Rembrandt House. **Mike's Bike Tours** provides an entertaining introduction to the city's sites and the surrounding countryside. Meet at the west entrance of the Rijksmuseum. *(Open daily June-Aug. 11:30pm and 4pm; Sept.-Oct. 12:30pm. 4hr. f37.)* The economical **Museumkaart** (f47.50, under 25 f17.5), gives discounts or admission to museums and transportation for a full year.

A visit to Amsterdam would be sinful without seeing the **Rijksmuseum,** and that's precisely why you'll have to use guerrilla fighting skills to get past the crowds to Rembrandt's famed militia portrait *The Night Watch. (Open daily 10am-5pm; f15.)* Slide shows every 25 minutes make it possible to handle the museum's art overload, which includes an impressive collection of the Dutch masters Vermeer, Frans Hals and Jan Steen. See how a painter's work can get better while he falls deeper into insanity at the renowned **van Gogh Museum,** where over 200 of the master's paintings are on display. *(Open daily 10am-5pm; closed until April 1999 for renovations. f15.)* The **Stedelijk Museum** of modern art, right next door, has an outstanding permanent collection, and is well worth a visit. *(Open daily Apr.-Oct. 11am-7pm; Nov.-Mar. 11am-5pm. f8.)* When you tire of high culture, visit the retired **Heineken Brewery,** nearby at Stadhouder-skade 78 (free beer *and* the f2 goes to charity). The presentation is super slick, and at the end uniformed servers give out samples. *(Tours M-F. Buy tickets at 9am for the 9:30am and 11am tours; at 11:15am for the 1pm and 2:30pm tours.)*

When you're through with the museums, lose the hordes in the narrow streets of the **Jordaan,** built as an artisan district in the Golden Age. Bounded roughly by Prinsengracht, Brouwersgracht, Marnixstr., and Lauriersgracht, the area holds small cafes, antique shops, and vine-laden buildings. You can also take refuge from Amsterdam's mobbed sights and seamy streets in **Begijnhof,** a beautifully maintained grassy courtyard surrounded by 18th-century buildings. To get there, walk down Kalverstr. and turn onto Begijnensteeg, a small side street between Kalverstr. 130 and 132. Spend a day people-watching in the grassy **Vondelpark.**

The **red-light district,** bounded by Warmoestr., Gelderskade, and Oude Doelenstr., is the vice sink of Europe; it will either repulse you or fulfill your wildest dreams. Pushers, porn shops, and live sex theaters do a brisk business. **Sex shows** (f10-50) usually consist of costumed, disaffected couples repeatedly acting out your "wildest" (choreographed) dreams. Red neon marks houses of legal ill repute. Unlike the illegal streetwalkers, these prostitutes have regular gynecological exams—but keep in mind that HIV/AIDS takes six months to detect. During the day, the red-light district is comparatively flaccid, with tourists (sometimes with children in tow) milling about, consulting their maps. As the sun goes down, the people get braver, and the area much more stimulating. Cops patrol the district until midnight, and there's a police station on Warmoestr. Women may feel uncomfortable walking through this area.

The area in and around the red-light district (the oldest part of the city) contains some of Amsterdam's most interesting sights. Amsterdam's former town hall, **Koninklijk Palace,** may be a symbol of the city's 17th-century commercialism, but its majesty is topped by the nearby **Magna Plaza,** today's homage to commercialism. *(Open M 11am-6pm, Tu-Sa 9:30am-6pm, Su 11am-5pm.)* The 14th-century **Oude Kerk,** 23 Oudekerkspl., has three 16th-century stained glass windows depicting scenes from Mary's life. The marblework hides a self-portrait of the organ's creator. **Rembrandthuis,** Jodenbreestr. 4-6, at the corner of the Oude Schans Canal, is where the master lived, worked, and taught until the house was confiscated by the city for taxes. *(Open M-Sa 10am-5pm, Tu until 9:30pm, Su 1-5pm. f7.50.)* It holds 250 of Rembrandt's etchings and dry points, as well as many of his tools and plates. The **Museum Amstelkring "Ons' Lieve Heer op Solder"** ("Our Lord in the Attic"), Oudezijds Voorburgwal 40, in the red-light district, dates from Reformation days, when Catholics were forbidden to practice their faith publicly. A former Catholic priest's house hides in an attic church. *(Open M-Sa 10am-5pm, Su 1-5pm. f7, students f5.)* A handsome 17th-century building, the **Joods-Portuguese Synagogue** at Jonas Daniël Meijerpl., near Waterloopl., was founded by Portuguese Jews expelled from their country. *(Open Su-F 10am-4pm. f2.)* Next door at Jonas Daniël Meijerpl. 2-4, the **Joods Historisch Museum,** has exhibits on Jewish history and culture. *(Open daily 11am-5pm. f8.)*

See sex in every way you dreamed possible (and many you didn't) to the tune of tasteful porno music at the **Amsterdam Sex Museum,** Damrak 18, near Centraal Station. *(Open daily 10am-11:30pm. f6, under 17 not admitted.)* To continue your "Only in Amsterdam" tour, visit the **Hash Marijuana Hemp Museum,** Oudezijds Achterburgwal 148—"if you come on the right day, you will see fat ripe buds glistening with the rich resin and smell air heavy with the fragrance of the crop. What an experience!" If you come on the wrong day, you may be subject to one of the frequent police raids. *(Open in summer daily 11am-10pm; off-season Su-W 11am-6pm, Th-Sa 11am-10pm. f6.)* Next door, **the Tattoo Museum,** Oudezijds Achterburgwal 130, displays the works of world-famous artists. *(Open Tu-Su noon-6pm; off-season until 5pm. f5.)*

The tiny space where the young journal-keeper hid with her family from the Nazis until their capture in 1944 can be seen at the **Anne Frank Huis,** Prinsengracht 263, west of the city center. *(Lines often 35-45min. Open M-Sa 9am-6:45pm, Su 10am-6:45pm; Sept.-May closes daily at 5pm. f12.)* While you're there, check out the **Homomonument,** a memorial to those persecuted for their sexual orientation. To the east of the red-light district, **newMetropolis,** Oosterdok 2, houses interactive science and technology exhibits. *(Open July-Aug. daily 10am-9pm; Sept.-June Su-Th 10am-6pm, F-Sa 10am-9pm.)* Farther out, the interesting **Tropenmuseum** (Museum of the Tropics), Linnaeusstr. 2, has a multimedia collection of artifacts and frequent film, food, and music festivals from Asia, Africa, and Latin America. *(Open M-F 10am-5pm, Tu until 9:30pm, Sa-Su noon-5pm. f12.)* Even more distant form the city center and to its Southeast lies the **Verzetsmuseum Amsterdam** (Resistance Museum), Lekstr. 63, which tells the story of the Nazi occupation of the Netherlands. To reach the museum, take trams 4 and 25. *(Open Tu-F 10am-5pm, Sa-Su and holidays 1-5pm. f5, free with Museumkaart.)*

Some of the most exciting art in Amsterdam is free—painted on doors, walls and trams. Check out the **Vrankrijk** building, Spuistr. 216, and the area around **Mr. Visserplein,** near Waterloopl. and the Hortus Botannicus, for evidence that graffiti is more than names and vulgar phrases. Continue your psychedelic survey at the **3D Hologram Store,** Grimburgwal 2. *(Open Tu-F noon-6pm, Sa noon-5:30pm, Su 1-5:30pm.)*

An open-air art market takes place in the **Spui** every Sunday where local and international artists present their oils, etchings, sculptures, and jewelry. *(Open Mar.-Dec. 10am-6pm.)* The Spui is also the site of a book market which can occasionally yield rare editions and 17th century Dutch romances (every F 10am-6pm). Pick up ancient stamps at the Poszegelmarkt on **Nieuwezijds Voorburgwal** (open W and Sa 1-4pm) and not-so-rare bulbs at the flower market on the **Singel** canal (open M-Sa 9:30am-5pm). Mill with the masses at the famous flea market on **Waterlooplein** where you can try your hand at bargaining for antiques, birds, or farming implements.

ENTERTAINMENT

Cafes and Bars

Amsterdam's finest cafes are the old, dark, wood-paneled *bruine kroegen* (brown cafes) of the **Jordaan,** where denizens gather under the nicotine-stained ceilings and dim brass lamps. **Leidseplein** is the liveliest nightspot, with coffeeshops and clubs galore. **Rembrandtsplein** is the place to watch soccer and sing with drunk revelers; just pretend you know the words (think German surfer trying to talk like a Valley girl—*"uitstekend* (excellent), dude"). **Prinsengracht** is flanked with pleasant outdoor cafes. Gay bars line **Reguliersdwarsstraat,** which connects Muntpl. and Rembrandtspl., and Kerkstr., five blocks north of Leidsepl. Most cafes open at 10 or 11am and close at 1am on Fridays and 2am Saturdays.

De Prins, Prinsengracht 124. A very lively student bar in the Jordaan. Open 11am-1am, F-Sa until 2am.

Cafe II Prinsen, Prinsenstr. 27, on edge of the Jordaan. Filled with upscale Dutch partygoers. Beer from f2.75. Open Su-Th 11am-1am, F-Sa 11am-2am.

Cafe de Tuin, Tweede Tuindwarsstr. 13 (open M-Th 10am-1am, F-Sa 10am-2am, Su 11am-1am), and **Cafe Sas,** Marnixstr. 79, (open Su-Th noon-1am, F-Sa until 2am), attract a young, artsy set. Cafe Sas often has live music on weekends.

Saarein, Elandstr. 119, is a (gay and straight) women-only bar in the Jordaan. Open M 8pm-1am, Tu-Th and Su 3pm-1am, F-Sa 3pm-2am.

Vrankrijk, Spuistr. 216. Revolutionary slogans, Marxist literature, punks and cheap beer can be found at this unmarked bar.

Grand Café Dulac, Haarlemserstr. 118. A fantasy from "1001 Nights," with erotic statues jumping out of every metallic corner. Open daily 4pm-1am or 2am.

The Sound Garden, Marnixstr. 164. Grunge cafe near the Christian Youth Hostel where you can recharge on angst before entering happyland. Open M-F 1pm-1am, Sa-Su 1pm-2am.

Café D'Oude Herbergh, Handboogstr. 19 at the end of Nieuwezijds Voorburgwal. Dutch twenty-somethings come here to drink, drink, drink. Open nightly 8pm-late.

April, Reguliersdwarsstr. 37, and **Havana,** Reguliersdwarsstr. 17-19, are hip gay bars. **The Other Side,** Reguliersdwarsstr. 6, attracts a younger crowd, also largely gay. All are open from 3 or 4pm until 1am weekdays and 2am weekends.

NETHERLANDS

Coffeeshops

Yes, the rumors are true: marijuana and hashish, though technically illegal, are so decriminalized that coffeeshops don't just sell coffee (unless one counts the green, leafy "mother's milk" and "super skunk" varieties). Shops are listed in the *Mellow Pages*. In general, hash is more common than marijuana here and comes in two varieties, black (like Afghan and Nepal) and blonde (like Moroccan). Black tends to be heavier and hits harder (f10-24 per gram). Dutch marijuana is the most common and is usually very good. It costs f12-15 per gram, f25-30 for a bag. The smaller the quantity, the smoother and more potent. The Dutch tend to mix tobacco with their pot, so joints are harsher on your lungs. Most places will supply rolling papers and filter tips. Avoid milkshakes, bonbons, and cakes ("space cakes") made with marijuana: their contents cannot be controlled, and ingestion has caused illness and paralysis.

Self-proclaimed cannabis experts and casual experimenters alike can find their niche among the hundreds of unique coffeeshops. The farther you travel from the touristed spots, the better and cheaper the establishments. People at shops are neither exceptionally welcoming nor unfriendly; they are simply…mellow. Acceptance of tourists depends on how much they blend in. Only tourists smoke from pipes; locals roll burnt, powdered hash into cigarettes with tobacco. Joints can also be bought for f7.50. Do not take pictures inside coffeehouses. Whatever approach you take, don't get too caught up in Amsterdam's narcotic quirk: use common sense, and remember that any experiment with drugs can be dangerous.

Dutch Flowers, Singel 387, close to the Spui circle and with a beautiful view of the canal, is the winner of the coveted "Highlife" cup. **La Tertulia,** Prinsengracht 312, in the Jordaan, defies any of your coffeeshop preconceptions; in this bright shop, Spanish music, plants and flowers envelop an indoor pond and waterfall. The laid-back **Homegrown Fantasy,** Nieuwezijds Voorburgwal 87a, offers an impressive selection of homegrown Dutch weed and well-designed bathrooms. Gloat about your Amsterdam experience to friends back home over email sent from **Tops,** Prinsengracht 480, near Leidsepl. (f3 for 15min.; open daily 11pm-1am, F-Sa until 3am). The most famous and touristy coffeeshops are **The Grasshopper,** Nieuwezijds Voorburgwal 57 (open Su-Th 9am-midnight, F-Sa 9am-1am), and **The Bulldog,** Oudezijds Voorburgwal 90 and on Leidsepl. (open Su-Th 9am-1am, F-Sa 9am-2am). **Barney's Coffeeshop,** Haarlemmerstr. 102, serves great meals (f7.50-12.50; open daily 7am-8pm).

Live Music

Amsterdam's large clubs occasionally feature some world-famous mainstream groups. The soul of the music scene, however, lies in the considerable variety of offerings at the dozens of smaller cafes and bars. The **Jazzlijn** (tel. 626 77 64) provides info on local concerts. The **A.U.B.,** Leidsepl. 26, has the "Pop & Jazz Uitlijst" and fliers of other free concerts. Many clubs inflate beer prices instead of charging a cover.

Melkweg, Lijnbaasgracht 234a (tel. 624 17 77; http://knoware.nl/melkweg/melkweg.html), in an old warehouse off Leidsepl., across from the police station. Amsterdam's legendary nightspot retains a cutting-edge aura despite the crowds. Live bands, theater, films, an art gallery (free W-Su 2-8pm), and a snack bar contribute to the multimedia sensory overload. "Tearoom" sells Amsterdam's leaves of choice. Cover for the bar f5 plus f4 monthly fee. Open W-Th and Su 7pm-2am, F-Sa 7pm-4am. Box office open M-F noon-5pm, Sa-Su 4-7pm, and while the club is open.

Paradiso, Weteringschans 6-8 (tel. 626 45 21; http://www.channels.nl/paradiso.html). Some of the foremost international punk, new-wave, and reggae bands play in this former church. Cover varies (f10-27). Shows start daily at 10pm.

Alto, Korte Leidsedwarsstr. 115, and the **Bourbon Sheets Jazz & Blues Cafe,** Leidse Kruisl-str. 6, (cover f2-5, open 9pm to 3-4am) have live blues, jazz or funk nightly.

De Kroeg, Lijnbaansgracht 163. Vibrant crowds writhe to reggae, salsa, rock, and blues. f5 cover on live music nights, f2.50 on DJ Fridays, periodic jam sessions (Mondays and Wednesdays) free. Open Su-Th 8pm-3am, F-Sa music starts at 10pm.

The Bimhuis, Oude Schans 73-77 (http://www.xs4all.nl/~bimhuis), near Waterloopl. The hub of Dutch jazz; more than 200 concerts held every year. Cover f10, students f7.50. Su-Tu free jam sessions. W-Sa concerts after 9pm.

NETHERLANDS

Winston Kingdom, Warmoesstr. 127 (cover f5-10; open Su-W 8pm-2am, Th-Sa until 3am) and the **Last Waterhole,** Oudezijds Arugsleeg 12 (Su-Th until 2am, F-Sa until 4am), both in the red-light district, offer nightly live music from acid rock to disco.

Odeon, Singel 460, near Leidsestr. Men in sharp suits and women in heels come here to groove. Cover f7.50, weekends f12.50. Opens at 10pm every night, until 4am F-Sa for dancing.

Dancing

Many nightclubs in Amsterdam charge a membership fee in addition to the normal cover, so the tab can be obscene. Be prepared for arrogant, cocky doormen who live to turn away tourists: be a beautiful woman or show up early. If you're really desperate, a f10-20 tip may make help them overlook your imperfections. There are expensive discos aplenty on Prinsengracht, near Leidsestr., and on Lange Leidsedwarsstr. Gay discos line Amstelstr.

MAZZO, Rozengracht 114, in the Jordaan. Artsy disco with constantly revolving DJs, music styles, display, and slideshow. Live music Tu Cover f7.50, weekends f10. Open Su-Th 11pm-4am, F-Sa 11pm-5am. No dress code.

Dansen bij Jansen, Handboogstr. 11, near the Spui. Near the university and popular among students (student ID officially required). Happy hour Su-W 11pm-midnight. Cover f4-5. Open Su-Th 11pm-4am, F-Sa 11pm-5am.

C.O.C., Rogenstr. 14 (tel. 623 40 79). Cultural center for gay men and women; sponsors weekly events. Friday night disco 11pm-4am. Saturday girls' cafe (8pm-midnight) and disco (11pm-3am). Sunday is Arabian disco night (8pm-12:30am).

RoXY, Singel 465. The hippest crowd in town busts a move to house. Obvious tourist attire rebuffed. Women-only "Pussy Lounge" Su 6pm-midnight. Cover W and Su f7.50, Th f10, F-Sa f12.50. Open W-Th around 11am-4am, F-Su 11am-5am.

iT, Amstelstr. 24, near Waterloopl. Clients tout this as one of the best and most decadent gay discos in Europe. Free to members, otherwise f15. Difficult to get into. Gay only on Sa. Open Th and Su 11pm-4am, F-Sa 11pm-5am.

Ministry, Reguliersdwarsstr. 12. The most popular gay disco, Saturday excluded. Expect to pay f15 cover. Open nightly 11pm-5am.

The Arena, 's-Gravesandestr. 51-53 (see **Accommodations,** p. 635). Housed in a former chapel; throws great parties on weekends. Friday techno, speed, and garage from 11pm. Saturdays, 70s, 80s, and dance from 9:30pm. Cover f12.50.

Mo' Music, Theater, Film, and Festivals Galore...

The VVV puts out *What's On* (f3.50) monthly, with comprehensive cultural listings. Also check out the free mini-magazine, *Boom Paper,* available at restaurants and cafes around the city and chock full of tourist info the VVV only wishes it had, or the free monthly *UITKRANT.* The monthly *Culture and Camp* (f5) gives info on gay venues and events. The fortnightly *Queer Fish* (f2.50) catalogues less mainstream concerts and parties. Also check the online www.aub.nl for "Culture in Amsterdam."

In the summer, there are free performances Wednesday through Sunday at the **Vondelpark Openluchttheater** (tel. 673 14 99); jazz and folk concerts dominate, but children's theater, rock bands, political music, and mime also grab the limelight. Check posters at park entrances. The **Muziektheater,** perched over the junction of the Amstel and the Oude Schans (tel. 625 54 55), hosts the **Netherlands Opera** and the **National Ballet.** The **Royal Concertgebouw Orchestra** is at the Concertgebouw on Van Baerlestr. is one of the world's finest (tickets from f25). Free classical concerts every Wednesday at 12:30pm. Organ concerts resound during the summer at **Westerkerk,** Prinsengracht 281 (W 8:15pm), where Rembrandt is buried. Concerts also happen at **Nieuwe Kerk,** on the Dam (f5-12.50), where Dutch monarchs are sworn in (they're not crowned).

When you're in the Vondelpark, see what's on at **The Vertigo** movie theater and cafe. The free **De Week Agenda** has comprehensive movie listings. Look for information on the **International Documentary Film Festival** in mid-December. Frequent English-language performances and cabarets are given at the theater/cafe **Suikerhof,** Prinsengracht 381 (tel. 22 75 71; open M-Sa from 5pm, Su from 2pm). Make reservations for any cultural event at the **Amsterdams Uit Buro** (AUB) ticketshop (tel. 621 12 11; open daily 10am-6pm) or at the VVV's theater desk, Stationspl. 10 (open M-Sa 10am-5pm). There's no escaping **Boom Chicago,** Leidepl. 12; their *Boom Paper* is ubiquitous. Here American actors perform improvised sketches taking cues from the audience (nightly at 8:15pm, doors open at 7pm). Reserve tickets (f25, f20 with *Boom Paper*) by calling 639 27 07 (box office open 10am-6pm). The restaurant serves American-style meals from noon to 11pm (f12-30) and is the only Amsterdam haunt to serve pitchers of beer (f19).

   The Queen's Day on April 30 gives the entire city an excuse to become a huge carnival. It is also the day of the year's largest flea market where you can buy and sell parrots, skulls, and glue sticks. The June **Holland Festival** of dance, drama, and music is closely followed by the **Summer Festival** of small theater companies in July (tickets f10-15; contact the Balie Theatre on Kleine cannabis at 623 29 04). On the first weekend in August, gay pride abounds in street parties along Warmoesstr., Amstel, Kerkstr., and Reguliersdwarsstr., and in the outrageously fun **Gay Pride Parade.** Call 625 83 75 for more info (daily 5am-midnight). During **Uitmarket** weekend at the end of August, hundreds of free concerts around the Dam Square, street theater, and a book market along the Nieuwezijds Voorburgwal transform the streets of Amsterdam into a brilliant and raucous party.

■ Near Amsterdam: Edam, and Hoorn

When you tire of free-living Amsterdam, discover quaint cottages, peaceful parks and canals, and lots of cheese and clogs in **Edam.** Holland's sleeping beauty lies just outside Amsterdam, accessible by NZH bus from Centraal Station (30min., 7 strips). The 15th-century **Grote Kerk,** or St. Nicholaaskerk, is the largest three-ridged church in Europe and has 30 exquisite stained-glass windows (open Apr.-Oct. daily 2-4:30pm). Farmers still bring their famed cheese to market by horse and boat on Wednesdays in July and August (10am-12:30pm). Rent a bike at **Ronald Schot,** Kleine Kerkstr. 9-11 (f12 per day), and head to the source yourself. At **Alida Hoeve,** Zeddewed 1, a traditional cheese factory across the street from the bike path as you head toward Volendam (pass the first touristy cheese factory you see), Edam cheese is still made by hand and the generous samples are free (open daily 9am-6pm). Farther down the path stands a towering **windmill.** For f1, you can climb the steep ladder to the top while it's turning (open Apr.-Aug. daily 9am-4pm). If you decide to crash for the night, the **VVV,** Kaisergracht 1 (tel. (0299) 31 51 25), will help you find a private room.

   A little farther from Amsterdam, **Hoorn** awaits on the edge of the **Ijsselmeer,** an inlet of the Atlantic that the ever-enterprising Dutch diked off in 1932 to form a freshwater sea. The town itself is charming, with frequent open-air markets and a picturesque harbor. If the weather cooperates, **swimming** and **sailing** in the Ijsselmeer can be the perfect tranquilizer after the frenzy of Amsterdam. The **tourist office,** Veemarkt 4 (tel. (0229) 21 83 44), organizes comprehensive walking tours. From the train station, turn left on Veemarkt (open M-F 9-11:30am and 12:30-4pm). **De Toorts (HI)** (tel. (0229) 21 42 56) has rooms right on the water. To get there, take bus 133, 137, or 147 to "Julianaplaen" (dorms f24.35, nonmembers f29.35; open July-Aug.).

■ Haarlem

Surrounded by fields of tulips, daffodils, and geraniums, Haarlem is home to the Renaissance facades and placid canals that inspired the Golden Age Dutch artists.

SIGHTS AND ENTERTAINMENT The local 17th- and 18th-century *hofjes* (almshouses for elderly women) feature elegant brickwork and grassy courtyards; notable among them are the secluded **Hofje van Bakenes,** Wijde Appelaarsteeg 11, near the Teylers Museum, and the **Hofje van Oirschot,** at the end of Kuisstr. where it becomes Barteljorisstr. These are inhabited private properties, so be respectful. From the station, Kruisweg leads to the **Grote Markt** and the glorious medieval **Stadhuis**

(Town Hall), originally the hunting lodge of the Count of Holland. When the Hall of Counts is not in use, sneak a peek at the lavish interior; ask at the reception desk. The **Grote Kerk** graces the opposite end of the Grote Markt and houses the Müller organ, which Mozart played at the age of 11. (Church open M-Sa 10am-4pm. f2, students f1. Free recitals May-Oct. Tu 8:15pm; July-Aug. also Th 3pm.)

From the church, walk down Damstr. to the Netherlands' oldest museum, the **Teylers Museum,** Spaarne 16, which lets you see what people in 1788 thought a museum should be: a blend of scientific instruments, fossils, coins, paintings, and drawings, including works by Raphael, Michelangelo, and Rembrandt (open Tu-Sa 10am-5pm, Su noon-5pm; f7.50). The legacy of Haarlem's brash portraitist Frans Hals lives on in the **Frans Hals Museum,** Groot Heiligland 62. Housed in a charming 17th-century almshouse, the collection includes Hals's imposing group portraits and a permanent collection of modern art (open M-Sa 11am-5pm, Su 1-5pm; f7-8). On Saturdays, a technicolor **flower and fruit market** fills the Grote Markt (open 9am-4pm).

PRACTICAL INFO, ACCOMMODATIONS, AND FOOD Haarlem is easily accessible from Amsterdam by **train** (f6.25) or by **bus** 80 from Marnixstr., near Leidsepl. (2 per hr., 6 strips). Five night buses (86) cruise from Amsterdam's Leidsepl. to Haarlem (12:42-3:20am). The VVV **tourist office,** Stationspl. 1 (tel. (0900) 616 16 00, f1 per min.; fax (023) 534 05 37; email vvv_zk@saturnus.nl; http://www.saturnus.nl/vvv_zk), sells an excellent map (f4), offers the informative *Holiday Magazine* (f2), and books rooms for a f4.50 fee (open M-F 9am-5:30pm, Sa 10am-4pm).

The lively **NJHC-herberg Jan Gijzen (HI),** Jan Gijzenpad 3 (tel. (023) 537 37 93), lies on the banks of a canal, next to a beautiful park, and has its own bar. Bus 2 ("Haarlem-Nord") will drive you the 3km from the station to the hostel; tell the driver your destination. (f24.75; nonmembers f29. Sheets f6.25. Reception 7am-midnight. Flexible midnight curfew. Open Mar.-Oct.) Haarlem has apparently not heard of budget hotels, but the VVV can find you a private room for a f9 fee (from f28). **Hotel Carillon,** Grote Markt 27 (tel. (023) 531 05 91), is ideally located if not ideally priced. (Singles f57.50-92; doubles f137. Breakfast included. Reception and bar open daily 7:30am-1am.) Cheap pensions are located in nearby Zandvoort (see **Near Haarlem,** below). A campground awaits at **De Liede,** Liewegje 17 (tel. (023) 33 23 60). Take bus 2 ("Zuiderpolder") and walk 10 minutes (f5-5.50 per person, f5 per tent; f2.50 tax per person in summer). **Pannekoekhuis De Smikkel,** Kruisweg 57, serves plump buttery pancakes (f12-14) with anything from bananas to seafood (open M-Sa noon-10pm, Su 2-10pm). For healthier fare, try out **Eko Eetcafe,** Zijlstr. 39, which serves a vegetarian plate for f17 and pizzas for f12-16.50 (open daily 5:30-9:30pm).

■ Near Haarlem

Haarlem is only 10 minutes by train (round-trip f4.25) from **Zandvoort,** a seaside town that boasts seven **nude beaches** along with more modest sands for the bashful (for more info call (023) 571 82 31). Zandvoort is also known for its casinos and circus. Cheap pensions and hotels abound, and the **VVV,** Schoolpl. 1 (tel. (023) 571 79 47), in the village center, a downhill walk from the beach and the station, sells a lodgings guide for f4. (Open Apr.-Sept. M-Sa 10am-12:30pm and 1:30pm-5pm; Oct.-Mar. Tu-F 10am-12:30pm and 1:30-4:30pm, Sa 10am-12:30pm and 1:30-3:30pm.) **Hotel-Pension Noordzee,** Hogeweg 15 (tel. (023) 571 31 27), is only 100m from the beach (singles f50; doubles f80). **Hotel van der Aar,** Brederodestr. 44 (tel. (023) 571 48 02), is a good second choice (singles f40; doubles f65; reception 8am-midnight). **Guest House Corper,** Koninginneweg 21 (tel./fax (023) 571 34 49), is 10 minutes from the beach (singles f50; doubles f80; triples f120).

Bloemendaal, a less revealing beach, accessible by bus 81 from the Haarlem train station (15min.), is famous for its stately mansions, peaceful sand dunes, and fields of flowers. An international **flower auction** is held year-round in the nearby town of **Aalsmeer** (auction open M-F 7:30-11am). From Haarlem, take bus 140. The **Frans Roozen Gardens** bloom with 500 different types of flowers and plants; summer flower shows are free. Bus 90 ("Den Haag") stops in front of the gardens (open July-

Oct. M-F 9am-5pm; tulip shows daily Apr.-May 8am-6pm). Bus 50 or 51 runs past some of Holland's famous flower fields. Daffodils blossom in early to late April, hyacinths in mid- to late April, and tulips from late April to mid-May. Haarlem is also often used as a base for the exploration of the magnificent **Keukenhof** gardens (see "Near Leiden: Lisse," p. 645).

■ Leiden

Rembrandt's birthplace and the site of the first Dutch tulips, Leiden occupies a special position in Holland because of its university, one of the oldest and most prestigious in Europe. Leiden brims with bookstores, bicycles, museums, and a few requisite windmills.

SIGHTS AND ENTERTAINMENT The **Rijksmuseum voor Volkenkunde** (National Museum of Ethnology), Steenstr. 1, one of the world's oldest anthropological museums, boasts a collection of fantastic artifacts from the Dutch East Indies (open Tu-F 10am-5pm, Sa-Su noon-5pm; f10, students f7.50). The **Rijksmuseum van Oudheden** (National Antiquities Museum), Rapenburg 28, harbors Egyptian mummies, exhibits on ancient Dutch history, and the lovingly restored Egyptian Temple of Taffeh, removed from the reservoir basin of the Aswan Dam (open Tu-Sa 10am-5pm, Su noon-5pm; f5). The university's 400-year-old garden, the **Hortus Botanicus,** Rapenburg 73, where the first Dutch tulips were grown, has a vast range of plants from all around the world. (Open Apr.-Sept. M-Sa 9am-5pm, Su 10am-5pm; Oct.-Mar. M-F 9am-5pm. Some greenhouses close at 4:30pm. f5.) Inspect the mechanical innards of a functioning windmill at the **Molenmuseum "De Valk,"** 2e Binnenvestgracht 1 (open Tu-Sa 10am-5pm, Su 1-5pm; f5, free with Museumkaart). The **Museum De Lakenhal,** Oude Singel 32, exhibits works by Rembrandt and Jan Steen. The **Leiden American Pilgrim Museum,** Beschuitsleeg 9, tells the story of the pilgrims who sought refuge in Leiden before sailing to America on the **Mayflower** (open W-Sa 1-5pm; f3).

PRACTICAL INFO, ACCOMMODATIONS, AND FOOD Leiden makes a good **rail** daytrip from Amsterdam (30min., f11.50) or the Hague (20min., f4.50). The **VVV Tourist Office,** Stationspl. 210 (tel. (0900) 222 23 33; fax (071) 512 53 18; http://www.leidenpromotie.nl), across the street and to the right of the train station, doles out maps (f1.25), and locates rooms in private homes (f4.50 fee). Their *Rembrandt Tour* (f3.50) and *Pilgrim Tour* (f1) brochures offer creative ways to see the town on foot, and their city guide has a long list of accommodations (open M-F 9am-5:30pm, Sa 10am-2pm). Due to a student housing crunch, finding inexpensive rooms may be difficult. Idyllic **NJHC-herberg De Duinark (HI),** Langevelderlaan 45 (tel. (0252) 37 29 20), is 18km from Leiden in Noordwijk, a five-minute walk from beautiful white-sand beaches. Take bus 60 or 61 to "Kappellebosiaan" or bus 61 to "Sancta Maria," and walk 15 minutes (f28.50, nonmembers f33.50; sheets f6.25; reception 8am-1am). The **Hotel Pension Witte Singel,** Witte Singel 80 (tel. (071) 512 45 92), offers immaculate rooms overlooking gardens and canals (singles f60; doubles f85-110).

The university *mensa* has Leiden's cheapest eats: **De Bak,** Kaiserstr. 23-25 (open mid-Aug. to late June M-F 5-7pm; dinner f7.50). **Cafe de Illegale,** Hooigracht 72, serves vegetarian and Dutch cuisine to an intellectual crowd (f15-22; open daily 5pm-midnight; kitchen closes at 10pm). The **Bruin Boon,** Stationsweg 1, is a convivial pub serving cheap snacks and lunches (under f10; open M-F 8am-11:30pm, Sa 9:30am-11:30pm, Su 10:30am-6:30pm). The **VIV** supermarket is opposite the station (open M-F 8am-8pm, Sa 8am-5pm). The **Duke,** Oude Singel 2, rounds up live jazz nightly at 9:30pm and open jam sessions on Sundays (open Su-F 7pm-1am, Sa 2pm-2am).

■ Near Leiden: Lisse

Arriving in Lisse, you'll feel like Dorothy landing in technicolor Oz. From late March to May, the **Keukenhof** garden becomes a kaleidoscope as over five million bulbs explode into life (f15; tickets sold until 6pm; Mar. 23-May 28 M-Su 8am-7:30pm). The **Museum Voor de Bloembollenstreek** chronicles the history and science of tulip raising (open Tu-Su 1-5pm; f4). Take bus 50 or 51 toward Lisse from the Haarlem train station; a combination bus and museum ticket bought at Centraal Station (f21) saves money. The **VVV** (tel. (02522) 41 42 62) is at Grachtweg 53 (open M noon-5pm, Tu-F 9am-5pm, Sa 9am-4pm). Look for petals in motion at the April **flower parade.**

■ The Hague (Den Haag)

The Hague, the Dutch seat of government, has the requisite parliament buildings, prestigious museums, parks, and even some great summer festivals. Most of the year, though, it lacks the vitality of its neighbors. Make it a day trip or stay in the nearby beachfront **Scheveningen.**

SIGHTS AND ENTERTAINMENT For snippets of Dutch politics, visit The Hague's **Binnenhof,** the Parliament complex. Guided tours leaving from Binnenhof 8a move on to the 13th-century **Ridderzaal** (Hall of Knights), and usually one or both of the chambers of the States General (open M-Sa 10am-4pm, last tour at 3:45pm; f5). Just outside the north entrance of the Binnenhof, the 17th-century **Mauritshuis** features an impressive collection of Dutch paintings, including Rembrandt's *The Anatomy Lesson* and Vermeer's *Lady with a Turban* (open Tu-Sa 10am-5pm, Su 11am-5pm; f12.50). The **Peace Palace,** the opulent home of the International Court of Justice at Carnegiepl., 10 minutes from the Binnenhof, was donated by Andrew Carnegie as he suffered a bout of Robber Baron guilt. The palace is usually closed when the Court is in session; call ahead to make sure it's open. (Tel. (070) 302 41 37. Tours M-F 10, 11am, 2, 3, and 4pm; Oct.-May last tour leaves at 3pm. f5.) The interesting **Madurodam** has miniatures of Dutch sites (open Apr.-Sept. daily 9am-10pm; f19.50).

The city streets empty out early—head to **Muziekcafe La Valletta,** Nwe. Schoolstr. 13a, a mellow jazz cafe that features live shows Thursday nights at 10pm (open daily 5pm-1am). The **CaDance,** in early November, attracts some of Europe's most flamboyant modern dance artists. **Parkpop,** the last weekend in June, is the largest free mainstream rock concert in Europe. The annual **North Sea Jazz Festival** brings four incredible days of the world's best jazz to The Hague (9-11 July in 1999).

PRACTICAL INFO, ACCOMMODATIONS, AND FOOD For **trains** (tel. (06) 92 92) which serve Amsterdam (1hr., f16.75) and Rotterdam (30min., one-way f7.25) use **Holland Spoor;** most others come and go at **Centraal Station.** Both have **lockers** (f4-6). *Stoptrein* and trams 9 and 12 run from Holland Spoor to Centraal Station. The **VVV Tourist Office,** Kon. Julianapl. 30 (info tel. (0900) 34 03 50 51; 0.75f per min.), in front of Centraal Station under the Hotel Sofitel, which distributes maps (f3), books rooms for a f4 fee, and publishes events listings (open M-F 8:30am-5:30pm, Sa 10am-5pm; July-Aug. also Su 11am-3pm).

The **Australian** embassy is at Carnegielaan 4 (tel. (070) 310 82 00; open M-F 9am-12:30pm and 2-5:30pm; visas mornings only). The **Canadian** embassy is at Sophialaan 7 (tel. (070) 361 41 11; open M-F 9am-1pm and 2-5:30pm). Kiwis head to the **New Zealand Immigration Service,** Carnegielaan 10 (tel. (070) 365 80 37; open M-F 9am-12:30pm and 1:30-5:30pm; F closes at 5pm). The **South African Consulate** is at Wassenarseweg 36 (tel. (070) 392 45 01; open daily 9am-noon). The **U.K.** embassy sits at Lange Voorhout 10 (tel. (070) 364 58 00; open M-F 9am-1pm and 2:15-5:30pm). Citizens of the U.S. call the **consulate** in Amsterdam (tel. (020) 664 56 61).

The **NJHC City Hostel,** Scheepmakerstr. 27 (tel. (070) 315 78 78; fax (070) 315 78 77), is one of the nicest in Holland. From Centraal Station take tram 1, 9, or 12 to "Rijswijkse." (Dorms f34.50; doubles f90; quads f158. Non-members add f5. Sheets and breakfast included.) Even more alluring quarters wait in nearby Scheveningen; the **VVV,** Gevers Deynootweg 1134 (tel. (06) 354 350 51), can give you an accommodations guide (open July-Aug. M-Sa 9am-noon; Sept.-June M-Sa 9am-5:30pm). **Hotel Pension Lobèl,** Haagsestr. 53 (tel. (06) 354 58 03) is five minutes from a sublime beach and huge casino. Take tram 1, 7, or 9 ("Scheveningen") from the station (3 strips), and tell the driver your destination (singles f65; doubles f125). **Hotel Schev-**

eningen, Gevers Deynootweg 2 (tel. (06) 354 70 03), has a shower and TV in each room (singles f50; larger rooms f35 per person). To reach the beachside campground **Recreatiecentrum Kijuduinpark,** Wijndaelerweg 25 (tel. (06) 325 23 64), take tram 3 from Centraal Station (f7.55 per person; f10 per tent; open Apr.-Sept.).

The bike ride from The Hague to Scheveningen (a town so difficult to pronounce correctly, it was used as a code word by the Dutch in World War II) is pleasant; **bike rental** for f8 per day is available at both Holland Spoor (tel. (070) 389 08 30) and the Centraal Station (tel. (070) 385 32 35). The VVV sells cycling maps (f8), but routes and nearby towns are clearly marked along paths. Cheap cafes line **Korte Poten,** a pedestrian section of the street connecting Centraal Station with the Binnenhof complex and **Denneweg,** which spills over with outdoor terraces. Tasty pizza and pasta (f10-15) are available at **Donatello's,** Molenstr. 8-10 (open daily 11am-10pm).

■ Delft

To gaze out over Delft's lilied canals from one of its stone footbridges is to behold the very images that local master Jan Vermeer immortalized on canvas over 300 years ago. The city has not lost its charm. A stroll down Delft's tree-lined canals and many-hued *markts* alone justifies the jaunt south from The Hague. Thursdays and Saturdays, when townspeople flood to the bustling marketplace, are the best days to visit.

SIGHTS AND ENTERTAINMENT Delft is renowned for its **Delftware,** the blue-on-white china developed in the 16th century to compete with the newly imported Chinese porcelain. You can gawk at the precious platters in the 17th-century factory **De Porceleyne Fles,** Rotterdamseweg 196, in south Delft, where there are hourly demonstrations. To get to the boutique, take bus 63, 121, or 129 from the station to "Jaffalaan" (open Apr.-Sept. M-Sa 9am-5pm, Su 9:30am-5pm; Oct.-Mar. M-Sa 9am-5pm; f5). Built in 1381, the **Nieuwe Kerk** looms over the central **Markt** and holds the mausoleum of Dutch liberator William of Orange, flanked by a statue of his dog, who starved to death out of despair after his master died (church open Apr.-Oct. M-Sa 9am-6pm; Nov.-Mar. M-F 11am-4pm, Sa 11am-5pm; f3). Ascend the church tower, as caretakers of the 48-bell *carillon* have done for six centuries, for a view of old Delft (tower closes 30min. earlier than the church; f3). Built in the 15th century as a nun's cloister, **Het Prinsenhof** at Sint Agathapl. was William's abode until a crazed Spanish sympathizer assassinated him in 1584. Today it exhibits paintings, tapestries, pottery, and contemporary art (open Tu-Sa 10am-5pm, Su 1-5pm; f5).

The immense cafe **Verderop,** Westuest 9, near the station, has inexpensive drinks and live music (open M-F 10am-1am, Sa-Su 2pm-2am; July-Aug. opens daily at 3pm). The **Straattheater festival** (2nd week in June) summons street performers from the city's every nook and cranny. The **Oude Stijl Jazz Festival** swings into Delft in the third week in August.

PRACTICAL INFO, ACCOMMODATIONS, AND FOOD Delft is one hour southwest of Amsterdam by **train,** with connections to The Hague (15min., f4) and Leiden (30min., f6.25). For train or **bus** info, call (0900) 92 92. The **VVV Tourist Office,** Markt 85 (tel. (015) 212 61 00), has hiking and cycling maps (f4-10) and books rooms for a f3.50 fee and a 10% deposit. (Open Apr.-Oct. M-F 9am-6pm, Sa 9am-5:30pm, Su 10am-3pm; Nov.-Mar. M-F 9am-5:30pm, Sa 9am-5pm.) From the station, cross the bridge and turn left. At the first traffic light, turn right and walk straight, following signs to the Markt. **Rondvaart Delft,** Koormkt. 113 (tel. (015) 212 63 85), offers canal rides (Apr.-Oct. 10:30am-5:30pm; f8.50, students f7.50). Delft has few budget accommodations. The sage's choice is unmarked **Van Leeuwen,** Achterom 143 (tel. (015) 212 37 16), overlooking a canal. Walk out straight from the station and turn right on Achterom street after crossing four canals (ring the bell; singles f35; doubles f70; excellent breakfast included). A few hotels dotting the Markt offer spiffy rooms at decent prices, including the nearby **Pension Van Domburg,** Voldersgracht 24 (tel. (015) 212 30 29; doubles f70). Delft also has a **campground** on Korftlaan (tel. (015)

213 00 40) in the Delftse Hout recreation area. (f25 per tent. Laundry facilities available. Reception May to mid-Sept. 9am-10pm; mid-Sept. to Apr. 9am-6pm.) Take bus 64 from the station to "Korftlaan."

Many inexpensive restaurants line **Volderstraat** and **Oude Delft,** so skip the tourists traps in the *Markt*. **Kleyweg's Stads-Koffyhuis,** Oude Delft 133-135, has an outdoor terrace overlooking a canal. Their sandwiches were voted the best *broodje* in the Netherlands (omelettes and salads from f8.25; open M-F 9am-7pm, Sa 9am-6pm). **Stads Pan,** down the street at Oude Delft 113-115, has multitudes of savory pancakes (f5-17; open Mar.-Oct. daily 11am-9pm; Nov.-Feb. closed Su).

■ Rotterdam

Rotterdam defies the stereotype of the sleepy Dutch town full of canals, clogs, and windmills—it is a seething urban conglomerate renowned for its striking (some might say hideous) modern architecture and enormous harbor. The stimulating pace of the city is heightened by its vibrant student population, which will gladly include you in its frenetic partying.

SIGHTS AND ENTERTAINMENT Much of Rotterdam's appeal lies in its futuristic, abstract architecture, heavily influenced by the de Stijl school. For a dramatic example of some recent, eccentric architecture, check out the freaky 1984 **cube houses** (Kijks-Kubus), designed by Piet Blom. To find them, take the metro to "Blaak," turn left, and look up (#70 offers tours; open Mar.-Oct. daily 11am-5pm; Nov.-Feb. F-Su 11am-5pm; f3.50). Perhaps the most powerful monument in the city is Ossip Zadkine's incredible **Monument for the Destroyed City,** a statue of an anguished man, his arms raised in self-defense. This vision vividly embodies the pain and terror of the 1940 bombing raid. The statue is near the Blaak, directly behind the **Prins Hendrik Mariteim Museum,** which displays a history of the Rotterdam harbor and its ship-building industry. The stately **Schielandshuis** (Historical Museum), Korte Hoogstr. 31, recounts the history of Rotterdam through painting, sculpture, and other artifacts (open Tu-F 10am-5pm, Sa-Su 11am-5pm; f6). For an astoundingly comprehensive collection of art, check out the **Museum Bogmans-van Bogningen,** Museumpark 18-20 (Metro: "Eendractspl." or tram 4 or 5). The vast museum includes Rubens, Van Gogh, and Magritte (open Tu-Sa 10am-5pm, Su 11am-5pm; f7.50).

Mellow **coffee shops** line Oude Binneweg and Nieuwe Binnenweg, but avoid the area west of **Dijkzigt.** A slightly older crowd chills at **LeVagabond,** Nieuwe Binnenweng 99A (open M-Sa noon-2am, Su 2pm-2am). For less talk and more sweat, check out one of Rotterdam's dance clubs. The most active spot, **Night Town,** West Kruiskade 28, hosts alternative and indie bands. Expect a f5 "membership fee" and f10-25 cover (open F-Sa 11pm-late). **Rotown,** Nieuwe Binnenweg 19, draws a large crowd with techno music and the occasional live band (band cover f10; open daily 11am-1am, F-Sa until 3am). Gay men and women disco at **Gay Palace,** Schiedamsesingel 139 (cover f5-10; open F and Sa 10pm-late). June in Rotterdam is especially festive, with the multicultural **Dunya** festival in the first week, shortly followed by the **International Poetry Festival.**

PRACTICAL INFO, ACCOMMODATIONS, AND FOOD All trains pass through **Centraal Station,** with daily connections to Amsterdam (1hr., f22.25), The Hague (20min., f7.25), and Utrecht (45min., f14.50). The **VVV tourist office** at Coolsingel 67 (tel. (0900) 403 40 65, 50¢ per min.), opposite the *Stadhuis,* books rooms (f2.50), makes theater and concert reservations, and offers tours (open M-Th and Sa 9:30am-6pm, F until 9pm, Su noon-5pm). **Use It,** Conradstr. 2 (tel. 240 9158; fax 240 9158; email use-it@stads.net), right of the Centraal Station, has free **email,** and free lockers for "young" backpackers (open M-Th, Sa 9:30am-6pm, F until 9pm, Su until 5pm). The comfy **NJHC City-Hostel Rotterdam (HI),** Rochussenstr. 107-109 (tel. 436 57 63; fax 436 55 69) has a cheerful staff, TV room, kitchen, and laundry. Take the metro to "Dijkzigt," or ride tram 4. (Dorms f29.50-34.50, nonmembers f5 extra; doubles with bath f75. Shower and breakfast included. Reception 7am-midnight.) For even cheaper accommodations, there's always the student-run **Sleep-In**, hidden away at Mauritsweg 29 (tel. 412 14 20; fax 414 32 56), with no sheets, blankets, pillows, or pretensions to luxury. (f19. Breakfast and showers included. Sheets f4. Bar downstairs. Reception 8am-10am and 4pm-1am. Open mid-June to mid-Aug.) To get to the **Hotel Bienvenue**, Spoorsingel 24 (tel. 466 93 94; fax 467 74 75), from the Centraal Station's back entrance, walk five minutes along the canal; the hotel is on the right. (Clean singles with TV f78; doubles f100-125; triples f156. Reception 7am-11pm.)

Most eating options cluster around **Nieuwe Binnenweg** or in the **Oude Haven**. The **Aya Eetcafe**, 's-Gravendijkwal 136, attracts a lively student crowd (menu f6-30). Linger over coffee at **Dudok**, Meent (sandwiches f6-9, spaghetti f12.50; open Su-F 8am-11pm, Sa until midnight). **De Consul**, Westeringracht 28, is the best choice for dinner (f12-15) and features a large university crowd (open Su-Tu 3pm-1am, W-Sa 3pm-4am). Buy groceries at **A&P**, Nieuwe Binneweg 30 (open M-Th 9am-8pm, F 9am-9pm, Su 9am-6pm).

■ Near Rotterdam: Gouda

Gouda ("HOW-da") is the quintessential Dutch town, complete with windmill, cheese, and canals. The **VVV** (tel. (0182) 51 36 66) is in the *Markt* (open M-F 9am-5pm, Sa 10am-4pm; June-Aug. also Su noon-3pm). A regional **cheese market** is held every Thursday morning in the summer (10am-12:30pm, last Th of June through the end of Aug.). Gouda's late Gothic splendor centers on the monstrous **St. John's Church**. Ravaged by everything from lightning to Reformation iconoclasts, it has managed to maintain a stunning collection of 16th-century stained-glass windows (open M-Sa Apr.-Oct. 9am-5pm; Nov.-Mar. 10am-4pm; f3, students f2). Across the street, **The Catharina Hospital and The Blackamoor** holds an enormous collection of early and contemporary Flemish art, period rooms (including a torture cell), and early surgical instruments (open M-Sa 10am-5pm, Su noon-5pm; f4.25, students f2.25). You can also climb inside a working windmill, **De Roode Leeuw** (open Th 9am-2pm, Sa 9am-4pm). The **Goudse Pottenbakkerij**, Peperstr. 76, has been producing the famous Gouda clay pipes since the 17th century (open M-F 9am-5pm, Sa 11am-5pm; free). Behind the factory, the **Het Trefpunt Hotel**, Westhaven 46 (tel. (01825) 128 79), has clean rooms overlooking a canal. (Singles f85; doubles f110; triples f150. Reception M-Sa 8am-11pm, Su 8am-7pm.) **Het Goudse Winkeltje**, Achter de Kerk 9a, across from the church, has great pancakes (f7-14; open Tu-Sa 9am-5pm).

▓ Utrecht

Utrecht, at the geographical center of the Netherlands, is defined by its pretty canals, grandiose cathedral, and leftist university. Students support a dynamic cultural scene.

SIGHTS AND ENTERTAINMENT If you arrive by train, you'll find yourself trapped in the middle of an ultramodern mall, the **Hoog Catharijne**. Its storefronts wait to devour wallets whole, but if you escape, Utrecht's old town lies only blocks away. At Utrecht's center rises the awe-inspiring, gothic **Domkerk**, begun in 1254 and finished 250 years later. The church's statues were defaced in the early 16th century by Calvinists who considered artistic representations of biblical figures to be sacrilegious. (Open May-Oct. M-F 10am-5pm; Oct.-May M-F 11am-4pm, Sa 10am-3:30pm, Su 2-4pm. Free.) The **Domtoren**, originally attached to the cathedral but freestanding since a malevolent medieval tornado blew away the church nave, is the highest tower in the Netherlands—on a clear day you can see Amsterdam. (Tower open Apr.-Oct. M-F 10am-5pm, Sa-Su noon-5pm. Guided tours on the hour. f5.50.) The **Pandhof**, the church's 15th-century cloister garden, has been converted into a rustic herb garden (open same hours as Domtoren; free). At the **Centraal Museum**, Agnietenstr. 1, you can marvel at a 9th-century Viking ship and the paintings of the Utrecht school (open Tu-Sa 10am-5pm, Su noon-5pm; f6). **Het Catharijneconvent**, Nieuwe Gracht

63, documents the progress of Christianity in the Netherlands with a collection of Dutch religious artwork (open Tu-F 10am-5pm, Sa-Su 11am-5pm; f7). **Van Speelklok tot Pierement,** Buurkerhof 10, displays musical instruments from the 18th century to the present (open Tu-Sa 10am-5pm, Su 1-5pm; f7.50).

Utrecht presents ample opportunity to get wild and let loose. Pick up a free copy of the *Vitagenda* from the VVV for info on weekly shows. **De Winkel van Sinkel,** Oude Gracht 158, combines a cafe, restaurant, bar, and dance hall in an 18th-century building by the water's edge (salads f10.50-15.50, sandwiches f8.50; food served 11am-10pm) and **Cafe Flitz,** Rozenstr. 15, is a lively place to drink and dance (open daily 8:30pm-late). A slightly mellower crowd chills at **Zeezicht,** Nobelstr. 2 (open daily 9am-2am) while the theater-cafe **De Bastaard,** Jansveld 17, serves up flavored coffees and liqueurs. **De Rose Wolk,** Jacobskerkhof, on the corner of Oude Gracht, and the **Homocafe Bodytalk,** Oude Gracht 64 (open M-Th 8pm-3am, F-Sa 8pm-5am, Su 4pm-4am) are popular gay hangouts. For more info on the gay scene, contact the **C.O.C.,** Oude Gracht 300 (tel. (030) 231 88 41; open M-F noon-5pm).

PRACTICAL INFO, ACCOMMODATIONS, AND FOOD   Utrecht is easily accessible by train from Amsterdam. The VVV **tourist office,** Vredenburg 90 (tel. (090) 04 14 14 14, 50¢ per min.; fax (030) 233 14 17; email vvv.utrecht@tref.nl), at the end of the shopping mall, charges f4.50 to locate lodgings. Follow signs from the train station (open M-F 9am-6pm, Sa 9am-4pm). Set in a majestic medieval manor house on the banks of the old Rhine, **Jeugdherberg Ridderhofstad (HI),** Rhijnauwenselaan 14 (tel. (030) 656 12 77; fax 657 10 65), offers a peaceful retreat. Take bus 40, 41 or 43 from Centraal Station (3 strips; tell the driver your destination), and walk 10 minutes. (f30, showers and breakfast included. Reception 7am-9:30am. Bar open 7am-12:30am.) **Pension Memory,** Pr. Magrietstr. 5 (tel. (030) 242 07 37; fax 242 07 37), is closer to the city center (singles f53-70; doubles f80-115). **Camping De Berekuil,** Ariënslaan 5-7 (tel. (030) 271 38 70), is not far from the center of town; take bus 57 (2 strips) from the station to the "Veemarkt" stop (f8 per person, f8 per tent).

Café De Baas, Lijnmarkt 8, across the canal from the Domtoren, features yummy vegetarian dishes (from f12.50) with occasional live music. (Open W 5pm-3am, Th-Sa 5pm-3am, Su 5pm-10pm. Kitchen closes at 8:30pm.) The restaurants on the Oude Gracht are atmospheric but costly. For traditional Dutch fare, try the **Pancake Bakery "de oude muntkelder,"** Oude Gracht 112 (pancakes f9-16; omelette f10-15; open daily noon-9:30pm). The hip **Toque Toque,** Oude Gracht 138, at Vinkenburgstr. serves up generous pasta dishes (f16.50; open M-F 10am-midnight, Sa 9am-midnight, Su noon-midnight).

■ Arnhem and Hoge Veluwe

Rebuilt after savage World War II bombings, **Arnhem,** 100km southeast of Amsterdam, is now a convenient base for the exploration of the impressive **Hoge Veluwe National Park,** a 13,000-acre preserve of woods, heath, dunes, red deer, and wild boars which shelters one of the finest modern art museums in all of Europe. This may well prove one of your trip's highlights. Take one of the free white **bikes** from the Koperen Kop **visitor center** to explore over 33km of paths which wind through woods, alongside ponds and amidst sand dunes. (Park open June-Aug. daily 8am-10pm; Sept. 9am-8pm; Oct. 9am-7pm; Nov.-Mar. 9am-5:30pm; Apr. 8am-8pm; May 8am-9pm. f7.) Tucked deep within the park and a 35-minute walk from the nearest entrance, the **Rijksmuseum Kröller-Müller** has an extensive collection of van Goghs, as well as works by Seurat, Mondrian, and many others. Another focal point is the museum's striking sculpture garden, one of the largest in Europe, with exceptional pieces by Rodin, Bourdelle, and Hepworth. (Museum open Tu-Su 10am-5pm. Sculpture garden open Apr.-Oct. 10am-4:30pm. f7.) The **Museonder,** at the visitor center, is the world's first underground museum, dedicated to the study of the subterranean ecosystem (open daily 10am-5pm; free).

The park is equally accessible from Arnhem and Apeldoorn (15km from both). From March through October, bus 12 (f7.50 or 5 strips) leaves from Arnhem train station, and stops at the museum and the visitors' center. After hours, bus 2 can also be taken to the Schaarvbergen stop to pick up bicycles. From Apeldoorn train station, take bus 110 (f6.75 or 4 strips); buses leave hourly between 9:40am and 4:10pm. **Burger's Zoo,** outside of town, has recreated spacious tropical and safari environments and rescued animals from tiny cubicles at other zoos (open daily in summer 9am-7pm; off-season 9am-sunset; f25). Take bus 3 from the station (30min.).

In Arnhem, the VVV **tourist office** (tel. (090) 02 02 40 75; fax 02 64 42 26 44), to the left of the station on Stationspl., finds lodgings and gives out park info (open M-F 9am-5:30pm, Sa 9am-4pm). The lively **Jeugdherberg Alteveer (HI),** Diepenbroeklaan 27 (tel. (026) 332 01 14), in a sylvan setting, offers basketball, volleyball, badminton, ping-pong, pool, and air-hockey facilities. Take bus 3 from the station toward Alteveer (3 strips), ask the driver to let you off at the hostel, and follow the signs. (f29.50, non-members f34.50; July-Aug. add f2 tourist tax. Breakfast included. Sheets f6.25. Reception 8am-11pm. Curfew midnight.) **Hotel-Pension Parkzicht,** Apeldoornsestr. 16 (tel. (026) 442 06 98), is a 15-minute walk from the station (singles f50; doubles f100; triples f135; breakfast included). Camp at **Kampeercentrum Arnhem,** Kemperberg-erweg 771 (tel. (026) 445 61 00), accessible by bus 2 "Haedaveld" (20min., 3 strips; f18.50 for 2 people, f13.50 for one; open Mar.-Sept.). **Apollo,** 4 Jansstr., serves cheap and spicy fast food (f3-5; open M-F 10am-8pm, Sa until 10pm). **Le Pistolet,** 38a Grote Oord, a sunny cafe in the heart of the city, offers a bit more class and excellent pasta (f17-23; open M-F noon-9pm, Sa-Su until 11:30pm). The **Luxor theater,** at Willenspl. 10, heats up with concerts (cover up to f20; open Th-Sa 11pm-5am).

■ Near Arnhem: Apeldoorn

In addition to providing access to De Hoge Veluwe, **Apeldoorn** is home to the **Museum Paleis Het Loo,** a magnificent palace from the 17th century (open Tu-Su 10am-5pm. f12.50). From Apeldoorn station, take bus 102 or 104 (10min., 2 strips). In Apeldoorn, the VVV **tourist office** sits next to the station at Stationstr. 72 (tel. (0900) 01 68 16 36; fax (055) 521 12 90). The staff books accommodations and has biking maps. (f7. Open Sept.-Apr. 25 M-F 9am-5:30pm, Sa 9am-1pm; Apr. 26-Sept. M-F 9am-6pm, Sa 9am-5pm.) **De Grote Beer (HI),** Asselsestr. 330 (tel. (055) 355 31 18; fax 355 38 11), is hidden in a quiet area of town but has a lively atmosphere and rents bikes for f12.50 per day. Take bus 4 or 7 ("Orden") from the train station (dorms f28-31; breakfast included; reception 8am-10pm; flexible midnight curfew).

■ Maastricht

Situated on the narrow strip of land between Belgium and Germany, Maastricht has seen its share of interstate rivalries, and centuries of foreign threats inspired an innovative defense system combining natural resources and hand-built fortifications. The city has since shed its armor and, with the passage of the 1991 Maastricht Treaty, become the symbol of a hopeful European unity. The **Saint Peter Caves,** a maze of more than 20,000 passages, were used as siege shelter as late as World War II. (1hr. tours July-Aug. daily every hour from 10:45am to 3:45pm, and in English at 2:15pm; Apr.-June and Sept.-Oct. daily at 12:30, 2, and 3pm; Jan.-Mar. and Oct.-Dec. W and F-Su at 2pm. f5.50.) The **Kazematten,** 10km of underground passageways constructed between 1575 and 1825, enabled locals to detect enemies and to carry out surprise attacks. (From Vrijtmarkt, go west toward Tongersepl., following the Waldeck Bastion signs. Mostly Dutch tours June 28-Aug. daily 12:30 and 2pm; Sept.-June 27 Su at 2pm). Maastricht's aboveground marvels include the beautiful **Basilica of Saint Servatius,** Keizer Karelplein, which contains 11th-century crypts and the country's largest bell (open Dec.-Mar. daily 10am-4pm; Sept.-Nov. 10am-5pm; July-Aug. 10am-6pm; f4). The **Onze Lieve Vrouwe Basiliek,** O.L. Vrouweplein, is a medieval basilica with ecclesiastical arts and crafts (open Easter-Oct. M-Sa 11am-5pm, Su 1-5pm; f3.50).

Arriving in Maastricht's Centraal Station, you'll end up on the eastern side, across the river from all of the action. Buses run frequently from the station across the river to the Markt. Most sights, bars, and restaurants are located in the pedestrian zone connecting the **Markt** to **Vrijthof Square** and **O.L. Vrouweplein.** The VVV **tourist office,** Kleine Staat 1 (tel. (043) 325 21 21), about a block south of the Markt at Het Dinghuis, books rooms for free and sells a map and a useful brochure (f2 each; open May-Oct. M-Sa 9am-6pm; Nov.-Apr. M-F 9am-6pm, Sa 9am-5pm). With a pool, tennis courts, and bar, the **HI Hostel Sportel de Dousberg,** Dousbergweg 4 (tel. (043) 346 67 77; fax 346 67 55), is 10 minutes from the station by bus 55 or 56 to "De Dousberg." (Su bus 28 toward Pottenberg; tell the driver your destination; 3 strips. Dorms f32-37; doubles f98. Breakfast included. Key deposit f10. Strict 1am curfew.) Sleep on the Maas River at **Botel Maastricht** (tel. (043) 321 90 23; fax (043) 325 79 98), moored at Maasbouleverd 95 (singles f57; tiny doubles f89; quads f160).

De Bobbel, Wolfstr. 32, is a charming cafe not far from the Vrijthof (meals from f10; open M-Sa 10am-midnight). Eat to your heart's content at **Stap in,** Kesselskade 61, where a three-course meal is f18.50 (open daily 10am-9pm). On Brusselstr., **Oase** features house music while **Kommel** offers live jazz (both open 8pm-late). A gay crowd mingles at **Trait d'Union** and **Rembrandt,** cafes located at Mkt. 32 and 38 respectively (both open daily 8pm-2am). The **C.O.C.** (tel. (043) 321 83 36) has more info on Maastricht's **gay scene.**

■ Groningen

Groningen, about two hours northeast of Amsterdam, is a vibrant university town whose flamboyant spirit is reflected in its eccentric museums and trendy cafes. While World War II bombing left most of the city in ruins, one building that survived is the **Martinitoren,** a 97m tower that weathered everything from German attacks to a victory celebration that got out of hand (open daily July-Sept. 11am-4:30pm; Apr.-June noon-4:30pm; Oct.-Mar. Sa-Su noon-4:30pm; f2.50). The **Groninger Museum,** a quirky pastel assemblage of squares, cylinders, and slag metal, literally forms a bridge between the central station and inner city. The uniqueness of the art—ranging from ancient Chinese to cutting-edge modern work—is reflected in exhibition titles like "Mutant Materials in Contemporary Design" (f10; open Tu-Su 10am-5pm). Groningen is also within easy biking distance from surrounding lakes and forests; rent a **bike** at the station (f8 per day) and buy a map at the VVV (f7). **Shiermonnikoog,** a peaceful island with bike paths and nature trails, is two hours away. Take bus 63 (every 2hr. from 8am-8pm, 10 strips) to the ferry (10min, f20; in summer f35 for bus and ferry).

To reach the VVV **tourist office,** Ged. Kattendiep 6 (tel. (0900) 20 23 30 50, f1 per min.; fax (050) 311 02 58), turn right out of the station, cross the bridge, and follow the signs. (Open M 1-6pm, Tu-F 9:30am-6pm, Sa 9am-5pm; July-Sept. also Su noon-4pm. Machine outside has f2.50 maps.) The funky **Simplon Youth Hotel,** Boteidiep 73 (tel. (050) 313 52 21; fax 313 30 27), has quirky ceiling art, laundry facilities, and a weight room. Take bus 1 or 2 from the station and ask the driver to show you the way (dorms f21.50; breakfast f6.50; linen f4.50). You can get a meal at the mellow **Ugly Duck** cafe, 28 Zwanestr., for only f12-15 (open M 4pm-2am, Tu-F noon-2am, Sa 11am-2am, Su 3pm-2am; kitchen closes 9pm).

Groningen's nightlife would make a metropolis twice its size proud. The hotspots are Poelstr. and Peperstr. (off the Groete Markt) and Zwanestr. (by the University). Dance till dawn at **The Palace,** Gelkingestr. 1, on the corner of the Markt (cover up to f10; open M-Sa 11pm-5am), or head to the intimate, candle-lit **Jazz Cafe de Spieghel,** Peperstr. 11, for live music (open daily until 5am). **El Rubio,** Zwanestr. 26, welcomes gay men and women with a relaxed atmosphere (open daily 4pm-3am).

■ Wadden Islands (Waddeneilanden)

Wadden means "mudflat" in Dutch. In summer, however, sand rather than mud defines the islands; sand beaches hide behind dune ridges with windblown manes of golden grass. Tulip-lined bike trails carve through vast, flat stretches of grazing land. The Wadden Islands are an idyllic retreat, especially from May to early July, before they are overrun by hordes of German and Dutch tourists.

Texel With a little planning, you can visit **Texel,** the southernmost and largest island, on a daytrip from Amsterdam. The island can be a voyeur's paradise, with two popular **nude beaches** (south of Den Hoorn and off De Cocksdorp at paal 28) and **bird watching.** You can only visit the **nature reserves** on a guided tour (2hr., f7.50). Book in advance from **Ecomare,** Ruyslaan 92 (tel. (0222) 31 77 41), in De Koog, and specify English-speaking tours not requiring rubber boots. Rent a **bike** at **Verhuurbedrijf Heijne,** across from the ferry stop at 't Horntje (f7.50 per day; open daily Apr.-Oct. 9am-9pm; Nov.-Mar. 9am-6pm) and pedal between the island's three major villages: the central **Den Burg,** the beach-front **De Koog,** and the more isolated, northern **De Cocksdrop.** Alternatively, a **Texel Ticket** allows unlimited one-day travel on the bus system (mid-June to mid-Sept.; f6).

To get to Texel from Amsterdam, take the train to Den Helder (70min., f20), then bus 3 from the station to the ferry. Boats leave at 35 minutes past the hour, every hour from 6am to 9pm daily (20min., last boat back 9:05pm, round-trip f10). The VVV **tourist office,** Den Burg, Emmaln 66 (tel. (0222) 31 47 41; fax 31 00 54; http:// www.texel.net), has camping and accommodation info and sells excellent hiking and walking maps (f6) as well as a birdwatcher's booklet (f5.50; open M-F 9am-6pm, Sa 9am-5pm; July-Aug. also Su 10am-1:30pm; Apr.-Nov. F until 9pm and Sa until 5:30pm). Both of Texel's **HI youth hostels** are immaculate and easily accessible from the ferry (tell the bus driver your destination). Take bus 29 to **Panorama,** Schansweg 7 (tel. (0222) 31 54 41; fax 31 38 89), which snuggles in a nature reserve 7km from the ferry and 3km from Den Burg center. (f28, nonmembers f34. Sheets f6.25. Midnight curfew, but night key available for f50 deposit.) Bus 28 goes to **De Eyercoogh,** Pontweg 106 (open to groups Apr. to mid-Oct., individuals July-Sept.; call Panorama for reservations). The three-star **Hotel de Merel,** Warmoestr. 22 (tel. (0222) 31 31 32), is around the corner from the main square in Den Burg (singles f66.25, 3 nights or fewer f73.75; doubles f102.50-117.50 for 2 nights or fewer). Numerous **campgrounds** cluster in De Koog (f4-7).

Sample the local seafood at **Theodorahoeve,** Kogerstr. 26 in Den Burg (open daily 11am-9pm). **De 12 Balcken Tavern,** Weverstr. 20 in Den Burg, is a snug and dimly lit pub that specializes in *'t Jutterje,* the island's wildly popular alcohol, blended from herbs and wheat (beer f2.75; open M-Sa 10am-2am, Su noon-2am). The second weekend in June, brings **RondeVan Texel,** the largest catamaran race in Europe and the culmination of a week-long **jazz festival** in Den Burg. Sate yourself with sea creatures during the last weekend in August at the **Tropical Sea Festival.**

The Friese Islands The four other islands (the Friese Islands) all have extensive dunes and wildlife sanctuaries. **Schiermonnikoog** and **Vlieland** are quiet, while **Terschelling** and **Ameland** offer more nightlife. On boat excursions to Vlieland from Texel, you must return the same day. Schiermonnikoog's VVV **tourist office,** on Reeweg (tel. (05195) 312 33), finds private rooms for a f35 fee (open M-F 9am-1pm and 2-6:30pm). Reserve ahead, even in the off season. You can stay at the **Terschelling Hostel (HI),** van Heusdenweg 39. (Tel. (0562) 44 23 38. Fax 44 33 12. f32, nonmembers f37. Breakfast included. Sheets f6.25. Reception 8am-midnight. Midnight curfew.) For Terschelling or Vlieland, take the main train line from Amsterdam to **Leeuwarden** (2½hr.), then continue to Harlingen (3hr., f35), where you can catch the ferry to either island (2hr., round-trip f37-42; bikes f17). To reach Ameland, take bus 66 from Leeuwarden (50min., 6 strips) to Holwerd and then the ferry (45min., round-trip f18). To reach Schiermonnikoog, take bus 51 from Lauwersoog where you catch the ferry (40min., round-trip f18). From May to September, ferries run among some of the islands, making it possible to see several in a few days. For more info, call the Ameland tourist office (tel. (0519) 54 20 20; open M-Sa 9am-5pm).

Norway (Norge)

US$1 =7.73kr (Norwegian kroner)	1kr = US$0.13
CDN$1= 5.09kr	1kr = CDN$0.20
UK£1 = 12.80kr	1kr = UK£0.08
IR£1 = 11.19kr	1kr = IR£0.09
AUS$1 = 4.56kr	1kr = AUS$0.22
NZ$1 = 3.94kr	1kr = NZ$0.25
SAR1 = 1.24kr	1kr = SAR0.81
Country Code: 47	International Dialing Prefix: 095

Norway is beautiful, rich, and modern. Its coast is long and jagged, extending to the northernmost point in Europe. Deep, still fjords cut famously into the land, bringing large numbers of its people under the influence of the sea. In the age of the Vikings, the country accumulated wealth by plundering. Fierce Norsemen spread across the Atlantic and "settled" communities in England, Ireland, and France. However, their pagan pillaging party subsided in the 10th century, when King Harald Hårfagre (the Fair-haired) unified the realm and Olav Haraldsson imported Christianity. Rune stones, stave churches, and preserved Viking ships still survive from this age, while sagas chronicle the Vikings' adventures and myths in rich poetry and epics.

After the Viking twilight, Norway was annexed first to Denmark, then Sweden, but the closing years of the 19th century spawned great national luminaries of art from Munch to Ibsen to Grieg. Independent from Sweden in 1905, Norway endured German occupation during World War II, but developed into a modern welfare state in the aftermath of the war. Today, the country is one of the most expensive in Europe, and citizens pay gargantuan taxes to maintain their social net. Norway's progressive social policies are coupled with a doggedly pro-whaling stance, which attracts disapproval abroad. The state-owned oil company, *Statoil*, is one of the world's greatest exporters of crude oil, and the black gold is injecting gobs of wealth into the national treasury. Most residents live in the bulge of southern Norway, but intrepid farmers and fishermen have carved out settlements as far north as Kirkeness on the Russian border, leaving the modern flavor of the capital Oslo behind.

GETTING THERE AND GETTING AROUND

Every coastal town of any significance from Oslo to Bergen has **ferry** service to Denmark, England, Germany, or the Netherlands (more frequent and expensive in summer and on weekends). Most travelers take the **train** to Oslo from Copenhagen (10hr., 3 per day, 790kr, under 26 650kr) or Stockholm (6hr., 2 per day, 675kr, under 26 525kr). **Eurail** is valid on all trains. The **Norway Railpass** grants unlimited travel within the country for three days (908kr), seven days (1304kr), or 14 days (1733kr) over the course of one month. The *buy-in-Scandinavia* **Scanrail Pass** allows five days within 15 (1420kr, under 26 1070kr) or 21 consecutive days (2200kr, under 26 1650kr) of unlimited rail travel through Scandinavia, as well as many free or discounted ferry rides and reduced bus fares in Norway. This differs from the *buy-outside-Scandinavia* **Scanrail Pass,** which offers five out of 15 days (US$182, under 26 US$137), 10 days out of one month (US$292, under 26 US$219), or 30 consecutive days (US$426, under 26 US$320) of unlimited travel. Foreign students sometimes get the discounts on domestic rail travel enjoyed by Norwegian students too. Off-peak green trains are always discounted.

No free brochure gives you a complete picture of the complex domestic transportation scene; you'll have to collect sheaves of free regional schedules, or ask at travel agencies, train stations, or tourist offices for a look at *Rutebok for Norge*. Norwegian trains run only as far North as Bodø, where buses take over. Trains far-

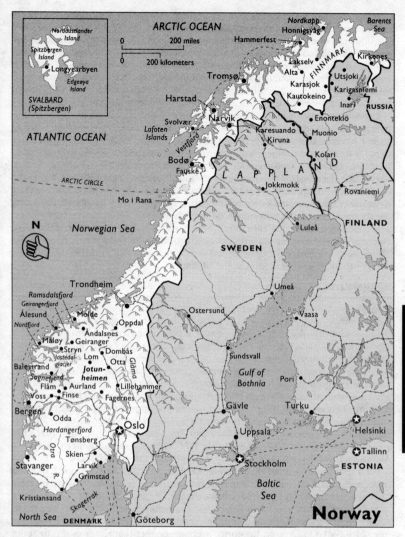

ARCTIC OCEAN

0 ———— 200 miles
0 ———— 200 kilometers

Nordaustlander Island
Spitzbergen Island
● Longyearbyen
Edgeøya Island

SVALBARD (Spitzbergen)

Barents Sea
Nordkapp
Honnigsvåg
Hammerfest
FINNMARK
Kirkenes
Lakselv
Alta
Tromsø
Karasjok
Utsjoki
Karigasniemi
Inari
Kautokeino
RUSSIA
Harstad
Svolvær
Narvik
Enontekiö
Lofoten Islands
Karesuando
Muonio
Kiruna
Vestfjord
Bodø
Kolari
Fauske
ATLANTIC OCEAN

ARCTIC CIRCLE

Mo i Rana
LAPPLAND
Jokkmokk
Rovaniemi

N

Norwegian Sea
SWEDEN
Luleå
FINLAND

Trondheim
Umeå
Romsdalsfjord
Geirangerfjord
Ålesund
Molde
Nordfjord
Oppdal
Østersund
Vaasa
Andalsnes
Geiranger
Måløy
Stryn
Dombås
Jostedal glacier
Lom
Otta
Sundsvall
Pori
Balestrand
Jotunheimen
Sognefjord
Flåm
Aurland
Lillehammer
Glåma
Gulf of Bothnia
Voss
Finse
Fagernes
Turku
Bergen
Odda
Gävle
Hardangerfjord
Tønsberg
Oslo
Uppsala
Helsinki
Otra R.
Skien
Tallinn
Stavanger
Larvik
ESTONIA
Kristiansand
Grimstad
Stockholm
Skagerrak
Baltic Sea
North Sea
DENMARK
Göteborg
Norway

ther north move along the Swedish rail line through Kiruna, which ends at Narvik on the Norwegian coast, on a line from Murmansk in Russia. Seat reservations are compulsory on many long-distance trains and all night trains (20kr). For a price, sleeping cars and couchettes are available on all night trains.

For those under 25 or students under 32, special youth fares make **flying** a viable option, often cheaper than the train. **Braathens SAFE** (tel. 67 58 60 00) and **SAS** (tel. 81 00 33 00) are the main airlines, and both offer domestic standby tickets (*chance billets*). Any trip which does not pass Trondheim but stays either north or south of it costs around 410kr one way (around 800kr if the trip involves both the northern and southern zones). A 71kr tax is added for trips from Oslo to the south. Tickets bought in the U.S. through the "Visit Norway Pass" from **Scanam World Tours** (tel. (800) 545-2204) should cost US$85 per short journey and US$170 per long (plus local taxes and a US$10 handling fee), but the service may change in 1999.

Buses are quite expensive (about 1kr per km), but are the only land option north of Bodø and in the fjords. **Norway Bussekspress** (tel. 23 00 24 40) operates 75% of the domestic bus routes and publishes a free, easy-to-follow book of schedules and prices. **Scanrail** and **InterRail** pass holders are entitled to a 50% discount on most bus routes, and students are entitled to a 25-50% discount on most routes—be insistent and follow the rules listed in the Norway Bussekspress booklet. Seats are guaranteed on routes operated by Norway Bussekspress. Bus passes valid for one (1375kr) or two (2200kr) weeks are a good deal for travelers exploring the fjords or the north.

Car ferries *(ferjer)* are usually much cheaper (and slower) than the many **hydrofoils** *(hurtigbåte)* that cruise the coasts and fjords; both often have student, Scanrail, and/or InterRail discounts. The **Hurtigruten** (the famed Coastal Steamer) takes six days for its fantastic voyage from Bergen to Kirkenes; each of the 34 stops en route have one northbound and one southbound departure per day. The Hurtigruten often have a free sleeping-bag room; cabins run from 100kr per night (50% off during the off-season). No railpass discounts are offered, and generally buses and trains will be more affordable. Cars and other vehicles are required to keep **headlights** on during the daytime. **Hitching** is notoriously difficult throughout Scandinavia. Many Norwegians hitch beyond the rail lines in northern Norway and the fjord areas of the west. Hitchers should bring several layers of clothing, rain gear, and a warm sleeping bag. Those using a sign have better odds, and many attempt to find a ride before or during a ferry trip to avoid getting stuck at the landing.

ESSENTIALS

Virtually every town, village, and pit stop in Norway has an ever-helpful **Turistinformasjon** office; look for a black lower-case **"i"** on a green sign. Try to go the night before you're planning to head out of town, as buses often leave early in the morning. Throughout July and the first half of August all tourist offices are open daily; most have reduced hours the rest of the year. Most businesses, including travel agents and ticket offices, close early during the summer, especially on Fridays and during August when Norwegians vacation. If a store closes at 3pm, get there by 2:45pm. **Banks** are generally open Monday through Friday from 8:15am to 3pm (during the winter until 3:30pm), Thursday until 5pm. Large post offices **exchange money,** usually charging a small commission and offering the best rates. Offices are generally open Monday through Friday 7am-6pm, Saturday 9am-3pm. Legal **holidays** include New Year's Eve and Day, Easter (April 9-10, 1999), Labor Day (May 1), Constitution Day (May 17), Ascension Day (May 13), Whit Monday (May 24), and Christmas (Dec. 25-27).

For a few weeks around the summer solstice (June 21), Norway north of Bodø basks in the midnight sun. You stand the best chance of seeing the **Northern Lights** between November and February above the Arctic Circle (although they are occasionally visible in the south). **Skiing** is best just before Easter, when the winter has slackened, and the sun returns after months of darkness. Oslo averages 63°F (18°C) in July, 24°F (-4°C) in January; up north, average summer temperatures dip to about 50°F (10°C) while winter temperatures are much the same as in the south. The north and the fjord country are wetter than the south and east.

Domestic and international **telephone** calls can butcher the budget in Norway. Pay phones take 1, 5, 10, and 20kr coins, and local calls require at least 3kr; buying a *telekort* (available in 35, 98, and 210kr denominations) card is more economical in the long-run. Calls from pay phones cost twice as much as from private lines, and between 10pm and 8am calls are 15-20% cheaper. To make collect international calls, dial 115, within Norway 117. **AT&T Direct's** number is 800 19 011; **MCI WorldPhone,** 800 19 912; **Sprint Access,** 800 198 77; **Canada Direct,** 800 19 111; **BT Direct,** 800 19 944; and **New Zealand Direct,** 800 128 53.

Norway is officially bilingual. The Danish-influenced *bokmål* Norwegian used in Oslo and a standardized language *(nynorsk)* based on dialects of rural western Norway are both taught in schools. Most Norwegians speak fluent English.

Yes/No	Ja/Ikke or Ne	yah/IK-eh, nay
Hello	Hallo	hah-LOH
Thank you	Takk	tak
Excuse me	Unnskyld	oon-SHOOLD
Do you speak English?	Kan du tale engelsk?	kan doo TA-leh ENG-elsk
I don't understand.	Jeg forstår ilke.	yay foh-STOH IK-eh
Help!	hjelpe!	YELP-eh

ACCOMMODATIONS AND CAMPING When in Norway, camp. Norwegian law allows you to camp for free anywhere you want on public land for two nights, provided you keep 150m from all buildings and fences and leave no traces of your frolicking. **Den Norske Turistforening** (DNT, the Norwegian Mountain Touring Association; tel. 22 82 28 22; http://www.turistforeningen.no) sells excellent maps, offers guided hiking trips, and maintains more than 300 **mountain huts** (*hytter*) throughout the country. (75-145kr per night; nonmembers 80kr extra. Membership can be purchased at a DNT office, huts, or tourist offices for 325kr, under 25 160kr.) Staffed huts, open during Easter and from late June to early September, serve full meals and are akin to hostels, but have a more attractive ambience and more Norwegian guests. Unstaffed huts are open from late February until mid-October; get the entrance key (100kr deposit required) from a DNT or tourist office. The DNT offices in Oslo (see p. 659) and Bergen (see p. 669) are particularly helpful.

The useful *Vandrerhjem i Norge* brochure lists prices, phone numbers, and more for Norway's 98 **HI youth hostels** (*vandrerhjem*). Beds run 70-165kr; breakfasts (45-60kr) are included in the price if mandatory (often the case). Most charge 35-40kr for bedsheets on the first night. Usually only rural or smaller hostels have curfews. Only a few are open year-round. Most tourist offices in Norway can book you a room in a private home (singles roughly 190kr, doubles 330kr). Official **campgrounds** charge 90-120kr per tent. Many also have two- to four-person cabins (450-800kr). Hot showers almost always cost extra.

FOOD AND DRINK Eating in Norway can be hazardous to your wallet; markets and bakeries will be your best company. The nationwide discount **REMA 1000** supermarkets generally have the best prices (usually open M-F 9am-8pm, Sa 9am-6pm). Join Norwegians at outdoor markets for good buys on fresh seafood and fruit. Many restaurants have inexpensive *dagens ret* (dish of the day) specials (60-70kr for a full meal); otherwise you're doing well to escape for less than 100kr. **Tips** are included. All-you-can-eat restaurant buffets abound in major cities and towns (pizza 47-69kr). Self-service *kafeterias* are a less expensive option. **Fish** in Norway—cod, salmon, and herring—is fresh, good, and cheap. National specialties include cheese (*ost;* try *Jarlsberg* and the brown goat cheese *geitost*), pork and veal meatballs (*kjøtkaker*) with boiled potatoes, and (for lusty carnivores) reindeer and controversial whale meat (*kval*). In the countryside, pick berries of all colors, sizes, and flavors, or sample a vendor's offerings. Come winter, delight in dried fish (*lutefisk*). In most Norwegian restaurants, **alcohol** is served only after 3pm and never on Sundays, although this is beginning to change, especially in the cities. Beer is *very* expensive (45kr for 0.5L is average in a bar). Alcohol is cheapest in supermarkets, but few towns permit the sale of alcohol outside of government operated liquor stores.

■ Oslo

In verdant, vibrant Oslo, even the bums dress well. The summer's Midnight Sun and the extraordinary reflected blue light in winter belie the gloomy shadows of natives Edvard Munch and Henrik Ibsen; here, everything is spotless, runs on time, and costs you your immortal soul—or at least an arm and a leg. The central strip, Karl Johans gate, and its many offshoots, are typified by classy cafes, cool coffeeshops, and beautiful Norwegians in tight clothing, while the numerous forests, islands, rivers, and lakes within the city limits hint at the splendor to be found farther west.

NORWAY

NORWAY

Oslo

ACCOMMODATIONS

D Albertine Hostel
A Coch's Pensjonant
B Ellingsens Pensjonant
F Haraldsheim Hostel
C KFUM (YMCA)
E Oslo Vineyard Hostel

Frederik Stangs gate
Gabels gate
Niels Juels gate

TO VIGELAND PARK
(TRAM 12, 15)

Molen Thorvns gate
Briskeby
Frogner
Heyerdahl
Frognervveien
Briskeby Alle
Hauxhausens gate

Framnesvn
Munkedamsveien
Drammensveien
Skovveien
Frognerveien
Oscars gate
Colbjørnsens gate
Riddervolds gate

Observatorie
Obstervatorgata
Cort Adelers gate
Huitfeldts gate
Ruseløkkveien
Inkognitogata
Parkveien
Løkkeveien
Nobel Institute

Munkedamsveien

Harbor of
Aker Brygge

Pipervika

Dokkveien

RADHUSPLASSEN

Dronning Mauds gate
Haakon VII's gate
Kronprinsens gate
Munkedamsveien

Royal
Palace

Akershusstranda

Akerhus Castle and Fortress

Radhuset
(City Hall)

R. Amundsens gate Frederiks
FRIDTJOF
NANSENS
PLASS
Stortingsgata
Universitetsgata
Tordenskiolds gate
Rosenkrantz'

Oslo
University
National
Gallery

TO A
St. Olavs gate

TO B
(TRAM 11, 13)

Christian Augusts gate

Pilestredet

Keysers gate

Munchs gate
Ullevalsveien

Akersgata
Nedre Vollgate
Akersgata
Karl Johans gate
PROFESSOR
ASCHEHOUGS
PLASS

Kongens gate
Radhusgata
Øvre Slottsgate
Nedre Slottsgata

Øvre Slottsgate

Revierkaia

Kongens gate
Glacisgata
Myntgata
Kongens gate
Tollbugata
Prinsens
Kirkegata
Sandidsmuseet

STORTORVET
Møllergata
Torggata

Grubbegata
YOUNGSTORGET
USE IT
Office

Dronningens gate
Skippergata
Fred. Olsens Gate
Strandgata

Oslo
Cathedral
Biskop Gunnerus' gate

Henrik Ibsens gate
Møllergata
Ber5t Ankers gate
Mariboes gate
Brugata

Bjørvika

Havnegata

Train
Station

Steners Gata
Storgata

Grønland
Breigata

Østerhaus gate
Hausmanns gate

TO E
(TRAM
15, 17)

TO F
(TRAM
10, 11)

TO C
(TRAM
10-12)

Nylandsveien
Schweigaards gate

ORIENTATION AND PRACTICAL INFORMATION

Running from *Sentralstasjon* (the central train station, also known as **Oslo S**) to the *Slottet* (Royal Palace), **Karl Johans gate** is Oslo's main boulevard. Virtually everything of interest to visitors clusters in the center of the city, around the **National Theater,** located at the end of the fountained **Slottsparken** and midway between the station and the palace. Oslo is conveniently dense, but weary travelers will appreciate the excellent public transport system of subways, trams, buses, and ferries. Don't be confused by the ubiquitous word "gate," which simply means "street" in Norwegian.

Flights: White SAS buses run every 15min. between **Fornebu Airport** and the city (20min., 40kr), with pickup/dropoff points at the bus station (track 9), the train station, Parliament, and the National Theater. Oslo to Fornebu M-F and Su 5:40am-9:40pm, Sa 6am-9:40pm. Fornebu to Oslo daily 7:30am-11:30pm. The slower bus 31 also runs to Fornebu (18kr).

Trains: Oslo Sentralstasjon (Central Station; tel. 81 50 08 88), known as the Oslo S. Book at least 1 day in advance and get a reduced fares (*minipriser*) any day but F or Su (to major cities only). Several trains run daily to Bergen (7-8hr., 530kr, *minipris* 390kr), Bodø (change at Trondheim; 17hr., 950kr, *minipris* 530kr), Lillehammer (2hr., 225kr), Stockholm (7hr., 584kr), and Trondheim (7-8hr., 610kr, *minipris* 390kr). A **customer card** (380kr, valid for 1yr.) entitles the holder to 50% discounts in the off season and 20% discounts in the high season. Ticket office open daily 6am-11pm; terminal open daily 4:30am-1:15am.

Buses: Norway Bussekspress, Schweigårdsgate 8 (tel. 23 00 24 40), in the Oslo Galleri Mall, behind and to the right as you exit the train station, sends buses scurrying throughout Norway (Bergen 580kr) and across Europe.

Ferries: Passenger ferries arrive at 2 different ports, one (Color Line) is a 20min. walk west of the train station, the other (Stena and DFDS) a 10min. walk due south from the station. Fares vary greatly with time, season, age, and cabin. **Color Line** (bookings tel. 22 94 44 44; fax 22 83 20 96) has daily ferries year-round to Kiel, Germany (20hr., 560-710kr) and Hirtshals, Denmark (12½hr., 450-580kr). Eurail, InterRail, and Scanrail passes generally offer 50% off. **DFDS Scandinavian Seaways** (tel. 22 41 90 90; fax 22 41 38 38) sails to Helsingborg, Sweden, and Copenhagen daily at 5pm (16hr. to Helsingborg, 17hr. to Copenhagen; 380-940kr in summer, higher Th-Sa). **Stena Lines** (tel. 22 33 50 00) has 1 daily run to Frederikshavn, Denmark (high season 390-450kr; 50% off with Eurail, InterRail, or Scanrail).

Public Transportation: Info at **Trafikanten** (tel. in Oslo 177), in front of the station. All forms (bus, tram, subway, and ferry) 18kr per trip; fines over 300kr for traveling without a valid ticket. A 24hr. **Dagskort** (day pass) costs 40kr; a **7-day card** costs 120kr; a **flexicard** allows 8 separate trips (105kr), and the Oslo Card (see below) grants unlimited travel on public transportation. Many buses, trams, and subways have late night schedules midnight to 5am. Ferries tend to stop service around 7-8pm.

Bike Rental: For more information on cycling in Norway contact the **Syklistenes Landsforening** (tel. 22 41 50 80).

Hitchhiking: Oslo is not a hitchhiker's paradise; the diligent reportedly go to gas stations and ask everyone stopping. Those heading southwest (E-18 to Kristiansand and Stavanger) take bus 31 or 32 to "Maritime." Hitchers to Bergen ride bus 161 "Skui" to the last stop. Hitchers heading for Trondheim hop on bus 32, 321, or Metro 5 to "Grorudkrysset" or bus 31 or 32 to "Aker Sykehus." Those going to Sweden take bus 81, 83, 85 to "Bekkeleget" or a local train "Ski" to "Nordstrand."

Tourist Offices: The **Main Tourist Office,** Vestbaneplassen 1 (tel. 82 06 01 00, outside Norway 22 83 00 50; fax 22 83 81 50; http://www.oslopro.no), in a yellow building behind the Rådhus. Free maps and guides. Sells the **Oslo Card,** which covers public transit and admission to nearly all sights for 1 day (150kr), 2 days (220kr), or 3 days (250kr). Open June-Aug. daily 9am-8pm; Sept.-May M-F 9am-4pm. The Oslo-only info center at **Oslo S** (central station) books rooms (open daily 8am-11pm). **Den Norske Turistforening,** Storgata 3 (tel. 22 82 28 22; fax 22 82 28 23), with an entrance around the corner on Olav V gate, rents mountain huts, sells trail maps, and has Norway-wide hiking info. Open M, W, and F 10am-4pm, Th 10am-6pm, Sa 10am-2pm. Youth-oriented **USE IT,** Møllergata 3 (tel. 22 41 51 32;

fax 22 42 63 71; http://www.unginfo.oslo.no), 4 blocks up Karl Johans gate from the station and then right, offers listings of cheap lodgings and restaurants, travel tips, and the invaluable *Streetwise* guide. Books rooms. Offers **Internet access.** Open July-Aug. M-F 7:30am-6pm, Sa 9am-2pm; Sept.-June M-F 11am-5pm.

Budget Travel: Kilroy Travels, Nedre Slottsgt. 23 (tel. 23 10 23 10; fax 22 11 13 48), and also at Universitetssenteret (tel. 22 85 32 40; fax 22 85 32 39; http://www.kilroytravels.com), has student and youth airline bargains. Open M-F 10am-6pm, Sa 10am-3pm. **Khan Travels Ltd.,** Brugate 3C (tel. 22 17 14 91; fax 22 17 12 48), offers competitive rates, especially on international flights.

Embassies/Consulates: Australian citizens should contact the **Australian consulate** (tel. 22 41 44 33 or 22 41 49 31; fax 22 42 26 83), or the Canadian embassy. **Canada,** Wergelandsveien 7, (tel. 22 46 69 55; fax 22 99 53 01). **Ireland,** Drammensveien 126A (tel. 22 56 33 10; fax 22 12 20 71). **New Zealand** (General Consul), Billengstadsletta 19B (tel. 22 13 20 00; fax 66 77 53 31). **South African consulate,** Drammensveien 88c (tel. 22 44 79 10; fax 22 44 39 75); consular service open M-F 9am-noon. **U.K.,** Thomas Heftyesgate 8 (tel. 23 13 27 00; fax 23 13 27 41). Open M-F 9am-4pm. **U.S.,** Drammensveien 18 (tel. 22 44 85 50; fax 22 56 27 51). Open M-F 9am-3pm; consular services 9am-noon.

Currency Exchange: Banks charge fees per check exchanged, so bring checks in large denominations. For changing small amounts (up to US$100), the best deal is at the AmEx offices (see below). Larger exchanges are best accomplished at the post offices (20kr charge for cash, 10kr per check; 20kr minimum). Rates outside the rail station are better than the rates inside the station. Open M-F 7am-6pm, Sa 9am-2pm. After-hours exchange at the central post office, the tourist and AmEx offices, in **Bankveksling,** in front of the train station (20kr per traveler's check). Open M-Sa 7am-9pm, Su 10am-5pm. Also at **Fornebu Airport,** International Arrivals Hall. Open M-Sa 6:30am-8pm, Su 7am-8pm.

American Express: Karl Johans gt. 33, N-0121 Oslo (tel. 22 98 37 20, emergencies 80 03 32 44). Open M-F 9am-5pm, Sa 10am-3pm; currency exchange open M-F 9am-9pm, Sa 9am-7pm, Su 2-7pm.

Luggage Storage: Train station lockers are 25kr for 24hr.

Bookstore: Tanum Libris, Karl Johans gt. 37-41 (tel. 22 41 11 00), in the Paléet. Good selection of English paperbacks. Open M-F 10am-8pm, Sa 10am-4pm. **Juul Møller Bøker,** 11 Nedre Slottsgate, is a smaller bookstore. Open M 10am-5pm, Tu-W and F 9am-5pm, Th 9am-6pm, Sa 10am-4pm.

Laundromat: Look for the word *Myntvaskeri.* **Selvbetjent Vask,** Ullevålsveien 15. Wash 30kr per 6kg, dry 20kr. Soap included. Open daily 8am-9pm.

Gay and Lesbian Services: The **Landsforeningen for Lesbiskog Homofil fri gjøring (LLH),** 2 St. Olavs plass (tel. 22 11 05 09; fax 22 20 24 05), provides an array of essential services and copies of *Blick* (30kr), a monthly gay and lesbian newspaper with daytime and nightlife listings. Open M-F 9am-4pm.

Travelers with Disabilities: The **Norwegian Association of the Disabled,** P.O. Box 9712 Grønland, 0134 Oslo (tel. 22 17 02 55; fax 22 17 61 77; email nhf@nhf.no), has general info. Most museums are wheelchair accessible and buses and trams can be used with a little help. From the tourist office get the essential *"Welcome to Oslo,"* a free, comprehensive guide for disabled visitors.

Emergencies: Ambulance, tel. 113. **Fire** and **Accidents,** tel. 110.

Police: tel. 112.

Crisis Lines: Rape Crisis Line, tel. 22 11 70 90. **AIDS info,** tel. 80 03 40 00. **Emotional Crisis Line,** tel. 22 11 70 80. **AA,** tel. 22 11 72 00.

24hr. Pharmacy: Jernbanetorvets Apotek (tel. 22 41 24 82), near the station.

Medical Assistance: Oslo Kommunale Legevakt, Storgata 40 (tel. 22 11 70 70). 24hr. emergency care.

Post Office: Dronningens gt. 15 (tel. 22 40 78 10); enter at Prinsens gt. *Poste Restante.* Open M-F 8am-6pm, Sa 10am-3pm. **Postal Code,** 0101 Oslo 1.

Internet Access: Use It office, Møllergata 3. Free (see **Tourist Offices,** p. 659). **Rådhuset** (town hall). Free; enter the building on the harborside entrance. **Velvet,** Nedre Slottsgate 2. 10kr per 30min. Open M-F 10am-6pm, Sa 10am-3pm.

Telephones and Faxes: Kongens gt. 21; enter at Prinsens gate. Fax service to North America or Europe 10kr plus 10kr per page. Open M-F 8:30am-8pm, Sa-Su 10am-5pm. Phone cards sold at kiosks and post offices.

ACCOMMODATIONS AND CAMPING

Hostels in Oslo fill up quickly in the summer—make reservations. **Use It** (see above) offers one of the best deals in town—private rooms, accessible by public transportation, though the later in the day you appear, the farther the trek from downtown (125kr, with sleeping bag 100kr). If you plan on a stay of a week or more, you may be able to sublet a university student dorm room (around 360kr per week plus deposit). For more info call **SiO** (tel. 22 85 33 76) or **OAS** (tel. 22 46 39 90). *Pensjonater* (pensions) are usually less expensive versions of hotels; call for reservations. Some hotels offer cheaper "last minute" prices on vacant rooms through the tourist office. In principle the Norwegian *allmansrett* gives you the right to camp anywhere, but effectively no one really camps on private lawns. You can camp in Oslo's forests for free.

Albertine Hostel, Storgata 55 (tel. 22 99 72 00; fax 22 99 72 20). 15min. north of the train station. Take tram 10, 11, 12, 15, or 17 to "Hausmanns gate" and the hostel will be 100m up Storgata on the left. New and beautifully furnished. Dorms 110kr; singles 240kr; doubles 330kr; quads 540kr. Open June 7-Aug.23. Sheets 35kr. Buffet breakfast 50kr. Kitchen. 24hr. reception.

Oslo Vandrerhjem Haraldsheim (HI), Haraldsheimveien 4 (tel. 22 15 50 43 or 22 22 29 65; fax 22 22 10 25). Take tram 10 or 11, or bus 31 or 32 to "Sinsenkrysset," and follow the signs across the field and up the hill. Pristine lounges with cable TV. No sleeping bags. Dorms 155kr, nonmembers 180kr; singles 260kr; doubles 370kr. Buffet breakfast included; lunch 70kr; dinner 90kr. Sheets 40kr. Kitchen. Laundry 40kr (soap included). 24hr. reception. Lockout 10am-3pm.

Ellingsens Pensjonat, Holtegata 25 (tel. 22 60 03 59; fax 22 60 99 21). Take tram 11, 13, or 19 to "Brisky," or walk 3km from the city center. Sign-less gray building is hard to spot but popular with backpackers. Singles 250kr; doubles 390kr; extra bed 100kr. Reception open M-F 7:30am-10:30pm, Sa-Su 8am-10:30pm. Cash only.

Oslo Vandrerhjem Holtekilen (HI), Michelets vei 55 (tel. 67 51 80 40; fax 67 59 12 30). Take bus 151/161, 251/252, or 261 to "Kveldsroveien" or the subway to "Stabekk." Popular, if somewhat far from the city center. Dorms 145kr; bed in a quad 155kr; singles 250kr; doubles 410kr; nonmembers 25kr extra. Breakfast included. Open early May to Aug. 24. Reserve ahead.

Cochs Pensjonat, Parkveien 25 (tel. 22 60 48 36; fax 22 46 54 02), at Hegdehaugsveien by the royal park. A 15min. walk from train station. Singles 310kr, with bath and kitchenette 390kr; doubles 420-580kr; quads 600-720kr.

Oslo Vineyard, Lillogata 5 (tel. 22 15 20 99). Take tram 12, 17 or bus 30 to "Grefsenveien," then turn left at the grocery store, cross Sandakerveiew, and follow the signs to the hostel. Bare bones, dare we say "monastic," church hostel. Kitchen. Dorms 105kr. No sleeping bags. 24hr. reception. Open July 7-Aug. 17.

OSI-Chalet (tel. 22 49 90 36), in the Nordmarka forest. Bus 41: "Sørhedalen School" (40min.), and then walk 1hr. Students in sleeping bags snooze in forest cottages. Call for directions, or get a map from Use It (see p. 659); pack some food. 125kr.

Camping: Ekeberg Camping, Ekebergveien 65 (tel. 22 19 85 68), about 3km from town. Take tram 18 or 19, or bus 34A from the train station. Marvelous view. Cooking facilities, grocery store. Tent and 2 people 115kr, showers included; tent and 4 people 160kr. Open May 25-Aug. Camping on the beach of Langøyene island (take boat 94), at **Langøyene Camping** (tel. 22 36 37 98), is cheaper. Tent and 2 people 60kr, extra person 30kr. Open June-Aug. **Bogstad Camping,** Ankerveien 117 (tel. 22 50 76 80), on Bogstand Lake is beautiful, if a bit far. Take bus 32 from the station (30min.) Tent and 2 people 115kr; tent and 4 people 170kr; extra person 30kr. 24hr. reception. **Free camping** in the forest north of town as long as you avoid public areas. Try the woods and lake at the end of the Sognsvann line (yes, those are naked Norwegians). Fires are not allowed. As always, exercise caution.

FOOD

For many, filling one's belly in Oslo consists of forming a cosmic union with grocery stores. Some of the most central are the **Rema 1000** at Torggata 2-G (open M-F 9am-7pm, Sa 9am-6pm) and the **Kiwi Supermarket** on Storgata (open M-Sa 8am-11pm). One must be a culinary strategist in Norway: take full advantage of your hostel's breakfast buffet. Vietnamese and Pakistani influences have multiplied veggie options in Oslo. **Seafood** offerings include freshly caught and boiled shrimp (0.5kg 25kr) from the fishing boats docked in the harbor behind the Rådhus.

Cafe Sult, Thorvald Meyersgt. 26, in the trendy 'hood of **Løka** north of the station. Norwegian salmon with feta salads 46-72kr; lunch 46-72kr; dinner 118-140kr. Open Tu-F 4pm-1am; Sa 11:30am-1am, Su 1pm-midnight.

Coco Chalet, Øvre Slottsgade 8. Hyggelig (cozy) and very popular, if somewhat pricey. Lunch 40-90kr. Salads 40-50kr. Dinner 79-149kr. Open M-Sa 11am-11pm.

Stortorvets Gjæstgiveru, Grensen 1. Traditional Norwegian cuisine in one of Oslo's oldest restaurant-pubs. Live jazz F and Sa. Lunch specials featuring salmon, herring, and mackerel 52-120kr. Open M-Th 10am-11pm, F-Sa 10am-1am.

Vegeta Vertshus, Munkedamsveien 3b, off Stortings gt. A vegetarian feast. All-you-can-strategically-engineer-onto-a-plate 79-114kr. 10% student discount. Buffet available daily 11am-11pm (50kr for students Tu-F 3-8pm).

Pasta Factory, Kristian IV gate 9. Filling pasta dishes with a fishy flair (85-119kr). Open daily 3-11pm. Bar open M-Th until midnight, F-Sa until 2am.

Børsen Café Stock Exchange, Nedre Vollgate 19. Drink prices change according to supply and demand. Watch for the rush when the "stock exchange" crashes. **Internet access** 20kr. Open W-Th 8pm-3:30am, F-Sa 8pm-5am.

Ett Glass, Rosenkrantz 11. The latest in chic. To keep your cool as well as your budget don't try for more than coffee (18kr) or a beer (40kr). Open Su-Tu noon-1:30am, W-Sa noon-2:30am. Also check out the ultra-trendy bar **XO** next door.

SIGHTS

To navigate Oslo's impressive array of sights, pick up the free *Oslo Official Guide,* which offers the most current information. Gustav Vigeland's powerful, masculine sculptures at **Frognerparken,** one of Norway's most visited attractions, depict each stage of the human life cycle; the park is a playground of grassy knolls, duck ponds, and tennis courts. *(Open 24hr. Free.)* To reach the park, take tram 12 or 15 to "Vigelandsparken." The **Munch Museum,** Tøyengata 53, has an outstanding collection of Edvard Munch's unsettling paintings, lithographs, and photographs. Take bus 20 or the subway to "Tøyen," or walk east from the train station for ten minutes. *(Open June 1-Sept. 15 daily 10am-6pm; Sept. 16-May 31 Tu-W and F-Sa 10am-4pm, Th and Su 10am-6pm. 50kr, students 20kr.)* Another of Munch's copies of "The Scream" is at the **Nasjonal Galleriet,** Universitetsgaten 13. *(Open M, W, and F 10am-4pm, Th 10am-8pm, Sa 10am-4pm, Su 11am-4pm. Free.)* Next door at the **University** you can see Munch's massive mural "Sun" paintings. *(Open M-F 9am-4pm. Free.)* The **Samtidsmuseet** (Museum of Contemporary Art), is at Bankplassen 4 *(Open Tu, W, and F 10am-5pm, Th 10am-8pm, Sa 11am-4pm, Su 11am-5pm. Free. Guided tours Tu-F noon, Sa-Su 2pm.)*

South of the **Nationaltheatret** on Fridtjof Nansens plass stands the towering **Rådhus.** The artists who painted the interior earned the pride of their compatriots by defying the Nazi occupiers; they were punished by deportation to prison camps. The Nobel Peace Prize ceremony takes place here each December 10. *(Open May-Aug. M-Sa 9am-5pm, Su noon-5pm.; Sept.-Apr. M-Sa 9am-4pm, Su noon-4pm. Admission 25kr. Free tours M-F at 10am, noon, and 2pm.)* See the changing of the guard (daily at 1:30pm) at the beautiful **Slottsparken,** the royal garden. The 17th-century **Oslo Damkirke** (cathedral) has stained glass windows designed by Emmanuel Vigeland. *(Open daily 10am-4pm. Free.)* **Akershus Castle and Fortress** was built in 1299 and transformed into a Renaissance palace by Christian IV. Explore the castle's underground passages, banquet halls, and dungeons and enjoy concerts on summer Sundays in the church at 2pm. *(Open Oct.-Apr. Su 12:30-4pm; May to mid-Sept. also M-Sa 10am-4pm. 20kr, students 10kr. English tours in summer at 11am, 1, and 3pm; spring and fall at 1 and 3pm.)* The poignant **Hjemmefrontmuseet** (Resistance Museum) in the fortress documents Norway's efforts to subvert Nazi occupation. *(Open June 15-Aug. M-Sa 10am-5pm, Su 11am-5pm; Sept.-June closes 1-2hr. earlier. 20kr.)*

The peninsula of **Bygdøy** is reached by the commuter ferry Bygdøyfergene (tel. 22 20 07 15) from pier 3 (every 40min., 18kr) or bus 30 from Nationaltheatret, and it houses five museums. The three vessels of the **Viking Ship Museum** include the 9th-century ring-prowed, dragon-keeled *Oseberg* burial barge. *(Open May-Aug. daily 9am-6pm; Sept. 11am-5pm; Apr. and Oct. 11am-4pm; Nov.-Mar. 11am-3pm. 30kr.)* At the ferry's second stop, Bygdøynes, the **Polar Ship "Fram"** chronicles the Arctic and Antarctic explorations of two of Norway's most famous, Fridtjof Nansen and Roald Amundsen. *(Open in summer daily 9am-5:45pm; off-season reduced hours. 25kr.)* The ethnologist Thor Heyerdahl's crafts **Kon-Tiki**, *Ra I*, and *Ra II* have their own museum, featuring the original *Kon-Tiki*, which set out in 1947 to prove that the first Polynesian settlers could have sailed from pre-Inca Peru. *(Open daily June-Aug. 9:30am-5:45pm; Sept. 10:30am-5pm; Oct.-Mar. 10:30am-4pm; Apr.-May 10:30am-5pm. 30kr.)* The **Folkemuseum** is a massive outdoor museum with houses and other structures from various eras and parts of the country. *(Open mid-May to mid-June and early to mid-Sept. daily 10am-5pm; mid-June to Aug. 10am-6pm; Jan. to mid-May and mid-Sept. to Dec. M-Sa 11am-3pm, Su 11am-4pm. 50kr.)* Dive into bracing water off the popular **Huk Beach,** about 1km from the Viking Ship Museum. Or, weather permitting, go bare at nude **Paradisbukten,** across the inlet.

Other islands in the inner Oslofjord also offer delightful, inexpensive daytrips. In summer, you can visit the ruins of a monastery on **Hovedøya; Langøyene** has Oslo's best beach. Boats leave from **Vippetangen,** reached by bus 29 (round-trip 36kr). Kayaks and canoes can be rented on the Akerselva river; ask at the tourist office.

For a great panorama of **Oslofjord** and the city, take subway 15 to the last stop on the Frognerseteren line, and walk to the ski jump **Holmenkollen** at the **Ski Museum,** which chronicles the history of skiing. *(Open July-Aug. daily 9am-10pm; June 9am-8pm; Apr.-May and Sept. 10am-5pm; Oct. and Mar. 10am-4pm. 50kr, students 35kr.)* A **simulator** outside recreates the adrenaline rush of a four-minute, 130km-per-hour downhill ski run—hold on tight! *(Same hours as museum. Admission 35kr, with the Oslo card 25kr.)* To bask in Norway's natural grandeur, take the Sognsvann subway from Nationaltheatret to the end of the line. Use It provides free trail maps; in winter, ask the tourist office about cross-country ski rental.

ENTERTAINMENT

What's on in Oslo, free at the tourist offices, details Oslo's "high culture," including the opera, Philharmonic, and theater. The hipper culture rag, *Natt og Dag,* free at USE IT and cafes, lists concerts and events. From late June to early September the **Norwegian Folklore Show** features all things folksy (tel. 22 83 45 10; 100kr). **Filmenshus,** Dronningsgate 16, is the center of Oslo's art film scene while more Hollywood type flicks are screened at **Saga Cinema,** Stortingsgata 28. Immigrant and minority Norwegians at **Nordic Black Theater,** Olaf Ryes plass 11 (tel. 22 38 12 62), stage socially critical productions in English. Big-name rock concerts take place at the **Rockefeller Music Hall,** Torggata (tel. 22 20 32 32; tickets 50-350kr).

In addition to the countless bars along **Karl Johans gate** and the **Aker Brygge** harbor complex, Oslo boasts a number of nightclubs with busy DJs and live music. Dance to the house, rock, and funk of **Barock,** Univeritetsgt. 26 (50kr weekend cover; open W-Su 9pm-3:30am) or the disco and lounge favorites of **Broadway,** Karl Johans gate 17 (weekend cover 50kr; open daily 9pm-3:30am). **So What!,** Grensen 9, is popular with a young, indie and beer-loving crowd (50kr concert cover, 2-3 times per week; open M-Th 2pm-2am, F-Sa 11pm-3:30am, Su 4pm-1am). **Sikamikanico,** 2 Møllergata, is *the* hip coffee bar in Oslo (DJs W-Sa and occasional live music; open daily 5pm-3:30am, Sept.-Apr. 11am-3:30am). Oslo's gay and lesbian crowd paints the town red at **Castro,** Kristian IV gate 7, a two-story dance club, and arguably the coolest bar, gay or straight, in Oslo (50kr weekend cover; open daily 9pm-3am; generally gay on weekdays, mixed crowd on weekends).

SOUTHERN NORWAY

Norway's southern coast substitutes serenity for drama. *Skjærgård,* archipelagos of water-worn rock hugging the shore, stretch from Oslo south and smooth to endless white beaches past Kristiansand. This coast is the country's premier summer holiday resort for Norwegians. Inland, green woods cover the high cliffs: fishing, hiking, rafting, and canoeing are popular summer options, and cross-country skiing reigns in winter. Two inland **train** lines with beautiful views run south from Oslo. The main branch extends through Kristiansand around to Stavanger; the other loops through Tønsberg to Skien before reconnecting with the main line at Nordagutu.

■ Kristiansand

Kristiansand, the town in Norway closest to the equator, attracts many glacier- and winter-weary Norwegian tourists to its beaches. The open-air **Vest-Agder Fylkesmuseum,** Vigeveien 23b, showcases 17th-century southern Norwegian farmhouses and traditional folk dancing. (Open M-Sa 10am-6pm; May 19-Sept. 14 also Su noon-6pm; Sept. 21-May 18 also Su noon-5pm. 20kr.) The remains of a Nazi bunker can be seen at the **Kristiansand Kanonenmuseum** (open June 11-Aug. daily 11am-6pm, May 1-June 10 and Sept. Th-Su 11am-6pm; 40kr).

Ferries run regularly from Kristiansand to the scenic Skerries (tiny islands and fjords) for 150kr; the tourist office has info. During the first weekend in July, Kristiansand hosts the **Quart Festival,** with hip-hop, rock, and pop acts like Björk and the Beastie Boys. The festival website (http://www.dagbladet.no/quart) has more info; you can also ask at the **tourist office** on Dronningensgt. 2 (tel. 38 12 13 14; http://www.sol.no/destinasjon-soerlandet), a five-block walk from the train station along Vestre Strandgt.; turn right as you leave the station and make a left on Dronningensgt. (Open June 2-Aug. 21 M-F 8am-7:30pm; June 27-Aug. 15 also Sa 8am-7:30pm; June 6-20 also Sa 8am-3pm and Su noon-7:3-pm. Rents **bikes.**) **Color Line ferries** (bookings tel. 38 07 88 88 or 81 00 08 11) float to Hirsthals, Denmark (2½-6hr., 3-4 per day, 200-370kr). Daily **trains** chug to Oslo (4½-5½hr., 400kr).

The **Kristiansand Youth Hostel (HI),** Skansen 8 (tel. 38 02 83 10; fax 38 02 75 05), is a 15-minute walk from the station (150kr, nonmembers 175kr; singles 310kr; breakfast included; reception open June 12-Aug. 15 24hrs.; Aug. 16-June 11 7-11am and 5-11pm). The **campground** (tel. 38 08 50 90), a 45-minute walk from town, calls itself *Roligheden* (Quiet Place), but this misnomer predated the motor homes and trailers (20kr per person, 100kr per tent; showers 5kr per 3min.; open June-Sept.15). The area around **Markensgata** is full of affordable bars, cafes, and restaurants. **Husholdnings,** on Gyldenløves gate in the old town, serves up authentic Norwegian cuisine. **Munch,** Kristian IV gate 1, is a lively pub.

■ Stavanger

Stavanger is a delightful port town with colorful Bergen-esque wooden fishing houses lining a busy pier and daily fish market. On the other side of the picture-perfect harbor is **Gamle Stavanger,** a restored neighborhood recalling 19th-century prosperity. The Gothic **Stavanger Domkirke** (cathedral) broods in medieval solemnity in Stavanger's modern center. (Open May 15-Sept. 15 M-Sa 10am-7pm, Su 1-6pm; late Sept. to early May M-F 10-11:45am and 12:15-2pm. Free.) The **Rogalund Kunstmuseum** (art museum) has a small but interesting collection (open Tu-F 10am-2pm, Sa 11am-2pm, Su 11am-5pm; 50kr, students 25kr). For the genealogical skinny on your Norwegian ancestors, check out the **Norwegian Emigration Centre,** Strandkaien 31, (tel. 51 55 88 60; open M-F 9am-3pm). Feel like a Norse god, command your sea-minions, and opiate the masses, but don't tumble over the edge of **Preikestolen** (Pulpit Rock) in nearby **Lysefjord,** one of Norway's postcard sweethearts. Take the 8:20 or

9:15am ferry to Tau (June 21-Sept. 7, 40min., 25kr), catch the waiting bus (40kr), and get ready for a serious two-hour hike on the marked paths (return bus 4:15pm).

The main **tourist office,** Roskildetorget 1 (tel. 51 85 92 00; fax 51 85 92 02), on the harbor next to the fish market, offers free maps, a town guide, and **currency exchange** (open June-Aug. daily 9am-8pm; Sept.-May M-F 9am-4pm, Sa 9am-2pm). **Flaggruten Catamarans** (tel. 51 86 87 80) run to **Bergen** (4hr., 2-4 per day, 480kr, students 240kr, 50% off with Scanrail). **Color Line** (tel. 51 52 45 45) runs ships three times weekly to **Newcastle,** England (18hr., July-Aug. 910kr and up; Sept.-June 295-460kr). **Trains** pull out of the station four times a day for Oslo (8hr., 650kr). The **Mosvangen Vandrerhjem (HI),** Ibsensgt. 21 (tel. 51 87 29 00; fax 51 87 06 30), has doubles, a kitchen, and free laundry (135kr, nonmembers 150kr). Next door sprawls **Mosvangen camping** (tel. 51 53 29 71; 60kr per tent, 10kr per person; open late May to early Sept.). Take bus 130, 78, or 97 (17kr) and ask to be dropped at the hostel or campground. The retro-hip **Cafe M,** Øvre Holegate 20, serves coffee (16kr) and affordable dishes (59kr) while **Armadillo,** across the street, has great music and a cigar bar (open M-Sa 8pm-1am). **Dickens Pub,** Skagenkaien 6, serves all-you-can-eat crab for around 80kr (open daily 11am-1:30am; live blues band Su nights). The daily **fish and fruit market** opposite the cathedral may also satisfy your seafood fantasies.

EASTERN NORWAY

■ Gudbrandsdalen, Rondane, and Dovrefjell

Two train lines shoot north from Oslo to Trondheim: the slower goes east through the Østerdalen valley and the town of Røros, the faster one through the **Gudbrandsdalen** valley, Lillehammer, Otta, and Dombås. Gudbrandsdalen is famous for its skiing, hiking, and canoeing, for its old churches and wooden houses, and for being the birthplace of brown *Gudbrandsdalsost* (a type of cheese). Lillehammer is the largest town and marks the southern edge of the region. Farther up the valley, the old, soft slopes of the mountain ranges of **Rondane** and **Dovrefjell** provide easy access to hiking and the more dramatic ranges farther west. Both regions have national parks.

Lillehammer In February 1994, the world learned that reindeer really do exist when Norway's second winter Olympic Games were hosted in Lillehammer and its neighboring towns. Despite the construction of several billion kroner (several hundred million dollars) worth of infrastructure, Lillehammer maintains a natural atmosphere; all the sports facilities were designed to be environmentally friendly, and the Olympic housing has been recycled for use by the army. Håkons Hall at the **Olympic Park** houses the **Norwegian Olympic Museum,** where you can relive Norway's athletic past (50kr; hall open M-F 8am-10pm, Sa 9am-6pm, Su 11am-10pm). In the square outside the hall, a **bobsled simulator** (35kr) gives your spinal cord a jolt. On the course itself, 15km north at Hunderfossen (tel. 61 27 75 50), you can reach speeds of up to 65mph in a wheeled bobsled (125kr). **Maihaugen** is an impressive, outdoor re-creation of 19th-century village life (70kr; 100kr for village and Olympic Park).

Daily **trains** run to Oslo (2½hr., 230kr), Åndalsnes (4hr., 330kr), and Trondheim (4½hr., 420kr). Most of Lillehammer's shops and restaurants are located on **Storgata,** which runs parallel to the hillside, two blocks uphill from the bus and train stations. The main **tourist office,** Elvegata 19 (tel. 61 25 92 99), at the end of a side street projecting off Storgata, stocks the *Lillehammer Accommodations* guide, which offers good info on hiking and *hytter* (cabins) in the popular **Sjusjøen** and **Nordseter** regions. (Office open mid-June to mid-Aug. M-Sa 9am-7pm, Su 11am-6pm; mid-Aug. to mid-June M-F 9am-4pm, Sa 10am-2pm.) The **Lillehammer Youth Hostel (HI)** (tel. 61 26 25 66), one of Norway's nicest hostels, is on the top floor of the train station, giving guests an 8am wake-up call when the station starts announcing departures. Each modern, clean room has its own bathroom (165kr, 140kr with Scanrail; breakfast included). **Gjeste Bu,** Gamleveien 110 (tel. 61 25 43 21; fax 61 25 43 21), one block north of Storgata, has three kitchens, free tea and coffee, and a non-smoking floor. (Sleeping bag accommodations 80kr; singles 175kr; doubles 250kr; triples 375kr. Sheets 40kr. Reception M-Sa 9am-11pm, Su and holidays 11am-11pm.) Try the popular lunch (49kr; 11am-3pm) or dinner (79kr; 3pm-10pm) special at **Nikkers** cafe/pub, just before the tourist office on Elvegata.

Otta and Dombås

The mountains of Rondane are quite accessible from **Otta** (1½hr. north of Lillehammer), which is also a springboard for the train-deficient fjord country. Spectacular **bus** routes snake from Otta across the Jotunheimen mountains to **Sogndal** on Sognefjord (5hr., 2 per day, 220kr) via **Lom** (7 per day, 59kr) and to **Stryn** on Nordfjord (3½hr., 4 per day, 205kr). Three or four buses leave weekdays from Otta to **Sjoa** (33kr). The **tourist office** (tel. 61 23 02 44), in the station, has info on the white water rafting on the Sjoa River and the Rondane hiking trails at nearby **Mysuseter** and **Høvringen.** (Open late June to early Aug. M-F 8:30am-7:30pm, Sa-Su 10am-6pm; mid-Aug. to mid-June M-F 8:30am-4pm.) Otta's **Guesthouse Sagatun,** Ottekra 1 (tel. 61 23 08 14), offers singles (160kr), doubles (250kr), and triples (375kr). The nearest **youth hostel** (tel. 61 23 62 00; fax 61 23 60 14) is in Sjoa, 11km south on the rail line (80kr, nonmembers 105kr; breakfast 50kr; reception 7am-11pm; open May-Sept.). The hostel houses a rafting company (day trip 690kr).

The slightly more challenging **Dovrefjell** range is best reached from **Dombås.** The train station perches on a hill above town. From there, go with gravity, and then cross the highway to enter the **tourist office** (tel. 61 24 14 44; fax 61 24 11 90; open daily June-Aug. 17 9am-8pm; Aug. 18-May 21 9am-4pm). The **Dombås Youth Hostel (HI)** (tel. 61 24 10 45) lies up the road from town, behind the massive parking lot. (15min. from train station. 105kr, nonmembers 130kr. Reception 8-10am and 4-10pm. Lockout 10am-4pm. Reserve ahead. Open mid-June to mid-Aug.) **Dombås Gård Hyltetun og Caravancamp** (tel. 61 24 10 26), 200m behind the tourist office, has four-person cabins (from 280kr) and tent sites (70kr; open May-Sept.).

■ Valdres and Jotunheimen

The **Valdres** valley ends in the highest mountain range in Europe north of the Alps, the jagged, reindeer-inhabited **Jotunheimen** massif. Even though only two of the several hundred peaks require technical gear to climb, the weather can be harsh and it snows at higher altitudes even in July. The DNT offices in Bergen and Oslo and tourist offices in the region overflow with maps and tips on trails and huts. **Gjendesheim,** an hour north of Fagernes by bus, is an excellent hiking base for the Jotunheimen. The DNT **hut** here provides a sleeping bag and lodging. From Gjendesheim, you can hike across the **Besseggen,** a spectacular ridge with an emerald green lake at 984m and a deep blue one at 1200m.

Fagernes

Though not particularly memorable, Fagernes holds an ideal central location for hiking, rafting or visiting medieval wooden stave-churches in the Valdres. Reach the town by **bus** from Gol on the Oslo-Bergen rail line (70min., 50kr, students 33% off), from Lillehammer (2hr., 95kr, students 33% off), or by *Valdresekspressen* bus from Oslo (3hr., 185kr). The **tourist office** (tel. 61 35 94 10), in the bus station, stocks the comprehensive *Valdres Summer Guide* or *Winter Guide.* (Open July to mid-Aug. M-F 8am-7pm, Sa 9am-6pm, Su 10am-6pm; late Aug. to June M-F 8am-4pm.) Ask at the tourist office about the **Folkemuseum** and the plethora of nearby **stave churches** (20-30kr each). The more rough 'n tumble should request a map and further info about the *Vardevandring* (watchtower hikes), which wind through most of the valley. The **Leira Youth Hostel (HI)** (tel. 61 36 20 25), Valdres Folkehøjskole, is 4km south of town (90kr, nonmembers 115kr; open May 25-Aug. 9). Ask the bus driver to drop you off at the hostel on your way into town.

Lom, Bøverdalen, Spiterstulen, and Turtagrø From Otta, the trip to **Lom** involves a breathtaking bus ride over the main massif of Jotunheimen (63kr). Lom's **tourist office** (tel. 61 21 29 90) is uphill and across the street from the bus stop. Pick up a copy of the brochure *Lom* and ask here about hiking in the nearby Jotunheimen Mountains. (Open June-July 9 daily 9am-6pm; July 10-Aug. 9 M-Sa 9am-9pm, Su 9am-7pm; Aug. 10-May M-F 9am-4pm.) While in Lom, visit the wonderful **wooden statue-church**, the oldest part of which dates from 1170. (Open daily May 20-June 15 and Aug. 15-Sept. 15 10am-4pm; June 16-Aug. 14 9am-9pm. 25kr.) Below the church churn the grey waters of glacier-fed **Bøvra River.** The two daily buses to Sogndal stop at **Bøverdalen,** 20km from Lom. There, stay at the **HI youth hostel.** (Tel. 61 21 20 64; fax 61 21 20 64. 75kr, nonmembers 100kr; breakfast 50kr. Reception 8am-10pm. Open May 25-Sept.) Both **Galdhøpiggen** (2469m) and **Glittertinden** (2464m), the highest points in Norway, can be reached without technical gear, but be prepared for snow. About 18km off Route 55, the **tourist chalet** (tel. 61 21 14 80) at **Spiterstulen** provides better access to Glittertinden (200kr, DNT members 150kr; camping 50kr). A **bus** runs daily (June 27-Aug. 16) from Lom at 8:35am and 4:25pm, returning from Spiterstulen at 10:30am and 5:25pm (round-trip 102kr). Southwest of Bøverdalen, the plateau between **Krossbu** and **Sognefjellhytta** is strewn with rock cairns tracing the way between snow-covered lakes; cross-country skiing is possible throughout the summer. Near **Turtagrø,** just above the tip of the Sognefjord system, is one of Norway's premier rock-climbing areas. From Sognefjellhytta, a steep five-hour path leads to **Fannaråkhytta** (2069m), the highest hut in the DNT system.

THE FJORDS AND WEST COUNTRY

Ten thousand years ago during the last Ice Age, glaciers scoured out huge, steep valleys at the edge of Norway, and when they melted, the sea rushed in, creating fjords. Buses and ferries wind through this scenic coastal region, which stretches from south of Bergen to Ålesund. Approaches to the fjords are infinite, and routes through them are plentiful; it is worthwhile to consult the tourist offices in Bergen or Oslo to plan your itinerary. Except for a small stretch on the Oslo-Bergen line, seeing the fjords from a train is impossible.

▓ Bergen

Vaunted as the "Gateway to the Fjords," Bergen is clean, compact, and stunningly beautiful. The city is surrounded by unblemished, forested mountains that rise steeply from the fjords. Yet the city was once Norway's capital and a center of trade in the Middle Ages, and still claims a prominent commercial and intellectual standing. A lively student population and a diversity of international influences make Bergen much more than just another scenic spot on the Norwegian coast.

ORIENTATION AND PRACTICAL INFORMATION

Bergen's train station lies several blocks above the gleaming harbor, at the top of the city center. Looking towards the water, **Bryggen** (the extension of Kong Oscars gate) and the town's most imposing mountain are to your right; most of the main buildings are to the left. The **Torget**—Bergen's famous outdoor market—is at the harbor's tip.

Trains: tel. 81 50 08 88 or 55 96 69 00. 3 trains head daily to Oslo (6½-7½hr., 500kr, 20kr seat reservations required) via Voss (1hr., 110kr) and Myrdal (1¾-2½hr., 165kr). Open daily 7am-11:50pm.

Buses: Bystasjonen, Strømgaten 8 (tel. 177). Service to neighboring areas, the Hardangerfjord district, Ålesund (470kr, students 25% off), and Oslo (575kr, students 25% off). Ticket office and information open M-F 7am-6pm, Sa 7am-2pm.

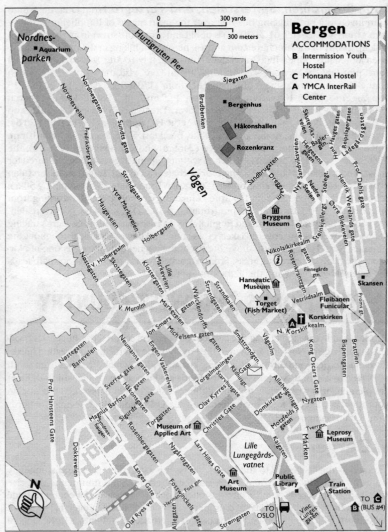

Bergen

ACCOMMODATIONS

B Intermission Youth Hostel
C Montana Hostel
A YMCA InterRail Center

Ferries: The **Hurtigruten,** which travels from Bergen to Kirkenes, leaves daily at 10:30pm from a separate harbor; inquire at the tourist office (full trip 3578kr; 50% student discount; cheaper Oct.-Apr.). International ships leave from Skoltegrunns-kaien, a 20min. walk past Bryggen along the right side of the harbor. **Fjord Line,** Rosenkrantz Gate 3 (tel. 55 54 88 00), runs ferries to Hanstholm, Denmark that depart M, W, and F at 4:30pm and arrive at 8am the next morning. (660-890kr; off-season 515kr; more expensive on F. Round-trip 10% discount; Aug.17-June 14 50% student discount.) **Smyril Line** (tel. 55 32 09 70; fax 55 96 02 72), with offices at Slottsgaten 1, departs June-Aug. Tu at 3pm for the Faroe Islands (24hr., 585-1800kr one-way), Iceland (40hr., 1283-3220kr one-way), and the Shetland Islands (11hr., 480-1430kr one-way). Student discount available. **Color Line** (tel. 81 00 08 11; fax 55 54 86 01), on Skoltegrunnskaien, sails to Newcastle via Stavanger and Hauge-sund (25hr.; Tu, W, and F in summer; 910kr, 50% off with student ID in winter).

Public Transportation: Yellow and red buses chauffeur you around the city (5-15kr per ride; free from the bus station into the center of town).

Tourist Office: Bryggen 7 (tel. 55 32 14 80; fax 55 32 14 64), on the harbor's right, just past the Torget. Helpful staff books rooms, exchanges currency, and sells the **Bergen Card,** which gets you admission to most museums plus other discounts (1-day 120kr, 2-day 190kr). The free *Bergen Guide* has the most up-to-date info. Ask for a photocopy of their suggested itineraries through the fjords. Luggage storage 10kr per piece per day. Open daily May and Sept. 9am-8pm; June-Aug. 8:30am-10pm; Oct.-Apr. M-Sa 9am-4pm. Train station branch open daily 7am-11pm. **DNT,** Tverrgaten 4-6 (tel. 55 32 22 30), off Marken, a pedestrian thoroughfare beginning at the railroad station and leading to the harbor, has info and sells detailed topological maps for all of Norway. Open M, W, and F 10am-4pm, Th until 6pm.

Currency Exchange: At the post office. After hours both tourist offices will change currency at 4% below the bank rate. No commission.

Luggage storage: In the train station. 20kr. Open daily 7am-11:50pm. Also ask at the tourist office.

Gay and Lesbian Services: Gay Movement, in the **Cafe Fincken,** Nygårdsgaten 2a (tel. 55 32 13 16). Open M-Sa noon-2:30am, Su 3pm-12:30am. **National Organization for Lesbian and Gay Liberation,** same address (tel. 55 31 21 39).

Emergencies: Ambulance, tel. 113. **Fire,** tel. 110.

Police: tel. 112.

Pharmacy: Apoteket Nordstjernen (tel. 55 31 68 84). Second floor of the bus station. Open M-Sa 8am-midnight, Su 9:30am-midnight.

Medical Assistance: 24hr. Accident Clinic, Vestre Strømkai 19 (tel. 55 32 11 20).

Post Office: tel. 55 54 15 00. A green building with a clock on Småstrand gate. Open M-F 8am-6pm, Sa 9am-3pm. **Postal Code:** N-5002.

Internet Access: Free at the **public library** *(bibliotek)* at Stromgata Vestre Stromkaien. Also try **Netropolis,** Theatergaten 20.

Telephones and Faxes: Tele Building, Byparken Starrhusegate 4, across Rådhusgate from the post office. Telephones and fax machines. Open M-F 9am-4pm.

ACCOMMODATIONS AND CAMPING

The tourist office books rooms (some with bathrooms) in private homes for a 15kr fee (20kr for 2 people; singles 160-200kr; doubles 250-350kr).

Intermission, Kalfarveien 8 (tel. 55 31 32 75). From the train station, head right from the exit, and right again on Kong Oscars gt., which mystically becomes Kalfarveien (5min.). Friendly staff, co-ed dorm with free sheets, blankets, ghost stories, tea and cookies, and laundry. Free waffles M and Th nights. Dorms 95kr. Breakfast 25kr; pack your own lunch for 15kr. Reception 7-11am and 5pm-midnight, F-Sa until 1am. Lockout 11am-5pm. Curfew 1am. Reserve ahead, or leave your name at the tourist office. Open mid-June to mid-Aug.

Montana Youth Hostel (HI), Johan Blyttsvei 30 (tel. 55 20 80 70; fax 55 20 80 75), is halfway up Mt. Ulriken, 5km from the city center. Take bus 4 ("Lægdene") from the central post office to "Montana" (15kr). Big dorms with bunk beds. Dorms 130-160kr; doubles with shower and bathroom 450kr. Breakfast included. Sheets 40kr. Wash and dry 20kr each. Kitchen use 5kr. Reception 24hr. Lockout 10am-3pm.

YMCA InterRail Center, Nedre Korskirkealmenningen 4 (tel. 55 31 72 52; fax 55 31 35 77). Single-sex and co-ed dorms. Kitchen, laundry, and piano. 100kr. Reception open daily 7am-1am. Lockout noon-4pm. Open June 15-Sept. 15.

Camping: Bergen Camping Park, Haukås om Åsane (tel. 55 24 88 08). 10kr per person, 60kr per tent. **Free camping** on the far side of the hills above town. Pick up a map or ask for further info at the DNT office in town.

FOOD

Bergen's culinary centerpiece is the **fish market** that springs up on Torget by the water (summer hours M-F 7am-4pm, Th until 7pm, Sa until 3pm; opens later in off-season). **Fellini,** Tverrgate, just off Marken, serves up Italian specialties and the best lunch deal in town (11am-5pm all pizzas 49kr; open daily 11am-midnight). Enjoy Norwegian cuisine and the older Bergen set at **Kaffistova til Ervingen,** Strandkaien 2B, on the second floor next to the harbor; it's cafeteria-style with a heavy emphasis on fish (*Dagens ret* (daily special) 65kr; open M-F 8am-7pm, Sa 8am-5pm, Su 11am-6pm). **Den Gode Klode,** Fosswinckelsgate 18, satisfies vegetarians in an elegant establishment with outdoor seating. (Salads from 30kr; *dagens ret* 60-70kr; students 10% off. Open M-F 11:30am-7pm, Sa 11:30am-5pm.) The **Dromedar Kaffebar,** next door, is a classy little place (open M-F 10am-10pm, Sa 11am-10pm, Su 1pm-10pm). The discount supermarket **Mekka** sprouts clones throughout the city; one lurks at Marken 3.

SIGHTS AND ENTERTAINMENT

Bergen, like the rest of Norway, is best seen on foot. The tourist office and bookstores sell *Round Bergen on Foot,* which details three walking tours with pictures, history, and anecdotes (29kr). As you gaze at the right side of the harbor from the Torget, you will see the pointed gables of **Bryggen,** a row of medieval buildings that has survived half a dozen disastrous fires and the explosion of a Nazi munitions ship in 1944. Listed by UNESCO as one of the world's most significant showcases of the Middle Ages, Bryggen also features restaurants and artsy-craftsy workshops. **Bryggens Museum,** 3 Dreggsalm, behind a small park at the end of the rows of Bryggen houses, displays old costumes, runic inscriptions, and scenes from life in old Norway. (Open May-Aug. daily 10am-5pm; Sept.-Apr. M-F 11am-3pm, Sa noon-3pm, Su noon-4pm. 20kr, students 10kr.) At the end of Bryggen stands the **Hanseatic Museum,** a preserved wooden house replete with secret compartments, mummified hanging fish, and an aura of affluent gloom from the days when German merchants controlled trade through Europe. (Open daily June-Aug. 9am-5pm; Sept.-May 11am-2pm. May-Sept. 35kr; Oct.-Apr. 20kr; guided tour of both museums 60kr.) The former city fortress, **Bergenhus,** teeters at the end of the quay, and the **Rosenkrantz Tower** stands adjacent in its late medieval splendor. **Håkonshallen,** built by Håkon Håkonsson in the 13th century, is what is left of the original castle. (Open daily May 15-Aug. 10am-4pm, guided tours of the hall and tower every hour; Sept.-May 14 noon-3pm; closed during the Bergen International Festival (see below). 15kr.)

Lose your head over the **Leprosy Museum,** Kong Oscars gate 59. Since 1970, the university has tastefully documented the history of the disease in a 19th-century hospital (open daily mid-May to Aug. 11am-3pm; 20kr). On the east shore of **Lille Lungegårdsvatnet,** a shimmering pond in the middle of town, the **Rasmus Meyer Collection** provides a extensive overview of Norwegian Naturalists, Impressionists, and Expressionists. Two buildings down the street, it is joined by the **Stenersens Collection,** with works by Munch and Picasso; both museums are branches of the **Bergen Art Museum.** (Open May 15-Sept. 15 M-Sa 10am-5pm, Su noon-6pm; Sept. 16-May 14 Tu-W and F 10am-3pm, Th noon-7pm, Sa 11am-4pm, Su noon-5pm. 35kr for both museums, 20kr Sept. 15-May 14.) Down the street the immaculately designed **West Norway Museum of Applied Art,** 9 Nordahl Brunsgate, highlights stunning 20th-century Norwegian design developments. (Open May 15-Sept. 14 Tu-Su 11am-4pm; Sept. 15-May 14 Tu-Sa noon-3pm, Th until 6pm, Su noon-4pm. 30kr, students 20kr.) **Gamle Bergen** (Old Bergen) is a rather touristy "village" and open-air museum of wooden buildings from the last century. Take city bus 20, 21, 22, or any red bus going to Sandviken to the first stop past the second tunnel (7min.) and then walk under the overpass, following the signs. (Houses open May 24-Aug. 9:30am-4:30pm. Hourly, obligatory guided tours 40kr, students 20kr.) Get wall-eyed with the sea-life at the **Bergen Aquarium,** Nordnesbakken 4, on the tip of the peninsula near the harbor entrance; take bus 4, or walk 15 minutes from the center. (Open daily May-Sept. 9am-8pm, feeding times 11am, 2pm, and 6pm; Oct.-April 10am-6pm, feeding times noon and 4pm. 55kr.) For an authentic taste of the city, stroll through Bergen's quieter, more residential neighborhoods. Explore the steep streets between the **Korskirken** (church) and the **Skansen** tower, and the **Sydneskleiben** and **Dragefjells-barker** neighborhoods near the university campus.

A vast archipelago lies to the west and towering mountains encroach on all other sides. Trails surrounding the city are sure to inspire awe. The **Fløibanen funicular** (lift) takes you to the top of Mount Fløyen, looming above the city. (M-F 7:30am-

11pm, Sa 8am-11pm; Su 9am-11pm; May-Aug. until midnight. One-way 15kr.) At the summit, you can enjoy the spectacular views, munch at the restaurant, or join up with one of the many **hiking trails** that lead up to the top of **Mt. Ulriken** (4hr. one-way), the highest peak above Bergen. A cable car also runs to the top of Mt. Ulriken every seven minutes (daily 9am-9pm, during winter 10am-sunset; round-trip 60kr). Free concerts are held at the top of Mt. Ulriken mid-May to mid-August (M-F 6pm); pick up a map of the hills above Bergen at the DNT office. From the Bergen bus station, take any bus to "Hopsbroen" ("Hop."), turn right, walk about 200m, then turn left, and walk for about 20 minutes to reach **Troldhaugen** (Troll Hill), the summer villa of Edvard Grieg, Norway's most famous composer. The house still contains many of Grieg's belongings, including his Steinway piano, which is used at summer concerts in neighboring **Troldsalen Hall** (tel. 55 91 17 91; open daily Apr. 18-Sept. 9am-6pm; 40kr; summer concerts W and Sa-Su, tickets at tourist information).

All stops are pulled out for the annual **Bergen International Festival** (tel. 55 21 61 50), a 12-day program of music, ballet, folklore, and drama, and the simultaneous **May Jazz Festival** in late May (tickets for both are generally expensive). The **Garage Bar,** at the corner of Nygårdsgaten and Christies gate, usually has live bands Fridays and Saturdays (cover varies); Wednesdays and Thursdays, check out the psychedelic dungeon (open daily until 3am). The milder scene is on at **Cafe Opera,** Engen 24, a mellow cafe/restaurant (try the reindeer roast with mountain cranberries, 89kr) with student theater on Thursday nights. It gets funky on Fridays and Saturdays with DJ dance music, surprise live concerts and "Club Eliassen" (no cover; open M-Th noon-2am, F noon-3am, Sa 11:30am-3am, Su 1pm-2am). **Miles Ahead,** 5 Torgata, hosts a popular disco (cover 60kr; open 10pm-3am), while **Rick's,** Veiten 3, combines the best of both worlds with a great bar and two discos upstairs (rock and pop; cover 50kr F-Sa after 10:30pm; open 10pm-3am).

■ Near Bergen

Virtually all of western Norway's **fjords** are accessible by daytripping ferries from Bergen. Most leave from the **Strandkaiterminalen** on the side of the harbor opposite Bryggen. **Flaggruten** (tel. 55 23 87 80) arranges daily boat and ferry excursions to **Hardangerfjord** (round-trip 290-595kr), while **Fylkesbaatane** (tel. 55 32 40 15) sends boats to towns on the **Sognefjord** (one way around 400kr) and up to **Nordfjord** (one way 500kr) with 50% student discounts. They also give day tours of Sognefjord and the Flåm valley (550kr). **Bergen Fjord Sightseeing** (tel. 55 25 90 00) offers tours of nearby fjords. (2-4hr. 150-250kr. 25% discount for students and InterRail holders. Tickets at tourist office or on the fish market pier.) **M/S Bruvik** (tel. 56 59 66 22) tours of nearby **Osterfjord** depart from the Bryggen Wharf (9hr.; 290kr; June 21-Aug. daily; Apr. 26-Oct. 4 Su only). One of the most popular and affordable day trips of the fjords is **Norway in a Nutshell,** which includes train, bus, and boat rides amidst the scenery (470kr round-trip from Bergen, 890kr from Oslo; 660kr between Bergen and Oslo).

■ Hardangerfjord

Slicing through one of Norway's fruit growing regions, the steep banks of the Hardangerfjord are lined with orchards and small farms. **Odda,** on the tip of Sørfjord, a slender branch of the main fjord, is the only "town" in the region. **Tourist offices** in Bergen and Odda (tel. 53 64 12 97) distribute the free *Hardanger Guide.* (Odda office open June 8-Aug. 16 M-F 10am-8pm, Sa 10am-5pm, Su 11am-6pm; Aug. 17-June 7 M-F 9am-3pm.) The comfortable **Odda Youth Hostel** (tel. 53 65 14 10) is at Bustetungata 2 (130kr, nonmembers 155kr; reception 5-10:30pm, 24hr. reception next door at the hotel). The area south of Odda on RV13, the main road, harbors many natural marvels, including the twin waterfalls of **Låtefoss.** For extended stays on the Hardangerfjord check out the towns of **Utne** or **Jondal.** The thunder of stampeding hikers can be heard in beautiful **Eidfjord,** 45km southeast of Voss on RV13, as they pass through this main gateway to **Hardangervidda,** Norway's largest national park. Duck into Eidfjord's **tourist office** (tel. 53 66 51 77) for an information refill. (Open

June 15-June 30 and Aug. 15-Aug. 30 M-Sa 9am-6pm; July-Aug. 14 M-F 9am-8pm, Sa 9am-6pm, Su noon-8pm; Sept.-Aug. 14 M-F 9am-3:30pm.) Walk 1km to see Vikings from 400-800 AD decaying at the **Viking Burial Place** in Hereid, or take the bus 20km to the one of Norway's most famous waterfalls, the 182m **Vøringstossen.** Ask the tourist office to find you a bed (from 50kr huts to 800kr hotel rooms) or try **Saebø Camping** (tel. 53 66 59 27; 10kr per person, 30kr per tent, 235kr per cabin).

■ Sognefjord

The deep, slender fingers of Sognefjord, the longest of the fjords (200km), penetrate all the way to the foot of the Jotunheimen mountains. A short ride north of the stunning Oslo-Bergen rail line, Sognefjord is ideal for those seeing Norway by train. A natural starting point deep in Sognefjord, **Flåm** is the only fjord town accessible by rail; the spectacular Flåm Railway runs from **Myrdal** (on the Oslo-Bergen line) to Flåm (50min., 11-13 per day, 80kr for railpass holders). If your legs can manage, you can also walk down to Flåm from Mydral (around 4hr.) and linger over the rainbow-capped waterfalls and snowy mountain vistas. Express boats also run between Flåm and Bergen (5hr., 2 per day, 410kr, 50% off with InterRail or ISIC). The post office, cafe, and train ticket office in Flåm coexist in the large building by the train station. The **tourist office** (tel. 57 63 21 06) dwells inside as well (open daily mid-June to mid-Aug. 8:30am-8:30pm; mid-Aug. to mid-June 9am-5pm). Fishing licenses (150kr per 24hr.) are available at **Flåm Camping and Hostel (HI)** (tel. 57 63 21 21; fax 57 63 23 80). To get there, cross to the side of the river opposite the train station and follow the road into the valley (95kr, nonmembers 120kr; tent and 1 person 60kr, 2 people 90kr; open May-Sept.). The **Heimly Pensjonat** (tel. 57 63 23 00) on the right bank of the fjord, offers sleeping bag accommodations for 125kr (reception 8am-midnight).

Wilderness junkies hop off the Oslo-Bergen train at **Finse,** just east of Myrdal, and hike north for three or four beautiful days down the Aurlandsdal Valley to **Aurland,** 10km from Flåm. You can sleep warmly all the way in evenly spaced DNT *hytter.* For maps, prices, and reservations, inquire at DNT in Oslo or Bergen. One of the most popular day **hikes** (8-10hr. one way) in Norway begins in Østerbø and runs through the Aurlandsdal Valley to Vassbydgi. Both endpoints can be reached by bus (3 per day, 34kr) from Aurland or Flåm. Buses also connect Aurland and Flåm (22kr). There is a fantastic view of the Aurland fjord a short hike up from **Otternes Bygdetun** (tel. 57 63 33 00), a unique cluster of 27 17th-century houses between the two towns (open mid-June to mid-Aug. 11am-6pm; 20kr). The **Aurland tourist office** (tel. 57 63 33 13) is at the highway junction (open May-Aug. M-F 9am-7pm, Sa-Su 10am-5pm; Sept.-Apr. M-F 8am-3:30pm). **Lunde Camping** (tel. 57 63 34 12), 1½km from town along the river, sprouts its quota of tents and caravans (15kr per person, 45kr per tent). Five hundred meters up the road, a trail branches to the left and offers a scenic, lung-searing four-hour hike to the top of **Prest** (1360m).

On the north side of Sognefjord, **Balestrand** is a groovy mid-way point between Flåm and Bergen or Nordfjord. Express boats whiz up the **Fjærland fjord** to Mundal (3 per day, round-trip 290kr). Buses (80kr) whisk passengers to two off-shoots of the **Jostedal glacier,** where guides await novices and experts (ask at any tourist office north of Bergen for schedules and prices). Buses stop en route at the new **Glacier Museum** (60kr), and return in time for riders to catch the boat back to Balestrand (bus fare included in express boat price). Those headed to Stryn from Mundal must plod 3km to the main highway and coordinate with the Sogndal-Skei buses (to Stryn 125kr, 50% ISIC discount). In Balestrand, the **tourist office** (tel. 57 69 12 55), near the quay, can help (open M-F 7:30am-9pm, Sa 7:30am-6:30pm, Su 8am-5:30pm). The Bergen **hydrofoils** serve Balestrand twice a day (3½hr., one-way 300kr, railpasses and ISIC 50% off). The gorgeous fjord-side **Kringsjå Hotel and Youth Hostel (HI)** (tel. 57 69 13 03) is 100m up the hill behind town. (160kr, nonmembers 190kr; doubles 190-220kr, nonmembers 220-250kr. Breakfast included. Kitchen. Laundry.) **Sjøtun camping** (tel. 57 69 12 23), 1km down the coastal road, provides tent sites and huts. (15kr

MCI Spoken Here

Worldwide Calling Made Simple

For more information or to apply for a Card call: **1-800-955-0925**

Outside the U.S., call MCI collect (reverse charge) at: **1-916-567-5151**

International Calling As Easy As Possible.

Calling Card

MCI

123 456 7890 1234
J.D. SMITH

WorldPhone

The MCI Card with WorldPhone Service is designed specifically to keep you in touch with the people that matter the most to you.

The MCI Card with WorldPhone Service....

- Provides access to the US and other countries worldwide.

- Gives you customer service 24 hours a day

- Connects you to operators who speak your language

- Provides you with MCI's low rates and no sign-up fees

For more information or to apply for a Card call:
1-800-955-0925

Outside the U.S., call MCI collect (reverse charge) at:
1-916-567-5151

Pick Up the Phone,
Pick Up the Miles.

You earn frequent flyer miles when you travel internationally, why not when you call internationally? Callers can earn frequent flyer miles if they sign up with one of MCI's airline partners:

- American Airlines
- Continental Airlines
- Delta Airlines
- Hawaiian Airlines
- Midwest Express Airlines
- Northwest Airlines
- Southwest Airlines
- United Airlines
- USAirways

Your MCI Worldphone Access Numbers

COUNTRY		WORLDPHONE TOLL-FREE ACCESS #
#Singapore		8000-112-112
#Slovak Republic (CC)		00421-00112
#Slovenia		080-8808
#South Africa (CC)		0800-99-0011
#Spain (CC)		900-99-0014
#Sri Lanka	(Outside of Colombo, dial 01 first)	440100
#St. Lucia ✝		1-800-888-8000
#St. Vincent		1-800-888-8000
#Sweden (CC) ♦		020-795-922
#Switzerland (CC) ♦		0800-89-0222
#Syria		0800
#Taiwan (CC) ♦		0080-13-4567
#Thailand ★		001-999-1-2001
#Trinidad & Tobago ✝		1-800-888-8000
#Turkey (CC) ♦		00-8001-1177
#Turks and Caicos ✝		1-800-888-8000
#Ukraine (CC) ✝		8▼10-013
#United Arab Emirates ♦		800-111
#United Kingdom (CC) To call using BT ■		0800-89-0222
	To call using C&W ■	0500-89-0222
#United States (CC)		1-800-888-8000
#Uruguay		000-412
#U.S. Virgin Islands (CC)		1-800-888-8000
#Vatican City (CC)		172-1022
#Venezuela (CC) ✝ ♦		800-1114-0
Vietnam ●		1201-1022
#Yemen		008-00-102

Automation available from most locations.
(CC)   Country-to-country calling available to/from most international locations.
◆   Limited availability.
▼   Wait for second dial tone.
■   International communications carrier.
★   When calling from public phones, use phones marked LADATEL.
●   Not available from public pay phones.
♦   Public phones may require deposit of coin or phone card for dial tone.
▲   Local service fee in U.S. currency required to complete call.
▲   Regulation does not permit intra-Japan calls.
✝   Available from most major cities

And, it's simple to call home.

1. Dial the WorldPhone toll-free access number of the country you're calling from (listed inside).

2. Follow the voice instructions in your language of choice or hold for a WorldPhone operator.
   - Enter or give the operator your MCI Card number or call collect.

3. Enter or give the WorldPhone operator your home number.

4. Share your adventures with your family!

The MCI Card with WorldPhone Service... The easy way to call when traveling worldwide.

MCI — Calling Card
123 456 7890 1234
J. D. SMITH
WorldPhone

COUNTRY	WORLDPHONE TOLL-FREE ACCESS #
American Samoa	633-2MCI (633-2624)
#Antigua	1-800-888-8000
(available from public card phones only)	#2
#Argentina (CC)	0800-5-1002
Aruba ÷	#2
#Australia (CC) ♦ To call using OPTUS ■	1-800-551-111
To call using TELSTRA ■	1-800-881-111
#Austria (CC) ♦	022-903-012
#Bahamas	1-800-888-8000
#Bahrain	800-002
#Barbados	1-800-888-8000
#Belarus (CC) From Brest, Vitebsk, Grodno, Minsk	8-800-103
From Gomel and Mogilev	8-10-800-103
#Belgium (CC) ♦	0800-10012
#Belize From Hotels	557
From Payphones	815
#Bermuda ÷	1-800-888-8000
#Bolivia (CC) ♦	0-800-2222
#Brazil (CC)	000-8012
#British Virgin Islands ÷	1-800-888-8000
#Brunei	800-011
#Bulgaria	00800-0001
#Canada (CC)	1-800-888-8000
#Cayman Islands	1-800-888-8000
#Chile (CC) To call using CTC ■	800-207-300
To call using ENTEL ■	800-360-180
#China ÷ For a Mandarin-speaking Operator	108-12
#Colombia (CC) ♦	980-16-0001
Collect Access in Spanish	980-16-1000
#Costa Rica ♦	0800-012-2222
Cote D'Ivoire	1001
#Croatia (CC) *	0800-22-0112
#Cyprus ♦	080-90000
#Czech Republic (CC) ♦	00-42-000112
#Denmark (CC) ♦	8001-0022
#Dominica	1-800-888-8000
#Dominican Republic Collect Access	1-800-888-8000
Collect Access in Spanish	1121
#Ecuador (CC) ÷	999-170
#Egypt (CC) ♦ (Outside of Cairo, dial 02 first)	355-5770
El Salvador	800-1767

FOLD

COUNTRY	WORLDPHONE TOLL-FREE ACCESS #
#Federated States of Micronesia	624
#Fiji	004-890-1002
#Finland (CC) ♦	08001-102-80
#France (CC) ♦	0800-99-0019
#French Antilles (CC) (includes Martinique, Guadeloupe)	0800-99-0019
#French Guiana (CC)	0-800-99-0019
#Gabon	00-195
#Germany (CC)	0-800-888-8000
#Greece (CC) ♦	00-800-1211
#Grenada ÷	1-800-888-8000
#Guam (CC)	1-800-888-8000
Guatemala ♦	99-99-189
Guyana	177
#Haiti ÷	193
Collect Access in French/Creole	190
#Honduras ÷	8000-122
#Hong Kong (CC) ♦	800-96-1121
#Hungary (CC) ♦	00▼800-01411
#Iceland (CC) ♦	800-9002
#India (CC) ♦	000-127
Collect Access	000-126
#Indonesia (CC) ♦	001-801-11
Iran ÷ (SPECIAL PHONES ONLY)	1-800-55-1001
#Ireland (CC) ♦	1-800-55-1001
#Israel (CC) ♦	1-800-940-2727
#Italy (CC) ♦	172-1022
#Jamaica (CC) Collect Access	1-800-888-8000
	873
#Japan (CC) ♦ (from special Hotels only)	0039-121▼
To call using KDD ■ (from public phones)	0066-55-121
To call using IDC ■	0044-11-121
To call using ITJ ■	18-800-001
#Jordan	8-800-131-4321
#Kazakhstan (CC)	080011
#Kenya ÷	009-14
#Korea ÷ To call using KT ■	00309-12
To call using DACOM ■	03669-14
To call using ONSE ■ Phone Booths÷	550-2255
Military Bases Press red button, 03, then ★	800-MCI (800-624)
#Kuwait	

FOLD

COUNTRY	WORLDPHONE TOLL-FREE ACCESS #
#Lebanon Collect Access	600-MCI (600-624)
#Liechtenstein (CC) ♦	0800-89-0222
#Luxembourg (CC)	0800-0112
#Macao	0800-131
#Macedonia (CC) ♦	99800-4266
#Malaysia (CC) ♦	1-800-80-0012
#Malta	0800-89-0120
#Marshall Islands	1-800-888-8000
#Mexico (CC) Avantel	01-800-021-8000
Telmex ▲	01-800-674-7000
Collect Access in Spanish	01-800-021-1000
#Monaco (CC) ♦	800-90-019
#Montserrat	1-800-888-8000
#Morocco	00-211-0012
#Netherlands (CC) ♦	0800-022-912
#Netherlands Antilles (CC) ÷	001-800-888-8000
#New Zealand (CC)	000-912
Nicaragua (CC) Collect Access in Spanish	166
(Outside of Managua, dial 02 first) From any public payphone	*2
#Norway (CC) ♦	800-19912
Pakistan	00-800-12-001
#Panama	108
Military Bases	2810-108
#Papua New Guinea (CC)	05-07-19140
#Paraguay ÷	00-812-800
Peru	0-800-500-10
#Philippines (CC) ♦ To call using PLDT ■	105-14
To call using PHILCOM ■	1026-14
Collect Access via PLDT in Filipino	105-15
Collect Access via ICC in Filipino	1237-77
#Poland (CC) ÷	00-800-111-21-22
#Portugal (CC) ÷	05-017-1234
#Puerto Rico (CC)	1-800-888-8000
#Qatar ★	0800-012-77
#Romania (CC) ÷	01-800-1800
#Russia (CC) ♦ ÷ To call using ROSTELCOM ■	747-3322
(For Russian speaking operator)	747-3320
To call using SOVINTEL ■	960-2222
#Saipan (CC) ÷	950-1022
#San Marino (CC) ♦	172-1022
#Saudi Arabia (CC) ÷	1-800-11

MEET TWO TRAVELERS
WHO JUST HAD A GOOD NIGHT'S SLEEP

SHE STAYED AT A HOSTEL

and with the money she saved on her accommodation, she had breakfast at a trendy café, toured the famous sights, saw a band at a local club and still had enough change left over to make a call home.

HE STAYED AT A HOTEL

and had enough money left over for a cup of coffee.

(no refills)

HOSTELLING
INTERNATIONAL

With a Hostelling International (HI) membership card you can access affordable accommodation at nearly 5,000 hostels in over 70 countries. So if you're planning a trip, get the HI card and join 4 million members worldwide who save every time they travel.

ORDER YOUR HI CARD BY CALLING 1-877-2-A-HOSTEL (PLEASE HAVE YOUR CREDIT CARD READY). FOR YOUR CONVENIENCE YOU CAN ORDER FOREIGN CURRENCY AT THE SAME TIME.

For all other inquiries or reservations, visit our website www.hiayh.org or phone 202-783-6161

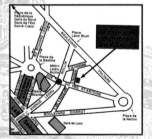

DON'T MISS

MIKE'S BIKE TOURS
OF
MUNICH

In **MUNICH:** At **11:30** & **4:00** **EVERY DAY** right under the tower of the **OLD TOWN HALL** at **MARIENPLATZ.**

June 1 to August 15 at **12:30** also for our all-inclusive 6-hour **EXTENDED TOUR** with 2 Beer Garden stops!

In March, and from Sept. 18 – Oct. 31 Standard Tour (4 hours) at **12:30 ONLY.**

MEETING POINT: MUNICH

AND
AMSTERDAM

In **AMSTERDAM:** At **11:30** & **4:00** **EVERY DAY** from May 15 until August 31 near the **WEST ENTRANCE** of the **RIJKSMUSEUM.**

April 15 to May 15 and from Sept. to mid-October at **12:30 ONLY.**

RAIN GEAR PROVIDED!

MEETING POINT: AMSTERDAM

FOR JUST $US 19 . . .

- 🚲 Brand New **SCHWINN CRUISERS!**
- 🚲 Not strenuous and only on **BIKE PATHS**
- 🚲 Super, entertaining and informative guides
- 🚲 Meet people and have a lot of **FUN**
- 🚲 See more, learn more, get **A LOT MORE** out of your stay
- 🚲 **INVEST** in your trip – **SATISFACTION GUARANTEED!**

Look for a brochure in your hotel or at Tourist Information when you get into town. Other info in Munich and Amsterdam sections of this book.

Reservations **NOT** necessary — Just show up!

If you're stuck for cash on your travels, don't panic. Millions of people trust Western Union to transfer money in minutes to 153 countries and over 45,000 locations worldwide. Our record of safety and reliability is second to none. So when you need money in a hurry, call Western Union.

WESTERN UNION | MONEY TRANSFER®

The fastest way to send money worldwide.®

per person; 25kr per tent; 2-person hut 125kr. Reception 9-10am, 6-7pm, and 9-10pm. Open June-Sept. 15.)

Ferries run from Flåm and Aurland west through narrow fjords to **Gudvangen** (2½hr., 4 per day, 130kr, 50% discount for InterRail and ISIC). From Gudvangen, buses (70min., 5-8 per day, 64kr, 50% ISIC discount) run up to **Voss,** east of Bergen on the Oslo rail line. By train get to Voss from Oslo (5 daily, 450kr) or Bergen (over 10 daily, 125kr). Voss is boss when it comes to winter sports, and the **Voss Adventure Center** (tel. 56 51 36 30) in a mini-golf hut behind the Park Hotel, books horsetrekking (90kr per hr.), white-water rafting (590kr for 4hr. trip), and tandem paragliding (600kr per hr.) trips, and rents bikes (30kr per hr., 150kr per day). More rafting can be organized through the **Voss Rafting Center** (tel. 56 51 05 25; http://www.bbb.no/rafting).

From the train station, turn left when you face the lake and bear right at the fork by the church to reach the **tourist office,** Hestavangen 10 (tel. 56 52 08 00; fax 56 52 08 01), which has info on accommodations and outdoor activities in the area (open May-Sept. M-Sa 9am-7pm, Su 2-7pm; Oct.-Apr. M-F 9am-4pm). Turning right from the station and trudging along the lakeside road brings you to Voss's large, modern **HI youth hostel** (tel. 56 51 20 17), where you can rent canoes, rowboats, and bikes (all 20kr per hr., 75kr per day), or relax in the sauna (dorms 165kr, nonmembers 190kr; reception 24hr.; open late Jan. to Apr. 15 and May2 22-Sept.). To reach the central **Voss Camping** (tel. 56 51 15 97 or 91 18 50 15), head left from the station, stick to the lake shore, and follow the avenue of trees that projects off towards the water (tents 60kr; bike rental 30kr per hour, 150kr per day; canoe and row boat rental).

■ Geirangerfjord

Though only 16km long, Geirangerfjord's gorgeous cliffs and waterfalls make it Norway's most sublime fjord. While cruising through the green-blue water, watch the drama of the **Seven Sisters,** the spurting and gushing of the **Suitor,** and the **Bridal Veil's** mist. A popular way to reach the fjord is to take the **Golden Route** bus, with spectacular views, incredibly steep inclines, and photographic pit-stops. Two buses depart daily to make the journey on the famous **Trollstigen** road that connects Åndalsnes with **Geiranger,** one of the fjord's sightseeing bases (3hr., 250kr, 50% discount for railpass holders). Over 3000 tourists trample the streets of Geiranger every day in summer, while an armada of ocean liners maintains a steady presence offshore.

If you find Geiranger too touristy, **hiking** opportunities abound in this charmed country. Especially notable are the path underneath the **Storseter waterfall** and the hikes to Flydalsjuvet Cliff, Skageflå farm, and Dalsnibba Mountain, which can be reached by the daily 10am bus from the church next to the hostel (12:45pm return; 90kr). Many of the tiny, now abandoned farms clinging to these cliffs could be reached only by ladders that were artfully yanked up when tax collectors passed by. The Geiranger **tourist office** (tel. 70 26 30 99), up from the landing, finds private rooms (from 200kr) for a 20kr fee (open late May to Aug. daily 9am-7pm). **Geiranger Camping** (tel. 70 26 31 20) is by the water 500m past the ferry dock (10kr per person, 50kr per tent; showers 5kr per 3min.; wheelchair accessible). To get to the **Vinjebakken Hostel** with its fantastic view of the fjord, follow the main road up the steep hillside behind town. (15min. walk, or ask the bus driver to drop you at the hostel. 120kr. Breakfast 50kr. Shower 10kr. Laundry 20kr. Checkout 11am. Reception 8-11am and 3pm-midnight. Open mid-June to mid-Aug.)

Geiranger Fjordservice (tel. 70 26 30 07) allows you to cruise the fjord's chilly waters. (1½hr. round-trip; 5 departures daily June-Aug. 10am-5:30pm, June 25-July 31 also 8pm.) Another way to see the fjord is to take the ferry connecting Geiranger with **Hellesylt,** the fjord's less touristy western base (1hr., 10 per day, 32kr, 50% discount with Scanrail). To reach Hellesylt from the south, leave from Stryn (2-3 buses per day, 70kr); from the north, start from Åndalsnes (partly via the Golden Route) or from Ålesund. Hikers head for the **Briksdal glacier** (3hr. round trip, glacier guides available) and the **Troll's Path.** The **tourist office** (tel. 70 26 50 52), right on the ferry landing, provides hiking maps (open daily mid-June to mid-Aug. 10am-4pm). The **Hellesylt Youth Hostel (HI)** (tel. 70 26 51 28; fax 70 26 36 57), up the steep hill along the road to Stranda (if coming by bus ask the driver to let you off in front of the hostel), has a great view; take the path up the right side of the waterfall that thunders through town, hang a right at the top, and walk along the road 300m. (The footpath leads else-where. 100kr, nonmembers 125k. Reception June-Aug. 8am-noon and 5-11pm; July 10-Aug. 10 24hr.). Walk 1km across the bridge from the dock and left to find **Helle-sylt Camping** (tel. 70 26 51 88; 15kr per person, 45kr per tent; fishing pole rental).

■ Åndalsnes and Ålesund

The mountains around Åndalsnes draw mountaineers, rock climbers, and casual hik-ers. Daily trains split off the Oslo-Trondheim line at Dombås (from Oslo 6hr., 520kr, *minipris* 290kr), and take off onto the roller-coaster **Rauma Line** which passes over stunning bridges and makes a U-turn inside the 1340m Stavems tunnel. The train passes Norway's ultimate mountaineering challenge, **Trollveggen**—the highest verti-cal rock wall in Europe—and the most notable peak in the area, **Romsdalshorn.** The Dombås-Åndalsnes buses parallel the train. An equally awesome approach is the diz-zying bus route up **Trollstigen** from Geiranger.

Åndalsnes At the mouth of the Rauma River and surrounded by a fantastic ring of serrated mountain peaks, Åndalsnes is a paradise for mountaineers and day hikers. The local **tourist office** (tel. 71 22 16 22; fax 71 22 16 82) is next to the train station. (Open mid-June to mid-Aug. daily 10am-7pm; mid-Aug. to mid-June M-F 10am-3:30pm; Aug. open Sa.) Get a list of **private accommodations** (doubles from 200kr) from the tourist office and call yourself to avoid the booking fee. To get to the **Åndal-snes Youth Hostel Setnes (HI)** (tel. 71 22 13 82), walk up Jernbaneg., take a left onto Storg. when the road ends, proceed to the traffic circle, stay right and go under the bridge, pass the gas stations, and cross the river (30min.). The hostel is one block far-ther, on the left. (Dorms 160kr; singles 260kr; doubles 395kr. Enormous pancake breakfast included. Reception 8-10am and 4-11pm. Open May 20-Sept. 10.) If the sky's clear, walk out to the field 500m behind the hostel, near the campsite, and watch the sunset. En route to the hostel, campers turn left after crossing the bridge, walk 1.3km along the road, and check in at the amazingly scenic **Åndalsnes Camp-ing.** (Tel. 71 22 16 29. 15kr per person, 45kr per tent, 4-bed huts from 150kr. **Bike rental** 100kr per day.) Between the hostel and campground, the **Norsk Tindemu-seum** houses legendary mountaineer Arne Randers Heen's collection of expedition paraphernalia, as well as exhibits on the few folk warped enough to parachute off Trollveggen (open June to mid-Aug. daily 1-5pm; other times on request; 30kr). Arne climbed Romsdalshorn for the 233rd time when he was 80 years old. Don't miss the chance to meet Mrs. Heen, who, at 80 years old, runs the museum, and who is quite well-known for climbing (and dancing) herself. Ask about paragliding (if you're into that sort of thing) at the tourist office. To hit the mountains, contact **Aak** (tel. 71 22 71 00), 4km east of town on the E9 back toward Dombås; they have beds (190kr) with showers and a fireplace and organize climbing clinics. Troll tours (tel. 90 65 04 16), leads 2-hour "potholing" (i.e. **spelunking**) trips in the nearby Blåmann caves. Dis-counted wool sweaters (400-900kr), hats and shawls can be found at the **Rauma Ull-varefabrikk** factory (5min. walk from the hostel). Call in advance (tel. 71 22 10 33).

Ålesund The largest city between Bergen and Trondheim, Ålesund (oh-les-oond) is renowned for its Art Nouveau architecture and beautiful cliffside location. For a view of the splendid city, the distant mountains, and the coastal ferries inching between islands, gasp up the 418 steps to the **Aksla** mountain viewpoint. Ålesund is accessible by **bus** (3 per day from Åndalsnes, 142kr, railpass 50% off), or by **Hurtigruten** which docks here daily. The **Sunnmøre Museum,** Borgundgavlen (10min. by bus 13, 14, 18, or 24; 15kr), displays local fishing boats from days of yore and a reconstructed Viking ship from around 800. (Open Jun. 15- Aug. 31 M-Sa 10am-5pm, Su noon-5pm; shorter hours off-season. 40kr, students 30kr.) Give the **Teater Fabrikken**, Molovcin 22 (Theatre Factory; tel. 70 10 04 10), a call to see if they've got any jazz or shows in English playing in their old wharf-side theatre. Commune with the fishes of the North Sea at the new **Atlantic Sea Park**, the largest aquarium in Scandinavia, built into its natural surroundings at Tueneset, 30km west of Ålesund (open daily June 1-Aug. 10am-6pm; Sept.-May 11am-4pm; 75kr). There's an old Viking site and 12th-century marble church on **Giske**, a short bus ride from Ålesund (route 64, 12 per day, 38kr). Ornithusiasts flock to the island of **Runde**, sanctuary to over 500,000 of our fine feathered friends. A hydrofoil land and a bus link Ålesund and Giske (2hr., M-F 3 per day, 104kr). Check with the tourist office for departure times; contact **Runde Vandrerhjem (HI)** (tel. 70 08 59 16) if you want to spend the night. **Mørebil** (tel. 70 25 16 88 or 70 27 06 00) has a full-day, round-trip tour of Geirangerfjord (bus to Hellesylt, ferry to Geiranger, bus back to Ålesund) for 280kr (1-2 per day).

The **tourist office** (tel. 70 12 12 02), on Keiser Wilhelms gate, is across from the bus station in the city hall (open June-Aug. M-F 8:30am-7pm, Sa 9am-5pm; Su 11am-5pm; Sept.-May M-F 9am-4pm). The **Ålesund Vandrerhjem**, Parkg. 14 (tel. 70 11 58 30), is a 5min. walk from the bus station (165kr; breakfast included; kitchen; free laundry). **Hansen Gaarden**, Kongensg. 14 (tel. 70 12 10 29), has spotless, spacious rooms. (Singles 200kr, doubles 280-310kr. Kitchen. Laundry 15kr. Reception 8am-9pm. Open mid-June-Aug. 20.) **Volsdalen Camping** (tel./fax 70 12 58 90) has the closest sites to town, 2km out along the main highway next to a beach. Take bus 13, 14, 18, or 24 (11kr), turn right off the highway, and follow the downhill road to the bottom of the stairs. Cross the road, turn right and cross the overpass, then turn left and walk 200m. (10kr per person, tents 90kr, cabins 290-490kr. Laundry 60kr. Reception 9am-9pm. Open May to mid-Sept.)

▓ Trondheim

Viking kings turned Trondheim into one of the most influential cities in Norway, but it's the slightly better-mannered 20,000 students who now give the city its flair—especially on weekend nights (Thursday included, of course). Fresh from celebrating its 1000th birthday, Trondheim will no doubt keep the good times rolling for the millennium to come.

SIGHTS AND ENTERTAINMENT Olav Tryggvason founded Trondheim in 997; his image presides over an outdoor market in the main town square, **Torget**. Local boy King Olav Haraldsson became Norway's patron saint after he fought to introduce Christianity. A steady stream of pilgrims prompted the construction of **Nidaros Cathedral**, Scandinavia's largest medieval structure, built over a holy well that sprang up beside St. Olav's grave. Site of all Norwegian coronations, the cathedral holds the crown jewels. (Open mid-June to mid-Aug. M-F 9am-6:15pm, Sa 9am-2pm, Su 1-4pm; reduced hours off-season. 20kr.) The view from the top of the 172-step spiral staircase in the tower is worth the 5kr (admission every 30min.). The 12th-century church is at the tail end of a renovation that began in 1869. Among the buildings that surround the church is the **Archbishop's Palace** and **Hjemmefrontmuseet**. (Army Museum. Palace open mid-June to Aug. M-F 10am-5pm, Sa 10am-3pm, Su noon-5pm. 20kr.) The Hjemmefrontmuseet chronicles the development of the army from Viking times to the present, and attempts to deal honestly with the issue of Nazi collaboration. (Open June-Aug. M-F 9am-3pm, Sa-Su 11am-4pm; Feb.-May and Sept.-Nov. Sa-Su 11am-4pm. 5kr.) Cross the **Gamle Bybro** (Old Town Bridge) and visit the old district on Innherredsveien, parallel to the river, for a taste of Trondheim of yore. On the hill across the river roosts the white 1681 **Kristiansten Fortress** with its splendid view of the city. If you don't feel like hiking up the hill, just pick up one of Trondheim's 200 free **city bicycles** (20kr deposit at bike stations sprinkled around town, though often the bikes are just left sitting around) and ride up the **bike lift** at the base of the Old Town Bridge. Pick up a key-card to operate the lift from the tourist office (100kr deposit). The **Trondhjems Kunst Museum**, Bispeg. 7B, next to the cathedral, has a new exhibit every month, though a permanent hallway is devoted to Edvard Munch, highlighted by the woodcuts *Lust* and *Jealousy* (open June-Aug. daily 10am-4pm; Sept.-May Tu-Su noon-4pm; 30kr, students 20kr). Bus 3 or 4 from Munkeg. will take you to the intriguing **Ringve Museum of Musical History.** Displays (with demonstrations) range from a one-stringed Ethiopian violin to the ornate Mozart Room. (Mandatory tours in English mid-June to mid-Aug. at 11am, 12:30, 2:30, and 4:30pm. 50kr, students 30kr.) Ferry over to **Munkholmen** (Monks' Island), an island monastery that became a prison fortress and then a quiet beach and picnic spot (round-trip 30kr; fortress 14kr). Boats depart daily from Ravnkloa hourly from 10am-6pm.

PRACTICAL INFO, ACCOMMODATIONS, AND FOOD The **train station** faces the center of town, which is circled by the Nid River. **Trains** arrive from Bodø (10-11hr., 2 per day, 680kr, *minipriser* 430kr), Oslo (7-8hr., 4 per day, 590kr), and Stockholm via Storlien (13hr., 2 per day, 718kr). **Long-distance buses** leave from the train station. The **airport** is 45km out of town and accessible via *flybussen* or train (44-50kr). All **city buses** leave from the Munkeg.-Dronningensg. intersection (17kr). From the train station, walk across the bridge, then six blocks on Søndreg., turn right on Kongensg., and continue to the main square and the **tourist office,** Munkeg. 19 (tel. 73 92 94 05). The office distributes the comprehensive *Trondheim Guide.* (Open June to mid-Aug. M-F 8:30am-10pm, Sa-Su 10am-8pm; late Aug. to May M-F 9am-4pm, Sa 9am-1pm.) **Trondheim's DNT** center, Munkeg. 64, 2nd fl. (tel. 73 52 38 08), above Paul's Tandoori Restaurant, provides information on huts and hiking trails to the north and south (open M-W and F 9am-4pm, Th 9am-6pm).

Trondheim has three options for budget lodging. The most unique is the **InterRail Center,** Elgeseterg. 1 (tel. 73 89 95 38; email tirc@stud.ntnu.no), which resides in the Studentersenter, a huge, red and round building known by students throughout Norway. From the station, cross the bridge, walk two blocks, turn right onto Olav Tryggvasonsg., then left on Prinsensg., walk seven blocks and cross the bridge; it will be on your left. Alternatively, take bus 41, 44, 46, 48, 49, 52, or 63 (17kr) to "Samfundet." Ask for a smaller room to avoid noisy groups. (Sleeping bag dorms 95kr. Breakfast included. Reception 7am-2am. Doorbell around back. Open from the last weekend in June until the last Tu in Aug.) The student-run center also offers free **Internet access,** serves the cheapest meal in town (39kr), and has a nice cafe and bar (beer 33kr). To reach the institutional **Trondheim Vandrerhjem (HI),** Weidemannsvei 41 (tel. 73 53 04 90), walk 15 minutes from the city center or ride bus 63 from the train station (160kr, nonmembers 185kr; breakfast included; sheets 45kr). Walk up Lillegårdsbabakken to reach the student-run **Singsaker Sommerhotell,** Rogertsg. 1 (tel. 73 89 31 00; fax 73 89 32 00), near the Kristiansten Fortress, which includes a grill and TV room. (Sleeping bag dorms 125kr; singles 255kr; doubles 400kr; triples 570kr. Sheets 30kr. Breakfast included. Open early June to late Aug.) **Sandmoen Camping** (tel. 72 88 61 35), 10km south of town, is the closest campsite; take bus 44 from the bus station to Sandbakken (100kr per tent; reception 24hr. in summer, 8am-10pm off-season). Sit for a while in **Bare Blåbær's** ("Just Blueberries") comfy couches at Nedre Bakklandet 5, in the old district—it was voted "Best Cafe in Trondheim" in 1997 (open daily until 1am, food served until 10pm Su-Th, until 11pm F-Sa). At **Café Gåsa,** Øvre Baklande 36, live peacocks glut the already overloaded atmosphere (dinners from 50kr). Nightlife centers around Nordre Gate and along Bratlørg.

NORTHERN NORWAY

Bodø and Narvik Its provincial charm obliterated in World War II, **Bodø** (BOO-deh) is today the northern terminus of the Norwegian rail line, the departure point for buses and boats to the Arctic, and not much else. Travelers generally flee quickly to their true destinations. There are two interesting trips outside of Bodø. The first is the quaint fishing village and trading post of **Kjerringøy** (40km north of Bodø). There's one round-trip bus per day (50kr). The second is the strongest maelstrom in the world, **Saltstraumen** (33km south of Bodø); pick up a tidal timetable from the tourist office to ensure you won't be disappointed (M-F 9-10 buses per day, Sa 6 buses, Su 2 buses; 43kr). For those under 25, daily stand-by **flights** to northern Norway from Oslo cost only 800kr. From Bodø they run 400kr. By **train**, Bodø is 10 hours north of Trondheim (680kr, 50% student fare). Two **buses** per day run north from Bodø to Narvik (7hr., 330kr, 50% railpass discount). The **tourist office**, Sjøg. 21 (tel. 75 52 60 00; fax 75 52 21 77), about five blocks toward the city center from the train station, doles out the all-encompassing *Bodø Guide*, rents bicycles (60kr per 24hr.), and books private accommodations for a 25kr fee (120-200kr. Open June-Aug. M-F 9am-8:30pm, Sa 10am-4pm and 6-8pm, Su noon-4pm and 6-8pm; Sept.-May M-F 9am-4pm.) The **Bodø Vandrerhjem Lokomotivet**, Sjøg. 55 (tel. 75 52 11 22; fax 75 52 11 22), is on the third floor of the train station and is relatively generic, though they've got singles (150kr) for just 10kr more than a dorm bed (140kr). (Sheets 35kr. Breakfast in the cafeteria downstairs 50kr. Laundry 60kr. Reception 24hr.) Cheap Norwegian victuals await in **Lövold's Kafeteria**, Tollbug. 9 (closed Su).

Undoubtedly, the most glorious aspects of **Narvik** are the approach and departure—from a distance, the city's metal buildings flicker beneath the awesome, looming mountains. Nordic nature in its untamed magnificence is yours on the **bus** north to Tromsø (4½hr., 283kr), the **hydrofoil** to Svolvær (Tu-F and Su, 263kr; 50% railpass discount), or the **train** to Kiruna in the Swedish Lappland (3hr., 2 per day, around 100kr). If you must stay in Narvik, contact the **youth hostel (HI)**, Havneg. 3 (tel. 76 94 25 98; reception 6-8pm and 11pm-noon).

■ Lofoten Islands

Made luscious by the Gulf Stream, the Lofoten Islands' jagged, green-gray mountains shelter fishing villages, farms, bird colonies, and happy sheep. The crystal clear water and mild climate make these islands a magical place to spend a few days or weeks. Rugged hikers and mountaineers will enjoy the network of trails covering the archipelago, but much of the islands' charm can be easily appreciated from a deck chair or cozy fireplace. As late as the 1950s, fisherfolk lived in the small *rorbuer*, yellow and red wooden shacks which cluster along the coast. Today, tourists book the *rorbuer* solid (90-125kr per person in a group of 4 or more). Call the local tourist office to book a *rorbuer* or get a copy of the brochure *Nordland 1999*, which is available at any tourist office from Bodø north, and which lists them, along with other accommodations. The *Lofoten Info-Guide 1998*, available at tourist offices in the Lofoten Islands, also furnishes information on ferries, buses, and sights.

Highway E10 binds the four largest of the islands—Vågen, Vestvågøy, Flakstad, and Moskenes—which point toward the tiny outlying isles of craggy **Værøy** and flat, puffin-thronged **Røst**. Both outlying islands have **HI hostels**. (On Røst, tel. 76 09 61 09 or 76 09 60 00. 100kr. On Værøy, tel. 76 09 53 52 or 76 09 53 75. 85kr, nonmembers 110kr.) Frequent **bus** and ferry connections are available from Bodø and Narvik, the two best mainland springboards to the islands. Bus service runs daily from Narvik to Svolvær (7hr., 330kr, 50% railpass discount) and from Bodø to Svolvær (10½hr., 385kr, 50% railpass discount). By **boat**, your best and cheapest bet is a car ferry from Bodø to Moskenes, which makes an impressive approach to the jagged isles (4hr., 4-5 per day, 108kr), and stops four times per week at Røst (120kr) and Værøy (95kr). Hydrofoils skim to Svolvær from Bodø (Su-F, 225kr) and from Narvik (Tu-F and Su, 263kr, 50% railpass discount). A final, slower approach, the Hurtigruten, connects Bodø with Stamsund (4½hr., 216kr) and Svolvær (6hr., 232kr) daily.

Bus service between the four major islands is frequent, but can be expensive. Only an InterRail pass grants a 50% discount on *internal* routes on the Lofoten Islands, but a Scanrail will get you a discount if your destination town has a rail connection. A student ID will get up to 50% off *any* route. Finally, many long routes in the islands are broken into several segments with connecting buses; for the best deal always ask for a ticket to your final destination and not a connecting stop. Internet information on the Lofoten Islands can be accessed at http://www.lofoten-info.no.

Moskenes and Flakstad

Moskenes and Flakstad Ferries to **Moskenes,** the southernmost of the larger Lofotens, dock at the town of the same name. The **tourist office** (tel. 76 09 15 99) in Moskenes, by the ferry landing, gives advice on rooms and sights (open June 1-18 and Aug. 14-31 M-F 10am-5pm; June 19-Aug. 13 daily 10am-7pm). A local bus whisks incoming ferry passengers 5km south to **Å** (pronounced Oh), a tiny fishing village at the end of the E10 Highway. Half of Å's buildings make up the **Norsk Fiskeværsmuseum,** an open-air museum documenting life in the old fishing days. (Open mid-June to mid-Aug. daily 11am-6pm; mid-Aug. to mid-June M-F 10am-3pm. Guided tours at 1pm. 55kr, students 30kr.) The **Å Vandrerhjen and Rorbuer** (tel. 76 09 11 21; fax 76 09 12 82) bunks travelers in quaint (but authentic) 19th-century buildings (125kr, nonmembers 150kr; laundry 40kr; reservations essential; open May-Sept.). The hostel also rents *rorbuer,* which are affordable for groups of four or more (550-1000kr). Fishing equipment, rowboats, and bikes are also for rent. To get to **Moskenes-Straumen Camping** (tel. 76 09 11 48), which overlooks the sea, follow E10 until it stops at the edge of Å (10kr per person, 50kr per tent, showers 5kr), or just **camp** free on the (sometimes soggy) shores of the snow-fed lake behind town. The enticing aroma of freshly baked cinnamon rolls (7kr) may draw you to the wood-fired **bakery** next to the hostel (open daily 7am-4pm). For some great excitement, get in touch with Bjorn Kennet for a speedboat day-tour of the powerful sea straumen and southern Lofoten (tel. 76 09 12 75 or 91 73 03 35; 350kr), or call the tourist office in Moskenes for information on a torchlit tour of Refsuika caves and their 3000 year-old drawings.

Moving north, the next large island is **Flakstad,** centered on the hamlet of **Ramberg.** Flakstad has perhaps the best hiking trails on the islands; get maps at the **tourist office** (tel. 76 09 34 50), which also books doubles from 120kr (open June 16-Aug. 31 daily 10am-7pm).

Vestvågøy and Austvågøy

Vestvågøy and Austvågøy The mountain-backed hamlet of **Stamsund** on **Vestvågøy,** the next island north, is also home to an **HI youth hostel** (tel. 76 08 93 34 or 94 53 91 29) where travelers from all over the world come for a night and remain for weeks. The benevolent ruler of this island utopia, Roar Justad, provides fishing gear (100kr deposit), rowboats (free), and mountain bikes (75kr per day). More sedate types enjoy the TV/VCR and food from the wood-stoves. (80kr per night. Laundry 30kr. *Rorbuer* 400-600kr. Wheelchair accessible. Open mid-Dec. to mid.-Oct.) A **tourist office** (tel. 76 08 97 92) is 1km down the main road near the coastal steamer dock and the Shell station (open mid-June to mid-Aug. daily 6-9:30pm). Four buses per day run north from Å to Leknes and Stamsund (88kr, 50% railpass discount), and on to Svolvær. On the bus route between Leknes and Svolvær lies **Borg,** the site of the largest Viking building ever found. The reconstructed longhouse holds a **Viking museum** staffed by costumed Norse folk who perform full-scale reenactments (open daily 10am-7pm; 70kr, students 56kr; Viking soup included).

Svolvær, on the northernmost island of **Austvågøy,** is the bland hub of beautiful Lofoten. The **tourist office** (tel. 76 07 30 00) is inside the large red building by the ferry dock (open July 1 to mid-Aug. M-F 9am-10pm, Sa 10am-8pm, Su 11am-10pm). **Svolvær Sjøhuscamping** (tel./fax 76 07 03 36) offers rooms in a structure on stilts above the harbor near the center; take the third right from Torget on Vestfjordg. going north from the tourist office (dorms 130kr; doubles 350kr; reception 8am-midnight). A bit more distant and even more interesting is the friendly **Marinepollen Sjøhus** (tel. 76 07 18 33), north along the E10 for 15 minutes until Jektveien on the right. (100kr; doubles 350kr. Free use of rowboat and fishing gear. Kitchen. Fridge in every room.) Call, and the owners may pick you up. Shop for groceries at **Rimi** on the corner of Torgg. and Storg. (open M-F 9am-8pm, Sa 9am-6pm).

■ Tromsø

Norway's fastest growing city, Tromsø makes many claims about its importance and uniqueness: "Gateway to the Arctic," "Paris of the North," "world's northernmost university city." After two winter months of perpetual darkness, the locals have to feel good about *something.* Still, Tromsø is the last city of note for those trudging even farther north, and the city does have a young, fun-loving student population, with more bars per capita than any other city in Norway.

SIGHTS AND ENTERTAINMENT The bizarre, some might even say hideous, modern **Arctic Cathedral** on the mainland has one of the largest stained glass windows in Europe, as well as clean white lines designed to blend with ice and snow. (Open May daily 3-6pm; June to mid-Aug. M-Sa 10am-8pm, Su 1-8pm; mid-Aug.to mid-Sept. daily 3-6pm. 15kr. Organ concerts W-F at 5pm. 10kr.) The **Tromsø Museum,** Lars Thøringsvei 10, features exhibits on the region's natural history and ethnographic displays on Sami culture. (Open June-Aug. daily 9am-9pm; Sept.-May M-F 8:30am-3:30pm, Sa noon-3pm, Su 11am-4pm. 20kr, students 10kr.) To reach the museum, take bus 28 from Smørtorget or 42 from the telephone center to the south end of the island (15kr). The **Polar Museum,** Søndre Tollbug. 11b, in a red warehouse on the wharf, details the history of hunting, exploration, and research in the high Arctic. (Open late May to early Sept. daily 11am-7pm; mid-Sept. to mid-May 11am-3pm. 30kr.) For a magnificent view of the city in the midnight sun (roughly May 20-July 22), take the **cable car** to the top of Tromsdalstind (daily 10am-5pm; in summer, weather permitting, until 1am; 55kr). Reach the cable car station on bus 28, or by walking across the enormous bridge over to the mainland.

To sample the nightlife, explore the west end of **Storgata** and its sidestreets. **Blå Rock Cafe,** Strandg. 14, has three floors of posters and rock paraphernalia. (0.5L beer 40kr. Large pizza 90kr, small 85kr. 25kr cover F and Sa nights. Open M-Th 11:30am-2am, F-Sa 11:30am-4am, Su 2pm-2am.) **Middags Kjelleren,** Strandg. 22, in a basement grotto on the corner of Strandskillet, has live rock or blues bands almost every night (40-50kr cover after 11pm; open M-Th 3pm-2am, F-Sa 3pm-4am, Su 6pm-2am).

PRACTICAL INFO, ACCOMMODATIONS, AND FOOD Three to four **buses** per day run south to Narvik (4½hr., 283kr), while two daily buses head to Alta (321kr; not including ferries, 41kr). Buses have a 50% Scanrail discount and leave from the parking lot below Roald Amundsens *plass,* near the water. The northbound Hurtigruten leaves daily at 6:30pm; the southbound at 1:30am (to Honningsvåg 720kr, Bodø 770kr). A standby **flight** from Oslo costs 800kr. The **tourist office,** Storg. 61/63 (tel. 77 61 00 00; fax 77 61 00 10), books rooms in private homes for a 25kr fee (singles from 170kr; doubles from 200kr), and will smother you with facts. From the bus station, walk up Kirkeg. away from the water, and turn left on Storg. (Open June to early Aug. M-F 8:30am-6pm, Sa-Su 10:30am-5pm; mid-Aug. to May M-F 8:30am-4pm.)

The **Elverhøy Youth Hostel (HI),** Gitta Jønnsons vei 4 (tel. 76 94 59 80), is a large student dorm; the rooms have kitchenettes. Take bus 24 at Storg. and Franz Langes gate downtown. (100kr, nonmembers 125kr; 200kr mandatory keys deposit. Reception 8-11am and 5-11pm. Open mid-June to mid-Aug.) To reach **Tromsdalen Camping** (tel. 77 63 80 30), walk across the river to Tromsdalen, 30 minutes from the town center, or spend 15kr and hop on bus 36. (90kr plus 10kr per person. 2- to 4-person huts 250-400kr. Reception 8am-11pm.) The unique dishes available at the arctic restaurant at **Vertshuset Skarven,** Strandtorget 1 (whale, seal, reindeer, and fresh arctic seafood), explain the priciness. (Beer 45kr. Appetizers from 55kr. Dinner from 120kr. Restaurant open daily 5-10:30pm; pub/cafe open daily noon-12:30am. Reservations a must.) More affordable specialties can be found at **Skarven,** Strandtorget 1, in an old stone building on the harbor (main dishes around 75kr). The atmosphere and pancakes of **Paletten,** Storg. 51, are both regional specialties. Grab a beer, or munch something in the cafe at **Amtmandens Datter** on Amtmannsg. (meals 50-100kr).

■ Finnmark

On most maps, Finnmark appears about as inviting as a walk-in freezer. The sun takes a permanent vacation from late November until late January; only the exquisite colors of the *aurora borealis* (Northern Lights) illuminate the frigid countryside. But in summer the snow-capped peaks, vast stretches of coastal tundra, and inland forest bask under the midnight sun, and the landscape becomes an arctic wonderland (beware the dense clouds of mosquitoes). The wilderness of **Finnmarksvidda** spreading east from Tromsø is Europe's largest, a highly popular hiking area dotted with tourist huts. The Oslo and Bergen DNT offices have maps, prices, and more info.

Buses run once or twice per day along the E6, the main highway around the top of Norway; spur lines branch south to Sweden and Finland. Both buses and the *Hurtigruten* are *very* expensive. Scanrailers get 50% off on *Nord-Norge Ekspressen* buses from Bodø to Kirkenes and reductions on some buses run by **FFR.** Some travelers find **hitchhiking** surprisingly successful, though traffic is light and distances are long. Thumbers bring a tent, a warm sleeping bag, and patience. If you're under 25, **flying** is the cheapest way to get to Finnmark. SAS offers 800kr standby *(Superhaik)* to Alta from any SAS destination south of Bodø. In summer, Widerøe Airlines will fly all ages between any two cities north of and including Tromsø for 400kr (make reservations); for those under 21, last-minute fares in Sweden (310 Swedish kr from Stockholm to Kiruna in Swedish Lapland) can be an even better option.

Alta and Hammerfest
Slate-gray mountains, towering cliffs, and an icy green sea make the road from Tromsø north to **Alta,** Finnmark's largest town, a spectacular bus route. One or two **buses** per day run to Tromsø (7-8hr., 300kr, not including 45kr ferries), Hammerfest (3hr., 160kr), Honningsvåg (5hr., 220kr with ferry), Karasjok (4hr., 265kr), and Kautokeino (3hr., 150kr), all 50% off with Scanrail discount.The town stretches along several kilometers of the main highway with two distinct centers. Arriving from the south, the first sign of approaching civilization is the **Alta Museum,** which displays Scandinavia's only prehistoric UNESCO World Heritage site: spectacular rock carvings 2500 to 6200 years old. A network of wooden boardwalks leads you to exposed boulders, on which red-painted figures hunt reindeer, boats navigate the fjords, and cows copulate. (Open June 15-Aug. 15 daily 8am-11pm; shorter hours off-season. 40kr, students 35kr; in winter 35kr, students 30kr.) Two kilometers farther along E6 is the old center, Bossekop, which houses the **tourist office** (Tel. 78 43 77 70. Open mid-July to late Aug. M-F 10am-6pm, Sa 10am-4pm; Su noon-4pm; June and late Aug. M-F 9am-5pm.) Ask about the daily four-hour tours to the nearby **Alta river canyon** (295kr; 5-person minimum), Europe's longest. The **bus station** lies 2km farther on the E6. The **Alta Vaudrerhjem** (tel. 78 43 44 09) mellows another 1km up the road; hang a left at the first traffic circle past the new center on E6, and follow the signs (115kr, nonmembers 130kr; 3 kitchens; reception 8-11am and 5-11pm). **Alta River Camping** (tel. 78 43 43 53) is 4km north of town on Route 94, accessible only by the twice-daily bus to Kautokeino or an hour-long hike. (15kr per person, 75kr per tent. 4-bed huts 350kr. Reception 9am-11pm. Open mid-June to mid-Aug.) Or try **Alta Strand Camping** (tel. 78 43 40 22) or **Wisløff Camping** (tel. 78 43 43 03). A city bus route (16kr) binds all of far-flung Alta, running along E6 from the Alta Museum to the **airport,** 3km east of the new center.

At **Hammerfest,** the world's northernmost town (only the "village" of Honnings-våg is farther north), you can become a member of the Royal and Ancient Polar Bear Society (est. 1963; 125kr) against the backdrop of parading fishing trawlers in the harbor and grazing reindeer in the streets. The *Hurtigruten* stops here for 1½ hours. Daily **buses** head south to Alta and north to Honningsvåg (4hr., 175kr). An express **boat** plies the waters to Honningsvåg twice daily (275kr). Contemplate the midnight sun and catch a good view of town from **Salen Hill,** a short, steep hike uphill from the **tourist office** (tel. 78 41 21 85), on Storg. across from the Hammerfest Hotel (open June-Aug. M-F 8am-7pm, Sa and Su 10am-5pm). From the bus station, walk into town and then follow the near lakeshore to reach the **youth hostel** (tel. 78 41 36 67, or 94 72 20 74; 100kr, nonmembers 125kr).

Poland (Polska)

US$1	= 3.76zł (złoty, or PLN)		1 zł =	US$0.26
CDN$1	= 2.41 zł		1 zł =	CDN$0.41
UK£1	= 6.18 zł		1 zł =	UK£0.16
IR£1	= 5.25 zł		1 zł =	IR£0.19
AUS$1	= 2.15 zł		1 zł =	AUS$0.46
NZ$1	= 1.86 zł		1 zł =	NZ$0.54
SAR1	= 0.59 zł		1 zł =	SAR1.69
DM1	= 2.09 zł		1 zł =	DM0.48

Country Phone Code: 48   **International Dialing Prefix: 00**

Poland's history might have been considerably less painful if the country itself were any less extraordinary. Graced with a fertile and varied landscape, from the amber-strewn shores of the Baltic in the north to the snow-capped peaks of the Tatra range in the south, Poland has also been home to one of the richest intellectual and literary legacies in modern Europe. Crippled by its neighbors from 1795 to 1918, destroyed in World War II, and oppressed under the Soviet thumb, this gem of Central Europe has been quick to assert itself as an important Western power, economically and otherwise. The western half of the country has benefited greatly from investment, and while prosperity has been slower in its eastern regions, Poland is likely to delight most any traveler with its color, historic sites, and rivers of powerful beer.

The native sons and daughters of Poland have a reputation as troublemakers and innovators. Mikołaj Kopernik, the son of a Toruń baker, attained fame by asserting that the earth revolves around the sun. In 1791, a parliament of nobles authored the world's second modern constitution. More recently, the selection of Karol Wojtyła (John Paul II) as the first Polish pope helped unify Polish Catholics and lent strength to the nascent Solidarity movement, the first independent worker's union in Eastern Europe. Polish poets have won the Nobel Prize in Literature twice in the last twenty years, and the first and most gracious of the 1989 Eastern European shakedowns unfolded in Poland; after political imprisonments failed to conquer Solidarity's charismatic leader Lech Wałęsa, he was elected president, a post he held until 1995. Poland's museums and cities remain a physical chronicle of these and other crazy happenings.

Even the pope sometimes kicks back with a copy of *Let's Go: Eastern Europe 1999* for the more detailed coverage of Poland therein.

GETTING THERE

Citizens of the U.S. and Ireland can visit Poland **visa-free** for up to 90 days; citizens of the U.K. can stay up to six months. Australians, Canadians, New Zealanders, and South Africans need **visas.** Single-entry visas (valid 90 days) are US$40 (students under 26 US$30), double-entry visas cost US$55 (students US$42), and 48-hour transit visas run US$20 (students US$15). If you need a visa, contact a Polish embassy (see **Government Information Offices,** p. 4). Processing takes four days (24hr. rush US$35).

LOT, British Airways, and Delta offer **flights** to Warsaw and Kraków from London, New York, Chicago, Toronto, and other cities. **Trains** and **buses** connect to all the neighboring countries, but **Eurail** is not valid in Poland. ALMATUR offers ISIC holders 25% off international fares for the Polish portion of the trip, sells **InterRail** passes, and, for those under 26, provides **Wasteels** tickets and **Eurotrain** passes that give 40% off international train travel. Discount tickets for those under 26 are also sold at major train stations and ORBIS offices. Thefts are a major problem on international overnight trains. **Ferries** run from Sweden and Denmark to Świnoujście and Gdańsk.

GETTING AROUND

PKP trains zip to most towns at bargain prices. In stations, *odjazdy* (departures) are posted in yellow and *przyjazdy* (arrivals) are in white. InterCity and *Ekspresowy* (express) trains are listed in red with "IC" or "Ex." *Pośpieszny* (direct in red), are almost as fast. *Osobowy* (in black), the slowest, are 35% cheaper. All *ekspresowy* and some *pośpieszny* need reservations; if you see a boxed R on the schedule, ask the clerk for a *miejscówka* ("myay-SOOV-ka"). Buy your ticket aboard the train for a surcharge, but find the *konduktor* before he or she finds you, or risk a fine. Tickets are only valid on the day for which they are issued.

PKS buses are cheapest and fastest for short trips. As with trains, red means fast and black means slow. Purchase advance tickets at the bus station. In the countryside, PKS markers (like yellow Mercedes-Benz logos) indicate bus stops, but drivers will often halt wherever you flag them down. Though legal, **hitching** is becoming increasingly dangerous for foreigners. *The Hitchhike Book,* sold by PTTK, includes an insurance policy, an ID card, and vouchers that qualify drivers for compensation.

ESSENTIALS

ORBIS, the Polish state travel bureau, sells international and domestic train tickets and international bus, plane, and ferry tickets. **ALMATUR,** the Polish student travel organization, sells ISIC cards and helps find university dorm rooms in summer. Both provide maps and brochures, as do **PTTK** and **IT** bureaus in every town. While private **tourist agencies'** prices are competitive, you should watch out for scams.

The Polish currency, **złoty** (plural *złote*), is fully convertible. For cash, private **kantor** offices (except those at the airport and train stations) offer better exchange rates than banks. **Bank PKO S.A.** accepts traveler's checks and gives MasterCard and Visa cash advances all over Poland. In 1995, the National Bank issued a new currency—learn the difference between old and new (posters at the airport and train stations show both), and never accept old currency.

Holidays include: January 1; Epiphany; Ash Wednesday; Holy Week and Catholic Easter; Labor Day (May 1); Constitution Day (May 3); Ascension Day (May 21); Corpus Christi (June 11); Assumption Day (Aug. 15); All Saints' Day (Nov. 1); Independence Day (Nov. 11); and Christmas (Dec. 25-26).

COMMUNICATION Mail is becoming increasingly efficient, though still plagued by theft. Airmail usually takes seven to 10 days to the U.S. For *Poste Restante,* put a "1" after the city name to ensure it goes to the main post office. Older pay **phones** use tokens (*żetony;* "A" for local calls and "C" for intercity calls); newer phones use **phone cards.** These phones have card slots and instructions in English. Both tokens and phone cards are available at any *poczta* (post office) as well as some kiosks. To reach an **AT&T Direct** operator, dial 010 480 01 11 (from outside Warsaw dial 0 and wait for a tone first); **BT Direct,** 00 800 441 11 44; **Canada Direct,** 00 800 111 4118; **MCI WorldPhone,** 010 480 02 22 or 00 800 111 21 22; and **Sprint Access,** 00 800 111 3115. To make a **collect call,** write the name of the city or country and the number plus *"Rozmowa 'R'"* on a slip of paper, hand it to a clerk, and be patient.

Many Poles speak at least a little English, German, or French. Polish spelling is phonetic and has some letters which don't belong to the Latin alphabet: *"ł"* sounds like a "w," *"ą"* is a nasal "o"; *"ę"* is a nasal "eh"; *"ó"* and *"u"* are equivalent to a short "oo"; and *"ż"* and *"rz"* are both like the "s" in pleasure. A dash above a consonant softens it. The language also has consonantal clusters: *"sz"* is "sh," *"cz"* is "ch," *"ch"* and *"h"* are equivalent to each other. When addressing a man, use the formal *"Pan,"* with a woman, use *"Pani."* The following chart lists important words and phrases in Polish:

Yes/No	Tak/Nie	tak/nyeh
Hello	Cześć	tcheshch
Please/You're welcome	Proszę	PROH-sheh
Thank you	Dziękuję	jeng-KOO-yeh
Where is...?	Gdzie jest...?	g-jeh yehst
Excuse me	Przepraszam	psheh-PRAH-sham
Do you speak English?	Czy Pan(i) mówi po anglicki?	tcheh PAHN (-ee) MOO-vee poh an-GLITS-kee
I don't understand	Nie rozumiem	nyeh roh-ZOO-myem
How much does this cost?	Ile to kosztuje?	EE-leh toh kosh-TOO-yeh
I'd like a...	Chciał(a) bym...	HCHOW (-ah) bim
Check, please.	Proszę rachunek	PROH-sheh rah-HOON-ehk
Help!	Na pomoc!	nah POH-motz

ACCOMMODATIONS AND CAMPING Grandmotherly **private room** owners smother travelers at train stations or outside tourist offices. Private rooms are usually safe, clean, and convenient, but sometimes far from city centers. Expect to pay about US$10 per person. **PTSM** is the national hostel organization. **HI youth hostels** (*schronisko młodzieżowe*) run from basic to divine; they're everywhere and run US$3 per night (less for "juniors" under 18 or 26, more for nonmembers). Hot water is standard. **University dorms** transform into spartan but cheap housing in July and August. Ask at ALMATUR; the Warsaw office can arrange stays in all major cities. **PTTK** runs a number of hotels called **Dom Turysty,** where you can stay in multi-bed rooms (US$2-5), as well as budget singles and doubles. Many towns have a **Biuro Zakwaterowań,** which arranges stays in private homes. Rooms come in three categories based on location and hot-water availability; category 1 is the best.

Campsites average US$2 per person, US$4 with a car. **Bungalows** are often available; a bed costs about US$5. *Polska Mapa Campingów* lists all campsites. ALMATUR also runs a number of sites in summer; ask for a list at one of their offices.

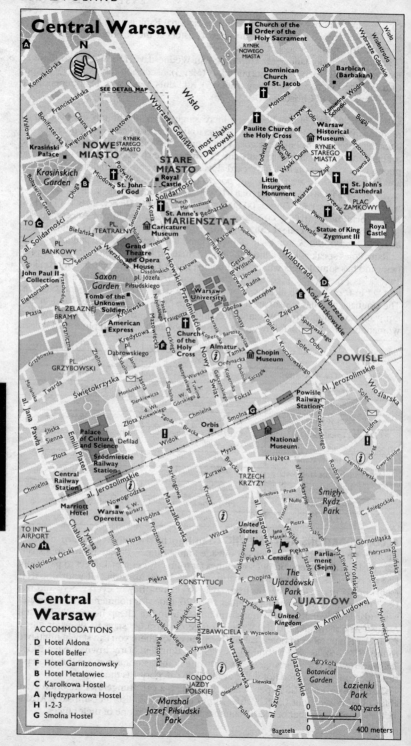

Central Warsaw

N

SEE DETAIL MAP

A

Konwiktorska
Franciszkańska
Bonifraterska
Świętojerska
Ciasna
Mostowa

NOWE MIASTO

RYNEK STAREGO MIASTA

Krasiński Palace

Krasińskich Garden

Długa

B

Miodowa
Podwale

St. John of God

STARE MIASTO

Royal Castle

al. Solidarności

Church Mariensztat

St. Anne's Bednarska

TO C

al. Solidarności

Bielańska

PL. BANKOWY

Senatorska Wierzbowa

John Paul II Collection

Elektoralna

Ptasia

PL. ŻELAZNEJ BRAMY

American Express

Graniczna

Grzybowska

PL. GRZYBOWSKI

Twarda

Świętokrzyska

al. Jana Pawła II

Śliska
Sienna
Złota
Chmielna

Marriott Hotel

TO INT'L AIRPORT AND

Tytusa Chałubińskiego

Wojciecha Oczki

PL. TEATRALNY

Caricature Museum

Grand Theatre and Opera House

Ossolińskich

Saxon Garden

Tomb of the Unknown Soldier

Królewska

Kredytowa

Dąbrowskiego

Zielna

Moniuszki
Sienkiewicza

d.W. Kniewskiego

Złota
Zgoda
Bracka

pl. Defilad

Palace of Culture and Science

Śródmieście Railway Station

Central Railway Station

al. Jerozolimskie

Nowogrodzka

S.W. Barbary

Warsaw Operetta

Wspólna

Hoża

Emilii Plater

Złota

Chmielna

MARIENSZTAT

pl. Józefa Piłsudskiego

Warsaw University

Church of the Holy Cross

Nowy Świat

Krakowskie Przedmieście

Traugutta

Ordynacka

Almatur

Chopin Museum

Tamka

Wareckia

Foksal

Smolna

Orbis

Widok

Mysia

Żurawia

Krucza

Bracka

PL. TRZECH KRZYŻY

Książęca

Wisła

most Śląsko-Dąbrowski

Wybrzeże Gdańskie

Wisłostrada

POWIŚLE

Powiśle Railway Station

National Museum

Al. Jerozolimskie

Wiślarska

Solec

Ludna

D Wybrzeże Kościuszkowskie

E Spasowskiego

Dobra

Zajęcza

Topiel i Kruczkowskiego

Smoleński

Czerniakowska

Rozbrat

Śmigły-Rydz Park

Górnośląska

Parkingowa
Marszałkowska

F. Nullo

Bolesława

Prusa

al. Na Skarpie

F. Chopina

Piotra

Jana Matejki

United States

Mokotowska

Piękna

Wilcza

PL. KONSTYTUCJI

Koszykowa

al. Róż

PL. ZBAWICIELA

al. Wyzwolenia

S. Noskowskiego

Śniadeckich

Lwowska

L. Waryńskiego

Jaworzyńska

RONDO JAZDY POLSKIEJ

Litewska

Polna

Marshal Józef Piłsudski Park

Bagatela

Rektorska

Canada

Parliament (Sejm)

The Ujazdowski Park

UJAZDÓW

United Kingdom

al. Armii Ludowej

Agrykola

Botanical Garden

Łazienki Park

Fabryczna

Kozmińska

Rozbrat

J.-H. Wrońskiego

Myśliwiecka

al. Ujazdowskie

Górnośląska

Ujazdowskie

Wiejska

Central Warsaw

ACCOMMODATIONS

D Hotel Aldona
E Hotel Belfer
F Hotel Garnizonowsky
B Hotel Metalowiec
C Karolkowa Hostel
A Międzyparkowa Hostel
H 1-2-3
G Smolna Hostel

POLAND

0 _____ 400 yards
0 _____ 400 meters

Detail map

✝ **Church of the Order of the Holy Sacrament**

RYNEK NOWEGO MIASTA

✝ **Dominican Church of St. Jacob**

✝ **Paulite Church of Holy Cross**

✝ Little Insurgent Monument

✝ Barbican (Barbakan)

Boleść
Mostowa
Krzywe Koło
Kamienne Schodki
Wodna
Bugaj
Brzozowa
Dawna

Warsaw Historical Museum

RYNEK STAREGO MIASTA

✝ **St. John's Cathedral**

PLAC ZAMKOWY

Statue of King Zygmunt III

Royal Castle

Podwale
Szeroki Dunaj
Wąski Dunaj
Piekarska
Rycerska
Piwna

Świętojańska

Wisła

Wisłostrada

Wybrzeże Gdańskie

FOOD AND DRINK Monks, merchants, invaders, and dynastic unions have all flavored Polish cuisine—a blend of hearty dishes drawing from French, Italian, and Jewish traditions. And while Polish food is often loaded with cholesterol, it is less starchy than Czech cuisine, and less fiery than that of Hungary or Bulgaria.

A Polish meal always starts with a soup. From a typical menu, you should be able to choose between *barszcz* (beet broth), *chłodnik* (a cold beet soup with buttermilk and hard-boiled eggs), *kapuśniak* (sauerkraut soup), *krupnik* (barley soup), and *żurek* (barley-flour soup loaded with eggs and sausage). *Bigos* (sauerkraut cooked with beef and mushrooms) and *flaczki* (tripe) can be eaten either as soup or entree.

More filling main courses include *gołąbki* (cabbage rolls stuffed with meat and rice), *kotlet schabowy* (pork chops), *kopytka* (potato dumplings topped with buttered bread crumbs), *naleśniki* (cream-topped pancakes filled with cottage cheese or jam), and *pierogi* (dumplings with various fillings—meat, potato, blueberry...).

Poland is bathed in beer, vodka, and spiced liquor. *Żywiec* is the favorite strong brew, and *EB* is its excellent, gentler brother. *Wódka* ranges from wheat to potato: *Wyborowa, Żytnia,* and *Polonez* usually decorate private bars, though the so-called *Kosher* is rumored to be top-notch. The herbal *Żubrówka* vodka comes with a blade of grass from the region where the bison roam. *Miód* and *krupnik*—two kinds of mead—were best loved by the gentry, and most idle grandmas make *nalewka na porzeczce* (black currant vodka).

■ Warsaw (Warszawa)

Once again the world's largest Polish city (a title long held by Chicago), Warsaw is quickly throwing off its Soviet legacy to emerge as an important international business center—witness the crop of new skyscrapers being built in the city center. Tourists come to take in the museums, listen to the concerts, and feast in the restaurants of the city that rebuilt itself from rubble—83 percent was destroyed during World War II. The university infuses Warsaw with young blood, keeping the energy high and the nightlife lively.

ORIENTATION AND PRACTICAL INFORMATION

Warsaw, the country's principal air and rail hub, spreads out in east-central Poland, about 150km from the Belarusian border. The **Śródmieście** (city center) and most points of interest lie on the west bank of the **Wisła River,** which bisects the city. Near the **Warszawa Centralna** train station, the intersection of **ul. Marszałkowska** and **Aleje Jerozolimskie** forms the center of the modern downtown and serves as a major bus and tram stop. Beyond, Al. Jerozolimskie extends east to **rondo Charles de Gaulle. Ul. Nowy Świat** runs north and then becomes **ul. Krakowskie Przedmieście,** which leads to the Old Town. A right at rondo Charles de Gaulle (coming from the station) puts you on **Al. Ujazdowskie,** which leads down embassy row to the Łazienki Palace. A good **map** of the whole city with bus, tram, and metro routes is essential.

Telephone Code: 022 for 6-digit numbers; 02 for 7-digit numbers.

Flights: Port Lotniczy Warszawa-Okęcie, ul. Żwirki i Wigury (tel. 650 30 00; staffed M-F 7:30am-6pm), commonly referred to as Terminal 1. Take bus 175 to the center (after 11pm, bus 611). Buy bus tickets at the Ruch kiosk in the departure hall or at the *kantor* outside (1.40zł, students 0.70zł, plus 1.40zł for a large suitcase or backpack). **Airport-City Bus** (5.60zł, students 2.80zł; luggage free) is a faster way to the center and back (daily 5:30am-11pm; M-F 3 per hr.; Sa-Su 2 per hr.). Buy tickets from the driver.

Trains: Warszawa Centralna, ul. Jerozolimskie 54 (tel. 25 50 00), in the center of town, is the most convenient stop. Most employees speak only Polish; write down where and when you want to go, and ask *"Który peron?"* to find your platform. To: Berlin (7-8hr., 100zł), Budapest (10hr., 192zł), Kiev (22-24hr., 120zł), Minsk (12hr., 110zł), Moscow (27-30hr., 220zł), Prague (12-14hr., 153zł), and Polish cities.

POLAND

Buses: PKS Warszawa Zachodnia, Al. Jerozolimskie 144 (tel. 94 33, info tel. 524 41 45), sends buses north and west of the city. Buses from **PKS Warszawa Stadion,** on the other side of the river, head to the east and south. Both stations are easily reached by taking the commuter train from the Warszawa Śródmieście station (next to Warszawa Centralna; 1.60zł). **Polski Express,** Al. Jana Pawła II (tel. 630 29 67), offers fast and comfortable bus service to Gdańsk (6hr., 30zł), Kraków (6hr., 25zł), Lublin (4hr., 18.50zł), and Szczecin (9½hr, 32zł).

Public Transportation: Bus and **tram** lines are marked on some city maps. Day trams and buses (including express lines) cost 1.40zł, night buses 3zł; large baggage costs 1.40zł per piece. Buy tickets at a Ruch kiosk or street vendor, and punch the end marked by the arrow in the machines on board. Warsaw's **metro** only connects the southern border of town with the center (1.40zł).

Taxis: Stands are marked by blue-and-white signs. For relatively cheap 24hr. taxi service, call 919 or 96 22. Taxi usually start at 3.60zł plus 1.40zł per km. At night, the rates are about 50% higher. Cabs frequently overcharge.

Tourist Offices: Warszawskie Centrum Informacji Turystycznej (WCIT), pl. Zamkowy 1B (tel. 635 18 81; fax 831 04 64), at the entrance to the Old Town. The friendly, busy staff runs an information line and provides maps, guidebooks, currency exchange, and hotel reservations. Pick up the *Warsaw Insider* (4zł), jammed with info, listings, and reviews. Open M-F 9am-8pm, Sa 10am-8pm, Su 11am-6pm. **Orbis,** ul. Bracka 16 (tel. 827 71 40 or 827 76 04), with an entrance on Al. Jerozolimskie near Nowy Świat, sells train, ferry, and bus tickets. Open M-F 8am-7pm, Sa 9am-3pm.

Embassies: Clustered around Al. Ujazdowskie. **Australia,** ul. Estońska 3/5 (tel. 617 60 81). Open M-Th 8:30am-1pm and 2-5pm. Visa section Piękna 2 open M-F 8:45am-1pm. **Belarus,** ul. Ateńska 67 (tel. 617 39 54). **Canada,** ul. Matejki 1/5 (tel. 629 80 51). Open M-F 8am-4:30pm. **Russia,** ul. Belwederska 49, bldg. C (tel. 621 34 53). Open W and F 8am-1pm. **Ukraine,** Al. Ujazdowskie 13 (tel. 629 32 01). **U.K.,** Al. Róż 1 (tel. 628 10 01). Open M-F 9am-noon and 2-4pm. **U.S.,** Al. Ujazdowskie 29/31 (tel. 628 30 41). Open M-F 8:30am-5pm.

Currency Exchange: Hotels, banks, tourist offices, and private *kantors* (which have slightly better rates) throughout the city exchange cash. The counters at the main train station and the airport departures area are open 24hr. **Bank PKO S.A.,** pl. Bankowy 2 (tel. 637 10 61), in the blue skyscraper, cashes AmEx and Visa traveler's checks for a 1% commission and gives MC and Visa cash advances. Branches throughout the city; all open M-F 8am-6pm. Cirrus/MC **ATMs** abound.

American Express: ul. Krakowskie Przedmieście 11 (tel. 635 20 02). Exchanges cash and traveler's checks with no commission. Also holds mail (send to box 159) and provides emergency cash advances for card members. Address mail to "American Express Travel" (PL 00-069). Open M-F 9am-6pm.

Luggage Storage: At the main train station, below the main hall. Lockers come in 3 sizes: "A" (5zł per day), "B" (7zł per day), and "C" (14zł per day). Open 24hr.

English Bookstore: American Bookstore, ul. Krakowskie Przedmieście 45 (tel. 826 01 61; fax 654 06 75). A fine selection of fiction, reference books, and periodicals. Open M-F 11am-7pm, Sa 11am-8pm, Su 11am-6pm.

Gay and Lesbian Hotline: tel. 628 52 22. The Lambda Center Information Line available both in English and Polish. Very friendly, very helpful, they'll tell you what's up and where. Tu and W 6-9pm, F 4-10pm. The Lambda Center has a new location at Tzernikowska 178 (room 16), but call ahead before visiting.

Laundromat: ul. Karmelicka 17 (tel. 831 73 17; call to reserve). Take bus 180 north from ul. Marszałkowska toward Żoliborz and get off at ul. Anielewicza. Bring your own detergent. Wash and dry 17.40zł. Open M-F 9am-5pm, Sa 9am-1pm.

Emergencies: Fire, tel. 998. **Ambulance,** tel. 999.

Police: tel. 997.

Crisis Lines: 24hr. Drugs, tel. 823 65 32, some English spoken. Open M-F 9am-5pm. **Mental Health,** tel. 295 813. **STDs,** 629 79 77.

24-Hour Pharmacy: Apteka Grabowski (tel. 825 13 72), at the central train station.

Medical Assistance: Medical Info Line, ul. Smolna 34/22 (tel. 827 89 62). Directs callers to private doctors and dentists. Open M-F 8am-8pm, Sa 8am-3pm. **24hr. service** and **ambulance,** ul. Hoża 56 (tel. 999 or 628 24 24).

POLAND

Post Office: ul. Świętokrzyska 31/33 (tel. 826 75 11). Take your ticket and await your turn. For stamps and letters, press "D." For packages, press "F." For *Poste Restante*, press "C" and head to *kasa* 12 or 13. Open 24hr. **Postal Code:** 00-001.
Internet Access: Cyberia Internet Cafe, ul. Krakowskie Przedmieście 4/6 (http://www.cyberia.com.pl). 12zł per hr. Open daily 9am-midnight.
Telephones: At the post office. Tokens and **phone cards** available. Open 24hr.

ACCOMMODATIONS AND CAMPING

Prices rise and rooms become scarce in July and August; call ahead. Differences in hotel prices often do not reflect differences in quality. For help finding private rooms, check in with **Syrena,** ul. Krucza 17 (tel. 628 75 40), off Al. Jerozolimskie (singles from 51zł; doubles from 74zł; open M-Sa 9am-7pm, Su 9am-5pm). WCIT (see **Practical Information,** above) can help find rooms.

Schronisko Młodzieżowe (HI), ul. Smolna 30, top floor (tel. 827 89 52), across from the National Museum. You can make the short walk from the train station, or take any tram headed east 3 stops to Nowy Świat. Price and location can't be beat. Regulations are enforced. Kitchen and baggage room. Only 2 showers. 16zł, nonmembers 22zł. Sheets 2.50zł. Lockout 10am-4pm. Curfew 11pm. 3-day max. stay.
Schronisko Młodzieżowe (HI), ul. Karolkowa 53a (tel. 632 88 29). Take tram 22 or 24 west from Al. Jerozolimskie or the train station; get off at "Okopowa" and go left on al. Solidarności; it will be on your right. Excellently maintained and uncrowded. Kitchen. Great showers. Lockout 10am-5pm. Curfew 11pm. Dorms 18zł, nonmembers 24zł; doubles 68zł; triples 72zł. Sheets 3.50zł.
Schronisko Młodzieżowe, ul. Międzyparkowa 4/6 (tel. 31 17 66), close to the river, between 2 parks. Take tram 2, 6, or 18 northbound from ul. Marszałkowska to "K.K.S. Polonia." The hostel is across the street as you continue down the road. The least formal of the hostels in town. Singles 9zł. Sheets 3zł. Curfew 11pm. Open April 15-Oct. 15.
Hotel Metalowiec, ul. Długa 29 (tel. 831 40 20; fax 635 31 38), 3 blocks away from the Old Town near the "Arsenał" stop. Very affordable and in a great location. Clean rooms. Singles 42zł; doubles 67zł; quads 81zł. Private bath 10zł extra.
Hotel Belfer, Wybrzeże Kościuszkowskie 31/33 (tel. 625 05 71, reservations 625 26 00; fax 625 26 00). From the train station, take any tram east to Most Poniatowskiego, then go north (with the river on your right) along Wisłostrada, which becomes Wybrzeże Kościuszkowskie. Comfortable rooms, some with views. Singles 80zł, with bath 112zł; doubles 108zł, with bath 152zł.
Hotel Aldona, Wybrzeże Kościuszkowskie (tel. 628 58 83). Same directions as Hotel Belfer. On a ship floating in the Wisła. A fun budget option, unless the thought of sleeping on a boat makes you queasy. Singles 55zł; doubles (bunk beds) 75zł.
Hotel Garnizonowy, ul. Mazowiecka 10 (tel. 682 20 65 or 682 20 69; tel./fax 827 23 65). A block from ul. Krakowskie Przedmieście off ul. Świętokrzyska, one of the nicest affordable hotels in the downtown area. Singles 95zł, with bath 180zł; doubles 130zł, with bath 220zł; triples 290zł; bed in a double 65zł, triple or quad 50zł.
Camping "123," ul. Bitwy Warszawskiej 1920r. 15/17 (tel. 822 91 21; tel./fax 823 37 48), by the main bus station. Take bus 127 to "Zachodnia" and cross the street at the traffic circle. Spacious and close to downtown. 9zł per person, children 4-10 6zł. Small tent space 7zł, large 8zł. Open year-round.

FOOD

Food stands line ul. Marszałkowska. You can blow your budget on roast duck or grilled salmon at any of Warsaw's finest, bunched around **Rynek Starego Miasta,** but proletarian cafeterias are much cheaper and more colorful. There is a **24-hour grocery** at the central train station; you can also do late-night shopping at **Delikatesy,** ul. Nowy Świat 53 (open 7am-5am). Fish, poultry, and meat is often sold by weight in restaurants; ask about the average weight to avoid a nasty surprise.

POLAND

Restaurants

Pod Samsonem, ul. Freta 3/5. Cheap eats on the way from Stare Miasto to Nowe, opposite Maria Skłodowska-Curie's museum. Polish-Jewish cuisine. *Cymes* salad 3zł. Iced tea (with ice!) 2zł. Open daily 10am-10pm.

Bar Uniwersytecki, ul. Krakowskie Przedmieście 16/18, next to the university under a yellow awning. As Polish as it gets. Salad 1.18zł; soups 0.75-1.30zł; pork chops 4.70zł. English menu. Open M-F 7am-8pm, Sa-Su 9am-5pm.

Bar Pod Barbakanem, ul. Mostowa 27/29, entrance on ul. Freta. A popular cafeteria-style eatery between Stare and Nowe Miasto. A full meal runs only 6zł. Long menu, English ones available. Open M-F 8am-6pm, Sa-Su 9am-5pm.

Bar Mleczny Familijny, ul. Nowy Świat 39. Traditional (fat) Polish (plentiful) food for the light wallet. *Pierogi* with meat 4zł. Open M-F 7am-8pm, Sa-Su 9am-5pm.

Zapiecek, ul. Piwna 34/36, at the corner of ul. Zapiecek in the Old Town. German ambiance and Polish cuisine. Veal 14zł. Outdoor dining. Open daily 11am-11pm.

Restauracja Boruta, ul. Freta 38, on Rynek Nowego Miasta. Dine outdoors or in. Roasted duck 26zł. Vegetarian menu. Open daily 11am until the last guest leaves.

Restauracja Ekologiczna "Nove Miasto," Rynek Nowego Miasta 13/15. Warsaw's first natural foods restaurant. Organically grown vegetarian main dishes 25-40zł. Encores of Polish beer (0.5L *Żywiec* 8zł) and German wine. Outdoor seating available. Live music nightly. Open daily 10am-midnight.

Cafes

Kawiarnia Bazyliszek, Rynek Starego Miasta 3/9. A fancy outdoor cafe amid the splendor of the Old Town. Coffee 5zł. Open daily 11am-11pm.

Gwiazdeczka, ul. Piwna 40/42, in the Old Town. The menu is full of snacks and coffees (3-8zł); beer and cocktails are also tempting. Open daily 9am-10pm.

Cyberia Internet Cafe, ul. Krakowskie Przedmieście 4/6 (tel. 828 1447; http://www.cyberia.com.pl). No signs to identify it, the cafe is next to Burger King (up the stairs and to the left). A little too Euro-chic for some tastes, but the coffee (7zł), which the helpful staff might make you buy to go with your time on the 'Net (see **Internet Access,** p. 687), is quite good. Open daily 9am-midnight.

SIGHTS

Razed beyond recognition during World War II, Warsaw was rebuilt from rubble by defiant and proud survivors. The city requires quite a bit of time to explore fully, since a few important sights are quite distant from the downtown area.

Stare Miasto, Nowe Miasto, and Trakt Królewski

Warsaw's postwar reconstruction shows its finest face in the narrow, cobbled streets and colorful facades of the **Stare Miasto** (Old Town), at the end of ul. Krakowskie Przedmieście. Right of the entrance to the Old Town stands the impressive **Zamek Królewski** (Royal Castle), burned down in 1939 but masterfully restored in the 1970s. Many residents of Warsaw risked their lives hiding the castle's priceless artworks during Nazi plundering, and the castle has since become a symbol of Polish patriotism. Past the Royal Castle, turn left onto ul. Świętojańska to reach the 14th-century **Katedra Św. Jana** (Cathedral of St. John), the oldest church in Warsaw. (*Open daylight hours.*) From here, Ul. Świętojańska takes you straight to the wonderfully restored Renaissance and Baroque houses of **Rynek Starego Miasta** (Old Town Square). Most of the houses surrounding the *rynek* were razed to their foundations during the Warsaw Uprising, but a few managed to survive World War II; the **house at #31** dates from the 14th century. The square now oozes with beer gardens and kitschy art.

Ul. Krzywe Koło leads from the square to **Barbakan** (Barbican), a rare example of 16th-century Polish fortifications, where street performers now sing folk music to entertain the crowds. Through the Barbican Gate, ul. Freta marks the edge of the **Nowe Miasto** (New Town), which, in spite of its name, is actually the second-oldest district in the city. The great physicist and chemist **Maria Skłodowska-Curie,** winner of two Nobel prizes, was born at ul. Freta 16 in 1867; the house is now a museum chronicling her life. (*Open Tu-Sa 10am-4pm, Su 10am-2pm. 2zl, students 1zl.*)

Lined with palaces and churches as well as hordes of tourists, the 4km **Trakt Królewski** (Royal Route) is the city's most attractive thoroughfare. The route begins on **plac Zamkowy** (Castle Square) in the Old Town and continues along **ul. Krakowskie Przedmieście.** Fryderyk Chopin gave his first public concert in the **Pałac Radziwiłłów** (a.k.a. **Pałac Namiestnikowski**) at #46/48, now the Polish White House. The Chopin theme continues at **Kościół Wizytek** (Church of the Visitation Nuns), one block down the street, where he was an organist. Much of his composing was done in the **Pałac Czapskich,** now home to the Academy of Fine Arts and the **Salonik Chopinów** (The Chopins' Drawing Room). *(Open M-F 10am-2pm. 1zl, students 0.50zl.)* If you really can't get enough of the mop-topped composer, waltz over to the **Muzeum Fryderyka Chopina** in Zamek Ostrogskich, ul. Okólnik 1; to get there, walk a few blocks down the street from the Academy, turn left onto ul. Ordynacka, and follow it to ul. Okólnik. *(Open May-Sept. M, W, and F 10am-5pm, Th noon-6pm, Sa-Su 10am-2pm; closed on holidays. 4zl, students 2zl.)*

In front of Kościól św. Krzyża, a complex of rebuilt palaces on the left belongs to **Uniwersytet Warszawski,** founded in 1816. The **Pomnik Mikołaja Kopernika** (Copernicus Monument), a permanent seat for the image of the famous astronomer, marks the end of ul. Krakowskie Przedmieście. The Royal Route, however, continues along **ulica Nowy Świat** (New World St.), a glorious street named for a working-class settlement of the 17th century. The street ends at the **Botanical Gardens,** on the left side of Al. Ujazdowskie, and the **Park Łazienki,** summer residence of the last Polish king. *(Botanical Gardens open M-Th 9am-8pm, F-Su 10am-8pm. 3zl, students 1.5zl.)* The striking Neoclassical **Pałac Łazienkowski,** also called **Pałac na Wodzie** (Palace on the Water) harbors galleries of 17th- and 18th-century art. *(Open Tu-Su 9:30am-4pm barring rain. 8zl, students 5zl. English tours 20zl.)*

Commercial District, the Ghetto, and Wilanów

Warsaw's commercial district lies southwest of the Old Town along ul. Marszałkowska. Here, at Al. Jerozolimskie 3, is the **Muzeum Narodowe** (National Museum), Poland's largest museum. *(Open Tu-W and F 10am-4pm, Th noon-5pm, Sa-Su 10am-5pm; 5zl, students 2.50zl, Sa free; closed M and days following public holidays.)* The galleries illustrate the evolution of Polish art over the centuries and also showcase medieval art and the works of German, Italian, and Dutch painters. Also in this part of town, the 70-story "Stalinist Gothic" **Pałac Kultury i Nauki** (Palace of Culture and Science), ul. Marszałkowska, is a fitting monument to Stalin—larger than life, omnipresent, and hideous. *(Open daily 9am-6pm; 7.50zl.)* Locals say the view from the top is exceptional, in large part because it doesn't include the palace itself. Below, **plac Defilad** (Parade Square) is the largest square in all of Europe, even bigger than Moscow's Red Square.

The modern Muranów (literally "walled") neighborhood of Warsaw holds few vestiges of what was once a community numbering nearly 400,000 Jews. At **Umschlagplatz,** a monument marks the spot where Nazis gathered 300,000 Jews for transport to death camps. A small section of the original **ghetto wall** still stands between two apartment buildings in the courtyard at ul. Sienna 55, just west of al. Jana Pawła II. The beautifully reconstructed **Nożyk Synagogue,** ul. Twarda 6, lies just north of the Pałac Kultury. On ul. Zamenhofa, look for the **Pomnik Bohaterów Ghetta** (Monument of the Ghetto Heroes). The **Cmentarz Żydowski** (Jewish Cemetery), in the western corner of the district, is a forest-covered treasure of gravestone craftsmanship. *(Open M-Th 9am-3pm, F 9am-1pm.)* **Muzeum Więzienia Pawiak,** ul. Dzielna 24/26, was a prison used by Nazis for the torture, execution, and imprisonment of over 100,000 Polish prisoners. *(Open W 9am-5pm, Th and Sa 9am-4pm, F 10am-5pm, and Su 10am-4pm. Children under 14 not admitted. Donation requested.)* Today, the museum carefully chronicles the events, and exhibits moving artwork, poetry, and religious artifacts created by the prisoners while they were there.

After his coronation in 1677, King Jan III Sobieski bought the village of Milanowo, had its existing mansion rebuilt into a Baroque-style palace, and named the new residence **Wilanów** (Villa Nova). The grounds were opened to visitors in 1805. Since then, the **Palac Wilanowski** has functioned both as a museum and as a residence for

POLAND

the highest-ranking guests of the Polish state. *(Palace open W-M 9:30am-2:30pm, Su 9:30am-4:30pm. 3zl, students 1zl.)* **Muzeum Plakatu** (Poster Museum), next to the palace, displays 50,000 posters from the last 100 years. *(Open Tu-Su 10am-3:30pm. 6zl, students 3zl.)* To get here, take bus 180 or express bus B from ul. Marszałkowska, or buses 122, 130, or 519 south to their end-stop, "Wilanów."

ENTERTAINMENT

Don't be fooled by people who tell you Warsaw doesn't have much nightlife outside the cafes of the Old Town and ul. Nowy Świat. Concerts fill the city year-round, and students energize several excellent clubs and bars on weekends.

Performances

Classical concerts fill the Gallery of Sculptures in **Stara Pomarańczarnia** near Pałac Łazienkowski on Sundays in June and July. Inquire about concerts at **Warszawskie Towarzystwo Muzyczne** (Warsaw Music Society), ul. Morskie Oko 2 (tel. 49 68 56; tickets available M-F 9am-3pm and before concerts). **Pomnik Chopina** (Chopin Monument), nearby in Park Łazienkowski, hosts free Sunday performances by classical artists (May-Oct. noon and 4pm). **Teatr Wielki**, pl. Teatralny 1 (tel. 826 32 87), Warsaw's main opera and ballet hall, offers performances almost daily. **Filharmonia Narodowa**, ul. Jasna 5 (tel. 826 72 81), gives regular concerts but is closed in summer. Classical music is also played in Zamek Królewski's **Sala Koncertowa**, pl. Zamkowy 4 (tel. 657 21 70; tickets sold Tu-Su 10am-3pm). Jazz, rock, and blues fans have quite a few options as well, especially in summer. **Sala Kongresowa** (tel. 620 49 80), in the Palace of Culture and Science, hosts excellent jazz and rock concerts.

Pubs and Nightclubs

Warsaw's pubs are popular with both trendy locals and visitors. Drinks are expensive, but many pubs compensate by offering live music. The nightclub and dance scene shifts frequently; posters around town are the best source for the latest info. Gay life is a bit underground here; the gay and lesbian hotline (tel. 628 52 22; Tu-W 6-9pm, F 4-10pm) has the latest info. *Inaczej* and *Filo* list gay establishments.

Morgan's, ul. Okólnik 1 (enter on ul. Tamka; tel. 826 81 38), under the Chopin Museum. A comfortable, friendly Irish pub with regulars who are actually Irish. Excellent Guinness (0.5L 12zł). Open daily noon until the last guest leaves.

Club Giovanni, ul. Krakowskie Przedmieście 24 (tel. 826 92 39), on the premises of Uniwersytet Warszawski, to the right and down the steps as you enter through the main gate. Popular with a low-key student crowd. A good, friendly hangout bar at all hours, complete with foosball and comfy leather chairs. Plenty of beer on tap (5zł). Open M-Th 10am-1am, F 10am-3am, Sa 1pm-3am, Su 1pm-1am.

The Irish Pub, ul. Miodowa 3. The name, decor, and beer are Irish, but the older clientele of revelers is local. Folk and country music nightly at 7:30pm. Open daily 9am until the last guest leaves.

Harenda Pub, ul. Krakowskie Przedmieście 4/6, at Hotel Harenda. Enter from ul. Karasia. Outdoor seating. The friendly crowd usually stays until closing, but don't go for a Polish lesson. 0.5L *Żywiec* 8.50zł. Open daily 8am-3am.

Park, al. Niepodległości 196. This international disco is one of the more popular student hangouts in Warsaw. Listen for the loud music through the trees. Polish rock Tu 8pm-2am, classic rock W 8pm-2am, metal and punk Th 8pm-2am, pop and rock F-Sa 9pm-3am, reggae Su 10pm-2am. Cover 8zł, students 4zł; F-Sa 16zł, 4zł.

Jazz Club Akwarium, ul. Emilii Plater 49. An older crowd enjoys the best live jazz in town. Schedule posted. Open daily 11am-11pm or later, F-Sa until 3am.

Paradise, at the corner of ul. Wawelska and ul. Żwirki i Wigury. Gay club at the grounds of the "Skra" sports complex. Disco on Friday and Saturday nights. A large, bright dance floor, mellow-out area, and patio if you need a breather. Men and women. Open Su-Th 10am-midnight, F-Sa 10am-5am.

POLAND

■ Łódź

A stroll down the pedestrian al. Piotrkowska among the beautiful historic buildings, busy shops, and student hangouts, makes one wonder why Łódź (WOODGE), Poland's second largest city, is so often unfairly overlooked. One block northwest of the monument at **plac Wolności**, which crowns the northern end of ul. Piotrkowska, stands the grandiose **Poznański Palace,** completely renovated as of August 1998. Walking four blocks south from the palace along ul. Gdańska brings you to **Muzeum Sztuki w Łodzi** (Łódź Fine Arts Museum), ul. Więckowskiego 36, home to 20th-century art by artists like Max Ernst and Piet Mondrian. (Open Tu 10am-5pm, W and F 11am-5pm, Th noon-7pm, Sa-Su 10am-4pm. 5zł, students 3zł, Tu-Th free.) The most affecting sight in Łódź, and one of the most beautiful, is the sprawling **Cmentarz Żydowski** (Jewish Cemetery). It is the largest in all of Europe, with more than 180,000 tombstones, many of them quite elaborate. (Open Su-F 9am-4pm, closed on Jewish holidays. 3zł admission goes toward maintenance; free for those visiting the graves of relatives.) Take tram 1, 15, or 19 north to the end of the line (30min.). Continue up the street to the first corner and make a sharp left turn onto the cobblestone ul. Zmienna before the car lot, and continue until the small gate in the wall. Near the entrance there's a memorial to the Jews killed in the Łódź Ghetto (Europe's largest), and signs lead the way to the **Pole Ghettowe** (Ghetto Fields).

Trains connect to Kraków (express 39zł) and Warsaw (2hr., express 39zł) from the main station on al. Piotrkowska. The **bus station**, attached to the main train station, sends buses to Kraków (5hr., 25zł), Warsaw (14zł), and Wrocław (4-5hr., 23zł). The **IT tourist office,** ul. Traugutta 18 (tel. (042) 633 72 99), in Dom Kultury, across al. Jana Kilińskiego from Łódź Fabryczna, has info on sights and accommodations (open M-F 8am-4pm, Sa 10am-2pm). A number of budget options are centrally located around ul. Piotrkowska. By the north end, the super-classy **Youth Hostel (HI),** ul. Legionów 27 (tel. (042) 633 03 65), provides newly renovated singles (20-35zł) and dorms (11-20zł; flexible curfew 10pm; lockout 10am-5pm). A little farther down the street, the wary budget traveler encounters **Hotel Garnizonowy,** ul. Legionów 81 (tel. 633 80 23), a large, simple place (dorms 21.40zł; singles 46zł; doubles 59zł; triples 73zł; quads 98zł). **Pizzeria "Solo,"** ul. Piotrkowska 41, serves a large variety of good pizzas as well as Greek salads (open M-Th 11am-9pm, F-Sa 11am-10pm, Su noon-9pm).

■ Gdańsk

Despite centuries of conflict, Gdańsk has flourished culturally and architecturally. Beautiful cathedrals tower over ornately decorated houses and artwork displayed in the streets—post-war reconstruction efforts have restored all but a few landmarks to their former majesty. This is also the city that witnessed the birth of the Polish solidarity movement under the leadership of Lech Wałęsa, an electrician in the shipyards.

ORIENTATION AND PRACTICAL INFORMATION

Gdańsk, Poland's principal port, lies on the Baltic Sea. From the Gdańsk Główny **train station,** the Old Town center lies a few blocks south, bordered on the west by **Wały Jagiellońskie** and on the east by **Stara Motława,** one of the Wisła's tributaries.

Telephone Code: 058.
Flights: Planes arrive at **Rebiechowo airport** (tel. 31 40 26), 22km south of the city. Bus B runs to the train station.
Trains: Info tel. 311 112. To: Berlin (7hr., 2 per day, 85zł), Kraków (6 per day, 33zł), Prague (15hr., 1 per day, 120zł), St. Petersburg (36hr., 1 per day, 250zł), and Warsaw (4hr., July-Aug. 14 per day, Sept.-June 6 per day, 23zł). **Commuter trains** run every 6-12min. to Gdynia (40min., 2.90zł) and Sopot (15min., 2.10zł). Punch your ticket at one of the *kasownik* machines before boarding.

POLAND

Buses: The station (tel. 32 15 32) is behind the train station through the underground passageway. To Malbork (1hr., 4.70zł) and Toruń (4hr., 17zł).

Ferries: Take the commuter rail to the Nowy Port terminal. To Oxelösund, near Stockholm (17hr., 170.20zł). Book through **Polferries Travel Office** (tel. 43 18 87; fax 43 65 74) or the **ORBIS** travel office (see below).

Public Transportation: Gdańsk has an extensive bus and tram system. 1.32zł for 30min; 2.64zł at night. Pay for large baggage as you would for yourself.

Taxis: It's a bird, it's a plane, it's…**Super Hallo Taxi,** tel. 91 91.

Tourist Offices: IT Gdańsk, ul. Długa 45 (tel. 31 93 27; fax 31 30 08), has info about sites and accommodations. Open daily 9am-6pm. **ORBIS,** ul. Heweliusza 22 (tel. 31 44 25), sells ferry, train, and plane tickets, and doubles as an **American Express** branch office. Open M-F 9am-5pm, Sa 10am-2pm.

Budget Travel: ALMATUR, Długi Targ 11, 2nd fl. (tel. 31 29 31; fax 31 78 18), in the Old Town center. The office sells ISICs and has youth and student hostel information. Open M-F 9am-5pm, Sa 10am-2pm.

Currency Exchange: At hotels, banks, *kantors,* and certain post offices throughout the city. Cirrus/Plus/MC/Visa **ATMs** are scattered throughout the city. **Bank Gdański,** Wały Jagiellońskie 14/16 (tel. 37 92 22), cashes traveler's checks for a 1% commission. AmEx/EC/MC/Visa advances without commission. Branch office at the train station. Open M-F 8am-6pm.

Luggage Storage: At the train station. 1zł plus 1% of baggage value. Open 24hr.

English Bookstore: English Books Unlimited, ul. Podmłyńska 10 (tel. 31 33 73). Look for the black and gold sign. Open M-F 10am-6pm, Sa 10am-3pm.

Emergencies: Fire, tel. 998. **Ambulance,** tel. 999. **AIDS,** 958.

Police: tel. 997.

24-Hour Pharmacy: At the train station.

Medical Assistance: Ambulance service, ul. Nowe Ogrody 1/7 (tel. 41 10 00). Emergency doctors at al. Zwycięstwa 49 (tel. 32 39 29 or 32 39 24), and ul. Pilotów 21 (tel. 47 82 51 or 56 69 95), in Gdańsk Zaspa. 24hr. facilities. Treats foreigners. 25zł per visit.

Post Office: ul. Długa 22 (tel. 38 91 39). **Fax** bureau. *Poste Restante* around the back. Open M-F 8am-8pm, Sa 9am-1pm. **Postal Code:** 80-800.

Telephones: Inside and outside the post office.

ACCOMMODATIONS AND FOOD

With Gdańsk's somewhat limited tourist infrastructure and increasing popularity, it is best to reserve well in advance, especially in summer. **Gdańsk-Tourist (Biuro Usług Turystycznych),** ul. Heweliusza 8 (tel. 31 26 34; fax 31 63 01), across from the train station, arranges stays in **private rooms** (singles 30zł; doubles around 50zł; open July-Aug. daily 8am-7pm; off-season M-Sa 9am-5pm). **Almatur,** Długi Targ 11 (tel. 31 29 31), directs travelers to student dorms in July and August (25zł per person).

Schronisko Młodzieżowe (HI), ul. Wałowa 21 (tel. 31 23 13). Cross the street in front of the train station, go up ul. Heweliusza, and turn left at ul. Łagiewniki. Most convenient of the hostels. 14-18zł, students 12-16zł. Sheets 2zł. Luggage storage 1zł. Reception on the 2nd fl. Lockout 10am-5pm. Curfew 10pm.

Schronisko Młodzieżowe (HI), ul. Grunwaldzka 244 (tel. 41 16 60). Take tram 6 to the end of the line or 12 north from the train station to where the tracks form a jughandle. Cross the tracks and follow the path to ul. Grunwaldzka. Immaculate and efficiently run. 12-17zł per bed. Sheets 2.50zł. Luggage storage 1zł. Reception 5pm-9pm. Lockout 10am-5pm. Curfew 10pm.

Hotel Zaułek, ul. Ogarna 107/108 (tel. 31 41 69). A good bet if hostels are full or you want more privacy. The hotel is a bit noisy, but well-located and clean, with comfortable beds. Singles 50zł; doubles 65zł; triples 70zł; quads 80zł.

For fresh produce, try the **Hala Targowa market** on ul. Pańska, in the shadows of St. Catherine's Church just off of Podwale Staromiejskie (open M-F 9am-6pm, first and last Sa of the month 9am-3pm). **Bar "Neptun,"** ul. Długa 33/34, serves hearty, home-style meat dishes alongside vegetarian meals in a cafeteria setting (meals 4zł; open M-F 7am-6pm, Sa 9am-5pm). **Pizzeria Napoli,** ul. Długa 62/63, lives up to its "Best in

Town" sign, with 30 varieties of tasty pizza (6-20zł) and spaghetti (12-17zł) and its prime people-watching location (open daily 11am-10pm). **Jagodzianka**, ul. Podw. Staromiejskie, sells delicious pastries (open M-F 6am-7pm, Sa 6am-5pm, Su 8am-4pm).

SIGHTS AND ENTERTAINMENT

Gdańsk was one of the first Polish cities to undergo an exhaustive postwar facelift. The handsome market square, **Długi Targ,** forms the physical and social center of the Old Town, where the original 16th-century facade of the **Dwór Artusa** looks out onto the **Fontanna Neptuna** (Neptune Fountain). Artists, musicians, and vendors now fill the square. Next to the fountain, the 14th-century **ratusz** (town hall) houses the **Muzeum Historii Gdańska** (Gdańsk Historical Museum); don't miss the fantastic Red Chamber with a ceiling covered with allegorical paintings by Baroque masters (open Tu-Th 10am-4pm, Su 11am-4pm; 4zł, students 2zł).

One block north of Długi Targ is the city's grandest house of worship, the 14th-century **Kościół Najświętszej Marii Panny** (St. Mary's). Almost completely rebuilt after World War II, the church is Poland's largest brick cathedral; trudge the 405 steps up the tower (open May to mid-Oct. daily 9am-5:30pm; 2zł). **Ul. Mariacka,** behind the church, may be Gdańsk's most beautiful street. Follow this tree-shaded lane and pass through the **Mariacka Gate** to reach the river. From here, head left along ul. Długie Pobrzeże to find the Gothic **Harbor Crane,** which set the masts on medieval ships.

On Plac Obrońców Poczty Polskiej, the **Old Post Office** was a rallying point for Polish resistance to the German invasion, and has since become a symbol of the city. Patriotism also runs high at the **Gdańsk Shipyard** and at the **monument to the 1970 uprising,** pl. Solidarności, just north of the center at the end of ul. Wały Piastowskie. Take a ferry to the island of **Westerplatte** to visit the site of the first shots of World War II; boats (tel. 31 49 26) leave from outside the Green Gate at the end of Długi Targ (1hr., Mar. 20-Nov. 15 9 per day, round-trip 24zł, students 15zł).

Along the left bank of the Stara Motława, a handful of pubs offer good beer and company after sunset. The turreted mansion at ul. Wały Jagiellońskie 1 is home to the student club **Żak,** your best bet on any weekend night. It has a movie theater (4-5zł), a pub downstairs, and a fashionably downtrodden cafe upstairs (pub and cafe open daily 2pm-2am). For billiards and jazz (or at least a jazzy atmosphere), head to the **Cotton Club** on ul. Złotników 25/29 (no cover; open daily 4pm-late). **Palowa,** ul. Długa 47, in the basement of the *ratusz*, is a popular pseudo-medieval cafe run by the students' union (open daily 10am-10pm). Follow signs down ul. Długa to **Irish Pub "Piwnica,"** ul. Podgarbary. The brick and wood setting of this cellar pub is perfect for a bowl of Irish stew (9zł) followed by a glass of "snake mix" (Guinness and cider; 6zł; open daily 1pm-midnight).

■ Near Gdańsk

Malbork Castle, in the unassuming town of the same name, became the focal point of the state established by the Teutonic Knights in the early 14th century. The castle withstood several sieges by the Prussians during this period, and for the next 300 years served as one of Poland's major arsenals. After sustaining heavy damage during World War II, the castle is currently being restored. (Castle open May-Sept. Tu-Su 9am-5pm; Oct.-Apr. 9am-2:30pm. Admission with 3hr. guided tour in Polish 12zł, students 7zł. English-speaking tour guide 90zł extra.) Malbork is 40 minutes from Gdańsk by **train** (25 per day, 7zł) and an hour away by **bus** (7 per day, 4.20zł). With your back to Malbork's train station, head right on ul. Dworcowa, then go left at the fork (direction "Elbląg" on the sign) up and around the corner to a traffic circle. Nearby is the **tourist office,** ul. Sienkiewicza 15 (tel. (055) 72 26 14; open M-F 10am-4:30pm, Sa 10am-2pm). A **youth hostel** is at ul. Żeromskiego 45 (tel. (055) 72 25 11).

Little **Frombork** is closely associated with the astronomer Mikołaj Kopernik (Copernicus), who lived and worked here from 1510 until his death in 1543. Follow the signs from the bus stop; once you cross the wooden bridge, the *kasa* on the left sells tickets to **Muzeum Kopernika,** the **cathedral,** and the **wieża** (tower). The museum houses copies of his revolutionary book, *De Revolutionibus Orbium Coelestium.* (Open May-Sept. Tu-Su 10am-5:30pm; Oct.-Apr. Tu-Su 9am-3:30pm. 1.20zł, students 0.70zł.) The 17th-century organ in the **cathedral** next door has a seven-second echo (open Tu-Sa 9:30am-5pm; 2zł, students 1zł). A climb up the tower provides a phenomenal view of the cathedral, the town, and the Wisła lagoon (open M 9:30am-5pm, Tu-Sa 9:30am-7:30pm; 2zł, students 1.20zł). Frombork is best reached by **bus** from Gdańsk (2hr., 6 per day, 7.20zł). Buy return tickets from the driver. The main **tourist office, Globus,** ul. Elbląska 2 (tel./fax (055) 73 54), sits in the *rynek,* at the end of the path from the train station (open daily 9am-7pm). To reach the **Youth Hostel Copernicus,** ul. Elbląska 11 (tel. (055) 74 53), follow the blue and white signs from the bus stop (8zł per bed, over 26 10zł; camping 4zł). **Dom Wycieczkowy PTTK,** ul. Krasickiego 2 (tel. (055) 72 52), has rooms (dorms 13zł; singles 22-29.60zł; doubles 45zł) and a **restaurant** (open daily 7am-9pm).

Just 15 minutes north of Gdańsk by commuter train (2zł), **Sopot** has miles of white beaches, the Baltic's longest pier (512m), renowned spas, a casino, and a growing number of cafes, pubs, and discos. The most popular and extensive sands spread along the end of ul. Monte Cassino. For tickets to the **Opera Leśna,** which hosts a mid-August rock and pop music festival, try **Orbis,** ul. Monte Cassino 49 (tel. (058) 51 41 42; open M-F 10am-6pm, Sa 10am-2pm). The **IT tourist office,** ul. Dworcowa 4 (tel. (058) 51 26 17), sells maps and helps find rooms (open M-F 8:30am-6pm, Sa-Su 9am-2pm). **Pub FM,** ul. Monte Cassino 36, has beer, food, and good company (open daily 1pm-1am). New discos and clubs like **Non-Stop** and **Fantom** rage by the pier.

■ Toruń

Toruń extols itself as the birthplace and childhood home of Mikołaj Kopernik, a.k.a. Copernicus—the man who "stopped the sun and moved the earth." After wandering its cobbled medieval streets, you might wonder why he ever left. The **Stare Miasto** (Old Town), commanding the right bank of the Wisła River, was constructed by the Teutonic Knights in the 13th century. Copernicus's birthplace, **Dom Kopernika,** ul. Kopernika 15/17, has been meticulously restored (open Tu-Su 10am-4pm; 3zł, students 2zł). The **ratusz** (town hall), Rynek Staromiejski 1, in the center of the tourist district, houses the **Muzeum Okręgowe** (Regional Museum), with a famous 16th-century portrait of Copernicus and works by modern Polish artists (open Tu-Su 10am-6pm; 3zł, students 2zł). A city-wide burghers' revolt in 1454 led to the destruction of the **Teutonic Knights' Castle,** but the ruins on ul. Przedzamcze are still impressive. The 50 ft. **Leaning Tower,** Pod Krzywą Wieżą 17, built in 1271 by a Teutonic knight as punishment for falling in love with a peasant girl, now deviates 5 ft. from the center at its top. Among the tall Gothic churches that dot the skyline, the **Bazylika Katedralna pw. św. św. Janów** (Cathedral of St. John the Baptist and St. John the Evangelist) is the most impressive. Built from the 13th to the 15th century, the church mixes Gothic, Baroque, and Rococo elements. From here, it's a short walk across the *rynek* to ul. Panny Marii and **Kościół Św. Marii** (Church of the Virgin Mary). At the end of a long day, stroll along **Bulwar Filadelfijski,** named for Toruń's sister city, Philadelphia, where fishermen and couples line the stone steps.

The Toruń Główny **train station,** across the Wisła River from the city center, serves Gdańsk (2½hr., 19zł), Poznań (2hr., 16zł), Szczecin (5hr., 23zł), and Warsaw (3hr., 20.40zł). The **IT tourist office,** ul. Piekary 37/39 (tel. (056) 62 10 93), offers helpful advice in English. Take city bus 22 or 27 (1.05zł; punch both ends; baggage requires its own ticket) to plac Rapackiego, the first stop across the river, and head through the little park area (open M and Sa 9am-4pm, Tu-F 9am-6pm, Su 9am-1pm; Sept.-Apr. closed Su). **Hotel Pod Orłem,** ul. Mostowa 17 (tel. (056) 210 96) has huge, comfortable rooms in a quiet corner of the city center (singles 80-115zł; doubles 90-130zł; triples 120-155zł). To reach **Dom Wycieczkowy,** ul. Legionów 24 (tel. (056) 238 55), take bus 10 outside the Old Town gate away from the river to the third stop (singles 40zł; doubles 48zł; triples 63zł).

Toruń's centuries-old calling card, sometimes covered with chocolate and even shaped like old Copernicus himself, is *pierniki* (gingerbread), sold at **Serdelek**, ul. Szeroka 19 (open M-F 8am-7pm, Sa 7am-7pm, Su 9am-3pm), and other grocery stores throughout the city. **Bar Mleczny**, ul. Różana 1, serves up primarily vegetarian traditional Polish dishes. *Naleśniki*, the house specialty, come with a multitude of fillings. Try them with blueberries and cream (*z jagodami i śmietaną*, 2.80zł; open M-F 9am-7pm, Sa 9am-4pm). **Pizzeria Browarna**, ul. Mostowa 17 (tel. 226 74), serves great pizza (6.50-14zł) and salads (6.50-10zł; open daily 11am-midnight).

■ Poznań

The provincial feel of Poznan (POSE-nine) belies its cosmopolitan offerings: the annual Trade Fair lures hundreds of businesspeople, international musicians enrich a lively music scene, and culinary and architectural marvels seduce tourists. Downtown, in the **Stary Rynek,** opulent 15th-century merchant homes surround the multicolored **ratusz** (town hall). Considered the finest secular monument of the Renaissance north of the Alps, the town hall now houses the **Muzeum Historii Poznania.** (Open M-Tu and Th-F 10am-4pm, W 11am-6pm, and Su 10am-3pm. 1zł, students 0.60zł, F free.) **Ul. Żydowska** (Jewish St.), the center of the pre-war Jewish district, begins behind the town hall, on the *rynek*'s northeast corner. On the other side of the square, the **Kościół Farny Marii Magdaleny** (Parish Church), resplendent with frescoes and pink marble, blesses the end of ul. Świętosławska (organ concerts M-Sa 12:15pm). On a less Catholic note, the **Museum of Historic Musical Instruments,** Stary Rynek 45/47, stars Chopin's piano and Polynesian and African instruments (open Tu and Sa 11am-5pm, W and F 10am-4pm, Su 10am-3pm; 1zł, students 0.60zł.).

The main **train station,** in the Old Town's southwest corner, serves Berlin (3hr., 93.40zł), Kraków (6hr., 24.60zł), Szczecin (3hr., 18.75zł), and Warsaw (3½hr., 29.40zł). The **bus station** is just 500m down the street. If you're not up for the 20-minute walk to the city center from the train station, take any tram heading down Św. Marcin (to the right) from the end of ul. Dworcowa, and get off at the corner of ul. Św. Marcin and al. Marcinkowskiego. The Glob-Tour **tourist office** (tel./fax (0618) 66 06 67), in the train station, offers maps, tourist info in English, and currency exchange (open 24hr.). **Centrum Informacji Turystycznej (IT),** Stary Ryenk 59 (tel. (0618) 852 61 56), sells maps (5zł) and provides info (in English) on budget lodgings (open M-F 9am-6pm, Sa 10am-2pm). The **youth hostel (HI),** ul. Berwińskiego 2/3 (tel. (0618) 66 36 80), has clean rooms; exit the train station through the tunnel toward McDonald's, turn left on ul. Głogowska, walk about two blocks, and turn right (12zł, nonmembers 15zł; reception 5-10:30pm; lockout 10am-5pm; curfew 11pm). **Hotel Royal,** ul. Sw. Marcin 75 (tel. (0618) 53 78 84; fax 51 79 31), a short walk from the *rynek*, has small but affordable rooms (singles 50-60zł; doubles 80zł).

For traditional Polish food at unbeatable prices, try **Bar Mleczny Pod Kuchcikiem,** ul. Św. Marcin 37 (open M-F 8am-7pm, Sa 8am-4pm, Su 10am-4pm). **Kebap Istanbuł,** ul. Głogowska 43, down the street from the train station, and at ul. Ratajczaka 21, has cheap Near Eastern fare (13-17zł; both open daily 10am-10pm). Pick up groceries at **Prospero,** ul. Wielka 18 (open 24hr.). **Stajenka Pegaza,** on the corner of ul. Fredry and ul. Wieniawskiego, has good beer and sudden musical uprisings. (Open M-F from 11am, Sa from noon, Su from 3pm, until the last guest leaves, around 2 or 3am.)

■ Kraków

Once tucked away behind the Iron Curtain, Kraków, recently chosen as a cultural capital of Europe, is now a trendy, international city. Although the city suffered little damage during World War II, the spectre of destruction is never far removed: the notorious Nowa Huta steelworks in Kraków's eastern suburb are a grim reminder of the Stalinist era, and the Auschwitz-Birkenau death camp lies only 70km to the west. Yet, it is perhaps precisely this combination of vitality and darkness that gives Kraków its uniquely dynamic atmosphere.

POLAND

Krakow: Stare Miasto

SEE ALSO COLOR INSERT

ACCOMMODATIONS

A Hotel Saski
B PTTK Dom Turysty

ORIENTATION AND PRACTICAL INFORMATION

The city fans outward in roughly concentric circles from the **Rynek Główny** (Main Market Square), at the heart of **Stare Miasto** (Old Town). The green belt of the **Planty** gardens rings Stare Miasto, and the **Wisła River** skims the southwest corner of **Wzgórze Wawelskie** (Wawel Hill). The **bus** and **train stations** are opposite each other 10 minutes northeast of the *rynek*. From the stations, head toward Hotel Europejski; the underpass leads diagonally across the street to the Planty. Across the gardens, follow **ul. Szpitalna** to the cathedral, then turn right to get to the *rynek*. Refer to this book's **color map** of central Kraków.

Telephone Code: 012.

Trains: Kraków Główny, pl. Kolejowy (tel. 624 54 39, info tel. 933). **Luggage storage.** To Berlin (8hr., 99zł), Bratislava (7hr., 92zł), Budapest (11hr., 134zł), Kiev (22hr., 158zł), Prague (8½hr., 129zł), Vienna (9hr., 132zł), and Warsaw (2½-4½hr., 26zł, express 44zł). **Kraków Plaszów** is a suburban station; take tram 3 or 13 into the city if stranded there.

Buses: ul. Worcella (info tel. 936), opposite the train station. **Sindbad** (tel. 421 02 40), in the main hall, sells tickets to international destinations. Open M-F 9am-5pm. To: Budapest (11hr., 80zł), Prague (11hr., 120zł), and Warsaw (6hr., 28zł).

Public Transportation: Buy tickets at kiosks and **tram** stops (1.20zł) and punch them on board. Large backpacks require their own tickets. Slight surcharge for tickets purchased on board. Express **buses** A, B, and C 2.25zł; night buses 2zł. Day passes 5zł; weekly passes 14zł. The fine for violating the system is 50zł.

Tourist Offices: Dexter, Rynek Główny 1/3 (tel. 421 77 06 or 421 30 51; fax 421 30 36). English-speaking staff organizes tours and offers free pamphlets on the town and cultural events. Open M-F 9am-6pm, Sa 9am-1pm. **Orbis,** Rynek Główny 41 (tel. 422 40 35), sells ferry, plane, bus, and train tickets. Open Apr.-Oct. M-F 8am-7pm, Sa 8:30am-3pm; off-season M-F 9am-6pm.

Currency Exchange: At *kantors*, Orbis offices, and hotels. *Kantors*, except the ones around the train and bus stations, usually have the best rates.

American Express: Rynek Główny 41 (tel. 422 91 80), in the Orbis office. Cashes and sells traveler's checks with no commission, replaces lost checks, holds mail, and accepts wired money. Open same hours as Orbis (see above).

Laundromat: ul. Piastowska 47, on the 1st floor of Hotel Piast. 3hr. drop-off available. Wash 5zł, dry 5zł. Open daily 10am-7pm.

Emergency: Fire, tel. 998. **Ambulance,** tel. 999.

Police: tel. 997.

Post Office: Main office ul. Westerplatte 20 (tel. 422 51 63, 422 86 48, or 422 24 97; fax 422 36 06). Open M-F 7:30am-8:30pm, Sa 9am-2pm, Su 9-11am. **Postal code:** 31-045.

Telephones: 24hr. phones at the main post office and at the office opposite the train station, ul. Lubicz 4 (tel. 422 14 85 or 422 86 35).

ACCOMMODATIONS AND CAMPING

Reservations are highly recommended in summer. Friendly neighborhood room-retriever **Waweltur**, ul. Pawia 8 (tel. 422 16 40; tel./fax 422 19 21), arranges private singles for 54zł and doubles for 80zł (open M-F 8am-8pm, Sa 8am-2pm). Other locals gladly rent rooms; watch for signs or solicitors in the train station. Be wary of owners hawking their "beautiful" rooms, though—see the room before paying.

Jan-Pol PTTK Dom Turysty, ul. Westerplatte 15 (tel. 422 95 00; fax 422 57 19), by the post office and near the *rynek*. The place to meet young travelers (and rowdy schoolchildren). Dorms remain unlocked, so use the hotel vault. You may only be allowed to arrange for a night at a time. 28zł. Reception 24hr.

Schronisko Młodzieżowe (HI), ul. Kościuszki 88 (tel. 422 19 51), inside the gates of a convent, a 20min. walk from the Old Town. Take tram 2 ("Salwator") from ul. Westerplatte to the last stop. Run by nuns in a heavenly setting, although school groups may detract from the serenity. 9.75zł, nonmembers 15zł. Sheets 2.50zł. Reception daily 8am-2pm and 5-11pm. Lockout 10am-5pm. Curfew 11pm.

Schronisko Młodzieżowe (HI), ul. Oleandry 4 (tel. 633 88 22). Take bus 119 north from the train station, and get off once the main drag turns into ul. Mickiewicza. Oleandry is parallel to Mickiewicza outside the Old Town. Cheap but dingy. Dorms 18-20zł; doubles 24zł per person. Flexible lockout 10am-5pm. Curfew midnight.

Hotel Piast, ul. Piastowska 47 (tel. 637 49 33 or 637 21 76). Take tram 4, 12, 13, or 40 westbound to "Wawel." Keep walking in the tram's direction to Piastowska and turn left. Popular with young foreigners who come to study Polish. Singles 40zł; doubles 60-88zł; triples with bath 99zł. Coin-op laundry.

Hotel Saski, ul. Sławkowska 3 (tel. 421 42 22; fax 421 48 30), close to the *rynek*. Comfortable and faded with an old-world atmosphere. Singles 100zł, with bath 160zł; doubles 130zł, with bath 220zł; triples 160zł, with bath 250zł.

Camping Krak, ul. Radzikowskiego 99 (tel. 637 21 22 or 637 29 57; fax 637 25 32). Take tram 4, 8, 12, or 40 to "Fizyków" and walk north. 9zł per person; cars 9.50zł; caravans 13zł. Open May 15-Sept. 30.

FOOD

There are 24-hour grocery stores in town including **Społem**, pl. Kolejowy, across from the train station. *Obwarzanki* (soft pretzels with poppy seeds), Kraków's street-stand specialty, sell for just 0.60zł. The eateries listed are near Rynek Główny.

Chimera, ul. Św. Anny 3. Popular with students between classes. Huge plate of creative, delicious salads 9zł. Smaller plates 6zł. Open daily 9am to 10 or 11pm.

Jadłodajnia u Stasi, ul. Mikołajska 16. A one-man show. Famous for its Polish dishes, such as *pierogi z serem* (cheese dumplings) and *pierogi z truskawkami* (strawberry dumplings). Open M-F 12:30pm until around 5pm.

Bar Mleczny Barcelona, ul. Piłsudskiego 1, across from Planty on the west side of Stare Miasto. A bastion of proletarian dining—a full meal for under 3zł. *Risotto z kurczaka* (rice with chicken; 3zł). Open M-F 8am-6pm, Sa 8am-4pm.

Cechowa, ul. Jagiellońska 11, a block west of the *rynek*. Crowded tables and chairs give a homey feel. Try their specialty, *śledź po krakowsku* (Kraków herring) for 4.50zł. Other traditional Polish dishes 3.50-17zł. Open daily 11am-10pm.

Vega Bar Restaurant, ul. św. Gertrudy 7. An elegantly taciturn vegetarian restaurant with two lace-draped pianos. Delicious menu includes cold salad, *pierogi* (3.80zł), *naleśniki* (3.80zł), and soups (2.50zł). Open daily 10am-9pm.

Prima Pizzeria, Sławkowska 3, just off the *rynek*. Standard but tasty thin-crust pizza. Small cheese pizza 6.20zł, large 7zł; with meat 8.50zł, large 9.50zł.

Pożegnania z Afryką (Out of Africa), ul. Św. Tomasza 21. A popular Polish coffee chain with an antique feel, a heady aroma, and an extensive selection of rich coffees (around 3.50zł for a small pot). **Imported coffee** beans sold in bulk. Open daily 10am-10pm.

SIGHTS

At the center of the Stare Miasto (Old Town) spreads **Rynek Główny,** one of the largest medieval market squares in Europe. In its northeast corner rise the asymmetrical towers of the **Kościół Mariacki** (Cathedral of St. Mary). *(Open daily noon-6pm. Altar 2.50zł, students 1.50zł.)* An interrupted *hejnał* (trumpet call) each hour from one tower recalls the death of a watchman warning the city of invading Tatars in 1241. The call has become Kraków's signature and is broadcast on national radio daily at noon. The deep blues and golds of the Baroque interior encase a 500-year-old carved-wood altarpiece. Diagonally across the square stands the lonely **Wieża Ratuszowa.** *(Town Hall Tower. Open M-F 10am-4:30pm, Sa-Su 10am-3:30pm. 1.50-3zł.)* Dividing the square in half, the yellow Italianate **Sukiennice** (Cloth Hall) is as mercantile now as it was in guild times; the ground floor contains an enormous trinket market. Upstairs, **Muzeum Narodowe** (National Museum) houses a gallery of 18th- and 19th-century Polish classics. *(Open Tu-Su 10am-3pm, Th until 5:30pm. 3zł, students 1.50zł.)* Kraków's **Uniwersytet Jagielloński** is the second-oldest university in Eastern Europe and names Copernicus among its alumni. The university's 15th-century **Collegium Maius,** west of the *rynek* on ul. Jagiellońska 15, has a Gothic courtyard and vaulted walkway. *(Open M-F 11am-2:30pm, Sa 11am-1:30pm.)*

  Zamek Wawelski (Wawel Castle) is one of the finest surviving pieces of Renaissance architecture in Poland. Begun in the 10th century, the castle contains 71 chambers, a magnificent sequence of 16th-century tapestries commissioned by the royal family, and a series of eight tapestries from Arras depicting the story of Noah's Ark. The **Crown Treasury** inside the castle features the sword used in the coronations of Polish kings. Also inside, the **Oriental Collection** boasts vases and an enormous and elaborately decorated 17th-century Turkish tent. The castle is undergoing renovations—not all the chambers are open to the public. A visitor's office sells English guidebooks. *(Office open M-Sa 8:45am-4pm, Su 10am-3pm. Royal Chambers (9zł, students 4zł), oriental collection (3 zł, students 1.50zł) and Treasury open Tu-F 9:30am-4:30pm, Su 9:30am-3pm, Su 10am-3pm. Admission free on W. Oct.-Mar. exhibits close at 3pm and are free Sa.)* Poland's monarchs were crowned and buried in the **Katedra Wawelska** (Cathedral) next door to the castle. *(Open May-Sept. M-Sa 9am-5:15pm, Su and holidays 12:15-5:30pm; off-season closes at 3pm. 5zł.)* Its former archbishop, Cardinal Karol Wojtyła, is now Pope John Paul II.

  South of the Old Town lies **Kazimierz,** the 600-year-old Jewish quarter. You can still see the remnants of what was once a large and vital community, including the beautiful **Remuh Cemetery,** ul. Szeroka 40 (open M-F 9am-4pm), and Kraków's only operating synagogue. In 1860-62, the Association of Progressive Israelis founded **Templ Synagoga,** ul. Miodowa 24, with its 36 splendid stained-glass windows. Poland's oldest synagogue, **Stara Synagoga,** ul. Szeroka 24, houses a small **museum.**

POLAND

(Open W-Th and Sa-Su 9am-3pm, F 11am-6pm. 5zł, students 2.50zł.) Close to the synagogue, the **Jewish bookstore Jordan,** ul. Szeroka 2, organizes tours of Kazimierz which trace the sites of *Schindler's List. (Open M-F 9am-6pm, Sa-Su 10am-6pm. English tours depart from the bookstore. 2-6hr. 20-40zł.)*

ENTERTAINMENT

The Dexter tourist office has info on cultural activities, while the **Cultural Information Center,** ul. św. Jana 2 (tel. 421 77 87; fax 421 77 31), sells a comprehensive monthly guide, *Karnet* (2zł), and tickets for upcoming events (open M-F 10am-7pm, Sa 11am-7pm). Student clubs romp from 8pm to midnight or 1am with a small cover.

U Louisa, Rynek Główny 13. Live jazz and blues on weekends. **Internet access** 4-6zł per hr. Beer 4-8zł. Open M-F 11am-2am, Sa-Su 11am-late.

Pub Pod Papugami (Under the Parrots), ul. Św. Jana 18. A quiet student crowd gathers around oddly low tables. Guinness 7.40zł. Open M-F noon-2am, Sa-Su 4pm-2am.

Jazz Club "U Muniaka," ul. Floriańska 3. Well-known jazzman invites his friends to jam. Weekend concerts with 15zł cover. Open daily 5pm to midnight or 1am.

Student Club, Rynek Główny 8. Very cheap, very laid back. Jazz on Tuesdays and disco on weekends. Usually open around 9am-2am.

Free Pub, ul. Sławkowska 4, through the archway and down the stairs on the right. Unmarked, easy to miss. Beer 4zł. Crowded after 2am, closes after everyone leaves.

■ Near Kraków: Auschwitz-Birkenau and Wieliczka

An estimated 1.5 million people, mostly Jews, were murdered and thousands more suffered in the Nazi concentration camps at **Auschwitz** (Oświęcim) and **Birkenau** (Brzezinka). Prisoners were originally kept at the smaller **Konzentrationslager Auschwitz I,** within the city limits. The camp itself is now a museum; barracks and crematoria hold displays detailing Nazi atrocities, and many nations whose citizens were killed here have erected their own exhibits or memorials. An English guidebook is sold at the entrance for 3zł. Begin your visit with the horrifying film, shot here by the Soviet Army on January 27, 1945. (Film shown daily; 1zł. Museum open June-Aug. daily 8am-7pm; May and Sept. 8am-6pm; Apr. and Oct. 8am-5pm; Mar. and Nov.-Dec. 15 8am-4pm; Dec. 16-Feb. 8am-3pm. Free. Children discouraged from visiting the museum.) **Konzentrationslager Auschwitz II-Birkenau,** in the countryside 3km from the original camp, is a well-marked 30-minute walk. Birkenau was built later in the war, when the Nazis decided that murdering prisoners was more important than putting them to work; this is a death camp in the strictest sense of the term. From April 15 to October 31, a bus shuttles to this site from the parking lot of the Auschwitz museum (every hour on the half-hour; 1zł). In the central watchtower, you can listen to recorded commentaries in 12 languages while getting a view of the immensity of the camp, which was mostly destroyed by the retreating Nazis—rows of chimneys, a few barracks, watchtowers, and, at the far end of the train tracks, gas chambers and crematoria. A pond in the far right corner is still slightly gray from the ashes deposited there half a century ago.

Buses run to Auschwitz-Birkenau from Kraków's central bus station (1½hr., 10 per day, 5.90zł); get off at "Muzeum Oświęcim." **Trains** leave from Kraków Główny (1¾hr., 4 per day, 5zł), although times are not particularly convenient. More trains run from Kraków's suburban Płaszów station. Tourist offices in Kraków also offer tours including transportation and knowledgeable guides. From the Oświęcim train station, buses 2, 3, 4, and 5 drop visitors off at the Museum Oświęcim bus stop, outside the driveway. By foot, turn right as you exit the station, go one block and turn left; the road stretches 1.6km to Auschwitz, which will be on the right.

Thirteen kilometers southeast of Kraków lies the 1000-year-old salt mine at **Wieliczka,** where Poles carved a 20-chapel complex in salt 100m underground. The most spectacular is **St. Kinga's Chapel.** The Wieliczka salt mine has been declared by UNESCO one of the 12 most priceless monuments in the world. (Open Apr. 15-Oct.

15 daily 7:30am-6:30pm; Oct.16-Apr. 14 8am-4pm. Obligatory guided tours 19zł, 9.50zł with ISIC; in English 1-5 per day, 21zł.) **Trains** travel to Wieliczka from Kraków (25min., 1 per hr., 1.50zł) and private **mini buses** depart from the little road between the train and bus stations (every 15min., 1.50zł). Once in Wieliczka, follow the tracks' former path and then the *"do kopalni"* (to the mine) signs. Local kiosks sell guide-books in English.

■ Częstochowa

Częstochowa (CHEN-sto-HO-va) is the Catholic Mecca of Poland. Every year, thou-sands make the pilgrimage to **Klasztor Paulinów** (Paulite Monastery) on top of Jasna Góra to catch glimpse of the miraculous **Czarna Madonna** (Black Madonna; c. 500-700), the most sacred of Polish icons. The monastery also houses a large **treasury** containing invaluable works of art, many of them donations of previous pilgrims: monstrances, chalices, crosses, liturgical vestments, and jewelry. (Chapel open daily 5am-9:30pm. The icon is displayed M-F 6am-noon and 1-9:30pm, Sa-Su 6am-1pm and 2-9:30pm. Treasury open daily 9am-5pm. Donations appreciated.)

Częstochowa is accessible by **train** from Kraków (2hr., 17.50zł), Warsaw (3hr., express 20zł), or Wrocław (4hr., 14zł). The WCIT **tourist office,** al. NMP 65 (tel. (034) 24 13 60; fax 24 34 12), provides a free map and hotel info (open M-F 9am-6pm, Sa-Su 10am-6pm). The popular **Dom Pielgrzyma im. Jana Pawla,** ul. Wyszyńskiego 1/31 (tel. (034) 24 70 11; fax 65 18 70), just outside the west gate of the monastery, has spacious rooms (singles with bath 45zł; doubles 50zł). Across the parking lot from the west gate of the monastery, **Camping Oleńka,** ul. Oleńki 10/30 (tel. (034) 24 74 95; fax 25 14 79), is a clean, sprawling complex (tent sites 7zł; bungalows 15-18zł per person). Students gather around the salad-laden tables of **Pod Gruszką,** al. NMP 37 (open daily 10am-10pm). The enormous **Supermarket Billa** sits across from the bus station at ul. Wolności (open M-F 9am-9pm, Sa 8am-8pm, Su 9am-4pm).

Between Częstochowa and Kraków, the fantastic **Trail of Eagles' Nests** follows a narrow 100km chain of crags tipped with the ruins of fortifications from the 12th century onwards. A **hiking trail** dotted with villages runs along the entire length. Bus 58 or 58bis from near the Częstochowa train station provides access to the 13th-cen-tury **Olsztyn Castle.** In Kraków or Częstochowa, **PTTK** can provide **hiking maps.**

The Black Madonna

Jasna Góra's pilgrimage tradition dates to the monastery's founding in 1382 when Prince Ladislaus II of Opole invited Paulite monks to Poland, giving them the Jasna Góra hill and the picture that has come to be known by its 20th-century appella-tion, the Black Madonna. According to tradition, the picture was painted by St. Luke on a plank of the table at which the Holy Family prayed and dined in Naza-reth, although it is most likely a 6th- or 7th-century Byzantine icon. The annual 5 million pilgrims to Częstochowa come to get a glimpse at the two scars she is said to bear in testimony to her miraculous powers. They are attributed to the mishap of thieves (said to be followers of the Czech reformer Jan Hus, but more likely political opponents of the monastery's patron, King Władysław). According to legend, the picture increased in weight under the thieves' efforts to such a degree that they were unable to carry it. In frustration, they slashed her face, immediately drawing a torrent of blood.

■ Lublin

A center for religious and social movements since it acted as the catalyst of the Polish Reformation and Counter-Reformation, Lublin was silenced during World War II. But the city regained a vibrant, bohemian flair after the war, when its Catholic university was the only institute of higher learning in Poland to maintain independence from the Communist government. The 19th-century facades of **ul. Krakowskie Przedmi-**

eście introduce the medieval **Stare Miasto** (Old Town). A stroll east from pl. Litewski leads to pl. Łokietka and the1827 **Nowy Ratusz** (New Town Hall), seat of Lublin's government. To the right starts ul. Królewska with the grand, 16th-century **Katedra Św. Jana Chrzciciela i Jana Ewangelisty** (Cathedral of St. John the Baptist and St. John the Evangelist), with frescoes and a gilded altar. To the left of the Nowy Ratusz runs **ul. Lubartowska,** the main artery of pre-war Lublin's Jewish district. **Plac Ofiar Getta** (Victims of the Ghetto Square), on the left of the street, centers around the **Monument to the Murdered Jews.** Ul. Krakowskie Przedmieście travels straight through pl. Łokietka to the **Brama Krakowska** (Kraków Gate), which houses **Oddział Historyczny Muzeum Lubelskiego** (Historical Division of the Lublin Museum), pl. Łokietka 3 (open W-Sa 9am-4pm; Su 9am-5pm; 1zł). Across the gate, ul. Bramowa leads to the **rynek,** lined with early Renaissance houses. In the middle of the *rynek* stands the Neoclassical **Stary Ratusz** (Old Town Hall). A walk along ul. Grodzka leads through the 15th-century **Brama Grodzka** (Grodzka Gate) to ul. Zamkowa, which runs to the massive **Zamek Lubelski** (Lublin Castle). Most of the structure was built in the 14th century, but was restored in the 19th century with a neo-Gothic exterior.

The Lublin Główny **train station,** pl. Dworcowy 1 (tel. (081) 532 02 19, info 933), south of the Old Town, sends trains to Kraków (4hr., 27.2zł) and Warsaw (2½hr., 19.6zł). **Buses** leave the station at ul. Tysiąclecia 4 (tel. (081) 77 66 49, info 934), near the Old Town, for Warsaw (3hr., 12zł). The **IT tourist office,** ul. Krakowskie Przedmieście 78 (tel. (081) 532 44 12), carries regional maps (4zł) and brochures (open M-F 9am-5pm, Sa 10am-2pm). **Orbis,** ul. Narutowicza 31/33 (tel. (081) 532 22 56; fax 532 15 30), handles plane, train, and bus tickets, and books hotel rooms (open May-July M-F 9am-6pm, Sa 10am-2pm). In summer, **university dorms** provide inexpensive rooms, although many are far from the city center; ask at the tourist offices. To get to **Schronisko Młodzieżowe (HI),** ul. Długosza 6a (tel. (081) 533 06 28), walk to the end of the Saxon Gardens and turn right onto ul. Długosza. (Dorms 14zł; triples 16zł per person. Sheets 4.50zł. Lockout 10am-5pm. Curfew 10pm.) **ZNP Dom Noclegowy,** ul. Akademicka (tel. (081) 533 82 85), is near the Katolicki Uniwersytet Lubelski (singles 36zł; doubles 44zł). From the Ogród Saski bus stop, cross the street and follow ul. Łopacińskiego until it turns into ul. Akademicka.

Jazz Pizza, ul. Krakowskie Przedmieście 55, serves delicious pizzas (6.50-8zł; open M-Sa 1:30pm-midnight, Su 3-10pm), and **Bar Staromiejski,** ul. Jezuicka 1, in the Old Town, has cheap cafeteria-style food (soups 1zł, *pierogi* 2.50zł; open M-F 8am-5pm, Sa-Su 8am-4pm). A few **grocery stores** line ul. Krakowskie Przedmieście, including the **24-hour Delikatesy Grota** at #13. Thanks to a student crowd, Lublin has an impressive number of pubs and an active music scene. The **Old Pub,** ul. Grodzka 8, serves drinks downstairs, and has a disco upstairs (open Su-Th 11am-10pm, F-Sa 11am-11pm).

■ Near Lublin: Majdanek

The largest concentration camp after Auschwitz, **Majdanek** lies only 4km from Lublin's city center. Because the Nazis did not have time to destroy the camp, **Państwowe Muzeum na Majdanku** (The Majdanek State Museum) contains original structures and houses chilling piles of ashes and prisoners' shoes. (Open May-Sept. Tu-Su 8am-6pm; Mar.-Apr. and Oct.-Nov. daily 8am-3pm. Free. Children under 14 not permitted.) Walking through the camp takes approximately two hours. The **information center** (tel. (081) 744 26 47 or 744 19 55) shows a 15-minute documentary. To get to Majdanek from Lublin, take eastbound bus 28 from the train station, tram 153 or 158 from Al. Racławickie, or the southbound tram 156 from ul. Królewska.

■ Kazimierz Dolny

Although this lovely, picturesque town was established by Kazimierz the Great in the 14th century, it's actually named in honor of Prince Kazimierz the Just, who in 1181 donated the settlement to a nunnery near Kraków. Hike up to the **castle tower,**

POLAND

which used to alert the residents to passing boats on which they could levy tolls (open Tu-Su 10am-5pm; castle ruins and tower 1zł). On your way down, take a left by the Zamek, cross the road, and head up the trail to **Three Crosses Hill** for an equally magnificent view. The crosses were erected as a monument to the people who died in a terrible 18th-century plague. At ul. Senatorska 11/13 you'll find the **Muzeum Sztuki Złotniczej** (Museum of Goldsmithery), as well as the Kamienica Lelejoska. The joint exhibit displays paintings inspired by the town alongside sparkling European silver, gold, and jewelry dating back to the 15th century.

Some **buses** pass on the way between Puławy and Lublin (1½hr., 1 per hr., 5.20zł); others zoom to Warsaw (3½hr., 7 per day, 10.40zł). When leaving Kazimierz by bus, don't assume that the driver will make the detour into the bus station—he or she may stop across the street just off the cobblestone **ul. Podzamcze.** If you've just arrived, continue up the incline two minutes to get to the *rynek*, which is on the left. The **PTTK tourist office,** Rynek 27 (tel. 81 00 46), sells divine little maps of town (2.50zł) and arranges private rooms. (Open May-Oct. M-F 8am-6pm, Sa-Su 10am-5:30pm; off-season M-F 8am-3pm, Sa-Su 10am-2pm.) The clean and conveniently located **Youth Hostel "Strażnica,"** ul. Senatorska 23a (tel. 81 04 27), sits only one block southwest of the *rynek*. Its 50 beds come in two- to 10-person rooms (dorms 15zł; doubles and triples 18zł per person; breakfast included; sheets 4zł).

■ Zakopane

Set in a valley surrounded by sky-high jagged peaks and soul-stirring alpine meadows, Zakopane buzzes with hikers and skiers clamoring to be a part of the great outdoors. Short mountain hikes are a specialty of **Tatrzański Park Narodowy** (Tatran National Park). Entrances to the park lie at the head of each trail (1zł, students 0.50zł). **Dolina Kościeliska** offers an easy day-hike and biking route in a valley along a stream; a bus shuttles from Zakopane west to Kiry (1.50-2zł), where the green trail begins. For more dramatic vistas, catch a bus to **Kuźnice** (1zł), 20 minutes south of central Zakopane, and hop on the **Kasprowy Wierch** cable car (round-trip 17zł, students 11zł). To conquer the **Czerwone Wierchy** (Red Peaks), follow the red trail that leads west from the top of the cable car route along the ridge that separates Poland and Slovakia. If you tire, four of the seven peaks along the way have paths descending to Zakopane.

The mountain lake **Morskie Oko** dazzles herds of tourists in the summer; to get there, take a bus from Zakopane's bus station (45min., 3zł) to Polana Palenica, then hike an easy 9km along the road. The **Dolina Pięciu Stawów Polskich** (Five-Lake Valley) hike, a 14-hour summer-only option starting from Kuźnice, and the **Rysy** hike to Poland's highest peak, are extremely demanding, but compensate with incredible views and sense of accomplishment. Before setting out, buy the map *Tatrzański Park Narodowy: Mapa turystyczna* at a local kiosk or bookstore.

The **train** and **bus stations** are across ul. Jagiellonska from each other, right next to the street's intersection with ul. Kosciuszki. Trains go to Kraków (3½hr.,18.31-23.29zł) and Warsaw (8hr., 30.13-39.43zł); buses travel to Budapest (8hr., 70zł), Kraków (2½hr., 10zł), Poprad, Slovakia (2½hr., 8zł), and Warsaw (8hr., 28.60zł). The **IT tourist office,** ul. Kościuszki 17 (tel. (018) 122 11; fax 660 51), at the intersection with ul. Sienkiewicza, sells maps and brochures and arranges private rooms (30zł per person; open daily 7am-9pm). **Usług Turystycznych,** ul. Krupówki 12 (tel. (018) 158 48; fax 124 29), arranges Tatra excursions (open in summer M-F 8am-4pm, Sa 8am-2pm, Su 8am-noon; off-season closed Su).

Watch for *"pokój"* (private room) signs (25-30zł with some haggling). To reach **Schronisko Młodzieżowe (HI),** ul. Nowotarska 45 (tel. (018) 662 03), walk down ul. Kościuszki toward town, then take the second right onto ul. Sienkiewicza and walk two blocks (dorms 15zł; HI card US$2 per night; curfew 11pm). **PTTK Dom Wycieczkowy,** ul. Zaruskiego 5 (tel. (018) 632 81), a large chalet in the town center, has spacious rooms and 24-hour hot water (15-30zł). If you make it to the Morskie Oko lake, **Schronisko Morskie Oko** (tel. (018) 776 09) is a gorgeous hostel in an ideal location (14-28zł; reserve ahead). Pitch a tent at **Camping Pod Krokwią,** ul.

Żeromskiego (tel. (018) 122 56; tents 7-10zł plus 8zł per person, 6zł per student; bungalows 22-25zł). **U Wandy**, ul. Sienkiewicza 10, off Kościuszki, has immense, tasty servings (chicken cutlet 8zł; open daily 2-6pm). **Grocery stores** line ul. Krupówki.

■ Wrocław

After decades of elaborate postwar rebuilding, only photographs recall the destruction of Wrocław (VROTS-wahv) during World War II. Now the city charms visitors with many bridges, lush parks, and restored 19th-century buildings. The oldest neighborhood, **Ostrów Tumski** (Cathedral Island), ages peacefully across the river from the center next to the **Botanical Gardens**, ul. Sienkiewicza 23 (open M-F 8am-6pm, Sa-Su 10am-6pm; 3zł; students 2zł). The stately **Katedra Św. Jana Chrzciciela** (Cathedral of St. John the Baptist) gives this part of town its dignified character. Inside, a nun will show you the amazing marble **Kaplica Św. Elżbiety** (Chapel of St. Elizabeth). Climb up the tower for a phenomenal view (open daily 10am-5:30pm; 3zł, students 2zł). The modern heart of the city, *Stare Miasto,* showcases the Renaissance and Gothic **ratusz** (town hall) on **Rynek Główny** (Main Market Sq.) and contains the **Historical Museum.** One exhibit focuses entirely on ul. Świdnicka, a street in central Wrocław so beautiful that the Germans tried to have its stones moved to their soil. (Open W-F 10am-4pm, Sa 11am-5pm, Su 10am-6pm; cashier closes 30min. earlier. 3zł, students 1.5zł, W free.) **Aula Leopoldina,** pl. Uniwersytecki 1, on the second floor of the main University building, is an 18th-century lecture hall with magnificent ceiling frescoes (open Th-Tu 10am-3:30pm; 2.50zł, students 1zł).

Trains arrive at ul. Piłsudskiego from Berlin (5½hr., 87zł), Budapest (12hr., 151zł), Kraków (4hr., 25zł), Prague (6½hr., 88zł), and Warsaw (5hr., 29zł). The **bus** station, ul. Sucha 1, behind the train station, serves Kraków (7hr., 30zł), Poznań (3hr., 26zł), and Warsaw (8hr., 31zł). The well-stocked **IT tourist office,** ul. Rynek 14 (tel. (071) 44 31 11 or 44 11 09; fax 44 29 62), has handy maps (2.50zł; open M-F 9am-5pm, Sa 10am-2pm). Speak with the staff about private rooms. The clean, safe **youth hostel (HI),** ul. Kołłątaja 20 (tel. (071) 343 88 56), is opposite the train station (13-18zł; lockout 10am-5pm; curfew 10pm). **Hotel Piast,** ul. Piłsudskiego 98 (tel. (071) 343 00 33), near the train station, has sinks in all rooms. Request a room that does not face the main street (singles 40-55zł; doubles 70zł; triples 90zł; quads 110zł).

Bar Vega, Rynek Ratusz 27a, serves tasty vegetarian dishes for less than 5zł (open M-F 8am-7pm, Sa-Su 9am-5pm), while **Bar Miś,** ul. Kuźnicza 48, offers cafeteria-style meals for 4-5zł (open M-F 7am-6pm, Sa 8am-5pm). There are several 24-hour grocery stores: **Delikatesy,** pl. Solny 8/9, is convenient to the *rynek*. For up to the nanosecond cultural info, pick up the free *Co jest grane* at the tourist office. With its Marilyn Monroe plastered walls and barstools/saddles, **Szalony Koń** (Crazy Horse), Rynek 36, is blissfully bad-ass. Next to the decadent artist's corner, **Kawiarnia "Pod Kalamburem,"** ul. Kuźnica 29a, the **Cyberkawiarnia** gives you a cup of coffee and an hour of **Internet access** for 6zł (open daily 10am-10pm).

Portugal

US $1 = 176.96$ (Portuguese escudos)	100$ = US $0.57
CDN $1 = 116.30$	100$ = CDN $0.86
UK £1 = 293.89$	100$ = UK £0.34
IR £1 = 256.73$	100$ = IR £0.39
AUS $1 = 104.70$	100$ = AUS $0.96
NZ $1 = 90.62$	100$ = NZ $1.10
SAR 1 = 28.50$	100$ = SAR 3.51
Country Code: 351	International Dialing Prefix: 00

Centuries ago, Portuguese explorers noticed that the Atlantic Ocean didn't swallow the sun every evening. Their ensuing revolutionary navigational and ship-building techniques allowed Vasco da Gama to sail around the Cape of Good Hope and Magellan to sail around the world. These discoveries also fed the country's prosperity, transforming art and architecture into the ornate and sometimes eccentric Manueline style. Following the Age of Discovery a period of decline set in, imbuing the culture with a nostalgia still reflected in the folk ballads of *fado*—fate. By 1580, Portugal had exhausted both its resources and its royal line, and after minimal resistance, the Spanish Hapsburg Philip II claimed the Portuguese throne. Independence wasn't regained until 1640, when the royal house of Bragança established itself by hooking up with England. An earthquake in 1755 reduced much of Lisbon to rubble, shaking the country's faith and economy so much that when Napoleon invaded in 1807, King Pedro III moved the court of his crumbling empire to Brazil.

Events in Portugal this century have proven no less turbulent. A parliamentary republic emerged in 1910, only to be overthrown by a 1926 military coup. Strongman António Salazar, an economist-turned-dictator, and his successor, Marcelo Caetano, ruled the country for the next 50 years, exploiting the domestic peasantry and African laborers under colonial rule. In 1974, a bloodless coup toppled the regime, prompting mass rejoicing—every Portuguese town now has its Rua 25 de Abril to honor the day. The new junta finally granted independence to Portugal's African holdings, but the ensuing civil wars in Mozambique and Angola set off a rush of immigration into an already unstable Portugal. In 1986, President Mario Soares and Prime Minister Cavaco Silva supervised Portugal's entry into the European Economic Community, and initiated a sometimes painful modernization drive. Portugal remains quite poor by European standards but is striving to catch up and should enter the European Monetary Union in 1999. Expo '98 is being held in Lisbon from May to September of 1998, and has prompted one of largest urban renewals, transforming a decaying industrial center into a thriving, beautified waterfront. All told, prospects for the future are especially bright given the influx in industry and vastly improved educational system. But some things seem destined never to change—the pristine beaches along the Atlantic seaboard, the plush landscape in the north, the wines of Porto, and the character and traditions which evolved over Portugal's rich history.

For more detailed, energetic, and sunny information on Portugal, grab a copy of *Let's Go: Spain & Portugal 1999*.

GETTING THERE AND GETTING AROUND

Citizens of the U.S., Canada, the U.K., and New Zealand can visit Portugal **visa-free** for up to 90 days. Citizens of Australia need only a passport as well, but must have a visa to cross into Spanish territory. Citizens of South Africa need a visa; contact the consulate in Pretoria at 201 Barkley Sq., 296 Walker St., Sunnyside 0002 (tel. (012) 341 55 01; fax 341 56 90).

Portugal

Rio Minho

Viana do Castelo

MINHO

Serra do Gerés

Bragança

Rio Cávado

TRÁS-OS-MONTES

Braga
Guimarães

Serra do Marão

Vila Real

DOURO LITORA

DOURO ALTO

Porto
(Oporto)

Rio Douro

BEIRA ALTA

Salamanca

Aveiro

Viseu

Rio Mondego

SPAIN

ATLANTIC OCEAN

BEIRA LITORA

COSTA VERDE

COSTA DA PRATA

Serra da Estrela

Guarda

Figueira da Foz

Coimbra

Serra da Gardunha

Leiria

BEIRA BAIXA

Batalha

Fátima

Castelo
Branco

Nazaré

Alcobaça

São Martinho do Porto

Tomar

ilhas Berlengas

Caldas da
Rainha

Cabo Carvoeiro

Óbidos

Castelo-
de Vide

Peniche

Serra do Aire

Marvão

Cáceres

ESTREMADURA

Santarém

Portalegre

RIBATEJO

Vila
Franca

Serra de São Mamede

Mafra

Sintra

Elvas

Mérida

Cascais

Lisbon

Estremoz

Estoril

Setúbal

ALTO ALENTEJO

Queluz

Évora

Cabo Espichel

Serra de Ossa

COSTA AZUL

Beja

Rio Guadiana

Sines

BAIXO ALENTEJO

COSTA DOURADA

Rio Mira

Mertola

N

Serra de Monchique

Portimão

ALGARVE

Cabo São Vicente

Silves

Tavira

Sagres

Lagos

Albufeira

Faro

Olhão

Vila Real de
Santo António

Golfo de Cádiz

The **airports** in Lisbon serves major European and North American cities; Lisbon and Porto are also accessible by daily **trains** from Madrid and Paris. **Eurail** is valid on the Portuguese national train system, but if you're planning to stay within the country, the reasonable fares and short distances may make a pass unnecessary. Be aware that posted schedules for trains and buses may be wrong, and that unless you have a Eurail pass, the return on round-trip tickets must be used by 3pm the next day. **Caminhos de Ferro Portugueses,** Portugal's national railway, operates throughout the country, but aside from the Braga-Porto-Coimbra-Lisbon line, the bus is better. **Rodoviária,** the national bus company, has recently been privatized and divided by region. These buses link just about every town, while private companies also operate regionally. Express coach service *(expressos)* between major cities is especially quick and convenient. **Hitchhiking** in Portugal is not reliable or safe enough to serve as a means of transportation, particularly as automobiles are relatively unsafe in Portugal, with its ill-kept smaller roads and reckless drivers.

ESSENTIALS

The national tourist board is the **Direção Geral do Turismo (DGT).** Their offices are in virtually every city; look for the **"Turismo"** sign. Services offered are similar to those in Spain. Finding an English speaker at bigger offices is usually no problem. The principal student travel agency is **TAGUS-Youth Student Travel.**

Portuguese **currency** is the escudo ($). Normal banking hours are weekdays from 8:30am to 3pm, but many close for lunch from around 11:45am to 1pm. Travelers checks are readily convertible. There are a decent number of **ATMs** throughout the country, and many establishments accept major credit cards.

A strongly Catholic country, Portugal recognizes many religious **holidays** and observances. Every town has its patron saint; their feast days are local holidays, accompanied by pilgrimages, village fairs, makeshift amusement parks, and closed shops. National festivals and holidays include *Semana Santa* (Mar. 29-Apr. 4), Liberty Day (Apr. 25), Labor Day (May 1), Corpus Christi (June 22), Feast of the Assumption (Aug. 15), Republic Day (Oct. 5), All Saints' Day (Nov. 1), Feast of the Immaculate Conception (Dec. 8), and Christmas.

COMMUNICATION **Airmail** usually takes 7-10 business days to reach North America. If you're sending a letter to Portugal, *Poste Restante* is available in nearly early town. The **phone system** in Portugal is currently being updated, and many numbers are gaining an extra digit. *Let's Go* lists all the known changes, but undoubtedly some numbers will change after the publication of this book. For a time, at least, you will probably be re-routed if you call the old number. **Phone booths** are located at phone offices, on the street, and in some post offices. Few pay phones accept coins; the competing **Telecom Portugal,** most common in Lisbon and Porto, and **Credifone,** most common everywhere else, phone booths use incompatible magnetic cards that are sold at drugstores, post offices, and elsewhere. For **directory assistance,** dial 118; for an **international operator,** dial 099 for Europe, 098 for intercontinental calls. For MCI's **WorldPhone,** dial 05 017 12 34; **AT&T Direct** 05 017 12 88; **Sprint Access** 05 017 18 77; **Canada Direct** 05 017 12 26; **BT Direct** 0800 800 440; **Australia Direct** 05 017 61 10; **New Zealand Direct** 05 017 64 00; and **SA Direct** 05 017 27 00. In an **emergency,** dial 112.

Portuguese is a Romance language similar to Spanish, but also accessible to those who know French or Italian. English, Spanish, and French are also widely spoken.

Yes/No	*sim/não*	seeng / now
Hello	*Olá*	oh-LAH
Please	*por favor*	poor fah-VOR
Thank you	*obrigado*	oh-bree-GAH-doo
Sorry	*desculpe*	dish-KOOL-peh
Do you speak English?	*Fala inglês?*	FAH-lah een-GLAYSH
I don't understand.	*Não compreendo*	now kohm-pree-AYN-doo
Where is...?	*Onde é que é...*	OHN-deh eh keh eh
How much does this cost?	*Quanto custa?*	KWAHN-too KOOSH-tah
Do you have a single/double room?	*Tem um quarto individual/ duple?*	tem oom KWAR-toe een-DE-vee-DU-ahl/DOO-play
Help!	*Socorro!*	so-ko-RO

ACCOMMODATIONS AND CAMPING **Movijovem** (tel. (1) 355 90 81 or 355 90 87; fax 352 14 66), the Portuguese Hostelling International affiliate, looks over the country's HI hostels. All bookings may be made here. To stay in a hostel, you must have an HI card (3000$); buy one in your home country or at Movijovem's office in Lisbon. A bargain bed in a *pousada de juventude* (not to be confused with plush *pousadas*) costs 1100-2500$ per night, slightly less off season (breakfast and sheets included).

Lunch or dinner usually costs 900$. Rates may be slightly higher for guests 26 or older. Check-in hours are 9am to noon and 6pm to midnight; some have lockouts from 10:30am to 6pm, and early curfews might cramp your style if you're planning a late night of club-hopping.

Pensões, also called *residencias,* will likely be your mainstay in Portugal; they're cheaper than hotels, and far more common than crowded hostels. All are rated by the government on a five-star scale, and are required to clearly display their category and legal price limits. During high season, it helps to book rooms around a month in advance, although travelers planning a week ahead will likely find a room. **Quartos** are rooms in private residences, sometimes the only choice in small or less touristed towns, particularly in southern Portugal. The tourist office can usually help you find them, and restaurant proprietors and bartenders often supply names and directions.

In Portugal, locals regard **camping** as a social activity more than anything else. Over 150 official campgrounds *(parques de campismo)* feature countless amenities and comforts; most have a supermarket and café, and many are beach-accessible or near rivers and pools. Given the facilities' quality and popularity, happy campers arrive early; urban and coastal parks may require reservations. Police have been cracking down on illegal camping, so don't try it, especially near official campgrounds. Big tourist offices stock the free *Portugal: Camping and Caravan Sites,* a handy guide to official campgrounds. Otherwise, write the **Federação Portuguesa de Campismo e Caravanismo,** Av. 5 de Outubro, 15-3, 950 Lisbon (tel. (1) 842 84 80; open 9:30am-12:30pm and 1:30-6:30pm).

FOOD AND DRINK Olive oil, garlic, herbs, and sea salt routinely season local specialties. The aromatic Portuguese cuisine is heavy on herbs and light on spices. Main dishes run a delectable gamut. Seafood lovers get their fix from *chocos grelhado* (grilled cuttlefish), *lulas grelhado* (grilled squid), *linguado grelhado* (grilled sole), *polvo* (boiled or grilled octopus), and *mexilhões* (mussels). Pork fiends indulge in *bife de porco à alentejana,* made with clams in a coriander sauce. Those who prefer chicken fork into *frango assado* (roasted on a spit) and *frango no churrasco* (grilled). The entire country feeds on *cozida à portuguesa* (boiled beef, pork, sausage, and vegetables) in winter. Portugal's favorite dessert is *pudim,* a rich caramel custard. Portuguese *vinho* (wine) costs a pittance by North American standards. Sparkling *vinho verde* (literally "green wine") comes in red and white versions. Excellent local table wines include Colares, Dão, Borba, Bairrada, Bucelas, and Periquita. Port, pressed (by feet) from the red grapes of the Douro Valley and fermented with a bit of brandy, is a fortified dessert in itself. A unique heating process gives Madeira wines their odd "cooked" flavor.

The Portuguese eat their main meal between noon and 2pm and supper between 9pm and midnight. Both meals entail at least three courses. Half portions *(meia dose)* cost more than half-price but are often more than adequate. The ubiquitous *prato do dia* (special of the day) and *menú* (appetizer, bread, entree, and dessert) satisfy hungry folks; the *ementa turistica* (tourist menu) is usually a way to rip off foreigners. Vegetarians will find a **mercado municipal** (open-air produce market) and at least one **supermercado** (supermarket) in every town. Most restaurants will add a 10% service charge to your bill, and couples typically leave around 150$ as a tip.

■ Lisbon (Lisboa)

Over 400 years ago, Lisbon was the center of the world's richest and farthest-reaching empire. Although the glorious Age of Discovery is part of the distant past, *Lisboetas* carefully preserve their traditions along with an urban and cosmopolitan atmosphere. The city continually renovates its historic monuments and meticulously maintains its black-and-white mosaic sidewalks, pastel facades, and cobbled, medieval alleys. Vintage streetcars weave between buses, motorcycles, cars, and pedestrians down broad avenues and narrow lanes.

PORTUGAL

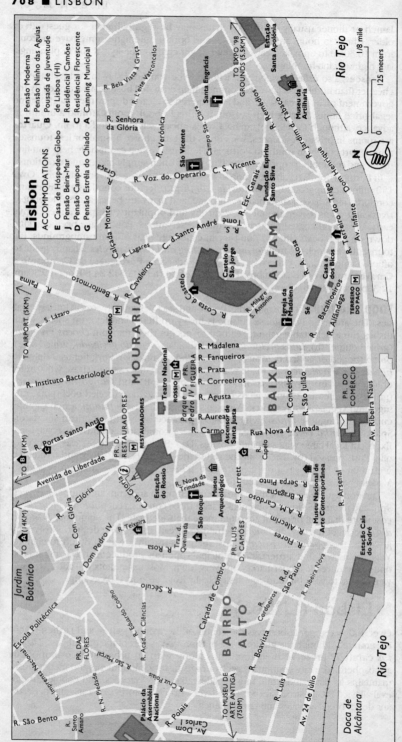

PORTUGAL

Lisbon

ACCOMMODATIONS

E Casa de Hóspedes Globo
J Pensão Beira-Mar
D Pensão Campos
G Pensão Estrêla do Chiado

H Pensão Moderna
I Pensão Ninho das Aguias
B Pousada de Juventude de Lisboa (HI)
F Residencial Camões
C Residencial Florescente
A Camping Municipal

Rio Tejo

1/8 mile
125 meters

N

TO EXPO 98 GROUNDS (5.5KM)

Estação Santa Apolónia

Museu da Artiharia

Santa Engrácia

R. Bela Vista d. Graça

R. Leite Vasconcelos

R. Verónica

Campo Sta. Clara

R. Senhora da Glória

R. Remédios

São Vicente

C. S. Vicente

R. Voz. do. Operario

Graça

R. Estc. Gerais

Fundação Espíritu Santo Silva

R. S. Tomé

Calçada Monte

C. d. Santo André

R. Lagares

ALFAMA

Castelo de São Jorge

R. A. Rosa

Casa a Bacalhoeiros dos Bicos

R. Cavaleiros

R. Costa d. Castelo

MOURARIA

R. Milagre S. Antonio

Igreja da Madalena

Sé

R. Alfandega

TERREIRO DO PAÇO

TO AIRPORT (5KM)

R. S. Lázaro

SOCORRO

R. Benformoso

Palma

R. Instituto Bacteriologico

R. Madalena

R. Fanqueiros

R. Prata

R. Correeiros

R. Agusta

R. Aurea

R. Carmo

R. Conceição

R. São Julião

BAIXA

PR. DO COMÉRCIO

Teatro Nacional

ROSSIO

PR. D. Pedro IV

Parque D.

RESTAURADORES

Ascensor de Santa Justa

Rua Nova d. Almada

Av. Ribeira Naus

TO B (1KM)

R. Portas Santo Antão

PR. D. RESTAURADORES

Estação do Rossio

R. Nova da Trindade

São Roque

Museu Arqueológico

R. Garrett

R. Capelo

R. Serpa Pinto

Museu Nacional de Arte Contemporânea

R. Arsenal

Avenida de Liberdade

TO A (1KM)

R. Con. Glória

R. Dom Pedro IV

R. Teixeira

Trav. R. Queimada

R. Rosa

PR. LUÍS D. CAMÕES

R. A.M. Cardoso

R. Alecrim

R. Flores

R. Bragança

R. Cardoso

Estação Cais do Sodré

Jardim Botânico

Escola Politécnica

Imprensa Nacional

PR. DAS FLORES

R. Acad. d. Ciências

R. Eduardo Coelho

R. Século

Calçada de Combro

BAIRRO ALTO

R. Boavista

R. Cordeiros

R. do. São Paulo

R. Ribeira Nova

Palácio da Assembleia Nacional

R. São Bento

R. Santo Amaro

R. N. Piedade

R. São Marçal

R. Cruz Polais

R. Poiais

R. Dom Carlos I

Av. Dom Carlos I

TO MUSEU DE ARTE ANTIGA (750M)

Av. 24 de Julho

Doca de Alcântara

Rio Tejo

ORIENTATION AND PRACTICAL INFORMATION

The three main *bairros* (neighborhoods) of the city center are the **Baixa** ("low" district, resting in the valley), the **Bairro Alto** (high district), and the **Alfama** (the oldest district). The Baixa, Lisbon's old business district, sits in the center of town. Its grid of small streets begins at the **Rossio** (also called the **Praça dom Pedro IV**) and ends at the **Praça do Comércio,** on the **Rio Tejo** (Tagus River). **Praça dos Restauradores,** where buses from the airport stop, lies just above the Baixa. From Pr. Restauradores, tree-lined **Avenida da Liberdade** runs uphill to the new business district, centered around **Praça do Marquês de Pombal.**

From the west side of the Baixa, the **Ascensor de Santa Justa,** an elegant, outdoor elevator, lifts you up to the **Bairro Alto's** ritzy shopping district, the **Chiado,** traversed by fashionable **Rua do Carmo** and **Rua Garrett.** Most of Bairro Alto, where young Portuguese come to party, is a mix of narrow streets, tropical parks, and Baroque churches. To the east of the Baixa, the **Alfama,** Lisbon's medieval Moorish quarter, has tiny whitewashed houses stacked along a labyrinth of narrow alleys and stairways beneath the **Castelo de São Jorge.**

Telephone Code: 01.

Flights: Aeroporto de Lisboa (tel. 840 20 60 or 849 63 50), on the northern outskirts of the city. Local buses 44 and 45 connect to the tourist office (20min., 150$); the express bus (AeroBus or 91; 430$) is faster. Taxis run 1300$, plus a 300$ flat fee for luggage. **TAP Air Portugal,** Pr. Marques de Pombal 3 (tel. 386 40 80), **Iberia,** Rua Rosa Araújo 2 (tel. 355 81 19), and the domestic **Portugália Airlines,** Av. Almirante Gago Coutinho 88 (tel. 848 66 93), are major airlines.

Trains: For info, call 888 40 25. **Estação Rossio,** between Pr. Restauradores and Pr. Dom Pedro IV, serves Sintra (185$) and western cities. **Estação Santa Apolónia,** Av. Infante D. Henrique, handles international, northern, and eastern lines. To: Coimbra (1300$), Madrid (8200$), and Paris (24,000$). **Estação Cais do Sodré,** just beyond the south end of R. Alecrim, serves Estoril and Cascais (180$) and a few other cities. **Estação Barreiro,** on the south bank of the Tejo (accessible by ferry), covers southern lines.

Buses: Rodoviária da Estremadura, Av. Casal Ribeiro 18 (tel. 55 77 15). M: Saldanha. From the metro station, walk to the Pr. Duque de Saldanha. To: Coimbra (2½hr., 1350$), Lagos (5hr., 2200$), Porto (4hr., 1900$). **Caima,** R. Bacalhoeiros 16 (tel. 887 50 61), runs to the Algarve, Porto (2000$), and Lagos (2400$).

Public Transportation: CARRIS buses (tel. 363 93 43 or 363 20 44) will take you virtually anywhere in the city for 150$. **Metro (M)** tickets cost 70$; a book of 10 tickets is 550$. The *bilhete de assinatura turístico* (tourist pass), good for unlimited public transportation travel, costs 430$ for 1 day, 1600$ for 4 days, or 2265$ for a week. The passes are sold in CARRIS booths (open daily 8am-8pm), located in most network train stations and the busier metro stations. **Trams** are old and ubiquitous, offering beautiful views of the harbor and older neighborhoods. Line 28 is good for sightseeing (stops in Pr. Comércio; 150$).

Taxis: Rádio Táxis de Lisboa (tel. 815 50 61), **Autocoope** (tel. 793 27 56), and **Teletáxi** (tel. 815 20 16) cover the city. Available 24hr. 300$ luggage fee.

Tourist Office: At Pr. Restauradores, try the Lisbon-specific **Municipal,** R. Jardin do Regidor 50 (tel. 343 36 72). **Palácio da Foz** (tel. 346 63 07 or 346 33 14) has info on Portugal. Bus schedules, *pensão* listings, and free map. Open daily 9am-8pm. **Branch** office at the airport. Open daily 6am-2am.

Budget Travel: Movijovem, Av. Duque d'Avila 37 (tel. 13 88 20), will make reservations at youth hostels throughout the country.

Embassies: Australians should contact their embassy in Paris (see **Embassies,** p. 287). **Canada,** Av. Liberdade 144, 4th fl. (tel. 347 48 92; fax 347 64 66). **Ireland,** R. da Imprensa à Estrela, 4th fl., Suite 1 (tel. 392 94 90; fax 397 73 63). **New Zealanders** should contact the U.K. Embassy in Lisbon or the New Zealand Embassy in Rome (see **Embassies,** p. 536). **South Africa,** Av. Luis Bivar 10, (tel. 353 50 41; fax 353 57 13; email SAfrican@mail.EUnet.pt). **U.K.,** R. São Bernardo 33 (tel.392 40 00; fax 392 41 86; Britembassy@mail.telepac.pt). **U.S.,** Av. Forças Armadas (tel. 727 33 00; fax 727 23 54).

PORTUGAL

Currency Exchange: Banks are open M-F 8:30-11:45am and 1-2:45pm. For a relatively low commission and decent rates, try **Cota Cámbio**, R. Áurea 283, 1 block off Pr. Dom Pedro IV in the Baixa. Estação Santa Apolónia branch of Banco Fonsecas and Burnay charges a high commission. **ATMs,** which offer the best exchange rates, line the streets of the Baixa.

American Express: Top Tours, Av. Duque de Loulé 108 (tel. 315 58 85). M: Rotunda. Exit toward R. Rodrigo Sampaio and walk up Av. Liberdade toward the Marquês de Pombal statue, then hang a right. This sole (and often crowded) Top Tours office handles all AmEx functions. Traveler's checks cashed and sold. Mail held. English spoken. Open M-F 9:30am-1pm and 2:30-6:30pm.

Luggage Storage: Estação Rossio. Lockers 450-600$ for 48hr. Open daily 6am-2am.

English Bookstore: Livraria Bertrand, R. Garrett 73 (tel. 342 19 41). Stock up on bestsellers and magazines. Open M-F 9am-7pm, Sa 9am-1pm.

Laundromat: Lavatax, R. Francisco Sanches 65A (tel. 812 33 92). M: Arroios. Wash and dry 1100$ per 5kg. Open Su-F 9am-1pm and 3-7pm, Sa 9am-noon.

Emergencies: tel. 112 anywhere in Portugal. **Fire,** tel. 342 22 22.

Police: R. Capelo 3 (tel. 346 61 41 or 347 56 38).

Medical Assistance: British Hospital, R. Saraiva de Carvalho 49 (tel. 395 50 67, for direct appointments 397 63 29).

Post Office: Correio (tel. 346 32 31) Pr. Comércio. Open for *Poste Restante*, telephones, and faxes M-F 8:30am-6:30pm. The **branch office** at Pr. Restauradores has the same services. Open daily 9am-6pm. **Postal Code:** 1100.

Internet Access: Ciber Chiado, Largo do Picadeiro 10 (tel. 346 67 22). Email access 900$ per hr. Open M-F 11am-6pm and 8pm-midnight, Sa 8pm-midnight.

Telephones: Ubiquitous. **Portugal Telecom,** Pr. Dom Pedro IV 68, has pay phones and booths for international calls. M: Rossio. **Phone cards** come in 50 units (875$) or 120 units (2100$); local calls consume at least 1 unit.

ACCOMMODATIONS AND CAMPING

Expect to pay about 3000-5000$ for a single and 6000-9000$ for a double: if the fee seems padded, request the printed price list. Most hotels are located in the center of town on **Av. da Liberdade,** while convenient budget *pensões* are in the **Baixa** along the **Rossio** and on **Ruas da Prata, dos Correeiros,** and **do Ouro.** Lodgings near the **Castelo de São Jorge** or in the **Bairro Alto** are quieter, closer to the sights, and more expensive. If the central accommodations are full, head east to the *pensões* along **Av. Almirante Reis.** Be cautious around the docks and the area near Cais de Sodné, and after dark in the *barrios;* many streets are isolated and poorly lit.

Pensão Campos, R. Jardim do Regedor 24, 3rd fl. (tel. 346 28 64), between Pr. Restauradores and R. Portas de Santo Antão. Comfortable rooms with well-scoured baths. Cool multilingual owner. Elevator whisks you up to the *pensão's* 12 rooms. Singles 3000$; doubles with shower 5500$; triples 6000$. Laundry 300$.

Casa de Hóspedes Globo, R. Teixeira 37 (tel. 346 22 79), on a small street across from the Parque São Pedro de Alcântra at the top of the funicular. Generally safe and convenient location. From the entrance to the park, cross the street to Tr. Cara and make a right onto R. Teixeira. Singles 2500$, with bath 4500$; doubles 5000-6000$. Prices drop 1000$ during the off season. Reservations recommended.

Pensão Ninho das Águias, R. Costa do Castelo 74 (tel. 886 70 08), down the street from the Teatro Taborda (behind the castle). This *pensão's* spectacular views of Lisbon are worth the long hike and additional staircase. Feels like home. Singles 5000$; doubles 7000$, with bath 8000$. Reserve ahead.

Pousada de Juventude de Lisboa (HI), R. Andrade Corvo 46 (tel. 353 26 96; fax 353 75 41). M: Picoas. Exit the metro station facing south, turn right, and walk one block. Huge, ultra-clean youth haven. In summer dorms 3000$; doubles 6000$. In winter dorms 1900$; doubles 4800$. Breakfast included. Lockers 250$. Reception 8am-midnight. Check-out 10:30am. Disabled access. Members only.

Pousada de Juventude de Catalazete (HI), Estrada Marginal (tel. 443 06 38), in the nearby coastal town of **Oeiras.** Take a train from Estação Cais do Sodré to Oeiras (20min., 155$). Exit through the train station underpass from the side of the train coming *from* Lisbon. Cross the street and follow signs to Lisbon and Cascais. At the intersection across from a bus stop (no street signs), make a left and go downhill along R. Filipa de Lencastre. At the underpass, go straight and follow HI signs to the INATEL complex. Members only. Dorms 2000$; doubles 4400$. Cheaper off-season. Breakfast included. Reception 8am-midnight. Curfew midnight. Reservations recommended.

Pensão Moderna, R. Correeiros 205, 4th fl. (tel. 346 08 18), 1 block off the south side of Pr. Figueira. A friendly family tends comfortable if rather noisy apartment-style rooms. Great location. Singles 3500$; doubles 6000$; triples 8000$.

Residêncial Florescente, R. Portas de Santo Antão 99 (tel. 342 66 09; fax 342 77 33), 1 block from Pr. Restauradores. The 72 impeccable, spacious rooms are luxurious by budget standards. Doubles with shower 7000$, with full bath 10,000$; triples 7000$, with bath 14000$; large room with full bath and A/C 12,000$.

Pensão Beira-Mar, Largo Terreiro do Trigo 16, 4th fl. (tel. 886 99 33; or call the owner, who speaks only Spanish, on his cell phone tel. 09 31 64 63 09). In a small square off Av. Infante Dom Henrique (the road parallel the Tejo). Dorms 6000$, with bath 6500$; triples 8000$. Laundry 3000$ per load. Reserve ahead.

Pensão Estrêla do Chiado, R. Garrett 29, 4th fl. (tel. 342 61 10). Spotless rooms, hot water, and large well-furnished singles. Rooms with verandas have castle views. Singles 3000$, with shower 4000$; doubles 5000$, with shower 5500$.

Residencial Camões, Tr. Poço da Cidade 38, 1st fl. (tel. 347 75 10; fax 346 40 48), off R. Misericórdia. A pristine set of rooms in the heart of the Bairro Alto party district. English spoken. Doubles 5000-8000$, with bath 9000$. Prices drop Oct.-June 500-1000$. Breakfast included. Reservations essential in summer.

Camping: *Portugal: Camping and Caravan Sites* is free from the tourist office.

Parque de Campismo Municipal de Lisboa (tel. 760 20 61; fax 760 74 74) is on the road to Benfica. Take bus 43 from the Rossio to the Parque Florestal Monsanto. Swimming pool and supermarket. 420$ per person, 355$ or more per tent (depending on size). Prices lower during winter.

FOOD

Lisbon has some of the least expensive restaurants and best wine of any European capital. A full dinner costs about 1800$ per person, and the *prato do dia* (special of the day) is often a great deal. Try the areas near the end of the port and bordering the Alfama in Baixa, or find the smaller eateries in the Bairro Alto. Lisbon reels with seafood specialties such as the local classic, *bacalhau cozido com grão e batatas* (cod with chick peas and boiled potatoes). Bus 40 runs to **Mercado Ribeira,** a market complex on Av. 24 de Julho, outside Cais do Sodré (open M-Sa sunrise-2pm). The smaller **Supermercado Celeiro,** Rua 1 de Dezembro 65, is centrally located (open M-F 8:30am-8pm, Sa 8:30am-7pm).

Restaurante João do Grão, R. dos Correeiros, 222. Chow down at one of Lisbon's most highly recommended eateries. House wine 295$. Main courses from 850$.

Restaurante Bonjardim, Tr. de Santo Antão 11, off Pr. Restauradores. Tasty roast chicken 1100$. Main courses 950-2800$. Open daily noon-11pm.

Cervejaria da Trindade, R. Nova Trindade 20C. 2 blocks down a side street that begins in front of the Igreja do São Roqua and parallels R. Misericórdia. Part beer hall, part restaurant. Daily *sugestões do chefe* (chef's suggestions) are budget finds. Open noon-2am.

Hua Ta Li, R. dos Bacalhoeiros 109-115A, near the Pr. Comércio. Great Chinese vegetarian options. *Menú* 1400$. Open daily noon-3:30pm and 6:30-11pm.

Celeiro, Rua 1 de Dezembro 65, take a right off the Rossio. Beneath a health food supermarket. Cafeteria-style salads, souffles, and sandwiches satisfy hungry herbivores. Main courses 200-570$. Open M-F 8:30am-8pm, Sa 8:30am-7pm.

Confeitaria Nacional, Praça da Figueira 18B. Succumb to sweet temptation with the *austríaca* (120$) at this famous *pastelaría.* Open M-Sa 10am-5pm.

SIGHTS

The **Rossio,** or **Praça Dom Pedro IV,** is the city's main square and the domain of drink-sipping tourists and heart-stopping traffic. At the north end of the *praça,* the **Teatro Nacional** marks the former site of the Palace of the Inquisition. Farther north, in **Praça dos Restauradores,** an obelisk and a bronze sculpture of the Spirit of Independence commemorate the 1640 "restoration" of Portugal's independence from Spain. The **Avenida da Liberdade,** one of the city's most elegant promenades, begins here and extends to the **Praça do Marquês do Pombal** in the center of a bustling commercial district. South of the Rossio, a grid of streets connects the town center and the river. This area, known as the **Baixa,** is crowded with pedestrians, upscale shops, and ice cream vendors.

Although it's just as easy to get from the Baixa to the Bairro Alto by walking, the classic way is to take the **Ascensor de Santa Justa,** built in 1902 inside a Gothic tower. *(Runs M-F 7am-11pm, Sa-Su 9am-11pm. 75$ each way.)* At the top, turn left and walk one block to Rua Garrett, the heart of the chic **Chiado** neighborhood. Nearby, on R. da Misericórdia, the **Igreja de São Roque** is noted for its **Capela de São João Baptista** (fourth from the left), a chapel ablaze with precious gems and metals. Continue up R. da Misericórdia, which becomes R. São Pedro de Alcântara, to reach Lisbon's most beautiful park, the **Parque de São Pedro de Alcântara.**

A half-hour walk down Av. Infante Santo leads to the **Museu Nacional de Arte Antiga,** R. Janelas Verdes, home to a representative collection of European paintings ranging from Gothic to 18th-century French masterpieces. *(Open Tu 2-6pm, W-Su 10am-6pm. 500$, students 250$.)* Buses 40 and 60 stop to the right of the museum exit and head back to the Baixa.

The **Alfama,** Lisbon's medieval quarter, was the lone neighborhood to survive the 1755 earthquake intact. Between the Alfama and the Baixa is the **Mouraria** (Moorish quarter), established after Dom Alfonso Henriques and the Crusaders expelled the Moors in 1147. Climb along the R. da Madalena (which runs north-south) to Largo Santo António da Sé, which changes names several times as you follow the tram tracks to the delicate **Igreja de Santo António da Sé.** *(Open daily 7:30am-7:30pm.)* The church was built in 1812 over the saint's alleged birthplace. In the square beyond sits the stolid 12th-century cathedral known as the **Sé.** *(Open M-Sa 9am-5pm, treasury 10am-5pm.)* From here, follow the signs for a winding uphill walk to the restored, lux-

---

The Many Lives of the Portuguese Feiras

While most nightlife in Lisbon revolves around the bars and *casas de fado,* those seeking more active revelry in June won't be disappointed. Open-air *feiras* (fairs)—smorgasbords of eating, drinking, live music, and dancing—abound. There's a lively one called *Oreal* at **Campo das Cebolas,** near the waterfront in the Alfama (open June M-F 10pm-1am, Sa-Su 10pm-3am). Don't miss the *feira* in the **Praça Camões** in the Bairro Alto (take the Elevador da Glória, or walk up R. Garrett), which goes until 3am every night in June. After savoring *farturas* (Portuguese donuts, 190$) and Sagres beer (200$), pick up your feet and join in the traditional Portuguese dancing. On the night of June 12, the streets become a mega-dance floor for the huge **Festa de Santo António**—banners are strung between streetlights and confetti falls like snow.

More commercial *feiras* combine shopping and cultural involvement. The open-air markets come in many varieties, and bargaining is the name of the game. Bookworms burrow for three glorious weeks in the **Feira do Livro** (in the Baixa from late May to early June). In June, the Alcântara holds the **Feira Internacional de Lisboa,** while in July and August the **Feira de Mar de Cascais** and the **Feira de Artesania de Estoril** take place near the casino.

Year-round *feiras* include the **Feira de Oeiras** for antiques on the fourth Sunday of every month, and the **Feira de Carcanelos** for clothes (Th 8am-2pm). Pack-rats should catch the **Feira da Ladra** (flea market), held at Campo de Santa Clara (Tu and Sa 7am-3pm). Take bus 12 or tram 28.

urious **Castelo de São Jorge,** which offers spectacular views of Lisbon and the ocean. *(Open daily Apr.-Sept. 9am-9pm; Oct.-Mar. 9am-7pm. Free.)* Built in the 5th century by the Visigoths, this castle was the royal family's palace from the 14th to the 16th century.

Belém is more of a suburb than a neighborhood of Lisbon. To get there, take tram 15 from Pr. do Comércio (20min., 150$) or the train from Estação Cais do Sodré (10min., 110$). From the train station, cross the tracks and street to get into town. Rising from the banks of the Tagus, **Mosteiro dos Jerónimos** celebrates the Age of Discovery and showcases Portugal's own Manueline style, combining Gothic forms with early Renaissance details. *(Open Tu-Su 10am-5pm. 400$, students 200$, Oct.-May 250$. Free for students on holidays and Su 10am-2pm. Cloisters open Tu-Su 10am-5pm. Free.)* Within the monastery complex is the **Museu da Marinha,** an intriguing ship museum. *(Open Tu-Su 10am-6pm. 400$, students 200$. Free Su 10am-2pm.)* A 10-minute walk along the coast from the monastery, the **Torre de Belém,** built to protect the seaward entrance of the Portuguese capital, rises from the Tagus's north bank and has a magnificent view of the coast. *(Open Tu-Su 10am-5pm; 400$, Oct.-May 250$, students 200$.)* Contemporary art buffs will bask in the glow of the gigantic, luminous **Centro Cultural de Belém** (http://www.fdescccb.pt), with four pavilions, several art galleries, and a huge auditorium for performances. *(Open daily 11am-8pm.)*

The reason to visit the residential suburb of **Queluz,** 14km west of Lisbon and about that far south of Sintra, is the amazing Rococo **Palácio Nacional de Queluz.** *(Open June-Sept. 10am-1pm and 2-5:30pm; Oct.-May 10am-1pm and 2-5pm. 400$, students and seniors 200$. Admission to garden 50$.)* Take the Sintra line from Estação Rossio and get off at the Queluz-Belas (not the Queluz-Massomá) stop (20min., departs every 15min., 120$). To reach the palace, turn left from the station, walk down Av. da República, and follow the signs; it's a 10-minute walk downhill.

ENTERTAINMENT

The *Agenda Cultura* (also at http://www.consiste.pt/agenda) and *Lisboa em,* available free from kiosks in the Rossio and at the tourist office, publish listings of concerts, movies, plays, exhibits, and bullfights. Lisbon's trademark is the heart-wrenching *fado,* an expressive art that combines elements of singing and narrative poetry. *Fadistas* perform sensational tales of lost loves and faded glory; their melancholy wailing is expressive of *saudade,* nostalgia and yearning. The Bairro Alto has many *fado* joints off **R. Misericórdia,** particularly on sidestreets radiating from the Museu de São Roque. Feel the knife twisting in your heart at **Adega Machado,** R. do Norte 91 (2500$ cover includes 2 drinks; open nightly 8pm-3am in summer; Nov.-May closed M), or **O Faia,** R. Baroca 54 (cover 2500$; open M-Sa 8pm-2am). Afterward, cheer up at the many bars and clubs around **Rua do Norte, Rua Diário Notícias,** and **Rua da Atalaia.**

Portas Largas, R. da Atalaia 105. Scrawl on the walls and hang with the locals. Opens at 10am, closes around 2:30am.

Solar do Vinho do Porto, R. São Pedro de Alcântara 45. Port tasting in a mature setting. Glasses 130-2800$. Open M-F 10am-11:30pm, Sa 11am-10:30pm.

Pé Sujo, Largo de St. Martinho 6-7, in the Alfama. Live Brazilian music nightly 11:30pm-2am. Try the killer Brazilian *caipirinha* (sugarcane alcohol, 700$), or, for the truly brave, a *caipirosca* (700$). Open Tu-Su 10pm-2am.

Termas D'Atalaia Bar, R. da Atalaia 108. One of the best, featuring drinks such as *orgasmo* and *sangue dos deuses* (blood of the gods; 400$). A waterfall flows down the front window. Open M-Sa 10pm-3:30am.

Memorial, R. Gustavo de Matos Sequeira 42A, 1 block south of R. Escola Politécnica in the Bairro Alto. This hip gay and lesbian disco-bar is far out—in every sense. Europop blasts from 10pm, but the fun starts after midnight. 1000$ cover (except M or Th) includes 2 beers or 1 mixed drink. Open Tu-Su 10pm-4am.

Frágil, R. da Atalaia 126/8, on the corner of R. da Atalaia and Tr. Queimada. A mixed gay/straight (but uniformly beautiful) crowd. Beer 600$. Hard liquor could empty your wallet. Open M-Sa 10:30pm-3:30am.

Os Três Pastorinhos, R. da Barroca 111-113. Funk, pop, soul, and disco merge into a dancing frenzy. Open Tu-Su 11pm-4am.

■ Near Lisbon: Sintra, Mafra, Estoril, and Cascais

After Lord Byron dubbed it "glorious Eden" in the epic poem *Childe Harold*, **Sintra** became a must for 19th-century aristocrats on the Grand Tour. Twentieth-century romantics trek 3km uphill to the architectural potpourri of the **Palácio da Pena**, a Bavarian castle with Arab minarets, Gothic turrets, Manueline windows, and a Renaissance dome. (Open Tu-Su 10am-6pm; in winter Tu-Su 2-4:30pm. 600$, students 400$; in winter 200$.) Signs point to the ruins of the **Castelo dos Mouros** (Moorish Castle), perched on the peaks towering over Sintra. Below, between the train station and the town center, looms the **Palácio Nacional de Sintra,** once the summer residence of Moorish sultans and their harems (open Th-Tu 10am-1pm and 2-5pm; 400$, students 200$). North of Sintra, the otherwise unremarkable town of **Mafra** is home to one of Portugal's most impressive sites, the **Palácio Nacional** complex, which incorporates a palace, royal library, Baroque church, and hospital (open W-M 10am-1pm and 2-5pm; 300$, students free). Reach Mafra from Sintra by train (1hr., 350$).

Sintra is accessible by **train** from Lisbon's Rossio station (45min., 180$). The **tourist office** (tel. (01) 923 11 57; fax 923 51 76) is at Pr. República (open June-Sept. daily 9am-8pm; Oct.-May 9am-7pm). Hike 3km uphill for the gorgeously situated **Pousada da Juventude de Sintra (HI)** (tel./fax (01) 924 12 10) in Sta. Eufémia (1200-1400$; reception 9am-noon and 6pm-midnight). The recently renovated **Pensão Nova Sintra,** Largo Afonso de Albuquerque 25 (tel. (01) 923 02 20) is closer (singles 2500-3200$; doubles 4500-5500$; reservations necessary).

Estoril and **Cascais,** 30 minutes west of Lisbon, are known as playgrounds for the rich and famous, but don't let that deter you from spending a day at their splendid beaches, although on weekends the bronzed-flesh to bronzed-sand ratio skyrockets. **Trains** to Cascais and Estoril leave from the Estação do Sodré in Lisbon (30min., 180$). Rodoviária **buses** run from Sintra's Av. Dr. Miguel Bombarda, across the street from the train station, to both towns (Cascais 1hr., 550$; Estoril 40min., 320$).

The Estoril **tourist office** (tel. (01) 466 38 13; fax 467 22 80), Arcada do Parque, across from the train station, offers detailed maps and schedules of local events (open M-Sa 9am-7pm, Su 10am-6pm). **Residencial Smart** is at R. Maestro Lacerda 6 (tel. (01) 468 21 64). To get there, follow Av. Marginal uphill past the Paris Hotel to the corner of Av. Bombeiros Voluntários and make a left. Walk 3 blocks uphill to R. Maestro Lacerda and follow this street for three blocks (doubles 5000-9000$; breakfast included).

The Cascais **tourist office,** Av. dos Combatentes 25 (tel. (01) 486 82 04), will find you a room (from 5000$; open June-Sept. 15 daily 9am-8pm; Sept. 16-May 9am-7pm). Indulge hummus cravings at **Joshua's Shoarma Grill,** R. Visconde da Luz 19, just uphill from the tourist office's back door (open M-F noon-4pm and 6pm-2am, Sa-Su 1pm-2am). Bus 403 takes you from Cascais to the jagged bluffs and spectacular views of **Cabo da Roca,** the westernmost point on the European continent (30min., 300$).

CENTRAL PORTUGAL

Jagged cliffs and whitewashed fishing villages line the Costa de Prata (Silver Coast) in **Estremadura,** with beaches to rival even the Algarve. Throngs of tourists fill the seafront Nazaré and Peniche, but smaller and less touristed towns pepper the coast, and the rugged Ilhas Berlingas lies offshore. The fertile region of the **Ribatejo** (banks of the Tejo) is perhaps the gentlest and greenest you will come across in Portugal. Although accommodations can sometimes be expensive in the smaller towns, camping is available, and both regions are connected by a reliable transportation network.

■ Tomar

For centuries the arcane Knights Templar—part monks, part Crusaders—schemed and plotted from Tomar, a small town straddling the Rio Nabão. It's worth trekking in from all corners of Portugal to explore the mysterious **Convento de Cristo** grounds, established in 1320 as a refuge for the disbanded Knights. An ornate octagonal canopy protects the high altar of the **Templo dos Templares,** modeled after the Holy Sepulchre in Jerusalem. The Knights supposedly attended mass here on horseback, each under one of the arches. Below two great stained glass windows stands the **Janela do Capítulo** (chapter window), a tribute to the Golden Age of Discoveries. The **Claustro dos Felipes,** one of Europe's masterpieces of Renaissance architecture, honors King Felipe II of Castile, crowned in Tomar as Felipe I of Portugal during Iberia's unification (1580-1640). To reach the complex, walk from the tourist office and take the second right, bear left at the fork, and follow the paved road up the mountain (open daily 9:30am-12:30pm and 2-5:30pm; 400$, students 200$). The **Museu Luso-Hebraíco,** in the 15th-century **Sinagoga do Arco** at R. Dr. Joaquim Jaquinto 73, is Portugal's most significant reminder of what was once one of Europe's great Jewish communities of the 15th century (open Th-Tu 9:30am-12:30pm and 2-6pm). Europe's largest matchbox collection lies in the **Museo dos Fósforos** in the Convento São Francisco (open Su-F 2-5pm; free).

The **Rio Nabão** divides Tomar; most accommodations and sights, as well as the train and bus stations, lie on the west bank. The **train station** (tel. (049) 31 28 15), on Av. Combatentes da Grande Guerra, serves Coimbra, Lisbon, and Porto. Most destinations require a transfer at Entrocamento; you can buy tickets for both parts of your trip here. **Buses** (tel. (049) 31 27 38) leave for Coimbra (2½hr., 1150$), Lagos (11hr., 2300$), Lisbon (2hr., 1200$), and Porto (4hr., 1400$). Tomar's **tourist office,** Av. Dr. Cândido Madureira (tel. (049) 32 34 27), offers a map and accommodations list. To reach the office from the train and bus stations, go through the small square onto Av. General Bernardo Raria. Continue for four blocks and turn left (open M-F 9:30am-6pm, Sa-Su 10am-1pm and 3-6pm).

Accommodations are fairly plentiful in Tomar, so try bargaining. **Residencial União,** R. Serpa Pinto 94 (tel. (049) 32 31 61; fax 32 12 99), halfway between Pr. República and the bridge, has bright, plush rooms, each with a shower or full bath, telephone, and TV. (Singles 3500-4500$; doubles 6000-6500$; triples 7500$. Breakfast included. Reserve ahead.) Camp at the thickly forested **Parque Municipal de Campismo** (tel. (049) 32 26 07; fax 32 10 26), on the river, across Ponte Velha near the stadium. (420$ per person, 200$ per tent. Free showers. Reception in summer 8am-8pm; off-season 9am-5pm.) Tomar is the picnic capital of Portugal—a section of the lush Parque Mouchão is set aside for just that purpose. The **market** on the corner of Av. Norton de Matos and R. Santa Iria, across the river, provides all the fixings (open M-Sa 8am-2pm, F until 5pm). **Restaurante Estrêla do Céu,** Pr. República 21, has daily lunch specials for 450$ (open Tu-Su 11am-midnight).

■ Santarém

The capital of the Ribatejo province, Santarém was once a flourishing medieval center of 15 convents, and is known today as the centerpiece of Portugal's Gothic style. The austere facade of the **Igreja do Seminário dos Jesuítas** dominates Praça Sá da Bandeira, the main square. Stone friezes carved like ropes separate each of the church's three stories, and Latin mottos embellish the lintels and doorways. If it is closed, enter the door to the right of the main entrance and ask Sr. Domingos to unlock it. In the chapel to the right of the severe **Igreja da Graça** is the tomb of Pedro Alvares Cabral, who discovered Brazil and was one of the few *conquistadores* who lived long enough to be buried in his homeland.

The main exhibit in the **Museu Arqueológico de São João do Alporão,** off R. São Martinho, is the elaborate Gothic tomb of Dom Duarte de Meneses, who was hacked apart while fighting the Muslims. The tomb contains all that his comrades could salvage from the battlefield—one tooth. (Open Tu-Su June-Sept. 10am-12:30pm and 2-6pm; Oct.-May 9am-12:30pm and 2-5:30pm. Free.) **Portas Do Sol,** at the end of Av. 5 de Outubro, is a garden paradise with fountains surrounded by old Moorish walls. Santarém's **sweets fair** ruins thousands of diets the last Wednesday to Sunday in April, and starting the first Friday in June, people flock for the 10-day orgy of bullfighting and horseracing at the **Feira Nacional de Agricultura** (Ribatejo Fair).

PORTUGAL

The **train station,** 2km outside town, serves Lisbon (1hr., 520$) and Tomar (1hr., 370$). The **bus station,** Av. Brasil, also serves Lisbon (1½hr., 1000$; *expressos* 1hr., 1450$) and major cities. The **tourist office,** R. Capelo Ivêns 6 (tel. (043) 33 33 18), elucidates bus and train schedules and finds rooms. (Open M 9am-12:30pm and 2-6pm, Tu-F 9am-7pm, Sa-Su 10am-12:30pm and 2:30-5:30pm.) Room prices increase 10 to 40% during the Ribatejo Fair. **Residencial Abidis,** R. Guilherme de Azevedo 4 (tel. (043) 220 17 or 220 18), around the corner from the tourist office, has soothing rooms (singles 3500-5000$; doubles 4500-7000$; breakfast included). Cramped rooms and medieval windows await travelers at the **Pensão do José** (a.k.a. Pensão da Dona Arminda), Trav. Froes 14 and 18 (tel. (043) 230 88). Go left as you exit Turismo, and take the first right (singles 2000$; doubles 3000-3500$).

■ Évora

From a rolling plain of cork tree groves and sunflower fields, Évora rises like a megalith on a hill. Portugal's foremost showpiece of medieval architecture, the town is also home to a Roman temple, Moorish arches, and a 16th-century university. Amid these monuments and museums, marble-floored shops display their wares and attract a steady (though not overwhelming) stream of tourists from Lisbon and the Algarve. The U.N. has taken notice and has granted the city World Heritage status for its cultural and architectural treasures.

ORIENTATION AND PRACTICAL INFORMATION

Évora is easily accessible by train from Lisbon, about 140km to the west. Near the edge of town, R. Dr. Baronha turns into **Rua República,** which leads to the main square, **Praça do Giraldo,** off which you'll find most monuments and lodgings. From the train station, it might be best to hail a taxi (400$) to reach the center; from the bus station, simply proceed uphill past the Igreja de São Francisco to the *praça*.

Telephone Code: 066.

Trains: From the *praça*, walk down R. República until it turns into R. Dr. Baronha; the **station** (tel. 221 25) is at the end of the road, 1½km from town. To Faro (6hr., 2 per day, 1430$) and Lisbon (3hr., 6 per day, 810$).

Buses: R. República (tel. 221 21), 5min. downhill from Praça Giraldo, opposite the Igreja de São Francisco. To Faro (5hr., 1470$), Lisbon (3hr., 5 per day, 1120$), and Porto (7hr., 2300$).

Tourist Office: Pr. Giraldo 73 (tel. 226 71). Helpful staff compensates for the illegible map by calling around until you have a room. Open Apr.-Sept. M-F 9am-7pm, Sa-Su 9am-12:30pm and 2-5:30pm; Oct.-Mar. daily 9am-12:30pm and 2-5:30pm.

Currency Exchange: There is a 24hr. exchange machine outside the tourist office.

Laundromat: Lavandaria Lavévora, Largo D'Alvaro Velho 6 (tel. 238 83), off R. Miguel Bombardo. 370$ per kg. Open M-F 9am-1pm and 3-7pm.

Emergency: tel. 112.

Police: R. Francisco Soares Lusitano (tel. 220 22), near the Roman temple.

Hospital: Largo Senhor da Pobreza (tel. 250 01), close to the city wall and the intersection with R. D. Augusto Eduardo Nunes.

Post Office: R. Olivença (tel. 264 39), 2 blocks north of Pr. Giraldo. Walk up R. João de Deus, pass under the aqueduct, and turn right uphill. Open for *Poste Restante*, mail, telephones, and faxes M-F 8:30am-6:30pm. **Postal Code:** 7000.

Internet Access: Ciber Évora, Rua Fria 7. Open daily 10:30am-10pm.

ACCOMMODATIONS, CAMPING, AND FOOD

Most *pensões* are located near the **Praça do Giraldo.** *Quartos,* rooms in private houses from 2000 to 4000$ per person, are pleasant alternatives to crowded *pensões* in the summer. Ask the tourist office to call around to find you a room.

Casa Palma, R. Bernando Mato 29-A (tel. 235 60), 3 blocks to the right from the tourist office. Pink frilly bedspreads in bright, well-furnished doubles. The singles are cheaper but dimmer. Singles 4000$; doubles 5500$; cheaper off-season.

Pensão Os Manueis, R. Raimundo 35 (tel. 228 61). Marble stairs lead to homey rooms lining a sun-roofed courtyard. Singles 3000-6500$; doubles 5000-7000$.

Pensão Giraldo, R. Mercadores 27 (tel. 258 33). From the tourist office, take a left, and then left 2 blocks later. Rooms have TV, winter heat, and either a sink, shower, or full bath. Singles 3900$; doubles 4800-7800$. Reserve ahead for the best rooms.

Orbitur's Parque de Campismo de Évora (tel. 251 90; fax 298 30). 3-star park on Estrada das Alcáçovas, which branches off the bottom of R. Raimundo. 20min. walk to town; 1 bus runs daily. Washing machines and a small market. 500$ per person, 400$ per tent; discounts Oct.-Mar. Showers 50$. Reception 8am-10pm.

Many passable budget restaurants cluster near the **Praça do Giraldo,** particularly along **R. Mercadores.** The **public market** sets up in the small square in front of Igreja de São Francisco and the public gardens, selling produce and cheeses. For other supplies, try **Maxigrula,** R. João de Deus 130 (open M-Sa 9am-7pm). **Restaurante A Choupana,** R. Mercadores 16-20, off Pr. Giraldo, has a snack bar on the left for a quick budget lunch. Sundries on table cost extra (meals 900-1300$; half-portions 600$; open daily 10am-2pm and 7-10pm). **Restaurante A Gruta,** Av. General Humberto Delgado 2, serves barbecued chicken buried under a heap of fries (half-chicken 650$). Exit Pr. Giraldo and pass by the bus station, follow R. República toward the train station, and turn right at the end of the park (open Su-F 11am-3pm and 5-10pm).

SIGHTS AND ENTERTAINMENT

Off the east side of the *praça,* R. 5 de Outubro leads to the colossal 12th-century **cathedral.** The 12 Apostles adorning the doorway are masterpieces of medieval Portuguese sculpture; inside, the **Museu de Arte Sacra** houses the cathedral's treasury and stunning 13th-century ivory *virgem do paraíso* (open Tu-Su 9am-noon and 2-5pm; cathedral free, cloister and museum 350$). Nearby, housed above Roman, Visigoth, and Moorish ruins, the **Museu de Évora** showcases a collection ranging from Roman tombs to 17th-century Virgin Mary polyptychs (open Tu-Su 10am-noon and 2-5pm; 250$, under 25 and seniors 125$). Across from the museum stands Évora's most famous monument, the 2nd-century **Templo de Diana,** honoring the Roman goddess of the moon, purity, and the hunt. The temple was used as a slaughterhouse for centuries, but now only a platform and 14 Corinthian columns remains.

Évora's best-kept secret is the 15th-century **Igreja de São João Evangelista,** facing the temple. The interior is covered with dazzling *azulejos,* but you must ask to see the church's hidden chambers (open Tu-Su 10am-noon and 2-5pm; 250$). Another standout is the **Igreja Real de São Francisco,** in its own square downhill from Pr. Giraldo. You might pause to admire the art, but the real show-stopper is the perverse **Capela de Ossos** (Chapel of Bones). Three tireless Franciscan monks ransacked assorted local graveyards for the remains of 5000 people to construct it. Enormous femurs and baby tibias neatly panel every inch of the walls, while rows of skulls line the capitals and ceiling vaults. (Open M-Sa 8:30am-1pm and 2:30-6pm, Su 10-11:30am and 2:30-6pm. Chapel closed during mass. Chapel 50$. Photos 100$.)

Although most of Évora tucks itself in with the sun, **Xeque-Mate,** R. Valdevinos 21, the second right off R. 5 de Outubro from the *praça,* and **Discoteca Slide,** R. Serpa Pinto 135, keep the music blaring until 2am. Only couples and single women need apply (cover 1000$). Évora's festival, the **Feira de São João,** keeps the town up all night with a huge Portuguese-style country fair during the last week of June.

ALGARVE

Once a quiet fishing backwater, Portugal's southern coast has now embraced commercial capitalism. In July and August, hordes of foreigners are lured by the Algarve's gorgeous sands, topless sunbathing, and exhilarating (and exhausting) nightlife. If you haven't reserved a room, ask at tourist offices and bars, keep your eyes peeled for signs, or take your chances with the room-pushers who accost incoming travelers at bus and train stations. **Faro,** the Algarve's capital, is at once a transportation hub and a provincial Portuguese city, to which trains chug from Lisbon (5hr., 6 per day, 2060$). In addition to the towns described here, many villages welcome budget travelers; notable among them are **Salema, Burgau, Sagres,** and the region between **Olhão** and the Spanish border. Reaching more remote towns and beaches is a snap, as EVA has extensive bus services with convenient schedules and low fares. The train costs less than the bus but only connects major coastal cities, and in some towns the station is a hike from the center.

■ Lagos

There isn't much more than beaches and bars in Lagos, but nobody's complaining. Whether soaking in the view from the cliffs, soaking in the sun on the beach, or simply soaking themselves in beers and cocktails, tourists here enjoy one of the backpacker party centers of Europe. To the west, natural tunnels through sheer cliffs connect sandy coves, while to the east, a 4km long beach spreads along the coast.

ORIENTATION AND PRACTICAL INFORMATION

Running the length of the river, **Avenida dos Descobrimentos** carries traffic in and out of the city. **Rua das Portas de Portugal** marks the gateway leading into **Praça Gil Eanes** and the town's glitzy tourist center. Most restaurants, accommodations, and services hover about the *praça* and **Rua 25 de Abril.**

Telephone Code: 082.

Trains: For info, call 76 29 87. The **station** is on the east edge of town, across the river from the bus station. To: Évora (6hr., 1740$) and Lisbon (6½hr., 2000$).

Buses: EVA (tel. 76 29 44), on the east edge of town, off. Av. dos Descobrimentos. To: Faro (2½hr., 670$), Lisbon (5hr., 2000-2500$), and Sagres (1hr., 445$).

Tourist Office: Largo Marquês de Pombal (tel. 76 30 31). Take the sidestreet R. Lina Leitão (off Pr. Gil Eanes), which leads to the Largo. A 20min. walk from the train station, 15min. from the bus station. Brochures, maps, transportation info, and a list of *quartos.* Open daily 9:30am-12:30pm and 2-5:30pm.

Currency Exchange: Commission-free exchange is available at the youth hostel.

Laundromat: Lavandaria Miele, Av. dos Descobrimentos 27. Wash and dry 1000$ per 5kg. Open M-F 9am-1pm and 3-7pm, Sa 9am-1pm.

Emergency: tel. 112. **Ambulance,** tel. 76 01 81 or 76 43 00.

Police: General Alberto Silva (tel. 76 26 30).

Medical Assistance: Hospital, R. Castelo dos Governadores (tel. 76 30 34), next to Igreja Santa María.

Post Office: R. Portas de Portugal (tel. 76 30 67), between Pr. Gil Eanes and the river. Open M-F 9am-6pm. For *Poste Restante,* make sure to label all letters "Estação Portas de Portugal." **Postal Code:** 8600.

ACCOMMODATIONS, CAMPING, AND FOOD

The youth hostel and most pensions fill up in summer, so reserve ahead. Rooms in *casa particulares* (private homes) go for 1000 to 3000$—try haggling.

Pousada de Juventude de Lagos (HI), R. Lançarote de Freitas 50 (tel./fax 76 19 70). From the train and bus stations, walk into town on Av. República and turn right up R. Portos de Portugal. Head into Pr. Gil Eanes and turn right up R. Garrett into Pr.

Luis de Camões, then take a left on R. Cândido dos Reis. At the bottom of the hill, take a left. *Hostal* heaven: comfy beds and beautiful grounds. Kitchen. Dorms 2000$; doubles with bath 4700$; cheaper off-season. Breakfast included. Reception 9am-1am. No curfew. Reserve ahead.

Residencial Rubi Mar, R. Barroca 70 (tel. 76 31 65, ask for David; fax 76 77 49), down R. 25 de Abril, then left on Senhora da Graça. Centrally located, but the 8 rooms go fast. Doubles 6000-7000$; cheaper off-season. Breakfast included.

Residencial Caravela, R. 25 de Abril 8 (tel. 76 33 61), has small but well-located rooms surrounding a courtyard. Singles 4000$; doubles 5500$, with bath 6000$; cheaper off-season. Breakfast included.

Camping: Parque de Campismo do Imulagos (tel. 76 00 31) is frustratingly far away but linked to Lagos by a free shuttle bus. 900$ per person, 450-640$ per tent. Reception 8am-10pm. Closer by, **Camping Trindade** charges 400$ per person with tent, 800$ without tent. Follow Av. dos Descobrimentos towards Sagres.

Casa Rosa, R. do Ferrador 22, has dozens of vegetarian dishes and all-you-can-eat specials; Mondays and Wednesdays have spaghetti and garlic bread for 850$ (open daily 9am-2pm and 7pm-3am). **Mullin's,** R. Cândido dos Reis 86, is a Lagos hot spot. Servers dance to the tables with huge portions of spicy food (chicken *piri-piri* smothered in hot sauce 1200$; open daily noon-2am). For supplies, hit the **mercado,** Av. dos Descobrimentos, five minutes from the town center, or **Supermercado São Toque,** R. Portas de Portugal, across from the post office (open July-Sept. daily 9am-5pm; Oct.-June M-F 9am-8pm, Sa 9am-2pm).

ENTERTAINMENT

Lagos's beaches are beautiful any way you look at them. Flat, smooth sands (crowded during the summer, pristine in the off season) stretch along the 4km long **Meia Praia,** across the river from town. For beautiful cliffs that hide less crowded beaches and caves (perfect to swim in and around), follow Av. Descobrimentos west until you reach the sign for **Praia do Pinhão** (about 5min.). From the beach, continue further on the paths and choose your own cove. The sculpted cliffs and grottoes of **Praia Dona Ana** appear on at least half of all Algarve postcards. For even more picturesque (and thinly populated) stretches, bike or hike your way west to **Praia do Camilo** and the grotto-speckled cliffs of **Ponta da Piedade.** There are relatively uncrowded sands between Lagos and Albufeira—try making **Portimão** your hub to explore them.

The streets of Lagos pick up as soon as the sun dips down. The area between Pr. Gil Eanes and Pr. Luis de Camões bursts with cafes. The area around R. Marreiros Netto, north of Pr. Gil Eanes and R. 25 de Abril, off the *praça*, forms the nightlife's center—bars and clubs run over until well past 5am, and club-hopping is more a profession than a pastime. North of the *praça*, **Garagem de José** (Joe's Garage), opposite Mullin's restaurant at R. 1 de Maio 78, will keep you on your toes from happy hour to early-morning tabletop-dancing. **Bad Moon Rising,** R. Marreiros Neto 50, jams to grunge and indie rock from 8pm to 4am, with a lively scam scene on the side. Stop by **Shots in the Dark,** R. 1 de Maio 16, to hang out with a younger backpacking crowd. Another hot watering hole is the **Calypso Bar,** R. 1 de Maio 22. Close to the water, bars scatter along R. 25 de Abril and its extension, R. Silva Lopes. **Sins,** R. Silva Lopes, has a friendly frat party atmosphere, with beer funneling and the infamous nine deadly sins (9 shots 4000$). A hopping gay bar, **The Last Resort,** is along R. Lançarote de Freitas and has live entertainment every Thursday night. Half a block up the street, the British pub **Taverna Velha** (The Old Tavern) hosts jolly happy hours with televised soccer matches.

■ Near Lagos: Sagres

Marooned atop a bleak, scrub-desert promontory on the barren southwest corner of Europe, Sagres's dramatic, desolate location discourages tour groups and upscale travelers—all the better for the town, which remains one of the most unspoiled destinations in the Algarve. Empty beaches, several open for nude bathing, fringe the peninsula. **Mareta** is at the bottom of the road from the center of town. Rock formations jut out into the ocean on both sides of the sandy crescent. The less popular **Tonel** is along the road east of town. Prince Henry the Navigator's polygonal **stone fortress** dominates the town in regal fashion. From this cliff-top outpost, Vasco da Gama, Magellan, Columbus, Diaz, and Cabral apprenticed in Henry's school of navigation. Six kilometers further west, the **Cabo de São Vicente,** once thought to be the end of the world, hangs onto the southwest tip of continental Europe.

Rodoviária **buses** (tel. (082) 76 29 44) run from Lagos (1hr., 4 per day, 445$); check the schedule to avoid getting stranded. The **tourist office** (tel. (082) 62 00 03), on Pr. República in the main square, recommends accommodations and events, rents **bikes** (2000$ per day), has bus and train schedules, and does laundry. It also organizes a **jeep tour** of the natural preserve (6500$, including lunch) and gives **scuba** advice (open daily 10am-7pm). The **market** is off R. Comandante Matoso; turn left off the main street at R. do Correio (open M-Sa 10am-8pm).

■ Albufeira

Those who come to Albufeira, the largest seaside resort in the Algarve, are hell-bent on relaxation. Of course, relaxation does not have to mean beaches and alcohol; Albufeira has preserved its graceful Moorish architecture in the old quarters of town, and a stroll out from the frenzied center affords a taste of genuine Portuguese culture. But who are we trying to kid? Albufeira's spectacular **beaches** range from the popular **Galé** and **São Rafael** west of town, to the central **Baleeira, Inatel,** and **Oura,** to the very chic **Falésia,** 10km east of town. Many small and relatively uncrowded beaches lie scattered among the *praias*—it pays to explore. The hottest clubs in town, **Disco Silvia's** and **Qué Pasa?,** face off on R. São Gonçalo de Lagos, near the east side of the beach. Other dandy mingling spots include the **Fastnet Bar** on R. Cândido dos Reis and the **Classic Bar** down the street. For more mellow nightlife, head east along the coast into the old town, where salsa tunes complement a stunning seaside view at **Cafe Latino,** on R. Latino Coelho.

The **train station** (tel. (089) 57 16 16), 6km inland, is accessible from town by bus (every hr., 180$). Albufeira is on the Lagos-Vila Real de Santo António line, with frequent departures to Faro (45min., 300$) and Lagos (1½hr., 480$). The **bus station** (tel. (089) 58 97 55) is at the entrance to town, up Av. Liberdade; walk downhill to reach the center. EVA buses head to Faro (1hr., 570$) and Lagos (1½hr., 850$). The **tourist office,** R. 5 de Outubro 5 (tel. (089) 58 52 79), has maps, brochures, and a list of *quartos* (open daily 9:30am-7pm). Many accommodations are booked from the last week in June through mid-September; if you can't find a room, ask for *quartos* around town or choose wisely among renters who meet you at the stations. The modern **Pensão Albufeirense,** R. Liberdade 18 (tel. (089) 51 20 79), one block downhill from the bus station, has comfortable rooms and a TV lounge (singles 3500$; doubles 5000$; open May-Sept.). **Pensão Silva,** R. 5 de Outubro (tel. (089) 51 26 69), near the tourist office, is in an old building with wood floors and chandeliers (singles 3000$; doubles 5000$; Oct.-May 2500$ and 4000$, respectively). **Parque de Campismo de Albufeira** (tel. (089) 58 98 70; fax 58 76 33), a few km outside town on the road to Ferreiras, has swimming pools, restaurants, tennis courts, a supermarket, and a hefty price tag (850$ per person, per car, and per tent). Budget restaurants spill across the old fishing harbor east of the main beach. Locals recommend **Tasca do Viegas,** R. Cais Herculano 2, where meat and fish dishes start at 800$ (open daily 11am-11pm).

Tavira White houses and palm trees fringe the banks of the slow Gilão River and Baroque churches glorify the hills above one of the loveliest communities in the Algarve. Most of Tavira's sights are planted along the side streets leading off Pr. República. Steps from the *praça* lead past the tourist office to the **Igreja da Misericórdia,** whose superb Renaissance doorway glowers with heads sprouting from twisting vines and candelabra. Just beyond, the remains of the city's **Castelo Mouro** (Moorish Castle) enclose the church **Santa Maria do Castelo** and a handsome garden. (Museum open M-F 8am-5:30pm, Sa-Su 10am-7:30pm. Church open daily 9am-8pm.) Local beaches, including **Pedras do Rei**, are close to town and accessible year-round. To reach the excellent beach on **Ilha da Tavira**, an island 2km away, take the Tavira-Quatro Águas bus from Pr. República to the ferry (10min., 13 per day, round-trip 100$; keep ticket stub for the return).

Tavira is easily reached from Faro by **bus** (1hr., 405$) and **train** (1hr., 300$). The **tourist office**, R. Galeria 9 (tel. (089) 32 25 11), off Pr. República, has maps and recommends accommodations. (Open daily 9:30am-7pm; off-season M-F 9:30am-7pm, Sa-Su 9:30am-12:30pm and 2-5:30pm.) Tavira has plenty of *pensões* and *quartos*. **Pensão Residencial Lagôas Bica,** R. Almirante Cândido dos Reis 24 (tel. (089) 222 52), on the far side of the river, has nicely furnished rooms, an outdoor patio, and a rooftop picnic area. From Pr. República, cross the bridge and continue straight down R. A. Cabreira; turn right and go down one block (singles 2500$; doubles 3500-5000$; less in winter). **Ilha de Tavira campground** (tel. (089) 32 35 05) sprawls on the island's beach (340$ per person, 510$ per tent; showers 100$; reception 24hr.; open Feb.-Sept.). Seek and ye shall find reasonably priced cafes and restaurants on Pr. República and opposite the garden on R. José Pires Padinha. **Churrasqueira "O Manuel,"** R. Almirante Cândido dos Reis 6, has food *pronto a comer* (ready to eat) and serves up *febres na brasa* (pork chops) and *entrecostos* (baby back ribs) for 700$ (open W-M 4pm-midnight).

NORTHERN PORTUGAL

Although their landscapes and shared Celtic past invite comparison with neighboring Galicia, the **Douro** and **Minho** regions are more populated and faster developing. South of the Rio Minho lies **Braga,** a busy commercial city whose concentration of religious architecture has earned it the title of "Portuguese Rome." Braga's people are considered by some the most pious, by others the most fanatic, and by all the most conservative in Portugal. Buses travel between Braga and Porto (1½hr., 640$).

Farther inland rises the rugged region of **Trás-os-Montes.** Train service is slow and rickety here, but hiking opportunities, especially in the natural reserves of the Parque Natural de Alvão, abound. Southward lies the region of the **Three Beiras. Beiras Litoral** to the west is swiftly modernizing and rests on the beautiful "Silver Coast." Farther east, however, the mountainous **Beira Alta** and **Beira Baixa** are among the least developed areas in Portugal. Throughout the Beiras, farmers cultivate grapes while silvery olive trees cloud the horizon.

■ Coimbra

Camouflage in Coimbra is easy—students and tourists shouldering backpacks blend harmoniously in and around town and at the renowned University of Coimbra. The charm of the city and its people have long since overshadowed Coimbra's infamous roles as center of the Inquisition and educator of Antònio Salazar, the notorious dictator of Portugal. Crew races, rowdy cafeteria halls, and swinging bars place Coimbra slightly on the wild side from September through May, but its youthful energy, diversity, and collection of medieval buildings welcome visitors year-round.

ORIENTATION AND PRACTICAL INFORMATION

Coimbra has two train stations connected by bus 5: **Coimbra-A,** in the lower town center, and **Coimbra-B,** 3km northwest of town. The lower town lies within the triangle formed by the river, **Largo da Portagem,** and **Praça 8 de Maio.** The university district perches atop the steep hill overlooking the lower town. Downhill, on the other side of the university, the **Praça da República** plays host to cafes, a shopping district, and the youth hostel.

Telephone Code: 039.

Trains: For info on either **station**, call 82 46 32, 83 49 98, or 83 41 27. Trains arriving in Coimbra will stop in Coimbra-B 1st and Coimbra-A 2nd. To: Figueira da Foz (1hr., every hr., 280$), Lisbon (3hr., 15 per day, 1300$), Paris (22hr., 1 per day, 23,000$), and Porto (3hr., 13 per day, 900$).

Buses: Av. Fernão Magalhães (tel. 48 40 45), on the university side of the river, 10min. out of town. To: Évora (6hr., 5 per day, 1850$), Faro (12hr., 4 per day, 2800$), Lisbon (3hr., 15 per day, 1250$), and Porto (6hr., 5 per day, 1200$).

Public Transportation: Buses and street cars handle inner-city traffic. Single tickets run 190$; a book of 10 costs 600$. Special tourist passes are also available. Tickets are sold in kiosks at Largo da Portagem and Pr. República.

Tourist Office: Largo Portagem (tel. 82 86 86 or 83 30 19; fax 82 55 76), 2 blocks upstream from Coimbra-A in a yellow building off the square. The skilled staff offers free maps and accommodations info. Open July-Oct. M-F 9am-7pm, Sa-Su 9am-1pm and 2:30-5:30pm; Oct.-Apr. M-F 9am-6pm, Sa-Su 10am-1pm.

Currency Exchange: Montepio Geral, C. Estrela, behind the tourist office. Decent rates. No charge for transactions less than 10,000$. Open M-F 8:30am-3pm.

Emergency: tel. 112.

Police: R. Olímpio Nicolau Rui Fernandes (tel. 82 20 22), facing the post office. Special division for foreigners on R. Venâncio Rodrigues 25 (tel. 82 40 45).

Hospital: Hospital da Universidade de Coimbra (tel. 40 05 00 or 40 04 00). Near the Cruz de Celas stop on line 29.

Post Office: R. Olímpio Nicolau Rui Fernandes (tel. 82 43 56), across from the police station. Open for *Poste Restante,* telephone, fax, and telegrams M-F 8:30am-6:30pm, Sa 9am-12:30pm. **Postal Code:** 3000.

Telephones: In post offices and at Largo Portagem 1.

ACCOMMODATIONS, CAMPING, AND FOOD

Decent *pensões* (most on side streets of **Avenida Fernão Magalhães**) start at 3500$ for doubles; pay less and pay the consequences. The hostel is an excellent choice if you have an HI card.

Residencia Moderna, R. Adelino Veiga 49 (tel. 82 54 13). Welcoming management will usher you into bright, comfortable rooms (many with terrace) in this *pensão* on a tiny pedestrian street. All with private bath, phone, A/C, and cable TV. Singles 3500-4500$; doubles 5500-6500$. Breakfast included.

Pousada de Juventude de Coimbra (HI), R. Henrique Seco 14 (tel./fax 82 29 55). From Coimbra-A or Largo Portagem, walk 20min. uphill along R. Olímpio Nicolau Rui Fernandes to Pr. República, then up R. Lourenço Azevedo (to the left of the park). Take the 2nd right. Alternatively, take bus 7, 8, 29, or 46 to Pr. República and walk the rest of the way. Recently renovated and welcoming. Dorms 1500$; doubles 4000-5000$; cheaper off-season. Breakfast included. Reception 9-10:30am and 6pm-midnight. Lockout all other times, but bag drop-off all day.

Pensão Rivoli, Pr. Comércio 27 (tel. 82 55 50), in a mercifully quiet pedestrian plaza 1 block downhill from R. Ferreira Borges. Well-furnished rooms are comfortably worn. Singles 2200$; doubles 5000$, with shower 5500$; triples 7000$.

Camping: Municipal Campground (tel. 70 14 97), corralled in a recreation complex ringed by noisy streets. Take bus 1 or 5 from Largo Portagem; enter the campground at the arch off Pr. 25 de Abril. 231$ per person, 163-174$ per tent. Showers included. Reception Apr.-Sept. 9am-10pm; Oct.-Mar. 9am-6pm.

For cheap eats, scout out **Rua Direita,** west off Pr. 8 de Maio, the side streets to the west of Pr. Comércio and Largo da Portagem, and the university district around **Praça da República.** Perhaps the best budget meal deal in the country awaits at the **UC Cantina,** the university's cafeteria. The cafeteria is located on the right side of R. Oliveiro Matos, about a half block downhill from the base of the steps leading from the university to Pr. República. An international student ID is (theoretically) needed to partake of meals for as little as 270$. **Churrasqueria do Mondego,** R. Sargento Mor 25, off R. Sota, serves a half-chicken for 350$ to a friendly student crowd (open daily noon-3pm and 6-10:30pm). The **Supermercado Minipreço** is in the lower town on R. António Granjo 6C; go left out of Coimbra-A and make another left (open M-Sa 9am-8pm). **Cafe Santa Cruz**, Pr. 8 de Maio, has seen better days, but it's still the most popular cafe in town (open daily 7am-2am).

SIGHTS AND ENTERTAINMENT

The best way to take in Coimbra's old town sights is to climb from the river up to the university—and quite a climb it is. Begin the ascent at the ancient **Arco de Almedina**, the remnant of a Moorish-era town wall. Up a narrow stone stairway looms the hulking, 12th-century, Romanesque **Sé Velha** (Old Cathedral). Tours leaving around noon explore the principal tombs and friezes while Gregorian chants echo in the background (open daily 9:30am-12:30pm and 2-5:30pm; cloisters 100$).

Enter the center of the university complex through the **Porta Férrea** (Iron Gate) off R. São Pedro. These buildings were Portugal's de facto royal palace when Coimbra was the capital of the kingdom. The staircase at the right leads up to the **Sala dos Capelos**, where portraits of Portugal's kings hang below a beautifully painted 17th-century ceiling (open daily 10am-noon and 2-5pm; free). Past the Baroque clock-tower are the **university chapel** and the 18th-century **university library** (library open daily 9:30am-noon and 2-5pm; 300$, students with ID free). The library holds 300,000 books from the 12th to 19th centuries in three gilded halls.

The **Igreja de Santa Cruz** (Church of the Holy Cross) on Pr. 8 de Maio, at the far end of R. Ferreira Borges in the lower town, is a 12th-century church with a splendid, barrel-vaulted **sacristía** (sacristy) and ornate **túmulos reals** (royal tombs) where the first two kings of Portugal lie buried (open daily 9am-noon and 3-6pm). Crossing the bridge in front of the other side of the river, you'll find the **Convento de Santa Clara-a-Velha**—smack on top of a swamp. The convent sinks a little deeper each year and today is more than half underground, but the **Convento de Santa Clara-a-Nova** (1649-1677), where Queen Isabel's 14th-century Gothic tomb and a new silver one rest, is standing firm (open daily 8:30am-12:30pm and 2-6:30pm; free). Swallow your pride and mingle with the minors at **Portugal dos Pequenitos**, between the new convent and the river bridge, with scaled-down reproductions of famous Portugese castles and monuments (open M-Sa 10am-5pm; 500$).

Nightlife gets highest honors in student-rich Coimbra. After free beer with dinner in the **U.C. Cantina**, enjoy a few bottles with the crowd at outdoor cafes around **Praça República**, which buzzes from midnight to 4am. Around the corner uphill is the disco **Via Latina**, R. Almeida Garret 1, near the Santa Cruz garden. Free-form *fado* singing resonates from **Bar 1910**, above a gymnasium on R. Simões Castro (beers about 200$; open until 4am).

Figueira da Foz

Halfway between Lisbon and Porto and only an hour from Coimbra, Figueira is one of the biggest (and seediest) party towns in Portugal. Those exhausted by their nights of debauchery collapse on Figueira's beach, which, at 1km by 3km, seems roomy even when packed. Nightlife takes off between 10pm and 2am, depending on the disco or bar, and continues all night. Jumping joints line **Avenida 25 de Abril** next to and above the tourist office. A lively student crowd gathers at **Bergantim**, R. Dr. António Lopes Guimarães, inland from the train station. Party at **CC Cafe**, just off the water at the end of the ramp. A happenin' crowd frequents **Bar 31**, a block away from the beach on R. Cândido dos Reis. The **casino** complex (tel. (033) 220 41) on R. Bernardo Lopes contains a **nightclub** (cover 1500$), **cinema** (500$), and **arcade**. Entry to the slot machines and bingo is free; you must be over 18 and show ID to gamble (casino open July-Aug. daily 4pm-4am; Sept.-June 3pm-3am). Figueira's party mode shifts from high gear to warp speed during the **Festa de São João** (June 6-July 9), featuring free public concerts every night.

Trains connect Figueira da Foz with Coimbra (1hr., 280$), Lisbon (3½hr., 1400$), and Porto (3hr., 1120$). The **tourist office** (tel. (033) 226 10; fax 285 49), on Av. 25 de Abril, next to the Aparthotel Atlântico, has a map and temporary luggage storage (open June-Sept. daily 9am-11pm; Oct.-May M-F 9am-12:30pm and 2-5:30pm). **Pen-**

são Central, R. Bernardo Lopes 36 (tel. (033) 223 08), down the street from the casino, has comfy rooms (singles 4500$; doubles 6000$; triples 7000$). Above an Indian restaurant, the **Pensão Residencial Bela Figueira,** R. Miguel Bombarda 13 (tel. (033) 227 28; fax 299 60), has singles (4500-6200$), doubles (5000-6950$), and triples (5000-7500$). **Parque Municipal de Campismo** (tel. (033) 327 42 or 330 33) beckons with an Olympic-size pool, tennis courts, and market. With the beach to your left, walk up Av. 25 de Abril and turn right at the roundabout on R. Alexandre Herculano. Then turn left at Parque Santa Catarina going up R. Joaquim Sotto-Mayor past Palácio Sotto-Mayor. A taxi from the station costs about 500$. (400$ per person; 300$ per tent and per car. Showers 100$. June-Sept. each party must be at least 2 people. Reception June-Sept. 8am-8pm; Oct.-May 8am-7pm. Quiet time midnight-7am.) For a great meal, try **Restaurante Rancho,** R. Miguel Bombarda 40-44, two blocks up from the tourist office (main courses 650-1100$; open M-Sa 11am-10pm).

■ Porto (Oporto)

Situated on a dramatic gorge cut by the Rio Douro and only 6km from the Atlantic, Porto, Portugal's second-largest city, is an attractive harbor town and the commercial center of the north. Granite church towers pierce the skyline, closely packed orange-tiled houses tumble down to the river, and three of Europe's most graceful bridges span the gorge above. For Henry the Navigator's 1415 invasion of Ceuta, residents here slaughtered their cattle, gave the meat to the Portuguese fleet, and kept only the entrails for themselves. The tasty dish *tripas à moda do Porto* commemorates this culinary self-sacrifice. Porto's real fame, however, springs from the taste of its *vinho.* Developed by English merchants in the early 18th century, the port wine industry across the River Douro in Vila Nova de Gaia drives the economy.

ORIENTATION AND PRACTICAL INFORMATION

Get ready to…get lost. Constant traffic and a chaotic maze of one-way streets disorient even veteran travelers; arm yourself with a map. At the heart of Porto is **Praça da Liberdade.** The **Estação São Bento** lies smack in the middle of town, just off Pr. Liberdade. The **Ribeira,** or Esplanade, district is a few blocks to the south, directly across the bridge from **Vila Nova de Gaia,** the wine house area.

Telephone Code: 02.

Flights: Aeroporto Francisco de Sá Carneiro (tel. 941 32 60 or 941 32 70). Take bus 44 and 56 from Pr. Lisboa. **TAP Air Portugal,** Pr. Mouzinho de Albuquerque 105 (tel. 948 22 91), flies to Lisbon and Madrid.

Trains: Estação de Campanhã (tel. 57 41 61), the main station, is east of the city center. To: Braga, via Nine (2hr., 450$), Coimbra (2½hr., 910$), Lisbon (4½hr., 1950$), Madrid via Entroncamento (12-13hr., 9100$), and Paris (28hr., 24,000$). **Estação de São Bento** (tel. 200 10 54), 1 block off Pr. Liberdade, receives local and regional trains. Buses run to Pr. Liberdade and beyond (every 30min., 170$).

Buses: If you know your destination, ask at Turismo and they'll direct you to a particular company—there is no central station. **Garagem Atlântico,** R. Alexandre Herculano 366 (tel. 200 69 54), serves Coimbra (1½hr., 1200$) and Lisbon (5½hr., 1900$). **Internorte,** Pr. Graliza 96 (tel. 69 32 20 or 48 75), makes trips to Spain, France, Belgium, Switzerland, Germany, and Luxembourg.

Public Transportation: Single trip ticket 160$, 1-day unlimited ticket 350$. Pre-purchase tickets for half price at the small kiosk on the corner, half a block downhill and across the street from the Estação de São Bento.

Tourist Office: R. Clube dos Fenianos 25, just off the top of Pr. Liberdade. The polyglot staff doles out maps. Open July-Sept. M-F 9am-7pm, Sa 9am-4pm, Su 10am-1pm; Oct.-June M-F 9:30am-5:30pm, Sa 9am-4pm.

Currency Exchange: ATMs line Pr. Liberdade and can be found throughout the city. Most banks on **Pr. Liberdade** offer currency exchange (open M-F 8:30am-3pm), and some have automatic currency exchange machines outside.

American Express: Top Tours, R. Alferes Malheiro 96 (tel. 208 27 85). Open M-F 9am-12:30pm and 2:30-6:30pm.
Emergency: tel. 112.
Police: R. Alexandre Herculano (tel. 200 68 21).
24-Hour Pharmacy: Dial 118 to find out which pharmacy is open.
Medical Assistance: Hospital de Santo António, R. Prof. Vicente José de Carvalho (tel. 200 52 41 or 200 73 54).
Post Office: Pr. General Humberto Delgado (tel. 31 98 77), next to the town hall. Open for *Poste Restante* (60$ per item), fax, phones, and stamps M-F 8am-9pm, Sa-Su 9am-6pm. **Postal Code:** 4000.
Telephones: Pr. Liberdade 62. Open daily 8am-11:30pm. Also at the post office.

ACCOMMODATIONS, CAMPING, AND FOOD

Most *pensões* lie west of Av. Aliados and on Rua de Fernandes Tomás and Rua Formosa, perpendicular to the Aliados Sq. Rates for singles can be criminal; shop around for a reasonable deal.

Residencial Paris, R. da Fábrica 27-9 (tel. 32 14 21). Cross Pr. Liberdade from the train station and turn left onto R. Dr. Artur de Magalhães Basto, which quickly turns into R. Fábrica. Friendly, English-speaking manager, large rooms, and lush garden. Singles 5000$; doubles 7000$. Reservations highly recommended.
Pensão São Marino, Pr. Carlos Alberto 59 (tel. 32 54 99). Facing town hall, go up the street on the left and take the 1st left onto R. Dr. Ricardo Jorge, which becomes R. Conceição; turn left onto R. Oliveiras and make a quick right onto Pr. Carlos Alberto. All rooms have a bath or shower. Singles 3000-4500$; doubles 4000-6500$; triples 4500-7000$; off-season 500$ less. Breakfast included.
Pousada de Juventude do Porto (HI), Paulo da Gama 551 (tel. 617 72 47). Take bus 3, 20, or 52 (10min., 160$) from the stop on the lower west end of Pr. Liberdade toward the river. After a right onto R. Júlio Dinis, get off at the 2nd traffic light. Cross the street and walk 1 block uphill; hang a left at the billboard. Lively social scene. Dorms 1800$; doubles with bath 5000$; cheaper off-season. Reception 9-11am and 6pm-midnight. Reservations highly recommended.
Camping: Prelada (tel. 81 26 16), R. Monte dos Burgos, Quinta da Prelada, 5km from the beach. Take bus 6 from Pr. Liberdade. 550$ per person, 475$ per tent and per car. **Salgueiros** (tel. 781 05 00), near Praia de Salgueiros in Vila Nova de Gaia, is harder to reach and has fewer amenities, but is closer to the surf. 200$ per person and per tent; 100$ per car. Open May-Sept.

Restaurant food costs more in Porto than in any other Portuguese city. Pick up produce and supplies at the **markets** that line Cais de Ribeira (open daily 8am-8pm) or at the **Mercado de Bolhão,** on the corner of R. Formosa and R. Sá de Bandeira (open M-F 8am-6pm, Sa 7am-1pm). If you can afford something more elegant, colorful and expensive restaurants border the river in the Ribeira district, particularly on **Cais da Ribeira, Rua Reboleira,** and **Rua de Cima do Muro.** Cheaper eateries surround the **Hospital de Santo António** and **Praça de Gomes Teixeira.** On a street parallel to Av. Aliados, **Churrasqueira Moura,** R. Almada 219, has dirt-cheap, solid meals (half portions 850$; full portions less than 1300$; open M-Sa 9am-10pm).

SIGHTS AND ENTERTAINMENT

Fortified on the hilltop south of the train station is Porto's pride and joy, the **cathedral,** situated in one of the city's oldest residential districts. It was built in the 12th and 13th centuries, and the Gothic, *azulejo*-covered cloister was added in the 14th century. The **Capela do Santíssimo Sacramento** to the left of the altar shines with solid silver and plated gold (open daily 9am-12:30pm and 2:30-6pm; cloister 200$).

Cash acquires cachet at the **Palácio da Bolsa** (Stock Exchange), R. Ferreira Borges, the epitome of 19th-century elegance. (Open Apr.-Oct. Tu-Sa 2-8pm, Sa-Su 10am-8pm; Nov.-Mar. Tu-Su 2-7pm. Tours 700$, students 550$. Main courtyard free.) Although tours are pricey, get a feel for its opulence by popping in to peer at the

PORTUGAL

Fine Wine, Port Gratis

Woe to the backpacker who has spent her last ducats on that pint of pissy ale! Let her dock her parched mouth and empty pockets in Porto where the fine and bounteous port wines are completely *gratuito* (free). As you'll learn while waiting impatiently for the tours to terminate and the toasting to begin, port was discovered when some enterprising English wine dealers added a strong brandy to cheap Portuguese wine to prevent it from souring *en route* to England. Nowadays, wine from grapes grown in the Douro Valley 100km west of Porto is mixed with 170 proof brandy and aged in barrels to yield port. The lodges are across the river in Vila Nova da Gaia—cross the lower level of the large bridge. A good starter is **Sandeman,** with costumed guides and high-quality port. **Cálem,** next door, has a less stilted tour, and the port's almost as good. At **Ferreira,** down the road from Sandeman, you'll learn about the famed *senhora* who built the Ferreira empire in the late 19th century. And finally, **Taylor's** wins the highly unscientific *Let's Go* poll for best port in Porto.

---

ornate courtyard ceiling. To get to the Bolsa, turn left out of the cathedral and follow the winding streets straight ahead to Travessa da Bainharia and Largo de Santo Domingos; the Bolsa is downhill on the right. From in front of the train station, follow R. Mouzinho da Silveira to the square. Next door to the Bolsa, the Gothic **Igreja de São Francisco** glitters with one of the most elaborate gilded wood interiors in Portugal. (Museum and church open Apr.-Oct. M-F 9am-6pm, Su 9am-5pm; Nov.-Mar. M-Sa 9am-5pm. 500$, students and seniors 250$.) Under the floor, thousands of human bones have been stored in the *osseria* in preparation for Judgement Day.

To get to Porto's rocky and polluted but popular **beach** in the ritzy Foz district, take bus 78 from P. Liberdade (one-way 160$) and jump off wherever you fancy. At the bottom of the hill on R. Alfândega, the **Ribeira** (Esplanade) skirts past a marvelous quay filled with shops and restaurants.

Back uphill rises the 82m **Torre dos Clérigos** (Tower of Clerics). Built in the mid-18th century and the city's most prominent landmark, its granite bell tower glimmers like a grand processional candle. Mount the 200 steps to view Porto and the Rio Douro Valley (open daily 10:30am-noon and 2-5pm; church free; tower 130$). For modern art in a lovely setting, visit the **Fundação Casa de Serralves (Museu de Arte Moderna),** a contemporary museum west of the town center on the way to the beach. The building crowns an impressive 44 acres of sculptured gardens, fountains, and even old farmland tumbling down toward the Douro River (museum open Tu-F 2-8pm, Sa-Su 10am-8pm; 300$, students 150$, Th free). Bus 78 leaves for the museum from Pr. Dom João I—ask the driver for the museum stop (about 30min. to R. Serralves, one-way 160$, buses return until midnight).

The place to party on weekend nights is the tirelessly fun **Ribeira,** where bars vibrate with the rhythms of Brazilian and Latin tunes. **Praça da Ribeira, Mura dos Bacalhoeiros,** and **Rua Alfândega** harbor most of the bars and pubs. Try **Pub O Muro,** Muro dos Bacalhoeiros 87-88, right above the riverside near the bridge going to the port wine houses. **Discoteca Swing,** on R. Júlio Dinis near the youth hostel, caters to a mixed gay-straight crowd (cover about 1000$).

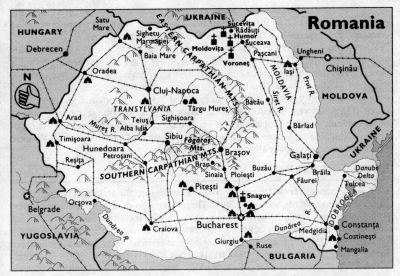

Romania (România)

US$1	= 8910 lei (ROL)		**1000 lei =**	**US$0.11**
CDN$1	= 5680 lei		**1000 lei =**	**CDN$0.18**
UK£1	= 14,900 lei		**1000 lei =**	**UK£0.07**
IR£1	= 12,600 lei		**1000 lei =**	**IR£0.08**
AUS$1	= 5030 lei		**1000 lei =**	**AUS$0.20**
NZ$1	= 4400 lei		**1000 lei =**	**NZ$0.23**
SAR1	= 1380 lei		**1000 lei =**	**SAR0.73**
DM1	= 5030 lei		**1000 lei =**	**DM0.20**

Country Phone Code: 40   **International Dialing Prefix: 00**

Ensconced within the mysterious Carpathian Mountains, Romanians preserve folk traditions abandoned in the rest of Europe centuries ago. The fortified towns of Transylvania still look like an array of medieval woodcuts, and the green hills of Moldavia remain as serene as the frescoes on their monastery walls. Sadly, more recent developments have come to overshadow the picturesque charm of these rural retreats: during Nicolae Ceauşescu's 24-year tyranny, Romania was the poorest and most totalitarian country in the Soviet Bloc, and industrial soot, a peculiarly communist gigantomania, and socialist concrete blocks still tarnish Bucharest and several other cities. The rebellion that destroyed Ceauşescu, in which he and his wife were summarily executed on Christmas Day, was by far the most vicious in Eastern Europe, but the country has not embraced the reformation of its system with the same zeal. The 1996 election was the first democratic transfer of power in Romania's history, but the people are still struggling with unemployment, corruption, and ignorance. Romania remains under-touristed and inexpensive, however, and the idiosyncratic, colorful buildings of its regional towns possess a magical, even cheerful, beauty.

For more thorough coverage of Romania, brave *Let's Go: Eastern Europe 1999*.

GETTING THERE

Citizens of the U.S. can visit Romania **visa-free** for up to 30 days, but citizens of Australia, Canada, Ireland, New Zealand, South Africa, and the U.K. all need visas. Single-entry (US$25) and multiple-entry (US$70) visas allow two- and six-month stays, respectively; a transit visa (US$25) is valid for four days. You can obtain a visa at the border with no additional fee. If you prefer to prepare in advance, contact an **embassy** or **consulate** (see **Government Information Offices,** p. 5).

You can **fly** into Bucharest on Air France, Alitalia, AUA, British Airways, Delta, Lufthansa, or TAROM. **TAROM** (Romanian Airlines) is currently renewing its aging fleet and also flies to most major European cities. Daily **trains** head from Bucharest via Budapest to Munich and Vienna. There are also direct trains to and from Moscow, Prague, Sofia, and Warsaw. To buy international tickets in Romania, go to the **CFR** office in larger towns. An ISIC will occasionally get you 50% off on domestic tickets, but technically the discount applies only to Romanian students. **Buses** connect major cities in Romania to Athens, Istanbul, Prague, Varna, and various cities in Western Europe. Buses are typically slow but fairly inexpensive.

GETTING AROUND

CFR sells domestic **train** tickets up to 24 hours before the train's departure. After that, only train stations will sell tickets. There is an info desk at all stations (staffers sometimes speak English), where you can inquire which counter sells tickets to your destination. The train timetable *Mersul Trenurilor* is incredibly useful in forming your plans (10,000 lei; instructions in English and French). **InterRail** is accepted, but **Eurail** is not. There are four types of trains: *InterCity* (IC), *rapid* or *expres* (in green), *accelerat* (red), and *personal* (black or blue). *InterCity* trains stop only at major cities. *Rapid* trains are the next fastest. *Personal* are slow, dirty, and stop at nearly every station. If taking an overnight train, opt for first class in a *vagon de dormir* (sleeping carriage). During holidays and in July and August, try to buy train tickets to the beach five days in advance. Use the extensive local **bus** system only when trains are not available; they are usually packed and poorly ventilated. Look for signs for the bus station *(autogară)* in each town. Hitchers report success, but consider the safety risks. A wave of the hand is the recognized sign; drivers generally expect a payment similar to the price of a train ticket.

ESSENTIALS

ONT (National Tourist Office) doesn't always give reliable information about the price and availability of cheap rooms. Branches in expensive hotels are often more useful than the main offices. The most common banknotes are 500, 1000, 5000, 10,000, 50,000, and the new 100,000 **lei.** Pay for everything in lei; when someone offers to take U.S. dollars directly, it's usually at a disadvantageous rate. Private **exchange bureaus** litter the country, but few take credit cards and traveler's checks. German and U.S. currencies are preferred, though others can be exchanged in some places. Whatever currency you have, know the going rates and commissions before exchanging anywhere. Unofficial currency exchange is illegal and risky; train stations demand special wariness. Don't hand over your money before you get your lei, and be especially careful afterward.

Many banks and businesses close on Friday afternoons. National **holidays** include: New Year's (Jan. 1-3), Orthodox Easter (3-4 days), Labor Day (May 1), Union Day (Dec. 1), and Christmas (Dec. 25-31).

Many Romanians hold conservative attitudes about sexuality; these attitudes may translate into harassment of gay and bisexual travelers, but affection is not uncommon between Romanian women. Homosexuality was only recently legalized in Romania. Be aware also that public **hygiene** in Romania will challenge Westerners. Most public restrooms lack soap, towels, and toilet paper, and even "privatized" public bathrooms that charge 300-500 lei may give you only a square of toilet paper. Feminine hygiene products are available in large cities. If you have to buy medicine in Romania, know what you're purchasing: *antinevralgic* for headaches, *piramidon* for colds and the flu, and *saprosan* for diarrhea. Condoms, available at drugstores and many vending kiosks, are called *prezervative.*

COMMUNICATION Orange and blue-and-orange **phones** take phone cards; other phones take coins. Unless you like the idea of carrying around a kilogram of coins, use a phone card, available at post and telephone offices in denominations of 20,000 and 50,000 lei. Rates per minute run around 5000 lei to most of Europe, and 9000 lei to the U.S. For **AT&T Direct,** dial 018 00 42 88; **MCI WorldPhone,** 018 00 18 00; **Sprint,** 018 00 08 77; **Canada Direct,** 018 00 50 00; **BT Direct,** 018 00 44 44. Some pay phones will cut off calling card calls after two or five minutes. **Local calls** cost 350-600 lei and can be made from any phone; **intercity** calls can be made from the new digital phones (orange and blue) or from old phones marked *telefon interurban*. Dial several times before giving up; a busy signal can just indicate a bad connection. In a small town, it may be necessary to a make a call with the help of an operator in a telephone office. It's no easy task (and it costs more), but it may be the only option. At the phone office, write down the destination, duration, and phone number for your call. Pay up front, and always ask for the rate per minute.

Romanian is a Romance language; travelers familiar with French, Italian, Spanish, or Portuguese can usually decipher public signs. Young Romanians often speak some English, and French or Russian are widely spoken by the older generation.

Yes/No	*Da/Nu*	dah/noo
Hello	*Bună ziua*	BOO-nuh zee-wah
Please	*Vă rog*	vuh rohg
Thank you	*Mulţumesc*	mool-tsoo-MESK
Excuse me	*Scuzaţi-mă*	skoo-ZAH-tz muh
Do you speak English?	*Vorbiţi englezeşţē?*	vor-BEE-tz ehng-leh-ZESH-teh
I don't understand	*Nu înţeleg*	noo ihn-TZEH-lehg
Where is...?	*Unde...?*	OON-deh
How much does this cost?	*Cît costă?*	kiht KOH-stuh
Do you have a vacancy?	*Aveţi camere libere?*	a-VETS CA-mer-eh LEE-ber-e
Check, please.	*Plata, vă rog*	PLAH-tah, VUH rohg
Help!	*Ajutor!*	AH-zhoot-or

ACCOMMODATIONS, CAMPING, FOOD, AND DRINK In general, **hotels** charge foreigners two to three times the price for Romanians. One-star hotels are iffy, corresponding to a mediocre youth hostel, two-star are decent, and three-star are good but expensive. If you go to the ONT office and ask for a room, you may get a price up to 50% lower than that quoted directly at the hotel. **Private accommodations** are a good idea; rooms run 50,000-80,000 lei, breakfast included. Hosts rarely speak English, and renting a room with someone else generally means sharing a bed. Always see the room and fix a price before you accept. Many towns reserve **university dorms** for foreign students at insanely low prices; ask local university officials or the ONT. **Campgrounds** are crowded, and their bathrooms are very often dirty.

An average homemade dish is probably better than the similar dish cooked at Romanian restaurants, so try to get an invitation. Lunch usually starts with a tasty soup, called *supă* or *ciorbă* (the latter is saltier and has vegetables), followed by a main dish (usually grilled pork, beef, or chicken) and dessert. Pork comes in several varieties, of which *muşchi* and *cotlet* are the best quality. Restaurants often quote prices for meats in lei per 100g and charge for every side order, including bread. Vegetarians will probably want to stick to salads. For dessert, *clătite* (crepes) or *papanaşi* (donuts with jam and sour cream) can be fantastic when they're fresh. Local specialties include *mămăligă* (cornmeal served with butter, cheese, and sour cream) and delicious *sarmale* (ground meat wrapped in grape or cabbage leaves). If you have to fend for yourself, private bakeries sell the best *pîine* (bread), and street vendors offer cheap *mititei* (garlicky barbecued ground meat; make sure the meat is fresh).

ROMANIA

Bucharest
ACCOMMODATIONS
D Hanul Manuc
B Hotel Cernuc
A Hotel Triumf
C Villa Helga Y. H.

Bucharest (București)

Bucharest bears the scars of Romania's political struggles. The city was known in the 19th century as "Little Paris" and "Pearl of the Balkans" for its beautiful boulevards, parks, and fine Neoclassical architecture. But Ceaușescu's government demolished historic neighborhoods in the area and replaced them with concrete housing, and today Bucharest is a somber ghost of its former self.

ORIENTATION AND PRACTICAL INFORMATION

Trains connect Bucharest, 60km north of the Danube, with most Eastern European capitals. From the main train station, take a left, then a right at (Magazin) Sora onto **Calea Griviței**, heading east, then take another right onto **Calea Victoriei** to reach the sights. Or walk another four blocks on strada Biserica Amzei, the continuation of

Griviței, to **bulevardul Magheru** (which becomes Bd. Bălcescu, then Bd. Brătianu), the main artery in Bucharest. The Metro and trolley 79 or 86 lead to Piața Romană, where Bd. Magheru starts.

Telephone code: 01.

Flights: Otopeni Airport (tel. 230 00 22), 16km from the city, handles international traffic. Bus 783 leaves for the airport from Piața Unirii every 1-1½hr. (7000 lei). From Otopeni, buses stop near the Hotel Intercontinental on Bd. Magheru. **Băneasa Airport** (tel. 232 00 20), linked with Piața Romană by bus 131 (1400 lei) and the train station by bus 205, handles domestic flights. Buy international tickets at the **CFR/TAROM office**, Str. Brezoiamu 10 (tel. 646 33 46). The **domestic** TAROM office, Piața Victoriei (tel. 659 41 85), sells domestic and international tickets. Both open M-F 7:30am-7:30pm, Sa 7:30am-1:30pm.

Trains: Gara de Nord (tel. 223 08 80) is the principal station. **Obor** (tel. 635 07 02), accessible by trolley 85 from Gara de Nord or 69 from Piață Universității, and **Băneasa** (tel. 222 48 56), accessible by bus 301 from Piață Romană, serve the Black Sea Coast. **Tickets** can be purchased in advance at **CFR**, Str. Brezoiamu 10 (tel. 614 55 28). Open M-F 8am-7pm, Sa 8am-noon. One or more trains per day serve Budapest (13hr., 295,000 lei), Istanbul (18hr., 208,000 lei), Kiev (17hr., 354,000 lei), and Sofia (10hr., 205,000 lei). Also to: Berlin, Moscow, Munich, Prague, and Vienna.

Buses: Filaret, Piața Gării Filaret 1 (tel. 336 06 92), and **Rahova,** Șos. Alexandriei 164 (tel. 220 44 10), are in the south suburbs; **Obor** and **Băneasa** train stations also contain bus stations. For international buses, the **Toros** bus line (tel. 638 24 24), outside Gara de Nord, sells tickets to Istanbul (leaving from Gara de Nord; 12-15hr., 200,000 lei). For buses to Athens, try **Liotsikas,** Bd. Cantemir 25, bloc 2B, apt. #38 (tel. 330 46 46; 20hr., 3 per week, US$65 or 600,000 lei). **Amad Touristik,** Str. Ankara 14, serves destinations in Western Europe (open M-F 9am-5pm; Sa 9am-2pm). International buses tend to be better than trains.

Public Transportation: Bus, trolley, and tram rides cost 1300 lei. Tickets, which must be punched, are sold at kiosks near most stops or on some buses. Buses are packed on busy routes—mind your valuables. The **Metro** runs daily 5am-midnight; keep your magnetic metro card to avoid unmerciful fines.

Tourist Offices: For decent help, head to the **ONT** office, Bd. Magheru 7 (tel. 614 07 59). From Piața Romană, walk down Magheru; ONT is on the right. The staff offers maps (10,000 lei), tours, and accommodations across Romania. Their private rooms run US$25-35 per person in the center. Open M-F 8am-8pm, Sa 8am-3pm, Su 8am-1pm. Major hotels also have ONT desks or private tourist desks.

Embassies: Canada, Str. Nicolae Iorga 36 (tel. 222 98 45), near Piața Romană. Open M-F 9am-5pm. **Russia,** Șos. Kiseleff 6 (tel. 617 13 19). Open M, W, and F 9am-1pm. Citizens of **Australia, Ireland,** and **New Zealand** should contact the **U.K.** embassy, Str. Jules Michelet 24 (tel. 312 03 03; fax 312 02 29). Open M-Th 8:30am-1pm and 2-5pm, F 8:30am-1:30pm. **U.S.,** Str. Snagov 26 (tel. 210 40 42, after-hours 210 01 49; fax 211 33 60). Open M-Th 8am-11:30am and 1-3pm, F 8-11:30am.

Currency Exchange: Use currency exchange offices instead of the black market. Banks often charge high commissions. For a better rate, try the **O.K. exchange bureaus,** 16 N. Bălcescu (open 24hr.; traveler's checks 4% commission, weekends 7%), and Bd. Magheru 33 (open M-F 8:30am-9:30pm, Sa 8:30am-8pm). **ATMs** are at major banks.

American Express: Bd. Magheru 43, 1st fl., #1 (tel. 223 12 04). Replaces lost cards and checks, but doesn't cash traveler's checks. Open M-F 9am-5pm, Sa 10am-1pm.

Luggage Storage: At Gara de Nord. 4800-9600 lei. Open 24hr.

Emergencies: Fire, tel. 981. **Ambulance,** tel. 961.

Police: tel. 955.

24-Hour Pharmacy: Șos. Colentina 1 (tel. 635 50 10), by the Bucur Obor Metro stop, and in Gara de Nord (tel. 222 91 55). Ring the bell at night. Info tel. 065 or 931.

Medical Assistance: Spitalul de Urgență, Calea Floreasca 8 (tel. 230 01 06). Near the Ștefan cel Mare Metro station.

Post Office: Str. Matei Millo 10 (tel. 613 03 87). Open M-F 7:30am-8pm, Sa 7:30am-2pm. *Poste Restante* is 3 doors down, next to Hotel Carpati. **Postal code:** 70154.

ROMANIA

Internet Access: Raffles, Calea Victoriei 25 (tel. 311 26 82), just south of Bd. Carol I. 8500 lei per 30min., email printing (4500 lei per page). Open M-F 10am-6pm.

Telephones: Orange **card phones** allow international calls from throughout the city. Try the train station and the **telephone office,** Calea Victoriei 37. Open M-F 7:30am-8pm, Sa 8am-2pm.

ACCOMMODATIONS

The ONT office on Bd. Magheru can arrange private rooms or hotel accommodations. During the school year, Romanian students will often share their drab rooms; try the student **dormitories** between the Grozăvești and the Semănătoarea Metro. It can be hard to find a decent hotel room for less than 200,000-300,000 lei per person.

Villa Helga Youth Hostel, Str. Salcâmilor 2 (tel. 610 22 14). Meet staffers at Gara de Nord or take bus 86, 79, or 133 from Piața Romană to Piața Galați (east along Bd. Dacia), then take a right on Str. V. Lascăr, a hard left on Str. Viitorului, and a right on Str. Salcâmilor. Friendly and funny staff provide free laundry and strong Romanian cigarettes. TV room. 102,000 lei per bed; breakfast included. Kitchen.

Hanul Manuc, Str. Iuliu Maniu 62-64 (tel. 613 14 15; fax 312 28 11). From Unirea and McDonald's in Piața Unirii, head straight along the north side of Piața Unirii and take the first right. Hanul Manuc is across from the church. Great rooms with luxurious decor and bath. Singles L265,000; doubles L490,000. Reserve 1 week ahead.

Hotel Triumf, Șos. Kiseleff 12 (tel. 222 31 72; fax 223 24 11). Take bus or trolley 131, 205, 301, or 331 (from Piața Lahovari) to Arcul de Triumf and walk south on Șos. Kiseleff. Singles 370,000-400,000 lei; doubles 540,000-600,000 lei.

Hotel Cerna, Str. Golescu 29 (tel. 637 40 87). A nice hotel next to Gara de Nord. Exit the station and turn right. Small but pleasant rooms. Singles 75,000-195,000 lei; doubles 105,000-300,000 lei; apartments 435,000 lei.

FOOD

Daily **open-air markets** offering all manner of veggies, fruits, meats, and cheese abound in Bucharest—good ones are at Piața Amzei, Piața Matache, and Piața Latina. **Vox Maris Supermarket,** at Piața Victoriei, is open 24 hours. When dining in a restaurant, be sure you're not ripped off; check the math. Fast-food restaurants like McDonald's are usually more expensive than a quality restaurant.

Cafe de la Joie, Str. Lipscani 80-82. From Piața Universității, walk down Bd. I.C. Babtianu and turn right on Str. Lipscani, then take the next left. French-style bistro. Salads 18,000 lei. Open M-Sa 6pm-2am or 3am.

Carul cu Bere, Str. Stavropoleos 5. Stuffed cabbage leaves with polenta 22,000 lei. Meals up to 46,000 lei. Folklore shows nightly at 8pm. Open daily 10am-1am.

Pescarul (The Fisherman), Bd. N. Bălcescu 9, across the street from Hotel Intercontinental at Piața Universității. Seafood 25,000-30,000 lei. Open M-Sa 10am-11pm.

Club Art Papillon, Str. Matei Voievod 66A, off Bd. Pache Protopopescu. Artsy hangout with music during the school year. Meat dishes under 20,000 lei. Open 24hr.

SIGHTS

In the heart of downtown is **Piața Universității,** home to the **National Theater.** Demonstrators perished fighting Ceaușescu's forces here on December 21, 1989, the day before his fall. In spring 1990, students declared the square a "Neo-Communist-free zone," and for almost two months their daily meetings here gathered tens of thousands of people. The government brought in miners to brutally end the demonstration in June. Today, crosses commemorate the martyrs.

From the fascinating 18th-century **St. John's Church** on Bd. Brătianu, continue down the boulevard to **Piața Unirii.** Ceaușescu drastically rearranged the square, but spared **Dealul Mitropoliei,** the small hill on the southwest side. Head up Str. Dealul Mitropoliei to find the headquarters of the Romanian Orthodox Church in one of the largest **cathedrals** in Romania. *(Open daily 8am-7pm.)* The cathedral flanks the Communist **parliament building,** now owned by the church. Left down Bd. Unirii from the Dealul is the world's second-largest building (after the Pentagon), the **Palatul Parla-mentului,** formerly **Casa Poporului** (People's House). Ceaușescu spent billions of dollars and destroyed historic neighborhoods for this private palace.

The oldest buildings in Bucharest are northwest of Piața Unirii, in the triangle between the river, Bd. Brătianu, and Bd. Kogălniceanu. Behind Hanul Manuc, in Piața Unirii, are the ruins of the old princely court, **Curtea Veche.** In the old town at the corner of Str. Stavropoleus and Calea Victoriei is the **Muzeul National de Istorie a României** (History Museum of Romania), Calea Victoriei 12; the Romanian treasures here include the famed *cloșca cu pui de aur* (golden hen and chicks) *(Open W-Su 10am-5pm.)* North of Piața Universitații, along Bd. N. Bălcescu, is the elegant **Ateneul Român,** the country's premier music hall and acoustically the continent's second best (after Milan). The concert hall's fresco depicts Romanian history from Dacia to World War I, but restoration work unfortunately prevents access to the interior. To the north, **Muzeul Colecțiilor de Artă,** Calea Victoriei 111, near Bd. Dacia, displays private collections of Romanian painting and temporary exhibits. *(Open W-Su 10am-6pm. 5000 lei, students 2500 lei, W free.)* Next door, **Muzeul Țăranului Român** (Peasant Museum) displays religious objects as well as textiles and folk crafts. *(Open Tu-Su 10am-6pm. Ticket booth closes at 5pm. 5000 lei, students 2000 lei.)*

On the other side of town, **Muzeul Național Cotroceni** (tel. 221 12 00) offers a tour of royal apartments. Originally built as a monastery, Cotroceni became home to Romania's crown prince Ferdinand. Call ahead to join a mandatory tour. *(Open M-F 9:30am-4pm. 25,000 lei, temporary exhibits 10,000 lei. English pamphlet 5000 lei.)* Near Parcul Herăstrău on Șos. Kiseleff stands **Arcul de Triumf,** built to celebrate Romania's independence from Turkey in 1877. It is accessible by bus 205, 301, and 331. The sidestreets between Piața Victoriei and Calea Dorobanților, with names like Paris, Washington, and Londra, brim with villas and houses typical of the beautiful Bucharest that was. Well-groomed **Cișmigiu Park** is, along with Herăstrău Park, the focal point for much of the city's social life. Elderly pensioners, young couples, chess whizzes, and football players abound.

ENTERTAINMENT

The magnificent **Ateneul** concert hall in Piața Revoluției (tel. 315 68 75) often hosts excellent concerts at affordable prices. Also check out the **Opera Română** (tel. 613 18 57) and the **Teatrul de Operetă** (tel. 613 63 48) near the **Teatrul Național** (tel. 613 91 75). Most shows are in Romanian. Some tickets are available one hour before show times, and managers may provide house seats. Bucharest hosts some of the biggest rock festivals this side of Berlin; inquire at the tourist office and keep your eyes peeled for posters detailing upcoming events. Whatever you do in the evening, pack a map and cab fare; the streets are poorly lit and buses are unreliable.

Dubliner Irish Pub, Bd. N. Titulescu 18. Pricey, but has Guinness, English-speakers, and celebrations of Irish holidays. Open daily noon-3am.

R1, R2, R3 ("Regie"), amid student dorms in the area between the Semănătoarea and Grozăvești metro stops. The most popular discos in town during the school year (Oct.-late June). Take the last metro (11:30pm) to Semănătoarea and let the noisy crowd through the maze of dorms lead you. Open daily Oct.-late June 9:30pm-4am; cover: men 10,000 lei, women Sa-Su 5000 lei, M-F free.

Hard 'n' Heavy, Str. Gabroveni 14 (tel. 615 08 12), down the street from Cafe de la Joie. Rock music draws those who've come to drink, dance, or hang out in the Old Town. 10,000 lei drink minimum. Open daily 8pm-5am.

Laptărie, at the National Theater; take the elevator to the top. Winter jazz concerts 15,000-30,000 lei; summer movies shown out on the terrace 5000 lei. Terrace open in summer daily 9:30pm-2am or 4am; bar open 10am-2am off-season.

Cafe Indigo, Str. Eforie 2. off Culea Victoriei. Jazz and blues make noise here every Tu, F, and Su during the school year, while a movie theater showing classic films operates during the day. Light meals around 15,000 lei. Open 24hr.

TRANSYLVANIA

Although it is a very Westernized region, the legends linking Transylvania with vampires and black magic take their cue from the architecture: the buildings here are tilted, jagged, and more sternly Gothic than anywhere else in Eastern Europe. Remarkably colorful in the day, in relief they rise forebodingly against the twilit sky.

■ Cluj-Napoca

Transylvania's unofficial capital and largest student center, Cluj is over 70% Romanian (including the ardently nationalist mayor) with a vocal Hungarian minority. A massive renovation of historic buildings has largely been completed, restoring Cluj to full splendor. To reach the center of town, take bus 3 or 4, left and across the street from the train station, to Piaţa Mihai Viteazul (round-trip 2400 lei); continue along the road and turn right on Bd. 21 Decembrie 1989 (which commemorates the victims of the 1989 revolution). By foot, cross the street and head down Str. Horea, which changes to Str. Gh. Doja after crossing the river. At the end of Str. Gh. Doja spreads the main drag, **Piaţa Unirii,** where the 80m Gothic steeple of the Catholic **Church of St. Michael** offers a magnificent city view. Near the cathedral stands the **equestrian statue of Mathias Rex,** a half-Hungarian, half-Romanian ruler in the 15th Century—the statue has become the emblem of ethnic tension in the city. The fanciest of the square's Hungarian palaces is **Bánffy Palace,** Piaţa Unirii 30, home to the **Art Museum** (open W-Su 10am-5pm; 6000 lei). From Piaţa Unirii, head to **Piaţa Avram Iancu,** along either busy Str. 21 Dec. 1989 or Bd. Eroilor. Tickets to the **National Theater and Opera** in the square are affordable (best seats 10,000 lei, students 2100 lei). Buy tickets at Piaţa Ştefan cel Mare 14 (tel. (064) 19 53 63; open daily 11am-5pm). Other sights to see include the **History Museum,** Str. Constantin Daicoviciu 2 (open Tu-Su 10:30am-4pm; 3000 lei), and the **Ethnographic Museum,** Str. Memorandumului 21 (open Tu-Su 9am-5pm; 3000 lei, students 1500 lei).

Cluj-Napoca is accessible by **train** from Braşov (4hr., 39,400 lei), Bucharest (7hr., 45,600 lei), Budapest (5-7hr., 205,000 lei), and Iaşi via Suceava (9hr., 45,600 lei). The **tourist office,** Piaţa Unirii 29 (tel. (064) 19 11 14), changes money and may be able to find you a room (US$9-20; open M-F 8am-6pm, Sa 9am-2pm). **OJT Feleacul,** Str. Memorandumului (tel. (064) 19 69 55), three blocks from Unirii, offers similar services (open M-F 8am-8pm, Sa-Su 9am-12:30pm). **Hotel Onix,** Str. Albini 12 (tel. (064) 41 40 76; fax 41 40 47), has gorgeous rooms with shower, phone, and color TV (singles and doubles 209,000 lei; breakfast included). Take bus 3 to "Albini." **Hotel Melody,** Piaţa Unirii 29 (tel. (064) 19 74 65), has a restaurant, sidewalk cafe, game room, and a very risqué cabaret show (nightly 11pm-midnight; doubles 150,000-250,000 lei). A **market** sprawls over Piaţa Mihai Viteazul during daylight. Climb Cetăţuie Hill to **Restaurant Panoramic,** Str. Şerpuitoare 31, for the view and follow the gravel path behind Hotel Transilvania away from the cross monument. Soup with dumplings, cream, and lemon (L7156) will wash away fatigue (open M 2:30pm-midnight, Tu-Su noon-1am). Relax at **Diesel,** Piaţa Unirii 15, a stylish jazz bar near St. Michael's Church (open 24hr.), or try **Bianco & Nero,** Universităţü 7-9, a popular disco.

■ Sighişoara

Of all the medieval towns in Transylvania, Sighişoara (see-ghee-SHWAH-rah) is perhaps the least spoiled and the most enchanting. Surrounded by mountains and crowning a green hill on the railroad line between Cluj and Braşov, Sighişoara's gilded steeples, old clock tower, and irregular tile roofs have survived centuries of attacks and natural disaster. You can enter the **Cetatea** (Citadel) through the **clock tower** off Str. O. Goga. The **history museum** inside offers an outstanding view of the area and a peek into the clock's mechanism (open Tu-F 9am-6pm, Sa-Su 9am-4pm; 6000 lei, students 3000 lei). From the clock tower, walk straight past Vlad Dracul's house and take a left at Str. Școlii to reach the 175-step **covered wooden staircase,** leading to the old Saxon **church** (closed for renovations). On the riverbank of the lower town is the 1937 black-and-white Orthodox **Catedrala Sfânta Treime.**

Trains run to Bucharest (4½hr., 11 per day, 33,600 lei), Cluj-Napoca (2½-3hr., 6 per day, 20,500 lei), and Brasov. To reach the center, take a right on Str. Libertații, a left on Str. Gării, veer left at the Russian cemetery, cross the footbridge over the river, and walk down the street behind Sigma. A right at the fork leads to the *Cetatea,* a left to the main Str. 1 Decembrie 1918. The **tourist office,** Str. 1 Decembrie 1918 10 (tel. (065) 77 10 72), helps find rooms, organizes tours, and sells English maps (3500 lei; open M-F 9am-5pm, Sa 9am-1pm). At the train station, a man may offer you a room at the new summer **Bobby's Hostel,** Str. Tache Ionescu 18 (tel. (065) 77 22 32); the company will likely be great—young people from all over stop here (dorms 50,000 lei; double 120,000 lei). **Hotel-Restaurant Non-Stop** (tel. (065) 77 59 01), across from the train station, has well-kept rooms and bathrooms (doubles 90,000 lei; breakfast 15,000 lei). In the *Cetatea,* **Restaurant Cetatea,** Piața Cositorarilor 5, boasts that the father of Count Dracula might have lived there (authentic Romanian meals 20,000-35,000 lei; open daily 10am-10pm).

■ Brașov

Brașov (BRA-shohv), rising from the foot of **Muntele Tâmpa,** provides an excellent base for excursions to the Carpathian mountains. Piața Sfatului and Str. Republicii in the Old Town are good places to begin an afternoon walking tour. The **Orthodox Cathedral** in the central *piața* was built in 1896 of marble and delicate gold. The **History Museum,** in the middle of the square, used to be a courthouse; legend holds that the condemned had to jump from its tower to their deaths (open Tu-Su 10am-6pm; 4000 lei, students 1000 lei). Uphill from the square along Str. Gh. Baritiu looms the Lutheran **Biserica Neagră** (Black Church), Romania's most celebrated Gothic church (open M-Sa 10am-3:30pm; 3000 lei). Str. Prundului behind the *poarta* leads to Piața Unirii's **Prima Școala Românescă** (Romania's First School) and the black-towered, icon-filled **Biserica Sfântu Nicolae.**

All Budapest-Bucharest **trains** stop in Brașov; the ride to Bucharest takes about three hours. To get to the town from the station, ride bus 4 ("Piața Unirii"; 1100 lei) to the main Piața Sfatului (10min.). The **bus station,** near the Hotel Aro-Palace, offers service to most major cities (open M-Sa 5:30am-8pm, Su 7am-7pm). Hotel Aro-Palace, Bd. Eroilor 9, offers **city maps** (6000 lei). From Piața Sfatului, walk right on Str. Mureșenilor and then left on Bd. Eroilor. If you have no luck with the private room hawkers at the train station, head to **Hotel Postăvarul,** Republicii 62 (tel. 14 43 30), which shares an entrance with Hotel Corona; enter under the Hotel Corona sign. (Singles 155,000 lei; doubles 220,000-292,000 lei; triples 330,000 lei; breakfast included.) A daily outdoor **market** on Str. Nicolae Bălescu provides famished hikers with tasty bread, cheese, and veggies. **Crama,** Piața Sfatului 12, in the 16th-century Hirschner house, welcomes guests with traditional dancing and serves excellent Romanian wine (meals from 9000 lei; open Tu-Su 7pm-2am).

■ Near Brașov: Bran, Poiana Brașov, Sinaia

Bran, 23km southwest of Brașov, is a picturesque town housing the famed **Castle of Vlad Țepeș,** ostensibly home to the count who inspired Bram Stoker's novel *Dracula.* Actually, Count Dracula had nothing at all to do with this castle, and neither did Bram Stoker (open Tu-Su 9am-4:30pm; 15,000 lei, students 10,000 lei). To get to Bran from Brașov, take bus 28 ("IAR Caminul") to "Gară Bartolomeu" (2200 lei), where the **bus** to Bran departs (45min., 2000 lei; if you ask in English it's usually more). To get to the castle, head down the main road (Str. Principal) back towards Brașov and take the first right. The **tourist office,** 395 Dr. Aurel Stoian (tel. (068) 23 66 42), is down the main road away from Brașov and to the right (open daily 8am-6pm).

Poiana Brașov is a mountain resort only 13km from Brașov, and perfect for hiking or skiing. Trails are accessible to the average hiker, and **Mt. Postăvarul** (1802m) has great views. **Buses** for Poiana Brașov leave the bus station in Brașov on Bd. Eroilor (2 per hr., 6:30am-midnight, 2700 lei; ticket valid for only 1hr. after purchase). Ask for "mașina de Poiana," or find bus 20 at the far end of the bus platform. The **tourist office** (tel. (068) 26 23 89) will suggest great day trips and help find accommodations. **Coliba Haiducilor** (The Outlaws' Hut; tel. 26 21 37), cloistered in the woods behind Hotel Teleferic, gets all its food from its own farm (salads and meat dishes 20,000-30,000 lei; open daily noon-midnight).

Sinaia is Romania's most celebrated year-round alpine resort. The immense **Caste-lul Peleș** (Peleș Castle), built in 1873, was the local monarch's summer residence (open W-Su 9am-3pm; 30,000 lei). Detailed maps of the trails surrounding Sinaia are available at most hotels. Obsessive hikers can try the **yellow stripe trail,** a strenuous 6hr. climb from Cota 2000 to the top of Omu (2505m). Others take the *telecabina* (cable car) to Cota 1400. **Trains** run almost every 2hr. to Brașov (1hr., 11,200 lei) and Bucharest (2hr., 19,300 lei for *accelerat*). Rooms here don't come cheap—try the three-star **Complex Economat** (tel. (044) 31 11 51).

■ Timișoara

Romania's westernmost city (just outside of Transylvania), Timișoara has always led Romania's cultural and economic change. Large and full of students, but quieter and cleaner than Bucharest, Timișoara remains brave and dynamic. The tourist hub revolves around Piața Victoriei, with the **Teatrul Național** and **Opera Timișoara** (Theater and Opera House) on one side, and **Catedrala Mitropolitană** on the other. The cathedral was built between 1936 and 1946 in Moldavian folk style, with a Byzantinesque rainbow-tiled roof (open 24hr.; free). Str. Alba Iulia travels from Piața Victoriei past numerous shops to **Piața Libertății,** the old city center. The old **town hall,** Piața Libertății 1, houses the **Art School.** Fashioned as a Baroque-Renaissance mix in the 1700s, it's the oldest edifice in Timișoara. On the left, Str. Ungureanu runs under the clock towers of the mustard-colored 1743 **Biserica Ortodoxă Sârbă** (Serbian Church), Str. Ungureanu 12 (open M-F 7:45-9am, Sa 4-6pm, Su 10am-12:30pm). Behind the church lies the **Piața Unirii,** where the lamp posts and pavement were designed to look turn-of-the-century. The **Old Prefecture** has a superb Baroque facade (under renovation). The water from the central fountain is said to be a remedy for stomach ailments. It tastes, accordingly, like medicine.

Trains run to Belgrade (4hr., round-trip 154,000 lei) and Budapest (5hr., round-trip 220,000 lei). The **tourist office, Colibri Travel and Tourism,** Bd. C. D. Loga 2 (tel./fax (056) 19 40 74), offers old, but still useful, free maps, and specializes in tours (open M-F 9am-5pm). Old **hotels** in Timișoara are cheap and decent. **Politehnicii,** Str. Ferdinand 2 (tel. (056) 19 68 50), has decent rooms in a good location (doubles 220,000 lei). **Hotel Central,** Str. Lenau 6 (tel. (056) 19 00 91), behind Muzeul Banat-ului, has clean rooms with TV, telephone, and wall tapestries (doubles with bath 180,000 lei). An **outdoor market** sits at the corner of Str. C. Brediceanu and Str. Paris, three blocks from Piața Libertății (open daily 7am-9pm, but slower on Su).

ROMANIAN MOLDOVA AND BUCOVINA

Eastern Romania, which before World War II included the neighboring Republic of Moldova, extends from the Carpathians to the Prut River. The northern landscape of green, gentle hills shelters some of Romania's most beautiful churches and villages.

ROMANIA

■ Iaşi

The intoxicating perfume of lindens floats among the famous churches and monuments of Iaşi, Romania's cultural center in the late 19th century. In those years, Iaşi's writers, nobles, and intellectuals filled the city with Neoclassical homes and palaces, and a century later tourists and local students still enjoy the clean, picturesque streets and homes. The massive neo-Gothic **Palatul Culturii** dominates monument-lined Bd. Ştefan cel Mare, which runs from Piaţa Unirii to Piaţa Ştefan cel Mare. The palace houses several museums. **Sala Voievozilor** (Voivodes' Hall), in the **Art Museum**, displays portraits of all Romanian rulers from Trajan (the Roman emperor) to King Carol II; also featured is the wall-sized *Execution of Horea*. The archeological section of the **Muzeul de Istorie** contains a rich and valuable display of the 5000-year-old Neolithic Cucuteni culture. The rest of the museum examines the more recent history of the region, but it grinds to a halt at the end of World War II and ignores the communist era (museums open Tu-Su 9am-6pm; 4000-5000 lei each, students half-price). A few meters up Bd. Ştefan cel Mare on the left stands the gorgeous **Trei Ierarhi** church, whose exterior walls display Moldavian, Romanian, and Turkish patterns in raised relief (open daily 9am-noon and 3-7pm; 3000 lei, students 1500 lei).

Frequent **trains** from Bucharest (6hr., 48,600 lei) deliver visitors to the station on Str. Silvestru. The **tourist office,** Str. A. Panu 29 (tel. (032) 11 43 64), near the Hotel Moldova, offers tours (in English US$20) and finds private rooms (70,000-100,000 lei; open M-F 8am-7:30pm, Sa 8am-1pm). A favorite among Americans, **Hotel Traian,** Piaţa Unirii 1 (tel. (032) 14 33 30), is Rococo and comfortable (singles 108,000 lei; doubles with bath 156,000 lei; breakfast included). Head to the basement of **Bolta Rece** (Cold Ceiling), Str. Rece 10, for the renowned pub in which great writers used to get sloshy (tasty meals up to 20,000-30,000 lei). Cheap food is also sold at the **market** at Piaţa Mihai Viteazul near the intersection of Str. Copou and Bd. Independenţei.

■ Suceava

Suceava has few monuments of its own, but serves as a useful base for exploring Bucovina's monasteries. The ruins of **Cetatea de Scaun** (Royal Fortress) spread in **Parcul Cetăţii,** east from Piaţa 22 Decembrie. Take a left on Bd. Ipătescu, a right on Str. Cetăţii, walk down the hill, and go up the path. The fortress was built around 1388, and withstood several sieges before falling to the Ottomans in 1675 (open daily 8am-9pm; free). The **History Museum,** Str. Ştefan cel Mare 33, contains a wax reconstruction of Ştefan cel Mare's throne room (open Tu-Su 10am-6pm; 12,000 lei).

Suceava lies 100km northwest of Iaşi near the foothills of the Carpathians. There are two train stations: **Suceava,** Str. Iorga 7, Cart. Burdujeni (tel. (030) 21 38 97), and **Suceava Nord,** Str. Gării 4 Cart. Iţcani. **Trains** run to Bucharest (6hr., 45,600 lei), Iaşi (2½hr., 20,900 lei), and Timişoara (12-13hr., 59,000 lei) several times daily. Buy tickets at **CFR,** Str. Bălcescu 8 (tel. (030) 21 43 35; open M-F 7am-8pm). The **bus station,** Str. Alecsandri 2 (tel. (030) 21 60 89), also serves Iaşi (3hr., 1 per day, 40,000 lei). **ONT,** Str. Bălcescu 2 (tel. 22 12 97), in the main square, sells maps (10,000 lei), arranges car tours of the monasteries (US$50-60 per day, driver included), and books rooms (open M-F 8am-4pm). Ask at **Bucovina Estur,** Str. Ştefan cel Mare 24 (tel. (030) 22 32 59), across the *piaţa* from the tourist office, for private rooms in the area (US$15). **Hotel Gloria** (formerly al Partidului), Str. V. Bumbac 4-8 (tel. 52 12 09), off Str. Nicolae Bălcescu, offers bright rooms with bath and color TV (singles L70,000; doubles L200,000; call 2-4 days ahead).

■ Near Suceava: Bukovina Monasteries

Bukovina's painted monasteries are hidden away among green hills and forests, near rustic farming villages. Built 500 years ago by Ştefan cel Mare and his successors, the small structures serenely mix Moldovan and Byzantine architecture, Romanian soul, and Christian dogma. When visiting, wear long sleeves and a long skirt or pants. Public transit is a nightmare, so consider one of the tours organized by **ONT** (see above).

The 15th-century **Voroneţ** monastery is among the most famous in the area. The monastery's frescoes are stupendous, and the *Last Judgment* mural a masterpiece. To get here from Suceava, go to Gura Humorului by train (1hr., 9 per day, 6600 lei) and then take a bus to Voroneţ (10min., M-F 4 per day, 1500 lei). To find the bus, turn right onto Str. Ştefan cel Mare as you exit the train station. **Moldovita** is the largest of the fortified painted monasteries, and its frescoes are among the best-preserved (L5000, students L300). Be sure to see the massive **religious tome** donated by Catherine the Great. From Suceava, take a train to Vama (1½-2hr.) and switch for the train to Vatra Moldoviţei (5th stop; 35min., 2 per day, L9100 for whole trip), 2km east of Moldoviţa. Beautiful in its simplicity, the 15th-century **Putna** monastery features the marble-canopied tomb of Ştefan cel Mare (open daily 9am-5pm; 5000 lei, students 1500 lei). It's also probably the best-kept and most accessible of the monasteries. For the scenic ride to Putna, catch a train from Suceava, 75km southeast (2½hr., 6 per day, 4600 lei). The last train leaves Putna in late afternoon. The monastery lies 2km from the station; exiting the platform, take a right, then a left at the first intersection, and keep walking. Quiet **lodging** can be found at **Cabana Putna** off the main road (30,000 lei per person; doubles 154,000 lei; breakfast included), which is also a bar-restaurant (meals under 30,000 lei).

Russia (Россия)

US$1 = 6R (Russian rubles)
Country Phone Code: 7

IR = US$0.17
International Dialing Prefix: 810

> The Russian ruble collapsed in August 1998 after several years of reasonable stability and went into a dive that has continued through September. The prices listed in this chapter were valid at US$1=6R, but where they will land is anyone's guess.

The paradoxes in which Russia currently exists go well beyond any of the clichés visited upon it by Western journalists. The question at the time of writing is how much longer Russia will be able to keep the oppositions so often harped on (rich and poor, old and new, exaggerated by the visible arrogance of the new rich) from descending into a nuclear-armed chaos. The collapse of the ruble and, with it, of the Russian economy in summer 1998 should have come as no surprise to anyone who saw that the decade of attempted reforms had done little to dent the system of graft into which Russian rubles have for centuries disappeared. Indeed, the surface historical continuities in Russia are remarkable; President Boris Yeltsin is a lot like Brezhnev is a lot like Nicholas I, and crooked, arrogant business-people are like Soviet officials are like Gogol's clerks, etc. Throughout it all, the Russian people have maintained what seems a mystical capacity for passivity untempered by indifference—unleashed into dialogue after years of imposed silence, many Russians now refuse to shut up.

Though the Soviets left little of beauty intact, and the bureaucratic hassle to which Russia still subjects tourists is outrageous, the country is in many ways an ideal destination for the budget traveler with the stomach for it—inexpensive and well-served by public transportation, with hundreds of neglected monasteries, kremlins, and churches. And there is a great deal to be said for a trip here out of pure curiosity: Russia is the European world turned inside out. After taking in Moscow's nightlife and Mt. Elbrus, the highest mountain in Europe, it is difficult to avoid sharing the conclusion of the 19th-century Slavophiles, that the rest of the continent is dross.

Now how much longer can you sit there without *Let's Go: Eastern Europe 1999?*

GETTING THERE

Russian **visas** require an invitation stating itinerary and dates of travel, and thus are inherently difficult to get without a contact in Russia. Fortunately, several organizations specialize in supplying invitations and/or visas for individual tourists. In Boston, U.S., **Info Travel,** 387 Harvard St., Brookline, MA 02146 (tel. (617) 566-2197; fax 734-8802; email infostudy@aol.com), provides invitations and visas to Russia from US$145. A more expensive but larger operation is **Russia House.** In the **U.S.,** they are at 1800 Connecticut Ave. NW, Washington, D.C. 20009 (tel. (202) 986-6010; fax 667-4244; email lozansky@aol.com). In **Russia,** contact them at 17 Leningradsky Prospekt, Moscow 125040 (tel. (095) 250 01 43; fax 250 25 03; email aum@glasnet.ru). Invitations and visas are available at fairly exorbitant prices (to Russia from $275; Ukraine $175; Belarus $175). **Traveler's Guest House,** Bolshaya Pereyaslavskaya 50, 10th fl., 129401 Moscow, Russia (tel. (095) 971 40 59 or 280 85 62; fax 280 76 86; email tgh@glas.apc.org), arranges visa invitations, will register you once you arrive, makes reservations, and gets train tickets. **Red Bear Tours/Russian Passport,** also known as **Russia-Rail Internet Travel Service,** Ste. 11A, 401 St. Kilda Rd., Melbourne 30004, Australia (tel. (3) 98 67 38 88, toll-free in Australia (800) 33 30 31; fax 98 67 10 55), provides invitations on the condition that you book accommodations with them. They also sell rail tickets for the Trans-Siberian/Manchurian/Mongolian and Silk routes and arranges assorted tours (email passport@werple.net.au; http://www.travelcentre.com.au or http://www.russia-rail.com). Also try **Host Families Association (HOFA),** 5-25 Tavricheskaya, 193015 St. Petersburg, Russia (tel./fax 812 275 19 92; email hofa@usa.net), which arranges homestays in more than 20 cities of the former Soviet Union, and provides visa invitations for HOFA guests to Russia, Ukraine, and Belarus (singles US$30; doubles US$50).

If you have received an invitation, apply for a visa at a Russian **embassy** or **consulate** (see **Government Information Offices,** p. 5). Send a photocopy of your invitation and the front pages of your passport, a completed application (contact the embassy or a travel agent for blanks), three photographs, a cover letter (with your name, arrival and departure dates, planned itinerary, birth date, and passport number), and the visa fee to the embassy or consulate. (2-week service US$65, 1-week US$75, 3-day US$105; prices change constantly, so check with the embassy.) Include a return envelope with postage. If you have even tentative plans to visit a city, have it

---

Every time we say goodbye, I cry a little

Unlike other countries, the former Soviet Union—touchingly—makes it much more difficult to exit than to enter. Throughout the former empire, especially at well-used border crossings like Brest, customs officials rarely smile at their new foreign acquaintance; instead, they frown theatrically before disappearing with your passport while the train changes wheels, the hope being that rich foreigners will chase around the train car flailing hard currency. If you happened to register with the appropriate visa office upon arrival, they will find another fault. Sit tight, take a short walk around town (Brest has a great restaurant), and your passport will be returned to you just before the train heads across to Poland, with a "don't do it again." Real offenses, however, will require varying levels of unofficial fine (US$20 should cover an expired visa, US$50-200 the lack of one entirely).

put on your visa, and get a visa for longer than you actually plan to stay. Most organizations will register your visa for you on arrival, but if not, go down to the central OVIR (ОВИР) office (in Moscow called УВИР) to register. This is also where you should attempt to extend your visa—good luck.

Rail travel from European capitals to Moscow and St. Petersburg is frequent. Check to see if you are going through Ukraine, for which you need a transit visa; sometimes you can get by with just a Russian visa. The Warsaw-Tallinn express goes through Lithuania instead. Finnord **buses** leave for St. Petersburg from Lahti, Finland (4 per day) and are cheaper than the trains.

Customs enforcement is arbitrary and unpredictable; one day they'll tear your pack apart, the next they'll just nod and dismiss you. At the border, politely answer the officials, but *do not* offer any information they don't specifically ask for. You will be given a **Customs Declaration Form** at the border on which to declare all your valuables and foreign currency. *Don't* lose it. Everything listed on the customs form must be on your person when you leave the country.

GETTING AROUND

In summer 1998, the U.S. State Department issued a travel advisory regarding bringing Global Positioning Systems (G.P.S.), cellular phones, and other radio transmission devices into Russia. Failure to register such devices can (and does) result in search, seizure, and arrest. Check http://travel.state.gov/travel_warnings.html for more info.

Foreigners are officially required to buy internal plane and train tickets at inflated Intourist prices. You must show your *dokumenty* (документы, i.e. passport) at the time of purchase, which makes it impossible to get the Russian rate. You can buy train tickets originating in a different city, but it is best to use Moscow or St. Petersburg as a base and make a series of round-trip journeys from there.

Russia boasts an extensive **rail** and **bus** network and a vast, not-so-reliable air system monopolized by the aging **Aeroflot.** A nascent Aeroflot alternative, **Transair,** services only select cities. Train compartments come in four **classes.** At the top is *lyuks* (люкс)—a place in a two-bunk cabin in the same car as second-class *koupeyny* (купейний), which has four bunks. The next class down is *platskartny* (плацкартный), an open car with 52 shorter, harder bunks. Women traveling alone can try to buy out a *lyuks* compartment for security, or can travel *platskartny* with the regular folk and depend on the crowds to shame would-be harassers into silence. *Platskartny* is also a good idea for the theft-ridden St. Petersburg-Moscow because these compartments won't be targeted for theft. It's a good idea to bring some food and drink to share with others on long journeys. All first and second class cars are equipped with *samovar*s dispensing scalding water, which can be used for soups, hot cocoa, and coffee. *Elektrichka* (**commuter rail,** marked on signs as пригородные поезда; *prigorodnye poezda*) has its own platforms at each station; buy tickets at the *kassa.* These are often packed, especially on weekends, so expect to stand.

Within Russian cities, overcrowded **buses, trams, trolleys,** and (in major metropolises) unbelievably efficient **metro** systems ferry citizens quickly and cheaply. In the metro, buy *zhetony* (жетоны; tokens) at the *kassa,* then drop them into machines that let you onto escalators. Magnetic strip cards have recently been introduced on the metro; you can buy one for 10 rides or more. There are regular buses and more comfortable express buses (marked with "Э"). On the express buses, pay the driver (US$0.42); otherwise, buy bus tickets at newsstands or in special kiosks and punch them on board. *Do not* buy them from the *babushki* at metro stations (they may be fake or invalid). Don't try to ride for free, especially in city centers; the system is energetic in searching out free riders, particularly during the last week of the month, and fines are high (US$60-120). When two lines intersect, there is often a different station name for each line. You'll want to know the words *vkhod* (вход; entrance), *vykhod* (выход; exit), *vykhod v gorod* (выход в город; exit to the city), and *perekhod* (переход; transfer to another line). Metro stations are marked above ground by a capital "M." Try to get the newest city map possible—stations and street names have changed in recent years.

Hailing a **taxi** is indistinguishable from hitchhiking. Almost all of those who stop will be private citizens trying make a little extra cash, although metered taxis are becoming available. Those seeking a ride stand off the curb and hold out a hand; when a car stops, riders name the destination before getting in. The driver will either refuse the destination and speed off, or nod his head, at which point haggling begins. Keep in mind that hitching is risky, and that non-Russian speakers *will* get ripped off.

ESSENTIALS

Be flexible. Expect airport delays, tour cancellations, hotel changes, cold showers, and bathrooms without toilet paper. The rules have changed so often no one really knows what they are anymore. Travel in Russia requires ample preparation. Pack carefully; bring your sense of humor and any Western goods you'll need. Most toiletries and such are available in Moscow and St. Petersburg for a price. Plastic bags and packs of tissue are indispensable. Roach traps can be a godsend in a dormitory.

Russia celebrates: January 1; Orthodox Christmas (Jan. 7); Defenders of the Motherland (Feb. 23); International Women's Day (Mar. 8); Orthodox Easter (Apr. 11); Labor Day (May 1-2); Victory Day (May 9); Independence Day (June 12); and Great October Socialist Revolution (Nov. 7).

Currency exchange in Russia is now easy—just find an *Obmen Valyuty* (Обмен валюты; currency exchange) sign. Besides U.S. dollars, many will change Deutschmarks, and some francs and British pounds, but few besides main branches will change traveler's checks or give cash advances on credit cards. Changing rubles back at the end of your trip is no problem, but the unstable exchange rate makes it best not to change large sums of money at once. *Do not* exchange money on the street.

COMMUNICATION There is neither rhyme nor reason to Russia's **mail service.** Delivery can take anywhere from two weeks to eternity. **AmEx** card- and traveler's check-holders can receive letters at their travel service bureaus in Moscow and St. Petersburg; this is usually more reliable than Russian mail. **DHL** has offices in Moscow and St. Petersburg; they are expensive but reliable.

Your best bet in Russia, even for local calls, is a fancy phone card. When making **intercity calls** from *mezhdugorodnye* (междугородные) phone booths, it will take a while, but you can usually get through. Dial 8, wait for the tone, then dial the city code. Direct **international** calls can be made from telephone offices and hotel rooms: dial 8, wait for the tone, then dial 10 and the country code. You cannot call collect, unless using AT&T service (same access number as listed below), which will cost your party dearly (to the U.S. US$8 1st min.; US$2.78 each additional min.). Prices for international calls vary greatly from city to city, from US$1.50 per minute (to the U.S.) up to US$4.17. To make calls from a telephone office, you can buy tokens or phone cards, or simply prepay your calls (depending on the city) and use the *mezhdugorodnye* telephones; be sure to press the *otvet* (ответ; reply) button when your party answers or you won't be heard. If there are no automatic phones, you must pay for your call at the counter and have it dialed for you by the operator. Several hotels in Moscow now have direct-dial booths operated by a special card or credit card. The cost is astronomical (at least US$6 per min. to the U.S.). For **AT&T Direct,** dial 755 50 42 in Moscow and dial 325 50 42 in St. Petersburg; **British Telecom,** dial 810 800 110 10 44; **Sprint,** dial 747 33 24 in Moscow. When calling from another city, dial 8-095 or 8-812 before these codes; you pay for the phone call to Moscow or St. Petersburg in addition to the international connection. For **Canada Direct,** dial 755 50 45 in Moscow, 747 33 25 in St. Petersburg. Calling into the country is much less frustrating. Most countries have direct dial to Moscow and St. Petersburg. For other cities, go through the international operator. In **emergencies,** call 01 for **fire,** 02 for **police,** and 03 for an **ambulance.**

LANGUAGE Though more and more people speak English in Russia, take some time to look over the Cyrillic alphabet. It's not as difficult as it looks and will make getting around and getting by immeasurably easier. The "r" in Russian is trilled.

Cyrillic	English	Pronunciation	Cyrillic	English	Pronunciation
А, а	a	St*a*lin	Р, р	r	*R*achel
Б, б	b	*B*yzantine	С, с	s	*C*ircuit board
В, в	v	The *V*illage People	Т, т	t	*T*itrate
Г, г	g	*G*oats	У, у	u	P*oo*dle
Д, д	d	*D*eliverance	Ф, ф	f	*F*abulous
Е, е	ye or e	*Ye*sterday	Х, х	kh	*Ch*utzpah (*hkh*)
Ё, ё	yo	*Ya*wn	Ц, ц	ts	Let'*s* Go
Ж, ж	zh	*Zh*irinovsky	Ч, ч	ch	Mun*ch*ies
З, з	z	*Z*ohra	Ш, ш	sh	*Ch*ivalry
И, и	i	Kath*l*een	Щ, щ	shch	Khru*shch*ev
Й, й	y	*Y*ak	Ъ, ъ	(hard)	(no sound)
К, к	k	*K*aren	Ы, ы	y	P*i*t
Л, л	l	*L*onging	Ь, ь	(soft)	(no sound)
М, м	m	*M*ara	Э, э	eh	*A*leksander
Н, н	n	*N*eanderthal	Ю, ю	yoo	*You*
О, о	o	*L*aw	Я, я	yah	*Ya*hoo!
П, п	p	*P*avement			

In the Slavic world, plurals of words are usually formed by adding "ы" or "и" at the end, so the plural of *matryoshka* is *matryoshki*. Note that улица (*ulitsa;* abbreviated ул.) means "street"; проспект (*prospekt;* пр.) means "avenue"; площадь (*ploshchad;* пл.) means "square"; and бульвар (*bulvar;* бул.) is "boulevard." Once you get the hang of the alphabet, you can pronounce most Russian words.

Yes/No	Да/Нет	dah/nyet
Hello	Добрый день	DOH-brih DYEN
Thank you	Спасибо	spa-SEE-bah
Please/You're welcome	Пожалуйсто	pa-ZHA-loo-sta
Excuse me.	Извините	eez-vee-NEET-yeh
Where is...?	Где...?	g-dyehÖ?
How much does this cost?	Сколько стоит?	SKOHL-ka STOH-yet?
I don't understand.	Я не понимаю	ya nee pa-nee-MAH-yoo
Do you speak English?	Вы говорите по английски?	vih go-vo-REE-tyeh po ahn-GLEE-ske?
Do you have a vacancy?	У вас есть свободный номер?	oo vahss yehst svah-BOD-niy NOH-meer
Help!	Помогите!	pah-mah-ZHEE-tyeh

ACCOMMODATIONS Western-style **youth hostels** have begun to appear in Russia; some arrange visas for your stay. Reserve well in advance, especially in summer. **Hotels** offer several classes of rooms. *Lux,* usually a two-room double with TV, phone, fridge, and bath, is most expensive. *Pol-lux* is a one-room single or double with TV, phone, and bath. Rooms with bath and no TV, if they exist, are cheaper. The lowest price rooms are *bez udobstv* (без удобств), which means one room with a sink. Many hotels have restaurants, often the fanciest eatery in town; all have at least a buffet or cafeteria—probably the worst food in town. Hot water—even all water— is sometimes turned off for pipe repair and conservation, and water only gets turned on once every two weeks due to shortages in parts of south Russia. Another cheap

RUSSIA

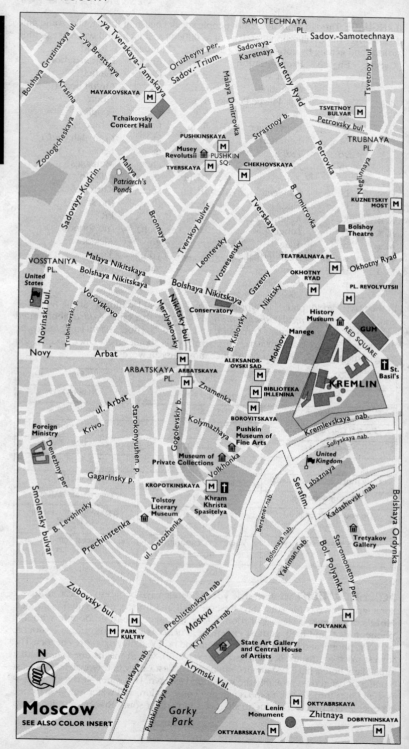

Moscow
SEE ALSO COLOR INSERT

option can be staying in a **university dorm;** many take in foreign students for US$10 per night. The rooms are livable, but don't expect sparkling bathrooms or reliable hot water. Make arrangements with an institute from your home country.

FOOD AND DRINK Russians look upon food principally for nourishment. The standard hotel dinner menu includes salat (салат), usually cucumbers or beets and potatoes with mayonnaise and sour cream; soup (суп), meat or cabbage; and *kuritsa* (курица; chicken) or *myaso* (мясо; meat), often turned into hamburger-like *kutlyety* (котлеты; meat). Ordering a number of *zakusky* (закуски; Russian appetizers) instead of a main dish can save money and add variety to your diet. Dessert is *morozhenoye* (мороженое; ice cream) and *koffye* (кофе) or *chai* (чай; tea). Russian cafes (кафе) are usually just bars. An empty *stolovaya* (столовая; cafeteria) could be unsanitary, but a full one will have good food cheap.

You can also buy food on the street or at a market. *Produkty* (Продукты) offer a variety of meats, cheeses, breads, and packaged goods; a *gastronom* (Гастроном) carries a smaller range of meat and dairy products; and an *universam* (Универсам) has the variety of a supermarket. The market (рынок; *rynok)* has abundant fruits and vegetables, meat, fresh milk, butter, honey, and cheese. Street vendors sometimes sell delicious *pirogi* (pies) or *khachipuri* (a Caucasian cheese specialty). Buy your booze in a foreign grocery store. In Moscow, make sure your Stolichnaya vodka has a bull jumping over a bottle on the cap; cheap vodka will give you a hangover like you've never known, and worse. If you can find a bottle of *Pertsovka,* don't pass it up.

Travelers are generally advised not to drink the water in Russia. While often potable in limited doses, its cleanliness is on the decrease. It is recommended that you boil your water for at least 10 minutes. A gamma globulin shot will lower your risk of hepatitis. For **medical emergencies,** leave the country or get to a St. Petersburg or Moscow clinic for foreigners.

■ Moscow (Москва)

Like very few cities on earth, Moscow has the audacity of place—a sense of itself on the persistent cusp of world history. Its most recent shift on the crest of the bubble economy has returned it to 19th-century magnificence—Stalin's gargantuan edifices now stand out like gay, monster-land anachronomisms amidst the restored pink-and-green of the new old city. And if one keeps to the 16th-century side-streets, it is possible, for the first time in decades, to glimpse what Napoleon saw: golden domes sparkling over the great mouthless mass of Asia.

But Moscow's circles, emanating from the Kremlin and spiraling into a crumbling wasteland on the peripheries, still suggest the permanent condition of its residents: destined to live on the margins of a system they don't understand and didn't authorize, flinging themselves into the city center only to return drab and wasted to their concrete blocks. Post-ideological, post-apocalyptic, post-whatever the hell you want, Moscow is in your face like the endless leather-jacketed hoods ever hanging about the darkened courtyards. Not such a big city that it doesn't care about you, but a city of ten million so small that everyone stares; a brutal, tiring capital, not so unsafe as it is maddening, Moscow at the millennium is most definitely the end of the world.

ORIENTATION AND PRACTICAL INFORMATION

A series of concentric rings radiates from the **Kremlin** (Кремль; *kreml*). The outermost ring road forms the city boundary, but most sights lie within the inner **Sadovoe koltso** (Садовое Кольцо; Garden Ring). **Krasnaya ploshchad** (Красная Площадь; **Red Square**) and the Kremlin mark the city center. Nearby begin Moscow's popular shopping streets: **Novy Arbat** (Новый Арбат), running west parallel to the Metro's blue lines, and **ul. Tverskaya** (Тверская), extending north along the green line. Ul. Tverskaya was formerly called ul. Gorkovo (Горького); the upper half, which leads to the Garden Ring, is now known as **ul. Pervaya Tverskaya-Yamskaya** (Первая Тверская-Ямская). If you familiarize yourself with the

Cyrillic alphabet and orient yourself by the **Metro,** it's difficult to get lost. An extensive city **map** (in Russian) can be bought for US$3.67 at **Torgovy Dom Biblio-Globus** (Myasnitskaya 6). A great English version of this map can be bought (also for US$3.67) at the book store **Slavyanka** (Славянка), ul. Kuznetsky Most 9. Many maps are outdated, so be sure to check that a recent year is clearly marked. Refer also to this book's **color maps** of the city and Metro.

Telephone Code: 095.

Flights: International flights arrive at **Sheremetyevo-2** (Шереметьево-2; tel. 956 46 66). M2: Rechnoy Vokzal. The van under the sign "автолайн" on the street in front of the train station picks up passengers every 10min. 7am-10pm for a 20min. ride to Sheremetyevo-2 (US$1.67). 24hr. Most flights to within the former USSR originate at **Vnukovo** (Внуково; tel. 436 21 09), **Bikovo** (Биково; tel. 558 47 38), **Domodedovo** (Домодедово; tel. 323 85 65), or **Sheremetyevo-I** (tel. 578 23 72). Buy tickets in *kassy* at the **Tsentralny Aerovokzal** (Центральный Аэровокзал; Central Airport Station), a 2-stop tram (23) or trolley (12 or 70) ride from M2: Aeroport. Express bus schedules are posted outside the station. Taxis will rip you off like you've never dreamed possible.

Trains: Buying a train ticket in Russia can be enormously frustrating. If you don't speak Russian you may want to buy the ticket through **Intourist** or your hotel. Tickets for longer trips can be purchased at the *Tsentralnoe Zhelezhnodorozhnoe Agenstvo* (Центраьное Железнодорожное Агенство; Central Train Agency), by Yaroslavsky Vokzal (M4: Komsomolskaya), window 10 or 11 (complete schedules posted; *kassy* open daily 8am-1pm and 2-7pm). After hours, try the 24hr. Intourist *kassy* on the 2nd floor of Leningradsky Vokzal (entrance 3, windows 19 and 20). Your ticket will tell you at which *vokzal* (вокзал; station) to catch your train. Tickets for local *elektrichka*s (local trains) should be bought at the *prisorodnye kassy* (пригородные кассы) in each station. Moscow's 9 train stations are arranged around the metro's circle line (M4). Trains to St. Petersburg depart from **Leningradsky Vokzal** (Ленинградский), Komsomolskaya pl. 3. M1,4: Komsomolskaya. **Kazansky Vokzal** (Казанский), Komsomolskaya pl. 2, opposite Leningradsky Vokzal, services the east and southeast, including Volgograd and Central Asia. **Yaroslavsky Vokzal** (Ярославский), Komsomolskaya pl. 5, sends trains to Siberia and the Far East (the Trans-Siberian Railroad; buy tickets 1-2 days in advance). **Paveletsky Vokzal** (Павелетский), Paveletskaya pl. 1, and **Kursky Vokzal** (Курский), ul. Zemlyenoy Val 29, 1, serve the Crimea, eastern Ukraine, Pyatigorsk. **Rizhsky Vokzal** (Рижский) Rizhkaya pl. To Rīga (16hr.) and Estonia. **Belorussky Vokzal** (Белорусский), pl. Tverskaya Zastava. To Warsaw (24hr.), Minsk (9-13hr.), and Kaliningrad. **Kievsky Vokzal** (Киевский), pl. Kievskovo Vokzala, sends trains to Bulgaria, Romania, Slovakia, and Kiev, Ukraine (15-17hr., US$20-30).

Public Transportation: The **Metro** is large, fast, and efficient—a work of art in urban planning. Passages between lines or stations are shown by a sign of a man walking up stairs. A station that serves more than 1 line will generally have more than 1 name. Trains run daily 6am-1am. Buy light green tokens (US$0.35) from the *kassy* inside the stations. **Bus** and **trolley** tickets are available in gray kiosks labeled "проездные билеты" and from the driver (US$0.25). Be sure to punch your ticket upon boarding—the fine for not doing so is US$1.67. *Edinye bilety* (единые билеты; calendar month passes) let you ride on any form of transportation (US$30). Monthly Metro passes are US$15. Purchase either from the *kassy*. Metro maps (in English and Russian) are in the front or back of this book.

Taxis: Look for a round sign with a green "T." If you don't speak Russian, you'll get ripped off. Ask around for the going rate and agree on a price before you get in. Be sure the meter is turned on.

Tourist Offices: Intourservice Central Excursion Bureau, Nikitsky per. 4A (Никитский; tel. 203 75 85 or 203 80 16; fax 200 12 43). M1: Okhotny Ryad. **Moskovsky Sputnik** (Московский спутник), Maly Ivanovsky per. 6, bldg. 2 (Малый Ивановский; tel. 924 03 17). M5 or 6: Kitai Gorod. Student travel, visas, and tickets. Open M-Th 9am-1pm and 2-6pm, F 9am-1pm and 2-7pm.

Budget Travel: Student Travel Agency Russia (STAR), 50 Bolshaya Pereyaslavskaya, 10th fl. (tel. 913 59 52; fax 280 90 30). Open M-F 10am-6pm.

Embassies: Most open M-F 9 or 9:30am-noon or 1pm; some also 1-5 or 6pm. **Australia,** Kropotkinsky per. 13 (Кропоткинский; tel. 956 60 70). M3: Smolenskaya. **Belarus,** ul. Maroseyka 1716 (Маросейка; tel. 924 70 31; fax 928 64 03). **Canada,** Starokonyushenny per. 23 (Староконюшенный; tel. 956 66 66). M1: Kropotkinskaya. Closed W. **Ireland,** Grokholsky per. 5 (Грохольский; tel. 742 09 07). M4 or 5: Prospekt Mira. **Lithuania,** Borisoglebsky per. 10 (Борисоглебский; tel. 291 26 43; fax 202 35 16). M3: Arbatskaya. **New Zealand,** ul. Povarskaya 44 (Поварская; tel. 956 35 79). M4 or 6: Krasnopresnenskaya. **South Africa,** Bolshoy Strochinovsky per. 22/25 (Большой Строчиновский; tel. 230 68 69). **U.K.,** nab. Sofiskaya 14 (Софиская; tel. 956 72 00; fax 956 74 20). M1, 3, or 8: Borovitskaya. Open M-F 9am-5pm. **Ukraine,** Leontevsky per. 18 (Леонтевский; formerly ul. Stanislavskovo; tel. 229 10 79, visa inquiries 229 69 22). M3: Tverskaya. **U.S.,** Novinsky 19/23 (Новинский; tel. 252 24 51, emergency tel. 230 20 01). M6: Krasnopresnenskaya.

Currency Exchange: Banks at almost every corner; check ads in English-language newspapers. The pamphlet *Moscow Express Directory,* updated biweekly and free in most luxury hotels, lists the addresses and phone numbers of many banks, as well as places to buy and cash traveler's checks. Nearly every bank and hotel has an **ATM;** a particularly useful and reliable ATM stands in the lobby of the Central Telegraph building (Visa/MC/Cirrus/Plus).

American Express: ul. Sadovaya-Kudrinskaya 21a (Садовая-Кудринская; tel. 755 90 00 or 755 90 04). M2: Mayakovskaya. Take a left onto ul. Bolshaya Sadovaya (Большая Садовая), which becomes ul. Sadovaya-Kudrinskaya. Travel assistance, mail, and banking services for members. **ATM** in lobby exchanges money 24hr. Office open M-F 9am-5pm, Sa 10am-2pm.

Laundromat: Traveler's Guest House (see p. 748) will do your laundry for US$4.17 per load. **California Cleaners,** Leninsky pr. 111/3 (tel. 956 52 84). Free pickup and delivery (tel. 497 00 05 or 497 00 11). Wash and dry US$3 per kg.

Emergencies: Ambulance, tel. 03. **Fire,** tel. 01. Try the centers for medical emergencies (below), call your embassy for passport and visa problems, and give up on legal retaliation. Call 299 11 80 to report offenses *by* the police (no coins needed from pay phones), or try the **U.S. embassy's emergency number,** tel. 230 20 01.

Police: tel. 02.

24-Hour Pharmacies: Leningradsky pr. 74 (Ленинградский; tel. 151 45 70). M2: Sokol. Also at Kutuzovsky pr. 14 (Кутузовский; tel. 243 16 01). M3: Kutuzovskaya.

Medical Assistance: American Medical Center, Vtoroy Tverskoy-Yamskoy per. 10 (2-ой Тверской-Ямской; tel. 956 33 66; fax 956 23 06). M2: Mayakovskaya. Most experienced Western medical clinic in Moscow (US$215 in hard currency per visit). Monthly membership US$55, students US$40. Open M-F 8am-8pm, Sa 9am-5pm; call first for pricier 24hr. service. Also **Mediclub Moscow,** Michurinsky pr. 56 (Мичуринский; tel. 931 50 18 or 931 53 18). M1: Prospekt Vernadskovo.

Express Mail: DHL, Radisson-Slavyanskaya, Berezhkovskaya nab. 2 (Бережковская; tel. 941 87 40). M3: Kievskaya. **GUM** (ГУМ) **business center** (бизнес-центр), 2nd fl. (tel. 921 09 11; fax 921 46 09). Open M-Sa 8am-8pm, Su 10am-5pm.

Post Offices: Moscow Central Telegraph, ul. Tverskaya 7, a few blocks from the Kremlin. Look for the globe and the digital clock out front. M1: Okhotny Ryad. Unreliable **international mail** service. Open M-F 8am-2pm and 3-9pm, Sa 8am-2pm and 3-7pm, Su 9am-2pm and 3-7pm. Address mail: "Москва 103009, POSTE RESTANTE, LARSSON, Måns." *Poste Restante* also at the **Gostinitsa Intourist post office,** ul. Tverskaya 3/5. Address mail "До востребования, К-600, Гостиница Интурист, ул. Тверская 3/5 Москва. Russia." To mail **packages,** bring them unwrapped to the Intourist post office (open M-F 9am-noon and 1-6pm) or to Myasnitskaya 26 (Мясницкая, formerly Kirova); they will be wrapped and mailed while you wait. **Postal Code:** 103009.

Telephones: Moscow Central Telegraph (see **Post Offices,** above). Open 24hr. Prepay at the counter. Calls to the U.S. and Australia cost approximately US$2.47 per min., to Europe US$1.05 per min. Do not call collect or use a calling card here; use the **international telephone cabinets** (международные телефоны; *mezhdunarodnye telefony*). Major hotels have direct-dial international phone booths at exorbitant prices (to the U.S. US$6-15 per min.). Local calls require plastic *zhetony* (жетоны; tokens), sold at some Metro stations or kiosks.

ACCOMMODATIONS

The concept of budget accommodations for student travelers has yet to arrive in Moscow. Options are slim, so in summer reservations are a must. Women holding signs in major rail stations will rent private rooms (сдаю комнату; *sdayu komnatu*) or apartments (сдаю квартиру; *sdayu kvartiru*) for as low as US$10 if you haggle.

Traveler's Guest House, ul. Bolshaya Pereyaslavskaya 50, 10th fl. (Большая Переяславская; tel. 280 90 30; fax 280 76 86; email tgh@glas.apc.org). M4 or 5: Prospekt Mira. Walk north along pr. Mira, take the 3rd right on Banny per. (Банный), and turn left at the end of the street. TGH is in the white, 12-story building across the street. If you arrive in Moscow speaking no Russian and knowing no one, TGH is all you'll ever need. Helpful, enthusiastic, English-speaking staff. Kitchen facilities, a laundry service, and a common room with TV and phone. Dorms US$18.67; singles US$37.33; doubles US$50. Reserve 1 week ahead. Retain copies of reservation forms and receipts. MC, Visa.

Galina's Flat, ul. Chaplygina 8, #35 (Чаплыгина; tel. 921 60 38). M1: Chistye Prudy. Head down bul. Chistoprudny (Чистопрудный) past the statue of Griboyedov (Грибоедов), take the 1st left onto Kharytonyevsky per. (Харитоньевский) just after the blue Kazakh Embassy, then the 2nd right. Go through the courtyard, turn right, and enter by the "Уникум" sign; the flat is on the 5th floor on the right-hand side. Friendly Galina and her sidekick Sergei welcome you to their homey apartment. The best deal in Moscow—hot showers, kitchen facilities, and safe location. 5-bed dorms US$9; doubles US$11 per person. Only 7 beds and a cot, so call ahead.

Gostinitsa Tsentralnaya (Гостиница Центральная), ul. Tverskaya 10 (tel. 229 89 57), next to Pizza Hut. M2, 6, or 8: Pushkinskaya. Standard Russian hotel with downstairs guard and floor women to keep your key. Shared bath, but all rooms have sinks. Singles US$37; doubles US$67. It's not much to look at, but the location, for the price, cannot be beat. MC, Visa.

American Academy of Foreign Languages, ul. Bolshaya Cheryomushkinskaya 17a (Большая Чермушкинская; tel. 129 43 00; fax 123 15 00). M5: Akademicheskaya. From the Metro station, turn left at the Ho Chi Minh sculpture and walk 15min. on ul. Dmitriya Ulyanova (Дмитрия Ульянова), then turn left on Bolshaya Cheryomushkinskaya. Trolley 26 also runs to the hotel from M5: Shabolovskaya; get off at "Shveinaya Fabrika Moskva" (15min., US$0.25). Beds US$10; 2-room "lux" suites US$67; "Half-lux" suites around US$58.33. Cash only.

Prakash Guesthouse, ul. Profsoyuznaya 83, kor. 1, 3rd fl. (Профсоюзная; tel. 334 82 01; fax 334 25 98). M5: Belyaevo. From the Metro, take the exit nearest the last car of the train and go all the way to the right of the *perekhod* (tunnel), exiting from the last stairway on the left-hand side. The guest house is a 16-story structure; enter through the 2nd entrance. Friendly if far. Shower, toilet in each room. Dorms US$15; singles US$30; doubles US$40. Breakfast US$5. Dinner US$10. Reception 7am-11pm or call; they'll meet you at the Metro. Cash only.

FOOD

Eating out in Moscow can be incredibly expensive, but it doesn't have to be. Prices are ridiculous along the main tourist streets and near big hotels, but walking just one block off the roads most traveled can make all the difference. Many restaurants list their prices in dollars, only so as not to constantly change their menus to keep up with inflation; payment is usually in rubles. Russians tend to eat late in the evening, so you can avoid crowds by eating earlier. Travelers who enter a university **cafeteria**, report being well rewarded with one or two well-prepared dishes at low prices. Scattered bread stands, rarer and rarer in central Moscow, are still an excellent choice: those with cabbage *(kapusta)* and meat *(myaso)* pies *(pirozhki)* for US$0.50-0.75 can be spotted on Tverskaya, while others sell delicious *khachipuri*, a sort of Caucasian cheese pastry, for a pittance. Moscow's first **McDonald's** continues the steady homogenization of world culture at ul. Bolshaya Bronnaya 29 (Большая Бронная).

Near the Kremlin

Moscow Bombay, Glinishchevsky per. 3 (Глинищевский; tel. 292 97 31), off ul. Tverskaya. M6: Pushkinskaya. English menu. Veggie options US$6.75. Tandoori chicken US$9. *Naan* US$2. Reserve ahead. Open daily noon-midnight.

La Cantina (Ла Кантина), ul. Tverskaya 5, on the right of Gostinitsa Intourist. M1: Okhotny Ryad. Carefully designed Mexican restaurant with a Russian flavor. Popular with tourists craving Spanish guitar bands. Nachos and chili US$8.33. Large chicken enchiladas a whopping US$14. Open daily 8am-midnight.

Blinchiki (Блинчики), a kiosk on Strastnoy bul. (Страстной), off ul. Tverskaya diagonally opposite McDonald's. Various *bliny* US$1.33-2.50. Open daily 10am-9pm.

Cafe Oladi (Оладьи), ul. Pushkinskaya 9, just past the Tchaikovsky Conservatory. The eponymous dish consists of small, sweet pancakes with jam or sour cream (US$1.33). Yum! Open daily 9am-8pm.

Around the City

Cafe Margarita (Кафе Маргарита), ul. Malaya Bronnaya 28, at the corner of Maly Kozikhinski per. (Малый Козихинский). An artistically painted door leads to this super-trendy cafe. *Bliny* with mushrooms US$8.33. Open daily 1pm-midnight. Live piano music after 7pm (cover US$2.50).

Guria, Komsomolsky pr. 7/3 (Комсомольский), on the corner of ul. Frunze, opposite St. Nicholas of the Weavers. M1 or 4: Park Kultury. Walk through a courtyard to the left. Delicious Georgian fare for some of the city's lowest prices. One of the hottest eateries for both locals and foreigners. *Satsivi* (turkey in walnut sauce; US$5). Main dishes US$5-7. No English menu. Open daily 11am-10pm.

Zaydi i poprobuy (Зайди и попробуй; Drop In and Try), pr. Mira 124 (Мира). M5: Rizhskaya, then take the trolley a couple of stops north. Entrance on Malaya Moskovskaya ul. (Малая Московская). Your favorite Russian cuisine, well prepared. Borsch US$1.75. Main dishes US$5-7. Open daily 11am-11:30pm.

Mama Zoya's, Sechenovsky per. 8 (Сеченовский). M1: Kropotkinskaya. Hearty, inexpensive Georgian cuisine and gypsy dancers who take requests. Extremely popular. Main dishes US$3.75-7. Open daily noon-11pm.

Starlight Diner, ul. Bolshaya Sadovaya (Большая Садовая). M2: Mayakovskaya. Also at ul. Korovy Val 9. M4: Octyabrskaya. Burgers US$5. Open 24hr.

Cafe Kitayskoy Kukhni (Кафе Китайской Кухни; Cafe of Chinese Cooking), ul. Krasnaya Presnya 30 (Красная Пресня). M6: Ulitsa 1905 goda. Turn left from the Metro stop; it's on the left marked by yellow lettering that lights up at night. Cheap Chinese food. There's no English menu; look at what the locals get and point. Fried emperor's chicken US$3.50. Dumplings US$6. Open daily 11am-11pm.

Markets and Supermarkets

As Georgians, Armenians, Uzbeks, and peasants cart their finest produce to Moscow, your best bet for fresh fruits and vegetables is a market. Wash fruit and vegetables before eating. The **central market** (M8: Tsvetnoy Bulvar), next to the Old Circus, has reopened after its recent reconstruction. The alternative is the **Rizhsky Market** (M5: Rizhskaya). Exit the Metro and keep turning left until you see it. Impromptu markets spring up around Metro stations; some of the best are at **Turgenevskaya, Kuznetsky Most, Aeroport, Baumanskaya,** and between **Novoslobodskaya** and **Mendeleevskaya.** In general, people appear with their goods around 10am and leave by 8pm. Produce, sold by the kilogram, is far cheaper than in the grocery stores.

Eliseyevsky Gastronom (Елисеевский), ul. Tverskaya 14. Moscow's most famous grocery store is packed with foreign goods. Its lines are long, but the prices are lower than in the hard currency supermarkets. Open M-F 8am-9pm, Sa 10am-7pm.

The Arbat Irish House, Novy Arbat 11, 2nd fl. (Новый Арбат). M3: Arbatskaya. Open M-Sa 9am-9pm, Su 10am-8pm. Well-stocked Russian supermarket **Novoarbatsky Gastronom** is downstairs. Open M-Sa 10am-9pm, Su 10am-8pm.

Dorogomilovo (Дорогомилого), ul. Boshaya Dorogomilovskaya 8 (Большая Дорогомиловокая). M4: Kievskaya. Left of McDonald's, across the park from Kievsky Vokzal. Considered the least expensive of the new supermarkets stocking Western foods. Minute Maid orange juice US$2. Open M-Sa 9am-9pm, Su 9am-7pm.

RUSSIA

SIGHTS

Moscow's sights reflect the city's strange history: the visitor can choose among 16th-century churches or Soviet-era museums, but there's little in between. Russia's capital suffers from the 200 years when St. Petersburg was the tsar's seat—there are no grand palaces, and the city's art museums, though impressive, pale in comparison with the Hermitage. Still, despite this gap, and despite the fact that the Soviet regime destroyed 80% of the city's pre-revolutionary splendor, the capital still packs in enough sights to occupy you for weeks.

Kremlin and Red Square

(Кремль; *kreml*) Like a spider in her web, the Kremlin, where Ivan the Terrible reigned with an iron fist and Stalin ruled the lands behind the Iron Curtain, sits geographically and historically in the center of Moscow. *(Kremlin open M-W and F-Su 10am-5pm. Entrance to grounds US$0.35. All cathedrals US$6.75, students US$3.35. Armory US$12.50, students US$6. Diamond Fund US$20. Shorts and large bags are not allowed, but bags can be checked for US$0.17. Buy tickets at the kassa in Aleksandr Gardens, on the west side of the kremlin, and enter through Borovitskaya gate tower in the southwest corner. English-speaking guides offer tours at outrageous prices, so don't forget to haggle. Local hotels also offer tours.)* Here Napoleon simmered while Moscow burned, and the Congress of People's Deputies dissolved itself in 1991, ending the USSR. The famous gold domes rise at **Cathedral Square.** The **Blagoveshchensky Sobor** (Благовещенский собор; Annunciation Cathedral) holds luminous icons by Andrei Rublyov and Theophanes the Greek. Across the way is the square **Arkhangelsky Sobor** (Архангельский Собор; Archangel Cathedral), the final resting place for many tsars prior to Peter the Great. The centerpiece of Cathedral Square is **Uspensky Sobor** (Усленский собор; Assumption Cathedral), where Ivan the Terrible's throne stands by the south wall. Behind Uspensky Sobor is **Patriarshy Dvorets** (Патриарший Дворец; Patriarch's Palace), site of the Museum of 17th-Century Russian Applied Art and Life and the 17th-century **Sobor Dvenadtsati Apostolov** (Собор Двенадцати Апостолов; Church of the Twelve Apostles), built to rival the extravagance of Ivan the Terrible's St. Basil's Cathedral.

Also in the Kremlin, the **Oruzheynaya i Vystavka Almaznovo Fonda** (Оружейная и Выставка Алмазного Фонда; Armory Museum and Diamond Fund) holds all the riches of the Russian Church and those of the State that are not in the Hermitage in St. Petersburg. Room 3 holds the legendary Fabergé eggs; each opens to reveal an impossibly intricate jewelled miniature. The Diamond Fund, an annex of the Armory, has still more glitter, including a 190-carat diamond once owned by Catherine the Great. **Aleksandrovsky Sad** (Александровский Сад; Aleksandr Gardens), where you buy tickets, is also a pleasant garden respite from the carbon monoxide fumes of central Moscow. At the north end, at the **Tomb of the Unknown Soldier,** an eternal flame burns in memory of millions killed in World War II.

There is nothing red about **Red Square** (Красная площадь; *krasnaya ploshchad*); *krasnaya* meant "beautiful" long before the Communists co-opted it. A 700m long lesson in history and culture, Red Square has been the site of everything from a giant farmer's market to public hangings to a renegade Cessna's landing. On one side, the **Kremlin** stands as the historical and religious center of Russia and the seat of the Communist Party for 70-odd years; on the other, **GUM,** once a market, then the world's largest purveyor of grim Soviet goods, has become a bona-fide shopping mall. At one end, **Pokrovsky Sobor** (Покровский Собор; St. Basil's Cathedral), the square's second-oldest building, rises high with its crazy-quilt onion domes; at the other the **History** and **Lenin Museums** are both closed for ideological repair. Indeed, Lenin's historical legacy has come into question, and his name and face have come down all over Moscow. The Party, so to speak, is over. But his mausoleum still stands in front of the Kremlin—patrolled by several scowling teenage draftees. Moscow's mayor has built a church to block the largest entrance to the square, ensuring that Communist parades will never again march through.

Churches, Monasteries, and Synagogues

When you can't take the grime and bedlam any more, escape to one of Moscow's quiet, beautiful churches or monasteries. Among the most famous is the **Novodevichy Monastyr** (Новодевичий Монастырь), near M1: Sportivnaya. *(Open W-M 10am-6pm. Cathedrals close at 5pm. Closed 1st M of each month. US$2.17, students US$1.83. Try to avoid coming on Su.)* You can't miss the high brick walls, golden domes, and tourist buses. The interior of the **Smolensky Sobor** (Смоленский Собор; Smolensk Cathedral), in the convent's center, is stunning. Due to staff shortages, it is closed in rainy weather, when only the museum, in a white building to the left, is open. Entrance to the grounds is US$0.33; to buy tickets to the other buildings, stop by the white *kassa* on the left once you enter through the gate. Turning right and down the street, the convent's **cemetery** cradles the graves of Gogol, Chekhov, Stanislavsky, Khrushchev, Shostakovich, Mayakovsky, Bulgakov, and other luminaries. *(Open daily 9am-7pm; in winter closes at 6pm.)* The gravestones are often creative representations—visual or symbolic—of the deceased. Buy cemetery tickets at the small kiosk across the street from the entrance; if you can figure out Cyrillic, the cemetery map is also useful.

Large, airy, and lovely, **Moscow Choral Synagogue,** Bolshoy Spasoglinishchevsky per. 10 (Большой Сласогинищевский; formerly ul. Arkhipova; M5 or 6: Kitai-Gorod), gives a very different feeling from Russia's other churches. *(Open daily 9:30am-6pm.)* To get here, head north on Solyansky proezd (Солянский Проезд), and then take the first left. The synagogue functioned under Soviet rule, although all but the bravest were deterred by the KGB agents who photographed anyone who entered. Regular services are held every morning and evening, during which women are not allowed downstairs and men must cover their heads.

An 18th-century ecclesiastic gem is the **Tserkov Ioanna Voina** (Церковь Иоанна Воина; Church of St. John the Warrior), ul. Bolshaya Yakimanka 54 (Большая Якиманка; formerly Dimitrova), named after the patron saint of the tsar's musketeers. *(M4 or 5: Oktyabrskaya. Open 24hr. Services Tu-Su 5pm.)* The inner south region is speckled with numerous, sometimes boarded-up churches. The magical **Yelokhovsky Cathedral,** ul. Spartakovskaya 15 (Спартаковская; M3: Baumanskaya), is Moscow's largest operational church. Built in 1845, the cathedral is a major administrative center of the Russian Orthodox Church.

The city's most controversial landmark is undoubtedly the enormous, gold-domed **Khram Khrista Spasitelya** (Храм Христа Спасителя; Cathedral of Christ the Savior; M1: Kropotkinskaya), between ul. Volkhonka (Волхонка) and the Moscow River. In 1934, Stalin had a cathedral here dynamited with the intention of erecting the tallest building in the world, but after his death Khrushchev turned the site into a popular outdoor swimming pool instead. By the early 90s, water vapor was damaging paintings at the nearby Pushkin Museum, so the pool was closed. In 1994-95 a controversy erupted over the site; in a mere three years, the Orthodox Church and Moscow's mayor raised funds to build the US$250 million cathedral that stands today.

The Arbat, Pushkin Square, the Patriarch's Ponds

At M3: Arbatskaya, the **Arbat,** a pedestrian shopping arcade, was once a showpiece of *glasnost* and a haven for political radicals, Hare Krishnas, street poets, and *metallisti* (heavy metal rockers). Now, it boasts a McDonald's, a Baskin Robbins, and the United Colors of Benetton. Up ul. Tverskaya from Red Square, **Pushkin Square** (M6: Pushkinskaya) is Moscow's favorite rendezvous spot. Amateur politicians gather to argue and hand out petitions, while missionary groups evangelize. All the major Russian news organizations are located in this region. Follow ul. Bolshaya Bronnaya, next to McDonald's, down to the bottom of the hill, turn right, and follow ul. Malaya Bronnaya to the **Patriarch's Ponds** (Патриаршие Пруды) where Mikhail Bulgakov's *The Master and Margarita* begins. This region, known as the **Margarita,** is popular with artsy students and old men playing dominoes by the shaded pond.

Parks and Pedestrians Areas

The best time to come to **Izmaylovskiy Park** (Измайловский Парк; M3: Izmaylovski Park) is late Sunday afternoon, when tired vendors at the colossal weekend market are willing to make a deal. *(Park open daily 9am-5:30pm.)* Everything is on sale here, from carpets, *matryoshki* (nesting dolls), and *samovars* to military uniforms and pins. Some stalls even take orders, with delivery in a week. Another respite from Moscow's chaos is the tsars's **Kolomenskoe Summer Residence,** on a wooded rise above the Moskva River. *(M2: Kolomenskaya. Grounds open daily 7am-10pm. Free. Museums open Tu-Su 11am-6pm. US$1.67-2.50 from the kassa.)* Follow the signs "к музею Коломенское." Walk about 400m south on ul. Novinka (Новинка) past the *kinoteatr* (Кинотеатр) and go right just before the long fence. Peter the Great's 1702 log cabin and Bratsk Prison, where the persecuted Archpriest Avvakum wrote his celebrated autobiography, have been moved here from Arkhangelsk and Siberia, respectively. **Tsaritsyno's** charming architecture was also designed for imperial whims. From M2: Orekhovo, exit "к парку" from the front of the train from the center. Take the main alley, directly before you when you exit, and follow it to the palaces. The park was conceived for Catherine the Great, canceled by her, and finally completed only two years ago. Many believe a curse, from Catherine's ill humor, still looms over the red and white buildings and ancient oak and linden trees.

The **Moscow State University** (МГУ; *Em Ghe Oo*), a hefty walk from M1: Universitet, lies within a single Stalinist edifice. To fully appreciate its size, you must go inside, which means persuading a student-friend to take you. Near MSU, in the **Lenin Hills** (a leafy enclave overlooking the city center), is one of the city's best viewing areas, from which you can see the **Luzhniki Sports Complex,** the **Lenin Stadium** (sites of the 1980 summer Olympics), and all of Moscow behind it.

Museums

The **Moscow Metro,** one of the most beautiful in the world, is well worth a look. All the stations are unique and those inside the ring line are quite elaborate, with mosaics, sculptures, and crazy chandeliers. Trains come every two minutes, so you can stay as short or long as you like. Stations Kievskaya, Mayakovskaya, and Ploshchad Revolutsii are particularly good, as are Novoslobodskaya and Mendeleevskaya. Note the atomic-model light fixtures in the Mendeleevskaya station (open daily 6am-1am).

Pushkin Museum of Fine Arts (Музей Изобразительных Искусств им. А.С. Пушкина; *Muzey Izobrazitelnykh Iskusstv im. A.C. Pushkina*), ul. Volkhonka 12 (Волхонка). M1: Kropotkinskaya. Russia's 2nd most famous art museum after the Hermitage in St. Petersburg. The Egyptian exhibit on the 1st floor and the French Impressionists (mainly Monets) are 2 major pilgrimage areas, but since the museum frequently rotates its large collection, spending time in each section is probably more advisable. Each floor has a detailed plan, and audio tours help guide the way (30min., US$2.50). Open Tu-Su 10am-7pm; *kassa* closes at 6pm. US$6.67, students US$3.33; keep ticket for entrance to the...

Museum of Private Collections, in the aqua building to the left of the entrance to the Pushkin. A wide collection of 19th- and 20th-century foreign and Russian art. Honors tickets from the Pushkin Museum.

Tretyakov Gallery (Третьяковская Галерея), Lavrushensky per. 10 (Лаврушенский). M7: Tretyakovskaya. Premier art gallery holds superb Russian paintings, sculptures, and a magnificent collection of icons. The *Mona Lisa* equivalent here is the 12th-century Vladimir icon *God and Mother,* taken from Constantinople. Open Tu-Su 10am-8pm. US$7.50, students US$4.33.

State Tretyakov Gallery (Государственная Третяковская Галерея; *Gosudarstvennaya Tretyakovskaya Galereya*), ul. Krymsky Val 10 (Крымский Вал). M4 or 5: Oktyabrskaya. This is the place for comprehensive exhibits on (recent) Russian artists; the top floor permanent collection on Socialist Realism is also worth a visit. Open Tu-Su 10am-8pm; *kassa* until 7pm. US$6, students US$3.33. The **Tsentralny Dom Khudozhnika** (Центральный Дом Художника; Central House of Artists) in the same building showcases cutting-edge Russian art and progressive historical exhibits. Open Tu-Su 11am-8pm. US$2.50.

Museum of the Revolution (Музей Революции; *Muzey Revolyutsii*), ul. Tverskaya 21. M6: Pushkinskaya. Covers everything *since* the revolution, with displays of myriad Soviet artifacts. Amazingly, this Soviet archive has moved with the times, adding statistics on the ill effects of socialism as well as eclectic documents such as those on 80s rock bands in the later rooms. The museum shop on the 1st floor is one of the best places to buy Soviet medals, old posters, and T-shirts with witty slogans like "The Party is Over" or "Хард Рок Кафе." Museum open Tu, Th, and Sa 10am-6pm, W 11am-7pm, Su 10am-5pm. US$1.33. English tour US$36.75.

Manege (Манеж), Manezhnaya Pl., a big yellow building with white columns west of the Kremlin. One-time riding school for the military, now the Central Exhibition Hall with interesting modern Russian exhibits. Enter from the north end, from the square. Open M-Sa noon-7pm.

Authors' Houses

Russians take immense pride in their formidable literary history, preserving authors' houses in their original state, down to the half-empty teacups on the mantelpiece. Each is guarded by a team of fiercely loyal *babushki*.

Lev Tolstoy Estate, ul. Lva Tolstovo 21 (Льва Толстого). M1 or 4: Park Kultury. One of the best-preserved house-museums in Moscow. The author lived and worked here between 1882 and 1901. Open Tu-Su 10am-6pm (*kassa* until 5pm); off-season 10am-3:30pm; closed last F of each month. US$3.33, students US$1.67.

Chekhov's House Museum, ul. Sadovaya-Kudrinskaya 6. M6: Barrikadnaya. Chekhov lived here from 1886 until 1890, both writing and receiving patients—but you won't get as much of a feel for the author/doctor as he did for the Russian psyche. Open Tu, Th, and Sa-Su 11am-6pm, W and F 2-8pm. *Kassa* closes 1hr. earlier. Closed M and last day of each month.

Gorky's Apartment, ul. Malaya Nikitskaya 6/2 (Малая Никитская; former Kachalova). M6: Pushkinskaya. A pilgrimage site more for its architectural interest (Art Nouveau) than for its collection of Maxim Gorky's possessions. Open W and F noon-7pm, Th and Sa-Su 10am-5pm. Closed the last Th of each month. Tours US$5-US$6.67. Wear the slippers.

ENTERTAINMENT

Moscow is a large, fast-paced city, and it has the entertainment options to prove it. From September to June, the city boasts good theater, ballet, and opera, as well as excellent orchestras. Tickets bought in advance can be very cheap. Those with no luck at the box office sometimes hang out outside the theater and look for scalpers.

Bolshoy Teatr (Большой Театр; tel. 292 00 50). M2: Teatralnaya Pl. Literally called "Big Theater." It is worth a trip; both the opera and ballet companies are still good, despite multiple defections abroad. The theater itself is pure pre-Revolutionary elegance. Daily performances Sept.-June at 7pm. Tickets US$0.83-12.50.

Maly Teatr (Малый Театр; tel. 923 26 21), just north of the Bolshoy on Teatralnaya Pl. The "Small Theater" shows a different drama production every night. Difficult for non-Russian speakers, but fun if you understand the language. *Kassa* open Tu-Su 12:30-3pm and 4-6:30pm. Daily performances at 7pm. Tickets US$0.83-6.

Moscow Operetta Theater, ul. Bolshaya Dmitrovka 6 (tel. 292 63 77), just east of the Bolshoy, completes the M2: Teatralnaya theater triumvirate. Famous operettas staged year-round. Performances begin at 7pm. Tickets US$0.83-6.

Tchaikovsky Conservatory's Great and Small Halls, ul. Gertsena 13 (tel. 229 94 36). M6: Pushkinskaya. Centrally located and big—even the small one. Concerts most days at 7pm; Su also 2pm. *Kassa* in big hall open daily noon-7pm. Buy tickets for the small hall (малый зал; *maly zal*) in the back rows for just US$0.83.

Taganka Theater (tel. 915 12 17). M4 or 6: Taganskaya. Directly across the street from the ring line exit. Avant-garde theater; shows renowned for their satirical value. Closed in summer. *Kassa* open daily 1-3pm and 5-7pm.

Great Moscow Circus, pr. Vernadskovo 7 (Вернадского; tel. 930 02 72). M1: Universitet. Used to be the greatest show on earth, then all the big stars defected, so it's the greatest show in Moscow. Performances Tu-F at 7pm, Sa-Su at 11:30am, 3pm, and 7pm. *Kassy* open daily 11am-3pm and 4-7pm. Tickets start at US$3.33.

Nightclubs and Bars

Moscow's nightlife is the most kickin' action this side of the Volga, and certainly the most varied—not to mention expensive and dangerous—in Eastern Europe. Check the weekend editions of the *Moscow Times* or the biweekly renegade paper, *The Exile,* for info on music festivals and the rapidly changing club scene. *The Moscow Times'* Friday pull-out section, *MT Out,* provides a synopsis of each week's events, as well as restaurant, bar, and club reviews.

Although Moscow's gay community is increasingly coming out of the closet, it is still not safe to appear openly gay. Many gay establishments are unmarked, while others have instituted a card-pass system for admission, meaning that unless you know someone from whom you can get a pass, you can't get in. Useful numbers are **Treugolnik** (Треуголник; general tel. 932 01 00), a gay-and-lesbian social and lobbying organization, and **AIDS Infoshare Russia** (tel. 110 24 60). Both carry info on gay and lesbian life in Russia.

The Hungry Duck, ul. Pushechnaya 9 (Пушечная; tel. 923 61 58). M1 or 6: Kuznetsky Most, then through the courtyard on your right. The most raucous mass-market meat market since the fall of the Roman Empire. Drunken teenagers dance on the bar and tend to fall off. Superlatives fail in the glare of its debauchery. Live music on weekends. Cover US$6.75 and beer US$6.75. Open daily noon-6am.

Krizis Zhanra, per. Ostrovskvo 22/4 (Островского). M1: Kropotkinskaya. It's set back from the street a bit; look for the nondescript door with the light. One of the best places in Moscow to grab a beer; great, moderately inexpensive food. Extremely popular with local and foreign students. Live concerts begin at 9pm. Arrive early. Open daily 11am-11pm. Occasional US$3.33 cover after 9pm.

Bednye Lyudi (Бедные Люди; Poor Folks), ul. Bolshaya Ordynka 11/6 (Большая Ордынка). M7: Tretyakovskaya. Loud hangout for young Russians and students from overseas. Salad US$3.33. *Pelmeni* US$7.50. Happy Hour 5-10pm: 2 beers US$3.33. Open daily 5pm-5am.

Trety Put (Третий Путь), ul. Pyatnitskaya 4 (Пятницкая). M7: Tretyakovskaya. Loft-turned-nightclub-and-bar, featuring a number of little rooms where you can watch videos, play chess, or dance to psychedelic music. Live house, techno, and experimental music. Cover hovers around US$5. Open daily 9pm-2am.

Moosehead Canadian Bar, ul. Bolshaya Polyanka 54 (Большая Полянка). M4: Dobryninskaya. Take a left coming out of the Metro on to Bolshaya Polyanka: Moosehead is in a little enclave on your left. Indoor and outdoor bars with live music on weekends and a full menu of food, beer, and mixed drinks. Happy Hour M-F 6pm-8pm with *Coors* 2-for-1. Open daily 11am-5am. 21 and older.

■ Near Moscow: Sergiev Posad (Сергиев Посад)

Sergiev Posad is one of Russia's most famous pilgrimage sights. Orthodox believers come to pray in the many colorful churches inside the small town's main sight, **Troitsko-Sergieva Lavra** (Троицко-Сергиева Лавра; St. Sergius's Trinity Monastery). The stunning monastery, founded in 1340, is again a religious center—the paths between the churches are dotted with monks in flowing robes. Although each of the churches is exquisite and worth a look, the opulence of Russian Orthodoxy is best visible inside the **Trinity Cathedral.** *Elektrichki* (commuter trains) run to Sergiev Posad from Moscow's Yaroslavsky Vokzal (30min., US$2).

■ Novgorod (Новгород)

Founded in the 9th century by Prince Rurik, Novgorod blossomed during the Middle Ages, at one time reaching almost twice its current population. Many of the 140 churches and 50 monasteries built between 1100 and 1500 have survived to this day.

SIGHTS AND ENTERTAINMENT Entering the oldest **kremlin** in Russia from the lakeside affords a panoramic view of the fortress's massive brick walls and the sandy lakeshore, as well as the **Novgorod horseman,** who commemorates the city's survival through the ages (kremlin open daily 6am-midnight; free). To the immediate right of the lakeside entrance, an array of bells stands at the base of the **belfry.** Continuing to the right past the sounds of a music school, walk straight to **Sofiysky Sobor** (Софийский Собор; St. Sophia's Cathedral), the religious pinnacle of any trip to Novgorod (open daily 8am-8pm; services 10am and 6pm; free). The oldest stone building in Russia, this 11th-century Byzantine cathedral is most imposing from the outside; the intricately carved Swedish west doors depict scenes from the Bible. Across the footbridge from the kremlin and to the right, **Yaroslavovo Dvorishche** (Ярославово Дворище; Yaroslav's Court) is the old market center and the original site of the palace of Novgorod princes. There are the remains of the 17th-century waterfront arcade, several churches from the 13th to 16th centuries, and the market gatehouse, which is now a museum. The **Yuriev Monastyr** (Юриев Монастырь), dating from 1030, is one of three working monasteries surrounding Novgorod (open W-M 7am-9pm). It is strikingly located in the middle of broad and windy marshes. Take bus 7 (US$0.25) from pl. Pobedy to the airport. Go left at the fork around a small church to see the monastery in front (US$1.67, students US$0.83; photography US$2).

PRACTICAL INFO, ACCOMMODATIONS, AND FOOD Trains run to Moscow (8hr., 1 per day, US$19.50) and St. Petersburg (5hr., 2 per day, US$7.50). Buy tickets at Intourist *kassa* #1 (open 24hr). Pr. Karla Marxa (Карла Маркса) runs from the train station to the earth walls that surround old Novgorod. The **tourist office,** ul. Meretskovo 2 (Мерецкого), on the left side of the square in front of the kremlin, organizes English tours of Novgorod (US$18.33) and the kremlin (US$6.67), but has no maps or brochures (open daily 9am-6pm). Purchase **maps** at **Gostinitsa Intourist,** from the kiosk at the kremlin's east side, or at the St. Petersburg youth hostel (US$4.17), but be warned that they haven't kept up with many changes in local street names. **Exchange currency** at ul. Velikaya 16 (Великая), inside Hotel Intourist. A **telephone office** can be found at pl. Pobedy, corner of ul. Gorkovo (Горыкого) and ul. Oktyabrskaya. The phones on the right are for direct calls—prepay for your call at the *kassa* and get a booth number. **Gostinitsa Roza Vetrov** (Гостиница Роза Ветров), ul. Novo-Luchanskaya 27 (Ново-Лучанская; formerly Komsomolskaya; tel. (81622) 720 33; fax 715 70), is a Russian Youth Hostel affiliate. From the station, go left onto Oktyabrskaya (Октябрьская). Continue around left where the road turns into ul. Aleksandra Germana (Александра Германа) and take a right onto ul. Novo-Luchanskaya. The hostel is on the right; the entrance is on the small street before it. Second floor rooms are worn but clean and bright with firm beds (as you enter, keep going right until the staircase). The staff speaks some English. (Doubles US$8.33 per person; triples US$6.67 per person; deluxe singles US$23.33. Reserve through the St. Petersburg International Youth Hostel (see p. 759) or the Russian Youth Hostel Association.) The few eateries with any kind of ambience cater to tourists and raise their prices accordingly. **Detinets** (Детинец; tel. (81622) 746 24), in a stone tower of the kremlin, serves traditional Russian cuisine. (Meals US$3.67-5. Open Tu-Su 11am-11pm, M noon-11pm. Tour groups fill the place; reservations recommended.)

RUSSIA

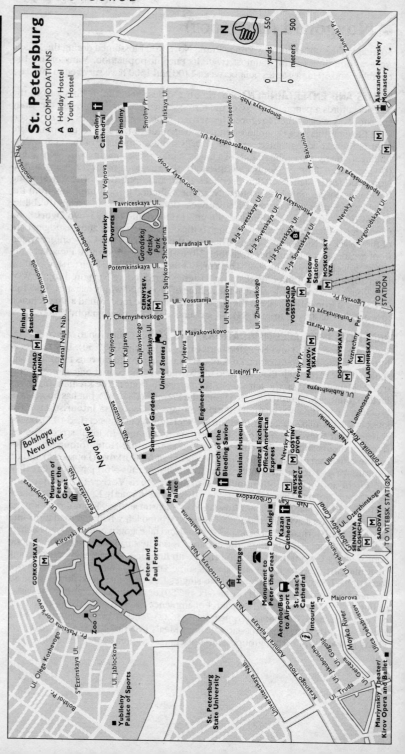

St. Petersburg

ACCOMMODATIONS
A Holiday Hostel
B Youth Hostel

Z

0 yards 550
0 meters 500

Smolny Cathedral
The Smolny
Tulskaya Ul.
Smolny Pr.
Ul. Vojnova
Suvorovsky Prosp.
Novgorodskaya Ul.
Sinopskaya Nab.
Pr. Bakunina
Moiseenko
Is폴komskaya Ul.
Nevsky Pr.
Mirgorodskaya Ul.
Alexander Nevsky Monastery
Znevskij Pr.

Tavriceskaya Ul.
Tavrichevsky Dvorets
Gorodskoj detskiy Park
Paradnaja Ul.
Potemkinskaya Ul.
Ul. Saltykova-Shchedrina
8-ja Sovetskaya Ul.
7-ja Sovetskaya Ul.
6-ja Sovetskaya Ul.
4-ja Sovetskaya Ul.
2-ja Sovetskaya Ul.
Mltninskaya Ul.
B
MOSKOVSKY VKZ.
Moscow Station
PROSCAD VOSSTANIJA
Ligovskij Pr.
TO BUS STATION

Finland Station
PLOSHCHAD LENINA
Arsenal Naja Nab.
Nab. R. obesera
Ul. Komsomola
CERNYSEV. SKAYA
Pr. Chernyshevskogo
Ul. Vojnova
Ul. Kaljaeva
Ul. Chajkovskogo
Furstadtskaya Ul.
United States
Ul. Ryleeva
Ul. Vosstanija
Ul. Mayakovskovo
Ul. Nekrasova
Ul. Zhukovskogo
Pushkinskaya Ul.
Ul. Marata
PROSCAD VOSSTANIJA
MAJAKOV. SKAYA
DOSTOEVSKAYA
Kuznechny Per.
VLADIMIRSKAYA

Litejnyj Pr.
Engineer's Castle
Summer Gardens
Church of the Bleeding Savior
Russian Museum
Central Exchange Office/American Express
Nevsky Pr.
GOSTINY DVOR
NEVSKY PROSPECT
Nevsky Pr.
Ul. Rubinshteyna
Ul. Lomonosova
Ul. Pomenki
FONTANKA River

Bolshaya Neva River
Neva River
Museum of Peter the Great
Nab. Kutuzova
Marble Palace
Nab. Kanala Gribojedova
Kazan Cathedral
Dom Knigi
Nab. Kan. Gribojedova
Ul. Plekhanova
GOSTINAYA PLOSHCHAD
SADOVAYA
TO VITEBSK STATION
Ul. Dzerzhinskogo

Ul. Kujbysheva
Ul. Kujbysheva
Peter and Paul Fortress
Monument to Peter the Great
Hermitage
St. Isaac's Cathedral
Aeroflot/Bus to Airport
Intourist
Pr. Majorova
Moyka River
Ul. Gogolja
Ul. Gercena

GORKOVSKAYA
Kirovski Pr.
Zoo
Pr. Maksima Gorkovo
Bolshoi Pr.
Ul. Olega Koshevogo
S'Ezzinskaya Ul.
Ul. Jablockova
Yubileiny Palace of Sports
Ul. Jakobicta
St. Petersburg State University
Universitetskaya Nab.
Krasnogo Flota Nab.
Admirali Tejskaja Nab.
Ul. Truda
Ul. Gogolja
Ul. Dekabristov
Marinsky Theater/Kirov Opera and Ballet
Borisorska Nab.

■ St. Petersburg (Санкт-Петербург)

Founded as Russia's new capital in 1703, St. Petersburg is a city forged of force. Peter the Great drove laborers to death by digging canals to drain the swamp on the Gulf of Finland, and then coerced his friends into building their palaces in the area. The land was strategically chosen to drag Russia away from Byzantium and make it turn westward. But St. Petersburg was also the birthplace of the 1917 revolution, which would turn Russia decisively away from the West. Petersburg's name has reflected the currents of its country's history: the German-sounding *Sankt Peterburg* was changed to Petrograd during World War I; after Lenin's death in 1924, the city was renamed Leningrad, only to reclaim St. Petersburg when Lenin fell out of favor. Yet it was Leningrad that suffered the 900-day siege in World War II, during which close to a million people died. Out of a turbulent and bloody history, the city has somehow persisted as Russia's cultural capital, home of Pushkin, Dostoevsky, one of the most famous art museums in the world, and a thriving alternative scene.

ORIENTATION AND PRACTICAL INFORMATION

St. Petersburg (often called "Petersburg" or "Peter") is in northwest Russia, a six-hour train ride east of Helsinki and nine hours northwest of Moscow. It sits on the mouth of the **Neva** (Нева) river, on the **Gulf of Finland** (Финский Залив, *Finsky Zaliv*). **Moscow train station** (Московский Вокзал; *Moskovsky Vokzal*) is located near the midpoint of the city's main thoroughfare, Nevsky pr. (Невский пр.), by metro station "pl. Vosstaniya" (пл. Восстания). Several canals run roughly parallel to the Neva river, and Nevsky pr. runs from the **Admiralteystvo** (Адмиралтейство) on the river to **Aleksandro-Nevskaya Lavra** (Александро-Невская Лавра; Aleksandr Nevsky Monastery). Across the river and to the north of the Admiralty is the city's historic heart, the **Petropavlovskaya Krepost** (Петропавловская Крепость; Peter and Paul Fortress). The area including Nevsky pr. is mainland St. Petersburg; the rest of the city consists of islands, the two largest being **Vasilevsky** (Васильевский) and **Petrogradsky** (Петроградский). Travelers should pick up a copy of the info-stuffed *Traveler's Yellow Pages for St. Petersburg* and glance at the three free English-language newspapers: *The St. Petersburg Times, Pulse,* and *Neva News.*

Telephone Code: 812

Flights: The main airport, **Pulkovo** (Пулково), has 2 terminals: Pulkovo-1 for domestic and Pulkovo-2 for international flights. From M2: "Moskovskaya," take bus 29 for Pulkovo-1, and bus 13 for Pulkovo-2. Hostels can usually arrange for you to be taken (or met) by taxi (usually US$30-40).

Trains: 4 main train stations for both daytrips and overnight coaches—check carefully which station you want. **Warsaw Station** (Варшавский Вокзал; *Varshavsky Vokzal*). M1: Baltiskaya (Балтийская). To Rīga (20hr., US$48.33), Tallinn (9hr., US$26.67), and Vilnius (15hr., US$38.17). **Vitebsk Station** (Витебский Вокзал; *Vitebsksky Vokzal*). M1: Pushkinskaya (Пушкинская). To: Kiev (27hr., US$45) and Odessa (36½hr., US$56.67). **Moscow Station** (Московский Вокзал; *Moskovsky Vokzal*). M1: Pl. Vosstaniya (пл. Восстания). To Moscow (6-8½hr., US$45.83) and Nizhny Novgorod (5hr., US$20). **Finland Station** (Финляндский Вокзал; *Finlandsky Vokzal*). M1: Pl. Lenina (пл. Ленина). To Helsinki (5½hr., US$55.83). The **Central Ticket Offices** for rail travel (Центральные Железнодорожные Кассы; *Tsentralny Zheleznodorozhnye Kassy*) are at Canal Griboedova 24 (кан. Грибоедова). Open M-Sa 8am-8pm, Su 8am-4pm. Foreign tourists must buy domestic tickets at **Intourist** windows 100-104 on the 2nd floor. Intourist also handles international tickets (windows 90-99). Info is at window 90; US$0.67 for each question asked. There are Intourist offices at each train station.

Buses: nab. Obvodnovo Kanala 36 (Обводного Канала). M4: Ligovsky pr. (Лиговский). From the Metro, take tram 19, 25, 44, or 49 or trolley 42 one stop until just across the canal. Facing the canal, go right along it for 2 long blocks. The station is on your right. Often cheaper and more comfortable than trains if you are traveling during the day. Buy tickets on the day you leave to avoid a US$0.50 surcharge; you can buy only one-way tickets. To Tallinn (6½hr., 2 per day, US$16.67) and Tartu (8hr., 1 per day, US$15.92). Baggage costs extra (US$0.33-0.83). Station open daily 5:30am-midnight. Advance ticket booth open 8am-2pm and 3-8pm.

Public Transportation: Buses, trams, and **trolleys** run fairly frequently, depending on the time of day. Read the stops posted on the outside of the bus. Trolleys 1, 5, and 22 go from pl. Vosstaniya to the bottom of Nevsky pr., near the Hermitage. Buses are often packed. The **Metro** (Метро) is an efficient, relatively safe method of exploring the city (daily 5:30am-12:30am). A Metro **token** (жетон; *zheton*) costs US$0.25 and also works in some phone booths for local calls. Bus, tram, and trolley *talony* (талоны; tickets) cost US$0.25; buy them from the driver. The fine for unpunched tickets is US$1.50 (not to mention great humiliation); they do check.

Tourist Offices: Sindbad Travel (FIYTO), 3rd Sovetskaya ul. 28 (3-я Советская; tel. 327 83 84; fax 329 80 19), in the International Hostel. Geared to students and budget travelers. Arranges plane, train, bus, and ferry tickets, and escorted package tours and adventure trips. 10-80% discounts on plane tickets. Open M-F 9:30am-5:30pm. **Ost-West Contact Service,** ul. Mayakovskovo 7 (Маяковского; tel. 327 34 16; fax 327 34 17). Free info, from clubs to pharmacies to airline tickets (international only). Staff arranges visas (US$7 per night, or US$60 for up to 3 month stays), homestays (US$20 in center, US$15 elsewhere), boat and bus tours, and theater tickets. Open M-F 10am-6pm, Sa noon-6pm.

Consulates: Canada, Malodetskoselsky pr. 32 (Малодетскосельский; tel. 325 84 48; fax 325 83 93). M1: Tekhnologichesky Institut. Open M-F 9am-1pm and 2-5pm. **U.K.,** pl. Proletarskoy Diktatury 5 (Пролетарской Диктатуры; tel. 325 60 36; fax 325 60 37). M1: Chernyshevskaya. Open M-F 9:30am-5:30pm. **U.S.,** ul. Furshtatskaya 15 (Фур штатская; tel. 275 17 01, 24hr. emergency tel. 274 86 92; fax 213 69 62). M1: Chernyshevskaya. Open M-F 9:15am-1pm and 2-5:30pm. Citizens of **Australia** and **New Zealand** should contact their embassies in Moscow but can use the U.K. consulate in an emergency.

Currency Exchange: Look for the обмен валюты *(Obmen Valyuty)* signs everywhere. **Central Exchange Office,** ul. Mikhailovskaya 4 (Михайловская), off Nevsky pr. and across from Grand Hotel Europe. M3: Gostiny Dvor (Гостиный Двор). Credit cards and traveler's checks accepted (3% commission). Expect a long wait and bring a picture ID. Open M-F 9am-1:30pm and 3-6pm, Sa-Su 9:30am-2pm and 3-6pm. Also at post offices. Keep receipts to change rubles back to dollars.

American Express: ul. Mikhailovskaya 1/7 (tel. 329 60 60; fax 329 60 61), in Grand Hotel Europe. Bank and currency exchange. Personal checks cashed and mail held for cardholders, but no packages. Send mail to: c/o American Express, P.O. Box 87, SF-53501, Lappeenranta, Finland. Open M-F 9am-5pm, Sa 9am-1pm.

Gay and Lesbian Information: St. Petersburg Gay and Lesbian Association, **KRYLYA** (КРЫЛЬЯ; wings), is the officially recognized organization. Call 312 31 80 or email krilija@ilga.org for information, help, or accommodations. English spoken.

Laundry Service: Pick-up laundry service (tel. 560 29 92). US$7.50 for 4.5kg, plus US$7.50 for delivery. Next-day service. Only Russian spoken.

Emergencies: 24hr. multilingual hotline for foreigners 164 97 87. Police and ambulance drivers do not speak English. Report crimes immediately to the consulate and the police station—bring a Russian speaker.

Pharmacy: The *apteka* at Nevsky pr. 22 stocks Russian and Western medicines (including giardia cure Tinidazole), as well as tampons. Open M-F 8am-9pm, Sa-Su 24hr. At night, enter through the back.

Medical Assistance: American Medical Center, ul. Serpukhovskaya 10 (Серпуховская; tel. 326 17 30, 24hr. emergency hotline 310 96 11; fax 326 17 31), near M1: Tekhnologichesky Institut (Технологический Институт). Western doctors. **Polyclinic #2,** Moskovsky pr. 22 (tel. 316 38 77), and **Hospital #20,** Gastello ul. 21 (Гастелло; tel. 108 40 90), treat foreigners.

Post Office: ul. Pochtamskaya 9 (Почтамтская). From Nevsky pr., west on ul. Malaya Morskaya (Малая Морская), which becomes ul. Pochtamskaya. 2 blocks past Isaakievsky Sobor on the right, just before an overhanging arch. Money exchange and telephones. Not reliable for international mail, but can be used within the former Soviet Union. **EMS** (Russian Express Mail) open M-F 9am-5pm. Post office open M-Sa 9am-7:30pm, Su 10am-5:30pm. **Postal Code:** 19000.

Express Mail: DHL, Izmaylovsky pr. 4 (Измайловский; tel. 326 64 00; fax 326 64 10). Open M-F 9am-6pm, Sa 10am-4pm. **Branch office** in the Nevsky Palace Hotel, Nevsky pr. 57 (tel. 325 61 00; fax 325 61 16). Open M-F 9am-6pm. **St. Petersburg Center of Business Communications** (tel. 312 20 85; fax 314 33 60) shares space with the Central Telephone Office and offers express mail. Open daily 9am-9pm.

Internet Access: Tetris (Тетрис) **Internet Cafe,** Chernyakhovskovo 33 (Черняховского; tel. 164 48 77; http://www.dux.ru). Full internet access and friendly, helpful staff. US$4.17 per hr. before 1pm, US$8.33 per hr. 1-9pm. Also at the **International Youth Hostel (HI)**; see **Accommodations,** below.

Telephones: Central Telephone and Telegraph, Bolshaya Morskaya ul. 3/5 (Большая Морская). Face the Admiralteystvo; it's right off Nevsky pr. near Palace Square. For **intercity calls,** use one of the *mezhdugorodny* (междугородный) phone booths at the Central Telephone office; they take special grooved *zhetony* (жетоны; tokens; US$0.40) sold across from the booths or prepay in the 3rd hall *kassa.* For long-distance calls, dial 8 and wait for the tone before proceeding. Open M-F 9am-12:30pm and 1-8pm; Su 9am-12:30pm and 1-5pm. Intercity calls can also be made from any public phone on the street that takes phone cards. 1 unit equals 1 min. of local calls. 54 units per min. to the U.S. Cards are available at the Central Telephone office or at newspaper kiosks. 25 units US$3.50, 400 units US$21.

There is no effective water purification system in St. Petersburg. Always boil tap water, dry your washed veggies, and stock up on bottled water.

ACCOMMODATIONS

Travelers can choose among deluxe new joint ventures, old Intourist dinosaurs, **hostels,** and **private apartments.** The International Hostel's *The Traveler's Yellow Pages* lists accommodation options. The **Host Families Association** (HOFA; tel./fax 275 19 92), based at the St. Petersburg Technical University, can arrange **homestays:** B&Bs in apartments less than 1km from a Metro station with a family guaranteed to have one English-speaking member. Perks besides room and breakfast will be billed. Given two to three weeks, HOFA will find you a bed in any major city in the CIS (singles US$25-30; doubles US$48-50).

Hostel "Holiday," ul. Mikhailova 1 (Михайлова; tel 542 73 64; fax 325 85 59; email postmaster@hostelling.spb.su; http://www.spb.ru/holiday). M1: Pl. Lenina. Exit at the Finland train station and turn left on ul. Komsomola (Комсомола), then right on ul. Mikhailova. Just before the river, turn left into a courtyard, then right. A "YH" adorns the wall ahead of you. Ring the bell. Entrance on the 3rd floor. Clean, pleasant rooms. Cafe. TV lounge. US$18.67 per person; doubles US$50. Breakfast and sheets included. Reception 9am-midnight. Reserve ahead.

International Youth Hostel (HI), 3-ya Sovetskaya ul. 28 (3-я Советская; tel. 329 80 18; fax 329 80 19; email ryh@ryh.spb.su; http://www.spb.ru/ryh). Housed in a restored 5-story building in the city center. Walk 3 blocks from M1: "Pl. Vosstaniya" along Suvorovsky pr. (Суворовский); turn right on 3-ya Sovetskaya ul. Clean, with basic Soviet furnishings. Kitchen. Laundry service US$41.17 for 4kg. **Cybercafe.** TV. Check-in by 1am. US$17.67 per person; nonmembers add US$2; discount with ISIC. Breakfast and sheets included. Reservations can be made internationally (U.S. tel. (310) 379-4316; fax 379-8420; email 71573.2010@compuserve.com; U.K. tel. (0171) 836 1036). MC and Visa accepted for abroad reservations only.

Petrovsky Hostel, ul. Baltiyskaya (Балтийская; tel. 252 75 63; fax 252 40 19). From M1: "Narvskaya," turn left on pr. Stachek (Стачек) to ul. Baltiskaya and turn left; it's a few blocks ahead on your left. Though a little ways from the center, this is a good, cheap option. Kitchen, common room, TV. Clean rooms for 2-3 people US$6.67 per person. Sheets not included. Check-in by midnight. Check-out 11am.

Hotel Olgino (Отель Олыгино), Primorskoye Shosse 18 (Приморское Шоссе; tel. 238 36 71; fax 238 34 63). M2: Chernaya Rechka, then bus 110 (20-25min.). Recently renovated hotel just outside the city. Saunas and horse rentals. Showers and kitchen. Singles US$35.17; doubles US$60. **Camping** US$8.

FOOD

Restaurants are expensive and menus are often only in Cyrillic, and top restaurants fill up fast. Even if pricier than state-owned stores, **markets** are a Russian experience. They stock fresh produce, meat, cheese, and occasionally prepared dishes, and require energy and bargaining on the part of all involved. Foreigners are often overcharged. The **covered market,** Kuznechny per. 3 (Кузнечьный), just around the corner from M1: "Vladimirskaya," and the **Maltsevski Rynok, ul.** Nekrasova 52 (Некрасова), at the top of Ligovsky pr. (Лиговский; M1: Pl. Vosstaniya), are the biggest and most exciting (both open M-Sa 8am-7pm, Su 8am-4pm). A **supermarket,** (Супермаркет), Nevsky pr. 48, is inside the Passazh building (Пассаж; M3: Gostiny Dvor; open M-Sa 10am-9pm, Su 11am-9pm).

Russian and Ethnic Cuisine

Pelmennaya "Alina" (Пелменная "Алина"), Suvorovsky pr. Serves the cheapest hearty food in town. Borscht US$1, salad US$0.50-1, *pelmeny* US$1.10. Open daily 10am-9pm. No English spoken.

Tblisi (Тблиси), ul. Sytninskaya 10 (Сытнинская). M2: Gorkovskaya. Wide variety of Georgian appetizers. *Tolma* (stuffed grape leaves) US$2.83. Lunch specials US$4.17 (daily noon-5pm). English menu. Open daily noon-11pm.

Green Crest (Грин Крест), Vladimirsky pr. 7 (Владимирский). M1: Vladimirskaya or M4: Dostoevskaya. An oasis for vegetarians: 12 varieties of fresh salads. Get them by scoops (100g for US$0.83). Mushroom pizza US$3. Open daily 9am-11:30pm.

Vetal (Веталь), Admiralteysky pr. 8 (Адмиралтейский). Go left 1 block at the bottom of Nevsky. Beautiful, traditional Russian restaurant. Hearty food and a location ideal for an after-dinner stroll down Nevsky. *Pelmeny* US$3-3.33, stuffed tomatoes US$3.17. Open daily 11am-midnight.

Tandoor (Тандур), Voznesensky pr. 2. On the corner of Admiraleysky pr., 2 blocks left from the bottom of Nevsky pr. Veggie options US$6.67-9. Lunch special US$15.50 (served noon-4pm). English menu. Open daily noon-11pm.

Fast Food and Cafes

Idiot (Идиот), nab. Moyki 82 (Мойки), about 200m along Moyki from Isaakievskaya pl. Tasteful, elegant cafe reproducing the atmosphere of a 17th-century salon. Pint of Baltica beer US$3. Happy hour 6:30-7:30pm. Open daily noon-11pm.

Kolobok (Коболок), ul. Chaykovskovo 40 (Чайкоского). M1: Chernyshevskaya. Delicious hot pirozhki to eat in or take out US$0.33-0.50. Open daily 7:30am-8pm.

Skazka (Сказка; Fairy Tale), 1-ya Sovetskaya 12. M1: pl. Vosstaniya. Combines the traditional Russian treat *bliny* (блины; US$1.08-1.25) with amicable Western service and unbeatable prices. Eat in or take out. Open 24hr.

The Brooklyn Bridge Cafe, nab. Moyki 106, near Teatralnaya pl. and Novaya Gollandia island, in the Lesgafta Institute. Manhattan "view." Caters to students and artists. Guinness US$4.17 per pint. Happy hour 5-8pm. Open daily 10am-10pm.

Minutka (Минутка), Nevsky pr. 20. Cheap, large sandwiches. Tuna sandwich US$5.58. Salads US$2.83-3.83. Open daily 10am-10pm.

SIGHTS

Hermitage, Russian Museum, and St. Isaac's Cathedral

Once comprising 225 paintings belonging to Catherine the Great, the State Hermitage Museum (Эрмитаж), Dvortsovaya nab. 34 (Дворцовая), now rivals the Louvre and the Prado in architectural, historical, and artistic magnificence. Housed in five opulent buildings—the **Winter Palace,** the **Little Hermitage,** the **Large Hermitage,** the **Hermitage Theater** (often closed), and the **New Hermitage,** it is the world's largest art collection. The whole museum cannot be absorbed in one visit—indeed, only 5% of the collection is on display at any one time. In the Winter Palace (Зимний Дворец; *Zimny Dvorets*), where the tsars reigned and entertained, is **Malachite Hall,** where Lenin's Bolshevik forces arrested Kerensky's government in October 1917. (*Open M-Sa 10:30am-6pm, Su 10:30am-5pm; cashier and upper floors until 1hr. before closing.*

Kassa located on the river side of the building. US$10, students free, cameras US$3.33, video US$10. Lines can be long, so come early or on a weekday.) If you wondered why the Revolution began here, the Palace's opulence may explain a few things.

The **Russian Museum** (Русский Музей; *Russky Muzey;* tel. 219 16 15; M3: Gostiny Dvor) is down ul. Mikhailova (Михайлова) past the Grand Hotel Europe. *(Open W-Su 10am-6pm, M 10am-5pm. Kassa closes at 5pm. US$8, students US$4, cameras US$4.16.)* Founded in 1898, this first public museum of Russian art houses the largest collection of national art outside Moscow's Tretyakov Gallery. The collection is arranged chronologically, featuring Russian folk art, 12th- to 17th-century icons, 18th- and 19th-century painting and sculpture, and often controversial modern art. While the building is being restored, enter through the basement in the right corner of the courtyard; go downstairs and turn left. Next to the *Russky Muzey,* the **Muzey Etnografii** (Музей Этнографии; Ethnographic Museum), has hands-on exhibits about the traditions, arts, and crafts of the former Soviet Republics. *(Open Tu-Su 11am-6pm. Kassa closes at 5pm. US$4, students US$2.50.)*

Behind the museum, the **Letny Sad i Dvorets** (Летний Сад и Дворец; Summer Gardens and Palace) are a lovely place to rest. They can be entered from the north or south and have long paths lined with marble busts of famous Russians. Peter's small **Summer Palace** in the northeast corner of the gardens was once part of a larger complex. Individuals must join tours given in Russian—after you buy your ticket, wait outside until they invite you in. *(Gardens open in summer daily 8am-11pm; off-season 8am-7pm. Free. Palace open W-M 11am-6pm. Closed the last M of the month. US$3.33, students US$1.67.)*

For an awe-inspiring view of the city's rooftops, climb to the dome of **St. Isaac's Cathedral** (Исаакиевский Собор; Isaakievski Sobor), Isaakievskaya pl. *(Open Th-Su 11am-7pm; colonnade open 11am-6pm. Kassa is to the right of the cathedral. US$8.33, students US$4.17. Colonnade US$3.33, students US$1.33. Foreigners buy tickets inside the church.)* From Nevsky pr., go left down Bolshaya Morskaya ul. A massive example of 19th-century civic-religious architecture designed by Auguste de Montferrand, the cathedral's dome is coated with almost 100kg of pure gold; in sunlight it shines from miles away. St. Isaac's took 40 years to finish, in part due to a superstition that the Romanov dynasty would fall with the cathedral's completion. In fact, the cathedral was completed in 1858, and the Romanovs lasted another 59 years. Some of Russia's greatest artists have worked on the murals and mosaics inside.

Despite the fact that the cathedral was the Nazi air force's "reference point #1" during World War II, the starving citizens of Leningrad planted cabbages in its square. Photographs of the cabbage-field are displayed at the "Leningrad During the War Years and the Siege" exhibit in **Rumyantsev House**, Angliskaya nab. 44 (Английская), along the embankment. *(Open Th-M 11am-5pm, Tu 11am-4pm. US$2.50.)*

Nevsky Prospekt and Environs

The Prospekt begins at the **Admiralteystvo** (Адмиралтейство; Admiralty), whose golden spire, painted black during World War II to disguise it from bombers, towers over the Admiralty Gardens and Palace Square. On the river side of Admiraleystvo stands Falconet's **Bronze Horseman**—the symbol of the city and its origins as a product of Peter the Great's will. **Palace Square** (Дворцовая Площадь; *Dvortsovaya Ploshchad*), is the expanse in front of the Winter Palace. Here Catherine was hailed as tsarina after she overthrew her husband, Tsar Peter III. On "Bloody Sunday" in 1905, Nicholas II's guards fired into a crowd of peaceful demonstrators here, the beginning of the Romanov's end. The site also saw the 1917 Revolution's storming of the Winter Palace. Gain insight into a national obsession at the **Muzey Pushkina** (Музей Пушкина), nab. Reki Moiki 12 (Реки Мойки), the yellow building just off Palace Square. *(Open W-M 11am-6pm; closed last F of the month. US$2 includes an English tour, students US$1.)* Russians *adore* native son Aleksandr Pushkin; they consider him greater than Shakespeare, and any Russian with more than a year of schooling can recite some of his verses.

The colossal edifice modeled after St. Peter's in Rome is the **Kazan Cathedral** (Казанский Собор; *Kazansky Sobor*). *(Open M-Tu and Th-F 11am-6pm, Sa-Su noon-6pm. Kassa closes at 5pm. US$2.83, students US$1.42. Morning services 9am, Su 10am.)* The **State Museum of the History of Religion**—formerly the Museum of the History of Religion and Atheism—has a gold cross that was restored in 1994. The few icons, robes, and bibles are displayed in glass cases, dwarfed by the interior of the cathedral—the real reason to pay the museum's entrance fee. The site of Tsar Aleksandr II's 1881 assassination, the colorful **Church of the Bleeding Savior** (Спас На Крови; *Spas Na Krovi;* a.k.a. the Savior on the Blood), has just reopened after 20 years of renovations, and its walls are covered with 7000 square feet of beautifully restored mosaics. *(Open daily 11am-7pm; Kassa closes 6pm. US$11.67, students US$1.17.)*

Ploshchad Ostrovskovo (Островского), just off Nevsky pr., close to M3: "Gostiny Dvor," holds a monument to Catherine the Great, surrounded by political and cultural figures of her reign. Russia's oldest theater, Aleksandrovsky (Александровский), built by architect Rossi in 1828, is behind Catherine's monument. The first production of Nikolai Gogol's *The Inspector General* was staged here in 1836.

Muzey Anny Akhmatovoy (Музей Анны Ахматовой), Fontanki 34 (Фонтанки), houses the famous poet's personal possessions. Enter at Liteyny pr. 51 (Литейный). *(Open Tu-Su 10:30am-5:30pm, closed last W of every month. US$0.67, students US$0.33.)* **Dostoevsky House** (Дом Достоевского; *Dom Dostoevskovo*) occupies the writer's apartment at Kuznechny per. 5/2 (Кузнечный), around the corner to the right from M1: "Vladimirskaya." The area resembles Dostoevsky's St. Petersburg, though diehard *Crime and Punishment* fans should check out Sennaya Pl. (Сенная)—the actual setting of the murder. *(Open Tu-Su 11am-6pm; kassa closes at 5:30pm. Closed last W of month. US$2.67, students US$1.33.)* Some of the bloodiest confrontations of the February Revolution took place at **Uprising Square** (Площадь Восстания; *Ploshchad Vosstaniya*), the halfway point of Nevsky pr., marked by the Moscow train station.

At the far end of Nevsky pr. directly opposite M3, 4: "Ploshchad Aleksandra Nevskovo," **Aleksandro-Nevskaya Lavra** (Александро-невская Лавра; Aleksandr Nevsky Monastery), is a major pilgrimage destination and a peaceful spot for a stroll. *(Open Su-W and F-Sa 10am-7pm. US$1.67, students US$0.83, photography US$0.67, video US$1.33; map of cemetery US$0.33.)* The monastery got its name and fame from Prince Aleksandr of Novgorod, whose body was moved here by Peter the Great in 1724. A cobblestone path lined with souvenir-sellers and beggars connects the monastery's cathedral and two cemeteries. The graveyard on the left is the 1716 **Lazarevskoye Kladbishche** (Лазаревское Кладбище; Lazarus Cemetery), the city's oldest. Across the way, on the right as you walk in, rests the younger, larger **Tikhvinskoye Kladbishche** (Тихвинское Кладбище; Tikhvin Cemetery)—its ground holds such famous names as Fyodor Dostoevsky. The **Blagoveshchenskaya Tserkov** (Благовещенская Церковь; Church of Annunciation), farther along the stone path on the left, was the original burial place of the Romanovs, who were then moved to Peter and Paul Cathedral (exhumation is possibly the only Russian government activity as popular as rewriting history). The church is currently under renovation. The **Troitsky Sobor** (Троицкий Собор; Trinity Cathedral) at the end of the path is still functioning. *(Services in the*

The Russian Museum

Like many museums in Eastern Europe, those in Russia charge foreigners much higher rates than natives. In desperation, some travelers don a fluffy fur hat, push the exact number of rubles for a Russian ticket toward the *babushka* at the *kassa*, and remain stoically mute. Go ahead and try it—it might work. Once inside, don't worry about forgetting to see anything—the *babushki* in each room will make sure of that. Many museums, with floors made of precious inlaid wood, will ask visitors to don *tapachki*, giant slippers that go over your shoes and transform the polished gallery floor into a veritable ice rink. There are no guardrails—only irreplaceable imperial china—to slow your slide. Make sure your slippers fit well, or you'll meet an unfortunate end on the stairs.

cathedral M-Sa 6am, 10am, and 5pm; Su 7am, 10am, and 5pm. Free during services; otherwise US$1.67, students US$0.83.) It is often possible to join English tours at the monastery.

The yellow, court-yarded **Menshikov Palace,** Universitetskaya nab. 15 (Университетская), is across the bridge north of the Admiralty to the left. *(Open Tu-Su 10:30am-4:30pm. US$5, students US$1.)* To truly understand the impact of World War II on St. Petersburg, go to the remote and chilling **Piskarovskoye Memorial Cemetery** (Пискаровское Мемориальное Кладбище; *Pisarkovskoye Memorialnoye Kladbishche*). Close to a million people died during the 900 days that the city was under German siege; this is their grave. The monument reads: "No one is forgotten; nothing is forgotten." Stop at M1: "Ploshchad Muzhestva" (Площадь Мужества) and go left to the street. Walk left, cross Nepokorennykh pr. (Непокоренных) and catch bus 123 from the shelter (7-10min.).

Peter and Paul Fortress

(Петропавловская Крепость; *Petropavlovskaya Krepost*) Across the river from the Hermitage, the fortress's spreading walls and golden spire beckon. In May 1703, a date now considered the birthday of St. Petersburg, construction on the fortress was begun. It was to be a defense against the Swedes, but Peter I defeated them before the fortress was finished. It now houses the gold-spired cathedral that gives the complex and several other museums its name. The icons in **Peter and Paul Cathedral** are currently under restoration, but you can see the graves of most of the tsars since Peter the Great. *(Open Th-M 11am-5pm, Tu 11am-4pm; closed last Tu of the month. US$3.08, students US$1.54. Graves open Th-M 10am-6pm, Tu 10am-5pm.)* **Trubetskoy Bastion** (Трубецкой Бастион), in the fortress's southwest corner, is a reconstruction of the prison where Peter the Great imprisoned and tortured his first son Aleksei. Dostoevsky, Gorky, Trotsky, and Lenin's older brother also spent time here (same opening hours as museum).

ENTERTAINMENT

St. Petersburg's famed White Nights lend the night sky a pale glow from mid-June to early July. During the third week in June, the city holds a series of outdoor evening concerts as part of the **White Nights Festival;** check kiosks and posters for more info. If you walk through the city during the White Nights (never do it alone!) and watch the bridges over the Neva go up at 1:30am, remember to walk on the same side of the river as your hotel—the bridges don't go back down until 3 or 4am. **Marinsky Teatr** (Марийнский Театр), Teatralnaya pl. 1 (Театральная; tel. 114 43 44; M4: Sadovaya (Садовая), then along canal Griboyedova and right onto the square), is one of the world's most famous ballet theaters. Pavlova, Nureyev, Nizhinsky, and Baryshnikov all started here. For two weeks in June, the theater hosts the White Nights Festival; tickets (US$1.67-10) are sold 10 days in advance (*kassa* open W-Su 11am-3pm and 4-7pm). Second to the Marinsky for opera and ballet, the **Maly Teatr** (Малый Театр), pl. Iskusstv 1 (Искусств; tel. 219 19 78), has the advantage of being open in July and August when the Marinsky is closed (*kassa* open daily 11am-3pm and 4-8pm). **Shostakovich Philharmonic Hall,** Mikhailovskaya ul. 2 (tel. 118 42 57), hosts classical and modern concerts (tickets from US$0.83).

During the pre-Gorbachev era, St. Petersburg was the heart of the underground music scene, and this is still evident today. Be careful going home late at night, especially if you've been drinking—loud, drunk foreigners might as well be carrying neon signs saying "rob me!" Clubs last no longer than college relationships; hostels can recommend the newest places. Or check the *St. Petersburg Times* and *Pulse* for ads. Soviet rock superstars like Kino and Igry got their starts at **St. Petersburg Rock Club** (Рок Клуб), ul. Rubinshtayna 13 (Рубинштейна; M4: Dostoevskaya; cover US$3.33-6.67). The place to dance to techno is **Tunnel,** in an old bomb shelter on Lyubyansky per (Любянский) between ul. Blokhina (Блохина) and Zverinskaya (Зверинская; cover US$5; open Th-Sa midnight-6am). **Moloko** (Молоко; Milk) Perekupnoy per. 12 (Перекупной; tel. 274 94 67), a small rock club, features various local bands and a young, friendly Russian crowd (beer US$1.08; open F-Sa 8-11:30pm; cover around

US$2.50). The sign-less **Jungle,** (tel. 238 80 33) ul. Blokhina 8 (Блохина), with its aquamarine door, is the city's newest gay club. Admission is based on membership, but foreigners are welcome; call ahead (cover US$3.67-US$8.33). **The Shamrock,** ul. Dekrabristov 27 (Декабристов), across from the Marinsky, serves pints of Guinness and Kilkenny (US$5) to prove its Irish mettle in the heart of Eastern Europe.

■ Near St. Petersburg

Ride the suburban *electrichka* trains any spring or summer weekend day and you will witness the Russian love of the countryside. Most Russians own or share a *dacha* outside the city. The tsars were no different; they, too, built country houses, and several of these places have been restored for tourists. They make particularly good daytrips from St. Petersburg. Do as the Russians do and bring a picnic lunch.

Peterhof (Петергоф), also known as Petrodvorets (Петродворец), is the most thoroughly restored of the palaces. The entire complex is 300 years old, and many of the tsars added to it or expanded existing palaces. The **Bolshoy Dvorets** (Большой Дворец; Grand Palace; tel. 427 95 27) was Peter's first residence here. From the more extensive but less well-kept **Lower Gardens,** the view up the cascade is stunning. One misstep activates the **joke fountains,** which splash unwitting victims. On the other side of the gardens stands **Monplaisir,** the graceful and elegant house in which Peter actually lived. (Parks open daily 9am-9pm. US$4.17, students US$2.08. Palace open Tu-Su 10:30am-6pm; closed last Tu of every month. US$8.33, students US$3.67; mandatory bag check US$17. Most museums open variable days 10:30am-5pm. Each of the other sites about US$6, students US$1.67.) Peterhof is an easy trip by *electrichka* (40min., every 15min., US$0.67) from the Baltisky Station at M1: "Baltiskaya" (Балтийская). The ticket office (Билетные Кассы) in the main courtyard sells round-trip tickets. Get off at Novy Peterhof (Новый Петергоф); walk left down the road for 15 minutes or take any bus (US$0.25) from the station to the stop after the cathedral.

South of the city 25km, **Tsarskoye Selo** (Царское Село; Tsar's Village) surrounds Catherine the Great's summer residence, **Ekaterinsky Dvorets,** a gorgeous azure, white, and gold Baroque palace (open W-M 10am-5pm, closed last M of every month; US$7.18, students US$3.58). The area was renamed "Pushkin" during the Soviet era, and Catherine's far-reaching artistic taste is visible throughout. Take any *electrichka* from Vitebsk Station; M1: "Pushkinskaya" (Пушкинская). Ask for "Detskoe Selo" or "Pushkin" (one-way US$0.50). From the station, it's a 15-minute walk, or 10 minutes on bus 371 or 382 (US$0.25). An easy bus ride from Tsarkoye Selo, **Pavlovsk** (Павловск) is a modest Classical contrast to Peterhof. Pavlovsk's biggest draw is one of the largest landscaped **parks** in the world (open daily 9am-8pm; US$2, students US$1). From St. Petersburg, take an *electrichka* from Vitebsk Station (M1: Pushkinskaya) to Pavlovsk (US$0.67); any train on platform 1, 2, or 3 is fine. Then take bus 370, 383, or 383A (US$0.25) to the palace (5 stops). Buses 370 and 383 also connect Pushkin and the Pavlovsk palace.

THE CAUCASUS (КАВКАЗ)

Foreigners are just beginning to discover the North Caucasus, a vacation mecca that Russians have treasured for centuries and the highest mountain range in Europe. You won't find many English speakers, though, or a tourist infrastructure to help you navigate. All paths lead through **Pyatigorsk** (Пятигорск), accessible by train from Kiev (31hr., 5 per week, US$41.67), Moscow (32hr., 3 per day, US$55), St. Petersburg (46hr., 1 per day, US$48.33), and Sochi (13hr., 1 per day, US$14.17). Buses connect Pyatigorsk to the rest of the Caucasus. To reach the **bus station,** take tram 1 or 4 to "Kraynyevo." If you're stuck in town for the night, crash at **Pyatigorsk State Universitiy Dorm #4,** up ul. Dvesti-Devyanosta-Pyaty Strelovoy Divizii (295 Стреловой Дивизии). From the Lermontovskaya rail stop (terminus of trams 4 and 2), walk up Strelovoy Divizii toward the Lermontov Duel Site. Ask for the *kommandant,* Galina Maksimovna (US$1.67 per person).

Before hiking the Caucasus, find out where the borders lie between Russia, Chechnya, and Georgia. Avoid crossing out of Russia at all costs and alert yourself to the political climate in the region.

Prielbrusye The valley below 5.6km high Mt. Elbrus contains numerous villages, camps, and settlements collectively referred to as Prielbrusye (Приэльбрусье). The highest-lying and most convenient are Terskol and Cheget. If you're planning to tackle Elbrus, the highest mountain in Europe, you should know what you're doing or take a guide who does. The area also affords plentiful hiking opportunities for the less ambitious. Pick up a **trail map** at the newsstand below Gostinitsa Cheget.

Getting to Prielbrusye takes a little work if you're not purchasing a packaged tour. **Buses** run from Pyatigorsk to Baksan (2hr., 9 per day, US$2.83) or Nalchik (2hr., 3 per day, US$2.83). From either, buses and **marshrutniye** (mini-buses) run to Terskol at least once per day. Baksan is closer, but Nalchik has a reasonable hostel, **Gostinitsa Bysym,** in the bus station if you arrive too late (unattractive singles US$11.67; doubles $13.33). The most pleasant and cost-effective housing in the Prielbrusye area is in private apartments (typically US$3.33-6.67). Ask at any store in Terskol, or head through the Turbaza Terskol gates and around to the five-story apartment complex in the woods below. If you need hot water more than twice a week, there are several hotels in the neighborhood. The **Gostinitsa Cheget** (tel. (86639) 713 39) is a short walk down the road from Terskol, with run-down but clean rooms (singles US$15.83; doubles US$11.33 or US$14.83 per person; triples US$10.33 per person).

Dombay Dombay (Домбай) is smaller, prettier, and filled with more butterflies than higher-altitude Cheget, but proves equally difficult to reach. A bus runs daily between Pyatigorsk and Teberda, 16km north of Dombay (5hr., US$6). From the Teberda bus station, three buses run daily to Dombay (40min., US$1). If the bus from Pyatigorsk arrives too late, a cheap hotel (20-30R) is in the Teberda bus station.

From the Dombay bus stop, cross the bridge to the *posyolok* (settlement), where private apartments can be rented from practically any *babushka* on the street (US$4-5 is reasonable; check for hot water and cooking gas), or continue winding to your right, where **Gostinitsa Gorniye Vershini** (tel. 582 30) offers adequate rooms with bath, and hot water at US$10 per place, or US$18 including three meals. The best dining option is **Kafe Airan,** below the hotel. One of the nicest short **hikes** begins as a continuation of the road through the village. After losing itself briefly in boulders, the trail climbs over a small waterfall, through deciduous forests, up to fantastically fragrant alpine meadows (1hr.), and continues from here. A longer, less steep trail starts as a continuation of the road above Gostinitsa Gorniye Vershiny. The first hour of the hike takes you to **Camp Alibek,** then continues through spectacular scenery to **Alibek Gap.** On both hikes, thousands of beautiful butterflies compete for attention with the alpine flora, including lilies, campanulas, and a few small orchids. **Hiking maps** are available at a kiosk below Gostinitsa Gorniye Vershini for 15R. A **gondola** ski-lift will take the weak and cowardly up above the tree-line for US$5 round-trip (open 8am-5pm).

Let Grandma on the Train

They push harder than anyone on the buses and metro. They bundle up to the ears on even the hottest days in scarves and winter coats, then strip down to teeny-weeny bikinis and sunbathe on the banks of the Neva. They are *babushki,* and they mean business. Technically, *babushka* means grandma, but under the Soviet system, when it became all right to be rude, Russians began using it as a generic term for elderly women. In any case, be warned: if a *babushka* gets on the metro, no matter how hardy she looks, and how weak and tired you feel, surrender your seat, or prepare for the verbal pummeling of a lifetime.

Slovakia (Slovensko)

US$1 = 35.70Sk (Slovak koruny)	10Sk = US$0.28
CDN$1 = 22.70Sk	10Sk = CDN$0.44
UK£1 = 59Sk	10Sk = UK£0.17
IR£1 = 50Sk	10Sk = IR£0.20
AUS$1 = 19.90Sk	10Sk = AUS$0.50
NZ$1 = 17.40Sk	10Sk = NZ$0.58
SAR1 = 5.35Sk	10Sk = SAR1.90
DM1 = 19.90Sk	10Sk = DM0.50
Country Phone Code: 421	**International Dialing Prefix: 00**

Survivor of nomadic invasions, Hungarian domination, and Soviet industrialization, Slovakia finally emerged as an independent country after the bloodless 1993 split with the Czech Republic. With rocky mountains to the north and forested hills in the center, Slovakia is covered with natural wonders—it's no surprise that hiking and skiing have become national pastimes. Castle ruins, relics of the defenses against Tatars and Turks, dot the countryside, and in smaller towns, even suburban factories have not compromised the old-time atmosphere. For a lesson in isolated rurality, take a deep swig of Slovak wine, put on some hiking boots, and enjoy the freedom.

For more on Slovakia's wacky adventures, get with *Let's Go: Eastern Europe 1999.*

GETTING THERE AND GETTING AROUND

Citizens of the U.S. and South Africa can visit Slovakia **visa-free** for up to 30 days; citizens of Ireland and Canada, 90 days; and citizens of the U.K., 180 days. Australians and New Zealanders need a 30-day, single-entry or transit visa (US$21), or a double-entry visa (US$32). (For the Slovak embassy in your country, see **Government Information Offices,** p. 5.) Submit your passport, cash or money order, as many visa applications as planned entries, and twice that many photos; processing takes two days.

International bus and rail links connect Slovakia to all of its neighbors. Many train stations operate **BIJ-Wasteels** offices, which offer 30% off tickets to European cities (except Prague) for those under 26. **EastRail** is valid in Slovakia, but **Eurail** is not. A *miestenka* (reservation; 7Sk) is required for international trips (including the Czech Republic). Buy tickets at windows marked with a boxed "R."

ŽSR is the national train company; every information desk has a copy of **Cestovný poriadok** (58Sk), the master schedule. *Odchody* (departures) and *príchody* (arrivals) are posted on yellow and white signs, respectively, but be sure to check revolving timetables. A reservation is needed for *expresný* trains and first-class seats, but not for *rychlík* (fast), *spešný* (semi-fast), or *osobný* (local) trains. In many hilly regions, **ČSAD** or **SAD buses** are the best and sometimes the only way to get around. Except for very long trips, buy tickets on the bus. Schedules have many complicated footnotes: "X" means weekdays only, "a" indicates Saturdays and Sundays only, and "r" and "k" exclude holidays. Numbers refer to days of the week on which the bus travels a given route—1 is Monday, 2 is Tuesday, and so forth. *Premava* means "including," and *nepremava* is equivalent to "except."

ESSENTIALS

The main tourist information offices form a loose conglomeration called **Asociácia Informačných Centier Slovenska (AICS),** complete with distinctive green logo. The offices are invariably on or near the town's main square, and the nearest one can often be found by dialing 186. After 1993, Slovakia hastily designed its own currency which is now the country's only legal tender. One hundred **halér** make up one **koruna (Sk). Všeobecná Úverová Banka (VÚB)** operates offices in even the smallest towns and cashes AmEx Traveler's Checks for a 1% fee. Most offices give MasterCard cash advances, and have Cirrus, Plus, MC, and Visa **ATMs.** Many **Slovenská Sporiteľňa** bureaus handle Visa cash advances and have Visa ATMs.

The Slovak Republic's **mail** service is efficient and modern. Almost every *pošta* (post office) provides **Express Mail Services,** but sending a package abroad requires a trip to a *colnice* (customs office). *Poste Restante* mail with a "1" after the city name will arrive at the main post office. Local **telephone** calls cost 2Sk; insert the coin after being connected. Phone cards (150Sk) are common; though sometimes frustrating, card phones are better than coin phones. For an **AT&T Direct** operator, dial 004 210 01 01; for **MCI WorldPhone,** 004 210 01 12; for **Sprint Access,** 004 218 71 87; for **Canada Direct,** 004 210 01 51; and for **BT Direct,** 004 210 44 01. In an **emergency,** dial 150 for **fire,** 158 for **police,** and 155 for an **ambulance.**

Slovak resembles Czech closely but the languages are not identical. The younger generation typically knows some English, but German is more widely understood.

Yes/no	*Áno/Nie*	AA-no/nyieh
Hello	*Dobrý deň*	DOH-bree dyeny
Please	*Prosím*	PROH-seem
Thank you	*Dakujem*	dyak-uh-yem
Do you speak English?	*Hovoríte po anglicky?*	HO-voh-ree-tyeh poh ahn-glits-kih
I don't understand.	*Nerozumiem*	nyeh-ro-zuh-miehm
Where is…?	*Kde je…?*	gdyeh yeh
How much does this cost?	*Coto stojí?*	KOH-to STOH-yee
I would like…	*Prosím si…*	PROH-seem sih
I'd like a (single room) (double room)	*Potrebujem (jednolužkovú izbu) (izbu pre dve osoby)*	poh-tre-buh-yem (yed-noh-loozh-koh-voo iz-buh) (iz-buh preh dveh oh-soh-bih)
Help!	*Pomoc!*	po-mots

Tap **water** is heavily chlorinated and may occasionally cause abdominal discomfort. Bottled water is available in grocery stores. A reciprocal Health Agreement between Slovakia and the U.K. entitles Brits to free medical care here.

ACCOMMODATIONS, CAMPING, FOOD, AND DRINK Cheap housing may be difficult to come by in Bratislava before student dorms open up in July. Popular summer destinations such as Slovensky Raj and Tatras fill quickly; you must reserve. **Juniorho-**

SLOVAKIA

Bratislava
ACCOMMODATIONS
A Pension Gremium
B YMCA na Slovensko
C Youth Hostel
D Youth Hostel Bernolak

tels (HI), though uncommon, are a step above the usual brand of hostel. In the mountains, **chaty** (mountain huts/chalets) range from plush quarters for 400Sk per night to a friendly bunk and outhouse for 100Sk. **Hotel** prices fall dramatically outside Bratislava and the High Tatras. **Pensions** are generally less expensive then hotels and are often nicer, especially when family run. **Campgrounds** lurk on the outskirts of most towns, and for travelers without tents, many offer bungalows. Sites range from basic to deluxe, and give good value. Camping in national parks is illegal.

Slovakia rose out of its 1000 year Hungarian captivity with a taste for paprika, spicy *gulaš,* and fine wines. The national dish, *bryndzove halušky,* knocks stomachs out with heavy dumplings smothered in a thick sauce of goat cheese. In fact, dumplings *(knedliky)* come with everything—fruit, gravy, and fried pork steak. If dumplings are not for you, most restaurants also serve potatoes *(zemiaky)* and french fries *(hranolky).* Slovakia's second favorite dish is *piroby,* a pasta-pocket usually filled with potato or *bryndza* cheese, with bits of bacon on top. *Pstruh* (trout) is also popular. Fine white wines are produced in the Small Carpathians northeast of Bratislava, especially around the town of Pezinok. *Riesling* and *Müller-Thurgau* grapes are typically used; quality varies greatly. You can enjoy these at a *vináreň* (wine hall). *Pivo* (beer) is served at a *pivnica* or *piváreň* (beer hall). Most **tip** by rounding up.

■ Bratislava

After 80 years of playing second fiddle to starlet Prague, Bratislava, a burgeoning city nestled between Vienna and Budapest on the Danube, has been thrust into a new role as the capital of Slovakia. The Baroque and Renaissance (and pedestrianized) city center is home to infinite cafes, talented street musicians, chic boutiques, and surprisingly stylish Bratislavans and expats. Lightly touristed in comparison with Vienna and Prague, this city of half a million merits a visit.

ORIENTATION AND PRACTICAL INFORMATION

Bratislava, on the banks of the Danube, is a proverbial stone's throw from the borders of Austria and Hungary. Avoid getting off at the **Nové Mesto** train station; **Hlavná stanica,** the main station, is closer to the center. To get downtown from Hlavná stanica, take tram 1 to "Poštová" at **nám. SNP,** the administrative center. Uršulínska leads to the tourist office. From the bus station, take bus 107 to **nám. J. Štúra** by the river. Go up Mostova, cross Hviezdoslavovo nám. onto Rybárska brána, and turn right at Hlavné nám. onto Kostolná. The tourist office is across Primaciálne nám.

Telephone Code: 7.

Trains: Bratislava Hlavná stanica (info tel. 204 44 84), north of town center. Go up Štefánikova, right onto Šancová, and left up the road that goes past the waiting buses. International tickets at counters 9-16. **Wasteels** office at front of station offers discounts to those under 26. Open M-F 8:30am-4pm. To: Berlin (11hr., 2837Sk, Wasteels 2127Sk), Budapest (3hr., 447Sk, Wasteels 335Sk), Kraków (8hr., 1301Sk, Wasteels 781Sk), Prague (5hr., 243Sk), Vienna (1hr., 239Sk), and Warsaw (8hr., 1313Sk, Wasteels 788Sk). **Lockers** 5Sk.

Buses: Mlynské nivy 31 (tel. 542 22 22), east of Old Town. To: Budapest (5hr., 350Sk), Prague (4½hr., 260Sk), and Vienna (1½hr., 340Sk). Check ticket for bus number (*č. aut);* several different buses may depart simultaneously. **Lockers** 5Sk.

Public Transportation: All daytime trips on **trams** and **buses** require a 7Sk ticket available at kiosks and orange automats found at most stops. Night buses have black and orange numbers in the 500s and cost 14Sk. Most trams pass by nám. SNP; most buses stop at the north base of Nový Most (bridge).

Hitchhiking: Those hitching to Vienna or to Hungary (via Győr) cross the SNP bridge and walk down Viedenská cesta. Those headed to Prague take bus 104 from the center to "Patronka." Hitching is legal and common, but not recommended.

Tourist Offices: Bratislavská Informačná Služba (BIS), Klobučnícka 2 (tel. 533 37 15 or 533 43 70; fax 533 27 08; email bis@isnet.sk; http://www.isnet.sk/bis). Sells maps (28Sk), gives city tours, and books rooms. Open M-F 8am-7pm, Sa-Su 8:30am-1:30pm. **Branches** in train station and at airport open daily 8am-6pm.

Embassies: Canada, Kolárska 4 (tel. 36 12 77). Open M and W 3-5pm. **South Africa,** Jančova 8 (tel. 531 15 82). Open M-F 9am-noon. In emergencies, **Irish** citizens and **Commonwealth** nationals should contact the **U.K.** embassy, Panská 16 (tel. 531 96 32; fax 531 00 02). **U.S.,** Hviezdoslavovo nám. 4 (tel. 533 08 61 or 533 33 38; after hours emergency tel. 09 01 70 36 66). Open M-F 8am-4:30pm (visas M-F 8-11:30am).

Currency Exchange: Všeobecná Úverová Banka (VÚB), Gorkého 9 (tel. 515 79 76), cashes traveler's checks (2% commission) and handles MC and Visa cash advances. Open M-W and F 8am-5pm, Th 8am-noon. An outdoor machine at Mostová 6 changes US$, DM, and UK£ into Sk for a 3% commission.

ATM: All over town. The one outside the Dunaj department store in nám. SNP takes Cirrus, Plus, MC, and Visa.

American Express: No office in Bratislava, but **Wings Travel Agency,** Františkánske nám. 3, Bratislava 81101 (tel. 533 55 36), cashes (2% commission) and sells (1% commission) traveler's checks and holds mail. Open M-F 10am-6pm, Sa 9am-noon.

24-Hour Pharmacy: At the corner of Gorkého and Lavrinská (tel 36 37 31).

Post Office: Main office at nám. SNP 35. *Poste Restante* at counter 6. Open M-F 7am-8pm, Sa 7am-6pm, Su 9am-2pm. **Postal Code:** 81000 Bratislava 1.

ACCOMMODATIONS AND CAMPING

In July and August, dorms open up for backpackers on their way to Vienna. Cheap rooms and beds are hard to find before early July, so book early and/or call ahead. **BIS** (see above) has addresses for private rooms (singles from 400Sk; doubles 600Sk).

Pension Gremium, Gorkého 11 (tel. 32 18 18; fax 533 06 53). From nám. SNP, turn left on Michalská. Left on Panská, right on Rybárska Brána, then left on Gorkého. Fluffy beds in the heart of Old Town; popular cafe downstairs. Only one single (890Sk) and 4 doubles (1290Sk), so call ahead. Breakfast included.

Youth Hostel Bernolak, Bernolákova 1 (tel. 39 77 23). From the train station, take bus 22, 23, or 210, or tram 3 to "Vazovova"; from the bus station take bus 37 or trolley 210 to "Račianské Mýto." Friendliest hostel in town with the best English. Spacious singles 480Sk; doubles 580Sk; triples 660Sk; all with showers and toilets. 10% discount for those with a Euro26, ISIC, or HI card. Open July-Aug.

YMCA na Slovenska, Karpatská 2 (tel. 39 80 05), only 500m from the train station. Walk the long lane out of the station and turn left on Šancova. Sterile, spacious rooms with less sterile showers. Bar and movie theater. Doubles, triples, and quints 200Sk per person. Check-out 9am. Usually booked months in advance; call ahead.

Youth Hostel, Wilsonova 6 (tel. 39 77 35). On the street parallel to Bernolákova (see YH Bernolak above). Rooms remarkable only for being cheap. Dorms 180Sk. 30% discount with Euro26, HI, or ISIC. Checkout 9am. Open July-Aug.

Camping: Autocamping Zlaté Piesky, Senecká cesta 2 (tel. 25 73 73), in suburban Trnávka by the lakeside. Take tram 2 or 4, or bus 118, to the last stop and cross the footbridge. 100Sk per person, 90Sk per tent. Bungalows 650-900Sk.

FOOD

Besides burgers, Bratislava's restaurants serve the region's spicy meat mixtures with West Slovakia's celebrated **Modra** wine. Find **markets** at Žilinská 5, near the train station, and outside Tesco's (open M-Sa 6am-4pm), and a **late-night deli** at Špitalská 45. For groceries, head to **Tesco's Potraviny,** Kamenné nám. 1 (open M-W 8am-7pm, Th 8am-8pm, F 8am-9pm, Sa 8am-5pm, Su 9am-5pm).

Prašná Bašta, Zámočnícka 11, off Michalská. Sheep cheese *halušky* (55Sk), fine onion soup (22Sk), and generous glasses of wine (10-16Sk). Dark alcoves full of funky sculptures inside, a leafy terrace outside. Open daily 11am-11pm.

Cafe London, Panská 17, in the British Council's courtyard. Serves up Anglophile nostalgia to expats and burger-and-sheep's-cheese-saturated travelers. Tuna salad, grilled cheese, and roast beef sandwiches 49-98Sk. Open M-F 9am-9pm.

Vegetarían Jedáleň, Laurinská 8. From nám. SNP, walk away from the castle and turn right. Young Slovak herbivores graze at this purely vegetarian lunch spot. Menu changes daily (50-100Sk). Open M-F 11am-3pm.

Corleone's, Hviezdoslavovo nám., on the north side. Italian *trattoria* that serves up delicious (if a little expensive) pizzas (79-189Sk). Open daily until midnight.

Bratislavaburg

The only thing more incomprehensible than a Slovak menu is a Bratislava menu at one of the city's ubiquitous burger stands. A cheeseburger costs less than a *hamburger so syrom* (hamburger with cheese) because, as the stand owner will explain with humiliating logic, a cheeseburger is made of cheese. A *pressburger* consists of bologna on a bun, and hamburgers are actually ham. Everything comes boiled (except the cheese) on a roll with cabbage, onions, and sauce.

SIGHTS AND ENTERTAINMENT

From **nám. SNP,** which commemorates the bloody Slovak National Uprising against the fascist Slovak state, walk left down Uršulínska to **Primaciálné nám.** The Neoclassical **Primaciálny Palác** (Primate's Palace) dates from 1781; Napoleon and Austrian Emperor Franz I signed the Peace of Pressburg here in 1805 (open Tu-Su 10am-5pm; 25Sk). The **Múzeum Histórie Mesta** (Town History Museum) is in the **Stará Radnica** (Old Town Hall), accessible from Primaciálné nám. Inside, past a wonderful 1:500 model of Bratislava, galleries display exhibits on the city's history (open Tu-Su 10am-5pm; 25Sk, students 10Sk). Stará Radnica fronts onto **Hlavné nám.**, the domain of tourists during the day and loud teenagers at night.

From Hlavné nám., walk left down Rybárska Brána until **Hviezdoslavovo nám.**, dominated at its eastern end by the 1886 **Slovenské Národné Divadlo** (Slovak National Theater). A left along the Dunaj leads to the **Slovenské Národné Múzeum**

(Slovak National Museum), Vajanského nábr. 2, which houses local archaeological finds, including casts of Neanderthal skeletons (open Tu-Su 9am-5pm; 20Sk). Also on the river, the **Slovak National Gallery,** Rázusovo nábr. 2, displays Slovak Gothic and Baroque art (open Tu-Su 10am-6pm; 25Sk, students 5Sk). The SNP suspension bridge spans the Dunaj, its reins held by a giant flying saucer (10Sk). From Rázusovo nábr., go right on the next-to-last street before the bridge to reach the fairly unspectacular **Dóm sv. Martina** (St. Martin's Cathedral), where the kings of Hungary were crowned for three centuries. Across the highway from the cathedral (use the pedestrian overpass), the road zooms over what used to be **Schlossberg,** the old Jewish quarter. The **Múzeum Židovskej Kultúry** (Museum of Jewish Culture), Židovská 17, preserves valuable fragments of a vanished population (open Su-F 11am-5pm; 35Sk). From the cathedral, go down Kapitulská, right onto Prepoštská, and left onto Michalská, a busy pedestrian street guarded by the **Michalská Brána** at the north end. Trot up to the top (open W-M 10am-5pm, last entrance 4:30; 25Sk).

From the banks of the Danube to the center's historic squares, the four-towered **Bratislavský hrad** (castle) is a visible landmark. Of strategic importance for more than a millennium, the castle's heyday was in the 18th century, when Maria Theresa held court here. The castle was burned down in 1811 and bombed during World War II, so what the visitor sees today is largely Communist-era restoration. There's also a **Historické Múzeum** (open Tu-Sa 9am-5pm; 30Sk).

For concert and theater schedules, pick up a copy of *Kám v Bratislave* at BIS. It's not in English, but the info is easy to decipher. Unfortunately, the Filharmonia and many theaters take their vacations in July and August. **Slovenská Filharmonia** plays regularly at Palackého ul. 2, which fronts onto Mostová; the box office is around the corner on Medená (tickets approx. 800-1000Sk; tel. 533 33 51; open M-F 1-5pm). **Národné Divadlo** (National Theater) tickets are sold at the box office at Laurinská 20 (around 50Sk; open M-F noon-6pm). If it takes more than theater to keep you entertained, call **West Bungee Jump Bratislava,** PKO Bratislava-Danube Bank (tel. 70 59 31) for a jump reservation (720Sk; ISIC and EURO26, 20% discount).

Bratislava's sleekest twenty-somethings gather at the **Alligator Club,** Laurinská 7, to hear live rock and blues bands (nightly at 7pm; *Gambrinus* 27Sk; open M-F 10am-midnight, Sa noon-midnight, Su noon-10pm). **Dubliner,** Sedlarská 6, Bratislava's *ersatz* Irish pub, has sewing machines for tables, a leaky roof, and a tremendously lively atmosphere as it fills up after dinner (open M-Sa 10am-1am, Su 11am-midnight). Connect at **Klub Internet,** Vajanského nábr. 2 (open M-F 9am-9pm, Sa-Su noon-9pm).

TATRY (THE TATRAS)

Slovaks take great pride in Vysoké Tatry, a mountainous mecca for hikers, skiers, and nature-lovers. The jagged **High Tatras** are one of the most compact mountain ranges in the world, and feature sky-scraping peaks, beautiful glacial lakes, and many excellent hiking trails. Electric trains and buses connect all the towns in the area.

Starý Smokovec

Starý Smokovec is the Vysoké Tatry's (High Tatras) most central resort town and one of the oldest. The neighboring hamlet Horný Smokovec offers cheap sleeps, making Starý Smokovec easily accessible to the budget traveler. The town itself is nothing much—the real draw is the network of **hiking** trails that lead to the quiet, rugged slopes of the Tatras. The funicular to **Hrebienok** (1285m) takes you to the hiking country's heart, and an easy 20-minute walk from there leads to the foaming **Cold Waterfall** *(Studeného Potoka)*. The eastward blue trail descends from the waterfall through the towering pines to **Tatranská Lomnica** (1½hr.). The long, red *"Tatranská magistrála"* trail travels west from Hrebienok through the chalet **Sliezsky dom** (1670m), to **Chata kapitána Moravku** (another chalet) ashore **Popradské pleso.** From here, descend to **Štrbské Pleso** (8hr. from Hrebienok). The truly ambitious can climb the stony, 2450m **Slavkovský štít** (about 8hr.).

The resort is easily reached from Poprad by TEŽ **trains** (30min., every 30min.-1hr., 10Sk). **Buses** to many mountain resorts stop in a parking lot east of the train station. **VKÚ sheet 113** (68-75Sk; essential for hiking) and weather info are cheerfully offered at the **Tatranská Informačná Kancelária** (tel. (0969) 423 34 40), in Dom Služieb, near the west end of the town's artery (open M-F 8am-5pm, Sa-Su 9am-1pm).

Horný Smokovec, 1km east along Starý's main street, offers affordable rooms and is home to **Slovakotourist** (tel. (0969) 42 30 31), whose English-speaking staff books mountain *chaty* (350-450Sk) and private rooms (250-300Sk). Further along the road (2 TEŽ stops toward Tatranská Lomnica), **Hotel Junior Vysoké Tatry** (tel. (0969) 42 26 61) has clean, basic rooms and a disco. (Singles 330Sk; doubles 610Sk; triples 760Sk; with ISIC or HI 200Sk per person. Breakfast included.) Other decent rooms are available at **Hotel Šport** (tel. (0969) 42 23 61), across the road from the tourist office (singles 490Sk; doubles 790Sk). **Grocery stores** clutter Starý Smokovec, with five on the main road near the bus and train stations.

Slovenský Raj

South of Starý Smokovec and on the other side of the Nízke Tatry lies the Slovenský Raj (Slovak Paradise) National Park. Fast-flowing streams have carved deep ravines into the limestone hills, and the whole region is smothered in pine forests. Nestled in a gorge on the shores of the man-made lake Palcmanská Maša, **Dedinky** is the largest of the towns on the Slovenský Raj's southern border. The easiest way to get there is to catch the **bus** from Poprad (1hr., 6 per day, 27Sk) heading for Rožňava, which stops at a junction 2km south of Dedinky. From there, follow the sign for Hotel Raj and the trail marked in green. Pick up a copy of **VKÚ sheet 124,** one of the excellent green hiking maps—make sure it's the 1998 third edition *(vydanie)*—at a tourist office or bookshop before entering the region (69-80Sk in Slovak, 100Sk in German). **Hotel Priehrada** (tel. 982 12; fax 982 21) has dated rooms with a view of the lake (200-225Sk per person; shared bath and toilets; lower prices Sept. to mid-Dec. and Apr.-June). One of the nicest hikes is the **Biele Vody** (White Waters; 1½hr.), which heads up one of the park's many rapids. From Hotel Priehrada in Dedinky, take the red trail to Biele Vody. The blue cascade trail will be on the left. It's one-way only and involves ladders, so there's no turning back once you start.

Liptovský Mikuláš

Liptovský Mikuláš (LIP-tov-skee mee-koo-LASH) is a drab town that provides easy access to the nearby Nízke Tatry (Low Tatras), which are much less crowded than their taller Carpathian cousins farther north. **Trains** run frequently to Poprad (40min.-1hr., 28-44Sk) and Bratislava (4hr., 12 per day, 158Sk). From the station, follow Štefánikova toward the gas station at the bus station's far end, then turn right onto Hodžu. The **tourist office** (tel. (0849) 224 18) in the main square has good hiking maps and helps arrange lodgings (open M-F 8am-7pm, Sa 8am-2pm, Su noon-7pm, shorter hours off-season). To hike **Mt. Ďumbier** (2043m), the region's highest peak, catch an early bus from platform 11 at Liptovský Mikuláš's bus station (next to the train station) to **Liptovský Ján Kúpele** (20min., 1 per hr., 10Sk) and hike the blue-marked trail up the Štiavnica river and onto the **Ďumbierske sedlo** (saddle) by **Chata generála M.R. Štefanika** (Gen. M.R. Štefanika hut; about 4hr.). Then follow the red path up to the summit (2hr.). Doubling back, but following the red signpost to **Chopok** (2024m), leads along the ridge to the neighboring peak (1½hr.), the second highest in the range. At the hut there, **Kammená chata,** you might be able to snag a bed (110Sk) as well as a *Martiner* draft beer (25Sk) and a mug of tea (10Sk). If staying in Liptovský Mikuláš, dead-central **Hotel Kriváň,** Štúrova 5 (tel. (0849) 52 24 14; fax 242 43), is a good bet (singles 350Sk; doubles 570Sk).

ŠARIŠ

Šariš once served as a borderland against Turkish and Saracen invasions, but now rests quietly tucked in the hills of East Slovakia. English is spoken widely here, but tourism has yet to make a significant appearance in these sleepy, religious towns.

■ Košice

Košice's Gothic and Renaissance center has managed to survive fires, revolutions, an Ottoman invasion, and the city's intense industrial development. **Hlavná** marks the heart of the Old Town. At its widest point is the towering **Dom sv. Alžbety** (Cathedral of St. Elizabeth), a conglomeration of nearly every style known to Western architecture and the final resting place of Rakóczi Ferenc II, Hungary's anti-Habsburg national hero. Built from stones discarded by the cathedral, the 19th-century **Jakabov Palác,** Mlynská 30, off Hlavná, was home to Czechoslovakia's president in the spring of 1945. Hlavná ends at Hviezdoslavova between the buildings of the **Východnoslovenské Múzeum** (East Slovak Museum). The museum has exhibits on the early inhabitants of the area, examples of the region's folk and religious art, and thousands of gold coins (open Tu-Sa 9am-5pm, Su 9am-1pm).

Košice's main **train station** is on Predstaničné nám. Trains run west to Bratislava (5hr., 212Sk) and Prague (9hr., 492Sk) and east to Kiev (12hr., 863Sk) and Lviv (6-8hr., 484Sk). North-south trains run to Budapest (4hr., 713Sk) and Kraków (6hr., 581Sk). The **tourist office,** Hlavná 8 (tel. (95) 186; fax 622 69 38), is near the station. (Open June-Sept. M-F 8am-6pm, Sa 9am-1pm; Oct.-May M-F 9am-5pm, Sa 9am-1pm.) **Tourist Hotel Metropol,** ul. Šturovà 32 (tel. (95) 625 59 48), is a godsend. Two stops by bus 11, 16, or 30 from the train/bus station (western direction) or a 15-minute walk along ul. Šturovà, you'll see a sign for Metropol on your left. Walk through the gate into a flower-filled large yard with a fountain, turn left, and go upstairs to the reception area (280Sk per person; shared bathrooms; reception 24hr.). A great restaurant, **K2,** is on the premises. **Hotel Európa,** Protifašistických Bojovníkov 1 (tel. (95) 622 38 97), across the park in front of the train station, is a 19th-century hotel with communal toilets and showers (singles 410-490Sk; doubles 650Sk). **Ajvega,** Orlia 10, off Mlynská, offers veggie pasta, pizza, and salads (open daily 11am-10pm).

■ Prešov

Magyars, Gypsies, and Rusins maintain their diverse traditions in Prešov, while clean-cut couples, black-clad widows, and Catholics flaunting their Sunday best complete the cultural mix. As **Hlavná** splits into two main branches, **Kostol sv. Mikuláša** (St. Nicholas's Cathedral) captures tourists' attention. The Gothic cathedral's distinctive turrets attest to the Saxon influence in Prešov during the late Middle Ages (open irregular hours). Beside the church at Hlavná 86, the 16th-century **Rákóczi Palace** now houses the eclectic **Vlastivedné múzeum** (City Museum), with exhibits on lace work and old fire trucks (open Tu-F 9am-noon and 12:30-5pm, Sa 9am-1pm, Su 1-5pm; 20Sk, students 10Sk). On the west side of Hlavná, the restored **Šarišská galéria** (Šariš Gallery) features exhibits of Slovak art. (Open Tu, W, and F 9am-5pm, Th 9am-6pm, Sa 9am-1pm, Su 1:30-5:30pm. 6Sk, students 2Sk, Su free.) Heading west from Hlavná, the narrow medieval street **Floriánova** leads to **Brána sv. Floriána** (St. Florian's Gate), a remnant of the town's early Renaissance fortification. In the northwest of the Old Town at Švermova 56 is an ornate **synagogue;** a monument outside commemorates the Jewish victims of fascist regimes.

Trains (tel. (91) 73 10 43) leave regularly for Bratislava via Kysak (4½hr., 212Sk) and Košice (50min., 18Sk); **buses** (tel. (91) 72 45 91) run to Košice (30-45min., 22Sk), Poprad (1½hr., 58Sk), and many smaller towns. The **tourist office,** Hlavná 67 (tel. (91) 14 69 09), provides town and hotel information (open M-F 7:30-11:30am and 12:30-4:30pm, Sa 9am-noon). Inexpensive rooms hide in Prešov's suburbs, and vacancies are common. **Turistická Ubytovaňa Sen,** Vajanského 65 (tel. (91) 73 31 70), offers a few rooms for 150Sk per person; call in advance and get directions. From the station, walk towards the town center, take the first left on Škultétyho, and a left again at Budovatelská to reach **Penzion Lineas,** Budovatelská 14 (tel. (91) 72 33 25, ext. 28), whose clean doubles include toilets and baths (450Sk). **Florianka,** Baštová 32, sits next to Slovakia's best hotel and restaurant management school, which explains the excellent food and service (meals 45-125Sk; open M-F 11am-9:30pm).

SLOVAKIA

Slovenia (Slovenija)

US$1	= 167Slt		100Slt =	US$0.59
CDN$1	= 108Slt		100Slt =	CDN$0.93
UK£1	= 280Slt		100Slt =	UK£0.36
IR£1	= 240Slt		100Slt =	IR£0.42
AUS$1	= 97Slt		100Slt =	AUS$1.03
NZ$1	= 84Slt		100Slt =	NZ$1.18
SAR1	= 27Slt		100Slt =	SAR3.76
DM1	= 96Slt		100Slt =	DM1.05
Country Phone Code: 386			**International Dialing Prefix: 00**	

Slovenia, the most prosperous of Yugoslavia's breakaway republics, has reveled in its independence, modernizing rapidly as it turns a hungry eye toward the West. For a country half Switzerland's size, Slovenia, on the "sunny side of the Alps," is extraordinarily diverse: in a day, you can breakfast on an Alpine peak, lunch under the Mediterranean sun, and dine in a vineyard on the Pannonian plains. Painters, bring extra amounts of green and white: Slovenia's pine-covered hills and mountains, which irresistibly attract hikers in the summer and skiers in the winter, won't disappoint you.

For more detailed coverage of Slovenia, check out *Let's Go: Eastern Europe 1999.*

GETTING THERE AND GETTING AROUND

Australian, Canadian, Irish, New Zealand, U.K., and U.S. citizens can visit visa-free for up to 90 days. South Africans need **visas** (US$35 for 3-month single-entry and transit; US$70 for 3-month multiple-entry). Apply by mail or in person to the embassy in your home country (see p. 5) with your passport and the fee in the form of a money order. Slovenia is easily accessible by car, train, or plane. Ljubljana has frequent and reliable international **train** connections, and discounts are sometimes available for travelers under 26; check at the Ljubljana station (look for the **BIJ-Wasteels** logo). Say *"vlak"* for train, *"prihodi vlakov"* for arrivals, and *"odhodi vlakov"* for departures. **Buses** are about 25% more expensive and usually slower, but run to some otherwise inaccessible places. Tickets are sold at the station or on board; put your luggage in the passenger compartment if possible. There are several international **airports:** commercial flights arrive at the **Ljubljana Airport** in Brnik, with regular bus service to the city center 25km away. The reformed national carrier—**Adria Airways**—flies to European capitals and Tel Aviv. Some **hitchers** report success in the countryside and near cities, but they advise avoiding December to January and July to August.

ESSENTIALS

Tourist offices are located in most major cities and tourist spots. The staff are generally helpful, speak English, provide basic information, and assist in finding accommodations. The national **currency** is the Slovenian tolar (Slt). Hard currency prices tend to be stable, but are usually set in Deutschmarks (DM) rather than US$. **Exchange offices** abound. **Banks** are usually open Monday to Friday 8am to 5pm and Saturday 8 to 11am. Rates vary, but tend to be better in cities. Some establishments charge no commission (a fact reflected in the rates). Major **credit cards** are widely accepted, particularly MC/Eurocard and Visa. **ATMs** exist only in Ljubljana.

Postal services are reliable. At the post office, buy a **phone card** (750Slt per 50 impulses, which yields 50 local calls or 1½min. to the U.S.). For **MCI WorldPhone,** call 080 88 08. Services from other carriers may become available in 1999. Operators will assist in connecting calls if you dial 90 in Ljubljana, Kranj, Maribor, and Nova Gorica, 900 elsewhere. Calling the U.S. is expensive (over US$6 per min.).

Most young people speak at least some English, but older folk are more likely to understand German or Italian. Slovene resembles other Slavic languages; "*č*," "*š*," and "*ž*" are pronounced as in Czech. The following phrases should get you started.

Yes/No	*Ja/Ne*	yah/neh
Hello	*Idravo*	ee-drah-voh
Thank you	*Hvala*	HVAA-lah
I am sorry	*oprostite*	oh-proh-stee-teh
Do you speak English?	*Govorite angleško?*	go-vo-REE-te ang-LEH-shko
I don't understand	*Ne razumem*	neh rah-ZOO-mehm
Where is...?	*Kje je...?*	kyeh ye
How much does this cost?	*Koliko to stane?*	koh-lee-koh toh stah-neh
I (feminine) would like a (single) (double) room.	*Rad (Rada) bi (enopostel-jno) (dvoposteljo) sobo*	rat (RAA-da) bi (e-no-POHS-tel-yno) (dvo-POHS-tel-yno) so-bo
Help!	*Na pomoč!*	nah poh-MOHCH

ACCOMMODATIONS, CAMPING, FOOD, AND DRINK At the height of tourist season, prices are steep and rooms scarce. Tourists tend to swarm in the mountains around July and August, but student rooms are generally available late June to early September. **Hotels** fall into five categories (L (deluxe), A, B, C, and D) and tend to be expensive. **Youth hostels** and **student dormitories** are cheap, but generally open only during summer. Usually, the best option is to rent **private rooms;** prices depend on location, but rarely exceed US$30. They're advertised on the street with *"sobe"* or *"Zimmer"* signs, or you can inquire at the tourist office. **Campgrounds** can also be crowded, but they are generally in excellent condition.

The best bet for mouth-watering, homestyle cooking is a *gostilna* or *gostišče* (interchangeable words for a restaurant with a country flavor, although a *gostišče* usually also rents rooms). A good national dish to start with is *jota,* a potato, bean, and sauerkraut soup. *Svinjska pečenka* (roast pork) is tasty, but **vegetarians** should look for *štruklji*—large, slightly sweet dumplings eaten as a main dish. The country's **wine** tradition, dating from antiquity, was fostered during the Middle Ages by monks and feudal lords. Look for familiar grape varieties on the label. *Renski Rizling* and *Šipon*

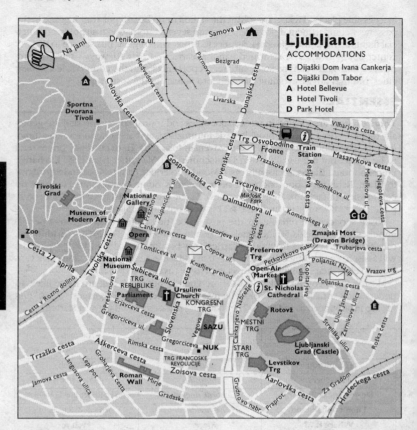

Ljubljana
ACCOMMODATIONS

E Dijaški Dom Ivana Cankerja
C Dijaški Dom Tabor
A Hotel Bellevue
B Hotel Tivoli
D Park Hotel

are popular whites. Slovenia produces many unique red wines, including the light
Cviček from the central region and the potent *Teran,* bottled on the coast. The art of
brewing is also centuries old in Slovenia; good beers include *Laško* and *Union.* For
something stronger, try *ganje,* a fruit brandy. Tap **water** is drinkable everywhere.

■ Ljubljana

If you are arriving in Ljubljana after some time in Central European Slavic countries,
the cost will stop you abruptly in your carefree currency tracks, and it will seem
strange to hear a Slavic language spoken in a country that seems so thoroughly Western European. Because it did not have its own school of architecture until the 20th
century, Ljubljana's style was heavily influenced by Vienna, where most of its talented students went to study. Still, drenched in Baroque elegance and swept with
weeping willows, its feel is exuberantly unique.

ORIENTATION AND PRACTICAL INFORMATION

The **train** and **bus stations** are on **Trg Osvobodilne Fronte (Trg O.F.),** north of
Stari Grad (Old Town). To reach the central square, exit the train station and
walk along **Resljeva cesta;** then bear right on **Trubarjeva cesta,** which leads to
Prešernov Trg. After crossing the **Tromostovje** (Triple Bridge), Stari Grad
emerges at the castle hill's base; the tourist office is on the left at the corner of
Stritarjeva ul. and Mačkova ul.

Telephone Code: 061.

Flights: The airport is in Brnik, 26km away. A shuttle runs to the airport from the major hotels (tel. (064) 64 08 39; 1500-2500Slt). Also public bus 7 and 17 (320Slt).

Trains: tel. 131 51 67. Several trains run each day to Budapest (10hr., 5370Slt), Munich (6hr., 8468Slt), Venice (6hr., 3000Slt), and Vienna (6hr., 6300Slt).

Buses: The **station** (tel. 133 61 36) neighbors the train station. To Budapest (8hr., 3 per week, 4590Slt) and Munich (6hr., 1-3 most days, 5215Slt).

Public Transportation: Buses run until midnight and cost 120Slt or one 75Slt token, available at post offices and newsstands. Passes are sold at **Ljubljanski Potniški Promet,** in the red kiosk situated in front of Slovenska cesta 55.

Tourist Office: Tourist Information Center (TIC), Stritarjeva 1 (tel. 133 01 11; fax 133 02 44). Free maps. Open M-F 8am-7pm, Sa 9am-5pm.

Embassies and Consulates: Australia, Trg Republike 3 (tel. 125 42 52; fax 126 47 21). **U.K.,** Trg Republike 3 (tel. 125 71 91; fax 125 01 74). Both open M-F 9am-noon. **U.S.,** Pražakova 4 (tel. 30 14 27; fax 30 14 01). Open M, W, and F 9am-noon.

Currency Exchange: Currency exchanges *(menjalnića)* abound. **Ljubljanska Bank,** Beethovnova 7, at the corner of Cankarjeva, cashes traveler's checks for no commission. Open M-F 9am-noon and 2-5pm, Sa 9am-noon and 3-6pm. **ATMs** are hard to find, but there is one in the Maximarket archway next to the travel office (Cirrus/EC/MC; open 24hr.).

Laundromat: Alba, Wolfova 12 (tel. 21 44 04). Open M-F 8am-6pm.

Emergencies: Fire, tel. 112. **Ambulance,** tel. 94.

Police: tel. 113.

Post Office: next to the train station. Open 24hr. *Poste Restante* at Pražakova 3 (tel. 31 45 84), 3 blocks south of the train station in a yellow building; enter in back. Open M-F 7am-8pm, Sa 7am-1pm. **Postal Code:** 1106.

ACCOMMODATIONS, CAMPING, AND FOOD

Don't expect Eastern European prices here. Room prices are often quoted in DM. Keep in mind that a nightly tourist tax is added to the bill (approx. 185Slt). **TIC** (see above) finds private singles (2000Slt) and doubles (4000-5400Slt).

Dijaški Dom Tabor, Vidovdanska 7 (tel. 31 60 69 or 32 10 67; fax 32 10 60). From the stations, head straight out along Resljeva, then left on Komenskega. Overall cleanliness, shared toilets and showers. 2600Slt per person, with ISIC 2200Slt. Generous breakfast included. Unenforced 10pm curfew. Open June 20-Aug. 28.

Dijaški Dom Ivana Cankarja, Poljanska 260-28 (tel. 133 51 77). Call for directions. 2000Slt per person. Breakfast 417Slt. Open July only.

Hotel Tivoli, Tivolska 30 (tel. 133 61 31 or 133 40 54; fax 30 26 71). Close to the train and bus stations. 31 well-kept rooms, with bath, TV, and phone. Singles 6600Slt; doubles 8300Slt.

Hotel Bellevue, Podgozdom 2 (tel. 133 40 49; fax 133 40 57), in Tivoli Park. Singles 3050Slt; doubles 6000Slt; triples 7900Slt. Breakfast included. Reception 24hr.

Park Hotel, Tabor 9 (tel. 133 13 06; fax 32 13 52), near Dom Tabor. Socialist and a bit shabby inside and out. Singles 5682-7000Slt; doubles 7164-8864Slt. Insist on the 20% student discount. Breakfast included.

Autocamp Ježica, Dunajska 270 (tel. 168 39 13; fax 168 39 12). Take bus 6 northbound from Slovenska ul. Swimming pool and tennis. 920Slt per person plus 170Slt per night. Bungalows 3300-4500Slt per person. Open year-round.

Bargain restaurants and colorful cafes line Mestni Trg and Stari Trg. **Šestica,** Slovenska 40, has a farmhouse kitchen, sun room, and garden terrace, and serves excellent Slovene food and wines at slightly upscale prices (menu from 900Slt, spaghetti Milano 550Slt; open daily 10am-midnight). **Gostilna Pri Pavli,** Stari trg 21, has *Ljubljanski zrzek* (steak Ljubljana style; 1000Slt), omelettes with ham and vegetables (600Slt), and spaghetti with mushrooms (550Slt) in a boxy, Eastern European setting (open M-F 7am-10pm, Sa 7am-3pm). Vodnikov Trg, near the cathedral, hosts a huge **outdoor market** (open M-Sa until 2pm).

SIGHTS AND ENTERTAINMENT

The best way to learn about the city may be to meet in front of the **rotovž** (city hall), Mestni trg 1, for the two-hour **walking tour** in English and Slovene (June-Sept. daily 5pm; Oct.-May Su 11am; 700Slt; students and seniors 500Slt). A **self-guided tour** is detailed in *Where?*, a monthly events brochure available free from tourist offices. In front of the *rotovž* spurts a fantastic fountain, embellished with allegorical sculptures of three rivers—the Ljubljanica, Sava, and Krka. A short walk form the *rotovž* across the **Tromostovje** (Triple Bridge) brings you to the main square, **Prešernov trg.** Christened in honor of the great Slovene poet France Prešeren, the square contains a Neoclassical **Frančiškanska cerkev** (Franciscan Church) built in the 17th century. From virtually anywhere in the Old Town, **Ljubljanski Grad** (Ljubljana Castle) is a short hike up the hill. The 12th-century castle is not as spectacular as the views of the city.

Trg Francoske Revolucije (French Revolution Square) and its immediate surroundings were once occupied by Teutonic Knights; the neighborhood is still called **Križanke,** the Slovene translation of their title. In the square, the Knights built a monastery which now hosts musical, theatrical, and dance performances during the **Ljubljana International Summer Festival** (mid-July to late Sept.). Ljubljana's museums cluster around the Slovene parliament buildings near Trg Republike. The **Narodni Muzej** (National Museum), Muzejska 1, has exhibits on archaeology, ethnography, and history (open Tu-W and F-Su 10am-6pm, Th until 8pm; 300Slt, students 200Slt), while the **Narodna Galerija** (National Gallery), Cankarjeva 20, displays Slovene art from the Middle Ages to the present (open Tu-Su 10am-6pm; 500Slt, students 300Slt, Sa afternoons free). Near the museums, **Tivoli park** offers some of the prettiest strolling grounds in the city.

The tourist office's *Where?* brochure is also the best source of info on music and dance. Cafes and bars line the streets of Old Town. **Nostalgija,** 9 Stari trg, is fantastically 1950s, from the rounded, triangular pale yellow and blue tables to the curtains over the bar (open M-Sa 9am-1am, Su 10am-1am). The ever-popular **K-4,** Kersnikova 4, remodeled every year, features a different music program every night; Sunday is gay night. **Eldorado,** Nazorjeva 6, is a Mexican restaurant by day and flashy club by night (cover F-Sa 1000Slt; open daily 11pm-4am). **Jazz Club Gajo,** Beethovnova 8, hosts free jazz concerts 2 to 4 days each week (open M-F 10am-2am).

■ Near Ljublijana: Postojna Caves

A single cavern of the two-million-year-old Postojnska Jama, which showcases an astonishing array of plant-like stalagmite columns, alabaster curtains of stone, gorges, rivers, and multi-colored stalactites, would justify a trip to Postojna. Follow the signs out of the center of town or ask anyone; the *jama* (cave), Jamska cesta 30 (tel. (061) 250 41), is 15 minutes northwest of the town. The obligatory tour (1½hr.) passes through only 20% of the 27km cave, but that's plenty (departs May-Sept. on the hr.; Oct.-Apr. on even hours; 1900Slt, students 950Slt). Bring a jacket to the chilly caves, or rent a cloak for 100Slt. You can reach the town of Postojna by **bus** (1hr., 720Slt) or **train** (1hr., 775Slt) from Ljubljana.

JULIJSKE ALPE (JULIAN ALPS)

The Southern Alps are not as high as their Austrian or Swiss counterparts, but they are no less beautiful. The mountains cover the northwest of Slovenia, peaking at 2864m on Mt. Triglav in the heart of the Triglav National Park. This mountain range is also the source of the Sava, one of the region's largest rivers.

Bled Green alpine hills, snow-covered peaks in the distance, an opaque lake, and a stately castle make Bled one of the most striking destinations in all Slovenia. Having drawn visitors for centuries, the present-day town is a resort of international renown. A stroll around the lake's 6km perimeter takes about two hours. On the island in the middle, a **church,** largely rebuilt in the 17th century, retains a unique pre-Romanesque apse. To get there, you can rent a boat for 1000Slt per hour, travel by **gondola** (round-trip 900Slt), or even swim. High above the water perches a picture-perfect 16th-century **castle.** The price of admission includes entry into an excellent **museum,** with art, furniture, and weaponry (open daily Mar.-Oct. 8am-7pm; Nov.-Feb. 9am-4pm; 400Slt). Numerous **paths** lead from the lake into the neighboring hills. The best one can be found by walking around the lake until the castle and the island are aligned—the path across the street takes about 45 minutes to climb.

Trains stop in Lesce, 5km from Bled on the Ljubljana-Salzburg-Munich line. From there, commuter buses (160Slt) run to Bled. You can travel directly to Bled by **bus** from Ljubljana (1½hr., 1 per hr., 790Slt). To rent **mountain bikes** (1500Slt per day), visit **Kompas Bled,** Ljubljanska cesta 4 (tel. (064) 74 15 15). For tourist info, head to **Turističko društvo,** Cesta svobode 15 (tel. 74 11 22), where you can pick up a copy of the illustrated *Bled Tourist News* (open M-Sa 8am-8pm, Su and holidays 10am-6pm). Kompas Bled seeks out **private** singles (2000Slt) and doubles (3400Stl; tourist tax DM1.85 per night). Stays of less than three nights cost 30% more. Finding a room yourself may save money; look for *"sobe"* signs on Prešernova cesta. The newly renovated **youth hostel,** Grajska cesta 17 (tel. (064) 782 30), is a jewel up the hill of Grajska cesta from the bus station; bear left at the Grad 1004 cafe and go 100m more (around 2400Slt, with ISIC 2000Slt). **Camping Zaka-Bled,** Cesta Svobode 13 (tel. (064) 74 11 17), asks 1400Slt per person (open Apr.-Oct.). Locals justly recommend **Gostilna pri Planincu,** Grajska cesta 8, visible from the bus station. This 1903 restaurant serves main dishes (900-1200Slt) until 10pm, pizzas (600-850Slt) until 10:30pm, and drinks until 11pm. If all else fails, try **Minimarket Śpecerija,** Ljubljanska 4 (open M-Sa 7am-7pm, Su 9am-noon).

Lake Bohinj (Bohinjsko Jezero)

Surrounded by the Triglav National Park and windy peaks, Bohinjsko Jezero is Slovenia's center for alpine tourism. There's plentiful **hiking** around the area—trips from the shores of the lake range from the casual to the nearly impossible. **Triglav,** the highest point in Slovenia, is a challenging two-day journey from town. The 2865m ascent may not seem extraordinary, but on a clear day the sea is visible from the summit. The most popular and accessible destination is **Slap Savica** (Savica Waterfall). The hike is only 20 minutes from the trailhead; just follow the signs and the people. Trails throughout Slovenia are well-marked with a white circle inside a red circle; look for the blaze on trees and rocks. Pick up maps of *Triglavski Narodni Park* and *Gorenjska* (around 1400Slt) from the tourist office. **Alpin Sport,** Ribčev Laz 53 (tel./fax (064) 72 34 86 or 65 00 36), near the bridge, has gear for hiking and water sports.

Five **trains** per day arrive in **Bohinjska Bistrica,** 6km from the water, from Ljubljana, most via Jesenice where you may have to change trains (2hr. direct). From there, take the bus to the lake. You can also reach the lake directly by **bus** from Bled (45min., 410Slt) or Ljubljana (2½hr., 1200Slt). Buses to "Bohinjsko Jezero" generally finish their routes in **Ribčev Laz;** the stop after the sign is most central. Buses marked "Bohinj Zlatorog" take you through Ribčev Laz to the village on the lake's west end, and a few buses climb all the way to the trailhead for the Savica waterfall. You should find everything you need on **Ribčev Laz** by the water's edge. The **tourist office,** Ribčev Laz 48 (tel. (064) 74 60 10; fax 72 33 30), arranges rooms for 1000 to 1900Slt per person, plus a 185Slt tax, with higher rates for stays of under three days (open July-Aug. daily 7am-9pm; Sept.-June M-Sa 8am-6pm, Su 9am-3pm). **Autokamp Zlatorog,** on the west side of the lake, has spaces for 900Slt (May-June and Aug.-Sept.) and 1500Slt (July-Aug.). **Gostišče Kramar,** Stara Fužina 3, is slung low over the lake; its wood-burning stove and cushioned wicker chairs hover scarcely a meter above the water. (pizzas 600-850Slt; grilled octopus 1100Slt). Follow the dirt path on your left after the stone bridge. The restaurant will appear after 10 minutes (open daily 11am-midnight). Stock up at the **Mercator supermarket** next to the tourist office (open M-Sa 7am-noon and 1:30-9pm, Su 7am-noon and 1:30-7pm).

Spain (España)

US$1	= 146.67ptas (pesetas, or ESP)		100ptas =	US$0.68
CDN$1	= 96.47ptas		100ptas =	CDN$1.04
UK£1	= 243.42ptas		100ptas =	UK£0.41
IR£1	= 212.64ptas		100ptas =	IR£0.47
AUS$1	= 86.72ptas		100ptas =	AUS$1.15
NZ$1	= 75.06ptas		100ptas =	NZ$1.33
SAR1	= 23.61ptas		100ptas =	SAR4.24
Country Code: 34			**International Dialing Prefix: 07**	

With a history that spans over 50 constitutions, an endless array of amorphous kingdoms controlled by Arabs, Visgoths, Germans, French, Celts, and indigenous peoples, Spain can only be described imprecisely—as a *mestizo* culture. Nine centuries of Roman rule left the empire's imprint in irrigation techniques, architecture, language, and its trademark use of olives and grapes. The Muslim invasion of 711 ushered in centuries of general religious toleration and the cultivation of classical Greek science and Eastern artistic traditions. Following the marriage of Fernando de Aragón and Isabel de Castilla and the fall of the Moorish Granada, Spain became a Catholic dominion. Soon after, Columbus, among others, was dispatched to the New World, and the country's Jews and Moors were cruelly expelled. Through savvy royal matchmaking, the Spanish Empire by the 16th century had become Europe's most powerful, encompassing modern-day Belgium and the Netherlands, as well as parts of Germany, Austria, Spain, Italy, and the American colonies.

Eventual Napoleonic occupation and incompetent government not only inspired Spanish colonies in the Americas to declare their independence, but also ushered in an era of nationalism and political unrest in Spain itself. Tensions arising from rapid industrialization in some areas and increasingly mounting nationalism were sparked by international depression, and erupted in the Spanish Civil War (1936-1939). Aided by Hitler and Mussolini, Francisco Franco emerged as the country's dictator and ruled until his death in 1975. Under King Juan Carlos, Franco's hand-picked successor, Spain has become a modern, stable, and democratic constitutional monarchy.

Still scintillating with noble flamenco dancers, graceful bullfighters, and five differ-ent spoken languages Spain doubles its population of 40 million yearly with an influx of tourists. Much of the crunch comes in July and August. This fact—and Andalusia's searing heat—counsel against traveling in summer in southern Spain; choose central or northern destinations whenever possible.

For more detailed coverage of Spain, grab *Let's Go: Spain & Portugal 1999.*

GETTING THERE AND GETTING AROUND

Travelers need legal **passports** or **visas** to enter and leave Spain. A passport allows U.S., Canadian, British, and New Zealand citizens to remain for 90 days. Australian and South African citizens need a visa to enter Spanish territory.

Airports in Madrid and Barcelona handle most of Spain's international air traffic. **Trains** chug over the border into France and connect with most major European cit-ies. Spanish trains are clean, somewhat punctual, and reasonably priced, although they ignore many small towns. The centralized rail network radiates from Madrid. **RENFE,** the Spanish national rail system, offers many types of services with a corre-sponding variety of prices. AVE trains are the fastest but currently run only between Madrid and Seville. *Talgos* are elegant low-slung trains that zip passengers in air-con-ditioned compartments. *Talgo 200s* are *talgo* trains on AVE rails; currently they offer some services out of Madrid. Talgo's long neglected cousin, *Intercity,* is cheaper, a bit dowdier, and operates some lines form Madrid. *Estrellas* are slow night trains with bunks. The commuter trains, *cercanías,* radiate from cities to suburbs and nearby *pueblos,* making frequent stops and usually lacking air-conditioning. Don't bother with *tranvía, semidirecto,* or *correo* trains—these are ludicrously slow.

The **Spain Flexipass** offers any three days of travel in a two-month period for US$180; additional days cost $40. The **Iberic Flexipass** offers any three days of unlim-ited travel in Iberia for a two-month period for US$198; additional days cost $43 (up to 7 more). See Rail Europe or other travel agencies on p. 29 for info on either pass. With a valid Carnet Joven, one can purchase a **Tarjeta Joven,** which allows unlimited travel for 7 consecutive days (19,000ptas), 15 consecutive days (23,000ptas), or 30 consecutive days (30,000ptas). Buy tickets within 60 days of departure at RENFE travel offices, train stations, and authorized travel agencies. Reservations are strongly advised. The only other train company in Spain is **FEVE,** which sluggishly but dependably runs trains between northern towns not served by RENFE.

More exhaustive, cheaper, and sometimes even faster than the rail network, **buses** are the only public transportation to isolated areas. Spain has a multitude of private companies rather than one national bus line, which makes trip planning an ordeal. **Transmediterránea** ferries (24hr. tel. 902 45 46 45; http://www.trasmediterra-nea.com) frequently shuttle back and forth between Tangier, Morocco and Tarifa, Gibraltar, and Algeciras. They also service the Balearic Islands and the Canary Islands.

Rental cars cost considerably less than in other European countries, but you must be over 21, have had a driver's license for at least one year, and be prepared to pay for expensive fuel. Renting from abroad is significantly less expensive than doing so once you have arrived in Spain. **Hitchhiking** is supposedly slow and can be danger-ous; it's reportedly best in the north and along the Mediterranean coast.

ESSENTIALS

Most towns have a centrally located **Oficina de Turismo** (tourist office, fondly called *Turismo*) that distributes information on sights, lodgings, and events, plus a free map here and there. Although most don't book accommodations, many *Turismos* keep a list of approved establishments or can point you to a *casa particular* (private room). **Viajes TIVE,** the national chain of student travel agencies, dispenses transportation info and peddles discount travel tickets, ISICs, and HI cards.

Spanish workers get started around 9am, close down the shop at 1:30 or 2pm for a loooong lunch, and go back around 4:30 or 5pm until 8pm. On Saturday, shops are usually open only in the morning, and Sunday is a day of rest for everyone except a few indispensables (tourist offices are not considered indispensable). **Banking** hours in Spain are Monday through Friday 9am to 2pm; from October 1 to May 31, banks are also open Saturday 9am to 1pm. Banks charge a minimum commission for currency exchange. Banco **Central Hispano,** marked by blue signs with a yellow seashell symbol, does not charge commission and offers good exchange rates.

Spain levies a **Value-Added Tax** (VAT, in Spain IVA) on all goods and services. The standard rate is 7%. Foreigners (non-EU) who have stayed in the EU less than 180 days can claim back the VAT paid on purchases which exceed 15ptas at the airport (ask shops to supply you with a tax return form). The tax on accommodations and other "services" is not refundable. Stores, restaurants, and lodgings include the IVA in their prices, unless otherwise noted. Most restaurants add a service charge to your bill. It's customary to round off the bill and leave the change as a **tip.** You should generally tip around 5%, more if the service is exceptional. Porters can be tipped 100-150ptas per bag, taxi drivers 5-10% of the meter fare (if they're nice).

The northwest is rightly called "wet" or "green" Spain, with a humid, temperate climate open to the sea and a lush, often thickly wooded landscape resembling the mountain areas of the south and east, where ranges are high enough to catch moisture. The interior's climate resembles that of Central Europe—long winters and, in the lowlands, torrid summers. The east and south coasts enjoy a Mediterranean climate. The northeast coast can be humid, but the southwest is the most sweltering, especially the Guadalquivir river basin (including Seville and Córdoba).

Men in Spain may be free with unwanted comments and gestures directed at women traveling alone. Women should be especially cautious in big cities and memorize the Spanish **emergency** phone number, 091 or 092. For additional travel tips, see **Women Travelers,** p. 23.

Holidays in Spain include: New Year's Day, Epiphany (Jan. 6), *Semana Santa* (Mar. 29-Apr. 4), May Day (May 1), Corpus Christi (June 22), July 25, Aug. 15, Oct. 12, Nov. 1, Dec. 6, Dec. 8, and Christmas. Some of these religious celebrations are no longer legal holidays, but business slows anyway and sometimes stops altogether. The *Semana Santa* (Holy Week), the week before Easter, sees much celebration, especially in Andalusia. Cities and towns strive to outdo one another with ardent displays of adoration. Bullfights are featured in most festivals from May to October.

COMMUNICATION An airmail letter *(por avión)* takes four to seven business days to reach the U.S. and Canada; service is faster to the U.K. and Ireland, slower to Australia and New Zealand. Standard postage is 87ptas. In Spain, Poste Restante is **Lista de Correos.** Most post offices also have fax service. Local phone calls cost 20ptas. Phone cards, sold in tobacconists in denominations of 1000 and 2000ptas, are more convenient than feeding tons of coins into a pay phone. Collect calls *(cobro revertido)* are billed according to pricier person-to-person *(persona a persona)* rates, but may still be cheaper than calls from hotels. Useful numbers include the **local operator,** 009; **directory assistance,** 1003; **national police,** 091; and local **police emergency,** 092. For **AT&T Direct,** dial 900 99 00 11; **MCI WorldPhone,** 900 99 00 14; **SprintExpress,** 900 99 00 13; **Canada Direct,** 900 99 00 15; **BT Direct,** 900 99 00 44; **Australia Direct,** 900 99 00 61; **Ireland Direct,** 900 99 03 53; and **NZ Direct,** 900 99 00 64.

There are five official **languages** in Spain, plus plenty of dialects, such as the Mallorquín of the Balearic Islands. Catalan is the language of choice in Catalonia, Valencian in Valencia. The non-Indo-European Basque (Euskera) language is spoken in north central Spain, and Galician (related to Portuguese) is spoken in the once-Celtic northwest, though both are minority languages even in their own dominions. Spanish (Castilian, or *castellano*) is spoken everywhere. In Spanish, "ll" is pronounced like the English "y," "j" and soft "g" (before "e" or "i") like the English "h," and "z" and soft "c" like "th." "H" is not pronounced.

Yes/no	*Sí/no*	see/no
Hello	*Hola*	OH-la
Please	*Por favor*	pohr fah-VOHR
Thank you	*Gracias*	GRAH-see as
Excuse me	*Con permiso*	con pehr-MEE-so
Do you speak English?	*¿Habla usted inglés?*	AH-blah oos-TED in-GLEHS
I don't understand.	*No entiendo*	no en-tee-EN-doh
I don't speak Spanish.	*No hablo español*	no AH-bloh es-pahn-YOL
Where is...?	*¿Dónde está...?*	DOHN-deh es-TAH...
How much does this cost?	*¿Cuánto cuesta?*	KWAHN-toh KWES-tah
I'd like...	*Quisiera...*	kee-see-EHR-ah
I would like a room.	*Quisiera un cuarto*	kee-see-EHR-ah oon KWAHR-toh
Help!	*¡Socorro!*	soh-KOHR-roh

ACCOMMODATIONS AND CAMPING REAJ, the Spanish Hostelling International (HI) affiliate, runs 165 youth hostels year-round. **HI cards** are required and are available for 1800ptas at youth hostels and from Spain's main national youth/travel company, TIVE. Reservations can be made through the central REAJ office (tel. 91 347 77 00; fax 91 401 81 60) or by direct calls to specific hostels.

Accommodations have many an alias in Spain; each name indicates a specific type of establishment. Cheapest and barest are *hospedajes* and *casas de huéspedes.* Higher in quality are *pensiones* and *fondas,* then *hostales,* then *hostal-residencias;* all three levels offer similar amenities and are budget travel staples. The highest priced accommodations are *hoteles,* often far beyond the reach of budget travelers.

Campgrounds are government-regulated and on a three-class system, rated and priced by the quality of amenities. Tourist offices stock the *Guía de Campings,* a fat guide to all official campgrounds in Spain. Alternate types of accommodations include *casas particulares* (private residences), *casas rurales* (rural cottages), *casas rústicas* (farmhouses), *refugios* (rustic huts in the mountains), *colegios mayores* (state university student dorms), and monasteries or convents.

FOOD AND DRINK Spaniards start their day with a breakfast of coffee or hot chocolate and *bollos* (rolls) or *churros* (lightly fried fritters). Dinner ("lunch" to Americans) is served between 2 and 3pm, and traditionally consists of several courses. Supper at home is light and eaten around 9pm. Supper out—also a light meal—begins later, usually around 10pm.

Some restaurants are "open" from 8am until 1 or 2am, but most only serve meals from 1 or 2 to 4pm and from 8pm until midnight. Each city's tourist office rates its restaurants with a row of forks, five forks indicating luxury. *Cafeterías* are rated by a row of up to three cups. Prices for a full meal start at about 800ptas in the cheapest bar-restaurants. Many places offer a *plato combinado* (combination platter—includes a main course and side dishes on a single plate, plus bread, and sometimes beverage—roughly 500-1000ptas) or a *menú del día* (two or three dishes, bread, beverage, and dessert—roughly 800-1500ptas).

Tasty *tapas* are ever so conducive to convivial good spirits. A *tasca*, or *taberna*, serves *tapas* at a counter; *mesones* bring them to the table. *Pinchos* are the north's equivalent of *tapas*. *Raciones* may equal an entree in size. *Bocadillos* are *tapas* served as a sandwich on a hunk of thick bread—often a viable substitute for lunch. Your fork may find its way into *champiñones al ajillo* (mushrooms in garlic sauce), *jamón serrano* (smoked ham), *atún* or *bonito* (tuna), *calamares fritos* (fried squid), *chorizo* (spicy sausage), *gambas* (shrimp), *ternera* (veal), and *lomo* (pork).

The most sophisticated and varied cuisines on the peninsula were developed in Catalonia, the Basque country, Navarre, and Galicia. Other regions make a good showing, though—Valencia claims *paella* (steamed saffron rice with chicken stock and an assortment of seafood), Andalusia presides over *gazpacho* (cold tomato-based soup), and Castile cooks a mean *tortilla de patata* (potato omelette).

Food is almost always washed down with alcohol, whether a glass of wine (*vino blanco* is white, *tinto* is red) or of beer *(cerveza)*. Beer is served in bottles or on draft. Aguila, Estrella, and San Miguel are fine national brands; Volldamm (Catalonia) and Alhambra (Andalusia) are fine regional brews. Rioja is a world-renowned grape-growing region, with especially good red wines; there are innumerable fine regional wines. *Sangría* is made of red wine, sugar, brandy, seltzer, and fruit. Another native beverage is *jerez* (sherry), from the city of the same name.

■ Madrid

The stately grandeur of Old Madrid's palaces and museums rapidly dissipates as one enters the smaller avenues and encounters the libertarian *joie de vivre* of its citizens. After decades of Franco's totalitarian repression, Madrid's youth burst out laughing and crying during the 1980s, an era known as *la Movida* ("Shift" or "Movement"), and they have yet to stop. Madrid's cultural renaissance has been led by its 200,000 students, who have taken over the streets, shed the decorous reserve of their predecessors, and captured the present. The newest generation, too young to recall the Franco years, seems neither cognizant of its city's historic landmarks nor preoccupied with the future, despite unemployment rates near 20 percent. Bright lights and a perpetual stream of cars and people blur the distinction between 4pm and 4am, and infinitely energized *madrileños* crowd bars and discos until dawn. Unlike much of the world, Madrid still works to live, not the reverse.

ORIENTATION AND PRACTICAL INFORMATION

The "Kilometro 0" marker in front of the police station signals the city's epicenter at **Puerta del Sol,** *the* transportation hub of the city. Most of Madrid's prominent points of interest lie within walking distance around Sol. Just west, close to the metro station, is the **Plaza Mayor.** This plaza has been happening since the 17th century; it now shares space with contemporary cafes and the churches and historical houses of Habsburg Madrid, the **Madrid de los Asturias.**

Farther west lies the reigning monument of the **Madrid de los Borbones** (Bourbon Madrid), the **Palacio Real.** This section of Madrid, also known as **Ópera,** has fantastic gardens and churches; in summer, it also attracts various music festivals. East of Sol, the **Museo del Prado** is on **Paseo del Prado.** The museum lies in the region of **Huertas,** once the literary district of Madrid and now the theatre district. Centered around **Plaza Santa Ana,** Huertas is bordered by **Calle Alcalá** to the north, Po. Prado to the east, Sol to the west, and C. Atocha to the south; it's crowded with some of the best hostel values in the city, as well as some of the best bars and cafes. East of the Po. Prado and behind the Museo del Prado awaits the lush **Parque del Buen Retiro.**

South of Sol lies another world-renowned center of art, the **Museo Reina Sofía.** The area around Metro stops **La Latina** and **Tirso de Molina** has less wealth and prestige, and fewer tourists, than the rest of Old Madrid. **El Rastro,** a gargantuan flea market, is staged here every Sunday morning. Finally, the area north of Sol is bordered by the grand avenue **Gran Vía,** running northwest to **Plaza de España.** The tall **Torre de**

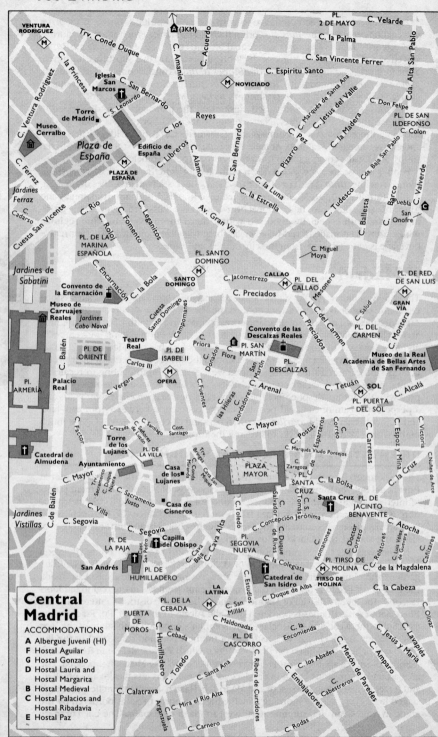

Central Madrid

ACCOMMODATIONS

A Albergue Juvenil (HI)
F Hostal Aguilar
G Hostal Gonzalo
D Hostal Lauria and
   Hostal Margarita
B Hostal Medieval
C Hostal Palacios and
   Hostal Ribadavia
E Hostal Paz

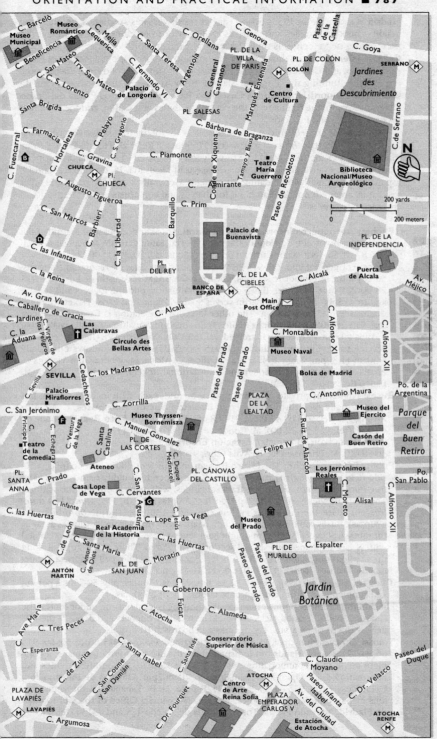

Madrid is the pride of 1950s Spain. Farther northwest lies **Argüelles,** an energetic neighborhood of families and students spilling over from **Moncloa,** the student district, whose nerve center is on C. Isaac Peral. Straight north of Gran Vía, linked by **Calle de Fuencarral,** are the three hyper-cool club and bar-hopping districts of **Malasaña, Bilbao,** and **Chueca,** where the nightlife never stops. Beyond Gran Vía lies modern Madrid. Running the length of Madrid, from **Atocha** in the south to **Plaza de Castilla** in the north, **Paseo de la Castellana-Paseo de Recoletos-Paseo del Prado** passes the Prado, the fountains at the plazas of **Cibeles** and **Colón,** and the elaborate skyscrapers beyond Pl. Colón.

The *Plano de Madrid,* free at tourist offices, is useful but index-less. For a comprehensive **map,** get the *Almax* at a newsstand (650ptas). Refer also to this book's **color map** of Madrid's metro. Madrid is extremely safe compared to other major European cities, but the Puerta del Sol, Pl. Dos de Mayo in Malasaña, Pl. de Chueca, and Pl. España are particularly intimidating late at night. Generally, avoid the parks and quiet residential areas after dark. Watch out for thieves and con artists in the Metro and on crowded city streets.

Flights: Aeropuerto Internacional de Barajas, 15km northeast of Madrid. Take the green **bus** to Pl. de Colón (380ptas). **Iberia,** Santa Cruz de Marcenado 2 (tel. 915 87 81 56), is a major carrier. For reservations, call 902 400 500 (24hr.).

Trains: For general info, call 913 28 90 20. Madrid has 2 *largo recorrido* (long distance) and 2 intermediate stations. **Estación Chamartín,** Agustín de Foxá (tel. 913 28 90 20). M: Chamartín. Bus 5 departs from just beyond the lockers and runs to and from Sol (45min.). Chamartín serves Spain, Lisbon, and Paris. Ticket windows open daily 6:45am-10:30pm. The other long-distance station is **Estación Atocha** (tel. 913 28 90 20). M: Atocha-Renfe. Trains head to Andalusia, Castilla la Mancha, Castilla y León, El Escorial, Extremadura, and Valencia. Also AVE (high-speed train) service to Seville via Córdoba (tel. 915 34 05 05). Ticket windows open daily 6:30am-11:30pm. The **RENFE Main Office,** C. Alcalá 44, where Gran Vía hits C. Alcalá, has schedules, national and international tickets, and plenty of info. M: Banco de España. Open M-F 9:30am-8pm.

Buses: Numerous private companies serve Madrid, each with its own station, but buses usually pass through the large **Estación Sur de Autobuses,** C. Méndez Alvaro, s/n (tel. 914 68 42 00 or 914 68 45 11). **Estación Auto Res,** Pl. Conde de Casal 6 (tel. 915 51 72 00). M: Conde de Casal. To Cuenca (2½hr., 1305ptas) and Salamanca (3¼hr., 1440ptas). **Estación Empresa Larrea,** Po. Florida 11 (tel. 915 30 48 00). M: Príncipe Pío. To Ávila (2hr., 910ptas).

Public Transportation: The **Metro** is clean and efficient. Rides cost 164ptas; a 10-ride ticket *(bonometro)* runs 670ptas. Trains operate roughly 6am-1:30am. The free *Plano del Metro* deciphers train schedules; wall maps abound in the stations. The more unwieldy *Plano de Transportes* (200ptas) and the free *Madrid en autobús* elucidate the city's **bus** system (bus fare 130ptas; 10-ride *bonobús* pass 670ptas). Buses run daily 6am-11:30pm. Night buses travel from Pl. Cibeles as far as the outskirts every 30min. midnight-3am, every hr. 3-6am. Night buses (labeled with N) are explained in a special section of the *Plano.* There are N stops all along the marked routes, not just in Pl. Cibeles. For more bus info, call **Empresa Municipal de Transportes (EMT)** at 914 06 88 10 (Spanish only).

Taxi: Tel. 914 45 90 08 or 914 47 32 32. Base fare is 170ptas, plus 50-75ptas per km and supplements. From city center to airport about 2500ptas.

Hitchhiking: Neither popular nor safe. Hitchhiking is legal only on minor routes; the Guardia Civil de Tráfico picks up would-be highway hitchers and deposits them at nearby towns or on a bus. Try the message boards at HI hostels.

Tourist Offices: Municipal, Pl. Mayor 3 (tel. 913 66 54 77 or 915 88 16 36; fax 913 66 54 77). M: Sol. Hands out indispensable city and transportation maps, a complete guide to accommodations, as well as *En Madrid,* a monthly activities and information guide.Open M-F 10am-8pm, Sa 10am-2pm. **Oficinas de Información,** C. Princesa 1 (tel. 915 41 23 25), off Pl. España. M: Pl. España. Has the same fabulous maps as the Municipal office. **Regional/Provincial Office of the Comunidad de Madrid,** Mercado Pta. de Toledo, Ronda de Toledo 1, stand #3134 (tel. 913 64

18 76). M: Pta. de Toledo. Brochures, transport info, and maps for towns in the Comunidad de Madrid. Open M-F 9am-7pm, Sa 9:30am-1:30pm. A **second office** is at C. Duque Medinaceli 2 (tel. 914 29 49 51, 914 29 31 71, or 914 29 37 05), just off Pl. Cortes. M: Sol. Open M-F 9am-7pm, Sa 9am-1pm. Other offices at **Estación Chamartín** (tel. 913 15 99 76) and the **airport** (tel. 913 05 86 56); both open M-F 8am-8pm, Sa 9am-1pm.

Embassies: Embassies open M-F; call for hours. **Australia,** Santa Engracia 120 (tel. 915 79 04 28; fax 914 42 53 62; email information@embaustralia.es; http://www.embaustralia.es). **Canada,** C. Núñez de Balboa 35 (tel. 914 31 43 00; fax 914 35 74 88; http://info.ic.gc.ca/Tourism). M: Velázquez. **New Zealand,** Pl. de la Lealtad 2 (tel. 915 23 02 26; fax 915 23 01 71). M: Banco de España. **South Africa,** Claudio Coello 91, 6th fl. (tel. 914 36 37 80; fax 915 77 74 14). **U.K.,** C. Fernando el Santo 16 (tel. 913 19 02 00; fax 913 08 10 33). M: Colón. **U.S.,** C. Serrano 75 (tel. 915 87 22 00; fax 915 87 23 03). M: Rubén Darío.

Currency Exchange: Banco Central Hispano charges no commission on traveler's checks and cash and offers the best rates on AmEx traveler's checks. Open in summer M-F 8:30am-2:30pm; off-season M-Th 8:30am-2:30pm, F-Sa 8:30am-1pm. **ATMs** are plentiful: use only the first 4 digits of your PIN code.

American Express: Pl. Cortes 2 (tel. 913 22 55 00 or, for main info, 915 72 03 03). M: Sevilla. Currency exchange. 1% cash and 2% traveler's check commission. No commission on AmEx traveler's checks. No min. charge. Mail held for 30 days and money wired. Open M-F 9am-5:30pm, Sa 9am-noon.

Luggage Storage: Estaciones de Chamartín and **Atocha.** Lockers 400-600ptas per day. Open daily 6:30am-12:30pm. **Estación Sur de Autobuses,** 800ptas.

Bookstores: FNAC, C. Preciados 28 (tel. 915 95 62 00). M: Callao. Open M-Sa 10am-9:30pm, Su noon-9:30pm.

Gay and Lesbian Services: Colectivo de Gais y Lesbianas de Madrid (COGAM), C. Fuencarral 37 (tel./fax 915 23 00 70). M: Gran Vía. Wide range of services and activities. Reception M-F 5-9pm; library open 7-9pm. **GAI-INFORM** (tel. 915 23 00 70), provides information in Spanish about gay associations, leisuretime activities, and health issues. Line staffed daily 5-9pm.

Laundromat: Lavandería Donoso Cortés, C. Donoso Cortés 17 (tel. 914 46 96 90). M: Quevedo. Self-service wash 600ptas. Open M-F 9am-2pm and 3:30-8pm, Sa 9am-2pm. **Maryland,** C. Meléndez Valdés 52 (tel. 915 43 30 41). M: Argüelles. Wash 725ptas, including detergent. Open M-F 10:30am-8pm, Sa 10am-2pm.

Emergency: tel. 091 or 092. **Ambulance,** tel. 061.

Police: C. Luna 17 (tel. 915 21 12 36). M: Callao.

Crisis Lines: AIDS Information, tel. 900 11 10 00; M-F 9am-2pm. **Alcohólicos Anónimos,** C. Juan Bravo 40-bis, 2nd fl. (tel. 913 09 19 47). **English-Language Help,** tel. 915 59 13 93; daily 7-11pm. **Rape Hotline,** tel. 915 74 01 10.

Medical Assistance: Anglo-American Medical Unit, Conde de Aranda 1, 1st fl. (tel. 914 35 18 23). M: Serrano or Retiro. Not an emergency clinic.

Post Office: Palacio de Comunicaciones, Pl. Cibeles (tel. 902 19 71 97). M: Banco de España. Information open M-F 8am-10pm or call 915 37 64 94. Open for stamps and certified mail M-F 8:30am-10pm, Sa 8:30am-8pm, Su 9:30am-1:30pm; for *Lista de Correos* M-F 8:30am-9:30pm, Sa 8:30am-8pm. English and French spoken at information desk. **Postal Code:** 28080.

Internet Access: Net Cafe, C. San Bernardo 81 (tel. 915 94 09 99). M: San Bernardo. One drink buys 1hr. Open M-Th 6pm-2am, F-Su 4pm-3am. **La Ciberteca,** C. General Perón 32 (tel. 915 56 56 03). M: Santiago Bernabeu. Open M-Sa 4-11pm.

Telephones: Telefónica, Gran Vía 34, at C. Valverde. M: Gran Vía.

ACCOMMODATIONS AND CAMPING

Demand for rooms rises dramatically in summer, so make reservations. Expect to pay 2400ptas per person for a typical *hostal* room, slightly less for a bed in a *pensión*. The centrally located **Puerta del Sol** zone crawls with tourists and hostels. The **Gran Vía** is a slightly louder and rougher part of town, while **Calle Fuencarral** is less expensive and closer to the nightlife of Malasaña and Chueca. For 300ptas, **Viajes Brújula,** Torre de Madrid, 6th fl., #14 (tel. 915 59 97 04 or 915 59 97 05; fax 915 48 46 24; M: "Pl.

España"), will book you a room, but you must go in person to specify desired prices and locations (HI hostels excluded; English spoken; open M-F 9am-7pm). **Branch offices** are at Estación Atocha at the AVE terminal (tel. 915 39 11 73; open daily 8am-10pm); Estación Chamartín (tel. 913 15 78 94; open daily 7:15am-11:30pm); and the airport bus terminal in Pl. Colón (tel. 915 75 96 80; open daily 8am-10pm).

Albergue Juvenil Santa Cruz de Marcenado (HI), C. Santa Cruz de Marcenado 28 (tel. 915 47 45 32; fax 915 48 11 96). M: Argüelles. From the Metro, walk 1 block down C. Alberto Aguilera away from C. Princesa, turn right on C. Serrano Jóve, then left on C. Santa Cruz de Marcenado. Members only, or buy an HI card (1800 ptas). Recently renovated facilities. 950ptas, over 26 1300ptas. Breakfast included. 3-day max. stay. Reception 9am-1:30am. Strict curfew 1:30am. Reserve in writing or arrive early. If you can't get a bed at Santa Cruz, **Hostal-Residencia La Montaña,** C. Juan Álvarez Mendizábal 44, 4th fl. (tel. 915 47 10 88), and the 4 other *pensiones* in the same building are a short jaunt away. From the HI, cross the busy C. Princesa, turn left, go right on C. Rey Francisco, then left on C. J. A. Mendizábal. Singles 1800-2000ptas; doubles 3400-3700ptas; triples 5100ptas.

Hostal Paz, C. Flora 4, 1st and 4th fl. (tel. 915 47 30 47). M: Ópera. On a quiet street parallel to C. Arenal, off C. Donados or C. Hileras. Firm beds in brilliant rooms—some overlooking a courtyard, others with access to a terrace. Satellite TV. A/C. Singles 2400ptas; doubles 3600ptas, with shower 4200ptas; triples with shower 5400ptas. Laundry 1000ptas. Reservations encouraged.

Hostal-Residencia Luz, C. Fuentes 10, 3rd fl. (tel. 915 42 07 59). M: Ópera. Sunny, inviting rooms in an elegant old building off C. Arenal. Satellite TV, fax service, and public phone. Singles 2500ptas; doubles 3700ptas; triples 5300ptas. Laundry 1000ptas. Discounts for stays of 15 days or more. 7% IVA not included.

Hostal Portugal, C. Flora 4, ground fl. (tel. 91 559 40 14). M: Ópera. Bright rooms, great location, and *cheap*—2000ptas per person.

Hostal Gonzalo, C. Cervantes 34, 3rd fl. (tel. 914 29 27 14). M: Antón Martín. Off C. León, which is off C. Atocha. Newly renovated by friendly proprietors. All rooms with TV, fans in summer. Singles 4000ptas; doubles 5200ptas. Ask about discounts.

Hostal Aguilar, C. San Jerónimo 32, 2nd fl. (tel. 914 29 59 26 or 914 29 36 61; fax 914 29 26 61). M: Sol. Very clean, modern rooms, all with telephone, A/C, coin-operated TV, and bath. Singles 3500ptas; doubles 5500ptas; triples 7000ptas.

Hostal Lauria, Gran Vía 50, 4th fl. (tel. 915 41 91 82; fax 915 41 91 88). M: Callao. Airy, ranch house feel. Tastefully sparse rooms with TVs and telephones. Singles 4000ptas; doubles 5200ptas; triples 7000ptas. 20% off stays longer than a week.

Hostal Margarita, Gran Vía, 50, 5th fl. (tel./fax 91 547 35 49). M: Callao. Ultra-comfortable rooms have oriental rugs and artwork. Use of kitchen and refrigerator. All with shower. Singles 4000ptas; doubles 4800ptas, with bath 5100ptas; triples 6750ptas. Laundry 1200ptas. Reservations recommended a week in advance.

Hostal Palacios and Hostal Ribadavia, C. Fuencarral 25, 1st-3rd fl. (tel. 915 31 10 58 or 915 31 48 47). M: Gran Vía. Both *hostales* are run by the same cheerful family. **Ribadavia** (3rd fl.) has pleasant, bright rooms with old furniture. **Palacios** (1st and 2nd fl.) flaunts brand new rooms, all with TV. Singles 2600-3000ptas; doubles 3800-4600ptas; triples 6900ptas; quads 7500ptas.

Hostal Abril, C. Fuencarral 39, 4th fl. (tel. 915 31 53 38). M: Tribunal or Gran Vía. Nice and simple. Singles 1900ptas, with shower 2200ptas, with bath 2500ptas; doubles 2900-3200ptas, with bath 3400ptas; triples 3100ptas, with bath 4300ptas.

Hostal Medieval, C. Fuencarral 46, 2nd fl. (tel. 915 22 25 49). M: Tribunal. On the corner of C. Augusto Figueroa. Don't think Dark Ages, think pink. Singles 3000ptas; doubles 4000-5000ptas; triples 6200ptas.

Tourist offices have details on the 13 or so **campsites** within 50km of Madrid. For further info, contact the Consejería de Educación de Juventud, C. Fernando el Católico (tel. 915 22 29 41). **Camping Osuna** (tel. 917 41 05 10; fax 913 20 63 65) is located on Av. Logroño Vicálvaro (8km). Take the Metro to Canillejas, cross the pedestrian overpass, walk through the parking lot, and turn right along the freeway (630ptas per person, per tent, and per car). **Camping Alpha** (tel. 916 95 80 69) hides on a shady site 12.4km down Ctra. de Andalucía in Getafe. From the Legazpi Metro station take bus 447, which stops next to the Nissan dealership (10min., every 30min. until

10pm). Ask the driver to let you off at the pedestrian overpass near the Amper building. Cross the bridge and walk 1.5km back toward Madrid along the busy highway (590ptas per person, 640ptas per tent). Both campgrounds have phones, showers, laundry, currency exchange, medical care, a bar, and a restaurant.

FOOD

In Madrid, it's not hard to fork it down without forking over too much; you can't walk a block without tripping over at least five *cafeterías,* where a sandwich, coffee, and dessert sell for around 600ptas. **Chueca** is the none-too-closeted gay/glam district, where scenesters crowd the chic gourmet joints and stalk the streets in platform shoes. **Calles Echegaray, Ventura de la Vega,** and **Manuel Fernández González** are its budget boulevards. **Argüelles** is full of moderately priced eateries.

In the following listings and in Madrid generally, a *restaurante* is open from 1 to 4pm and 8pm to midnight unless otherwise noted. Establishments such as *mesones, cafeterías, bares, cafés, terrazas,* and *tabernas* include a bar and serve drinks and *tapas* all day until midnight. Some close on Sundays. Keep in mind the following buzz words for quicker, cheaper *madrileño* fare: *bocadillo* (350-400ptas), a sandwich on a french roll; *sandwich* (about 300ptas), a sandwich on sliced bread, usually grilled; *croissant* (250ptas); *ración* (300-600ptas), a plate of meat, cheese, or some other finger food served with bread; and *empanada* (200-300ptas), a puff pastry generally filled with tuna.

Fresh produce in the center of Madrid is scarce—your best bet is to walk around a residential area like Argüelles for neighborhood markets. Vegetarians may shrink a size. For **groceries,** the **Mercado de San Miguel,** on Pl. San Miguel, just off the northwest corner of Pl. Mayor, is a spectacle (open M-Th 9:30am-2pm and 5:30-8:30pm, F-Sa 9am-2:30pm and 5:30-9pm), but **%Dia,** right behind the Mercado de San Miguel, is cheap. Excellent pastry shops and delis line the streets. The sublime **Horno La Santiaguesa,** C. Mayor 73, sells everything from *empanadas* to chocolate and candy.

El Estragón, Costanilla de S. Andrés 10, Pl. Raja. M: La Latina. Uphill off C. Segovia, facing La Capilla del Obispo. Vegetarian food that will make die-hard meat-eaters reconsider. *Menú* 1750ptas.

Museo del Jamón, C. San Jerónimo 6. M: Sol. 5 other locations throughout the city. Succulent Iberian ham served up in any and every form your piggish little heart could possibly desire. Open M-Sa 9am-12:30am, Su 10am-12:30am.

Casa Botín, C. Cuchilleros 17 (tel. 913 66 42 17). M: Sol. The best restaurant in Madrid, maybe all of Spain, and worth the ducats. Founded in 1725, it's the oldest restaurant in the world, according to Guinness. Hemingway, a patron, wrote about it in *A Clean, Well-lighted Place.* Reservations recommended.

El Tazumal, C. Madera 36. M. Tribunal. From the station, walk down to C. Espiritú Santo, turn right then left at C. Madera. Tasty and unique *salvadoreño.* Main courses 275-1300ptas. Open W-M 1:30-4:30pm and 8pm-midnight.

Cáscaras, C. Ventura Rodríguez 7. M: Ventura Rodríguez. Sleek interior that kind of looks like a tortilla, which is what they serve (725-955ptas). Vegetarian dishes 675-935ptas. Breakfast and non-vegetarian fare as well.

El 26 de Libertad, C. Libertad 26, off C. las Infantas. M: Chueca. Spectacular lunch *menú* (1250ptas) in a restaurant with art gallery decor. Dinner *menú* 2500ptas.

La Tarterie, C. Cardenal Cisneros 24, off C. Luchana, which is off Glorieta de Bilbao. M: Bilbao. This restaurant/art gallery likes to consider itself an art gallery/restaurant and is full of experimental art and skinny artists. Great quiches (675ptas), salads (650ptas), and pizzas (775-1050ptas).

Gula Gula, C. Infantes 5 (tel. 915 22 87 64), off C. Echegaray near C. Huertas. M: Antón Martin. Food is fun! This place has lost its mind. *Spectáculos,* Su at 11pm, might include storytellers or drag queens. Another branch is at Gran Via 1 (tel. 915 22 87 64), near C. Accacá. Make reservations on weekends.

Restaurante Integral Artemisa, C. Ventura de la Vega 4, off C. San Jerónimo. M: Sol. Tasty veggie food unspoiled by nicotine (no smoking). All proceeds from W dinners go to humanitarian organizations. Main courses 1175-2595ptas. *Menú* 1200ptas. Non-vegetarian courses 1200-1600ptas.

El Granero de Lavapiés, C. Argumosa 10. M: Lavapiés. Old-World charm. Gazpacho 475ptas. Vegetarian *menú* 1200ptas. Open daily 1-4pm.

La Farfalla, C. Santa María 17. M: Antón Martín, 1 block south following C. Huertas. La Farfalla's specialty is Argentine-style grilled meat (1100-1750ptas), but true love is one unforgettable mouthful of their thin-crust pizza: *erótica* or *exquisita* 700ptas. Open Su-Th until 3am, F-Sa until 4am.

Costa Del Sol, opposite C. Valverde. M: Gran Vía. A well-kept secret. Deliciously inexpensive meat and loads of it. Salads 250-450ptas. *Carnes* 400-875ptas. Lunchtime *menú* 1000ptas.

Nabucco, C. Hortaleza 108, a few blocks off Pl. Santa Bárbara. M: Alonso Martínez or Chueca. Upscale clientele, excellent food, and affordable prices. Pizzas 730-935ptas. Pasta 825-975ptas. Salads 590-875ptas.

SIGHTS

Madrid, large as it may seem at first, is a walker's city. A lounger's city, too—when panting for a break from the museums or a retreat from the summer's scorching heat, head for the shade at the Parque del Retiro or any sidewalk cafe.

From Plaza Mayor to Puerta de Toledo

The Habsburgs' elegant black-slate roofs and spindly, pagoda-like towers top the arcaded **Plaza Mayor.** It was completed in 1620 for Felipe III; his statue also dates from the 17th century, although it took the city until 1847 to install it. The days of public executions and bullfights are now but ghosts haunting the plaza's lively cafes. This most picturesque part of Old Madrid is not far from smaller and quieter **Plaza de la Villa.** The **Torre de los Lujanes,** a 15th-century building on the eastern side of the plaza, is the sole remnant of the once lavish residence of the Lujanes family. The characteristically Habsburg 17th-century **Ayuntamiento** (or Casa de la Villa), on the plaza, was both the mayor's home and the city jail. South of Pl. Mayor on C. Toledo looms **Iglesia de San Isidro,** a 17th-century church dedicated to Madrid's patron saint; the remains of San Isidro landed here after being tossed from church to church. *(M: Latina. Open for mass only.)* The church served as the cathedral of Madrid from the late 19th century until the Catedral de la Almudena was consecrated in 1993.

Between Sol and Paseo del Prado

In Madrid, only the Prado surpasses the collection of the **Museo de la Real Academia de Bellas Artes de San Fernando,** C. Alcalá 13. *(M: Sol or Sevilla. Open Tu-F 9am-7pm, Sa-M 9am-2:30pm. 400ptas, students 200ptas, Sa-Su free.)* Masterpieces in the collection include Velázquez's portraits of Felipe IV and Mariana de Austria and Goya's *La Tirana.* In the same building, the **Calcografía Real** (Royal Print and Drawing Collection) organizes excellent temporary exhibitions. *(Free with museum admission.)*

The Retiro and Jerónimos

Parque del Retiro, Madrid's top picnic and suntanning zone, was originally intended to be a *buen retiro* (nice retreat) for Felipe IV. The palace burned down, but the **Museo del Ejército** remains, featuring interesting military paraphernalia. The **Estanque Grande,** a rectangular lake in the middle of the park, has become its social center. Ricardo Velázquez built the steel and glass **Palacio de Cristal,** south of the lake by the boat rental center, to exhibit Philippine flowers; it now hosts a variety of art shows. A few steps away, the **Palacio de Velázquez** (named after Ricardo; tel. 915 73 62 45), north of the *estanque,* exhibits works in conjunction with the Museo de Arte Reina Sofía. Fernando and Isabel were crowned and King Alfonso XIII married at the **Iglesia de San Jerónimo.** *(Open daily 8am-1:30pm and 5-8:30pm.)*

Triángulo de Arte

Don't miss the **Paseo del Arte** ticket that grants patrons unlimited access to the Museo del Prado, Colección Thyssen-Bornemisza, and Centro de Arte Reina Sofía for 1050ptas. Spain's premier museum, and one of Europe's finest, the **Museo del Prado** is on Po. Prado at Pl. Cánovas del Castillo. *(M: Banco de España or Atocha. Open Tu-Sa 9am-7pm, Su 9am-2pm. 500ptas, students 250ptas, Sa 2:30-7pm and all day Su free.)* This

Neoclassical building has sheltered the royal painting collection since the time of Fernando VII, who cared precious little for art and plenty about making an impression at home and abroad. Over 3000 paintings, many collected by Spanish monarchs between 1400 and 1700, include Spanish and foreign masterpieces. The Prado has a formidable stash of Italian works by greats including Titian, Raphael, Tintoretto, and Botticelli. The Spanish Hapsburgs' long reign over the Netherlands resulted in the strong Flemish collection, with Van Dyck, Roger van der Weyden, Albrecht Dürer, Peter Breughel the Elder, and Rubens. This is also *the* place for Velásquez and Goya fanatics. The museum is laid out in a fairly logical fashion, and rooms are numbered, but it can be easy to lose sight of the forest for the groves of Goyas once within. Guides to the Prado can be helpful and informative; they vary in size and detail, ranging from 150ptas "greatest hits" brochures to weighty 2000ptas tomes packed with serious art criticism.

Picasso's *Guernica* is the centerpiece of the **Museo Nacional Centro de Arte Reina Sofía,** a collection of 20th-century art at C. Santa Isabel 52, near the south end of Po. Prado. *(M: Atocha. Open M and W-Sa 10am-9pm, Su 10am-2:30pm. 500ptas, students 250ptas, Sa after 2:30pm and Su all day free.)* When Germans bombed the Basque town of Guernica for the Fascists in Spain's Civil War, Picasso painted this huge work of distorted figures in agony to denounce the bloodshed. When asked by Nazi officials if he was responsible for the painting, Picasso answered "No, you are." He gave the canvas to New York's Museum of Modern Art on condition that it return to Spain when democracy was restored. Works by Miró, Julio González, Juan Gris, Picasso, and Dalí illustrate the essential role of Spanish artists in the Cubist and Surrealist movements.

The **Museo Thyssen-Bornemizsa,** on the corner of Po. Prado and C. San Jerónimo, is an 18th-century palace with a collection of art ranging from the Old Masters to major 20th-century figures. *(M: Banco de España. Open Tu-Su 10am-7pm; last admission 6:30pm. 600ptas, with ISIC 400ptas.)*

The Palacio Real and Environs

With 20 square km of tapestry and a huge candelabra, the luxurious **Palacio Real** was built for the first Bourbon King, Felipe V, to replace the burned-down Alcázar. *(M: Ópera. Palace open, except during royal visits, Apr.-Sept. M-Sa 9am-6pm, Su 9am-3pm; Oct.-Mar. M-Sa 9:30am-5pm, Su 9am-2pm. 950ptas, students 850ptas, with 40min. guided tour in Spanish 950ptas. W free for EU citizens. Arrive early to avoid lines.)* The shell of the palace took 40 years to complete, and interior decoration of its 2000 rooms dragged on for a century. To see the collection of porcelain, tapestries, furniture, armor, and art, take a guided tour or stroll around. The palace faces the **Plaza de Oriente,** a square with statues of monarchs nearby. To the northwest are the serene **Jardines de Sabatini,** the park of choice for romantics. The view of the **Campo del Moro** is straight out of a fairy tale. In the heart of downtown, the **Convento de las Descalzas Reales,** Pl. Descalzas, between Pl. Callao and Sol, sheltered royal widows for a few centuries and acquired an exceptional collection of religious artwork. *(M: Callao or Sol. Compulsory 45min. tour in Spanish. Open Tu-Th and Sa 10:30am-12:45pm and 4-6pm, F 10:30am-12:45pm, Su 11am-1:45pm. 650ptas, students 250ptas, W free for EU citizens.)*

Casa de Campo

Catch the *teleférico* (cable car; 360ptas) down to the city's largest park, the **Casa de Campo.** *(M: Batán. Park open daily 11am-9pm; off-season Sa-Su noon-8pm.)* Woods, a municipal pool, a zoo, and an amusement park all conspire to leave the city far behind. Don't attempt to explore the entire park on foot; it's so large it makes Madrid's center look like a clearing in the woods. The Madrid **zoo** is a five-minute walk from the amusement park.

El Pardo

Built as a hunting lodge for Carlos I in 1547, **El Pardo** was subsequently enlarged by generations of Habsburg and Bourbon royalty into the magnificent country palace that stands today. *(Open Apr.-Sept. M-F 9:30am-6pm, Su 9:25am-1:40pm; Oct.-Mar. M-F 10:30am-5pm, Su 9:55am-1:40pm. Compulsory 45min. guided tour in Spanish. 650ptas, stu-*

dents 250ptas, W free for EU citizens. Catch bus 601 from the stop in front of the Ejército del Aire building above M: Moncloa. 15min., 150ptas each way.) Renowned for its collection of tapestries—several of which were designed by Goya—El Pardo also holds a little-known Velázquez depicting a deer slain by Felipe IV. Franco resided here from 1940-1975, and the palace is still the official reception site for distinguished foreign visitors. The palace's **chapel** and the nearby **Casita del Príncipe** are free.

ENTERTAINMENT

Enormously proud of their nightlife, residents of Madrid will tell you with a straight face that they were bored in Paris and New York. The weekly *Guía del Ocio* (125ptas) carries comprehensive entertainment listings; the free municipal tourist office's *En Madrid* is less thorough, but still helpful.

Nightlife

Spaniards get on average one less hour of sleep than other Europeans, and people in Madrid claim to need even less than that. Some clubs don't even bother opening until 4 or 5am; warm up for the night's activities at one of Madrid's many **classic cafes.** Ceiling frescoes and a marble nudes add style to the **Cafe Circulo de Bellas Artes,** C. Alcalá 42 (M: Banco de España; cover 100ptas; coffee 200ptas). **Cafe Gijón,** Po. Recoletos 21 (M: Colón), has both a breezy terrace and a smoky bar-restaurant. Long a favorite of the literati, this cafe has become an official historic site (coffee 300ptas; open daily 9am-1:30am).

As the sun sets and bathes the streets in gold, **terrazas** and **chiringuitos** (outdoor cafes/bars) spill across sidewalks all over Madrid. Enjoy a glass of wine at **Plaza Mayor** while digesting the tourist office's brochures. **Calle Bailén,** by the Viaducto, has spectacular views of flaming sunsets and couples equally aflame. **Paseo Castellana, Paseo Recoletos,** and **Paseo Prado** are fashionable areas, hence a bit pricey. **El Viso,** between Po. Castellana and C. María de Molina, is a pre-war garden city within the city. Villas, walled gardens, and winding streets exude a charming village-like aura. Hippies, intellectuals, bohemians, street musicians, and junkies quaff drinks in the shade of umbrellas and trees at **Plaza 2 de Mayo** and **Plaza Olavide. Chueca** is home to an outrageous, mostly male, gay scene.

For **clubs and discos,** life begins at 3am. Many discos have "afternoon" sessions for teens (cover 250-1000ptas; usually 7-midnight); but the "night" sessions (lasting until dawn) are when to really let your hair down. Don't be surprised if at 5:30am there's still a line of people waiting to get in. Cover *(entrada)* can get as high as 2000ptas; men may be charged up to 500ptas more than women. The cover often includes a drink. The hippest clubs change quickly, so consult the *Guía de Ocio* or ask around.

Kapital, C. Atocha 125. M: Atocha. A block off Po. Prado. One of the most extreme results of *La Movida,* this place strives to impress. 2 dance floors, a sky-light lounge, and tons of bars amount to a total of seven floors. Cover 1200ptas. Includes 2 drinks if you have their invite from the tourist office, 1 drink without. Don't lose your ticket or they'll fine you 5000ptas when you leave. Drinks 800-1000ptas. Open Th 12:30-6am, F-Su 6-11pm and 12:30-6am.

Joy Eslava, C. Arenal 11. M: Sol or Ópera. A 3-tiered theater turned disco. Young crowd of all types grooves to disco, techno, R&B, and salsa. Cover 1500-2000ptas includes 1 drink. Open M-Th 11:30pm-dawn, F-Sa 7-10:15pm and 11:30pm-5:30am.

Las Noches de Babel, Ronda de Toledo 1. M: Puerta de Toledo. *Pijolandia*—where sleek young "beautiful people" in tight clothes wiggle to funk and house around a vegetable decor. Open daily 10pm-6am.

Refugio, C. Dr. Cortezo 1. M: Tirso de Molina. The most outrageous gay men's scene in the…you decide. Cover 1000ptas. Open Tu-Su midnight-morning.

Heaven, C. Veneras 2. M: Santo Domingo. Heavenly party at 8am. **After-hours.** Cover 1000ptas. Drinks 600-900ptas. Open Sa-Su 6-10:30am.

Azúcar, Po. Reina Cristina 7. M: Atocha. The only place up to date on top Latin American rhythms. No sneakers. Salsa classes daily 9:30-11pm. Cover 1200ptas, Sa 1500ptas. Open M-Th 11pm-5am, F-Sa 11pm-6:30am, Su 8pm-5am.

Tierra, Cabarello de Gracia 20. M: Gran Vía. Off C. Montera, but best to go over 1 block to C. Peligios. Black interior with psychedelic glow-in-the-dark design plays host to wicked good house. Beer 500ptas. Open Th-Sa midnight-4:30am.

Soul Kitchen, Mesoneros Romanos 13. M: Gran Vía or Callao, where *"la música es funky."* The only hip-hop club. A hangout for basketball players in Madrid. Women alone may feel uncomfortable. Cover 1000-2000ptas. Open W-Sa midnight-5:30am.

No Se Lo Digas a Nadie, C. Ventura de la Vega 7, next to Pl. Santa Ana. M: Sevilla. Not the best kept secret in Madrid. Billiards upstairs. Drinks 500-800ptas. Live mellow music starts around 12:15am.

Kasbah, C. Santa Maria 17. M: Antón Martín. Dazed aliens and other funked-out decorations look on as house DJs spin some of the best jungle and techno in Madrid. On Sunday, amateurs are invited to give it a whirl. Beer 300ptas. No cover.

Film, Theater, and Music

The **Parque del Retiro** sometimes shows free movies at 11pm. The state-subsidized *filmoteca,* in the renovated Art Deco **Ciné Doré,** C. Santa Isabel 3 (tel. 913 69 11 25; M: Antón Martín), is the best for repertory cinema (tickets 200-400ptas). Subtitled films are shown in many private theaters, including **Alphaville** and **Renoir**—check the *v.o.* (for *versión original)* listings in entertainment guides. **Huertas,** east of Sol, is the theater district. In July and August, **Plaza Mayor, Plaza de Lavapiés,** and **Plaza Villa de París** host frequent plays. Theater-goers can consult magazines published by state-sponsored theaters, such as **Teatro Español, Teatro de la Comedia,** and the city's superb **Teatro María Guerrero.** The **Centro Cultural de la Villa,** Pl. Colón (tel. 915 75 60 80; M: Colón or Serrano), is a major performance center (tickets 2000ptas). The **Auditorio Nacional,** C. Príncipe de Vergara 146 (tel. 913 37 01 00; M: Cruz del Rayo), hosts the finest classical performances (800-4200ptas). **Flamenco** is tourist-oriented and expensive. If you must, try **Casa Patas,** C. Cañizares 10 (tel. 913 69 04 96; flamenco starts at midnight Th-Sa).

Sports

Spanish sports fans go ballistic for **fútbol** (soccer). Every Sunday and some Saturdays between September and June, one of two local teams plays at home. **Real Madrid** plays at Estadio Santiago Bernabeu, Po. Castellana 104 (tel. 914 57 11 12; M: Lima). **Atlético de Madrid** plays at Estadio Vicente Calderón, C. Virgen del Puerto 67 (tel. 366 47 07; M: Pirámides or Marqués de Vadillos). **Corridas** (bullfights) are held during the Festival of San Isidro and every Sunday in summer, less frequently the rest of the year. The season lasts from March to October, signaled by posters in bars and cafes (especially on C. Victoria, off C. San Jerónimo). **Plaza de las Ventas,** C. Alcalá 237 (tel. 913 56 22 00; M: Ventas), east of central Madrid, is the biggest ring in Spain. Tickets are 450-15,200ptas.

■ Near Madrid: El Escorial, El Valle de los Caídos, and Aranjuez

They called **El Escorial** (tel. 918 90 59 03, 918 90 59 04, or 918 66 02 38) the eighth wonder of the world, and they were right. The fascinating complex includes a monastery, two palaces, a church, two pantheons, a magnificent library, and innumerable artistic treasures. El Escorial is located near the charming town of **San Lorenzo,** within easy striking distance of Madrid. *Don't* come on Monday, when the whole complex and most of the town shut down. (Entire complex is open Tu-Su Apr.-Sept. 10am-7pm; Oct.-Mar. 10am-6pm. Last admission to palaces, pantheons, and museums 1hr. before closing. Monastery 850ptas, students 350ptas, guided tour 950ptas, W free for EU citizens. *Casitas* 325ptas.)

To avoid the worst of the crowds, enter El Escorial by the traditional gateway on the west side (C. Floridablanca), then stop into the **Museo de Arquitectura.** It has an outstanding exhibition on the construction of El Escorial, with some wooden models of 16th-century machinery and the buildings themselves. The **Museo de Pintura** holds a collection of masterpieces by Bosch, Dürer, El Greco, Titian, Tintoretto,

Velázquez, Zurbarán, Van Dyck, Rubens, and others. The **Monasterio de San Lorenzo del Escorial** was a gift from Felipe II to God, the people, and himself, commemorating his victory over the French at the battle of San Quintín in 1557. The **Palacio Real** includes the *Salón del Trono* (Throne Room) and two dwellings in one—Felipe II's spartan 16th-century apartments and the more luxurious 18th-century rooms of Carlos III and Carlos IV. The astonishing **Panteón Real** (known affectionately as *el pudridero,* the rotting chamber) was another brainchild of Felipe II. Although he didn't live to see it finished, he's buried here with Carlos I and most of their royal descendants.

The easiest way to get to El Escorial from Madrid is by bus. Autocarres Herranz **buses** pull right up to the kiosk outside the "Moncloa" Metro station (buy a ticket here) and whisk travelers to El Escorial's **Plaza Virgen de Gracia.** The Pl. Virgen is in the center of town, close to the **tourist office**, C. Floridablanca 10 (tel. 918 90 15 54; open M-Sa 10am-6pm). Confirm your return ticket before boarding the bus for Madrid at the **bar/casino**, C. Rey 27 (tel. 918 90 41 00), around the corner from Pl. Virgen de Gracia. **Trains** arrive at Ctra. Estación, 2km from town, and shuttle buses run frequently to Pl. Virgen. Trains run to Madrid's Atocha and Chamartín stations (1hr., round-trip 780ptas).

In a previously untouched valley of the Sierra de Guadarrama, 8km north of El Escorial, Franco built the overpowering monument of **Santa Cruz del Valle de los Caídos** (Valley of the Fallen) as a memorial to those who gave their lives in the Civil War. Naturally, the massive granite cross was meant to honor only those who died "serving *Dios* and *España*," i.e. the fascist Nationalists. The high altar, directly underneath the mammoth cross and statues, is testimony to modern Spain's view of Franco; despite the fact that Franco lies buried underneath, there is no mention of his **tomb** in tourist literature. El Valle de los Caídos is accessible only via El Escorial. **Autocares Herranz** runs one **bus** to the monument (15min., leaves El Escorial Tu-Su 3:15pm and returns 5:30pm, round-trip plus admission 870ptas; funicular not included).

Aranjuez's stately **Palacio Real** warrants a day trip from Madrid. The white brick marvel features finely worked Vatican mosaics in marble, chandeliers and mirrors from the La Granja crystal factory, Buen Retiro porcelain, Flemish tapestries, and ornate French clocks. (Open Tu-Sa June-Sept. 10am-6:15pm; Oct.-May 10am-5:15pm. Compulsory tour in Spanish 650ptas, students 250ptas, W free for EU citizens.) The city is famed for its strawberries and asparagus, and for its beautiful, humid gardens. River walkways run from the **Jardín de la Isla,** which sprouts banana trees and a mythological statue garden, to the huge **Jardín del Príncipe** (open daily June-Sept. 8am-8:30pm; Oct.-May 8am-6:30pm; free). The **train station** (tel. 918 91 02 02) is a pleasant 10-minute walk from the center of town and serves Madrid (45min., 480ptas) and Toledo (30min., 320ptas). Frequent **buses** run to Madrid (1hr., 390ptas) from the station at C. Infantas 8 (tel. 918 91 01 83). The **tourist office** (tel. 918 91 04 27), in Pl. San Antonio, has brochures and maps (open M-F 10am-2pm and 4-6pm).

■ Toledo

Cervantes called Toledo a "rocky gravity, glory of Spain and light of her cities." Successively a Roman settlement, capital of the Visigothic kingdom, stronghold of the Emirate of Córdoba, and imperial city under Carlos V, medieval Toledo became the European capital for the study of natural sciences, the Bible, and languages. Synonymous with cultural tolerance, the city exemplified the Spanish *convivencia* (coexistence of Christian, Islamic, and Jewish cultures), as represented by the ubiquitous churches, synagogues, and mosques. The arts continue to flourish, and the city is famous for *damascene* swords and knives (black steel inlaid with gold) and *mazapán* (marzipan). Toledo's cultural tolerance is tried today by tacky gift shops and busloads of tourists, but a nighttime lull brings quiet to the streets.

ORIENTATION AND PRACTICAL INFORMATION

Despite the well-labeled streets and the map dispensed by the tourist office, you *will get lost* in Toledo; the city could not be more labyrinthine if it contained an actual Minotaur. Many major sights are near or atop the central hill, which is basically circular. To get to **Plaza de Zocodóver** in the center of town, take bus 5 or 6 (115ptas) from the bus or train station.

Trains: Paseo de la Rosa 2 (tel. 925 22 30 99), opposite the Puente de Azarquiel. Its only line runs to Madrid's Atocha (1½hr., 7-9 per day, 630ptas), passing through Aranjuez (35min., 320ptas). To get elsewhere, transfer in Madrid or Aranjuez.

Buses: (tel. 925 21 58 50), 5min. from the city gate (from Pl. Zocodóver, take C. Armas). To Cuenca (3hr., 1300ptas) and Madrid (1½hr., 580ptas). Call **SAMAR** for buses to Valencia (tel. 925 22 39 15 or 925 22 12 17).

Tourist Office: (tel. 925 22 08 43; fax 925 25 26 48), just outside the Puerta Nueva de Bisagra, on the north side of town. From Pl. Zocodóver, take C. Armas, the main street with many name changes downhill and through the gates (Puertas de Bisagra); the office is across the intersection (15min.). From the train station, turn right and take the busy right-hand fork across the bridge (Puente de Azarquiel); follow the city walls until reaching the plaza. The office is across the road, outside the walls. Open M-F 9am-7pm (off-season until 6pm), Sa 9am-7pm, Su 9am-3pm.

Emergency: 092.

Police: Local police, Avda. Portugal (tel. 925 21 34 00).

Internet Access: Scorpions, on Pintor Matías Moreno, next to Monasterio San Juan de los Reyes. 100ptas per 7min. Open M-F 10am-2:30am, Sa-Su noon-2:30am.

Post Office: C. Plata 1 (tel. 925 22 36 11), off Pl. Zocodóver via C. Comercio and then C. Toledo. All services, including Lista de Correos. Open M-F 8:30am-9pm, Sa 9am-2pm. **Postal Code:** 45070.

ACCOMMODATIONS, CAMPING, AND FOOD

Finding a bed during the summer, especially on weekends, can be a hassle. The tourist office provides an invaluable list of hotels, *hostales,* and *pensiones*.

Residencia Juvenil San Servando (HI), Castillo San Servando (tel. 925 22 45 54). From the train station, cross the street, turn left, then immediately right up Callejón del Hospital. When the steps reach a road, turn right, then right again following the signs to Hospital Provincial (10min.). Not the 14th-century castle—the annex. If alone at night, take a cab. 1100ptas, over 26 1350ptas. Reception 7am-11:50pm. Curfew 11:50pm. No reservations. Closed various times during the year; call ahead.

Pensión Nuncio Viejo, C. Nuncio Viejo 19, 3rd fl. (tel. 925 22 81 78), on a street leading off the cathedral. Rooms are a bit cramped and dim, but your new mom is a great cook. Singles 1300ptas; doubles 2900ptas, with bath 3200ptas. Breakfast 225ptas. Lunch and dinner 850ptas each.

Pensión Castilla, C. Recoletos 6 (tel. 925 25 63 18) up an alley off C. Armas. Comfortable and spacious doubles make you feel right at home, as does owner Teresa. Singles 2200ptas; doubles with bath 3900ptas.

Pensión Descalzos, C. Descalzos 30 (tel. 925 22 28 88), down the steps off Po. San Cristóbal or down the Bajada Descalzos near the Casa del Greco. Singles 2500ptas; doubles 3500ptas, with bath or shower 5600ptas; triples with bath 7290ptas. Low season: 2200ptas; 3200ptas; 5400ptas; 7560ptas. Closed Feb.

La Belviseña, Cuesta del Can 5 (tel. 925 22 00 67). From the Zocodóver, walk down the Cuesta Carlos V (a.k.a. Cuesta del Alcázar), past the Alcázar and through the small plaza beyond. Take C. Gran Moscardo—the street left of the hotel—and turn right on C. Soledad. Veer right and go left on C. San Miguel until you get to C. San Justo. Turn left and go uphill. Cuesta del Can is on the right. The cheapest *pensión* in Toledo. The Ritz it's not, but still clean. Singles 1200ptas; doubles 2300ptas.

Camping: Camping El Greco (tel. 925 22 00 90), 1½km from town on the road away from Madrid (C-502). Bus 7 (from Pl. Zocodóver) stops at the entrance. Wooded and shady first-class site between the Tajo and an olive grove. 575ptas per person (children 475ptas), 590ptas per tent, 550ptas per car. 7% IVA not included.

Toledo grinds almonds into marzipan delights of every shape and size, from colorful fruity nuggets to half-moon cookies. If the pocket allows, dining out in Toledo could be an ecstatic culinary experience; *menús* hover between 1400 and 1600ptas. Regional specialties include *perdiz* (fowl), *venado* (venison), and *carcamusas* (mystery meat). Near the cathedral, the vegetarian-friendly **Restaurante Armiño,** C. Tendillas 8, serves Spanish *menús* for lunch (875ptas) and Italian specialties for dinner (750-900ptas; open daily 1-5pm and 8pm-midnight). **Restaurante El Zoco,** C. Bacrio Rey 1, is reasonably priced and attractive (*menú* 800-1500ptas; open daily 1:30-4pm and 8-10:30pm). Pick up groceries at **Frutería-Pan,** C. Real Arrabal, opposite the tourist office (open M-F 9am-10pm), or try the **market** in Pl. Mayor, behind the cathedral (M-Sa 8:30am-2pm).

SIGHTS AND ENTERTAINMENT

South and uphill from Pl. Zocodóver is the **Alcázar,** Toledo's most formidable landmark. The site was a stronghold of Visigoths, Muslims, and Christians, each rebuilding it in their own style. Little remains of the 16th-century structure built by Carlos V; the building was largely reduced to rubble during the Civil War, as besieged Fascist troops held out against heavy Republican bombardment. Don't miss the room where the father-son drama of the Moscardós took place. You can also visit the dark, windowless basement refuge where over 500 civilians hid during the siege (open Tu-Su 10am-2pm; 125ptas, W free for EU citizens). To the west, the grandiose **cathedral,** with five naves, delicate stained glass, and ostentation throughout, soars from the city center. Noteworthy features of the cathedral include the 14th-century Gothic *Virgen Blanca* (White Virgin) by the entrance, and above all, Narciso Tomés's 1732 *Transparente,* a whirlpool of Spanish Baroque architecture, sculpture, and painting. The **Sacristía** hoards 18 El Grecos and two Van Dycks. (Cathedral open July-Aug. M-Sa 10:30am-1pm and 3:30-7pm, Su 10am-1:30pm and 4-7pm; Sept.-June closes 1hr. earlier. 500ptas; buy tickets at the store opposite the entrance.)

El Greco, the artist formerly known as Domenico Theotocopuli, lived most of his life in Toledo, and locales throughout town display his work. On the west side of town, the **Iglesia de San Tomé** houses El Greco's amazing *El entierro del Conde de Orgaz.* (The Burial of Count Orgaz. Open Tu-Sa 10am-6:45pm. 150ptas.) Downhill and to the left, there's also the **Casa Museo de El Greco,** C. Levi 3. This oddly arranged museum has 19 works of El Greco, including a copy of the *Vista y plano de Toledo.* (Landscape of Toledo. Open Tu-Sa 10am-2pm and 4-6pm, Su 10am-2pm. Admission 200ptas, students free. Sa afternoons and Su free.)

Two synagogues, both in the **Old Jewish Quarter** on the west side, are all that remain of what was once Spain's largest Jewish community. The 1366 **Sinagoga del Tránsito** is a simple building with Mudéjar plasterwork and an intricately designed wood ceiling. Inside, the **Museo Sefardí** is packed with artifacts including a *torá.* (Open Tu-Sa 10am-1:45pm and 4-5:45pm, Su 10am-1:45pm. 400ptas, students 200ptas; Sa after 4pm and Su free.) Built in 1180, the **Sinagoga de Santa María la Blanca,** down the street, was originally meant to be a mosque, but was then purchased by Jews, used as the city's principle synagogue, and was converted into a church in 1492 (open daily 10am-1:45pm and 3:45-5:45pm; 150ptas). At the far western edge of the city stands the Franciscan **Iglesia de San Juan de los Reyes,** a bright cloister with views of the surrounding hills. (Open daily 10am-1:45pm and 2:30-6:45pm. Closes an hour earlier in winter. 150ptas.)

Toledo loves **Corpus Christi,** celebrated the eighth Sunday after Easter. During the rest of the year, nightlife thrives at **Calle de Santa Fe,** east of Pl. Zocodóver (through the arch) and **Calle de la Sillería** and **Calle de los Alfileritos,** both west of Pl. Zocodóver. **Zaida,** in the Centro Comercial Miradero, downhill from Pl. Zocodóver, is a hotspot for dancing.

■ Cuenca

Perched atop a hill, tall Cuenca overlooks the two rivers that confine it and the stunning rock formations they created. The enchanting old city safeguards Cuenca's **casas colgadas** (hanging houses). Down C. Obispo, they dangle over the riverbanks as precariously today as they did six centuries ago. Inside one of the *casas* at Pl. Ciudad de Ronda, the **Museo de Arte Abstracto Español** displays important works by recent Spanish artists. (Open M-F 11am-2pm and 4-6pm, Sa 11am-2pm and 4-8pm, Su 11am-2:30pm. 500ptas, students 250ptas.) Down C. Obispo Valero, the **Museo de Cuenca** is a treasure-trove of archeological finds, including Visigoth jewelry (open Tu-Sa 9am-2pm and 4-6pm, Su 11am-2pm; 200ptas, students 100ptas). Perhaps the most beautiful of the museums along this short street is the **Museo Diocesano.** Exhibits are imaginatively displayed and include Juan de Borgoña's *retablo* from local Convento de San Pablo and two El Grecos. (Open Tu-F 11am-2pm and 4-6pm, Sa 11am-2pm and 4-8pm, Su 11am-2pm. 200ptas.) Cuenca's **cathedral** is the only Anglo-Norman Gothic cathedral in Spain. A 1724 fire cut short the latest attempt to build a front, leaving the current exterior incomplete. (Open daily in summer 10:30am-2pm and 5-8pm; off-season 10:30am-2pm and 4-6pm. Free.)

Trains chug from Po. del Ferrocarril (tel. 969 22 07 20) to Madrid (2½-3hr., 1355ptas) and Valencia (2¾-3¾hr., 1490ptas). **Buses** roll from C. Fermín Caballero 20 (tel. 969 22 70 87), down the street from the train station, to Madrid (2½hr., 1305-1600ptas) and Toledo (3hr., M-F at 5:30am, 1600ptas). To get to **Plaza Mayor** in the old city from either station, go left until you hit the first bus shelter and take bus 1 or 2 to the last stop (80ptas). The **Municipal Tourist Office,** Plaza Mayor 1 (tel. 969 23 21 19), has maps, listings of accommodations, and hiking and excursion routes (open daily 9:30am-2pm and 4-6pm). Cheap, adequate rooms collect in the new city, while rooms on the hill exact a bit more money. **Hostal-Residencia Posada de San José,** C. Julián Romero 4 (tel. 969 21 13 00; fax 969 23 03 65), just up the street from the cathedral, gives deluxe treatment with cushy beds, historic echoes, and gorgeous views. (Singles 2600ptas, with shower 4300ptas; doubles 4300-8400ptas; triples 5800-11,000ptas; prices may vary. Reserve 2-3 weeks in advance.) **Pensión Cuenca,** Av. República Argentina 8, 2nd floor (tel. 969 21 25 74), along Hurtado de Mendoza from the train or bus station (singles 1600-1900ptas; doubles 2300-3500ptas), and **Pensión Central,** C. Alonso Chirino 7, 2nd floor (tel. 969 21 15 11), off C. Carretería (singles 1400ptas; doubles 2100-2500ptas; triples 3450ptas), provide comfortable accommodations at good prices. Budget eateries line **C. Cervantes** and **C. República Argentina.** A former convent, **Posada de San José,** C. Julian Romero 4, boasts spectacular views and delicious regional *tapas* (open Tu-Su 6-10:30pm).

■ Segovia

Segovia represents Castile at its best—a magnificent castle, an impressive cathedral, and twisting alleyways filled with the aromas of *sopa castellano* and *cochinillo asado* (roast suckling pig).

SIGHTS AND ENTERTAINMENT The **acueducto romano** is constructed out of some 200,000 blocks of granite—without any mortar to hold them together. View it at its maximum height (28.9m) from Plaza del Azoguejo, or catch its profile from the steps on the left side of the plaza. Amazingly, the Romans' feat of engineering, restored by the monarchy in the 15th century, was still in use 50 years ago.

The **Alcázar,** an archetypal late-medieval castle and site of Isabel's coronation in 1474, occupies the north end of the old quarter. The castle is filled with trappings of its bloody, royal past. The **Sala de Armas** holds a veritable arsenal of medieval weaponry, while the **Sala de Reyes** is adorned with wood and gold inlay sculptures of the monarchs of Asturias, Castilla, and León. (Alcázar open daily Apr.-Sept. 10am-7pm; Oct.-Mar. 10am-6pm. 375ptas, seniors 250ptas.) Commissioned by Carlos I in 1525, the **cathedral** towers above Pl. Mayor in the center of town. Inside, the **Sala Capitu-**

lar (chapter house), hung with well-preserved tapestries, displays a silver and gold chariot and various crucifixes and chalices. The **museum** collection includes Coello's *La duda de Santo Tomás,* and a series of Francisco de Solis's 17th-century paintings on marble depicting the Passion of Christ (open daily Apr.-Oct. 9:15am-6:45pm; Nov.-Mar. 9:30am-5:45pm; 250ptas).

Pl. Mayor and its tributaries reign at night, crammed with **cafes** and **bars.** Pl. Azoguejo and C. Carmen, down near the aqueduct, are filled with bars as well; for **clubs,** head to C. de Ruiz de Alda, off Pl. Azoguejo.

PRACTICAL INFO, ACCOMMODATIONS, AND FOOD Rail lines to Segovia are limited, but **trains** do run frequently from the station on Po. Obispo Quesada to Madrid (2hr., 9 per day, 765ptas). From Po. Ezequiel González 12, **buses** trek to Ávila (1hr., 555ptas), Madrid (2hr., 765ptas), and Salamanca (3hr., 1245ptas). The helpful **municipal tourist office,** Pl. Mayor 10 (tel 921 46 03 34), is in front of the bus stop, on the corner opposite the cathedral (open daily 10am-2pm and 5-8pm).

During the summer, finding an *hostal* room can be a nightmare; book ahead and be prepared to pay at least 2500ptas. The **regional tourist office,** Pl. Azoguejo 1 (tel. 921 44 03 02), has lists of accommodations (open daily 10am-8pm). The **Residencia Juvenil "Emperador Teodosio" (HI),** Av. Conde de Sepúlveda (tel. 921 44 11 11 or 921 44 10 47), is only open to travelers in July and August, when its hotel-like doubles and triples, all with private baths, make it extremely popular. From the bus station, turn right on C. Ezequiel González, which becomes Av. Conde Sepúlveda (1450ptas, under 26 1000ptas). **Hostal Juan Bravo,** C. Juan Bravo 12, 2nd fl. (tel. 921 46 34 13), on the main thoroughfare in the old town, has bright rooms that stay cool in the summer (doubles 3800-4800ptas; triples 5000-6500ptas). Centrally located **Pensión Ferri,** C. Escuderos 10 (tel. 921 46 09 57), off Pl. Mayor, has clean rooms (singles 1350ptas; doubles 2300ptas; showers 300ptas). **Camping Acueducto,** Ctra. Nacional 601, km 112 (tel. 921 42 50 00), 2km toward La Granja, is an adequate site in the shadow of the Sierra de Guadarrama. Take the Autobus Urbano from Pl. Azoguejo to Nueva Segovia (500ptas per person and per tent).

Segovia is famed for sublimely tender roast suckling pig *(cochinillo asado)* and lamb, but steer clear of pricey Pl. Mayor and Pl. Azoguejo. **Bar-Mesón Cueva de San Estéban,** Valdeláguila 15, off Pl. San Estéban and C. Escuderos, serves a 900ptas *menú* (open daily 10am-midnight).

■ Near Segovia: La Granja de San Ildefonso

The royal palace and grounds of **La Granja,** 9km southeast of Segovia, were commissioned by Felipe V, the first Bourbon King in Spain, who detested the Hapsburgs' austere El Escorial. The "Versailles of Spain," La Granja was one of four royal summer retreats (with El Pardo, El Escorial, and Aranjuez), and far and away the most extravagant. Marble, lace curtains, and lavish crystal chandeliers (made in San Ildefonso's renowned crystal factory) liven up the palace. (Open June-Sept. Tu-Su 10am-6pm; Oct.-Mar. Tu-Sa 10am-1:30pm and 3-5pm, Su 10am-2pm; Apr.-May Tu-F 10am-1:30pm and 3-5pm, Sa-Su 10am-6pm. 650ptas, students 250ptas, W free for EU citizens.) Frequent **buses** arrive at La Granja from Segovia (20min., 200ptas round-trip).

■ Ávila

The walled city of Ávila revives nostalgia for medieval times, when crowds gathered around *juglares* listening to epic verses like *El Cid,* and chivalry reigned. Less crowded and touristy than Toledo or Cuenca, Ávila offers nearly as many sights and keeps cool on its rocky escarpment in the summer while the plain swelters below.

SIGHTS AND ENTERTAINMENT Construction of the **murallas medievales,** the oldest and best preserved medieval walls in Spain, began in 1090. Eighty-two massive towers reinforce the 3m thick *murallas.* To walk on the walls, head to Puerta del Alcázar. (Open in summer Tu-Su 11am-1:30pm and 5-7:30pm; off-season Tu-Su

10:30am-3:30pm. 200ptas.) Some believe that the profile of the **cathedral** looming over the watchtowers inspired St. Teresa's metaphor of the soul as a diamond castle. Begun in the late 12th century, the cathedral participated in Ávila's defense system and recalls the turbulent centuries of the *Reconquista.* (Cathedral open daily Apr.-Oct. 10am-1pm and 3:30-6pm; Nov.-Mar. 10am-1:30pm and 3:30-5:30pm. 250ptas.)

St. Teresa's admirers built the 17th-century **Convento de Santa Teresa** on the site of her childhood home. Next door, the **Sala de Reliquias** holds relics, including her right ring finger, the sole of her sandal, and her flagellation cord. (Church open daily May-Sept. 9:30am-1:30pm and 3:30-9pm; Oct.-Apr. 9:30am-1:30pm and 3:30-8:30pm. Sala de Reliquias open daily 9:30am-1:30pm and 3:30-7:30pm. Free.) Most of St. Teresa's mystical experiences took place during the 30 years she spent in the **Monasterio de la Encarnación,** a short distance outside the city walls. The mandatory guided tour (in Spanish, 10-15min.) visits her tiny cell. (Open daily in summer 10am-1pm and 4-7pm; off-season 10am-1pm and 3:30-6pm. 150ptas.)

PRACTICAL INFO, ACCOMMODATIONS, AND FOOD Trains leave the station at Av. José Antonio (tel. 920 25 02 02), for Madrid (2hr., 835-1500ptas) and Villalba, for transfer to Salamanca (2hr., 835ptas) and Segovia (1hr., 980ptas). To reach Pl. Santa Teresa from the train station, follow Av. José Antonio to C. Isaac Peral, which leads to C. Duque de Alba; turn left and continue. The **bus station,** Av. Madrid 2 (tel. 920 22 01 54), on the northeast side of town, serves Madrid (1½hr., 910ptas), Salamanca (1½hr., 700ptas), and Segovia (1hr., 555ptas). To reach Pl. Santa Teresa from the station, cross the street and walk down C. Duque de Alba. Ávila's **tourist office** is at Pl. Catedral 4 (tel. 920 21 13 87); from Pl. Santa Teresa, walk through the main gate and turn right at C. Alemania (open daily 10am-2pm and 4-7pm).

Lodgings in Ávila are plentiful and reasonably priced. Attractive, comfortable **Pensión Continental,** Pl. Catedral 6 (tel. 920 21 15 02; fax 25 16 91), is right next to the tourist office. (Singles 2200ptas; doubles 3700-4500ptas; triples 5500-6700ptas. 7% IVA not included.) **Pensión Santa Ana,** C. Alfonso Montalvo 2 (tel. 920 22 00 63), has spacious rooms (singles 2500ptas; doubles 4000ptas; triples 4500ptas).

The city has won fame for its *ternera de Ávila* (veal) and *mollejas* (sweetbread). The *yemas de Santa Teresa* or *yemas de Ávila,* local confections made of egg yolks and honey, and *vino de Cebreros,* a smooth regional wine, are also delectable. Every Friday (10am-2pm), a **market** in Pl. Victoria sells foodstuffs at low prices. **Plaza de la Victoria** is a center of budget dining. **Restaurante El Grande,** Pl. Santa Teresa 8, is a big, popular family-style restaurant with outdoor seating on the plaza (*raciones* 375-800ptas; *menú* 1250ptas; open noon-4pm and 8pm-midnight).

■ Salamanca

For centuries the "hand of Salamanca," the brass knocker on the doors of the city, has welcomed students, scholars, rogues, royals, and saints. Bustling Salamanca is famed for its 13th-century university—the oldest in Spain—and for its architecture of warm golden sandstone.

SIGHTS AND ENTERTAINMENT Nowhere is Salamanca's architectural fame more apparent than in **Plaza Mayor,** in which all styles—Roman, Gothic, Renaissance, and Baroque—are carved out of the characteristic stone. Between the almost 100 arches hang medallions with bas-reliefs of famous Spaniards, from El Cid to Franco. The 15th-century **Casa de las Conchas** (House of Shells) is adorned by rows of scallop shells chiseled in sandstone. The house is now a public library, but the courtyard is open to tourists (open M-F 9am-9pm, Sa 9am-2pm and 4-7pm, Su 10am-2pm and 4-7pm; free). Enter the **Universidad,** founded in 1218, from the Patio de las Escuelas, off C. Libreros. The university's **entryway** is one of the best examples of Spanish Plateresque, a style named for the filigree work of *plateros* (silversmiths). The smallish frog carved on a skull is said to represent the dankness of prison life and to bring good luck on exams. If you spot the frog without help, you'll be married within the year.

The walls are marked by students' initials in bold red, painted in an ink of bull's blood, olive oil, and herbs. Inside the **Escuelas Menores,** the *Cielo de Salamanca,* a 15th-century fresco of the zodiac, is preserved in the **University Museum.** (Open M-F 9:30am-1:30pm and 4-7:30pm, Sa 9:30am-1:30pm and 4-7pm, Su 10am-1:30pm.)

Follow Rua Mayor south from Pl. Mayor; the *vieja* (old) and *nueva* (new) cathedrals sit together just past Pl. Anaya. Begun in 1513 to accommodate the growing tide of Catholics, the spindly spires of the Late Gothic **Catedral Nueva** weren't finished until 1733. The Romanesque **Catedral Vieja** (1140) has a striking cupola with depictions of apocalyptic angels separating the sinners from the saved. The cathedral **museum** houses a Mudéjar Salinas organ, one of the oldest organs in Europe. (Cathedrals open daily Apr.-Sept. 9am-2pm and 4-8pm; Oct.-Mar. 9am-1pm and 4-6pm. *Vieja,* cloister, and museum 300ptas. *Nueva* free.)

Lugares, a free pamphlet at the tourist office and some bars, lists everything from movies to bus schedules. **Plaza Mayor** is the social center of town; people overflow from the plaza as far west as San Vicente. Student nightlife also concentrates on **Calle Bordadores,** the **Gran Vía,** and side streets. **Camelot,** C. Bordedores 3, is a monastery-turned-club, packed with converts looking to be defrocked. **El Corrillo Cafe,** C. Meléndez 14-18, has live jazz for the ultra-hip in a neon setting (cover 1000ptas for performances). For a more relaxed setting, **Birdland,** C. Azafranal 57, by Pl. España, has jazz greats. A gay and straight clientele grooves under black lights at **Submarino,** C. San Justo 27, built in an old submarine.

PRACTICAL INFO, ACCOMMODATIONS, AND FOOD Most sights and budget accommodations lie south of the central **Plaza Mayor. Trains** chug from Po. Estación Ferrocarril (tel. 923 12 02 02) to Ávila (2hr., 835ptas), Barcelona (11½hr., 6000ptas), Madrid (3½hr., 1625ptas), and the transportation hub Valladolid (1400ptas). **Buses** run to Ávila (1-2hr., 820ptas), Madrid (2½-3hr., 2210-2690ptas), León (3hr., 1675ptas), and Segovia (3hr., 1245ptas). To get to the city center from the train station, catch bus 1; from the bus station, take bus 4. Both buses go to Gran Vía, a block from Pl. Mercado (next to Pl. Mayor). The helpful **tourist office** is at Pl. Mayor 14. (Tel. 923 21 83 42. Open M-Sa 9:30am-2pm and 4:30-6:30pm, Su 10am-2pm and 4:30-6:30pm.) During the summer, students sometimes offer maps and accommodations listings at **information booths** in Plaza Anaya and both stations.

The abundance of students means many rooms. Cheap *pensiones* abound on the side streets off Pl. Mayor, especially on **Calle Meléndez,** just south of the plaza. One of the best bargains for *duo* travelers, **Pensión Marina,** C. Doctrinos 4, 3rd fl. (tel. 923 21 65 69), between C. Compañía and C. Prado, boasts mammoth TV lounges (doubles 2700ptas; showers 200ptas). **Pensión Las Vegas,** C. Meléndez 13 (tel. 923 21 87 49), has comfy beds and lots of plants. (Singles 1300-1500ptas; doubles 2500-3000ptas; triples 4000-4500ptas. Showers 150ptas.) For camping, head 4km toward Madrid to reach **Regio** (tel. 923 13 88 88), on the Ctra. Salamanca (425ptas per person, 375-425ptas per tent).

Every clique has its favorite cafe in Plaza Mayor; each hangout serves the same moderately good food at a standard, slightly inflated price. A slew of bar-restaurants line the streets between the plaza and the university, where a full meal costs no more than 1000ptas. **Restaurante El Bardo,** C. Compañía 8, between the Casa de Conchas and the Clerecía, is a traditional Spanish restaurant with a lively bar downstairs (main courses 1000-1800ptas; open daily 10am-5pm and 7pm-1am). **Pans & Company,** C. Rua Mayor 26, will teach you the Spanish word for "fast food" as you chow down on their tasty *bocadillos,* including some vegetarian (395-485ptas). **Simago,** C. Toro 82, has a downstairs **supermarket** (open M-Sa 9:30am-8:30pm).

■ Near Salamanca: Ciudad Rodrigo and Mérida

A medieval town characterized by fabulous masonry and honey-colored stone, **Ciudad Rodrigo** rises from the plains near the Portuguese border. The **cathedral** is the town's masterpiece. The cloister alone, with biblical and mythological scenes illustrated in intricate stonework, justifies the trip from Salamanca. Fascinating figures festoon the columns—making love, playing peek-a-boo, or nibbling body parts. The cathedral's **museum** is filled with strange and thrilling old pieces, including an ancient clavichord, the ornate "ballot box" used to determine the cathedral's hierarchy, and Velázquez's *Llanto de Adam y Eva por Ariel muerto*. (Cathedral open daily 9:30am-1:30pm and 4-8pm. Free. Cloister and museum open daily 10am-1pm and 4-6pm. 200ptas. Mandatory guided tour in Spanish.) Eight **buses** per day (3-5 on weekends) arrive from Salamanca (1¼hr., 715ptas).

Mérida, with the most Roman ruins in all of Spain, merits a trip to its aquaducts, hippodrome, arena, amphitheater, and world-class **Museo Romano.** (On C.P.M. Plano. Open daily 10am-2pm; in summer also Tu-Sa 5-7pm; in winter also Tu-Sa 4-6pm. 400ptas, students 200ptas, Sa afternoon and Su free.) Over the wide, shallow Río Gaudiana, the **Puente Romano** is still the main entrance to town. Most monuments are free on Saturday afternoons and Sunday mornings; otherwise buy a combined ticket (750ptas, EU students 375ptas) to visit the 6000-seat **Teatro Romano** and the 16,000-seat **Anfiteatro Romano,** as well as the Moorish fortress **Alcazaba.** Four **buses** per day run from Mérida to Salamanca (5hr., 2320ptas).

■ León

The blue stained-glass windows of León's cathedral have earned the city the nickname *La Ciudad Azul* (the Blue City). But you won't catch the inhabitants of this lively, friendly town singing the blues; rather, the *leonses* (literally, "lions") exude a fierce local pride.

SIGHTS AND ENTERTAINMENT The 13th-century Gothic **cathedral,** La Pulchra Leonina, is arguably the most beautiful in Spain (open daily 8:30am-1:30pm and 4-8pm; 700ptas). Its stained-glass windows alone will justify your trip to León. The cathedral's **museo** includes gruesome Renaissance wonders. (Open M-F 9:30am-2pm and 4-7:30pm, Sa 9:30am-2pm; off-season closes 30min. earlier. 450ptas.) The **Basílica de San Isidoro** was dedicated in the 11th century to San Isidoro of Sevilla, whose remains were brought to León while Muslims ruled the south. The corpses of León's royal family rest in the **Panteón Real,** whose ceilings are covered with vibrant frescoes. (Open daily July-Aug. 9am-2pm and 3-8pm; Sept.-June 10am-1:30pm and 4-6:30pm. 350ptas.) The **Museo de León,** Pl. San Marcos, holds an extensive archaeological collection with pieces dating from the Paleolithic era. (Open Tu-Sa 10am-2pm and 5-8:30pm, Su 10am-2pm. 200ptas, students, seniors, and weekends free.)

For the "early" part of the night, the *barrio húmedo* (drinker's neighborhood) around **Plaza San Martín** sweats with bars, discos, and techno-pop. After 2am, the crowds stagger to **Calles Lancia** and **Conde de Guillén,** both heavily populated with discos and bars. **Fiestas** commemorating St. John and St. Peter enliven a week-long celebration (June 21-30) including a *corrida de toros* (bullfight).

PRACTICAL INFO, ACCOMMODATIONS, AND FOOD **Trains** leave from Av. Astorga 2 (info tel. (987) 27 02 02), across the river from Pl. Guzmán el Bueno, for La Coruña (7hr., 3200-4400ptas), Madrid (4½-5½hr., 3190-3500ptas), and other locales. The ticket office is at C. Carmen 4 (tel. (987) 22 05 25). **Buses** (tel. (987) 21 10 00) depart from the Estación de Autobuses, Po. Ingeniero Saenz de Miera, for Madrid (4½hr., 2550ptas). León's **tourist office** is at Pl. Regla 3 (tel. (987) 23 70 82; fax 27 33 91), in front of the cathedral. (Open M-F 10am-2pm and 5-7:30pm, Sa 10am-2pm and 4:30-8:30pm, Su 10am-2pm.) For lodging, look on Av. Roma, Av. Ordoño II, and Av. República Argentina, which lead into the new town from Pl. Guzmán el Bueno. The **Consejo de Europa (HI),** Po. Parque 2 (tel. (987) 20 02 06), behind Pl. Toros, was recently renovated. (Dorms 850ptas, over 26 1000ptas. Breakfast 300ptas. Open late June to Aug. Call ahead.) The chatty proprietors of **Hostal Oviedo,** Av. Roma 26, 2nd fl. (tel. (987) 22 22 36), offer huge rooms, many with sinks and terraces (singles 1900ptas; doubles 3000ptas; triples 4500ptas). The spotless **Condado,** Av. República

SPAIN

Argentina 28 (tel. (987) 20 61 60), has airy rooms in shades of brown and red (singles 1500-1800ptas; doubles 2000-2400ptas; showers 250ptas).

Eateries cluster by the cathedral, on the small streets off Av. Generalísimo Franco, and at Pl. San Martín near Pl. Mayor. Gourmet and vegetarian dishes abound at **Calle Ancha,** C. Generalísimo Franco, between C. General Mola and C. Conde Luna (*menú* 900ptas; open daily 8am-1:30am). The **Cafetería-Restaurante Catedral,** by the cathedral at C. Mariano Dominguez Berrueta 17, serves monumental portions (*menú* 1100ptas; open daily 1-4pm and 8-11pm, closed Tu and W afternoon). **Lleras, 38,** C. Burgos Nuevo, is a jazzy restaurant with a 1050ptas *menú* (open daily 1-5pm and after 8pm). You can also find fresh produce at **Mercado Municipal del Conde,** Pl. Conde, off C. General Mola (open M-Sa 9am-3:30pm).

■ Burgos

Despite its small size, the chestnut-colored city of Burgos has figured prominently in Spain's history, first through the exploits of native son Rodrigo Díaz de Vivar (El Cid) and later as the capital of the Castile kingdom in the 15th century. The hard-line politics that justified El Cid's expulsion were revived in the 20th century when General Franco stationed his Nationalist headquarters here during the Civil War, but today the city hosts international brigades of pilgrims and enjoys peaceful riverside games, a nightly *paseo,* and a Bacchanalian nightlife invigorated by the university.

SIGHTS AND ENTERTAINMENT The magnificent **cathedral** dominates the city (open daily 9:30am-1pm and 4-7pm; 400ptas, students 200ptas). The 13th-century Gothic north facade is stark in comparison to the intricate 15th-century towers and 16th-century *Puerta de la Pellejería.* Beneath the glass skylight of the **Capilla Mayor,** El Cid's bones and those of his wife Jimena commingle serenely. Before leaving the cathedral, look for the fly catcher high up near the main door. As the hour strikes, the strange creature imitates the gawking crowds below. The ruins of a **medieval castle** crown the hilltop behind the cathedral. If you're not already panting from the climb, the view will take your breath away.

After the cathedral, the **Estatua del Cid** in Pl. General Primo de Rivera is Burgos's most venerated landmark. El Cid won his fame in battle against the Moors, and the medieval poem celebrating his life, *Cantar de Mío Cid,* is considered the first great work in the Castilian language. Burgos tradition compels its youth to climb the statue and fondle the testicles of El Cid's horse to ensure their own strength, courage, and fame. Just up C. Santander on the other side of the statue, the restored **Casa del Cordón,** where Columbus met Ferdinand and Isabel after his second trip to America, glows in the sunshine. Nearby, the **Museo de Pintura Marceliano Santa María** (a.k.a. the **Monasterio de San Juan**) features landscapes and portraits by Marceliano Santa María, a 20th-century local artist (open Tu-Sa 10am-2pm and 5-8pm, Su 10am-2pm; closed holidays; free).

After dinner, bars on C. San Juan and C. Puebla fill up with merrymakers aiming for an early start (try **Marmedi** on C. Puebla). By 11pm a steady hum rises up from **La Pécora,** where startling numbers of teenagers swarm. When the "early" bars close at 4 or 5am, head to **Las Bernardas,** the general area circumscribed by C. Las Calzadas, C. Belorado, and Av. General Yagüe, for "la penúltima"—the perpetual second-to-last drink. During the last week of June, Burgos celebrates its patron saints Peter and Paul with concerts, parades, fireworks, bullfights, and dances.

PRACTICAL INFO, ACCOMMODATIONS, AND FOOD Burgos, 240km north of Madrid, is divided by Río Arlanzón. The train and bus stations are on the south side, while the cathedral and sights are to the north. **Trains** (tel. 947 20 35 60) roll into the station at the end of Av. Conde Guadalhorce, across the river from Pl. Castilla, from Barcelona (8hr., 4800ptas), Madrid (3½hr., 2945ptas), San Sebastián (4hr., 2180ptas), and Santiago (8hr., 4500ptas). **RENFE,** C. Moneda 21 (tel. 947 20 91 31), sells tickets. **Buses** leave C. Miranda 4 (tel. 947 28 88 55), just off Pl. Vega, to Barcelona (7½hr.,

4960ptas), Madrid (3hr., 1920ptas), and Pamplona (3½hr., 1900ptas). From the train or bus station, reach the **tourist office,** Pl. Alonso Martínez 7 (tel. 947 20 31 25), next to the Capitanía General building, by crossing the river, turning right onto Av. del Generalísimo Franco (which becomes Paseo del Espolón), then following C. Santander (open M-F 9am-2pm and 5-7pm, Sa-Su and holidays 10am-2pm and 5-8pm).

Reservations are crucial during late June and early July. Scout the streets near **Plaza Alonso Martínez** and **Calle San Juan** for a room. **Pensión Peña,** C. Puebla 18 (tel. 947 20 63 23), has small, elegant rooms (singles 1500-1600ptas; doubles 2700-2800ptas). **Hostal Victoria,** C. San Juan 3 (tel. 947 20 15 42), has simple rooms with sinks (singles 2300ptas; doubles 3500ptas; triples 4500ptas; quads 6000ptas). A dim stairway leads to the warm and friendly **Hostal Hidalgo,** C. Almirante Bonifaz 14 (tel. 947 20 34 81), off C. San Juan (singles 1800ptas; doubles 3200ptas; triples 4500ptas; quads 6000ptas). Vegetarians take heed—Burgos specializes in meat, meat, and more meat. **Gaia Comedor Vegetariano,** C. San Francisco 31, serves gazpacho in a New Age atmosphere (open M-F 1:30-4pm). **La Riojana,** C. Arellanos 10, is a haven for the famished (*menú* 900ptas; open daily noon-1am). **Mercado de Abastos (Norte),** near Pl. España, and **Mercado de Abastos (Sur),** on C. Miranda near the bus station, have pungent market wares (open M-Sa 7am-3pm; Mercado Norte also F 5:30-8pm).

▓ Úbeda

Fifteen minutes from Baeza and two hours from Granada and Córdoba, the cobbled streets of Úbeda's monumental district dip between ivy-covered medieval walls and venerable churches and palaces. The **Hospital de Santiago** lists cultural events and houses a modern art museum (museum open M-F 8am-3pm and 3:30-10pm, Sa 8am-3pm; 225ptas). The **barrio antiguo** (ancient quarter), stretching downhill from Pl. Andalucía and centered at the **Plaza Vázquez de Molina,** holds well-preserved Spanish Renaissance architecture. Two stone lions guard the **Palacio de las Cadenas,** now the city hall, and across the pathway is the Gothic **Colegiata de Santa María de los Reales Alcázares,** whose chapels are embellished by wrought iron grilles. The **Sacra Capilla del Salvador** sits at the far end of the plaza (open M-F 6-7pm; free). Uphill, the **Museo Arqueológico,** C. Cervantes 6, narrates Úbeda's history through prehistoric, Roman, Moorish, and Castillian times (open Tu-Sa 10am-2pm, 4-7pm; free). A walk all the way downhill leads to a stunning view of the olive-laden **Guadalquivir valley** and the ruins of the **muralla,** a "wall of God" built by the Moors.

There is no train service to Úbeda; the nearest station is **Estación Linares-Baeza** (tel. 953 65 02 02). **Buses** leave from C. San José 6 (tel. 953 75 21 57) for Córdoba (2½hr., 3 per day, 1305ptas), Granada (2-3hr., 7 per day, 1400ptas), and Seville (5hr., 3 per day, 2555ptas). The **tourist office** in the **Centro Cultural Hospital de Santiago,** Obispo Cobos (tel./fax 953 75 08 97), between the bus station and Pl. Andalucía, offers a map in English (open M-F 9am-2:30pm, Sa 11am-1:30pm). The **Hostal Castillo,** Av. Ramón y Cajal 20 (tel. 953 75 04 30 or 75 12 18), has comfortable rooms and a popular bar (singles 2000-2300ptas; doubles 3000-4300ptas; add 300-400ptas in high season). Calle Rastro, leading from Pl. Andalucía, has many *terrazas* with entrees around 600ptas. **Restaurante Castillo-Victoria,** inside Hostal Castillo (see above), serves up the best deals in town (menu 1000ptas). The **market** is down C. San Fernando from Pl. Andalucía (M-Sa 7am-2:30pm).

GALICIA (GALIZA)

▓ Santiago de Compostela

Embraced by the Ríos Tambre and Ulla, Santiago was founded in 813 when, according to legend, a tomb containing the remains of the apostle St. James was found in the area. The city soon became one of Christianity's great holy sites. Many believed that the arduous journey to Santiago's glorious cathedral would halve their time in purgatory. Today, sunburnt pilgrims, street musicians, and tourists fill the granite streets, awed by Santiago's magnificence.

ORIENTATION AND PRACTICAL INFORMATION

The **cathedral** marks the center of the old city, which sits higher than the new city. Three streets lead directly to the cathedral from the south side of town, where the train station is located: **Rúa do Franco** (Calle del Franco), **Rúa do Vilar** (Calle del Vilar), and **Rúa Nova** (Calle Nueva). From the train station, turn right at the top of the stairs and take C. Hórreo to **Praza de Galiza** (do *not* take Av. de Lugo). One block ahead is **Calle Bautizatos**, from which the three cathedral-bound streets spring. From the bus station, take bus 10 to Pr. Galiza (every 15-20min., 90ptas).

Trains: R. Hórreo (tel. 981 52 02 02). Open M-Sa 7am-9pm, Su 7am-1pm. To: La Coruña (1hr., 500-575ptas), León (6½hr., 2800-3300ptas), Madrid (8hr., 4600-5600ptas), and Vigo (2hr., 750-865ptas).

Buses: Estación Central de Autobuses, C. San Cayetano (tel. 981 58 77 00). Nothing central about it, but bus 10 leaves every 20min. from the R. Montero Río side of Pr. Galiza for the station (90ptas). Info open daily 6am-10pm. **ALSA** (tel. 981 58 61 33) runs to Bilbao (9½hr., 6300ptas), Madrid (8-9hr., 5010ptas), and San Sebastián (6hr., 6910ptas). **Castromil** (tel. 981 58 90 90) serves La Coruña (1½hr., 650-820ptas) and Pontevedra (1½hr., 620ptas), among others.

Tourist Office: R. Vilar (tel. 981 58 40 81), in the old town. Open M-F 10am-2pm and 4-7pm, Sa 11am-2pm and 5-7pm, Su and festival days 11am-2pm. **Branch** in the Modernist structure in the center island of Pr. Galiza. Open M-F 10am-2pm and 5-8pm; in summer also Sa 11am-2pm.

Budget Travel: TIVE, Plazuela del Matadero (tel. 981 57 24 26). Turn right up R. Fonte Santo Antonio from Pr. Galiza. Train, bus, and plane tickets for international destinations. ISIC 700ptas. HI cards 500ptas. Open M-F 9am-2pm.

American Express: Ultratur Viajes, Av. Figueroa 6 (tel. 981 58 70 00). Open M-F 9:30am-2pm and 4:30-7pm, Sa 10am-12:30pm.

Luggage Storage: At the train station. Lockers 400ptas. Open daily 7:30am-11pm. Also at the bus station. 80ptas per bag. Open daily 8am-10pm.

Laundromat: Lavandería Lobato, C. Santiago de Chile 7 (tel. 981 59 99 54).

Emergency: tel. 091 or 092.

Police: Guardia Civil, tel. 981 58 22 66 or 981 58 16 11.

Medical Assistance: Hospital Xeral, C. Galeras (tel. 981 54 00 00).

Post Office: Travesa de Fonseca (tel. 981 58 12 52; fax 981 56 32 88), on the corner of R. Franco. Open for stamps, faxes, and *Lista de Correos* M-F 8:30am-8:30pm, Sa 9:30am-2pm. **Postal Code:** 15080.

Internet Access: Zum Zum, C. Rep. de El Salvador 28 (tel. 981 59 97 45). A friendly cybercafe in the heart of the new city. 200ptas per 30min. Open daily noon-3am.

ACCOMMODATIONS, CAMPING, AND FOOD

Hospedajes and *pensiones* multiply around **Rúa do Vilar** and **Calle Raiña,** and hand-drawn *"habitaciones"* signs are just about everywhere else.

Hospedaje Ramos, C. Raíña 18, 2nd fl. (tel. 981 58 18 59), above a restaurant. Spacious rooms in a great location. Singles 1600-1750ptas; doubles 3000-3500ptas.

Hospedaje Itatti, Pl. Mazarelos 1 (tel. 981 58 06 29). From Pr. Galiza, take a right onto R. Fonte San Antonio, then the 1st left up a diagonal granite street. Sunny doubles and sweet prices. Doubles 1150ptas, with bath 3500ptas. Call ahead.

Hospedaje Sofia, C. Cardenal Paya 16 (tel. 981 58 51 50). Enter the restaurant on the ground floor and head upstairs. Spic 'n' span rooms ensure a comfortable stay. Singles 2500ptas; doubles 3600-4000ptas; cheaper off-season.

Hospedaje Santa Cruz, R. Vilar 42, 2nd fl. (tel. 981 58 28 15). Big windows overlook the most popular street in Santiago. In summer singles 2000ptas; doubles 2500ptas. Off-season singles 1500ptas; doubles 3000ptas.

Camping: Camping As Cancelas, R. 25 de Xullo 35 (tel. 981 58 02 66), 2km from the cathedral on the north edge of town. Take bus 6 or 9. Laundry, a supermarket, and a pool on site. 475ptas per person, car, and tent. Open year-round.

Santiago is a budget diner's dream. Its open-air **market** is a sight; produce carts, meat stalls, and baskets of cheeses line the streets from Pr. San Felix to Convento de San Augustín (open M-Sa 7:30am-2pm). Most restaurants in the old town lie south of the cathedral, on **Rúa do Villar, Rúa Franco,** and **Calle Raíña.** Near the market and Pl. San Augustín, **Casa Manolo,** R. Traviesa 27, has the best deal in town (*menú* 750ptas; open M-F 1-4pm and 8pm-midnight). **Cabaliño do Demo,** R. Aller Ulloa 7, is a chic, cheery vegetarian restaurant (*menú del día* 850ptas; open daily 2-4pm and 9-12pm).

SIGHTS AND ENTERTAINMENT

The entire old town has been designated a national monument, but the centerpiece is the **cathedral.** Modern pilgrims congregate around the altar, and during mass, every candle is lit and every pew filled to bursting. The cathedral's four entrances open onto four plazas: Platerías, Quintana, Obradoiro, and Azabaxería. Consecrated in 1211, the cathedral later acquired Gothic chapels in the apse and transept, a 15th-century dome, a 16th-century cloister, and a Baroque facade called the **Obradoiro,** which sends two exquisitely ornate towers soaring above the city. Encased in the Obradoiro, the **Pórtico de la Gloria** is considered the crowning achievement of Spanish Romanesque sculpture. Inside, St. James's revered remains lie beneath the high altar in a silver coffer, while his bejeweled bust sits above. Across Pr. Obradoiro, the long facade of the former **Pazo de Raxoi** (Royal Palace) shines with gold-accented balconies and Neoclassical columns. Everything you ever wanted to know (and more) about traditional Galician living awaits at the **Museo de Pobo Gallego,** just past the Porto de Camino inside the Gothic Convento de Santo Domingo de Bonavad. (Open daily 10am-1pm and 4-7pm. 200ptas, Su free).

Santiago offers an eclectic mix of entertainment. The newspaper *El Correo Gallego* (125ptas) lists art exhibits and concert info. At night, crowds flood cellars throughout the city, and bars on **Rúas Nova, Vilar,** and **Franco** are packed all night. (Cover for men 500-800ptas; women generally free. Most open 11pm-4am; the action starts well after midnight.) From July 18 to 31, Santiago's **fiestas** enliven the city.

Pilgrims' Progress

One starry night in 813, a lonely hermit trudged through the hills on the way to his hermitage. Suddenly, bright visions revealed the long-forgotten tomb of the Apostle James ("Santiago" in Spanish). Around this *campus stellae* (Latin for "field of stars"), the cathedral of Santiago de Compostela was built. Since the 12th century, thousands (including King Ferdinand and Queen Isabella, Francis of Assisi, Pope John Paul II, and Shirley MacLaine) have traveled the 900km of the **Camino de Santiago.** Clever Benedictine monks built monasteries to host pilgrims along the *camino,* giving rise to large-scale international tourism, and making Santiago's cathedral the world's most frequented Christian shrine. The scallop-edged conch shell, used to dip water from streams on the way, has become a symbol of the Camino de Santiago; pilgrims are easily spotted by the shells tied to their backpacks and by their crook-necked walking sticks. *Peregrinos* must cover 100km on foot or horse (200km on bike) to receive an official certificate of pilgrimage completion from the cathedral. A network of shelters offers free lodging and stamps the "pilgrims' passports" which provide evidence of completion. For info and free route guides, contact the **Officinal de Acogida del Peregrino,** R. Vilar 1 (tel. 981 56 24 19), in the Casa del Deán. At 30km per day, it takes about a month to walk the entire *camino.* The year 1999 has been designated an **Año Santo** for Santiago. Various special activities will take place throughout the year, culminating on July 24, when the Pope comes to open the *puerta sacra.*

SPAIN

■ Rías Altas

If Galicia is the forgotten corner of Spain, then the small *rías* of the Costa de la Muerte are the forgotten corner of Galicia. Beaches here are arguably the emptiest, cleanest, and loveliest in all of Spain. Bus service to the smaller towns and isolated beaches is infrequent or nonexistent.

La Coruña and Environs North of Santiago, the Rías Altas stretch their watery fingers into the land from the province of Lugo down to Cabo Finisterre. In the misty mountains of Galicia the weather is anything but predictable, but views are spectacular year-round. Thanks to a healthy burst of summer tourism, the Rías Altas have modern conveniences to complement a relatively unspoiled coastline.

La Coruña, an ideal base for exploration of the region, boasts stellar nightlife, a historic old town, and pleasant beaches. **Trains** leave from Pr. San Cristóbal (tel. 981 15 02 02) for Santiago (1hr., 500-565ptas) and Vigo (3hr., 1200-1370ptas). **Buses** serve the Rías Altas and surrounding area from C. Caballeros (tel. 981 23 96 44), across Av. Alcalde Molina from the train station. Buses 1 and 1A (105ptas each) run from the train and bus stations to the tourist office. The **tourist office,** Dársena de la Marina (tel. 981 22 18 22), has tips on trips to the Rías Altas (open M-F 9am-2pm and 4:30-6:30pm, Sa 10:30am-1pm). The best place to look for a room is one block back from Avenida Marina, near the tourist office. C. Riego de Agua and the surrounding area always have rooms. **Hospedaje María Pita,** C. Riego de Agua 38, 3rd fl. (tel. 981 22 11 87), has cheery rooms and pristine bathrooms (doubles 2200-2700ptas).

The Rías Altas beckon with their relatively unspoiled coastline. Where tourists seldom tread, ferny rainforests give way to soft, empty beaches along **Rías de Cedeira** and **Viveiro.** Buses and a few FEVE trains run inland to Viveiro from El Ferrol, but the sporadic coastal bus is preferable—you can always hop off if you see a place you like.

PICOS DE EUROPA

Intrepid mountaineers, novice trekkers, and even idle admirers flock to the Picos, the most notable section of the **Cordillera Cantábrica** mountain range, which extends across northern Spain. Other European ranges may be higher, but few match the beauty of the Picos de Europa's abrupt and jagged profile.

Most trails in the Picos traverse the region's north-south axis between **Arenas de Cabrales** and **Fuente Dé.** The bus company **ALSA** and its subsidiary **Económicos** are the best way to get around. The Oviedo (tel. 985 21 33 85) and Cangas de Onís (tel. 985 84 80 05) tourist offices stock schedules. For general info on the park, contact the **Picos de Europa National Park Visitors Center,** Casa Dago, Av. Dovadonga 43, Cangas de Onís, Asturias, 33550 (tel. 985 84 86 14). Often only campers can find beds during July and August, and even this can be touch and go—many campgrounds and **refugios** (cabins with bunks but not blankets) fill up in high season. **Albergues** are ancient, non-heated buildings with bunks and access to cold water, and **casas** have hot water and wood stoves. In any case, you should bring a sleeping bag. Make reservations at *hostales* or *pensiones* in June or earlier. In a jam, tourist offices can help you find a bed in a private residence. Small towns often do not have ATM machines or supermarkets, so stock up in Oviedo. If you set off from the bus alone (not recommended), leave a copy of your planned route so a rescue squad can be alerted if you don't return or call by a certain time. Always pack **warm clothes** and **rain gear.** If a heavy mist descends *en route* (as often happens), don't continue unless you know exactly where you're going. Just be patient and wait for the mist to clear.

Cosmopolitan **Oviedo** is a good base for excursions to the Picos de Europa. **Trains** (tel. 985 24 33 64 or 985 25 02 02) run from C. Uría, at the junction with Av. Santander, to Barcelona (13hr., 6000ptas), León (2½hr., 850-1470ptas), and Madrid (6½-8hr., 4200ptas). **ALSA** sends **buses** from Pl. General Primo de Rivera 1 (tel. 985 28 12 00), unmarked, on the lower level of a shopping arcade, to Barcelona (12hr.,

4850ptas), Burgos (4hr., 1640ptas), León (2hr., 1010ptas), and Madrid (6hr., 3700-5800ptas). **Económicos (EASA),** C. Jerónimo Ibrán 1 (tel. 985 29 00 39), runs to Arenas de Cabrales (2¼hr., 950ptas), Cangas de Onís (1½hr., 670ptas), and Covadonga (1¾hr., 790ptas), all near the Picos. Significantly fewer buses run on weekends.

The English-speaking **tourist office** at Pl. Alfonso II (tel. 985 21 33 85) has maps and advice on Picos treks (open M-F 9:30am-1:30pm and 4:30-6:30pm, Sa 9am-2pm, Su 11am-2pm). Robin Walker's *Picos de Europa* is a good **English guidebook** to the trails and towns of the area. Organizations devoted to activities and accommodations in the Picos include the **TIVE** travel agency, C. Calvo Sotelo 5 (tel. 985 23 60 58; open M-F 8am-3pm); **Dirección Regional de la Juventud,** C. Calvo Sotelo 5 (tel. 985 23 11 12; open M-F 10am-1pm); **ICONA,** C. Arquitecto Reguera 13, 2nd fl. (tel. 985 24 14 12); **Dirección Regional de Deportes,** Pl. España (tel. 985 27 23 47); and **Oxígeno,** C. Manuel Pedregal (tel. 985 22 79 75).

A plethora of *pensiones* pack Oviedo's new city near the transport stations. Try **C. Uría, C. Campoamor** (1 block east), and **C. Nueve de Mayo** (a continuation of C. Manuel Pedregal, 1 block farther east). Near the cathedral, try C. Jovellanos. Across from the hospital, **Residencia Juvenil Ramón Menéndez Pidal,** C. Julián Clavería 14 (tel. 985 23 20 54), has a few rooms for 750ptas per person (over 26 1000ptas). Call first, then take bus 2 from C. Uría. **Pensión Pomar,** C. Jovellanos 7 (tel. 985 22 27 91), provides super-clean, airy rooms (singles 1500-2000ptas; doubles 3000-3500ptas; triples 4500ptas). **Pensión Riesgo,** C. Nueve de Mayo 16, 1st fl. (tel. 985 21 89 45), has simple rooms (singles 1800ptas; doubles 3500ptas). **Pensión Martinez,** C. Jovellanos 5 (tel. 985 21 53 44), has clean rooms with sinks and communal bathrooms (singles 1600ptas; doubles and triples 3000ptas). A posh indoor **market** with an **ATM** is on C. Fontán, off Pl. Mayor (open M-Sa 8am-8pm). For groceries, try **El Corte Inglés** at C. General Alorza, opposite the ALSA station, and C. Uría (open M-Sa 10am-9:30pm).

BASQUE COUNTRY

■ Bilbao (Bilbo)

Graced by the marvelous new Guggenheim Museum, **Bilbao** is gaining its rightful place on the tourist itinerary. Centuries of prosperity give Bilbao a distinctly "bourgeois" feel—from the medieval *casco viejo* to the wide and grandiose 19th-century boulevards and buildings to the modern-day urban sprawl.

SIGHTS AND ENTERTAINMENT Constructed mainly out of titanium, limestone, and glass, Frank O. Gehry's **Guggenheim Museum Bibao,** Av. Abandoibarra 2 (tel. 944 35 90 80), is breathtaking. (Open Tu-Su 11am-8pm. 700ptas, students and seniors 350ptas. Free English-speaking guided tours Tu-F 1pm and 4pm, Sa-Su 4pm; sign up 30min. before at Info Desk.) The exterior undulating curves contain constantly changing exhibits drawn from the Guggenheim Foundation's collection. Follow Almeda de Mazarro to the ivy-covered **Museo de Bellas Artes,** Pl. Museo 2; an impressive collection ranges from 12th to 20th-century Spanish and Flemish holdings to numerous canvases by Basque painters (open Tu-Sa 10am-1:30pm and 4-7:30pm, Su 10am-2pm; free). The **Museo Vásco,** C. Cruz 4, housed in a beautiful cloister, has displays on Basque hand-weaving, blacksmithing, and life on the sea. The museum is in the old city; walk past Pensión de la Fuente away from C. Correo to Pl. Miguel de Unamuno, then to C. Cruz. (Open Tu-Sa 10am-1:30pm and 4-7pm, Su 10:30am-1:30pm. 300ptas, students 150ptas, Th free.)

In Bilbao's **casco viejo** (old town) people spill out into the streets to tipple *txikitos,* small glasses of regional beer or wine. Youngsters also jam **C. Licenciado Poza** and **C. Barrencalle.** A mellower scene rests at the city's elegant 19th-century cafes like **Cafe Boulevard,** C. Arenal 3. For afternoon entertainment, hop on the Metro to reach the **beaches** at **Plencia** or at **Sopelana,** north of the city. **Getxo** also lies near the waves;

its suspension bridge fords the river, leading to a spate of all-night bars. Revelers who miss the midnight train will need to take a taxi home (2000-2500ptas). Beginning the weekend after August 15, the city explodes for two weeks with music, theater, bullfights, and fireworks for its **Semana Grande** *fiesta.*

PRACTICAL INFO, ACCOMMODATIONS, AND FOOD Bilbao has three **train stations. RENFE** at **Estación de Abando/del Noret,** Pl. España (info tel. 944 23 86 23), serves Barcelona (9½-11hr., 4800-5000ptas), Madrid (6-9hr., 4100-4300ptas), Salamanca (5½-6½hr., 3400ptas), and Seville via Madrid (12hr., 13,600ptas). Most **bus** companies are based at **Terminbus terminal,** C. Gurtubay 1 (tel. 944 39 50 77). **PESA** (tel. 944 24 88 99) serves San Sebastián (1¼hr., 1060ptas). **ANSA,** C. Autonomía 17 (tel. 944 44 31 00), serves Burgos (2hr., 1420ptas) and Madrid (4½hr., 3245ptas). From any of the stations, navigate toward the Gran Vía, leading to Pl. España and the **Puente del Arenal** bridge, which links the new town with the *casco viejo.* Across the bridge, the **tourist office** (tel. 944 16 00 22; fax 944 16 81 68) helps sort out the transportation system and gives out an excellent map (open M-F 9am-2pm and 4-7:30pm, Sa 9am-2pm, Su 10am-2pm). Cyberphiles connect at **Cybercafe Antxi,** Luis Briñas 13 (250ptas per 30min.; open M-F 9am-1:30pm and 4-9:30pm).

 Plaza Arriaga and nearby **Calle Arenal** are good starting points for hunting budget pensions; the tourist office has a list of options. To find **Pensión de la Fuente,** C. Sombrería 2 (tel. 944 16 99 89), from C. Arenal, turn right on C. Correo and walk two blocks, then turn left. The pension offers pleasant rooms and big furniture (singles 1700-2000ptas; doubles 3000-4000ptas). From Pl. Arriga, take C. Bidebarrieta and turn left onto C. Lotería for clean rooms at the **Pensión Ladero,** C. Lotería 1, 4th floor (tel. 944 15 09 32; singles 2000ptas; doubles 3000ptas). Restaurants and bars in the *casco viejo* are crowded but offer hearty local dishes. Dining spots in the modern quarter offer more variety and comfort, but not nearly as much flavor. **Mercado de la Ribera,** on the bank of the river heading left from the tourist office, is the biggest indoor market in Europe. It's worth a trip even if you're not eating. (Open M-Sa 8am-2pm; June 15-Sept. 15 also F 4:30-7:30pm; Sept. 16-June 14 also M-F 4:30-7pm.)

■ San Sebastián (Donostia)

Glittering on the shores of the Cantabrian Sea, San Sebastián welcomes visitors with broad boulevards, garden avenues, ornate buildings, and radiant beaches. The *parte viejai* claims to have the most bars per square meter in the world, where locals and vacationers merrily down *pintxos* and *txacoli.* The gorgeous beaches and mountains that bookend the city demand appreciation.

ORIENTATION AND PRACTICAL INFORMATION

The Río Urumea splits San Sebastián in two. The city center, many monuments, and the two most popular beaches are on the west side of the river, on a peninsula. Inland on the peninsula is the **parte vieja** (old city), where the nightlife rages, and budget accommodations and restaurants cluster. To the south is the **Catedral del Buen Pastor.** East of the river lies the **RENFE station,** the **Barrio de Gros,** and **Playa de la Zurriola.** The west and east are connected by three bridges. To get to the *parte vieja* from the train station, head straight to Puente María Cristina, cross the bridge, and then turn right and walk four blocks north to Av. Libertad. Turn left and follow it to the port; the *parte vieja* fans out to the right. From the **bus station,** south of the city in Plaza de Pío XII, turn right (north) onto Av. Sancho el Sabio and follow it into the *parte vieja,* or simply take bus 28 from the station.

 Trains: RENFE, Estación del Norte, Po. Francia (tel. 943 28 30 89 or 943 28 35 99), on the east side of Puente María Cristina. To: Barcelona (9hr., 4700ptas), Burgos (3½hr., 2500ptas), Madrid (8hr., 4800ptas), and Paris (8-11hr., 11,000ptas; change at Hendaye, France). Open daily 7am-11pm.

Buses: Several private companies run from different points in the city; most pass through the station on Pl. Pío XII. **PESA,** Av. Sancho el Sabio 33 (tel. 902 10 12 10 or 943 47 30 85). To Bilbao (1¼hr., 1060ptas). **Continental Auto,** Av. Sancho el Sabio 31 (tel. 943 46 90 74). To Madrid (6hr., 3685ptas). **Irbarsa,** Po. Vizcaya 16 (tel. 943 45 75 00), sends buses to Barcelona (7hr., 2450ptas). **La Roncalesa,** Po. de Vízcaya 16 (tel. 943 46 10 64), runs to Pamplona (1hr., 750ptas).

Public Transportation: Bus tickets are 105ptas. Call 943 28 71 00 for routes.

Tourist Office: Centro de Atracción y Turismo, C. Reina Regente (tel. 943 48 11 66; fax 943 48 11 72), in the Teatro Victoria Eugenia. From the train station, turn right immediately after crossing Puente María Cristina; C. Reina Regente is on the left where Puente Zurriola crosses the river. English-speaking staff distributes indexed map, transit, and accommodations info. Open June-Sept. M-Sa 8am-8pm, Su 10am-1pm; Oct.-May M-Sa 9am-2pm and 3:30-7pm.

Currency Exchange: Banco Central Hispano, Av. Libertad 17. Open M-F 8:30am-2pm; in winter also Sa 8:30am-1pm. **ATMs** dot the city.

Luggage Storage: At RENFE station. 400ptas per day. Open daily 7am-11pm.

Laundromat: Lavomatique, C. Iñigo 13 off C. San Juan. Wash 575ptas; dry 400ptas. Open M-F 10am-1pm and 4-7pm, Sa-Su 10am-1pm.

Emergency: tel. 088.

Police: C. Easo 41 (tel. 943 45 00 00).

Medical Assistance: Casa de Socorro, Bengoetxea 4 (tel. 943 44 06 33). **Red Cross Hospital,** C. Matía 7 (tel. 943 27 22 22).

Post Office: C. Urdaneta (tel. 943 46 49 14; fax 943 45 07 94), just south of the cathedral. Open M-F 8:30am-8:30pm, Sa 9:30am-2pm. **Postal Code:** 20007.

Internet Access: Elaurre Cibercafe, C. Urbiata 12 (tel. 943 44 00 90). 250ptas per 15min., 400ptas per 30min., 700ptas per hr. Open M-Sa 10am-10pm.

ACCOMMODATIONS AND CAMPING

Rooms are scarce in July and August—particularly during *San Fermines* (July 6-14) and *Semana Grande* (the week of Aug. 15). Prices are also higher during *Semana Santa*. Budget options cluster both in the **parte vieja** and around the **cathedral.** The tourist office has lists of rooms, and most *pensión* owners know *casas particulares* that take in guests.

Pensión Amaiur, C. 31 de Agosto 44, 2nd fl. (tel. 943 42 96 54). From Alameda del Boulevard, go up C. San Jerónimo and turn left. Floral rooms and delightful owner. Doubles 3000-5000ptas; triples 3800-6500. *Let's Go* discount 300ptas.

Albergue Juvenil la Sirena (HI), Po. Igueldo 25 (tel. 943 31 02 68; fax 943 21 40 90), near the beach at the far west end of the city. Bus 5 takes you one street past the hostel on C. Matia. Bus 24 runs from train and bus stations to Av. Zumalacárregui (stop in front of the San Sebastián Hotel); from there, turn left at the end of the street that angles toward the mountain (Av. Brunei). Luggage storage, laundry facilities, and kitchen. Members or ISIC card-holders only. 1885ptas, over 26 2145ptas. Off-season prices 250-325ptas cheaper. Breakfast included. Reception closed 11am-3pm. Curfew in summer 2am; off-season Su-Th midnight, F-Sa 2am.

Pensión Loinaz, C. San Lorenzo 17 (tel. 943 42 67 14). Attentive, English-speaking owners have bright rooms that will make you want to stay forever. Doubles 2700-4700ptas; triples 3800-6200ptas. *Let's Go* discount. Laundry 1000ptas.

Pensión San Lorenzo, C. San Lorenzo 2 (tel. 943 42 55 16), a right off C. Narrica from Alameda del Boulevard, on the corner of C. San Juan. Cozy rooms. Use the kitchen, which serves as a chatty community center. 1200-2000ptas per person.

Pensión Larrea, C. Narrica 21 (tel. 943 42 26 94). Simple rooms and spotless bathrooms. Singles 2500-3000ptas; doubles 3500-5000ptas; triples 5000-6000ptas.

Pensión Urkia, C. Urbieta 12, 3rd. fl. (tel. 943 42 44 36), bordering the cathedral on the west side. Upscale and lovely. Singles 3000; doubles 3745-5300ptas.

Pensión La Perla, C. Loiola 10, 2nd fl. (tel. 943 42 81 23), the street directly ahead of the cathedral. Attractive rooms. Singles 3225-4000ptas; doubles 3750-6000ptas.

FOOD

Pinchos (*pintxos* in Basque) are a religion here, usually chased with the fizzy regional wine, *txacoli*. Worship at the *pincho* altar and you will surely be rewarded in the afterlife. Bars in the lively old city spread an array of enticing tidbits on toothpicks or bread. In the harbor, many small places serve tangy sardines with strong, slightly bitter *sidra* (cider), another regional specialty.

Masses of restaurants and bars line **Calle Fermín Calbetón.** Farmers sell fresh produce on tables outside the **Mercado de la Bretxa,** on Alameda del Boulevard at C. San Juan. For history's greatest *pinchos* tour, start at **Bar La Cepa,** C. 31 de Agosto 7-9, which has exquisite peppers and a host of other delicacies (*pinchos* 160-325ptas, lunch *menú* 1700ptas). Then continue to **Bar Intza,** C. Esterlines 12, for mussels stuffed with spinach and cheese (150ptas each; open daily 10am-4pm and 6:30-11:30pm, later on weekends). **Bar Juantxo,** C. Embeltrán 6, in the *parte vieja,* sells an estimated 1000 *bocadillos* per day (275-465ptas, *pinchos* 130ptas; open daily 8:30am-midnight). **Santa Lucia,** C. Puerto 6, has large portions at low prices (open daily 8:30am-9pm), and **Caravanseri Cafe,** on Pl. Buen Pastor at C. San Bartolomé 1, has veggie options (open M-Sa 8am-12:30am, Su 10am-midnight). For groceries, **Todo Todo 3,** C. Serrano Anguta, between C. Zumalacárregui and C. Matia, is near the hostel (open M-Sa 9am-9pm, Su 10am-2pm), and **Super Todo Todo,** on Alameda del Boulevard, is near the *parte vieja* (open M-Sa 8:30am-2:30pm and 5-9pm, Su 10am-2pm).

SIGHTS AND ENTERTAINMENT

The view of the bay is spectacular on weekends after dark, when the base of Isla Santa Clara is lit by banks of floodlights. The top of **Monte Igueldo,** at the bay's far side, provides the best view. A **funicular** makes the climb from the base of the mountain. At the other end of the bay, paths wind through the cool, shady woods of **Monte Urgull.** The overgrown **Castillo de Santa Cruz de la Mota** crowns the summit with cannons and a chapel (castle open daily in summer 8am-8pm; off-season 8am-6pm). **Paseo Nuevo,** starting at the end of the port, circles the base of Monte Urgull, bringing you close enough to the waves to feel the spray. At one end of the road, the **Museo de San Telmo,** housed in a former Dominican monastery, has an array of Basque funerary artifacts, some El Grecos, and contemporary art. (Open Tu-Sa 10:30am-1:30pm and 4-8pm, Su 10am-2pm. 350ptas, students 200ptas.)

Movie stars and directors own the streets for a week in September during the **Festival Internacional de Cine,** deemed among the four most important in the world. For info about this year's film festival, call 943 48 12 12, fax 943 48 12 12, or write to Apartados de Correos 397, 20080 San Sebastián. San Sebastián's five-day **Festival de Jazz** is also one of Europe's most ambitious. For information on the 1999 festival, contact the Oficina del Festival de Jazz, C. Camino 2, 20004 San Sebastián (tel. 943 48 11 79; http://www.jazzaldia.com). The week of August 15, **Semana Grande** (Big Week) is ablaze with concerts, movies, and an international fireworks festival.

What the Devil are they Txpeaking?

Linguists still cannot pinpoint the origin of *euskera,* an agglutinate non-Indo-European language. Its commonalties with Caucasian and African tongues regarding root structures suggest that prehistoric Basques may have migrated from the Caucasus through Africa. Historically referred to by other Spaniards as *la lengua del diablo* (the devil's tongue), *euskera* has come to symbolize cultural self-determination. Only half a million natives speak the language, chiefly in País Vasco regions Guipúzcoa and Vizcaya, and northern Navarra. Franco banned *euskera* and forbade parents to give their children Basque names. Today, usage spreads through *ikastolas* (all-Basque schools), TV, and Basque publications. As a result, mostly the young and elderly speak the language. Younger generations listen to rock music in *euskera,* converse normally in the language, and give their kids traditional names such as Iñaki, Idoya, and Estibaliz.

The **parte vieja** pulls out all the stops after dark. On C. Fermín Calbetón, **Bars Tas-Tas, Sariketa,** and **Txalupa** are human zoos and virtually impassable after dark. Techno fans head to the sleek, black bars of **Akerbeltz** and **Etxe Kalte,** on C. Mari near the port. The city's small but mighty disco scene starts thumping at **Ku,** atop Monte Igueldo (opens nightly at 8pm). Many crowd along the beach at **Bataplán,** Po de la Concha (cover with drink 2000ptas; opens nightly at midnight).

■ Near San Sebastián: Hondarribia

Less than an hour east of San Sebastián by bus, the refreshingly simple **Hondarribia** stretches along the Txingudi Bay, flaunting a silky-smooth beach and brightly painted houses. The gorgeous stone-and-timber *casco antiguo,* centered around Carlos V's imposing palace in Pl. Armas (now a *parador*—peek inside), provides welcome relief from Coppertone fumes. The **beach,** which lies at the far end of town past the fisherman's marina and at the end of a long seaside walk, can become ridiculously crowded in the peak days of summer, although it's still pleasantly calm through June.

The entire bay, containing both Hondarribia and Irún, is called **Bidasoa. Interurbanos buses** (tel. 943 64 13 02) run to San Sebastián from C. Zuluaga (45min., 195ptas). The English-speaking staff at the regional **tourist office, Bidasoa Turismo,** C. Javier Ugarte 6 (tel. 943 64 54 58), on Pl. San Cristóbal, doles out maps and lodging lists. (Open July-Aug. daily 10am-8pm; Sept.-June M-F 9am-1:30pm and 4-6:30pm, Sa 10am-2pm.) In summer, reservations for accommodations are key; call ahead. The modern **Albergue Juan Sebastián Elcano (HI),** Ctra. Faro (tel. 943 64 15 50; fax 943 64 00 28), sits on a hillside overlooking the sea. From the bus stop, head to the beach on C. Itsasargi. Bear left at the coast and continue to the traffic circle, then turn left and follow signs uphill to the hostel. (Members only! HI cards for sale. Dorms 1200ptas, over 30 1800ptas. Sheets 110ptas. 3-night max. stay when full. Curfew midnight; doors open at 1 and 2am. Reception 9am-noon and 4-7pm. Reserve 1 day ahead.) Several **markets** spill onto on C. San Pedro, three blocks inland from the port. Try C. Mayor (Nagusia) in the *casco antiguo* for various *menús del día.*

Hondaribbia offers several excursion possibilities. Six km up Av. Monte Jaizkibel, **Monte Jaizkibel,** the highest mountain on the Costa Cantábrica, guards the **Santuario de Guadalupe.** The environs offer mind-blasting views of the coast; on a clear day you can see as far as Bayonne, France, 45km away. **Boats** (tel. 943 61 64 47) shuttle 5km to Hendaye, a French town with a bigger beach. They leave from the pier at the end of C. Domingo Egia, off La Marina (every 15min., reduced service in winter, 200ptas).

NAVARRA AND ARAGÓN

■ Pamplona (Iruña)

At Pamplona's bullring, a statue of Ernest Hemingway welcomes *aficionados* and rowdy partiers to eight days of dancing, drinking, and dashing. **Los San Fermines** (July 6-14) is better known to English speakers as "The Running of the Bulls." The ritual dates back to the 14th century, when it served the practical function of getting the bulls from their corrals to the bullring. At noon on July 6, the mayor kicks off the craziness by lighting the first rocket, the *chupinazad,* from the Ayuntamiento's balcony. A barbaric howl explodes from eager *sanferministas* below, and within minutes the *casco antiguo* is flooded with singing and dancing. The *peñas,* societies more concerned with beer than bulls, lead the brouhaha.

SIGHTS AND ENCIERRO The **encierro** (the actual running of the bulls) takes place at 8am every morning; hyper-adrenalized and hung-over men flee from the bulls that charge 825m down the streets to the bull ring (Plaza de Toros). The race lasts less than three minutes when the bulls stay together; isolated bulls are equally dangerous, since they run into the crowds. *Let's Go* strongly recommends that you enjoy the festivities only as a spectator. In recent years, surging numbers of inexperienced foreigners have joined the run and crowded the course, increasing the risks for everyone involved. Travelers who decide to participate should watch an *encierro* first, and avoid running with the dangerous, enormous weekend bunch. It is not wise to cower in a doorway; you can be trapped and killed. Many more are injured at the end of the course, where a narrow opening rudely interrupts the bravado. If you fall, stay down and protect yourself by curling up into the fetal position. Runners must get to the course by 7:30am; many recommend getting there at 6am. If you want to participate, but are not confident in your running ability, line up by the Plaza de Toros before 7:30am and run in before the bulls are even in sight. Then you can "play" with the bulls in a mass of people. Bullfight spectators should arrive around 6:45am to experience the crowd heating up for the *encierro*. Buying tickets for the **Grada** section of the bull ring may be a good idea (arrive before 7am; 450ptas, Sa-Su 600ptas).

After the taurine track meet, the hoopla moves into the streets with dancing in the alleys, wild parades, and a no-holds-barred party on **Plaza Castillo.** At the corner of C. Navarréria and C. Carmen, in front of Casa Santa Cecilia, a number of people die each year jumping from a fountain. Nearby towns sponsor *encierros* too: **Tudela** during the week surrounding July 24, **Estella** the Friday before the first Sunday in August, **Tafalla** the week of August 15, and **Sangüesa** the week of September 11.

Pamplona shows a different but no less enchanting side during the other 51 weeks of the year. Graffiti and posters from several Basque Nationalist and Separatist movements are offset by acres of tranquil parks and a well-regarded university. The pentagonal **Ciudadela,** with a duck pond, deer park, and gravel paths, sprawls next to the delicious **Jardines de la Taconera.** Throughout the year, Pl. Castillo is the city's social heart, with people of all ages congregating in and around its bars and cafes. Hemingway's favorite was **Cafe-Bar Iruña**—the backdrop for *The Sun Also Rises.*

PRACTICAL INFO, ACCOMMODATIONS, AND FOOD Pamplona is miserably connected by rail. Although **trains** do run to Barcelona (6-8hr., 4100ptas), Madrid (5hr., 4100ptas), and San Sebastián (2hr., 1400-1500ptas), it is better to take **buses** from the station on C. Conde Oliveto (tel. 948 22 38 54), at the corner of C. Yanguas y Miranda. Nearly 20 companies compete to fill their buses to Barcelona (5½hr., 2090ptas), Bilbao (2hr., 1535ptas), San Sebastián (1hr., 750ptas), and many other towns. The **tourist office,** C. Duque de Ahumada 3 (tel. 948 22 07 41; fax 948 21 14 62), offers a map, bus info, and a guide to the festivities. From Pl. Castillo, take Av. Carlos III one block, turn left on C. Duque de Ahumada, and cross C. Espoz y Mina. (Open July-Aug. M-Sa 10am-2pm and 4-7pm, Su 10am-2pm; Sept.-June M-F 10am-2pm and 4-7pm, Sa 10am-2pm; during *San Fermines* daily 10am-5pm.)

And now for a lesson in supply and demand: diehard *sanferministas* book their rooms up to a year in advance; in most cases, you must reserve at least two months ahead and pay up-front rates two to four times higher than those listed here. Check newspapers *(Diario de Navarra)* for **private rooms,** but be wary of people offering couches and floor space at the train and bus stations. Many who can't find rooms reportedly take quick naps during the day or sleep outside on the lawns of the Ciudadela and the Pl. Fueros; do this only if you can sleep in a group and protect your belongings. **Luggage storage** is available at the stations.

When the bulls stop running, take C. Chapitela, make the first right on C. Mercaderes, turn right, then turn left at a 45° angle for **Pensión Santa Cecilia,** C. Navarrería 17 (tel. 948 22 22 30), for good prices (singles 2500ptas; doubles 3700-4000ptas; during *San Fermines* 4000ptas per person). For a spartan room at **Fonda La Aragonesa,** San Nicolás 22 (tel. 948 22 34 28), use the reception desk at Hostal Berán across the street (singles 2000ptas; doubles 3000ptas). With several floors of beds and quick turnover, the **Fonda La Montañesa,** C. San Gregorio 2 (tel. 948 22 43 80), is worth a try (1400-1500ptas; *San Fermines* up to 4000ptas per person). Four La Montañesa buses per day run from Pl. Toros to **Camping Ezcaba** (tel. 948 33 16 65; 450ptas per person and per tent; open June-Oct.). Look on C. Navarrería, the neighborhood of Pensión Santa Cecilia, around Pl. San Fransisco, and C. Descalzos near Po. Ronda for frenzied feeding. **Restaurante Sarasate,** C. San Nicolás 19-21, has great vegetarian food (lunch *menú* 1200ptas; open M-Th 1:15-4pm and 8-11pm, F-Sa 1:15-4pm and 9-11pm). The supermarket **Vendi** is at the corner of C. Hilarión Eslava and C. Mayor (open M-F 9am-2pm and 5:30-7:30pm, Sa 9am-2pm; *San Fermines* M-Sa 9am-2pm).

Jaca For centuries, Santiago-bound pilgrims crossed the Pyrenees into Spain, crashed in Jaca for the night, and left by dawn. They had the right idea. Today's travelers sleep here on their way to the hiking and skiing trails of the Aragonese Pyrenees. Buses run from downtown to the train station 30 minutes before each train leaves, stopping at the Ayuntamiento on C. Mayor or (if closed) at the taxi stop, and at the bus station. The **train station,** at C. Estación, serves Madrid (7hr., 4100ptas) and Zaragoza (3¼hr., 1900ptas). **La Oscense** (tel. 974 35 50 60) sends **buses** to Pamplona (2hr., 855ptas), Zaragoza (2¼hr., 1450ptas), and elsewhere. The **tourist office,** Av. Regimiento Galicia 2 (tel. 974 36 00 98), left off C. Mayor, has hiking advice and a map. (Open July-Aug. M-F 9am-2pm and 4:30-8pm, Sa 10am-1:30pm and 5-8pm, Su 10am-1:30pm; Sept.-June M-F 9am-1:30pm and 4:30-7pm, Sa 10am-1pm and 5-7pm.)

Jaca's *hostales* and *pensiones* are mainly grouped around C. Mayor and the cathedral. The **Albergue Juvenil Escuelas Pías (HI),** is at Av. Perimetral 6 (tel. 974 36 05 36). From C. Mayor, make a left on Regimiento de Galicia and another left on C. Perimetral. Follow the driveway on the right side of the road to the left of the metal sculpture until you reach the bungalows (1300ptas, over 26 1750ptas; nonmembers add 400ptas; midnight curfew). **Hostal Paris,** Pl. San Pedro 4 (tel. 974 36 10 20), a left off Av. Jacetania as you face *ciudadela,* has doubles for 3300 to 3600ptas. Camp at **Peña Oroel** (tel. 974 36 02 15), 3½km down the road to Sabiñánigo. (650ptas per person, per tent, and per car. Open during *Semana Santa* and mid-June to mid-Sept.)

■ Parque Nacional de Ordesa y Monte Perdido

Well-maintained trails, idyllic forests, jagged rock faces, snow-covered peaks, rushing rivers, and alpine meadows make up the **Parque Nacional de Ordesa y Monte Perdido,** just south of the French border. Though the valleys of Ordesa, Añisclo, Escuaín, and Pineta are more accessible than they used to be, excursions into the park still require patience and careful planning. From **Jaca,** La Oscense (tel. 974 35 50 60) sends **buses** to Sabiñánigo (30min., 110ptas); from **Sabiñánigo,** Empresa Hudebus (tel. 974 21 32 77) runs to Torla daily at 11am (55min., 355ptas); and from **Torla,** you can reach **Ordesa** by bus (July-Aug. only, round-trip 200ptas), taxi (tel. 974 48 62 43; 1500-2000ptas), or foot (8km). All **trains** on the Zaragoza-Huesca-Jaca line stop in Sabiñánigo. If you only have a day to spend in Ordesa, the **Soaso Circle** is the most practical hike, especially for novices. If you prefer a private mountain climb to a communal, multilingual parade, try the **Circo Cotatuero** or **Circo Carriata** hikes (2-3hr. each). More experienced hikers brave the **Torla-Gavarnie** trail, a six-hour haul (one-way) all the way to Gavarnie, France, or the 10-hour **Ordesa-Gavarnie** trail.

The **Editorial Alpina** guide is a must for any of these hikes; buy it at the souvenir shop by the parking lot (675ptas) or the supermarket down the street (600ptas). At the park entrance, the **Visitor Center "El Parador"** sells maps (400ptas) and has hiking info (open daily July-Aug. 9am-1pm and 3:30-7pm). Opposite the Refugio L'Atalaya in Torla, the **Compañia de Ordesa** (tel. 974 48 64 17), on C. Francia, rents mountain bikes and organizes excursions. Many **refugios** (mountain huts, usually without facilities) allow overnight stays; the 120-bed **Refugio Góriz** (tel. 974 34 12 01), about four hours from the parking lot, has winter heating and meager hot showers (950ptas). Get a *refugio* preview in Torla, at the 31-bunk room of the **Refugio L'Atalaya,** C. Francia 45 (tel. 974 48 60 22; 1000ptas per person). The newer **Refugio Briet,** across the street (tel. 974 48 62 21), has similar facilities (1000ptas). Both **Camping San Anton** (tel. 974 48 60 63) and **Camping Río Ara** (tel. 974 48 62 48) are 445ptas per person and per tent (open Apr.-Oct.). In between is the more upscale **Camping Ordesa.** (Tel. 974 48 61 46. 600ptas per person, 630ptas per tent; tax not included. 30% discount off season. Open Apr.-Oct.)

SPAIN

SPAIN

Central Barcelona

SEE ALSO COLOR INSERT

ACCOMMODATIONS

L Albergue de
  Juventud Kabul
M Alberg Juvenil Palau
  and Casa de
  Huéspedes Mari-Luz
K Hostal-Albergue
  Fernando
N Hostal Avinyó
E Hostal Fontanella
I Hostal Malda
G Hostal Residencia
  Lausanne and
  Pensión Nevada

C Hostal Residencia
  Oliva
H Hostal-Residencia
  Rembrandt
B Hostal-Residencia
  Windsor
J Hotel Don Rey
  Jaime I
F Hotel Toledano/
  Hostal Residencial
  Capitol
A Pensión San Medin
D Residencia
  Australia

CATALONIA (CATALUNYA, CATALUÑA)

■ Barcelona

Sanguine and self-possessed, Barcelona has swaggered into the spotlight and won the world's attention. The 1992 Olympics, creating a space-age village where a slum had stood only a few years before, consummated the city's recent rise to glory. Barcelona has long reached up and away from its more provincial home country: since the late 1800s, when *modernista* (Art Nouveau) architects studded the city with brilliantly daring buildings and parks, Barcelona has reigned as the world's premier showcase of avant-garde architecture. Today, amidst more traditional European tree-lined avenues, a vibrant port, and a serpentine old town, Antoni Gaudí's fantastic flights of fancy battle for attention with the 90s return of the avant-garde—in the form of stylish shoes and carefully angled, glassy, millennium-ready museums and malls. As an unprecedented tourist boom sucks in the bulk of Spain's Eurail circuiteers, hostel vacancies are becoming scarce. Reserve early, dress well, and prepare yourself for a circus.

ORIENTATION AND PRACTICAL INFORMATION

On Spain's Mediterranean coast 200km from the French border, Barcelona slopes gently upward from the harbor to the mountains—on most avenues, this should help you get your bearings. From the harbor, **Las Ramblas** proceeds directly to **Pl. Catalunya,** the city's center, site of the **city tourist office** and **El Corte Inglés** department store (both dispense El Corte Inglés' **free map**). To the right of Las Ramblas lies **Barri Gòtic,** enclosed on the other side by **Vía Laietana.** Beyond Vía Laietana lies the **Ribera,** which touches **Parc de la Ciutadella** and **Estació de França.** Past Parc de la Ciutadella is the **Vila Olímpica,** with its two new towers (the tallest buildings in Barcelona) and a shiny assortment of malls and hotels. On the left side of Las Ramblas rises **Montjuïc,** a picturesque hill crammed with tourist attractions.

From Pl. Catalunya, fanning up toward the mountains away from Las Ramblas, the **Eixample** is bordered along its lower edge by the **Gran Vía de les Corts Catalanes** and bisected by **Passeig de Gràcia,** with its numerous shops and cafes. **Avinguda Diagonal** marks the upper limit of the grid-planned neighborhoods, separating the Eixample from **Gràcia,** an older neighborhood in the foothills of the mountains that encircle Barcelona. In this mountain range, the peak of **Tibidabo,** the highest point in Barcelona, provides the most privileged area from which to view the city. For more detail, refer to this book's **color maps** of the city and Metro.

Pickpocketing is the only common crime in Barcelona. **El Raval,** on your left side while ascending Las Ramblas, is not safe for lone walkers at night; you should also watch your belongings in **Plaça Reial,** on the opposite side of Las Ramblas.

Airport: El Prat de Llobregat (tel. 932 98 38 38), 12km southwest of Barcelona. The most convenient way to Plaça Catalunya (the center of town) or Estació-Sants is by **Aerobus** (40min., every 15min., 475ptas; from the airport to Pl. Catalunya M-F 6am-10:55pm and Sa-Su 6:30am-10:55pm; to the airport from Pl. Catalunya M-F 5:30am-10:20pm, Sa-Su 6am-10:20pm). A late-night bus (marked "EN") travels from the airport to Pl. Espanya from 6:20am-2:40am; the bus returns to the airport from Pl. Espanya (at Av. Reina María Cristina and the Gran Vía) from 7am-3:15am. A **taxi** costs 2500-3500ptas. **Iberia,** Pg. Gràcia 30 (tel. 934 01 22 81, reservations 902 40 05 00), flies to many destinations across Europe.

Trains: Call **RENFE** (tel. 934 90 02 02, international 934 90 11 22) for train info. **Estació Sants,** Pl. Països Catalans (tel. 934 90 24 00), is the main station. M: Sants-Estació. To: Madrid (7hr., 5900-7000ptas), Milan (13hr.), Paris (11hr.), Seville (12hr., 6700-7700ptas), and Valencia (4hr., 3500-4200ptas). Open daily 6:10am-11pm. **Estació França,** Av. Marqués de L'Argentera. M: Barceloneta. Serves a few domestic and international destinations. Open daily 7am-10pm.

Buses: Most buses arrive at the **Estació del Nord,** C. Ali-bei, 80 (tel. 932 65 65 08). M: Arc de Triomf. **Enatcar** (tel. 932 45 25 28) serves Madrid (8hr., 2690ptas) and Valencia (4½hr., 2690ptas). **Linebús** (tel. 932 65 07 00) travels to London (25hr., 13,800ptas) and Paris (14hr., 11,700ptas). 10% discount for travelers under 26. **Sarfa** (tel. 932 65 11 58) sends buses to Costa Brava beach towns. **Julià Vía,** C. Viriato (tel. 490 40 00), to the right of Estació-Sants, connects to Amsterdam, Frankfurt (19hr., 14,550ptas), and Marseille (10hr., 6300ptas).

Ferries: Transmediterránea, Estació Marítima-Moll Barcelona (tel. 902 45 46 45). M: Drassanes. From Las Ramblas, Columbus points the way. Open M-F 9am-1:30pm and 4:30-7pm, Sa 9am-1pm. In summer there are voyages most days to: Mallorca (8hr.), Menorca (8hr.), and Ibiza (8hr.). Summer fares run 6660-8150ptas one-way.

Public Transportation: tel. 934 12 00 00; for handicapped transportation call 934 12 44 44. **Metro (M)** and **bus** rides cost 140ptas; 10-ride T2 Metro pass 720ptas; 10-ride T1 combo pass 775ptas. Riding without a receipt carries a hefty 5000ptas **fine.** Metro open M-Th 5am-11pm, F-Sa 5am-1am, Su 6am-midnight. Day buses usually run daily 5am-10pm; night buses 11pm-4am.

Taxis: tel. 933 30 03 00 or 933 00 11 00. 295ptas base rate, then 92-107ptas per km.

Car Rental: Docar, C. Montnegre, 18 (24hr. tel. 933 22 90 08; fax 934 39 81 19). Free delivery and pickup. Base price 3000ptas per day including insurance, 19ptas each additional km. Open M-F 9am-2pm and 4-8pm, Sa 9am-2pm.

Hitchhiking: Those who hitch to France often take the Metro to Fabra i Puig, then Av. Meridiana to reach A-7. Those en route to Tarragona and Valencia take bus 7 from Rambla Catalunya on the side Gran Vía side. *Autopista* access lies near here. Hitchhiking on *autopistas* (toll roads, marked by the letter A) is illegal. Hitchhiking is permitted (although not recommended) on national highways (marked by N). **Barnastop,** C. Sant Ramon 29 (tel. 934 43 06 32), at Non de Rambla. M: Liceu. Matches drivers with riders. Driver's fee is 3ptas per km in Spain, 4ptas per km outside Spain. Open M-F 11am-2pm and 5-7pm, Sa noon-2pm.

Tourist Offices: For **general city info** call 10 10 (one-time 130ptas charge); on-line, head to http://www.bcn.es. **Turisme de Barcelona,** Pl. Catalunya (tel. 933 04 31 34 or 902 31 12 82). Multilingual advice, tons of maps and pamphlets, and currency exchange. **Branch office** at Pl. Països Catalans (tel. 93 491 44 31). M: Sants-Estació. Barcelona info only. Open in summer daily 8am-8pm; off-season M-F 8am-8pm, Sa-Su 8am-2pm. For info on Catalunya, try **Centre d'Informació Turística de Catalunya-Palau Robert,** Pg. de Gràcia 107 (tel. 932 38 40 00; http://www.gencat.es/probert). M: Diagonal. Open M-Sa 10am-7pm. **Airport branch,** International Terminal, left of customs. Open M-Sa 9:30am-8:30pm, Su 9:30am-3pm.

Budget Travel: Wasteels, Pl. Catalunya-Estació RENFE (tel. 933 01 18 81; fax 933 01 18 53). M: Catalunya. In the Metro/RENFE terminal. Air and train discounts for students. Open M-F 8:30am-8:30pm, Sa 10am-1pm. **Centre d'Informació: Assesorament per a Joves,** C. Ferrán 32 (tel. 934 02 78 00 or 934 02 78 01). Free advice, travel library, and events bulletin board. Open M-F 10am-2pm and 4-8pm.

Consulates: Australia, Gran Vía Carlos III 98, 9th fl. (tel. 933 30 94 96; fax 934 11 09 04). **Canada,** Passeig de Gracia 77, 3rd fl. (tel. 932 15 07 04; fax 934 87 91 17). **New Zealand,** Traversa de Gracia 64, 4th fl. (tel. 932 09 03 99; fax 932 02 08 90). **South Africa,** Teodora Lamadrid 7-11 (tel. 934 18 64 45; fax 934 18 05 38). Consulates open M-F. **U.K.,** Av. Diagonal 477, Edif. Torre Barcelona (tel. 934 19 90 44; fax 934 05 24 11). **U.S.,** Pg. Reina Elisenda 23 (tel. 932 80 22 27; fax 932 05 52 06).

American Express: Pg. Gràcia 101 (tel. 900 99 44 26, 24hr. tel. 915 72 03 03; fax 934 15 37 00). M: Diagonal. The entrance is around the corner on C. Rosselló. Mail held free for cardholders. Open M-F 9:30am-6pm, Sa 10am-noon. **ATM** outside.

Currency Exchange: Find the best rates at **banks** (open M-F 8:30am-2pm). **Banco Central Hispano,** Las Ramblas at C. Boqueria, is best for AmEx traveler's checks. **Banco de Espanya** in Pl. Catalunya and the AmEx office charge no commission. On Su, try **Estació Sants** (tel. 934 90 77 70). Open daily 8am-10pm.

Luggage Storage: Estació Sants, lockers 400-600ptas. Open daily 5:30am-11:30pm. **Estació França,** same prices. Open daily 6am-11pm. **Estació del Nord,** lockers 300-600ptas. Open 24hr.

English Bookstores: LAIE, Av. Pau Claris 85 (tel. 933 18 17 39), 1 block from the Gran Vía. M: Urquinaona or Pl. Catalunya. Open M-Sa 10am-9pm.

Gay and Lesbian Organization: Coordinadora Gay Lesbiana, C. Les Carolines 13 (tel. 93 237 08 69, toll free tel. 900 60 16 01). Line staffed daily 6-10pm.

Laundromat: Tintoreria San Pablo, C. San Pau 105 (tel. 933 29 42 49). Wash, dry, and fold 1600ptas, do-it-yourself for 1200ptas. Open M-F 9am-1pm and 4-8pm.

Emergency: tel. 092 or 091.

Police: Las Ramblas, 43 (tel. 933 01 90 60), across from Pl. Real, next to C. Nou de la Rambla. M: Liceu. English spoken.

Medical Assistance: Médicos de Urgencia, C. Pelai 40 (tel. 934 12 12 12). M: Catalunya. Dial 061 for **ambulance.**

Post Office: Pl. Antoni López (tel. 933 18 38 31), at the foot of Vía Laietana. M: Jaume I or Barceloneta. Open for *Lista de Correos* (general delivery) M-F 8am-9pm, Sa 9am-2pm. **Postal Code:** 08002.

Internet Access: El Cafe de Internet, Gran Vía de les Corts Catalanes 656 (tel. 934 12 19 15). M: Pg. Gracia. Trendy restaurant offers access for 600ptas per 30min., 800ptas per hr. with student ID. Open M-W 10am-midnight and Th-Sa 10am-2am.

Telephones: Phones and **fax** service at Estació Sants (tel./fax 934 90 76 50). M: Sants-Estació. Open daily 9am-10:15pm. **Directory assistance** tel. 1003.

ACCOMMODATIONS AND CAMPING

Although *hostales* and *pensiones* abound, reservations are essential in summer, when tourists flood the city. Most accommodations have some rooms with splendid balconies onto the street and others with windows onto stuffy interior patios. Ask for an exterior room if you value sunlight and breeze. Barcelona's *albergues* offer basic lodgings at low prices, but ask to see your room before you sign your night away.

Youth Hostels

Albergue de Juventud Kabul, Pl. Reial 17 (tel. 933 18 51 90). M: Liceu. Head toward the port on Las Ramblas, and turn left after C. Ferrán to enter Pl. Reial. Kabul is at the near right corner. Social atmosphere—beer vending machines and satellite TV. 1500ptas. Sheets 200ptas. Laundry 800ptas. Free lockers. 5-night max. stay. Reception 24hr. The area is fairly safe, but police urge caution at night.

Alberg Juvenil Palau (HI), C. Palau 6 (tel. 934 12 50 80). M: Jaume I. 1 block from Pl. Sant Jaume; take C. Ciutat to C. Templaris, then take the 2nd left. Full kitchen. Showers available 8-11am and 4-10pm. 1300ptas. Sheets 150ptas. Breakfast included. 5-night max. stay. Reception 7am-3am. Curfew 3am.

Ciutat Vella: Barri Gòtic and El Raval

Barcelona's *ciutat vella* (old quarter) has a wealth of affordable rooms. Police patrol the area, but be aware of your possessions and surroundings on Las Ramblas.

Hostal-Albergue Fernando, C. Ferrán 31 (tel. 933 01 79 93). M: Liceu. One of the best deals in the Barri Gòtic—it sparkles with cleanliness. Dorm bed 1600ptas; doubles with bath 5000ptas; triples with bath 5500ptas.

Hostal Avinyo, C. Avinyó 42 (tel. 933 18 79 45 or 933 01 75 70; fax 933 18 68 93). M: Drassanes. Clean, cheery rooms with either street-side balconies or windows onto a tranquil central courtyard. Singles 1700ptas; doubles 2600-3800ptas; triples 3900-5700ptas; quads 5200-7600ptas. Prices vary with season and length of stay.

Pensión Francia, C. Rera Palau 4 (tel. 933 19 03 76). M: Barceloneta. From the Metro, head toward town, crossing Pl. Palau, then turn right on Marqués de l'Argentera, and C. Rera Palau is the 2nd left. Brand-new wooden furniture and a mini-library of English books. Singles 1600ptas; doubles 2700-5000ptas; triples 3900ptas; quads 4500ptas. Breakfast 275ptas. Keys for 24hr. entry.

Hostal Residencia Rembrandt, C. Portaferrisa 23 (tel./fax 933 18 10 11). M: Liceu. As you walk up Las Ramblas (away from the ocean), Portaferrisa is on your right. Clean *hostal* with large windows. Singles 2700ptas; doubles 4000ptas, with shower 4500ptas, with bath 5000ptas; triples 7000ptas. Breakfast 350ptas.

Casa de Huéspedes Mari-Luz, C. Palau 4 (tel. 933 17 34 63), 1 block from Pl. Sant Jaume. M: Jaume I or Liceu. Take C. Ciutat to C. Templaris, then take the 2nd left. After dark it's safer not to approach on C. Escudellers. 1500ptas. Laundry 800ptas per load. Kitchen. Lockers in rooms. Keys for 24hr. entry.

Hostal Malda, C. Pí 5 (tel. 933 17 30 02). M: Liceu. Take C. Portaferrissa (on the right with your back to the sea) from Las Ramblas. C. Pí is your fourth right. *Hostal* is directly above the Cine Malda. Offers simple rooms and a dining room with travel library. Singles 1500ptas; doubles 2500ptas; triples 3500ptas.

Hotel Rey Don Jaime I, C. Jaume I 11 (tel. 933 10 62 08). M: Jaume I. Every bed has a double mattress, every room a bathroom and telephone, and every luxury a price. Singles 4000ptas; doubles 5800ptas; triples 6900ptas. Reception 24hr.

Citat Vella: Near Plaça de Catalunya

A bit pricier than in the Barri Gòtic, accommodations here are safer, more modern, and close to the action (and rumble) of Las Ramblas. The Metro stop is Pl. Catalunya.

Pensión L'Isard, C. Tallers 82 (tel. 933 02 51 83), near MACBA, the new contemporary art museum. M: Universitat. Take Pelai exit from the metro, take a left at the end of the block, then a quick left at the pharmacy. Tidy rooms with balconies. Singles 1900ptas; doubles 3700-4700ptas; triples 4800ptas. Keys for 24hr. entry.

Hostal Fontanella, Vía Laietana 71 (tel./fax 933 17 59 43). From Pl. Catalunya, go 3 blocks past El Corte Inglés and hang a right. Hotel-quality beds and baths. Singles 2900ptas, with bath 3800ptas; doubles 4800-6600ptas. Reservations with deposit.

Residencia Australia, Ronda Universitat 11 (tel. 933 17 41 77). M: Universitat. María. Embroidered sheets and curtains, a spotless bathroom, and ceiling fans in rooms. Singles 2800ptas; doubles 4000-4800ptas. Prices do not include 7% IVA.

Hostal Residencia Lausanne, Av. Portal de L'Angel 24 (tel. 933 02 11 39). Couches and chairs in many rooms, new wallpaper, renovated baths, and a TV lounge. Singles 2500ptas; doubles 3500-5000ptas; triples 6000-7500ptas.

Hotel Toledano/Hostal Residencia Capitol, Las Ramblas 138 (tel. 933 01 08 72; fax 934 12 31 42). Near the top of Las Ramblas. All rooms have cable TV and phones; some have balconies with a panoramic views. English-speaking owner. 4th-floor *hostal:* singles 2900ptas; doubles 4600-5200ptas; triples 5900-6500ptas; quads 6800-7400ptas. Higher prices in 5th-floor hotel. Add 7% IVA. Reception 24hr.

Hostal Plaza, C. Fontanella 18 (tel./fax 933 01 01 39). Calle Fontanella stems right out of Pl. Catalunya at El Corte Inglés. Phone, fax, TV, and Internet access (600ptas per 30min.), kitchen. Singles 3500-4000ptas; doubles 5000-6000ptas. Laundry 1500ptas. Reception closed 2-5pm.

Pensión Nevada, Av. Portal de L'Angel 16 (tel. 933 02 31 01), just past Hostal Residencia Lausanne. Great location. Singles 3700ptas; doubles 5400ptas. No heat. Keys for 24hr. entry.

The Eixample

The most beautiful and safest *hostales* are located along wide, safe *avingudas* in the newer part of town. Most have elevators and huge entryways with colorful tiles.

Hostal Residencia Oliva, Pg. Gràcia 32, 4th fl. (tel. 934 88 01 62 or 934 88 17 89), on the intersection of C. Disputació. M: Pg. Gràcia. The Aerobus drops you off. Posh woodwork and color TVs in rooms. Singles 3100ptas; doubles 5700-6700ptas.

Hostal Residencia Palacios, Gran Vía de les Corts Catalanes 629, 2nd fl. (tel./fax 933 01 37 92). M: Pg. Gràcia. An excellent choice with well-furnished rooms. Singles 2700-3750ptas; doubles 4000-5250ptas. 7% IVA not included. Breakfast 350ptas. Laundry (wash and dry) 1000ptas.

Hostal Residencia Windsor, Rambla Catalunya 84 (tel. 93 215 11 98), near the intersection of C. Mallorca. M: Pg. Gràcia. Aristocratic *hostal* with good location, though a bit far up into L'Eixample. Ask for a balcony room. Singles 3500-4300ptas; doubles 6000-7100ptas. 7% IVA not included. Laundry 600ptas.

Gràcia

Berlitz Spanish won't help in this Catalan-dominated area five to ten minutes north of Av. Diagonal. The accommodations listed here are small and well-kept, and neighborhood bars and *pastelerías* remain relatively undiscovered.

Pensión San Medín, C. Gran de Gràcia 125 (tel. 932 17 30 68; fax 934 15 44 10). M: Fontana. Excellent family-run *pensión.* Each room has fine furniture and a phone. Common room with TV. Singles 2500-3500ptas; doubles 4500-5800ptas.

Hostal Bonavista, C. Bonavista 21 (tel. 932 37 37 57). M: Diagonal. Walk toward the fountain at the end of Pg. Gràcia and make your first right; *hostal* is just off the traffic circle. Well-kept rooms and a nice common *salón.* Singles 2200ptas; doubles 3300-300ptas. Showers 300ptas. Keys for entry 24hr. No reservations.

Camping

Although there is no camping in Barcelona, intercity buses (190ptas) run to these locations in 20 to 45 minutes: **El Toro Bravo** (tel. 936 37 34 62), 11km south of Barcelona, accessible by buses L94 (summer only) and L95 from Pl. Catalunya or Pl. Espanya (630ptas per person, 700ptas per tent); and **Filipinas** (24hr. tel. 936 58 28 95; 650ptas per person, 700ptas per tent), 1km down the road from El Toro Bravo.

FOOD

For the cheapest meals, be on the lookout for 850 to 950ptas *menús* posted in the restaurants in the Barri Gòtic. Small, family owned eateries serve basic but satisfying dishes. Closer to the port, bars and cafes get more crowded and harried, whereas on Rbla. Catalunya leisurely *al fresco* meals are an expensive excuse for people-watching. Be aware that food options shrink drastically in August, when restauranteurs and bar owners close up shop and take their vacations. Barcelona offers such Catalan specialities as *merluza* (whitefish), *butifarra con judías blancas* (sausage with white beans), *berenjenas rellenas* (eggplant casserole), and *crema catalana* (similar to *crème brulée*). *Torrades,* toasted bread rubbed with olive oil, garlic, and tomato, are a Catalan delight not to be missed. **La Boqueria** (officially the Mercat de Sant Josep), off Rambla Sant Josep 89, vends fresh fish and produce (open M-Sa 9am-9pm).

Restaurante Bidasoa, C. Serra 21. M: Drassanes. Take the 3rd left off C. Josep Anselm Clavé as you head from Las Ramblas. 43 permutations of soups, salads, and meat and fish items, all under 600ptas or so. Open Tu-Su noon-midnight, but no food between 3:30-8pm. Closed Aug.

La Fonda, C. Escudellers 10. M: Drassanes or Liceu. C. Escudellers stems into Barri Gòtic from Las Ramblas between Liceu and Drassanes. Catalan cuisine with fancy tablecloth-and-crystal presentation. Deceptively cheap at 390-995ptas plus 7% IVA. Open daily 1-3:30pm and 8:30-11:30pm.

Irati, C. Cardenal Casanyes 17. An excellent Basque *tapas* bar that attracts droves of hungry *tapas*-seekers. All *tapas* 130ptas. Open Tu-Sa noon-midnight, Su noon-5pm, but *tapas* only noon-3pm and 7-11pm.

Bar Restaurante Los Toreros, C. Xuclá 3-5, on a narrow alley between C. Fortuny and C. Carme, both off Las Ramblas. M: Catalunya. Traditional Spanish food—4-course *menú* for 875ptas. Open Tu-Sa 9am-midnight, Su 9am-5pm.

Nou Celler, C. Princesa 16. M: Jaume I. From the Metro, cross Vía Laietana from Pl. Angel. Calle Jaume becomes C. Princesa. Authentic Catalan specialties. *Menú* 1000ptas. Open M-F 8am-midnight, Su 8am-4pm. Closed June· 15-July 15.

ba-ba-reeba, Pg. Gràcia 28. M: Pg. Gràcia. Offers a wide selection of *tapas* and Catalonian *pa* (bread). Ba-ba is chi-chi, but not too expensive. Outdoor dining on the *passeig* available. Open daily 8am-2pm.

Taverna El Glop, C. Sant Lluís 24. Near the Joanic Metro stop off C. Escorial. This 2-story rustic tavern has become super-popular with the locals for its *chorizo* (Spanish sausage). Open Oct.-Aug. Tu-Su 1-4pm and 8pm-1am. Also at C. Montmary 49.

Els Quatre Gats, C. Montsió 3. M: Catalunya. From the metro, go down Av. Portal de L'Angel and take the 2nd left. *Modernista*-designed hangout of Picasso, who created the famous menu (on display at Museu Picasso). Good place for a beer and some *tapas.* Live music 9pm-1am. Open M-Sa 8am-2am, Su 5pm-2am.

Comme-Bio, Gran Vía de les Corts Catalanes 603, just off Rambla Catalunya. M: Catalunya. Groceries in front, food and drink in back. The all-veggie menu is quite creative. Open M-Sa 9am-midnight, Su noon-midnight.

El Tastavins, C. Ramon y Cajal, near Pl. Sol. M: Joanic. Admire work by local artists (and caricatures of the owners) while scarfing down traditional Catalan fare. Afternoon *menú* 850ptas. Open Tu-Sa 9:30am-5pm and 8:30pm-1am, Su 12:30-5pm.

SIGHTS

Barcelona's *modernista* treasures stand above all else—the Ruta del Modernisme passes are the best way to go (see below). Las Ramblas, everyone's favorite street, and the lovely Barri Gòtic are the traditional tourist areas, but don't neglect other vibrant neighborhoods outside the Ciutat Vella. The wide avenues of L'Eixample, the Gaudí delights in Parc Güell, the panoramic city views from Montjuïc and Tibidabo, and the dramatic Port Olímpic and harborside areas all have much to offer.

Ruta del Modernisme passes (1200ptas, students 750ptas) allow privileged and economical access to Barcelona's architectural masterpieces. The pass, good for a month, allows entrance to Casa Batlló, Casa Amatller, Casa Lleó Morera (inaccessible without pass), Palau Guell, Sagrada Familia, Casa Milá, Palau de la Música, Casa-Museu Gaudí, Fundació Antoni Tápies, and Museu d'Art Modern. Passes are sold in the Palau Güell (see below) or at Casa Lleó Morera on Pg. Grácia. During the summer, the air conditioned **Bus Turístic** (marked #100) stops at 21 points of interest; a 1700ptas full-day pass allows you to get on and off freely. The best way to approach this macro-museum of Catalan architecture is with two handy pamphlet guides available free at the tourist office, *Discovering Modernist Art in Catalonia* and *Gaudí.*

Ciutat Vella: Las Ramblas and Barri Gòtic

The broad pedestrian lane of **Las Ramblas** is a veritable urban carnival: street performers dance flamenco, fortune-tellers survey palms, and merchants hawk their wares. The tree-lined lane runs from Pl. Catalunya to the Monument de Colom at the port. Half-way down, **Joan Miró's** pavement mosaic brightens Pl. Boqueria. At the corner of C. Sant Pau, the **Gran Teatre del Liceu** was one of Europe's leading stages before a fire gutted it in 1994. It will reopen in 1999. At the far end of C. Sant Pau, Barcelona's oldest Romanesque church, the 10th-century **Església de Sant Pau,** stands in stark contrast to its setting in the former red-light district, El Raval. *(Visiting hours M-F 5-8pm.)* The newly-restored **Palau Güell,** C. Nou de la Rambla 3-5, two streets down from Teatre Liceu on the right, attracts visitors with its fascinating architecture. At the port end of Las Ramblas, the **Monument a Colom** towers over the city. *(Elevator to the top open June-Sept. daily 9am-8:30pm; shorter hours off-season. 250ptas.)*

Marvelous Modernisme

In the late 19th and early 20th centuries, Barcelona's flourishing bourgeoisie commissioned a new class of architects to build their houses, reshaping the face of the Eixample neighborhood with Modernista architecture that employed revolutionary shapes, materials, and spaces to reflect the signs and symbols of Catalunya. Antoni Gaudí's serpentine rooftops, warrior-like chimneys, and skeletal facades are perhaps the most famous examples of this new style, *Modernisme* (often described as a Catalan version of Art Nouveau). A staunch nationalist, Gaudí incorporated in his organic architecture a vast array of Catalan symbols and myths. Gaudí designed every feature of his buildings, down to the undulating furniture, colorful ceramic mosaics, and elaborate light fixtures that fill his boisterous buildings. Even his methods were unconventional; Gaudí designed the vault of the Colònia Güell by hanging sand bags from a wire model of the ceiling, the inversion of which was perfectly balanced against structural stress. Although most of Gaudí's creations seem fantastical upon first glance, many, such as the attic of La Pedrera, which regulates heat with its vaulted ceilings, are architectural breakthroughs that have since been imitated only by advanced computer technology. Fellow Modernista luminaries include **Luis Domènech i Montaner,** noted for his profusely decorated surfaces, and **Josep Puig i Cadafalch,** who developed an antiquarian style uniting local and foreign traditions.

Palaces, cathedrals, and Roman ruins make the **Barri Gòtic** (located between Las Ramblas and Vía Laietana) a monument to Barcelona's past. Countless souvenir stands and bars now diminish the medieval charm, but also give the area a liveliness it would otherwise lack. Since Roman times, the handsome **Plaça de Sant Jaume** has been the city's political center. The *plaça* is dominated by two of Catalonia's most important buildings: the **Palau de la Generalitat** (seat of Catalonia's autonomous government) and the **Ajuntament,** the Spanish government's seat of power. (*Call 934 02 73 64 or 934 02 73 00 to visit. Open Sa-Su 10am-2pm. Free.*) The Gothic **Església Catedral de la Santa Creu** is in Plaça de la Seu, up C. Bisbe next to the Generalitat (look for the cathedral's high-flying jagged spires). The cathedral's cloister has magnolias growing in the middle and geese waddling around the periphery. (*Cathedral open M-F 8am-1:30pm and 4-7:30pm, Sa-Su 8am-1:30pm and 5-7:30pm. Cloister opens at daily 9am. Entrance to choral chamber 125ptas.*) On the opposite side of the cathedral, on C. Comtes, is the **Palau Reial** (Royal Palace). Inside, the **Museu Frederic Marès** holds the sculptor's idiosyncratic personal collection, and the **Museu d'Historia de la Ciutat** displays the ruins of a Roman colony. (*Marès museum open Tu-Sa 10am-5pm, Su 10am-2am; 300ptas, students 150ptas. History museum open July-Sept. Tu-Sa 10am-8pm, Su 10am-2pm; Oct.-June Tu-Sa 10am-2pm and 4-8pm, Su 10am-2pm; 500ptas, students 250ptas. W afternoons both free.*)

Barri de la Ribera, Parc de la Ciutadella, and vila Olímpica

The venerated **Barri de la Ribera** section of the old city grew with Barcelona's development as a major sea power during the Middle Ages. During the "Bourbon Tyranny" (as it is known locally), however, Felipe V burned much of the neighborhood. The remaining neighborhood has since evolved into the Ciutat Vella's bohemian nucleus. The Gothic **Església Santa María del Mar,** on Pl. Santa María, survived the era and today represents the pinnacle of Catalan Gothic design. Off Pg. Born, #15 C. Montcada features the famous **Museu Picasso,** housed in the medieval **Palau Berenguer d'Agüilar.** It is the most comprehensive exhibition of Picasso's early works; the two rooms devoted to studies and renditions of Velázquez's *Las Meninas* is the *museu's* centerpiece (*Open Tu-Sa 10am-8pm, Su 10am-3pm. 600ptas, students 300ptas, under 16 free.*) At #25, the **Galeria Maeght,** one of several prestigious art galleries on the block, is in a medieval palace. (*Open Tu-Sa 10am-2pm and 4-8pm.*)

The **Parc de la Ciutadella,** where Felipe incarcerated Barcelona's influential citizens and later the site of the 1888 Universal Exposition, now harbors a lake with rowboats for rent, Gaudí and friends' **Cascada** fountains, several museums, and a zoo. On Pl. Armes, outside the park, the **Museu d'Art Modern** showcases 20th-century Catalan artists. (*Open Tu-Sa 10am-7pm, Su 10am-2:30pm. 500ptas, students 250ptas.*)

The **Vila Olímpica,** beyond the east side of the zoo, was built from the ground up (on top of what was once a poor neighborhood) to house 15,000 athletes and entertain millions of tourists for the 25th Summer Olympiad in 1992. Now a yuppie village, the area contains several public parks, a shopping center, and an in-line skate rental.

The Eixample

The 1859 demolition of Barcelona's medieval walls symbolically ushered in a *Renaixença* (Renaissance) of Catalan culture. Catalan architect Ildefons Cerdà's design for a new Barcelona included a grid of squares softened by the cropped corners of streets, forming octagonal intersections. Meanwhile, the flourishing bourgeoisie commissioned a new wave of architects to build their houses, reshaping the face of the Eixample with *modernista* architecture. Gaudí's serpentine rooftops, warrior-like chimneys, and skeletal facades are the most famous of Barcelona's modernist gems.

The odd-numbered side of Pg. Gràcia is popularly known as *la manzana de la discordia* (block of discord), referring to the aesthetic competition of its buildings. Situated between C. Aragò and Consell de Cent, it offers an overview of the peak of the modernist movement. The bottom two floors of the facade of **Casa Lleó i Morera,** by Domènech i Montaner, were destroyed to house a store, but the upper floors sprout flowers and winged monsters. Puig i Cadafalch opted for a cubical pattern on the facade of **Casa Amatller** at #41. Gaudí's balconies ripple and tiles sparkle on **Casa Batlló,** #43. The rooftop is a scaly representation of Catalunya's patron Sant Jordi slaying a dragon. The central hallway and variegated blue-tiled stairway are open to the public, but only holders of the *Ruta del Modernisme* pass (available two doors down at Casa Lleó Morera) can enter the *casa principal* (main apartment).

Many modernist buffs argue that the **Casa Milà** apartment building (popularly known as **La Pedrera**—Stone Quarry), Pg. Gràcia 92, is Antoni Gaudí's masterpiece, with intricate ironwork around the balconies and egg-shaped window panes in the front gate. *(Open daily 10am-8pm. One guided tour per day: M-F 6pm, Sa-Su 11am. 500ptas, students 300 ptas—or better, buy your Ruta del Modernisme multi-pass.)* Only Gaudí's genius could draw tourists to a half-finished church, the **Temple Expiatori de la Sagrada Família,** on C. Marina between C. Mallorca and C. Provença (M: Sagrada Familia). *(Open Sept. and Mar. 9am-7pm; Jan.-Feb. and Oct.-Dec. 9am-6pm; Apr.-Aug. 9am-8pm. Guided visits 4pm and 5:30pm. Church and museum 800ptas. Elevator 200ptas.)* The church's three planned facades symbolize Jesus' nativity, passion, and glory; only the first is finished. Elevators and symmetrical staircases lead to its towers, bridges, and crannies.

Montjuïc

Overlooking the harbor and the city, with a Jewish cemetery buried underneath, **Montjuïc** (mountain of the Jews) and its **fortress** served as strategic posts for Barcelona's ruling classes for centuries before Franco made it one of his "interrogation" headquarters. Bus 61 (every 10min.) leaves for the *mont* from Pl. Espanya (M: Espanya) at Av. Reina María Cristina. The **Fonts Luminoses** (Illuminated Fountains) lining Av. Reina María Cristina put on a dazzling show in the evening, lighting up the **Palau Nacional**. The palace was designed in the "international style" by German architect Pavelló Mies van der Rohe as his country's 1929 Expo pavilion. Across the hillside, **Poble Espanyol** features replicas of famous sights from every Spanish region: a Plaza Mayor (with a self-service cafeteria), a Plazuela de la Iglesia, and so on. *(Open Su 9am-midnight, M 9am-8pm, Tu-Th 9am-2am, F-Sa 9am-4am. 500ptas.)*

In 1929, Barcelona inaugurated the **Estadi Olímpic de Montjuïc** in its bid for the 1932 Olympic games. About 100m down the road from the Olympic stadium is the **Fundació Joan Miró,** with works from all periods of Miró's career. *(Open in summer M-W and F-Sa 10am-8pm, Th 10am-9:30pm, Su 10am-2:30pm; slightly reduced hours in winter. 700ptas, students 400ptas.)*

Gràcia

Located just beyond the Eixample (M: Fontana or Lesseps), lovely, little-visited **Gràcia** is more of a living, breathing neighborhood than most of the stops on Barcelona's tourist conga line. It charms as it confuses, with narrow alleys and numerous plazas. The **Torre del Reloj** (Clocktower), on popular **Plaça Rius i Taulet,** is an emblem of the Revolution of 1868. **Plaça del Diamant,** on nearby C. Astúries, was made famous by Mercè Rodoreda's eponymous novel. Gràcia's best is **Plaça del Sol,** to which local youths swarm each night. Cafes and bars skirt its edge, and the air is one of vitality and activism. Protest graffiti, signs, and banners touching on issues from Catalan independence to the Zapatista uprising in Chiapas fill the streets and plazas. Cruise the streets coming off **Gran de Gràcia,** as well as **Plaça del Sol,** for nighttime diversions. Gran de Gràcia eventually leads to **Plaça de Lesseps.**

Parc Güell and Tibidabo

On a hill just north of the Gràcia district lies one of Barcelona's greatest treasures—perhaps the world's most enchanting public park. *(Open May-Aug. daily 10am-9pm; Apr. and Sept. 10am-8pm; Mar. and Oct. 10am-7pm; Nov.-Feb. 10am-6pm. Free.)* Gaudí intended Parc Güell (after Eusebi Güell, its commissioner) to be a garden city, its multicolored dwarfish houses and sparkling ceramic-mosaic stairways to house the city's elite. When only two people signed on, it became a park. Inside, an elegant white staircase adorned with patterned tiles and a multicolored salamander leads to a pavilion supported by 86 pillars. In the back of the park, sweeping elevated paths, supported by columns shaped like palm trees, swerve through large hedges and prehistoric plants. Bus 24 from Pg. Gràcia reaches the upper park.

You can survey the Pyrenees and the ocean from atop **Tibidabo,** Barcelona's highest point. It derives its odd name from the devil's promise to Jesus, "All this I will give to you (*tibi dabo* in Latin) if you fall down and worship me." Tibidabo's huge **Temple del Sagrat Cor** is mainly a tourist trap, but the view of Montserrat and the Pyrenees from the bust of Jesus is worth the elevator ride (75ptas). To reach the mountain top, either wait 15 minutes for the *tramvia blau* streetcar (Tramvia runs daily 9:05am-9:35pm; Oct.-May Sa-Su only; 135ptas) or walk up Av. Tibidabo in almost the same time. At the top of the street, you have to take a funicular (300ptas).

ENTERTAINMENT

Every evening around 5pm, people stroll along Las Ramblas, Pg. Gràcia, and the sea—nightlife in Barcelona starts then and there, and winds down about 14 hours later. After *siesta,* the masses roll into Las Ramblas to browse magic shows and periodical stands or stroll the portside *moll;* youngsters mill around Portal l'Angel and Portaferrissa, displaying the latest fashions. To recharge, the theater crowd makes conversation in cafes and *tapas* bars around Liceu, and foreign 20-somethings order *copas* in Pl. Reial. Farther away from the Barri Gòtic, well-off adults cruise L'Eixample, while bona fide Barcelonan students head for the bars and cafes in Gràcia. The bar scene begins around 9pm; the discos start bumping around 2am. The best source of info on fun things to do is the weekly *Guía del Ocio* (125ptas, available at newsstands).

Music and Film

The **Gran Teatre del Liceu** (see **Sights,** p. 819), Rambla de Caputxins 61, will supposedly reopen in 1999. At the **Palau de la Música Catalana,** an extraordinary brick *modernista* building on C. Francesc de Paula 2 (tel. 932 68 10 00), off Vía Laietana near Pl. Urquinaona, concerts cover all varieties of symphonic and choral music. Ask about free winter concerts (Tu nights) and the October music festival. (Tickets 1000-3500ptas. Box office open M-F 10am-9pm, Sa 3-9pm, Su from 1hr. prior to the concert. Tours are offered daily around 2 and 3pm. 300ptas, free with a *Ruta del Modernisme* pass.) The **Grec-Barcelona** summer festival (http://www.grecbcn.com) turns Barcelona into a theater, musical, and dance extravaganza from June to mid-August. Some of the major venues (the **Teatro Grec** and the **Convent de Sant Augusti**) are open-air theaters. Tickets can be purchased at the Pl. Catalunya **tourist office** (tickets sold Tu, W, and F 6-10pm, Th and Sa 4-10pm, Su 3-7pm).

Films are popular in Barcelona; besides Spanish and Catalan features, you should be able to find a Hollywood classic or the hot recent flick in English. Check the schedule of the **Filmoteca,** Av. Sarrià 33 (tel. 934 10 75 90; M: Hospital Clínic), run by the Generalitat, for classic, cult, exotic, and otherwise exceptional films (always subtitled if not a Castilian- or Catalan-language film; 400ptas).

Discos and Bars

The evening *passeig* (stroll) is divided into two shifts: the post-siesta burst (around 5-7pm), and a second wave after dinner (perhaps 9-11pm), fueled by alcohol. After the bars wind down around 2am, crowds flood the discos till morning. Bouncers can be finicky, and what's hip varies from day to day.

Las Ramblas and Barri Gótic: La Oveja Negra, Sitges 5. M: Catalunya. From Pl. Catalunya, down Las Ramblas and the first right at C. Tallers; C. Sitges is the first left. The most popular tavern in town, where locals fraternize over pitchers of beer and foosball. Open M-Th 9am-2:30am, F 9am-3:30am, Sa-Su 5pm-3:30am. **Schilling,** C. Ferrán 23. M: Liceu. You'll have to push to find a seat in this chic, popular bar. Mixed gay and straight. Open M-F 9am-2am, Sa-Su 11am-2am. **Harlem Jazz Club,** C. Comtesa de Sobradiel 8. M: Liceu. Between the Pl. Reial and Vía Laietana. Jazz and a variety of other live music. Open daily 10pm-4am (but doesn't start hopping 'til past midnight). Su-Th free, Sa 500ptas with drink. **Bar Almirall,** C. Joaquim Costa 33. A dark red cave with a decaying ceiling and weathered couches. They serve *absenta,* the licorice-flavored liquor banned in France for its eerie effects on the minds of Impressionist painters. Open Su-Th 7pm-2am, F-Sa 7pm-3am.

Eixample: Velòdrom, C. Muntaner 213. M: Diagonal. Pre-party crowd. Students meet to drink in cushioned booths and shoot pool in a weather-worn hangout. Open M-Sa 6pm-2am. **La Bodegueta,** on the corner of Rbla. Catalunya and Provença, a block away from La Pedrera. M: Diagonal. In the hours before dinner, this wine bar hops with chic Barcelonans sampling local wines and *cavas* with their cheese and pate. Dress for success. Open M-Sa noon-1am.

Montjuïc: Poble Espanyol, Av. Marqués de Comillas. M: Pl. Espanya. 12 restaurants, 15 bars, 3 *bares-musicales,* and a large *discoteca* called **Le Fou.** Touristy, but quite a show. Dancing starts at around 1:30am, and usually doesn't end until 9am. Open in summer nightly; in winter Th-Sa. **Firestiu,** Pl. del Universo. M: Espanya. An incredibly popular open-air complex with a medley of bars, bungee-jumping, carnival games, and outdoor dancing. Open June 5-Aug. 29 Th-Sa 10pm-4:30am. 1000ptas includes one drink. Free before midnight.

Port Olímpic: Nestled next to Barcelona's *platjas,* the Olympic Village brims with glitzy restaurants that give way to throngs of dance fiends, from the merely light-of-foot to the crackpot *discotecarios.* Twenty or so *bares-musicales* occupy the strip, but many revelers choose to dance on the port itself. Things begin at midnight and wind down at 6am. From the metro stop Ciutadella-Vila Olímpica (L4), walk down C. Marina toward the twin towers.

Maremagnum (the ultra-modern mall complex at **Port Vell**): At 1am the adults leave, the children go to bed, and the older kids party. Maremagnum spots are not cheap—expect to pay at least 600ptas for a beer. **Sub 34.3,** on the middle floor of Maremagnum. Ride a submarine into the depths of the ocean, grind to American pop, and swill 800ptas drafts, all at once. Open Su-Th 11pm-4am, F-Sa 11pm-5am.

■ Near Barcelona: Montserrat

Northwest of Barcelona, the **Montserrat** mountain range—legendary site of the Holy Grail and inspiration of Wagner's *Parsifal*—juts out from the flat Río Llobregat valley. In the 10th century, a wandering mountaineer had a blinding vision of the Virgin Mary here, and the site is now a major pilgrimage center, second in Spain only to Santiago de Compostela. The **basílica** stands above Pl. Creu and looks out onto Pl. Santa Noría (open daily 7:30am-8:30pm). Plaça Santa María also boasts the **Museu de Montserrat,** which exhibits a sweeping range of art—from Israeli Torahs to paintings by El Greco, Caravaggio, and Picasso (open daily 9:30am-7pm; 500ptas, students 300ptas). A visit to Montserrat without a meditative walk along the ridge of what Maragall called "the mountain of a hundred peaks" would be a sin. From Pl. Creu, the Santa Cova **funicular** descends to paths winding along the sides of the mountain to ancient hermitages (every 20min., 350ptas). Take the St. Joan funicular up for more inspirational views of Montserrat (every 20min., 875ptas). The dilapidated **St. Joan monastery** and **shrine** are only a 20-minute tromp away, but the real prize is the **Sant Jerónim** peak, with its mystical views of Montserrat's celebrated rock formations.

RENFE trains (tel. 932 05 15 15) to Montserrat leave from M: Espanya in Barcelona (1hr., every hr. 6am-9pm, 1145ptas, same-day round-trip 1785ptas); be sure to get off at the Aeri de Montserrat stop, *not* Olesa de Montserrat. Trains leaving Barcelona on odd hours (destined for Manresa) go direct to Aeri de Montserrat; if you take an even-hour train (destined for Igualada), you must change at Martorell-Enllaç. The train stops at the base of the mountain, where you can take the heartstopping **Aeri cable car** up to the monastery (every 15min. 10am-1:45pm and 2:20-6:35pm, price included in train fares; otherwise 600ptas, round-trip 900ptas). Upon exiting the upper cable car station, turn left and walk up 100m to reach **Plaça Creu,** Montserrat's tourist-oriented commercial area. For details on daily religious services and navigating your way through the mountains, go to the **info booth** in **Plaça Creu** (tel. 938 35 02 51, ext. 586). If you choose to spend the night, apartments for up to ten are available through **Administació de les Cel.les** (tel. 938 35 02 01; fax 938 35 06 59), found in the far plaza. The office runs three *hostales* and a three-star hotel. **Abat Marcet** is the newest and nicest of the lot (singles 3975-4250ptas; doubles 4225-4500ptas). As food options are less than thrilling, the prudent beat a path to the *pastissería* and *autoservei* **supermarket,** on the right as you go up Pl. Creu, which carry baked goods and groceries to appreciate on the quiet mountain paths (open Su-F 9am-6:45pm, Sa 9am-7:45pm). The best place to dine in town is the informal **Bar de la Plaça,** in the far plaza (open Su-F 9:30am-7:30pm, Sa 9:30am-8pm).

■ Sitges

Long considered a watered-down Ibiza, Sitges has better, closer beaches than the notorious Balearic hotspot, and on mainland Spain, you won't find much crazier beach-oriented nightlife than this. The **beach** is 10 minutes by foot from the train station; walking to the right as you face the water brings you to quieter shore areas. On C. Fonollar, the **Museu Cau Ferrat** houses a veritable shrine to Modernist painting, glass, and metalwork. (Open June 22-Sept. 10 Tu-Sa 9:30am-2pm and 4-9pm, Su 9:30am-2pm; off-season reduced hours. 500ptas, students 250ptas.) Late night bacchanalia clusters around **Carrer Primer de Maig,** which runs directly from the beach. The wild things are at **Atlántida,** Scetor Terramar, and **Pachá,** Pg. Sant Didac, in nearby Vallipenda. Buses run from C. Primer de Maig to both locations (midnight-4am).

Sitges celebrates its holidays with style. On June 6, for the **Festa de Corpus Christi,** the city overflows with intricate carpets woven of hundreds of thousand of flowers. Papier-mâché creatures dance in the streets from August 23 to 25 for the **Festa Major.** Yet nothing compares to the **Carnaval** during the first week of Lent, when Spaniards of every ilk crash town for a frenzy of dancing, outrageous costumes, and vats of alcohol. Ask the tourist office about other Sitges revelries.

Trains (tel. 934 90 02 02) link Sitges to Barcelona-Sants and M: "Gràcia" (40min., every 15min., 305-350ptas). To get to the **tourist office,** Pg. Vilafranca (tel. 938 94 42 51; fax 938 94 43 05), from the station, turn right on C. Salvador Mirabent Pareta and go downhill. (Open July-Aug. daily 9am-9pm; mid-Sept. to June M-F 9am-2pm and 4-6:30pm, Sa 10am-1pm.) They have a super map and plenty of info. Accommodations are expensive in Sitges: it's best to make it a daytrip from Barcelona. If you must stay, **Hostal Parelladas,** C. Parelladas 11 (tel. 938 94 08 01), is one block from the beach (singles 2500ptas; doubles 5200ptas).

■ Girona (Gerona)

A world-class city waiting patiently for the world to notice, Girona rules its namesake province from the banks of the gorgeous Riu Onyar. The city is really two in one: a hushed medieval masterpiece of stone alleyways on one river bank, and a thriving modern city on the other. Girona was founded by the Romans, but owes more to the renowned *cabalistas de Girona,* who for centuries spread the teachings of Kabbalah (mystical Judaism) in the West. Still a cultural center and home to a large university, the city is a magnet for artists, intellectuals, and activists.

SIGHTS AND ENTERTAINMENT Most of Girona's sights are in the old city across the Riu Onyar from the train station. The **Pont de Pedra** connects the two banks and leads directly into the old quarter by way of Carreras Ciutadans, Carreras Peralta, and Forçà. **El Call,** a medieval Jewish neighborhood, begins at C. Sant Llorenç; take a right off C. Forçà into a narrow alleyway. A thriving community during the Middle Ages, it was virtually wiped out by the 1492 expulsion, mass emigration, conversion, and the Inquisition. The entrance to **Centre Bonastruc Ça Porta,** the probable site of the last synagogue in Girona, is off C. Sant Llorenç about halfway up the hill. (Open June-Oct. M-Sa 10am-8pm, Su 10am-3pm; Nov.-May M-Sa 10am-6pm, Su 10am-2pm. Free.) The center now serves as a museum linking the baths, butcher shop, and synagogue, all of which surround a serene patio. Farther uphill on C. Forçà and around the corner to the right, Girona's Gothic **cathedral** rises up a record-breaking 90 Rococo steps from its *plaça.* The northern **Torre de Charlemany** is the only structure which remains from the 11th century; the cavernous interior has the world's widest Gothic nave (22m). In the trapezoidal cloister, the **Tesoro Capitular** hoards some of Girona's most precious possessions, including the intricate and animated **Tapis de la Creació,** which takes up the entire wall of Room IV. Woven in the 11th or 12th century, its illustrations depict the cycle of creation and biblical scenes. (Cathedral and museum open Tu-Su 10am-2pm and 4-7pm; Sept.-June closed Su 4-7pm. 400ptas.)

Girona takes its evening *passeig* seriously. The **Rambla** is the place to see and be seen, gossip, politic, flirt, and dance. Some summer Fridays see spontaneous *sardanas,* traditional Catalan dances involving 10 to 12 musicians, who serenade a ring of dancers. After the *passeig* there's dinner, and after dinner there's bar-hopping, when the throngs move to the newer part of the city. Bars near **Plaça Ferran el Catòlic** draw big crowds, but during the summer, **Parc de la Devesa,** across the river from the old town and several blocks to the left, has all the cachet, and often live music as well. Of Girona's four discos, the mightiest is **La Sala de Cel,** C. Pedret 118, off Pl. Sant Pere in the northern quarter of the city (cover 2000ptas, includes 2 drinks; open Sept.-July Th-Su nights). Artsy folk mill around bars and cafes in the old quarter.

PRACTICAL INFO, ACCOMMODATIONS, AND FOOD Girona is the Costa Brava's transport center: all trains on the Barcelona-Portbou-Cerbère line stop here, and scores of buses travel daily to the Costa Brava and nearby cities. Girona is also an ideal base for exploring the Catalan Pyrenees. The RENFE and bus terminals are off **Carrer de Barcelona** on the modern side of town. **Trains** (tel. 972 20 70 93) chug to Barcelona (1¼hr., 880ptas), Figueras (30min., 330-370ptas), Madrid (9-10½hr., 5400-6500ptas), Valencia (5hr., 4600ptas), and Zaragoza (5-6hr., 3700-4700ptas). **Buses** (tel. 972 21 23 19) depart from around the corner from the train station. **Sarfa** (tel. 972 20 17 96) travels to Tossa de Mar (1hr., 625ptas). The **tourist office,** Rambla de la Llibertat 1 (tel. 972 22 65 75; fax 972 22 66 12), directly on the left as you cross Pont de Pedra from the new town, is an oasis for the directionally dehydrated (open M-F 8am-8pm, Sa 8am-2pm and 4-8pm, Su 9am-2pm). There is also a **branch office** at the train station (tel. 972 21 62 96; open July-Aug. M-F 8:30am-1:30pm). Connect to the web at **Ciberxuxes,** C. Carme 55 (tel. 972 22 61 91), one block before the English bookstore (open daily July-Sept. 3-10pm; Oct.-June 8am-midnight).

Rooms are hardest to find in June and August. **Alberg-Residència Cerverí de Girona (HI),** C. Ciutadans 9 (tel. 972 21 81 21; fax 972 21 20 23), lies in the heart of the old quarter on the street running left after Pont de Pedra. A college dorm most of the year, the building is ultra-modern inside. (1700ptas, over 25 2275ptas. Breakfast included. Sheets 350ptas.) Next door, the **Pensió Viladomat,** C. Ciutadans 5 (tel 972 20 31 76), has neat and well-furnished rooms (singles 2000ptas; doubles 4000-6000ptas). **Cafe Le Bistrot,** Pujada Sant Domènec 4, packs in the locals and young lovers for a lunchtime *menú* (1200ptas) as well as pizzas and crepes. (475-675ptas. Open M-Sa 1pm-midnight, later on weekends, Su 7pm-midnight. Kitchen closed 4-8pm.) Enjoy *torradas* (delectable toasts with toppings; 500-1300ptas for 2 or 3) with the local student crowd at **Cafe la Torrada,** C. Ciutadans 18, a block from the youth hostel (open M-F 9am-11pm; in winter also Sa 7pm-midnight).

■ Near Girona: Tossa de Mar and Figueras

Tossa de Mar is a touristy resort on the lower part of the Costa Brava, about 40km north of Barcelona. All four of Tossa's **beaches** are worth a visit, as are the **calas** (small bays) accessible by foot. Beaches aside, inside the **Vila Vella** (old town), a spiral of medieval alleys leads to the Plaça Pintor J. Roig y Soler, where the **Museu Municipal** displays Roman artifacts and early 20th-century artwork (open Tu-Su June-Sept. 10am-7pm; Oct.-May 10am-1pm and 3-6pm; 200ptas). **Bus** service is frequent in summer from Barcelona (12 per day) and Girona (1-2 per day), but is so limited during low- and mid-season that travelers may wish to head for **Lloret de Mar** (8km south) and catch the bus (20min.) from there to Tossa. The **tourist office** (tel. 972 34 01 08; fax 972 34 07 12), in the bus terminal at the corner of Av. Ferran Agulló and Av. Pelegrí, has a well-indexed city map. (Open June 15-Sept. 15 M-Sa 9am-9pm, Su 10am-1pm; May and Oct. M-Sa 10am-1pm and 4-8pm; rest of year M-F 10am-1pm and 4-

7pm, Sa 10am-1pm.) **Can Lluna,** C. Roqueta 20 (tel. 972 34 03 65), is an amazing budget find: immaculate rooms with private baths and a rooftop terrace with a heart-stopping view of Tossa (1750-1900ptas; breakfast included; call ahead). Camp at **Can Martí** (tel. 972 34 08 51; fax 972 34 24 61), at the end of Rbla. Pau Casals. (July-Aug. 750ptas per person, 755ptas per tent; off-season 600ptas per person, 650ptas per tent. Open late May to mid-Sept.) The *paella* at **Restaurant Marina,** C. Tarull 6, is as good as it gets (*menú* 950ptas, *paella menú* 1250ptas). **Bar La Pirata,** C. Portal 32, has outdoor seating overlooking the sea (open Apr.-Oct. 10am-3am).

In 1974 Salvador Dalí built a museum for his works in his native, beachless **Figueras,** 36km north of Girona. Ever since, melting clocks have meant fast bucks. Transformed from an old municipal theater, the **Teatre-Museu Dalí,** in Pl. Gala i S. Dalí, parades the artist's capricious projects: erotically nightmarish drawings, extra-terrestrial landscapes, and even a personal rock collection. (Open July-Sept. daily 9am-7:15pm; Oct.-June Tu-Su 10:30am-5:15pm. July-Sept. 1000ptas, students 800ptas; Oct.-June 800ptas, 600ptas.) **Trains** (tel. 972 20 70 93) run to Barcelona (1½hr., 1085-1240ptas) and Girona (30min., 320-350ptas). **Barcelona Bus** (tel. 972 50 50 29) trucks to Barcelona (2¼hr., 1375ptas) and Girona (1hr., 415ptas). The **tourist office** (tel. 972 50 31 55) on Pl. del Sol offers a good city map, list of accommodations, and ranking of restaurants. (Open July-Aug. M-Sa 9am-9pm, Su 9am-2pm and 4-6pm; Easter-June and Oct. M-F 8:30am-3pm and 4:30-8pm, Sa 9:30am-1:30pm and 3:30-6:30pm; Sept. and Nov.-Easter M-F 8:30am-3pm.) **Alberg Tramuntana (HI),** C. Anicet de Pagès 2 (tel. 972 50 12 13; fax 972 67 38 08), provides bike rentals and friendly hosts. (1700ptas, over 25 2275ptas; cheaper off-season. Members only, but they sell HI cards. Reception 8-10am and 4pm-midnight. Lockout M-F 10am-4pm, Sa-Su 10am-5pm. Curfew midnight, but in summer opens briefly at 1 and 2am. Reserve 1 month ahead through Barcelona office at 934 03 83 63, or call the hostel 2-3 days before arrival. Closed Oct. 15-30, mid-Jan. to mid-Feb., and Su and M in winter.)

■ Catalan Pyrenees

Jagged green mountains, simple Romanesque churches, and tranquil towns attract a select group of tourists to the Catalan Pyrenees. Those who make their way away from the coast will discover the beautiful National Park, L'Aigüestortes i Estany de Sant Maurici, and excellent outdoor adventure opportunities in both sun and snow. The *Snow in Catalonia* guide (free at tourist offices) and *SKI.España* map are especially useful for skiers. **Editorial Alpina** publishes indispensable topographical maps bound in red booklets; ask at the tourist offices.

Val d'Aran

Some of the most dazzling peaks in the Catalan Pyrenees cluster in the province's northwest corner, around the **Val d'Aran.** The area is best known as one of chic ski resorts; there are about 80 alpine trails, as well as a few cross-country ones, winding down the surrounding peaks. **Vielha** is only 12km from the ski resort **Bac-quiera-Beret.** A shuttle bus connects the two in high season; check the tourist office for schedules. For **skiing info** and reservations, contact the Oficeria de Baquiera-Berey (tel. 973 64 44 55; fax 973 64 44 88), or the Vielha tourist office (see below).

Alsina Graells (tel. 973 26 85 00) runs **buses** to Vielha from Lérida (3hr., 1500ptas) that continue on to Barcelona (5½hr., 3320ptas). The **tourist office** hangs one block upriver from the *plaça* on C. Sarriulèra 6 (tel. 973 64 01 10; fax 973 64 05 37). The multilingual staff handles spacey hikers, wanna-be skiers, and uptight Romanesque-seekers with equal aplomb. (Open July-Sept. 15 daily 9am-1pm and 4-8pm; Sept. 16-May 30 M-Sa 10am-1pm and 4:30-7:30pm.) The outdoor company **Camins,** Av. Pas d'Arro 5 (tel. 973 64 24 44; fax 973 64 24 97), organizes treks into the Aigüestortes National Park and surrounding mountains (from 2000ptas), leads rafting and horse-back trips, and rents mountain bikes (2500ptas per day). Ask about winter activities. Several inexpensive *pensiones* cluster at the end of Camin Reiau, off Pg. Libertat. The best of the bunch is **Casa Vicenta,** Camin Reiau 3 (tel. 973 64 08 19), with sparkling rooms (singles 3000ptas; doubles 5000ptas; breakfast included).

BALEARIC ISLANDS (ISLAS BALEARES)

Every year, discos, ancient history, and beaches—especially beaches—draw nearly 2 million of the hippest Europeans to the Balearic Islands, 100km off the east coast of Spain. Mallorca is home to the province's capital, **Palma,** as well as limestone cliffs, countless orchards, and clear turquoise waters. **Ibiza,** a counter-culture haven since the 1960s, is the entertainment and style capital of the islands; it also boasts an active gay community. The smaller, less-touristed islands like **Menorca** offer empty white beaches, hidden coves, and mysterious Bronze Age megaliths.

Charters are the cheapest and quickest means of round-trip travel to the islands; check newspaper ads or travel agencies. **Scheduled flights** are easier to book. Frequent departures soar from cities throughout Europe. On **Iberia/Aviaco Airlines** (tel. 902 40 05 00), round-trip student fares from Barcelona to Palma, Menorca, or Ibiza run 17,000-20,000ptas. From Madrid to Ibiza, Palma, or Menorca, flights cost 25,000-30,000ptas. **Transmediterránea ships** (tel. 902 45 46 45; http://www.transmediterranea.com) leave from Barcelona, Estació Marítima Moll Sant Bertrán (tel. 93 295 91 34), and Valencia, Estació Marítima, Pta. de Valencia (tel. 963 67 06 44). Any travel agent in Spain can book seats to Palma, Mahón, and Ibiza; high-season prices run 6660-8150ptas one-way. **Flebasa** (tel. 902 16 01 80), sends ferries to Ibiza (3-4½hr., 1 per day) that continue to Palma (4500ptas) from Denia, on the FEVE rail line between Valencia and Alicante. In summer, the ferry ticket can be supplemented with a bus connection from Valencia, Alicante, or Madrid for 350ptas extra. **Buquebus** (tel. 902 41 42 42 or 934 81 73 60) has just begun super-fast catamaran service between Barcelona and Palma (4hr., 2 per day, one-way 8150ptas, cars 18,560).

Flying is the best way to **island-hop. Iberia** flies from Palma to Ibiza (20min., 3-4 per day, from 7800ptas) and Mahón, Menorca (20min., 2-3 per day, from 7800ptas). Iberia also flies from Menorca to Ibiza (2-3 per day, 14,000ptas), but the stopover in Palma can last up to four hours. Planes fill a couple of days in advance in summer, so make reservations. Seafarers between the islands sail Transmediterránea, whose **ships** connect Palma with Ibiza (2½-4½hr., 2-6 per week, 3330-5210ptas) and Mahón (6½hr., 1 per week, 3330ptas). There is no Mahón-Ibiza connection. **Trasmapi** (tel. 971 31 20 71), owned by Flebasa, links Ibiza and Formentera (25min., 12 per day). **Bus** fares between cities in Mallorca, Menorca, and Ibiza range from 200-700ptas each way. **Car** rental runs 4500ptas, **moped** rental 2700ptas, and **bike** rental 1000ptas per day.

Mallorca

Mallorca subscribes to a simple theorem—more hotels, more tourists, more money. Yet amid the tourism, jagged cliffs line the north coast, and lazy calm bays and caves scoop into the rest of the coast. The capital of the province, **Palma** is a showy Balearic upstart; its streets hustle with conspicuously consuming shoppers, and the town boasts a swinging nightlife. Though better **beaches** spread throughout the expanse of the island, decent ones are a mere bus ride from Palma. The beach at **El Arenal** (Platja de Palma, bus 15), 11km to the southeast, is popular. The equally crowded **Palma Nova** and **Illetes** beaches (buses 21 and 3, respectively) are 15 and 9km southwest. The tourist office (see below) distributes a list of over 40 nearby beaches, so take your pick—the smaller and lesser known, the better. Every Friday, *El Día de Mundo* newspaper (125ptas) includes numerous listings of bars and discos all over Mallorca. Palma nightlife centers in the **El Terreno** area, with many nightclubs on Pl. Gomilia and along C. Joan Miró. Good drinks complement elegant furniture and piles of fresh fruit and flowers at **ABACO**, C. Sant Joan 1, in the Barri Gòtic near the waterfront (fruit shakes 1100ptas, potent cocktails from 1900ptas). The divine **Baccus**, on C. Lluís Fábregas 2, attracts lively lesbian and gay hedonists (open nightly until 3am). **BCM** in nearby **Magaluf** is supposedly the biggest nightclub in Europe. (Playa-Sol bus company sends last bus at 8pm; return on bus 10 at 6:45am. Taxi from Palma 1800ptas. Cover 2000-2500ptas. Open 11pm-6am.)

In Palma, the **tourist office,** C. Sant Dominic 11 (tel. 971 72 40 90; email turisme@palma.es), offers island info, a map, and bus and train schedules (open M-F 9am-8pm, Sa 9am-1pm). The **Hostal Cuba,** C. San Magín 1 (tel. 971 73 81 59), at C. Argentina, has clean, simple rooms right on the edge of the town center (singles 1500ptas; doubles 3000ptas-3500ptas; triples 5000ptas). **Hostal Bonany,** C. Almirante Cerevera 5 (tel. 971 73 79 24), **Hostal Apuntadores,** C. Apuntadores 8 (tel. 971 71 34 91), and **Hostal Pons,** Carrer del Vi 8 (tel. 971 72 26 58), all offer clean rooms and a good location (singles 2000-2400ptas; doubles 3500-4200ptas).

Menorca Menorca's raw beaches, rustic landscape, and well-preserved ancient monuments spark the diverse interests of ecologists, sun worshippers, and photographers. Prices here are generally higher and tourists fewer in comparison with the other Balearics. Perched atop a steep bluff, **Mahón** (Maó) is the island's principal gateway. Its **tourist office,** Pl. s'Esplanada 40 (tel. 971 36 37 90; http://www.menorca.com), has bus schedules and a good, free **map** (open M-F 8:30am-7:30pm, Sa 9am-2pm). **Hostal La Isla,** C. Santa Catalina 4 (tel. 971 36 64 92), is a pleasant family-run bar-restaurant-hotel with spanking clean rooms and friendly service (singles 2200ptas; doubles 4100ptas; breakfast 300ptas). Take C. Concepció from Pl. Miranda. Bar-cafes around **Plazas Constitució, Reial,** and **s'Esplanada** serve filling *platos combinados* (450-850ptas) to rows and rows of sidewalk tables.

Several **beaches** are accessible by bus from Mahón; many of the best require a vehicle, sometimes legwork, but they're worth the extra hassle. **Es Grau** is a small bay about 8km north of Mahón, popular with Menorcan locals. Roca Triay buses leave from C. Vasallo in Mahón (6 per day, 10:15am-6:15pm). Once at Es Grau, catch a boat out to the **Illa d'en Colom,** a tiny island with more beaches that is generally quiet until July (tickets on sale at Bar C'an Bernat at the beach). **Cap de Favàrtix** is an area far more tranquil than the beaten-path beaches. From Mahón, take a moped or car in the direction of Es Gran/Fornells, turn off the highway at Favàrtix (9km), pass through farmlands, and break off from the bushy-edged roadway through an open gate to sink your toes in your very own black sand cove.

Ciutadella (Ciudadela), the island's other town, combines Mediterranean stucco and medieval cobblestone with a tranquility that eludes Máhon. Buses and ferries connect the two towns. Once there, stay at **Hotel Geminis,** C. Josepa Rossinyol 4 (tel. 971 38 58 96; fax 971 38 36 83), or **Hostal Residencia Oasis,** C. Sant Isidre 33 (tel. 971 38 21 97). **Cala Bosch,** whose jagged cliffs plummet into clear pale-blue water, is a perfect backdrop for a refreshing dip in the Mediterranean. Take the Torres bus from Ciutadella (13-16 per day, 8:15am-10:30pm).

Ibiza Only recently a hippie enclave, Ibiza's summer camp for disco fiends and high fashion victims evokes a sense of new-age decadence. Although its thriving gay community lends credence to Ibiza's self-image as a "tolerant" center, the island's high cost of touring precludes true diversity. No beach is within quick walking distance, but **Platja de Talamanca, Platja des Duros, Platja de Ses Figures,** and **Platja Figueredes** are no farther than 20 minutes away by bike. At nightfall, even the clothing stores (open until 1am) dazzle with throbbing music and flashing lights. Jazz wails through the smoky air of **Arteca,** on C. Bisbe Azara. On C. Virgen, **Capricios** has an outdoor terrace, while **Bar Galerie** and **Exis** are a bit livelier. A great scene for people-watching is the **Dôme Bar,** Carrer d'Alfons XII, off C. Virgen. Above, **Incognito** and **Angelo's,** with mostly gay crowds, look down on the crazy fashion scene. Ibiza's **disco** scene is world famous and ever changing. **Privelege,** Urbanización San Rafael, on the road to San Antonio, is a mini village with double-digit bars (open June-Sept. daily midnight-7am), while **Pachá,** Pg. Perimetral, a 20-minute walk from the port, features a playful atmosphere with palm trees and terraces (open daily 11pm-7am). **El Divino,** Puerto Ibiza Nueva, hosts extravagant parties (cover 3000ptas; open mid-June to mid-Sept. nightly 1:30-6am). Gay nightlife hovers around **Calle Virgen** and the part of Dalt Vila closest to the port. The **Discobús** runs to and from the major hotspots (midnight-6:30am; 225ptas).

The **tourist office,** C. Antoni Riquer 2 (tel. 971 30 19 00; http://www.ibizaon-line.com), right on the water, gives out good maps, especially for hiking, and a complete bus schedule (open M-F 9:30am-1:30pm and 5-7pm, Sa 10:30am-1pm). Decent, cheap accommodations in Ibiza are rare. "CH," which stands for **casa de huéspedes,** marks many doorways, but often the owner must be reached through the phone number tacked on the door. The sun and breeze have done wonders for the **Hostal Residencia Sol y Brisa,** Av. Bartomeu v. Ramón 15 (tel. 971 31 08 18; fax 971 30 30 32), parallel to Pg. Vara de Rey (singles 1800-2200ptas; doubles 3000-4000ptas). **Hostal La Marina,** C. Andenes del Puerto 4 (tel. 971 31 01 72), across from Estació Marítima, is conveniently located (singles 2000ptas; doubles 3300-6500ptas).

VALENCIA

Valencia's rich soil has earned the region its nickname: "Huerta de España" (Spain's Orchard). Dunes, sandbars, jagged promontories, and lagoons mark the coast's grand bay, and lovely fountains and pools grace the cities' carefully landscaped gardens.

▪ Valencia

Valencia is a stylish, cosmopolitan, and business-oriented nerve center, a striking contrast to its surrounding orchards and brown, speckled mountain ranges. Parks and gardens soothe the city's congested environment, and soft-sanded beaches nearby complement its kinetic day and nightlife. Unique architectural surprises hide behind the crowded city center, but the presence of modern montrosities like the Ayuntamiento discredits Valencia's bid for architectural fame.

ORIENTATION AND PRACTICAL INFORMATION

From the train station, near the city center, **Avenida Marquéz de Sotelo** runs to **Plaza del Ayuntamiento,** where the city tourist office is located. The avenue then splits into **Avenida Maria Cristina,** leading to the Central Market, and **Carrer de Sant Vicent,** leading to **Plaza de la Reina** and the cathedral. The *casco antiguo* (ancient quarter), nestled into a bend in the riverbed, contains almost everything of interest.

Flights: The airport is 15km southwest of the city (tel. 963 70 95 00). *Cercanías* trains run to and from the train station (32min., every 30min. 7am-10pm, 145ptas).

Trains: Estación del Nord, C. Xàtiva 24. Ticket windows open 7am-9pm. **RENFE** (24hr. tel. 96 352 02 02) to Barcelona (4-6hr., 11 per day, 3200ptas), Madrid (5-7½hr., departs every 1½hr., 4400ptas), and Seville (9hr., 2 per day, 5200ptas).

Buses: Estación Terminal d'Autobuses, Av. Menéndez Pidal 13 (tel. 963 49 72 22), across the river. Take bus 8 (105ptas) from Pl. Ayuntamiento or walk northwest from the center. To Barcelona (4½hr., 2900ptas) and Madrid (4-5hr., 2845-3145ptas). Eurolines also runs international service from here.

Ferries: Trasmediterránea, Estació Marítima (Valencia port tel. 963 67 06 44, general tel. 902 45 46 45). Bus 4 from Pl. Ayuntamiento. To Menorca, Mallorca, and Ibiza. Buy tickets at a travel agency, or at the port office on the day of departure.

Public Transportation: EMT Buses (tel. 963 52 83 99). Half leave from Pl. Ayuntamiento 22. Buy tickets aboard or at newsstands (110ptas, 10-ride 695ptas).

Tourist Offices: Regional office (tel. 963 52 85 73), inside the train station. Pamphlets and maps. Open M-F 9am-6:30pm. **City office,** Pl. Ayuntamiento 1 (tel. 963 51 04 17). Dedicated staff, info on museums and cultural happenings. Open M-F 8:30am-2:15pm and 4:15-6:15pm, Sa 9am-12:45pm.

Currency Exchange: Banco Central Hispano (tel. 96 159 85 00), across the street, offers decent exchange rates. 24hr. **ATMs** everywhere.

American Express: Duna Viajes, C. Cirilo Amorós 88 (tel. 963 74 15 62; fax 963 34 57 00), next to Pl. América on the edge of Río Turia. No commission on AmEx Traveler's Checks. Mail held. Open in summer M-F 10am-2pm and 5-8pm, Sa 10am-2pm; off-season M-F 9:30am-1:30pm and 4:30-7:30pm.

Emergency: Call 091 or 092. **Ambulance,** 085.
Police: Guardia Civil, tel. 062. **Policía Local,** tel. 963 62 10 12.
Hospital: Hospital Clínico Universitario, Av. Blasco Ibañez 17 (tel. 963 86 26 00), at the corner of C. Dr. Ferrer. Take bus 70 or 81 from Pl. Ayuntamiento. An English-speaking doctor is often on duty.
24-Hour Pharmacy: Check listing in the local paper *Levante* (125ptas) or check the *farmacias de guardia* schedule posted outside any pharmacy.
Post Office: Pl. Ayuntamiento 24 (tel. 963 51 67.50). Open M-F 8:30am-8:30pm, Sa 9:30am-2pm. **Postal Code:** 46080.
Internet Access: In El Corte Inglés and shopping center **Nuevo Centro.** Follow along the edge of the river north and cross the river at Puente de las Glorias Valencianas. Open daily 10am-9pm.

ACCOMMODATIONS

The business of Valencia is business, not tourism, so rooms are plentiful during the summer. The best options cluster around **Pl. del Ayuntamiento** and **Pl. del Mercado.** Avoid the areas by the *barrio chino* (red-light district) around Pl. Pilar.

Alberg Colegio "La Paz" (HI), Av. Puerto 69 (tel. 963 69 01 52), nearly halfway between the city and the port. Take bus 19 from Pl. Ayuntamiento (next to Citibank); it's the 3rd stop on Av. Puerto. 2-4 people and a bathroom in every room. Members only. Dorms 1100ptas, with full board 2500ptas; over 26 dorms 1600ptas, with full board 3000ptas. Breakfast included. Sheets 400ptas for 5 days. Reception 9am-2pm and 5pm-midnight. Curfew 1-2am. Open July-Sept. 15.

Pensión Paris, C. Salvá 12 (tel. 963 52 67 66). From Pl. Ayuntamiento turn right at C. Barcas, left at C. Poeta Querol, and right onto C. Salvá. 13 spotless rooms with angelic white curtains and balconies. A bargain. Singles 2200ptas; doubles 3200ptas, with shower 3800ptas, with bath 4200ptas; triples 4700ptas.

Hostal-Residencia Universal, C. Barcas 5 (tel. 96 351 53 84), off the plaza. 3 floors of spacious rooms with balconies, ornate ceilings, and new sinks. Singles 2000ptas; doubles 3000ptas, with shower 3600ptas; triples 4200ptas.

Hostal El Rincón, C. Carda 11 (tel. 963 91 60 83). From Pl. Ayuntamiento, Pl. Mercado extends past the market building; its continuation is C. Carda. The 54-room hostel was once a medieval lodging for wayfarers. Rooms with private bath are nicer. Singles 1500-2000ptas; doubles 2800-3600ptas.

FOOD

Celebrated as the birthplace of *paella,* Valencia boasts 200 rice specialties. Another regional favorite is *horchata,* a sweet, milky-white drink pressed from local *chufas* (earth almonds). Fresh fish, meat, and fruit sell at the **Mercado Central** on Pl. Mercado (open M-Th 7am-2pm, F 7am-2pm and 5-8:30pm, Sa 7am-3pm).

Restaurante La Utielana, Pl. Picadero Dos Aguas 3. Take C. Barcelonina off Pl. Ayuntamiento, turn left at its end into and across Pl. Rodrigo Botet, make a right onto C. Procida, and duck into a little alley/plaza on the left called Pl. Picadero Dos Aguas (look for the Utielana sign). Ideal service; all items under 825ptas. A/C. Open Sept.-July M-F 1:15-4pm and 9-11pm, Sa 1:15-4pm.

La Lluna, C. Sant Ramón, in El Carme district. A veggie restaurant to moon over. A 4-course *menú* and whole-grain bread served only weekday afternoons (850ptas) under refreshing A/C. Juices 260ptas. Open M-Sa 1:30-4pm and 8:30-11:30pm.

La Pappardella, C. Bordadores 5. Facing the cathedral, look right. A lively, chic crowd enjoys deliciously fresh pasta dishes (800-1100ptas) on the outdoor terrace. Nice inexpensive wine selection. Open W-M 2-4:30pm and 9pm-midnight.

SIGHTS AND ENTERTAINMENT

Most of the sights line the **Río Turia** or cluster near **Plaza de la Reina.** The Aragonese began the **cathedral** in Pl. Reina shortly after the *Reconquista* (open daily 7:30am-1pm and 4:30-8:30pm; free). Seized by a fit of Romantic hyperbole, or maybe just ver-

SPAIN

tigo, French novelist Victor Hugo counted 300 bell towers in the city from the **Micalet** (cathedral tower)—actually there are about 100 (open daily 10am-1pm and 4:30-7pm; reduced hours off-season; 100ptas). The **Museo de la Catedral** squeezes many treasures into very little space. Check out a Holy Grail, two Goyas, and an tabernacle made from 1200kg of gold, silver, platinum, emeralds, and sapphires. (Open Mar.-Nov. M-F 10am-1pm and 4:30-7pm, Sa 10am-1pm; Dec.-Feb. M-Sa 10am-1pm. 200ptas.) In Plaza del Mercado, the old **Lonja de la Seda** (Silk Exchange) is a prime example of Valencian Gothic architecture (open Tu-F 9am-2pm and 4-8pm, Sa-Su 9am-1:30pm; free).

On C. Sant Pius V, the **Museu Provincial de Belles Artes** displays superb 14th- to 16th-century Valencian primitives and works by later Spanish and foreign masters—a Hieronymous Bosch triptych, El Greco's *San Juan Bautista*, Velázquez's self-portrait, and a slew of Goyas. (Open Oct.-July Tu-Sa 10am-2:15pm and 4-7:30pm, Su 10am-2:15pm; Aug. Tu-Su 10am-2:15pm. Free.) Across the river and to the west, the **Instituto València de Arte Moderno (IVAM),** C. Guillem de Castro 118, has a collection of abstract sculptures by Julio González and temporary exhibits of cutting-edge photography (open Tu-Su 10am-7pm; 350ptas, students 175ptas).

For botanical diversion, the city maintains impressive **parks** on the outskirts of the historic district. Taxonomists marvel at the **Jardín Botànico,** C. Beato Gaspar Bono 6, on the western end of Río Turia (open Tu-Su 10am-9pm; 50ptas). This university-maintained, open-air garden cultivates 43,000 plants of 300 precisely labeled species from around the world. One block farther, Valencia shows the world what should be done with dry riverbeds; a series of pillared public recreation areas mark the banks of the now diverted Río Turia. Sand seekers will find the **beaches** close to Valencia overcrowded. Most accessible are **Las Arenas** and **Malvarrosa,** both on bus 19's route from Pl. Ayuntamiento (in summer also bus 20, 21, and 22).

Bars and pubs around the **El Carme** district, just beyond the market, pick up around 11:30pm. Follow Pl. Mercado and C. Bolsería (bearing right) to Pl. Tossal, where outdoor terraces, upbeat music, and *agua de Valencia* (orange juice, champagne, and vodka) entertain the masses. **Bar Sant Jaume** and **Cafe Infanta,** both in Pl. Tossal, stay lively late into the night. **Plaza Cánovas del Castillo** and **Plaza de los Fueros** also buzz until the disco hour. American students and expats frequent two Irish pubs in town. One is **Finnegan's** at Pl. Reina in front of, and to the right of, the cathedral. Discos dominate the university area, particularly on **Avenida Blasco Ibañez.** Young twentysomethings begin dancing at the pubs off Av. Ibañez at **Plaza Xúquer.** Walk around the Pl. Xúquer pubs to pick up discounted passes to the discos. **Caballito de Mar,** C. Eugenia Viñes 22 at Playa de Malvarrosa, is hugely popular.

Valencia's most illustrious traditional event is undoubtedly **Las Fallas,** March 12 to 19. The city's neighborhoods compete to build the most elaborate and satirical papier-mâché effigy; over 300 such *ninots* spring up in the streets. Parades, bullfights, fireworks, and dancing add to the festivities, and on the final day—*la nit del foc* (fire night)—all the *ninots* burn together in one last, clamorous release.

■ Near Valencia: Gandía

Before its beaches became so popular, **Gandía** was best known as the hangout of the refined and powerful Borjas family. The **train station,** on Marqués de Campo, serves Valencia (1hr., every 30min., 480ptas). The **tourist office** (tel. 962 87 77 88), opposite the station, has a detailed map and accommodations listings. (Open in summer M-F 10am-2pm and 4:30-7:30pm, Sa 10am-1:30pm; off-season M-F 10am-2pm and 4-7pm; Sa 10am-2pm.) A **branch office** (tel. 962 84 24 07) is at the beach at Pg. Marítim. Flattery doesn't do justice to **Alberg Mar i Vent (HI),** C. Doctor Fleming (tel. 962 83 17 48), a hostel/beachfront resort in Platja de Piles 10km south of Gandía. Take the **La Amistad bus** (tel. 962 87 44 10) from the right of the train station (105ptas). Water laps at the door, and the hostel offers an outdoor patio, basketball court, and bike and windsurfer rental. (800ptas, with breakfast 900ptas; over 26 1100ptas, 1400ptas. 3-day max. stay. No alcohol. Curfew Su-Th 2am, F-Sa 4am. Open Feb. 15-Dec. 15.)

■ Alicante (Alacant)

Sun-drenched Alicante has somehow been chiseled into a gem, the most redeeming sort of resort town: it quietly charms as it dutifully entertains. Although a multifaceted nightlife energizes the city, Alicante's famous, mosaic-lined waterside Esplanada is almost relaxing at sunset. High above the rows of sun-darkened bodies, the ancient *castillo*, spared by Franco when Alicante was the last Republican city to fall in the Civil War, guards the wicked tangle of streets in the cobblestoned *casco antiguo*.

ORIENTATION AND PRACTICAL INFORMATION

Avenida la Estación runs from the train station and becomes **Avenida Alfonso X el Sabio** after passing through **Plaza de los Luceros**. **Esplanada d'Espanya** stretches along the waterfront between **Rambla Méndez Núñez** and **Avenida Federico Soto**, which reach back up to Av. Alfonso X el Sabio, forming a box of streets where nearly all services cluster.

Flights: Aeroport Internacional El Altet (tel. 966 91 90 00), 10km from town. **Alcoyana** (tel. 965 16 79 11) sends bus C-6 to the airport (every 40min. from Pl. Luceros and the airport, 105ptas). The tourist office has a schedule.

Trains: RENFE, Estació Término (tel. 965 92 02 02), on Av. Salamanca, west of the city center. Info open daily 7am-midnight. To: Barcelona (4½-6hr., 3600-4200ptas), Madrid (4hr., 3200-4700ptas), Murcia (1½hr., 500-590ptas), and Valencia (2hr., 2600ptas). **Ferrocarriles de la Generalitat Valenciana,** Estació de la Marina, Av. Villajoyosa 2 (tel. 965 26 27 31), is a 15min. walk down Esplanada d'Espanya, away from Rambla Méndez Núñez; or, take bus G from the bus station and Corte Inglés. Local service along the Costa Blanca.

Buses: C. Portugal 17 (tel. 965 13 07 00). To reach Esplanada d'Espanya, turn left on Carrer d'Italia and take the 3rd right on Av. Dr. Gadea, and then left at the waterfront. **UBESA** (tel. 965 13 01 43) runs to Valencia (1960ptas). **Enatcar** (tel. 965 13 06 73) serves Barcelona (8hr., 4590ptas), Granada (6hr., 3325ptas), Madrid (6½hr., 2895ptas), Málaga (8hr., 4435ptas), and Seville (10hr., 5740ptas).

Ferries: Boats float to Ibiza, Palma, and back from nearby **Dénia. Flebasa Lines** (tel. 965 78 40 11) is in Puerto de Dénia. **Pitra car ferries** (tel. 971 19 10 68) depart from Estació Marítime (tel. 966 42 31 20) in Dénia.

Tourist Office: Regional office, Esplanada d'Espanya 2 (tel. 965 20 00 00; fax 965 20 02 43). Info on the entire coast and city. Open M-F 10am-8pm, Sa 10am-2pm and 3-8pm. A **branch office** is located at the airport (tel. 965 28 50 11).

Budget Travel: TIVE, Av. Aguilera 1 (tel. 965 90 07 70), near the train station off Av. Oscar Esplá. ISIC 700ptas. HI card 1800ptas. Open M-F 9am-1:30pm.

Emergency: dial 091.

Police: Comisaría, C. Médico Pascual Pérez 27 (tel. 965 14 22 22).

Medical Services: Hospital General, Maestro Alonzo 109 (tel. 965 93 89 99).

Post Office: Pl. Gabriel Miró 7 (tel. 965 21 99 84), off C. Sant Ferran. *Lista de Correos.* Open M-F 8am-9pm, Sa 9am-2pm. **Postal Code:** 03000.

Internet Access: On the corner of C. Gravina and C. San Telmo, 1 block from the Pl. Ayuntamiento. Hefty 250ptas per 15min. Open M-Sa 9am-1:30pm and 3-6pm.

ACCOMMODATIONS, CAMPING, AND FOOD

Although there seem to be *pensiones* and *casas de huéspedes* on every corner, the number of clean rooms is considerably smaller. The tourist office keeps accommodations listings. Stay away from most places along C. San Fernando and around the Església de Santa María, and opt instead for the newer section of town.

Pensión Les Monges Palace, C. Monjas 2 (tel. 965 21 50 46), behind the Ayuntamiento. In the center of the historic district a few blocks from the beach. Budget traveler's dream. A/C (600ptas per day). Winter heating. Singles 1700-3000ptas; doubles 3000-4500ptas; triples 5000-5500ptas.

Residencia Universitaria (HI), Av. Orihuela 59 (tel. 965 11 30 44). Take bus G (100ptas) to the last stop, directly behind the large *residencia.* Individual rooms, private bath, and A/C. 800ptas per person, with breakfast 900ptas; over 26 1100ptas, 1400ptas. Members only. 3-day max. stay. Rooms scarce Sept.-June.

Habitaciones México, C. General Primo de Rivera 10 (tel. 965 20 93 07), off the end of Av. Alfonso X El Sabio. Pristine rooms. **Internet access.** Singles 1900ptas; doubles 3200-3800ptas; triples 4500ptas. Laundry service 900ptas per load.

Camping: Playa Mutxavista (tel. 965 65 45 26), 2nd class site near the beach. Take bus C-1. 530ptas per person and per tent. Open year-round.

Small family-run joints in the old city (between the cathedral and the steps to the castle) are quieter and often cheaper than the restaurants on the pedestrian thoroughfare. The most popular *terrazas* stuff **Calle San Francisco** locals with cheap *menús* and *tapas;* natives also devour *tapas* in the **Calle Mayor. Capitol,** C. Bazan 45, between Alfonso El Sabio and the Esplanada, serves an appetizing 1150ptas *menú* all day (open M-F 1-4:30pm and 8-11pm, Sa 1-4:30pm). For some of the best *tapas* in town, head to **La Taberna del Gormet,** C. San Fernando 10. Restaurant courses are pricey, but the *tapas* at the lively bar are particularly delicious and reasonably priced (open daily noon-midnight). The neighborhood grill **La Venta del Lobo,** C. San Fernando 48, two blocks toward the center from Av. Dr. Gadea, has a four-course *menú* all day (1075ptas; open Tu-Sa 1-4pm and 8:30pm-midnight, Su 1-5pm). The **market** near Av. Alfonso X El Sabio keeps picnickers happy (open M-Sa 8am-2pm).

SIGHTS AND ENTERTAINMENT

Built by the Carthaginians and recently reconstructed, the 200m high **Castell de Santa Bárbara** has a dry moat, a dungeon, an ammunition storeroom, and an amazing view of Alicante (open daily Apr.-Sept. 10am-7:30pm; Oct.-Mar. 9am-6:30pm; free). A paved road from the old section of Alicante leads to the top; most people take the elevator (400ptas) from a hidden entrance on Av. Jovellanos, across the street from the beach. Bronze Age dowries and Roman statues mingle in the **Museu Arqueológic de la Diputación,** Av. Estación 6 (open M-F 10am-6pm; free). Skipping ahead a few centuries, a crowd of Valencian Modernist pieces, along with Mirós, Picassos, Kandinskys, and Calders, fraternize in the **Museu de Arte del Siglo XX La Asegurada,** at the east end of C. Mayor. (Open Tu-Sa Oct.-Apr. 10am-1pm and 5-8pm; May-Sept. 10:30am-1pm and 6-9pm. Free.) If Alicante's beach doesn't suit you, hop on bus C-1 in Pl. Espanya and bus S from either Pl. Espanya or Pl. Mar (105ptas) or board the Alicante-Denia train (20min., 105ptas) for 6km long **Playa de San Juan.** For more privacy and even more flesh visit **Platja del Saladar** in Urbanova. Buses from the Alicante bus station run to Urbanova (20min., 100ptas).

Warm-weather nightlife centers on the **Platja de Sant Joan.** In July and August, **Ferrocarriles de la Generalitat Valenciana** runs special **Trensnochador** night trains from Estació de la Marina to several points along the beach (every hr. 9pm-7am, 100-700ptas). Pick up a schedule (with cover charge discounts) at the tourist office. **Voy Voy,** on Av. Niza at the "Discotecas" night train stop, has disco inside and out (beer from 350ptas; open nightly until 6am). The **Copity** disco, on Av. Condomina, is a long walk or short taxi ride from the "Condomina" stop. The "Disco Benidorm" stop (round-trip 650ptas), in package-tour crazy Benidorm, has hard-core *discotecas* like **Penélope, Pachá, KM,** and **Insomnia** (open nightly until 9am; cover from 1500ptas).

For those in search of parties closer to home, Alicante offers its own popular *discotecas* and bars. In the old town, **El Barne,** students hop from one *bar-musical* to the next. Popular with both gay and straight dancers is **Celestial Copas** on C. San Pascual. **Rosé** on C. San. Juan Bosco also attracts a gay crowd, while **Desdén** on C. Santo Tomás attracts huge numbers of Americans. On the Esplanada, at Pl. Canelejas, a **petit Pachá** welcomes those who do not brave the bigger brother in Benidorm.

From June 20 to 24, hedonistic celebrations erupt for the **Festival de Sant Joan.** *Fogueres* (symbolic or satiric effigies) are paraded around town, then burned in a *cremá* on the 24th, but the revelry continues with breathtaking and hazardous nightly fireworks and lights and decorations along the streets. Ask the tourist office about summer concerts and performances honoring Alicante's patron saint, Virgen del Demedio.

ANDALUSIA (ANDALUCÍA)

Andalusia derives its spirit from a mix of cultures. Greeks, Phoenicians, and Romans colonized and traded in the region, but the most enduring influences were left by Arabs, who arrived in 711. Under Moorish rule, which lasted until 1492, Seville and Granada reached the pinnacle of Islamic arts, and Córdoba matured into the most culturally influential Islamic city of the western Caliphate. The Moors perfected a distinctly *Andalucían* architectural style marked by cool patios and the alternation of red brick and white stone, and sparked the European Renaissance by reintroducing the wisdom and science of Classical Greece and the Near East. The dark legacy of Andalusia is its failure to progress economically; stagnant industrialization and severe drought have mired the region in indefinite recession. At the same time, residents believe the good life is possible with good food, good drink, and spirited company.

■ Seville (Sevilla)

Site of a Roman acropolis, seat of Moorish culture, focal point of the Spanish Renaissance, and guardian angel of traditional Andalusian culture, Seville has never failed to spark the imagination. Jean Cocteau included it with Venice and Beijing in his trio of magical cities, and Bizet, Mozart, and Rossini wrote operas inspired by the metropolis. The 16th-century maxim *"Qui non ha visto Sevilla non ha visto maravilla"*—one who has not seen Seville has not seen a marvel—remains true today.

ORIENTATION AND PRACTICAL INFORMATION

Río Guadalquivir flows roughly north-south through Seville. Most of the city, including the alleyways of the old **Barrio de Santa Cruz,** is on the east bank; the historic and proud **Barrio de Triana** and the modern, middle-class **Barrio de los Remedios** occupy the west bank. The **cathedral,** next to Barrio de Santa Cruz, is Seville's centerpiece. **Avenida de la Constitución,** home of the tourist office and other agencies, runs alongside the cathedral. **El Centro,** a busy commercial pedestrian zone, lies north of the cathedral where Av. Constitución hits **Plaza Nueva.**

To reach El Centro from **Estación Santa Justa,** catch bus 27, which heads to **Plaza de la Encarnacíon.** To get to Barrio Santa Cruz and the cathedral, first take bus C1, C2, or 70 to Santa Justa and the main bus station at Prado de San Sebastián. Beware; Seville is the Spanish capital of pickpocketing and car theft. The city has become safer in recent years, but if you value your stuff, don't leave it unattended or in a locked car.

Flights: Aeropuerto San Pablo (tel. 954 67 29 81 or 954 67 52 10), 12km from town on Ctra. Madrid. A taxi from the center of town costs about 2000ptas. **Los Amarillos** runs a bus (750ptas) from outside the Hotel Alfonso XIII in the Puerta de Jerez (approx. 1 per hr. 6:15am-10:30pm; call 954 41 52 01 for schedule).
Trains: Estación Santa Justa, Av. Kansas City (tel. 954 54 03 03, reservations tel. 954 54 02 02). Buses C1 and C2 link this station to the Prado de San Sebastián bus station, stopping on Av. Kansas City, left as you exit the train station. **RENFE,** C. Zaragoza 29 (tel. 954 22 26 93), near Pl. Nueva. Open M-F 9am-1:15pm and 4-7pm. **AVE** to: Córdoba (45min., 2700ptas) and Madrid (2½hr., 7000-9500ptas). **Talgo** to: Cádiz (2hr., 1200ptas), Granada (4hr., 2280ptas), and Málaga (3hr., 2055ptas).
Buses: The older **Prado de San Sebastián,** C. José María Osborne 11 (tel. 954 41 71 11), serves mainly Andalusia. **Transportes Alsina Graells** (tel. 954 41 88 11). To: Córdoba (2hr., 1200ptas), Granada (3hr., 2400ptas), and Málaga (2½hr., 1850ptas). **Transportes Comes** (tel. 954 41 68 58). To Algeciras (3½hr., 2100ptas), Cádiz (1½hr., 1300ptas), and Jerez de la Frontera (2hr., 875ptas). **Enatcar-Bacoma** (tel.

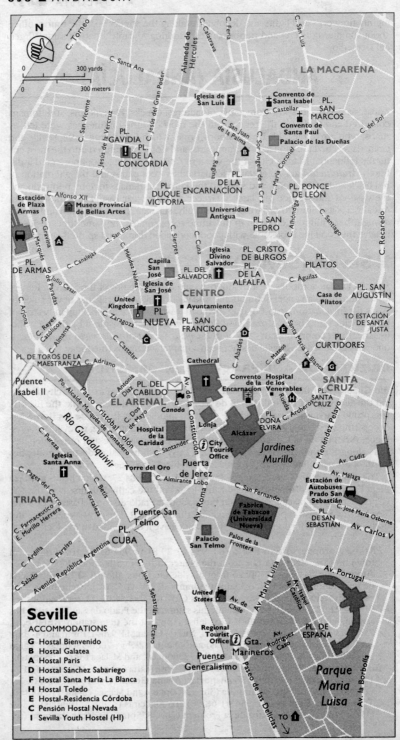

Seville

ACCOMMODATIONS

G Hostal Bienvenido
B Hostal Galatea
A Hostal Paris
D Hostal Sánchez Sabariego
F Hostal Santa María La Blanca
H Hostal Toledo
E Hostal-Residencia Córdoba
C Pensión Hostal Nevada
I Sevilla Youth Hostel (HI)

954 41 46 60). To Barcelona (16hr., 8820 ptas). **Los Amarillos** (tel. 954 41 52 01). To Arcos de la Frontera (2hr., 905ptas) and Marbella (3hr., 1820ptas). The newer station at **Plaza de Armas** (tel. 954 90 80 40), on the riverbank where Puente Cristo de la Expiración meets C. Arjona, serves destinations outside Andalusia and Spain. **Socibus** (tel. 954 90 11 60; fax 954 90 16 92). To Madrid (6hr., 2715ptas).

Tourist Offices: Junta de Andalucía, Av. Constitución 21B (tel. 954 22 14 04; fax 954 22 97 53), 1 block south of the cathedral. An absolute must. Open M-F 9am-7pm, Sa 10am-2pm and 5-7pm, Su 10am-2pm. **Municipal office,** Po. Delicias 9 (tel. 954 23 44 65), opposite Parque de María Luísa by Puente del Generalísimo. Open M-F 9am-6:30pm.

Currency Exchange: Banco Central Hispano, C. Sierpes 55 (tel. 954 56 26 84), exchanges cash at good rates with no commission. Open M-F 8:30am-2:30pm.

American Express: Pl. Nueva 7 (tel. 954 21 16 17), changes cash and AmEx Traveler's Checks without commission, holds mail, and offers emergency services for cardmembers. Open M-F 9:30am-1:30pm and 4:30-7:30pm, Sa 10am-1pm.

Luggage Storage: At the Prado de San Sebastián bus station. 250ptas. Open daily 6:30am-10pm. At the newer bus station at Plaza de Armas, 300ptas. Also at Santa Justa train station. 300-500ptas.

Laundromat: Lavandería Robledo, C. F. Sánchez Bedoya 18 (tel. 954 21 81 32), 1 block west of the cathedral, across Av. Constitución. Wash and dry 950ptas per 5kg. Open M-F 10am-2pm and 5-8pm.

Emergency: tel. 091 or 092.

Police: Av. Paseo de las Delicias 15 (tel. 954 61 54 50).

24-Hour Pharmacy: 5-6 pharmacies open each night, all night, on a rotating basis. Check list posted at any pharmacy in the city.

Medical Assistance: Ambulatorio Esperanza Macarena (tel. 954 42 01 05). **Hospital Universitario Virgen Macarena,** Av. Dr. Fedriani (tel. 954 24 81 81).

Post Office: Av. Constitución 32 (tel. 954 21 64 76), across from the cathedral. Open for stamps, *Lista de Correos,* and faxes M-F 8:30am-8:30pm, Sa 9:30am-2pm. **Postal Code:** 41808.

Internet Access: Cibercenter, C. Julio Cesar 8 (tel. 954 22 88 99), off C. Reyes Católizos. 1000ptas per hr., 15min. minimum. Open daily 9am-9pm.

ACCOMMODATIONS AND CAMPING

Rooms vanish and prices soar during *Semana Santa* and the *Feria de Abril;* reserve ahead. Check out the **Barrio de Santa Cruz,** especially on C. Fabiola and C. Archeros, and around the quiet backstreets near the Pl. de Armas. Also try the *casco viejo* of **El Centro,** a disorienting array of narrow streets radiating from Pl. de la Encarnación.

Sevilla Youth Hostel (HI), C. Isaac Peral 2 (tel. 954 61 31 50; fax 954 61 31 58). Take bus 34 from Prado de San Sebastián, which stops behind the hostel just after Po. Delicias. Bright, white, and disinfected. 1300ptas, over 26 1800ptas. Nonmembers 300ptas extra for 6 nights to become members. Wheelchair accessible.

Hostal Sánchez Sabariego, C. Corral del Rey 23 (tel. 954 21 44 70), on the continuation of C. Argote de Molina, northeast of the cathedral. Follow signs to Hostel Sierpes. Friendly little hostel with antique furniture and spacious rooms. A/C upstairs. Singles 3000ptas; doubles 5000-7000ptas; prices somewhat negotiable.

Hostal Paris, C. San Pedro Mártir 14 (tel. 954 22 98 61; fax 954 21 96 45), off C. Gravina. New, clean, and classy. Bath, A/C, TV. For comforts, one of the best values in town. Singles 3500ptas; doubles 5000-6000ptas. Ask about student discounts.

Hostal-Residencia Córdoba, C. Farnesio 12 (tel. 954 22 74 98), off C. Fabiola. Recently renovated with a beautiful indoor patio. A/C in all rooms. Singles 2800-3800ptas; doubles 4500-8000ptas. Front door locked 3-6:30am.

Hostal Galetea, C. San Juan de la Palma 4 (tel. 954 56 35 64; fax 954 56 35 17). From the west end of Pl. Encarnación, take C. Regina, then turn right. Clean rooms with fans. Singles 3200ptas; doubles 4900-5600ptas; cheaper off-season.

Hostal Toledo, C. Santa Teresa 15 (tel. 954 21 53 35), off C. Ximénez de Enciso, which is perpendicular to C. Sta. María la Blanca. Just west of Jardines de Murillo. Quiet, comfortable hostel houses researchers using the Archivo de Indias. Singles 2675-3200ptas; doubles 5350ptas. Private baths. Curfew 1am.

Hostal Santa María La Blanca, C. Sta. María La Blanca 28 (tel. 954 42 11 74). Gregarious owner offers one of the few bargains in the Sta. Cruz district. Each room has a fan. Singles 1500-2000ptas; doubles and triples 1500-2000ptas.

Hostal Bienvenido, C. Archeros 14 (tel. 954 41 36 55), near Pl. Curtidores. English-speaking owner welcomes you to spacious doubles with balconies and small singles with big windows. 3rd fl. is oven-like July-Aug. Singles 1800-2000ptas; doubles and triples 1500-1800ptas per person.

Pensión Hostal Nevada, C. Gamazo 28 (tel. 954 22 53 40), in El Arenal. From Pl. Nueva, take C. Barcelona and turn right on C. Gamazo. Naturally cool courtyard. Sleek leather sofas. Singles 2200-3500ptas; doubles 4000-6000ptas.

Camping Sevilla, Ctra. Madrid-Cádiz, km 534 (tel. 954 51 43 79), 12km out of town near the airport. From Est. Prado de San Sebastián, take bus 70, which stops 800m away at Parque Alcosa. Grassy sites, hot showers, supermarket, and swimming pool. 460ptas per person, per car, and per tent. Children 375ptas.

FOOD

Sevillians offset the merciless midday sun by keeping their cuisine light—the town claims to be the birthplace of *tapas*. Popular venues for *el tapeo* (*tapas*-bar hopping) hide out in **Triana** and in **Barrio Santa Cruza** and **El Arenal** around the bullring. More casual still are Seville's bountiful markets. Buy renowned jams, pastries, and candies from convent kitchens or the stores in **Plaza Cabildo** off Av. Constitución. **Mercado del Arenal,** near the bullring on C. Pastor y Leandro, between C. Almansa and C. Arenal, has fresh produce, *toro de lidia* (fresh bull meat), and screaming vendors. Merchants also hawk excellent fresh produce, fish, meat, and baked goods at **Mercadillo de la Encarnación** (both open M-Sa 9am-2pm). **El Corte Inglés,** Pl. Duque de la Victoria 7, has a huge basement supermarket (open M-Sa 10am-9:30pm). For better prices, try **%Día,** C. San Juan de Ávila, on Pl. Gavídia, around the corner from El Corte Inglés (open M-F 9:30am-2pm and 6:30-9pm, Sa 9am-1pm).

Restaurante-Bar El Baratillo/Casa Chari, C. Pavia 12 (tel. 954 22 96 51), on a tiny street off C. Dos de Mayo. Friendly owner, early 80s posters, and rock-bottom prices. *Menú* 500ptas. *Platos combinados* 450-750ptas. Call ahead for homemade *paella* and drinks (2500ptas for 2). Open M-F 8am-10pm, Sa noon-5pm.

Jalea Real, Sor Angela de la Cruz 37. From Pl. Encarnación, head 150m east on C. Laraña, and turn left just before Iglesia de San Pedro. Young, hip vegetarian restaurant with interesting salads and homemade desserts. Delectable spinach crepe 675ptas. Lunch *menú* 1250ptas. Open M-Sa 1:30-5pm and 8:30-11:30pm.

Bodega Santa Cruz, C. Rodrigo Caro 1. Take C. Mateos Gago from the fountain by the cathedral to the 1st corner on the right. Casual and crowded. Varied and tasty *tapas* 175-200ptas. Beer 125ptas. Mega-watt A/C. Open daily 8am-midnight.

Casa Cuesta, C. Castilla 3-5, north of Puente Isabel II, 1 block inland. A bit expensive but worth it. Popular with locals. *Pescado* 900-1700ptas. *Cola de toro* (bull's tail) 1700ptas. Open for lunch and dinner, especially popular on weekends.

Bodega Sierpes, C. Azofaifo 9, off C. Sierpes. Specializes in cheap, enormous portions of chicken eaten outside in a *terraza*. *Gazpacho* in a glass 150ptas. Half-chicken, bread, salad, and beverage 775ptas. Open W-M 11am-midnight.

La Ortiga, C. Procurador 19, off C. Castilla. Health food bar/patio in a theater. All-organic *tapas ecológicas* (225ptas). Open M-Sa from 8pm; off-season from 5pm.

Café-Bar Jerusalem, C. Salado 6, at C. Virgen de las Huertas. Meat and cheese *shoarma* called a *bocadillo hebreo* (bread, lettuce, roast pork, holland cheese, hebrew spices) ain't kosher but sure is tasty (400-625ptas). Open daily 8pm-3am.

Bodegón Alfonso XII, C. Alfonso XII 33, near the Museo de Bellas Artes. Breakfast with eggs, ham, and coffee (or beer) around 425ptas. *Menú del día* 800ptas. Open M-Sa 8am-10:30pm.

SIGHTS

Christians razed an Almohad mosque to clear space for Seville's cathedral in 1401, leaving only the famed **La Giralda** minaret. The tower and its twins in Marrakech and Rabat are the oldest and largest surviving Almohad minarets. The **cathedral,** which took over a century to complete and stands as the largest Gothic edifice in the world, is by far Seville's most impressive sight. *(Cathedral complex and Giralda open M-Sa 10:30am-6pm, Su 2-7pm. Tickets sold until 1hr. before closing. 700ptas, students and senior citizens 200ptas, under 12 free; Su free.)* To demonstrate their religious fervor, the conquerors constructed a church so great that, in their own words, "those who come after us will take us for madmen." The **retablo mayor** (altarpiece), the largest in the world, is a golden wall of intricately wrought figurines, depicting 36 biblical scenes. By circling the choir, you will approach a monument to **Cristóbal Colón** (Christopher Columbus). His black and gold coffin-bearers represent the eternally grateful kings of Castilla, León, Aragón, and Navarra. Farther on and to the right stands the cathedral's most precious museum, the **Sacristía Mayor,** which holds Riberas, Murillos, and a glittering Corpus Christi icon, **la Custodia processional.** Outside the cathedral proper, on the north end, the **Patio de Los Naranjos** (orange trees) evokes the bygone days of the Arab Caliphate.

The 9th-century walls of the **Alcázar**—the oldest palace still used by European royalty—face the south side of the cathedral. *(Open Tu-Sa 9:30am-7pm, Su 9:30am-5pm. 600ptas, students, seniors, and under 12 free.)* Within, the *Patio de las Muñecas* (Courtyard of the Dolls) remains from the Moorish era. Of later Christian additions to the palace, the most exceptional are the *Patio de las Doncellas* (Maids' Court), with foliated archways, glistening tilework, and a central fountain, and the golden-domed *Salón de los Embajadores* where Fernando and Isabel welcomed Columbus upon his return from America. The 16th-century **Casa Lonja**, between the cathedral and the Alcázar, was built by Felipe II as a commercial exchange for American trade. In 1785 it was turned into the **Archivo General de las Indias** (Archive of the Indies), a collection of over 44,000 documents relating to the conquest of the "New World." *(Access to documents restricted to scholars. Exhibits open M-F 10am-1pm. Free.)* Highlights include letters from Columbus to Fernando and Isabel.

King Fernando III forced Jews fleeing Toledo to live in the **Barrio de Santa Cruz,** now a neighborhood of winding alleys, wrought-iron gates, and fountained courtyards. Northeast of Barrio Santa Cruz off Pl. Pilatos, the **Casa de Pilatos** is a palace of plenty—Roman antiques, Renaissance and Baroque paintings, period furniture, and several courtyards. *(Open daily 9am-7pm. 1000ptas.)* The **Museo Provincial de Bellas Artes,** Pl. Museo 9, houses Spain's finest collection of Seville School painters (especially Murillo, Leal, and Zurbarán) as well as works by El Greco and Dutch master Jan Breughel. *(Open W-Sa 9am-8pm, Tu 3-8pm, Su 9am-3pm. 250ptas, EU citizens free.)* Flanking the west end of the 12th-century walls in the northeast of the city, the **Basílica Macarena** houses the venerated image of *La Virgen de la Macarena,* which is featured in Holy Week processions. *(Open daily 9:30am-1pm and 5-9pm. Free.)* Across the river and north of Triana, the **Centro Andaluz de Arte Contemporáneo,** in the Cartuja district, houses works by such 20th-century favorites as Miró. *(Open Tu-Sa 10am-9pm, Su 10am-3pm. 300ptas, EU citizens free; Tu free.)*

ENTERTAINMENT

The tourist office distributes *El Giraldillo,* a free monthly magazine with complete entertainment listings. Popular bars cluster around **Plaza Alfalfa** and **Plaza Salvador** in El Centro, **Calle Mateos Gago** near the cathedral, **Calle Adriano** by the bullring, and **Calle Betis** across the river in Triana. Summer crowds sweep towards the river in hopes of a pleasant breeze. A trio of bars (popular with exchange students) line C. Betis: **Alambique, Mú Dáquí,** and **Big Ben.** On the other bank and downstream on Po. Delicias, near Parque María Luisa, **Alfonso, Libano,** and **Chile** are popular *chiringuitos* (beach bars). There's always a crowd at **Bar Capote,** Po. Cristóbal Colón, beside Puente Isabel II (open M-Th until 4am, later F-Sa with live music; DJs W-Th. Beer 200ptas). A number of sandy summer dance floors open up in **Puerta Triana,** upstream from Triana on the old Expo '92 grounds. There is usually no cover (crowds build around 3am). In winter time, bar-hoppers stick to El Centro around Pl. Alfalfa and Pl. Salvador. The most popular disco is ultra-chic **Catedral,** Cuesta Rosario off of Pl. Salvador (expect a cover charge). Other popular spots cluster on **Avenida**

SPAIN

de la Raza, parallel to the river off Puente de las Delicias. The **gay** scene is coming out strong in Seville: popular disco-bars include **Isbiliyya,** Po. de Colón 2, and **To Ca Me,** C. Reyes Católicos 25 (both open nightly until 4am). The liveliest gay disco in town is **Itaca,** C. Amor de Dios in El Centro. (Open until 5am weeknights, later on weekends; shows W at 1am. Knock on the door to be let in.)

On the west edge of Barrio Santa Cruz, **Los Gallos,** Pl. Santa Cruz 11 (tel. 954 21 69 81), performs the flashiest *flamenco* in town. To get a ticket (much less a good seat) arrive early (cover and drink 3000ptas). Several booths on C. Sierpes, C. Velázquez, and Pl. Toros sell **bullfight** tickets (anywhere from 3000-13,000ptas). For current information on dates and prices, call 954 22 35 06. Seville's world-famous **Semana Santa** (Holy Week) festival lasts from Palm Sunday to Good Friday (Mar. 28-Apr. 2 in 1999). Penitents in hoods guide bejeweled floats lit by hundreds of candles through the streets. The city explodes during the six-day **Feria de Abril** (April Fair), which began as a 19th-century popular revolt against foreign influence. The party rages through the night with circuses, bullfights, and flamenco shows.

■ Near Seville: Cádiz, Jerez de la Frontera, and Arcos de la Frontera

Located on the southeast corner of the Iberian peninsula, **Cádiz** claims to be the oldest city in Western Europe—and one of Spain's most progressive. Cádiz's inhabitants drafted a liberal (although ignored) constitution in 1812 and fought fiercely against the Fascists in the 1936-39 Civil War. Socially, the city rocks: summer nightlife centers on the beach, while the **Carnaval** (Feb. 6-16) makes New Orleans's Mardi Gras look like Thursday night bingo. The **tourist office,** Pl. San Juan de Dios 11 (tel. 956 24 10 01), provides a free map (open M-F 9am-2pm and 5-8pm). *Hostales* huddle around the harbor, in Pl. San Juan de Dios, and behind it on C. Marqués de Cádiz. At C. Marqués de Cádiz 6, the **Hostal Colón** (tel. 956 28 53 51) is squeaky clean and colorful (singles 2000ptas), and the **Hostal Marqués,** #1 (tel. 956 28 58 54), has newly renovated rooms (singles 1800ptas). The manager of **Hostal Cádiz,** C. Feduchy 20 (tel. 956 28 58 01), has tips on restaurants and nightlife (1500-2000ptas per person).

Unremarkable in appearance, **Jerez de la Frontera** is the cradle of three staples of Andalusian culture: *flamenco,* Carthusian horses, and above all, *vino de jerez*—better known as sherry. You can visit *bodegas* (wine cellars) throughout Jerez de la Frontera. **Williams and Humbert, Ltd.** (tel. 956 34 65 39; 300 ptas), **Harvey's of Bristol** (tel. 956 15 10 02; 325ptas), and **B. Domecq** (tel. 956 15 15 00; 325ptas) have multilingual tour guides who distill the complete sherry-making process as you sip free samples (call ahead for tour hours and for reservations, often required). Avoid visiting in August, when many *bodegas* close down for the annual hangover. The **Fiestas de la Bulería** in September celebrates the town's *flamenco* tradition. **Trains** roll to Cádiz (45min., 365ptas) and Seville (1½hr., 735ptas). The **tourist office,** C. Larga 39 (tel. 956 33 11 50), has info on *bodega* tours and festivals. (Open in summer M-F 8am-2pm and 5-8pm, Sa 10am-2pm; in winter M-F 8am-3pm and 4-7pm, Sa 10am-2pm and 5-7pm.) Finding a bed in Jerez is as easy as finding sherry. Look along **Calle Medina,** near the bus station, and **Calle Arcos,** which intersects C. Medina at Pl. Romero Martínez. To reach the **Albergue Juvenil (HI),** Av. Carrero Blanco 30 (tel. 956 14 39 01), walk 25 minutes from downtown, or take bus L-8 near the bus station (every 15min., 125ptas) or bus L-1 from Pl. Arenal. The hostel has a pool, library, TV room, tennis and basketball courts, and spacious doubles (800-1300ptas, over 26 1100-1800ptas; nonmembers 300ptas extra). *Tapas*-hoppers bounce all around **Plaza del Arenal,** and northeast on Av. Alcalde Alvaro Domecq around **Plaza del Caballo.**

The road to **Arcos de la Frontera** snakes through fields of sunflowers and sherry-grape vines; the city itself is a maze of little white houses, alleyways, medieval ruins, and stone arches. The most beautiful sight might just be the view from **Plaza Cabildo.** In this square stands the **Iglesia de Santa María,** built in 1553, with its well-preserved wall painting from the 14th century (open daily 10am-1pm and 4-7pm; 150ptas). T.G. Comes **buses** (tel. 956 70 20 15) travel to Cádiz (1½hr., 670ptas) and Jerez (280ptas), while Los Amarillos (tel. 956 70 02 57) jaunts to Jerez (15min.,

295ptas) and Seville (2hr., 905ptas). The **tourist office** at Pl. Cabildo (tel. 956 70 22 64) offers a detailed map of the old city and essential info. (Open in summer M-Sa 10am-2pm and 5-8pm, Su 11am-2pm; off-season M-Sa 9am-2pm and 5-7pm.) **Hostal Callejón de las Monjas,** C. Dean Espinosa 4 (tel. 956 70 23 02 or 956 70 43 88), offers roomy, cool accommodations (singles and doubles 3500-4500ptas).

■ Córdoba

A Spaniard well versed in regional subtleties once made the following distinction between Córdoba and her more flamboyant Andalusian sister to the west: "Seville is a young girl, gay, laughing, provoking—but Córdoba...Córdoba is a dear old lady." Córdoba does indeed show a dignity and refinement befitting a city known less for joviality than for breadth of mind. Romanization brought the incomparable playwright and philosopher Seneca here. During Islamic rule (711-1263) the city emerged as an intellectual powerhouse and the capital of the Western Caliphate. No where else in Spain are remnants of Islamic, Jewish, and Catholic civilizations so well mixed.

ORIENTATION AND PRACTICAL INFORMATION

Córdoba sits atop the Andalusian triangle (north of Seville and Granada), about halfway between Madrid and Gibraltar. The city's more modern and commercial northern half extends from the train station on **Avenida de América** down to **Plaza de las Tendillas** in the center of the city. The older, more touristy, maze-like southern half, known as the **Judería** (old Jewish quarter), extends from Pl. Tendillas down to the banks of the Guadalquivir, winding past the Mezquita and Alcázar.

Trains: Av. América (tel. 957 49 02 02). To: Algeciras (5hr., 2220-3270ptas), Cádiz (2½-3hr., 1960-4000ptas), Granada via Bobadilla, Madrid (2-6hr., 3500-7000ptas), Málaga (2¼-3hr., 1535-2200ptas), and Seville (45min.-1¼hr., 890-2700ptas). For international tickets, contact **RENFE,** Ronda de los Tejares 10 (tel. 957 47 58 84).

Buses: The main bus station is at C. Diego Serrano 14. **Alsina-Graells Sur** (tel. 957 23 64 74), off C. Noguer, covers most of Andalusia. To: Granada (3hr., 1765ptas), Málaga (3-3½hr., 1500ptas), Marbella (4hr., 2085ptas), and Seville (2hr., 1200ptas). **Bacoma** (tel. 957 45 65 14), travels to Barcelona, Murcia, and Valencia (1 per day). **Socibus** (tel. 902 22 92 92) provides exceptionally cheap service to Madrid (4½hr., 1540ptas), departing from Camino de los Sastres in front of Hotel Melia. **Autocares Priego** (tel. 957 29 01 58) runs anywhere on the Sierra Cordobesa; **Empresa Carrera** (tel. 957 23 14 01) serves the Campiña Cordobesa; and **Empresa Ramírez** (tel. 957 41 01 00) runs to nearby towns and camping sites.

Tourist Office: Junta de Andalucía, C. Torrijos 10 (tel. 957 47 12 35; fax 957 49 17 78), on the west side of the Mezquita. Bubbly English-speaking staff provides abundant info on Córdoba and Andalusia as well as a free map. Open M-Sa in summer 9:30am-8pm; in winter 9:30am to 6 or 7pm.

Luggage Storage: At the train station and main bus station. 300-600ptas per locker.

Emergency: tel. 091 or 092. **Ambulance,** tel. 061.

Medical Assistance: Red Cross Hospital, Po. Victoria (tel. 957 29 34 11).

Post Office: C. Cruz Conde 15, just north of Pl. Tendillas. Open for *Lista de Correos* M-F 8:30am-8:30pm, Sa 9:30am-2pm. **Postal Code:** 14070.

Internet Access: El Navegante Cafe Internet, C. Llanos del Pretorio 1 (tel. 957 49 75 36), off Av. de America, near the train station. 250ptas per 15min., 350ptas per 30min., 600ptas per hr. Open daily 8am-3:30pm and 8pm-3am.

ACCOMMODATIONS AND CAMPING

Accommodations cluster near the train station, in and around the Judería, and off the Pl. Tendillas. Most are crowded during *Semana Santa* and in summer.

Residencia Juvenil Córdoba (HI), Pl. Juda Leví (tel. 957 29 01 66; fax 957 29 05 00), next to the municipal tourist office. Huge, modern, and antiseptic. 1300ptas, over 26 1800ptas; nonmembers 300ptas extra. A/C. No curfew. Call ahead in the summer and confirm a day before arriving.

Hotel/Hostal Maestre, C. Romer Barros 16 (tel./fax 957 47 53 95, reservations tel. 957 47 24 10). From the Mezquita, follow the river east to Pl. Potro, walk uphill and take a left (10min.). Newly renovated rooms ranging from intimate *hostal* to modern hotel with A/C and TV to spacious apartments with kitchens. In *hostal:* singles 2000-2500ptas; doubles 4000-5000ptas; all with bath. In hotel: doubles 5000-6000ptas. Apartments 7000-8000ptas.

Huéspedes Martínez Rücker, Martínez Rücker 14 (tel. 957 47 25 62), just east of the Mezquita. Comfortable patio. All rooms have quiet fans. Singles 1500ptas; doubles 3000-3500ptas; larger rooms 1500ptas per person.

Hostal-Residencia Séneca, C. Conde y Luque 7 (tel./fax 957 47 32 34), 2 blocks north of the Mezquita; follow C. Céspedes. All rooms have fans. Singles 2000ptas; doubles 3600ptas, with bath 4600ptas. Breakfast 450ptas. 1000ptas for A/C.

Camping: Municipal, Av. Brillante (tel. 957 28 21 65). From the train station, turn left on Av. América, left again at Av. Brillante, and then walk 2km uphill. Alternatively, take bus 10 or 11, both of which leave from Av. Cervantes near the station and run to the campsite. Public pool. 560ptas per person, per tent, and per car.

FOOD

The famous Mezquita attracts nearly as many high-priced eateries as Muhammad does followers, but a five-minute walk north, west, or east yields local specialities at reasonable prices. **Calle Doctor Fleming,** demarcating the west side of the Judería, is sprinkled with little *mesones* dispatching *platos combinados* for a moderate 600ptas. Student-priced eateries await in **Barrio Cruz Conde,** around Av. de Menéndez Pidal. Join locals at the outdoor cafes around **Plaza Tendillas,** or pick up snacks and groceries downstairs at supermercado **Simago,** C. Jesús María, half a block south of Pl. Tendillas (open M-Sa 9am-9pm).

Sociedad de Plateros, C. San Francisco 6, between C. San Francisco and the top end of Pl. Potro. Casual and tasty. *Tapas* 150-200ptas. Fresh fish daily. Bar open Tu-Su 8am-4pm and 7pm-2am. Meals served 1-4pm and 8pm-midnight.

Taberna San Miguel, Pl. San Miguel 1, 1 block north of Pl. Tendillas. Classic *tapas* joint with bullfighting decor, always packed during lunchtime. *Tapas* 230-275ptas, *raciones* 750-1500ptas. Open M-Sa noon-4pm and 8pm-midnight. Closed Aug.

Taberna Las Comedias, C. Veláquez Bosco 12. Intimate setting for relaxing with *una copa.* Handpainted furniture and tiny rooms. Open daily 11:30am-late.

SIGHTS AND ENTERTAINMENT

Begun in 784, the **Mezquita** was intended to surpass all other mosques in grandeur. Over the next two centuries, the spectacular building was gradually enlarged, making it for a time the largest mosque in the world. Inside, past the impressive **Patio de los Naranjos,** 850 pink and blue marble, alabaster, and stone columns support hundreds of red and white striped two-tiered arches. At the far end of the Mezquita lies the **Capilla Villaviciosa,** where Caliphal vaulting, greatly influential in later Spanish architecture, appears for the first time. Intricate gold, pink, and blue marble Byzantine mosaics given by Emperor Constantine VII shimmer across the arches of the **Mihrab,** the dome where the Muslims guarded the Koran. Additions such as the church transept and choir dome were added after the mosque became a church in 1236. (Open M-Sa 10am-7pm, Su 2-7pm; in winter, Mezquita closes between 5:30 and 6:30pm. 750ptas. Free during mass, held M-F 8:30-10am; Su 9:30am-1:30pm.)

The area known as **Judería,** just north of the Mezquita, is the historically Jewish quarter of the city. Tucked away on C. Judíos, the small **Sinagoga** is one of only three synagogues remaining in Spain. (Open Tu-Sa 10am-2pm and 3:30-5:30pm, Su 10:30am-1pm. 50ptas, EU citizens free.) Just west of the Mezquita and closer to the river lies the **Alcázar.** The palace was constructed for the Catholic monarchs in 1328 during the conquest of Granada, and later served as headquarters for the Inquisition. The walls of the Alcázar enclose a manicured hedge garden and a museum displaying Roman mosaics. (Open May-Sept. Tu-Sa 10am-2pm and 6-8pm, Su 9:30am-3pm; Oct.-Apr. Tu-Sa 10am-2pm and 4:30-6:30pm, Su 9:30am-3pm. Illuminated gardens open

SPAIN

8pm-midnight. 425ptas, F free.) The **Museo Taurino y de Arte Cordobés,** Pl. Maimonides, displays the heads of bulls who killed matadors and other unfortunates. (Open May-Sept. Tu-Sa 10am-2pm and 6-8pm, Su 9:30am-3pm; Oct.-Apr. M-Sa 10am-2pm and 5-7pm, Su 9:30am-3pm. 425ptas, F free.)

For *flamenco,* try the **Tablao Cardenal,** C. Torrijos 10 (tel. 957 48 33 20), facing the Mezquita (shows M-Sa 10:30pm; 2800ptas, including 1 drink). During the **Festival de los Patios** in early May, the city erupts with classical music concerts, *flamenco* dances, and a city-wide decorated *patio* contest. Late May brings the **Feria de Nuestra Señora de la Salud,** with lively dancing and non-stop drinking for an entire week. From the first weekend in June until the heat subsides, the **Brillante** barrio (uphill from and north of Av. América or a 500-900ptas cab ride) is the place to be: the Sierra is cool, the beer cold, and the prices low. Around 4am, Cordoban youth head to **Kachao,** a huge disco and *terraza* outside the city along Ctra. Santa María de Trassierra. In winter, pubs around **Plaza de las Tendillas** are a safe bet.

■ Near Córdoba: Medina Azahara

Built in the Sierra Morena by Abderramán III for his favorite wife, the 10th-century **Medina Azahara** (tel. 957 32 91 30) was considered one of the greatest palaces of its time. Before excavations in 1910, the existence of the site had been mere rumor; today the *medina* is one of Spain's most impressive archaeological finds. (Open May-Sept. Tu-Sa 10am-2pm and 6-8:30pm; Oct.-Apr. Tu-Sa 10am-2pm and 4-6:30pm, Su 10am-2pm. 250ptas, EU citizens free.) Reaching Medina Azahara takes some effort; first call ahead to make sure it's open. The O-1 **bus** (info tel. 957 25 57 00) leaves from Av. República Argentina for Cruce Medina Azahara (about 1 per hr., 6:30am-10:30pm, 100ptas); from there it's a 35-minute walk mostly uphill.

■ Granada

"There is nothing crueler in life than to be blind in Granada," proclaims an inscription above the majestic red-clay Alhambra, the fortress which the Moors held until 1492, when ruler Boabdil lost the city to Catholic monarchs Fernando and Isabel. The last Muslim stronghold in Spain, Granada's mosques were destroyed, but the Albaicín, a maze of Moorish houses and twisting alleys, remains Spain's best-preserved Arab settlement. Not to be outdone by the artistry of the Alhambra, Fernando and Isabel built their own magnificent Renaissance cathedral and royal chapel in the city. Today the Moors and Christians still vie with each other—but only for visitors' attention.

ORIENTATION AND PRACTICAL INFORMATION

To reach the city center from **RENFE station,** walk 3 blocks up Av. Andaluces to Av. Constitución, and take bus 3, 4, 5, 6, 9, or 11. From the bus station, take bus 3 (120ptas). The geographic center of Granada is the small **Plaza de Isabel la Católica,** the intersection of the city's two main arteries, **Calle de los Reyes Católicos** and **Gran Vía de Colón.** Two short blocks uphill on C. Reyes Católicos sits **Plaza Nueva,** framed by Renaissance buildings, hotels, and restaurants. Downhill, also along C. Reyes Católicos, lie **Plaza del Carmen,** site of the **Ayuntamiento,** and **Puerta Real.** The **Alhambra** commands the steep hill up from Pl. Nueva.

Trains: RENFE Station, Av. Andaluces (tel. 958 27 12 72). From Pl. Isabel la Católica, follow Gran Vía de Colón to the end, then bear left on Av. Constitución. Turn left on Av. Andaluces. To: Barcelona (12-13hr., 6400ptas), Cádiz (7hr., 2000ptas), Madrid (5hr., 3200ptas), and Seville (4-5hr., 2575ptas).

Buses: A new bus station sits on the outskirts of Granada on Ctra. de Madrid. **Bacoma** (tel. 958 15 75 57) serves Alicante (6hr., 3335ptas), Barcelona (14hr., 7830ptas), and Valencia (8hr., 4855ptas). **Alsina Graells** (tel. 958 18 50 10), sends buses to Algeciras (5hr., 2485ptas), Cádiz (4hr., 3700ptas), Córdoba (3hr., 1780ptas), Madrid (5hr., 1945ptas), and Seville (3hr., 2400ptas). Bus 3 goes from the station to Av. Constitución, Gran Vía, and Pl. Isabel la Católica.

Tourist Office: Pl. Mariana Pineda 10 (tel. 958 22 66 88; fax 958 22 89 16). From Pta. Real, turn right on C. Angel Ganivet, and right again 2 blocks later. Helpful staff has free maps. Open M-F 9:30am-7pm, Sa 10am-2pm. **Branch office** at C. Mariana Pineda (tel. 958 22 10 22; fax 958 22 39 27). Open M-Sa 9am-7pm, Su 10am-2pm.

Currency Exchange: Banco Central Hispano, Gran Vía de Colón 3, exchanges money and traveler's checks without commission. Open M-F 9am-2pm.

American Express: C. Reyes Católicos 31 (tel. 958 22 45 12). Holds mail. Open M-F 9:30am-1:30pm and 2-8pm, Sa 10am-2pm and 3-7pm, Su 9am-2pm.

Luggage Storage: At the train and bus stations. 400ptas. Open 4-9pm.

Laundromat, C. La Paz 19. Wash 400ptas, dry 100ptas per 15min. Open M-F 9:30am-2pm and 4:30-8:30pm, Sa 9am-2pm.

Police: C. Duquesa, 21 (tel. 958 24 81 00). English spoken.

Medical Services: Clínica de San Cecilio, C. Doctor Oloriz 16 (tel. 958 28 02 00).

Red Cross: C. Escorianza 8 (tel. 958 22 22 22, 958 22 20 24, or 958 22 21 66).

Post Office: Puerta Real (tel. 958 22 48 35; fax 958 22 36 41), between Acera de Darro and C. Angel Ganivet. Open for stamps and *Lista de Correos* M-F 8:30am-8:30pm, Sa 9:30am-2pm. **Faxes** sent and received. **Postal Code:** 18009.

Internet Access: Net, C. Santa Ecolástica 13. 150ptas per 15min. 400ptas per hr. Open M-Sa 9am-11pm, Su 4-11pm.

ACCOMMODATIONS, CAMPING, AND FOOD

Granada has even more cheap accommodations than *fútbol* fans. Lodgings pose a problem only during *Semana Santa* (Holy Week; the week before Easter), when you should call ahead.

Albergue Juvenil Granada (HI), Ramón y Cajal, 2 (tel. 958 27 26 38 or 958 28 43 06; fax 958 28 52 85). Take bus 11 from the center or bus 10 from the bus station and ask the driver to stop at "El Estadio de la Juventud." Spacious and comfortable. 1300ptas, over 26 1600ptas. Nonmembers add 300ptas. Limited wheelchair access.

Hostal Residencia Britz, Cuesta de Gomérez 1 (tel. 958 22 36 52). On the corner of Pl. Nueva. Large rooms with luxurious beds and green-tiled bathrooms. Singles 2300ptas; doubles 3500ptas, with bath 5000ptas. 6% discount for *Let's Go* readers if you pay in cash and are courteous. Reception 24hr. MC, V.

Hostal Gomérez, Cuesta de Gomérez 10 (tel. 958 22 44 37). Clean rooms with firm beds. Singles 1500ptas; doubles 2500ptas; triples 3500ptas. Offers a 100-200ptas discount to *Let's Go*ers during off-season.

Hospedaje Almohada, C. Postigo de Zarate 4 (tel. 958 20 74 46). Walk 1 block from Pl. Trinidad along C. Duquesa and turn right on C. Málaga; it's at the top and has no sign. A successful experiment in communal living. Singles 1800ptas; doubles 3500ptas. Longer stays 33,000-36,000ptas per month. Laundry 500ptas.

Hostal-Residencia Lisboa, Pl. Carmen 29 (tel. 958 22 14 13 or 958 22 14 14; fax 958 22 14 87). Take C. Reyes Católicos from Pl. Isabel la Católica; Pl. Carmen is on the left. Well-furnished rooms have phones and fans. Singles 2600-3900ptas; doubles 3900-5400ptas; triples 5200-7200ptas.

Hostal Residencia Zacatín, C. Ermita 11 (tel. 958 22 11 55). Enter through the Alcaicería from C. Reyes Católicos (C. Ermita is on the left). Rooms are amply sized and baths are immense. Singles 1600-2400ptas; doubles 2800-4000ptas.

Hostal Gran Vía, Gran Vía de Colón 17 (tel. 958 27 92 12), about 4 blocks from Pl. Isabel la Católica. Clean rooms with a pristine shower in each single (2500ptas). Doubles 3000-4000ptas; triples with bath 5000ptas.

Sierra Nevada, Av. Madrid 107 (tel. 958 15 00 62); take bus 3 or 10. Shady trees, nice facilities, and free showers. 560ptas per person and per tent. Open Mar.-Oct.

Cheap, tasty, and healthy Middle Eastern cuisine is available in and around the Albaicín. Near Pl. Nueva, the usual fare of *menús* awaits. Picnickers and vegetarians can collect fresh fruit and veggies at the **market** on C. San Agustín. Pick up groceries at **Supermercado T. Mariscal,** C. Genil (open M-Sa 9:30am-2pm and M-F 5-9pm). **La Nueva Bodega,** C. Cetti-Meriem 9, on a small side street off C. Elvira out of Pl. Nueva, is popular with locals and tourists (*menú* 825-1400ptas; *bocadillos* 300ptas; open daily noon-midnight). **Bodega Mancha** and **Bodega Castañeda,** both in the alleyways left of C. Reyes Católicos leading from Pl. Nueva, offer *bocadillos* and *tapas* (under

300ptas), and lots of wine and sherry (125-200ptas; open daily noon-4pm and 6pm-1am). **Naturi Albaicín,** C. Calderería Nueva 10, has excellent vegetarian cuisine (open Sa-Th 1-4pm and 7-11pm, F 7-11pm).

SIGHTS AND ENTERTAINMENT

Against the silvery backdrop of the Sierra Nevada, the Christians drove the first Naz-arite King Alhamar from the Albaicín to a more strategic location on the hill overlooking Granada. The **Alhambra** is the name for this hill and the sprawling palace-fortress atop it. Here King Alhamar built a fortress called the **Alcazaba,** the oldest section of the complex, and the great Moorish rulers Yusuf I (1333-1354) and Mohammed V (1354-1391) constructed the **Alcázar** (Royal Palace). After the Christian *Reconquista* drove the Moors from Spain, Fernando and Isabel respectfully restored the Alcázar, never suspecting that, two generations later, Emperor Carlos V would demolish part of it to make way for his **Palacio de Carlos V.** Although it is glaringly incongruous amidst all the Moorish splendor, the Palacio is one of the most beautiful Renaissance buildings in Spain. Up the hill past the Alhambra's main entrance is the lush palace greenery of the **Generalife,** the spacious summer retreat of the sultans. Canals, fountains, and water jets criss-cross the gardens. To reach the complex, follow Cuesta de Gomérez from Pl. Nueva. (Alhambra open Apr.-Sept. M-Sa 9am-8pm, Su 9am-6pm; Oct.-Mar. M-Sa 9am-5:45pm. 750ptas. Entry limited to 8400 visitors daily, so go early. Open in summer also Tu, Th, and Sa 10pm-midnight; off-season Sa 8-10pm.)

Back down from heaven, in the town proper, is the **Capilla Real** (Royal Chapel), Fernando and Isabel's private chapel. Isabel's private **art collection,** including royal jewels and 15th-century Flemish and German masterpieces, is exhibited next door in the sacristy. (Open Apr.-Sept. M-Sa 10:30am-1pm and 4-7pm; Oct.-Mar. M-Sa 10:30am-1pm and 3:30-6:30pm, Su 11am-1pm. 300ptas.) The adjacent **cathedral** dwarfs the Capilla Real. The first purely Renaissance cathedral in Spain boasts massive Corinthian pillars supporting an astonishingly high vaulted nave. (Open daily Apr.-Sept. 10am-1:30pm and 4-7pm; Oct.-Mar. 10am-1:30pm and 3:30-6:30pm. Closed Su mornings. 300ptas includes admission to the museum.) Don't miss the **Albaicín,** the old Arab quarter, where the Moors built their first fortresses. The best way to explore the maze is to proceed along Carrera del Darro off Pl. Nueva, climb up Cuesta del Chapiz on the left, and then wander through Muslim ramparts, cisterns, and gates. Be cautious here at night.

Entertainment listings are near the back of the daily paper, the *Ideal* (120ptas), under the heading *Cine y Espectáculos;* the Friday supplement lists even more bars, concerts, and special events. The *Guía del Ocio* (100ptas), sold at newsstands, lists the city's clubs, pubs, and cafes. **Eschavira,** C. Postigo de la Cuna (tel. 958 20 32 62), in an alley off C. Azacayes, is *the* place to go for flamenco, jazz, and flamenco-jazz fusion (call for a schedule). Pubs and bars cluster in three areas: Campo de Principe, the Albaicín, and the small streets off C. Pedro Antonio de Alarcón. Outside **El 22,** close to Pl. Nueva, at the top of Calderería Nueva, a young throng of vacationers with beer bottles lounge on the steps of Placeta San Gregorio. Teetotalers can lounge the night away in the candle-lit pillowed dens of **Jardín de los Sueños,** on C. Calderería Nueva, while sipping exotic *infusions* for 250ptas. **Babylon,** Placeta Sillería 5, off C. Reyes Católicos before Pl. Nueva, pumps reggae, hip-hop, and funk. Avoid the **Cuevas Gitanas de Sacromonte** (gypsy caves), a snare for tourists.

■ Near Granada: La Cartuja

On the outskirts of Granada stands **La Cartuja** (tel. 958 16 19 32), a 16th-century Carthusian monastery and pinnacle of Baroque artistry in Granada. (Open Apr.-Sept. M-Sa 10am-1pm and 4-8pm, Su 10am-noon; Oct.-Mar. M-Sa 10am-1pm and 3:30-6pm, Su 10am-noon. 300ptas.) Marble with rich brown tones and swirling forms (a stone unique to nearby Lanjarón) marks the sacristy of Saint Bruno. To reach the monastery, take bus 8 from the front of the cathedral.

■ Costa del Sol

Costa del Sol has sold its soul to the Devil, and now he's starting to collect. Artifice covers its once-natural charms as chic promenades and hotels seal off small towns from the shoreline. Although the Costa del Sol officially extends from Tarifa in the southwest to Cabo de Gata east of Almería, the name most often refers to the resorts from Marbella to Motril (directly south of Granada). Post-industrial Málaga divides the Costa in two. To the southeast, the Costa is built up and water washes against concrete, while to the northeast, the hills dip straight to the ocean, resulting in rocky and less popular beaches. Nothing can take away the coast's major attraction: eight months of spring and four of summer each year. Prices double in high season, and visitors should make reservations or be ready for a search. Some sleep on the beaches, but this is not a wise option, particularly for solo travelers and women. Alternatively, ask around for *casas particulares*. June is the best time to visit, when summer weather has come to town but most vacationers haven't.

Málaga Birthplace of Picasso, and once celebrated by Hans Christian Andersen and native poet Vicente Aleixandre, **Málaga** has since lost some of its gleam. While dinginess and an infamy for petty thievery have soured the city, Málaga is still a critical Andalusian transportation hub. The 11th-century **Alcazaba** was built as a palace for Moorish kings; its attached **Museo Arqueológico** is currently closed for renovations (Alcazaba open W-M 9:30am-8pm). Diehard fans can visit **Picasso's birthplace** in Pl. Merced; call for info on special exhibitions, concerts, and lectures (tel. 952 21 50 05; open M-Sa 10am-2pm and 6-9pm, Su 10am-2pm; free).

Trains (tel. 952 36 02 02) roll to Barcelona (13hr., 6700ptas), Córdoba (2½hr., 2100ptas), Madrid (4hr., 8000ptas), Seville (3hr., 1800ptas), and Torremolinos (20min., 150ptas). To get to the station, take bus 3 at Po. Parque or bus 4 at Pl. Marina. Nearby on Po. Tilos, **buses** (tel. 952 35 00 61) leave the station for Granada (2hr., 1200ptas), Madrid (7hr., 2800ptas), Marbella (1½hr., 575ptas), Seville (3hr., 2200ptas), and many other cities. The **tourist office,** Pasaje de Chinitas 4 (tel. 952 21 34 45), provides the basics (open July-Sept. M-F 9am-7pm, Sa-Su 9am-1pm; Oct.-June M-F 9am-2pm, Sa 9am-1pm).

Most budget accommodations are between **Plaza Marina** and **Plaza de la Constitución,** but the rooms are generally somewhat run-down. After dark, be particularly wary of Alameda de Colón, El Perchel (towards the river from the stations), Cruz de Molnillo (near the market), and La Esperanza/Santo Domingo (up the river from El Corte Inglés). **Hostal La Palma,** C. Martínez 7 (tel. 952 22 67 72), has clean but noisy old rooms (singles 2000-2500ptas; doubles 3500ptas; triples and quads 1100ptas per person). **Pension Córdoba,** C. Bolsa 11 (tel. 952 21 44 69), off C. Molina Lario, has antique furniture and spotless common bathrooms (singles 1500ptas; doubles 2700ptas). Seafood restaurants cluster in the beachfront district **El Pedregalejo** (40min. walk or bus 11 from Pl. La Marina, 115ptas). **La Cancela,** C. Jose Denis Belgrano 5, off C. Granada, will tempt the most finicky eater (*menú* 1425ptas; open daily 1-4:30pm and 8-11:30pm; closed W nights). The boardwalk bars of **El Pedregalejo** overflow in summer; the bars between C. Comedias and C. Granada hop year-round.

Marbella Save your *pesetas* for glamorous Marbella, the jewel of the Costa del Sol. You will be rewarded with beckoning waiters, fabulous window shopping in the **casco antiguo** (old town), and glimpses of the flashy and famous along the city's beaches. Although no one comes here for the sights, the maze of cobbled alleyways and ancient façades merits a stroll. The **Museo del Grabado Español Contemporano,** C. Hospital Bazán, displays works by Miró and Picasso (open M-F 10:15am-2pm and 5:30-8:30pm; 300ptas). With 22km of beach, Marbella offers a variety of sizzling settings, from below the chic promenade to **Playa de las Chapas,** 10km east via the Fuengirola bus. The sand is generally gritty and scorching, but the human landscape is scenic, to say the least. Because of the towering mountains nearby, Marbella's winter temperatures tend to be warmer than Malaga's, and beach season goes on and on. Take buses from along Av. Richard Soriano to "San Pedro" (125ptas) to reach the opulent and trendy **Puerto Banús.** Buffered by imposing white yachts and rows of boutiques and fancy restaurants, *this* is where the Beautiful People are. The port is frequented by the likes of Sean Connery, Richard Gere, Elton John, and King Fahd of Saudi Arabia, and throngs of Euro-chicks roaming the marina in search of rich prospects. If you find star-gazing a waste of a perfectly good life, kick back at **Sinatra Bar,** on the first row, and drink in the views, among other things. The Moroccan coast is visible on exceptionally clear days.

Back in town, Marbella's **nightlife** is unrivaled; beaches don't fill up until three in the afternoon because people are just waking up—the night is yet young at 4am. In the *casco antiguo,* action brews along C. Peral. A mellower ambience suffuses the **Townhouse Bar,** C. Alamo, on an alley off C. Nueva (opens at 10pm). A young, international crowd socializes in bar **Kashmir,** C. Rafina 8, off C. Aduar (opens at 10pm). Toward morning, the city's entire young population swarms to the **Puerto Deportivo** ("The Port"), an amusement park of disco-bars and clubs.

From the new station atop Avenida Trapiche, s/n (tel. 952 76 44 00), **buses** leave for Granada (4½hr., 1735ptas), Málaga (1½hr., 570ptas), and Seville (4hr., 1820ptas). To get to the town center, walk left, make the first right onto Av. Trapiche, and follow any downhill route to **Avenida Ramón y Cajal.** From here, C. Peral curves up and around the *casco antiguo.* The **tourist office** (tel. 952 77 14 42) is at C. Glorieta de la Fontanilla, fronting the shore (open in summer M-F 9am-9pm; in winter 10am-8pm, Sa 10am-2pm). Another office is located in Pl. Naranjos (tel. 952 82 35 50; same hours). The *casco antiguo* around Pl. Naranjos is loaded with quick-filling *hostales.* Several cheap guest houses line **Calles Ancha, San Francisco, Aduar,** and **de los Caballeros,** all of which are uphill off C. Huerta Chica. The **Albergue Juvenil (HI),** Av. Trapiche 2 (tel. 952 77 14 91; fax 952 86 32 27), is just downhill from the station, only slightly removed from the action. Facilities include a TV room, basketball court, and pool (800-1300ptas, over 26 1100-1800ptas). **Hostal del Pilar,** C. Mesoncillo 4 (tel. 952 82 99 36), off C. Peral, an extension of C. Huerta Chica, or off C. San Francisco if approaching from the bus station, is run by a multilingual staff (mattresses on the roof (if warm) from 1000ptas; otherwise from 1500ptas). **Bar El Gallo,** C. Lobatas 44, serves cheap, delicious food (open daily 9am-midnight). The corner of C. Pablo Casals and Av. Fontanilla has a **24-hour minimarket.**

■ Gibraltar

The gateway to the Atlantic, **Gibraltar** soothes homesick Brits with fish 'n chips, while all the other expats go batty over the tax-free cigarettes (90p per pack). Britain and Spain have long hotly contested the enclave, and the town is a multicultural mix of religions and linguistic groups. It's a tourist trap, but worth a daytrip—stand on the Rock to say that you've done it. From the northern tip of the massif known as **Top of the Rock,** there's a remarkable view of Iberia and the Straits of Gibraltar. Cable cars carry visitors from the southern end of Main St. to the Top of the Rock, stopping at **Apes' Den,** where a colony of monkeys clamber lithely about the rocks. The ruins of a Moorish wall crumble down the road from the cable car station to the south, where the spooky chambers of **St. Michael's Cave** have been cut into the rock. (Cable car M-Sa 9:30am-5:45pm. Last tickets sold 5:15pm. Round-trip £4.90. Ticket includes St. Michael's Cave and the Apes' Den.) From the southern tip of Gibraltar, **Europa Point** commands a view of the straits; on a clear day you can see all the way to Morocco. Take bus 3 or 1b from Line Wall Rd., off Main St., to the end (every 15min., 40p).

Gibraltar is considered a foreign destination from Spain, and although *pesetas* are accepted everywhere (except in pay phones), the pound sterling is clearly preferred. From Spain, dial 9567 (from the Cádiz province 7) to access **telephone** numbers in Gibraltar. From Britain dial (00) 350; from the US (011) 350. The **USA Direct** code is 88 00. **Buses** run to **La Línea,** the nearest Spanish town on the border, from Algeciras (40min., 220ptas), Granada (6hr., 2390ptas), Málaga (3¼hr., 1225ptas), and Seville (6hr., 2500ptas). The **tourist office,** at Duke of Kent House, Cathedral Square (tel. 749 50), hands out a free map (open M-F 9am-5:30pm). Gibraltar pales in comparison with the rest of the coast, but if you do stay overnight, try **Emille Youth Hostel**

Gibraltar, Line Wall Rd. (tel. 511 06; dorms £10) or **Queen's Hotel,** 1 Boyd St. (tel. 740 00; singles £18-24; twins £14-20; ask about *Let's Go* discounts).

The Leanse, 7 Bomb House Lane, off Main St., serves kosher, international cuisine in a cozy setting (open Su-Th 11:30am-3pm and 7:30pm-midnight, F 11:30am-3:30pm). Main St. is dotted with lively **pubs.** Busybodies enjoy people-watching (and occasional live music) at the **Angry Friar,** also known as **The Convent,** 287 Main St. across from the Governor's Residence. (Open daily 9:30am-midnight, weekends until 1am; food served 10am-4pm and 6:30-8:30pm.)

Algeciras On the Spanish side of the Bahía de Algeciras, Algeciras has some pleasant older areas, but most tourists see only the dingy port, which offers easy access to Gibraltar and Morocco. The Empresa Portillo **bus station,** Av. Virgen del Carmen 15 (tel. 956 65 10 55), serves Granada (5hr., 2455ptas), Málaga (3hr., 1290ptas), Marbella (1½hr., 760ptas), and other cities; **trains** chug to Granada (5½hr., 2325-2520ptas) from the station on Ctra. Cádiz. During the summer, **ferries** leave hourly for Ceuta (1½hr., 1884ptas) and Tangier (2½hr., 3200ptas per person, 9900ptas per car). Eurail holders get a 20% discount. The **tourist office,** C. Juan de la Cierva (tel. 956 57 26 36), is the tube-shaped pink and red building (open M-F 9am-2pm). Convenient lodgings bunch around **Calle José Santacana,** parallel to Av. Marina and one block inland, and **Calle Duque de Almodóvar,** two blocks farther from the water. Or try the **Hostal Residencia Versalles,** C. Moutero Rios 12 (tel. 956 65 42 11 or 956 65 43 00), off C. Cayetanodel Toro (singles 1900-2500ptas; doubles 3000-3500ptas).

Sweden (Sverige)

US$1	= 7.96kr (Swedish kronor)		1kr =	US$0.13
CDN$1	= 5.25kr		1kr =	CDN$0.19
UK£1	= 13.19kr		1kr =	UK£0.08
IR£1	= 11.53kr		1kr =	IR£0.09
AUS$1	= 4.70kr		1kr =	AUS$0.21
NZ$1	= 4.06kr		1kr =	NZ$0.25
SAR1	= 1.27kr		1kr =	SAR0.79
Country Code: 46			**International Dialing Prefix: 009**	

When the celebrated Swedish entertainer Jonas Gardell named his last hit show *På besök i Mellanmjölks Land* (On Tour in the Land of 2% Milk), he was poking fun at the Swedish concept of *lagom* (moderation). The idea implies that life should be lived somewhere between wealth and poverty, ecstasy and depression, whole milk and skim. The reputation of the *lagom* Swede runs anywhere from the complaint that Swedes are sober, boring, unemotional folk to praise for Volvo's sleek designs and Swedes' skill in international conflict resolution. Yet Sweden is, in fact, a country of dramatic extremes: even the Scandinavian weather silently defies the *lagom* stereotype; while the summer sun never sets, it seems to disappear almost entirely in the winter. Over 2400km long, Sweden stretches from the mountainous arctic reaches of Kiruna down to the flat, temperate farmland and white-sand beaches of Skåne and Småland in the south. While Dalarna, Värmland, and Norrland counties evoke images of quiet woods, folk music, and rustic country Midsummer celebration, the capital city of Stockholm shines as a thoroughly cosmopolitan center.

The contrast of natural and geographical extremes is reflected also in Sweden's social, political, and cultural landscape. Sweden's mythic early history of violent Viking conflict and conquest has given way to a successful experiment with egalitarian socialism and a succession of international peacekeepers: Alfred Nobel established his prizes for peaceful contributions to humanity; Raoul Wallenberg clambered over the roofs of Nazi trains to hand out Swedish passports that saved thousands of Jews from concentration camps; U.N. Secretary General Dag Hammarskjöld was awarded the Nobel Peace Prize posthumously; and late Prime Minister Olof Palme marched against the Vietnam War, sheltered American draft resisters, and was later assassinated for his peace efforts. Culturally, Sweden is thought of as the land of oompah folk fiddlers and hurdy-gurdy accordions, but film director Ingmar Berman and playwright August Strindberg gained fame for their dark sophistication, and Lasse Hallström's films, like *My Life as a Dog,* show a range of Swedish humor and drama.

GETTING THERE AND GETTING AROUND

Sweden is easily accessible by boat or train from Denmark and Germany, by ferry from Poland and Finland, and by train and bus from Norway and Finland. Trains are reliable and frequent in the southern half of Sweden; in the north, long-distance buses are often a better option. The *buy-in-Scandinavia* **Scanrail Pass** allows five days within 15 (1550kr, under 26 1200kr, seniors 1400kr) or 21 consecutive days (2350kr, under 26 1800kr, seniors 2100kr) of unlimited rail travel through Sweden, Norway, Denmark, and Finland, as well as free or discounted ferry rides. This differs from the *buy-outside-of-Scandinavia* **Scanrail Pass** offering five of 15 days (US$182, under 26 US$137), 10 of 21 days (US$292, under 26 US$219), or one month (US$426, under 26 US$320) of unlimited travel. For reservations and schedule information, dial toll free (020) 75 75 75 (press "1" for domestic travel; "2" for international trips) throughout Sweden. **Eurail** is valid in Sweden. Reservations (30kr) are technically required on all journeys over 150km and actually required on all X2000 express trains (125kr).

For travelers under 26, **SAS** offers a special standby fare of 200kr (one-way) on **flights** between Stockholm and other Swedish cities (tel. (020) 727 727, outside Sweden (08) 797 50 80). Buy your ticket from automatic ticket machines at airports at least 20 minutes before departure. **Hitching** can be slow near major cities but picks up in the north. Everyone must wear seatbelts; headlights must always be on. Sweden is a biker's heaven: paths cover most of the country, particularly in the south, and you can complete a trip of Sweden on the hostel-spotted **Sverigeleden bike route.** Contact the Svenska Turistföreningen (STF, see **Essentials,** below) for more info.

ESSENTIALS

Swedish **tourist offices** have info on local activities and can help you find rooms. Most **banks** are open weekdays until 3pm (sometimes later in Stockholm); exchange rates are constant, but commissions vary. Exchange checks in large denominations; there's often a 35-50kr commission per check. Many **post offices** double as banks. **Phones** need at least 2kr, but almost all accept only Telefonkort (phone cards), available at newsstands and post offices in denominations of 30, 60, or 120 units (35kr, 60kr, and 100kr). Traffic lights click slow for "don't walk" and fast for "walk" to help vision-impaired pedestrians. For **AT&T Direct,** dial 020 79 56 11; **MCI WorldPhone** 020 79 59 22; **Sprint Access** 020 79 90 11; **Canada Direct** 020 79 90 15; **BT Direct** 020 79 91 44; **NZ Direct** 020 79 84 31. For **emergency help,** dial 112. Almost all Swedes speak some English, and those under 50 are usually fluent. Sweden leads the world in facilities for people with disabilities.

Sweden's public **holidays** include January 1, Epiphany (Jan. 6), Easter (Apr. 10-13), Labor Day (May 1), Ascension Day (May 13), Whit Sunday and Monday (May 23-24), Midsummer Day (June 26), All Saints Day (Nov. 6), and Christmas (Dec. 24-26). **Midsummer** incites family frolicking and bacchanalian dancing around maypoles. July and August bring two special festivals, the *surströmming* (rotten herring) and eel parties. *Surströmming* is prepared by letting fish ferment (or rot), after which it is tinned and sold. In mid-August, the **Stockholm Water Festival** features fireworks, market stalls, and outdoor cafes. Plan ahead for holidays, especially around Midsummer, as many transportation lines shut down and some hotels close.

Yes/No	*Ja/Nej*	yaa/ney
Hello	*Goddag/Hallå*	goo-DAAG
Thank you	*Tack*	TUCK
Excuse me.	*Ursäkta*	ur-SAK-ta
Do you speak English?	*Pratar du Engelska?*	PRAH-tar du en-GELL-ska
I don't speak Swedish.	*Jag pratar inte Svenska.*	yaag PRAH-tar IN-te SVAN-ska
I would like a single/double.	*Jag vill ha en enkel/dubbel.*	yaag vill HAA-ain EN-kel/DUB-bel
Help!	*Hjälp!*	YELP

ACCOMMODATIONS AND CAMPING Sweden's extensive network of **youth hostels** *(vandrarhem),* at 95kr-150kr per night, are the best deals for the budget traveler, though their increasing popularity with Swedish families, as well as with foreign visitors (both young and not-so-young) means that many cheaper hotels are beginning to offer reduced-service rooms at prices competitive with the hostel, especially for groups of three or more. Die-hard hostelers will not be disappointed, though: the 300-odd HI-affiliated hostels run by the **Svenska Turistföreningen (STF)** are invariably top-notch (non-members pay 40kr extra per night). Private hostels are, with few exceptions, very good as well. Most hostels have kitchen facilities, laundry, a common area with a TV, and family room. Receptions are usually open 8 to 10am and 5 to 9 or 10pm (shorter hours in winter). Hostels fill up quickly in the summer; reserve in advance by calling the hostel or the STF headquarters in Stockholm (tel. (08) 463 22 70). Tourist offices often book beds in hostels for no fee, and if you arrive in the off season and the local hostel is closed (a problem in the north and in smaller towns), can help you find a room in a private home (100kr-250kr). Bringing your own sheets (even if you plan on using a sleeping bag) will save you the 30-50kr per night that hostels charge for rentals. All STF hostels sell **Hostelling International (HI)** memberships for 240kr (additional family members 75kr) or give HI cards valid in Sweden that will make you a member after paying full price six times in Swedish hostels. The free *Swedish Youth and Family Hostels* lists all STF hostels with phone and fax numbers, has a map, and is available at STF hostels. STF also manages mountain huts in the northern wilds with 10-80 beds which cost 155-195kr in high season (non-members 195-245kr). Huts are very popular; plan ahead.

Many **campgrounds** (80-110kr per site) also offer *stugor* (cottages) for around 85-175kr per person. International Camping Cards are not valid in Sweden. Get a Swedish Camping Card (good for 1yr.) along with the free booklet *Camping i Sverige* (60kr per family) from **Sveriges Campingvärdars Riksförbund (SCR),** Box 255, 451 17 Uddevalla (email ck@camping.se) or from any SCR campground. You may walk or camp for one or two nights anywhere on public or privately owned land—except

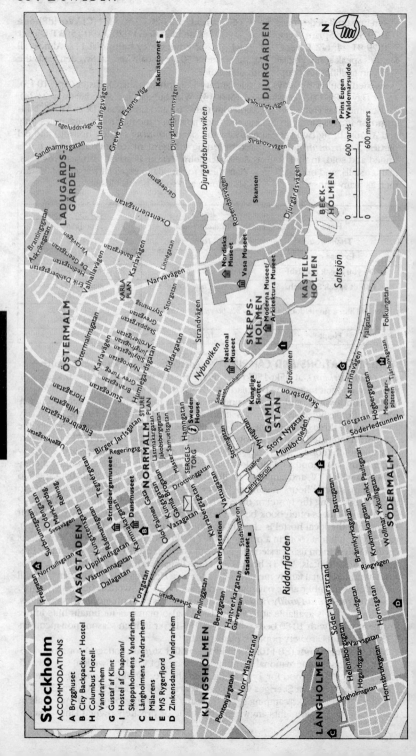

N

Stockholm
ACCOMMODATIONS

A Brygghuset
B City Backpackers' Hostel
H Columbus Hocell-
   Vandrarhem
G Gustaf af Klint
I Hostel af Chapman/
   Skeppsholmens Vandrarhem
C Långholmens Vandrarhem
F Mälarens
E M/S Rygerfjord
D Zinkensdamm Vandrarhem

LADUGÅRDS
GÄRDET

DJURGÅRDEN

Prins Eugen
Waldemarsudde

600 yards
600 meters

BECK-
HOLMEN

Saltsjön

ÖSTERMALM

KARLA
PLAN

Nordiska
Museet

Vasa Museet

Moderna Museet/
Arkitektura Museet

KASTELL-
HOLMEN

SKEPPS-
HOLMEN

National
Museet

VASASTADEN

Strindbergsmuseet

Dansmuseet

NORRMALM

STURE
PLAN

Sweden
House

SERGELS
TORG

Kungliga
Slottet

GAMLA
STAN

Skeppsbron

Centralstation

Stadshuset

Riddarfjärden

SÖDERMALM

KUNGSHOLMEN

Söder Mälarstrand

LÅNGHOLMEN

Ringvägen

gardens and farmland—as long as you respect the flora, fauna, and the owner's privacy. Don't camp within sight of a dwelling for more than a day or two without asking the landowner's permission, and always pack out all garbage. Pick up the brochure **Right (and Wrongs) of Public Access in Sweden** from the STF or from tourist offices, or call the Swedish Environmental Protection Agency at (08) 698 10 00 for more info. Summer days are pleasant—around 20°C (68°F) in the south, 16°C (61°F) in the north—but nights can get chilly, around 10°C (50°F) in the south, 5°C (41°F) in the north. Winters last nine months, and are frequently below -5°C (23°F).

FOOD AND DRINK   Food is very expensive in restaurants and not much cheaper in grocery stores. Rely on supermarkets and outdoor fruit and vegetable markets. Ubiquitous stands provide the most kebabs for your kronor (25-35kr for meat, rice, and veggies). Potatoes are the national staple; these and other dishes are invariably smothered with dill. Try tasty milk products like *messmör* (spreadable cheese) and *filmjölk,* a fluid yogurt. When you tire of groceries, seek out restaurants offering an affordable **dagens rätt** (40-60kr), a daily special including an entree, salad, bread, and drink, often all-you-can-eat and usually available only at lunch. A real beer *(starköl)* costs 10-15kr in stores and 30-50kr per pint in city pubs. The cheaper, weaker *lättöl* (beer up to 3.5%) can be purchased at supermarkets and convenience stores for 8-12kr per 0.5L. Though the drinking age is 18, bars and many night clubs have age restrictions as high as 25 (usually less strictly enforced earlier in the night); you must be 20 to buy alcohol from the state-run Systembolaget stores, which monopolize the sale of hard booze (wine from 40kr per bottle, liquor 115kr per 0.35L; open M-F; expect long lines on F).

■ Stockholm

Sweden's capital is a city at peace with itself. Striking modern architecture coexists unselfconsciously with centuries-old castles and warships; the trendiest young hipsters don't find it incongruous to be friendly and helpful; and the whole place seems immune to the social ills faced by every other modern city. Situated on an archipelago, the Jewel of Scandinavia lives up to its moniker: waterways wend through the city that launched ABBA and the Cardigans, and the relentless summer sun allows Stockholm's cobblestoned streets, world-class museums, chic cafes, and nightclubs to shine around the clock.

ORIENTATION AND PRACTICAL INFORMATION

Stockholm is built on seven islands at the junction of **Lake Mälaren,** to the west, and the **Baltic Sea,** to the east. The northern island is divided into two sections: **Norrmalm**—home to the Central Station and the shopping district on Drottningg.—and **Östermalm,** home to the elegant waterfront **Strandvägen** and much of the nightlife fanning out from **Stureplan Square.** The largely residential western island, **Kungsholmen,** is home to the **Stadshuset** (city hall) and grassy beaches. The southern island of **Södermalm,** formerly Stockholm's slum, hosts cafes, artists, and the extensive gay scene. Södermalm's little sister-island, **Långholmen,** is a nature preserve, while the island of **Djurgården** is a veritable nature-playground and site of the Nordiska Museet and the Vasa Museet. At the center of these five islands is **Gamla Stan** (Old Town) island, which fans out from the main thoroughfare, **Västerlånggatan.** Gamla Stan's neighboring island **Skeppsholmen** (best reached via Norrmalm), harbors the **Moderna Museet.** The extensive, efficient **tunnelbana** (subway; also **T-bana**) links the islands, but you can easily walk between the sites clustering around the center.

Telephone Code: 08.
Flights: Arlanda Airport (tel. 797 60 00), 45km north of the city. **Flygbussar** buses (tel. 600 10 00) run between the airport and Cityterminalen (35min., every 15min. 4:30am-10pm, 60kr, public transport passes not valid). Public transit bus 583 goes between the airport and T-bana: "Märsta." (1 hr., 35kr or 5 coupons; SL pass valid. Buy one on arrival at the Pressbyrån if you don't plan to buy a Stockholm card.)

Trains: Centralstation. T-bana: T-Centralen. **Train info and reservations:** Tel. (020) 75 75 75 (toll-free), 6am-11pm, press 1 for travel within Sweden, 2 for international travel. To Berlin (18hr., 2 per day, 1008kr, under 25 730kr), Copenhagen (7-9hr., 6 per day, 527kr, under 25 371kr), and Oslo (6-8hr., 2 per day, 604kr, under 25 422kr). 50% discount with Reslust card if you buy your ticket 7 days in advance. Reservations mandatory on X2000 high-speed trains (30kr, in summer 125kr), recommended even for local trips during the summer (30kr). **Luggage storage** 40kr per day. **Lockers** 15-30kr for 24 hr. **Showers** 30kr.

Buses: Cityterminalen, upstairs from Centralstation. **Terminal service** (tel. 762 59 97): buses to the airport (60kr) and the Gotland ferries (50kr). **Bus Stop** (tel. 440 85 70) sells tickets for international and longer domestic routes: Copenhagen (10hr., 6 per week, 390kr), Göteborg (7-8hr., 8 per day, 260kr, under 21 190kr), Malmö (10hr., 6-7 per day, 330kr, under 20 240kr).

Ferries: Silja Line, Kungsg. 2 (tel. 22 21 40), sails overnight to Helsinki (14 hr., 1 per day, 450-550kr, 50% off with Scanrail, 65% off with Eurail; book ahead), Mariehamn (5hr., 1 per day, 99kr, 50% off with Scanrail, free with Eurail), and Åbo (Turku), Finland (10-11hr., 2 per day, 200-335kr, 50% off with Scanrail, free with Eurail). To get to Silja's ferry terminal, take the T-bana to "Gärdet" and walk toward the water, or take the Silja bus (14kr) from City terminalen. **Viking Line** also sails to Helsinki (15hr., 1 per day, 350-425kr, 50% off with Scanrail, free with Eurail), Mariehamn (5hr., 1 per day, 80-120kr, 50% off with rail passes), and Åbo (12hr., 2 per day, 100-120kr, free with Eurail). The Viking Line terminal is at Stadsgården on the northeast coast of Södermalm. T-bana: Slussen. **Destination Gotland** (booking tel. 20 10 20) sails to Visby, Gotland from Nynäshamn, 1hr. south of the city (commuter train from City Terminalen 16kr, free with SL pass). Ferry: 5hr., 140kr; students, seniors, and children 90kr. More on summer weekends. High-speed catamaran: 2½hrs; 240kr, students, seniors and children 155kr.

Public Transportation: SL office (tel. 600 10 00) at Sergels Torg. Open M-F 7am-9pm, Sa-Su 8am-9pm. T-bana: T-Centralen. Walk-in office open M-Th 8:30am-6:30pm, F 8:30am-5:30pm. Most in-town destinations cost 2 coupons (14kr, 1hr. unlimited bus/subway transfer). **Rabattkuponger** (95kr), books of 20 coupons, are sold at Pressbyrån news agents. **SL Tourist Card** (Turistkort), valid on buses, subways, commuter trains, and the trams and ferries to Djurgården, costs 60kr for 24hr., 120kr for 72hr. Subway (T-bana) runs roughly 5am-12:30am. After hours, it is replaced by night buses. Check schedules on bus-stop kiosks.

Taxis: Rather high fares. Try to agree on a price before you get in, as locals do. 345kr from the airport to the center. **Taxi Stockholm** (tel. 15 00 00), **Taxicard** (tel. 97 00 00), and **Taxi Kurir** (tel. 30 00 00).

Bike Rental: Skepp & Hoj (tel. 660 57 57) on Djurgårdsbron. 150kr per day, 500kr per week. Rollerblades same prices. Open daily 9am-10pm.

Hitchhiking: Risky (as always) and unreliable. Waiting on highways is illegal. Those headed south take the T-bana to the gas station on Kungens Kurva in Skärholmen. Those going north take bus 52 to Sveaplan and stand on Sveav. at Norrtull.

Tourist Offices: Sweden House, Hamng. 27 (tel. 789 24 90; fax 789 24 91; email info@stoinfo.se; http://www.stoinfo.se), in the northeast corner of Kungsträdgården. From Centralstation, walk up Klarabergsg. to Sergels Torg (the plaza with the 50ft. glass tower), then bear right on Hamng. Books hostels (15kr) and hotels (40kr). Has the free *Stockholm this Week* and maps; sells the **Stockholm-skortet,** which provides free museum entrance and public transportation (24hr., 199kr; 48hr., 398kr; 72hr., 498kr; ages 7-17 25kr per day, limit 2 children per adult card). Tourist info open June-Aug. M-F 8am-6pm, Sa-Su 9am-5pm; Sept.-May M-F 9am-6pm, Sa-Su 10am-3pm; telephone hours to 9pm year-round. **Hotellcentralen** (tel. 789 24 25; fax 791 86 66; email hotels@stoinfo.se), at the train station, books hotels (40kr) and hostels (15kr) throughout Scandinavia. Comprehensive color city map 15kr. Open daily June-Aug. 7am-9pm; May and Sept. 8am-7pm; Oct.-Apr. 9am-6pm. Radio Stockholm International (89.6 FM) has daily tourist info in English.

Embassies: Australia, Sergels Torg 12 (tel. 613 29 00, 24hr. emergency line 020 79 84 80; fax 24 74 14). **Canada,** Tegelbacken 4 (tel. 453 30 00, 24hr. line (070) 549 34 63; fax 24 24 91). **Ireland,** Östermalmsg. 97 (tel. 661 80 05). **South Africa,** Linnég. 76 (tel. 24 39 50; fax 660 71 36). **U.K.,** Skarpög. 6-8 (tel. 671 90 00; fax 662 99 89). **U.S.,** Strandv. 101 (tel. 783 53 00, 24hr. line 783 53 10; fax 661 19 64). **New Zealand,** contact The Hague embassy (tel. +31 (70) 346 93 24 or 363 29 83).

Currency Exchange: Forex in Centralstation (tel. 411 67 34; open daily 7am-9pm), in Cityterminalen (tel. 21 42 80; open M-F 8am-7pm, Sa 8am-5pm), and in the tourist office in Sverigehuset (tel. 20 03 89). 15kr commission per traveler's check, 20kr commission on cash.

American Express: Norrlandsg. 21 (tel. 411 05 40, 24hr. refund assistance (020) 79 51 55; fax 796 95 33). T-bana: Östermalmstorg. Walk up Jakobsbergsg. to Norrlandsg.; it's on the far side of the street. No fee for cashing AmEx Traveller's Cheques; 20kr fee for cash exchange. Open M-F 9am-5pm, Sa 10am-1pm.

Bookstore: Akademibokhandeln, at Mäster Samuelsg. 32 (tel. 613 61 00), Sergels Torg 12 (tel. 411 59 90), and at the university campus's Allhuset Student Union, Universitetsv. (tel. 15 18 65). Open June-Aug. M-F 9:30am-6pm, Sa 10am-3pm; Sept.-May M-F 10am-4pm, Sa 10am-4pm.

Gay and Lesbian Services: RFSL, the Riksförbundet för Sexuellt Likaberättigande (Swedish Federation for Sexual Equality), Sveav. 57 (tel. 736 02 19; http://www.rfsl.se). T-bana: Rådmansg. Organizes support services. Features a bookstore, **Rosa Rummet,** a cafe, **Café G,** and distributes *Queer Xtra (QX)*, with bar, club, and events guide. Open M-F noon-8pm, Sa-Su 1-6pm.

Emergencies: Ambulance, fire, and **police,** tel. 112.

Crisis Lines: Suicide and Crisis Hotline, tel. 463 91 00. 24hr. Often busy; keep trying. **Womens' Helpline,** Kvinnojouren (tel. 644 09 25).

Pharmacy: Look for the green and white "Apotek" signs. **Apotek C. W. Scheele,** Klarabergsg. 64, at the overpass over Vasag. T-bana: T-Centralen. Open 24hr.

Medical Assistance: tel. 463 91 00.

Police: Police headquarters are at Agneg. 33-37 (tel. 401 00 00), on Kungsholmen. Another station is at Bryggarg. 19, north of Centralstation (tel. 454 81 30).

Post Office: In Centralstation (tel. 781 24 25). Open M-F 7am-10pm, Sa-Su 10am-7pm. Also at Drottningg. 53 (tel. 781 46 82). Open M-F 9am-6pm, Sa 10am-1pm. **Postal Code:** 101 10 Stockholm 1.

Internet Access: Free at annex to main library, **Stadsbibliotek,** Odeng. 59 (T-bana: Odenplan; open M-F 11am-5pm; 20min. drop-in or call 50 83 11 30 to book a computer for 1hr.). Also at **Café Access** (tel. 50 83 14 89) in the basement the Kulturhuset building. 20kr per 30min., 40kr with coffee and pastry. Open Tu-F 11am-6pm, Sa 11am-4pm, Su noon-4pm.

Telephones: Telecenter, at Centralstation, assists with international calls and sells phone cards for 30, 60, and 120 units (30, 60, and 100kr). Open M-Sa 8am-9pm, Su 10am-5pm. You can also buy phone cards at **Pressbyrån** stores (especially at T-bana stations) or at **Telia Butiken,** Kungsg. 36, behind Hötorget. **National directory assistance:** 07975.

ACCOMMODATIONS AND CAMPING

Hostels (Vandrarhem)

Summer demands reservations (often accepted by email), and many HI hostels limit stays to five nights. If you haven't booked ahead, arrive early—around 7am. Check-out time is usually 10am. Almost all hostels offer a breakfast buffet for 40-50kr.

Columbus Hotell-Vandrarhem, Tjärhovsg. 11 (tel. 644 17 17; fax 702 07 64; email columbus@algonet.se). Three blocks east of T-bana: "Medborgarplatsen" in the heart of Södermalm. This former brewery, prison, and plague hospital is a dream city hostel: clean, modern, bright, and spacious. 135kr in rooms of 3-6; singles 310kr; doubles 350kr. Breakfast 50kr. Higher prices for hotel. Kitchen facility. Free lockers in most rooms. No max. stay. Reception 24hr. No curfew.

What the Hell is a Botel?!

Stockholm's several boat-hostels, sometimes dubiously dubbed "botels," offer a novel solution to the compact city's tight real estate situation. If the cramped quarters and lack of facilities aren't too bothersome, their great locations and nautical charm can make for a delightful stay. Just be sure to request a room on the water side of the boat, or traffic noise will make your sea-faring fantasy seem a little less plausible....

SWEDEN

Mälarens, Södermalarstrand, Kajplats 6 (tel. 644 43 85; fax 641 37 33; email info@icts.se). The classiest of the floating hostels, with newly renovated rooms on two boats. Dorms 130kr; doubles 390kr; quads 700kr. Reception 8am-4pm and 6pm-11pm, later on weekends. Check-out 9am. No curfew.

Långholmens Vandrarhem (HI), Gamla Kronohäktet (tel. 668 05 10; fax 720 85 75; email vandrarhem@langholmen.com), on Långholmen Island. From T-bana: "Hornstull," walk north on Långholmsg., turn left (before the bridge) onto Högalidsg., then right on Bergsundsg. over the bridge onto Långholmen, then follow the "Kronohäktet" signs. 2-4 beds per converted prison cell. Think Alcatraz. Very cool. 150kr; nonmembers 190kr; sheets 40kr. Reception 24hr. No curfew or lockout.

Brygghuset, Norrtullsg. 12N (tel. 31 24 24; fax 31 02 06). Two blocks north of T-bana: "Odenplan;" 15min. walk from city center. Big, bright, clean, wheelchair accessible rooms. Ping-pong and TV area. 3-8 bed dorms 130kr; doubles 320kr. Small kitchen. Reception daily 8am-noon and 3-10pm. Lockout noon-3pm. Hostel closes at 2am, but get a key (20kr charge). Cash only. Open June to mid-Sept.

City Backpackers' Vandrarhem, Barnhusg. 16 (tel. 20 69 20; fax 10 04 64). Exit Centralstation, walk left on Vasag. until it forks. Barnhusg. is the 1st street on your right. Renovations sometime in 1999 will give the hostel a new entrance and address around the corner on Upplandsg. 2A. Clean, well-located, and run by super-friendly former backpackers. Dorms 150-175kr; doubles 430kr. Reception daily June-Sept. 9am-8pm; Oct.-May 9am-7pm. No curfew or lockout.

Hostel af Chapman/Skeppsholmens Vandrarhem (HI) (tel. 679 50 15 or 679 50 17; fax 611 71 55). Take bus 65 from T-Centralen. The af Chapman is a full-rigger sailing ship moored majestically off Skeppsholmen Island, in front of the less mythic (but roomier) on-shore hostel. The location can't be beat, and the on-shore kitchen, TV room and pool table are for guests of both hostels. Some non-reservable beds available daily at 7:15am. Dorm 100kr; single 130kr; doubles 300kr; nonmembers add 40kr per person. Reception 24hr. 2am curfew on boat.

M/S Rygerfjord, Södermälarstrand Kajplats 12 (tel. 84 08 30; fax 84 07 30; email hotell@rygerfjord.se; http://www.rygerfjord.se). T-bana: Mariatorget. Exit towards Mariatorget, follow Torkel Knutssonsg. down to the water and look for the sign. Features plenty of cozy rooms and in summer, an on deck bar until 1am. Dorm 130kr; singles 385kr; doubles 485kr. Reception 7am-1am. No curfew.

Gustaf af Klint, Stadsgårdskajen 153 (tel. 640 40 77, 640 40 78; fax 640 64 16). A former Navy ship moored 200m east of T-bana: "Slussen" (lower exit). Slightly cramped dorms 110kr; cabins 130kr; doubles 300kr. Breakfast 40kr. Free lockers. Laundry 25kr. Reception in summer 24hr. No curfew. Open all year. MC, V.

Zinkensdamm Vandrarhem (HI), Zinkens Väg 20 (tel. 616 81 00; fax 616 81 20). From T-bana: "Zinkensdamm," head south on Ringv. 3 blocks, then turn right on Zinkens Väg. Peaceful, comfortable hostel on Södermalm, frequented more by families than by youths. TV, sauna (25kr), restaurant, and pub. 130kr, nonmembers 170kr. Kitchen. Lockers in rooms. Reception 24hr. No curfew or lockout.

Camping

Be sure to bring insect repellent to ward off the infamous Swedish mosquitoes. An SL bus pass (or Stockholm Card) will get you to and from the city most economically.

Ängby Camping, Blackebergsv. 24 (tel. 37 04 20; fax 37 82 26). Year-round wooded campground on Lake Mälaren. T-bana: "Ängbyplan," then follow signs for ½km. 110kr. Reception daily 7am-11pm.

Bredäng Camping (tel. 97 70 71; fax 708 72 62), 10km southwest of the city center near Lake Mälaren. T-bana: Bredäng. You can also take the ferry from nearby Mälarhöjdsbadet to Stockholm City Hall or Drottningholm. Follow signs down stairs, past the big apartment complex, and parallel to the train tracks along Stora Sällskapets väg to the campsite (7-10min.). Store, laundry, and running water. 145kr per tent; 4-bed cabins with kitchen from 400kr. Reception Mar.-Oct. 7am-11pm.

FOOD

Stockholm's restaurants reflect the city's increasing ethnic diversity, but local cuisine is well worth tracking down. The cheapest options are the *dagens rätt* lunch specials (45-80kr) that many restaurants offer between 11:30am and 3pm. For groceries, look for the ubiquitous green signs of the **Konsum Supermarket** chain, at Odeng. 65, Sveav. 70, Vasag. 22, and in Gamla Stan at Järntorget 80 (all open daily 10am-9pm). **Hötorget** square hosts an open-air fruit **market** (M-Sa 10am-5pm). The three-story **Kungshallen food court,** across the street at Kungsg. 44, offers cafes, delis, and fastfood (lunch or dinner 25-85kr; open daily 11am-11pm).

Herman's Hermitage, Stora Nyg. 11, in Gamla Stan; **Herman's Höjdare,** Fjällg. 23A, in Söder. Superlative vegetarian and vegan fare. The Söder branch has a great cliff top view to go with its all-you-can-eat buffet (55kr lunch, 68kr dinner); at Gamla Stan, weekday lunch is 60kr. (Söder open noon-9pm, summer 11am-11pm; Gamla Stan open M-F 11am-6pm, Sa-Su 11am-8pm, summer daily 11am-8pm.)

Collage, Smålandsg. 2. T-bana: Östermalmstorg., exit towards Stureplan. The ultimate budget place for dinner. Extensive buffet (served 6:30-9:30pm) 32kr. Get discount tickets for cheap drinks until 10pm. Show up early, then dance off your dinner at the disco after 11pm (see **Entertainment,** p. 860).

Café Pierrot, Götg. 68, in Söder. Cool under-20 set lounges beneath chandeliers and original artwork. Coffee & dessert 30kr. Open noon-11pm, summer 6pm-midnight.

Jerusalems Kebab, Götg. 59. Look for the flashing neon rooster. Cheap, tasty kebab and falafel (10kr), near Götg.'s many pubs and clubs. Open 24hr.

Café Art, Västerlångg. 60, in Gamla Stan. Former medieval wine cellar; one of the hippest cafes in the old town. Sandwiches around 40kr, salads around 30kr, great Swedish pastries 15-20kr. Open daily 11am-11pm.

Pauli's Café, Dramaten 2 trappen, Nybroplan. T-bana: Kungsträdgården. Fantastic cafe restaurant on the terrace-level second floor of Dramaten, the National Theater. Daily summer lunch buffet of Swedish delicacies 70kr (served 11:30am-2:30pm).

SIGHTS

Towering above Stockholm's skyline is the regal **Stadshuset** (City Hall), Handverkarg. 1 (T-bana: Rådhuset). *(Open for guided tours only: June.-Aug. 10am, 11am, noon, and 2pm; May-Oct. and Apr. 10am and noon; Sept. 10am, noon, and 2pm. Tower open May-Sept. 10am-noon. Tower 15kr, with tour 40kr.)* Emblematic of 1920s Swedish architecture and the symbol of Stockholm, its exterior tower provides a great aerial view of the city. The interior boasts municipal Viking chambers, the marbled **Blå Hallen** (Blue Hall), where the annual Nobel Prize Celebration is held, and the glittering mosaic-tiled **Gyllene Hallen** (Gold Hall), where the Nobels, nobles, and other notables dance the rest of the night away. To cool off, take the plunge into the water off Stadshuset lawn; the water downtown is clean enough to swim and even fish in.

Across the water from Stadshuset is **Gamla Stan,** the medieval center of Stockholm. Its winding, catacombed streets of Västerlångg., Stora Nyg., and Österlångg. are packed with cafes, shops, and restaurants. Gamla Stan is also home to the commanding **Kungliga Slottet,** winter home of the Swedish royal family, and site of the daily changing of the guard; tours of the Versailles-like interiors reveal the royal chambers. *(Open June-Aug., daily 10am-4pm; Sept.-May Tu-Su noon-3pm. 50kr, students 25kr. Guard changes June-Aug. M-Sa 12:10pm, Su 1:10pm; Sept.-May W and Sa 12:10pm, Su 1:10pm.)* The palace's **Skattkammaren** (Royal Treasury) houses the crown jewels, including the sword of Sweden's first king, the legendary Gustav Vasa, who unified Sweden in 1523. *(Same hours as palace. 40kr, students 25kr; combined ticket 80kr, students 50kr.)*

At the top of Gamla Stan's winding streets is **Stortorget** (town square), where the annual **Julmarknad** (Christmas Fair) serves hot *glögg* (spiced wine) and Swedish handicrafts for your Christmas list. Behind the square towers the 700-year-old **Storkyrkan** (cathedral), site of royal weddings and home of the dramatic medieval sculpture of Stockholm's patron Saint Göran slaying the dragon. *(Open daily mid-May to Sept. 9am-6pm; Oct.-Apr. 9am-4pm. 10kr.)* For more info on Gamla Stan, visit **Turistbyrå,** in the Passagen (off-street gallery) at Västerlångg. 66 (tel. 20 00 68), or take one of their daily English **tours** which leave from behind the cathedral (7pm; 40kr).

Stockholm's many museums are far different from dusty collections of Scando-esoterica. The lush island of Djurgården, a national park in the heart of the city, houses a number of museums. **Skansen,** an open-air museum with historical buildings from all over Sweden, is a great way to survey Sweden's history and architecture. *(Open daily May 9am-*

8pm; June-Aug. 9am-10pm; Sept-Oct. 9am-5pm; Nov.-Dec. 9am-6pm. 55kr.) There are daily concerts and performances in colorful *folkdräkt* (folk costumes) as well as seasonal events such as the annual Julmarknad (Christmas Market), St. Lucia Dagen (Dec. 13; St. Lucia Day, the beginning of Swedish Christmas), and Midsummer (June 20-22). From the corner of Drottningg. and Klarabergsg. in Sergels Torg square (T-bana: T-Centralen), take bus 44 or 47. Also on Djurgården, the extraordinary **Vasa Museet** houses a mammoth wooden Vasa warship that sank before getting out of the harbor on its maiden voyage in 1628. *(Open late June to mid-Aug. daily 9:30am-7pm; late Aug. to early June M-Tu and Th-Su 10am-5pm, W 10am-8pm. 50kr, students 35kr.)* Next door, the castle-like **Nordiska Museet** (Nordic Museum) presents an innovative exhibit on Swedish history from the Viking age to the modern era of Volvo, ABBA, and Electrolux. *(Open June-Aug. Tu 11am-9pm, W-F 11am-5pm, Sa-Su 10am-5pm; Sept-May Tu-W and F-Su 11am-5pm, Th 11am-9pm. 60kr, students 30kr.)* Former home of 19th- and 20th-century painter Prince Eugen, the **Prins Eugens Waldemarsudde** is now a museum with more Larssons, Janssons, Zorns, and of course, Eugens, than you can shake a paintbrush at. *(Open Sept-May Tu-Su 11am-4pm; June-Aug., Tu and Th 11am-8pm, W and F-Su 11am-5pm. 50kr, students 30kr.)* The museum's seaside grounds also house a collection of sculptures including works by Hasselberg and Rodin. The **National Museet,** Blasieholmskajen (T-bana: Kungsträdgården), houses an impressive collection of paintings and sculpture with some of Sweden's most famous works, including Carl Larsson's 19th-century Nationalist Viking murals and paintings by Anders Zorn, Prins Eugen, Eugen Jansson, and Edvard Munch. *(Open May-June 5 Tu 11am-8pm, W-Su 11am-5pm; June 6-May, Tu and Th 11am-8pm, W and F-Su 11am-5pm. 60kr, students 30kr.)* Just across the Skeppsholmsbron on Skeppsholmen are the **Moderna Museet** (http://www.modernamuseet.se) and **Arkitekturmuseet,** housed in a brand new building by Spanish architect Rafael Moneo. *(Open Tu-Th 11am-10pm, F-Su 11am-6pm. Moderna 60kr, students and seniors 40kr. Arkitektura 40kr, students and seniors 25kr. Combined ticket 75kr, students and seniors 60kr. Under 16 free.)* The Moderna Museet, whose collection is as extensive and striking as the new space, will feature several major exhibitions in 1999, including the first Rodchenko retrospective in 20 years. For literary pilgrims, the **Strindbergsmuseet,** Drottningg. 85 (T-bana: Rådmansg.), sponsors exhibitions, films, and lectures in the last home of dramatist August Strindberg. *(Open Tu-F 11am-4pm, Sa-Su noon-4pm; June-Aug Tu until 7pm. 35kr, students and seniors 20kr.)*

The 530 foot tall **Kaknästornet** (TV tower) (tel. 789 24 35) offers 360° views of the city and archipelago from its indoor and outdoor observation decks and cafe. *(Open May-Aug. 9am-10pm; Sept-Apr. 10am-9pm. 20kr.)* Take bus 69 from downtown or walk over from Djurgården.

ENTERTAINMENT

For up-to-date info on the latest events, check out *Stockholm this Week* (published monthly), *N&D* (Night and Day), or *Dagens Nyheter*'s weekly Swedish-language supplement, *DN På Stan* (all free at the tourist office).

Stockholm's beautiful people and their admirers party until 5am at the many nightclubs and bars around Stureplan in Östermalm (T-bana: Östermalmtorg). Be prepared to pay steep cover charges and wait in long lines. The scene on Södermalm (Söder to the locals), Stockholm's answer to London's SoHo or New York's Greenwich Village, is a little rougher around the edges, but more relaxed, interesting, and inexpensive (though most establishments there close around 1am). The bars and cafes lining Götg. make a good point of departure (T-bana: Slussen or Medborgplatsen). New cafes and bars are also sprouting up in the up-and-coming neighborhoods of Vasastaden (T-bana: Sankt Eriksplan) and Kungsholmen (T-bana: Rådhuset). Stockholm's compactness and the excellent night bus service means revelers can partake of any or all of these scenes in a single night.

See the informative monthly *QX (Queer Extra)* for a last-minute guide to gay entertainment and nightlife, much of which can be found on Söder. The three stages of the national theater, **Dramaten,** Nybroplan (tel. 667 0680), feature Swedish- and English-language performances of Strindberg and other Scandinavian and international playwrights (80-350kr), while the **Operan** (tel. 24 82 40) offers opera and ballet (70-350kr). Ask for the cheaper student and rush seats. The **Konserthuset** at Hötorget (tel. 10 21 10) features classical music concerts from the Stockholm Philharmoniker (symphony orchestra). Concerts are also held at the **Globen** arena (tel. 60 034 00; 50-300kr). Pop music venues include **Skansen** (tel. 57 89 00 05) and the stage at **Gröna Lund** (tel. 670 76 00), Djurgården's huge outdoor Tivoli amusement park. (Open late Apr. to early Sept. Su noon-10pm, M noon-11pm, Tu-Sa noon-midnight. Park 40kr. Concert tickets 125-300kr.) Check theater and concert listings in *Stockholm this Week*, then visit Sweden House or call BiljettDirekt (tel. 077 170 70 70) for tickets.

Catch a film at the 18-theater **Sergel Filmstaden** (tel. 789 60 60) on Hötorget (70kr), or for smaller art-house releases, head to the **Röda Lilla Kvarn** cinema, Biblioteksg. 5 (tel. 789 60 60; T-bana: Östermalmtorget, exit "Stureplan"). English-language films are subtitled, not dubbed.

Stockholm's festivals include: the world-class **Jazz and Blues Festsival** at Skansen (early July but not every year); the **Stockholm Water Festival,** a week-long aqua party and carnival (mid-August; tel. 10 23 03); the two-week **Strindberg Festival** (late Aug. or early Sept.; tel. 34 14 01); and the annual gay pride **Homo Festival** (late July; tel. 736 02 10). Skansen and Gamla Stan also host celebrations for many national holidays, including Nobel Dagen (Dec. 10), St. Lucia Dagen (Dec. 13), Christmas (Dec. 25), Midsummer (June 20-22), and Flag Day (June 6).

Alcohol is very expensive at bars (35-55kr per beer) but available cheaply (10-15kr per 0.5L of beer) at one of the ubiquitous **Systembolaget** state liquor stores (open M-F 9am-5pm). Lighter beer (up to 3.5% alcohol) is also available in supermarkets at around 10kr per beer.

Bröderna Olssons Garlic and Shots, Folkungag. 84, in Söder across from the Columbus Hostel. T-bana: Medborgarplatsen. Electric atmosphere and funky downstairs vodka bar. Pick out a delicious appetizer from the bar menu and wash it down with garlic-flavored beer or one of more than 100 esoteric shots (33kr, many available without garlic). Great DJs on weekends. Hilariously bad Swedish music on Thursdays. No cover. Open 5pm-1am (kitchen closes at 11pm).

Fasching, Kungsg. 63 (tel. 21 62 67; http://www.fasching.se). T-bana: T-Centralen. One of the best jazz clubs in Europe. Live jazz, Latin, blues, funk, fusion, and world music from Swedish and international groups in a funky loft-like space. Leave your neon club-kid synthetics at home and think black. Cover varies by artist (70-250kr). Open 8pm-midnight. F-Sa from midnight-3am the club is used as a regular disco.

Tranan, Karlbergsv. 14, in Vastaden, across the street from T-bana: Odenplan. A young, hip (but not oppressively so) crowd gathers at this trendy, sit-down bar to hear sweet beats and sip pricey drinks. The Chemical Brothers have been known to play here as "secret guests" when in town. Beer 45kr, mixed drinks 62kr. Age 23 and up. No cover. Open 5pm-1am.

Sturecompagniet, Stureg. 4. T-bana: Östermalmstorg. In the center of Stureplan square, the heart of Östermalm's nightlife. Ultra-chic 3-level restaurant, bar, and disco. Expect long lines. Cover 60kr. Open M-W noon-midnight, Th-Sa noon-5am.

Collage, Smålandsg. T-bana: Östermalmstorg. Great dance floor with techno-pop. Women 20 and up, men 22 and up. Cover F-Sa 30kr after 9:30pm. Disco open M-Th 10:30pm-3am, F-Su 10:30pm-5am. See **Food,** p. 858.

Patricia, Stadsgården. T-bana: Slussen. A floating bar-restaurant-nightclub aboard a former luxury yacht. Techno disco below decks, and open-air bars on deck. Sunday after midnight is the popular queer night. Women 23 and up, men 25 and up. Cover F-Sa 60kr, Su 40kr. Open W-Th 6:30pm-1am, F-Su 7pm-5am.

Mingel, Sveavägen 47. Gay club at **Hemingway's** restaurant on Sa nights. Along with Sundays at Patricia, a staple of the gay scene. Th-Sa 10pm-3am.

Bitch Girl Club, Stockholm's rotating lesbian club with a mixed crowd of lipstick lesbians and baby butch women with attitude. Call 720 52 05 or check *QX* for dates and locations.

SWEDEN

■ Near Stockholm

The peninsulas and islands of Stockholm's surrounding *skärgård* (archipelago) offer many opportunities to swim, sail, fish, and explore. To the west, **Björkö** (not to be confused with the island of the same name to the northeast) was a Viking trade center; Swedes first encountered Christianity in 829 in its capital, Birka. Today you can visit the excavation sites, burial mounds, and a Viking museum. **Strömma Kanalbolaget ferries** (tel. 23 33 75) leave from Stadshusbron near the Stadshuset at 10am and return at 3:45pm (round-trip 195kr). Built by King Gustav Vasa, **Waxholm's** mighty 16th-century fortress and museum are closer to central Stockholm. Contact Strömma Kanalbolaget or **Waxholmsbolaget** (tel. 679 58 30) about trips out (1½hr., round-trip 90kr) from both ferry terminals on Strömkajen on Nybroplan in central Stockholm, or take buses 670-678 from central station (45min., free with SL pass).

Just 45 minutes away by ferry, the Swedish royal family makes their summer home at the exquisite Versailles-inspired **Drottningholm.** (Open daily May 11am-4:30pm; June-Aug. 10am-4:30pm; Sept. noon-3:30pm. 40kr, students 20kr.) Lush Baroque gardens and extravagant Rococo interiors echo with the ghosts of elegant Drottning (Queen) Larisa Ulrika, for whom the palace was a wedding gift. Catch the free half-hourly English tour of the palace's **theater** and watch the original stage machinery produce thunderstorm effects (theater tours 40kr, students 10kr). Enjoy a ballet or opera for 85-410kr (tel. 660 82 25). **Kina Slott,** Drottningholm's Chinese pavilion, was an 18th-century royal summer cottage. (Open May-Aug. daily 11am-4:30pm; Sept. noon-3:30pm; Oct. 1-3:30pm. 40kr, students 200kr.) Get to Drottningholm via hourly **Strömma Kanalbolaget ferries** (May-Sept. daily 10am-6pm) from Stadshusbron (round-trip 70kr), or on less palatial **buses 301-323** from T-bana: "Brommaplan."

Little can compare to the tranquil islands of the **outer skärgård.** Longer stays in the area's 20 hostels must be booked months ahead, but the odd night may still be available on short notice, and is worth planning a special trip around. Better still, bring a tent and enjoy free camping courtesy of the law of the right of common access (see p. 853) on any island except Sandhamm (some islands are also in military protection zones and are not open to foreigners). The Waxholmsbolaget ferry company serves even the tiniest of islands and offers the **Båtluffarkortet** card (a bargain 250kr), good for 16 days of sailings. The excursions shop at Sweden House in Stockholm (Hamng. 27) sells the ferry pass and has info on hostels, camping, and kayak or canoe rentals.

Once the home of Swedish sculptor Carl Milles, **Millesgården,** nestled in the suburb of **Lidingö,** is now a beautiful museum with a large collection of classical and medieval European sculpture. The most intriguing works, however, are Milles' own, perched on terraces throughout the grounds. Take T-bana to "Ropsten" and then bus 201, 202, 204-206, or 212 (21kr) to "Torsviks" and follow the signs. (Open May-Sept. daily 10am-5pm; Oct.-Apr. Tu-Su noon-4pm. 50kr, students and seniors 35kr.)

Built in 1380 on Lake Mälarens by the Lord High Chancellor Bo Jonsson Grip, **Gripsholm Castle** looms majestically over the bucolic hamlet of **Mariefred.** The interior of the castle is adorned with portraits and its original Renaissance wall paintings and furniture. (Open May-Aug. daily 10am-8pm; Sept. Tu-Sa 10am-3pm; Oct.-Apr. Sa-Su noon-3pm. 40kr, students 20kr.) A short walk from the castle is **Grafikeus Hus,** once the royal barn, now a print-making workshop (open daily 11am-5pm; 40kr, students 20kr). Take the train to Läggesta, then hop on bus 303 (15kr) to Mariefred (1hr. total). Ask the driver to drop you off at the castle. The M/S Mariefred steamboat (tel. (0152) 296 86), from Klara Mälarstrand in Stockholm, also goes to Mariefred (3hr., mid-June to mid-Aug. at 10am, 140kr).

■ Gotland

Gotland, 300km from Stockholm, Sweden's largest island is a favorite with vacationing Swedes for its green meadows, light-housed cliffs, white sand beaches, and cobblestoned capital, **Visby.** Visby's wall (the oldest medieval monument in Scandinavia) may well have kept the Danes at bay, but it hasn't done much against the tourists.

Unless you're dying to stock up on t-shirts and baubles, the town itself is best left behind for a more remote corner of the island. Pleasant day-trips from Visby include visits to the mystical monoliths on **Fårö**, off the northern tip of the island (bus 21, 2hr.), the blazing beaches of **Tofta,** about 15km south of Visby (bus 31, 21 min.), or the calcified cliffs of **Hoburgen** at the island's southernmost tip (bus 11, 2½hr.).

Destination Gotland ferries (tel. (0498) 20 10 20) sail to Visby from Nynäshamn (south of Stockholm, 5-6hr., catamaran 2½hr.) or Oskarshamn (north of Kalmar, 4-6hr.). Fares are highest on weekends (185kr, catamaran 375kr) and cheapest during the week (140kr, catamaran 240kr; students 90kr and 140kr). During the winter (Oct.-May) there is one ferry per day from each terminal, in summer (June-Sept.) two to five per day. A Scanrail pass earns 50% off. Nynäshamn is linked to Stockholm by **bus** from Cityterminalen (1hr., 60kr) and by *pendeltåg* (commuter train) from Centralstation (45min., 35kr; *rabattk-uponger* and SL passes valid). Oskarshamn is linked to Kalmar by bus (1½hr., 75kr) and by train. To book ferry transport or to get regional tourist info in Stockholm, contact Gotland's satellite tourist center, **Gotland City,** Kungsg. 57A (tel. (08) 406 15 00; fax 406 15 90; open M-F 9:30am-6pm, Sa 10am-2pm).

Once you reach Gotland, find the helpful **tourist office,** Hamng. 4 (tel. (0498) 20 17 00; fax 20 17 17), a 10-minute walk left from the ferry terminal. (Open June-Aug. M-F 7am-7pm, Sa-Su 7am-6pm; Mar.-Apr. M-F 10am-noon and 1-3pm; May M-F 8am-5pm, Sa-Su 10am-4pm.) The office offers detailed maps of Gotland and Visby (25-65kr) and the helpful *Gotlands Guiden* (free). **Gotlands Turist-center,** Färjeleden 3 (tel. (0498) 27 90 95; fax 21 29 20) will help you find a room. (Open May-Sept. M-F 8am-6pm, Sa-Su 10am-6pm; Oct.-Apr. M-F 8am-4pm.) Private rooms inside Visby's walls cost 285kr for singles and 425kr for doubles (outside the city walls 240kr and 380kr). Pick up a bus timetable at the ferry terminal or at the Visby **bus station,** Kung Magnusväg 1 (tel. (0498) 21 41 12). Buses on the island cost 11-42kr, and carry bikes for an extra 20kr. If you have a few days, **cycling** is the best way to explore Gotland's flat terrain with its extensive paths and bike-friendly motorways. **O'Hoj Cykeluthyrning,** across the street from the ferry terminal, rents bikes (55-100kr per day, 275-500kr per week; open daily 7am-6pm). Contact the Turistcenter (see above) for more info on the 34 hostels, camp-grounds, and bike rentals located elsewhere on the island.

If you need to stay in Visby, the convenient **Visby Fängelse Vandrarhem,** Skeps-bron 1 (tel. (0498) 20 60 50; fax 20 51 10), just across from the ferry terminal, was a maximum security prison until 1998. Sweet dreams. (150kr per person in doubles. Reception 10am-4pm, call to arrange arrivals outside those hours.) Otherwise, explore the island's many offerings, and take full advantage of the right of common access (see p. 853). Before you leave town, pack a picnic lunch from **Rimi supermarket,** Stenkumlav. 36 (open daily 8am-10pm).

SOUTHERN SWEDEN

Islands and skerries line both the east and west coasts of Sweden; the southwest **Småland** coastline, between Västervik and Kalmar, is particularly scenic, while the western **Halland** coast between Göteborg and Helsingborg is scattered with small resort towns. From **Helsingborg** in northern Skåne, trains bound for Copenhagen cross on ferries to Helsingør in Denmark; reach Helsingborg by SJ train or by pågatåg (from Malmö or Lund 65kr). **Trelleborg,** in southern Skåne, sees several ferries per day off to Saßnitz (railpasses valid) and Travemünde in Germany; take an SJ train or bus from Malmö (48kr). From **Ystad,** also in southern Skåne, ferries serve Bornholm. Reach Ystad by pågatåg (from Malmö 63kr).

■ Kalmar

Nesting on the deep blue Baltic waters, Kalmar is home to the stunning Renaissance castle **Kalmar Slott,** the site of the inception of 1397 Kalmar Union, an attempt to unite the kingdoms of Denmark, Norway, Sweden, and Finland. (Open daily June-Aug. 10am-6pm; Apr.-May and Sept. 10am-4pm; Oct.-Mar. the second weekend of each month 11am-4pm. 60kr, students 30kr.) The baroque **Kalmar Domkyrka,** in the center of town on Stortorget (the main square), enjoys all the splendor of a major cathedral, but, alas, is *sans* bishop (open daily 9am-6pm; free organ concerts W at noon). The **Kalmar Läns Museum,** Skeppsbrog. 51, houses relics from the wreckage of the 17th-century warship, **Kronan,** which was twice the size of Stockholm's *Vasa,* and met a more glorious end when it sank in a 1676 battle against the Danish. (Open daily mid-June to mid-Aug. 10am-6pm; late Aug. to early June 10am-4pm; 50kr, students 20kr.) The **Kalmar Konstmuseum,** Slottsv. 1D, houses a collection of Scandinavian art emphasizing local masters. (Open late May to early Sept. M-F 10am-5pm, Sa-Su 11am-5pm; mid-Sept. to mid-May also M-F 7-9pm. 30kr, students 20kr.) In the nearby towns, collectively dubbed **Glasriket** (Kingdom of Crystal), exquisite hand-blown crystal, such as **Orrefors** (tel. (0481) 341 95) and **Kosta Boda** (tel. (0481) 240 30), are produced by the artisans depicted in the movie *My Life as a Dog* (both open M-F 9am-5pm, Sa 10am-4pm). Bus 138 or 101 (1hr., 70kr) from Kalmar's train station.

Kalmar's **train station** and **bus terminal** lie just south of town, across the bay from the castle. To reach the helpful **tourist office,** Larmg. 6 (tel. (0480) 153 50; fax 174 53), from the train station, go right on Stationsg. and at the small park make a left onto Ölandsg. It provides free maps and book rooms for 190kr. (50kr fee. Open June-Aug. M-F 9am-9pm, Sa 9am-5pm, Su 1-6pm; May and Sept. M-F 9am-5pm, Sa 10am-1pm; Jan.-Apr. M-F 9am-5pm.) To get to the **Kalmar Vandrarhem (HI),** Rappeg. 1 (tel. (0480) 129 28; fax 882 93), on the island of Angö, walk from the tourist office north on Larmg., go right on Fiskareg. until it becomes Angöleden, cross the bridge and cruise—the hostel is on the right just before the next bridge (130kr, nonmembers 170kr; reception daily 7:30-10am and 4:30-10pm). **Stensö Camping** (tel. (0480) 888 03), is in a nature reserve 2km south of Kalmar (95-120kr; reception 8am-10pm; open Apr.-Oct.). Restaurants cluster around **Larmtorget.** In summer, the outdoor **Teatervallen,** behind the theater on Larmtorget, is a busy post-cafe destination.

In view of Kalmar's coast, the vacation island of **Öland** stretches over 100km of green fields, white sand beaches, and lakes. The royal family roosts here on holiday, and Crown Princess Victoria's birthday, **Victoriadagen** (July 14), is celebrated island-wide. Commoners flock to the beaches of **Löttorp** and **Böda** in the north and **Grönhögen** and **Ottenby** in the south. **Buses** 101 and 105 leave from in front of the train station (60-100kr) for Öland. Öland's **tourist office** (tel. (0485) 386 21) is in Färjestaden. If you stay here, **Vandrarhem Borgholm,** Rosenfors (tel. (0485) 107 56), and **Vandrarhem Böda** (tel. (0485) 220 38) on Melböda in Löttorp, await.

■ Malmö

Malmö (mahl-MER), the country's third-largest city, is often used as no more than a gateway, but with its beautiful squares **Stortorget** and **Lilla Torg,** the city has its own appeal. Both the inspiring **Rooseum,** Gasverksg. 22 (open Tu-W and F-Su 11am-5pm, Th until 8pm; 30kr), and the **Malmö Konsthall,** St. Johannesg. 7 (free), house modern art exhibits. The **Form Design Center,** Lilla Torg 9, highlights the Swedish design work made famous by IKEA, Volvo, Saab, and Electrolux (open Tu-F 11am-5pm, Sa 10am-4pm, Su noon-4pm; closed Su in July; free). In Malmö's west end, **Slottsparken** (Castle Park) contains **Malmöhus,** a collection of museums housed in the castle at the park's center (open daily June-Aug. 10am-4pm; Sept.-May noon-4pm; 40kr).

The **train station** and **harbor** lie just north of the Old Town. Pilen (tel. (040) 23 44 11) has **ferry** service to Copenhagen (45min., 59kr); **trains** arrive from Göteborg (3½hr., 395kr, under 25 275kr) and Stockholm (4½-6hr., 560kr, under 25 395kr). The **tourist office** in the train station has free maps and the useful *Malmö this Month.* (Open June-Aug. M-F 9am-7pm, Sa-Su 10am-3pm; Sept.-May M-F 9am-5pm, Sa 10am-

2pm.) **Forex,** next door, exchanges money and cashes traveler's checks (open daily 8am-9pm). From the train station or boat terminal, cross Mälarbron bridge and take a right on Västerg. to the hostel **City Vandrarhem,** Västerg. 9. (Tel. (040) 23 56 40; fax 30 40 98. 125kr. Reception 8:30-11am and 4-11pm. Open June-Aug.) **Sibbarp Camping,** Strandg. 101 (tel. (040) 15 51 65; fax 15 97 77), is at the end of bus route 12B (tents 110kr). While Lilla Torg is filled with trendy cafes, your wallet will thank you for feasting at **Cafe Siesta,** Hjorttackeg. 1 (*dagens rätt* 50kr; open M-Sa 10am-midnight, Su noon-midnight). On weekends, head out to **Slakthuset** (Slaughterhouse), Carlsg. 12A, a giant disco that earns its meat market name. (3 dance floors. Ice rink. Women 20 and over, men 23 and over. Cover 70kr. Open F-Sa midnight-5am.)

■ Lund

What Oxford and Cambridge are to England, Uppsala and Lund are to Sweden. Lund University's antagonism with its scholarly northern neighbors in Uppsala has inspired countless pranks, drag shows, and drinkfests in Lund's bright streets..To see the last 400 years of Lund's antics, check out the comical **Studentmuseet Arkivet,** Sandg. 2 (open Tu 4-8pm, W 4-6pm; 20kr). For more information on student life, including cheap, fun nightlife, contact **Student Info** on the ground floor of the student union (*akademiska föreningen* or AF; Sept.-May M-F 10am-4pm) or visit the "What's Up?" page at http://www.lu.se/intsek. The university campus is north of the town's ancient **cathedral,** an impressive 900-year-old reminder of the time when Lund was the religious epicenter of Scandinavia. (Open M-Tu and F 8am-6pm, W-Th 8am-7pm, Sa 9:30am-5pm, Su 9:30am-6pm. Guided English tours M-Sa 3pm. Free organ concerts Su 10am.) **Kulturen,** Tegnérplatsen, is an open-air museum with 17th- and 18th- century Swedish homes, churches and history displays (open May-Sept. daily 11am-5pm; Oct.-Apr. Tu-Su noon-4pm; 40kr).

Lund is easily accessible from Malmö on most **SJ trains** and by pagatågen, the local trains (10min., 30kr, railpasses valid). Lund's **tourist office,** Kyrkog. 11 (tel. (046) 35 50 40; fax 12 59 63), across from the cathedral, books rooms. (175kr, 50kr fee. Open June-Aug. M-F 10am-6pm, Sa-Su 10am-2pm; Sept. and May M-F 10am-5pm, Sa 10am-2pm; Oct.-Apr. M-F 10am-5pm.) Rest your tired limbs at the delightful **HI Hostel Tåget** (The Train), Vävareg. 22 (tel. (046) 14 28 20; fax 32 05 68), with authentic sleeping cars from the 1940s. Take the overpass to the park side of the station (100kr, nonmembers 140kr; reception daily 8-10am and 5-8pm). If you've missed "the train," try to find a bed in Malmö—the run-down **Lastrada Vandrarhem,** is just as far and is not recommended. Pitch your tent at **Källby Camping** (tel. (046) 35 51 88). Take bus 1 ("Klostergården") and ask to be let off at the campground (30kr per tent; kitchen, swimming pool, and sauna; open early June to mid-Aug.).

Mårtenstorget features a fresh fruit and vegetable **market** (open M-Sa 7am-2:30pm). **Govindas,** Bredg. 28, cooks up an all-day, eat-'til-you-can't buffet of Indian vegetarian food (50kr; students 45kr; open M-Th 11:30am-5pm, F-Sa 11:30am-3pm). **Mejeriet,** Stora Söderg. 64, packs a bar, movie theater, and concert hall into a former dairy (hours vary with shows, call (046) 12 38 11 for info).

■ Varberg

Located between Göteborg and Malmö, coastal Varberg beckons with expansive white sand beaches and the spectacular **Varberg Fortress,** overlooking the sky-blue waters of the Kattegatt. Although you can't explore the castle on your own, tours are offered from mid-June to mid-August (hourly from 11am-4pm; 20kr). Just south of town, the shallow bay of **Apelviken** offers some of the best **windsurfing** and **surfing** in northern Europe. **Surfer's Paradise,** Söderg. 22 (tel. (0340) 67 70 55) rents gear and gives tips (seasonal hours, call ahead). For those who would rather explore the gorgeous beaches, **BF Cykel,** Östra Langg. 47, rents bikes (70kr per day; open M-F 9:30am-6pm, Sa 9:30am-2pm). In the second week of August, the fortress hosts a **medieval festival.**

Trains arrive from Göteborg (1hr., 100kr, under 25 70kr) and from Malmö (2hr., 290kr, under 25 205kr). The **tourist office** (tel. (0340) 887 70; fax 61 11 95), in Brunnsparken, offers maps and books rooms in hotels, hostels, and private homes. From the train station, walk right on Västra Vallg. for four blocks. (Open mid-June to mid-Aug. M-Sa 9am-7pm, Su 3-7pm; shorter hours off-season.) The bright rooms of **Varbergs Fästning Vandrarhem** (tel. (0340) 887 88), inside the fortress itself will make you forget it was used as the **Crown Jail** from 1852-1931. Being locked up was never this fun (unless you're into that), nor this popular; book ahead. (Reception open daily June-Aug. 8-10am and 5-9pm, call ahead at other times of the year. Dorms 135kr, small singles 130kr. Cash only.) If you're acquitted, there's usually room at **Skeppsgårdens Vandrarhem,** Krabbesväg 4 (tel. (0340) 130 35 or (070) 321 30 35 while desk is closed; fax (0340) 103 95). From the train station, continue on Västra Vallg. past the tourist office, go right on Lasarettsg., then left on Knut Porses väg (150kr, includes breakfast; reception open daily 8am-noon and 3-7pm). On the beach, **Apelvikens Camping** (tel. (0340) 141 78; fax 104 22) will let you stake out a tent site for 150kr (off-season 115kr; open late Mar. to Sept.). The **Mignan Cafe,** Drottningg. 23, and **Majas Cafe** on Kungsg., both just off Stortorget (the main square), offer fantastic breakfasts (around 40kr) and daily lunch specials (around 50kr). **Sophia och Uscars** and their second floor disco **Gustavs,** Norrg. 16, offer live jazz, rock, and stand-up comedy as well as dancing (open Th-Su 9pm-2am).

■ Göteborg (Gothenburg)

The long-time hub of Swedish industry and the country's second largest city, Göteborg (YUH-ta-boy) is a city with a job to do. Here, culture, history, and style for its own sake aren't always on display, and university students fuel an active but easygoing cafe scene. The Göteborgare think of themselves as more welcoming than their counterparts in Stockholm, whom they contemptuously call *Nollåtor* (zeroeights), after Stockholm's area code.

PRACTICAL INFORMATION

Trains arrive at Centralstation on their way to Malmö (3½hr., 11 per day, 395kr, under 25 275kr), Oslo (4½hr., 3 per day, 401kr, under 25 280kr), and Stockholm (3½-5hr., 10 per day, 505kr, under 25 355kr). The station also offers **lockers** (15-30kr for 24hr.) and **showers** (25kr). **Stena Line ferries** (tel. (031) 704 00 00; fax 85 85 95) sail to Frederikshavn, Denmark (3hr., 15 per day, 80kr) and to Kiel, Germany (14hr., 820kr). **SeaCat hydrofoils** (tel. (031) 775 08 00; fax 12 60 90) whisk to Frederikshavn (1hr. 45min., 4 per day, 100-120kr). **Scandinavian Seaways** (tel. (031) 65 06 50) sails to Newcastle, England (22hr.; 1125kr, year-round starting Feb. 1999). Göteborg is a compact city, but the weary can ride **Stadstrafiken trams** and **buses** (16kr; midnight-5am 32kr; 24hr. pass 40kr but not valid midnight-5am).

The main **tourist office,** Kungsportsplatsen 2 (tel. (031) 10 07 40; fax 13 21 84; email info@gbg-co.se; http://www.gbg-co.se), provides free maps, copies of the *Göteborg Guide* and *What's on in Göteborg,* and **Göteborg Cards,** which grant free public transportation and free entry or discounts for many attractions (74kr for 24hr.). Exit to Drottningtorget from the train station, and cross the square to the big pink Radisson hotel. At the right end of this building, follow Östra Larmag. for five minutes to Kungsportspl. (Open daily late June to early Aug. 9am-8pm; early June and late Aug. 9am-6pm; May M-F 9am-6pm, Sa-Su 10am-2pm; Sept.-Apr. M-F 9am-5pm, Sa 10am-2pm.) **Currency exchange** is available at the Forex shops at Centralstation (20kr commission per traveler's check, 30kr for cash; open daily 8am-9pm). The **American Express office** (tel. (031) 13 07 12) is located in the Nyman & Schultz travel agency at Drottningg. 14B (open June-Aug. 8:15am-4:30pm; Sept.-May 10am-1pm and 1:30-4pm). **Internet access** is free at the city library (stadsbibliotek) on Götaplatsen (open M-Th and Sa-Su 10am-8pm, F 10am-6pm).

ACCOMMODATIONS, CAMPING, AND FOOD

The seamen who shacked up in the historic building that is now the **Stigbergsliden Hostel (HI),** Stigbergsliden 10 (tel. (031) 24 16 20; fax 24 65 20; email vandrarhem.stigbergsliden@swipnet.se), used to fight over jobs in the building's courtyard. Today, backpackers duke it out for the chance to stay in this well-appointed and comfy hostel. Take tram 3, 4, or 9 to "Stigbergstorget" and walk down the hill. (Dorms 110kr; singles 185kr; doubles 240kr; nonmembers add 40kr. Reception 8-10am and 4-10pm.) **Slottskogens Hostel (HI),** Vegag. 21 (tel. (031) 42 65 20; fax 14 21 02; email mail@slottskogenvh.se), has gorgeous, brand-new facilities and clean, spacious rooms. Take tram 1 or 2 to "Olivedalsg." and walk uphill to Vegag. New dorms will be open for summer 1999 for 90kr. (3-6 bed dorms 110kr; singles 185kr; nonmembers add 40kr. Kitchen, sauna, bike rental. Reception daily 8am-noon and 3-10pm.) Docked at Packhuskajen harbor among the ships of the Maritime Museum and in view of the opera house, **M/S Seaside** (tel. (031) 10 59 70; fax 711 60 35), in a former Norwegian motorship, is well worth the 100kr—if you don't get seasick. From the train station, take tram 5 to "Lilla Bommen" and then walk left along the pier. (12-bed dorms 100kr; singles 250kr. Reception daily 8-11am and 5-9pm. Check-in 4pm-9pm. No curfew or phone reservations.) Pitch your tent at **Kärralund Camping,** Olbersg. (tel. (031) 84 02 00; fax 84 05 00). Tram 5: "Welanderg.," then east on Olbersg. (130kr per tent; rooms 110kr, nonmembers 150kr; reception 7am-11pm).

In the summer, **Kajskjul 8** (Warehouse 8) on Parkhuskajen, next to the Maritime Centrum, is transformed into an open air restaurant where visitors sample fruits of the sea, then party all night (open late June to mid-Aug. noon-3am; 60kr cover after 10pm). **Solrosen,** Käponjargen 4A, serves up an all-you-can-eat buffet of tasty vegetarian and vegan fare for 45-60kr. (Open mid-June to July M-Sa 4pm-1am; Aug. to early June M-Sa 11:30am-1am. Kitchen closes at 10:30pm.)

SIGHTS AND ENTERTAINMENT

On arriving at Centralstation, travelers will find themselves in Nordstaden, north of most of the action. To the south, just across Drottningtorget (main square) and the Hamn canal is the touristy island of **Inom Vallgraven.** Across one more canal and extending west are **Vasastaden,** the student grotto, and **Haga,** the old city. Kungsport Avenyn, the city's main drag, stretches from Kungsportsplatsen all the way up to **Götaplatsen,** site of the regal **Konstmuseet** and Carl Milles' famous **sculpture-fountain** of Poseidon. Göteborg's more conservative citizens were uncomfortable with Milles' original design, which featured a more virile Poseidon wielding his member like a mighty trident. Milles compromised by replacing the trident with a large fish, squirming out of Posiedon's hand. The Konstmuseet houses the largest collection of Nordic art in Scandinavia. (Open May-Aug. M-F 11am-4pm, Sa-Su 11am-5pm; Sept.-Apr. Tu and Th-F 11am-4pm, W 11am-9pm, Sa-Su 11am-5pm. 35kr.)

Hasselblad Center, also on Götaplatsen, has excellent photo exhibitions (open May-Aug. M-F 11am-4pm, Sa-Su 11am-5pm). The **Göteborgs Operan,** Lilla Bommen (tel. tickets (031) 13 13 00; tours 10 80 50), mimics a ship at full mast. Even for the opera-allergic, this award-winning building is worth a look on your way to the **Göteborg Maritime Centrum,** which features a large number of docked ships and sailing vessels which you can board and tour. (Open daily Mar.-Apr. and Sept.-Nov. 10am-4pm; May-June and Aug. 10am-6pm; July 10am-9pm. 50kr.) **Stadsmuseet,** the city museum at Norra Hamng. 12, houses exhibits on the city's industrial past and its post-industrial rebirth, as well as remains of a Viking ship (open June-Aug. daily 11am-4pm; Sept.-Apr. Tu and Th-Su 11am-4pm, W 11am-8pm; 40kr, students 10kr).

Göteborgs Skärgård (Archipelago) is a summer paradise for beach-goers and sailors. Pick up a free copy of the *Skärgårds Guiden* at the tourist office. For a simple one-day excursion to the Skärgården, **Vrångö** island offers a secluded and serene beach; take tram 4 to "Saltholmen," then a ferry to the island. Bus transfers are valid on the ferries. Call **Styrsöbolaget Ferry Line** (tel. (031) 69 64 00) for info. To rise above it all, climb the bell tower of **Masthuggskyrkan,** a 20th-century church with the best view of the city. (Bus 85 from Lilla Torget, or tram 4 to Fjällg. Open M-F 9am-3pm, Sa 9:30am-1:30pm.)

Göteborg also has a thriving theater and classical music scene—check the tourist office's free *What's on in Göteborg* for events. For live music, from jazz and blues to hip-hop, try **Nefertiti,** Hvitfeldtsplatsen 6 (tel. (031) 711 15 33; http://www.nefertiti.se) downstairs in a stone building just over the canal from Haga (open Tu-Su 9pm-late; cover varies). The queer set heads to **Disco Touch,** located at RFSL Göteborg (the Göteborg Gay Center; club open W 9pm-1am, F 9pm-2am, Sa 9pm-3am).

CENTRAL SWEDEN

■ Uppsala

Once a hotbed of pagan spirituality and the cradle of Swedish civilization, Uppsala is now a Nordic Oxbridge, sheltering the 20,000 students of Sweden's oldest university. Scandinavia's largest cathedral, the magnificent **Domkyrka,** where Swedish monarchs were crowned, looms just over the river (open daily 8am-6pm; tours in English June-Aug. M-Sa 1pm). The university museum, **Gustavianum,** across from the Domkyrka, lodges the **Anatomical Theater**—the site of 18th-century public human dissections. (Open June-Aug. daily 11am-4pm, Th until 9pm; Sept.-May noon-3pm; 40kr, students 20kr.) For university events, scope the bulletin board at the home of the Silver Bible, the **Carolina Rediviva Library,** Övre Slottsg. at Drottningg. The debate still rages over whether **Gamla Uppsala** (Old Uppsala), 4km north of the city center, was the site of a legendary pagan temple. Little remains save huge burial mounds of monarchs and **Gamla Uppsala Kyrka,** one of Sweden's oldest churches (open daily Apr.-Sept. 9am-6pm; Oct.-Mar. 9am-4pm; free). Take bus 2, 20, 24, or 54 (14kr) north from Dragarbrunnsg. (return within 1½hr. to re-use ticket). After exhausting Uppsala, you can hop the boat to **Skokloster,** a dazzling Baroque palace built between 1654-1676 (open May-Sept. daily 7am-5pm; 60kr, students 40kr). The boat departs in summer Tu-Su at 11:45am and returns at 5:30pm from Islandsbron on Östra Åg. and Munkg. (round-trip 105kr).

Trains from Stockholm's Centralstation run to Uppsala about hourly (40min., 65kr, under 25 50kr). The **tourist office,** Fyristorg 8 (tel. (018) 27 48 00; fax 13 28 95; email tb@utkab.se). From the train station, walk right on Kungsg., left on St. Persg., and cross the bridge (open M-F 10am-6pm, Sa 10am-3pm, summer also Su noon-4pm). The pleasant **Basic Hotel,** Kungsg. 27, has a bathroom, shower, and kitchenette in each room (150kr; reception M-F 7am-11pm, Sa-Su 8am-10pm). For peaceful, newly-renovated rooms, try **Sunnersta Herrgård (HI),** Sunnerstav. 24 (tel. (018) 32 42 20), 6km south of town. Take bus 20 or 50 from Dragarbrunnsg. to Herrgårdsv. (16kr), then walk two blocks behind the kiosk, turn left, and walk 50m (150kr, nonmembers 190kr; reception 8-10am and 5-9pm; open May-Aug.). **Fyrishov Camping,** Idrottsg. 2 (tel. (018) 27 49 60; fax 24 43 33), off Svartbäcksg., is 2km from the city center. Take bus 4 to "Fyrishov" (tents 75kr; 4-5 bed huts June 1-Aug. 8 400kr; reception 7am-11pm). **Max and Marie,** Drottningg. 7, serves up a veggie buffet daily for 55kr (students 50kr). Good bets after dark are **Fellini,** Svartbäcksg. 7, a loud student rock and blues bar (open M-Sa 11am-1am); the moody **Fredman's,** which features live R&B, blues, and rock Wednesday to Saturday (open Su-Tu 5pm-1am; W-Sa 5pm-2am; cover 20kr-100kr; age 20 and over); and the popular nightclub **Sten Sture & Co.,** Nedre Slottsg. 3 (open W-Sa 11pm-2am).

■ Dalarna

Swedes get misty-eyed just talking about Dalarna, close to southern Sweden and yet part of the northern wilderness. This popular vacation spot is Sweden's *Smultronstället*—a secret spot where one goes to commune with nature, one's self, and one's significant other. Scores of Swedes summer here in tidy red and white farmhouses in the woods. The **Siljansleden,** a 340km cycling and hiking trail, winds its way through forests and over mountains around Lake Siljan, which is enjoyed for its swimming, boating, and fishing. **Trains** run from Stockholm via Uppsala to Borlänge, and from there either northeast to Falun or northwest to Leksand, Rättvik, and Mora. If you wish to be near Lake Siljan around **Midsummer** (June 20-22), reserve a bed months in advance and know that many bus and train lines shut down.

Leksand
More than 20,000 people flock to this small town above the lake to take part in the Midsummer festivities, featuring a maypole, folk music, and the **Siljan-srodden,** a two-week series of churchboat competitions on Lake Siljan to revive the tradition of rowing to church. The annual **Musik vid Siljan** festival in Leksand and Rättvik (the first week of July) has classical and folk music from all over the earth (tel. (0248) 105 72; 30-200kr). The **tourist office** (tel. (0247) 803 00; fax 018 40; http://www.siljan-dalarna.com), attached to the Leksand train station, has more details. (Open mid-June to mid-Aug. M-F 9am-8pm, Sa-Su 10am-8pm; mid-Aug. to mid-June M-F 9am-5pm, Sa 10am-1pm.) From Leksand's quay there are breezy summer **cruises** on the *M/S Gustaf Wasa* a few times a day to Rättvik and Mora (tel. (010) 252 32 92 or (070) 542 10 25; 2-4hr., 80-120kr).

Accommodations are often hard to come by (packed for Midsummer), but the tourist office can find you a private room for a 25kr fee (doubles from 265kr). Try the **Solvi SMU-gård** (tel. (0247) 100 90), Rättviksv. 60, a few minutes from the station. A combination campground, lodge, and country kitchen, the main building is a red farmhouse. (100kr per bed, tents 80kr. Reception 7:30am-9:30pm. Open mid-June to mid-Aug.) Otherwise, call **STF hostel (HI)** (tel. (0247) 152 50), 2.5km from the train station, and ask for directions. A 20-minute walk along the road toward Tällberg brings you to swimming and camping at **Camping Stugby** (tel./fax (0247) 803 13; 100kr per tent). Hit **Leksands Kebab & Pizza,** Norsg. 23, for substantial pizza (from 30kr; open M-Sa 11am-11pm, Su noon-11pm). Delicatessen items can be found at the **Mårtas** supermarket, Leksandsv. 5 (open M-Sa 9am-8pm, Su 10am-8pm).

Mora
Head north by bus to **Mora,** perhaps the nicest of the Siljan villages and home to artist Anders Zorn (1860-1920), most famous for painting large, naked women. See his collection and house at the **Zornmuseet,** Vasag. 36. (Museum open May-Sept. M-Sa 9am-5pm, Su 11am-5pm; Oct-Apr. M-Sa noon-5pm, Su 1-4pm. 30kr, students 25kr. Guided tours of the house 35kr, students 30kr.) The legendary red wooden *dalahäst* horses are hand-made in **Nusnäs,** 10km east of Mora (bus 108, 20min., 13kr), but their celebrity has come at a price: brothers Nils and Grannas Olsson (tel. (0250) 372 00 and 372 50 respectively) now inhabit a house divided and run competing factories which you can tour for free. (Open June to mid-Aug. M-F 9am-6pm, Sa-Su 9am-4pm; mid-Aug. to May M-F 8am-4pm, Sa 10am-1pm.)

The **Inlandsbanan** train route (see **Lappland,** p. 872) begins in Mora, with a train leaving at 7:50am from the "Morastrand" train station (Mora-Östersund 160kr; Mora-Gällivare 480kr) and arriving at Östersund at 1:45pm; another train leaves Östersund at 7:05am and arrives at Gällivare at 9:50pm (Midsummer to early August only). The **tourist office** (tel. (0250) 265 50 or 945 11), which books rooms in private homes for a 25kr. fee (135kr-155kr per person) is in Mora's "central" train station, but the

---

Midsummer Madness

For Midsummer (June 20) Swedes emerge from the woodwork to welcome the sun after a long and dark winter. Groups of families, villages, and amorous youngsters erect and dance around the **Midsommarstång,** a cross-shaped pole with two rings dangling from the ends. Its phallic construction symbolizes the fertilization of the soil it is staked in, and thoughts of other fertilization abound as girls place flowers under their pillows to induce dreams of their future spouses. The largest celebrations are in Dalarna, where alcohol and pickled herring flow freely and people flood the city for a two-day party. Keep Midsummer in mind while planning a trip—most transportation lines and establishments are closed.

Morastrand stop is closer to civilization. (Open mid-June to mid-Aug. M-F 9am-8pm, Sa-Su 10am-8pm; mid-Aug. to mid-June M-F 9am-5pm, Sa 10am-2pm.) Mora's **youth hostel (HI),** Fredsg. 6 (tel. (0250) 381 96; fax 381 95) is 500m from the Morastrand station; go right on the main road and cross the street when you see the sign for "Målkull Ann's Cafe," which functions as an office for the hostel outside of reception hours. (130kr, nonmembers 170kr. Reception 8-10am and 5-7pm. No credit cards; wheelchair accessible.) For cheap grub, browse the bakeries on **Kyrkogatan,** or load up on supplies at the **Hemköp supermarket,** also on Kyrkog. (Open M-F 9:30am-7pm, Sa 9:30am-3pm, Su noon-4pm.) The best *dagens rätt* in town is the very Swedish all-you-can-eat buffet (55kr, open daily 11am-3pm) at the **Mora Hotell,** on Hamng.

■ Östersund

At the edge of the serene Lake Storsjön, Östersund is a natural stopover from Trondheim for travelers heading to or from Norway and a required one for those riding the length of the Inlandsbanan. **Lake Storsjön** is home to a cousin of the Loch Ness monster, which King Oscar II and a crew of Norwegian whalers tried unsuccessfully to capture in 1894. See their harpoons at the **Jamtli museum,** north of the city center on Kyrkg. The museum also features Sami photography, crafts, Viking paintings, and people dressed in period clothing living and working in the buildings of an open-air museum. (Open June-Aug. daily 11am-5pm; Sept.-May Tu 11am-9pm, W-Su 11am-5pm. 80kr.) Rent a bike at **Cykelogen,** Kyrkg. 45 (tel. (063) 12 20 80), for 100kr per day (open M-F 10am-1pm and 2-6pm, Sa 10am-2pm), and let gravity draw you over the footbridge to **Frösön Island,** once thought to be the dwelling of Viking gods.

Trains run west to Trondheim (5½hr., 300kr), south to Stockholm (6hr., 497kr), as well as north into Lappland. The **tourist office,** Rådhusg. 44 (tel. (063) 14 40 01), has city maps (free-55kr), and books rooms for no fee (open June-Aug. M-Sa 9am-9pm, Su 10am-7pm; Sept.-May M-F 8am-5pm). From the train station, walk up the hill on your left and continue down Prästg.; hang a right up Postgränd one block. Östersund's splendid **HI youth hostel** (tel. (063) 13 91 00 or 10 23 43) is 600m from the railroad station on Södra Gröng., and has kitchenettes and TVs in all rooms (doubles only; call for directions; reception 8-10am and 5-9pm). Wild strawberries grow on the thatched roof of **Frösötornets Härbärge hostel** (tel. (063) 51 57 67), at the top of a 176m ski slope overlooking the city. Take bus 5 from the city center (last one 8:22pm; no buses Sunday) or endure a hellish climb (reception 9am-9pm; 125kr; showers 1kr per 2min; open May-Oct). Take bus 2, 6, or 9 to **Östersunds Camping** (tel. (063) 14 46 15) at Fritidsbyn (camping spaces 90kr). You'll find Mexican and Creole cuisine in the old-fashioned Swedish interior of **Brunkullans Restaurang,** Postgränd 5, with its 65kr lunch buffet (open M-F 11am-11pm, Sa 2-11pm, Su 5-11pm; buffet M-F 11am-2pm). An even cheaper option is the supermarket **Hemköp** at 56 Kyrkg. (open M-F 9am-7pm, Sa 9am-4pm, Su noon-5pm).

THE BALTIC COAST

Sweden's Baltic coast can be gentle and dramatic, rural and sophisticated, lively and peacefully remote. The beautiful, unblemished stretch of coastline south of Örnsköldsvik contrasts with Umeå, one of the world's northernmost university towns.

Gävle A survivor of three major fires in its 550-year history, the city of Gävle bursts with lilacs and pansies in summer and thrives year-round amidst the charm of old-world cobblestone and enchanting gardens. Gävle centers on the **Gävleån River,** with **Gamla Gefle** (old city) on the south bank. Perhaps built a little too close to the river, the 17th-century church, **Heliga Trefaldighetskyrkan,** is slowly leaning into the muck. The **Galleri Gunnar Cyrén,** Nedre Bergsg. 11 (open Sept.-June Tu-Sa noon-5pm; free), holds work by Gunnar Cyrén, who designed the 1991 Nobel Peace prize plates. The **Länsmuseet Gävleborg**, S. Strandg. 20, contains art by Cyrén and other Swedes (open Tu and Th-F 10am-4pm, W 10am-9pm, Sa-Su 1-5pm; 25kr).

Trains run regularly from Stockholm through Uppsala (2hr.). To get to the **tourist office**, Drottningg. 37 (tel. (026) 14 74 30), exit the train station straight ahead to Drottningg.; the office is on the right. (Open June-Aug. M-F 9am-6pm, Sa 9am-2pm, Su 11am-4pm; Sept.-May M-F 9am-5pm). The **Vandrarhem Gävle (HI)**, S. Rådmansg. 1 (tel. (026) 62 17 45), has clean rooms and a secluded garden for guests (120kr, nonmembers 160kr; reception 8-10am and 5-7pm.) Bus 5 will take you to the quality waterfront hostel **Vandrarhem Engeltofta (HI)** (tel. (026) 961 60; fax 960 55; 110kr, nonmembers 150kr) or to **Engesberg Camping** (tel. (960) 990 25; tents 75kr, nonmembers 85kr; reception 8am-10pm; open May-Aug.). For the hostel, get off at "Engeltofta" (15min., 13kr); for the camp-ground, "Engesberg" (20min., 20kr). The open-air **market** in the Stortorget sells fresh fruit and vegetables and is surrounded by cafes and restaurants. Good, cheap grub can be found at **Tennstopet**, Nyg. 38 (open M-Sa 9am-10pm, Su noon-10pm). At night, the best places to hit are on S. and N. Kungsg., near the river.

Hiking, swimming, and fishing are just a ferry-ride away from Gävle on the island of **Limön**. Ferries leave from the tourist boat dock on S. Skeppsboron. Local smoked herring can be eaten straight from the curing barrels at **Böna**, a fishing village northeast of Gävle. Take bus 5 from Gävle (20min., 20kr).

Örnsköldsvik

Off the beaten track and main train route is Örnsköldsvik (Urn-SHULDS-vik; Ö-vik to the locals), surrounded by mountains with ski jumps and a harbor filled with tiny islands waiting to be explored. The 130km **Höga Kusten Leden** (High Coast Trail) links Ö-vik with Veda in the south, and winds along the most beautiful, dramatic section of Sweden's Baltic coast. Pick up the trail guide at the tourist office (25kr) for information on transportation links and huts along the way. Several day hikes are also conveniently near—the **Yellow Trail** loops an easy 6km. A journey to the **Ulvön Islands** is an easy excursion to the land of fermented Baltic herring. Throughout the north island are scenic **hiking trails,** the toughest leading to the peak of Lotsberget Mountain. The *M/S Otilia* leaves Örnsköldsvik at 9:30am and returns at 3pm (2½hr., round-trip 100kr). The same ferry stops en route at the island of **Trysunda**, which also has beautiful hiking trails and a beach in Björnviken. (1½h; leaves Ö-vik at 9:30am, Tvysunda at 3:40pm; round trip 70kr). **Gene Fornby**, a 2000-year-old settlement discovered 6km from Ö-vik, has been rebuilt to look as it did as an Iron Age village in the year 500 (50kr, children 20kr; open late June to early Aug. daily 11am-5pm; tours on the hour from 1-4pm).

Buses run to Örnsköldsvik from Umeå (2hr., 90kr) and Östersund (4½hr., 210kr). Örnsköldsvik's **tourist office**, Nyg. 18 (tel. (0660) 125 37; fax 881 23), has maps and info about hiking and daytrips to nearby islands. It also books private rooms (150kr) and cottages (200kr) for a 50kr fee (open mid-June to mid-Aug. M-F 9am-7pm, Sa 9am-3pm, Su 10am-3pm; mid-Aug. to mid-June M-F 9am-5pm, Sa 9am-1pm). To get there, walk up the steps behind the bus station, follow Fabriksg. to Nyg., then make a left. The youth hostel **STF Vandrarhem Örnsköldsvik (HI)**, Högsnäsgården pl. 1980 (tel./fax (0660) 702 44), is a 15-minute ride into the cow-pie-scented countryside. (Bus 42, 19kr; weekdays last bus leaves from the bus station at 9pm. Reception in summer 9-10am and 5-7pm; off-season 9-10am. Members 110kr, nonmembers 150kr.) **Cafe Lilla Paris,** Storg. 22, has sandwiches for 15-25kr (open M-F 7:30am-5pm, Sa 10am-3pm).

Umeå

Umeå (OOM-eh-oh), the largest city in northern Sweden, is a lively and fast growing university town at the mouth of the Ume Älv river. Adventurous souls head for the 30km **Umeleden** bike trail, which snakes past old hydropower stations, gardens, restaurants, and **Baggböle Herrgård,** a delightful cafe in a 19th-century mansion (open Tu-Su noon-8pm). A bridge upriver allows for a more manageable 15km loop. **Oves Cykelservice**, Storg. 87 (tel. (090) 12 61 91), rents bikes to said adventurous souls (40kr per day; open M-F 8am-5pm).

Trains run to Umeå from Boden (5hr.), Luleå (6hr.), and Stockholm (11hr.), but the faster route north is by **bus** to Luleå (4½hr., 149kr). **Silja Line** ferries (tel. (090) 71 44 00) sail to Vaasa, Finland, and can often be huge, floating parties buoyed by duty-free booze. To get to the **tourist office,** Renmarkstorget 15 (tel. (090) 16 16 16), walk down Rådhusesplanaden across from the train station and turn right on Skolg.; it has a list of contacts for private rooms starting at 150kr. (Open June-Aug. M-F 8am-8pm, Sa 10am-5pm, Su 11am-5pm; Sept.-May M-F 8am-6pm.) The **HI youth hostel,** V. Esplanaden 10 (tel. (090) 77 16 50; fax 77 16 95), is a short walk from the train station; go straight up Rådhusesplanaden, take a right on Skolg., then left on V. Esplanaden. (110kr-130kr, nonmembers 150kr-170kr. Reception 8am-11am and 5-10pm. Laundry.) From June to late August, quiet singles in a student dorm can be had for 145kr at **Vandrarhem 57,** O. Norrlandsg. 57 (tel. (090) 77 78 05). Camp at **Nydala Lake** (tel. (090) 16 16 60); bus 81 (13kr) goes straight to the campgrounds in summer (tents 90kr with mandatory 49kr camping card; reception 8am-10pm).

Picnickers of all stripes are advised to pick up the delicious, filling sandwich of the day from **Catarina's,** Vasag. 11 just off Vasaplan (40kr including drink; open M-F 11am-6pm, Sa 11am-3pm). Unbelievers can pick out their own ingredients at the ICA **supermarket,** Vastra Norvlomolsg. 29. At night, students congregate at the **Mucky Duck Pub** on Vasaplan.

LAPPLAND

Those "Southerners" living south of the Arctic Circle imagine that Lappland consists of reindeer herds roaming through dense forest, thick snow, unrelenting darkness, and bitter cold for half the year and perpetual light for the other half—and you know what? They're right. While mining has encroached upon previously virgin land, the lure here is still nature, from swampy birch and pine forests in the vast lowlands to the spectacular rounded mountains that rise to meet the Norwegian border. Swedish Lappland is home to 20,000 reindeer-tending **Sami** ("Lapps" is derogatory), descendants of the prehistoric inhabitants of Scandinavia. Their language and culture live on even as modern Sami use helicopters and snowmobiles to herd their reindeer.

Flying north is a good time-saver; enjoy youth standby fares on **Transwede** (tel. (020) 225 225; under 24 only; Stockholm-Gällivare 340kr) or **SAS** (tel. (020) 727 727, outside Sweden (08) 797 50 80; under 26 only; Stockholm-Kiruna 200kr at automatic ticket machines in the airport). There are two **rail routes** to Lappland. The **coastal route** runs from Stockholm through Boden, Gällivare, and Kiruna to Narvik, Norway, along the **Malmbanan** (2 per day in either direction, 19hr., 602kr, under 25 423kr). In summer, the privately-run Inlandsbanan travels from Mora to Gällivare, stopping for photo-ops with wildlife and for passengers to jump into the Arctic circle. Traveling the entire length requires an overnight stopover in Östersund. (One per day. Mora-Gällivare June-Aug. 480kr. 14-day unlimited travel 700kr. Runs late June to mid-Aug.) **Buses,** most of which do not accept railpasses, are the only way to smaller towns and often the easiest way to larger ones. Call (020) 47 00 47 for schedules.

Two daily trains go from Luleå to Narvik, Norway (6½hr.) stopping in Gällivare, Kiruna, and Abisko. One or two buses a day (2½hr., 125kr) links Kiruna to **Karesuando** on the Finnish border. From there, continue to Skibotn, Norway, or Kilpisjärvi and Muonio, Finland. Finland is also accessible by bus from **Boden.** Railpasses are valid on all **buses** from Boden to **Haparanda,** on the Finnish border. At Haparanda, stay at the **HI youth hostel,** Strandg. 26 (tel. (0922) 611 71; reception 7am-9pm; 110kr, non-members 150kr). Remember that Finland is one time zone ahead.

Luleå At the mouth of the **Lule Älv** (Lule River) lies Luleå (LOOL-eh-oh), a small university town with a laid-back atmosphere and plenty of natural beauty. The 15th-century church town **Gammelstad** is a UNESCO World Heritage site, and rural locals embark on a weekly pilgrimage to its 400-odd cottages. Take bus 8, 9, or 32 (20kr. Church open in summer M-Sa 8:30am-6pm, Su 9am-8pm, in winter call 20 30 00 dur-

ing business hours for the key). Ask at the **tourist office,** Storg. 43 (tel. (0920) 29 35 00 or 29 35 05), about exploring the uninhabited islands of the **Luleå archipelago,** either by ferry or by rented canoe or kayak. The office will also book you into a hostel or private room (200-500kr) for no fee. From the train station, cross Prästg., walk diagonally across the park, cross Hermalingsg., and tromp up Storg. (Open in summer M-F 9am-7pm, Sa-Su 10am-4pm; off-season M-F 10am-6pm, Sa 10am-2pm.)

The peaceful **Örnviks Youth Hostel (HI),** Örnviksv. 87 (tel. (0920) 25 23 25), is set in a nature reserve 6km from the city center. Take bus 6 (20kr) and ask the driver to drop you off after the bridge, then cross the road, walk back towards the bridge, and follow the path into the field on your right. At night, buses go to the front door. (100-120kr, non-members 140-160kr. Reception 7am-11pm. Kitchen. Wheel chair accessible.) **EFS Sundet** (tel. (0920) 25 20 74) is the closest campground; take bus 6 (75kr per tent, 2-bed cabins 300kr; open 9:30am-9:30pm). Trendy yet affordable, **Café Pimpinella,** Storg. 40, is a bar at night (*dagens rätt* 59kr; open until 3am on F and Sa, closed Su). Summer nightlife revolves around **Sommarmix,** in the Luleå Stads Hotell, Storg. 17. (Cover Su-F 40kr, before 10:30pm 20kr, Sa 60kr, before 10:30pm 40kr. Open Tu-Sa 7pm-3am.)

Jokkmokk

One of the only reasons to stop in Jokkmokk is its outstanding museum of indigenous Sami culture, **Ájtte,** Kyrkog. 3, complete with an alpine flower garden. (Open mid-June to late Aug. M-F 9am-7pm, Sa-Su 11am-6pm; late Aug. to mid-June M-F 9am-4pm, Sa-Su noon-4pm; Oct.-Apr. closed Saturday; 40kr, under 18 free.) **Buses** to Jokkmokk run from Gällivare (1½hr., 5 per day, Sa-Su 1 per day, 75kr) and from Boden (2hr., 3 per day, 95kr) in the south. From Jokkmokk, buses run to **Kvikkjokk,** a good place to enter the vast western wilderness (2hr., 95kr). Ask the **tourist office,** Stortorget 4 (tel. (0971) 121 40), about hikes and tours of the reconstructed Stone Age village of **Vuollerim,** 45km east of Jokkmokk. The office keeps a list of private rooms (125-150kr per person), stores luggage (15kr), rents bikes (10kr per hour, 50kr per day), and sells mountain maps (open June-Aug. daily 9am-7pm; Sept.-May M-F 8:30am-4pm). The **Åsgard Vandrarhem (HI),** Åsg. 20 (tel. (0971) 559 77), which has a kitchen and sauna, is across from the tourist office on Åsg. (100-120kr, nonmembers 140-160kr. Reception in summer 7-10am and 5-8pm; in winter 5pm-7pm). **Skogskojan** (tel. (0971) 103 97; fax 108 31), a six-bed, bring-your-own-drinking-water log cabin, features a creekside wood-fired sauna and lies just a 10-minute walk from the tourist office (80kr per person). The **campsite,** which rents boats and bikes, is 3km outside town at **Jokkmokks Turistcenter** (tel. (0971) 123 70). To get there, hike east on Storg. (Tents 70kr for cardholders; mandatory camping card 49kr. 4-bed cabins 595kr. Reception 7am-11pm.)

Gällivare

Spend some time underground in the mining town of **Gällivare** (YELL-i-var-ay). Geological amusements abound, and you can tour the **copper and iron mines** in summer. From mid-June to mid-August, tours to the copper mines leave from the tourist office at 2pm (3hr., 160kr). Iron mine tours leave from the tourist office at 10am (160kr, children under 12 excluded; open early July to early Aug.). Or take a gentle day hike up 820m **Dundret mountain.** The **tourist office** (tel. (0970) 166 60) is at Storg. 16; from the train station, turn right onto the main road, walk up the hill and cross through the parking lot. (Open mid-June to mid-Aug. M-F 9am-8pm, Sa-Su 10am-6pm; mid-Aug. to May M-F 9am-5pm.) The **HI youth hostel** (tel. (0970) 143 80; fax 165 86) offers acceptable accomodations and camping, and is a five-minute walk from the station. Cross the bridge over the tracks heading away from town, then take the one over the river (120kr, nonmembers 160kr; reception 8-10am, 5-7pm and 9:30-11pm). **Gällivare Camping** (tel. (0970) 165 75) is 1.5km from the station (75kr per tent; open June-early Sept.).

■ Northwest Hiking Regions

Beginning in snow-melting July, northwest Sweden attracts hikers from all over Europe to its impeccably preserved national parks. The most popular trail is the **Kungsleden,** stretching from Abisko on the Norwegian border south for 500km to Hemavan. The marked trails have cabins, usually 10-20km apart. Good for novices, the **Padjelanta** trail, which runs from Kvikkjokk west through Staloluokta, up into the mountains, and ends in Ritsem, is the way into Sweden's largest national park. If you're coming from Sweden, take a bus from Jokkmokk to Kvikkjokk (2hr., 95kr), or from Kereine to Abisko or Nikkaluokta for the easiest access.

Organized **day trips** leave from the Abisko **Turistation** (tel. (0980) 402 00; fax 401 40). Excursions include a hike through Kårsavagge and the surrounding waterfalls (4hr., 60kr), a tour of the Stordalen blossoming wetland (7hr., 100kr), a tour of Klövjetur on Siberian huskies (90kr), and an exploration of the Kåppasjåkka caves (6hr., 140kr). All **trains** between Kiruna and Narvik stop in Abisko.

This is rugged country, and there may be snow as late as July. Bring food, maps, raingear, and warm clothing, and always leave a copy of your route with someone in town—make sure that you'll be missed if you don't make it back on time. Mosquitoes in these regions swarm in thick clouds, and since many eco-unfriendly brands are banned, plan to buy some strong stuff in Lappland before your hike. Contact **STF** (Svenska Turistföreningen) before heading north (see p. 853). STF runs most of the mountain stations and huts and publishes essential hiking guides. Many sections of trails, in particular from Abisko to Kvikkjokk, have HI-staffed **cabins** 8-21km apart (170-195kr, nonmembers 220-245kr).

To climb Sweden's highest peak, **Kebnekaise** (2117m), take a bus from Kiruna to Nikkaluokta (1hr., 2 per day, 63kr) and hike 19km to the mountain cabin. From there, you can reach the summit in a day. You can connect back to the Kungsleden Trail via Singisturgorna from the bottom of Kebnekaise. **Sarek,** the most dangerous and difficult of the area parks, is touted as Europe's last virgin wilderness (no trails or huts). It is also accessible from Kvikkjokk, Saltoluokta, and Ritsem. Pick up *Sarek—Myth and Reality* at any northern tourist office.

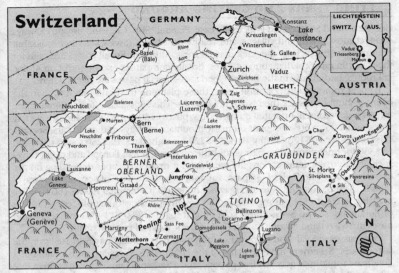

Switzerland (Svizzera, Suisse, Die Schweiz)

US$1 = 1.41SFr (Swiss francs)
CDN$1 = 0.93SFr
UK£1 = 2.35SFr
IR£1 = 2.05SFr
AUS$1 = 0.84SFr
NZ$1 = 0.72SFr
SAR1 = 0.23SFr
Country Code: 41

1SFr = US$0.71
1SFr = CDN$1.08
1SFr = UK£0.43
1SFr = IR£0.49
1SFr = AUS$1.19
1SFr = NZ$1.39
1SFr = SAR4.35
International Dialing Prefix: 00

Divided by impassable Alpine giants and united by neither language nor religion, Switzerland is remarkably diverse for a nation so stable. What is now a confederation of 23 cantons (and 3 sub-cantons) began as only three cantons in 1291. Swiss politics have an old-fashioned feel; approximately 3000 local communes retain a great deal of power, and major policy disputes are occasionally settled by national referenda. Official neutrality since 1815 has kept the ravages of war away from this postcard-perfect haven, but recent news suggests that Swiss bankers may have been a little too neutral in accepting gold and money from all sources in the 1930s and 1940s. For good and for ill, social stability has nurtured the growth of Big Money in the flashy banking centers of Geneva and Zurich. Reaction against bourgeois prosperity has also given birth to Dadaism, a rambunctious contemporary squatter culture, and one of the world's most pervasive ecological movements.

One aspect of Switzerland will likely always overshadow whatever internal divisions exist—the majestic Alps. Keats, Shelley, and Byron glorified the mountains in their Romantic poetry, while others have fallen silent against a landscape that defies words. Snow-capped peaks lord over half the country's area, enticing hikers, skiers, bikers, and paragliders from around the globe to one of the most finely tuned tourist industries in the world. Victorian scholar John Ruskin called the Alps "the great cathedrals of the earth." You're welcome to worship here—if you can spare the cash.

Let's Go: Austria and Switzerland 1999 provides updated and comprehensive info on indoor and outdoor activities throughout the country.

GETTING THERE AND GETTING AROUND

Getting around Switzerland is gleefully easy. Federal (SBB, CFF) and private **railways** connect most towns and villages, and yellow post buses (Swisspass often valid, but not Eurailpasses) pick up the slack in rural areas. Although **Eurail** passes are valid for the state-run railways that connect cities, private companies exert control on Alpine rail routes, particularly in the Berner Oberland—special passes are needed here.

To beat ruinous transportation costs, those planning to spend much time in the country should consider the myriad rail options. The **Swisspass** offers unlimited free travel on government-operated trains, ferries, buses in 30 Swiss cities, and private railways, and a 25 to 50% discount on many mountain railways and cable cars. Second-class prices are US$176 for four days, US$220 for eight days, US$256 for 15 days, and US$350 for one month. The pass is sold abroad through Rail Europe and major travel agencies; in major train stations in Switzerland it may be cheaper depending on the exchange rate. The **Swiss Flexipass,** valid for any three days of second-class travel within 15 days, costs US$176 and may not be worth it. **Regional Passes** (50-175SFr), available in eight different regions, can be bought in major tourist offices by holders of Eurailpasses. The **Swiss Card,** sold only abroad, offers 50% off most trains and buses in Switzerland for one month (US$96). For national rail info, dial 157 22 22.

Swisspasses are valid on many buses, although pass holders pay 5 to 10SFr on the faster buses. **Steamers** traverse many of the larger lakes. Fares are no bargain, but a Eurailpass sometimes gets you free passage, and a Swisspass almost always wins a free ride. **Cycling,** though strenuous, is a splendid way to see the country; rental at most stations is 22 to 24SFr or slightly more per day (return to any station). With sufficient stamina, overland **walking and hiking** can be the most enjoyable ways to see Switzerland. **Hitching** is difficult and risky as always.

ESSENTIALS

Switzerland is quadrilingual: French is spoken in the west, Italian in the south, Romansh (a close relative of Latin) in parts of the canton of Graubünden, and Swiss German (*Schwyzerdütsch,* a dialect nearly incomprehensible to other German speakers) everywhere else. Most people know at least three languages, including High German and English. **Tourist offices** (*Verkehrsbüro* or *Kurverein*) in every Swiss city locate rooms, distribute maps, and suggest hiking and biking routes. A fat green "i" marks all official tourist offices. The **Anglo-phone** (tel. 157 50 14) provides info and English-speaking doctor referrals (1.40SFr per min.).

Currency exchange is easiest in train stations; rates are comparable to those at banks. **Local calls** cost 60 centimes. Post offices provide the easiest way to make collect **calls abroad.** Ask for a *Zurückrufen,* or return call, and you will receive a card with a number on it. Make the call and tell your party to call you back at that number; at the end of the conversation, you pay just for the original call. For **AT&T Direct,** dial 0 800 89 00 11; **MCI WorldPhone** 0800 89 02 22; **Sprint Access** 0800 89 97 77; **Canada Direct** 0800 155 83 30; **BT Direct** 0800 55 25 44; and **New Zealand Direct** 0800 83 80 15. Dial 111 for **information** (including directory assistance and train schedules), and 191 or 114 for an English-speaking **international operator.** The **police** emergency number is 117, **fire** emergency is 118, **medical** emergency is 144.

Most stores are open Monday through Friday from 8am to 6:30pm with a break from noon to 2pm, and Saturday mornings. In cities, shops also close Monday mornings. Museums close on Mondays. The country closes down for **national holidays** on January 1, Good Friday (Apr. 2 in 1999), Easter Monday (Apr. 4), Ascension (May 13), Whit Monday (June 1), August 1, and Christmas (Dec. 25-26).

Switzerland is justifiably proud of its reputation for great **skiing** and **hiking.** Contrary to popular belief, skiing in Switzerland is often less expensive than in the U.S., if you avoid the pricey resorts. Ski passes are valid for transportation to, from, and on lifts (30-50SFr per day, 100-300SFr per week). A week of lift tickets, equipment rental, lessons, lodging, and *demi-pension* (half-pension; breakfast plus one other meal, usually dinner) averages 500SFr. Summer skiing is no longer as prevalent as it once was, but it's still available in Zermatt, Saas Fee, Les Diablerets, and on the Diavolezza in Pontresina. Over 45,000km of hiking trails lace the entire country. Trails are marked by bands of white-red-white; yellow signs give directions and traveling times. Tourist offices offer maps and info on hiking preparation and safety.

ACCOMMODATIONS, CAMPING, FOOD, AND DRINK True to legend, all things Swiss are meticulous, orderly, efficient, and expensive. The uniformly cheery **HI Jugendherbergen** (hostels) are bright, clean, and open to all ages (US$5-30; breakfast and sheets included). **Hotels** are generally pretty pricey. In smaller towns, *Zimmer frei* (private rooms) abound; the tourist office can supply a list and make reservations. Wherever you stay, be sure to ask for a **guest card,** which often grants discounts to local attractions and transportation. As befits a country so blessed by Mother Nature, Switzerland blossoms with over 1200 **campgrounds,** and the prices are welcome relief in a very expensive country (7-10SFr per person, 5-12SFr per tent). You must obtain permission from landowners to camp on private property; camping along roads and in public areas is forbidden. **Swiss Alpine Club (SAC) huts** are modest and extremely practical for those interested in trekking in higher, more remote areas. Bunk rooms sleep 10 to 20 weary hikers and provide blankets. SAC huts are open to all, but SAC members get discounts. (An average one-night stay is 20-25SFr, nonmembers 30SFr.) Those serious about conquering the summits should contact SAC, Sektion Zermatt, Haus Dolomite, CH-3920 Zermatt, Switzerland (tel. (028) 67 26 10).

The Swiss are hardly culinary daredevils, but they're very good at what they do. In French Switzerland, try the cheese specialties; *fondue* is always excellent, as is *raclette* (melted cheese with pickled onions and boiled new potatoes). Swiss-German food is heartier. Try *Züricher Geschnetzeltes* (veal strips in a delicious cream sauce) and *Rösti* (hashbrowned potato with onion). Of course, *Lindt* chocolate is a perennial favorite, especially in its home city of Zurich. **Migros** supermarket cafeterias and **Co-op** centers are the budgeteer's choices for self-service dining.

GERMAN SWITZERLAND

■ Zurich (Zürich)

Switzerland has a bank for every 1200 people, and about half of those banks are in Zurich, where battalions of ballyhooed and Bally-shoed executives charge daily to the world's preeminent gold exchange and fourth-largest stock exchange. Yet there is more to Zurich than money. A radical spirit has been apparent since the firebrand Ulrich Zwingli led the Swiss Protestant Reformation in the 16th century. Revolution brewed again in 1916, when artistic and philosophical radicalism shook the town's institutions: James Joyce toiled away on *Ulysses*, the Dadaists pushed the limits of the ridiculous at the Cabaret Voltaire, and Russian exile Vladimir Lenin, unhappily situated next door to the raucous cabaret, read Marx and bided his time.

ORIENTATION AND PRACTICAL INFORMATION

Zurich sits smack in the middle of northern Switzerland. The **Limmat River** splits the city in two on its way to the Zürichsee. From the train station, **Bahnhofstraße** runs south, parallel to the river, through much of the **Altstadt** (old city) and past countless banks and shops. Most of the activity in Zurich is confined to this relatively small, walkable area. For weary travelers, trams criss-cross the city; buy the 24-hour Tageskarte if you plan to ride several times (7.20SFr), or pay 2.10SFr for individual rides.

Telephone Code: 01.
Trains: The **Hauptbahnhof** (main train station), at the northern terminus of Bahnhofstr., has connections to Basel (1hr., 30SFr), Bern (1¼hr., 42SFr), Geneva (3hr., 74SFr), Lugano (3hr., 59SFr), and Lucerne (1hr., 20SFr).

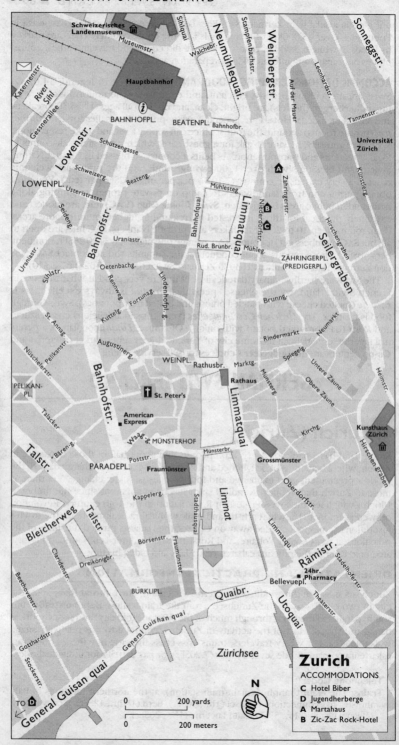

SWITZERLAND

Schweizerisches
Landesmuseum
Museumstr.

Hauptbahnhof

BAHNHOFPL.   BEATENPL. Bahnhofbr.

Sihlquai   Neumühlequai.   Stampfenbachser.   Weinbergstr.   Sonneggstr.

Walchebr.   Auf der Mauer   Leonhardstr.   Tannenstr.

Kasernenstr.   River Sihl   Gessneralle   Schützengasse   Schweizerg.   Beateng.   Universität Zürich

LOWENPL. Usteristrasse   Mühlesteg   Niederdorfstr.   Zähringerstr.   Kunslerg.   Hirschengraben

Lowenstr.   Seidens.   Uraniastr.   Bahnhofquai   Limmatquai   Mühleg.   Rud. Brunbr.   ZÄHRINGERPL. (PREDIGERPL.)   Seilergraben

Uraniastr.   Sihlstr.   Oetenbachg.   Rennweg.   Fortunag.   Lindenhofpl. g.   Brunng.   Rindermarkt   Neumarkt

St. Annag.   Pelikanstr.   Kürtelg.   Augustinerg.   WEINPL. Rathusbr.   Marktg.   Spiegelg.   Untere Zäune   Heimstr.

Nüschelerstr.   Talacker   Bären-g.   Waag.   MÜNSTERHOF   Rathaus   Münsserg.   Obere Zäune   Kirchg.   Kunsthaus Zürich

PELIKAN-PL.   Bahnhofstr.   St. Peter's   American Express   Münsterbr.   Grossmünster   Oberdorfstr.   Hirschen graben

Talstr.   Poststr.   PARADEPL.   Fraumünster   Kappelerg.   Limmat   Limmatqu.   Rämistr.   Stadelhoferstr.

Bleicherweg   Talstr.   Clardenstr.   Börsenstr.   Fraumünster   24hr. Pharmacy   Bellevuepl.   Theaterstr.

Dreikönigbr.   BÜRKLIPL.   Quaibr.   Utoquai

Beethovenstr.   Gotthardstr.   Stockerstr.   General Guisan quai   Zürichsee

TO 🅓   General Guishan quai

N

0   200 yards
0   200 meters

Zurich
ACCOMMODATIONS
C Hotel Biber
D Jugendherberge
A Martahaus
B Zic-Zac Rock-Hotel

Bike Rental: At the baggage counter in the train station. 19SFr per day; add 6SFr if you leave it at another station. Open daily 6:45am-7:45pm. Bikes are available for free at Oerlikon, (tel. 336 36 13), Altstetten (tel. 336 36 14), and Hauptbahnhof (tel. 323 48 58) with a passport and 20SFr deposit.

Hitchhiking: Hitchers heading west reportedly take streetcar 4 to "Werdhölzli," and those heading east reportedly take streetcar 9 or 14 to "Bahnhof Wiedikon."

Tourist Office: Bahnhofpl. 15 (tel. 211 40 00, hotel reservation service 215 40 40; fax 215 40 44; email zhtourismus@access.ch; http://www.zurichtourism.ch); exit the train station to Bahnhofpl. and walk to the left. The reservation desk finds rooms. Wade through the crowd for copies of *Zürich News* and *Zürich Next*. Open Apr.-Oct. M-F 8:30am-9:30pm, Sa-Su 8:30am-8:30pm; Nov.-Mar. M-F 8:30am-7:30pm, Sa-Su 8:30am-6:30pm.

Consulates: Australian, Canadian, Irish, and **South African** citizens should contact the Bern embassies (see p. 883). **New Zealand's** consulate is in Geneva (tel. (022) 734 95 30; fax 734 30 62). **U.K.,** Minervastr. 117 (tel. 383 65 60; fax 383 65 61). Open M-F 9am-noon. **U.S.,** Dufourstr. 101 (tel. 422 25 66). Open M-F 10am-1pm.

Currency Exchange: The train station rates are the same as those at banks. Open daily 6:30am-10:45pm. Also try **Credit Suisse** or **Swiss Bank** on Bahnhofstr.

American Express: Uraniastr. 14, CH-8023 (tel. 228 77 77). Mail held and checks cashed. **ATM.** Open M-F 8:30am-6pm, Sa 9am-1pm. Traveler's check toll-free **emergency line** (tel. 08 00 55 01 00).

Laundromat: Self-Service Wachari, Weinbergstr. 37, Müllerstr. 55, and Badenstr. 655. Wash and dry 5kg for 10.20SFr. Open M-Sa 7am-10pm, Su 10:30am-10pm.

Emergency: Ambulance, tel. 144. **Medical Emergency,** tel. 261 61 00.

Police: tel. 117.

24hr. Pharmacy: Theaterstr. 14 (tel. 252 56 00), on Bellevuepl.

Post Office: Main office at Kasernenstr. 95/97. Open for *Poste Restante* M-F 7:30am-8pm, Sa 8am-4pm. Address to: Sihlpost, Kasernenstr., Postlagernde Briefe, CH-8021 Zürich. **Postal Code:** CH-8021.

Internet Access: Internet Cafe, Uraniastr. 3 (tel. 210 33 11), 0.25SFr per min., 15SFr per hr. Open M 10am-6pm, Tu-Th 10am-midnight, F-Sa 10am-2am, Su 10am-11pm.

ACCOMMODATIONS AND CAMPING

Expensive as Zurich can be, there are a few budget accommodations available. Hostels are often somewhat distant from the town center, but easily accessible with Zurich's extensive public transportation system. Reserve at least a day in advance.

Jugendherberge Zürich (HI), Mutschellenstr. 114 (tel. 482 35 44; fax 480 17 27). Take tram 7 ("Wollishofen") to "Morgental" and walk 5 min. Huge, orderly, and impeccably clean. 29SFr, nonmembers 34SFr; doubles 88SFr, nonmembers 98SFr. Showers, sheets, and breakfast included. Huge dinner 11SFr. Reception 24hr.

The City Backpacker-Hotel Biber, Niederdorfstr. 5 (tel. 251 90 15; fax 251 90 24), in the heart of the *Altstadt*. Boasts a rooftop deck and a helpful staff. Dorms 29SFr; singles 65SFr; doubles 88SFr. Showers included. Sheets 3SFr. Laundry 9SFr. **Internet access** 2SFr per 10min. Reception daily 8am-noon and 3-10pm.

Justinus heim Zürich, Freudenbergstr. 146 (tel. 361 38 06; fax 362 29 82). Take tram 9 or 10 to "Seilbahn Rigiblick," and then take the hillside tram up to the end station. Student-run hotel with spectacular views. Singles 35SFr, with shower 50-60SFr; doubles 80-100SFr; breakfast included. Reception daily 8am-9pm.

Zic-Zac Rock-hotel, Mankeg 7 (tel. 261 21 81; fax 261 21 75), in the heart of the *Altstadt*. Uniquely designed rooms, from the "Rolling Stones" to the "Bryan Adams." Singles 65-85SFr; doubles 110-130SFr; breakfast included. Reception 24hr.

Martahaus, Zähringerstr. 36 (tel. 251 45 50; fax 251 45 40). Take a left from the station, cross the Balinkofbrücke, and take the second right after Limmatquai. Prime river location near the nightlife. Dorms 34SFr. Singles 62-68SFr; doubles 94-100SFr. Showers and breakfast included. Reception 24hr.

Studenthaus, Rötelstr. 100 (tel. 361 23 13). Take tram 11 to "Bucheggpl." and walk downhill 5min. on Rötelstr. Student housing turns into backpacker haven from July 15-Oct. 15. Beautiful views. Singles 45SFr; doubles 60SFr. Kitchen and laundry.

Camping Seebucht, Seestr. 559 (tel. 482 16 12; fax 482 16 60). Take tram 7 to "Wollishofen," walk downhill towards the lakeside, then turn right on Seestr. Or take bus 161 or 165 from Bürklipl. to "Stadt Grente." 8.50SFr per person; 12SFr per tent. Reception daily 7:30am-noon and 3-10pm. Open early May to late Sept.

FOOD

Zurich boasts over 1300 restaurants, but few cater to budget travelers. The cheapest meals can be found at *Würstli* kiosks or fruit and vegetable stands. **Co-op Super Center** is a super-huge market stretching from the Limmat River all the way to the train station. Watch for free promotional treats (open M-F 7am-8pm, Sa 7am-4pm).

Mensa der Universität Zürich, Rämistr. 71. Take streetcar 6 from Bahnhofpl. to "ETH Zentrum" for stunningly edible food. Meals 7.50SFr with ISIC, salads 6SFr. Open July 15-Oct. 21 M-F 11am-2pm; Oct. 22-July 14 M-F and alternate Sa 11am-2:30pm and 5-7:30pm. Mensa B is open M-F 6:30am-7:30pm and 2 Sa per month. **Mensa Polyterrasse,** just down the street at #101, has the same food and prices.
Zeughauskeller, Bahnhofstr. 28a, near Paradepl. Handsome *Biergarten* serving Swiss specialties. *Rösti* and bratwurst for 5-30SFr. Open M-Sa 11:30am-10pm.
Restaurant Raclette-Stube, Zähringerstr. 16. Swiss fondues at their richest, largest, and cheapest. All-you-can-eat fondue for 28.50SFr. Open daily 6-10:30pm.
Rheinfelder Bierhalle, Niederdorfstr. 76. Local crowd enjoys the self-proclaimed "cheapest beer in town." Entrees 11-30SFr. Open daily 9am-midnight.
Gleich, Seefeldstr. 9. Completely vegetarian restaurant and bakery provides an oasis of green. Salads 4-7SFr; entrees 10-14SFr. Open M-F 6am-9pm, Sa 7:30am-4pm.
Sprüngli Confiserie Cafe, Paradepl. A Zurich landmark, founded by one of the original makers of Lindt chocolate. Exquisite confections. Cafe open M-F 7:30am-6:30pm, Sa 7:30am-5:30pm. Confectionery open M-F 7:30am-8pm, Sa 8am-4pm.

SIGHTS AND ENTERTAINMENT

Stately and colorful, the **Bahnhofstraße** runs from the station to the Zürichsee; trees lining each side of the street shade shoppers on this causeway of capitalism. **Paradeplatz,** about halfway down Bahnhofstr., marks the center of the city. Two giant cathedrals face each other from opposite sides of the river in the *Altstadt.* To the east loom the twin towers of the **Grossmünster,** a Romanesque cathedral built by Charlemagne. Zwingli spearheaded the Swiss Reformation with tirades from the pulpit here (open daily Mar. 15-Oct. 9am-6pm; Nov.-Mar. 14 10am-4pm). On the left bank rises the 13th-century **Fraumünster,** with stained-glass scenes by Marc Chagall. The nearby **St. Peter's Church** has the largest clockface in Europe.

Yes I said yes I will Yes take tram 6, 9, or 10 to "ETH" uphill from the university to reach the grave of author **James Joyce,** in the Fluntern Cemetery. (Open daily May-Aug. 7am-8pm; Mar.-Apr. and Sept.-Oct. 7am-7pm; Nov.-Feb. 8am-5pm. Free.) Next door, the **Zürich Zoo,** Zürichbergstr. 221, features over 2000 species. (Take tram 5 or 6. Open daily Mar.-Oct. 8am-6pm; Nov.-Feb. 8am-5pm. 14SFr, students 7SFr.) The **Kunsthaus Zürich,** Heimpl. 1 at Rämistr., houses a stunning collection of 15th- and 20th-century art (open Tu-Th 10am-9pm, F-Su 10am-5pm. 4SFr, students 3SFr, Su free). The **E.G. Bunrie Collection,** Zollikerstr. 172 (tel. 422 00 86) holds a prestigious collection of French Impressionists (open Tu and F 2-5pm, W 5-8pm; 9SFr, students 3SFr). Satisfying both intellectual and caffeine cravings, the **Johann Jacobs Museum: Collection on the Cultural History of Coffee,** Seestr. 204, offers visitors a free cup of coffee at the end of the exhibits (open F-Sa 2-5pm, Su 10-5pm; free).

Nightlife revolves around Niederdorfstr., Münsterg., and Limmatquai, where cafes and bars overflow with people until the wee hours of the morning. Women may be uncomfortable walking alone near the strip clubs of Niederdorfstr. The tiny, crowded **Casa Bar,** Münsterg. 30, has first-rate live jazz (beer from 9.50SFr; no cover; open daily 7pm-2am). **Castel DADA,** Münsterg. 26, on the site of the original Cabaret Voltaire, is now a lively bar and disco (open daily 6pm-2am, F-Sa 8pm-2am, disco open until 4am). Thornton Wilder and Lenin used to get sloshed at the posh **Bar Odeon,** Limmatquai 2, Bellevuepl. (beers from 6SFr; open daily 7am-2am, F-Sa until 4am).

■ St. Gallen

St. Gallen may well be a tourist's dream come true. Here, you can alternately feed your Dark Ages cobblestone fetish and satiate your urge for sweaty, student-fueled nightlife. Book lovers gasp at the sight of the city's main attraction, the **Stiftsbibliotek** (Abbey Library), with a collection of 2000 manuscripts. (Open Apr.-Nov. M-Sa 9am-noon and 1:30-5pm, Su 10am-noon and 1:30-4pm.; Dec.-Mar. M-Sa 9am-noon and 1:30-4pm.) The Abbey's **Kathedrale St. Gallen** was founded in the 8th century but took its present form in the mid-18th century. **Museumstraße** has several museums of interest. The **Historical Museum** at #50 displays artifacts from Switzerland and outside Europe (open Tu-Sa 10am-noon and 2-5pm, Su 10am-5pm; 6SFr, students 2SFr). The **Kunstmuseum** at #32 juxtaposes the modern art of Lasker and Sengantinit on the top floor with works by more traditional 19th- and 20th-century artists like Monet and Giacometti (open Tu-Sa 10am-noon and 2-5pm, Su 10am-5pm; 6SFr, students 2SFr). In late June, the **Open Air St. Gallen Music Festival,** features such artists as the Beastie Boys, Garbage, and Cypress Hill (tickets 139SFr; info tel. (071) 223 41 01).

Trains run from Bahnhofpl. to Bern (2½hr., 59SFr), Munich (3hr., 60SFr, under 26 49SFr), and Zurich (1hr., 26SFr). The **tourist office,** Bahnhofpl. 1a (tel. (071) 227 37 37; fax 227 37 67), makes free hotel reservations and provides a **city tour.** From the train station, cross straight through the bus stop and past the fountain on the left. (Tours June 12-Sept. M, W, and F 2:30pm. 15SFr. Office open M-F 9am-noon and 1-6pm, Sa 9am-noon.) Find **Internet access** at **Media Lounge,** 10 Katerineng. (12SFr per hr.; open M-F 9am-9pm, Sa 9am-5pm). Perched on a hill overlooking St. Gallen, the **Jugendherberge St. Gallen (HI),** Jüchstr. 25 (tel. (071) 245 47 77), is clean and quiet, and has a terrace, billiards, and a library. From the train station, take the *Trogenerbahn* from the smaller Appenzeller/Trogener station to the right. (Dorms 20.50-23SFr; singles 54.50-57SFr; doubles 59-64SFr. Reception M-Sa 7-10am and 5-10:30pm, Su 6-10:30pm. Closed Dec. 15-Mar. 7.) **Hotel Elite,** Metzgerg. 9-11 (tel. (071) 222 12 36), has simple, airy rooms (singles 60-90SFr; doubles 90-140SFr; breakfast included). **Christina's,** Weberg. 9, is an indigo-tinted Swedish bar/restaurant with exotic veggie specialties from 17SFr (open Tu-Th 9:30am-11:30pm, F-Sa 9:30am-12:30am, Su 10am-11:30pm).

■ Lucerne (Luzern)

The sunrise over Lucerne's most acclaimed peak, the 2132m **Mount Pilatus,** has hypnotized hikers and artists for centuries. These are the mountains that inspired the likes of Twain, Wagner, and Goethe. When clouds obscure the view, Lucerne's extraordinary museums, medieval streets, and painted bridges provide an equally rewarding afternoon of sightseeing and exploration.

SIGHTS AND ENTERTAINMENT Much of Lucerne's tourist culture thrives on the Vierwaldstättersee and the cobblestone streets lining the Reuss River in the **Altstadt** (Old Town). The area is known for its frescoed houses and *oriel* windows. The 660-year-old **Kapellbrücke,** a famous wooden-roofed bridge running from the train station to the *Altstadt,* is ornately decorated with Swiss historical scenes. Down the river, the covered **Spreuerbrücke** is adorned with Kaspar Meglinger's eerie *Totentanz* (Dance of Death) paintings. For a magnificent view of Lucerne, climb the ramparts of the medieval city. At the base of the cliff on Denkmalstr., the melancholy **Lion of Lucerne** honors the Swiss Guard who died defending Marie Antoinette in Revolutionary Paris. Mark Twain called it "the most mournful and moving piece of stone in the world."

Lucerne's outstanding museums include the **Picasso Museum,** Am Rhyn Haus, Furreng. 21, which chronicles the artist's life in photos by David Duncan. (Open daily Apr.-Oct. 10am-6pm; Nov.-Mar. 11am-1pm and 2-4pm. 6SFr, students 3SFr.) The **Verkehrshaus der Schweiz** (Transport Museum), Lidostr. 5, features a planetarium, Imax shows, and a virtual-reality exhibit (open daily Apr. 4-Oct. 9am-6pm; Nov.-Mar. 10am-5pm; 18SFr, students 16SFr). The **Natur-Museum,** Kasernenpl. 6, details Lucerne's pre-history and offers "hands-on" exhibits (open Tu-Sa 10am-noon and 2-5pm, Su 10am-5pm; 5SFr, students 4SFr). The **Richard Wagner Museum,** Wagnerweg 27, in Wagner's secluded sylvan home, displays the composer's letters, scores, and instruments (open Mar. 15-Nov. 30 Tu-Su 10am-noon and 2-5pm; 5SFr, students 4SFr).

To gaze from Mt. Pilatus, get a boat to Alpnachstad and ascend by the steepest **cogwheel train** in the world. On a clear day you can see to Italy, but save your money if it's cloudy. Return by cable car to Kriens and bus to Lucerne (round-trip 77SFr, with Eurail 40SFr). Forbidden until the 17th century for fear of Pilatus's angry ghost, climbing Mt. Pilatus is now legal. The trails require sturdy hiking boots and at least five hours. The **Seepark,** 15 minutes right of the train station, allows a lakeside dip.

Nightlife concentrates in the *Altstadt*'s crowded corridors. **Hexenkessel,** Haldenstr. 21, styles itself as a witch's haunt (open daily 9pm-2:30am; required beer 7Sfr).

PRACTICAL INFO, ACCOMMODATIONS, AND FOOD The **tourist office,** Frankenstr. 1 (tel. (041) 410 71 71; fax 410 73 34), leads walking tours of the city, and sojourns to the top of Mt. Pilatus. (Open Apr.-Oct. M-F 8:30am-6pm, Sa 9am-5pm, Su 9am-1pm; Nov.-Mar. M-F 8:30am-noon and 2-6pm, Sa 9am-1pm.) Lucerne sends **trains** to Basel (1¼hr., 30SFr), Bern (1¼hr., 31SFr), Geneva (3¼hr., 65SFr), Interlaken (2hr., 25SFr), Lausanne (2½hr., 55SFr), and Zurich (1hr., 19.40SFr). The train station also **rents bikes** (22SFr per day).

Backpackers, Alpenquai 42 (tel. (041) 360 04 20; fax 360 04 42), across the concrete bridge from Inseli-Quai, has rooms with balconies (21.50-26.50SFr; sheets 2SFr; reception 7:30-11am and 4-11pm). Hop on bus 18: "Jugendherberge" to get to the **Jugendherberge (HI),** Sedelstr. 12 (tel. (041) 420 88 00; fax 420 56 16). After 7:30pm, take bus 1 to "Schlossberg" and walk 15 minutes down Friedentalstr. (Dorms 30.50SFr. Lockers, sheets, shower, and breakfast included. Reception 7-10am and 2pm-midnight.) The **Tourist Hotel Luzern,** St. Karliquai 12 (tel. (041) 410 24 74; fax 410 84 14), is by the river. From the station, go underground, exit the complex to the *Altstadt,* walk left along the river, cross the second covered bridge, then left on St. Karliquai. (Reception 7am-10:30pm. Dorms 31-36SFr, students 28-33SFr; doubles 98-108SFr.) **Privatpension Panorama,** Kapuzinerweg 9 (tel. (041) 420 67 01; fax 420 67 30), overlooks the *Altstadt* (singles 45SFr; doubles 70-90SFr; breakfast included). Take bus 2 ("Würzenbach") to "Verkehrshaus" or to **Camping Lido,** Lidostr. 8. (Tel. (041) 370 21 46; fax 370 21 45. 6.50SFr per person, 3SFr per tent. Reception 9am-noon and 3-8pm; July-Aug. 8am-10pm. Open Mar. 15-Oct.)

Saturday morning markets along the river offer fresh goods for an inexpensive picnic, but the restaurants in supermarkets and department stores offer the cheapest meals in town. The restaurant at **EPA,** at Rösslig. and Mühlenpl., has delicious, healthy 8-50SFr *menus.* **Krone,** Rösslig. 15, serves good food cafeteria-style (all sandwiches under 8SFr; food served 10am-9pm).

▓ Bern (Berne)

Although Bern has been Switzerland's capital since 1848, don't expect fast tracks and screeching cars. Parliament is in session only four times a year, and politics is considered part-time work. Indeed, you'll probably see more suitors than suits in Bern: the city is known for Toblerone, flowers, bears, and its decidedly romantic design.

SIGHTS AND ENTERTAINMENT The massive **Bundeshaus** dominates the Aare river and hides the politicians in the **Parlamentsgebäude.** (45min. tour every hr. 9-11am and 2-4pm, except when Parliament is in session. You can arrange to watch sessions by calling ahead: (031) 322 85 22.) From the state house, Kockerg. and Herreng. lead to the 15th-century Protestant **Münster.** The imagination of the late-Gothic period runs riot in the portal sculpture of the Last Judgment. (Open Easter-Oct. Tu-Sa 10am-5pm, Su 11am-5pm; Nov.-Easter Tu-F 10am-noon and 2-4pm, Sa 10am-noon and 2-5pm, Su 11am-2pm. Tower closes 30min. before the church. 3SFr.) Head down Münstergp., take a right, then left on Kramg. to reach the 13th-century **Zytglogge** (clock tower), which performs four minutes before the hour. The Bärengrabenbrücke leads to the **Bärengraben** (bear pits), which have held bears since the 15th century (open daily Apr.-Sept. 8am-6pm; Oct.-Mar. 9am-4pm). A walk south along the Aare (or bus 19 to "Tierpark") leads to the **Dählhölzli Städtischer Tierpark** (Zoo), Tierparkweg 1 (open daily in summer 8am-6pm; in winter 9am-4:30pm; 7SFr, students 5SFr).

Several **museums** cluster at **Helvetiaplatz** across the **Kirchenfeldbrücke** (tram 3 or 5); the tourist office and museum cashiers sell day tickets (*Tageskarte;* 7SFr, students 5SFr) good at many but not all museums. The **Kunstmuseum**, Hodlerstr. 8-12, near Lorrainebrücke, has the world's largest Klee collection (over 2500 works), plus Kandinsky, Braque, Picasso, and Giacometti (open Tu 10am-9pm, W-Su 10am-5pm; 6SFr, students 4SFr, *Tageskarte* not valid). **Bernisches Historische Museum**, Helvetiapl. 5, has everything from a witty Dance of Death to an astonishing Islamic collection (open Tu-Su 10am-5pm; 5SFr, students 3SFr, Sa free). The **Swiss Alpine Museum**, Helvetiapl. 4, has spell-binding models of Swiss mountains and geology. (Open M 2-5pm, Tu-Su 10am-5pm; closed mid-Oct. to mid-May Tu-Su noon-2pm. 5SFr, students 3SFr.) **Albert Einstein's House**, Kramg. 49, is a small apartment good for a relatively brief visit (open Feb.-Nov. Tu-F 10am-5pm, Sa 10am-4pm; 3SFr, *Tageskarte* not valid).

The **Berner Altstadtsommer** comes to life in July and August with dance and music in the *Altstadt's* squares. July's **Gurten Festival** attracts big names (contact the tourist office or check http://www.gurtenfestival.ch). At night, head to the bars and cafes along the Bärenpl., or to Bern's oldest wine cellar: the **Klötzlikeller Weine Stube**, Gerechtigkeitsg. 62, which resounds with talk and the songs of patrons (open Tu-Sa 4pm-12:30am). The **Art Cafe**, Gurteng. 3, is a cafe by day and a smoky bar by night (open M-Th 7am-12:30pm, F-Sa 7am-7pm and 8pm-2:30am, Su 6pm-12:30am).

PRACTICAL INFO, ACCOMMODATIONS, AND FOOD

Bern sits diplomatically at the juncture of the French- and German-speaking areas of the country. Most of medieval Bern lies in front of the train station and nestled along the Aare River. Drug users may lurk around the Parliament park and terraces at night. **Bern Tourismus** (tel. (031) 328 12 12; fax 312 12 33), in the train station, has maps and the event guide *Bern Aktuell*, and books rooms for a 3SFr fee (open June-Sept. daily 9am-8:30pm; Oct.-May M-Sa 9am-6:30pm, Su 10am-5pm). The **Hauptbahnhof** (train info tel. (031) 157 22 22) serves Geneva (2hr., 48SFr), Interlaken (1hr., 24SFr), Lucerne (1½hr., 31SFr), Munich (5¾hr., 115SFr), Paris (4½hr., 76SFr), Prague (12½hr., 163SFr), and Zurich (1½hr., 42SFr). **SVB** bus/tram visitor's cards (24hr. ticket 6SFr) are available downstairs at the train station. Free **bike rental** at Blubike, Casinopl. (tel. (031) 311 22 34), with 20SFr and ID deposit; reserve ahead. **Embassies: Australia**, Alpenstr. 29 (tel. 351 01 43); **Canada**, Kirchenfeldstr. 88 (tel. 352 63 81); **Ireland**, Kirchenfeldstr. 68 (tel. 352 14 42); **South Africa**, Jungfraustr. 1 (tel. 352 20 11); **U.K.**, Thunstr. 50 (tel. 352 50 21); **U.S.**, Jubiläumsstr. 93 (tel. 357 70 11).

Bern's shortage of inexpensive hotels thwarts budget travelers; cheap accommodations are rare even outside the city. Reserve ahead. To reach **Jugendherberge (HI)**, Weiherg. 4 (tel. (031) 311 63 16; fax 312 52 40), from the station, cross the tram lines and go down Christoffelg. Take the road by the Park Cafe down to Weiherg., following the signs. (19.25SFr. Laundry 6SFr. 3-night max. Reception 7-9:30am and 5pm-midnight; in summer 3pm-midnight. Curfew midnight.) The new **Landhaus Hotel**, Altenbergstr. 4/6 (tel. (031) 331 41 66; fax 332 69 04), has river views, a kitchen, and **Internet access**. Take bus 12 ("Schlosshalde") to "Bärengraben" and walk down to the Aare on the left (dorms 30SFr; doubles 110SFr-160SFr; breakfast 7SFr; bedding 5SFr; laundry 4-6SFr). Calm, comfortable **Pension Martahaus**, Wyttenbachstr. 22a (tel. (031) 332 41 35; fax 333 33 86), is in a quiet suburb. Take bus 20 to "Gewerbeschule," then take your first right. (Singles 60-90SFr; doubles 95-120SFr; triples 120-150SFr. Breakfast included. Laundry 8SFr. Reception 7am-9pm, live-in night-porter.) Ride streetcar 9 to "Wabern" (last stop) to camp under the stars at **Camping Eichholz**, Strandweg 49 (tel. (031) 961 26 02), near the zoo. (6.90SFr, students 5.50SFr; 5-8.50SFr per tent; doubles 15SFr; shower 1SFr. Open May-Sept.)

SWITZERLAND

The lively **Bärenplatz** overflows with cafes and restaurants; its daily **fruit and vegetable market** is open May to October 8am-6pm (year-round Tu and Sa on Bundespl.). **Manora,** Bubenbergpl. 5A, has tasty salads, fruits, and main courses (open M-Sa 7am-10:45pm, Su from 9am). The bustling **Cafe des Pyrénées,** Kornhauspl. 17, has inventive sandwiches (calamari 6.50SFr; open M-F 9am-12:30am, Sa 8am-5pm). **Cafe Bubenberg Vegi,** Bubenbergpl. 8, is a vegetarian's dream come true (Indian dishes 18-24SFr; open Aug.-June daily 8:30am-10:30pm; July closed Su).

■ Interlaken

Less than an hour by train from Bern, Interlaken provides access to the mountains, the Brienzersee and Thunersee, and to train lines throughout Switzerland. But with few tourist attractions and many more tourists than Swiss, the town functions better as a base than as a destination. Sign up at any hostel for activities run by **Adventure World,** Kirchgasse 18 (tel. (033) 826 77 11), Interlaken's main "adventure coordinator." On the water, there's **river rafting** (half-day 85SFr) and **canyoning** down waterfalls (half-day 85SFr). On land, **rock climbing** (half-day 75SFr) affords the opportunity to grapple with the Alps. In the air, enjoy **tandem paragliding** (half-day 140-200SFr) or experience **bungee jumping** from Schilthorn (100m 100SFr; 180m 225SFr, one previous jump required). Combination packages are available (155-333SFr).

Interlaken lies at the base of a steep valley that offers incredible (if difficult) **hikes.** The half-day climb up **Harderklum** (1322m) brings you touchably close to the white wall of the Jungfrau, Eiger, and Mönch peaks, towering 3700m over Interlaken.

PRACTICAL INFO, ACCOMMODATIONS, AND FOOD Interlaken has two train stations. The **Westbahnhof** (tel. (033) 826 47 50) borders the Thunersee in the center of town, while the **Ostbahnhof** (tel. (033) 822 27 92) is on the Brienzersee. Trains arrive from Basel (54SFr), Bern (24SFr), Geneva (60SFr), and Zurich (60SFr). The main **tourist office,** Höheweg 37 (tel. (033) 822 21 21), in the Hotel Metropole near Westbahnhof, provides free maps and schedules. (Open July-Aug. M-F 8am-noon and 1:30-6:30pm, Sa 8am-5pm, Su 5-7pm; Sept.-June M-F 8am-noon and 2-6pm, Sa 8am-noon.) **Bicycles** can be rented at the train stations (25-30SFr per day).

Finding a place to sleep is easy. Take bus 5 to "Hotel Sonne" and backtrack one minute to **Balmer's Herberge,** Haupstr. 23 (tel. (033) 822 19 61; fax 823 32 61), which draws a primarily American crowd with its frat-party atmosphere. From Westbahnhof go left, veer right onto Bahnhofstr., turn right on Centralstr., and follow the signs. Sign in and return at 5pm, when beds are assigned (no reservations). The hostel provides bike rental, laundry (8SFr per load), a bar, a store, and more. (Dorms 19-22SFr; doubles 56SFr; triples 72SFr; quads 96SFr. Reception in summer 6:30am-noon and 4:30-11pm; off-season 6:30-9am and 4:30-11pm. Breakfast included.) **Backpackers Villa Sonnenhof,** Alpenstr. 16 (tel. (033) 826 71 71; fax 826 71 72), at the corner of Höhenmatte, offers warm beds with million-dollar views of the Jungfrau and Silberhorn. (27SFr, 30SFr to face the Jungfrau; doubles 33SFr, with shower 43SFr. Breakfast, lockers, and kitchen (nice kitchen, too) included. Reception 7:30-11am and 4-9pm. No curfew.) **Heidi's Garni-Hotel Beyeler,** Bernastr. 37 (tel./fax (033) 822 90 30), is a family-run hotel on a quiet and convenient street (doubles 60-75SFr; triples 93SFr; quads 100-124SFr). Just across the river from Ostbahnhof is **Camping Sackgut** (tel. (033) 824 44 34; 7.60SFr per person, 6.50-14SFr per tent; open May-Sept.). **Camping Jungfraublick** (tel. (033) 822 44 14; fax 822 16 19) is five minutes past Balmer's on Gsteigstr. and has splendid views (7-12SFr per person; open May-Sept.).

Interlaken is filled with overpriced restaurants, but some across the river in old Interlaken are cheaper. Hostels also often serve cheap food. Stock up for hikes at the **Migros supermarket** across from Westbahnhof (open M-Th 7:30am-6:30pm, F 7:30am-9pm, Sa 7:30am-4pm). Revelers head to **Buddy's,** Höheweg 33, for beer (3.20-5.30SFr) and email (6SFr per 15min.; open daily 10am-12:30am). Some then stumble to **Johnny's Dancing Club,** Höheweg 92, in the Hotel Carlton (open Tu-Su 9:30pm-2:30am) or **Brasserie 17,** Rosenstr. 17, for live samba, jazz, and pop (open M-Sa 8:30am-12:30am, Su 3pm-12:30am). Every summer, Interlaken also stages an unforgettable performance of Schiller's *Wilhelm Tell* (call (033) 822 37 23 for ticket info).

■ Near Interlaken: Thunersee and Brienzersee

You can appreciate Berner Oberland's calm waters and stark mountain peaks by cruising on Interlaken's lakes, the **Thunersee** (to the west) and the **Brienzersee** (to the east). Ferries on Thunersee are free with Eurail, Swisspass, and Berner Oberland passes, while day passes for area ferry, bus, and train travel can be bought at Interlaken's station (July-Aug. 42SF; June and Sept. 32SFr).

The **Beatushöhlen**, caves with stalactites, waterfalls, and the ancient cell of St. Beatus, are reachable by bus 21 from Interlaken to Thun (caves open Apr.-Oct. daily 10:30am-5pm; 14SFr, students 12SFr). The walk back to Interlaken takes two hours. Across the lake in Spiez, **Spiez Castle** features fabulous woodwork, a stunning tower view, and a rose garden. (Open July-Aug. M 2-6pm, Tu-Su 10am-6pm; Apr.-June and Sept.-Oct. M 2-5pm, Tu-Su 10am-5pm. 4SFr, students 3SFr.) Get to Spiez by **boat** from Thun or Interlaken or by **train** from Bern, Thun, or Interlaken West. The towns of **Spiez** and **Thun** have **tourist offices** adjacent to the train stations (Spiez tel. (033) 654 20 20; Thun tel. (033) 222 23 40). Accommodations on the lake are hard to find; ask at the tourist offices about private rooms. Campgrounds are numerous; in Spiez, take the bus to Mustermattli to reach **Panorama Rossen** (tel. (033) 654 43 77), in Aeschi (5.50SFr; showers 1SFr; tents 7-8SFr; open May-Sept.).

The **Brienzersee** is more rugged and less developed. The town of **Brienz** has escaped tourism and makes a serene daytrip (from Interlaken 1¼hr. and 12.40SFr by boat or 20min. by train). On the outskirts of town, the **Ballenberg Swiss Open-Air Museum** is a 50-hectare park displaying traditional rural dwellings from every region of Switzerland. The park is an hour's walk from the train station, but a **bus** (round-trip 5.60SFr) connects the two every hour (open mid-Apr. to Nov. daily 10am-5pm; 14SFr, students 12SFr). The **tourist office** (tel. (033) 952 80 80; fax 952 80 88), across from the train station, gives tips to hikers of all experience levels. (Open July-Aug. M-F 8am-6:30pm, Sa 9am-noon and 4-6pm; Sept.-June M-F 8am-noon and 2-6pm; May-June and Sept.-Oct. also Sa 8am-noon.) From the train station, cross the tracks, face the lake, turn left, and trace the lake for 15 minutes to reach the rustic **Brienz Jugendherberge (HI)**, Strandweg 10 (tel. (033) 951 11 52; fax 951 22 60). The hostel rents **bikes** (12SFr per day) to its guests (dorms 21-23SFr; doubles 51-56SFr; reception 8-10am and 5-10pm). Along the same stretch sprawl **Camping Seegärtli** (tel. (033) 951 13 51; 7SFr per person, 5-7SFr per tent; open Apr.-Oct.) and **Camping Aaregg** (tel. (033) 951 18 43; fax 951 43 24; 9.20SFr per person, 13SFr per tent; open Apr.-Oct.).

▓ Jungfrau Region

The most famous (and most visited) region of the Berner Oberland, the Jungfrau area has attracted tourists for hundreds of years with glorious hiking trails and perennially snow-capped peaks. As the birthplace of skiing (or so locals claim), the area offers some of the most challenging slopes in Switzerland. Transportation throughout the area is, unfortunately, scandalously expensive. **Berner Oberland Bahn,** which runs mountain trains linking Interlaken to the valleys, often grants only minor price reductions to Swiss- and Eurailpass holders. Of uncertain value is the 15-day **Berner Oberland Regional Pass** (200Fr, with Swisspass or Half-Fare card 160SFr, Eurailpass not valid), which gives free travel for five days on many railways and cable cars (e.g. Rothorn, Schynige Platte, First, Niesen) after 10 days of travel at half-price. A seven-day variation is available for 160SFr, offering 50% off for four days and the remaining days free. Both are available at train stations or any tourist office.

The best way to see the Alps, of course, is to **hike.** Maps for hikers are available from nearly every tourist office. Trails are clearly marked by bright yellow signs indicating the estimated time to nearby destinations ("Std." is short for *Stunden,* or hours). Climbers should pack sunglasses, water, raingear, and a sweater, and follow standard safety procedures; the Alps are unkind to the underprepared. There are several types of **ski passes** for the Oberland, from 52SFr for one day and 95SFr for two. All passes include transportation to and from the lifts, and can be purchased at tourist offices or at chair lifts. **Balmer's Herberge** in Interlaken (see above) offers expert advice on skiing in the area, as well as discounts on ski and snowboard rental. Call or ask at the desk for more details. Ski rental is available throughout the valleys. The **ski schools** in **Wengen** (tel. (033) 855 20 22) and **Mürren** (tel. (033) 855 12 47) supply information on classes. Call (033) 157 45 06 for **weather information,** and check out conditions on the TVs in tourist offices and large hotels.

Grindelwald

Grindelwald is a skier's and climber's dream. Ride Europe's longest chairlift up the **Männlichen** for a great view of the Eiger, Mönch, and Jungfrau (28SFr, round-trip 45SFr, Swisspass 25% off, Eurail 50% off). **First** mountain (same price; Swisspass/Eurail 25% off) has idyllic scenery and spectacular hiking. The **tourist office** (tel. (036) 854 12 12; fax 854 12 10), in the Sport-Zentrum, has hiking maps and skiing info and finds private rooms. (25-50SFr. Open July-Aug. M-F 8am-7pm, Sa 8am-5pm, Su 9-11am and 3-5pm; Sept.-June M-F 8am-noon and 2-6pm, Sa 8am-noon and 2-5pm.) The **Bergführerbüro** (Mountain Guide Office; tel. (036) 853 52 00) on Hauptstr., has **hiking** info (open June-Oct. M-Sa 9am-noon and 3-6pm, Su 4-6pm).

The **Jugendherberge (HI)** (tel. (036) 853 10 09; fax 853 50 29) is undoubtedly one of the best in Switzerland. Go left from the station (5-7min.), right and uphill at the tiny brown sign, and left at the fork by the blue SJH sign (29.50SFr first night, thereafter 27SFr; doubles and quads 32-45SFr). The newly renovated **Mountain Hostel** (tel. (036) 853 39 00; fax 853 47 30), at the Grund station, simply gleams (dorms 29-34SFr; doubles 78-88SFr; breakfast included). **Gletscherdorf** (tel. (036) 853 14 29; fax 853 31 29) is the closest campsite. From the station, turn right, take first right after the tourist office, and then the third left (9SFr per person, 4-9SFr per tent). **Camping Eigernordwand** (tel. (036) 853 42 27) is across the river and to the left of the Grund station (9.50SFr per person, 7-8SFr per tent). The budget-minded buy provisions at the **Co-op** across from the tourist office (open M-F 8am-6:30pm, Sa 8am-4pm).

Lauterbrunnen Valley

Beautiful **Lauterbrunnen** derives its name from the 72 waterfalls that plummet down the sheer walls of the narrow, glacier-cut valley. The **tourist office** (tel. (033) 855 19 55) is 200m left of the station on the main street. (Open M-F 8am-noon and 2-6pm; July-Aug. also Sa 9am-noon and 3-7pm, Su 9am-3pm.) The brand new **Valley Hostel** (tel. (033) 855 20 08) is on the left off the main street, downhill, past the Co-op on the right. 20SFr dorms include showers, sheets, and kitchen access; the hostel has one double (44SFr). Impressive **Camping Jungfrau** (tel. (033) 856 20 10; fax 856 20 20), up the main street from the station toward the large waterfall, has cheap beds, kitchens, showers, lounges, and a store (8-10SFr per person, 6-15SFr per tent; dorms 18SFr). **Camping Schützenbach** (tel. (033) 855 12 68; fax 855 12 75) has communal bathrooms, and laundry and kitchen facilities (6SFr per person, 11SFr per tent; dorms 16-19SFr). Follow the signs toward Trümmelbach from the station (15min.). Lauterbrunnen's **Co-op** roosts next to the post office.

When you're ready to move on, an easy 40-minute hike leads to the fabulous **Trümmelbach Falls,** 10 consecutive glacier-bed chutes that gush up to 20,000L of water per second and generate mighty winds. Explore via tunnels, footbridges, and underground funiculars. (Open July-Aug. 8:30am-6pm; Apr.-June and Sept.-Nov. 9am-5pm. 10SFr, with Jungfrau region visitor's card 9SFr.) Follow signs along the river to **Stechelberg,** where cable cars leave for Gimmelwald (7.20SFr), Mürren (14SFr), Birg (33.20SFr), and Schilthorn (48SFr). First two free with Swisspass; Eurailpass 25% off all four destinations. If you stop at **Mürren,** ask at the tourist office (tel. (036) 856 86 86; fax 856 86 96) in the sports center (10min. from the Schilthorn cable car station, 5min. left of the train station, off the right fork) about private rooms, hiking trails, and skiing prices. (Open July-Aug. M-F 9am-noon and 1-6:30pm, Sa 1-6:30pm, Su 1-5:30pm; Sept.-June M-F 9am-noon and 2-5pm.) Next door to the **Gimmelwald** cable car station is the hiker's mecca: the rustic, inexpensive, and friendly **Mountain Hostel** (tel. (036) 855 17 04; 15SFr; kitchen access). Beds fill fast; only same-day reservations are accepted (after 10am). Bring food—Gimmelwald has no co-ops. If this hostel is full, head back to the hostels in Lauterbrunnen or Mürren.

■ Zermatt and the Matterhorn

A trick of the valley blocks out the great Alpine summits surrounding **Zermatt,** allowing the **Matterhorn** (4478m), orange at dawn and cloud-shrouded much of the time, to rise alone above the town. To climb this beast, you need a mountain of money, rock climbing experience, and a courageous heart; the hike takes two days and hiring a guide costs over 670SFr. Fortunately, you can hike miles of sign-posted paths around Zermatt without grave danger to life or wallet. Find out more at the **Bergführerbüro** (Mountaineering Office; tel. (027) 966 24 66), five minutes from the train station up Bahnhofstr. (open July-Sept. M-F 8:30am-noon and 4-7pm, Sa 4-7pm, Su 10am-noon and 4-7pm). The **tourist office** (tel. (027) 967 01 81; fax 967 01 85), adjacent to the station, provides skiing and hiking maps. (Open mid-June to mid-Oct. M-Sa 8:30am-6pm, Su 9:30am-noon and 4-6:30pm; mid-Oct. to mid-June M-Sa 8:30am-noon and 1:30-7pm.) Sturdy boots, warm clothing, and raingear are essential. For a spectacular glimpse of the Matterhorn and its splendid valleys, climb to **Hörnlihütte,** the base camp for ascents of the Matterhorn, a grueling 4 to 5 hour hike past the tiny lake **Schwarzsee** from Zermatt. The less zealous can take a cable car to Schwarzsee (round-trip 29.50SFr). Zermatt has more summer **ski trails** than any other Alpine resort—36 square km of year-round runs between 3900m and 2900m. In winter, downhill ski passes cost 60SFr for a day, and discounts are available for longer stays. For more time on the slopes, rent gear in town a day ahead. Most ski shops are open Monday through Saturday 8am to noon and 2 to 7pm and charge about 43SFr (10% off for hostelers at ROC Sport on Kirchstr.). For **alpine rescue,** call (027) 967 20 00.

Cars have been outlawed in Zermatt—the only way in is the hourly BVZ (Brig-Visp-Zermatt) **rail line.** The **Jugendherberge (HI),** Winkelmatten (tel. (027) 967 23 20; fax 967 53 06), provides a view of The Mountain from the bedroom windows, but it's a 15-minute trek uphill (37.50-40SFr). From the train station, walk to the right down the main street, turn left at the church, cross the river, and take the second street to the right. Closer to the station, **Hotel Bahnhof** (tel. (027) 967 24 06; fax 967 72 16), on Bahnhofstr. just past the Gornergratbahn, feels like a rustic cabin (dorms 26-28SFr; singles 40-50SFr; doubles 71-79SFr). The lone campground is **Camping Matterhorn Zermatt** (tel. (027) 967 39 21), a five-minute walk left down Bahnhofstr. from the station (8SFr, showers included; reception May-Sept. 8:30-10am and 5:15-7pm). **The Pipe Surfers' Cantina,** on Kirchstr., dishes out Mexican food (open daily in summer 11am-1am; in winter 3pm-2am). Zermatt's oldest restaurant, the **Cafe du Pont,** at the end of Bahnhofstr., serves hearty Alpine fare (open 9am-midnight; food served 11am-3pm and 5-10pm; closed Nov. and May).

■ Saas Fee

Nicknamed "the pearl of the Alps," Saas Fee is situated in a hanging valley above the Saastal and snuggles among 13 4000m peaks. One of the peaks is the **Dom** (4545m), the second highest mountain in Switzerland. Summer **skiers** can enjoy 20km of runs and a stupendous Alpine view, but in winter an immense network of lifts opens (day ski passes 56SFr). Stores in the **Swiss Rentasport System** offer good rates (skis or snowboard and boots 43SFr per day). In summer, turn to **hiking;** the **Alpine Guide's office** (tel. (027) 957 44 64) by the church has a selection of climbs for both amateurs and experts (open M-Sa 9:30am-noon and 3-6pm).

A **post bus** runs every hour to **Visp** (1hr., 13.20SFr), which connects to Lausanne and elsewhere, and **Stalden Saas** (35min., 10.40SFr), which connects to Zermatt for another 30SFr. Reserve a place on all buses starting at Saas Fee at least two hours before departure (call (027) 957 19 45 or stop by the station). The staff of the **tourist office** (tel. (027) 958 18 58; fax 957 18 60), across from the bus station, reserves rooms (10SFr), and dispenses seasonal information and hiking advice. (Open high-season July to mid-Sept. and mid-Dec. to mid-Apr. M-F 8:30am-noon and 2-6:30pm, Sa 8am-7pm, Su 9am-noon and 3-6pm; low-season mid-Sept. to mid-Dec and mid-Apr. to June M-Sa 8:30am-noon and 2-6pm, Su 10am-noon and 4-6pm.) The budget-minded

SWITZERLAND

willing to sacrifice comfort can find a bargain in the basement of **Hotel Garni Imseng** (tel. (027) 958 12 58, fax 958 12 55). From the station, head down the main street, left of the tourist office, then turn left and pass the church (20SFr; sheets 3.50SFr; buffet breakfast 15SFr). One of the town's better values is **Pension Garni Mascotte** and its two sister chalets (tel. (027) 957 27 24; fax 957 12 16). With your back to the station, head down the road opposite you just left of the tourist office. At the first large street, turn right and continue up the hill for 200m (dorms 27-55SFr; breakfast included; open mid-Dec. to Apr. and July-Sept.). **Spaghetteria da Rasso,** two minutes to the left of the pharmacy, has 14 variations on spaghetti (13-24SFr; open 10am-11:30pm most days; closed May-June).

Buna Saira!

Switzerland's oft-forgotten fourth national language, Romansh, is spoken only in the province of Graubünden, where it is an official cantonal language along with German and Italian. Up until about 1850, it was the most spoken language in the canton. By 1880, Romansh speakers dropped to 39.8% of the population, a percentage that kept dropping, then leveled out as the primary language for 23.6% of the residents in Graubünden. In some villages like S-chanf, Romansh speakers are in the majority, and even in large towns like Chur they form a quarter of the population. All Romansh speakers (except toddlers) are fully bilingual. Romansh is taught in the schools, and its speakers support five Romansh newspapers and 13-14 hours of TV broadcast time in Romansh. The language is fully supported by the Swiss government, but its survival is threatened by the fact that its speakers are divided by at least four major dialects that arose from the mountain isolation of many high-altitude villages. Romansh didn't become a written language until the 16th-century, when people began publishing catechisms and tracts on preserving Romansh identity (already!). Now, Romansh has a small literature of its own and translations of everything from the Bible to Asterix comics. Maybe when you're traveling through Switzerland, you'll overhear someone calling out, "Bun di!" (hello), "grazia" (thank you), or even "Tge bel che ti es!" (how beautiful you are!).

FRENCH SWITZERLAND

■ Basel (Bâle)

Perched on the Rhine a stone's throw from France and Germany, Basel (rhymes with "nozzle") exemplifies the cultural diversity of Northern Switzerland; it is neither French nor German, but takes from both to create a distinct character all its own. A beautiful city with a charming cobblestone *Altstadt,* Basel's medieval image subtly masks the vibrance of a modern university town.

ORIENTATION AND PRACTICAL INFORMATION

On the left bank of the Rhine, the **Gross-Basel** part of town, where most sights are located, rests in two hills separated by the valley of the Birsig; on the right bank lies **Klein-Basel.** Be sure to pick up a city **map** (0.50SFr) at either tourist office.

Telephone Code: 061.
Trains: 3 stations. The **French (SNCF;** tel. 156 10 56) and **Swiss (SBB;** tel. 157 22 22) stations are in Centralbahnpl., near the *Altstadt;* trains from Germany arrive at the **DB** station across the Rhine down Riehenstr. (tel. 690 11 11). To: Bern (1hr., 34SFr), Geneva (3hr., 67SFr), Lausanne (2½hr., 57SFr), Paris (5hr., 70SFr), Rome (7hr., 135SFr), Vienna (10hr., 126SFr), and Zurich (1hr., 30SFr).
Buses: The DB station sends buses to Germany, while the SBB and SNCF stations run to Germany and France.

Public Transportation: Trams and buses operate from 5:45am-11:45pm. Most sights are within zone 10. 1-zone tickets cost 2.60SFr; day-tickets cost 7.40SFr.

Bike Rental: In the train station. 25SFr per day. Open M-Su 7am-8:30pm.

Tourist Office, Schifflände 5 (tel. 268 68 68; fax 268 68 70). Take tram 1 (from the SBB station) to "Schifflände"; the office is on the river, near the Mittlere Bridge. Lists of museums, cultural events, and suggested walking tours. Open M-F 8:30am-6pm, Sa 10am-4pm. Hotel reservations (10SFr) here or at the **branch office** (tel. 271 36 84; fax 272 93 42), located at the SBB station. Open M-F 8:30am-7pm, Sa 8:30am-12:30pm and 1:30-6pm, Su 10am-4pm.

Currency Exchange: Rates uniform city-wide; SBB station open daily 6am-9pm.

Emergency: Medical Assistance, tel. 144. All lines have English speakers.

Police: tel. 117.

Hotlines: Helping Hand, tel. 143. **Rape Crisis Hotline,** tel. 261 89 89.

Post Office: Rüdeng 1. Tram 1 or 8: "Marktpl." Open M-F 7:30am-6pm, Sa 8am-12:30pm. **Postal Codes:** CH-4000 to CH-4051.

ACCOMMODATIONS AND CAMPING

Only one crowded hostel and very few hotels even remotely approach budget status; reserve a room ahead of time. The truly desperate can try **Stadthof,** Gerbergasse 84 (tel. 261 87 11), at Barfüsserpl., which has showerless rooms in extremely limited numbers (singles 60-75SFr).

Jugendherberge (HI), St. Alban-Kirchrain 10 (tel. 272 05 72; fax 272 08 33). Tram 2 to "Kunstmuseum" and 5min. down St. Albangraben, passing St. Albanchurch. Very peaceful and within 2min. of 5 museums. Dorms 26.80SFr the 1st night, then 24.30SFr; singles 56.70SFr; doubles 37.80SFr, 35.30SFr. Breakfast, showers, and sheets included. Dinner 11SFr. **Laundry** 8SFr. Reception 7-10am and 2pm-midnight. Check-out 7-10am. Curfew midnight. Reservations recommended.

Hotel-Pension Steinenschanze, Steinengraben 69 (tel. 272 53 53; fax 272 45 73). From the SBB station, turn left on Centralbahnstr. toward Heuwage-Viadukt, and walk straight ahead. Amenities make up for the higher price. Singles from 105-160SFr, under 25 with ISIC 55SFr. Doubles from 150SFr; under 25 with ISIC 150-240SFr. Breakfast and shower included. 3-day max. stay. Reception 24hr.

Hecht am Rhein, Rheing. 8 (tel. 691 22 20; fax 681 07 88). Singles 70-80SFr; doubles 120-130SFr. Breakfast included. Reception 7am-6pm. Women traveling alone may not feel safe in this neighborhood.

Camping: Camp Waldhort, Heideweg 16 (tel. 711 64 29), in Reinach. Take tram 11 to "Landhof," then backtrack 200m toward Basel. 7SFr per person, 4-6SFr per tent. Reception 8am-12:15pm and 2:30-10pm. Open Mar.-Oct.

FOOD

Basel is a university town, so relatively cheap eateries are fairly numerous, even in the heart of the city. Check out cafes and weekday morning fruit, vegetable, and baked goods stalls on **Marktplatz.** Shop for groceries at **Migros,** Clarapl., or at the **Co-op** center opposite the train station.

Hirscheneck, Lindenberg 23. Cross the Wettsteinbrücke and take the first left. A left-of-center restaurant/bar where dreadlocks and piercings prevail. Features vegetarian dishes. *Menu* 15SFr. Open M 5pm-midnight, Tu-Th 9am-midnight, F 9am-1am, Sa 2pm-1am, Su 10am-midnight.

Zum Schnabel, Trillengässlein 2. From *Marktplatz,* walk a block on Hutg., then left onto Schnabelg. Comfy restaurant serves well-prepared German dishes. 12.80SFr meal will fill you up. Open daily 8am-midnight.

Topas Kosher Restaurant, Leimenstr. 24 (tel. 206 95 00). Kosher deli. Main courses 13-28SFr. Open Su, Tu, and Th 11:30am-2pm and 6:30-9pm, F 11:30am-2pm. Call one day ahead for Sa lunch and F dinner.

SIGHTS AND ENTERTAINMENT

The **Münster,** the crown jewel of Basel's medieval buildings, was built on the site of a Celtic town and Roman fort. (Cathedral open in summer M-F 10am-5pm, Sa 10am-noon and 2-4pm; Su 1-5pm; after July 1 Sa 10am-5pm; off-season M-Sa 11am-4pm, Su 2-4pm. Free.) The church holds Erasmus's tomb, but the red sandstone facade steals the show with hundreds of figures in pious acts ranging from trumpet-playing to dragon-slaying. The Münster **tower** boasts the best view of **Klein Basel,** the Rhine, and the Black Forest (2SFr). Toward Barfüsserpl. on Steinenberg, the **Jean Tinguely Fountain** memorializes modern chaos. Nearby Freiestr., the main shopping avenue, leads to the *Marktplatz* and the **Rathaus** (City Hall). This gaudy building was erected in the early 1500s to celebrate Basel's entry into the Confederation. **St. Alban-Tor** by the hostel is one of the three remaining towers of the **Old City Wall.**

Basel's 30 **museums** feature everything from medieval medicine to Monteverdi cars. The (deservedly) best known is the **Kunstmuseum** (Museum of Fine Arts), St. Alban-Graben 16 (tel. 271 08 28; streetcar 2 from the station), established in the 17th century, with works by Matisse, Chagall, Picasso, and Dalí (open Tu-Su 10am-5pm, W until 9pm; 7SFr, students 5SFr, Su free). For more modern works, try the **Museum für Gegenwartskunst** (Museum of Contemporary Art), St. Alban-Rheinweg 60, by the youth hostel (open Tu-Su 11am-5pm; 7SFr, students 5SFr). The **Museum der Kulturen Basel** (Museum of Ethnology), Augustinerg. 2, just off Munsterpl., has an off-beat collection of exotic art (open Mar.-Aug. Tu-Su 10am-5pm, W until 9pm; 6SFr, students 4SFr).

Barfüsserplatz is a good place to start bar-hopping, though drinks just about everywhere are quite expensive. **Atlantis,** Klosterburg 13, is a large bar that sways to salsa, reggae, blues, and rock (cover 5-7SFr; open Su-Th 10am-midnight, F-Sa 10am-1am). **Brauerei Fischerstube,** Rheing. 45, Basel's smallest brewery, brews four of the best beers in town (open M-Th 10am-midnight, F-Sa 10am-1am, Su 5pm-midnight). **Caveau Mövenpick Wine Pub,** Grünpfahlg. 4, by the post office, is a sophisticated change from the bar scene (wine 4.40-10SFr per glass; open M-Sa 11am-midnight). The annual Basel blow-out is the **Fasnacht** carnival, the week of February 22 in 1999, when revelers wear masks to scare away winter.

Lizard Lunacy

In 1529, Basel's residents enthusiastically joined the Reformation and threw out the bishop, but they kept his *crozier* (staff) as the town's emblem. The staff shares this honor with the basilisk (Basel-isk), a creature part bat, part dragon, and part rooster, which spawned what may have been the world's first and only public trial and execution of a chicken. In 1474, a hen allegedly laid an egg on a dung heap under a full moon, an action sure to hatch the horrible creature. The bird was tried, found guilty, and beheaded, and the egg was ceremonially burnt.

■ Neuchâtel

Perhaps at a loss for words, Alexandre Dumas once likened Neuchâtel to a city carved out of a block of butter. Although he was obviously referring to the unique yellow stone that makes up a large part of the city's architecture, Dumas could easily be mistaken these days as an overly appreciative fan of the calorie-laden treats in the local *pâtisseries.* But even after the visual and gastronomical novelty has worn off, Neuchâtel possesses a remarkable medieval beauty. The **château** and neighboring **Eglise Collégiale,** featuring a 1372 **Cenotaph,** dominate the town from their hilltop perches. (Church open daily 8am-6pm; guided tours on the next-to-last F of each month. Free concerts on the last F.) The wonderful **Tour des Prisons** is just an arrow-shot away on rue Jehanne-de-Hochberg, and its **tower** provides a magnificent view (tower open Apr.-Sept.). Lock your traveling companion in one of the tiny wooden cells used in 1848 (0.50SFr). Take a bus to the **Fromagerie Les Martel** cheese factory in nearby Les Ponts-de-Martel for a free tour, and sample the product for a nominal fee (call

'032) 937 16 to sign up for a tour), or travel 10 minutes by train to nearby Cressier to taste the wine at local vineyards. More wine-tasting takes place in Neuchâtel at the three-day **Wine Festival** during the last weekend in September.

Trains connect Neuchâtel to Basel (1½hr., 35SFr), Bern (40min., 16.60SFr), Interlaken (2hr., 39SFr), and Geneva (1½hr., 41SFr). The helpful **tourist office** (tel. (032) 889 68 90; fax 889 62 96; email neuchatel@tourisme.etatne.ch; http://www.etatne.ch), Hôtel des Postes, is two blocks to the left of Pl. Pury if you're facing the lake. (Open July-Aug. M-Sa 9am-7pm; Su 4-7pm; Sept.-June M-F 9am-noon and 1:30-5:30pm, Sa 9am-noon.) The excellent **Oasis Neuchâtel,** rue de Suchiez 35 (tel. '032) 731 31 90; fax 730 37 09), boasts fine views of the lake. From the station, take bus 6 to pl. Pury, walk in front of the kiosk, and take bus 1 ("Cormondrèche") to "Vauseyon." From there, head uphill and follow pedestrian signs up a flight of stairs; then turn right and the hostel will be up the road to your left (20-22.50SFr; reception daily 8-10am and 5-9pm; no curfew; reserve ahead in July and Aug.). If the Oasis is full, check the *Hotel Restaurant* guide, free at the tourist office, for inexpensive options in nearby towns.

The student hang-out **Crêperie Bach et Buck,** av. du Premier-Mars 22, offers crepes (and only crepes) for under 10SFr. (Open M-Th 11:30am-2pm and 5:30-10pm, F 11:30am-2pm and 5:30-11:30pm, Sa 11:30am-11:30pm, Su 5-10pm.) If you hanker for something else, the unassuming bistro **Chauffrage Compris** serves up a hearty *plat du jour* (open M-Th 6am-1am, F-Sa 6am-2am, Su 2-11pm). Keep on keepin' on until 4am at the **Casino de la Rotonde,** a sprawling nightclub complex at fbg. du Lac 14 (beer 3-5SFr; open M-Sa 10pm; cover around 10SFr).

■ Geneva (Genève)

"I detest Geneva," muttered Napoleon Bonaparte in 1798, "they know English too well." They still do. Two-thirds of Geneva's population are foreign-born or transplants from other regions of Switzerland, and the city is a hybrid of cultures. The large concentration of international banks and multinational organizations preserves the intricate melange—quite a contrast to Switzerland's other, mostly homogeneous towns. Yet modern internationalism contrasts with past isolationism. Geneva's citizens have a long and belligerent tradition of doing battle to protect their political and religious independence, and it wasn't until the Enlightenment that Madame de Staël's salons won out over Calvinist intolerance.

ORIENTATION AND PRACTICAL INFORMATION

Genevois sun themselves on the western shore of **Lac Léman** (Lake Geneva), in southwestern Switzerland. In the city's *vieille ville,* cobbled streets and quiet squares surround the **Cathédrale de St-Pierre** and the **university.** Heading north, banks, bistros, and boutiques line the **Rhône river.** The United Nations, the Red Cross, and other international bodies overlook the city in a northern suburb. Carry your passport with you at all times; the French border is close and regional buses often cross it.

Telephone Code: 022.

Flights: Cointrin Airport (tel. 717 71 11) is naturally one of Swissair's hubs. Direct flights to New York, Paris, London, Amsterdam, and Rome.

Trains: Gare Cornavin, pl. Cornavin. To: **Basel** (2¾hr., every hr., 67SFr), **Bern** (1¾hr., every hr., 48SFr), **Interlaken** (3hr., every hr., 60SFr), **Lausanne** (40min., every 20min., 19.40SFr), **Montreux** (1hr., every hr., 27SFr), **Paris** (3½hr., 6 per day, 80SFr plus reservation fee, under 26 20% off), **Rome** (10hr., 1 per day, 122SFr, under 26 20% off), **Zurich** (3hr., every hr., 74SFr). Settle down and wait at the busy reservation and information office (open M-F 8:30am-7pm, Sa 9am-5:30pm). Train schedules at http://www.sbb.ch.

Ferries: Hugely popular **CGN ferries** (tel. 732 39 16) depart from the quai du Mont-Blanc at the foot of rue des Alpes for Lausanne (3hr.) and Montreux (4½hr.). Round-trip tickets (32-50SFr) include the option of returning by train.

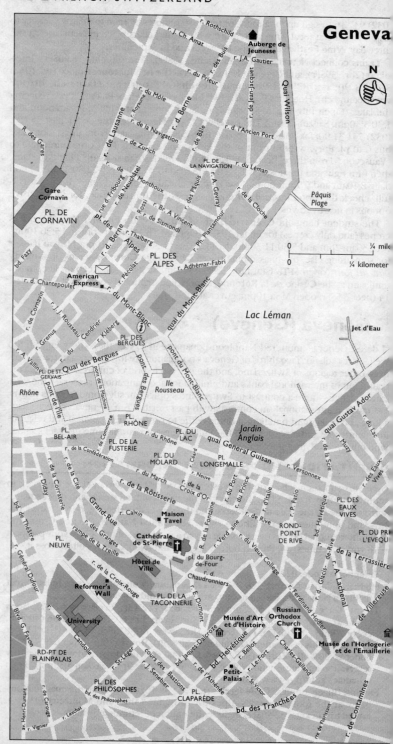

Geneva

N

Auberge de Jeunesse

r. Rothschild
r. J. Ch. Amat
r. des Buis
r. J.A. Gautier
r. du Prieur
r. de Jean-Jacquet
Quai Wilson
r. du Môle
r. Royaume
r. de la Navigation
r. d' Berne
r. de Bâle
r. d. l'Ancien Port
r. de Lausanne
r. de Neuchâtel
Monthoux
r. de Zurich
PL. DE LA NAVIGATION
r. du Léman
Gare Cornavin
rue d. Fribourg
r. Rossi
r. B. A. Vincent
r. des Pâquis
r. A. Gevray
r. de la Cloche
PL. DE CORNAVIN
PL. des
r. de Sismondi
r. Ph. Plantamour
Pâquis Plage
R. des Gares
r. d. Berne
r. Thalberg
PL. DES ALPES
r. Pécolat
r. Adhémar-Fabri
bd. Fazy
r. d. Chantepoulet
American Express ✉
r. de Cornavin
r. J.J. Rousseau Cendrier
r. Kléberg
quai du Mont-Blanc
Lac Léman
Jet d'Eau
r. A. Vallin
r. Grenus
r. du
PL. DES BERGUES ℹ
pont du Mont-Blanc
PL. DE ST. GERVAIS
Quai des Bergues
pont de la Machine
Ile Rousseau
Rhône
pont de l'Ile
pont des Bergues
PL. RHÔNE
Jardin Anglais
quai Gustav Ador
quai du Lac
PL. BEL-AIR
r. de Commerce
PL. DE LA FUSTERIE
PL. DU RHÔNE
r. du Rhône
PL. DU LAC
quai General Guisan
r. de la Scie
r. Mury
r. des Eaux-Vives
r. de la Confederation
PL. DU MOLARD
r. Céard
Pl. LONGEMALLE
r. Versonnex
r. de la Corraterie
r. de la Cité
r. du March
r. de la Croix d'Or
r. Neuve
r. du Port
r. du Prince
r. d'Italie
PL. DES EAUX VIVES
r. Didäy
r. de la Rôtisserie
r. de Rive
r. P. Fatio
bd. Helvétique
PL. DU PRE L'EVEQU
Grand-Rue
r. Calvin
r. de la Fontaine
r. Verdaine
r. du Vieux Collège
ROND-POINT DE RIVE
r. de la Terrassière
r. des Granges
Maison Tavel
r. d. Glacis-de-Rive
r. A. Lachenal
rampe de la Treille
Cathédrale de St-Pierre ✝
r. de Villereuse
PL. NEUVE
Hôtel de Ville
pl. du Bourg-de-Four
r. d. Chaudronniers
r. Ferdinand Hodler
r. de la Croix-Rouge
PL. DE LA TACONNERIE
Reformer's Wall
r. E. Dumont
University
r. de Candolle
Musée d'Art et d'Histoire 🏛
Russian Orthodox Church ✝
r. de Contamines
RD-PT DE PLAINPALAIS
r. St-Léger
cours des Bastions
bd. Jaques-Dalcroze
bd. Helvétique
r. Bellot
r. Charles-Galland
Musée de l'Horlogerie et de l'Emaillerie 🏛
PL. DES PHILOSOPHES
bd. des Philosophes
r. J. Senebier
r. de l'Athénée
Petit-Palais
r. Le-Fort
r. St-Victor
PL CLAPARÈDE
r. Lechat
av. Henri-Dumant
r. de Carouge
r. Vignier
bd. des Tranchées
r. de Florisant
bd. G. Favon
r. Genéral Dufour
blvd de Théatre

0   ¼ mile
0   ¼ kilometer

SWITZERLAND

Public Transportation: Transport Publics Genevois (tel. 308 34 34), next to the tourist office in Gare Cornavin, provides a free but confusing map of the local bus routes called *Le Réseau.* Open 6:15am-8pm. 2.20SFr buys 1hr. of unlimited travel on any bus; 3 stops or less cost 1.50SFr. Best bet is a full-day pass for 5SFr. Swisspass valid on buses; Eurailpass not valid. Buy multi-fare and day tickets at the train station, others at automatic vendors at every stop. Stamp multi-use tickets before boarding or suffer 60SFr fines if caught. Buses run daily roughly 5:30am-midnight.

Bike Rental: Behind the train station, **Genève Route,** pl. Montbrillant 17 (tel. 740 13 43), has 28 free bikes available. A 50SFr deposit is required; 250SFr fine if bike is lost or stolen. Open 7:30am-9:30pm.

Hitchhiking: Those headed to Germany or northern Switzerland take bus 4/44 to "Jardin Botanique." Those headed to France take bus 4/44 to "Palettes" then line D to "St. Julien." In summer, **Telstop** has ride lists in front of the CAR info booth.

Tourist Offices: Must-haves are the city map; *Info Jeunes/Young People;* and *Genève pratique.* The **main office,** rue du Mont-Blanc 3 (tel. 909 70 00; fax 929 70 11; email info@geneve-tourisme.ch; http://www.geneve-tourisme.ch), lies 1min. from the Mont-Blanc bus station and 5min. to the right of the train station. Books hotel rooms for a 5SFr fee and offers **walking tours.** Open June 15-Sept. 15 M-F 8am-6pm, Sa-Su 9am-6pm; Sept. 16-June 14 M-Sa 9am-6pm. Mobile, backpacker-oriented **Centre d'Accueil et de Renseignements (CAR)** (tel. 731 46 47), parks during the summer at the top of rue du Mont-Blanc after the pedestrian underpass beneath Gare Cornavin. Open June 16-Sept. 6 daily 9:30am-11pm. Last resort— **Anglo-phone** (tel. 157 50 14), a 24hr. hotline (in English; 2.13SFr per min.).

Currency Exchange: Throughout town. **Gare Cornavin** has good rates, no commission on traveler's checks, and will advance cash on MC, Visa, AmEx. Open 6:45am-9:30pm. **ATMs,** offering the best rates of all, dot Geneva.

American Express: rue du Mont-Blanc 7, P.O. Box 1032, CH-1211 Geneva 01 (tel. 731 76 00; fax 732 72 11). Mail held. All banking services; reasonable exchange rates. Hotel (30SFr) and train (20SFr) reservations. Open in summer M-F 8:30am-6pm, Sa 9am-noon; in winter M-F 8:30am-5:30pm, Sa 9am-noon.

Gay and Lesbian Organization: Dialogai, rue de la Navigation 11-13, (tel. 906 40 40; fax 906 40 44; http://www.hivnet.ch/dialogai). Publishes *Dialogai,* a guide to Switzerland's gay scene. Mostly men; women are welcome. Open M-Tu, F 3-6pm, W 3-10pm. **Centre Femmes Natalie Barney** (women only), av. Peschier 30, CH-1211, Geneva 25 (tel. 789 26 00). Similar services to Dialogai, but smaller and lesbian-oriented. 24hr. answering machine; phone answered W 6-8pm.

Laundromat: Salon Lavoir St. Gervais, rue Vallin 9 (tel. 731 26 46), off pl. St. Gervais. Open M-Sa 7:30am-9pm, Su 10am-9pm. **En 5 Sec SA,** rue Cornavin 5 (tel. 73 23 25), just 2 min. from Gare Cornavin.

Emergencies: Fire, tel. 118. **Ambulance,** tel. 144.

Police: tel. 117, rue Pecolat 5, next to the post office.

Rape Crisis Hotline: Viol-Secours (tel. 345 20 20). Open M 4-11pm, Tu 2-6pm, W and F 9am-noon, Th 2-9pm.

Medical Assistance: Hôpital Cantonal, rue Micheli-du-Crest 24 (tel. 372 33 11). Door 2 is for emergency care, Door 3 for outpatients. Walk-in clinics dot the city.

Post Office: Poste Centrale, rue de Mont-Blanc 18, a block from Gare Cornavin in the stately Hôtel des Postes. Open M-F 7:30am-6pm, Sa 8-11am. Address *Poste Restante* to CH-1211, Genève 1 Mont-Blanc. **Postal Code:** CH-1211.

Internet Access: Cafe Video ROM, Galerie de la Gare (tel. 901 16 21). Surf for 5SFr per hr. Open M-Th 11am-8:30pm, F-Sa 11am-10pm, Su 1-8:30pm.

ACCOMMODATIONS AND CAMPING

You can usually find dorm beds and hostel rooms in Geneva, but hotels fill quickly, so reserve in advance. If the places listed below are booked, try one of the 50 others listed in the free *Info Jeunes,* which you can pick up at the tourist office.

Auberge de Jeunesse (HI), rue Rothschild 28-30 (tel. 732 62 60; fax 738 39 87). Walk 15min. left from the station down rue de Lausanne and then turn right on rue Rothschild. Bus 1 ("Wilson") stops right in front of the hostel. Find a comfortable bunk at the last minute. Singles 23SFr; doubles 70SFr; nonmembers add 5SFR.

Artamis—Geneva's Guerrilla Artist Colony

What do you do when you're a young artist in Geneva and have no place to work? If there's 300 others like you, you shut down the tourist industry until the city gives you a place of your own. That's what happened in the summer of 1996 when a group of artists staged a sit-in demonstration at place du Bourg-de-Four just below the Cathédrale de St-Pierre. They ripped up pavement, built bonfires, and confused the hell out of tourists for six days until the city capitulated and granted them a no-rent lease for an abandoned industrial park on the left bank, now called Artamis (tel. 320 39 30; http://www.artamis.org). You'll find it at 12 rue de Strand, on the 2 and 10 bus lines (Palladium). Rising from the wreckage of an old factory, this ten building complex now houses a vibrant mix of art workshops, theaters, and an Internet cafe (5SFr per hr.). Electronic music enthusiasts should stop by the Database building, housing a recording studio where many of the top house, goa, and jungle DJs in the area come to experiment and exchange ideas. Some of their efforts are on Internet stream radio at http://www.basic.ch. All facilities and the main phone line (with info on performances and events) are open 4pm to 2am.

Showers, sheets, and breakfast included. Reception in summer 6:30-10am and 4pm-midnight; in winter 6:30-10am and 5pm-midnight. Curfew midnight.

Cité Universitaire, av. Miremont 46 (tel. 839 22 11; fax 839 22 23). From pl. de 22 Cantons take bus 3 ("Crêts-de-Champel") to the last stop. Institutional college housing with a disco (Th and Sa all-night dancing, free to residents), ping-pong, and **Internet access** (5SFr per hr.). Dorms (July-Sept. only) 16SFr; singles 36SFr; doubles 52SFr. Hall showers included. Reception M-F 8am-noon and 2-10pm, Sa-Su 8am-noon and 6-10pm. Lockout 10am-6pm. Curfew 11pm for dorm residents.

Centre St-Boniface, av. du Mail 14 (tel. 322 26 00; fax 322 26 01). Bus 1 or 4/44 ("Voirets") to "Cirque" or tram 13, then continue down av. du Mail. Just minutes from the *vieille ville*. Singles (mid-July to late Sept. only) 39-45SFr; doubles (mid-July to late Sept. only) 57-62SFr. Reception M-F 9am-noon, 4-7pm. Reserve ahead.

Hotel Pension St-Victor, rue François-le-Fort 1 (tel. 346 17 18; fax 346 10 46; email stvictor@iprolink.ch; http://geneva.yop.ch/hotels/smp). Bus 1, 3, or 5 to "pl. Claparède." Manager lets guests use **Internet** (1SFr per 5min.). Singles from 65SFr; doubles from 98SFr; triples from 120SFr. Breakfast included. Reservations imperative. Reception 7:30am-8pm.

Forget-Me-Not, rue Vignier 8 (tel. 320 93 55; fax 781 46 45). Bus 4/44 or tram 12 to "Plainpalais," walk down av. Dunant, and turn left on rue Vignier. Cement high-rise above a pool hall. Dorms 25SFr; singles 50SFr; doubles 80SFr. Breakfast included. Slightly more expensive "hotel" rooms: singles 60SFr; doubles with shower 110SFr. Reception M-F 9am-9pm, Sa 10am-4pm; call if arriving after 10pm. No curfew.

Camping: Pointe-à-la-Bise TCS, Chemin de la Bise (tel. 752 12 96). Bus 9 to "Rive" then bus E (north) to "Bise" (about 7km). 1 person 12SFr, 2 people 17.50SFr. No tents provided. Reception 8am-noon and 2-8pm. Open Apr.-Oct. 31.

FOOD

You can find anything from sushi to *paella* in Geneva, but you may need a banker's salary to foot the bill. For a quick bite, shop at the **supermarkets** on virtually every corner of the city, or try one of the many university **cafeterias** listed in *Info Jeunes*. *Patisseries* and pasta/pizza parlors permeate **Place du Bourg-de-Four,** below Cathédrale de St-Pierre, as do some of the best cafes.

Restaurant Manora, rue de Cornavin 4, 3min. from the station on the right in the Placette Dept. Store. Self-serve restaurant with a fresh, varied, high-quality selection. Salads (big bowl 4SFr), fresh juices (4SFr), and entrees cooked on the spot for you (from 11SFr). Wheelchair accessible. Open M-Sa 7am-9pm, Su 9am-9pm.

Le Rozzel, Grand-Rue 18. Breton-style *crêperie* in the *vieille ville*. Large dinner crepes 7-17SFr; dessert crepes 5-14SFr. Open 7:45am-8:30pm.

La Crise, rue de Chantepoulet 13. From the station, go right on rue de Cornavin and turn left on rue de Chantepoulet. Quiche and a plate full of veggies for a mere 6SFr; beer or wine 3SFr. Open M-F 6am-7:15pm, Sa 6am-3pm.

Auberge de Saviese, rue du Pâquis 20. Bus 1 to Monthoux. Traditional Swiss specialties here in a rustic interior. *Plats du jour* (13-14SFr); *fondue au cognac* (19SFr). Open M-F 11:30am-11pm, Sa-Su 6pm-11pm.

Sunset, rue St-Léger 3, off pl. des Philosophes. Try the *pita au champignons* (15SFr) with local vegetarians. Open M-F 7:30am-7pm.

SIGHTS AND ENTERTAINMENT

A visit to the *vieille ville* should start at the **Cathédrale de St-Pierre,** where John Calvin preached against indulgences and the extravagance of the 16th-century papacy. Climb the 157-step **north tower** for a view of the old town. (Cathedral open June-Sept. M-F 9am-7pm, Su 11am-7pm; Oct. and Mar.-May M-Sa 10am-noon and 2-5pm, Su 11am-12:30pm and 1:30-5pm. Tower closes 30min. earlier and costs 3SFr.) As you leave the cathedral, stroll along quai Gustave-Ardor, by the lakefront, to the 140m high plume of water from the **Jet-d'Eau;** at any given time (Mar.-Oct.), the world's highest fountain keeps seven tons of water aloft. The nearby **Jardin Anglais** pays homage to Geneva's watch industry with the much-touted **floral clock.**

Farther inland, walk along **Grand-Rue** takes you to the commemorative plaque at #40, birthplace of philosopher Jean-Jacques Rousseau. Check out the stony gazes of Calvin, Cromwell, and company along **Le Mur des Réformatuers,** facing the Promenade des Bastions. Bearded monks shuffle about inside the **Russian Orthodox Church** on rue Toepffer, near the Musée d'Art et d'Histoire (1SFr). And if you have time for just one art museum in Geneva, go to the **Petit-Palais,** terrasse St-Victor 2, off bd. Helvétique, a beautiful mansion full of works by Picasso, Renoir, and Gaugin among others (open M-F 10am-6pm, Sa-Su 10am-5pm; 10SFr, students 5SFr). Take bus 17 to "Petit Palais" or bus 1, 3, or 5 to "Claparède."

A veritable sub-city of organizational headquarters awaits on the *rive droite,* a 15-minute walk from the train station. At the headquarters of the International Red Cross, the excellent **International Red Cross and Red Crescent Museum,** av. de la Paix 17 (bus 8, F, V, or Z to "Appia" or "Ariana"), is *Let's Go's* surprise pick as the best museum in Geneva. The museum reflects on the organization's work with powerful displays and videos (open W-M 10am-5pm; 10SFr, students 5SFr). The rather dull guided tour of the **United Nations** (info tel. 907 45 60), at the end of rue Montbrillant, pales before the constant traffic of international diplomats, brightly clothed in native garb. (Open daily July-Aug. 9am-6pm; Apr.-June and Sept.-Oct. 10am-noon and 2-4pm; Nov.-Mar. M-F 10am-noon and 2-4pm. 8.50SFr, seniors and students 6.50SFr.)

Two **beaches** front the lake: *Genevois* frequent the laid-back **Pâquis Plage** at quai du Mont-Blanc (1SFr), while upscale **Genève Plage** (6SFr) offers a waterslide, volleyball, and an Olympic-size pool.

Pick up *Genève Agenda* at the tourist office to plan your fun. Summer nightlife offerings center on lakeside quais, cafes in **pl. du Bourg-de-Four,** and in the village of **Carouge** (tram 12 to "pl. du Marché"). Befriend a native to find this week's **squat bar,** a moving party that attracts a trendy and artsy crowd. Get funky or get sloshed (beer

Late Night Workouts

Geneva can be an expensive place to party for locals as for tourists, especially now that unemployment is running around 10%. Groups of twenty-somethings have lately taken to moving into vacant buildings where they live communally as squatters. To raise money for electricity and basic expenses, they run **squat bars,** selling some of the cheapest drinks in Geneva. Essentially roving parties, squat bars attract the artsy set and electronic music, jungle, and house fans. They also attract the notice of local authorities after neighbors complain of noise, so most squat bars move around a lot, meaning that in order to find them you have to be in the know. To find the latest, make friends with a native or bartender, or else look for posters on the left bank.

3-5SFr) at **Demi-Lune Café,** rue Etienne Dumot 3, in the *vieille ville*. **Au Chat Noir,** rue Vautier 13, Carouge, has live music nightly (open M-Th 6pm-4am, F 6pm-5am, Sa 9pm-5am, Su 9pm-4am). Put on a clean shirt and be nice to the bouncer to get into **Call My Agency/RDV,** route de St. Julien 7, Carouge, a late night dance club with a mixed gay-straight crowd (open F-Sa 2-5am). In the morning, join a student crowd for breakfast and beer, at **La Clémence,** pl. du Bourg-de-Four 20 (beer 4-8SFr; open M-F 7am-1am, Sa-Su until 2am). **Post Café,** rue de Berne 7, is a tiny bar that draws a huge, largely anglophone crowd (open daily 6:30am-2am).

In July and August, **Cinélac** shows movies on a screen over the lake near Genève Plage. **Free Jazz concerts** take place on Wednesday and Friday nights at 8:30pm at the Théâtre de Verdure in Parc de la Grange. *The* party in Geneva is **L'Escalade,** commemorating the dramatic repulse of the invading Savoyard troops from the city walls. The revelry lasts a full weekend in mid-December. Summer festivals include the biggest celebration of **American Independence Day** outside the U.S., and the **Fêtes de Genève,** an international music and art celebration.

■ Lausanne

The story of Lausanne is really a tale of two cities. The *vieille ville* is cosmopolitan and businesslike; the lakefront at Ouchy is lazy and more than a bit decadent. In its past, this lush Alpine valley was the haunt of literary luminaries such as Dickens, Thackery, and T.S. Eliot (who wrote *The Waste Land* beside Lake Léman). Today Lausanne charms visitors with its natural beauty, unique museums, vibrant nightlife, and magnificent parks.

SIGHTS AND ENTERTAINMENT Although the medieval town center is referred to as the *vieille ville,* the true old city may be found at the waterfront, where archaeological digs have unearthed the 2000-year-old remains of the **Vicus de Lousonna.** To stroll through the foundations of a temple, forum, and many villas, take bus 2 to "Bois de Vaux" and follow the signs for the ruins. Move forward through time to the **Cathédrale,** consecrated in 1275 by Pope Gregory X, by taking bus 16 to "Cathédrale" or by walking up the covered stairs to the top of the hill. Climb the 61m tower for spectacular views of the city, lake, and mountains beyond. (Cathedral open daily July to mid-Sept. 7am-7pm; mid-Sept. to June 7am-5pm. Free guided tours July-Sept. (tel. (021) 323 84 34). Tower open daily 8:30-11:30am and 1:30-5:30pm; 2SFr.) The macabre **Collection de l'Art Brut,** av. Bergières 11 (tel. (021) 647 54 35; bus 2 or 3 to "Jomini"), features chilling works by the criminally insane, the institutionalized, and other "non-artists" (open Tu-Su 11am-1pm and 2-6pm; 6SFr, students and seniors 4SFr). The **Musée Olympique,** quai d'Ouchy 1 (tel. 621 65 11), is a high-tech temple to modern Olympians, with a smaller exhibit on the ancient games. Revisit any moment (on video) in modern Olympic history. (Open May-Sept. M-W and F-Su 10am-7pm, Th until 8pm; Oct.-Apr. Tu-W and F-Su 10am-6pm, Th until 8pm. 14.5SFr, students 95SFr.) Complete your tour of Lausanne with the splendid waterfront and city parks in Ouchy. The **quai de Belgique** and **la Place de la Navigation** are lakeside promenades flanked by flowers, gardens, and fountains; the best beach area is in the **Bellerive Complex.** (Bus 2 to "Bellerive." Open daily mid-May to Aug. 9:30am-dusk. 4.50SFr, students and seniors 3SFr; 0.50SFr discount after 5pm.)

The *vieille ville* springs to life in the first half of July with theater and dance events, most free, during the **Festival de la Cité.** For drinks and entertainment, check out the bar-lined **pl. St-François.** Pulse-pounding dance parties surround the chill-out room at **The Mad,** rte. de Geneve 23. (Cover F-Sa 20SFr before midnight, 25SFr after. Ask a member in line for an invitation and get in free. Open W-Su 11pm-5am; gay night Su.)

PRACTICAL INFO, ACCOMMODATIONS, AND FOOD Frequent **trains** serve Basel (2½hr., 57SFr), Geneva (40min., 19.40SFr), Montreux (20min., 8.40SFr), Zurich (2½hr., 62SFr), and other cities; visit the station at pl. de la Gare 9 (open daily 7am-9pm) or call (021) 157 22 22 for more info. The **tourist office** (tel. (021) 617 73 73;

email information@lausanne-tourisme.ch; http://www.lausanne.tourisme.ch), in the train station, gives out the free *Plan Officiel* (city map and guide to public transport) and the *Welcome to Lausanne* booklet (a wealth of info, including accommodation lists), and makes hotel reservations for 4-6SFr. (Open daily Apr.-Sept. 9am-8pm; Oct.-Mar. 9am-7pm. Similar office in the "Ouchy" metro station.) The office also sells museum passports (26SFr for a 3-day pass; students and seniors 20SFr) which give visitors free entry to all museums, use of public transportation, and admission to one art film at the **Cinémathéque Suisse,** allée E. Ansemat 3 (tel. (021) 331 01 00). A vast, barracks-like but comfortable complex, **Jeunotel,** Chemin du Bois-de-vaux 36 (tel. (021) 626 02 22; fax 626 02 26), is Lausanne's only official youth hostel. Take bus 2 ("Bourdonette") to "Bois-de-Vaux," then cross the street and follow the signs. (Dorms 24-36SFr; singles 50SFr, with shower 73SFr; doubles 72SFr, with shower 88SFR; quads 108SFr. Breakfast 3SFr. MC, V. Reception 24hr. Reservations recommended in summer.) **Hotel "Le Chalet,"** av. d'Ouchy 49 (tel. (021) 616 52 06), has a limited number of rooms in a gardened 19th-century chalet. Take the metro or bus 2 to "Jordils." (Singles 62SFr; doubles 87SFr; smaller rooms 48SFr. Breakfast 8SFr. Reception open daily noon-10:30pm.) To get to the lakeside **Camping de Vidy** (tel. (021) 624 31), take bus 2 to "Bois-de-Vaux," then cross the street and go down the Chemin du Bois-de-Vaux past Jeunotel and underneath the overpass. The reception office is straight across Rte. de Vidy. A restaurant and supermarket are close by. (6.50SFr, students 6SFr; tents 7-11SFr; 1- to 2-person bungalows 54SFr; 3- to 4-person bungalows 86SFr; city tax 1.20SFr per person and 1.40SFr per car. Showers included. Wheelchair access. Reception daily 8am-12:30pm and 5pm-8pm.)

Many Lausanne restaurants are just spectator sports for the budget traveler. Visit produce **markets** Monday and Thursday mornings at bd. de Grancy, Wednesday and Saturday mornings on rue de Bourg behind the Eglise St.-François, Friday mornings at rue du Petit-Chêne off pl. St-François, and Sunday at Ouchy (open Apr. to mid-Oct. 8am-8pm). **Manora,** pl. St-François 17, under the Zürich Bank sign, is a popular self-service restaurant with fantastic salad, fruit, and dessert bars. (*Menus du jour* 7-15SFr. Open M-Sa 7am-10:30pm, Su 9am-10:30pm; hot food served 11am-10pm.) The **Crêperie d'Ouchy,** pl. du Port 7, just outside the Ouchy metro station, serves up crepes by the lake (4-17SFr; open spring 11am-11pm, summer 9am-midnight, fall 11am-8pm, winter 11am-7pm). **Au Couscous,** rue Enning 2, at the top of rue de Bourg, serves fashionable, vegetarian-friendly Maghreb and Tunisian cuisine (14-24SFr; open Su-Th 6pm-1am, F-Sa until 2am).

■ Montreux

Montreux is postcard Switzerland at its swanky, but genteel, best. The crystal-blue water of Lac Léman and the snow-capped Alps are a photographer's dream, and can be seen with breathtaking perfection from **St-Vincent,** the parish church, on rue de Temple. Montreux's 13th-century savoy fortress, **Château de Chillon,** features all the comforts of home—prison cells, a torture chamber, a weapons room—and inspired narratives by Rousseau and Hugo, as well as Lord Byron's *The Prisoner of Chillon.* (Open daily July-Aug. 9am-6pm; Apr.-June and Sept. 9am-5:45pm; Oct. 10am-4:45pm; Nov.-Feb. 10am-noon and 1:30-4pm; Mar. 10am-noon and 1:30-4:45pm. 7SFr, students 5.50SFr.) The main attraction, however, is the world-famous **Montreux Jazz Festival,** one of the biggest parties in Europe, which lasts for 15 days starting the first Friday in July. Contact the tourist office months in advance for info and tickets (26-129SFr). The **booking desk** (tel. (041) 900 55 56 78; http://www.montreuxjazz.com) is open 24hr. The Jazz Boutique opens its info hotline (tel. (021) 963 82 82) in mid-March. The postal address for ticket orders is Grand-Rue 100, CP1325, CH-1820 Montreux. Tickets are also available from Société de Banque Suisse ticket counters, the Swiss National Tourist Offices at 608 Fifth Ave., New York, NY 10020 (tel. (212) 757-5944), and Swiss Court, London W1V 8EE (tel. (0171) 287 81 37). During the festival, **Jazz Off** offers 500 hours of free open-air concerts.

Trains roll frequently into the station on av. des Alpes from Bern (1½hr., 37SFr), Geneva (1hr., 27SFr), and Lausanne (20min., 8.40SFr). Direct trains also go to Aigle, Brig, Martigny, and Sion, and through the mountains of Gstaad. Montreux's **tourist office,** pl. du Débarcadère (tel. (021) 962 84 84; fax 963 78 95; email tourism@montreux.ch; http://www.montreux.ch), sits on the lake. Descend the stairs opposite the train station and head left on Grand-Rue. The office is set back on the right hand side (open daily June-Aug. 9am-7pm; Sept.-May 9am-noon and 1:30-6pm). The best budget option is the **Riviera Lodge,** Pl. du Marché 5 (tel. (021) 923 80 40; fax 923 80 41), 20 minutes by city bus 1 to Vevey (dorms 20SFr; doubles 70SFr; reception 7:30-10am and 4:30-6:30pm). Otherwise, walk along the lake for 20 minutes to the **Auberge de Jeunesse Montreux (HI),** passage de l'Auberge 8 (tel. (021) 963 49 34; fax 969 27 29), or take bus 1 ("Villeneuve") to "Territet" and follow the signs downhill. Despite the rumbling trains above, visitors pack the hostel for its view of the lake, so make reservations. (27SFr first night, then 24.90SFr; doubles 72-80SFr, then 67.80SFr; nonmembers add 5Sfr. Breakfast and sheets included. Reception Apr.-Sept. 7-10am and 4-11pm; Oct.-Mar. 7:30-9:30am and 5-10pm. Check-out 9:30am. Lockout 10am-5pm. Curfew midnight; groups and families can request a key. Wheelchair accessible.) Nearby **Villeneuve** has lakeside camping at **Les Horizons Bleus** (tel. (021) 960 15 47). Take bus 1 to Villeneuve, then walk along the lake to the left (7SFr per person, 4.50-11SFr per tent; tax 1SFr; showers free; reception 8am-10pm).

Lakeside dining is sadly unaffordable. **The White Horse,** 28 Grand Rue, has inexpensive, good food, despite its claim to be an authentic English pub (open M-Sa 11am-1am, Su 3pm-midnight, food served until 11pm). The **Marché de Montreux,** pl. du Marché, is a covered outdoor market (open F 7am-3pm).

From late August to early October, the **Montreux-Vevey Festival International de Musique et d'Art Lyrique** (tickets 15-180SFr) reigns, featuring philharmonics from Moscow to Memphis. Write to the Office of the Classical Music Festival, rue du Théâtre 5, 1st Floor, Case Postale 162, CH-1820 Montreux 2 (tel. (021) 966 80 20; fax 963 25 06). Check out the **Mayfair Cafe,** across from the tourist office, where a young crowd grooves to DJs on weekends (open Su-Th 8am-midnight, F-Sa until 2am). One of the jazz festival venues, **Duke's,** Grand-Rue 97, approximates the festive spirit year-round. (Beer 6-7.50SFr. Open Su-Th until 2am, F-Sa until 4am, during Jazz Festival until 6am. Happy hour 6-10pm.)

■ Near Montreux: Gstaad

Lying at the juncture of four Alpine valleys, Gstaad is in the heart of ski country. But as small Alpine villages go, Gstaad is an anomaly. While its neighbor, Saanen, has a goat for a mascot, Gstaad's emblems are its glitzy five-star hotels and designer boutiques. The main reason to come to Gstaad is for its superlative sports scene, including hard-core **mountain bike** and **hiking** trails (the tourist office has a helpful map and guide) and, most notably, **skiing.** With 250km of runs and 69 lifts, the town generally has something open from mid-December through April. The **Top Card ski pass** (tel. (033) 748 82 82; fax 748 82 60; email ski.gstaad@gstaad.ch; http://www.skigstaad.ch) is 50SFr for one day on all sectors. More limited passes are slightly cheaper.

Gstaad's very friendly, well-organized **tourist office** (tel. (033) 748 81 81, for direct reservations 748 81 84; fax 748 81 83; email tvsl@gstaad.ch; http://www.gstaad.ch) is just past the railway bridge on the main road to the right of the station and publishes a list of budget accommodations. (Open July-Aug. M-F 8:30am-6:30pm, Sa 9am-6pm, Su 2-6pm; Sept.-June M-F 8:30am-noon and 2-6pm, Sa 9am-noon.) The **Jugendherberge** (tel. (033) 744 13 43), 2 mi. away in Saanen, is a godsend. From Gstaad, take the train (every hr., 2.40SFr) or post bus (every hr., 2.40SFr). (Dorms 22.90-25.40SFr; doubles 30.90-33.40SFr. Breakfast, sheets, and showers included. Reception 7-10am and 5-10pm. Closed Nov.-Dec.) **Camping Bellerive** (tel. (033) 744 63 30) rests between Gstaad and Saanen (6.40-7.50SFr, 5.30SFr per tent). Budget diners should take advantage of the **Co-op,** left on the main street from the train station. (Restaurant open M-Th 8am-6:30pm, F 8am-10pm, Sa 8am-4pm, Su 9am-5pm. Supermarket open M-Th 7:30am-6:30pm, F 8am-12:15pm and 1:30-8pm, Sa 8am-4pm, Su 9am-5pm.)

ITALIAN SWITZERLAND (TICINO)

The Italian-speaking canton of Ticino (Tessin, in German and French) is renowned for its refreshing mix of Swiss efficiency and Italian *dolce vita*. Language is not the only thing that sets this region apart from the rest of Switzerland. The white and charred-wood chalets of the Graubünden and Berner Oberland fade away, replaced by jasmine-laced villas and the bright colors of Italian *gelato*. Lush, almost Mediterranean vegetation, emerald lakes, and shaded castles render Ticino's hilly countryside as romantic as its famed resorts, Lugano and Locarno.

■ Lugano

Lugano, Switzerland's third-largest banking center, hides from German Switzerland in the crevassed bay between San Salvatore and Monte Brè. Warmed by a Mediterranean climate, Lugano's shady streets are lined with tiles, climbing vines, and blood-red wildflowers. The leafy frescoes of the 16th-century **Cathedral San Lorenzo,** just below the train station, gleam through centuries of dust. **Basilica Sacro Cuore,** on corso Elevezia, and the **Chiesa Santa Maria degli Angioli,** on P. B. Luini, both feature striking frescoes as well. A variety of museums offers rainy day amusement. The statues from Samoa, Papua-New Guinea, and Africa in the **Museo delle Culture Extraeuropee,** 324 via Cortivo, on the footpath to Gandria in the Villa Helenum, provide a break from the usual paintings and cuckoo clocks (open Mar. 5-Oct. Tu-Su 10am-5pm; 5SFr, students 3SFr). Lugano's waterfront parks are ideal places to spend a few hours. Hiking in the region is supplemented by adrenaline-intensive activities ranging from skiing (full-day 89SFr) to paragliding (150SFr) to "canyoning" down waterfalls (85SFr) to rock-climbing (85SFr), all arranged by **ASBEST Adventure Company,** via Basilea 28, CH-6900 Lugano (tel. (091) 966 11 14; fax 966 12 13).

Trains (tel. (091) 157 22 22) go to Basel (4½hr., 77SFr), Locarno (1hr., 16SFr), Milan (1½hr., 14SFr), and Zurich (3hr., 59SFr). The **tourist office,** 5 riva Albertolli (tel. (091) 921 46 64; fax 922 76 53), has maps and books rooms for a 4SFr fee. (Open Apr.-Oct. M-F 9am-6:30pm, Sa 9am-12:30pm and 1:30-5pm, Su 10am-2pm; Nov.-Mar. M-Sa 9am-12:30pm and 1:30-5pm.) **Hotel Montarina,** 1 via Montarina (tel. (091) 966 72 72), is a converted luxury villa with a swimming pool, natural caverns, and lush jasmine grounds. Walk 200m right from the station, cross the tracks, and walk one minute uphill. (Dorms 20SFr; singles 45-65SFr; doubles 80-120SFr. Reception 9am-8:30pm. Open Mar.-Dec.) **Ostello della Gioventù (HI),** Lugano-Savosa (*not* downtown Lugano), 13 via Cantonale (tel. (091) 966 27 28; fax 928 23 63), is like a villa resort with bunk beds. Take bus 5 to "Crocifisso" (6th stop), then backtrack a bit and go left up via Cantonale. (Dorms 17SFr; singles 32-42SFr; doubles 46-60SFr. Reception 7am-noon and 3-10pm. Curfew 10pm. Open mid-Mar. to Oct.) There are five **campsites** in nearby **Agno.** Take the Ferrovia-Lugano-Ponte-Tresa (FLP) train across the street from the station (all 7.50SFr per person, 4-15SFr per tent; open Apr.-Oct.).

Lugano's many outdoor restaurants and cafes pay homage to the canton's Italian heritage. **La Tinèra,** 2 via dei Gorini, is a low-lit, romantic, underground restaurant with authentic Ticinese ambience (daily specials 10-15SFr; open M-Sa 11am-3pm and 5:30-10pm). **Pestalozzi,** 9 P. Indipendenza, offers vegetarian dishes from 10.50SFr (open M-Sa 11am-9:30pm), while **Ristorante Cantinone,** in P. Cioccaro, does pasta and pizza for 10.50 to 18SFr (open daily 9pm-midnight). Shop at **Migros,** 15 via Pretoria, in the center of town, or around the corner from the hostel. The arcades of the *città vecchia* (old city) come alive at night, and the outdoor cafes of the P. della Riforma are especially vital. The **Pave Pub,** riva Albertolli 1, pours out an English pub atmosphere (beer 4-5SFr; open daily 11am-1am). **Mango Club,** 8 P. Dante, gets spicy with salsa and techno (open daily from 11pm).

■ Locarno

On the shores of Lago Maggiore, Locarno basks in warm near-Mediterranean breezes and bright Italian sun, with luxuriant palm trees replacing the ruggedness of the Alps. Above the city towers the striking church, **Madonna del Sasso** (Madonna of the Rock). The lady of the house, the Madonna, is in the museum next door, as are masterpieces by Ciseri and Raphael. (Grounds open daily Mar.-Oct. 7am-10pm; Nov.-Feb. 7am-9pm. Museum open Apr.-Oct. M-F 2-5pm, Su 10am-noon and 2-5pm. Museum 2.50SFr, students 1.50SFr.) For eleven days in August, the huge **International Film Festival** hits town—check their website (http://www.pardo.ch) for info.

To reach the **tourist office** (tel. (091) 751 03 33), Largo Zorzi, on P. Grande, walk diagonally to the right from the train station, cross via della Stazione, follow this street through the pedestrian walkway, and then cross the street on your left. The office is in the same building as the casino (open mid-Mar. to mid-Oct. M-F 8:30am-7pm, Sa-Su 10am-4pm; mid-Oct. to mid-Mar. M-F 9am-12:30pm and 2-6pm). To reach the new **Palagiovani Youth Hostel (HI),** 18 via Varenna (tel. (091) 756 15 00; fax 756 15 01) from the station, turn left, follow via alla Romogna to P. Grande, cross the square and turn right on via B. Rusca to P.S. Francisco, then take via Varenna to the hostel (HI signs point the way from via B. Rusca on). This former convent now has its own pop music radio station upstairs. (30-42SFr; non-members add 5SFr. Sheets and buffet breakfast included. Kitchen, laundry, and bike rental. Reception 7-10am and 3-11pm.) **Pensione Città Vecchia,** 13 via Toretta (tel./fax (091) 751 45 54), has great prices and location (22SFr; singles 33SFr; reception 8am-9pm; open Mar.-Oct.).

Turkey (Türkiye)

US$1 = 270,700TL (Turkish Lira)	100,000TL = US$0.36
CDN$1 = 180,322TL	100,000TL = CDN$0.55
UK£1 = 446,221 TL	100,000TL = UK£0.22
IR£1 = 382,647TL	100,000TL = IR£0.26
AUS$1 = 166,277TL	100,000TL = AUS$0.60
NZ$1 = 139,694TL	100,000TL = NZ$0.72
SAR1 = 43,275TL	100,000TL = SAR2.30
Country Code: 90	International Dialing Prefix: 00

> Exchange rates were calculated during the summer of 1998. Inflation can be as high as 100%, and thus these rates can change dramatically. Prices are listed in U.S. dollars for consistency, though these are likely to fluctuate somewhat.

Merely 77 years old, The Turkish Republic is an infant in a world of long-standing democracies. Falling somewhere outside of the European nation-state model and existing as an alienated outsider in the Middle East, Turkey is an anomaly in both Europe and Asia. A lengthy laundry list of civilizations has left inestimable physical and cultural imprints on this country whose infinite complexity is both its virtue and its burden. For the traveler, Turkey offers a fabulously rich artistic, cultural, and natural reservoir to explore.

Following the creation of the Eastern Roman Empire in Byzantium (renamed "Constantinople"), Asia Minor became the center of Greek Orthodox Christian culture, an empire stretching from the Balkans through Greece to the Levant and Egypt. The Selçuk Turks held sway from the 11th to the 14th centuries. The Ottomans ruled their vast empire of Turkey (and parts of the Eastern Mediterranean) from the early 1400s to the end of World War I. Centuries of intrigue and European power play culminated in disastrous military defeats of the late 19th century, wherein the Ottomans lost the majority of their territory. Modern Turkey's existence is due to early 20th-century leader Mustafa Kemal (Atatürk), who expelled foreign armies. Equating modernization with Westernization, Atatürk abolished the Ottoman Caliphate, romanized the alphabet, outlawed Muslim tribunals, and set up a democratic government.

Today, Turkey's major cities and its western coast exhibit a cosmopolitan, secular, and Westernized character, while in more remote areas to the north and east, traditional Islamic customs and attitudes prevail. In the late 1970s, democracy began to falter as street warfare erupted in Istanbul, and Turkey began its period of occupation in North Cyprus. In early 1995, Turkey was conditionally accepted into the European Customs Union, but some of the conditions have still not been met. Meanwhile, Turkey has sought economic opportunity in the East with Muslim former Soviet republics. In June 1996 Tansu Çiller formed a coalition government with Necmettin Erbakan, the Fundamentalist Islam leader of the Welfare Party, but Erbakan resigned in 1997, and was officially barred from all political activity in early 1998. Questions about whether Turkey will continue on its secular course remain at the forefront of the European consciousness.

For a true Turkish delight, consult the all-new, first ever, *Let's Go Turkey 1999*.

GETTING THERE

Turkish entrance visas must be purchased at all Turkish ports by Americans (US$45), British (£10), Irish (IR£15), and other internationals. **Bus** travel is one of the cheapest methods of getting to Turkey. **Eurolines,** 4 Cardiff Rd., Luton LU1 1PP (tel. (01582) 40 45 11), in the U.K., operates buses to Turkey. Although **trains** link Turkey to major cities (such as Athens and Vienna) in other European countries, they are not the most convenient way to travel: **Eurail** is *not* valid in Turkey, and the Turkish rail system is very antiquated and inefficient. Always ask for a top bunk and wrap your luggage straps around your limbs when you sleep.

Ferries travel between Turkey and Greece, North Cyprus, Italy, southern France, and Israel. Reservations are recommended for many **ferries,** which run on irregular schedules. If you come into Turkey by boat, expect to pay a US$11 Turkish port tax. Most countries also charge a port tax for exit (from Greece: US$17). Check in at least two hours in advance. Bring toilet paper, motion sickness medication, and food. From Çeşme, an **Ertürk** ferry offers service to Chios, Greece (45min., May-June 3-4 per week; July-Apr. 1 per week). Prices are US$25 one-way, same-day return US$30, open round-trip US$35. Ferries also run from Kuşadası to Samos (5hr., daily 8am and 5pm, US$25) and from Rhodes to Marmaris (one-way 10,000dr, round-trip 12,000dr), Limassol, Cyprus (17hr., 2 per week, 18,500-22,000dr), and Haifa, Israel (36hr., 2 per week, 28,500-33,000dr). Limassol and Haifa services give student and youth discounts of 20%. **Hydrofoils** (Flying Dolphins) run more frequently than ferries, at twice the speed, but cost twice as much. If you have **flown** to Greece on a European charter flight, you cannot travel to Turkey.

GETTING AROUND

All road travel within Turkey is considered risky. Deaths per vehicle kilometer are much higher in Turkey than elsewhere in Europe. However, frequent and cheap buses run between all sizeable cities, and are generally the most convenient mode of transportation. In the interest of safety, you should always opt for the most expensive buses, which tend to be newer, better-maintained, and have well-paid, well-rested drivers.

Many bus lines provide a 10% ISIC discount to students who ask. These more expensive companies usually offer pleasant amenities including larger seats, air-conditioning, a toilet, and tea. Reputable companies include **Varan Tours, Nevtur, Ulusoy, Kamıl Koç, Pamukkale,** and **Çanakkale Seyahat.** The trade-off for inexpensive **trains** (10% student discount) is the long rides. **Shared taxis,** known as *dolmuş,* usually vans, fill gaps left by the bus system and follow fixed routes. They are almost as cheap as buses and leave whenever they fill up (*dolmuş* means "stuffed"). You can get on and off *dolmuş* whenever you like. Those who **hitchhike** generally pay half what the trip would cost by bus. The hitching signal is a waving hand, but *Let's Go* urges you to consider the safety risks. The reputable **Turkish Airlines** has direct flights once or twice weekly from Istanbul to Trabzon, Van, Diyarbakır, Erzurum, Izmir, and Ankara, among other places. Domestic flights average US$80 one-way, but passengers 12 to 24 years old may receive a discount. **Ferries** do not serve the west coast, but a **Turkish Maritime Lines** cruise ship sails from Istanbul to Izmir (21hr., 1 per week).

ESSENTIALS

Turkish government **tourist offices** and tourist police exist in most major cities and resort areas. Some English, German, or French is usually spoken. They help find accommodations and often provide the usual slew of services without charge. In places without an official office, travel agents often serve the same function.

ATM cards provide the best exchange rates and are useful in major cities, particularly if your home bank's system is compatible with Cirrus or Plus. Currency exchange offices are common in most areas, and banks can provide exchange services as well. Find out about the surcharge beforehand; some banks charge high rates, and it is best to exchange larger sums to minimize additional fees. Persistent haggling in shops, over accommodations, and over some transportation fares can save you money. Examine what you buy at bazaars carefully; exporting antiques is a jailable offense, even if you play ignorant. If you're caught doing drugs in Turkey, you're screwed. Horror stories of lengthy prison sentences and dealer-informers are true; embassies are utterly helpless in all cases. Turkish law also provides for "guilt by association"—those in the company of a person caught are subject to prosecution.

Everything closes on the national **holidays:** January 1, January 29 to February 1, April 7 to 10, April 23, May 1, August 30, and October 29. During Ramadan (*Ramazan* in Turkish; starting Dec. 19 in 1998, Dec. 10 in 1999, and Nov. 28 in 2000), a one-month fasting period, pious Muslims abstain from eating, drinking, smoking, or sex between dawn and sunset. Businesses may have shorter hours, few restaurants are open at that time, and public eating is inappropriate. There are many hotel vacancies during this period. Large celebrations mark Ramadan's conclusion; at that time bus and train tickets and hotel rooms may be scarce. During *Kurban Bayramı* (the Festival of Sacrifice; March 28 in 1999), similar disruption occurs.

Museums and archaeological sites in Turkey are open Tuesday through Sunday 9am to 5pm. At all state-run museums, students with **ISICs** receive 50% off. Entrance to many museums is free with a **GO25** (FIYTO) youth card. Bank, post office, and Tourist office hours are usually 8:30am to 12:30pm and 1:30 to 5:30pm.

COMMUNICATION Turkey's **post offices (PTTs)** are typically open from 8:30am to 12:30pm and 1:30 to 5:30pm; offices in resort towns and central post offices in larger towns keep longer hours. Address *Poste Restante (Postrestant)* to the *Merkez Postanesi* (Central Post Office) in the destination city. Make sure to include the postal code. Turkey has a surprisingly good phone system, and all but the smallest village is accessible by phone. All area codes have three digits and all phone numbers have seven. Make international calls at post offices, or buy a phone card *(telekart)*. Phone cards are easy and convenient in most of the country, and are available at kiosks in denominations of 30, 60, and 100 units. New phones accept *telekart*, while old ones require tokens *(jeton)*. Card phones have directions in English, Turkish, German, and French. For **directory assistance** in Turkey, dial 118. For operator assistance dial 131, and for an **international operator,** dial 115. To make a **collect call,** contact an operator in the destination country. To make a calling card call, dial the access number for your company. Callers to the U.S. can dial 00 800 122 77 for an **AT&T Direct** operator. For **MCI World Phone,** dial 00 800 111 77; for **Sprint Access,** dial 00 800 144 77. To call **Canada Direct,** dial 00 800 16 67 77; **BT Direct,** 00 800 44 11 77; **Ireland Direct,** 00 800 353 11 77; **Australia Direct,** 00 800 61 11 77. Pay phones usually terminate calling card calls after three minutes.

It's rarely hard to find English-speakers in well-touristed areas. Off the beaten track, sign language and a pocket dictionary usually suffice. Remember that in Turkey a raise of the chin, sometimes accompanied by a clicking noise made with the tongue, means "no"; waving a hand up and down at you, palm toward the ground, means "come," not "good-bye." The habit of snapping the fingers of one hand and then slapping the top of the other fist is considered obscene

TURKEY

Yes/No	*Evet/Hayır*	EH-vet/HIGH-yuhr
Hello	*Merhaba*	MEHR-hah-bah
Please	*Lütfen*	LEWT-fen
Thank you	*Teşekkürler*	teh-shehk-keur-LEHR
Pardon me	*Affedersiniz*	ahf-feh-DEHR-see-neez
Do you speak English?	*İngilizce biliyor musunuz?*	EEN-ghee-leez-jeh bee-lee-YOHR-moo-soo-nooz
I don't speak Turkish.	*Türkçe bilmiyorum.*	TEWRK-cheh BEEHL-mee-yohr-oom
Where is…?	*…nerede?*	NEHR-eh-deh
Help!	*İmdat!*	EEEm-Daht!

HEALTH, SAFETY, AND CLIMATE Toiletries are cheap and readily available in Turkey, although tampons may be difficult to find. Always carry toilet paper; expect to encounter quite a number of pit toilets. The most significant health concerns in Turkey are parasites and other gastro-intestinal ailments. You should never drink unbottled water that you have not purified yourself—the risk of contracting diarrhea or other diseases is high. Also avoid the untreated water in uncooked fruits and vegetables and ice cubes. Stay away from ground beef, any sort of uncooked meat including raw shellfish, unpasteurized milk, and sauces containing raw eggs. In the event that you get diarrhea or food poisoning, see **On-the-Road Ailments**, p. 21. Dial 112 for **emergency medical service.** There are rumors that the Cukorova/Amikova area of southeastern Anatolia occasionally produces cases of malaria. For safety reasons, *Let's Go* does not recommend travel to the affected regions, but if you go, start a course of anti-malaria pills early.

Before setting out for southeastern Turkey, become fully informed on the latest developments and travel advisories. Though beautiful and fascinating, most of the area is under martial law, and while many cities present only moderate danger to foreign travelers, those areas engaged in ongoing conflict should be avoided. Access to Mt. Ararat is officially prohibited, and *Let's Go* does not recommend travel to **Diyarbakır** or **Batman** due to Kurd-related violence. Throughout eastern Anatolia, stay in main urban areas, avoiding the surrounding hills, and be sure not to travel at night since most roads close before sunset.

Women traveling in Turkey may have a less pleasant experience than men. In sparsely touristed areas, women should dress conservatively. Always wear a bra and avoid short shorts and tank tops; in the east, wear long skirts and sleeves, even a head scarf. If you feel threatened, visible and audible anger—particularly in public—can be a deterrent. Holler "eem-DAHT" (help) if the situation gets out of hand. The **emergency police number** is 155. Invest in secure accommodations, especially ones with the word *"aile"* (family-style) in their names. Your best bet is to not travel alone.

Climate in Turkey varies substantially. The Mediterranean and Aegean coasts are known for being extremely hot and dry during July and August; in central and eastern Anatolia, winter cold and summer heat are severe. Coastal regions are generally most pleasant and least crowded in the spring and autumn. The Black Sea Coast, moderate almost all year, contains areas where rain falls 200 days per year.

ACCOMMODATIONS, CAMPING, AND FOOD A night's budget accommodation averages US$5-8. Make sure your hotel has water before paying; when traveling in winter, check for heating. Don't expect toilet paper or towels in low-budget hotels. Most Turkish towns have a *hamam,* or bathhouse, where you can get a steam bath for US$3. *Hamamlar* schedule different times for men and women. It is not wise for women traveling alone to visit the *hamam.* **Camping** is popular in Turkey, and cheap campgrounds abound (around US$2 per person), although many official ones still aren't registered with the Ministry of Culture and Tourism. Official government campsites are open from April or May to October.

Turkish cuisine is rich and varied. Meat is generally emphasized, though vegetarian options are available; ask if you have specific needs. Certain staple items like *çoban salatası* (shepherd's salad), *mercimek çorbası* (lentil soup), rice pilaf, and *yoğurt* are not listed on *lokanta* (restaurant) menus; their availability is understood. You can't usually bargain in restaurants unless you order fish. Tourists who prefer water to soft drinks at meals should buy bottled spring water cheaply at a corner grocery store and bring it along. *Kebap,* the most famous of Turkish dishes, means any food broiled or roasted in small pieces. Usually involving lamb or chicken, *kebap* cooking ranges from skewer (*şiş*) or spit (*döner*) broiling to oven roasting. After *kebap,* the most popular food served are the medallion-sized, spiced meatballs (*köfte*). *Et* is the generic word for meat: lamb is *kuzu,* veal *dana eti.* Chicken, usually known as *tavuk,* becomes *piliç* when roasted. Over 8333km of coastline inspire Turks to cook *kılıç* (swordfish), *kalkan* (turbot), *hamsi* (anchovies), *kalamar* (squid), *karides* (shrimp), and *midye* (mussels). **Vegetarians** often choose to subsist on Turkey's wide variety of *meze* (appetizers). *İmambayıldı,* a cold concoction of split eggplant, tomatoes, onions, and olive oil, literally means "the priest fainted" (from its delicious taste). One cannot talk about Turkish food without mentioning *dolma*—yes, stuffed, like the taxis. *Dolma* can consist of peppers, grape leaves, or eggplant stuffed with rice, served hot or cold, with or without meat. Turkish **tea** (*çay*) is served hot, with sugar. Specify a level of sweetness for your *kahve* (coffee): *sade* (unsweetened), *orta* (medium-sweet), or *şekerli* (sweet). Ice-cold *rakı,* an aniseed liquor tasting like licorice, is Turkey's **national drink.** Customarily mixed in equal parts with water, which clouds it, *rakı* has acquired the name "lion's milk." There's an endless array of **sweet things**—*baklava,* a flaky pastry jammed with nuts and soaked in honey; *kadayıf,* a shredded-wheat dough filled with nuts and sugar; and *helva,* a crumbly sesame and honey loaf. Of course, there's always the delicious Turkish Delight (*lokum*) and Turkish marzipan (*acıbadem kurabiyesi*).

■ Istanbul

Straddling two continents and almost three millennia of history, Istanbul exists on an incomprehensible scale. Having withstood innumerable demographic shifts, devastating wars, natural disasters, and foreign occupations, the city is naturally comprised of a bizarre mix of civilizations, a composition evident not only in architecture and religious practice, but in customs and cultural quirks as well. In the 1001 dramas of contrast and complement, black-veiled women link arms with their scantily clad daughters on the city's tiny, winding streets, and Istanbul's noveau riche wear Harley Davidson boots to parade through dusty markets filled with street merchants and peddlers selling gold, spices, and aphrodisiacs. A perennial port city, Istanbul is unselfconsciously international, a sprawling behemoth whose multi-dimensional sections encompass travelers from West and East.

ORIENTATION AND PRACTICAL INFORMATION

Waterways divide Istanbul into three sections. The **Bosphorus Strait** (Boğaziçi) separates Asia from Europe. The Turks call the western, European side of Istanbul **Avrupa** and the eastern, Asian side **Asya.** Most of the historical sites, markets, mosques, and museums are located in the area south of the **Golden Horn** known as **Haliç.** The main boulevard—leading west from **Sultanahmet** towards the university, the Grand Bazaar, and Aksaray—changes names from Divan Yolu to Ordu Caddesi as it heads toward Aksaray.

Budget travelers converge in **Sultanahmet,** the area around the Aya Sofia mosque. From airport, catch Havaş bus to Aksaray, then catch an "Eminönü"-bound tram to Sultanahmet; alternatively, split a cab with three friends (about US$3 per person). To reach **Taksim Square** from Sultanahmet, take bus 61b from Beyazit to Taksim; or take the tram ("Zeytiuburnu") to Yusutpaşa, go up onto the overpass, head left, and catch a Taksim-bound bus from the stop at the bottom. To reach **Eminönü** from Sultanahmet, tram it to the end of the line, or walk (20min.) along the tram line.

TURKEY

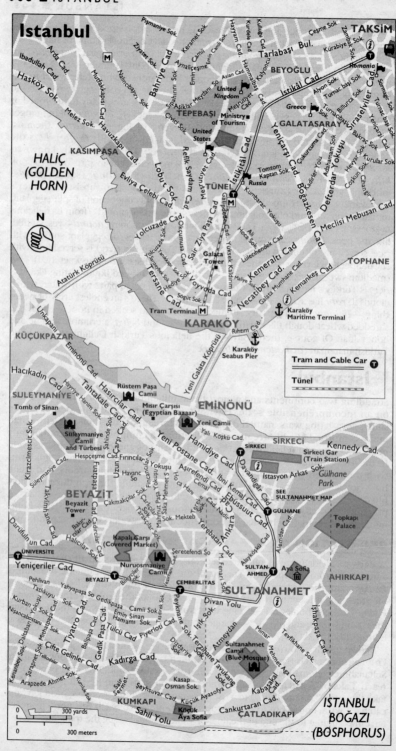

Istanbul

TURKEY

HALİÇ (GOLDEN HORN)

N

TAKSİM

BEYOĞLU

TEPEBAŞI

KASIMPAŞA

United Kingdom

Ministry of Tourism

United States

GALATASARAY

Greece

Russia

TÜNEL

Galata Tower

Romania

TOPHANE

Atatürk Köprüsü

Tram Terminal

KARAKÖY

Karaköy Maritime Terminal

Karaköy Seabus Pier

KÜÇÜKPAZAR

Tram and Cable Car **T**

Tünel

SÜLEYMANİYE

Tomb of Sinan

Rüstem Paşa Camii

Mısır Çarşısı (Egyptian Bazaar)

Yeni Camii

EMİNÖNÜ

SİRKECİ

Süleymaniye Camii and Türbesi

Kennedy Cad.

Sirkeci Gar (Train Station)

GÜLHANE

Gülhane Park

SEE SULTANAHMET MAP

BEYAZIT

Beyazit Tower

Topkapı Palace

Kapalı Çarşı (Covered Market)

Nuruosmaniye Camii

ÜNİVERSİTE

Yeniçeriler Cad.

BEYAZIT

ÇEMBERLİTAS

SULTANAHMET

Aya Sofia

AHIRKAPI

Divan Yolu

Sultanahmet Camii (Blue Mosque)

KUMKAPI

Küçük Aya Sofia

ÇATLADIKAPI

0   300 yards

0   300 meters

İSTANBUL BOĞAZI (BOSPHORUS)

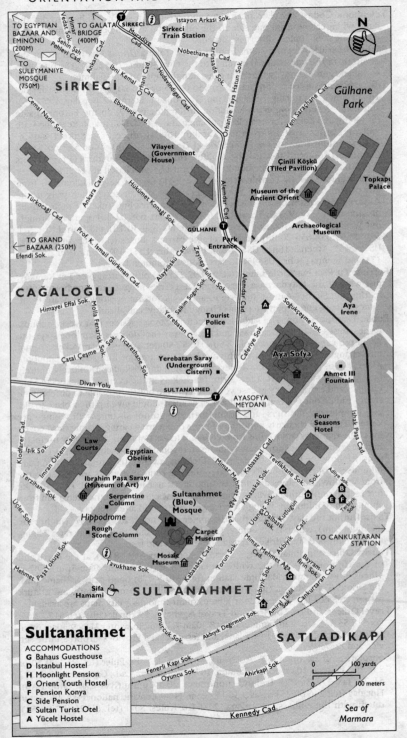

TO EGYPTIAN BAZAAR AND EMINÖNÜ (200M)

TO GALATA BRIDGE (400M)

TO SULEYMANIYE MOSQUE (750M)

SİRKECİ

Istayon Arkası Sok.

SİRKECİ
Sirkeci Train Station

Nöbethane Cad.

Vilayet (Government House)

Gülhane Park

Çinili Köşkü (Tiled Pavilion)

Museum of the Ancient Orient

Topkapı Palace

Archaeological Museum

TO GRAND BAZAAR (250M)

GÜLHANE
Park Entrance

CAĞALOĞLU

Tourist Police

Yerebatan Saray (Underground Cistern)

Aya İrene

Aya Sofya

Ahmet III Fountain

Divan Yolu

SULTANAHMED

AYASOFYA MEYDANI

Four Seasons Hotel

Law Courts

Egyptian Obelisk

İbrahim Paşa Sarayı (Museum of Art)

Serpentine Column

Hippodrome

Rough Stone Column

Sultanahmet (Blue) Mosque

Carpet Museum

Mosaic Museum

TO CANKURTARAN STATION

Şifa Hamamı

SULTANAHMET

SATLADIKAPI

Sultanahmet

ACCOMMODATIONS
- **G** Bahaus Guesthouse
- **D** Istanbul Hostel
- **H** Moonlight Pension
- **B** Orient Youth Hostel
- **F** Pension Konya
- **C** Side Pension
- **E** Sultan Turist Otel
- **A** Yücelt Hostel

Kennedy Cad.

Sea of Marmara

0   100 yards
0   100 meters

TURKEY

Telephone Codes: 212 (European side) and 216 (Asian side); you have to dial the code when calling from one side to the other. The listings below assume a (212) telephone code, unless otherwise noted.

Flights: Atatürk Airport, 30km from the city. Take a *Havaş* bus from either the domestic or the international terminal to the city (30min., US$2.50). The bus stops at Şişhane and Aksaray, where you can catch the tram to Sultanahmet.

Trains: Haydarpaşa Station (tel. (216) 336 04 75 or 336 20 63), on the Asian side. Ticket office open daily 7:30am-11pm. To: Ankara, Edirne (2 per day, US$2.75), and İzmir. A ferry connects the station to Karaköy pier 7, on the European side (50¢). Buy rail tickets for Anatolia in advance at the **TCDD** (Turkish Republic State Railway) office upstairs from the Karaköy tourist office or at Sirkeci station. Europe-bound trains leave from **Sirkeci Gar** (tel. 527 00 50 or 527 00 51) in Eminönü (downhill toward the Golden Horn from Sultanahmet) for Athens (US$70) and Vienna. Europe-bound tickets must be purchased at the Sirkeci Gar.

Buses: Esenler Otobüs Terminal (tel. 658 00 36) in Esenler, several kilometers from downtown. Take the tram to **Yusufpaşa** (1 stop past Aksaray), then walk to the **Aksaray Metro station,** on the broad Adnan Menderes Bul. Take the metro to the *otogar* stop (35¢). **Varan Tours** (tel. 658 02 77; fax 658 02 80) operates throughout Western Europe. **Ulusoy** (tel. 658 30 00; fax 658 30 10) and **Kamıl Koç** (tel. 658 20 00; fax 658 20 08) are also reliable carriers. Buses leave for Ankara (6hr., US$12-15), Athens (16hr., US$24-27), Bursa (4hr., US$8-10), İzmir (9hr., US$14-17), and Vienna (36hr., US$95). Reservations recommended.

Ferries: Turkish Maritime Lines (tel. 249 92 22) has offices near pier 7 at Karaköy, just west of the **Haydarpaşa** ferry terminal. Ferries leave from Sarayburnu; after exiting the Sirkeci station, turn right, and walk for 5min. along the waterfront. Times, prices, and departure points change regularly; call ahead.

Public Transportation: The **Akbil** is an electronic ticket system that works on most ferries, buses, trams, all seabuses, and the subway (not *dolmuş*). For long stays, the **Akbil tab** can give discounts of 15-50% (US$2.50 deposit). Regular tickets are not interchangeable. It's best to catch your **bus** from a major hub such as Eminönü, Aksaray (Yosuf Paşa tram stop), Beyazit, Taksim, and Üsküdar. Don't rely entirely on Akbil—be sure to have a few spare bus tickets in the event of unexpected bus changes and extra money in case you take a private bus (impossible to differentiate from a public one). When riding the bus, women should give up their place to elderly people and mothers, and young men should not sit unless all women are seated. This is particularly important if the women are wearing Islamic head coverings. The **tramvay** (tram) runs from Eminönü to Zeytinburnu, and is very useful for finding your way back to Sultanahmet, even if you don't actually take it, as you can simply follow the tracks (30¢ per ride). **Dolmuş,** a venerated Turkish tradition, are minibuses that run along a fixed local route. The route endpoints are posted in the front window, but stops are neither announced nor fully executed. *Dolmuş,* like ferries, run only during daylight hours, while buses, trams, and the metro run from about 5pm to midnight, though service gets pretty thin after sunset.

Taxis: During the day, be sure that the meter does not read *"geceleri"* (night rate, midnight-8am), which is 50% more. One light on the meter means day rate; 2 lights means night rate. Taxi drivers tend to be reckless and fast.

Tourist Offices: In Sultanahmet, 3 Divan Yolu (tel./fax 518 18 02), at the north end of the Hippodrome, in the white metal cubicle (open daily 9am-5pm). Other offices in the Karaköy Maritime Station (tel. 249 57 76; open daily 8:30am-5pm), the Sirkeci Train Station (tel. 511 58 88; open daily 8:30am-5:30pm), and Atatürk Airport (tel. 663 07 93; open 24hr.). Free country and poor city maps are available.

Travel Offices: Indigo Tourism and Travel Agency, 24 Akbıyık Cad. (tel. 517 72 66; fax 518 53 33). Open in summer daily 8:30am-7:30pm; in winter M-Sa 9:30am-6pm. Sells GO25 cards (US$5), bus, plane, and ferry tickets. Provides airport shuttle service and *Poste Restante.*

Consulates: All are open M-F. **Australia,** 58 Tepecik Yolu, Etiler (tel. 257 70 50 or 257 70 51); visas 10am-noon. **Canada,** 107/3 Büyükdere Cad., Gayrettepe (tel. 272 51 74; fax 272 34 27). **Ireland** (honorary), 26-a Cumhuriyet Cad., Mobil Altı, Elmadağ (tel. 246 60 25); visas 9:30-11:30am. **New Zealand** nationals should get in touch with the embassy in Ankara, 24/1 Kız Kulesi Sok. (tel. (312) 467 90 54).

South Africa, 106 Büyükdere Cad., Esentepe (tel. 275 47 93; fax 288 25 04); visas 9am-noon. **U.K.,** 34 Meşrutiyet Cad., Beyoğlu/Tepebaşı (tel. 293 75 40; fax 245 49 89); visas 8:30am-noon. **U.S.,** 104-108 Meşrutiyet Cad., Tepebaşı (tel. 251 36 02; fax 251 32 18); visas 8:30-11am.

Currency exchange: Most banks don't charge a commission; currency exchange counters open M-F 8:30am-noon and 1:30-5pm. **ATMs** are scattered over the city.

American Express: Türk Express, 91 Cumhuriyet Cad., 2nd fl. (tel. 230 15 15), uphill from Taksim Sq. Handles lost checks and cards as well as other related business, including *Poste Restante*, but does not give cash advances or accept wired money—Turkish law requires it be done through a bank. Open M-F 9am-6pm.

International Bookstores: International Press Büfe, 91 İstiklâl Cad., offers international printed media at low prices.

Laundromats: Star Laundry, 18 Akbıyık Cad. (tel. 638 23 02), below Star Pension in Sultanahmet. Wash and dry US$1.25 per kg., 2kg min. Open daily 8am-10pm.

Emergency: dial 155 from any phone.

Tourist Police: In Sultanahmet, at the beginning of Yerebatan Cad. **24-hour hotline,** tel. 527 45 03 or 528 53 69; fax 512 76 76.

Hospitals: The **German Hospital,** 119 Sıraselviler Cad., Taksim (tel. 293 21 50), hosts a multilingual staff and is convenient for Sultanahmet hostelers.

Post Offices: The most convenient PTT office to Sultanahmet is the booth opposite the entrance to Aya Sofia. **Main branch** in Sirkeci, 25 Büyük Postane Sok. Stamp and currency exchange services open 8:30am-7pm. 24hr. phones. **Sirkeci postal code:** 5270050 and 5270051.

Telephones: Card phones are the most convenient. Cards have 30, 60, or 100 *kontür* (credits). One credit lasts 2-10 seconds during international calls.

ACCOMMODATIONS AND CAMPING

Istanbul's budget accommodations are concentrated in the **Sultanahmet** district, just steps away from the city's most awe-inspiring sights; the listings below concentrate on that area. Hotels in **Lâleli** are the center of prostitution in Istanbul and should be avoided. Rates rise by 20% in July and August.

Orient Youth Hostel, 13 Akbıyık Cad. (tel. 517 94 93; fax 518 38 94), near Topkapı Palace. It's always happy hour at this friendly backpacker magnet; from 8-10pm the bar hosts Turkey's biggest Australian invasion since Gallipoli. Email access, cable TVs, luggage storage, and 24hr. hot water. Bring toilet paper. Dorms US$7; doubles US$16; quads US$36; outside (only when full) US$3. Breakfast included.

Sultan Turist Otel, 3 Terbıyık Sok. (tel. 516 92 60; fax 517 16 26), Fez Travel Office at entrance. Around the corner from the Orient Hostel. Immaculate rooms. Great views from the roof restaurant/bar; happy hour 5-8pm (beer US$1.50). Safe-deposit and laundry services. Dorms US$7; singles US$15; doubles US$20; triples US$24.

Yücelt Hostel, 6/1 Caferiye Cad. (tel. 513 61 50 or 513 61 51; fax 512 76 28). Rundown facilities and non-competitive prices but social atmosphere. The lucky may find hot water. Luggage storage. Transport to airport through in-house travel agency (US$5). Dorms US$7; singles US$13; doubles US$20; triples US$18; outside (only when full) US$4. Breakfast US$1. 10% discount for *Let's Go* readers.

Moonlight Pension, Akbıyık Cad. 87 (tel. 517 54 29 or 518 85 36; fax 516 24 80). Good, clean rooms, and an extremely kind, helpful staff. Nice rooftop views, bar, and communal kitchen with 24hr. free *çay.* Dorms US$7; doubles US$20.

Istanbul Hostel, 35 Kutlu Gün Sok. (tel. 516 93 86; fax 516 93 84), right down the hill from the Four Seasons Hotel. Recently opened with immaculate rooms. Hot water morning and night. Happy hour 6:30-9:30pm. Dorms US$8; singles US$25.

Pension Konya (tel. 517 36 77), right across from Poem Guesthouse on Tevbıyık Sok. The cheapest place in Sultanahmet, bar none. Singles US$5; doubles US$7.

Cordial House, 29 Peykhane Sok., Divan Yolu (tel. 518 05 76; fax 516 41 08; email cordial@dominet.in.com.tr). Combination hotel/hostel in nearby Çemberlitaş. Dorms US$6-8; singles US$20; doubles US$24; triples US$36.

Side Pension/Hotel Side, 20 Utangaç Sok. (tel./fax 517 65 90), near the entrance of the Four Seasons hotel. 24hr. hot water. Pension singles US$20; doubles US$25; triples US$35. Hotel singles US$35; doubles US$45; triples US$55.

Bahaus Guesthouse, 11 Bayram Fırını Sok., Akbıyık Cad. (tel. 517 66 97; fax 517 66 97). Terrace view of the Bosphorus. Singles US$15; doubles US$25-30; triples US$35-40; basement US$5. Breakfast included. 10% discount for *Let's Go* readers.

Camping: Londra Camping (tel. 560 4200), on Londra Asfaltı Süt Sanayi Karşısı, 1km from the airport, along a noisy highway. No bus stop; take a taxi. Includes cafeteria, bar, and showers. US$3 per person, US$2 per tent; bungalows US$14.

FOOD

Istanbul's restaurants, like the city's clubs and bars, all stick by the golden rule that if it's well advertised or easy to find, it's not worth doing. Much better meals can be had on İstiklâl Cad. and around **Taksim** than in the touristy Sultanahmet. To get to İstiklâl Cad. from Sultanahmet, follow the tram lines to Sirkeci, take a left, and follow the water, crossing the Galata Bridge and taking a left onto the first major thoroughfare; the Tünel station will be on your immediate right. The Tünel mini-metro will take you to İstiklâl Cad. (20¢), or you can take the 15-minute walk, an good idea if you plan to explore Taksim's nightlife later on.

Another important and lamentably overlooked area of the city's cuisine is food sold by **street vendors.** The ubiquitous, sesame-sprinkled **simit** (rings) are bread rings with crispy crusts and soft insides. Baked, flame-broiled, or boiled corn on the cob is pretty universal. **Vişne suyu** (sour cherry juice) is sold by vendors in Ottoman costume, with big steel teapots on their backs. Great **leblebi** (roasted and salted chickpeas) costs 20-30¢ per serving. **Dondurma** (Turkish ice cream) stands are all over the place. A large and fresh selection of produce can be found in the city's various **open-air markets,** the best being the daily one in Beşiktaş, near Barbaros Cad.

Dârüzziyâfe, behind the Sultanahmet Camii on the Hippodrome. The mellow atmosphere and attentive service compensate for the plethora of tour groups. The *Süleymaniye Çorbası* (meat and veggie soup; US$1.75) is a must. Meals US$12-15. Open noon-11pm. Sister restaurant at 6 Şifahane Cad. in the Süleymaniye Mosque.

Afacan, İstiklâl Cad. 2 locations, one at the top end by the movie theater and the other past the Galatasaray Lisesi at the other end. Seriously good stuff. Bottom restaurant open 8am-11pm; top open 10am-midnight.

House of Medusa Restaurant, Yerebatan Cad. 19 Muhteremefendi Sok., on a cross street off Divan Yolu. Excellent Turkish cuisine in the 1st fl. garden (open in summer), the 3rd fl. divan area, and a 4th fl. bar. Open daily 8am-midnight.

Bereket, on İstiklâl Cad. heading downhill, is on the left before the Galatasaray Lisesi. Not to be confused with Bereket Halk Döner. Open 9am-11:30pm.

Doy-Doy, 13 Şifa Hamamı Sok. Easily the best and cheapest of Sultanahmet's cheap eats. Tasty *kebap*s and salads (US$3.50 and under). Open 8:30am-late.

Şampiyon, Balık Pazarı. Believed throughout Turkey to prepare the best *kokoreç* in the country. Tripe is grilled, then cooked with spices and tomatoes. Try the *çeyrek ekmek kokoreç,* which is the smallest portion (US$1.50). Open 8:30am-midnight.

Cumhuriyet Meyhanesi, at the far end of the fish market. At night, Turkey's intelligensia discusses politics and culture here. Open daily 10am-1am, possibly later.

Med Cezir, 16 Tevkifhane Sok., across from the Four Seasons Hotel. Big Turkish breakfasts (US$3-4), and a pleasant cafe at night. Open 8:30am-midnight.

Pudding Shop, 6 Divan Yolu, was a major pitstop on the Hippie Trail to the Far and Middle East in 1970s. The *creme caramel* and *keşkül* (vanilla pudding) are sure to please, each for US$1. The cappuccino rocks at only US$1.

SIGHTS

IN SULTANAHMET For over 1500 years, the **Aya Sofia** has endured as Istanbul's most embattled landmark, having suffered such hardships as the cruelty of gravity, attacks of vicious crusaders, and a second-rate repainting just 10 years ago. *(Museum open Tu-Su 9:30am-4:30pm, gallery open Tu-Su 9:30-11:30am and 1-4pm. US$3.30, students US$1.30.)* Intended to cement Justinian's Imperial authority and to regain civic control, the church was designed and built by the mathematicians Anthemius of Tralles and Isodorus of Miletus. After five years of construction, the exterior of the church was painted blood red to serve as an unambiguous warning to would-be revolutionaries. At 7570 square meters with a height of 55.6 meters, it was the grandest building in the world when it opened in 537. Twenty years later, an earthquake revealed a fatal miscalculation on the part of the original architects, bringing the dome crashing to the ground. Isador the Younger, nephew of Isadorus, completed the reconstruction in 563 after adding clumsy exterior buttresses to support the new dome. The church then began its millennium-long tenure as the most impressive building of the Byzantine world. During the Fourth Crusade, soldiers looted the holy relics, destroyed the exquisite carvings, and seated a prostitute on the patriarch's throne in order to ridicule the Eastern Church. Mehmet the Conqueror converted Aya Sofia to a mosque, which it remained until 1932, when Atatürk established it as a museum.

The **mihrab,** the calligraphy-adorned portal pointing towards Mecca, stands awkwardly in the **apse,** a space which obviously housed the altar during the mosque's Orthodox incarnation. The elaborate marble square in the floor marks the spot where Byzantine emperors were once crowned. The **gallery** contains Byzantine mosaics recovered from beneath a thick layer of Ottoman plaster, as well as the famed **sweating pillar** that has a hole for your finger to collect the odd drop of water, believed to possess healing powers. At the end of the row of mosaics is a depiction of Jesus with the Empress Zoe and Constantine Monomachus. The story goes that each time one of Zoe's husbands died, his face would be carved out of the mosaic and the new husband's face would replace it.

Located between the Hippodrome and Aya Sofia, the six-minareted, multi-domed structure is, of course, the **Blue Mosque,** or **Sultanahmet Camii.** *(Open Tu-Sa 8:25am-12:45pm, 1:40-4:40pm, and 5:35-6:40pm. Please be courteous—don't attempt to visit during prayer times, and remember to dress appropriately.)* Completed in 1617, it was Sultan Ahmet's response to the architectural challenge of Aya Sofia. Where the Blue Mosque falls short in sheer enormity, it compensates with a beautifully coherent and balanced design structure. Follow the signs for the "visitor entrance" to find yourself directly under the giant İznik-tiled hemispheres. The four giant columns, or "elephant feet," that support the main dome, are exquisitely decorated with Kütahya tiles in characteristically Ottoman floral and geometric patterns. Constructed in honor of Sultan Ahmet's position as the sixth sultan after the Turkish conquest of Istanbul, the **six minarets** are the primary source of the mosque's fame. Only the mosque at Mecca had six minarets at the time of the Blue Mosque's construction, and the thought of equalling that sacred edifice was considered heretical. Sultan Ahmet obviated this difficulty by financing the construction of a seventh minaret at Mecca.

Few sites conjure images of the glory of Byzantine Constantinople like the **Hippodrome,** behind the Blue Mosque. The tall, northernmost column with hieroglyphics is the **Dikili Taş,** the **Egyptian Obelisk** erected by the Pharoah Thutmosis III in 1500 BC and brought from Egypt to Constantinople in the 4th century by Emperor Theodosius I. The subterranean bronze stump is all that remains of the **Serpentine Column,** a particularly impressive piece of Imperial plunder. Originally placed at the Oracle of Delphi, the statue consisted of three intertwined snakes whose heads pointed in different directions until Mehmet I conquered the city and decapitated one of them. The southernmost column is the deteriorating **Column of Constantine,** whose original gold-plated bronze tiling was looted by members of the Fourth Crusade during the sack of Constantinople. On the east side of Hippodrome along Atmeydanı Sok. is **İbrahim Paşa Sarayı,** the **Museum of Turkish and Islamic Art.** *(Museum and cafe open Tu-Su 9am-4:30pm. US$2, students US$1.20.)* This superb museum and former prison features a large, well-organized Islamic art collection.

Sultanahmet's most mysterious, otherworldly attraction is the oft-overlooked **Yerebatan Saray,** or the Underground Cistern. *(Open daily 9am-5:30pm. US$2, students US$1.75.)* The underground "palace" is actually a vast underground cavern whose shallow water eerily reflects the images of its 336 supporting columns, all illuminated by colored ambient lighting.

TURKEY

TOPKAPI PALACE Towering over the high ground at the tip of the old city and hidden behind walls up to 12m high stands **Topkapı Sarayı** (Topkapı Palace), the nerve center of the Ottoman Empire from the 15th through 19th centuries. (*Museum open Su-M and W-Sa 9am-4:30pm. US$4, students US$2.75.*) Offering unparalleled insights into the wealth (the Spoonmaker's Diamond), excess (the sultan's bathroom), cruelty (the Harem, which housed the deaf mutes who served as court executioners), and artistic vitality that characterized the Ottoman Empire at its peak, the Topkapı is a fascinating complex. Built by **Mehmet the Conqueror** between 1458 and 1465, the palace morphed into an Imperial residence during the reign of **Suleyman the Magnificent.** The palace is divided into four courts, all surrounded by the palace walls: the first is a park-like courtyard; the second is the bulk of the palace proper; the third court is the site of the palace school; and the fourth court houses a set of pavilions with amazing views of the Sea of Marmara over the forest canopy of Gülhane. The main entrance is on Babıhümayun Cad., the cobblestone street off Aya Sofia square.

In the **second court,** beyond the colonnade on the right, the **Imperial kitchens,** with their distinctive conical and vaulted chimneys, house collections of porcelain and silver. The **silver and European porcelain collections** are worth visiting if only to pay homage to the herniated spirits of those who had to carry the stuff in. The **Chinese and Japanese porcelain collection** is among the largest in the world, featuring pieces from all the major Chinese porcelain eras.

The **third court,** officially known as **Enderun** (inside), is accessible through the **Gate of Felicity,** which, like everything else in the palace, has a pseudonym. The gate was also referred to as Akağalar Kapısı (White Eunuchs' Gate), suggesting that, minor surgery aside, the lives of the eunuchs were far from incomplete. The **costumes collection** traces the evolution of Imperial costumes—the sheer size of Süleyman's robe clearly shows the girth, if not the breadth, of his magnificence. In the **Palace Treasury,** you'll find the chain mail armor of Murat IV, the legendary Topkapı dagger, and all 86 karats of the **Spoonmaker's Diamond,** so called because it was once traded to a spoonmaker in exchange for three spoons. The **Hall of the Treasury** houses 37 portraits, one for each of the 37 sultans. The **Treasure Dormitory** next door displays a sizeable collection of Islamic Art cataloging the evolution of Selçuk and Mamluke art, particularly calligraphy. On the other side of the courtyard is the **Pavilion of Holy Relics,** housing the booty taken by Selim the Grim. The edifice is lavishly covered from floor to dome in blue İznik tile, with the names of God and Muhammed on calligraphic seals. The room on the left features the staff of Moses, several hairs of Muhammed's beard, and a rather angry letter penned by the Prophet asking a Coptic chieftain to convert to Islam.

If Topkapı can be thought of as the nerve center of the Ottoman Empire, then the **fourth courtyard** certainly qualifies as the pleasure center, as it was amongst these pavilions, gardens, and fountains that the (in)famous merriments and sordid garden parties of the Tulip Period took place. The **Circumcision Room,** an octagonal chamber that overhangs the edge of the pavillion, built by Ibrahim the Mad. Young princes would be clipped into adulthood in this chamber lined with beautiful İznik tiles.

Cashing in at US$2 per head on the plethora of associations of debauchery and intrigue conjured by the word **Harem,** the Topkapı admissions ticket doesn't cover a tour of this, the museum's most popular attraction next to the Spoonmaker's Diamond. (*Open Su and M and W-Sa. Mandatory tours leave every 30min. 9:30am-3:30pm. US$2.*) The Harem was the home of the sultan and his family and breaks down quite nicely into three main sections: the Eunuchs' section; the Womens' section; and the Sultan's section. The women's section of the Harem, begins with the chambers of the **Valide Sultan,** the sultan's mother. Easily the most powerful of the Harem women, the Valide Sultan exerted a great deal of influence on her son. Roxelana, the wife of Süleyman the Magnificent, induced her husband to kill his first son in order to pave the way for the accession of Selim the Sot. If a concubine attracted the sultan's affections or the sultan were sufficiently attracted to her as to spend a night with her, she would be promoted to *odalisque*.

GRAND BAZAAR AND AROUND Consisting of over 4000 shops, several banks, mosques, police stations, and restaurants, the enormous **Grand Bazaar (Kapalı Çarşısı)** could be a city onto itself. *(Open M-Sa 9am-7pm; http://www.grand-bazaar.com.)* The enormous Kapalı Çarşısı forms the entrance to the massive mercantile sprawl that starts at Çemberlitaş and covers the hill down to Eminönü, ending at the Mısır Çarşısı (Egyptian Spice Bazaar) and the Golden Horn waterfront. This colorful, chaotic, labyrinthine world combines all the best and worst of shopping in Turkey—Byzantine-style icons on red velvet, Turkish daggers, embroidered pillows, amber jewelry, silver flintlock guns with mother-of-pearl handles, musical instruments, chess sets, hand puppets, and the ubiquitous evil-eye keychains, ornaments, and jewelry. Through banter and barter, haggle and hassle, a day spent at the Kapalı Çarşısı is bound to tempt, titillate, and tantalize even the most experienced traveler.

The Grand Bazaar is undoubtedly a tourist trap in many respects. However, it has served Istanbul's native population for centuries, providing locals with a convenient one-stop shopping spot and a trading extravaganza. Both swindles and bargains are easy to come by, and if you use good judgement and savvy, you might even take home a great find. If you plan to bargain, decide on your price beforehand. In order to make sure that your first offer isn't insulting, don't offer much less than half of the asking price. Your target price should be somewhere in between your first offer and their stated price. Be wary of buying anything expensive whose value rests on a promise of age or authenticity.

The **Mısır Çarşısı (Egyptian Spice Bazaar)** in Eminönü once handled customs and excises, but today the 80 or so vendors in the L-shaped building sell a mind-boggling array of spices, aphrodisiacs, gold, tea, sticky sweets, honeycomb, nuts, dried fruit, and a bit of unlicensed soccer team merchandise. The bazaar's high-vaulted ceilings, saffron- and curry-scented air, and relative lack of tourists and tourist-related merchandise lend it an atmosphere and integrity that the Covered Bazaar doesn't even approach. Vendors even give away free samples.

Want Some New Threads?

Carpet and *kilim* buying in Turkey is a task for the expert bargainer. Merchandise is always overpriced, sometimes by as much as 50%, but the high quality can make it worth your while. "Shop around" is an understatement—you should seek out advice from several carpet/*kilim* vendors who speak English (as most do). The Grand Bazaar in Istanbul has the most exorbitant prices, so beware. The name of the game is bargaining, so don't be afraid to stick by your bid if you know it's fair. Always get several independent opinions on the value of a carpet before you buy. Be sure to flip the carpet over to feel for knots (if you cannot feel any, it is probably machine made). Also, pull out a strand from the carpet and burn it; if it smells like wool, you know it is real. Be careful not to leave the store without a copy of insurance and shipping contracts, as well as a certificate of guarantee.

ELSEWHERE In Beyazit, the large mosque with four minarets at the north end of Istanbul University is **Süleymaniye Camii,** one of architect Mimar Sinan's three great masterpieces (the other two being Şehzade Camii in Istanbul and Selimiye Camii in Edirne). The **Süleymaniye Complex,** a set of Ottoman buildings in the vicinity of the mosque, includes several tombs, an imaret (soup kitchen), and several medreses. Passing through the graveyard brings you to the two **royal tombs,** decorated in the same fashion, the sultan's tomb being the more impressive. *(Open Tu-Su 9:30am-4:30pm. 50¢ donation.)* Süleyman's tomb incorporates all three of Sinan's decorative signatures: İznik tiles, stained glass, and painted patterns.

At the far wester end of the Golden Horn, the necropolis of **Eyüp,** a major Muslim pilgrimage site, houses the tomb of Eyüp (Job), a companion of Muhammed who died during the first Arab siege of Constantinople. Today, Eyüp is mostly a religious site, with Quran shops, the Eyüp Mosque, and lovely, spacious cemeteries. Dress modestly and avoid traveling in packs, making excessive hand gestures, or drinking alcohol in the open.

TURKEY

Ferries from Eminönü or Kabataş travel to four of the beautiful, undeveloped islands in the **Princes Isles.** Look for signs saying "Sirkeci Adalar" (round-trip US$2.50). **Büyükada** is the largest and most enjoyable of the islands, offering pine-forested scenery, swimming spots, and peaceful walks. Ask for directions to the path to the stone-covered **beach,** the cleanest swimming hole on the island, and about **hiking** trails—hiking is forbidden in some places. There are no cars or buses on the island; the main forms of transportation are **walking, biking,** or a **horse-and-buggy ride** (horse-and-buggy prices run US$2.50-15; bike rentals about US$2.50 per hr.). The **Ideal Aile Pansion,** 14 Kadıyoran Cad. (tel. (216) 382 68 57) costs US$10.

ENTERTAINMENT

Turkish Baths

Not all have designated female attendants; women should specifically request female washers. Self service is always an option, a desire for which is best indicated by showing the attendants your bar of soap and wash cloth.

Çemberlitaş Hamamı, 8 Verzirhan Cad. (tel. 522 7974), is just a soap-slide away from the Çemberlitaş tram stop. Touristy, but one of the better spots in terms of cleanliness and service. Built by Sinan in 1584, it's also one of the most beautiful, with both the men's and women's sections under identical large domes with marble interiors. Bath US$14, with massage US$18; with ISIC US$8, US$12.

Mihrimah Hamamı (tel. 523 0487), right next to Mihrimah Mosque on Fevzi Paşa Cad., about 50m from Edirnekapı. Large, quiet, clean, and cheap. Men's section open 7am-midnight; women's section 9am-7pm. Bath US$3.75, massage US$3.

Çinli Hamamı, in Fatih on Itfaiye Cad., near the end with the butcher shops. Excellent, non-touristy option. Both sections open 9am-8pm. Bath US$4, massage US$4.

The Hamam

It is worth your while to visit a *hamam* (Turkish bath) at least once in Turkey. Because of the Islamic emphasis on cleanliness (pious Muslims perform ablutions before each of the day's 5 prayers), the baths have been a part of daily life since medieval times. They also function as social centers, especially for women, who customarily were not expected to leave the house often. Men and women use separate bath houses or the same place on different days. A sign on the door may indicate the schedule for women (*kadınlar)* and men (*erkekler).*

Enter the bath house, deposit your clothes and lock your valuables in a cubicle (*camekan),* don the provided towel (*peştemal),* and proceed to the warm main room (*hararet)* with its large, heated stone (*göbek taşı).* Bring your own shampoo, soap, and towel, or pay to use theirs. Bathe yourself at the basins (*kurnas)* lining the walls, pouring the water over yourself with the provided bowl. Basins should only be shared by friends, and soapsuds should be kept clear of the basin water. Take care not to douse your neighbors, as they might have just finished a ritual cleansing; a chance splash would oblige them to repeat the entire process.

You usually pay extra to be washed and receive a **massage.** Typically, masseuse and client are of the same gender; females may request a female masseuse if they wish to be on the safe side. The massage can be harder than Westerners are accustomed to; *"lütfen daha yumuşak"* (gentler please) is a useful phrase to know. The *kese* (abrasive mitt) is used to strip excess skin cells beyond imagining; you can also buy your own at pharmacies. Following the massage and *kese,* you will usually be sponged gently and shampooed. After reaching optimum cleanliness, you can return to your cubicle, order a drink (good for rehydration), and relax before returning to the dusty streets outside.

Men should never drop their *peştemal;* cleaning one's lower half is therefore tricky, but not impossible. Turkish women frequently strip naked in the bath, but it's a good idea to wear underwear under your *peştemal* until you can gauge the sensibilities of a given *hamam.*

TURKEY

Nightlife

Turkish nightlife options generally fall into one of three categories. The first includes male-only *çay* houses, backgammon parlors, and dancing shows. Women, though usually not prohibited, are unwelcome, and should avoid these places. They tend to be dingy, poorly lit, and can even be somewhat unsafe for men as well. *Let's Go* does not recommend patronage of this sort of establishment. The second category includes **rock bars** and **backpacker bars.** Rock bars tend to be fine, clean fun; don't be deceived by the prevalent Def Leppard and Bon Jovi musical fare. Backpacker bars, are concentrated in the Sultanahmet area and tend to be associated with hostels. The third category of nightlife is that of **clubs,** many of which don't list their addresses and move from unlisted locations in Taksim in the winter to unlisted open-air summer locations scattered throughout the city. Random, uninformed attempts at club hopping are ill advised, largely because they tend to prove fruitless.

The action is generally centered **Taksım Square and İstiklâl Caddesi** area, where the bar scene starts at about 8pm or so and finishes at about 2 or 3am, whereas the clubs and *"clup"* shut down a few hours later.

Vivaçı Bar, Meşelik Sok., off İstiklâl Cad. by Triada Church. Open-air rooftop bar/*pastanesi* with a truly staggering view of the Greek church off Taksim Square.

Jazz Cafe, Haşnun Galip Sok., off Büyük Parmakkapı Sok. One of the coolest places in Istanbul, and not just because of the A/C. The music, usually jazz, is always good and occasionally live. Happy hour daily 5-7pm. Open daily 10am-2am.

Madrid Bar, Ipek Sok., off Küçük Parmakkapı Sok. off İstiklâl Cad. Small, mellow, and cozy. The cheapest pint in Taksim (US$1.25). Open daily 8pm-2:30am.

Kemancı, 3 locations on Siraselviler Cad. The "New Kemancı" houses 2 clubs in a passage marked "Sanat Evi." Upstairs is a decent **disco.** Open 11pm-late. Cover US$15. Downstairs is the fabled **rock bar,** where high-schoolers and young college students watch cover bands. Cover US$8, includes 1 free drink. 50m down Siraselviler away from Taksim Square is the **Old Kemancı,** where an older crowd chugs cheap beer (US$1.75) and headbangs to Iron Maiden. Open 5pm-2am.

Caravan Pub/Cafe is in the fruit market beside the Çiçek Pasaji off İstiklâl Cad. Loud, cavernous, and cheap, this is where Turks consummate their love affair with heavy metal. Beer US$2. Open 7pm-late; live music until 1am.

■ Edirne

An easy *dolmuş* ride from the Greek and Bulgarian borders, **Edirne** nourished the genius of Sinan, the quintessential Ottoman architect. His masterpiece, the **Selimiye Camii** (Selim's Mosque), presides over the city with 71m minarets and 999 windows. The vast interior, ornately decorated from dome to floor, is even more impressive. Edirne's other major sight is the **Beyazıt Complex,** a spiritual and physical welfare facility a couple of kilometers from town. The centerpiece is the **Beyazıt Camii,** a beautiful, single-domed mosque surrounded by multi-domed buildings that were designed to be schools, storehouses, and asylums. To make the long but scenic trek, walk along Talat Paşa Cad. to the river (don't cross it), then turn right and walk along the dirt path. After about 10 minutes you will see a bridge on your left; cross it, and walk another five minutes until you see the mosque. Back in town, you may want to relax in one of Edirne's excellent **Turkish baths.** Sinan's 16th-century **Sokollu Hamamı,** beside the Üç Şerefeli Camii, combines superior service with inspiring architecture. (Open daily 7am-11pm for men; 9am-6pm for women. US$2.80, with massage US$7.) Those less interested in cleanliness can get down and dirty when the annual **Kirkpinar Grease Wrestling Festival** comes to town in the last week of June.

Buses arrive from Ankara (10hr., US$20), Bursa (US$9.50), and Istanbul (3hr., US$7.50); when you arrive at the *otogar,* walk across the street and take a *dolmuş* into Edirne. The **tourist office,** 17 Talat Paşa Cad. (tel. (284) 213 92 08), about 200m west of the Eski Camii, gives out free maps (open June-Aug. daily 9am-6pm). The wonderful **Hotel Kervansaray** (tel. (284) 225 21 95 or 212 61 19; fax 225 04 62), along Hürriyet Meydanı, built in the 16th century as a resting place for camel cara-

TURKEY

vans, now has small but comfortable rooms with bath, TV, and phone. The call to prayer that resonates down the corridors at 4:30am will no doubt fill you with the joy of this Turkish tradition (singles US$30; doubles US$60; triples US$90; breakfast included). **Efe Hotel,** 13 Maarif Cad. (tel. (284) 213 61 66 or 213 64 66), has spotless rooms with modern bathrooms (singles US$24; doubles US$30; breakfast included). A few doors down is **Hotel Aksaray** (tel. (284) 225 39 01), with cheaper but more basic rooms (singles US$5; doubles US$9). Don't leave Edirne without taking *çay* (small US$0.20, large US$0.35) at **Sera Park Cafe,** on Selimiye Meydari in the park between Selimiye Camii and Eski Camii.

■ Bursa

Along with Konya, Bursa is one of Turkey's two holy cities of pilgrimage. Although the city is now an industrial center and wealthy resort area, the well preserved Ottoman monuments scattered throughout town and the thermal baths in the **Çekirge** (Grasshopper) district remain excellent attractions. Despite their names, **Yeşil Camii** (Green Mosque) and **Yeşil Türbe** (Green Mausoleum), in the eastern part of town, feature rich turquoise and cobalt blue Iznik tiles (open daily 8:30am-noon and 1-5:30pm; off-season 8am-5pm). Nearby, the **Turkish and Islamic Art Museum,** including the **Ethnographic Museum,** houses 16th-century ivory boxes, costumes and musical instruments of the dervishes, exquisite bath tools, and other exhibits (open daily 8:30am-noon and 1-5pm; US$1, students US$0.60). Built in the Turkish style common before the conquest of Constantinople, the **Ulu Camii** (Great Mosque) was commissioned by Beyazıt to commemorate his victory in Nikopolis in 1396. It's said that Beyazıt vowed to build 20 mosques if he won the war, but later skimped by just building Ulu Camii's 20 domes. To get to the **Eski Kaplıca** (Old Springs) bathing complex, built by Justinian in the 6th century, take the Çekirge *dolmuş* and get off at the Kervansaray Hotel. After a long day of travel, ask for the "rubbing" and have your skin treated with a special cloth. (Open daily 7am-11pm. Entrance to baths US$7.50. Rubbing and massage US$3 each.)

Mt. Uludağ (Mt. Olympus), home of Turkey's leading ski resort, gives the city its nickname, "Green Bursa." To reach the **Uludağ cable car** station, take a bus marked "Teleferik" (US$0.35) from Pevon l at the main station on Atatürk Cad. in Bursa. The cable car runs to the mid-station (every 40min., round-trip US$8), and from the mid-station to Sarıalan. Plan for a cool climate, changing weather, and high-priced hotels.

Bursa is accessible by **ferry** from Istanbul (US$2.50); the ferries land in Yalova, where you can hop on a *dolmuş* or bus. **Buses** arrive from Istanbul's Esenler Bus Station (4hr., US$7) and connect to Ankara, Izmir, and other cities. To reach the center of town from the bus station, take a minibus to the Santral Garaj, then a bus or *dolmuş* marked "Heykel" and get off at Ulu Camii. The **tourist office** (tel. (224) 220 18 48) is near the *heykel* (a huge statue of Atatürk) and down the stairs by the big fountain (open June-Sept. daily 8:30am-7:30pm; Oct.-May M-F 8:30am-6:30pm). **Çeşmeli Otel** (tel. (224) 224 15 11), on Gümüşçeken Cad. near the covered bazaar, has very clean rooms (singles US$12-15; doubles US$20-24). **Otel Deniz,** 19 Tahtakale Cad. (tel. (224) 222 92 38), has comfortable rooms around a courtyard (singles US$10; doubles US$15). Bursa is home to *İskender kebap,* a yogurt, tomato, and lamb dish you can sample at many restaurants between the Atatürk statue and the *Yeşil Camii.* **Kebapçı İskender,** on Atatürk Blv., claims to have invented the *İskender kebap* (US$3.15).

AEGEAN COAST

With a rich collection of classical ruins and a sinuous coastline that conceals sublime beaches, the once tranquil Aegean Coast is becoming an increasingly popular destination. No legal barriers prevent tourists from traveling from the Greek islands to Turkey, though some travelers have reported complications and high port taxes.

■ Gallipoli to Troy

Gallipoli (Gelibolu) Across the Dardanelles, on the European side, lies the battlefield of **Gallipoli,** known as Gelibolu in Turkish. In 1915-16, Allied forces sent wave after wave of Australian, New Zealander, and British troops against the highly fortified Turkish positions here and suffered brutal losses. This battle launched its hero **Atatürk,** on a rapid rise to his status as Turkey's founding father. Thousands of Australians and New Zealanders make pilgrimages to war cemeteries here, where over half a million men were killed, and 22,000 Allied dead lie buried. To tour the battle sights and memorials try **Ana-Tur,** Cumhuriyet Meydani Özay İşhani Kat. 2, No. 30 (tel. (286) 271 58 42 or 217 07 71), or **Troyanzac Travel Agency** (tel. (286) 217 58 47; fax 217 58 49), both based in Çanakkale. Next door to the Saros Otel (see below) in **Eceabat,** the **Down Under Travel Agency** (tel. (286) 814 24 31; fax 814 24 30) runs daily tours for US$13. Bring a bathing suit, as many tours stop for a dip at **Brighton Beach.** To explore on your own, take a *dolmuş* from Eceabat, accessible by frequent ferries from Çanakkale (US$0.80), to the **Kabatep Müzesi** (open daily 8:30am-noon and 1-5:30pm; US$0.75). From the museum, it is 4km to **ANZAC Cove,** and 7km uphill to the Australian **Lone Pine Memorial.** From here, walk to the highest point on the peninsula, **Çanakbayırı**—the ground taken by Atatürk. Today, the **New Zealand Memorial** shares space with Atatürk's statued image.

Gallipoli Town, known for its quiet atmosphere, excellent seafood, and sandy beach, makes a relaxing base for touring the nearby battlefields. Gallipoli is connected by Radar Tur **buses** (tel. (286) 566 64 24) to Istanbul (8 per day, US$7) and Izmir (3 per day, US$8). The bus station is in the **Liman Meydani** square, where hotels, restaurants, and taxis cluster. If you walk from the square across the bridge next to the old watch tower, you will come to the **Yilmaz Hotel,** right on the square at 8 Liman Mevkii (tel. (286) 566 12 56, 566 35 98 or 566 35 95), which offers singles (US$8) and daily tours of the battlefields (US$28). In Eceabat, the **Saros Otel,** 39 Topçular Sok. (tel. (286) 814 10 65), has clean singles with bath (US$5), a restaurant, **Internet access,** and an extremely helpful English-speaking staff.

Çanakkale Blessed with inexpensive accommodations and bus connections to major cities and sights, **Çanakkale** is an easy base from which to explore Gallipoli and Troy. As many Australian and New Zealander troops lost their lives in nearby Gallipoli during World War I, Aussies and Kiwis are particularly welcome. A handful of pubs cater to those nationals. **Buses** arrive often from Bursa (5½hr., US$8.15), Istanbul (5hr., US$10.75), Izmir (5hr., US$8.75), and other cities. From the bus station, take a left out the main doors, then the next right onto Demircioğlu Cad. (following the "feribot" sign), and continue to the docks. The **tourist office,** 67 İskele Meydanı (tel./fax (286) 217 11 87), is on your left (open daily 8:30am-7:30pm). A peaceful garden awaits at **Yellow Rose Pension,** 5 Yeni Sok. (tel./fax (286) 217 33 43), around a corner from the clock tower (singles US$5; doubles US$10; triples US$15).

Troy (Truva) The site slept under a blanket of mythology until Heinrich Schliemann, millionaire-*cum*-archaeologist, uncovered the ancient city 32km south of Çanakkale to prove that Homeric stories were not merely fiction. The remaining Bronze Age fortifications are remarkably well-preserved. Nine distinct strata have been identified and are explained in the **Excavation House.** (Site and house open in summer daily 8am-7:30pm; off-season 8am-5pm. US$2, students US$0.80.) Take a *dolmuş* (US$1) from the station in Çanakkale, and ask it to wait while you explore. **Anzac House** (tel. 217 54 82) leads tours leaving at 9am (US$8). Arrive by 8:30am and bring plenty of water.

Black, White, and Read with Envy

In ancient times, only the library in Alexandria surpassed Pergamon's, which contained over 200,000 volumes in repositories all over the city. So great was Alexandria's jealousy of the Pergamenes' literary hoard that they made what they thought was a brilliant strategic move: they limited the flow of Egyptian papyrus to Pergamon. The Pergamenes countered by writing all subsequent volumes on parchment pages made from goat hide, an exponentially more durable, more manageable medium. However, the scheming Alexandrians were foiled but temporarily. After the Alexandrian library burned down, Marc Antony and his boys plundered Pergamon's shelves and presented the pilfered publications, as a token of his love, to Cleopatra to replace the charred editions. In 640, the ill-fated collection was put to the torch by the Caliph Omar: if the books agreed with the Qu'ran, Omar argued, they were superfluous, and if they disagreed with the Qu'ran, they were heretical and fit for combustion.

■ Pergamon to Çeşme

Pergamon The hilltop city of Pergamon was a dazzling center of cultural activity with one of the richest libraries in the ancient world. Today, ruins spread over 30,000 acres, but many attractions cluster around two principal sites: the **Acropolis,** which looms majestically above the town, and the **Asclepion** (medical center) in the valley below. An impressive portion of the Asclepion remains, including a marble colonnade, theater, and healing rooms. (Both sites open daily in summer 8:30am-7pm; off-season 8:30am-5:30pm. Admission to each US$2, with ISIC US$1.25.) The ruins of a huge gymnasium, a Roman circus, several temples, and the lavishly frescoed **House of Attalus** are also scattered about. The most notable attraction is the mammoth **amphitheater,** capable of seating 10,000 spectators. On your way to the **Royal Palaces,** try to land one of three coins on top of the column inside the **wishing well.** Pergamon gazes across the river at the pleasant, modern town of **Bergama,** where buses travel to and from Istanbul (9hr., US$16) and Izmir (1½hr.,US$2). Bergama's **tourist office** (tel. (232) 633 18 62) is a 1km walk to the right from the main bus station (open Apr.-Sept. daily 8:30am-7pm; Oct.-Mar. M-Sa 8:30am-5:30pm). **Pension Athena** (tel. (232) 633 34 20), on the road beyond İstiklal Meydanı in a restored Ottoman house, boasts "Not the best, but we're trying to get there." Chalk one up for honest advertising (US$6, with shower US$8; 10% *Let's Go* discount; laundry US$6).

Izmir From the rubble of the 1922 Turkish War of Independence, **Izmir,** formerly ancient **Smyrna,** has risen to become Turkey's third largest city. Industrial fumes now linger over parts of the city, but amid the concrete buildings of the Anafartalar Cad., *çay salonu* (teahouses), the cries of children and street vendors, and a full-fledged **bazaar** (open M-Sa 8am-8pm) provide energy and excitement. Izmir's **Archaeological Museum,** near Konak Sq., displays statues of Poseidon and Demeter, among other antiquities (open Tu-Su 8:30am-5:30pm; US$2, students US$1). In late June and early July, an **international festival** brings folk and classical music to Izmir, Çeşme, and Ephesus (for info, call Pozitif at (232) 249 75 70 or the Hilton Hotel at (232) 441 60 61). Many budget hotels and cheap restaurants, along with several bus company offices and the **Basmane train station,** are located around **9 Eylül Meydanı,** the center of the Basmane district. You can take city bus 47, 50, 51, 52, 53, 465, or 501 to the Basmane district from **Yeni Garaj,** Izmir's principal bus station for municipal and inter-city travel. **Buses** run to Bursa (5hr., US$6), Istanbul (9hr., US$19), and many other cities. The **tourist office,** 1/1D Gazi Osman Paşa Blvd. (tel. (232) 484 21 47 or 489 92 78; fax 489 92 78), near the Hilton Hotel, has maps and info. (Open M-F 8:30am-5:30pm, July-Aug. until 7pm; Sa 9am-5pm.) **Güzel Izmir Hotel,** 1368 Sok. No. 8 (tel. (232) 483 50 69 or 484 66 93), has clean rooms with showers (singles US$8; doubles US$16). Most rooms at **Otel Divan,** 1369 Sok No. 56 (tel. (232) 483 36 75; fax 483 22 43), have TV, toilet, and shower (all beds US$7.20).

Çeşme The popular seaside resort of Çeşme lies one hour west of Izmir. **Buses** leave every half hour from the Üçkuyular bus lot in Izmir (US$2). **Ertürk Tourism** (tel. (232) 712 67 68) sends ferries from Çeşme to Chios in Greece (July-Sept. daily; May-June 3-5 per week; US$20 port tax upon leaving Greece). The **tourist office** (tel. (232) 712 66 53) is across from the castle and caravanserai. (Open in summer M-F 8:30am-7pm, Sa-Su 8:30am-5pm; off-season daily 8:30am-5:30pm.) **Tarhan Pension,** Musalla Mah., 9 Çarşı Sok. (tel. (232) 712 65 99), has hot-water showers and comfy rooms (singles US$6; doubles US$12; triples US$18; breakfast US$2), while the family-style **Tani Pension,** Musalla Mah., 15 Çarşı Sok. (tel. (232) 712 62 38), has clean rooms and a terrace (singles US$6; doubles US$12; triples US$18).

■ Kuşadası

Located some 95km south of Izmir, Kuşadası has something to offer almost every traveler. Its extensive daily **bazaar** overflows with leather goods, Turkish carpets, and other wares. Overcrowded but clean **beaches** are a short distance away by *dolmuş*, as is the gorgeous **Dilek National Park,** a great place for canyon climbing, picnicking, and swimming (the park has 4 beautiful beaches). By night, this former fishing village comes alive with cafes, bars, and dance clubs. The nearby towns of Ephesus, Selçuk, Priene, Miletus, and Didyma are convenient daytrips.

You must pay a US$10 port tax upon entering (generally best paid in US$ to avoid commissions and weak exchange rates). **Ferries** run to Samos, Greece daily in summer (2 per week off-season). Contact **Ekol Travel** (tel. (256) 614 92 55 or 614 55 91), and flash *Let's Go* for a discount. The main **bus station** is about 2km east of the port area, but frequent *dolmuş* connect it with the city center. Buses run to Ankara (10hr., US$16.70), Bodrum (2½hr., US$6), and Istanbul (11hr., US$15). The **tourist office,** No. 13 Liman Cad. (tel. (256) 614 11 03), is on the corner of Liman Cad. and Güvercin Ada Sok (open daily in summer 8am-6pm; in winter M-F 8am-noon and 1:30-5:30pm). To get there from the bus station, take a taxi.

Use discretion when dealing with the hustlers who meet buses and ferries and offer "bargain accommodations." You'll find many cheap pensions along **Aslanlar Cad.** and **Aydinlik Cad. Hotel Rose,** 7 Aslanlar Cad. (tel. (256) 612 25 88; fax 614 11 11), has a bar, **Internet access,** laundry service, free luggage storage, and transport to Ephesus. (Dorms US$4; rooms US$5-8; roof accommodations US$2.50. 10% off for students; 15% *Let's Go* discount.) Down the street from Hotel Rose, **Park Pension,** 17 Aslanlar Cad. (tel. (256) 614 39 17 or 612 69 12), offers comfort in colorful rooms (rooms US$6-8; breakfast included; reserve ahead). **Kaylon Hotel,** Kibris Cad. No. 7 (tel. (256) 614 33 46), offers comfortable rooms (US$5) and pick-up service from the bus station. Bring your sleeping bag and tent to **Onder** (tel. (256) 614 24 13) or **Yat Camping** (tel. (256) 614 13 33), 2km north of town on Atatürk Blv. (US$2.40 per person, US$1.60 per tent, caravans US$1.60). There are many cheap restaurants along **Kahramanlar Cad.** and its alley tributaries. The madness of the nightclubs on **Barlar Sok,** parallel to Kahramanlar Cad., spills into the streets (many open until 4am).

■ Near Kuşadası: Ephesus (Efes) and Selçuk

For an archaeological fix, search no farther than **Ephesus** (Efes), where ruins from the Roman and early Christian era are extensive and well preserved. If you see Ephesus on your own, you'll approach the ruins from the road between Kuşadası and Selçuk; your first glimpse of the site will be the outskirts of the ancient city. The most important of these remains is the **Vedius Gymnasium,** to the left as you proceed down the road to the main entrance. Farther along lies an enormous **stadium** (the seats were removed to build the Byzantine city walls). Once you pass through the main entrance, marvel at the **Arcadian Street,** a magnificent, colonnaded marble avenue. Uphill, the imposing ruins of the **Temple of Hadrian** dominate the right side of the road. Farther up the hill are the ruins of the exquisite **Fountain of Trajan.** To get to Ephesus from the Kuşadası bus station, take a *dolmuş* to Selçuk, and tell the driver you want to get off at Ephesus. From the Selçuk train station, take any *dolmuş* towards Kuşadası. Guided tours of the ruins are expensive (about US$15-25); instead, get a good guidebook at the entrance (US$5) and tour the site on your own (open daily 8am-6pm; US$4, free with ISIC).

The authentic "Turkishness" of the small and beautiful **Selçuk** has made it both preferable to Kuşadası and aggressively touristed.The colossal and comparatively unadvertised **Basilica of Saint John** was constructed in the 6th century under the Byzantine emperor Justinian (open daily 8am-6pm; US$1.40, free with ISIC). The **Temple of Artemis**, one of the seven wonders of the ancient world, used to be the largest temple on the planet; now a lone reconstructed column twists toward the heavens. Selçuk's **Ephesus Museum** holds most of the archaeological finds unearthed in the region since World War II (open daily 8:30am-noon and 1-5:30pm; US$1.50, free with ISIC). It is easy to escape the town's commercial fervor by exploring the breathtaking landscape surrounding town.

The **train** and **bus stations** send *dolmuş* to Kuşadası and buses to Izmir (US$1.50). About four blocks down Atatürk Cad., the **tourist office,** Atatürk Mah. Agora Çarşısı, 35-6 Mirza Karşısı (tel. (232) 892 63 28), provides free maps. (Open in summer M-F 8:30am-noon and 1-5:30pm; off-season 9am-noon and 1-5pm.) **Barim Pansiyon I,** Müze Arkası Sok. (tel. (232) 892 69 23), behind the Ephesus Museum off Turgutreis Cad., has cool, quiet rooms and a Tahiti-like decor (US$6). Also behind the museum, the friendly **Australian New Zealand Pension,** 7 Prof. Miltner Sok. (tel. (232) 892 60 50), has a lively garden (dorms US$4; private rooms US$5-8; 15% *Let's Go* discount). Outdoor seating and excellent views of Selçuk Castle await at **Özdamar Restaurant,** Atatürk Mah. Cengiz Topel Cad. No. 65 (open daily 9am-midnight).

■ Pamukkale and Aphrodisias

Whether as **Pamukkale** (Cotton Castle) or ancient Hierapolis (Holy City), this village has been drawing the weary to its thermal springs for over 23 centuries. The Turkish name refers to the amazing snow-white cliff surface, accreted over millennia from the calcium-rich mineral water that drips down through terraced pools (site open 24hr.; US$3, students US$2). Don't leave Pamukkale without a dip in the warm, fizzy **sacred fountain** at the Pamukkale Motel (tel. 272 20 24; open for pool use daily 8am-8pm; US$4 per 2hr.). Most of the direct **buses** that run to Pamukkale leave from Selçuk and Kuşadası (4½hr., 5-6 per day, US$4.50). From Pamukkale, there are buses to Bodrum (5hr., US$6.25), Cappadocia (10hr., US$14), and Selçuk and Kuşadası (4½hr., US$6). Facing the road leading to the Pamukkale Motel, the **tourist office** (tel. 272 20 77) is about 200m to the right (open daily 8am-7:30pm; off-season M-F 8am-5pm). **Koray Hotel,** 27 Fevzi Çakmak Cad. (tel. 272 23 00; fax 272 20 95), has rooms facing a beautiful garden and a thermal water pool. All rooms with bathroom and shower (singles US$12; doubles US$16; breakfast US$2). **Öztürk Pension,** 29 Fevzi Çakmak Cad. (tel. 272 21 16 or 272 26 27), has rooms for US$6 per person.

In ancient times, **Aphrodisias** (Geyre) gained fame for its exquisite sculptures; it evolved into a metropolis after Pergamon became Roman. Particularly worth seeing are the Greek **stadium** (capacity 30,000), the **tetrapylon** (gateway), and the elegant **Temple of Aphrodite.** (Site and museum open daily in summer 8:30am-7pm; site closes at 7:30pm. Open in winter 8:30am-5pm. US$2.40 per site, students US$1.20.) The easiest way to see the ruins is as a daytrip from Pamukkale; **buses** leave at 10am and return at 5pm (2hr., round-trip US$6.70).

■ Bodrum

Bodrum, Herodotus's home town, is a nexus of divine beaches, forests, and quaint little islands known for their exquisite swimming coves. Turn left onto Kirkateyn Sok. from Neyzen Tevfik Cad. to reach the scanty remains of the **Mausoleum of Halicarnassus,** yet another of the seven wonders of the ancient world (open Tu-Su 8am-noon and 1-5:30pm; US$1.60, students US$1). Guarding the harbor, the **fortress,** built on an acropolis, now houses Bodrum's **Museum of Underwater Archaeology,** a unique assortment of shipwreck flotsam from sites along the surrounding coastline. (Fortress open Tu-Su 8am-noon and 1-5pm. US$3.40, students US$2. Museum open Tu-F 10am-noon and 2-4pm. US$1.60, students US$1.) Nightlife in Bodrum rages all week long. Despite the high cover, your destination should be the large open-air **Halicarnassus Disco,** at the end of Cumhuriyet Cad., 1.5km from the center of town. This mammoth disco entertains the crowd with great music, laser lights, and lots of alcohol (cover US$16; open until the early morning). Another hotspot is the **Red Lion Bar,** 137 Cumhuriyet Cad. (no cover).

The **tourist office,** 12 Barış Meydanı (tel. (252) 316 10 91), at the foot of the castle, has room listings and free brochures with maps (open Apr.-Oct. daily 8:30am-7:30pm; Nov.-Mar. M-F 8am-noon and 1-5pm). Pensions are plentiful, but reservations are wise. Solo travelers may need to find a roommate in the high season. Tucked off Atatürk Cad., the **Ekimo Pension,** 11 Ushı Sok. (tel./fax (252) 316 55 60), has tidy, quaint rooms. **Polyanna Pension,** 5 Ortanca Sok. (tel. (252) 316 15 28), a side street just before the Halicarnassis Disco end of Cumhuriyet Cad., offers clean rooms with toilets and showers (doubles US$16). Bodrum is famous for its seafood, especially octopus and squid. The centrally located **Karadeniz Restaurant,** 15 Hilmi Uran Mey., off Cumhuriyet Cad., serves excellent Turkish pizza (US$4-7; open 24hr.)

■ Near Bodrum: The Bodrum Peninsula

Bodrum's popularity among Turks stems from its location at the head of the enchanting **Bodrum Peninsula** and its rousing nightlife. A few of the beaches on the southern coast of the peninsula are accessible only by tour boats, which leave from the front of Bodrum's castle (daily 9-11am, returning 5-6pm). Itineraries for the tours vary widely (check the tour schedule at the dock); some popular destinations include the **Akfaryo, Kara Ada** (Black Island), and the beaches at **Camel Bay** and **Bağla.** Boat trips cost around US$12 and include lunch. In summer, boats also leave daily from the castle to tranquil **Orak Island.** These are some of the best swimming spots on the peninsula, but there are few budget accommodations nearby. Daytrips are your best bet. **Gölköy** and **Türkbükü,** once idyllic villages, are now hives for Turkish tourists. **Gümüşlük** is a tiny seaside paradise at the western tip of the Bodrum Peninsula, whose sparkling vistas, cool sea breezes, and relaxed atmosphere make it a welcome escape from the frenetic hedonism of Bodrum.

MEDITERRANEAN COAST

Reaching from the edges of Greece to the Syrian border, Turkey's Mediterranean coast is alternately chic, garish, and remote. Pine forests, hidden coves, and beaches line the stretch between Fethiye and Antalya. Accommodations along the west segment are cheap, and excellent seafood abounds. Farther east, swatches of sand and concrete dotted with castles and ruins mark the shore dubbed the "Turquoise Coast."

■ Marmaris and the Datça Peninsula

Urban **Marmaris** is easily accessible from Rhodes and serves as a good base for exploring in the southern Aegean and Mediterranean coasts. Its small **castle,** built by Süleyman the Magnificent in 1522, is a worth a visit. **Ferries** (1hr., Tu and F 9:30am, round-trip US$43) and **hydrofoils** (50min., daily 9:30am and 4:30pm, US$40) travel to Rhodes; contact **Yeşil Marmairis** for more info (tel. (252) 412 10 33 or 412 22 90; fax 412 07 78). Frequent **buses** run to Bodrum (3hr., US$6), Izmir (5hr., US$10), and many other cities. If you're facing the Atatürk statue at the harbor, the **tourist office,** 2 İskele Meydanı (tel. (252) 412 72 77), is about 250m to the left (open in summer daily 8:30am-7:30pm; off-season M-F 8:30am-5pm).

The **Interyouth Hostel,** Tepe Mah. #45 42nd Sok. (tel. (252) 412 36 87; fax 412 78 23), is one of the most professionally run hostels on the coast. There is a less appealing copycat on the outskirts of town; to get to the real Interyouth Hostel from the Atatürk statue, go straight up Ulusal Egemenlik Bd., look for signs, and take a right. (Dorms US$5; private rooms US$13; US$1 discount with ISIC, IYH, or GO25. **Internet access** US$4 per hr.) To reach **Maltepe Pansiyon,** 64 Sokak No. 7 (tel. (252) 412

16 29), from the statue, walk to G. Mustafa Muğlali Cad., take the second left, then left again 25m from the Grand Cafe (doubles US$16). For food, try the **bazaar,** where several affordable restaurants await (meals US$1-2), or **Özyiğut Restaurant,** Tepe Mah. 53 Çarşı İçi No. 21, which serves no-frills Turkish meals. At night, head to the row of pubs behind the tourist office, or to **Greenhouse** or **Backstreet,** both on Bar St.

From Marmaris, hop on a bus to the resplendent **Datça Peninsula** (2hr., US$4). Boats depart from Bodrum (2hr., M, W, and F 9am and 5pm, round-trip US$16), as do hydrofoils (45min., daily 11am and 5pm, round-trip US$20). **Mandalina Pensiyon** (tel. (252) 712 49 95), on Yali Cad., has airy, modern rooms with toilets ($8 per person). From the harbor off Yali Cad., turn right and walk along the shore about 150m to find **Ilıca Camping** (tel. (252) 712 34 00; US$4 per person; bungalows US$8 per person).

The ancient city of **Caunos,** home to an impressive Roman bath, theater, and church, is located by the river leading out of nearby Lake Küyceğiz. The ruins are accessible by daytrip from **Dalyan,** Köyceğiz, and other nearby locations. If you decide to stay in beautiful Dalyan, the **Kristal Pansiyon** (tel. (252) 284 22 63 or 284 31 53) provides palatial rooms, all-important screened windows, and an excellent view of the Lycean rock tombs (singles US$7; doubles US$14; breakfast included). You can also camp in Köyceğiz at **Anatolia Camping** (US$3 per person, US$2.50 per tent, US$3 per caravan) or in Dalyan at **Dalyan Camping** (tel. (252) 248 41 57; US$4-8). Bring mosquito repellent.

CENTRAL TURKEY

The high, dry mountain ranges of Central Anatolia form Turkey's bread basket. While the Aegean and Mediterranean coasts suffer from rampant tourism, this beautiful region boasts some of the country's most authentic, hospitable towns and villages.

■ Ankara

Though less charming and European than Istanbul, Ankara is also less pretentious—it buzzes with a current of real life, urgency, and industry found nowhere else in Turkey. Catch the city on a sunny summer day, and you may find it livelier and more engaging than its reputation suggests.

SIGHTS AND ENTERTAINMENT The fantastic **Anadolu Medeniyetleri Müzesi** (Museum of Anatolian Civilizations) lies at the foot of the citadel that dominates the old town. Walk to the top of Hisarpark Cad., turn right at the Citadel steps (without ascending), and follow the Citadel boundaries. The museum's unique setting—a restored 15th-century Ottoman *han* (inn) and *bedesten* (covered bazaar)—complements the world-class collection of astoundingly old artifacts inside (open Tu-Su 8:30am-5:15pm; US$2.40, students US$1.60). Completed in 1987, the pure white **Kocatepe Mosque** is one of the world's largest and most beautiful. Don't leave town without visiting **Anıt Kabir,** Atatürk's mausoleum (open M 1:30-5pm, Tu-Su 9am-5pm; free). The structure, nearly a kilometer long, houses Atatürk's sarcophagus and many personal effects. To get there, take Ankaray to Tandoğan and follow the Anıt Kabir signs. When you reach an unmarked entrance guarded by two soldiers, it's a 10-minute uphill walk to the mausoleum entrance.

At night, bars in Kızılay fill with students after the coffeeshops close, but manic dancers head to the **nightclubs** and discos scattered around Kavaklidere, Gaziosmanpaşa, and Çankaya. Pub life centers on two streets: **İnkilâp Sok.** and the livelier **Bayındır Sok.,** two and three blocks to the left of Kızılay Sq. as you look south. Beer flows freely at the crowded **Büyük Ekspress,** 12/A Bayındır Sok.

PRACTICAL INFO, ACCOMMODATIONS, AND FOOD The **train** station *(gar)* is 1½km southwest of Ulus Sq.; trains travel to Istanbul and Izmir (US$6-16 each). The **bus** terminal *(Otogar),* in Söğütözü 5km west of Kızılay, is connected to all points in the city by local buses, *dolmuş,* and taxis. Buses depart frequently for Konya (3½hr., US$7.20), Istanbul (7½hr., US$10.50), and Izmir (8½hr., US$14). The **tourist office,** 121 Gazi Mustafa Kemal Blv. (tel. (312) 488 70 07 or 231 55 72), directly outside the Maltepe stop on Ankaray, gives out free maps (open daily 9am-6:30pm). There is a **branch office** at the airport (open 24hr.). **Embassies** in Ankara include: **Australia,** 83 Nenehatun Cad., Gaziomanpaşa (tel. (312) 446 11 80); **Bulgaria,** 124 Atatürk Blv. (tel. (312) 426 74 55); **Canada,** 75 Nenehatun Cad. (tel. (312) 436 12 75); **Greece,** 9-11 Zia Ül-Rahman Cad., Gaziomanpaşa (tel. (312) 436 88 60); **New Zealand,** 13/4 İran Cad., Kavaklıdere (tel. (312) 467 90 56); **South Africa,** 27 Filistin Sok., Gaziomanpaşa (tel. (312) 446 40 56); **U.K.,** 46A Şehit Ersan Cad., Çankaya (tel. (312) 468 62 30); and **U.S.,** 110 Atatürk Blv. (tel. (312) 468 61 10).

Of the two main accommodations centers, Ulus is cheaper, but Kızılay is safer and cleaner. Going south along Atatürk Blv., take the fourth left after the McDonald's and the third right onto Selanik Cad. to reach peaceful **Otel Ertan,** 70 Selanik Cad. (tel. (312) 418 40 84), convenient to Kızılay nightlife (singles US$15; doubles US$28). **M.E.B. Özel Çağdaş Erkek Öğrenci Yurt,** 15 Neyzen Tevfik Sok., Maltepe (tel. (312) 232 29 54 or 232 29 55), between G.M.K. Blv. and Gençlik Cad., is a co-ed hostel June through August. Coming out of the Demirtepe Ankaray stop onto G.M.K. Blv., make a right (away from the tourist office) uphill onto Neyzen Tevfik Sok (US$12).

Kızılay has many mid-range restaurants and cafes; Gençlike Park has cheaper eateries, and the Citadel and Kavaklıdere more upscale establishments. In Kızılay, **Göksu Restaurant,** 22/A Bayındur Sok., has excellent Turkish and European food at surprisingly low prices. Near the citadel is the **Zenger Paşa Konağı,** 13 Doyran Sok., a restaurant and museum in a beautifully restored Ottoman house (lamb chops US$6). The **Gıma supermarket** is on Anafartalar Cad. in Ulus and Atatürk Bul. in Kızılay.

CAPPADOCIA

The Biblical land of Tabal, later named Katpatukya ("Land of the Beautiful Horses") under the Persian Empire (585-332 BC), is known today as Cappadocia (Kapadokya). Early Christians dug homes and churches and the Byzantines developed vast underground cities in the **tufa,** a soft rock formed from hardened volcanic ash and lava. Part of Cappadocia's otherworldly appearance stems from its "moonscapes," where stairs, windows, and sentry holes have been carved into the already eerily-eroded rock. If you can only spare a day or two, it is probably easiest to stay in Göreme, see the spectacular Open Air Museum, and then take a day trip to the underground cities of Derinkuyu and Kaymaklı (many local companies run a full-day tour to the Ihlara Valley; US$25). **Transportation** in the region includes minibuses, guided tours, and horse (about US$85 per hr.), bike, moped, and car rentals from any of the numerous agencies in Ürgüp and Göreme. A minibus runs from the Ürgüp *otogar* to Göreme, Çavuşin, Zelve, and Avanos. Guided tours of Cappadocia's major sites are available from agencies in Göreme and Ürgüp (US$20-35, ISIC discounts).

Nevşehir Although **Nevşehir** is not especially interesting, it is the region's transportation hub. Even if you buy what looks like a direct bus ticket from Göreme or Ürgüp, what you are really getting is probably a *servis* shuttle to Nevşehir and then a regular bus onward from there. Also, the only public transportation available to Aksaray, Penhkuyu, and Kaymakılı from Ürgüp and Göreme is through Nevşehir. Don't stay here if you have time to take a *servis* bus to Göreme or Ürgüp, which are more interesting. **Dolmuş** leave from outside the tourist office for most parts of Cappadocia and also stop at the main bus station. At the *otogar,* buses leave for Ankara (4hr., 12 per day, US$6), Istanbul (11hr., 6 per day, US$14), and Izmir (12hr., 2 per day, US$14). From Lale Cad., outside the Göreme and Nevşehir ticket agencies, turn left at the intersection and you will see the **tourist office** (tel. (384) 213 36 59), which offers free maps and brochures (open M-F 8am-5:30pm and Sa-Su 9:30am-5:30pm; English spoken). If you find yourself needing to spend the night in Nevşehir, try the **Epok**

Otel, 39 Atatürk Blv. (tel. (384) 213 11 68 or 213 14 87; fax 213 16 42), with well-furnished rooms, private showers, and an in-house restaurant (singles US$14; doubles US$24; breakfast included). Many places along the main street serve *kebap* and *lahmacun* (Turkish pizza) for under US$3.

Cappadocia contains almost 200 **underground cities,** all carved from *tufa.* **Kaymaklı** and **Derinkuyu** are the two largest, about 30 minutes and 45 minutes from Göreme by *dolmuş* respectively, with a connection in Nevşehir (both sites open daily 8am-7pm, off season 8am-5pm; US$2, students US$1.20). *Dolmuş* (US$0.30) run to Nevşehir every 30 minutes (6:30am-7pm) and then go on to the underground cities for an additional US$0.75. Remember, these cities were designed to foil potential trespassers, who would fall to their deaths from sudden drops hidden behind corners. Both cities have uncharted tunnels, so be careful and know that red arrows lead down, blue arrows up.

■ Göreme

Göreme is conveniently located, easy to navigate, and places an emphasis on doing things in caves—most bars and discos are subterranean. Many restaurants and virtually all pensions offer one or more "cave rooms." Göreme also makes a good base for exploring the Rose Valley and the Pigeon Valley.

SIGHTS AND ENTERTAINMENT The most impressive concentration of sights in the region is at the **Open-Air Museum,** 1km out of Göreme on the Ürgüp road, containing six Byzantine churches, a convent, and a kitchen/refectory (museum open 8am-6:30pm; Sept.-Oct. closes at 6pm; US$5, students US$3). The **Rose Valley,** between Göreme and Çavuşin, provides terrain and atmosphere for wonderful **hikes** through eerie landscapes of fairy chimneys and bizarre multicolored rock formations. Tour groups don't come here, so you'll have the place all to yourself. From Göreme, take the first left on the road to the Open Air Museum, walk for five minutes, then go right; you'll be rewarded with a magnificent vista. Descend into the valley from here. After wandering off the several paths and getting lost from time to time, you'll eventually end up in **Çavuşin.** The Avanos-Nevşehir bus and the Avanos-Zelve-Göreme-Ürgüp minibus back to Göreme are available until 6pm, departing every 30 minutes (weekends every hr.). After that, a taxi from Çavuşin costs roughly US$4. **Escape Bar,** located in a converted donkey barn below the giant fairy chimney with the Turkish flag, features bellydancing nightly (open until morning).

PRACTICAL INFO, ACCOMMODATIONS, AND FOOD Göreme's **bus station** in the main square contains the hotel-run cooperative, a **tourist office** (tel. (384) 271 23 16 or 271 2317; fax 271 25 69), which only provides info on lodgings. The government of Göreme has set the prices for the town's hostels according to the following scale: dorm beds US$5; private singles US$6, with shower US$8; but establishments designated as starred hotels can charge higher rates. **Köse Pansiyon** (tel. (384) 279 22 44; fax 274 25 77), just past and behind the PTT, offers a dorm, 4 triples, and 6 doubles. The excellent **Paradise Pansiyon** (tel./fax (384) 271 22 48), is located on the road to the Open Air Museum (Turkish breakfast US$1.60). **Ufuk Motel and Pension** (tel. (384) 271 21 57), next door to Paradise, offers 4 cave rooms and 11 regular rooms. **Kaya Camping** (tel. (384) 343 31 00), a 5 to 10 minute walk uphill from the museum, has a superb view of the opposite valley (US$3.20 per person, US$1.60 per tent). **Orient,** opposite the Yüksel Motel, features mostly Turkish food in a cave atmosphere (main courses US$1.20; vegetarian dishes and *saç tava* US$3.50, 5-course special US$4.75). **Cafe Dociş,** to the left as you exit the *otogar,* has Turkish *mantı* (ravioli), American movies shown until 8pm, happy hour from 7-8pm (large beer US$0.80), and free (but slow) **Internet access** (open until 1am).

■ Ürgüp

Less of a tourist resort and more compact than Göreme, **Ürgüp** emerges from a collage of bizarre rock formations and early Christian dwellings interspersed among sunny vineyards and old Greek mansions. Göreme is an easy 10-minute *dolmuş* ride away, and Ürgüp's *otogar* and rental agencies offer access to most Cappadocian points of interest. At the **otogar** on Güllüce Cad., buses leave for Ankara (5hr., US$8) and Istanbul (12hr., US$14). You may direct any bus schedule-related questions to the helpful and English-speaking Aydın Altan at **Nevtur** (tel. (384) 341 43 02 or 341 33 30) in the *otogar*. The extremely informative Ürgüp **tourist office** (tel. (384) 341 40 59), inside the garden on Kayseri Cad., provides maps, bus schedules, and helps arrange tours (open daily Apr.-Oct. 8am-7pm or later; Nov.-Mar. 8am-5:30pm).

The main square is 20m down the road from the bus station, marked by a bath house and an Atatürk statue. The road forks uphill into two smaller roads, both full of pensions and hotels. **Hotel Asia Minor** (tel. (384) 341 46 45), behind the Atatürk statue, is a beautiful 150-year-old Greek mansion with reproductions of rock church frescoes on the lobby walls and a lovely garden (singles with bath US$10-16; breakfast included). **Hotel Akuzun** (tel. (384) 341 38 69 or 341 38 66), across the street from Hotel Asia Minor, has friendly service and modern facilities, including a restaurant (singles US$16-20; doubles US$32-40). The local specialty is called *tandir*—cooked in an underground clay charcoal oven similar to the Indian tandoori. *Tandir* specialties include *sebze güveç* (eggplant and other vegetables), *kiremit kebap* (lamb or chicken cooked with onion, tomato, mushroom, and cheese), and *kuru fasulye* (pinto beans, tomato, and onion). **Cappadocia Restaurant,** a few blocks from the center of town on Kongre Salonu Yanı Cad., makes a mean *dolma* for US$1.50 and has veggie options.

The connoisseur may be aware that Cappadocia is one of Turkey's major viticultural regions, with its center in Ürgüp. Just uphill from Hotel Surban, the renowned **Turasan Winery,** supplier of 98% of Cappadocia's wines, offers free tours and tastings in its rock-carved wine cellar. Several wine shops around the main square also offer free tastings. You may also want to drop in at the coed **Tarihi Şehir Hamamı** in the main square for a complete bath with massage/scrub and sauna (US$5; open daily 7am-11pm). A combination of Turks and tourists heads to the **Armağan Disco,** across the street from the Kapadokya Market (under the "Born To Be Free" neon sign), where disco tunes and Turkish pop occasionally precede a belly-dance act. They also have several (relatively) quiet stone-cut rooms with divans and carpets, making Armağan the most conducive of Ürgüp's nighttime establishments to privacy and coherent conversation.

Talking Turkey

The Turkish language is incredibly expressive, full of idioms and metaphors used to colorfully explain different aspects of the human experience. *Turşu gibiyim* literally means "I am like a pickle," and is used to describe a state of complete exhaustion. *Tavuk gibiyim,* or "I am like a chicken," is said by someone who goes to bed very early. If you are completely shocked by something unexpected, you should say *eşekten karpuz düşmüş olduğum,* to explain that you were like the watermelon that fell from the donkey's back. When feeling distracted and preoccupied, you should explain yourself with *midiye çikariyorum,* to let everyone know that you are busy digging for mussels. When confronted with some sort of unpleasant surprise, an exasperated "what the hell?" can be replaced with a simple *battı balık yan gider,* an exclamation that sunken fish go sideways. After a fantastic meal, you should thank your hostess effusively with *herkes harika, sadece kuş sütü yoktu,* and she will understand that everything was wonderful and only the bird's milk was missing.

Ukraine (Україна)

US$1	= 2.25hv (hryvny)	1hv =	US$0.44
CDN$1	= 1.44hv	1hv =	CDN$0.69
UK£1	= 3.77hv	1hv =	UK£0.27
IR£1	= 3.20hv	1hv =	IR£0.31
AUS$1	= 1.28hv	1hv =	AUS$0.78
NZ$1	= 1.11hv	1hv =	NZ$0.87
SAR1	= 0.35hv	1hv =	SAR2.85
DM1	= 1.28hv	1hv =	DM0.78

Country Phone Code: 380   **International Dialing Prefix: 810**

Even by the standards of a newly crazed Eastern Europe, huge, unhinged Ukraine is anarchic and dour. Kiev, for centuries the cradle of Russian culture, finds itself besieged on the one side by the western region of the country, with its Uniate congregations in lavish Polish cathedrals, its bold rhetoric of Ukrainian nationalism, and its traditional affinity for Europe; and on the other hand by the lovely Crimean peninsula, whose predominantly Russian population clamors for increased autonomy and looks toward the big neighbor to the north. East-central Ukraine, meanwhile, is an industrial wasteland and home to the infamous, still functioning Chernobyl nuclear power plant. There is nothing quaint or pretty about a nation in as deep a crisis as Ukraine's, but it does make the rest of Europe seem too modern, superficial, even a little dull. One need not depart from any beaten path, because—apart from an ugly and expensive Intourist trail—there is none. Awful as this sounds, Ukrainian financial troubles mean dirt-cheap transportation and accommodations. Quality museums in the cities cost nothing and are empty; in western Ukraine, medieval castles are still huge, dark, and unsupervised; and the rolling, endless plains of wheat and sunflowers in the country's center, and the Black Sea off the coast of Yalta, even after years of Soviet tourism, retain an untouchable natural magnificence. There are treasures here, but you'll have to find them yourself, because Ukraine, with enough troubles of its own, isn't inclined to play host.

For more detailed coverage of Ukraine, refer to *Let's Go: Eastern Europe 1999.*

GETTING THERE

Foreign travelers arriving in Ukraine must have not only a **visa,** but also an **invitation** from a citizen or official organization or a tourist voucher from a travel agency. Regular visa processing at an embassy (invitation in hand) takes up to nine days and costs US$50 (double-entry US$80); three-day rush, available to citizens of Australia, Canada, Great Britain, Ireland, New Zealand, and South Africa, but *not* the United States, costs US$80 (double-entry US$120). For more info, contact an **embassy** (see **Government Information Offices,** p. 7). Some private organizations, such as **Russia House** (U.S. tel. (202) 986-6010; fax 667-4244), arrange visas and invitations. **Host Families Association,** 5-25 Tavricheskaya, 193015 St. Petersburg, Russia (tel./fax +7 (812) 275 19 92; email alexei@hofak.hop.stu.neva.ru), provides invitations for HOFA guests.

If you arrive at the **Kiev airport** without a visa, you can buy a **tourist voucher,** which will then permit you to buy a visa. This allows you to go through customs, where you must declare all valuables and foreign currency to facilitate leaving the country. Carry a copy of your invitation and letters of introduction at all times. Within three days of your arrival in Ukraine, you should check into a hotel or register with the hall of nightmares that is the **Office of Visas and Registration (OVIR),** in Kiev at bulv. Tarasa Shevchenka 34 (Тараса Шевченка), or in police stations in smaller cities (US$10). Visas may also be extended here. Your visa not only lets you in; it also allows you to leave. *Do not lose it.*

Air Ukraine International (in the U.S., tel. (312) 337-0004) flies from European capitals, Chicago, New York, and Washington. Swiss Air, Air France, ČSA, Lufthansa, LOT, Malév, and SAS also fly to Kiev. **Trains** run to Ukraine from all neighboring states. When coming from the west, prepare for a two-hour stop at the border. **Ferries** cross the Black Sea from Odessa and Yalta to Istanbul.

GETTING AROUND

Trains are dirt cheap, reasonably comfortable, and go everywhere. Getting tickets, however, can drive you batty. Try to buy tickets two or three days in advance. You may be told there are no more seats when only the first two classes are full; ask about the other classes as well. Conductors are often willing to seat those without tickets (charging the ticket price and pocketing the money), and scalpers sell what are usually valid tickets. **Buses** are more expensive but best for short distances. Buy tickets at the regular ticket windows (the night before in large cities).

Taxis overcharge everyone; agree on a price before getting in. State taxis (with checkered signs) are supplemented by unregulated "private transport," which is at your own risk. Both can be hailed by holding the hand at a downward salute.

ESSENTIALS

Technically, the breakup of the Soviet Union brought about the demise of the state travel agency, **Intourist,** which was responsible for foreigners traveling to Ukraine. Nonetheless, they still have an office in every city, sometimes under another name. It's not a bad idea to register with your embassy once you arrive in Ukraine. Besides making the process of recovering lost passports much quicker, the embassy staff may be able to offer important information on travel in Ukraine.

UKRAINE

On September 2, 1996, Ukraine replaced **karbovanets** (Krb; a.k.a. kupon) with a new currency, **hryvnia** (hv; гривна), which eradicated five zeroes—each hryvnia (pl. hryvny) is worth 100,000 karbovantsi. Hotels usually request hryvny, only occasionally asking for dollars. International train tickets are usually sold partly in hryvny, partly in dollars. **Exchange** of US$ and DM is fairly simple and can be done at Обнім Валюты *(Obmin Valyut)* kiosks. Exchange of other currencies is difficult; **traveler's checks** are not accepted but can be changed to dollars at small commissions in almost every city. **X-Change Points,** in major cities, have Western Union and give Visa cash advances. *Don't* give your money to private money exchangers lurking by kiosks.

COMMUNICATION Telephones are struggling out of the Dark Ages. Order international calls at the post office for the cheapest rates. In Kiev, **Utel** (Ukraine telephone) produces electronic **phonecards.** Utel's new technology lets you make collect calls from some phones; dial 27 10 36 and ask for an "ITNT" (AT&T) operator. **AT&T Direct** (tel. (8) 100 11—wait for another tone after the 8); **BT Direct** (tel. (8) 10 04 41); **Canada Direct** (tel. (8) 100 17); **MCI Direct** (tel. (8) 100 13); and **Sprint Direct** (tel. (8) 100 15) are available from Utel and private phones. **Local calls** cost 0.10-0.30hv from any gray pay phone in most cities. In Lviv, buy tokens at the post office or at kiosks. **Mail** is cheap but slow (at least 2-3 weeks from Kiev to any foreign destination). DHL is available, however, in Kiev, Odessa, and Lviv. In case of **fire,** dial 01; to reach the **police,** call 02; and for an **ambulance,** dial 03.

Ease your trip with a few Ukrainian or Russian phrases (see **Russia: Essentials,** p. 743). Ukrainian or sometimes Polish is preferred in the West, but Russian is still more common in Crimea and most of Eastern Ukraine, even Kiev. The Ukrainian alphabet resembles Russian with only a few character and pronunciation differences. Ukrainian adds "і" (*ee* sound) and "ї" (*yee* sound)—"и" is closest to "*sit*." The "г" (hard g) has been reintroduced since independence but is not widely used, and the "г," pronounced "g" in Russian, comes out like an "h."

Yes/No	Так/Ні	tak/nee
Hello	Добрий день	DOH-bree dehn
Please	Прошу	PRO-shoo
Thank you	Дякую	DYA-kou-yoo
Excuse me	Выбачте	VIH-bach-te
Do you speak English?	Вы говорите по-англиськи?	vih ho-VOR-ih-te poh-anh-lih-skih
I don't understand	Я не розумію	ya ne roh-zoo-MEE-yu
Where?	Де?	deh
How much?	Скільки?	SKEEL-kih
I'd like...	Я хочу...	ya KHO-choo
Help!	Поможіт	poh-moh-ZHEET

ACCOMMODATIONS, CAMPING, AND FOOD Hotels fall into two categories, "hotels" and "tourist bases" called "Турбаза" (TOOR-bah-zah). The latter usually form part of a complex aimed at motoring tourists but are otherwise nearly indistinguishable from hotels. Hotel prices in Kiev are astronomical, but singles run anywhere from 5hv to 90hv per night in the rest of the country. Check your bill carefully. Your passport may be kept for the duration of your stay. Conditions are usually adequate, although you'll need your own toilet paper (buy it at kiosks or markets), and hot water is a rare gift. Do not leave valuables in your room unattended. Most cities have a **campground** on the edge of town. These old Soviet complexes can be quite posh, with saunas and restaurants. Free camping is illegal. **Private rooms** are available through overseas agencies and bargaining at the train station (10hv per person).

Ukraine is simply not going to make your tummy happy. New, fancy restaurants (main dishes from 15-60hv) are popping up to accommodate tourists and the few Ukrainians who can afford them. There are few choices between these and *stolovayas* that are dying bastions of cheap, hot food. Most restauranteurs' reactions to **vegetarians** are hostile, and the meat-free menu rarely has more than 'shrooms (гриби; *hribi*). Produce is sold by the kilogram in jam-packed **markets** filling enormous warehouses. **State food stores** are classified by content. *Hastronom* (Гастроном) sells everything, but concentrates on packaged goods. *Moloko* (Молоко) offers milk products. *Ovochi-frukty* (Овочі-Фрукты) sells fruits and vegetables, often preserved in large jars. *Myaso* (Мясо) has meat, *Hlib* (Хліб) bread, *Kolbasy* (Колбаси) sausage, and *Ryba* (Риба) fish. **Liquor,** available everywhere, is very cheap. A half-liter of *Stolichnaya* costs about 3hv and is generally tastier than the moonshine *(samohonka)*.

■ Kiev (Київ)

Straddling the wide Dnipro River and layered with hills and greenery, Kiev is a becoming city, but it hasn't yet figured out how to become a thriving capital(ist) metropolis. Once the USSR's third city, and now Ukraine's center for everything, Kiev should share the vibrance and vivacity that other newly liberated Eastern European cities possess. But, alas, with hesitant foreign investment, stagnant political reform, and a struggling population that lives day-to-day, Kiev does not radiate progress. This lull can be a virtue, not a vice, providing a comfortable and un-touristed environment in which to enjoy its rich, though crumbling, melange of medieval cathedrals and 19th-century façades.

ORIENTATION AND PRACTICAL INFORMATION

Almost all attractions and services lie on the right bank of the Dnipro River, in western Kiev. The metro consists of three intersecting lines: blue (MB), green (MG), and red (MR). The train station is at MR: Vokzalna (Вокзальна). Two metro stops away, **Khreshchatik** (Хрещатик), a busy boulevard, satisfies most tourist needs except housing. The center of Kiev is vul. Khreshchatik's **Maydan Nezalezhnosti** (Майдан Незалежності), a fountain-filled fun spot next to the post office.

Telephone Code: 044.
Flights: Kiev-Borispil Airport receives international flights. A **city bus** (2.50hv) runs to MR: Livoberezhna (Лівобережна), across the river from central Kiev (every 2hr.).
Trains: Kiev-Passazhirski (Київ-Пассажирський), Vokzalna pl. (Вокзальна). MR: Vokzalna or tram 2. Buy international **tickets** at Intourist window 10, 2nd fl. Open daily 8am-1pm, 2-7pm, and 8pm-7am. To: Budapest (12hr., 192hv); Lviv (12hr., 14-21hv); Moscow (15-17hr., 43-63hv); Odessa (19hr., 16hv); Prague (34hr., 197hv); and Warsaw (15hr., 82hv).
Buses: Tsentralny Avtovokzal (Центральний Автовокзал), Moskovska pl. 3 (Московська; tel. 265 04 30). Long-distance destinations. To: Kharkiv (2 per day, 17hv); Minsk (2 per day, 21hv); and Moscow (2 per day, 42hv). **Pivdenna** (Південна), pr. Akademyka Hlushkova 3 (Академика Глушкова; tel. 263 40 04), connects to Odessa, and **Podil** (Поділ), vul. Nyzhny Val 15a (Нижній Вал), services Crimea. Buy tickets at **Central Bus Terminal,** Lesi Ukrainky 14 (tel. 225 20 66).
Public Transportation: Kiev's **Metro** has 3 intersecting lines. Buy tokens at the "Каса" *(Kasa)* for 0.30hv or a monthly pass from a numbered kiosk for 10hv (good on all public transport). Tickets for **trams, trolleys,** and **buses** are sold at kiosks (0.30hv) and must be punched on board.
Tourist Office: Intercity Travel, vul. Hospitalna 4, #304 (Госпітальна; tel. 294 31 11; fax 220 54 46), inside Hotel Rus (Готел Рус). Open M-F 9am-8pm, Sa 10am-4pm. *Kiev Pocket* guides are available in the lobby downstairs (10hv). **Hotel Kyivska's lobby** (Київська), behind Hotel Rus at vul. Hospitalna 12, also has info. Both hotels are at MB: Respublikansky stadion (Республиканський стадіон).
Embassies: Australia, vul. Kominternu 18 (Комінтерну; tel. 225 75 86). **Belarus,** vul. Yanvarskogo Vosstaniya 6 (Январского Восстанія; tel. 290 02 01). **Canada,** vul.

Yaroslaviv Val 31 (Ярославів Вал; tel. 464 11 44). **Russia,** pr. Kutuzova 8 (Кутузова; tel. 294 79 36). **South Africa** (tel. 227 71 72). **U.K.,** vul. Desyatynna 6 (tel. 462 00 11; fax 462 00 13). Open M-F 9am-noon. **U.S.,** vul. Y. Kotsyubinskoho 10 (Ю. Коцюбинського; tel. 244 73 49, emergency tel. 216 38 05). Open M-F 2-5pm. Citizens of **Ireland** and **New Zealand** should contact the U.K. embassy.

Currency Exchange: Look for *Obmin-Valyut* (Обмін-Валют) windows on every street and in every cafe-bar. They usually take only US$ and DM and don't deal in traveler's checks or credit card advances. For those services, try a bank.

Emergencies: Fire, tel. 01. **Ambulance,** tel. 03.

Police: tel. 02.

Medical Assistance: Emergency Care Center, vul. Mechnikova 1 (tel. 22 42 02 or 227 92 30), also has a **dental clinic** (tel. 227 42 40). The **U.S. Embassy** (see **Embassies,** above) has a list of recommended hospitals.

Post Office: vul. Khreshchatik 22, next to Maidan Nezalezhnosti (Майдан Незалежності). *Poste Restante* at counters 29-30. Open M-Sa 8am-8pm, Su 9am-7pm. **Postal Code:** 252 001.

Telephones: Mizhmisky Perehovorny Punkt (Мижміський Перегорний Пункт), at the post office, or **Telefon-Telefaks** (Телефон-Телефакс) around the corner (entry on Khreshchatik). Both offices open 24hr. They insist they can't dial AT&T or MCI operators, but Utel phones will do the trick. Buy **Utel phonecards** (10, 20, or 40hv) from the post office and upscale hotels.

ACCOMMODATIONS AND FOOD

Kiev's hotel prices, aimed at exploitative foreign businesspeople, seem rude at best, but cheap lodgings await on the distant horizons. **Diane Sadovnikov**—a former missionary living and working here—and her husband Yuri find accommodations in a private apartment (45-75hv), with a family, or in a hotel/dorm. They also arrange invitations (US$30; tel./fax 558 10 58; call or fax between 9am-5pm 1 month in advance). The **Grazhdanski Aviatski Institut Student Hotel,** vul. Nizhinska 29E (Ніжіньска; tel. 484 90 59), is an unbeatable deal if you don't mind the trek. From behind MR: Vokzalna, ride 5 stops on tram 1 or 7 to *Hramatna*. Walk back a block and a half, swing a right onto vul. Nyzhinska, and cross the first big intersection diagonally left into the block complex. Pass the first house, turn left, and walk along the wavy path behind block "Д," until "Гостиница ФПК" appears above the entrance to building 29E (singles 15hv; doubles 25hv). **Hostinitsa Druzhba** (Дружба), bulv. Druzhby Narodiv 5 (Дружби Народів; director's tel. 268 33 87; reservations fax 268 33 00) is the cheapest hotel in Kiev, the bathrooms work, and it's on a metro line (MB: Libidska; singles 85-115hv; doubles 120-168hv). Walk straight out of the metro stop for 100m and turn left at the overpass onto the major road; the hostel is 100m up on the left. **Hostinitsa Bratislava** (Братіслава), vul. Malyshka 1 (Малішка; tel. 551 76 44), has pleasant rooms and clean bathrooms. (MR: Darnytsya. Singles with bath US$54; doubles with bath US$85. Breakfast included. English spoken.)

Most restaurants in Kiev cater to foreigners or the newly rich; with few exceptions meals cost 12hv and up even at cheaper restaurants. Supermarkets such as **7/24,** vul. Baseina 1/2 (Басеїна; open 24hr.), are convenient but more expensive than markets and smaller shops. **Pantagruel** (Пантагрюель; tel 228 81 42), vul. Lysenko 1 (Лисенко), right next to MG: Zoloty Vorota, serves delicious, authentic Italian food (live music F-Sa 8-10pm; open Su-Th 11am-11pm, F-Sa 11am-2am; reserve ahead). Go for some tasty Lebanese dishes at **Montannya Snack** (Монтання Снак), vul. Volodimyrska 68. (Володимирська. MB: Ploshcha Lva Tolstoho. Open M-F noon-11pm, Sa-Su noon-midnight.) **Cafe Panorama** (Кафе Панорама) lies down Andryivsky uzviz, 25m past St. Andrew's Church, and up the steep wooden steps on the right, with glorious views from its perch above Kiev and quiet outdoor seating (food served; open daily in summer noon-11pm). **Bessarabsky Rynok** (Бессарабский Ринок), vul. Khreshchatik and bulv. Shevchenka (Шевченка), is a large **market** (open M 7am-5pm, Tu-Su 7am-7pm).

UKRAINE

SIGHTS AND ENTERTAINMENT

Downtown Kiev lies on **vul. Khreshchatyk** (Хрещатик), a broad commercial avenue built largely after World War II but not marred by the stereotypical Soviet bleakness. Book venders, musicians, and angel-headed hipsters gather at **Maidan Nezalezhnosti** (Independence Plaza, formerly October Revolution Square), encircled by large fountains and emerging market forces. Head up Sofiyska vul. (Софіївська вул.) beyond the plaza to reach the golden onion domes, decorated facades, and 11th-century Byzantine icons of the **St. Sophia Monastery Complex,** once the centerpiece of mighty Kievan Rus, the site of Rus's first library, and even now the country's symbolic focal point. (Open F-Tu 10am-5:30pm, W 10am-5pm. 6hv. Architectural museum inside, as well as exhibitions, each an additional 1hv, students 0.50hv. 1hr. tours: foreigners 10hv, students 3hv. Cameras 10hv.) If there are no protesters gathered under the equestrian statue of **Bohdan Khmelnitsky,** who led the 17th-century uprising against Polish rule, you'll be able to head past the crumbling facades of Rilsky prov. (Рильський пров.) to vul. Volodimyrska (Володимирьська) to ancient, winding **Andrivsky uzviz,** lined with cafes, souvenir vendors, and galleries. **St. Andrew's Cathedral** looms proudly over the street and is a favorite with artists in it for the money. From the end of the street near Volodimirska, a scenic **funicular** goes back to upper Kiev (every 5min. daily 6:30am-11pm, 0.30hv).

The **Zolotoi Vorota** (Золотои Ворота; Golden Gates) have marked the entrance to Kiev since 1037 and are down Volodimyrska on the other side of St. Sophia's. Farther down, Volodimyrska runs into bulv. Tarasa Shevchenka (бул. Тараса Шевченка), one of Kiev's more pleasant streets, sweeping past many-domed **Volodimyrsky Cathedral,** built to commemorate 900 years of Christianity in Kiev. Pleasant Khreshchatyk Park lies overlooking the Dniepr at the end of vul. Khreshchatyk.

Kiev's oldest and holiest religious site is the mysterious **Kievo-Pecherska Lavra** (Київо-Печерська Лавра; Kiev-Pechery Monastery; MR: Arsenalna), once the center of Orthodox Christianity. Its monks were mummified and entombed in the **caves.** Buy a candle as you enter if you want to see anything. Women should cover their heads and shoulders; men should wear pants. When in the caves, you're supposed to look only at the monks whose palms are facing up (open W-M 9-11:30am and 1-4pm). The 18th-century **Velyka lavrska dzvinytsya** (Велика лаврська дзвіниця; Great Cave Bell Tower; open daily 9:30am-8pm; 2.5hv, students 1hv) and the 12th-century **Troitska Nadzramna Tserkva** (Троїцка надзрамна церква; Holy Trinity Church) on the grounds are particularly worth visiting. (Complex open daily 9:30am-7pm; in winter until 6pm. Ticket for all churches and exhibitions (but not museums) 8hv, students 4hv. English guides 2-3hv.)

Club Sofia, vul. Sofiivska 7 (Софіївська), off Maydan Nezalezhnosti, is a smoky cellar jam-packed with young artists, intellectuals, foreigners, and Ukrainians (open daily noon-1am). The hot new **Dinamo Luks Disco,** vul. Hrushevsky 3, is *the* place for groovin' up the dance floor, and it's right in the center. Bring your money (F-Sa men 30hv, women 15hv) and your disco-going clothes, and don't arrive before 11pm.

"Beeznesmen"

Wild rumors of the Ukrainian (and Russian) mafia loom large in other parts of the world, and truth be told, the mafia is a strong presence. The average traveler minding his or her own business, however, shouldn't be affected (unless his or her business is starting his or her own business). A tip for spotting these law-despising, tax-sheltering, Ukraine-exploiting folk: if you see a man with a flat-top and an Adidas sweat suit, talking on a cell phone, get out of a BMW, you shouldn't jump to conclusions in this PC age, but neither should you step on his toes and yell, "Hey, did you get run over by a lawnmower, or what, you sissy?"

■ Lviv (Львів)

Lviv's cobblestone alleys lead past towering spires, hulking homes, and several centuries of artistic and architectural achievement. These monuments see few of the tourists so familiar to other Austro-Hungarian cities like Kraków and Prague, but the vendors, storekeepers, and cafe owners on the streets below are ready and waiting.

SIGHTS AND ENTERTAINMENT Lviv's historical center is best seen on foot; start on prosp. Svobody (Свободи), next to the ornate Neoclassical **Opera and Ballet Theater** (Театра Опери та Балету), which opens onto a pedestrian mall. The **Mickiewicz statue,** honoring the Polish poet and patriot, is the site of concerts and political discussions. The **Natsionalny Muzey** (Національний Музей) at pr. Svobody 20, displays excellent 19th- and 20th-century Ukranian paintings (open M-W 11am-5pm, Sa-Su noon-6pm; 1hv, students 0.50hv, M students free). **Pl. Rynok** (Ринок), the historic market square, is the true heart of the city. On adjacent pl. Katedralna (Катедральна) rises the Polish **Roman Catholic Cathedral** (open M-Sa 6am-noon and 6-8pm, Su 6am-3pm and 5:30-8pm). The polished interior of **Preobrazhenska Tserkva** (Преображенська церква; Transfiguration Church), a block off Lesy Ukrainky, is definitely worth a peek. At the top of vul. Virmenska 35, the new **Kulturno-Mystetsky Tsentr "Dzyha"** (Культурно-Мистецький Центр "Дзига"; Art-Cultural Center "Dzyha"; tel. (0322) 72 74 20) holds funky exhibits of mostly contemporary art—sculptures, paintings, photos, and prints (open 10am-9pm; free). Once a week, usually Sa or Su, concerts are held here; look for notices in the building. Friday night is jazz night. To catch a performance at the **Opera** or the **Symphony,** vul. Tchaikovskoho, visit the ticket windows (театральни каси; *teatralny kasy*) at pr. Svobody 37 (open M-Sa 10am-1pm and 2:30-6pm). At night, shabbily dressed artsy types do shots while arguing with the sophisticated black-clad wine-sippers at **Club-Cafe Lyalka** (Клуб-Кафе Лялька), vul. Halytska 1 (Галицького; cover 2hv; open M-Th 11am-11pm, F-Su 11am-1 or 2am).

PRACTICAL INFO, ACCOMMODATIONS, AND FOOD The **train station,** at the end of Vokzalna vul. (Вокзальна), serves Kiev (11-16hr., 20-25hv), Moscow (29hr., 67hv), and Warsaw (13hr., 50hv). Buy **bus** tickets to Poland (Kraków 7-9hr., 34hv) at the station on the edge of town at vul. Stryska (Стрийська). The **travel bureau** in the Hotel George is the best place to plan a tour or gather info about the city (open daily 9am-noon and 2-6pm). The **Hotel George** (Готель Жорж), pl. Mitskievycha 1 (Міцкевича; tel. (0322) 72 59 52), is a restored turn-of-the-century luxury hotel; take tram 1 from the train station to "Дорошенка." (Singles 37-47hv, with bath 135hv; doubles 52hv, with bath 140hv. Breakfast included.) **Hotel Lviv,** ul. 700 Lvova 7 (tel. 79 22 70), a few blocks north of pr. Svobody, has spartan rooms (singles 30-54hv; doubles 30-84hv). Lviv is full of quick eateries serving Ukrainian fast food (beef and potatoes, borscht, etc.), especially around pl. Rynok. The most convenient **market** is behind the flower stands across from St. Andrew's Church. **Mediviya** (Медівія), vul. Krakivska 17, not far from pl. Rynok, serves fresh Ukrainian food at low prices (open daily 10am-10pm). **Skifya** (Скіфія), vul. Shevchenka 10, through the grocery into the dimly lit cellar, serves miraculously meat-less pitas (beef pitas also; open 11am-8pm).

■ Yalta (Ялта)

Yalta has weathered its perennial popularity remarkably well. There still remain spots where the wood and stone houses, the narrow tree-hung streets, the encircling gray-green mountains, and a glimpse of the sparkling sea recall the Yalta of Chekhov, Rachmaninov, and Tolstoy.

SIGHTS AND ENTERTAINMENT Strolling along the promenade is a favorite pastime after a hard day of sunbathing. Get off the trolleybus at **Sovetskaya pl.** (Советская) and walk 100m down **Moskovskaya ul.** (Московская) to reach the sea.

Author and playwright **Anton Chekhov** called Yalta home for the last five years of his life, and his house and garden at ul. Kirova 112 (Кирова) are now a museum (open Tu-Su 10am-5:15pm; 4hv, students 2hv). Bus 8 takes you there every 40 minutes from the *Kinoteatr Spartak* (Кинотеатр Спартак) stop on Pushkinskaya ul. (Пушкинская). Chekhov also built a *dacha* in lovely **Gurzuf** (Гурзуф), 45 minutes away by ferry. Ferries also run every 40 minutes to **Livadia** (Лівадія), site of the **Veliky Palats** (Великий Дворец; Great Palace), Nicholas II's ornate summer palace. In 1945, Churchill, Roosevelt, and Stalin met here during the "Yalta" Conference to finalize post-war spheres of influence (palace open daily in summer 10am-6pm; winter Th-Tu 10am-4pm; 6hv, students 3hv). The most extravagant *dacha* in Greater Yalta—**Palats Vorontsova** (open May-Sept. daily 9am-5pm; Oct.-Apr. closed M and F)—resides in the nearby city of **Alupka** (Алупка), where you can also take a **cable car** (runs F-W 9am-6pm; round-trip 10hv). The ferry for Livadia continues to Alupka (1½hr., 3.50hv); buy tickets from window #3 on the pier for all three destinations. Many **hiking trails** begin in Yalta; consult the *Polyana Skazok* (Поляна Сказок) campground (see below) for advice on reaching the **Uchan-Su waterfall** and other wonders.

PRACTICAL INFO, ACCOMMODATIONS, AND FOOD To get to Yalta, take a **train** to Simferopol from Kiev (16hr., 36hv), Moscow (26hr., 64hv), or Odessa (14hr., 18hv), and then get on one of the frequent **trolleybuses** to Yalta (4.08hv). Tickets for buses to nearby points can be purchased on board or at the **bus station,** Moskovskaya ul. 57; across the street is the **trolley station.** In the city, trolley 1 is most useful (0.20hv on board). The prices at Yalta's hotels have recently increased dramatically. The best deal is to book ahead or get a room from one of the elderly women at the bus station. The prices at **Gostinitsa Krym** (Гостиница Крым), Moskovskaya ul. 1/6 (tel. (0654) 32 60 01 or 32 78 73), with its small, clean rooms and hall shower and bath, can't be beaten for a downtown hotel (singles 20hv; doubles 31hv; 2.55hv registration fee). **Massandra** (Массандра), ul. Drazhinskovo 48 (Дражинского; tel. (0654) 35 25 91), is 15 minutes from the center (doubles 14-32hv per bed). For a beautiful campground with showers and kitchen, trek to **Motel-Camping Polyana Skazok,** ul. Kirova 167 (Кірова; tel. (0654) 39 52 19). Take bus 11, 26, or 27 from the station's upper platform to "Polyana Skazok" and walk 20 minutes uphill (no tents allowed; bungalows for two 16hv; motel doubles 40-60hv). For traditional Russian food, try **Cafe Siren** (Кафе Сирень), ul. Roosevelta 6 (Рузвелта), with its freshly made *borscht, kasha, kakdet,* and *kompot* (full meal 3-4hv; open daily 8am-9pm), or the **Cafe Krym** (Крым), Moskovskaya ul. 1/2 (full meal 3hv; open daily 7am-8pm).

■ Odessa (Odesa; Одесса)

A port city built to Baroque splendor with the help of Catherine's imperial patronage, sunny Odessa is the hometown of Isaac Babel. It still retains, in a lazily crumbling way, the flavor of his difficult, hilarious stories about the city's Jewish mobsters.

SIGHTS AND ENTERTAINMENT The pedestrian **Deribasovskaya ul.** (Дерибасовская), the port city's commercial center, is home to performers, artists, and a thriving cafe culture. Turn left on Rishelevskaya (Ришельевская) to find the **Opera and Ballet Theater,** a spectacular circular edifice towering over the surrounding gardens. Tickets for nightly shows run 1 to 5hv at the box office next door (open daily 10:30am-5pm, Sa until 4pm). The nearby **Muzey morskovo flotu** (Музей морского флота; Museum of the Black Sea Fleet), ul. Lanzheronovskaya 6 (Ланжероновская), boasts a unique collection, with dozens of models of old ships in what was once a luxurious club for 19th-century aristocratic dandies (open F-W 10am-3pm; 2hv, children 1hv; Russian tour 8hv). Shady **ul. Primorskaya** (ул. Приморская) is the most popular spot for strolling and people-watching. Down Primorskaya, a statue of the **Duc de Richelieu,** the city's founder, gazes toward the **Potemkin Stairs** (Потемкинская Лестница; *Potemkinskaya lestnitsa*). Director Sergei Eisenstein used these stairs in his epic 1925 film *Battleship Potemkin,* and the name has stuck. Beyond the steps is **Morskoy Vokzal,** the port, renovated into shininess by the Italians and graced by a hideous golden baby in the parking lot. The rock used to build Odessa was mined under the city, forming the world's longest series of **catacombs** on the outskirts. During the Nazi occupation, the **resistance** was based here, and the city has set up an excellent **museum** re-creating their camp. For tours in English, contact Ekskurzi Byuro (tel. (0482) 25 28 74), at the corner of Preobrazhenskaya (Преображенская) and Malaya Arnantskaya (Малая Арнантская). The coast is accessible on foot or by public transit. **Delfin** (Дельфин), on the edge of the park, and **Arkadiya** (Аркадия), the city's most popular, with wide stretches of sand, can be reached by trolley 5 or bus 129.

PRACTICAL INFO, ACCOMMODATIONS, AND FOOD You can leave Odessa by **train** for Kiev (12hr., 34hv), Lviv (15hr., 30hv), and Moscow (26hr., 101hv). The station lies on pl. Privokzalnaya (Привокзальная), at the south end of ul. Pushkinskaya (Пушкинская). Tram 2, 3, or 12 takes you along ul. Preobrazhenskaya to the west end of ul. Deribasovskaya; from there, take a right onto ul. Pushkinskaya. The **bus** station, ul. Dzerzhinskovo 58 (Дзержинского), along the tram 5 and 15 lines, also serves Kiev (11hr., 27hv). The office on the 2nd floor of **Hotel Krasnaya,** ul. Pushkinskaya 17 (tel. (0482) 25 75 20), will be happy to offer advice and info on tours of the catacombs and the city (open daily 9am-5pm). You must register at the **Office of Visas and International Registration (ОВИР),** Krasny Pereulok 5 (Красный Переулок; tel. (0482) 25 89 74; US$10), and keep the registration card to avoid a heavy "fine" at the border.

Accommodations are few and far between in Odessa. Private **apartments** are by far the cheapest option (from US$3 per person), but they tend to be far from the center. Train-station hawkers are recognizable by their signs—some variation on "Сдаю Комнату." Ask *"Skolko?"* (Сколько; how much?). Bargain for a better price than US$10. **Odessa State University Dormitories,** ul. Dovzhenko 9B, have clean rooms with shared kitchen and shower (10hv per bed). It is essential to call Irina Kolegaeva, the university dean, before you come (tel. (0482) 21 87 60; fax 63 32 66). If you can't reach her by phone, stop by her office at ul. Mayakovskaya 7 (Маяковская). **Pasazh** (Пасаж), ul. Preobrazhenskaya 34 (tel. (0482) 22 48 49), has pleasant, boxy little rooms (singles 35-65hv; doubles 60-75hv). Ul. Deribasovskaya teems with outdoor *pivo* and cutlet cafes. Point to what you want at the friendly Ukrainian **Kartoplyanki** (Картоплянки), ul. Ekaterininskaya 3 (Екатерининская; dishes US$1-2; open daily 8am-10pm). The party town of the former USSR never sleeps—ul. Deribasovskaya hops all night with music ranging from Euro-techno to Slavic folk. Check out the legendary **Gambrinus** (Гамбринус), at #31 (open 10am-11pm).

Yugoslavia (Југославија)

US$1	= 10DIN (dinar)	1DIN =	US$0.10
CDN$1	= 6.45DIN	1DIN =	CDN$0.16
UK£1	= 17DIN	1DIN =	UK£0.06
IR£1	= 14.30DIN	1DIN =	IR£0.07
AUS$1	= 5.90DIN	1DIN =	AUS$0.17
NZ$1	= 5.30DIN	1DIN =	NZ$0.20
SAR1	= 1.60DIN	1DIN =	SAR0.63
DM1	= 5.30DIN	1DIN =	DM0.19
Country Phone Code: 381		**International Dialing Prefix: 99**	

Yugoslavia has been born again three times: in 1929, 1946, and most recently in 1992, after four of its six constituent republics peeled away to independence. And there's no telling how long this latest incarnation will last. Kosovo, central to Serbian national mythology but now 90% Albanian, is being shelled into oblivion but also, perhaps, independence, while NATO continues to consider intervention. Vojbodina, to the north, where memories of Turkish occupation are few, and coastal Montenegro, packed with resorts and desperate for the return of Western tourists, hanker after their lost autonomy. Many Yugoslavs are eager to engage visitors in conversations about current affairs, and the tenor of these conversations can range from interesting and informative to profoundly uncomfortable. But few destinations in Europe are more politically compelling, if nothing else, and most Serbs and Montenegrans are quick to help visitors in any way possible.

In spring and summer 1998, the U.S. Department of State issued a series of warnings against travel in the southern Serbian province of Kosovo, where tensions between ethnic Albanians, who make up a 90% majority, and Yugoslav police forces have frequently erupted in violence and military action. Recent economic sanctions against Serbia and Montenegro, as well as a European ban on Yugoslav Airlines, may create delays or hostility toward tourists. While Belgrade and Novi Sad, remain worthwhile travel destinations, *Let's Go* does not recommend travel to Kosovo.

For more information on Yugoslavia, see *Let's Go: Eastern Europe 1999.*

ESSENTIALS

Visas (US$45 for Americans, US$22 for other citizens) are required of nationals from Australia, Canada, Ireland, New Zealand, South Africa, the U.K., and the U.S. Visa processing usually takes seven working days. Citizens of Ireland and Great Britain require letters of invitation to support their visa. Do not expect to receive a visa on the border. Entrants are required to declare the amount of cash they are bringing into the country and take no more out of the country than the amount on the entry receipt.

Belgrade is the main entry point, and is accessible by plane, train, bus, and car. **Yugoslavia Airlines (YAT)** flies into Belgrade, as well as European carriers including Lufthansa, British Airways, SwissAir, Air France, and LOT airlines. **Trains** are designated *brzi* (fast) or *putnički* (slow); reservations are generally required for couchettes and international trains, which come from Budapest, Thessaloniki, Skopje, Sofia, and Istanbul. **Buses** are more far reaching and less expensive.

With the exception of the tourist center in Belgrade, most **tourist offices** are geared toward organizing tours for locals going abroad and offer little info for international travelers. Most brochures are long out of date. State-run **hotels** dominate the accommodations scene in Serbia and Montenegro; you will have to leave your passport at the desk when you register, but you will regain it when you leave. **Private rooms** are few and far between. **Camping** is an option along the Danube and the Adriatic coast.

Yugoslav dinars (subdivided into the para; 100 para = 1 dinar) come in denominations of one, five, 10, and 20. While all transactions are legally supposed to take place in local currency, many establishments take Deutschmarks. Banks, hotels, and exchange booths (especially in Belgrade) offer exchange services; remember to get rid of excess dinars before you leave. Bring enough cash to cover your trip; restocking is difficult and can only be done in Belgrade. In theory, you can cash **AmEx** checks at several banks in Belgrade, but economic sanctions in the summer of 1998 have made this impossible. A growing number of establishments accept **credit cards.**

Poste Restante services are only available in Belgrade. **Post offices** have yellow PTT (ПТТ) signs. Telephones are coin- or card-operated; telephone coins, available at post offices, are cheaper and more convenient. The only place to make an **international call** is at the main post office in Belgrade. **You cannot make collect calls** from Yugoslavia. Emergency numbers are 93 for **fire,** 92 for **police,** 94 for **medical emergency.**

■ Belgrade (Београд)

Belgrade, the heart and soul of Serbia, offers unique insight into the character of a nation that has monopolized media headlines for ten years. Economic sanctions have made Belgrade a cheap destination, but political conditions can give visitors the somewhat awkward feeling of being goodwill ambassadors from hostile nations. For the most part, however, tourists are welcomed warmly.

SIGHTS AND ENTERTAINMENT Serbia's tumultuous history is documented in the **Narodni Muzej** (National Museum), Trg Republike (open Tu-W and F-Sa 10am-5pm, Th noon-8pm, Su 10am-2pm; 5dn, students 2dn). Past the fountains across the square begins **Knez Mihaila,** a commercial street lined with shops, restaurants, and galleries. The **Saborna,** home to the patriarchate of the Serbian Orthodox Church, lies just off

Knez Mihaila at Kralj Petra/7 Jula (Краља Петра/7 Јула; open daily 7am-8pm; free). The most notable landmark in Belgrade is the well-preserved ruin of the huge fortress **Kalemedan,** which consists of Upper and Lower cities. The first is a popular park, while the second, a gang hangout, should be avoided at night. The huge **Vojni Muzej** (Military Museum), inside the fortress, is perhaps the best place for visitors to learn about Serbian history (open Tu-Su 8:30am-4:30pm; 4dn; English guidebook 10dn).

Other worthwhile places to visit lie across the Sava River in Novi Beograd and Zamun. The **Muzej Savremene Umetnosti** (Museum of Contemporary Art), Ušće Save bb, is a must (bus 15 or 84; open W-M 10am-6pm; free). The old town of **Zemun,** northwest along the Danube, was built in the Austro-Hungarian style. The 18th-century Orthodox **Sveti Nikola** sits at the base of Sindelićeva and harbors exquisite religious artworks (open daily 9am-1pm and 5-7pm). In the basement of the Technical University building, **KST** (Club of Technical Students), Bulevar Revolucije 73, rocks nightly with friendly bartenders and 8dn beer (cover 10dn).

PRACTICAL INFO, ACCOMMODATIONS, AND FOOD The **Aerodrum Beograd** (airport; tel. (011) 60 55 55) is 25km west of Belgrade. **Trains** run from the Glavna železnička stanica (tel. (011) 62 94 00) to Sofia (10hr., 250dn), Zagreb (17hr., 320dn), and elsewhere. **Buses** (station tel. (011) 63 62 99) are faster, cheaper, and offer more destinations; a master schedule is posted on the wall. The excellent TIC **tourist office** (tel. (011) 63 56 22), in the pedestrian underground passage at the north end of Terazije, dispenses information and maps and books accommodations (open M-F 9am-8pm, Sa 9am-4pm). The **Australian** embassy is at Čika Ljubina (tel. (011) 62 46 55); **Canadian,** Kneza Miloša 75 (tel. (011) 64 46 66, emergency tel. 64 45 47); **U.K.,** Generala Ždanova 46 (tel. (011) 64 50 55); and **U.S.,** Kneza Miloša 50 (tel. (011) 64 56 55). **New Zealanders** should contact their embassy in Bonn (Bundeskanzlerpl. 2-10; tel. (49) 228 22 80 70). In June 1998, Belgrade **banks** were unable to cash traveler's checks due to economic sanctions; check the situation before you go. The exchange rates for DM should be uniform across the city. The **post office,** Takouska 2, has **telephones** (office open M-Sa 8am-8pm; phones open daily 7am-10pm). The **Internet** will keep you up to speed with shifting political currents at **Dom Omladine,** Makedonska 22 (tel. (011) 324 82 02; open M-F 10am-10pm, Sa-Su 2-10pm; 8dn per hr.).

The tourist office can help you find rooms, or try **Hotel Beograd,** Balkanska 52 (tel. (011) 64 53 61), which has new, clean singles for 200dn. **Hotel DOM,** Kralja Milutina 54 (tel. (011) 68 56 96), is in a leafy, quiet part of town (singles 244dn; reception 24hr.). The gastronomical center is the area called **Skadarlija,** where classy locals dine. Common folk can get the cheaper version at the bottom end of the street. **Pivnica Aleksandar,** Cetinjska 15, serves chicken wings (45dn per kg) and beer (a dangerous 10dn per L) on picnic tables outdoors. **Grmeč,** Makedonska 32, features excellent Yugoslavian cuisine.

■ Novi Sad (Нови Сад)

Unlike Belgrade, Novi Sad spent many more years as an Austro-Hungarian city than as a Turkish one, and signs of this are everywhere—from the abundance of Catholic churches to the natty dress of elderly Hungarian men to the many Germanic facades. The most impressive building in Novi Sad is the well-preserved Austro-Hungarian fortress **Petrovaradin** (Петроварадин), built in 1786 at the orders of Maria Teresa (subterranean military galleries open M-Sa 9am-4pm). To get there, walk to the eastern end of Dunavska; the fortress is across the Danube on the right. **Trains** (info tel. (21) 44 32 00; open 24hr.) go to: Belgrade (1½hr., 6 per day, 18dn), Budapest (5hr., 5 per day, 300dn), Skopje (9hr., 1 per day, 278dn), and Sofia (11hr., 1 per day, 262dn). **City buses** run to the center—tickets can be purchased for 3dn from kiosks or on board—but the walk takes only 20 minutes and provides a chance to drop off your belongings at **Fontana** (Фонтана), Pašićeva 17 (tel. (21) 61 27 60), with large singles and opulent bathrooms for just 170dn. Fontana also houses one of Novi Sad's favorite special-occasion restaurants. Busy **Jevrejska** leads to a number of restaurants.

Index

Thanks to Our Readers...

Mano Aaron, CA; Jean-Marc Abela, CAN; George Adams, NH; Bob & Susan Adams, GA; Deborah Adeyanju, NY; Rita Alexander, MI; Shani Amory-Claxton, NY; Kate Anderson, AUS; Lindsey Anderson, ENG; Viki Anderson, NY; Ray Andrews, JPN; Robin J. Andrus, NJ; L. Asurmendi, CA; Anthony Atkinson, ENG; Deborah Bacek, GA; Jeffrey Bagdade, MI; Mark Baker, UK; Mary Baker, TN; Jeff Barkoff, PA; Regina Barsanti, NY; Ethan Beeler, MA; Damao Bell, CA; Rya Ben-Shir, IL; Susan Bennerstrom, WA; Marla Benton, CAN; Matthew Berenson, OR; Walter Bergstrom, OR; Caryl Bird, ENG; Charlotte Blanc, NY; Jeremy Boley, EL SAL; Oliver Bradley, GER; A.Braurstein, CO; Philip R. Brazil, WA; Henrik Brockdorff, DMK; Tony Bronco, NJ; Eileen Brouillard, SC; Mary Brown, ENG; Tom Brown, CA; Elizabeth Buckius, CO; Sue Buckley, UK; Christine Burer, SWITZ; Norman Butler, MO; Brett Carroll, WA; Susan Caswell, ISR; Carlos Cersosimo, ITA; Barbara Crary Chase, WA; Stella Cherry Carbost, SCOT; Oi Ling Cheung, HK; Simon Chinn, ENG; Charles Cho, AUS; Carolyn R. Christie, AUS; Emma Church, ENG; Kelley Coblentz, IN; Cathy Cohan, PA; Phyllis Cole, TX; Karina Collins, SWITZ; Michael Cox, TX; Mike Craig, MD; Rene Crusto, LA; Claudine D'Anjou, CAN; Lizz Daniels, CAN; Simon Davies, SCOT; Samantha Davis, AUS; Leah Davis, TX; Stephanie Dickman, MN; Philipp Dittrich,GER; Tim Donovan, NH; Reed Drew, OR; Wendy Duncan, SCOT; Melissa Dunlap, VA; P.A. Emery, UK; GCL Emery, SAF; Louise Evans, AUS; Christine Farr, AUS; David Fattel, NJ; Vivian Feen, MD; David Ferraro, SPN; Sue Ferrick, CO; Philip Fielden, UK; Nancy Fintel, FL; Jody Finver, FL; D. Ross Fisher, CAN; Abigail Flack, IL; Elizabeth Foster, NY; Bonnie Fritz, CAN; J. Fuson, OR; Michael K. Gasuad, NY; Raad German, TX; Mark Gilbert, NY; Betsy Gilliland, CA; Ana Goshko, NY; Patrick Goyenneche, CAN; David Greene, NY; Jennifer Griffin, ENG; Janet & Jeremy Griffith, ENG; Nanci Guartofierro, NY; Denise Guillemette, MA; Ilona Haayer, HON; Joseph Habboushe, PA; John Haddon, CA; Ladislav Hanka, MI; Michael Hanke, CA; Avital Harari, TX; Channing Hardy, KY; Patrick Harris, CA; Denise Hasher, PA; Jackie Hattori, UK; Guthrie Hebenstreit, ROM; Therase Hill, AUS; Denise Hines, NJ; Cheryl Horne, ENG; Julie Howell, IL; Naomi Hsu, NJ; Mark Hudgkinson, ENG; Brenda Humphrey, NC; Kelly Hunt, NY; Daman Irby, AUT; Bill Irwin, NY; Andrea B. Jackson, PA; John Jacobsen, FL; Pat Johanson, MD; Fuckhead Jones, MA; J. Jones, AUS; Sharon Jones, MI; Craig Jones, CA; Wayne Jones, ENG; Jamie Kagan, NJ; Mirko Kaiser, GER; Scott Kauffman, NY; John Keanie, NIRE; Barbara Keary, FL; Jamie Kehoe, AUS; Alistair Kernick, SAF; Daihi Kielle, SWITZ; John Knutsen, CA; Rebecca Koepke, NY; Jeannine Kolb, ME; Elze Kollen, NETH; Lorne Korman, CAN; Robin Kortright, CAN; Isel Krinsky, CAN; George Landers, ENG; Jodie Lanthois, AUS; Roger Latzgo, PA; A. Lavery, AZ; Joan Lea, ENG; Lorraine Lee, NY; Phoebe Leed, MA; Tammy Leeper, CA; Paul Lejeune, ENG; Yee-Leng Leong, CA; Sam Levene, CAN; Robin Levin, PA; Christianna Lewis, PA; Ernesto Licata, ITA; Wolfgang Lischtansky, AUT; Michelle Little, CAN; Dee Littrell, CA; Maria Lobosco, UK; Netii Ross, ITA; Didier Look, CAN; Alice Lorenzotti, MA; David Love, PA; Briege Mac Donagh, IRE; Brooke Madigan, NY; Helen Maltby, FL; Shyama Marchesi, ITA; Domenico Maria, ITA; Natasha Markovic, AUS; Edward Marshall, ECU; Rachel Marshall, TX; Kate Maynard, UK; Agnes McCann, IRE; Susan McGowan, NY; Brandi McGunigal, CAN; Neville McLean, NZ; Marty McLendon, MS; Matthew Melko, OH; Barry Mendelson, CA; Eric Middendorf, OH; Nancy Mike, AZ; Coren Milbury, NH; Margaret Mill, NY; David H. Miller, TX; Ralph Miller, NV; Susan Miller, CO; Larry Moeller, MI; Richard Moore, ENG; Anne & Andrea Mosher, MA; J. L. Mourne, TX; Athanassios Moustakas, GER; Laurel Naversen, ENG; Suzanne Neil, IA; Deborah Nickles, PA; Pieter & Agnes Noels, BEL; Werner Norr, GER; Ruth J. Nye, ENG; Heidi O'Brien, WA; Sherry O'Cain, SC; Aibhan O'Connor, IRE; Kevin O'Connor, CA; Margaret O'Rielly, IRE; Daniel O'Rourke, CA; Krissy Oechslin, OH; Johan Oelofse, SAF; Quinn Okamoto, CA; Juan Ramon Olaizola, SPN; Laura Onorato, NM; Bill Orkin, IL; K. Owusu-Agyenang, UK; Anne Paananen, SWD; Jenine Padget, AUS; Frank Pado, TX; G. Pajkich, Washington, DC; J. Parker, CA; Marian Parnat, AUS; Sandra Swift Parrino, NY; Iris Patten, NY; M. Pavini, CT; David Pawielski, MN; Jenny Pawson, ENG; Colin Peak, AUS; Marius Penderis, ENG; Jo-an Peters, AZ; Barbara Phillips, NY; Romain Picard, Washington, DC; Pati Pike, ENG; Mark Pollock, SWITZ; Minnie Adele Potter, FL; Martin Potter, ENG; Claudia Praetel, ENG; Bill Press, Washington, DC; David Prince, NC; Andrea Pronko, OH; C. Robert Pryor, OH; Phu Quy, VTNM; Adrian Rainbow, ENG; John Raven, AUS; Lynn Reddringer, VA; John Rennie, NZ; Ruth B.Robinson, FL; John & Adelaida Romagnoli, CA; Eva Romano, FRA; Mark A. Roscoe, NETH; Yolanda & Jason Ross, CAN; Sharee Rowe, NY; W. Suzanne Rowell, NY; Vic Roych, AZ; John Russell, ENG; Jennifer Ruth, OK; William Sabino, NJ; Hideki Saito, JPN; Frank Schaer, HUN; Jeff Schultz, WI; Floretta Seeland-Connally, IL; Colette Shoulders, FRA; Shireen Sills, ITA; Virginia Simon, AUS; Beth Simon, NY; Gary Simpson, AUS; Barbara & Allen Sisarsky, GA; Alon Siton, ISR; Kathy Skeie, CA; Robyn Skillecorn, AUS; Erik & Kathy Skon, MN; Stine Skorpen, NOR; Philip Smart, CAN; Colin Smit, ENG; Kenneth Smith, DE; Caleb Smith, CA; Geoffrey Smith, TX; John Snyder, NC; Kathrin Speidel, GER; Lani Steele, PHIL; Julie Stelbracht, PA; Margaret Stires, TN; Donald Stumpf, NY; Samuel Suffern, TN; Michael Swerdlow, ENG; Brian Talley, TX; Serene-Marie Terrell, NY; B. Larry Thilson, CAN; J. Pelham Thomas, NC; Wright Thompson, ITA; Christine Timm, NY; Melinda Tong, HK; M. Tritica, AUS; Melanie Tritz, CAN; Mark Trop, FL; Chris Troxel, AZ; Rozana Tsiknaki, GRC; Lois Turner, NZ; Nicole Virgil, IL; Blondie Vucich, CO; Wendy Wan, SAF; Carrie & Simon Wedgwood, ENG; Frederick Weibgen, NJ; Richard Weil, MN; Alan Weissberg, OH; Ryan Wells, OH; Jill Wester, GER; Clinton White, AL; Gael White, CAN; Melanie Whitfield, SCOT; Bryn Williams, CAN; Amanda Williams, CAN; Wendy Willis, CAN; Sasha Wilson, NY; Kendra Wilson, CA; Olivia Wiseman, ENG; Gerry Wood, CAN; Kelly Wooten, ENG; Robert Worsley, ENG; C.A.Wright, ENG; Caroline Wright, ENG; Mary H. Yuhasz, CO; Margaret Zimmerman, WA.

Researcher-Writers

Tom Davidson *Denmark, Sweden*
Tom rode the high of the Scandinavian midsummer through Sweden and Denmark, documenting both the hottest nightspots and the minutiae of Nordic culture. Racing through a challenging itinerary, his prose was brilliant and incisive, his work amazingly thorough (what other RW would follow up on ancient Viking graffiti while in Istanbul?). Last seen: pillaging the small coastal towns of the Côte d'Azur.

Greg Halpern *Iceland, Norway*
Outdoorsman extraordinaire, Greg took to the trails, and discovered that in Scandinavia, even an 80-year-old woman with a plastic hip can give you a run for your money. Skiing down mountainsides in his tennis shoes, and hunting puffins with his bare hands, Greg covered Iceland and Norway from top to bottom, never missing a beat or neglecting a piece of hard info. Days after emerging from Iceland's lunar interior, Greg was off leading excursions into the White Mountains.

Bede Sheppard *Estonia, Finland*
A native New Zealander, this associate editor of *Let's Go: Eastern Europe 1998* brought his expertise to bear on Estonia and Finland. Bede's copy was impeccably formatted, his research outstanding, and his candy pink and piscine. His command of Finnish allowed him an inside view of the region not many could match. Now on the table for our venerable Bede: the Continent. The Sorbonne is his already.

Manjari Mahajan *Belgium, Luxembourg, the Netherlands*
Having traveled extensively through her native India, Benelux was a breeze for Manjari. In the height of the tourist season, through the red lights of Amsterdam, Manjari sought out the Low Countries' quieter spots while also hitting the nightlife hard. Never deterred, she climbed through windows and sunk boats to get her way—and the guide's coverage improved accordingly.

Linas Alšėnas	*Latvia, Lithuania, Warsaw*
Andreea Balan	*Romania*
Judith Batalion	*Vienna, Lower Austria, Carinthia*
Amy Beck	*Normandy, Brittany, Rennes nightlife*
Justyna Beinek	*Zakopane, Eastern Slovakia*
Marya Cohen	*Andalusía*
Kathleen Conroy	*Counties Cork, Kerry, Limerick, Tipperary, Waterford*
Daryn David	*Aegean and Mediterranean Coasts*
Laura Beth Deason	*Paris*
Daniel Engber	*Salzburg, Tyrol, Western Austria*
Melissa Enriquez	*Madrid, Extremadura, Castilla La Mancha, Castilla y León, Portugal*
Andras Forgacs	*Budapest*
Christa Franklin	*South and Southwest England, Heart of England, East Anglia*
Adriane Giebel	*Loire Valley, Poitou-Charentes, Limousin, Scotland*
Kata Gellen	*Berlin, Brandenburg, Niedersachsen, Sachsen-Anhalt, Hessen*
Breeze K. Giannasio	*Tuscany, Sardinia*
Melissa Gibson	*Czech and Slovak Republics, Western/Southern Hungary*
Kristin Glover	*Bulgaria, Northern Hungary, Danube Bend*
Robin Goldstein	*Barcelona, Catalunya, Islas Baleares, Valencia, Murcia*
Nick Grandy	*Heart of England, Central and North England, Scotland*
Adam 'Waka' Green	*Rome*
Rachel Greenblatt	*London*
Brady Gunderson	*Cyprus, Dodecanese*
Brenna Haysom	*Aquitaine, Pays Basque, Languedoc, Gascony, Nîmes*

James Higbie	*The Caucasus*
Mercedes Hinton	*Paris*
Max Hirsh	*Berlin, Mecklen*
Valerie Hletko	*Slovenia, Croatia, Southern Poland*
Daniel Horwitz	*Counties Armagh, Cavan, Clare, Fermanagh, Galway, Leitrim, Mayo, Monaghan, Roscommon, Sligo, Tyrone*
Sara Houghteling	*Corsica, The Côte d'Azur, The Rhône Valley*
M. Daniel Hughes, Jr.	*Malta*
Ben Jackson	*Scotland, London*
Sarah Jacoby	*Castilla y León, La Rioja, Navarra, País Vasco, Aragón, Andorra, Catalunya*
Jamie L. Jones	*Rheinland-Pfalz, Nordrhein-Westfalen, Niedersachsen, Hessen*
Ashley Kircher	*Cyclades, Sporades, Northeast Aegean Islands*
Jeremy Kurzyniec	*Peloponnese, Sterea Ellada, Ionians*
Michele Lee	*Attica, Saronic Gulf Islands, Crete*
Nora F. Lehmann	*Lombardy, Piedmont, Liguria, Emilia-Romagna*
Christopher Leighton	*Counties Carlow, Dublin, Kildare, Kilkenny, Logford, Meath, Waterford, Westmeath, Wexford, Wicklow*
Dan Levi	*Eastern Turkey*
Darryl Li	*Cappodocia, Eastern Mediterranean, North Cyprus*
Winnie Li	*Frankfurt, Baden-Württemberg, Allgäu Alps, Rheinland-Pfalz*
Anna Medvedovsky	*Northern France, Alsace-Lorraine, Champagne*
Matthew JT Murray	*Rome*
Deirdre O'Dwyer	*Counties Antrim, Derry, Down, Louth*
Masi Osseo-Asare	*Castilla y Léon, Galicia, Asturias, Cantabria*
Michael J. Passante	*Abruzzo, Molise, Campania, Apulia, Basilicata*
Dáša Pejchar	*Bayern*
Sarah Petty	*St. Petersburg Region, Kaliningrad, Western/Northern Poland*
Nick Pinto	*Thrace, Black Sea Coast, Ankara*
Adam Reilly	*Bosnia-Herzegovina, Dubrovnik, Yugoslavia, Macedonia*
Peter Richards	*Belarus, Ukraine, Eastern Poland*
Justine Sadoff	*Scotland*
Charles Savage	*Geneva, Neuchâtel, Italian Switzerland*
Melina Shannon-DiPietro	*Calabria, Sicily*
Stuart Shapley	*Istanbul, Aegean Coast*
Matthew Sigel	*Alps, Lyon and the Auvergne, Burgundy, Franche-Comté*
Daryl Sng	*Wales, Central and North England*
Natasha Sokol	*Portugal*
Nick Stephanopoulos	*Northern Greece, Corfu*
Sharmila Surianarain	*Zurich, Bern, Liechtenstein*
Shatema Threadcraft	*Rome*
Bulbul Tiwari	*Paris*
Daniel Tobey	*Trentino, Veneto, Emilia-Romagna*
Mike Weller	*Sachsen, Thüringen, Halle*
Christopher White	*Moscow*
Tobie Whitman	*London*

Acknowledgments

The Europe guide has always depended on the expertise and good will of the editors of *Let's Go*'s country and city guides. This year, we were privileged to work with an outstanding group. Always helpful and considerate but also fun and supportive, each did his or her part to make our lives easier. Thank you Shanya, Jenny, Brina, Alex L., Olivia, Christina, Justin, Erica, Doug, Rachel K., Ben P., Keith, Penelope, Christian, Saadi, Semra, Katie, Elena, Ethan, Nicole, Alex D., Stefania, Whitney, Jessica, Bruce, Brian, and Anna. The production team was awesome: Heath, Maryanthe, and Dan V. bailed us out time and time again. Derek, Dan L., and Matt, the ever-helpful map folks, vastly improved the look of this year's guide. Anne monitored our stress levels and kept us cool and healthy; Rachel F. reassured us. Our researchers—Tom, Greg, Bede, and Manjari—all did excellent work. And what would we have done without our intern and hired guns? Masha was unbelievably generous with her time, and Jordan never missed a town (even in Ireland). Lisa, Ben H., and RobeSpeier all helped out immeasurably, above and beyond their own responsibilities. Adam H. caught that last diacritic. We owe a special debt of gratitude to Måns, who was there every step of the way, keeping us on track and upbeat; Keith, Christian, and Ben, who saved us—and entertained us—down the home stretch; Rachel and Alex L., who were always there; Heath, who held the techno-demons (oh, they're out there, all right) at bay just long enough; and Dan, benevolent Production dictator, who typeset this monster.

Alex thanks: Karen and Elizabeth—you made the job a joy. Without Karen's attention to detail and phenomenal devotion to this book, we'd be a mess of lost papers with an underlined GI. Without Elizabeth's enthusiasm, focus, and speed, we'd be stuck somewhere in Slovenia. Måns, man—thanks for being with us through all of this. Ben—for being on top of everything, for keeping the office crazy ... it *was* the best. Rachel—I think everyone in the pod owes their productivity to you. You were an example. Bruce—for sharing a little of life. Heath—yah, dude! Keith—I can't help but feel selfish for roping you into this; you made this summer so much more worthwhile. Debbie—for putting up with me through all of this. Mom, Dad, Michael—for love and support from afar.

Karen thanks: Alex, the most considerate and capable editor imaginable, for patience with his shrinking chair. Elizabeth, a fast and flawless copy editor, for lively wit and the perfect turn of phrase. Måns, for stability and an eye for italicized em-dashes. Ben P. for high spirits, Keith for street cred, and Rachel for pod sanity. Nic for use of the beanbag. Maps and Production for help burning the midnight oil. Z-haus for roller coasters. Dan for fine company and good advice I should have taken. Ben H. and Matt for being themselves. Leora for wise words and laughs. Christina for helping me make it through the summer. Redcords for unfailing support. Mostly: Mom, Dad, Kevin, and Christopher, for reminding me what's important. I love you best of all.

Elizabeth thanks: Alex—for his continual revisions, well-traveled sensibilities, utter devotion to Belgium, and extensive jazz collection. Karen—for her unflagging critical eye and her determination to keep the office working around the clock. To Måns for his fascination with grammatical quirks. Special thanks go to the Eastern Europeans of contradictions—the mellow yet efficient Rachel, the crochety yet earnest Keith, and the occasionally bizarre yet always entertaining Benjamin. Thanks to Tim and Tracey, for our summer cooking experiments. And finally, thanks to Mom and Dad, ever ready with emergency cash and brownies, Alex and Andy, for their have-book-will-travel attitude, and Mimi, who always reminds me how fun life can be.

Staff

★Let's Go 1999 Reader Questionnaire★

Please fill this out and return it to **Let's Go, St. Martin's Press**, 175 Fifth Ave., New York, NY 10010-7848. All respondents will receive a free subscription to *The Yellowjacket*, the Let's Go Newsletter. You can find a more extensive version of this survey on the web at http://www.letsgo.com.

Name: _____

Address: _____

City: _____ State: _____ Zip/Postal Code: _____

Email: _____ Which book(s) did you use?_____

How old are you? under 19   19-24   25-34   35-44   45-54   55 or over

Are you (circle one)   in high school   in college   in graduate school
    employed   retired   between jobs

Have you used Let's Go before? yes no   **Would you use it again?** yes no

How did you first hear about Let's Go? friend   store clerk   television
    bookstore display   advertisement/promotion   review   other

Why did you choose Let's Go (circle up to two)? reputation budget focus
    price   writing style   annual updating   other: _____

Which other guides have you used, if any? Fodor's   Footprint Handbooks
    Frommer's $-a-day   Lonely Planet   Moon Guides   Rick Steve's
    Rough Guides   UpClose   other: _____

Which guide do you prefer? _____

**Please rank each of the following parts of Let's Go 1 to 5 (1=needs
    improvement, 5=perfect).** packaging/cover   practical information
    accommodations   food   cultural introduction   sights
    practical introduction ("Essentials")   directions   entertainment
    gay/lesbian information   maps   other: _____

**How would you like to see the books improved? (continue on separate page,
    if necessary)**_____

_____

How long was your trip?   one week   two weeks   three weeks
    one month   two months or more

Which countries did you visit? _____

What was your average daily budget, not including flights? _____

Have you traveled extensively before?   yes   no

Do you buy a separate map when you visit a foreign city?   yes   no

Have you used a Let's Go Map Guide?   yes   no

If you have, would you recommend them to others?   yes   no

Have you visited Let's Go's website?   yes no

What would you like to see included on Let's Go's website? _____

_____

What percentage of your trip planning did you do on the Web? _____

Would you use a Let's Go: recreational (e.g. skiing) guide gay/lesbian guide
    adventure/trekking guide   phrasebook   general travel information guide

**Which of the following destinations do you hope to visit in the next three to
    five years (circle one)?** Canada Argentina Perú Kenya Middle East
    Caribbean   Scandinavia   other: _____

Where did you buy your guidebook?   Internet   independent bookstore
    chain bookstore   college bookstore   travel store   other: _____

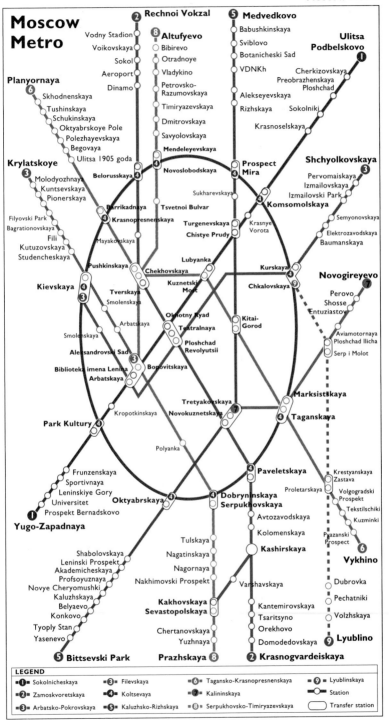

Moscow Metro

Moscow Metro

Moscow

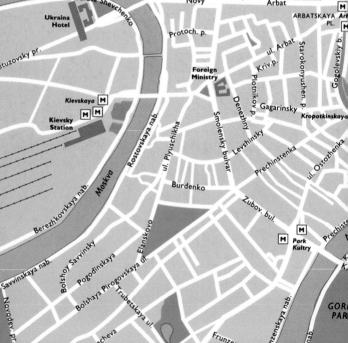

Khodynskaya

Presnensky Val

Tishinsky per.

Bolshaya Gruzinskaya ul.

Brestskaya ul.

Pervaya Tverskaya-Yamskaya

Krasina

Oruzh

Sado

ul. 1905 Goda

Sergeya Makeeva

Ultisa 1905 Goda Ⓜ

Zoologicheskaya

Yar. Gasheka

Pu

Krasnaya Presnya

Malaya

Tver

Trekhgor. Val

ZOO PARK

Shmitovsky pr.

Barrikadnaya Ⓜ

Sadovaya-Kudrin.

Bronnaya

Mantulinskaya

Krasnopresnenskaya Ⓜ

VOSSTANIYA PL.

Bol. Nikitskaya ul.

NIKITSKIE VOROTA PL.

Tver

Rochdelskaya

Mezhdnarodnaya Hotel

Konyushkovskaya

U.S. Embassy

Povarskaya

Merzlyakovsky

Kalashny p.

Krasnopresnenskaya nab.

Novinski bul.

Trubnikovsky p.

Tarasa Shevchenko

Novy

Arbat

ARBATSKAYA PL.

Arb

Ⓜ

Gogolevsky b.

Ukraina Hotel

Protoch. p.

ul. Arbat

Kriv. p.

Starokonyushen. p.

Ⓜ

Kutuzovsky pr.

Foreign Ministry

Piotnikov p.

Gagarinsky

Kropotkinskaya

Kievskaya Ⓜ

Denezhny

Smolensky bulvar

Levshinsky

Prechinstenka

ul. Ostozhenka

Kievsky Station

Ⓜ Ⓜ

Rostovskaya nab.

ul. Plyuschikha

Burdenko

Moskva

Zubov. bul.

Berezhkovskaya nab.

Bolshoy Savvinsky

Pogodinskaya

Elanskovo

Ⓜ **Park Kultry**

Prechis

Savvinskaya nab.

Bolshaya Pirogovskaya

Trubetskaya ul.

K

Novodev. pr.

ul. Usacheva

Frynzenskaya Ⓜ

Frunzenskaya 1.

Frunzenskaya nab.

Pushkinskaya nab.

Novodevich Convent and Cemetary

Ⓜ **Sportivnaya**

Ⓜ

Dovatora

Efremova

Komsomolsky Frunzen-skaya 3

Frunzen-skaya

Frunzenskaya 2.

GOR PA

Moscow

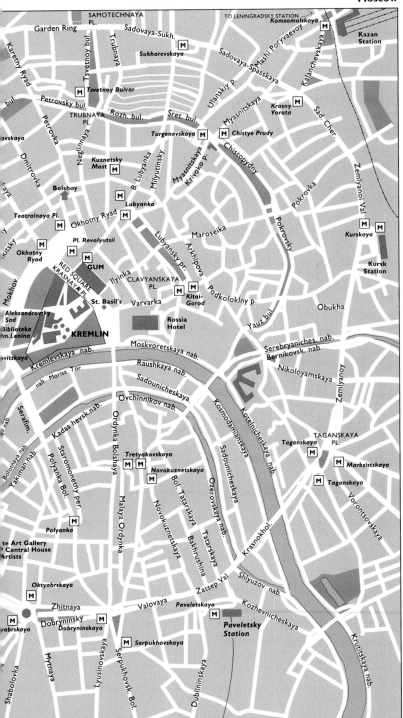

SAMOTECHNAYA PL.

Garden Ring
Sadovaya-Sukh.

TO LENINGRADSKY STATION →
Komsomolskaya

Kazan Station

Karetny Ryad

Tsvetnoy bul.

Trubnaya

Sukharevskaya

Sadovaya-Spasskaya

Mashi Poryvaevoy

Kalanchevskaya

Tsvetnoy Bulvar

Petrovsky bul.

Ulanskiy p.

Myasnitskaya

Krasny Vorota

Sad. Cher.

Zemlyanoi Val

Petrovka

Rozh. bul.

TRUBNAYA PL.

Sret. bul.

Chistopydny

Kurskaya

Dmitrovka

Neglinnaya

Kuznetsky Most

B. Lubyanka

Milyutinsky

Myasnitskaya

Krivoko p.

Turgenevskaya

Chistye Prudy

Pokrovka

Kursk Station

Bolshoy

Lubyanka

Pokrovsky

Teatralnaya Pl.

Okhotny Ryad

Maroseika

Lubyansky pr.

Arkhipova

Okhotny Ryad

Pl. Revolyutsii

GUM

RED SQUARE
KRASNAYA PL.

Ilyinka

CLAVYANSKAYA PL.

Podkoloklny p.

Obukha

Kitai-Gorod

St. Basil's

Varvarka

Yauz bul.

Aleksandrovsky Sad

Biblioteka
Im. Lenina

KREMLIN

Rossia Hotel

Serebryaniches. nab.
Bernikovsk. nab.

Kremlevskaya nab.

Moskvoretskaya nab.

Nikoloyamskaya

nab. Morisa Tor.

Raushskaya nab.

Zemlyanoy

Serafim

Kadas hevsk.nab.

Sadounicheskaya

Ovchinnikov nab.

Kosmodamianskaya

Kotelnicheskaya nab.

TAGANSKAYA PL.

Bolotnaya nab.

Yakimanka

Staromonetny per.

Ordynka Bolshaya

Tretyakovskaya

Novokuznetskaya

Sadounicheskaya

Ozerovskaya nab.

Taganskaya

Marksistskaya

Taganskaya

Polyanka Bol.

Malaya Ordynka

Novokuznetskaya

Bol. Tatarskaya

Novokuznetskaya

Tatarskaya

Bakhtrushina

Krasnokhol.

Vorontsovskaya

Polyanka

Polyanka

te Art Gallery
Central House
Artists

Oktyabrskaya

Zhitnaya

Zatsep. Val

Valovaya

Paveletskaya

Kozhevnicheskaya

Shlyuzov. nab.

Paveletsky Station

Dobryninsky

Dobryninskaya

Lyusinovskaya

Serpukhovskaya

Dublininskaya

Krutitskaya nab.

yabrskaya

Myntnaya

Serpukhovsk. Bol.

Shabolovka

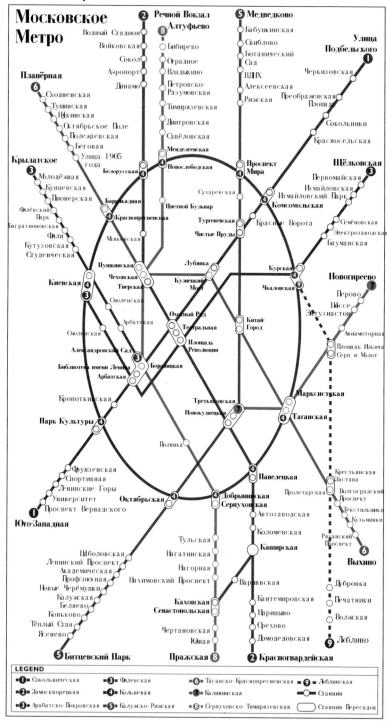

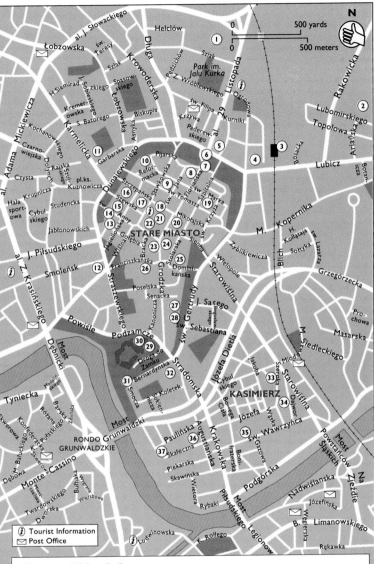

Prague

Prague

American Express, **23**
Anešský klášter, **22**
Basilica sv. Jiří (Basilica of St. George), **5**
Canadian Embassy, **1**
Chrám sv. Mikuláše (St. Nicholas Church), **8**
Chrám sv. Víta (St. Vitus's Cathedral), **3**
Florenc bus station, **20**
Hlavní nádraží (Main train station), **14**
Kafka's grave, **24**
Karlův most (Charles Bridge), **11**
Lobkovický palác, **6**
Main post office, **21**
Masarykovo nádraží, **19**
Matka Boží před Týnem (Týn Church), **17**
Národní divadlo (National Theater), **12**
Národní galérie (National Gallery), **2**
Národní muzeum (National Museum), **13**
Panna Maria Sněžná (Church of Our Lady of the Snows), **15**
Panna Maria Vítězna (Church of Our Lady Victorious), **10**
Powder Tower, **18**
Staroměstská radnice (Old Town Hall), **16**
Starý královský palác (Old Royal Palace), **4**
U.K. Embassy, **7**
U.S. Embassy, **9**

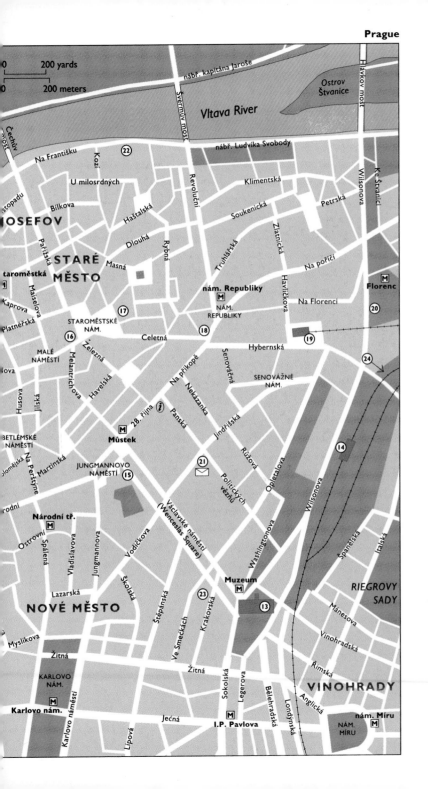

Prague

Central Budapest

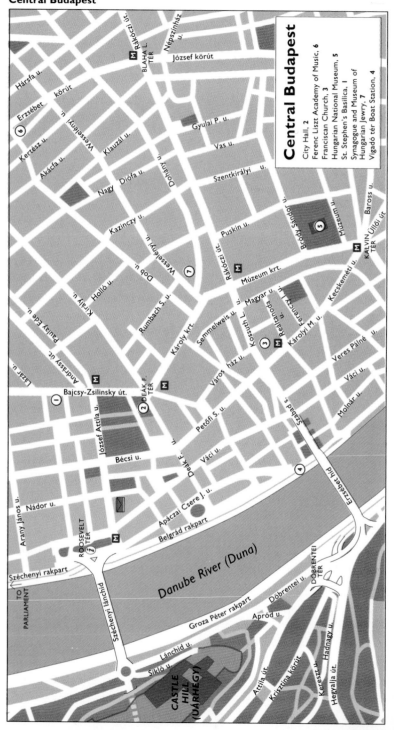

Central Budapest

City Hall, 2
Ferenc Liszt Academy of Music, 6
Franciscan Church, 3
Hungarian National Museum, 5
St. Stephen's Basilica, 1
Synagogue and Museum of
Hungarian Jewry, 7
Vigadó tér Boat Station, 4

Berlin Transit

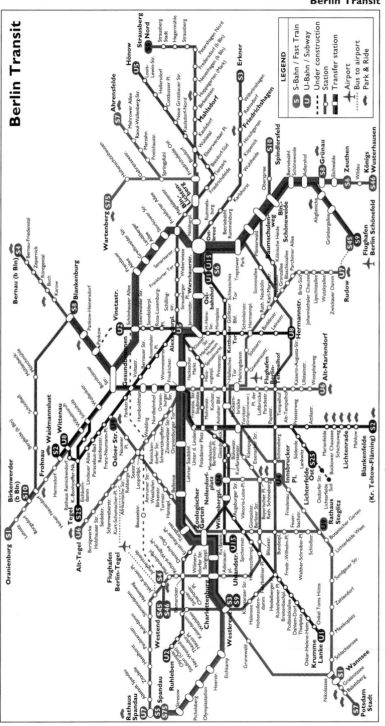

Munich Transit

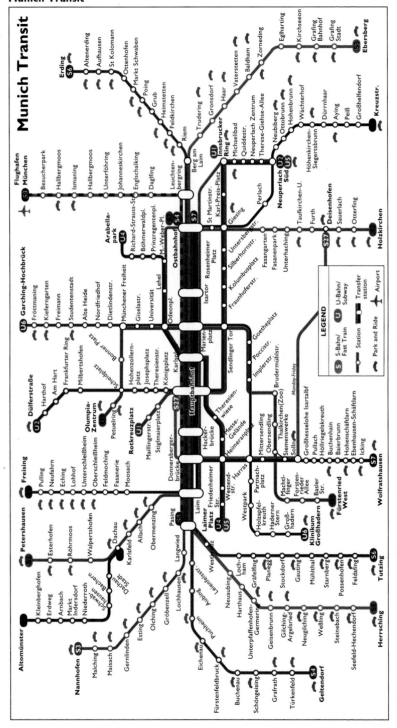

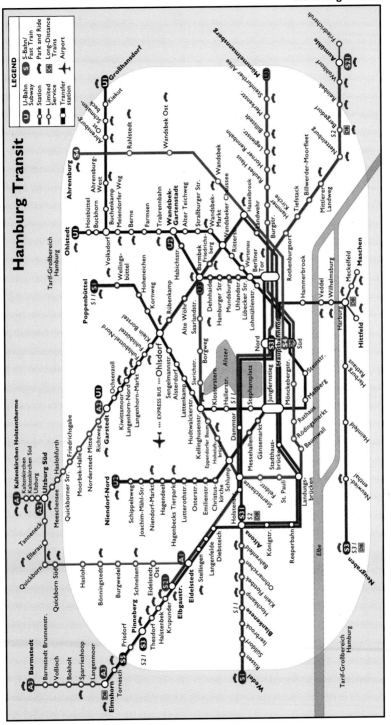

Hamburg Transit

Frankfurt Transit

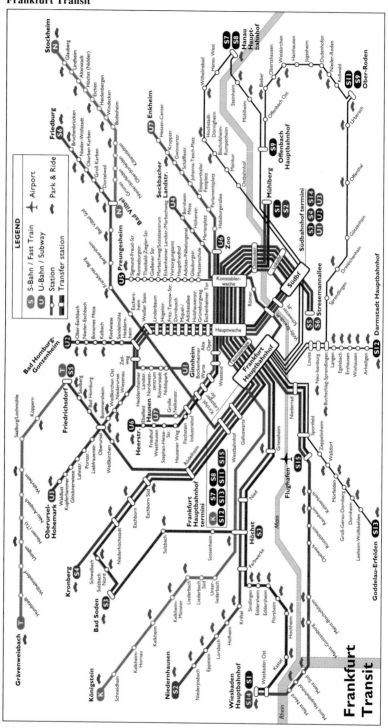

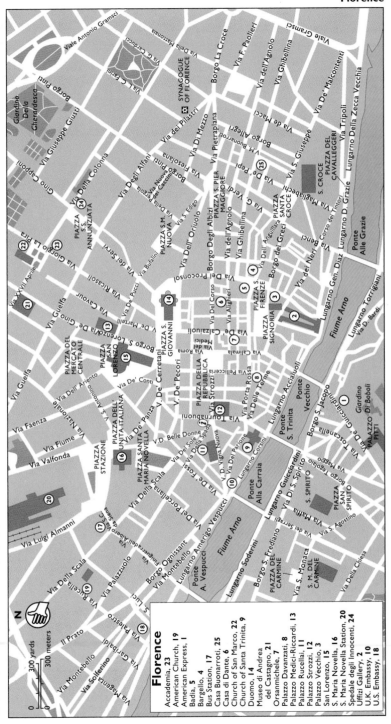

Florence

Accademia, 23
American Church, 19
American Express, 1
Badia, 5
Bargello, 4
Bus Station, 17
Casa Buonarroti, 25
Casa di Dante, 6
Church of San Marco, 22
Church of Santa Trinita, 9
Duomo, 14
Museo di Andrea
   del Castagno, 21
Orsanmichele, 7
Palazzo Davanzati, 8
Palazzo Medici-Riccardi, 13
Palazzo Rucellai, 11
Palazzo Strozzi, 12
Palazzo Vecchio, 3
San Lorenzo, 15
S. Maria Novella, 16
S. Maria Novella Station, 20
Spedale degli Innocenti, 24
Uffizi Gallery, 2
U.K. Embassy, 10
U.S. Embassy, 18

Venice

TO MAINLAND

Ponte della Libertà

CANNARE

Rio di S. Girolamo

Rio del Battello

CAMPO DEL GHETTO

Canale di Cannareggio

C. Riello

R. terrà d Leonard

CAMPO SAN GEREMIA

Lista di Spagna

Canal Grande

Ponte Scalzi

Riva d.Biasio

Lista d. Bari

Fondamenta di Santa Lucia

S. Simeon Piccolo

SANTA CR

Canale di Chiara

F.d.

Rio Marin

CAMP DEI MOR

Corte Canal

C. d. Lacca

R. di S

Canale Scomenzera

Rio terra dei Pensieri

Rio Saccherre

Rio della

CAMPO S. ROCCO

SANTA CR

Rio Foscari

F.Minotto

Nuovo

CAMPO DI SAN MARGHERITA

Rio d. Santa Margherita

Rio di S. Barnaba

Calle Avogaria

Rio d. Ognissanti

DORSODUR

Fondamenta della Zattere

Canale della Giudecca

Venice

Amex, **3**
Campo dei Frari, **10**
Campo S. Giorgio, **12**
Campo SS. Giovanni e Paolo, **13**
Campo San Salvaatore, **7**
Church of S. Maria Della Salute, **9**
Church of S. Maria Formosa, **14**
Church of San Zaccaria, **11**
Gallerie dell' Accademia, **8**
Hospital (Ospedale Civili), **20**
IYHF, **4**
Palazzo Ducale (Doge's Palace), **6**
Piazza San Marco, **5**
Piazzale Roma, **18**
Ponte Rialto, **21**
Post Office, **2**
Questura di Venezia, **19**
Teatro Goldoni, **15**
Tourist Office (APT),
  Piazza San Marco, **16**
Tourist Office (APT),
  Stazione S. Lucia, **17**
Train Station, **1**

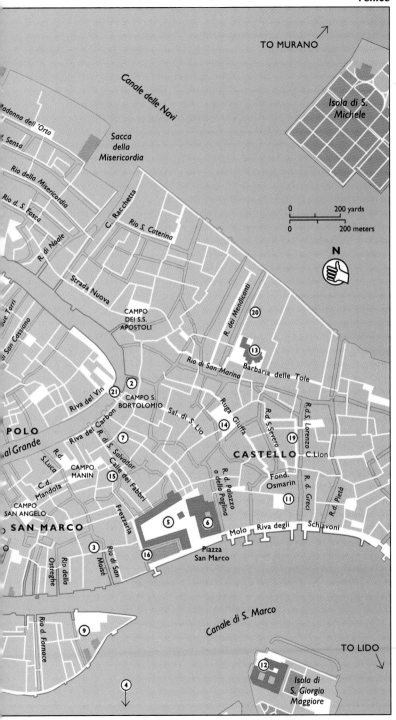

Milan

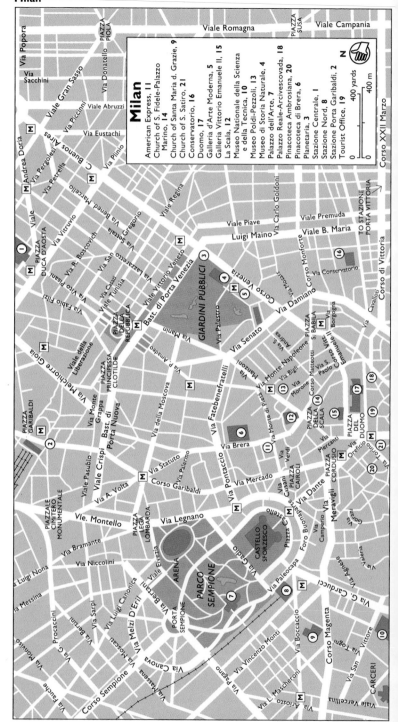

Milan

American Express, **11**
Church of S. Fidele-Palazzo Marino, **14**
Church of Santa Maria d. Grazie, **9**
Church of S. Satiro, **21**
Conservatorio, **16**
Duomo, **17**
Galleria d'Arte Moderna, **5**
Galleria Vittorio Emanuele II, **15**
La Scala, **12**
Museo Nazionale della Scienza e della Tecnica, **10**
Museo Poldi-Pezzoli, **13**
Museo di Storia Naturale, **4**
Palazzo dell'Arte, **7**
Palazzo Reale-Arcivescovada, **18**
Pinacoteca Ambrosiana, **20**
Pinacoteca di Brera, **6**
Planetaria, **3**
Stazione Centrale, **1**
Stazione Nord, **8**
Stazione Porta Garibaldi, **2**
Tourist Office, **19**

0 ___ 400 yards
0 ___ 400 m

Barcelona Metro

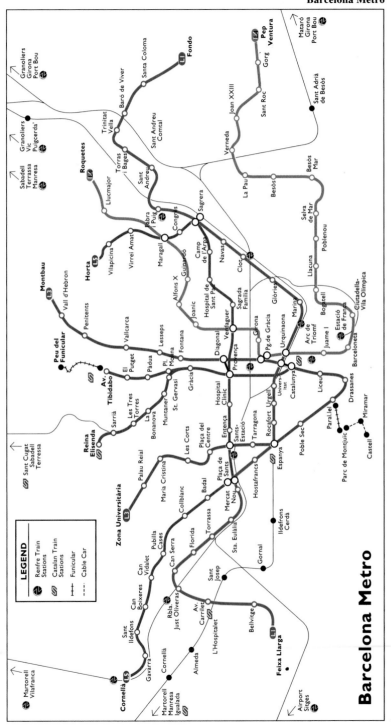

Barcelona Metro

Madrid Metro

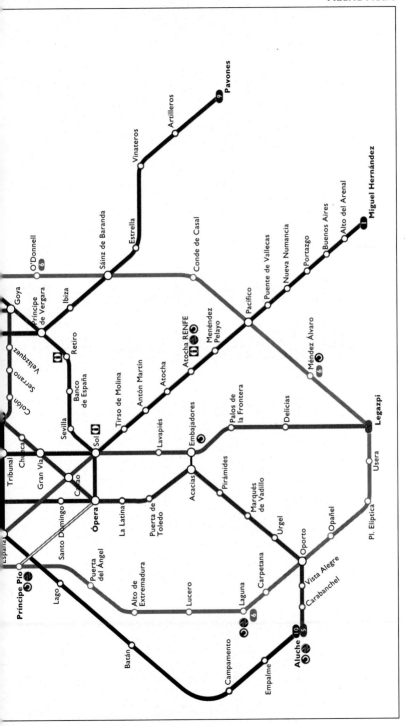

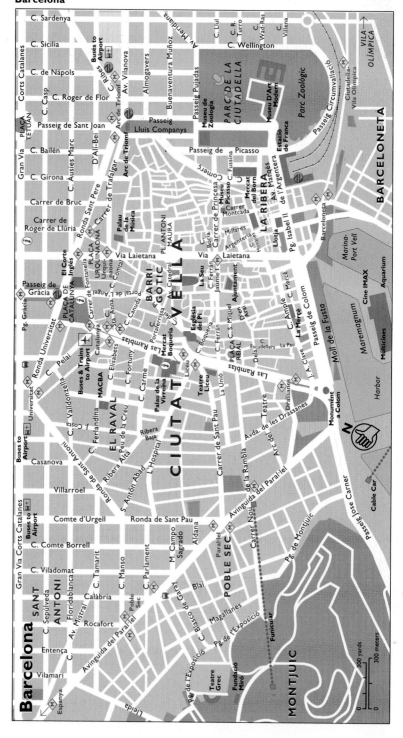